PETERSON'S GRADUATE PROGRAMS IN THE PHYSICAL SCIENCES, MATHEMATICS, AGRICULTURAL SCIENCES, THE ENVIRONMENT & NATURAL RESOURCES

2013

PETERSON'S
Publishing

About Peterson's Publishing

Peterson's Publishing provides the accurate, dependable, high-quality education content and guidance you need to succeed. No matter where you are on your academic or professional path, you can rely on Peterson's print and digital publications for the most up-to-date education exploration data, expert test-prep tools, and top-notch career success resources—everything you need to achieve your goals.

Visit us online at **www.petersonspublishing.com** and let Peterson's help you achieve your goals.

For more information, contact Peterson's Publishing, 2000 Lenox Drive, Lawrenceville, NJ 08648; 800-338-3282 Ext. 54229; or find us on the World Wide Web at www.petersonspublishing.com.

Bernadette Webster, Managing Editor; Jill C. Schwartz, Editor; Ken Britschge, Research Project Manager; Amanda Ortiz, Amy L. Weber, Research Associates; Phyllis Johnson, Software Engineer; Ray Golaszewski, Publishing Operations Manager; Linda M. Williams, Composition Manager; Carrie Hansen, Christine Lucht, Bailey Williams, Client Fulfillment Team

ISSN 1093-8443
ISBN-13: 978-0-7689-3623-0
ISBN-10: 0-7689-3623-3

Printed in the United States of America

10 9 8 7 6 5 4 3 2 1   15 14 13

Forty-seventh Edition

By producing this book on recycled paper (40% post-consumer waste) 46 trees were saved.

Sustainability—Its Importance to Peterson's Publishing

What does sustainability mean to Peterson's Publishing? As a leading publisher, we are aware that out business has a direct impact on vital resources—most especially the trees that are used to make out books. Peterson's Publishing is proud that its products are certified to the Sustainable Forestry Initiative (SFI) chain-of-custody standard and that all of its books are printed on paper that is 40 percent post-consumer waste using vegetable-based ink.

Being a part of the Sustainable Forestry Initiative (SFI) means that all of out vendors—from paper suppliers to printers—have undergone rigorous audits to demonstrate that they are maintaining a sustainable environment.

Peterson's Publishing continuously strives to find new ways to incorporate sustainability throughout all aspects of its business.

CONTENTS

CONTENTS

vi   facebook.com/petersonspublishing

Peterson's Graduate Programs in the Physical Sciences, Mathematics, Agricultural Sciences, the Environment & Natural Resources 2013

A Note from the Peterson's Editors

The six volumes of Peterson's *Graduate and Professional Programs*, the only annually updated reference work of its kind, provide wideranging information on the graduate and professional programs offered by accredited colleges and universities in the United States, U.S. territories, and Canada and by those institutions outside the United States that are accredited by U.S. accrediting bodies. Nearly 36,000 individual academic and professional programs at more than 2,200 institutions are listed. Peterson's *Graduate and Professional Programs* have been used for more than forty years by prospective graduate and professional students, placement counselors, faculty advisers, and all others interested in postbaccalaureate education.

Graduate & Professional Programs: An Overview contains information on institutions as a whole, while the other books in the series are devoted to specific academic and professional fields:

> *Graduate Programs in the Humanities, Arts & Social Sciences*
> *Graduate Programs in the Biological/Biomedical Sciences & Health-Related Medical Professions*
> *Graduate Programs in the Physical Sciences, Mathematics, Agricultural Sciences, the Environment & Natural Resources*
> *Graduate Programs in Engineering & Applied Sciences*
> *Graduate Programs in Business, Education, Information Studies, Law & Social Work*

The books may be used individually or as a set. For example, if you have chosen a field of study but do not know what institution you want to attend or if you have a college or university in mind but have not chosen an academic field of study, it is best to begin with the Overview guide.

Graduate & Professional Programs: An Overview presents several directories to help you identify programs of study that might interest you; you can then research those programs further in the other books in the series by using the Directory of Graduate and Professional Programs by Field, which lists 500 fields and gives the names of those institutions that offer graduate degree programs in each.

For geographical or financial reasons, you may be interested in attending a particular institution and will want to know what it has to offer. You should turn to the Directory of Institutions and Their Offerings, which lists the degree programs available at each institution. As in the Directory of Graduate and Professional Programs by Field, the level of degrees offered is also indicated. All books in the series include advice on graduate education, including topics such as admissions tests, financial aid, and accreditation. **The Graduate Adviser** includes two essays and information about accreditation. The first essay, "The Admissions Process," discusses general admission requirements, admission tests, factors to consider when selecting a graduate school or program, when and how to apply, and how admission decisions are made. Special information for international students and tips for minority students are also included. The second essay, "Financial Support," is an overview of the broad range of support available at the graduate level. Fellowships, scholarships, and grants; assistantships and internships; federal and private loan programs, as well as Federal Work-Study; and the GI bill are detailed. This essay concludes with advice on applying for need-based financial aid. "Accreditation and Accrediting Agencies" gives information on accreditation and its purpose and lists institutional accrediting agencies first and then specialized accrediting agencies relevant to each volume's specific fields of study.

With information on more than 44,000 graduate programs in more than 500 disciplines, Peterson's *Graduate and Professional Programs* give you all the information you need about the programs that are of interest to you in three formats: **Profiles** (capsule summaries of basic information), **Displays** (information that an institution or program wants to emphasize), and **Close-Ups** (written by administrators, with more expansive information than the **Profiles**, emphasizing different aspects of the programs). By using these various formats of program information, coupled with **Appendixes** and **Indexes** covering directories and subject areas for all six books, you will find that these guides provide the most comprehensive, accurate, and up-to-date graduate study information available.

Find Us on Facebook®

Join the grad school conversation on Facebook® at www.facebook.com/petersonspublishing. Peterson's expert resources are available to help you as you search for the right graduate program for you.

Peterson's publishes a full line of resources with information you need to guide you through the graduate admissions process. Peterson's publications can be found at college libraries and career centers and your local bookstore or library—or visit us on the Web at www.petersonspublishing.com. Peterson's books are now also available as eBooks.

Colleges and universities will be pleased to know that Peterson's helped you in your selection. Admissions staff members are more than happy to answer questions, address specific problems, and help in any way they can. The editors at Peterson's wish you great success in your graduate program search!

THE GRADUATE ADVISER

The Admissions Process

Generalizations about graduate admissions practices are not always helpful because each institution has its own set of guidelines and procedures. Nevertheless, some broad statements can be made about the admissions process that may help you plan your strategy.

Factors Involved in Selecting a Graduate School or Program

Selecting a graduate school and a specific program of study is a complex matter. Quality of the faculty; program and course offerings; the nature, size, and location of the institution; admission requirements; cost; and the availability of financial assistance are among the many factors that affect one's choice of institution. Other considerations are job placement and achievements of the program's graduates and the institution's resources, such as libraries, laboratories, and computer facilities. If you are to make the best possible choice, you need to learn as much as you can about the schools and programs you are considering before you apply.

The following steps may help you narrow your choices.

- Talk to alumni of the programs or institutions you are considering to get their impressions of how well they were prepared for work in their fields of study.
- Remember that graduate school requirements change, so be sure to get the most up-to-date information possible.
- Talk to department faculty members and the graduate adviser at your undergraduate institution. They often have information about programs of study at other institutions.
- Visit the Web sites of the graduate schools in which you are interested to request a graduate catalog. Contact the department chair in your chosen field of study for additional information about the department and the field.
- Visit as many campuses as possible. Call ahead for an appointment with the graduate adviser in your field of interest and be sure to check out the facilities and talk to students.

General Requirements

Graduate schools and departments have requirements that applicants for admission must meet. Typically, these requirements include undergraduate transcripts (which provide information about undergraduate grade point average and course work applied toward a major), admission test scores, and letters of recommendation. Most graduate programs also ask for an essay or personal statement that describes your personal reasons for seeking graduate study. In some fields, such as art and music, portfolios or auditions may be required in addition to other evidence of talent. Some institutions require that the applicant have an undergraduate degree in the same subject as the intended graduate major.

Most institutions evaluate each applicant on the basis of the applicant's total record, and the weight accorded any given factor varies widely from institution to institution and from program to program.

The Application Process

You should begin the application process at least one year before you expect to begin your graduate study. Find out the application deadline for each institution (many are provided in the **Profile** section of this guide). Go to the institution's Web site and find out if you can apply online. If not, request a paper application form. Fill out this form thoroughly and neatly. Assume that the school needs all the information it is requesting and that the admissions officer will be sensitive to the neatness and overall quality of what you submit. Do not supply more information than the school requires.

The institution may ask at least one question that will require a threeor four-paragraph answer. Compose your response on the assumption that the admissions officer is interested in both what you think and how you express yourself. Keep your statement brief and to the point, but, at the same time, include all pertinent information about your past experiences and your educational goals. Individual statements vary greatly in style and content, which helps admissions officers differentiate among applicants. Many graduate departments give considerable weight to the statement in making their admissions decisions, so be sure to take the time to prepare a thoughtful and concise statement.

If recommendations are a part of the admissions requirements, carefully choose the individuals you ask to write them. It is generally best to ask current or former professors to write the recommendations, provided they are able to attest to your intellectual ability and motivation for doing the work required of a graduate student. It is advisable to provide stamped, preaddressed envelopes to people being asked to submit recommendations on your behalf.

Completed applications, including references, transcripts, and admission test scores, should be received at the institution by the specified date.

Be advised that institutions do not usually make admissions decisions until all materials have been received. Enclose a self-addressed postcard with your application, requesting confirmation of receipt. Allow at least ten days for the return of the postcard before making further inquiries.

If you plan to apply for financial support, it is imperative that you file your application early.

ADMISSION TESTS

The major testing program used in graduate admissions is the Graduate Record Examinations (GRE) testing program, sponsored by the GRE Board and administered by Educational Testing Service, Princeton, New Jersey.

The Graduate Record Examinations testing program consists of a General Test and eight Subject Tests. The General Test measures critical thinking, verbal reasoning, quantitative reasoning, and analytical writing skills. It is offered as an Internet-based test (iBT) in the United States, Canada, and many other countries.

The Graduate Record Examinations testing program consists of the revised General Test and eight Subject Tests. The GRE® revised General Test, introduced in August 2011, features a new test-taker friendly design and new question types. It reflects the kind of thinking students need to do in graduate or business school and demonstrates that students are indeed ready for graduate-level work.

- **Verbal Reasoning**—Measures ability to analyze and evaluate written material and synthesize information obtained from it, analyze relationships among component parts of sentences, and recognize relationships among words and concepts.
- **Quantitative Reasoning**—Measures problem-solving ability, focusing on basic concepts of arithmetic, algebra, geometry, and data analysis.
- **Analytical Writing**—Measures critical thinking and analytical writing skills, specifically the ability to articulate and support complex ideas clearly and effectively.

The GRE® revised General Test is available at about 700 test centers in more than 160 countries. It is offered as a computer-based test year-round at most locations around the world and as a paper-based test up to three times a year in areas where computer-based testing is not available.

Three scores are reported on the revised General Test:

1. A **Verbal Reasoning score** is reported on a 130–170 score scale, in 1-point increments.

2 A **Quantitative Reasoning score** is reported on a 130–170 score scale, in 1-point increments.

3 An **Analytical Writing score** is reported on a 0–6 score level, in half-point increments.

The GRE Subject Tests measure achievement and assume undergraduate majors or extensive background in the following eight disciplines:

- Biochemistry, Cell and Molecular Biology
- Biology
- Chemistry
- Computer Science
- Literature in English
- Mathematics
- Physics
- Psychology

The Subject Tests are available three times per year as paper-based administrations around the world. Testing time is approximately 2 hours and 50 minutes. You can obtain more information about the GRE by visiting the ETS Web site at www.ets.org or consulting the *GRE Information and Registration Bulletin*. The *Bulletin* can be obtained at many undergraduate colleges. You can also download it from the ETS Web site or obtain it by contacting Graduate Record Examinations, Educational Testing Service, P.O. Box 6000, Princeton, NJ 08541-6000; phone: 609-771-7670.

If you expect to apply for admission to a program that requires any of the GRE tests, you should select a test date well in advance of the application deadline. Scores on the computer-based General Test are reported within ten to fifteen days; scores on the paper-based Subject Tests are reported within six weeks.

Another testing program, the Miller Analogies Test (MAT), is administered at more than 500 Controlled Testing Centers, licensed by Harcourt Assessment, Inc., in the United States, Canada, and other countries. The MAT computer-based test is now available. Testing time is 60 minutes. The test consists of 120 partial analogies. You can obtain the *Candidate Information Booklet,* which contains a list of test centers and instructions for taking the test, from http://www.milleranalogies.com or by calling 800-622-3231 (toll-free).

Check the specific requirements of the programs to which you are applying.

How Admission Decisions Are Made

The program you apply to is directly involved in the admissions process. Although the final decision is usually made by the graduate dean (or an associate) or the faculty admissions committee, recommendations from faculty members in your intended field are important. At some institutions, an interview is incorporated into the decision process.

A Special Note for International Students

In addition to the steps already described, there are some special considerations for international students who intend to apply for graduate study in the United States. All graduate schools require an indication of competence in English. The purpose of the Test of English as a Foreign Language (TOEFL) is to evaluate the English proficiency of people who are nonnative speakers of English and want to study at colleges and universities where English is the language of instruction. The TOEFL is administered by Educational Testing Service (ETS) under the general direction of a policy board established by the College Board and the Graduate Record Examinations Board.

The TOEFL iBT assesses the four basic language skills: listening, reading, writing, and speaking. It was administered for the first time in September 2005, and ETS continues to introduce the TOEFL iBT in selected cities. The Internet-based test is administered at secure, official test centers. The testing time is approximately 4 hours. Because the TOEFL iBT includes a speaking section, the Test of Spoken English (TSE) is no longer needed.

The TOEFL is also offered in the paper-based format in areas of the world where Internet-based testing is not available. The paper-based TOEFL consists of three sections—listening comprehension, structure and written expression, and reading comprehension. The testing time is approximately 3 hours. The Test of Written English (TWE) is also given. The TWE is a 30-minute essay that measures the examinee's ability to compose in English. Examinees receive a TWE score separate from their TOEFL score. The *Information Bulletin* contains information on local fees and registration procedures.

The TOEFL® paper-based test (TOEFL PBT) began being phased out in mid-2012. For those who may have taken the TOEFL PBT, scores remain valid for two years after the test date. The Test of Written English (TWE) is also given. The TWE is a 30-minute essay that measures the examinee's ability to compose in English. Examinees receive a TWE score separate from their TOEFL score. The Information Bulletin contains information on local fees and registration procedures.

Additional information and registration materials are available from TOEFL Services, Educational Testing Service, P.O. Box 6151, Princeton, New Jersey 08541-6151. Phone: 609-771-7100. Web site: www.toefl.org.

International students should apply especially early because of the number of steps required to complete the admissions process. Furthermore, many United States graduate schools have a limited number of spaces for international students, and many more students apply than the schools can accommodate.

International students may find financial assistance from institutions very limited. The U.S. government requires international applicants to submit a certification of support, which is a statement attesting to the applicant's financial resources. In addition, international students *must* have health insurance coverage.

Tips for Minority Students

Indicators of a university's values in terms of diversity are found both in its recruitment programs and its resources directed to student success. Important questions: Does the institution vigorously recruit minorities for its graduate programs? Is there funding available to help with the costs associated with visiting the school? Are minorities represented in the institution's brochures or Web site or on their faculty rolls? What campus-based resources or services (including assistance in locating housing or career counseling and placement) are available? Is funding available to members of underrepresented groups?

At the program level, it is particularly important for minority students to investigate the "climate" of a program under consideration. How many minority students are enrolled and how many have graduated? What opportunities are there to work with diverse faculty and mentors whose research interests match yours? How are conflicts resolved or concerns addressed? How interested are faculty in building strong and supportive relations with students? "Climate" concerns should be addressed by posing questions to various individuals, including faculty members, current students, and alumni.

Information is also available through various organizations, such as the Hispanic Association of Colleges & Universities (HACU), and publications such as *Diverse Issues in Higher Education* and *Hispanic Outlook* magazine. There are also books devoted to this topic, such as *The Multicultural Student's Guide to Colleges* by Robert Mitchell.

4 facebook.com/petersonspublishing

Peterson's Graduate Programs in the Physical Sciences, Mathematics, Agricultural Sciences, the Environment & Natural Resources 2013

Financial Support

The range of financial support at the graduate level is very broad. The following descriptions will give you a general idea of what you might expect and what will be expected of you as a financial support recipient.

Fellowships, Scholarships, and Grants

These are usually outright awards of a few hundred to many thousands of dollars with no service to the institution required in return. Fellowships and scholarships are usually awarded on the basis of merit and are highly competitive. Grants are made on the basis of financial need or special talent in a field of study. Many fellowships, scholarships, and grants not only cover tuition, fees, and supplies but also include stipends for living expenses with allowances for dependents. However, the terms of each should be examined because some do not permit recipients to supplement their income with outside work. Fellowships, scholarships, and grants may vary in the number of years for which they are awarded.

In addition to the availability of these funds at the university or program level, many excellent fellowship programs are available at the national level and may be applied for before and during enrollment in a graduate program. A listing of many of these programs can be found at the Council of Graduate Schools' Web site: http://www. cgsnet.org. There is a wealth of information in the "Programs" and "Awards" sections.

Assistantships and Internships

Many graduate students receive financial support through assistantships, particularly involving teaching or research duties. It is important to recognize that such appointments should not be viewed simply as employment relationships but rather should constitute an integral and important part of a student's graduate education. As such, the appointments should be accompanied by strong faculty mentoring and increasingly responsible apprenticeship experiences. The specific nature of these appointments in a given program should be considered in selecting that graduate program.

TEACHING ASSISTANTSHIPS

These usually provide a salary and full or partial tuition remission and may also provide health benefits. Unlike fellowships, scholarships, and grants, which require no service to the institution, teaching assistantships require recipients to provide the institution with a specific amount of undergraduate teaching, ideally related to the student's field of study. Some teaching assistants are limited to grading papers, compiling bibliographies, taking notes, or monitoring laboratories. At some graduate schools, teaching assistants must carry lighter course loads than regular full-time students.

RESEARCH ASSISTANTSHIPS

These are very similar to teaching assistantships in the manner in which financial assistance is provided. The difference is that recipients are given basic research assignments in their disciplines rather than teaching responsibilities. The work required is normally related to the student's field of study; in most instances, the assistantship supports the student's thesis or dissertation research.

ADMINISTRATIVE INTERNSHIPS

These are similar to assistantships in application of financial assistance funds, but the student is given an assignment on a part-time basis, usually as a special assistant with one of the university's administrative offices. The assignment may not necessarily be directly related to the recipient's discipline.

RESIDENCE HALL AND COUNSELING ASSISTANTSHIPS

These assistantships are frequently assigned to graduate students in psychology, counseling, and social work, but they may be offered to students in other disciplines, especially if the student has worked in this capacity during his or her undergraduate years. Duties can vary from being available in a dean's office for a specific number of hours for consultation with undergraduates to living in campus residences and being responsible for both counseling and administrative tasks or advising student activity groups. Residence hall assistantships often include a room and board allowance and, in some cases, tuition assistance and stipends. Contact the Housing and Student Life Office for more information.

Health Insurance

The availability and affordability of health insurance is an important issue and one that should be considered in an applicant's choice of institution and program. While often included with assistantships and fellowships, this is not always the case and, even if provided, the benefits may be limited. It is important to note that the U.S. government requires international students to have health insurance.

The GI Bill

This provides financial assistance for students who are veterans of the United States armed forces. If you are a veteran, contact your local Veterans Administration office to determine your eligibility and to get full details about benefits. There are a number of programs that offer educational benefits to current military enlistees. Some states have tuition assistance programs for members of the National Guard. Contact the VA office at the college for more information.

Federal Work-Study Program (FWS)

Employment is another way some students finance their graduate studies. The federally funded Federal Work-Study Program provides eligible students with employment opportunities, usually in public and private nonprofit organizations. Federal funds pay up to 75 percent of the wages, with the remainder paid by the employing agency. FWS is available to graduate students who demonstrate financial need. Not all schools have these funds, and some only award them to undergraduates. Each school sets its application deadline and workstudy earnings limits. Wages vary and are related to the type of work done. You must file the Free Application for Federal Student Aid (FAFSA) to be eligible for this program.

Loans

Many graduate students borrow to finance their graduate programs when other sources of assistance (which do not have to be repaid) prove insufficient. You should always read and understand the terms of any loan program before submitting your application.

FEDERAL DIRECT LOANS

Federal Direct Stafford Loans. The Federal Direct Stafford Loan Program offers 6.8 percent interest rate loans to students with the Department of Education acting as the lender.

There are two components of the Federal Stafford Loan program. Under the *subsidized* component (for loans with enrollment prior to July 1, 2012) of the program, the federal government pays the interest on the loan while you are enrolled in graduate school on at least a half-time basis, as well as during any period of deferment. Under the *unsubsidized* component of the program, you pay the interest on the loan from the day proceeds are issued. Eligibility for the federal subsidy is based on demonstrated financial need as determined by the financial aid office from the information you provide on the FAFSA. A cosigner is not required, since the loan is not based on creditworthiness.

Although *unsubsidized* Federal Direct Stafford Loans may not be as desirable as *subsidized* Federal Direct Stafford Loans from the student's perspective, they are a useful source of support for those who may not qualify for the subsidized loans or who need additional financial assistance.

Graduate students may borrow up to $20,500 per year through the Direct Stafford Loan Program, up to a cumulative maximum of $138,500, including undergraduate borrowing. This may include up to $8,500 in *subsidized* Direct Stafford Loans annually, depending on eligibility, up to a cumulative maximum of $65,500, including undergraduate borrowing. The amount of the loan borrowed through the *unsubsidized* Direct Stafford Loan Program equals the total amount of the loan (as much as $20,500) minus your eligibility for a *subsidized* Direct Loan (as much as $8,500). You may borrow up to the cost of attendance at the school in which you are enrolled or will attend, minus estimated financial assistance from other federal, state, and private sources, up to a maximum of $20,500.

Direct Stafford Graduate Loans made on or after July 1, 2006, carry a fixed interest rate of 6.8% both for in-school and in-repayment borrowers.

A fee is deducted from the loan proceeds upon disbursement. Loans with a first disbursement on or after July 1, 2010 but before July 1, 2012, have a borrower origination fee of 1 percent. For loans disbursed after July 1, 2012, these fee deductions no longer apply. The Budget Control Act of 2011, signed into law on August 2, 2011, eliminates Direct Subsidized Loan eligibility for graduate and professional students for periods of enrollment beginning on or after July 1, 2012 and terminates the authority of the Department of Education to offer most repayment incentives to Direct Loan borrowers for loans disbursed on or after July 1, 2012.

Under the *subsidized* Federal Direct Stafford Loan Program, repayment begins six months after your last date of enrollment on at least a half-time basis. Under the *unsubsidized* program, repayment of interest begins within thirty days from disbursement of the loan proceeds, and repayment of the principal begins six months after your last enrollment on at least a half-time basis. Some borrowers may choose to defer interest payments while they are in school. The accrued interest is added to the loan balance when the borrower begins repayment. There are several repayment options.

Federal Perkins Loans. The Federal Perkins Loan is available to students demonstrating financial need and is administered directly by the school. Not all schools have these funds, and some may award them to undergraduates only. Eligibility is determined from the information you provide on the FAFSA. The school will notify you of your eligibility.

Eligible graduate students may borrow up to $6,000 per year, up to a maximum of $40,000, including undergraduate borrowing (even if your previous Perkins Loans have been repaid). The interest rate for Federal Perkins Loans is 5 percent, and no interest accrues while you remain in school at least half-time. There are no guarantee, loan, or disbursement fees. Repayment begins nine months after your last date of enrollment on at least a half-time basis and may extend over a maximum of ten years with no prepayment penalty.

Federal Direct Graduate PLUS Loans. Effective July 1, 2006, graduate and professional students are eligible for Graduate PLUS loans. This program allows students to borrow up to the cost of attendance, less any other aid received. These loans have a fixed interest rate of 7.9 percent, and interest begins to accrue at the time of disbursement. The PLUS loans do involve a credit check; a PLUS borrower may obtain a loan with a cosigner if his or her credit is not good enough. Grad PLUS loans may be deferred while a student in school and for the six months following a drop below half-time enrollment. For more information, contact your college financial aid office.

Deferring Your Federal Loan Repayments. If you borrowed under the Federal Direct Stafford Loan Program, Federal Direct PLUS Loan Program, or the Federal Perkins Loan Program for previous under-

graduate or graduate study, your payments may be deferred when you return to graduate school, depending on when you borrowed and under which program.

There are other deferment options available if you are temporarily unable to repay your loan. Information about these deferments is provided at your entrance and exit interviews. If you believe you are eligible for a deferment of your loan payments, you must contact your lender or loan servicer to request a deferment. The deferment must be filed prior to the time your payment is due, and it must be refiled when it expires if you remain eligible for deferment at that time.

SUPPLEMENTAL (PRIVATE) LOANS

Many lending institutions offer supplemental loan programs and other financing plans, such as the ones described here, to students seeking additional assistance in meeting their education expenses. Some loan programs target all types of graduate students; others are designed specifically for business, law, or medical students. In addition, you can use private loans not specifically designed for education to help finance your graduate degree.

If you are considering borrowing through a supplemental or private loan program, you should carefully consider the terms and be sure to "read the fine print." Check with the program sponsor for the most current terms that will be applicable to the amounts you intend to borrow for graduate study. Most supplemental loan programs for graduate study offer unsubsidized, credit-based loans. In general, a credit-ready borrower is one who has a satisfactory credit history or no credit history at all. A creditworthy borrower generally must pass a credit test to be eligible to borrow or act as a cosigner for the loan funds.

Many supplemental loan programs have minimum and maximum annual loan limits. Some offer amounts equal to the cost of attendance minus any other aid you will receive for graduate study. If you are planning to borrow for several years of graduate study, consider whether there is a cumulative or aggregate limit on the amount you may borrow. Often this cumulative or aggregate limit will include any amounts you borrowed and have not repaid for undergraduate or previous graduate study.

The combination of the annual interest rate, loan fees, and the repayment terms you choose will determine how much you will repay over time. Compare these features in combination before you decide which loan program to use. Some loans offer interest rates that are adjusted monthly, some quarterly, some annually. Some offer interest rates that are lower during the in-school, grace, and deferment periods and then increase when you begin repayment. Some programs include a loan "origination" fee, which is usually deducted from the principal amount you receive when the loan is disbursed and must be repaid along with the interest and other principal when you graduate, withdraw from school, or drop below half-time study. Sometimes the loan fees are reduced if you borrow with a qualified cosigner. Some programs allow you to defer interest and/or principal payments while you are enrolled in graduate school. Many programs allow you to capitalize your interest payments; the interest due on your loan is added to the outstanding balance of your loan, so you don't have to repay immediately, but this increases the amount you owe. Other programs allow you to pay the interest as you go, which reduces the amount you later have to repay. The private loan market is very competitive, and your financial aid office can help you evaluate these programs.

Applying for Need-Based Financial Aid

Schools that award federal and institutional financial assistance based on need will require you to complete the FAFSA and, in some cases, an institutional financial aid application.

If you are applying for federal student assistance, you **must** complete the FAFSA. A service of the U.S. Department of Education, the FAFSA is free to all applicants. Most applicants apply online at www.fafsa.ed.gov. Paper applications are available at the financial aid office of your local college.

After your FAFSA information has been processed, you will receive a Student Aid Report (SAR). If you provided an e-mail address on the

6 facebook.com/petersonspublishing

Peterson's Graduate Programs in the Physical Sciences, Mathematics, Agricultural Sciences, the Environment & Natural Resources 2013

FAFSA, this will be sent to you electronically; otherwise, it will be mailed to your home address.

Follow the instructions on the SAR if you need to correct information reported on your original application. If your situation changes after you file your FAFSA, contact your financial aid officer to discuss amending your information. You can also appeal your financial aid award if you have extenuating circumstances.

If you would like more information on federal student financial aid, visit the FAFSA Web site or download the most recent version of *Funding Education Beyond High School: The Guide to Federal Student Aid* at http://studentaid.ed.gov/students/publications/student_guide/index.html. This guide is also available in Spanish.

The U.S. Department of Education also has a toll-free number for questions concerning federal student aid programs. The number is 1-800-4-FED AID (1-800-433-3243). If you are hearing impaired, call toll-free, 1-800-730-8913.

Summary

Remember that these are generalized statements about financial assistance at the graduate level. Because each institution allots its aid differently, you should communicate directly with the school and the specific department of interest to you. It is not unusual, for example, to find that an endowment vested within a specific department supports one or more fellowships. You may fit its requirements and specifications precisely.

Peterson's Graduate Programs in the Physical Sciences, Mathematics, Agricultural Sciences, the Environment & Natural Resources 2013

facebook.com/petersonspublishing **7**

Accreditation and Accrediting Agencies

Colleges and universities in the United States, and their individual academic and professional programs, are accredited by nongovernmental agencies concerned with monitoring the quality of education in this country. Agencies with both regional and national jurisdictions grant accreditation to institutions as a whole, while specialized bodies acting on a nationwide basis—often national professional associations— grant accreditation to departments and programs in specific fields.

Institutional and specialized accrediting agencies share the same basic concerns: the purpose an academic unit—whether university or program—has set for itself and how well it fulfills that purpose, the adequacy of its financial and other resources, the quality of its academic offerings, and the level of services it provides. Agencies that grant institutional accreditation take a broader view, of course, and examine university-wide or college-wide services with which a specialized agency may not concern itself.

Both types of agencies follow the same general procedures when considering an application for accreditation. The academic unit prepares a self-evaluation, focusing on the concerns mentioned above and usually including an assessment of both its strengths and weaknesses; a team of representatives of the accrediting body reviews this evaluation, visits the campus, and makes its own report; and finally, the accrediting body makes a decision on the application. Often, even when accreditation is granted, the agency makes a recommendation regarding how the institution or program can improve. All institutions and programs are also reviewed every few years to determine whether they continue to meet established standards; if they do not, they may lose their accreditation.

Accrediting agencies themselves are reviewed and evaluated periodically by the U.S. Department of Education and the Council for Higher Education Accreditation (CHEA). Recognized agencies adhere to certain standards and practices, and their authority in matters of accreditation is widely accepted in the educational community.

This does not mean, however, that accreditation is a simple matter, either for schools wishing to become accredited or for students deciding where to apply. Indeed, in certain fields the very meaning and methods of accreditation are the subject of a good deal of debate. For their part, those applying to graduate school should be aware of the safeguards provided by regional accreditation, especially in terms of degree acceptance and institutional longevity. Beyond this, applicants should understand the role that specialized accreditation plays in their field, as this varies considerably from one discipline to another. In certain professional fields, it is necessary to have graduated from a program that is accredited in order to be eligible for a license to practice, and in some fields the federal government also makes this a hiring requirement. In other disciplines, however, accreditation is not as essential, and there can be excellent programs that are not accredited. In fact, some programs choose not to seek accreditation, although most do.

Institutions and programs that present themselves for accreditation are sometimes granted the status of candidate for accreditation, or what is known as "preaccreditation." This may happen, for example, when an academic unit is too new to have met all the requirements for accreditation. Such status signifies initial recognition and indicates that the school or program in question is working to fulfill all requirements; it does not, however, guarantee that accreditation will be granted.

Institutional Accrediting Agencies—Regional

MIDDLE STATES ASSOCIATION OF COLLEGES AND SCHOOLS
Accredits institutions in Delaware, District of Columbia, Maryland, New Jersey, New York, Pennsylvania, Puerto Rico, and the Virgin Islands.
Dr. Elizabeth Sibolski, President
Middle States Commission on Higher Education
3624 Market Street, Second Floor West
Philadelphia, Pennsylvania 19104
Phone: 267-284-5000
Fax: 215-662-5501
E-mail: info@msche.org
Web: www.msche.org

NEW ENGLAND ASSOCIATION OF SCHOOLS AND COLLEGES
Accredits institutions in Connecticut, Maine, Massachusetts, New Hampshire, Rhode Island, and Vermont.
Barbara E. Brittingham, Director
Commission on Institutions of Higher Education
209 Burlington Road, Suite 201
Bedford, Massachusetts 01730-1433
Phone: 781-271-0022
Fax: 781-271-0950
E-mail: kwillis@neasc.org
Web: http://cihe.neasc.org

NORTH CENTRAL ASSOCIATION OF COLLEGES AND SCHOOLS
Accredits institutions in Arizona, Arkansas, Colorado, Illinois, Indiana, Iowa, Kansas, Michigan, Minnesota, Missouri, Nebraska, New Mexico, North Dakota, Ohio, Oklahoma, South Dakota, West Virginia, Wisconsin, and Wyoming.
Dr. Sylvia Manning, President
The Higher Learning Commission
230 South LaSalle Street, Suite 7-500
Chicago, Illinois 60604-1413
Phone: 312-263-0456
Fax: 312-263-7462
E-mail: smanning@hlcommission.org
Web: www.ncahlc.org

NORTHWEST COMMISSION ON COLLEGES AND UNIVERSITIES
Accredits institutions in Alaska, Idaho, Montana, Nevada, Oregon, Utah, and Washington.
Dr. Sandra E. Elman, President
8060 165th Avenue, NE, Suite 100
Redmond, Washington 98052
Phone: 425-558-4224
Fax: 425-376-0596
E-mail: selman@nwccu.org
Web: www.nwccu.org

SOUTHERN ASSOCIATION OF COLLEGES AND SCHOOLS
Accredits institutions in Alabama, Florida, Georgia, Kentucky, Louisiana, Mississippi, North Carolina, South Carolina, Tennessee, Texas, and Virginia.
Belle S. Wheelan, President
Commission on Colleges
1866 Southern Lane
Decatur, Georgia 30033-4097
Phone: 404-679-4500
Fax: 404-679-4558
E-mail: questions@sacscoc.org
Web: www.sacscoc.org

WESTERN ASSOCIATION OF SCHOOLS AND COLLEGES
Accredits institutions in California, Guam, and Hawaii.
Ralph A. Wolff, President and Executive Director
Accrediting Commission for Senior Colleges and Universities
985 Atlantic Avenue, Suite 100
Alameda, California 94501
Phone: 510-748-9001
Fax: 510-748-9797
E-mail: wascsr@wascsenior.org
Web: www.wascweb.org/org

Institutional Accrediting Agencies—Other

ACCREDITING COUNCIL FOR INDEPENDENT COLLEGES AND SCHOOLS
Albert C. Gray, Ph.D., Executive Director and CEO
750 First Street, NE, Suite 980
Washington, DC 20002-4241
Phone: 202-336-6780
Fax: 202-842-2593
E-mail: info@acics.org
Web: www.acics.org

DISTANCE EDUCATION AND TRAINING COUNCIL (DETC)
Accrediting Commission
Michael P. Lambert, Executive Director
1601 18th Street, NW, Suite 2
Washington, DC 20009
Phone: 202-234-5100
Fax: 202-332-1386
E-mail: Brianna@detc.org
Web: www.detc.org

Specialized Accrediting Agencies

ACUPUNCTURE AND ORIENTAL MEDICINE
William W. Goding, M.Ed., RRT, Interim Executive Director
Accreditation Commission for Acupuncture and Oriental Medicine
14502 Greenview Drive, Suite 300B
Laurel, Maryland 20708
Phone: 301-313-0855
Fax: 301-313-0912
E-mail: coordinator@acaom.org
Web: www.acaom.org

ART AND DESIGN
Samuel Hope, Executive Director
Karen P. Moynahan, Associate Director
National Association of Schools of Art and Design (NASAD)
Commission on Accreditation
11250 Roger Bacon Drive, Suite 21
Reston, Virginia 20190-5243
Phone: 703-437-0700
Fax: 703-437-6312
E-mail: info@arts-accredit.org
Web: http://nasad.arts-accredit.org/

BUSINESS
Jerry Trapnell, Executive Vice President/Chief Accreditation Officer
AACSB International--The Association to Advance Collegiate Schools of Business
777 South Harbour Island Boulevard, Suite 750
Tampa, Florida 33602
Phone: 813-769-6500
Fax: 813-769-6559
E-mail: jerryt@aacsb.edu
Web: www.aacsb.edu

CHIROPRACTIC
S. Ray Bennett, Director of Accreditation Services
Council on Chiropractic Education (CCE) Commission on Accreditation
8049 North 85th Way
Scottsdale, Arizona 85258-4321
Phone: 480-443-8877
Fax: 480-483-7333
E-mail: cce@cce-usa.org
Web: www.cce-usa.org

CLINICAL LABORATORY SCIENCES
Dianne M. Cearlock, Ph.D., Chief Executive Officer
National Accrediting Agency for Clinical Laboratory Sciences
5600 North River Road, Suite 720
Rosemont, Illinois 60018-5119
Phone: 773-714-8880
Fax: 773-714-8886
E-mail: info@naacls.org
Web: www.naacls.org

CLINICAL PASTORAL EDUCATION
Deryck Durston, Interim Executive Director
Association for Clinical Pastoral Education, Inc.
1549 Claremont Road, Suite 103
Decatur, Georgia 30033-4611
Phone: 404-320-1472
Fax: 404-320-0849
E-mail: acpe@acpe.edu
Web: www.acpe.edu

DANCE
Samuel Hope, Executive Director
Karen P. Moynahan, Associate Director
National Association of Schools of Dance (NASD) Commission on Accreditation
11250 Roger Bacon Drive, Suite 21
Reston, Virginia 20190-5248
Phone: 703-437-0700
Fax: 703-437-6312
E-mail: info@arts-accredit.org
Web: http://nasd.arts-accredit.org

DENTISTRY
Anthony Ziebert, Director
Commission on Dental Accreditation
American Dental Association
211 East Chicago Avenue, Suite 1900
Chicago, Illinois 60611
Phone: 312-440-4643
E-mail: accreditation@ada.org
Web: www.ada.org

DIETETICS
Ulric K. Chung, Ph.D., Executive Director
American Dietetic Association
Commission on Accreditation for Dietetics Education (CADE-ADA)
120 South Riverside Plaza, Suite 2000
Chicago, Illinois 60606-6995
Phone: 800-877-1600
Fax: 312-899-4817
E-mail: cade@eatright.org
Web: www.eatright.org/cade

ENGINEERING
Michael Milligan, Ph.D., PE, Executive Director
Accreditation Board for Engineering and Technology, Inc. (ABET)
111 Market Place, Suite 1050
Baltimore, Maryland 21202
Phone: 410-347-7700
Fax: 410-625-2238
E-mail: accreditation@abet.org
Web: www.abet.org

FORESTRY
Carol L. Redelsheimer
Director of Science and Education
5400 Grosvenor Lane
Bethesda, Maryland 20814-2198
Phone: 301-897-8720 Ext. 123
Fax: 301-897-3690
E-mail: redelsheimerc@safnet.org
Web: www.safnet.org

10 facebook.com/petersonspublishing

Peterson's Graduate Programs in the Physical Sciences, Mathematics, Agricultural Sciences, the Environment & Natural Resources 2013

HEALTH SERVICES ADMINISTRATION
Commission on Accreditation of Healthcare Management Education (CAHME)
John S. Lloyd, President and CEO
2111 Wilson Boulevard, Suite 700
Arlington, Virginia 22201
Phone: 703-351-5010
Fax: 703-991-5989
E-mail: info@cahme.org
Web: www.cahme.org

INTERIOR DESIGN
Holly Mattson, Executive Director
Council for Interior Design Accreditation
206 Grandview Avenue, Suite 350
Grand Rapids, Michigan 49503-4014
Phone: 616-458-0400
Fax: 616-458-0460
E-mail: info@accredit-id.org
Web: www.accredit-id.org

JOURNALISM AND MASS COMMUNICATIONS
Susanne Shaw, Executive Director
Accrediting Council on Education in Journalism and Mass Communications (ACEJMC) School of Journalism
Stauffer-Flint Hall
University of Kansas
1435 Jayhawk Boulevard
Lawrence, Kansas 66045-7575
Phone: 785-864-3973
Fax: 785-864-5225
E-mail: sshaw@ku.edu
Web: www2.ku.edu/~acejmc

LANDSCAPE ARCHITECTURE
Ronald C. Leighton, Executive Director
Landscape Architectural Accreditation Board (LAAB)
American Society of Landscape Architects (ASLA)
636 Eye Street, NW
Washington, DC 20001-3736
Phone: 202-898-2444
Fax: 202-898-1185
E-mail: info@asla.org
Web: www.asla.org

LAW
Hulett H. Askew, Consultant on Legal Education
American Bar Association
321 North Clark Street, 21st Floor
Chicago, Illinois 60654
Phone: 312-988-6738
Fax: 312-988-5681
E-mail: legaled@americanbar.org
Web: www.abanet.org/legaled/

LIBRARY
Karen O'Brien, Director
Office for Accreditation
American Library Association
50 East Huron Street
Chicago, Illinois 60611
Phone: 800-545-2433 Ext. 2432
Fax: 312-280-2433
E-mail: accred@ala.org
Web: www.ala.org/accreditation/

MARRIAGE AND FAMILY THERAPY
Tanya A. Tamarkin, Director of Educational Affairs
Commission on Accreditation for Marriage and Family Therapy Education
American Association for Marriage and Family Therapy
112 South Alfred Street
Alexandria, Virginia 22314-3061
Phone: 703-838-9808
Fax: 703-838-9805
E-mail: coamfte@aamft.org
Web: www.aamft.org

MEDICAL ILLUSTRATION
Commission on Accreditation of Allied Health Education Programs (CAAHEP)
Kathleen Megivern, Executive Director
1361 Park Street
Clearwater, Florida 33756
Phone: 727-210-2350
Fax: 727-210-2354
E-mail: mail@caahep.org
Web: www.caahep.org

MEDICINE
Liaison Committee on Medical Education (LCME)
In odd-numbered years beginning each July 1, contact:
Barbara Barzansky, Ph.D., LCME Secretary
American Medical Association
Council on Medical Education
515 North State Street
Chicago, Illinois 60654
Phone: 312-464-4933
Fax: 312-464-5830
E-mail: cme@aamc.org
Web: www.ama-assn.org

In even-numbered years beginning each July 1, contact:
Dan Hunt, M.D., LCME Secretary
Association of American Medical Colleges
2450 N Street, NW Washington, DC 20037
Phone: 202-828-0596
Fax: 202-828-1125
E-mail: dhunt@aamc.org
Web: www.lcme.org

MUSIC
Samuel Hope, Executive Director
Karen P. Moynahan, Associate Director
National Association of Schools of Music (NASM)
Commission on Accreditation
11250 Roger Bacon Drive, Suite 21
Reston, Virginia 20190-5248
Phone: 703-437-0700
Fax: 703-437-6312
E-mail: info@arts-accredit.org
Web: http://nasm.arts-accredit.org/

NATUROPATHIC MEDICINE
Daniel Seitz, J.D., Ed.D., Executive Director
Council on Naturopathic Medical Education
P.O. Box 178
Great Barrington, Massachusetts 01230
Phone: 413-528-8877
Fax: 413-528-8880
E-mail: council@cnme.org
Web: www.cnme.org

Peterson's Graduate Programs in the Physical Sciences, Mathematics, Agricultural Sciences, the Environment & Natural Resources 2013

facebook.com/petersonspublishing **11**

NURSE ANESTHESIA
Francis R. Gerbasi, Executive Director
Council on Accreditation of Nurse Anesthesia Educational Programs
American Association of Nurse Anesthetists
222 South Prospect Avenue, Suite 304
Park Ridge, Illinois 60068
Phone: 847-692-7050 Ext. 1154
Fax: 847-692-6968
E-mail: fgerbasi@aana.com
Web: http://home.coa.us.com

NURSE EDUCATION
Jennifer L. Butlin, Director
Commission on Collegiate Nursing Education (CCNE)
One Dupont Circle, NW, Suite 530
Washington, DC 20036-1120
Phone: 202-887-6791
Fax: 202-887-8476
E-mail: jbutlin@aacn.nche.edu
Web: www.aacn.nche.edu/accreditation

NURSE MIDWIFERY
Lorrie Kaplan, Executive Director
Accreditation Commission for Midwifery Education
American College of Nurse-Midwives
Nurse-Midwifery Program
8403 Colesville Road, Suite 1550
Silver Spring, Maryland 20910
Phone: 240-485-1800
Fax: 240-485-1818
E-mail: lkaplan@acnm.org
Web: www.midwife.org/acme.cfm

Jo Anne Myers-Ciecko, MPH, Executive Director
Midwifery Education Accreditation Council
P.O. Box 984
La Conner, Washington 98257
Phone: 360-466-2080
Fax: 480-907-2936
E-mail: info@meacschools.org
Web: www.meacschools.org

NURSE PRACTITIONER
Gay Johnson, Acting CEO
National Association of Nurse Practitioners in Women's Health
Council on Accreditation
505 C Street, NE Washington, DC 20002
Phone: 202-543-9693 Ext. 1
Fax: 202-543-9858
E-mail: info@npwh.org
Web: www.npwh.org

NURSING
Sharon J. Tanner, Ed.D., RN, Executive Director
National League for Nursing Accrediting Commission (NLNAC)
3343 Peachtree Road, NE, Suite 500
Atlanta, Georgia 30326
Phone: 404-975-5000
Fax: 404-975-5020
E-mail: nlnac@nlnac.org
Web: www.nlnac.org

OCCUPATIONAL THERAPY
Neil Harvison, Ph.D., OTR/L
Director of Accreditation and Academic Affairs
The American Occupational Therapy Association
4720 Montgomery Lane
P.O. Box 31220
Bethesda, Maryland 20824-1220
Phone: 301-652-2682 Ext. 2912
Fax: 301-652-7711
E-mail: accred@aota.org
Web: www.aota.org

OPTOMETRY
Joyce L. Urbeck, Administrative Director
Accreditation Council on Optometric Education
American Optometric Association (AOA)
243 North Lindbergh Boulevard
St. Louis, Missouri 63141
Phone: 314-991-4000 Ext. 246
Fax: 314-991-4101
E-mail: acoe@aoa.org
Web: www.theacoe.org

OSTEOPATHIC MEDICINE
Konrad C. Miskowicz-Retz, Ph.D., CAE
Director, Department of Education
Commission on Osteopathic College Accreditation
American Osteopathic Association
142 East Ontario Street
Chicago, Illinois 60611
Phone: 312-202-8048
Fax: 312-202-8202
E-mail: kretz@osteopathic.org
Web: www.osteopathic.org

PHARMACY
Peter H. Vlasses, Executive Director
Accreditation Council for Pharmacy Education
20 North Clark Street, Suite 2500
Chicago, Illinois 60602-5109
Phone: 312-664-3575
Fax: 312-664-4652
E-mail: csinfo@acpe-accredit.org
Web: www.acpe-accredit.org

PHYSICAL THERAPY
Mary Jane Harris, Director
Commission on Accreditation in Physical Therapy Education
(CAPTE)
American Physical Therapy Association (APTA)
1111 North Fairfax Street
Alexandria, Virginia 22314
Phone: 703-706-3245
Fax: 703-706-3387
E-mail: accreditation@apta.org
Web: www.capteonline.org

PHYSICIAN ASSISTANT STUDIES
John E. McCarty, Executive Director
Accreditation Review Commission on Education for the
Physician Assistant, Inc. (ARC-PA)
12000 Findley Road, Suite 150
Johns Creek, Georgia 30097
Phone: 770-476-1224
Fax: 770-476-1738
E-mail: arc-pa@arc-pa.org
Web: www.arc-pa.org

PLANNING
Shonagh Merits, Executive Director
American Institute of Certified Planners/Association of Collegiate
Schools of Planning/American Planning Association
Planning Accreditation Board (PAB)
53 W. Jackson Boulevard, Suite 1315
Chicago, Illinois 60604
Phone: 312-334-1271
Fax: 312-334-1273
E-mail: smerits@planningaccreditationboard.org
Web: www.planningaccreditationboard.org

12 facebook.com/petersonspublishing

*Peterson's Graduate Programs in the Physical Sciences, Mathematics,
Agricultural Sciences, the Environment & Natural Resources 2013*

PODIATRIC MEDICINE

Alan R. Tinkleman, Executive Director
Council on Podiatric Medical Education (CPME)
American Podiatric Medical Association
9312 Old Georgetown Road
Bethesda, Maryland 20814-1621
Phone: 301-571-9200
Fax: 301-571-4903
E-mail: artinkleman@apma.org
Web: www.cpme.org

PSYCHOLOGY AND COUNSELING

Susan Zlotlow, Executive Director
Office of Program Consultation and Accreditation
American Psychological Association
750 First Street, NE Washington, DC 20002-4242
Phone: 202-336-5979
Fax: 202-336-5978
E-mail: apaaccred@apa.org
Web: www.apa.org/ed/accreditation

Carol L. Bobby, Executive Director
Council for Accreditation of Counseling and Related Educational
Programs (CACREP)
1001 North Fairfax Street, Suite 510
Alexandria, Virginia 22314
Phone: 703-535-5990
Fax: 703-739-6209
E-mail: cacrep@cacrep.org
Web: www.cacrep.org

PUBLIC AFFAIRS AND ADMINISTRATION

Crystal Calarusse, Executive Director Commission on Peer Review and
Accreditation
National Association of Schools of Public Affairs and Administration
1029 Vermont Avenue, NW, Suite 1100
Washington, DC 20005
Phone: 202-628-8965
Fax: 202-626-4978
E-mail: copra@naspaa.org
Web: www.naspaa.org

PUBLIC HEALTH

Laura Rasar King, M.P.H., CHES, Executive Director
Council on Education for Public Health
800 Eye Street, NW, Suite 202
Washington, DC 20001-3710
Phone: 202-789-1050
Fax: 202-789-1895
E-mail: Lking@ceph.org
Web: www.ceph.org

REHABILITATION EDUCATION

Dr. Tom Evenson, Executive Director
Council on Rehabilitation Education (CORE)
Commission on Standards and Accreditation
1699 Woodfield Road, Suite 300
Schaumburg, Illinois 60173
Phone: 847-944-1345
Fax: 847-944-1324
E-mail: evenson@unt.edu
Web: www.core-rehab.org

SOCIAL WORK

Stephen M. Holloway, Director of Accreditation
Commission on Accreditation
Council on Social Work Education
1701 Duke Street, Suite 200
Alexandria, Virginia 22314
Phone: 703-683-8080
Fax: 703-683-8099
E-mail: sholloway@cswe.org
Web: www.cswe.org

SPEECH-LANGUAGE PATHOLOGY AND AUDIOLOGY

Patrima L. Tice, Director of Credentialing
American Speech-Language-Hearing Association
Council on Academic Accreditation in Audiology and SpeechLanguage
Pathology
2200 Research Boulevard
Rockville, Maryland 20850-3289
Phone: 301-296-5796
Fax: 301-296-8750
E-mail: ptice@asha.org
Web: www.asha.org/academic/accreditation/default.htm

TECHNOLOGY

Michale S. McComis, Ed.D., Executive Director
Accrediting Commission of Career Schools and Colleges
2101 Wilson Boulevard, Suite 302
Arlington, Virginia 22201
Phone: 703-247-4212
Fax: 703-247-4533
E-mail: mccomis@accsc.org
Web: www.accsc.org

TEACHER EDUCATION

James G. Cibulka, President
National Council for Accreditation of Teacher Education
2010 Massachusetts Avenue, NW, Suite 500
Washington, DC 20036-1023
Phone: 202-466-7496
Fax: 202-296-6620
E-mail: ncate@ncate.org
Web: www.ncate.org

Mark LaCelle-Peterson, President
Teacher Education Accreditation Council (TEAC) Accreditation
Committee
One Dupont Circle, Suite 320
Washington, DC 20036-0110
Phone: 202-831-0400
Fax: 202-831-3013
E-mail: teac@teac.org
Web: www.teac.org

THEATER

Samuel Hope, Executive Director
Karen P. Moynahan, Associate Director National Association of Schools
of Theatre Commission on Accreditation
11250 Roger Bacon Drive, Suite 21
Reston, Virginia 20190
Phone: 703-437-0700
Fax: 703-437-6312
E-mail: info@arts-accredit.org
Web: http://nast.arts-accredit.org/

Peterson's Graduate Programs in the Physical Sciences, Mathematics,
Agricultural Sciences, the Environment & Natural Resources 2013

facebook.com/petersonspublishing **13**

THEOLOGY

Bernard Fryshman, Executive Vice President
Association of Advanced Rabbinical and Talmudic Schools (AARTS)
Accreditation Commission
11 Broadway, Suite 405
New York, New York 10004
Phone: 212-363-1991
Fax: 212-533-5335
E-mail: BFryshman@nyit.edu

Daniel O. Aleshire, Executive Director
Association of Theological Schools in the United States and
Canada (ATS) Commission on Accrediting
10 Summit Park Drive
Pittsburgh, Pennsylvania 15275-1110
Phone: 412-788-6505
Fax: 412-788-6510
E-mail: ats@ats.edu
Web: www.ats.edu

Paul Boatner, President
Transnational Association of Christian Colleges and
Schools (TRACS) Accreditation Commission
15935 Forest Road
Forest, Virginia 24551
Phone: 434-525-9539
Fax: 434-525-9538
E-mail: info@tracs.org
Web: www.tracs.org

VETERINARY MEDICINE

Dave Granstrom, Executive Director
Education and Research Division
American Veterinary Medical Association (AVMA)
Council on Education
1931 North Meacham Road, Suite 100
Schaumburg, Illinois 60173
Phone: 847-925-8070 Ext. 6674
Fax: 847-925-9329
E-mail: info@avma.org
Web: www.avma.org

14 facebook.com/petersonspublishing

Peterson's Graduate Programs in the Physical Sciences, Mathematics,
Agricultural Sciences, the Environment & Natural Resources 2013

How to Use These Guides

As you identify the particular programs and institutions that interest you, you can use both the *Graduate & Professional Programs: An Overview* volume and the specialized volumes in the series to obtain detailed information.

- *Graduate Programs in the Physical Sciences, Mathematics, Agricultural Sciences, the Environment & Natural Resources*
- *Graduate Programs in Engineering & Applied Sciences*
- *Graduate Programs the Humanities, Arts & Social Sciences*
- *Graduate Programs in the Biological/Biomedical Sciences & Health-Related Professions*
- *Graduate Programs in Business, Education, Information Studies, Law & Social Work*

Each of the specialized volumes in the series is divided into sections that contain one or more directories devoted to programs in a particular field. If you do not find a directory devoted to your field of interest in a specific volume, consult "Directories and Subject Areas" (located at the end of each volume). After you have identified the correct volume, consult the "Directories and Subject Areas in This Book" index, which shows (as does the more general directory) what directories cover subjects not specifically named in a directory or section title.

Each of the specialized volumes in the series has a number of general directories. These directories have entries for the largest unit at an institution granting graduate degrees in that field. For example, the general Engineering and Applied Sciences directory in the *Graduate Programs in Engineering & Applied Sciences* volume consists of **Profiles** for colleges, schools, and departments of engineering and applied sciences.

General directories are followed by other directories, or sections, that give more detailed information about programs in particular areas of the general field that has been covered. The general Engineering and Applied Sciences directory, in the previous example, is followed by nineteen sections with directories in specific areas of engineering, such as Chemical Engineering, Industrial/Management Engineering, and Mechanical Engineering.

Because of the broad nature of many fields, any system of organization is bound to involve a certain amount of overlap. Environmental studies, for example, is a field whose various aspects are studied in several types of departments and schools. Readers interested in such studies will find information on relevant programs in the *Graduate Programs in the Biological/Biomedical Sciences & Health-Related Professions* volume under Ecology and Environmental Biology and Environmental and Occupational Health; in the *Graduate Programs in the Physical Sciences, Mathematics, Agricultural Sciences, the Environment & Natural Resources* volume under Environmental Management and Policy and Natural Resources; and in the *Graduate Programs in Engineering & Applied Sciences* volume under Energy Management and Policy and Environmental Engineering. To help you find all of the programs of interest to you, the introduction to each section within the specialized volumes includes, if applicable, a paragraph suggesting other sections and directories with information on related areas of study.

Directory of Institutions with Programs in the Physical Sciences, Mathematics, Agricultural Sciences, the Environment & Natural Resources

This directory lists institutions in alphabetical order and includes beneath each name the academic fields in which each institution offers graduate programs. The degree level in each field is also indicated, provided

that the institution has supplied that information in response to Peterson's Annual Survey of Graduate and Professional Institutions.

An M indicates that a master's degree program is offered; a D indicates that a doctoral degree program is offered; a P indicates that the first professional degree is offered; an O signifies that other advanced degrees (e.g., certificates or specialist degrees) are offered; and an * (asterisk) indicates that a **Close-Up** and/or **Display** is located in this volume. See the index, "Close-Ups and Displays," for the specific page number.

Profiles of Academic and Professional Programs in the Specialized Volumes

Each section of **Profiles** has a table of contents that lists the Program Directories, **Displays**, and **Close-Ups**. Program Directories consist of the **Profiles** of programs in the relevant fields, with **Displays** following if programs have chosen to include them. **Close-Ups,** which are more individualized statements, again if programs have chosen to submit them, are also listed.

The **Profiles** found in the 500 directories in the specialized volumes provide basic data about the graduate units in capsule form for quick reference. To make these directories as useful as possible, **Profiles** are generally listed for an institution's smallest academic unit within a subject area. In other words, if an institution has a College of Liberal Arts that administers many related programs, the **Profile** for the individual program (e.g., Program in History), not the entire College, appears in the directory.

There are some programs that do not fit into any current directory and are not given individual **Profiles**. The directory structure is reviewed annually in order to keep this number to a minimum and to accommodate major trends in graduate education.

The following outline describes the **Profile** information found in the guides and explains how best to use that information. Any item that does not apply to or was not provided by a graduate unit is omitted from its listing. The format of the **Profiles** is constant, making it easy to compare one institution with another and one program with another.

Identifying Information. The institution's name, in boldface type, is followed by a complete listing of the administrative structure for that field of study. (For example, University of Akron, Buchtel College of Arts and Sciences, Department of Theoretical and Applied Mathematics, Program in Mathematics.) The last unit listed is the one to which all information in the **Profile** pertains. The institution's city, state, and zip code follow.

Offerings. Each field of study offered by the unit is listed with all postbaccalaureate degrees awarded. Degrees that are not preceded by a specific concentration are awarded in the general field listed in the unit name. Frequently, fields of study are broken down into subspecializations, and those appear following the degrees awarded; for example, "Offerings in secondary education (M.Ed.), including English education, mathematics education, science education." Students enrolled in the M.Ed. program would be able to specialize in any of the three fields mentioned.

Professional Accreditation. Some **Profiles** indicate whether a program is professionally accredited. Because it is possible for a program to receive or lose professional accreditation at any time, students entering fields in which accreditation is important to a career should verify the status of programs by contacting either the chairperson or the appropriate accrediting association.

Jointly Offered Degrees. Explanatory statements concerning programs that are offered in cooperation with other institutions are included in the list of degrees offered. This occurs most commonly on a regional basis (for example, two state universities offering a cooperative Ph.D. in special education) or where the specialized nature of the institutions encourages joint efforts (a J.D./M.B.A. offered by a law school at an institution with no formal business programs and an institution with a business school but lacking a law school). Only programs that are truly cooperative are listed; those involving only limited course work at another institution are not. Interested students should contact the heads of such units for further information.

Part-Time and Evening/Weekend Programs. When information regarding the availability of part-time or evening/weekend study appears in the **Profile**, it means that students are able to earn a degree exclusively through such study.

Postbaccalaureate Distance Learning Degrees. A post-baccalaureate distance learning degree program signifies that course requirements can be fulfilled with minimal or no on-campus study.

Faculty. Figures on the number of faculty members actively involved with graduate students through teaching or research are separated into full- and part-time as well as men and women whenever the information has been supplied.

Students. Figures for the number of students enrolled in graduate and professional programs pertain to the semester of highest enrollment from the 2011–12 academic year. These figures are broken down into full- and part-time and men and women whenever the data have been supplied. Information on the number of matriculated students enrolled in the unit who are members of a minority group or are international students appears here. The average age of the matriculated students is followed by the number of applicants, the percentage accepted, and the number enrolled for fall 2011.

Degrees Awarded. The number of degrees awarded in the calendar year is listed. Many doctoral programs offer a terminal master's degree if students leave the program after completing only part of the requirements for a doctoral degree; that is indicated here. All degrees are classified into one of four types: master's, doctoral, first professional, and other advanced degrees. A unit may award one or several degrees at a given level; however, the data are only collected by type and may therefore represent several different degree programs.

Degree Requirements. The information in this section is also broken down by type of degree, and all information for a degree level pertains to all degrees of that type unless otherwise specified. Degree requirements are collected in a simplified form to provide some very basic information on the nature of the program and on foreign language, thesis or dissertation, comprehensive exam, and registration requirements. Many units also provide a short list of additional requirements, such as fieldwork or an internship. For complete information on graduation requirements, contact the graduate school or program directly.

Entrance Requirements. Entrance requirements are broken down into the four degree levels of master's, doctoral, first professional, and other advanced degrees. Within each level, information may be provided in two basic categories: entrance exams and other requirements. The entrance exams are identified by the standard acronyms used by the testing agencies, unless they are not well known. Other entrance requirements are quite varied, but they often contain an undergraduate or graduate grade point average (GPA). Unless otherwise stated, the GPA is calculated on a 4.0 scale and is listed as a minimum required for admission. Additional exam requirements/recommendations for international students may be listed here. Application deadlines for domestic and international students, the application fee, and whether electronic applications are accepted may be listed here. Note that the deadline should be used for reference only; these dates are subject to change, and students interested in applying should always contact the graduate unit directly about application procedures and deadlines.

Expenses. The typical cost of study for the 2011–12 academic year is given in two basic categories: tuition and fees. Cost of study may be quite complex at a graduate institution. There are often sliding scales for part-time study, a different cost for first-year students, and other variables that make it impossible to completely cover the cost of study for each graduate program. To provide the most usable information, figures are given for full-time study for a full year where available and for part-time study in terms of a per-unit rate (per credit, per semester hour, etc.). Occasionally, variances may be noted in tuition and fees for reasons such as the type of program, whether courses are taken during the day or evening, whether courses are at the master's or doctoral level, or other institution-specific reasons. Expenses are usually subject to change; for exact costs at any given time, contact your chosen schools and programs directly. Keep in mind that the tuition of Canadian institutions is usually given in Canadian dollars.

Financial Support. This section contains data on the number of awards administered by the institution and given to graduate students during the 2011–12 academic year. The first figure given represents the total number of students receiving financial support enrolled in that unit. If the unit has provided information on graduate appointments, these are broken down into three major categories: fellowships give money to graduate students to cover the cost of study and living expenses and are not based on a work obligation or research commitment, research assistantships provide stipends to graduate students for assistance in a formal research project with a faculty member, and teaching assistantships provide stipends to graduate students for teaching or for assisting faculty members in teaching undergraduate classes. Within each category, figures are given for the total number of awards, the average yearly amount per award, and whether full or partial tuition reimbursements are awarded. In addition to graduate appointments, the availability of several other financial aid sources is covered in this section. Tuition waivers are routinely part of a graduate appointment, but units sometimes waive part or all of a student's tuition even if a graduate appointment is not available. Federal WorkStudy is made available to students who demonstrate need and meet the federal guidelines; this form of aid normally includes 10 or more hours of work per week in an office of the institution. Institutionally sponsored loans are low-interest loans available to graduate students to cover both educational and living expenses. Career-related internships or fieldwork offer money to students who are participating in a formal off-campus research project or practicum. Grants, scholarships, traineeships, unspecified assistantships, and other awards may also be noted. The availability of financial support to part-time students is also indicated here.

Some programs list the financial aid application deadline and the forms that need to be completed for students to be eligible for financial awards. There are two forms: FAFSA, the Free Application for Federal Student Aid, which is required for federal aid, and the CSS PROFILE®.

Faculty Research. Each unit has the opportunity to list several keyword phrases describing the current research involving faculty members and graduate students. Space limitations prevent the unit from listing complete information on all research programs. The total expenditure for funded research from the previous academic year may also be included.

Unit Head and Application Contact. The head of the graduate program for each unit is listed with academic title and telephone and fax numbers and e-mail address if available. In addition to the unit head, many graduate programs list a separate contact for application and admission information, which follows the listing for the unit head. If no unit head or application contact is given, you should contact the overall institution for information on graduate admissions.

Displays and Close-Ups

The **Displays** and **Close-Ups** are supplementary insertions submitted by deans, chairs, and other administrators who wish to offer an additional, more individualized statement to readers. A number of graduate school and program administrators have attached a **Display** ad near the **Profile** listing. Here you will find information that an institution or program wants to emphasize. The **Close-Ups** are by their very nature more expansive and flexible than the **Profiles**, and the administrators who have written them may emphasize different aspects of their programs. All of the **Close-Ups** are organized in the same way (with the exception of a few that describe research and training opportunities instead of degree programs), and in each one you will find information on the same basic topics, such as programs of study, research facilities, tuition and fees, financial aid, and application procedures. If an institution or program has submitted a **Close-Up**, a boldface cross-reference appears below its **Profile**. As with the **Displays**, all of the **Close-Ups** in the guides have been submitted by choice; the absence of a **Display** or **Close-Up** does not reflect any type of editorial judgment on the part of Peterson's, and their presence in the guides should not be taken as an indication of status, quality, or approval. Statements regarding a university's objectives and accomplish-

16 facebook.com/petersonspublishing

Peterson's Graduate Programs in the Physical Sciences, Mathematics, Agricultural Sciences, the Environment & Natural Resources 2013

ments are a reflection of its own beliefs and are not the opinions of the Peterson's editors.

Appendixes

This section contains two appendixes. The first, "Institutional Changes Since the 2012 Edition," lists institutions that have closed, merged, or changed their name or status since the last edition of the guides. The second, "Abbreviations Used in the Guides," gives abbreviations of degree names, along with what those abbreviations stand for. These appendixes are identical in all six volumes of *Peterson's Graduate and Professional Programs*.

Indexes

There are three indexes presented here. The first index, "Close-Ups and Displays," gives page references for all programs that have chosen to place **Close-Ups** and **Displays** in this volume. It is arranged alphabetically by institution; within institutions, the arrangement is alphabetical by subject area. It is not an index to all programs in the book's directories of **Profiles**; readers must refer to the directories themselves for **Profile** information on programs that have not submitted the additional, more individualized statements. The second index, "Directories and Subject Areas in Other Books in This Series", gives book references for the directories in the specialized volumes and also includes cross-references for subject area names not used in the directory structure, for example, "Computing Technology (see Computer Science)." The third index, "Directories and Subject Areas in This Book," gives page references for the directories in this volume and cross-references for subject area names not used in this volume's directory structure.

Data Collection Procedures

The information published in the directories and **Profiles** of all the books is collected through Peterson's Annual Survey of Graduate and Professional Institutions. The survey is sent each spring to nearly 2,400 institutions offering postbaccalaureate degree programs, including accredited institutions in the United States, U.S. territories, and Canada and those institutions outside the United States that are accredited by U.S. accrediting bodies. Deans and other administrators complete these surveys, providing information on programs in the 500 academic and professional fields covered in the guides as well as overall institutional information. While every effort has been made to ensure the accuracy and completeness of the data, information is sometimes unavailable or changes occur after publication deadlines. All usable information received in time for publication has been included. The omission of any particular item from a directory or **Profile** signifies either that the item is not applicable to the institution or program or that information was not available. **Profiles** of programs scheduled to begin during the 2012–13 academic year cannot, obviously, include statistics on enrollment or, in many cases, the number of faculty members. If no usable data were submitted by an institution, its name, address, and program name appear in order to indicate the availability of graduate work.

Criteria for Inclusion in This Guide

To be included in this guide, an institution must have full accreditation or be a candidate for accreditation (preaccreditation) status by an institutional or specialized accrediting body recognized by the U.S. Department of Education or the Council for Higher Education Accreditation (CHEA). Institutional accrediting bodies, which review each institution as a whole, include the six regional associations of schools and colleges (Middle States, New England, North Central, Northwest, Southern, and Western), each of which is responsible for a specified portion of the United States and its territories. Other institutional accrediting bodies are national in scope and accredit specific kinds of institutions (e.g., Bible colleges, independent colleges, and rabbinical and Talmudic schools). Program registration by the New York State Board of Regents is considered to be the equivalent of institutional accreditation, since the board requires that all programs offered by an institution meet its standards before recognition is granted. A Canadian institution must be chartered and authorized to grant degrees by the provincial government, affiliated with a chartered institution, or accredited by a recognized U.S. accrediting body. This guide also includes institutions outside the United States that are accredited by these U.S. accrediting bodies. There are recognized specialized or professional accrediting bodies in more than fifty different fields, each of which is authorized to accredit institutions or specific programs in its particular field. For specialized institutions that offer programs in one field only, we designate this to be the equivalent of institutional accreditation. A full explanation of the accrediting process and complete information on recognized institutional (regional and national) and specialized accrediting bodies can be found online at www.chea.org or at www.ed.gov/admins/finaid/accred/index.html.

Peterson's Graduate Programs in the Physical Sciences, Mathematics, Agricultural Sciences, the Environment & Natural Resources 2013

facebook.com/petersonspublishing **17**

DIRECTORY OF INSTITUTIONS WITH PROGRAMS IN THE PHYSICAL SCIENCES, MATHEMATICS, AGRICULTURAL SCIENCES, THE ENVIRONMENT & NATURAL RESOURCES

ACADIA UNIVERSITY
Applied Mathematics	M
Chemistry	M
Geology	M
Statistics	M

ADELPHI UNIVERSITY
Environmental Management and Policy	M*

AIR FORCE INSTITUTE OF TECHNOLOGY
Applied Mathematics	M,D
Applied Physics	M,D
Astrophysics	M,D
Environmental Management and Policy	M
Optical Sciences	M,D
Planetary and Space Sciences	M,D

ALABAMA AGRICULTURAL AND MECHANICAL UNIVERSITY
Agricultural Sciences— General	M,D
Agronomy and Soil Sciences	M,D
Applied Physics	M,D
Food Science and Technology	M,D
Optical Sciences	M,D
Physics	M,D
Plant Sciences	M,D

ALABAMA STATE UNIVERSITY
Environmental Sciences	M,D
Geology	M,D
Geosciences	M,D
Mathematics	M,O

ALASKA PACIFIC UNIVERSITY
Environmental Sciences	M

ALBANY STATE UNIVERSITY
Water Resources	M

ALCORN STATE UNIVERSITY
Agricultural Sciences— General	M
Agronomy and Soil Sciences	M
Animal Sciences	M

AMERICAN PUBLIC UNIVERSITY SYSTEM
Environmental Management and Policy	M
Fish, Game, and Wildlife Management	M
Marine Affairs	M
Planetary and Space Sciences	M

AMERICAN UNIVERSITY
Applied Statistics	M,O
Environmental Management and Policy	M,D,O
Environmental Sciences	M,O
Mathematics	M,O
Natural Resources	M,D,O
Statistics	M,O

THE AMERICAN UNIVERSITY IN CAIRO
Chemistry	M

AMERICAN UNIVERSITY OF BEIRUT
Agronomy and Soil Sciences	M
Animal Sciences	M
Aquaculture	M
Biostatistics	M
Chemistry	M
Computational Sciences	M
Environmental Management and Policy	M

Environmental Sciences	M,D
Food Science and Technology	M
Geology	M
Mathematics	M
Physics	M
Plant Sciences	M
Statistics	M

ANDREWS UNIVERSITY
Mathematics	M

ANGELO STATE UNIVERSITY
Agricultural Sciences— General	M
Animal Sciences	M

ANTIOCH UNIVERSITY NEW ENGLAND
Environmental Management and Policy	M,D
Environmental Sciences	M,D

ANTIOCH UNIVERSITY SEATTLE
Environmental Management and Policy	M

APPALACHIAN STATE UNIVERSITY
Environmental Management and Policy	M
Mathematics	M

AQUINAS COLLEGE
Environmental Management and Policy	M

ARIZONA STATE UNIVERSITY
Applied Mathematics	M,D,O
Astrophysics	M,D
Atmospheric Sciences	M,D,O
Chemistry	M,D
Environmental Management and Policy	M
Environmental Sciences	M,D,O
Geology	M,D
Geosciences	M,D
Mathematics	M,D
Physics	M,D
Planetary and Space Sciences	M,D
Statistics	M,D,O

ARKANSAS STATE UNIVERSITY
Agricultural Sciences— General	M,O
Chemistry	M,O
Environmental Sciences	M,D
Mathematics	M

ARKANSAS TECH UNIVERSITY
Fish, Game, and Wildlife Management	M

AUBURN UNIVERSITY
Agricultural Sciences— General	M,D
Agronomy and Soil Sciences	M,D
Analytical Chemistry	M,D
Animal Sciences	M,D
Applied Mathematics	M,D
Aquaculture	M,D
Chemistry	M,D
Fish, Game, and Wildlife Management	M,D
Food Science and Technology	M,D,O
Forestry	M,D
Geology	M
Horticulture	M,D
Hydrology	M,D
Inorganic Chemistry	M,D
Mathematics	M,D
Natural Resources	M,D
Organic Chemistry	M,D

Physical Chemistry	M,D
Physics	M,D
Statistics	M,D

AURORA UNIVERSITY
Mathematics	M

BALL STATE UNIVERSITY
Chemistry	M
Environmental Sciences	D
Geology	M
Mathematics	M
Natural Resources	M
Physics	M
Statistics	M

BARD COLLEGE
Atmospheric Sciences	M,O
Environmental Management and Policy	M,O

BAYLOR UNIVERSITY
Chemistry	M,D
Environmental Management and Policy	M
Environmental Sciences	D
Geology	M,D
Geosciences	M,D
Limnology	M,D
Mathematics	M,D
Physics	M,D
Statistics	M,D

BEMIDJI STATE UNIVERSITY
Environmental Management and Policy	M
Mathematics	M

BERNARD M. BARUCH COLLEGE OF THE CITY UNIVERSITY OF NEW YORK
Mathematical and Computational Finance	M
Statistics	M

BOISE STATE UNIVERSITY
Animal Sciences	M
Environmental Management and Policy	M
Geology	M,D
Geophysics	M,D
Geosciences	M

BOSTON COLLEGE
Chemistry	M,D
Geology	M
Geophysics	M
Inorganic Chemistry	M,D
Mathematics	D
Organic Chemistry	M,D
Physical Chemistry	M,D
Physics	M,D

BOSTON UNIVERSITY
Astronomy	M,D
Biostatistics	M,D
Chemistry	M,D
Environmental Management and Policy	M,D,O
Food Science and Technology	M
Geosciences	M,D
Mathematical and Computational Finance	M,D
Mathematics	M,D
Photonics	M,D
Physics	M,D

BOWIE STATE UNIVERSITY
Applied Mathematics	M

BOWLING GREEN STATE UNIVERSITY
Applied Statistics	M,D

Chemistry	M,D
Geology	M
Geophysics	M
Mathematics	M,D
Physics	M
Statistics	M,D

BRADLEY UNIVERSITY
Chemistry	M

BRANDEIS UNIVERSITY
Chemistry	M,D
Inorganic Chemistry	M,D
Mathematics	M,D,O
Organic Chemistry	M,D
Physical Chemistry	M,D
Physics	M,D

BRIGHAM YOUNG UNIVERSITY
Agricultural Sciences— General	M,D
Analytical Chemistry	M,D
Animal Sciences	M,D
Applied Statistics	M
Astronomy	M,D
Chemistry	M,D
Environmental Sciences	M,D
Fish, Game, and Wildlife Management	M,D
Food Science and Technology	M
Geology	M,D
Mathematics	M,D
Physics	M,D
Plant Sciences	M,D
Statistics	M

BROCK UNIVERSITY
Chemistry	M,D
Geosciences	M
Mathematics	M
Physics	M
Statistics	M

BROOKLYN COLLEGE OF THE CITY UNIVERSITY OF NEW YORK
Chemistry	M,D
Geology	M,D
Geosciences	M,O
Mathematics	M,D
Physics	M,D

BROWN UNIVERSITY
Applied Mathematics	M,D
Biostatistics	M,D
Chemistry	M,D
Geosciences	M,D
Mathematics	M,D
Physics	M,D

BRYN MAWR COLLEGE
Chemistry	M,D
Mathematics	M,D
Physics	M,D

BUCKNELL UNIVERSITY
Chemistry	M
Mathematics	M

BUFFALO STATE COLLEGE, STATE UNIVERSITY OF NEW YORK
Chemistry	M

CALIFORNIA INSTITUTE OF TECHNOLOGY
Applied Mathematics	M,D
Applied Physics	M,D
Astronomy	D
Chemistry	M,D
Computational Sciences	M,D
Environmental Sciences	M,D
Geochemistry	M,D
Geology	M,D
Geophysics	M,D

20 facebook.com/petersonspublishing

Petersons Graduate Programs in the Physical Sciences, Mathematics,
Agricultural Sciences, the Environment & Natural Resources 2013

Mathematics	D
Physics	D
Planetary and Space Sciences	M,D

CALIFORNIA POLYTECHNIC STATE UNIVERSITY, SAN LUIS OBISPO

Agricultural Sciences—General	M
Chemistry	M
Forestry	M
Mathematics	M
Natural Resources	M

CALIFORNIA STATE POLYTECHNIC UNIVERSITY, POMONA

Agricultural Sciences—General	M
Applied Mathematics	M
Chemistry	M
Environmental Sciences	M
Mathematics	M

CALIFORNIA STATE UNIVERSITY, BAKERSFIELD

Geology	M,O
Hydrogeology	M,O
Hydrology	M,O

CALIFORNIA STATE UNIVERSITY CHANNEL ISLANDS

Mathematics	M

CALIFORNIA STATE UNIVERSITY, CHICO

Environmental Management and Policy	M
Environmental Sciences	M
Geology	M
Geosciences	M
Hydrogeology	M
Hydrology	M

CALIFORNIA STATE UNIVERSITY, DOMINGUEZ HILLS

Environmental Sciences	M

CALIFORNIA STATE UNIVERSITY, EAST BAY

Applied Mathematics	M
Applied Statistics	M
Biostatistics	M
Chemistry	M
Environmental Sciences	M
Geology	M
Marine Sciences	M
Mathematics	M
Statistics	M

CALIFORNIA STATE UNIVERSITY, FRESNO

Animal Sciences	M
Chemistry	M
Food Science and Technology	M
Geology	M
Marine Sciences	M
Mathematics	M
Physics	M
Plant Sciences	M
Viticulture and Enology	M

CALIFORNIA STATE UNIVERSITY, FULLERTON

Applied Mathematics	M
Chemistry	M
Environmental Management and Policy	M
Environmental Sciences	M
Geochemistry	M
Geology	M

Mathematics	M
Physics	M

CALIFORNIA STATE UNIVERSITY, LONG BEACH

Applied Mathematics	M,D
Applied Statistics	M
Chemistry	M
Food Science and Technology	M
Geology	M
Geophysics	M
Mathematics	M
Physics	M

CALIFORNIA STATE UNIVERSITY, LOS ANGELES

Analytical Chemistry	M
Applied Mathematics	M
Chemistry	M
Geology	M
Inorganic Chemistry	M
Mathematics	M
Organic Chemistry	M
Physical Chemistry	M
Physics	M

CALIFORNIA STATE UNIVERSITY, MONTEREY BAY

Marine Sciences	M
Water Resources	M

CALIFORNIA STATE UNIVERSITY, NORTHRIDGE

Applied Mathematics	M
Chemistry	M
Environmental Sciences	M
Geology	M
Mathematics	M
Physics	M

CALIFORNIA STATE UNIVERSITY, SACRAMENTO

Chemistry	M
Marine Sciences	M
Mathematics	M
Statistics	M

CALIFORNIA STATE UNIVERSITY, SAN BERNARDINO

Chemistry	M
Environmental Sciences	M
Mathematics	M

CALIFORNIA STATE UNIVERSITY, SAN MARCOS

Mathematics	M

CARLETON UNIVERSITY

Chemistry	M,D
Geosciences	M,D
Mathematics	M,D
Physics	M,D

CARNEGIE MELLON UNIVERSITY

Applied Mathematics	M,D
Applied Physics	M,D
Chemistry	M,D
Computational Sciences	D
Inorganic Chemistry	M,D
Mathematical and Computational Finance	M,D
Mathematics	M,D
Organic Chemistry	M,D
Physics	M,D
Statistics	M,D
Theoretical Chemistry	M,D

CASE WESTERN RESERVE UNIVERSITY

Applied Mathematics	M,D
Astronomy	M,D

Biostatistics	M,D
Chemistry	M,D
Geology	M,D
Geosciences	M,D
Mathematics	M,D
Physics	M,D
Statistics	M,D

THE CATHOLIC UNIVERSITY OF AMERICA

Physics	M,D

CENTRAL CONNECTICUT STATE UNIVERSITY

Chemistry	M,O
Geosciences	M,O
Mathematics	M,O
Physics	M,O
Statistics	M,O

CENTRAL EUROPEAN UNIVERSITY

Applied Mathematics	M,D
Environmental Management and Policy	M,D
Mathematics	M,D

CENTRAL MICHIGAN UNIVERSITY

Chemistry	M
Mathematics	M,D
Physics	M,D

CENTRAL WASHINGTON UNIVERSITY

Chemistry	M
Geology	M
Mathematics	M
Natural Resources	M

CHAPMAN UNIVERSITY

Computational Sciences	M
Food Science and Technology	M
Geosciences	M

CHICAGO STATE UNIVERSITY

Mathematics	M

CHRISTOPHER NEWPORT UNIVERSITY

Applied Physics	M
Chemistry	M
Environmental Sciences	M
Physics	M

CITY COLLEGE OF THE CITY UNIVERSITY OF NEW YORK

Atmospheric Sciences	M,D
Chemistry	M,D
Environmental Sciences	M,D
Geosciences	M,D
Mathematics	M
Physics	M,D

CLAREMONT GRADUATE UNIVERSITY

Applied Mathematics	M,D
Computational Sciences	M,D
Mathematics	M,D
Statistics	M,D

CLARION UNIVERSITY OF PENNSYLVANIA

Environmental Sciences	M

CLARK ATLANTA UNIVERSITY

Chemistry	M,D
Mathematics	M
Physics	M

CLARKSON UNIVERSITY

Chemistry	M,D
Environmental Management and Policy	M
Environmental Sciences	M,D
Mathematics	M,D
Physics	M,D

CLARK UNIVERSITY

Chemistry	M,D
Environmental Management and Policy	M
Physics	M,D

CLEMSON UNIVERSITY

Agricultural Sciences—General	M,D
Animal Sciences	M,D
Applied Mathematics	M,D
Aquaculture	M,D
Astronomy	M,D
Astrophysics	M,D
Atmospheric Sciences	M,D
Chemistry	M,D
Computational Sciences	M,D
Environmental Management and Policy	M,D
Environmental Sciences	M,D
Fish, Game, and Wildlife Management	M,D
Food Science and Technology	M,D
Forestry	M,D
Hydrogeology	M
Mathematics	M,D
Physics	M,D
Plant Sciences	M,D
Statistics	M,D

CLEVELAND STATE UNIVERSITY

Analytical Chemistry	M,D
Chemistry	M,D
Condensed Matter Physics	M
Environmental Management and Policy	M,O
Environmental Sciences	M,D
Inorganic Chemistry	M,D
Mathematics	M
Optical Sciences	M
Organic Chemistry	M,D
Physical Chemistry	M,D
Physics	M

COASTAL CAROLINA UNIVERSITY

Marine Sciences	M

THE COLLEGE AT BROCKPORT, STATE UNIVERSITY OF NEW YORK

Environmental Sciences	M
Mathematics	M

COLLEGE OF CHARLESTON

Environmental Sciences	M
Marine Sciences	M
Mathematics	M,O

COLLEGE OF STATEN ISLAND OF THE CITY UNIVERSITY OF NEW YORK

Environmental Sciences	M

COLLEGE OF THE ATLANTIC

Environmental Management and Policy	M

THE COLLEGE OF WILLIAM AND MARY

Chemistry	M
Computational Sciences	M
Marine Sciences	M,D
Physics	M,D

---

*M—master's degree; P—first professional degree; D—doctorate; O—other advanced degree; *—Close-Up and/or Display*

Petersons Graduate Programs in the Physical Sciences, Mathematics, Agricultural Sciences, the Environment & Natural Resources 2013

facebook.com/petersonspublishing **21**

COLORADO SCHOOL OF MINES

Applied Physics	M,D
Chemistry	M,D
Environmental Sciences	M,D
Geochemistry	M,D
Geology	M,D
Geophysics	M,D
Mathematics	M,D
Physics	M,D

COLORADO STATE UNIVERSITY

Agricultural Sciences— General	M,D
Agronomy and Soil Sciences	M,D
Animal Sciences	M,D
Atmospheric Sciences	M,D
Chemistry	M,D
Fish, Game, and Wildlife Management	M,D
Food Science and Technology	M,D
Forestry	M,D
Geosciences	M,D
Horticulture	M,D
Hydrology	M,D
Mathematics	M,D
Natural Resources	M,D
Physics	M,D
Plant Sciences	M,D
Range Science	M,D
Statistics	M,D
Water Resources	M,D

COLORADO STATE UNIVERSITY–PUEBLO

Chemistry	M

COLUMBIA UNIVERSITY

Applied Mathematics	M,D,O
Applied Physics	M,D,O
Astronomy	M,D
Atmospheric Sciences	M,D
Biostatistics	M,D
Chemical Physics	M,D
Chemistry	M,D
Environmental Management and Policy	M
Environmental Sciences	M
Geochemistry	M,D
Geodetic Sciences	M,D
Geophysics	M,D
Geosciences	M,D
Inorganic Chemistry	M,D
Mathematics	M,D
Meteorology	M
Oceanography	M,D
Organic Chemistry	M,D
Physics	M,D
Planetary and Space Sciences	M,D
Statistics	M,D

COLUMBUS STATE UNIVERSITY

Environmental Sciences	M

CONCORDIA UNIVERSITY (CANADA)

Chemistry	M,D
Environmental Management and Policy	M,O
Mathematics	M,D
Physics	M,D

CORNELL UNIVERSITY

Agronomy and Soil Sciences	M,D
Analytical Chemistry	D
Animal Sciences	M,D
Applied Mathematics	M,D
Applied Physics	M,D
Applied Statistics	M,D
Astronomy	D
Astrophysics	D
Atmospheric Sciences	M,D
Biometry	M,D
Chemical Physics	D
Chemistry	D
Computational Sciences	M,D
Environmental Management and Policy	M,D
Environmental Sciences	M,D
Fish, Game, and Wildlife Management	M,D
Food Science and Technology	M,D
Forestry	M,D
Geochemistry	M,D
Geology	M,D
Geophysics	M,D
Geosciences	M,D
Horticulture	M,D
Hydrology	M,D
Inorganic Chemistry	D
Limnology	D
Marine Geology	M,D
Marine Sciences	M,D
Mathematics	D
Mineralogy	M,D
Natural Resources	M,D
Oceanography	D
Organic Chemistry	D
Paleontology	M,D
Physical Chemistry	D
Physics	M,D
Planetary and Space Sciences	D
Plant Sciences	M,D
Statistics	M,D
Theoretical Chemistry	D
Theoretical Physics	M,D

CREIGHTON UNIVERSITY

Atmospheric Sciences	M
Physics	M

DALHOUSIE UNIVERSITY

Agricultural Sciences— General	M
Applied Mathematics	M,D
Chemistry	M,D
Environmental Management and Policy	M
Food Science and Technology	M,D
Geosciences	M,D
Marine Affairs	M
Mathematics	M,D
Natural Resources	M
Oceanography	M,D
Physics	M,D
Statistics	M,D

DARTMOUTH COLLEGE

Astronomy	M,D
Chemistry	D
Geosciences	M,D
Mathematics	D
Physics	M,D

DELAWARE STATE UNIVERSITY

Applied Mathematics	M,D
Chemistry	M
Mathematics	M
Natural Resources	M
Optical Sciences	M,D
Physics	M,D
Plant Sciences	M
Theoretical Physics	D

DEPAUL UNIVERSITY

Applied Mathematics	M,O
Applied Physics	M
Applied Statistics	M,O
Chemistry	M
Mathematical and Computational Finance	M,D
Mathematics	M,O
Physics	M

DOWLING COLLEGE

Mathematics	M

DREW UNIVERSITY

Chemistry	M
Physics	M

DREXEL UNIVERSITY

Biostatistics	M,D,O
Chemistry	M,D
Environmental Management and Policy	M
Environmental Sciences	M,D
Food Science and Technology	M
Hydrology	M,D
Mathematics	M,D
Physics	M,D

DUKE UNIVERSITY

Biostatistics	M
Chemistry	D
Environmental Management and Policy	M,D
Environmental Sciences	M,D
Forestry	M
Geology	M,D
Marine Affairs	M
Marine Sciences	M
Mathematics	D
Natural Resources	M,D
Optical Sciences	M
Paleontology	D
Photonics	M
Physics	M,D
Statistics	D
Water Resources	M

DUQUESNE UNIVERSITY

Chemistry	M,D
Environmental Management and Policy	M,O
Environmental Sciences	M,O
Mathematics	M

EAST CAROLINA UNIVERSITY

Applied Physics	M,D
Chemistry	M
Geology	M,O
Hydrogeology	M,O
Mathematics	M,O
Physics	M,D
Statistics	M,O

EASTERN ILLINOIS UNIVERSITY

Chemistry	M
Mathematics	M

EASTERN KENTUCKY UNIVERSITY

Chemistry	M
Geology	M,D
Mathematics	M

EASTERN MICHIGAN UNIVERSITY

Applied Statistics	M
Chemistry	M
Geosciences	M
Mathematics	M
Physics	M
Water Resources	M,O

EASTERN NEW MEXICO UNIVERSITY

Analytical Chemistry	M
Chemistry	M
Inorganic Chemistry	M
Mathematics	M
Organic Chemistry	M
Physical Chemistry	M

EASTERN WASHINGTON UNIVERSITY

Mathematics	M

EAST TENNESSEE STATE UNIVERSITY

Biostatistics	M,O
Chemistry	M
Geosciences	M
Mathematics	M
Paleontology	M

ÉCOLE POLYTECHNIQUE DE MONTRÉAL

Applied Mathematics	M,D,O
Optical Sciences	M,D,O

ELIZABETH CITY STATE UNIVERSITY

Mathematics	M

EMORY UNIVERSITY

Biostatistics	M,D
Chemistry	D
Computational Sciences	D
Mathematics	M,D
Physics	D
Theoretical Physics	D

EMPORIA STATE UNIVERSITY

Geosciences	M,O
Mathematics	M

THE EVERGREEN STATE COLLEGE

Environmental Management and Policy	M

FAIRFIELD UNIVERSITY

Mathematics	M

FAIRLEIGH DICKINSON UNIVERSITY, COLLEGE AT FLORHAM

Chemistry	M

FAIRLEIGH DICKINSON UNIVERSITY, METROPOLITAN CAMPUS

Chemistry	M
Mathematics	M

FAYETTEVILLE STATE UNIVERSITY

Mathematics	M

FISK UNIVERSITY

Chemistry	M
Physics	M

FLORIDA AGRICULTURAL AND MECHANICAL UNIVERSITY

Chemistry	M
Environmental Sciences	M,D
Physics	M,D

FLORIDA ATLANTIC UNIVERSITY

Applied Mathematics	M,D
Chemistry	M,D
Environmental Management and Policy	M,O
Environmental Sciences	M
Geology	M,D
Geosciences	M,D
Mathematics	M,D
Physics	M,D
Statistics	M,D

FLORIDA GULF COAST UNIVERSITY

Environmental Management and Policy	M
Environmental Sciences	M

FLORIDA INSTITUTE OF TECHNOLOGY

Applied Mathematics	M,D
Chemistry	M,D
Environmental Management and Policy	M,D
Environmental Sciences	M,D
Marine Sciences	M,D
Meteorology	M,D

Oceanography	M,D
Physics	M,D
Planetary and Space Sciences	M,D

FLORIDA INTERNATIONAL UNIVERSITY

Biostatistics	M,D
Chemistry	M,D
Environmental Management and Policy	M
Environmental Sciences	M
Geosciences	M,D
Mathematics	M
Physics	M,D
Statistics	M

FLORIDA STATE UNIVERSITY

Analytical Chemistry	M,D
Applied Mathematics	M,D
Applied Statistics	M,D
Atmospheric Sciences	M,D
Biostatistics	M,D
Chemistry	M,D
Computational Sciences	M,D
Environmental Sciences	M,D
Food Science and Technology	M,D
Geology	M,D
Geophysics	D
Geosciences	M,D
Inorganic Chemistry	M,D
Marine Sciences	M,D
Mathematical and Computational Finance	M,D
Mathematics	M,D
Meteorology	M,D
Oceanography	M,D
Organic Chemistry	M,D
Physical Chemistry	M,D
Physics	M,D
Statistics	M,D,O

FORT HAYS STATE UNIVERSITY

Geology	M
Geosciences	M

FORT VALLEY STATE UNIVERSITY

Animal Sciences	M

FRAMINGHAM STATE UNIVERSITY

Food Science and Technology	M

FRIENDS UNIVERSITY

Environmental Sciences	M

FROSTBURG STATE UNIVERSITY

Fish, Game, and Wildlife Management	M

FURMAN UNIVERSITY

Chemistry	M

GANNON UNIVERSITY

Environmental Sciences	M,O

GEORGE MASON UNIVERSITY

Applied Physics	M,D,O
Atmospheric Sciences	D
Biostatistics	M,O
Chemistry	M,D
Computational Sciences	M,D,O
Environmental Management and Policy	M,D,O
Environmental Sciences	M,D,O
Geosciences	M,D,O
Mathematics	M,D,O
Physics	M,D,O
Statistics	M,D,O

GEORGETOWN UNIVERSITY

Analytical Chemistry	D

Biostatistics	M
Chemistry	D
Inorganic Chemistry	D
Mathematics	M
Organic Chemistry	D
Physical Chemistry	D
Statistics	M
Theoretical Chemistry	D

THE GEORGE WASHINGTON UNIVERSITY

Analytical Chemistry	M,D
Applied Mathematics	M,D
Biostatistics	M,D
Chemistry	M,D
Environmental Management and Policy	M
Inorganic Chemistry	M,D
Mathematics	M,D
Organic Chemistry	M,D
Physical Chemistry	M,D
Physics	M,D
Statistics	M,D,O

GEORGIA HEALTH SCIENCES UNIVERSITY

Biostatistics	M,D

GEORGIA INSTITUTE OF TECHNOLOGY

Applied Mathematics	M,D
Atmospheric Sciences	M,D
Chemistry	M,D
Environmental Management and Policy	M,D
Environmental Sciences	M,D
Geochemistry	M,D
Geophysics	M,D
Geosciences	M,D
Marine Sciences	M,D
Mathematical and Computational Finance	M,D
Mathematics	M,D
Meteorology	M,D
Natural Resources	M,D
Oceanography	M,D
Physics	M,D
Planetary and Space Sciences	M,D
Statistics	M,D

GEORGIAN COURT UNIVERSITY

Mathematics	M,O

GEORGIA SOUTHERN UNIVERSITY

Biostatistics	M,D
Mathematics	M

GEORGIA STATE UNIVERSITY

Astronomy	D
Chemistry	M,D
Geology	M
Geosciences	M,O
Hydrogeology	M,O
Mathematics	M,D
Physics	M,D
Statistics	M,D

GODDARD COLLEGE

Environmental Management and Policy	M

GOVERNORS STATE UNIVERSITY

Analytical Chemistry	M

GRADUATE SCHOOL AND UNIVERSITY CENTER OF THE CITY UNIVERSITY OF NEW YORK

Chemistry	D
Environmental Sciences	D
Geosciences	D

Mathematics	D
Physics	D

GRAND VALLEY STATE UNIVERSITY

Biostatistics	M

GREEN MOUNTAIN COLLEGE

Environmental Management and Policy	M

HAMPTON UNIVERSITY

Applied Mathematics	M
Atmospheric Sciences	M,D
Chemistry	M
Computational Sciences	M
Physics	M,D
Planetary and Space Sciences	M,D
Statistics	M

HARDIN-SIMMONS UNIVERSITY

Environmental Management and Policy	M
Mathematics	M,D

HARVARD UNIVERSITY

Applied Mathematics	M,D
Applied Physics	M,D
Astronomy	D
Astrophysics	D
Biostatistics	M,D
Chemical Physics	D
Chemistry	D*
Environmental Management and Policy	M,O
Environmental Sciences	M,D
Forestry	M
Geosciences	M,D
Inorganic Chemistry	D
Mathematics	D
Organic Chemistry	D
Physical Chemistry	D
Physics	D
Planetary and Space Sciences	M,D
Statistics	M,D
Theoretical Physics	D

HAWAI`I PACIFIC UNIVERSITY

Marine Sciences	M*

HOFSTRA UNIVERSITY

Chemistry	M,O
Geology	M,O
Geosciences	M,O
Physics	M,O

HOWARD UNIVERSITY

Analytical Chemistry	M,D
Applied Mathematics	M,D
Atmospheric Sciences	M,D
Chemistry	M,D
Environmental Sciences	M,D
Inorganic Chemistry	M,D
Mathematics	M,D
Organic Chemistry	M,D
Physical Chemistry	M,D
Physics	M,D

HUMBOLDT STATE UNIVERSITY

Environmental Management and Policy	M
Environmental Sciences	M
Fish, Game, and Wildlife Management	M
Forestry	M
Geology	M
Natural Resources	M
Water Resources	M

HUNTER COLLEGE OF THE CITY UNIVERSITY OF NEW YORK

Applied Mathematics	M
Biostatistics	M
Chemistry	M,D
Environmental Sciences	M,O
Geosciences	M,O
Mathematics	M
Physics	M,D

ICR GRADUATE SCHOOL

Astrophysics	M
Geology	M
Geophysics	M

IDAHO STATE UNIVERSITY

Applied Physics	M,D
Chemistry	M
Environmental Management and Policy	M
Environmental Sciences	M,O
Geology	M,O
Geophysics	M,O
Geosciences	M,O
Hydrology	M,O
Mathematics	M,D
Physics	M,D

ILLINOIS INSTITUTE OF TECHNOLOGY

Analytical Chemistry	M,D
Applied Mathematics	M,D
Chemistry	M,D
Environmental Management and Policy	M
Food Science and Technology	M
Mathematical and Computational Finance	M
Physics	M,D

ILLINOIS STATE UNIVERSITY

Agricultural Sciences— General	M
Chemistry	M
Hydrogeology	M
Hydrology	M
Mathematics	M
Plant Sciences	M,D

INDIANA STATE UNIVERSITY

Mathematics	M

INDIANA UNIVERSITY BLOOMINGTON

Analytical Chemistry	M,D
Applied Mathematics	M,D
Applied Statistics	M,D
Astronomy	M,D
Astrophysics	M,D
Biostatistics	M,D
Chemistry	M,D
Environmental Management and Policy	M,D,O
Environmental Sciences	M,D
Geochemistry	M,D
Geology	M,D
Geophysics	M,D
Geosciences	M,D
Hydrogeology	M,D
Inorganic Chemistry	M,D
Mathematics	M,D
Mineralogy	M,D
Organic Chemistry	M,D
Physical Chemistry	M,D
Physics	M,D
Statistics	M,D

INDIANA UNIVERSITY OF PENNSYLVANIA

Applied Mathematics	M
Chemistry	M
Environmental Management and Policy	M

---

*M—master's degree; P—first professional degree; D—doctorate; O—other advanced degree; *—Close-Up and/or Display*

Petersons Graduate Programs in the Physical Sciences, Mathematics, Agricultural Sciences, the Environment & Natural Resources 2013

facebook.com/petersonspublishing **23**

Mathematics	M
Physics	M

INDIANA UNIVERSITY–PURDUE UNIVERSITY FORT WAYNE

Applied Mathematics	M,O
Applied Statistics	M,O
Mathematics	M,O

INDIANA UNIVERSITY–PURDUE UNIVERSITY INDIANAPOLIS

Applied Mathematics	M,D
Applied Statistics	M
Biostatistics	D
Chemistry	M,D
Geology	M,D
Geosciences	M,D
Mathematics	M,D
Physics	M,D
Statistics	D

INDIANA UNIVERSITY SOUTH BEND

Applied Mathematics	M

INSTITUTO TECNOLOGICO DE SANTO DOMINGO

Environmental Management and Policy	M,D,O
Environmental Sciences	M,D,O
Marine Sciences	M,D,O
Mathematics	M,D,O
Natural Resources	M,D,O

INSTITUTO TECNOLÓGICO Y DE ESTUDIOS SUPERIORES DE MONTERREY, CAMPUS CIUDAD DE MÉXICO

Environmental Sciences	M,D

INSTITUTO TECNOLÓGICO Y DE ESTUDIOS SUPERIORES DE MONTERREY, CAMPUS ESTADO DE MÉXICO

Environmental Management and Policy	M,D

INSTITUTO TECNOLÓGICO Y DE ESTUDIOS SUPERIORES DE MONTERREY, CAMPUS IRAPUATO

Environmental Management and Policy	M,D

INSTITUTO TECNOLÓGICO Y DE ESTUDIOS SUPERIORES DE MONTERREY, CAMPUS MONTERREY

Agricultural Sciences— General	M,D
Applied Statistics	M,D
Chemistry	M,D
Organic Chemistry	M,D

INTER AMERICAN UNIVERSITY OF PUERTO RICO, METROPOLITAN CAMPUS

Environmental Management and Policy	M

INTER AMERICAN UNIVERSITY OF PUERTO RICO, SAN GERMÁN CAMPUS

Environmental Sciences	M

IOWA STATE UNIVERSITY OF SCIENCE AND TECHNOLOGY

Agricultural Sciences— General	M,D
Agronomy and Soil Sciences	M,D
Analytical Chemistry	D
Animal Sciences	M,D
Applied Mathematics	M,D

Applied Physics	M,D
Astrophysics	M,D
Biostatistics	M,D
Chemistry	M,D
Condensed Matter Physics	M,D
Environmental Sciences	M,D
Fish, Game, and Wildlife Management	M,D
Food Science and Technology	M,D
Forestry	M,D
Geology	M,D
Geosciences	M,D
Horticulture	M,D
Inorganic Chemistry	M,D
Mathematics	M,D
Meteorology	M,D
Natural Resources	M,D
Organic Chemistry	M,D
Physical Chemistry	M,D
Physics	M,D
Plant Sciences	M,D
Statistics	M,D

JACKSON STATE UNIVERSITY

Chemistry	M,D
Environmental Sciences	M,D
Mathematics	M

JACKSONVILLE STATE UNIVERSITY

Mathematics	M

JACKSONVILLE UNIVERSITY

Marine Sciences	M

JAMES MADISON UNIVERSITY

Mathematics	M
Statistics	M

JOHN CARROLL UNIVERSITY

Mathematics	M

THE JOHNS HOPKINS UNIVERSITY

Applied Mathematics	M,D,O
Applied Physics	M,O
Astronomy	D
Biostatistics	M,D
Chemistry	D
Environmental Management and Policy	M,O
Environmental Sciences	M
Geosciences	M,D
Mathematical and Computational Finance	M,D
Mathematics	D
Physics	D
Statistics	M,D

KANSAS STATE UNIVERSITY

Agricultural Sciences— General	M,D
Agronomy and Soil Sciences	M,D
Analytical Chemistry	M,D
Animal Sciences	M,D
Chemistry	M,D
Food Science and Technology	M,D
Geology	M
Horticulture	M,D
Inorganic Chemistry	M,D
Mathematics	M,D
Organic Chemistry	M,D
Physical Chemistry	M,D
Plant Sciences	M,D
Range Science	M,D
Statistics	M,D

KEAN UNIVERSITY

Environmental Management and Policy	M

KENNESAW STATE UNIVERSITY

Applied Statistics	M

KENT STATE UNIVERSITY

Analytical Chemistry	M,D
Applied Mathematics	M,D
Chemical Physics	M,D
Chemistry	M,D*
Geology	M,D
Inorganic Chemistry	M,D
Mathematics	M,D
Organic Chemistry	M,D
Physical Chemistry	M,D
Physics	M,D

KENTUCKY STATE UNIVERSITY

Aquaculture	M
Environmental Management and Policy	M

LAKEHEAD UNIVERSITY

Chemistry	M
Forestry	M,D
Geology	M
Mathematics	M
Physics	M

LAMAR UNIVERSITY

Chemistry	M
Environmental Management and Policy	M,D
Mathematics	M

LAURENTIAN UNIVERSITY

Analytical Chemistry	M
Applied Physics	M
Chemistry	M
Environmental Sciences	M
Geology	M,D
Natural Resources	M,D
Organic Chemistry	M
Physical Chemistry	M
Theoretical Chemistry	M

LEHIGH UNIVERSITY

Applied Mathematics	M,D
Chemistry	M,D
Computational Sciences	M,D
Environmental Management and Policy	M,O
Environmental Sciences	M,D
Geology	M,D
Geosciences	M,D
Mathematics	M,D
Photonics	M,D
Physics	M,D
Statistics	M,D

LEHMAN COLLEGE OF THE CITY UNIVERSITY OF NEW YORK

Mathematics	M
Plant Sciences	D

LOMA LINDA UNIVERSITY

Biostatistics	M,D,O
Geosciences	M,D

LONG ISLAND UNIVERSITY–BROOKLYN CAMPUS

Chemistry	M

LONG ISLAND UNIVERSITY– C. W. POST CAMPUS

Applied Mathematics	M
Environmental Management and Policy	M
Geosciences	M
Mathematics	M

LOUISIANA STATE UNIVERSITY AND AGRICULTURAL AND MECHANICAL COLLEGE

Agricultural Sciences— General	M,D
Agronomy and Soil Sciences	M,D
Animal Sciences	M,D

Applied Statistics	M
Astronomy	M,D
Astrophysics	M,D
Chemistry	M,D
Environmental Management and Policy	M
Environmental Sciences	M,D
Fish, Game, and Wildlife Management	M,D
Food Science and Technology	M,D
Forestry	M,D
Geology	M,D
Geophysics	M,D
Horticulture	M,D
Marine Affairs	M,D
Mathematics	M,D
Natural Resources	M,D
Oceanography	M,D
Physics	M,D
Statistics	M

LOUISIANA STATE UNIVERSITY HEALTH SCIENCES CENTER

Biostatistics	M,D

LOUISIANA TECH UNIVERSITY

Chemistry	M
Mathematics	M
Physics	M,D
Statistics	M

LOYOLA MARYMOUNT UNIVERSITY

Environmental Sciences	M

LOYOLA UNIVERSITY CHICAGO

Applied Statistics	M
Chemistry	M,D
Mathematics	M
Statistics	M

MARQUETTE UNIVERSITY

Analytical Chemistry	M,D
Chemical Physics	M,D
Chemistry	M,D
Computational Sciences	M,D
Inorganic Chemistry	M,D
Mathematics	M,D
Organic Chemistry	M,D
Physical Chemistry	M,D
Water Resources	M,D,O

MARSHALL UNIVERSITY

Chemistry	M
Environmental Sciences	M
Mathematics	M
Physics	M

MARYLHURST UNIVERSITY

Environmental Management and Policy	M
Natural Resources	M

MASSACHUSETTS COLLEGE OF PHARMACY AND HEALTH SCIENCES

Chemistry	M,D

MASSACHUSETTS INSTITUTE OF TECHNOLOGY

Atmospheric Sciences	M,D
Chemistry	D
Computational Sciences	M
Environmental Sciences	M,D,O
Geochemistry	M,D
Geology	M,D
Geophysics	M,D
Geosciences	M,D
Hydrology	M,D,O
Inorganic Chemistry	D
Marine Geology	M,D
Mathematics	D
Oceanography	M,D,O
Organic Chemistry	M,D,O

24 facebook.com/petersonspublishing

Petersons Graduate Programs in the Physical Sciences, Mathematics, Agricultural Sciences, the Environment & Natural Resources 2013

Physical Chemistry	D
Physics	M,D
Planetary and Space Sciences	M,D

MCGILL UNIVERSITY

Agricultural Sciences— General	M,D,O
Agronomy and Soil Sciences	M,D
Animal Sciences	M,D
Applied Mathematics	M,D
Atmospheric Sciences	M,D
Biostatistics	M,D,O
Chemistry	M,D
Computational Sciences	M,D
Environmental Management and Policy	M,D
Fish, Game, and Wildlife Management	M,D
Food Science and Technology	M,D
Forestry	M,D
Geosciences	M,D
Mathematics	M,D
Meteorology	M,D
Natural Resources	M,D
Oceanography	M,D
Physics	M,D
Planetary and Space Sciences	M,D
Plant Sciences	M,D,O
Statistics	M,D,O

MCMASTER UNIVERSITY

Analytical Chemistry	M,D
Applied Statistics	M
Astrophysics	D
Chemical Physics	M,D
Chemistry	M,D
Geochemistry	M,D
Geology	M,D
Geosciences	M,D
Inorganic Chemistry	M,D
Mathematics	M,D
Organic Chemistry	M,D
Physical Chemistry	M,D
Physics	D
Statistics	M

MCNEESE STATE UNIVERSITY

Agricultural Sciences— General	M
Chemistry	M
Environmental Sciences	M
Mathematics	M
Statistics	M

MEDICAL COLLEGE OF WISCONSIN

Biostatistics	D

MEDICAL UNIVERSITY OF SOUTH CAROLINA

Biostatistics	M,D
Marine Sciences	D

MEMORIAL UNIVERSITY OF NEWFOUNDLAND

Aquaculture	M
Chemistry	M,D
Computational Sciences	M
Condensed Matter Physics	M,D
Environmental Sciences	M
Fish, Game, and Wildlife Management	M,O
Food Science and Technology	M,D
Geology	M,D
Geophysics	M,D
Geosciences	M,D
Marine Affairs	M,D,O
Marine Sciences	M,O
Mathematics	M,D
Oceanography	M,D
Physics	M,D
Statistics	M,D

MERCER UNIVERSITY

Environmental Sciences	M

MIAMI UNIVERSITY

Chemistry	M,D
Computational Sciences	M
Environmental Sciences	M
Geology	M,D
Mathematics	M
Physics	M
Plant Sciences	M,D
Statistics	M

MICHIGAN STATE UNIVERSITY

Agricultural Sciences— General	M,D
Agronomy and Soil Sciences	M,D
Animal Sciences	M,D
Applied Mathematics	M,D
Applied Statistics	M,D
Astronomy	M,D
Astrophysics	M,D
Chemical Physics	M,D
Chemistry	M,D
Environmental Sciences	M,D
Fish, Game, and Wildlife Management	M,D
Food Science and Technology	M,D
Forestry	M,D
Geosciences	M,D
Horticulture	M,D
Mathematics	M,D
Natural Resources	M,D
Physics	M,D
Plant Sciences	M,D
Statistics	M,D

MICHIGAN TECHNOLOGICAL UNIVERSITY

Atmospheric Sciences	D
Chemistry	M,D
Computational Sciences	D
Environmental Management and Policy	M,D
Forestry	M,D
Geology	M,D
Geophysics	M,D
Mathematics	M,D
Physics	M,D

MIDDLE TENNESSEE STATE UNIVERSITY

Biostatistics	M
Chemistry	M,D
Geosciences	O
Mathematics	M,D

MILLERSVILLE UNIVERSITY OF PENNSYLVANIA

Atmospheric Sciences	M
Meteorology	M

MINNESOTA STATE UNIVERSITY MANKATO

Astronomy	M
Environmental Sciences	M
Mathematics	M
Physics	M
Statistics	M

MISSISSIPPI COLLEGE

Chemistry	M
Mathematics	M

MISSISSIPPI STATE UNIVERSITY

Agricultural Sciences— General	M,D
Agronomy and Soil Sciences	M
Animal Sciences	M,D
Atmospheric Sciences	M,D
Chemistry	M,D
Fish, Game, and Wildlife Management	M,D

Food Science and Technology	M,D
Forestry	M,D
Geology	M,D
Geosciences	M,D
Horticulture	M
Mathematics	M,D
Meteorology	M,D
Physics	M,D
Plant Sciences	M
Statistics	M,D

MISSOURI STATE UNIVERSITY

Agricultural Sciences— General	M
Chemistry	M
Environmental Management and Policy	M
Geology	M
Geosciences	M
Mathematics	M
Natural Resources	M
Plant Sciences	M

MISSOURI UNIVERSITY OF SCIENCE AND TECHNOLOGY

Applied Mathematics	M,D
Chemistry	M,D
Geochemistry	M,D
Geology	M,D
Geophysics	M,D
Hydrology	M,D
Mathematics	M,D
Physics	M,D
Statistics	M,D
Water Resources	M,D

MISSOURI WESTERN STATE UNIVERSITY

Chemistry	M

MONMOUTH UNIVERSITY

Mathematical and Computational Finance	M

MONTANA STATE UNIVERSITY

Agricultural Sciences— General	M,D
Animal Sciences	M,D
Chemistry	M,D
Environmental Sciences	M,D
Fish, Game, and Wildlife Management	M,D
Geosciences	M,D
Mathematics	M,D
Natural Resources	M
Physics	M,D
Plant Sciences	M,D
Range Science	M,D
Statistics	M,D

MONTANA TECH OF THE UNIVERSITY OF MONTANA

Geochemistry	M
Geology	M
Geosciences	M
Hydrogeology	M

MONTCLAIR STATE UNIVERSITY

Applied Mathematics	M
Chemistry	M
Environmental Management and Policy	M,D
Environmental Sciences	M
Geosciences	M
Mathematics	M
Statistics	M

MONTEREY INSTITUTE OF INTERNATIONAL STUDIES

Environmental Management and Policy	M

MOREHEAD STATE UNIVERSITY

Agricultural Sciences— General	M
Environmental Management and Policy	M

MORGAN STATE UNIVERSITY

Chemistry	M
Mathematics	M

MOUNT ALLISON UNIVERSITY

Chemistry	M

MURRAY STATE UNIVERSITY

Agricultural Sciences— General	M
Chemistry	M
Environmental Sciences	M
Geosciences	M
Hydrology	M
Mathematics	M
Statistics	M

NAROPA UNIVERSITY

Environmental Management and Policy	M

NAVAL POSTGRADUATE SCHOOL

Acoustics	M,D
Applied Mathematics	M,D
Applied Physics	M,D,O
Meteorology	M,D
Oceanography	M,D
Physics	M,D

NEW JERSEY INSTITUTE OF TECHNOLOGY

Applied Mathematics	M
Applied Physics	M,D
Applied Statistics	M
Biostatistics	M
Chemistry	M,D
Environmental Management and Policy	M
Environmental Sciences	M,D
Mathematical and Computational Finance	M
Mathematics	D

NEW MEXICO HIGHLANDS UNIVERSITY

Chemistry	M
Fish, Game, and Wildlife Management	M

NEW MEXICO INSTITUTE OF MINING AND TECHNOLOGY

Applied Mathematics	M,D
Astrophysics	M,D
Atmospheric Sciences	M,D
Chemistry	M,D
Geochemistry	M,D
Geology	M,D
Geophysics	M,D
Geosciences	M,D
Hydrology	M,D
Mathematical Physics	M,D
Mathematics	M,D
Physics	M,D
Statistics	M,D

NEW MEXICO STATE UNIVERSITY

Agricultural Sciences— General	M
Animal Sciences	M,D
Applied Statistics	M,D
Astronomy	M,D
Astrophysics	M,D
Chemistry	M,D
Environmental Sciences	M,D
Fish, Game, and Wildlife Management	M

*M—master's degree; P—first professional degree; D—doctorate; O—other advanced degree; *—Close-Up and/or Display*

Petersons Graduate Programs in the Physical Sciences, Mathematics, Agricultural Sciences, the Environment & Natural Resources 2013

facebook.com/petersonspublishing **25**

Food Science and Technology M
Geology | M
Horticulture | M,D
Hydrology | M,D
Mathematics | M,D
Physics | M,D
Plant Sciences | M,D
Range Science | M,D

THE NEW SCHOOL
Environmental Management
and Policy | M

NEW YORK INSTITUTE OF TECHNOLOGY
Environmental Management
and Policy | M,O

NEW YORK UNIVERSITY
Chemistry | M,D
Environmental Management
and Policy | M
Food Science and Technology M,D
Mathematical and
Computational Finance | M,D
Mathematics | M,D
Physics | M,D
Statistics | M,D

NICHOLLS STATE UNIVERSITY
Mathematics | M

NORFOLK STATE UNIVERSITY
Optical Sciences | M

NORTH CAROLINA AGRICULTURAL AND TECHNICAL STATE UNIVERSITY
Agricultural Sciences—
General | M
Agronomy and Soil Sciences | M
Animal Sciences | M
Applied Mathematics | M
Chemistry | M,D
Computational Sciences | M
Environmental Sciences | M
Mathematics | M
Optical Sciences | M,D
Physics | M
Plant Sciences | M

NORTH CAROLINA CENTRAL UNIVERSITY
Applied Mathematics | M
Chemistry | M
Geosciences | M
Mathematics | M
Physics | M

NORTH CAROLINA STATE UNIVERSITY
Agricultural Sciences—
General | M,D,O
Agronomy and Soil Sciences | M,D
Animal Sciences | M,D
Applied Mathematics | M,D
Atmospheric Sciences | M,D
Biomathematics | M,D
Chemistry | M,D
Fish, Game, and Wildlife
Management | M,D
Food Science and Technology M,D
Forestry | M,D
Geosciences | M,D
Horticulture | M,D,O
Marine Sciences | M,D
Mathematical and
Computational Finance | M
Mathematics | M,D
Meteorology | M,D
Natural Resources | M,D
Oceanography | M,D
Physics | M,D
Statistics | M,D

NORTH DAKOTA STATE UNIVERSITY
Agricultural Sciences—
General | M,D
Agronomy and Soil Sciences | M,D
Animal Sciences | M,D
Applied Mathematics | M,D
Applied Statistics | M,D,O
Chemistry | M,D
Environmental Sciences | M,D
Food Science and Technology M,D
Mathematics | M,D
Natural Resources | M,D
Physics | M,D
Plant Sciences | M,D
Range Science | M,D
Statistics | M,D,O

NORTHEASTERN ILLINOIS UNIVERSITY
Chemistry | M
Environmental Management
and Policy | M
Mathematics | M

NORTHEASTERN UNIVERSITY
Analytical Chemistry | M,D
Applied Mathematics | M,D
Chemistry | M,D
Inorganic Chemistry | M,D
Mathematics | M,D
Organic Chemistry | M,D
Physical Chemistry | M,D
Physics | M,D

NORTHERN ARIZONA UNIVERSITY
Applied Physics | M
Applied Statistics | M,O
Atmospheric Sciences | M,D
Chemistry | M
Environmental Management
and Policy | M,D
Environmental Sciences | M,D
Forestry | M,D
Geology | M,D
Mathematics | M,O
Meteorology | M,D
Physics | M
Statistics | M,O

NORTHERN ILLINOIS UNIVERSITY
Chemistry | M,D
Geology | M,D
Mathematics | M,D
Physics | M,D
Statistics | M

NORTHWESTERN UNIVERSITY
Applied Mathematics | M,D
Astronomy | M,D
Astrophysics | M,D
Chemistry | D
Geology | M,D
Geosciences | M,D
Mathematics | D
Physics | M,D
Statistics | M,D

NORTHWEST MISSOURI STATE UNIVERSITY
Agricultural Sciences—
General | M

NOVA SCOTIA AGRICULTURAL COLLEGE
Agricultural Sciences—
General | M
Agronomy and Soil Sciences | M
Animal Sciences | M
Aquaculture | M
Environmental Management
and Policy | M
Environmental Sciences | M
Food Science and Technology M

Horticulture | M
Water Resources | M

NOVA SOUTHEASTERN UNIVERSITY
Environmental Sciences | M,D
Marine Affairs | M,D
Marine Sciences | M,D
Oceanography | M,D

OAKLAND UNIVERSITY
Applied Mathematics | M,D
Applied Statistics | M
Chemistry | M,D
Environmental Sciences | M,D
Mathematics | M
Physics | M,D
Statistics | O

THE OHIO STATE UNIVERSITY
Agricultural Sciences—
General | M,D
Agronomy and Soil Sciences | M,D
Animal Sciences | M,D
Astronomy | M,D
Atmospheric Sciences | M,D
Biostatistics | M,D
Chemical Physics | M,D
Chemistry | M,D
Environmental Sciences | M,D
Food Science and Technology M,D
Geodetic Sciences | M,D
Geology | M,D
Horticulture | M,D
Mathematics | M,D
Natural Resources | M,D
Optical Sciences | M,D
Physics | M,D
Statistics | M,D

OHIO UNIVERSITY
Astronomy | M,D
Environmental Management
and Policy | M
Geochemistry | M
Geology | M
Geophysics | M
Hydrogeology | M
Mathematics | M,D
Physics | M,D*

OKLAHOMA STATE UNIVERSITY
Agricultural Sciences—
General | M,D
Agronomy and Soil Sciences | M,D
Animal Sciences | M,D
Applied Mathematics | M,D
Chemistry | M,D
Environmental Sciences | M,D,O
Food Science and Technology M,D
Forestry | M,D
Geology | M,D
Horticulture | M,D
Mathematics | M,D
Natural Resources | M,D
Photonics | M,D,O
Physics | M,D
Plant Sciences | M,D,O
Statistics | M,D

OLD DOMINION UNIVERSITY
Analytical Chemistry | M,D
Chemistry | M,D
Marine Affairs | M
Mathematics | M,D
Oceanography | M,D
Organic Chemistry | M,D
Physical Chemistry | M,D
Physics | M,D

OREGON HEALTH & SCIENCE UNIVERSITY
Biostatistics | M,O
Environmental Sciences | M,D

OREGON STATE UNIVERSITY
Agricultural Sciences—
General | M,D
Agronomy and Soil Sciences | M,D
Analytical Chemistry | M,D
Animal Sciences | M,D
Applied Physics | M,D
Atmospheric Sciences | M,D
Biostatistics | M
Chemistry | M,D
Environmental Sciences | M,D
Fish, Game, and Wildlife
Management | M,D
Food Science and Technology M,D
Forestry | M,D
Geology | M,D
Geophysics | M,D
Geosciences | M,D
Horticulture | M,D
Inorganic Chemistry | M,D
Marine Affairs | M
Marine Sciences | M
Mathematics | M,D
Oceanography | M,D
Organic Chemistry | M,D
Physical Chemistry | M,D
Physics | M,D
Range Science | M,D
Statistics | M,D

PACE UNIVERSITY
Environmental Management
and Policy | M
Environmental Sciences | M

PENN STATE HARRISBURG
Environmental Sciences | M

PENN STATE UNIVERSITY PARK
Acoustics | M,D
Agricultural Sciences—
General | M,D,O
Agronomy and Soil Sciences | M,D
Animal Sciences | M,D
Applied Mathematics | M,D
Astronomy | M,D
Astrophysics | M,D
Chemistry | M,D
Environmental Management
and Policy | M
Environmental Sciences | M
Fish, Game, and Wildlife
Management | M,D
Food Science and Technology M,D
Forestry | M,D
Geosciences | M,D
Horticulture | M,D
Mathematics | M,D
Meteorology | M,D
Physics | M,D
Statistics | M,D

PITTSBURG STATE UNIVERSITY
Applied Physics | M
Chemistry | M
Mathematics | M
Physics | M

PLYMOUTH STATE UNIVERSITY
Environmental Management
and Policy | M
Meteorology | M

POINT PARK UNIVERSITY
Environmental Management
and Policy | M

POLYTECHNIC INSTITUTE OF NEW YORK UNIVERSITY
Applied Physics | M,D
Chemistry | M,D
Environmental Sciences | M
Mathematical and
Computational Finance | M,O
Mathematics | M,D

Petersons Graduate Programs in the Physical Sciences, Mathematics, Agricultural Sciences, the Environment & Natural Resources 2013

POLYTECHNIC INSTITUTE OF NYU, LONG ISLAND GRADUATE CENTER
Chemistry — M

POLYTECHNIC INSTITUTE OF NYU, WESTCHESTER GRADUATE CENTER
Chemistry — M

POLYTECHNIC UNIVERSITY OF PUERTO RICO
Environmental Management and Policy — M

POLYTECHNIC UNIVERSITY OF PUERTO RICO, MIAMI CAMPUS
Environmental Management and Policy — M

POLYTECHNIC UNIVERSITY OF PUERTO RICO, ORLANDO CAMPUS
Environmental Management and Policy — M

PONTIFICAL CATHOLIC UNIVERSITY OF PUERTO RICO
Chemistry — M
Environmental Sciences — M

PORTLAND STATE UNIVERSITY
Chemistry — M,D
Environmental Management and Policy — M,D
Environmental Sciences — M,D
Geology — M,D
Mathematics — M,D,O
Physics — M,D
Statistics — M,D

PRAIRIE VIEW A&M UNIVERSITY
Agricultural Sciences— General — M
Agronomy and Soil Sciences — M
Animal Sciences — M
Chemistry — M
Mathematics — M

PRESCOTT COLLEGE
Environmental Management and Policy — M

PRINCETON UNIVERSITY
Applied Mathematics — D
Astronomy — D
Astrophysics — D
Atmospheric Sciences — D
Chemistry — M,D*
Computational Sciences — D
Geosciences — D
Mathematics — D
Oceanography — D
Photonics — D
Physics — D
Plasma Physics — D

PURDUE UNIVERSITY
Agricultural Sciences— General — M,D
Agronomy and Soil Sciences — M,D
Analytical Chemistry — M,D
Animal Sciences — M,D
Aquaculture — M,D
Atmospheric Sciences — M,D
Chemistry — M,D
Computational Sciences — D
Environmental Management and Policy — M,D
Fish, Game, and Wildlife Management — M,D

Food Science and Technology — M,D
Forestry — M,D
Geosciences — M,D
Horticulture — M,D
Inorganic Chemistry — M,D
Mathematics — M,D
Natural Resources — M,D
Organic Chemistry — M,D
Physical Chemistry — M,D
Physics — M,D
Plant Sciences — D
Statistics — M,D

PURDUE UNIVERSITY CALUMET
Mathematics — M

QUEENS COLLEGE OF THE CITY UNIVERSITY OF NEW YORK
Chemistry — M
Environmental Sciences — M
Geology — M
Mathematics — M
Physics — M,D

QUEEN'S UNIVERSITY AT KINGSTON
Chemistry — M,D
Geology — M,D
Mathematics — M,D
Physics — M,D
Statistics — M,D

RENSSELAER POLYTECHNIC INSTITUTE
Acoustics — M,D
Analytical Chemistry — M,D
Applied Mathematics — M
Chemistry — M,D
Environmental Management and Policy — M,D
Geology — M,D
Inorganic Chemistry — M,D
Mathematics — M,D
Organic Chemistry — M,D
Physical Chemistry — M,D
Physics — M,D

RHODE ISLAND COLLEGE
Mathematics — M,O

RICE UNIVERSITY
Applied Mathematics — M,D
Applied Physics — M,D
Astronomy — M,D
Biostatistics — M,D
Chemistry — M,D
Computational Sciences — M,D
Environmental Management and Policy — M
Environmental Sciences — M,D
Geophysics — M
Geosciences — M,D
Inorganic Chemistry — M,D
Mathematical and Computational Finance — M,D
Mathematics — D
Organic Chemistry — M,D
Physical Chemistry — M,D
Physics — M,D
Statistics — M,D

THE RICHARD STOCKTON COLLEGE OF NEW JERSEY
Computational Sciences — M
Environmental Sciences — M

RIVIER UNIVERSITY
Mathematics — M

ROCHESTER INSTITUTE OF TECHNOLOGY
Applied Mathematics — M

Applied Statistics — M,O
Astrophysics — M,D
Chemistry — M
Environmental Management and Policy — M
Environmental Sciences — M
Optical Sciences — M,D
Statistics — M,O

ROOSEVELT UNIVERSITY
Chemistry — M
Mathematics — M

ROSE-HULMAN INSTITUTE OF TECHNOLOGY
Optical Sciences — M

ROWAN UNIVERSITY
Mathematics — M

ROYAL MILITARY COLLEGE OF CANADA
Chemistry — M,D
Environmental Sciences — M,D
Mathematics — M
Physics — M

ROYAL ROADS UNIVERSITY
Environmental Management and Policy — M,O

RUTGERS, THE STATE UNIVERSITY OF NEW JERSEY, CAMDEN
Applied Mathematics — M
Chemistry — M
Mathematics — M

RUTGERS, THE STATE UNIVERSITY OF NEW JERSEY, NEWARK
Analytical Chemistry — M,D
Applied Physics — M,D
Chemistry — M,D
Environmental Sciences — M,D
Geology — M
Inorganic Chemistry — M,D
Mathematics — D
Organic Chemistry — M,D
Physical Chemistry — M,D

RUTGERS, THE STATE UNIVERSITY OF NEW JERSEY, NEW BRUNSWICK
Animal Sciences — M,D
Applied Mathematics — M,D
Applied Statistics — M,D
Astronomy — M,D
Atmospheric Sciences — M,D
Biostatistics — M,D
Chemistry — M,D
Condensed Matter Physics — M,D
Environmental Sciences — M,D
Food Science and Technology — M,D
Geology — M,D
Horticulture — M,D
Inorganic Chemistry — M,D
Mathematics — M,D
Oceanography — M,D
Organic Chemistry — M,D
Physical Chemistry — M,D
Physics — M,D
Statistics — M,D
Theoretical Physics — M,D
Water Resources — M,D

SACRED HEART UNIVERSITY
Chemistry — M
Environmental Management and Policy — M

ST. CLOUD STATE UNIVERSITY
Applied Statistics — M
Environmental Management and Policy — M
Mathematics — M

ST. EDWARD'S UNIVERSITY
Environmental Management and Policy — M

ST. FRANCIS XAVIER UNIVERSITY
Chemistry — M
Geology — M
Geosciences — M
Physics — M

ST. JOHN'S UNIVERSITY (NY)
Chemistry — M

SAINT JOSEPH'S UNIVERSITY
Mathematics — M,O

SAINT LOUIS UNIVERSITY
Chemistry — M,D
Geophysics — M,D
Geosciences — M,D
Mathematics — M,D
Meteorology — M,D

SAINT MARY'S UNIVERSITY (CANADA)
Astronomy — M,D

ST. THOMAS UNIVERSITY
Geosciences — M,D,O
Planetary and Space Sciences — M,D,O

SALEM STATE UNIVERSITY
Mathematics — M

SAMFORD UNIVERSITY
Environmental Management and Policy — M

SAM HOUSTON STATE UNIVERSITY
Agricultural Sciences— General — M
Chemistry — M
Computational Sciences — M
Mathematics — M
Statistics — M

SAN DIEGO STATE UNIVERSITY
Applied Mathematics — M
Astronomy — M
Biometry — M
Biostatistics — M,D
Chemistry — M,D
Computational Sciences — M,D
Geology — M
Mathematics — M,D
Physics — M
Statistics — M

SAN FRANCISCO STATE UNIVERSITY
Chemistry — M
Environmental Management and Policy — M
Geosciences — M
Marine Sciences — M
Mathematics — M
Natural Resources — M
Physics — M

SAN JOSE STATE UNIVERSITY
Applied Mathematics — M

M—master's degree; P—first professional degree; D—doctorate; O—other advanced degree; *—Close-Up and/or Display

Petersons Graduate Programs in the Physical Sciences, Mathematics, Agricultural Sciences, the Environment & Natural Resources 2013

facebook.com/petersonspublishing   **27**

Chemistry	M
Environmental Management and Policy	M
Geology	M
Marine Sciences	M
Mathematics	M
Meteorology	M
Physics	M
Statistics	M

SANTA CLARA UNIVERSITY

Applied Mathematics	M

SAVANNAH STATE UNIVERSITY

Marine Sciences	M

THE SCRIPPS RESEARCH INSTITUTE

Chemistry	D

SETON HALL UNIVERSITY

Analytical Chemistry	M,D
Chemistry	M,D
Inorganic Chemistry	M,D
Organic Chemistry	M,D
Physical Chemistry	M,D

SHIPPENSBURG UNIVERSITY OF PENNSYLVANIA

Environmental Management and Policy	M

SIMON FRASER UNIVERSITY

Applied Mathematics	M,D
Chemical Physics	M,D
Chemistry	M,D
Computational Sciences	M,D
Environmental Management and Policy	M,D
Geosciences	M,D
Mathematics	M,D
Physics	M,D
Statistics	M,D

SLIPPERY ROCK UNIVERSITY OF PENNSYLVANIA

Environmental Management and Policy	M

SMITH COLLEGE

Chemistry	M
Mathematics	O

SOUTH DAKOTA SCHOOL OF MINES AND TECHNOLOGY

Atmospheric Sciences	M,D
Environmental Sciences	D
Geology	M,D
Paleontology	M,D
Physics	M,D

SOUTH DAKOTA STATE UNIVERSITY

Agricultural Sciences— General	M,D
Agronomy and Soil Sciences	M,D
Animal Sciences	M,D
Chemistry	M,D
Computational Sciences	M,D
Fish, Game, and Wildlife Management	M,D
Food Science and Technology	M,D
Geosciences	D
Mathematics	M,D
Physics	M
Plant Sciences	M,D
Statistics	M,D

SOUTHEAST MISSOURI STATE UNIVERSITY

Chemistry	M
Environmental Management and Policy	M

Environmental Sciences	M
Mathematics	M

SOUTHERN ARKANSAS UNIVERSITY–MAGNOLIA

Agricultural Sciences— General	M

SOUTHERN CONNECTICUT STATE UNIVERSITY

Chemistry	M
Mathematics	M

SOUTHERN ILLINOIS UNIVERSITY CARBONDALE

Agricultural Sciences— General	M
Agronomy and Soil Sciences	M
Animal Sciences	M
Applied Physics	M,D
Chemistry	M,D
Environmental Management and Policy	M,D
Environmental Sciences	D
Forestry	M
Geology	M,D
Horticulture	M
Mathematics	M,D
Physics	M,D
Plant Sciences	M
Statistics	M,D

SOUTHERN ILLINOIS UNIVERSITY EDWARDSVILLE

Chemistry	M
Computational Sciences	M
Environmental Management and Policy	M
Environmental Sciences	M
Mathematics	M
Statistics	M

SOUTHERN METHODIST UNIVERSITY

Applied Mathematics	M,D
Chemistry	M,D
Computational Sciences	M,D
Environmental Sciences	M,D
Geology	M,D
Geophysics	M,D
Mathematics	M,D
Physics	M,D
Statistics	M,D

SOUTHERN OREGON UNIVERSITY

Applied Mathematics	M

SOUTHERN UNIVERSITY AND AGRICULTURAL AND MECHANICAL COLLEGE

Agricultural Sciences— General	M
Analytical Chemistry	M
Chemistry	M
Environmental Sciences	M
Forestry	M
Inorganic Chemistry	M
Mathematics	M
Organic Chemistry	M
Physical Chemistry	M
Physics	M

STANFORD UNIVERSITY

Applied Physics	M,D
Chemistry	D
Computational Sciences	M,D
Environmental Management and Policy	M
Environmental Sciences	M,D,O
Geophysics	M,D
Geosciences	M,D,O
Mathematical and Computational Finance	M,D
Mathematics	M,D

Physics	D
Statistics	M,D

STATE UNIVERSITY OF NEW YORK AT BINGHAMTON

Analytical Chemistry	M,D
Applied Physics	M,D
Chemistry	M,D
Geology	M,D
Inorganic Chemistry	M,D
Mathematics	M,D
Organic Chemistry	M,D
Physical Chemistry	M,D
Physics	M,D
Statistics	M,D

STATE UNIVERSITY OF NEW YORK AT FREDONIA

Chemistry	M
Mathematics	M

STATE UNIVERSITY OF NEW YORK AT NEW PALTZ

Chemistry	M
Geosciences	M

STATE UNIVERSITY OF NEW YORK AT OSWEGO

Chemistry	M

STATE UNIVERSITY OF NEW YORK COLLEGE AT CORTLAND

Mathematics	M

STATE UNIVERSITY OF NEW YORK COLLEGE AT ONEONTA

Geosciences	M

STATE UNIVERSITY OF NEW YORK COLLEGE AT POTSDAM

Mathematics	M

STATE UNIVERSITY OF NEW YORK COLLEGE OF ENVIRONMENTAL SCIENCE AND FORESTRY

Chemistry	M,D
Environmental Management and Policy	M,D
Environmental Sciences	M,D
Fish, Game, and Wildlife Management	M,D
Forestry	M,D
Geodetic Sciences	M,D
Natural Resources	M,D
Organic Chemistry	M,D
Plant Sciences	M,D
Water Resources	M,D

STEPHEN F. AUSTIN STATE UNIVERSITY

Chemistry	M
Environmental Sciences	M
Forestry	M,D
Geology	M
Mathematics	M
Physics	M
Statistics	M

STEVENS INSTITUTE OF TECHNOLOGY

Analytical Chemistry	M,D,O
Applied Mathematics	M
Applied Statistics	O
Chemistry	M,D,O
Hydrology	M,D,O
Marine Affairs	M
Mathematics	M,D
Organic Chemistry	M,D,O
Photonics	M,D,O
Physical Chemistry	M,D,O
Physics	M,D,O
Statistics	M,O

STONY BROOK UNIVERSITY, STATE UNIVERSITY OF NEW YORK

Applied Mathematics	M,D
Astronomy	D
Atmospheric Sciences	M,D
Chemistry	M,D
Environmental Management and Policy	M,O
Geosciences	M,D
Marine Affairs	M
Marine Sciences	M,D
Mathematics	M,D
Physics	M,D
Statistics	M,D

SUL ROSS STATE UNIVERSITY

Animal Sciences	M
Fish, Game, and Wildlife Management	M
Geology	M
Range Science	M

SYRACUSE UNIVERSITY

Applied Statistics	M
Chemistry	M,D
Geology	M,D
Mathematics	M,D
Physics	M,D

TARLETON STATE UNIVERSITY

Agricultural Sciences— General	M
Environmental Sciences	M
Mathematics	M

TAYLOR UNIVERSITY

Environmental Sciences	M

TEMPLE UNIVERSITY

Applied Mathematics	M,D
Chemistry	M,D
Computational Sciences	M,D
Geology	M
Mathematics	M,D
Physics	M,D
Statistics	M,D

TENNESSEE STATE UNIVERSITY

Agricultural Sciences— General	M
Chemistry	M
Mathematics	M

TENNESSEE TECHNOLOGICAL UNIVERSITY

Chemistry	M,D
Environmental Sciences	D
Fish, Game, and Wildlife Management	M
Mathematics	M

TEXAS A&M INTERNATIONAL UNIVERSITY

Mathematics	M

TEXAS A&M UNIVERSITY

Agricultural Sciences— General	M,D
Agronomy and Soil Sciences	M,D
Animal Sciences	M,D
Applied Physics	M,D
Chemistry	M,D
Fish, Game, and Wildlife Management	M,D
Food Science and Technology	M,D
Forestry	M,D
Geology	M,D
Geophysics	M,D
Horticulture	M,D
Mathematics	M,D
Meteorology	M,D
Natural Resources	M,D
Oceanography	M,D

Petersons Graduate Programs in the Physical Sciences, Mathematics, Agricultural Sciences, the Environment & Natural Resources 2013

Physics	M,D
Plant Sciences	M,D
Range Science	M,D
Statistics	M,D

TEXAS A&M UNIVERSITY AT GALVESTON

Marine Sciences	M

TEXAS A&M UNIVERSITY–COMMERCE

Agricultural Sciences— General	M
Chemistry	M
Environmental Sciences	M,O
Mathematics	M
Physics	M

TEXAS A&M UNIVERSITY–CORPUS CHRISTI

Applied Mathematics	M
Aquaculture	M
Environmental Sciences	M
Marine Sciences	D
Mathematics	M

TEXAS A&M UNIVERSITY–KINGSVILLE

Agricultural Sciences— General	M,D
Agronomy and Soil Sciences	M,D
Animal Sciences	M
Chemistry	M
Fish, Game, and Wildlife Management	M,D
Geology	M
Mathematics	M
Plant Sciences	M,D
Range Science	M

TEXAS CHRISTIAN UNIVERSITY

Applied Mathematics	M,D
Astrophysics	M,D
Chemistry	M,D
Environmental Management and Policy	M
Environmental Sciences	M
Geology	M
Inorganic Chemistry	M,D
Mathematics	M,D
Organic Chemistry	M,D
Physical Chemistry	M,D
Physics	M,D

TEXAS SOUTHERN UNIVERSITY

Chemistry	M
Environmental Management and Policy	M,D
Mathematics	M

TEXAS STATE UNIVERSITY–SAN MARCOS

Applied Mathematics	M
Chemistry	M
Environmental Management and Policy	M
Fish, Game, and Wildlife Management	M
Mathematics	M,D
Physics	M

TEXAS TECH UNIVERSITY

Agricultural Sciences— General	M,D
Agronomy and Soil Sciences	M,D
Animal Sciences	M,D
Applied Physics	M,D
Atmospheric Sciences	M,D
Chemistry	M,D
Environmental Management and Policy	D
Environmental Sciences	M,D

Fish, Game, and Wildlife Management	M,D
Food Science and Technology	M,D
Geosciences	M,D
Horticulture	M,D
Mathematics	M,D
Natural Resources	M,D
Physics	M,D
Plant Sciences	M,D
Range Science	M,D
Statistics	M,D

TEXAS WOMAN'S UNIVERSITY

Chemistry	M
Food Science and Technology	M,D
Mathematics	M

THOMPSON RIVERS UNIVERSITY

Environmental Sciences	M

TOWSON UNIVERSITY

Applied Mathematics	M
Applied Physics	M
Environmental Management and Policy	M
Environmental Sciences	M,O

TRENT UNIVERSITY

Chemistry	M
Environmental Management and Policy	M,D
Physics	M

TROPICAL AGRICULTURE RESEARCH AND HIGHER EDUCATION CENTER

Agricultural Sciences— General	M,D
Environmental Management and Policy	M,D
Forestry	M,D
Water Resources	M,D

TROY UNIVERSITY

Environmental Management and Policy	M

TUFTS UNIVERSITY

Analytical Chemistry	M,D
Animal Sciences	M
Biostatistics	M,D
Chemistry	M,D
Environmental Management and Policy	M,D,O
Environmental Sciences	M,D
Inorganic Chemistry	M,D
Mathematics	M,D
Organic Chemistry	M,D
Physical Chemistry	M,D
Physics	M,D

TULANE UNIVERSITY

Applied Mathematics	M,D
Biostatistics	M,D
Chemistry	M,D
Mathematics	M,D
Physics	D
Statistics	M,D

TUSKEGEE UNIVERSITY

Agronomy and Soil Sciences	M
Animal Sciences	M
Chemistry	M
Environmental Sciences	M
Food Science and Technology	M
Plant Sciences	M

UNIVERSIDAD AUTONOMA DE GUADALAJARA

Environmental Management and Policy	M,D

UNIVERSIDAD DE LAS AMÉRICAS–PUEBLA

Food Science and Technology	M

UNIVERSIDAD DEL TURABO

Chemistry	M,D
Environmental Management and Policy	M,D
Environmental Sciences	M,D

UNIVERSIDAD METROPOLITANA

Environmental Management and Policy	M
Natural Resources	M

UNIVERSIDAD NACIONAL PEDRO HENRIQUEZ URENA

Agricultural Sciences— General	M
Animal Sciences	M
Environmental Sciences	M
Horticulture	M
Natural Resources	M

UNIVERSITÉ DE MONCTON

Astronomy	M
Chemistry	M
Food Science and Technology	M
Mathematics	M
Physics	M

UNIVERSITÉ DE MONTRÉAL

Chemistry	M,D
Environmental Management and Policy	O
Mathematical and Computational Finance	M,D,O
Mathematics	M,D,O
Physics	M,D
Statistics	M,D,O

UNIVERSITÉ DE SHERBROOKE

Chemistry	M,D,O
Environmental Sciences	M,O
Mathematics	M,D
Physics	M,D

UNIVERSITÉ DU QUÉBEC À CHICOUTIMI

Environmental Management and Policy	M
Geosciences	M
Mineralogy	D

UNIVERSITÉ DU QUÉBEC À MONTRÉAL

Atmospheric Sciences	M,D,O
Chemistry	M,D
Environmental Sciences	M,D,O
Geology	M,D,O
Geosciences	M,D,O
Mathematics	M,D
Meteorology	M,D,O
Mineralogy	M,D,O
Natural Resources	M,D,O

UNIVERSITÉ DU QUÉBEC À RIMOUSKI

Fish, Game, and Wildlife Management	M,D,O
Marine Affairs	M,O
Oceanography	M,D

UNIVERSITÉ DU QUÉBEC À TROIS-RIVIÈRES

Chemistry	M
Environmental Sciences	M,D
Mathematics	M
Physics	M,D

UNIVERSITÉ DU QUÉBEC EN ABITIBI-TÉMISCAMINGUE

Environmental Sciences	M,D
Forestry	M,D
Natural Resources	M,D

UNIVERSITÉ DU QUÉBEC, INSTITUT NATIONAL DE LA RECHERCHE SCIENTIFIQUE

Environmental Management and Policy	M,D
Geosciences	M,D
Hydrology	M,D

UNIVERSITÉ LAVAL

Agricultural Sciences— General	M,D,O
Agronomy and Soil Sciences	M,D
Animal Sciences	M,D
Chemistry	M,D
Environmental Management and Policy	M,D,O
Environmental Sciences	M,D
Food Science and Technology	M,D
Forestry	M,D
Geodetic Sciences	M,D
Geology	M,D
Geosciences	M,D
Mathematics	M,D
Oceanography	D
Physics	M,D
Statistics	M

UNIVERSITY AT ALBANY, STATE UNIVERSITY OF NEW YORK

Atmospheric Sciences	M,D
Biostatistics	M,D
Chemistry	M,D
Environmental Management and Policy	M
Environmental Sciences	M
Geology	M,D
Geosciences	M,D
Mathematics	M,D
Physics	M,D
Statistics	M,D,O

UNIVERSITY AT BUFFALO, THE STATE UNIVERSITY OF NEW YORK

Biostatistics	M,D
Chemistry	M,D
Computational Sciences	O
Environmental Sciences	M,D,O
Geology	M,D
Geosciences	M,D,O
Mathematics	M,D
Physics	M,D

THE UNIVERSITY OF AKRON

Applied Mathematics	M,D
Chemistry	M,D
Geology	M
Geophysics	M
Geosciences	M
Mathematics	M
Physics	M
Statistics	M

THE UNIVERSITY OF ALABAMA

Applied Mathematics	M,D
Applied Statistics	M,D
Chemistry	M,D
Geology	M,D
Mathematics	M,D
Physics	M,D

THE UNIVERSITY OF ALABAMA AT BIRMINGHAM

Applied Mathematics	D
Biostatistics	M,D
Chemistry	M,D

*M—master's degree; P—first professional degree; D—doctorate; O—other advanced degree; *—Close-Up and/or Display*

Petersons Graduate Programs in the Physical Sciences, Mathematics, Agricultural Sciences, the Environment & Natural Resources 2013

facebook.com/petersonspublishing **29**

Mathematics	M
Physics	M,D

THE UNIVERSITY OF ALABAMA IN HUNTSVILLE

Applied Mathematics	M,D
Atmospheric Sciences	M,D
Chemistry	M
Environmental Sciences	M,D
Geosciences	M,D
Mathematics	M,D
Optical Sciences	M,D
Photonics	M,D
Physics	M,D

UNIVERSITY OF ALASKA ANCHORAGE

Environmental Sciences	M

UNIVERSITY OF ALASKA FAIRBANKS

Astrophysics	M,D
Atmospheric Sciences	M,D
Chemistry	M,D
Computational Sciences	M,D
Environmental Management and Policy	M,D
Environmental Sciences	M,D
Fish, Game, and Wildlife Management	M,D
Geology	M,D
Geophysics	M,D
Limnology	M,D
Marine Sciences	M,D
Mathematics	M,D,O
Natural Resources	M,D
Oceanography	M,D
Physics	M,D
Statistics	M,D,O
Water Resources	M,D

UNIVERSITY OF ALBERTA

Agricultural Sciences— General	M,D
Agronomy and Soil Sciences	M,D
Applied Mathematics	M,D,O
Astrophysics	M,D
Biostatistics	M,D,O
Chemistry	M,D
Condensed Matter Physics	M,D
Environmental Management and Policy	M,D
Environmental Sciences	M,D
Forestry	M,D
Geophysics	M,D
Geosciences	M,D
Mathematical and Computational Finance	M,D,O
Mathematical Physics	M,D,O
Mathematics	M,D,O
Natural Resources	M,D
Physics	M,D
Statistics	M,D,O

THE UNIVERSITY OF ARIZONA

Agricultural Sciences— General	M,D
Agronomy and Soil Sciences	M,D
Animal Sciences	M,D
Applied Mathematics	M,D
Applied Physics	M
Astronomy	M,D
Atmospheric Sciences	M,D
Biostatistics	D
Chemistry	D
Environmental Sciences	M,D
Fish, Game, and Wildlife Management	M,D
Forestry	M,D
Geosciences	M,D
Hydrology	M,D
Mathematics	M,D
Natural Resources	M,D
Optical Sciences	M,D
Physics	M,D
Planetary and Space Sciences	M,D

Plant Sciences	M,D
Range Science	M,D
Statistics	M,D
Water Resources	M,D

UNIVERSITY OF ARKANSAS

Agricultural Sciences— General	M,D
Agronomy and Soil Sciences	M,D
Animal Sciences	M,D
Applied Physics	M,D
Chemistry	M,D
Food Science and Technology	M,D
Geology	M
Horticulture	M
Mathematics	M,D
Photonics	M,D
Physics	M,D
Planetary and Space Sciences	M,D
Plant Sciences	D
Statistics	M

UNIVERSITY OF ARKANSAS AT LITTLE ROCK

Applied Mathematics	M,O
Applied Statistics	M,O
Chemistry	M
Geosciences	O
Mathematics	M,O

UNIVERSITY OF ARKANSAS AT MONTICELLO

Forestry	M
Natural Resources	M

UNIVERSITY OF ARKANSAS AT PINE BLUFF

Aquaculture	M
Fish, Game, and Wildlife Management	M

THE UNIVERSITY OF BRITISH COLUMBIA

Agricultural Sciences— General	M,D
Agronomy and Soil Sciences	M,D
Animal Sciences	M,D
Applied Mathematics	M,D
Astronomy	M,D
Atmospheric Sciences	M,D
Chemistry	M,D
Food Science and Technology	M,D
Forestry	M,D
Geology	M,D
Geophysics	M,D
Marine Sciences	M,D
Mathematics	M,D
Natural Resources	M,D
Oceanography	M,D
Physics	M,D
Plant Sciences	M,D
Statistics	M,D

UNIVERSITY OF CALGARY

Analytical Chemistry	M,D
Astronomy	M,D
Chemistry	M,D
Environmental Management and Policy	M,D,O
Geology	M,D
Geophysics	M,D
Inorganic Chemistry	M,D
Mathematics	M,D
Organic Chemistry	M,D
Physical Chemistry	M,D
Physics	M,D
Statistics	M,D
Theoretical Chemistry	M,D

UNIVERSITY OF CALIFORNIA, BERKELEY

Applied Mathematics	D
Astrophysics	D
Biostatistics	M,D
Chemistry	D

Environmental Management and Policy	M,D,O
Environmental Sciences	M,D
Forestry	M,D
Geology	M,D
Geophysics	M,D
Mathematics	M,D
Natural Resources	M,D
Physics	D
Range Science	M
Statistics	M,D

UNIVERSITY OF CALIFORNIA, DAVIS

Agricultural Sciences— General	M
Agronomy and Soil Sciences	M,D
Animal Sciences	M,D
Applied Mathematics	M,D
Atmospheric Sciences	M,D
Biostatistics	M,D
Chemistry	M,D
Environmental Sciences	M,D
Food Science and Technology	M,D
Geology	M,D
Horticulture	M
Hydrology	M,D
Mathematics	M,D
Physics	M,D
Statistics	M,D
Viticulture and Enology	M,D

UNIVERSITY OF CALIFORNIA, IRVINE

Chemistry	M,D
Geosciences	M,D
Mathematics	M,D
Physics	M,D
Statistics	M,D

UNIVERSITY OF CALIFORNIA, LOS ANGELES

Astronomy	M,D
Astrophysics	M,D
Atmospheric Sciences	M,D
Biomathematics	M,D
Biostatistics	M,D
Chemistry	M,D
Environmental Sciences	M,D
Geochemistry	M,D
Geology	M,D
Geophysics	M,D
Geosciences	M,D
Mathematics	M,D
Physics	M,D
Planetary and Space Sciences	M,D
Statistics	M,D

UNIVERSITY OF CALIFORNIA, MERCED

Applied Mathematics	M,D
Chemistry	M,D
Environmental Sciences	M,D
Physics	M,D

UNIVERSITY OF CALIFORNIA, RIVERSIDE

Agronomy and Soil Sciences	M,D
Applied Statistics	M,D
Chemistry	M,D
Environmental Sciences	M,D
Geology	M,D
Mathematics	M,D
Physics	M,D
Plant Sciences	M,D
Statistics	M,D
Water Resources	M,D

UNIVERSITY OF CALIFORNIA, SAN DIEGO

Applied Mathematics	M,D
Applied Physics	M,D
Chemistry	M,D
Geosciences	D
Marine Sciences	M

Mathematics	M,D
Oceanography	D
Photonics	M,D
Physics	M,D
Statistics	M,D

UNIVERSITY OF CALIFORNIA, SAN FRANCISCO

Chemistry	D

UNIVERSITY OF CALIFORNIA, SANTA BARBARA

Applied Mathematics	M,D
Applied Statistics	M,D
Chemistry	M,D
Computational Sciences	M,D
Environmental Management and Policy	M,D
Environmental Sciences	M,D
Geology	M,D
Geophysics	M,D
Geosciences	M,D
Marine Sciences	M,D
Mathematical and Computational Finance	M,D
Mathematics	M,D
Photonics	M,D
Physics	D
Statistics	M,D

UNIVERSITY OF CALIFORNIA, SANTA CRUZ

Applied Mathematics	M,D
Astronomy	D
Astrophysics	D
Chemistry	M,D
Environmental Management and Policy	D
Geosciences	M,D
Marine Sciences	M,D
Mathematics	M,D
Physics	M,D
Planetary and Space Sciences	M,D
Statistics	M,D

UNIVERSITY OF CENTRAL ARKANSAS

Applied Mathematics	M
Mathematics	M

UNIVERSITY OF CENTRAL FLORIDA

Applied Mathematics	M,D,O
Chemistry	M,D,O
Mathematics	M,D,O
Optical Sciences	M,D
Photonics	M,D
Physics	M,D
Statistics	M,O

UNIVERSITY OF CENTRAL MISSOURI

Applied Mathematics	M,D
Environmental Management and Policy	M,D
Mathematics	M,D

UNIVERSITY OF CENTRAL OKLAHOMA

Applied Mathematics	M
Chemistry	M
Mathematics	M
Physics	M
Statistics	M

UNIVERSITY OF CHICAGO

Applied Mathematics	M,D
Astronomy	M,D
Astrophysics	M,D
Atmospheric Sciences	M,D
Chemistry	D
Environmental Management and Policy	M,D
Environmental Sciences	M,D

Petersons Graduate Programs in the Physical Sciences, Mathematics, Agricultural Sciences, the Environment & Natural Resources 2013

Geochemistry	M,D
Geophysics	M,D
Geosciences	M,D
Mathematical and Computational Finance	M
Mathematics	M,D
Paleontology	M,D
Physics	M,D
Planetary and Space Sciences	M,D
Statistics	M,D,O

UNIVERSITY OF CINCINNATI

Analytical Chemistry	M,D
Applied Mathematics	M,D
Biostatistics	M,D
Chemistry	M,D
Environmental Sciences	M,D
Geology	M,D
Inorganic Chemistry	M,D
Mathematics	M,D
Organic Chemistry	M,D
Physical Chemistry	M,D
Physics	M,D
Statistics	M,D

UNIVERSITY OF COLORADO AT COLORADO SPRINGS

Applied Mathematics	M,D
Chemistry	M
Environmental Sciences	M
Mathematics	M,D
Physics	M

UNIVERSITY OF COLORADO BOULDER

Applied Mathematics	M,D
Astrophysics	M,D
Atmospheric Sciences	M,D
Chemical Physics	M,D
Chemistry	M,D
Environmental Management and Policy	M,D
Geology	M,D
Geophysics	M,D
Hydrology	M,D
Mathematical Physics	M,D
Mathematics	M,D
Oceanography	M,D
Optical Sciences	M,D
Physics	M,D
Plasma Physics	M,D

UNIVERSITY OF COLORADO DENVER

Applied Mathematics	M,D
Applied Statistics	M,D
Biostatistics	M,D
Chemistry	M
Computational Sciences	M,D
Environmental Management and Policy	M,D
Environmental Sciences	M
Hydrology	M,D
Mathematics	M,D
Statistics	M,D
Water Resources	M

UNIVERSITY OF CONNECTICUT

Agricultural Sciences— General	M,D
Agronomy and Soil Sciences	M,D
Animal Sciences	M,D
Applied Mathematics	M
Chemistry	M,D
Geology	M,D
Marine Sciences	M,D
Mathematical and Computational Finance	M
Mathematics	M,D
Natural Resources	M,D
Oceanography	M,D
Physics	M,D
Plant Sciences	M,D
Statistics	M,D

UNIVERSITY OF DAYTON

Applied Mathematics	M
Chemistry	M
Environmental Management and Policy	M,D
Mathematical and Computational Finance	M
Optical Sciences	M,D

UNIVERSITY OF DELAWARE

Agricultural Sciences— General	M,D
Agronomy and Soil Sciences	M,D
Animal Sciences	M,D
Applied Mathematics	M,D
Astronomy	M,D
Chemistry	M,D
Environmental Management and Policy	M,D
Fish, Game, and Wildlife Management	M,D
Food Science and Technology	M,D
Geology	M,D
Horticulture	M
Marine Affairs	M,D
Marine Geology	M,D
Marine Sciences	M,D
Mathematics	M,D
Natural Resources	M
Oceanography	M,D
Physics	M,D
Plant Sciences	M,D
Statistics	M

UNIVERSITY OF DENVER

Applied Physics	M,D
Astronomy	M,D
Chemistry	M,D
Environmental Management and Policy	M,O
Mathematics	M,D
Natural Resources	M,O
Physics	M,D
Statistics	M,D,O

UNIVERSITY OF DETROIT MERCY

Chemistry	M

THE UNIVERSITY OF FINDLAY

Environmental Management and Policy	M

UNIVERSITY OF FLORIDA

Agricultural Sciences— General	M,D
Agronomy and Soil Sciences	M,D
Animal Sciences	M,D
Aquaculture	M,D
Astronomy	M,D
Biostatistics	M,D
Chemistry	M,D
Fish, Game, and Wildlife Management	M,D
Food Science and Technology	M,D
Forestry	M,D
Geology	M,D
Geosciences	M,D
Horticulture	M,D
Hydrology	M,D
Limnology	M,D
Marine Sciences	M,D
Mathematics	M,D
Natural Resources	M,D
Physics	M,D
Plant Sciences	D
Statistics	M,D
Water Resources	M,D

UNIVERSITY OF GEORGIA

Agricultural Sciences— General	M,D
Agronomy and Soil Sciences	M,D
Analytical Chemistry	M,D
Animal Sciences	M,D

Applied Mathematics	M,D
Chemistry	M,D
Food Science and Technology	M,D
Forestry	M,D
Geology	M,D
Horticulture	M,D
Inorganic Chemistry	M,D
Marine Sciences	M,D
Mathematics	M,D
Natural Resources	M,D
Organic Chemistry	M,D
Physical Chemistry	M,D
Physics	M,D
Plant Sciences	M,D
Statistics	M,D

UNIVERSITY OF GUAM

Environmental Sciences	M

UNIVERSITY OF GUELPH

Agricultural Sciences— General	M,D,O
Agronomy and Soil Sciences	M,D
Animal Sciences	M,D
Applied Mathematics	M,D
Applied Statistics	M,D
Aquaculture	M
Atmospheric Sciences	M,D
Chemistry	M,D
Environmental Management and Policy	M,D
Environmental Sciences	M,D
Food Science and Technology	M,D
Horticulture	M,D
Mathematics	M,D
Natural Resources	M,D
Physics	M,D
Statistics	M,D

UNIVERSITY OF HAWAII AT HILO

Environmental Sciences	M

UNIVERSITY OF HAWAII AT MANOA

Agricultural Sciences— General	M,D
Animal Sciences	M
Astronomy	M,D
Chemistry	M,D
Environmental Management and Policy	M,D,O
Food Science and Technology	M
Geochemistry	M,D
Geology	M,D
Geophysics	M,D
Horticulture	M,D
Hydrogeology	M,D
Marine Geology	M,D
Marine Sciences	O
Mathematics	M,D
Meteorology	M,D
Natural Resources	M,D
Oceanography	M,D
Physics	M,D
Planetary and Space Sciences	M,D
Plant Sciences	M,D

UNIVERSITY OF HOUSTON

Applied Mathematics	M,D
Atmospheric Sciences	M,D
Chemistry	M,D
Geology	M,D
Geophysics	M,D
Mathematics	M,D
Physics	M,D
Planetary and Space Sciences	M,D

UNIVERSITY OF HOUSTON–CLEAR LAKE

Chemistry	M
Environmental Management and Policy	M

Environmental Sciences	M
Mathematics	M
Physics	M
Statistics	M

UNIVERSITY OF IDAHO

Agronomy and Soil Sciences	M,D
Animal Sciences	M,D
Chemistry	M,D
Environmental Sciences	M,D
Fish, Game, and Wildlife Management	M,D
Food Science and Technology	M,D
Geology	M,D
Hydrology	M
Mathematics	M,D
Natural Resources	M,D
Physics	M,D
Plant Sciences	M,D
Statistics	M
Water Resources	M,D

UNIVERSITY OF ILLINOIS AT CHICAGO

Applied Mathematics	M,D
Biostatistics	M,D
Chemistry	M,D
Geology	M,D
Geosciences	M,D
Mathematical and Computational Finance	M,D
Mathematics	M,D
Physics	M,D
Statistics	M,D

UNIVERSITY OF ILLINOIS AT SPRINGFIELD

Environmental Management and Policy	M
Environmental Sciences	M

UNIVERSITY OF ILLINOIS AT URBANA–CHAMPAIGN

Agricultural Sciences— General	M
Agronomy and Soil Sciences	M,D
Animal Sciences	M,D
Applied Mathematics	M,D
Applied Statistics	M,D
Astronomy	M,D
Atmospheric Sciences	M,D
Chemical Physics	M,D
Chemistry	M,D
Environmental Sciences	M,D
Food Science and Technology	M,D
Geology	M,D
Geosciences	M,D
Mathematics	M,D
Natural Resources	M,D
Physics	M,D
Statistics	M,D

THE UNIVERSITY OF IOWA

Applied Mathematics	D
Astronomy	M
Biostatistics	M,D
Chemistry	M,D
Computational Sciences	D
Geosciences	M,D
Mathematics	M,D
Physics	M,D
Statistics	M,D,O

THE UNIVERSITY OF KANSAS

Astronomy	M,D
Atmospheric Sciences	M,D
Biostatistics	M,D
Chemistry	M,D
Computational Sciences	M,D
Environmental Sciences	M,D
Geology	M,D
Mathematics	M,D
Physics	M,D

*M—master's degree; P—first professional degree; D—doctorate; O—other advanced degree; *—Close-Up and/or Display*

Petersons Graduate Programs in the Physical Sciences, Mathematics, Agricultural Sciences, the Environment & Natural Resources 2013

facebook.com/petersonspublishing   **31**

UNIVERSITY OF KENTUCKY

Agricultural Sciences— General	M,D
Agronomy and Soil Sciences	M,D
Animal Sciences	M,D
Applied Mathematics	M,D
Astronomy	M,D
Chemistry	M,D
Forestry	M
Geology	M,D
Mathematics	M,D
Physics	M,D
Plant Sciences	M
Statistics	M,D

UNIVERSITY OF LETHBRIDGE

Agricultural Sciences— General	M,D
Chemistry	M,D
Computational Sciences	M,D
Environmental Sciences	M,D
Mathematics	M,D
Physics	M,D

UNIVERSITY OF LOUISIANA AT LAFAYETTE

Geology	M
Mathematics	M,D
Physics	M

UNIVERSITY OF LOUISVILLE

Analytical Chemistry	M,D
Applied Mathematics	M,D
Biostatistics	M,D
Chemical Physics	M,D
Chemistry	M,D
Inorganic Chemistry	M,D
Mathematics	M,D
Organic Chemistry	M,D
Physical Chemistry	M,D
Physics	M,D

UNIVERSITY OF MAINE

Agricultural Sciences— General	M,D,O
Agronomy and Soil Sciences	M,D
Animal Sciences	M
Astronomy	M
Chemistry	M,D
Environmental Management and Policy	M,D
Environmental Sciences	M,D
Fish, Game, and Wildlife Management	M,D
Food Science and Technology	M,D
Forestry	M,D
Geology	M,D
Geosciences	M,D
Horticulture	M
Marine Affairs	M
Marine Sciences	M,D
Mathematics	M
Natural Resources	M,D
Oceanography	M,D
Physics	M,D
Plant Sciences	M,D
Water Resources	M,D

THE UNIVERSITY OF MANCHESTER

Analytical Chemistry	M,D
Applied Mathematics	M,D
Astronomy	M,D
Astrophysics	M,D
Atmospheric Sciences	M,D
Chemistry	M,D
Condensed Matter Physics	M,D
Environmental Management and Policy	M,D
Environmental Sciences	M,D
Geochemistry	M,D
Geosciences	M,D
Inorganic Chemistry	M,D
Mathematical and Computational Finance	M,D
Mathematics	M,D
Natural Resources	M,D

Organic Chemistry	M,D
Paleontology	M,D
Physical Chemistry	M,D
Physics	M,D
Plant Sciences	M,D
Statistics	M,D
Theoretical Chemistry	M,D
Theoretical Physics	M,D

UNIVERSITY OF MANITOBA

Agricultural Sciences— General	M,D
Agronomy and Soil Sciences	M,D
Animal Sciences	M,D
Chemistry	M,D
Computational Sciences	M
Environmental Sciences	M,D
Food Science and Technology	M,D
Geology	M,D
Geophysics	M,D
Horticulture	M,D
Mathematics	M,D
Natural Resources	M,D
Physics	M,D
Plant Sciences	M,D
Statistics	M,D

UNIVERSITY OF MARYLAND, BALTIMORE

Biostatistics	M,D
Environmental Sciences	M,D
Marine Sciences	M,D

UNIVERSITY OF MARYLAND, BALTIMORE COUNTY

Applied Mathematics	M,D
Applied Physics	M,D
Atmospheric Sciences	M,D
Biostatistics	M,D
Chemistry	M,D,O
Environmental Management and Policy	M,D
Environmental Sciences	M,D
Marine Sciences	M,D
Physics	M,D
Planetary and Space Sciences	M
Statistics	M,D

UNIVERSITY OF MARYLAND, COLLEGE PARK

Agricultural Sciences— General	M,D
Analytical Chemistry	M,D
Animal Sciences	M,D
Applied Mathematics	M,D
Astronomy	M,D
Biostatistics	M,D
Chemical Physics	M,D
Chemistry	M,D
Environmental Sciences	M,D
Food Science and Technology	M,D
Geology	M,D
Horticulture	M,D
Inorganic Chemistry	M,D
Marine Sciences	M,D
Mathematics	M,D
Meteorology	M,D
Natural Resources	M,D
Oceanography	M,D
Organic Chemistry	M,D
Physical Chemistry	M,D
Physics	M,D
Statistics	M,D

UNIVERSITY OF MARYLAND EASTERN SHORE

Agricultural Sciences— General	M,D
Environmental Sciences	M,D
Food Science and Technology	M,D
Marine Sciences	M,D

UNIVERSITY OF MARYLAND UNIVERSITY COLLEGE

Environmental Management and Policy	M,O

UNIVERSITY OF MASSACHUSETTS AMHERST

Agronomy and Soil Sciences	M,D
Animal Sciences	M,D
Applied Mathematics	M,D
Astronomy	M,D
Biostatistics	M,D
Chemistry	M,D
Environmental Management and Policy	M,D
Fish, Game, and Wildlife Management	M,D
Food Science and Technology	M,D
Forestry	M,D
Geosciences	M,D
Marine Sciences	M,D
Mathematics	M,D
Physics	M,D
Plant Sciences	M,D
Statistics	M,D
Water Resources	M,D

UNIVERSITY OF MASSACHUSETTS BOSTON

Applied Physics	M
Chemistry	M
Environmental Sciences	D
Marine Sciences	D

UNIVERSITY OF MASSACHUSETTS DARTMOUTH

Acoustics	M,D,O
Chemistry	M,D
Environmental Management and Policy	M,O
Physics	M

UNIVERSITY OF MASSACHUSETTS LOWELL

Analytical Chemistry	M,D
Applied Mathematics	M,D
Applied Physics	M,D
Atmospheric Sciences	M,D
Chemistry	M,D
Computational Sciences	M,D
Environmental Management and Policy	M,D,O
Environmental Sciences	M,D,O
Inorganic Chemistry	M,D
Mathematics	M,D
Optical Sciences	M,D
Organic Chemistry	M,D
Physics	M,D

UNIVERSITY OF MEDICINE AND DENTISTRY OF NEW JERSEY

Biostatistics	M,D,O
Environmental Sciences	D

UNIVERSITY OF MEMPHIS

Analytical Chemistry	M,D
Applied Mathematics	M,D
Applied Statistics	M,D
Biostatistics	M
Chemistry	M,D
Geology	M,D,O
Geophysics	M,D,O
Inorganic Chemistry	M,D
Mathematics	M,D
Organic Chemistry	M,D
Physical Chemistry	M,D
Physics	M
Statistics	M,D

UNIVERSITY OF MIAMI

Chemistry	M,D
Environmental Management and Policy	M,D
Fish, Game, and Wildlife Management	M,D
Geophysics	M,D

Inorganic Chemistry	M,D
Marine Affairs	M
Marine Geology	M,D
Marine Sciences	M,D
Mathematics	M,D
Meteorology	M,D
Oceanography	M,D
Organic Chemistry	M,D
Physical Chemistry	M,D
Physics	M,D

UNIVERSITY OF MICHIGAN

Analytical Chemistry	D
Applied Physics	D
Applied Statistics	M,D
Astronomy	D
Astrophysics	D
Atmospheric Sciences	M,D
Biostatistics	M,D
Chemistry	D
Environmental Management and Policy	M,D
Environmental Sciences	M,D
Inorganic Chemistry	D
Marine Sciences	M,D
Mathematics	M,D
Natural Resources	M,D,O
Organic Chemistry	D
Physical Chemistry	D
Physics	M,D
Planetary and Space Sciences	M,D
Statistics	M,D

UNIVERSITY OF MICHIGAN–DEARBORN

Applied Mathematics	M
Computational Sciences	M
Environmental Sciences	M

UNIVERSITY OF MINNESOTA, DULUTH

Applied Mathematics	M
Chemistry	M
Computational Sciences	M
Geology	M,D
Physics	M

UNIVERSITY OF MINNESOTA, TWIN CITIES CAMPUS

Agricultural Sciences— General	M,D
Agronomy and Soil Sciences	M,D
Animal Sciences	M,D
Astrophysics	M,D
Biostatistics	M,D
Chemistry	M,D
Computational Sciences	M,D
Environmental Management and Policy	M
Food Science and Technology	M,D
Geology	M,D
Geophysics	M,D
Mathematics	M,D,O
Natural Resources	M,D
Physics	M,D
Plant Sciences	M,D
Statistics	M,D
Water Resources	M,D

UNIVERSITY OF MISSISSIPPI

Chemistry	M,D
Mathematics	M,D
Physics	M,D

UNIVERSITY OF MISSOURI

Agricultural Sciences— General	M,D,O
Agronomy and Soil Sciences	M,D
Analytical Chemistry	M,D
Animal Sciences	M,D
Applied Mathematics	M
Astronomy	M,D
Atmospheric Sciences	M,D
Chemistry	M,D
Fish, Game, and Wildlife Management	M,D,O

Petersons Graduate Programs in the Physical Sciences, Mathematics, Agricultural Sciences, the Environment & Natural Resources 2013

Food Science and Technology M,D
Forestry M,D
Geology M,D
Horticulture M,D
Inorganic Chemistry M,D
Mathematics M,D
Natural Resources M
Organic Chemistry M,D
Physical Chemistry M,D
Physics M,D
Plant Sciences M,D
Statistics M,D

UNIVERSITY OF MISSOURI–KANSAS CITY
Analytical Chemistry M,D
Chemistry M,D
Geology M,D
Geosciences M,D
Inorganic Chemistry M,D
Mathematics M,D
Organic Chemistry M,D
Physical Chemistry M,D
Physics M,D
Statistics M,D

UNIVERSITY OF MISSOURI–ST. LOUIS
Applied Mathematics M,D
Applied Physics M,D
Chemistry M,D
Inorganic Chemistry M,D
Mathematics M,D
Organic Chemistry M,D
Physical Chemistry M,D
Physics M,D

THE UNIVERSITY OF MONTANA
Analytical Chemistry M,D
Chemistry M,D
Environmental Management and Policy M
Environmental Sciences M
Fish, Game, and Wildlife Management M,D
Forestry M,D
Geology M,D
Geosciences M,D
Inorganic Chemistry M,D
Mathematics M,D
Natural Resources M,D
Organic Chemistry M,D
Physical Chemistry M,D

UNIVERSITY OF NEBRASKA AT OMAHA
Mathematics M

UNIVERSITY OF NEBRASKA–LINCOLN
Agricultural Sciences— General M,D
Agronomy and Soil Sciences M,D
Analytical Chemistry M,D
Animal Sciences M,D
Astronomy M,D
Chemistry M,D
Food Science and Technology M,D
Geosciences M,D
Horticulture M,D
Inorganic Chemistry M,D
Mathematics M,D
Natural Resources M,D
Organic Chemistry M,D
Physical Chemistry M,D
Physics M,D
Statistics M,D

UNIVERSITY OF NEVADA, LAS VEGAS
Astronomy M,D
Chemistry M,D
Environmental Sciences M,D,O
Geosciences M,D

Mathematics M,D
Physics M,D
Water Resources M

UNIVERSITY OF NEVADA, RENO
Agricultural Sciences— General M,D
Animal Sciences M
Atmospheric Sciences M,D
Chemical Physics D
Chemistry M,D
Environmental Management and Policy M
Environmental Sciences M,D
Geochemistry M,D
Geology M,D
Geophysics M,D
Hydrogeology M,D
Hydrology M,D
Mathematics M
Physics M,D

UNIVERSITY OF NEW BRUNSWICK FREDERICTON
Chemistry M,D
Environmental Management and Policy M,D
Forestry M,D
Geodetic Sciences M,D,O
Geology M,D
Hydrology M,D
Mathematics M,D
Physics M,D
Statistics M,D
Water Resources M,D

UNIVERSITY OF NEW BRUNSWICK SAINT JOHN
Natural Resources M

UNIVERSITY OF NEW ENGLAND
Marine Sciences M

UNIVERSITY OF NEW HAMPSHIRE
Animal Sciences M,D
Applied Mathematics M,D,O
Chemistry M,D
Environmental Management and Policy M
Fish, Game, and Wildlife Management M
Forestry M
Geology M
Geosciences M
Hydrology M
Marine Sciences M
Mathematics M,D,O
Natural Resources M,D
Oceanography M,D,O
Physics M,D
Statistics M,D,O
Water Resources M

UNIVERSITY OF NEW HAVEN
Environmental Management and Policy M,O
Environmental Sciences M,O
Geosciences M,O

UNIVERSITY OF NEW MEXICO
Chemistry M,D
Computational Sciences O
Environmental Management and Policy M
Geosciences M,D
Mathematics M,D
Natural Resources M,D
Optical Sciences M,D
Photonics M,D
Physics M,D
Planetary and Space Sciences M,D
Statistics M,D
Water Resources M

UNIVERSITY OF NEW ORLEANS
Chemistry M,D
Environmental Sciences M
Geosciences M
Mathematics M
Physics M,D

THE UNIVERSITY OF NORTH CAROLINA AT CHAPEL HILL
Astronomy M,D
Astrophysics M,D
Atmospheric Sciences M,D
Biostatistics M,D
Chemistry M,D
Environmental Management and Policy M,D
Environmental Sciences M,D
Geology M,D
Marine Sciences M,D
Mathematics M,D
Physics M,D
Statistics M,D

THE UNIVERSITY OF NORTH CAROLINA AT CHARLOTTE
Applied Mathematics M,D
Applied Physics M,D
Chemistry M,D
Geosciences M,D
Mathematical and Computational Finance M
Mathematics M,D
Optical Sciences M,D

THE UNIVERSITY OF NORTH CAROLINA AT GREENSBORO
Chemistry M
Mathematics M,D

THE UNIVERSITY OF NORTH CAROLINA WILMINGTON
Chemistry M
Environmental Management and Policy M
Geology M
Geosciences M
Marine Sciences M,D
Mathematics M
Statistics M

UNIVERSITY OF NORTH DAKOTA
Atmospheric Sciences M,D
Chemistry M,D
Fish, Game, and Wildlife Management M,D
Geology M,D
Geosciences M,D
Mathematics M
Physics M,D
Planetary and Space Sciences M

UNIVERSITY OF NORTHERN BRITISH COLUMBIA
Environmental Management and Policy M,D,O
Mathematics M,D,O
Natural Resources M,D,O

UNIVERSITY OF NORTHERN COLORADO
Applied Statistics M,D
Chemistry M,D
Geosciences M
Mathematics M,D

UNIVERSITY OF NORTHERN IOWA
Applied Mathematics M
Applied Physics M
Chemistry M
Environmental Sciences M
Geosciences M
Mathematics M

Natural Resources M
Physics M

UNIVERSITY OF NORTH FLORIDA
Mathematics M
Statistics M

UNIVERSITY OF NORTH TEXAS
Chemistry M,D
Environmental Sciences M,D
Mathematics M,D
Physics M,D

UNIVERSITY OF NORTH TEXAS HEALTH SCIENCE CENTER AT FORT WORTH
Biostatistics M,D

UNIVERSITY OF NOTRE DAME
Applied Mathematics M,D
Applied Statistics M,D
Chemistry M,D
Computational Sciences M,D
Geosciences M,D
Inorganic Chemistry M,D
Mathematical and Computational Finance M,D
Mathematics M,D
Organic Chemistry M,D
Physical Chemistry M,D
Physics M,D
Statistics M,D

UNIVERSITY OF OKLAHOMA
Chemistry M,D
Environmental Sciences M,D
Geology M,D
Geophysics M,D
Mathematics M,D*
Meteorology M,D
Natural Resources M,D
Physics M,D

UNIVERSITY OF OKLAHOMA HEALTH SCIENCES CENTER
Biostatistics M,D

UNIVERSITY OF OREGON
Chemistry M,D
Environmental Management and Policy M,D
Geology M,D
Mathematics M,D
Physics M,D

UNIVERSITY OF OTTAWA
Chemistry M,D
Geosciences M,D
Mathematics M,D
Physics M,D
Statistics M,D

UNIVERSITY OF PENNSYLVANIA
Applied Mathematics D
Biostatistics M,D
Chemistry M,D
Computational Sciences D
Environmental Management and Policy M
Environmental Sciences M,D
Geosciences M,D
Mathematics M,D
Physics M,D
Statistics M,D

UNIVERSITY OF PITTSBURGH
Applied Mathematics M,D
Applied Statistics M,D
Biostatistics M,D
Chemistry M,D
Environmental Management and Policy M

---

*M—master's degree; P—first professional degree; D—doctorate; O—other advanced degree; *—Close-Up and/or Display*

Petersons Graduate Programs in the Physical Sciences, Mathematics, Agricultural Sciences, the Environment & Natural Resources 2013

facebook.com/petersonspublishing **33**

Geology	M,D
Mathematics	M,D
Physics	M,D
Planetary and Space Sciences	M,D
Statistics	M,D

UNIVERSITY OF PRINCE EDWARD ISLAND

Chemistry	M

UNIVERSITY OF PUERTO RICO, MAYAG\U00FC EZ CAMPUS

Agricultural Sciences— General	M
Agronomy and Soil Sciences	M
Animal Sciences	M
Applied Mathematics	M
Chemistry	M,D
Computational Sciences	M
Food Science and Technology	M
Geology	M
Horticulture	M
Marine Sciences	M,D
Mathematics	M
Physics	M
Statistics	M

UNIVERSITY OF PUERTO RICO, MEDICAL SCIENCES CAMPUS

Biostatistics	M

UNIVERSITY OF PUERTO RICO, R\U00ED O PIEDRAS

Chemistry	M,D
Environmental Management and Policy	M
Environmental Sciences	M,D
Mathematics	M,D
Physics	M,D

UNIVERSITY OF REGINA

Analytical Chemistry	M,D
Chemistry	M,D
Geology	M,D
Inorganic Chemistry	M,D
Mathematics	M,D
Organic Chemistry	M,D
Physics	M,D
Statistics	M,D
Theoretical Chemistry	M,D

UNIVERSITY OF RHODE ISLAND

Animal Sciences	M,D
Applied Mathematics	M,D,O
Aquaculture	M,D
Chemistry	M,D
Environmental Management and Policy	M,D
Environmental Sciences	M,D
Fish, Game, and Wildlife Management	M,D
Food Science and Technology	M,D
Geosciences	M,D
Marine Affairs	M,D
Marine Sciences	M,D
Mathematics	M,D
Natural Resources	M,D
Oceanography	M,D
Physics	M,D
Plant Sciences	M,D
Statistics	M,D,O

UNIVERSITY OF ROCHESTER

Astronomy	M,D
Biostatistics	M
Chemistry	D
Environmental Management and Policy	M
Geology	M,D
Geosciences	M,D
Mathematics	D
Optical Sciences	M,D
Physics	M,D
Statistics	M,D

UNIVERSITY OF SAINT FRANCIS (IN)

Environmental Sciences	M

UNIVERSITY OF SAINT JOSEPH

Chemistry	M

UNIVERSITY OF SAN DIEGO

Marine Affairs	M
Marine Sciences	M

UNIVERSITY OF SAN FRANCISCO

Chemistry	M
Natural Resources	M

UNIVERSITY OF SASKATCHEWAN

Agricultural Sciences— General	M,D,O
Agronomy and Soil Sciences	M,D,O
Animal Sciences	M,D
Chemistry	M,D
Environmental Sciences	M,D
Food Science and Technology	M,D
Geology	M,D,O
Mathematics	M,D
Physics	M,D
Plant Sciences	M,D
Statistics	M,D

THE UNIVERSITY OF SCRANTON

Chemistry	M

UNIVERSITY OF SOUTH AFRICA

Agricultural Sciences— General	M,D
Environmental Management and Policy	M,D
Environmental Sciences	M,D
Horticulture	M,D
Natural Resources	M,D
Statistics	M,D

UNIVERSITY OF SOUTH ALABAMA

Marine Sciences	M,D
Mathematics	M

UNIVERSITY OF SOUTH CAROLINA

Applied Statistics	M,D,O
Astronomy	M,D
Biostatistics	M,D
Chemistry	M,D
Environmental Management and Policy	M
Geology	M,D
Geosciences	M,D
Marine Sciences	M,D
Mathematics	M,D
Physics	M,D
Statistics	M,D,O

THE UNIVERSITY OF SOUTH DAKOTA

Chemistry	M,D
Computational Sciences	M,D
Mathematics	M
Physics	M,D
Statistics	M,D

UNIVERSITY OF SOUTHERN CALIFORNIA

Applied Mathematics	M,D
Biostatistics	M,D*
Chemistry	D
Food Science and Technology	M,D,O
Geosciences	M,D
Marine Sciences	M,D
Mathematical and Computational Finance	M,D
Mathematics	M,D
Oceanography	M,D
Physical Chemistry	D
Physics	M,D

Statistics	M,D
Water Resources	M,D,O

UNIVERSITY OF SOUTHERN MAINE

Statistics	M

UNIVERSITY OF SOUTHERN MISSISSIPPI

Analytical Chemistry	M,D
Biostatistics	M
Chemistry	M,D
Computational Sciences	M,D
Geology	M,D
Hydrology	M,D
Inorganic Chemistry	M,D
Marine Sciences	M,D
Mathematics	M,D
Organic Chemistry	M,D
Physical Chemistry	M,D
Physics	M,D

UNIVERSITY OF SOUTH FLORIDA

Analytical Chemistry	M,D
Applied Physics	M,D
Biostatistics	M,D
Chemistry	M,D
Environmental Management and Policy	M,D
Environmental Sciences	M,D
Geology	M,D
Inorganic Chemistry	M,D
Marine Sciences	M,D
Mathematics	M,D
Oceanography	M,D
Organic Chemistry	M,D
Physical Chemistry	M,D
Physics	M,D
Statistics	M,D

UNIVERSITY OF SOUTH FLORIDA–ST. PETERSBURG CAMPUS

Environmental Management and Policy	M
Environmental Sciences	M

THE UNIVERSITY OF TENNESSEE

Agricultural Sciences— General	M,D
Analytical Chemistry	M,D
Animal Sciences	M,D
Applied Mathematics	M,D
Chemical Physics	M,D
Chemistry	M,D
Environmental Management and Policy	M,D
Fish, Game, and Wildlife Management	M
Food Science and Technology	M,D
Forestry	M
Geology	M,D
Inorganic Chemistry	M,D
Mathematics	M,D
Organic Chemistry	M,D
Physical Chemistry	M,D
Physics	M,D
Plant Sciences	M
Statistics	M,D
Theoretical Chemistry	M,D

THE UNIVERSITY OF TENNESSEE AT CHATTANOOGA

Computational Sciences	M,D
Environmental Sciences	M

THE UNIVERSITY OF TENNESSEE AT MARTIN

Agricultural Sciences— General	M
Food Science and Technology	M

THE UNIVERSITY OF TENNESSEE SPACE INSTITUTE

Physics	M,D

THE UNIVERSITY OF TEXAS AT ARLINGTON

Applied Mathematics	M,D
Chemistry	M,D
Environmental Sciences	M,D
Geology	M,D
Mathematics	M,D
Physics	M,D

THE UNIVERSITY OF TEXAS AT AUSTIN

Analytical Chemistry	D
Applied Mathematics	M,D
Applied Physics	M,D
Astronomy	M,D
Chemistry	D
Computational Sciences	M,D
Environmental Management and Policy	M
Geology	M,D
Geosciences	M,D
Inorganic Chemistry	D
Marine Sciences	M,D
Mathematics	M,D
Natural Resources	M
Organic Chemistry	D
Physical Chemistry	D
Physics	M,D
Statistics	M

THE UNIVERSITY OF TEXAS AT BROWNSVILLE

Mathematics	M
Physics	M

THE UNIVERSITY OF TEXAS AT DALLAS

Applied Mathematics	M,D
Chemistry	M,D
Geochemistry	M,D
Geophysics	M,D
Geosciences	M,D
Hydrogeology	M,D
Mathematics	M,D
Paleontology	M,D
Physics	M,D
Statistics	M,D

THE UNIVERSITY OF TEXAS AT EL PASO

Chemistry	M,D
Computational Sciences	M,D
Environmental Sciences	M,D
Geology	M,D
Geophysics	M
Mathematics	M
Physics	M
Statistics	M

THE UNIVERSITY OF TEXAS AT SAN ANTONIO

Applied Mathematics	M
Applied Statistics	M,D
Chemistry	M,D
Environmental Sciences	M,D
Geology	M
Mathematics	M
Physics	M,D
Statistics	M,D

THE UNIVERSITY OF TEXAS AT TYLER

Mathematics	M

THE UNIVERSITY OF TEXAS HEALTH SCIENCE CENTER AT HOUSTON

Biomathematics	M,D
Biostatistics	M,D

THE UNIVERSITY OF TEXAS OF THE PERMIAN BASIN

Geology	M

34 facebook.com/petersonspublishing

Petersons Graduate Programs in the Physical Sciences, Mathematics, Agricultural Sciences, the Environment & Natural Resources 2013

THE UNIVERSITY OF TEXAS–PAN AMERICAN
Chemistry — M
Mathematics — M

UNIVERSITY OF THE DISTRICT OF COLUMBIA
Applied Statistics — M

UNIVERSITY OF THE INCARNATE WORD
Mathematics — M
Statistics — M

UNIVERSITY OF THE PACIFIC
Water Resources — M,D

UNIVERSITY OF THE SCIENCES IN PHILADELPHIA
Chemistry — M,D

UNIVERSITY OF THE VIRGIN ISLANDS
Environmental Sciences — M
Marine Sciences — M

THE UNIVERSITY OF TOLEDO
Analytical Chemistry — M,D
Applied Mathematics — M,D
Astrophysics — M,D
Biostatistics — M,O
Chemistry — M,D
Environmental Sciences — M,D
Geology — M,D
Inorganic Chemistry — M,D
Mathematics — M,D
Organic Chemistry — M,D
Physical Chemistry — M,D
Physics — M,D
Statistics — M,D

UNIVERSITY OF TORONTO
Astronomy — M,D
Astrophysics — M,D
Biostatistics — M,D
Chemistry — M,D
Environmental Sciences — M,D
Forestry — M,D
Geology — M,D
Mathematical and Computational Finance — M
Mathematics — M,D
Physics — M,D
Statistics — M,D

UNIVERSITY OF TULSA
Applied Mathematics
Chemistry — M,D
Geosciences — M,D
Mathematics — M
Physics — M

UNIVERSITY OF UTAH
Atmospheric Sciences — M,D
Biostatistics — M,D
Chemical Physics — M,D
Chemistry — M,D
Computational Sciences — M
Environmental Sciences — M
Geology — M,D
Geophysics — M,D
Mathematics — M,D
Physics — M,D
Statistics — M,D

UNIVERSITY OF VERMONT
Agricultural Sciences—
   General — M,D
Agronomy and Soil Sciences — M,D
Animal Sciences — M,D
Biostatistics — M

Chemistry — M
Food Science and Technology — D
Forestry — M,D
Geology — M
Horticulture — M,D
Mathematics — M,D
Natural Resources — M,D
Physics — M
Plant Sciences — M,D
Statistics — M

UNIVERSITY OF VICTORIA
Astronomy — M,D
Astrophysics — M,D
Chemistry — M,D
Condensed Matter Physics — M,D
Geophysics — M,D
Geosciences — M,D
Mathematics — M,D
Oceanography — M,D
Physics — M,D
Statistics — M,D
Theoretical Physics — M,D

UNIVERSITY OF VIRGINIA
Astronomy — M,D
Chemistry — M,D
Environmental Sciences — M,D
Mathematics — M,D
Physics — M,D
Statistics — M,D

UNIVERSITY OF WASHINGTON
Applied Mathematics — M,D
Applied Physics — M,D
Astronomy — M,D
Atmospheric Sciences — M,D
Biostatistics — M,D
Chemistry — M,D
Computational Sciences — M,D
Environmental Management and Policy — M,D
Fish, Game, and Wildlife Management — M,D
Forestry — M,D
Geology — M,D
Geophysics — M,D
Horticulture — M,D
Hydrology — M,D
Marine Affairs — M,O
Marine Geology — M,D
Mathematics — M,D
Natural Resources — M,D
Oceanography — M,D
Physics — M,D
Statistics — M,D

UNIVERSITY OF WATERLOO
Applied Mathematics — M,D
Biostatistics — M,D
Chemistry — M,D
Environmental Management and Policy — M
Geosciences — M,D
Mathematics — M,D
Physics — M,D
Statistics — M,D

THE UNIVERSITY OF WESTERN ONTARIO
Applied Mathematics — M,D
Astronomy — M,D
Biostatistics — M,D
Chemistry — M,D
Environmental Sciences — M,D
Geology — M,D
Geophysics — M,D
Geosciences — M,D
Mathematics — M,D
Physics — M,D
Plant Sciences — M,D
Statistics — M,D

UNIVERSITY OF WEST FLORIDA
Applied Statistics — M
Environmental Sciences — M
Marine Affairs — M
Mathematics — M

UNIVERSITY OF WEST GEORGIA
Applied Mathematics — M
Mathematics — M

UNIVERSITY OF WINDSOR
Chemistry — M,D
Environmental Sciences — M,D
Geosciences — M,D
Mathematics — M,D
Physics — M,D
Statistics — M,D

UNIVERSITY OF WISCONSIN–GREEN BAY
Environmental Management and Policy — M
Environmental Sciences — M

UNIVERSITY OF WISCONSIN–LA CROSSE
Marine Sciences — M

UNIVERSITY OF WISCONSIN–MADISON
Agricultural Sciences—
   General — M,D
Agronomy and Soil Sciences — M,D
Animal Sciences — M,D
Astronomy — D
Atmospheric Sciences — M,D
Biometry — M
Chemistry — M,D
Environmental Sciences — M,D
Fish, Game, and Wildlife Management — M,D
Food Science and Technology — M,D
Forestry — M,D
Geology — M,D
Geophysics — M,D
Horticulture — M,D
Limnology — M,D
Marine Sciences — M,D
Mathematics — D
Natural Resources — M,D
Oceanography — M,D
Physics — M,D
Plant Sciences — M,D
Statistics — M,D
Water Resources — M

UNIVERSITY OF WISCONSIN–MILWAUKEE
Chemistry — M,D
Geochemistry — M,D
Geology — M,D
Mathematics — M,D
Physics — M,D
Water Resources — M,D

UNIVERSITY OF WISCONSIN–RIVER FALLS
Agricultural Sciences—
   General — M

UNIVERSITY OF WISCONSIN–STEVENS POINT
Natural Resources — M

UNIVERSITY OF WISCONSIN–STOUT
Food Science and Technology — M

UNIVERSITY OF WYOMING
Agricultural Sciences—
   General — M,D

Agronomy and Soil Sciences — M,D
Animal Sciences — M,D
Atmospheric Sciences — M,D
Chemistry — M,D
Food Science and Technology — M
Geology — M,D
Geophysics — M,D
Mathematics — M,D
Natural Resources — M,D
Range Science — M,D
Statistics — M,D
Water Resources — M,D

UTAH STATE UNIVERSITY
Agricultural Sciences—
   General — M,D
Agronomy and Soil Sciences — M,D
Animal Sciences — M,D
Applied Mathematics — M,D
Chemistry — M,D
Environmental Management and Policy — M,D
Fish, Game, and Wildlife Management — M,D
Food Science and Technology — M,D
Forestry — M,D
Geology — M
Mathematics — M,D
Meteorology — M,D
Natural Resources — M
Physics — M,D
Plant Sciences — M,D
Range Science — M,D
Statistics — M,D
Water Resources — M,D

VANDERBILT UNIVERSITY
Analytical Chemistry — M,D
Astronomy — M,D
Chemistry — M,D
Environmental Management and Policy — M,D
Environmental Sciences — M
Inorganic Chemistry — M,D
Mathematics — M,D
Organic Chemistry — M,D
Physical Chemistry — M,D
Physics — M,D
Theoretical Chemistry — M,D

VERMONT LAW SCHOOL
Environmental Management and Policy — M

VILLANOVA UNIVERSITY
Applied Statistics — M
Chemistry — M
Mathematics — M

VIRGINIA COMMONWEALTH UNIVERSITY
Analytical Chemistry — M,D
Applied Mathematics — M
Applied Physics — M
Biostatistics — M,D
Chemical Physics — M,D
Chemistry — M,D
Environmental Management and Policy — M
Inorganic Chemistry — M,D
Mathematics — M
Organic Chemistry — M,D
Physical Chemistry — M,D
Physics — M
Statistics — M,D

VIRGINIA POLYTECHNIC INSTITUTE AND STATE UNIVERSITY
Agricultural Sciences—
   General — M,D,O
Agronomy and Soil Sciences — M,D
Animal Sciences — M,D
Chemistry — M,D

*M—master's degree; P—first professional degree; D—doctorate; O—other advanced degree; *—Close-Up and/or Display*

Petersons Graduate Programs in the Physical Sciences, Mathematics,
Agricultural Sciences, the Environment & Natural Resources 2013

facebook.com/petersonspublishing **35**

Environmental Management
  and Policy — M,D,O
Environmental Sciences — M,D,O
Fish, Game, and Wildlife
  Management — M,D
Food Science and Technology — M,D,O
Forestry — M,D,O
Geosciences — M,D
Horticulture — M,D
Hydrology — M,D,O
Mathematics — M,D
Natural Resources — M,O
Physics — M,D
Statistics — M,D
Water Resources — M,D,O

VIRGINIA STATE UNIVERSITY
Agricultural Sciences—
  General — M
Mathematics — M
Physics — M
Plant Sciences — M

WAKE FOREST UNIVERSITY
Analytical Chemistry — M,D
Chemistry — M,D
Inorganic Chemistry — M,D
Mathematics — M
Organic Chemistry — M,D
Physical Chemistry — M,D
Physics — M,D

WASHINGTON STATE UNIVERSITY
Agricultural Sciences—
  General — M
Agronomy and Soil Sciences — M,D
Animal Sciences — M,D
Applied Mathematics — M,D
Applied Statistics — M
Chemistry — M,D
Environmental Sciences — M,D
Food Science and Technology — M,D
Geology — M,D
Horticulture — M,D
Mathematics — M,D
Natural Resources — M,D
Physics — M,D
Statistics — M

WASHINGTON STATE UNIVERSITY TRI-CITIES
Chemistry — M,D
Environmental Sciences — M,D
Natural Resources — M,D

WASHINGTON STATE UNIVERSITY VANCOUVER
Environmental Sciences — M

WASHINGTON UNIVERSITY IN ST. LOUIS
Biostatistics — M,O
Chemistry — D
Geosciences — M,D
Mathematics — M,D
Physics — D
Planetary and Space
  Sciences — M,D
Statistics — M,D

WAYNE STATE UNIVERSITY
Applied Mathematics — M,D
Chemistry — M,D
Food Science and Technology — M,D
Geology — M
Mathematics — M,D

Physics — M,D
Statistics — M,D

WEBSTER UNIVERSITY
Environmental Management
  and Policy — M,D,O

WESLEYAN UNIVERSITY
Astronomy — M
Chemical Physics — M,D
Chemistry — M,D
Environmental Sciences — M
Geosciences — M
Inorganic Chemistry — M,D
Mathematics — M,D*
Organic Chemistry — M,D
Physics — M,D
Theoretical Chemistry — M,D

WESLEY COLLEGE
Environmental Management
  and Policy — M

WEST CHESTER UNIVERSITY OF PENNSYLVANIA
Applied Statistics — M,O
Astronomy — M,O
Chemistry — O
Geology — M,O
Geosciences — M,O
Mathematics — M,O
Planetary and Space
  Sciences — M,O

WESTERN CAROLINA UNIVERSITY
Chemistry — M
Mathematics — M

WESTERN CONNECTICUT STATE UNIVERSITY
Environmental Sciences — M
Geosciences — M
Mathematics — M
Planetary and Space
  Sciences — M

WESTERN ILLINOIS UNIVERSITY
Applied Mathematics — M,O
Chemistry — M
Mathematics — M,O
Physics — M

WESTERN KENTUCKY UNIVERSITY
Agricultural Sciences—
  General — M
Chemistry — M
Computational Sciences — M
Geology — M
Geosciences — M
Mathematics — M
Physics — M

WESTERN MICHIGAN UNIVERSITY
Applied Mathematics — M
Chemistry — M,D
Computational Sciences — M
Geosciences — M,D
Mathematics — M,D
Physics — M,D
Statistics — M,D

WESTERN WASHINGTON UNIVERSITY
Chemistry — M
Environmental Sciences — M
Geology — M
Marine Sciences — M
Mathematics — M

WEST TEXAS A&M UNIVERSITY
Agricultural Sciences—
  General — M,D
Animal Sciences — M
Chemistry — M
Environmental Sciences — M
Mathematics — M
Plant Sciences — M

WEST VIRGINIA UNIVERSITY
Agricultural Sciences—
  General — M,D
Agronomy and Soil Sciences — D
Analytical Chemistry — M,D
Animal Sciences — M,D
Applied Mathematics — M,D
Applied Physics — M,D
Chemical Physics — M,D
Chemistry — M,D
Condensed Matter Physics — M,D
Environmental Management
  and Policy — M,D
Fish, Game, and Wildlife
  Management — M
Food Science and Technology — M,D
Forestry — M,D
Geology — M,D
Geophysics — M,D
Horticulture — M,D
Hydrogeology — M,D
Inorganic Chemistry — M,D
Mathematics — M,D
Natural Resources — M,D
Organic Chemistry — M,D
Paleontology — M,D
Physical Chemistry — M,D
Physics — M,D
Plant Sciences — D
Plasma Physics — M,D
Statistics — M,D
Theoretical Chemistry — M,D
Theoretical Physics — M,D

WICHITA STATE UNIVERSITY
Applied Mathematics — M,D
Chemistry — M,D
Environmental Sciences — M
Geology — M
Mathematics — M,D

WILFRID LAURIER UNIVERSITY
Chemistry — M
Environmental Management
  and Policy — M,D
Environmental Sciences — M,D
Mathematics — M

WILKES UNIVERSITY
Mathematics — M

WILLAMETTE UNIVERSITY
Environmental Management
  and Policy — M

WILMINGTON UNIVERSITY
Environmental Management
  and Policy — M,D

WOODS HOLE OCEANOGRAPHIC INSTITUTION
Marine Geology — D
Oceanography — D

WORCESTER POLYTECHNIC INSTITUTE
Applied Mathematics — M,D,O
Applied Statistics — M,D,O
Chemistry — M,D
Mathematics — M,D,O
Physics — M,D

WRIGHT STATE UNIVERSITY
Applied Mathematics — M
Applied Statistics — M
Chemistry — M
Environmental Sciences — M,D
Geology — M
Geophysics — M
Mathematics — M
Physics — M

YALE UNIVERSITY
Applied Mathematics — M,D
Applied Physics — M,D
Astronomy — M,D
Astrophysics — M,D
Atmospheric Sciences — D
Biostatistics — M,D
Chemistry — D
Environmental Management
  and Policy — M,D
Environmental Sciences — M,D
Forestry — M,D
Geochemistry — D
Geology — D
Geophysics — D
Geosciences — D
Inorganic Chemistry — D
Mathematics — M,D
Meteorology — D
Oceanography — D
Organic Chemistry — D
Paleontology — D
Physical Chemistry — D
Physics — D
Planetary and Space
  Sciences — M,D
Statistics — M,D
Theoretical Chemistry — D

YORK UNIVERSITY
Applied Mathematics — M,D
Astronomy — M,D
Chemistry — M,D
Environmental Management
  and Policy — M,D
Geosciences — M,D
Mathematics — M,D
Physics — M,D
Planetary and Space
  Sciences — M,D
Statistics — M,D

YOUNGSTOWN STATE UNIVERSITY
Analytical Chemistry — M
Applied Mathematics — M
Chemistry — M
Environmental Management
  and Policy — M,O
Inorganic Chemistry — M
Mathematics — M
Organic Chemistry — M
Physical Chemistry — M
Statistics — M

36 facebook.com/petersonspublishing

Petersons Graduate Programs in the Physical Sciences, Mathematics,
Agricultural Sciences, the Environment & Natural Resources 2013

ACADEMIC AND PROFESSIONAL PROGRAMS IN THE PHYSICAL SCIENCES

Section 1
Astronomy and Astrophysics

This section contains a directory of institutions offering graduate work in astronomy and astrophysics. Additional information about programs listed in the directory but not augmented by an in-depth entry may be obtained by writing directly to the dean of a graduate school or chair of a department at the address given in the directory.

For programs offering related work, see also in this book *Geosciences, Meteorology and Atmospheric Sciences,* and *Physics.* In the other guides in this series:

Graduate Programs in the Biological/Biomedical Sciences & Health-Related Medical Professions
See *Biological and Biomedical Sciences* and *Biophysics*

Graduate Programs in Engineering & Applied Sciences
See *Aerospace/Aeronautical Engineering, Energy and Power Engineering (Nuclear Engineering), Engineering and Applied Sciences,* and *Mechanical Engineering and Mechanics*

CONTENTS

Astronomy

Boston University, Graduate School of Arts and Sciences, Department of Astronomy, Boston, MA 02215. Offers MA, PhD. *Students:* 41 full-time (21 women); includes 8 minority (1 American Indian or Alaska Native, non-Hispanic/Latino; 3 Asian, non-Hispanic/Latino; 3 Hispanic/Latino; 1 Two or more races, non-Hispanic/Latino), 24 international. Average age 28. 89 applicants, 13% accepted, 5 enrolled. In 2011, 8 master's awarded. Terminal master's awarded for partial completion of doctoral program. *Degree requirements:* For master's, one foreign language, comprehensive exam, thesis or alternative; for doctorate, one foreign language, comprehensive exam, thesis/dissertation. *Entrance requirements:* For master's and doctorate, GRE General Test, GRE Subject Test (physics), 3 letters of recommendation. Additional exam requirements/recommendations for international students: Required—TOEFL (minimum score 550 paper-based; 213 computer-based). *Application deadline:* For fall admission, 12/15 for domestic and international students. Application fee: $70. *Expenses: Tuition:* Full-time $40,848; part-time $1276 per credit hour. *Required fees:* $572; $286 per semester. *Financial support:* In 2011–12, 1 fellowship with full tuition reimbursement (averaging $19,800 per year), 29 research assistantships with full tuition reimbursements (averaging $19,300 per year), 9 teaching assistantships with full tuition reimbursements (averaging $19,300 per year) were awarded; Federal Work-Study and unspecified assistantships also available. Support available to part-time students. Financial award application deadline: 12/15; financial award applicants required to submit FAFSA. *Unit head:* Tereasa Brainerd, Chairman, 617-353-7412, Fax: 617-353-6463, E-mail: brainerd@bu.edu. *Application contact:* John-Albert Mosely, Department Administrator, 617-363-2625, Fax: 617-353-5704, E-mail: jmosely@bu.edu. Web site: http://www.bu.edu/dbin/astronomy.

Brigham Young University, Graduate Studies, College of Physical and Mathematical Sciences, Department of Physics and Astronomy, Provo, UT 84602-1001. Offers physics (MS, PhD); physics and astronomy (PhD). Part-time programs available. *Faculty:* 29 full-time (2 women). *Students:* 36 full-time (4 women); includes 5 minority (3 Asian, non-Hispanic/Latino; 2 Hispanic/Latino). Average age 29. 22 applicants, 55% accepted, 8 enrolled. In 2011, 7 master's, 4 doctorates awarded. Terminal master's awarded for partial completion of doctoral program. *Degree requirements:* For master's, thesis; for doctorate, thesis/dissertation, qualifying exam. *Entrance requirements:* For master's and doctorate, GRE Subject Test (physics), GRE General Test, minimum GPA of 3.0 in last 60 hours, ecclesiastical endorsement. Additional exam requirements/recommendations for international students: Required—TOEFL (minimum score 580 paper-based; 85 iBT), IELTS (minimum score 7). *Application deadline:* For fall admission, 1/15 priority date for domestic students, 1/15 for international students. Application fee: $50. Electronic applications accepted. Full-time tuition for non-LDS students: $11,520 per year; $640 per credit. *Expenses: Tuition:* Full-time $5760; part-time $320 per credit. Tuition and fees vary according to student's religious affiliation. *Financial support:* In 2011–12, 35 students received support, including 18 research assistantships with full tuition reimbursements available (averaging $20,490 per year), 17 teaching assistantships with full tuition reimbursements available (averaging $19,485 per year); fellowships with full tuition reimbursements available, institutionally sponsored loans, and tuition waivers (full) also available. Support available to part-time students. Financial award application deadline: 1/15. *Faculty research:* Acoustics; atomic, molecular, and optical physics; theoretical and mathematical physics; condensed matter; astrophysics and plasma. *Total annual research expenditures:* $1.7 million. *Unit head:* Dr. Ross L. Spencer, Chair, 801-422-2341, Fax: 801-422-0553, E-mail: ross_spencer@byu.edu. *Application contact:* Dr. J. Ward Moody, Graduate Coordinator, 801-422-4347, Fax: 801-422-0553, E-mail: jmoody@byu.edu. Web site: http://physics.byu.edu/.

California Institute of Technology, Division of Physics, Mathematics and Astronomy, Department of Astronomy, Pasadena, CA 91125-0001. Offers PhD. *Degree requirements:* For doctorate, one foreign language, thesis/dissertation, candidacy and final exams. *Entrance requirements:* For doctorate, GRE General Test, GRE Subject Test. Additional exam requirements/recommendations for international students: Required—TOEFL. *Faculty research:* Observational and theoretical astrophysics, cosmology, radio astronomy, solar physics.

Case Western Reserve University, School of Graduate Studies, Department of Astronomy, Cleveland, OH 44106. Offers MS, PhD. Part-time programs available. *Faculty:* 4 full-time (2 women), 2 part-time/adjunct (1 woman). *Students:* 3 full-time (0 women), 1 international. Average age 26. 24 applicants, 25% accepted, 2 enrolled. In 2011, 1 doctorate awarded. *Degree requirements:* For doctorate, comprehensive exam, thesis/dissertation.·*Entrance requirements:* For doctorate, GRE General Test, GRE Subject Test (physics). Additional exam requirements/recommendations for international students: Required—TOEFL (minimum score 577 paper-based; 213 computer-based; 90 iBT), IELTS (minimum score 7). *Application deadline:* For fall admission, 1/1 for domestic students. Applications are processed on a rolling basis. Application fee: $50. Electronic applications accepted. *Financial support:* Fellowships and research assistantships available. Financial award application deadline: 2/15; financial award applicants required to submit FAFSA. *Faculty research:* Optical observational astronomy, highand low-dispersion spectroscopy, theoretical astrophysics, galactic structure. *Unit head:*

Prof. James Christopher Mihos, Chair, 216-368-3729, Fax: 216-368-5406, E-mail: mihos@case.edu. *Application contact:* Agnes Torontalli, Department Assistant, 216-368-3728, Fax: 216-368-5406, E-mail: agnes@case.edu. Web site: http://burro.astr.case.edu/dept/.

Clemson University, Graduate School, College of Engineering and Science, Department of Physics and Astronomy, Clemson, SC 29634. Offers physics (MS, PhD), including astronomy and astrophysics, atmospheric physics, biophysics. Part-time programs available. *Faculty:* 27 full-time (3 women). *Students:* 67 full-time (21 women); includes 3 minority (2 Black or African American, non-Hispanic/Latino; 1 Hispanic/Latino), 27 international. Average age 27. 133 applicants, 75% accepted, 31 enrolled. In 2011, 4 master's, 6 doctorates awarded. Terminal master's awarded for partial completion of doctoral program. *Degree requirements:* For master's, thesis or alternative; for doctorate, thesis/dissertation. *Entrance requirements:* For master's and doctorate, GRE General Test. Additional exam requirements/recommendations for international students: Required—TOEFL. *Application deadline:* For fall admission, 1/15 priority date for domestic students; for spring admission, 9/15 priority date for domestic students. Applications are processed on a rolling basis. Application fee: $70 ($80 for international students). Electronic applications accepted. *Financial support:* In 2011–12, 58 students received support, including 1 fellowship with full and partial tuition reimbursement available (averaging $8,000 per year), 24 research assistantships with partial tuition reimbursements available (averaging $13,653 per year), 50 teaching assistantships with partial tuition reimbursements available (averaging $13,265 per year); career-related internships or fieldwork, institutionally sponsored loans, scholarships/grants, health care benefits, and unspecified assistantships also available. Support available to part-time students. Financial award application deadline: 6/1; financial award applicants required to submit FAFSA. *Faculty research:* Radiation physics, solid-state physics, nuclear physics, radar and lidar studies of atmosphere. *Total annual research expenditures:* $2.6 million. *Unit head:* Dr. Peter Barnes, Chair, 864-656-3419, Fax: 864-656-0805, E-mail: peterb@clemson.edu. *Application contact:* Graduate Coordinator, 864-656-6702, Fax: 864-656-0805, E-mail: physgradinfo-l@clemson.edu. Web site: http://physicsnt.clemson.edu/.

Columbia University, Graduate School of Arts and Sciences, Division of Natural Sciences, Department of Astronomy, New York, NY 10027. Offers M Phil, MA, PhD. Part-time programs available. *Degree requirements:* For doctorate, thesis/dissertation. *Entrance requirements:* For master's and doctorate, GRE General Test, major in astronomy or physics. Additional exam requirements/recommendations for international students: Required—TOEFL. *Faculty research:* Theoretical astrophysics, x-ray astronomy, radio astronomy.

Cornell University, Graduate School, Graduate Fields of Arts and Sciences, Field of Astronomy and Space Sciences, Ithaca, NY 14853-0001. Offers astronomy (PhD); astrophysics (PhD); general space sciences (PhD); infrared astronomy (PhD); planetary studies (PhD); radio astronomy (PhD); radiophysics (PhD); theoretical astrophysics (PhD). *Faculty:* 27 full-time (2 women). *Students:* 32 full-time (11 women); includes 5 minority (3 Asian, non-Hispanic/Latino; 2 Hispanic/Latino), 9 international. Average age 26. 101 applicants, 30% accepted, 11 enrolled. In 2011, 5 doctorates awarded. *Degree requirements:* For doctorate, comprehensive exam, thesis/dissertation. *Entrance requirements:* For doctorate, GRE General Test, GRE Subject Test (physics), 3 letters of recommendation. Additional exam requirements/recommendations for international students: Required—TOEFL (minimum score 600 paper-based; 250 computer-based; 77 iBT). *Application deadline:* For fall admission, 1/15 for domestic students. Application fee: $95. Electronic applications accepted. *Financial support:* In 2011–12, 5 fellowships with full tuition reimbursements, 15 research assistantships with full tuition reimbursements, 10 teaching assistantships with full tuition reimbursements were awarded; institutionally sponsored loans, scholarships/grants, health care benefits, tuition waivers (full and partial), and unspecified assistantships also available. Financial award applicants required to submit FAFSA. *Faculty research:* Observational astrophysics, planetary sciences, cosmology, instrumentation, gravitational astrophysics. *Unit head:* Director of Graduate Studies, 607-255-4341. *Application contact:* Graduate Field Assistant, 607-255-4341, E-mail: oconnor@astro.cornell.edu. Web site: http://www.gradschool.cornell.edu/fields.php?id-24&a-2.

Dartmouth College, Arts and Sciences Graduate Programs, Department of Physics and Astronomy, Hanover, NH 03755. Offers MS, PhD. Terminal master's awarded for partial completion of doctoral program. *Degree requirements:* For master's, thesis; for doctorate, thesis/dissertation. *Entrance requirements:* For master's and doctorate, GRE General Test, GRE Subject Test. Additional exam requirements/recommendations for international students: Required—TOEFL. *Faculty research:* Matter physics, plasma and beam physics, space physics, astronomy, cosmology.

Georgia State University, College of Arts and Sciences, Department of Physics and Astronomy, Program in Astronomy, Atlanta, GA 30302-3083. Offers PhD. *Degree requirements:* For doctorate, 2 foreign languages, thesis/dissertation, exam. *Entrance requirements:* For doctorate, GRE General Test, GRE Subject Test. Additional exam requirements/recommendations for international students:

Required—TOEFL. Electronic applications accepted. *Faculty research:* Extragalactic photometry, theoretical astrophysics, young stellar objects.

Harvard University, Graduate School of Arts and Sciences, Department of Astronomy, Cambridge, MA 02138. Offers astronomy (PhD); astrophysics (PhD). *Degree requirements:* For doctorate, thesis/dissertation, paper, research project, 2 semesters of teaching. *Entrance requirements:* For doctorate, GRE General Test, GRE Subject Test (physics). Additional exam requirements/recommendations for international students: Required—TOEFL. Electronic applications accepted. *Expenses:* Tuition: Full-time $36,304. *Required fees:* $1186. Full-time tuition and fees vary according to program. *Faculty research:* Atomic and molecular physics, electromagnetism, solar physics, nuclear physics, fluid dynamics.

Indiana University Bloomington, University Graduate School, College of Arts and Sciences, Department of Astronomy, Bloomington, IN 47405-7000. Offers astronomy (MA, PhD); astrophysics (PhD). *Faculty:* 9 full-time (5 women), 2 part-time/adjunct (0 women). *Students:* 23 full-time (8 women); includes 4 minority (1 American Indian or Alaska Native, non-Hispanic/Latino; 1 Asian, non-Hispanic/Latino; 1 Hispanic/Latino; 1 Two or more races, non-Hispanic/Latino). 43 applicants, 19% accepted, 3 enrolled. In 2011, 5 master's, 4 doctorates awarded. Terminal master's awarded for partial completion of doctoral program. *Degree requirements:* For master's, thesis or alternative, oral exam; for doctorate, comprehensive exam, thesis/dissertation, oral defense. *Entrance requirements:* For master's and doctorate, GRE General Test, GRE Subject Test (physics), BA or BS in science. Additional exam requirements/recommendations for international students: Required—TOEFL. *Application deadline:* For fall admission, 1/15 for domestic students, 12/1 for international students; for spring admission, 9/1 for domestic students. Application fee: $55 ($65 for international students). Electronic applications accepted. *Financial support:* In 2011–12, 18 students received support, including 3 fellowships with full tuition reimbursements available (averaging $14,333 per year), 7 research assistantships with full tuition reimbursements available (averaging $19,850 per year), 8 teaching assistantships with full tuition reimbursements available (averaging $17,950 per year); scholarships/grants, health care benefits, and unspecified assistantships also available. Financial award application deadline: 1/15. *Faculty research:* Stellar and galaxy dynamics, stellar chemical abundances, galaxy evolution, observational cosmology. *Total annual research expenditures:* $772,980. *Unit head:* Dr. John Salzer, Chair, 812-855-6911, Fax: 812-855-8725, E-mail: josalzer@indiana.edu. *Application contact:* Julie Wilson, Graduate Secretary, 812-855-6911, Fax: 812-855-8725, E-mail: jaw@indiana.edu. Web site: http://www.astro.indiana.edu/.

The Johns Hopkins University, Zanvyl Krieger School of Arts and Sciences, Henry A. Rowland Department of Physics and Astronomy, Baltimore, MD 21218-2699. Offers astronomy (PhD); physics (PhD). *Degree requirements:* For doctorate, comprehensive exam, thesis/dissertation, minimum Baverage on required coursework. *Entrance requirements:* For doctorate, GRE General Test, GRE Subject Test. Additional exam requirements/recommendations for international students: Required—TOEFL (minimum score 600 paper-based; 250 computer-based; 100 iBT), IELTS. Electronic applications accepted. *Faculty research:* High-energy physics, condensed-matter, astrophysics, particle and experimental physics, plasma physics.

Louisiana State University and Agricultural and Mechanical College, Graduate School, College of Science, Department of Physics and Astronomy, Baton Rouge, LA 70803. Offers astronomy (PhD); astrophysics (PhD); medical physics (MS); physics (MS, PhD). *Faculty:* 47 full-time (5 women), 2 part-time/adjunct (0 women). *Students:* 106 full-time (23 women), 1 part-time (0 women); includes 5 minority (3 Black or African American, non-Hispanic/Latino; 2 Hispanic/Latino), 49 international. Average age 27. 166 applicants, 14% accepted, 21 enrolled. In 2011, 5 master's, 11 doctorates awarded. Terminal master's awarded for partial completion of doctoral program. *Degree requirements:* For master's, thesis or alternative; for doctorate, thesis/dissertation. *Entrance requirements:* For master's and doctorate, GRE General Test, minimum GPA of 3.0. Additional exam requirements/recommendations for international students: Required—TOEFL (minimum score 550 paper-based; 213 computer-based; 79 iBT) or IELTS (minimum score 6.5). *Application deadline:* For fall admission, 1/25 priority date for domestic students, 5/15 for international students; for spring admission, 10/15 for international students. Applications are processed on a rolling basis. Application fee: $50 ($70 for international students). Electronic applications accepted. *Financial support:* In 2011–12, 107 students received support, including 8 fellowships with full tuition reimbursements available (averaging $19,566 per year), 57 research assistantships with full and partial tuition reimbursements available (averaging $22,634 per year), 39 teaching assistantships with full and partial tuition reimbursements available (averaging $19,774 per year); Federal Work-Study, institutionally sponsored loans, health care benefits, tuition waivers (full and partial), and unspecified assistantships also available. Financial award application deadline: 3/15; financial award applicants required to submit FAFSA. *Faculty research:* Experimentation and numerical relativity, condensed matter astrophysics, quantum computing, medical physics. *Total annual research expenditures:* $8.1 million. *Unit head:* Dr. Michael Cherry, Chair, 225-578-2262, Fax: 225-578-5855, E-mail: cherry@phys.lsu.edu. *Application contact:* Arnell Dangerfield, Administrative Coordinator, 225-578-1193, Fax: 225-578-5855, E-mail: adanger@lsu.edu. Web site: http://www.phys.lsu.edu/.

Michigan State University, The Graduate School, College of Natural Science, Department of Physics and Astronomy, East Lansing, MI 48824. Offers astrophysics and astronomy (MS, PhD); physics (MS, PhD). *Entrance requirements:* Additional exam requirements/recommendations for international students: Required—TOEFL (minimum score 550 paper-based; 213 computer-based), Michigan State University ELT (minimum score 85), Michigan English Language Assessment Battery (minimum score 83). Electronic applications accepted. *Faculty research:* Nuclear and accelerator physics, high energy physics, condensed matter physics, biophysics, astrophysics and astronomy.

Minnesota State University Mankato, College of Graduate Studies, College of Science, Engineering and Technology, Department of Physics and Astronomy, Mankato, MN 56001. Offers MS. *Students:* 7 full-time (0 women), 3 part-time (0 women). *Degree requirements:* For master's, one foreign language, comprehensive exam, thesis or alternative. *Entrance requirements:* For master's, minimum GPA of 3.0 during previous 2 years, recommendation letters. Additional exam requirements/recommendations for international students: Required—TOEFL. *Application deadline:* For fall admission, 7/1 priority date for domestic students; for spring admission, 11/1 for domestic students. Applications are processed on a rolling basis. Application fee: $40. Electronic applications accepted. *Financial support:* Research assistantships, teaching assistantships with full tuition reimbursements, Federal Work-Study, and unspecified assistantships available. Support available to part-time students. Financial award application deadline: 3/15; financial award applicants required to submit FAFSA. *Unit head:* Dr. Youwen Xu, Chairperson, 507-389-5742. *Application contact:* 507-389-2321, E-mail: grad@mnsu.edu. Web site: http://cset.mnsu.edu/pa/.

New Mexico State University, Graduate School, College of Arts and Sciences, Department of Astronomy, Las Cruces, NM 88003-8001. Offers MS, PhD. Part-time programs available. *Faculty:* 10 full-time (2 women), 1 (woman) part-time/adjunct. *Students:* 30 full-time (12 women), 3 part-time (1 woman); includes 1 minority (Asian, non-Hispanic/Latino), 1 international. Average age 28. 40 applicants, 13% accepted, 5 enrolled. In 2011, 5 master's, 4 doctorates awarded. Terminal master's awarded for partial completion of doctoral program. *Degree requirements:* For master's, comprehensive exam (for some programs), thesis (for some programs); for doctorate, comprehensive exam, thesis/dissertation. *Entrance requirements:* For master's and doctorate, GRE General Test, GRE Subject Test (advanced physics). Additional exam requirements/recommendations for international students: Required—TOEFL (minimum score 550 paper-based; 79 iBT), IELTS (minimum score 6.5). *Application deadline:* For fall admission, 2/1 priority date for domestic students, 2/15 for international students. Applications are processed on a rolling basis. Application fee: $40 ($50 for international students). Electronic applications accepted. *Expenses:* Tuition, state resident: full-time $5004; part-time $208.50 per credit. Tuition, nonresident: full-time $17,446; part-time $726.90 per credit. *Financial support:* In 2011–12, 11 fellowships (averaging $12,083 per year), 15 research assistantships with tuition reimbursements (averaging $17,509 per year), 11 teaching assistantships with partial tuition reimbursements (averaging $20,768 per year) were awarded; scholarships/grants, health care benefits, and unspecified assistantships also available. Financial award application deadline: 3/1. *Faculty research:* Planetary systems, solar and stellar physics, stellar populations, galaxies, interstellar medium. *Total annual research expenditures:* $4.9 million. *Unit head:* Dr. Jon Holtzman, Head, 575-646-8181, Fax: 575-646-1602, E-mail: holtz@nmsu.edu. *Application contact:* Dr. Nancy Chanover, Coordinator, 575-646-2567, Fax: 575-646-1602, E-mail: gradapps@astronomy.nmsu.edu. Web site: http://astronomy.nmsu.edu/.

Northwestern University, The Graduate School, Judd A. and Marjorie Weinberg College of Arts and Sciences, Department of Physics and Astronomy, Evanston, IL 60208. Offers astrophysics (PhD); physics (MS, PhD). Admissions and degrees offered through The Graduate School. *Degree requirements:* For doctorate, thesis/dissertation, qualifying exam. *Entrance requirements:* For doctorate, GRE General Test, GRE Subject Test. Additional exam requirements/recommendations for international students: Required—TOEFL. *Faculty research:* Nuclear and particle physics, condensed-matter physics, nonlinear physics, astrophysics.

The Ohio State University, Graduate School, College of Arts and Sciences, Division of Natural and Mathematical Sciences, Department of Astronomy, Columbus, OH 43210. Offers MS, PhD. *Faculty:* 16. *Students:* 13 full-time (3 women), 10 part-time (4 women); includes 2 minority (both Two or more races, non-Hispanic/Latino), 6 international. Average age 25. In 2011, 7 master's, 2 doctorates awarded. *Degree requirements:* For master's, comprehensive exam, thesis; for doctorate, comprehensive exam, thesis/dissertation. *Entrance requirements:* For master's and doctorate, GRE General Test, GRE Subject Test (physics). Additional exam requirements/recommendations for international students: Required—TOEFL (minimum score 550 paper-based; 250 computer-based; 79 iBT), Michigan English Language Assessment Battery (minimum score 82). *Application deadline:* For fall admission, 8/15 priority date for domestic students, 7/1 for international students; for winter admission, 12/1 priority date for domestic students, 11/1 for international students; for spring admission, 3/1 priority date for domestic students, 2/1 for international students. Applications are processed on a rolling basis. Application fee: $40 ($50 for international students). Electronic applications accepted. *Expenses:* Tuition, state resident: full-time $11,400. Tuition, nonresident: full-time $28,125. Tuition and fees vary according to course load, degree level, campus/location and program. *Financial support:* Fellowships, research assistantships, teaching assistantships, Federal Work-

Peterson's Graduate Programs in the Physical Sciences, Mathematics, Agricultural Sciences, the Environment & Natural Resources 2013

facebook.com/petersonspublishing   **41**

SECTION 1: ASTRONOMY AND ASTROPHYSICS

Astronomy

Study, and institutionally sponsored loans available. Support available to part-time students. *Unit head:* Bradley M. Peterson, Chair, 614-292-2022, E-mail: peterson.12@osu.edu. *Application contact:* Todd Thompson, Graduate Admissions Chair, 614-292-1773, Fax: 614-292-2928, E-mail: gradchair@astronomy.ohio-state.edu. Web site: http://www.astronomy.ohio-state.edu/.

Ohio University, Graduate College, College of Arts and Sciences, Department of Physics and Astronomy, Athens, OH 45701. Offers astronomy (MS, PhD); physics (MS, PhD). *Faculty:* 27 full-time (3 women), 5 part-time/adjunct (1 woman). *Students:* 81 full-time (27 women); includes 1 minority (Hispanic/Latino), 66 international. Average age 27. 114 applicants, 29% accepted, 14 enrolled. In 2011, 5 master's, 13 doctorates awarded. Terminal master's awarded for partial completion of doctoral program. *Entrance requirements:* For master's and doctorate, minimum GPA of 3.0. Additional exam requirements/recommendations for international students: Required—TOEFL (minimum score 600 paper-based; 250 computer-based; 100 iBT), IELTS (minimum score 7), TWE (minimum score 4). *Application deadline:* For fall admission, 2/1 priority date for domestic students, 2/1 for international students. Applications are processed on a rolling basis. Electronic applications accepted. Application fee is waived when completed online. *Financial support:* In 2011–12, 1 fellowship with full tuition reimbursement (averaging $24,007 per year), 51 research assistantships with full tuition reimbursements (averaging $24,007 per year), 29 teaching assistantships with full tuition reimbursements (averaging $21,825 per year) were awarded; scholarships/grants and unspecified assistantships also available. Financial award application deadline: 4/1. *Faculty research:* Nuclear physics, condensed-matter physics, nonlinear systems, astrophysics, biophysics. *Total annual research expenditures:* $3.2 million. *Unit head:* Dr. David Ingram, Chair, 740-593-0336, Fax: 740-593-0433, E-mail: ingram@ohio.edu. *Application contact:* Dr. Marcus Boettcher, Graduate Admissions Chair, 740-593-1714, Fax: 740-593-0433, E-mail: gradapp@phy.ohiou.edu. Web site: http://www.phy.ohiou.edu/.

See Display on page 248 and Close-Up on page 273.

Penn State University Park, Graduate School, Eberly College of Science, Department of Astronomy and Astrophysics, State College, University Park, PA 16802-1503. Offers MS, PhD. *Unit head:* Dr. Daniel J. Larson, Dean, 814-865-9591, Fax: 814-865-3634. *Application contact:* Cynthia E. Nicosia, Director, Graduate Enrollment Services, 814-865-1795, Fax: 814-865-4627, E-mail: cey1@psu.edu. Web site: http://www.astro.psu.edu/.

Princeton University, Graduate School, Department of Astrophysical Sciences, Princeton, NJ 08544-1019. Offers astronomy (PhD); plasma physics (PhD). *Degree requirements:* For doctorate, thesis/dissertation. *Entrance requirements:* For doctorate, GRE General Test, GRE Subject Test (physics). Additional exam requirements/recommendations for international students: Required—TOEFL (minimum score 600 paper-based; 250 computer-based). Electronic applications accepted. *Faculty research:* Theoretical astrophysics, cosmology, galaxy formation, galactic dynamics, interstellar and intergalactic matter.

Rice University, Graduate Programs, Wiess School of Natural Sciences, Department of Physics and Astronomy, Houston, TX 77251-1892. Offers nanoscale physics (MS); physics and astronomy (PhD); science teaching (MST). Part-time programs available. *Degree requirements:* For master's, thesis (for some programs); for doctorate, thesis/dissertation, minimum B average. *Entrance requirements:* For master's, GRE General Test; for doctorate, GRE General Test, GRE Subject Test. Additional exam requirements/recommendations for international students: Required—TOEFL (minimum score 600 paper-based; 250 computer-based; 90 iBT). Electronic applications accepted. *Faculty research:* Optical physics; ultra cold atoms; membrane electr-statics, peptides, proteins and lipids; solar astrophysics; stellar activity; magnetic fields; young stars.

Rutgers, The State University of New Jersey, New Brunswick, Graduate School-New Brunswick, Department of Physics and Astronomy, Piscataway, NJ 08854-8097. Offers astronomy (MS, PhD); biophysics (PhD); condensed matter physics (MS, PhD); elementary particle physics (MS, PhD); intermediate energy nuclear physics (MS); nuclear physics (MS, PhD); physics (MST); surface science (PhD); theoretical physics (MS, PhD). Part-time programs available. Terminal master's awarded for partial completion of doctoral program. *Degree requirements:* For master's, comprehensive exam, thesis or alternative; for doctorate, comprehensive exam, thesis/dissertation. *Entrance requirements:* For master's and doctorate, GRE General Test, GRE Subject Test. Additional exam requirements/recommendations for international students: Required—TOEFL (minimum score 560 paper-based). Electronic applications accepted. *Faculty research:* Astronomy, high energy, condensed matter, surface, nuclear physics.

Saint Mary's University, Faculty of Science, Department of Astronomy and Physics, Halifax, NS B3H 3C3, Canada. Offers astronomy (M Sc, PhD). Part-time programs available. *Degree requirements:* For master's, thesis optional; for doctorate, comprehensive exam, thesis/dissertation. *Entrance requirements:* For master's, honors degree with minimum GPA of 3.0. Additional exam requirements/recommendations for international students: Required—TOEFL. *Faculty research:* Young stellar objects, interstellar medium, star clusters, galactic structure, early-type galaxies.

San Diego State University, Graduate and Research Affairs, College of Sciences, Department of Astronomy, San Diego, CA 92182. Offers MS. *Degree requirements:* For master's, thesis. *Entrance requirements:* For master's, GRE

General Test, letters of reference. Additional exam requirements/recommendations for international students: Required—TOEFL. Electronic applications accepted. *Faculty research:* CCD, classical and dwarf novae, photometry, interactive binaries.

Stony Brook University, State University of New York, Graduate School, College of Arts and Sciences, Department of Physics and Astronomy, Program in Astronomy, Stony Brook, NY 11794. Offers PhD. *Degree requirements:* For doctorate, thesis/dissertation. *Entrance requirements:* For doctorate, GRE General Test, minimum GPA of 3.0. Additional exam requirements/recommendations for international students: Required—TOEFL.

Université de Moncton, Faculty of Sciences, Department of Physics and Astronomy, Moncton, NB E1A 3E9, Canada. Offers M Sc. Part-time programs available. *Degree requirements:* For master's, thesis. *Entrance requirements:* For master's, proficiency in French. Electronic applications accepted. *Faculty research:* Thin films, optical properties, solar selective surfaces, microgravity and photonic materials.

The University of Arizona, College of Science, Department of Astronomy, Tucson, AZ 85721. Offers MS, PhD. *Faculty:* 24 full-time (4 women), 3 part-time/adjunct (0 women). *Students:* 38 full-time (13 women), 4 part-time (1 woman); includes 3 minority (1 Hispanic/Latino; 2 Two or more races, non-Hispanic/Latino), 8 international. Average age 27. 116 applicants, 12% accepted, 4 enrolled. In 2011, 4 master's, 7 doctorates awarded. *Degree requirements:* For doctorate, thesis/dissertation. *Entrance requirements:* For doctorate, GRE General Test, GRE Subject Test (physics), minimum GPA of 3.5, 3 letters of recommendation. Additional exam requirements/recommendations for international students: Required—TOEFL (minimum score 550 paper-based; 213 computer-based; 79 iBT). *Application deadline:* For fall admission, 1/15 for domestic students, 12/1 for international students. Applications are processed on a rolling basis. Application fee: $75. Electronic applications accepted. *Expenses:* Tuition, state resident: full-time $10,840. Tuition, nonresident: full-time $25,802. *Financial support:* In 2011–12, 47 research assistantships with full tuition reimbursements (averaging $23,605 per year), 3 teaching assistantships with full tuition reimbursements (averaging $22,770 per year) were awarded; scholarships/grants, health care benefits, and unspecified assistantships also available. *Faculty research:* Astrophysics, submillimeter astronomy, infrared astronomy, NICMOS, SIRTF. *Total annual research expenditures:* $77.7 million. *Unit head:* Dr. Peter A. Strittmatter, Head, 520-621-6524, Fax: 520-621-1532, E-mail: pstrittm@as.arizona.edu. *Application contact:* Erin L. Carlson, Administrative Associate, 520-621-6538, Fax: 520-621-1532, E-mail: ecarlson@as.arizona.edu. Web site: http://www.as.arizona.edu.

The University of British Columbia, Faculty of Science, Program in Astronomy, Vancouver, BC V6T 1Z1, Canada. Offers M Sc, PhD.

University of Calgary, Faculty of Graduate Studies, Faculty of Science, Department of Physics and Astronomy, Calgary, AB T2N 1N4, Canada. Offers M Sc, PhD. Part-time programs available. *Degree requirements:* For master's, thesis; for doctorate, thesis/dissertation, oral candidacy exam, written qualifying exam. *Entrance requirements:* For master's and doctorate, GRE General Test, GRE Subject Test. Additional exam requirements/recommendations for international students: Required—TOEFL (minimum score 550 paper-based; 213 computer-based). Electronic applications accepted. *Faculty research:* Astronomy and astrophysics, mass spectrometry, atmospheric physics, space physics, medical physics.

University of California, Los Angeles, Graduate Division, College of Letters and Science, Department of Physics and Astronomy, Program in Astronomy, Los Angeles, CA 90095. Offers MAT, MS, PhD. *Students:* 25 full-time (15 women); includes 2 minority (both Asian, non-Hispanic/Latino), 2 international. Average age 25. 85 applicants, 28% accepted, 7 enrolled. In 2011, 4 master's, 3 doctorates awarded. Terminal master's awarded for partial completion of doctoral program. *Degree requirements:* For master's, comprehensive exam; for doctorate, thesis/dissertation, oral and written qualifying exams. *Entrance requirements:* For master's, GRE General Test, GRE Subject Test (physics), minimum GPA of 3.0, statement of purpose, BS in related field; for doctorate, GRE General Test, GRE Subject Test (physics), BS in related field, minimum undergraduate GPA of 3.0. *Application deadline:* For fall admission, 12/15 for domestic and international students. Application fee: $70 ($90 for international students). Electronic applications accepted. *Financial support:* In 2011–12, 8 fellowships with full and partial tuition reimbursements, 19 research assistantships with full and partial tuition reimbursements, 6 teaching assistantships with full and partial tuition reimbursements were awarded; Federal Work-Study, institutionally sponsored loans, scholarships/grants, health care benefits, tuition waivers (full and partial), and unspecified assistantships also available. Financial award application deadline: 3/1; financial award applicants required to submit FAFSA. *Unit head:* Dr. James Rosenzweig, Chair, 310-206-4541, E-mail: rosenzweig@physics.ucla.edu. *Application contact:* Carol Finn, Graduate Counselor, 310-825-2307, E-mail: apply@physics.ucla.edu. Web site: http://www.physics.ucla.edu.

University of California, Santa Cruz, Division of Graduate Studies, Division of Physical and Biological Sciences, Department of Astronomy and Astrophysics, Santa Cruz, CA 95064. Offers PhD. *Degree requirements:* For doctorate, one foreign language, thesis/dissertation, qualifying exam. *Entrance requirements:* For doctorate, GRE General Test, GRE Subject Test. Additional exam requirements/recommendations for international students: Required—TOEFL (minimum score 550 paper-based; 220 computer-based; 83 iBT);

Recommended—IELTS (minimum score 8). Electronic applications accepted. *Faculty research:* Solar system and the Milky Way to the most distant galaxies in the Universe, fundamental questions of cosmology.

University of Chicago, Division of the Physical Sciences, Department of Astronomy and Astrophysics, Chicago, IL 60637-1513. Offers MS, PhD. Terminal master's awarded for partial completion of doctoral program. *Degree requirements:* For master's, comprehensive exam, thesis optional, candidacy exam; for doctorate, comprehensive exam, thesis/dissertation, dissertation for publication. *Entrance requirements:* For master's, department candidacy examination, minimum GPA of 3.0; for doctorate, GRE General Test, GRE Subject Test, minimum GPA of 3.0. Additional exam requirements/recommendations for international students: Required—TOEFL (minimum score 600 paper-based; 250 computer-based); Recommended—IELTS. Electronic applications accepted. *Faculty research:* Quasi-stellar object absorption lines, fluid dynamics, interstellar matter, particle physics, cosmology.

University of Delaware, College of Arts and Sciences, Department of Physics and Astronomy, Newark, DE 19716. Offers MS, PhD. Part-time programs available. Terminal master's awarded for partial completion of doctoral program. *Degree requirements:* For master's, thesis; for doctorate, thesis/dissertation. *Entrance requirements:* For master's and doctorate, GRE General Test, GRE Subject Test. Additional exam requirements/recommendations for international students: Required—TOEFL (minimum score 600 paper-based; 250 computer-based). Electronic applications accepted. *Faculty research:* Magnetoresistance and magnetic materials, ultrafast optical phenomena, superfluidity, elementary particle physics, stellar atmospheres and interiors.

University of Denver, Faculty of Natural Sciences and Mathematics, Department of Physics and Astronomy, Denver, CO 80208. Offers applied physics (MS); physics (MS, PhD). Part-time programs available. *Faculty:* 10 full-time (3 women), 5 part-time/adjunct (0 women). *Students:* 8 full-time (3 women), 9 part-time (3 women); includes 1 minority (Hispanic/Latino), 2 international. Average age 29. 36 applicants, 19% accepted, 6 enrolled. In 2011, 1 master's, 1 doctorate awarded. Terminal master's awarded for partial completion of doctoral program. *Median time to degree:* Of those who began their doctoral program in fall 2003, 100% received their degree in 8 years or less. *Degree requirements:* For master's, thesis optional; for doctorate, thesis/dissertation. *Entrance requirements:* For master's and doctorate, GRE General Test, GRE Subject Test in physics (strongly preferred), three letters of recommendation, personal statement. Additional exam requirements/recommendations for international students: Required—TOEFL (minimum score 550 paper-based; 80 iBT). *Application deadline:* For fall admission, 3/1 priority date for domestic students. Applications are processed on a rolling basis. Application fee: $60. Electronic applications accepted. *Financial support:* In 2011–12, 15 students received support, including 10 research assistantships with full and partial tuition reimbursements available (averaging $19,300 per year), 10 teaching assistantships with full and partial tuition reimbursements available (averaging $17,370 per year); career-related internships or fieldwork, Federal Work-Study, institutionally sponsored loans, scholarships/grants, and unspecified assistantships also available. Support available to part-time students. Financial award application deadline: 2/15; financial award applicants required to submit FAFSA. *Faculty research:* Atomic and molecular beams and collisions, infrared astronomy, acoustic emission from stressed solids, nano materials. *Unit head:* Dr. Davor Balzar, Chair, 303-871-2238, E-mail: davor.balzar@du.edu. *Application contact:* Barbara Stephen, Assistant to the Chair, 303-871-2238, E-mail: barbara.stephen@du.edu. Web site: http://www.physics.du.edu.

University of Florida, Graduate School, College of Liberal Arts and Sciences, Department of Astronomy, Gainesville, FL 32611. Offers MS, MST, PhD. *Faculty:* 21 full-time (3 women). *Students:* 35 full-time (10 women); includes 2 minority (both Hispanic/Latino), 14 international. Average age 28. 87 applicants, 29% accepted, 6 enrolled. In 2011, 5 master's, 8 doctorates awarded. *Degree requirements:* For doctorate, one foreign language, comprehensive exam, thesis/dissertation. *Entrance requirements:* For master's and doctorate, GRE General Test, GRE Subject Test (physics), minimum GPA of 3.0. Additional exam requirements/recommendations for international students: Required—TOEFL (minimum score 550 paper-based; 213 computer-based; 80 iBT), IELTS (minimum score 6). *Application deadline:* For fall admission, 1/20 for domestic and international students. Applications are processed on a rolling basis. Application fee: $30. Electronic applications accepted. *Financial support:* Fellowships, research assistantships, teaching assistantships, tuition waivers (full), and unspecified assistantships available. Financial award application deadline: 1/31; financial award applicants required to submit FAFSA. *Faculty research:* Solar systems, stars and stellar populations, star formation and interstellar medium, structure and evolution of galaxies, extragalactic astronomy and cosmology, extrasolar planets and instrumentation. *Unit head:* Dr. Rafael Guzman, Chair, 352-392-2052 Ext. 212, Fax: 352-392-5089, E-mail: guzman@astro.ufl.edu. *Application contact:* Dr. Anthony H. Gonzalez, Graduate Coordinator, 352-392-2052 Ext. 233, Fax: 352-392-5089, E-mail: anthony@astro.ufl.edu. Web site: http://www.astro.ufl.edu/.

University of Hawaii at Manoa, Graduate Division, College of Natural Sciences, Department of Physics and Astronomy, Program in Astronomy, Honolulu, HI 96822. Offers MS, PhD. Part-time programs available. *Degree requirements:* For master's, thesis optional; for doctorate, comprehensive exam, thesis/dissertation. *Entrance requirements:* For master's and doctorate, GRE General Test. Additional exam requirements/recommendations for international students:

Required—TOEFL (minimum score 560 paper-based; 220 computer-based; 83 iBT), IELTS (minimum score 5).

University of Illinois at Urbana–Champaign, Graduate College, College of Liberal Arts and Sciences, Department of Astronomy, Champaign, IL 61820. Offers astronomy (PhD). *Faculty:* 12 full-time (1 woman). *Students:* 15 full-time (7 women), 10 part-time (6 women); includes 3 minority (2 Asian, non-Hispanic/Latino; 1 Hispanic/Latino), 13 international. 58 applicants, 12% accepted, 3 enrolled. In 2011, 5 master's, 5 doctorates awarded. *Entrance requirements:* For master's and doctorate, GRE General Test, minimum GPA of 3.0. Additional exam requirements/recommendations for international students: Required—TOEFL (minimum score 550 paper-based; 213 computer-based). *Application deadline:* Applications are processed on a rolling basis. Application fee: $75 ($90 for international students). Electronic applications accepted. *Financial support:* In 2011–12, 1 fellowship, 18 research assistantships, 11 teaching assistantships were awarded; tuition waivers (full and partial) also available. *Unit head:* Charles Gammie, Chair, 217-333-8646, Fax: 217-244-7638, E-mail: gammie@illinois.edu. *Application contact:* Jeri Cochran, Administrative Assistant, 217-333-9784, Fax: 217-244-7638, E-mail: jcochran@illinois.edu. Web site: http://www.astro.illinois.edu.

The University of Iowa, Graduate College, College of Liberal Arts and Sciences, Department of Physics and Astronomy, Program in Astronomy, Iowa City, IA 52242-1316. Offers MS. *Degree requirements:* For master's, thesis optional, exam. *Entrance requirements:* For master's, GRE General Test, minimum GPA of 3.0. Additional exam requirements/recommendations for international students: Required—TOEFL (minimum score 550 paper-based; 213 computer-based; 81 iBT). Electronic applications accepted.

The University of Kansas, Graduate Studies, College of Liberal Arts and Sciences, Department of Physics and Astronomy, Lawrence, KS 66045. Offers computational physics and astronomy (MS); physics (MS, PhD). *Faculty:* 25 full-time (4 women). *Students:* 42 full-time (9 women), 4 part-time (1 woman); includes 3 minority (1 Black or African American, non-Hispanic/Latino; 1 Hispanic/Latino; 1 Two or more races, non-Hispanic/Latino), 11 international. Average age 29. 59 applicants, 41% accepted, 12 enrolled. In 2011, 3 master's, 4 doctorates awarded. Terminal master's awarded for partial completion of doctoral program. *Degree requirements:* For master's, thesis (for some programs); for doctorate, comprehensive exam, thesis/dissertation, computer skills, communication skills. *Entrance requirements:* For master's and doctorate, GRE Subject Test (physics), undergraduate degree. Additional exam requirements/recommendations for international students: Required—TOEFL (minimum score 20 computer-based; 20 iBT). *Application deadline:* For fall admission, 4/1 priority date for domestic students, 4/1 for international students; for spring admission, 11/15 for domestic and international students. Applications are processed on a rolling basis. Application fee: $55 ($65 for international students). Electronic applications accepted. Tuition and fees vary according to course load, campus/location, program and reciprocity agreements. *Financial support:* Fellowships with full and partial tuition reimbursements, research assistantships with full and partial tuition reimbursements, teaching assistantships with full and partial tuition reimbursements, health care benefits, and unspecified assistantships available. Financial award application deadline: 4/1; financial award applicants required to submit FAFSA. *Faculty research:* Condensed-matter, cosmology, elementary particles, nuclear physics, space physics, astrophysics, astrobiology, biophysics, high energy. *Unit head:* Dr. Stephen J. Sanders, Chair, 785-864-4626, Fax: 785-864-5262. *Application contact:* Teri Leahy, Graduate Coordinator, 785-864-1225, Fax: 785-864-5262, E-mail: tleahy@ku.edu. Web site: http://www.physics.ku.edu.

University of Kentucky, Graduate School, College of Arts and Sciences, Program in Physics and Astronomy, Lexington, KY 40506-0032. Offers physics (MS, PhD). *Degree requirements:* For master's, comprehensive exam, thesis optional; for doctorate, comprehensive exam, thesis/dissertation. *Entrance requirements:* For master's, GRE General Test, minimum undergraduate GPA of 2.75; for doctorate, GRE General Test, minimum graduate GPA of 3.0. Additional exam requirements/recommendations for international students: Required—TOEFL (minimum score 550 paper-based; 213 computer-based). Electronic applications accepted. *Faculty research:* Astrophysics, active galactic nuclei, and radio astronomy; Rydbert atoms, and electron scattering; TOF spectroscopy, hyperon interactions and muons; particle theory, lattice gauge theory, quark, and skyrmion models.

University of Maine, Graduate School, College of Education and Human Development, Interdisciplinary Program in Teaching, Orono, ME 04469. Offers earth sciences (MST); generalist (MST); mathematics (MST); physics and astronomy (MST). *Students:* 8 full-time (6 women), 13 part-time (10 women); includes 1 minority (American Indian or Alaska Native, non-Hispanic/Latino). Average age 40. 2 applicants, 50% accepted, 1 enrolled. In 2011, 6 master's awarded. *Entrance requirements:* For master's, GRE General Test, MAT. Application fee: $65. *Expenses:* Tuition, state resident: full-time $5016. Tuition, nonresident: full-time $14,424. *Unit head:* Dr. Susan McKay, Director, 207-581-1016. *Application contact:* Scott G. Delcourt, Associate Dean of the Graduate School, 207-581-3291, Fax: 207-581-3232, E-mail: graduate@maine.edu. Web site: http://www2.umaine.edu/graduate/.

The University of Manchester, School of Physics and Astronomy, Manchester, United Kingdom. Offers astronomy and astrophysics (M Sc, PhD); biological physics (M Sc, PhD); condensed matter physics (M Sc, PhD); nonlinear and liquid crystals physics (M Sc, PhD); nuclear physics (M Sc, PhD); particle physics

Peterson's Graduate Programs in the Physical Sciences, Mathematics, Agricultural Sciences, the Environment & Natural Resources 2013

facebook.com/petersonspublishing **43**

Astronomy

(M Sc, PhD); photon physics (M Sc, PhD); physics (M Sc, PhD); theoretical physics (M Sc, PhD).

University of Maryland, College Park, Academic Affairs, College of Computer, Mathematical and Natural Sciences, Department of Astronomy, College Park, MD 20742. Offers MS, PhD. Part-time and evening/weekend programs available. *Faculty:* 86 full-time (18 women), 14 part-time/adjunct (3 women). *Students:* 37 full-time (14 women), 1 (woman) part-time; includes 3 minority (all Asian, non-Hispanic/Latino), 11 international. 146 applicants, 16% accepted, 8 enrolled. In 2011, 8 master's, 4 doctorates awarded. Terminal master's awarded for partial completion of doctoral program. *Degree requirements:* For master's, thesis or alternative, written exam; for doctorate, thesis/dissertation, research project. *Entrance requirements:* For master's, GRE General Test, GRE Subject Test (physics), minimum GPA of 3.0, 3 letters of recommendation; for doctorate, GRE General Test, GRE Subject Test (physics), 3 letters of recommendation. *Application deadline:* For fall admission, 1/15 for domestic and international students. Applications are processed on a rolling basis. Application fee: $75. Electronic applications accepted. *Expenses: Tuition, area resident:* Part-time $525 per credit hour. Tuition, state resident: part-time $525 per credit hour. Tuition, nonresident: part-time $1131 per credit hour. *Required fees:* $386.31 per term. Tuition and fees vary according to program. *Financial support:* In 2011–12, 1 fellowship with full tuition reimbursement (averaging $20,440 per year), 23 research assistantships with tuition reimbursements (averaging $21,325 per year), 14 teaching assistantships with tuition reimbursements (averaging $19,090 per year) were awarded; career-related internships or fieldwork, Federal Work-Study, and scholarships/grants also available. Support available to part-time students. Financial award applicants required to submit FAFSA. *Faculty research:* Solar radio astronomy, plasma and high-energy astrophysics, galactic and extragalactic astronomy. *Total annual research expenditures:* $23.6 million. *Unit head:* Stuart N. Vogel, Chair, 301-405-1508, Fax: 301-314-9067, E-mail: svogel@umd.edu. *Application contact:* Dr. Charles A. Caramello, Dean of Graduate School, 301-405-0358, Fax: 301-314-9305, E-mail: ccaramel@umd.edu.

University of Massachusetts Amherst, Graduate School, College of Natural Sciences, Department of Astronomy, Amherst, MA 01003. Offers MS, PhD. Part-time programs available. *Faculty:* 18 full-time (3 women). *Students:* 21 full-time (5 women); includes 2 minority (1 American Indian or Alaska Native, non-Hispanic/Latino; 1 Hispanic/Latino), 8 international. Average age 27. 55 applicants, 24% accepted, 4 enrolled. In 2011, 1 master's, 5 doctorates awarded. Terminal master's awarded for partial completion of doctoral program. *Degree requirements:* For master's, thesis or alternative; for doctorate, comprehensive exam, thesis/dissertation. *Entrance requirements:* For master's and doctorate, GRE General Test, GRE Subject Test (physics). Additional exam requirements/recommendations for international students: Required—TOEFL (minimum score 550 paper-based; 213 computer-based; 80 iBT), IELTS (minimum score 6.5). *Application deadline:* For fall admission, 2/1 for domestic and international students; for spring admission, 10/1 for domestic and international students. Applications are processed on a rolling basis. Application fee: $50 ($65 for international students). Electronic applications accepted. Tuition and fees vary according to course load, campus/location and program. *Financial support:* Fellowships with full and partial tuition reimbursements, research assistantships with full and partial tuition reimbursements, teaching assistantships with full and partial tuition reimbursements, career-related internships or fieldwork, Federal Work-Study, scholarships/grants, traineeships, health care benefits, tuition waivers (full and partial), and unspecified assistantships available. Support available to part-time students. Financial award application deadline: 2/1. *Unit head:* Dr. William M. Irvine, Graduate Program Director, 413-545-2194, Fax: 413-545-4223. *Application contact:* Lindsay DeSantis, Interim Supervisor of Admissions, 413-545-0722, Fax: 413-577-0010, E-mail: gradadm@grad.umass.edu. Web site: http://www-astro.phast.umass.edu/.

University of Michigan, Horace H. Rackham School of Graduate Studies, College of Literature, Science, and the Arts, Department of Astronomy, Ann Arbor, MI 48109-1042. Offers astronomy and astrophysics (PhD). *Faculty:* 21 full-time (6 women). *Students:* 26 full-time (10 women); includes 4 minority (all Asian, non-Hispanic/Latino). In 2011, 5 degrees awarded. Terminal master's awarded for partial completion of doctoral program. *Median time to degree:* Of those who began their doctoral program in fall 2003, 99% received their degree in 8 years or less. *Degree requirements:* For doctorate, thesis/dissertation, oral defense of dissertation, preliminary exam. *Entrance requirements:* For doctorate, GRE General Test, GRE Subject Test (physics). Additional exam requirements/recommendations for international students: Required—TOEFL. *Application deadline:* For fall admission, 1/4 for domestic and international students. Application fee: $65 ($75 for international students). Electronic applications accepted. *Financial support:* In 2011–12, 5 fellowships with full tuition reimbursements (averaging $22,800 per year), 23 research assistantships with full tuition reimbursements (averaging $22,800 per year), 13 teaching assistantships with full tuition reimbursements (averaging $22,800 per year) were awarded; institutionally sponsored loans, scholarships/grants, health care benefits, and unspecified assistantships also available. Financial award applicants required to submit FAFSA. *Faculty research:* Extragalactic and galactic astronomy, cosmology, star and planet formation, high energy astrophysics. *Total annual research expenditures:* $2.1 million. *Unit head:* Dr. Joel Bregman, Chair and Professor, 734-764-3440, Fax: 734-763-6317, E-mail: jbregman@umich.edu. *Application contact:* Brian M. Cox, Administrative Assistant, 734-764-3440, Fax: 734-763-6317, E-mail: bmcox@umich.edu. Web site: http://www.astro.lsa.umich.edu/.

University of Missouri, Graduate School, College of Arts and Sciences, Department of Physics and Astronomy, Columbia, MO 65211. Offers MS, PhD. *Faculty:* 27 full-time (8 women), 1 (woman) part-time/adjunct. *Students:* 32 full-time (3 women), 21 part-time (5 women); includes 4 minority (1 Asian, non-Hispanic/Latino; 1 Hispanic/Latino; 2 Two or more races, non-Hispanic/Latino), 29 international. Average age 28. 85 applicants, 13% accepted, 10 enrolled. In 2011, 6 master's, 8 doctorates awarded. Terminal master's awarded for partial completion of doctoral program. *Degree requirements:* For doctorate, one foreign language, comprehensive exam, thesis/dissertation. *Entrance requirements:* For master's and doctorate, GRE General Test, minimum GPA of 3.0. Additional exam requirements/recommendations for international students: Required—TOEFL (minimum score 550 paper-based; 213 computer-based; 80 iBT). *Application deadline:* For fall admission, 3/15 priority date for domestic students. Applications are processed on a rolling basis. Application fee: $55 ($75 for international students). Electronic applications accepted. *Expenses:* Tuition, state resident: full-time $5881. Tuition, nonresident: full-time $15,183. *Required fees:* $952. Tuition and fees vary according to campus/location and program. *Financial support:* In 2011–12, 35 research assistantships with full tuition reimbursements, 10 teaching assistantships with full tuition reimbursements were awarded; institutionally sponsored loans, health care benefits, and unspecified assistantships also available. *Faculty research:* Experimental and theoretical condensed-matter physics, biological physics, astronomy/astrophysics. *Unit head:* Dr. Peter Pfeifer, Department Chair, 573-882-2335, E-mail: pfeiferp@missouri.edu. *Application contact:* Dr. Carsten Ullrich, Director of Graduate Studies, 573-882-3335, E-mail: ullrichc@missouri.edu. Web site: http://physics.missouri.edu/graduate/.

University of Nebraska–Lincoln, Graduate College, College of Arts and Sciences, Department of Physics and Astronomy, Lincoln, NE 68588. Offers astronomy (MS, PhD); physics (MS, PhD). *Degree requirements:* For master's, thesis optional; for doctorate, comprehensive exam, thesis/dissertation. *Entrance requirements:* For master's and doctorate, GRE General Test. Additional exam requirements/recommendations for international students: Required—TOEFL (minimum score 550 paper-based; 213 computer-based). Electronic applications accepted. *Faculty research:* Electromagnetics of solids and thin films, photoionization, ion collisions with atoms, molecules and surfaces, nanostructures.

University of Nevada, Las Vegas, Graduate College, College of Science, Department of Physics, Las Vegas, NV 89154-4002. Offers astronomy (MS, PhD); physics (MS, PhD). Part-time programs available. *Faculty:* 20 full-time (3 women), 7 part-time/adjunct (3 women). *Students:* 2 full-time (0 women), 13 part-time (1 woman), 4 international. Average age 29. 10 applicants, 20% accepted, 0 enrolled. In 2011, 3 master's, 5 doctorates awarded. *Degree requirements:* For master's, thesis, oral exam; for doctorate, comprehensive exam, thesis/dissertation. *Entrance requirements:* For master's and doctorate, GRE General Test. Additional exam requirements/recommendations for international students: Required—TOEFL (minimum score 550 paper-based; 213 computer-based; 80 iBT), IELTS (minimum score 7). *Application deadline:* For fall admission, 8/1 priority date for domestic students, 5/1 for international students; for spring admission, 10/1 priority date for domestic students, 10/1 for international students. Applications are processed on a rolling basis. Application fee: $60 ($95 for international students). Electronic applications accepted. *Financial support:* In 2011–12, 15 students received support, including 1 research assistantship with partial tuition reimbursement available (averaging $33,892 per year), 14 teaching assistantships with partial tuition reimbursements available (averaging $14,882 per year); institutionally sponsored loans, scholarships/grants, health care benefits, and unspecified assistantships also available. Financial award application deadline: 3/1. *Faculty research:* Gamma-ray bursters astrophysics, cosmology and dark matter astrophysics, experimental high pressure physics, theoretical condensed matter physics, laser-plasma atomic physics. *Total annual research expenditures:* $4.4 million. *Unit head:* Dr. Tao Pang, Chair/Professor, 702-895-4454, Fax: 702-895-0804, E-mail: pang@physics.unlv.edu. *Application contact:* Graduate College Admissions Evaluator, 702-895-3320, Fax: 702-895-4180, E-mail: gradcollege@unlv.edu. Web site: http://www.physics.unlv.edu/graduate.html.

The University of North Carolina at Chapel Hill, Graduate School, College of Arts and Sciences, Department of Physics and Astronomy, Chapel Hill, NC 27599. Offers physics (MS, PhD). Terminal master's awarded for partial completion of doctoral program. *Degree requirements:* For master's, comprehensive exam; for doctorate, comprehensive exam, thesis/dissertation. *Entrance requirements:* For master's and doctorate, GRE General Test, minimum GPA of 3.0. Electronic applications accepted. *Faculty research:* Observational astronomy, fullerenes, polarized beams, nanotubes, nucleosynthesis in stars and supernovae, superstring theory, ballistic transport in semiconductors, gravitation.

University of Rochester, School of Arts and Sciences, Department of Physics and Astronomy, Rochester, NY 14627. Offers physics (MA, MS, PhD); physics and astronomy (PhD). Part-time programs available. *Faculty:* 26 full-time (3 women). *Students:* 105 full-time (23 women), 2 part-time (0 women); includes 8 minority (4 Asian, non-Hispanic/Latino; 4 Hispanic/Latino), 43 international. 354 applicants, 15% accepted, 10 enrolled. In 2011, 22 master's, 4 doctorates awarded. Terminal master's awarded for partial completion of doctoral program. *Degree requirements:* For master's, comprehensive exam, thesis (for some programs); for doctorate, comprehensive exam, thesis/dissertation, qualifying exam. *Entrance requirements:* For master's and doctorate, GRE General Test.

44 facebook.com/petersonspublishing

Peterson's Graduate Programs in the Physical Sciences, Mathematics, Agricultural Sciences, the Environment & Natural Resources 2013

Additional exam requirements/recommendations for international students: Required—TOEFL. *Application deadline:* For fall admission, 1/15 priority date for domestic students. Application fee: $0. *Expenses: Tuition:* Full-time $41,040. *Financial support:* Fellowships, research assistantships, teaching assistantships, and tuition waivers (full and partial) available. Financial award application deadline: 2/1. *Faculty research:* Astronomy and astrophysics, biological physics, condensed matter physics, high energy/nuclear physics, quantum optics. *Unit head:* Nicholas P. Bigelow, Chair, 585-275-4344. *Application contact:* Laura Blumkin, Graduate Coordinator, 585-275-4356, E-mail: laurablumkin@pas.rochester.edu. Web site: http://www.pas.rochester.edu/urpas/pages/graduate/gradprograms.

University of South Carolina, The Graduate School, College of Arts and Sciences, Department of Physics and Astronomy, Columbia, SC 29208. Offers IMA, MAT, MS, PSM, PhD. IMA and MAT offered in cooperation with the College of Education. Part-time programs available. Terminal master's awarded for partial completion of doctoral program. *Degree requirements:* For master's, comprehensive exam, thesis; for doctorate, one foreign language, comprehensive exam, thesis/dissertation. *Entrance requirements:* For master's and doctorate, GRE General Test, GRE Subject Test. Additional exam requirements/recommendations for international students: Required—TOEFL (minimum score 570 paper-based; 230 computer-based; 75 iBT). Electronic applications accepted. *Faculty research:* Condensed matter, intermediate-energy nuclear physics, foundations of quantum mechanics, astronomy/astrophysics.

The University of Texas at Austin, Graduate School, College of Natural Sciences, Department of Astronomy, Austin, TX 78712-1111. Offers MA, PhD. *Entrance requirements:* For master's and doctorate, GRE General Test, GRE Subject Test (physics). Additional exam requirements/recommendations for international students: Required—TOEFL. *Application deadline:* For fall admission, 1/15 priority date for domestic students. Application fee: $50 ($75 for international students). Electronic applications accepted. *Financial support:* Fellowships, research assistantships, and teaching assistantships available. Financial award application deadline: 1/15. *Faculty research:* Stars, interstellar medium, galaxies, planetary astronomy, cosmology. *Unit head:* Daniel Jaffe, Chair, 512-471-3302, E-mail: chair@astro.as.utexas.edu. *Application contact:* Eiichiro Komatsu, Graduate Advisor, 512-471-1483, E-mail: komatsu@astro.as.utexas.edu. Web site: http://www.as.utexas.edu/.

University of Toronto, School of Graduate Studies, Faculty of Arts and Science, Department of Astronomy and Astrophysics, Toronto, ON M5S 1A1, Canada. Offers M Sc, PhD. Part-time programs available. *Degree requirements:* For doctorate, thesis/dissertation, qualifying exam, thesis defense. *Entrance requirements:* For master's, minimum B average, bachelor's degree in astronomy or equivalent, 3 letters of reference; for doctorate, GRE General Test, minimum B+ average, master's degree in astronomy or equivalent, demonstrated research competence, 3 letters of reference. Additional exam requirements/recommendations for international students: Required—TOEFL (minimum score 580 paper-based; 93 iBT), TWE (minimum score 4). Electronic applications accepted.

University of Victoria, Faculty of Graduate Studies, Faculty of Science, Department of Physics and Astronomy, Victoria, BC V8W 2Y2, Canada. Offers astronomy and astrophysics (M Sc, PhD); condensed matter physics (M Sc, PhD); experimental particle physics (M Sc, PhD); medical physics (M Sc, PhD); ocean physics (M Sc, PhD); theoretical physics (M Sc, PhD). *Degree requirements:* For master's, thesis; for doctorate, comprehensive exam, thesis/dissertation, candidacy exam. *Entrance requirements:* For master's and doctorate, GRE. Additional exam requirements/recommendations for international students: Required—TOEFL (minimum score 575 paper-based; 233 computer-based), IELTS (minimum score 7). Electronic applications accepted. *Faculty research:* Old stellar populations; observational cosmology and large scale structure; cp violation; atlas.

University of Virginia, College and Graduate School of Arts and Sciences, Department of Astronomy, Charlottesville, VA 22903. Offers MS, PhD. *Faculty:* 14 full-time (2 women). *Students:* 32 full-time (11 women), 11 international. Average age 25. 105 applicants, 34% accepted, 4 enrolled. In 2011, 6 master's, 5 doctorates awarded. *Degree requirements:* For master's, comprehensive exam, thesis or alternative; for doctorate, comprehensive exam, thesis/dissertation. *Entrance requirements:* For master's and doctorate, GRE General Test, GRE Subject Test. Additional exam requirements/recommendations for international students: Required—TOEFL (minimum score 650 paper-based; 250 computer-based; 90 iBT), IELTS (minimum score 7). *Application deadline:* For fall admission, 12/31 for domestic and international students. Applications are processed on a rolling basis. Application fee: $60. Electronic applications accepted. *Financial support:* Fellowships, research assistantships, and teaching assistantships available. Financial award application deadline: 12/3; financial award applicants required to submit FAFSA. *Unit head:* John Hawley, Chair, 434-924-7494, Fax: 434-924-3104, E-mail: jh8h@virginia.edu. *Application contact:* Craig Sarazin, Chair, Graduate Admissions, 434-924-7494, Fax: 434-924-3104, E-mail: gradadm@mail.astro.virginia.edu. Web site: http://www.astro.virginia.edu/.

University of Washington, Graduate School, College of Arts and Sciences, Department of Astronomy, Seattle, WA 98195. Offers MS, PhD. Terminal master's awarded for partial completion of doctoral program. *Degree requirements:* For doctorate, thesis/dissertation. *Entrance requirements:* For master's and doctorate, GRE General Test, GRE Subject Test, minimum GPA of 3.0. Additional exam requirements/recommendations for international students: Required—TOEFL. *Faculty research:* Solar system dust, space astronomy, high-energy astrophysics, galactic and extragalactic astronomy, stellar astrophysics.

The University of Western Ontario, Faculty of Graduate Studies, Physical Sciences Division, Department of Physics and Astronomy, Program in Astronomy, London, ON N6A 5B8, Canada. Offers M Sc, PhD. Terminal master's awarded for partial completion of doctoral program. *Degree requirements:* For master's, thesis optional; for doctorate, comprehensive exam, thesis/dissertation. *Entrance requirements:* For master's, GRE Subject Test (physics), honors B Sc degree, minimum B average (Canadian), A (international); for doctorate, M Sc degree, minimum B average (Canadian), A (international). Additional exam requirements/recommendations for international students: Required—TOEFL (minimum score 580 paper-based; 237 computer-based). *Faculty research:* Observational and theoretical astrophysics spectroscopy, photometry, spectro-polarimetry, variable stars, cosmology.

University of Wisconsin–Madison, Graduate School, College of Letters and Science, Department of Astronomy, Madison, WI 53706-1380. Offers PhD. *Degree requirements:* For doctorate, comprehensive exam, thesis/dissertation. *Entrance requirements:* For doctorate, GRE General Test, GRE Subject Test (physics), bachelor's degree in related field. Additional exam requirements/recommendations for international students: Required—TOEFL. Electronic applications accepted. *Expenses:* Tuition, state resident: full-time $10,296; part-time $643.51 per credit. Tuition, nonresident: full-time $24,054; part-time $1503.40 per credit. *Required fees:* $70.06 per credit. Tuition and fees vary according to course load, campus/location, program and reciprocity agreements. *Faculty research:* Kinematics, evolution of galaxies, cosmic distance, scale and large-scale structures, interstellar intergalactic medium, star formation and evolution, solar system chemistry and dynamics.

Vanderbilt University, Graduate School, Department of Physics and Astronomy, Nashville, TN 37240-1001. Offers astronomy (MS); physics (MA, MAT, MS, PhD). *Faculty:* 34 full-time (4 women), 2 part-time/adjunct (0 women). *Students:* 78 full-time (20 women), 3 part-time (0 women); includes 13 minority (6 Black or African American, non-Hispanic/Latino; 1 Asian, non-Hispanic/Latino; 4 Hispanic/Latino; 2 Two or more races, non-Hispanic/Latino), 22 international. Average age 28. 171 applicants, 25% accepted, 15 enrolled. In 2011, 8 master's, 4 doctorates awarded. *Degree requirements:* For master's, thesis; for doctorate, comprehensive exam, thesis/dissertation, final and qualifying exams. *Entrance requirements:* For master's, GRE General Test; for doctorate, GRE General Test, GRE Subject Test. Additional exam requirements/recommendations for international students: Required—TOEFL (minimum score 570 paper-based; 230 computer-based; 88 iBT). *Application deadline:* For fall admission, 1/15 for domestic and international students. Application fee: $0. Electronic applications accepted. *Financial support:* Fellowships with full and partial tuition reimbursements, research assistantships with full tuition reimbursements, teaching assistantships with full tuition reimbursements, career-related internships or fieldwork, Federal Work-Study, and institutionally sponsored loans available. Financial award application deadline: 1/15; financial award applicants required to submit CSS PROFILE or FAFSA. *Faculty research:* Experimental and theoretical physics, free electron laser, living-state physics, heavy-ion physics, nuclear structure. *Unit head:* Dr. Robert J. Scherrer, Chair, 615-322-2828, Fax: 615-343-7263, E-mail: robert.scherrer@vanderbilt.edu. *Application contact:* Dr. Julia Velkovska, Director of Graduate Studies, 615-322-0656, Fax: 615-343-7263, E-mail: julia.velkovska@vanderbilt.edu. Web site: http://www.vanderbilt.edu/physics/.

Wesleyan University, Graduate Programs, Department of Astronomy, Middletown, CT 06459. Offers MA. *Degree requirements:* For master's, thesis. *Entrance requirements:* For master's, GRE General Test, GRE Subject Test. Additional exam requirements/recommendations for international students: Required—TOEFL. Electronic applications accepted. *Faculty research:* Observational-theoretical astronomy and astrophysics.

West Chester University of Pennsylvania, College of Arts and Sciences, Department of Geology and Astronomy, West Chester, PA 19383. Offers earth-space science (Teaching Certificate); general science (Teaching Certificate); geoscience (MA). Part-time and evening/weekend programs available. *Faculty:* 6 part-time/adjunct (1 woman). *Students:* 6 full-time (3 women), 17 part-time (6 women); includes 1 minority (Black or African American, non-Hispanic/Latino). Average age 32. 8 applicants, 88% accepted, 5 enrolled. In 2011, 4 degrees awarded. *Degree requirements:* For master's, comprehensive exam (for some programs), thesis or alternative. *Entrance requirements:* For master's, minimum GPA of 2.5. Additional exam requirements/recommendations for international students: Required—TOEFL (minimum score 550 paper-based; 213 computer-based; 80 iBT). *Application deadline:* For fall admission, 4/15 priority date for domestic students, 3/15 for international students; for spring admission, 10/15 priority date for domestic students, 9/1 for international students. Applications are processed on a rolling basis. Application fee: $45. Electronic applications accepted. *Expenses:* Tuition, state resident: full-time $7488; part-time $416 per credit. Tuition, nonresident: full-time $11,232; part-time $624 per credit. *Required fees:* $1784.64; $67.59 per credit. Tuition and fees vary according to program. *Financial support:* Unspecified assistantships available. Support available to part-time students. Financial award application deadline: 2/15; financial award applicants required to submit FAFSA. *Faculty research:* Geoscience education, environmental geology, energy and sustainability, astronomy, meteorology. *Unit*

Peterson's Graduate Programs in the Physical Sciences, Mathematics, Agricultural Sciences, the Environment & Natural Resources 2013

facebook.com/petersonspublishing **45**

Astronomy

head: Dr. Lee Anne Srogi, Chair, 610-436-2727, Fax: 610-436-3036, E-mail: lsrogi@wcupa.edu. *Application contact:* Dr. Martin Helmke, Graduate Coordinator, 610-436-3565, Fax: 610-436-3036, E-mail: mhelmke@wcupa.edu. Web site: http://www.wcupa.edu/_academics/sch_cas.esc/.

Yale University, Graduate School of Arts and Sciences, Department of Astronomy, New Haven, CT 06520. Offers astronomy (PhD); solar and terrestrial physics (PhD). *Degree requirements:* For doctorate, thesis/dissertation. *Entrance requirements:* For doctorate, GRE General Test, GRE Subject Test (physics).

York University, Faculty of Graduate Studies, Faculty of Science and Engineering, Program in Physics and Astronomy, Toronto, ON M3J 1P3, Canada. Offers M Sc, PhD. Part-time and evening/weekend programs available. *Degree requirements:* For master's, thesis or alternative; for doctorate, comprehensive exam, thesis/dissertation. Electronic applications accepted.

Astrophysics

Air Force Institute of Technology, Graduate School of Engineering and Management, Department of Engineering Physics, Dayton, OH 45433-7765. Offers applied physics (MS, PhD); electro-optics (MS, PhD); materials science (PhD); nuclear engineering (MS, PhD); space physics (MS). Part-time programs available. *Degree requirements:* For master's, thesis; for doctorate, thesis/dissertation. *Entrance requirements:* For master's and doctorate, GRE General Test, minimum GPA of 3.0, U.S. citizenship. *Faculty research:* High-energy lasers, space physics, nuclear weapon effects, semiconductor physics.

Arizona State University, College of Liberal Arts and Sciences, School of Earth and Space Exploration, Tempe, AZ 85287-1404. Offers astrophysics (MS, PhD); exploration systems design (PhD); geological sciences (MS, PhD). PhD in exploration systems design is offered in collaboration with the Fulton Schools of Engineering. Terminal master's awarded for partial completion of doctoral program. *Degree requirements:* For master's, thesis, interactive Program of Study (iPOS) submitted before completing 50 percent of required credit hours; for doctorate, thesis/dissertation, interactive Program of Study (iPOS) submitted before completing 50 percent of required credit hours. *Entrance requirements:* For master's and doctorate, GRE, minimum GPA of 3.0 or equivalent in last 2 years of work leading to bachelor's degree. Additional exam requirements/recommendations for international students: Required—TOEFL (minimum score 80 iBT), TOEFL, IELTS, or Pearson Test of English. Electronic applications accepted.

Clemson University, Graduate School, College of Engineering and Science, Department of Physics and Astronomy, Clemson, SC 29634. Offers physics (MS, PhD), including astronomy and astrophysics, atmospheric physics, biophysics. Part-time programs available. *Faculty:* 27 full-time (3 women). *Students:* 67 full-time (21 women); includes 3 minority (2 Black or African American, non-Hispanic/Latino; 1 Hispanic/Latino), 27 international. Average age 27. 133 applicants, 75% accepted, 31 enrolled. In 2011, 4 master's, 6 doctorates awarded. Terminal master's awarded for partial completion of doctoral program. *Degree requirements:* For master's, thesis or alternative; for doctorate, thesis/dissertation. *Entrance requirements:* For master's and doctorate, GRE General Test. Additional exam requirements/recommendations for international students: Required—TOEFL. *Application deadline:* For fall admission, 1/15 priority date for domestic students; for spring admission, 9/15 priority date for domestic students. Applications are processed on a rolling basis. Application fee: $70 ($80 for international students). Electronic applications accepted. *Financial support:* In 2011–12, 58 students received support, including 1 fellowship with full and partial tuition reimbursement available (averaging $8,000 per year), 24 research assistantships with partial tuition reimbursements available (averaging $13,653 per year), 50 teaching assistantships with partial tuition reimbursements available (averaging $13,265 per year); career-related internships or fieldwork, institutionally sponsored loans, scholarships/grants, health care benefits, and unspecified assistantships also available. Support available to part-time students. Financial award application deadline: 6/1; financial award applicants required to submit FAFSA. *Faculty research:* Radiation physics, solid-state physics, nuclear physics, radar and lidar studies of atmosphere. *Total annual research expenditures:* $2.6 million. *Unit head:* Dr. Peter Barnes, Chair, 864-656-3419, Fax: 864-656-0805, E-mail: peterb@clemson.edu. *Application contact:* Graduate Coordinator, 864-656-6702, Fax: 864-656-0805, E-mail: physgradinfo-l@clemson.edu. Web site: http://physicsnt.clemson.edu/.

Cornell University, Graduate School, Graduate Fields of Arts and Sciences, Field of Astronomy and Space Sciences, Ithaca, NY 14853-0001. Offers astronomy (PhD); astrophysics (PhD); general space sciences (PhD); infrared astronomy (PhD); planetary studies (PhD); radio astronomy (PhD); radiophysics (PhD); theoretical astrophysics (PhD). *Faculty:* 27 full-time (2 women). *Students:* 32 full-time (11 women); includes 5 minority (3 Asian, non-Hispanic/Latino; 2 Hispanic/Latino), 9 international. Average age 26. 101 applicants, 30% accepted, 11 enrolled. In 2011, 5 doctorates awarded. *Degree requirements:* For doctorate, comprehensive exam, thesis/dissertation. *Entrance requirements:* For doctorate, GRE General Test, GRE Subject Test (physics), 3 letters of recommendation. Additional exam requirements/recommendations for international students: Required—TOEFL (minimum score 600 paper-based; 250 computer-based; 77 iBT). *Application deadline:* For fall admission, 1/15 for domestic students. Application fee: $95. Electronic applications accepted. *Financial support:* In 2011–12, 5 fellowships with full tuition reimbursements, 15 research assistantships with full tuition reimbursements, 10 teaching assistantships with full tuition reimbursements were awarded; institutionally sponsored loans, scholarships/grants, health care benefits, tuition waivers (full and partial), and unspecified assistantships also available. Financial award applicants required to submit FAFSA. *Faculty research:* Observational astrophysics, planetary sciences, cosmology, instrumentation, gravitational astrophysics. *Unit head:* Director of Graduate Studies, 607-255-4341. *Application contact:* Graduate Field Assistant, 607-255-4341, E-mail: oconnor@astro.cornell.edu. Web site: http://www.gradschool.cornell.edu/fields.php?id-24&a-2.

Harvard University, Graduate School of Arts and Sciences, Department of Astronomy, Cambridge, MA 02138. Offers astronomy (PhD); astrophysics (PhD). *Degree requirements:* For doctorate, thesis/dissertation, paper, research project, 2 semesters of teaching. *Entrance requirements:* For doctorate, GRE General Test, GRE Subject Test (physics). Additional exam requirements/recommendations for international students: Required—TOEFL. Electronic applications accepted. *Expenses: Tuition:* Full-time $36,304. *Required fees:* $1186. Full-time tuition and fees vary according to program. *Faculty research:* Atomic and molecular physics, electromagnetism, solar physics, nuclear physics, fluid dynamics.

ICR Graduate School, Graduate Programs, Santee, CA 92071. Offers astro/geophysics (MS); biology (MS); geology (MS); science education (MS). Part-time programs available. *Degree requirements:* For master's, comprehensive exam (for some programs), thesis (for some programs). *Entrance requirements:* For master's, minimum undergraduate GPA of 3.0, bachelor's degree in science or science education. *Faculty research:* Age of the earth, limits of variation, catastrophe, optimum methods for teaching.

Indiana University Bloomington, University Graduate School, College of Arts and Sciences, Department of Astronomy, Bloomington, IN 47405-7000. Offers astronomy (MA, PhD); astrophysics (PhD). *Faculty:* 9 full-time (5 women), 2 part-time/adjunct (0 women). *Students:* 23 full-time (8 women); includes 4 minority (1 American Indian or Alaska Native, non-Hispanic/Latino; 1 Asian, non-Hispanic/Latino; 1 Hispanic/Latino; 1 Two or more races, non-Hispanic/Latino). 43 applicants, 19% accepted, 3 enrolled. In 2011, 5 master's, 4 doctorates awarded. Terminal master's awarded for partial completion of doctoral program. *Degree requirements:* For master's, thesis or alternative, oral exam; for doctorate, comprehensive exam, thesis/dissertation, oral defense. *Entrance requirements:* For master's and doctorate, GRE General Test, GRE Subject Test (physics), BA or BS in science. Additional exam requirements/recommendations for international students: Required—TOEFL. *Application deadline:* For fall admission, 1/15 for domestic students, 12/1 for international students; for spring admission, 9/1 for domestic students. Application fee: $55 ($65 for international students). Electronic applications accepted. *Financial support:* In 2011–12, 18 students received support, including 3 fellowships with full tuition reimbursements available (averaging $14,333 per year), 7 research assistantships with full tuition reimbursements available (averaging $19,850 per year), 8 teaching assistantships with full tuition reimbursements available (averaging $17,950 per year); scholarships/grants, health care benefits, and unspecified assistantships also available. Financial award application deadline: 1/15. *Faculty research:* Stellar and galaxy dynamics, stellar chemical abundances, galaxy evolution, observational cosmology. *Total annual research expenditures:* $772,980. *Unit head:* Dr. John Salzer, Chair, 812-855-6911, Fax: 812-855-8725, E-mail: josalzer@indiana.edu. *Application contact:* Julie Wilson, Graduate Secretary, 812-855-6911, Fax: 812-855-8725, E-mail: jaw@indiana.edu. Web site: http://www.astro.indiana.edu/.

Iowa State University of Science and Technology, Department of Physics and Astronomy, Ames, IA 50011-3160. Offers applied physics (MS, PhD); astrophysics (MS, PhD); condensed matter physics (MS, PhD); high energy physics (MS, PhD); nuclear physics (MS, PhD); physics (MS, PhD). *Degree requirements:* For master's, thesis (for some programs); for doctorate, thesis/dissertation. *Entrance requirements:* For master's and doctorate, GRE General Test, GRE Subject Test (physics). Additional exam requirements/recommendations for international students: Required—TOEFL (minimum score 550 paper-based; 79 iBT), IELTS (minimum score 6.5). *Application deadline:* For fall admission, 2/15 priority date for domestic students, 2/15 for international students; for spring admission, 10/15 for domestic and international students. Applications are processed on a rolling basis. Application fee: $40 ($90 for international students). Electronic applications accepted. *Financial support:* Application deadline: 2/15. *Faculty research:* Condensed-matter physics, including superconductivity and new materials; high-energy and nuclear physics;

46 facebook.com/petersonspublishing

Peterson's Graduate Programs in the Physical Sciences, Mathematics, Agricultural Sciences, the Environment & Natural Resources 2013

astronomy and astrophysics; atmospheric and environmental physics. *Total annual research expenditures:* $8.8 million. *Unit head:* Dr. Steve Kawaler, Director of Graduate Education, 515-294-5870, Fax: 515-294-6027, E-mail: physastro@iastate.edu. *Application contact:* Lori Hockett, Application Contact, 515-294-5870, E-mail: phys_astro@iastate.edu. Web site: http://www.physics.iastate.edu/.

Iowa State University of Science and Technology, Program in Astrophysics, Ames, IA 50011-3160. Offers MS, PhD. *Entrance requirements:* For master's and doctorate, GRE. Additional exam requirements/recommendations for international students: Required—TOEFL (minimum score 550 paper-based; 79 iBT), IELTS (minimum score 6.5). *Application deadline:* For fall admission, 2/15 for domestic students; for spring admission, 10/15 for domestic students. *Unit head:* Dr. Steven Kawaler, Director of Graduate Education, 515-294-5870, E-mail: physastro@iastate.edu. *Application contact:* Lori Hockett, Application Contact, 515-294-5870, Fax: 515-294-6027, E-mail: physastro@iastate.edu. Web site: http://www.physastro@iastate.edu.

Louisiana State University and Agricultural and Mechanical College, Graduate School, College of Science, Department of Physics and Astronomy, Baton Rouge, LA 70803. Offers astronomy (PhD); astrophysics (PhD); medical physics (MS); physics (MS, PhD). *Faculty:* 47 full-time (5 women), 2 part-time/adjunct (0 women). *Students:* 106 full-time (23 women), 1 part-time (0 women); includes 5 minority (3 Black or African American, non-Hispanic/Latino; 2 Hispanic/Latino), 49 international. Average age 27. 166 applicants, 14% accepted, 21 enrolled. In 2011, 5 master's, 11 doctorates awarded. Terminal master's awarded for partial completion of doctoral program. *Degree requirements:* For master's, thesis or alternative; for doctorate, thesis/dissertation. *Entrance requirements:* For master's and doctorate, GRE General Test, minimum GPA of 3.0. Additional exam requirements/recommendations for international students: Required—TOEFL (minimum score 550 paper-based; 213 computer-based; 79 iBT) or IELTS (minimum score 6.5). *Application deadline:* For fall admission, 1/25 priority date for domestic students, 5/15 for international students; for spring admission, 10/15 for international students. Applications are processed on a rolling basis. Application fee: $50 ($70 for international students). Electronic applications accepted. *Financial support:* In 2011–12, 107 students received support, including 8 fellowships with full tuition reimbursements available (averaging $19,566 per year), 57 research assistantships with full and partial tuition reimbursements available (averaging $22,634 per year), 39 teaching assistantships with full and partial tuition reimbursements available (averaging $19,774 per year); Federal Work-Study, institutionally sponsored loans, health care benefits, tuition waivers (full and partial), and unspecified assistantships also available. Financial award application deadline: 3/15; financial award applicants required to submit FAFSA. *Faculty research:* Experimentation and numerical relativity, condensed matter astrophysics, quantum computing, medical physics. *Total annual research expenditures:* $8.1 million. *Unit head:* Dr. Michael Cherry, Chair, 225-578-2262, Fax: 225-578-5855, E-mail: cherry@phys.lsu.edu. *Application contact:* Arnell Dangerfield, Administrative Coordinator, 225-578-1193, Fax: 225-578-5855, E-mail: adanger@lsu.edu. Web site: http://www.phys.lsu.edu/.

McMaster University, School of Graduate Studies, Faculty of Science, Department of Physics and Astronomy, Hamilton, ON L8S 4M2, Canada. Offers astrophysics (PhD); physics (PhD). Part-time programs available. *Degree requirements:* For doctorate, comprehensive exam, thesis/dissertation. *Entrance requirements:* For doctorate, minimum B+ average. Additional exam requirements/recommendations for international students: Required—TOEFL (minimum score 550 paper-based; 213 computer-based). *Faculty research:* Condensed matter, astrophysics, nuclear, medical, nonlinear dynamics.

Michigan State University, The Graduate School, College of Natural Science, Department of Physics and Astronomy, East Lansing, MI 48824. Offers astrophysics and astronomy (MS, PhD); physics (MS, PhD). *Entrance requirements:* Additional exam requirements/recommendations for international students: Required—TOEFL (minimum score 550 paper-based; 213 computer-based), Michigan State University ELT (minimum score 85), Michigan English Language Assessment Battery (minimum score 83). Electronic applications accepted. *Faculty research:* Nuclear and accelerator physics, high energy physics, condensed matter physics, biophysics, astrophysics and astronomy.

New Mexico Institute of Mining and Technology, Graduate Studies, Department of Physics, Socorro, NM 87801. Offers astrophysics (PhD); atmospheric physics (PhD); instrumentation (MS); mathematical physics (PhD); physics (MS). *Faculty:* 14 full-time (2 women), 19 part-time/adjunct (2 women). *Students:* 30 full-time (12 women), 2 part-time (1 woman); includes 1 minority (Asian, non-Hispanic/Latino), 3 international. Average age 28. 28 applicants, 50% accepted, 5 enrolled. In 2011, 5 master's, 3 doctorates awarded. *Degree requirements:* For master's, thesis optional; for doctorate, thesis/dissertation. *Entrance requirements:* For master's, GRE General Test; for doctorate, GRE General Test, GRE Subject Test. Additional exam requirements/recommendations for international students: Required—TOEFL (minimum score 540 paper-based; 207 computer-based). *Application deadline:* For fall admission, 3/1 priority date for domestic students; for spring admission, 6/1 for domestic students. Applications are processed on a rolling basis. Application fee: $16 ($30 for international students). *Expenses:* Tuition, state resident: full-time $4849; part-time $269.41 per credit hour. Tuition, nonresident: full-time $16,041; part-time $891.15 per credit hour. *Required fees:* $622; $65 per credit hour. $20 per semester. Part-time tuition and fees vary according to course load. *Financial support:* In 2011–12, 18 research assistantships (averaging $38,918 per year),

11 teaching assistantships with full and partial tuition reimbursements (averaging $35,099 per year) were awarded; fellowships, Federal Work-Study, institutionally sponsored loans, and unspecified assistantships also available. Financial award application deadline: 3/1; financial award applicants required to submit CSS PROFILE or FAFSA. *Faculty research:* Cloud physics, stellar and extragalactic processes. *Unit head:* Dr. Kenneth Eack, Chairman, 575-835-5328, Fax: 575-835-5707, E-mail: dwestpfa@nmt.edu. *Application contact:* Dr. Lorie Liebrock, Dean of Graduate Studies, 575-835-5513, Fax: 575-835-5476, E-mail: graduate@nmt.edu. Web site: http://www.physics.nmt.edu/.

New Mexico State University, Graduate School, College of Arts and Sciences, Department of Physics, Las Cruces, NM 88003-8001. Offers physics (MS, PhD); space physics (MS). Part-time programs available. *Faculty:* 14 full-time (1 woman), 3 part-time/adjunct (0 women). *Students:* 34 full-time (7 women), 3 part-time (0 women); includes 3 minority (all Hispanic/Latino), 26 international. Average age 30. 20 applicants, 55% accepted, 8 enrolled. In 2011, 4 master's, 5 doctorates awarded. Terminal master's awarded for partial completion of doctoral program. *Degree requirements:* For master's, comprehensive exam, thesis optional, written qualifying exam; for doctorate, comprehensive exam, thesis or dissertation. *Entrance requirements:* For master's and doctorate, GRE General Test, GRE Subject Test. Additional exam requirements/recommendations for international students: Required—TOEFL (minimum score 550 paper-based; 79 iBT), IELTS (minimum score 6.5). *Application deadline:* For fall admission, 2/15 priority date for domestic students, 2/15 for international students; for spring admission, 9/1 priority date for domestic students, 9/1 for international students. Applications are processed on a rolling basis. Application fee: $40 ($50 for international students). Electronic applications accepted. *Expenses:* Tuition, state resident: full-time $5004; part-time $208.50 per credit. Tuition, nonresident: full-time $17,446; part-time $726.90 per credit. *Financial support:* In 2011–12, 2 fellowships with partial tuition reimbursements (averaging $16,800 per year), 13 research assistantships (averaging $25,125 per year), 17 teaching assistantships (averaging $26,670 per year) were awarded; scholarships/grants, health care benefits, tuition waivers (partial), and unspecified assistantships also available. Financial award application deadline: 2/15; financial award applicants required to submit FAFSA. *Faculty research:* Nuclear and particle physics, optics, materials science, geophysics, physics education, atmospheric physics. *Total annual research expenditures:* $1.5 million. *Unit head:* Dr. Stefan Zollner, Head, 575-646-7627, Fax: 575-646-1934, E-mail: zollner@nmsu.edu. *Application contact:* Dr. Vassilios Papavassiliou, 575-646-3831, Fax: 575-646-1934, E-mail: graduate_advisor@physics.nmsu.edu. Web site: http://physics.nmsu.edu.

Northwestern University, The Graduate School, Judd A. and Marjorie Weinberg College of Arts and Sciences, Department of Physics and Astronomy, Evanston, IL 60208. Offers astrophysics (PhD); physics (MS, PhD). Admissions and degrees offered through The Graduate School. *Degree requirements:* For doctorate, thesis/dissertation, qualifying exam. *Entrance requirements:* For doctorate, GRE General Test, GRE Subject Test. Additional exam requirements/recommendations for international students: Required—TOEFL. *Faculty research:* Nuclear and particle physics, condensed-matter physics, nonlinear physics, astrophysics.

Penn State University Park, Graduate School, Eberly College of Science, Department of Astronomy and Astrophysics, State College, University Park, PA 16802-1503. Offers MS, PhD. *Unit head:* Dr. Daniel J. Larson, Dean, 814-865-9591, Fax: 814-865-3634. *Application contact:* Cynthia E. Nicosia, Director, Graduate Enrollment Services, 814-865-1795, Fax: 814-865-4627, E-mail: cey1@psu.edu. Web site: http://www.astro.psu.edu/.

Princeton University, Graduate School, Depártment of Astrophysical Sciences, Princeton, NJ 08544-1019. Offers astronomy (PhD); plasma physics (PhD). *Degree requirements:* For doctorate, thesis/dissertation. *Entrance requirements:* For doctorate, GRE General Test, GRE Subject Test (physics). Additional exam requirements/recommendations for international students: Required—TOEFL (minimum score 600 paper-based; 250 computer-based). Electronic applications accepted. *Faculty research:* Theoretical astrophysics, cosmology, galaxy formation, galactic dynamics, interstellar and intergalactic matter.

Rochester Institute of Technology, Graduate Enrollment Services, College of Science, Graduate Studies in Astrophysical Sciences and Technology, Rochester, NY 14623-5603. Offers MS, PhD. *Students:* 12 full-time (3 women); includes 2 minority (1 Black or African American, non-Hispanic/Latino; 1 Hispanic/Latino), 3 international. Average age 31. 30 applicants, 23% accepted, 2 enrolled. In 2011, 3 degrees awarded. Terminal master's awarded for partial completion of doctoral program. *Degree requirements:* For master's, comprehensive exam, thesis. *Entrance requirements:* For master's, GRE. Additional exam requirements/recommendations for international students: Required—TOEFL (minimum score 550 paper-based; 213 computer-based; 79 iBT) or IELTS (minimum score 6.5). *Application deadline:* For fall admission, 1/15 priority date for domestic students, 1/15 for international students. Application fee: $50. *Expenses:* Tuition: Full-time $34,659; part-time $963 per credit hour. *Required fees:* $228; $76 per quarter. *Financial support:* Fellowships with full and partial tuition reimbursements, research assistantships with full and partial tuition reimbursements, teaching assistantships with full and partial tuition reimbursements, Federal Work-Study, scholarships/grants, health care benefits, and unspecified assistantships available. *Faculty research:* Supermassive black holes, dark energy, gravitational waves, supernovae, massive stars, the galactic center, star formation, clusters of galaxies, active galactic nuclei, astro-informatics, computational astrophysics, instrument and detector development. *Unit head:* Dr. Andrew Robinson, Graduate

Peterson's Graduate Programs in the Physical Sciences, Mathematics, Agricultural Sciences, the Environment & Natural Resources 2013

facebook.com/petersonspublishing **47**

Astrophysics

Program Director, 585-475-2726, E-mail: axrsps@rit.edu. *Application contact:* Diane Ellison, Assistant Vice President, Graduate Enrollment Services, 585-475-2229, Fax: 585-475-7164, E-mail: gradinfo@rit.edu. Web site: http://www.rit.edu/cos/astrophysics/.

Texas Christian University, College of Science and Engineering, Department of Physics and Astronomy, Fort Worth, TX 76129-0002. Offers physics (MA, MS, PhD), including astrophysics (PhD), business (PhD), physics (PhD); PhD/MBA. *Faculty:* 7 full-time, 1 part-time/adjunct. *Students:* 3 full-time (1 woman), 13 part-time (4 women); includes 2 minority (1 Asian, non-Hispanic/Latino; 1 Hispanic/Latino), 7 international. Average age 27. 7 applicants, 71% accepted, 5 enrolled. In 2011, 1 master's, 2 doctorates awarded. Terminal master's awarded for partial completion of doctoral program. *Degree requirements:* For master's, comprehensive exam, thesis; for doctorate, comprehensive exam, thesis/dissertation, paper submitted to scientific journal. *Entrance requirements:* For master's and doctorate, GRE General Test, minimum GPA of 3.0. Additional exam requirements/recommendations for international students: Required—TOEFL (minimum score 600 paper-based). *Application deadline:* For fall admission, 2/1 for domestic and international students; for spring admission, 10/1 for domestic and international students. Applications are processed on a rolling basis. Application fee: $60. Electronic applications accepted. *Expenses: Tuition:* Full-time $20,250; part-time $1125 per credit hour. Part-time tuition and fees vary according to course load and program. *Financial support:* In 2011–12, 11 teaching assistantships with full tuition reimbursements (averaging $19,500 per year) were awarded; tuition waivers also available. Financial award application deadline: 2/1. *Unit head:* Dr. William R. Graham, Chairperson, 817-257-7375 Ext. 6383, Fax: 817-257-7742, E-mail: w.graham@tcu.edu. *Application contact:* Dr. Yuri Strzhemechny, Associate Professor, 817-257-7375 Ext. 5793, Fax: 817-257-7742, E-mail: y.strzhemechny@tcu.edu. Web site: http://www.phys.tcu.edu/grad_program.asp.

University of Alaska Fairbanks, College of Natural Sciences and Mathematics, Department of Physics, Fairbanks, AK 99775-5920. Offers computational physics (MS); physics (MAT, MS, PhD); space physics (MS, PhD). Part-time programs available. *Faculty:* 9 full-time (2 women), 3 part-time (0 women); includes 3 minority (1 American Indian or Alaska Native, non-Hispanic/Latino; 1 Asian, non-Hispanic/Latino; 1 Hispanic/Latino), 8 international. Average age 29. 18 applicants, 28% accepted, 5 enrolled. In 2011, 1 master's, 2 doctorates awarded. Terminal master's awarded for partial completion of doctoral program. *Degree requirements:* For master's, comprehensive exam, thesis or alternative; for doctorate, comprehensive exam, thesis/dissertation, oral defense. *Entrance requirements:* Additional exam requirements/recommendations for international students: Required—TOEFL (minimum score 550 paper-based; 213 computer-based; 80 iBT). *Application deadline:* For fall admission, 6/1 for domestic students, 3/1 for international students; for spring admission, 10/15 for domestic students, 9/1 for international students. Applications are processed on a rolling basis. Application fee: $60. Electronic applications accepted. *Expenses:* Tuition, state resident: full-time $6696; part-time $372 per credit. Tuition, nonresident: full-time $13,680; part-time $760 per credit. Tuition and fees vary according to course load and reciprocity agreements. *Financial support:* In 2011–12, 17 research assistantships with tuition reimbursements (averaging $14,039 per year), 8 teaching assistantships with tuition reimbursements (averaging $7,927 per year) were awarded; fellowships with tuition reimbursements, Federal Work-Study, scholarships/grants, health care benefits, and unspecified assistantships also available. Support available to part-time students. Financial award application deadline: 2/15; financial award applicants required to submit FAFSA. *Faculty research:* Atmospheric and ionospheric radar studies, space plasma theory, magnetospheric dynamics, space weather and auroral studies, turbulence and complex systems. *Unit head:* Ataur Chowdhury, Chair, 907-474-7339, Fax: 907-474-6130, E-mail: physics@uaf.edu. *Application contact:* Mike Earnest, Director of Admissions, 907-474-7500, Fax: 907-474-5379, E-mail: admissions@uaf.edu. Web site: http://www.uaf.edu/physics/.

University of Alberta, Faculty of Graduate Studies and Research, Department of Physics, Edmonton, AB T6G 2E1, Canada. Offers astrophysics (M Sc, PhD); condensed matter (M Sc, PhD); geophysics (M Sc, PhD); medical physics (M Sc, PhD); subatomic physics (M Sc, PhD). *Degree requirements:* For master's, thesis; for doctorate, thesis/dissertation. *Entrance requirements:* For master's and doctorate, minimum GPA of 7.0 on a 9.0 scale. Additional exam requirements/recommendations for international students: Required—TOEFL. *Faculty research:* Cosmology, astroparticle physics, high-intermediate energy, magnetism, superconductivity.

University of California, Berkeley, Graduate Division, College of Letters and Science, Department of Astrophysics, Berkeley, CA 94720-1500. Offers PhD. *Degree requirements:* For doctorate, thesis/dissertation, qualifying exam. *Entrance requirements:* For doctorate, GRE General Test, GRE Subject Test, minimum GPA of 3.0, 3 letters of recommendation. *Faculty research:* Theory, cosmology, radio astronomy, extra solar planets, infrared instrumentation.

University of California, Los Angeles, Graduate Division, College of Letters and Science, Department of Earth and Space Sciences, Program in Geophysics and Space Physics, Los Angeles, CA 90095. Offers MS, PhD. *Students:* 38 full-time (18 women); includes 5 minority (1 Black or African American, non-Hispanic/Latino; 3 Asian, non-Hispanic/Latino; 1 Two or more races, non-Hispanic/Latino), 14 international. Average age 27. 65 applicants, 20% accepted, 10 enrolled. In 2011, 4 master's, 3 doctorates awarded. Terminal master's awarded for partial completion of doctoral program. *Degree requirements:* For master's,

comprehensive exams or thesis; for doctorate, thesis/dissertation, oral and written qualifying exams. *Entrance requirements:* For master's, GRE General Test, minimum GPA of 3.0, bachelor's degree in related field; for doctorate, GRE General Test, minimum undergraduate GPA of 3.0, bachelor's degree in related field. *Application deadline:* For fall admission, 1/15 for domestic and international students. Application fee: $70 ($90 for international students). Electronic applications accepted. *Financial support:* In 2011–12, 28 fellowships with full and partial tuition reimbursements, 27 research assistantships with full and partial tuition reimbursements, 8 teaching assistantships with full and partial tuition reimbursements were awarded; Federal Work-Study, institutionally sponsored loans, scholarships/grants, health care benefits, tuition waivers (full and partial), and unspecified assistantships also available. Financial award application deadline: 3/1; financial award applicants required to submit FAFSA. *Unit head:* Dr. Craig E. Manning, Chair, 310-206-3290, E-mail: manning@ess.ucla.edu. *Application contact:* Departmental Office, 310-825-3917, E-mail: holbrook@ess.ucla.edu. Web site: http://www.ess.ucla.edu/.

University of California, Santa Cruz, Division of Graduate Studies, Division of Physical and Biological Sciences, Department of Astronomy and Astrophysics, Santa Cruz, CA 95064. Offers PhD. *Degree requirements:* For doctorate, one foreign language, thesis/dissertation, qualifying exam. *Entrance requirements:* For doctorate, GRE General Test, GRE Subject Test. Additional exam requirements/recommendations for international students: Required—TOEFL (minimum score 550 paper-based; 220 computer-based; 83 iBT); Recommended—IELTS (minimum score 8). Electronic applications accepted. *Faculty research:* Solar system and the Milky Way to the most distant galaxies in the Universe, fundamental questions of cosmology.

University of Chicago, Division of the Physical Sciences, Department of Astronomy and Astrophysics, Chicago, IL 60637-1513. Offers MS, PhD. Terminal master's awarded for partial completion of doctoral program. *Degree requirements:* For master's, comprehensive exam, thesis optional, candidacy exam; for doctorate, comprehensive exam, thesis/dissertation, dissertation for publication. *Entrance requirements:* For master's, department candidacy examination, minimum GPA of 3.0; for doctorate, GRE General Test, GRE Subject Test, minimum GPA of 3.0. Additional exam requirements/recommendations for international students: Required—TOEFL (minimum score 600 paper-based; 250 computer-based); Recommended—IELTS. Electronic applications accepted. *Faculty research:* Quasi-stellar object absorption lines, fluid dynamics, interstellar matter, particle physics, cosmology.

University of Colorado Boulder, Graduate School, College of Arts and Sciences, Department of Astrophysical and Planetary Sciences, Boulder, CO 80309. Offers astrophysics (MS, PhD); planetary science (MS, PhD). *Faculty:* 22 full-time (3 women). *Students:* 52 full-time (15 women), 2 part-time (1 woman); includes 4 minority (1 Black or African American, non-Hispanic/Latino; 1 American Indian or Alaska Native, non-Hispanic/Latino; 2 Asian, non-Hispanic/Latino), 7 international. Average age 26. 185 applicants, 18% accepted, 14 enrolled. In 2011, 5 master's, 7 doctorates awarded. Terminal master's awarded for partial completion of doctoral program. *Degree requirements:* For master's, comprehensive exam, thesis or alternative; for doctorate, one foreign language, thesis/dissertation. *Entrance requirements:* For master's, GRE General Test, GRE Subject Test, minimum undergraduate GPA of 3.0; for doctorate, GRE General Test, GRE Subject Test. *Application deadline:* For fall admission, 1/15 priority date for domestic students, 12/1 for international students. Applications are processed on a rolling basis. Application fee: $50 ($60 for international students). Electronic applications accepted. *Financial support:* In 2011–12, 55 students received support, including 34 fellowships (averaging $12,309 per year), 27 research assistantships with full and partial tuition reimbursements available (averaging $25,858 per year), 8 teaching assistantships with full and partial tuition reimbursements available (averaging $22,262 per year); institutionally sponsored loans, scholarships/grants, health care benefits, and unspecified assistantships also available. Financial award application deadline: 1/15; financial award applicants required to submit FAFSA. *Faculty research:* Stellar and extragalactic astrophysics cosmology, space astronomy, planetary science. *Total annual research expenditures:* $41.3 million. *Application contact:* E-mail: apsgradsec@colorado.edu. Web site: http://aps.colorado.edu/.

The University of Manchester, School of Physics and Astronomy, Manchester, United Kingdom. Offers astronomy and astrophysics (M Sc, PhD); biological physics (M Sc, PhD); condensed matter physics (M Sc, PhD); nonlinear and liquid crystals physics (M Sc, PhD); nuclear physics (M Sc, PhD); particle physics (M Sc, PhD); photon physics (M Sc, PhD); physics (M Sc, PhD); theoretical physics (M Sc, PhD).

University of Michigan, Horace H. Rackham School of Graduate Studies, College of Literature, Science, and the Arts, Department of Astronomy, Ann Arbor, MI 48109-1042. Offers astronomy and astrophysics (PhD). *Faculty:* 21 full-time (6 women). *Students:* 26 full-time (10 women); includes 4 minority (all Asian, non-Hispanic/Latino). In 2011, 5 degrees awarded. Terminal master's awarded for partial completion of doctoral program. *Median time to degree:* Of those who began their doctoral program in fall 2003, 99% received their degree in 8 years or less. *Degree requirements:* For doctorate, thesis/dissertation, oral defense of dissertation, preliminary exam. *Entrance requirements:* For doctorate, GRE General Test, GRE Subject Test (physics). Additional exam requirements/recommendations for international students: Required—TOEFL. *Application deadline:* For fall admission, 1/4 for domestic and international students. Application fee: $65 ($75 for international students). Electronic applications accepted. *Financial support:* In 2011–12, 5 fellowships with full tuition reimbursements (averaging $22,800 per year), 23 research assistantships with full tuition reimbursements (averaging $22,800 per year), 13 teaching assistantships with full tuition reimbursements (averaging $22,800 per year) were awarded; institutionally sponsored loans, scholarships/grants, health care benefits, and unspecified assistantships also available. Financial award applicants required to submit FAFSA. *Faculty research:* Extragalactic and galactic astronomy, cosmology, star and planet formation, high energy astrophysics. *Total annual research expenditures:* $2.1 million. *Unit head:* Dr. Joel Bregman, Chair and Professor, 734-764-3440, Fax: 734-763-6317, E-mail: jbregman@umich.edu. *Application contact:* Brian M. Cox, Administrative Assistant, 734-764-3440, Fax: 734-763-6317, E-mail: bmcox@umich.edu. Web site: http://www.astro.lsa.umich.edu/.

University of Minnesota, Twin Cities Campus, College of Science and Engineering, School of Physics and Astronomy, Program in Astrophysics, Minneapolis, MN 55455-0213. Offers MS, PhD. *Students:* 17 full-time (2 women); includes 1 minority (Asian, non-Hispanic/Latino), 3 international. Terminal master's awarded for partial completion of doctoral program. *Degree requirements:* For master's, thesis optional; for doctorate, thesis/dissertation. *Entrance requirements:* For master's and doctorate, GRE General Test, GRE Subject Test. Additional exam requirements/recommendations for international students: Required—TOEFL. *Application deadline:* For fall admission, 1/10 for domestic students. Applications are processed on a rolling basis. Application fee: $75 ($95 for international students). *Financial support:* Fellowships with tuition reimbursements, research assistantships with tuition reimbursements, and teaching assistantships with tuition reimbursements available. *Faculty research:* Evolution of stars and galaxies; the interstellar medium; cosmology; observational, optical, infrared, and radio astronomy; computational astrophysics. *Application contact:* Director of Graduate Studies, E-mail: grad-req@astro.umn.edu. Web site: http://www.astro.umn.edu.

The University of North Carolina at Chapel Hill, Graduate School, College of Arts and Sciences, Department of Physics and Astronomy, Chapel Hill, NC 27599. Offers physics (MS, PhD). Terminal master's awarded for partial completion of doctoral program. *Degree requirements:* For master's, comprehensive exam; for doctorate, comprehensive exam, thesis/dissertation. *Entrance requirements:* For master's and doctorate, GRE General Test, minimum GPA of 3.0. Electronic applications accepted. *Faculty research:* Observational astronomy, fullerenes, polarized beams, nanotubes, nucleosynthesis in stars and supernovae, superstring theory, ballistic transport in semiconductors, gravitation.

The University of Toledo, College of Graduate Studies, College of Natural Sciences and Mathematics, Department of Physics and Astronomy, Toledo, OH 43606-3390. Offers physics (MS, PhD), including astrophysics (PhD), materials science (PhD), medical physics (PhD). *Faculty:* 26. *Students:* 65 full-time (13 women), 3 part-time (0 women); includes 1 minority (Asian, non-Hispanic/Latino), 24 international. Average age 29. 94 applicants, 15% accepted, 13 enrolled. In 2011, 2 master's, 8 doctorates awarded. *Degree requirements:* For master's, thesis; for doctorate, thesis/dissertation, departmental qualifying exam. *Entrance requirements:* For master's and doctorate, GRE General Test, GRE Subject Test, minimum cumulative point-hour ratio of 2.7 for all previous academic work, three letters of recommendation, statement of purpose, transcripts from all prior institutions attended. Additional exam requirements/recommendations for international students: Required—TOEFL (minimum score 550 paper-based; 213 computer-based; 80 iBT), IELTS (minimum score 6.5). *Application deadline:* For fall admission, 1/15 priority date for domestic students, 1/15 for international students. Applications are processed on a rolling basis. Application fee: $45 ($75 for international students). Electronic applications accepted. *Financial support:* In 2011–12, 47 research assistantships with full and partial tuition reimbursements (averaging $17,484 per year), 22 teaching assistantships with full and partial tuition reimbursements (averaging $19,131 per year) were awarded; Federal Work-Study, institutionally sponsored loans, scholarships/grants, tuition waivers (full), and unspecified assistantships also available. Support available to part-time students. *Faculty research:* Atomic physics, solid-state physics, materials science, astrophysics. *Unit head:* Dr. Lawrence Anderson-Huang, Chair, 419-530-7257, E-mail: lawrence.anderson@utoledo.edu. *Application contact:* Graduate School Office, 419-530-4723, Fax: 419-537-4724, E-mail: grdsch@utnet.utoledo.edu. Web site: http://www.utoledo.edu/nsm/.

University of Toronto, School of Graduate Studies, Faculty of Arts and Science, Department of Astronomy and Astrophysics, Toronto, ON M5S 1A1, Canada. Offers M Sc, PhD. Part-time programs available. *Degree requirements:* For doctorate, thesis/dissertation, qualifying exam, thesis defense. *Entrance requirements:* For master's, minimum B average, bachelor's degree in astronomy or equivalent, 3 letters of reference; for doctorate, GRE General Test, minimum B+ average, master's degree in astronomy or equivalent, demonstrated research competence, 3 letters of reference. Additional exam requirements/recommendations for international students: Required—TOEFL (minimum score 580 paper-based; 93 iBT), TWE (minimum score 4). Electronic applications accepted.

University of Victoria, Faculty of Graduate Studies, Faculty of Science, Department of Physics and Astronomy, Victoria, BC V8W 2Y2, Canada. Offers astronomy and astrophysics (M Sc, PhD); condensed matter physics (M Sc, PhD); experimental particle physics (M Sc, PhD); medical physics (M Sc, PhD); ocean physics (M Sc, PhD); theoretical physics (M Sc, PhD). *Degree requirements:* For master's, thesis; for doctorate, comprehensive exam, thesis/dissertation, candidacy exam. *Entrance requirements:* For master's and doctorate, GRE. Additional exam requirements/recommendations for international students: Required—TOEFL (minimum score 575 paper-based; 233 computer-based), IELTS (minimum score 7). Electronic applications accepted. *Faculty research:* Old stellar populations; observational cosmology and large scale structure; cp violation; atlas.

Yale University, Graduate School of Arts and Sciences, Department of Astronomy, New Haven, CT 06520. Offers astronomy (PhD); solar and terrestrial physics (PhD). *Degree requirements:* For doctorate, thesis/dissertation. *Entrance requirements:* For doctorate, GRE General Test, GRE Subject Test (physics).

Peterson's Graduate Programs in the Physical Sciences, Mathematics, Agricultural Sciences, the Environment & Natural Resources 2013

facebook.com/petersonspublishing **49**

Section 2
Chemistry

This section contains a directory of institutions offering graduate work in chemistry, followed by in-depth entries submitted by institutions that chose to prepare detailed program descriptions. Additional information about programs listed in the directory but not augmented by an in-depth entry may be obtained by writing directly to the dean of a graduate school or chair of a department at the address given in the directory.

For programs offering related work, see also in this book *Geosciences* and *Physics*. In the other guides in this series:

Graduate Programs in the Biological/Biomedical Sciences & Health-Related Medical Professions

See *Biological and Biomedical Sciences, Biochemistry, Biophysics, Nutrition, Pharmacology and Toxicology,* and *Pharmacy and Pharmaceutical Sciences*

Graduate Programs in Engineering & Applied Sciences

See *Engineering and Applied Sciences; Agricultural Engineering; Chemical Engineering; Geological, Mineral/Mining, and Petroleum Engineering; Materials Sciences and Engineering;* and *Pharmaceutical Engineering*

CONTENTS

Analytical Chemistry

Auburn University, Graduate School, College of Sciences and Mathematics, Department of Chemistry and Biochemistry, Auburn University, AL 36849. Offers analytical chemistry (MS, PhD); biochemistry (MS, PhD); inorganic chemistry (MS, PhD); organic chemistry (MS, PhD); physical chemistry (MS, PhD). Part-time programs available. *Faculty:* 28 full-time (5 women), 1 part-time/adjunct (0 women). *Students:* 37 full-time (14 women), 30 part-time (15 women); includes 6 minority (3 Black or African American, non-Hispanic/Latino; 1 American Indian or Alaska Native, non-Hispanic/Latino; 1 Asian, non-Hispanic/Latino; 1 Hispanic/Latino), 41 international. Average age 28. 38 applicants, 39% accepted, 12 enrolled. In 2011, 1 master's, 9 doctorates awarded. *Degree requirements:* For master's, thesis (for some programs); for doctorate, thesis/dissertation, oral and written exams. *Entrance requirements:* For master's and doctorate, GRE General Test. *Application deadline:* For fall admission, 7/7 for domestic students; for spring admission, 11/24 for domestic students. Applications are processed on a rolling basis. Application fee: $50 ($60 for international students). Electronic applications accepted. *Expenses:* Tuition, state resident: full-time $7290; part-time $405 per credit hour. Tuition, nonresident: full-time $21,870; part-time $1215 per credit hour. *International tuition:* $22,000 full-time. *Required fees:* $1402. *Financial support:* Fellowships, research assistantships, and teaching assistantships available. Financial award application deadline: 3/15; financial award applicants required to submit FAFSA. *Unit head:* Dr. J. V. Ortiz, Chair, 334-844-4043, Fax: 334-844-4043. *Application contact:* Dr. George Flowers, Dean of the Graduate School, 334-844-2125. Web site: http://www.auburn.edu/cosam/departments/chemistry/.

Brigham Young University, Graduate Studies, College of Physical and Mathematical Sciences, Department of Chemistry and Biochemistry, Provo, UT 84602. Offers biochemistry (MS, PhD); chemistry (MS, PhD). *Faculty:* 33 full-time (2 women). *Students:* 104 full-time (39 women); includes 3 minority (2 Asian, non-Hispanic/Latino; 1 Native Hawaiian or other Pacific Islander, non-Hispanic/Latino), 53 international. Average age 28. 93 applicants, 41% accepted, 19 enrolled. In 2011, 5 master's, 11 doctorates awarded. *Median time to degree:* Of those who began their doctoral program in fall 2003, 50% received their degree in 8 years or less. *Degree requirements:* For master's, thesis; for doctorate, comprehensive exam, thesis/dissertation, qualifying exam. *Entrance requirements:* For master's and doctorate, GRE General Test, minimum GPA of 3.0 in last 60 hours. Additional exam requirements/recommendations for international students: Required—TOEFL (minimum score 580 paper-based; 237 computer-based; 85 iBT), IELTS (minimum score 7); Recommended—TWE. *Application deadline:* For fall admission, 2/1 priority date for domestic students, 2/1 for international students. Applications are processed on a rolling basis. Application fee: $50. Electronic applications accepted. Full-time tuition for non-LDS students: $11,520 per year; $640 per credit. *Expenses: Tuition:* Full-time $5760; part-time $320 per credit. Tuition and fees vary according to student's religious affiliation. *Financial support:* In 2011–12, 104 students received support, including 10 fellowships with full tuition reimbursements available (averaging $21,250 per year), 59 research assistantships with full tuition reimbursements available (averaging $21,250 per year), 35 teaching assistantships with full tuition reimbursements available (averaging $21,250 per year); institutionally sponsored loans, scholarships/grants, health care benefits, tuition waivers (full), and unspecified assistantships also available. Financial award application deadline: 2/1. *Faculty research:* Separation science, molecular recognition, organic synthesis and biomedical application, biochemistry and molecular biology, molecular spectroscopy. *Total annual research expenditures:* $5.6 million. *Unit head:* Dr. Gregory F. Burton, Chair, 801-422-4917, Fax: 801-422-0153, E-mail: gburton@byu.edu. *Application contact:* Dr. Paul B. Farnsworth, Graduate Coordinator, 801-422-6502, Fax: 801-422-0153, E-mail: pbfarnsw@byu.edu. Web site: http://www.chem.byu.edu/.

California State University, Los Angeles, Graduate Studies, College of Natural and Social Sciences, Department of Chemistry and Biochemistry, Los Angeles, CA 90032-8530. Offers analytical chemistry (MS); biochemistry (MS); chemistry (MS); inorganic chemistry (MS); organic chemistry (MS); physical chemistry (MS). Part-time and evening/weekend programs available. *Faculty:* 4 part-time/adjunct (1 woman). *Students:* 22 full-time (14 women), 24 part-time (11 women); includes 30 minority (4 Black or African American, non-Hispanic/Latino; 7 Asian, non-Hispanic/Latino; 19 Hispanic/Latino), 7 international. Average age 29. 60 applicants, 48% accepted, 17 enrolled. In 2011, 15 master's awarded. *Degree requirements:* For master's, one foreign language, comprehensive exam or thesis. *Entrance requirements:* Additional exam requirements/recommendations for international students: Required—TOEFL. *Application deadline:* For fall admission, 5/1 for domestic and international students. Applications are processed on a rolling basis. Application fee: $55. *Expenses:* Tuition, state resident: full-time $8225. *Financial support:* Federal Work-Study available. Support available to part-time students. Financial award application deadline: 3/1. *Faculty research:* Intercalation of heavy metal, carborane chemistry, conductive polymers and fabrics, titanium reagents, computer modeling and synthesis. *Unit head:* Dr. Robert L. Vellanoweth, Chair, 323-343-2300, Fax: 323-343-6490, E-mail: rvellan@calstatela.edu. *Application contact:* Dr. Karin Brown, Acting Associate Dean of Graduate Studies, 323-343-3820 Ext. 3827, Fax: 323-343-5653, E-mail: kbrown5@calstatela.edu. Web site: http://www.calstatela.edu/dept/chem/index.htm.

Cleveland State University, College of Graduate Studies, College of Sciences and Health Professions, Department of Chemistry, Cleveland, OH 44115. Offers analytical chemistry (MS); clinical chemistry (MS); clinical/bioanalytical chemistry (PhD), including cellular and molecular medicine, clinical chemistry, clinical/bioanalytical chemistry; environmental chemistry (MS); inorganic chemistry (MS); pharmaceutical/organic chemistry (MS); physical chemistry (MS). Part-time and evening/weekend programs available. *Faculty:* 12 full-time (0 women). *Students:* 17 full-time (8 women), 87 part-time (36 women); includes 6 minority (5 Black or African American, non-Hispanic/Latino; 1 Asian, non-Hispanic/Latino), 74 international. Average age 27. 143 applicants, 59% accepted, 22 enrolled. In 2011, 14 master's, 10 doctorates awarded. *Median time to degree:* Of those who began their doctoral program in fall 2003, 67% received their degree in 8 years or less. *Degree requirements:* For master's, thesis optional; for doctorate, comprehensive exam, thesis/dissertation. *Entrance requirements:* For master's and doctorate, GRE General Test. Additional exam requirements/recommendations for international students: Required—TOEFL (minimum score 525 paper-based; 197 computer-based; 65 iBT). *Application deadline:* For fall admission, 1/15 priority date for domestic students, 1/15 for international students. Applications are processed on a rolling basis. Application fee: $30. Electronic applications accepted. *Expenses:* Tuition, state resident: full-time $6416; part-time $494 per credit hour. Tuition, nonresident: full-time $12,074; part-time $929 per credit hour. *Financial support:* In 2011–12, 44 students received support, including 5 fellowships with full tuition reimbursements available (averaging $30,000 per year), 13 research assistantships with full tuition reimbursements available (averaging $20,000 per year), 24 teaching assistantships with full tuition reimbursements available (averaging $18,500 per year); scholarships/grants and unspecified assistantships also available. Financial award application deadline: 1/15. *Faculty research:* Bioanalytical techniques and molecular diagnostics, glycoproteomics and antithrombotic agents, drug discovery and innovation, analytical pharmacology, inflammatory disease research. *Total annual research expenditures:* $3 million. *Unit head:* Dr. David J. Anderson, Interim Chair, 216-687-2467, Fax: 216-687-9298, E-mail: d.anderson@csuohio.edu. *Application contact:* Richelle P. Emery, Administrative Coordinator, 216-687-2457, Fax: 216-687-9298, E-mail: r.emery@csuohio.edu. Web site: http://www.csuohio.edu/chemistry/.

Cornell University, Graduate School, Graduate Fields of Arts and Sciences, Field of Chemistry and Chemical Biology, Ithaca, NY 14853-0001. Offers analytical chemistry (PhD); bio-organic chemistry (PhD); biophysical chemistry (PhD); chemical biology (PhD); chemical physics (PhD); inorganic chemistry (PhD); materials chemistry (PhD); organic chemistry (PhD); organometallic chemistry (PhD); physical chemistry (PhD); polymer chemistry (PhD); theoretical chemistry (PhD). *Faculty:* 46 full-time (3 women). *Students:* 151 full-time (67 women); includes 16 minority (13 Asian, non-Hispanic/Latino; 2 Hispanic/Latino; 1 Two or more races, non-Hispanic/Latino), 48 international. Average age 25. 297 applicants, 35% accepted, 29 enrolled. In 2011, 22 doctorates awarded. *Degree requirements:* For doctorate, comprehensive exam, thesis/dissertation. *Entrance requirements:* For doctorate, GRE General Test, GRE Subject Test (chemistry), 3 letters of recommendation. Additional exam requirements/recommendations for international students: Required—TOEFL (minimum score 600 paper-based; 250 computer-based; 77 iBT). *Application deadline:* For fall admission, 1/10 for domestic students. Application fee: $95. Electronic applications accepted. *Financial support:* In 2011–12, 21 fellowships with full tuition reimbursements, 63 research assistantships with full tuition reimbursements, 59 teaching assistantships with full tuition reimbursements were awarded; institutionally sponsored loans, scholarships/grants, health care benefits, tuition waivers (full and partial), and unspecified assistantships also available. Financial award applicants required to submit FAFSA. *Faculty research:* Analytical, organic, inorganic, physical, materials, chemical biology. *Unit head:* Director of Graduate Studies, 607-255-4139, Fax: 607-255-4137. *Application contact:* Graduate Field Assistant, 607-255-4139, Fax: 607-255-4137, E-mail: chemgrad@cornell.edu. Web site: http://www.gradschool.cornell.edu/fields.php?id-26&a-2.

Eastern New Mexico University, Graduate School, College of Liberal Arts and Sciences, Department of Physical Sciences, Portales, NM 88130. Offers chemistry (MS), including analytical, biochemistry, inorganic, organic, physical. Part-time programs available. *Faculty:* 6 full-time (0 women). *Students:* 11 part-time (5 women), 9 international. Average age 25. 25 applicants, 44% accepted, 4 enrolled. In 2011, 5 master's awarded. *Degree requirements:* For master's, thesis optional, seminar, oral and written comprehensive exams. *Entrance requirements:* For master's, ACS placement examination, minimum GPA of 3.0; 2 letters of recommendation; personal statement of career goals; bachelor's degree with one year minimum each of general, organic, and analytical chemistry. Additional exam requirements/recommendations for international students: Required—TOEFL (minimum score 550 paper-based; 213 computer-based; 79 iBT), IELTS (minimum score 6). *Application deadline:* For fall admission, 7/20 priority date for domestic students, 6/20 for international students; for spring admission, 12/15 priority date for domestic students, 11/15 for international students. Applications are processed on a rolling basis. Application fee: $10. Electronic applications accepted. *Financial support:* In 2011–12, 1 research assistantship with partial tuition reimbursement (averaging $8,500 per year), 10 teaching assistantships

52 facebook.com/petersonspublishing

Peterson's Graduate Programs in the Physical Sciences, Mathematics, Agricultural Sciences, the Environment & Natural Resources 2013

with partial tuition reimbursements (averaging $8,500 per year) were awarded; career-related internships or fieldwork and unspecified assistantships also available. Support available to part-time students. Financial award application deadline: 3/1; financial award applicants required to submit FAFSA. *Faculty research:* Synfuel, electrochemistry, protein chemistry. *Unit head:* Dr. Juacho Yan, Graduate Coordinator, 575-562-2494, Fax: 575-562-2192, E-mail: juacho.yan@enmu.edu. *Application contact:* Sharon Potter, Department Secretary, Biology and Physical Sciences, 575-562-2174, Fax: 575-562-2192, E-mail: sharon.potter@enmu.edu. Web site: http://liberal-arts.enmu.edu/sciences/grad-chemistry.shtml.

Florida State University, The Graduate School, College of Arts and Sciences, Department of Chemistry and Biochemistry, Tallahassee, FL 32306-4390. Offers analytical chemistry (MS, PhD); biochemistry (MS, PhD); inorganic chemistry (MS, PhD); materials chemistry (PhD); organic chemistry (MS, PhD); physical chemistry (MS, PhD). *Faculty:* 35 full-time (5 women), 1 (woman) part-time/adjunct. *Students:* 138 full-time (52 women), 8 part-time (1 woman); includes 14 minority (6 Black or African American, non-Hispanic/Latino; 3 Asian, non-Hispanic/Latino; 2 Hispanic/Latino; 3 Two or more races, non-Hispanic/Latino), 63 international. Average age 25. 147 applicants, 40% accepted, 28 enrolled. In 2011, 10 master's, 24 doctorates awarded. Terminal master's awarded for partial completion of doctoral program. *Median time to degree:* Of those who began their doctoral program in fall 2003, 58% received their degree in 8 years or less. *Degree requirements:* For master's, comprehensive exam (for some programs), thesis (for some programs); for doctorate, comprehensive exam (for some programs), thesis/dissertation. *Entrance requirements:* For master's and doctorate, GRE General Test, minimum B average in undergraduate course work. Additional exam requirements/recommendations for international students: Required—TOEFL (minimum score 550 paper-based; 213 computer-based; 80 iBT). *Application deadline:* For fall admission, 12/15 priority date for domestic students, 12/15 for international students; for spring admission, 9/15 for domestic and international students. Applications are processed on a rolling basis. Application fee: $30. Electronic applications accepted. *Expenses:* Contact institution. *Financial support:* In 2011–12, 140 students received support, including fellowships with full tuition reimbursements available (averaging $20,000 per year), 50 research assistantships with full tuition reimbursements available (averaging $20,000 per year), 100 teaching assistantships with full tuition reimbursements available (averaging $20,000 per year). Financial award application deadline: 12/15; financial award applicants required to submit FAFSA. *Faculty research:* Materials synthesis including polymers, natural products; catalysis, NMR; mass spectrometry; optical spectroscopy, scattering techniques, computational chemistry, separation technology; nanostructured materials including metallic, semiconducting and magnetic nanocrystals; nanoscience interfaced with biology; supramolecular materials for solar energy conversion. *Total annual research expenditures:* $9.9 million. *Unit head:* Dr. Timothy Logan, Chairman, 850-644-1244, Fax: 850-644-8281, E-mail: gradinfo@chem.fsu.edu. *Application contact:* Dr. Michael Shatruk, Chair, Graduate Admissions Committee, 888-525-9286, Fax: 850-644-0465, E-mail: gradinfo@chem.fsu.edu. Web site: http://www.chem.fsu.edu/.

Georgetown University, Graduate School of Arts and Sciences, Department of Chemistry, Washington, DC 20057. Offers analytical chemistry (PhD); biochemistry (PhD); computational chemistry (PhD); inorganic chemistry (PhD); materials chemistry (PhD); organic chemistry (PhD); physical chemistry (PhD); theoretical chemistry (PhD). Terminal master's awarded for partial completion of doctoral program. *Degree requirements:* For doctorate, comprehensive exam, thesis/dissertation. *Entrance requirements:* For doctorate, GRE General Test. Additional exam requirements/recommendations for international students: Required—TOEFL.

The George Washington University, Columbian College of Arts and Sciences, Department of Chemistry, Washington, DC 20052. Offers analytical chemistry (MS, PhD); inorganic chemistry (MS, PhD); materials science (MS, PhD); organic chemistry (MS, PhD); physical chemistry (MS, PhD). Part-time and evening/weekend programs available. *Faculty:* 16 full-time (5 women), 5 part-time/adjunct (2 women). *Students:* 22 full-time (10 women), 10 part-time (7 women); includes 4 minority (3 Asian, non-Hispanic/Latino; 1 Hispanic/Latino), 7 international. Average age 27. 55 applicants, 42% accepted, 8 enrolled. In 2011, 4 master's, 3 doctorates awarded. Terminal master's awarded for partial completion of doctoral program. *Degree requirements:* For master's, comprehensive exam, thesis or alternative; for doctorate, thesis/dissertation, general exam. *Entrance requirements:* For master's and doctorate, GRE General Test, interview, minimum GPA of 3.0. Additional exam requirements/recommendations for international students: Required—TOEFL (minimum score 550 paper-based; 213 computer-based; 80 iBT). *Application deadline:* For fall admission, 1/15 priority date for domestic students, 1/15 for international students; for spring admission, 9/1 priority date for domestic students, 9/1 for international students. Applications are processed on a rolling basis. Application fee: $75. Electronic applications accepted. *Financial support:* In 2011–12, 27 students received support. Fellowships with tuition reimbursements available, research assistantships, teaching assistantships with tuition reimbursements available, Federal Work-Study, and tuition waivers available. Financial award application deadline: 1/15. *Unit head:* Dr. Michael King, Chair, 202-994-6488. *Application contact:* Information Contact, 202-994-6121, E-mail: gwchem@gwu.edu. Web site: http://www.gwu.edu/~gwchem/.

Governors State University, College of Arts and Sciences, Program in Analytical Chemistry, University Park, IL 60484. Offers MS. Part-time and evening/weekend programs available. *Students:* 34 full-time (20 women), 28 part-time (9 women); includes 13 minority (6 Black or African American, non-Hispanic/Latino; 5 Asian, non-Hispanic/Latino; 2 Hispanic/Latino), 42 international. Average age 29. *Degree requirements:* For master's, thesis or alternative. *Application deadline:* For fall admission, 7/15 priority date for domestic students; for spring admission, 11/10 for domestic students. Applications are processed on a rolling basis. Application fee: $25. *Financial support:* Career-related internships or fieldwork, Federal Work-Study, institutionally sponsored loans, and scholarships/grants available. Support available to part-time students. Financial award application deadline: 5/1. *Faculty research:* Electrochemistry, photochemistry, spectrochemistry, biochemistry. *Unit head:* Dr. James Howley, Chair, Division of Liberal Arts, 708-534-7893. *Application contact:* Yakeea Daniels, Interim Director of Admission, 708-534-4510, E-mail: ydaniels@govst.edu.

Howard University, Graduate School, Department of Chemistry, Washington, DC 20059-0002. Offers analytical chemistry (MS, PhD); atmospheric (MS, PhD); biochemistry (MS, PhD); environmental (MS, PhD); inorganic chemistry (MS, PhD); organic chemistry (MS, PhD); physical chemistry (MS, PhD). Terminal master's awarded for partial completion of doctoral program. *Degree requirements:* For master's, comprehensive exam, thesis, teaching experience; for doctorate, comprehensive exam, thesis/dissertation, teaching experience. *Entrance requirements:* For master's, GRE General Test, minimum GPA of 2.7; for doctorate, GRE General Test, minimum GPA of 3.0. Additional exam requirements/recommendations for international students: Required—TOEFL. Electronic applications accepted. *Faculty research:* Synthetic organics, materials, natural products, mass spectrometry.

Illinois Institute of Technology, Graduate College, College of Science and Letters, Department of Biological, Chemical and Physical Sciences, Chemistry Division, Chicago, IL 60616. Offers analytical chemistry (M Ch); chemistry (M Chem, MS, PhD); materials and chemical synthesis (M Ch). Part-time and evening/weekend programs available. Postbaccalaureate distance learning degree programs offered (no on-campus study). Terminal master's awarded for partial completion of doctoral program. *Degree requirements:* For master's, comprehensive exam, thesis (for some programs); for doctorate, comprehensive exam, thesis/dissertation. *Entrance requirements:* For master's, GRE General Test (minimum score 1000 Quantitative and Verbal, 2.5 Analytical Writing), minimum undergraduate GPA of 3.0; for doctorate, GRE General Test (minimum score 1100 Quantitative and Verbal, 3.0 Analytical Writing), GRE Subject Test, minimum undergraduate GPA of 3.0. Additional exam requirements/recommendations for international students: Required—TOEFL (minimum score 523 paper-based; 213 computer-based; 70 iBT); Recommended—IELTS. Electronic applications accepted. *Faculty research:* Synthesis and analysis of inorganic nanoparticles; synthetic and mechanistic organic chemistry; synthesis of penicillin-related compounds; design, synthesis and property studies of nanomaterials for applications in chemical sensing, energy storage and biomedical usage; scanning probe microscopy.

Indiana University Bloomington, University Graduate School, College of Arts and Sciences, Department of Chemistry, Bloomington, IN 47405. Offers analytical chemistry (PhD); chemical biology chemistry (PhD); chemistry (MAT); inorganic chemistry (PhD); materials chemistry (PhD); organic chemistry (PhD); physical chemistry (PhD). *Faculty:* 42 full-time (4 women). *Students:* 200 full-time (82 women), 3 part-time (0 women); includes 18 minority (7 Black or African American, non-Hispanic/Latino; 8 Asian, non-Hispanic/Latino; 1 Hispanic/Latino; 1 Native Hawaiian or other Pacific Islander, non-Hispanic/Latino; 1 Two or more races, non-Hispanic/Latino), 63 international. Average age 27. 290 applicants, 49% accepted, 46 enrolled. In 2011, 11 master's, 20 doctorates awarded. Terminal master's awarded for partial completion of doctoral program. *Median time to degree:* Of those who began their doctoral program in fall 2003, 49% received their degree in 8 years or less. *Degree requirements:* For master's, thesis; for doctorate, thesis/dissertation. *Entrance requirements:* For master's and doctorate, GRE General Test, GRE Subject Test. Additional exam requirements/recommendations for international students: Required—TOEFL. *Application deadline:* For fall admission, 1/15 priority date for domestic students, 12/15 for international students. Applications are processed on a rolling basis. Application fee: $55 ($65 for international students). *Financial support:* In 2011–12, 200 students received support, including 10 fellowships with full tuition reimbursements available, 76 research assistantships with full tuition reimbursements available, 111 teaching assistantships with full tuition reimbursements available; Federal Work-Study and institutionally sponsored loans also available. *Faculty research:* Synthesis of complex natural products, organic reaction mechanisms, organic electrochemistry, transitive-metal chemistry, solid-state and surface chemistry. *Total annual research expenditures:* $7.7 million. *Unit head:* David Giedroc, Chairperson, 812-855-6239, E-mail: chemchair@indiana.edu. *Application contact:* Daniel Mindiola, Director of Graduate Admissions, 812-855-2069, Fax: 812-855-8385, E-mail: mindiola@indiana.edu. Web site: http://www.chem.indiana.edu/.

Iowa State University of Science and Technology, Program in Analytical Chemistry, Ames, IA 50011-3011. Offers PhD. *Entrance requirements:* For doctorate, official academic transcripts, resume, three letters of recommendation. Additional exam requirements/recommendations for international students: Required—TOEFL (minimum score 570 paper-based; 89 iBT), IELTS (minimum score 6.5). *Application deadline:* For fall admission, 2/1 for domestic and

Peterson's Graduate Programs in the Physical Sciences, Mathematics, Agricultural Sciences, the Environment & Natural Resources 2013

facebook.com/petersonspublishing **53**

international students. Electronic applications accepted. *Unit head:* Theresa Windus, Director of Graduate Education, 515-294-2436, Fax: 515-294-0105, E-mail: chemgrad@iastate.edu. *Application contact:* Lynette Edsall, Application Contact, 515-294-7810, Fax: 515-294-0105, E-mail: grad_admissions@iastate.edu.

Kansas State University, Graduate School, College of Arts and Sciences, Department of Chemistry, Manhattan, KS 66506. Offers analytical chemistry (MS); biological chemistry (MS); chemistry (PhD); inorganic chemistry (MS); materials chemistry (MS); organic chemistry (MS); physical chemistry (MS). *Faculty:* 17 full-time (2 women). *Students:* 63 full-time (28 women), 4 part-time (0 women); includes 2 minority (1 Black or African American, non-Hispanic/Latino; 1 Asian, non-Hispanic/Latino), 55 international. Average age 28. 119 applicants, 34% accepted, 15 enrolled. In 2011, 2 master's, 10 doctorates awarded. Terminal master's awarded for partial completion of doctoral program. *Degree requirements:* For master's, thesis; for doctorate, thesis/dissertation. *Entrance requirements:* For master's and doctorate, GRE, minimum GPA of 3.0. Additional exam requirements/recommendations for international students: Required—TOEFL (minimum score 550 paper-based; 213 computer-based). *Application deadline:* For fall admission, 2/1 priority date for domestic students, 2/1 for international students; for spring admission, 8/1 priority date for domestic students, 8/1 for international students. Applications are processed on a rolling basis. Application fee: $40 ($55 for international students). Electronic applications accepted. *Financial support:* In 2011–12, 39 research assistantships (averaging $18,182 per year), 24 teaching assistantships with full tuition reimbursements (averaging $18,106 per year) were awarded; institutionally sponsored loans and scholarships/grants also available. Support available to part-time students. Financial award application deadline: 3/1; financial award applicants required to submit FAFSA. *Faculty research:* Inorganic chemistry, organic and biological chemistry, analytical chemistry, physical chemistry, materials chemistry and nanotechnology. *Total annual research expenditures:* $2.4 million. *Unit head:* Eric Maatta, Head, 785-532-6665, Fax: 785-532-6666, E-mail: eam@ksu.edu. *Application contact:* Christer Aakeroy, Director, 785-532-6096, Fax: 785-532-6666, E-mail: aakeroy@ksu.edu. Web site: http://www.k-state.edu/chem/.

Kent State University, College of Arts and Sciences, Department of Chemistry and Biochemistry, Kent, OH 44242-0001. Offers analytical chemistry (MS, PhD); biochemistry (MS, PhD); chemistry (MA); inorganic chemistry (MS, PhD); organic chemistry (MS, PhD); physical chemistry (MS, PhD). Terminal master's awarded for partial completion of doctoral program. *Degree requirements:* For master's, comprehensive exam, thesis; for doctorate, comprehensive exam, thesis/dissertation. *Entrance requirements:* For master's and doctorate, placement exam, GRE General Test, GRE Subject Test (recommended), minimum GPA of 2.75. Additional exam requirements/recommendations for international students: Required—TOEFL (minimum score 525 paper-based; 71 iBT). Electronic applications accepted. *Expenses:* Tuition, state resident: full-time $8136; part-time $452 per credit hour. Tuition, nonresident: full-time $14,292; part-time $794 per credit hour. *Faculty research:* Biological chemistry, materials chemistry, molecular spectroscopy.

See Display on page 70 and Close-Up on page 127.

Laurentian University, School of Graduate Studies and Research, Programme in Chemistry and Biochemistry, Sudbury, ON P3E 2C6, Canada. Offers analytical chemistry (M Sc); biochemistry (M Sc); environmental chemistry (M Sc); organic chemistry (M Sc); physical/theoretical chemistry (M Sc). Part-time programs available. *Degree requirements:* For master's, thesis or alternative. *Entrance requirements:* For master's, honors degree with minimum second class. *Faculty research:* Cell cycle checkpoints, kinetic modeling, toxicology to metal stress, quantum chemistry, biogeochemistry metal speciation.

Marquette University, Graduate School, College of Arts and Sciences, Department of Chemistry, Milwaukee, WI 53201-1881. Offers analytical chemistry (MS, PhD); bioanalytical chemistry (MS, PhD); biophysical chemistry (MS, PhD); chemical physics (MS, PhD); inorganic chemistry (MS, PhD); organic chemistry (MS, PhD); physical chemistry (MS, PhD). Part-time programs available. *Faculty:* 29 full-time (4 women), 1 (woman) part-time/adjunct. *Students:* 42 full-time (11 women), 2 part-time (0 women); includes 5 minority (2 Black or African American, non-Hispanic/Latino; 3 Asian, non-Hispanic/Latino), 31 international. Average age 29. 18 applicants, 100% accepted, 10 enrolled. In 2011, 5 master's, 7 doctorates awarded. Terminal master's awarded for partial completion of doctoral program. *Degree requirements:* For master's, comprehensive exam; for doctorate, thesis/dissertation, cumulative exams. *Entrance requirements:* For master's and doctorate, official transcripts from all current and previous colleges/universities except Marquette, three letters of recommendation from individuals familiar with the applicant's academic work. Additional exam requirements/recommendations for international students: Required—TOEFL (minimum score 530 paper-based; 78 computer-based). *Application deadline:* Applications are processed on a rolling basis. Application fee: $50. Electronic applications accepted. *Expenses: Tuition:* Full-time $17,010; part-time $945 per credit hour. Tuition and fees vary according to program. *Financial support:* In 2011–12, 41 students received support, including 2 fellowships (averaging $17,134 per year), 30 teaching assistantships with full tuition reimbursements available (averaging $20,295 per year); research assistantships, scholarships/grants, health care benefits, tuition waivers (full and partial), and unspecified assistantships also available. Support available to part-time students. Financial award application deadline: 2/15. *Faculty research:* Inorganic complexes, laser Raman spectroscopy, organic synthesis, synthetic bioinorganic chemistry, electro-active organic molecules. *Total annual research*

expenditures: $2.1 million. *Unit head:* Dr. Michael Ryan, Chair, 414-288-3537, Fax: 414-288-7066. *Application contact:* Dr. Mark Steinmetz, Director of Graduate Studies, 414-288-7374, Fax: 414-288-7066. Web site: http://www.marquette.edu/chem/graduate.shtml.

McMaster University, School of Graduate Studies, Faculty of Science, Department of Chemistry, Hamilton, ON L8S 4M2, Canada. Offers analytical chemistry (M Sc, PhD); chemical physics (M Sc, PhD); chemistry (M Sc, PhD); inorganic chemistry (M Sc, PhD); organic chemistry (M Sc, PhD); physical chemistry (M Sc, PhD); polymer chemistry (M Sc, PhD). Part-time programs available. Terminal master's awarded for partial completion of doctoral program. *Degree requirements:* For master's, thesis; for doctorate, comprehensive exam, thesis/dissertation. *Entrance requirements:* For master's, minimum B+ average. Additional exam requirements/recommendations for international students: Required—TOEFL (minimum score 550 paper-based; 213 computer-based).

Northeastern University, College of Science, Department of Chemistry and Chemical Biology, Boston, MA 02115-5096. Offers analytical chemistry (PhD); chemistry (MS, PhD); inorganic chemistry (PhD); organic chemistry (PhD); physical chemistry (PhD). Part-time and evening/weekend programs available. *Faculty:* 24 full-time, 7 part-time/adjunct. *Students:* 98 full-time (58 women), 31 part-time (15 women). 190 applicants, 32% accepted, 34 enrolled. In 2011, 16 master's, 6 doctorates awarded. Terminal master's awarded for partial completion of doctoral program. *Degree requirements:* For master's, thesis (for some programs); for doctorate, thesis/dissertation, qualifying exam in specialty area. *Entrance requirements:* Additional exam requirements/recommendations for international students: Required—TOEFL. *Application deadline:* For fall admission, 2/1 priority date for domestic students, 2/1 for international students. Applications are processed on a rolling basis. Application fee: $50. Electronic applications accepted. *Financial support:* In 2011–12, 41 research assistantships with tuition reimbursements (averaging $18,285 per year), 38 teaching assistantships with tuition reimbursements (averaging $18,285 per year) were awarded; fellowships with tuition reimbursements, career-related internships or fieldwork, Federal Work-Study, scholarships/grants, tuition waivers (partial), and unspecified assistantships also available. Financial award application deadline: 3/1; financial award applicants required to submit FAFSA. *Faculty research:* Bioanalysis, bioorganic and medicinal chemistry, biophysical chemistry, nanomaterials, proteonics. *Unit head:* Dr. Robert Hanson, Graduate Coordinator, 617-373-3313, Fax: 617-373-8795, E-mail: chemistry-grad-info@neu.edu. *Application contact:* Jo-Anne Dickinson, Admissions Contact, 617-373-5990, Fax: 617-373-7281, E-mail: gsas@neu.edu. Web site: http://www.northeastern.edu/chem/.

Old Dominion University, College of Sciences, Program in Chemistry, Norfolk, VA 23529. Offers analytical chemistry (MS); biochemistry (MS); chemistry (PhD); environmental chemistry (MS); organic chemistry (MS); physical chemistry (MS). Part-time and evening/weekend programs available. *Faculty:* 14 full-time (5 women), 2 part-time/adjunct (0 women). *Students:* 34 full-time (17 women), 2 part-time (1 woman); includes 2 minority (1 Black or African American, non-Hispanic/Latino; 1 Asian, non-Hispanic/Latino), 17 international. Average age 28. 35 applicants, 60% accepted, 8 enrolled. In 2011, 3 master's, 2 doctorates awarded. *Degree requirements:* For master's, comprehensive exam, thesis. *Entrance requirements:* For master's, GRE General Test, minimum GPA of 3.0 in major, 2.5 overall; for doctorate, GRE General Test. Additional exam requirements/recommendations for international students: Required—TOEFL. *Application deadline:* For fall admission, 7/1 for domestic students, 1/15 for international students; for spring admission, 11/1 for domestic students, 8/15 for international students. Applications are processed on a rolling basis. Application fee: $30. Electronic applications accepted. *Expenses:* Tuition, state resident: full-time $9096; part-time $379 per credit. Tuition, nonresident: full-time $23,064; part-time $961 per credit. *Required fees:* $127 per semester. One-time fee: $50. *Financial support:* In 2011–12, 6 students received support, including fellowships (averaging $18,000 per year), research assistantships with tuition reimbursements available (averaging $21,000 per year), teaching assistantships with tuition reimbursements available (averaging $18,000 per year); career-related internships or fieldwork, scholarships/grants, and unspecified assistantships also available. Financial award application deadline: 2/15; financial award applicants required to submit FAFSA. *Faculty research:* Biogeochemistry, materials chemistry, bioanalytical chemistry, computational chemistry, organic chemistry. *Total annual research expenditures:* $2.6 million. *Unit head:* Dr. Craig A. Bayse, Graduate Program Director, 757-683-4097, Fax: 757-683-4628, E-mail: chemgpd@odu.edu. *Application contact:* Valerie DeCosta, Grants and Graduate Program Assistant, 757-683-6979, Fax: 757-683-4628, E-mail: chemgpd@odu.edu.

Oregon State University, Graduate School, College of Science, Department of Chemistry, Corvallis, OR 97331. Offers analytical chemistry (MS, PhD); chemistry (MA, MAIS); inorganic chemistry (MS, PhD); nuclear and radiation chemistry (MS, PhD); organic chemistry (MS, PhD); physical chemistry (MS, PhD). Part-time programs available. Terminal master's awarded for partial completion of doctoral program. *Degree requirements:* For master's, one foreign language, thesis; for doctorate, one foreign language, thesis/dissertation. *Entrance requirements:* For master's and doctorate, minimum GPA of 3.0 in last 90 hours of course work. Additional exam requirements/recommendations for international students: Required—TOEFL. *Faculty research:* Solid state chemistry, enzyme reaction mechanisms, structure and dynamics of gas molecules, chemiluminescence, nonlinear optical spectroscopy.

54 facebook.com/petersonspublishing

Peterson's Graduate Programs in the Physical Sciences, Mathematics, Agricultural Sciences, the Environment & Natural Resources 2013

Purdue University, Graduate School, College of Science, Department of Chemistry, West Lafayette, IN 47907. Offers analytical chemistry (MS, PhD); biochemistry (MS, PhD); chemical education (MS, PhD); inorganic chemistry (MS, PhD); organic chemistry (MS, PhD); physical chemistry (MS, PhD). *Faculty:* 47 full-time (16 women), 6 part-time/adjunct (0 women). *Students:* 275 full-time (103 women), 33 part-time (10 women); includes 38 minority (19 Black or African American, non-Hispanic/Latino; 6 Asian, non-Hispanic/Latino; 12 Hispanic/Latino; 1 Two or more races, non-Hispanic/Latino), 94 international. Average age 27. 777 applicants, 26% accepted, 62 enrolled. In 2011, 4 master's, 67 doctorates awarded. Terminal master's awarded for partial completion of doctoral program. *Degree requirements:* For master's, thesis; for doctorate, comprehensive exam, thesis/dissertation. *Entrance requirements:* For master's and doctorate, minimum undergraduate GPA of 3.0. Additional exam requirements/recommendations for international students: Required—TOEFL (minimum score 550 computer-based; 77 iBT); Recommended—TWE. *Application deadline:* For fall admission, 2/15 priority date for domestic students, 1/1 for international students. Applications are processed on a rolling basis. Application fee: $60 ($75 for international students). Electronic applications accepted. *Financial support:* In 2011–12, 2 fellowships with partial tuition reimbursements (averaging $18,000 per year), 55 teaching assistantships with partial tuition reimbursements (averaging $18,000 per year) were awarded; research assistantships with partial tuition reimbursements and tuition waivers (partial) also available. Support available to part-time students. Financial award applicants required to submit FAFSA. *Unit head:* Dr. Paul B. Shepson, Head, 765-494-5203, E-mail: pshepson@purdue.edu. *Application contact:* Betty L. Hatfield, Director of Graduate Admissions, 765-494-5208, E-mail: bettyh@purdue.edu.

Rensselaer Polytechnic Institute, Graduate School, School of Science, Program in Chemistry, Troy, NY 12180-3590. Offers analytical chemistry (MS, PhD); biochemistry (MS, PhD); inorganic chemistry (MS, PhD); organic chemistry (MS, PhD); physical chemistry (MS, PhD); polymer chemistry (MS, PhD). Part-time and evening/weekend programs available. Terminal master's awarded for partial completion of doctoral program. *Degree requirements:* For master's, thesis (for some programs); for doctorate, comprehensive exam, thesis/dissertation. *Entrance requirements:* For master's, GRE General Test, GRE Subject Test (strongly recommended); for doctorate, GRE General Test, GRE Subject Test (chemistry or biochemistry strongly recommended). Additional exam requirements/recommendations for international students: Required—TOEFL (minimum score 570 paper-based; 230 computer-based; 88 iBT). Electronic applications accepted. *Faculty research:* Synthetic polymer and biopolymer chemistry, physical chemistry of polymeric systems, bioanalytical chemistry, synthetic and computational drug design, protein folding and protein design.

Rutgers, The State University of New Jersey, Newark, Graduate School, Program in Chemistry, Newark, NJ 07102. Offers analytical chemistry (MS, PhD); biochemistry (MS, PhD); inorganic chemistry (MS, PhD); organic chemistry (MS, PhD); physical chemistry (MS, PhD). Part-time and evening/weekend programs available. Terminal master's awarded for partial completion of doctoral program. *Degree requirements:* For master's, thesis optional, cumulative exams; for doctorate, thesis/dissertation, exams, research proposal. *Entrance requirements:* For master's and doctorate, GRE General Test, minimum undergraduate B average. Additional exam requirements/recommendations for international students: Required—TOEFL. Electronic applications accepted. *Faculty research:* Medicinal chemistry, natural products, isotope effects, biophysics and biorganic approaches to enzyme mechanisms, organic and organometallic synthesis.

Seton Hall University, College of Arts and Sciences, Department of Chemistry and Biochemistry, South Orange, NJ 07079-2697. Offers analytical chemistry (MS, PhD); biochemistry (MS, PhD); chemistry (MS); inorganic chemistry (MS, PhD); organic chemistry (MS, PhD); physical chemistry (MS, PhD). Part-time and evening/weekend programs available. Terminal master's awarded for partial completion of doctoral program. *Degree requirements:* For master's, thesis optional; for doctorate, comprehensive exam, thesis/dissertation. *Entrance requirements:* Additional exam requirements/recommendations for international students: Required—TOEFL. Electronic applications accepted. *Expenses: Tuition:* Part-time $1033 per credit hour. *Required fees:* $85 per semester. *Faculty research:* DNA metal reactions; chromatography; bioinorganic, biophysical, organometallic, polymer chemistry; heterogeneous catalyst; synthetic organic and carbohydrate chemistry.

Southern University and Agricultural and Mechanical College, Graduate School, College of Sciences, Department of Chemistry, Baton Rouge, LA 70813. Offers analytical chemistry (MS); biochemistry (MS); environmental sciences (MS); inorganic chemistry (MS); organic chemistry (MS); physical chemistry (MS). *Degree requirements:* For master's, thesis. *Entrance requirements:* For master's, GMAT or GRE General Test. Additional exam requirements/recommendations for international students: Required—TOEFL (minimum score 525 paper-based; 193 computer-based). *Faculty research:* Synthesis of macrocyclic ligands, latex accelerators, anticancer drugs, biosensors, absorption isotheums, isolation of specific enzymes from plants.

State University of New York at Binghamton, Graduate School, School of Arts and Sciences, Department of Chemistry, Binghamton, NY 13902-6000. Offers analytical chemistry (PhD); chemistry (MA, MS); inorganic chemistry (PhD); organic chemistry (PhD); physical chemistry (PhD). Part-time programs available. *Faculty:* 16 full-time (5 women), 2 part-time/adjunct (both women). *Students:* 24 full-time (8 women), 32 part-time (13 women); includes 5 minority (2 Black or African American, non-Hispanic/Latino; 1 Hispanic/Latino; 2 Native Hawaiian or other Pacific Islander, non-Hispanic/Latino), 36 international. Average age 28. 39 applicants, 36% accepted, 10 enrolled. In 2011, 3 master's, 6 doctorates awarded. Terminal master's awarded for partial completion of doctoral program. *Degree requirements:* For master's, thesis or alternative, oral exam, seminar presentation; for doctorate, thesis/dissertation, cumulative exams. *Entrance requirements:* For master's and doctorate, GRE General Test, GRE Subject Test. Additional exam requirements/recommendations for international students: Required—TOEFL (minimum score 550 paper-based; 213 computer-based; 80 iBT). *Application deadline:* For fall admission, 1/15 priority date for domestic students, 1/15 for international students; for spring admission, 10/15 priority date for domestic students, 10/15 for international students. Applications are processed on a rolling basis. Application fee: $60. Electronic applications accepted. *Financial support:* In 2011–12, 9 fellowships with full tuition reimbursements (averaging $18,000 per year), 13 research assistantships with full tuition reimbursements (averaging $18,000 per year), 35 teaching assistantships with full tuition reimbursements (averaging $18,000 per year) were awarded; career-related internships or fieldwork, Federal Work-Study, institutionally sponsored loans, scholarships/grants, health care benefits, tuition waivers (full), and unspecified assistantships also available. Financial award application deadline: 2/15; financial award applicants required to submit FAFSA. *Unit head:* Dr. Wayne E. Jones, Chairperson, 607-777-2421, E-mail: wjones@binghamton.edu. *Application contact:* Catherine Smith, Recruiting and Admissions Coordinator, 607-777-2151, Fax: 607-777-2501, E-mail: cmsmith@binghamton.edu.

Stevens Institute of Technology, Graduate School, Charles V. Schaefer Jr. School of Engineering, Department of Chemistry, Chemical Biology and Biomedical Engineering, Hoboken, NJ 07030. Offers analytical chemistry (PhD, Certificate); bioinformatics (PhD, Certificate); biomedical chemistry (Certificate); biomedical engineering (M Eng, Certificate); chemical biology (MS, PhD, Certificate); chemical physiology (Certificate); chemistry (MS, PhD); organic chemistry (PhD); physical chemistry (PhD); polymer chemistry (PhD, Certificate). Part-time and evening/weekend programs available. Postbaccalaureate distance learning degree programs offered (no on-campus study). Terminal master's awarded for partial completion of doctoral program. *Degree requirements:* For master's, thesis or alternative; for doctorate, one foreign language, thesis/dissertation; for Certificate, project or thesis. *Entrance requirements:* Additional exam requirements/recommendations for international students: Required—TOEFL. Electronic applications accepted. *Faculty research:* Biochemical reaction engineering, polymerization engineering, reactor design, biochemical process control and synthesis.

Tufts University, Graduate School of Arts and Sciences, Department of Chemistry, Medford, MA 02155. Offers analytical chemistry (MS, PhD); bioorganic chemistry (MS, PhD); environmental chemistry (MS, PhD); inorganic chemistry (MS, PhD); organic chemistry (MS, PhD); physical chemistry (MS, PhD). *Students:* 75 full-time (33 women); includes 7 minority (1 Black or African American, non-Hispanic/Latino; 5 Asian, non-Hispanic/Latino; 1 Hispanic/Latino), 25 international. 88 applicants, 59% accepted, 16 enrolled. In 2011, 5 master's, 8 doctorates awarded. Terminal master's awarded for partial completion of doctoral program. *Degree requirements:* For master's, thesis optional; for doctorate, thesis/dissertation. *Entrance requirements:* For master's and doctorate, GRE General Test, GRE Subject Test. Additional exam requirements/recommendations for international students: Required—TOEFL (minimum score 600 paper-based; 250 computer-based; 80 iBT). *Application deadline:* For fall admission, 1/15 for domestic students, 12/15 for international students; for spring admission, 10/15 for domestic students, 9/15 for international students. Applications are processed on a rolling basis. Application fee: $75. Electronic applications accepted. *Expenses: Tuition:* Full-time $41,208; part-time $1030 per credit hour. Full-time tuition and fees vary according to degree level, program and student level. Part-time tuition and fees vary according to course load. *Financial support:* Fellowships, research assistantships with full tuition reimbursements, teaching assistantships with full tuition reimbursements, Federal Work-Study, scholarships/grants, tuition waivers (partial), and unspecified assistantships available. Financial award application deadline: 1/15; financial award applicants required to submit FAFSA. *Unit head:* Arthur Utz, Chair, 617-627-3441. *Application contact:* Deborah D'Andrea, Information Contact, 617-627-3441, Fax: 617-627-3443. Web site: http://chem.tufts.edu/.

University of Calgary, Faculty of Graduate Studies, Faculty of Science, Department of Chemistry, Calgary, AB T2N 1N4, Canada. Offers analytical chemistry (M Sc, PhD); applied chemistry (M Sc, PhD); inorganic chemistry (M Sc, PhD); organic chemistry (M Sc, PhD); physical chemistry (M Sc, PhD); polymer chemistry (M Sc, PhD); theoretical chemistry (M Sc, PhD). *Degree requirements:* For master's, thesis; for doctorate, thesis/dissertation, candidacy exam. *Entrance requirements:* For master's, minimum GPA of 3.0; for doctorate, honors B Sc degree with minimum GPA of 3.7 or M Sc with minimum GPA of 3.3. Additional exam requirements/recommendations for international students: Required—TOEFL (minimum score 580 paper-based; 237 computer-based). Electronic applications accepted. *Faculty research:* Chemical analysis, chemical dynamics, synthesis theory.

University of Cincinnati, Graduate School, McMicken College of Arts and Sciences, Department of Chemistry, Cincinnati, OH 45221. Offers analytical chemistry (MS, PhD); biochemistry (MS, PhD); inorganic chemistry (MS, PhD); organic chemistry (MS, PhD); physical chemistry (MS, PhD); polymer chemistry (MS, PhD); sensors (PhD). Part-time and evening/weekend programs available.

Peterson's Graduate Programs in the Physical Sciences, Mathematics, Agricultural Sciences, the Environment & Natural Resources 2013

facebook.com/petersonspublishing **55**

Terminal master's awarded for partial completion of doctoral program. *Degree requirements:* For master's, thesis optional; for doctorate, comprehensive exam, thesis/dissertation. *Entrance requirements:* For master's and doctorate, GRE General Test. Additional exam requirements/recommendations for international students: Required—TOEFL (minimum score 580 paper-based; 237 computer-based). Electronic applications accepted. *Faculty research:* Biomedical chemistry, laser chemistry, surface science, chemical sensors, synthesis.

University of Georgia, Franklin College of Arts and Sciences, Department of Chemistry, Athens, GA 30602. Offers analytical chemistry (MS, PhD); inorganic chemistry (MS, PhD); organic chemistry (MS, PhD); physical chemistry (MS, PhD). *Faculty:* 26 full-time (2 women). *Students:* 153 full-time (53 women), 6 part-time (2 women); includes 21 minority (6 Black or African American, non-Hispanic/Latino; 12 Asian, non-Hispanic/Latino; 1 Hispanic/Latino; 2 Two or more races, non-Hispanic/Latino), 60 international. Average age 27. 175 applicants, 41% accepted, 38 enrolled. In 2011, 7 master's, 22 doctorates awarded. Terminal master's awarded for partial completion of doctoral program. *Median time to degree:* Of those who began their doctoral program in fall 2003, 100% received their degree in 8 years or less. *Degree requirements:* For master's, thesis; for doctorate, one foreign language, thesis/dissertation. *Entrance requirements:* For master's and doctorate, GRE General Test. Additional exam requirements/recommendations for international students: Required—TOEFL (minimum score 213 computer-based). *Application deadline:* For fall admission, 7/1 priority date for domestic students; for spring admission, 11/15 for domestic students. Application fee: $50. Electronic applications accepted. *Financial support:* Fellowships, research assistantships, teaching assistantships, and unspecified assistantships available. *Unit head:* Dr. Jon Amster, Head, 706-542-2726, E-mail: jamster@uga.edu. *Application contact:* Dr. Jeffrey L. Urbauer, Graduate Coordinator, 706-542-7922, E-mail: urbauer@uga.edu. Web site: http://www.chem.uga.edu/.

University of Louisville, Graduate School, College of Arts and Sciences, Department of Chemistry, Louisville, KY 40292-0001. Offers analytical chemistry (MS, PhD); biochemistry (MS, PhD); chemical physics (PhD); inorganic chemistry (MS, PhD); organic chemistry (MS, PhD); physical chemistry (MS, PhD). Terminal master's awarded for partial completion of doctoral program. *Degree requirements:* For master's, variable foreign language requirement, comprehensive exam, thesis optional; for doctorate, variable foreign language requirement, comprehensive exam, thesis/dissertation. *Entrance requirements:* For master's and doctorate, BA or BS coursework. Additional exam requirements/recommendations for international students: Required—TOEFL. Electronic applications accepted. *Expenses:* Tuition, state resident: full-time $9692; part-time $539 per credit hour. Tuition, nonresident: full-time $20,168; part-time $1121 per credit hour. Tuition and fees vary according to program and reciprocity agreements. *Faculty research:* Computational chemistry, biophysics nuclear magnetic resonance, synthetic organic chemistry, synthetic inorganic chemistry, medicinal chemistry, protein chemistry, enzymology, nanochemistry, electrochemistry, analytical chemistry, synthetic biology, bioinformatics.

The University of Manchester, School of Chemical Engineering and Analytical Science, Manchester, United Kingdom. Offers biocatalysis (M Phil, PhD); chemical engineering (M Phil, PhD); chemical engineering and analytical science (M Phil, D Eng, PhD); colloids, crystals, interfaces and materials (M Phil, PhD); environment and sustainable technology (M Phil, PhD); instrumentation (M Phil, PhD); multi-scale modeling (M Phil, PhD); process integration (M Phil, PhD); systems biology (M Phil, PhD).

University of Maryland, College Park, Academic Affairs, College of Computer, Mathematical and Natural Sciences, Department of Chemistry and Biochemistry, Chemistry Program, College Park, MD 20742. Offers analytical chemistry (MS, PhD); inorganic chemistry (MS, PhD); organic chemistry (MS, PhD); physical chemistry (MS, PhD). Part-time and evening/weekend programs available. *Students:* 115 full-time (59 women), 4 part-time (1 woman); includes 20 minority (12 Black or African American, non-Hispanic/Latino; 4 Asian, non-Hispanic/Latino; 2 Hispanic/Latino; 2 Two or more races, non-Hispanic/Latino), 52 international. 335 applicants, 8% accepted, 18 enrolled. In 2011, 11 master's, 15 doctorates awarded. Terminal master's awarded for partial completion of doctoral program. *Median time to degree:* Of those who began their doctoral program in fall 2003, 63% received their degree in 8 years or less. *Degree requirements:* For master's, thesis optional; for doctorate, thesis/dissertation, 2 seminar presentations, oral exam. *Entrance requirements:* For master's and doctorate, GRE General Test, GRE Subject Test (recommended), minimum GPA of 3.0, 3 letters of recommendation. Additional exam requirements/recommendations for international students: Required—TOEFL. *Application deadline:* For fall admission, 2/1 for domestic and international students; for spring admission, 6/1 for domestic and international students. Applications are processed on a rolling basis. Application fee: $75. Electronic applications accepted. *Expenses: Tuition, area resident:* Part-time $525 per credit hour. Tuition, state resident: part-time $525 per credit hour. Tuition, nonresident: part-time $1131 per credit hour. *Required fees:* $386.31 per term. Tuition and fees vary according to program. *Financial support:* In 2011–12, 9 fellowships with full and partial tuition reimbursements (averaging $25,360 per year), 46 research assistantships (averaging $19,791 per year), 59 teaching assistantships (averaging $19,243 per year) were awarded. Financial award applicants required to submit FAFSA. *Faculty research:* Environmental chemistry, nuclear chemistry, lunar and environmental analysis, x-ray crystallography. *Unit head:* Dr. Michael Doyle, Chairperson, 301-405-1795, Fax: 301-314-2779, E-mail: mdoyle3@umd.edu.

Application contact: Dr. Charles A. Caramello, Dean of Graduate School, 301-405-0358, Fax: 301-314-9305.

University of Massachusetts Lowell, College of Sciences, Department of Chemistry, Lowell, MA 01854-2881. Offers analytical chemistry (PhD); biochemistry (PhD); chemistry (MS, PhD); environmental studies (PhD); green chemistry (PhD); inorganic chemistry (PhD); organic chemistry (PhD); polymer science (MS). Terminal master's awarded for partial completion of doctoral program. *Degree requirements:* For master's, thesis; for doctorate, 2 foreign languages, thesis/dissertation. *Entrance requirements:* For master's and doctorate, GRE General Test. Electronic applications accepted.

University of Memphis, Graduate School, College of Arts and Sciences, Department of Chemistry, Memphis, TN 38152. Offers analytical chemistry (MS, PhD); computational chemistry (MS, PhD); inorganic chemistry (MS, PhD); organic chemistry (MS, PhD); physical chemistry (MS, PhD). Part-time programs available. Terminal master's awarded for partial completion of doctoral program. *Degree requirements:* For master's, comprehensive exam, thesis or alternative; for doctorate, comprehensive exam, thesis/dissertation. *Entrance requirements:* For master's and doctorate, GRE General Test, admission to Graduate School plus 32 undergraduate hours in chemistry. Additional exam requirements/recommendations for international students: Required—TOEFL. Electronic applications accepted. *Faculty research:* Computational chemistry, materials chemistry, organic/polymer synthesis, drug design/delivery, water chemistry.

University of Michigan, Horace H. Rackham School of Graduate Studies, College of Literature, Science, and the Arts, Department of Chemistry, Ann Arbor, MI 48109-1055. Offers analytical chemistry (PhD); chemical biology (PhD); inorganic chemistry (PhD); material chemistry (PhD); organic chemistry (PhD); physical chemistry (PhD). *Faculty:* 39 full-time (9 women). *Students:* 221 full-time (114 women); includes 24 minority (1 Black or African American, non-Hispanic/Latino; 15 Asian, non-Hispanic/Latino; 4 Hispanic/Latino; 4 Two or more races, non-Hispanic/Latino), 66 international. Average age 26. 608 applicants, 27% accepted, 39 enrolled. In 2011, 39 doctorates awarded. *Degree requirements:* For doctorate, thesis/dissertation, oral defense of dissertation, organic cumulative proficiency exams. *Entrance requirements:* For doctorate, GRE General Test, GRE Subject Test (recommended), 3 letters of recommendation. Additional exam requirements/recommendations for international students: Required—TOEFL (minimum score 560 paper-based; 220 computer-based; 84 iBT). *Application deadline:* For fall admission, 12/31 for domestic students, 12/15 for international students. Applications are processed on a rolling basis. Application fee: $0 ($75 for international students). Electronic applications accepted. *Financial support:* In 2011–12, 221 students received support, including 25 fellowships with full tuition reimbursements available (averaging $26,553 per year), 86 research assistantships with full tuition reimbursements available (averaging $26,553 per year), 110 teaching assistantships with full tuition reimbursements available (averaging $26,553 per year); career-related internships or fieldwork, scholarships/grants, traineeships, health care benefits, and unspecified assistantships also available. *Faculty research:* Biological catalysis, protein engineering, chemical sensors, de novo metalloprotein design, supramolecular architecture. *Unit head:* Dr. Carol A. Fierke, Chair, 734-763-9681, Fax: 734-647-4847. *Application contact:* Margarita Bekiares, Graduate Program Coordinator, 734-764-7278, Fax: 734-647-4865, E-mail: chemadmissions@umich.edu. Web site: http://www.umich.edu/~michchem/.

University of Missouri, Graduate School, College of Arts and Sciences, Department of Chemistry, Columbia, MO 65211. Offers analytical chemistry (MS, PhD); inorganic chemistry (MS, PhD); organic chemistry (MS, PhD); physical chemistry (MS, PhD). *Faculty:* 22 full-time (4 women), 1 part-time/adjunct (0 women). *Students:* 102 full-time (38 women), 10 part-time (6 women); includes 7 minority (3 Black or African American, non-Hispanic/Latino; 2 Asian, non-Hispanic/Latino; 1 Hispanic/Latino; 1 Two or more races, non-Hispanic/Latino), 53 international. Average age 27. 98 applicants, 28% accepted, 24 enrolled. In 2011, 2 master's, 5 doctorates awarded. *Degree requirements:* For master's, thesis; for doctorate, one foreign language, comprehensive exam, thesis/dissertation. *Entrance requirements:* For master's, GRE General Test, minimum GPA of 3.0; for doctorate, GRE General Test (minimum score: Verbal 450, Quantitative 600, Analytical 3), minimum GPA of 3.0. Additional exam requirements/recommendations for international students: Required—TOEFL (minimum score 600 paper-based; 250 computer-based; 100 iBT). *Application deadline:* For fall admission, 4/1 priority date for domestic students; for winter admission, 10/15 for domestic students. Applications are processed on a rolling basis. Application fee: $55 ($75 for international students). Electronic applications accepted. *Expenses:* Tuition, state resident: full-time $5881. Tuition, nonresident: full-time $15,183. *Required fees:* $952. Tuition and fees vary according to campus/location and program. *Financial support:* In 2011–12, 9 fellowships with full tuition reimbursements, 15 research assistantships with full tuition reimbursements, 78 teaching assistantships with full tuition reimbursements were awarded; institutionally sponsored loans, traineeships, health care benefits, and unspecified assistantships also available. *Faculty research:* Analytical, organic, biological, physical, inorganic and radiochemistry. *Unit head:* Dr. Jerry Atwood, Department Chair, 573-882-8374, E-mail: atwoodj@missouri.edu. *Application contact:* Jerry Brightwell, Administrative Assistant, 573-884-6832, E-mail: brightwellj@missouri.edu. Web site: http://chemistry.missouri.edu/.

University of Missouri–Kansas City, College of Arts and Sciences, Department of Chemistry, Kansas City, MO 64110-2499. Offers analytical chemistry (MS, PhD); inorganic chemistry (MS, PhD); organic chemistry (MS, PhD); physical

56 facebook.com/petersonspublishing

Peterson's Graduate Programs in the Physical Sciences, Mathematics, Agricultural Sciences, the Environment & Natural Resources 2013

chemistry (MS, PhD); polymer chemistry (MS, PhD). PhD (interdisciplinary) offered through the School of Graduate Studies. Part-time and evening/weekend programs available. *Faculty:* 16 full-time (3 women), 1 part-time/adjunct (0 women). *Students:* 1 (woman) part-time; minority (Black or African American, non-Hispanic/Latino). Average age 30. 28 applicants, 32% accepted, 0 enrolled. In 2011, 2 degrees awarded. *Degree requirements:* For master's, thesis (for some programs); for doctorate, thesis/dissertation. *Entrance requirements:* For master's, equivalent of American Chemical Society approved bachelor's degree in chemistry; for doctorate, GRE General Test, equivalent of American Chemical Society approved bachelor's degree in chemistry. Additional exam requirements/recommendations for international students: Required—TOEFL (minimum score 550 paper-based; 213 computer-based; 80 iBT), TWE. *Application deadline:* For fall admission, 4/15 for domestic and international students; for spring admission, 10/15 for domestic and international students. Applications are processed on a rolling basis. Application fee: $45 ($50 for international students). Electronic applications accepted. *Expenses:* Tuition, state resident: full-time $5798; part-time $322.10 per credit hour. Tuition, nonresident: full-time $14,969; part-time $831.60 per credit hour. *Required fees:* $93.51 per credit hour. *Financial support:* In 2011–12, 9 research assistantships with partial tuition reimbursements (averaging $19,119 per year), 14 teaching assistantships with partial tuition reimbursements (averaging $17,187 per year) were awarded; Federal Work-Study, institutionally sponsored loans, and scholarships/grants also available. Support available to part-time students. Financial award application deadline: 3/1; financial award applicants required to submit FAFSA. *Faculty research:* Molecular spectroscopy, characterization and synthesis of materials and compounds, computational chemistry, natural products, drug delivery systems and anti-tumor agents. *Unit head:* Dr. Kathleen V. Kilway, Chair, 816-235-2289, Fax: 816-235-5502. *Application contact:* Graduate Recruiting Committee, 816-235-2272, Fax: 816-235-5502, E-mail: umkc-chemdept@umkc.edu. Web site: http://cas.umkc.edu/chem/.

The University of Montana, Graduate School, College of Arts and Sciences, Department of Chemistry and Biochemistry, Missoula, MT 59812-0002. Offers chemistry (MS, PhD), including environmental/analytical chemistry, inorganic chemistry, organic chemistry, physical chemistry. Terminal master's awarded for partial completion of doctoral program. *Degree requirements:* For master's, thesis (for some programs); for doctorate, thesis/dissertation. *Entrance requirements:* For master's and doctorate, GRE General Test. Additional exam requirements/recommendations for international students: Required—TOEFL (minimum score 575 paper-based; 230 computer-based). *Faculty research:* Reaction mechanisms and kinetics, inorganic and organic synthesis, analytical chemistry, natural products.

University of Nebraska–Lincoln, Graduate College, College of Arts and Sciences, Department of Chemistry, Lincoln, NE 68588. Offers analytical chemistry (PhD); biochemistry (PhD); chemistry (MS); inorganic chemistry (PhD); materials chemistry (PhD); organic chemistry (PhD); physical chemistry (PhD). *Degree requirements:* For master's, one foreign language, thesis optional, departmental qualifying exam; for doctorate, one foreign language, comprehensive exam, thesis/dissertation, departmental qualifying exams. *Entrance requirements:* For master's and doctorate, GRE. Additional exam requirements/recommendations for international students: Required—TOEFL (minimum score 550 paper-based; 213 computer-based). Electronic applications accepted. *Faculty research:* Bioorganic and bioinorganic chemistry, biophysical and bioanalytical chemistry, structure-function of DNA and proteins, organometallics, mass spectrometry.

University of Regina, Faculty of Graduate Studies and Research, Faculty of Science, Department of Chemistry and Biochemistry, Regina, SK S4S 0A2, Canada. Offers analytical/environmental chemistry (M Sc, PhD); biophysics of biological interfaces (M Sc, PhD); enzymology/chemical biology (M Sc, PhD); inorganic/organometallic chemistry (M Sc, PhD); signal transduction and mechanisms of cancer cell regulation (M Sc, PhD); supramolecular organic photochemistry and photophysics (M Sc, PhD); synthetic organic chemistry (M Sc, PhD); theoretical/computational chemistry (M Sc, PhD). *Faculty:* 12 full-time (2 women). *Students:* 13 full-time (4 women), 1 (woman) part-time. 22 applicants, 50% accepted. In 2011, 1 master's, 2 doctorates awarded. *Degree requirements:* For master's, thesis; for doctorate, thesis/dissertation. *Entrance requirements:* Additional exam requirements/recommendations for international students: Required—TOEFL (minimum score 580 paper-based; 80 iBT), IELTS (minimum score 6.5). *Application deadline:* Applications are processed on a rolling basis. Application fee: $100. Electronic applications accepted. *Financial support:* In 2011–12, 3 fellowships (averaging $6,500 per year), 1 research assistantship (averaging $5,500 per year), 7 teaching assistantships (averaging $2,298 per year) were awarded; scholarships/grants also available. Financial award application deadline: 6/15. *Faculty research:* Asymmetric synthesis and methodology, theoretical and computational chemistry, biophysical biochemistry, analytical and environmental chemistry, chemical biology. *Unit head:* Dr. Lynn Mihichuk, Head, 306-585-4793, Fax: 306-337-2409, E-mail: lynn.mihichuk@uregina.ca. *Application contact:* Dr. Tanya Dahms, Graduate Program Coordinator, 306-585-4246, Fax: 306-337-2409, E-mail: tanya.dahms@uregina.ca. Web site: http://www.chem.uregina.ca/.

University of Southern Mississippi, Graduate School, College of Science and Technology, Department of Chemistry and Biochemistry, Hattiesburg, MS 39406-0001. Offers analytical chemistry (MS, PhD); biochemistry (MS, PhD); inorganic chemistry (MS, PhD); organic chemistry (MS, PhD); physical chemistry (MS,

PhD). *Faculty:* 16 full-time (4 women). *Students:* 22 full-time (9 women), 4 part-time (3 women); includes 1 minority (Black or African American, non-Hispanic/Latino), 9 international. Average age 29. 43 applicants, 19% accepted, 5 enrolled. In 2011, 1 master's, 4 doctorates awarded. *Degree requirements:* For master's, comprehensive exam, thesis; for doctorate, comprehensive exam, thesis/dissertation. *Entrance requirements:* For master's, GRE General Test, minimum GPA of 2.75 in last 60 hours; for doctorate, GRE General Test, minimum GPA of 3.5. Additional exam requirements/recommendations for international students: Required—TOEFL, IELTS. *Application deadline:* For fall admission, 3/1 priority date for domestic students, 3/1 for international students. Applications are processed on a rolling basis. Application fee: $50. *Financial support:* In 2011–12, 3 research assistantships with full tuition reimbursements (averaging $17,000 per year), 19 teaching assistantships with full tuition reimbursements (averaging $20,700 per year) were awarded; fellowships, Federal Work-Study, institutionally sponsored loans, scholarships/grants, health care benefits, and unspecified assistantships also available. Support available to part-time students. Financial award application deadline: 3/15; financial award applicants required to submit FAFSA. *Faculty research:* Plant biochemistry, photo chemistry, polymer chemistry, x-ray analysis, enzyme chemistry. *Unit head:* Dr. Sabine Heinhorst, Chair, 601-266-4701, Fax: 601-266-6075. *Application contact:* Dr. Sabine Heinhorst, Graduate Coordinator, 601-266-4702, Fax: 601-266-6075. Web site: http://www.usm.edu/graduateschool/table.php.

University of South Florida, Graduate School, College of Arts and Sciences, Department of Chemistry, Tampa, FL 33620-9951. Offers analytical chemistry (MS, PhD); biochemistry (MS, PhD); computational chemistry (MS, PhD); environmental chemistry (MS, PhD); inorganic chemistry (MS, PhD); organic chemistry (MS); physical chemistry (MS, PhD); polymer chemistry (PhD). Part-time programs available. *Faculty:* 25 full-time (4 women), 9 part-time/adjunct (1 woman). *Students:* 118 full-time (46 women), 14 part-time (7 women); includes 28 minority (8 Black or African American, non-Hispanic/Latino; 11 Asian, non-Hispanic/Latino; 9 Hispanic/Latino), 58 international. Average age 29. 127 applicants, 31% accepted, 19 enrolled. In 2011, 3 master's, 16 doctorates awarded. Terminal master's awarded for partial completion of doctoral program. *Degree requirements:* For master's, comprehensive exam, thesis (for some programs); for doctorate, comprehensive exam, thesis/dissertation. *Entrance requirements:* For master's and doctorate, GRE General Test, minimum GPA of 3.0. Additional exam requirements/recommendations for international students: Required—TOEFL (minimum score 550 paper-based; 213 computer-based; 79 iBT) or IELTS (minimum score 6.5). *Application deadline:* For fall admission, 2/15 priority date for domestic students, 1/2 for international students; for spring admission, 10/1 priority date for domestic students, 6/1 for international students. Applications are processed on a rolling basis. Application fee: $30. Electronic applications accepted. *Financial support:* In 2011–12, 136 students received support, including 28 research assistantships with tuition reimbursements available (averaging $15,020 per year), 108 teaching assistantships with tuition reimbursements available (averaging $15,164 per year); unspecified assistantships also available. Financial award application deadline: 6/30. *Faculty research:* Synthesis, bio-organic chemistry, bioinorganic chemistry, environmental chemistry, NMR. *Total annual research expenditures:* $3.1 million. *Unit head:* Dr. Randy Larsen, Chairperson, 813-974-4129, Fax: 813-974-3203, E-mail: rlarsen@cas.usf.edu. *Application contact:* Patricia Muisener, Director, 813-974-1730, Fax: 813-974-3203, E-mail: muisener@cas.usf.edu. Web site: http://chemistry.usf.edu/.

The University of Tennessee, Graduate School, College of Arts and Sciences, Department of Chemistry, Knoxville, TN 37996. Offers analytical chemistry (MS, PhD); chemical physics (PhD); environmental chemistry (MS, PhD); inorganic chemistry (MS, PhD); organic chemistry (MS, PhD); physical chemistry (MS, PhD); polymer chemistry (MS, PhD); theoretical chemistry (PhD). Part-time programs available. Terminal master's awarded for partial completion of doctoral program. *Degree requirements:* For master's, thesis; for doctorate, thesis/dissertation. *Entrance requirements:* For master's and doctorate, GRE General Test, minimum GPA of 2.7. Additional exam requirements/recommendations for international students: Required—TOEFL. Electronic applications accepted. *Expenses:* Tuition, state resident: full-time $8332; part-time $464 per credit hour. Tuition, nonresident: full-time $25,174; part-time $1400 per credit hour. *Required fees:* $1162; $56 per credit hour. Tuition and fees vary according to program.

The University of Texas at Austin, Graduate School, College of Natural Sciences, Department of Chemistry and Biochemistry, Austin, TX 78712-1111. Offers analytical chemistry (PhD); biochemistry (PhD); inorganic chemistry (PhD); organic chemistry (PhD); physical chemistry (PhD). *Entrance requirements:* For doctorate, GRE General Test. Application fee: $50 ($75 for international students). *Financial support:* Fellowships, research assistantships, teaching assistantships, and scholarships/grants available. Financial award application deadline: 2/1. *Unit head:* Dr. Richard M. Crooks, Chairman, 512-475-8674, E-mail: crooks@cm.utexas.edu. *Application contact:* Dr. Jennifer S. Brodbelt, Graduate Admissions Chair, 512-471-0028, E-mail: jbrodbelt@cm.utexas.edu. Web site: http://www.cm.utexas.edu/.

The University of Toledo, College of Graduate Studies, College of Natural Sciences and Mathematics, Department of Chemistry, Toledo, OH 43606-3390. Offers analytical chemistry (MS, PhD); biological chemistry (MS, PhD); inorganic chemistry (MS, PhD); organic chemistry (MS, PhD); physical chemistry (MS, PhD). Part-time programs available. *Faculty:* 22. *Students:* 56 full-time (18 women), 18 part-time (10 women); includes 4 minority (1 Black or African

Peterson's Graduate Programs in the Physical Sciences, Mathematics, Agricultural Sciences, the Environment & Natural Resources 2013

facebook.com/petersonspublishing **57**

American, non-Hispanic/Latino; 1 Asian, non-Hispanic/Latino; 2 Hispanic/Latino), 43 international. Average age 27. 111 applicants, 17% accepted, 16 enrolled. In 2011, 4 master's, 6 doctorates awarded. *Degree requirements:* For master's, thesis (for some programs); for doctorate, thesis/dissertation. *Entrance requirements:* For master's and doctorate, GRE General Test, GRE Subject Test, minimum cumulative point-hour ratio of 2.7 for all previous academic work, three letters of recommendation, statement of purpose, transcripts from all prior institutions attended. Additional exam requirements/recommendations for international students: Required—TOEFL (minimum score 550 paper-based; 213 computer-based; 80 iBT), IELTS (minimum score 6.5). *Application deadline:* For fall admission, 1/15 priority date for domestic students, 1/15 for international students. Applications are processed on a rolling basis. Application fee: $45 ($75 for international students). Electronic applications accepted. *Financial support:* In 2011–12, 24 research assistantships with full and partial tuition reimbursements (averaging $17,218 per year) were awarded; fellowships with tuition reimbursements, Federal Work-Study, institutionally sponsored loans, scholarships/grants, tuition waivers (full), and unspecified assistantships also available. Support available to part-time students. *Faculty research:* Enzymology, materials chemistry, crystallography, theoretical chemistry. *Unit head:* Dr. Alan Pinkerton, Chair, 419-530-7902, Fax: 419-530-4033, E-mail: alan.pinkerton@utoledo.edu. *Application contact:* Graduate School Office, 419-530-4723, Fax: 419-530-4724, E-mail: grdsch@utnet.utoledo.edu. Web site: http://www.utoledo.edu/nsm/.

Vanderbilt University, Graduate School, Department of Chemistry, Nashville, TN 37240-1001. Offers analytical chemistry (MAT, MS, PhD); inorganic chemistry (MAT, MS, PhD); organic chemistry (MAT, MS, PhD); physical chemistry (MAT, MS, PhD); theoretical chemistry (MAT, MS, PhD). *Faculty:* 21 full-time (3 women). *Students:* 114 full-time (43 women), 2 part-time (0 women); includes 16 minority (6 Black or African American, non-Hispanic/Latino; 1 American Indian or Alaska Native, non-Hispanic/Latino; 3 Asian, non-Hispanic/Latino; 1 Hispanic/Latino; 5 Two or more races, non-Hispanic/Latino), 18 international. Average age 26. 420 applicants, 12% accepted, 18 enrolled. In 2011, 4 master's, 17 doctorates awarded. Terminal master's awarded for partial completion of doctoral program. *Degree requirements:* For master's, thesis; for doctorate, thesis/dissertation, area, qualifying, and final exams. *Entrance requirements:* For master's and doctorate, GRE General Test, GRE Subject Test (recommended). Additional exam requirements/recommendations for international students: Required—TOEFL (minimum score 570 paper-based; 230 computer-based; 88 iBT). *Application deadline:* For fall admission, 1/15 for domestic and international students. Application fee: $0. Electronic applications accepted. *Financial support:* Fellowships with full and partial tuition reimbursements, research assistantships with full tuition reimbursements, teaching assistantships with full tuition reimbursements, Federal Work-Study, institutionally sponsored loans, scholarships/grants, traineeships, and health care benefits available. Financial award application deadline: 1/15; financial award applicants required to submit CSS PROFILE or FAFSA. *Faculty research:* Chemical synthesis; mechanistic, theoretical, bioorganic, analytical, and spectroscopic chemistry. *Unit head:* Dr. Mike P. Stone, Chair, 615-322-2589, Fax: 615-343-1234, E-mail: michael.p.stone@vanderbilt.edu. *Application contact:* Dr. Carmelo J. Rizzo, Director of Graduate Studies, 615-322-6100, Fax: 615-343-1234, E-mail: c.j.rizzo@vanderbilt.edu. Web site: http://www.vanderbilt.edu/AnS/Chemistry/grad/.

Virginia Commonwealth University, Graduate School, College of Humanities and Sciences, Department of Chemistry, Richmond, VA 23284-9005. Offers analytical chemistry (MS, PhD); chemical physics (PhD); inorganic chemistry (MS, PhD); organic chemistry (MS, PhD); physical chemistry (MS, PhD). Part-time programs available. *Students:* 49 full-time (20 women), 19 part-time (8 women); includes 10 minority (3 Black or African American, non-Hispanic/Latino; 5 Asian, non-Hispanic/Latino; 1 Hispanic/Latino; 1 Two or more races, non-Hispanic/Latino), 26 international. 56 applicants, 41% accepted, 11 enrolled. In 2011, 3

master's, 8 doctorates awarded. Terminal master's awarded for partial completion of doctoral program. *Degree requirements:* For master's, thesis; for doctorate, thesis/dissertation, comprehensive cumulative exams, research proposal. *Entrance requirements:* For master's, GRE General Test, 30 undergraduate credits in chemistry; for doctorate, GRE General Test. Additional exam requirements/recommendations for international students: Required—TOEFL (minimum score 600 paper-based; 250 computer-based; 100 iBT) or IELTS (minimum score 6.5). *Application deadline:* For fall admission, 3/15 for domestic students; for spring admission, 11/15 for domestic students. Applications are processed on a rolling basis. Application fee: $50. Electronic applications accepted. *Expenses:* Tuition, state resident: full-time $9133; part-time $507 per credit. Tuition, nonresident: full-time $18,777; part-time $1043 per credit. *Required fees:* $77 per credit. Tuition and fees vary according to degree level, campus/location, program and student level. *Financial support:* Fellowships, research assistantships, teaching assistantships, career-related internships or fieldwork, and institutionally sponsored loans available. Support available to part-time students. Financial award application deadline: 7/1; financial award applicants required to submit FAFSA. *Faculty research:* Physical, organic, inorganic, analytical, and polymer chemistry; chemical physics. *Unit head:* Dr. Scott Gronert, Chair, 804-828-1298, Fax: 804-828-8599, E-mail: sgronert@vcu.edu. *Application contact:* Dr. Maryanne M. Collinson, Chair, Graduate Recruiting and Admissions Committee, 804-828-7509, E-mail: mselshal@vcu.edu. Web site: http://www.has.vcu.edu/che/.

Wake Forest University, Graduate School of Arts and Sciences, Department of Chemistry, Winston-Salem, NC 27109. Offers analytical chemistry (MS, PhD); inorganic chemistry (MS, PhD); organic chemistry (MS, PhD); physical chemistry (MS, PhD). Part-time programs available. *Degree requirements:* For master's, one foreign language, comprehensive exam, thesis; for doctorate, 2 foreign languages, comprehensive exam, thesis/dissertation. *Entrance requirements:* For master's and doctorate, GRE General Test. Additional exam requirements/recommendations for international students: Required—TOEFL (minimum score 213 computer-based). Electronic applications accepted.

West Virginia University, Eberly College of Arts and Sciences, Department of Chemistry, Morgantown, WV 26506. Offers analytical chemistry (MS, PhD); inorganic chemistry (MS, PhD); organic chemistry (MS, PhD); physical chemistry (MS, PhD); theoretical chemistry (MS, PhD). Part-time programs available. Postbaccalaureate distance learning degree programs offered (no on-campus study). Terminal master's awarded for partial completion of doctoral program. *Degree requirements:* For master's, thesis; for doctorate, thesis/dissertation. *Entrance requirements:* For master's, GRE General Test, GRE Subject Test (recommended), minimum GPA of 2.5; for doctorate, GRE General Test, GRE Subject Test (recommended), minimum GPA of 2.75. Additional exam requirements/recommendations for international students: Required—TOEFL. Electronic applications accepted. *Faculty research:* Analysis of proteins, drug interactions, solids and effluents by advanced separation methods; new synthetic strategies for complex organic molecules; synthesis and structural characterization of metal complexes for polymerization catalysis, nonlinear science, spectroscopy.

Youngstown State University, Graduate School, College of Science, Technology, Engineering and Mathematics, Department of Chemistry, Youngstown, OH 44555-0001. Offers analytical chemistry (MS); biochemistry (MS); chemistry education (MS); inorganic chemistry (MS); organic chemistry (MS); physical chemistry (MS). Part-time programs available. *Degree requirements:* For master's, thesis. *Entrance requirements:* For master's, bachelor's degree in chemistry, minimum GPA of 2.7. Additional exam requirements/recommendations for international students: Required—TOEFL. *Faculty research:* Analysis of antioxidants, chromatography, defects and disorder in crystalline oxides, hydrogen bonding, novel organic and organometallic materials.

Chemistry

Acadia University, Faculty of Pure and Applied Science, Department of Chemistry, Wolfville, NS B4P 2R6, Canada. Offers M Sc. *Degree requirements:* For master's, thesis. *Entrance requirements:* Additional exam requirements/recommendations for international students: Required—TOEFL (minimum score 580 paper-based; 237 computer-based; 93 iBT), IELTS (minimum score 6.5). *Faculty research:* Atmospheric chemistry, chemical kinetics, bioelectrochemistry of proteins, self-assembling monolayers.

The American University in Cairo, School of Sciences and Engineering, Department of Chemistry, Cairo, Egypt. Offers food chemistry (M Chem). *Degree requirements:* For master's, thesis. *Entrance requirements:* For master's, bachelor's degree in chemistry or related discipline with minimum GPA of 3.0. *Expenses: Tuition:* Part-time $932 per credit hour. Tuition and fees vary according to course load, degree level and program. *Unit head:* Dr. Adham Ramadan, Chair, 20-2-2615-2926. *Application contact:* Wesley Clark, Director of North American

Admissions and Financial Aid, 212-646-810-9433 Ext. 4547, E-mail: wclark@aucnyo.edu. Web site: http://www.aucegypt.edu/sse/chem/.

American University of Beirut, Graduate Programs, Faculty of Arts and Sciences, Beirut, Lebanon. Offers anthropology (MA); Arabic language and literature (MA); archaeology (MA); biology (MS); chemistry (MS); computational science (MS); computer science (MS); economics (MA); education (MA); English language (MA); English literature (MA); environmental policy planning (MSES); financial economics (MAFE); geology (MS); history (MA); mathematics (MA, MS); Middle Eastern studies (MA); philosophy (MA); physics (MS); political studies (MA); psychology (MA); public administration (MA); sociology (MA); statistics (MA, MS). Part-time programs available. *Faculty:* 154 full-time (44 women), 12 part-time/adjunct (2 women). *Students:* 180 full-time (122 women), 240 part-time (158 women). Average age 25. 336 applicants, 47% accepted, 86 enrolled. In 2011, 57 master's awarded. *Degree requirements:* For master's, one foreign language, comprehensive exam, thesis (for some programs). *Entrance requirements:* For master's, GRE, letter of recommendation. Additional exam requirements/ recommendations for international students: Required—TOEFL (minimum score 600 paper-based; 250 computer-based; 97 iBT), IELTS (minimum score 7). *Application deadline:* For fall admission, 4/30 for domestic and international students; for spring admission, 11/1 for domestic and international students. Application fee: $50. *Expenses: Tuition:* Full-time $12,780; part-time $710 per credit. *Required fees:* $528; $528 per credit. Tuition and fees vary according to course load and program. *Financial support:* In 2011–12, 33 students received support. Career-related internships or fieldwork, institutionally sponsored loans, scholarships/grants, health care benefits, and unspecified assistantships available. Financial award application deadline: 2/4; financial award applicants required to submit FAFSA. *Faculty research:* History of composition studies, syntax of Arabic dialects, Oscar Wilde, decadence, Middle Eastern and international politics, neural mechanisms of creativity and consciousness, personality and psycho-socio-cultural-spiritual correlates of negative and positive mental health, philosophy of mind, metaphysics, micropaleontology and stratigraphy, geochemistry, mineralogy and petrology, tectonophysics, Abbasid, Ottoman and Russian history, landscape, Bronze and Iron Age archaeology. *Unit head:* Dr. Patrick McGreevy, Dean, 961-1374374 Ext. 3800, Fax: 961-1744461, E-mail: pm07@aub.edu.lb. *Application contact:* Dr. Salim Kanaan, Director, Admissions Office, 961-1350000 Ext. 2594, Fax: 961-1750775, E-mail: sk00@aub.edu.lb. Web site: http://staff.aub.edu.lb/~webfas.

Arizona State University, College of Liberal Arts and Sciences, Department of Chemistry and Biochemistry, Tempe, AZ 85287-1604. Offers biochemistry (MS, PhD); chemistry (MS, PhD); nanoscience (PSM). Terminal master's awarded for partial completion of doctoral program. *Degree requirements:* For master's, thesis, interactive Program of Study (iPOS) submitted before completing 50 percent of required credit hours; for doctorate, comprehensive exam, thesis/dissertation, interactive Program of Study (iPOS) submitted before completing 50 percent of required credit hours. *Entrance requirements:* For master's and doctorate, GRE, minimum GPA of 3.0 or equivalent in last 2 years of work leading to bachelor's degree. Additional exam requirements/recommendations for international students: Required—TOEFL (minimum score 80 iBT), TOEFL, IELTS, or Pearson Test of English. Electronic applications accepted.

Arkansas State University, Graduate School, College of Sciences and Mathematics, Department of Chemistry and Physics, Jonesboro, State University, AR 72467. Offers chemistry (MS); chemistry education (MSE, SCCT). Part-time programs available. *Faculty:* 12 full-time (1 woman). *Students:* 2 full-time (1 woman), 12 part-time (5 women); includes 2 minority (both Black or African American, non-Hispanic/Latino), 6 international. Average age 27. 13 applicants, 85% accepted, 3 enrolled. In 2011, 10 master's awarded. *Degree requirements:* For master's, comprehensive exam, thesis or alternative; for SCCT, comprehensive exam. *Entrance requirements:* For master's, GRE General Test or MAT, appropriate bachelor's degree, official transcript, immunization records, valid teaching certificate (for MSE); for SCCT, GRE General Test or MAT, interview, master's degree, official transcript, immunization records. Additional exam requirements/recommendations for international students: Required—TOEFL (minimum score 550 paper-based; 213 computer-based; 79 iBT), IELTS (minimum score 6), PTE: Pearson Test of English Academic (minimum score 56). *Application deadline:* For fall admission, 7/1 for domestic and international students; for spring admission, 11/15 for domestic students, 11/14 for international students. Applications are processed on a rolling basis. Application fee: $30 ($40 for international students). Electronic applications accepted. *Expenses:* Tuition, state resident: full-time $4044; part-time $225 per credit hour. Tuition, nonresident: full-time $8087; part-time $449 per credit hour. *Required fees:* $936; $52 per credit hour. $25 per term. One-time fee: $30. Tuition and fees vary according to course load and program. *Financial support:* In 2011–12, 6 students received support. Teaching assistantships, career-related internships or fieldwork, scholarships/grants, and unspecified assistantships available. Financial award application deadline: 7/1; financial award applicants required to submit FAFSA. *Unit head:* Dr. William Burns, Interim Chair, 870-972-3086, Fax: 870-972-3089, E-mail: wburns@astate.edu. *Application contact:* Dr. Andrew Sustich, Dean of the Graduate School, 870-972-3029, Fax: 870-972-3857, E-mail: sustich@astate.edu. Web site: http://www.astate.edu/a/scimath/chemistryphysics/.

Auburn University, Graduate School, College of Sciences and Mathematics, Department of Chemistry and Biochemistry, Auburn University, AL 36849. Offers analytical chemistry (MS, PhD); biochemistry (MS, PhD); inorganic chemistry (MS, PhD); organic chemistry (MS, PhD); physical chemistry (MS, PhD). Part-time programs available. *Faculty:* 28 full-time (5 women), 1 part-time/adjunct (0 women). *Students:* 37 full-time (14 women), 30 part-time (15 women); includes 6 minority (3 Black or African American, non-Hispanic/Latino; 1 American Indian or Alaska Native, non-Hispanic/Latino; 1 Asian, non-Hispanic/Latino; 1 Hispanic/Latino), 41 international. Average age 28. 38 applicants, 39% accepted, 12 enrolled. In 2011, 1 master's, 9 doctorates awarded. *Degree requirements:* For master's, thesis (for some programs); for doctorate, thesis/dissertation, oral and written exams. *Entrance requirements:* For master's and doctorate, GRE General Test. *Application deadline:* For fall admission, 7/7 for domestic students; for spring admission, 11/24 for domestic students. Applications are processed on a rolling basis. Application fee: $50 ($60 for international students). Electronic applications accepted. *Expenses:* Tuition, state resident: full-time $7290; part-time $405 per credit hour. Tuition, nonresident: full-time $21,870; part-time $1215 per credit hour. *International tuition:* $22,000 full-time. *Required fees:* $1402. *Financial support:* Fellowships, research assistantships, and teaching assistantships available. Financial award application deadline: 3/15; financial award applicants

required to submit FAFSA. *Unit head:* Dr. J. V. Ortiz, Chair, 334-844-4043, Fax: 334-844-4043. *Application contact:* Dr. George Flowers, Dean of the Graduate School, 334-844-2125. Web site: http://www.auburn.edu/cosam/departments/chemistry/.

Ball State University, Graduate School, College of Sciences and Humanities, Department of Chemistry, Muncie, IN 47306-1099. Offers MA, MS. *Faculty:* 22 full-time (8 women). *Students:* 1 full-time (0 women), 13 part-time (8 women), 1 international. Average age 22. 29 applicants, 38% accepted, 4 enrolled. In 2011, 5 master's awarded. *Entrance requirements:* For master's, GRE General Test. Application fee: $50. Tuition and fees vary according to program and reciprocity agreements. *Financial support:* In 2011–12, 14 students received support, including 13 teaching assistantships with full and partial tuition reimbursements available (averaging $4,520 per year); research assistantships with full tuition reimbursements available also available. Financial award application deadline: 3/1. *Faculty research:* Synthetic and analytical chemistry, biochemistry, theoretical chemistry. *Unit head:* Dr. Patti Lang, Interim Chair, 765-285-8060, Fax: 765-285-2351, E-mail: plang@bsu.edu. *Application contact:* Dr. James Poole, Associate Provost for Research and Dean of the Graduate School, 765-285-8071, E-mail: jpoole@bsu.edu. Web site: http://www.bsu.edu/csh/chemistry/.

Baylor University, Graduate School, College of Arts and Sciences, Department of Chemistry and Biochemistry, Waco, TX 76798. Offers chemistry (MS, PhD). Part-time programs available. *Faculty:* 14 full-time (2 women). *Students:* 52 full-time (25 women); includes 6 minority (2 Asian, non-Hispanic/Latino; 2 Hispanic/Latino; 2 Two or more races, non-Hispanic/Latino), 17 international. In 2011, 1 master's, 3 doctorates awarded. Terminal master's awarded for partial completion of doctoral program. *Degree requirements:* For master's, thesis; for doctorate, comprehensive exam, thesis/dissertation. *Entrance requirements:* For master's and doctorate, GRE General Test, GRE Subject Test. Additional exam requirements/recommendations for international students: Required—TOEFL. *Application deadline:* For fall admission, 8/1 for domestic students. Applications are processed on a rolling basis. Application fee: $25. *Financial support:* In 2011–12, 20 students received support. Fellowships, research assistantships, teaching assistantships, Federal Work-Study, institutionally sponsored loans, and tuition waivers (full) available. Support available to part-time students. *Unit head:* Dr. Charles Garner, Graduate Program Director, 254-710-6862, Fax: 254-710-2403, E-mail: charles_garner@baylor.edu. *Application contact:* Nancy Kallas, Administrative Assistant, 254-710-6844, Fax: 254-710-2403, E-mail: nancy_kallas@baylor.edu. Web site: http://www.baylor.edu/chemistry/.

Boston College, Graduate School of Arts and Sciences, Department of Chemistry, Chestnut Hill, MA 02467-3800. Offers biochemistry (PhD); inorganic chemistry (PhD); organic chemistry (PhD); physical chemistry (PhD); science education (MST). *Degree requirements:* For doctorate, thesis/dissertation, qualifying exam. *Entrance requirements:* For doctorate, GRE General Test, GRE Subject Test. Additional exam requirements/recommendations for international students: Required—TOEFL (minimum score 600 paper-based; 250 computer-based; 100 iBT). Electronic applications accepted.

Boston University, Graduate School of Arts and Sciences, Department of Chemistry, Boston, MA 02215. Offers MA, PhD. *Students:* 126 full-time (53 women); includes 14 minority (2 American Indian or Alaska Native, non-Hispanic/Latino; 8 Asian, non-Hispanic/Latino; 4 Hispanic/Latino), 50 international. Average age 26. 250 applicants, 32% accepted, 32 enrolled. In 2011, 23 master's, 11 doctorates awarded. Terminal master's awarded for partial completion of doctoral program. *Degree requirements:* For master's, one foreign language; for doctorate, one foreign language, comprehensive exam, thesis/dissertation. *Entrance requirements:* For master's and doctorate, GRE General Test, GRE Subject Test (recommended), 3 letters of recommendation. Additional exam requirements/recommendations for international students: Required—TOEFL (minimum score 550 paper-based; 213 computer-based). *Application deadline:* For fall admission, 1/1 for domestic and international students. Application fee: $70. Electronic applications accepted. *Expenses: Tuition:* Full-time $40,848; part-time $1276 per credit hour. *Required fees:* $572; $286 per semester. *Financial support:* In 2011–12, 3 fellowships with full tuition reimbursements (averaging $19,800 per year), 55 research assistantships with full tuition reimbursements (averaging $19,300 per year), 61 teaching assistantships with full tuition reimbursements (averaging $19,300 per year) were awarded; Federal Work-Study, scholarships/grants, and tuition waivers (full) also available. Support available to part-time students. Financial award application deadline: 1/1; financial award applicants required to submit FAFSA. *Unit head:* John Straub, Chairman, 617-353-2498, Fax: 617-353-6466, E-mail: straub@bu.edu. *Application contact:* Sarah Satgunam, Academic Administrator, 617-353-2503, Fax: 617-353-6466, E-mail: scoenen@bu.edu. Web site: http://www.bu.edu/chemistry/.

Bowling Green State University, Graduate College, College of Arts and Sciences, Center for Photochemical Sciences, Bowling Green, OH 43403. Offers PhD. *Degree requirements:* For doctorate, comprehensive exam, thesis/dissertation. *Entrance requirements:* For doctorate, GRE General Test. Additional exam requirements/recommendations for international students: Required—TOEFL. Electronic applications accepted. *Faculty research:* Laser-initiated photopolymerization, spectroscopic and kinetic studies, optoelectronics of semiconductor multiple quantum wells, electron transfer processes, carotenoid pigments.

Bowling Green State University, Graduate College, College of Arts and Sciences, Department of Chemistry, Bowling Green, OH 43403. Offers MAT, MS.

Peterson's Graduate Programs in the Physical Sciences, Mathematics, Agricultural Sciences, the Environment & Natural Resources 2013

facebook.com/petersonspublishing **59**

Chemistry

Part-time programs available. *Degree requirements:* For master's, thesis or alternative. *Entrance requirements:* For master's, GRE General Test. Additional exam requirements/recommendations for international students: Required—TOEFL. Electronic applications accepted. *Faculty research:* Organic, inorganic, physical, and analytical chemistry; biochemistry; surface science.

Bradley University, Graduate School, College of Liberal Arts and Sciences, Department of Chemistry and Biochemistry, Peoria, IL 61625-0002. Offers chemistry (MS). Part-time and evening/weekend programs available. *Degree requirements:* For master's, comprehensive exam, thesis. *Entrance requirements:* For master's, 2 letters of recommendation. Additional exam requirements/recommendations for international students: Required—TOEFL (minimum score 550 paper-based; 213 computer-based; 79 iBT).

Brandeis University, Graduate School of Arts and Sciences, Department of Chemistry, Waltham, MA 02454. Offers inorganic chemistry (MS, PhD); organic chemistry (MS, PhD); physical chemistry (MS, PhD). Terminal master's awarded for partial completion of doctoral program. *Degree requirements:* For master's, thesis, 1 year of residency; for doctorate, one foreign language, thesis/dissertation, 3 years of residency, 2 seminars, qualifying exams. *Entrance requirements:* For master's and doctorate, GRE General Test, resume, letters of recommendation. Additional exam requirements/recommendations for international students: Required—TOEFL (minimum score 600 paper-based; 250 computer-based; 100 iBT); Recommended—IELTS (minimum score 7). Electronic applications accepted. *Faculty research:* Oscillating chemical reactions, molecular recognition systems, protein crystallography, synthesis of natural product spectroscopy and magnetic resonance.

Brigham Young University, Graduate Studies, College of Physical and Mathematical Sciences, Department of Chemistry and Biochemistry, Provo, UT 84602. Offers biochemistry (MS, PhD); chemistry (MS, PhD). *Faculty:* 33 full-time (2 women). *Students:* 104 full-time (39 women); includes 3 minority (2 Asian, non-Hispanic/Latino; 1 Native Hawaiian or other Pacific Islander, non-Hispanic/Latino), 53 international. Average age 28. 93 applicants, 41% accepted, 19 enrolled. In 2011, 5 master's, 11 doctorates awarded. *Median time to degree:* Of those who began their doctoral program in fall 2003, 50% received their degree in 8 years or less. *Degree requirements:* For master's, thesis; for doctorate, comprehensive exam, thesis/dissertation, qualifying exam. *Entrance requirements:* For master's and doctorate, GRE General Test, minimum GPA of 3.0 in last 60 hours. Additional exam requirements/recommendations for international students: Required—TOEFL (minimum score 580 paper-based; 237 computer-based; 85 iBT), IELTS (minimum score 7); Recommended—TWE. *Application deadline:* For fall admission, 2/1 priority date for domestic students, 2/1 for international students. Applications are processed on a rolling basis. Application fee: $50. Electronic applications accepted. Full-time tuition for non-LDS students: $11,520 per year; $640 per credit. *Expenses: Tuition:* Full-time $5760; part-time $320 per credit. Tuition and fees vary according to student's religious affiliation. *Financial support:* In 2011–12, 104 students received support, including 10 fellowships with full tuition reimbursements available (averaging $21,250 per year), 59 research assistantships with full tuition reimbursements available (averaging $21,250 per year), 35 teaching assistantships with full tuition reimbursements available (averaging $21,250 per year); institutionally sponsored loans, scholarships/grants, health care benefits, tuition waivers (full), and unspecified assistantships also available. Financial award application deadline: 2/1. *Faculty research:* Separation science, molecular recognition, organic synthesis and biomedical application, biochemistry and molecular biology, molecular spectroscopy. *Total annual research expenditures:* $5.6 million. *Unit head:* Dr. Gregory F. Burton, Chair, 801-422-4917, Fax: 801-422-0153, E-mail: gburton@byu.edu. *Application contact:* Dr. Paul B. Farnsworth, Graduate Coordinator, 801-422-6502, Fax: 801-422-0153, E-mail: pbfarnsw@byu.edu. Web site: http://www.chem.byu.edu/.

Brock University, Faculty of Graduate Studies, Faculty of Mathematics and Science, Program in Chemistry, St. Catharines, ON L2S 3A1, Canada. Offers M Sc, PhD. Part-time programs available. *Degree requirements:* For master's, thesis; for doctorate, thesis/dissertation. *Entrance requirements:* For master's, honors B Sc in chemistry; for doctorate, M Sc. Additional exam requirements/recommendations for international students: Required—TOEFL (minimum score 550 paper-based; 213 computer-based; 80 iBT), IELTS (minimum score 6.5), TWE (minimum score 4). Electronic applications accepted. *Faculty research:* Bioorganic chemistry, trace element analysis, organic synthesis, electrochemistry, structural inorganic chemistry.

Brooklyn College of the City University of New York, Division of Graduate Studies, Department of Chemistry, Brooklyn, NY 11210-2889. Offers MA, PhD. Part-time programs available. *Degree requirements:* For master's, one foreign language, thesis or alternative, 30 credits. *Entrance requirements:* For master's, 2 letters of recommendation. Additional exam requirements/recommendations for international students: Required—TOEFL (minimum score 500 paper-based; 173 computer-based; 61 iBT). Electronic applications accepted.

Brooklyn College of the City University of New York, Division of Graduate Studies, School of Education, Program in Middle Childhood Education (Science), Brooklyn, NY 11210-2889. Offers biology (MA); chemistry (MA); earth science (MA); general science (MA); physics (MA). Part-time and evening/weekend programs available. *Entrance requirements:* For master's, LAST, interview, previous course work in education and mathematics, resume, 2 letters of recommendation, essay. Additional exam requirements/recommendations for international students: Required—TOEFL (minimum score 500 paper-based; 173

computer-based; 61 iBT). Electronic applications accepted. *Faculty research:* Geometric thinking, mastery of basic facts, problem-solving strategies, history of mathematics.

Brown University, Graduate School, Department of Chemistry, Providence, RI 02912. Offers biochemistry (PhD); chemistry (AM, Sc M, PhD). *Degree requirements:* For master's, thesis; for doctorate, one foreign language, thesis/dissertation, cumulative exam.

Bryn Mawr College, Graduate School of Arts and Sciences, Department of Chemistry, Bryn Mawr, PA 19010-2899. Offers MA, PhD. *Faculty:* 6. *Students:* 4 full-time (3 women), 7 part-time (3 women). Average age 28. 11 applicants, 45% accepted, 3 enrolled. In 2011, 2 degrees awarded. *Degree requirements:* For master's, one foreign language, thesis; for doctorate, 2 foreign languages, comprehensive exam, thesis/dissertation. *Entrance requirements:* For master's and doctorate, GRE General Test, GRE Subject Test. Additional exam requirements/recommendations for international students: Required—TOEFL (minimum score 600 paper-based; 250 computer-based). *Application deadline:* For fall admission, 1/3 for domestic and international students. Application fee: $50. *Expenses: Tuition:* Full-time $34,110; part-time $4500 per unit. *Financial support:* In 2011–12, 1 research assistantship with full tuition reimbursement (averaging $15,000 per year), 4 teaching assistantships with partial tuition reimbursements (averaging $14,000 per year) were awarded; Federal Work-Study, scholarships/grants, and tuition waivers (partial) also available. Support available to part-time students. Financial award application deadline: 1/3. *Unit head:* Dr. William Malachowski, Chair, 610-526-5104. *Application contact:* Lea R. Miller, Secretary, 610-526-5072, Fax: 610-526-5076, E-mail: lrmiller@brynmawr.edu.

Bucknell University, Graduate Studies, College of Arts and Sciences, Department of Chemistry, Lewisburg, PA 17837. Offers MA, MS. *Faculty:* 12 full-time (3 women). *Students:* 7 full-time (2 women), 1 international. 17 applicants, 47% accepted, 5 enrolled. In 2011, 5 master's awarded. *Degree requirements:* For master's, thesis. *Entrance requirements:* For master's, GRE General Test, GRE Subject Test, minimum GPA of 3.0. Additional exam requirements/recommendations for international students: Required—TOEFL (minimum score 600 paper-based). *Application deadline:* For fall admission, 2/1 priority date for domestic students, 1/1 for international students. Application fee: $25. *Financial support:* In 2011–12, 7 students received support, including 8 research assistantships with full tuition reimbursements available (averaging $10,000 per year); scholarships/grants, tuition waivers (partial), and unspecified assistantships also available. Financial award application deadline: 2/1. *Unit head:* Dr. Eric Tillman, Head, 570-577-3258. *Application contact:* Gretchen H. Fegley, Coordinator, 570-577-3655, Fax: 570-577-3760, E-mail: gfegley@bucknell.edu. Web site: http://www.bucknell.edu/chemistry.

Buffalo State College, State University of New York, The Graduate School, Faculty of Natural and Social Sciences, Department of Chemistry, Buffalo, NY 14222-1095. Offers chemistry (MA); secondary education (MS Ed), including chemistry. Part-time and evening/weekend programs available. *Degree requirements:* For master's, thesis (for some programs), project. *Entrance requirements:* For master's, minimum GPA of 2.6, New York teaching certificate (MS Ed). Additional exam requirements/recommendations for international students: Required—TOEFL (minimum score 550 paper-based; 213 computer-based).

California Institute of Technology, Division of Chemistry and Chemical Engineering, Program in Chemistry, Pasadena, CA 91125-0001. Offers MS, PhD. Part-time and evening/weekend programs available. Postbaccalaureate distance learning degree programs offered (minimal on-campus study). *Faculty:* 30 full-time (5 women). *Students:* 211 full-time (80 women). Average age 26. 367 applicants, 25% accepted, 27 enrolled. In 2011, 4 master's, 32 doctorates awarded. Terminal master's awarded for partial completion of doctoral program. *Degree requirements:* For master's, thesis; for doctorate, thesis/dissertation. *Entrance requirements:* Additional exam requirements/recommendations for international students: Required—TOEFL; Recommended—IELTS, TWE. *Application deadline:* For fall admission, 1/1 for domestic and international students. Application fee: $80. Electronic applications accepted. *Financial support:* Fellowships, research assistantships, teaching assistantships, Federal Work-Study, institutionally sponsored loans, scholarships/grants, traineeships, health care benefits, and unspecified assistantships available. Financial award application deadline: 1/1. *Unit head:* Prof. Jacqueline K. Barton, Chair, Chemistry and Chemical Engineering, 626-395-3646, Fax: 626-568-8824, E-mail: jkbarton@caltech.edu. *Application contact:* Agnes Tong, Option Secretary, 626-395-6111, E-mail: agnest@caltech.edu. Web site: http://chemistry.caltech.edu/.

California Polytechnic State University, San Luis Obispo, College of Science and Mathematics, Department of Chemistry and Biochemistry, San Luis Obispo, CA 93407. Offers polymers and coating science (MS). Part-time programs available. *Faculty:* 1 full-time (0 women). *Students:* 2 full-time (1 woman), 3 part-time (0 women); includes 2 minority (both Asian, non-Hispanic/Latino). Average age 24. 5 applicants, 40% accepted, 1 enrolled. In 2011, 3 master's awarded. *Degree requirements:* For master's, comprehensive exam (for some programs), thesis (for some programs), comprehensive oral exam. *Entrance requirements:* For master's, minimum GPA of 2.5 in last 90 quarter units of course work. Additional exam requirements/recommendations for international students: Required—TOEFL (minimum score 550 paper-based; 213 computer-based) or IELTS (minimum score 6). *Application deadline:* For fall admission, 7/1 for

60 facebook.com/petersonspublishing

Peterson's Graduate Programs in the Physical Sciences, Mathematics, Agricultural Sciences, the Environment & Natural Resources 2013

domestic students, 11/30 for international students; for winter admission, 11/1 for domestic students, 6/30 for international students; for spring admission, 2/1 for domestic students. Applications are processed on a rolling basis. Application fee: $55. Electronic applications accepted. *Expenses:* Tuition, state resident: full-time $6738. Tuition, nonresident: full-time $17,898. *Required fees:* $2449. *Financial support:* Fellowships, research assistantships, career-related internships or fieldwork, Federal Work-Study, and scholarships/grants available. Support available to part-time students. Financial award application deadline: 3/2; financial award applicants required to submit FAFSA. *Faculty research:* Polymer physical chemistry and analysis, polymer synthesis, coatings formulation. *Unit head:* Dr. Ray Fernando, Graduate Coordinator, 805-756-2395, Fax: 805-756-5500, E-mail: rhfernan@calpoly.edu. *Application contact:* Dr. James Maraviglia, Associate Vice Provost for Marketing and Enrollment Development, 805-756-2311, Fax: 805-756-5400, E-mail: admissions@calpoly.edu. Web site: http://polymerscoatings.calpoly.edu/graduate.htm.

California State Polytechnic University, Pomona, Academic Affairs, College of Science, Program in Chemistry, Pomona, CA 91768-2557. Offers MS. Part-time programs available. *Students:* 4 full-time (all women), 8 part-time (3 women); includes 4 minority (1 Asian, non-Hispanic/Latino; 2 Hispanic/Latino; 1 Two or more races, non-Hispanic/Latino), 3 international. Average age 27. 43 applicants, 19% accepted, 3 enrolled. In 2011, 10 master's awarded. *Degree requirements:* For master's, thesis. *Entrance requirements:* For master's, GRE General Test. *Application deadline:* For fall admission, 5/1 priority date for domestic students; for winter admission, 10/15 priority date for domestic students; for spring admission, 1/20 priority date for domestic students. Applications are processed on a rolling basis. Application fee: $55. Electronic applications accepted. *Expenses:* Tuition, state resident: full-time $6738. Tuition, nonresident: full-time $12,300. *Required fees:* $657. Tuition and fees vary according to course load and program. *Financial support:* In 2011–12, 2 students received support. Career-related internships or fieldwork, Federal Work-Study, and institutionally sponsored loans available. Support available to part-time students. Financial award application deadline: 3/2; financial award applicants required to submit FAFSA. *Unit head:* Dr. Tim C. Corcoran, Graduate Coordinator, 909-869-3660, Fax: 909-869-4344, E-mail: tccorcoran@csupomona.edu. *Application contact:* Deborah L. Brandon, Executive Director, Admissions and Outreach, 909-869-3427, Fax: 909-869-5315, E-mail: dlbrandon@csupomona.edu. Web site: http://www.csupomona.edu/~chemistry/grad/index.htm.

California State University, East Bay, Office of Academic Programs and Graduate Studies, College of Science, Department of Chemistry, Hayward, CA 94542-3000. Offers biochemistry (MS); chemistry (MS). *Faculty:* 3 full-time (2 women), 2 part-time/adjunct (1 woman). *Students:* 23 full-time (14 women), 31 part-time (19 women); includes 24 minority (3 Black or African American, non-Hispanic/Latino; 18 Asian, non-Hispanic/Latino; 3 Hispanic/Latino), 15 international. Average age 28. 57 applicants, 68% accepted, 22 enrolled. In 2011, 13 master's awarded. *Degree requirements:* For master's, comprehensive exam or thesis. *Entrance requirements:* For master's, minimum GPA of 2.6 in field during previous 2 years of course work. Additional exam requirements/recommendations for international students: Required—TOEFL (minimum score 550 paper-based; 213 computer-based). *Application deadline:* For fall admission, 6/30 for domestic and international students. Application fee: $55. Electronic applications accepted. *Expenses:* Tuition, state resident: full-time $6738; part-time $1302 per quarter. Tuition, nonresident: full-time $12,690; part-time $2294 per quarter. *Required fees:* $449 per quarter. Tuition and fees vary according to degree level, program and reciprocity agreements. *Financial support:* Fellowships, career-related internships or fieldwork, Federal Work-Study, institutionally sponsored loans, and scholarships/grants available. Support available to part-time students. Financial award application deadline: 3/2; financial award applicants required to submit FAFSA. *Unit head:* Dr. Ann McPartland, Chair, 510-885-3452, Fax: 510-885-4675, E-mail: ann.mcpartland@csueastbay.edu. *Application contact:* Prof. Chul Kim, Chemistry Graduate Advisor, 510-885-3490, Fax: 510-885-4675, E-mail: chul.kim@csueastbay.edu. Web site: http://www20.csueastbay.edu/csci/departments/chemistry.

California State University, Fresno, Division of Graduate Studies, College of Science and Mathematics, Department of Chemistry, Fresno, CA 93740-8027. Offers MS. Part-time programs available. *Degree requirements:* For master's, thesis or alternative. *Entrance requirements:* For master's, GRE General Test, minimum GPA of 2.5. Additional exam requirements/recommendations for international students: Required—TOEFL. Electronic applications accepted. *Faculty research:* Genetics, viticulture, DNA, soils, molecular modeling, analysis of quinone.

California State University, Fullerton, Graduate Studies, College of Natural Science and Mathematics, Department of Chemistry and Biochemistry, Fullerton, CA 92834-9480. Offers chemistry (MS); geochemistry (MS). Part-time programs available. *Students:* 3 full-time (1 woman), 19 part-time (8 women); includes 6 minority (4 Asian, non-Hispanic/Latino; 2 Hispanic/Latino), 1 international. Average age 29. 38 applicants, 45% accepted, 4 enrolled. In 2011, 5 master's awarded. *Degree requirements:* For master's, thesis, departmental qualifying exam. *Entrance requirements:* For master's, minimum GPA of 2.5 in last 60 units of course work, major in chemistry or related field. Application fee: $55. *Financial support:* Research assistantships, teaching assistantships, career-related internships or fieldwork, Federal Work-Study, institutionally sponsored loans, and scholarships/grants available. Support available to part-time students. Financial award application deadline: 3/1; financial award applicants required to submit

FAFSA. *Unit head:* Dr. Christopher Meyer, Chair, 657-278-3621. *Application contact:* Admissions/Applications, 657-278-2371.

California State University, Long Beach, Graduate Studies, College of Natural Sciences and Mathematics, Department of Chemistry and Biochemistry, Long Beach, CA 90840. Offers biochemistry (MS); chemistry (MS). Part-time programs available. *Faculty:* 15 full-time (3 women). *Students:* 12 full-time (5 women), 24 part-time (10 women); includes 13 minority (7 Asian, non-Hispanic/Latino; 6 Hispanic/Latino), 6 international. Average age 26. 75 applicants, 16% accepted, 10 enrolled. In 2011, 5 master's awarded. *Degree requirements:* For master's, thesis, departmental qualifying exam. *Application deadline:* For fall admission, 6/1 for domestic students. Applications are processed on a rolling basis. Application fee: $55. Electronic applications accepted. *Financial support:* Research assistantships, teaching assistantships, Federal Work-Study, institutionally sponsored loans, scholarships/grants, and unspecified assistantships available. Financial award application deadline: 3/2. *Faculty research:* Enzymology, organic synthesis, molecular modeling, environmental chemistry, reaction kinetics. *Unit head:* Dr. Jeffrey Cohlberg, Chair, 562-985-4944, Fax: 562-985-8557, E-mail: cohlberg@csulb.edu. *Application contact:* Dr. Lijuan Li, Graduate Advisor, 562-985-5068, Fax: 562-985-8557, E-mail: lli@csulb.edu.

California State University, Los Angeles, Graduate Studies, College of Natural and Social Sciences, Department of Chemistry and Biochemistry, Los Angeles, CA 90032-8530. Offers analytical chemistry (MS); biochemistry (MS); chemistry (MS); inorganic chemistry (MS); organic chemistry (MS); physical chemistry (MS). Part-time and evening/weekend programs available. *Faculty:* 4 part-time/adjunct (1 woman). *Students:* 22 full-time (14 women), 24 part-time (11 women); includes 30 minority (4 Black or African American, non-Hispanic/Latino; 7 Asian, non-Hispanic/Latino; 19 Hispanic/Latino), 7 international. Average age 29. 60 applicants, 48% accepted, 17 enrolled. In 2011, 15 master's awarded. *Degree requirements:* For master's, one foreign language, comprehensive exam or thesis. *Entrance requirements:* Additional exam requirements/recommendations for international students: Required—TOEFL. *Application deadline:* For fall admission, 5/1 for domestic and international students. Applications are processed on a rolling basis. Application fee: $55. *Expenses:* Tuition, state resident: full-time $8225. *Financial support:* Federal Work-Study available. Support available to part-time students. Financial award application deadline: 3/1. *Faculty research:* Intercalation of heavy metal, carborane chemistry, conductive polymers and fabrics, titanium reagents, computer modeling and synthesis. *Unit head:* Dr. Robert L. Vellanoweth, Chair, 323-343-2300, Fax: 323-343-6490, E-mail: rvellan@calstatela.edu. *Application contact:* Dr. Karin Brown, Acting Associate Dean of Graduate Studies, 323-343-3820 Ext. 3827, Fax: 323-343-5653, E-mail: kbrown5@calstatela.edu. Web site: http://www.calstatela.edu/dept/chem/index.htm.

California State University, Northridge, Graduate Studies, College of Science and Mathematics, Department of Chemistry and Biochemistry, Northridge, CA 91330. Offers biochemistry (MS); chemistry (MS), including chemistry, environmental chemistry. *Degree requirements:* For master's, thesis. *Entrance requirements:* For master's, GRE General Test or minimum GPA of 3.0. Additional exam requirements/recommendations for international students: Required—TOEFL. Electronic applications accepted.

California State University, Sacramento, Office of Graduate Studies, College of Natural Sciences and Mathematics, Department of Chemistry, Sacramento, CA 95819-6057. Offers MS. Part-time programs available. *Faculty:* 15 full-time (7 women), 9 part-time/adjunct (2 women). *Students:* 2 full-time, 31 part-time; includes 17 minority (1 Black or African American, non-Hispanic/Latino; 1 American Indian or Alaska Native, non-Hispanic/Latino; 7 Asian, non-Hispanic/Latino; 2 Hispanic/Latino; 3 Native Hawaiian or other Pacific Islander, non-Hispanic/Latino; 3 Two or more races, non-Hispanic/Latino). Average age 31. 30 applicants, 40% accepted, 9 enrolled. In 2011, 4 master's awarded. *Degree requirements:* For master's, thesis or project; qualifying exam; writing proficiency exam. *Entrance requirements:* For master's, minimum GPA of 2.5 during previous 2 years of course work, BA in chemistry or equivalent. Additional exam requirements/recommendations for international students: Required—TOEFL. *Application deadline:* For fall admission, 3/1 for domestic and international students; for spring admission, 9/30 for international students. Applications are processed on a rolling basis. Application fee: $55. Electronic applications accepted. *Financial support:* Career-related internships or fieldwork and Federal Work-Study available. Support available to part-time students. Financial award application deadline: 3/1; financial award applicants required to submit FAFSA. *Unit head:* Linda Roberts, Chair, 916-278-6684, Fax: 916-278-4986, E-mail: robertssim@csus.edu. *Application contact:* Jose Martinez, Outreach and Graduate Diversity Coordinator, 916-278-6470, Fax: 916-278-5669, E-mail: martinj@skymail.csus.edu. Web site: http://www.csus.edu/chem.

California State University, San Bernardino, Graduate Studies, College of Social and Behavioral Sciences, Program in Environmental Sciences, San Bernardino, CA 92407-2397. Offers MS. *Students:* 15 full-time (7 women), 7 part-time (4 women); includes 8 minority (3 Asian, non-Hispanic/Latino; 4 Hispanic/Latino; 1 Two or more races, non-Hispanic/Latino), 1 international. Average age 27. 10 applicants, 80% accepted, 6 enrolled. In 2011, 5 master's awarded. *Expenses:* Tuition, state resident: full-time $7356. Tuition, nonresident: full-time $7356. *Required fees:* $1077. Tuition and fees vary according to program. *Unit head:* Dr. Brett Stanley, Chair, 909-537-3313, E-mail: bstanley@csusb.edu. *Application contact:* Sandra Kamusikiri, Associate Vice-President/Dean of Graduate Studies, 909-537-5058, E-mail: skamusik@csusb.edu.

Peterson's Graduate Programs in the Physical Sciences, Mathematics, Agricultural Sciences, the Environment & Natural Resources 2013

facebook.com/petersonspublishing **61**

Chemistry

Carleton University, Faculty of Graduate Studies, Faculty of Science, Department of Chemistry, Ottawa, ON K1S 5B6, Canada. Offers M Sc, PhD. Programs offered jointly with University of Ottawa. *Degree requirements:* For master's, thesis; for doctorate, comprehensive exam, thesis/dissertation. *Entrance requirements:* For master's, honors degree; for doctorate, M Sc. Additional exam requirements/recommendations for international students: Required—TOEFL. *Faculty research:* Bioorganic chemistry, analytical toxicology, theoretical and physical chemistry, inorganic chemistry.

Carnegie Mellon University, Mellon College of Science, Department of Chemistry, Pittsburgh, PA 15213-3891. Offers biotechnology and management (MS); chemistry (PhD), including bioinorganic, bioorganic, organic and materials, biophysics and spectroscopy, computational and theoretical, polymer; colloids, polymers and surfaces (MS). Part-time programs available. Terminal master's awarded for partial completion of doctoral program. *Degree requirements:* For doctorate, thesis/dissertation, departmental qualifying and oral exams, teaching experience. *Entrance requirements:* For master's, GRE General Test; for doctorate, GRE General Test, GRE Subject Test. Additional exam requirements/recommendations for international students: Required—TOEFL. Electronic applications accepted. *Faculty research:* Physical and theoretical chemistry, chemical synthesis, biophysical/bioinorganic chemistry.

Case Western Reserve University, School of Graduate Studies, Department of Chemistry, Cleveland, OH 44106. Offers MS, PhD. Part-time programs available. *Faculty:* 21 full-time (5 women). *Students:* 89 full-time (37 women); includes 4 minority (all Asian, non-Hispanic/Latino), 56 international. Average age 27. 276 applicants, 15% accepted, 23 enrolled. In 2011, 4 master's, 14 doctorates awarded. Terminal master's awarded for partial completion of doctoral program. *Degree requirements:* For master's, thesis optional; for doctorate, thesis/dissertation. *Entrance requirements:* For master's and doctorate, GRE General Test, GRE Subject Test. Additional exam requirements/recommendations for international students: Required—TOEFL (minimum score 577 paper-based; 213 computer-based; 90 iBT); Recommended—IELTS (minimum score 7). *Application deadline:* For fall admission, 12/1 priority date for domestic students. Applications are processed on a rolling basis. Application fee: $8. Electronic applications accepted. *Financial support:* Fellowships, research assistantships, teaching assistantships, and unspecified assistantships available. Financial award application deadline: 2/15. *Faculty research:* Electrochemistry, synthetic chemistry, chemistry of life process, spectroscopy, kinetics. *Unit head:* Mary Barkley, Chair, 216-368-3622, Fax: 216-368-3006, E-mail: mary.barkley@case.edu. *Application contact:* Julie Ilhan, Graduate Affairs Coordinator, 216-368-5030, Fax: 216-368-3006, E-mail: julie.ilhan@case.edu. Web site: http://www.case.edu/artsci/chem/.

Central Connecticut State University, School of Graduate Studies, School of Arts and Sciences, Department of Chemistry and Biochemistry, New Britain, CT 06050-4010. Offers natural sciences (MS). Part-time and evening/weekend programs available. *Students:* 1 (woman) part-time. 1 applicant, 100% accepted, 1 enrolled. *Degree requirements:* For master's, comprehensive exam, thesis or alternative; for Certificate, qualifying exam. *Entrance requirements:* For master's, minimum undergraduate GPA of 2.7. Additional exam requirements/recommendations for international students: Required—TOEFL (minimum score 550 paper-based; 213 computer-based). *Application deadline:* For fall admission, 6/1 for domestic students, 5/1 for international students; for spring admission, 11/1 for domestic and international students. Applications are processed on a rolling basis. Application fee: $50. Electronic applications accepted. *Expenses: Tuition,* area resident: Full-time $5137; part-time $482 per credit. Tuition, state resident: full-time $7707; part-time $494 per credit. Tuition, nonresident: full-time $14,311; part-time $494 per credit. *Required fees:* $3865. One-time fee: $62 part-time. *Unit head:* Dr. Thomas Burkholder, Chair, 860-832-2675, E-mail: burkholder@ccsu.edu. *Application contact:* Patricia Gardner, Associate Director of Graduate Studies, 860-832-2350, Fax: 860-832-2352, E-mail: graduateadmissions@ccsu.edu. Web site: http://www.chemistry.ccsu.edu/.

Central Michigan University, College of Graduate Studies, College of Science and Technology, Department of Chemistry, Mount Pleasant, MI 48859. Offers chemistry (MS); teaching chemistry (MA), including teaching college chemistry, teaching high school chemistry. Part-time programs available. *Degree requirements:* For master's, comprehensive exam, thesis or alternative. *Entrance requirements:* For master's, GRE. Electronic applications accepted. *Faculty research:* Analytical and organic-inorganic chemistry, biochemistry, catalysis, dendrimer and polymer studies, nanotechnology.

Central Washington University, Graduate Studies and Research, College of the Sciences, Department of Chemistry, Ellensburg, WA 98926. Offers MS. Part-time programs available. *Faculty:* 12 full-time (4 women). *Students:* 3 full-time (0 women), 1 (woman) part-time. 5 applicants, 80% accepted, 4 enrolled. *Degree requirements:* For master's, thesis. *Entrance requirements:* For master's, GRE General Test, minimum GPA of 3.0. Additional exam requirements/recommendations for international students: Required—TOEFL (minimum score 550 paper-based; 213 computer-based; 79 iBT), IELTS (minimum score 6.5). *Application deadline:* For fall admission, 2/1 for domestic students; for winter admission, 10/1 for domestic students; for spring admission, 1/1 for domestic students. Applications are processed on a rolling basis. Application fee: $50. Electronic applications accepted. *Expenses:* Tuition, state resident: full-time $8112; part-time $270 per credit. Tuition, nonresident: full-time $18,069; part-time $602 per credit. *Required fees:* $924. *Financial support:* In 2011–12, 7 teaching assistantships with full and partial tuition reimbursements (averaging $9,234 per year) were awarded; career-related internships or fieldwork, Federal Work-Study, and health care benefits also available. Financial award application deadline: 3/1; financial award applicants required to submit FAFSA. *Unit head:* Dr. Levente Fabry-Asztalos, Program Director, 509-963-2887, Fax: 509-963-1050, E-mail: fabryl@cwu.edu. *Application contact:* Justine Eason, Admissions Program Coordinator, 509-963-3103, Fax: 509-963-1799, E-mail: masters@cwu.edu.

Christopher Newport University, Graduate Studies, Department of Teacher Preparation, Newport News, VA 23606-2998. Offers art (PK-12) (MAT); biology (6-12) (MAT); chemistry (6-12) (MAT); computer science (6-12) (MAT); elementary (PK-6) (MAT); English (6-12) (MAT); English as second language (PK-12) (MAT); French (PK-12) (MAT); history and social science (6-12) (MAT); mathematics (6-12) (MAT); music (PK-12) (MAT), including choral, instrumental; physics (6-12) (MAT); Spanish (PK-12) (MAT). Part-time and evening/weekend programs available. *Degree requirements:* For master's, comprehensive exam, thesis or alternative. *Entrance requirements:* For master's, PRAXIS I, minimum GPA of 3.0. Additional exam requirements/recommendations for international students: Required—TOEFL (minimum score 580 paper-based; 237 computer-based; 92 iBT). Electronic applications accepted. *Faculty research:* Early literacy development, instructional innovations, professional teaching standards, multicultural issues, aesthetic education.

City College of the City University of New York, Graduate School, College of Liberal Arts and Science, Division of Science, Department of Chemistry, Program in Chemistry, New York, NY 10031-9198. Offers MA, PhD. PhD program offered jointly with Graduate School and University Center of the City University of New York. Terminal master's awarded for partial completion of doctoral program. *Degree requirements:* For doctorate, one foreign language, thesis/dissertation. *Entrance requirements:* For master's and doctorate, GRE. Additional exam requirements/recommendations for international students: Required—TOEFL (minimum score 500 paper-based; 173 computer-based). *Faculty research:* Laser spectroscopy, bioorganic chemistry, polymer chemistry and crystallography, electroanalytical chemistry, ESR of metal clusters.

Clark Atlanta University, School of Arts and Sciences, Department of Chemistry, Atlanta, GA 30314. Offers MS, PhD. Part-time programs available. *Faculty:* 6 full-time (0 women). *Students:* 9 full-time (6 women), 17 part-time (9 women); includes 20 minority (19 Black or African American, non-Hispanic/Latino; 1 American Indian or Alaska Native, non-Hispanic/Latino), 3 international. Average age 30. 4 applicants, 100% accepted, 0 enrolled. In 2011, 1 degree awarded. *Degree requirements:* For master's, one foreign language, thesis; for doctorate, 2 foreign languages, thesis/dissertation. *Entrance requirements:* For master's, GRE General Test, minimum GPA of 2.5; for doctorate, GRE General Test, GRE Subject Test, minimum graduate GPA of 3.0. Additional exam requirements/recommendations for international students: Required—TOEFL (minimum score 500 paper-based; 173 computer-based; 61 iBT). *Application deadline:* For fall admission, 4/1 for domestic and international students; for spring admission, 11/1 for domestic and international students. Applications are processed on a rolling basis. Application fee: $40 ($55 for international students). *Expenses: Tuition:* Full-time $13,572; part-time $754 per credit hour. *Required fees:* $806; $403 per semester. *Financial support:* In 2011–12, 6 teaching assistantships were awarded; fellowships, research assistantships, career-related internships or fieldwork, Federal Work-Study, scholarships/grants, traineeships, and unspecified assistantships also available. Support available to part-time students. Financial award application deadline: 4/30; financial award applicants required to submit FAFSA. *Unit head:* Dr. Cass Parker, Chairperson, 404-880-6858, E-mail: cparker@cau.edu. *Application contact:* Michelle Clark-Davis, Graduate Program Admissions, 404-880-6605, E-mail: cauadmissions@cau.edu.

Clarkson University, Graduate School, School of Arts and Sciences, Department of Chemistry and Biomolecular Science, Potsdam, NY 13699. Offers chemistry (MS, PhD). Part-time programs available. *Faculty:* 23 full-time (4 women), 2 part-time/adjunct (both women). *Students:* 41 full-time (14 women), 24 international. Average age 26. 38 applicants, 79% accepted, 10 enrolled. In 2011, 1 master's, 6 doctorates awarded. *Degree requirements:* For doctorate, comprehensive exam, thesis/dissertation, departmental qualifying exam. *Entrance requirements:* For master's and doctorate, GRE, transcripts of all college coursework, three letters of recommendation; resume and personal statement (recommended). Additional exam requirements/recommendations for international students: Required—TOEFL, TSE recommended. *Application deadline:* For fall admission, 1/30 priority date for domestic students, 1/30 for international students; for spring admission, 9/1 priority date for domestic students, 9/1 for international students. Applications are processed on a rolling basis. Application fee: $25 ($35 for international students). Electronic applications accepted. *Expenses: Tuition:* Full-time $14,376; part-time $1198 per credit hour. *Required fees:* $295 per semester. *Financial support:* In 2011–12, 37 students received support, including 2 fellowships with full tuition reimbursements available (averaging $21,999 per year), 16 research assistantships with full tuition reimbursements available (averaging $21,999 per year), 21 teaching assistantships with full tuition reimbursements available (averaging $21,999 per year); scholarships/grants, tuition waivers (partial), and unspecified assistantships also available. *Faculty research:* Enzyme logic systems, inorganic nanoparticle, biomagnetic glasses, engineered abrasives, chemical catalysis. *Total annual research expenditures:* $2.1 million. *Unit head:* Dr. Phillip Christiansen, Chair, 315-268-2389, Fax: 315-268-6610, E-mail: pac@clarkson.edu. *Application contact:* Jennifer Reed, Graduate School Coordinator, School of Arts and

62 facebook.com/petersonspublishing

Peterson's Graduate Programs in the Physical Sciences, Mathematics, Agricultural Sciences, the Environment & Natural Resources 2013

Sciences, 315-268-3802, Fax: 315-268-3989, E-mail: sciencegrad@clarkson.edu. Web site: http://www.clarkson.edu/biosci_chemistry/.

Clark University, Graduate School, Department of Chemistry, Worcester, MA 01610-1477. Offers MA, PhD. *Faculty:* 10 full-time (2 women). *Students:* 15 full-time (4 women); includes 1 minority (Asian, non-Hispanic/Latino), 10 international. Average age 27. 24 applicants, 38% accepted, 2 enrolled. In 2011, 3 master's, 1 doctorate awarded. Terminal master's awarded for partial completion of doctoral program. *Degree requirements:* For master's, thesis or alternative; for doctorate, one foreign language, thesis/dissertation. *Entrance requirements:* For master's and doctorate, GRE General Test. Additional exam requirements/recommendations for international students: Required—TOEFL. *Application deadline:* For fall admission, 2/15 priority date for domestic students. Applications are processed on a rolling basis. Application fee: $50. *Expenses: Tuition:* Full-time $37,000; part-time $1156 per credit hour. *Financial support:* In 2011–12, fellowships with tuition reimbursements (averaging $19,825 per year), 6 research assistantships with full tuition reimbursements (averaging $19,825 per year), 8 teaching assistantships with full tuition reimbursements (averaging $19,825 per year) were awarded; tuition waivers (full) also available. *Faculty research:* Nuclear chemistry, molecular biology simulation, NMR studies, biochemistry, protein folding mechanisms. *Total annual research expenditures:* $550,000. *Unit head:* Dr. Frederick Greenaway, Chair, 508-793-7116. *Application contact:* Rene Baril, Department Secretary, 528-793-7173, Fax: 528-793-8861, E-mail: chemistry@clarku.edu. Web site: http://www.clarku.edu/departments/chemistry/graduate/index.cfm.

Clemson University, Graduate School, College of Engineering and Science, Department of Chemistry, Clemson, SC 29634. Offers MS, PhD. *Faculty:* 33 full-time (4 women), 6 part-time/adjunct (2 women). *Students:* 91 full-time (35 women), 6 part-time (4 women); includes 10 minority (4 Black or African American, non-Hispanic/Latino; 4 Asian, non-Hispanic/Latino; 1 Hispanic/Latino; 1 Two or more races, non-Hispanic/Latino), 46 international. Average age 29. 163 applicants, 31% accepted, 19 enrolled. In 2011, 5 master's, 14 doctorates awarded. *Degree requirements:* For master's, one foreign language, thesis; for doctorate, one foreign language, thesis/dissertation. *Entrance requirements:* For master's and doctorate, GRE General Test. Additional exam requirements/recommendations for international students: Required—TOEFL. *Application deadline:* For fall admission, 3/1 for domestic students, 4/15 for international students; for spring admission, 9/15 for international students. Applications are processed on a rolling basis. Application fee: $70 ($80 for international students). Electronic applications accepted. *Financial support:* In 2011–12, 92 students received support, including 2 fellowships with full and partial tuition reimbursements available (averaging $6,500 per year), 29 research assistantships with partial tuition reimbursements available (averaging $15,727 per year), 77 teaching assistantships with partial tuition reimbursements available (averaging $18,872 per year); career-related internships or fieldwork, institutionally sponsored loans, scholarships/grants, health care benefits, and unspecified assistantships also available. Support available to part-time students. Financial award applicants required to submit FAFSA. *Faculty research:* Fluorine chemistry, organic synthetic methods and natural products, metal and non-metal clusters, analytical spectroscopies, polymers. *Total annual research expenditures:* $2.7 million. *Unit head:* Dr. Stephen E. Creager, Chair, 864-656-3065, Fax: 864-656-6613, E-mail: screage@clemson.edu. *Application contact:* Dr. Steve Stuart, Coordinator, 864-656-5013, Fax: 864-656-6613, E-mail: ss@clemson.edu. Web site: http://chemistry.clemson.edu/.

Cleveland State University, College of Graduate Studies, College of Sciences and Health Professions, Department of Chemistry, Cleveland, OH 44115. Offers analytical chemistry (MS); clinical chemistry (MS); clinical/bioanalytical chemistry (PhD), including cellular and molecular medicine, clinical chemistry, clinical/bioanalytical chemistry; environmental chemistry (MS); inorganic chemistry (MS); pharmaceutical/organic chemistry (MS); physical chemistry (MS). Part-time and evening/weekend programs available. *Faculty:* 12 full-time (0 women). *Students:* 17 full-time (8 women), 87 part-time (36 women); includes 6 minority (5 Black or African American, non-Hispanic/Latino; 1 Asian, non-Hispanic/Latino), 74 international. Average age 27. 143 applicants, 59% accepted, 22 enrolled. In 2011, 14 master's, 10 doctorates awarded. *Median time to degree:* Of those who began their doctoral program in fall 2003, 67% received their degree in 8 years or less. *Degree requirements:* For master's, thesis optional; for doctorate, comprehensive exam, thesis/dissertation. *Entrance requirements:* For master's and doctorate, GRE General Test. Additional exam requirements/recommendations for international students: Required—TOEFL (minimum score 525 paper-based; 197 computer-based; 65 iBT). *Application deadline:* For fall admission, 1/15 priority date for domestic students, 1/15 for international students. Applications are processed on a rolling basis. Application fee: $30. Electronic applications accepted. *Expenses:* Tuition, state resident: full-time $6416; part-time $494 per credit hour. Tuition, nonresident: full-time $12,074; part-time $929 per credit hour. *Financial support:* In 2011–12, 44 students received support, including 5 fellowships with full tuition reimbursements available (averaging $30,000 per year), 13 research assistantships with full tuition reimbursements available (averaging $20,000 per year), 24 teaching assistantships with full tuition reimbursements available (averaging $18,500 per year); scholarships/grants and unspecified assistantships also available. Financial award application deadline: 1/15. *Faculty research:* Bioanalytical techniques and molecular diagnostics, glycoproteomics and antithrombotic agents, drug discovery and innovation, analytical pharmacology, inflammatory disease research. *Total annual research expenditures:* $3 million. *Unit head:* Dr. David J. Anderson, Interim Chair, 216-

687-2467, Fax: 216-687-9298, E-mail: d.anderson@csuohio.edu. *Application contact:* Richelle P. Emery, Administrative Coordinator, 216-687-2457, Fax: 216-687-9298, E-mail: r.emery@csuohio.edu. Web site: http://www.csuohio.edu/chemistry/.

The College of William and Mary, Faculty of Arts and Sciences, Department of Chemistry, Williamsburg, VA 23187-8795. Offers MA, MS. *Faculty:* 16 full-time (4 women), 3 part-time/adjunct (0 women). *Students:* 8 full-time (4 women), 2 part-time (0 women); includes 1 minority (Black or African American, non-Hispanic/Latino), 1 international. Average age 24. 18 applicants, 39% accepted, 6 enrolled. In 2011, 7 master's awarded. *Degree requirements:* For master's, comprehensive exam, thesis (for some programs). *Entrance requirements:* For master's, GRE, minimum GPA of 2.5. Additional exam requirements/recommendations for international students: Required—TOEFL. *Application deadline:* For fall admission, 3/1 priority date for domestic students, 3/1 for international students. Applications are processed on a rolling basis. Application fee: $45. Electronic applications accepted. *Expenses:* Tuition, state resident: full-time $6400; part-time $365 per credit hour. Tuition, nonresident: full-time $19,720; part-time $985 per credit hour. *Required fees:* $4562. *Financial support:* In 2011–12, 10 students received support, including 2 research assistantships with full tuition reimbursements available (averaging $15,300 per year), 6 teaching assistantships with full tuition reimbursements available (averaging $15,300 per year); health care benefits and unspecified assistantships also available. Financial award application deadline: 5/1; financial award applicants required to submit FAFSA. *Faculty research:* Organic, physical, polymer and analytic chemistry; biochemistry. *Total annual research expenditures:* $711,372. *Unit head:* Dr. Chris Abelt, Chair, 757-221-2540, Fax: 757-221-2715, E-mail: cjabel@wm.edu. *Application contact:* Dr. Deborah C. Bebout, Graduate Director, 757-221-2558, Fax: 757-221-2715, E-mail: dcbebo@wm.edu. Web site: http://www.wm.edu/as/chemistry.

Colorado School of Mines, Graduate School, Department of Chemistry and Geochemistry, Program in Chemistry, Golden, CO 80401-1887. Offers applied chemistry (PhD); chemistry (MS). Part-time programs available. *Students:* 43 full-time (15 women), 2 part-time (1 woman); includes 5 minority (3 Asian, non-Hispanic/Latino; 2 Hispanic/Latino), 13 international. Average age 28. 57 applicants, 26% accepted, 5 enrolled. In 2011, 3 master's, 2 doctorates awarded. *Degree requirements:* For master's, thesis (for some programs); for doctorate, comprehensive exam, thesis/dissertation. *Entrance requirements:* For master's and doctorate, GRE General Test. Additional exam requirements/recommendations for international students: Required—TOEFL (minimum score 550 paper-based; 213 computer-based; 80 iBT). *Application deadline:* For fall admission, 1/15 priority date for domestic students, 1/15 for international students; for spring admission, 10/15 priority date for domestic students, 10/15 for international students. Application fee: $50 ($70 for international students). Electronic applications accepted. *Expenses:* Tuition, state resident: full-time $12,585; part-time $699 per credit. Tuition, nonresident: full-time $27,270; part-time $1516 per credit. *Required fees:* $1864.20; $670 per semester. *Financial support:* In 2011–12, fellowships with full tuition reimbursements (averaging $20,000 per year), research assistantships with full tuition reimbursements (averaging $20,000 per year), teaching assistantships with full tuition reimbursements (averaging $20,000 per year) were awarded; scholarships/grants, health care benefits, and unspecified assistantships also available. Financial award application deadline: 1/15; financial award applicants required to submit FAFSA. *Unit head:* Dr. Dan Knauss, Department Head, 303-273-3625 Ext. 303, Fax: 303-273-3629. *Application contact:* Prof. Tina Voelker, Associate Professor, 303-273-3152, Fax: 303-273-3629, E-mail: tvoelker@mines.edu. Web site: http://chemistry.mines.edu.

Colorado State University, Graduate School, College of Natural Sciences, Department of Chemistry, Fort Collins, CO 80523-1872. Offers MS, PhD. Postbaccalaureate distance learning degree programs offered (no on-campus study). *Faculty:* 28 full-time (9 women). *Students:* 58 full-time (24 women), 89 part-time (34 women); includes 18 minority (1 Black or African American, non-Hispanic/Latino; 6 Asian, non-Hispanic/Latino; 6 Hispanic/Latino; 5 Two or more races, non-Hispanic/Latino), 11 international. Average age 27. 53 applicants, 60% accepted, 31 enrolled. In 2011, 6 master's, 17 doctorates awarded. Terminal master's awarded for partial completion of doctoral program. *Degree requirements:* For master's, comprehensive exam (for some programs), thesis (for some programs); for doctorate, thesis/dissertation, oral comprehensive exam. *Entrance requirements:* For master's, GRE General Test, minimum GPA of 3.0; 3 letters of recommendation; for doctorate, GRE General Test, minimum GPA of 3.0; 2 transcripts; 3 letters of recommendation; statement of purpose. Additional exam requirements/recommendations for international students: Required—TOEFL (minimum score 550 paper-based; 213 computer-based; 80 iBT). *Application deadline:* For fall admission, 2/1 priority date for domestic students, 2/1 for international students; for spring admission, 9/15 priority date for domestic students, 9/15 for international students. Applications are processed on a rolling basis. Application fee: $50. Electronic applications accepted. *Expenses:* Tuition, state resident: full-time $7992. Tuition, nonresident: full-time $19,592. *Required fees:* $1735; $58 per credit. *Financial support:* In 2011–12, 40 fellowships (averaging $24,277 per year), 88 research assistantships with full tuition reimbursements (averaging $14,807 per year), 71 teaching assistantships with full tuition reimbursements (averaging $14,013 per year) were awarded; health care benefits also available. Financial award application deadline: 1/15; financial award applicants required to submit FAFSA. *Faculty research:* Analytical chemistry, inorganic chemistry, organic chemistry, physical chemistry, materials and

Peterson's Graduate Programs in the Physical Sciences, Mathematics, Agricultural Sciences, the Environment & Natural Resources 2013

facebook.com/petersonspublishing **63**

Chemistry

biological chemistry. *Total annual research expenditures:* $7.2 million. *Unit head:* Dr. Ellen R. Fisher, Department Head, 970-491-6292, Fax: 970-491-1801, E-mail: ellen.fisher@colostate.edu. *Application contact:* Kathy Gibson, Graduate Contact, 970-491-0502, Fax: 970-491-1801, E-mail: kathy.gibson@colostate.edu. Web site: http://www.chem.colostate.edu/.

Colorado State University–Pueblo, College of Science and Mathematics, Pueblo, CO 81001-4901. Offers applied natural science (MS), including biochemistry, biology, chemistry. Part-time and evening/weekend programs available. *Degree requirements:* For master's, comprehensive exam (for some programs), thesis (for some programs), internship report (if non-thesis). *Entrance requirements:* For master's, GRE General Test (minimum score 1000), 2 letters of reference, minimum GPA of 3.0. Additional exam requirements/recommendations for international students: Required—TOEFL (minimum score 500 paper-based; 173 computer-based), IELTS (minimum score 5). *Faculty research:* Fungal cell walls, molecular biology, bioactive materials synthesis, atomic force microscopy-surface chemistry, nanoscience.

Columbia University, Graduate School of Arts and Sciences, Division of Natural Sciences, Department of Chemistry, New York, NY 10027. Offers chemical physics (M Phil, PhD); inorganic chemistry (M Phil, MA, PhD); organic chemistry (M Phil, MA, PhD); MD/PhD. *Degree requirements:* For master's, one foreign language, teaching experience, oral/written exams (M Phil); for doctorate, one foreign language, thesis/dissertation. *Entrance requirements:* For master's and doctorate, GRE General Test, GRE Subject Test. Additional exam requirements/recommendations for international students: Required—TOEFL. *Faculty research:* Biophysics.

Concordia University, School of Graduate Studies, Faculty of Arts and Science, Department of Chemistry and Biochemistry, Montréal, QC H3G 1M8, Canada. Offers chemistry (M Sc, PhD). *Degree requirements:* For master's, thesis; for doctorate, thesis/dissertation. *Entrance requirements:* For master's, honors degree in chemistry; for doctorate, M Sc in biochemistry, biology, or chemistry. *Faculty research:* Bioanalytical, bio-organic, and inorganic chemistry; materials and solid-state chemistry.

Cornell University, Graduate School, Graduate Fields of Arts and Sciences, Field of Chemistry and Chemical Biology, Ithaca, NY 14853-0001. Offers analytical chemistry (PhD); bio-organic chemistry (PhD); biophysical chemistry (PhD); chemical biology (PhD); chemical physics (PhD); inorganic chemistry (PhD); materials chemistry (PhD); organic chemistry (PhD); organometallic chemistry (PhD); physical chemistry (PhD); polymer chemistry (PhD); theoretical chemistry (PhD). *Faculty:* 46 full-time (3 women). *Students:* 151 full-time (67 women); includes 16 minority (13 Asian, non-Hispanic/Latino; 2 Hispanic/Latino; 1 Two or more races, non-Hispanic/Latino), 48 international. Average age 25. 297 applicants, 35% accepted, 29 enrolled. In 2011, 22 doctorates awarded. *Degree requirements:* For doctorate, comprehensive exam, thesis/dissertation. *Entrance requirements:* For doctorate, GRE General Test, GRE Subject Test (chemistry), 3 letters of recommendation. Additional exam requirements/recommendations for international students: Required—TOEFL (minimum score 600 paper-based; 250 computer-based; 77 iBT). *Application deadline:* For fall admission, 1/10 for domestic students. Application fee: $95. Electronic applications accepted. *Financial support:* In 2011–12, 21 fellowships with full tuition reimbursements, 63 research assistantships with full tuition reimbursements, 59 teaching assistantships with full tuition reimbursements were awarded; institutionally sponsored loans, scholarships/grants, health care benefits, tuition waivers (full and partial), and unspecified assistantships also available. Financial award applicants required to submit FAFSA. *Faculty research:* Analytical, organic, inorganic, physical, materials, chemical biology. *Unit head:* Director of Graduate Studies, 607-255-4139, Fax: 607-255-4137. *Application contact:* Graduate Field Assistant, 607-255-4139, Fax: 607-255-4137, E-mail: chemgrad@cornell.edu. Web site: http://www.gradschool.cornell.edu/fields.php?id-26&a-2.

Dalhousie University, Faculty of Science, Department of Chemistry, Halifax, NS B3H 4R2, Canada. Offers M Sc, PhD. Part-time programs available. Terminal master's awarded for partial completion of doctoral program. *Degree requirements:* For master's, thesis; for doctorate, thesis/dissertation. *Entrance requirements:* Additional exam requirements/recommendations for international students: Required—TOEFL (minimum score 600 paper-based; 237 computer-based; 92 iBT), IELTS (minimum score 7). Electronic applications accepted. *Faculty research:* Analytical, inorganic, organic, physical, and theoretical chemistry.

Dartmouth College, Arts and Sciences Graduate Programs, Department of Chemistry, Hanover, NH 03755. Offers PhD. *Degree requirements:* For doctorate, thesis/dissertation, departmental qualifying exams. *Entrance requirements:* For doctorate, GRE General Test, GRE Subject Test. Additional exam requirements/recommendations for international students: Required—TOEFL. Electronic applications accepted. *Faculty research:* Organic and polymer synthesis, bioinorganic chemistry, magnetic resonance parameters.

Delaware State University, Graduate Programs, Department of Chemistry, Program in Chemistry, Dover, DE 19901-2277. Offers MS. *Entrance requirements:* For master's, GRE. Additional exam requirements/recommendations for international students: Required—TOEFL (minimum score 550 paper-based). Electronic applications accepted.

DePaul University, College of Science and Health, Department of Chemistry, Chicago, IL 60614. Offers biochemistry (MS); chemistry (MS); polymer chemistry

and coatings technology (MS). Part-time and evening/weekend programs available. *Faculty:* 13 full-time (7 women), 4 part-time/adjunct (1 woman). *Students:* 11 full-time (6 women), 3 part-time (2 women); includes 5 minority (1 Asian, non-Hispanic/Latino; 3 Hispanic/Latino; 1 Two or more races, non-Hispanic/Latino), 1 international. Average age 26. 6 applicants, 100% accepted, 4 enrolled. In 2011, 2 master's awarded. *Degree requirements:* For master's, thesis (for some programs), oral exam (for select programs). *Entrance requirements:* For master's, GRE Subject Test (chemistry), GRE General Test, BS in chemistry or equivalent. Additional exam requirements/recommendations for international students: Required—TOEFL (minimum score 590 paper-based; 243 computer-based). *Application deadline:* For fall admission, 7/15 for domestic students, 5/1 for international students; for winter admission, 11/15 for domestic students, 9/1 for international students; for spring admission, 2/15 for domestic students, 12/1 for international students. Applications are processed on a rolling basis. Application fee: $40. Electronic applications accepted. *Financial support:* In 2011–12, 4 students received support, including 6 teaching assistantships with partial tuition reimbursements available (averaging $9,000 per year). Financial award application deadline: 6/1. *Faculty research:* Computational chemistry, organic synthesis, inorganic synthesis, polymer synthesis, biochemistry. *Total annual research expenditures:* $30,000. *Unit head:* Dr. Richard F. Niedziela, Chair, 773-325-7307, Fax: 773-325-7421, E-mail: rniedzie@condor.depaul.edu. *Application contact:* Dr. Matthew Dintzner, Director of Graduate Studies, 773-325-4726, Fax: 773-325-7421, E-mail: mdintzne@depaul.edu. Web site: http://chemistry.depaul.edu.

Drew University, Caspersen School of Graduate Studies, Program in Education, Madison, NJ 07940-1493. Offers biology (MAT); chemistry (MAT); English (MAT); French (MAT); Italian (MAT); math (MAT); physics (MAT); social studies (MAT); Spanish (MAT); theatre arts (MAT). Part-time programs available. *Entrance requirements:* For master's, transcripts, personal statement, recommendations. Additional exam requirements/recommendations for international students: Required—TOEFL, TWE. *Expenses:* Contact institution.

Drexel University, College of Arts and Sciences, Department of Chemistry, Philadelphia, PA 19104-2875. Offers MS, PhD. Part-time programs available. Terminal master's awarded for partial completion of doctoral program. *Degree requirements:* For master's, thesis optional; for doctorate, one foreign language, thesis/dissertation. *Entrance requirements:* For master's and doctorate, GRE. Additional exam requirements/recommendations for international students: Required—TOEFL. Electronic applications accepted. *Faculty research:* Inorganic, analytical, organic, physical, and atmospheric polymer chemistry.

Duke University, Graduate School, Department of Chemistry, Durham, NC 27708. Offers PhD. *Faculty:* 23 full-time. *Students:* 99 full-time (46 women); includes 3 minority (2 Black or African American, non-Hispanic/Latino; 1 Hispanic/Latino), 50 international. 250 applicants, 26% accepted, 26 enrolled. In 2011, 16 doctorates awarded. *Degree requirements:* For doctorate, one foreign language, thesis/dissertation. *Entrance requirements:* For doctorate, GRE General Test, GRE Subject Test (recommended). Additional exam requirements/recommendations for international students: Required—TOEFL (minimum score 550 paper-based; 213 computer-based; 83 iBT), IELTS (minimum score 7). *Application deadline:* For fall admission, 12/8 priority date for domestic students, 12/8 for international students. Application fee: $75. Electronic applications accepted. *Expenses: Tuition:* Full-time $40,720. *Required fees:* $3107. *Financial support:* Fellowships, research assistantships, and teaching assistantships available. Financial award application deadline: 12/8. *Unit head:* Baldwin Steve, Director of Graduate Studies, 919-660-1503, Fax: 919-660-1605, E-mail: caroline.morris@duke.edu. *Application contact:* Elizabeth Hutton, Director of Admissions, 919-684-3913, Fax: 919-684-2277, E-mail: grad-admissions@duke.edu. Web site: http://www.chem.duke.edu/graduates/.

Duquesne University, Bayer School of Natural and Environmental Sciences, Department of Chemistry and Biochemistry, Pittsburgh, PA 15282-0001. Offers chemistry (MS, PhD). Part-time programs available. *Faculty:* 16 full-time (5 women), 17 part-time/adjunct (8 women). *Students:* 45 full-time (19 women), 3 part-time (0 women); includes 5 minority (3 Black or African American, non-Hispanic/Latino; 1 Asian, non-Hispanic/Latino; 1 Two or more races, non-Hispanic/Latino), 12 international. Average age 28. 50 applicants, 38% accepted, 4 enrolled. In 2011, 2 master's, 6 doctorates awarded. Terminal master's awarded for partial completion of doctoral program. *Degree requirements:* For master's, thesis (for some programs); for doctorate, thesis/dissertation. *Entrance requirements:* For master's, GRE General Test, BS in chemistry or related field, 3 letters of recommendation, official transcripts, statement of purpose; for doctorate, GRE General Test, BS in chemistry or related field, statement of purpose, official transcripts, 3 letters of recommendation with recommendation forms. Additional exam requirements/recommendations for international students: Required—TOEFL (minimum score 100 iBT). *Application deadline:* For fall admission, 2/15 priority date for domestic students, 2/15 for international students; for spring admission, 10/1 priority date for domestic students, 10/1 for international students. Applications are processed on a rolling basis. Application fee: $0 ($40 for international students). Electronic applications accepted. *Expenses:* Contact institution. *Financial support:* In 2011–12, 43 students received support, including 1 fellowship with tuition reimbursement available (averaging $22,100 per year), 11 research assistantships with full tuition reimbursements available (averaging $21,850 per year), 28 teaching assistantships with full tuition reimbursements available (averaging $21,850 per year); scholarships/grants and unspecified assistantships also available. Financial award application deadline: 5/31. *Faculty*

64 facebook.com/petersonspublishing

Peterson's Graduate Programs in the Physical Sciences, Mathematics, Agricultural Sciences, the Environment & Natural Resources 2013

research: Computational physical chemistry, bioinorganic chemistry, analytical chemistry, biophysics, synthetic organic chemistry. *Unit head:* Dr. Ralph Wheeler, Chair, 412-396-6341, Fax: 412-396-5683, E-mail: wheeler7@duq.edu. *Application contact:* Heather Costello, Graduate Academic Advisor, 412-396-6339, Fax: 412-396-4881, E-mail: costelloh@duq.edu. Web site: http://www.science.duq.edu/.

East Carolina University, Graduate School, Thomas Harriot College of Arts and Sciences, Department of Chemistry, Greenville, NC 27858-4353. Offers MS. Part-time programs available. *Degree requirements:* For master's, one foreign language, comprehensive exam, thesis. *Entrance requirements:* For master's, GRE General Test. Additional exam requirements/recommendations for international students: Required—TOEFL. *Application deadline:* For fall admission, 6/1 priority date for domestic students; for spring admission, 10/15 for domestic students. Applications are processed on a rolling basis. Application fee: $50. *Expenses:* Tuition, state resident: full-time $3557; part-time $444.63 per semester hour. Tuition, nonresident: full-time $14,351; part-time $1793.88 per semester hour. *Required fees:* $2016; $252 per semester hour. Part-time tuition and fees vary according to course load, campus/location and program. *Financial support:* Teaching assistantships and Federal Work-Study available. Financial award application deadline: 6/1. *Faculty research:* Organometallic, natural-product syntheses; chemometrics; electroanalytical method development; microcomputer adaptations for handicapped students. *Unit head:* Dr. Ricky Hicks, Chair, 252-328-9710, E-mail: hicksr@ecu.edu. Web site: http://www.ecu.edu/cs-cas/chem/Graduate-Program.cfm.

Eastern Illinois University, Graduate School, College of Sciences, Department of Chemistry, Charleston, IL 61920-3099. Offers MS. *Degree requirements:* For master's, thesis. *Entrance requirements:* For master's, GRE General Test. *Expenses:* Tuition, state resident: part-time $279 per credit hour. Tuition, nonresident: part-time $670 per credit hour. *Required fees:* $179.07 per credit hour. $1253 per semester.

Eastern Kentucky University, The Graduate School, College of Arts and Sciences, Department of Chemistry, Richmond, KY 40475-3102. Offers MS. Part-time and evening/weekend programs available. *Entrance requirements:* For master's, GRE General Test, minimum GPA of 2.5. *Faculty research:* Organic synthesis, surface chemistry, inorganic chemistry, analytical chemistry.

Eastern Michigan University, Graduate School, College of Arts and Sciences, Department of Chemistry, Ypsilanti, MI 48197. Offers MS. Part-time and evening/weekend programs available. *Faculty:* 21 full-time (9 women). *Students:* 3 full-time (all women), 27 part-time (16 women), 18 international. Average age 29. 64 applicants, 27% accepted, 7 enrolled. In 2011, 11 degrees awarded. *Degree requirements:* For master's, thesis. *Entrance requirements:* For master's, GRE General Test. Additional exam requirements/recommendations for international students: Required—TOEFL. *Application deadline:* For fall admission, 8/1 for domestic students, 5/1 for international students; for winter admission, 12/1 for domestic students, 8/1 for international students; for spring admission, 4/1 for domestic students, 3/1 for international students. Applications are processed on a rolling basis. Application fee: $35. *Expenses:* Tuition, state resident: full-time $10,367; part-time $432 per credit hour. Tuition, nonresident: full-time $20,435; part-time $851 per credit hour. *Required fees:* $39 per credit hour. $46 per semester. One-time fee: $100. Tuition and fees vary according to course level, degree level and reciprocity agreements. *Financial support:* Fellowships, research assistantships with full tuition reimbursements, teaching assistantships with full tuition reimbursements, career-related internships or fieldwork, Federal Work-Study, institutionally sponsored loans, scholarships/grants, tuition waivers (partial), and unspecified assistantships available. Support available to part-time students. Financial award applicants required to submit FAFSA. *Unit head:* Dr. Ross Nord, Department Head, 734-487-0106, Fax: 734-487-1496, E-mail: ross.nord@emich.edu. *Application contact:* Dr. Timothy Brewer, Graduate Coordinator, 734-487-9613, Fax: 734-487-1496, E-mail: tbrewer@emich.edu. Web site: http://www.emich.edu/public/chemistry/chmhome.htm.

Eastern New Mexico University, Graduate School, College of Liberal Arts and Sciences, Department of Physical Sciences, Portales, NM 88130. Offers chemistry (MS), including analytical, biochemistry, inorganic, organic, physical. Part-time programs available. *Faculty:* 6 full-time (0 women). *Students:* 11 part-time (5 women), 9 international. Average age 25. 25 applicants, 44% accepted, 4 enrolled. In 2011, 5 master's awarded. *Degree requirements:* For master's, thesis optional, seminar, oral and written comprehensive exams. *Entrance requirements:* For master's, ACS placement examination, minimum GPA of 3.0; 2 letters of recommendation; personal statement of career goals; bachelor's degree with one year minimum each of general, organic, and analytical chemistry. Additional exam requirements/recommendations for international students: Required—TOEFL (minimum score 550 paper-based; 213 computer-based; 79 iBT), IELTS (minimum score 6). *Application deadline:* For fall admission, 7/20 priority date for domestic students, 6/20 for international students; for spring admission, 12/15 priority date for domestic students, 11/15 for international students. Applications are processed on a rolling basis. Application fee: $10. Electronic applications accepted. *Financial support:* In 2011–12, 1 research assistantship with partial tuition reimbursement (averaging $8,500 per year), 10 teaching assistantships with partial tuition reimbursements (averaging $8,500 per year) were awarded; career-related internships or fieldwork and unspecified assistantships also available. Support available to part-time students. Financial award application deadline: 3/1; financial award applicants required to submit FAFSA. *Faculty*

research: Synfuel, electrochemistry, protein chemistry. *Unit head:* Dr. Juacho Yan, Graduate Coordinator, 575-562-2494, Fax: 575-562-2192, E-mail: juacho.yan@enmu.edu. *Application contact:* Sharon Potter, Department Secretary, Biology and Physical Sciences, 575-562-2174, Fax: 575-562-2192, E-mail: sharon.potter@enmu.edu. Web site: http://liberal-arts.enmu.edu/sciences/grad-chemistry.shtml.

East Tennessee State University, School of Graduate Studies, College of Arts and Sciences, Department of Chemistry, Johnson City, TN 37614. Offers MS. Part-time and evening/weekend programs available. *Faculty:* 9 full-time (2 women). *Students:* 15 full-time (5 women), 4 part-time (3 women); includes 4 minority (1 Black or African American, non-Hispanic/Latino; 1 American Indian or Alaska Native, non-Hispanic/Latino; 1 Asian, non-Hispanic/Latino; 1 Two or more races, non-Hispanic/Latino), 11 international. Average age 27. 45 applicants, 51% accepted, 14 enrolled. In 2011, 11 master's awarded. *Degree requirements:* For master's, comprehensive exam, thesis. *Entrance requirements:* Additional exam requirements/recommendations for international students: Required—TOEFL (minimum score 550 paper-based; 213 computer-based; 79 iBT). *Application deadline:* For fall admission, 6/1 for domestic students, 4/30 for international students; for spring admission, 11/1 for domestic students, 9/30 for international students. Application fee: $35 ($45 for international students). Electronic applications accepted. *Expenses:* Tuition, state resident: full-time $7312; part-time $350 per credit hour. Tuition, nonresident: full-time $18,490; part-time $621 per credit hour. *Required fees:* $63 per credit hour. Tuition and fees vary according to course load and program. *Financial support:* In 2011–12, 17 students received support, including 16 teaching assistantships with full and partial tuition reimbursements available (averaging $8,300 per year); career-related internships or fieldwork, institutionally sponsored loans, scholarships/grants, and unspecified assistantships also available. Financial award application deadline: 7/1; financial award applicants required to submit FAFSA. *Faculty research:* Development of luminescence techniques for chemical analysis, new functional materials and biosensor technology, synthesis of theoretically significant organic molecules and synthetic metals, synthesis and study of phosphatase enzyme models. *Total annual research expenditures:* $39,000. *Unit head:* Dr. Cassandra Eagle, Chair, 423-439-4347, Fax: 423-439-5835, E-mail: eaglec@etsu.edu. *Application contact:* Gail Powers, Graduate Specialist, 423-439-4703, Fax: 423-439-5624, E-mail: powersg@etsu.edu.

Emory University, Laney Graduate School, Department of Chemistry, Atlanta, GA 30322-1100. Offers PhD. *Faculty:* 19 full-time (1 woman), 4 part-time/adjunct (0 women). *Students:* 157 full-time (66 women); includes 74 minority (9 Black or African American, non-Hispanic/Latino; 1 American Indian or Alaska Native, non-Hispanic/Latino; 59 Asian, non-Hispanic/Latino; 5 Hispanic/Latino). 401 applicants, 20% accepted, 35 enrolled. In 2011, 13 doctorates awarded. *Degree requirements:* For doctorate, comprehensive exam, thesis/dissertation. *Entrance requirements:* For doctorate, GRE General Test, 3 letters of recommendation, curriculum vitae. Additional exam requirements/recommendations for international students: Required—TOEFL. *Application deadline:* For fall admission, 1/3 priority date for domestic students, 1/3 for international students. Electronic applications accepted. *Expenses:* Tuition: Full-time $34,800. *Required fees:* $1300. *Financial support:* In 2011–12, 15 fellowships with full tuition reimbursements (averaging $26,000 per year), 75 research assistantships with full tuition reimbursements (averaging $21,000 per year), 60 teaching assistantships with full tuition reimbursements (averaging $21,000 per year) were awarded; Federal Work-Study, institutionally sponsored loans, scholarships/grants, and health care benefits also available. Financial award application deadline: 1/3; financial award applicants required to submit FAFSA. *Faculty research:* Organometallic synthesis and catalysis, synthesis of natural products, x-ray crystallography, mass spectrometry, analytical neurochemistry. *Total annual research expenditures:* $5.1 million. *Unit head:* Prof. David Lynn, Chair, 404-727-9348. *Application contact:* Prof. Vincent Conticello, Director of Graduate Studies, 404-727-2779, Fax: 404-727-6586, E-mail: vcontic@emory.edu. Web site: http://www.chemistry.emory.edu/.

Fairleigh Dickinson University, College at Florham, Maxwell Becton College of Arts and Sciences, Department of Chemistry and Geological Sciences, Program in Chemistry, Madison, NJ 07940-1099. Offers MS.

Fairleigh Dickinson University, Metropolitan Campus, University College: Arts, Sciences, and Professional Studies, School of Natural Sciences, Program in Chemistry, Teaneck, NJ 07666-1914. Offers MS.

Fairleigh Dickinson University, Metropolitan Campus, University College: Arts, Sciences, and Professional Studies, School of Natural Sciences, Program in Cosmetic Science, Teaneck, NJ 07666-1914. Offers MS.

Fisk University, Division of Graduate Studies, Department of Chemistry, Nashville, TN 37208-3051. Offers MA. Part-time programs available. *Degree requirements:* For master's, comprehensive exam, thesis. *Entrance requirements:* For master's, GRE General Test, minimum GPA of 3.0. Electronic applications accepted. *Faculty research:* Environmental studies, lithium compound synthesis, HIU compound synthesis.

Florida Agricultural and Mechanical University, Division of Graduate Studies, Research, and Continuing Education, College of Arts and Sciences, Department of Chemistry, Tallahassee, FL 32307-3200. Offers MS. *Degree requirements:* For master's, comprehensive exam, thesis optional. *Entrance requirements:* For master's, GRE General Test, minimum GPA of 3.0.

Peterson's Graduate Programs in the Physical Sciences, Mathematics, Agricultural Sciences, the Environment & Natural Resources 2013

facebook.com/petersonspublishing **65**

Chemistry

Florida Atlantic University, Charles E. Schmidt College of Science, Department of Chemistry and Biochemistry, Boca Raton, FL 33431-0991. Offers chemistry (MS, MST, PhD). Part-time programs available. *Faculty:* 13 full-time (1 woman), 1 (woman) part-time/adjunct. *Students:* 29 full-time (14 women), 10 part-time (6 women); includes 4 minority (1 Black or African American, non-Hispanic/Latino; 1 Asian, non-Hispanic/Latino; 2 Hispanic/Latino), 16 international. Average age 27. 38 applicants, 18% accepted, 4 enrolled. In 2011, 3 master's, 3 doctorates awarded. Terminal master's awarded for partial completion of doctoral program. *Degree requirements:* For master's, thesis; for doctorate, comprehensive exam, thesis/dissertation. *Entrance requirements:* For master's, GRE General Test, minimum GPA of 3.0; for doctorate, GRE, minimum GPA of 3.0. Additional exam requirements/recommendations for international students: Required—TOEFL. *Application deadline:* For fall admission, 7/1 priority date for domestic students, 2/15 for international students; for spring admission, 11/1 priority date for domestic students, 7/15 for international students. Applications are processed on a rolling basis. Application fee: $30. *Expenses: Tuition, area resident:* Part-time $343.02 per credit hour. Tuition, state resident: full-time $8232. Tuition, nonresident: full-time $23,931; part-time $997.14 per credit hour. *Financial support:* Fellowships, research assistantships with full tuition reimbursements, teaching assistantships with full tuition reimbursements, and Federal Work-Study available. *Faculty research:* Polymer synthesis and characterization, spectroscopy, geochemistry, environmental chemistry, biomedical chemistry. *Unit head:* Dr. Cyril Parkanyi, Chair, 561-297-2093, Fax: 561-297-2759, E-mail: parkanyi@fau.edu. *Application contact:* Dr. Salvatore D. Lepore, Professor, 561-297-0330, Fax: 561-297-2759, E-mail: slepore@fau.edu. Web site: http://www.science.fau.edu/chemistry/.

Florida Institute of Technology, Graduate Programs, College of Science, Department of Chemistry, Melbourne, FL 32901-6975. Offers biochemistry (MS); chemistry (MS, PhD). Part-time programs available. *Faculty:* 5 full-time (0 women). *Students:* 44 full-time (22 women), 1 (woman) part-time; includes 1 minority (Black or African American, non-Hispanic/Latino), 34 international. Average age 29. 79 applicants, 57% accepted, 13 enrolled. In 2011, 1 degree awarded. Terminal master's awarded for partial completion of doctoral program. *Median time to degree:* Of those who began their doctoral program in fall 2003, 100% received their degree in 8 years or less. *Degree requirements:* For master's, comprehensive exam, research proposal, thesis and oral examination in defense of the thesis, proficiency examination; for doctorate, comprehensive exam, thesis/dissertation, oral defense of dissertation, dissertation research publishable to standards, complete original research study. *Entrance requirements:* For master's, proficiency exams, minimum GPA of 3.0; for doctorate, minimum GPA of 3.3, resume, 3 letters of recommendation, statement of objectives. Additional exam requirements/recommendations for international students: Required—TOEFL (minimum score 550 paper-based; 213 computer-based; 79 iBT). *Application deadline:* For fall admission, 4/1 for international students; for spring admission, 9/30 for international students. Applications are processed on a rolling basis. Electronic applications accepted. *Expenses: Tuition:* Full-time $19,620; part-time $1090 per credit hour. Tuition and fees vary according to campus/location. *Financial support:* In 2011–12, 4 research assistantships with full and partial tuition reimbursements (averaging $11,704 per year), 15 teaching assistantships with full and partial tuition reimbursements (averaging $10,318 per year) were awarded; career-related internships or fieldwork, institutionally sponsored loans, tuition waivers (partial), unspecified assistantships, and tuition remissions also available. Support available to part-time students. Financial award application deadline: 3/1; financial award applicants required to submit FAFSA. *Faculty research:* Energy storage applications, marine and organic chemistry, stereochemistry, medicinal chemistry, environmental chemistry. *Total annual research expenditures:* $772,720. *Unit head:* Dr. Michael W. Babich, Department Head, 321-674-8046, Fax: 321-674-8951, E-mail: babich@fit.edu. *Application contact:* Cheryl A. Brown, Associate Director of Graduate Admissions, 321-674-7581, Fax: 321-723-9468, E-mail: cbrown@fit.edu. Web site: http://cos.fit.edu/chemistry/.

Florida International University, College of Arts and Sciences, Department of Chemistry, Chemistry Program, Miami, FL 33199. Offers MS, PhD. *Degree requirements:* For master's, thesis; for doctorate, comprehensive exam, thesis/dissertation. *Entrance requirements:* For master's and doctorate, GRE, minimum GPA of 3.0, 3 letters of recommendation. Additional exam requirements/recommendations for international students: Required—TOEFL (minimum score 550 paper-based; 213 computer-based). Electronic applications accepted.

Florida State University, The Graduate School, College of Arts and Sciences, Department of Chemistry and Biochemistry, Tallahassee, FL 32306-4390. Offers analytical chemistry (MS, PhD); biochemistry (MS, PhD); inorganic chemistry (MS, PhD); materials chemistry (MS, PhD); organic chemistry (MS, PhD); physical chemistry (MS, PhD). *Faculty:* 35 full-time (5 women), 1 (woman) part-time/adjunct. *Students:* 138 full-time (52 women), 8 part-time (1 woman); includes 14 minority (6 Black or African American, non-Hispanic/Latino; 3 Asian, non-Hispanic/Latino; 2 Hispanic/Latino; 3 Two or more races, non-Hispanic/Latino), 63 international. Average age 25. 147 applicants, 40% accepted, 28 enrolled. In 2011, 10 master's, 24 doctorates awarded. Terminal master's awarded for partial completion of doctoral program. *Median time to degree:* Of those who began their doctoral program in fall 2003, 58% received their degree in 8 years or less. *Degree requirements:* For master's, comprehensive exam (for some programs), thesis (for some programs); for doctorate, comprehensive exam (for some programs), thesis/dissertation. *Entrance requirements:* For master's and doctorate, GRE General Test, minimum B average in undergraduate course work. Additional exam requirements/recommendations for international students:

Required—TOEFL (minimum score 550 paper-based; 213 computer-based; 80 iBT). *Application deadline:* For fall admission, 12/15 priority date for domestic students, 12/15 for international students; for spring admission, 9/15 for domestic and international students. Applications are processed on a rolling basis. Application fee: $30. Electronic applications accepted. *Expenses:* Contact institution. *Financial support:* In 2011–12, 140 students received support, including fellowships with full tuition reimbursements available (averaging $20,000 per year), 50 research assistantships with full tuition reimbursements available (averaging $20,000 per year), 100 teaching assistantships with full tuition reimbursements available (averaging $20,000 per year). Financial award application deadline: 12/15; financial award applicants required to submit FAFSA. *Faculty research:* Materials synthesis including polymers, natural products; catalysis, NMR; mass spectrometry; optical spectroscopy, scattering techniques, computational chemistry, separation technology; nanostructured materials including metallic, semiconducting and magnetic nanocrystals; nanoscience interfaced with biology; supramolecular materials for solar energy conversion. *Total annual research expenditures:* $9.9 million. *Unit head:* Dr. Timothy Logan, Chairman, 850-644-1244, Fax: 850-644-8281, E-mail: gradinfo@chem.fsu.edu. *Application contact:* Dr. Michael Shatruk, Chair, Graduate Admissions Committee, 888-525-9286, Fax: 850-644-0465, E-mail: gradinfo@chem.fsu.edu. Web site: http://www.chem.fsu.edu/.

Furman University, Graduate Division, Department of Chemistry, Greenville, SC 29613. Offers MS. *Faculty:* 9 full-time (3 women). *Students:* 5 full-time (1 woman); includes 2 minority (1 Black or African American, non-Hispanic/Latino; 1 Asian, non-Hispanic/Latino). Average age 23. In 2011, 6 master's awarded. *Degree requirements:* For master's, comprehensive exam, thesis. *Entrance requirements:* For master's, GRE General Test, GRE Subject Test. *Application deadline:* For fall admission, 8/1 for domestic and international students; for spring admission, 12/10 for domestic and international students. Applications are processed on a rolling basis. Application fee: $50. *Financial support:* In 2011–12, 3 fellowships (averaging $4,350 per year) were awarded; research assistantships, scholarships/grants, and unspecified assistantships also available. Financial award application deadline: 7/1; financial award applicants required to submit FAFSA. *Faculty research:* Computer-assisted chemical analysis, DNA-metal interactions, laser-initiated reactions, nucleic acid chemistry and biochemistry. *Unit head:* Dr. Lon B. Knight, Jr., Professor, 864-294-3372, Fax: 864-294-3559, E-mail: lon.knight@furman.edu. *Application contact:* Myra Crumley, Information Contact, 864-294-2056, Fax: 864-294-3559, E-mail: myra.crumley@furman.edu.

George Mason University, College of Science, Department of Chemistry and Biochemistry, Fairfax, VA 22030. Offers chemistry (MS); chemistry and biochemistry (PhD). *Faculty:* 17 full-time (3 women), 5 part-time/adjunct (3 women). *Students:* 20 full-time (7 women), 31 part-time (14 women); includes 17 minority (3 Black or African American, non-Hispanic/Latino; 1 American Indian or Alaska Native, non-Hispanic/Latino; 10 Asian, non-Hispanic/Latino; 3 Hispanic/Latino), 5 international. Average age 29. 58 applicants, 50% accepted, 11 enrolled. In 2011, 14 master's, 1 doctorate awarded. *Degree requirements:* For master's, thesis or alternative. *Entrance requirements:* For master's, GRE, bachelor's degree in related field; 2 official copies of transcripts; expanded goals statement; 3 letters of recommendation; resume for those whose bachelor's degree is 5 years or older; for doctorate, GRE, undergraduate degree in related field; BS with minimum GPA of 3.0; 3 letters of recommendation; 2 copies of official transcripts; expanded goals statement; resume. Additional exam requirements/recommendations for international students: Required—TOEFL (minimum score 570 paper-based; 230 computer-based; 88 iBT), IELTS, Pearson Test of English. *Application deadline:* For fall admission, 4/15 priority date for domestic students; for spring admission, 11/1 priority date for domestic students. Application fee: $65 ($80 for international students). Electronic applications accepted. *Expenses:* Tuition, state resident: full-time $8750; part-time $364.58 per credit. Tuition, nonresident: full-time $24,092; part-time $1003.83 per credit. *Required fees:* $2514; $104.75 per credit. *Financial support:* In 2011–12, 15 students received support, including 1 fellowship with full tuition reimbursement available (averaging $18,000 per year), 1 research assistantship with full and partial tuition reimbursement available (averaging $11,329 per year), 13 teaching assistantships with full and partial tuition reimbursements available (averaging $16,002 per year); career-related internships or fieldwork, Federal Work-Study, scholarships/grants, unspecified assistantships, and health care benefits (full-time research or teaching assistantship recipients) also available. Financial award application deadline: 3/1; financial award applicants required to submit FAFSA. *Total annual research expenditures:* $61,378. *Unit head:* John A. Schreifels, Chair, 703-993-1082, Fax: 703-993-1055, E-mail: jschreif@gmu.edu. *Application contact:* Mery Tucker, Administrative Specialist, 703-993-1070, Fax: 703-993-1055, E-mail: mtucker2@gmu.edu. Web site: http://chemistry.gmu.edu/.

Georgetown University, Graduate School of Arts and Sciences, Department of Chemistry, Washington, DC 20057. Offers analytical chemistry (PhD); biochemistry (PhD); computational chemistry (PhD); inorganic chemistry (PhD); materials chemistry (PhD); organic chemistry (PhD); physical chemistry (PhD); theoretical chemistry (PhD). Terminal master's awarded for partial completion of doctoral program. *Degree requirements:* For doctorate, comprehensive exam, thesis/dissertation. *Entrance requirements:* For doctorate, GRE General Test. Additional exam requirements/recommendations for international students: Required—TOEFL.

The George Washington University, Columbian College of Arts and Sciences, Department of Chemistry, Washington, DC 20052. Offers analytical chemistry

66 facebook.com/petersonspublishing

Peterson's Graduate Programs in the Physical Sciences, Mathematics, Agricultural Sciences, the Environment & Natural Resources 2013

(MS, PhD); inorganic chemistry (MS, PhD); materials science (MS, PhD); organic chemistry (MS, PhD); physical chemistry (MS, PhD). Part-time and evening/weekend programs available. *Faculty:* 16 full-time (5 women), 5 part-time/adjunct (2 women). *Students:* 22 full-time (10 women), 10 part-time (7 women); includes 4 minority (3 Asian, non-Hispanic/Latino; 1 Hispanic/Latino), 7 international. Average age 27. 55 applicants, 42% accepted, 8 enrolled. In 2011, 4 master's, 3 doctorates awarded. Terminal master's awarded for partial completion of doctoral program. *Degree requirements:* For master's, comprehensive exam, thesis or alternative; for doctorate, thesis/dissertation, general exam. *Entrance requirements:* For master's and doctorate, GRE General Test, interview, minimum GPA of 3.0. Additional exam requirements/recommendations for international students: Required—TOEFL (minimum score 550 paper-based; 213 computer-based; 80 iBT). *Application deadline:* For fall admission, 1/15 priority date for domestic students, 1/15 for international students; for spring admission, 9/1 priority date for domestic students, 9/1 for international students. Applications are processed on a rolling basis. Application fee: $75. Electronic applications accepted. *Financial support:* In 2011–12, 27 students received support. Fellowships with tuition reimbursements available, research assistantships, teaching assistantships with tuition reimbursements available, Federal Work-Study, and tuition waivers available. Financial award application deadline: 1/15. *Unit head:* Dr. Michael King, Chair, 202-994-6488. *Application contact:* Information Contact, 202-994-6121, E-mail: gwchem@gwu.edu. Web site: http://www.gwu.edu/~gwchem/.

Georgia Institute of Technology, Graduate Studies and Research, College of Sciences, School of Chemistry and Biochemistry, Atlanta, GA 30332-0001. Offers MS, MS Chem, PhD. Terminal master's awarded for partial completion of doctoral program. *Degree requirements:* For master's, thesis (for some programs); for doctorate, thesis/dissertation. *Entrance requirements:* For master's and doctorate, GRE General Test, GRE Subject Test, minimum GPA of 2.7. Additional exam requirements/recommendations for international students: Required—TOEFL. Electronic applications accepted. *Faculty research:* Inorganic, organic, physical, and analytical chemistry.

Georgia State University, College of Arts and Sciences, Department of Chemistry, Atlanta, GA 30302-3083. Offers MS, PhD. Part-time programs available. Terminal master's awarded for partial completion of doctoral program. *Degree requirements:* For master's, one foreign language, comprehensive exam, thesis or alternative, oral defense or approved non-thesis paper; for doctorate, one foreign language, comprehensive exam, thesis/dissertation, oral defense. *Entrance requirements:* For master's, GRE General Test; for doctorate, GRE General Test, 3 letters of recommendation, departmental supplemental form. Additional exam requirements/recommendations for international students: Required—TOEFL (minimum score 550 paper-based; 213 computer-based; 90

iBT). Electronic applications accepted. *Faculty research:* RNA/DNA, enzymology, drug design/discovery, biochemical-biophysical studies.

Graduate School and University Center of the City University of New York, Graduate Studies, Program in Chemistry, New York, NY 10016-4039. Offers PhD. *Degree requirements:* For doctorate, one foreign language, thesis/dissertation. *Entrance requirements:* For doctorate, GRE General Test. Additional exam requirements/recommendations for international students: Required—TOEFL. Electronic applications accepted.

Hampton University, Graduate College, Department of Chemistry, Hampton, VA 23668. Offers MS. Part-time and evening/weekend programs available. *Degree requirements:* For master's, thesis. *Entrance requirements:* For master's, GRE General Test.

Harvard University, Graduate School of Arts and Sciences, Department of Chemistry and Chemical Biology, Cambridge, MA 02138. Offers biochemical chemistry (PhD); inorganic chemistry (PhD); organic chemistry (PhD); physical chemistry (PhD). *Degree requirements:* For doctorate, thesis/dissertation, cumulative exams. *Entrance requirements:* For doctorate, GRE General Test, GRE Subject Test. Additional exam requirements/recommendations for international students: Required—TOEFL. *Expenses: Tuition:* Full-time $36,304. *Required fees:* $1186. Full-time tuition and fees vary according to program.

See Display below and Close-Up on page 125.

Hofstra University, School of Education, Health, and Human Services, Programs in Teaching Secondary Education, Hempstead, NY 11549. Offers business education (MS Ed); education technology (Advanced Certificate); English education (MA, MS Ed); foreign language and TESOL (MS Ed); foreign language education (MA, MS Ed), including French, German, Russian, Spanish; mathematics education (MA, MS Ed); science education (MA, MS Ed), including biology, chemistry, earth science, geology, physics; secondary education (Advanced Certificate); social studies education (MA, MS Ed). Part-time and evening/weekend programs available. Postbaccalaureate distance learning degree programs offered (minimal on-campus study). *Students:* 72 full-time (47 women), 51 part-time (30 women); includes 21 minority (9 Black or African American, non-Hispanic/Latino; 7 Asian, non-Hispanic/Latino; 5 Hispanic/Latino). Average age 28. 103 applicants, 91% accepted, 41 enrolled. In 2011, 86 master's, 6 other advanced degrees awarded. *Degree requirements:* For master's, one foreign language, comprehensive exam (for some programs), thesis (for some programs), exit project, electronic portfolio, student teaching, fieldwork, curriculum project, minimum GPA of 3.0; for Advanced Certificate, 3 foreign languages, comprehensive exam (for some programs), thesis project, minimum GPA of 3.0. *Entrance requirements:* For master's, 2 letters of recommendation, teacher certification (MA), essay; for Advanced Certificate, 2 letters of recommendation, essay. Additional exam requirements/recommendations for international students:

Peterson's Graduate Programs in the Physical Sciences, Mathematics, Agricultural Sciences, the Environment & Natural Resources 2013

facebook.com/petersonspublishing **67**

Chemistry

Required—TOEFL (minimum score 550 paper-based; 213 computer-based; 80 iBT). *Application deadline:* Applications are processed on a rolling basis. Application fee: $70 ($75 for international students). Electronic applications accepted. *Expenses: Tuition:* Full-time $18,990; part-time $1055 per credit hour. *Required fees:* $970. Tuition and fees vary according to program. *Financial support:* In 2011–12, 90 students received support, including 13 fellowships with full and partial tuition reimbursements available (averaging $3,202 per year), 1 research assistantship with full and partial tuition reimbursement available (averaging $11,645 per year); career-related internships or fieldwork, Federal Work-Study, institutionally sponsored loans, scholarships/grants, tuition waivers (full and partial), and unspecified assistantships also available. Support available to part-time students. Financial award applicants required to submit FAFSA. *Faculty research:* Appropriate content and pedagogy in secondary school disciplines, appropriate pedagogy in secondary school disciplines, adolescent development, secondary school organization, alternative secondary school programs. *Unit head:* Dr. Esther Fusco, Chairperson, 516-463-7704, Fax: 516-463-6196, E-mail: catezf@hofstra.edu. *Application contact:* Carol Drummer, Dean of Graduate Admissions, 516-463-4876, Fax: 516-463-4664, E-mail: gradstudent@hofstra.edu. Web site: http://www.hofstra.edu/education/.

Howard University, Graduate School, Department of Chemistry, Washington, DC 20059-0002. Offers analytical chemistry (MS, PhD); atmospheric (MS, PhD); biochemistry (MS, PhD); environmental (MS, PhD); inorganic chemistry (MS, PhD); organic chemistry (MS, PhD); physical chemistry (MS, PhD). Terminal master's awarded for partial completion of doctoral program. *Degree requirements:* For master's, comprehensive exam, thesis, teaching experience; for doctorate, comprehensive exam, thesis/dissertation, teaching experience. *Entrance requirements:* For master's, GRE General Test, minimum GPA of 2.7; for doctorate, GRE General Test, minimum GPA of 3.0. Additional exam requirements/recommendations for international students: Required—TOEFL. Electronic applications accepted. *Faculty research:* Synthetic organics, materials, natural products, mass spectrometry.

Hunter College of the City University of New York, Graduate School, School of Arts and Sciences, Department of Chemistry, New York, NY 10021-5085. Offers biochemistry (MA, PhD); chemistry (PhD). Part-time programs available. *Faculty:* 3 full-time (2 women). *Students:* 3 full-time (0 women), 10 part-time (7 women); includes 5 minority (1 Black or African American, non-Hispanic/Latino; 3 Asian, non-Hispanic/Latino; 1 Hispanic/Latino), 3 international. Average age 26. 13 applicants, 54% accepted, 6 enrolled. In 2011, 11 master's awarded. *Degree requirements:* For master's, comprehensive exam or, thesis. *Entrance requirements:* For master's, GRE General Test, 1 year of course work in chemistry, quantitative analysis, organic chemistry, physical chemistry, biology, biochemistry lecture and laboratory. Additional exam requirements/recommendations for international students: Required—TOEFL. *Application deadline:* For fall admission, 4/1 for domestic students; for spring admission, 11/1 for domestic students. Application fee: $125. *Expenses:* Tuition, state resident: full-time $8210; part-time $345 per credit. Tuition, nonresident: full-time $15,360; part-time $640 per credit. *Required fees:* $280 per semester. One-time fee: $125. Tuition and fees vary according to class time, campus/location and program. *Financial support:* Teaching assistantships and tuition waivers (partial) available. Support available to part-time students. *Faculty research:* Theoretical chemistry, vibrational optical activity, Raman spectroscopy. *Unit head:* Dr. Gary J. Quigley, Chairperson, 212-772-5330, E-mail: gary.quilgley@hunter.cuny.edu. *Application contact:* William Zlata, Director for Graduate Admissions, 212-772-4482, Fax: 212-650-3336, E-mail: admissions@hunter.cuny.edu.

Idaho State University, Office of Graduate Studies, College of Science and Engineering, Department of Chemistry, Pocatello, ID 83209-8023. Offers MNS, MS. MS students must enter as undergraduates. Part-time programs available. *Degree requirements:* For master's, comprehensive exam, thesis (for some programs). *Entrance requirements:* For master's, GRE General Test, minimum GPA of 3.0 in all upper-division classes; 1 semester of calculus, inorganic chemistry, and analytical chemistry; 1 year of physics, organic chemistry and physical chemistry. Additional exam requirements/recommendations for international students: Required—TOEFL (minimum score 550 paper-based; 213 computer-based; 80 iBT). Electronic applications accepted. *Faculty research:* Low temperature plasma, organic chemistry, physical chemistry, inorganic chemistry, analytical chemistry.

Illinois Institute of Technology, Graduate College, College of Science and Letters, Department of Biological, Chemical and Physical Sciences, Chemistry Division, Chicago, IL 60616. Offers analytical chemistry (M Ch); chemistry (M Chem, MS, PhD); materials and chemical synthesis (M Ch). Part-time and evening/weekend programs available. Postbaccalaureate distance learning degree programs offered (no on-campus study). Terminal master's awarded for partial completion of doctoral program. *Degree requirements:* For master's, comprehensive exam, thesis (for some programs); for doctorate, comprehensive exam, thesis/dissertation. *Entrance requirements:* For master's, GRE General Test (minimum score 1000 Quantitative and Verbal, 2.5 Analytical Writing), minimum undergraduate GPA of 3.0; for doctorate, GRE General Test (minimum score 1100 Quantitative and Verbal, 3.0 Analytical Writing), GRE Subject Test, minimum undergraduate GPA of 3.0. Additional exam requirements/recommendations for international students: Required—TOEFL (minimum score 523 paper-based; 213 computer-based; 70 iBT); Recommended—IELTS. Electronic applications accepted. *Faculty research:* Synthesis and analysis of inorganic nanoparticles; synthetic and mechanistic organic chemistry; synthesis of

penicillin-related compounds; design, synthesis and property studies of nanomaterials for applications in chemical sensing, energy storage and biomedical usage; scanning probe microscopy.

Illinois State University, Graduate School, College of Arts and Sciences, Department of Chemistry, Normal, IL 61790-2200. Offers MS. *Degree requirements:* For master's, thesis. *Entrance requirements:* For master's, GRE General Test, minimum GPA of 2.6 in last 60 hours of course work. *Faculty research:* Solid-state and solution behavior of lanthanide scorpionates and porphyrinoids; CAREER: Versatile Vanadium: biology, materials science and education through its diverse coordinator carbaporphyrins and other highly modified porphyrinoid systems; oxadiazines: structurally novel templates for catalytic asymmetric synthesis.

Indiana University Bloomington, University Graduate School, College of Arts and Sciences, Department of Chemistry, Bloomington, IN 47405. Offers analytical chemistry (PhD); chemical biology chemistry (PhD); chemistry (MAT); inorganic chemistry (PhD); materials chemistry (PhD); organic chemistry (PhD); physical chemistry (PhD). *Faculty:* 42 full-time (4 women). *Students:* 200 full-time (82 women), 3 part-time (0 women); includes 18 minority (7 Black or African American, non-Hispanic/Latino; 8 Asian, non-Hispanic/Latino; 1 Hispanic/Latino; 1 Native Hawaiian or other Pacific Islander, non-Hispanic/Latino; 1 Two or more races, non-Hispanic/Latino), 63 international. Average age 27. 290 applicants, 49% accepted, 46 enrolled. In 2011, 11 master's, 20 doctorates awarded. Terminal master's awarded for partial completion of doctoral program. *Median time to degree:* Of those who began their doctoral program in fall 2003, 49% received their degree in 8 years or less. *Degree requirements:* For master's, thesis; for doctorate, thesis/dissertation. *Entrance requirements:* For master's and doctorate, GRE General Test, GRE Subject Test. Additional exam requirements/recommendations for international students: Required—TOEFL. *Application deadline:* For fall admission, 1/15 priority date for domestic students, 12/15 for international students. Applications are processed on a rolling basis. Application fee: $55 ($65 for international students). *Financial support:* In 2011–12, 200 students received support, including 10 fellowships with full tuition reimbursements available, 76 research assistantships with full tuition reimbursements available, 111 teaching assistantships with full tuition reimbursements available; Federal Work-Study and institutionally sponsored loans also available. *Faculty research:* Synthesis of complex natural products, organic reaction mechanisms, organic electrochemistry, transitive-metal chemistry, solid-state and surface chemistry. *Total annual research expenditures:* $7.7 million. *Unit head:* David Giedroc, Chairperson, 812-855-6239, E-mail: chemchair@indiana.edu. *Application contact:* Daniel Mindiola, Director of Graduate Admissions, 812-855-2069, Fax: 812-855-8385, E-mail: mindiola@indiana.edu. Web site: http://www.chem.indiana.edu/.

Indiana University of Pennsylvania, School of Graduate Studies and Research, College of Natural Sciences and Mathematics, Department of Chemistry, MA Program in Chemistry, Indiana, PA 15705-1087. Offers MA. Part-time programs available. *Faculty:* 7 full-time (3 women). *Students:* 2 full-time (0 women), 1 part-time (0 women), 1 international. Average age 33. 4 applicants, 50% accepted, 2 enrolled. In 2011, 1 master's awarded. *Degree requirements:* For master's, thesis optional. *Entrance requirements:* For master's, 2 letters of recommendation. Additional exam requirements/recommendations for international students: Required—TOEFL (minimum score 540 paper-based; 207 computer-based). *Application deadline:* Applications are processed on a rolling basis. Application fee: $50. Electronic applications accepted. *Expenses:* Tuition, state resident: full-time $7488; part-time $416 per credit. Tuition, nonresident: full-time $11,232; part-time $624 per credit. *Required fees:* $2070; $192.20 per credit. $90 per semester. *Financial support:* Research assistantships with full and partial tuition reimbursements available. Financial award application deadline: 4/15; financial award applicants required to submit FAFSA. *Unit head:* Dr. Keith Kyler, Graduate Coordinator, 724-357-5702, E-mail: keith.kyler@iup.edu. *Application contact:* Dr. Lawrence Kupchella, Graduate Coordinator, 724-357-5702, E-mail: lkup@iup.edu. Web site: http://www.iup.edu/upper.aspx?id=90471.

Indiana University of Pennsylvania, School of Graduate Studies and Research, College of Natural Sciences and Mathematics, Department of Chemistry, MS Program in Chemistry, Indiana, PA 15705-1087. Offers MS. *Faculty:* 7 full-time (3 women). *Students:* 12 full-time (4 women); includes 3 minority (1 Black or African American, non-Hispanic/Latino; 2 Asian, non-Hispanic/Latino), 1 international. Average age 25. 31 applicants, 65% accepted, 5 enrolled. In 2011, 5 master's awarded. *Degree requirements:* For master's, thesis. *Entrance requirements:* For master's, 2 letters of recommendation. Additional exam requirements/recommendations for international students: Required—TOEFL (minimum score 540 paper-based; 207 computer-based). *Application deadline:* Applications are processed on a rolling basis. Application fee: $50. Electronic applications accepted. *Expenses:* Tuition, state resident: full-time $7488; part-time $416 per credit. Tuition, nonresident: full-time $11,232; part-time $624 per credit. *Required fees:* $2070; $192.20 per credit. $90 per semester. *Financial support:* In 2011–12, 4 research assistantships (averaging $2,783 per year) were awarded. *Unit head:* Dr. John C. Woolcock, Chairperson, 724-357-2361. *Application contact:* Dr. Lawrence Kupchella, Graduate Coordinator, 724-357-5702, E-mail: lkup@iup.edu. Web site: http://www.iup.edu/upper.aspx?id=49407.

Indiana University–Purdue University Indianapolis, School of Science, Department of Chemistry and Chemical Biology, Indianapolis, IN 46202-2896. Offers MS, PhD, MD/PhD. MD/PhD offered jointly with Indiana University School of Medicine and Purdue University. Part-time and evening/weekend programs available. *Faculty:* 10 full-time (2 women). *Students:* 21 full-time (11 women), 22 part-time (10 women); includes 4 minority (1 Asian, non-Hispanic/Latino; 1 Hispanic/Latino; 2 Two or more races, non-Hispanic/Latino), 7 international. Average age 31. 21 applicants, 71% accepted, 15 enrolled. In 2011, 8 master's awarded. Terminal master's awarded for partial completion of doctoral program. *Degree requirements:* For master's, thesis (for some programs); for doctorate, thesis/dissertation. *Entrance requirements:* For master's and doctorate, minimum GPA of 3.0. Additional exam requirements/recommendations for international students: Required—TOEFL. *Application deadline:* Applications are processed on a rolling basis. Application fee: $55 ($65 for international students). *Financial support:* In 2011–12, fellowships with partial tuition reimbursements (averaging $13,500 per year), teaching assistantships with partial tuition reimbursements (averaging $17,440 per year) were awarded; research assistantships with partial tuition reimbursements, career-related internships or fieldwork, institutionally sponsored loans, tuition waivers (partial), and cooperative positions also available. Financial award application deadline: 3/1. *Faculty research:* Analytical, biological, inorganic, organic, and physical chemistry. *Total annual research expenditures:* $1.6 million. *Unit head:* Jay A. Siegel, Chair, 317-274-6872. *Application contact:* Eric Long, Associate Chair, 317-274-6888, Fax: 317-274-4701, E-mail: long@chem.iupui.edu. Web site: http://www.chem.iupui.edu/.

Instituto Tecnológico y de Estudios Superiores de Monterrey, Campus Monterrey, Graduate and Research Division, Program in Natural and Social Sciences, Monterrey, Mexico. Offers biotechnology (MS); chemistry (MS, PhD); communications (MS); education (MA). Part-time programs available. *Degree requirements:* For master's, one foreign language, thesis; for doctorate, one foreign language, thesis/dissertation. *Entrance requirements:* For master's, EXADEP; for doctorate, EXADEP, master's degree in related field. Additional exam requirements/recommendations for international students: Required—TOEFL. *Faculty research:* Cultural industries, mineral substances, bioremediation, food processing, CQ in industrial chemical processing.

Iowa State University of Science and Technology, Department of Chemistry, Ames, IA 50011-3011. Offers MS, PhD. *Degree requirements:* For master's, thesis; for doctorate, thesis/dissertation. *Entrance requirements:* Additional exam requirements/recommendations for international students: Required—TOEFL (minimum score 570 paper-based; 89 iBT), IELTS (minimum score 6.5). *Application deadline:* For fall admission, 2/1 priority date for domestic students, 2/1 for international students. Application fee: $40 ($90 for international students). Electronic applications accepted. *Unit head:* Dr. Theresa Windus, Director of Graduate Education, 515-294-2436, Fax: 515-294-0105, E-mail: chemgrad@iastate.edu. *Application contact:* Lynette Edsall, Application Contact, 800-521-2436, Fax: 515-294-0105, E-mail: chemgrad@iastate.edu. Web site: http://www.chem.iastate.edu/.

Jackson State University, Graduate School, College of Science, Engineering and Technology, Department of Chemistry and Biochemistry, Jackson, MS 39217. Offers MS, PhD. Part-time and evening/weekend programs available. *Degree requirements:* For master's, comprehensive exam, thesis; for doctorate, comprehensive exam, thesis/dissertation. *Entrance requirements:* For master's, GRE General Test; for doctorate, MAT. Additional exam requirements/recommendations for international students: Required—TOEFL (minimum score 520 paper-based; 195 computer-based; 67 iBT). *Faculty research:* Electrochemical and spectroscopic studies on charge transfer and energy transfer processes, spectroscopy of trapped molecular ions, respirable mine dust.

The Johns Hopkins University, Zanvyl Krieger School of Arts and Sciences, Chemistry-Biology Interface Program, Baltimore, MD 21218-2699. Offers PhD. Terminal master's awarded for partial completion of doctoral program. *Degree requirements:* For doctorate, comprehensive exam, thesis/dissertation, 8 one-semester courses, literature seminar, research proposal. *Entrance requirements:* For doctorate, GRE General Test, GRE Subject Test in biochemistry, cell and molecular biology, biology or chemistry (strongly recommended), 3 letters of recommendation, interview. Electronic applications accepted. *Faculty research:* Enzyme mechanisms, inhibitors, and metabolic pathways; DNA replication, damaged, and repair; using small molecules to probe signal transduction, gene regulation, angiogenesis, and other biological processes; synthetic methods and medicinal chemistry; synthetic modeling of metalloenzymes.

The Johns Hopkins University, Zanvyl Krieger School of Arts and Sciences, Department of Chemistry, Baltimore, MD 21218-2699. Offers PhD. Terminal master's awarded for partial completion of doctoral program. *Degree requirements:* For doctorate, comprehensive exam, thesis/dissertation, 8 one-semester courses, literature seminar. *Entrance requirements:* For doctorate, GRE General Test, GRE Subject Test. Additional exam requirements/recommendations for international students: Required—TOEFL (minimum score 600 paper-based; 250 computer-based), IELTS. Electronic applications accepted. *Faculty research:* Experimental physical, biophysical, inorganic/materials, organic/bioorganic theoretical.

Kansas State University, Graduate School, College of Arts and Sciences, Department of Chemistry, Manhattan, KS 66506. Offers analytical chemistry (MS); biological chemistry (MS); chemistry (PhD); inorganic chemistry (MS); materials chemistry (MS); organic chemistry (MS); physical chemistry (MS). *Faculty:* 17 full-time (2 women). *Students:* 63 full-time (28 women), 4 part-time (0 women); includes 2 minority (1 Black or African American, non-Hispanic/Latino; 1 Asian, non-Hispanic/Latino), 55 international. Average age 28. 119 applicants, 34% accepted, 15 enrolled. In 2011, 2 master's, 10 doctorates awarded. Terminal

master's awarded for partial completion of doctoral program. *Degree requirements:* For master's, thesis; for doctorate, thesis/dissertation. *Entrance requirements:* For master's and doctorate, GRE, minimum GPA of 3.0. Additional exam requirements/recommendations for international students: Required—TOEFL (minimum score 550 paper-based; 213 computer-based). *Application deadline:* For fall admission, 2/1 priority date for domestic students, 2/1 for international students; for spring admission, 8/1 priority date for domestic students, 8/1 for international students. Applications are processed on a rolling basis. Application fee: $40 ($55 for international students). Electronic applications accepted. *Financial support:* In 2011–12, 39 research assistantships (averaging $18,182 per year), 24 teaching assistantships with full tuition reimbursements (averaging $18,106 per year) were awarded; institutionally sponsored loans and scholarships/grants also available. Support available to part-time students. Financial award application deadline: 3/1; financial award applicants required to submit FAFSA. *Faculty research:* Inorganic chemistry, organic and biological chemistry, analytical chemistry, physical chemistry, materials chemistry and nanotechnology. *Total annual research expenditures:* $2.4 million. *Unit head:* Eric Maatta, Head, 785-532-6665, Fax: 785-532-6666, E-mail: eam@ksu.edu. *Application contact:* Christer Aakeroy, Director, 785-532-6096, Fax: 785-532-6666, E-mail: aakeroy@ksu.edu. Web site: http://www.k-state.edu/chem/.

Kent State University, College of Arts and Sciences, Department of Chemistry and Biochemistry, Kent, OH 44242-0001. Offers analytical chemistry (MS, PhD); biochemistry (MS, PhD); chemistry (MA); inorganic chemistry (MS, PhD); organic chemistry (MS, PhD); physical chemistry (MS, PhD). Terminal master's awarded for partial completion of doctoral program. *Degree requirements:* For master's, comprehensive exam, thesis; for doctorate, comprehensive exam, thesis/dissertation. *Entrance requirements:* For master's and doctorate, placement exam, GRE General Test, GRE Subject Test (recommended), minimum GPA of 2.75. Additional exam requirements/recommendations for international students: Required—TOEFL (minimum score 525 paper-based; 71 iBT). Electronic applications accepted. *Expenses:* Tuition, state resident: full-time $8136; part-time $452 per credit hour. Tuition, nonresident: full-time $14,292; part-time $794 per credit hour. *Faculty research:* Biological chemistry, materials chemistry, molecular spectroscopy.

See Display on next page and Close-Up on page 127.

Lakehead University, Graduate Studies, Faculty of Social Sciences and Humanities, Department of Chemistry, Thunder Bay, ON P7B 5E1, Canada. Offers M Sc. Part-time and evening/weekend programs available. *Degree requirements:* For master's, thesis, oral examination. *Entrance requirements:* For master's, minimum B+ average. Additional exam requirements/recommendations for international students: Required—TOEFL. *Faculty research:* Physical inorganic chemistry, photochemistry, physical chemistry.

Lamar University, College of Graduate Studies, College of Arts and Sciences, Department of Chemistry and Biochemistry, Beaumont, TX 77710. Offers chemistry (MS). Part-time programs available. *Faculty:* 9 full-time (3 women). *Students:* 66 full-time (25 women), 9 part-time (4 women); includes 2 minority (1 Black or African American, non-Hispanic/Latino; 1 Hispanic/Latino), 69 international. Average age 24. 103 applicants, 83% accepted, 33 enrolled. In 2011, 13 master's awarded. *Degree requirements:* For master's, thesis, practicum. *Entrance requirements:* For master's, GRE General Test, minimum GPA of 2.5 in last 60 hours of course work. Additional exam requirements/recommendations for international students: Required—TOEFL, TWE. *Application deadline:* For fall admission, 8/1 for domestic students, 7/1 for international students; for spring admission, 12/1 for domestic students, 11/1 for international students. Applications are processed on a rolling basis. Application fee: $25 ($50 for international students). *Expenses:* Tuition, state resident: full-time $5430; part-time $272 per credit hour. Tuition, nonresident: full-time $11,540; part-time $577 per credit hour. *Required fees:* $1916. *Financial support:* In 2011–12, 6 students received support, including 5 teaching assistantships with partial tuition reimbursements available (averaging $9,000 per year); tuition waivers (partial) and unspecified assistantships also available. Financial award application deadline: 4/1. *Faculty research:* Environmental chemistry, surface chemistry, polymer chemistry, organic synthesis, computational chemistry. *Unit head:* Dr. Richard S. Lumpkin, Chair, 409-880-8267, Fax: 409-880-8270, E-mail: lumpkines@hal.lamar.edu. *Application contact:* Dr. Paul Bernazzani, Graduate Advisor, 409-880-8272, Fax: 409-880-8270, E-mail: bernazzapx@hal.lamar.edu.

Laurentian University, School of Graduate Studies and Research, Programme in Chemistry and Biochemistry, Sudbury, ON P3E 2C6, Canada. Offers analytical chemistry (M Sc); biochemistry (M Sc); environmental chemistry (M Sc); organic chemistry (M Sc); physical/theoretical chemistry (M Sc). Part-time programs available. *Degree requirements:* For master's, thesis or alternative. *Entrance requirements:* For master's, honors degree with minimum second class. *Faculty research:* Cell cycle checkpoints, kinetic modeling, toxicology to metal stress, quantum chemistry, biogeochemistry metal speciation.

Lehigh University, College of Arts and Sciences, Department of Chemistry, Bethlehem, PA 18015. Offers MS, PhD. Part-time programs available. Postbaccalaureate distance learning degree programs offered (no on-campus study). *Faculty:* 16 full-time (2 women), 2 part-time/adjunct (1 woman). *Students:* 38 full-time (19 women), 74 part-time (35 women); includes 12 minority (4 Black or African American, non-Hispanic/Latino; 1 American Indian or Alaska Native, non-Hispanic/Latino; 6 Asian, non-Hispanic/Latino; 1 Hispanic/Latino), 13 international. Average age 30. 93 applicants, 32% accepted, 26 enrolled. In 2011,

Peterson's Graduate Programs in the Physical Sciences, Mathematics, Agricultural Sciences, the Environment & Natural Resources 2013

facebook.com/petersonspublishing **69**

Chemistry

41 master's, 8 doctorates awarded. Terminal master's awarded for partial completion of doctoral program. *Degree requirements:* For master's, comprehensive exam, thesis; for doctorate, comprehensive exam, thesis/dissertation. *Entrance requirements:* Additional exam requirements/recommendations for international students: Required—TOEFL (minimum score 230 computer-based; 85 iBT). *Application deadline:* For fall admission, 1/15 priority date for domestic students, 1/15 for international students. Applications are processed on a rolling basis. Application fee: $75. Electronic applications accepted. *Financial support:* In 2011–12, 3 fellowships with full tuition reimbursements (averaging $25,000 per year), 8 research assistantships with full tuition reimbursements (averaging $25,000 per year), 19 teaching assistantships with full tuition reimbursements (averaging $25,000 per year) were awarded; career-related internships or fieldwork, Federal Work-Study, institutionally sponsored loans, scholarships/grants, tuition waivers (full and partial), and unspecified assistantships also available. Support available to part-time students. Financial award application deadline: 1/15. *Faculty research:* Materials chemistry, biological chemistry, surface chemistry, nano science. *Total annual research expenditures:* $3.1 million. *Unit head:* Prof. Robert A. Flowers, II, Professor/Chair, 610-758-3470, Fax: 610-758-6536, E-mail: rof2@lehigh.edu. *Application contact:* Dr. Rebecca Miller, Graduate Coordinator, 610-758-3471, Fax: 610-758-6536, E-mail: inluchem@lehigh.edu. Web site: http://www.lehigh.edu/chemistry.

Long Island University–Brooklyn Campus, Richard L. Conolly College of Liberal Arts and Sciences, Department of Chemistry, Brooklyn, NY 11201-8423. Offers MS. Part-time and evening/weekend programs available. *Degree requirements:* For master's, thesis or alternative. *Entrance requirements:* For master's, 2 letters of recommendation. Additional exam requirements/recommendations for international students: Required—TOEFL (minimum score 500 paper-based; 173 computer-based). Electronic applications accepted. *Faculty research:* Clinical chemistry, free radicals, heats of hydrogenation.

Louisiana State University and Agricultural and Mechanical College, Graduate School, College of Science, Department of Chemistry, Baton Rouge, LA 70803. Offers MS, PhD. Part-time programs available. *Faculty:* 27 full-time (6 women). *Students:* 152 full-time (63 women), 9 part-time (5 women); includes 43 minority (32 Black or African American, non-Hispanic/Latino; 6 Asian, non-Hispanic/Latino; 4 Hispanic/Latino; 1 Two or more races, non-Hispanic/Latino), 67 international. Average age 28. 157 applicants, 32% accepted, 31 enrolled. In 2011, 4 master's, 19 doctorates awarded. Terminal master's awarded for partial completion of doctoral program. *Degree requirements:* For master's, thesis (for some programs); for doctorate, thesis/dissertation, general exam. *Entrance requirements:* For master's and doctorate, GRE General Test, minimum GPA of 3.0. Additional exam requirements/recommendations for international students: Required—TOEFL (minimum score 550 paper-based; 213 computer-based; 79 iBT) or IELTS (minimum score 6.5). *Application deadline:* For fall admission, 3/1 priority date for domestic students, 5/15 for international students; for spring admission, 8/1 for domestic students, 10/15 for international students. Applications are processed on a rolling basis. Application fee: $25. Electronic applications accepted. *Financial support:* In 2011–12, 154 students received support, including 18 fellowships with full tuition reimbursements available (averaging $21,760 per year), 58 research assistantships with full and partial tuition reimbursements available (averaging $22,215 per year), 73 teaching assistantships with full and partial tuition reimbursements available (averaging $22,077 per year); career-related internships or fieldwork, Federal Work-Study, scholarships/grants, traineeships, and unspecified assistantships also available. Support available to part-time students. Financial award application deadline: 7/1; financial award applicants required to submit FAFSA. *Faculty research:* Materials, biological, environmental. *Total annual research expenditures:* $7.4 million. *Unit head:* Dr. Andrew Maverick, Chair, 225-578-3465, Fax: 225-578-3458, E-mail: maverick@lsu.edu. *Application contact:* Dr. John Pojman, Director of Graduate Studies, 225-578-7202, Fax: 225-578-3458, E-mail: japojman@lsu.edu. Web site: http://chemistry.lsu.edu/.

Louisiana Tech University, Graduate School, College of Engineering and Science, Department of Chemistry, Ruston, LA 71272. Offers MS. Part-time programs available. *Degree requirements:* For master's, thesis. *Entrance requirements:* For master's, GRE General Test, minimum GPA of 3.0 in last 60 hours. Additional exam requirements/recommendations for international students: Required—TOEFL. *Faculty research:* Vibrational spectroscopy, quantum studies of chemical reactions, enzyme kinetics, synthesis of transition metal compounds, NMR spectrometry.

Loyola University Chicago, Graduate School, Department of Chemistry, Chicago, IL 60660. Offers MS, PhD. Part-time and evening/weekend programs available. *Faculty:* 14 full-time (2 women). *Students:* 32 full-time (15 women), 8 part-time (3 women); includes 8 minority (3 Black or African American, non-Hispanic/Latino; 3 Asian, non-Hispanic/Latino; 1 Native Hawaiian or other Pacific Islander, non-Hispanic/Latino; 1 Two or more races, non-Hispanic/Latino), 7 international. Average age 29. 67 applicants, 31% accepted, 10 enrolled. In 2011, 6 master's, 1 doctorate awarded. Terminal master's awarded for partial completion of doctoral program. *Degree requirements:* For master's, thesis (for some programs); for doctorate, comprehensive exam, thesis/dissertation. *Entrance requirements:* For master's and doctorate, GRE General Test, GRE Subject Test. Additional exam requirements/recommendations for international students: Required—TOEFL (minimum score 550 paper-based; 213 computer-based). *Application deadline:* For fall admission, 8/1 priority date for domestic students; for spring admission, 12/1 for domestic students. Applications are

70 facebook.com/petersonspublishing

Peterson's Graduate Programs in the Physical Sciences, Mathematics, Agricultural Sciences, the Environment & Natural Resources 2013

processed on a rolling basis. Application fee: $50. Electronic applications accepted. Application fee is waived when completed online. *Expenses: Tuition:* Full-time $15,660; part-time $870 per credit hour. *Required fees:* $125 per semester. Tuition and fees vary according to course load and program. *Financial support:* In 2011–12, 19 students received support, including 3 fellowships with full tuition reimbursements available (averaging $22,000 per year), 6 research assistantships with full and partial tuition reimbursements available (averaging $22,000 per year), 16 teaching assistantships with full tuition reimbursements available (averaging $22,000 per year); Federal Work-Study, scholarships/grants, traineeships, and unspecified assistantships also available. Financial award application deadline: 2/1; financial award applicants required to submit FAFSA. *Faculty research:* Magnetic resonance of membrane/protein systems, organometallic catalysis, novel synthesis of natural products. *Total annual research expenditures:* $682,510. *Unit head:* Dr. Duarte Freitas, Chair, 773-508-7045, Fax: 773-508-3086, E-mail: dfreita@luc.edu. *Application contact:* Stacey N. Lind, Graduate Program Coordinator, 773-508-3104, Fax: 773-508-3086, E-mail: slind@luc.edu. Web site: http://www.luc.edu/chemistry/.

Marquette University, Graduate School, College of Arts and Sciences, Department of Chemistry, Milwaukee, WI 53201-1881. Offers analytical chemistry (MS, PhD); bioanalytical chemistry (MS, PhD); biophysical chemistry (MS, PhD); chemical physics (MS, PhD); inorganic chemistry (MS, PhD); organic chemistry (MS, PhD); physical chemistry (MS, PhD). Part-time programs available. *Faculty:* 29 full-time (4 women), 1 (woman) part-time/adjunct. *Students:* 42 full-time (11 women), 2 part-time (0 women); includes 5 minority (2 Black or African American, non-Hispanic/Latino; 3 Asian, non-Hispanic/Latino), 31 international. Average age 29. 18 applicants, 100% accepted, 10 enrolled. In 2011, 5 master's, 7 doctorates awarded. Terminal master's awarded for partial completion of doctoral program. *Degree requirements:* For master's, comprehensive exam; for doctorate, thesis/dissertation, cumulative exams. *Entrance requirements:* For master's and doctorate, official transcripts from all current and previous colleges/universities except Marquette, three letters of recommendation from individuals familiar with the applicant's academic work. Additional exam requirements/recommendations for international students: Required—TOEFL (minimum score 530 paper-based; 78 computer-based). *Application deadline:* Applications are processed on a rolling basis. Application fee: $50. Electronic applications accepted. *Expenses: Tuition:* Full-time $17,010; part-time $945 per credit hour. Tuition and fees vary according to program. *Financial support:* In 2011–12, 41 students received support, including 2 fellowships (averaging $17,134 per year), 30 teaching assistantships with full tuition reimbursements available (averaging $20,295 per year); research assistantships, scholarships/grants, health care benefits, tuition waivers (full and partial), and unspecified assistantships also available. Support available to part-time students. Financial award application deadline: 2/15. *Faculty research:* Inorganic complexes, laser Raman spectroscopy, organic synthesis, synthetic bioinorganic chemistry, electro-active organic molecules. *Total annual research expenditures:* $2.1 million. *Unit head:* Dr. Michael Ryan, Chair, 414-288-3537, Fax: 414-288-7066. *Application contact:* Dr. Mark Steinmetz, Director of Graduate Studies, 414-288-7374, Fax: 414-288-7066. Web site: http://www.marquette.edu/chem/graduate.shtml.

Marshall University, Academic Affairs Division, College of Science, Department of Chemistry, Huntington, WV 25755. Offers MS. *Faculty:* 10 full-time (3 women). *Students:* 3 full-time (1 women), 1 (woman) part-time, 1 international. Average age 29. In 2011, 3 master's awarded. *Degree requirements:* For master's, thesis. Application fee: $40. *Financial support:* Career-related internships or fieldwork available. *Unit head:* Dr. Michael Casteliani, Chairperson, 304-696-6486, E-mail: castella@marshall.edu. *Application contact:* Dr. John Hubbard, Information Contact, 304-696-2430, Fax: 304-746-1902, E-mail: hubbard@marshall.edu.

Massachusetts College of Pharmacy and Health Sciences, Graduate Studies, Program in Medicinal Chemistry, Boston, MA 02115-5896. Offers MS, PhD. *Students:* 5 full-time (1 woman), 1 (woman) part-time, all international. Average age 29. 14 applicants, 21% accepted, 1 enrolled. In 2011, 2 master's awarded. Terminal master's awarded for partial completion of doctoral program. *Degree requirements:* For master's, thesis, oral defense of thesis; for doctorate, one foreign language, comprehensive exam, thesis/dissertation, oral defense of dissertation, qualifying exam. *Entrance requirements:* For master's and doctorate, GRE General Test, minimum GPA of 3.0. Additional exam requirements/recommendations for international students: Required—TOEFL (minimum score 550 paper-based; 213 computer-based; 79 iBT). *Application deadline:* For fall admission, 2/1 priority date for domestic students, 2/1 for international students. Application fee: $70. Electronic applications accepted. *Expenses: Tuition:* Full-time $30,200; part-time $945 per credit hour. *Financial support:* Fellowships with partial tuition reimbursements, research assistantships with partial tuition reimbursements, teaching assistantships with full tuition reimbursements, tuition waivers (partial), and unspecified assistantships available. Financial award application deadline: 3/15. *Faculty research:* Analytical chemistry, medicinal chemistry, organic chemistry, neurochemistry. *Unit head:* Dr. Ahmed Mehanna, Professor, 617-732-2955, E-mail: ahmed.mehanna@mcphs.edu. *Application contact:* Brian Barilone, Coordinator of Graduate Admission, 617-879-5032, E-mail: admissions@mcphs.edu.

Massachusetts Institute of Technology, School of Science, Department of Chemistry, Cambridge, MA 02139. Offers biological chemistry (PhD, Sc D); inorganic chemistry (PhD, Sc D); organic chemistry (PhD, Sc D); physical chemistry (PhD, Sc D). *Faculty:* 26 full-time (5 women). *Students:* 221 full-time (73 women), 1 (woman) part-time; includes 48 minority (5 Black or African American,

non-Hispanic/Latino; 1 American Indian or Alaska Native, non-Hispanic/Latino; 24 Asian, non-Hispanic/Latino; 14 Hispanic/Latino; 4 Two or more races, non-Hispanic/Latino), 64 international. Average age 25. 570 applicants, 20% accepted, 43 enrolled. In 2011, 45 doctorates awarded. *Degree requirements:* For doctorate, comprehensive exam, thesis/dissertation. *Entrance requirements:* For doctorate, GRE General Test. Additional exam requirements/recommendations for international students: Required—IELTS (minimum score 7); Recommended—TOEFL (minimum score 600 paper-based; 250 computer-based). *Application deadline:* For fall admission, 12/15 for domestic and international students. Application fee: $75. Electronic applications accepted. *Expenses: Tuition:* Full-time $40,460; part-time $630 per credit hour. *Required fees:* $272. *Financial support:* In 2011–12, 216 students received support, including 79 fellowships (averaging $34,800 per year), 127 research assistantships (averaging $31,400 per year), 16 teaching assistantships (averaging $32,600 per year); Federal Work-Study, institutionally sponsored loans, scholarships/grants, traineeships, health care benefits, and unspecified assistantships also available. *Faculty research:* Synthetic organic and organometallic chemistry including catalysis; biological chemistry including bioorganic chemistry; physical chemistry including chemical dynamics and biophysical chemistry; inorganic chemistry including synthesis, catalysis, bioinorganic and physical inorganic chemistry; materials chemistry including surface science, nanoscience and polymers. *Total annual research expenditures:* $31.1 million. *Unit head:* Prof. Sylvia T. Ceyer, Head, 617-253-1803, Fax: 617-258-7500. *Application contact:* Graduate Administrator, 617-253-1845, Fax: 617-258-0241, E-mail: chemgradeducation@mit.edu. Web site: http://web.mit.edu/chemistry/www/.

McGill University, Faculty of Graduate and Postdoctoral Studies, Faculty of Science, Department of Chemistry, Montréal, QC H3A 2T5, Canada. Offers chemical biology (M Sc, PhD); chemistry (M Sc, PhD).

McMaster University, School of Graduate Studies, Faculty of Science, Department of Chemistry, Hamilton, ON L8S 4M2, Canada. Offers analytical chemistry (M Sc, PhD); chemical physics (M Sc, PhD); chemistry (M Sc, PhD); inorganic chemistry (M Sc, PhD); organic chemistry (M Sc, PhD); physical chemistry (M Sc, PhD); polymer chemistry (M Sc, PhD). Part-time programs available. Terminal master's awarded for partial completion of doctoral program. *Degree requirements:* For master's, thesis; for doctorate, comprehensive exam, thesis/dissertation. *Entrance requirements:* For master's, minimum B+ average. Additional exam requirements/recommendations for international students: Required—TOEFL (minimum score 550 paper-based; 213 computer-based).

McNeese State University, Doré School of Graduate Studies, College of Science, Department of Chemistry, Program in Environmental and Chemical Sciences, Lake Charles, LA 70609. Offers chemistry (MS); chemistry/environmental science education (MS). Evening/weekend programs available. *Faculty:* 4 full-time (0 women). *Students:* 15 full-time (6 women), 2 part-time (1 woman); includes 4 minority (3 Black or African American, non-Hispanic/Latino; 1 Asian, non-Hispanic/Latino), 11 international. In 2011, 6 master's awarded. *Degree requirements:* For master's, comprehensive exam, thesis or alternative. *Entrance requirements:* For master's, GRE. *Application deadline:* For fall admission, 5/15 priority date for domestic students, 5/15 for international students; for spring admission, 10/15 priority date for domestic students, 10/15 for international students. Applications are processed on a rolling basis. Application fee: $20 ($30 for international students). *Expenses:* Tuition, state resident: part-time $519 per credit hour. Tuition and fees vary according to course load. *Financial support:* Application deadline: 5/1. *Unit head:* Dr. Bruce C. Wyman, Coordinator, 337-475-5669, Fax: 337-475-5677, E-mail: wyman@mcneese.edu. *Application contact:* Dr. Bruce C. Wyman, Coordinator, 337-475-5669, Fax: 337-475-5677, E-mail: wyman@mcneese.edu.

Memorial University of Newfoundland, School of Graduate Studies, Department of Chemistry, St. John's, NL A1C 5S7, Canada. Offers chemistry (M Sc, PhD); instrumental analysis (M Sc). Part-time programs available. *Degree requirements:* For master's, thesis, research seminar, American Chemical Society Exam; for doctorate, comprehensive exam, thesis/dissertation, seminars, oral thesis defense, American Chemical Society Exam. *Entrance requirements:* For master's, B Sc or honors degree in chemistry (preferred); for doctorate, master's degree in chemistry or honors bachelor's degree. Electronic applications accepted. *Faculty research:* Analytical/environmental chemistry; medicinal electrochemistry; inorganic, marine, organic, physical, and theoretical/computational chemistry, environmental science and instrumental analysis.

Miami University, College of Arts and Science, Department of Chemistry and Biochemistry, Oxford, OH 45056. Offers MS, PhD. *Students:* 67 full-time (32 women), 1 part-time (0 women); includes 5 minority (1 Black or African American, non-Hispanic/Latino; 3 Asian, non-Hispanic/Latino; 1 Hispanic/Latino), 30 international. Average age 26. In 2011, 3 master's, 4 doctorates awarded. *Entrance requirements:* For master's, GRE General Test; GRE Subject Test (recommended), minimum undergraduate GPA of 3.0 during previous 2 years or 2.75 overall; for doctorate, GRE General Test, minimum undergraduate GPA of 2.75, 3.0 graduate. Additional exam requirements/recommendations for international students: Required—TOEFL. *Application deadline:* Applications are processed on a rolling basis. Application fee: $50. Electronic applications accepted. *Expenses:* Tuition, state resident: full-time $12,023; part-time $501 per credit hour. Tuition, nonresident: full-time $26,554; part-time $1107 per credit hour. *Required fees:* $528. *Financial support:* Fellowships with full tuition reimbursements, research assistantships with full tuition reimbursements,

Peterson's Graduate Programs in the Physical Sciences, Mathematics, Agricultural Sciences, the Environment & Natural Resources 2013

facebook.com/petersonspublishing **71**

teaching assistantships with full tuition reimbursements, Federal Work-Study, institutionally sponsored loans, tuition waivers (full), and unspecified assistantships available. Financial award application deadline: 2/15; financial award applicants required to submit FAFSA. *Unit head:* Dr. Chris Makaroff, Chair, 513-529-1659, E-mail: makaroca@muohio.edu. *Application contact:* Dr. Stacey Lowery Bretz, Professor, 513-529-3731, E-mail: bretzsl@muohio.edu. Web site: http://chemistry.muohio.edu/.

Michigan State University, The Graduate School, College of Natural Science, Department of Chemistry, East Lansing, MI 48824. Offers chemical physics (PhD); chemistry (MS, PhD); chemistry-environmental toxicology (PhD); computational chemistry (MS). *Entrance requirements:* Additional exam requirements/recommendations for international students: Required—TOEFL. Electronic applications accepted. *Faculty research:* Analytical chemistry, inorganic and organic chemistry, nuclear chemistry, physical chemistry, theoretical and computational chemistry.

Michigan State University, National Superconducting Cyclotron Laboratory, East Lansing, MI 48824. Offers chemistry (PhD); physics (PhD).

Michigan Technological University, Graduate School, College of Sciences and Arts, Department of Chemistry, Houghton, MI 49931. Offers MS, PhD. Part-time programs available. *Faculty:* 23 full-time (8 women), 1 part-time/adjunct (0 women). *Students:* 33 full-time (18 women), 4 part-time (0 women); includes 2 minority (both Black or African American, non-Hispanic/Latino), 25 international. Average age 27. 106 applicants, 13% accepted, 9 enrolled. In 2011, 2 master's, 3 doctorates awarded. Terminal master's awarded for partial completion of doctoral program. *Degree requirements:* For master's, comprehensive exam (for some programs), thesis (for some programs); for doctorate, comprehensive exam, thesis/dissertation. *Entrance requirements:* For master's and doctorate, GRE, statement of purpose, official transcripts, 3 letters of recommendation. Additional exam requirements/recommendations for international students: Required—TOEFL (minimum score 79 iBT) or IELTS. *Application deadline:* Applications are processed on a rolling basis. Electronic applications accepted. *Expenses:* Tuition, state resident: full-time $12,636; part-time $702 per credit. Tuition, nonresident: full-time $12,636; part-time $702 per credit. *Required fees:* $226; $226 per year. *Financial support:* In 2011–12, 32 students received support, including fellowships with full tuition reimbursements available (averaging $6,065 per year), 2 research assistantships with full tuition reimbursements available (averaging $6,065 per year), 26 teaching assistantships with full tuition reimbursements available (averaging $6,065 per year); career-related internships or fieldwork, Federal Work-Study, scholarships/grants, health care benefits, tuition waivers (partial), unspecified assistantships, and cooperative program also available. Financial award applicants required to submit FAFSA. *Faculty research:* Inorganic chemistry, physical/theoretical chemistry, bio/organic chemistry, polymer/materials chemistry, analytical/environmental chemistry. *Total annual research expenditures:* $534,022. *Unit head:* Dr. Sarah A. Green, Chair, 906-487-2048, Fax: 906-487-2061, E-mail: sgreen@mtu.edu. *Application contact:* Celine Grace, Graduate Program Assistant, 906-487-2048, Fax: 906-487-2061, E-mail: cegrace@mtu.edu. Web site: http://www.chemistry.mtu.edu/.

Middle Tennessee State University, College of Graduate Studies, College of Basic and Applied Sciences, Department of Chemistry, Murfreesboro, TN 37132. Offers MS, DA. Part-time and evening/weekend programs available. Postbaccalaureate distance learning degree programs offered. *Faculty:* 23 full-time (5 women). *Students:* 30 part-time (15 women); includes 14 minority (5 Black or African American, non-Hispanic/Latino; 9 Asian, non-Hispanic/Latino). Average age 28. 47 applicants, 38% accepted. In 2011, 3 master's, 1 doctorate awarded. *Degree requirements:* For master's, comprehensive exam, thesis. *Entrance requirements:* For master's and doctorate, GRE. Additional exam requirements/recommendations for international students: Required—TOEFL (minimum score 525 paper-based; 195 computer-based; 71 iBT) or IELTS (minimum score 6). *Application deadline:* For fall admission, 6/1 for domestic and international students. Applications are processed on a rolling basis. Application fee: $25 ($30 for international students). Electronic applications accepted. *Expenses:* Tuition, state resident: full-time $10,008. Tuition, nonresident: full-time $25,056. *Financial support:* In 2011–12, 25 students received support. Tuition waivers available. Support available to part-time students. Financial award application deadline: 5/1; financial award applicants required to submit FAFSA. *Faculty research:* Chemical education. *Unit head:* Dr. Paul G. Van Patten, Chair, 615-898-2956, Fax: 615-494-7693. *Application contact:* Dr. Michael D. Allen, Dean and Vice Provost for Research, 615-898-2840, Fax: 615-904-8020, E-mail: michael.allen@mtsu.edu.

Mississippi College, Graduate School, College of Arts and Sciences, School of Science and Mathematics, Department of Chemistry and Biochemistry, Clinton, MS 39058. Offers MCS, MS. Part-time programs available. *Degree requirements:* For master's, comprehensive exam, thesis (for some programs). *Entrance requirements:* For master's, GRE. Additional exam requirements/recommendations for international students: Recommended—TOEFL, IELTS. Electronic applications accepted.

Mississippi State University, College of Arts and Sciences, Department of Chemistry, Mississippi State, MS 39762. Offers MS, PhD. MA program only available online. *Faculty:* 12 full-time (0 women), 1 part-time/adjunct (0 women). *Students:* 51 full-time (18 women), 8 part-time (2 women); includes 3 minority (1 Black or African American, non-Hispanic/Latino; 1 Asian, non-Hispanic/Latino; 1 Hispanic/Latino), 45 international. Average age 30. 132 applicants, 11% accepted, 12 enrolled. In 2011, 4 master's, 6 doctorates awarded. Terminal

master's awarded for partial completion of doctoral program. *Degree requirements:* For master's, thesis, comprehensive oral or written exam; for doctorate, thesis/dissertation, comprehensive oral or written exam. *Entrance requirements:* For master's, minimum GPA of 2.75 on last two years of undergraduate courses; for doctorate, minimum GPA of 2.75. Additional exam requirements/recommendations for international students: Required—TOEFL (minimum score 475 paper-based; 153 computer-based). *Application deadline:* For fall admission, 7/1 for domestic students, 5/1 for international students; for spring admission, 11/1 for domestic students, 9/1 for international students. Applications are processed on a rolling basis. Application fee: $40. Electronic applications accepted. *Expenses:* Tuition, state resident: full-time $5805; part-time $322.50 per credit hour. Tuition, nonresident: full-time $14,670; part-time $815 per credit hour. *Financial support:* In 2011–12, 5 research assistantships with full tuition reimbursements (averaging $16,851 per year), 42 teaching assistantships with full tuition reimbursements (averaging $17,529 per year) were awarded; Federal Work-Study, institutionally sponsored loans, scholarships/grants, and unspecified assistantships also available. Financial award application deadline: 4/1; financial award applicants required to submit FAFSA. *Faculty research:* Spectroscopy, fluorometry, organic and inorganic synthesis, electrochemistry. *Total annual research expenditures:* $4.3 million. *Unit head:* Dr. Edwin A. Lewis, Department Head, 662-325-3584, Fax: 662-325-1618, E-mail: elewis@chemistry.msstate.edu. *Application contact:* Dr. Stephen Foster, Graduate Coordinator, 662-325-8854, E-mail: grad@chemistry.msstate.edu. Web site: http://www.chemistry.msstate.edu/graduate/.

Missouri State University, Graduate College, College of Natural and Applied Sciences, Department of Chemistry, Springfield, MO 65897. Offers chemistry (MS); natural and applied science (MNAS), including chemistry (MNAS, MS Ed); secondary education (MS Ed), including chemistry (MNAS, MS Ed). Part-time programs available. *Students:* 15 full-time (2 women), 7 part-time (3 women); includes 1 minority (Black or African American, non-Hispanic/Latino), 6 international. Average age 31. 16 applicants, 38% accepted, 4 enrolled. In 2011, 5 master's awarded. *Degree requirements:* For master's, comprehensive exam, thesis. *Entrance requirements:* For master's, GRE General Test (MS, MNAS), minimum undergraduate GPA of 3.0 (MS and MNAS), 9-12 teacher certification (MS Ed). Additional exam requirements/recommendations for international students: Required—TOEFL (minimum score 550 paper-based; 213 computer-based; 79 iBT). *Application deadline:* For fall admission, 7/20 priority date for domestic students, 5/1 for international students; for spring admission, 12/20 priority date for domestic students, 9/1 for international students. Applications are processed on a rolling basis. Application fee: $35 ($50 for international students). Electronic applications accepted. *Expenses:* Tuition, state resident: full-time $4086; part-time $227 per credit hour. Tuition, nonresident: full-time $8172; part-time $454 per credit hour. *Required fees:* $275 per semester. Tuition and fees vary according to course load, campus/location and program. *Financial support:* In 2011–12, 1 research assistantship with full tuition reimbursement (averaging $8,865 per year), 4 teaching assistantships with full tuition reimbursements (averaging $9,730 per year) were awarded; Federal Work-Study, institutionally sponsored loans, scholarships/grants, and unspecified assistantships also available. Financial award application deadline: 3/31; financial award applicants required to submit FAFSA. *Faculty research:* Polyethylene glycol derivatives, electrochemiluminescence of environmental systems, enzymology, environmental organic pollutants, DNA repair via NMR. *Unit head:* Dr. Alan Schick, Department Head, 417-836-5506, Fax: 417-836-5507, E-mail: chemistry@missouristate.edu. *Application contact:* Misty Stewart, Coordinator of Graduate Recruitment, 417-836-6079, Fax: 417-836-6200, E-mail: mistystewart@missouristate.edu. Web site: http://chemistry.missouristate.edu/.

Missouri University of Science and Technology, Graduate School, Department of Chemistry, Rolla, MO 65409. Offers MS, MST, PhD. Terminal master's awarded for partial completion of doctoral program. *Degree requirements:* For doctorate, one foreign language, thesis/dissertation. *Entrance requirements:* For master's, GRE (minimum score 600 quantitative, 3 writing), minimum GPA of 3.0; for doctorate, GRE (minimum score: quantitative 600, writing 3.5), minimum GPA of 3.0. Additional exam requirements/recommendations for international students: Required—TOEFL (minimum score 550 paper-based; 213 computer-based). Electronic applications accepted. *Faculty research:* Structure and properties of materials; bioanalytical, environmental, and polymer chemistry.

Missouri Western State University, Program in Applied Science, St. Joseph, MO 64507-2294. Offers chemistry (MAS); engineering technology management (MAS); human factors and usability testing (MAS); information technology management (MAS). Part-time programs available. *Application deadline:* For fall admission, 7/15 for domestic and international students; for spring admission, 10/1 for domestic and international students. Electronic applications accepted. *Expenses:* Tuition, state resident: full-time $4697; part-time $261 per credit hour. Tuition, nonresident: full-time $9355; part-time $520 per credit hour. *Required fees:* $343; $19.10 per credit hour. $30 per semester. Tuition and fees vary according to course load. *Application contact:* Dr. Brian C. Cronk, Dean of the Graduate School, 816-271-4394, E-mail: graduate@missouriwestern.edu.

Montana State University, College of Graduate Studies, College of Letters and Science, Department of Chemistry and Biochemistry, Bozeman, MT 59717. Offers biochemistry (MS, PhD); chemistry (MS, PhD). Part-time programs available. *Degree requirements:* For master's, comprehensive exam, thesis (for some

72 facebook.com/petersonspublishing

Peterson's Graduate Programs in the Physical Sciences, Mathematics, Agricultural Sciences, the Environment & Natural Resources 2013

programs); for doctorate, comprehensive exam, thesis/dissertation. *Entrance requirements:* For master's and doctorate, GRE General Test, transcripts, letter of recommendation. Additional exam requirements/recommendations for international students: Required—TOEFL (minimum score 550 paper-based; 213 computer-based). Electronic applications accepted. *Faculty research:* Proteomics, nano-materials chemistry, computational chemistry, optical spectroscopy, photochemistry,.

Montclair State University, The Graduate School, College of Science and Mathematics, Department of Chemistry and Biochemistry, Program in Chemistry, Montclair, NJ 07043-1624. Offers MS. *Students:* 8 full-time (4 women), 10 part-time (8 women); includes 3 minority (1 Black or African American, non-Hispanic/Latino; 2 Hispanic/Latino), 1 international. Average age 28. 29 applicants, 17% accepted, 4 enrolled. In 2011, 13 master's awarded. *Degree requirements:* For master's, thesis. *Entrance requirements:* For master's, GRE General Test, 24 undergraduate credits in chemistry, 2 letters of recommendation, essay. Additional exam requirements/recommendations for international students: Required—TOEFL (minimum score 83 iBT), IELTS (minimum score 6.5). *Application deadline:* Applications are processed on a rolling basis. Application fee: $60. Electronic applications accepted. *Financial support:* Federal Work-Study, scholarships/grants, and unspecified assistantships available. Support available to part-time students. Financial award application deadline: 3/1; financial award applicants required to submit FAFSA. *Faculty research:* Computational chemistry, nanochemistry, pharmaceutical biochemistry, medicinal chemistry, biophysical chemistry. *Unit head:* Dr. Marc Kasner, Chair, 973-655-6864. *Application contact:* Amy Aiello, Executive Director of The Graduate School, 973-655-5147, Fax: 973-973-7869, E-mail: graduate.school@montclair.edu. Web site: http://www.montclair.edu/csam/chemistry-biochemistry/graduate-programs/master-science-chemistry/.

Morgan State University, School of Graduate Studies, School of Computer, Mathematical, and Natural Sciences, Department of Chemistry, Baltimore, MD 21251. Offers MS. *Degree requirements:* For master's, comprehensive exam, thesis, oral defense of thesis. *Entrance requirements:* For master's, GRE General Test, minimum GPA of 2.5.

Mount Allison University, Department of Chemistry, Sackville, NB E4L 1E4, Canada. Offers M Sc. *Degree requirements:* For master's, thesis. *Entrance requirements:* For master's, honors degree in chemistry. *Faculty research:* Biophysical chemistry of model biomembranes, organic synthesis, fast-reaction kinetics, physical chemistry of micelles.

Murray State University, College of Science, Engineering and Technology, Program in Chemistry, Murray, KY 42071. Offers MS. Part-time programs available. *Degree requirements:* For master's, comprehensive exam (for some programs), thesis (for some programs). *Entrance requirements:* For master's, GRE General Test. Additional exam requirements/recommendations for international students: Required—TOEFL. *Faculty research:* Environmental, organic, biochemistry, analytical.

New Jersey Institute of Technology, Office of Graduate Studies, College of Science and Liberal Arts, Department of Chemistry and Environmental Science, Program in Chemistry, Newark, NJ 07102. Offers MS, PhD. Part-time and evening/weekend programs available. *Students:* 32 full-time (19 women), 13 part-time (7 women); includes 7 minority (2 Black or African American, non-Hispanic/Latino; 4 Asian, non-Hispanic/Latino; 1 Hispanic/Latino), 30 international. Average age 27. 77 applicants, 47% accepted, 11 enrolled. In 2011, 10 master's, 3 doctorates awarded. Terminal master's awarded for partial completion of doctoral program. *Degree requirements:* For master's, thesis optional; for doctorate, thesis/dissertation. *Entrance requirements:* For master's, GRE General Test; for doctorate, GRE General Test, minimum graduate GPA of 3.5. Additional exam requirements/recommendations for international students: Required—TOEFL (minimum score 550 paper-based; 213 computer-based; 79 iBT). *Application deadline:* For fall admission, 6/1 priority date for domestic students, 5/1 for international students; for spring admission, 11/15 priority date for domestic students, 11/15 for international students. Applications are processed on a rolling basis. Application fee: $65. Electronic applications accepted. *Expenses:* Tuition, state resident: full-time $7980; part-time $867 per credit. Tuition, nonresident: full-time $11,336; part-time $1196 per credit. *Required fees:* $230 per credit. *Financial support:* Fellowships with full and partial tuition reimbursements, research assistantships with full and partial tuition reimbursements, teaching assistantships with full and partial tuition reimbursements, career-related internships or fieldwork, Federal Work-Study, institutionally sponsored loans, and unspecified assistantships available. Financial award application deadline: 1/15. *Faculty research:* Medical instrumentation, prosthesis design, biodegradation of hazardous waste, orthopedic biomechanics, image processing. *Unit head:* Dr. Somenath Mitra, Chair, 973-596-5611, E-mail: somenath.mitra@njit.edu. *Application contact:* Kathryn Kelly, Director of Admissions, 973-596-3300, Fax: 973-596-3461, E-mail: admissions@njit.edu.

New Mexico Highlands University, Graduate Studies, College of Arts and Sciences, Department of Biology, Chemistry, Natural Resource Management, Las Vegas, NM 87701. Offers chemistry (MS); life science (MS). Part-time programs available. *Faculty:* 14 full-time (6 women). *Students:* 21 full-time (7 women), 8 part-time (2 women); includes 16 minority (1 American Indian or Alaska Native, non-Hispanic/Latino; 15 Hispanic/Latino), 11 international. Average age 29. 30 applicants, 80% accepted, 10 enrolled. In 2011, 10 master's awarded. *Degree requirements:* For master's, comprehensive exam, thesis. *Entrance requirements:*

For master's, minimum undergraduate GPA of 3.0. Additional exam requirements/recommendations for international students: Required—TOEFL (minimum score 540 paper-based; 207 computer-based). *Application deadline:* For fall admission, 8/1 priority date for domestic students. Applications are processed on a rolling basis. Application fee: $15. *Expenses:* Tuition, state resident: full-time $2767; part-time $146 per credit hour. Tuition, nonresident: full-time $4879; part-time $234 per credit hour. *International tuition:* $5436 full-time. *Required fees:* $737. *Financial support:* In 2011–12, 17 students received support. Career-related internships or fieldwork, Federal Work-Study, institutionally sponsored loans, scholarships/grants, tuition waivers (full and partial), and unspecified assistantships available. Support available to part-time students. Financial award application deadline: 3/1. *Faculty research:* Invasive organisms in managed and wildland ecosystems, juniper and pinyon ecology and management, vegetation and community structure, big game management, quantitative forestry. *Unit head:* Dr. Mary Shaw, Department Head, 505-454-3407, E-mail: shaw_mary@nmhu.edu. *Application contact:* Diane Trujillo, Administrative Assistant, Graduate Studies, 505-454-3266, Fax: 505-426-2117, E-mail: dtrujillo@nmhu.edu.

New Mexico Institute of Mining and Technology, Graduate Studies, Department of Chemistry, Socorro, NM 87801. Offers MS, PhD. Part-time programs available. *Faculty:* 7 full-time (1 woman). *Students:* 15 full-time (5 women); includes 8 minority (1 Black or African American, non-Hispanic/Latino; 4 Asian, non-Hispanic/Latino; 2 Hispanic/Latino; 1 Two or more races, non-Hispanic/Latino). Average age 29. 19 applicants, 37% accepted, 4 enrolled. In 2011, 1 master's, 2 doctorates awarded. *Degree requirements:* For master's, thesis; for doctorate, thesis/dissertation. *Entrance requirements:* For master's, GRE General Test; for doctorate, GRE General Test, GRE Subject Test. Additional exam requirements/recommendations for international students: Required—TOEFL (minimum score 540 paper-based; 207 computer-based). *Application deadline:* For fall admission, 3/1 priority date for domestic students; for spring admission, 6/1 priority date for domestic students. Applications are processed on a rolling basis. Application fee: $16 ($30 for international students). Electronic applications accepted. *Expenses:* Tuition, state resident: full-time $4849; part-time $269.41 per credit hour. Tuition, nonresident: full-time $16,041; part-time $891.15 per credit hour. *Required fees:* $622; $65 per credit hour. $20 per semester. Part-time tuition and fees vary according to course load. *Financial support:* In 2011–12, 2 research assistantships (averaging $30,327 per year), 14 teaching assistantships with full and partial tuition reimbursements (averaging $32,990 per year) were awarded; fellowships, Federal Work-Study, institutionally sponsored loans, and unspecified assistantships also available. Financial award application deadline: 3/1; financial award applicants required to submit CSS PROFILE or FAFSA. *Faculty research:* Organic, analytical, environmental, and explosives chemistry. *Unit head:* Dr. Alexander Kornienko, Chair, 575-835-5263, Fax: 575-835-5364, E-mail: akornien@nmt.edu. *Application contact:* Dr. Lorie Liebrock, Dean of Graduate Studies, 575-835-5513, Fax: 575-835-5476, E-mail: graduate@nmt.edu. Web site: http://infohost.nmt.edu/~chem/.

New Mexico State University, Graduate School, College of Arts and Sciences, Department of Chemistry and Biochemistry, Las Cruces, NM 88003-8001. Offers chemistry (MS, PhD). Part-time programs available. *Faculty:* 18 full-time (3 women). *Students:* 46 full-time (10 women), 3 part-time (1 woman); includes 7 minority (1 American Indian or Alaska Native, non-Hispanic/Latino; 1 Asian, non-Hispanic/Latino; 4 Hispanic/Latino; 1 Native Hawaiian or other Pacific Islander, non-Hispanic/Latino), 36 international. Average age 31. 22 applicants, 23% accepted, 3 enrolled. In 2011, 8 master's, 3 doctorates awarded. *Degree requirements:* For master's, comprehensive exam, thesis; for doctorate, comprehensive exam, thesis/dissertation. *Entrance requirements:* For master's and doctorate, GRE, BS in chemistry or biochemistry, minimum GPA of 3.0. Additional exam requirements/recommendations for international students: Required—TOEFL (minimum score 550 paper-based; 0 computer-based; 79 iBT), IELTS (minimum score 6.5). *Application deadline:* For fall admission, 7/1 priority date for domestic students, 3/1 for international students; for spring admission, 11/1 for domestic students. Applications are processed on a rolling basis. Application fee: $40 ($50 for international students). Electronic applications accepted. *Expenses:* Tuition, state resident: full-time $5004; part-time $208.50 per credit. Tuition, nonresident: full-time $17,446; part-time $726.90 per credit. *Financial support:* In 2011–12, 8 fellowships (averaging $3,866 per year), 18 research assistantships (averaging $28,478 per year), 25 teaching assistantships (averaging $27,356 per year) were awarded; career-related internships or fieldwork, Federal Work-Study, health care benefits, and unspecified assistantships also available. Support available to part-time students. Financial award application deadline: 4/1. *Faculty research:* Clays, surfaces, and water structure; electroanalytical and environmental chemistry; organometallic synthesis and organobiomimetics; molecular genetics, DNA recombination mechanisms, and NMR spectroscopy of protein interactions; spectroscopy and reaction kinetics. *Total annual research expenditures:* $7.1 million. *Unit head:* Dr. William Quintana, Head, 575-646-5877, Fax: 575-646-2649, E-mail: wquintan@nmsu.edu. *Application contact:* Dr. Jeremy M. Smith, Associate Professor, Chemistry, 575-646-3346, Fax: 575-646-2649, E-mail: jesmith@nmsu.edu. Web site: http://www.chemistry.nmsu.edu/.

New York University, Graduate School of Arts and Science, Department of Chemistry, New York, NY 10012-1019. Offers MS, PhD. *Faculty:* 23 full-time (1 woman). *Students:* 111 full-time (44 women), 3 part-time (1 woman); includes 12 minority (1 Black or African American, non-Hispanic/Latino; 6 Asian, non-Hispanic/Latino; 4 Hispanic/Latino; 1 Two or more races, non-Hispanic/Latino), 71 international. Average age 27. 165 applicants, 37% accepted, 31 enrolled. In

Peterson's Graduate Programs in the Physical Sciences, Mathematics, Agricultural Sciences, the Environment & Natural Resources 2013

facebook.com/petersonspublishing **73**

Chemistry

2011, 20 master's, 7 doctorates awarded. *Degree requirements:* For master's, thesis or alternative; for doctorate, one foreign language, thesis/dissertation. *Entrance requirements:* For master's and doctorate, GRE General Test, GRE Subject Test. Additional exam requirements/recommendations for international students: Required—TOEFL. *Application deadline:* For fall admission, 12/12 for domestic and international students. Application fee: $90. *Financial support:* Fellowships with tuition reimbursements, research assistantships with tuition reimbursements, teaching assistantships with tuition reimbursements, career-related internships or fieldwork, Federal Work-Study, institutionally sponsored loans, scholarships/grants, health care benefits, and unspecified assistantships available. Financial award application deadline: 12/12; financial award applicants required to submit FAFSA. *Faculty research:* Biomolecular chemistry, theoretical and computational chemistry, physical chemistry, nanotechnology, bio-organic chemistry. *Unit head:* Michael Ward, Chair, 212-998-8400, Fax: 212-260-7905, E-mail: grad.chem@nyu.edu. *Application contact:* Marcus Weck, Director of Graduate Studies, 212-998-8400, Fax: 212-260-7905, E-mail: grad.chem@nyu.edu. Web site: http://www.nyu.edu/pages/chemistry/.

North Carolina Agricultural and Technical State University, School of Graduate Studies, College of Arts and Sciences, Department of Chemistry, Greensboro, NC 27411. Offers MS, PhD. Part-time and evening/weekend programs available. *Degree requirements:* For master's, comprehensive exam, thesis or alternative, qualifying exam. *Entrance requirements:* For master's, GRE General Test, minimum GPA of 3.0. *Faculty research:* Tobacco pesticides.

North Carolina Central University, Division of Academic Affairs, College of Science and Technology, Department of Chemistry, Durham, NC 27707-3129. Offers MS. *Degree requirements:* For master's, one foreign language, comprehensive exam, thesis. *Entrance requirements:* For master's, GRE, minimum GPA of 3.0 in major, 2.5 overall. Additional exam requirements/recommendations for international students: Required—TOEFL.

North Carolina State University, Graduate School, College of Physical and Mathematical Sciences, Department of Chemistry, Raleigh, NC 27695. Offers MS, PhD. Part-time programs available. Terminal master's awarded for partial completion of doctoral program. *Degree requirements:* For master's, thesis (for some programs); for doctorate, thesis/dissertation. *Entrance requirements:* For master's and doctorate, GRE General Test (recommended). Electronic applications accepted. *Faculty research:* Biological chemistry, electrochemistry, organic/inorganic materials, natural products, organometallics.

North Dakota State University, College of Graduate and Interdisciplinary Studies, College of Science and Mathematics, Department of Biochemistry and Molecular Biology, Program in Chemistry, Fargo, ND 58108. Offers MS, PhD. *Students:* 36 full-time (11 women), 1 part-time; includes 1 minority (Two or more races, non-Hispanic/Latino), 18 international. 51 applicants, 35% accepted, 7 enrolled. In 2011, 1 master's, 2 doctorates awarded. Application fee: $35. *Unit head:* Dr. Gregory Cook, Chair, 701-231-8694, Fax: 701-231-8831, E-mail: gregory.cook@ndsu.edu.

Northeastern Illinois University, Graduate College, College of Arts and Sciences, Department of Chemistry, Program in Chemistry, Chicago, IL 60625-4699. Offers MS. Part-time and evening/weekend programs available. *Degree requirements:* For master's, comprehensive exam, final exam or thesis. *Entrance requirements:* For master's, 2 semesters of chemistry, calculus, organic chemistry, physical chemistry, and physics; 1 semester analytic chemistry; minimum GPA of 2.75. Additional exam requirements/recommendations for international students: Required—TOEFL (minimum score 550 paper-based; 213 computer-based; 79 iBT). Electronic applications accepted. *Faculty research:* Liquid chromatographic separation of pharmaceuticals, Diels-Alder reaction products, organogermanium chemistry, mass spectroscopy.

Northeastern University, College of Science, Department of Chemistry and Chemical Biology, Boston, MA 02115-5096. Offers analytical chemistry (PhD); chemistry (MS, PhD); inorganic chemistry (PhD); organic chemistry (PhD); physical chemistry (PhD). Part-time and evening/weekend programs available. *Faculty:* 24 full-time, 7 part-time/adjunct. *Students:* 98 full-time (58 women), 31 part-time (15 women). 190 applicants, 32% accepted, 34 enrolled. In 2011, 16 master's, 6 doctorates awarded. Terminal master's awarded for partial completion of doctoral program. *Degree requirements:* For master's, thesis (for some programs); for doctorate, thesis/dissertation, qualifying exam in specialty area. *Entrance requirements:* Additional exam requirements/recommendations for international students: Required—TOEFL. *Application deadline:* For fall admission, 2/1 priority date for domestic students, 2/1 for international students. Applications are processed on a rolling basis. Application fee: $50. Electronic applications accepted. *Financial support:* In 2011–12, 41 research assistantships with tuition reimbursements (averaging $18,285 per year), 38 teaching assistantships with tuition reimbursements (averaging $18,285 per year) were awarded; fellowships with tuition reimbursements, career-related internships or fieldwork, Federal Work-Study, scholarships/grants, tuition waivers (partial), and unspecified assistantships also available. Financial award application deadline: 3/1; financial award applicants required to submit FAFSA. *Faculty research:* Bioanalysis, biorganic and medicinal chemistry, biophysical chemistry, nanomaterials, proteonics. *Unit head:* Dr. Robert Hanson, Graduate Coordinator, 617-373-3313, Fax: 617-373-8795, E-mail: chemistry-grad-info@neu.edu. *Application contact:* Jo-Anne Dickinson, Admissions Contact, 617-373-5990, Fax: 617-373-7281, E-mail: gsas@neu.edu. Web site: http://www.northeastern.edu/chem/.

Northern Arizona University, Graduate College, College of Engineering, Forestry and Natural Sciences, Department of Chemistry and Biochemistry, Flagstaff, AZ 86011. Offers chemistry (MS). Part-time programs available. *Faculty:* 21 full-time (10 women). *Students:* 16 full-time (12 women), 5 part-time (2 women); includes 4 minority (3 American Indian or Alaska Native, non-Hispanic/Latino; 1 Asian, non-Hispanic/Latino), 2 international. Average age 27. 18 applicants, 33% accepted, 6 enrolled. In 2011, 3 degrees awarded. *Degree requirements:* For master's, thesis. *Entrance requirements:* For master's, minimum GPA of 3.0. Additional exam requirements/recommendations for international students: Required—TOEFL (minimum score 550 paper-based; 213 computer-based; 80 iBT), IELTS (minimum score 7). *Application deadline:* For fall admission, 3/1 priority date for domestic students, 3/1 for international students; for spring admission, 10/1 priority date for domestic students, 10/1 for international students. Applications are processed on a rolling basis. Application fee: $65. Electronic applications accepted. *Expenses:* Tuition, state resident: full-time $7190; part-time $355 per credit hour. Tuition, nonresident: full-time $18,092; part-time $1005 per credit hour. *Required fees:* $818; $328 per semester. *Financial support:* In 2011–12, 6 research assistantships with partial tuition reimbursements (averaging $9,874 per year), 7 teaching assistantships with partial tuition reimbursements (averaging $12,390 per year) were awarded; Federal Work-Study, scholarships/grants, health care benefits, tuition waivers (full and partial), and unspecified assistantships also available. Financial award applicants required to submit FAFSA. *Faculty research:* Biochemistry of exercise, organic and inorganic mechanism studies, inhibition of ice mutation, polymer separation. *Total annual research expenditures:* $261,191. *Unit head:* Dr. Cindy Browder, Chair, 928-523-9062, E-mail: cindy.browder@nau.edu. *Application contact:* Julie Gillette, Administrative Associate, 928-523-7079, Fax: 928-523-8111, E-mail: chemistry@nau.edu. Web site: http://nau.edu/cefns/natsci/biochem/.

Northern Illinois University, Graduate School, College of Liberal Arts and Sciences, Department of Chemistry and Biochemistry, De Kalb, IL 60115-2854. Offers chemistry (MS, PhD). *Faculty:* 16 full-time (1 woman), 3 part-time/adjunct (1 woman). *Students:* 40 full-time (21 women), 4 part-time (3 women); includes 5 minority (2 Black or African American, non-Hispanic/Latino; 2 Asian, non-Hispanic/Latino; 1 Two or more races, non-Hispanic/Latino), 15 international. Average age 26. 82 applicants, 34% accepted, 11 enrolled. In 2011, 3 master's, 3 doctorates awarded. Terminal master's awarded for partial completion of doctoral program. *Degree requirements:* For master's, comprehensive exam, thesis optional, research seminar; for doctorate, one foreign language, thesis/dissertation, candidacy exam, dissertation defense, research seminar. *Entrance requirements:* For master's, GRE General Test, bachelor's degree in mathematics or science, minimum GPA of 2.75; for doctorate, GRE General Test, bachelor's degree in mathematics or science; minimum undergraduate GPA of 2.75, 3.2 graduate. Additional exam requirements/recommendations for international students: Required—TOEFL (minimum score 550 paper-based; 213 computer-based). *Application deadline:* For fall admission, 6/1 for domestic students, 5/1 for international students; for spring admission, 11/1 for domestic students, 10/1 for international students. Applications are processed on a rolling basis. Application fee: $40. Electronic applications accepted. *Financial support:* In 2011–12, 10 research assistantships with full tuition reimbursements, 32 teaching assistantships with full tuition reimbursements were awarded; fellowships with full tuition reimbursements, career-related internships or fieldwork, Federal Work-Study, scholarships/grants, tuition waivers (full), and unspecified assistantships also available. Support available to part-time students. Financial award applicants required to submit FAFSA. *Faculty research:* Viscoelastic properties of polymers, lig and buding tocytochrome coxidases, computational inorganic chemistry, chemistry of organosilanes. *Unit head:* Dr. Jon Carnahan, Chair, 815-753-1181, Fax: 815-753-4802, E-mail: carnahan@niu.edu. *Application contact:* Graduate School Office, 815-753-0395, E-mail: gradsch@niu.edu. Web site: http://www.chembio.niu.edu/.

Northwestern University, The Graduate School, Judd A. and Marjorie Weinberg College of Arts and Sciences, Department of Chemistry, Evanston, IL 60208. Offers PhD. Admissions and degrees offered through The Graduate School. *Degree requirements:* For doctorate, thesis/dissertation. *Entrance requirements:* For doctorate, GRE General Test, GRE Subject Test (chemistry). Additional exam requirements/recommendations for international students: Required—TOEFL. Electronic applications accepted. *Faculty research:* Inorganic, organic, physical, environmental, materials, and chemistry of life processes.

Oakland University, Graduate Study and Lifelong Learning, College of Arts and Sciences, Department of Chemistry, Rochester, MI 48309-4401. Offers biological sciences: health and environmental chemistry (PhD); chemistry (MS). *Degree requirements:* For master's, thesis; for doctorate, thesis/dissertation. *Entrance requirements:* For master's, minimum GPA of 3.0 for unconditional admission; for doctorate, GRE Subject Test, minimum GPA of 3.0 for unconditional admission. Additional exam requirements/recommendations for international students: Required—TOEFL (minimum score 550 paper-based; 213 computer-based). Electronic applications accepted. *Faculty research:* Chemistry of free radical species generated from biological intermediates; fate of toxic organic compounds in the environment; electroanalytical and surface chemistry at solid/liquid interface; computational modeling of intermolecular interactions and surface phenomena; metabolism and biological activity of modified fatty acids and xenobiotic carboxylic acids; physiologic and pathologic mechanisms that modulate immune responses.

74 facebook.com/petersonspublishing

Peterson's Graduate Programs in the Physical Sciences, Mathematics, Agricultural Sciences, the Environment & Natural Resources 2013

The Ohio State University, Graduate School, College of Arts and Sciences, Division of Natural and Mathematical Sciences, Departments of Chemistry and Biochemistry, Columbus, OH 43210. Offers biochemistry (MS); chemistry (MS, PhD). *Faculty:* 45. *Students:* 76 full-time (24 women), 144 part-time (54 women); includes 21 minority (6 Black or African American, non-Hispanic/Latino; 1 American Indian or Alaska Native, non-Hispanic/Latino; 8 Asian, non-Hispanic/Latino; 4 Hispanic/Latino; 2 Two or more races, non-Hispanic/Latino), 111 international. Average age 26. In 2011, 15 master's, 35 doctorates awarded. *Degree requirements:* For master's, thesis optional; for doctorate, thesis/dissertation. *Entrance requirements:* For master's and doctorate, GRE General Test, GRE Subject Test (chemistry). Additional exam requirements/recommendations for international students: Required—TOEFL (minimum score 550 paper-based; 250 computer-based; 79 iBT), Michigan English Language Assessment Battery (minimum score 82). *Application deadline:* For fall admission, 8/15 priority date for domestic students, 7/1 for international students; for winter admission, 12/1 priority date for domestic students, 11/1 for international students; for spring admission, 3/1 priority date for domestic students, 2/1 for international students. Applications are processed on a rolling basis. Application fee: $40 ($50 for international students). Electronic applications accepted. *Expenses:* Tuition, state resident: full-time $11,400. Tuition, nonresident: full-time $28,125. Tuition and fees vary according to course load, degree level, campus/location and program. *Financial support:* Fellowships, research assistantships, teaching assistantships, Federal Work-Study, and institutionally sponsored loans available. Support available to part-time students. *Unit head:* Dr. Susan V. Olesik, Chair, 614-292-0733, E-mail: olesik.1@osu.edu. *Application contact:* Dr. Claudia Turro, Vice Chair, 614-292-8917, Fax: 614-292-1685, E-mail: turro.1@osu.edu. Web site: https://chemistry.osu.edu/.

Oklahoma State University, College of Arts and Sciences, Department of Chemistry, Stillwater, OK 74078. Offers MS, PhD. *Faculty:* 22 full-time (3 women). *Students:* 7 full-time (2 women), 57 part-time (24 women); includes 3 minority (2 Black or African American, non-Hispanic/Latino; 1 Asian, non-Hispanic/Latino), 43 international. Average age 29. 109 applicants, 13% accepted, 9 enrolled. In 2011, 2 master's, 4 doctorates awarded. *Degree requirements:* For master's, thesis; for doctorate, comprehensive exam, thesis/dissertation. *Entrance requirements:* For master's and doctorate, GRE or GMAT. Additional exam requirements/recommendations for international students: Required—TOEFL (minimum score 550 paper-based; 79 iBT). *Application deadline:* For fall admission, 3/1 for international students; for spring admission, 8/1 for international students. Applications are processed on a rolling basis. Application fee: $40 ($75 for international students). Electronic applications accepted. *Expenses:* Tuition, state resident: full-time $4044; part-time $168.50 per credit hour. Tuition, nonresident: full-time $16,008; part-time $667 per credit hour. *Required fees:* $2122; $88.45 per credit hour. One-time fee: $50. Tuition and fees vary according to course load and campus/location. *Financial support:* In 2011–12, 25 research assistantships (averaging $17,063 per year), 40 teaching assistantships (averaging $17,941 per year) were awarded; career-related internships or fieldwork, Federal Work-Study, scholarships/grants, health care benefits, tuition waivers (partial), and unspecified assistantships also available. Support available to part-time students. Financial award application deadline: 3/1; financial award applicants required to submit FAFSA. *Faculty research:* Materials science, surface chemistry, and nanoparticles; theoretical physical chemistry; synthetic and medicinal chemistry; bioanalytical chemistry; electromagnetic (UV, VIS, IR, Raman), mass, and x-ray spectroscopes. *Unit head:* Dr. Frank Blum, Interim Head, 405-744-5920, Fax: 405-744-6007. *Application contact:* Dr. Sheryl Tucker, Dean, 405-744-7099, Fax: 405-744-0355, E-mail: grad-i@okstate.edu. Web site: http://chemistry.okstate.edu.

Old Dominion University, College of Sciences, Program in Chemistry, Norfolk, VA 23529. Offers analytical chemistry (MS); biochemistry (MS); chemistry (PhD); environmental chemistry (MS); organic chemistry (MS); physical chemistry (MS). Part-time and evening/weekend programs available. *Faculty:* 14 full-time (5 women), 2 part-time/adjunct (0 women). *Students:* 34 full-time (17 women), 2 part-time (1 woman); includes 2 minority (1 Black or African American, non-Hispanic/Latino; 1 Asian, non-Hispanic/Latino), 17 international. Average age 28. 35 applicants, 60% accepted, 8 enrolled. In 2011, 3 master's, 2 doctorates awarded. *Degree requirements:* For master's, comprehensive exam, thesis. *Entrance requirements:* For master's, GRE General Test, minimum GPA of 3.0 in major, 2.5 overall; for doctorate, GRE General Test. Additional exam requirements/recommendations for international students: Required—TOEFL. *Application deadline:* For fall admission, 7/1 for domestic students, 1/15 for international students; for spring admission, 11/1 for domestic students, 8/15 for international students. Applications are processed on a rolling basis. Application fee: $30. Electronic applications accepted. *Expenses:* Tuition, state resident: full-time $9096; part-time $379 per credit. Tuition, nonresident: full-time $23,064; part-time $961 per credit. *Required fees:* $127 per semester. One-time fee: $50. *Financial support:* In 2011–12, 6 students received support, including fellowships (averaging $18,000 per year), research assistantships with tuition reimbursements available (averaging $21,000 per year), teaching assistantships with tuition reimbursements available (averaging $18,000 per year); career-related internships or fieldwork, scholarships/grants, and unspecified assistantships also available. Financial award application deadline: 2/15; financial award applicants required to submit FAFSA. *Faculty research:* Biogeochemistry, materials chemistry, bioanalytical chemistry, computational chemistry, organic chemistry. *Total annual research expenditures:* $2.6 million. *Unit head:* Dr. Craig A. Bayse, Graduate Program Director, 757-683-4097, Fax: 757-683-4628, E-mail: chemgpd@odu.edu. *Application contact:* Valerie DeCosta, Grants and Graduate Program Assistant, 757-683-6979, Fax: 757-683-4628, E-mail: chemgpd@odu.edu.

Old Dominion University, Darden College of Education, Programs in Secondary Education, Norfolk, VA 23529. Offers biology (MS Ed); chemistry (MS Ed); English (MS Ed); instructional technology (MS Ed); library science (MS Ed); secondary education (MS Ed). *Accreditation:* NCATE. Part-time and evening/weekend programs available. Postbaccalaureate distance learning degree programs offered (minimal on-campus study). *Faculty:* 20 full-time (16 women). *Students:* 82 full-time (49 women), 95 part-time (63 women); includes 37 minority (21 Black or African American, non-Hispanic/Latino; 3 Asian, non-Hispanic/Latino; 8 Hispanic/Latino; 5 Two or more races, non-Hispanic/Latino), 1 international. Average age 32. 67 applicants, 79% accepted, 53 enrolled. In 2011, 84 degrees awarded. *Degree requirements:* For master's, comprehensive exam, thesis. *Entrance requirements:* For master's, GRE General Test or MAT, PRAXIS I (for licensure), minimum GPA of 2.8, teaching certificate. Additional exam requirements/recommendations for international students: Required—TOEFL. *Application deadline:* For fall admission, 6/1 for domestic and international students; for winter admission, 11/1 for domestic and international students; for spring admission, 3/1 for domestic and international students. Applications are processed on a rolling basis. Application fee: $50. Electronic applications accepted. *Expenses:* Tuition, state resident: full-time $9096; part-time $379 per credit. Tuition, nonresident: full-time $23,064; part-time $961 per credit. *Required fees:* $127 per semester. One-time fee: $50. *Financial support:* In 2011–12, 56 students received support, including fellowships (averaging $15,000 per year), 2 research assistantships with tuition reimbursements available (averaging $9,000 per year), 3 teaching assistantships with tuition reimbursements available (averaging $12,500 per year); career-related internships or fieldwork, Federal Work-Study, institutionally sponsored loans, scholarships/grants, and tuition waivers (partial) also available. Support available to part-time students. Financial award application deadline: 2/15; financial award applicants required to submit FAFSA. *Faculty research:* Use of technology, writing project for teachers, geography teaching, reading. *Unit head:* Dr. Robert Lucking, Graduate Program Director, 757-683-5545, Fax: 757-683-5862, E-mail: rlucking@odu.edu. *Application contact:* William Heffelfinger, Director of Graduate Admissions, 757-683-5554, Fax: 757-683-3255, E-mail: gradadmit@odu.edu. Web site: http://education.odu.edu/eci/secondary/.

Oregon State University, Graduate School, College of Science, Department of Chemistry, Corvallis, OR 97331. Offers analytical chemistry (MS, PhD); chemistry (MA, MAIS); inorganic chemistry (MS, PhD); nuclear and radiation chemistry (MS, PhD); organic chemistry (MS, PhD); physical chemistry (MS, PhD). Part-time programs available. Terminal master's awarded for partial completion of doctoral program. *Degree requirements:* For master's, one foreign language, thesis; for doctorate, one foreign language, thesis/dissertation. *Entrance requirements:* For master's and doctorate, minimum GPA of 3.0 in last 90 hours of course work. Additional exam requirements/recommendations for international students: Required—TOEFL. *Faculty research:* Solid state chemistry, enzyme reaction mechanisms, structure and dynamics of gas molecules, chemiluminescence, nonlinear optical spectroscopy.

Penn State University Park, Graduate School, Eberly College of Science, Department of Chemistry, State College, University Park, PA 16802-1503. Offers MS, PhD. *Unit head:* Dr. Ayusman Sen, Head, 814-865-1383, Fax: 814-863-8403, E-mail: axs20@psu.edu. *Application contact:* Dana Coval-Dinant, Graduate Student Recruiting Manager, 814-865-1383, Fax: 814-865-3228, E-mail: dmc6@psu.edu. Web site: http://www.chem.psu.edu/.

Pittsburg State University, Graduate School, College of Arts and Sciences, Department of Chemistry, Pittsburg, KS 66762. Offers MS. *Degree requirements:* For master's, thesis or alternative.

Polytechnic Institute of New York University, Department of Chemical and Biological Sciences, Major in Chemistry, Brooklyn, NY 11201-2990. Offers MS. Part-time and evening/weekend programs available. *Students:* 16 full-time (7 women), 8 part-time (5 women); includes 3 minority (all Asian, non-Hispanic/Latino), 16 international. Average age 29. 51 applicants, 43% accepted, 10 enrolled. In 2011, 7 degrees awarded. *Degree requirements:* For master's, comprehensive exam (for some programs), thesis (for some programs). *Entrance requirements:* For master's, GRE General Test, GRE Subject Test. Additional exam requirements/recommendations for international students: Required—TOEFL (minimum score 550 paper-based; 213 computer-based; 80 iBT); Recommended—IELTS (minimum score 6.5). *Application deadline:* For fall admission, 7/31 priority date for domestic students, 4/30 for international students; for spring admission, 12/31 priority date for domestic students, 10/30 for international students. Applications are processed on a rolling basis. Application fee: $75. Electronic applications accepted. *Expenses:* Tuition: Full-time $22,464; part-time $1248 per credit. *Required fees:* $501 per semester. *Financial support:* Fellowships, research assistantships, teaching assistantships, institutionally sponsored loans, scholarships/grants, and unspecified assistantships available. Support available to part-time students. Financial award applicants required to submit FAFSA. *Faculty research:* Optical rotation of light by plastic films, supramolecular chemistry, unusual stereochemical opportunities, polyaniline copolymers. *Unit head:* Dr. Bruce Garetz, Department Head, 718-260-3287, E-mail: bgaretz@poly.edu. *Application contact:* JeanCarlo Bonilla, Director, Graduate Enrollment Management, 718-260-3182, Fax: 718-260-3624, E-mail: gradinfo@poly.edu.

Peterson's Graduate Programs in the Physical Sciences, Mathematics, Agricultural Sciences, the Environment & Natural Resources 2013

facebook.com/petersonspublishing **75**

Chemistry

Polytechnic Institute of New York University, Department of Chemical and Biological Sciences, Major in Materials Chemistry, Brooklyn, NY 11201-2990. Offers PhD. Part-time and evening/weekend programs available. *Students:* 8 full-time (1 woman), 11 part-time (4 women); includes 2 minority (both Asian, non-Hispanic/Latino), 14 international. 22 applicants, 23% accepted, 3 enrolled. In 2011, 1 degree awarded. *Median time to degree:* Of those who began their doctoral program in fall 2003, 100% received their degree in 8 years or less. *Degree requirements:* For doctorate, comprehensive exam, thesis/dissertation. *Entrance requirements:* Additional exam requirements/recommendations for international students: Required—TOEFL (minimum score 550 paper-based; 213 computer-based; 80 iBT); Recommended—IELTS (minimum score 6.5). *Application deadline:* For fall admission, 7/31 priority date for domestic students, 4/30 for international students; for spring admission, 12/31 priority date for domestic students, 10/30 for international students. Applications are processed on a rolling basis. Application fee: $75. Electronic applications accepted. *Expenses: Tuition:* Full-time $22,464; part-time $1248 per credit. *Required fees:* $501 per semester. *Financial support:* Fellowships, research assistantships, teaching assistantships, institutionally sponsored loans, scholarships/grants, and unspecified assistantships available. Support available to part-time students. Financial award applicants required to submit .FAFSA. *Unit head:* Dr. Bruce Garetz, Department Head, 718-260-3287, E-mail: bgaretz@poly.edu. *Application contact:* JeanCarlo Bonilla, Director, Graduate Enrollment Management, 718-260-3182, Fax: 718-260-3624, E-mail: gradinfo@poly.edu.

Polytechnic Institute of NYU, Long Island Graduate Center, Graduate Programs, Department of Chemical and Biological Sciences, Major in Chemistry, Melville, NY 11747. Offers MS. *Students:* 17 applicants, 82% accepted, 13 enrolled. *Degree requirements:* For master's, comprehensive exam (for some programs), thesis (for some programs). *Entrance requirements:* Additional exam requirements/recommendations for international students: Required—TOEFL (minimum score 550 paper-based; 213 computer-based; 80 iBT); Recommended—IELTS (minimum score 6.5). *Application deadline:* For fall admission, 7/31 priority date for domestic students, 4/30 for international students; for spring admission, 12/31 priority date for domestic students, 11/30 for international students. Applications are processed on a rolling basis. Application fee: $75. Electronic applications accepted. *Financial support:* Institutionally sponsored loans, scholarships/grants, and unspecified assistantships available. Support available to part-time students. *Unit head:* Prof. Bruce A. Garetz, Department Head, 718-260-3287, E-mail: bgaretz@poly.edu. *Application contact:* JeanCarlo Bonilla, Director of Graduate Enrollment Management, 718-260-3182, Fax: 718-260-3624, E-mail: gradinfo@poly.edu.

Polytechnic Institute of NYU, Westchester Graduate Center, Graduate Programs, Department of Chemical and Biological Sciences, Major in Chemistry, Hawthorne, NY 10532-1507. Offers MS. *Degree requirements:* For master's, comprehensive exam (for some programs), thesis (for some programs). *Entrance requirements:* Additional exam requirements/recommendations for international students: Required—TOEFL (minimum score 550 paper-based; 213 computer-based; 80 iBT); Recommended—IELTS (minimum score 6.5). *Application deadline:* For fall admission, 7/31 priority date for domestic students, 4/30 for international students; for spring admission, 12/31 priority date for domestic students, 11/30 for international students. Applications are processed on a rolling basis. Application fee: $75. Electronic applications accepted. *Financial support:* Institutionally sponsored loans, scholarships/grants, and unspecified assistantships available. Support available to part-time students. *Unit head:* Dr. Bruce A. Garetz, Department Head, 718-260-3287, E-mail: bgaretz@poly.edu. *Application contact:* JeanCarlo Bonilla, Director of Graduate Enrollment Management, 718-260-3182, Fax: 718-260-3624, E-mail: gradinfo@poly.edu.

Pontifical Catholic University of Puerto Rico, College of Sciences, Department of Chemistry, Ponce, PR 00717-0777. Offers MS. Part-time and evening/weekend programs available. *Degree requirements:* For master's, thesis. *Entrance requirements:* For master's, GRE General Test, 2 letters of recommendation, minimum GPA of 3.0, minimum 37 credits in chemistry. Electronic applications accepted.

Portland State University, Graduate Studies, College of Liberal Arts and Sciences, Department of Chemistry, Portland, OR 97207-0751. Offers MA, MS, PhD. Part-time programs available. *Degree requirements:* For master's, one foreign language, thesis; for doctorate, one foreign language, thesis/dissertation, cumulative exams, seminar presentations. *Entrance requirements:* For master's, GRE General Test, GRE Subject Test, minimum GPA of 3.0 in upper-division course work or 2.75 overall, 2 letters of recommendation. Additional exam requirements/recommendations for international students: Required—TOEFL (minimum score 550 paper-based; 213 computer-based). *Faculty research:* Synthetic inorganic chemistry, atmospheric chemistry, organic photochemistry, enzymology, analytical chemistry.

Prairie View A&M University, College of Arts and Sciences, Department of Chemistry, Prairie View, TX 77446-0519. Offers MS. Part-time and evening/weekend programs available. *Degree requirements:* For master's, thesis. *Entrance requirements:* For master's, GRE General Test. Additional exam requirements/recommendations for international students: Recommended—TOEFL. Electronic applications accepted. *Faculty research:* Material science, environmental characterization (surface phenomena), activation of plasminogens, polymer modifications, organic synthesis.

Princeton University, Graduate School, Department of Chemistry, Princeton, NJ 08544-1019. Offers chemistry (PhD); industrial chemistry (MS). *Degree requirements:* For doctorate, thesis/dissertation, general exams. *Entrance requirements:* For master's, GRE General Test; for doctorate, GRE General Test, GRE Subject Test (recommended). Additional exam requirements/ recommendations for international students: Required—TOEFL (minimum score 250 computer-based). Electronic applications accepted. *Faculty research:* Chemistry of interfaces, organic synthesis, organometallic chemistry, inorganic reactions, biostructural chemistry.

See Display on next page and Close-Up on page 131.

Purdue University, Graduate School, College of Science, Department of Chemistry, West Lafayette, IN 47907. Offers analytical chemistry (MS, PhD); biochemistry (MS, PhD); chemical education (MS, PhD); inorganic chemistry (MS, PhD); organic chemistry (MS, PhD); physical chemistry (MS, PhD). *Faculty:* 47 full-time (16 women), 6 part-time/adjunct (0 women). *Students:* 275 full-time (103 women), 33 part-time (10 women); includes 38 minority (19 Black or African American, non-Hispanic/Latino; 6 Asian, non-Hispanic/Latino; 12 Hispanic/Latino; 1 Two or more races, non-Hispanic/Latino), 94 international. Average age 27. 777 applicants, 26% accepted, 62 enrolled. In 2011, 4 master's, 67 doctorates awarded. Terminal master's awarded for partial completion of doctoral program. *Degree requirements:* For master's, thesis; for doctorate, comprehensive exam, thesis/dissertation. *Entrance requirements:* For master's and doctorate, minimum undergraduate GPA of 3.0. Additional exam requirements/recommendations for international students: Required—TOEFL (minimum score 550 computer-based; 77 iBT); Recommended—TWE. *Application deadline:* For fall admission, 2/15 priority date for domestic students, 1/1 for international students. Applications are processed on a rolling basis. Application fee: $60 ($75 for international students). Electronic applications accepted. *Financial support:* In 2011–12, 2 fellowships with partial tuition reimbursements (averaging $18,000 per year), 55 teaching assistantships with partial tuition reimbursements (averaging $18,000 per year) were awarded; research assistantships with partial tuition reimbursements and tuition waivers (partial) also available. Support available to part-time students. Financial award applicants required to submit FAFSA. *Unit head:* Dr. Paul B. Shepson, Head, 765-494-5203, E-mail: pshepson@purdue.edu. *Application contact:* Betty L. Hatfield, Director of Graduate Admissions, 765-494-5208, E-mail: bettyh@purdue.edu.

Queens College of the City University of New York, Division of Graduate Studies, Mathematics and Natural Sciences Division, Department of Chemistry and Biochemistry, Flushing, NY 11367-1597. Offers biochemistry (MA); chemistry (MA). Part-time and evening/weekend programs available. *Faculty:* 14 full-time (4 women). *Students:* 3 full-time (1 woman), 14 part-time (3 women); includes 9 minority (1 Black or African American, non-Hispanic/Latino; 5 Asian, non-Hispanic/Latino; 3 Hispanic/Latino), 3 international. 13 applicants, 38% accepted, 2 enrolled. In 2011, 3 master's awarded. *Degree requirements:* For master's, comprehensive exam. *Entrance requirements:* For master's, GRE, previous course work in calculus and physics, minimum GPA of 3.0. Additional exam requirements/recommendations for international students: Required—TOEFL. *Application deadline:* For fall admission, 4/1 for domestic students; for spring admission, 11/1 for domestic students. Applications are processed on a rolling basis. Application fee: $125. *Expenses:* Tuition, state resident: part-time $345 per credit. Tuition, nonresident: part-time $640 per credit. *Required fees:* $145.25 per semester. *Financial support:* Career-related internships or fieldwork, Federal Work-Study, institutionally sponsored loans, and tuition waivers (partial) available. Support available to part-time students. Financial award application deadline: 4/1; financial award applicants required to submit FAFSA. *Unit head:* Dr. William Hersh, Chairperson, 718-997-4144. *Application contact:* Graduate Adviser, 718-997-4100.

Queen's University at Kingston, School of Graduate Studies and Research, Faculty of Arts and Sciences, Department of Chemistry, Kingston, ON K7L 3N6, Canada. Offers M Sc, PhD. Part-time programs available. *Degree requirements:* For master's, thesis (for some programs); for doctorate, comprehensive exam, thesis/dissertation. *Entrance requirements:* Additional exam requirements/ recommendations for international students: Required—TOEFL (minimum score 580 paper-based). *Faculty research:* Medicinal/biological chemistry, materials chemistry, environmental/analytical chemistry, theoretical/computational chemistry.

Rensselaer Polytechnic Institute, Graduate School, School of Science, Program in Chemistry, Troy, NY 12180-3590. Offers analytical chemistry (MS, PhD); biochemistry (MS, PhD); inorganic chemistry (MS, PhD); organic chemistry (MS, PhD); physical chemistry (MS, PhD); polymer chemistry (MS, PhD). Part-time and evening/weekend programs available. Terminal master's awarded for partial completion of doctoral program. *Degree requirements:* For master's, thesis (for some programs); for doctorate, comprehensive exam, thesis/dissertation. *Entrance requirements:* For master's, GRE General Test, GRE Subject Test (strongly recommended); for doctorate, GRE General Test, GRE Subject Test (chemistry or biochemistry strongly recommended). Additional exam requirements/recommendations for international students: Required—TOEFL (minimum score 570 paper-based; 230 computer-based; 88 iBT). Electronic applications accepted. *Faculty research:* Synthetic polymer and biopolymer chemistry, physical chemistry of polymeric systems, bioanalytical chemistry, synthetic and computational drug design, protein folding and protein design.

Peterson's Graduate Programs in the Physical Sciences, Mathematics, Agricultural Sciences, the Environment & Natural Resources 2013

Rice University, Graduate Programs, Wiess School of Natural Sciences, Department of Chemistry, Houston, TX 77251-1892. Offers chemistry (MA); inorganic chemistry (PhD); organic chemistry (PhD); physical chemistry (PhD). Terminal master's awarded for partial completion of doctoral program. *Degree requirements:* For master's, thesis; for doctorate, thesis/dissertation. *Entrance requirements:* For master's and doctorate, GRE General Test, minimum GPA of 3.0. Additional exam requirements/recommendations for international students: Required—TOEFL (minimum score 600 paper-based; 250 computer-based; 90 iBT). Electronic applications accepted. *Faculty research:* Nanoscience, biomaterials, nanobioinformatics, fullerene pharmaceuticals.

Rochester Institute of Technology, Graduate Enrollment Services, College of Science, Department of Chemistry, Rochester, NY 14623-5603. Offers MS. Part-time and evening/weekend programs available. Postbaccalaureate distance learning degree programs offered (minimal on-campus study). *Students:* 10 full-time (4 women), 7 part-time (5 women), 4 international. Average age 26. 25 applicants, 60% accepted, 9 enrolled. In 2011, 5 degrees awarded. *Degree requirements:* For master's, thesis. *Entrance requirements:* For master's, GRE, minimum GPA of 3.0. Additional exam requirements/recommendations for international students: Required—TOEFL (minimum score 550 paper-based; 213 computer-based; 79 iBT) or IELTS (minimum score 6.5). *Application deadline:* For fall admission, 2/15 priority date for domestic students, 2/15 for international students; for winter admission, 11/1 for domestic students; for spring admission, 2/1 for domestic students. Applications are processed on a rolling basis. Application fee: $50. Electronic applications accepted. *Expenses: Tuition:* Full-time $34,659; part-time $963 per credit hour. *Required fees:* $228; $76 per quarter. *Financial support:* Fellowships with full and partial tuition reimbursements, research assistantships with full and partial tuition reimbursements, teaching assistantships with full and partial tuition reimbursements, career-related internships or fieldwork, scholarships/grants, and unspecified assistantships available. Support available to part-time students. Financial award applicants required to submit FAFSA. *Faculty research:* Organic polymer chemistry, magnetic resonance and imaging, inorganic coordination polymers, biophysical chemistry, physical polymer chemistry. *Unit head:* Dr. Paul Rosenberg, Department Head, 585-475-2497, Fax: 585-475-7800, E-mail: lprsch@rit.edu. *Application contact:* Diane Ellison, Assistant Vice President, Graduate Enrollment Services, 585-475-2229, Fax: 585-475-7164, E-mail: gradinfo@rit.edu. Web site: http://www.rit.edu/cos/chemistry/department_info.html.

Roosevelt University, Graduate Division, College of Arts and Sciences, Department of Biological, Chemical, and Physical Sciences, Chicago, IL 60605. Offers biotechnology and chemical science (MS). Part-time and evening/weekend programs available. *Degree requirements:* For master's, thesis optional. *Entrance requirements:* For master's, minimum GPA of 2.7, undergraduate course work in science and mathematics. *Faculty research:* Phase-transfer catalysts, bioinorganic chemistry, long chain dicarboxylic acids, organosilicon compounds, spectroscopic studies.

Royal Military College of Canada, Division of Graduate Studies and Research, Science Division, Department of Chemistry and Chemical and Materials Engineering, Kingston, ON K7K 7B4, Canada. Offers chemical engineering (M Eng, MA Sc, PhD); chemistry (M Sc, PhD). *Degree requirements:* For master's, thesis; for doctorate, comprehensive exam, thesis/dissertation. *Entrance requirements:* For master's, honour's degree with second-class standing; for doctorate, master's degree. Electronic applications accepted.

Rutgers, The State University of New Jersey, Camden, Graduate School of Arts and Sciences, Program in Chemistry, Camden, NJ 08102. Offers MS. Part-time and evening/weekend programs available. *Degree requirements:* For master's, comprehensive exam, thesis (for some programs), 30 credits. *Entrance requirements:* For master's, GRE (for assistantships), 3 letters of recommendation; statement of personal, professional and academic goals; chemistry or related undergraduate degree (preferred). Additional exam requirements/recommendations for international students: Required—TOEFL, IELTS; Recommended—TWE. Electronic applications accepted. *Faculty research:* Organic and inorganic synthesis, enzyme biochemistry, trace metal analysis, theoretical and molecular modeling.

Rutgers, The State University of New Jersey, Newark, Graduate School, Program in Chemistry, Newark, NJ 07102. Offers analytical chemistry (MS, PhD); biochemistry (MS, PhD); inorganic chemistry (MS, PhD); organic chemistry (MS, PhD); physical chemistry (MS, PhD). Part-time and evening/weekend programs available. Terminal master's awarded for partial completion of doctoral program. *Degree requirements:* For master's, thesis optional, cumulative exams; for doctorate, thesis/dissertation, exams, research proposal. *Entrance requirements:* For master's and doctorate, GRE General Test, minimum undergraduate B average. Additional exam requirements/recommendations for international students: Required—TOEFL. Electronic applications accepted. *Faculty research:* Medicinal chemistry, natural products, isotope effects, biophysics and biorganic approaches to enzyme mechanisms, organic and organometallic synthesis.

Rutgers, The State University of New Jersey, New Brunswick, Graduate School-New Brunswick, Department of Chemistry and Chemical Biology, Piscataway, NJ 08854-8097. Offers biological chemistry (MS, PhD); inorganic chemistry (MS, PhD); organic chemistry (MS, PhD); physical chemistry (MS, PhD). Part-time and evening/weekend programs available. Terminal master's awarded for partial completion of doctoral program. *Degree requirements:* For master's, thesis or alternative, exam; for doctorate, thesis/dissertation, 1 year residency. *Entrance requirements:* For master's and doctorate, GRE General Test, GRE Subject Test. Additional exam requirements/recommendations for

▼ PRINCETON UNIVERSITY
DEPARTMENT OF CHEMISTRY

chemistry.princeton.edu

Peterson's Graduate Programs in the Physical Sciences, Mathematics, Agricultural Sciences, the Environment & Natural Resources 2013

Chemistry

international students: Required—TOEFL. Electronic applications accepted. *Faculty research:* Biophysical organic/bioorganic, inorganic/bioinorganic, theoretical, and solid-state/surface chemistry.

Rutgers, The State University of New Jersey, New Brunswick, Graduate School-New Brunswick, Department of Environmental Sciences, Piscataway, NJ 08854-8097. Offers air pollution and resources (MS, PhD); aquatic biology (MS, PhD); aquatic chemistry (MS, PhD); atmospheric science (MS, PhD); chemistry and physics of aerosol and hydrosol systems (MS, PhD); environmental chemistry (MS, PhD); environmental microbiology (MS, PhD); environmental toxicology (PhD); exposure assessment (PhD); fate and effects of pollutants (MS, PhD); pollution prevention and control (MS, PhD); water and wastewater treatment (MS, PhD); water resources (MS, PhD). Terminal master's awarded for partial completion of doctoral program. *Degree requirements:* For master's, comprehensive exam, thesis or alternative, oral final exam; for doctorate, comprehensive exam, thesis/dissertation, thesis defense, qualifying exam. *Entrance requirements:* For master's and doctorate, GRE General Test. Additional exam requirements/recommendations for international students: Required—TOEFL. Electronic applications accepted. *Faculty research:* Biological waste treatment; contaminant fate and transport; air, soil and water quality.

Sacred Heart University, Graduate Programs, College of Arts and Sciences, Department of Chemistry, Fairfield, CT 06825-1000. Offers MS. Part-time and evening/weekend programs available. *Degree requirements:* For master's, thesis optional. *Entrance requirements:* For master's, bachelor's degree in related area, minimum GPA of 2.75. Additional exam requirements/recommendations for international students: Required—TOEFL (minimum score 550 paper-based; 213 computer-based; 75 iBT). Electronic applications accepted.

St. Francis Xavier University, Graduate Studies, Department of Chemistry, Antigonish, NS B2G 2W5, Canada. Offers M Sc. *Degree requirements:* For master's, thesis. *Entrance requirements:* Additional exam requirements/recommendations for international students: Required—TOEFL (minimum score 580 paper-based; 236 computer-based). *Faculty research:* Photoelectron spectroscopy, synthesis and properties of surfactants, nucleic acid synthesis, transition metal chemistry, colloids.

St. John's University, St. John's College of Liberal Arts and Sciences, Department of Chemistry, Queens, NY 11439. Offers MS. Part-time and evening/weekend programs available. *Students:* 10 full-time (6 women), 11 part-time (7 women); includes 8 minority (1 Black or African American, non-Hispanic/Latino; 2 Asian, non-Hispanic/Latino; 3 Hispanic/Latino; 2 Two or more races, non-Hispanic/Latino), 10 international. Average age 29. 26 applicants, 46% accepted, 5 enrolled. In 2011, 5 master's awarded. *Degree requirements:* For master's, comprehensive exam, thesis optional. *Entrance requirements:* For master's, minimum GPA of 3.0 (overall); 3.5 (in chemistry). Additional exam requirements/recommendations for international students: Required—TOEFL (minimum score 600 paper-based; 250 computer-based; 100 iBT), IELTS (minimum score 5.5). *Application deadline:* For fall admission, 5/1 priority date for domestic students, 5/1 for international students; for spring admission, 11/1 priority date for domestic students, 11/1 for international students. Applications are processed on a rolling basis. Application fee: $70. Electronic applications accepted. *Expenses: Tuition:* Full-time $18,000; part-time $1000 per credit. *Required fees:* $170 per semester. Tuition and fees vary according to program. *Financial support:* Research assistantships, teaching assistantships, and scholarships/grants available. Support available to part-time students. Financial award application deadline: 3/1; financial award applicants required to submit FAFSA. *Faculty research:* Synthesis and reactions of a-lactams, NMR spectroscopy or nucleosides, analytical chemistry, environment chemistry and photochemistry of transition metal complexes. *Unit head:* Dr. Richard Rosso, Chair, 718-990-5216, E-mail: rossor@stjohns.edu. *Application contact:* Robert Medrano, Director of Graduate Admission, 718-990-1601, Fax: 718-990-5686, E-mail: gradhelp@stjohns.edu.

Saint Louis University, Graduate Education, College of Arts and Sciences and Graduate Education, Department of Chemistry, St. Louis, MO 63103-2097. Offers MS, MS-R, PhD. Part-time and evening/weekend programs available. *Degree requirements:* For master's, thesis; for doctorate, comprehensive exam, thesis/dissertation. *Entrance requirements:* For master's, letters of recommendation, resume, interview; for doctorate, letters of recommendation, resumé, interview, transcripts, goal statement. Additional exam requirements/recommendations for international students: Required—TOEFL (minimum score 550 paper-based; 213 computer-based; 80 iBT). Electronic applications accepted. *Faculty research:* Photochemistry, energy, materials, biomaterials, nanomaterials.

Sam Houston State University, College of Sciences, Department of Chemistry, Huntsville, TX 77341. Offers MS. Part-time programs available. *Faculty:* 9 full-time (1 woman). *Students:* 10 full-time (6 women), 1 part-time (0 women); includes 2 minority (1 Asian, non-Hispanic/Latino; 1 Hispanic/Latino), 7 international. Average age 26. 18 applicants, 39% accepted, 6 enrolled. In 2011, 1 master's awarded. *Degree requirements:* For master's, thesis (for some programs). *Entrance requirements:* For master's, GRE General Test. Additional exam requirements/recommendations for international students: Required—TOEFL (minimum score 550 paper-based; 213 computer-based; 79 iBT). *Application deadline:* For fall admission, 8/1 for domestic students, 6/25 for international students; for spring admission, 12/1 for domestic students, 11/12 for international students. Applications are processed on a rolling basis. Application fee: $45 ($75 for international students). Electronic applications accepted. *Expenses:* Tuition, state resident: full-time $4420; part-time $221 per credit hour. Tuition,

nonresident: full-time $10,680; part-time $534 per credit hour. *Required fees:* $329 per credit hour. *Financial support:* Research assistantships, teaching assistantships, Federal Work-Study, institutionally sponsored loans, and tuition waivers (partial) available. Support available to part-time students. Financial award application deadline: 5/31; financial award applicants required to submit FAFSA. *Unit head:* Dr. Rick Norman, Chair, 936-294-1527, Fax: 936-294-4996, E-mail: chm_ren@shsu.edu. *Application contact:* Dr. Thomas Chasteen, Advisor, 936-294-1971, E-mail: chm_tgc@shsu.edu. Web site: http://www.shsu.edu/~chemistry/.

San Diego State University, Graduate and Research Affairs, College of Sciences, Department of Chemistry and Biochemistry, San Diego, CA 92182. Offers MA, MS, PhD. PhD offered jointly with University of California, San Diego. Terminal master's awarded for partial completion of doctoral program. *Degree requirements:* For doctorate, thesis/dissertation. *Entrance requirements:* For master's, GRE General Test, bachelor's degree in related field, 3 letters of reference; for doctorate, GRE General Test, GRE Subject Test. Additional exam requirements/recommendations for international students: Required—TOEFL. Electronic applications accepted. *Faculty research:* Nonlinear, laser, and electrochemistry; surface reaction dynamics; catalysis, synthesis, and organometallics; proteins, enzymology, and gene expression regulation.

San Francisco State University, Division of Graduate Studies, College of Science and Engineering, Department of Chemistry and Biochemistry, San Francisco, CA 94132-1722. Offers chemistry (MS), including biochemistry. Part-time programs available. *Application deadline:* Applications are processed on a rolling basis. Electronic applications accepted. *Unit head:* Dr. Jane DeWitt, Chair, 415-338-1288, Fax: 415-338-2384, E-mail: gradchem@sfsu.edu. *Application contact:* Dr. Bruce Manning, Graduate Coordinator, 415-338-1288, Fax: 415-338-2384, E-mail: bmanning@sfsu.edu. Web site: http://lewis.sfsu.edu.

San Jose State University, Graduate Studies and Research, College of Science, Department of Chemistry, San Jose, CA 95192-0001. Offers MA, MS. Part-time and evening/weekend programs available. *Degree requirements:* For master's, thesis or alternative. *Entrance requirements:* For master's, GRE. Electronic applications accepted. *Faculty research:* Intercalated compounds, organic/biochemical reaction mechanisms, complexing agents in biochemistry, DNA repair, metabolic inhibitors.

The Scripps Research Institute, Kellogg School of Science and Technology, La Jolla, CA 92037. Offers chemical and biological sciences (PhD). *Degree requirements:* For doctorate, thesis/dissertation. *Entrance requirements:* For doctorate, GRE General Test, GRE Subject Test, 3 letters of recommendation. Additional exam requirements/recommendations for international students: Required—TOEFL. Electronic applications accepted. *Faculty research:* Molecular structure and function, plant biology, immunology, bioorganic chemistry and molecular design, synthetic organic chemistry and natural product synthesis.

Seton Hall University, College of Arts and Sciences, Department of Chemistry and Biochemistry, South Orange, NJ 07079-2697. Offers analytical chemistry (MS, PhD); biochemistry (MS, PhD); chemistry (MS); inorganic chemistry (MS, PhD); organic chemistry (MS, PhD); physical chemistry (MS, PhD). Part-time and evening/weekend programs available. Terminal master's awarded for partial completion of doctoral program. *Degree requirements:* For master's, thesis optional; for doctorate, comprehensive exam, thesis/dissertation. *Entrance requirements:* Additional exam requirements/recommendations for international students: Required—TOEFL. Electronic applications accepted. *Expenses: Tuition:* Part-time $1033 per credit hour. *Required fees:* $85 per semester. *Faculty research:* DNA metal reactions; chromatography; bioinorganic, biophysical, organometallic, polymer chemistry; heterogeneous catalyst; synthetic organic and carbohydrate chemistry.

Simon Fraser University, Graduate Studies, Faculty of Science, Department of Chemistry, Burnaby, BC V5A 1S6, Canada. Offers chemical physics (PhD); chemistry (PhD). *Degree requirements:* For master's, thesis; for doctorate, thesis/dissertation. *Entrance requirements:* For master's, minimum GPA of 3.0. Additional exam requirements/recommendations for international students: Required—TOEFL (minimum score 600 paper-based; 250 computer-based; 100 iBT). Electronic applications accepted. *Faculty research:* Organic chemistry, nuclear chemistry, physical chemistry, inorganic chemistry, theoretical chemistry.

Smith College, Graduate and Special Programs, Department of Chemistry, Northampton, MA 01063. Offers MAT. Part-time programs available. *Faculty:* 9 full-time (6 women). *Students:* 1 (woman) part-time. Average age 33. *Entrance requirements:* For master's, GRE General Test. Additional exam requirements/recommendations for international students: Required—TOEFL (minimum score 590 paper-based; 243 computer-based; 97 iBT). *Application deadline:* For fall admission, 4/1 for domestic students, 1/15 for international students; for spring admission, 12/1 for domestic students. Application fee: $60. *Expenses: Tuition:* Full-time $14,925; part-time $1245 per credit. *Financial support:* Career-related internships or fieldwork and institutionally sponsored loans available. Support available to part-time students. Financial award application deadline: 1/15; financial award applicants required to submit CSS PROFILE or FAFSA. *Unit head:* Kate Queeney, Chair, 413-585-3835, E-mail: kqueeney@smith.edu. *Application contact:* Ruth Morgan, Administrative Assistant, 413-585-3050, Fax: 413-585-3054, E-mail: gradstdy@smith.edu. Web site: http://www.science.smith.edu/departments/chem/.

78 facebook.com/petersonspublishing

Peterson's Graduate Programs in the Physical Sciences, Mathematics, Agricultural Sciences, the Environment & Natural Resources 2013

South Dakota State University, Graduate School, College of Arts and Science, Department of Chemistry, Brookings, SD 57007. Offers MS, PhD. *Degree requirements:* For master's, thesis, oral exam; for doctorate, thesis/dissertation, preliminary oral and written exams, research tool. *Entrance requirements:* For master's and doctorate, bachelor's degree in chemistry or closely related discipline. Additional exam requirements/recommendations for international students: Required—TOEFL (minimum score 580 paper-based; 237 computer-based; 92 iBT). *Faculty research:* Environmental chemistry, computational chemistry, organic synthesis and photochemistry, novel material development and characterization.

Southeast Missouri State University, School of Graduate Studies, Department of Chemistry, Cape Girardeau, MO 63701-4799. Offers MNS. Fall semester admission only. Part-time programs available. *Faculty:* 8 full-time (1 woman). *Students:* 13 full-time (4 women), 4 part-time (2 women); includes 1 minority (Asian, non-Hispanic/Latino), 13 international. Average age 25. 37 applicants, 32% accepted, 4 enrolled. In 2011, 7 master's awarded. *Degree requirements:* For master's, comprehensive exam (for some programs), thesis (for some programs), either thesis and oral defense, or research paper and comprehensive exam. *Entrance requirements:* For master's, GRE General Test, minimum undergraduate GPA of 2.5, 2.75 in last 30 semester hours of undergraduate science or math courses; 2 letters of recommendation; minimum C grade in selected chemistry courses. Additional exam requirements/recommendations for international students: Required—TOEFL (minimum score 550 paper-based; 213 computer-based; 79 iBT); Recommended—IELTS (minimum score 6). *Application deadline:* For fall admission, 8/1 for domestic students, 7/1 for international students. Applications are processed on a rolling basis. Application fee: $30 ($40 for international students). Electronic applications accepted. *Expenses:* Tuition, state resident: full-time $4896; part-time $272 per credit hour. Tuition, nonresident: full-time $8649; part-time $480.50 per credit hour. *Financial support:* In 2011–12, 13 students received support, including 6 teaching assistantships with full tuition reimbursements available (averaging $7,600 per year); career-related internships or fieldwork, Federal Work-Study, scholarships/grants, tuition waivers (full), and unspecified assistantships also available. Financial award application deadline: 6/30; financial award applicants required to submit FAFSA. *Faculty research:* Crystallography, trace metal detection, electrochemistry of metalloporphyrins, organic reactions with supported reagents, synthesis of molecules of biological interest. *Unit head:* Dr. Philip W. Crawford, Chairperson and Professor, 573-651-2166, Fax: 573-986-2508, E-mail: pcrawford@semo.edu. *Application contact:* Alisa Aleen McFerron, Assistant Director of Admissions for Operations, 573-651-5937, Fax: 573-651-5936, E-mail: amcferron@semo.edu. Web site: http://www.semo.edu/chemistry/.

Southern Connecticut State University, School of Graduate Studies, School of Arts and Sciences, Department of Chemistry, New Haven, CT 06515-1355. Offers MS. Part-time and evening/weekend programs available. *Faculty:* 4 full-time (0 women). *Students:* 1 (woman) full-time, 4 part-time (2 women); includes 1 minority (Asian, non-Hispanic/Latino), 1 international. 18 applicants, 28% accepted, 1 enrolled. In 2011, 5 master's awarded. *Degree requirements:* For master's, thesis or alternative. *Entrance requirements:* For master's, interview, undergraduate work in chemistry. *Application deadline:* Applications are processed on a rolling basis. Application fee: $50. Electronic applications accepted. *Expenses:* Tuition, state resident: full-time $5137; part-time $413 per credit. *Required fees:* $4008; $55 per term. *Financial support:* Teaching assistantships available. Financial award application deadline: 4/15; financial award applicants required to submit FAFSA. *Unit head:* Dr. Gregory Kowalczyk, Chairperson, 203-392-6268, Fax: 203-392-6396, E-mail: kowalczykg1@southernct.edu. *Application contact:* Dr. Robert Snyder, Graduate Coordinator, 203-392-6263, E-mail: snyderr1@southernct.edu.

Southern Illinois University Carbondale, Graduate School, College of Science, Department of Chemistry and Biochemistry, Carbondale, IL 62901-4701. Offers MS, PhD. Part-time programs available. *Faculty:* 18 full-time (1 woman), 2 part-time/adjunct (0 women). *Students:* 49 full-time (24 women), 9 part-time (3 women); includes 1 minority (Black or African American, non-Hispanic/Latino), 37 international. Average age 25. 59 applicants, 10% accepted, 4 enrolled. In 2011, 2 master's, 4 doctorates awarded. Terminal master's awarded for partial completion of doctoral program. *Degree requirements:* For master's, one foreign language, thesis; for doctorate, variable foreign language requirement, thesis/dissertation. *Entrance requirements:* For master's, minimum GPA of 2.7; for doctorate, GRE General Test, minimum GPA of 3.25. Additional exam requirements/recommendations for international students: Required—TOEFL. *Application deadline:* Applications are processed on a rolling basis. Application fee: $0. *Financial support:* In 2011–12, 17 research assistantships with full tuition reimbursements, 23 teaching assistantships with full tuition reimbursements were awarded; fellowships with full tuition reimbursements, Federal Work-Study, institutionally sponsored loans, and tuition waivers (full) also available. Support available to part-time students. *Faculty research:* Materials, separations, computational chemistry, synthetics. *Total annual research expenditures:* $1 million. *Unit head:* Gary Kinsel, Chair, 618-453-6482, Fax: 618-453-6408. *Application contact:* Kristen Burton, Office Specialist, 618-453-6494, Fax: 618-453-6408, E-mail: kburton@chem.siu.edu.

Southern Illinois University Edwardsville, Graduate School, College of Arts and Sciences, Department of Chemistry, Edwardsville, IL 62026. Offers MS. Part-time and evening/weekend programs available. *Faculty:* 17 full-time (3 women). *Students:* 11 full-time (6 women), 23 part-time (8 women); includes 1 minority (Two or more races, non-Hispanic/Latino), 12 international. 46 applicants, 22% accepted. In 2011, 15 master's awarded. *Degree requirements:* For master's, thesis (for some programs), research paper. *Entrance requirements:* Additional exam requirements/recommendations for international students: Required—TOEFL (minimum score 550 paper-based; 213 computer-based; 79 iBT), IELTS (minimum score 6.5). *Application deadline:* For fall admission, 7/22 for domestic students, 6/1 for international students; for spring admission, 12/9 for domestic students, 10/1 for international students. Applications are processed on a rolling basis. Application fee: $30. Electronic applications accepted. Tuition and fees vary according to course load and program. *Financial support:* In 2011–12, 3 teaching assistantships with full tuition reimbursements (averaging $9,927 per year) were awarded; fellowships with full tuition reimbursements, research assistantships with full tuition reimbursements, institutionally sponsored loans, scholarships/grants, and unspecified assistantships also available. Financial award application deadline: 3/1; financial award applicants required to submit FAFSA. *Unit head:* Dr. Yun Lu, Program Director, 618-650-2042, E-mail: yulu@siue.edu. *Application contact:* Michelle Robinson, Coordinator of Graduate Recruitment, 618-650-2811, Fax: 618-650-3523, E-mail: michero@siue.edu. Web site: http://www.siue.edu/artsandsciences/chemistry/.

Southern Methodist University, Dedman College, Department of Chemistry, Dallas, TX 75275-0314. Offers MS, PhD. Terminal master's awarded for partial completion of doctoral program. *Degree requirements:* For master's, thesis; for doctorate, comprehensive exam, thesis/dissertation. *Entrance requirements:* For master's, GRE General Test, bachelor's degree in chemistry, minimum GPA of 3.0; for doctorate, GRE General Test, bachelor's degree in chemistry or closely related field, minimum GPA of 3.0. Additional exam requirements/recommendations for international students: Required—TOEFL (minimum score 550 paper-based; 213 computer-based; 80 iBT). Electronic applications accepted. *Faculty research:* Materials/polymer, medicinal/bioorganic, theoretical and computational, organic/inorganic/organometallic synthesis, inorganic polymer chemistry.

Southern University and Agricultural and Mechanical College, Graduate School, College of Sciences, Department of Chemistry, Baton Rouge, LA 70813. Offers analytical chemistry (MS); biochemistry (MS); environmental sciences (MS); inorganic chemistry (MS); organic chemistry (MS); physical chemistry (MS). *Degree requirements:* For master's, thesis. *Entrance requirements:* For master's, GMAT or GRE General Test. Additional exam requirements/recommendations for international students: Required—TOEFL (minimum score 525 paper-based; 193 computer-based). *Faculty research:* Synthesis of macrocyclic ligands, latex accelerators, anticancer drugs, biosensors, absorption isotheums, isolation of specific enzymes from plants.

Stanford University, School of Humanities and Sciences, Department of Chemistry, Stanford, CA 94305-5080. Offers PhD. *Degree requirements:* For doctorate, thesis/dissertation. *Entrance requirements:* For doctorate, GRE General Test, GRE Subject Test. Additional exam requirements/recommendations for international students: Required—TOEFL. Electronic applications accepted. *Expenses: Tuition:* Full-time $40,050; part-time $890 per credit.

State University of New York at Binghamton, Graduate School, School of Arts and Sciences, Department of Chemistry, Binghamton, NY 13902-6000. Offers analytical chemistry (PhD); chemistry (MA, MS); inorganic chemistry (PhD); organic chemistry (PhD); physical chemistry (PhD). Part-time programs available. *Faculty:* 16 full-time (5 women), 2 part-time/adjunct (both women). *Students:* 24 full-time (8 women), 32 part-time (13 women); includes 5 minority (2 Black or African American, non-Hispanic/Latino; 1 Hispanic/Latino; 2 Native Hawaiian or other Pacific Islander, non-Hispanic/Latino), 36 international. Average age 28. 39 applicants, 36% accepted, 10 enrolled. In 2011, 3 master's, 6 doctorates awarded. Terminal master's awarded for partial completion of doctoral program. *Degree requirements:* For master's, thesis or alternative, oral exam, seminar presentation; for doctorate, thesis/dissertation, cumulative exams. *Entrance requirements:* For master's and doctorate, GRE General Test, GRE Subject Test. Additional exam requirements/recommendations for international students: Required—TOEFL (minimum score 550 paper-based; 213 computer-based; 80 iBT). *Application deadline:* For fall admission, 1/15 priority date for domestic students, 1/15 for international students; for spring admission, 10/15 priority date for domestic students, 10/15 for international students. Applications are processed on a rolling basis. Application fee: $60. Electronic applications accepted. *Financial support:* In 2011–12, 9 fellowships with full tuition reimbursements (averaging $18,000 per year), 13 research assistantships with full tuition reimbursements (averaging $18,000 per year), 35 teaching assistantships with full tuition reimbursements (averaging $18,000 per year) were awarded; career-related internships or fieldwork, Federal Work-Study, institutionally sponsored loans, scholarships/grants, health care benefits, tuition waivers (full), and unspecified assistantships also available. Financial award application deadline: 2/15; financial award applicants required to submit FAFSA. *Unit head:* Dr. Wayne E. Jones, Chairperson, 607-777-2421, E-mail: wjones@binghamton.edu. *Application contact:* Catherine Smith, Recruiting and Admissions Coordinator, 607-777-2151, Fax: 607-777-2501, E-mail: cmsmith@binghamton.edu.

State University of New York at Fredonia, Graduate Studies, Department of Chemistry and Biochemistry, Fredonia, NY 14063-1136. Offers chemistry (MS); curriculum and instruction science education (MS Ed). Part-time and evening/weekend programs available. *Degree requirements:* For master's, thesis optional.

Peterson's Graduate Programs in the Physical Sciences, Mathematics, Agricultural Sciences, the Environment & Natural Resources 2013

facebook.com/petersonspublishing **79**

Chemistry

Expenses: Tuition, state resident: full-time $6666; part-time $370 per credit hour. Tuition, nonresident: full-time $11,376; part-time $632 per credit hour. *Required fees:* $1059.30; $58.85 per credit hour. Tuition and fees vary according to course load.

State University of New York at New Paltz, Graduate School, School of Education, Department of Secondary Education, New Paltz, NY 12561. Offers adolescence education: biology (MAT, MS Ed); adolescence education: chemistry (MAT, MS Ed); adolescence education: earth science (MAT, MS Ed); adolescence education: English (MAT, MS Ed); adolescence education: French (MAT, MS Ed); adolescence education: social studies (MAT, MS Ed); adolescence education: Spanish (MAT, MS Ed); second language education (MS Ed). *Accreditation:* NCATE. Part-time and evening/weekend programs available. *Faculty:* 18 full-time (10 women), 2 part-time/adjunct (both women). *Students:* 79 full-time (48 women), 76 part-time (55 women); includes 30 minority (3 Black or African American, non-Hispanic/Latino; 2 Asian, non-Hispanic/Latino; 22 Hispanic/Latino; 3 Two or more races, non-Hispanic/Latino), 1 international. Average age 32. 127 applicants, 69% accepted, 64 enrolled. In 2011, 73 master's awarded. *Degree requirements:* For master's, comprehensive exam (for some programs), portfolio. *Entrance requirements:* For master's, minimum GPA of 3.0, New York state teaching certificate (MS Ed). Additional exam requirements/recommendations for international students: Required—TOEFL (minimum score 550 paper-based; 213 computer-based; 80 iBT), IELTS (minimum score 6.5). *Application deadline:* For fall admission, 3/1 priority date for domestic students, 3/1 for international students; for spring admission, 10/1 priority date for domestic students, 10/1 for international students. Application fee: $50. Electronic applications accepted. *Expenses:* Tuition, state resident: full-time $8870; part-time $370 per credit. Tuition, nonresident: full-time $15,160; part-time $632 per credit. *Required fees:* $1188; $34 per credit; $184 per semester. *Financial support:* In 2011–12, 13 students received support, including 3 fellowships with partial tuition reimbursements available (averaging $7,000 per year); Federal Work-Study, institutionally sponsored loans, and tuition waivers (full) also available. Financial award application deadline: 8/1; financial award applicants required to submit FAFSA. *Unit head:* Dr. Devon Duhaney, Chair, 845-257-2850, E-mail: duhaneyd@newpaltz.edu. *Application contact:* Caroline Murphy, Graduate Admissions Advisor, 845-257-3285, Fax: 845-257-3284, E-mail: gradschool@newpaltz.edu. Web site: http://www.newpaltz.edu/secondaryed/.

State University of New York at Oswego, Graduate Studies, College of Liberal Arts and Sciences, Department of Chemistry, Oswego, NY 13126. Offers MS. Part-time programs available. *Degree requirements:* For master's, comprehensive exam, thesis. *Entrance requirements:* For master's, GRE General Test, GRE Subject Test, BA or BS in chemistry. Additional exam requirements/recommendations for international students: Required—TOEFL (minimum score 560 paper-based; 220 computer-based).

State University of New York College of Environmental Science and Forestry, Department of Chemistry, Syracuse, NY 13210-2779. Offers biochemistry (MPS, MS, PhD); environmental chemistry (MPS, MS, PhD); organic chemistry of natural products (MPS, MS, PhD); polymer chemistry (MPS, MS, PhD). *Degree requirements:* For master's, thesis; for doctorate, comprehensive exam, thesis/dissertation. *Entrance requirements:* For master's and doctorate, GRE General Test, GRE Subject Test, minimum GPA of 3.0. Additional exam requirements/recommendations for international students: Required—TOEFL (minimum score 550 paper-based; 213 computer-based; 80 iBT), IELTS (minimum score 6). *Application deadline:* For fall admission, 2/1 priority date for domestic students, 2/1 for international students; for spring admission, 11/1 priority date for domestic students, 11/1 for international students. Applications are processed on a rolling basis. Application fee: $60. Electronic applications accepted. *Expenses:* Tuition, state resident: full-time $8870; part-time $370 per credit hour. Tuition, nonresident: full-time $15,160; part-time $632 per credit hour. *Required fees:* $60; $370 per credit hour. $350 per semester. One-time fee: $85. *Financial support:* Fellowships with full tuition reimbursements, research assistantships with full tuition reimbursements, teaching assistantships with full tuition reimbursements, Federal Work-Study, institutionally sponsored loans, scholarships/grants, health care benefits, and unspecified assistantships available. Financial award application deadline: 6/30; financial award applicants required to submit FAFSA. *Faculty research:* Polymer chemistry, biochemistry. *Total annual research expenditures:* $1.8 million. *Unit head:* Prof. Gregory Boyer, Chair, 315-470-6825, Fax: 315-470-6856, E-mail: glboyer@esf.edu. *Application contact:* Scott Shannon, Associate Provost for Instruction/Dean of the Graduate School, 315-470-6599, Fax: 315-470-6978, E-mail: sshannon@esf.edu. Web site: http://www.esf.edu/chemistry.

Stephen F. Austin State University, Graduate School, College of Sciences and Mathematics, Department of Chemistry, Nacogdoches, TX 75962. Offers MS. Part-time programs available. *Degree requirements:* For master's, comprehensive exam. *Entrance requirements:* For master's, GRE General Test, minimum GPA of 2.8 in last 60 hours, 2.5 overall. Additional exam requirements/recommendations for international students: Required—TOEFL. *Faculty research:* Synthesis and chemistry of ferrate ion, properties of fluoroberyllates, polymer chemistry.

Stevens Institute of Technology, Graduate School, Charles V. Schaefer Jr. School of Engineering, Department of Chemistry, Chemical Biology and Biomedical Engineering, Hoboken, NJ 07030. Offers analytical chemistry (PhD, Certificate); bioinformatics (PhD, Certificate); biomedical chemistry (Certificate); biomedical engineering (M Eng, Certificate); chemical biology (MS, PhD, Certificate); chemical physiology (Certificate); chemistry (MS, PhD); organic chemistry (PhD); physical chemistry (PhD); polymer chemistry (PhD, Certificate). Part-time and evening/weekend programs available. Postbaccalaureate distance learning degree programs offered (no on-campus study). Terminal master's awarded for partial completion of doctoral program. *Degree requirements:* For master's, thesis or alternative; for doctorate, one foreign language, thesis/dissertation; for Certificate, project or thesis. *Entrance requirements:* Additional exam requirements/recommendations for international students: Required—TOEFL. Electronic applications accepted. *Faculty research:* Biochemical reaction engineering, polymerization engineering, reactor design, biochemical process control and synthesis.

Stony Brook University, State University of New York, Graduate School, College of Arts and Sciences, Department of Chemistry, Stony Brook, NY 11794. Offers MS, PhD. Terminal master's awarded for partial completion of doctoral program. *Degree requirements:* For master's, thesis; for doctorate, one foreign language, thesis/dissertation. *Entrance requirements:* For master's and doctorate, GRE General Test. Additional exam requirements/recommendations for international students: Required—TOEFL.

Syracuse University, College of Arts and Sciences, Program in Chemistry, Syracuse, NY 13244. Offers MS, PhD. *Students:* 84 full-time (40 women), 4 part-time (2 women); includes 9 minority (2 Black or African American, non-Hispanic/Latino; 3 Asian, non-Hispanic/Latino; 3 Hispanic/Latino; 1 Two or more races, non-Hispanic/Latino), 24 international. Average age 25. 92 applicants, 58% accepted, 26 enrolled. In 2011, 5 master's, 7 doctorates awarded. *Degree requirements:* For master's, comprehensive exam, thesis (for some programs); for doctorate, comprehensive exam, thesis/dissertation. *Entrance requirements:* For master's and doctorate, GRE General Test. Additional exam requirements/recommendations for international students: Required—TOEFL (minimum score 100 iBT). *Application deadline:* For fall admission, 2/1 priority date for domestic students, 2/1 for international students. Application fee: $75. Electronic applications accepted. *Expenses:* Tuition: Part-time $1206 per credit. *Financial support:* Fellowships with full tuition reimbursements, research assistantships with full and partial tuition reimbursements, and teaching assistantships with full and partial tuition reimbursements available. Financial award application deadline: 1/1; financial award applicants required to submit FAFSA. *Faculty research:* Synthetic organic chemistry, biophysical spectroscopy, solid state in organic chemistry, biochemistry, organometallic chemistry. *Unit head:* Dr. Karin Ruhlandt, Chair, 315-443-4109, Fax: 315-443-4070. *Application contact:* Joyce Lagoe, Information Contact, 315-443-4109, E-mail: jalagoe@syr.edu. Web site: http://www-che.syr.edu/.

Temple University, College of Science and Technology, Department of Chemistry, Philadelphia, PA 19122-6096. Offers MA, PhD. Evening/weekend programs available. *Faculty:* 18 full-time (4 women). *Students:* 92 full-time (31 women), 11 part-time (5 women); includes 8 minority (1 Black or African American, non-Hispanic/Latino; 7 Asian, non-Hispanic/Latino), 58 international. Average age 28. 69 applicants, 26% accepted, 12 enrolled. In 2011, 6 master's, 12 doctorates awarded. Terminal master's awarded for partial completion of doctoral program. *Degree requirements:* For master's, thesis (for some programs); for doctorate, thesis/dissertation, teaching experience. *Entrance requirements:* For master's and doctorate, GRE General Test, minimum GPA of 3.0. Additional exam requirements/recommendations for international students: Required—TOEFL (minimum score 550 paper-based; 213 computer-based; 79 iBT). *Application deadline:* For fall admission, 2/15 for domestic students, 12/15 for international students; for spring admission, 9/15 for domestic students, 8/1 for international students. Applications are processed on a rolling basis. Application fee: $50. Electronic applications accepted. *Expenses:* Tuition, state resident: full-time $12,366; part-time $687 per credit hour. Tuition, nonresident: full-time $17,298; part-time $961 per credit hour. *Required fees:* $590; $213 per year. *Financial support:* Fellowships, research assistantships, and teaching assistantships available. Financial award application deadline: 1/15; financial award applicants required to submit FAFSA. *Faculty research:* Polymers, nonlinear optics, natural products, materials science, enantioselective synthesis. *Unit head:* Dr. Robert Levis, Chair, 215-204-5241, Fax: 215-204-1532, E-mail: rjlevis@temple.edu. *Application contact:* Tara Schumacher, Coordinator of Outreach, 215-204-6575, Fax: 215-204-8781, E-mail: tara.schumacher@temple.edu. Web site: http://www.temple.edu/chemistry.

Tennessee State University, The School of Graduate Studies and Research, College of Arts and Sciences, Department of Chemistry, Nashville, TN 37209-1561. Offers MS. Part-time programs available. *Degree requirements:* For master's, thesis optional. *Entrance requirements:* For master's, GRE General Test. Electronic applications accepted.

Tennessee Technological University, Graduate School, College of Arts and Sciences, Department of Chemistry, Cookeville, TN 38505. Offers MS. Part-time programs available. *Faculty:* 16 full-time (1 woman). *Students:* 10 full-time (3 women), 7 part-time (2 women); includes 2 minority (1 Black or African American, non-Hispanic/Latino; 1 Asian, non-Hispanic/Latino), 11 international. Average age 28. 37 applicants, 19% accepted, 6 enrolled. In 2011, 4 master's awarded. *Degree requirements:* For master's, thesis. *Entrance requirements:* For master's, GRE. Additional exam requirements/recommendations for international students: Required—TOEFL (minimum score 550 paper-based; 79 iBT), IELTS (minimum score 5.5), PTE Academic. *Application deadline:* For fall admission, 8/1 for domestic students, 5/1 for international students; for spring admission, 12/1 for domestic students, 10/1 for international students. Application fee: $25 ($30 for international students). Electronic applications accepted. *Expenses:* Tuition, state

Peterson's Graduate Programs in the Physical Sciences, Mathematics, Agricultural Sciences, the Environment & Natural Resources 2013

resident: full-time $8094; part-time $422 per credit hour. Tuition, nonresident: full-time $20,574; part-time $1046 per credit hour. *Financial support:* In 2011–12, 1 research assistantship (averaging $10,000 per year), 6 teaching assistantships (averaging $7,500 per year) were awarded; career-related internships or fieldwork also available. Financial award application deadline: 4/1. *Unit head:* Dr. Jeffrey Boles, Interim Chairperson, 931-372-3421, Fax: 931-372-3434, E-mail: jboles@tntech.edu. *Application contact:* Shelia K. Kendrick, Coordinator of Graduate Admissions, 931-372-3808, Fax: 931-372-3497, E-mail: skendrick@tntech.edu.

Tennessee Technological University, Graduate School, College of Arts and Sciences, Department of Environmental Sciences, Cookeville, TN 38505. Offers biology (PhD); chemistry (PhD). Part-time programs available. *Students:* 4 full-time (2 women), 12 part-time (5 women); includes 3 minority (1 Black or African American, non-Hispanic/Latino; 1 American Indian or Alaska Native, non-Hispanic/Latino; 1 Hispanic/Latino), 4 international. 8 applicants, 50% accepted, 2 enrolled. In 2011, 1 doctorate awarded. *Degree requirements:* For doctorate, comprehensive exam, thesis/dissertation. *Entrance requirements:* For doctorate, GRE. Additional exam requirements/recommendations for international students: Required—TOEFL (minimum score 550 paper-based; 79 iBT), IELTS (minimum score 5.5), PTE Academic. *Application deadline:* For fall admission, 8/1 for domestic students, 5/1 for international students; for spring admission, 12/1 for domestic students, 10/2 for international students. Application fee: $25 ($30 for international students). Electronic applications accepted. *Expenses:* Tuition, state resident: full-time $8094; part-time $422 per credit hour. Tuition, nonresident: full-time $20,574; part-time $1046 per credit hour. *Financial support:* In 2011–12, 5 research assistantships (averaging $10,000 per year), 3 teaching assistantships (averaging $10,000 per year) were awarded; fellowships also available. Financial award application deadline: 4/1. *Application contact:* Shelia K. Kendrick, Coordinator of Graduate Admissions, 931-372-3808, Fax: 931-372-3497, E-mail: skendrick@tntech.edu.

Texas A&M University, College of Science, Department of Chemistry, College Station, TX 77843. Offers MS, PhD. *Faculty:* 44. *Students:* 276 full-time (102 women), 6 part-time (2 women); includes 32 minority (7 Black or African American, non-Hispanic/Latino; 1 American Indian or Alaska Native, non-Hispanic/Latino; 9 Asian, non-Hispanic/Latino; 14 Hispanic/Latino; 1 Two or more races, non-Hispanic/Latino), 142 international. Average age 24. In 2011, 7 master's, 33 doctorates awarded. Terminal master's awarded for partial completion of doctoral program. *Degree requirements:* For master's, thesis; for doctorate, thesis/dissertation. *Entrance requirements:* For master's and doctorate, GRE General Test. Additional exam requirements/recommendations for international students: Required—TOEFL. *Application deadline:* For fall admission, 3/1 priority date for domestic students. Applications are processed on a rolling basis. Electronic applications accepted. *Expenses:* Tuition, state resident: full-time $5437; part-time $226.55 per credit hour. Tuition, nonresident: full-time $12,949; part-time $539.55 per credit hour. *Required fees:* $2741. *Financial support:* In 2011–12, fellowships with full tuition reimbursements (averaging $21,600 per year), research assistantships with full tuition reimbursements (averaging $18,600 per year), teaching assistantships with full tuition reimbursements (averaging $18,600 per year) were awarded. Financial award application deadline: 3/1; financial award applicants required to submit FAFSA. *Faculty research:* Biological chemistry, spectroscopy, structure and bonding, reactions and mechanisms, theoretical chemistry. *Unit head:* Dr. David Russell, Head, 979-845-3345, E-mail: russell@chem.tamu.edu. *Application contact:* Dr. Michael P. Rosynek, Graduate Advisor, 979-845-2233, Fax: 979-845-4719, E-mail: rosynek@chem.tamu.edu. Web site: http://www.chem.tamu.edu/.

Texas A&M University–Commerce, Graduate School, College of Science, Engineering and Agriculture, Department of Chemistry, Commerce, TX 75429-3011. Offers M Ed, MS. Part-time programs available. *Degree requirements:* For master's, comprehensive exam, thesis (for some programs). *Entrance requirements:* For master's, GRE General Test. Electronic applications accepted. *Faculty research:* Analytical organic.

Texas A&M University–Kingsville, College of Graduate Studies, College of Arts and Sciences, Department of Chemistry, Kingsville, TX 78363. Offers MS. Part-time programs available. *Degree requirements:* For master's, comprehensive exam, thesis or alternative. *Entrance requirements:* For master's, GRE General Test, minimum GPA of 3.0. Additional exam requirements/recommendations for international students: Required—TOEFL. *Faculty research:* Organic heterocycles, amino alcohol complexes, rare earth arsine complexes.

Texas Christian University, College of Science and Engineering, Department of Chemistry, Fort Worth, TX 76129. Offers biochemistry (MS, PhD); chemistry (MA); inorganic (MS, PhD); organic (MS, PhD); physical (MS, PhD). Part-time programs available. *Faculty:* 11 full-time (2 women). *Students:* 4 full-time (2 women), 16 part-time (10 women); includes 3 minority (1 Asian, non-Hispanic/Latino; 2 Hispanic/Latino), 11 international. Average age 27. 5 applicants, 100% accepted, 4 enrolled. In 2011, 1 master's, 3 doctorates awarded. *Degree requirements:* For master's, thesis; for doctorate, thesis/dissertation, literature seminar, cumulative exams, research progress report, original proposal. *Entrance requirements:* For master's and doctorate, GRE General Test. Additional exam requirements/recommendations for international students: Required—TOEFL. *Application deadline:* For fall admission, 3/1 priority date for domestic students, 3/1 for international students; for spring admission, 9/1 priority date for domestic students, 9/1 for international students. Application fee: $50. Electronic applications accepted. *Expenses:* Tuition: Full-time $20,250; part-time $1125 per credit hour. Part-time tuition and fees vary according to course load and program.

Financial support: In 2011–12, 11 students received support, including 11 teaching assistantships with full tuition reimbursements available; tuition waivers (full and partial) and unspecified assistantships also available. Financial award application deadline: 3/1. *Faculty research:* Phase transitions and transport properties of bio/macromolecular solutions, nanoscale biomaterials, electronic structure theory, synthetic methodology and total synthesis of natural products, chemistry and biology of (bio)polymers. *Unit head:* Dr. Robert Neilson, Chairperson/Professor, 817-257-7345, Fax: 817-257-5851, E-mail: r.neilson@tcu.edu. *Application contact:* Dr. Sergei V. Dzyuba, Director of Graduate Studies/Assistant Professor, 817-257-6218, Fax: 817-257-5851, E-mail: s.dzyuba@tcu.edu. Web site: http://www.chm.tcu.edu/.

Texas Southern University, School of Science and Technology, Department of Chemistry, Houston, TX 77004-4584. Offers MS. *Degree requirements:* For master's, one foreign language, comprehensive exam, thesis. *Entrance requirements:* For master's, GRE General Test, minimum GPA of 2.5. Additional exam requirements/recommendations for international students: Required—TOEFL. Electronic applications accepted. *Faculty research:* Analytical and physical chemistry, geochemistry, inorganic chemistry, biochemistry, organic chemistry.

Texas State University–San Marcos, Graduate School, College of Science and Engineering, Department of Chemistry and Biochemistry, Program in Chemistry, San Marcos, TX 78666. Offers MA, MS. *Faculty:* 7 full-time (2 women). *Students:* 13 full-time (5 women), 7 part-time (2 women); includes 2 minority (both Black or African American, non-Hispanic/Latino), 4 international. Average age 27. 21 applicants, 43% accepted, 8 enrolled. In 2011, 5 master's awarded. *Degree requirements:* For master's, comprehensive exam, thesis (for some programs). *Entrance requirements:* For master's, minimum GPA of 2.75 in last 60 hours of course work. Additional exam requirements/recommendations for international students: Required—TOEFL (minimum score 550 paper-based; 213 computer-based; 78 iBT). *Application deadline:* For fall admission, 6/15 for domestic students, 6/1 for international students; for spring admission, 10/15 for domestic students, 10/1 for international students. Applications are processed on a rolling basis. Application fee: $40 ($90 for international students). *Expenses:* Tuition, state resident: full-time $6408; part-time $3204 per semester. Tuition, nonresident: full-time $14,832; part-time $7416 per semester. *Required fees:* $1824; $912 per semester. Tuition and fees vary according to course load. *Financial support:* In 2011–12, 18 students received support, including 7 teaching assistantships (averaging $4,844 per year); research assistantships, career-related internships or fieldwork, Federal Work-Study, institutionally sponsored loans, scholarships/grants, health care benefits, and unspecified assistantships also available. Support available to part-time students. Financial award application deadline: 4/1; financial award applicants required to submit FAFSA. *Unit head:* Dr. Chad Booth, Graduate Advisor, 512-245-2156, Fax: 512-245-2374, E-mail: chadbooth@txstate.edu. *Application contact:* Dr. J. Michael Willoughby, Dean of Graduate School, 512-245-2581, Fax: 512-245-8365, E-mail: gradcollege@txstate.edu. Web site: http://www.txstate.edu/chemistry/.

Texas Tech University, Graduate School, College of Arts and Sciences, Department of Chemistry and Biochemistry, Lubbock, TX 79409. Offers chemistry (MS, PhD). Part-time programs available. *Faculty:* 26 full-time (3 women). *Students:* 90 full-time (41 women), 4 part-time (2 women); includes 7 minority (2 Black or African American, non-Hispanic/Latino; 1 Asian, non-Hispanic/Latino; 4 Hispanic/Latino), 70 international. Average age 27. 131 applicants, 37% accepted, 24 enrolled. In 2011, 16 master's, 9 doctorates awarded. *Degree requirements:* For master's, thesis; for doctorate, thesis/dissertation. *Entrance requirements:* For master's and doctorate, GRE General Test, diagnostic examination in area of specialization. Additional exam requirements/recommendations for international students: Required—TOEFL (minimum score 550 paper-based; 213 computer-based; 79 iBT). *Application deadline:* For fall admission, 6/1 priority date for domestic students, 1/15 for international students; for spring admission, 9/1 priority date for domestic students, 6/15 for international students. Applications are processed on a rolling basis. Application fee: $50 ($75 for international students). Electronic applications accepted. *Expenses:* Tuition, state resident: full-time $5899; part-time $245.80 per credit hour. Tuition, nonresident: full-time $13,411; part-time $558.80 per credit hour. *Required fees:* $2680.60; $86.50 per credit hour. $920.30 per semester. *Financial support:* In 2011–12, 9 students received support. Application deadline: 4/15; applicants required to submit FAFSA. *Faculty research:* Theoretical and computational chemistry, plant biochemistry and chemical biology, materials and supramolecular chemistry, nanotechnology, spectroscopic analysis. *Total annual research expenditures:* $4.5 million. *Unit head:* Dr. Carol Korzeniewski, Chair, 806-742-3067, Fax: 806-742-1289, E-mail: carol.korzeniewski@ttu.edu. *Application contact:* Carly Jenkins, Senior Business Assistant, 806-742-3057, Fax: 806-742-4890, E-mail: carly.jenkins@ttu.edu. Web site: http://www.depts.ttu.edu/chemistry/.

Texas Woman's University, Graduate School, College of Arts and Sciences, Department of Chemistry and Biochemistry, Denton, TX 76201. Offers chemistry (MS). Part-time programs available. *Faculty:* 5 full-time (2 women). *Students:* 4 full-time (2 women), 7 part-time (6 women); includes 2 minority (1 Black or African American, non-Hispanic/Latino; 1 Hispanic/Latino), 2 international. Average age 28. 9 applicants, 44% accepted, 4 enrolled. In 2011, 3 master's awarded. *Degree requirements:* For master's, comprehensive exam, thesis. *Entrance requirements:* For master's, GRE General Test (preferred minimum score 146 [400 old version] verbal, 146 [550 old version] quantitative), 2 reference contacts. Additional exam

Peterson's Graduate Programs in the Physical Sciences, Mathematics, Agricultural Sciences, the Environment & Natural Resources 2013

facebook.com/petersonspublishing **81**

Chemistry

requirements/recommendations for international students: Required—TOEFL (minimum score 550 paper-based; 213 computer-based; 79 iBT). *Application deadline:* For fall admission, 7/1 priority date for domestic students, 3/1 for international students; for spring admission, 12/1 priority date for domestic students, 7/1 for international students. Applications are processed on a rolling basis. Application fee: $50 ($75 for international students). Electronic applications accepted. *Expenses:* Tuition, state resident: full-time $3834; part-time $213 per credit hour. Tuition, nonresident: full-time $9468; part-time $526 per credit hour. *Required fees:* $213 per credit hour. Tuition and fees vary according to course load. *Financial support:* In 2011–12, 4 students received support, including 11 research assistantships (averaging $13,248 per year), teaching assistantships (averaging $13,248 per year); career-related internships or fieldwork, Federal Work-Study, institutionally sponsored loans, scholarships/grants, traineeships, health care benefits, and unspecified assistantships also available. Support available to part-time students. Financial award application deadline: 3/1; financial award applicants required to submit FAFSA. *Faculty research:* Glutathione synthetase, conformational properties of DNA quadruplexes, constriction and analysis of aqueous enzyme phase diagrams, development of metallopolymers, basic chemical research. *Total annual research expenditures:* $107,820. *Unit head:* Dr. Richard Sheardy, Chair, 940-898-2551, Fax: 940-898-2548, E-mail: chemistry@twu.edu. *Application contact:* Dr. Samuel Wheeler, Assistant Director of Admissions, 940-898-3188, Fax: 940-898-3081, E-mail: wheelersr@twu.edu. Web site: http://www.twu.edu/chemistry-biochemistry/.

Trent University, Graduate Studies, Program in Applications of Modeling in the Natural and Social Sciences, Department of Chemistry, Peterborough, ON K9J 7B8, Canada. Offers M Sc. Part-time programs available. *Degree requirements:* For master's, thesis. *Entrance requirements:* For master's, honours degree. *Faculty research:* Synthetic-organic chemistry, mass spectrometry and ion storage.

Tufts University, Graduate School of Arts and Sciences, Department of Chemistry, Medford, MA 02155. Offers analytical chemistry (MS, PhD); bioorganic chemistry (MS, PhD); environmental chemistry (MS, PhD); inorganic chemistry (MS, PhD); organic chemistry (MS, PhD); physical chemistry (MS, PhD). *Students:* 75 full-time (33 women); includes 7 minority (1 Black or African American, non-Hispanic/Latino; 5 Asian, non-Hispanic/Latino; 1 Hispanic/Latino), 25 international. 88 applicants, 59% accepted, 16 enrolled. In 2011, 5 master's, 8 doctorates awarded. Terminal master's awarded for partial completion of doctoral program. *Degree requirements:* For master's, thesis optional; for doctorate, thesis/dissertation. *Entrance requirements:* For master's and doctorate, GRE General Test, GRE Subject Test. Additional exam requirements/ recommendations for international students: Required—TOEFL (minimum score 600 paper-based; 250 computer-based; 80 iBT). *Application deadline:* For fall admission, 1/15 for domestic students, 12/15 for international students; for spring admission, 10/15 for domestic students, 9/15 for international students. Applications are processed on a rolling basis. Application fee: $75. Electronic applications accepted. *Expenses: Tuition:* Full-time $41,208; part-time $1030 per credit hour. Full-time tuition and fees vary according to degree level, program and student level. Part-time tuition and fees vary according to course load. *Financial support:* Fellowships, research assistantships with full tuition reimbursements, teaching assistantships with full tuition reimbursements, Federal Work-Study, scholarships/grants, tuition waivers (partial), and unspecified assistantships available. Financial award application deadline: 1/15; financial award applicants required to submit FAFSA. *Unit head:* Arthur Utz, Chair, 617-627-3441. *Application contact:* Deborah D'Andrea, Information Contact, 617-627-3441, Fax: 617-627-3443. Web site: http://chem.tufts.edu/.

Tulane University, School of Science and Engineering, Department of Chemistry, New Orleans, LA 70118-5669. Offers MS, PhD. Terminal master's awarded for partial completion of doctoral program. *Degree requirements:* For master's, thesis; for doctorate, thesis/dissertation. *Entrance requirements:* For master's, GRE General Test, minimum B average in undergraduate course work; for doctorate, GRE General Test. Additional exam requirements/ recommendations for international students: Required—TOEFL. Electronic applications accepted. *Faculty research:* Enzyme mechanisms, organic synthesis, photochemistry, theory of polymer dynamics.

Tuskegee University, Graduate Programs, College of Agricultural, Environmental and Natural Sciences, Department of Chemistry, Tuskegee, AL 36088. Offers MS. *Faculty:* 6 full-time (1 woman). *Students:* 7 full-time (6 women); includes 5 minority (all Black or African American, non-Hispanic/Latino), 2 international. Average age 31. In 2011, 4 master's awarded. *Degree requirements:* For master's, thesis. *Entrance requirements:* For master's, GRE General Test. Additional exam requirements/recommendations for international students: Required—TOEFL (minimum score 500 paper-based; 69 computer-based). *Application deadline:* For fall admission, 7/15 for domestic students. Applications are processed on a rolling basis. Application fee: $25 ($35 for international students). *Expenses: Tuition:* Full-time $17,070; part-time $705 per credit hour. *Financial support:* Fellowships, teaching assistantships, Federal Work-Study, and institutionally sponsored loans available. Support available to part-time students. Financial award application deadline: 4/15. *Unit head:* Dr. Gregory Pritchett, Head, 334-727-8836. *Application contact:* Dr. Robert L. Laney, Jr., Vice President/Director of Admissions and Enrollment Management, 334-727-8580, Fax: 334-727-5750, E-mail: planey@tuskegee.edu.

Universidad del Turabo, Graduate Programs, Programs in Science and Technology, Gurabo, PR 00778-3030. Offers environmental analysis (MSE),

including environmental chemistry; environmental management (MSE), including pollution management; environmental science (D Sc), including environmental biology. *Students:* 8 full-time (4 women), 101 part-time (68 women); includes 101 minority (all Hispanic/Latino). Average age 39. 58 applicants, 76% accepted, 39 enrolled. In 2011, 16 master's, 3 doctorates awarded. *Entrance requirements:* For master's, GRE, EXADEP, interview. *Application deadline:* For fall admission, 8/5 for domestic students. Application fee: $25. *Unit head:* David Mendez, Head, 787-743-7979. *Application contact:* Virginia Gonzalez, Admissions Officer, 787-746-3009.

Université de Moncton, Faculty of Sciences, Department of Chemistry and Biochemistry, Moncton, NB E1A 3E9, Canada. Offers biochemistry (M Sc); chemistry (M Sc). Part-time programs available. *Degree requirements:* For master's, one foreign language, thesis. *Entrance requirements:* For master's, minimum GPA of 3.0. Electronic applications accepted. *Faculty research:* Environmental contaminants, natural products-synthesis, nutraceutical, organic catalysis, molecular biology of cancer.

Université de Montréal, Faculty of Arts and Sciences, Department of Chemistry, Montréal, QC H3C 3J7, Canada. Offers M Sc, PhD. *Degree requirements:* For master's, thesis; for doctorate, thesis/dissertation, general exam. *Entrance requirements:* For master's, B Sc in chemistry or the equivalent; for doctorate, M Sc in chemistry or equivalent. Electronic applications accepted. *Faculty research:* Analytical, inorganic, physical, and organic chemistry.

Université de Sherbrooke, Faculty of Sciences, Department of Chemistry, Sherbrooke, QC J1K 2R1, Canada. Offers M Sc, PhD, Diploma. *Degree requirements:* For master's, thesis; for doctorate, thesis/dissertation. *Entrance requirements:* For doctorate, master's degree. Electronic applications accepted. *Faculty research:* Organic, electro-, theoretical, and physical chemistry.

Université du Québec à Montréal, Graduate Programs, Program in Chemistry, Montréal, QC H3C 3P8, Canada. Offers M Sc, PhD. M Sc offered jointly with Université du Québec à Trois-Rivières. Part-time programs available. *Degree requirements:* For master's, thesis. *Entrance requirements:* For master's, appropriate bachelor's degree or equivalent and proficiency in French.

Université du Québec à Trois-Rivières, Graduate Programs, Program in Chemistry, Trois-Rivières, QC G9A 5H7, Canada. Offers M Sc. Part-time programs available. *Degree requirements:* For master's, thesis. *Entrance requirements:* For master's, appropriate bachelor's degree, proficiency in French.

Université Laval, Faculty of Sciences and Engineering, Department of Chemistry, Programs in Chemistry, Québec, QC G1K 7P4, Canada. Offers M Sc, PhD. Part-time programs available. Terminal master's awarded for partial completion of doctoral program. *Degree requirements:* For master's, thesis; for doctorate, comprehensive exam, thesis/dissertation. *Entrance requirements:* For master's and doctorate, knowledge of French, comprehension of written English. Electronic applications accepted.

University at Albany, State University of New York, College of Arts and Sciences, Department of Chemistry, Albany, NY 12222-0001. Offers MS, PhD. *Degree requirements:* For master's, one foreign language, thesis, major field exam; for doctorate, 2 foreign languages, thesis/dissertation, cumulative exams, oral proposition. *Entrance requirements:* For doctorate, GRE. Additional exam requirements/recommendations for international students: Required—TOEFL (minimum score 550 paper-based; 213 computer-based). Electronic applications accepted. *Faculty research:* Synthetic, organic, and inorganic chemistry; polymer chemistry; ESR and NMR spectroscopy; theoretical chemistry; physical biochemistry.

University at Albany, State University of New York, School of Public Health, Department of Environmental Health Sciences, Albany, NY 12222-0001. Offers environmental and analytical chemistry (MS, PhD); environmental and occupational health (MS, PhD); toxicology (MS, PhD). *Degree requirements:* For master's, thesis; for doctorate, comprehensive exam, thesis/dissertation. *Entrance requirements:* For master's and doctorate, GRE General Test, GRE Subject Test, 3 letters of reference. Additional exam requirements/recommendations for international students: Required—TOEFL (minimum score 600 paper-based; 213 computer-based). Electronic applications accepted. *Faculty research:* Xenobiotic metabolism, neurotoxicity of halogenated hydrocarbons, pharmac/toxicogenomics, environmental analytical chemistry.

University at Buffalo, the State University of New York, Graduate School, College of Arts and Sciences, Department of Chemistry, Buffalo, NY 14260. Offers chemistry (MA, PhD); medicinal chemistry (MS, PhD). Part-time programs available. *Faculty:* 30 full-time (4 women), 1 (woman) part-time/adjunct. *Students:* 142 full-time (54 women); includes 17 minority (8 Black or African American, non-Hispanic/Latino; 4 Asian, non-Hispanic/Latino; 5 Hispanic/Latino), 43 international. Average age 26. 235 applicants, 25% accepted, 24 enrolled. In 2011, 11 master's, 15 doctorates awarded. Terminal master's awarded for partial completion of doctoral program. *Degree requirements:* For master's, thesis or alternative, project; for doctorate, thesis/dissertation, synopsis proposal. *Entrance requirements:* For master's and doctorate, GRE General Test. Additional exam requirements/recommendations for international students: Required—TOEFL (minimum score 550 paper-based; 213 computer-based; 79 iBT). *Application deadline:* For fall admission, 3/1 priority date for domestic students, 3/1 for international students; for spring admission, 11/1 priority date for domestic students. Applications are processed on a rolling basis. Application fee: $75. Electronic applications accepted. *Financial support:* In 2011–12, 3 students

82 facebook.com/petersonspublishing

Peterson's Graduate Programs in the Physical Sciences, Mathematics, Agricultural Sciences, the Environment & Natural Resources 2013

received support, including 3 fellowships with full tuition reimbursements available (averaging $22,080 per year), 34 research assistantships with full tuition reimbursements available (averaging $22,080 per year), 83 teaching assistantships with full tuition reimbursements available (averaging $22,080 per year); Federal Work-Study, institutionally sponsored loans, and unspecified assistantships also available. Financial award application deadline: 6/15; financial award applicants required to submit FAFSA. *Faculty research:* Synthesis, measurements, structure theory, translation. *Total annual research expenditures:* $1.8 million. *Unit head:* Dr. Luis A. Colon, Chairman, 716-645-6824, Fax: 716-645-6963, E-mail: chechair@buffalo.edu. *Application contact:* Dr. Steven T. Diver, Director of Graduate Studies, 716-645-4208, Fax: 716-645-6963, E-mail: diver@buffalo.edu. Web site: http://www.chem.buffalo.edu/.

The University of Akron, Graduate School, Buchtel College of Arts and Sciences, Department of Chemistry, Akron, OH 44325. Offers MS, PhD. Part-time and evening/weekend programs available. *Faculty:* 18 full-time (2 women), 5 part-time/adjunct (4 women). *Students:* 56 full-time (26 women), 2 part-time (both women); includes 3 minority (2 Black or African American, non-Hispanic/Latino; 1 Hispanic/Latino), 32 international. Average age 29. 94 applicants, 12% accepted, 8 enrolled. In 2011, 1 master's, 13 doctorates awarded. Terminal master's awarded for partial completion of doctoral program. *Degree requirements:* For master's, thesis, seminar presentation; for doctorate, comprehensive exam, thesis/dissertation, cumulative exams, oral exam, defense of dissertation. *Entrance requirements:* For master's, baccalaureate degree in chemistry, biochemistry, or a related field, minimum GPA of 2.75, 3 letters of recommendation, statement of purpose; for doctorate, baccalaureate degree in chemistry, biochemistry, or a related field, minimum GPA of 2.75, three letters of recommendation, statement of purpose. Additional exam requirements/recommendations for international students: Required—TOEFL (minimum score 550 paper-based; 213 computer-based; 79 iBT). *Application deadline:* For fall admission, 6/1 for domestic and international students; for spring admission, 11/15 for domestic and international students. Application fee: $30 ($40 for international students). *Expenses:* Tuition, state resident: full-time $7038; part-time $391 per credit hour. Tuition, nonresident: full-time $12,051; part-time $670 per credit hour. *Required fees:* $1274; $34 per credit hour. *Financial support:* In 2011–12, 9 research assistantships with full tuition reimbursements, 42 teaching assistantships with full tuition reimbursements were awarded; tuition waivers (partial) also available. *Faculty research:* NMR and mass spectrometric characterization of biological and synthetic polymers, synthesis and characterization of new organic and inorganic material, metals in medicine, enzymalogy of gene regulation, high-resolution spectroscopy and ultrafast characterization of organic materials. *Total annual research expenditures:* $726,895. *Unit head:* Dr. Kim Calvo, Chair, 330-972-6135, E-mail: kcalvo@uakron.edu. *Application contact:* Dr. Mark Tausig, Associate Dean, 330-972-6266, Fax: 330-972-6475, E-mail: mtausig@uakron.edu. Web site: http://www.uakron.edu/chemistry/.

The University of Alabama, Graduate School, College of Arts and Sciences, Department of Chemistry, Tuscaloosa, AL 35487-0336. Offers MS, PhD. *Faculty:* 22 full-time (1 woman). *Students:* 85 full-time (35 women), 8 part-time (4 women); includes 12 minority (9 Black or African American, non-Hispanic/Latino; 1 Asian, non-Hispanic/Latino; 2 Hispanic/Latino), 28 international. Average age 28. 145 applicants, 34% accepted, 21 enrolled. In 2011, 7 master's, 7 doctorates awarded. Terminal master's awarded for partial completion of doctoral program. *Median time to degree:* Of those who began their doctoral program in fall 2003, 57% received their degree in 8 years or less. *Degree requirements:* For master's, comprehensive exam, thesis (for some programs), literature seminar; for doctorate, comprehensive exam, thesis/dissertation, exams, research proposal, oral defense. *Entrance requirements:* For master's, GRE, minimum GPA of 3.0; for doctorate, GRE General Test, MAT, minimum GPA of 3.0. Additional exam requirements/recommendations for international students: Required—Pearson Test of English (minimum score 59); Recommended—TOEFL (minimum score 550 paper-based; 213 computer-based; 79 iBT), IELTS (minimum score 6.5). *Application deadline:* Applications are processed on a rolling basis. Application fee: $50 ($60 for international students). Electronic applications accepted. *Expenses:* Tuition, state resident: full-time $8600. Tuition, nonresident: full-time $21,900. *Financial support:* In 2011–12, 13 fellowships with full tuition reimbursements (averaging $21,900 per year), 26 research assistantships with full tuition reimbursements (averaging $21,900 per year), 45 teaching assistantships with full tuition reimbursements (averaging $21,900 per year) were awarded; career-related internships or fieldwork, scholarships/grants, health care benefits, and unspecified assistantships also available. *Faculty research:* Molecular synthesis and assembly, materials and measurements for alternative energy, electronic and magnetic nanomaterials, biochemical processes and biomaterials, environmental and green chemistry. *Total annual research expenditures:* $4 million. *Unit head:* Dr. Kevin H. Shaughnessy, Associate Professor and Chair of Chemistry, 205-348-8436, Fax: 205-348-9104, E-mail: kshaughn@bama.ua.edu. *Application contact:* Dr. Shane C. Street, Associate Professor and Director of Graduate Recruiting, 205-348-5957, Fax: 205-348-9104, E-mail: sstreet@bama.ua.edu. Web site: http://www.bama.ua.edu/~chem/.

The University of Alabama at Birmingham, College of Arts and Sciences, Program in Chemistry, Birmingham, AL 35294. Offers MS, PhD. *Degree requirements:* For master's, thesis (for some programs); for doctorate, thesis/dissertation. *Entrance requirements:* For master's and doctorate, GRE General Test. Additional exam requirements/recommendations for international students: Required—TOEFL. *Application deadline:* Applications are processed on a rolling basis. *Expenses:* Tuition, state resident: full-time $5922; part-time $309 per hour. Tuition, nonresident: full-time $13,428; part-time $726 per hour. Tuition and fees vary according to program. *Financial support:* Fellowships with full tuition reimbursements, research assistantships with full tuition reimbursements, teaching assistantships with full tuition reimbursements, career-related internships or fieldwork, Federal Work-Study, institutionally sponsored loans, health care benefits, and unspecified assistantships available. Support available to part-time students. Financial award application deadline: 5/1; financial award applicants required to submit FAFSA. *Faculty research:* Drug discovery and synthesis, structural biochemistry and physical biochemistry, synthesis and characterization of advanced materials and polymers. *Total annual research expenditures:* $707,000. *Unit head:* Dr. David E. Graves, Chair, 205-975-5381, Fax: 205-934-2543, E-mail: dgraves@uab.edu. Web site: http://www.chem.uab.edu.

The University of Alabama in Huntsville, School of Graduate Studies, College of Science, Department of Chemistry, Huntsville, AL 35899. Offers chemistry (MS); education (MS). Part-time and evening/weekend programs available. *Faculty:* 11 full-time (1 woman). *Students:* 13 full-time (9 women), 5 part-time (3 women); includes 7 minority (4 Black or African American, non-Hispanic/Latino; 1 American Indian or Alaska Native, non-Hispanic/Latino; 1 Asian, non-Hispanic/Latino; 1 Two or more races, non-Hispanic/Latino), 2 international. Average age 28. 10 applicants, 60% accepted, 5 enrolled. In 2011, 4 master's awarded. *Degree requirements:* For master's, comprehensive exam, thesis or alternative, oral and written exams. *Entrance requirements:* For master's, GRE General Test, minimum GPA of 3.0. Additional exam requirements/recommendations for international students: Required—TOEFL (minimum score 550 paper-based; 213 computer-based; 62 iBT). *Application deadline:* For fall admission, 7/15 for domestic students, 4/1 for international students; for spring admission, 11/30 for domestic students, 9/1 for international students. Applications are processed on a rolling basis. Application fee: $40 ($50 for international students). Electronic applications accepted. *Expenses:* Tuition, state resident: full-time $7830; part-time $473.50 per credit. Tuition, nonresident: full-time $18,748; part-time $1128.33 per credit. Tuition and fees vary according to course load and program. *Financial support:* In 2011–12, 12 students received support, including 12 teaching assistantships with full tuition reimbursements available (averaging $11,121 per year); career-related internships or fieldwork, Federal Work-Study, institutionally sponsored loans, scholarships/grants, health care benefits, tuition waivers, and unspecified assistantships also available. Support available to part-time students. Financial award application deadline: 4/1; financial award applicants required to submit FAFSA. *Faculty research:* Kinetics and bonding, organic nonlinear optical materials, x-ray crystallography, crystal growth in space, polymers, Raman spectroscopy. *Total annual research expenditures:* $1.5 million. *Unit head:* Dr. William Setzer, Chair, 256-824-6153, Fax: 256-824-6349, E-mail: setzerw@uah.edu. *Application contact:* Kim Gray, Graduate Studies Admissions Coordinator, 256-824-6002, Fax: 256-824-6405, E-mail: deangrad@uah.edu. Web site: http://chemistry.uah.edu.

University of Alaska Fairbanks, College of Natural Sciences and Mathematics, Department of Chemistry and Biochemistry, Fairbanks, AK 99775-6160. Offers biochemistry and molecular biology (MS, PhD); chemistry (MA, MS); environmental chemistry (MS, PhD). Part-time programs available. *Faculty:* 7 full-time (0 women). *Students:* 26 full-time (11 women), 5 part-time (3 women); includes 4 minority (1 American Indian or Alaska Native, non-Hispanic/Latino; 2 Asian, non-Hispanic/Latino; 1 Hispanic/Latino), 7 international. Average age 27. 28 applicants, 29% accepted, 6 enrolled. In 2011, 4 master's, 3 doctorates awarded. *Degree requirements:* For master's, comprehensive exam, thesis or alternative; for doctorate, comprehensive exam, thesis/dissertation, oral defense. *Entrance requirements:* Additional exam requirements/recommendations for international students: Required—TOEFL (minimum score 550 paper-based; 213 computer-based). *Application deadline:* For fall admission, 6/1 for domestic students, 3/1 for international students; for spring admission, 10/15 for domestic students, 9/1 for international students. Applications are processed on a rolling basis. Application fee: $60. Electronic applications accepted. *Expenses:* Tuition, state resident: full-time $6696; part-time $372 per credit. Tuition, nonresident: full-time $13,680; part-time $760 per credit. Tuition and fees vary according to course load and reciprocity agreements. *Financial support:* In 2011–12, 8 research assistantships with tuition reimbursements (averaging $12,759 per year), 16 teaching assistantships with tuition reimbursements (averaging $17,112 per year) were awarded; fellowships with tuition reimbursements, Federal Work-Study, scholarships/grants, health care benefits, and unspecified assistantships also available. Support available to part-time students. Financial award application deadline: 7/1; financial award applicants required to submit FAFSA. *Faculty research:* Atmospheric aerosols, cold adaptation, hibernation and neuroprotection, liganogated ion channels, arctic contaminants. *Unit head:* Bill Simpson, Department Chair, 907-474-5510, Fax: 907-474-5640, E-mail: fychem@uaf.edu. *Application contact:* Mike Earnest, Director of Admissions, 907-474-7500, Fax: 907-474-5379, E-mail: admissions@uaf.edu. Web site: http://www.uaf.edu/chem.

University of Alberta, Faculty of Graduate Studies and Research, Department of Chemistry, Edmonton, AB T6G 2E1, Canada. Offers M Sc, PhD. Part-time programs available. Terminal master's awarded for partial completion of doctoral program. *Degree requirements:* For master's, thesis; for doctorate, thesis/dissertation. *Entrance requirements:* For master's and doctorate, minimum GPA of 6.5 on 9.0 scale. *Expenses:* Contact institution. *Faculty research:* Synthetic inorganic and organic chemistry, chemical biology and biochemical analysis,

Peterson's Graduate Programs in the Physical Sciences, Mathematics, Agricultural Sciences, the Environment & Natural Resources 2013

facebook.com/petersonpublishing **83**

Chemistry

materials and surface chemistry, spectroscopy and instrumentation, computational chemistry.

The University of Arizona, College of Science, Department of Chemistry and Biochemistry, Tucson, AZ 85721. Offers biochemistry (PhD); chemistry (PhD). Part-time programs available. *Faculty:* 34 full-time (7 women), 4 part-time/adjunct (2 women). *Students:* 193 full-time (86 women), 12 part-time (4 women); includes 22 minority (1 Black or African American, non-Hispanic/Latino; 2 American Indian or Alaska Native, non-Hispanic/Latino; 10 Hispanic/Latino; 1 Native Hawaiian or other Pacific Islander, non-Hispanic/Latino; 8 Two or more races, non-Hispanic/Latino), 78 international. Average age 29. 124 applicants, 31% accepted, 34 enrolled. In 2011, 31 doctorates awarded. *Degree requirements:* For doctorate, comprehensive exam, thesis/dissertation. *Entrance requirements:* For doctorate, GRE General Test, 3 letters of recommendation, statement of purpose. Additional exam requirements/recommendations for international students: Required—TOEFL (minimum score 550 paper-based; 213 computer-based; 79 iBT). *Application deadline:* For fall admission, 2/1 for domestic students, 1/1 for international students; for spring admission, 10/15 for domestic and international students. Applications are processed on a rolling basis. Application fee: $75. Electronic applications accepted. *Expenses:* Tuition, state resident: full-time $10,840. Tuition, nonresident: full-time $25,802. *Financial support:* In 2011–12, 56 research assistantships with full tuition reimbursements (averaging $24,349 per year), 107 teaching assistantships with full tuition reimbursements (averaging $24,878 per year) were awarded; institutionally sponsored loans, scholarships/grants, health care benefits, tuition waivers (partial), and unspecified assistantships also available. Financial award applicants required to submit FAFSA. *Faculty research:* Analytical, inorganic, organic, physical chemistry, biological chemistry. *Total annual research expenditures:* $14.7 million. *Unit head:* Dr. Vicki Wysocki, Head, 520-621-2628, Fax: 520-621-8407, E-mail: vwysocki@u.arizona.edu. *Application contact:* Lori Boyd, 800-545-5814, Fax: 520-621-8407, E-mail: chemistry@arizona.edu. Web site: http://www.chem.arizona.edu/.

University of Arkansas, Graduate School, J. William Fulbright College of Arts and Sciences, Department of Chemistry and Biochemistry, Fayetteville, AR 72701-1201. Offers chemistry (MS, PhD). *Students:* 18 full-time (9 women), 38 part-time (12 women); includes 2 minority (1 Asian, non-Hispanic/Latino; 1 Two or more races, non-Hispanic/Latino), 22 international. In 2011, 2 master's, 11 doctorates awarded. *Degree requirements:* For master's, one foreign language, thesis; for doctorate, one foreign language, thesis/dissertation. *Application deadline:* For fall admission, 4/1 for international students; for spring admission, 10/1 for international students. Applications are processed on a rolling basis. Application fee: $40 ($50 for international students). Electronic applications accepted. *Financial support:* In 2011–12, 17 research assistantships, 32 teaching assistantships were awarded; fellowships with tuition reimbursements, career-related internships or fieldwork, and Federal Work-Study also available. Support available to part-time students. Financial award application deadline: 4/1; financial award applicants required to submit FAFSA. *Unit head:* Dr. Bob Gawley, Departmental Chairperson, 479-575-4601, Fax: 479-575-4049, E-mail: cheminfo@uark.edu. *Application contact:* Graduate Admissions, 479-575-6246, Fax: 479-575-5908, E-mail: gradinfo@uark.edu. Web site: http://chemistry.uark.edu/.

University of Arkansas at Little Rock, Graduate School, College of Science and Mathematics, Department of Chemistry, Little Rock, AR 72204-1099. Offers MA, MS. Part-time and evening/weekend programs available. *Degree requirements:* For master's, thesis (MS). *Entrance requirements:* For master's, minimum GPA of 2.7.

The University of British Columbia, Faculty of Science, Program in Chemistry, Vancouver, BC V6T 1Z1, Canada. Offers M Sc, PhD. Terminal master's awarded for partial completion of doctoral program. *Degree requirements:* For master's, thesis; for doctorate, comprehensive exam, thesis/dissertation. *Entrance requirements:* For master's and doctorate, GRE General Test, GRE Subject Test. Additional exam requirements/recommendations for international students: Required—TOEFL (minimum score 580 paper-based; 237 computer-based). Electronic applications accepted. *Faculty research:* Organic, physical, analytical, inorganic, and bio-chemical projects.

University of Calgary, Faculty of Graduate Studies, Faculty of Science, Department of Chemistry, Calgary, AB T2N 1N4, Canada. Offers analytical chemistry (M Sc, PhD); applied chemistry (M Sc, PhD); inorganic chemistry (M Sc, PhD); organic chemistry (M Sc, PhD); physical chemistry (M Sc, PhD); polymer chemistry (M Sc, PhD); theoretical chemistry (M Sc, PhD). *Degree requirements:* For master's, thesis; for doctorate, thesis/dissertation, candidacy exam. *Entrance requirements:* For master's, minimum GPA of 3.0; for doctorate, honors B Sc degree with minimum GPA of 3.7 or M Sc with minimum GPA of 3.3. Additional exam requirements/recommendations for international students: Required—TOEFL (minimum score 580 paper-based; 237 computer-based). Electronic applications accepted. *Faculty research:* Chemical analysis, chemical dynamics, synthesis theory.

University of California, Berkeley, Graduate Division, College of Chemistry, Department of Chemistry, Berkeley, CA 94720-1500. Offers PhD. *Degree requirements:* For doctorate, thesis/dissertation, qualifying exam. *Entrance requirements:* For doctorate, GRE General Test, GRE Subject Test, minimum GPA of 3.0, 3 letters of recommendation. Additional exam requirements/recommendations for international students: Required—TOEFL. Electronic

applications accepted. *Faculty research:* Analytical bioinorganic, bio-organic, biophysical environmental, inorganic and organometallic.

University of California, Davis, Graduate Studies, Graduate Group in Agricultural and Environmental Chemistry, Davis, CA 95616. Offers MS, PhD. *Degree requirements:* For master's, thesis; for doctorate, thesis/dissertation. *Entrance requirements:* For master's and doctorate, GRE General Test, minimum GPA of 3.0. Additional exam requirements/recommendations for international students: Required—TOEFL (minimum score 550 paper-based; 213 computer-based). Electronic applications accepted.

University of California, Davis, Graduate Studies, Program in Chemistry, Davis, CA 95616. Offers MS, PhD. Terminal master's awarded for partial completion of doctoral program. *Degree requirements:* For master's, thesis; for doctorate, thesis/dissertation. *Entrance requirements:* For master's, minimum GPA of 3.0; for doctorate, GRE, minimum GPA of 3.0. Additional exam requirements/recommendations for international students: Required—TOEFL (minimum score 550 paper-based; 213 computer-based). Electronic applications accepted. *Faculty research:* Analytical, biological, organic, inorganic, and theoretical chemistry.

University of California, Irvine, School of Physical Sciences, Department of Chemistry, Irvine, CA 92697. Offers chemical and material physics (PhD); chemical and materials physics (MS); chemistry (MS, PhD). *Students:* 193 full-time (84 women), 2 part-time (1 woman); includes 40 minority (27 Asian, non-Hispanic/Latino; 10 Hispanic/Latino; 3 Two or more races, non-Hispanic/Latino), 31 international. Average age 26. 319 applicants, 41% accepted, 43 enrolled. In 2011, 24 master's, 40 doctorates awarded. *Degree requirements:* For doctorate, thesis/dissertation. *Entrance requirements:* For master's and doctorate, GRE General Test, GRE Subject Test, minimum GPA of 3.0. Additional exam requirements/recommendations for international students: Required—TOEFL (minimum score 550 paper-based; 213 computer-based). *Application deadline:* For fall admission, 1/15 priority date for domestic students, 1/15 for international students. Applications are processed on a rolling basis. Application fee: $80 ($100 for international students). Electronic applications accepted. *Financial support:* Fellowships, research assistantships with full tuition reimbursements, teaching assistantships, institutionally sponsored loans, traineeships, health care benefits, and unspecified assistantships available. Financial award application deadline: 3/1; financial award applicants required to submit FAFSA. *Faculty research:* Analytical, organic, inorganic, physical, and atmospheric chemistry; biogeochemistry and climate; synthetic chemistry. *Unit head:* Dr. Scott Rychnovsky, Chair, 949-824-8292, Fax: 949-824-6379, E-mail: srychnov@uci.edu. *Application contact:* Jaime M. Albano, Graduate Affairs Officer, 949-824-4261, Fax: 949-824-8571, E-mail: jmalbano@uci.edu. Web site: http://www.chem.uci.edu/.

University of California, Los Angeles, Graduate Division, College of Letters and Science, Department of Chemistry and Biochemistry, Program in Chemistry, Los Angeles, CA 90095. Offers MS, PhD. *Students:* 216 full-time (72 women); includes 70 minority (3 Black or African American, non-Hispanic/Latino; 39 Asian, non-Hispanic/Latino; 23 Hispanic/Latino; 5 Two or more races, non-Hispanic/Latino), 39 international. Average age 26. 336 applicants, 44% accepted, 43 enrolled. In 2011, 25 master's, 26 doctorates awarded. Terminal master's awarded for partial completion of doctoral program. *Degree requirements:* For master's, comprehensive exam or thesis; for doctorate, thesis/dissertation, oral and written exams, 1 year teaching experience. *Entrance requirements:* For master's, GRE General Test, GRE Subject Test, minimum GPA of 3.0; for doctorate, GRE General Test, GRE Subject Test, minimum undergraduate GPA of 3.0. *Application deadline:* For fall admission, 1/15 for domestic and international students. Application fee: $70 ($90 for international students). Electronic applications accepted. *Financial support:* In 2011–12, 217 fellowships with full and partial tuition reimbursements, 144 research assistantships with full and partial tuition reimbursements, 146 teaching assistantships with full and partial tuition reimbursements were awarded; Federal Work-Study, scholarships/grants, health care benefits, tuition waivers (full and partial), and unspecified assistantships also available. Financial award applicants required to submit FAFSA. *Unit head:* Dr. Albert Courey, 310-825-2530, E-mail: courey@chem.ucla.edu. *Application contact:* Departmental Office, 310-825-1490, E-mail: chemgrad@chem.ucla.edu. Web site: http://www.chem.ucla.edu.

University of California, Merced, Division of Graduate Studies, School of Natural Sciences, Merced, CA 95343. Offers applied mathematics (MS, PhD); biological engineering and small-scale technologies (MS, PhD); environmental systems (MS, PhD); mechanical engineering and applied mechanics (MS, PhD); physics and chemistry (PhD); quantitative and systems biology (MS, PhD). *Unit head:* Dr. Samuel J. Traina, Dean, 209-228-4723, Fax: 209-228-6906, E-mail: grad.dean@ucmerced.edu. *Application contact:* Tsu Ya, Graduate Admissions and Academic Services Manager, 209-228-4723, Fax: 209-228-6906, E-mail: tya@ucmerced.edu.

University of California, Riverside, Graduate Division, Department of Chemistry, Riverside, CA 92521-0403. Offers MS, PhD. *Faculty:* 28 full-time (5 women). *Students:* 114 full-time (35 women); includes 21 minority (3 Black or African American, non-Hispanic/Latino; 6 Asian, non-Hispanic/Latino; 11 Hispanic/Latino; 1 Native Hawaiian or other Pacific Islander, non-Hispanic/Latino), 40 international. Average age 27. 230 applicants, 17% accepted, 20 enrolled. In 2011, 10 master's, 22 doctorates awarded. Terminal master's awarded for partial completion of doctoral program. *Degree requirements:* For master's, qualifying

84 facebook.com/petersonspublishing

Peterson's Graduate Programs in the Physical Sciences, Mathematics, Agricultural Sciences, the Environment & Natural Resources 2013

exams or thesis; for doctorate, thesis/dissertation, qualifying exams, 3 quarters of teaching experience, research proposition. *Entrance requirements:* For master's and doctorate, GRE General Test, minimum GPA of 3.0. Additional exam requirements/recommendations for international students: Required—TOEFL (minimum score 550 paper-based; 213 computer-based; 80 iBT). *Application deadline:* For fall admission, 1/5 for domestic and international students; for winter admission, 12/1 for domestic students, 4/1 for international students; for spring admission, 3/1 for domestic students, 10/1 for international students. Applications are processed on a rolling basis. Application fee: $100. Electronic applications accepted. *Financial support:* In 2011–12, 113 students received support, including 13 fellowships with full tuition reimbursements available (averaging $16,348 per year), 32 research assistantships with full tuition reimbursements available (averaging $23,579 per year), 68 teaching assistantships with full tuition reimbursements available (averaging $23,079 per year); career-related internships or fieldwork, Federal Work-Study, institutionally sponsored loans, and tuition waivers (full and partial) also available. Financial award application deadline: 2/1; financial award applicants required to submit FAFSA. *Faculty research:* Analytical, inorganic, organic, and physical chemistry; chemical physics. *Total annual research expenditures:* $4.8 million. *Unit head:* Prof. Eric L. Chronister, Chair, 951-827-3288, Fax: 951-827-4713, E-mail: eric.chronister@ucr.edu. *Application contact:* Prof. Christopher J. Bardeen, Graduate Advisor, 951-827-2723, Fax: 951-827-4713, E-mail: christopher.bardeen@ucr.edu. Web site: http://www.chem.ucr.edu/.

University of California, San Diego, Office of Graduate Studies, Department of Chemistry and Biochemistry, La Jolla, CA 92093. Offers chemistry (MS, PhD). *Degree requirements:* For doctorate, thesis/dissertation. *Entrance requirements:* For doctorate, GRE General Test, GRE Subject Test. Electronic applications accepted.

University of California, San Francisco, School of Pharmacy and Graduate Division, Chemistry and Chemical Biology Graduate Program, San Francisco, CA 94143. Offers PhD. *Faculty:* 45 full-time (11 women). *Students:* 52 full-time (30 women); includes 17 minority (4 Black or African American, non-Hispanic/Latino; 8 Asian, non-Hispanic/Latino; 5 Hispanic/Latino), 4 international. Average age 27. 95 applicants, 23% accepted, 7 enrolled. In 2011, 7 degrees awarded. *Median time to degree:* Of those who began their doctoral program in fall 2003, 100% received their degree in 8 years or less. *Degree requirements:* For doctorate, thesis/dissertation. *Entrance requirements:* For doctorate, GRE General Test, GRE Subject Test, minimum GPA of 3.0. Additional exam requirements/recommendations for international students: Required—TOEFL (minimum score 550 paper-based; 213 computer-based; 80 iBT). *Application deadline:* For fall admission, 12/1 for domestic and international students. Applications are processed on a rolling basis. Application fee: $80 ($100 for international students). Electronic applications accepted. *Financial support:* In 2011–12, 52 students received support, including 9 fellowships with full tuition reimbursements available (averaging $29,500 per year), 43 research assistantships with full tuition reimbursements available (averaging $29,500 per year); teaching assistantships with partial tuition reimbursements available, institutionally sponsored loans, scholarships/grants, traineeships, and tuition waivers (full) also available. Financial award application deadline: 5/15. *Faculty research:* Biochemistry, macromolecular structure, cellular and molecular pharmacology, physical chemistry and computational biology, synthetic chemistry. *Unit head:* Dr. Charles S. Craik, Director, 415-476-8146, E-mail: craik@cgl.ucsf.edu. *Application contact:* Julia Molla, Senior Administrative Analyst, 415-476-1914, Fax: 415-514-1546, E-mail: julia.molla@ucsf.edu. Web site: http://ccb.ucsf.edu/.

University of California, Santa Barbara, Graduate Division, College of Letters and Sciences, Division of Mathematics, Life, and Physical Sciences, Department of Chemistry and Biochemistry, Santa Barbara, CA 93106-9510. Offers chemistry (MA, MS, PhD). *Faculty:* 35 full-time (8 women), 3 part-time/adjunct (0 women). *Students:* 147 full-time (42 women); includes 23 minority (2 Black or African American, non-Hispanic/Latino; 1 American Indian or Alaska Native, non-Hispanic/Latino; 14 Asian, non-Hispanic/Latino; 6 Hispanic/Latino), 25 international. Average age 27. 242 applicants, 48% accepted, 37 enrolled. In 2011, 7 master's, 30 doctorates awarded. Terminal master's awarded for partial completion of doctoral program. *Median time to degree:* Of those who began their doctoral program in fall 2003, 58% received their degree in 8 years or less. *Degree requirements:* For master's, comprehensive exam (for some programs), thesis (for some programs), annual faculty committee meetings; for doctorate, comprehensive exam, thesis/dissertation, annual faculty committee meetings; minimum 1 year teaching experience. *Entrance requirements:* For master's and doctorate, GRE, 3 letters of recommendation, statement of purpose, personal achievements essay, resume/curriculum vitae, transcripts. Additional exam requirements/recommendations for international students: Required—TOEFL (minimum score 550 paper-based; 213 computer-based; 80 iBT), IELTS (minimum score 7). *Application deadline:* For fall admission, 12/15 priority date for domestic students, 12/15 for international students. Application fee: $80 ($100 for international students). Electronic applications accepted. *Expenses:* Tuition, state resident: full-time $12,192. Tuition, nonresident: full-time $27,294. *Required fees:* $764.13. *Financial support:* In 2011–12, 115 students received support, including 103 fellowships with full and partial tuition reimbursements available (averaging $7,407 per year), 24 research assistantships with full and partial tuition reimbursements available (averaging $12,735 per year), 87 teaching assistantships with full and partial tuition reimbursements available (averaging $17,309 per year); career-related internships or fieldwork, Federal Work-Study, institutionally sponsored loans, scholarships/grants, traineeships, health care

benefits, tuition waivers (full and partial), and unspecified assistantships also available. Support available to part-time students. Financial award application deadline: 12/15; financial award applicants required to submit FAFSA. *Faculty research:* Organic, inorganic, physical, and materials chemistry, biochemistry. *Unit head:* Dr. Fredrick W. Dahlquist, Department Chair, 805-893-5326, Fax: 805-893-4120, E-mail: dahlquist@chem.ucsb.edu. *Application contact:* Mallarie A. Stevens, Graduate Program Advisor/Student Affairs Manager, 805-893-5675, Fax: 805-893-4120, E-mail: gradprog@chem.ucsb.edu. Web site: http://www.chem.ucsb.edu/.

University of California, Santa Cruz, Division of Graduate Studies, Division of Physical and Biological Sciences, Department of Chemistry and Biochemistry, Santa Cruz, CA 95064. Offers MS, PhD. *Degree requirements:* For master's, thesis optional; for doctorate, one foreign language, thesis/dissertation, qualifying exam. *Entrance requirements:* For master's and doctorate, GRE General Test, GRE Subject Test. Additional exam requirements/recommendations for international students: Required—TOEFL (minimum score 570 paper-based; 230 computer-based; 89 iBT); Recommended—IELTS (minimum score 8). Electronic applications accepted. *Faculty research:* Marine chemistry; biochemistry; inorganic, organic, and physical chemistry.

University of Central Florida, College of Sciences, Department of Chemistry, Orlando, FL 32816. Offers chemistry (MS, PhD); computer forensics (Certificate). Part-time and evening/weekend programs available. *Faculty:* 28 full-time (1 woman), 6 part-time/adjunct (3 women). *Students:* 70 full-time (31 women), 23 part-time (5 women); includes 27 minority (3 Black or African American, non-Hispanic/Latino; 9 Asian, non-Hispanic/Latino; 14 Hispanic/Latino; 1 Two or more races, non-Hispanic/Latino), 20 international. Average age 31. 86 applicants, 57% accepted, 21 enrolled. In 2011, 5 master's, 13 doctorates, 8 other advanced degrees awarded. *Degree requirements:* For master's, thesis, final exam. *Entrance requirements:* For master's, GRE General Test, minimum GPA of 3.0 in last 60 hours. Additional exam requirements/recommendations for international students: Required—TOEFL. *Application deadline:* For fall admission, 7/15 for domestic students; for spring admission, 12/1 for domestic students. Application fee: $30. Electronic applications accepted. *Expenses:* Tuition, state resident: part-time $277.08 per credit hour. Tuition, nonresident: part-time $277.08 per credit hour. Part-time tuition and fees vary according to degree level and program. *Financial support:* In 2011–12, 58 students received support, including 1 fellowship with partial tuition reimbursements available (averaging $5,400 per year), 18 research assistantships with partial tuition reimbursements available (averaging $9,200 per year), 50 teaching assistantships with partial tuition reimbursements available (averaging $10,800 per year); career-related internships or fieldwork, Federal Work-Study, institutionally sponsored loans, tuition waivers (partial), and unspecified assistantships also available. Financial award application deadline: 3/1; financial award applicants required to submit FAFSA. *Faculty research:* Physical and synthetic organic chemistry, lasers, polymers, biochemical action of pesticides, environmental analysis. *Unit head:* Dr. Kevin D. Belfield, Chair, 407-823-2246, Fax: 407-823-2252, E-mail: belfield@ucf.edu. *Application contact:* Barbara Rodriguez, Director, Admissions and Registration, 407-823-2766, Fax: 407-823-6442, E-mail: gradadmissions@ucf.edu. Web site: http://chemistry.cos.ucf.edu/.

University of Central Oklahoma, College of Graduate Studies and Research, College of Mathematics and Science, Department of Chemistry, Edmond, OK 73034-5209. Offers MS. Part-time programs available. *Faculty:* 3 full-time (1 woman), 3 part-time/adjunct (0 women). *Students:* 16 full-time (11 women), 24 part-time (21 women); includes 9 minority (3 Black or African American, non-Hispanic/Latino; 2 Asian, non-Hispanic/Latino; 4 Hispanic/Latino), 1 international. Average age 28. In 2011, 18 master's awarded. *Entrance requirements:* For master's, GRE General Test. *Application deadline:* For fall admission, 7/1 for international students; for spring admission, 11/1 for international students. Applications are processed on a rolling basis. Application fee: $25. Electronic applications accepted. *Expenses:* Tuition, state resident: full-time $3901; part-time $218.30 per credit hour. Tuition, nonresident: full-time $9198; part-time $511.20 per credit hour. Tuition and fees vary according to program. *Financial support:* Application deadline: 3/31; applicants required to submit FAFSA. *Unit head:* Dr. Cheryl Frech, Chairperson, 405-974-5476. *Application contact:* Dr. John Garic, Interim Dean, Graduate College, 405-974-3341, Fax: 405-974-3852, E-mail: gradcoll@ucok.edu.

University of Chicago, Division of the Physical Sciences, Department of Chemistry, Chicago, IL 60637-1513. Offers PhD. *Faculty:* 23 full-time (2 women). *Students:* 175 full-time (45 women); includes 16 minority (1 Black or African American, non-Hispanic/Latino; 12 Asian, non-Hispanic/Latino; 3 Hispanic/Latino), 90 international. Average age 24. 412 applicants, 27% accepted, 32 enrolled. In 2011, 29 doctorates awarded. *Degree requirements:* For doctorate, comprehensive exam, thesis/dissertation. *Entrance requirements:* For doctorate, GRE General Test, GRE Subject Test. Additional exam requirements/recommendations for international students: Required—TOEFL (minimum score 600 paper-based; 205 computer-based; 104 iBT), IELTS (minimum score 7). *Application deadline:* For fall admission, 12/31 for domestic and international students. Applications are processed on a rolling basis. Application fee: $55. Electronic applications accepted. *Expenses:* Contact institution. *Financial support:* In 2011–12, 17 fellowships with full tuition reimbursements (averaging $26,749 per year), 120 research assistantships with full tuition reimbursements (averaging $29,148 per year), 38 teaching assistantships with full tuition reimbursements (averaging $31,764 per year) were awarded; institutionally sponsored loans,

Peterson's Graduate Programs in the Physical Sciences, Mathematics, Agricultural Sciences, the Environment & Natural Resources 2013

facebook.com/petersonspublishing **85**

Chemistry

scholarships/grants, traineeships, health care benefits, and unspecified assistantships also available. Financial award application deadline: 12/31; financial award applicants required to submit FAFSA. *Faculty research:* Organic, inorganic, physical, biological chemistry. *Total annual research expenditures:* $16.4 million. *Unit head:* Dr. Richard F. Jordan, Chairman, 773-702-8639, Fax: 773-702-6594, E-mail: chem-chair@uchicago.edu. *Application contact:* Dr. Vera Dragisich, Executive Officer, 773-702-7250, Fax: 773-702-6594, E-mail: v-dragisich@uchicago.edu. Web site: http://chemistry.uchicago.edu/.

University of Cincinnati, Graduate School, McMicken College of Arts and Sciences, Department of Chemistry, Cincinnati, OH 45221. Offers analytical chemistry (MS, PhD); biochemistry (MS, PhD); inorganic chemistry (MS, PhD); organic chemistry (MS, PhD); physical chemistry (MS, PhD); polymer chemistry (MS, PhD); sensors (PhD). Part-time and evening/weekend programs available. Terminal master's awarded for partial completion of doctoral program. *Degree requirements:* For master's, thesis optional; for doctorate, comprehensive exam, thesis/dissertation. *Entrance requirements:* For master's and doctorate, GRE General Test. Additional exam requirements/recommendations for international students: Required—TOEFL (minimum score 580 paper-based; 237 computer-based). Electronic applications accepted. *Faculty research:* Biomedical chemistry, laser chemistry, surface science, chemical sensors, synthesis.

University of Colorado at Colorado Springs, College of Letters, Arts and Sciences, Master of Sciences Program, Colorado Springs, CO 80933-7150. Offers applied science bioscience (M Sc); applied science physics (M Sc); biology (M Sc); chemistry (M Sc); health promotion (M Sc); mathematics (M Sc); physics (M Sc); sports medicine (M Sc); sports nutrition (M Sc). Part-time programs available. *Students:* 13 full-time (5 women), 11 part-time (6 women); includes 3 minority (2 Asian, non-Hispanic/Latino; 1 Hispanic/Latino). Average age 33. 15 applicants, 53% accepted, 3 enrolled. In 2011, 39 degrees awarded. *Degree requirements:* For master's, thesis or alternative. *Entrance requirements:* For master's, minimum GPA of 2.75. Additional exam requirements/recommendations for international students: Recommended—TOEFL. *Application deadline:* For fall admission, 6/1 priority date for domestic students; for spring admission, 12/1 for domestic students. Application fee: $60 ($75 for international students). *Expenses:* Contact institution. *Financial support:* In 2011–12, 5 students received support. Fellowships, research assistantships, teaching assistantships, career-related internships or fieldwork, Federal Work-Study, and scholarships/grants available. Support available to part-time students. Financial award application deadline: 3/1; financial award applicants required to submit FAFSA. *Faculty research:* Biomechanics and physiology of elite athletic training, genetic engineering in yeast and bacteria including phage display and DNA repair, immunology and cell biology, synthetic organic chemistry. *Unit head:* Dr. Tom Christensen, Dean, 719-255-4550, Fax: 719-255-4200, E-mail: tchriste@uccs.edu. *Application contact:* Taryn Bailey, Information Contact, 719-255-3702, Fax: 719-255-3037, E-mail: gradinfo@uccs.edu.

University of Colorado Boulder, Graduate School, College of Arts and Sciences, Department of Chemistry and Biochemistry, Boulder, CO 80309. Offers biochemistry (PhD); chemistry (MS). *Faculty:* 40 full-time (7 women). *Students:* 210 full-time (83 women), 2 part-time; includes 20 minority (3 Black or African American, non-Hispanic/Latino; 7 Asian, non-Hispanic/Latino; 9 Hispanic/Latino; 1 Two or more races, non-Hispanic/Latino), 38 international. Average age 27. 451 applicants, 10% accepted, 42 enrolled. In 2011, 3 master's, 26 doctorates awarded. Terminal master's awarded for partial completion of doctoral program. *Degree requirements:* For master's, comprehensive exam or thesis; for doctorate, comprehensive exam, thesis/dissertation, cumulative exam. *Entrance requirements:* For master's, GRE General Test, GRE Subject Test, minimum undergraduate GPA of 2.75; for doctorate, GRE General Test, GRE Subject Test, minimum GPA of 3.0. *Application deadline:* For fall admission, 1/15 priority date for domestic students, 1/15 for international students. Applications are processed on a rolling basis. Application fee: $50 ($60 for international students). Electronic applications accepted. *Financial support:* In 2011–12, 265 students received support, including 119 fellowships (averaging $8,382 per year), 125 research assistantships with full and partial tuition reimbursements available (averaging $21,743 per year), 53 teaching assistantships with full and partial tuition reimbursements available (averaging $20,060 per year); institutionally sponsored loans, scholarships/grants, health care benefits, and unspecified assistantships also available. Financial award applicants required to submit FAFSA. *Faculty research:* Analytical, atmospheric, biochemistry, biophysical, chemical physics, environmental, inorganic, organic and physical chemistry. *Total annual research expenditures:* $26.7 million. *Application contact:* E-mail: gradassist.chembiochem@colorado.edu. Web site: http://chem.colorado.edu.

University of Colorado Denver, College of Liberal Arts and Sciences, Department of Chemistry, Denver, CO 80217. Offers MS. Part-time programs available. *Faculty:* 12 full-time (3 women). *Students:* 12 full-time (4 women), 7 part-time; includes 7 minority (1 Black or African American, non-Hispanic/Latino; 4 Asian, non-Hispanic/Latino; 2 Hispanic/Latino). Average age 29. 16 applicants, 50% accepted, 6 enrolled. In 2011, 2 master's awarded. *Degree requirements:* For master's, comprehensive exam, thesis or alternative, 30-33 credit hours. *Entrance requirements:* For master's, GRE General Test and GRE Subject Test in chemistry (recommended), undergraduate degree in chemistry, including two semesters of organic, analytical and physical chemistry, with laboratories, and one semester of inorganic chemistry; minimum undergraduate GPA of 3.0. Additional exam requirements/recommendations for international students: Required—TOEFL (minimum score 525 paper-based; 197 computer-based).

Application deadline: For fall admission, 7/22 priority date for domestic students; for spring admission, 12/1 priority date for domestic students. Applications are processed on a rolling basis. Application fee: $50 ($75 for international students). Electronic applications accepted. *Financial support:* Research assistantships, teaching assistantships, and Federal Work-Study available. Financial award application deadline: 4/1; financial award applicants required to submit FAFSA. *Faculty research:* Enzymology of proteinases, computational chemistry, metal-organic coordination and materials chemistry, environmental chemistry, materials chemistry. *Unit head:* Dr. Mark Anderson, Professor and Chair, 303-352-3530, Fax: 303-556-4776, E-mail: mark.anderson@ucdenver.edu. *Application contact:* Laura Cuellar, Program Assistant, 303-556-3259, Fax: 303-556-4776, E-mail: laura.cuellar@ucdenver.edu. Web site: http://www.ucdenver.edu/academics/colleges/CLAS/Departments/chemistry/Pages/Chemistry.aspx.

University of Connecticut, Graduate School, College of Liberal Arts and Sciences, Department of Chemistry, Storrs, CT 06269. Offers MS, PhD. Terminal master's awarded for partial completion of doctoral program. *Degree requirements:* For master's, comprehensive exam; for doctorate, thesis/dissertation. *Entrance requirements:* For master's and doctorate, GRE General Test, GRE Subject Test. Additional exam requirements/recommendations for international students: Required—TOEFL (minimum score 550 paper-based; 213 computer-based). Electronic applications accepted.

University of Dayton, Department of Chemistry, Dayton, OH 45469-1300. Offers MS. Part-time programs available. *Faculty:* 9 full-time (0 women). *Students:* 5 full-time (4 women), 3 part-time (1 woman), 7 international. Average age 24. 39 applicants, 23% accepted, 5 enrolled. In 2011, 2 degrees awarded. *Degree requirements:* For master's, thesis and 30 credit hours (21 course and 9 research) or 30 hours course credit. *Entrance requirements:* For master's, GRE, American Chemical Society standardized exams, BS in chemistry or closely-related discipline. Additional exam requirements/recommendations for international students: Required—TOEFL (minimum score 550 paper-based; 213 computer-based; 80 iBT), TWE. *Application deadline:* For fall admission, 3/1 priority date for domestic students, 3/1 for international students; for winter admission, 7/1 for international students; for spring admission, 1/1 for international students. Applications are processed on a rolling basis. Application fee: $0. Electronic applications accepted. *Expenses: Tuition:* Full-time $8400; part-time $700 per credit hour. *Required fees:* $25 per semester. Tuition and fees vary according to degree level. *Financial support:* In 2011–12, 8 teaching assistantships with full tuition reimbursements (averaging $11,694 per year) were awarded; institutionally sponsored loans, health care benefits, and unspecified assistantships also available. Financial award applicants required to submit FAFSA. *Faculty research:* Organic synthesis, medicinal chemistry, enzyme purification, physical organic, materials chemistry and nanotechnology. *Total annual research expenditures:* $20,000. *Unit head:* Dr. Mark Masthay, Chair, 937-229-2631, E-mail: mmasthay1@udayton.edu. *Application contact:* Dr. Kevin Church, Graduate Program Director, 937-229-2659, E-mail: kchurch1@udayton.edu.

University of Delaware, College of Arts and Sciences, Department of Chemistry and Biochemistry, Newark, DE 19716. Offers biochemistry (MA, MS, PhD); chemistry (MA, MS, PhD). Part-time programs available. Terminal master's awarded for partial completion of doctoral program. *Degree requirements:* For master's, one foreign language, thesis (for some programs); for doctorate, one foreign language, thesis/dissertation, cumulative exam. *Entrance requirements:* For master's and doctorate, GRE General Test. Additional exam requirements/recommendations for international students: Required—TOEFL (minimum score 600 paper-based; 260 computer-based). Electronic applications accepted. *Faculty research:* Micro-organisms, bone, cancer metastasis, developmental biology, cell biology, molecular biology.

University of Denver, Faculty of Natural Sciences and Mathematics, Department of Chemistry and Biochemistry, Denver, CO 80208. Offers MA, MS, PhD. Part-time programs available. *Faculty:* 16 full-time (2 women), 4 part-time/adjunct (1 woman). *Students:* 13 full-time (9 women), 12 part-time (6 women); includes 1 minority (Black or African American, non-Hispanic/Latino), 11 international. Average age 28. 41 applicants, 41% accepted, 10 enrolled. In 2011, 1 degree awarded. Terminal master's awarded for partial completion of doctoral program. *Median time to degree:* Of those who began their doctoral program in fall 2003, 100% received their degree in 8 years or less. *Degree requirements:* For master's, comprehensive exam (for some programs), thesis; for doctorate, comprehensive exam, thesis/dissertation. *Entrance requirements:* For master's, GRE General Test (for MS). Additional exam requirements/recommendations for international students: Required—TOEFL (minimum score 550 paper-based; 80 iBT). *Application deadline:* For fall admission, 3/1 priority date for domestic students. Applications are processed on a rolling basis. Application fee: $60. Electronic applications accepted. *Financial support:* In 2011–12, 19 students received support, including 12 research assistantships with full and partial tuition reimbursements available (averaging $19,300 per year), 13 teaching assistantships with full and partial tuition reimbursements available (averaging $18,310 per year); career-related internships or fieldwork, Federal Work-Study, institutionally sponsored loans, and scholarships/grants also available. Support available to part-time students. Financial award application deadline: 2/15; financial award applicants required to submit FAFSA. *Faculty research:* Atmospheric chemistry, magnetic resonance, molecular spectroscopy, laser photolysis, biophysical chemistry. *Unit head:* Dr. Sandra S. Eaton, Chair, 303-871-3100, Fax: 303-871-2254, E-mail: seaton@du.edu. *Application contact:*

Information Contact, 303-871-2435, Fax: 303-871-2254, E-mail: cheminfo@du.edu. Web site: http://www.du.edu/nsm/departments/chemistryandbiochemistry/.

University of Detroit Mercy, College of Engineering and Science, Department of Chemistry and Biochemistry, Detroit, MI 48221. Offers chemistry (MS). Evening/weekend programs available. *Degree requirements:* For master's, thesis. *Entrance requirements:* For master's, GRE General Test, minimum GPA of 3.0. *Faculty research:* Polymer and physical chemistry, industrial aspects of chemistry.

University of Florida, Graduate School, College of Liberal Arts and Sciences, Department of Chemistry, Gainesville, FL 32611. Offers chemistry (MS, MST); clinical and translational science (PhD); imaging science and technology (PhD). *Faculty:* 43 full-time (7 women), 2 part-time/adjunct (0 women). *Students:* 261 full-time (99 women), 8 part-time (4 women); includes 24 minority (7 Black or African American, non-Hispanic/Latino; 11 Asian, non-Hispanic/Latino; 6 Hispanic/Latino), 163 international. Average age 28. 654 applicants, 17% accepted, 50 enrolled. In 2011, 21 master's, 39 doctorates awarded. Terminal master's awarded for partial completion of doctoral program. *Degree requirements:* For master's, thesis; for doctorate, comprehensive exam, thesis/dissertation. *Entrance requirements:* For master's and doctorate, GRE General Test, minimum GPA of 3.0. Additional exam requirements/recommendations for international students: Required—TOEFL (minimum score 550 paper-based; 213 computer-based; 80 iBT), IELTS (minimum score 6). *Application deadline:* For fall admission, 1/1 priority date for domestic students, 1/1 for international students; for spring admission, 9/1 for domestic and international students. Applications are processed on a rolling basis. Application fee: $30. Electronic applications accepted. *Financial support:* Fellowships, research assistantships, teaching assistantships, institutionally sponsored loans, and unspecified assistantships available. Financial award applicants required to submit FAFSA. *Faculty research:* Organic, analytical, physical, inorganic, and biological chemistry. *Unit head:* Dr. Daniel R. Talham, Chair, 352-392-5266, Fax: 352-392-3255, E-mail: chair@chem.ufl.edu. *Application contact:* Dr. Ben Smith, Graduate Coordinator, 352-392-0256, Fax: 352-392-8758, E-mail: bwsmith@chem.ufl.edu. Web site: http://web.chem.ufl.edu/.

University of Georgia, Franklin College of Arts and Sciences, Department of Chemistry, Athens, GA 30602. Offers analytical chemistry (MS, PhD); inorganic chemistry (MS, PhD); organic chemistry (MS, PhD); physical chemistry (MS, PhD). *Faculty:* 26 full-time (2 women). *Students:* 153 full-time (53 women), 6 part-time (2 women); includes 21 minority (6 Black or African American, non-Hispanic/Latino; 12 Asian, non-Hispanic/Latino; 1 Hispanic/Latino; 2 Two or more races, non-Hispanic/Latino), 60 international. Average age 27. 175 applicants, 41% accepted, 38 enrolled. In 2011, 7 master's, 22 doctorates awarded. Terminal master's awarded for partial completion of doctoral program. *Median time to degree:* Of those who began their doctoral program in fall 2003, 100% received their degree in 8 years or less. *Degree requirements:* For master's, thesis; for doctorate, one foreign language, thesis/dissertation. *Entrance requirements:* For master's and doctorate, GRE General Test. Additional exam requirements/recommendations for international students: Required—TOEFL (minimum score 213 computer-based). *Application deadline:* For fall admission, 7/1 priority date for domestic students; for spring admission, 11/15 for domestic students. Application fee: $50. Electronic applications accepted. *Financial support:* Fellowships, research assistantships, teaching assistantships, and unspecified assistantships available. *Unit head:* Dr. Jon Amster, Head, 706-542-2726, E-mail: jamster@uga.edu. *Application contact:* Dr. Jeffrey L. Urbauer, Graduate Coordinator, 706-542-7922, E-mail: urbauer@uga.edu. Web site: http://www.chem.uga.edu/.

University of Guelph, Graduate Studies, College of Physical and Engineering Science, Guelph-Waterloo Centre for Graduate Work in Chemistry and Biochemistry, Guelph, ON N1G 2W1, Canada. Offers M Sc, PhD. M Sc, PhD offered jointly with University of Waterloo. Part-time programs available. *Degree requirements:* For master's, thesis; for doctorate, thesis/dissertation. *Faculty research:* Inorganic, analytical, biological, physical/theoretical, polymer, and organic chemistry.

University of Hawaii at Manoa, Graduate Division, College of Natural Sciences, Department of Chemistry, Honolulu, HI 96822. Offers MS, PhD. Part-time programs available. *Degree requirements:* For master's, comprehensive exam, thesis; for doctorate, comprehensive exam, thesis/dissertation. *Entrance requirements:* For master's and doctorate, GRE General Test, GRE Subject Test. Additional exam requirements/recommendations for international students: Required—TOEFL (minimum score 500 paper-based; 173 computer-based; 61 iBT), IELTS (minimum score 5). *Faculty research:* Marine natural products, biophysical spectroscopy, zeolites, organometallic hydrides, new visual pigments, theory of surfaces.

University of Houston, College of Natural Sciences and Mathematics, Department of Chemistry, Houston, TX 77204. Offers MA, PhD. Part-time programs available. Terminal master's awarded for partial completion of doctoral program. *Degree requirements:* For master's, thesis; for doctorate, thesis/dissertation, oral presentation. *Entrance requirements:* For master's and doctorate, GRE General Test. Additional exam requirements/recommendations for international students: Required—TOEFL (minimum score 79 iBT), IELTS (minimum score 6.5). Electronic applications accepted. *Faculty research:* Materials, molecular design, surface science, structural chemistry, synthesis.

University of Houston–Clear Lake, School of Science and Computer Engineering, Program in Chemistry, Houston, TX 77058-1098. Offers MS. Part-

time and evening/weekend programs available. *Entrance requirements:* For master's, GRE General Test. Additional exam requirements/recommendations for international students: Required—TOEFL (minimum score 550 paper-based; 213 computer-based).

University of Idaho, College of Graduate Studies, College of Science, Department of Chemistry, Moscow, ID 83844-2343. Offers MS, PhD. *Faculty:* 10 full-time, 1 part-time/adjunct. *Students:* 32 full-time, 4 part-time. Average age 30. In 2011, 9 doctorates awarded. *Degree requirements:* For master's, thesis or alternative; for doctorate, one foreign language, thesis/dissertation. *Entrance requirements:* For master's, minimum GPA of 2.8; for doctorate, minimum undergraduate GPA of 2.8, 3.0 graduate. *Application deadline:* For fall admission, 8/1 for domestic students; for spring admission, 12/15 for domestic students. Applications are processed on a rolling basis. Application fee: $60. Electronic applications accepted. *Expenses:* Tuition, state resident: full-time $3874; part-time $334 per credit hour. Tuition, nonresident: full-time $16,394; part-time $861 per credit hour. *Required fees:* $2808; $99 per credit hour. Tuition and fees vary according to program. *Financial support:* Fellowships, research assistantships, and teaching assistantships available. Financial award applicants required to submit FAFSA. *Faculty research:* Analytical chemistry, inorganic chemistry, organic chemistry, physical chemistry. *Unit head:* Dr. Ray von Wandruska, Chair, 208-885-6552, E-mail: chemoff@uidaho.edu. *Application contact:* Erick Larson, Director of Graduate Admissions, 208-885-4723, E-mail: gadms@uidaho.edu. Web site: http://www.uidaho.edu/sci/chem.

University of Illinois at Chicago, College of Pharmacy and Graduate College, Graduate Programs in Pharmacy, Chicago, IL 60607-7128. Offers biopharmaceutical sciences (PhD); forensic science (MS); medicinal chemistry (MS, PhD); pharmacognosy (MS, PhD); pharmacy administration (MS, PhD). Terminal master's awarded for partial completion of doctoral program. *Degree requirements:* For master's, variable foreign language requirement, thesis; for doctorate, variable foreign language requirement, thesis/dissertation. *Entrance requirements:* For master's and doctorate, GRE General Test. Additional exam requirements/recommendations for international students: Required—TOEFL. Electronic applications accepted. *Expenses:* Contact institution.

University of Illinois at Chicago, Graduate College, College of Liberal Arts and Sciences, Department of Chemistry, Chicago, IL 60607-7128. Offers MS, PhD. Part-time programs available. Terminal master's awarded for partial completion of doctoral program. *Degree requirements:* For master's, thesis or cumulative exam; for doctorate, one foreign language, thesis/dissertation, cumulative exams. *Entrance requirements:* For master's and doctorate, GRE Subject Test, minimum GPA of 3.0. Additional exam requirements/recommendations for international students: Required—TOEFL. Electronic applications accepted.

University of Illinois at Urbana–Champaign, Graduate College, College of Liberal Arts and Sciences, School of Chemical Sciences, Department of Chemistry, Champaign, IL 61820. Offers astrochemistry (PhD); chemical physics (PhD); chemistry (MA, MS, PhD); teaching of chemistry (MS); MS/JD; MS/MBA. *Faculty:* 29 full-time (5 women), 1 part-time/adjunct (0 women). *Students:* 279 full-time (95 women), 5 part-time (1 woman); includes 39 minority (4 Black or African American, non-Hispanic/Latino; 1 American Indian or Alaska Native, non-Hispanic/Latino; 19 Asian, non-Hispanic/Latino; 7 Hispanic/Latino; 8 Two or more races, non-Hispanic/Latino), 73 international. 476 applicants, 15% accepted, 71 enrolled. In 2011, 14 master's, 56 doctorates awarded. *Entrance requirements:* For master's and doctorate, GRE General Test, GRE Subject Test, minimum GPA of 3.0. Additional exam requirements/recommendations for international students: Required—TOEFL (minimum score 580 paper-based; 237 computer-based). *Application deadline:* Applications are processed on a rolling basis. Application fee: $75 ($90 for international students). Electronic applications accepted. *Financial support:* In 2011–12, 114 fellowships, 162 research assistantships, 167 teaching assistantships were awarded; tuition waivers (full and partial) also available. *Unit head:* Steven C. Zimmerman, Head, 217-333-6655, Fax: 217-244-5943, E-mail: sczimmer@illinois.edu. *Application contact:* Krista Smith, Program Coordinator, 217-244-4844, Fax: 217-244-5943, E-mail: kristasm@illinois.edu. Web site: http://chemistry.illinois.edu/.

The University of Iowa, Graduate College, College of Liberal Arts and Sciences, Department of Chemistry, Iowa City, IA 52242-1316. Offers MS, PhD. *Degree requirements:* For master's, thesis optional, exam; for doctorate, comprehensive exam, thesis/dissertation. *Entrance requirements:* For master's and doctorate, GRE General Test, minimum GPA of 3.0. Additional exam requirements/recommendations for international students: Required—TOEFL (minimum score 550 paper-based; 213 computer-based; 81 iBT). Electronic applications accepted.

The University of Kansas, Graduate Studies, College of Liberal Arts and Sciences, Department of Chemistry, Lawrence, KS 66045. Offers MS, PhD. *Faculty:* 29. *Students:* 103 full-time (45 women), 3 part-time (2 women); includes 7 minority (3 Asian, non-Hispanic/Latino; 2 Hispanic/Latino; 2 Two or more races, non-Hispanic/Latino), 31 international. Average age 27. 211 applicants, 18% accepted, 20 enrolled. In 2011, 2 master's, 9 doctorates awarded. *Degree requirements:* For master's, thesis; for doctorate, comprehensive exam, thesis/dissertation. *Entrance requirements:* For master's and doctorate, GRE General Test. Additional exam requirements/recommendations for international students: Required—TOEFL. *Application deadline:* For fall admission, 2/1 priority date for domestic students, 2/1 for international students; for spring admission, 9/1 priority date for domestic students, 7/1 for international students. Applications are processed on a rolling basis. Application fee: $55 ($65 for international students).

Peterson's Graduate Programs in the Physical Sciences, Mathematics, Agricultural Sciences, the Environment & Natural Resources 2013

facebook.com/petersonspublishing **87**

Chemistry

Electronic applications accepted. Tuition and fees vary according to course load, campus/location, program and reciprocity agreements. *Financial support:* Fellowships with full tuition reimbursements, research assistantships with full and partial tuition reimbursements, teaching assistantships with full and partial tuition reimbursements, scholarships/grants, traineeships, tuition waivers (full), and unspecified assistantships available. Financial award application deadline: 4/15. *Faculty research:* Organometallic and inorganic synthetic methodology, bioanalytical chemistry, computational materials science, proteomics, biophysical chemistry. *Unit head:* Prof. Craig E. Lunte, Chair, 785-864-4670, Fax: 785-864-5396, E-mail: clunte@ku.edu. *Application contact:* Prof. Brian B. Laird, Associate Chair for Graduate Studies, 785-864-4632, Fax: 785-864-5396, E-mail: blaird@ku.edu. Web site: http://www.chem.ku.edu/.

University of Kentucky, Graduate School, College of Arts and Sciences, Program in Chemistry, Lexington, KY 40506-0032. Offers MS, PhD. Part-time programs available. Terminal master's awarded for partial completion of doctoral program. *Degree requirements:* For master's, comprehensive exam, thesis optional; for doctorate, comprehensive exam, thesis/dissertation. *Entrance requirements:* For master's, GRE General Test, minimum undergraduate GPA of 2.75; for doctorate, GRE General Test, minimum graduate GPA of 3.0. Additional exam requirements/recommendations for international students: Required—TOEFL (minimum score 550 paper-based; 213 computer-based). Electronic applications accepted. *Faculty research:* Analytical, inorganic, organic, and physical chemistry; biological chemistry; nuclear chemistry; radiochemistry; materials chemistry.

University of Lethbridge, School of Graduate Studies, Lethbridge, AB T1K 3M4, Canada. Offers accounting (MScM); addictions counseling (M Sc); agricultural biotechnology (M Sc); agricultural studies (M Sc, MA); anthropology (MA); archaeology (MA); art (MA, MFA); biochemistry (M Sc); biological sciences (M Sc); biomolecular science (PhD); biosystems and biodiversity (PhD); Canadian studies (MA); chemistry (M Sc); computer science (M Sc); computer science and geographical information science (M Sc); counseling psychology (M Ed); dramatic arts (MA); earth, space, and physical science (PhD); economics (MA); educational leadership (M Ed); English (MA); environmental science (M Sc); evolution and behavior (PhD); exercise science (M Sc); finance (MScM); French (MA); French/German (MA); French/Spanish (MA); general education (M Ed); general management (MScM); geography (M Sc, MA); German (MA); health science (M Sc); history (MA); human resource management and labour relations (MScM); individualized multidisciplinary (M Sc, MA); information systems (MScM); international management (MScM); kinesiology (M Sc, MA); management (M Sc, MA); marketing (MScM); mathematics (M Sc); music (M Mus, MA); Native American studies (MA); neuroscience (M Sc, PhD); new media (MA); nursing (M Sc); philosophy (MA); physics (M Sc); policy and strategy (MScM); political science (MA); psychology (M Sc, MA); religious studies (MA); social sciences (MA); sociology (MA); theatre and dramatic arts (MFA); theoretical and computational science (PhD); urban and regional studies (MA); women's studies (MA). Part-time and evening/weekend programs available. *Degree requirements:* For doctorate, comprehensive exam, thesis/dissertation. *Entrance requirements:* For master's, GMAT (M Sc in management), bachelor's degree in related field, minimum GPA of 3.0 during previous 20 graded semester courses, 2 years teaching or related experience (M Ed); for doctorate, master's degree, minimum graduate GPA of 3.5. Additional exam requirements/recommendations for international students: Required—TOEFL. *Faculty research:* Movement and brain plasticity, gibberellin physiology, photosynthesis, carbon cycling, molecular properties of main-group ring components.

University of Louisville, Graduate School, College of Arts and Sciences, Department of Chemistry, Louisville, KY 40292-0001. Offers analytical chemistry (MS, PhD); biochemistry (MS, PhD); chemical physics (PhD); inorganic chemistry (MS, PhD); organic chemistry (MS, PhD); physical chemistry (MS, PhD). Terminal master's awarded for partial completion of doctoral program. *Degree requirements:* For master's, variable foreign language requirement, comprehensive exam, thesis optional; for doctorate, variable foreign language requirement, comprehensive exam, thesis/dissertation. *Entrance requirements:* For master's and doctorate, BA or BS coursework. Additional exam requirements/recommendations for international students: Required—TOEFL. Electronic applications accepted. *Expenses:* Tuition, state resident: full-time $9692; part-time $539 per credit hour. Tuition, nonresident: full-time $20,168; part-time $1121 per credit hour. Tuition and fees vary according to program and reciprocity agreements. *Faculty research:* Computational chemistry, biophysics nuclear magnetic resonance, synthetic organic chemistry, synthetic inorganic chemistry, medicinal chemistry, protein chemistry, enzymology, nanochemistry, electrochemistry, analytical chemistry, synthetic biology, bioinformatics.

University of Maine, Graduate School, College of Liberal Arts and Sciences, Department of Chemistry, Orono, ME 04469. Offers MS, PhD. *Faculty:* 12 full-time (3 women), 1 part-time/adjunct (0 women). *Students:* 18 full-time (8 women), 6 part-time (1 woman); includes 2 minority (1 American Indian or Alaska Native, non-Hispanic/Latino; 1 Asian, non-Hispanic/Latino), 13 international. Average age 30. 25 applicants, 24% accepted, 6 enrolled. In 2011, 3 master's, 4 doctorates awarded. Terminal master's awarded for partial completion of doctoral program. *Degree requirements:* For master's, thesis; for doctorate, thesis/dissertation, oral exam. *Entrance requirements:* For master's and doctorate, GRE General Test. Additional exam requirements/recommendations for international students: Required—TOEFL. *Application deadline:* For fall admission, 2/1 priority date for domestic students. Applications are processed on a rolling basis. Application fee:

$65. Electronic applications accepted. *Expenses:* Tuition, state resident: full-time $5016. Tuition, nonresident: full-time $14,424. *Financial support:* In 2011–12, 2 research assistantships with full tuition reimbursements (averaging $12,900 per year), 15 teaching assistantships with full tuition reimbursements (averaging $17,184 per year) were awarded; tuition waivers (full and partial) also available. Financial award application deadline: 3/1. *Faculty research:* Quantum mechanics, insect chemistry, organic synthesis. *Unit head:* Dr. Francois Amar, Chair, 207-581-1196. *Application contact:* Scott G. Delcourt, Associate Dean of the Graduate School, 207-581-3291, Fax: 207-581-3232, E-mail: graduate@maine.edu. Web site: http://www2.umaine.edu/graduate/.

The University of Manchester, School of Chemical Engineering and Analytical Science, Manchester, United Kingdom. Offers biocatalysis (M Phil, PhD); chemical engineering (M Phil, PhD); chemical engineering and analytical science (M Phil, D Eng, PhD); colloids, crystals, interfaces and materials (M Phil, PhD); environment and sustainable technology (M Phil, PhD); instrumentation (M Phil, PhD); multi-scale modeling (M Phil, PhD); process integration (M Phil, PhD); systems biology (M Phil, PhD).

The University of Manchester, School of Chemistry, Manchester, United Kingdom. Offers biological chemistry (PhD); chemistry (M Ent, M Phil, M Sc, D Ent, PhD); inorganic chemistry (PhD); materials chemistry (PhD); nanoscience (PhD); nuclear fission (PhD); organic chemistry (PhD); physical chemistry (PhD); theoretical chemistry (PhD).

The University of Manchester, School of Earth, Atmospheric and Environmental Sciences, Manchester, United Kingdom. Offers atmospheric sciences (M Phil, M Sc, PhD); basin studies and petroleum geosciences (M Phil, M Sc, PhD); earth, atmospheric and environmental sciences (M Phil, M Sc, PhD); environmental geochemistry and cosmochemistry (M Phil, M Sc, PhD); isotope geochemistry and cosmochemistry (M Phil, M Sc, PhD); paleontology (M Phil, M Sc, PhD); physics and chemistry of minerals and fluids (M Phil, M Sc, PhD); structural and petrological geosciences (M Phil, M Sc, PhD).

University of Manitoba, Faculty of Graduate Studies, Faculty of Science, Department of Chemistry, Winnipeg, MB R3T 2N2, Canada. Offers M Sc, PhD. *Degree requirements:* For master's, thesis; for doctorate, one foreign language, thesis/dissertation.

University of Maryland, Baltimore County, Graduate School, College of Arts, Humanities and Social Sciences, Department of Education, Program in Teaching, Baltimore, MD 21250. Offers early childhood education (MAT); elementary education (MAT); secondary education (MAT), including social studies; secondary education (MAT), including art, biology, chemistry, dance, earth/space science, English, foreign language, mathematics, music, physics, theatre. Part-time and evening/weekend programs available. *Faculty:* 24 full-time (18 women), 25 part-time/adjunct (19 women). *Students:* 46 full-time (35 women), 64 part-time (39 women); includes 24 minority (8 Black or African American, non-Hispanic/Latino; 7 Asian, non-Hispanic/Latino; 6 Hispanic/Latino; 1 Native Hawaiian or other Pacific Islander, non-Hispanic/Latino; 2 Two or more races, non-Hispanic/Latino), 4 international. Average age 31. 88 applicants, 57% accepted, 39 enrolled. In 2011, 106 master's awarded. *Degree requirements:* For master's, comprehensive exam (for some programs), thesis (for some programs). *Entrance requirements:* For master's, PRAXIS I or GRE (minimum score of 1000), minimum GPA of 3.0. Additional exam requirements/recommendations for international students: Required—TOEFL. *Application deadline:* For fall admission, 6/1 for domestic students; for spring admission, 11/1 for domestic students. Applications are processed on a rolling basis. Application fee: $50. Electronic applications accepted. *Financial support:* In 2011–12, 6 students received support, including teaching assistantships with full and partial tuition reimbursements available (averaging $12,000 per year); career-related internships or fieldwork, Federal Work-Study, scholarships/grants, tuition waivers, and unspecified assistantships also available. Financial award application deadline: 3/1. *Faculty research:* STEM teacher education, culturally sensitive pedagogy, ESOL/bilingual education, early childhood education, language, literacy and culture. *Unit head:* Dr. Susan M. Blunck, Graduate Program Director, 410-455-2869, Fax: 410-455-3986, E-mail: blunck@umbc.edu. *Application contact:* Cheryl Johnson, 410-455-3388, E-mail: blackwel@umbc.edu. Web site: http://www.umbc.edu/education/.

University of Maryland, Baltimore County, Graduate School, College of Natural and Mathematical Sciences, Department of Chemistry and Biochemistry, Baltimore, MD 21250. Offers biochemistry (PhD); chemistry (MS, PhD); chemistry and biochemistry (Postbaccalaureate Certificate). Part-time programs available. *Faculty:* 77 full-time (11 women). *Students:* 90 full-time (51 women), 2 part-time (0 women); includes 24 minority (10 Black or African American, non-Hispanic/Latino; 1 American Indian or Alaska Native, non-Hispanic/Latino; 6 Asian, non-Hispanic/Latino; 6 Hispanic/Latino; 1 Two or more races, non-Hispanic/Latino), 26 international. Average age 27. 142 applicants, 30% accepted, 27 enrolled. In 2011, 4 master's, 5 doctorates awarded. Terminal master's awarded for partial completion of doctoral program. *Degree requirements:* For master's, comprehensive exam (for some programs), thesis (for some programs); for doctorate, comprehensive exam, thesis/dissertation. *Entrance requirements:* For master's, GRE General Test, minimum GPA of 3.0; for doctorate, GRE General Test, GRE Subject Test (recommended), minimum GPA of 3.0. Additional exam requirements/recommendations for international students: Required—TOEFL (minimum score 550 paper-based; 213 computer-based). *Application deadline:* For fall admission, 6/1 priority date for domestic students, 1/1 for international students; for spring admission, 11/1 priority date for domestic students, 5/1 for

88 facebook.com/petersonspublishing

Peterson's Graduate Programs in the Physical Sciences, Mathematics, Agricultural Sciences, the Environment & Natural Resources 2013

international students. Applications are processed on a rolling basis. Application fee: $50. Electronic applications accepted. *Financial support:* In 2011–12, 13 fellowships with full tuition reimbursements (averaging $24,000 per year), 41 research assistantships with full tuition reimbursements (averaging $21,000 per year), 35 teaching assistantships with full tuition reimbursements (averaging $21,000 per year) were awarded; health care benefits also available. *Faculty research:* Protein structures, bio-organic chemistry, enzyme catalysis, molecular biology, metabolism. *Total annual research expenditures:* $3.3 million. *Unit head:* Dr. Dale R. Whalen, Director, Graduate Program, 410-455-2491, Fax: 410-455-2608, E-mail: chemgrad@umbc.edu. *Application contact:* Patricia Gagne, Graduate Coordinator, 410-455-2491, Fax: 410-455-2608, E-mail: pgagne1@umbc.edu. Web site: http://www.umbc.edu/chem.

University of Maryland, College Park, Academic Affairs, College of Computer, Mathematical and Natural Sciences, Department of Chemistry and Biochemistry, Chemistry Program, College Park, MD 20742. Offers analytical chemistry (MS, PhD); inorganic chemistry (MS, PhD); organic chemistry (MS, PhD); physical chemistry (MS, PhD). Part-time and evening/weekend programs available. *Students:* 115 full-time (59 women), 4 part-time (1 woman); includes 20 minority (12 Black or African American, non-Hispanic/Latino; 4 Asian, non-Hispanic/Latino; 2 Hispanic/Latino; 2 Two or more races, non-Hispanic/Latino), 52 international. 335 applicants, 8% accepted, 18 enrolled. In 2011, 11 master's, 15 doctorates awarded. Terminal master's awarded for partial completion of doctoral program. *Median time to degree:* Of those who began their doctoral program in fall 2003, 63% received their degree in 8 years or less. *Degree requirements:* For master's, thesis optional; for doctorate, thesis/dissertation, 2 seminar presentations, oral exam. *Entrance requirements:* For master's and doctorate, GRE General Test, GRE Subject Test (recommended), minimum GPA of 3.0, 3 letters of recommendation. Additional exam requirements/recommendations for international students: Required—TOEFL. *Application deadline:* For fall admission, 2/1 for domestic and international students; for spring admission, 6/1 for domestic and international students. Applications are processed on a rolling basis. Application fee: $75. Electronic applications accepted. *Expenses: Tuition, area resident:* Part-time $525 per credit hour. Tuition, state resident: part-time $525 per credit hour. Tuition, nonresident: part-time $1131 per credit hour. *Required fees:* $386.31 per term. Tuition and fees vary according to program. *Financial support:* In 2011–12, 9 fellowships with full and partial tuition reimbursements (averaging $25,360 per year), 46 research assistantships (averaging $19,791 per year), 59 teaching assistantships (averaging $19,243 per year) were awarded. Financial award applicants required to submit FAFSA. *Faculty research:* Environmental chemistry, nuclear chemistry, lunar and environmental analysis, x-ray crystallography. *Unit head:* Dr. Michael Doyle, Chairperson, 301-405-1795, Fax: 301-314-2779, E-mail: mdoyle3@umd.edu. *Application contact:* Dr. Charles A. Caramello, Dean of Graduate School, 301-405-0358, Fax: 301-314-9305.

University of Massachusetts Amherst, Graduate School, College of Natural Sciences, Department of Chemistry, Amherst, MA 01003. Offers MS, PhD. Part-time programs available. *Faculty:* 30 full-time (5 women). *Students:* 141 full-time (55 women), 1 (woman) part-time; includes 16 minority (8 Black or African American, non-Hispanic/Latino; 3 Asian, non-Hispanic/Latino; 5 Hispanic/Latino), 81 international. Average age 27. 298 applicants, 30% accepted, 27 enrolled. In 2011, 7 master's, 16 doctorates awarded. Terminal master's awarded for partial completion of doctoral program. *Degree requirements:* For master's, thesis (for some programs); for doctorate, comprehensive exam, thesis/dissertation. *Entrance requirements:* For master's and doctorate, GRE General Test. Additional exam requirements/recommendations for international students: Required—TOEFL (minimum score 550 paper-based; 213 computer-based; 80 iBT), IELTS (minimum score 6.5). *Application deadline:* For fall admission, 1/15 for domestic and international students. Applications are processed on a rolling basis. Application fee: $50 ($65 for international students). Electronic applications accepted. Tuition and fees vary according to course load, campus/location and program. *Financial support:* Fellowships with full and partial tuition reimbursements, research assistantships with full and partial tuition reimbursements, teaching assistantships with full and partial tuition reimbursements, career-related internships or fieldwork, Federal Work-Study, scholarships/grants, traineeships, health care benefits, tuition waivers (full), and unspecified assistantships available. Support available to part-time students. Financial award application deadline: 1/15; financial award applicants required to submit FAFSA. *Unit head:* Dr. Igor Kaltashov, Graduate Program Director, 413-545-2664, Fax: 413-545-4490. *Application contact:* Lindsay DeSantis, Interim Supervisor of Admissions, 413-545-0722, Fax: 413-577-0010, E-mail: gradadm@grad.umass.edu. Web site: http://www.chem.umass.edu/.

University of Massachusetts Boston, Office of Graduate Studies, College of Science and Mathematics, Program in Chemistry, Boston, MA 02125-3393. Offers MS. Part-time and evening/weekend programs available. *Degree requirements:* For master's, comprehensive exam, thesis, oral exams. *Entrance requirements:* For master's, GRE General Test, GRE Subject Test, minimum GPA of 2.75. *Faculty research:* Synthesis and mechanisms of organic nitrogen compounds, application of spin resonance in the study of structure and dynamics, chemical education and teacher training, new synthetic reagents, structural study of inorganic solids by infrared and Raman spectroscopy.

University of Massachusetts Dartmouth, Graduate School, College of Arts and Sciences, Department of Chemistry, North Dartmouth, MA 02747-2300. Offers MS, PhD. Part-time programs available. *Faculty:* 15 full-time (3 women), 2 part-time/adjunct (1 woman). *Students:* 19 full-time (10 women), 8 part-time (4 women); includes 1 minority (Hispanic/Latino), 17 international. Average age 27. 20 applicants, 70% accepted, 8 enrolled. In 2011, 6 degrees awarded. *Degree requirements:* For master's, comprehensive exam (for some programs), thesis or alternative; for doctorate, thesis/dissertation (for some programs). *Entrance requirements:* For master's, GRE (recommended), 2 letters of recommendation, resume, statement of intent; for doctorate, GRE, 2 letters of recommendation, resume, statement of intent. Additional exam requirements/recommendations for international students: Required—TOEFL (minimum score 550 paper-based). *Application deadline:* For fall admission, 3/15 for domestic students, 2/15 for international students; for spring admission, 11/1 for domestic students, 10/1 for international students. Application fee: $40 ($60 for international students). Electronic applications accepted. *Expenses:* Tuition, state resident: full-time $2071; part-time $86.29 per credit. Tuition, nonresident: full-time $8099; part-time $337.46 per credit. *Required fees:* $438.58 per credit. Part-time tuition and fees vary according to class time, course load, degree level and reciprocity agreements. *Financial support:* In 2011–12, 1 fellowship with full tuition reimbursement (averaging $8,000 per year), 5 research assistantships with full tuition reimbursements (averaging $10,820 per year), 18 teaching assistantships with full tuition reimbursements (averaging $10,282 per year) were awarded; Federal Work-Study also available. Support available to part-time students. Financial award application deadline: 3/1; financial award applicants required to submit FAFSA. *Faculty research:* Inorganic chemistry, biochemical kinetics, photochemistry, ion-molecule reactions, atmosphere chemistry. *Total annual research expenditures:* $1.3 million. *Unit head:* Dr. Yuegang Zuo, Graduate Program Director, 508-999-8959, Fax: 508-999-9167, E-mail: yzuo@umassd.edu. *Application contact:* Elan Turcotte-Shamski, Graduate Admissions Officer, 508-999-8604, Fax: 508-999-8183, E-mail: graduate@umassd.edu. Web site: http://www.umassd.edu/cas/chemistry/graduateprograms/.

University of Massachusetts Lowell, College of Sciences, Department of Chemistry, Lowell, MA 01854-2881. Offers analytical chemistry (PhD); biochemistry (PhD); chemistry (MS, PhD); environmental studies (PhD); green chemistry (PhD); inorganic chemistry (PhD); organic chemistry (PhD); polymer science (MS). Terminal master's awarded for partial completion of doctoral program. *Degree requirements:* For master's, thesis; for doctorate, 2 foreign languages, thesis/dissertation. *Entrance requirements:* For master's and doctorate, GRE General Test. Electronic applications accepted.

University of Memphis, Graduate School, College of Arts and Sciences, Department of Chemistry, Memphis, TN 38152. Offers analytical chemistry (MS, PhD); computational chemistry (MS, PhD); inorganic chemistry (MS, PhD); organic chemistry (MS, PhD); physical chemistry (MS, PhD). Part-time programs available. Terminal master's awarded for partial completion of doctoral program. *Degree requirements:* For master's, comprehensive exam, thesis or alternative; for doctorate, comprehensive exam, thesis/dissertation. *Entrance requirements:* For master's and doctorate, GRE General Test, admission to Graduate School plus 32 undergraduate hours in chemistry. Additional exam requirements/recommendations for international students: Required—TOEFL. Electronic applications accepted. *Faculty research:* Computational chemistry, materials chemistry, organic/polymer synthesis, drug design/delivery, water chemistry.

University of Miami, Graduate School, College of Arts and Sciences, Department of Chemistry, Coral Gables, FL 33124. Offers chemistry (MS); inorganic chemistry (PhD); organic chemistry (PhD); physical chemistry (PhD). Terminal master's awarded for partial completion of doctoral program. *Degree requirements:* For master's, comprehensive exam; for doctorate, comprehensive exam, thesis/dissertation. *Entrance requirements:* For master's and doctorate, GRE General Test. Additional exam requirements/recommendations for international students: Required—TOEFL (minimum score 550 paper-based; 213 computer-based). Electronic applications accepted. *Faculty research:* Supramolecular chemistry, electrochemistry, surface chemistry, catalysis, organometalic.

University of Michigan, Horace H. Rackham School of Graduate Studies, College of Literature, Science, and the Arts, Department of Chemistry, Ann Arbor, MI 48109-1055. Offers analytical chemistry (PhD); chemical biology (PhD); inorganic chemistry (PhD); material chemistry (PhD); organic chemistry (PhD); physical chemistry (PhD). *Faculty:* 39 full-time (9 women). *Students:* 221 full-time (114 women); includes 24 minority (1 Black or African American, non-Hispanic/Latino; 15 Asian, non-Hispanic/Latino; 4 Hispanic/Latino; 4 Two or more races, non-Hispanic/Latino), 66 international. Average age 26. 608 applicants, 27% accepted, 39 enrolled. In 2011, 39 doctorates awarded. *Degree requirements:* For doctorate, thesis/dissertation, oral defense of dissertation, organic cumulative proficiency exams. *Entrance requirements:* For doctorate, GRE General Test, GRE Subject Test (recommended), 3 letters of recommendation. Additional exam requirements/recommendations for international students: Required—TOEFL (minimum score 560 paper-based; 220 computer-based; 84 iBT). *Application deadline:* For fall admission, 12/31 for domestic students, 12/15 for international students. Applications are processed on a rolling basis. Application fee: $0 ($75 for international students). Electronic applications accepted. *Financial support:* In 2011–12, 221 students received support, including 25 fellowships with full tuition reimbursements available (averaging $26,553 per year), 86 research assistantships with full tuition reimbursements available (averaging $26,553 per year), 110 teaching assistantships with full tuition reimbursements available (averaging $26,553 per year); career-related internships or fieldwork, scholarships/grants, traineeships, health care benefits, and unspecified

Peterson's Graduate Programs in the Physical Sciences, Mathematics, Agricultural Sciences, the Environment & Natural Resources 2013

facebook.com/petersonspublishing **89**

Chemistry

assistantships also available. *Faculty research:* Biological catalysis, protein engineering, chemical sensors, de novo metalloprotein design, supramolecular architecture. *Unit head:* Dr. Carol A. Fierke, Chair, 734-763-9681, Fax: 734-647-4847. *Application contact:* Margarita Bekiares, Graduate Program Coordinator, 734-764-7278, Fax: 734-647-4865, E-mail: chemadmissions@umich.edu. Web site: http://www.umich.edu/~michchem/.

University of Minnesota, Duluth, Graduate School, Swenson College of Science and Engineering, Department of Chemistry and Biochemistry, Duluth, MN 55812-2496. Offers MS. Part-time programs available. *Degree requirements:* For master's, thesis. *Entrance requirements:* For master's, bachelor's degree in chemistry, minimum GPA of 3.0. Additional exam requirements/recommendations for international students: Required—TOEFL (minimum score 550 paper-based; 213 computer-based; 79 iBT), IELTS (minimum score 6.5). *Faculty research:* Physical, inorganic, organic, and analytical chemistry; biochemistry and molecular biology.

University of Minnesota, Twin Cities Campus, College of Science and Engineering, Department of Chemistry, Minneapolis, MN 55455-0213. Offers MS, PhD. Part-time programs available. *Faculty:* 36 full-time (7 women). *Students:* 223 (79 women); includes 10 minority (5 Asian, non-Hispanic/Latino; 5 Hispanic/Latino), 69 international. Terminal master's awarded for partial completion of doctoral program. *Degree requirements:* For master's, thesis or alternative; for doctorate, thesis/dissertation, preliminary candidacy exams. *Entrance requirements:* For master's and doctorate, GRE General Test. Additional exam requirements/recommendations for international students: Required—TOEFL. *Application deadline:* Applications are processed on a rolling basis. Application fee: $75 ($95 for international students). *Financial support:* Fellowships, research assistantships, and teaching assistantships available. *Faculty research:* Analytical, biological, inorganic, organic, and physical chemistry. *Application contact:* Director of Graduate Studies, E-mail: chmapply@umn.edu. Web site: http://www.chem.umn.edu/.

University of Minnesota, Twin Cities Campus, School of Public Health, Division of Environmental Health Sciences, Area in Environmental Chemistry, Minneapolis, MN 55455-0213. Offers MS, PhD. *Degree requirements:* For doctorate, thesis/dissertation. *Entrance requirements:* For master's and doctorate, GRE General Test. Electronic applications accepted.

University of Mississippi, Graduate School, College of Liberal Arts, Department of Chemistry and Biochemistry, Oxford, University, MS 38677. Offers MS, DA, PhD. *Students:* 39 full-time (15 women), 1 part-time (0 women); includes 11 minority (6 Black or African American, non-Hispanic/Latino; 1 Asian, non-Hispanic/Latino; 2 Hispanic/Latino; 2 Two or more races, non-Hispanic/Latino), 18 international. In 2011, 3 master's, 1 doctorate awarded. *Degree requirements:* For master's, thesis; for doctorate, one foreign language, thesis/dissertation. *Entrance requirements:* For master's, GRE General Test, minimum GPA of 3.0; for doctorate, GRE General Test. Additional exam requirements/recommendations for international students: Required—TOEFL. *Application deadline:* For fall admission, 4/1 for domestic students; for spring admission, 10/1 for domestic students. Applications are processed on a rolling basis. Application fee: $25. Electronic applications accepted. *Financial support:* Scholarships/grants available. Financial award application deadline: 3/1; financial award applicants required to submit FAFSA. *Unit head:* Dr. Charles Hussey, Chairman, 662-915-7301, Fax: 662-915-7300, E-mail: chemistry@olemiss.edu. *Application contact:* Dr. Christy M. Wyandt, Associate Dean, 662-915-7474, Fax: 662-915-7577, E-mail: cwyandt@olemiss.edu.

University of Missouri, Graduate School, College of Arts and Sciences, Department of Chemistry, Columbia, MO 65211. Offers analytical chemistry (MS, PhD); inorganic chemistry (MS, PhD); organic chemistry (MS, PhD); physical chemistry (MS, PhD). *Faculty:* 22 full-time (4 women), 1 part-time/adjunct (0 women). *Students:* 102 full-time (38 women), 10 part-time (6 women); includes 7 minority (3 Black or African American, non-Hispanic/Latino; 2 Asian, non-Hispanic/Latino; 1 Hispanic/Latino; 1 Two or more races, non-Hispanic/Latino), 53 international. Average age 27. 98 applicants, 28% accepted, 24 enrolled. In 2011, 2 master's, 5 doctorates awarded. *Degree requirements:* For master's, thesis; for doctorate, one foreign language, comprehensive exam, thesis/dissertation. *Entrance requirements:* For master's, GRE General Test, minimum GPA of 3.0; for doctorate, GRE General Test (minimum score: Verbal 450, Quantitative 600, Analytical 3), minimum GPA of 3.0. Additional exam requirements/recommendations for international students: Required—TOEFL (minimum score 600 paper-based; 250 computer-based; 100 iBT). *Application deadline:* For fall admission, 4/1 priority date for domestic students; for winter admission, 10/15 for domestic students. Applications are processed on a rolling basis. Application fee: $55 ($75 for international students). Electronic applications accepted. *Expenses:* Tuition, state resident: full-time $5881. Tuition, nonresident: full-time $15,183. *Required fees:* $952. Tuition and fees vary according to campus/location and program. *Financial support:* In 2011–12, 9 fellowships with full tuition reimbursements, 15 research assistantships with full tuition reimbursements, 78 teaching assistantships with full tuition reimbursements were awarded; institutionally sponsored loans, traineeships, health care benefits, and unspecified assistantships also available. *Faculty research:* Analytical, organic, biological, physical, inorganic and radiochemistry. *Unit head:* Dr. Jerry Atwood, Department Chair, 573-882-8374, E-mail: atwoodj@missouri.edu. *Application contact:* Jerry Brightwell, Administrative Assistant, 573-884-6832, E-mail: brightwellj@missouri.edu. Web site: http://chemistry.missouri.edu/.

University of Missouri–Kansas City, College of Arts and Sciences, Department of Chemistry, Kansas City, MO 64110-2499. Offers analytical chemistry (MS, PhD); inorganic chemistry (MS, PhD); organic chemistry (MS, PhD); physical chemistry (MS, PhD); polymer chemistry (MS, PhD). PhD (interdisciplinary) offered through the School of Graduate Studies. Part-time and evening/weekend programs available. *Faculty:* 16 full-time (3 women), 1 part-time/adjunct (0 women). *Students:* 1 (woman) part-time; minority (Black or African American, non-Hispanic/Latino). Average age 30. 28 applicants, 32% accepted, 0 enrolled. In 2011, 2 degrees awarded. *Degree requirements:* For master's, thesis (for some programs); for doctorate, thesis/dissertation. *Entrance requirements:* For master's, equivalent of American Chemical Society approved bachelor's degree in chemistry; for doctorate, GRE General Test, equivalent of American Chemical Society approved bachelor's degree in chemistry. Additional exam requirements/recommendations for international students: Required—TOEFL (minimum score 550 paper-based; 213 computer-based; 80 iBT), TWE. *Application deadline:* For fall admission, 4/15 for domestic and international students; for spring admission, 10/15 for domestic and international students. Applications are processed on a rolling basis. Application fee: $45 ($50 for international students). Electronic applications accepted. *Expenses:* Tuition, state resident: full-time $5798; part-time $322.10 per credit hour. Tuition, nonresident: full-time $14,969; part-time $831.60 per credit hour. *Required fees:* $93.51 per credit hour. *Financial support:* In 2011–12, 9 research assistantships with partial tuition reimbursements (averaging $19,119 per year), 14 teaching assistantships with partial tuition reimbursements (averaging $17,187 per year) were awarded; Federal Work-Study, institutionally sponsored loans, and scholarships/grants also available. Support available to part-time students. Financial award application deadline: 3/1; financial award applicants required to submit FAFSA. *Faculty research:* Molecular spectroscopy, characterization and synthesis of materials and compounds, computational chemistry, natural products, drug delivery systems and anti-tumor agents. *Unit head:* Dr. Kathleen V. Kilway, Chair, 816-235-2289, Fax: 816-235-5502. *Application contact:* Graduate Recruiting Committee, 816-235-2272, Fax: 816-235-5502, E-mail: umkc-chemdept@umkc.edu. Web site: http://cas.umkc.edu/chem/.

University of Missouri–St. Louis, College of Arts and Sciences, Department of Chemistry and Biochemistry, St. Louis, MO 63121. Offers chemistry (MS, PhD), including biochemistry, inorganic chemistry, organic chemistry, physical chemistry. Part-time and evening/weekend programs available. *Faculty:* 18 full-time (3 women), 4 part-time/adjunct (1 woman). *Students:* 37 full-time (18 women), 28 part-time (11 women); includes 4 minority (1 Black or African American, non-Hispanic/Latino; 2 Asian, non-Hispanic/Latino; 1 Hispanic/Latino), 22 international. Average age 30. 73 applicants, 30% accepted, 11 enrolled. In 2011, 16 master's, 4 doctorates awarded. Terminal master's awarded for partial completion of doctoral program. *Degree requirements:* For master's, thesis optional; for doctorate, thesis/dissertation. *Entrance requirements:* For master's, 2 letters of recommendation; for doctorate, GRE General Test, 3 letters of recommendation. Additional exam requirements/recommendations for international students: Required—TOEFL (minimum score 550 paper-based; 213 computer-based). *Application deadline:* For fall admission, 7/1 priority date for domestic students, 7/1 for international students; for spring admission, 12/1 priority date for domestic students, 12/1 for international students. Applications are processed on a rolling basis. Application fee: $35 ($40 for international students). Electronic applications accepted. *Expenses:* Tuition, state resident: full-time $6273; part-time $3866 per year. Tuition, nonresident: full-time $14,969; part-time $9980 per year. *Required fees:* $315 per year. *Financial support:* In 2011–12, 19 research assistantships with full and partial tuition reimbursements (averaging $13,500 per year), 19 teaching assistantships with full and partial tuition reimbursements (averaging $13,500 per year) were awarded; fellowships with full and partial tuition reimbursements also available. *Faculty research:* Metalloborane chemistry, serum transferrin chemistry, natural products chemistry, organic synthesis. *Unit head:* Dr. Janet Wilking, Director of Graduate Studies, 314-516-5311, Fax: 314-516-5342, E-mail: gradchem@umsl.edu. *Application contact:* Graduate Admissions, 314-516-5458, Fax: 314-516-6996, E-mail: gradadm@umsl.edu. Web site: http://www.umsl.edu/chemistry/.

The University of Montana, Graduate School, College of Arts and Sciences, Department of Chemistry and Biochemistry, Missoula, MT 59812-0002. Offers chemistry (MS, PhD), including environmental/analytical chemistry, inorganic chemistry, organic chemistry, physical chemistry. Terminal master's awarded for partial completion of doctoral program. *Degree requirements:* For master's, thesis (for some programs); for doctorate, thesis/dissertation. *Entrance requirements:* For master's and doctorate, GRE General Test. Additional exam requirements/recommendations for international students: Required—TOEFL (minimum score 575 paper-based; 230 computer-based). *Faculty research:* Reaction mechanisms and kinetics, inorganic and organic synthesis, analytical chemistry, natural products.

University of Nebraska–Lincoln, Graduate College, College of Arts and Sciences, Department of Chemistry, Lincoln, NE 68588. Offers analytical chemistry (PhD); biochemistry (PhD); chemistry (MS); inorganic chemistry (PhD); materials chemistry (PhD); organic chemistry (PhD); physical chemistry (PhD). *Degree requirements:* For master's, one foreign language, thesis optional, departmental qualifying exam; for doctorate, one foreign language, comprehensive exam, thesis/dissertation, departmental qualifying exams. *Entrance requirements:* For master's and doctorate, GRE. Additional exam requirements/recommendations for international students: Required—TOEFL (minimum score 550 paper-based; 213 computer-based). Electronic applications

90 facebook.com/petersonspublishing

Peterson's Graduate Programs in the Physical Sciences, Mathematics, Agricultural Sciences, the Environment & Natural Resources 2013

accepted. *Faculty research:* Bioorganic and bioinorganic chemistry, biophysical and bioanalytical chemistry, structure-function of DNA and proteins, organometallics, mass spectrometry.

University of Nevada, Las Vegas, Graduate College, College of Science, Department of Chemistry, Las Vegas, NV 89154-4003. Offers biochemistry (MS); chemistry (MS, PhD); radiochemistry (PhD). Part-time programs available. *Faculty:* 15 full-time (2 women), 6 part-time/adjunct (1 woman). *Students:* 10 full-time (3 women), 34 part-time (18 women); includes 7 minority (2 Black or African American, non-Hispanic/Latino; 2 Asian, non-Hispanic/Latino; 1 Hispanic/Latino; 2 Two or more races, non-Hispanic/Latino), 9 international. Average age 30. 22 applicants, 41% accepted, 5 enrolled. In 2011, 3 master's, 7 doctorates awarded. *Degree requirements:* For master's, thesis. *Entrance requirements:* For master's and doctorate, GRE General Test. Additional exam requirements/recommendations for international students: Required—TOEFL (minimum score 550 paper-based; 213 computer-based; 80 iBT), IELTS (minimum score 7). *Application deadline:* For fall admission, 2/1 priority date for domestic students, 5/1 for international students; for spring admission, 10/1 priority date for domestic students, 10/1 for international students. Applications are processed on a rolling basis. Application fee: $60 ($95 for international students). Electronic applications accepted. *Financial support:* In 2011–12, 44 students received support, including 33 research assistantships with partial tuition reimbursements available (averaging $13,346 per year), 11 teaching assistantships with partial tuition reimbursements available (averaging $16,397 per year); institutionally sponsored loans, scholarships/grants, health care benefits, and unspecified assistantships also available. Financial award application deadline: 3/1. *Faculty research:* Material science, biochemistry, chemical education, physical chemistry and theoretical computation, analytical and organic chemistry. *Total annual research expenditures:* $2.4 million. *Unit head:* Dr. Dennis Lindle, Chair/Professor, 702-895-4426, Fax: 702-895-4072, E-mail: lindle@unlv.nevada.edu. *Application contact:* Graduate Coordinator, 702-895-3320, Fax: 702-895-4180, E-mail: gradcollege@unlv.edu. Web site: http://sciences.unlv.edu/Chemistry/index.htm.

University of Nevada, Reno, Graduate School, College of Science, Department of Chemistry, Reno, NV 89557. Offers MS, PhD. Terminal master's awarded for partial completion of doctoral program. *Degree requirements:* For master's, thesis; for doctorate, one foreign language, thesis/dissertation. *Entrance requirements:* For master's, GRE, minimum GPA of 2.75; for doctorate, GRE, minimum GPA of 3.0. Additional exam requirements/recommendations for international students: Required—TOEFL (minimum score 500 paper-based; 173 computer-based; 61 iBT), IELTS (minimum score 6). Electronic applications accepted. *Faculty research:* Organic/inorganic chemistry, physical chemistry, chemical chemistry, physics, organometallic chemistry .

University of New Brunswick Fredericton, School of Graduate Studies, Faculty of Science, Department of Chemistry, Fredericton, NB E3B 5A3, Canada. Offers M Sc, PhD. *Faculty:* 14 full-time (1 woman). *Students:* 41 full-time (22 women), 3 part-time (1 woman); includes 10 minority (1 Black or African American, non-Hispanic/Latino; 9 Asian, non-Hispanic/Latino). In 2011, 5 master's, 3 doctorates awarded. Terminal master's awarded for partial completion of doctoral program. *Degree requirements:* For master's, thesis; for doctorate, comprehensive exam, thesis/dissertation. *Entrance requirements:* For master's and doctorate, minimum GPA of 3.0. Additional exam requirements/recommendations for international students: Required—TOEFL, IELTS. *Application deadline:* For fall admission, 3/1 priority date for domestic students. Application fee: $50 Canadian dollars. *Financial support:* In 2011–12, 4 fellowships (averaging $18,000 per year), 33 research assistantships (averaging $1,595 per year), 36 teaching assistantships (averaging $3,800 per year) were awarded; scholarships/grants also available. *Faculty research:* Electrochemistry, synthetic inorganic and organic chemistry, molecular spectroscopy, computational and theoretical chemistry, catalytic processes, materials chemistry, supramolecular chemistry, chemical energy storage and conversion. *Total annual research expenditures:* $1.1 million. *Unit head:* Dr. Ajit Thakkar, Director of Graduate Studies, 506-461-9629, Fax: 506-453-4981, E-mail: ajit@unb.ca. *Application contact:* Krista Coy, Graduate Secretary, 506-453-4781, Fax: 506-453-4981, E-mail: coyy@unb.ca. Web site: http://www.unb.ca/fredericton/science/chem/.

University of New Hampshire, Graduate School, College of Engineering and Physical Sciences, Department of Chemistry, Durham, NH 03824. Offers chemistry (MS, MST, PhD); chemistry education (PhD). *Faculty:* 28 full-time (17 women). *Students:* 40 full-time (18 women), 10 part-time (4 women); includes 3 minority (2 Hispanic/Latino; 1 Two or more races, non-Hispanic/Latino), 18 international. Average age 28. 68 applicants, 44% accepted, 12 enrolled. In 2011, 5 master's, 3 doctorates awarded. Terminal master's awarded for partial completion of doctoral program. *Degree requirements:* For master's, thesis; for doctorate, one foreign language, thesis/dissertation. *Entrance requirements:* Additional exam requirements/recommendations for international students: Required—TOEFL (minimum score 550 paper-based; 213 computer-based; 80 iBT). *Application deadline:* For fall admission, 4/1 priority date for domestic students, 4/1 for international students; for spring admission, 12/1 for domestic students. Applications are processed on a rolling basis. Application fee: $65. *Expenses:* Tuition, state resident: full-time $12,360; part-time $687 per credit hour. Tuition, nonresident: full-time $25,680; part-time $1058 per credit hour. *International tuition:* $29,550 full-time. *Required fees:* $1666; $833 per course. $416.50 per semester. Tuition and fees vary according to course load and degree level. *Financial support:* In 2011–12, 48 students received support, including 2 fellowships, 8 research assistantships, 35 teaching assistantships; Federal Work-

Study, scholarships/grants, and tuition waivers (full and partial) also available. Support available to part-time students. Financial award application deadline: 2/15. *Faculty research:* Analytical, physical, organic, and inorganic chemistry. *Unit head:* Dr. Chuck Zercher, Chairperson, 603-862-1550. *Application contact:* Cindi Rohwer, Coordinator, 603-862-1550, E-mail: chem.dept@unh.edu. Web site: http://www.unh.edu/chemistry/.

University of New Mexico, Graduate School, College of Arts and Sciences, Department of Chemistry and Chemical Biology, Albuquerque, NM 87131-2039. Offers MS, PhD. *Faculty:* 17 full-time (3 women), 3 part-time/adjunct (1 woman). *Students:* 40 full-time (13 women), 5 part-time (1 woman); includes 1 minority (Hispanic/Latino), 28 international. Average age 31. 25 applicants, 56% accepted, 13 enrolled. In 2011, 3 master's, 8 doctorates awarded. Terminal master's awarded for partial completion of doctoral program. *Median time to degree:* Of those who began their doctoral program in fall 2003, 100% received their degree in 8 years or less. *Degree requirements:* For master's, comprehensive exam, thesis (for some programs); for doctorate, comprehensive exam, thesis/dissertation. *Entrance requirements:* For master's and doctorate, department exams. Additional exam requirements/recommendations for international students: Required—TOEFL (minimum score 550 paper-based; 213 computer-based; 79 iBT). *Application deadline:* For fall admission, 2/1 for domestic and international students. Applications are processed on a rolling basis. Application fee: $50 ($100 for international students). *Financial support:* In 2011–12, 50 students received support, including 11 fellowships (averaging $986 per year), 33 research assistantships with tuition reimbursements available (averaging $11,215 per year), 30 teaching assistantships (averaging $15,341 per year); scholarships/grants, health care benefits, and unspecified assistantships also available. Financial award application deadline: 2/1; financial award applicants required to submit FAFSA. *Faculty research:* Materials, inorganic, organic, physical, and biological chemistry. *Total annual research expenditures:* $1.8 million. *Unit head:* Dr. Stephen Cabaniss, Chair, 505-277-6655, Fax: 505-277-2609, E-mail: cabaniss@unm.edu. *Application contact:* Coordinator, Program Advisement, 505-277-6655, Fax: 505-277-2609, E-mail: kamc@unm.edu. Web site: http://chemistry.unm.edu/.

University of New Orleans, Graduate School, College of Sciences, Department of Chemistry, New Orleans, LA 70148. Offers MS, PhD. *Degree requirements:* For master's, variable foreign language requirement, thesis, departmental qualifying exam; for doctorate, variable foreign language requirement, thesis/dissertation, departmental qualifying exam. *Entrance requirements:* For master's and doctorate, GRE General Test. Additional exam requirements/recommendations for international students: Required—TOEFL (minimum score 550 paper-based; 213 computer-based; 79 iBT). Electronic applications accepted. *Faculty research:* Synthesis and reactions of novel compounds, high-temperature kinetics, calculations of molecular electrostatic potentials, structures and reactions of metal complexes.

The University of North Carolina at Chapel Hill, Graduate School, College of Arts and Sciences, Department of Chemistry, Chapel Hill, NC 27599. Offers MA, MS, PhD. *Degree requirements:* For master's, comprehensive exam, thesis (for some programs); for doctorate, comprehensive exam, thesis/dissertation. *Entrance requirements:* For master's and doctorate, GRE General Test, GRE Subject Test, minimum GPA of 3.0.

The University of North Carolina at Charlotte, Graduate School, College of Liberal Arts and Sciences, Department of Chemistry, Charlotte, NC 28223-0001. Offers chemistry (MS); nanoscale science (PhD). Part-time programs available. *Faculty:* 18 full-time (3 women), 1 part-time/adjunct. *Students:* 14 full-time (3 women), 22 part-time (11 women); includes 5 minority (4 Black or African American, non-Hispanic/Latino; 1 Asian, non-Hispanic/Latino), 3 international. Average age 25. 39 applicants, 41% accepted, 12 enrolled. In 2011, 7 degrees awarded. Terminal master's awarded for partial completion of doctoral program. *Degree requirements:* For master's, thesis; for doctorate, thesis/dissertation. *Entrance requirements:* For master's, GRE General Test or MAT, minimum GPA of 3.0 in undergraduate major, 2.75 overall. Additional exam requirements/recommendations for international students: Required—TOEFL (minimum score 557 paper-based; 220 computer-based; 83 iBT). *Application deadline:* For fall admission, 7/1 for domestic students, 5/1 for international students; for spring admission, 11/1 for domestic students, 10/1 for international students. Applications are processed on a rolling basis. Application fee: $65 ($75 for international students). Electronic applications accepted. *Expenses:* Tuition, state resident: full-time $3689. Tuition, nonresident: full-time $15,226. *Required fees:* $2198. Tuition and fees vary according to course load and program. *Financial support:* In 2011–12, 24 students received support, including 3 research assistantships (averaging $8,167 per year), 21 teaching assistantships (averaging $14,798 per year); fellowships, career-related internships or fieldwork, Federal Work-Study, institutionally sponsored loans, scholarships/grants, and unspecified assistantships also available. Support available to part-time students. Financial award application deadline: 4/1; financial award applicants required to submit FAFSA. *Faculty research:* Biophysical organic chemistry and biochemistry; polymers, biomaterials and nanostructures; materials chemistry; synthetic organic and inorganic chemistry; bioanalytical chemistry. *Total annual research expenditures:* $578,228. *Unit head:* Dr. Bernadette T. Donovan-Merkert, Chair, 704-687-4436, Fax: 704-687-3151, E-mail: bdonovan@uncc.edu. *Application contact:* Kathy B. Giddings, Director of Graduate Admissions, 704-687-5503, Fax: 704-687-3279, E-mail: gradadm@uncc.edu. Web site: http://www.chem.uncc.edu/.

Peterson's Graduate Programs in the Physical Sciences, Mathematics, Agricultural Sciences, the Environment & Natural Resources 2013

facebook.com/petersonspublishing **91**

Chemistry

The University of North Carolina at Greensboro, Graduate School, College of Arts and Sciences, Department of Chemistry and Biochemistry, Greensboro, NC 27412-5001. Offers biochemistry (MS); chemistry (MS). *Degree requirements:* For master's, one foreign language, thesis. *Entrance requirements:* For master's, GRE General Test. Additional exam requirements/recommendations for international students: Required—TOEFL. Electronic applications accepted. *Faculty research:* Synthesis of novel cyclopentadienes, molybdenum hydroxylase-cata ladder polymers, vinyl silicones.

The University of North Carolina Wilmington, College of Arts and Sciences, Department of Chemistry and Biochemistry, Wilmington, NC 28403-3297. Offers MS. Part-time programs available. *Degree requirements:* For master's, comprehensive exam, thesis. *Entrance requirements:* For master's, GRE General Test, minimum B average in undergraduate major. Additional exam requirements/recommendations for international students: Required—TOEFL (minimum score 550 paper-based; 217 computer-based; 79 iBT), IELTS (minimum score 6.5).

University of North Dakota, Graduate School, College of Arts and Sciences, Department of Chemistry, Grand Forks, ND 58202. Offers MS, PhD. Terminal master's awarded for partial completion of doctoral program. *Degree requirements:* For master's, thesis, final exam; for doctorate, comprehensive exam, thesis/dissertation, final exam. *Entrance requirements:* For master's and doctorate, GRE General Test, GRE Subject Test, minimum GPA of 3.0. Additional exam requirements/recommendations for international students: Required—TOEFL (minimum score 550 paper-based; 213 computer-based; 79 iBT), IELTS (minimum score 6.5). Electronic applications accepted. *Faculty research:* Synthetic and structural organometallic chemistry, photochemistry, theoretical chemistry, chromatographic chemistry, x-ray crystallography.

University of Northern Colorado, Graduate School, College of Natural and Health Sciences, Department of Chemistry and Biochemistry, Greeley, CO 80639. Offers chemical education (MS, PhD); chemistry (MS). Part-time programs available. *Degree requirements:* For master's, comprehensive exam, thesis or alternative; for doctorate, comprehensive exam, thesis/dissertation. *Entrance requirements:* For master's, 3 letters of reference; for doctorate, GRE General Test, 3 letters of reference. Electronic applications accepted.

University of Northern Iowa, Graduate College, College of Humanities, Arts and Sciences, Department of Chemistry, Cedar Falls, IA 50614. Offers applied chemistry and biochemistry (PSM); chemistry (MA, MS). Part-time programs available. *Students:* 2 full-time (0 women), 1 part-time (0 women). 16 applicants, 19% accepted, 0 enrolled. In 2011, 4 master's awarded. *Degree requirements:* For master's, comprehensive exam (for some programs), thesis (for some programs). *Entrance requirements:* For master's, minimum GPA of 3.0, 3 letters of recommendation. Additional exam requirements/recommendations for international students: Required—TOEFL (minimum score 500 paper-based; 180 computer-based; 61 iBT). *Application deadline:* For fall admission, 8/1 priority date for domestic students. Applications are processed on a rolling basis. Application fee: $50 ($70 for international students). Electronic applications accepted. *Expenses:* Tuition, state resident: full-time $7476. Tuition, nonresident: full-time $16,410. *Required fees:* $942. *Financial support:* Career-related internships or fieldwork, Federal Work-Study, scholarships/grants, and tuition waivers (full and partial) available. Support available to part-time students. Financial award application deadline: 2/1. *Unit head:* Dr. William S. Harwood, Head, 319-273-2437, Fax: 319-273-7127, E-mail: bill.harwood@uni.edu. *Application contact:* Laurie S. Russell, Record Analyst, 319-273-2623, Fax: 319-273-2885, E-mail: laurie.russell@uni.edu. Web site: http://www.chem.uni.edu/.

University of North Texas, Toulouse Graduate School, College of Arts and Sciences, Department of Chemistry, Denton, TX 76203. Offers MS, PhD. Part-time and evening/weekend programs available. Terminal master's awarded for partial completion of doctoral program. *Degree requirements:* For master's, comprehensive exam, thesis (for some programs); for doctorate, one foreign language, comprehensive exam, thesis/dissertation. *Entrance requirements:* For master's, GRE General Test, 2 letters of recommendation; for doctorate, GRE General Test, 2 letters of recommendation, transcripts, statement of purpose. Additional exam requirements/recommendations for international students: Recommended—TOEFL (minimum score 550 paper-based; 213 computer-based). *Expenses:* Tuition, state resident: part-time $100 per credit hour. Tuition, nonresident: part-time $413 per credit hour. *Faculty research:* Analytical, inorganic, physical, and organic chemistry and materials.

University of Notre Dame, Graduate School, College of Science, Department of Chemistry and Biochemistry, Notre Dame, IN 46556. Offers biochemistry (MS, PhD); inorganic chemistry (MS, PhD); organic chemistry (MS, PhD); physical chemistry (MS, PhD). Terminal master's awarded for partial completion of doctoral program. *Degree requirements:* For master's, comprehensive exam, thesis; for doctorate, thesis/dissertation, qualifying exam. *Entrance requirements:* For master's and doctorate, GRE General Test, GRE Subject Test (strongly recommended). Additional exam requirements/recommendations for international students: Required—TOEFL (minimum score 600 paper-based; 250 computer-based; 80 iBT). Electronic applications accepted. *Faculty research:* Reaction design and mechanistic studies; reactive intermediates; synthesis, structure and reactivity of organometallic cluster complexes and biologically active natural products; bioorganic chemistry; enzymology.

University of Oklahoma, College of Arts and Sciences, Department of Chemistry and Biochemistry, Norman, OK 73019. Offers chemistry and biochemistry (MS, PhD), including bioinformatics, cellular and behavioral neurobiology (PhD), chemistry. Part-time programs available. *Faculty:* 27 full-time (6 women). *Students:* 67 full-time (25 women), 22 part-time (9 women); includes 15 minority (5 Black or African American, non-Hispanic/Latino; 1 American Indian or Alaska Native, non-Hispanic/Latino; 3 Asian, non-Hispanic/Latino; 4 Hispanic/Latino; 2 Two or more races, non-Hispanic/Latino), 40 international. Average age 28. 92 applicants, 17% accepted, 15 enrolled. In 2011, 17 master's, 17 doctorates awarded. Terminal master's awarded for partial completion of doctoral program. *Degree requirements:* For master's, thesis optional; for doctorate, thesis/dissertation. *Entrance requirements:* For master's, GRE, BS in chemistry; for doctorate, GRE. Additional exam requirements/recommendations for international students: Required—TOEFL (minimum score 550 paper-based; 79 iBT). *Application deadline:* For fall admission, 4/1 priority date for domestic students, 3/1 for international students; for spring admission, 9/1 priority date for domestic students, 9/1 for international students. Applications are processed on a rolling basis. Application fee: $40 ($90 for international students). Electronic applications accepted. *Expenses:* Tuition, state resident: full-time $4087; part-time $170.30 per credit hour. Tuition, nonresident: full-time $14,875; part-time $619.80 per credit hour. *Required fees:* $2659; $100.25 per credit hour. Tuition and fees vary according to course load and degree level. *Financial support:* In 2011–12, 89 students received support, including 1 fellowship with full tuition reimbursement available (averaging $5,000 per year), 19 research assistantships with partial tuition reimbursements available (averaging $15,794 per year), 58 teaching assistantships with partial tuition reimbursements available (averaging $16,776 per year); scholarships/grants, tuition waivers (full), and unspecified assistantships also available. Financial award applicants required to submit FAFSA. *Faculty research:* Structural biology, synthesis and catalysis, biomaterials, membrane biochemistry, genomics. *Total annual research expenditures:* $7 million. *Unit head:* Dr. George Richter-Addo, Chair, 405-325-4811, Fax: 405-325-6111, E-mail: grichteraddo@ou.edu. *Application contact:* Angelika Tietz, Graduate Program Assistant, 405-325-4811 Ext. 62946, Fax: 405-325-6111, E-mail: atietz@ou.edu. Web site: http://chem.ou.edu.

University of Oregon, Graduate School, College of Arts and Sciences, Department of Chemistry, Eugene, OR 97403. Offers biochemistry (MA, MS, PhD); chemistry (MA, MS, PhD). Terminal master's awarded for partial completion of doctoral program. *Degree requirements:* For doctorate, thesis/dissertation. *Entrance requirements:* For master's and doctorate, GRE General Test, minimum GPA of 3.0. Additional exam requirements/recommendations for international students: Required—TOEFL. *Faculty research:* Organic chemistry, organometallic chemistry, inorganic chemistry, physical chemistry, materials science, biochemistry, chemical physics, molecular or cell biology.

University of Ottawa, Faculty of Graduate and Postdoctoral Studies, Faculty of Science, Ottawa-Carleton Chemistry Institute, Ottawa, ON K1N 6N5, Canada. Offers M Sc, PhD. M Sc, PhD offered jointly with Carleton University. *Degree requirements:* For master's, thesis, seminar; for doctorate, comprehensive exam, thesis/dissertation, 2 seminars. *Entrance requirements:* For master's, honors B Sc degree or equivalent, minimum B average; for doctorate, honors B Sc with minimum B average or M Sc in chemistry with minimum B+ average. Electronic applications accepted. *Faculty research:* Organic chemistry, physical chemistry, inorganic chemistry.

University of Pennsylvania, School of Arts and Sciences, Graduate Group in Chemistry, Philadelphia, PA 19104. Offers MS, PhD. *Faculty:* 30 full-time (5 women), 10 part-time/adjunct (0 women). *Students:* 173 full-time (83 women), 1 part-time (0 women); includes 17 minority (3 Black or African American, non-Hispanic/Latino; 9 Asian, non-Hispanic/Latino; 5 Hispanic/Latino), 80 international. 478 applicants, 31% accepted, 36 enrolled. In 2011, 25 master's, 26 doctorates awarded. *Degree requirements:* For doctorate, thesis/dissertation. *Entrance requirements:* For doctorate, GRE General Test, GRE Subject Test, previous graduate course work in organic, inorganic, and physical chemistry, and general physics, each with a lab, as well as differential and integral calculus. Additional exam requirements/recommendations for international students: Required—TOEFL. *Application deadline:* For fall admission, 12/1 priority date for domestic students. Application fee: $70. Electronic applications accepted. *Expenses: Tuition:* Full-time $26,660; part-time $4944 per course. *Required fees:* $2318; $291 per course. Tuition and fees vary according to course load, degree level and program. *Financial support:* Fellowships, research assistantships, teaching assistantships, institutionally sponsored loans, scholarships/grants, traineeships, health care benefits, and unspecified assistantships available. Financial award application deadline: 12/15. *Unit head:* Gary A. Molander, Department Chair, 215-573-8604, E-mail: gmolandr@sas.upenn.edu. *Application contact:* 215-898-8317, E-mail: web@chem.upenn.edu.

University of Pittsburgh, Dietrich School of Arts and Sciences, Department of Chemistry, Pittsburgh, PA 15260. Offers MS, PhD. Part-time and evening/weekend programs available. *Faculty:* 31 full-time (4 women), 14 part-time/adjunct (3 women). *Students:* 204 full-time (58 women), 3 part-time (2 women); includes 4 minority (2 Asian, non-Hispanic/Latino; 2 Hispanic/Latino), 91 international. Average age 24. 391 applicants, 38% accepted, 42 enrolled. In 2011, 11 master's, 21 doctorates awarded. Terminal master's awarded for partial completion of doctoral program. *Degree requirements:* For master's, comprehensive exam, thesis; for doctorate, comprehensive exam, thesis/dissertation. *Entrance requirements:* For master's and doctorate, GRE General Test, GRE Subject Test. Additional exam requirements/recommendations for international students: Required—TOEFL (minimum score 600 paper-based; 250 computer-based; 100 iBT). *Application deadline:* For fall admission, 2/1 priority

92 facebook.com/petersonspublishing

Peterson's Graduate Programs in the Physical Sciences, Mathematics, Agricultural Sciences, the Environment & Natural Resources 2013

date for domestic students, 2/1 for international students. Applications are processed on a rolling basis. Application fee: $50. Electronic applications accepted. *Expenses:* Tuition, state resident: full-time $18,774; part-time $760 per credit. Tuition, nonresident: full-time $30,736; part-time $1258 per credit. *Required fees:* $740; $200 per term. Tuition and fees vary according to program. *Financial support:* In 2011–12, 204 students received support, including 10 fellowships with tuition reimbursements available (averaging $26,955 per year), 125 research assistantships with tuition reimbursements available (averaging $23,265 per year), 70 teaching assistantships with tuition reimbursements available (averaging $23,745 per year); Federal Work-Study, scholarships/grants, health care benefits, and unspecified assistantships also available. Financial award application deadline: 2/1. *Faculty research:* Analytical, biological, inorganic and materials including nanostructured materials, organic, physical and theoretical. *Total annual research expenditures:* $10.1 million. *Unit head:* Dr. David H. Waldeck, Chairman, 412-624-0415, Fax: 412-624-1649, E-mail: chemchr@pitt.edu. *Application contact:* Fran Nagy, Graduate Program Administrator, 412-624-8501, Fax: 412-624-8611, E-mail: fnagy@pitt.edu. Web site: http://www.chem.pitt.edu.

University of Prince Edward Island, Faculty of Science, Charlottetown, PE C1A 4P3, Canada. Offers biology (M Sc); chemistry (M Sc). *Degree requirements:* For master's, thesis. *Entrance requirements:* Additional exam requirements/recommendations for international students: Required—TOEFL (minimum score 550 paper-based; 213 computer-based; 80 iBT), Canadian Academic English Language Assessment, Michigan English Language Assessment Battery, Canadian Test of English for Scholars and Trainees. *Faculty research:* Ecology and wildlife biology, molecular, genetics and biotechnology, organametallic, bio-organic, supramolecular and synthetic organic chemistry, neurobiology and stoke materials science.

University of Puerto Rico, Mayagüez Campus, Graduate Studies, College of Arts and Sciences, Department of Chemistry, Mayagüez, PR 00681-9000. Offers chemistry (MS, PhD). Part-time programs available. *Students:* 80 full-time (46 women), 1 (woman) part-time; includes 55 minority (all Hispanic/Latino), 26 international. 18 applicants, 72% accepted, 11 enrolled. In 2011, 5 master's, 7 doctorates awarded. *Degree requirements:* For master's, one foreign language, comprehensive exam, thesis; for doctorate, comprehensive exam, thesis/dissertation. *Entrance requirements:* For master's, GRE, BS in chemistry or the equivalent. *Application deadline:* For fall admission, 2/15 for domestic and international students; for spring admission, 9/15 for domestic and international students. Applications are processed on a rolling basis. Application fee: $25. Tuition and fees vary according to course level and course load. *Financial support:* In 2011–12, 1 fellowship, 31 research assistantships (averaging $15,000 per year), 63 teaching assistantships (averaging $8,500 per year) were awarded; Federal Work-Study and institutionally sponsored loans also available. *Faculty research:* Biochemistry, spectroscopy, food chemistry, physical chemistry, electrochemistry. *Unit head:* Dr. Rene Vieta, Director, 787-265-5458, Fax: 787-265-3849, E-mail: rene.vieta@upr.edu. Web site: http://www.uprm.edu/wquim/.

University of Puerto Rico, Río Piedras, College of Natural Sciences, Department of Chemistry, San Juan, PR 00931-3300. Offers MS, PhD. Part-time programs available. *Degree requirements:* For master's, one foreign language, comprehensive exam, thesis; for doctorate, one foreign language, comprehensive exam, thesis/dissertation. *Entrance requirements:* For master's, GRE General Test, GRE Subject Test, interview, minimum GPA of 3.0, letter of recommendation; for doctorate, GRE General Test, GRE Subject Test, minimum GPA of 3.0, letter of recommendation. Additional exam requirements/recommendations for international students: Required—TOEFL.

University of Regina, Faculty of Graduate Studies and Research, Faculty of Science, Department of Chemistry and Biochemistry, Regina, SK S4S 0A2, Canada. Offers analytical/environmental chemistry (M Sc, PhD); biophysics of biological interfaces (M Sc, PhD); enzymology/chemical biology (M Sc, PhD); inorganic/organometallic chemistry (M Sc, PhD); signal transduction and mechanisms of cancer cell regulation (M Sc, PhD); supramolecular organic photochemistry and photophysics (M Sc, PhD); synthetic organic chemistry (M Sc, PhD); theoretical/computational chemistry (M Sc, PhD). *Faculty:* 12 full-time (2 women). *Students:* 13 full-time (4 women), 1 (woman) part-time. 22 applicants, 50% accepted. In 2011, 1 master's, 2 doctorates awarded. *Degree requirements:* For master's, thesis; for doctorate, thesis/dissertation. *Entrance requirements:* Additional exam requirements/recommendations for international students: Required—TOEFL (minimum score 580 paper-based; 80 iBT), IELTS (minimum score 6.5). *Application deadline:* Applications are processed on a rolling basis. Application fee: $100. Electronic applications accepted. *Financial support:* In 2011–12, 3 fellowships (averaging $6,500 per year), 1 research assistantship (averaging $5,500 per year), 7 teaching assistantships (averaging $2,298 per year) were awarded; scholarships/grants also available. Financial award application deadline: 6/15. *Faculty research:* Asymmetric synthesis and methodology, theoretical and computational chemistry, biophysical biochemistry, analytical and environmental chemistry, chemical biology. *Unit head:* Dr. Lynn Mihichuk, Head, 306-585-4793, Fax: 306-337-2409, E-mail: lynn.mihichuk@uregina.ca. *Application contact:* Dr. Tanya Dahms, Graduate Program Coordinator, 306-585-4246, Fax: 306-337-2409, E-mail: tanya.dahms@uregina.ca. Web site: http://www.chem.uregina.ca/.

University of Rhode Island, Graduate School, College of Arts and Sciences, Department of Chemistry, Kingston, RI 02881. Offers MS, PhD. Part-time and evening/weekend programs available. *Faculty:* 17 full-time (5 women). *Students:* 42 full-time (20 women), 10 part-time (3 women); includes 6 minority (2 Black or African American, non-Hispanic/Latino; 4 Asian, non-Hispanic/Latino; 12 international. In 2011, 4 master's, 7 doctorates awarded. *Degree requirements:* For master's, comprehensive exam (for some programs), thesis optional; for doctorate, comprehensive exam, thesis/dissertation. *Entrance requirements:* For master's and doctorate, GRE (for graduates of non-U.S. universities), 2 letters of recommendation. Additional exam requirements/recommendations for international students: Required—TOEFL (minimum score 550 paper-based; 213 computer-based). *Application deadline:* For fall admission, 7/15 for domestic students, 1/15 for international students; for spring admission, 11/15 for domestic students, 9/15 for international students. Application fee: $65. Electronic applications accepted. *Expenses:* Tuition, state resident: full-time $10,432; part-time $580 per credit hour. Tuition, nonresident: full-time $23,130; part-time $1285 per credit hour. *Required fees:* $1362; $36 per credit hour. $35 per semester. One-time fee: $130. *Financial support:* In 2011–12, 7 research assistantships with full and partial tuition reimbursements (averaging $7,166 per year), 30 teaching assistantships with full and partial tuition reimbursements (averaging $11,841 per year) were awarded. Financial award applicants required to submit FAFSA. *Faculty research:* Analytical chemistry, biochemistry, analytical/nanoscience, materials/analytical, theoretical chemistry. *Unit head:* Dr. William Euler, Chairperson, 401-874-5090, Fax: 401-874-5072, E-mail: weuler@chm.uri.edu. *Application contact:* Nasser H. Zawia, Dean of the Graduate School, 401-874-5909, Fax: 401-874-5787, E-mail: nzawia@uri.edu. Web site: http://www.chm.uri.edu/index.php.

University of Rochester, School of Arts and Sciences, Department of Chemistry, Rochester, NY 14627. Offers PhD. *Faculty:* 20 full-time (2 women). *Students:* 110 full-time (43 women), 3 part-time (2 women); includes 10 minority (2 American Indian or Alaska Native, non-Hispanic/Latino; 4 Asian, non-Hispanic/Latino; 1 Hispanic/Latino; 3 Two or more races, non-Hispanic/Latino), 28 international. 361 applicants, 18% accepted, 16 enrolled. In 2011, 11 doctorates awarded. Terminal master's awarded for partial completion of doctoral program. *Degree requirements:* For doctorate, thesis/dissertation, qualifying exam. *Entrance requirements:* For doctorate, GRE General Test, undergraduate transcript, three letters of recommendation. Additional exam requirements/recommendations for international students: Required—TOEFL. *Application deadline:* For fall admission, 1/15 for domestic students. Application fee: $0. Electronic applications accepted. *Expenses: Tuition:* Full-time $41,040. *Financial support:* Fellowships, research assistantships, teaching assistantships, and tuition waivers (full and partial) available. Financial award application deadline: 1/15. *Faculty research:* Organic, inorganic, physical, biological, theoretical. *Unit head:* Robert K. Boeckman, Jr., Chair, 585-275-4229. *Application contact:* Robin Cooley, Graduate Studies Coordinator, 585-275-0635. Web site: http://www.chem.rochester.edu/.

University of Saint Joseph, Department of Chemistry, West Hartford, CT 06117-2700. Offers biochemistry (MS); chemistry (MS). Part-time and evening/weekend programs available. Postbaccalaureate distance learning degree programs offered. *Students:* 33 part-time (20 women); includes 8 minority (3 Black or African American, non-Hispanic/Latino; 2 Asian, non-Hispanic/Latino; 3 Hispanic/Latino). Average age 30. *Degree requirements:* For master's, comprehensive exam, thesis optional. *Entrance requirements:* For master's, 2 letters of recommendation. *Application deadline:* Applications are processed on a rolling basis. Application fee: $50. Electronic applications accepted. Application fee is waived when completed online. *Expenses: Tuition:* Part-time $670 per credit. *Required fees:* $40 per credit. Tuition and fees vary according to course load, degree level, campus/location and program. *Financial support:* Career-related internships or fieldwork and unspecified assistantships available. Support available to part-time students. Financial award applicants required to submit FAFSA. *Application contact:* Graduate Admissions Office, 860-231-5261, E-mail: graduate@usj.edu.

University of San Francisco, College of Arts and Sciences, Chemistry Program, San Francisco, CA 94117-1080. Offers MS. Part-time and evening/weekend programs available. *Faculty:* 1 full-time (0 women). *Students:* 13 full-time (5 women); includes 3 minority (2 Asian, non-Hispanic/Latino; 1 Native Hawaiian or other Pacific Islander, non-Hispanic/Latino), 3 international. Average age 25. 44 applicants, 16% accepted, 4 enrolled. In 2011, 2 master's awarded. *Degree requirements:* For master's, thesis. *Entrance requirements:* For master's, GRE General Test, GRE Subject Test, BS in chemistry or related field. *Application deadline:* Applications are processed on a rolling basis. Application fee: $55 ($65 for international students). *Expenses: Tuition:* Full-time $20,070; part-time $1115 per unit. Tuition and fees vary according to course load, campus/location and program. *Financial support:* In 2011–12, 13 students received support. Fellowships, research assistantships, teaching assistantships, career-related internships or fieldwork, Federal Work-Study, institutionally sponsored loans, and tuition waivers (partial) available. Support available to part-time students. Financial award application deadline: 3/2; financial award applicants required to submit FAFSA. *Faculty research:* Organic photochemistry, genetics of chromatic adaptation, electron transfer processes in solution, metabolism of protein hormones. *Total annual research expenditures:* $75,000. *Unit head:* Dr. Jeff Curtis, Chair, 415-422-6157, Fax: 415-422-5157. *Application contact:* Information Contact, 415-422-5135, Fax: 415-422-2217, E-mail: asgraduate@usfca.edu. Web site: http://www.usfca.edu/artsci/chemg/.

University of Saskatchewan, College of Graduate Studies and Research, College of Arts and Science, Department of Chemistry, Saskatoon, SK S7N 5A2,

Peterson's Graduate Programs in the Physical Sciences, Mathematics, Agricultural Sciences, the Environment & Natural Resources 2013

facebook.com/petersonspublishing **93**

Chemistry

Canada. Offers M Sc, PhD. *Degree requirements:* For master's, thesis; for doctorate, comprehensive exam (for some programs), thesis/dissertation. *Entrance requirements:* Additional exam requirements/recommendations for international students: Required—TOEFL (minimum score 80 iBT); Recommended—IELTS (minimum score 6.5). Electronic applications accepted.

The University of Scranton, College of Graduate and Continuing Education, Department of Chemistry, Program in Chemistry, Scranton, PA 18510. Offers MA, MS. Part-time and evening/weekend programs available. *Faculty:* 10 full-time (3 women), 1 part-time/adjunct (0 women). *Students:* 6 full-time (4 women), 5 part-time (4 women), 3 international. Average age 30. 23 applicants, 70% accepted. In 2011, 1 master's awarded. *Degree requirements:* For master's, comprehensive exam (for some programs), thesis (for some programs), capstone experience. *Entrance requirements:* For master's, minimum GPA of 2.75. Additional exam requirements/recommendations for international students: Required—TOEFL (minimum score 500 paper-based; 173 computer-based), IELTS (minimum score 5.5). *Application deadline:* Applications are processed on a rolling basis. Application fee: $0. *Financial support:* Fellowships, teaching assistantships, career-related internships or fieldwork, Federal Work-Study, and unspecified assistantships available. Support available to part-time students. Financial award application deadline: 3/1. *Unit head:* Dr. Christopher A. Baumann, Director, 570-941-6389, Fax: 570-941-7510, E-mail: cab@scranton.edu. *Application contact:* Dr. Christopher A. Baumann, Director, 570-941-6389, Fax: 570-941-7510, E-mail: cab@scranton.edu.

The University of Scranton, College of Graduate and Continuing Education, Department of Chemistry, Program in Clinical Chemistry, Scranton, PA 18510. Offers MA, MS. Part-time and evening/weekend programs available. *Faculty:* 10 full-time (3 women), 1 part-time/adjunct (0 women). *Students:* 14 full-time (11 women), 5 part-time (3 women), 8 international. Average age 24. 23 applicants, 83% accepted. In 2011, 2 master's awarded. *Degree requirements:* For master's, comprehensive exam (for some programs), thesis (for some programs), capstone experience. *Entrance requirements:* For master's, minimum GPA of 2.75. Additional exam requirements/recommendations for international students: Required—TOEFL (minimum score 500 paper-based; 173 computer-based), IELTS (minimum score 5.5). *Application deadline:* Applications are processed on a rolling basis. Application fee: $0. *Financial support:* Fellowships, teaching assistantships, career-related internships or fieldwork, Federal Work-Study, and unspecified assistantships available. Support available to part-time students. Financial award application deadline: 3/1. *Unit head:* Dr. Christopher A. Baumann, Director, 570-941-6389, Fax: 570-941-7510, E-mail: cab@scranton.edu. *Application contact:* Dr. Christopher A. Baumann, Director, 570-941-6389, Fax: 570-941-7510, E-mail: cab@scranton.edu.

University of South Carolina, The Graduate School, College of Arts and Sciences, Department of Chemistry and Biochemistry, Columbia, SC 29208. Offers IMA, MAT, MS, PhD. IMA and MAT offered in cooperation with the College of Education. Part-time programs available. Terminal master's awarded for partial completion of doctoral program. *Degree requirements:* For master's, comprehensive exam, thesis; for doctorate, comprehensive exam, thesis/dissertation. *Entrance requirements:* For master's and doctorate, GRE General Test. Additional exam requirements/recommendations for international students: Required—TOEFL. Electronic applications accepted. *Faculty research:* Spectroscopy, crystallography, organic and organometallic synthesis, analytical chemistry, materials.

The University of South Dakota, Graduate School, College of Arts and Sciences, Department of Chemistry, Vermillion, SD 57069-2390. Offers MNS, MS, PhD. *Degree requirements:* For master's, comprehensive exam, thesis. *Entrance requirements:* For master's, minimum GPA of 2.7; for doctorate, GRE, minimum GPA of 2.7. Additional exam requirements/recommendations for international students: Required—TOEFL (minimum score 550 paper-based; 213 computer-based; 79 iBT). Electronic applications accepted. *Expenses:* Tuition: state resident: full-time $3118.50; part-time $173.25 per credit hour. Tuition, nonresident: full-time $6601; part-time $366.70 per credit hour. *Required fees:* $2268; $126 per credit hour. Tuition and fees vary according to program. *Faculty research:* Electrochemistry, photochemistry, inorganic synthesis, environmental and solid-state chemistry.

University of Southern California, Graduate School, Dana and David Dornsife College of Letters, Arts and Sciences, Department of Chemistry, Los Angeles, CA 90089. Offers chemistry (PhD); physical chemistry (PhD). Terminal master's awarded for partial completion of doctoral program. *Degree requirements:* For doctorate, thesis/dissertation. *Entrance requirements:* For doctorate, GRE General Test. Additional exam requirements/recommendations for international students: Required—TOEFL. Electronic applications accepted. *Faculty research:* Biological chemistry, inorganic chemistry, organic chemistry, physical chemistry, theoretical chemistry.

University of Southern Mississippi, Graduate School, College of Science and Technology, Department of Chemistry and Biochemistry, Hattiesburg, MS 39406-0001. Offers analytical chemistry (MS, PhD); biochemistry (MS, PhD); inorganic chemistry (MS, PhD); organic chemistry (MS, PhD); physical chemistry (MS, PhD). *Faculty:* 16 full-time (4 women). *Students:* 22 full-time (9 women), 4 part-time (3 women); includes 1 minority (Black or African American, non-Hispanic/Latino), 9 international. Average age 29. 43 applicants, 19% accepted, 5 enrolled. In 2011, 1 master's, 4 doctorates awarded. *Degree requirements:* For master's, comprehensive exam, thesis; for doctorate, comprehensive exam, thesis/dissertation. *Entrance requirements:* For master's, GRE General Test, minimum GPA of 2.75 in last 60 hours; for doctorate, GRE General Test, minimum GPA of 3.5. Additional exam requirements/recommendations for international students: Required—TOEFL, IELTS. *Application deadline:* For fall admission, 3/1 priority date for domestic students, 3/1 for international students. Applications are processed on a rolling basis. Application fee: $50. *Financial support:* In 2011–12, 3 research assistantships with full tuition reimbursements (averaging $17,000 per year), 19 teaching assistantships with full tuition reimbursements (averaging $20,700 per year) were awarded; fellowships, Federal Work-Study, institutionally sponsored loans, scholarships/grants, health care benefits, and unspecified assistantships also available. Support available to part-time students. Financial award application deadline: 3/15; financial award applicants required to submit FAFSA. *Faculty research:* Plant biochemistry, photo chemistry, polymer chemistry, x-ray analysis, enzyme chemistry. *Unit head:* Dr. Sabine Heinhorst, Chair, 601-266-4701, Fax: 601-266-6075. *Application contact:* Dr. Sabine Heinhorst, Graduate Coordinator, 601-266-4702, Fax: 601-266-6075. Web site: http://www.usm.edu/graduateschool/table.php.

University of South Florida, Graduate School, College of Arts and Sciences, Department of Chemistry, Tampa, FL 33620-9951. Offers analytical chemistry (MS, PhD); biochemistry (MS, PhD); computational chemistry (MS, PhD); environmental chemistry (MS, PhD); inorganic chemistry (MS, PhD); organic chemistry (MS); physical chemistry (MS, PhD); polymer chemistry (PhD). Part-time programs available. *Faculty:* 25 full-time (4 women), 9 part-time/adjunct (1 woman). *Students:* 118 full-time (46 women), 14 part-time (7 women); includes 28 minority (8 Black or African American, non-Hispanic/Latino; 11 Asian, non-Hispanic/Latino; 9 Hispanic/Latino), 58 international. Average age 29. 127 applicants, 31% accepted, 19 enrolled. In 2011, 3 master's, 16 doctorates awarded. Terminal master's awarded for partial completion of doctoral program. *Degree requirements:* For master's, comprehensive exam, thesis (for some programs); for doctorate, comprehensive exam, thesis/dissertation. *Entrance requirements:* For master's and doctorate, GRE General Test, minimum GPA of 3.0. Additional exam requirements/recommendations for international students: Required—TOEFL (minimum score 550 paper-based; 213 computer-based; 79 iBT) or IELTS (minimum score 6.5). *Application deadline:* For fall admission, 2/15 priority date for domestic students, 1/2 for international students; for spring admission, 10/1 priority date for domestic students, 6/1 for international students. Applications are processed on a rolling basis. Application fee: $30. Electronic applications accepted. *Financial support:* In 2011–12, 136 students received support, including 28 research assistantships with tuition reimbursements available (averaging $15,020 per year), 108 teaching assistantships with tuition reimbursements available (averaging $15,164 per year); unspecified assistantships also available. Financial award application deadline: 6/30. *Faculty research:* Synthesis, bio-organic chemistry, bioinorganic chemistry, environmental chemistry, NMR. *Total annual research expenditures:* $3.1 million. *Unit head:* Dr. Randy Larsen, Chairperson, 813-974-4129, Fax: 813-974-3203, E-mail: rlarsen@cas.usf.edu. *Application contact:* Patricia Muisener, Director, 813-974-1730, Fax: 813-974-3203, E-mail: muisener@cas.usf.edu. Web site: http://chemistry.usf.edu/.

The University of Tennessee, Graduate School, College of Arts and Sciences, Department of Chemistry, Knoxville, TN 37996. Offers analytical chemistry (MS, PhD); chemical physics (PhD); environmental chemistry (MS, PhD); inorganic chemistry (MS, PhD); organic chemistry (MS, PhD); physical chemistry (MS, PhD); polymer chemistry (MS, PhD); theoretical chemistry (PhD). Part-time programs available. Terminal master's awarded for partial completion of doctoral program. *Degree requirements:* For master's, thesis; for doctorate, thesis/dissertation. *Entrance requirements:* For master's and doctorate, GRE General Test, minimum GPA of 2.7. Additional exam requirements/recommendations for international students: Required—TOEFL. Electronic applications accepted. *Expenses:* Tuition, state resident: full-time $8332; part-time $464 per credit hour. Tuition, nonresident: full-time $25,174; part-time $1400 per credit hour. *Required fees:* $1162; $56 per credit hour. Tuition and fees vary according to program.

The University of Texas at Arlington, Graduate School, College of Science, Department of Chemistry and Biochemistry, Arlington, TX 76019. Offers chemistry (MS, PhD). Part-time programs available. *Faculty:* 19 full-time (1 woman), 1 part-time/adjunct (0 women). *Students:* 60 full-time (26 women), 14 part-time (9 women); includes 10 minority (2 Black or African American, non-Hispanic/Latino; 4 Asian, non-Hispanic/Latino; 3 Hispanic/Latino; 1 Native Hawaiian or other Pacific Islander, non-Hispanic/Latino), 42 international. 89 applicants, 21% accepted, 8 enrolled. In 2011, 3 master's, 11 doctorates awarded. Terminal master's awarded for partial completion of doctoral program. *Degree requirements:* For master's, comprehensive exam (for some programs), thesis optional; for doctorate, comprehensive exam, thesis/dissertation, internship, oral defense of dissertation. *Entrance requirements:* For master's and doctorate, GRE General Test, minimum GPA of 3.0 in last 60 hours of course work; BS in STEM field (preferably chemistry or biochemistry) or equivalent 4-year minimum program. Additional exam requirements/recommendations for international students: Required—TOEFL (minimum score 550 paper-based; 213 computer-based; 80 iBT). *Application deadline:* For fall admission, 3/1 for domestic and international students; for spring admission, 10/15 for domestic students, 9/15 for international students. Applications are processed on a rolling basis. Application fee: $40 ($70 for international students). Electronic applications accepted. *Financial support:* In 2011–12, 4 fellowships (averaging $1,000 per year), 25 research assistantships with partial tuition reimbursements (averaging $21,000 per year), 31 teaching assistantships with full and partial tuition reimbursements

94 facebook.com/petersonspublishing

Peterson's Graduate Programs in the Physical Sciences, Mathematics, Agricultural Sciences, the Environment & Natural Resources 2013

(averaging $20,000 per year) were awarded; career-related internships or fieldwork, Federal Work-Study, institutionally sponsored loans, scholarships/grants, health care benefits, tuition waivers (partial), and unspecified assistantships also available. Financial award application deadline: 6/1; financial award applicants required to submit FAFSA. *Unit head:* Dr. Rasika Dias, Chairman, 817-272-3171, Fax: 817-272-3808, E-mail: dias@uta.edu. *Application contact:* Jacob McKeever, Academic Advisor II, 817-272-2750, Fax: 817-272-3808, E-mail: jacobm@uta.edu. Web site: http://www.uta.edu/chemistry/.

The University of Texas at Austin, Graduate School, College of Natural Sciences, Department of Chemistry and Biochemistry, Austin, TX 78712-1111. Offers analytical chemistry (PhD); biochemistry (PhD); inorganic chemistry (PhD); organic chemistry (PhD); physical chemistry (PhD). *Entrance requirements:* For doctorate, GRE General Test. Application fee: $50 ($75 for international students). *Financial support:* Fellowships, research assistantships, teaching assistantships, and scholarships/grants available. Financial award application deadline: 2/1. *Unit head:* Dr. Richard M. Crooks, Chairman, 512-475-8674, E-mail: crooks@cm.utexas.edu. *Application contact:* Dr. Jennifer S. Brodbelt, Graduate Admissions Chair, 512-471-0028, E-mail: jbrodbelt@cm.utexas.edu. Web site: http://www.cm.utexas.edu/.

The University of Texas at Dallas, School of Natural Sciences and Mathematics, Department of Chemistry, Richardson, TX 75080. Offers MS, PhD. Part-time and evening/weekend programs available. *Faculty:* 17 full-time (2 women), 1 part-time/adjunct (0 women). *Students:* 59 full-time (27 women), 7 part-time (4 women); includes 9 minority (5 Asian, non-Hispanic/Latino; 4 Hispanic/Latino), 42 international. Average age 29. 119 applicants, 20% accepted, 21 enrolled. In 2011, 6 master's, 6 doctorates awarded. *Degree requirements:* For master's, thesis or internship; for doctorate, comprehensive exam, thesis/dissertation, research practica. *Entrance requirements:* For master's and doctorate, GRE General Test, minimum GPA of 3.0 in upper-level course work in field. Additional exam requirements/recommendations for international students: Required—TOEFL (minimum score 600 paper-based; 250 computer-based). *Application deadline:* For fall admission, 7/15 for domestic students, 5/1 for international students; for spring admission, 11/15 for domestic students, 9/1 for international students. Applications are processed on a rolling basis. Application fee: $50 ($100 for international students). Electronic applications accepted. *Expenses:* Tuition, state resident: full-time $11,170; part-time $620.56 per credit hour. Tuition, nonresident: full-time $20,212; part-time $1122.89 per credit hour. *Financial support:* In 2011–12, 59 students received support, including 30 research assistantships with partial tuition reimbursements available (averaging $21,900 per year), 27 teaching assistantships with partial tuition reimbursements available (averaging $15,699 per year); career-related internships or fieldwork, Federal Work-Study, institutionally sponsored loans, scholarships/grants, and unspecified assistantships also available. Support available to part-time students. Financial award application deadline: 4/30; financial award applicants required to submit FAFSA. *Faculty research:* Advanced nano-materials; novel MR imaging agents; peptidomimetics to treat diabetes; semiconducting polymers for organic electronics; macrocyclic receptors for catalysis, medicine, materials science; electroactive polymers. *Unit head:* Dr. John P. Ferraris, Department Head, 972-883-2901, Fax: 972-883-2925, E-mail: chemistry@utdallas.edu. *Application contact:* Dr. Inga H. Musselman, Associate Department Head, 972-883-2706, Fax: 972-883-2925, E-mail: imusselm@utdallas.edu. Web site: http://www.utdallas.edu/chemistry/.

The University of Texas at El Paso, Graduate School, College of Science, Department of Chemistry, El Paso, TX 79968-0001. Offers MS, PhD. Part-time and evening/weekend programs available. *Students:* 39 (15 women); includes 15 minority (all Hispanic/Latino), 22 international. Average age 34. 15 applicants, 60% accepted, 4 enrolled. In 2011, 2 master's, 2 doctorates awarded. *Degree requirements:* For master's, thesis; for doctorate, thesis/dissertation. *Entrance requirements:* For master's, GRE, minimum GPA of 3.0; for doctorate, GRE, letters of recommendation. Additional exam requirements/recommendations for international students: Required—TOEFL; Recommended—IELTS. *Application deadline:* For fall admission, 8/1 priority date for domestic students, 3/1 for international students; for spring admission, 11/1 priority date for domestic students, 9/1 for international students. Applications are processed on a rolling basis. Application fee: $45 ($80 for international students). Electronic applications accepted. *Financial support:* In 2011–12, research assistantships with partial tuition reimbursements (averaging $20,250 per year), teaching assistantships with partial tuition reimbursements (averaging $16,200 per year) were awarded; fellowships with partial tuition reimbursements, institutionally sponsored loans, scholarships/grants, health care benefits, tuition waivers (partial), and unspecified assistantships also available. Support available to part-time students. Financial award application deadline: 3/15; financial award applicants required to submit FAFSA. *Unit head:* Dr. Jorge Gardea-Torresdey, Chairperson, 915-747-5359, Fax: 915-747-5748, E-mail: jgardea@utep.edu. *Application contact:* Dr. Benjamin Flores, Interim Dean of the Graduate School, 915-747-5491, Fax: 915-747-5788, E-mail: bflores@utep.edu. Web site: http://science.utep.edu/chemistry/.

The University of Texas at San Antonio, College of Sciences, Department of Chemistry, San Antonio, TX 78249-0617. Offers MS, PhD. *Faculty:* 13 full-time (1 woman), 2 part-time/adjunct (0 women). *Students:* 31 full-time (16 women), 18 part-time (4 women); includes 12 minority (1 Black or African American, non-Hispanic/Latino; 1 Asian, non-Hispanic/Latino; 7 Hispanic/Latino; 3 Two or more races, non-Hispanic/Latino), 17 international. Average age 29. 57 applicants, 39% accepted, 16 enrolled. In 2011, 3 master's, 1 doctorate awarded. *Degree*

requirements: For master's, comprehensive exam, thesis optional; for doctorate, comprehensive exam, thesis/dissertation. *Entrance requirements:* For master's, GRE General Test, minimum GPA of 3.0 in all undergraduate chemistry courses, 2 letters of recommendation; for doctorate, GRE, official transcripts from all colleges and universities attended, resume or curriculum vitae, at least 2 letters of recommendation, statement of purpose. Additional exam requirements/recommendations for international students: Required—TOEFL (minimum score 500 paper-based; 61 iBT), IELTS (minimum score 5). *Application deadline:* For fall admission, 7/1 for domestic students, 4/1 for international students; for spring admission, 11/1 for domestic students, 9/1 for international students. Application fee: $45 ($85 for international students). *Expenses:* Tuition, state resident: full-time $3148; part-time $2176 per semester. Tuition, nonresident: full-time $8782; part-time $5932 per semester. *Required fees:* $719 per semester. *Financial support:* In 2011–12, 48 students received support, including 12 fellowships with full tuition reimbursements available (averaging $21,000 per year), 12 research assistantships with full tuition reimbursements available (averaging $25,000 per year), 24 teaching assistantships with full tuition reimbursements available (averaging $13,000 per year). *Faculty research:* Medicinal chemistry, biosensors, mass spectrometry, organic synthesis, enzymatic mechanisms. *Total annual research expenditures:* $1.7 million. *Unit head:* Dr. Waldemar Gorski, Department Chair, 210-458-5469, Fax: 210-458-7428, E-mail: waldemar.gorski@utsa.edu. *Application contact:* Dr. Stephan Bach, Graduate Advisor of Record, 210-458-6896, Fax: 210-458-7428, E-mail: stephan.bach@utsa.edu.

The University of Texas–Pan American, College of Science and Mathematics, Department of Chemistry, Edinburg, TX 78539. Offers MS, MSIS. Tuition and fees vary according to course load, program and student level. *Unit head:* Dr. Narayan Bhat, Chair, 956-665-3373, E-mail: nbhat@utpa.edu. Web site: http://portal.utpa.edu/utpa_main/daa_home/cosm_home/chem_home/chem_grad.

University of the Sciences in Philadelphia, College of Graduate Studies, Program in Chemistry, Biochemistry and Pharmacognosy, Philadelphia, PA 19104-4495. Offers biochemistry (MS, PhD); chemistry (MS, PhD); pharmacognosy (MS, PhD). Part-time programs available. *Degree requirements:* For master's, thesis, qualifying exams; for doctorate, comprehensive exam, thesis/dissertation, qualifying exams. *Entrance requirements:* For master's and doctorate, GRE General Test, GRE Subject Test. Additional exam requirements/recommendations for international students: Required—TOEFL, TWE. *Expenses:* Contact institution. *Faculty research:* Organic and medicinal synthesis, mass spectroscopy use in protein analysis, study of analogues of taxol, cholesteryl esters.

The University of Toledo, College of Graduate Studies, College of Natural Sciences and Mathematics, Department of Chemistry, Toledo, OH 43606-3390. Offers analytical chemistry (MS, PhD); biological chemistry (MS, PhD); inorganic chemistry (MS, PhD); organic chemistry (MS, PhD); physical chemistry (MS, PhD). Part-time programs available. *Faculty:* 22. *Students:* 56 full-time (18 women), 18 part-time (10 women); includes 4 minority (1 Black or African American, non-Hispanic/Latino; 1 Asian, non-Hispanic/Latino; 2 Hispanic/Latino), 43 international. Average age 27. 111 applicants, 17% accepted, 16 enrolled. In 2011, 4 master's, 6 doctorates awarded. *Degree requirements:* For master's, thesis (for some programs); for doctorate, thesis/dissertation. *Entrance requirements:* For master's and doctorate, GRE General Test, GRE Subject Test, minimum cumulative point-hour ratio of 2.7 for all previous academic work, three letters of recommendation, statement of purpose, transcripts from all prior institutions attended. Additional exam requirements/recommendations for international students: Required—TOEFL (minimum score 550 paper-based; 213 computer-based; 80 iBT), IELTS (minimum score 6.5). *Application deadline:* For fall admission, 1/15 priority date for domestic students, 1/15 for international students. Applications are processed on a rolling basis. Application fee: $45 ($75 for international students). Electronic applications accepted. *Financial support:* In 2011–12, 24 research assistantships with full and partial tuition reimbursements (averaging $17,218 per year) were awarded; fellowships with tuition reimbursements, Federal Work-Study, institutionally sponsored loans, scholarships/grants, tuition waivers (full), and unspecified assistantships also available. Support available to part-time students. *Faculty research:* Enzymology, materials chemistry, crystallography, theoretical chemistry. *Unit head:* Dr. Alan Pinkerton, Chair, 419-530-7902, Fax: 419-530-4033, E-mail: alan.pinkerton@utoledo.edu. *Application contact:* Graduate School Office, 419-530-4723, Fax: 419-530-4724, E-mail: grdsch@utnet.utoledo.edu. Web site: http://www.utoledo.edu/nsm/.

University of Toronto, School of Graduate Studies, Faculty of Arts and Science, Department of Chemistry, Toronto, ON M5S 1A1, Canada. Offers M Sc, PhD. *Degree requirements:* For master's, thesis; for doctorate, thesis/dissertation, oral exam, thesis defense. *Entrance requirements:* For master's, bachelor's degree in chemistry or a related field; for doctorate, master's degree in chemistry or a related field. Additional exam requirements/recommendations for international students: Required—TOEFL (minimum score 580 paper-based; 93 iBT), TWE (minimum score 4). Electronic applications accepted.

University of Tulsa, Graduate School, College of Engineering and Natural Sciences, Department of Chemistry and Biochemistry, Program in Chemistry, Tulsa, OK 74104-3189. Offers MS, PhD. Part-time programs available. *Faculty:* 10 full-time (1 woman). *Students:* 12 full-time (3 women), 1 part-time (0 women), 4 international. Average age 31. 24 applicants, 71% accepted, 4 enrolled. In 2011, 2 master's awarded. Terminal master's awarded for partial completion of doctoral program. *Degree requirements:* For master's, thesis (for some programs).

Peterson's Graduate Programs in the Physical Sciences, Mathematics, Agricultural Sciences, the Environment & Natural Resources 2013

facebook.com/petersonspublishing **95**

Chemistry

Entrance requirements: For master's, GRE General Test. Additional exam requirements/recommendations for international students: Required—TOEFL (minimum score 550 paper-based; 213 computer-based; 80 iBT), IELTS (minimum score 6). *Application deadline:* Applications are processed on a rolling basis. Application fee: $40. Electronic applications accepted. *Expenses: Tuition:* Full-time $17,748; part-time $986 per hour. *Required fees:* $5 per contact hour. $75 per semester. Tuition and fees vary according to program. *Financial support:* In 2011–12, 13 students received support, including 3 fellowships (averaging $1,458 per year), 6 research assistantships with full tuition reimbursements available (averaging $12,826 per year), 8 teaching assistantships with full tuition reimbursements available (averaging $12,583 per year); career-related internships or fieldwork, Federal Work-Study, scholarships/grants, health care benefits, tuition waivers (full and partial), and unspecified assistantships also available. Support available to part-time students. Financial award application deadline: 2/1; financial award applicants required to submit FAFSA. *Total annual research expenditures:* $4.3 million. *Unit head:* Dr. Dale C. Teeters, Chairperson, 918-631-2515, Fax: 918-631-3404, E-mail: dale-teeters@utulsa.edu. *Application contact:* Dr. Kenneth Roberts, Advisor, 918-631-3090, Fax: 918-631-3404, E-mail: kproberts@utulsa.edu. Web site: http://www.chemistry.utulsa.edu/.

University of Utah, Graduate School, College of Science, Department of Chemistry, Salt Lake City, UT 84112-0850. Offers chemical physics (PhD); chemistry (M Phil, MA, MS, PhD); science teacher education (MS). Part-time programs available. Postbaccalaureate distance learning degree programs offered. *Faculty:* 35 full-time (7 women). *Students:* 144 full-time (43 women), 40 part-time (15 women); includes 6 minority (1 Black or African American, non-Hispanic/Latino; 3 Asian, non-Hispanic/Latino; 1 Hispanic/Latino; 1 Two or more races, non-Hispanic/Latino), 54 international. Average age 28. 311 applicants, 28% accepted, 35 enrolled. In 2011, 10 master's, 21 doctorates awarded. Terminal master's awarded for partial completion of doctoral program. *Median time to degree:* Of those who began their doctoral program in fall 2003, 100% received their degree in 8 years or less. *Degree requirements:* For master's, thesis optional, 20 hours course work, 10 hours research; for doctorate, thesis/dissertation, 18 hours course work, 14 hours research. *Entrance requirements:* For master's and doctorate, GRE General Test, minimum GPA of 3.0. Additional exam requirements/recommendations for international students: Required—TOEFL (minimum score 620 paper-based; 260 computer-based; 105 iBT). *Application deadline:* For fall admission, 4/1 for domestic students, 2/1 for international students; for spring admission, 11/1 for domestic and international students. Application fee: $55 ($65 for international students). Electronic applications accepted. *Financial support:* In 2011–12, 1 fellowship with tuition reimbursement (averaging $22,000 per year), 128 research assistantships with tuition reimbursements (averaging $22,500 per year), 55 teaching assistantships with tuition reimbursements (averaging $22,000 per year) were awarded; scholarships/grants and tuition waivers (full) also available. Financial award application deadline: 4/1; financial award applicants required to submit FAFSA. *Faculty research:* Biological, theoretical, inorganic, organic, and physical-analytical chemistry. *Total annual research expenditures:* $13.3 million. *Unit head:* Dr. Henry S. White, Chair, 801-585-6256, Fax: 801-581-8433, E-mail: chair@chemistry.utah.edu. *Application contact:* Jo Hoovey, Graduate Coordinator, 801-581-4393, Fax: 801-581-5408, E-mail: jhoovey@chem.utah.edu. Web site: http://www.chem.utah.edu/.

University of Vermont, Graduate College, College of Arts and Sciences, Department of Chemistry, Burlington, VT 05405. Offers chemistry (MS, PhD). *Students:* 42 (17 women); includes 4 minority (1 American Indian or Alaska Native, non-Hispanic/Latino; 2 Asian, non-Hispanic/Latino; 1 Hispanic/Latino), 13 international. 70 applicants, 31% accepted, 7 enrolled. In 2011, 4 doctorates awarded. *Degree requirements:* For master's, one foreign language, thesis; for doctorate, 2 foreign languages, thesis/dissertation. *Entrance requirements:* For master's and doctorate, GRE General Test. Additional exam requirements/recommendations for international students: Required—TOEFL (minimum score 550 paper-based; 213 computer-based; 80 iBT). *Application deadline:* For fall admission, 4/1 priority date for domestic students, 4/1 for international students. Applications are processed on a rolling basis. Application fee: $40. Electronic applications accepted. *Financial support:* Fellowships, research assistantships, and teaching assistantships available. Financial award application deadline: 3/1. *Unit head:* Dr. Dwight Matthews, Chairperson, 802-656-2594. *Application contact:* Dr. Rory Waterman, Coordinator, 802-656-2594.

University of Victoria, Faculty of Graduate Studies, Faculty of Science, Department of Chemistry, Victoria, BC V8W 2Y2, Canada. Offers M Sc, PhD. *Degree requirements:* For master's, thesis; for doctorate, thesis/dissertation, candidacy exam. *Entrance requirements:* For master's and doctorate, GRE Subject Test. Additional exam requirements/recommendations for international students: Required—TOEFL (minimum score 575 paper-based; 233 computer-based), IELTS (minimum score 7). Electronic applications accepted. *Faculty research:* Laser spectroscopy and dynamics; inorganic, organic, and organometallic synthesis; electro and surface chemistry.

University of Virginia, College and Graduate School of Arts and Sciences, Department of Chemistry, Charlottesville, VA 22903. Offers MA, MS, PhD. *Faculty:* 25 full-time (3 women). *Students:* 95 full-time (43 women); includes 8 minority (1 Black or African American, non-Hispanic/Latino; 7 Asian, non-Hispanic/Latino), 28 international. Average age 24. 289 applicants, 24% accepted, 21 enrolled. In 2011, 5 master's, 21 doctorates awarded. *Degree requirements:* For master's, comprehensive exam, thesis; for doctorate,

comprehensive exam, thesis/dissertation. *Entrance requirements:* For master's and doctorate, GRE General Test; GRE Subject Test (recommended). Additional exam requirements/recommendations for international students: Required—TOEFL (minimum score 600 paper-based; 250 computer-based; 90 iBT), IELTS (minimum score 7). *Application deadline:* For fall admission, 2/1 for domestic and international students. Application fee: $60. Electronic applications accepted. *Financial support:* Fellowships and teaching assistantships available. Financial award applicants required to submit FAFSA. *Unit head:* Dean Harman, Chairman, 434-924-3344, Fax: 434-924-3710, E-mail: chem@virginia.edu. *Application contact:* Susan Marshall, Graduate Studies Administrative Assistant, 434-924-7014, Fax: 434-924-6737, E-mail: sem8h@virginia.edu. Web site: http://www.virginia.edu/chem/.

University of Washington, Graduate School, College of Arts and Sciences, Department of Chemistry, Seattle, WA 98195. Offers MS, PhD. Terminal master's awarded for partial completion of doctoral program. *Degree requirements:* For master's, thesis (for some programs); for doctorate, thesis/dissertation. *Entrance requirements:* For master's and doctorate, GRE Subject Test, minimum GPA of 3.0. Additional exam requirements/recommendations for international students: Required—TOEFL. *Faculty research:* Biopolymers, material science and nanotechnology, organometallic chemistry, analytical chemistry, bioorganic chemistry.

University of Waterloo, Graduate Studies, Faculty of Science, Guelph-Waterloo Centre for Graduate Work in Chemistry and Biochemistry, Waterloo, ON N2L 3G1, Canada. Offers M Sc, PhD. M Sc, PhD offered jointly with University of Guelph. Part-time programs available. *Degree requirements:* For master's and doctorate, project or thesis. *Entrance requirements:* For master's, GRE, honors degree, minimum B average; for doctorate, GRE, master's degree, minimum B average. Additional exam requirements/recommendations for international students: Required—TOEFL, TWE. Electronic applications accepted. *Faculty research:* Polymer, physical, inorganic, organic, and theoretical chemistry.

The University of Western Ontario, Faculty of Graduate Studies, Physical Sciences Division, Department of Chemistry, London, ON N6A 5B8, Canada. Offers M Sc, PhD. *Degree requirements:* For master's, thesis; for doctorate, thesis/dissertation. *Entrance requirements:* For master's, minimum B+ average, honors B Sc in chemistry; for doctorate, M Sc or equivalent in chemistry. Additional exam requirements/recommendations for international students: Required—TOEFL (paper-based 570; computer-based 230) or IELTS (paper-based 6). *Faculty research:* Materials, inorganic, organic, physical and theoretical chemistry.

University of Windsor, Faculty of Graduate Studies, Faculty of Science, Department of Chemistry and Biochemistry, Windsor, ON N9B 3P4, Canada. Offers M Sc, PhD. Part-time programs available. *Degree requirements:* For master's, thesis; for doctorate, comprehensive exam, thesis/dissertation. *Entrance requirements:* For master's and doctorate, minimum B average. Additional exam requirements/recommendations for international students: Required—TOEFL (minimum score 560 paper-based; 220 computer-based). Electronic applications accepted. *Faculty research:* Molecular biology/recombinant DNA techniques (PCR, cloning mutagenesis), No/02 detectors, western immunoblotting and detection, CD/NMR protein/peptide structure determination, confocal/electron microscopes.

University of Wisconsin–Madison, Graduate School, College of Engineering, Program in Environmental Chemistry and Technology, Madison, WI 53706. Offers MS, PhD. Part-time programs available. *Faculty:* 17 full-time (3 women). *Students:* 9 full-time (5 women); includes 1 minority (Hispanic/Latino), 1 international. 58 applicants, 0% accepted, 0 enrolled. Terminal master's awarded for partial completion of doctoral program. *Degree requirements:* For master's, thesis or alternative; for doctorate, thesis/dissertation. *Entrance requirements:* For master's and doctorate, GRE General Test. Additional exam requirements/recommendations for international students: Required—TOEFL. *Application deadline:* For fall admission, 1/1 priority date for domestic students, 1/1 for international students. Application fee: $45. Electronic applications accepted. *Expenses:* Tuition, state resident: full-time $10,296; part-time $643.51 per credit. Tuition, nonresident: full-time $24,054; part-time $1503.40 per credit. *Required fees:* $70.06 per credit. Tuition and fees vary according to course load, campus/location, program and reciprocity agreements. *Financial support:* In 2011–12, fellowships with full tuition reimbursements (averaging $20,100 per year), 10 research assistantships with full tuition reimbursements (averaging $20,100 per year) were awarded; Federal Work-Study and institutionally sponsored loans also available. Financial award application deadline: 1/1. *Faculty research:* Chemical limnology, chemical remediation, geochemistry, photocatalysis, water quality. *Total annual research expenditures:* $1 million. *Unit head:* Dr. Marc A. Anderson, Chair, 608-263-3264, E-mail: nanopor@wisc.edu. *Application contact:* Mary Possin, Student Services Coordinator, 608-263-3264, Fax: 608-265-2340, E-mail: mcpossin@wisc.edu. Web site: http://www.engr.edu/interd/wcp/.

University of Wisconsin–Madison, Graduate School, College of Letters and Science, Department of Chemistry, Madison, WI 53706-1380. Offers MS, PhD. Part-time programs available. Terminal master's awarded for partial completion of doctoral program. *Degree requirements:* For master's, thesis (for some programs); for doctorate, thesis/dissertation, cumulative exams, research proposal, seminar. *Entrance requirements:* For master's and doctorate, GRE, minimum GPA of 3.0. Additional exam requirements/recommendations for international students: Required—TOEFL. Electronic applications accepted.

96 facebook.com/petersonspublishing

Peterson's Graduate Programs in the Physical Sciences, Mathematics, Agricultural Sciences, the Environment & Natural Resources 2013

Expenses: Tuition, state resident: full-time $10,296; part-time $643.51 per credit. Tuition, nonresident: full-time $24,054; part-time $1503.40 per credit. *Required fees:* $70.06 per credit. Tuition and fees vary according to course load, campus/location, program and reciprocity agreements. *Faculty research:* Analytical, inorganic, organic, physical, and macromolecular chemistry.

University of Wisconsin–Milwaukee, Graduate School, College of Letters and Sciences, Department of Chemistry, Milwaukee, WI 53201-0413. Offers biogeochemistry (PhD); chemistry (MS, PhD). *Faculty:* 20 full-time (4 women). *Students:* 58 full-time (25 women), 16 part-time (8 women); includes 12 minority (2 Black or African American, non-Hispanic/Latino; 5 Asian, non-Hispanic/Latino; 4 Hispanic/Latino; 1 Two or more races, non-Hispanic/Latino), 7 international. Average age 32. 46 applicants, 30% accepted, 9 enrolled. In 2011, 4 master's, 6 doctorates awarded. *Degree requirements:* For master's, thesis or alternative; for doctorate, thesis/dissertation. *Entrance requirements:* For doctorate, GRE General Test. Additional exam requirements/recommendations for international students: Required—TOEFL (minimum score 600 paper-based; 79 iBT), IELTS (minimum score 6.5). *Application deadline:* For fall admission, 1/1 priority date for domestic students; for spring admission, 9/1 for domestic students. Applications are processed on a rolling basis. Application fee: $56 ($96 for international students). One-time fee: $506.10 full-time. Tuition and fees vary according to course load and reciprocity agreements. *Financial support:* In 2011–12, 3 fellowships, 30 research assistantships, 46 teaching assistantships were awarded; career-related internships or fieldwork, unspecified assistantships, and project assistantships also available. Support available to part-time students. Financial award application deadline: 4/15; financial award applicants required to submit FAFSA. *Faculty research:* Analytical chemistry, biochemistry, inorganic chemistry, organic chemistry, physical chemistry. *Total annual research expenditures:* $4 million. *Unit head:* Peter Geissinger, Department Chair, 414-229-5230, Fax: 414-229-5530, E-mail: geissing@uwm.edu. *Application contact:* General Information Contact, 414-229-4982, Fax: 414-229-6967, E-mail: gradschool@uwm.edu. Web site: http://www.uwm.edu/dept/chemistry/.

University of Wyoming, College of Arts and Sciences, Department of Chemistry, Laramie, WY 82070. Offers MS, PhD. *Degree requirements:* For master's, thesis; for doctorate, thesis/dissertation. *Entrance requirements:* For master's and doctorate, GRE General Test, minimum GPA of 3.0. Additional exam requirements/recommendations for international students: Required—TOEFL (minimum score 600 paper-based). Electronic applications accepted. *Faculty research:* Organic chemistry, inorganic chemistry, analytical chemistry, physical chemistry.

Utah State University, School of Graduate Studies, College of Science, Department of Chemistry and Biochemistry, Logan, UT 84322. Offers biochemistry (MS, PhD); chemistry (MS, PhD). Part-time programs available. Terminal master's awarded for partial completion of doctoral program. *Degree requirements:* For master's, thesis, oral and written exams; for doctorate, thesis/dissertation, oral and written exams. *Entrance requirements:* For master's and doctorate, GRE General Test, minimum GPA of 3.0. Additional exam requirements/recommendations for international students: Required—TOEFL. *Faculty research:* Analytical, inorganic, organic, and physical chemistry; iron in asbestos chemistry and carcinogenicity; dicopper complexes; photothermal spectrometry; metal molecule clusters.

Vanderbilt University, Graduate School, Department of Chemistry, Nashville, TN 37240-1001. Offers analytical chemistry (MAT, MS, PhD); inorganic chemistry (MAT, MS, PhD); organic chemistry (MAT, MS, PhD); physical chemistry (MAT, MS, PhD); theoretical chemistry (MAT, MS, PhD). *Faculty:* 21 full-time (3 women). *Students:* 114 full-time (43 women), 2 part-time (0 women); includes 16 minority (6 Black or African American, non-Hispanic/Latino; 1 American Indian or Alaska Native, non-Hispanic/Latino; 3 Asian, non-Hispanic/Latino; 1 Hispanic/Latino; 5 Two or more races, non-Hispanic/Latino), 18 international. Average age 26. 420 applicants, 12% accepted, 18 enrolled. In 2011, 4 master's, 17 doctorates awarded. Terminal master's awarded for partial completion of doctoral program. *Degree requirements:* For master's, thesis; for doctorate, thesis/dissertation, area, qualifying, and final exams. *Entrance requirements:* For master's and doctorate, GRE General Test, GRE Subject Test (recommended). Additional exam requirements/recommendations for international students: Required—TOEFL (minimum score 570 paper-based; 230 computer-based; 88 iBT). *Application deadline:* For fall admission, 1/15 for domestic and international students. Application fee: $0. Electronic applications accepted. *Financial support:* Fellowships with full and partial tuition reimbursements, research assistantships with full tuition reimbursements, teaching assistantships with full tuition reimbursements, Federal Work-Study, institutionally sponsored loans, scholarships/grants, traineeships, and health care benefits available. Financial award application deadline: 1/15; financial award applicants required to submit CSS PROFILE or FAFSA. *Faculty research:* Chemical synthesis; mechanistic, theoretical, bioorganic, analytical, and spectroscopic chemistry. *Unit head:* Dr. Mike P. Stone, Chair, 615-322-2589, Fax: 615-343-1234, E-mail: michael.p.stone@vanderbilt.edu. *Application contact:* Dr. Carmelo J. Rizzo, Director of Graduate Studies, 615-322-6100, Fax: 615-343-1234, E-mail: c.j.rizzo@vanderbilt.edu. Web site: http://www.vanderbilt.edu/AnS/Chemistry/grad/.

Villanova University, Graduate School of Liberal Arts and Sciences, Department of Chemistry, Villanova, PA 19085-1699. Offers MS. Part-time and evening/weekend programs available. *Faculty:* 5 full-time (0 women), 1 part-time/adjunct (0 women). *Students:* 23 full-time (10 women), 11 part-time (4 women); includes 6 minority (1 Black or African American, non-Hispanic/Latino; 2 Asian, non-Hispanic/Latino; 1 Hispanic/Latino; 1 Native Hawaiian or other Pacific Islander, non-Hispanic/Latino; 1 Two or more races, non-Hispanic/Latino), 2 international. Average age 26. 38 applicants, 50% accepted, 10 enrolled. In 2011, 9 master's awarded. *Degree requirements:* For master's, comprehensive exam (for some programs), thesis (for some programs). *Entrance requirements:* For master's, GRE General Test, minimum GPA of 3.0. Additional exam requirements/recommendations for international students: Required—TOEFL. *Application deadline:* For fall admission, 5/1 for international students; for spring admission, 10/15 for international students. Applications are processed on a rolling basis. Application fee: $50. Electronic applications accepted. *Expenses:* Contact institution. *Financial support:* Research assistantships, teaching assistantships, scholarships/grants, and unspecified assistantships available. Financial award applicants required to submit FAFSA. *Unit head:* Dr. Barry Selinsky, Chair, 610-519-4840. *Application contact:* Dean, Graduate School of Liberal Arts and Sciences. Web site: http://www.villanova.edu/artsci/chemistry/graduate/.

Virginia Commonwealth University, Graduate School, College of Humanities and Sciences, Department of Chemistry, Richmond, VA 23284-9005. Offers analytical chemistry (MS, PhD); chemical physics (PhD); inorganic chemistry (MS, PhD); organic chemistry (MS, PhD); physical chemistry (MS, PhD). Part-time programs available. *Students:* 49 full-time (20 women), 19 part-time (8 women); includes 10 minority (3 Black or African American, non-Hispanic/Latino; 5 Asian, non-Hispanic/Latino; 1 Hispanic/Latino; 1 Two or more races, non-Hispanic/Latino), 26 international. 56 applicants, 41% accepted, 11 enrolled. In 2011, 3 master's, 8 doctorates awarded. Terminal master's awarded for partial completion of doctoral program. *Degree requirements:* For master's, thesis; for doctorate, thesis/dissertation, comprehensive cumulative exams, research proposal. *Entrance requirements:* For master's, GRE General Test, 30 undergraduate credits in chemistry; for doctorate, GRE General Test. Additional exam requirements/recommendations for international students: Required—TOEFL (minimum score 600 paper-based; 250 computer-based; 100 iBT) or IELTS (minimum score 6.5). *Application deadline:* For fall admission, 3/15 for domestic students; for spring admission, 11/15 for domestic students. Applications are processed on a rolling basis. Application fee: $50. Electronic applications accepted. *Expenses:* Tuition, state resident: full-time $9133; part-time $507 per credit. Tuition, nonresident: full-time $18,777; part-time $1043 per credit. *Required fees:* $77 per credit. Tuition and fees vary according to degree level, campus/location, program and student level. *Financial support:* Fellowships, research assistantships, teaching assistantships, career-related internships or fieldwork, and institutionally sponsored loans available. Support available to part-time students. Financial award application deadline: 7/1; financial award applicants required to submit FAFSA. *Faculty research:* Physical, organic, inorganic, analytical, and polymer chemistry; chemical physics. *Unit head:* Dr. Scott Gronert, Chair, 804-828-1298, Fax: 804-828-8599, E-mail: sgronert@vcu.edu. *Application contact:* Dr. Maryanne M. Collinson, Chair, Graduate Recruiting and Admissions Committee, 804-828-7509, E-mail: mselshal@vcu.edu. Web site: http://www.has.vcu.edu/che/.

Virginia Polytechnic Institute and State University, Graduate School, College of Science, Department of Chemistry, Blacksburg, VA 24061. Offers MS, PhD. *Degree requirements:* For master's, comprehensive exam (for some programs), thesis (for some programs); for doctorate, comprehensive exam (for some programs), thesis/dissertation (for some programs). *Entrance requirements:* For master's and doctorate, GRE. Additional exam requirements/recommendations for international students: Required—TOEFL (minimum score 550 paper-based; 213 computer-based). *Application deadline:* For fall admission, 7/1 for domestic and international students; for spring admission, 12/1 for domestic and international students. Applications are processed on a rolling basis. Application fee: $65. Electronic applications accepted. *Expenses:* Tuition, state resident: full-time $10,048; part-time $558.25 per credit hour. Tuition, nonresident: full-time $19,497; part-time $1083.25 per credit hour. *Required fees:* $405 per semester. Tuition and fees vary according to course load, campus/location and program. *Financial support:* Fellowships with full tuition reimbursements, research assistantships with full tuition reimbursements, teaching assistantships with full tuition reimbursements, career-related internships or fieldwork, Federal Work-Study, scholarships/grants, health care benefits, and unspecified assistantships available. Financial award application deadline: 1/15. *Faculty research:* Analytical, inorganic, organic, physical, and polymer chemistry. *Unit head:* Dr. James M. Tanko, Unit Head, 540-231-6687, Fax: 540-231-3255, E-mail: jtanko@vt.edu. *Application contact:* Paul Deck, Information Contact, 540-231-3254, Fax: 540-231-3255, E-mail: pdeck@vt.edu. Web site: http://www.chem.vt.edu/grad/index.html.

Wake Forest University, Graduate School of Arts and Sciences, Department of Chemistry, Winston-Salem, NC 27109. Offers analytical chemistry (MS, PhD); inorganic chemistry (MS, PhD); organic chemistry (MS, PhD); physical chemistry (MS, PhD). Part-time programs available. *Degree requirements:* For master's, one foreign language, comprehensive exam, thesis; for doctorate, 2 foreign languages, comprehensive exam, thesis/dissertation. *Entrance requirements:* For master's and doctorate, GRE General Test. Additional exam requirements/recommendations for international students: Required—TOEFL (minimum score 213 computer-based). Electronic applications accepted.

Washington State University, Graduate School, College of Sciences, Department of Chemistry, Pullman, WA 99164. Offers MS, PhD. *Faculty:* 25. *Students:* 90 full-time (31 women), 9 part-time (2 women); includes 9 minority (5

Peterson's Graduate Programs in the Physical Sciences, Mathematics, Agricultural Sciences, the Environment & Natural Resources 2013

facebook.com/petersonspublishing **97**

Chemistry

Asian, non-Hispanic/Latino; 3 Hispanic/Latino; 1 Two or more races, non-Hispanic/Latino), 22 international. Average age 28. 189 applicants, 15% accepted, 16 enrolled. In 2011, 7 master's, 9 doctorates awarded. Terminal master's awarded for partial completion of doctoral program. *Degree requirements:* For master's, comprehensive exam (for some programs), thesis (for some programs), oral exam, teaching experience; for doctorate, comprehensive exam, thesis/dissertation, oral exam, written exam. *Entrance requirements:* For master's and doctorate, GRE General Test, GRE Subject Test (recommended), transcripts from each post-secondary school attended (photocopies acceptable); three letters of recommendation. Additional exam requirements/recommendations for international students: Required—TOEFL. *Application deadline:* For fall admission, 3/1 priority date for domestic students, 3/1 for international students; for spring admission, 10/1 priority date for domestic students, 7/1 for international students. Applications are processed on a rolling basis. Application fee: $75. *Financial support:* In 2011–12, 3 fellowships (averaging $8,977 per year), 12 research assistantships with full and partial tuition reimbursements (averaging $13,917 per year), 23 teaching assistantships with full and partial tuition reimbursements (averaging $13,056 per year) were awarded; career-related internships or fieldwork, Federal Work-Study, institutionally sponsored loans, scholarships/grants, health care benefits, and unspecified assistantships also available. Financial award application deadline: 2/15; financial award applicants required to submit FAFSA. *Faculty research:* Environmental chemistry, materials chemistry, radio chemistry, bio-organic, computational chemistry. *Unit head:* Kerry W. Hipps, Chair, 509-335-8866, Fax: 509-335-8867, E-mail: chemistry@wsu.edu. *Application contact:* Graduate School Admissions, 800-GRADWSU, Fax: 509-335-1949, E-mail: gradsch@wsu.edu. Web site: http://www.chem.wsu.edu/.

Washington State University Tri-Cities, Graduate Programs, Program in Chemistry, Richland, WA 99354. Offers MS, PhD. *Faculty:* 25. *Students:* 2 full-time (1 woman), 6 part-time (1 woman). Average age 31. 6 applicants, 17% accepted, 1 enrolled. In 2011, 2 master's awarded. Terminal master's awarded for partial completion of doctoral program. *Degree requirements:* For master's, comprehensive exam (for some programs), thesis; for doctorate, comprehensive exam, thesis/dissertation. *Entrance requirements:* For master's and doctorate, GRE, minimum GPA of 3.0, 3 letters of recommendation. Additional exam requirements/recommendations for international students: Required—TOEFL. *Application deadline:* For fall admission, 3/1 priority date for domestic students, 3/1 for international students; for spring admission, 10/1 priority date for domestic students, 7/1 for international students. Applications are processed on a rolling basis. Application fee: $75. *Financial support:* In 2011–12, 1 student received support. Career-related internships or fieldwork, Federal Work-Study, institutionally sponsored loans, scholarships/grants, health care benefits, and unspecified assistantships available. Financial award application deadline: 2/15; financial award applicants required to submit FAFSA. *Unit head:* Dr. Kerry Hipps, Chair, 509-335-3442. *Application contact:* Bonnie Bates, Academic Coordinator, 509-372-7171, Fax: 509-335-1949, E-mail: bbates@tricity.wsu.edu. Web site: http://www.tricity.wsu.edu/science/chemistry.html.

Washington University in St. Louis, Graduate School of Arts and Sciences, Department of Chemistry, St. Louis, MO 63130-4899. Offers PhD. Terminal master's awarded for partial completion of doctoral program. *Degree requirements:* For doctorate, thesis/dissertation. *Entrance requirements:* For doctorate, GRE General Test, GRE Subject Test. Electronic applications accepted.

Wayne State University, College of Liberal Arts and Sciences, Department of Chemistry, Detroit, MI 48202. Offers MA, MS, PhD. *Students:* 140 full-time (67 women), 2 part-time (0 women); includes 12 minority (3 Black or African American, non-Hispanic/Latino; 1 American Indian or Alaska Native, non-Hispanic/Latino; 6 Asian, non-Hispanic/Latino; 2 Hispanic/Latino), 95 international. Average age 28. 442 applicants, 18% accepted, 32 enrolled. In 2011, 9 master's, 25 doctorates awarded. *Degree requirements:* For master's, thesis (for some programs), oral exam; for doctorate, thesis/dissertation, oral exam. *Entrance requirements:* Additional exam requirements/recommendations for international students: Required—TOEFL (minimum score 550 paper-based; 213 computer-based); Recommended—TWE (minimum score 5.5). *Application deadline:* For fall admission, 2/10 priority date for domestic students, 2/10 for international students; for winter admission, 10/1 priority date for domestic students, 9/1 for international students; for spring admission, 2/1 priority date for domestic students, 1/1 for international students. Applications are processed on a rolling basis. Application fee: $50. Electronic applications accepted. *Expenses:* Tuition, state resident: part-time $512.85 per credit. Tuition, nonresident: part-time $1132.65 per credit. *Required fees:* $26.60 per credit. $199.65 per semester. Tuition and fees vary according to course load and program. *Financial support:* In 2011–12, 110 students received support, including 5 fellowships with full tuition reimbursements available (averaging $20,598 per year), 47 research assistantships with tuition reimbursements available (averaging $19,481 per year), 83 teaching assistantships with tuition reimbursements available (averaging $19,516 per year); scholarships/grants, health care benefits, and unspecified assistantships also available. Financial award application deadline: 7/1. *Faculty research:* Natural products synthesis, molecular biology, molecular mechanics calculations, organometallic chemistry, experimental physical chemistry. *Total annual research expenditures:* $6.9 million. *Unit head:* Dr. James Rigby, Chair, 313-577-3472, Fax: 313-577-8822, E-mail: aa392@wayne.edu. *Application contact:* Dr. Charles Winter, Graduate Director, 313-577-5224, E-mail: chw@chem.wayne.edu. Web site: http://www.science.wayne.edu/~chem/.

Wesleyan University, Graduate Programs, Department of Chemistry, Middletown, CT 06459. Offers biochemistry (MA, PhD); chemical physics (MA, PhD); inorganic chemistry (MA, PhD); organic chemistry (MA, PhD); physical chemistry (MA, PhD); theoretical chemistry (MA, PhD). Terminal master's awarded for partial completion of doctoral program. *Degree requirements:* For master's, thesis, proposal; for doctorate, thesis/dissertation, proposal. *Entrance requirements:* For doctorate, GRE General Test, 3 recommendations. Additional exam requirements/recommendations for international students: Required—TOEFL. Electronic applications accepted.

West Chester University of Pennsylvania, College of Arts and Sciences, Department of Chemistry, West Chester, PA 19383. Offers Teaching Certificate. *Students:* 1 full-time (0 women). Average age 23. 1 applicant, 100% accepted, 1 enrolled. *Degree requirements:* For Teaching Certificate, minimum overall GPA of 3.0, PRAXIS I and Chemistry PRAXIS. *Entrance requirements:* For degree, minimum GPA of 2.8 in most recent 48 credits. Additional exam requirements/recommendations for international students: Required—TOEFL (minimum score 550 paper-based; 213 computer-based; 80 iBT). *Application deadline:* For fall admission, 4/15 priority date for domestic students, 3/15 for international students; for spring admission, 10/15 priority date for domestic students, 9/1 for international students. Applications are processed on a rolling basis. Application fee: $451. Electronic applications accepted. *Expenses:* Tuition, state resident: full-time $7488; part-time $416 per credit. Tuition, nonresident: full-time $11,232; part-time $624 per credit. *Required fees:* $1784.64; $67.59 per credit. Tuition and fees vary according to program. *Financial support:* Unspecified assistantships available. Support available to part-time students. Financial award application deadline: 2/15; financial award applicants required to submit FAFSA. *Unit head:* Dr. Blaise Frost, Chair, 610-436-2526, E-mail: bfrost@wcupa.edu. *Application contact:* Dr. John Townsend, Secondary Education Advisor, 610-436-1063, E-mail: jtownsend@wcupa.edu. Web site: http://www.wcupa.edu/_academics/sch_cas.che/.

Western Carolina University, Graduate School, College of Arts and Sciences, Department of Chemistry and Physics, Cullowhee, NC 28723. Offers chemistry (MS). *Students:* 9 full-time (4 women), 1 part-time (0 women), 1 international. Average age 24. 14 applicants, 71% accepted, 4 enrolled. In 2011, 5 master's awarded. *Degree requirements:* For master's, thesis. *Entrance requirements:* For master's, GRE General Test, undergraduate science degree with minimum GPA of 3.0, 3 letters of recommendation. Additional exam requirements/recommendations for international students: Required—TOEFL (minimum score 550 paper-based; 270 computer-based; 79 iBT). *Application deadline:* For fall admission, 5/1 priority date for domestic students; for spring admission, 9/1 priority date for domestic students. Applications are processed on a rolling basis. Application fee: $50. *Expenses:* Tuition, state resident: full-time $3348. Tuition, nonresident: full-time $12,933. *Required fees:* $3155. *Financial support:* Fellowships, research assistantships with full and partial tuition reimbursements, teaching assistantships with full and partial tuition reimbursements, career-related internships or fieldwork, institutionally sponsored loans, scholarships/grants, and unspecified assistantships available. Financial award application deadline: 3/31; financial award applicants required to submit FAFSA. *Faculty research:* Trace metal analysis, metal waste reduction, supramolecular chemistry, free radical biophysical chemistry. *Unit head:* Dr. Cynthia Atterholt, Head, 828-227-7260, Fax: 828-227-7393, E-mail: atterholt@email.wcu.edu. *Application contact:* Admissions Specialist for Chemistry, 828-227-7398, Fax: 828-227-7480, E-mail: gradsch@email.wcu.edu. Web site: http://www.wcu.edu/as/chemphys/chemphys.html.

Western Illinois University, School of Graduate Studies, College of Arts and Sciences, Department of Chemistry, Macomb, IL 61455-1390. Offers MS. Part-time programs available. *Students:* 43 full-time (17 women), 36 international. Average age 23. 137 applicants, 30% accepted. In 2011, 22 master's awarded. *Degree requirements:* For master's, thesis or alternative. *Entrance requirements:* Additional exam requirements/recommendations for international students: Required—TOEFL (minimum score 530 paper-based; 71 iBT). *Application deadline:* Applications are processed on a rolling basis. Application fee: $30. Electronic applications accepted. *Expenses:* Tuition, state resident: part-time $281.16 per credit hour. Tuition, nonresident: part-time $562.32 per credit hour. Part-time tuition and fees vary according to campus/location and reciprocity agreements. *Financial support:* In 2011–12, 21 students received support, including 3 research assistantships with full tuition reimbursements available (averaging $7,360 per year), 18 teaching assistantships with full tuition reimbursements available (averaging $8,480 per year). Financial award applicants required to submit FAFSA. *Unit head:* Dr. Rose McConnell, Chairperson, 309-298-1538. *Application contact:* Nancy Parsons, Interim Associate Provost and Director of Graduate Studies, 309-298-1806, Fax: 309-298-2345, E-mail: grad-office@wiu.edu. Web site: http://wiu.edu/chemistry.

Western Kentucky University, Graduate Studies, Ogden College of Science and Engineering, Department of Chemistry, Bowling Green, KY 42101. Offers MA Ed, MS. *Degree requirements:* For master's, comprehensive exam, thesis. *Entrance requirements:* For master's, GRE General Test, minimum GPA of 2.75. Additional exam requirements/recommendations for international students: Required—TOEFL (minimum score 555 paper-based; 213 computer-based). *Faculty research:* Catatonic surfactants, directed orthometalation reactions, thermal stability and degradation mechanisms, co-firing refused derived fuels, laser fluorescence.

Western Michigan University, Graduate College, College of Arts and Sciences, Department of Chemistry, Kalamazoo, MI 49008. Offers MS, PhD. *Degree*

98 facebook.com/petersonspublishing

Peterson's Graduate Programs in the Physical Sciences, Mathematics, Agricultural Sciences, the Environment & Natural Resources 2013

requirements: For master's, thesis, departmental qualifying and oral exams; for doctorate, thesis/dissertation.

Western Michigan University, Graduate College, College of Arts and Sciences, Mallinson Institute for Science Education, Kalamazoo, MI 49008. Offers science education (MA, PhD); science education: biological sciences (PhD); science education: chemistry (PhD); science education: geosciences (PhD); science education: physical geography (PhD); science education: physics (PhD). *Degree requirements:* For doctorate, thesis/dissertation, oral and written exams. *Entrance requirements:* For master's, undergraduate degree in a science or science education, teacher certification (or appropriate education courses); for doctorate, GRE General Test, master's degree in a science or science education. Additional exam requirements/recommendations for international students: Recommended—TOEFL. Electronic applications accepted. *Faculty research:* History and philosophy of science, curriculum and instruction, science content learning, college science teaching and learning, social and cultural factors in science education.

Western Washington University, Graduate School, College of Sciences and Technology, Department of Chemistry, Bellingham, WA 98225-5996. Offers MS. Part-time programs available. *Degree requirements:* For master's, thesis (for some programs). *Entrance requirements:* For master's, GRE General Test, minimum GPA of 3.0 in last 60 semester hours or last 90 quarter hours. Additional exam requirements/recommendations for international students: Required—TOEFL (minimum score 567 paper-based; 227 computer-based). Electronic applications accepted. *Faculty research:* Bio-, organic, inorganic, physical, analytical chemistry.

West Texas A&M University, College of Agriculture, Nursing, and Natural Sciences, Department of Mathematics, Physical Sciences and Engineering Technology, Program in Chemistry, Canyon, TX 79016-0001. Offers MS. Part-time programs available. *Degree requirements:* For master's, comprehensive exam, thesis optional. *Entrance requirements:* For master's, GRE General Test. Additional exam requirements/recommendations for international students: Required—TOEFL (minimum score 550 paper-based). Electronic applications accepted. *Faculty research:* Biochemistry; inorganic, organic, and physical chemistry; vibrational spectroscopy; magnetic susceptibilities; carbene chemistry.

West Virginia University, Eberly College of Arts and Sciences, Department of Chemistry, Morgantown, WV 26506. Offers analytical chemistry (MS, PhD); inorganic chemistry (MS, PhD); organic chemistry (MS, PhD); physical chemistry (MS, PhD); theoretical chemistry (MS, PhD). Part-time programs available. Postbaccalaureate distance learning degree programs offered (no on-campus study). Terminal master's awarded for partial completion of doctoral program. *Degree requirements:* For master's, thesis; for doctorate, thesis/dissertation. *Entrance requirements:* For master's, GRE General Test, GRE Subject Test (recommended), minimum GPA of 2.5; for doctorate, GRE General Test, GRE Subject Test (recommended), minimum GPA of 2.75. Additional exam requirements/recommendations for international students: Required—TOEFL. Electronic applications accepted. *Faculty research:* Analysis of proteins, drug interactions, solids and effluents by advanced separation methods; new synthetic strategies for complex organic molecules; synthesis and structural characterization of metal complexes for polymerization catalysis, nonlinear science, spectroscopy.

Wichita State University, Graduate School, Fairmount College of Liberal Arts and Sciences, Department of Chemistry, Wichita, KS 67260. Offers MS, PhD. *Expenses:* Tuition, state resident: full-time $4746; part-time $263.65 per credit. Tuition, nonresident: full-time $11,669; part-time $648.30 per credit. *Unit head:* Dr. David Eichhorn, Chair, 316-978-3120, Fax: 316-978-3431, E-mail: david.eichhorn@wichita.edu. *Application contact:* Dr. Dennis Burns, Graduate Coordinator, 316-978-3120, E-mail: dennis.burns@wichita.edu. Web site: http://www.wichita.edu/.

Wilfrid Laurier University, Faculty of Graduate and Postdoctoral Studies, Faculty of Science, Department of Chemistry, Waterloo, ON N2L 3C5, Canada. Offers M Sc. *Degree requirements:* For master's, thesis. *Entrance requirements:* For master's, honors degree or equivalent in chemistry, biochemistry or a related discipline; minimum B average in last two full-time undergraduate years.

Additional exam requirements/recommendations for international students: Required—TOEFL (minimum score 89 iBT). Electronic applications accepted. *Faculty research:* Cold regions water science, biophysical methods, biochemistry, nanochemistry.

Worcester Polytechnic Institute, Graduate Studies and Research, Department of Chemistry and Biochemistry, Worcester, MA 01609-2280. Offers biochemistry (MS, PhD); chemistry (MS, PhD). Evening/weekend programs available. *Faculty:* 8 full-time (1 woman), 1 part-time/adjunct (0 women). *Students:* 14 full-time (5 women), 16 part-time (4 women); includes 5 minority (3 Asian, non-Hispanic/Latino; 1 Hispanic/Latino; 1 Two or more races, non-Hispanic/Latino), 7 international. 37 applicants, 16% accepted, 3 enrolled. In 2011, 5 degrees awarded. *Degree requirements:* For master's, thesis; for doctorate, comprehensive exam, thesis/dissertation. *Entrance requirements:* For master's and doctorate, GRE General Test, 3 letters of recommendation, statement of purpose. Additional exam requirements/recommendations for international students: Required—TOEFL (minimum score 563 paper-based; 223 computer-based; 84 iBT), IELTS (minimum score 7). *Application deadline:* For fall admission, 1/1 priority date for domestic students, 1/1 for international students; for spring admission, 10/1 priority date for domestic students, 10/1 for international students. Applications are processed on a rolling basis. Application fee: $70. Electronic applications accepted. *Financial support:* Research assistantships, teaching assistantships, career-related internships or fieldwork, institutionally sponsored loans, scholarships/grants, and unspecified assistantships available. Financial award application deadline: 1/1; financial award applicants required to submit FAFSA. *Faculty research:* Catalysis experimental and computational protein biophysics, biological metals, synthetic methods, surface chemistry, computational chemistry. *Unit head:* Dr. Arne Gericke, Department Head, 508-831-5371, Fax: 508-831-5933, E-mail: agericke@wpi.edu. *Application contact:* Dr. George Kaminski, Graduate Coordinator, 508-831-5371, Fax: 508-831-5933, E-mail: gkaminski@wpi.edu. Web site: http://www.wpi.edu/Academics/Depts/Chemistry/.

Wright State University, School of Graduate Studies, College of Science and Mathematics, Department of Chemistry, Dayton, OH 45435. Offers chemistry (MS); environmental sciences (MS). Part-time and evening/weekend programs available. *Degree requirements:* For master's, oral defense of thesis, seminar. *Entrance requirements:* Additional exam requirements/recommendations for international students: Required—TOEFL. *Faculty research:* Polymer synthesis and characterization, laser kinetics, organic and inorganic synthesis, analytical and environmental chemistry.

Yale University, Graduate School of Arts and Sciences, Department of Chemistry, New Haven, CT 06520. Offers biophysical chemistry (PhD); inorganic chemistry (PhD); organic chemistry (PhD); physical and theoretical chemistry (PhD). *Degree requirements:* For doctorate, thesis/dissertation. *Entrance requirements:* For doctorate, GRE General Test, GRE Subject Test. Additional exam requirements/recommendations for international students: Required—TOEFL.

York University, Faculty of Graduate Studies, Faculty of Science and Engineering, Program in Chemistry, Toronto, ON M3J 1P3, Canada. Offers M Sc, PhD. Part-time and evening/weekend programs available. *Degree requirements:* For master's, thesis or alternative; for doctorate, thesis/dissertation. Electronic applications accepted.

Youngstown State University, Graduate School, College of Science, Technology, Engineering and Mathematics, Department of Chemistry, Youngstown, OH 44555-0001. Offers analytical chemistry (MS); biochemistry (MS); chemistry education (MS); inorganic chemistry (MS); organic chemistry (MS); physical chemistry (MS). Part-time programs available. *Degree requirements:* For master's, thesis. *Entrance requirements:* For master's, bachelor's degree in chemistry, minimum GPA of 2.7. Additional exam requirements/recommendations for international students: Required—TOEFL. *Faculty research:* Analysis of antioxidants, chromatography, defects and disorder in crystalline oxides, hydrogen bonding, novel organic and organometallic materials.

Inorganic Chemistry

Auburn University, Graduate School, College of Sciences and Mathematics, Department of Chemistry and Biochemistry, Auburn University, AL 36849. Offers analytical chemistry (MS, PhD); biochemistry (MS, PhD); inorganic chemistry (MS, PhD); organic chemistry (MS, PhD); physical chemistry (MS, PhD). Part-time programs available. *Faculty:* 28 full-time (5 women), 1 part-time/adjunct (0 women). *Students:* 37 full-time (14 women), 30 part-time (15 women); includes 6 minority (3 Black or African American, non-Hispanic/Latino; 1 American Indian or Alaska Native, non-Hispanic/Latino; 1 Asian, non-Hispanic/Latino; 1 Hispanic/Latino), 41 international. Average age 28. 38 applicants, 39% accepted, 12 enrolled. In 2011, 1 master's, 9 doctorates awarded. *Degree requirements:* For master's, thesis (for some programs); for doctorate, thesis/dissertation, oral and

written exams. *Entrance requirements:* For master's and doctorate, GRE General Test. *Application deadline:* For fall admission, 7/7 for domestic students; for spring admission, 11/24 for domestic students. Applications are processed on a rolling basis. Application fee: $50 ($60 for international students). Electronic applications accepted. *Expenses:* Tuition, state resident: full-time $7290; part-time $405 per credit hour. Tuition, nonresident: full-time $21,870; part-time $1215 per credit hour. International tuition: $22,000 full-time. Required fees: $1402. *Financial support:* Fellowships, research assistantships, and teaching assistantships available. Financial award application deadline: 3/15; financial award applicants required to submit FAFSA. *Unit head:* Dr. J. V. Ortiz, Chair, 334-844-4043, Fax: 334-844-4043. *Application contact:* Dr. George Flowers, Dean of the Graduate

Peterson's Graduate Programs in the Physical Sciences, Mathematics, Agricultural Sciences, the Environment & Natural Resources 2013

facebook.com/petersonspublishing   **99**

School, 334-844-2125. Web site: http://www.auburn.edu/cosam/departments/chemistry/.

Boston College, Graduate School of Arts and Sciences, Department of Chemistry, Chestnut Hill, MA 02467-3800. Offers biochemistry (PhD); inorganic chemistry (PhD); organic chemistry (PhD); physical chemistry (PhD); science education (MST). *Degree requirements:* For doctorate, thesis/dissertation, qualifying exam. *Entrance requirements:* For doctorate, GRE General Test, GRE Subject Test. Additional exam requirements/recommendations for international students: Required—TOEFL (minimum score 600 paper-based; 250 computer-based; 100 iBT). Electronic applications accepted.

Brandeis University, Graduate School of Arts and Sciences, Department of Chemistry, Waltham, MA 02454. Offers inorganic chemistry (MS, PhD); organic chemistry (MS, PhD); physical chemistry (MS, PhD). Terminal master's awarded for partial completion of doctoral program. *Degree requirements:* For master's, thesis, 1 year of residency; for doctorate, one foreign language, thesis/dissertation, 3 years of residency, 2 seminars, qualifying exams. *Entrance requirements:* For master's and doctorate, GRE General Test, resume, letters of recommendation. Additional exam requirements/recommendations for international students: Required—TOEFL (minimum score 600 paper-based; 250 computer-based; 100 iBT); Recommended—IELTS (minimum score 7). Electronic applications accepted. *Faculty research:* Oscillating chemical reactions, molecular recognition systems, protein crystallography, synthesis of natural product spectroscopy and magnetic resonance.

California State University, Los Angeles, Graduate Studies, College of Natural and Social Sciences, Department of Chemistry and Biochemistry, Los Angeles, CA 90032-8530. Offers analytical chemistry (MS); biochemistry (MS); chemistry (MS); inorganic chemistry (MS); organic chemistry (MS); physical chemistry (MS). Part-time and evening/weekend programs available. *Faculty:* 4 part-time/adjunct (1 woman). *Students:* 22 full-time (14 women), 24 part-time (11 women); includes 30 minority (4 Black or African American, non-Hispanic/Latino; 7 Asian, non-Hispanic/Latino; 19 Hispanic/Latino), 7 international. Average age 29. 60 applicants, 48% accepted, 17 enrolled. In 2011, 15 master's awarded. *Degree requirements:* For master's, one foreign language, comprehensive exam or thesis. *Entrance requirements:* Additional exam requirements/recommendations for international students: Required—TOEFL. *Application deadline:* For fall admission, 5/1 for domestic and international students. Applications are processed on a rolling basis. Application fee: $55. *Expenses:* Tuition, state resident: full-time $8225. *Financial support:* Federal Work-Study available. Support available to part-time students. Financial award application deadline: 3/1. *Faculty research:* Intercalation of heavy metal, carborane chemistry, conductive polymers and fabrics, titanium reagents, computer modeling and synthesis. *Unit head:* Dr. Robert L. Vellanoweth, Chair, 323-343-2300, Fax: 323-343-6490, E-mail: rvellan@calstatela.edu. *Application contact:* Dr. Karin Brown, Acting Associate Dean of Graduate Studies, 323-343-3820 Ext. 3827, Fax: 323-343-5653, E-mail: kbrown5@calstatela.edu. Web site: http://www.calstatela.edu/dept/chem/index.htm.

Carnegie Mellon University, Mellon College of Science, Department of Chemistry, Pittsburgh, PA 15213-3891. Offers biotechnology and management (MS); chemistry (PhD), including bioinorganic, bioorganic, organic and materials, biophysics and spectroscopy, computational and theoretical, polymer; colloids, polymers and surfaces (MS). Part-time programs available. Terminal master's awarded for partial completion of doctoral program. *Degree requirements:* For doctorate, thesis/dissertation, departmental qualifying and oral exams, teaching experience. *Entrance requirements:* For master's, GRE General Test; for doctorate, GRE General Test, GRE Subject Test. Additional exam requirements/recommendations for international students: Required—TOEFL. Electronic applications accepted. *Faculty research:* Physical and theoretical chemistry, chemical synthesis, biophysical/bioinorganic chemistry.

Cleveland State University, College of Graduate Studies, College of Sciences and Health Professions, Department of Chemistry, Cleveland, OH 44115. Offers analytical chemistry (MS); clinical chemistry (MS); clinical/bioanalytical chemistry (PhD), including cellular and molecular medicine, clinical chemistry, clinical/bioanalytical chemistry; environmental chemistry (MS); inorganic chemistry (MS); pharmaceutical/organic chemistry (MS); physical chemistry (MS). Part-time and evening/weekend programs available. *Faculty:* 12 full-time (0 women). *Students:* 17 full-time (8 women), 87 part-time (36 women); includes 6 minority (5 Black or African American, non-Hispanic/Latino; 1 Asian, non-Hispanic/Latino), 74 international. Average age 27. 143 applicants, 59% accepted, 22 enrolled. In 2011, 14 master's, 10 doctorates awarded. *Median time to degree:* Of those who began their doctoral program in fall 2003, 67% received their degree in 8 years or less. *Degree requirements:* For master's, thesis optional; for doctorate, comprehensive exam, thesis/dissertation. *Entrance requirements:* For master's and doctorate, GRE General Test. Additional exam requirements/recommendations for international students: Required—TOEFL (minimum score 525 paper-based; 197 computer-based; 65 iBT). *Application deadline:* For fall admission, 1/15 priority date for domestic students, 1/15 for international students. Applications are processed on a rolling basis. Application fee: $30. Electronic applications accepted. *Expenses:* Tuition, state resident: full-time $6416; part-time $494 per credit hour. Tuition, nonresident: full-time $12,074; part-time $929 per credit hour. *Financial support:* In 2011–12, 44 students received support, including 5 fellowships with full tuition reimbursements available (averaging $30,000 per year), 13 research assistantships with full tuition reimbursements available (averaging $20,000 per year), 24 teaching assistantships with full tuition reimbursements available (averaging $18,500 per year); scholarships/grants and unspecified assistantships also available. Financial award application deadline: 1/15. *Faculty research:* Bioanalytical techniques and molecular diagnostics, glycoproteomics and antithrombotic agents, drug discovery and innovation, analytical pharmacology, inflammatory disease research. *Total annual research expenditures:* $3 million. *Unit head:* Dr. David J. Anderson, Interim Chair, 216-687-2467, Fax: 216-687-9298, E-mail: d.anderson@csuohio.edu. *Application contact:* Richelle P. Emery, Administrative Coordinator, 216-687-2457, Fax: 216-687-9298, E-mail: r.emery@csuohio.edu. Web site: http://www.csuohio.edu/chemistry/.

Columbia University, Graduate School of Arts and Sciences, Division of Natural Sciences, Department of Chemistry, New York, NY 10027. Offers chemical physics (M Phil, PhD); inorganic chemistry (M Phil, MA, PhD); organic chemistry (M Phil, MA, PhD); MD/PhD. *Degree requirements:* For master's, one foreign language, teaching experience, oral/written exams (M Phil); for doctorate, one foreign language, thesis/dissertation. *Entrance requirements:* For master's and doctorate, GRE General Test, GRE Subject Test. Additional exam requirements/recommendations for international students: Required—TOEFL. *Faculty research:* Biophysics.

Cornell University, Graduate School, Graduate Fields of Arts and Sciences, Field of Chemistry and Chemical Biology, Ithaca, NY 14853-0001. Offers analytical chemistry (PhD); bio-organic chemistry (PhD); biophysical chemistry (PhD); chemical biology (PhD); chemical physics (PhD); inorganic chemistry (PhD); materials chemistry (PhD); organic chemistry (PhD); organometallic chemistry (PhD); physical chemistry (PhD); polymer chemistry (PhD); theoretical chemistry (PhD). *Faculty:* 46 full-time (3 women). *Students:* 151 full-time (67 women); includes 16 minority (13 Asian, non-Hispanic/Latino; 2 Hispanic/Latino; 1 Two or more races, non-Hispanic/Latino), 48 international. Average age 25. 297 applicants, 35% accepted, 29 enrolled. In 2011, 22 doctorates awarded. *Degree requirements:* For doctorate, comprehensive exam, thesis/dissertation. *Entrance requirements:* For doctorate, GRE General Test, GRE Subject Test (chemistry), 3 letters of recommendation. Additional exam requirements/recommendations for international students: Required—TOEFL (minimum score 600 paper-based; 250 computer-based; 77 iBT). *Application deadline:* For fall admission, 1/10 for domestic students. Application fee: $95. Electronic applications accepted. *Financial support:* In 2011–12, 21 fellowships with full tuition reimbursements, 63 research assistantships with full tuition reimbursements, 59 teaching assistantships with full tuition reimbursements were awarded; institutionally sponsored loans, scholarships/grants, health care benefits, tuition waivers (full and partial), and unspecified assistantships also available. Financial award applicants required to submit FAFSA. *Faculty research:* Analytical, organic, inorganic, physical, materials, chemical biology. *Unit head:* Director of Graduate Studies, 607-255-4139, Fax: 607-255-4137. *Application contact:* Graduate Field Assistant, 607-255-4139, Fax: 607-255-4137, E-mail: chemgrad@cornell.edu. Web site: http://www.gradschool.cornell.edu/fields.php?id-26&a-2.

Eastern New Mexico University, Graduate School, College of Liberal Arts and Sciences, Department of Physical Sciences, Portales, NM 88130. Offers chemistry (MS), including analytical, biochemistry, inorganic, organic, physical. Part-time programs available. *Faculty:* 6 full-time (0 women). *Students:* 11 part-time (5 women), 9 international. Average age 25. 25 applicants, 44% accepted, 4 enrolled. In 2011, 5 master's awarded. *Degree requirements:* For master's, thesis optional, seminar, oral and written comprehensive exams. *Entrance requirements:* For master's, ACS placement examination, minimum GPA of 3.0; 2 letters of recommendation; personal statement of career goals; bachelor's degree with one year minimum each of general, organic, and analytical chemistry. Additional exam requirements/recommendations for international students: Required—TOEFL (minimum score 550 paper-based; 213 computer-based; 79 iBT), IELTS (minimum score 6). *Application deadline:* For fall admission, 7/20 priority date for domestic students, 6/20 for international students; for spring admission, 12/15 priority date for domestic students, 11/15 for international students. Applications are processed on a rolling basis. Application fee: $10. Electronic applications accepted. *Financial support:* In 2011–12, 1 research assistantship with partial tuition reimbursement (averaging $8,500 per year), 10 teaching assistantships with partial tuition reimbursements (averaging $8,500 per year) were awarded; career-related internships or fieldwork and unspecified assistantships also available. Support available to part-time students. Financial award application deadline: 3/1; financial award applicants required to submit FAFSA. *Faculty research:* Synfuel, electrochemistry, protein chemistry. *Unit head:* Dr. Juacho Yan, Graduate Coordinator, 575-562-2494, Fax: 575-562-2192, E-mail: juacho.yan@enmu.edu. *Application contact:* Sharon Potter, Department Secretary, Biology and Physical Sciences, 575-562-2174, Fax: 575-562-2192, E-mail: sharon.potter@enmu.edu. Web site: http://liberal-arts.enmu.edu/sciences/grad-chemistry.shtml.

Florida State University, The Graduate School, College of Arts and Sciences, Department of Chemistry and Biochemistry, Tallahassee, FL 32306-4390. Offers analytical chemistry (MS, PhD); biochemistry (MS, PhD); inorganic chemistry (MS, PhD); materials chemistry (PhD); organic chemistry (MS, PhD); physical chemistry (MS, PhD). *Faculty:* 35 full-time (5 women), 1 (woman) part-time/adjunct. *Students:* 138 full-time (52 women), 8 part-time (1 woman); includes 14 minority (6 Black or African American, non-Hispanic/Latino; 3 Asian, non-Hispanic/Latino; 2 Hispanic/Latino; 3 Two or more races, non-Hispanic/Latino), 63 international. Average age 25. 147 applicants, 40% accepted, 28 enrolled. In 2011, 10 master's, 24 doctorates awarded. Terminal master's awarded for partial

100 facebook.com/petersonspublishing

Peterson's Graduate Programs in the Physical Sciences, Mathematics, Agricultural Sciences, the Environment & Natural Resources 2013

completion of doctoral program. *Median time to degree:* Of those who began their doctoral program in fall 2003, 58% received their degree in 8 years or less. *Degree requirements:* For master's, comprehensive exam (for some programs), thesis (for some programs); for doctorate, comprehensive exam (for some programs), thesis/dissertation. *Entrance requirements:* For master's and doctorate, GRE General Test, minimum B average in undergraduate course work. Additional exam requirements/recommendations for international students: Required—TOEFL (minimum score 550 paper-based; 213 computer-based; 80 iBT). *Application deadline:* For fall admission, 12/15 priority date for domestic students, 12/15 for international students; for spring admission, 9/15 for domestic and international students. Applications are processed on a rolling basis. Application fee: $30. Electronic applications accepted. *Expenses:* Contact institution. *Financial support:* In 2011–12, 140 students received support, including fellowships with full tuition reimbursements available (averaging $20,000 per year), 50 research assistantships with full tuition reimbursements available (averaging $20,000 per year), 100 teaching assistantships with full tuition reimbursements available (averaging $20,000 per year). Financial award application deadline: 12/15; financial award applicants required to submit FAFSA. *Faculty research:* Materials synthesis including polymers, natural products; catalysis, NMR; mass spectrometry; optical spectroscopy, scattering techniques, computational chemistry, separation technology; nanostructured materials including metallic, semiconducting and magnetic nanocrystals; nanoscience interfaced with biology; supramolecular materials for solar energy conversion. *Total annual research expenditures:* $9.9 million. *Unit head:* Dr. Timothy Logan, Chairman, 850-644-1244, Fax: 850-644-8281, E-mail: gradinfo@chem.fsu.edu. *Application contact:* Dr. Michael Shatruk, Chair, Graduate Admissions Committee, 888-525-9286, Fax: 850-644-0465, E-mail: gradinfo@chem.fsu.edu. Web site: http://www.chem.fsu.edu/.

Georgetown University, Graduate School of Arts and Sciences, Department of Chemistry, Washington, DC 20057. Offers analytical chemistry (PhD); biochemistry (PhD); computational chemistry (PhD); inorganic chemistry (PhD); materials chemistry (PhD); organic chemistry (PhD); physical chemistry (PhD); theoretical chemistry (PhD). Terminal master's awarded for partial completion of doctoral program. *Degree requirements:* For doctorate, comprehensive exam, thesis/dissertation. *Entrance requirements:* For doctorate, GRE General Test. Additional exam requirements/recommendations for international students: Required—TOEFL.

The George Washington University, Columbian College of Arts and Sciences, Department of Chemistry, Washington, DC 20052. Offers analytical chemistry (MS, PhD); inorganic chemistry (MS, PhD); materials science (MS, PhD); organic chemistry (MS, PhD); physical chemistry (MS, PhD). Part-time and evening/weekend programs available. *Faculty:* 16 full-time (5 women), 5 part-time/adjunct (2 women). *Students:* 22 full-time (10 women), 10 part-time (7 women); includes 4 minority (3 Asian, non-Hispanic/Latino; 1 Hispanic/Latino), 7 international. Average age 27. 55 applicants, 42% accepted, 8 enrolled. In 2011, 4 master's, 3 doctorates awarded. Terminal master's awarded for partial completion of doctoral program. *Degree requirements:* For master's, comprehensive exam, thesis or alternative; for doctorate, thesis/dissertation, general exam. *Entrance requirements:* For master's and doctorate, GRE General Test, interview, minimum GPA of 3.0. Additional exam requirements/recommendations for international students: Required—TOEFL (minimum score 550 paper-based; 213 computer-based; 80 iBT). *Application deadline:* For fall admission, 1/15 priority date for domestic students, 1/15 for international students; for spring admission, 9/1 priority date for domestic students, 9/1 for international students. Applications are processed on a rolling basis. Application fee: $75. Electronic applications accepted. *Financial support:* In 2011–12, 27 students received support. Fellowships with tuition reimbursements available, research assistantships, teaching assistantships with tuition reimbursements available, Federal Work-Study, and tuition waivers available. Financial award application deadline: 1/15. *Unit head:* Dr. Michael King, Chair, 202-994-6488. *Application contact:* Information Contact, 202-994-6121, E-mail: gwchem@gwu.edu. Web site: http://www.gwu.edu/~gwchem/.

Harvard University, Graduate School of Arts and Sciences, Department of Chemistry and Chemical Biology, Cambridge, MA 02138. Offers biochemical chemistry (PhD); inorganic chemistry (PhD); organic chemistry (PhD); physical chemistry (PhD). *Degree requirements:* For doctorate, thesis/dissertation, cumulative exams. *Entrance requirements:* For doctorate, GRE General Test, GRE Subject Test. Additional exam requirements/recommendations for international students: Required—TOEFL. *Expenses: Tuition:* Full-time $36,304. *Required fees:* $1186. Full-time tuition and fees vary according to program.

See Display on page 67 and Close-Up on page 125.

Howard University, Graduate School, Department of Chemistry, Washington, DC 20059-0002. Offers analytical chemistry (MS, PhD); atmospheric (MS, PhD); biochemistry (MS, PhD); environmental (MS, PhD); inorganic chemistry (MS, PhD); organic chemistry (MS, PhD); physical chemistry (MS, PhD). Terminal master's awarded for partial completion of doctoral program. *Degree requirements:* For master's, comprehensive exam, thesis, teaching experience; for doctorate, comprehensive exam, thesis/dissertation, teaching experience. *Entrance requirements:* For master's, GRE General Test, minimum GPA of 2.7; for doctorate, GRE General Test, minimum GPA of 3.0. Additional exam requirements/recommendations for international students: Required—TOEFL. Electronic applications accepted. *Faculty research:* Synthetic organics, materials, natural products, mass spectrometry.

Indiana University Bloomington, University Graduate School, College of Arts and Sciences, Department of Chemistry, Bloomington, IN 47405. Offers analytical chemistry (PhD); chemical biology chemistry (PhD); chemistry (MAT); inorganic chemistry (PhD); materials chemistry (PhD); organic chemistry (PhD); physical chemistry (PhD). *Faculty:* 42 full-time (4 women). *Students:* 200 full-time (82 women), 3 part-time (0 women); includes 18 minority (7 Black or African American, non-Hispanic/Latino; 8 Asian, non-Hispanic/Latino; 1 Hispanic/Latino; 1 Native Hawaiian or other Pacific Islander, non-Hispanic/Latino; 1 Two or more races, non-Hispanic/Latino), 63 international. Average age 27. 290 applicants, 49% accepted, 46 enrolled. In 2011, 11 master's, 20 doctorates awarded. Terminal master's awarded for partial completion of doctoral program. *Median time to degree:* Of those who began their doctoral program in fall 2003, 49% received their degree in 8 years or less. *Degree requirements:* For master's, thesis; for doctorate, thesis/dissertation. *Entrance requirements:* For master's and doctorate, GRE General Test, GRE Subject Test. Additional exam requirements/recommendations for international students: Required—TOEFL. *Application deadline:* For fall admission, 1/15 priority date for domestic students, 12/15 for international students. Applications are processed on a rolling basis. Application fee: $55 ($65 for international students). *Financial support:* In 2011–12, 200 students received support, including 10 fellowships with full tuition reimbursements available, 76 research assistantships with full tuition reimbursements available, 111 teaching assistantships with full tuition reimbursements available; Federal Work-Study and institutionally sponsored loans also available. *Faculty research:* Synthesis of complex natural products, organic reaction mechanisms, organic electrochemistry, transitive-metal chemistry, solid-state and surface chemistry. *Total annual research expenditures:* $7.7 million. *Unit head:* David Giedroc, Chairperson, 812-855-6239, E-mail: chemchair@indiana.edu. *Application contact:* Daniel Mindiola, Director of Graduate Admissions, 812-855-2069, Fax: 812-855-8385, E-mail: mindiola@indiana.edu. Web site: http://www.chem.indiana.edu/.

Iowa State University of Science and Technology, Program in Inorganic Chemistry, Ames, IA 50011-3011. Offers MS, PhD. *Entrance requirements:* Additional exam requirements/recommendations for international students: Required—TOEFL (minimum score 570 paper-based; 89 iBT), IELTS (minimum score 6.5). *Application deadline:* For fall admission, 2/1 for domestic students. Electronic applications accepted. *Unit head:* Theresa Windus, Director of Graduate Education, 515-294-2436, Fax: 515-294-0105, E-mail: chemgrad@iastate.edu. *Application contact:* Lynette Edsall, Application Contact, 515-294-7810, Fax: 515-294-0105, E-mail: chemgrad@iastate.edu. Web site: http://www.chem.iastate.edu.

Kansas State University, Graduate School, College of Arts and Sciences, Department of Chemistry, Manhattan, KS 66506. Offers analytical chemistry (MS); biological chemistry (MS); chemistry (PhD); inorganic chemistry (MS); materials chemistry (MS); organic chemistry (MS); physical chemistry (MS). *Faculty:* 17 full-time (2 women). *Students:* 63 full-time (28 women), 4 part-time (0 women); includes 2 minority (1 Black or African American, non-Hispanic/Latino; 1 Asian, non-Hispanic/Latino), 55 international. Average age 28. 119 applicants, 34% accepted, 15 enrolled. In 2011, 2 master's, 10 doctorates awarded. Terminal master's awarded for partial completion of doctoral program. *Degree requirements:* For master's, thesis; for doctorate, thesis/dissertation. *Entrance requirements:* For master's and doctorate, GRE, minimum GPA of 3.0. Additional exam requirements/recommendations for international students: Required—TOEFL (minimum score 550 paper-based; 213 computer-based). *Application deadline:* For fall admission, 2/1 priority date for domestic students, 2/1 for international students; for spring admission, 8/1 priority date for domestic students, 8/1 for international students. Applications are processed on a rolling basis. Application fee: $40 ($55 for international students). Electronic applications accepted. *Financial support:* In 2011–12, 39 research assistantships (averaging $18,182 per year), 24 teaching assistantships with full tuition reimbursements (averaging $18,106 per year) were awarded; institutionally sponsored loans and scholarships/grants also available. Support available to part-time students. Financial award application deadline: 3/1; financial award applicants required to submit FAFSA. *Faculty research:* Inorganic chemistry, organic and biological chemistry, analytical chemistry, physical chemistry, materials chemistry and nanotechnology. *Total annual research expenditures:* $2.4 million. *Unit head:* Eric Maatta, Head, 785-532-6665, Fax: 785-532-6666, E-mail: eam@ksu.edu. *Application contact:* Christer Aakeroy, Director, 785-532-6096, Fax: 785-532-6666, E-mail: aakeroy@ksu.edu. Web site: http://www.k-state.edu/chem/.

Kent State University, College of Arts and Sciences, Department of Chemistry and Biochemistry, Kent, OH 44242-0001. Offers analytical chemistry (MS, PhD); biochemistry (MS, PhD); chemistry (MA); inorganic chemistry (MS, PhD); organic chemistry (MS, PhD); physical chemistry (MS, PhD). Terminal master's awarded for partial completion of doctoral program. *Degree requirements:* For master's, comprehensive exam, thesis; for doctorate, comprehensive exam, thesis/dissertation. *Entrance requirements:* For master's and doctorate, placement exam, GRE General Test, GRE Subject Test (recommended), minimum GPA of 2.75. Additional exam requirements/recommendations for international students: Required—TOEFL (minimum score 525 paper-based; 71 iBT). Electronic applications accepted. *Expenses:* Tuition, state resident: full-time $8136; part-time $452 per credit hour. Tuition, nonresident: full-time $14,292; part-time $794 per credit hour. *Faculty research:* Biological chemistry, materials chemistry, molecular spectroscopy.

See Display on page 70 and Close-Up on page 127.

Peterson's Graduate Programs in the Physical Sciences, Mathematics, Agricultural Sciences, the Environment & Natural Resources 2013

facebook.com/petersonspublishing **101**

Inorganic Chemistry

Marquette University, Graduate School, College of Arts and Sciences, Department of Chemistry, Milwaukee, WI 53201-1881. Offers analytical chemistry (MS, PhD); bioanalytical chemistry (MS, PhD); biophysical chemistry (MS, PhD); chemical physics (MS, PhD); inorganic chemistry (MS, PhD); organic chemistry (MS, PhD); physical chemistry (MS, PhD). Part-time programs available. *Faculty:* 29 full-time (4 women), 1 (woman) part-time/adjunct. *Students:* 42 full-time (11 women), 2 part-time (0 women); includes 5 minority (2 Black or African American, non-Hispanic/Latino; 3 Asian, non-Hispanic/Latino), 31 international. Average age 29. 18 applicants, 100% accepted, 10 enrolled. In 2011, 5 master's, 7 doctorates awarded. Terminal master's awarded for partial completion of doctoral program. *Degree requirements:* For master's, comprehensive exam; for doctorate, thesis/dissertation, cumulative exams. *Entrance requirements:* For master's and doctorate, official transcripts from all current and previous colleges/universities except Marquette, three letters of recommendation from individuals familiar with the applicant's academic work. Additional exam requirements/recommendations for international students: Required—TOEFL (minimum score 530 paper-based; 78 computer-based). *Application deadline:* Applications are processed on a rolling basis. Application fee: $50. Electronic applications accepted. *Expenses: Tuition:* Full-time $17,010; part-time $945 per credit hour. Tuition and fees vary according to program. *Financial support:* In 2011–12, 41 students received support, including 2 fellowships (averaging $17,134 per year), 30 teaching assistantships with full tuition reimbursements available (averaging $20,295 per year); research assistantships, scholarships/grants, health care benefits, tuition waivers (full and partial), and unspecified assistantships also available. Support available to part-time students. Financial award application deadline: 2/15. *Faculty research:* Inorganic complexes, laser Raman spectroscopy, organic synthesis, synthetic bioinorganic chemistry, electro-active organic molecules. *Total annual research expenditures:* $2.1 million. *Unit head:* Dr. Michael Ryan, Chair, 414-288-3537, Fax: 414-288-7066. *Application contact:* Dr. Mark Steinmetz, Director of Graduate Studies, 414-288-7374, Fax: 414-288-7066. Web site: http://www.marquette.edu/chem/graduate.shtml.

Massachusetts Institute of Technology, School of Science, Department of Chemistry, Cambridge, MA 02139. Offers biological chemistry (PhD, Sc D); inorganic chemistry (PhD, Sc D); organic chemistry (PhD, Sc D); physical chemistry (PhD, Sc D). *Faculty:* 26 full-time (5 women). *Students:* 221 full-time (73 women), 1 (woman) part-time; includes 48 minority (5 Black or African American, non-Hispanic/Latino; 1 American Indian or Alaska Native, non-Hispanic/Latino; 24 Asian, non-Hispanic/Latino; 14 Hispanic/Latino; 4 Two or more races, non-Hispanic/Latino), 64 international. Average age 25. 570 applicants, 20% accepted, 43 enrolled. In 2011, 45 doctorates awarded. *Degree requirements:* For doctorate, comprehensive exam, thesis/dissertation. *Entrance requirements:* For doctorate, GRE General Test. Additional exam requirements/recommendations for international students: Required—IELTS (minimum score 7); Recommended—TOEFL (minimum score 600 paper-based; 250 computer-based). *Application deadline:* For fall admission, 12/15 for domestic and international students. Application fee: $75. Electronic applications accepted. *Expenses: Tuition:* Full-time $40,460; part-time $630 per credit hour. *Required fees:* $272. *Financial support:* In 2011–12, 216 students received support, including 79 fellowships (averaging $34,800 per year), 127 research assistantships (averaging $31,400 per year), 16 teaching assistantships (averaging $32,600 per year); Federal Work-Study, institutionally sponsored loans, scholarships/grants, traineeships, health care benefits, and unspecified assistantships also available. *Faculty research:* Synthetic organic and organometallic chemistry including catalysis; biological chemistry including bioorganic chemistry; physical chemistry including chemical dynamics and biophysical chemistry; inorganic chemistry including synthesis, catalysis, bioinorganic and physical inorganic chemistry; materials chemistry including surface science, nanoscience and polymers. *Total annual research expenditures:* $31.1 million. *Unit head:* Prof. Sylvia T. Ceyer, Head, 617-253-1803, Fax: 617-258-7500. *Application contact:* Graduate Administrator, 617-253-1845, Fax: 617-258-0241, E-mail: chemgradeducation@mit.edu. Web site: http://web.mit.edu/chemistry/www/.

McMaster University, School of Graduate Studies, Faculty of Science, Department of Chemistry, Hamilton, ON L8S 4M2, Canada. Offers analytical chemistry (M Sc, PhD); chemical physics (M Sc, PhD); chemistry (M Sc, PhD); inorganic chemistry (M Sc, PhD); organic chemistry (M Sc, PhD); physical chemistry (M Sc, PhD); polymer chemistry (M Sc, PhD). Part-time programs available. Terminal master's awarded for partial completion of doctoral program. *Degree requirements:* For master's, thesis; for doctorate, comprehensive exam, thesis/dissertation. *Entrance requirements:* For master's, minimum B+ average. Additional exam requirements/recommendations for international students: Required—TOEFL (minimum score 550 paper-based; 213 computer-based).

Northeastern University, College of Science, Department of Chemistry and Chemical Biology, Boston, MA 02115-5096. Offers analytical chemistry (PhD); chemistry (MS, PhD); inorganic chemistry (PhD); organic chemistry (PhD); physical chemistry (PhD). Part-time and evening/weekend programs available. *Faculty:* 24 full-time, 7 part-time/adjunct. *Students:* 98 full-time (58 women), 31 part-time (15 women). 190 applicants, 32% accepted, 34 enrolled. In 2011, 16 master's, 6 doctorates awarded. Terminal master's awarded for partial completion of doctoral program. *Degree requirements:* For master's, thesis (for some programs); for doctorate, thesis/dissertation, qualifying exam in specialty area. *Entrance requirements:* Additional exam requirements/recommendations for international students: Required—TOEFL. *Application deadline:* For fall admission, 2/1 priority date for domestic students, 2/1 for international students. Applications are processed on a rolling basis. Application fee: $50. Electronic applications accepted. *Financial support:* In 2011–12, 41 research assistantships with tuition reimbursements (averaging $18,285 per year), 38 teaching assistantships with tuition reimbursements (averaging $18,285 per year) were awarded; fellowships with tuition reimbursements, career-related internships or fieldwork, Federal Work-Study, scholarships/grants, tuition waivers (partial), and unspecified assistantships also available. Financial award application deadline: 3/1; financial award applicants required to submit FAFSA. *Faculty research:* Bioanalysis, bioorganic and medicinal chemistry, biophysical chemistry, nanomaterials, proteonics. *Unit head:* Dr. Robert Hanson, Graduate Coordinator, 617-373-3313, Fax: 617-373-8795, E-mail: chemistry-grad-info@neu.edu. *Application contact:* Jo-Anne Dickinson, Admissions Contact, 617-373-5990, Fax: 617-373-7281, E-mail: gsas@neu.edu. Web site: http://www.northeastern.edu/chem/.

Oregon State University, Graduate School, College of Science, Department of Chemistry, Corvallis, OR 97331. Offers analytical chemistry (MS, PhD); chemistry (MA, MAIS); inorganic chemistry (MS, PhD); nuclear and radiation chemistry (MS, PhD); organic chemistry (MS, PhD); physical chemistry (MS, PhD). Part-time programs available. Terminal master's awarded for partial completion of doctoral program. *Degree requirements:* For master's, one foreign language, thesis; for doctorate, one foreign language, thesis/dissertation. *Entrance requirements:* For master's and doctorate, minimum GPA of 3.0 in last 90 hours of course work. Additional exam requirements/recommendations for international students: Required—TOEFL. *Faculty research:* Solid state chemistry, enzyme reaction mechanisms, structure and dynamics of gas molecules, chemiluminescence, nonlinear optical spectroscopy.

Purdue University, Graduate School, College of Science, Department of Chemistry, West Lafayette, IN 47907. Offers analytical chemistry (MS, PhD); biochemistry (MS, PhD); chemical education (MS, PhD); inorganic chemistry (MS, PhD); organic chemistry (MS, PhD); physical chemistry (MS, PhD). *Faculty:* 47 full-time (16 women), 6 part-time/adjunct (0 women). *Students:* 275 full-time (103 women), 33 part-time (10 women); includes 38 minority (19 Black or African American, non-Hispanic/Latino; 6 Asian, non-Hispanic/Latino; 12 Hispanic/Latino; 1 Two or more races, non-Hispanic/Latino), 94 international. Average age 27. 777 applicants, 26% accepted, 62 enrolled. In 2011, 4 master's, 67 doctorates awarded. Terminal master's awarded for partial completion of doctoral program. *Degree requirements:* For master's, thesis; for doctorate, comprehensive exam, thesis/dissertation. *Entrance requirements:* For master's and doctorate, minimum undergraduate GPA of 3.0. Additional exam requirements/recommendations for international students: Required—TOEFL (minimum score 550 computer-based; 77 iBT); Recommended—TWE. *Application deadline:* For fall admission, 2/15 priority date for domestic students, 1/1 for international students. Applications are processed on a rolling basis. Application fee: $60 ($75 for international students). Electronic applications accepted. *Financial support:* In 2011–12, 2 fellowships with partial tuition reimbursements (averaging $18,000 per year), 55 teaching assistantships with partial tuition reimbursements (averaging $18,000 per year) were awarded; research assistantships with partial tuition reimbursements and tuition waivers (partial) also available. Support available to part-time students. Financial award applicants required to submit FAFSA. *Unit head:* Dr. Paul B. Shepson, Head, 765-494-5203, E-mail: pshepson@purdue.edu. *Application contact:* Betty L.. Hatfield, Director of Graduate Admissions, 765-494-5208, E-mail: bettyh@purdue.edu.

Rensselaer Polytechnic Institute, Graduate School, School of Science, Program in Chemistry, Troy, NY 12180-3590. Offers analytical chemistry (MS, PhD); biochemistry (MS, PhD); inorganic chemistry (MS, PhD); organic chemistry (MS, PhD); physical chemistry (MS, PhD); polymer chemistry (MS, PhD). Part-time and evening/weekend programs available. Terminal master's awarded for partial completion of doctoral program. *Degree requirements:* For master's, thesis (for some programs); for doctorate, comprehensive exam, thesis/dissertation. *Entrance requirements:* For master's, GRE General Test, GRE Subject Test (strongly recommended); for doctorate, GRE General Test, GRE Subject Test (chemistry or biochemistry strongly recommended). Additional exam requirements/recommendations for international students: Required—TOEFL (minimum score 570 paper-based; 230 computer-based; 88 iBT). Electronic applications accepted. *Faculty research:* Synthetic polymer and biopolymer chemistry, physical chemistry of polymeric systems, bioanalytical chemistry, synthetic and computational drug design, protein folding and protein design.

Rice University, Graduate Programs, Wiess School of Natural Sciences, Department of Chemistry, Houston, TX 77251-1892. Offers chemistry (MA); inorganic chemistry (PhD); organic chemistry (PhD); physical chemistry (PhD). Terminal master's awarded for partial completion of doctoral program. *Degree requirements:* For master's, thesis; for doctorate, thesis/dissertation. *Entrance requirements:* For master's and doctorate, GRE General Test, minimum GPA of 3.0. Additional exam requirements/recommendations for international students: Required—TOEFL (minimum score 600 paper-based; 250 computer-based; 90 iBT). Electronic applications accepted. *Faculty research:* Nanoscience, biomaterials, nanobioinformatics, fullerene pharmaceuticals.

Rutgers, The State University of New Jersey, Newark, Graduate School, Program in Chemistry, Newark, NJ 07102. Offers analytical chemistry (MS, PhD); biochemistry (MS, PhD); inorganic chemistry (MS, PhD); organic chemistry (MS, PhD); physical chemistry (MS, PhD). Part-time and evening/weekend programs available. Terminal master's awarded for partial completion of doctoral program. *Degree requirements:* For master's, thesis optional, cumulative exams; for doctorate, thesis/dissertation, exams, research proposal. *Entrance requirements:* For master's and doctorate, GRE General Test, minimum undergraduate B average. Additional exam requirements/recommendations for international students: Required—TOEFL. Electronic applications accepted. *Faculty research:* Medicinal chemistry, natural products, isotope effects, biophysics and biorganic approaches to enzyme mechanisms, organic and organometallic synthesis.

Rutgers, The State University of New Jersey, New Brunswick, Graduate School-New Brunswick, Department of Chemistry and Chemical Biology, Piscataway, NJ 08854-8097. Offers biological chemistry (MS, PhD); inorganic chemistry (MS, PhD); organic chemistry (MS, PhD); physical chemistry (MS, PhD). Part-time and evening/weekend programs available. Terminal master's awarded for partial completion of doctoral program. *Degree requirements:* For master's, thesis or alternative, exam; for doctorate, thesis/dissertation, 1 year residency. *Entrance requirements:* For master's and doctorate, GRE General Test, GRE Subject Test. Additional exam requirements/recommendations for international students: Required—TOEFL. Electronic applications accepted. *Faculty research:* Biophysical organic/bioorganic, inorganic/bioinorganic, theoretical, and solid-state/surface chemistry.

Seton Hall University, College of Arts and Sciences, Department of Chemistry and Biochemistry, South Orange, NJ 07079-2697. Offers analytical chemistry (MS, PhD); biochemistry (MS, PhD); chemistry (MS); inorganic chemistry (MS, PhD); organic chemistry (MS, PhD); physical chemistry (MS, PhD). Part-time and evening/weekend programs available. Terminal master's awarded for partial completion of doctoral program. *Degree requirements:* For master's, thesis optional; for doctorate, comprehensive exam, thesis/dissertation. *Entrance requirements:* Additional exam requirements/recommendations for international students: Required—TOEFL. Electronic applications accepted. *Expenses: Tuition:* Part-time $1033 per credit hour. *Required fees:* $85 per semester. *Faculty research:* DNA metal reactions; chromatography; bioinorganic, biophysical, organometallic, polymer chemistry; heterogeneous catalyst; synthetic organic and carbohydrate chemistry.

Southern University and Agricultural and Mechanical College, Graduate School, College of Sciences, Department of Chemistry, Baton Rouge, LA 70813. Offers analytical chemistry (MS); biochemistry (MS); environmental sciences (MS); inorganic chemistry (MS); organic chemistry (MS); physical chemistry (MS). *Degree requirements:* For master's, thesis. *Entrance requirements:* For master's, GMAT or GRE General Test. Additional exam requirements/recommendations for international students: Required—TOEFL (minimum score 525 paper-based; 193 computer-based). *Faculty research:* Synthesis of macrocyclic ligands, latex accelerators, anticancer drugs, biosensors, absorption isotheums, isolation of specific enzymes from plants.

State University of New York at Binghamton, Graduate School, School of Arts and Sciences, Department of Chemistry, Binghamton, NY 13902-6000. Offers analytical chemistry (PhD); chemistry (MA, MS); inorganic chemistry (PhD); organic chemistry (PhD); physical chemistry (PhD). Part-time programs available. *Faculty:* 16 full-time (5 women), 2 part-time/adjunct (both women). *Students:* 24 full-time (8 women), 32 part-time (13 women); includes 5 minority (2 Black or African American, non-Hispanic/Latino; 1 Hispanic/Latino; 2 Native Hawaiian or other Pacific Islander, non-Hispanic/Latino), 36 international. Average age 28. 39 applicants, 36% accepted, 10 enrolled. In 2011, 3 master's, 6 doctorates awarded. Terminal master's awarded for partial completion of doctoral program. *Degree requirements:* For master's, thesis or alternative, oral exam, seminar presentation; for doctorate, thesis/dissertation, cumulative exams. *Entrance requirements:* For master's and doctorate, GRE General Test, GRE Subject Test. Additional exam requirements/recommendations for international students: Required—TOEFL (minimum score 550 paper-based; 213 computer-based; 80 iBT). *Application deadline:* For fall admission, 1/15 priority date for domestic students, 1/15 for international students; for spring admission, 10/15 priority date for domestic students, 10/15 for international students. Applications are processed on a rolling basis. Application fee: $60. Electronic applications accepted. *Financial support:* In 2011–12, 9 fellowships with full tuition reimbursements (averaging $18,000 per year), 13 research assistantships with full tuition reimbursements (averaging $18,000 per year), 35 teaching assistantships with full tuition reimbursements (averaging $18,000 per year) were awarded; career-related internships or fieldwork, Federal Work-Study, institutionally sponsored loans, scholarships/grants, health care benefits, tuition waivers (full), and unspecified assistantships also available. Financial award application deadline: 2/15; financial award applicants required to submit FAFSA. *Unit head:* Dr. Wayne E. Jones, Chairperson, 607-777-2421, E-mail: wjones@binghamton.edu. *Application contact:* Catherine Smith, Recruiting and Admissions Coordinator, 607-777-2151, Fax: 607-777-2501, E-mail: cmsmith@binghamton.edu.

Texas Christian University, College of Science and Engineering, Department of Chemistry, Fort Worth, TX 76129. Offers biochemistry (MS, PhD); chemistry (MA); inorganic (MS, PhD); organic (MS, PhD); physical (MS, PhD). Part-time programs available. *Faculty:* 11 full-time (2 women). *Students:* 4 full-time (2 women), 16 part-time (10 women); includes 3 minority (1 Asian, non-Hispanic/Latino; 2 Hispanic/Latino), 11 international. Average age 27. 5 applicants, 100% accepted, 4 enrolled. In 2011, 1 master's, 3 doctorates awarded. *Degree requirements:* For master's, thesis; for doctorate, thesis/dissertation, literature seminar, cumulative exams, research progress report, original proposal. *Entrance requirements:* For master's and doctorate, GRE General Test. Additional exam requirements/recommendations for international students: Required—TOEFL.

Application deadline: For fall admission, 3/1 priority date for domestic students, 3/1 for international students; for spring admission, 9/1 priority date for domestic students, 9/1 for international students. Application fee: $50. Electronic applications accepted. *Expenses: Tuition:* Full-time $20,250; part-time $1125 per credit hour. Part-time tuition and fees vary according to course load and program. *Financial support:* In 2011–12, 11 students received support, including 11 teaching assistantships with full tuition reimbursements available; tuition waivers (full and partial) and unspecified assistantships also available. Financial award application deadline: 3/1. *Faculty research:* Phase transitions and transport properties of bio/macromolecular solutions, nanoscale biomaterials, electronic structure theory, synthetic methodology and total synthesis of natural products, chemistry and biology of (bio)polymers. *Unit head:* Dr. Robert Neilson, Chairperson/Professor, 817-257-7345, Fax: 817-257-5851, E-mail: r.neilson@tcu.edu. *Application contact:* Dr. Sergei V. Dzyuba, Director of Graduate Studies/Assistant Professor, 817-257-6218, Fax: 817-257-5851, E-mail: s.dzyuba@tcu.edu. Web site: http://www.chm.tcu.edu/.

Tufts University, Graduate School of Arts and Sciences, Department of Chemistry, Medford, MA 02155. Offers analytical chemistry (MS, PhD); bioorganic chemistry (MS, PhD); environmental chemistry (MS, PhD); inorganic chemistry (MS, PhD); organic chemistry (MS, PhD); physical chemistry (MS, PhD). *Students:* 75 full-time (33 women); includes 7 minority (1 Black or African American, non-Hispanic/Latino; 5 Asian, non-Hispanic/Latino; 1 Hispanic/Latino), 25 international. 88 applicants, 59% accepted, 16 enrolled. In 2011, 5 master's, 8 doctorates awarded. Terminal master's awarded for partial completion of doctoral program. *Degree requirements:* For master's, thesis optional; for doctorate, thesis/dissertation. *Entrance requirements:* For master's and doctorate, GRE General Test, GRE Subject Test. Additional exam requirements/recommendations for international students: Required—TOEFL (minimum score 600 paper-based; 250 computer-based; 80 iBT). *Application deadline:* For fall admission, 1/15 for domestic students, 12/15 for international students; for spring admission, 10/15 for domestic students, 9/15 for international students. Applications are processed on a rolling basis. Application fee: $75. Electronic applications accepted. *Expenses: Tuition:* Full-time $41,208; part-time $1030 per credit hour. Full-time tuition and fees vary according to degree level, program and student level. Part-time tuition and fees vary according to course load. *Financial support:* Fellowships, research assistantships with full tuition reimbursements, teaching assistantships with full tuition reimbursements, Federal Work-Study, scholarships/grants, tuition waivers (partial), and unspecified assistantships available. Financial award application deadline: 1/15; financial award applicants required to submit FAFSA. *Unit head:* Arthur Utz, Chair, 617-627-3441. *Application contact:* Deborah D'Andrea, Information Contact, 617-627-3441, Fax: 617-627-3443. Web site: http://chem.tufts.edu/.

University of Calgary, Faculty of Graduate Studies, Faculty of Science, Department of Chemistry, Calgary, AB T2N 1N4, Canada. Offers analytical chemistry (M Sc, PhD); applied chemistry (M Sc, PhD); inorganic chemistry (M Sc, PhD); organic chemistry (M Sc, PhD); physical chemistry (M Sc, PhD); polymer chemistry (M Sc, PhD); theoretical chemistry (M Sc, PhD). *Degree requirements:* For master's, thesis; for doctorate, thesis/dissertation, candidacy exam. *Entrance requirements:* For master's, minimum GPA of 3.0; for doctorate, honors B Sc degree with minimum GPA of 3.7 or M Sc with minimum GPA of 3.3. Additional exam requirements/recommendations for international students: Required—TOEFL (minimum score 580 paper-based; 237 computer-based). Electronic applications accepted. *Faculty research:* Chemical analysis, chemical dynamics, synthesis theory.

University of Cincinnati, Graduate School, McMicken College of Arts and Sciences, Department of Chemistry, Cincinnati, OH 45221. Offers analytical chemistry (MS, PhD); biochemistry (MS, PhD); inorganic chemistry (MS, PhD); organic chemistry (MS, PhD); physical chemistry (MS, PhD); polymer chemistry (MS, PhD); sensors (PhD). Part-time and evening/weekend programs available. Terminal master's awarded for partial completion of doctoral program. *Degree requirements:* For master's, thesis optional; for doctorate, comprehensive exam, thesis/dissertation. *Entrance requirements:* For master's and doctorate, GRE General Test. Additional exam requirements/recommendations for international students: Required—TOEFL (minimum score 580 paper-based; 237 computer-based). Electronic applications accepted. *Faculty research:* Biomedical chemistry, laser chemistry, surface science, chemical sensors, synthesis.

University of Georgia, Franklin College of Arts and Sciences, Department of Chemistry, Athens, GA 30602. Offers analytical chemistry (MS, PhD); inorganic chemistry (MS, PhD); organic chemistry (MS, PhD); physical chemistry (MS, PhD). *Faculty:* 26 full-time (2 women). *Students:* 153 full-time (53 women), 6 part-time (2 women); includes 21 minority (6 Black or African American, non-Hispanic/Latino; 12 Asian, non-Hispanic/Latino; 1 Hispanic/Latino; 2 Two or more races, non-Hispanic/Latino), 60 international. Average age 27. 175 applicants, 41% accepted, 38 enrolled. In 2011, 7 master's, 22 doctorates awarded. Terminal master's awarded for partial completion of doctoral program. *Median time to degree:* Of those who began their doctoral program in fall 2003, 100% received their degree in 8 years or less. *Degree requirements:* For master's, thesis; for doctorate, one foreign language, thesis/dissertation. *Entrance requirements:* For master's and doctorate, GRE General Test. Additional exam requirements/recommendations for international students: Required—TOEFL (minimum score 213 computer-based). *Application deadline:* For fall admission, 7/1 priority date for domestic students; for spring admission, 11/15 for domestic students. Application fee: $50. Electronic applications accepted. *Financial support:* Fellowships,

Peterson's Graduate Programs in the Physical Sciences, Mathematics, Agricultural Sciences, the Environment & Natural Resources 2013

facebook.com/petersonspublishing **103**

Inorganic Chemistry

research assistantships, teaching assistantships, and unspecified assistantships available. *Unit head:* Dr. Jon Amster, Head, 706-542-2726, E-mail: jamster@uga.edu. *Application contact:* Dr. Jeffrey L. Urbauer, Graduate Coordinator, 706-542-7922, E-mail: urbauer@uga.edu. Web site: http://www.chem.uga.edu/.

University of Louisville, Graduate School, College of Arts and Sciences, Department of Chemistry, Louisville, KY 40292-0001. Offers analytical chemistry (MS, PhD); biochemistry (MS, PhD); chemical physics (PhD); inorganic chemistry (MS, PhD); organic chemistry (MS, PhD); physical chemistry (MS, PhD). Terminal master's awarded for partial completion of doctoral program. *Degree requirements:* For master's, variable foreign language requirement, comprehensive exam, thesis optional; for doctorate, variable foreign language requirement, comprehensive exam, thesis/dissertation. *Entrance requirements:* For master's and doctorate, BA or BS coursework. Additional exam requirements/recommendations for international students: Required—TOEFL. Electronic applications accepted. *Expenses:* Tuition, state resident: full-time $9692; part-time $539 per credit hour. Tuition, nonresident: full-time $20,168; part-time $1121 per credit hour. Tuition and fees vary according to program and reciprocity agreements. *Faculty research:* Computational chemistry, biophysics nuclear magnetic resonance, synthetic organic chemistry, synthetic inorganic chemistry, medicinal chemistry, protein chemistry, enzymology, nanochemistry, electrochemistry, analytical chemistry, synthetic biology, bioinformatics.

The University of Manchester, School of Chemistry, Manchester, United Kingdom. Offers biological chemistry (PhD); chemistry (M Ent, M Phil, M Sc, D Ent, PhD); inorganic chemistry (PhD); materials chemistry (PhD); nanoscience (PhD); nuclear fission (PhD); organic chemistry (PhD); physical chemistry (PhD); theoretical chemistry (PhD).

University of Maryland, College Park, Academic Affairs, College of Computer, Mathematical and Natural Sciences, Department of Chemistry and Biochemistry, Chemistry Program, College Park, MD 20742. Offers analytical chemistry (MS, PhD); inorganic chemistry (MS, PhD); organic chemistry (MS, PhD); physical chemistry (MS, PhD). Part-time and evening/weekend programs available. *Students:* 115 full-time (59 women), 4 part-time (1 woman); includes 20 minority (12 Black or African American, non-Hispanic/Latino; 4 Asian, non-Hispanic/Latino; 2 Hispanic/Latino; 2 Two or more races, non-Hispanic/Latino), 52 international. 335 applicants, 8% accepted, 18 enrolled. In 2011, 11 master's, 15 doctorates awarded. Terminal master's awarded for partial completion of doctoral program. *Median time to degree:* Of those who began their doctoral program in fall 2003, 63% received their degree in 8 years or less. *Degree requirements:* For master's, thesis optional; for doctorate, thesis/dissertation, 2 seminar presentations, oral exam. *Entrance requirements:* For master's and doctorate, GRE General Test, GRE Subject Test (recommended), minimum GPA of 3.0, 3 letters of recommendation. Additional exam requirements/recommendations for international students: Required—TOEFL. *Application deadline:* For fall admission, 2/1 for domestic and international students; for spring admission, 6/1 for domestic and international students. Applications are processed on a rolling basis. Application fee: $75. Electronic applications accepted. *Expenses: Tuition, area resident:* Part-time $525 per credit hour. Tuition, state resident: part-time $525 per credit hour. Tuition, nonresident: part-time $1131 per credit hour. *Required fees:* $386.31 per term. Tuition and fees vary according to program. *Financial support:* In 2011–12, 9 fellowships with full and partial tuition reimbursements (averaging $25,360 per year), 46 research assistantships (averaging $19,791 per year), 59 teaching assistantships (averaging $19,243 per year) were awarded. Financial award applicants required to submit FAFSA. *Faculty research:* Environmental chemistry, nuclear chemistry, lunar and environmental analysis, x-ray crystallography. *Unit head:* Dr. Michael Doyle, Chairperson, 301-405-1795, Fax: 301-314-2779, E-mail: mdoyle3@umd.edu. *Application contact:* Dr. Charles A. Caramello, Dean of Graduate School, 301-405-0358, Fax: 301-314-9305.

University of Massachusetts Lowell, College of Sciences, Department of Chemistry, Lowell, MA 01854-2881. Offers analytical chemistry (PhD); biochemistry (PhD); chemistry (MS, PhD); environmental studies (PhD); green chemistry (PhD); inorganic chemistry (PhD); organic chemistry (PhD); polymer science (MS). Terminal master's awarded for partial completion of doctoral program. *Degree requirements:* For master's, thesis; for doctorate, 2 foreign languages, thesis/dissertation. *Entrance requirements:* For master's and doctorate, GRE General Test. Electronic applications accepted.

University of Memphis, Graduate School, College of Arts and Sciences, Department of Chemistry, Memphis, TN 38152. Offers analytical chemistry (MS, PhD); computational chemistry (MS, PhD); inorganic chemistry (MS, PhD); organic chemistry (MS, PhD); physical chemistry (MS, PhD). Part-time programs available. Terminal master's awarded for partial completion of doctoral program. *Degree requirements:* For master's, comprehensive exam, thesis or alternative; for doctorate, comprehensive exam, thesis/dissertation. *Entrance requirements:* For master's and doctorate, GRE General Test, admission to Graduate School plus 32 undergraduate hours in chemistry. Additional exam requirements/recommendations for international students: Required—TOEFL. Electronic applications accepted. *Faculty research:* Computational chemistry, materials chemistry, organic/polymer synthesis, drug design/delivery, water chemistry.

University of Miami, Graduate School, College of Arts and Sciences, Department of Chemistry, Coral Gables, FL 33124. Offers chemistry (MS); inorganic chemistry (PhD); organic chemistry (PhD); physical chemistry (PhD). Terminal master's awarded for partial completion of doctoral program. *Degree*

requirements: For master's, comprehensive exam; for doctorate, comprehensive exam, thesis/dissertation. *Entrance requirements:* For master's and doctorate, GRE General Test. Additional exam requirements/recommendations for international students: Required—TOEFL (minimum score 550 paper-based; 213 computer-based). Electronic applications accepted. *Faculty research:* Supramolecular chemistry, electrochemistry, surface chemistry, catalysis, organometalic.

University of Michigan, Horace H. Rackham School of Graduate Studies, College of Literature, Science, and the Arts, Department of Chemistry, Ann Arbor, MI 48109-1055. Offers analytical chemistry (PhD); chemical biology (PhD); inorganic chemistry (PhD); material chemistry (PhD); organic chemistry (PhD); physical chemistry (PhD). *Faculty:* 39 full-time (9 women). *Students:* 221 full-time (114 women); includes 24 minority (1 Black or African American, non-Hispanic/Latino; 15 Asian, non-Hispanic/Latino; 4 Hispanic/Latino; 4 Two or more races, non-Hispanic/Latino), 66 international. Average age 26. 608 applicants, 27% accepted, 39 enrolled. In 2011, 39 doctorates awarded. *Degree requirements:* For doctorate, thesis/dissertation, oral defense of dissertation, organic cumulative proficiency exams. *Entrance requirements:* For doctorate, GRE General Test, GRE Subject Test (recommended), 3 letters of recommendation. Additional exam requirements/recommendations for international students: Required—TOEFL (minimum score 560 paper-based; 220 computer-based; 84 iBT). *Application deadline:* For fall admission, 12/31 for domestic students, 12/15 for international students. Applications are processed on a rolling basis. Application fee: $0 ($75 for international students). Electronic applications accepted. *Financial support:* In 2011–12, 221 students received support; including 25 fellowships with full tuition reimbursements available (averaging $26,553 per year), 86 research assistantships with full tuition reimbursements available (averaging $26,553 per year), 110 teaching assistantships with full tuition reimbursements available (averaging $26,553 per year); career-related internships or fieldwork, scholarships/grants, traineeships, health care benefits, and unspecified assistantships also available. *Faculty research:* Biological catalysis, protein engineering, chemical sensors, de novo metalloprotein design, supramolecular architecture. *Unit head:* Dr. Carol A. Fierke, Chair, 734-763-9681, Fax: 734-647-4847. *Application contact:* Margarita Bekiares, Graduate Program Coordinator, 734-764-7278, Fax: 734-647-4865, E-mail: chemadmissions@umich.edu. Web site: http://www.umich.edu/~michchem/.

University of Missouri, Graduate School, College of Arts and Sciences, Department of Chemistry, Columbia, MO 65211. Offers analytical chemistry (MS, PhD); inorganic chemistry (MS, PhD); organic chemistry (MS, PhD); physical chemistry (MS, PhD). *Faculty:* 22 full-time (4 women), 1 part-time/adjunct (0 women). *Students:* 102 full-time (38 women), 10 part-time (6 women); includes 7 minority (3 Black or African American, non-Hispanic/Latino; 2 Asian, non-Hispanic/Latino; 1 Hispanic/Latino; 1 Two or more races, non-Hispanic/Latino), 53 international. Average age 27. 98 applicants, 28% accepted, 24 enrolled. In 2011, 2 master's, 5 doctorates awarded. *Degree requirements:* For master's, thesis; for doctorate, one foreign language, comprehensive exam, thesis/dissertation. *Entrance requirements:* For master's, GRE General Test, minimum GPA of 3.0; for doctorate, GRE General Test (minimum score: Verbal 450, Quantitative 600, Analytical 3), minimum GPA of 3.0. Additional exam requirements/recommendations for international students: Required—TOEFL (minimum score 600 paper-based; 250 computer-based; 100 iBT). *Application deadline:* For fall admission, 4/1 priority date for domestic students; for winter admission, 10/15 for domestic students. Applications are processed on a rolling basis. Application fee: $55 ($75 for international students). Electronic applications accepted. *Expenses:* Tuition, state resident: full-time $5881. Tuition, nonresident: full-time $15,183. *Required fees:* $952. Tuition and fees vary according to campus/location and program. *Financial support:* In 2011–12, 9 fellowships with full tuition reimbursements, 15 research assistantships with full tuition reimbursements, 78 teaching assistantships with full tuition reimbursements were awarded; institutionally sponsored loans, traineeships, health care benefits, and unspecified assistantships also available. *Faculty research:* Analytical, organic, biological, physical, inorganic and radiochemistry. *Unit head:* Dr. Jerry Atwood, Department Chair, 573-882-8374, E-mail: atwoodj@missouri.edu. *Application contact:* Jerry Brightwell, Administrative Assistant, 573-884-6832, E-mail: brightwellj@missouri.edu. Web site: http://chemistry.missouri.edu/.

University of Missouri–Kansas City, College of Arts and Sciences, Department of Chemistry, Kansas City, MO 64110-2499. Offers analytical chemistry (MS, PhD); inorganic chemistry (MS, PhD); organic chemistry (MS, PhD); physical chemistry (MS, PhD); polymer chemistry (MS, PhD). PhD (interdisciplinary) offered through the School of Graduate Studies. Part-time and evening/weekend programs available. *Faculty:* 16 full-time (3 women), 1 part-time/adjunct (0 women). *Students:* 1 (woman) part-time; minority (Black or African American, non-Hispanic/Latino). Average age 30. 28 applicants, 32% accepted, 0 enrolled. In 2011, 2 degrees awarded. *Degree requirements:* For master's, thesis (for some programs); for doctorate, thesis/dissertation. *Entrance requirements:* For master's, equivalent of American Chemical Society approved bachelor's degree in chemistry; for doctorate, GRE General Test, equivalent of American Chemical Society approved bachelor's degree in chemistry. Additional exam requirements/recommendations for international students: Required—TOEFL (minimum score 550 paper-based; 213 computer-based; 80 iBT), TWE. *Application deadline:* For fall admission, 4/15 for domestic and international students; for spring admission, 10/15 for domestic and international students. Applications are processed on a rolling basis. Application fee: $45 ($50 for international students). Electronic applications accepted. *Expenses:* Tuition, state resident: full-time $5798; part-

104 facebook.com/petersonspublishing

Peterson's Graduate Programs in the Physical Sciences, Mathematics, Agricultural Sciences, the Environment & Natural Resources 2013

time $322.10 per credit hour. Tuition, nonresident: full-time $14,969; part-time $831.60 per credit hour. *Required fees:* $93.51 per credit hour. *Financial support:* In 2011–12, 9 research assistantships with partial tuition reimbursements (averaging $19,119 per year), 14 teaching assistantships with partial tuition reimbursements (averaging $17,187 per year) were awarded; Federal Work-Study, institutionally sponsored loans, and scholarships/grants also available. Support available to part-time students. Financial award application deadline: 3/1; financial award applicants required to submit FAFSA. *Faculty research:* Molecular spectroscopy, characterization and synthesis of materials and compounds, computational chemistry, natural products, drug delivery systems and anti-tumor agents. *Unit head:* Dr. Kathleen V. Kilway, Chair, 816-235-2289, Fax: 816-235-5502. *Application contact:* Graduate Recruiting Committee, 816-235-2272, Fax: 816-235-5502, E-mail: umkc-chemdept@umkc.edu. Web site: http://cas.umkc.edu/chem/.

University of Missouri–St. Louis, College of Arts and Sciences, Department of Chemistry and Biochemistry, St. Louis, MO 63121. Offers chemistry (MS, PhD), including biochemistry, inorganic chemistry, organic chemistry, physical chemistry. Part-time and evening/weekend programs available. *Faculty:* 18 full-time (3 women), 4 part-time/adjunct (1 woman). *Students:* 37 full-time (18 women), 28 part-time (11 women); includes 4 minority (1 Black or African American, non-Hispanic/Latino; 2 Asian, non-Hispanic/Latino; 1 Hispanic/Latino), 22 international. Average age 30. 73 applicants, 30% accepted, 11 enrolled. In 2011, 16 master's, 4 doctorates awarded. Terminal master's awarded for partial completion of doctoral program. *Degree requirements:* For master's, thesis optional; for doctorate, thesis/dissertation. *Entrance requirements:* For master's, 2 letters of recommendation; for doctorate, GRE General Test, 3 letters of recommendation. Additional exam requirements/recommendations for international students: Required—TOEFL (minimum score 550 paper-based; 213 computer-based). *Application deadline:* For fall admission, 7/1 priority date for domestic students, 7/1 for international students; for spring admission, 12/1 priority date for domestic students, 12/1 for international students. Applications are processed on a rolling basis. Application fee: $35 ($40 for international students). Electronic applications accepted. *Expenses:* Tuition, state resident: full-time $6273; part-time $3866 per year. Tuition, nonresident: full-time $14,969; part-time $9980 per year. *Required fees:* $315 per year. *Financial support:* In 2011–12, 19 research assistantships with full and partial tuition reimbursements (averaging $13,500 per year), 19 teaching assistantships with full and partial tuition reimbursements (averaging $13,500 per year) were awarded; fellowships with full and partial tuition reimbursements also available. *Faculty research:* Metallaborane chemistry, serum transferrin chemistry, natural products chemistry, organic synthesis. *Unit head:* Dr. Janet Wilking, Director of Graduate Studies, 314-516-5311, Fax: 314-516-5342, E-mail: gradchem@umsl.edu. *Application contact:* Graduate Admissions, 314-516-5458, Fax: 314-516-6996, E-mail: gradadm@umsl.edu. Web site: http://www.umsl.edu/chemistry/.

The University of Montana, Graduate School, College of Arts and Sciences, Department of Chemistry and Biochemistry, Missoula, MT 59812-0002. Offers chemistry (MS, PhD), including environmental/analytical chemistry, inorganic chemistry, organic chemistry, physical chemistry. Terminal master's awarded for partial completion of doctoral program. *Degree requirements:* For master's, thesis (for some programs); for doctorate, thesis/dissertation. *Entrance requirements:* For master's and doctorate, GRE General Test. Additional exam requirements/recommendations for international students: Required—TOEFL (minimum score 575 paper-based; 230 computer-based). *Faculty research:* Reaction mechanisms and kinetics, inorganic and organic synthesis, analytical chemistry, natural products.

University of Nebraska–Lincoln, Graduate College, College of Arts and Sciences, Department of Chemistry, Lincoln, NE 68588. Offers analytical chemistry (PhD); biochemistry (PhD); chemistry (MS); inorganic chemistry (PhD); materials chemistry (PhD); organic chemistry (PhD); physical chemistry (PhD). *Degree requirements:* For master's, one foreign language, thesis optional, departmental qualifying exam; for doctorate, one foreign language, comprehensive exam, thesis/dissertation, departmental qualifying exams. *Entrance requirements:* For master's and doctorate, GRE. Additional exam requirements/recommendations for international students: Required—TOEFL (minimum score 550 paper-based; 213 computer-based). Electronic applications accepted. *Faculty research:* Bioorganic and bioinorganic chemistry, biophysical and bioanalytical chemistry, structure-function of DNA and proteins, organometallics, mass spectrometry.

University of Notre Dame, Graduate School, College of Science, Department of Chemistry and Biochemistry, Notre Dame, IN 46556. Offers biochemistry (MS, PhD); inorganic chemistry (MS, PhD); organic chemistry (MS, PhD); physical chemistry (MS, PhD). Terminal master's awarded for partial completion of doctoral program. *Degree requirements:* For master's, comprehensive exam, thesis; for doctorate, thesis/dissertation, qualifying exam. *Entrance requirements:* For master's and doctorate, GRE General Test, GRE Subject Test (strongly recommended). Additional exam requirements/recommendations for international students: Required—TOEFL (minimum score 600 paper-based; 250 computer-based; 80 iBT). Electronic applications accepted. *Faculty research:* Reaction design and mechanistic studies; reactive intermediates; synthesis, structure and reactivity of organometallic cluster complexes and biologically active natural products; bioorganic chemistry; enzymology.

University of Regina, Faculty of Graduate Studies and Research, Faculty of Science, Department of Chemistry and Biochemistry, Regina, SK S4S 0A2, Canada. Offers analytical/environmental chemistry (M Sc, PhD); biophysics of biological interfaces (M Sc, PhD); enzymology/chemical biology (M Sc, PhD); inorganic/organometallic chemistry (M Sc, PhD); signal transduction and mechanisms of cancer cell regulation (M Sc, PhD); supramolecular organic photochemistry and photophysics (M Sc, PhD); synthetic organic chemistry (M Sc, PhD); theoretical/computational chemistry (M Sc, PhD). *Faculty:* 12 full-time (2 women). *Students:* 13 full-time (4 women), 1 (woman) part-time. 22 applicants, 50% accepted. In 2011, 1 master's, 2 doctorates awarded. *Degree requirements:* For master's, thesis; for doctorate, thesis/dissertation. *Entrance requirements:* Additional exam requirements/recommendations for international students: Required—TOEFL (minimum score 580 paper-based; 80 iBT), IELTS (minimum score 6.5). *Application deadline:* Applications are processed on a rolling basis. Application fee: $100. Electronic applications accepted. *Financial support:* In 2011–12, 3 fellowships (averaging $6,500 per year), 1 research assistantship (averaging $5,500 per year), 7 teaching assistantships (averaging $2,298 per year) were awarded; scholarships/grants also available. Financial award application deadline: 6/15. *Faculty research:* Asymmetric synthesis and methodology, theoretical and computational chemistry, biophysical biochemistry, analytical and environmental chemistry, chemical biology. *Unit head:* Dr. Lynn Mihichuk, Head, 306-585-4793, Fax: 306-337-2409, E-mail: lynn.mihichuk@uregina.ca. *Application contact:* Dr. Tanya Dahms, Graduate Program Coordinator, 306-585-4246, Fax: 306-337-2409, E-mail: tanya.dahms@uregina.ca. Web site: http://www.chem.uregina.ca/.

University of Southern Mississippi, Graduate School, College of Science and Technology, Department of Chemistry and Biochemistry, Hattiesburg, MS 39406-0001. Offers analytical chemistry (MS, PhD); biochemistry (MS, PhD); inorganic chemistry (MS, PhD); organic chemistry (MS, PhD); physical chemistry (MS, PhD). *Faculty:* 16 full-time (4 women). *Students:* 22 full-time (9 women), 4 part-time (3 women); includes 1 minority (Black or African American, non-Hispanic/Latino), 9 international. Average age 29. 43 applicants, 19% accepted, 5 enrolled. In 2011, 1 master's, 4 doctorates awarded. *Degree requirements:* For master's, comprehensive exam, thesis; for doctorate, comprehensive exam, thesis/dissertation. *Entrance requirements:* For master's, GRE General Test, minimum GPA of 2.75 in last 60 hours; for doctorate, GRE General Test, minimum GPA of 3.5. Additional exam requirements/recommendations for international students: Required—TOEFL, IELTS. *Application deadline:* For fall admission, 3/1 priority date for domestic students, 3/1 for international students. Applications are processed on a rolling basis. Application fee: $50. *Financial support:* In 2011–12, 3 research assistantships with full tuition reimbursements (averaging $17,000 per year), 19 teaching assistantships with full tuition reimbursements (averaging $20,700 per year) were awarded; fellowships, Federal Work-Study, institutionally sponsored loans, scholarships/grants, health care benefits, and unspecified assistantships also available. Support available to part-time students. Financial award application deadline: 3/15; financial award applicants required to submit FAFSA. *Faculty research:* Plant biochemistry, photo chemistry, polymer chemistry, x-ray analysis, enzyme chemistry. *Unit head:* Dr. Sabine Heinhorst, Chair, 601-266-4701, Fax: 601-266-6075. *Application contact:* Dr. Sabine Heinhorst, Graduate Coordinator, 601-266-4702, Fax: 601-266-6075. Web site: http://www.usm.edu/graduateschool/table.php.

University of South Florida, Graduate School, College of Arts and Sciences, Department of Chemistry, Tampa, FL 33620-9951. Offers analytical chemistry (MS, PhD); biochemistry (MS, PhD); computational chemistry (MS, PhD); environmental chemistry (MS, PhD); inorganic chemistry (MS, PhD); organic chemistry (MS); physical chemistry (MS, PhD); polymer chemistry (PhD). Part-time programs available. *Faculty:* 25 full-time (4 women), 9 part-time/adjunct (1 woman). *Students:* 118 full-time (46 women), 14 part-time (7 women); includes 28 minority (8 Black or African American, non-Hispanic/Latino; 11 Asian, non-Hispanic/Latino; 9 Hispanic/Latino), 58 international. Average age 29. 127 applicants, 31% accepted, 19 enrolled. In 2011, 3 master's, 16 doctorates awarded. Terminal master's awarded for partial completion of doctoral program. *Degree requirements:* For master's, comprehensive exam, thesis (for some programs); for doctorate, comprehensive exam, thesis/dissertation. *Entrance requirements:* For master's and doctorate, GRE General Test, minimum GPA of 3.0. Additional exam requirements/recommendations for international students: Required—TOEFL (minimum score 550 paper-based; 213 computer-based; 79 iBT) or IELTS (minimum score 6.5). *Application deadline:* For fall admission, 2/15 priority date for domestic students, 1/2 for international students; for spring admission, 10/1 priority date for domestic students, 6/1 for international students. Applications are processed on a rolling basis. Application fee: $30. Electronic applications accepted. *Financial support:* In 2011–12, 136 students received support, including 28 research assistantships with tuition reimbursements available (averaging $15,020 per year), 108 teaching assistantships with tuition reimbursements available (averaging $15,164 per year); unspecified assistantships also available. Financial award application deadline: 6/30. *Faculty research:* Synthesis, bio-organic chemistry, bioinorganic chemistry, environmental chemistry, NMR. *Total annual research expenditures:* $3.1 million. *Unit head:* Dr. Randy Larsen, Chairperson, 813-974-4129, Fax: 813-974-3203, E-mail: rlarsen@cas.usf.edu. *Application contact:* Patricia Muisener, Director, 813-974-1730, Fax: 813-974-3203, E-mail: muisener@cas.usf.edu. Web site: http://chemistry.usf.edu/.

The University of Tennessee, Graduate School, College of Arts and Sciences, Department of Chemistry, Knoxville, TN 37996. Offers analytical chemistry (MS, PhD); chemical physics (PhD); environmental chemistry (MS, PhD); inorganic chemistry (MS, PhD); organic chemistry (MS, PhD); physical chemistry (MS,

Peterson's Graduate Programs in the Physical Sciences, Mathematics, Agricultural Sciences, the Environment & Natural Resources 2013

facebook.com/petersonspublishing   **105**

Inorganic Chemistry

PhD); polymer chemistry (MS, PhD); theoretical chemistry (PhD). Part-time programs available. Terminal master's awarded for partial completion of doctoral program. *Degree requirements:* For master's, thesis; for doctorate, thesis/dissertation. *Entrance requirements:* For master's and doctorate, GRE General Test, minimum GPA of 2.7. Additional exam requirements/recommendations for international students: Required—TOEFL. Electronic applications accepted. *Expenses:* Tuition, state resident: full-time $8332; part-time $464 per credit hour. Tuition, nonresident: full-time $25,174; part-time $1400 per credit hour. *Required fees:* $1162; $56 per credit hour. Tuition and fees vary according to program.

The University of Texas at Austin, Graduate School, College of Natural Sciences, Department of Chemistry and Biochemistry, Austin, TX 78712-1111. Offers analytical chemistry (PhD); biochemistry (PhD); inorganic chemistry (PhD); organic chemistry (PhD); physical chemistry (PhD). *Entrance requirements:* For doctorate, GRE General Test. Application fee: $50 ($75 for international students). *Financial support:* Fellowships, research assistantships, teaching assistantships, and scholarships/grants available. Financial award application deadline: 2/1. *Unit head:* Dr. Richard M. Crooks, Chairman, 512-475-8674, E-mail: crooks@cm.utexas.edu. *Application contact:* Dr. Jennifer S. Brodbelt, Graduate Admissions Chair, 512-471-0028, E-mail: jbrodbelt@cm.utexas.edu. Web site: http://www.cm.utexas.edu/.

The University of Toledo, College of Graduate Studies, College of Natural Sciences and Mathematics, Department of Chemistry, Toledo, OH 43606-3390. Offers analytical chemistry (MS, PhD); biological chemistry (MS, PhD); inorganic chemistry (MS, PhD); organic chemistry (MS, PhD); physical chemistry (MS, PhD). Part-time programs available. *Faculty:* 22. *Students:* 56 full-time (18 women), 18 part-time (10 women); includes 4 minority (1 Black or African American, non-Hispanic/Latino; 1 Asian, non-Hispanic/Latino; 2 Hispanic/Latino), 43 international. Average age 27. 111 applicants, 17% accepted, 16 enrolled. In 2011, 4 master's, 6 doctorates awarded. *Degree requirements:* For master's, thesis (for some programs); for doctorate, thesis/dissertation. *Entrance requirements:* For master's and doctorate, GRE General Test, GRE Subject Test, minimum cumulative point-hour ratio of 2.7 for all previous academic work, three letters of recommendation, statement of purpose, transcripts from all prior institutions attended. Additional exam requirements/recommendations for international students: Required—TOEFL (minimum score 550 paper-based; 213 computer-based; 80 iBT), IELTS (minimum score 6.5). *Application deadline:* For fall admission, 1/15 priority date for domestic students, 1/15 for international students. Applications are processed on a rolling basis. Application fee: $45 ($75 for international students). Electronic applications accepted. *Financial support:* In 2011–12, 24 research assistantships with full and partial tuition reimbursements (averaging $17,218 per year) were awarded; fellowships with tuition reimbursements, Federal Work-Study, institutionally sponsored loans, scholarships/grants, tuition waivers (full), and unspecified assistantships also available. Support available to part-time students. *Faculty research:* Enzymology, materials chemistry, crystallography, theoretical chemistry. *Unit head:* Dr. Alan Pinkerton, Chair, 419-530-7902, Fax: 419-530-4033, E-mail: alan.pinkerton@utoledo.edu. *Application contact:* Graduate School Office, 419-530-4723, Fax: 419-530-4724, E-mail: grdsch@utnet.utoledo.edu. Web site: http://www.utoledo.edu/nsm/.

Vanderbilt University, Graduate School, Department of Chemistry, Nashville, TN 37240-1001. Offers analytical chemistry (MAT, MS, PhD); inorganic chemistry (MAT, MS, PhD); organic chemistry (MAT, MS, PhD); physical chemistry (MAT, MS, PhD); theoretical chemistry (MAT, MS, PhD). *Faculty:* 21 full-time (3 women). *Students:* 114 full-time (43 women), 2 part-time (0 women); includes 16 minority (6 Black or African American, non-Hispanic/Latino; 1 American Indian or Alaska Native, non-Hispanic/Latino; 3 Asian, non-Hispanic/Latino; 1 Hispanic/Latino; 5 Two or more races, non-Hispanic/Latino), 18 international. Average age 26. 420 applicants, 12% accepted, 18 enrolled. In 2011, 4 master's, 17 doctorates awarded. Terminal master's awarded for partial completion of doctoral program. *Degree requirements:* For master's, thesis; for doctorate, thesis/dissertation, area, qualifying, and final exams. *Entrance requirements:* For master's and doctorate, GRE General Test, GRE Subject Test (recommended). Additional exam requirements/recommendations for international students: Required—TOEFL (minimum score 570 paper-based; 230 computer-based; 88 iBT). *Application deadline:* For fall admission, 1/15 for domestic and international students. Application fee: $0. Electronic applications accepted. *Financial support:* Fellowships with full and partial tuition reimbursements, research assistantships with full tuition reimbursements, teaching assistantships with full tuition reimbursements, Federal Work-Study, institutionally sponsored loans, scholarships/grants, traineeships, and health care benefits available. Financial award application deadline: 1/15; financial award applicants required to submit CSS PROFILE or FAFSA. *Faculty research:* Chemical synthesis; mechanistic, theoretical, bioorganic, analytical, and spectroscopic chemistry. *Unit head:* Dr. Mike P. Stone, Chair, 615-322-2589, Fax: 615-343-1234, E-mail: michael.p.stone@vanderbilt.edu. *Application contact:* Dr. Carmelo J. Rizzo, Director of Graduate Studies, 615-322-6100, Fax: 615-343-1234, E-mail: c.j.rizzo@vanderbilt.edu. Web site: http://www.vanderbilt.edu/AnS/Chemistry/grad/.

Virginia Commonwealth University, Graduate School, College of Humanities and Sciences, Department of Chemistry, Richmond, VA 23284-9005. Offers analytical chemistry (MS, PhD); chemical physics (PhD); inorganic chemistry (MS,

PhD); organic chemistry (MS, PhD); physical chemistry (MS, PhD). Part-time programs available. *Students:* 49 full-time (20 women), 19 part-time (8 women); includes 10 minority (3 Black or African American, non-Hispanic/Latino; 5 Asian, non-Hispanic/Latino; 1 Hispanic/Latino; 1 Two or more races, non-Hispanic/Latino), 26 international. 56 applicants, 41% accepted, 11 enrolled. In 2011, 3 master's, 8 doctorates awarded. Terminal master's awarded for partial completion of doctoral program. *Degree requirements:* For master's, thesis; for doctorate, thesis/dissertation, comprehensive cumulative exams, research proposal. *Entrance requirements:* For master's, GRE General Test, 30 undergraduate credits in chemistry; for doctorate, GRE General Test. Additional exam requirements/recommendations for international students: Required—TOEFL (minimum score 600 paper-based; 250 computer-based; 100 iBT) or IELTS (minimum score 6.5). *Application deadline:* For fall admission, 3/15 for domestic students; for spring admission, 11/15 for domestic students. Applications are processed on a rolling basis. Application fee: $50. Electronic applications accepted. *Expenses:* Tuition, state resident: full-time $9133; part-time $507 per credit. Tuition, nonresident: full-time $18,777; part-time $1043 per credit. *Required fees:* $77 per credit. Tuition and fees vary according to degree level, campus/location, program and student level. *Financial support:* Fellowships, research assistantships, teaching assistantships, career-related internships or fieldwork, and institutionally sponsored loans available. Support available to part-time students. Financial award application deadline: 7/1; financial award applicants required to submit FAFSA. *Faculty research:* Physical, organic, inorganic, analytical, and polymer chemistry; chemical physics. *Unit head:* Dr. Scott Gronert, Chair, 804-828-1298, Fax: 804-828-8599, E-mail: sgronert@vcu.edu. *Application contact:* Dr. Maryanne M. Collinson, Chair, Graduate Recruiting and Admissions Committee, 804-828-7509, E-mail: mselshal@vcu.edu. Web site: http://www.has.vcu.edu/che/.

Wake Forest University, Graduate School of Arts and Sciences, Department of Chemistry, Winston-Salem, NC 27109. Offers analytical chemistry (MS, PhD); inorganic chemistry (MS, PhD); organic chemistry (MS, PhD); physical chemistry (MS, PhD). Part-time programs available. *Degree requirements:* For master's, one foreign language, comprehensive exam, thesis; for doctorate, 2 foreign languages, comprehensive exam, thesis/dissertation. *Entrance requirements:* For master's and doctorate, GRE General Test. Additional exam requirements/recommendations for international students: Required—TOEFL (minimum score 213 computer-based). Electronic applications accepted.

Wesleyan University, Graduate Programs, Department of Chemistry, Middletown, CT 06459. Offers biochemistry (MA, PhD); chemical physics (MA, PhD); inorganic chemistry (MA, PhD); organic chemistry (MA, PhD); physical chemistry (MA, PhD); theoretical chemistry (MA, PhD). Terminal master's awarded for partial completion of doctoral program. *Degree requirements:* For master's, thesis, proposal; for doctorate, thesis/dissertation, proposal. *Entrance requirements:* For doctorate, GRE General Test, 3 recommendations. Additional exam requirements/recommendations for international students: Required—TOEFL. Electronic applications accepted.

West Virginia University, Eberly College of Arts and Sciences, Department of Chemistry, Morgantown, WV 26506. Offers analytical chemistry (MS, PhD); inorganic chemistry (MS, PhD); organic chemistry (MS, PhD); physical chemistry (MS, PhD); theoretical chemistry (MS, PhD). Part-time programs available. Postbaccalaureate distance learning degree programs offered (no on-campus study). Terminal master's awarded for partial completion of doctoral program. *Degree requirements:* For master's, thesis; for doctorate, thesis/dissertation. *Entrance requirements:* For master's, GRE General Test, GRE Subject Test (recommended), minimum GPA of 2.5; for doctorate, GRE General Test, GRE Subject Test (recommended), minimum GPA of 2.75. Additional exam requirements/recommendations for international students: Required—TOEFL. Electronic applications accepted. *Faculty research:* Analysis of proteins, drug interactions, solids and effluents by advanced separation methods; new synthetic strategies for complex organic molecules; synthesis and structural characterization of metal complexes for polymerization catalysis, nonlinear science, spectroscopy.

Yale University, Graduate School of Arts and Sciences, Department of Chemistry, New Haven, CT 06520. Offers biophysical chemistry (PhD); inorganic chemistry (PhD); organic chemistry (PhD); physical and theoretical chemistry (PhD). *Degree requirements:* For doctorate, thesis/dissertation. *Entrance requirements:* For doctorate, GRE General Test, GRE Subject Test. Additional exam requirements/recommendations for international students: Required—TOEFL.

Youngstown State University, Graduate School, College of Science, Technology, Engineering and Mathematics, Department of Chemistry, Youngstown, OH 44555-0001. Offers analytical chemistry (MS); biochemistry (MS); chemistry education (MS); inorganic chemistry (MS); organic chemistry (MS); physical chemistry (MS). Part-time programs available. *Degree requirements:* For master's, thesis. *Entrance requirements:* For master's, bachelor's degree in chemistry, minimum GPA of 2.7. Additional exam requirements/recommendations for international students: Required—TOEFL. *Faculty research:* Analysis of antioxidants, chromatography, defects and disorder in crystalline oxides, hydrogen bonding, novel organic and organometallic materials.

106 facebook.com/petersonspublishing

Peterson's Graduate Programs in the Physical Sciences, Mathematics, Agricultural Sciences, the Environment & Natural Resources 2013

Organic Chemistry

Auburn University, Graduate School, College of Sciences and Mathematics, Department of Chemistry and Biochemistry, Auburn University, AL 36849. Offers analytical chemistry (MS, PhD); biochemistry (MS, PhD); inorganic chemistry (MS, PhD); organic chemistry (MS, PhD); physical chemistry (MS, PhD). Part-time programs available. *Faculty:* 28 full-time (5 women), 1 part-time/adjunct (0 women). *Students:* 37 full-time (14 women), 30 part-time (15 women); includes 6 minority (3 Black or African American, non-Hispanic/Latino; 1 American Indian or Alaska Native, non-Hispanic/Latino; 1 Asian, non-Hispanic/Latino; 1 Hispanic/Latino), 41 international. Average age 28. 38 applicants, 39% accepted, 12 enrolled. In 2011, 1 master's, 9 doctorates awarded. *Degree requirements:* For master's, thesis (for some programs); for doctorate, thesis/dissertation, oral and written exams. *Entrance requirements:* For master's and doctorate, GRE General Test. *Application deadline:* For fall admission, 7/7 for domestic students; for spring admission, 11/24 for domestic students. Applications are processed on a rolling basis. Application fee: $50 ($60 for international students). Electronic applications accepted. *Expenses:* Tuition, state resident: full-time $7290; part-time $405 per credit hour. Tuition, nonresident: full-time $21,870; part-time $1215 per credit hour. *International tuition:* $22,000 full-time. *Required fees:* $1402. *Financial support:* Fellowships, research assistantships, and teaching assistantships available. Financial award application deadline: 3/15; financial award applicants required to submit FAFSA. *Unit head:* Dr. J. V. Ortiz, Chair, 334-844-4043, Fax: 334-844-4043. *Application contact:* Dr. George Flowers, Dean of the Graduate School, 334-844-2125. Web site: http://www.auburn.edu/cosam/departments/chemistry/.

Boston College, Graduate School of Arts and Sciences, Department of Chemistry, Chestnut Hill, MA 02467-3800. Offers biochemistry (PhD); inorganic chemistry (PhD); organic chemistry (PhD); physical chemistry (PhD); science education (MST). *Degree requirements:* For doctorate, thesis/dissertation, qualifying exam. *Entrance requirements:* For doctorate, GRE General Test, GRE Subject Test. Additional exam requirements/recommendations for international students: Required—TOEFL (minimum score 600 paper-based; 250 computer-based; 100 iBT). Electronic applications accepted.

Brandeis University, Graduate School of Arts and Sciences, Department of Chemistry, Waltham, MA 02454. Offers inorganic chemistry (MS, PhD); organic chemistry (MS, PhD); physical chemistry (MS, PhD). Terminal master's awarded for partial completion of doctoral program. *Degree requirements:* For master's, thesis, 1 year of residency; for doctorate, one foreign language, thesis/dissertation, 3 years of residency, 2 seminars, qualifying exams. *Entrance requirements:* For master's and doctorate, GRE General Test, resume, letters of recommendation. Additional exam requirements/recommendations for international students: Required—TOEFL (minimum score 600 paper-based; 250 computer-based; 100 iBT); Recommended—IELTS (minimum score 7). Electronic applications accepted. *Faculty research:* Oscillating chemical reactions, molecular recognition systems, protein crystallography, synthesis of natural product spectroscopy and magnetic resonance.

California State University, Los Angeles, Graduate Studies, College of Natural and Social Sciences, Department of Chemistry and Biochemistry, Los Angeles, CA 90032-8530. Offers analytical chemistry (MS); biochemistry (MS); chemistry (MS); inorganic chemistry (MS); organic chemistry (MS); physical chemistry (MS). Part-time and evening/weekend programs available. *Faculty:* 4 part-time/adjunct (1 woman). *Students:* 22 full-time (14 women), 24 part-time (11 women); includes 30 minority (4 Black or African American, non-Hispanic/Latino; 7 Asian, non-Hispanic/Latino; 19 Hispanic/Latino), 7 international. Average age 29. 60 applicants, 48% accepted, 17 enrolled. In 2011, 15 master's awarded. *Degree requirements:* For master's, one foreign language, comprehensive exam or thesis. *Entrance requirements:* Additional exam requirements/recommendations for international students: Required—TOEFL. *Application deadline:* For fall admission, 5/1 for domestic and international students. Applications are processed on a rolling basis. Application fee: $55. *Expenses:* Tuition, state resident: full-time $8225. *Financial support:* Federal Work-Study available. Support available to part-time students. Financial award application deadline: 3/1. *Faculty research:* Intercalation of heavy metal, carborane chemistry, conductive polymers and fabrics, titanium reagents, computer modeling and synthesis. *Unit head:* Dr. Robert L. Vellanoweth, Chair, 323-343-2300, Fax: 323-343-6490, E-mail: rvellan@calstatela.edu. *Application contact:* Dr. Karin Brown, Acting Associate Dean of Graduate Studies, 323-343-3820 Ext. 3827, Fax: 323-343-5653, E-mail: kbrown5@calstatela.edu. Web site: http://www.calstatela.edu/dept/chem/index.htm.

Carnegie Mellon University, Mellon College of Science, Department of Chemistry, Pittsburgh, PA 15213-3891. Offers biotechnology and management (MS); chemistry (PhD), including bioinorganic, bioorganic, organic and materials, biophysics and spectroscopy, computational and theoretical, polymer; colloids, polymers and surfaces (MS). Part-time programs available. Terminal master's awarded for partial completion of doctoral program. *Degree requirements:* For doctorate, thesis/dissertation, departmental qualifying and oral exams, teaching experience. *Entrance requirements:* For master's, GRE General Test; for doctorate, GRE General Test, GRE Subject Test. Additional exam requirements/recommendations for international students: Required—TOEFL. Electronic

applications accepted. *Faculty research:* Physical and theoretical chemistry, chemical synthesis, biophysical/bioinorganic chemistry.

Cleveland State University, College of Graduate Studies, College of Sciences and Health Professions, Department of Chemistry, Cleveland, OH 44115. Offers analytical chemistry (MS); clinical chemistry (MS); clinical/bioanalytical chemistry (PhD), including cellular and molecular medicine, clinical chemistry, clinical/bioanalytical chemistry; environmental chemistry (MS); inorganic chemistry (MS); pharmaceutical/organic chemistry (MS); physical chemistry (MS). Part-time and evening/weekend programs available. *Faculty:* 12 full-time (0 women). *Students:* 17 full-time (8 women), 87 part-time (36 women); includes 6 minority (5 Black or African American, non-Hispanic/Latino; 1 Asian, non-Hispanic/Latino), 74 international. Average age 27. 143 applicants, 59% accepted, 22 enrolled. In 2011, 14 master's, 10 doctorates awarded. *Median time to degree:* Of those who began their doctoral program in fall 2003, 67% received their degree in 8 years or less. *Degree requirements:* For master's, thesis optional; for doctorate, comprehensive exam, thesis/dissertation. *Entrance requirements:* For master's and doctorate, GRE General Test. Additional exam requirements/recommendations for international students: Required—TOEFL (minimum score 525 paper-based; 197 computer-based; 65 iBT). *Application deadline:* For fall admission, 1/15 priority date for domestic students, 1/15 for international students. Applications are processed on a rolling basis. Application fee: $30. Electronic applications accepted. *Expenses:* Tuition, state resident: full-time $6416; part-time $494 per credit hour. Tuition, nonresident: full-time $12,074; part-time $929 per credit hour. *Financial support:* In 2011–12, 44 students received support, including 5 fellowships with full tuition reimbursements available (averaging $30,000 per year), 13 research assistantships with full tuition reimbursements available (averaging $20,000 per year), 24 teaching assistantships with full tuition reimbursements available (averaging $18,500 per year); scholarships/grants and unspecified assistantships also available. Financial award application deadline: 1/15. *Faculty research:* Bioanalytical techniques and molecular diagnostics, glycoproteomics and antithrombotic agents, drug discovery and innovation, analytical pharmacology, inflammatory disease research. *Total annual research expenditures:* $3 million. *Unit head:* Dr. David J. Anderson, Interim Chair, 216-687-2467, Fax: 216-687-9298, E-mail: d.anderson@csuohio.edu. *Application contact:* Richelle P. Emery, Administrative Coordinator, 216-687-2457, Fax: 216-687-9298, E-mail: r.emery@csuohio.edu. Web site: http://www.csuohio.edu/chemistry/.

Columbia University, Graduate School of Arts and Sciences, Division of Natural Sciences, Department of Chemistry, New York, NY 10027. Offers chemical physics (M Phil, PhD); inorganic chemistry (M Phil, MA, PhD); organic chemistry (M Phil, MA, PhD); MD/PhD. *Degree requirements:* For master's, one foreign language, teaching experience, oral/written exams (M Phil); for doctorate, one foreign language, thesis/dissertation. *Entrance requirements:* For master's and doctorate, GRE General Test, GRE Subject Test. Additional exam requirements/recommendations for international students: Required—TOEFL. *Faculty research:* Biophysics.

Cornell University, Graduate School, Graduate Fields of Arts and Sciences, Field of Chemistry and Chemical Biology, Ithaca, NY 14853-0001. Offers analytical chemistry (PhD); bio-organic chemistry (PhD); biophysical chemistry (PhD); chemical biology (PhD); chemical physics (PhD); inorganic chemistry (PhD); materials chemistry (PhD); organic chemistry (PhD); organometallic chemistry (PhD); physical chemistry (PhD); polymer chemistry (PhD); theoretical chemistry (PhD). *Faculty:* 46 full-time (3 women). *Students:* 151 full-time (67 women); includes 16 minority (13 Asian, non-Hispanic/Latino; 2 Hispanic/Latino; 1 Two or more races, non-Hispanic/Latino), 48 international. Average age 25. 297 applicants, 35% accepted, 29 enrolled. In 2011, 22 doctorates awarded. *Degree requirements:* For doctorate, comprehensive exam, thesis/dissertation. *Entrance requirements:* For doctorate, GRE General Test, GRE Subject Test (chemistry), 3 letters of recommendation. Additional exam requirements/recommendations for international students: Required—TOEFL (minimum score 600 paper-based; 250 computer-based; 77 iBT). *Application deadline:* For fall admission, 1/10 for domestic students. Application fee: $95. Electronic applications accepted. *Financial support:* In 2011–12, 21 fellowships with full tuition reimbursements, 63 research assistantships with full tuition reimbursements, 59 teaching assistantships with full tuition reimbursements were awarded; institutionally sponsored loans, scholarships/grants, health care benefits, tuition waivers (full and partial), and unspecified assistantships also available. Financial award applicants required to submit FAFSA. *Faculty research:* Analytical, organic, inorganic, physical, materials, chemical biology. *Unit head:* Director of Graduate Studies, 607-255-4139, Fax: 607-255-4137. *Application contact:* Graduate Field Assistant, 607-255-4139, Fax: 607-255-4137, E-mail: chemgrad@cornell.edu. Web site: http://www.gradschool.cornell.edu/fields.php?id-26&a-2.

Eastern New Mexico University, Graduate School, College of Liberal Arts and Sciences, Department of Physical Sciences, Portales, NM 88130. Offers chemistry (MS), including analytical, biochemistry, inorganic, organic, physical. Part-time programs available. *Faculty:* 6 full-time (0 women). *Students:* 11 part-time (5 women), 9 international. Average age 25. 25 applicants, 44% accepted, 4 enrolled. In 2011, 5 master's awarded. *Degree requirements:* For master's, thesis

Peterson's Graduate Programs in the Physical Sciences, Mathematics, Agricultural Sciences, the Environment & Natural Resources 2013

facebook.com/petersonspublishing   **107**

Organic Chemistry

optional, seminar, oral and written comprehensive exams. *Entrance requirements:* For master's, ACS placement examination, minimum GPA of 3.0; 2 letters of recommendation; personal statement of career goals; bachelor's degree with one year minimum each of general, organic, and analytical chemistry. Additional exam requirements/recommendations for international students: Required—TOEFL (minimum score 550 paper-based; 213 computer-based; 79 iBT), IELTS (minimum score 6). *Application deadline:* For fall admission, 7/20 priority date for domestic students, 6/20 for international students; for spring admission, 12/15 priority date for domestic students, 11/15 for international students. Applications are processed on a rolling basis. Application fee: $10. Electronic applications accepted. *Financial support:* In 2011–12, 1 research assistantship with partial tuition reimbursement (averaging $8,500 per year), 10 teaching assistantships with partial tuition reimbursements (averaging $8,500 per year) were awarded; career-related internships or fieldwork and unspecified assistantships also available. Support available to part-time students. Financial award application deadline: 3/1; financial award applicants required to submit FAFSA. *Faculty research:* Synfuel, electrochemistry, protein chemistry. *Unit head:* Dr. Juacho Yan, Graduate Coordinator, 575-562-2494, Fax: 575-562-2192, E-mail: juacho.yan@enmu.edu. *Application contact:* Sharon Potter, Department Secretary, Biology and Physical Sciences, 575-562-2174, Fax: 575-562-2192, E-mail: sharon.potter@enmu.edu. Web site: http://liberal-arts.enmu.edu/sciences/grad-chemistry.shtml.

Florida State University, The Graduate School, College of Arts and Sciences, Department of Chemistry and Biochemistry, Tallahassee, FL 32306-4390. Offers analytical chemistry (MS, PhD); biochemistry (MS, PhD); inorganic chemistry (MS, PhD); materials chemistry (PhD); organic chemistry (MS, PhD); physical chemistry (MS, PhD). *Faculty:* 35 full-time (5 women), 1 (woman) part-time/adjunct. *Students:* 138 full-time (52 women), 8 part-time (1 woman); includes 14 minority (6 Black or African American, non-Hispanic/Latino; 3 Asian, non-Hispanic/Latino; 2 Hispanic/Latino; 3 Two or more races, non-Hispanic/Latino), 63 international. Average age 25. 147 applicants, 40% accepted, 28 enrolled. In 2011, 10 master's, 24 doctorates awarded. Terminal master's awarded for partial completion of doctoral program. *Median time to degree:* Of those who began their doctoral program in fall 2003, 58% received their degree in 8 years or less. *Degree requirements:* For master's, comprehensive exam (for some programs), thesis (for some programs); for doctorate, comprehensive exam (for some programs), thesis/dissertation. *Entrance requirements:* For master's and doctorate, GRE General Test, minimum B average in undergraduate course work. Additional exam requirements/recommendations for international students: Required—TOEFL (minimum score 550 paper-based; 213 computer-based; 80 iBT). *Application deadline:* For fall admission, 12/15 priority date for domestic students, 12/15 for international students; for spring admission, 9/15 for domestic and international students. Applications are processed on a rolling basis. Application fee: $30. Electronic applications accepted. *Expenses:* Contact institution. *Financial support:* In 2011–12, 140 students received support, including fellowships with full tuition reimbursements available (averaging $20,000 per year), 50 research assistantships with full tuition reimbursements available (averaging $20,000 per year), 100 teaching assistantships with full tuition reimbursements available (averaging $20,000 per year). Financial award application deadline: 12/15; financial award applicants required to submit FAFSA. *Faculty research:* Materials synthesis including polymers, natural products; catalysis, NMR; mass spectrometry; optical spectroscopy, scattering techniques; computational chemistry, separation technology; nanostructured materials including metallic, semiconducting and magnetic nanocrystals; nanoscience interfaced with biology; supramolecular materials for solar energy conversion. *Total annual research expenditures:* $9.9 million. *Unit head:* Dr. Timothy Logan, Chairman, 850-644-1244, Fax: 850-644-8281, E-mail: gradinfo@chem.fsu.edu. *Application contact:* Dr. Michael Shatruk, Chair, Graduate Admissions Committee, 888-525-9286, Fax: 850-644-0465, E-mail: gradinfo@chem.fsu.edu. Web site: http://www.chem.fsu.edu/.

Georgetown University, Graduate School of Arts and Sciences, Department of Chemistry, Washington, DC 20057. Offers analytical chemistry (PhD); biochemistry (PhD); computational chemistry (PhD); inorganic chemistry (PhD); materials chemistry (PhD); organic chemistry (PhD); physical chemistry (PhD); theoretical chemistry (PhD). Terminal master's awarded for partial completion of doctoral program. *Degree requirements:* For doctorate, comprehensive exam, thesis/dissertation. *Entrance requirements:* For doctorate, GRE General Test. Additional exam requirements/recommendations for international students: Required—TOEFL.

The George Washington University, Columbian College of Arts and Sciences, Department of Chemistry, Washington, DC 20052. Offers analytical chemistry (MS, PhD); inorganic chemistry (MS, PhD); materials science (MS, PhD); organic chemistry (MS, PhD); physical chemistry (MS, PhD). Part-time and evening/weekend programs available. *Faculty:* 16 full-time (5 women), 5 part-time/adjunct (2 women). *Students:* 22 full-time (10 women), 10 part-time (7 women); includes 4 minority (3 Asian, non-Hispanic/Latino; 1 Hispanic/Latino), 7 international. Average age 27. 55 applicants, 42% accepted, 8 enrolled. In 2011, 4 master's, 3 doctorates awarded. Terminal master's awarded for partial completion of doctoral program. *Degree requirements:* For master's, comprehensive exam, thesis or alternative; for doctorate, thesis/dissertation, general exam. *Entrance requirements:* For master's and doctorate, GRE General Test, interview, minimum GPA of 3.0. Additional exam requirements/recommendations for international students: Required—TOEFL (minimum score 550 paper-based; 213 computer-based; 80 iBT). *Application deadline:* For fall admission, 1/15 priority date for

domestic students, 1/15 for international students; for spring admission, 9/1 priority date for domestic students, 9/1 for international students. Applications are processed on a rolling basis. Application fee: $75. Electronic applications accepted. *Financial support:* In 2011–12, 27 students received support. Fellowships with tuition reimbursements available, research assistantships, teaching assistantships with tuition reimbursements available, Federal Work-Study, and tuition waivers available. Financial award application deadline: 1/15. *Unit head:* Dr. Michael King, Chair, 202-994-6488. *Application contact:* Information Contact, 202-994-6121, E-mail: gwchem@gwu.edu. Web site: http://www.gwu.edu/~gwchem/.

Harvard University, Graduate School of Arts and Sciences, Department of Chemistry and Chemical Biology, Cambridge, MA 02138. Offers biochemical chemistry (PhD); inorganic chemistry (PhD); organic chemistry (PhD); physical chemistry (PhD). *Degree requirements:* For doctorate, thesis/dissertation, cumulative exams. *Entrance requirements:* For doctorate, GRE General Test, GRE Subject Test. Additional exam requirements/recommendations for international students: Required—TOEFL. *Expenses: Tuition:* Full-time $36,304. *Required fees:* $1186. Full-time tuition and fees vary according to program.

See Display on page 67 and Close-Up on page 125.

Howard University, Graduate School, Department of Chemistry, Washington, DC 20059-0002. Offers analytical chemistry (MS, PhD); atmospheric (MS, PhD); biochemistry (MS, PhD); environmental (MS, PhD); inorganic chemistry (MS, PhD); organic chemistry (MS, PhD); physical chemistry (MS, PhD). Terminal master's awarded for partial completion of doctoral program. *Degree requirements:* For master's, comprehensive exam, thesis, teaching experience; for doctorate, comprehensive exam, thesis/dissertation, teaching experience. *Entrance requirements:* For master's, GRE General Test, minimum GPA of 2.7; for doctorate, GRE General Test, minimum GPA of 3.0. Additional exam requirements/recommendations for international students: Required—TOEFL. Electronic applications accepted. *Faculty research:* Synthetic organics, materials, natural products, mass spectrometry.

Indiana University Bloomington, University Graduate School, College of Arts and Sciences, Department of Chemistry, Bloomington, IN 47405. Offers analytical chemistry (PhD); chemical biology chemistry (PhD); chemistry (MAT); inorganic chemistry (PhD); materials chemistry (PhD); organic chemistry (PhD); physical chemistry (PhD). *Faculty:* 42 full-time (4 women). *Students:* 200 full-time (82 women), 3 part-time (0 women); includes 18 minority (7 Black or African American, non-Hispanic/Latino; 8 Asian, non-Hispanic/Latino; 1 Hispanic/Latino; 1 Native Hawaiian or other Pacific Islander, non-Hispanic/Latino; 1 Two or more races, non-Hispanic/Latino), 63 international. Average age 27. 290 applicants, 49% accepted, 46 enrolled. In 2011, 11 master's, 20 doctorates awarded. Terminal master's awarded for partial completion of doctoral program. *Median time to degree:* Of those who began their doctoral program in fall 2003, 49% received their degree in 8 years or less. *Degree requirements:* For master's, thesis; for doctorate, thesis/dissertation. *Entrance requirements:* For master's and doctorate, GRE General Test, GRE Subject Test. Additional exam requirements/recommendations for international students: Required—TOEFL. *Application deadline:* For fall admission, 1/15 priority date for domestic students, 12/15 for international students. Applications are processed on a rolling basis. Application fee: $55 ($65 for international students). *Financial support:* In 2011–12, 200 students received support, including 10 fellowships with full tuition reimbursements available, 76 research assistantships with full tuition reimbursements available, 111 teaching assistantships with full tuition reimbursements available; Federal Work-Study and institutionally sponsored loans also available. *Faculty research:* Synthesis of complex natural products, organic reaction mechanisms, organic electrochemistry, transitive-metal chemistry, solid-state and surface chemistry. *Total annual research expenditures:* $7.7 million. *Unit head:* David Giedroc, Chairperson, 812-855-6239, E-mail: chemchair@indiana.edu. *Application contact:* Daniel Mindiola, Director of Graduate Admissions, 812-855-2069, Fax: 812-855-8385, E-mail: mindiola@indiana.edu. Web site: http://www.chem.indiana.edu/.

Instituto Tecnológico y de Estudios Superiores de Monterrey, Campus Monterrey, Graduate and Research Division, Program in Natural and Social Sciences, Monterrey, Mexico. Offers biotechnology (MS); chemistry (MS, PhD); communications (MS); education (MA). Part-time programs available. *Degree requirements:* For master's, one foreign language, thesis; for doctorate, one foreign language, thesis/dissertation. *Entrance requirements:* For master's, EXADEP; for doctorate, EXADEP, master's degree in related field. Additional exam requirements/recommendations for international students: Required—TOEFL. *Faculty research:* Cultural industries, mineral substances, bioremediation, food processing, CQ in industrial chemical processing.

Iowa State University of Science and Technology, Program in Organic Chemistry, Ames, IA 50011-3011. Offers MS, PhD. *Entrance requirements:* Additional exam requirements/recommendations for international students: Required—TOEFL (minimum score 570 paper-based; 89 iBT), IELTS (minimum score 6.5). *Application deadline:* For fall admission, 2/1 for domestic students. Electronic applications accepted. *Unit head:* Theresa Windus, Director of Graduate Education, 800-521-2436, Fax: 515-294-0105, E-mail: chemgrad@iastate.edu. *Application contact:* Lynette Edsall, Application Contact, 515-294-2436, Fax: 515-294-0105, E-mail: grad_admissions@iastate.edu. Web site: http://www.chem.iastate.edu.

Kansas State University, Graduate School, College of Arts and Sciences, Department of Chemistry, Manhattan, KS 66506. Offers analytical chemistry (MS); biological chemistry (MS); chemistry (PhD); inorganic chemistry (MS); materials chemistry (MS); organic chemistry (MS); physical chemistry (MS). *Faculty:* 17 full-time (2 women). *Students:* 63 full-time (28 women), 4 part-time (0 women); includes 2 minority (1 Black or African American, non-Hispanic/Latino; 1 Asian, non-Hispanic/Latino, 55 international. Average age 28. 119 applicants, 34% accepted, 15 enrolled. In 2011, 2 master's, 10 doctorates awarded. Terminal master's awarded for partial completion of doctoral program. *Degree requirements:* For master's, thesis; for doctorate, thesis/dissertation. *Entrance requirements:* For master's and doctorate, GRE, minimum GPA of 3.0. Additional exam requirements/recommendations for international students: Required—TOEFL (minimum score 550 paper-based; 213 computer-based). *Application deadline:* For fall admission, 2/1 priority date for domestic students, 2/1 for international students; for spring admission, 8/1 priority date for domestic students, 8/1 for international students. Applications are processed on a rolling basis. Application fee: $40 ($55 for international students). Electronic applications accepted. *Financial support:* In 2011–12, 39 research assistantships (averaging $18,182 per year), 24 teaching assistantships with full tuition reimbursements (averaging $18,106 per year) were awarded; institutionally sponsored loans and scholarships/grants also available. Support available to part-time students. Financial award application deadline: 3/1; financial award applicants required to submit FAFSA. *Faculty research:* Inorganic chemistry, organic and biological chemistry, analytical chemistry, physical chemistry, materials chemistry and nanotechnology. *Total annual research expenditures:* $2.4 million. *Unit head:* Eric Maatta, Head, 785-532-6665, Fax: 785-532-6666, E-mail: eam@ksu.edu. *Application contact:* Christer Aakeroy, Director, 785-532-6096, Fax: 785-532-6666, E-mail: aakeroy@ksu.edu. Web site: http://www.k-state.edu/chem/.

Kent State University, College of Arts and Sciences, Department of Chemistry and Biochemistry, Kent, OH 44242-0001. Offers analytical chemistry (MS, PhD); biochemistry (MS, PhD); chemistry (MA); inorganic chemistry (MS, PhD); organic chemistry (MS, PhD); physical chemistry (MS, PhD). Terminal master's awarded for partial completion of doctoral program. *Degree requirements:* For master's, comprehensive exam, thesis; for doctorate, comprehensive exam, thesis/ dissertation. *Entrance requirements:* For master's and doctorate, placement exam, GRE General Test, GRE Subject Test (recommended), minimum GPA of 2.75. Additional exam requirements/recommendations for international students: Required—TOEFL (minimum score 525 paper-based; 71 iBT). Electronic applications accepted. *Expenses:* Tuition, state resident: full-time $8136; part-time $452 per credit hour. Tuition, nonresident: full-time $14,292; part-time $794 per credit hour. *Faculty research:* Biological chemistry, materials chemistry, molecular spectroscopy.

See Display on page 70 and Close-Up on page 127.

Laurentian University, School of Graduate Studies and Research, Programme in Chemistry and Biochemistry, Sudbury, ON P3E 2C6, Canada. Offers analytical chemistry (M Sc); biochemistry (M Sc); environmental chemistry (M Sc); organic chemistry (M Sc); physical/theoretical chemistry (M Sc). Part-time programs available. *Degree requirements:* For master's, thesis or alternative. *Entrance requirements:* For master's, honors degree with minimum second class. *Faculty research:* Cell cycle checkpoints, kinetic modeling, toxicology to metal stress, quantum chemistry, biogeochemistry metal speciation.

Marquette University, Graduate School, College of Arts and Sciences, Department of Chemistry, Milwaukee, WI 53201-1881. Offers analytical chemistry (MS, PhD); bioanalytical chemistry (MS, PhD); biophysical chemistry (MS, PhD); chemical physics (MS, PhD); inorganic chemistry (MS, PhD); organic chemistry (MS, PhD); physical chemistry (MS, PhD). Part-time programs available. *Faculty:* 29 full-time (4 women), 1 (woman) part-time/adjunct. *Students:* 42 full-time (11 women), 2 part-time (0 women); includes 5 minority (2 Black or African American, non-Hispanic/Latino; 3 Asian, non-Hispanic/Latino), 31 international. Average age 29. 18 applicants, 100% accepted, 10 enrolled. In 2011, 5 master's, 7 doctorates awarded. Terminal master's awarded for partial completion of doctoral program. *Degree requirements:* For master's, comprehensive exam; for doctorate, thesis/ dissertation, cumulative exams. *Entrance requirements:* For master's and doctorate, official transcripts from all current and previous colleges/universities except Marquette, three letters of recommendation from individuals familiar with the applicant's academic work. Additional exam requirements/recommendations for international students: Required—TOEFL (minimum score 530 paper-based; 78 computer-based). *Application deadline:* Applications are processed on a rolling basis. Application fee: $50. Electronic applications accepted. *Expenses: Tuition:* Full-time $17,010; part-time $945 per credit hour. Tuition and fees vary according to program. *Financial support:* In 2011–12, 41 students received support, including 2 fellowships (averaging $17,134 per year), 30 teaching assistantships with full tuition reimbursements available (averaging $20,295 per year); research assistantships, scholarships/grants, health care benefits, tuition waivers (full and partial), and unspecified assistantships also available. Support available to part-time students. Financial award application deadline: 2/15. *Faculty research:* Inorganic complexes, laser Raman spectroscopy, organic synthesis, synthetic bioinorganic chemistry, electro-active organic molecules. *Total annual research expenditures:* $2.1 million. *Unit head:* Dr. Michael Ryan, Chair, 414-288-3537, Fax: 414-288-7066. *Application contact:* Dr. Mark Steinmetz, Director of Graduate Studies, 414-288-7374, Fax: 414-288-7066. Web site: http://www.marquette.edu/ chem/graduate.shtml.

Massachusetts Institute of Technology, School of Engineering, Department of Civil and Environmental Engineering, Cambridge, MA 02139. Offers biological oceanography (PhD, Sc D); chemical oceanography (PhD, Sc D); civil and environmental engineering (PhD, Sc D); civil and environmental systems (PhD, Sc D); civil engineering (PhD, Sc D, CE); coastal engineering (PhD, Sc D); construction engineering and management (PhD, Sc D); environmental and water quality engineering (M Eng); environmental biology (PhD, Sc D); environmental chemistry (PhD, Sc D); environmental engineering (PhD, Sc D); environmental fluid mechanics (PhD, Sc D); environmental science and engineering (SM); geotechnical and geoenvironmental engineering (PhD, Sc D); geotechnology (M Eng); high-performance structures (M Eng); hydrology (PhD, Sc D); information technology (PhD, Sc D); mechanics (SM); oceanographic engineering (PhD, Sc D); structures and materials (PhD, Sc D); transportation (M Eng, PhD, Sc D); SM/MBA. *Faculty:* 35 full-time (6 women), 1 part-time/adjunct (0 women). *Students:* 216 full-time (80 women); includes 30 minority (4 Black or African American, non-Hispanic/Latino; 13 Asian, non-Hispanic/Latino; 8 Hispanic/Latino; 5 Two or more races, non-Hispanic/Latino), 110 international. Average age 27. 589 applicants, 26% accepted, 91 enrolled. In 2011, 62 master's, 14 doctorates awarded. *Degree requirements:* For master's and CE, thesis; for doctorate, comprehensive exam, thesis/dissertation. *Entrance requirements:* For master's and doctorate, GRE General Test. Additional exam requirements/ recommendations for international students: Required—TOEFL (minimum score 577 paper-based; 233 computer-based; 90 iBT), IELTS (minimum score 7). *Application deadline:* For fall admission, 12/15 for domestic and international students. Application fee: $75. Electronic applications accepted. *Expenses: Tuition:* Full-time $40,460; part-time $630 per credit hour. *Required fees:* $272. *Financial support:* In 2011–12, 180 students received support, including 51 fellowships (averaging $30,800 per year), 110 research assistantships (averaging $29,500 per year), 19 teaching assistantships (averaging $29,500 per year); career-related internships or fieldwork, Federal Work-Study, institutionally sponsored loans, scholarships/grants, health care benefits, and unspecified assistantships also available. *Faculty research:* Environmental chemistry, environmental fluid mechanics and coastal engineering, environmental microbiology, geotechnical engineering and geomechanics, hydrology and hydroclimatology, infrastructure systems, mechanics of materials and structures, transportation systems. *Total annual research expenditures:* $17.7 million. *Unit head:* Prof. Andrew Whittle, Head, 617-253-7101. *Application contact:* Patricia Glidden, Graduate Admissions Coordinator, 617-253-7119, Fax: 617-258-6775, E-mail: cee-admissions@mit.edu. Web site: http://cee.mit.edu/.

Massachusetts Institute of Technology, School of Science, Department of Chemistry, Cambridge, MA 02139. Offers biological chemistry (PhD, Sc D); inorganic chemistry (PhD, Sc D); organic chemistry (PhD, Sc D); physical chemistry (PhD, Sc D). *Faculty:* 26 full-time (5 women). *Students:* 221 full-time (73 women), 1 (woman) part-time; includes 48 minority (5 Black or African American, non-Hispanic/Latino; 1 American Indian or Alaska Native, non-Hispanic/Latino; 24 Asian, non-Hispanic/Latino; 14 Hispanic/Latino; 4 Two or more races, non-Hispanic/Latino), 64 international. Average age 25. 570 applicants, 20% accepted, 43 enrolled. In 2011, 45 doctorates awarded. *Degree requirements:* For doctorate, comprehensive exam, thesis/dissertation. *Entrance requirements:* For doctorate, GRE General Test. Additional exam requirements/recommendations for international students: Required—IELTS (minimum score 7); Recommended—TOEFL (minimum score 600 paper-based; 250 computer-based). *Application deadline:* For fall admission, 12/15 for domestic and international students. Application fee: $75. Electronic applications accepted. *Expenses: Tuition:* Full-time $40,460; part-time $630 per credit hour. *Required fees:* $272. *Financial support:* In 2011–12, 216 students received support, including 79 fellowships (averaging $34,800 per year), 127 research assistantships (averaging $31,400 per year), 16 teaching assistantships (averaging $32,600 per year); Federal Work-Study, institutionally sponsored loans, scholarships/grants, traineeships, health care benefits, and unspecified assistantships also available. *Faculty research:* Synthetic organic and organometallic chemistry including catalysis; biological chemistry including bioorganic chemistry; physical chemistry including chemical dynamics and biophysical chemistry; inorganic chemistry including synthesis, catalysis, bioinorganic and physical inorganic chemistry; materials chemistry including surface science, nanoscience and polymers. *Total annual research expenditures:* $31.1 million. *Unit head:* Prof. Sylvia T. Ceyer, Head, 617-253-1803, Fax: 617-258-7500. *Application contact:* Graduate Administrator, 617-253-1845, Fax: 617-258-0241, E-mail: chemgradeducation@mit.edu. Web site: http://web.mit.edu/ chemistry/www/.

McMaster University, School of Graduate Studies, Faculty of Science, Department of Chemistry, Hamilton, ON L8S 4M2, Canada. Offers analytical chemistry (M Sc, PhD); chemical physics (M Sc, PhD); chemistry (M Sc, PhD); inorganic chemistry (M Sc, PhD); organic chemistry (M Sc, PhD); physical chemistry (M Sc, PhD); polymer chemistry (M Sc, PhD). Part-time programs available. Terminal master's awarded for partial completion of doctoral program. *Degree requirements:* For master's, thesis; for doctorate, comprehensive exam, thesis/dissertation. *Entrance requirements:* For master's, minimum B+ average. Additional exam requirements/recommendations for international students: Required—TOEFL (minimum score 550 paper-based; 213 computer-based).

Northeastern University, College of Science, Department of Chemistry and Chemical Biology, Boston, MA 02115-5096. Offers analytical chemistry (PhD); chemistry (MS, PhD); inorganic chemistry (PhD); organic chemistry (PhD); physical chemistry (PhD). Part-time and evening/weekend programs available.

Peterson's Graduate Programs in the Physical Sciences, Mathematics, Agricultural Sciences, the Environment & Natural Resources 2013

facebook.com/petersonspublishing   **109**

Organic Chemistry

Faculty: 24 full-time, 7 part-time/adjunct. *Students:* 98 full-time (58 women), 31 part-time (15 women). 190 applicants, 32% accepted, 34 enrolled. In 2011, 16 master's, 6 doctorates awarded. Terminal master's awarded for partial completion of doctoral program. *Degree requirements:* For master's, thesis (for some programs); for doctorate, thesis/dissertation, qualifying exam in specialty area. *Entrance requirements:* Additional exam requirements/recommendations for international students: Required—TOEFL. *Application deadline:* For fall admission, 2/1 priority date for domestic students, 2/1 for international students. Applications are processed on a rolling basis. Application fee: $50. Electronic applications accepted. *Financial support:* In 2011–12, 41 research assistantships with tuition reimbursements (averaging $18,285 per year), 38 teaching assistantships with tuition reimbursements (averaging $18,285 per year) were awarded; fellowships with tuition reimbursements, career-related internships or fieldwork, Federal Work-Study, scholarships/grants, tuition waivers (partial), and unspecified assistantships also available. Financial award application deadline: 3/1; financial award applicants required to submit FAFSA. *Faculty research:* Bioanalysis, bioorganic and medicinal chemistry, biophysical chemistry, nanomaterials, proteonics. *Unit head:* Dr. Robert Hanson, Graduate Coordinator, 617-373-3313, Fax: 617-373-8795, E-mail: chemistry-grad-info@neu.edu. *Application contact:* Jo-Anne Dickinson, Admissions Contact, 617-373-5990, Fax: 617-373-7281, E-mail: gsas@neu.edu. Web site: http://www.northeastern.edu/chem/.

Old Dominion University, College of Sciences, Program in Chemistry, Norfolk, VA 23529. Offers analytical chemistry (MS); biochemistry (MS); chemistry (PhD); environmental chemistry (MS); organic chemistry (MS); physical chemistry (MS). Part-time and evening/weekend programs available. *Faculty:* 14 full-time (5 women), 2 part-time/adjunct (0 women). *Students:* 34 full-time (17 women), 2 part-time (1 woman); includes 2 minority (1 Black or African American, non-Hispanic/Latino; 1 Asian, non-Hispanic/Latino), 17 international. Average age 28. 35 applicants, 60% accepted, 8 enrolled. In 2011, 3 master's, 2 doctorates awarded. *Degree requirements:* For master's, comprehensive exam, thesis. *Entrance requirements:* For master's, GRE General Test, minimum GPA of 3.0 in major, 2.5 overall; for doctorate, GRE General Test. Additional exam requirements/recommendations for international students: Required—TOEFL. *Application deadline:* For fall admission, 7/1 for domestic students, 1/15 for international students; for spring admission, 11/1 for domestic students, 8/15 for international students. Applications are processed on a rolling basis. Application fee: $30. Electronic applications accepted. *Expenses:* Tuition, state resident: full-time $9096; part-time $379 per credit. Tuition, nonresident: full-time $23,064; part-time $961 per credit. *Required fees:* $127 per semester. One-time fee: $50. *Financial support:* In 2011–12, 6 students received support, including fellowships (averaging $18,000 per year), research assistantships with tuition reimbursements available (averaging $21,000 per year), teaching assistantships with tuition reimbursements available (averaging $18,000 per year); career-related internships or fieldwork, scholarships/grants, and unspecified assistantships also available. Financial award application deadline: 2/15; financial award applicants required to submit FAFSA. *Faculty research:* Biogeochemistry, materials chemistry, bioanalytical chemistry, computational chemistry, organic chemistry. *Total annual research expenditures:* $2.6 million. *Unit head:* Dr. Craig A. Bayse, Graduate Program Director, 757-683-4097, Fax: 757-683-4628, E-mail: chemgpd@odu.edu. *Application contact:* Valerie DeCosta, Grants and Graduate Program Assistant, 757-683-6979, Fax: 757-683-4628, E-mail: chemgpd@odu.edu.

Oregon State University, Graduate School, College of Science, Department of Chemistry, Corvallis, OR 97331. Offers analytical chemistry (MS, PhD); chemistry (MA, MAIS); inorganic chemistry (MS, PhD); nuclear and radiation chemistry (MS, PhD); organic chemistry (MS, PhD); physical chemistry (MS, PhD). Part-time programs available. Terminal master's awarded for partial completion of doctoral program. *Degree requirements:* For master's, one foreign language, thesis; for doctorate, one foreign language, thesis/dissertation. *Entrance requirements:* For master's and doctorate, minimum GPA of 3.0 in last 90 hours of course work. Additional exam requirements/recommendations for international students: Required—TOEFL. *Faculty research:* Solid state chemistry, enzyme reaction mechanisms, structure and dynamics of gas molecules, chemiluminescence, nonlinear optical spectroscopy.

Purdue University, Graduate School, College of Science, Department of Chemistry, West Lafayette, IN 47907. Offers analytical chemistry (MS, PhD); biochemistry (MS, PhD); chemical education (MS, PhD); inorganic chemistry (MS, PhD); organic chemistry (MS, PhD); physical chemistry (MS, PhD). *Faculty:* 47 full-time (16 women), 6 part-time/adjunct (0 women). *Students:* 275 full-time (103 women), 33 part-time (10 women); includes 38 minority (19 Black or African American, non-Hispanic/Latino; 6 Asian, non-Hispanic/Latino; 12 Hispanic/Latino; 1 Two or more races, non-Hispanic/Latino), 94 international. Average age 27. 777 applicants, 26% accepted, 62 enrolled. In 2011, 4 master's, 67 doctorates awarded. Terminal master's awarded for partial completion of doctoral program. *Degree requirements:* For master's, thesis; for doctorate, comprehensive exam, thesis/dissertation. *Entrance requirements:* For master's and doctorate, minimum undergraduate GPA of 3.0. Additional exam requirements/recommendations for international students: Required—TOEFL (minimum score 550 computer-based; 77 iBT); Recommended—TWE. *Application deadline:* For fall admission, 2/15 priority date for domestic students, 1/1 for international students. Applications are processed on a rolling basis. Application fee: $60 ($75 for international students). Electronic applications accepted. *Financial support:* In 2011–12, 2 fellowships with partial tuition reimbursements (averaging $18,000 per year), 55 teaching assistantships with partial tuition reimbursements (averaging $18,000 per year) were awarded; research assistantships with partial tuition reimbursements and tuition waivers (partial) also available. Support available to part-time students. Financial award applicants required to submit FAFSA. *Unit head:* Dr. Paul B. Shepson, Head, 765-494-5203, E-mail: pshepson@purdue.edu. *Application contact:* Betty L.. Hatfield, Director of Graduate Admissions, 765-494-5208, E-mail: bettyh@purdue.edu.

Rensselaer Polytechnic Institute, Graduate School, School of Science, Program in Chemistry, Troy, NY 12180-3590. Offers analytical chemistry (MS, PhD); biochemistry (MS, PhD); inorganic chemistry (MS, PhD); organic chemistry (MS, PhD); physical chemistry (MS, PhD); polymer chemistry (MS, PhD). Part-time and evening/weekend programs available. Terminal master's awarded for partial completion of doctoral program. *Degree requirements:* For master's, thesis (for some programs); for doctorate, comprehensive exam, thesis/dissertation. *Entrance requirements:* For master's, GRE General Test, GRE Subject Test (strongly recommended); for doctorate, GRE General Test, GRE Subject Test (chemistry or biochemistry strongly recommended). Additional exam requirements/recommendations for international students: Required—TOEFL (minimum score 570 paper-based; 230 computer-based; 88 iBT). Electronic applications accepted. *Faculty research:* Synthetic polymer and biopolymer chemistry, physical chemistry of polymeric systems, bioanalytical chemistry, synthetic and computational drug design, protein folding and protein design.

Rice University, Graduate Programs, Wiess School of Natural Sciences, Department of Chemistry, Houston, TX 77251-1892. Offers chemistry (MA); inorganic chemistry (PhD); organic chemistry (PhD); physical chemistry (PhD). Terminal master's awarded for partial completion of doctoral program. *Degree requirements:* For master's, thesis; for doctorate, thesis/dissertation. *Entrance requirements:* For master's and doctorate, GRE General Test, minimum GPA of 3.0. Additional exam requirements/recommendations for international students: Required—TOEFL (minimum score 600 paper-based; 250 computer-based; 90 iBT). Electronic applications accepted. *Faculty research:* Nanoscience, biomaterials, nanobioinformatics, fullerene pharmaceuticals.

Rutgers, The State University of New Jersey, Newark, Graduate School, Program in Chemistry, Newark, NJ 07102. Offers analytical chemistry (MS, PhD); biochemistry (MS, PhD); inorganic chemistry (MS, PhD); organic chemistry (MS, PhD); physical chemistry (MS, PhD). Part-time and evening/weekend programs available. Terminal master's awarded for partial completion of doctoral program. *Degree requirements:* For master's, thesis optional, cumulative exams; for doctorate, thesis/dissertation, exams, research proposal. *Entrance requirements:* For master's and doctorate, GRE General Test, minimum undergraduate B average. Additional exam requirements/recommendations for international students: Required—TOEFL. Electronic applications accepted. *Faculty research:* Medicinal chemistry, natural products, isotope effects, biophysics and biorganic approaches to enzyme mechanisms, organic and organometallic synthesis.

Rutgers, The State University of New Jersey, New Brunswick, Graduate School-New Brunswick, Department of Chemistry and Chemical Biology, Piscataway, NJ 08854-8097. Offers biological chemistry (MS, PhD); inorganic chemistry (MS, PhD); organic chemistry (MS, PhD); physical chemistry (MS, PhD). Part-time and evening/weekend programs available. Terminal master's awarded for partial completion of doctoral program. *Degree requirements:* For master's, thesis or alternative, exam; for doctorate, thesis/dissertation, 1 year residency. *Entrance requirements:* For master's and doctorate, GRE General Test, GRE Subject Test. Additional exam requirements/recommendations for international students: Required—TOEFL. Electronic applications accepted. *Faculty research:* Biophysical organic/bioorganic, inorganic/bioinorganic, theoretical, and solid-state/surface chemistry.

Seton Hall University, College of Arts and Sciences, Department of Chemistry and Biochemistry, South Orange, NJ 07079-2697. Offers analytical chemistry (MS, PhD); biochemistry (MS, PhD); chemistry (MS); inorganic chemistry (MS, PhD); organic chemistry (MS, PhD); physical chemistry (MS, PhD). Part-time and evening/weekend programs available. Terminal master's awarded for partial completion of doctoral program. *Degree requirements:* For master's, thesis optional; for doctorate, comprehensive exam, thesis/dissertation. *Entrance requirements:* Additional exam requirements/recommendations for international students: Required—TOEFL. Electronic applications accepted. *Expenses:* Tuition: Part-time $1033 per credit hour. *Required fees:* $85 per semester. *Faculty research:* DNA metal reactions; chromatography; bioinorganic, biophysical, organometallic, polymer chemistry; heterogeneous catalyst; synthetic organic and carbohydrate chemistry.

Southern University and Agricultural and Mechanical College, Graduate School, College of Sciences, Department of Chemistry, Baton Rouge, LA 70813. Offers analytical chemistry (MS); biochemistry (MS); environmental sciences (MS); inorganic chemistry (MS); organic chemistry (MS); physical chemistry (MS). *Degree requirements:* For master's, thesis. *Entrance requirements:* For master's, GMAT or GRE General Test. Additional exam requirements/recommendations for international students: Required—TOEFL (minimum score 525 paper-based; 193 computer-based). *Faculty research:* Synthesis of macrocyclic ligands, latex accelerators, anticancer drugs, biosensors, absorption isotheums, isolation of specific enzymes from plants.

State University of New York at Binghamton, Graduate School, School of Arts and Sciences, Department of Chemistry, Binghamton, NY 13902-6000. Offers analytical chemistry (PhD); chemistry (MA, MS); inorganic chemistry (PhD);

110 facebook.com/petersonspublishing

Peterson's Graduate Programs in the Physical Sciences, Mathematics, Agricultural Sciences, the Environment & Natural Resources 2013

organic chemistry (PhD); physical chemistry (PhD). Part-time programs available. *Faculty:* 16 full-time (5 women), 2 part-time/adjunct (both women). *Students:* 24 full-time (8 women), 32 part-time (13 women); includes 5 minority (2 Black or African American, non-Hispanic/Latino; 1 Hispanic/Latino; 2 Native Hawaiian or other Pacific Islander, non-Hispanic/Latino), 36 international. Average age 28. 39 applicants, 36% accepted, 10 enrolled. In 2011, 3 master's, 6 doctorates awarded. Terminal master's awarded for partial completion of doctoral program. *Degree requirements:* For master's, thesis or alternative, oral exam, seminar presentation; for doctorate, thesis/dissertation, cumulative exams. *Entrance requirements:* For master's and doctorate, GRE General Test, GRE Subject Test. Additional exam requirements/recommendations for international students: Required—TOEFL (minimum score 550 paper-based; 213 computer-based; 80 iBT). *Application deadline:* For fall admission, 1/15 priority date for domestic students, 1/15 for international students; for spring admission, 10/15 priority date for domestic students, 10/15 for international students. Applications are processed on a rolling basis. Application fee: $60. Electronic applications accepted. *Financial support:* In 2011–12, 9 fellowships with full tuition reimbursements (averaging $18,000 per year), 13 research assistantships with full tuition reimbursements (averaging $18,000 per year), 35 teaching assistantships with full tuition reimbursements (averaging $18,000 per year) were awarded; career-related internships or fieldwork, Federal Work-Study, institutionally sponsored loans, scholarships/grants, health care benefits, tuition waivers (full), and unspecified assistantships also available. Financial award application deadline: 2/15; financial award applicants required to submit FAFSA. *Unit head:* Dr. Wayne E. Jones, Chairperson, 607-777-2421, E-mail: wjones@binghamton.edu. *Application contact:* Catherine Smith, Recruiting and Admissions Coordinator, 607-777-2151, Fax: 607-777-2501, E-mail: cmsmith@binghamton.edu.

State University of New York College of Environmental Science and Forestry, Department of Chemistry, Syracuse, NY 13210-2779. Offers biochemistry (MPS, MS, PhD); environmental chemistry (MPS, MS, PhD); organic chemistry of natural products (MPS, MS, PhD); polymer chemistry (MPS, MS, PhD). *Degree requirements:* For master's, thesis; for doctorate, comprehensive exam, thesis/dissertation. *Entrance requirements:* For master's and doctorate, GRE General Test, GRE Subject Test, minimum GPA of 3.0. Additional exam requirements/recommendations for international students: Required—TOEFL (minimum score 550 paper-based; 213 computer-based; 80 iBT), IELTS (minimum score 6). *Application deadline:* For fall admission, 2/1 priority date for domestic students, 2/1 for international students; for spring admission, 11/1 priority date for domestic students, 11/1 for international students. Applications are processed on a rolling basis. Application fee: $60. Electronic applications accepted. *Expenses:* Tuition, state resident: full-time $8870; part-time $370 per credit hour. Tuition, nonresident: full-time $15,160; part-time $632 per credit hour. *Required fees:* $60; $370 per credit hour. $350 per semester. One-time fee: $85. *Financial support:* Fellowships with full tuition reimbursements, research assistantships with full tuition reimbursements, teaching assistantships with full tuition reimbursements, Federal Work-Study, institutionally sponsored loans, scholarships/grants, health care benefits, and unspecified assistantships available. Financial award application deadline: 6/30; financial award applicants required to submit FAFSA. *Faculty research:* Polymer chemistry, biochemistry. *Total annual research expenditures:* $1.8 million. *Unit head:* Prof. Gregory Boyer, Chair, 315-470-6825, Fax: 315-470-6856, E-mail: glboyer@esf.edu. *Application contact:* Scott Shannon, Associate Provost for Instruction/Dean of the Graduate School, 315-470-6599, Fax: 315-470-6978, E-mail: sshannon@esf.edu. Web site: http://www.esf.edu/chemistry.

Stevens Institute of Technology, Graduate School, Charles V. Schaefer Jr. School of Engineering, Department of Chemistry, Chemical Biology and Biomedical Engineering, Hoboken, NJ 07030. Offers analytical chemistry (PhD, Certificate); bioinformatics (PhD, Certificate); biomedical chemistry (Certificate); biomedical engineering (M Eng, Certificate); chemical biology (MS, PhD, Certificate); chemical physiology (Certificate); chemistry (MS, PhD); organic chemistry (PhD); physical chemistry (PhD); polymer chemistry (PhD, Certificate). Part-time and evening/weekend programs available. Postbaccalaureate distance learning degree programs offered (no on-campus study). Terminal master's awarded for partial completion of doctoral program. *Degree requirements:* For master's, thesis or alternative; for doctorate, one foreign language, thesis/dissertation; for Certificate, project or thesis. *Entrance requirements:* Additional exam requirements/recommendations for international students: Required—TOEFL. Electronic applications accepted. *Faculty research:* Biochemical reaction engineering, polymerization engineering, reactor design, biochemical process control and synthesis.

Texas Christian University, College of Science and Engineering, Department of Chemistry, Fort Worth, TX 76129. Offers biochemistry (MS, PhD); chemistry (MA); inorganic (MS, PhD); organic (MS, PhD); physical (MS, PhD). Part-time programs available. *Faculty:* 11 full-time (2 women). *Students:* 4 full-time (2 women), 16 part-time (10 women); includes 3 minority (1 Asian, non-Hispanic/Latino; 2 Hispanic/Latino), 11 international. Average age 27. 5 applicants, 100% accepted, 4 enrolled. In 2011, 1 master's, 3 doctorates awarded. *Degree requirements:* For master's, thesis; for doctorate, thesis/dissertation, literature seminar, cumulative exams, research progress report, original proposal. *Entrance requirements:* For master's and doctorate, GRE General Test. Additional exam requirements/recommendations for international students: Required—TOEFL. *Application deadline:* For fall admission, 3/1 priority date for domestic students, 3/1 for international students; for spring admission, 9/1 priority date for domestic

students, 9/1 for international students. Application fee: $50. Electronic applications accepted. *Expenses: Tuition:* Full-time $20,250; part-time $1125 per credit hour. Part-time tuition and fees vary according to course load and program. *Financial support:* In 2011–12, 11 students received support, including 11 teaching assistantships with full tuition reimbursements available; tuition waivers (full and partial) and unspecified assistantships also available. Financial award application deadline: 3/1. *Faculty research:* Phase transitions and transport properties of bio/macromolecular solutions, nanoscale biomaterials, electronic structure theory, synthetic methodology and total synthesis of natural products, chemistry and biology of (bio)polymers. *Unit head:* Dr. Robert Neilson, Chairperson/Professor, 817-257-7345, Fax: 817-257-5851, E-mail: r.neilson@tcu.edu. *Application contact:* Dr. Sergei V. Dzyuba, Director of Graduate Studies/Assistant Professor, 817-257-6218, Fax: 817-257-5851, E-mail: s.dzyuba@tcu.edu. Web site: http://www.chm.tcu.edu/.

Tufts University, Graduate School of Arts and Sciences, Department of Chemistry, Medford, MA 02155. Offers analytical chemistry (MS, PhD); bioorganic chemistry (MS, PhD); environmental chemistry (MS, PhD); inorganic chemistry (MS, PhD); organic chemistry (MS, PhD); physical chemistry (MS, PhD). *Students:* 75 full-time (33 women); includes 7 minority (1 Black or African American, non-Hispanic/Latino; 5 Asian, non-Hispanic/Latino; 1 Hispanic/Latino), 25 international. 88 applicants, 59% accepted, 16 enrolled. In 2011, 5 master's, 8 doctorates awarded. Terminal master's awarded for partial completion of doctoral program. *Degree requirements:* For master's, thesis optional; for doctorate, thesis/dissertation. *Entrance requirements:* For master's and doctorate, GRE General Test, GRE Subject Test. Additional exam requirements/recommendations for international students: Required—TOEFL (minimum score 600 paper-based; 250 computer-based; 80 iBT). *Application deadline:* For fall admission, 1/15 for domestic students, 12/15 for international students; for spring admission, 10/15 for domestic students, 9/15 for international students. Applications are processed on a rolling basis. Application fee: $75. Electronic applications accepted. *Expenses: Tuition:* Full-time $41,208; part-time $1030 per credit hour. Full-time tuition and fees vary according to degree level, program and student level. Part-time tuition and fees vary according to course load. *Financial support:* Fellowships, research assistantships with full tuition reimbursements, teaching assistantships with full tuition reimbursements, Federal Work-Study, scholarships/grants, tuition waivers (partial), and unspecified assistantships available. Financial award application deadline: 1/15; financial award applicants required to submit FAFSA. *Unit head:* Arthur Utz, Chair, 617-627-3441. *Application contact:* Deborah D'Andrea, Information Contact, 617-627-3441, Fax: 617-627-3443. Web site: http://chem.tufts.edu/.

University of Calgary, Faculty of Graduate Studies, Faculty of Science, Department of Chemistry, Calgary, AB T2N 1N4, Canada. Offers analytical chemistry (M Sc, PhD); applied chemistry (M Sc, PhD); inorganic chemistry (M Sc, PhD); organic chemistry (M Sc, PhD); physical chemistry (M Sc, PhD); polymer chemistry (M Sc, PhD); theoretical chemistry (M Sc, PhD). *Degree requirements:* For master's, thesis; for doctorate, thesis/dissertation, candidacy exam. *Entrance requirements:* For master's, minimum GPA of 3.0; for doctorate, honors B Sc degree with minimum GPA of 3.7 or M Sc with minimum GPA of 3.3. Additional exam requirements/recommendations for international students: Required—TOEFL (minimum score 580 paper-based; 237 computer-based). Electronic applications accepted. *Faculty research:* Chemical analysis, chemical dynamics, synthesis theory.

University of Cincinnati, Graduate School, McMicken College of Arts and Sciences, Department of Chemistry, Cincinnati, OH 45221. Offers analytical chemistry (MS, PhD); biochemistry (MS, PhD); inorganic chemistry (MS, PhD); organic chemistry (MS, PhD); physical chemistry (MS, PhD); polymer chemistry (MS, PhD); sensors (PhD). Part-time and evening/weekend programs available. Terminal master's awarded for partial completion of doctoral program. *Degree requirements:* For master's, thesis optional; for doctorate, comprehensive exam, thesis/dissertation. *Entrance requirements:* For master's and doctorate, GRE General Test. Additional exam requirements/recommendations for international students: Required—TOEFL (minimum score 580 paper-based; 237 computer-based). Electronic applications accepted. *Faculty research:* Biomedical chemistry, laser chemistry, surface science, chemical sensors, synthesis.

University of Georgia, Franklin College of Arts and Sciences, Department of Chemistry, Athens, GA 30602. Offers analytical chemistry (MS, PhD); inorganic chemistry (MS, PhD); organic chemistry (MS, PhD); physical chemistry (MS, PhD). *Faculty:* 26 full-time (2 women). *Students:* 153 full-time (53 women), 6 part-time (2 women); includes 21 minority (6 Black or African American, non-Hispanic/Latino; 12 Asian, non-Hispanic/Latino; 1 Hispanic/Latino; 2 Two or more races, non-Hispanic/Latino), 60 international. Average age 27. 175 applicants, 41% accepted, 38 enrolled. In 2011, 7 master's, 22 doctorates awarded. Terminal master's awarded for partial completion of doctoral program. *Median time to degree:* Of those who began their doctoral program in fall 2003, 100% received their degree in 8 years or less. *Degree requirements:* For master's, thesis; for doctorate, one foreign language, thesis/dissertation. *Entrance requirements:* For master's and doctorate, GRE General Test. Additional exam requirements/recommendations for international students: Required—TOEFL (minimum score 213 computer-based). *Application deadline:* For fall admission, 7/1 priority date for domestic students; for spring admission, 11/15 for domestic students. Application fee: $50. Electronic applications accepted. *Financial support:* Fellowships, research assistantships, teaching assistantships, and unspecified assistantships available. *Unit head:* Dr. Jon Amster, Head, 706-542-2726, E-mail: jamster@

Peterson's Graduate Programs in the Physical Sciences, Mathematics, Agricultural Sciences, the Environment & Natural Resources 2013

facebook.com/petersonspublishing **111**

Organic Chemistry

uga.edu. *Application contact:* Dr. Jeffrey L. Urbauer, Graduate Coordinator, 706-542-7922, E-mail: urbauer@uga.edu. Web site: http://www.chem.uga.edu/.

University of Louisville, Graduate School, College of Arts and Sciences, Department of Chemistry, Louisville, KY 40292-0001. Offers analytical chemistry (MS, PhD); biochemistry (MS, PhD); chemical physics (PhD); inorganic chemistry (MS, PhD); organic chemistry (MS, PhD); physical chemistry (MS, PhD). Terminal master's awarded for partial completion of doctoral program. *Degree requirements:* For master's, variable foreign language requirement, comprehensive exam, thesis optional; for doctorate, variable foreign language requirement, comprehensive exam, thesis/dissertation. *Entrance requirements:* For master's and doctorate, BA or BS coursework. Additional exam requirements/recommendations for international students: Required—TOEFL. Electronic applications accepted. *Expenses:* Tuition, state resident: full-time $9692; part-time $539 per credit hour. Tuition, nonresident: full-time $20,168; part-time $1121 per credit hour. Tuition and fees vary according to program and reciprocity agreements. *Faculty research:* Computational chemistry, biophysics nuclear magnetic resonance, synthetic organic chemistry, synthetic inorganic chemistry, medicinal chemistry, protein chemistry, enzymology, nanochemistry, electrochemistry, analytical chemistry, synthetic biology, bioinformatics.

The University of Manchester, School of Chemistry, Manchester, United Kingdom. Offers biological chemistry (PhD); chemistry (M Ent, M Phil, M Sc, D Ent, PhD); inorganic chemistry (PhD); materials chemistry (PhD); nanoscience (PhD); nuclear fission (PhD); organic chemistry (PhD); physical chemistry (PhD); theoretical chemistry (PhD).

University of Maryland, College Park, Academic Affairs, College of Computer, Mathematical and Natural Sciences, Department of Chemistry and Biochemistry, Chemistry Program, College Park, MD 20742. Offers analytical chemistry (MS, PhD); inorganic chemistry (MS, PhD); organic chemistry (MS, PhD); physical chemistry (MS, PhD). Part-time and evening/weekend programs available. *Students:* 115 full-time (59 women), 4 part-time (1 woman); includes 20 minority (12 Black or African American, non-Hispanic/Latino; 4 Asian, non-Hispanic/Latino; 2 Hispanic/Latino; 2 Two or more races, non-Hispanic/Latino), 52 international. 335 applicants, 8% accepted, 18 enrolled. In 2011, 11 master's, 15 doctorates awarded. Terminal master's awarded for partial completion of doctoral program. *Median time to degree:* Of those who began their doctoral program in fall 2003, 63% received their degree in 8 years or less. *Degree requirements:* For master's, thesis optional; for doctorate, thesis/dissertation, 2 seminar presentations, oral exam. *Entrance requirements:* For master's and doctorate, GRE General Test, GRE Subject Test (recommended), minimum GPA of 3.0, 3 letters of recommendation. Additional exam requirements/recommendations for international students: Required—TOEFL. *Application deadline:* For fall admission, 2/1 for domestic and international students; for spring admission, 6/1 for domestic and international students. Applications are processed on a rolling basis. Application fee: $75. Electronic applications accepted. *Expenses:* Tuition, area resident: Part-time $525 per credit hour. Tuition, state resident: part-time $525 per credit hour. Tuition, nonresident: part-time $1131 per credit hour. *Required fees:* $386.31 per term. Tuition and fees vary according to program. *Financial support:* In 2011–12, 9 fellowships with full and partial tuition reimbursements (averaging $25,360 per year), 46 research assistantships (averaging $19,791 per year), 59 teaching assistantships (averaging $19,243 per year) were awarded. Financial award applicants required to submit FAFSA. *Faculty research:* Environmental chemistry, nuclear chemistry, lunar and environmental analysis, x-ray crystallography. *Unit head:* Dr. Michael Doyle, Chairperson, 301-405-1795, Fax: 301-314-2779, E-mail: mdoyle3@umd.edu. *Application contact:* Dr. Charles A. Caramello, Dean of Graduate School, 301-405-0358, Fax: 301-314-9305.

University of Massachusetts Lowell, College of Sciences, Department of Chemistry, Lowell, MA 01854-2881. Offers analytical chemistry (PhD); biochemistry (PhD); chemistry (MS, PhD); environmental studies (PhD); green chemistry (PhD); inorganic chemistry (PhD); organic chemistry (PhD); polymer science (MS). Terminal master's awarded for partial completion of doctoral program. *Degree requirements:* For master's, thesis; for doctorate, 2 foreign languages, thesis/dissertation. *Entrance requirements:* For master's and doctorate, GRE General Test. Electronic applications accepted.

University of Memphis, Graduate School, College of Arts and Sciences, Department of Chemistry, Memphis, TN 38152. Offers analytical chemistry (MS, PhD); computational chemistry (MS, PhD); inorganic chemistry (MS, PhD); organic chemistry (MS, PhD); physical chemistry (MS, PhD). Part-time programs available. Terminal master's awarded for partial completion of doctoral program. *Degree requirements:* For master's, comprehensive exam, thesis or alternative; for doctorate, comprehensive exam, thesis/dissertation. *Entrance requirements:* For master's and doctorate, GRE General Test, admission to Graduate School plus 32 undergraduate hours in chemistry. Additional exam requirements/recommendations for international students: Required—TOEFL. Electronic applications accepted. *Faculty research:* Computational chemistry, materials chemistry, organic/polymer synthesis, drug design/delivery, water chemistry.

University of Miami, Graduate School, College of Arts and Sciences, Department of Chemistry, Coral Gables, FL 33124. Offers chemistry (MS); inorganic chemistry (PhD); organic chemistry (PhD); physical chemistry (PhD). Terminal master's awarded for partial completion of doctoral program. *Degree requirements:* For master's, comprehensive exam; for doctorate, comprehensive exam, thesis/dissertation. *Entrance requirements:* For master's and doctorate, GRE General Test. Additional exam requirements/recommendations for international students: Required—TOEFL (minimum score 550 paper-based; 213 computer-based). Electronic applications accepted. *Faculty research:* Supramolecular chemistry, electrochemistry, surface chemistry, catalysis, organometalic.

University of Michigan, Horace H. Rackham School of Graduate Studies, College of Literature, Science, and the Arts, Department of Chemistry, Ann Arbor, MI 48109-1055. Offers analytical chemistry (PhD); chemical biology (PhD); inorganic chemistry (PhD); material chemistry (PhD); organic chemistry (PhD); physical chemistry (PhD). *Faculty:* 39 full-time (9 women). *Students:* 221 full-time (114 women); includes 24 minority (1 Black or African American, non-Hispanic/Latino; 15 Asian, non-Hispanic/Latino; 4 Hispanic/Latino; 4 Two or more races, non-Hispanic/Latino), 66 international. Average age 26. 608 applicants, 27% accepted, 39 enrolled. In 2011, 39 doctorates awarded. *Degree requirements:* For doctorate, thesis/dissertation, oral defense of dissertation, organic cumulative proficiency exams. *Entrance requirements:* For doctorate, GRE General Test, GRE Subject Test (recommended), 3 letters of recommendation. Additional exam requirements/recommendations for international students: Required—TOEFL (minimum score 560 paper-based; 220 computer-based; 84 iBT). *Application deadline:* For fall admission, 12/31 for domestic students, 12/15 for international students. Applications are processed on a rolling basis. Application fee: $0 ($75 for international students). Electronic applications accepted. *Financial support:* In 2011–12, 221 students received support, including 25 fellowships with full tuition reimbursements available (averaging $26,553 per year), 86 research assistantships with full tuition reimbursements available (averaging $26,553 per year), 110 teaching assistantships with full tuition reimbursements available (averaging $26,553 per year); career-related internships or fieldwork, scholarships/grants, traineeships, health care benefits, and unspecified assistantships also available. *Faculty research:* Biological catalysis, protein engineering, chemical sensors, de novo metalloprotein design, supramolecular architecture. *Unit head:* Dr. Carol A. Fierke, Chair, 734-763-9681, Fax: 734-647-4847. *Application contact:* Margarita Bekiares, Graduate Program Coordinator, 734-764-7278, Fax: 734-647-4865, E-mail: chemadmissions@umich.edu. Web site: http://www.umich.edu/~michchem/.

University of Missouri, Graduate School, College of Arts and Sciences, Department of Chemistry, Columbia, MO 65211. Offers analytical chemistry (MS, PhD); inorganic chemistry (MS, PhD); organic chemistry (MS, PhD); physical chemistry (MS, PhD). *Faculty:* 22 full-time (4 women), 1 part-time/adjunct (0 women). *Students:* 102 full-time (38 women), 10 part-time (6 women); includes 7 minority (3 Black or African American, non-Hispanic/Latino; 2 Asian, non-Hispanic/Latino; 1 Hispanic/Latino; 1 Two or more races, non-Hispanic/Latino), 53 international. Average age 27. 98 applicants, 28% accepted, 24 enrolled. In 2011, 2 master's, 5 doctorates awarded. *Degree requirements:* For master's, thesis; for doctorate, one foreign language, comprehensive exam, thesis/dissertation. *Entrance requirements:* For master's, GRE General Test, minimum GPA of 3.0; for doctorate, GRE General Test (minimum score: Verbal 450, Quantitative 600, Analytical 3), minimum GPA of 3.0. Additional exam requirements/recommendations for international students: Required—TOEFL (minimum score 600 paper-based; 250 computer-based; 100 iBT). *Application deadline:* For fall admission, 4/1 priority date for domestic students; for winter admission, 10/15 for domestic students. Applications are processed on a rolling basis. Application fee: $55 ($75 for international students). Electronic applications accepted. *Expenses:* Tuition, state resident: full-time $5881. Tuition, nonresident: full-time $15,183. *Required fees:* $952. Tuition and fees vary according to campus/location and program. *Financial support:* In 2011–12, 9 fellowships with full tuition reimbursements, 15 research assistantships with full tuition reimbursements, 78 teaching assistantships with full tuition reimbursements were awarded; institutionally sponsored loans, traineeships, health care benefits, and unspecified assistantships also available. *Faculty research:* Analytical, organic, biological, physical, inorganic and radiochemistry. *Unit head:* Dr. Jerry Atwood, Department Chair, 573-882-8374, E-mail: atwoodj@missouri.edu. *Application contact:* Jerry Brightwell, Administrative Assistant, 573-884-6832, E-mail: brightwellj@missouri.edu. Web site: http://chemistry.missouri.edu/.

University of Missouri–Kansas City, College of Arts and Sciences, Department of Chemistry, Kansas City, MO 64110-2499. Offers analytical chemistry (MS, PhD); inorganic chemistry (MS, PhD); organic chemistry (MS, PhD); physical chemistry (MS, PhD); polymer chemistry (MS, PhD). PhD (interdisciplinary) offered through the School of Graduate Studies. Part-time and evening/weekend programs available. *Faculty:* 16 full-time (3 women), 1 part-time/adjunct (0 women). *Students:* 1 (woman) part-time; minority (Black or African American, non-Hispanic/Latino). Average age 30. 28 applicants, 32% accepted, 0 enrolled. In 2011, 2 degrees awarded. *Degree requirements:* For master's, thesis (for some programs); for doctorate, thesis/dissertation. *Entrance requirements:* For master's, equivalent of American Chemical Society approved bachelor's degree in chemistry; for doctorate, GRE General Test, equivalent of American Chemical Society approved bachelor's degree in chemistry. Additional exam requirements/recommendations for international students: Required—TOEFL (minimum score 550 paper-based; 213 computer-based; 80 iBT), TWE. *Application deadline:* For fall admission, 4/15 for domestic and international students; for spring admission, 10/15 for domestic and international students. Applications are processed on a rolling basis. Application fee: $45 ($50 for international students). Electronic applications accepted. *Expenses:* Tuition, state resident: full-time $5798; part-time $322.10 per credit hour. Tuition, nonresident: full-time $14,969; part-time $831.60 per credit hour. *Required fees:* $93.51 per credit hour. *Financial support:*

In 2011–12, 9 research assistantships with partial tuition reimbursements (averaging $19,119 per year), 14 teaching assistantships with partial tuition reimbursements (averaging $17,187 per year) were awarded; Federal Work-Study, institutionally sponsored loans, and scholarships/grants also available. Support available to part-time students. Financial award application deadline: 3/1; financial award applicants required to submit FAFSA. *Faculty research:* Molecular spectroscopy, characterization and synthesis of materials and compounds, computational chemistry, natural products, drug delivery systems and anti-tumor agents. *Unit head:* Dr. Kathleen V. Kilway, Chair, 816-235-2289, Fax: 816-235-5502. *Application contact:* Graduate Recruiting Committee, 816-235-2272, Fax: 816-235-5502. E-mail: umkc-chemdept@umkc.edu. Web site: http://cas.umkc.edu/chem/.

University of Missouri–St. Louis, College of Arts and Sciences, Department of Chemistry and Biochemistry, St. Louis, MO 63121. Offers chemistry (MS, PhD), including biochemistry, inorganic chemistry, organic chemistry, physical chemistry. Part-time and evening/weekend programs available. *Faculty:* 18 full-time (3 women), 4 part-time/adjunct (1 woman). *Students:* 37 full-time (18 women), 28 part-time (11 women); includes 4 minority (1 Black or African American, non-Hispanic/Latino; 2 Asian, non-Hispanic/Latino; 1 Hispanic/Latino), 22 international. Average age 30. 73 applicants, 30% accepted, 11 enrolled. In 2011, 16 master's, 4 doctorates awarded. Terminal master's awarded for partial completion of doctoral program. *Degree requirements:* For master's, thesis optional; for doctorate, thesis/dissertation. *Entrance requirements:* For master's, 2 letters of recommendation; for doctorate, GRE General Test, 3 letters of recommendation. Additional exam requirements/recommendations for international students: Required—TOEFL (minimum score 550 paper-based; 213 computer-based). *Application deadline:* For fall admission, 7/1 priority date for domestic students, 7/1 for international students; for spring admission, 12/1 priority date for domestic students, 12/1 for international students. Applications are processed on a rolling basis. Application fee: $35 ($40 for international students). Electronic applications accepted. *Expenses:* Tuition, state resident: full-time $6273; part-time $3866 per year. Tuition, nonresident: full-time $14,969; part-time $9980 per year. *Required fees:* $315 per year. *Financial support:* In 2011–12, 19 research assistantships with full and partial tuition reimbursements (averaging $13,500 per year), 19 teaching assistantships with full and partial tuition reimbursements (averaging $13,500 per year) were awarded; fellowships with full and partial tuition reimbursements also available. *Faculty research:* Metalloborane chemistry, serum transferrin chemistry, natural products chemistry, organic synthesis. *Unit head:* Dr. Janet Wilking, Director of Graduate Studies, 314-516-5311, Fax: 314-516-5342, E-mail: gradchem@umsl.edu. *Application contact:* Graduate Admissions, 314-516-5458, Fax: 314-516-6996, E-mail: gradadm@umsl.edu. Web site: http://www.umsl.edu/chemistry/.

The University of Montana, Graduate School, College of Arts and Sciences, Department of Chemistry and Biochemistry, Missoula, MT 59812-0002. Offers chemistry (MS, PhD), including environmental/analytical chemistry, inorganic chemistry, organic chemistry, physical chemistry. Terminal master's awarded for partial completion of doctoral program. *Degree requirements:* For master's, thesis (for some programs); for doctorate, thesis/dissertation. *Entrance requirements:* For master's and doctorate, GRE General Test. Additional exam requirements/recommendations for international students: Required—TOEFL (minimum score 575 paper-based; 230 computer-based). *Faculty research:* Reaction mechanisms and kinetics, inorganic and organic synthesis, analytical chemistry, natural products.

University of Nebraska–Lincoln, Graduate College, College of Arts and Sciences, Department of Chemistry, Lincoln, NE 68588. Offers analytical chemistry (PhD); biochemistry (PhD); chemistry (MS); inorganic chemistry (PhD); materials chemistry (PhD); organic chemistry (PhD); physical chemistry (PhD). *Degree requirements:* For master's, one foreign language, thesis optional, departmental qualifying exam; for doctorate, one foreign language, comprehensive exam, thesis/dissertation, departmental qualifying exams. *Entrance requirements:* For master's and doctorate, GRE. Additional exam requirements/recommendations for international students: Required—TOEFL (minimum score 550 paper-based; 213 computer-based). Electronic applications accepted. *Faculty research:* Bioorganic and bioinorganic chemistry, biophysical and bioanalytical chemistry, structure-function of DNA and proteins, organometallics, mass spectrometry.

University of Notre Dame, Graduate School, College of Science, Department of Chemistry and Biochemistry, Notre Dame, IN 46556. Offers biochemistry (MS, PhD); inorganic chemistry (MS, PhD); organic chemistry (MS, PhD); physical chemistry (MS, PhD). Terminal master's awarded for partial completion of doctoral program. *Degree requirements:* For master's, comprehensive exam, thesis; for doctorate, thesis/dissertation, qualifying exam. *Entrance requirements:* For master's and doctorate, GRE General Test, GRE Subject Test (strongly recommended). Additional exam requirements/recommendations for international students: Required—TOEFL (minimum score 600 paper-based; 250 computer-based; 80 iBT). Electronic applications accepted. *Faculty research:* Reaction design and mechanistic studies; reactive intermediates; synthesis, structure and reactivity of organometallic cluster complexes and biologically active natural products; bioorganic chemistry; enzymology.

University of Regina, Faculty of Graduate Studies and Research, Faculty of Science, Department of Chemistry and Biochemistry, Regina, SK S4S 0A2, Canada. Offers analytical/environmental chemistry (M Sc, PhD); biophysics of biological interfaces (M Sc, PhD); enzymology/chemical biology (M Sc, PhD); inorganic/organometallic chemistry (M Sc, PhD); signal transduction and mechanisms of cancer cell regulation (M Sc, PhD); supramolecular organic photochemistry and photophysics (M Sc, PhD); synthetic organic chemistry (M Sc, PhD); theoretical/computational chemistry (M Sc, PhD). *Faculty:* 12 full-time (2 women). *Students:* 13 full-time (4 women), 1 (woman) part-time. 22 applicants, 50% accepted. In 2011, 1 master's, 2 doctorates awarded. *Degree requirements:* For master's, thesis; for doctorate, thesis/dissertation. *Entrance requirements:* Additional exam requirements/recommendations for international students: Required—TOEFL (minimum score 580 paper-based; 80 iBT), IELTS (minimum score 6.5). *Application deadline:* Applications are processed on a rolling basis. Application fee: $100. Electronic applications accepted. *Financial support:* In 2011–12, 3 fellowships (averaging $6,500 per year), 1 research assistantship (averaging $5,500 per year), 7 teaching assistantships (averaging $2,298 per year) were awarded; scholarships/grants also available. Financial award application deadline: 6/15. *Faculty research:* Asymmetric synthesis and methodology, theoretical and computational chemistry, biophysical biochemistry, analytical and environmental chemistry, chemical biology. *Unit head:* Dr. Lynn Mihichuk, Head, 306-585-4793, Fax: 306-337-2409, E-mail: lynn.mihichuk@uregina.ca. *Application contact:* Dr. Tanya Dahms, Graduate Program Coordinator, 306-585-4246, Fax: 306-337-2409, E-mail: tanya.dahms@uregina.ca. Web site: http://www.chem.uregina.ca/.

University of Southern Mississippi, Graduate School, College of Science and Technology, Department of Chemistry and Biochemistry, Hattiesburg, MS 39406-0001. Offers analytical chemistry (MS, PhD); biochemistry (MS, PhD); inorganic chemistry (MS, PhD); organic chemistry (MS, PhD); physical chemistry (MS, PhD). *Faculty:* 16 full-time (4 women). *Students:* 22 full-time (9 women), 4 part-time (3 women); includes 1 minority (Black or African American, non-Hispanic/Latino), 9 international. Average age 29. 43 applicants, 19% accepted, 5 enrolled. In 2011, 1 master's, 4 doctorates awarded. *Degree requirements:* For master's, comprehensive exam, thesis; for doctorate, comprehensive exam, thesis/dissertation. *Entrance requirements:* For master's, GRE General Test, minimum GPA of 2.75 in last 60 hours; for doctorate, GRE General Test, minimum GPA of 3.5. Additional exam requirements/recommendations for international students: Required—TOEFL, IELTS. *Application deadline:* For fall admission, 3/1 priority date for domestic students, 3/1 for international students. Applications are processed on a rolling basis. Application fee: $50. *Financial support:* In 2011–12, 3 research assistantships with full tuition reimbursements (averaging $17,000 per year), 19 teaching assistantships with full tuition reimbursements (averaging $20,700 per year) were awarded; fellowships, Federal Work-Study, institutionally sponsored loans, scholarships/grants, health care benefits, and unspecified assistantships also available. Support available to part-time students. Financial award application deadline: 3/15; financial award applicants required to submit FAFSA. *Faculty research:* Plant biochemistry, photo chemistry, polymer chemistry, x-ray analysis, enzyme chemistry. *Unit head:* Dr. Sabine Heinhorst, Chair, 601-266-4701, Fax: 601-266-6075. *Application contact:* Dr. Sabine Heinhorst, Graduate Coordinator, 601-266-4702, Fax: 601-266-6075. Web site: http://www.usm.edu/graduateschool/table.php.

University of South Florida, Graduate School, College of Arts and Sciences, Department of Chemistry, Tampa, FL 33620-9951. Offers analytical chemistry (MS, PhD); biochemistry (MS, PhD); computational chemistry (MS, PhD); environmental chemistry (MS, PhD); inorganic chemistry (MS, PhD); organic chemistry (MS); physical chemistry (MS, PhD); polymer chemistry (PhD). Part-time programs available. *Faculty:* 25 full-time (4 women), 9 part-time/adjunct (1 woman). *Students:* 118 full-time (46 women), 14 part-time (7 women); includes 28 minority (8 Black or African American, non-Hispanic/Latino; 11 Asian, non-Hispanic/Latino; 9 Hispanic/Latino), 58 international. Average age 29. 127 applicants, 31% accepted, 19 enrolled. In 2011, 3 master's, 16 doctorates awarded. Terminal master's awarded for partial completion of doctoral program. *Degree requirements:* For master's, comprehensive exam, thesis (for some programs); for doctorate, comprehensive exam, thesis/dissertation. *Entrance requirements:* For master's and doctorate, GRE General Test, minimum GPA of 3.0. Additional exam requirements/recommendations for international students: Required—TOEFL (minimum score 550 paper-based; 213 computer-based; 79 iBT) or IELTS (minimum score 6.5). *Application deadline:* For fall admission, 2/15 priority date for domestic students, 1/2 for international students; for spring admission, 10/1 priority date for domestic students, 6/1 for international students. Applications are processed on a rolling basis. Application fee: $30. Electronic applications accepted. *Financial support:* In 2011–12, 136 students received support, including 28 research assistantships with tuition reimbursements available (averaging $15,020 per year), 108 teaching assistantships with tuition reimbursements available (averaging $15,164 per year); unspecified assistantships also available. Financial award application deadline: 6/30. *Faculty research:* Synthesis, bio-organic chemistry, bioinorganic chemistry, environmental chemistry, NMR. *Total annual research expenditures:* $3.1 million. *Unit head:* Dr. Randy Larsen, Chairperson, 813-974-4129, Fax: 813-974-3203, E-mail: rlarsen@cas.usf.edu. *Application contact:* Patricia Muisener, Director, 813-974-1730, Fax: 813-974-3203, E-mail: muisener@cas.usf.edu. Web site: http://chemistry.usf.edu/.

The University of Tennessee, Graduate School, College of Arts and Sciences, Department of Chemistry, Knoxville, TN 37996. Offers analytical chemistry (MS, PhD); chemical physics (PhD); environmental chemistry (MS, PhD); inorganic chemistry (MS, PhD); organic chemistry (MS, PhD); physical chemistry (MS, PhD); polymer chemistry (MS, PhD); theoretical chemistry (PhD). Part-time programs available. Terminal master's awarded for partial completion of doctoral

Peterson's Graduate Programs in the Physical Sciences, Mathematics, Agricultural Sciences, the Environment & Natural Resources 2013

facebook.com/petersonspublishing **113**

program. *Degree requirements:* For master's, thesis; for doctorate, thesis/ dissertation. *Entrance requirements:* For master's and doctorate, GRE General Test, minimum GPA of 2.7. Additional exam requirements/recommendations for international students: Required—TOEFL. Electronic applications accepted. *Expenses:* Tuition, state resident: full-time $8332; part-time $464 per credit hour. Tuition, nonresident: full-time $25,174; part-time $1400 per credit hour. *Required fees:* $1162; $56 per credit hour. Tuition and fees vary according to program.

The University of Texas at Austin, Graduate School, College of Natural Sciences, Department of Chemistry and Biochemistry, Austin, TX 78712-1111. Offers analytical chemistry (PhD); biochemistry (PhD); inorganic chemistry (PhD); organic chemistry (PhD); physical chemistry (PhD). *Entrance requirements:* For doctorate, GRE General Test. Application fee: $50 ($75 for international students). *Financial support:* Fellowships, research assistantships, teaching assistantships, and scholarships/grants available. Financial award application deadline: 2/1. *Unit head:* Dr. Richard M. Crooks, Chairman, 512-475-8674, E-mail: crooks@cm.utexas.edu. *Application contact:* Dr. Jennifer S. Brodbelt, Graduate Admissions Chair, 512-471-0028, E-mail: jbrodbelt@cm.utexas.edu. Web site: http://www.cm.utexas.edu/.

The University of Toledo, College of Graduate Studies, College of Natural Sciences and Mathematics, Department of Chemistry, Toledo, OH 43606-3390. Offers analytical chemistry (MS, PhD); biological chemistry (MS, PhD); inorganic chemistry (MS, PhD); organic chemistry (MS, PhD); physical chemistry (MS, PhD). Part-time programs available. *Faculty:* 22. *Students:* 56 full-time (18 women), 18 part-time (10 women); includes 4 minority (1 Black or African American, non-Hispanic/Latino; 1 Asian, non-Hispanic/Latino; 2 Hispanic/Latino), 43 international. Average age 27. 111 applicants, 17% accepted, 16 enrolled. In 2011, 4 master's, 6 doctorates awarded. *Degree requirements:* For master's, thesis (for some programs); for doctorate, thesis/dissertation. *Entrance requirements:* For master's and doctorate, GRE General Test, GRE Subject Test, minimum cumulative point-hour ratio of 2.7 for all previous academic work, three letters of recommendation, statement of purpose, transcripts from all prior institutions attended. Additional exam requirements/recommendations for international students: Required—TOEFL (minimum score 550 paper-based; 213 computer-based; 80 iBT), IELTS (minimum score 6.5). *Application deadline:* For fall admission, 1/15 priority date for domestic students, 1/15 for international students. Applications are processed on a rolling basis. Application fee: $45 ($75 for international students). Electronic applications accepted. *Financial support:* In 2011–12, 24 research assistantships with full and partial tuition reimbursements (averaging $17,218 per year) were awarded; fellowships with tuition reimbursements, Federal Work-Study, institutionally sponsored loans, scholarships/grants, tuition waivers (full), and unspecified assistantships also available. Support available to part-time students. *Faculty research:* Enzymology, materials chemistry, crystallography, theoretical chemistry. *Unit head:* Dr. Alan Pinkerton, Chair, 419-530-7902, Fax: 419-530-4033, E-mail: alan.pinkerton@utoledo.edu. *Application contact:* Graduate School Office, 419-530-4723, Fax: 419-530-4724, E-mail: grdsch@utnet.utoledo.edu. Web site: http://www.utoledo.edu/nsm/.

Vanderbilt University, Graduate School, Department of Chemistry, Nashville, TN 37240-1001. Offers analytical chemistry (MAT, MS, PhD); inorganic chemistry (MAT, MS, PhD); organic chemistry (MAT, MS, PhD); physical chemistry (MAT, MS, PhD); theoretical chemistry (MAT, MS, PhD). *Faculty:* 21 full-time (3 women). *Students:* 114 full-time (43 women), 2 part-time (0 women); includes 16 minority (6 Black or African American, non-Hispanic/Latino; 1 American Indian or Alaska Native, non-Hispanic/Latino; 3 Asian, non-Hispanic/Latino; 1 Hispanic/Latino; 5 Two or more races, non-Hispanic/Latino), 18 international. Average age 26. 420 applicants, 12% accepted, 18 enrolled. In 2011, 4 master's, 17 doctorates awarded. Terminal master's awarded for partial completion of doctoral program. *Degree requirements:* For master's, thesis; for doctorate, thesis/dissertation, area, qualifying, and final exams. *Entrance requirements:* For master's and doctorate, GRE General Test, GRE Subject Test (recommended). Additional exam requirements/recommendations for international students: Required—TOEFL (minimum score 570 paper-based; 230 computer-based; 88 iBT). *Application deadline:* For fall admission, 1/15 for domestic and international students. Application fee: $0. Electronic applications accepted. *Financial support:* Fellowships with full and partial tuition reimbursements, research assistantships with full tuition reimbursements, teaching assistantships with full tuition reimbursements, Federal Work-Study, institutionally sponsored loans, scholarships/grants, traineeships, and health care benefits available. Financial award application deadline: 1/15; financial award applicants required to submit CSS PROFILE or FAFSA. *Faculty research:* Chemical synthesis; mechanistic, theoretical, bioorganic, analytical, and spectroscopic chemistry. *Unit head:* Dr. Mike P. Stone, Chair, 615-322-2589, Fax: 615-343-1234, E-mail: michael.p.stone@vanderbilt.edu. *Application contact:* Dr. Carmelo J. Rizzo, Director of Graduate Studies, 615-322-6100, Fax: 615-343-1234, E-mail: c.j.rizzo@vanderbilt.edu. Web site: http://www.vanderbilt.edu/AnS/Chemistry/grad/.

Virginia Commonwealth University, Graduate School, College of Humanities and Sciences, Department of Chemistry, Richmond, VA 23284-9005. Offers analytical chemistry (MS, PhD); chemical physics (PhD); inorganic chemistry (MS, PhD); organic chemistry (MS, PhD); physical chemistry (MS, PhD). Part-time programs available. *Students:* 49 full-time (20 women), 19 part-time (8 women); includes 10 minority (3 Black or African American, non-Hispanic/Latino; 5 Asian, non-Hispanic/Latino; 1 Hispanic/Latino; 1 Two or more races, non-Hispanic/Latino), 26 international. 56 applicants, 41% accepted, 11 enrolled. In 2011, 3 master's, 8 doctorates awarded. Terminal master's awarded for partial completion of doctoral program. *Degree requirements:* For master's, thesis; for doctorate, thesis/dissertation, comprehensive cumulative exams, research proposal. *Entrance requirements:* For master's, GRE General Test, 30 undergraduate credits in chemistry; for doctorate, GRE General Test. Additional exam requirements/recommendations for international students: Required—TOEFL (minimum score 600 paper-based; 250 computer-based; 100 iBT) or IELTS (minimum score 6.5). *Application deadline:* For fall admission, 3/15 for domestic students; for spring admission, 11/15 for domestic students. Applications are processed on a rolling basis. Application fee: $50. Electronic applications accepted. *Expenses:* Tuition, state resident: full-time $9133; part-time $507 per credit. Tuition, nonresident: full-time $18,777; part-time $1043 per credit. *Required fees:* $77 per credit. Tuition and fees vary according to degree level, campus/location, program and student level. *Financial support:* Fellowships, research assistantships, teaching assistantships, career-related internships or fieldwork, and institutionally sponsored loans available. Support available to part-time students. Financial award application deadline: 7/1; financial award applicants required to submit FAFSA. *Faculty research:* Physical, organic, inorganic, analytical, and polymer chemistry; chemical physics. *Unit head:* Dr. Scott Gronert, Chair, 804-828-1298, Fax: 804-828-8599, E-mail: sgronert@vcu.edu. *Application contact:* Dr. Maryanne M. Collinson, Chair, Graduate Recruiting and Admissions Committee, 804-828-7509, E-mail: mselshal@vcu.edu. Web site: http://www.has.vcu.edu/che/.

Wake Forest University, Graduate School of Arts and Sciences, Department of Chemistry, Winston-Salem, NC 27109. Offers analytical chemistry (MS, PhD); inorganic chemistry (MS, PhD); organic chemistry (MS, PhD); physical chemistry (MS, PhD). Part-time programs available. *Degree requirements:* For master's, one foreign language, comprehensive exam, thesis; for doctorate, 2 foreign languages, comprehensive exam, thesis/dissertation. *Entrance requirements:* For master's and doctorate, GRE General Test. Additional exam requirements/ recommendations for international students: Required—TOEFL (minimum score 213 computer-based). Electronic applications accepted.

Wesleyan University, Graduate Programs, Department of Chemistry, Middletown, CT 06459. Offers biochemistry (MA, PhD); chemical physics (MA, PhD); inorganic chemistry (MA, PhD); organic chemistry (MA, PhD); physical chemistry (MA, PhD); theoretical chemistry (MA, PhD). Terminal master's awarded for partial completion of doctoral program. *Degree requirements:* For master's, thesis, proposal; for doctorate, thesis/dissertation, proposal. *Entrance requirements:* For doctorate, GRE General Test, 3 recommendations. Additional exam requirements/recommendations for international students: Required—TOEFL. Electronic applications accepted.

West Virginia University, Eberly College of Arts and Sciences, Department of Chemistry, Morgantown, WV 26506. Offers analytical chemistry (MS, PhD); inorganic chemistry (MS, PhD); organic chemistry (MS, PhD); physical chemistry (MS, PhD); theoretical chemistry (MS, PhD). Part-time programs available. Postbaccalaureate distance learning degree programs offered (no on-campus study). Terminal master's awarded for partial completion of doctoral program. *Degree requirements:* For master's, thesis; for doctorate, thesis/dissertation. *Entrance requirements:* For master's, GRE General Test, GRE Subject Test (recommended), minimum GPA of 2.5; for doctorate, GRE General Test, GRE Subject Test (recommended), minimum GPA of 2.75. Additional exam requirements/recommendations for international students: Required—TOEFL. Electronic applications accepted. *Faculty research:* Analysis of proteins, drug interactions, solids and effluents by advanced separation methods; new synthetic strategies for complex organic molecules; synthesis and structural characterization of metal complexes for polymerization catalysis, nonlinear science, spectroscopy.

Yale University, Graduate School of Arts and Sciences, Department of Chemistry, New Haven, CT 06520. Offers biophysical chemistry (PhD); inorganic chemistry (PhD); organic chemistry (PhD); physical and theoretical chemistry (PhD). *Degree requirements:* For doctorate, thesis/dissertation. *Entrance requirements:* For doctorate, GRE General Test, GRE Subject Test. Additional exam requirements/recommendations for international students: Required—TOEFL.

Youngstown State University, Graduate School, College of Science, Technology, Engineering and Mathematics, Department of Chemistry, Youngstown, OH 44555-0001. Offers analytical chemistry (MS); biochemistry (MS); chemistry education (MS); inorganic chemistry (MS); organic chemistry (MS); physical chemistry (MS). Part-time programs available. *Degree requirements:* For master's, thesis. *Entrance requirements:* For master's, bachelor's degree in chemistry, minimum GPA of 2.7. Additional exam requirements/recommendations for international students: Required—TOEFL. *Faculty research:* Analysis of antioxidants, chromatography, defects and disorder in crystalline oxides, hydrogen bonding, novel organic and organometallic materials.

Peterson's Graduate Programs in the Physical Sciences, Mathematics, Agricultural Sciences, the Environment & Natural Resources 2013

Physical Chemistry

Auburn University, Graduate School, College of Sciences and Mathematics, Department of Chemistry and Biochemistry, Auburn University, AL 36849. Offers analytical chemistry (MS, PhD); biochemistry (MS, PhD); inorganic chemistry (MS, PhD); organic chemistry (MS, PhD); physical chemistry (MS, PhD). Part-time programs available. *Faculty:* 28 full-time (5 women), 1 part-time/adjunct (0 women). *Students:* 37 full-time (14 women), 30 part-time (15 women); includes 6 minority (3 Black or African American, non-Hispanic/Latino; 1 American Indian or Alaska Native, non-Hispanic/Latino; 1 Asian, non-Hispanic/Latino; 1 Hispanic/Latino), 41 international. Average age 28. 38 applicants, 39% accepted, 12 enrolled. In 2011, 1 master's, 9 doctorates awarded. *Degree requirements:* For master's, thesis (for some programs); for doctorate, thesis/dissertation, oral and written exams. *Entrance requirements:* For master's and doctorate, GRE General Test. *Application deadline:* For fall admission, 7/7 for domestic students; for spring admission, 11/24 for domestic students. Applications are processed on a rolling basis. Application fee: $50 ($60 for international students). Electronic applications accepted. *Expenses:* Tuition, state resident: full-time $7290; part-time $405 per credit hour. Tuition, nonresident: full-time $21,870; part-time $1215 per credit hour. *International tuition:* $22,000 full-time. *Required fees:* $1402. *Financial support:* Fellowships, research assistantships, and teaching assistantships available. Financial award application deadline: 3/15; financial award applicants required to submit FAFSA. *Unit head:* Dr. J. V. Ortiz, Chair, 334-844-4043, Fax: 334-844-4043. *Application contact:* Dr. George Flowers, Dean of the Graduate School, 334-844-2125. Web site: http://www.auburn.edu/cosam/departments/chemistry/.

Boston College, Graduate School of Arts and Sciences, Department of Chemistry, Chestnut Hill, MA 02467-3800. Offers biochemistry (PhD); inorganic chemistry (PhD); organic chemistry (PhD); physical chemistry (PhD); science education (MST). *Degree requirements:* For doctorate, thesis/dissertation, qualifying exam. *Entrance requirements:* For doctorate, GRE General Test, GRE Subject Test. Additional exam requirements/recommendations for international students: Required—TOEFL (minimum score 600 paper-based; 250 computer-based; 100 iBT). Electronic applications accepted.

Brandeis University, Graduate School of Arts and Sciences, Department of Chemistry, Waltham, MA 02454. Offers inorganic chemistry (MS, PhD); organic chemistry (MS, PhD); physical chemistry (MS, PhD). Terminal master's awarded for partial completion of doctoral program. *Degree requirements:* For master's, thesis, 1 year of residency; for doctorate, one foreign language, thesis/dissertation, 3 years of residency, 2 seminars, qualifying exams. *Entrance requirements:* For master's and doctorate, GRE General Test, resume, letters of recommendation. Additional exam requirements/recommendations for international students: Required—TOEFL (minimum score 600 paper-based; 250 computer-based; 100 iBT); Recommended—IELTS (minimum score 7). Electronic applications accepted. *Faculty research:* Oscillating chemical reactions, molecular recognition systems, protein crystallography, synthesis of natural product spectroscopy and magnetic resonance.

California State University, Los Angeles, Graduate Studies, College of Natural and Social Sciences, Department of Chemistry and Biochemistry, Los Angeles, CA 90032-8530. Offers analytical chemistry (MS); biochemistry (MS); chemistry (MS); inorganic chemistry (MS); organic chemistry (MS); physical chemistry (MS). Part-time and evening/weekend programs available. *Faculty:* 4 part-time/adjunct (1 woman). *Students:* 22 full-time (14 women), 24 part-time (11 women); includes 30 minority (4 Black or African American, non-Hispanic/Latino; 7 Asian, non-Hispanic/Latino; 19 Hispanic/Latino), 7 international. Average age 29. 60 applicants, 48% accepted, 17 enrolled. In 2011, 15 master's awarded. *Degree requirements:* For master's, one foreign language, comprehensive exam or thesis. *Entrance requirements:* Additional exam requirements/recommendations for international students: Required—TOEFL. *Application deadline:* For fall admission, 5/1 for domestic and international students. Applications are processed on a rolling basis. Application fee: $55. *Expenses:* Tuition, state resident: full-time $8225. *Financial support:* Federal Work-Study available. Support available to part-time students. Financial award application deadline: 3/1. *Faculty research:* Intercalation of heavy metal, carborane chemistry, conductive polymers and fabrics, titanium reagents, computer modeling and synthesis. *Unit head:* Dr. Robert L. Vellanoweth, Chair, 323-343-2300, Fax: 323-343-6490, E-mail: rvellan@calstatela.edu. *Application contact:* Dr. Karin Brown, Acting Associate Dean of Graduate Studies, 323-343-3820 Ext. 3827, Fax: 323-343-5653, E-mail: kbrown5@calstatela.edu. Web site: http://www.calstatela.edu/dept/chem/index.htm.

Cleveland State University, College of Graduate Studies, College of Sciences and Health Professions, Department of Chemistry, Cleveland, OH 44115. Offers analytical chemistry (MS); clinical chemistry (MS); clinical/bioanalytical chemistry (PhD), including cellular and molecular medicine, clinical chemistry, clinical/bioanalytical chemistry; environmental chemistry (MS); inorganic chemistry (MS); pharmaceutical/organic chemistry (MS); physical chemistry (MS). Part-time and evening/weekend programs available. *Faculty:* 12 full-time (0 women). *Students:* 17 full-time (8 women), 87 part-time (36 women); includes 6 minority (5 Black or African American, non-Hispanic/Latino; 1 Asian, non-Hispanic/Latino), 74 international. Average age 27. 143 applicants, 59% accepted, 22 enrolled. In

2011, 14 master's, 10 doctorates awarded. *Median time to degree:* Of those who began their doctoral program in fall 2003, 67% received their degree in 8 years or less. *Degree requirements:* For master's, thesis optional; for doctorate, comprehensive exam, thesis/dissertation. *Entrance requirements:* For master's and doctorate, GRE General Test. Additional exam requirements/recommendations for international students: Required—TOEFL (minimum score 525 paper-based; 197 computer-based; 65 iBT). *Application deadline:* For fall admission, 1/15 priority date for domestic students, 1/15 for international students. Applications are processed on a rolling basis. Application fee: $30. Electronic applications accepted. *Expenses:* Tuition, state resident: full-time $6416; part-time $494 per credit hour. Tuition, nonresident: full-time $12,074; part-time $929 per credit hour. *Financial support:* In 2011–12, 44 students received support, including 5 fellowships with full tuition reimbursements available (averaging $30,000 per year), 13 research assistantships with full tuition reimbursements available (averaging $20,000 per year), 24 teaching assistantships with full tuition reimbursements available (averaging $18,500 per year); scholarships/grants and unspecified assistantships also available. Financial award application deadline: 1/15. *Faculty research:* Bioanalytical techniques and molecular diagnostics, glycoproteomics and antithrombotic agents, drug discovery and innovation, analytical pharmacology, inflammatory disease research. *Total annual research expenditures:* $3 million. *Unit head:* Dr. David J. Anderson, Interim Chair, 216-687-2467, Fax: 216-687-9298, E-mail: d.anderson@csuohio.edu. *Application contact:* Richelle P. Emery, Administrative Coordinator, 216-687-2457, Fax: 216-687-9298, E-mail: r.emery@csuohio.edu. Web site: http://www.csuohio.edu/chemistry/.

Cornell University, Graduate School, Graduate Fields of Arts and Sciences, Field of Chemistry and Chemical Biology, Ithaca, NY 14853-0001. Offers analytical chemistry (PhD); bio-organic chemistry (PhD); biophysical chemistry (PhD); chemical biology (PhD); chemical physics (PhD); inorganic chemistry (PhD); materials chemistry (PhD); organic chemistry (PhD); organometallic chemistry (PhD); physical chemistry (PhD); polymer chemistry (PhD); theoretical chemistry (PhD). *Faculty:* 46 full-time (3 women). *Students:* 151 full-time (67 women); includes 16 minority (13 Asian, non-Hispanic/Latino; 2 Hispanic/Latino; 1 Two or more races, non-Hispanic/Latino), 48 international. Average age 25. 297 applicants, 35% accepted, 29 enrolled. In 2011, 22 doctorates awarded. *Degree requirements:* For doctorate, comprehensive exam, thesis/dissertation. *Entrance requirements:* For doctorate, GRE General Test, GRE Subject Test (chemistry), 3 letters of recommendation. Additional exam requirements/recommendations for international students: Required—TOEFL (minimum score 600 paper-based; 250 computer-based; 77 iBT). *Application deadline:* For fall admission, 1/10 for domestic students. Application fee: $95. Electronic applications accepted. *Financial support:* In 2011–12, 21 fellowships with full tuition reimbursements, 63 research assistantships with full tuition reimbursements, 59 teaching assistantships with full tuition reimbursements were awarded; institutionally sponsored loans, scholarships/grants, health care benefits, tuition waivers (full and partial), and unspecified assistantships also available. Financial award applicants required to submit FAFSA. *Faculty research:* Analytical, organic, inorganic, physical, materials, chemical biology. *Unit head:* Director of Graduate Studies, 607-255-4139, Fax: 607-255-4137. *Application contact:* Graduate Field Assistant, 607-255-4139, Fax: 607-255-4137, E-mail: chemgrad@cornell.edu. Web site: http://www.gradschool.cornell.edu/fields.php?id-26&a-2.

Eastern New Mexico University, Graduate School, College of Liberal Arts and Sciences, Department of Physical Sciences, Portales, NM 88130. Offers chemistry (MS), including analytical, biochemistry, inorganic, organic, physical. Part-time programs available. *Faculty:* 6 full-time (0 women). *Students:* 11 part-time (5 women), 9 international. Average age 25. 25 applicants, 44% accepted, 4 enrolled. In 2011, 5 master's awarded. *Degree requirements:* For master's, thesis optional, seminar, oral and written comprehensive exams. *Entrance requirements:* For master's, ACS placement examination, minimum GPA of 3.0; 2 letters of recommendation; personal statement of career goals; bachelor's degree with one year minimum each of general, organic, and analytical chemistry. Additional exam requirements/recommendations for international students: Required—TOEFL (minimum score 550 paper-based; 213 computer-based; 79 iBT), IELTS (minimum score 6). *Application deadline:* For fall admission, 7/20 priority date for domestic students, 6/20 for international students; for spring admission, 12/15 priority date for domestic students, 11/15 for international students. Applications are processed on a rolling basis. Application fee: $10. Electronic applications accepted. *Financial support:* In 2011–12, 1 research assistantship with partial tuition reimbursement (averaging $8,500 per year), 10 teaching assistantships with partial tuition reimbursements (averaging $8,500 per year) were awarded; career-related internships or fieldwork and unspecified assistantships also available. Support available to part-time students. Financial award application deadline: 3/1; financial award applicants required to submit FAFSA. *Faculty research:* Synfuel, electrochemistry, protein chemistry. *Unit head:* Dr. Juacho Yan, Graduate Coordinator, 575-562-2494, Fax: 575-562-2192, E-mail: juacho.yan@enmu.edu. *Application contact:* Sharon Potter, Department Secretary, Biology and Physical Sciences, 575-562-2174, Fax: 575-562-2192, E-mail: sharon.potter@enmu.edu. Web site: http://liberal-arts.enmu.edu/sciences/grad-chemistry.shtml.

Peterson's Graduate Programs in the Physical Sciences, Mathematics, Agricultural Sciences, the Environment & Natural Resources 2013

facebook.com/petersonspublishing **115**

Physical Chemistry

Florida State University, The Graduate School, College of Arts and Sciences, Department of Chemistry and Biochemistry, Tallahassee, FL 32306-4390. Offers analytical chemistry (MS, PhD); biochemistry (MS, PhD); inorganic chemistry (MS, PhD); materials chemistry (PhD); organic chemistry (MS, PhD); physical chemistry (MS, PhD). *Faculty:* 35 full-time (5 women), 1 (woman) part-time/adjunct. *Students:* 138 full-time (52 women), 8 part-time (1 woman); includes 14 minority (6 Black or African American, non-Hispanic/Latino; 3 Asian, non-Hispanic/Latino; 2 Hispanic/Latino; 3 Two or more races, non-Hispanic/Latino), 63 international. Average age 25. 147 applicants, 40% accepted, 28 enrolled. In 2011, 10 master's, 24 doctorates awarded. Terminal master's awarded for partial completion of doctoral program. *Median time to degree:* Of those who began their doctoral program in fall 2003, 58% received their degree in 8 years or less. *Degree requirements:* For master's, comprehensive exam (for some programs), thesis (for some programs); for doctorate, comprehensive exam (for some programs), thesis/dissertation. *Entrance requirements:* For master's and doctorate, GRE General Test, minimum B average in undergraduate course work. Additional exam requirements/recommendations for international students: Required—TOEFL (minimum score 550 paper-based; 213 computer-based; 80 iBT). *Application deadline:* For fall admission, 12/15 priority date for domestic students, 12/15 for international students; for spring admission, 9/15 for domestic and international students. Applications are processed on a rolling basis. Application fee: $30. Electronic applications accepted. *Expenses:* Contact institution. *Financial support:* In 2011–12, 140 students received support, including fellowships with full tuition reimbursements available (averaging $20,000 per year), 50 research assistantships with full tuition reimbursements available (averaging $20,000 per year), 100 teaching assistantships with full tuition reimbursements available (averaging $20,000 per year). Financial award application deadline: 12/15; financial award applicants required to submit FAFSA. *Faculty research:* Materials synthesis including polymers, natural products; catalysis, NMR; mass spectrometry; optical spectroscopy, scattering techniques, computational chemistry, separation technology; nanostructured materials including metallic, semiconducting and magnetic nanocrystals; nanoscience interfaced with biology; supramolecular materials for solar energy conversion. *Total annual research expenditures:* $9.9 million. *Unit head:* Dr. Timothy Logan, Chairman, 850-644-1244, Fax: 850-644-8281, E-mail: gradinfo@chem.fsu.edu. *Application contact:* Dr. Michael Shatruk, Chair, Graduate Admissions Committee, 888-525-9286, Fax: 850-644-0465, E-mail: gradinfo@chem.fsu.edu. Web site: http://www.chem.fsu.edu/.

Georgetown University, Graduate School of Arts and Sciences, Department of Chemistry, Washington, DC 20057. Offers analytical chemistry (PhD); biochemistry (PhD); computational chemistry (PhD); inorganic chemistry (PhD); materials chemistry (PhD); organic chemistry (PhD); physical chemistry (PhD); theoretical chemistry (PhD). Terminal master's awarded for partial completion of doctoral program. *Degree requirements:* For doctorate, comprehensive exam, thesis/dissertation. *Entrance requirements:* For doctorate, GRE General Test. Additional exam requirements/recommendations for international students: Required—TOEFL.

The George Washington University, Columbian College of Arts and Sciences, Department of Chemistry, Washington, DC 20052. Offers analytical chemistry (MS, PhD); inorganic chemistry (MS, PhD); materials science (MS, PhD); organic chemistry (MS, PhD); physical chemistry (MS, PhD). Part-time and evening/weekend programs available. *Faculty:* 16 full-time (5 women), 5 part-time/adjunct (2 women). *Students:* 22 full-time (10 women), 10 part-time (7 women); includes 4 minority (3 Asian, non-Hispanic/Latino; 1 Hispanic/Latino), 7 international. Average age 27. 55 applicants, 42% accepted, 8 enrolled. In 2011, 4 master's, 3 doctorates awarded. Terminal master's awarded for partial completion of doctoral program. *Degree requirements:* For master's, comprehensive exam, thesis or alternative; for doctorate, thesis/dissertation, general exam. *Entrance requirements:* For master's and doctorate, GRE General Test, interview, minimum GPA of 3.0. Additional exam requirements/recommendations for international students: Required—TOEFL (minimum score 550 paper-based; 213 computer-based; 80 iBT). *Application deadline:* For fall admission, 1/15 priority date for domestic students, 1/15 for international students; for spring admission, 9/1 priority date for domestic students, 9/1 for international students. Applications are processed on a rolling basis. Application fee: $75. Electronic applications accepted. *Financial support:* In 2011–12, 27 students received support. Fellowships with tuition reimbursements available, research assistantships, teaching assistantships with tuition reimbursements available, Federal Work-Study, and tuition waivers available. Financial award application deadline: 1/15. *Unit head:* Dr. Michael King, Chair, 202-994-6488. *Application contact:* Information Contact, 202-994-6121, E-mail: gwchem@gwu.edu. Web site: http://www.gwu.edu/~gwchem/.

Harvard University, Graduate School of Arts and Sciences, Department of Chemistry and Chemical Biology, Cambridge, MA 02138. Offers biochemical chemistry (PhD); inorganic chemistry (PhD); organic chemistry (PhD); physical chemistry (PhD). *Degree requirements:* For doctorate, thesis/dissertation, cumulative exams. *Entrance requirements:* For doctorate, GRE General Test, GRE Subject Test. Additional exam requirements/recommendations for international students: Required—TOEFL. *Expenses:* Tuition: Full-time $36,304. *Required fees:* $1186. Full-time tuition and fees vary according to program.

See Display on page 67 and Close-Up on page 125.

Howard University, Graduate School, Department of Chemistry, Washington, DC 20059-0002. Offers analytical chemistry (MS, PhD); atmospheric (MS, PhD);

biochemistry (MS, PhD); environmental (MS, PhD); inorganic chemistry (MS, PhD); organic chemistry (MS, PhD); physical chemistry (MS, PhD). Terminal master's awarded for partial completion of doctoral program. *Degree requirements:* For master's, comprehensive exam, thesis, teaching experience; for doctorate, comprehensive exam, thesis/dissertation, teaching experience. *Entrance requirements:* For master's, GRE General Test, minimum GPA of 2.7; for doctorate, GRE General Test, minimum GPA of 3.0. Additional exam requirements/recommendations for international students: Required—TOEFL. Electronic applications accepted. *Faculty research:* Synthetic organics, materials, natural products, mass spectrometry.

Indiana University Bloomington, University Graduate School, College of Arts and Sciences, Department of Chemistry, Bloomington, IN 47405. Offers analytical chemistry (PhD); chemical biology chemistry (PhD); chemistry (MAT); inorganic chemistry (PhD); materials chemistry (PhD); organic chemistry (PhD); physical chemistry (PhD). *Faculty:* 42 full-time (4 women). *Students:* 200 full-time (82 women), 3 part-time (0 women); includes 18 minority (7 Black or African American, non-Hispanic/Latino; 8 Asian, non-Hispanic/Latino; 1 Hispanic/Latino; 1 Native Hawaiian or other Pacific Islander, non-Hispanic/Latino; 1 Two or more races, non-Hispanic/Latino), 63 international. Average age 27. 290 applicants, 49% accepted, 46 enrolled. In 2011, 11 master's, 20 doctorates awarded. Terminal master's awarded for partial completion of doctoral program. *Median time to degree:* Of those who began their doctoral program in fall 2003, 49% received their degree in 8 years or less. *Degree requirements:* For master's, thesis; for doctorate, thesis/dissertation. *Entrance requirements:* For master's and doctorate, GRE General Test, GRE Subject Test. Additional exam requirements/recommendations for international students: Required—TOEFL. *Application deadline:* For fall admission, 1/15 priority date for domestic students, 12/15 for international students. Applications are processed on a rolling basis. Application fee: $55 ($65 for international students). *Financial support:* In 2011–12, 200 students received support, including 10 fellowships with full tuition reimbursements available, 76 research assistantships with full tuition reimbursements available, 111 teaching assistantships with full tuition reimbursements available; Federal Work-Study and institutionally sponsored loans also available. *Faculty research:* Synthesis of complex natural products, organic reaction mechanisms, organic electrochemistry, transitive-metal chemistry, solid-state and surface chemistry. *Total annual research expenditures:* $7.7 million. *Unit head:* David Giedroc, Chairperson, 812-855-6239, E-mail: chemchair@indiana.edu. *Application contact:* Daniel Mindiola, Director of Graduate Admissions, 812-855-2069, Fax: 812-855-8385, E-mail: mindiola@indiana.edu. Web site: http://www.chem.indiana.edu/.

Iowa State University of Science and Technology, Program in Physical Chemistry, Ames, IA 50011-3011. Offers MS, PhD. *Entrance requirements:* Additional exam requirements/recommendations for international students: Required—TOEFL (minimum score 570 paper-based; 89 iBT), IELTS (minimum score 6.5). *Application deadline:* For fall admission, 2/1 for domestic students. Electronic applications accepted. *Unit head:* Theresa Windus, Director of Graduate Education, 800-521-2436, Fax: 515-294-0105, E-mail: chemgrad@iastate.edu. *Application contact:* Lynette Edsall, Application Contact, 800-521-2436, Fax: 515-294-0105, E-mail: grad_admissions@iastate.edu. Web site: http://www.chem.iastate.edu.

Kansas State University, Graduate School, College of Arts and Sciences, Department of Chemistry, Manhattan, KS 66506. Offers analytical chemistry (MS); biological chemistry (MS); chemistry (PhD); inorganic chemistry (MS); materials chemistry (MS); organic chemistry (MS); physical chemistry (MS). *Faculty:* 17 full-time (2 women). *Students:* 63 full-time (28 women), 4 part-time (0 women); includes 2 minority (1 Black or African American, non-Hispanic/Latino; 1 Asian, non-Hispanic/Latino), 55 international. Average age 28. 119 applicants, 34% accepted, 15 enrolled. In 2011, 2 master's, 10 doctorates awarded. Terminal master's awarded for partial completion of doctoral program. *Degree requirements:* For master's, thesis; for doctorate, thesis/dissertation. *Entrance requirements:* For master's and doctorate, GRE, minimum GPA of 3.0. Additional exam requirements/recommendations for international students: Required—TOEFL (minimum score 550 paper-based; 213 computer-based). *Application deadline:* For fall admission, 2/1 priority date for domestic students, 2/1 for international students; for spring admission, 8/1 priority date for domestic students, 8/1 for international students. Applications are processed on a rolling basis. Application fee: $40 ($55 for international students). Electronic applications accepted. *Financial support:* In 2011–12, 39 research assistantships (averaging $18,182 per year), 24 teaching assistantships with full tuition reimbursements (averaging $18,106 per year) were awarded; institutionally sponsored loans and scholarships/grants also available. Support available to part-time students. Financial award application deadline: 3/1; financial award applicants required to submit FAFSA. *Faculty research:* Inorganic chemistry, organic and biological chemistry, analytical chemistry, physical chemistry, materials chemistry and nanotechnology. *Total annual research expenditures:* $2.4 million. *Unit head:* Eric Maatta, Head, 785-532-6665, Fax: 785-532-6666, E-mail: eam@ksu.edu. *Application contact:* Christer Aakeroy, Director, 785-532-6096, Fax: 785-532-6666, E-mail: aakeroy@ksu.edu. Web site: http://www.k-state.edu/chem/.

Kent State University, College of Arts and Sciences, Department of Chemistry and Biochemistry, Kent, OH 44242-0001. Offers analytical chemistry (MS, PhD); biochemistry (MS, PhD); chemistry (MA); inorganic chemistry (MS, PhD); organic chemistry (MS, PhD); physical chemistry (MS, PhD). Terminal master's awarded for partial completion of doctoral program. *Degree requirements:* For master's,

116 facebook.com/petersonspublishing

Peterson's Graduate Programs in the Physical Sciences, Mathematics, Agricultural Sciences, the Environment & Natural Resources 2013

comprehensive exam, thesis; for doctorate, comprehensive exam, thesis/dissertation. *Entrance requirements:* For master's and doctorate, placement exam, GRE General Test, GRE Subject Test (recommended), minimum GPA of 2.75. Additional exam requirements/recommendations for international students: Required—TOEFL (minimum score 525 paper-based; 71 iBT). Electronic applications accepted. *Expenses:* Tuition, state resident: full-time $8136; part-time $452 per credit hour. Tuition, nonresident: full-time $14,292; part-time $794 per credit hour. *Faculty research:* Biological chemistry, materials chemistry, molecular spectroscopy.

See Display on page 70 and Close-Up on page 127.

Laurentian University, School of Graduate Studies and Research, Programme in Chemistry and Biochemistry, Sudbury, ON P3E 2C6, Canada. Offers analytical chemistry (M Sc); biochemistry (M Sc); environmental chemistry (M Sc); organic chemistry (M Sc); physical/theoretical chemistry (M Sc). Part-time programs available. *Degree requirements:* For master's, thesis or alternative. *Entrance requirements:* For master's, honors degree with minimum second class. *Faculty research:* Cell cycle checkpoints, kinetic modeling, toxicology to metal stress, quantum chemistry, biogeochemistry metal speciation.

Marquette University, Graduate School, College of Arts and Sciences, Department of Chemistry, Milwaukee, WI 53201-1881. Offers analytical chemistry (MS, PhD); bioanalytical chemistry (MS, PhD); biophysical chemistry (MS, PhD); chemical physics (MS, PhD); inorganic chemistry (MS, PhD); organic chemistry (MS, PhD); physical chemistry (MS, PhD). Part-time programs available. *Faculty:* 29 full-time (4 women), 1 (woman) part-time/adjunct. *Students:* 42 full-time (11 women), 2 part-time (0 women); includes 5 minority (2 Black or African American, non-Hispanic/Latino; 3 Asian, non-Hispanic/Latino), 31 international. Average age 29. 18 applicants, 100% accepted, 10 enrolled. In 2011, 5 master's, 7 doctorates awarded. Terminal master's awarded for partial completion of doctoral program. *Degree requirements:* For master's, comprehensive exam; for doctorate, thesis/dissertation, cumulative exams. *Entrance requirements:* For master's and doctorate, official transcripts from all current and previous colleges/universities except Marquette, three letters of recommendation from individuals familiar with the applicant's academic work. Additional exam requirements/recommendations for international students: Required—TOEFL (minimum score 530 paper-based; 78 computer-based). *Application deadline:* Applications are processed on a rolling basis. Application fee: $50. Electronic applications accepted. *Expenses: Tuition:* Full-time $17,010; part-time $945 per credit hour. Tuition and fees vary according to program. *Financial support:* In 2011–12, 41 students received support, including 2 fellowships (averaging $17,134 per year), 30 teaching assistantships with full tuition reimbursements available (averaging $20,295 per year); research assistantships, scholarships/grants, health care benefits, tuition waivers (full and partial), and unspecified assistantships also available. Support available to part-time students. Financial award application deadline: 2/15. *Faculty research:* Inorganic complexes, laser Raman spectroscopy, organic synthesis, synthetic bioinorganic chemistry, electro-active organic molecules. *Total annual research expenditures:* $2.1 million. *Unit head:* Dr. Michael Ryan, Chair, 414-288-3537, Fax: 414-288-7066. *Application contact:* Dr. Mark Steinmetz, Director of Graduate Studies, 414-288-7374, Fax: 414-288-7066. Web site: http://www.marquette.edu/chem/graduate.shtml.

Massachusetts Institute of Technology, School of Science, Department of Chemistry, Cambridge, MA 02139. Offers biological chemistry (PhD, Sc D); inorganic chemistry (PhD, Sc D); organic chemistry (PhD, Sc D); physical chemistry (PhD, Sc D). *Faculty:* 26 full-time (5 women). *Students:* 221 full-time (73 women), 1 (woman) part-time; includes 48 minority (5 Black or African American, non-Hispanic/Latino; 1 American Indian or Alaska Native, non-Hispanic/Latino; 24 Asian, non-Hispanic/Latino; 14 Hispanic/Latino; 4 Two or more races, non-Hispanic/Latino), 64 international. Average age 25. 570 applicants, 20% accepted, 43 enrolled. In 2011, 45 doctorates awarded. *Degree requirements:* For doctorate, comprehensive exam, thesis/dissertation. *Entrance requirements:* For doctorate, GRE General Test. Additional exam requirements/recommendations for international students: Required—IELTS (minimum score 7); Recommended—TOEFL (minimum score 600 paper-based; 250 computer-based). *Application deadline:* For fall admission, 12/15 for domestic and international students. Application fee: $75. Electronic applications accepted. *Expenses: Tuition:* Full-time $40,460; part-time $630 per credit hour. *Required fees:* $272. *Financial support:* In 2011–12, 216 students received support, including 79 fellowships (averaging $34,800 per year), 127 research assistantships (averaging $31,400 per year), 16 teaching assistantships (averaging $32,600 per year); Federal Work-Study, institutionally sponsored loans, scholarships/grants, traineeships, health care benefits, and unspecified assistantships also available. *Faculty research:* Synthetic organic and organometallic chemistry including catalysis; biological chemistry including bioorganic chemistry; physical chemistry including chemical dynamics and biophysical chemistry; inorganic chemistry including synthesis, catalysis, bioinorganic and physical inorganic chemistry; materials chemistry including surface science, nanoscience and polymers. *Total annual research expenditures:* $31.1 million. *Unit head:* Prof. Sylvia T. Ceyer, Head, 617-253-1803, Fax: 617-258-7500. *Application contact:* Graduate Administrator, 617-253-1845, Fax: 617-258-0241, E-mail: chemgradeducation@mit.edu. Web site: http://web.mit.edu/chemistry/www/.

McMaster University, School of Graduate Studies, Faculty of Science, Department of Chemistry, Hamilton, ON L8S 4M2, Canada. Offers analytical chemistry (M Sc, PhD); chemical physics (M Sc, PhD); chemistry (M Sc, PhD);

inorganic chemistry (M Sc, PhD); organic chemistry (M Sc, PhD); physical chemistry (M Sc, PhD); polymer chemistry (M Sc, PhD). Part-time programs available. Terminal master's awarded for partial completion of doctoral program. *Degree requirements:* For master's, thesis; for doctorate, comprehensive exam, thesis/dissertation. *Entrance requirements:* For master's, minimum B+ average. Additional exam requirements/recommendations for international students: Required—TOEFL (minimum score 550 paper-based; 213 computer-based).

Northeastern University, College of Science, Department of Chemistry and Chemical Biology, Boston, MA 02115-5096. Offers analytical chemistry (PhD); chemistry (MS, PhD); inorganic chemistry (PhD); organic chemistry (PhD); physical chemistry (PhD). Part-time and evening/weekend programs available. *Faculty:* 24 full-time, 7 part-time/adjunct. *Students:* 98 full-time (58 women), 31 part-time (15 women). 190 applicants, 32% accepted, 34 enrolled. In 2011, 16 master's, 6 doctorates awarded. Terminal master's awarded for partial completion of doctoral program. *Degree requirements:* For master's, thesis (for some programs); for doctorate, thesis/dissertation, qualifying exam in specialty area. *Entrance requirements:* Additional exam requirements/recommendations for international students: Required—TOEFL. *Application deadline:* For fall admission, 2/1 priority date for domestic students, 2/1 for international students. Applications are processed on a rolling basis. Application fee: $50. Electronic applications accepted. *Financial support:* In 2011–12, 41 research assistantships with tuition reimbursements (averaging $18,285 per year), 38 teaching assistantships with tuition reimbursements (averaging $18,285 per year) were awarded; fellowships with tuition reimbursements, career-related internships or fieldwork, Federal Work-Study, scholarships/grants, tuition waivers (partial), and unspecified assistantships also available. Financial award application deadline: 3/1; financial award applicants required to submit FAFSA. *Faculty research:* Bioanalysis, biorganic and medicinal chemistry, biophysical chemistry, nanomaterials, proteonics. *Unit head:* Dr. Robert Hanson, Graduate Coordinator, 617-373-3313, Fax: 617-373-8795, E-mail: chemistry-grad-info@neu.edu. *Application contact:* Jo-Anne Dickinson, Admissions Contact, 617-373-5990, Fax: 617-373-7281, E-mail: gsas@neu.edu. Web site: http://www.northeastern.edu/chem/.

Old Dominion University, College of Sciences, Program in Chemistry, Norfolk, VA 23529. Offers analytical chemistry (MS); biochemistry (MS); chemistry (PhD); environmental chemistry (MS); organic chemistry (MS); physical chemistry (MS). Part-time and evening/weekend programs available. *Faculty:* 14 full-time (5 women), 2 part-time/adjunct (0 women). *Students:* 34 full-time (17 women), 2 part-time (1 woman); includes 2 minority (1 Black or African American, non-Hispanic/Latino; 1 Asian, non-Hispanic/Latino), 17 international. Average age 28. 35 applicants, 60% accepted, 8 enrolled. In 2011, 3 master's, 2 doctorates awarded. *Degree requirements:* For master's, comprehensive exam, thesis. *Entrance requirements:* For master's, GRE General Test, minimum GPA of 3.0 in major, 2.5 overall; for doctorate, GRE General Test. Additional exam requirements/recommendations for international students: Required—TOEFL. *Application deadline:* For fall admission, 7/1 for domestic students, 1/15 for international students; for spring admission, 11/1 for domestic students, 8/15 for international students. Applications are processed on a rolling basis. Application fee: $30. Electronic applications accepted. *Expenses:* Tuition, state resident: full-time $9096; part-time $379 per credit. Tuition, nonresident: full-time $23,064; part-time $961 per credit. *Required fees:* $127 per semester. One-time fee: $50. *Financial support:* In 2011–12, 6 students received support, including fellowships (averaging $18,000 per year), research assistantships with tuition reimbursements available (averaging $21,000 per year), teaching assistantships with tuition reimbursements available (averaging $18,000 per year); career-related internships or fieldwork, scholarships/grants, and unspecified assistantships also available. Financial award application deadline: 2/15; financial award applicants required to submit FAFSA. *Faculty research:* Biogeochemistry, materials chemistry, bioanalytical chemistry, computational chemistry, organic chemistry. *Total annual research expenditures:* $2.6 million. *Unit head:* Dr. Craig A. Bayse, Graduate Program Director, 757-683-4097, Fax: 757-683-4628, E-mail: chemgpd@odu.edu. *Application contact:* Valerie DeCosta, Grants and Graduate Program Assistant, 757-683-6979, Fax: 757-683-4628, E-mail: chemgpd@odu.edu.

Oregon State University, Graduate School, College of Science, Department of Chemistry, Corvallis, OR 97331. Offers analytical chemistry (MS, PhD); chemistry (MA, MAIS); inorganic chemistry (MS, PhD); nuclear and radiation chemistry (MS, PhD); organic chemistry (MS, PhD); physical chemistry (MS, PhD). Part-time programs available. Terminal master's awarded for partial completion of doctoral program. *Degree requirements:* For master's, one foreign language, thesis; for doctorate, one foreign language, thesis/dissertation. *Entrance requirements:* For master's and doctorate, minimum GPA of 3.0 in last 90 hours of course work. Additional exam requirements/recommendations for international students: Required—TOEFL. *Faculty research:* Solid state chemistry, enzyme reaction mechanisms, structure and dynamics of gas molecules, chemiluminescence, nonlinear optical spectroscopy.

Purdue University, Graduate School, College of Science, Department of Chemistry, West Lafayette, IN 47907. Offers analytical chemistry (MS, PhD); biochemistry (MS, PhD); chemical education (MS, PhD); inorganic chemistry (MS, PhD); organic chemistry (MS, PhD); physical chemistry (MS, PhD). *Faculty:* 47 full-time (16 women), 6 part-time/adjunct (0 women). *Students:* 275 full-time (103 women), 33 part-time (10 women); includes 38 minority (19 Black or African American, non-Hispanic/Latino; 6 Asian, non-Hispanic/Latino; 12 Hispanic/Latino;

Peterson's Graduate Programs in the Physical Sciences, Mathematics, Agricultural Sciences, the Environment & Natural Resources 2013

facebook.com/petersonspublishing **117**

SECTION 2: CHEMISTRY

Physical Chemistry

1 Two or more races, non-Hispanic/Latino), 94 international. Average age 27. 777 applicants, 26% accepted, 62 enrolled. In 2011, 4 master's, 67 doctorates awarded. Terminal master's awarded for partial completion of doctoral program. *Degree requirements:* For master's, thesis; for doctorate, comprehensive exam, thesis/dissertation. *Entrance requirements:* For master's and doctorate, minimum undergraduate GPA of 3.0. Additional exam requirements/recommendations for international students: Required—TOEFL (minimum score 550 computer-based; 77 iBT); Recommended—TWE. *Application deadline:* For fall admission, 2/15 priority date for domestic students, 1/1 for international students. Applications are processed on a rolling basis. Application fee: $60 ($75 for international students). Electronic applications accepted. *Financial support:* In 2011–12, 2 fellowships with partial tuition reimbursements (averaging $18,000 per year), 55 teaching assistantships with partial tuition reimbursements (averaging $18,000 per year) were awarded; research assistantships with partial tuition reimbursements and tuition waivers (partial) also available. Support available to part-time students. Financial award applicants required to submit FAFSA. *Unit head:* Dr. Paul B. Shepson, Head, 765-494-5203, E-mail: pshepson@purdue.edu. *Application contact:* Betty L.. Hatfield, Director of Graduate Admissions, 765-494-5208, E-mail: bettyh@purdue.edu.

Rensselaer Polytechnic Institute, Graduate School, School of Science, Program in Chemistry, Troy, NY 12180-3590. Offers analytical chemistry (MS, PhD); biochemistry (MS, PhD); inorganic chemistry (MS, PhD); organic chemistry (MS, PhD); physical chemistry (MS, PhD); polymer chemistry (MS, PhD). Part-time and evening/weekend programs available. Terminal master's awarded for partial completion of doctoral program. *Degree requirements:* For master's, thesis (for some programs); for doctorate, comprehensive exam, thesis/dissertation. *Entrance requirements:* For master's, GRE General Test, GRE Subject Test (strongly recommended); for doctorate, GRE General Test, GRE Subject Test (chemistry or biochemistry strongly recommended). Additional exam requirements/recommendations for international students: Required—TOEFL (minimum score 570 paper-based; 230 computer-based; 88 iBT). Electronic applications accepted. *Faculty research:* Synthetic polymer and biopolymer chemistry, physical chemistry of polymeric systems, bioanalytical chemistry, synthetic and computational drug design, protein folding and protein design.

Rice University, Graduate Programs, Wiess School of Natural Sciences, Department of Chemistry, Houston, TX 77251-1892. Offers chemistry (MA); inorganic chemistry (PhD); organic chemistry (PhD); physical chemistry (PhD). Terminal master's awarded for partial completion of doctoral program. *Degree requirements:* For master's, thesis; for doctorate, thesis/dissertation. *Entrance requirements:* For master's and doctorate, GRE General Test, minimum GPA of 3.0. Additional exam requirements/recommendations for international students: Required—TOEFL (minimum score 600 paper-based; 250 computer-based; 90 iBT). Electronic applications accepted. *Faculty research:* Nanoscience, biomaterials, nanobioinformatics, fullerene pharmaceuticals.

Rutgers, The State University of New Jersey, Newark, Graduate School, Program in Chemistry, Newark, NJ 07102. Offers analytical chemistry (MS, PhD); biochemistry (MS, PhD); inorganic chemistry (MS, PhD); organic chemistry (MS, PhD); physical chemistry (MS, PhD). Part-time and evening/weekend programs available. Terminal master's awarded for partial completion of doctoral program. *Degree requirements:* For master's, thesis optional, cumulative exams; for doctorate, thesis/dissertation, exams, research proposal. *Entrance requirements:* For master's and doctorate, GRE General Test, minimum undergraduate B average. Additional exam requirements/recommendations for international students: Required—TOEFL. Electronic applications accepted. *Faculty research:* Medicinal chemistry, natural products, isotope effects, biophysics and biorganic approaches to enzyme mechanisms, organic and organometallic synthesis.

Rutgers, The State University of New Jersey, New Brunswick, Graduate School-New Brunswick, Department of Chemistry and Chemical Biology, Piscataway, NJ 08854-8097. Offers biological chemistry (MS, PhD); inorganic chemistry (MS, PhD); organic chemistry (MS, PhD); physical chemistry (MS, PhD). Part-time and evening/weekend programs available. Terminal master's awarded for partial completion of doctoral program. *Degree requirements:* For master's, thesis or alternative, exam; for doctorate, thesis/dissertation, 1 year residency. *Entrance requirements:* For master's and doctorate, GRE General Test, GRE Subject Test. Additional exam requirements/recommendations for international students: Required—TOEFL. Electronic applications accepted. *Faculty research:* Biophysical organic/bioorganic, inorganic/bioinorganic, theoretical, and solid-state/surface chemistry.

Seton Hall University, College of Arts and Sciences, Department of Chemistry and Biochemistry, South Orange, NJ 07079-2697. Offers analytical chemistry (MS, PhD); biochemistry (MS, PhD); chemistry (MS); inorganic chemistry (MS, PhD); organic chemistry (MS, PhD); physical chemistry (MS, PhD). Part-time and evening/weekend programs available. Terminal master's awarded for partial completion of doctoral program. *Degree requirements:* For master's, thesis optional; for doctorate, comprehensive exam, thesis/dissertation. *Entrance requirements:* Additional exam requirements/recommendations for international students: Required—TOEFL. Electronic applications accepted. *Expenses:* Tuition: Part-time $1033 per credit hour. *Required fees:* $85 per semester. *Faculty research:* DNA metal reactions; chromatography; bioinorganic, biophysical, organometallic, polymer chemistry; heterogeneous catalyst; synthetic organic and carbohydrate chemistry.

Southern University and Agricultural and Mechanical College, Graduate School, College of Sciences, Department of Chemistry, Baton Rouge, LA 70813. Offers analytical chemistry (MS); biochemistry (MS); environmental sciences (MS); inorganic chemistry (MS); organic chemistry (MS); physical chemistry (MS). *Degree requirements:* For master's, thesis. *Entrance requirements:* For master's, GMAT or GRE General Test. Additional exam requirements/recommendations for international students: Required—TOEFL (minimum score 525 paper-based; 193 computer-based). *Faculty research:* Synthesis of macrocyclic ligands, latex accelerators, anticancer drugs, biosensors, absorption isotheums, isolation of specific enzymes from plants.

State University of New York at Binghamton, Graduate School, School of Arts and Sciences, Department of Chemistry, Binghamton, NY 13902-6000. Offers analytical chemistry (PhD); chemistry (MA, MS); inorganic chemistry (PhD); organic chemistry (PhD); physical chemistry (PhD). Part-time programs available. *Faculty:* 16 full-time (5 women), 2 part-time/adjunct (both women). *Students:* 24 full-time (8 women), 32 part-time (13 women); includes 5 minority (2 Black or African American, non-Hispanic/Latino; 1 Hispanic/Latino; 2 Native Hawaiian or other Pacific Islander, non-Hispanic/Latino), 36 international. Average age 28. 39 applicants, 36% accepted, 10 enrolled. In 2011, 3 master's, 6 doctorates awarded. Terminal master's awarded for partial completion of doctoral program. *Degree requirements:* For master's, thesis or alternative, oral exam, seminar presentation; for doctorate, thesis/dissertation, cumulative exams. *Entrance requirements:* For master's and doctorate, GRE General Test, GRE Subject Test. Additional exam requirements/recommendations for international students: Required—TOEFL (minimum score 550 paper-based; 213 computer-based; 80 iBT). *Application deadline:* For fall admission, 1/15 priority date for domestic students, 1/15 for international students; for spring admission, 10/15 priority date for domestic students, 10/15 for international students. Applications are processed on a rolling basis. Application fee: $60. Electronic applications accepted. *Financial support:* In 2011–12, 9 fellowships with full tuition reimbursements (averaging $18,000 per year), 13 research assistantships with full tuition reimbursements (averaging $18,000 per year), 35 teaching assistantships with full tuition reimbursements (averaging $18,000 per year) were awarded; career-related internships or fieldwork, Federal Work-Study, institutionally sponsored loans, scholarships/grants, health care benefits, tuition waivers (full), and unspecified assistantships also available. Financial award application deadline: 2/15; financial award applicants required to submit FAFSA. *Unit head:* Dr. Wayne E. Jones, Chairperson, 607-777-2421, E-mail: wjones@binghamton.edu. *Application contact:* Catherine Smith, Recruiting and Admissions Coordinator, 607-777-2151, Fax: 607-777-2501, E-mail: cmsmith@binghamton.edu.

Stevens Institute of Technology, Graduate School, Charles V. Schaefer Jr. School of Engineering, Department of Chemistry, Chemical Biology and Biomedical Engineering, Hoboken, NJ 07030. Offers analytical chemistry (PhD, Certificate); bioinformatics (PhD, Certificate); biomedical chemistry (Certificate); biomedical engineering (M Eng, Certificate); chemical biology (MS, PhD, Certificate); chemical physiology (Certificate); chemistry (MS, PhD); organic chemistry (PhD); physical chemistry (PhD); polymer chemistry (PhD, Certificate). Part-time and evening/weekend programs available. Postbaccalaureate distance learning degree programs offered (no on-campus study). Terminal master's awarded for partial completion of doctoral program. *Degree requirements:* For master's, thesis or alternative; for doctorate, one foreign language, thesis/dissertation; for Certificate, project or thesis. *Entrance requirements:* Additional exam requirements/recommendations for international students: Required—TOEFL. Electronic applications accepted. *Faculty research:* Biochemical reaction engineering, polymerization engineering, reactor design, biochemical process control and synthesis.

Texas Christian University, College of Science and Engineering, Department of Chemistry, Fort Worth, TX 76129. Offers biochemistry (MS, PhD); chemistry (MA); inorganic (MS, PhD); organic (MS, PhD); physical (MS, PhD). Part-time programs available. *Faculty:* 11 full-time (2 women). *Students:* 4 full-time (2 women), 16 part-time (10 women); includes 3 minority (1 Asian, non-Hispanic/Latino; 2 Hispanic/Latino), 11 international. Average age 27. 5 applicants, 100% accepted, 4 enrolled. In 2011, 1 master's, 3 doctorates awarded. *Degree requirements:* For master's, thesis; for doctorate, thesis/dissertation, literature seminar, cumulative exams, research progress report, original proposal. *Entrance requirements:* For master's and doctorate, GRE General Test. Additional exam requirements/recommendations for international students: Required—TOEFL. *Application deadline:* For fall admission, 3/1 priority date for domestic students, 3/1 for international students; for spring admission, 9/1 priority date for domestic students, 9/1 for international students. Application fee: $50. Electronic applications accepted. *Expenses:* Tuition: Full-time $20,250; part-time $1125 per credit hour. Part-time tuition and fees vary according to course load and program. *Financial support:* In 2011–12, 11 students received support, including 11 teaching assistantships with full tuition reimbursements available; tuition waivers (full and partial) and unspecified assistantships also available. Financial award application deadline: 3/1. *Faculty research:* Phase transitions and transport properties of bio/macromolecular solutions, nanoscale biomaterials, electronic structure theory, synthetic methodology and total synthesis of natural products, chemistry and biology of (bio)polymers. *Unit head:* Dr. Robert Neilson, Chairperson/Professor, 817-257-7345, Fax: 817-257-5851, E-mail: r.neilson@tcu.edu. *Application contact:* Dr. Sergei V. Dzyuba, Director of Graduate Studies/Assistant Professor, 817-257-6218, Fax: 817-257-5851, E-mail: s.dzyuba@tcu.edu. Web site: http://www.chm.tcu.edu/.

Tufts University, Graduate School of Arts and Sciences, Department of Chemistry, Medford, MA 02155. Offers analytical chemistry (MS, PhD); bioorganic chemistry (MS, PhD); environmental chemistry (MS, PhD); inorganic chemistry (MS, PhD); organic chemistry (MS, PhD); physical chemistry (MS, PhD). *Students:* 75 full-time (33 women); includes 7 minority (1 Black or African American, non-Hispanic/Latino; 5 Asian, non-Hispanic/Latino; 1 Hispanic/Latino), 25 international. 88 applicants, 59% accepted, 16 enrolled. In 2011, 5 master's, 8 doctorates awarded. Terminal master's awarded for partial completion of doctoral program. *Degree requirements:* For master's, thesis optional; for doctorate, thesis/dissertation. *Entrance requirements:* For master's and doctorate, GRE General Test, GRE Subject Test. Additional exam requirements/recommendations for international students: Required—TOEFL (minimum score 600 paper-based; 250 computer-based; 80 iBT). *Application deadline:* For fall admission, 1/15 for domestic students, 12/15 for international students; for spring admission, 10/15 for domestic students, 9/15 for international students. Applications are processed on a rolling basis. Application fee: $75. Electronic applications accepted. *Expenses: Tuition:* Full-time $41,208; part-time $1030 per credit hour. Full-time tuition and fees vary according to degree level, program and student level. Part-time tuition and fees vary according to course load. *Financial support:* Fellowships, research assistantships with full tuition reimbursements, teaching assistantships with full tuition reimbursements, Federal Work-Study, scholarships/grants, tuition waivers (partial), and unspecified assistantships available. Financial award application deadline: 1/15; financial award applicants required to submit FAFSA. *Unit head:* Arthur Utz, Chair, 617-627-3441. *Application contact:* Deborah D'Andrea, Information Contact, 617-627-3441, Fax: 617-627-3443. Web site: http://chem.tufts.edu/.

University of Calgary, Faculty of Graduate Studies, Faculty of Science, Department of Chemistry, Calgary, AB T2N 1N4, Canada. Offers analytical chemistry (M Sc, PhD); applied chemistry (M Sc, PhD); inorganic chemistry (M Sc, PhD); organic chemistry (M Sc, PhD); physical chemistry (M Sc, PhD); polymer chemistry (M Sc, PhD); theoretical chemistry (M Sc, PhD). *Degree requirements:* For master's, thesis; for doctorate, thesis/dissertation, candidacy exam. *Entrance requirements:* For master's, minimum GPA of 3.0; for doctorate, honors B Sc degree with minimum GPA of 3.7 or M Sc with minimum GPA of 3.3. Additional exam requirements/recommendations for international students: Required—TOEFL (minimum score 580 paper-based; 237 computer-based). Electronic applications accepted. *Faculty research:* Chemical analysis, chemical dynamics, synthesis theory.

University of Cincinnati, Graduate School, McMicken College of Arts and Sciences, Department of Chemistry, Cincinnati, OH 45221. Offers analytical chemistry (MS, PhD); biochemistry (MS, PhD); inorganic chemistry (MS, PhD); organic chemistry (MS, PhD); physical chemistry (MS, PhD); polymer chemistry (MS, PhD); sensors (PhD). Part-time and evening/weekend programs available. Terminal master's awarded for partial completion of doctoral program. *Degree requirements:* For master's, thesis optional; for doctorate, comprehensive exam, thesis/dissertation. *Entrance requirements:* For master's and doctorate, GRE General Test. Additional exam requirements/recommendations for international students: Required—TOEFL (minimum score 580 paper-based; 237 computer-based). Electronic applications accepted. *Faculty research:* Biomedical chemistry, laser chemistry, surface science, chemical sensors, synthesis.

University of Georgia, Franklin College of Arts and Sciences, Department of Chemistry, Athens, GA 30602. Offers analytical chemistry (MS, PhD); inorganic chemistry (MS, PhD); organic chemistry (MS, PhD); physical chemistry (MS, PhD). *Faculty:* 26 full-time (2 women). *Students:* 153 full-time (53 women), 6 part-time (2 women); includes 21 minority (6 Black or African American, non-Hispanic/Latino; 12 Asian, non-Hispanic/Latino; 1 Hispanic/Latino; 2 Two or more races, non-Hispanic/Latino), 60 international. Average age 27. 175 applicants, 41% accepted, 38 enrolled. In 2011, 7 master's, 22 doctorates awarded. Terminal master's awarded for partial completion of doctoral program. *Median time to degree:* Of those who began their doctoral program in fall 2003, 100% received their degree in 8 years or less. *Degree requirements:* For master's, thesis; for doctorate, one foreign language, thesis/dissertation. *Entrance requirements:* For master's and doctorate, GRE General Test. Additional exam requirements/recommendations for international students: Required—TOEFL (minimum score 213 computer-based). *Application deadline:* For fall admission, 7/1 priority date for domestic students; for spring admission, 11/15 for domestic students. Application fee: $50. Electronic applications accepted. *Financial support:* Fellowships, research assistantships, teaching assistantships, and unspecified assistantships available. *Unit head:* Dr. Jon Amster, Head, 706-542-2726, E-mail: jamster@uga.edu. *Application contact:* Dr. Jeffrey L. Urbauer, Graduate Coordinator, 706-542-7922, E-mail: urbauer@uga.edu. Web site: http://www.chem.uga.edu/.

University of Louisville, Graduate School, College of Arts and Sciences, Department of Chemistry, Louisville, KY 40292-0001. Offers analytical chemistry (MS, PhD); biochemistry (MS, PhD); chemical physics (PhD); inorganic chemistry (MS, PhD); organic chemistry (MS, PhD); physical chemistry (MS, PhD). Terminal master's awarded for partial completion of doctoral program. *Degree requirements:* For master's, variable foreign language requirement, comprehensive exam, thesis optional; for doctorate, variable foreign language requirement, comprehensive exam, thesis/dissertation. *Entrance requirements:* For master's and doctorate, BA or BS coursework. Additional exam requirements/recommendations for international students: Required—TOEFL. Electronic applications accepted. *Expenses:* Tuition, state resident: full-time $9692; part-time $539 per credit hour. Tuition, nonresident: full-time $20,168; part-time $1121 per credit hour. Tuition and fees vary according to program and reciprocity agreements. *Faculty research:* Computational chemistry, biophysics nuclear magnetic resonance, synthetic organic chemistry, synthetic inorganic chemistry, medicinal chemistry, protein chemistry, enzymology, nanochemistry, electrochemistry, analytical chemistry, synthetic biology, bioinformatics.

The University of Manchester, School of Chemistry, Manchester, United Kingdom. Offers biological chemistry (PhD); chemistry (M Ent, M Phil, M Sc, D Ent, PhD); inorganic chemistry (PhD); materials chemistry (PhD); nanoscience (PhD); nuclear fission (PhD); organic chemistry (PhD); physical chemistry (PhD); theoretical chemistry (PhD).

University of Maryland, College Park, Academic Affairs, College of Computer, Mathematical and Natural Sciences, Department of Chemistry and Biochemistry, Chemistry Program, College Park, MD 20742. Offers analytical chemistry (MS, PhD); inorganic chemistry (MS, PhD); organic chemistry (MS, PhD); physical chemistry (MS, PhD). Part-time and evening/weekend programs available. *Students:* 115 full-time (59 women), 4 part-time (1 woman); includes 20 minority (12 Black or African American, non-Hispanic/Latino; 4 Asian, non-Hispanic/Latino; 2 Hispanic/Latino; 2 Two or more races, non-Hispanic/Latino), 52 international. 335 applicants, 8% accepted, 18 enrolled. In 2011, 11 master's, 15 doctorates awarded. Terminal master's awarded for partial completion of doctoral program. *Median time to degree:* Of those who began their doctoral program in fall 2003, 63% received their degree in 8 years or less. *Degree requirements:* For master's, thesis optional; for doctorate, thesis/dissertation, 2 seminar presentations, oral exam. *Entrance requirements:* For master's and doctorate, GRE General Test, GRE Subject Test (recommended), minimum GPA of 3.0, 3 letters of recommendation. Additional exam requirements/recommendations for international students: Required—TOEFL. *Application deadline:* For fall admission, 2/1 for domestic and international students; for spring admission, 6/1 for domestic and international students. Applications are processed on a rolling basis. Application fee: $75. Electronic applications accepted. *Expenses: Tuition, area resident:* Part-time $525 per credit hour. Tuition, state resident: part-time $525 per credit hour. Tuition, nonresident: part-time $1131 per credit hour. *Required fees:* $386.31 per term. Tuition and fees vary according to program. *Financial support:* In 2011–12, 9 fellowships with full and partial tuition reimbursements (averaging $25,360 per year), 46 research assistantships (averaging $19,791 per year), 59 teaching assistantships (averaging $19,243 per year) were awarded. Financial award applicants required to submit FAFSA. *Faculty research:* Environmental chemistry, nuclear chemistry, lunar and environmental analysis, x-ray crystallography. *Unit head:* Dr. Michael Doyle, Chairperson, 301-405-1795, Fax: 301-314-2779, E-mail: mdoyle3@umd.edu. *Application contact:* Dr. Charles A. Caramello, Dean of Graduate School, 301-405-0358, Fax: 301-314-9305.

University of Memphis, Graduate School, College of Arts and Sciences, Department of Chemistry, Memphis, TN 38152. Offers analytical chemistry (MS, PhD); computational chemistry (MS, PhD); inorganic chemistry (MS, PhD); organic chemistry (MS, PhD); physical chemistry (MS, PhD). Part-time programs available. Terminal master's awarded for partial completion of doctoral program. *Degree requirements:* For master's, comprehensive exam, thesis or alternative; for doctorate, comprehensive exam, thesis/dissertation. *Entrance requirements:* For master's and doctorate, GRE General Test, admission to Graduate School plus 32 undergraduate hours in chemistry. Additional exam requirements/recommendations for international students: Required—TOEFL. Electronic applications accepted. *Faculty research:* Computational chemistry, materials chemistry, organic/polymer synthesis, drug design/delivery, water chemistry.

University of Miami, Graduate School, College of Arts and Sciences, Department of Chemistry, Coral Gables, FL 33124. Offers chemistry (MS); inorganic chemistry (PhD); organic chemistry (PhD); physical chemistry (PhD). Terminal master's awarded for partial completion of doctoral program. *Degree requirements:* For master's, comprehensive exam; for doctorate, comprehensive exam, thesis/dissertation. *Entrance requirements:* For master's and doctorate, GRE General Test. Additional exam requirements/recommendations for international students: Required—TOEFL (minimum score 550 paper-based; 213 computer-based). Electronic applications accepted. *Faculty research:* Supramolecular chemistry, electrochemistry, surface chemistry, catalysis, organometalic.

University of Michigan, Horace H. Rackham School of Graduate Studies, College of Literature, Science, and the Arts, Department of Chemistry, Ann Arbor, MI 48109-1055. Offers analytical chemistry (PhD); chemical biology (PhD); inorganic chemistry (PhD); material chemistry (PhD); organic chemistry (PhD); physical chemistry (PhD). *Faculty:* 39 full-time (9 women). *Students:* 221 full-time (114 women); includes 24 minority (1 Black or African American, non-Hispanic/Latino; 15 Asian, non-Hispanic/Latino; 4 Hispanic/Latino; 4 Two or more races, non-Hispanic/Latino), 66 international. Average age 26. 608 applicants, 27% accepted, 39 enrolled. In 2011, 39 doctorates awarded. *Degree requirements:* For doctorate, thesis/dissertation, oral defense of dissertation, organic cumulative proficiency exams. *Entrance requirements:* For doctorate, GRE General Test, GRE Subject Test (recommended), 3 letters of recommendation. Additional exam requirements/recommendations for international students: Required—TOEFL (minimum score 560 paper-based; 220 computer-based; 84 iBT). *Application deadline:* For fall admission, 12/31 for domestic students, 12/15 for international students. Applications are processed on a rolling basis. Application fee: $0 ($75 for international students). Electronic applications accepted. *Financial support:* In 2011–12, 221 students received support, including 25 fellowships with full tuition

Peterson's Graduate Programs in the Physical Sciences, Mathematics, Agricultural Sciences, the Environment & Natural Resources 2013

facebook.com/petersonspublishing **119**

Physical Chemistry

reimbursements available · (averaging $26,553 per year), 86 research assistantships with full tuition reimbursements available (averaging $26,553 per year), 110 teaching assistantships with full tuition reimbursements available (averaging $26,553 per year); career-related internships or fieldwork, scholarships/grants, traineeships, health care benefits, and unspecified assistantships also available. *Faculty research:* Biological catalysis, protein engineering, chemical sensors, de novo metalloprotein design, supramolecular architecture. *Unit head:* Dr. Carol A. Fierke, Chair, 734-763-9681, Fax: 734-647-4847. *Application contact:* Margarita Bekiares, Graduate Program Coordinator, 734-764-7278, Fax: 734-647-4865, E-mail: chemadmissions@umich.edu. Web site: http://www.umich.edu/~michchem/.

University of Missouri, Graduate School, College of Arts and Sciences, Department of Chemistry, Columbia, MO 65211. Offers analytical chemistry (MS, PhD); inorganic chemistry (MS, PhD); organic chemistry (MS, PhD); physical chemistry (MS, PhD). *Faculty:* 22 full-time (4 women), 1 part-time/adjunct (0 women). *Students:* 102 full-time (38 women), 10 part-time (6 women); includes 7 minority (3 Black or African American, non-Hispanic/Latino; 2 Asian, non-Hispanic/Latino; 1 Hispanic/Latino; 1 Two or more races, non-Hispanic/Latino), 53 international. Average age 27. 98 applicants, 28% accepted, 24 enrolled. In 2011, 2 master's, 5 doctorates awarded. *Degree requirements:* For master's, thesis; for doctorate, one foreign language, comprehensive exam, thesis/dissertation. *Entrance requirements:* For master's, GRE General Test, minimum GPA of 3.0; for doctorate, GRE General Test (minimum score: Verbal 450, Quantitative 600, Analytical 3), minimum GPA of 3.0. Additional exam requirements/recommendations for international students: Required—TOEFL (minimum score 600 paper-based; 250 computer-based; 100 iBT). *Application deadline:* For fall admission, 4/1 priority date for domestic students; for winter admission, 10/15 for domestic students. Applications are processed on a rolling basis. Application fee: $55 ($75 for international students). Electronic applications accepted. *Expenses:* Tuition, state resident: full-time $5881. Tuition, nonresident: full-time $15,183. Required fees: $952. Tuition and fees vary according to campus/location and program. *Financial support:* In 2011–12, 9 fellowships with full tuition reimbursements, 15 research assistantships with full tuition reimbursements, 78 teaching assistantships with full tuition reimbursements were awarded; institutionally sponsored loans, traineeships, health care benefits, and unspecified assistantships also available. *Faculty research:* Analytical, organic, biological, physical, inorganic and radiochemistry. *Unit head:* Dr. Jerry Atwood, Department Chair, 573-882-8374, E-mail: atwoodj@missouri.edu. *Application contact:* Jerry Brightwell, Administrative Assistant, 573-884-6832, E-mail: brightwellj@missouri.edu. Web site: http://chemistry.missouri.edu/.

University of Missouri–Kansas City, College of Arts and Sciences, Department of Chemistry, Kansas City, MO 64110-2499. Offers analytical chemistry (MS, PhD); inorganic chemistry (MS, PhD); organic chemistry (MS, PhD); physical chemistry (MS, PhD); polymer chemistry (MS, PhD). PhD (interdisciplinary) offered through the School of Graduate Studies. Part-time and evening/weekend programs available. *Faculty:* 16 full-time (3 women), 1 part-time/adjunct (0 women). *Students:* 1 (woman) part-time; minority (Black or African American, non-Hispanic/Latino). Average age 30. 28 applicants, 32% accepted, 0 enrolled. In 2011, 2 degrees awarded. *Degree requirements:* For master's, thesis (for some programs); for doctorate, thesis/dissertation. *Entrance requirements:* For master's, equivalent of American Chemical Society approved bachelor's degree in chemistry; for doctorate, GRE General Test, equivalent of American Chemical Society approved bachelor's degree in chemistry. Additional exam requirements/recommendations for international students: Required—TOEFL (minimum score 550 paper-based; 213 computer-based; 80 iBT), TWE. *Application deadline:* For fall admission, 4/15 for domestic and international students; for spring admission, 10/15 for domestic and international students. Applications are processed on a rolling basis. Application fee: $45 ($50 for international students). Electronic applications accepted. *Expenses:* Tuition, state resident: full-time $5798; part-time $322.10 per credit hour. Tuition, nonresident: full-time $14,969; part-time $831.60 per credit hour. Required fees: $93.51 per credit hour. *Financial support:* In 2011–12, 9 research assistantships with partial tuition reimbursements (averaging $19,119 per year), 14 teaching assistantships with partial tuition reimbursements (averaging $17,187 per year) were awarded; Federal Work-Study, institutionally sponsored loans, and scholarships/grants also available. Support available to part-time students. Financial award application deadline: 3/1; financial award applicants required to submit FAFSA. *Faculty research:* Molecular spectroscopy, characterization and synthesis of materials and compounds, computational chemistry, natural products, drug delivery systems and anti-tumor agents. *Unit head:* Dr. Kathleen V. Kilway, Chair, 816-235-2289, Fax: 816-235-5502. *Application contact:* Graduate Recruiting Committee, 816-235-2272, Fax: 816-235-5502, E-mail: umkc-chemdept@umkc.edu. Web site: http://cas.umkc.edu/chem/.

University of Missouri–St. Louis, College of Arts and Sciences, Department of Chemistry and Biochemistry, St. Louis, MO 63121. Offers chemistry (MS, PhD), including biochemistry, inorganic, organic, physical chemistry. Part-time and evening/weekend programs available. *Faculty:* 18 full-time (3 women), 4 part-time/adjunct (1 woman). *Students:* 37 full-time (18 women), 28 part-time (11 women); includes 4 minority (1 Black or African American, non-Hispanic/Latino; 2 Asian, non-Hispanic/Latino; 1 Hispanic/Latino), 22 international. Average age 30. 73 applicants, 30% accepted, 11 enrolled. In 2011, 16 master's, 4 doctorates awarded. Terminal master's awarded for partial completion of doctoral program. *Degree requirements:* For master's, thesis optional; for doctorate, thesis/dissertation. *Entrance requirements:* For master's, 2

letters of recommendation; for doctorate, GRE General Test, 3 letters of recommendation. Additional exam requirements/recommendations for international students: Required—TOEFL (minimum score 550 paper-based; 213 computer-based). *Application deadline:* For fall admission, 7/1 priority date for domestic students, 7/1 for international students; for spring admission, 12/1 priority date for domestic students, 12/1 for international students. Applications are processed on a rolling basis. Application fee: $35 ($40 for international students). Electronic applications accepted. *Expenses:* Tuition, state resident: full-time $6273; part-time $3866 per year. Tuition, nonresident: full-time $14,969; part-time $9980 per year. Required fees: $315 per year. *Financial support:* In 2011–12, 19 research assistantships with full and partial tuition reimbursements (averaging $13,500 per year), 19 teaching assistantships with full and partial tuition reimbursements (averaging $13,500 per year) were awarded; fellowships with full and partial tuition reimbursements also available. *Faculty research:* Metalloborane chemistry, serum transferrin chemistry, natural products chemistry, organic synthesis. *Unit head:* Dr. Janet Wilking, Director of Graduate Studies, 314-516-5311, Fax: 314-516-5342, E-mail: gradchem@umsl.edu. *Application contact:* Graduate Admissions, 314-516-5458, Fax: 314-516-6996, E-mail: gradadm@umsl.edu. Web site: http://www.umsl.edu/chemistry/.

The University of Montana, Graduate School, College of Arts and Sciences, Department of Chemistry and Biochemistry, Missoula, MT 59812-0002. Offers chemistry (MS, PhD), including environmental/analytical chemistry, inorganic chemistry, organic chemistry, physical chemistry. Terminal master's awarded for partial completion of doctoral program. *Degree requirements:* For master's, thesis (for some programs); for doctorate, thesis/dissertation. *Entrance requirements:* For master's and doctorate, GRE General Test. Additional exam requirements/recommendations for international students: Required—TOEFL (minimum score 575 paper-based; 230 computer-based). *Faculty research:* Reaction mechanisms and kinetics, inorganic and organic synthesis, analytical chemistry, natural products.

University of Nebraska–Lincoln, Graduate College, College of Arts and Sciences, Department of Chemistry, Lincoln, NE 68588. Offers analytical chemistry (PhD); biochemistry (PhD); chemistry (MS); inorganic chemistry (PhD); materials chemistry (PhD); organic chemistry (PhD); physical chemistry (PhD). *Degree requirements:* For master's, one foreign language, thesis optional, departmental qualifying exam; for doctorate, one foreign language, comprehensive exam, thesis/dissertation, departmental qualifying exams. *Entrance requirements:* For master's and doctorate, GRE. Additional exam requirements/recommendations for international students: Required—TOEFL (minimum score 550 paper-based; 213 computer-based). Electronic applications accepted. *Faculty research:* Bioorganic and bioinorganic chemistry, biophysical and bioanalytical chemistry, structure-function of DNA and proteins, organometallics, mass spectrometry.

University of Notre Dame, Graduate School, College of Science, Department of Chemistry and Biochemistry, Notre Dame, IN 46556. Offers biochemistry (MS, PhD); inorganic chemistry (MS, PhD); organic chemistry (MS, PhD); physical chemistry (MS, PhD). Terminal master's awarded for partial completion of doctoral program. *Degree requirements:* For master's, comprehensive exam, thesis; for doctorate, thesis/dissertation, qualifying exam. *Entrance requirements:* For master's and doctorate, GRE General Test, GRE Subject Test (strongly recommended). Additional exam requirements/recommendations for international students: Required—TOEFL (minimum score 600 paper-based; 250 computer-based; 80 iBT). Electronic applications accepted. *Faculty research:* Reaction design and mechanistic studies; reactive intermediates; synthesis, structure and reactivity of organometallic cluster complexes and biologically active natural products; bioorganic chemistry; enzymology.

University of Southern California, Graduate School, Dana and David Dornsife College of Letters, Arts and Sciences, Department of Chemistry, Los Angeles, CA 90089. Offers chemistry (PhD); physical chemistry (PhD). Terminal master's awarded for partial completion of doctoral program. *Degree requirements:* For doctorate, thesis/dissertation. *Entrance requirements:* For doctorate, GRE General Test. Additional exam requirements/recommendations for international students: Required—TOEFL. Electronic applications accepted. *Faculty research:* Biological chemistry, inorganic chemistry, organic chemistry, physical chemistry, theoretical chemistry.

University of Southern Mississippi, Graduate School, College of Science and Technology, Department of Chemistry and Biochemistry, Hattiesburg, MS 39406-0001. Offers analytical chemistry (MS, PhD); biochemistry (MS, PhD); inorganic chemistry (MS, PhD); organic chemistry (MS, PhD); physical chemistry (MS, PhD). *Faculty:* 16 full-time (4 women), 4 part-time (3 women); includes 1 minority (Black or African American, non-Hispanic/Latino), 9 international. Average age 29. 43 applicants, 19% accepted, 5 enrolled. In 2011, 1 master's, 4 doctorates awarded. *Degree requirements:* For master's, comprehensive exam, thesis; for doctorate, comprehensive exam, thesis/dissertation. *Entrance requirements:* For master's, GRE General Test, minimum GPA of 2.75 in last 60 hours; for doctorate, GRE General Test, minimum GPA of 3.5. Additional exam requirements/recommendations for international students: Required—TOEFL, IELTS. *Application deadline:* For fall admission, 3/1 priority date for domestic students, 3/1 for international students. Applications are processed on a rolling basis. Application fee: $50. *Financial support:* In 2011–12, 3 research assistantships with full tuition reimbursements (averaging $17,000 per year), 19 teaching assistantships with full tuition reimbursements (averaging $20,700 per year) were awarded; fellowships, Federal Work-Study, institutionally sponsored loans, scholarships/grants, health care benefits, and unspecified assistantships also available. Support available to part-time students. Financial award application deadline: 3/15; financial award applicants required to submit FAFSA. *Faculty research:* Plant biochemistry, photo chemistry, polymer chemistry, x-ray analysis, enzyme chemistry. *Unit head:* Dr. Sabine Heinhorst, Chair, 601-266-4701, Fax: 601-266-6075. *Application contact:* Dr. Sabine Heinhorst, Graduate Coordinator, 601-266-4702, Fax: 601-266-6075. Web site: http://www.usm.edu/graduateschool/table.php.

University of South Florida, Graduate School, College of Arts and Sciences, Department of Chemistry, Tampa, FL 33620-9951. Offers analytical chemistry (MS, PhD); biochemistry (MS, PhD); computational chemistry (MS, PhD); environmental chemistry (MS, PhD); inorganic chemistry (MS, PhD); organic chemistry (MS); physical chemistry (MS, PhD); polymer chemistry (PhD). Part-time programs available. *Faculty:* 25 full-time (4 women), 9 part-time/adjunct (1 woman). *Students:* 118 full-time (46 women), 14 part-time (7 women); includes 28 minority (8 Black or African American, non-Hispanic/Latino; 11 Asian, non-Hispanic/Latino; 9 Hispanic/Latino), 58 international. Average age 29. 127 applicants, 31% accepted, 19 enrolled. In 2011, 3 master's, 16 doctorates awarded. Terminal master's awarded for partial completion of doctoral program. *Degree requirements:* For master's, comprehensive exam, thesis (for some programs); for doctorate, comprehensive exam, thesis/dissertation. *Entrance requirements:* For master's and doctorate, GRE General Test, minimum GPA of 3.0. Additional exam requirements/recommendations for international students: Required—TOEFL (minimum score 550 paper-based; 213 computer-based; 79 iBT) or IELTS (minimum score 6.5). *Application deadline:* For fall admission, 2/15 priority date for domestic students, 1/2 for international students; for spring admission, 10/1 priority date for domestic students, 6/1 for international students. Applications are processed on a rolling basis. Application fee: $30. Electronic applications accepted. *Financial support:* In 2011–12, 136 students received support, including 28 research assistantships with tuition reimbursements available (averaging $15,020 per year), 108 teaching assistantships with tuition reimbursements available (averaging $15,164 per year); unspecified assistantships also available. Financial award application deadline: 6/30. *Faculty research:* Synthesis, bio-organic chemistry, bioinorganic chemistry, environmental chemistry, NMR. *Total annual research expenditures:* $3.1 million. *Unit head:* Dr. Randy Larsen, Chairperson, 813-974-4129, Fax: 813-974-3203, E-mail: rlarsen@cas.usf.edu. *Application contact:* Patricia Muisener, Director, 813-974-1730, Fax: 813-974-3203, E-mail: muisener@cas.usf.edu. Web site: http://chemistry.usf.edu/.

The University of Tennessee, Graduate School, College of Arts and Sciences, Department of Chemistry, Knoxville, TN 37996. Offers analytical chemistry (MS, PhD); chemical physics (PhD); environmental chemistry (MS, PhD); inorganic chemistry (MS, PhD); organic chemistry (MS, PhD); physical chemistry (MS, PhD); polymer chemistry (MS, PhD); theoretical chemistry (PhD). Part-time programs available. Terminal master's awarded for partial completion of doctoral program. *Degree requirements:* For master's, thesis; for doctorate, thesis/dissertation. *Entrance requirements:* For master's and doctorate, GRE General Test, minimum GPA of 2.7. Additional exam requirements/recommendations for international students: Required—TOEFL. Electronic applications accepted. *Expenses:* Tuition, state resident: full-time $8332; part-time $464 per credit hour. Tuition, nonresident: full-time $25,174; part-time $1400 per credit hour. *Required fees:* $1162; $56 per credit hour. Tuition and fees vary according to program.

The University of Texas at Austin, Graduate School, College of Natural Sciences, Department of Chemistry and Biochemistry, Austin, TX 78712-1111. Offers analytical chemistry (PhD); biochemistry (PhD); inorganic chemistry (PhD); organic chemistry (PhD); physical chemistry (PhD). *Entrance requirements:* For doctorate, GRE General Test. Application fee: $50 ($75 for international students). *Financial support:* Fellowships, research assistantships, teaching assistantships, and scholarships/grants available. Financial award application deadline: 2/1. *Unit head:* Dr. Richard M. Crooks, Chairman, 512-475-8674, E-mail: crooks@cm.utexas.edu. *Application contact:* Dr. Jennifer S. Brodbelt, Graduate Admissions Chair, 512-471-0028, E-mail: jbrodbelt@cm.utexas.edu. Web site: http://www.cm.utexas.edu/.

The University of Toledo, College of Graduate Studies, College of Natural Sciences and Mathematics, Department of Chemistry, Toledo, OH 43606-3390. Offers analytical chemistry (MS, PhD); biological chemistry (MS, PhD); inorganic chemistry (MS, PhD); organic chemistry (MS, PhD); physical chemistry (MS, PhD). Part-time programs available. *Faculty:* 22. *Students:* 56 full-time (18 women), 18 part-time (10 women); includes 4 minority (1 Black or African American, non-Hispanic/Latino; 1 Asian, non-Hispanic/Latino; 2 Hispanic/Latino), 43 international. Average age 27. 111 applicants, 17% accepted, 16 enrolled. In 2011, 4 master's, 6 doctorates awarded. *Degree requirements:* For master's, thesis (for some programs); for doctorate, thesis/dissertation. *Entrance requirements:* For master's and doctorate, GRE General Test, GRE Subject Test, minimum cumulative point-hour ratio of 2.7 for all previous academic work, three letters of recommendation, statement of purpose, transcripts from all prior institutions attended. Additional exam requirements/recommendations for international students: Required—TOEFL (minimum score 550 paper-based; 213 computer-based; 80 iBT), IELTS (minimum score 6.5). *Application deadline:* For fall admission, 1/15 priority date for domestic students, 1/15 for international students. Applications are processed on a rolling basis. Application fee: $45 ($75 for international students). Electronic applications accepted. *Financial support:* In 2011–12, 24 research assistantships with full and partial tuition reimbursements

(averaging $17,218 per year) were awarded; fellowships with tuition reimbursements, Federal Work-Study, institutionally sponsored loans, scholarships/grants, tuition waivers (full), and unspecified assistantships also available. Support available to part-time students. *Faculty research:* Enzymology, materials chemistry, crystallography, theoretical chemistry. *Unit head:* Dr. Alan Pinkerton, Chair, 419-530-7902, Fax: 419-530-4033, E-mail: alan.pinkerton@utoledo.edu. *Application contact:* Graduate School Office, 419-530-4723, Fax: 419-530-4724, E-mail: grdsch@utnet.utoledo.edu. Web site: http://www.utoledo.edu/nsm/.

Vanderbilt University, Graduate School, Department of Chemistry, Nashville, TN 37240-1001. Offers analytical chemistry (MAT, MS, PhD); inorganic chemistry (MAT, MS, PhD); organic chemistry (MAT, MS, PhD); physical chemistry (MAT, MS, PhD); theoretical chemistry (MAT, MS, PhD). *Faculty:* 21 full-time (3 women). *Students:* 114 full-time (43 women), 2 part-time (0 women); includes 16 minority (6 Black or African American, non-Hispanic/Latino; 1 American Indian or Alaska Native, non-Hispanic/Latino; 3 Asian, non-Hispanic/Latino; 1 Hispanic/Latino; 5 Two or more races, non-Hispanic/Latino), 18 international. Average age 26. 420 applicants, 12% accepted, 18 enrolled. In 2011, 4 master's, 17 doctorates awarded. Terminal master's awarded for partial completion of doctoral program. *Degree requirements:* For master's, thesis; for doctorate, thesis/dissertation, area, qualifying, and final exams. *Entrance requirements:* For master's and doctorate, GRE General Test, GRE Subject Test (recommended). Additional exam requirements/recommendations for international students: Required—TOEFL (minimum score 570 paper-based; 230 computer-based; 88 iBT). *Application deadline:* For fall admission, 1/15 for domestic and international students. Application fee: $0. Electronic applications accepted. *Financial support:* Fellowships with full and partial tuition reimbursements, research assistantships with full tuition reimbursements, teaching assistantships with full tuition reimbursements, Federal Work-Study, institutionally sponsored loans, scholarships/grants, traineeships, and health care benefits available. Financial award application deadline: 1/15; financial award applicants required to submit CSS PROFILE or FAFSA. *Faculty research:* Chemical synthesis; mechanistic, theoretical, bioorganic, analytical, and spectroscopic chemistry. *Unit head:* Dr. Mike P. Stone, Chair, 615-322-2589, Fax: 615-343-1234, E-mail: michael.p.stone@vanderbilt.edu. *Application contact:* Dr. Carmelo J. Rizzo, Director of Graduate Studies, 615-322-6100, Fax: 615-343-1234, E-mail: c.j.rizzo@vanderbilt.edu. Web site: http://www.vanderbilt.edu/AnS/Chemistry/grad/.

Virginia Commonwealth University, Graduate School, College of Humanities and Sciences, Department of Chemistry, Richmond, VA 23284-9005. Offers analytical chemistry (MS, PhD); chemical physics (PhD); inorganic chemistry (MS, PhD); organic chemistry (MS, PhD); physical chemistry (MS, PhD). Part-time programs available. *Students:* 49 full-time (20 women), 19 part-time (8 women); includes 10 minority (3 Black or African American, non-Hispanic/Latino; 5 Asian, non-Hispanic/Latino; 1 Hispanic/Latino; 1 Two or more races, non-Hispanic/Latino), 26 international. 56 applicants, 41% accepted, 11 enrolled. In 2011, 3 master's, 8 doctorates awarded. Terminal master's awarded for partial completion of doctoral program. *Degree requirements:* For master's, thesis; for doctorate, thesis/dissertation, comprehensive cumulative exams, research proposal. *Entrance requirements:* For master's, GRE General Test, 30 undergraduate credits in chemistry; for doctorate, GRE General Test. Additional exam requirements/recommendations for international students: Required—TOEFL (minimum score 600 paper-based; 250 computer-based; 100 iBT) or IELTS (minimum score 6.5). *Application deadline:* For fall admission, 3/15 for domestic students; for spring admission, 11/15 for domestic students. Applications are processed on a rolling basis. Application fee: $50. Electronic applications accepted. *Expenses:* Tuition, state resident: full-time $9133; part-time $507 per credit. Tuition, nonresident: full-time $18,777; part-time $1043 per credit. *Required fees:* $77 per credit. Tuition and fees vary according to degree level, campus/location, program and student level. *Financial support:* Fellowships, research assistantships, teaching assistantships, career-related internships or fieldwork, and institutionally sponsored loans available. Support available to part-time students. Financial award application deadline: 7/1; financial award applicants required to submit FAFSA. *Faculty research:* Physical, organic, inorganic, analytical, and polymer chemistry; chemical physics. *Unit head:* Dr. Scott Gronert, Chair, 804-828-1298, Fax: 804-828-8599, E-mail: sgronert@vcu.edu. *Application contact:* Dr. Maryanne M. Collinson, Chair, Graduate Recruiting and Admissions Committee, 804-828-7509, E-mail: mselshal@vcu.edu. Web site: http://www.has.vcu.edu/che/.

Wake Forest University, Graduate School of Arts and Sciences, Department of Chemistry, Winston-Salem, NC 27109. Offers analytical chemistry (MS, PhD); inorganic chemistry (MS, PhD); organic chemistry (MS, PhD); physical chemistry (MS, PhD). Part-time programs available. *Degree requirements:* For master's, one foreign language, comprehensive exam, thesis; for doctorate, 2 foreign languages, comprehensive exam, thesis/dissertation. *Entrance requirements:* For master's and doctorate, GRE General Test. Additional exam requirements/recommendations for international students: Required—TOEFL (minimum score 213 computer-based). Electronic applications accepted.

West Virginia University, Eberly College of Arts and Sciences, Department of Chemistry, Morgantown, WV 26506. Offers analytical chemistry (MS, PhD); inorganic chemistry (MS, PhD); organic chemistry (MS, PhD); physical chemistry (MS, PhD); theoretical chemistry (MS, PhD). Part-time programs available. Postbaccalaureate distance learning degree programs offered (no on-campus

Peterson's Graduate Programs in the Physical Sciences, Mathematics, Agricultural Sciences, the Environment & Natural Resources 2013

facebook.com/petersonspublishing **121**

study). Terminal master's awarded for partial completion of doctoral program. *Degree requirements:* For master's, thesis; for doctorate, thesis/dissertation. *Entrance requirements:* For master's, GRE General Test, GRE Subject Test (recommended), minimum GPA of 2.5; for doctorate, GRE General Test, GRE Subject Test (recommended), minimum GPA of 2.75. Additional exam requirements/recommendations for international students: Required—TOEFL. Electronic applications accepted. *Faculty research:* Analysis of proteins, drug interactions, solids and effluents by advanced separation methods; new synthetic strategies for complex organic molecules; synthesis and structural characterization of metal complexes for polymerization catalysis, nonlinear science, spectroscopy.

Yale University, Graduate School of Arts and Sciences, Department of Chemistry, New Haven, CT 06520. Offers biophysical chemistry (PhD); inorganic chemistry (PhD); organic chemistry (PhD); physical and theoretical chemistry (PhD). *Degree requirements:* For doctorate, thesis/dissertation. *Entrance*

requirements: For doctorate, GRE General Test, GRE Subject Test. Additional exam requirements/recommendations for international students: Required—TOEFL.

Youngstown State University, Graduate School, College of Science, Technology, Engineering and Mathematics, Department of Chemistry, Youngstown, OH 44555-0001. Offers analytical chemistry (MS); biochemistry (MS); chemistry education (MS); inorganic chemistry (MS); organic chemistry (MS); physical chemistry (MS). Part-time programs available. *Degree requirements:* For master's, thesis. *Entrance requirements:* For master's, bachelor's degree in chemistry, minimum GPA of 2.7. Additional exam requirements/recommendations for international students: Required—TOEFL. *Faculty research:* Analysis of antioxidants, chromatography, defects and disorder in crystalline oxides, hydrogen bonding, novel organic and organometallic materials.

Theoretical Chemistry

Carnegie Mellon University, Mellon College of Science, Department of Chemistry, Pittsburgh, PA 15213-3891. Offers biotechnology and management (MS); chemistry (PhD), including bioinorganic, bioorganic, organic and materials, biophysics and spectroscopy, computational and theoretical, polymer; colloids, polymers and surfaces (MS). Part-time programs available. Terminal master's awarded for partial completion of doctoral program. *Degree requirements:* For doctorate, thesis/dissertation, departmental qualifying and oral exams, teaching experience. *Entrance requirements:* For master's, GRE General Test; for doctorate, GRE General Test, GRE Subject Test. Additional exam requirements/recommendations for international students: Required—TOEFL. Electronic applications accepted. *Faculty research:* Physical and theoretical chemistry, chemical synthesis, biophysical/bioinorganic chemistry.

Cornell University, Graduate School, Graduate Fields of Arts and Sciences, Field of Chemistry and Chemical Biology, Ithaca, NY 14853-0001. Offers analytical chemistry (PhD); bio-organic chemistry (PhD); biophysical chemistry (PhD); chemical biology (PhD); chemical physics (PhD); inorganic chemistry (PhD); materials chemistry (PhD); organic chemistry (PhD); organometallic chemistry (PhD); physical chemistry (PhD); polymer chemistry (PhD); theoretical chemistry (PhD). *Faculty:* 46 full-time (3 women). *Students:* 151 full-time (67 women); includes 16 minority (13 Asian, non-Hispanic/Latino; 2 Hispanic/Latino; 1 Two or more races, non-Hispanic/Latino), 48 international. Average age 25. 297 applicants, 35% accepted, 29 enrolled. In 2011, 22 doctorates awarded. *Degree requirements:* For doctorate, comprehensive exam, thesis/dissertation. *Entrance requirements:* For doctorate, GRE General Test, GRE Subject Test (chemistry), 3 letters of recommendation. Additional exam requirements/recommendations for international students: Required—TOEFL (minimum score 600 paper-based; 250 computer-based; 77 iBT). *Application deadline:* For fall admission, 1/10 for domestic students. Application fee: $95. Electronic applications accepted. *Financial support:* In 2011–12, 21 fellowships with full tuition reimbursements, 63 research assistantships with full tuition reimbursements, 59 teaching assistantships with full tuition reimbursements were awarded; institutionally sponsored loans, scholarships/grants, health care benefits, tuition waivers (full and partial), and unspecified assistantships also available. Financial award applicants required to submit FAFSA. *Faculty research:* Analytical, organic, inorganic, physical, materials, chemical biology. *Unit head:* Director of Graduate Studies, 607-255-4139, Fax: 607-255-4137. *Application contact:* Graduate Field Assistant, 607-255-4139, Fax: 607-255-4137, E-mail: chemgrad@cornell.edu. Web site: http://www.gradschool.cornell.edu/fields.php?id-26&a-2.

Georgetown University, Graduate School of Arts and Sciences, Department of Chemistry, Washington, DC 20057. Offers analytical chemistry (PhD); biochemistry (PhD); computational chemistry (PhD); inorganic chemistry (PhD); materials chemistry (PhD); organic chemistry (PhD); physical chemistry (PhD); theoretical chemistry (PhD). Terminal master's awarded for partial completion of doctoral program. *Degree requirements:* For doctorate, comprehensive exam, thesis/dissertation. *Entrance requirements:* For doctorate, GRE General Test. Additional exam requirements/recommendations for international students: Required—TOEFL.

Laurentian University, School of Graduate Studies and Research, Programme in Chemistry and Biochemistry, Sudbury, ON P3E 2C6, Canada. Offers analytical chemistry (M Sc); biochemistry (M Sc); environmental chemistry (M Sc); organic chemistry (M Sc); physical/theoretical chemistry (M Sc). Part-time programs available. *Degree requirements:* For master's, thesis or alternative. *Entrance requirements:* For master's, honors degree with minimum second class. *Faculty research:* Cell cycle checkpoints, kinetic modeling, toxicology to metal stress, quantum chemistry, biogeochemistry metal speciation.

University of Calgary, Faculty of Graduate Studies, Faculty of Science, Department of Chemistry, Calgary, AB T2N 1N4, Canada. Offers analytical chemistry (M Sc, PhD); applied chemistry (M Sc, PhD); inorganic chemistry (M Sc, PhD); organic chemistry (M Sc, PhD); physical chemistry (M Sc, PhD);

polymer chemistry (M Sc, PhD); theoretical chemistry (M Sc, PhD). *Degree requirements:* For master's, thesis; for doctorate, thesis/dissertation, candidacy exam. *Entrance requirements:* For master's, minimum GPA of 3.0; for doctorate, honors B Sc degree with minimum GPA of 3.7 or M Sc with minimum GPA of 3.3. Additional exam requirements/recommendations for international students: Required—TOEFL (minimum score 580 paper-based; 237 computer-based). Electronic applications accepted. *Faculty research:* Chemical analysis, chemical dynamics, synthesis theory.

The University of Manchester, School of Chemistry, Manchester, United Kingdom. Offers biological chemistry (PhD); chemistry (M Ent, M Phil, M Sc, D Ent, PhD); inorganic chemistry (PhD); materials chemistry (PhD); nanoscience (PhD); nuclear fission (PhD); organic chemistry (PhD); physical chemistry (PhD); theoretical chemistry (PhD).

University of Regina, Faculty of Graduate Studies and Research, Faculty of Science, Department of Chemistry and Biochemistry, Regina, SK S4S 0A2, Canada. Offers analytical/environmental chemistry (M Sc, PhD); biophysics of biological interfaces (M Sc, PhD); enzymology/chemical biology (M Sc, PhD); inorganic/organometallic chemistry (M Sc, PhD); signal transduction and mechanisms of cancer cell regulation (M Sc, PhD); supramolecular organic photochemistry and photophysics (M Sc, PhD); synthetic organic chemistry (M Sc, PhD); theoretical/computational chemistry (M Sc, PhD). *Faculty:* 12 full-time (2 women). *Students:* 13 full-time (4 women), 1 (woman) part-time. 22 applicants, 50% accepted. In 2011, 1 master's, 2 doctorates awarded. *Degree requirements:* For master's, thesis; for doctorate, thesis/dissertation. *Entrance requirements:* Additional exam requirements/recommendations for international students: Required—TOEFL (minimum score 580 paper-based; 80 iBT), IELTS (minimum score 6.5). *Application deadline:* Applications are processed on a rolling basis. Application fee: $100. Electronic applications accepted. *Financial support:* In 2011–12, 3 fellowships (averaging $6,500 per year), 1 research assistantship (averaging $5,500 per year), 7 teaching assistantships (averaging $2,298 per year) were awarded; scholarships/grants also available. Financial award application deadline: 6/15. *Faculty research:* Asymmetric synthesis and methodology, theoretical and computational chemistry, biophysical biochemistry, analytical and environmental chemistry, chemical biology. *Unit head:* Dr. Lynn Mihichuk, Head, 306-585-4793, Fax: 306-337-2409, E-mail: lynn.mihichuk@uregina.ca. *Application contact:* Dr. Tanya Dahms, Graduate Program Coordinator, 306-585-4246, Fax: 306-337-2409, E-mail: tanya.dahms@uregina.ca. Web site: http://www.chem.uregina.ca/.

The University of Tennessee, Graduate School, College of Arts and Sciences, Department of Chemistry, Knoxville, TN 37996. Offers analytical chemistry (MS, PhD); chemical physics (PhD); environmental chemistry (MS, PhD); inorganic chemistry (MS, PhD); organic chemistry (MS, PhD); physical chemistry (MS, PhD); polymer chemistry (MS, PhD); theoretical chemistry (PhD). Part-time programs available. Terminal master's awarded for partial completion of doctoral program. *Degree requirements:* For master's, thesis; for doctorate, thesis/dissertation. *Entrance requirements:* For master's and doctorate, GRE General Test, minimum GPA of 2.7. Additional exam requirements/recommendations for international students: Required—TOEFL. Electronic applications accepted. *Expenses:* Tuition, state resident: full-time $8332; part-time $464 per credit hour. Tuition, nonresident: full-time $25,174; part-time $1400 per credit hour. *Required fees:* $1162; $56 per credit hour. Tuition and fees vary according to program.

Vanderbilt University, Graduate School, Department of Chemistry, Nashville, TN 37240-1001. Offers analytical chemistry (MAT, MS, PhD); inorganic chemistry (MAT, MS, PhD); organic chemistry (MAT, MS, PhD); physical chemistry (MAT, MS, PhD); theoretical chemistry (MAT, MS, PhD). *Faculty:* 21 full-time (3 women). *Students:* 114 full-time (43 women), 2 part-time (0 women); includes 16 minority (6 Black or African American, non-Hispanic/Latino; 1 American Indian or Alaska Native, non-Hispanic/Latino; 3 Asian, non-Hispanic/Latino; 1 Hispanic/Latino; 5 Two or more races, non-Hispanic/Latino), 18 international. Average age 26. 420

122 facebook.com/petersonspublishing

Peterson's Graduate Programs in the Physical Sciences, Mathematics, Agricultural Sciences, the Environment & Natural Resources 2013

applicants, 12% accepted, 18 enrolled. In 2011, 4 master's, 17 doctorates awarded. Terminal master's awarded for partial completion of doctoral program. *Degree requirements:* For master's, thesis; for doctorate, thesis/dissertation, area, qualifying, and final exams. *Entrance requirements:* For master's and doctorate, GRE General Test, GRE Subject Test (recommended). Additional exam requirements/recommendations for international students: Required—TOEFL (minimum score 570 paper-based; 230 computer-based; 88 iBT). *Application deadline:* For fall admission, 1/15 for domestic and international students. Application fee: $0. Electronic applications accepted. *Financial support:* Fellowships with full and partial tuition reimbursements, research assistantships with full tuition reimbursements, teaching assistantships with full tuition reimbursements, Federal Work-Study, institutionally sponsored loans, scholarships/grants, traineeships, and health care benefits available. Financial award application deadline: 1/15; financial award applicants required to submit CSS PROFILE or FAFSA. *Faculty research:* Chemical synthesis; mechanistic, theoretical, bioorganic, analytical, and spectroscopic chemistry. *Unit head:* Dr. Mike P. Stone, Chair, 615-322-2589, Fax: 615-343-1234, E-mail: michael.p.stone@vanderbilt.edu. *Application contact:* Dr. Carmelo J. Rizzo, Director of Graduate Studies, 615-322-6100, Fax: 615-343-1234, E-mail: c.j.rizzo@vanderbilt.edu. Web site: http://www.vanderbilt.edu/AnS/Chemistry/grad/.

Wesleyan University, Graduate Programs, Department of Chemistry, Middletown, CT 06459. Offers biochemistry (MA, PhD); chemical physics (MA, PhD); inorganic chemistry (MA, PhD); organic chemistry (MA, PhD); physical chemistry (MA, PhD); theoretical chemistry (MA, PhD). Terminal master's awarded for partial completion of doctoral program. *Degree requirements:* For master's, thesis, proposal; for doctorate, thesis/dissertation, proposal. *Entrance*

requirements: For doctorate, GRE General Test, 3 recommendations. Additional exam requirements/recommendations for international students: Required—TOEFL. Electronic applications accepted.

West Virginia University, Eberly College of Arts and Sciences, Department of Chemistry, Morgantown, WV 26506. Offers analytical chemistry (MS, PhD); inorganic chemistry (MS, PhD); organic chemistry (MS, PhD); physical chemistry (MS, PhD); theoretical chemistry (MS, PhD). Part-time programs available. Postbaccalaureate distance learning degree programs offered (no on-campus study). Terminal master's awarded for partial completion of doctoral program. *Degree requirements:* For master's, thesis; for doctorate, thesis/dissertation. *Entrance requirements:* For master's, GRE General Test, GRE Subject Test (recommended), minimum GPA of 2.5; for doctorate, GRE General Test, GRE Subject Test (recommended), minimum GPA of 2.75. Additional exam requirements/recommendations for international students: Required—TOEFL. Electronic applications accepted. *Faculty research:* Analysis of proteins, drug interactions, solids and effluents by advanced separation methods; new synthetic strategies for complex organic molecules; synthesis and structural characterization of metal complexes for polymerization catalysis, nonlinear science, spectroscopy.

Yale University, Graduate School of Arts and Sciences, Department of Chemistry, New Haven, CT 06520. Offers biophysical chemistry (PhD); inorganic chemistry (PhD); organic chemistry (PhD); physical and theoretical chemistry (PhD). *Degree requirements:* For doctorate, thesis/dissertation. *Entrance requirements:* For doctorate, GRE General Test, GRE Subject Test. Additional exam requirements/recommendations for international students: Required—TOEFL.

Peterson's Graduate Programs in the Physical Sciences, Mathematics, Agricultural Sciences, the Environment & Natural Resources 2013

facebook.com/petersonspublishing **123**

HARVARD UNIVERSITY
Department of Chemistry and Chemical Biology

Programs of Study

The Department of Chemistry and Chemical Biology offers a program of study that leads to the degree of Doctor of Philosophy (Ph.D.) in chemistry in the special fields of biological, inorganic, organic, and physical chemistry. An interdepartmental Ph.D. program in chemical physics is also available. Upon entering the program, students formulate a plan of study in consultation with a Curriculum Advising Committee. Students must obtain honor grades in four advanced half courses (five for chemical physics). The course work is usually expected to be completed by the end of the second year of study. Students are expected to present and defend an independent research proposal anytime from the first semester of their second year through the end of their fourth year (June 30). Although the curriculum for the Ph.D. degree includes the course, research proposal, and oral defense requirements, the majority of the graduate student's time and energy is devoted to original investigations in a chosen field of research. Students are expected to join a research group in their second semester of residence, but no later than the third. The Ph.D. dissertation is based on independent scholarly research, which, upon conclusion, is defended in an oral examination before a Ph.D. committee. The preparation of a satisfactory thesis normally requires at least four years of full-time research.

Research Facilities

Departmental research facilities are located in six buildings on the historic main Harvard campus: Mallinckrodt, Conant, Converse, Naito, Bauer, and the Mallinckrodt/Hoffman "Link." These laboratories are adjacent to the Departments of Stem Cell and Regenerative Biology, Molecular and Cellular Biology, Organismic and Evolutionary Biology, Physics, Earth and Planetary Sciences, the Centers for Systems Biology and Brain Science, and the School of Engineering and Applied Sciences. Also nearby is the Science Center, which houses Mathematics, Statistics, and History of Science but is devoted primarily to undergraduate teaching facilities. In addition to the faculty research labs, the Chemistry and Chemical Biology complex contains facilities for analytical instrumentation (NMR, MS, X-ray Crystallography, and X-ray Diffractometry), a library, and computer workstations for molecular modeling and chemical information retrieval. A machine shop, electronics shop, and facilities for biological mass spectrometry, protein structure determination, materials synthesis, nanofabrication, and imaging are available in adjacent departments. Nearly all CCB faculty members are affiliated with multiple cross-departmental programs and research centers at Harvard.

Financial Aid

The Department of Chemistry and Chemical Biology meets the financial needs of its graduate students through Departmental scholarships, Departmental fellowships, teaching fellowships, research assistantships, and independent outside fellowships. Financial support is awarded on a twelve-month basis, enabling students to pursue their research throughout the year. Tuition is afforded to all graduate students in good standing for the tenure of the Ph.D. program.

Cost of Study

As stated in the Financial Aid section, tuition is waived for all Ph.D. students in good standing.

Living and Housing Costs

Dormitory rooms for single students are available, with costs (excluding meals) that ranged from $6106 for a single room to $8756 for a two-room suite in 2012–13. Married and single students may apply for apartments managed by Harvard Planning and Real Estate. The monthly costs are studio apartment, $992–$1734; one-bedroom apartment, $1472–$2184; two-bedroom apartment, $1874–$2836; and three-bedroom apartment, $2232–$4137. There are also many privately owned apartments nearby and within commuting distance.

Student Group

The Graduate School of Arts and Sciences (GSAS) has an enrollment of approximately 4,000 graduate students. There are approximately 170 students in the Department of Chemistry and Chemical Biology, 43 percent of whom are international students.

Student Outcomes

In 2011, 0 percent of the Ph.D. recipients entered positions in academia, 25 percent accepted permanent positions in industry, 68 percent conducted postdoctoral research before accepting permanent positions in academia or industry, and 7 percent pursued other directions.

Location

Cambridge, a city of over 100,000, is just minutes from Boston. It is a scientific and intellectual center, teeming with activities in all areas of creativity and study. The Cambridge/Boston area is a major cultural center, with its many public and university museums, theaters, symphony, and numerous private, special interest, and historical collections and performances. New England abounds in possibilities for recreational pursuits, from camping, hiking, and skiing in the mountains of New Hampshire and Vermont to swimming, sailing, fishing, and surfing on the seashores of Cape Cod and Maine.

The University

Harvard College was established in 1636, and its charter, which still guides the University, was granted in 1650. An early brochure, published in 1643, justified the College's existence: "To advance Learning and perpetuate it to Posterity...." Today, Harvard University, with its network of graduate and professional schools, occupies a noteworthy position in the academic world, and the Department of Chemistry and Chemical Biology offers an educational program in keeping with the University's long-standing record of achievement.

Applying

Applications for admission to study for the Ph.D. degree in chemistry may be accessed at the GSAS Web site at http://www.gsas.harvard.edu/apply/apply.php. Applications are accepted online from students who have received a bachelor's degree or equivalent.

The application process should begin during the summer or fall of the year preceding desired entrance. Completed online applications and any paper supporting materials should be submitted to the GSAS Admissions Office by December 1, though this date may vary slightly from year to year.

Correspondence and Information

Graduate Admissions Office
Department of Chemistry and Chemical Biology
Harvard University
12 Oxford Street
Cambridge, Massachusetts 02138
United States
Phone: 617-496-3208
E-mail: admissions@chemistry.harvard.edu
Web site: http://www.chem.harvard.edu

THE FACULTY AND THEIR RESEARCH

Joanna Aizenberg, Gordon McKay Professor of Materials Science, Susan S. and Kenneth L. Wallach Professor at the Radcliffe Institute for Advanced Study, and Professor of Chemistry and Chemical Biology; Ph.D., Weizmann (Israel), 1996. Biomimetic inorganic materials synthesis, self-assembly, crystal engineering, surface chemistry, nanofabrication, biomaterials, biomechanics, biooptics.

James G. Anderson, Philip S. Weld Professor of Atmospheric Chemistry; Ph.D., Colorado, 1970. Chemical reactivity of radical and radical-molecule systems; chemical catalysis sustained by free radical chain reactions in the earth's stratosphere and troposphere; mechanistic links between chemistry, radiation, and dynamics in the atmosphere that control climate; high-accuracy satellite observations for testing and systematic improvement of climate forecasts.

Alan Aspuru-Guzik, Associate Professor of Chemistry and Chemical Biology; Ph.D., Berkeley, 2004. Theoretical physical chemistry; quantum

Peterson's Graduate Programs in the Physical Sciences, Mathematics, Agricultural Sciences, the Environment & Natural Resources 2013

facebook.com/petersonspublishing **125**

computation and its application to chemistry problems; development of electronic structure methods for atoms and molecules: density functional theory and quantum Monte Carlo; theoretical understanding and design of renewable energy materials.

Emily Balskus, Assistant Professor of Chemistry and Chemical Biology; Ph.D., Harvard, 2008. The elucidation and study of biosynthetic pathways and enzymes as well as the development of synthetic methods that are compatible with microbial chemistry.

Theodore A. Betley, Associate Professor of Chemistry and Chemical Biology; Ph.D., Caltech, 2005. Synthetic inorganic chemistry targeting chemical energy conversion, structure and reactivity of polymetallic and organometallic compounds.

Adam E. Cohen, Professor of Chemistry and Chemical Biology and of Physics; Ph.D., Cambridge, 2003; Ph.D., Stanford, 2007. Single-molecule spectroscopy and biophysics; Brownian motion and feedback control; electrokinetics, polymer physics, fluctuation-induced forces; nonequilibrium van der Waals/Casimir forces; instrumentation.

Cynthia M. Friend, Theodore William Richards Professor of Chemistry and Professor of Materials Science; Ph.D., Berkeley, 1981. Surface chemistry: heterogeneous catalysis, nanostructure growth, environmental chemistry, laser-assisted materials processing, heterogeneous chemistry relevant to origins of life, chemical sensor technology.

Roy Gerald Gordon, Thomas Dudley Cabot Professor of Chemistry; Ph.D., Harvard, 1964. Intermolecular forces, transport processes, and molecular motion; theory of crystal structures and phase transitions, kinetics of crystal growth; solar energy, chemical vapor deposition; synthesis of inorganic precursors to new materials, thin films and their applications to microelectronics and solar cells.

Eric J. Heller, Professor of Chemistry and Physics; Ph.D., Harvard, 1973. Few-body quantum mechanics, scattering theory, and quantum chaos; physics of semiconductor devices, ultracold molecular collisions, and nonadiabatic interactions in molecules and gases.

Eric N. Jacobsen, Sheldon Emery Professor of Chemistry; Ph.D., Berkeley, 1986. Mechanistic and synthetic organic chemistry; development of new synthetic methods with emphasis on asymmetric catalysis; physical-organic studies of reactivity and recognition phenomena in homogeneous catalysis; stereoselective synthesis of natural products.

Daniel Kahne, Professor of Chemistry and Chemical Biology and Professor of Biological Chemistry and Molecular Pharmacology; Ph.D., Columbia, 1986. Synthetic organic chemistry and its applications to problems in chemistry and biology.

Charles M. Lieber, Mark Hyman Jr. Professor of Chemistry; Ph.D., Stanford, 1985. Chemistry and physics of materials with an emphasis on nanoscale systems; rational synthesis of new nanoscale building blocks and nanostructured solids; development of methodologies for hierarchical assembly of nanoscale building blocks into complex and functional systems; investigation of fundamental electronic, optical, and optoelectronic properties of nanoscale materials; design and development of nanoelectronics and nanophotonic systems, with emphasis on electrically based biological detection, digital and quantum computing, and photonic systems.

David R. Liu, Professor of Chemistry and Chemical Biology and Howard Hughes Medical Institute Investigator; Ph.D., Berkeley, 1999. Organic chemistry and chemical biology of molecular evolution, nucleic acid–templated organic synthesis, reaction discovery, protein and nucleic acid evolution and engineering, synthetic polymer evolution; generally, effective molarity-based approaches to controlling reactivity and evolution-based approaches to the discovery of functional synthetic and biological molecules.

Andrew G. Myers, Professor of Chemistry and Chemical Biology and Amory Houghton Professor of Chemistry; Ph.D., Harvard, 1985. Synthesis and study of complex natural products; development of synthetic methodology.

Daniel G. Nocera, Patterson Rockwood Professor of Energy; Ph.D., Caltech, 1984. Chemistry of renewable energy, solar energy conversion and storage, biological energy conversion with emphasis on mechanisms derived from proton-coupled electron transfer, applications of photochemistry including the development of nanocrystal-bioconjugate constructs for metabolic profiling of living systems, the physics of highly correlated systems derived from spin frustration.

Erin O'Shea, Professor of Molecular and Cellular Biology and of Chemistry and Chemical Biology, Howard Hughes Medical Institute Investigator, and Director of the Center for Systems Biology; Ph.D., MIT, 1992. Systems-level and molecular analysis of signaling pathways; transcriptional regulatory network architecture, function, and evolution; regulation and mechanism of oscillation of a circadian clock.

Hongkun Park, Professor of Chemistry and Chemical Biology and Professor of Physics; Ph.D., Stanford, 1996. Physics and chemistry of nanostructured materials; development of neuro-electronic interface; electron transport through individual molecules, nanowires, and nanotubes; single-molecule optoelectronics; synthesis and characterization of transition-metal-oxide and chalcogenide nanostructures; interrogation of complex neural networks using optical and electronic techniques.

Tobias Ritter, Professor of Chemistry and Chemical Biology; Ph.D., Swiss Federal Institute of Technology, 2004. Synthetic organic and organometallic chemistry, development of new synthetic methods based on transition-metal catalysis, stereoselective synthesis of biologically active natural and unnatural products.

Alan Saghatelian, Associate Professor of Chemistry and Chemical Biology; Ph.D., California, San Diego (Scripps), 2002. Development and application of global metabolite profiling (metabolomics) as a general discovery tool for chemical biology, elucidation of molecules and metabolic pathways that control phenotype at the cellular and physiological level.

Stuart L. Schreiber, Morris Loeb Professor of Chemistry and Chemical Biology and Howard Hughes Medical Institute Investigator; Ph.D., Harvard, 1981. Development of diversity-oriented synthesis, chemical genetics, and ChemBank; application to an understanding of cell circuitry and disease biology.

Matthew D. Shair, Professor of Chemistry and Chemical Biology; Ph.D., Columbia, 1995. Synthesis of small molecules that have interesting biological functions and elucidation of their cellular mechanisms; development of organic synthesis.

Eugene I. Shakhnovich, Professor of Chemistry and Chemical Biology; Ph.D., Moscow, 1984. Theoretical biomolecular science, including protein folding, theory of molecular evolution, structural bioinformatics, rational drug design, populational genomics, other complex systems including complex polymers and spin glasses.

Gregory L. Verdine, Erving Professor of Chemistry; Ph.D., Columbia, 1986. Protein-nucleic acid interactions, transcriptional regulation, X-ray crystallography, structure and function of DNA-processing enzymes, discovery of novel ligands to peptide receptors.

George M. Whitesides, Woodford L. and Ann A. Flowers University Professor; Ph.D., Caltech, 1964. Physical organic chemistry, materials science, biophysics, complexity, surface science, microfluidics, self-assembly, microtechnology and nanotechnology, cell-surface biochemistry.

Xiaoliang Sunney Xie, Professor; Ph.D., California, San Diego, 1990. Single-molecule spectroscopy and dynamics, molecular interaction and chemical dynamics in biological systems, live cell imaging.

Xiaowei Zhuang, Professor of Chemistry and Chemical Biology and of Physics and Howard Hughes Medical Institute Investigator; Ph.D., Berkeley, 1996. Investigating complex biological processes at the single-molecule level, live cell imaging, development of new techniques for single-molecule sensing and imaging.

Affiliate Members of the Department of Chemistry and Chemical Biology

Jon Clardy, Professor of Biological Chemistry and Molecular Pharmacology (Medical School); Ph.D., Harvard, 1969. Discovery of biologically active small molecules using DNA-based approaches or high-throughput screening and chemical analysis, protein structure and enzymology, functioning of small molecules as carriers of biological information, new biosynthetic pathways, new microbial biology.

Efthimios Kaxiras, Gordon McKay Professor of Applied Physics and Professor of Physics (SEAS); Ph.D., MIT, 1987. Development of computational methodologies for coupling spatial and temporal scales; optical and electronic properties for nucleic acids, melanin, and flavonoids; structure and properties of carbon and other nanotubes, surface nanowires and nanodots, and graphene nanoflakes; effect of chemical impurities on the large-scale mechanical behavior of solids.

Suzanne Walker, Professor of Microbiology and Molecular Genetics (Medical School); Ph.D., Princeton, 1992. Chemical biology: synthetic organic chemistry applied to the study of biochemical molecules, enzymology, mechanism of action of antibiotics.

Christopher Walsh, Hamilton Kuhn Professor of Biological Chemistry and Molecular Pharmacology (Medical School); Ph.D., Rockefeller, 1970. Molecular basis of biological catalysis, with focus on the structure and function of enzymes; biosynthesis and mechanism of action of antibiotics and bacterial siderophores.

126 facebook.com/petersonspublishing

Peterson's Graduate Programs in the Physical Sciences, Mathematics, Agricultural Sciences, the Environment & Natural Resources 2013

KENT STATE UNIVERSITY
Department of Chemistry and Biochemistry

Programs of Study

The Department of Chemistry and Biochemistry offers programs leading to the Master of Science (M.S.) and Doctor of Philosophy (Ph.D.) degrees in the traditional divisions of analytical, inorganic, organic, and physical chemistry and biochemistry. A variety of interdisciplinary areas are covered in bioanalytical chemistry, bioinorganic chemistry, biophysics, and molecular/cell biology. Faculty members also have research interests in the specialty areas of liquid crystals, photonic materials, spectroscopy, nanomaterials, separations, and surface science.

Graduate students are required to complete a program of core courses in their area of specialization and at least one (for M.S. candidates) or two (for Ph.D. candidates) elective courses in other areas of chemistry. The extraordinary breadth of the program gives students considerable flexibility in curriculum design, ensuring a modern and dynamic graduate education. At the end of the second year, doctoral students must pass a written examination in their field of specialization and defend an original research proposal for their dissertation. Students typically complete their doctoral program with their thesis defense after 4.5 years.

Research Facilities

Kent State University is home to excellent research facilities. The chemistry department has advanced NMR, X-ray, mass spectrometry, and proteomics core facilities. Research laboratories are located primarily in Williams Hall and the attached Science Research Laboratory. In addition, excellent materials' characterization facilities and one of the largest academic clean room facilities in the nation are housed in the nearby Liquid Crystal Institute. A confocal microscopy core facility located in the biology department is also available to chemistry students. Williams Hall houses two large lecture halls, classrooms, undergraduate and research laboratories, the Chemistry-Physics Library, chemical stockrooms, and glass and electronics shops. A machine shop, which is jointly operated with the physics department, is located in adjoining Smith Hall. Spectrometers include 500-MHz, 400-MHz (solids), and 300-MHz high-resolution NMR instruments; electrospray, MALDI-TOF, LC/ESI, protein chip SELDI mass spectrometers; various high-end FT-IR spectrometers, including a focal plane array FT-IR microscope for spectroscopic imaging; photon-counting fluorometer; circular dichroism; ESR, FPLC, UV/visible spectrometers; AA/AE equipment; and an EDX-700 energy dispersive X-ray spectrometer. An X-ray facility includes a Siemens D5000 Powder diffractometer and a Bruker AXS CCD instrument for single-crystal structural elucidation. Equipment available in specialty areas includes a microwave spectrometer, an LCQ electrospray mass spectrometer with MS/MS capability, a phosphorimager, Microcal VP DSC and ITC calorimeters, Bruker Vector 33 FTIR-NIR, Jobin Yvon Raman spectrometer with inverted microscope, laser tweezer instrumentation, particle sizer, Cary Eclipse fluorescence spectrophotometer, MF^2 Jobin Yvon fluorescence lifetime spectrometer, fluorescence correlation spectrometer, ThermoFinnigan Polaris Q115W GC-MS, a BAS electrochemical analyzer, various preparative centrifuges, a molecular dynamic Typhoon 8600 imaging system, and PCR and DNA sequencing and cell culture facilities. Individual research groups in the Department of Chemistry and Biochemistry maintain a variety of computer systems, including PCs and workstations. High-performance computing is made possible with access to the Ohio Supercomputer Center, which maintains Cray T94, Cray T3E, IBM SP2, and SGI Origin 2000 supercomputers. The Department has advanced molecular modeling facilities, including Cerius, Felix, Hyperchem, InsightII/Discover, Macromodel, and Spartan packages for modeling surfaces and interfaces, polymers, proteins, and nucleic acids, as well as facilities for performing ab initio calculations of molecular properties and molecular dynamics. A 3-D immersive classroom equipped with a rear projection system that generates 6' x 7' three-dimensional images when viewed with shutter glasses is available in Williams Hall and is frequently used for a variety of graduate classes. The University Library provides online access to virtually all chemical/biochemical journals as well as a broad variety of chemical databases, including the Chemical Abstracts SciFinder Service.

Financial Aid

Graduate students are generously supported through teaching and research assistantships as well as University fellowships. Students in good academic standing are guaranteed appointments for periods of at least 4½ years (Ph.D. candidates) or 2½ years (M.S. candidates). Stipends for 2011–12 range from $18,000 (M.S.) to $20,000 (Ph.D.) for a twelve-month appointment. A $1010 credit is made toward the University's health insurance plan. First-year bonuses and renewable merit fellowships providing an additional $2500 per year are available to outstanding doctoral applicants. In addition, first-year bonuses of $1250 are available for highly talented students pursuing their Ph.D. in physical chemistry. Advanced Ph.D. students are typically funded through research assistantships ($20,000 or higher) provided by their respective advisors.

Cost of Study

Graduate tuition and fees for the 2012–13 academic year are $7232, for which a tuition scholarship is provided.

Living and Housing Costs

Rooms in the graduate hall of residence are $2515 to $3360 per semester; married students' apartments may be rented for $669 to $699 per month (all utilities included). Information concerning off-campus housing may be obtained from the University housing office. Costs vary widely, but apartments typically rent for $500 to $600 per month.

Student Group

The ethnically diverse and highly talented chemistry graduate student population currently numbers about 50. There are approximately 23,000 students enrolled at the main campus of Kent State University; 12,000 additional students attend the seven regional campuses.

Location

Kent, a college town of about 28,000, is located 35 miles southeast of Cleveland and 12 miles east of Akron in a peaceful suburban setting. Kent offers the cultural advantages of a major metropolitan complex as well as the relaxed pace of semirural living. There are a number of music (e.g., Kent State's folk festival and free chamber music concerts in the summer), theater, and visual art groups at the University and in the community. Blossom Music Center, the summer home of the Cleveland Orchestra and the site of Kent State's cooperative programs in art, music, and theater, is only 15 miles from the main campus. This beautiful outdoor concert venue is also the site for many critically acclaimed rock concerts throughout the summer months. The newly expanded Akron and Cleveland art museums are within easy reach of the campus. Cleveland is also the home of the world-renowned Rock and Roll Hall of Fame and several professional sport teams. There are a wide variety of recreational facilities available on the campus and within the local area, including West Branch State Park and the Cuyahoga Valley National Park. Nearby Lake Erie and its beaches offer

Peterson's Graduate Programs in the Physical Sciences, Mathematics, Agricultural Sciences, the Environment & Natural Resources 2013

facebook.com/petersonspublishing **127**

a broad range of water recreational activities. Winter activities include ice skating as well as downhill and cross-country skiing. Kent State's state-of-the-art recreation and wellness center is available for graduate students free of charge.

The University

Established in 1910, Kent State University is one of Ohio's largest and oldest state universities. The campus contains 820 acres of wooded hillsides plus an airport and an eighteen-hole golf course. There are approximately 100 buildings on the main campus. Bachelor's, master's, and doctoral degrees are offered in more than thirty subject areas. The full-time faculty numbers approximately 1,200.

Applying

The online application system for the graduate program is located at: http://www.kent.edu/admissions/apply/. To ensure full consideration, candidates for admission for the upcoming fall semester should make certain that all their application material is received by the University no later than January 10. However, applications will be accepted until all positions are filled. In the case that late applications cannot be considered for fall admission, they will be automatically considered for admission the following spring semester. A limited number of positions are available for spring admission. Candidates should ensure that their application package is complete no later than September 1.

Application material must include all pertinent transcripts, general GRE exam, personal statement, three letters of recommendation, and a CV/resume. Domestic applicants can send all application materials to: Research and Graduate Studies, Office of Graduate Services, 16 Cartwright Hall, Kent State University, P. O. Box 5190, Kent, Ohio 44242-0001.

Foreign students must also provide TOEFL or IELTS exam scores. The minimum cutoff for the TOEFL is 525 on the paper-based exam, and 71 on the Internet-based test. The minimum cutoff for the IELTS is a score of six. Although the subject GRE is not required, candidates are encouraged to provide a subject GRE to strengthen their file. International applicants can send all application materials to: Office of International Affairs, Kent State University, 106 Van Campen Hall, 21 Loop Road, Kent, Ohio 44242, U.S.A.

Correspondence and Information

General Correspondence:
Graduate Coordinator
Department of Chemistry and Biochemistry
Kent State University
Kent, Ohio 44242
Phone: 330-672-2032
Fax: 330-672-3816
E-mail: chemgc@kent.edu
Web site: http://www.kent.edu/chemistry

THE FACULTY AND THEIR RESEARCH

Research groups are supported through grants awarded by the National Science Foundation, the National Institutes of Health, the Department of Energy, the Department of Defense, and other federal and state funding agencies.

Soumitra Basu, Assistant Professor; Ph.D., Thomas Jefferson, 1996. Biochemistry: molecular modulation of RNA function, anticancer therapeutics using RNAi, alternative translation modes with implications for tumor angiogenesis, chemical modification of RNA, toxicoribonomics.

Nicola E. Brasch, Associate Professor; Ph.D., Otago (New Zealand), 1994. Bioinorganic and medicinal chemistry; vitamin B_{12} and the B_{12}-dependent enzyme reactions; vanadium chemistry; inorganic drug delivery systems; synthesis, kinetics, and mechanism.

Scott D. Bunge, Assistant Professor; Ph.D., Georgia Tech, 2001. Inorganic chemistry: molecular design, organometallics, coordination chemistry, air-sensitive synthesis, catalysis, X-ray crystallography, thin films, nanomaterials.

Bansidhar Datta, Associate Professor; Ph.D., Nebraska–Lincoln, 1989. Biochemistry and molecular biology: mechanism of protein synthesis initiation in mammals; studies of posttranslational modifications, such as O-glycosylation and phosphorylation of translational regulator, p67; molecular cloning of translational regulatory proteins; studies of the evolutionary origins of the regulatory/structural domains in p67.

Roger B. Gregory, Professor; Ph.D., Sheffield (England), 1980. Biochemistry: protein conformational dynamics; the characterization of dynamic substructures in proteins; protein hydration and glass transition behavior; proteomics: development and application of high-sensitivity methods for protein characterization, including protein-protein interactions and protein chemical modifications.

Songping D. Huang, Associate Professor; Ph.D., Michigan State, 1993. Inorganic chemistry: molecule-based magnetic and nonlinear optical materials, organic conductors and superconductors, novel microporous and mesoporous materials, synthesis and crystal growth of metal oxides and chalcogenides.

Mietek Jaroniec, Professor; Ph.D., Lublin (Poland), 1976. Physical/analytical/materials chemistry: adsorption and chromatography at the gas/solid and liquid/solid interface; synthesis and modification of adsorbents, catalysts, and chromatographic packings with tailored surface and structural properties; self-assembled organic-inorganic nanomaterials; ordered mesoporous carbons synthesized via templating and imprinting methods; characterization of nanoporous materials.

Anatoly K. Khitrin, Associate Professor; Ph.D., Institute of Chemical Physics, Russian Academy of Sciences, 1985: Physical chemistry: NMR techniques, theory of magnetic resonance, material science, quantum computing and microimaging.

Hanbin Mao, Assistant Professor; Ph.D., Texas A&M, 2003. Bioanalytical and biophysical chemistry: micro total analysis systems ("lab-on-a-chip"), laser and magnetic tweezers, single-molecule DNA and DNA-protein interactions, drug-screening.

Paul Sampson, Professor; Ph.D., Birmingham (England), 1983. Synthetic organic chemistry: development of new synthetic methods; synthetic (stereoselective) organofluorine chemistry, with applications to the synthesis of fluorinated liquid crystals and carbohydrate analogs; development of new organometallic synthons as building blocks for organic synthesis.

Alexander J. Seed, Associate Professor; Ph.D., Hull (England), 1995. Organic chemistry, design, synthesis, and physical characterization of liquid crystals; ferroelectric, antiferroelectric, and high-twisting power materials for optical applications; new heterocyclic synthetic methodology.

Diane Stroup, Associate Professor; Ph.D., Ohio State, 1992. Biochemistry: control of mammalian gene expression by regulation of transcriptional and posttranscriptional processes, study of nuclear hormone receptors and signal transduction events.

Chun-che Tsai, Professor; Ph.D., Indiana, 1968. Biochemistry: interaction of drugs with nucleic acids; structure and activity of anticancer drugs, antiviral agents, antibiotic drugs, and interferon inducers; structure and biological function relationships; X-ray diffraction; quantitative structure-activity relationships (QSAR); molecular and drug design.

Michael J. Tubergen, Associate Professor; Ph.D., Chicago, 1991. Physical chemistry: high-resolution microwave spectroscopy

128 facebook.com/petersonspublishing

Peterson's Graduate Programs in the Physical Sciences, Mathematics, Agricultural Sciences, the Environment & Natural Resources 2013

for molecular structure determination of hydrogen-bonded complexes and biological molecules.

Robert J. Twieg, Distinguished Professor; Ph.D., Berkeley, 1976. Organic chemistry and materials science: development of organic and polymeric materials with novel electronic and optoelectronic properties, including nonlinear optical chromophores, photorefractive chromophores, organic semiconductors, fluorescent tags, and liquid crystals, with emphasis on applications and durability issues.

John L. West, Professor; Ph.D., Carnegie Mellon, 1980. Physical chemistry: materials science; liquid crystal polymer formulations for display applications, basic studies of liquid crystal alignment.

SELECTED PUBLICATIONS

Basu, S., and S. A. Strobel. Identification of specific monovalent metal ion binding sites within RNA. *Methods* 122:264–75, 2001.

Basu, S., A. Szewczak, M. Cocco, and S. A. Strobel. Direct detection of specific monovalent metal ion binding to a DNA G-quartet by ^{205}Tl NMR. *J. Am. Chem. Soc.* 122:3240–1, 2000.

Basu, S., and S. A. Strobel. Thiophilic metal ion rescue of phosphorothioate interference within the Tetrahymena ribozyme P4-P6 domain. *RNA* 5:1399–407, 1999.

Hannibal, L., C. A. Smith, D. W. Jacobsen, and **N. E. Brasch.** Nitroxylcob(III)alamin: Synthesis and X-ray structural characterization. *Angew. Chem.* 46:5140, 2007.

Hannibal, L., et al. **(N. E. Brasch).** X-ray structural characterization of imidazolylcobalamin and histidinylcobalamin: Cobalamin models for aquacobalamin bound to the B_{12} transporter protein transcobalamin. *Inorg. Chem.* 46:3613, 2007.

Mukherjee, R., et al. **(N. E. Brasch).** Structural and spectroscopic evidence for the formation of trinuclear and tetranuclear V(III)/carboxylate complexes of acetate and related derivatives in aqueous solution. *Inorg. Chem.* 46:1575, 2007.

Bunge, S. D., J. A. Bertke, and T. L. Cleland. Synthesis, structure, and reactivity of low-coordinate 1,1,3,3-tetraethylguanidinate complexes. *Inorg. Chem.* 48(16):8037–43, 2009.

Bunge, S. D., J. A. Ocana, T. L. Cleland, and J. L. Steele. Synthetic, structural, and theoretical investigation of guanidinate complexes containing planar Cu_6 cores. *Inorg. Chem.* 48(11):4619–21, 2009.

Monegan, J. D., and **S. D. Bunge.** Structurally characterized 1,1,3,3-tetramethylguanidine solvated magnesium aryloxide complexes: [Mg(μ-OEt)(DBP)(H-TMG)]₂, [Mg(μ-OBc)(DBP)(H-TMG)]₂, [Mg(μ-TMBA)(DBP)(H-TMG)]₂, [Mg(μ-DPP)(DBP)(H-TMG)]₂, [Mg(BMP)₂(H-TMG)₂], [Mg(O-2,6-Ph₂C₆H₃)₂(H-TMG)₂]. *Inorg. Chem.* 48(7):3248–56, 2009.

Datta, B., et al. Autoproteolysis of rat p67 generates several peptide fragments: The N-terminal fragment, p26, is required for the protection of eIF2 alpha from phosphorylation. *Biochemistry* 46(11):3465, 2007.

Ghosh A., et al. **(B. Datta).** The N-terminal lysine residue-rich domain II and the 340-430 amino acid segment of eukaryotic initiation factor 2-associated glycoprotein p67 are the binding sites for the gamma subunit of eIF2. *Exp. Cell Res.* 312(16):3184, 2006.

Datta, B., et al. The binding between p67 and eukaryotic initiation factor 2 plays important roles in the protection of eIF2 alpha from phosphorylation by kinases. *Arch. Biochem. Biophys.* 452(2):138, 2006.

Roh, J. H., et al. **(R. B. Gregory).** Influence of hydration on the dynamics of lysozyme. *Biophys. J.* 91(7):2573, 2006.

Roh, J. H., et al. **(R. B. Gregory).** Onsets of anharmonicity in protein dynamics. *Phys. Rev. Lett.* 95(3): 038101, 2005.

Gregory, R. B. Protein hydration and glass transitions. In *The Properties of Water in Foods*, pp. 55–99, ed. D. Reid. New York: Chapman-Hall, 1997.

Fu, D. W., et al. **(S. D. Huang).** Dielectric anisotropy of a homochiral trinuclear nickel(II) complex. *J. Am. Chem. Soc.* 129(17):5346, 2007.

Ye, Q., et al. **(S. D. Huang).** Ferroelectric metal-organic framework with a high dielectric constant. *J. Am. Chem. Soc.* 128(20):6554, 2006.

Vanchura, B. A., et al. **(S. D. Huang).** Direct synthesis of mesostructured lamellar molybdenum disulfides using a molten neutral n-alkylamine as the solvent and template. *J. Am. Chem. Soc.* 124(41):12090, 2002.

Celer, E. B., and **M. Jaroniec.** Temperature-programmed microwave-assisted synthesis of SBA-15 ordered mesoporous silica. *J. Am. Chem. Soc.* 128(44):14408, 2006.

Gierszal, K. P., and **M. Jaroniec.** Carbons with extremely large volume of uniform mesopores synthesized by carbonization of phenolic resin film formed on colloidal silica template. *J. Am. Chem. Soc.* 128(31):10026, 2006.

Jaroniec, M. Materials science: Organosilica the conciliator. *Nature* 442(7103):638, 2006.

Lee, J. S., T. Adams, and **A. K. Khitrin.** Experimental demonstration of a stimulated polarization wave in a chain of nuclear spins. *New J. Phys.* 9(4): 83, 2007.

Lee, J. S., and **A. K. Khitrin.** Constant-time method for measuring internuclear distances in static powders. *J. Magn. Reson.* 186:327, 2007.

Lee, J. S., and **A. K. Khitrin.** NMR quantum toys. *Concepts Magn. Reson.* 30A:194, 2007.

Luchette, P., N. Abiy, and **H. Mao.** Microanalysis of clouding process at the single droplet level. *Sensor. Actuator. B Chem.* 128:154–60, 2007.

Mao, H., et al. Temperature control methods in a laser-tweezers system. *Biophys. J.* 89:1308, 2005.

Mao, H., P. Cremer, and M. Manson. A versatile, sensitive microfluidic assay for bacterial chemotaxis. *Proc. Natl. Acad. Sci. U.S.A.* 100:5449, 2003.

Chumachenko, N., and **P. Sampson.** Synthesis of beta-hydroxy sulfones via opening of hydrophilic epoxides with zinc sulfinates in aqueous media. *Tetrahedron* 62(18):4540, 2006.

Novikov, Y. Y., and **P. Sampson.** 1-bromo-1-lithioethene: A practical reagent in organic synthesis. *J. Org. Chem.* 70(25):10247, 2005.

Chumachenko, N., **P. Sampson,** A. D. Hunter, and M. Zeller. -acyloxysulfonyl tethers for intramolecular Diels-Alder cycloaddition reactions. *Org. Lett.* 7:3203, 2005.

Sybo, B., et al. **(P. Sampson** and **A. J. Seed).** 1,3,4-Thiadiazole-2-carboxylate esters: New synthetic methodology for the preparation of an elusive family of self-organizing materials. *J. Mater. Chem.* 17(32):3406–11, 2007.

Seed, A. J. Synthesis of self-organizing mesogenic materials containing a sulfur-based five-membered heterocyclic core. *Chem. Soc. Rev.* 36(12):2046–69, 2007.

McCoy, B. K., et al. **(A. J. Seed).** Smectic-C^* phase with two coexistent helical pitch values and a first-order smectic-C^* to smectic-C^* transition. *Phys. Rev. E* 75(5-1): 051706, 2007.

Docherty, J., et al. **(C. C. Tsai).** In vivo anti-herpes simplex virus activity of resveratrol, a cyclin dependent kinase gene inhibitor. *Antivir. Res.* 57(3):86, 2003.

Tsai, C. C., et al. In vivo and in vitro antiherpetic effects of hydroxytolans. *Antivir. Res.* 57(3):87, 2003.

Nassiri, M. R., et al. **(C. C. Tsai).** The activity of Mg2+ and poly r(A-U) against HIV-I. *Antivir. Res.* 46(1):32, 2000.

Tubergen, M. J., et al. Rotational spectra and conformational structures of 1-phenyl-2-propanol, methamphetamine, and 1-phenyl-2-propanone. *J. Phys. Chem. A* 110(49):13188, 2006.

Tubergen, M. J., et al. Rotational spectra, nuclear quadrupole hyperfine tensors, and conformational structures of the mustard gas simulent 2-chloroethyl ethyl sulfide. *J. Mol. Spectros.* 233(2):180, 2005.

Tubergen, M. J., C. R. Torok, and R. J. Lavrich. Effect of solvent on molecular conformation: Microwave spectra and structures of 2-aminoethanol van der Waals complexes. *J. Chem. Phys.* 119:8397–403, 2003.

Wang, H., et al. **(R. J. Twieg).** The influence of tetrahydroquinoline rings in dicyanomethylenedihydrofuran (DCDHF) single-molecule fluorophores. *Tetrahedron* 63(1):103, 2007.

Lu, Z. K., et al. **(R. J. Twieg).** Long-wavelength analogue of PRODAN: Synthesis and properties of Anthradan, a fluorophore with a 2,6-donor-acceptor anthracene structure. *J. Org. Chem.* 71(26):9651, 2006.

Ellman, B., et al. **(R. J. Twieg).** High mobility, low dispersion hole transport in 1,4-diiodobenzene. *Adv. Mater.* 18(17):2284, 2006.

Li, F. H., et al. **(J. West).** Orientational coupling amplification in ferroelectric nematic colloids. *Phys. Rev. Lett.* 97(14): 147801, 2006.

Buyuktanir, E. A., et al. **(J. L. West).** Field-induced polymer wall formation in a bistable smectic-A liquid crystal display. *Appl. Phys. Lett.* 89(3): 031101, 2006.

West, J. L., et al. Colloidal particles at a nematic-isotropic interface: Effects of confinement. *Eur. Phys. J. E* 20(2):237, 2006.

Peterson's Graduate Programs in the Physical Sciences, Mathematics, Agricultural Sciences, the Environment & Natural Resources 2013

facebook.com/petersonspublishing **129**

PRINCETON UNIVERSITY
Department of Chemistry

Programs of Study

The Department of Chemistry offers a program of study leading to the degree of Doctor of Philosophy (Ph.D.). The graduate program emphasizes research, and students enter a research group by the end of the first semester. Students are required to take six graduate courses in chemistry and allied areas, satisfying at least four of ten areas of distribution, and are expected to participate in the active lecture and seminar programs throughout their graduate careers.

Early in the second year, students take a general examination that consists of an oral defense of a thesis-related subject. Presentation of an original research proposal, unrelated to the thesis research, is also required. Upon satisfactory completion of these steps, students advance to candidacy for the degree of Doctor of Philosophy in chemistry. The degree is awarded primarily on the basis of a thesis describing original research in one of the areas of chemistry. The normal length of the entire Ph.D. program is five years.

Interdisciplinary programs of graduate study are also offered, in cooperation with other science departments at Princeton University, including neuroscience, the Princeton Environmental Institute, and the Princeton Institute for the Science and Technology of Materials.

Research Facilities

In the fall of 2010, the department moved to the new, state-of-the-art Frick Chemistry Laboratory, designed by the award-winning, London-based Hopkins Architects. The building has been described as a cathedral to science. It is adjacent to the departments of physics, molecular biology, and mathematics, as well as the Lewis-Siegler Genomics Institute and the new neuroscience and psychology building which is scheduled for completion in spring 2013. A wide variety of research instrumentation is available, both in the departmental instrument facility and in individual faculty members' laboratories. Shared core facilities include NMR; ESR; mass spectrometry (high-resolution and gas chromatograph integrated); and visible, ultraviolet, and infrared spectrometers. Recent instrument acquisitions include three 500 MHz NMRs with cryoprobes and autosamplers, a high resolution ESI-TOF mass spectrometer, an LC-interfaced Q-TOF mass spectrometer for proteomics studies, a fast LC-triple quadrupole mass spectrometer, and a suite of bench-top FT-IR spectrometers for routine analysis. There is research equipment for ultrahigh vacuum surface studies, including electron diffraction and electron spectroscopy equipment. Tunable and fixed wavelength laser sources, gas and liquid chromatographic equipment, X-ray diffraction facilities, and controlled atmosphere dry boxes also are available to students.

Financial Aid

All admitted students receive funding during the normal period of study, usually five years. This funding covers tuition, health insurance, and a maintenance allowance, typically in the form of assistantships in instruction or research. In 2012–13, students earn $23,650 to $27,400 during the ten-month academic year, plus a summer stipend of $5000. First-year graduate students are not required to teach, as they receive fellowship funds that allow them to concentrate on course work.

Cost of Study

See the Financial Aid section.

Living and Housing Costs

Rooms at the Graduate College cost from $4380 to $7569 for the 2012–13 academic year of thirty-five weeks. Several meal plans are available, priced from $3150 to $5705. University apartments for both single and married students currently rent for $733 to $1788 per month. Accommodations are also available in the surrounding community.

Student Group

The total number of graduate students in chemistry is approximately 150. Postdoctoral students number about 110. A wide variety of academic, ethnic, and national backgrounds is represented among these students.

Location

Princeton University and the surrounding community together provide an ideal environment for learning and research. Princeton—noted for its highly collaborative ethos and the proximity of the engineering, physics, mathematics, and molecular biology departments, together with the DOE Princeton Plasma Physics Lab and the Institute for Advanced Study—offers valuable associates, supplementary facilities, and diverse sources of specialist knowledge. Many pharmaceutical and science-based companies have research laboratories near Princeton, leading to fruitful collaborations, seminars and lecture series, and employment opportunities after graduation.

The nearby concentration of elite institutions and large corporations, coupled with the commutability of New York City and Philadelphia, make Princeton a unique community of highly educated, professionals. Although it is a small town (population less than 27,500), the intellectual and cultural offerings rival the number and variety found in large cities, with the advantage of having everything within easy walking or bicycling distance. Attractions include a Tony Award–winning regional theater; a very active local arts council and public library; annual opera and jazz festivals; ongoing orchestral, chamber, and choral performances; and artisanal dining as well as fabled New Jersey diners. Scientific seminars and other symposia across the University bring prominent visitors from every field of endeavor.

Princeton's surrounding landscape offers great places for walking, hiking, bicycling, birding, canoeing, and outdoor discovery. Graduate students also enjoy free access to the University's athletic facilities which include the fitness center, indoor pools, a skating rink, and tennis and squash courts.

The University

Princeton University was founded in 1746 as the College of New Jersey. At its 150th anniversary in 1896, the trustees changed the name to Princeton University. The Graduate School was organized in 1901 and has since won international recognition in mathematics, the natural sciences, philosophy, and the humanities.

Applying

Application instructions, including the online application, are available at http://www.princeton.edu/gradschool/admission/. The application deadline for the Department of Chemistry is December 1 for all applicants. All applications must be completed online and accompanied by an application fee, which is $90 for applications in fall of 2012 for admission in fall of 2013. There is no spring admission period.

Admission consideration is given to all candidates without regard to race, color, national origin, religion, sex, or handicap.

Correspondence and Information

Meghan Krause, Graduate Administrator
Department of Chemistry
Frick Chemistry Laboratory
Princeton University
Princeton, New Jersey 08544
Phone: 609-258-4116
E-mail: mkrause@princeton.edu
Web site: http://www.princeton.edu/chemistry

THE FACULTY AND THEIR RESEARCH

The faculty members represent all major areas of chemistry, and there is much interdisciplinary and collaborative research both within the Department and with other departments and programs in the University. The following list briefly indicates the areas of interest of each professor.

S. L. Bernasek. Chemical physics of surfaces: basic studies of chemisorption on well-characterized transition-metal surfaces using electron diffraction and electron spectroscopy, surface reaction dynamics, heterogeneous catalysis.

A. B. Bocarsly. Inorganic materials chemistry, chemistry of alternate energy systems, chemical mitigation of carbon dioxide, electrochemistry, photochemistry, semiconductor photoelectrochemistry, coordination chemistry.

R. Car. Chemical physics and materials science; electronic structure theory and ab initio molecular dynamics; computer modeling and simulation of solids, liquids, disordered systems, and molecular structures; structural phase transitions and chemical reactions.

J. Carey. Biophysical chemistry: protein and nucleic acid structure, function, and interactions; protein folding and stability.

R. J. Cava. Materials chemistry; synthesis of new oxide, intermetallic, pnictide, and chalcogenide compounds, and characterization of their crystal structures and electronic and magnetic properties.

G. Chan. Development of new techniques for electronic structure theory using approaches that bridge quantum chemistry, condensed matter, and quantum information.

P. J. Chirik. Inorganic, organometallic, and organic chemistry: Base metal catalysis directed toward commodity and fine chemical synthesis, energy-efficient methods for N_2 functionalization and understanding electronic structure of redox-active metal-ligand complexes.

Peterson's Graduate Programs in the Physical Sciences, Mathematics, Agricultural Sciences, the Environment & Natural Resources 2013

facebook.com/petersonspublishing   **131**

Princeton University

A. G. Doyle. Organic and organometallic chemistry: discovery and development of new catalytic routes to chiral building blocks of importance in the enantioselective synthesis of natural products, pharmaceuticals, materials.

D. Fiedler. Chemical biology, bioinorganic chemistry: signaling functions of small molecule second messengers.

J. T. Groves. Bioorganic and bioinorganic chemistry, synthetic and mechanistic studies of reactions of biological interest, transition metal redox catalysis, models and mimics of metalloenzymes, biochemical mechanisms of protein nitration, the chemical biology of iron acquisition by siderophores and models of biological membranes.

M. Hecht. Biochemistry and chemical biology, protein folding and misfolding, protein design, synthetic biology, Alzheimer's disease.

R. Knowles. Synthetic organic chemistry, with an emphasis on stereoselective catalysis, unconventional redox processes, molecular recognition, and complex target.

D. W. C. MacMillan. Organic synthesis and catalysis: new concepts in synthetic organic chemistry involving organocatalysis, organo-cascade catalysis, metal-mediated catalysis, and total synthesis of natural products and pharmaceuticals.

T. W. Muir. Organic chemistry, biochemistry, and cell biology: investigating the physiochemical basis of protein function in complex systems of biomedical interest with new chemical biology technologies.

J. Rabinowitz. Biochemical kinetics, cellular metabolism, chemical basis of complex biological processes.

H. Rabitz. Physical chemistry, biomolecular modeling, laser control of molecular processes, molecular collisions, theory of chemical reactions, time- and space-dependent molecular manipulation.

C. E. Schutt. Structural biology, structure and function of proteins and cellular organelles, X-ray crystallography.

J. Schwartz. Organometallic chemistry, surface and interface organic and inorganic chemistry and their applications to biomaterials and electronic materials.

A. Selloni. Computational physics and chemistry and modeling of materials; structural, electronic, and dynamic properties of semiconductor and oxide surfaces; chemisorption and surface reactions.

M. F. Semmelhack. Organometallic and electrogenerated intermediates in organic synthesis, synthesis of unusual ring systems in natural and unnatural molecules.

Z. G. Soos. Chemical physics, electronic states of conjugated polymers and ion-radical solids, paramagnetic and charge transfer excitons, one-dimensional models.

E. J. Sorensen. Organic chemistry: chemical synthesis of bioactive natural products and molecular probes for biological research, bioinspired strategies for chemical synthesis, architectural self-constructions and novel methods for synthesis.

S. Torquato. Statistical mechanics and materials science; theory and computer simulations of disordered heterogeneous materials, liquids, amorphous solids, and biological materials; optimization in materials science; simulations of peptide binding; modeling the growth of tumors.

H. Yang. Physical chemistry, reaction dynamics in complex systems, development and application of single-molecule spectroscopy and methods to elucidate functional consequences in protein conformational dynamics in vitro and in living cells, self assembly of biological macromolecules and nanostructures, biofuels and basic sciences in sustainable energy solutions.

Associated Faculty

B. Bassler, Department of Molecular Biology. Cell-to-cell communication in bacteria.

E. A. Carter, Department of Mechanical and Aerospace Engineering and of Applied and Computational Mathematics. Development of quantum mechanics-based methods to predict behavior of molecules and materials, with applications to combustion chemistry, nanoscale physics, and materials science, with a new emphasis on alternative energy research.

F. M. Hughson, Department of Molecular Biology. Biochemical and X-ray crystallographic studies of intracellular trafficking and bacterial quorum sensing.

B. Koel, Department of Chemical and Biological Engineering. Surface chemistry and interfacial processes: heterogeneous catalysis of hydrocarbon conversion, solar photochemistry, electrocatalytic processes, fuel cells, plasma-surface interactions, environmental remediation by iron nanoparticles.

M. Llinas, Department of Molecular Biology. Cellular metabolism, biochemistry, genomics, microbiology, parasitology.

M. C. McAlpine. Department of Mechanical and Aerospace Engineering. Materials science: nanotechnology and biomaterials-enabled approaches to addressing fundamental problems in medicine, energy, and flexible electronics.

F. M. M. Morel, Department of Geosciences. Environmental chemistry, trace metal geochemistry, metals-biota interactions.

S. M. Myneni, Department of Geosciences. Environmental chemistry, ion hydration and complexation, interfacial chemistry, X-ray spectroscopy.

J. Stock, Department of Molecular Biology. Protein chemistry, cell biology, pharmacology.

The new Frick Chemistry Laboratory has been described as a cathedral to science.

SELECTED PUBLICATIONS

Swem, L. R., D. S. Swem, N. S. Wingreen, and **B. L. Bassler.** Deducing receptor signaling parameters from in vivo analysis: LuxN/AI-1 quorum sensing in *Vibrio harveyi. Cell* 134:461–73, 2008.

Higgins, D. A., et al. **(B. L. Bassler).** The major *Vibrio cholerae* autoinducer and its role in virulence factor production. *Nature* 450:883–6, 2007.

Neiditch, M. B., et al. **(B. L. Bassler).** Ligand-induced asymmetry in histidine sensor kinase complex regulates quorum sensing. *Cell* 126:1095–108, 2006.

Lenz, D. H., et al. **(B. L. Bassler).** The small RNA chaperone Hfq and multiple small RNAs control quorum sensing in *Vibrio harveyi* and *Vibrio cholerae. Cell* 118:69–82, 2004.

Miller, M. B., et al. **(B. L. Bassler).** Parallel quorum sensing systems converge to regulate virulence in *Vibrio cholerae. Cell* 110: 303–14, 2002.

Zhong, Y.-L. and **S. L. Bernasek.** Mild and efficient functionalization of hydrogen-terminated Si(111) via sonochemical activated hydrosilylation. *J. Am. Chem. Soc.* 133:8118–21, 2011.

Tao, F. and **S. L. Bernasek.** Thermally-driven switch of binding configuration of 3-pyrroline on Si(111)-7×7. *J. Phys. Chem. C* 115:2020–25, 2011.

Bhargava, G., T. A. Ramanarayanan, and **S. L. Bernasek.** Imidazole-Fe interaction in an aqueous chloride medium: Effect of cathodic reduction of the native oxide. *Langmuir* 26:215–9, 2010.

Dickerson, P. N., A. M. Hibberd, N. Oncel, and **S. L. Bernasek.** Hydrogen-bonding vs. van der Waals interactions in self-assembled monolayers of substituted isophthalic acids. *Langmuir* 26:18155–61, 2010.

Tao, F., G.-Q. Xu, and **S. L. Bernasek.** Electronic and structural factors in modification and functionalization of clean and passivated semiconductor surfaces with aromatic systems. *Chem. Rev.* 109:3991–4024, 2009.

Bocarsly, A. B. and D. M. P. Mingos, eds. *Fuel Cells and Hydrogen Storage.* 1st ed. Berlin: Springer, 2011.

Morris, A. J., R. T. McGibbon, and **A. B. Bocarsly.** Electrocatalytic carbon dioxide activation: The rate-determining step of pyridinium-catalyzed CO_2 reduction. *Chem. Sus. Chem.* 4:191–6, 2011.

Cole, E. B., et al. **(A. B. Bocarsly).** Using a one-electron shuttle for the multielectron reduction of CO_2 to methanol: Kinetic, mechanistic, and structural insights. *J. Am. Chem. Soc.* 132:11539–51, 2010.

Burgess, C. M., N. Yao, and **A. B. Bocarsly.** Stabilizing cyanosols: Amorphous cyanide bridged transition metal polymer nanoparticles. *J. Mat. Chem.* 19(46):8846–55, 2009.

Barton, E. E., D. M. Rampulla, and **A. B. Bocarsly.** Selective solar-driven reduction of CO_2 to methanol using a catalyzed p-GaP based photoelectrochemical cell. *J. Am. Chem. Soc.* 130(20):6342–4, 2008.

Strawn, R., et al. **(J. Carey).** Symmetric allosteric mechanism of hexameric *Escherichia coli* arginine repressor exploits competition between L-arginine ligands and resident arginine residues. *PLoS Computational Biology* 6(6):e1000801, 2010.

Lapkouski, M., et al. **(J. Carey).** Structure of the motor subunit of type I restriction-modification complex EcoR124I. *Nat. Struct. Mol. Biol.* 16:94–5, 2008.

Carey, J., et al. WrbA bridges bacterial flavodoxins and eukaryotic NAD(P)H:quinone oxidoreductases. *Protein Sci.* 16(10):2301–5, 2007.

Keith, J. A. and **E. A. Carter.** Theoretical insights into pyridinium-based photoelectrocatalytic reduction of CO_2. *J. Am. Chem. Soc.* 134:7580–3, 2012.

Krisiloff, D. B. and **E. A. Carter.** Approximately size extensive local multireference singles and doubles configuration interaction. *Phys. Chem. Chem. Phys.* 14:7710–17, 2012.

Xia, J., C. Huang, I. Shin, and **E. A. Carter.** Can orbital-free density functional theory simulate molecules? *J. Chem. Phys.* 136:084102, 2012.

Pavone, M., A. M. Ritzmann, and **E. A. Carter.** Quantum-mechanics-based design principles for solid oxide fuel cell cathode materials. *Energy Environ. Sci.* 4:4933–7, 2011.

Huang, C. and **E. A. Carter.** Potential-functional embedding theory for molecules and materials. *J. Chem. Phys.* 135:194104, 2011.

Climent-Pascual, E., et. al. **(R. J. Cava).** Spin 1/2 delafossite honeycomb compound Cu_5SbO_6. *Inorg. Chem.* 51:557–65, 2012.

Dutton, S. E., et. al. **(R. J. Cava).** Quantum spin liquid in frustrated one-dimensional $LiCuSbO_4$. *Phys. Rev. Lett.* 108:87206, 2012.

Ji, Huiwen, et. al. **(R. J. Cava).** Bulk intergrowth of a topological insulator with a room-temperature ferromagnet. *Phys. Rev. B* 85:165313, 2012.

Allred, J. M., L. M. Wang, P. Khalifah, and **R. J. Cava.** $Na_{27}Ru_{14}O_{48}$: A new mixed-valence sodium ruthenate with magnetic heptameric plaquettes. *J. Solid State Chem.* 184:44–51, 2011.

Climent-Pascual, E. et. al. **(R. J. Cava).** Polymorphism in $BaPb_{1-x}Bi_xO_3$ at the superconducting composition. *Phys. Rev. B Condens. Matter* 83:174512, 2011.

Chan, G. K.-L. and S. Sharma. The density matrix renormalization group in quantum chemistry. *Ann. Rev. Phys. Chem.* 62:465–81, 2011.

Yang, J., Y. Kurashige, F. Manby, and **G. K.-L. Chan.** Tensor factorizations of local second-order Moller-Plesset theory. *J. Chem. Phys.* 134:044123, 2011.

Zgid, D. and **G. K.-L. Chan.** Dynamical mean-field theory from a quantum chemical perspective. *J. Chem. Phys.* 134:094115, 2011.

Neuscamman, E., T. Yanai, and **G. K.-L. Chan.** A review of canonical transformation theory. *Int. Rev. Phys. Chem.* 29:231–71, 2010.

Changlani, H., J. Kinder, C. J. Umrigar, and **G. K.-L. Chan.** Approximating strongly correlated wavefunctions with correlator product states. *Phys. Rev. B Condens. Matter* 80:245116, 2010.

Semproni, S. P., C Milsmann, and **P. J. Chirik.** Structure and reactivity of a hafnocene μ-nitrido prepared from dinitrogen cleavage. *Angew. Chem. Int. Ed.* 51:5213–6, 2012.

Monfette, S., Z. R. Turner, S. P. Semproni, and **P. J. Chirik.** Enantiopure C_2-symmetric bis(imino)pyridine cobalt complexes for asymmetric alkene hydrogenation. *J. Am. Chem. Soc.* 134:4561–4, 2012.

Tondreau, A. M., et al. **(P. J. Chirik).** Iron catalysts for selective anti-Markovnikov alkene hydrosilylation using tertiary silanes. *Science* 335:567–70, 2012.

Bowman, A. C., et al. **(P. J. Chirik).** Synthesis and electronic structure determination of N-alkyl-substituted bis(imino)pyridine iron imides exhibiting spin cross behavior. *J. Am. Chem. Soc.* 133:17353–69, 2011.

Russell, S. K., E. Lobkovsky, and **P. J. Chirik.** Iron-catalyzed intermolecular [2π-2π] cycloaddition. *J. Am. Chem. Soc.* 133:8858–61, 2011.

Huang, C.-Y. (Dennis) and **A. G. Doyle.** Nickel-catalyzed negishi alkylations of styrenyl aziridines. *J. Am. Chem. Soc.* 134:9541–4, 2012.

Katcher, M. H., A. Sha, and **A. G. Doyle.** Palladium-catalyzed regio- and enantioselective fluorination of acyclic allylic halides. *J. Am. Chem. Soc.* 133:15902–5, 2011.

Kalow, J. A. and **A. G. Doyle.** Mechanistic investigations of cooperative catalysis in the enantioselective fluorination of epoxides. *J. Am. Chem. Soc.* 133:16001–2, 2011.

Nielsen, D. K. and **A. G. Doyle.** Nickel-catalyzed cross-coupling of styrenyl epoxides with boronic acids. *Angew. Chem. Int. Ed.* 50:6056–9, 2011.

Graham, T. J. A. and **A. G. Doyle.** Transition metal-catalyzed cross coupling with *N*-acyliminium ions derived from quinolines and isoquinolines. *Chem. Sci.* 2:980–4, 2011.

Fiedler, D., et al. Functional organization of the S. cerevisiae phosphorylation network. *Cell* 136:952–63, 2009.

Okuzumi, T.,et al. **(D. Fiedler).** Inhibitor hijacking of Akt activation. *Nat. Chem. Biol.* 5:484–93, 2009.

Fiedler, D., H. Van Halbeek, R. G. Bergman, and K. N. Raymond. Supramolecular catalysis of unimolecular rearrangements: Substrate scope and mechanistic insights. *J. Am. Chem. Soc.* 128:10240–52, 2006.

Fiedler, D., R. G. Bergman, and K. N. Raymond. Stabilization of reactive organometallic intermediates inside a self-assembled nanoscale host. *Angew. Chem. Int. Ed.* 45:745–8, 2006.

Fiedler, D., R. G. Bergman, and K. N. Raymond. Supramolecular catalysis of a unimolecular transformation: Aza-cope rearrangement within a self-assembled host. *Angew. Chem. Int. Ed.* 43, 6748–51, 2004.

Bell, S. R., and **J. T. Groves.** A highly reactive P450 model compound I. *J. Am. Chem. Soc.* 131(28):9640–1, 2009.

Su, J., and **J.T. Groves.** Direct detection of the oxygen rebound intermediates, ferryl Mb and NO_2, in the reaction of metMyoglobin with peroxynitrite. *J. Am. Chem. Soc.* 131(36):12979–88, 2009.

Austin, R. N., et al. **(J. T. Groves).** Cage escape competes with geminate recombination during alkane hydroxylation by the diiron oxygenase AlkB. *Angew. Chem.* 47(28):5232–4, 2008.

Jin, N., M. Ibrahim, T. G. Spiro, and **J.T. Groves.** Trans-dioxo manganese(V) porphyrins. *J. Am. Chem. Soc.* 129(41):12416–7, 2007.

Chen, J., A. H. Armstrong, A. N. Koehler, and **M. H. Hecht.** Small molecule microarrays enable the discovery of compounds that bind the Alzheimer's A peptide and reduce its cytotoxicity. *J. Am. Chem. Soc.* 132:17015–22, 2010.

Cherny, I., M. Korolev, A. N. Koehler , and **M. H. Hecht.** Proteins from an unevolved library of *de novo* designed sequences bind a range of small molecules. *ACS Synth. Bio.* 1:130–8, 2012.

Patel, S. C. and **M. H. Hecht.** Directed evolution of the peroxidase activity of a *de novo*-designed protein. *Protein Eng. Des. Sel.* 2012. doi:10.1093/protein/gzs025.

Arai, R., et al. **(M. H. Hecht).** Domain-swapped dimeric structure of a stable and functional *de novo* four-helix bundle protein, WA20. *J. Phys. Chem. B.* 116:6789–97, 2012.

Fisher, M. A., et al. **(M. H. Hecht).** De novo designed proteins from a library of artificial sequences function in *Escherichia coli* and enable cell growth. *PLoS One* 6(1):e15364, 2011.

Chen, G., et al. **(F. M. Hughson).** A strategy for antagonizing quorum sensing. *Mol. Cell* 42(2):199–209, 2011.

Lees, J. A., C. K. Yip, T. Walz, and **F. M. Hughson.** Molecular organization of the COG vesicle tethering complex. *Nat. Struct. Biol.* 17:1292–7, 2010.

Richardson, B.C., et al. **(F. M. Hughson).** Structural basis for a human glycosylation disorder caused by mutation of the COG4 gene. *Proc. Natl. Acad. Sci. USA* 106(32):13329–34, 2009.

Kelly, R.C., et al. **(F. M. Hughson).** The *Vibrio cholerae* quorum-sensing autoinducer CAI-1: Analysis of the biosynthetic enzyme CqsA. *Nat. Chem. Biol.* 5(12):891–5, 2009.

Ren, Y., et al. **(F. M. Hughson).** A structure-based mechanism for vesicle capture by the multisubunit tethering complex Dsl1. *Cell* 139:1119–29, 2009.

He, Q., et al. **(B. E. Koel).** Electrochemical and spectroscopic study of novel Cu and Fe-based catalysts for oxygen reduction in alkaline media. *J. Power Sourc.* 213:169–79, 2012.

Yan, W., R. Vasic, A. Frenkel, and **B. E. Koel.** Intraparticle reduction of arsenite (As(III)) by nanoscale zerovalent iron (nZVI) investigated with in situ X-ray absorption spectroscopy. *Environ. Sci. Tech.* 46(13):7018–26, 2012.

Yang, X., et al. **(B. E. Koel).** Nanofaceted C/Re(11-21): Fabrication, structure, and template for synthesizing nanostructured model pt electrocatalyst for hydrogen evolution reaction. *ACS Nano* 6(2):1404–9, 2012.

Kim, J., J. Fu, S. Podkolzin, and **B. E. Koel.** Studies of ethylene oxide adsorption on Pt–Sn alloys with TPD, HREELS, UPS, and DFT calculations. *J. Phys. Chem. C* 114(40):17238–47, 2010.

Koel, B. E., Structure, characterization, and reactivity of Pt–Sn surface alloys. In *Model Systems in Catalysis: Single Crystals to Supported Enzyme Mimics,* ed. R. M. Rioux. Berlin: Springer, 2010.

MacMillan, D. W. C. The advent and development of organocatalysis. *Nature* 455:304–8, 2008.

Nicewicz, D. and **D. W. C. MacMillan.** Merging photoredox catalysis with organocatalysis: The direct asymmetric alkylation of aldehydes. *Science* 322:77–80, 2008.

Beeson, T. D. et al. **(D. W. C. MacMillan).** Enantioselective organocatalysis using SOMO activation. *Science* 316:582–5, 2007.

Northrup, A. B. and **D. W. C. MacMillan.** Two-step synthesis of carbohydrates by selective aldol reactions. *Science* 305:1752–5, 2004.

Ahrendt, K. A., C. J. Borths, and **D. W. C. MacMillan.** New strategies for organic catalysis: The first highly enantioselective organocatalytic Diels-Alder reaction. *J. Am. Chem. Soc.* 122:4243–4, 2000.

Nguyen, T. D., et al. **(M. C. McAlpine).** Piezoelectric nanoribbons for monitoring cellular deformations. *Nature Nanotech.,* 2012. doi:10.1038/nnano.2012.112.

Mannoor, M. S., et al. **(M. C. McAlpine).** Graphene-based wireless bacteria detection on tooth enamel. *Nat. Commun.* 3:763, 2012.

Cui, Y., S. N. Kim, R. R. Naik, and **M. C. McAlpine.** Biomimetic peptide nanosensors. *Accounts Chem. Res.* 45(5): 696–704, 2012.

Qi, Y., J et al. **(M. C. McAlpine).** Enhanced piezoelectricity and stretchability in energy harvesting devices fabricated from buckled PZT ribbons. *Nano Letters* 11(3):1331–6, 2011.

McAlpine, M. C., H. Ahmad, D. Wang, and J. R. Heath. Highly ordered nanowire arrays on plastic substrates for ultrasensitive flexible chemical sensors. *Nat. Mater.* 6:379–84, 2007.

Peterson's Graduate Programs in the Physical Sciences, Mathematics, Agricultural Sciences, the Environment & Natural Resources 2013

facebook.com/petersonspublishing **133**

Princeton University

Aristilde, L., Y. Xu, and **F. M. M. Morel**. Weak organic ligands enhance zinc uptake in marine phytoplankton. *Environmental Science & Technology* 46(10):5438–45, 2012.

Hopkinson, B. M., C. L. Dupont, A. E. Allen, and **F. M. M. Morel**. Efficiency of the CO$_2$-concentrating mechanism of diatoms. *Proc. Natl. Acad. Sci. Unit. States Am.* 108(10):38930–7, 2011.

Schaefer, J .K., et al. **(F. M. M. Morel)**. Active transport, substrate specificity, and methylation of Hg(II) in anaerobic bacteria. *Proc. Natl. Acad. Sci. Unit. States Am.* 108(21):8714–9, 2011.

Shi, D., Y. Xu, B. M. Hopkinson, and **F. M. M. Morel**. Effect of ocean acidification on iron availability to marine phytoplankton. *Science* 327:676–9, 2010.

Xu Y., et al. **(F. M. M. Morel)**. Structure and metal exchange in the cadmium carbonic anhydrase of marine diatoms. *Nature* 452:56–62, 2008.

Shah, N. H., et al. **(T. W. Muir)**. Ultrafast protein splicing is common among cyanobacterial split inteins: Implications for protein engineering. *J. Am. Chem. Soc.* 134(28):11338–41, 2012.

Fierz, B., et al. **(T. W. Muir)**. Histone H2B ubiquitylation disrupts local and higher-order chromatin compaction. *Nat. Chem. Biol.* 7(2):113–9, 2011.

Kee, J. M., B. Villani, L. R. Carpenter, and **T. W. Muir**. Development of stable phosphohistidine analogues. *J. Am. Chem. Soc.* 132(41):14327–9, 2010.

Vila-Perelló, M. and **T. W. Muir**. Biological applications of protein splicing. *Cell* 143(2):191–200, 2010.

McGinty R. K., et al. **(T. W. Muir)**. Chemically ubiquitylated histone H2B stimulates hDot1L-mediated intranucleosomal methylation. *Nature* 453(7196):812–6, 2008.

Kamphorst, J. J., et al. **(J. D. Rabinowitz)**. Liquid chromatography-high resolution mass spectrometry analysis of fatty acid metabolism. *Anal. Chem.* 83(23): 9114–22, 2011.

Doucette, C. D., D. J. Schwab, N. S. Wingreen, and **J. D. Rabinowitz**. α-ketoglutarate coordinates carbon and nitrogen utilization via enzyme I inhibition. *Nat. Chem. Biol.* 7(12):894–901, 2011.

Vastag, L., et al. **(J. D. Rabinowitz)**. (2011). Divergent effects of human cytomegalovirus and herpes simplex virus-1 on cellular metabolism. *PLoS Pathogens* 7(7):e1002124, 2011.

Clasquin, M. F., et al. **(J. D. Rabinowitz)**. Riboneogenesis in yeast. *Cell* 145(6):969–80, 2011.

Rabinowitz, J. D. and E. White. Autophagy and metabolism. *Science* 330(6009):1344–8, 2010.

Feng, X. J., J. Sanchis, M. T. Reetz, and **H. Rabitz**. Enhancing the efficiency of directed evolution in focused enzyme libraries by the adaptive substituent reordering. *Chem. Eur. J.* 18(18):5646–54, 2012.

Brif, C., R. Chakrabarti, and **H. Rabitz**. Control of quantum phenomena. In *Advances in Chemical Physics, Volume 148*, eds. S. Rice and A. Dinner. Hoboken, New Jersey: John Wiley & Sons, Inc., 2012.

Feng, X. J., et al. **(H. Rabitz)**. Global optimality of fitness landscapes in evolution. *Chem. Sci.* 3(3):900–6, 2012.

Roslund, J., et al. **(H. Rabitz)**. Resolution of strongly competitive product channels with optimal dynamic discrimination: Application to flavins. *J. Chem. Phys.* 134(3):034511, 2011.

Moore, K. W., et al. **(H. Rabitz)**. Why is chemical synthesis and property optimization easier than expected? *Phys. Chem. Chem. Phys.* 13(21):10048–70, 2011.

Lassing, I., et al. **(C. Schutt)**. Tropomyosin is a tetramer under physiological salt conditions. *Cytoskeleton* 67(9):599–607, 2010.

Grenklo, S., et al. **(C. Schutt)**. Tropomyosin assembly intermediates in the control of microfilament system turnover. *Eur. J. Cell Biol.* 87:905–20, 2008.

Lovelace, J.J., et al. **(C. Schutt)**. Protein crystals can be incommensurately modulated. J. Appl. *Crystallogr.* 41:600–5, 2008.

Lindberg U., et al. **(C. Schutt)**. The microfilament system and malignancy. *Semin. Canc. Biol.* 18(1):2–11, 2008.

Lassing, I., et al. **(C. Schutt)**. Molecular and structural basis for redox regulation of beta-actin. *J. Mol. Biol.* 370(2):331–48, 2007.

Cattani-Scholz, A., et al. **(J. Schwartz)**. Molecular architecture: Construction of self-assembled organophosphonate duplexes and their electrochemical characterization. *Langmuir* 28(20):7889–96, 2012.

Chiang, C., et al. **(J. Schwartz)**. A new surface derivatization strategy for combinatorial analysis of cell response to mixtures of protein domains. *Langmuir* 28(1):548–56, 2012.

Auernhammer, M., et al. **(J. Schwartz)**. Surface functionalization of 6H-SiC using organophosphonate monolayers. *Appl. Phys. Lett.* 100(10):101601, 2012.

Avasthi. S., et al. **(J. Schwartz)**. Electronic structure and band alignment of 9,10-phenanthrenequinone passivated silicon surfaces. *Surf. Sci.* 605:1308–12, 2011.

Liao, K.-C., et al. **(J. Schwartz)**. Designed organophosphonate self-assembled monolayers enhance device performance of pentacene-based organic thin-film transistors. *Adv. Mater.* 22(28):3081–5, 2010.

Di Valentin, D. and **A. Selloni**. Bulk and surface polarons in photoexcited anatase TiO$_2$. *J. Phys. Chem.* Lett. 2(17):2223–8, 2011.

Cheng, H. and **A. Selloni**. Hydroxide ions at the water/anatase TiO$_2$(101) interface: Structure and electronic states from first principles molecular dynamics. *Langmuir* 26(13):11518–25, 2010.

Zipoli, F., R. Car, M. H. Cohen, and **A. Selloni**. Simulation of electrocatalytic hydrogen production by a bioinspired catalyst anchored to a pyrite electrode. *J. Am. Chem. Soc.* 132(25):8593–601, 2010.

De Angelis, F., et al. **(A. Selloni)**. Influence of the sensitizer adsorption mode on the open-circuit potential of dye-sensitized solar cells. *Nano Letters* 7(10):3189–95, 2007.

Aschauer, U. and **A. Selloni**. Structure of the rutile TiO$_2$(011) surface in an aqueous environment. *Phys. Rev. Lett.* 106(16):166102–6, 2011.

Miller, S. T., et al. **(M. F. Semmelhack and F. M. Hughson)**. Salmonella typhimurium recognizes a chemically distinct form of the bacterial quorum sensing signal AI-2. *Mol. Cell* 15:677–87, 2004.

Semmelhack, M. F., and R. J. Hooley. Palladium-catalyzed hydrostannylations of highly hindered acetyolenes in hexane. *Tetrahedron Lett.* 44:5737–9, 2003.

Semmelhack, M. F., L. Wu, **R. A. Pascal Jr.**, and D. M. Ho. Conformational control in activation of an enediyne. *J. Am. Chem. Soc.* 125:10496–7, 2003.

D'Avino, G., et al. **(Z. G. Soos)**. Anomalous dispersion of optical phonons at the neutral-ionic transition: Evidence from diffuse X-ray scattering. *Phys. Rev. Lett.* 99(15):156407, 2007.

Bewick, S. A., and **Z. G. Soos**. Peierls transitions in ionic organic charge-transfer crystals with spin and charge degrees of freedom. *J. Phys. Chem. B* 110(38):18748–57, 2006.

Kim, J., J. S. Schneekloth, Jr., and **E. J. Sorensen**. A chemical synthesis of 11-methoxy mitragynine pseudoindoxyl featuring the interrupted Ugi reaction. *Chem. Sci.* 3(9), 2849–2852, 2012.

Guerrero, C. A. and **E. J. Sorensen**. Concise, stereocontrolled synthesis of the citrinadin B core architecture. *Org. Lett.* 13(19):5164–7, 2011.

Xie, H., et al. **(E. J. Sorensen)**. The catalytic asymmetric Diels-Alder reactions and post-cycloaddition reductive transpositions of 1-hydrazinodienes. *Chem. Eur. J.* 17(40):11131–4, 2011.

Lotesta, S. D., et al. **(E. J. Sorensen)**. Expanding the pleuromutilin class of antibiotics by de novo chemical synthesis. *Chem. Sci.* 2:1258–61, 2011.

Shipe, W. D. and **E. J. Sorensen**. Convergent, enantioselective synthesis of guanacastepenes A and E featuring a selective cyclobutane fragmentation. *J. Am. Chem. Soc.* 128(21):7025–35, 2006.

Li, Z., and **J. B. Stock**. Protein carboxyl methylation and the biochemistry of memory. *Biol. Chem.* 390(11):1087–96, 2009.

Xing, Y., et al. **(J. B. Stock)**. .Structural mechanism of demethylation and inactivation of protein phosphatase 2A. *Cell* 133(1):154–63, 2008.

Gordon, J. S., et al. **(J. B. Stock)**. Topical N-acetyl-S-farnesyl-L-cysteine inhibits mouse skin inflammation, and unlike dexamethasone, its effects are restricted to the application site. *J. Invest. Dermatol.* 128(3):643–54, 2008.

Torquato, S. Effect of dimensionality on the continuum percolation of overlapping hyperspheres and hypercubes. *J. Chem. Phys.* 136:054106, 2012.

Torquato, S. Toward an Ising model of cancer and beyond. *Phys. Biol.* 8:015017, 2011.

Torquato, S., and Y. Jiao. Dense packings of the Platonic and Archimedean solids. *Nature* 460:876–9, 2009.

Batten, R. D., F. H. Stillinger, and **S. Torquato**. Interactions leading to disordered ground states and unusual low-temperature behavior. *Phys. Rev. E* 80(3):031105–29, 2009.

Torquato, S., and Y. Jiao. Dense packings of polyhedra: Platonic and Archimedean solids. *Phys. Rev. E* 80:041104–35, 2009.

Hanson, J. A., et al. **(H. Yang)**. Structural distributions from single-molecule measurements as a tool for molecular mechanics. *Chem. Phys.* 396:61–7, 2012.

Hsia, C.-H., A. Wuttig, and **H. Yang**. An accessible approach to preparing water-soluble Mn2+-doped (CdSSe)ZnS (core)shell nanocrystals for ratiometric temperature sensing. *ACS Nano* 5(12):9511–22, 2011.

Yang, J.-M., **H. Yang**, and L. Lin. Quantum dot nano thermometers reveal heterogeneous local thermogenesis in living cells. *ACS Nano* 5(6):5067–71, 2011.

Tan, Y.-W. and **H. Yang**. Seeing the forest for the trees: Fluorescence studies of single enzymes in the context of ensemble experiments. *Phys. Chem. Chem. Phys.* 13:1709–21, 2011.

Section 3
Geosciences

This section contains a directory of institutions offering graduate work in geosciences. Additional information about programs listed in the directory but not augmented by an in-depth entry may be obtained by writing directly to the dean of a graduate school or chair of a department at the address given in the directory.

For programs offering related work, see all other areas in this book. In the other guides in this series:

Graduate Programs in the Humanities, Arts & Social Sciences

See *Geography*

Graduate Programs in the Biological/Biomedical Sciences & Health-Related Medical Professions

See *Biological and Biomedical Sciences, Biophysics,* and *Botany and Plant Biology*

Graduate Programs in Engineering & Applied Sciences

See *Aerospace/Aeronautical Engineering; Agricultural Engineering and Bioengineering; Civil and Environmental Engineering; Energy and Power Engineering (Nuclear Engineering); Engineering and Applied Sciences; Geological, Mineral/Mining, and Petroleum Engineering;* and *Mechanical Engineering and Mechanics*

CONTENTS

Program Directories

Geochemistry

California Institute of Technology, Division of Geological and Planetary Sciences, Pasadena, CA 91125-0001. Offers environmental science and engineering (MS, PhD); geobiology (MS, PhD); geochemistry (MS, PhD); geology (MS, PhD); geophysics (MS, PhD); planetary science (MS, PhD). *Faculty:* 42 full-time (8 women). *Students:* 102 full-time (48 women); includes 10 minority (2 Black or African American, non-Hispanic/Latino; 7 Asian, non-Hispanic/Latino; 1 Hispanic/Latino), 28 international. Average age 26. 188 applicants, 23% accepted, 21 enrolled. In 2011, 11 master's, 12 doctorates awarded. *Degree requirements:* For doctorate, thesis/dissertation. *Entrance requirements:* For doctorate, GRE General Test. Additional exam requirements/recommendations for international students: Required—TOEFL; Recommended—IELTS, TWE. *Application deadline:* For fall admission, 1/1 for domestic and international students. Application fee: $80. Electronic applications accepted. *Financial support:* In 2011–12, 75 students received support, including 16 fellowships with full tuition reimbursements available (averaging $28,000 per year); 86 research assistantships with full tuition reimbursements available (averaging $28,000 per year); teaching assistantships with full tuition reimbursements available, institutionally sponsored loans, scholarships/grants, health care benefits, and unspecified assistantships also available. Financial award applicants required to submit FAFSA. *Faculty research:* Planetary surfaces, evolution of anaerobic respiratory processes, structural geology and tectonics, theoretical and numerical seismology, global biogeochemical cycles. *Unit head:* Dr. Kenneth A. Farley, Chairman, 626-395-6111, Fax: 626-795-6028, E-mail: dianb@gps.caltech.edu. *Application contact:* Dr. Robert W. Clayton, Academic Officer, 626-395-6909, Fax: 626-795-6028, E-mail: dianb@gps.caltech.edu. Web site: http://www.gps.caltech.edu/.

California State University, Fullerton, Graduate Studies, College of Natural Science and Mathematics, Department of Chemistry and Biochemistry, Fullerton, CA 92834-9480. Offers chemistry (MS); geochemistry (MS). Part-time programs available. *Students:* 3 full-time (1 woman), 19 part-time (8 women); includes 6 minority (4 Asian, non-Hispanic/Latino; 2 Hispanic/Latino), 1 international. Average age 29. 38 applicants, 45% accepted, 4 enrolled. In 2011, 5 master's awarded. *Degree requirements:* For master's, thesis, departmental qualifying exam. *Entrance requirements:* For master's, minimum GPA of 2.5 in last 60 units of course work, major in chemistry or related field. Application fee: $55. *Financial support:* Research assistantships, teaching assistantships, career-related internships or fieldwork, Federal Work-Study, institutionally sponsored loans, and scholarships/grants available. Support available to part-time students. Financial award application deadline: 3/1; financial award applicants required to submit FAFSA. *Unit head:* Dr. Christopher Meyer, Chair, 657-278-3621. *Application contact:* Admissions/Applications, 657-278-2371.

Colorado School of Mines, Graduate School, Department of Chemistry and Geochemistry and Department of Geology and Geological Engineering, Program in Geochemistry, Golden, CO 80401-1887. Offers MS, PhD. Part-time programs available. *Students:* 6 full-time (4 women). Average age 29. 24 applicants, 13% accepted, 1 enrolled. *Degree requirements:* For master's, thesis (for some programs); for doctorate, comprehensive exam, thesis/dissertation. *Entrance requirements:* For master's and doctorate, GRE General Test. Additional exam requirements/recommendations for international students: Required—TOEFL (minimum score 550 paper-based; 213 computer-based; 80 iBT). *Application deadline:* For fall admission, 1/15 for domestic and international students; for spring admission, 10/15 priority date for domestic students, 10/15 for international students. Application fee: $50 ($70 for international students). Electronic applications accepted. *Expenses:* Tuition, state resident: full-time $12,585; part-time $699 per credit. Tuition, nonresident: full-time $27,270; part-time $1516 per credit. *Required fees:* $1864.20; $670 per semester. *Financial support:* In 2011–12, fellowships with full tuition reimbursements (averaging $20,000 per year), research assistantships with full tuition reimbursements (averaging $20,000 per year), teaching assistantships with full tuition reimbursements (averaging $20,000 per year) were awarded; scholarships/grants, health care benefits, and unspecified assistantships also available. Financial award application deadline: 1/15; financial award applicants required to submit FAFSA. *Faculty research:* Geochemical analysis, organic geochemistry, hydrochemical systems, environmental microbiology, process control programming. *Unit head:* Dr. Dan Knauss, Department Head, 303-273-3625, Fax: 303-273-3629, E-mail: dknauss@mines.edu. *Application contact:* Tina Voelker, Associate Professor, 303-273-3152, Fax: 303-273-3629, E-mail: tvoelker@mines.edu. Web site: http://geochem.mines.edu.

Colorado School of Mines, Graduate School, Department of Geology and Geological Engineering, Golden, CO 80401-1887. Offers geochemistry (MS, PMS, PhD); geological engineering (ME, MS, PhD); geology (MS, PhD). Part-time programs available. *Faculty:* 22 full-time (7 women), 4 part-time/adjunct (2 women). *Students:* 147 full-time (51 women), 31 part-time (11 women); includes 15 minority (2 Black or African American, non-Hispanic/Latino; 2 American Indian or Alaska Native, non-Hispanic/Latino; 2 Asian, non-Hispanic/Latino; 8 Hispanic/Latino; 1 Two or more races, non-Hispanic/Latino), 29 international. Average age 30. 241 applicants, 55% accepted, 55 enrolled. In 2011, 26 master's, 1 doctorate awarded. *Degree requirements:* For master's, thesis (for some programs); for

doctorate, comprehensive exam, thesis/dissertation. *Entrance requirements:* For master's and doctorate, GRE General Test. Additional exam requirements/recommendations for international students: Required—TOEFL (minimum score 550 paper-based; 213 computer-based; 80 iBT). *Application deadline:* For fall admission, 1/15 for domestic and international students; for spring admission, 10/15 for domestic and international students. Application fee: $50 ($70 for international students). Electronic applications accepted. *Expenses:* Tuition, state resident: full-time $12,585; part-time $699 per credit. Tuition, nonresident: full-time $27,270; part-time $1516 per credit. *Required fees:* $1864.20; $670 per semester. *Financial support:* In 2011–12, 79 students received support, including 14 fellowships with full tuition reimbursements available (averaging $20,000 per year), 47 research assistantships with full tuition reimbursements available (averaging $20,000 per year), 18 teaching assistantships with full tuition reimbursements available (averaging $20,000 per year); scholarships/grants, health care benefits, and unspecified assistantships also available. Financial award application deadline: 1/15; financial award applicants required to submit FAFSA. *Faculty research:* Predictive sediment modeling, petrophysics, aquifer-contaminant flow modeling, water-rock interactions, geotechnical engineering. *Total annual research expenditures:* $3.3 million. *Unit head:* Dr. John Humphrey, Head, 303-273-3819, Fax: 303-273-3859, E-mail: jhumphre@mines.edu. *Application contact:* Dr. Christian Shorey, Lecturer, 303-273-3556, Fax: 303-273-3859, E-mail: cshorey@mines.edu. Web site: http://geology.mines.edu.

Columbia University, Graduate School of Arts and Sciences, Division of Natural Sciences, Department of Earth and Environmental Sciences, New York, NY 10027. Offers geochemistry (M Phil, MA, PhD); geodetic sciences (M Phil, MA, PhD); geophysics (M Phil, MA, PhD); oceanography (M Phil, MA, PhD). *Degree requirements:* For master's, thesis or alternative, fieldwork, written exam; for doctorate, one foreign language, thesis/dissertation. *Entrance requirements:* For master's and doctorate, GRE General Test, GRE Subject Test, major in natural or physical science. Additional exam requirements/recommendations for international students: Required—TOEFL. *Faculty research:* Structural geology and stratigraphy, petrology, paleontology, rare gas, isotope and aqueous geochemistry.

Cornell University, Graduate School, Graduate Fields of Engineering, Field of Geological Sciences, Ithaca, NY 14853. Offers economic geology (M Eng, MS, PhD); engineering geology (M Eng, MS, PhD); environmental geophysics (M Eng, MS, PhD); general geology (M Eng, MS, PhD); geobiology (M Eng, MS, PhD); geochemistry and isotope geology (M Eng, MS, PhD); geohydrology (M Eng, MS, PhD); geomorphology (M Eng, MS, PhD); geophysics (M Eng, MS, PhD); geotectonics (M Eng, MS, PhD); marine geology (MS, PhD); mineralogy (M Eng, MS, PhD); paleontology (M Eng, MS, PhD); petroleum geology (M Eng, MS, PhD); petrology (M Eng, MS, PhD); planetary geology (M Eng, MS, PhD); Precambrian geology (M Eng, MS, PhD); Quaternary geology (M Eng, MS, PhD); rock mechanics (M Eng, MS, PhD); sedimentology (M Eng, MS, PhD); seismology (M Eng, MS, PhD); stratigraphy (M Eng, MS, PhD); structural geology (M Eng, MS, PhD). *Faculty:* 37 full-time (5 women). *Students:* 41 full-time (19 women); includes 5 minority (2 Asian, non-Hispanic/Latino; 3 Hispanic/Latino), 7 international. Average age 27. 74 applicants, 19% accepted, 9 enrolled. In 2011, 3 master's, 3 doctorates awarded. *Degree requirements:* For master's, thesis (MS); for doctorate, comprehensive exam, thesis/dissertation. *Entrance requirements:* For master's and doctorate, GRE General Test, 3 letters of recommendation. Additional exam requirements/recommendations for international students: Required—TOEFL (minimum score 550 paper-based; 213 computer-based; 77 iBT). *Application deadline:* For fall admission, 1/15 priority date for domestic students. Applications are processed on a rolling basis. Application fee: $95. Electronic applications accepted. *Financial support:* In 2011–12, 25 students received support, including 7 fellowships with full tuition reimbursements available, 19 research assistantships with full tuition reimbursements available, 8 teaching assistantships with full tuition reimbursements available; institutionally sponsored loans, scholarships/grants, health care benefits, tuition waivers (full and partial), and unspecified assistantships also available. Financial award applicants required to submit FAFSA. *Faculty research:* Geophysics, structural geology, petrology, geochemistry, geodynamics. *Unit head:* Director of Graduate Studies, 607-255-5466, Fax: 607-254-4780. *Application contact:* Graduate Field Assistant, 607-255-5466, Fax: 607-254-4780, E-mail: gradprog@geology.cornell.edu. Web site: http://www.gradschool.cornell.edu/fields.php?id-30&a-2.

Georgia Institute of Technology, Graduate Studies and Research, College of Sciences, School of Earth and Atmospheric Sciences, Atlanta, GA 30332-0340. Offers atmospheric chemistry, aerosols and clouds (MS, PhD); dynamics of weather and climate (MS, PhD); geochemistry (MS, PhD); geophysics (MS, PhD); oceanography (MS, PhD); paleoclimate (MS, PhD); planetary science (MS, PhD); remote sensing (MS, PhD). Part-time programs available. Terminal master's awarded for partial completion of doctoral program. *Degree requirements:* For master's, thesis or alternative; for doctorate, comprehensive exam, thesis/dissertation. *Entrance requirements:* For master's, GRE, letters of recommendation; for doctorate, GRE, academic transcripts, letters of recommendation, personal statement. Additional exam requirements/

recommendations for international students: Required—TOEFL (minimum score 550 paper-based; 213 computer-based; 79 iBT). *Faculty research:* Geophysics; atmospheric chemistry, aerosols and clouds; dynamics of weather and climate; geochemistry; oceanography; paleoclimate; planetary science; remote sensing.

Indiana University Bloomington, University Graduate School, College of Arts and Sciences, Department of Geological Sciences, Bloomington, IN 47405-7000. Offers biogeochemistry (MS, PhD); economic geology (MS, PhD); geobiology (MS, PhD); geophysics, structural geology and tectonics (MS, PhD); hydrogeology (MS, PhD); mineralogy (MS, PhD); stratigraphy and sedimentology (MS, PhD). *Faculty:* 17 full-time (1 woman). *Students:* 60 full-time (26 women), 2 part-time (0 women); includes 5 minority (2 Black or African American, non-Hispanic/Latino; 1 Hispanic/Latino; 2 Two or more races, non-Hispanic/Latino), 18 international. Average age 29. 44 applicants, 55% accepted, 18 enrolled. In 2011, 11 master's, 6 doctorates awarded. Terminal master's awarded for partial completion of doctoral program. *Degree requirements:* For master's, thesis or alternative; for doctorate, comprehensive exam, thesis/dissertation. *Entrance requirements:* For master's and doctorate, GRE General Test. Additional exam requirements/recommendations for international students: Required—TOEFL. *Application deadline:* For fall admission, 1/15 priority date for domestic students, 12/15 for international students; for spring admission, 9/1 priority date for domestic students, 9/1 for international students. Applications are processed on a rolling basis. Application fee: $55 ($65 for international students). *Financial support:* In 2011–12, fellowships with full tuition reimbursements (averaging $17,300 per year), research assistantships with full tuition reimbursements (averaging $16,370 per year), teaching assistantships with full tuition reimbursements (averaging $15,150 per year) were awarded; career-related internships or fieldwork, Federal Work-Study, and institutionally sponsored loans also available. *Faculty research:* Geophysics, geochemistry, hydrogeology, geobiology, planetary science. *Total annual research expenditures:* $644,299. *Unit head:* Simon Brassell, Chair, 812-855-5581, Fax: 812-855-7899, E-mail: geochair@indiana.edu. *Application contact:* Mary Iverson, Graduate Secretary, 812-855-7214, Fax: 812-855-7899, E-mail: miverson@indiana.edu. Web site: http://www.indiana.edu/~geosci/.

Massachusetts Institute of Technology, School of Science, Department of Earth, Atmospheric, and Planetary Sciences, Cambridge, MA 02139. Offers atmospheric chemistry (PhD, Sc D); atmospheric science (SM, PhD, Sc D); chemical oceanography (SM, PhD, Sc D); climate physics and chemistry (SM, PhD, Sc D); earth and planetary sciences (SM); geochemistry (PhD, Sc D); geology (PhD, Sc D); geophysics (PhD, Sc D); marine geology and geophysics (SM, PhD, Sc D); physical oceanography (SM, PhD, Sc D); planetary sciences (PhD, Sc D). *Faculty:* 33 full-time (6 women). *Students:* 175 full-time (81 women); includes 21 minority (3 Black or African American, non-Hispanic/Latino; 1 American Indian or Alaska Native, non-Hispanic/Latino; 8 Asian, non-Hispanic/Latino; 4 Hispanic/Latino; 5 Two or more races, non-Hispanic/Latino), 58 international. Average age 26. 241 applicants, 28% accepted, 43 enrolled. In 2011, 6 master's, 16 doctorates awarded. Terminal master's awarded for partial completion of doctoral program. *Degree requirements:* For master's, thesis; for doctorate, comprehensive exam, thesis/dissertation. *Entrance requirements:* For master's, GRE General Test; for doctorate, GRE General Test, GRE Subject Test (chemistry or physics for planetary science area). Additional exam requirements/recommendations for international students: Required—TOEFL (minimum score 577 paper-based; 233 computer-based; 91 iBT), IELTS (minimum score 7). *Application deadline:* For fall admission, 1/5 for domestic and international students; for spring admission, 11/1 for domestic and international students. Application fee: $75. Electronic applications accepted. *Expenses:* Tuition: Full-time $40,460; part-time $630 per credit hour. *Required fees:* $272. *Financial support:* In 2011–12, 125 students received support, including 68 fellowships (averaging $32,200 per year), 94 research assistantships (averaging $31,900 per year), 10 teaching assistantships (averaging $30,000 per year); Federal Work-Study, institutionally sponsored loans, scholarships/grants, health care benefits, and unspecified assistantships also available. *Faculty research:* Formation, dynamics and evolution of planetary systems; origin, composition, structure and dynamics of the atmospheres, oceans, surfaces and interiors of the Earth and other planets; evolution and interaction of the physical, chemical, geological and biological components of the Earth system; characterization of past, present and potential future climates and the causes and consequences of climate change; interplay of energy and the environment. *Total annual research expenditures:* $26.2 million. *Unit head:* Prof. Robert van der Hilst, Head, 617-253-2127, Fax: 617-253-8298, E-mail: eapsinfo@mit.edu. *Application contact:* EAPS Education Office, 617-253-3381, Fax: 617-253-8298, E-mail: eapsinfo@mit.edu. Web site: http://eapsweb.mit.edu/.

McMaster University, School of Graduate Studies, Faculty of Science, School of Geography and Earth Sciences, Hamilton, ON L8S 4M2, Canada. Offers geochemistry (PhD); geology (M Sc, PhD); human geography (MA, PhD); physical geography (M Sc, PhD). Part-time programs available. Terminal master's awarded for partial completion of doctoral program. *Degree requirements:* For master's, thesis; for doctorate, comprehensive exam, thesis/dissertation. *Entrance requirements:* For master's, minimum B+ average. Additional exam requirements/recommendations for international students: Required—TOEFL (minimum score 550 paper-based; 213 computer-based).

Missouri University of Science and Technology, Graduate School, Department of Geological Sciences and Engineering, Rolla, MO 65409. Offers geological engineering (MS, DE, PhD); geology and geophysics (MS, PhD),

including geochemistry, geology, geophysics, groundwater and environmental geology; petroleum engineering (MS, DE, PhD). Part-time programs available. *Degree requirements:* For master's, thesis optional; for doctorate, comprehensive exam, thesis/dissertation. *Entrance requirements:* For master's, GRE General Test (minimum score 600 quantitative, writing 3.5), minimum GPA of 3.0 in last 4 semesters; for doctorate, GRE General Test (minimum: Q 600, GRE WR 3.5). Additional exam requirements/recommendations for international students: Required—TOEFL. Electronic applications accepted. *Faculty research:* Digital image processing and geographic information systems, mineralogy, igneous and sedimentary petrology-geochemistry, sedimentology groundwater hydrology and contaminant transport.

Montana Tech of The University of Montana, Graduate School, Geosciences Programs, Butte, MT 59701-8997. Offers geochemistry (MS); geological engineering (MS); geology (MS); geophysical engineering (MS); hydrogeological engineering (MS); hydrogeology (MS). Part-time programs available. *Faculty:* 16 full-time (4 women), 4 part-time/adjunct (0 women). *Students:* 16 full-time (7 women), 12 part-time (6 women); includes 2 minority (1 Black or African American, non-Hispanic/Latino; 1 American Indian or Alaska Native, non-Hispanic/Latino), 1 international. 23 applicants, 65% accepted, 13 enrolled. In 2011, 9 master's awarded. *Degree requirements:* For master's, comprehensive exam (for some programs), thesis (for some programs). *Entrance requirements:* For master's, GRE General Test, minimum GPA of 3.0. Additional exam requirements/recommendations for international students: Required—TOEFL (minimum score 525 paper-based; 195 computer-based; 71 iBT). *Application deadline:* For fall admission, 4/1 priority date for domestic students, 3/1 for international students; for spring admission, 10/1 priority date for domestic students, 7/1 for international students. Applications are processed on a rolling basis. Application fee: $30. Electronic applications accepted. *Financial support:* In 2011–12, 15 students received support, including 10 teaching assistantships with partial tuition reimbursements available (averaging $5,000 per year); research assistantships with partial tuition reimbursements available, career-related internships or fieldwork, tuition waivers (full and partial), and unspecified assistantships also available. Financial award application deadline: 4/1; financial award applicants required to submit FAFSA. *Faculty research:* Water resource development, seismic processing, petroleum reservoir characterization, environmental geochemistry, geologic mapping. *Unit head:* Dr. Mary MacLaughlin, Department Head, 406-496-4655, Fax: 406-496-4260, E-mail: mmaclaughlin@mtech.edu. *Application contact:* Fred Sullivan, Administrator, Graduate School, 406-496-4304, Fax: 406-496-4710, E-mail: fsullivan@mtech.edu. Web site: http://www.mtech.edu/academics/gradschool/degreeprograms/degrees.htm.

New Mexico Institute of Mining and Technology, Graduate Studies, Department of Earth and Environmental Science, Program in Geochemistry, Socorro, NM 87801. Offers MS, PhD. *Students:* 2 full-time (0 women), 2 part-time (1 woman). Average age 27. In 2011, 1 degree awarded. *Expenses:* Tuition, state resident: full-time $4849; part-time $269.41 per credit hour. Tuition, nonresident: full-time $16,041; part-time $891.15 per credit hour. *Required fees:* $622; $65 per credit hour. $20 per semester. Part-time tuition and fees vary according to course load. *Unit head:* Dr. Gary Axen, Chair, 575-835-5178, Fax: 575-835-6436, E-mail: gaxen@ees.nmt.edu. *Application contact:* Dr. Lorie Liebrock, Dean of Graduate Studies, 575-835-5513, Fax: 575-835-5476, E-mail: graduate@nmt.edu.

Ohio University, Graduate College, College of Arts and Sciences, Department of Geological Sciences, Athens, OH 45701-2979. Offers environmental geochemistry (MS); environmental geology (MS); environmental/hydrology (MS); geology (MS); geology education (MS); geomorphology/surficial processes (MS); geophysics (MS); hydrogeology (MS); sedimentology (MS); structure/tectonics (MS). Part-time programs available. *Students:* 19 full-time (10 women). 14 applicants, 64% accepted, 9 enrolled. In 2011, 8 master's awarded. *Degree requirements:* For master's, thesis. *Entrance requirements:* Additional exam requirements/recommendations for international students: Required—TOEFL (minimum score 550 paper-based; 80 iBT) or IELTS (minimum score 6.5). *Application deadline:* For fall admission, 2/1 priority date for domestic students, 2/1 for international students. Application fee: $50 ($55 for international students). Electronic applications accepted. *Financial support:* Research assistantships with full tuition reimbursements, teaching assistantships with full tuition reimbursements, Federal Work-Study, institutionally sponsored loans, scholarships/grants, tuition waivers (partial), and unspecified assistantships available. Financial award application deadline: 2/1. *Faculty research:* Geoscience education, tectonics, fluvial geomorphology, invertebrate paleontology, mine/hydrology. *Total annual research expenditures:* $649,020. *Unit head:* Dr. Gregory Nadon, Chair, 740-593-4212, Fax: 740-593-0486, E-mail: nadon@ohio.edu. *Application contact:* Dr. Keith Milam, Graduate Chair, 740-593-1106, Fax: 740-593-0486, E-mail: milamk@ohio.edu. Web site: http://www.ohiou.edu/geology/.

University of California, Los Angeles, Graduate Division, College of Letters and Science, Department of Earth and Space Sciences, Program in Geochemistry, Los Angeles, CA 90095. Offers MS, PhD. *Students:* 10 full-time (6 women); includes 2 minority (1 Black or African American, non-Hispanic/Latino; 1 American Indian or Alaska Native, non-Hispanic/Latino), 1 international. Average age 32. 18 applicants, 22% accepted, 2 enrolled. In 2011, 4 master's, 3 doctorates awarded. Terminal master's awarded for partial completion of doctoral program. *Degree requirements:* For master's, comprehensive exams or thesis; for doctorate, thesis/dissertation, oral and written qualifying exams. *Entrance requirements:* For

Peterson's Graduate Programs in the Physical Sciences, Mathematics, Agricultural Sciences, the Environment & Natural Resources 2013

facebook.com/petersonspublishing **137**

Geodetic Sciences

master's, GRE General Test, minimum GPA of 3.0, bachelor's degree in related field; for doctorate, GRE General Test, minimum undergraduate GPA of 3.0, bachelor's degree in related field. *Application deadline:* For fall admission, 1/15 for domestic and international students. Application fee: $70 ($90 for international students). Electronic applications accepted. *Financial support:* In 2011–12, 12 fellowships with full and partial tuition reimbursements, 12 research assistantships with full and partial tuition reimbursements, 6 teaching assistantships with full and partial tuition reimbursements were awarded; Federal Work-Study, institutionally sponsored loans, scholarships/grants, health care benefits, tuition waivers (full and partial), and unspecified assistantships also available. Financial award application deadline: 3/1; financial award applicants required to submit FAFSA. *Unit head:* Dr. Craig E. Manning, 310-825-1475, E-mail: manning@ess.ucla.edu. *Application contact:* Department Office, 310-825-3917, E-mail: holbrook@ess.ucla.edu. Web site: http://www.ess.ucla.edu/.

University of Chicago, Division of the Physical Sciences, Department of the Geophysical Sciences, Chicago, IL 60637-1513. Offers atmospheric sciences (SM, PhD); cosmochemistry (PhD); earth sciences (SM, PhD); paleobiology (PhD); planetary and space sciences (SM, PhD). *Faculty:* 24 full-time (3 women). *Students:* 38 full-time (16 women); includes 2 minority (both Hispanic/Latino), 16 international. Average age 26. 68 applicants, 28% accepted, 10 enrolled. In 2011, 2 master's, 5 doctorates awarded. Terminal master's awarded for partial completion of doctoral program. *Degree requirements:* For master's, thesis, seminar; for doctorate, variable foreign language requirement, comprehensive exam, thesis/dissertation. *Entrance requirements:* For doctorate, GRE General Test. Additional exam requirements/recommendations for international students: Required—TOEFL (minimum score 600 paper-based; 250 computer-based; 96 iBT), IELTS (minimum score 7). *Application deadline:* For fall admission, 1/9 for domestic students, 1/10 for international students. Application fee: $55. Electronic applications accepted. *Financial support:* In 2011–12, research assistantships with full tuition reimbursements (averaging $26,500 per year), teaching assistantships with full tuition reimbursements (averaging $27,000 per year) were awarded; fellowships, Federal Work-Study, institutionally sponsored loans, scholarships/grants, tuition waivers (partial), and unspecified assistantships also available. Financial award application deadline: 1/9. *Faculty research:* Climatology, evolutionary paleontology, cosmochemistry, geochemistry, oceanic sciences. *Unit head:* Dr. Michael Foote, Chairman, 773-702-8102, Fax: 773-702-9505. *Application contact:* David J. Taylor, Graduate Student Services Coordinator, 773-702-8180, Fax: 773-702-9505, E-mail: info@geosci.uchicago.edu. Web site: http://geosci.uchicago.edu/.

University of Hawaii at Manoa, Graduate Division, School of Ocean and Earth Science and Technology, Department of Geology and Geophysics, Honolulu, HI 96822. Offers high-pressure geophysics and geochemistry (MS, PhD); hydrogeology and engineering geology (MS, PhD); marine geology and geophysics (MS, PhD); planetary geosciences and remote sensing (MS, PhD); seismology and solid-earth geophysics (MS, PhD); volcanology, petrology, and geochemistry (MS, PhD). Part-time programs available. Terminal master's awarded for partial completion of doctoral program. *Degree requirements:* For master's, thesis optional; for doctorate, comprehensive exam, thesis/dissertation. *Entrance requirements:* For master's and doctorate, GRE General Test, minimum GPA of 3.0. Additional exam requirements/recommendations for international students: Required—TOEFL (minimum score 580 paper-based; 237 computer-based; 92 iBT), IELTS (minimum score 5).

The University of Manchester, School of Earth, Atmospheric and Environmental Sciences, Manchester, United Kingdom. Offers atmospheric sciences (M Phil, M Sc, PhD); basin studies and petroleum geosciences (M Phil, M Sc, PhD); earth, atmospheric and environmental sciences (M Phil, M Sc, PhD); environmental geochemistry and cosmochemistry (M Phil, M Sc, PhD); isotope geochemistry and cosmochemistry (M Phil, M Sc, PhD); paleontology (M Phil, M Sc, PhD); physics and chemistry of minerals and fluids (M Phil, M Sc, PhD); structural and petrological geosciences (M Phil, M Sc, PhD).

University of Nevada, Reno, Graduate School, College of Science, Mackay School of Earth Sciences and Engineering, Department of Geological Sciences, Program in Geochemistry, Reno, NV 89557. Offers MS, PhD. Terminal master's awarded for partial completion of doctoral program. *Degree requirements:* For master's, thesis optional; for doctorate, thesis/dissertation. *Entrance requirements:* For master's, GRE General Test, minimum GPA of 2.75; for doctorate, GRE General Test, minimum GPA of 3.0. Additional exam requirements/recommendations for international students: Required—TOEFL (minimum score 500 paper-based; 173 computer-based; 61 iBT), IELTS (minimum score 6). Electronic applications accepted.

The University of Texas at Dallas, School of Natural Sciences and Mathematics, Department of Geosciences, Richardson, TX 75080. Offers geochemistry (MS, PhD); geophysics (MS, PhD); geospatial information sciences (MS, PhD); hydrogeology (MS, PhD); sedimentary, stratigraphy, paleontology (PhD); stratigraphy, paleontology (MS); structural geology and tectonics (MS, PhD). Part-time and evening/weekend programs available. *Faculty:* 10 full-time (1 woman). *Students:* 39 full-time (13 women), 20 part-time (7 women); includes 8 minority (2 Black or African American, non-Hispanic/Latino; 4 Asian, non-Hispanic/Latino; 2 Hispanic/Latino), 18 international. Average age 32. 67 applicants, 39% accepted, 14 enrolled. In 2011, 8 master's, 3 doctorates awarded. *Degree requirements:* For master's, thesis optional; for doctorate, thesis/dissertation. *Entrance requirements:* For master's and doctorate, GRE General Test, minimum GPA of 3.0 in upper-level course work in field. Additional exam requirements/recommendations for international students: Required—TOEFL (minimum score 550 paper-based; 215 computer-based). *Application deadline:* For fall admission, 7/15 for domestic students, 5/1 for international students; for spring admission, 11/15 for domestic students, 9/1 for international students. Applications are processed on a rolling basis. Application fee: $50 ($100 for international students). Electronic applications accepted. *Expenses:* Tuition, state resident: full-time $11,170; part-time $620.56 per credit hour. Tuition, nonresident: full-time $20,212; part-time $1122.89 per credit hour. *Financial support:* In 2011–12, 32 students received support, including 13 research assistantships with partial tuition reimbursements available (averaging $21,462 per year), 15 teaching assistantships with partial tuition reimbursements available (averaging $15,800 per year); career-related internships or fieldwork, Federal Work-Study, institutionally sponsored loans, scholarships/grants, and unspecified assistantships also available. Support available to part-time students. Financial award application deadline: 4/30; financial award applicants required to submit FAFSA. *Faculty research:* Cybermapping, GPS applications for geophysics and geology, seismology and ground-penetrating radar, numerical modeling, signal processing and inverse modeling techniques in seismology. *Unit head:* Dr. John Oldow, Department Head, 972-883-2401, Fax: 972-883-2537, E-mail: geosciences@utdallas.edu. *Application contact:* Dr. John W. Geissman, Graduate Advisor, 972-883-2406, Fax: 972-883-2537, E-mail: geissman@utdallas.edu. Web site: http://www.utdallas.edu/geosciences.

University of Wisconsin–Milwaukee, Graduate School, College of Letters and Sciences, Department of Chemistry, Milwaukee, WI 53201-0413. Offers biogeochemistry (PhD); chemistry (MS, PhD). *Faculty:* 20 full-time (4 women). *Students:* 58 full-time (25 women), 16 part-time (8 women); includes 12 minority (2 Black or African American, non-Hispanic/Latino; 5 Asian, non-Hispanic/Latino; 4 Hispanic/Latino; 1 Two or more races, non-Hispanic/Latino), 7 international. Average age 32. 46 applicants, 30% accepted, 9 enrolled. In 2011, 4 master's, 6 doctorates awarded. *Degree requirements:* For master's, thesis or alternative; for doctorate, thesis/dissertation. *Entrance requirements:* For doctorate, GRE General Test. Additional exam requirements/recommendations for international students: Required—TOEFL (minimum score 600 paper-based; 79 iBT), IELTS (minimum score 6.5). *Application deadline:* For fall admission, 1/1 priority date for domestic students; for spring admission, 9/1 for domestic students. Applications are processed on a rolling basis. Application fee: $56 ($96 for international students). One-time fee: $506.10 full-time. Tuition and fees vary according to course load and reciprocity agreements. *Financial support:* In 2011–12, 3 fellowships, 30 research assistantships, 46 teaching assistantships were awarded; career-related internships or fieldwork, unspecified assistantships, and project assistantships also available. Support available to part-time students. Financial award application deadline: 4/15; financial award applicants required to submit FAFSA. *Faculty research:* Analytical chemistry, biochemistry, inorganic chemistry, organic chemistry, physical chemistry. *Total annual research expenditures:* $4 million. *Unit head:* Peter Geissinger, Department Chair, 414-229-5230, Fax: 414-229-5530, E-mail: geissing@uwm.edu. *Application contact:* General Information Contact, 414-229-4982, Fax: 414-229-6967, E-mail: gradschool@uwm.edu. Web site: http://www.uwm.edu/dept/chemistry/.

Yale University, Graduate School of Arts and Sciences, Department of Geology and Geophysics, New Haven, CT 06520. Offers biogeochemistry (PhD); climate dynamics (PhD); geochemistry (PhD); geophysics (PhD); meteorology (PhD); oceanography (PhD); paleontology (PhD); paleooceanography (PhD); petrology (PhD); tectonics (PhD). *Degree requirements:* For doctorate, thesis/dissertation. *Entrance requirements:* For doctorate, GRE General Test. Additional exam requirements/recommendations for international students: Required—TOEFL.

Geodetic Sciences

Columbia University, Graduate School of Arts and Sciences, Division of Natural Sciences, Department of Earth and Environmental Sciences, New York, NY 10027. Offers geochemistry (M Phil, MA, PhD); geodetic sciences (M Phil, MA, PhD); geophysics (M Phil, MA, PhD); oceanography (M Phil, MA, PhD). *Degree requirements:* For master's, thesis or alternative, fieldwork, written exam; for doctorate, one foreign language, thesis/dissertation. *Entrance requirements:* For master's and doctorate, GRE General Test, GRE Subject Test, major in natural or physical science. Additional exam requirements/recommendations for international science. Required—TOEFL. *Faculty research:* Structural geology

138 facebook.com/petersonspublishing

Peterson's Graduate Programs in the Physical Sciences, Mathematics, Agricultural Sciences, the Environment & Natural Resources 2013

and stratigraphy, petrology, paleontology, rare gas, isotope and aqueous geochemistry.

The Ohio State University, Graduate School, College of Arts and Sciences, Division of Natural and Mathematical Sciences, School of Earth Sciences, Columbus, OH 43210. Offers geodetic science (MS); geological sciences (MS, PhD). *Faculty:* 28. *Students:* 25 full-time (7 women), 18 part-time (10 women); includes 4 minority (3 Hispanic/Latino; 1 Two or more races, non-Hispanic/Latino), 2 international. Average age 28. In 2011, 8 master's, 2 doctorates awarded. *Degree requirements:* For master's, thesis; for doctorate, thesis/dissertation. *Entrance requirements:* For master's and doctorate, GRE. Additional exam requirements/recommendations for international students: Required—TOEFL (minimum score 600 paper-based; 250 computer-based), Michigan English Language Assessment Battery (minimum score 82). *Application deadline:* For fall admission, 8/15 priority date for domestic students, 7/1 for international students; for winter admission, 12/1 priority date for domestic students, 11/1 for international students; for spring admission, 3/1 priority date for domestic students, 2/1 for international students. Applications are processed on a rolling basis. Application fee: $40 ($50 for international students). Electronic applications accepted. *Expenses:* Tuition, state resident: full-time $11,400. Tuition, nonresident: full-time $28,125. Tuition and fees vary according to course load, degree level, campus/location and program. *Unit head:* W. Berry Lyons, Director, 614-688-3241, Fax: 614-292-7688, E-mail: lyons.142@osu.edu. *Application contact:* Graduate Admissions, 614-292-9444, Fax: 614-292-3895, E-mail: domestic.grad@osu.edu. Web site: http://www.earthsciences.osu.edu/.

The Ohio State University, Graduate School, College of Engineering, Department of Civil and Environmental Engineering and Geodetic Science, Columbus, OH 43210. Offers civil engineering (MS, PhD); geodetic science and surveying (MS, PhD). *Faculty:* 20. *Students:* 66 full-time (23 women), 41 part-time (3 women); includes 8 minority (1 Black or African American, non-Hispanic/Latino; 2 Asian, non-Hispanic/Latino; 3 Hispanic/Latino; 2 Two or more races, non-Hispanic/Latino), 58 international. Average age 27. In 2011, 28 master's, 5 doctorates awarded. *Entrance requirements:* Additional exam requirements/recommendations for international students: Required—TOEFL (minimum score 550 paper-based; 79 iBT), Michigan English Language Assessment Battery (minimum score 82). *Expenses:* Tuition, state resident: full-time $11,400. Tuition, nonresident: full-time $28,125. Tuition and fees vary according to course load, degree level, campus/location and program. *Unit head:* Dr. Carolyn J. Merry, Chair, 614-292-3455, Fax: 614-292-8062, E-mail: merry.1@osu.edu. *Application contact:* Graduate Admissions, 614-292-6301, Fax: 614-292-3656, E-mail: gradadmissions@osu.edu. Web site: http://ceg.osu.edu/.

State University of New York College of Environmental Science and Forestry, Department of Environmental Resources Engineering, Syracuse, NY 13210-2779. Offers ecological engineering (MS, PhD); environmental and resources engineering (MPS, MS, PhD); environmental management (MPS); geospatial information science and engineering (MS, PhD); mapping sciences (MPS); water resources engineering (MS, PhD). *Degree requirements:* For master's, thesis (for some programs); for doctorate, comprehensive exam, thesis/dissertation. *Entrance requirements:* For master's and doctorate, GRE General Test, minimum GPA of 3.0. Additional exam requirements/recommendations for international students: Required—TOEFL (minimum score 550 paper-based; 213 computer-based; 80 iBT), IELTS (minimum score 6). *Application deadline:* For fall admission, 2/1 priority date for domestic students, 2/1 for international students; for spring admission, 11/1 priority date for domestic students, 11/1 for international students. Applications are processed on a rolling basis. Application fee: $60. *Expenses:* Tuition, state resident: full-time $8870; part-time $370 per credit hour. Tuition, nonresident: full-time $15,160; part-time $632 per credit hour. *Required fees:* $60; $370 per credit hour. $350 per semester. One-time fee: $85. *Financial support:* Fellowships with full and partial tuition reimbursements, research assistantships with full and partial tuition reimbursements, teaching assistantships with full and partial tuition reimbursements, Federal Work-Study, institutionally sponsored loans, scholarships/grants, health care benefits, and unspecified assistantships available. Financial award application deadline: 6/30; financial award applicants required to submit FAFSA. *Faculty research:* Forest engineering, paper science and engineering, wood products engineering. *Total annual research expenditures:* $968,412. *Unit head:* Dr. Theodore Endreny, Chair, 315-470-6565, Fax: 315-470-6958, E-mail: te@esf.edu. *Application contact:* Dr. Dudley J. Raynal, Dean, Instruction and Graduate Studies, 315-470-6599, Fax: 315-470-6978, E-mail: esfgrad@esf.edu. Web site: http://www.esf.edu/ere.

Université Laval, Faculty of Forestry, Geography and Geomatics, Department of Geomatics Sciences, Programs in Geomatics Sciences, Québec, QC G1K 7P4, Canada. Offers M Sc, PhD. Terminal master's awarded for partial completion of doctoral program. *Degree requirements:* For master's, thesis (for some programs); for doctorate, comprehensive exam, thesis/dissertation. *Entrance requirements:* For master's and doctorate, knowledge of French and English. Electronic applications accepted.

University of New Brunswick Fredericton, School of Graduate Studies, Faculty of Engineering, Department of Geodesy and Geomatics, Fredericton, NB E3B 5A3, Canada. Offers land information management (Diploma); mapping, charting and geodesy (Diploma); surveying engineering (M Eng, M Sc E, PhD). *Faculty:* 9 full-time (1 woman), 13 part-time/adjunct (1 woman). *Students:* 37 full-time (6 women), 6 part-time (0 women). In 2011, 10 master's awarded. *Degree requirements:* For master's, thesis; for doctorate, comprehensive exam, thesis/dissertation, qualifying exam. *Entrance requirements:* For master's and doctorate, minimum GPA of 3.0. Additional exam requirements/recommendations for international students: Required—TOEFL (minimum score 580 paper-based), TWE (minimum score 4). *Application deadline:* For fall admission, 3/1 priority date for domestic students. Applications are processed on a rolling basis. Application fee: $50 Canadian dollars. *Financial support:* In 2011–12, 23 research assistantships, 22 teaching assistantships were awarded; fellowships also available. *Faculty research:* Remote sensing, ocean mapping, land administration. *Unit head:* Dr. Sue Nichols, Director of Graduate Studies, 506-453-5141, Fax: 506-453-4943, E-mail: nichols@unb.ca. *Application contact:* Sylvia Whitaker, Graduate Secretary, 506-458-7085, Fax: 506-453-4943, E-mail: swhitake@unb.ca. Web site: http://www.gge.unb.ca/.

Geology

Acadia University, Faculty of Pure and Applied Science, Department of Earth and Environmental Science, Wolfville, NS B4P 2R6, Canada. Offers M Sc. *Degree requirements:* For master's, thesis. *Entrance requirements:* For master's, BSC (honours) in geology or equivalent. Additional exam requirements/recommendations for international students: Required—TOEFL (minimum score 580 paper-based; 237 computer-based; 93 iBT), IELTS (minimum score 6.5). *Faculty research:* Igneous, metamorphic, and Quaternary geology; stratigraphy; remote sensing; tectonics, carbonate sedimentology.

Alabama State University, Department of Earth and Environmental Sciences, Montgomery, AL 36101-0271. Offers MS, PhD. *Faculty:* 9 full-time. *Degree requirements:* For master's, one foreign language, thesis or alternative; for doctorate, one foreign language, thesis/dissertation. *Entrance requirements:* For master's, GRE General Test, minimum B average in undergraduate course work; for doctorate, GRE General Test. Additional exam requirements/recommendations for international students: Required—TOEFL. *Application deadline:* For fall admission, 2/1 for domestic and international students. Application fee: $45. Electronic applications accepted. *Financial support:* Research assistantships with full tuition reimbursements, teaching assistantships with full tuition reimbursements, career-related internships or fieldwork, Federal Work-Study, and institutionally sponsored loans available. Financial award application deadline: 2/1. *Faculty research:* Sedimentation, isotopes, biogeochemistry, marine geology, structural geology. *Unit head:* Dr. Stephen Nelson, Chair, 504-862-3194, Fax: 504-865-5199, E-mail: snelson@tulane.edu. *Application contact:* Dr. Doris Screws, Dean of Graduate Studies, 334-229-4274, Fax: 334-229-4928, E-mail: dscrews@alasu.edu.

American University of Beirut, Graduate Programs, Faculty of Arts and Sciences, Beirut, Lebanon. Offers anthropology (MA); Arabic language and literature (MA); archaeology (MA); biology (MS); chemistry (MS); computational science (MS); computer science (MS); economics (MA); education (MA); English language (MA); English literature (MA); environmental policy planning (MSES); financial economics (MAFE); geology (MS); history (MA); mathematics (MA, MS); Middle Eastern studies (MA); philosophy (MA); physics (MS); political studies (MA); psychology (MA); public administration (MA); sociology (MA); statistics (MA, MS). Part-time programs available. *Faculty:* 154 full-time (44 women), 12 part-time/adjunct (2 women). *Students:* 180 full-time (122 women), 240 part-time (158 women). Average age 25. 336 applicants, 47% accepted, 86 enrolled. In 2011, 57 master's awarded. *Degree requirements:* For master's, one foreign language, comprehensive exam, thesis (for some programs). *Entrance requirements:* For master's, GRE, letter of recommendation. Additional exam requirements/recommendations for international students: Required—TOEFL (minimum score 600 paper-based; 250 computer-based; 97 iBT), IELTS (minimum score 7). *Application deadline:* For fall admission, 4/30 for domestic and international students; for spring admission, 11/1 for domestic and international students. Application fee: $50. *Expenses: Tuition:* Full-time $12,780; part-time $710 per credit. *Required fees:* $528; $528 per credit. Tuition and fees vary according to course load and program. *Financial support:* In 2011–12, 33 students received support. Career-related internships or fieldwork, institutionally sponsored loans, scholarships/grants, health care benefits, and unspecified assistantships available. Financial award application deadline: 2/4; financial award applicants required to submit FAFSA. *Faculty research:* History of composition studies, syntax of Arabic dialects, Oscar Wilde, decadence, Middle Eastern and international politics, neural mechanisms of creativity and consciousness,

Peterson's Graduate Programs in the Physical Sciences, Mathematics, Agricultural Sciences, the Environment & Natural Resources 2013

facebook.com/petersonspublishing **139**

Geology

personality and psycho-socio-cultural-spiritual correlates of negative and positive mental health, philosophy of mind, metaphysics, micropaleontology and stratigraphy, geochemistry, mineralogy and petrology, tectonophysics, Abbasid, Ottoman and Russian history, landscape, Bronze and Iron Age archaeology. *Unit head:* Dr. Patrick McGreevy, Dean, 961-1374374 Ext. 3800, Fax: 961-1744461, E-mail: pm07@aub.edu.lb. *Application contact:* Dr. Salim Kanaan, Director, Admissions Office, 961-1350000 Ext. 2594, Fax: 961-1750775, E-mail: sk00@aub.edu.lb. Web site: http://staff.aub.edu.lb/~webfas.

Arizona State University, College of Liberal Arts and Sciences, School of Earth and Space Exploration, Tempe, AZ 85287-1404. Offers astrophysics (MS, PhD); exploration systems design (PhD); geological sciences (MS, PhD). PhD in exploration systems design is offered in collaboration with the Fulton Schools of Engineering. Terminal master's awarded for partial completion of doctoral program. *Degree requirements:* For master's, thesis, interactive Program of Study (iPOS) submitted before completing 50 percent of required credit hours; for doctorate, thesis/dissertation, interactive Program of Study (iPOS) submitted before completing 50 percent of required credit hours. *Entrance requirements:* For master's and doctorate, GRE, minimum GPA of 3.0 or equivalent in last 2 years of work leading to bachelor's degree. Additional exam requirements/recommendations for international students: Required—TOEFL (minimum score 80 iBT), TOEFL, IELTS, or Pearson Test of English. Electronic applications accepted.

Auburn University, Graduate School, College of Sciences and Mathematics, Department of Geology and Geography, Auburn University, AL 36849. Offers geography (MS); geology (MS). Part-time programs available. *Faculty:* 11 full-time (2 women). *Students:* 16 full-time (7 women), 17 part-time (4 women); includes 1 minority (American Indian or Alaska Native, non-Hispanic/Latino), 7 international. Average age 28. 23 applicants, 48% accepted, 9 enrolled. In 2011, 5 master's awarded. *Degree requirements:* For master's, computer language or geographic information systems, field camp. *Entrance requirements:* For master's, GRE General Test. *Application deadline:* For fall admission, 7/7 for domestic students; for spring admission, 11/24 for domestic students. Applications are processed on a rolling basis. Application fee: $50 ($60 for international students). Electronic applications accepted. *Expenses:* Tuition, state resident: full-time $7290; part-time $405 per credit hour. Tuition, nonresident: full-time $21,870; part-time $1215 per credit hour. *International tuition:* $22,000 full-time. *Required fees:* $1402. *Financial support:* Research assistantships, teaching assistantships, and Federal Work-Study available. Support available to part-time students. Financial award application deadline: 3/15; financial award applicants required to submit FAFSA. *Faculty research:* Empirical magma dynamics and melt migration, ore mineralogy, role of terrestrial plant biomass in deposition, metamorphic petrology and isotope geochemistry, reef development, crinoid topology. *Unit head:* Dr. Charles E. Savrda, Chair, 334-844-4282. *Application contact:* Dr. George Flowers, Dean of the Graduate School, 334-844-2125.

Ball State University, Graduate School, College of Sciences and Humanities, Department of Geology, Muncie, IN 47306-1099. Offers MA, MS. *Faculty:* 6 full-time (2 women). *Students:* 6 full-time (5 women), 8 part-time (3 women); includes 1 minority (Hispanic/Latino), 2 international. Average age 39. 11 applicants, 73% accepted, 6 enrolled. In 2011, 1 master's awarded. *Degree requirements:* For master's, thesis (for some programs). *Entrance requirements:* For master's, GRE General Test. Application fee: $50. Tuition and fees vary according to program and reciprocity agreements. *Financial support:* In 2011–12, 8 students received support, including 8 teaching assistantships with full tuition reimbursements available (averaging $14,044 per year); research assistantships and career-related internships or fieldwork also available. Financial award application deadline: 3/1. *Faculty research:* Environmental geology, geophysics, stratigraphy. *Unit head:* Scott Rice-Snow, Interim Chairman. *Application contact:* Dr. Kirsten Nicholson. Web site: http://www.bsu.edu/geology/.

Baylor University, Graduate School, College of Arts and Sciences, Department of Geology, Waco, TX 76798. Offers earth science (MA); geology (MS, PhD). *Faculty:* 12 full-time (1 woman). *Students:* 26 full-time (11 women), 4 part-time (2 women); includes 2 minority (1 American Indian or Alaska Native, non-Hispanic/Latino; 1 Asian, non-Hispanic/Latino), 4 international. In 2011, 6 master's, 1 doctorate awarded. *Degree requirements:* For master's, thesis; for doctorate, thesis/dissertation. *Entrance requirements:* For master's and doctorate, GRE General Test. *Application deadline:* For fall admission, 3/15 priority date for domestic students. Applications are processed on a rolling basis. Application fee: $25. *Financial support:* In 2011–12, 18 teaching assistantships were awarded; Federal Work-Study and institutionally sponsored loans also available. *Faculty research:* Petroleum geology, geophysics, engineering geology, hydrogeology. *Unit head:* Dr. Steve Dworkin, Graduate Program Director, 254-710-2186, Fax: 254-710-2673, E-mail: steve_dworkin@baylor.edu. *Application contact:* Paulette Penney, Administrative Assistant, 254-710-2361, Fax: 254-710-3870, E-mail: paulette_penney@baylor.edu. Web site: http://www.baylor.edu/geology/.

Boise State University, Graduate College, College of Arts and Sciences, Department of Geosciences, Program in Geology, Boise, ID 83725-0399. Offers MS, PhD. Part-time programs available. *Degree requirements:* For master's, thesis. *Entrance requirements:* For master's, GRE General Test, BS in related field, minimum GPA of 3.0. Electronic applications accepted.

Boston College, Graduate School of Arts and Sciences, Department of Earth and Environmental Sciences, Chestnut Hill, MA 02467-3800. Offers MS, MBA/MS. *Degree requirements:* For master's, thesis. *Entrance requirements:* For master's, GRE General Test, GRE Subject Test. Additional exam requirements/recommendations for international students: Required—TOEFL (minimum score 600 paper-based; 250 computer-based; 100 iBT). Electronic applications accepted. *Faculty research:* Coastal and marine geology, experimental sedimentology, geomagnetism, igneous petrology, paleontology.

Bowling Green State University, Graduate College, College of Arts and Sciences, Department of Geology, Bowling Green, OH 43403. Offers MS. Part-time programs available. *Degree requirements:* For master's, thesis. *Entrance requirements:* For master's, GRE General Test. Additional exam requirements/recommendations for international students: Required—TOEFL. Electronic applications accepted. *Faculty research:* Remote sensing, environmental geology, geological information systems, structural geology, geochemistry.

Brigham Young University, Graduate Studies, College of Physical and Mathematical Sciences, Department of Geological Sciences, Provo, UT 84602-1001. Offers MS. *Faculty:* 16 full-time (2 women), 1 part-time/adjunct (0 women). *Students:* 14 full-time (4 women), 13 part-time (3 women); includes 2 minority (1 American Indian or Alaska Native, non-Hispanic/Latino; 1 Asian, non-Hispanic/Latino). Average age 27. 19 applicants, 63% accepted, 8 enrolled. In 2011, 12 master's awarded. *Degree requirements:* For master's, thesis. *Entrance requirements:* For master's, GRE General Test, minimum GPA of 3.0 in last 60 hours of course work. Additional exam requirements/recommendations for international students: Required—TOEFL. *Application deadline:* For fall admission, 2/1 priority date for domestic students, 2/1 for international students; for winter admission, 9/15 priority date for domestic students, 9/15 for international students. Applications are processed on a rolling basis. Application fee: $50. Full-time tuition for non-LDS students: $11,520 per year; $640 per credit. *Expenses: Tuition:* Full-time $5760; part-time $320 per credit. Tuition and fees vary according to student's religious affiliation. *Financial support:* In 2011–12, 27 students received support, including 3 research assistantships with partial tuition reimbursements available (averaging $17,920 per year), 24 teaching assistantships with partial tuition reimbursements available (averaging $17,920 per year); career-related internships or fieldwork, institutionally sponsored loans, scholarships/grants, and tuition waivers (partial) also available. Financial award application deadline: 2/1. *Faculty research:* Regional tectonics, hydrogeochemistry, crystal chemistry and crystallography, stratigraphy, environmental geophysics, petrology. *Total annual research expenditures:* $112,000. *Unit head:* Dr. Scott Ritter, Chairman, 801-422-4239, Fax: 801-422-0267, E-mail: scott_ritter@byu.edu. *Application contact:* Dr. Michael J. Dorais, Graduate Coordinator, 801-422-1347, Fax: 801-422-0267, E-mail: michael_dorais@byu.edu. Web site: http://www.geology.byu.edu/.

Brooklyn College of the City University of New York, Division of Graduate Studies, Department of Earth and Environmental Sciences, Brooklyn, NY 11210-2889. Offers MA, PhD. Evening/weekend programs available. Terminal master's awarded for partial completion of doctoral program. *Degree requirements:* For master's, comprehensive exam, thesis or alternative, qualifying exams, 30 credits. *Entrance requirements:* For master's, bachelor's degree in geology or equivalent, 2 letters of recommendation; for doctorate, GRE. Additional exam requirements/recommendations for international students: Required—TOEFL (minimum score 550 paper-based; 213 computer-based; 79 iBT). Electronic applications accepted. *Faculty research:* Geochemistry, petrology, tectonophysics, hydrogeology, sedimentary geology, environmental geology.

California Institute of Technology, Division of Geological and Planetary Sciences, Pasadena, CA 91125-0001. Offers environmental science and engineering (MS, PhD); geobiology (MS, PhD); geochemistry (MS, PhD); geology (MS, PhD); geophysics (MS, PhD); planetary science (MS, PhD). *Faculty:* 42 full-time (8 women). *Students:* 102 full-time (48 women); includes 10 minority (2 Black or African American, non-Hispanic/Latino; 7 Asian, non-Hispanic/Latino; 1 Hispanic/Latino), 28 international. Average age 26. 188 applicants, 23% accepted, 21 enrolled. In 2011, 11 master's, 12 doctorates awarded. *Degree requirements:* For doctorate, thesis/dissertation. *Entrance requirements:* For doctorate, GRE General Test. Additional exam requirements/recommendations for international students: Required—TOEFL; Recommended—IELTS, TWE. *Application deadline:* For fall admission, 1/1 for domestic and international students. Application fee: $80. Electronic applications accepted. *Financial support:* In 2011–12, 75 students received support, including 16 fellowships with full tuition reimbursements available (averaging $28,000 per year), 86 research assistantships with full tuition reimbursements available (averaging $28,000 per year); teaching assistantships with full tuition reimbursements available, institutionally sponsored loans, scholarships/grants, health care benefits, and unspecified assistantships also available. Financial award applicants required to submit FAFSA. *Faculty research:* Planetary surfaces, evolution of anaerobic respiratory processes, structural geology and tectonics, theoretical and numerical seismology, global biogeochemical cycles. *Unit head:* Dr. Kenneth A. Farley, Chairman, 626-395-6111, Fax: 626-795-6028, E-mail: dianb@gps.caltech.edu. *Application contact:* Dr. Robert W. Clayton, Academic Officer, 626-395-6909, Fax: 626-795-6028, E-mail: dianb@gps.caltech.edu. Web site: http://www.gps.caltech.edu/.

California State University, Bakersfield, Division of Graduate Studies, School of Natural Sciences, Mathematics, and Engineering, Program in Geology, Bakersfield, CA 93311. Offers geology (MS); hydrogeology (MS, Postbaccalaureate Certificate); petroleum geology (MS). Part-time and evening/weekend programs available. *Degree requirements:* For master's, thesis. *Entrance requirements:* For master's, GRE General Test, BS in geology.

140 facebook.com/petersonspublishing

Peterson's Graduate Programs in the Physical Sciences, Mathematics, Agricultural Sciences, the Environment & Natural Resources 2013

Application deadline: Applications are processed on a rolling basis. Application fee: $55. *Expenses: Required fees:* $1302 per unit. Part-time tuition and fees vary according to course load and program. *Financial support:* Teaching assistantships, career-related internships or fieldwork, institutionally sponsored loans, and scholarships/grants available. *Unit head:* Dr. Dirk Baron, Department Chair, 661-664-3044, Fax: 661-664-2040, E-mail: dbaron@csub.edu.

California State University, Chico, Office of Graduate Studies, College of Natural Sciences, Department of Geological and Environmental Sciences, Chico, CA 95929-0722. Offers environmental science (MS); geosciences (MS), including hydrology/hydrogeology. Part-time programs available. *Faculty:* 3 full-time (1 woman), 2 part-time/adjunct (0 women). *Students:* 10 full-time (1 woman), 8 part-time (2 women); includes 3 minority (1 Asian, non-Hispanic/Latino; 2 Hispanic/Latino). Average age 31. 35 applicants, 46% accepted, 7 enrolled. *Degree requirements:* For master's, thesis or internship. *Entrance requirements:* For master's, GRE General Test, two letters of recommendation, faculty mentor, statement of purpose. Additional exam requirements/recommendations for international students: Required—TOEFL (minimum score 550 paper-based; 213 computer-based; 80 iBT), IELTS (minimum score 6.5), Pearson Test of English (minimum score 59). *Application deadline:* For fall admission, 3/1 priority date for domestic students, 3/1 for international students; for spring admission, 9/15 priority date for domestic students, 9/15 for international students. Application fee: $55. Electronic applications accepted. Tuition and fees vary according to class time, course load and degree level. *Financial support:* Fellowships, teaching assistantships, career-related internships or fieldwork, and scholarships/grants available. Financial award application deadline: 3/1; financial award applicants required to submit FAFSA. *Unit head:* Dr. David L. Brown, Chair, 530-898-5262, Fax: 530-898-5234, E-mail: geos@csuchico.edu. *Application contact:* Judy L. Rice, Graduate Admissions Coordinator, 530-898-5416, Fax: 530-898-3342, E-mail: jlrice@csuchico.edu. Web site: http://www.csuchico.edu/geos/index.shtml.

California State University, East Bay, Office of Academic Programs and Graduate Studies, College of Science, Department of Earth and Environmental Sciences, Hayward, CA 94542-3000. Offers geology (MS), including environmental geology, geology. Part-time and evening/weekend programs available. *Faculty:* 1 full-time (0 women), 1 part-time/adjunct (0 women). *Students:* 3 full-time (2 women), 12 part-time (5 women); includes 2 minority (1 Asian, non-Hispanic/Latino; 1 Hispanic/Latino). Average age 37. 9 applicants, 56% accepted, 3 enrolled. *Degree requirements:* For master's, thesis or project. *Entrance requirements:* For master's, GRE, minimum GPA of 2.75 in field, 2.5 overall; 2 letters of recommendation. Additional exam requirements/recommendations for international students: Required—TOEFL (minimum score 550 paper-based; 213 computer-based). *Application deadline:* For fall admission, 6/30 for domestic and international students. Application fee: $55. Electronic applications accepted. *Expenses:* Tuition, state resident: full-time $6738; part-time $1302 per quarter. Tuition, nonresident: full-time $12,690; part-time $2294 per quarter. *Required fees:* $449 per quarter. Tuition and fees vary according to degree level, program and reciprocity agreements. *Financial support:* Career-related internships or fieldwork, Federal Work-Study, and institutionally sponsored loans available. Support available to part-time students. Financial award application deadline: 3/2; financial award applicants required to submit FAFSA. *Faculty research:* Hydrology, seismic activity; origins of life. *Unit head:* Dr. Jeffery Seitz, Chair, 510-885-3486, Fax: 510-885-2526, E-mail: jeff.seitz@csueastbay.edu. *Application contact:* Prof. Mitchell Craig, Geology Graduate Advisor, 510-885-3425, Fax: 510-885-2526, E-mail: mitchell.craig@csueastbay.edu. Web site: http://www20.csueastbay.edu/csci/departments/earth/.

California State University, Fresno, Division of Graduate Studies, College of Science and Mathematics, Department of Earth and Environmental Sciences, Fresno, CA 93740-8027. Offers geology (MS). Part-time programs available. *Degree requirements:* For master's, thesis. *Entrance requirements:* For master's, GRE General Test, undergraduate geology degree, minimum GPA of 2.7. Additional exam requirements/recommendations for international students: Required—TOEFL. Electronic applications accepted. *Faculty research:* Water drainage, pollution, cartography, creek restoration, nitrate contamination.

California State University, Fullerton, Graduate Studies, College of Natural Science and Mathematics, Department of Geological Sciences, Fullerton, CA 92834-9480. Offers MS. Part-time programs available. *Students:* 2 full-time (both women), 8 part-time (4 women); includes 2 minority (both Hispanic/Latino), 1 international. Average age 30. 15 applicants, 33% accepted, 4 enrolled. In 2011, 5 master's awarded. *Degree requirements:* For master's, thesis. *Entrance requirements:* For master's, bachelor's degree in geology, minimum GPA of 3.0 in geology courses. Application fee: $55. *Financial support:* Research assistantships, teaching assistantships, career-related internships or fieldwork, Federal Work-Study, institutionally sponsored loans, and scholarships/grants available. Support available to part-time students. Financial award application deadline: 3/1; financial award applicants required to submit FAFSA. *Unit head:* Dr. David Bowman, Chair, 657-278-3882. *Application contact:* Admissions/Applications, 657-278-2371.

California State University, Long Beach, Graduate Studies, College of Natural Sciences and Mathematics, Department of Geological Sciences, Long Beach, CA 90840. Offers geology (MS); geophysics (MS). Part-time programs available. *Faculty:* 8 full-time (2 women). *Students:* 17 full-time (8 women), 26 part-time (12 women); includes 11 minority (1 Black or African American, non-Hispanic/Latino; 1 American Indian or Alaska Native, non-Hispanic/Latino; 1 Asian, non-Hispanic/Latino; 5 Hispanic/Latino; 1 Native Hawaiian or other Pacific Islander, non-Hispanic/Latino; 2 Two or more races, non-Hispanic/Latino), 3 international. Average age 30. 26 applicants, 50% accepted, 11 enrolled. In 2011, 2 master's awarded. *Degree requirements:* For master's, thesis. *Entrance requirements:* For master's, GRE General Test. *Application deadline:* For fall admission, 7/1 for domestic students. Applications are processed on a rolling basis. Application fee: $55. Electronic applications accepted. *Financial support:* Research assistantships, teaching assistantships, Federal Work-Study, institutionally sponsored loans, and scholarships/grants available. Financial award application deadline: 3/2. *Faculty research:* Paleontology, geophysics, structural geology, organic geochemistry, sedimentary geology. *Unit head:* Robert D. Francis, Chair, 562-985-4929, Fax: 562-985-8638, E-mail: rfrancis@csulb.edu. *Application contact:* Gregory Holk, Graduate Advisor, 562-985-5006, Fax: 562-985-8638, E-mail: gholk@csulb.edu.

California State University, Los Angeles, Graduate Studies, College of Natural and Social Sciences, Department of Geological Sciences, Los Angeles, CA 90032-8530. Offers MS. Program offered jointly with California State University, Northridge. Part-time and evening/weekend programs available. *Faculty:* 3 part-time/adjunct (0 women). *Students:* 14 full-time (10 women), 15 part-time (7 women); includes 18 minority (7 Asian, non-Hispanic/Latino; 9 Hispanic/Latino; 2 Two or more races, non-Hispanic/Latino), 2 international. Average age 29. 28 applicants, 39% accepted, 11 enrolled. In 2011, 5 master's awarded. *Degree requirements:* For master's, comprehensive exam or thesis. *Entrance requirements:* Additional exam requirements/recommendations for international students: Required—TOEFL (minimum score 500 paper-based; 173 computer-based). *Application deadline:* For fall admission, 5/1 for domestic and international students. Applications are processed on a rolling basis. Application fee: $55. Electronic applications accepted. *Expenses:* Tuition, state resident: full-time $8225. *Financial support:* Federal Work-Study available. Support available to part-time students. Financial award application deadline: 3/1. *Unit head:* Dr. Ali Modarres, Chair, 323-343-2435, Fax: 323-343-5609, E-mail: amodarr@calstatela.edu. *Application contact:* Dr. Karin Brown, Acting Associate Dean of Graduate Studies, 323-343-3820, Fax: 323-343-5653, E-mail: kbrown5@calstatela.edu. Web site: http://www.calstatela.edu/dept/geology/index.htm.

California State University, Northridge, Graduate Studies, College of Science and Mathematics, Department of Geological Sciences, Northridge, CA 91330. Offers geology (MS). Part-time and evening/weekend programs available. *Degree requirements:* For master's, thesis. *Entrance requirements:* For master's, GRE General Test, minimum GPA of 2.75. Additional exam requirements/recommendations for international students: Required—TOEFL. *Faculty research:* Petrology of California Miocene volcanics, sedimentology of California Miocene formations, Eocene gastropods, structure of White/Inyo Mountains, seismology of Californian and Mexican earthquakes.

Case Western Reserve University, School of Graduate Studies, Earth, Environmental, and Planetary Sciences, Cleveland, OH 44106. Offers MS, PhD. Part-time programs available. *Faculty:* 7 full-time (1 woman), 7 part-time/adjunct (1 woman). *Students:* 6 full-time (3 women), 2 international. Average age 30. 10 applicants, 10% accepted, 1 enrolled. In 2011, 1 degree awarded. Terminal master's awarded for partial completion of doctoral program. *Degree requirements:* For master's, thesis or alternative; for doctorate, thesis/dissertation. *Entrance requirements:* For master's and doctorate, GRE General Test, GRE Subject Test. Additional exam requirements/recommendations for international students: Required—TOEFL (minimum score 577 paper-based; 213 computer-based; 90 iBT); Recommended—IELTS (minimum score 7). *Application deadline:* For fall admission, 1/15 priority date for domestic students; for spring admission, 11/15 for domestic students. Applications are processed on a rolling basis. Application fee: $50. Electronic applications accepted. *Financial support:* Research assistantships, teaching assistantships, Federal Work-Study, and tuition waivers (partial) available. Support available to part-time students. Financial award application deadline: 1/15; financial award applicants required to submit FAFSA. *Faculty research:* Geochemistry, hydrology, ecology, geomorphology, planetary science, stratigraphy and basin analysis, igneous petrology. *Unit head:* Gerald Matisoff, Chairman, 216-368-3677, Fax: 216-368-3691, E-mail: gerald.matisoff@case.edu. *Application contact:* James Van Orman, Chair, Graduate Admission Committee, 216-368-3690, Fax: 216-368-3691, E-mail: james.vanorman@case.edu. Web site: http://geology.cwru.edu/.

Central Washington University, Graduate Studies and Research, College of the Sciences, Department of Geological Sciences, Ellensburg, WA 98926. Offers MS. Part-time programs available. *Faculty:* 16 full-time (8 women). *Students:* 11 full-time (4 women), 3 part-time (2 women). 27 applicants, 56% accepted, 14 enrolled. In 2011, 5 master's awarded. *Degree requirements:* For master's, thesis. *Entrance requirements:* For master's, GRE General Test, minimum GPA of 3.0. Additional exam requirements/recommendations for international students: Required—TOEFL (minimum score 550 paper-based; 213 computer-based; 79 iBT) or IELTS. *Application deadline:* For fall admission, 2/1 priority date for domestic students; for winter admission, 10/1 for domestic students; for spring admission, 1/1 for domestic students. Applications are processed on a rolling basis. Application fee: $50. Electronic applications accepted. *Expenses:* Tuition, state resident: full-time $8112; part-time $270 per credit. Tuition, nonresident: full-time $18,069; part-time $602 per credit. *Required fees:* $924. *Financial support:* In 2011–12, 2 research assistantships with full and partial tuition reimbursements (averaging $9,234 per year), 8 teaching assistantships with full and partial tuition reimbursements (averaging $9,234 per year) were awarded; career-related internships or fieldwork, Federal Work-Study, health care benefits,

Peterson's Graduate Programs in the Physical Sciences, Mathematics, Agricultural Sciences, the Environment & Natural Resources 2013

facebook.com/petersonspublishing **141**

Geology

and unspecified assistantships also available. Financial award application deadline: 3/1; financial award applicants required to submit FAFSA. *Unit head:* Dr. Christopher Mattinson, Graduate Coordinator, 509-963-2702. *Application contact:* Justine Eason, Admissions Program Coordinator, 509-963-3103, Fax: 509-963-1799, E-mail: masters@cwu.edu. Web site: http://www.geology.cwu.edu/.

Colorado School of Mines, Graduate School, Department of Geology and Geological Engineering, Golden, CO 80401-1887. Offers geochemistry (MS, PMS, PhD); geological engineering (ME, MS, PhD); geology (MS, PhD). Part-time programs available. *Faculty:* 22 full-time (7 women), 4 part-time/adjunct (2 women). *Students:* 147 full-time (51 women), 31 part-time (11 women); includes 15 minority (2 Black or African American, non-Hispanic/Latino; 2 American Indian or Alaska Native, non-Hispanic/Latino; 2 Asian, non-Hispanic/Latino; 8 Hispanic/Latino; 1 Two or more races, non-Hispanic/Latino), 29 international. Average age 30. 241 applicants, 55% accepted, 55 enrolled. In 2011, 26 master's, 1 doctorate awarded. *Degree requirements:* For master's, thesis (for some programs); for doctorate, comprehensive exam, thesis/dissertation. *Entrance requirements:* For master's and doctorate, GRE General Test. Additional exam requirements/recommendations for international students: Required—TOEFL (minimum score 550 paper-based; 213 computer-based; 80 iBT). *Application deadline:* For fall admission, 1/15 for domestic and international students; for spring admission, 10/15 for domestic and international students. Application fee: $50 ($70 for international students). Electronic applications accepted. *Expenses:* Tuition, state resident: full-time $12,585; part-time $699 per credit. Tuition, nonresident: full-time $27,270; part-time $1516 per credit. *Required fees:* $1864.20; $670 per semester. *Financial support:* In 2011–12, 79 students received support, including 14 fellowships with full tuition reimbursements available (averaging $20,000 per year), 47 research assistantships with full tuition reimbursements available (averaging $20,000 per year), 18 teaching assistantships with full tuition reimbursements available (averaging $20,000 per year); scholarships/grants, health care benefits, and unspecified assistantships also available. Financial award application deadline: 1/15; financial award applicants required to submit FAFSA. *Faculty research:* Predictive sediment modeling, petrophysics, aquifer-contaminant flow modeling, water-rock interactions, geotechnical engineering. *Total annual research expenditures:* $3.3 million. *Unit head:* Dr. John Humphrey, Head, 303-273-3819, Fax: 303-273-3859, E-mail: jhumphre@mines.edu. *Application contact:* Dr. Christian Shorey, Lecturer, 303-273-3556, Fax: 303-273-3859, E-mail: cshorey@mines.edu. Web site: http://geology.mines.edu.

Cornell University, Graduate School, Graduate Fields of Engineering, Field of Geological Sciences, Ithaca, NY 14853. Offers economic geology (M Eng, MS, PhD); engineering geology (M Eng, MS, PhD); environmental geophysics (M Eng, MS, PhD); general geology (M Eng, MS, PhD); geobiology (M Eng, MS, PhD); geochemistry and isotope geology (M Eng, MS, PhD); geohydrology (M Eng, MS, PhD); geomorphology (M Eng, MS, PhD); geophysics (M Eng, MS, PhD); geotectonics (M Eng, MS, PhD); marine geology (MS, PhD); mineralogy (M Eng, MS, PhD); paleontology (M Eng, MS, PhD); petroleum geology (M Eng, MS, PhD); petrology (M Eng, MS, PhD); planetary geology (M Eng, MS, PhD); Precambrian geology (M Eng, MS, PhD); Quaternary geology (M Eng, MS, PhD); rock mechanics (M Eng, MS, PhD); sedimentology (M Eng, MS, PhD); seismology (M Eng, MS, PhD); stratigraphy (M Eng, MS, PhD); structural geology (M Eng, MS, PhD). *Faculty:* 37 full-time (5 women). *Students:* 41 full-time (19 women); includes 5 minority (2 Asian, non-Hispanic/Latino; 3 Hispanic/Latino), 7 international. Average age 27. 74 applicants, 19% accepted, 9 enrolled. In 2011, 3 master's, 3 doctorates awarded. *Degree requirements:* For master's, thesis (MS); for doctorate, comprehensive exam, thesis/dissertation. *Entrance requirements:* For master's and doctorate, GRE General Test, 3 letters of recommendation. Additional exam requirements/recommendations for international students: Required—TOEFL (minimum score 550 paper-based; 213 computer-based; 77 iBT). *Application deadline:* For fall admission, 1/15 priority date for domestic students. Applications are processed on a rolling basis. Application fee: $95. Electronic applications accepted. *Financial support:* In 2011–12, 25 students received support, including 7 fellowships with full tuition reimbursements available, 19 research assistantships with full tuition reimbursements available, 8 teaching assistantships with full tuition reimbursements available; institutionally sponsored loans, scholarships/grants, health care benefits, tuition waivers (full and partial), and unspecified assistantships also available. Financial award applicants required to submit FAFSA. *Faculty research:* Geophysics, structural geology, petrology, geochemistry, geodynamics. *Unit head:* Director of Graduate Studies, 607-255-5466, Fax: 607-254-4780. *Application contact:* Graduate Field Assistant, 607-255-5466, Fax: 607-254-4780, E-mail: gradprog@geology.cornell.edu. Web site: http://www.gradschool.cornell.edu/fields.php?id-30&a-2.

Duke University, Graduate School, Division of Earth and Ocean Sciences, Durham, NC 27708. Offers MS, PhD. Part-time programs available. *Faculty:* 11 full-time. *Students:* 19 full-time (10 women); includes 1 minority (Asian, non-Hispanic/Latino), 4 international. 27 applicants, 19% accepted, 2 enrolled. In 2011, 4 degrees awarded. Terminal master's awarded for partial completion of doctoral program. *Degree requirements:* For master's, thesis; for doctorate, thesis/dissertation. *Entrance requirements:* For master's and doctorate, GRE General Test. Additional exam requirements/recommendations for international students: Required—TOEFL (minimum score 550 paper-based; 213 computer-based; 83 iBT), IELTS (minimum score 7). *Application deadline:* For fall admission, 12/8 priority date for domestic students, 12/8 for international students; for spring admission, 10/15 for domestic and international students. Application fee: $75. Electronic applications accepted. *Expenses: Tuition:* Full-time $40,720.

Required fees: $3107. *Financial support:* Fellowships, research assistantships, teaching assistantships, and Federal Work-Study available. Financial award application deadline: 12/8. *Unit head:* Alan Boudreau, Director of Graduate Studies, 919-681-4426, Fax: 919-684-5833, E-mail: cabrera@duke.edu. *Application contact:* Elizabeth Hutton, Director of Admissions, 919-684-3913, Fax: 919-684-2277, E-mail: grad-admissions@duke.edu. Web site: http://www.nicholas.duke.edu/eos/.

East Carolina University, Graduate School, Thomas Harriot College of Arts and Sciences, Department of Geology, Greenville, NC 27858-4353. Offers geology (MS); hydrogeology and environmental geology (Certificate). Part-time programs available. *Degree requirements:* For master's, one foreign language, comprehensive exam, thesis. *Entrance requirements:* For master's, GRE General Test. Additional exam requirements/recommendations for international students: Required—TOEFL. *Application deadline:* For fall admission, 6/1 priority date for domestic students; for spring admission, 10/15 for domestic students. Applications are processed on a rolling basis. Application fee: $50. *Expenses:* Tuition, state resident: full-time $3557; part-time $444.63 per semester hour. Tuition, nonresident: full-time $14,351; part-time $1793.88 per semester hour. *Required fees:* $2016; $252 per semester hour. Part-time tuition and fees vary according to course load, campus/location and program. *Financial support:* Research assistantships with partial tuition reimbursements and teaching assistantships with partial tuition reimbursements available. Support available to part-time students. Financial award application deadline: 6/1. *Unit head:* Dr. Stephen Culver, Chair, 252-328-6360, Fax: 252-328-4391, E-mail: culvers@ecu.edu. *Application contact:* Dean of Graduate School, 252-328-6012, Fax: 252-328-6071, E-mail: gradschool@ecu.edu. Web site: http://www.ecu.edu/geology/.

Eastern Kentucky University, The Graduate School, College of Arts and Sciences, Department of Earth Sciences, Richmond, KY 40475-3102. Offers geology (MS, PhD). PhD program offered jointly with University of Kentucky. Part-time programs available. *Degree requirements:* For master's, thesis. *Entrance requirements:* For master's, GRE General Test, minimum GPA of 2.5. *Faculty research:* Hydrogeology, sedimentary geology, geochemistry, environmental geology, tectonics.

Florida Atlantic University, Charles E. Schmidt College of Science, Department of Geosciences, Boca Raton, FL 33431-0991. Offers geography (MA); geology (MS); geosciences (PhD). Part-time programs available. *Faculty:* 11 full-time (3 women), 2 part-time/adjunct (0 women). *Students:* 29 full-time (18 women), 11 part-time (5 women); includes 4 minority (1 Asian, non-Hispanic/Latino; 3 Hispanic/Latino), 2 international. Average age 37. 22 applicants, 64% accepted, 8 enrolled. In 2011, 8 master's awarded. *Degree requirements:* For master's, thesis (for some programs). *Entrance requirements:* For master's, GRE General Test, minimum GPA of 3.0. *Application deadline:* For fall admission, 3/15 for domestic and international students; for spring admission, 10/15 for domestic and international students. Applications are processed on a rolling basis. Application fee: $30. Electronic applications accepted. *Expenses: Tuition, area resident:* Part-time $343.02 per credit hour. Tuition, state resident: full-time $8232. Tuition, nonresident: full-time $23,931; part-time $997.14 per credit hour. *Financial support:* Research assistantships with partial tuition reimbursements, teaching assistantships with partial tuition reimbursements, career-related internships or fieldwork, Federal Work-Study, institutionally sponsored loans, and unspecified assistantships available. *Faculty research:* GIS applications, paleontology, hydrogeology, economic development. *Unit head:* Dr. Russell Ivy, Chair, 561-297-3295, Fax: 561-297-2745, E-mail: ivy@fau.edu. *Application contact:* Dr. David Warburton, Graduate Coordinator, 561-297-3312, Fax: 561-297-2745, E-mail: warburto@fau.edu. Web site: http://www.geosciences.fau.edu/.

Florida State University, The Graduate School, College of Arts and Sciences, Department of Earth, Ocean and Atmospheric Science, Program in Geological Sciences, Tallahassee, FL 32306. Offers MS, PhD. *Faculty:* 12 full-time (1 woman). *Students:* 29 full-time (17 women), 5 part-time (4 women). Average age 27. *Degree requirements:* For master's, thesis; for doctorate, thesis/dissertation. *Entrance requirements:* For master's and doctorate, GRE General Test, minimum GPA of 3.0. Additional exam requirements/recommendations for international students: Required—TOEFL (minimum score 550 paper-based; 80 iBT). *Application deadline:* For fall admission, 3/1 priority date for domestic students, 3/1 for international students; for spring admission, 8/1 priority date for domestic students, 8/1 for international students. Applications are processed on a rolling basis. Application fee: $30. Electronic applications accepted. *Expenses:* Tuition, state resident: full-time $9474; part-time $350.88 per credit hour. Tuition, nonresident: full-time $16,236; part-time $601.34 per credit hour. *Required fees:* $630 per semester. One-time fee: $20. Tuition and fees vary according to course load and campus/location. *Financial support:* In 2011–12, 23 students received support. Fellowships, research assistantships, teaching assistantships, career-related internships or fieldwork, and Federal Work-Study available. Financial award application deadline: 2/7; financial award applicants required to submit FAFSA. *Faculty research:* Appalachian and collisional tectonics, surface and groundwater hydrogeology, micropaleontology, isotope and trace element geochemistry, coastal and estuarine studies. *Total annual research expenditures:* $2.3 million. *Unit head:* Dr. Lynn Dudley, Chairman, 850-644-3864, Fax: 850-644-4214, E-mail: ldudley@fsu.edu. *Application contact:* Sharon R. Wynn, Student Coordinator, 850-644-5860, Fax: 850-644-4214, E-mail: srwynn@fsu.edu. Web site: http://www.gly.fsu.edu.

Fort Hays State University, Graduate School, College of Arts and Sciences, Department of Geosciences, Program in Geosciences, Hays, KS 67601-4099.

142 facebook.com/petersonspublishing

Peterson's Graduate Programs in the Physical Sciences, Mathematics, Agricultural Sciences, the Environment & Natural Resources 2013

Offers geography (MS); geology (MS). *Degree requirements:* For master's, comprehensive exam, thesis. *Entrance requirements:* For master's, GRE General Test. Additional exam requirements/recommendations for international students: Required—TOEFL (minimum score 550 paper-based; 213 computer-based). Electronic applications accepted. *Faculty research:* Cretaceous and late Cenozoic stratigraphy, sedimentation, paleontology.

Georgia State University, College of Arts and Sciences, Department of Geosciences, Program in Geology, Atlanta, GA 30302-3083. Offers MA. *Degree requirements:* For master's, one foreign language, comprehensive exam (for some programs), thesis or alternative. *Entrance requirements:* For master's, GRE General Test, minimum GPA of 2.75. Additional exam requirements/ recommendations for international students: Required—TOEFL.

Hofstra University, School of Education, Health, and Human Services, Programs in Teaching Secondary Education, Hempstead, NY 11549. Offers business education (MS Ed); education technology (Advanced Certificate); English education (MA, MS Ed); foreign language and TESOL (MS Ed); foreign language education (MA, MS Ed), including French, German, Russian, Spanish; mathematics education (MA, MS Ed); science education (MA, MS Ed), including biology, chemistry, earth science, geology, physics; secondary education (Advanced Certificate); social studies education (MA, MS Ed). Part-time and evening/weekend programs available. Postbaccalaureate distance learning degree programs offered (minimal on-campus study). *Students:* 72 full-time (47 women), 51 part-time (30 women); includes 21 minority (9 Black or African American, non-Hispanic/Latino; 7 Asian, non-Hispanic/Latino; 5 Hispanic/Latino). Average age 28. 103 applicants, 91% accepted, 41 enrolled. In 2011, 86 master's, 6 other advanced degrees awarded. *Degree requirements:* For master's, one foreign language, comprehensive exam (for some programs), thesis (for some programs), exit project, electronic portfolio, student teaching, fieldwork, curriculum project, minimum GPA of 3.0; for Advanced Certificate, 3 foreign languages, comprehensive exam (for some programs), thesis project, minimum GPA of 3.0. *Entrance requirements:* For master's, 2 letters of recommendation, teacher certification (MA), essay; for Advanced Certificate, 2 letters of recommendation, essay. Additional exam requirements/recommendations for international students: Required—TOEFL (minimum score 550 paper-based; 213 computer-based; 80 iBT). *Application deadline:* Applications are processed on a rolling basis. Application fee: $70 ($75 for international students). Electronic applications accepted. *Expenses: Tuition:* Full-time $18,990; part-time $1055 per credit hour. *Required fees:* $970. Tuition and fees vary according to program. *Financial support:* In 2011–12, 90 students received support, including 13 fellowships with full and partial tuition reimbursements available (averaging $3,202 per year), 1 research assistantship with full and partial tuition reimbursement available (averaging $11,645 per year); career-related internships or fieldwork, Federal Work-Study, institutionally sponsored loans, scholarships/grants, tuition waivers (full and partial), and unspecified assistantships also available. Support available to part-time students. Financial award applicants required to submit FAFSA. *Faculty research:* Appropriate content and pedagogy in secondary school disciplines, appropriate pedagogy in secondary school disciplines, adolescent development, secondary school organization, alternative secondary school programs. *Unit head:* Dr. Esther Fusco, Chairperson, 516-463-7704, Fax: 516-463-6196, E-mail: catezf@hofstra.edu. *Application contact:* Carol Drummer, Dean of Graduate Admissions, 516-463-4876, Fax: 516-463-4664, E-mail: gradstudent@hofstra.edu. Web site: http://www.hofstra.edu/education/.

Humboldt State University, Academic Programs, College of Natural Resources and Sciences, Programs in Environmental Systems, Arcata, CA 95521-8299. Offers environmental systems (MS), including energy, environment and society, environmental resources engineering, geology, math modeling. *Students:* 32 full-time (12 women), 4 part-time (2 women); includes 5 minority (1 Black or African American, non-Hispanic/Latino; 1 Asian, non-Hispanic/Latino; 1 Hispanic/Latino; 2 Two or more races, non-Hispanic/Latino), 3 international. Average age 28. 58 applicants, 36% accepted, 13 enrolled. In 2011, 12 master's awarded. *Degree requirements:* For master's, thesis. *Entrance requirements:* For master's, GRE, appropriate bachelor's degree, minimum GPA of 2.5, 3 letters of recommendation. Additional exam requirements/recommendations for international students: Required—TOEFL. *Application deadline:* For fall admission, 2/15 for domestic students; for spring admission, 10/15 for domestic students. Applications are processed on a rolling basis. Application fee: $55. *Expenses:* Tuition, state resident: full-time $6734. Tuition, nonresident: full-time $15,662; part-time $372 per credit. *Required fees:* $903. Tuition and fees vary according to program. *Financial support:* Application deadline: 3/1; applicants required to submit FAFSA. *Faculty research:* Mathematical modeling, international development technology, geology, environmental resources engineering. *Unit head:* Dr. Chris Dugaw, Chair, 707-826-4251, Fax: 707-826-4145, E-mail: dugaw@humboldt.edu. *Application contact:* Dr. Dale Oliver, Coordinator, 707-826-4921, Fax: 707-826-3140, E-mail: dale.oliver@humboldt.edu.

ICR Graduate School, Graduate Programs, Santee, CA 92071. Offers astro/ geophysics (MS); biology (MS); geology (MS); science education (MS). Part-time programs available. *Degree requirements:* For master's, comprehensive exam (for some programs), thesis (for some programs). *Entrance requirements:* For master's, minimum undergraduate GPA of 3.0, bachelor's degree in science or science education. *Faculty research:* Age of the earth, limits of variation, catastrophe, optimum methods for teaching.

Idaho State University, Office of Graduate Studies, College of Science and Engineering, Department of Geosciences, Pocatello, ID 83209-8072. Offers

geographic information science (MS); geology (MNS, MS); geology with emphasis in environmental geoscience (MS); geophysics/hydrology/geology (MS); geotechnology (Postbaccalaureate Certificate). Part-time programs available. *Degree requirements:* For master's, comprehensive exam, thesis, oral colloquium; for Postbaccalaureate Certificate, thesis optional, minimum 19 credits. *Entrance requirements:* For master's, GRE General Test (minimum 50th percentile in 2 sections), 3 letters of recommendation; for Postbaccalaureate Certificate, GRE General Test, 3 letters of recommendation, bachelor's degree, statement of goals. Additional exam requirements/recommendations for international students: Required—TOEFL (minimum score 550 paper-based; 213 computer-based; 80 iBT). Electronic applications accepted. *Faculty research:* Quantitative field mapping and sampling: microscopic, geochemical, and isotopic analysis of rocks, minerals and water; remote sensing, geographic information systems, and global positioning systems: environmental and watershed management; surficial and fluvial processes: landscape change; regional tectonics, structural geology; planetary geology.

Indiana University Bloomington, University Graduate School, College of Arts and Sciences, Department of Geological Sciences, Bloomington, IN 47405-7000. Offers biogeochemistry (MS, PhD); economic geology (MS, PhD); geobiology (MS, PhD); geophysics, structural geology and tectonics (MS, PhD); hydrogeology (MS, PhD); mineralogy (MS, PhD); stratigraphy and sedimentology (MS, PhD). *Faculty:* 17 full-time (1 woman). *Students:* 60 full-time (26 women), 2 part-time (0 women); includes 5 minority (2 Black or African American, non-Hispanic/Latino; 1 Hispanic/Latino; 2 Two or more races, non-Hispanic/Latino), 18 international. Average age 29. 44 applicants, 55% accepted, 18 enrolled. In 2011, 11 master's, 6 doctorates awarded. Terminal master's awarded for partial completion of doctoral program. *Degree requirements:* For master's, thesis or alternative; for doctorate, comprehensive exam, thesis/dissertation. *Entrance requirements:* For master's and doctorate, GRE General Test. Additional exam requirements/recommendations for international students: Required—TOEFL. *Application deadline:* For fall admission, 1/15 priority date for domestic students, 12/15 for international students; for spring admission, 9/1 priority date for domestic students, 9/1 for international students. Applications are processed on a rolling basis. Application fee: $55 ($65 for international students). *Financial support:* In 2011–12, fellowships with full tuition reimbursements (averaging $17,300 per year), research assistantships with full tuition reimbursements (averaging $16,370 per year), teaching assistantships with full tuition reimbursements (averaging $15,150 per year) were awarded; career-related internships or fieldwork, Federal Work-Study, and institutionally sponsored loans also available. *Faculty research:* Geophysics, geochemistry, hydrogeology, geobiology, planetary science. Total annual research expenditures: $644,299. *Unit head:* Simon Brassell, Chair, 812-855-5581, Fax: 812-855-7899, E-mail: geochair@indiana.edu. *Application contact:* Mary Iverson, Graduate Secretary, 812-855-7214, Fax: 812-855-7899, E-mail: miverson@indiana.edu. Web site: http://www.indiana.edu/~geosci/.

Indiana University–Purdue University Indianapolis, School of Science, Department of Earth Sciences, Indianapolis, IN 46202-3272. Offers applied earth sciences (PhD); geology (MS). Part-time and evening/weekend programs available. *Faculty:* 8 full-time (2 women). *Students:* 10 full-time (6 women), 11 part-time (5 women); includes 1 minority (American Indian or Alaska Native, non-Hispanic/Latino), 8 international. Average age 29. 31 applicants, 45% accepted, 14 enrolled. In 2011, 7 master's awarded. *Degree requirements:* For master's, thesis (for some programs). *Entrance requirements:* For master's, GRE General Test, minimum GPA of 3.0. Application fee: $55 ($65 for international students). *Financial support:* In 2011–12, fellowships with full tuition reimbursements (averaging $12,000 per year), teaching assistantships with full tuition reimbursements (averaging $12,103 per year) were awarded; research assistantships with full tuition reimbursements and scholarships/grants also available. Financial award application deadline: 3/1. *Faculty research:* Wetland hydrology, groundwater contamination, soils, sedimentology, sediment chemistry. *Unit head:* Gabriel Filippelli, Chair, 317-274-7484, Fax: 317-274-7966. *Application contact:* Lenore P. Tedesco, Associate Professor, 317-274-7484, Fax: 317-274-7966, E-mail: ltedesco@iupui.edu. Web site: http://www.geology.iupui.edu/.

Iowa State University of Science and Technology, Department of Geological and Atmospheric Sciences, Ames, IA 50011-3212. Offers earth science (MS, PhD); environmental science (MS, PhD); geology (MS, PhD); meteorology (MS, PhD). *Degree requirements:* For master's, thesis (for some programs); for doctorate, thesis/dissertation. *Entrance requirements:* For master's and doctorate, GRE General Test. Additional exam requirements/recommendations for international students: Required—TOEFL (minimum score 550 paper-based; 79 iBT), IELTS (minimum score 6.5). *Application deadline:* For fall admission, 1/1 priority date for domestic students. Application fee: $40 ($90 for international students). Electronic applications accepted. *Unit head:* Dr. Carl E. Jacobson, Director of Graduate Education, 515-294-8048, Fax: 515-294-6049, E-mail: geology@iastate.edu. *Application contact:* Neal Iverson, Information Contact, 515-294-8048, Fax: 515-294-6049, E-mail: geology@iastate.edu. Web site: http://www.ge-at.iastate.edu/.

Kansas State University, Graduate School, College of Arts and Sciences, Department of Geology, Manhattan, KS 66506. Offers MS. *Faculty:* 9 full-time (0 women), 2 part-time/adjunct (0 women). *Students:* 15 full-time (5 women), 5 part-time (0 women); includes 4 minority (2 Black or African American, non-Hispanic/ Latino; 1 Hispanic/Latino; 1 Two or more races, non-Hispanic/Latino), 3 international. Average age 26. 21 applicants, 71% accepted, 7 enrolled. In 2011, 6

Peterson's Graduate Programs in the Physical Sciences, Mathematics, Agricultural Sciences, the Environment & Natural Resources 2013

facebook.com/petersonspublishing **143**

Geology

master's awarded. *Degree requirements:* For master's, thesis. *Entrance requirements:* For master's, GRE General Test. Additional exam requirements/recommendations for international students: Required—TOEFL. *Application deadline:* For fall admission, 2/1 priority date for domestic students, 2/1 for international students; for spring admission, 8/1 priority date for domestic students, 8/1 for international students. Applications are processed on a rolling basis. Application fee: $40 ($55 for international students). Electronic applications accepted. *Financial support:* In 2011–12, 10 students received support, including 4 research assistantships (averaging $16,875 per year), 10 teaching assistantships with full tuition reimbursements available (averaging $10,469 per year); career-related internships or fieldwork, institutionally sponsored loans, scholarships/grants, unspecified assistantships, and GTA stipends, departmental scholarships also available. Support available to part-time students. Financial award application deadline: 3/1; financial award applicants required to submit FAFSA. *Faculty research:* Chemical hydrogeology, petroleum geology, exploration seismic and near surface geophysics, Late Pleistocene geochronology, igneous petrology, volcanology, climate change, tidal sedimentation processes, luminescence dating, biomineralization. *Total annual research expenditures:* $165,415. *Unit head:* Dr. George Clark, Head, 785-532-2242, Fax: 785-532-5159, E-mail: grc@ksu.edu. *Application contact:* Dr. Matthew Brueseke, Interim Director of Domestic Graduate Studies, 785-532-1908, Fax: 785-532-5159, E-mail: brueseke@ksu.edu. Web site: http://www.k-state.edu/geology/.

Kent State University, College of Arts and Sciences, Department of Geology, Kent, OH 44242-0001. Offers applied geology (PhD); geology (MS). *Degree requirements:* For master's, thesis; for doctorate, one foreign language, thesis/dissertation. *Entrance requirements:* For master's, minimum GPA of 2.75; for doctorate, GRE General Test, GRE Subject Test, minimum GPA of 3.0. Additional exam requirements/recommendations for international students: Required—TOEFL (minimum score 575 paper-based; 232 computer-based). Electronic applications accepted. *Expenses:* Tuition, state resident: full-time $8136; part-time $452 per credit hour. Tuition, nonresident: full-time $14,292; part-time $794 per credit hour. *Faculty research:* Groundwater, surface water, engineering geology, paleontology, structural geology.

Lakehead University, Graduate Studies, Department of Geology, Thunder Bay, ON P7B 5E1, Canada. Offers M Sc. Part-time and evening/weekend programs available. *Degree requirements:* For master's, thesis, department seminar, oral exam. *Entrance requirements:* For master's, minimum B average, honours bachelors degree in geology. Additional exam requirements/recommendations for international students: Required—TOEFL. *Faculty research:* Rock physics, sedimentology, mineralogy and economic geology, geochemistry, petrology of alkaline rocks.

Laurentian University, School of Graduate Studies and Research, Programme in Geology (Earth Sciences), Sudbury, ON P3E 2C6, Canada. Offers geology (M Sc); mineral deposits and precambrian geology (PhD); mineral exploration (M Sc). Part-time programs available. *Degree requirements:* For master's, thesis. *Entrance requirements:* For master's, honors degree with second class or better. *Faculty research:* Localization and metallogenesis of Ni-Cu-(PGE) sulfide mineralization in the Thompson Nickel Belt, mapping lithology and ore-grade and monitoring dissolved organic carbon in lakes using remote sensing, global reefs, volcanic effects on VMS deposits.

Lehigh University, College of Arts and Sciences, Department of Earth and Environmental Sciences, Bethlehem, PA 18015. Offers MS, PhD. *Faculty:* 15 full-time (2 women). *Students:* 27 full-time (11 women), 3 part-time (1 woman), 3 international. Average age 27. 38 applicants, 18% accepted, 7 enrolled. In 2011, 3 master's, 1 doctorate awarded. Terminal master's awarded for partial completion of doctoral program. *Degree requirements:* For master's, thesis; for doctorate, thesis/dissertation. *Entrance requirements:* For master's and doctorate, GRE General Test, transcripts, recommendation letters, research statement, faculty advocates. Additional exam requirements/recommendations for international students: Required—TOEFL (minimum score 85 iBT). *Application deadline:* For fall admission, 1/1 for domestic and international students. Applications are processed on a rolling basis. Application fee: $75. Electronic applications accepted. *Financial support:* In 2011–12, 13 students received support, including 3 fellowships with full tuition reimbursements available (averaging $24,500 per year), 10 research assistantships with full tuition reimbursements available (averaging $24,500 per year), 10 teaching assistantships with full tuition reimbursements available (averaging $24,500 per year); career-related internships or fieldwork, Federal Work-Study, institutionally sponsored loans, scholarships/grants, tuition waivers (full and partial), and unspecified assistantships also available. Support available to part-time students. Financial award application deadline: 1/1. *Faculty research:* Tectonics, surficial processes, ecology, environmental change. *Total annual research expenditures:* $1 million. *Unit head:* Dr. Frank J. Pazzaglia, Chairman, 610-758-3667, Fax: 610-758-3677, E-mail: fjp3@lehigh.edu. *Application contact:* Dr. Stephen Peters, Graduate Coordinator, 610-758-3957, Fax: 610-758-3677, E-mail: scp2@lehigh.edu. Web site: http://www.ees.lehigh.edu/.

Louisiana State University and Agricultural and Mechanical College, Graduate School, College of Science, Department of Geology and Geophysics, Baton Rouge, LA 70803. Offers MS, PhD. *Faculty:* 14 full-time (4 women). *Students:* 49 full-time (23 women), 9 part-time (0 women); includes 4 minority (2 Black or African American, non-Hispanic/Latino; 1 Hispanic/Latino; 1 Two or more races, non-Hispanic/Latino), 12 international. Average age 26. 68 applicants, 32%

accepted, 18 enrolled. In 2011, 14 master's, 3 doctorates awarded. Terminal master's awarded for partial completion of doctoral program. *Degree requirements:* For master's, thesis; for doctorate, thesis/dissertation. *Entrance requirements:* For master's and doctorate, GRE General Test, minimum GPA of 3.0. Additional exam requirements/recommendations for international students: Required—TOEFL (minimum score 550 paper-based; 213 computer-based; 79 iBT) or IELTS (minimum score 6.5). *Application deadline:* For fall admission, 1/25 priority date for domestic students, 5/15 for international students; for spring admission, 10/15 for international students. Applications are processed on a rolling basis. Application fee: $50 ($70 for international students). Electronic applications accepted. *Financial support:* In 2011–12, 47 students received support, including 1 fellowship with full tuition reimbursement available (averaging $30,477 per year), 24 research assistantships with full and partial tuition reimbursements available (averaging $19,406 per year), 18 teaching assistantships with full and partial tuition reimbursements available (averaging $14,191 per year); career-related internships or fieldwork, Federal Work-Study, institutionally sponsored loans, health care benefits, tuition waivers (full and partial), and unspecified assistantships also available. Financial award application deadline: 3/15; financial award applicants required to submit FAFSA. *Faculty research:* Geophysics, sedimentology, geochemistry, geomicrobiology, tectonics. *Total annual research expenditures:* $785,748. *Unit head:* Dr. Carol Wicks, Chair, 225-578-3353, Fax: 225-578-2302, E-mail: cwicks@lsu.edu. *Application contact:* Dr. Sam Bentley, Graduate Adviser, 225-578-5735, E-mail: sjb@lsu.edu. Web site: http://www.geol.lsu.edu/.

Massachusetts Institute of Technology, School of Science, Department of Earth, Atmospheric, and Planetary Sciences, Cambridge, MA 02139. Offers atmospheric chemistry (PhD, Sc D); atmospheric science (SM, PhD, Sc D); chemical oceanography (SM, PhD, Sc D); climate physics and chemistry (SM, PhD, Sc D); earth and planetary sciences (SM); geochemistry (PhD, Sc D); geology (PhD, Sc D); geophysics (PhD, Sc D); marine geology and geophysics (SM, PhD, Sc D); physical oceanography (SM, PhD, Sc D); planetary sciences (PhD, Sc D). *Faculty:* 33 full-time (6 women). *Students:* 175 full-time (81 women); includes 21 minority (3 Black or African American, non-Hispanic/Latino; 1 American Indian or Alaska Native, non-Hispanic/Latino; 8 Asian, non-Hispanic/Latino; 4 Hispanic/Latino; 5 Two or more races, non-Hispanic/Latino), 58 international. Average age 26. 241 applicants, 28% accepted, 43 enrolled. In 2011, 6 master's, 16 doctorates awarded. Terminal master's awarded for partial completion of doctoral program. *Degree requirements:* For master's, thesis; for doctorate, comprehensive exam, thesis/dissertation. *Entrance requirements:* For master's, GRE General Test; for doctorate, GRE General Test, GRE Subject Test (chemistry or physics for planetary science area). Additional exam requirements/recommendations for international students: Required—TOEFL (minimum score 577 paper-based; 233 computer-based; 91 iBT), IELTS (minimum score 7). *Application deadline:* For fall admission, 1/5 for domestic and international students; for spring admission, 11/1 for domestic and international students. Application fee: $75. Electronic applications accepted. *Expenses: Tuition:* Full-time $40,460; part-time $630 per credit hour. *Required fees:* $272. *Financial support:* In 2011–12, 125 students received support, including 68 fellowships (averaging $32,200 per year), 94 research assistantships (averaging $31,900 per year), 10 teaching assistantships (averaging $30,000 per year); Federal Work-Study, institutionally sponsored loans, scholarships/grants, health care benefits, and unspecified assistantships also available. *Faculty research:* Formation, dynamics and evolution of planetary systems; origin, composition, structure and dynamics of the atmospheres, oceans, surfaces and interiors of the Earth and other planets; evolution and interaction of the physical, chemical, geological and biological components of the Earth system; characterization of past, present and potential future climates and the causes and consequences of climate change; interplay of energy and the environment. *Total annual research expenditures:* $26.2 million. *Unit head:* Prof. Robert van der Hilst, Head, 617-253-2127, Fax: 617-253-8298, E-mail: eapsinfo@mit.edu. *Application contact:* EAPS Education Office, 617-253-3381, Fax: 617-253-8298, E-mail: eapsinfo@mit.edu. Web site: http://eapsweb.mit.edu/.

McMaster University, School of Graduate Studies, Faculty of Science, School of Geography and Earth Sciences, Hamilton, ON L8S 4M2, Canada. Offers geochemistry (PhD); geology (M Sc, PhD); human geography (MA, PhD); physical geography (M Sc, PhD). Part-time programs available. Terminal master's awarded for partial completion of doctoral program. *Degree requirements:* For master's, thesis; for doctorate, comprehensive exam, thesis/dissertation. *Entrance requirements:* For master's, minimum B+ average. Additional exam requirements/recommendations for international students: Required—TOEFL (minimum score 550 paper-based; 213 computer-based).

Memorial University of Newfoundland, School of Graduate Studies, Department of Earth Sciences, St. John's, NL A1C 5S7, Canada. Offers geology (M Sc, PhD); geophysics (M Sc, PhD). Part-time programs available. *Degree requirements:* For master's, thesis; for doctorate, comprehensive exam, thesis/dissertation, oral thesis defense, entry evaluation. *Entrance requirements:* For master's, honors B Sc; for doctorate, M Sc. Electronic applications accepted. *Faculty research:* Geochemistry, sedimentology, paleoceanography and global change, mineral deposits, petroleum geology, hydrology.

Miami University, College of Arts and Science, Department of Geology, Oxford, OH 45056. Offers MA, MS, PhD. Part-time programs available. *Students:* 31 full-time (17 women); includes 3 minority (1 Black or African American, non-Hispanic/Latino; 1 Asian, non-Hispanic/Latino; 1 Two or more races, non-Hispanic/Latino),

12 international. Average age 28. In 2011, 3 master's, 2 doctorates awarded. *Entrance requirements:* For master's, GRE, minimum undergraduate GPA of 3.0 during previous 2 years or 2.75 overall; for doctorate, GRE General Test, GRE Subject Test, minimum GPA of 2.75 (undergraduate) or 3.0 (graduate). Additional exam requirements/recommendations for international students: Required—TOEFL. *Application deadline:* For fall admission, 2/1 for domestic and international students. Application fee: $50. *Expenses:* Tuition, state resident: full-time $12,023; part-time $501 per credit hour. Tuition, nonresident: full-time $26,554; part-time $1107 per credit hour. *Required fees:* $528. *Financial support:* Fellowships with full tuition reimbursements, research assistantships with full tuition reimbursements, teaching assistantships with full tuition reimbursements, Federal Work-Study, institutionally sponsored loans, health care benefits, tuition waivers (full), and unspecified assistantships available. Financial award application deadline: 2/15; financial award applicants required to submit FAFSA. *Unit head:* Dr. William Hart, Department Chair and Professor, 513-529-3216, Fax: 513-529-1542, E-mail: hartwk@muohio.edu. *Application contact:* Dr. Elisabeth Widom, Director of Graduate Studies, 513-529-5048, E-mail: widome@muohio.edu. Web site: http://www.units.muohio.edu/geology/.

Michigan Technological University, Graduate School, College of Engineering, Department of Geological and Mining Engineering and Sciences, Houghton, MI 49931. Offers geological engineering (MS, PhD); geology (MS, PhD); geophysics (MS, PhD); mining engineering (MS, PhD). Part-time programs available. *Faculty:* 20 full-time (2 women), 21 part-time/adjunct (1 woman). *Students:* 52 full-time (28 women), 8 part-time (3 women); includes 3 minority (all Hispanic/Latino), 20 international. Average age 29. 114 applicants, 33% accepted, 15 enrolled. In 2011, 10 master's, 1 doctorate awarded. Terminal master's awarded for partial completion of doctoral program. *Degree requirements:* For master's, comprehensive exam (for some programs), thesis (for some programs); for doctorate, comprehensive exam, thesis/dissertation. *Entrance requirements:* For master's and doctorate, GRE, statement of purpose, official transcripts, 3 letters of recommendation. Additional exam requirements/recommendations for international students: Required—TOEFL (minimum score 79 iBT) or IELTS. *Application deadline:* Applications are processed on a rolling basis. Electronic applications accepted. *Expenses:* Tuition, state resident: full-time $12,636; part-time $702 per credit. Tuition, nonresident: full-time $12,636; part-time $702 per credit. *Required fees:* $226; $226 per year. *Financial support:* In 2011–12, 45 students received support, including 4 fellowships with full tuition reimbursements available (averaging $6,065 per year), 22 research assistantships with full tuition reimbursements available (averaging $6,065 per year), teaching assistantships with full tuition reimbursements available (averaging $6,065 per year); career-related internships or fieldwork, Federal Work-Study, scholarships/grants, health care benefits, tuition waivers (partial), unspecified assistantships, and cooperative program also available. Financial award applicants required to submit FAFSA. *Faculty research:* Volcanic hazards and volcanic clouds, oil and gas exploration and development, groundwater measurement and modeling, geophysics, environmental paleomagnetism. *Total annual research expenditures:* $1.3 million. *Unit head:* Dr. Wayne D. Pennington, Chair, 906-487-3573, Fax: 906-487-3371, E-mail: wayne@mtu.edu. *Application contact:* Amie S. Ledgerwood, Secretary 5, 906-487-2531, Fax: 906-487-3371, E-mail: asledger@mtu.edu. Web site: http://www.mtu.edu/geo/.

Mississippi State University, College of Arts and Sciences, Department of Geosciences, Mississippi State, MS 39762. Offers applied meteorology (MS); broadcast meteorology (MS); earth and atmospheric science (PhD); environmental geoscience (MS); geography (MS); geology (MS); geospatial sciences (MS); professional meteorology/climatology (MS); teachers in geoscience (MS). Postbaccalaureate distance learning degree programs offered (no on-campus study). *Faculty:* 19 full-time (3 women), 2 part-time/adjunct (0 women). *Students:* 72 full-time (27 women), 279 part-time (127 women); includes 40 minority (12 Black or African American, non-Hispanic/Latino; 4 American Indian or Alaska Native, non-Hispanic/Latino; 6 Asian, non-Hispanic/Latino; 14 Hispanic/Latino; 4 Two or more races, non-Hispanic/Latino), 10 international. Average age 35. 228 applicants, 77% accepted, 144 enrolled. In 2011, 89 master's awarded. *Degree requirements:* For master's, thesis (for some programs), comprehensive oral or written exam. *Entrance requirements:* For master's, GRE (for on-campus applicants), minimum undergraduate GPA of 2.75. Additional exam requirements/recommendations for international students: Required—TOEFL (minimum score 475 paper-based; 153 computer-based; 53 iBT); Recommended—IELTS (minimum score 4.5). *Application deadline:* For fall admission, 7/1 for domestic students, 5/1 for international students; for spring admission, 11/1 for domestic students, 9/1 for international students. Applications are processed on a rolling basis. Application fee: $40. Electronic applications accepted. *Expenses:* Tuition, state resident: full-time $5805; part-time $322.50 per credit hour. Tuition, nonresident: full-time $14,670; part-time $815 per credit hour. *Financial support:* In 2011–12, 13 research assistantships with full tuition reimbursements (averaging $20,746 per year), 31 teaching assistantships with full tuition reimbursements (averaging $14,151 per year) were awarded; Federal Work-Study, institutionally sponsored loans, scholarships/grants, tuition waivers (partial), and unspecified assistantships also available. Financial award application deadline: 4/1; financial award applicants required to submit FAFSA. *Faculty research:* Climatology, hydrogeology, sedimentology, meteorology. *Total annual research expenditures:* $6.2 million. *Unit head:* Dr. Darrel Schmitz, Professor and Head, 662-325-3915, Fax: 662-325-9423, E-mail: schmitz@geosci.msstate.edu. *Application contact:* Dr. Christopher P. Dewey, Associate Professor/Graduate Coordinator, 662-325-2909, Fax: 662-325-9423, E-mail: cpd4@msstate.edu. Web site: http://www.msstate.edu/dept/geosciences/.

Missouri State University, Graduate College, College of Natural and Applied Sciences, Department of Geography, Geology, and Planning, Springfield, MO 65897. Offers geospatial sciences (MS, MS Ed), including earth science (MS Ed), geology (MS), human geography and planning (MS), physical geography (MS Ed); natural and applied science (MNAS), including geography, geology and planning; secondary education (MS Ed), including geography. Part-time and evening/weekend programs available. *Faculty:* 19 full-time (4 women). *Students:* 19 full-time (9 women), 12 part-time (7 women), 2 international. Average age 31. 20 applicants, 80% accepted, 11 enrolled. In 2011, 15 master's awarded. *Degree requirements:* For master's, comprehensive exam, thesis (for some programs). *Entrance requirements:* For master's, GRE General Test (MS, MNAS), minimum undergraduate GPA of 3.0 (MS, MNAS), 9-12 teacher certification (MS Ed). Additional exam requirements/recommendations for international students: Required—TOEFL (minimum score 550 paper-based; 213 computer-based; 79 iBT). *Application deadline:* For fall admission, 7/20 priority date for domestic students, 5/1 for international students; for spring admission, 12/20 priority date for domestic students, 9/1 for international students. Applications are processed on a rolling basis. Application fee: $35 ($50 for international students). Electronic applications accepted. *Expenses:* Tuition, state resident: full-time $4086; part-time $227 per credit hour. Tuition, nonresident: full-time $8172; part-time $454 per credit hour. *Required fees:* $275 per semester. Tuition and fees vary according to course load, campus/location and program. *Financial support:* In 2011–12, 3 research assistantships with full tuition reimbursements (averaging $8,000 per year), 9 teaching assistantships with full tuition reimbursements (averaging $8,000 per year) were awarded; career-related internships or fieldwork, Federal Work-Study, institutionally sponsored loans, scholarships/grants, and unspecified assistantships also available. Financial award application deadline: 3/31; financial award applicants required to submit FAFSA. *Faculty research:* Stratigraphy and ancient meteorite impacts, environmental geochemistry of karst, hyperspectral image processing, water quality, small town planning. *Unit head:* Dr. Thomas Plymate, Head, 417-836-5800, Fax: 417-836-6934, E-mail: tomplymate@missouristate.edu. *Application contact:* Misty Stewart, Coordinator of Graduate Recruitment, 417-836-6079, Fax: 417-836-6200, E-mail: mistystewart@missouristate.edu. Web site: http://geosciences.missouristate.edu/

Missouri University of Science and Technology, Graduate School, Department of Geological Sciences and Engineering, Rolla, MO 65409. Offers geological engineering (MS, DE, PhD); geology and geophysics (MS, PhD), including geochemistry, geology, geophysics, groundwater and environmental geology; petroleum engineering (MS, DE, PhD). Part-time programs available. *Degree requirements:* For master's, thesis optional; for doctorate, comprehensive exam, thesis/dissertation. *Entrance requirements:* For master's, GRE General Test (minimum score 600 quantitative, writing 3.5), minimum GPA of 3.0 in last 4 semesters; for doctorate, GRE General Test (minimum: Q 600, GRE WR 3.5). Additional exam requirements/recommendations for international students: Required—TOEFL. Electronic applications accepted. *Faculty research:* Digital image processing and geographic information systems, mineralogy, igneous and sedimentary petrology-geochemistry, sedimentology groundwater hydrology and contaminant transport.

Montana Tech of The University of Montana, Graduate School, Geosciences Programs, Butte, MT 59701-8997. Offers geochemistry (MS); geological engineering (MS); geology (MS); geophysical engineering (MS); hydrogeological engineering (MS); hydrogeology (MS). Part-time programs available. *Faculty:* 16 full-time (4 women), 4 part-time/adjunct (0 women). *Students:* 16 full-time (7 women), 12 part-time (6 women); includes 2 minority (1 Black or African American, non-Hispanic/Latino; 1 American Indian or Alaska Native, non-Hispanic/Latino), 1 international. 23 applicants, 65% accepted, 13 enrolled. In 2011, 9 master's awarded. *Degree requirements:* For master's, comprehensive exam (for some programs), thesis (for some programs). *Entrance requirements:* For master's, GRE General Test, minimum GPA of 3.0. Additional exam requirements/recommendations for international students: Required—TOEFL (minimum score 525 paper-based; 195 computer-based; 71 iBT). *Application deadline:* For fall admission, 4/1 priority date for domestic students, 3/1 for international students; for spring admission, 10/1 priority date for domestic students, 7/1 for international students. Applications are processed on a rolling basis. Application fee: $30. Electronic applications accepted. *Financial support:* In 2011–12, 15 students received support, including 10 teaching assistantships with partial tuition reimbursements available (averaging $5,000 per year); research assistantships with partial tuition reimbursements available, career-related internships or fieldwork, tuition waivers (full and partial), and unspecified assistantships also available. Financial award application deadline: 4/1; financial award applicants required to submit FAFSA. *Faculty research:* Water resource development, seismic processing, petroleum reservoir characterization, environmental geochemistry, geologic mapping. *Unit head:* Dr. Mary MacLaughlin, Department Head, 406-496-4655, Fax: 406-496-4260, E-mail: mmaclaughlin@mtech.edu. *Application contact:* Fred Sullivan, Administrator, Graduate School, 406-496-4304, Fax: 406-496-4710, E-mail: fsullivan@mtech.edu. Web site: http://www.mtech.edu/academics/gradschool/degreeprograms/degrees.htm.

New Mexico Institute of Mining and Technology, Graduate Studies, Department of Earth and Environmental Science, Program in Geology, Socorro,

Peterson's Graduate Programs in the Physical Sciences, Mathematics, Agricultural Sciences, the Environment & Natural Resources 2013

facebook.com/petersonspublishing **145**

Geology

NM 87801. Offers MS, PhD. *Students:* 29 full-time (13 women), 5 part-time (4 women); includes 5 minority (2 American Indian or Alaska Native, non-Hispanic/Latino; 2 Hispanic/Latino; 1 Two or more races, non-Hispanic/Latino), 2 international. Average age 28. In 2011, 2 master's, 4 doctorates awarded. *Degree requirements:* For master's, thesis optional; for doctorate, thesis/dissertation. *Entrance requirements:* For master's, GRE General Test; for doctorate, GRE General Test, GRE Subject Test. Additional exam requirements/recommendations for international students: Required—TOEFL (minimum score 540 paper-based; 207 computer-based). *Application deadline:* For fall admission, 3/1 priority date for domestic students; for spring admission, 6/1 for domestic students. Applications are processed on a rolling basis. Application fee: $16 ($30 for international students). Electronic applications accepted. *Expenses:* Tuition, state resident: full-time $4849; part-time $269.41 per credit hour. Tuition, nonresident: full-time $16,041; part-time $891.15 per credit hour. *Required fees:* $622; $65 per credit hour. $20 per semester. Part-time tuition and fees vary according to course load. *Financial support:* Federal Work-Study, institutionally sponsored loans, and unspecified assistantships available. Financial award application deadline: 3/1; financial award applicants required to submit CSS PROFILE or FAFSA. *Faculty research:* Care and karst topography, soil/water chemistry and properties, geochemistry of ore deposits. *Unit head:* Dr. Andrew Campbell, Coordinator, 575-835-5327, Fax: 575-835-6436, E-mail: campbell@nmt.edu. *Application contact:* Dr. Lorie Liebrock, Dean of Graduate Studies, 575-835-5513, Fax: 575-835-5476, E-mail: graduate@nmt.edu.

New Mexico State University, Graduate School, College of Arts and Sciences, Department of Geological Sciences, Las Cruces, NM 88003-8001. Offers MS. Part-time programs available. *Faculty:* 6 full-time (2 women). *Students:* 14 full-time (6 women), 9 part-time (2 women). Average age 27. 23 applicants, 96% accepted, 6 enrolled. In 2011, 7 master's awarded. *Degree requirements:* For master's, thesis. *Entrance requirements:* For master's, GRE General Test, BS in geology or the equivalent. Additional exam requirements/recommendations for international students: Required—TOEFL (minimum score 550 paper-based; 0 computer-based; 79 iBT), IELTS (minimum score 6.5). *Application deadline:* For fall admission, 7/1 priority date for domestic students, 7/1 for international students; for spring admission, 11/1 priority date for domestic students, 11/1 for international students. Applications are processed on a rolling basis. Application fee: $40 ($50 for international students). Electronic applications accepted. *Expenses:* Tuition, state resident: full-time $5004; part-time $208.50 per credit. Tuition, nonresident: full-time $17,446; part-time $726.90 per credit. *Financial support:* In 2011–12, 6 students received support, including 12 teaching assistantships with partial tuition reimbursements available (averaging $27,860 per year); research assistantships with full tuition reimbursements available, career-related internships or fieldwork, Federal Work-Study, institutionally sponsored loans, scholarships/grants, health care benefits, and unspecified assistantships also available. Support available to part-time students. Financial award application deadline: 2/15; financial award applicants required to submit FAFSA. *Faculty research:* Geochemistry, tectonics, sedimentology, stratigraphy, igneous petrology. *Total annual research expenditures:* $421,130. *Unit head:* Dr. Nancy J. McMillan, Head, 575-646-5000, Fax: 575-646-1056, E-mail: nmcmilla@nmsu.edu. *Application contact:* Dr. Nancy McMillan, Head, 575-646-5000, Fax: 575-646-1056, E-mail: nmcmilla@nmsu.edu. Web site: http://www.nmsu.edu/~geology/.

Northern Arizona University, Graduate College, College of Engineering, Forestry and Natural Sciences, School of Earth Sciences and Environmental Sustainability, Flagstaff, AZ 86011. Offers climate science and solutions (MS); earth science (MS); earth sciences and environmental sustainability (PhD); environmental sciences and policy (MS); geology (MS). *Faculty:* 27 full-time (9 women). *Students:* 67 full-time (32 women), 11 part-time (3 women); includes 6 minority (3 American Indian or Alaska Native, non-Hispanic/Latino; 3 Hispanic/Latino), 2 international. 149 applicants, 23% accepted, 30 enrolled. In 2011, 16 degrees awarded. *Degree requirements:* For master's, comprehensive exam (for some programs), thesis (for some programs). *Entrance requirements:* Additional exam requirements/recommendations for international students: Required—TOEFL (minimum score 550 paper-based; 213 computer-based; 80 iBT), IELTS (minimum score 7). *Application deadline:* For fall admission, 2/1 priority date for domestic students, 2/1 for international students. Applications are processed on a rolling basis. Application fee: $65. Electronic applications accepted. *Expenses:* Tuition, state resident: full-time $7190; part-time $355 per credit hour. Tuition, nonresident: full-time $18,092; part-time $1005 per credit hour. *Required fees:* $818; $328 per semester. *Financial support:* In 2011–12, 6 fellowships, 7 research assistantships with partial tuition reimbursements (averaging $12,866 per year), 28 teaching assistantships with partial tuition reimbursements (averaging $12,477 per year) were awarded; career-related internships or fieldwork, Federal Work-Study, scholarships/grants, health care benefits, tuition waivers (full and partial), and unspecified assistantships also available. Financial award applicants required to submit FAFSA. *Unit head:* Dr. Abe Springer, Director, 928-523-7198. *Application contact:* Mark Aasmundstad, Coordinator, 928-523-9333, Fax: 928-523-7432, E-mail: mark.aasmundstad@nau.edu. Web site: http://nau.edu/cefns/natsci/seses/.

Northern Illinois University, Graduate School, College of Liberal Arts and Sciences, Department of Geology and Environmental Geosciences, De Kalb, IL 60115-2854. Offers geology (MS, PhD). Part-time programs available. *Faculty:* 11 full-time (1 woman), 1 (woman) part-time/adjunct. *Students:* 19 full-time (6 women), 16 part-time (6 women), 5 international. 22 applicants, 59% accepted, 5 enrolled. In 2011, 4 master's, 2 doctorates awarded. Terminal

master's awarded for partial completion of doctoral program. *Degree requirements:* For master's, comprehensive exam, thesis optional, research seminar; for doctorate, thesis/dissertation, candidacy exam, dissertation defense, internship, research seminar. *Entrance requirements:* For master's, GRE General Test, bachelor's degree in engineering or science, minimum GPA of 2.75; for doctorate, GRE General Test, bachelor's or master's degree in engineering or science, minimum graduate GPA of 3.2. Additional exam requirements/recommendations for international students: Required—TOEFL (minimum score 550 paper-based; 213 computer-based). *Application deadline:* For fall admission, 6/1 for domestic students, 5/1 for international students; for spring admission, 11/1 for domestic students, 10/1 for international students. Applications are processed on a rolling basis. Application fee: $40. Electronic applications accepted. *Financial support:* In 2011–12, 5 research assistantships with full tuition reimbursements, 20 teaching assistantships with full tuition reimbursements were awarded; fellowships with full tuition reimbursements, career-related internships or fieldwork, Federal Work-Study, scholarships/grants, tuition waivers (full), and unspecified assistantships also available. Support available to part-time students. Financial award applicants required to submit FAFSA. *Faculty research:* Micropaleontology, environmental geochemistry, glacial geology, igneous petrology, statistical analyses of fracture networks. *Unit head:* Dr. Colin Booth, Chair, 815-753-0523, Fax: 815-753-1945, E-mail: cbooth@niu.edu. *Application contact:* Dr. Mark Fischer, Graduate Program Director, 815-753-7939, E-mail: mfischer@niu.edu. Web site: http://jove.geol.niu.edu/.

Northwestern University, The Graduate School, Judd A. and Marjorie Weinberg College of Arts and Sciences, Department of Geological Sciences, Evanston, IL 60208. Offers MS, PhD. Admissions and degrees offered through The Graduate School. Part-time programs available. *Degree requirements:* For doctorate, thesis/dissertation. *Entrance requirements:* For master's and doctorate, GRE General Test. Additional exam requirements/recommendations for international students: Required—TOEFL. Electronic applications accepted.

The Ohio State University, Graduate School, College of Arts and Sciences, Division of Natural and Mathematical Sciences, School of Earth Sciences, Columbus, OH 43210. Offers geodetic science (MS); geological sciences (MS, PhD). *Faculty:* 28. *Students:* 25 full-time (7 women), 18 part-time (10 women); includes 4 minority (3 Hispanic/Latino; 1 Two or more races, non-Hispanic/Latino), 2 international. Average age 28. In 2011, 8 master's, 2 doctorates awarded. *Degree requirements:* For master's, thesis; for doctorate, thesis/dissertation. *Entrance requirements:* For master's and doctorate, GRE. Additional exam requirements/recommendations for international students: Required—TOEFL (minimum score 600 paper-based; 250 computer-based), Michigan English Language Assessment Battery (minimum score 82). *Application deadline:* For fall admission, 8/15 priority date for domestic students, 7/1 for international students; for winter admission, 12/1 priority date for domestic students, 11/1 for international students; for spring admission, 3/1 priority date for domestic students, 2/1 for international students. Applications are processed on a rolling basis. Application fee: $40 ($50 for international students). Electronic applications accepted. *Expenses:* Tuition, state resident: full-time $11,400. Tuition, nonresident: full-time $28,125. Tuition and fees vary according to course load, degree level, campus/location and program. *Unit head:* W. Berry Lyons, Director, 614-688-3241, Fax: 614-292-7688, E-mail: lyons.142@osu.edu. *Application contact:* Graduate Admissions, 614-292-9444, Fax: 614-292-3895, E-mail: domestic.grad@osu.edu. Web site: http://www.earthsciences.osu.edu/.

Ohio University, Graduate College, College of Arts and Sciences, Department of Geological Sciences, Athens, OH 45701-2979. Offers environmental geochemistry (MS); environmental geology (MS); environmental/hydrology (MS); geology (MS); geology education (MS); geomorphology/surficial processes (MS); geophysics (MS); hydrogeology (MS); sedimentology (MS); structure/tectonics (MS). Part-time programs available. *Students:* 19 full-time (10 women). 14 applicants, 64% accepted, 9 enrolled. In 2011, 8 master's awarded. *Degree requirements:* For master's, thesis. *Entrance requirements:* Additional exam requirements/recommendations for international students: Required—TOEFL (minimum score 550 paper-based; 80 iBT) or IELTS (minimum score 6.5). *Application deadline:* For fall admission, 2/1 priority date for domestic students, 2/1 for international students. Application fee: $50 ($55 for international students). Electronic applications accepted. *Financial support:* Research assistantships with full tuition reimbursements, teaching assistantships with full tuition reimbursements, Federal Work-Study, institutionally sponsored loans, scholarships/grants, tuition waivers (partial), and unspecified assistantships available. Financial award application deadline: 2/1. *Faculty research:* Geoscience education, tectonics, fluvial geomorphology, invertebrate paleontology, mine/hydrology. *Total annual research expenditures:* $649,020. *Unit head:* Dr. Gregory Nadon, Chair, 740-593-4212, Fax: 740-593-0486, E-mail: nadon@ohio.edu. *Application contact:* Dr. Keith Milam, Graduate Chair, 740-593-1106, Fax: 740-593-0486, E-mail: milamk@ohio.edu. Web site: http://www.ohiou.edu/geology/.

Oklahoma State University, College of Arts and Sciences, School of Geology, Stillwater, OK 74078. Offers MS, PhD. *Faculty:* 11 full-time (2 women), 1 (woman) part-time/adjunct. *Students:* 37 full-time (8 women), 23 part-time (8 women); includes 7 minority (1 Black or African American, non-Hispanic/Latino; 1 American Indian or Alaska Native, non-Hispanic/Latino; 2 Hispanic/Latino; 3 Two or more races, non-Hispanic/Latino), 16 international. Average age 29. 79 applicants, 28% accepted, 10 enrolled. In 2011, 14 degrees awarded. *Degree requirements:* For master's, thesis; for doctorate, comprehensive exam, thesis/dissertation.

Entrance requirements: For master's, GRE; for doctorate, GRE. Additional exam requirements/recommendations for international students: Required—TOEFL (minimum score 550 paper-based; 79 iBT). *Application deadline:* For fall admission, 3/1 for international students; for spring admission, 8/1 for international students. Applications are processed on a rolling basis. Application fee: $40 ($75 for international students). Electronic applications accepted. *Expenses:* Tuition, state resident: full-time $4044; part-time $168.50 per credit hour. Tuition, nonresident: full-time $16,008; part-time $667 per credit hour. *Required fees:* $2122; $88.45 per credit hour. One-time fee: $50. Tuition and fees vary according to course load and campus/location. *Financial support:* In 2011–12, 10 research assistantships (averaging $12,272 per year), 21 teaching assistantships (averaging $8,070 per year) were awarded; career-related internships or fieldwork, Federal Work-Study, scholarships/grants, health care benefits, tuition waivers (partial), and unspecified assistantships also available. Support available to part-time students. Financial award application deadline: 3/1; financial award applicants required to submit FAFSA. *Faculty research:* Groundwater hydrology, petroleum geology. *Unit head:* Dr. Jay Gregg, Head, 405-744-6358, Fax: 405-744-7841. *Application contact:* Dr. Sheryl Tucker, Dean, 405-744-7099, Fax: 405-744-0355, E-mail: grad-i@okstate.edu. Web site: http://geology.okstate.edu.

Oregon State University, Graduate School, College of Science, Department of Geosciences, Program in Geology, Corvallis, OR 97331. Offers MA, MAIS, MS, PhD. Part-time programs available. Terminal master's awarded for partial completion of doctoral program. *Degree requirements:* For master's, variable foreign language requirement, thesis; for doctorate, one foreign language, thesis/dissertation. *Entrance requirements:* For master's and doctorate, GRE General Test, GRE Subject Test, minimum GPA of 3.0 in last 90 hours. Additional exam requirements/recommendations for international students: Required—TOEFL. *Faculty research:* Hydrogeology, geomorphology, ocean geology, geochemistry, earthquake geology.

Portland State University, Graduate Studies, College of Liberal Arts and Sciences, Department of Geology, Portland, OR 97207-0751. Offers environmental sciences and resources (PhD); geology (MA, MS); science/geology (MAT, MST). Part-time programs available. *Degree requirements:* For master's, comprehensive exam, thesis, field comprehensive; for doctorate, thesis/dissertation, 2 years of residency. *Entrance requirements:* For master's, GRE General Test, GRE Subject Test, BA/BS in geology, minimum GPA of 3.0 in upper-division course work or 2.75 overall. Additional exam requirements/recommendations for international students: Required—TOEFL (minimum score 550 paper-based; 213 computer-based). *Faculty research:* Sediment transport, volcanic environmental geology, coastal and fluvial processes.

Queens College of the City University of New York, Division of Graduate Studies, Mathematics and Natural Sciences Division, School of Earth and Environmental Sciences, Flushing, NY 11367-1597. Offers MA. Part-time and evening/weekend programs available. *Faculty:* 14 full-time (4 women). *Students:* 1 full-time (0 women), 19 part-time (9 women); includes 3 minority (1 Asian, non-Hispanic/Latino; 2 Hispanic/Latino), 1 international. 13 applicants, 38% accepted, 3 enrolled. In 2011, 3 master's awarded. *Degree requirements:* For master's, comprehensive exam, thesis. *Entrance requirements:* For master's, GRE, previous course work in calculus, physics, and chemistry; minimum GPA of 3.0. Additional exam requirements/recommendations for international students: Required—TOEFL. *Application deadline:* For fall admission, 4/1 for domestic students; for spring admission, 11/1 for domestic students. Applications are processed on a rolling basis. Application fee: $125. *Expenses:* Tuition, state resident: part-time $345 per credit. Tuition, nonresident: part-time $640 per credit. *Required fees:* $145.25 per semester. *Financial support:* Career-related internships or fieldwork, Federal Work-Study, institutionally sponsored loans, tuition waivers (partial), and unspecified assistantships available. Support available to part-time students. Financial award application deadline: 4/1; financial award applicants required to submit FAFSA. *Faculty research:* Sedimentology/stratigraphy, paleontology, field petrology. *Unit head:* Dr. Yan Zheng, Chairperson, 718-997-3300. *Application contact:* Dr. Hannes Brueckner, Graduate Adviser, 718-997-3300, E-mail: hannes_brueckner@qc.edu.

Queen's University at Kingston, School of Graduate Studies and Research, Faculty of Arts and Sciences, Department of Geological Sciences and Geological Engineering, Kingston, ON K7L 3N6, Canada. Offers M Sc, M Sc Eng, PhD. Part-time programs available. *Degree requirements:* For master's, thesis (for some programs); for doctorate, comprehensive exam, thesis/dissertation. *Entrance requirements:* Additional exam requirements/recommendations for international students: Required—TOEFL. *Faculty research:* Geochemistry, sedimentology, geophysics, economic geology, structural geology.

Rensselaer Polytechnic Institute, Graduate School, School of Science, Program in Geology, Troy, NY 12180-3590. Offers MS, PhD. Part-time programs available. Terminal master's awarded for partial completion of doctoral program. *Degree requirements:* For master's, comprehensive exam, thesis (for some programs); for doctorate, comprehensive exam, thesis/dissertation. *Entrance requirements:* For master's and doctorate, GRE General Test. Additional exam requirements/recommendations for international students: Required—TOEFL. Electronic applications accepted. *Faculty research:* Geochemistry, petrology, geophysics, environmental geochemistry, planetary geology.

Rutgers, The State University of New Jersey, Newark, Graduate School, Program in Environmental Geology, Newark, NJ 07102. Offers MS. Part-time and evening/weekend programs available. *Degree requirements:* For master's,

comprehensive exam, thesis optional. *Entrance requirements:* For master's, GRE General Test, minimum B average. Electronic applications accepted. *Faculty research:* Environmental geology, plate tectonics, geoarchaeology, geophysics, mineralogy-petrology.

Rutgers, The State University of New Jersey, New Brunswick, Graduate School-New Brunswick, Department of Earth and Planetary Sciences, Piscataway, NJ 08854-8097. Offers geological sciences (MS, PhD). Part-time programs available. *Degree requirements:* For master's, thesis; for doctorate, comprehensive exam, thesis/dissertation. *Entrance requirements:* For master's and doctorate, GRE General Test, GRE Subject Test (recommended). Electronic applications accepted. *Faculty research:* Basin analysis, volcanology, quaternary studies, engineering geophysics, marine geology, biogeochemistry and paleoceanography.

St. Francis Xavier University, Graduate Studies, Department of Earth Sciences, Antigonish, NS B2G 2W5, Canada. Offers M Sc. *Degree requirements:* For master's, thesis. *Entrance requirements:* Additional exam requirements/recommendations for international students: Required—TOEFL (minimum score 580 paper-based; 236 computer-based). *Faculty research:* Environmental earth sciences, global change tectonics, paleoclimatology, crustal fluids.

San Diego State University, Graduate and Research Affairs, College of Sciences, Department of Geological Sciences, San Diego, CA 92182. Offers MS. Part-time programs available. *Degree requirements:* For master's, thesis. *Entrance requirements:* For master's, GRE General Test, bachelor's degree in related field, 2 letters of reference. Additional exam requirements/recommendations for international students: Required—TOEFL. Electronic applications accepted. *Faculty research:* Earthquakes, hydrology, meteorological analysis and tomography studies.

San Jose State University, Graduate Studies and Research, College of Science, Department of Geology, San Jose, CA 95192-0001. Offers MS. *Degree requirements:* For master's, thesis. *Entrance requirements:* For master's, GRE. Electronic applications accepted.

South Dakota School of Mines and Technology, Graduate Division, Department of Geology and Geological Engineering, Rapid City, SD 57701-3995. Offers geology and geological engineering (MS, PhD); paleontology (MS). Part-time programs available. *Degree requirements:* For master's, thesis; for doctorate, thesis/dissertation. *Entrance requirements:* For master's and doctorate, GRE General Test, GRE Subject Test. Additional exam requirements/recommendations for international students: Required—TOEFL, TWE. Electronic applications accepted. *Faculty research:* Contaminants in soil, nitrate leaching, environmental changes, fracture formations, greenhouse effect.

Southern Illinois University Carbondale, Graduate School, College of Science, Department of Geology, Carbondale, IL 62901-4701. Offers environmental resources and policy (PhD); geology (MS, PhD). *Faculty:* 12 full-time (0 women). *Students:* 22 full-time (10 women), 43 part-time (9 women); includes 6 minority (3 Black or African American, non-Hispanic/Latino; 2 American Indian or Alaska Native, non-Hispanic/Latino; 1 Hispanic/Latino), 11 international. Average age 25. 46 applicants, 37% accepted, 16 enrolled. In 2011, 11 master's, 4 doctorates awarded. *Degree requirements:* For master's, thesis; for doctorate, one foreign language, thesis/dissertation. *Entrance requirements:* For master's, GRE, minimum GPA of 2.7; for doctorate, GRE General Test, minimum GPA of 3.25. Additional exam requirements/recommendations for international students: Required—TOEFL. *Application deadline:* For fall admission, 2/15 priority date for domestic students. Applications are processed on a rolling basis. Application fee: $20. *Financial support:* In 2011–12, 17 students received support. Fellowships with full tuition reimbursements available, research assistantships with full tuition reimbursements available, teaching assistantships with full tuition reimbursements available, Federal Work-Study, institutionally sponsored loans, and tuition waivers (full) available. Support available to part-time students. *Total annual research expenditures:* $720,000. *Unit head:* Dr. Steven Esling, Chair, 618-453-3351, Fax: 618-453-7393, E-mail: esling@geo.siu.edu. *Application contact:* Sharon Simons, Office Specialist, 618-453-3351, E-mail: simons@geo.siu.edu.

Southern Methodist University, Dedman College, Department of Earth Sciences, Program in Geology, Dallas, TX 75275. Offers MS, PhD. Part-time programs available. *Degree requirements:* For master's, thesis, qualifying exam; for doctorate, thesis/dissertation, qualifying exam. *Entrance requirements:* For master's and doctorate, GRE General Test, minimum GPA of 3.0, letters of recommendation. Additional exam requirements/recommendations for international students: Required—TOEFL. *Faculty research:* Geothermal, paleontology, environmental, stable isotope geochemistry.

State University of New York at Binghamton, Graduate School, School of Arts and Sciences, Department of Geological Sciences, Binghamton, NY 13902-6000. Offers MA, PhD. Part-time programs available. *Faculty:* 12 full-time (1 woman). *Students:* 11 full-time (3 women), 19 part-time (9 women); includes 2 minority (1 Hispanic/Latino; 1 Native Hawaiian or other Pacific Islander, non-Hispanic/Latino), 3 international. Average age 31. 21 applicants, 52% accepted, 5 enrolled. In 2011, 1 master's, 1 doctorate awarded. Terminal master's awarded for partial completion of doctoral program. *Degree requirements:* For master's, thesis or alternative; for doctorate, variable foreign language requirement, thesis/dissertation, departmental qualifying exam. *Entrance requirements:* For master's and doctorate, GRE General Test, GRE Subject Test. Additional exam

Peterson's Graduate Programs in the Physical Sciences, Mathematics, Agricultural Sciences, the Environment & Natural Resources 2013

facebook.com/petersonspublishing **147**

Geology

requirements/recommendations for international students: Required—TOEFL (minimum score 550 paper-based; 213 computer-based; 80 iBT). *Application deadline:* For fall admission, 2/15 priority date for domestic students, 2/15 for international students; for spring admission, 9/15 priority date for domestic students, 9/15 for international students. Applications are processed on a rolling basis. Application fee: $60. Electronic applications accepted. *Financial support:* In 2011–12, 16 students received support, including 2 fellowships with full tuition reimbursements available (averaging $15,000 per year), 3 research assistantships with full tuition reimbursements available (averaging $10,000 per year), 9 teaching assistantships with full tuition reimbursements available (averaging $15,500 per year); career-related internships or fieldwork, Federal Work-Study, institutionally sponsored loans, scholarships/grants, health care benefits, tuition waivers (full and partial), and unspecified assistantships also available. Financial award application deadline: 2/15; financial award applicants required to submit FAFSA. *Unit head:* Dr. Robert Demicco, Chairperson, 607-777-2604, E-mail: demicco@binghamton.edu. *Application contact:* Catherine Smith, Recruiting and Admissions Coordinator, 607-777-2151, Fax: 607-777-2501, E-mail: cmsmith@binghamton.edu.

Stephen F. Austin State University, Graduate School, College of Sciences and Mathematics, Department of Geology, Nacogdoches, TX 75962. Offers MS, MSNS. *Degree requirements:* For master's, comprehensive exam. *Entrance requirements:* For master's, GRE General Test, minimum GPA of 2.8 in last 60 hours, 2.5 overall. Additional exam requirements/recommendations for international students: Required—TOEFL. *Faculty research:* Stratigraphy of Kaibab limestone, Utah; structure of Ouachita Mountains, Arkansas; groundwater chemistry of Carrizo Sand, Texas.

Sul Ross State University, School of Arts and Sciences, Department of Earth and Physical Sciences, Alpine, TX 79832. Offers MS. Part-time programs available. *Degree requirements:* For master's, thesis optional. *Entrance requirements:* For master's, GRE General Test, minimum GPA of 2.5 in last 60 hours of undergraduate work.

Syracuse University, College of Arts and Sciences, Program in Earth Sciences, Syracuse, NY 13244. Offers MA, MS, PhD. Part-time programs available. *Students:* 22 full-time (9 women), 7 part-time (4 women); includes 1 minority (Asian, non-Hispanic/Latino), 6 international. Average age 28. 48 applicants, 31% accepted, 9 enrolled. In 2011, 2 master's, 4 doctorates awarded. *Degree requirements:* For master's, thesis (for some programs), research tool; for doctorate, thesis/dissertation, 2 research tools. *Entrance requirements:* For master's and doctorate, GRE General Test, GRE Subject Test. Additional exam requirements/recommendations for international students: Required—TOEFL (minimum score 100 iBT). *Application deadline:* For fall admission, 1/15 priority date for domestic students, 1/15 for international students. Application fee: $75. Electronic applications accepted. *Expenses: Tuition:* Part-time $1206 per credit. *Financial support:* Fellowships with full tuition reimbursements, research assistantships with full tuition reimbursements, teaching assistantships with full and partial tuition reimbursements, and tuition waivers (partial) available. Financial award application deadline: 1/1; financial award applicants required to submit FAFSA. *Unit head:* Dr. Jeff Karson, Chair, 315-443-7976, Fax: 315-443-3363, E-mail: jakarson@syr.edu. *Application contact:* Jolene Fitch, Information Contact, 315-443-2672, E-mail: jofitch@syr.edu.

Temple University, College of Science and Technology, Department of Earth and Environmental Science, Philadelphia, PA 19122-6096. Offers MS. *Faculty:* 8 full-time (2 women). *Students:* 11 full-time (2 women); includes 1 minority (Black or African American, non-Hispanic/Latino). Average age 26. 4 applicants, 100% accepted, 4 enrolled. In 2011, 9 master's awarded. *Degree requirements:* For master's, thesis, qualifying exam. *Entrance requirements:* For master's, GRE General Test, minimum GPA of 3.0. Additional exam requirements/recommendations for international students: Required—TOEFL (minimum score 550 paper-based; 213 computer-based; 79 iBT). *Application deadline:* For fall admission, 2/1 for domestic students, 12/15 for international students; for spring admission, 10/1 for domestic students, 8/1 for international students. Application fee: $50. Electronic applications accepted. *Expenses:* Tuition, state resident: full-time $12,366; part-time $687 per credit hour. Tuition, nonresident: full-time $17,298; part-time $961 per credit hour. *Required fees:* $590; $213 per year. *Financial support:* Fellowships, research assistantships with full tuition reimbursements, teaching assistantships with full tuition reimbursements, and scholarships/grants available. Financial award application deadline: 1/15; financial award applicants required to submit FAFSA. *Faculty research:* Hydraulic modeling, environmental geochemistry and geophysics, paleosas, cyclic stratigraphy, materials research. *Unit head:* Dr. David Grandstaff, Chair, 215-204-8227, Fax: 215-204-3496, E-mail: ees@temple.edu. *Application contact:* Tara Schumacher, Coordinator of Outreach, 215-204-6575, Fax: 215-204-8781, E-mail: tara.schumacher@temple.edu. Web site: https://ees.cst.temple.edu/.

Texas A&M University, College of Geosciences, Department of Geology and Geophysics, College Station, TX 77843. Offers geology (MS, PhD); geophysics (MS, PhD). *Faculty:* 31. *Students:* 108 full-time (43 women), 18 part-time (9 women); includes 12 minority (2 Black or African American, non-Hispanic/Latino; 4 Asian, non-Hispanic/Latino; 5 Hispanic/Latino; 1 Two or more races, non-Hispanic/Latino), 46 international. Average age 31. In 2011, 16 master's, 4 doctorates awarded. *Degree requirements:* For master's, thesis; for doctorate, thesis/dissertation. *Entrance requirements:* For master's and doctorate, GRE General Test. Additional exam requirements/recommendations for international students: Required—TOEFL. *Application deadline:* For fall admission, 3/1 priority

date for domestic students, 1/15 for international students; for spring admission, 10/1 priority date for domestic students, 8/15 for international students. Applications are processed on a rolling basis. Application fee: $50 ($75 for international students). Electronic applications accepted. *Expenses:* Tuition, state resident: full-time $5437; part-time $226.55 per credit hour. Tuition, nonresident: full-time $12,949; part-time $539.55 per credit hour. *Required fees:* $2741. *Financial support:* In 2011–12, fellowships with partial tuition reimbursements (averaging $1,000 per year), research assistantships with partial tuition reimbursements (averaging $11,925 per year), teaching assistantships with partial tuition reimbursements (averaging $11,925 per year) were awarded; Federal Work-Study, institutionally sponsored loans, scholarships/grants, tuition waivers (partial), and unspecified assistantships also available. Financial award application deadline: 3/1; financial award applicants required to submit FAFSA. *Faculty research:* Environmental and engineering geology and geophysics, petroleum geology, tectonophysics, geochemistry. *Unit head:* Dr. Rick Giardino, Head, 979-845-3224, E-mail: giardino@geo.tamu.edu. *Application contact:* Graduate Admissions, 979-845-1044, E-mail: admissions@tamu.edu. Web site: http://geoweb.tamu.edu.

Texas A&M University–Kingsville, College of Graduate Studies, College of Arts and Sciences, Department of Geosciences, Kingsville, TX 78363. Offers applied geology (MS). Part-time and evening/weekend programs available. *Degree requirements:* For master's, comprehensive exam, thesis. *Entrance requirements:* For master's, GRE General Test, minimum GPA of 3.0. Additional exam requirements/recommendations for international students: Required—TOEFL. *Faculty research:* Stratigraphy and sedimentology of modern coastal sediments, sandstone diagnosis, vertebrate paleontology, structural geology.

Texas Christian University, College of Science and Engineering, School of Geology, Energy and the Environment, Fort Worth, TX 76129-0002. Offers environmental management (MEM); environmental science (MA, MS); geology (MS). Part-time programs available. *Faculty:* 6 full-time (1 woman), 1 part-time/adjunct. *Students:* 9 full-time (3 women), 30 part-time (15 women); includes 3 minority (all Hispanic/Latino), 1 international. Average age 27. 24 applicants, 88% accepted, 12 enrolled. In 2011, 15 master's awarded. *Degree requirements:* For master's, comprehensive exam (for some programs), thesis (for some programs). *Entrance requirements:* For master's, GRE. Additional exam requirements/recommendations for international students: Required—TOEFL (minimum score 550 paper-based; 213 computer-based; 80 iBT). *Application deadline:* For fall admission, 2/28 priority date for domestic students, 2/28 for international students. Application fee: $60. *Expenses: Tuition:* Full-time $20,250; part-time $1125 per credit hour. Part-time tuition and fees vary according to course load and program. *Financial support:* In 2011–12, 15 teaching assistantships with full tuition reimbursements (averaging $15,000 per year) were awarded. Financial award application deadline: 2/28. *Unit head:* Dr. Phil Hartman, Dean, 817-257-7727, E-mail: p.hartman@tcu.edu. *Application contact:* Dr. Magnus Rittby, Associate Dean for Administration and Graduate Programs, 817-257-7729, Fax: 817-257-7736, E-mail: m.rittby@tcu.edu.

Université du Québec à Montréal, Graduate Programs, Prógram in Earth Sciences, Montreal, QC H3C 3P8, Canada. Offers earth sciences (M Sc); mineral resources (PhD); non-renewable resources (DESS). Part-time programs available. Terminal master's awarded for partial completion of doctoral program. *Degree requirements:* For master's, thesis (for some programs); for doctorate, thesis/dissertation. *Entrance requirements:* For master's, appropriate bachelor's degree or equivalent, proficiency in French. *Faculty research:* Economic geology, structural geology, geochemistry, Quaternary geology, isotopic geochemistry.

Université Laval, Faculty of Sciences and Engineering, Department of Geology and Geological Engineering, Québec, QC G1K 7P4, Canada. Offers earth sciences (M Sc, PhD), including earth sciences, environmental technologies (M Sc); geology (M Sc, PhD). Terminal master's awarded for partial completion of doctoral program. *Degree requirements:* For master's, thesis (for some programs); for doctorate, comprehensive exam, thesis/dissertation. *Entrance requirements:* For master's and doctorate, knowledge of French. Electronic applications accepted. *Faculty research:* Engineering, economics, regional geology.

University at Albany, State University of New York, College of Arts and Sciences, Department of Earth and Atmospheric Sciences, Albany, NY 12222-0001. Offers atmospheric science (MS, PhD); geology (MS, PhD). *Degree requirements:* For master's, one foreign language, comprehensive exam, thesis; for doctorate, 2 foreign languages, comprehensive exam, thesis/dissertation, oral exams. *Entrance requirements:* For master's and doctorate, GRE General Test. Additional exam requirements/recommendations for international students: Required—TOEFL (minimum score 550 paper-based; 213 computer-based). Electronic applications accepted. *Faculty research:* Environmental geochemistry, tectonics, mesoscale meteorology, atmospheric chemistry.

University at Buffalo, the State University of New York, Graduate School, College of Arts and Sciences, Department of Geology, Buffalo, NY 14260. Offers MA, MS, PhD. Part-time programs available. *Faculty:* 14 full-time (6 women), 1 part-time/adjunct (0 women). *Students:* 60 full-time (23 women); includes 3 minority (1 American Indian or Alaska Native, non-Hispanic/Latino; 2 Hispanic/Latino), 12 international. Average age 26. 63 applicants, 57% accepted, 24 enrolled. In 2011, 8 degrees awarded. *Degree requirements:* For master's, project or thesis; for doctorate, thesis/dissertation, dissertation defense. *Entrance requirements:* For master's and doctorate, GRE General Test. Additional exam requirements/recommendations for international students: Required—TOEFL (minimum score 550 paper-based; 213 computer-based; 79 iBT). *Application deadline:* For fall admission, 2/1 priority date for domestic students, 2/1 for international students; for spring admission, 10/1 priority date for domestic students, 10/1 for international students. Applications are processed on a rolling basis. Application fee: $75. Electronic applications accepted. *Financial support:* In 2011–12, 31 students received support, including 7 fellowships with full tuition reimbursements available (averaging $6,000 per year), 16 research assistantships with full tuition reimbursements available (averaging $15,500 per year), 15 teaching assistantships with full tuition reimbursements available (averaging $15,500 per year); Federal Work-Study, scholarships/grants, health care benefits, and unspecified assistantships also available. Financial award application deadline: 2/1; financial award applicants required to submit FAFSA. *Faculty research:* Environmental geology, hydrogeology, geochemistry, fractured rocks, volcanology. *Total annual research expenditures:* $2.1 million. *Unit head:* Dr. Richelle M. Allen-King, Professor and Chair, 716-645-3489, Fax: 716-645-3999, E-mail: geology@buffalo.edu. *Application contact:* Dr. Eliza Calder, Director of Graduate Studies, 716-645-4329, Fax: 716-645-3999, E-mail: ecalder@buffalo.edu. Web site: http://www.geology.buffalo.edu/.

The University of Akron, Graduate School, Buchtel College of Arts and Sciences, Department of Geology and Environmental Science, Akron, OH 44325. Offers earth science (MS); environmental geology (MS); geographic information science (MS); geology (MS); geophysics (MS). Part-time programs available. *Faculty:* 16 full-time (5 women), 5 part-time/adjunct (2 women). *Students:* 19 full-time (9 women), 1 part-time (0 women). Average age 29. 24 applicants, 79% accepted, 7 enrolled. In 2011, 6 master's awarded. *Degree requirements:* For master's, comprehensive exam, thesis, seminar, proficiency exam. *Entrance requirements:* For master's, minimum GPA of 2.75, three letters of recommendation, statement of purpose. Additional exam requirements/recommendations for international students: Required—TOEFL (minimum score 550 paper-based; 213 computer-based; 79 iBT). *Application deadline:* Applications are processed on a rolling basis. Application fee: $30 ($40 for international students). Electronic applications accepted. *Expenses:* Tuition, state resident: full-time $7038; part-time $391 per credit hour. Tuition, nonresident: full-time $12,051; part-time $670 per credit hour. *Required fees:* $1274; $34 per credit hour. *Financial support:* In 2011–12, 1 research assistantship with full tuition reimbursement, 13 teaching assistantships with full tuition reimbursements were awarded. *Faculty research:* Terrestrial environmental change, Karst hydrogeology, lacustrine paleoenvironments, environmental magnetism and geophysics. *Total annual research expenditures:* $172,387. *Unit head:* Dr. John Szabo, Chair, 330-972-8039, E-mail: jszabo@uakron.edu. *Application contact:* Dr. LaVerne Friberg, Director of Graduate Studies, 330-972-8046, E-mail: lfribe1@uakron.edu. Web site: http://www.uakron.edu/geology/.

The University of Alabama, Graduate School, College of Arts and Sciences, Department of Geological Sciences, Tuscaloosa, AL 35487. Offers MS, PhD. *Faculty:* 14 full-time (5 women). *Students:* 41 full-time (13 women), 14 part-time (3 women); includes 3 minority (1 Black or African American, non-Hispanic/Latino; 1 Asian, non-Hispanic/Latino; 1 Two or more races, non-Hispanic/Latino), 16 international. Average age 29. 38 applicants, 66% accepted, 14 enrolled. In 2011, 6 master's, 3 doctorates awarded. Terminal master's awarded for partial completion of doctoral program. *Degree requirements:* For master's, comprehensive exam, thesis; for doctorate, comprehensive exam, thesis/dissertation. *Entrance requirements:* For master's and doctorate, GRE. Additional exam requirements/recommendations for international students: Required—TOEFL (minimum score 550 paper-based; 213 computer-based; 79 iBT). *Application deadline:* For fall admission, 3/1 priority date for domestic students, 3/1 for international students; for spring admission, 10/1 priority date for domestic students, 10/1 for international students. Applications are processed on a rolling basis. Application fee: $50 ($60 for international students). Electronic applications accepted. *Expenses:* Tuition, state resident: full-time $8600. Tuition, nonresident: full-time $21,900. *Financial support:* In 2011–12, 11 research assistantships with full tuition reimbursements (averaging $13,595 per year), 29 teaching assistantships with full tuition reimbursements (averaging $13,365 per year) were awarded; career-related internships or fieldwork, Federal Work-Study, and institutionally sponsored loans also available. *Faculty research:* Structure, petrology, stratigraphy, geochemistry, hydrogeology, geophysics. *Total annual research expenditures:* $1.1 million. *Unit head:* Dr. Harold H. Stowell, Chairperson and Professor, 205-348-5095, E-mail: hstowell@wgs.geo.ua.edu. *Application contact:* Dr. Andrew Mark Goodliffe, Graduate Program Director, 205-348-7167, E-mail: amg@ua.edu. Web site: http://www.geo.ua.edu/.

University of Alaska Fairbanks, College of Natural Sciences and Mathematics, Department of Geology and Geophysics, Fairbanks, AK 99775-5780. Offers geology (MS, PhD), including economic geology (PhD), petroleum geology (MS), quaternary geology (PhD), remote sensing, volcanology (PhD); geophysics (MS, PhD), including remote sensing, snow, ice, and permafrost geophysics (MS), solid-earth geophysics (MS). Part-time programs available. *Faculty:* 12 full-time (5 women). *Students:* 60 full-time (27 women), 12 part-time (5 women); includes 5 minority (1 Hispanic/Latino; 4 Two or more races, non-Hispanic/Latino), 23 international. Average age 29. 89 applicants, 18% accepted, 15 enrolled. In 2011, 7 master's, 2 doctorates awarded. Terminal master's awarded for partial completion of doctoral program. *Degree requirements:* For master's, comprehensive exam, thesis, oral exam, oral defense; for doctorate, comprehensive exam, thesis/dissertation, oral exam, oral defense. *Entrance requirements:* For master's and doctorate, GRE General Test. Additional exam

requirements/recommendations for international students: Required—TOEFL (minimum score 550 paper-based; 213 computer-based; 79 iBT). *Application deadline:* For fall admission, 6/1 for domestic students, 3/1 for international students; for spring admission, 10/15 for domestic students, 9/1 for international students. Applications are processed on a rolling basis. Application fee: $60. Electronic applications accepted. *Expenses:* Tuition, state resident: full-time $6696; part-time $372 per credit. Tuition, nonresident: full-time $13,680; part-time $760 per credit. Tuition and fees vary according to course load and reciprocity agreements. *Financial support:* In 2011–12, 42 research assistantships with tuition reimbursements (averaging $14,177 per year), 7 teaching assistantships with tuition reimbursements (averaging $9,807 per year) were awarded; fellowships with tuition reimbursements, Federal Work-Study, scholarships/grants, health care benefits, and unspecified assistantships also available. Support available to part-time students. Financial award application deadline: 2/15; financial award applicants required to submit FAFSA. *Faculty research:* Glacial surging, volcanology, geochronology, impact cratering, permafrost geophysics. *Total annual research expenditures:* $23,000. *Unit head:* Dr. Benard Coakley, Department Chair, 907-474-7565, Fax: 907-474-5163, E-mail: geology@uaf.edu. *Application contact:* Mike Earnest, Director of Admissions, 907-474-7500, Fax: 907-474-5379, E-mail: admissions@uaf.edu. Web site: http://www.uaf.edu/geology/.

University of Arkansas, Graduate School, J. William Fulbright College of Arts and Sciences, Department of Geosciences, Program in Geology, Fayetteville, AR 72701-1201. Offers MS. Part-time programs available. *Students:* 17 full-time (3 women), 8 part-time (5 women); includes 3 minority (1 Black or African American, non-Hispanic/Latino; 1 Hispanic/Latino; 1 Two or more races, non-Hispanic/Latino), 1 international. In 2011, 7 master's awarded. *Degree requirements:* For master's, thesis. *Application deadline:* For fall admission, 4/1 for international students; for spring admission, 10/1 for international students. Applications are processed on a rolling basis. Application fee: $40 ($50 for international students). Electronic applications accepted. *Financial support:* In 2011–12, 1 research assistantship, 10 teaching assistantships were awarded; fellowships, career-related internships or fieldwork, and Federal Work-Study also available. Support available to part-time students. Financial award application deadline: 4/1; financial award applicants required to submit FAFSA. *Unit head:* Dr. Ralph Davis, Graduate Coordinator, 479-575-3355, Fax: 479-575-3469, E-mail: ralphd@uark.edu. *Application contact:* Dr. Doy Zachry, Graduate Admissions, 479-575-2785, E-mail: dzachry@uark.edu. Web site: http://geosciences.uark.edu/.

The University of British Columbia, Faculty of Science, Department of Earth and Ocean Sciences, Vancouver, BC V6T 1Z4, Canada. Offers atmospheric science (M Sc, PhD); geological engineering (M Eng, MA Sc, PhD); geological sciences (M Sc, PhD); geophysics (M Sc, MA Sc, PhD); oceanography (M Sc, PhD). *Degree requirements:* For master's, thesis (for some programs); for doctorate, comprehensive exam, thesis/dissertation. *Entrance requirements:* Additional exam requirements/recommendations for international students: Required—TOEFL (minimum score 600 paper-based; 250 computer-based; 100 iBT). Electronic applications accepted. *Faculty research:* Oceans and atmosphere, environmental earth science, hydro geology, mineral deposits, geophysics.

University of Calgary, Faculty of Graduate Studies, Faculty of Science, Department of Geology and Geophysics, Calgary, AB T2N 1N4, Canada. Offers geology (M Sc, PhD); geophysics (M Sc, PhD). Part-time programs available. Terminal master's awarded for partial completion of doctoral program. *Degree requirements:* For master's, thesis; for doctorate, thesis/dissertation, candidacy exam. *Entrance requirements:* For master's, B Sc; for doctorate, honors B Sc or M Sc. Additional exam requirements/recommendations for international students: Required—TOEFL. Electronic applications accepted. *Faculty research:* Geochemistry, petrology, paleontology, stratigraphy, exploration and solid-earth geophysics.

University of California, Berkeley, Graduate Division, College of Letters and Science, Department of Earth and Planetary Science, Berkeley, CA 94720-1500. Offers geology (MA, MS, PhD); geophysics (MA, MS, PhD). Terminal master's awarded for partial completion of doctoral program. *Degree requirements:* For master's, oral exam (MA), thesis (MS); for doctorate, comprehensive exam, thesis/dissertation, candidacy exams. *Entrance requirements:* For master's and doctorate, GRE General Test, minimum GPA of 3.0, 3 letters of recommendation. Additional exam requirements/recommendations for international students: Required—TOEFL. *Faculty research:* Tectonics, environmental geology, high-pressure geophysics and seismology, economic geology, geochemistry.

University of California, Davis, Graduate Studies, Program in Geology, Davis, CA 95616. Offers MS, PhD. Terminal master's awarded for partial completion of doctoral program. *Degree requirements:* For master's, thesis; for doctorate, thesis/dissertation. *Entrance requirements:* For master's and doctorate, GRE General Test, GRE Subject Test, minimum GPA of 3.0. Additional exam requirements/recommendations for international students: Required—TOEFL (minimum score 550 paper-based; 213 computer-based). Electronic applications accepted. *Faculty research:* Petrology, paleontology, geophysics, sedimentology, structure/tectonics.

University of California, Los Angeles, Graduate Division, College of Letters and Science, Department of Earth and Space Sciences, Program in Geology, Los Angeles, CA 90095. Offers MS, PhD. *Students:* 22 full-time (10 women); includes 6 minority (1 Black or African American, non-Hispanic/Latino; 3 Asian, non-

Peterson's Graduate Programs in the Physical Sciences, Mathematics, Agricultural Sciences, the Environment & Natural Resources 2013

facebook.com/petersonspublishing **149**

Hispanic/Latino; 1 Hispanic/Latino; 1 Two or more races, non-Hispanic/Latino), 2 international. Average age 28. 38 applicants, 47% accepted, 8 enrolled. In 2011, 1 master's, 1 doctorate awarded. Terminal master's awarded for partial completion of doctoral program. *Degree requirements:* For master's, comprehensive exams or thesis; for doctorate, thesis/dissertation, oral and written qualifying exams. *Entrance requirements:* For master's, GRE General Test, minimum GPA of 3.0, bachelor's degree in related field; for doctorate, GRE General Test, minimum undergraduate GPA of 3.0, bachelor's degree in related field. *Application deadline:* For fall admission, 1/15 for domestic and international students. Application fee: $70 ($90 for international students). Electronic applications accepted. *Financial support:* In 2011–12, 17 fellowships with full and partial tuition reimbursements, 12 research assistantships with full and partial tuition reimbursements, 15 teaching assistantships with full and partial tuition reimbursements were awarded; Federal Work-Study, institutionally sponsored loans, scholarships/grants, health care benefits, tuition waivers (full and partial), and unspecified assistantships also available. Financial award application deadline: 3/1; financial award applicants required to submit FAFSA. *Unit head:* Dr. Craig E. Manning, Chair, 310-206-3290, E-mail: manning@ess.ucla.edu. *Application contact:* Department Office, 310-825-3917, E-mail: holbrook@ess.ucla.edu. Web site: http://www.ess.ucla.edu.

University of California, Riverside, Graduate Division, Department of Earth Sciences, Riverside, CA 92521-0102. Offers geological sciences (MS, PhD). *Faculty:* 34 full-time (15 women). *Students:* 31 full-time (10 women); includes 2 minority (both Hispanic/Latino), 2 international. Average age 30. In 2011, 2 doctorates awarded. Terminal master's awarded for partial completion of doctoral program. *Degree requirements:* For master's, thesis, final oral exam; for doctorate, thesis/dissertation, qualifying exams, final oral exam. *Entrance requirements:* For master's and doctorate, GRE General Test, minimum GPA of 3.2. Additional exam requirements/recommendations for international students: Required—TOEFL (minimum score 550 paper-based; 213 computer-based; 80 iBT). *Application deadline:* For fall admission, 5/1 for domestic students, 2/1 for international students; for winter admission, 9/1 for domestic students, 7/1 for international students; for spring admission, 12/1 for domestic students, 10/1 for international students. Applications are processed on a rolling basis. Application fee: $80 ($100 for international students). Electronic applications accepted. *Financial support:* In 2011–12, fellowships with full and partial tuition reimbursements (averaging $12,000 per year), research assistantships with full and partial tuition reimbursements (averaging $16,000 per year), teaching assistantships with full and partial tuition reimbursements (averaging $16,500 per year) were awarded; career-related internships or fieldwork, Federal Work-Study, institutionally sponsored loans, health care benefits, tuition waivers (full and partial), and unspecified assistantships also available. Financial award application deadline: 1/5; financial award applicants required to submit FAFSA. *Faculty research:* Applied and solid earth geophysics, tectonic geomorphology, fluid-rock interaction, paleobiology-ecology, sedimentary-geochemistry. *Unit head:* Dr. Richard Minnich, Chair, 951-827-5515, Fax: 951-827-4324, E-mail: richard.minnich@ucr.edu. *Application contact:* John Herring, Graduate Program Assistant, 951-827-3435, Fax: 951-827-4324, E-mail: geology@ucr.edu. Web site: http://vortex.ucr.edu/esdocs/gradstud.html.

University of California, Santa Barbara, Graduate Division, College of Letters and Sciences, Division of Mathematics, Life, and Physical Sciences, Department of Earth Science, Santa Barbara, CA 93106-9620. Offers geological sciences (MS, PhD); geophysics (MS). *Faculty:* 20 full-time (3 women). *Students:* 43 full-time (16 women); includes 8 minority (1 American Indian or Alaska Native, non-Hispanic/Latino; 2 Asian, non-Hispanic/Latino; 5 Hispanic/Latino), 5 international. Average age 27. 83 applicants, 16% accepted, 8 enrolled. In 2011, 10 master's, 3 doctorates awarded. Terminal master's awarded for partial completion of doctoral program. *Median time to degree:* Of those who began their doctoral program in fall 2003, 64% received their degree in 8 years or less. *Degree requirements:* For master's, comprehensive exam, thesis, 30 units; for doctorate, comprehensive exam, thesis/dissertation, 30 units, oral qualifying exam. *Entrance requirements:* For master's and doctorate, GRE General Test. Additional exam requirements/recommendations for international students: Required—TOEFL (minimum score 550 paper-based; 80 iBT), IELTS (minimum score 7). *Application deadline:* For fall admission, 1/1 for domestic and international students. Application fee: $80 ($100 for international students). Electronic applications accepted. *Expenses:* Tuition, state resident: full-time $12,192. Tuition, nonresident: full-time $27,294. *Required fees:* $764.13. *Financial support:* In 2011–12, 38 students received support, including 34 fellowships with full and partial tuition reimbursements available (averaging $12,566 per year), 22 research assistantships with full and partial tuition reimbursements available (averaging $7,362 per year), 28 teaching assistantships with full and partial tuition reimbursements available (averaging $7,234 per year); tuition waivers (full and partial) also available. Financial award application deadline: 1/1; financial award applicants required to submit CSS PROFILE or FAFSA. *Faculty research:* Geology, geomaterials and earth's structure; geomorphology, tectonics; geophysics, seismology; paleoclimate, paleoceanography and geochemistry; paleobiology, evolution and paleontology. *Unit head:* Dr. Douglas Burbank, Chair, 805-893-7858, Fax: 805-893-2314, E-mail: burbank@eri.ucsb.edu. *Application contact:* Hannah Smit, Graduate Program Assistant, 805-893-3329, Fax: 805-893-2314, E-mail: hsmit@geol.ucsb.edu. Web site: http://www.geol.ucsb.edu/.

University of Cincinnati, Graduate School, McMicken College of Arts and Sciences, Department of Geology, Cincinnati, OH 45221. Offers MS, PhD. Part-time programs available. *Degree requirements:* For master's, thesis; for doctorate,

comprehensive exam, thesis/dissertation. *Entrance requirements:* For master's and doctorate, GRE General Test, 1 year of course work in physics, chemistry, and calculus. Additional exam requirements/recommendations for international students: Required—TOEFL. Electronic applications accepted. *Faculty research:* Paleobiology, sequence stratigraphy, earth systems history, quaternary, groundwater.

University of Colorado Boulder, Graduate School, College of Arts and Sciences, Department of Geological Sciences, Boulder, CO 80309. Offers geology (MS, PhD); geophysics (PhD). *Faculty:* 29 full-time (8 women). *Students:* 69 full-time (41 women), 18 part-time (7 women); includes 6 minority (2 American Indian or Alaska Native, non-Hispanic/Latino; 2 Hispanic/Latino; 2 Two or more races, non-Hispanic/Latino), 6 international. Average age 29. 236 applicants, 12% accepted, 23 enrolled. In 2011, 15 master's, 7 doctorates awarded. Terminal master's awarded for partial completion of doctoral program. *Degree requirements:* For master's, comprehensive exam, thesis; for doctorate, comprehensive exam, thesis/dissertation. *Entrance requirements:* For master's, GRE General Test, minimum undergraduate GPA of 3.0; for doctorate, GRE General Test, minimum GPA of 2.75. *Application deadline:* For fall admission, 12/15 priority date for domestic students, 12/1 for international students. Application fee: $50 ($60 for international students). Electronic applications accepted. *Financial support:* In 2011–12, 109 students received support, including 62 fellowships (averaging $7,337 per year), 38 research assistantships with full and partial tuition reimbursements available (averaging $21,321 per year), 23 teaching assistantships with full and partial tuition reimbursements available (averaging $19,046 per year); institutionally sponsored loans, scholarships/grants, health care benefits, and unspecified assistantships also available. Financial award application deadline: 1/15; financial award applicants required to submit FAFSA. *Faculty research:* Sedimentology, stratigraphy, economic geology of mineral deposits, fossil fuels, hydrogeology and water resources, geophysics, isotope geology, paleobiology, mineralogy, remote sensing. *Total annual research expenditures:* $6.8 million. *Application contact:* E-mail: geolinfo@colorado.edu. Web site: http://www.colorado.edu/GeolSci.

University of Connecticut, Graduate School, College of Liberal Arts and Sciences, Center for Integrative Geosciences, Storrs, CT 06269. Offers geological sciences (MS, PhD). *Degree requirements:* For doctorate, thesis/dissertation. *Entrance requirements:* For master's and doctorate, GRE General Test. Additional exam requirements/recommendations for international students: Required—TOEFL (minimum score 550 paper-based; 213 computer-based). Electronic applications accepted.

University of Delaware, College of Earth, Ocean, and Environment, Department of Geological Sciences, Newark, DE 19716. Offers MA, PhD.

University of Florida, Graduate School, College of Liberal Arts and Sciences, Department of Geological Sciences, Gainesville, FL 32611. Offers hydrologic sciences (MS, MST, PhD); tropical conservation and development (MS, MST, PhD); wetland sciences (MS, MST, PhD). *Faculty:* 17 full-time (3 women). *Students:* 38 full-time (17 women), 3 part-time (2 women); includes 1 minority (Hispanic/Latino), 11 international. Average age 30. 63 applicants, 32% accepted, 11 enrolled. In 2011, 6 master's, 2 doctorates awarded. Terminal master's awarded for partial completion of doctoral program. *Degree requirements:* For master's, thesis (for some programs); for doctorate, one foreign language, thesis/dissertation. *Entrance requirements:* For master's, GRE General Test (minimum score of 1000), minimum GPA of 3.0; for doctorate, GRE General Test (minimum score of 1100), minimum GPA of 3.0. Additional exam requirements/recommendations for international students: Required—TOEFL (minimum score 550 paper-based; 213 computer-based; 80 iBT), IELTS (minimum score 6). *Application deadline:* For fall admission, 1/15 for domestic students; for spring admission, 10/1 for domestic students. Applications are processed on a rolling basis. Application fee: $30. Electronic applications accepted. *Financial support:* In 2011–12, 4 fellowships with full tuition reimbursements, 19 research assistantships with full tuition reimbursements (averaging $16,810 per year), 16 teaching assistantships with full tuition reimbursements (averaging $15,290 per year) were awarded; career-related internships or fieldwork, Federal Work-Study, institutionally sponsored loans, and scholarships/grants also available. Support available to part-time students. Financial award application deadline: 3/1; financial award applicants required to submit FAFSA. *Faculty research:* Paleoclimatology, tectonophysics, petrochemistry, marine geology, geochemistry, hydrology. *Unit head:* Dr. Michael R. Perfit, Chair, 352-392-2231, Fax: 352-392-9294, E-mail: mperfit@ufl.edu. *Application contact:* Dr. John Jaeger, Graduate Coordinator, 352-392-2231, Fax: 352-392-9294, E-mail: jmjaeger@ufl.edu. Web site: http://web.geology.ufl.edu/.

University of Georgia, Franklin College of Arts and Sciences, Department of Geology, Athens, GA 30602. Offers MS, PhD. *Faculty:* 15 full-time (3 women), 1 part-time/adjunct (0 women). *Students:* 21 full-time (12 women), 6 part-time (3 women), 1 international. Average age 29. 40 applicants, 40% accepted, 7 enrolled. In 2011, 11 master's, 1 doctorate awarded. *Degree requirements:* For master's, thesis; for doctorate, one foreign language, thesis/dissertation. *Entrance requirements:* For master's and doctorate, GRE General Test. *Application deadline:* For fall admission, 7/1 priority date for domestic students; for spring admission, 11/15 for domestic students. Application fee: $50. Electronic applications accepted. *Financial support:* Fellowships, research assistantships, teaching assistantships, and unspecified assistantships available. *Unit head:* Dr. Michael F. Roden, Head, 706-542-2652, Fax: 706-542-2425, E-mail: mroden@uga.edu. *Application contact:* Dr. Steven M. Holland, Graduate Coordinator, 706-

150 facebook.com/petersonspublishing

Peterson's Graduate Programs in the Physical Sciences, Mathematics, Agricultural Sciences, the Environment & Natural Resources 2013

542-0424, Fax: 706-542-2425, E-mail: stratum@uga.edu. Web site: http://www.gly.uga.edu/.

University of Hawaii at Manoa, Graduate Division, School of Ocean and Earth Science and Technology, Department of Geology and Geophysics, Honolulu, HI 96822. Offers high-pressure geophysics and geochemistry (MS, PhD); hydrogeology and engineering geology (MS, PhD); marine geology and geophysics (MS, PhD); planetary geosciences and remote sensing (MS, PhD); seismology and solid-earth geophysics (MS, PhD); volcanology, petrology, and geochemistry (MS, PhD). Part-time programs available. Terminal master's awarded for partial completion of doctoral program. *Degree requirements:* For master's, thesis optional; for doctorate, comprehensive exam, thesis/dissertation. *Entrance requirements:* For master's and doctorate, GRE General Test, minimum GPA of 3.0. Additional exam requirements/recommendations for international students: Required—TOEFL (minimum score 580 paper-based; 237 computer-based; 92 iBT), IELTS (minimum score 5).

University of Houston, College of Natural Sciences and Mathematics, Department of Earth and Atmospheric Sciences, Houston, TX 77204. Offers atmospheric science (PhD); geology (MA, PhD); geophysics (PhD). Part-time programs available. *Degree requirements:* For master's, thesis; for doctorate, comprehensive exam, thesis/dissertation. *Entrance requirements:* For master's and doctorate, GRE General Test. Additional exam requirements/recommendations for international students: Required—TOEFL (minimum score 550 paper-based; 213 computer-based; 79 iBT), IELTS (minimum score 6.5). Electronic applications accepted. *Faculty research:* Atmospherics sciences, seismic and solid earth geophysics, tectonics, environmental hydrochemistry, carbonates, micropaleontology, structure and tectonics, petroleum geology.

University of Idaho, College of Graduate Studies, College of Science, Department of Geological Sciences, Program in Geology, Moscow, ID 83844-2282. Offers MS, PhD. *Students:* 21 full-time, 9 part-time. Average age 30. In 2011, 3 master's, 1 doctorate awarded. *Entrance requirements:* For master's, minimum GPA of 2.8. *Application deadline:* For fall admission, 8/1 for domestic students; for spring admission, 12/15 for domestic students. Applications are processed on a rolling basis. Application fee: $60. Electronic applications accepted. *Expenses:* Tuition, state resident: full-time $3874; part-time $334 per credit hour. Tuition, nonresident: full-time $16,394; part-time $861 per credit hour. *Required fees:* $2808; $99 per credit hour. Tuition and fees vary according to program. *Financial support:* Applicants required to submit FAFSA. *Unit head:* Dr. Mickey Gunter, Head, 208-885-6491, E-mail: geology@uidaho.edu. *Application contact:* Erick Larson, Director of Graduate Admissions, 208-885-4723, E-mail: gadms@uidaho.edu. Web site: http://www.uidaho.edu/sci/geology/academics/graduateprogram.

University of Illinois at Chicago, Graduate College, College of Liberal Arts and Sciences, Department of Earth and Environmental Sciences, Chicago, IL 60607-7128. Offers MS, PhD. *Degree requirements:* For master's, thesis; for doctorate, thesis/dissertation. *Entrance requirements:* For master's and doctorate, GRE General Test, minimum GPA of 2.75. Additional exam requirements/recommendations for international students: Required—TOEFL. Electronic applications accepted.

University of Illinois at Urbana–Champaign, Graduate College, College of Liberal Arts and Sciences, School of Earth, Society and Environment, Department of Geology, Champaign, IL 61820. Offers geology (MS, PhD); teaching of earth sciences (MS). *Faculty:* 12 full-time (3 women). *Students:* 21 full-time (10 women), 4 part-time (all women); includes 1 minority (Asian, non-Hispanic/Latino), 10 international. 53 applicants, 17% accepted, 5 enrolled. In 2011, 6 master's, 1 doctorate awarded. Terminal master's awarded for partial completion of doctoral program. *Entrance requirements:* For master's and doctorate, GRE General Test, minimum GPA of 3.0. Additional exam requirements/recommendations for international students: Required—TOEFL. *Application deadline:* Applications are processed on a rolling basis. Application fee: $75 ($90 for international students). Electronic applications accepted. *Financial support:* In 2011–12, 4 fellowships, 17 research assistantships, 12 teaching assistantships were awarded; Federal Work-Study and tuition waivers (full and partial) also available. *Faculty research:* Hydrogeology, structure/tectonics, mineral science. *Unit head:* Thomas M. Johnson, Head, 217-244-2002, Fax: 217-244-4996, E-mail: tmjohnsn@illinois.edu. *Application contact:* Marilyn K. Whalen, Office Administrator, 217-333-3542, Fax: 217-244-4996, E-mail: mkt@illinois.edu. Web site: http://www.geology.illinois.edu/.

The University of Kansas, Graduate Studies, College of Liberal Arts and Sciences, Department of Geology, Lawrence, KS 66045. Offers MS, PhD. PhD offered jointly with Kansas State University. *Students:* 69 full-time (24 women), 22 part-time (9 women); includes 15 minority (3 American Indian or Alaska Native, non-Hispanic/Latino; 8 Hispanic/Latino; 4 Two or more races, non-Hispanic/Latino), 11 international. Average age 28. 98 applicants, 45% accepted, 17 enrolled. In 2011, 10 master's, 2 doctorates awarded. *Degree requirements:* For master's, thesis or alternative; for doctorate, comprehensive exam, thesis/dissertation. *Entrance requirements:* For master's and doctorate, GRE General Test, 3 letters of recommendation. Additional exam requirements/recommendations for international students: Required—TOEFL. *Application deadline:* For fall admission, 2/1 priority date for domestic students, 2/1 for international students; for spring admission, 10/31 priority date for domestic students, 10/31 for international students. Applications are processed on a rolling basis. Application fee: $45 ($55 for international students). Electronic applications

accepted. Tuition and fees vary according to course load, campus/location, program and reciprocity agreements. *Financial support:* Fellowships with full and partial tuition reimbursements, research assistantships with full and partial tuition reimbursements, teaching assistantships with full and partial tuition reimbursements, and unspecified assistantships available. Financial award application deadline: 2/1. *Faculty research:* Sedimentology, paleontology, tectonics, geophysics, hydrogeology. *Unit head:* Luis A. Gonzalez, Chair, 785-864-4974, Fax: 785-864-2743, E-mail: lgonzlez@ku.edu. *Application contact:* Yolanda G. Davis, Graduate Coordinator, 785-864-4975, Fax: 785-864-5276, E-mail: yolanda@ku.edu. Web site: http://www.geo.ku.edu.

University of Kentucky, Graduate School, College of Arts and Sciences, Program in Geology, Lexington, KY 40506-0032. Offers MS, PhD. *Degree requirements:* .For master's, comprehensive exam, thesis; for doctorate, comprehensive exam, thesis/dissertation. *Entrance requirements:* For master's, GRE General Test, minimum undergraduate GPA of 2.75; for doctorate, GRE General Test, minimum graduate GPA of 3.0. Additional exam requirements/recommendations for international students: Required—TOEFL (minimum score 550 paper-based; 213 computer-based). Electronic applications accepted. *Faculty research:* Structure tectonics, geophysics, stratigraphy, hydrogeology, coal geology.

University of Louisiana at Lafayette, College of Sciences, Department of Geology, Lafayette, LA 70504. Offers MS. Part-time programs available. *Degree requirements:* For master's, comprehensive exam, thesis. *Entrance requirements:* For master's, GRE General Test, minimum GPA of 2.75. Additional exam requirements/recommendations for international students: Required—TOEFL (minimum score 550 paper-based; 213 computer-based). Electronic applications accepted. *Faculty research:* Aquifer contamination, coastal erosion, geochemistry of peat, petroleum geology and geophysics, remote sensing and geographic information systems applications.

University of Maine, Graduate School, Climate Change Institute, Orono, ME 04469. Offers MS. Part-time programs available. *Students:* 5 full-time (4 women), 2 part-time (both women), 2 international. Average age 26. 12 applicants, 50% accepted, 2 enrolled. In 2011, 5 master's awarded. *Degree requirements:* For master's, thesis. *Entrance requirements:* For master's, GRE General Test. Additional exam requirements/recommendations for international students: Required—TOEFL. *Application deadline:* For fall admission, 2/1 priority date for domestic students. Applications are processed on a rolling basis. Application fee: $65. Electronic applications accepted. *Expenses:* Tuition, state resident: full-time $5016. Tuition, nonresident: full-time $14,424. *Financial support:* In 2011–12, 14 research assistantships with full tuition reimbursements (averaging $14,780 per year), 2 teaching assistantships with full tuition reimbursements (averaging $13,600 per year) were awarded. Financial award application deadline: 3/1. *Faculty research:* Geology, glacial geology, anthropology. *Total annual research expenditures:* $143,097. *Unit head:* Dr. Paul Mayewski, Director, 207-581-3019, Fax: 207-581-1203. *Application contact:* Scott G. Delcourt, Associate Dean of the Graduate School, 207-581-3291, Fax: 207-581-3232, E-mail: graduate@maine.edu. Web site: http://www2.umaine.edu/graduate/.

University of Maine, Graduate School, College of Natural Sciences, Forestry, and Agriculture, Department of Earth Sciences, Orono, ME 04469. Offers water resources (MS, PhD). Part-time programs available. *Faculty:* 9 full-time (2 women), 3 part-time/adjunct (0 women). *Students:* 23 full-time (12 women), 10 part-time (5 women), 3 international. Average age 28. 32 applicants, 66% accepted, 17 enrolled. In 2011, 6 master's, 4 doctorates awarded. *Degree requirements:* For master's, thesis; for doctorate, one foreign language, thesis/dissertation. *Entrance requirements:* For master's and doctorate, GRE General Test. Additional exam requirements/recommendations for international students: Required—TOEFL. *Application deadline:* For fall admission, 2/1 priority date for domestic students. Applications are processed on a rolling basis. Application fee: $65. Electronic applications accepted. *Expenses:* Tuition, state resident: full-time $5016. Tuition, nonresident: full-time $14,424. *Financial support:* In 2011–12, 5 research assistantships with full tuition reimbursements (averaging $16,950 per year), 6 teaching assistantships with full tuition reimbursements (averaging $13,600 per year) were awarded; Federal Work-Study, institutionally sponsored loans, and tuition waivers (full and partial) also available. Financial award application deadline: 3/1. *Faculty research:* Appalachian bedrock geology, Quaternary studies, marine geology. *Unit head:* Dr. Joseph Kelley, Chair, 207-581-2162, Fax: 207-581-2202. *Application contact:* Scott G. Delcourt, Associate Dean of the Graduate School, 207-581-3291, Fax: 207-581-3232, E-mail: graduate@maine.edu. Web site: http://www2.umaine.edu/graduate/.

University of Manitoba, Faculty of Graduate Studies, Clayton H. Riddell Faculty of Environment, Earth, and Resources, Department of Geological Sciences, Winnipeg, MB R3T 2N2, Canada. Offers geology (M Sc, PhD); geophysics (M Sc, PhD). *Degree requirements:* For master's, thesis; for doctorate, thesis/dissertation. *Entrance requirements:* For master's and doctorate, GRE General Test, GRE Subject Test (geology), minimum GPA of 3.0. Additional exam requirements/recommendations for international students: Required—TOEFL.

University of Maryland, College Park, Academic Affairs, College of Computer, Mathematical and Natural Sciences, Department of Geology, College Park, MD 20742. Offers MS, PhD. *Faculty:* 33 full-time (6 women), 3 part-time/adjunct (2 women). *Students:* 37 full-time (18 women); includes 5 minority (1 Black or African American, non-Hispanic/Latino; 1 Asian, non-Hispanic/Latino; 3 Hispanic/Latino), 10 international. 71 applicants, 34% accepted, 13 enrolled. In 2011, 2 master's, 3

Peterson's Graduate Programs in the Physical Sciences, Mathematics, Agricultural Sciences, the Environment & Natural Resources 2013

facebook.com/petersonspublishing **151**

Geology

doctorates awarded. *Degree requirements:* For master's, thesis, oral defense; for doctorate, thesis/dissertation. *Entrance requirements:* For master's, GRE General Test, minimum GPA of 3.0, 3 letters of recommendation; for doctorate, GRE General Test, 3 letters of recommendation. Additional exam requirements/recommendations for international students: Required—TOEFL. *Application deadline:* For fall admission, 3/15 for domestic students, 2/1 for international students; for spring admission, 10/15 for domestic students, 6/1 for international students. Applications are processed on a rolling basis. Application fee: $75. Electronic applications accepted. *Expenses: Tuition, area resident:* Part-time $525 per credit hour. Tuition, state resident: part-time $525 per credit hour. Tuition, nonresident: part-time $1131 per credit hour. *Required fees:* $386.31 per term. Tuition and fees vary according to program. *Financial support:* In 2011–12, 1 fellowship with full tuition reimbursement (averaging $15,008 per year), 5 research assistantships (averaging $20,177 per year), 28 teaching assistantships (averaging $19,964 per year) were awarded; Federal Work-Study and scholarships/grants also available. Support available to part-time students. Financial award application deadline: 2/15; financial award applicants required to submit FAFSA. *Total annual research expenditures:* $2.8 million. *Unit head:* Roberta Rudnick, Chair, 301-405-4065, Fax: 301-314-9661, E-mail: rudnick@umd.edu. *Application contact:* Dr. Charles A. Caramello, Dean of Graduate School, 301-405-0358, Fax: 301-314-9305.

University of Memphis, Graduate School, College of Arts and Sciences, Department of Earth Sciences, Memphis, TN 38152. Offers archaeology (MS); earth sciences (PhD); geographic information systems (Graduate Certificate); geography (MA, MS); geology (MS); geophysics (MS); interdisciplinary (MS). Part-time and evening/weekend programs available. Terminal master's awarded for partial completion of doctoral program. *Degree requirements:* For master's, comprehensive exam, thesis, seminar presentation; for doctorate, thesis/dissertation. *Entrance requirements:* For master's, GRE General Test, 3 letters of recommendation, statement of research interests; for doctorate, GRE General Test, 2 letters of recommendation, resume, personal statement. Additional exam requirements/recommendations for international students: Required—TOEFL (minimum score 550 paper-based; 210 computer-based). Electronic applications accepted. *Faculty research:* Hazards, active tectonics, geophysics, hydrology and water resources, spatial analysis.

University of Minnesota, Duluth, Graduate School, Swenson College of Science and Engineering, Department of Geological Sciences, Duluth, MN 55812-2496. Offers MS, PhD. PhD offered jointly with University of Minnesota, Twin Cities Campus. Part-time programs available. *Degree requirements:* For master's, thesis, final oral exam, written and oral research proposal. *Entrance requirements:* For master's, GRE General Test, minimum GPA of 3.0. Additional exam requirements/recommendations for international students: Required—TOEFL (minimum score 550 paper-based; 213 computer-based). Electronic applications accepted. *Faculty research:* Surface processes, tectonics, planetary geology, paleoclimate, petrology.

University of Minnesota, Twin Cities Campus, College of Science and Engineering, Department of Earth Sciences, Minneapolis, MN 55455-0213. Offers MS, PhD. *Faculty:* 22 full-time (4 women). *Students:* 60 (27 women); includes 7 minority (1 Black or African American, non-Hispanic/Latino; 2 American Indian or Alaska Native, non-Hispanic/Latino; 4 Hispanic/Latino), 11 international. Terminal master's awarded for partial completion of doctoral program. *Degree requirements:* For master's, thesis; for doctorate, thesis/dissertation. *Entrance requirements:* For master's and doctorate, GRE General Test, 3 letters of recommendation. Additional exam requirements/recommendations for international students: Required—TOEFL (minimum score 550 paper-based; 213 computer-based). *Application deadline:* For fall admission, 1/8 for domestic and international students. Application fee: $75 ($95 for international students). Electronic applications accepted. *Financial support:* Fellowships, research assistantships, teaching assistantships, health care benefits, and unspecified assistantships available. *Faculty research:* Geology, geophysics, geochemistry, geobiology, climate and environmental geosciences. *Application contact:* Sharon Kressler, Student Services Specialist, E-mail: kress004@umn.edu. Web site: http://www.geo.umn.edu/.

University of Missouri, Graduate School, College of Arts and Sciences, Department of Geological Sciences, Columbia, MO 65211. Offers MS, PhD. *Faculty:* 10 full-time (3 women), 1 part-time/adjunct (0 women). *Students:* 33 full-time (12 women), 3 part-time (0 women), 17 international. Average age 28. 35 applicants, 46% accepted, 11 enrolled. In 2011, 8 master's, 1 doctorate awarded. *Degree requirements:* For master's, thesis; for doctorate, variable foreign language requirement, thesis/dissertation. *Entrance requirements:* For master's and doctorate, GRE General Test, minimum GPA of 3.0. Additional exam requirements/recommendations for international students: Required—TOEFL (minimum score 530 paper-based; 197 computer-based; 71 iBT). *Application deadline:* For fall admission, 2/15 priority date for domestic students. Applications are processed on a rolling basis. Application fee: $55 ($75 for international students). Electronic applications accepted. *Expenses:* Tuition, state resident: full-time $5881. Tuition, nonresident: full-time $15,183. *Required fees:* $952. Tuition and fees vary according to campus/location and program. *Financial support:* In 2011–12, 2 fellowships with full tuition reimbursements, 17 research assistantships with full tuition reimbursements, 13 teaching assistantships with full tuition reimbursements were awarded; institutionally sponsored loans, health care benefits, and unspecified assistantships also available. *Faculty research:* Geochemistry, tectonics, economic geology, biogeochemistry, geophysics. *Unit*

head: Dr. Kevin L. Shelton, Department Chair, 573-882-6568, E-mail: sheltonkl@missouri.edu. *Application contact:* Alice Thompson, Administrative Assistant, 573-882-6785, E-mail: thompsonae@missouri.edu. Web site: http://geology.missouri.edu/degree/grad.html.

University of Missouri–Kansas City, College of Arts and Sciences, Department of Geosciences, Kansas City, MO 64110-2499. Offers environmental and urban geosciences (MS); geosciences (PhD). PhD (interdisciplinary) offered through the School of Graduate Studies. Part-time programs available. *Faculty:* 10 full-time (3 women), 5 part-time/adjunct (0 women). *Students:* 5 full-time (1 woman), 29 part-time (12 women); includes 1 minority (Hispanic/Latino), 5 international. Average age 34. 19 applicants, 63% accepted, 9 enrolled. In 2011, 3 degrees awarded. *Degree requirements:* For master's, thesis; for doctorate, thesis/dissertation, qualifying exam. *Entrance requirements:* For master's, GRE General Test, minimum GPA of 3.0. Additional exam requirements/recommendations for international students: Required—TOEFL (minimum score 550 paper-based; 213 computer-based; 80 iBT). *Application deadline:* For fall admission, 3/15 priority date for domestic students, 3/15 for international students. Applications are processed on a rolling basis. Application fee: $45 ($50 for international students). Electronic applications accepted. *Expenses:* Tuition, state resident: full-time $5798; part-time $322.10 per credit hour. Tuition, nonresident: full-time $14,969; part-time $831.60 per credit hour. *Required fees:* $93.51 per credit hour. *Financial support:* In 2011–12, 3 research assistantships with partial tuition reimbursements (averaging $10,400 per year), 17 teaching assistantships with partial tuition reimbursements (averaging $12,134 per year) were awarded; Federal Work-Study, institutionally sponsored loans, and tuition waivers (full and partial) also available. Support available to part-time students. Financial award application deadline: 3/1; financial award applicants required to submit FAFSA. *Faculty research:* Neotectonics and applied geophysics, environmental geosciences, urban geoscience, geoinformatics-remote sensing, atmospheric research. *Unit head:* Dr. Jimmy Adegoke, Chair, 816-235-1334, Fax: 816-235-5535, E-mail: adegokej@umkc.edu. *Application contact:* Dr. Jejung Lee, Associate Professor, 816-235-6495, Fax: 816-235-5535, E-mail: leej@umkc.edu. Web site: http://cas.umkc.edu/geo/.

The University of Montana, Graduate School, College of Arts and Sciences, Department of Geology, Missoula, MT 59812-0002. Offers applied geoscience (PhD); geology (MS, PhD). *Degree requirements:* For doctorate, thesis/dissertation. *Entrance requirements:* For master's and doctorate, GRE General Test. Additional exam requirements/recommendations for international students: Required—TOEFL (minimum score 525 paper-based; 197 computer-based). *Faculty research:* Environmental geoscience, regional structure and tectonics, groundwater geology, petrology, mineral deposits.

University of Nevada, Reno, Graduate School, College of Science, Mackay School of Earth Sciences and Engineering, Department of Geological Sciences, Program in Geology, Reno, NV 89557. Offers MS, PhD. Terminal master's awarded for partial completion of doctoral program. *Degree requirements:* For master's, thesis optional; for doctorate, thesis/dissertation. *Entrance requirements:* For master's, GRE General Test, minimum GPA of 2.75; for doctorate, GRE General Test, minimum GPA of 3.0. Additional exam requirements/recommendations for international students: Required—TOEFL (minimum score 500 paper-based; 173 computer-based; 61 iBT), IELTS (minimum score 6). Electronic applications accepted. *Faculty research:* Mineral exploration, geochemistry, hydrology.

University of New Brunswick Fredericton, School of Graduate Studies, Faculty of Science, Department of Earth Sciences, Fredericton, NB E3B 5A3, Canada. Offers M Sc, PhD. Part-time programs available. *Faculty:* 10 full-time (0 women). *Students:* 26 full-time (11 women), 6 part-time (4 women). In 2011, 2 master's, 1 doctorate awarded. *Degree requirements:* For master's, thesis; for doctorate, thesis/dissertation. *Entrance requirements:* For master's, minimum GPA of 3.0, B Sc in earth sciences or related subject; for doctorate, minimum GPA of 3.0; M Sc in earth science or related subject. Additional exam requirements/recommendations for international students: Required—TOEFL, IELTS, TWE. *Application deadline:* For fall admission, 3/1 priority date for domestic students. Applications are processed on a rolling basis. Application fee: $50 Canadian dollars. *Financial support:* In 2011–12, 21 fellowships, 26 research assistantships (averaging $1,160 per year), 26 teaching assistantships (averaging $2,016 per year) were awarded. *Faculty research:* Hydrogeology, glacial geology, petrology, paleontology, aqueous and hydrothermal geochemistry. *Total annual research expenditures:* $133,936. *Unit head:* Dr. David Keighley, Director of Graduate Studies, 506-453-5196, Fax: 506-453-5055, E-mail: keig@unb.ca. *Application contact:* Christine Lodge, 506-453-4803, Fax: 506-453-5055, E-mail: lodge@unb.ca. Web site: http://www.unb.ca/fredericton/science/geology.

University of New Hampshire, Graduate School, College of Engineering and Physical Sciences, Department of Earth Sciences, Durham, NH 03824. Offers geology (MS); hydrology (MS). *Faculty:* 17 full-time (5 women). *Students:* 21 full-time (11 women), 13 part-time (6 women); includes 3 minority (2 Black or African American, non-Hispanic/Latino; 1 Asian, non-Hispanic/Latino), 5 international. Average age 27. 60 applicants, 58% accepted, 12 enrolled. In 2011, 10 master's awarded. *Degree requirements:* For master's, thesis. *Entrance requirements:* For master's, GRE General Test. Additional exam requirements/recommendations for international students: Required—TOEFL (minimum score 550 paper-based; 213 computer-based; 80 iBT). *Application deadline:* For fall admission, 4/1 priority date for domestic students, 4/1 for international students; for spring admission, 12/1 for domestic students. Applications are processed on a rolling basis.

Application fee: $65. Electronic applications accepted. *Expenses:* Tuition, state resident: full-time $12,360; part-time $687 per credit hour. Tuition, nonresident: full-time $25,680; part-time $1058 per credit hour. *International tuition:* $29,550 full-time. *Required fees:* $1666; $833 per course. $416.50 per semester. Tuition and fees vary according to course load and degree level. *Financial support:* In 2011–12, 24 students received support, including 12 research assistantships, 8 teaching assistantships; fellowships, career-related internships or fieldwork, Federal Work-Study, scholarships/grants, and tuition waivers (full and partial) also available. Support available to part-time students. Financial award application deadline: 2/15. *Unit head:* Dr. Will Clyde, Chairperson, 603-862-1718, E-mail: earth.sciences@unh.edu. *Application contact:* Sue Clark, Administrative Assistant, 603-862-1718, E-mail: earth.sciences@unh.edu. Web site: http://www.unh.edu/esci/.

The University of North Carolina at Chapel Hill, Graduate School, College of Arts and Sciences, Department of Geological Sciences, Chapel Hill, NC 27599. Offers MS, PhD. *Degree requirements:* For master's, comprehensive exam, thesis; for doctorate, one foreign language, comprehensive exam, thesis/dissertation. *Entrance requirements:* For master's and doctorate, GRE General Test, minimum GPA of 3.0. Electronic applications accepted. *Faculty research:* Paleoceanography, igneous petrology, paleontology, geophysics, structural geology.

The University of North Carolina Wilmington, College of Arts and Sciences, Department of Geography and Geology, Wilmington, NC 28403-3297. Offers geology (MS); marine science (MS). *Degree requirements:* For master's, comprehensive exam, thesis. *Entrance requirements:* For master's, GRE General Test, GRE Subject Test, minimum B average in undergraduate major and basic prerequisite geology courses.

University of North Dakota, Graduate School, School of Engineering and Mines, Department of Geology, Grand Forks, ND 58202. Offers MA, MS, PhD. *Degree requirements:* For master's, thesis, final exam; for doctorate, one foreign language, comprehensive exam, thesis/dissertation, final exam. *Entrance requirements:* For master's and doctorate, GRE General Test, minimum GPA of 3.0. Additional exam requirements/recommendations for international students: Required—TOEFL (minimum score 550 paper-based; 213 computer-based; 79 iBT), IELTS (minimum score 6.5). Electronic applications accepted. *Faculty research:* Hydrogeology, environmental geology, geological engineering, sedimentology, geomorphology.

University of Oklahoma, College of Earth and Energy, ConocoPhillips School of Geology and Geophysics, Program in Geology, Norman, OK 73019. Offers MS, PhD. Part-time programs available. *Students:* 44 full-time (10 women), 28 part-time (8 women); includes 4 minority (2 American Indian or Alaska Native, non-Hispanic/Latino; 1 Hispanic/Latino; 1 Two or more races, non-Hispanic/Latino), 26 international. Average age 28. 103 applicants, 21% accepted, 16 enrolled. In 2011, 22 master's, 1 doctorate awarded. *Degree requirements:* For master's, comprehensive exam, thesis; for doctorate, one foreign language, thesis/dissertation, general exam. *Entrance requirements:* For master's, GRE General Test, bachelor's degree in geology; for doctorate, GRE General Test. Additional exam requirements/recommendations for international students: Required—TOEFL (minimum score 550 paper-based; 79 iBT). *Application deadline:* For fall admission, 2/1 priority date for domestic students, 3/1 for international students; for spring admission, 9/1 for domestic and international students. Applications are processed on a rolling basis. Application fee: $40 ($90 for international students). Electronic applications accepted. *Expenses:* Tuition, state resident: full-time $4087; part-time $170.30 per credit hour. Tuition, nonresident: full-time $14,875; part-time $619.80 per credit hour. *Required fees:* $2659; $100.25 per credit hour. Tuition and fees vary according to course load and degree level. *Financial support:* In 2011–12, 58 students received support. Scholarships/grants and unspecified assistantships available. Financial award applicants required to submit FAFSA. *Faculty research:* Earth systems, lithospheric dynamics, energy, geochemistry, and geophysics. *Unit head:* Dr. Douglas Elmore, Director and Associate Provost, 405-325-3253, Fax: 405-325-3140, E-mail: delmore@ou.edu. *Application contact:* Donna S. Mullins, Coordinator for Administrative Student Services and Corporate Recruiting, 405-325-3255, Fax: 405-325-3140, E-mail: dsmullins@ou.edu. Web site: http://geology.ou.edu.

University of Oregon, Graduate School, College of Arts and Sciences, Department of Geological Sciences, Eugene, OR 97403. Offers MA, MS, PhD. *Degree requirements:* For master's, foreign language (MA). *Entrance requirements:* For master's and doctorate, GRE General Test, GRE Subject Test.

University of Pittsburgh, Dietrich School of Arts and Sciences, Department of Geology and Planetary Science, Pittsburgh, PA 15260-3332. Offers geographical information systems (Pro-MS); geology and planetary science (MS, PhD). Part-time programs available. *Faculty:* 7 full-time (2 women), 3 part-time/adjunct (1 woman). *Students:* 24 full-time (11 women), 8 part-time (4 women), 1 international. Average age 30. 27 applicants, 48% accepted, 5 enrolled. In 2011, 5 master's, 5 doctorates awarded. *Degree requirements:* For master's, thesis, oral thesis defense; for doctorate, comprehensive exam, thesis/dissertation, oral dissertation defense. *Entrance requirements:* For master's and doctorate, GRE General Test. Additional exam requirements/recommendations for international students: Required—TOEFL (minimum score 550 paper-based; 213 computer-based; 80 iBT). *Application deadline:* For fall admission, 1/15 priority date for domestic students, 1/15 for international students. Applications are processed on a rolling basis. Application fee: $50. Electronic applications accepted. *Expenses:*

Tuition, state resident: full-time $18,774; part-time $760 per credit. Tuition, nonresident: full-time $30,736; part-time $1258 per credit. *Required fees:* $740; $200 per term. Tuition and fees vary according to program. *Financial support:* In 2011–12, 21 students received support, including 2 fellowships with full tuition reimbursements available (averaging $19,165 per year), 9 research assistantships with full and partial tuition reimbursements available (averaging $14,400 per year), 9 teaching assistantships with full and partial tuition reimbursements available (averaging $16,145 per year); career-related internships or fieldwork, Federal Work-Study, institutionally sponsored loans, scholarships/grants, health care benefits, and tuition waivers (full and partial) also available. Support available to part-time students. Financial award application deadline: 1/15; financial award applicants required to submit FAFSA. *Faculty research:* Geographical information systems, hydrology, low temperature geochemistry, volcanology, paleoclimatology. *Total annual research expenditures:* $1.6 million. *Unit head:* Dr. William Harbert, Chair, 412-624-8783, Fax: 412-624-3914, E-mail: harbert@pitt.edu. *Application contact:* Dr. Rosemary Capo, Director of Graduate Studies, 412-624-8873, Fax: 412-624-3914, E-mail: rcapo@pitt.edu. Web site: http://www.geology.pitt.edu/.

University of Puerto Rico, Mayagüez Campus, Graduate Studies, College of Arts and Sciences, Department of Geology, Mayagüez, PR 00681-9000. Offers MS. Part-time programs available. *Students:* 17 full-time (10 women); all minorities (all Hispanic/Latino). 5 applicants, 40% accepted, 2 enrolled. *Degree requirements:* For master's, comprehensive exam, thesis. *Entrance requirements:* For master's, GRE General Test, BS in geology or the equivalent; minimum GPA of 2.8. *Application deadline:* For fall admission, 2/15 for domestic and international students; for spring admission, 9/15 for domestic and international students. Applications are processed on a rolling basis. Application fee: $25. Tuition and fees vary according to course level and course load. *Financial support:* In 2011–12, 14 students received support, including 7 research assistantships (averaging $15,000 per year), 7 teaching assistantships (averaging $8,500 per year). *Faculty research:* Seismology, applied geophysics, geographic information systems, environmental remote sensing, petrology. *Total annual research expenditures:* $363,164. *Unit head:* Dr. Lizzette Rodriguez, Interim Director, 787-832-4040 Ext. 3000, E-mail: lizzette.rodriguez1@upr.edu. *Application contact:* Marsha Irizarry, 787-832-4040 Ext. 2414, Fax: 787-265-3845, E-mail: irizarrym@uprm.edu. Web site: http://geology.uprm.edu.

University of Regina, Faculty of Graduate Studies and Research, Faculty of Science, Department of Geology, Regina, SK S4S 0A2, Canada. Offers M Sc, PhD. PhD program offered on a special case basis. *Faculty:* 9 full-time (4 women). *Students:* 13 full-time (7 women), 5 part-time (3 women). 8 applicants, 75% accepted. In 2011, 3 degrees awarded. *Degree requirements:* For master's, thesis; for doctorate, thesis/dissertation. *Entrance requirements:* Additional exam requirements/recommendations for international students: Required—TOEFL (minimum score 580 paper-based; 80 iBT), IELTS (minimum score 6.5). *Application deadline:* Applications are processed on a rolling basis. Application fee: $100. Electronic applications accepted. *Financial support:* In 2011–12, 2 fellowships (averaging $6,500 per year), 1 research assistantship (averaging $5,500 per year), 2 teaching assistantships (averaging $2,298 per year) were awarded; scholarships/grants also available. Financial award application deadline: 6/15. *Faculty research:* Quaternary and economic geology; volcanology; organic, igneous, and metamorphic petrology; carbonate sedimentology and basin analysis; mineralogy. *Unit head:* Dr. Hairuo Qing, Head, 306-585-4677, Fax: 306-585-5433, E-mail: hairuo.qing@uregina.ca. *Application contact:* Dr. Kathryn Bethune, Graduate Program Coordinator, 306-585-4270, Fax: 306-585-5433, E-mail: kathryn.bethune@uregina.ca. Web site: http://www.uregina.ca/geology/.

University of Rochester, School of Arts and Sciences, Department of Earth and Environmental Sciences, Rochester, NY 14627. Offers MS, PhD. *Faculty:* 7 full-time (2 women). *Students:* 9 full-time (4 women), 4 international. 44 applicants, 16% accepted, 3 enrolled. In 2011, 6 master's, 2 doctorates awarded. *Degree requirements:* For doctorate, thesis/dissertation, qualifying exam. *Entrance requirements:* For master's and doctorate, GRE General Test. Additional exam requirements/recommendations for international students: Required—TOEFL. *Application deadline:* For fall admission, 2/1 priority date for domestic students. Application fee: $0. Electronic applications accepted. *Expenses: Tuition:* Full-time $41,040. *Financial support:* Fellowships, research assistantships, teaching assistantships, career-related internships or fieldwork, and tuition waivers (full and partial) available. Financial award application deadline: 2/1. *Faculty research:* Geochemistry and environmental sciences; paleomagnetism, structure and tectonics. *Unit head:* Carmala Garzione, Chair, 585-275-5713, E-mail: carmala.garzione@rochester.edu. *Application contact:* Kathy Lutz, Secretary, 585-275-5713, E-mail: kathy@ur.rochester.edu. Web site: http://www.ees.rochester.edu/.

University of Saskatchewan, College of Graduate Studies and Research, College of Arts and Science and College of Engineering, Department of Geological Sciences, Saskatoon, SK S7N 5A2, Canada. Offers M Sc, PhD, Diploma. *Degree requirements:* For master's, thesis; for doctorate, comprehensive exam (for some programs), thesis/dissertation. *Entrance requirements:* Additional exam requirements/recommendations for international students: Required—TOEFL (minimum score 80 iBT); Recommended—IELTS (minimum score 6.5). Electronic applications accepted.

University of South Carolina, The Graduate School, College of Arts and Sciences, Department of Geological Sciences, Columbia, SC 29208. Offers MS, PhD. Terminal master's awarded for partial completion of doctoral program.

Peterson's Graduate Programs in the Physical Sciences, Mathematics, Agricultural Sciences, the Environment & Natural Resources 2013

facebook.com/petersonspublishing **153**

Geology

Degree requirements: For master's, thesis; for doctorate, comprehensive exam, thesis/dissertation, published paper. *Entrance requirements:* For master's and doctorate, GRE General Test. Additional exam requirements/recommendations for international students: Required—TOEFL (minimum score 570 paper-based; 230 computer-based; 75 iBT). Electronic applications accepted. *Faculty research:* Environmental geology, tectonics, petrology, coastal processes, paleoclimatology.

University of Southern Mississippi, Graduate School, College of Science and Technology, Department of Geography and Geology, Hattiesburg, MS 39406-0001. Offers geography (MS, PhD); geology (MS). Part-time programs available. *Faculty:* 11 full-time (2 women), 1 part-time/adjunct (0 women). *Students:* 17 full-time (1 woman), 16 part-time (4 women); includes 1 minority (Two or more races, non-Hispanic/Latino). Average age 34. 18 applicants, 72% accepted, 8 enrolled. In 2011, 4 degrees awarded. *Degree requirements:* For master's, comprehensive exam, thesis (for some programs), internships; for doctorate, comprehensive exam, thesis/dissertation. *Entrance requirements:* For master's, GMAT, GRE General Test, minimum GPA of 3.0 for last 60 hours; for doctorate, GRE, minimum GPA of 3.5. Additional exam requirements/recommendations for international students: Required—TOEFL, IELTS. *Application deadline:* For fall admission, 3/15 for domestic and international students; for spring admission, 1/3 for domestic students. Applications are processed on a rolling basis. Application fee: $50. Electronic applications accepted. *Financial support:* In 2011–12, 1 research assistantship with tuition reimbursement (averaging $18,000 per year), 8 teaching assistantships with full tuition reimbursements (averaging $8,700 per year) were awarded; fellowships with full tuition reimbursements, career-related internships or fieldwork, Federal Work-Study, scholarships/grants, health care benefits, and unspecified assistantships also available. Financial award application deadline: 3/15; financial award applicants required to submit FAFSA. *Faculty research:* City and regional planning, geographic techniques, physical geography, human geography. *Unit head:* Dr. Clifton Dixon, Chair, 601-266-4729, Fax: 601-266-6219, E-mail: c.dixon@usm.edu. *Application contact:* Dr. Clifton Dixon, Director, Graduate Studies, 601-266-4729, Fax: 601-266-6219. Web site: http://www.usm.edu/graduateschool/table.php.

University of South Florida, Graduate School, College of Arts and Sciences, Department of Geology, Tampa, FL 33620-9951. Offers MS, PhD. Part-time programs available. *Faculty:* 15 full-time (2 women), 9 part-time/adjunct (2 women). *Students:* 43 full-time (17 women), 20 part-time (7 women); includes 4 minority (2 Black or African American, non-Hispanic/Latino; 1 Asian, non-Hispanic/Latino; 1 Two or more races, non-Hispanic/Latino), 10 international. Average age 34. 50 applicants, 36% accepted, 13 enrolled. In 2011, 4 master's, 8 doctorates awarded. *Degree requirements:* For master's, comprehensive exam, thesis (for some programs); for doctorate, comprehensive exam, thesis/dissertation. *Entrance requirements:* For master's and doctorate, GRE General Test, minimum GPA of 3.0, three letters of recommendation, personal statement. Additional exam requirements/recommendations for international students: Required—TOEFL (minimum score 550 paper-based; 213 computer-based; 79 iBT) or IELTS (minimum score 6.5). *Application deadline:* For fall admission, 2/15 for domestic students, 1/2 for international students; for spring admission, 10/15 for domestic students, 6/1 for international students. Application fee: $30. Electronic applications accepted. *Financial support:* In 2011–12, 41 students received support, including 13 research assistantships (averaging $14,983 per year), 28 teaching assistantships with tuition reimbursements available (averaging $14,592 per year); unspecified assistantships also available. Financial award application deadline: 6/30; financial award applicants required to submit FAFSA. *Total annual research expenditures:* $1.6 million. *Unit head:* Dr. Jeffrey Ryan, Chairperson, 813-974-1598, Fax: 813-974-2654, E-mail: ryan@usf.edu. *Application contact:* Dr. Ping Wang, Graduate Director, 813-974-9170, Fax: 813-974-2654, E-mail: pwang@usf.edu. Web site: http://geology.usf.edu/.

The University of Tennessee, Graduate School, College of Arts and Sciences, Department of Geological Sciences, Knoxville, TN 37996. Offers geology (MS, PhD). Part-time programs available. *Degree requirements:* For master's, thesis; for doctorate, one foreign language, thesis/dissertation. *Entrance requirements:* For master's and doctorate, GRE General Test, minimum GPA of 2.7. Additional exam requirements/recommendations for international students: Required—TOEFL. Electronic applications accepted. *Expenses:* Tuition, state resident: full-time $8332; part-time $464 per credit hour. Tuition, nonresident: full-time $25,174; part-time $1400 per credit hour. *Required fees:* $1162; $56 per credit hour. Tuition and fees vary according to program.

The University of Texas at Arlington, Graduate School, College of Science, Department of Earth and Environmental Sciences, Program in Environmental and Earth Sciences, Arlington, TX 76019. Offers environmental science (MS, PhD); geology (MS, PhD). Part-time and evening/weekend programs available. *Faculty:* 5 full-time (0 women), 1 part-time/adjunct (0 women). *Students:* 22 full-time (13 women), 25 part-time (12 women); includes 9 minority (2 Black or African American, non-Hispanic/Latino; 1 American Indian or Alaska Native, non-Hispanic/Latino; 2 Asian, non-Hispanic/Latino; 4 Hispanic/Latino), 11 international. 23 applicants, 74% accepted, 10 enrolled. In 2011, 11 master's, 1 doctorate awarded. Terminal master's awarded for partial completion of doctoral program. *Degree requirements:* For master's, thesis optional; for doctorate, comprehensive exam, thesis/dissertation. *Entrance requirements:* For master's, GRE General Test. Additional exam requirements/recommendations for international students: Required—TOEFL (minimum score 550 paper-based; 213 computer-based). *Application deadline:* Applications are processed on a rolling basis. Application fee: $35 ($50 for international students). Electronic applications

accepted. *Financial support:* In 2011–12, 4 fellowships (averaging $1,000 per year), 7 teaching assistantships (averaging $14,700 per year) were awarded; career-related internships or fieldwork, Federal Work-Study, institutionally sponsored loans, scholarships/grants, health care benefits, and unspecified assistantships also available. Financial award applicants required to submit FAFSA. *Unit head:* Dr. John S. Wickham, Chair, 817-272-2987, Fax: 817-272-2628, E-mail: wickham@uta.edu. *Application contact:* Dr. Andrew Hunt, Graduate Advisor, 817-272-2987, Fax: 817-272-2628, E-mail: hunt@uta.edu. Web site: http://www.uta.edu/ees.

The University of Texas at Austin, Graduate School, Jackson School of Geosciences, Austin, TX 78712-1111. Offers MA, MS, PhD. Part-time programs available. *Degree requirements:* For master's, report (MA), thesis (MS); for doctorate, thesis/dissertation. *Entrance requirements:* For master's and doctorate, GRE General Test. *Application deadline:* For fall admission, 2/1 priority date for domestic students; for spring admission, 10/1 for domestic students. Application fee: $50 ($75 for international students). Electronic applications accepted. *Financial support:* Fellowships with partial tuition reimbursements, research assistantships with partial tuition reimbursements, teaching assistantships with partial tuition reimbursements, career-related internships or fieldwork, Federal Work-Study, and institutionally sponsored loans available. Financial award application deadline: 2/1. *Faculty research:* Sedimentary geology, geophysics, hydrogeology, structure/tectonics, vertebrate paleontology. *Unit head:* Dr. Sharon Mosher, Dean, 512-471-6048, E-mail: smosher@jsg.utexas.edu. *Application contact:* Jesus Garcia, Senior Academic Advisor, 512-471-8472, E-mail: jgar5@mail.utexas.edu. Web site: http://www.jsg.utexas.edu/.

The University of Texas at El Paso, Graduate School, College of Science, Department of Geological Sciences, El Paso, TX 79968-0001. Offers geological sciences (MS, PhD); geophysics (MS). Part-time and evening/weekend programs available. *Students:* 73 (32 women); includes 24 minority (1 Black or African American, non-Hispanic/Latino; 3 Asian, non-Hispanic/Latino; 20 Hispanic/Latino), 20 international. Average age 34. 32 applicants, 56% accepted, 16 enrolled. In 2011, 3 master's, 4 doctorates awarded. *Degree requirements:* For master's, thesis; for doctorate, one foreign language, thesis/dissertation. *Entrance requirements:* For master's, GRE, minimum GPA of 3.0, BS in geology or equivalent; for doctorate, GRE, minimum GPA of 3.0, MS in geology or equivalent. Additional exam requirements/recommendations for international students: Required—TOEFL. *Application deadline:* For fall admission, 7/1 priority date for domestic students, 3/1 for international students; for spring admission, 11/1 priority date for domestic students, 9/1 for international students. Applications are processed on a rolling basis. Application fee: $15 ($65 for international students). Electronic applications accepted. *Financial support:* In 2011–12, 36 students received support, including research assistantships with partial tuition reimbursements available (averaging $21,812 per year), teaching assistantships with partial tuition reimbursements available (averaging $17,450 per year); fellowships with partial tuition reimbursements available, career-related internships or fieldwork, institutionally sponsored loans, scholarships/grants, and tuition waivers (partial) also available. Support available to part-time students. Financial award application deadline: 3/15; financial award applicants required to submit FAFSA. *Unit head:* Aaron A. Velasco, Chair, 915-747-5501, Fax: 915-747-5073, E-mail: velasco@geo.utep.edu. *Application contact:* Dr. Benjamin Flores, Interim Dean of the Graduate School, 915-747-5491, Fax: 915-747-5788, E-mail: bflores@utep.edu.

The University of Texas at San Antonio, College of Sciences, Department of Geological Sciences, San Antonio, TX 78249-0617. Offers MS. Part-time programs available. *Faculty:* 9 full-time (3 women), 4 part-time/adjunct (0 women). *Students:* 16 full-time (9 women), 9 part-time (2 women); includes 4 minority (1 Asian, non-Hispanic/Latino; 2 Hispanic/Latino; 1 Two or more races, non-Hispanic/Latino), 4 international. Average age 30. 22 applicants, 86% accepted, 10 enrolled. In 2011, 2 master's awarded. *Degree requirements:* For master's, comprehensive exam, thesis (for some programs). *Entrance requirements:* For master's, GRE General Test, three letters of recommendation, statement of research interest. Additional exam requirements/recommendations for international students: Required—TOEFL (minimum score 500 paper-based; 61 iBT), IELTS (minimum score 5). *Application deadline:* For fall admission, 7/1 for domestic students, 4/1 for international students; for spring admission, 11/1 for domestic students, 9/1 for international students. Application fee: $45 ($85 for international students). *Expenses:* Tuition, state resident: full-time $3148; part-time $2176 per semester. Tuition, nonresident: full-time $8782; part-time $5932 per semester. *Required fees:* $719 per semester. *Financial support:* Tuition waivers available. *Faculty research:* Low temperature geochemistry, aqueous geochemistry, hydrogeology, groundwater modeling, stratigraphy, carbonate petrology, paleontology, micropaleontolory, remote sensing, GIS, geoinformatics, tectonics, structural geology, metamorphic petrology, geochronology, sediment transports, methodology. *Unit head:* Dr. Alan R. Dutton, Department Chair, 210-458-4455, Fax: 210-458-4469, E-mail: alan.dutton@utsa.edu. *Application contact:* Graduate Advisor of Record, 210-458-4455, Fax: 210-458-4469, E-mail: geosciences@utsa.edu. Web site: http://www.utsa.edu/geosci/.

The University of Texas of the Permian Basin, Office of Graduate Studies, College of Arts and Sciences, Department of Physical Sciences, Program in Geology, Odessa, TX 79762-0001. Offers MS. *Degree requirements:* For master's, comprehensive exam, thesis or alternative. *Entrance requirements:* For master's, GRE General Test. Additional exam requirements/recommendations for international students: Required—TOEFL (minimum score 550 paper-based; 213 computer-based).

The University of Toledo, College of Graduate Studies, College of Natural Sciences and Mathematics, Department of Environmental Sciences, Toledo, OH 43606-3390. Offers biology (MS, PhD), including ecology. Part-time programs available. *Faculty:* 26. *Students:* 9 full-time (4 women), 2 part-time (1 woman); includes 1 minority (Black or African American, non-Hispanic/Latino), 1 international. Average age 30. 9 applicants, 56% accepted, 5 enrolled. In 2011, 3 master's awarded. *Degree requirements:* For master's, thesis (for some programs). *Entrance requirements:* For master's, GRE General Test, minimum cumulative point-hour ratio of 2.7 for all previous academic work, three letters of recommendation, statement of purpose, transcripts from all prior institutions attended. Additional exam requirements/recommendations for international students: Required—TOEFL (minimum score 550 paper-based; 213 computer-based; 80 iBT), IELTS (minimum score 6.5). *Application deadline:* For fall admission, 1/15 priority date for domestic students, 1/15 for international students. Applications are processed on a rolling basis. Application fee: $45 ($75 for international students). Electronic applications accepted. *Financial support:* In 2011–12, 5 research assistantships with full and partial tuition reimbursements (averaging $18,126 per year), 12 teaching assistantships with full and partial tuition reimbursements (averaging $12,850 per year) were awarded; Federal Work-Study, institutionally sponsored loans, scholarships/grants, tuition waivers (full), and unspecified assistantships also available. Support available to part-time students. *Faculty research:* Environmental geochemistry, geophysics, petrology and mineralogy, paleontology, geohydrology. *Unit head:* Dr. Timothy G. Fisher, Chair, 419-530-2883, E-mail: timothy.fisher@utoledo.edu. *Application contact:* Graduate School Office, 419-530-4723, Fax: 419-530-4724, E-mail: grdsch@utnet.utoledo.edu. Web site: http://www.utoledo.edu/nsm/.

University of Toronto, School of Graduate Studies, Faculty of Arts and Science, Department of Geology, Toronto, ON M5S 1A1, Canada. Offers M Sc, MA Sc, PhD. Part-time programs available. *Degree requirements:* For master's, thesis (for some programs); for doctorate, thesis/dissertation. *Entrance requirements:* For master's, B Sc, BA Sc, or equivalent; letters of reference; for doctorate, M Sc or equivalent, minimum B+ average, letters of reference. Additional exam requirements/recommendations for international students: Required—TOEFL (minimum score 580 paper-based; 93 iBT), TWE (minimum score 4). Electronic applications accepted.

University of Utah, Graduate School, College of Mines and Earth Sciences, Department of Geology and Geophysics, Salt Lake City, UT 84112. Offers environmental engineering (ME, MS, PhD); geological engineering (ME, MS, PhD); geology (MS, PhD); geophysics (MS, PhD). *Faculty:* 22 full-time (5 women), 4 part-time/adjunct (0 women). *Students:* 55 full-time (16 women), 28 part-time (9 women); includes 2 minority (both Asian, non-Hispanic/Latino), 16 international. Average age 30. 174 applicants, 17% accepted, 21 enrolled. In 2011, 13 master's, 3 doctorates awarded. Terminal master's awarded for partial completion of doctoral program. *Median time to degree:* Of those who began their doctoral program in fall 2003, 76% received their degree in 8 years or less. *Degree requirements:* For master's, comprehensive exam, thesis; for doctorate, thesis/dissertation, qualifying exam (written and oral). *Entrance requirements:* For master's and doctorate, GRE General Test, minimum GPA of 3.25. Additional exam requirements/recommendations for international students: Required—TOEFL (minimum score 500 paper-based; 173 computer-based). *Application deadline:* For fall admission, 1/15 priority date for domestic students, 1/15 for international students. Applications are processed on a rolling basis. Application fee: $55 ($65 for international students). Electronic applications accepted. *Financial support:* In 2011–12, 22 students received support, including 10 fellowships with full tuition reimbursements available (averaging $15,000 per year), 40 research assistantships with full tuition reimbursements available (averaging $22,000 per year), 14 teaching assistantships with full tuition reimbursements available (averaging $15,000 per year); career-related internships or fieldwork, institutionally sponsored loans, scholarships/grants, unspecified assistantships, and stipends also available. Financial award application deadline: 1/15; financial award applicants required to submit FAFSA. *Faculty research:* Igneous, metamorphic, and sedimentary petrology; ore deposits; aqueous geochemistry; isotope geochemistry; heat flow. *Total annual research expenditures:* $3.3 million. *Unit head:* Dr. Kip Solomon, Chair, 801-581-7231, Fax: 801-581-7065, E-mail: kip.solomon@utah.edu. *Application contact:* Dr. Cari L. Johnson, Director of Graduate Studies, 801-585-3782, Fax: 801-581-7065, E-mail: cari.johnson@utah.edu. Web site: http://www.earth.utah.edu/.

University of Vermont, Graduate College, College of Arts and Sciences, Department of Geology, Burlington, VT 05405. Offers MS. *Students:* 12 (7 women); includes 1 minority (Hispanic/Latino), 1 international. 34 applicants, 24% accepted, 4 enrolled. In 2011, 3 master's awarded. *Degree requirements:* For master's, thesis. *Entrance requirements:* For master's, GRE General Test. Additional exam requirements/recommendations for international students: Required—TOEFL (minimum score 550 paper-based; 213 computer-based; 80 iBT). *Application deadline:* For fall admission, 2/15 priority date for domestic students, 2/15 for international students. Applications are processed on a rolling basis. Application fee: $40. Electronic applications accepted. *Financial support:* Research assistantships and teaching assistantships available. Financial award application deadline: 3/1. *Faculty research:* Mineralogy, lake sediments, structural geology. *Unit head:* Dr. Andrea Lini, Chairperson, 802-656-3396. *Application contact:* Prof. Laura Webb, Coordinator, 802-656-3396.

University of Washington, Graduate School, College of the Environment, Department of Earth and Space Sciences, Seattle, WA 98195. Offers geology (MS, PhD); geophysics (MS, PhD). *Degree requirements:* For master's, thesis or alternative, departmental qualifying exam, final exam; for doctorate, thesis/dissertation, departmental qualifying exam, general and final exams. *Entrance requirements:* For master's and doctorate, GRE General Test, minimum GPA of 3.0. Additional exam requirements/recommendations for international students: Required—TOEFL (minimum score 580 paper-based). Electronic applications accepted.

The University of Western Ontario, Faculty of Graduate Studies, Physical Sciences Division, Department of Earth Sciences, London, ON N6A 5B8, Canada. Offers environment and sustainability (MES); geology (M Sc, PhD); geology and environmental science (M Sc, PhD); geophysics (M Sc, PhD); geophysics and environmental science (M Sc, PhD). *Degree requirements:* For master's, thesis; for doctorate, thesis/dissertation, qualifying exam. *Entrance requirements:* For master's, honors in B Sc; for doctorate, M Sc. Additional exam requirements/recommendations for international students: Required—TOEFL. *Faculty research:* Geophysics, geochemistry, paleontology, sedimentation/stratigraphy, glaciology/quaternary.

University of Wisconsin–Madison, Graduate School, College of Letters and Science, Department of Geology and Geophysics, Program in Geology, Madison, WI 53706-1380. Offers MS, PhD. *Degree requirements:* For master's, thesis; for doctorate, one foreign language, thesis/dissertation. *Entrance requirements:* For master's and doctorate, GRE General Test. *Expenses:* Tuition, state resident: full-time $10,296; part-time $643.51 per credit. Tuition, nonresident: full-time $24,054; part-time $1503.40 per credit. *Required fees:* $70.06 per credit. Tuition and fees vary according to course load, campus/location, program and reciprocity agreements.

University of Wisconsin–Milwaukee, Graduate School, College of Letters and Sciences, Department of Geosciences, Milwaukee, WI 53201-0413. Offers geological sciences (MS, PhD). *Faculty:* 8 full-time (2 women). *Students:* 14 full-time (8 women), 11 part-time (4 women); includes 1 minority (Two or more races, non-Hispanic/Latino), 1 international. Average age 32. 22 applicants, 82% accepted, 7 enrolled. In 2011, 8 degrees awarded. *Degree requirements:* For master's, thesis; for doctorate, one foreign language, thesis/dissertation. *Entrance requirements:* For master's, GRE General Test, minimum GPA of 3.0; for doctorate, GRE General Test, master's degree. Additional exam requirements/recommendations for international students: Required—TOEFL (minimum score 550 paper-based; 79 iBT), IELTS (minimum score 6.5). *Application deadline:* For fall admission, 1/1 priority date for domestic students; for spring admission, 9/1 for domestic students. Applications are processed on a rolling basis. Application fee: $56 ($96 for international students). Electronic applications accepted. One-time fee: $506.10 full-time. Tuition and fees vary according to course load and reciprocity agreements. *Financial support:* In 2011–12, 4 research assistantships, 11 teaching assistantships were awarded; career-related internships or fieldwork and unspecified assistantships also available. Support available to part-time students. Financial award application deadline: 4/15; financial award applicants required to submit FAFSA. *Faculty research:* Geology, geosciences, geophysics, hydrogeology, paleontology. *Total annual research expenditures:* $690,970. *Unit head:* John Isbell, Department Chair, 414-229-2877, E-mail: jisbell@uwm.edu. *Application contact:* General Information Contact, 414-229-4982, Fax: 414-229-6967, E-mail: gradschool@uwm.edu. Web site: http://www.uwm.edu/dept/geosciences/.

University of Wyoming, College of Arts and Sciences, Department of Geology and Geophysics, Laramie, WY 82070. Offers geology (MS, PhD); geophysics (MS, PhD). Part-time programs available. *Degree requirements:* For master's, comprehensive exam, thesis; for doctorate, comprehensive exam, thesis/dissertation. *Entrance requirements:* For master's and doctorate, GRE General Test, minimum GPA of 3.0. *Faculty research:* Low-temp geochemistry, geohydrology, paleontology, structure/tectonics, sedimentation and petroleum geology, petrology, geophysics/seismology.

Utah State University, School of Graduate Studies, College of Science, Department of Geology, Logan, UT 84322. Offers MS. *Degree requirements:* For master's, thesis. *Entrance requirements:* For master's, GRE General Test, minimum GPA of 3.0. Additional exam requirements/recommendations for international students: Required—TOEFL. *Faculty research:* Sedimentary geology, structural geology, regional tectonics, hydrogeology petrology.

Washington State University, Graduate School, College of Sciences, School of Earth and Environmental Sciences, Department of Geology, Pullman, WA 99164. Offers MS, PhD. *Faculty:* 9. *Students:* 21 full-time (9 women), 8 part-time (2 women); includes 1 minority (Two or more races, non-Hispanic/Latino). Average age 30. 42 applicants, 43% accepted, 8 enrolled. In 2011, 3 master's, 3 doctorates awarded. *Degree requirements:* For master's, comprehensive exam (for some programs), thesis, oral exam; for doctorate, one foreign language, comprehensive exam, thesis/dissertation, oral exam, written exam. *Entrance requirements:* For master's and doctorate, GRE General Test, official copies of college transcripts, minimum GPA of 3.0, 3 letters of recommendation. Additional exam requirements/recommendations for international students: Required—TOEFL (minimum score 560 paper-based; 220 computer-based). *Application deadline:* For fall admission, 1/10 priority date for domestic students, 1/10 for international students; for spring admission, 7/1 priority date for domestic students, 7/1 for international students. Applications are processed on a rolling

Peterson's Graduate Programs in the Physical Sciences, Mathematics, Agricultural Sciences, the Environment & Natural Resources 2013

facebook.com/petersonspublishing **155**

basis. Application fee: $75. Electronic applications accepted. *Financial support:* In 2011–12, 4 fellowships (averaging $2,700 per year), 5 research assistantships with full and partial tuition reimbursements (averaging $13,917 per year), 18 teaching assistantships with full and partial tuition reimbursements (averaging $13,056 per year) were awarded; career-related internships or fieldwork, Federal Work-Study, institutionally sponsored loans, and scholarships/grants also available. Financial award application deadline: 2/1; financial award applicants required to submit FAFSA. *Faculty research:* Genesis of ore deposits, geohydrology of the Pacific Northwest, geochemistry and petrology of plateau basalts. *Total annual research expenditures:* $358,000. *Unit head:* Dr. John A. Wolff, Acting Director, 509-335-2825, Fax: 509-335-7816, E-mail: jawolff@mail.wsu.edu. *Application contact:* Graduate School Admissions, 800-GRADWSU, Fax: 509-335-1949, E-mail: gradsch@wsu.edu.

Wayne State University, College of Liberal Arts and Sciences, Department of Geology, Detroit, MI 48202. Offers MS. *Students:* 5 full-time (2 women), 1 (woman) part-time. Average age 27. 9 applicants, 44% accepted, 3 enrolled. In 2011, 1 master's awarded. *Degree requirements:* For master's, thesis. *Entrance requirements:* For master's, GRE General Test, undergraduate major in geology or strong background in geology-supported courses, minimum GPA of 3.0, three letters of recommendation. Additional exam requirements/recommendations for international students: Required—TOEFL (minimum score 550 paper-based; 213 computer-based); Recommended—TWE (minimum score 5.5). *Application deadline:* For fall admission, 6/1 priority date for domestic students, 5/1 for international students; for winter admission, 10/1 priority date for domestic students, 9/1 for international students; for spring admission, 2/1 priority date for domestic students, 10/1 for international students. Applications are processed on a rolling basis. Application fee: $50. Electronic applications accepted. *Expenses:* Tuition, state resident: part-time $512.85 per credit. Tuition, nonresident: part-time $1132.65 per credit. *Required fees:* $26.60 per credit. $199.65 per semester. Tuition and fees vary according to course load and program. *Financial support:* In 2011–12, 2 students received support, including 2 research assistantships with full and partial tuition reimbursements available (averaging $17,391 per year), 1 teaching assistantship with full and partial tuition reimbursement available (averaging $17,391 per year); fellowships with full and partial tuition reimbursements available, scholarships/grants, health care benefits, and unspecified assistantships also available. Support available to part-time students. *Faculty research:* Glacial geology of Southeastern Michigan; applications of U-Th-series, cosmogenic and anthrogenic radionuclides as tracers and chronometers in the environment; geochemical exploration of ore deposits using trace-elemental and stable isotopic (light-elemental) analytical tools; fate and transport of groundwater contaminants in glacial sediments; environmental radioactivity and geochronology. *Total annual research expenditures:* $320,982. *Unit head:* Dr. David Njus, Professor and Acting Chair, 313-577-3105, E-mail: ad5348@wayne.edu. *Application contact:* Dr. Mark Baskaran, 313-577-2506, E-mail: baskaran@wayne.edu. Web site: http://www.clas.wayne.edu/geology/.

West Chester University of Pennsylvania, College of Arts and Sciences, Department of Geology and Astronomy, West Chester, PA 19383. Offers earth-space science (Teaching Certificate); general science (Teaching Certificate); geoscience (MA). Part-time and evening/weekend programs available. *Faculty:* 6 part-time/adjunct (1 woman). *Students:* 6 full-time (3 women), 17 part-time (6 women); includes 1 minority (Black or African American, non-Hispanic/Latino). Average age 32. 8 applicants, 88% accepted, 5 enrolled. In 2011, 4 degrees awarded. *Degree requirements:* For master's, comprehensive exam (for some programs), thesis or alternative. *Entrance requirements:* For master's, minimum GPA of 2.5. Additional exam requirements/recommendations for international students: Required—TOEFL (minimum score 550 paper-based; 213 computer-based; 80 iBT). *Application deadline:* For fall admission, 4/15 priority date for domestic students, 3/15 for international students; for spring admission, 10/15 priority date for domestic students, 9/1 for international students. Applications are processed on a rolling basis. Application fee: $45. Electronic applications accepted. *Expenses:* Tuition, state resident: full-time $7488; part-time $416 per credit. Tuition, nonresident: full-time $11,232; part-time $624 per credit. *Required*

fees: $1784.64; $67.59 per credit. Tuition and fees vary according to program. *Financial support:* Unspecified assistantships available. Support available to part-time students. Financial award application deadline: 2/15; financial award applicants required to submit FAFSA. *Faculty research:* Geoscience education, environmental geology, energy and sustainability, astronomy, meteorology. *Unit head:* Dr. Lee Anne Srogi, Chair; 610-436-2727, Fax: 610-436-3036, E-mail: lsrogi@wcupa.edu. *Application contact:* Dr. Martin Helmke, Graduate Coordinator, 610-436-3565, Fax: 610-436-3036, E-mail: mhelmke@wcupa.edu. Web site: http://www.wcupa.edu/_academics/sch_cas.esc/.

Western Kentucky University, Graduate Studies, Ogden College of Science and Engineering, Department of Geography and Geology, Bowling Green, KY 42101. Offers geoscience (MS). *Degree requirements:* For master's, comprehensive exam, thesis or alternative. *Entrance requirements:* For master's, GRE General Test, minimum GPA of 2.75. Additional exam requirements/recommendations for international students: Required—TOEFL (minimum score 555 paper-based; 213 computer-based; 79 iBT). *Faculty research:* Hydroclimatology, electronic data sets, groundwater, sinkhole liquification potential, meteorological analysis.

Western Washington University, Graduate School, College of Sciences and Technology, Department of Geology, Bellingham, WA 98225-5996. Offers MS. Part-time programs available. *Degree requirements:* For master's, thesis. *Entrance requirements:* For master's, GRE General Test, minimum GPA of 3.0 in last 60 semester hours or last 90 quarter hours. Additional exam requirements/recommendations for international students: Required—TOEFL (minimum score 567 paper-based; 227 computer-based). Electronic applications accepted. *Faculty research:* Structure/tectonics; sedimentary, glacial and quaternary geomorphology; igneous and metamorphic petrology; hydrology, geophysics.

West Virginia University, Eberly College of Arts and Sciences, Department of Geology and Geography, Program in Geology, Morgantown, WV 26506. Offers geomorphology (MS, PhD); geophysics (MS, PhD); hydrogeology (MS, PhD); paleontology (MS, PhD); petroleum geology (PhD); petrology (MS, PhD); stratigraphy (MS, PhD); structure (MS, PhD). Part-time programs available. Terminal master's awarded for partial completion of doctoral program. *Degree requirements:* For master's, thesis (for some programs); for doctorate, comprehensive exam, thesis/dissertation. *Entrance requirements:* For master's, GRE General Test, minimum GPA of 2.5; for doctorate, GRE General Test, minimum GPA of 3.3. Additional exam requirements/recommendations for international students: Required—TOEFL.

Wichita State University, Graduate School, Fairmount College of Liberal Arts and Sciences, Department of Geology, Wichita, KS 67260. Offers earth, environmental, and physical sciences (MS). Part-time programs available. *Expenses:* Tuition, state resident: full-time $4746; part-time $263.65 per credit. Tuition, nonresident: full-time $11,669; part-time $648.30 per credit. *Unit head:* Dr. William Parcell, Chair, 316-978-3140, E-mail: william.parcell@wichita.edu. *Application contact:* Dr. Collette Burke, Graduate Coordinator for EEPS Program, 316-978-3140, E-mail: collette.burke@wichita.edu. Web site: http://www.wichita.edu/.

Wright State University, School of Graduate Studies, College of Science and Mathematics, Department of Earth and Environmental Sciences, Program in Geological Sciences, Dayton, OH 45435. Offers MS. Part-time programs available. *Degree requirements:* For master's, thesis. *Entrance requirements:* Additional exam requirements/recommendations for international students: Required—TOEFL.

Yale University, Graduate School of Arts and Sciences, Department of Geology and Geophysics, New Haven, CT 06520. Offers biogeochemistry (PhD); climate dynamics (PhD); geochemistry (PhD); geophysics (PhD); meteorology (PhD); oceanography (PhD); paleontology (PhD); paleooceanography (PhD); petrology (PhD); tectonics (PhD). *Degree requirements:* For doctorate, thesis/dissertation. *Entrance requirements:* For doctorate, GRE General Test. Additional exam requirements/recommendations for international students: Required—TOEFL.

Geophysics

Boise State University, Graduate College, College of Arts and Sciences, Department of Geosciences, Master's Program in Geophysics, Boise, ID 83725-0399. Offers MS. Part-time programs available. *Degree requirements:* For master's, thesis. *Entrance requirements:* For master's, GRE General Test, minimum GPA of 3.0, BS in related field. Additional exam requirements/recommendations for international students: Required—TOEFL. Electronic applications accepted. *Faculty research:* Shallow seismic profile, seismic hazard, tectonics, hazardous waste disposal.

Boise State University, Graduate College, College of Arts and Sciences, Department of Geosciences, Program in Geophysics, Boise, ID 83725-0399. Offers PhD. Part-time programs available. *Degree requirements:* For doctorate, comprehensive exam, thesis/dissertation. *Entrance requirements:* For doctorate, GRE General Test. Electronic applications accepted.

Boston College, Graduate School of Arts and Sciences, Department of Earth and Environmental Sciences, Chestnut Hill, MA 02467-3800. Offers MS, MBA/MS. *Degree requirements:* For master's, thesis. *Entrance requirements:* For master's, GRE General Test, GRE Subject Test. Additional exam requirements/recommendations for international students: Required—TOEFL (minimum score 600 paper-based; 250 computer-based; 100 iBT). Electronic applications accepted. *Faculty research:* Coastal and marine geology, experimental sedimentology, geomagnetism, igneous petrology, paleontology.

Bowling Green State University, Graduate College, College of Arts and Sciences, Department of Physics and Astronomy, Bowling Green, OH 43403. Offers geophysics (MS); physics (MAT, MS). *Degree requirements:* For master's, thesis or alternative. *Entrance requirements:* For master's, GRE General Test. Additional exam requirements/recommendations for international students:

156 facebook.com/petersonspublishing

Peterson's Graduate Programs in the Physical Sciences, Mathematics, Agricultural Sciences, the Environment & Natural Resources 2013

Required—TOEFL. Electronic applications accepted. *Faculty research:* Computational physics, solid-state physics, materials science, theoretical physics.

California Institute of Technology, Division of Geological and Planetary Sciences, Pasadena, CA 91125-0001. Offers environmental science and engineering (MS, PhD); geobiology (MS, PhD); geochemistry (MS, PhD); geology (MS, PhD); geophysics (MS, PhD); planetary science (MS, PhD). *Faculty:* 42 full-time (8 women). *Students:* 102 full-time (48 women); includes 10 minority (2 Black or African American, non-Hispanic/Latino; 7 Asian, non-Hispanic/Latino; 1 Hispanic/Latino), 28 international. Average age 26. 188 applicants, 23% accepted, 21 enrolled. In 2011, 11 master's, 12 doctorates awarded. *Degree requirements:* For doctorate, thesis/dissertation. *Entrance requirements:* For doctorate, GRE General Test. Additional exam requirements/recommendations for international students: Required—TOEFL; Recommended—IELTS, TWE. *Application deadline:* For fall admission, 1/1 for domestic and international students. Application fee: $80. Electronic applications accepted. *Financial support:* In 2011–12, 75 students received support, including 16 fellowships with full tuition reimbursements available (averaging $28,000 per year), 86 research assistantships with full tuition reimbursements available (averaging $28,000 per year); teaching assistantships with full tuition reimbursements available, institutionally sponsored loans, scholarships/grants, health care benefits, and unspecified assistantships also available. Financial award applicants required to submit FAFSA. *Faculty research:* Planetary surfaces, evolution of anaerobic respiratory processes, structural geology and tectonics, theoretical and numerical seismology, global biogeochemical cycles. *Unit head:* Dr. Kenneth A. Farley, Chairman, 626-395-6111, Fax: 626-795-6028, E-mail: dianb@gps.caltech.edu. *Application contact:* Dr. Robert W. Clayton, Academic Officer, 626-395-6909, Fax: 626-795-6028, E-mail: dianb@gps.caltech.edu. Web site: http://www.gps.caltech.edu/.

California State University, Long Beach, Graduate Studies, College of Natural Sciences and Mathematics, Department of Geological Sciences, Long Beach, CA 90840. Offers geology (MS); geophysics (MS). Part-time programs available. *Faculty:* 8 full-time (2 women). *Students:* 17 full-time (8 women), 26 part-time (12 women); includes 11 minority (1 Black or African American, non-Hispanic/Latino; 1 American Indian or Alaska Native, non-Hispanic/Latino; 1 Asian, non-Hispanic/Latino; 5 Hispanic/Latino; 1 Native Hawaiian or other Pacific Islander, non-Hispanic/Latino; 2 Two or more races, non-Hispanic/Latino), 3 international. Average age 30. 26 applicants, 50% accepted, 11 enrolled. In 2011, 2 master's awarded. *Degree requirements:* For master's, thesis. *Entrance requirements:* For master's, GRE General Test. *Application deadline:* For fall admission, 7/1 for domestic students. Applications are processed on a rolling basis. Application fee: $55. Electronic applications accepted. *Financial support:* Research assistantships, teaching assistantships, Federal Work-Study, institutionally sponsored loans, and scholarships/grants available. Financial award application deadline: 3/2. *Faculty research:* Paleontology, geophysics, structural geology, organic geochemistry, sedimentary geology. *Unit head:* Robert D. Francis, Chair, 562-985-4929, Fax: 562-985-8638, E-mail: rfrancis@csulb.edu. *Application contact:* Gregory Holk, Graduate Advisor, 562-985-5006, Fax: 562-985-8638, E-mail: gholk@csulb.edu.

Colorado School of Mines, Graduate School, Department of Geophysics, Golden, CO 80401-1887. Offers geophysical engineering (ME, MS, PhD); geophysics (MS, PhD); mineral exploration and mining geosciences (PMS). Part-time programs available. *Faculty:* 18 full-time (1 woman), 2 part-time/adjunct (0 women). *Students:* 85 full-time (28 women), 7 part-time (2 women); includes 9 minority (1 American Indian or Alaska Native, non-Hispanic/Latino; 3 Asian, non-Hispanic/Latino; 5 Hispanic/Latino), 47 international. Average age 28. 163 applicants, 24% accepted, 28 enrolled. In 2011, 14 master's, 3 doctorates awarded. *Degree requirements:* For master's, thesis (for some programs); for doctorate, one foreign language, comprehensive exam, thesis/dissertation, oral exams. *Entrance requirements:* For master's and doctorate, GRE General Test. Additional exam requirements/recommendations for international students: Required—TOEFL (minimum score 550 paper-based; 213 computer-based; 80 iBT). *Application deadline:* For fall admission, 1/15 for domestic and international students; for spring admission, 10/15 for domestic and international students. Application fee: $50 ($70 for international students). Electronic applications accepted. *Expenses:* Tuition, state resident: full-time $12,585; part-time $699 per credit. Tuition, nonresident: full-time $27,270; part-time $1516 per credit. *Required fees:* $1864.20; $670 per semester. *Financial support:* In 2011–12, 74 students received support, including 7 fellowships with full tuition reimbursements available (averaging $20,000 per year), 60 research assistantships with full tuition reimbursements available (averaging $20,000 per year), 7 teaching assistantships with full tuition reimbursements available (averaging $20,000 per year); scholarships/grants, health care benefits, and unspecified assistantships also available. Financial award application deadline: 1/15; financial award applicants required to submit FAFSA. *Faculty research:* Seismic exploration, gravity and geomagnetic fields, electrical mapping and sounding, bore hole measurements, environmental physics. *Total annual research expenditures:* $4.3 million. *Unit head:* Dr. Terence K. Young, Head, 303-273-3454, Fax: 303-273-3478, E-mail: tkyoung@mines.edu. *Application contact:* Michelle Szobody, Office Manager, 303-273-3935, Fax: 303-273-3478, E-mail: mszobody@mines.edu. Web site: http://geophysics.mines.edu.

Columbia University, Graduate School of Arts and Sciences, Division of Natural Sciences, Department of Earth and Environmental Sciences, New York, NY 10027. Offers geochemistry (M Phil, MA, PhD); geodetic sciences (M Phil, MA, PhD); geophysics (M Phil, MA, PhD); oceanography (M Phil, MA, PhD). *Degree requirements:* For master's, thesis or alternative, fieldwork, written exam; for doctorate, one foreign language, thesis/dissertation. *Entrance requirements:* For master's and doctorate, GRE General Test, GRE Subject Test, major in natural or physical science. Additional exam requirements/recommendations for international students: Required—TOEFL. *Faculty research:* Structural geology and stratigraphy, petrology, paleontology, rare gas, isotope and aqueous geochemistry.

Cornell University, Graduate School, Graduate Fields of Engineering, Field of Geological Sciences, Ithaca, NY 14853. Offers economic geology (M Eng, MS, PhD); engineering geology (M Eng, MS, PhD); environmental geophysics (M Eng, MS, PhD); general geology (M Eng, MS, PhD); geobiology (M Eng, MS, PhD); geochemistry and isotope geology (M Eng, MS, PhD); geohydrology (M Eng, MS, PhD); geomorphology (M Eng, MS, PhD); geophysics (M Eng, MS, PhD); geotectonics (M Eng, MS, PhD); marine geology (MS, PhD); mineralogy (M Eng, MS, PhD); paleontology (M Eng, MS, PhD); petroleum geology (M Eng, MS, PhD); petrology (M Eng, MS, PhD); planetary geology (M Eng, MS, PhD); Precambrian geology (M Eng, MS, PhD); Quaternary geology (M Eng, MS, PhD); rock mechanics (M Eng, MS, PhD); sedimentology (M Eng, MS, PhD); seismology (M Eng, MS, PhD); stratigraphy (M Eng, MS, PhD); structural geology (M Eng, MS, PhD). *Faculty:* 37 full-time (5 women). *Students:* 41 full-time (19 women); includes 5 minority (2 Asian, non-Hispanic/Latino; 3 Hispanic/Latino), 7 international. Average age 27. 74 applicants, 19% accepted, 9 enrolled. In 2011, 3 master's, 3 doctorates awarded. *Degree requirements:* For master's, thesis (MS); for doctorate, comprehensive exam, thesis/dissertation. *Entrance requirements:* For master's and doctorate, GRE General Test, 3 letters of recommendation. Additional exam requirements/recommendations for international students: Required—TOEFL (minimum score 550 paper-based; 213 computer-based; 77 iBT). *Application deadline:* For fall admission, 1/15 priority date for domestic students. Applications are processed on a rolling basis. Application fee: $95. Electronic applications accepted. *Financial support:* In 2011–12, 25 students received support, including 7 fellowships with full tuition reimbursements available, 19 research assistantships with full tuition reimbursements available, 8 teaching assistantships with full tuition reimbursements available; institutionally sponsored loans, scholarships/grants, health care benefits, tuition waivers (full and partial), and unspecified assistantships also available. Financial award applicants required to submit FAFSA. *Faculty research:* Geophysics, structural geology, petrology, geochemistry, geodynamics. *Unit head:* Director of Graduate Studies, 607-255-5466, Fax: 607-254-4780. *Application contact:* Graduate Field Assistant, 607-255-5466, Fax: 607-254-4780, E-mail: gradprog@geology.cornell.edu. Web site: http://www.gradschool.cornell.edu/fields.php?id-30&a-2.

Florida State University, The Graduate School, College of Arts and Sciences, Interdisciplinary Program in Geophysical Fluid Dynamics, Tallahassee, FL 32306. Offers PhD. *Faculty:* 18 full-time (2 women). *Students:* 8 full-time (3 women), 3 part-time (0 women), 4 international. Average age 30. 5 applicants, 80% accepted, 4 enrolled. *Degree requirements:* For doctorate, thesis/dissertation, departmental qualifying exam. *Entrance requirements:* For doctorate, GRE General Test, GRE Subject Test, minimum GPA of 3.0. Additional exam requirements/recommendations for international students: Required—TOEFL (minimum score 550 paper-based; 80 iBT). *Application deadline:* For fall admission, 3/30 for domestic and international students. Application fee: $30. Electronic applications accepted. *Expenses:* Tuition, state resident: full-time $9474; part-time $350.88 per credit hour. Tuition, nonresident: full-time $16,236; part-time $601.34 per credit hour. *Required fees:* $630 per semester. One-time fee: $20. Tuition and fees vary according to course load and campus/location. *Financial support:* In 2011–12, 1 research assistantship (averaging $21,500 per year) was awarded; fellowships and unspecified assistantships also available. Financial award applicants required to submit FAFSA. *Faculty research:* Hurricane dynamics, convection, air-sea interaction, wave-mean flow interaction, numerical models. *Total annual research expenditures:* $369,802. *Unit head:* Dr. Kevin Speer, Director, 850-645-5625, Fax: 850-644-8972, E-mail: kspeer@ocean.fsu.edu. *Application contact:* Vijaya Challa, Academic Coordinator, 850-644-5594, Fax: 850-644-8972, E-mail: vijaya@gfdi.fsu.edu. Web site: http://www.gfdphd.fsu.edu/.

Georgia Institute of Technology, Graduate Studies and Research, College of Sciences, School of Earth and Atmospheric Sciences, Atlanta, GA 30332-0340. Offers atmospheric chemistry, aerosols and clouds (MS, PhD); dynamics of weather and climate (MS, PhD); geochemistry (MS, PhD); geophysics (MS, PhD); oceanography (MS, PhD); paleoclimate (MS, PhD); planetary science (MS, PhD); remote sensing (MS, PhD). Part-time programs available. Terminal master's awarded for partial completion of doctoral program. *Degree requirements:* For master's, thesis or alternative; for doctorate, comprehensive exam, thesis/dissertation. *Entrance requirements:* For master's, GRE, letters of recommendation; for doctorate, GRE, academic transcripts, letters of recommendation, personal statement. Additional exam requirements/recommendations for international students: Required—TOEFL (minimum score 550 paper-based; 213 computer-based; 79 iBT). *Faculty research:* Geophysics; atmospheric chemistry, aerosols and clouds; dynamics of weather and climate; geochemistry; oceanography; paleoclimate; planetary science; remote sensing.

ICR Graduate School, Graduate Programs, Santee, CA 92071. Offers astro/geophysics (MS); biology (MS); geology (MS); science education (MS). Part-time programs available. *Degree requirements:* For master's, comprehensive exam

Peterson's Graduate Programs in the Physical Sciences, Mathematics, Agricultural Sciences, the Environment & Natural Resources 2013

facebook.com/petersonspublishing **157**

(for some programs), thesis (for some programs). *Entrance requirements:* For master's, minimum undergraduate GPA of 3.0, bachelor's degree in science or science education. *Faculty research:* Age of the earth, limits of variation, catastrophe, optimum methods for teaching.

Idaho State University, Office of Graduate Studies, College of Science and Engineering, Department of Geosciences, Pocatello, ID 83209-8072. Offers geographic information science (MS); geology (MNS, MS); geology with emphasis in environmental geoscience (MS); geophysics/hydrology/geology (MS); geotechnology (Postbaccalaureate Certificate). Part-time programs available. *Degree requirements:* For master's, comprehensive exam, thesis, oral colloquium; for Postbaccalaureate Certificate, thesis optional, minimum 19 credits. *Entrance requirements:* For master's, GRE General Test (minimum 50th percentile in 2 sections), 3 letters of recommendation; for Postbaccalaureate Certificate, GRE General Test, 3 letters of recommendation, bachelor's degree, statement of goals. Additional exam requirements/recommendations for international students: Required—TOEFL (minimum score 550 paper-based; 213 computer-based; 80 iBT). Electronic applications accepted. *Faculty research:* Quantitative field mapping and sampling: microscopic, geochemical, and isotopic analysis of rocks, minerals and water; remote sensing, geographic information systems, and global positioning systems: environmental and watershed management; surficial and fluvial processes: landscape change; regional tectonics, structural geology; planetary geology.

Indiana University Bloomington, University Graduate School, College of Arts and Sciences, Department of Geological Sciences, Bloomington, IN 47405-7000. Offers biogeochemistry (MS, PhD); economic geology (MS, PhD); geobiology (MS, PhD); geophysics, structural geology and tectonics (MS, PhD); hydrogeology (MS, PhD); mineralogy (MS, PhD); stratigraphy and sedimentology (MS, PhD). *Faculty:* 17 full-time (1 woman). *Students:* 60 full-time (26 women), 2 part-time (0 women); includes 5 minority (2 Black or African American, non-Hispanic/Latino; 1 Hispanic/Latino; 2 Two or more races, non-Hispanic/Latino), 18 international. Average age 29. 44 applicants, 55% accepted, 18 enrolled. In 2011, 11 master's, 6 doctorates awarded. Terminal master's awarded for partial completion of doctoral program. *Degree requirements:* For master's, thesis or alternative; for doctorate, comprehensive exam, thesis/dissertation. *Entrance requirements:* For master's and doctorate, GRE General Test. Additional exam requirements/recommendations for international students: Required—TOEFL. *Application deadline:* For fall admission, 1/15 priority date for domestic students, 12/15 for international students; for spring admission, 9/1 priority date for domestic students, 9/1 for international students. Applications are processed on a rolling basis. Application fee: $55 ($65 for international students). *Financial support:* In 2011–12, fellowships with full tuition reimbursements (averaging $17,300 per year), research assistantships with full tuition reimbursements (averaging $16,370 per year), teaching assistantships with full tuition reimbursements (averaging $15,150 per year) were awarded; career-related internships or fieldwork, Federal Work-Study, and institutionally sponsored loans also available. *Faculty research:* Geophysics, geochemistry, hydrogeology, geobiology, planetary science. *Total annual research expenditures:* $644,299. *Unit head:* Simon Brassell, Chair, 812-855-5581, Fax: 812-855-7899, E-mail: geochair@indiana.edu. *Application contact:* Mary Iverson, Graduate Secretary, 812-855-7214, Fax: 812-855-7899, E-mail: miverson@indiana.edu. Web site: http://www.indiana.edu/~geosci/.

Louisiana State University and Agricultural and Mechanical College, Graduate School, College of Science, Department of Geology and Geophysics, Baton Rouge, LA 70803. Offers MS, PhD. *Faculty:* 14 full-time (4 women). *Students:* 49 full-time (23 women), 9 part-time (0 women); includes 4 minority (2 Black or African American, non-Hispanic/Latino; 1 Hispanic/Latino; 1 Two or more races, non-Hispanic/Latino), 12 international. Average age 26. 68 applicants, 32% accepted, 18 enrolled. In 2011, 14 master's, 3 doctorates awarded. Terminal master's awarded for partial completion of doctoral program. *Degree requirements:* For master's, thesis; for doctorate, thesis/dissertation. *Entrance requirements:* For master's and doctorate, GRE General Test, minimum GPA of 3.0. Additional exam requirements/recommendations for international students: Required—TOEFL (minimum score 550 paper-based; 213 computer-based; 79 iBT) or IELTS (minimum score 6.5). *Application deadline:* For fall admission, 1/25 priority date for domestic students, 5/15 for international students; for spring admission, 10/15 for international students. Applications are processed on a rolling basis. Application fee: $50 ($70 for international students). Electronic applications accepted. *Financial support:* In 2011–12, 47 students received support, including 1 fellowship with full tuition reimbursement available (averaging $30,477 per year), 24 research assistantships with full and partial tuition reimbursements available (averaging $19,406 per year), 18 teaching assistantships with full and partial tuition reimbursements available (averaging $14,191 per year); career-related internships or fieldwork, Federal Work-Study, institutionally sponsored loans, health care benefits, tuition waivers (full and partial), and unspecified assistantships also available. Financial award application deadline: 3/15; financial award applicants required to submit FAFSA. *Faculty research:* Geophysics, sedimentology, geochemistry, geomicrobiology, tectonics. *Total annual research expenditures:* $785,748. *Unit head:* Dr. Carol Wicks, Chair, 225-578-3353, Fax: 225-578-2302, E-mail: cwicks@lsu.edu. *Application contact:* Dr. Sam Bentley, Graduate Adviser, 225-578-5735, E-mail: sjb@lsu.edu. Web site: http://www.geol.lsu.edu/.

Massachusetts Institute of Technology, School of Science, Department of Earth, Atmospheric, and Planetary Sciences, Cambridge, MA 02139. Offers atmospheric chemistry (PhD, Sc D); atmospheric science (SM, PhD, Sc D); chemical oceanography (SM, PhD, Sc D); climate physics and chemistry (SM, PhD, Sc D); earth and planetary sciences (SM); geochemistry (PhD, Sc D); geology (PhD, Sc D); geophysics (PhD, Sc D); marine geology and geophysics (SM, PhD, Sc D); physical oceanography (SM, PhD, Sc D); planetary sciences (PhD, Sc D). *Faculty:* 33 full-time (6 women). *Students:* 175 full-time (81 women); includes 21 minority (3 Black or African American, non-Hispanic/Latino; 1 American Indian or Alaska Native, non-Hispanic/Latino; 8 Asian, non-Hispanic/Latino; 4 Hispanic/Latino; 5 Two or more races, non-Hispanic/Latino), 58 international. Average age 26. 241 applicants, 28% accepted, 43 enrolled. In 2011, 6 master's, 16 doctorates awarded. Terminal master's awarded for partial completion of doctoral program. *Degree requirements:* For master's, thesis; for doctorate, comprehensive exam, thesis/dissertation. *Entrance requirements:* For master's, GRE General Test; for doctorate, GRE General Test, GRE Subject Test (chemistry or physics for planetary science area). Additional exam requirements/recommendations for international students: Required—TOEFL (minimum score 577 paper-based; 233 computer-based; 91 iBT), IELTS (minimum score 7). *Application deadline:* For fall admission, 1/5 for domestic and international students; for spring admission, 11/1 for domestic and international students. Application fee: $75. Electronic applications accepted. *Expenses: Tuition:* Full-time $40,460; part-time $630 per credit hour. *Required fees:* $272. *Financial support:* In 2011–12, 125 students received support, including 68 fellowships (averaging $32,200 per year), 94 research assistantships (averaging $31,900 per year), 10 teaching assistantships (averaging $30,000 per year); Federal Work-Study, institutionally sponsored loans, scholarships/grants, health care benefits, and unspecified assistantships also available. *Faculty research:* Formation, dynamics and evolution of planetary systems; origin, composition, structure and dynamics of the atmospheres, oceans, surfaces and interiors of the Earth and other planets; evolution and interaction of the physical, chemical, geological and biological components of the Earth system; characterization of past, present and potential future climates and the causes and consequences of climate change; interplay of energy and the environment. *Total annual research expenditures:* $26.2 million. *Unit head:* Prof. Robert van der Hilst, Head, 617-253-2127, Fax: 617-253-8298, E-mail: eapsinfo@mit.edu. *Application contact:* EAPS Education Office, 617-253-3381, Fax: 617-253-8298, E-mail: eapsinfo@mit.edu. Web site: http://eapsweb.mit.edu/.

Memorial University of Newfoundland, School of Graduate Studies, Department of Earth Sciences, St. John's, NL A1C 5S7, Canada. Offers geology (M Sc, PhD); geophysics (M Sc, PhD). Part-time programs available. *Degree requirements:* For master's, thesis; for doctorate, comprehensive exam, thesis/dissertation, oral thesis defense, entry evaluation. *Entrance requirements:* For master's, honors B Sc; for doctorate, M Sc. Electronic applications accepted. *Faculty research:* Geochemistry, sedimentology, paleoceanography and global change, mineral deposits, petroleum geology, hydrology.

Michigan Technological University, Graduate School, College of Engineering, Department of Geological and Mining Engineering and Sciences, Houghton, MI 49931. Offers geological engineering (MS, PhD); geology (MS, PhD); geophysics (MS, PhD); mining engineering (MS, PhD). Part-time programs available. *Faculty:* 20 full-time (2 women), 21 part-time/adjunct (1 woman). *Students:* 52 full-time (28 women), 8 part-time (3 women); includes 3 minority (all Hispanic/Latino), 20 international. Average age 29. 114 applicants, 33% accepted, 15 enrolled. In 2011, 10 master's, 1 doctorate awarded. Terminal master's awarded for partial completion of doctoral program. *Degree requirements:* For master's, comprehensive exam (for some programs), thesis (for some programs); for doctorate, comprehensive exam, thesis/dissertation. *Entrance requirements:* For master's and doctorate, GRE, statement of purpose, official transcripts, 3 letters of recommendation. Additional exam requirements/recommendations for international students: Required—TOEFL (minimum score 79 iBT) or IELTS. *Application deadline:* Applications are processed on a rolling basis. Electronic applications accepted. *Expenses: Tuition,* state resident: full-time $12,636; part-time $702 per credit. Tuition, nonresident: full-time $12,636; part-time $702 per credit. *Required fees:* $226; $226 per year. *Financial support:* In 2011–12, 45 students received support, including 4 fellowships with full tuition reimbursements available (averaging $6,065 per year), 22 research assistantships with full tuition reimbursements available (averaging $6,065 per year), teaching assistantships with full tuition reimbursements available (averaging $6,065 per year); career-related internships or fieldwork, Federal Work-Study, scholarships/grants, health care benefits, tuition waivers (partial), unspecified assistantships, and cooperative program also available. Financial award applicants required to submit FAFSA. *Faculty research:* Volcanic hazards and volcanic clouds, oil and gas exploration and development, groundwater measurement and modeling, geophysics, environmental paleomagnetism. *Total annual research expenditures:* $1.3 million. *Unit head:* Dr. Wayne D. Pennington, Chair, 906-487-3573, Fax: 906-487-3371, E-mail: wayne@mtu.edu. *Application contact:* Amie S. Ledgerwood, Secretary 5, 906-487-2531, Fax: 906-487-3371, E-mail: asledger@mtu.edu. Web site: http://www.mtu.edu/geo/.

Missouri University of Science and Technology, Graduate School, Department of Geological Sciences and Engineering, Rolla, MO 65409. Offers geological engineering (MS, DE, PhD); geology and geophysics (MS, PhD), including geochemistry, geology, geophysics, groundwater and environmental geology; petroleum engineering (MS, DE, PhD). Part-time programs available. *Degree requirements:* For master's, thesis optional; for doctorate, comprehensive exam, thesis/dissertation. *Entrance requirements:* For master's, GRE General Test (minimum score 600 quantitative, writing 3.5), minimum GPA of 3.0 in last 4

158 facebook.com/petersonspublishing

Peterson's Graduate Programs in the Physical Sciences, Mathematics, Agricultural Sciences, the Environment & Natural Resources 2013

semesters; for doctorate, GRE General Test (minimum: Q 600, GRE WR 3.5). Additional exam requirements/recommendations for international students: Required—TOEFL. Electronic applications accepted. *Faculty research:* Digital image processing and geographic information systems, mineralogy, igneous and sedimentary petrology-geochemistry, sedimentology groundwater hydrology and contaminant transport.

New Mexico Institute of Mining and Technology, Graduate Studies, Department of Earth and Environmental Science, Program in Geophysics, Socorro, NM 87801. Offers MS, PhD. *Students:* 11 full-time (7 women), 1 (woman) part-time, 2 international. Average age 28. In 2011, 2 degrees awarded. *Degree requirements:* For master's, thesis optional; for doctorate, thesis/ dissertation. *Entrance requirements:* For master's, GRE General Test; for doctorate, GRE General Test, GRE Subject Test. Additional exam requirements/ recommendations for international students: Required—TOEFL (minimum score 540 paper-based; 207 computer-based). *Application deadline:* For fall admission, 3/1 priority date for domestic students; for spring admission, 6/1 for domestic students. Applications are processed on a rolling basis. Application fee: $16 ($30 for international students). *Expenses:* Tuition, state resident: full-time $4849; part-time $269.41 per credit hour. Tuition, nonresident: full-time $16,041; part-time $891.15 per credit hour. *Required fees:* $622; $65 per credit hour. $20 per semester. Part-time tuition and fees vary according to course load. *Financial support:* Federal Work-Study, institutionally sponsored loans, and unspecified assistantships available. Financial award application deadline: 3/1; financial award applicants required to submit CSS PROFILE or FAFSA. *Faculty research:* Earthquake and volcanic seismology, subduction zone tectonics, network seismology, physical properties of sediments in fault zones. *Unit head:* Dr. Richard Aster, Coordinator, 575-835-5924, Fax: 575-835-6436, E-mail: aster@ nmt.edu. *Application contact:* Dr. Lorie Liebrock, Dean of Graduate Studies, 575-835-5513, Fax: 575-835-5476, E-mail: graduate@nmt.edu.

Ohio University, Graduate College, College of Arts and Sciences, Department of Geological Sciences, Athens, OH 45701-2979. Offers environmental geochemistry (MS); environmental geology (MS); environmental/hydrology (MS); geology (MS); geology education (MS); geomorphology/surficial processes (MS); geophysics (MS); hydrogeology (MS); sedimentology (MS); structure/tectonics (MS). Part-time programs available. *Students:* 19 full-time (10 women). 14 applicants, 64% accepted, 9 enrolled. In 2011, 8 master's awarded. *Degree requirements:* For master's, thesis. *Entrance requirements:* Additional exam requirements/recommendations for international students: Required—TOEFL (minimum score 550 paper-based; 80 iBT) or IELTS (minimum score 6.5). *Application deadline:* For fall admission, 2/1 priority date for domestic students, 2/ 1 for international students. Application fee: $50 ($55 for international students). Electronic applications accepted. *Financial support:* Research assistantships with full tuition reimbursements, teaching assistantships with full tuition reimbursements, Federal Work-Study, institutionally sponsored loans, scholarships/grants, tuition waivers (partial), and unspecified assistantships available. Financial award application deadline: 2/1. *Faculty research:* Geoscience education, tectonics, fluvial geomorphology, invertebrate paleontology, mine/hydrology. *Total annual research expenditures:* $649,020. *Unit head:* Dr. Gregory Nadon, Chair, 740-593-4212, Fax: 740-593-0486, E-mail: nadon@ohio.edu. *Application contact:* Dr. Keith Milam, Graduate Chair, 740-593-1106, Fax: 740-593-0486, E-mail: milamk@ohio.edu. Web site: http:// www.ohiou.edu/geology/.

Oregon State University, Graduate School, College of Oceanic and Atmospheric Sciences, Program in Geophysics, Corvallis, OR 97331. Offers MA, MS, PhD. Terminal master's awarded for partial completion of doctoral program. *Degree requirements:* For master's, thesis optional; for doctorate, thesis/dissertation. *Entrance requirements:* For master's and doctorate, GRE General Test, minimum GPA of 3.0 in last 90 hours. Additional exam requirements/recommendations for international students: Required—TOEFL. *Faculty research:* Seismic waves; gravitational, geothermal, and electromagnetic fields; rock magnetism; paleomagnetism.

Rice University, Graduate Programs, Wiess School–Professional Science Master's Programs, Professional Master's Program in Subsurface Geosciences, Houston, TX 77251-1892. Offers geophysics (MS). Part-time programs available. *Degree requirements:* For master's, internship. *Entrance requirements:* For master's, GRE, letters of recommendation (4). Additional exam requirements/ recommendations for international students: Required—TOEFL (minimum score 600 paper-based; 250 computer-based; 90 iBT). Electronic applications accepted. *Faculty research:* Seismology, geodynamics, wave propagation, bio-geochemistry, remote sensing.

Saint Louis University, Graduate Education, College of Arts and Sciences, Department of Earth and Atmospheric Sciences, St. Louis, MO 63103-2097. Offers geophysics (PhD); geoscience (MS); meteorology (M Pr Met, MS-R, PhD). Part-time programs available. *Degree requirements:* For master's, thesis (for some programs), comprehensive oral exam; for doctorate, thesis/dissertation, preliminary exams. *Entrance requirements:* For master's, GRE General Test, letters of recommendation, resume; for doctorate, GRE General Test, letters of recommendation, resumé, goal statement, transcripts. Additional exam requirements/recommendations for international students: Required—TOEFL (minimum score 525 paper-based; 194 computer-based). Electronic applications accepted. *Faculty research:* Structural geology, mesoscale meteorology and severe storms, weather and climate change prediction.

Southern Methodist University, Dedman College, Department of Earth Sciences, Program in Applied Geophysics, Dallas, TX 75275. Offers MS. Part-time programs available. *Degree requirements:* For master's, thesis optional, qualifying exam. *Entrance requirements:* For master's, GRE General Test, minimum GPA of 3.0, letters of recommendation. Additional exam requirements/ recommendations for international students: Required—TOEFL. *Faculty research:* Geothermal energy, seismology.

Southern Methodist University, Dedman College, Department of Earth Sciences, Program in Geophysics, Dallas, TX 75275. Offers MS, PhD. Part-time programs available. *Degree requirements:* For master's, thesis (for some programs), qualifying exam; for doctorate, thesis/dissertation, qualifying exam. *Entrance requirements:* For master's and doctorate, GRE General Test, minimum GPA of 3.0, letters of recommendation. Additional exam requirements/ recommendations for international students: Required—TOEFL. *Faculty research:* Seismology, heat flow, tectonics.

Stanford University, School of Earth Sciences, Department of Geophysics, Stanford, CA 94305-9991. Offers MS, PhD. Terminal master's awarded for partial completion of doctoral program. *Degree requirements:* For master's, thesis; for doctorate, thesis/dissertation. *Entrance requirements:* For master's and doctorate, GRE General Test. Additional exam requirements/recommendations for international students: Required—TOEFL. Electronic applications accepted. *Expenses: Tuition:* Full-time $40,050; part-time $890 per credit.

Texas A&M University, College of Geosciences, Department of Geology and Geophysics, College Station, TX 77843. Offers geology (MS, PhD); geophysics (MS, PhD). *Faculty:* 31. *Students:* 108 full-time (43 women), 18 part-time (9 women); includes 12 minority (2 Black or African American, non-Hispanic/Latino; 4 Asian, non-Hispanic/Latino; 5 Hispanic/Latino; 1 Two or more races, non-Hispanic/Latino), 46 international. Average age 31. In 2011, 16 master's, 4 doctorates awarded. *Degree requirements:* For master's, thesis; for doctorate, thesis/dissertation. *Entrance requirements:* For master's and doctorate, GRE General Test. Additional exam requirements/recommendations for international students: Required—TOEFL. *Application deadline:* For fall admission, 3/1 priority date for domestic students, 1/15 for international students; for spring admission, 10/1 priority date for domestic students, 8/15 for international students. Applications are processed on a rolling basis. Application fee: $50 ($75 for international students). Electronic applications accepted. *Expenses:* Tuition, state resident: full-time $5437; part-time $226.55 per credit hour. Tuition, nonresident: full-time $12,949; part-time $539.55 per credit hour. *Required fees:* $2741. *Financial support:* In 2011–12, fellowships with partial tuition reimbursements (averaging $1,000 per year), research assistantships with partial tuition reimbursements (averaging $11,925 per year), teaching assistantships with partial tuition reimbursements (averaging $11,925 per year) were awarded; Federal Work-Study, institutionally sponsored loans, scholarships/grants, tuition waivers (partial), and unspecified assistantships also available. Financial award application deadline: 3/1; financial award applicants required to submit FAFSA. *Faculty research:* Environmental and engineering geology and geophysics, petroleum geology, tectonophysics, geochemistry. *Unit head:* Dr. Rick Giardino, Head, 979-845-3224, E-mail: giardino@geo.tamu.edu. *Application contact:* Graduate Admissions, 979-845-1044, E-mail: admissions@tamu.edu. Web site: http://geoweb.tamu.edu.

The University of Akron, Graduate School, Buchtel College of Arts and Sciences, Department of Geology and Environmental Science, Program in Geophysics, Akron, OH 44325. Offers MS. *Students:* 1 (woman) full-time. Average age 49. 3 applicants, 67% accepted, 0 enrolled. *Degree requirements:* For master's, comprehensive exam, thesis, seminar, proficiency exam. *Entrance requirements:* For master's, minimum GPA of 2.75, letters of recommendation, statement of purpose. Additional exam requirements/recommendations for international students: Required—TOEFL (minimum score 550 paper-based; 213 computer-based; 79 iBT). *Application deadline:* Applications are processed on a rolling basis. Application fee: $30 ($40 for international students). Electronic applications accepted. *Expenses:* Tuition, state resident: full-time $7038; part-time $391 per credit hour. Tuition, nonresident: full-time $12,051; part-time $670 per credit hour. *Required fees:* $1274; $34 per credit hour. *Unit head:* Dr. LaVerne Friberg, Director of Graduate Studies, 330-972-8046, E-mail: lfribe1@uakron.edu. *Application contact:* Dr. LaVerne Friberg, Director of Graduate Studies, 330-972-8046, E-mail: lfribe1@uakron.edu.

University of Alaska Fairbanks, College of Natural Sciences and Mathematics, Department of Geology and Geophysics, Fairbanks, AK 99775-5780. Offers geology (MS, PhD), including economic geology (PhD), petroleum geology (MS), quaternary geology (PhD), remote sensing, volcanology (PhD); geophysics (MS, PhD), including remote sensing, snow, ice, and permafrost geophysics (MS), solid-earth geophysics (MS). Part-time programs available. *Faculty:* 12 full-time (5 women). *Students:* 60 full-time (27 women), 12 part-time (5 women); includes 5 minority (1 Hispanic/Latino; 4 Two or more races, non-Hispanic/Latino), 23 international. Average age 29. 89 applicants, 18% accepted, 15 enrolled. In 2011, 7 master's, 2 doctorates awarded. Terminal master's awarded for partial completion of doctoral program. *Degree requirements:* For master's, comprehensive exam, thesis, oral exam, oral defense; for doctorate, comprehensive exam, thesis/dissertation, oral exam, oral defense. *Entrance requirements:* For master's and doctorate, GRE General Test. Additional exam requirements/recommendations for international students: Required—TOEFL (minimum score 550 paper-based; 213 computer-based). *Application deadline:* For fall admission, 6/1 for domestic students, 3/1 for international students; for

Peterson's Graduate Programs in the Physical Sciences, Mathematics, Agricultural Sciences, the Environment & Natural Resources 2013

facebook.com/petersonspublishing **159**

spring admission, 10/15 for domestic students, 9/1 for international students. Applications are processed on a rolling basis. Application fee: $60. Electronic applications accepted. *Expenses:* Tuition, state resident: full-time $6696; part-time $372 per credit. Tuition, nonresident: full-time $13,680; part-time $760 per credit. Tuition and fees vary according to course load and reciprocity agreements. *Financial support:* In 2011–12, 42 research assistantships with tuition reimbursements (averaging $14,177 per year), 7 teaching assistantships with tuition reimbursements (averaging $9,807 per year) were awarded; fellowships with tuition reimbursements, Federal Work-Study, scholarships/grants, health care benefits, and unspecified assistantships also available. Support available to part-time students. Financial award application deadline: 2/15; financial award applicants required to submit FAFSA. *Faculty research:* Glacial surging, volcanology, geochronology, impact cratering, permafrost geophysics. *Total annual research expenditures:* $23,000. *Unit head:* Dr. Benard Coakley, Department Chair, 907-474-7565, Fax: 907-474-5163, E-mail: geology@uaf.edu. *Application contact:* Mike Earnest, Director of Admissions, 907-474-7500, Fax: 907-474-5379, E-mail: admissions@uaf.edu. Web site: http://www.uaf.edu/geology/.

University of Alberta, Faculty of Graduate Studies and Research, Department of Physics, Edmonton, AB T6G 2E1, Canada. Offers astrophysics (M Sc, PhD); condensed matter (M Sc, PhD); geophysics (M Sc, PhD); medical physics (M Sc, PhD); subatomic physics (M Sc, PhD). *Degree requirements:* For master's, thesis; for doctorate, thesis/dissertation. *Entrance requirements:* For master's and doctorate, minimum GPA of 7.0 on a 9.0 scale. Additional exam requirements/recommendations for international students: Required—TOEFL. *Faculty research:* Cosmology, astroparticle physics, high-intermediate energy, magnetism, superconductivity.

The University of British Columbia, Faculty of Science, Department of Earth and Ocean Sciences, Vancouver, BC V6T 1Z4, Canada. Offers atmospheric science (M Sc, PhD); geological engineering (M Eng, MA Sc, PhD); geological sciences (M Sc, PhD); geophysics (M Sc, MA Sc, PhD); oceanography (M Sc, PhD). *Degree requirements:* For master's, thesis (for some programs); for doctorate, comprehensive exam, thesis/dissertation. *Entrance requirements:* Additional exam requirements/recommendations for international students: Required—TOEFL (minimum score 600 paper-based; 250 computer-based; 100 iBT). Electronic applications accepted. *Faculty research:* Oceans and atmosphere, environmental earth science, hydro geology, mineral deposits, geophysics.

University of Calgary, Faculty of Graduate Studies, Faculty of Science, Department of Geology and Geophysics, Calgary, AB T2N 1N4, Canada. Offers geology (M Sc, PhD); geophysics (M Sc, PhD). Part-time programs available. Terminal master's awarded for partial completion of doctoral program. *Degree requirements:* For master's, thesis; for doctorate, thesis/dissertation, candidacy exam. *Entrance requirements:* For master's, B Sc; for doctorate, honors B Sc or M Sc. Additional exam requirements/recommendations for international students: Required—TOEFL. Electronic applications accepted. *Faculty research:* Geochemistry, petrology, paleontology, stratigraphy, exploration and solid-earth geophysics.

University of California, Berkeley, Graduate Division, College of Letters and Science, Department of Earth and Planetary Science, Berkeley, CA 94720-1500. Offers geology (MA, MS, PhD); geophysics (MA, MS, PhD). Terminal master's awarded for partial completion of doctoral program. *Degree requirements:* For master's, oral exam (MA), thesis (MS); for doctorate, comprehensive exam, thesis/dissertation, candidacy exams. *Entrance requirements:* For master's and doctorate, GRE General Test, minimum GPA of 3.0, 3 letters of recommendation. Additional exam requirements/recommendations for international students: Required—TOEFL. *Faculty research:* Tectonics, environmental geology, high-pressure geophysics and seismology, economic geology, geochemistry.

University of California, Los Angeles, Graduate Division, College of Letters and Science, Department of Earth and Space Sciences, Program in Geophysics and Space Physics, Los Angeles, CA 90095. Offers MS, PhD. *Students:* 38 full-time (18 women); includes 5 minority (1 Black or African American, non-Hispanic/Latino; 3 Asian, non-Hispanic/Latino; 1 Two or more races, non-Hispanic/Latino), 14 international. Average age 27. 65 applicants, 20% accepted, 10 enrolled. In 2011, 4 master's, 3 doctorates awarded. Terminal master's awarded for partial completion of doctoral program. *Degree requirements:* For master's, comprehensive exams or thesis; for doctorate, thesis/dissertation, oral and written qualifying exams. *Entrance requirements:* For master's, GRE General Test, minimum GPA of 3.0, bachelor's degree in related field; for doctorate, GRE General Test, minimum undergraduate GPA of 3.0, bachelor's degree in related field. *Application deadline:* For fall admission, 1/15 for domestic and international students. Application fee: $70 ($90 for international students). Electronic applications accepted. *Financial support:* In 2011–12, 28 fellowships with full and partial tuition reimbursements, 27 research assistantships with full and partial tuition reimbursements, 8 teaching assistantships with full and partial tuition reimbursements were awarded; Federal Work-Study, institutionally sponsored loans, scholarships/grants, health care benefits, tuition waivers (full and partial), and unspecified assistantships also available. Financial award application deadline: 3/1; financial award applicants required to submit FAFSA. *Unit head:* Dr. Craig E. Manning, Chair, 310-206-3290, E-mail: manning@ess.ucla.edu. *Application contact:* Departmental Office, 310-825-3917, E-mail: holbrook@ess.ucla.edu. Web site: http://www.ess.ucla.edu/.

University of California, Santa Barbara, Graduate Division, College of Letters and Sciences, Division of Mathematics, Life, and Physical Sciences, Department of Earth Science, Santa Barbara, CA 93106-9620. Offers geological sciences (MS, PhD); geophysics (MS). *Faculty:* 20 full-time (3 women). *Students:* 43 full-time (16 women); includes 8 minority (1 American Indian or Alaska Native, non-Hispanic/Latino; 2 Asian, non-Hispanic/Latino; 5 Hispanic/Latino), 5 international. Average age 27. 83 applicants, 16% accepted, 8 enrolled. In 2011, 10 master's, 3 doctorates awarded. Terminal master's awarded for partial completion of doctoral program. *Median time to degree:* Of those who began their doctoral program in fall 2003, 64% received their degree in 8 years or less. *Degree requirements:* For master's, comprehensive exam, thesis, 30 units; for doctorate, comprehensive exam, thesis/dissertation, 30 units, oral qualifying exam. *Entrance requirements:* For master's and doctorate, GRE General Test. Additional exam requirements/recommendations for international students: Required—TOEFL (minimum score 550 paper-based; 80 iBT), IELTS (minimum score 7). *Application deadline:* For fall admission, 1/1 for domestic and international students. Application fee: $80 ($100 for international students). Electronic applications accepted. *Expenses:* Tuition, state resident: full-time $12,192. Tuition, nonresident: full-time $27,294. *Required fees:* $764.13. *Financial support:* In 2011–12, 38 students received support, including 34 fellowships with full and partial tuition reimbursements available (averaging $12,566 per year), 22 research assistantships with full and partial tuition reimbursements available (averaging $7,362 per year), 28 teaching assistantships with full and partial tuition reimbursements available (averaging $7,234 per year); tuition waivers (full and partial) also available. Financial award application deadline: 1/1; financial award applicants required to submit CSS PROFILE or FAFSA. *Faculty research:* Geology, geomaterials and earth's structure; geomorphology, tectonics; geophysics, seismology; paleoclimate, paleoceanography and geochemistry; paleobiology, evolution and paleontology. *Unit head:* Dr. Douglas Burbank, Chair, 805-893-7858, Fax: 805-893-2314, E-mail: burbank@eri.ucsb.edu. *Application contact:* Hannah Smit, Graduate Program Assistant, 805-893-3329, Fax: 805-893-2314, E-mail: hsmit@geol.ucsb.edu. Web site: http://www.geol.ucsb.edu/.

University of Chicago, Division of the Physical Sciences, Department of the Geophysical Sciences, Chicago, IL 60637-1513. Offers atmospheric sciences (SM, PhD); cosmochemistry (PhD); earth sciences (SM, PhD); paleobiology (PhD); planetary and space sciences (SM, PhD). *Faculty:* 24 full-time (3 women). *Students:* 38 full-time (16 women); includes 2 minority (both Hispanic/Latino), 16 international. Average age 26. 68 applicants, 28% accepted, 10 enrolled. In 2011, 2 master's, 5 doctorates awarded. Terminal master's awarded for partial completion of doctoral program. *Degree requirements:* For master's, thesis, seminar; for doctorate, variable foreign language requirement, comprehensive exam, thesis/dissertation. *Entrance requirements:* For doctorate, GRE General Test. Additional exam requirements/recommendations for international students: Required—TOEFL (minimum score 600 paper-based; 250 computer-based; 96 iBT), IELTS (minimum score 7). *Application deadline:* For fall admission, 1/9 for domestic students, 1/10 for international students. Application fee: $55. Electronic applications accepted. *Financial support:* In 2011–12, research assistantships with full tuition reimbursements (averaging $26,500 per year), teaching assistantships with full tuition reimbursements (averaging $27,000 per year) were awarded; fellowships, Federal Work-Study, institutionally sponsored loans, scholarships/grants, tuition waivers (partial), and unspecified assistantships also available. Financial award application deadline: 1/9. *Faculty research:* Climatology, evolutionary paleontology, cosmochemistry, geochemistry, oceanic sciences. *Unit head:* Dr. Michael Foote, Chairman, 773-702-8102, Fax: 773-702-9505. *Application contact:* David J. Taylor, Graduate Student Services Coordinator, 773-702-8180, Fax: 773-702-9505, E-mail: info@geosci.uchicago.edu. Web site: http://geosci.uchicago.edu/.

University of Colorado Boulder, Graduate School, College of Arts and Sciences, Department of Geological Sciences, Boulder, CO 80309. Offers geology (MS, PhD); geophysics (PhD). *Faculty:* 29 full-time (8 women). *Students:* 69 full-time (41 women), 18 part-time (7 women); includes 6 minority (2 American Indian or Alaska Native, non-Hispanic/Latino; 2 Hispanic/Latino; 2 Two or more races, non-Hispanic/Latino), 6 international. Average age 29. 236 applicants, 12% accepted, 23 enrolled. In 2011, 15 master's, 7 doctorates awarded. Terminal master's awarded for partial completion of doctoral program. *Degree requirements:* For master's, comprehensive exam, thesis; for doctorate, comprehensive exam, thesis/dissertation. *Entrance requirements:* For master's, GRE General Test, minimum undergraduate GPA of 3.0; for doctorate, GRE General Test, minimum GPA of 2.75. *Application deadline:* For fall admission, 12/15 priority date for domestic students, 12/1 for international students. Application fee: $50 ($60 for international students). Electronic applications accepted. *Financial support:* In 2011–12, 109 students received support, including 62 fellowships (averaging $7,337 per year), 38 research assistantships with full and partial tuition reimbursements available (averaging $21,321 per year), 23 teaching assistantships with full and partial tuition reimbursements available (averaging $19,046 per year); institutionally sponsored loans, scholarships/grants, health care benefits, and unspecified assistantships also available. Financial award application deadline: 1/15; financial award applicants required to submit FAFSA. *Faculty research:* Sedimentology, stratigraphy, economic geology of mineral deposits, fossil fuels, hydrogeology and water resources, geophysics, isotope geology, paleobiology, mineralogy, remote sensing. *Total annual research expenditures:* $6.8 million. *Application contact:* E-mail: geolinfo@colorado.edu. Web site: http://www.colorado.edu/GeolSci.

160 facebook.com/petersonspublishing

Peterson's Graduate Programs in the Physical Sciences, Mathematics, Agricultural Sciences, the Environment & Natural Resources 2013

University of Colorado Boulder, Graduate School, College of Arts and Sciences, Department of Physics, Boulder, CO 80309. Offers chemical physics (PhD); geophysics (PhD); liquid crystal science and technology (PhD); mathematical physics (PhD); medical physics (PhD); optical sciences and engineering (PhD); physics (MS, PhD). *Faculty:* 51 full-time (7 women). *Students:* 157 full-time (28 women), 66 part-time (11 women); includes 11 minority (6 Asian, non-Hispanic/Latino; 5 Hispanic/Latino), 75 international. Average age 26. 551 applicants, 25% accepted, 47 enrolled. In 2011, 29 master's, 28 doctorates awarded. Terminal master's awarded for partial completion of doctoral program. *Degree requirements:* For master's, comprehensive exam, thesis or alternative; for doctorate, comprehensive exam, thesis/dissertation. *Entrance requirements:* For master's and doctorate, GRE General Test, GRE Subject Test, minimum undergraduate GPA of 3.0. Additional exam requirements/recommendations for international students: Required—TOEFL. *Application deadline:* For fall admission, 1/15 priority date for domestic students, 1/15 for international students. Applications are processed on a rolling basis. Application fee: $50 ($60 for international students). Electronic applications accepted. *Financial support:* In 2011–12, 216 students received support, including 85 fellowships (averaging $9,233 per year), 131 research assistantships with full and partial tuition reimbursements available (averaging $24,425 per year), 31 teaching assistantships with full and partial tuition reimbursements available (averaging $20,162 per year); institutionally sponsored loans, scholarships/grants, health care benefits, and unspecified assistantships also available. Financial award application deadline: 1/15; financial award applicants required to submit FAFSA. *Faculty research:* Atomic and molecular physics, nuclear physics, condensed matter, elementary particle physics, laser or optical physics, plasma physics, geophysics, OSEP, astrophysics and chemical physics. *Total annual research expenditures:* $26.1 million. *Application contact:* E-mail: physics@colorado.edu. Web site: http://physics.colorado.edu/.

University of Hawaii at Manoa, Graduate Division, School of Ocean and Earth Science and Technology, Department of Geology and Geophysics, Honolulu, HI 96822. Offers high-pressure geophysics and geochemistry (MS, PhD); hydrogeology and engineering geology (MS, PhD); marine geology and geophysics (MS, PhD); planetary geosciences and remote sensing (MS, PhD); seismology and solid-earth geophysics (MS, PhD); volcanology, petrology, and geochemistry (MS, PhD). Part-time programs available. Terminal master's awarded for partial completion of doctoral program. *Degree requirements:* For master's, thesis optional; for doctorate, comprehensive exam, thesis/dissertation. *Entrance requirements:* For master's and doctorate, GRE General Test, minimum GPA of 3.0. Additional exam requirements/recommendations for international students: Required—TOEFL (minimum score 580 paper-based; 237 computer-based; 92 iBT), IELTS (minimum score 5).

University of Houston, College of Natural Sciences and Mathematics, Department of Earth and Atmospheric Sciences, Houston, TX 77204. Offers atmospheric science (PhD); geology (MA, PhD); geophysics (PhD). Part-time programs available. *Degree requirements:* For master's, thesis; for doctorate, comprehensive exam, thesis/dissertation. *Entrance requirements:* For master's and doctorate, GRE General Test. Additional exam requirements/recommendations for international students: Required—TOEFL (minimum score 550 paper-based; 213 computer-based; 79 iBT), IELTS (minimum score 6.5). Electronic applications accepted. *Faculty research:* Atmospherics sciences, seismic and solid earth geophysics, tectonics, environmental hydrochemistry, carbonates, micropaleontology, structure and tectonics, petroleum geology.

University of Manitoba, Faculty of Graduate Studies, Clayton H. Riddell Faculty of Environment, Earth, and Resources, Department of Geological Sciences, Winnipeg, MB R3T 2N2, Canada. Offers geology (M Sc, PhD); geophysics (M Sc, PhD). *Degree requirements:* For master's, thesis; for doctorate, thesis/dissertation. *Entrance requirements:* For master's and doctorate, GRE General Test, GRE Subject Test (geology), minimum GPA of 3.0. Additional exam requirements/recommendations for international students: Required—TOEFL.

University of Memphis, Graduate School, College of Arts and Sciences, Department of Earth Sciences, Memphis, TN 38152. Offers archaeology (MS); earth sciences (PhD); geographic information systems (Graduate Certificate); geography (MA, MS); geology (MS); geophysics (MS); interdisciplinary (MS). Part-time and evening/weekend programs available. Terminal master's awarded for partial completion of doctoral program. *Degree requirements:* For master's, comprehensive exam, thesis, seminar presentation; for doctorate, thesis/dissertation. *Entrance requirements:* For master's, GRE General Test, 3 letters of recommendation, statement of research interests; for doctorate, GRE General Test, 2 letters of recommendation, resume, personal statement. Additional exam requirements/recommendations for international students: Required—TOEFL (minimum score 550 paper-based; 210 computer-based). Electronic applications accepted. *Faculty research:* Hazards, active tectonics, geophysics, hydrology and water resources, spatial analysis.

University of Miami, Graduate School, Rosenstiel School of Marine and Atmospheric Science, Division of Marine Geology and Geophysics, Coral Gables, FL 33124. Offers MS, PhD. Terminal master's awarded for partial completion of doctoral program. *Degree requirements:* For master's, comprehensive exam, thesis; for doctorate, comprehensive exam, thesis/dissertation. *Entrance requirements:* For master's and doctorate, GRE General Test. Additional exam requirements/recommendations for international students: Required—TOEFL (minimum score 550 paper-based; 213 computer-based). Electronic applications

accepted. *Faculty research:* Carbonate sedimentology, low-temperature geochemistry, paleoceanography, geodesy and tectonics.

University of Minnesota, Twin Cities Campus, College of Science and Engineering, Department of Earth Sciences, Minneapolis, MN 55455-0213. Offers MS, PhD. *Faculty:* 22 full-time (4 women). *Students:* 60 (27 women); includes 7 minority (1 Black or African American, non-Hispanic/Latino; 2 American Indian or Alaska Native, non-Hispanic/Latino; 4 Hispanic/Latino), 11 international. Terminal master's awarded for partial completion of doctoral program. *Degree requirements:* For master's, thesis; for doctorate, thesis/dissertation. *Entrance requirements:* For master's and doctorate, GRE General Test, 3 letters of recommendation. Additional exam requirements/recommendations for international students: Required—TOEFL (minimum score 550 paper-based; 213 computer-based). *Application deadline:* For fall admission, 1/8 for domestic and international students. Application fee: $75 ($95 for international students). Electronic applications accepted. *Financial support:* Fellowships, research assistantships, teaching assistantships, health care benefits, and unspecified assistantships available. *Faculty research:* Geology, geophysics, geochemistry, geobiology, climate and environmental geosciences. *Application contact:* Sharon Kressler, Student Services Specialist, E-mail: kress004@umn.edu. Web site: http://www.geo.umn.edu/.

University of Nevada, Reno, Graduate School, College of Science, Mackay School of Earth Sciences and Engineering, Department of Geological Sciences, Program in Geophysics, Reno, NV 89557. Offers MS, PhD. Terminal master's awarded for partial completion of doctoral program. *Degree requirements:* For master's, thesis optional; for doctorate, thesis/dissertation. *Entrance requirements:* For master's, GRE General Test, minimum GPA of 2.75; for doctorate, GRE General Test, minimum GPA of 3.0. Additional exam requirements/recommendations for international students: Required—TOEFL (minimum score 500 paper-based; 173 computer-based; 61 iBT), IELTS (minimum score 6). Electronic applications accepted. *Faculty research:* Geophysics exploration, seismology, remote sensing.

University of Oklahoma, College of Earth and Energy, ConocoPhillips School of Geology and Geophysics, Program in Geophysics, Norman, OK 73019. Offers MS, PhD. Part-time programs available. *Students:* 22 full-time (4 women), 8 part-time (1 woman); includes 3 minority (1 Asian, non-Hispanic/Latino; 2 Hispanic/Latino), 20 international. Average age 28. 62 applicants, 23% accepted, 9 enrolled. In 2011, 12 master's, 1 doctorate awarded. *Degree requirements:* For master's, comprehensive exam, thesis. *Entrance requirements:* For master's, GRE General Test. Additional exam requirements/recommendations for international students: Required—TOEFL (minimum score 550 paper-based; 79 iBT). *Application deadline:* For fall admission, 2/1 priority date for domestic students, 3/1 for international students; for spring admission, 9/1 for domestic and international students. Applications are processed on a rolling basis. Application fee: $40 ($90 for international students). Electronic applications accepted. *Expenses:* Tuition, state resident: full-time $4087; part-time $170.30 per credit hour. Tuition, nonresident: full-time $14,875; part-time $619.80 per credit hour. *Required fees:* $2659; $100.25 per credit hour. Tuition and fees vary according to course load and degree level. *Financial support:* In 2011–12, 30 students received support. Scholarships/grants and unspecified assistantships available. Financial award applicants required to submit FAFSA. *Faculty research:* Lithospheric structure and evolution, basin studies, outcrop-scale investigations of sand-bodies in Turbidite channels. *Unit head:* Doug Elmore, Associate Provost/Director, 405-325-3253, Fax: 405-325-3140, E-mail: delmore@ou.edu. *Application contact:* Donna S. Mullins, Coordinator of Administrative Student Services and Corporate Recruiting, 405-325-3255, Fax: 405-325-3140, E-mail: dsmullins@ou.edu. Web site: http://geology.ou.edu.

The University of Texas at Dallas, School of Natural Sciences and Mathematics, Department of Geosciences, Richardson, TX 75080. Offers geochemistry (MS, PhD); geophysics (MS, PhD); geospatial information sciences (MS, PhD); hydrogeology (MS, PhD); sedimentary, stratigraphy, paleontology (PhD); stratigraphy, paleontology (MS); structural geology and tectonics (MS, PhD). Part-time and evening/weekend programs available. *Faculty:* 10 full-time (1 woman). *Students:* 39 full-time (13 women), 20 part-time (7 women); includes 8 minority (2 Black or African American, non-Hispanic/Latino; 4 Asian, non-Hispanic/Latino; 2 Hispanic/Latino), 18 international. Average age 32. 67 applicants, 39% accepted, 14 enrolled. In 2011, 8 master's, 3 doctorates awarded. *Degree requirements:* For master's, thesis optional; for doctorate, thesis/dissertation. *Entrance requirements:* For master's and doctorate, GRE General Test, minimum GPA of 3.0 in upper-level course work in field. Additional exam requirements/recommendations for international students: Required—TOEFL (minimum score 550 paper-based; 215 computer-based). *Application deadline:* For fall admission, 7/15 for domestic students, 5/1 for international students; for spring admission, 11/15 for domestic students, 9/1 for international students. Applications are processed on a rolling basis. Application fee: $50 ($100 for international students). Electronic applications accepted. *Expenses:* Tuition, state resident: full-time $11,170; part-time $620.56 per credit hour. Tuition, nonresident: full-time $20,212; part-time $1122.89 per credit hour. *Financial support:* In 2011–12, 32 students received support, including 13 research assistantships with partial tuition reimbursements available (averaging $21,462 per year), 15 teaching assistantships with partial tuition reimbursements available (averaging $15,800 per year); career-related internships or fieldwork, Federal Work-Study, institutionally sponsored loans, scholarships/grants, and unspecified assistantships also available. Support available to part-time students. Financial

Peterson's Graduate Programs in the Physical Sciences, Mathematics, Agricultural Sciences, the Environment & Natural Resources 2013

facebook.com/petersonspublishing   **161**

award application deadline: 4/30; financial award applicants required to submit FAFSA. *Faculty research:* Cybermapping, GPS applications for geophysics and geology, seismology and ground-penetrating radar, numerical modeling, signal processing and inverse modeling techniques in seismology. *Unit head:* Dr. John Oldow, Department Head, 972-883-2401, Fax: 972-883-2537, E-mail: geosciences@utdallas.edu. *Application contact:* Dr. John W. Geissman, Graduate Advisor, 972-883-2406, Fax: 972-883-2537, E-mail: geissman@utdallas.edu. Web site: http://www.utdallas.edu/geosciences.

The University of Texas at El Paso, Graduate School, College of Science, Department of Geological Sciences, Program in Geophysics, El Paso, TX 79968-0001. Offers MS. Part-time and evening/weekend programs available. *Students:* 6 (2 women); includes 3 minority (1 Asian, non-Hispanic/Latino; 2 Hispanic/Latino), 2 international. Average age 34. In 2011, 1 master's awarded. *Degree requirements:* For master's, thesis. *Entrance requirements:* For master's, minimum GPA of 3.0, letters of recommendation. Additional exam requirements/recommendations for international students: Required—TOEFL; Recommended—IELTS. *Application deadline:* For fall admission, 8/1 priority date for domestic students, 3/1 for international students; for spring admission, 11/1 priority date for domestic students, 9/3 for international students. Applications are processed on a rolling basis. Application fee: $45 ($80 for international students). Electronic applications accepted. *Financial support:* In 2011–12, research assistantships with partial tuition reimbursements (averaging $21,812 per year), teaching assistantships with partial tuition reimbursements (averaging $17,450 per year) were awarded; fellowships with partial tuition reimbursements, institutionally sponsored loans, scholarships/grants, health care benefits, tuition waivers (partial), and unspecified assistantships also available. Support available to part-time students. Financial award application deadline: 3/15; financial award applicants required to submit FAFSA. *Unit head:* Dr. Diane Doser, Coordinator, 915-747-5501, Fax: 915-747-5073, E-mail: doser@utep.edu. *Application contact:* Dr. Benjamin Flores, Interim Dean of the Graduate School, 915-747-5491, Fax: 915-747-5788, E-mail: bflores@utep.edu.

University of Utah, Graduate School, College of Mines and Earth Sciences, Department of Geology and Geophysics, Salt Lake City, UT 84112. Offers environmental engineering (ME, MS, PhD); geological engineering (ME, MS, PhD); geology (MS, PhD); geophysics (MS, PhD). *Faculty:* 22 full-time (5 women), 4 part-time/adjunct (0 women). *Students:* 55 full-time (16 women), 28 part-time (9 women); includes 2 minority (both Asian, non-Hispanic/Latino), 16 international. Average age 30. 174 applicants, 17% accepted, 21 enrolled. In 2011, 13 master's, 3 doctorates awarded. Terminal master's awarded for partial completion of doctoral program. *Median time to degree:* Of those who began their doctoral program in fall 2003, 76% received their degree in 8 years or less. *Degree requirements:* For master's, comprehensive exam, thesis; for doctorate, thesis/dissertation, qualifying exam (written and oral). *Entrance requirements:* For master's and doctorate, GRE General Test, minimum GPA of 3.25. Additional exam requirements/recommendations for international students: Required—TOEFL (minimum score 500 paper-based; 173 computer-based). *Application deadline:* For fall admission, 1/15 priority date for domestic students, 1/15 for international students. Applications are processed on a rolling basis. Application fee: $55 ($65 for international students). Electronic applications accepted. *Financial support:* In 2011–12, 22 students received support, including 10 fellowships with full tuition reimbursements available (averaging $15,000 per year), 40 research assistantships with full tuition reimbursements available (averaging $22,000 per year), 14 teaching assistantships with full tuition reimbursements available (averaging $15,000 per year); career-related internships or fieldwork, institutionally sponsored loans, scholarships/grants, unspecified assistantships, and stipends also available. Financial award application deadline: 1/15; financial award applicants required to submit FAFSA. *Faculty research:* Igneous, metamorphic, and sedimentary petrology; ore deposits; aqueous geochemistry; isotope geochemistry; heat flow. *Total annual research expenditures:* $3.3 million. *Unit head:* Dr. Kip Solomon, Chair, 801-581-7231, Fax: 801-581-7065, E-mail: kip.solomon@utah.edu. *Application contact:* Dr. Cari L. Johnson, Director of Graduate Studies, 801-585-3782, Fax: 801-581-7065, E-mail: cari.johnson@utah.edu. Web site: http://www.earth.utah.edu/.

University of Victoria, Faculty of Graduate Studies, Faculty of Science, Department of Physics and Astronomy, Victoria, BC V8W 2Y2, Canada. Offers astronomy and astrophysics (M Sc, PhD); condensed matter physics (M Sc, PhD); experimental particle physics (M Sc, PhD); medical physics (M Sc, PhD); ocean physics (M Sc, PhD); theoretical physics (M Sc, PhD). *Degree requirements:* For master's, thesis; for doctorate, comprehensive exam, thesis/

dissertation, candidacy exam. *Entrance requirements:* For master's and doctorate, GRE. Additional exam requirements/recommendations for international students: Required—TOEFL (minimum score 575 paper-based; 233 computer-based), IELTS (minimum score 7). Electronic applications accepted. *Faculty research:* Old stellar populations; observational cosmology and large scale structure; cp violation; atlas.

University of Washington, Graduate School, College of the Environment, Department of Earth and Space Sciences, Seattle, WA 98195. Offers geology (MS, PhD); geophysics (MS, PhD). *Degree requirements:* For master's, thesis or alternative, departmental qualifying exam, final exam; for doctorate, thesis/dissertation, departmental qualifying exam, general and final exams. *Entrance requirements:* For master's and doctorate, GRE General Test, minimum GPA of 3.0. Additional exam requirements/recommendations for international students: Required—TOEFL (minimum score 580 paper-based). Electronic applications accepted.

The University of Western Ontario, Faculty of Graduate Studies, Physical Sciences Division, Department of Earth Sciences, London, ON N6A 5B8, Canada. Offers environment and sustainability (MES); geology (M Sc, PhD); geology and environmental science (M Sc, PhD); geophysics (M Sc, PhD); geophysics and environmental science (M Sc, PhD). *Degree requirements:* For master's, thesis; for doctorate, thesis/dissertation, qualifying exam. *Entrance requirements:* For master's, honors in B Sc; for doctorate, M Sc. Additional exam requirements/recommendations for international students: Required—TOEFL. *Faculty research:* Geophysics, geochemistry, paleontology, sedimentology/stratigraphy, glaciology/quaternary.

University of Wisconsin–Madison, Graduate School, College of Letters and Science, Department of Geology and Geophysics, Program in Geophysics, Madison, WI 53706-1380. Offers MS, PhD. *Degree requirements:* For master's, thesis; for doctorate, one foreign language, thesis/dissertation. *Entrance requirements:* For master's and doctorate, GRE General Test. *Expenses:* Tuition, state resident: full-time $10,296; part-time $643.51 per credit. Tuition, nonresident: full-time $24,054; part-time $1503.40 per credit. *Required fees:* $70.06 per credit. Tuition and fees vary according to course load, campus/location, program and reciprocity agreements.

University of Wyoming, College of Arts and Sciences, Department of Geology and Geophysics, Laramie, WY 82070. Offers geology (MS, PhD); geophysics (MS, PhD). Part-time programs available. *Degree requirements:* For master's, comprehensive exam, thesis; for doctorate, comprehensive exam, thesis/dissertation. *Entrance requirements:* For master's and doctorate, GRE General Test, minimum GPA of 3.0. *Faculty research:* Low-temp geochemistry, geohydrology, paleontology, structure/tectonics, sedimentation and petroleum geology, petrology, geophysics/seismology.

West Virginia University, Eberly College of Arts and Sciences, Department of Geology and Geography, Program in Geology, Morgantown, WV 26506. Offers geomorphology (MS, PhD); geophysics (MS, PhD); hydrogeology (MS, PhD); paleontology (MS, PhD); petroleum geology (PhD); petrology (MS, PhD); stratigraphy (MS, PhD); structure (MS, PhD). Part-time programs available. Terminal master's awarded for partial completion of doctoral program. *Degree requirements:* For master's, thesis (for some programs); for doctorate, comprehensive exam, thesis/dissertation. *Entrance requirements:* For master's, GRE General Test, minimum GPA of 2.5; for doctorate, GRE General Test, minimum GPA of 3.3. Additional exam requirements/recommendations for international students: Required—TOEFL.

Wright State University, School of Graduate Studies, College of Science and Mathematics, Department of Physics, Program in Physics, Dayton, OH 45435. Offers geophysics (MS); medical physics (MS). Part-time and evening/weekend programs available. *Degree requirements:* For master's, thesis. *Entrance requirements:* Additional exam requirements/recommendations for international students: Required—TOEFL. *Faculty research:* Solid-state physics, optics, geophysics.

Yale University, Graduate School of Arts and Sciences, Department of Geology and Geophysics, New Haven, CT 06520. Offers biogeochemistry (PhD); climate dynamics (PhD); geochemistry (PhD); geophysics (PhD); meteorology (PhD); oceanography (PhD); paleontology (PhD); paleooceanography (PhD); petrology (PhD); tectonics (PhD). *Degree requirements:* For doctorate, thesis/dissertation. *Entrance requirements:* For doctorate, GRE General Test. Additional exam requirements/recommendations for international students: Required—TOEFL.

Geosciences

Alabama State University, Department of Earth and Environmental Sciences, Montgomery, AL 36101-0271. Offers MS, PhD. *Faculty:* 9 full-time. *Degree requirements:* For master's, one foreign language, thesis or alternative; for doctorate, one foreign language, thesis/dissertation. *Entrance requirements:* For master's, GRE General Test, minimum B average in undergraduate course work; for doctorate, GRE General Test. Additional exam requirements/

recommendations for international students: Required—TOEFL. *Application deadline:* For fall admission, 2/1 for domestic and international students. Application fee: $45. Electronic applications accepted. *Financial support:* Research assistantships with full tuition reimbursements, teaching assistantships with full tuition reimbursements, career-related internships or fieldwork, Federal Work-Study, and institutionally sponsored loans available. Financial award

162 facebook.com/petersonspublishing

Peterson's Graduate Programs in the Physical Sciences, Mathematics, Agricultural Sciences, the Environment & Natural Resources 2013

application deadline: 2/1. *Faculty research:* Sedimentation, isotopes, biogeochemistry, marine geology, structural geology. *Unit head:* Dr. Stephen Nelson, Chair, 504-862-3194, Fax: 504-865-5199, E-mail: snelson@tulane.edu. *Application contact:* Dr. Doris Screws, Dean of Graduate Studies, 334-229-4274, Fax: 334-229-4928, E-mail: dscrews@alasu.edu.

Arizona State University, College of Liberal Arts and Sciences, School of Earth and Space Exploration, Tempe, AZ 85287-1404. Offers astrophysics (MS, PhD); exploration systems design (PhD); geological sciences (MS, PhD). PhD in exploration systems design is offered in collaboration with the Fulton Schools of Engineering. Terminal master's awarded for partial completion of doctoral program. *Degree requirements:* For master's, thesis, interactive Program of Study (iPOS) submitted before completing 50 percent of required credit hours; for doctorate, thesis/dissertation, interactive Program of Study (iPOS) submitted before completing 50 percent of required credit hours. *Entrance requirements:* For master's and doctorate, GRE, minimum GPA of 3.0 or equivalent in last 2 years of work leading to bachelor's degree. Additional exam requirements/recommendations for international students: Required—TOEFL (minimum score 80 iBT), TOEFL, IELTS, or Pearson Test of English. Electronic applications accepted.

Baylor University, Graduate School, College of Arts and Sciences, Department of Geology, Waco, TX 76798. Offers earth science (MA); geology (MS, PhD). *Faculty:* 12 full-time (1 woman). *Students:* 26 full-time (11 women), 4 part-time (2 women); includes 2 minority (1 American Indian or Alaska Native, non-Hispanic/Latino; 1 Asian, non-Hispanic/Latino), 4 international. In 2011, 6 master's, 1 doctorate awarded. *Degree requirements:* For master's, thesis; for doctorate, thesis/dissertation. *Entrance requirements:* For master's and doctorate, GRE General Test. *Application deadline:* For fall admission, 3/15 priority date for domestic students. Applications are processed on a rolling basis. Application fee: $25. *Financial support:* In 2011–12, 18 teaching assistantships were awarded; Federal Work-Study and institutionally sponsored loans also available. *Faculty research:* Petroleum geology, geophysics, engineering geology, hydrogeology. *Unit head:* Dr. Steve Dworkin, Graduate Program Director, 254-710-2186, Fax: 254-710-2673, E-mail: steve_dworkin@baylor.edu. *Application contact:* Paulette Penney, Administrative Assistant, 254-710-2361, Fax: 254-710-3870, E-mail: paulette_penney@baylor.edu. Web site: http://www.baylor.edu/geology/.

Baylor University, Graduate School, College of Arts and Sciences, The Institute of Ecological, Earth and Environmental Sciences, Waco, TX 76798. Offers PhD. *Students:* 8 full-time (3 women); includes 2 minority (1 Hispanic/Latino; 1 Two or more races, non-Hispanic/Latino), 5 international. *Unit head:* Dr. Joseph D. White, Director, 254-710-2911, E-mail: joseph_d_white@baylor.edu. *Application contact:* Suzanne Keener, Administrative Assistant, 254-710-3588, Fax: 254-710-3870. Web site: http://www.baylor.edu/TIEEES/.

Boise State University, Graduate College, College of Arts and Sciences, Department of Geosciences, Program in Earth Science, Boise, ID 83725-0399. Offers MS. Part-time programs available. *Degree requirements:* For master's, thesis. *Entrance requirements:* For master's, GRE General Test, minimum GPA of 3.0, BS in related field. Electronic applications accepted.

Boston University, Graduate School of Arts and Sciences, Department of Earth Sciences, Boston, MA 02215. Offers MA, PhD. *Students:* 28 full-time (19 women), 1 part-time (0 women); includes 1 minority (Asian, non-Hispanic/Latino), 5 international. Average age 27. 87 applicants, 9% accepted, 5 enrolled. In 2011, 3 master's, 3 doctorates awarded. Terminal master's awarded for partial completion of doctoral program. *Degree requirements:* For master's, one foreign language, comprehensive exam, thesis; for doctorate, one foreign language, comprehensive exam, thesis/dissertation. *Entrance requirements:* For master's and doctorate, GRE General Test, 3 letters of recommendation. Additional exam requirements/recommendations for international students: Required—TOEFL (minimum score 550 paper-based; 213 computer-based). *Application deadline:* For fall admission, 1/15 for domestic and international students; for spring admission, 10/15 for domestic and international students. Application fee: $70. Electronic applications accepted. *Expenses: Tuition:* Full-time $40,848; part-time $1276 per credit hour. *Required fees:* $572; $286 per semester. *Financial support:* In 2011–12, 1 fellowship with full tuition reimbursement (averaging $19,800 per year), 15 research assistantships with full tuition reimbursements (averaging $19,300 per year), 8 teaching assistantships with full tuition reimbursements were awarded; Federal Work-Study and unspecified assistantships also available. Support available to part-time students. Financial award application deadline: 1/15; financial award applicants required to submit FAFSA. *Unit head:* Mark Friedl, Chairman, 617-353-5745, Fax: 617-353-3290, E-mail: friedl@bu.edu. *Application contact:* Christian Cole, Department Administrator, 617-353-2529, Fax: 617-353-3290, E-mail: ccole@bu.edu. Web site: http://www.bu.edu/es/.

Brock University, Faculty of Graduate Studies, Faculty of Mathematics and Science, Program in Earth Sciences, St. Catharines, ON L2S 3A1, Canada. Offers M Sc. Part-time programs available. *Degree requirements:* For master's, thesis. *Entrance requirements:* For master's, honors B Sc in earth sciences. Additional exam requirements/recommendations for international students: Required—TOEFL (minimum score 550 paper-based; 213 computer-based; 80 iBT), IELTS (minimum score 6.5), TWE (minimum score 4). Electronic applications accepted. *Faculty research:* Clastic sedimentology, environmental geology, geochemistry, micropaleontology, structural geology.

Brooklyn College of the City University of New York, Division of Graduate Studies, School of Education, Program in Adolescence Education and Special Subjects, Brooklyn, NY 11210-2889. Offers adolescence science education (MAT); art teacher (MA); biology teacher (MA); chemistry teacher (MA); earth science teacher (MAT); English teacher (MA); French teacher (MA); health and nutrition sciences: health teacher (MS Ed); mathematics teacher (MA); music education (CAS); music teacher (MA); physical education teacher (MS Ed); physics teacher (MA); social studies teacher (MA); Spanish teacher (MA). Part-time and evening/weekend programs available. *Degree requirements:* For master's, comprehensive exam (for some programs), thesis (for some programs). *Entrance requirements:* For master's, LAST, previous course work in education, resume, 2 letters of recommendation, essay. Additional exam requirements/recommendations for international students: Required—TOEFL (minimum score 500 paper-based; 173 computer-based; 61 iBT). Electronic applications accepted. *Faculty research:* Interdisciplinary education, semiotics, discourse analysis, autobiography, teacher identity.

Brooklyn College of the City University of New York, Division of Graduate Studies, School of Education, Program in Middle Childhood Education (Science), Brooklyn, NY 11210-2889. Offers biology (MA); chemistry (MA); earth science (MA); general science (MA); physics (MA). Part-time and evening/weekend programs available. *Entrance requirements:* For master's, LAST, interview, previous course work in education and mathematics, resume, 2 letters of recommendation, essay. Additional exam requirements/recommendations for international students: Required—TOEFL (minimum score 500 paper-based; 173 computer-based; 61 iBT). Electronic applications accepted. *Faculty research:* Geometric thinking, mastery of basic facts, problem-solving strategies, history of mathematics.

Brown University, Graduate School, Department of Geological Sciences, Providence, RI 02912. Offers MA, Sc M, PhD. *Degree requirements:* For doctorate, thesis/dissertation, 1 semester of teaching experience, preliminary exam. *Faculty research:* Geochemistry, mineral kinetics, igneous and metamorphic petrology, tectonophysics including geophysics and structural geology, paleoclimatology, paleoceanography, sedimentation, planetary geology.

California State University, Chico, Office of Graduate Studies, College of Natural Sciences, Department of Geological and Environmental Sciences, Program in Geosciences, Chico, CA 95929-0722. Offers hydrology/hydrogeology (MS). Part-time programs available. *Students:* 3 full-time (0 women), 5 part-time (1 woman); includes 1 minority (Hispanic/Latino). Average age 31. 9 applicants, 56% accepted, 3 enrolled. In 2011, 1 master's awarded. *Degree requirements:* For master's, thesis, oral exam. *Entrance requirements:* For master's, GRE, faculty mentor, statement of purpose. Additional exam requirements/recommendations for international students: Required—TOEFL (minimum score 550 paper-based; 213 computer-based; 80 iBT), IELTS (minimum score 6.5), Pearson Test of English (minimum score 59). *Application deadline:* For fall admission, 3/1 priority date for domestic students, 3/1 for international students; for spring admission, 9/15 priority date for domestic students, 9/15 for international students. Application fee: $55. Electronic applications accepted. Tuition and fees vary according to class time, course load and degree level. *Financial support:* Fellowships, research assistantships, teaching assistantships, and career-related internships or fieldwork available. *Unit head:* Dr. David L. Brown, Chair, 530-898-5262, Fax: 530-898-5234, E-mail: geos@csuchico.edu. *Application contact:* Judy L. Rice, Graduate Admissions Coordinator, 530-898-5416, Fax: 530-898-3342, E-mail: jlrice@csuchico.edu. Web site: http://catalog.csuchico.edu/viewer/12/GEOS.html.

Carleton University, Faculty of Graduate Studies, Faculty of Science, Department of Earth Sciences, Ottawa, ON K1S 5B6, Canada. Offers M Sc, PhD. Programs offered jointly with University of Ottawa. *Degree requirements:* For master's, thesis, seminar; for doctorate, comprehensive exam, thesis/dissertation, seminar. *Entrance requirements:* For master's, honors degree in science; for doctorate, M Sc. Additional exam requirements/recommendations for international students: Required—TOEFL. *Faculty research:* Resource geology, geophysics, basin analysis, lithosphere dynamics.

Case Western Reserve University, School of Graduate Studies, Earth, Environmental, and Planetary Sciences, Cleveland, OH 44106. Offers MS, PhD. Part-time programs available. *Faculty:* 7 full-time (1 woman), 7 part-time/adjunct (1 woman). *Students:* 6 full-time (3 women), 2 international. Average age 30. 10 applicants, 10% accepted, 1 enrolled. In 2011, 1 degree awarded. Terminal master's awarded for partial completion of doctoral program. *Degree requirements:* For master's, thesis or alternative; for doctorate, thesis/dissertation. *Entrance requirements:* For master's and doctorate, GRE General Test, GRE Subject Test. Additional exam requirements/recommendations for international students: Required—TOEFL (minimum score 577 paper-based; 213 computer-based; 90 iBT); Recommended—IELTS (minimum score 7). *Application deadline:* For fall admission, 1/15 priority date for domestic students; for spring admission, 11/15 for domestic students. Applications are processed on a rolling basis. Application fee: $50. Electronic applications accepted. *Financial support:* Research assistantships, teaching assistantships, Federal Work-Study, and tuition waivers (partial) available. Support available to part-time students. Financial award application deadline: 1/15; financial award applicants required to submit FAFSA. *Faculty research:* Geochemistry, hydrology, ecology, geomorphology, planetary science, stratigraphy and basin analysis, igneous petrology. *Unit head:* Gerald Matisoff, Chairman, 216-368-3677, Fax: 216-368-3691, E-mail: gerald.matisoff@case.edu. *Application contact:* James Van Orman, Chair, Graduate Admission Committee, 216-368-3690, Fax: 216-368-3691, E-mail: james.vanorman@case.edu. Web site: http://geology.cwru.edu/.

Peterson's Graduate Programs in the Physical Sciences, Mathematics, Agricultural Sciences, the Environment & Natural Resources 2013

facebook.com/petersonspublishing **163**

Geosciences

Central Connecticut State University, School of Graduate Studies, School of Arts and Sciences, Department of Physics and Earth Science, New Britain, CT 06050-4010. Offers natural sciences (MS); science education (Certificate). Part-time and evening/weekend programs available. *Faculty:* 11 full-time (4 women), 17 part-time/adjunct (3 women). *Students:* 1 full-time (0 women), 9 part-time (6 women); includes 1 minority (Asian, non-Hispanic/Latino). Average age 38. 5 applicants, 80% accepted, 2 enrolled. In 2011, 7 master's awarded. *Degree requirements:* For master's, comprehensive exam, thesis or alternative; for Certificate, qualifying exam. *Entrance requirements:* For master's, minimum undergraduate GPA of 2.7. Additional exam requirements/recommendations for international students: Required—TOEFL (minimum score 550 paper-based; 213 computer-based). *Application deadline:* For fall admission, 6/1 for domestic students, 5/1 for international students; for spring admission, 11/1 for domestic and international students. Applications are processed on a rolling basis. Application fee: $50. Electronic applications accepted. *Expenses: Tuition, area resident:* Full-time $5137; part-time $482 per credit. Tuition, state resident: full-time $7707; part-time $494 per credit. Tuition, nonresident: full-time $14,311; part-time $494 per credit. *Required fees:* $3865. One-time fee: $62 part-time. *Financial support:* In 2011–12, 1 student received support. Career-related internships or fieldwork, Federal Work-Study, scholarships/grants, and unspecified assistantships available. Support available to part-time students. Financial award application deadline: 4/15; financial award applicants required to submit FAFSA. *Faculty research:* Elementary/secondary science education, particle and solid states, weather patterns, planetary studies. *Unit head:* Dr. Steven Newman, Chair, 860-832-2930, E-mail: newman@ccsu.edu. *Application contact:* Patricia Gardner, Associate Director of Graduate Studies, 860-832-2350, Fax: 860-832-2352, E-mail: graduateadmissions@ccsu.edu. Web site: http://www.physics.ccsu.edu/.

Chapman University, Schmid College of Science and Technology, Program in Hazards, Global and Environmental Change, Orange, CA 92866. Offers MS. *Faculty:* 16 full-time (1 woman), 1 part-time/adjunct (0 women). *Students:* 8 full-time (2 women), 6 part-time (2 women); includes 4 minority (3 Hispanic/Latino; 1 Native Hawaiian or other Pacific Islander, non-Hispanic/Latino), 4 international. Average age 27. 13 applicants, 85% accepted, 9 enrolled. *Entrance requirements:* Additional exam requirements/recommendations for international students: Required—TOEFL (minimum score 550 paper-based; 213 computer-based; 80 iBT). Tuition and fees vary according to degree level and program. *Financial support:* Fellowships, Federal Work-Study, and scholarships/grants available. Financial award applicants required to submit FAFSA. *Unit head:* Dr. Menas Kafatos, Dean, 714-628-7223, E-mail: jhill@chapman.edu. *Application contact:* Saundra Hoover, Director of Graduate Admissions, 714-997-6786, Fax: 714-997-6713, E-mail: shoover@chapman.edu. Web site: http://www.chapman.edu/SCS/EES/MSHGEC.asp.

City College of the City University of New York, Graduate School, College of Liberal Arts and Science, Division of Science, Department of Earth and Atmospheric Sciences, New York, NY 10031-9198. Offers earth and environmental science (PhD); earth systems science (MA). PhD program offered jointly with Graduate School and University Center of the City University of New York. *Degree requirements:* For master's, comprehensive exam, thesis. *Entrance requirements:* Additional exam requirements/recommendations for international students: Required—TOEFL (minimum score 500 paper-based; 61 iBT). Electronic applications accepted. *Faculty research:* Water resources, high-temperature geochemistry, sedimentary basin analysis, tectonics.

Colorado State University, Graduate School, Warner College of Natural Resources, Department of Geosciences, Fort Collins, CO 80523-1482. Offers earth sciences (PhD); geosciences (MS). Part-time programs available. *Faculty:* 11 full-time (4 women). *Students:* 30 full-time (13 women), 31 part-time (15 women); includes 5 minority (1 American Indian or Alaska Native, non-Hispanic/Latino; 1 Asian, non-Hispanic/Latino; 2 Hispanic/Latino; 1 Two or more races, non-Hispanic/Latino), 7 international. Average age 30. 72 applicants, 43% accepted, 16 enrolled. In 2011, 6 master's, 2 doctorates awarded. *Degree requirements:* For master's, thesis; for doctorate, comprehensive exam, thesis/dissertation. *Entrance requirements:* For master's and doctorate, GRE General Test, minimum GPA of 3.0, letters of recommendation. Additional exam requirements/recommendations for international students: Required—TOEFL (minimum score 550 paper-based; 213 computer-based; 80 iBT); Recommended—IELTS (minimum score 6). *Application deadline:* For fall admission, 2/15 priority date for domestic students, 2/15 for international students; for spring admission, 7/15 priority date for domestic students, 7/15 for international students. Applications are processed on a rolling basis. Application fee: $50. Electronic applications accepted. *Expenses: Tuition, state resident:* full-time $7992. Tuition, nonresident: full-time $19,592. *Required fees:* $1735; $58 per credit. *Financial support:* In 2011–12, 33 students received support, including 2 fellowships (averaging $27,452 per year), 22 research assistantships with full tuition reimbursements available (averaging $13,028 per year), 9 teaching assistantships with full tuition reimbursements available (averaging $8,333 per year); scholarships/grants also available. Financial award application deadline: 2/15; financial award applicants required to submit FAFSA. *Faculty research:* Snow, surface, and groundwater hydrology; fluvial geomorphology; geographic information systems; geochemistry; chemical weathering. *Total annual research expenditures:* $1.6 million. *Unit head:* Dr. Sally J. Sutton, Head, 970-491-5995, Fax: 970-491-6307, E-mail: sally.sutton@colostate.edu. *Application contact:* Sharon Gale, Graduate Contact, 970-491-5661, Fax: 970-491-6307, E-mail:

sharon.gale@colostate.edu. Web site: http://warnercnr.colostate.edu/geosciences-home/.

Columbia University, Graduate School of Arts and Sciences, Division of Natural Sciences, Department of Earth and Environmental Sciences, New York, NY 10027. Offers geochemistry (M Phil, MA, PhD); geodetic sciences (M Phil, MA, PhD); geophysics (M Phil, MA, PhD); oceanography (M Phil, MA, PhD). *Degree requirements:* For master's, thesis or alternative, fieldwork, written exam; for doctorate, one foreign language, thesis/dissertation. *Entrance requirements:* For master's and doctorate, GRE General Test, GRE Subject Test, major in natural or physical science. Additional exam requirements/recommendations for international students: Required—TOEFL. *Faculty research:* Structural geology and stratigraphy, petrology, paleontology, rare gas, isotope and aqueous geochemistry.

Cornell University, Graduate School, Graduate Fields of Engineering, Field of Geological Sciences, Ithaca, NY 14853. Offers economic geology (M Eng, MS, PhD); engineering geology (M Eng, MS, PhD); environmental geophysics (M Eng, MS, PhD); general geology (M Eng, MS, PhD); geobiology (M Eng, MS, PhD); geochemistry and isotope geology (M Eng, MS, PhD); geohydrology (M Eng, MS, PhD); geomorphology (M Eng, MS, PhD); geophysics (M Eng, MS, PhD); geotectonics (M Eng, MS, PhD); marine geology (MS, PhD); mineralogy (M Eng, MS, PhD); paleontology (M Eng, MS, PhD); petroleum geology (M Eng, MS, PhD); petrology (M Eng, MS, PhD); planetary geology (M Eng, MS, PhD); Precambrian geology (M Eng, MS, PhD); Quaternary geology (M Eng, MS, PhD); rock mechanics (M Eng, MS, PhD); sedimentology (M Eng, MS, PhD); seismology (M Eng, MS, PhD); stratigraphy (M Eng, MS, PhD); structural geology (M Eng, MS, PhD). *Faculty:* 37 full-time (5 women). *Students:* 41 full-time (19 women); includes 5 minority (2 Asian, non-Hispanic/Latino; 3 Hispanic/Latino), 7 international. Average age 27. 74 applicants, 19% accepted, 9 enrolled. In 2011, 3 master's, 3 doctorates awarded. *Degree requirements:* For master's, thesis (MS); for doctorate, comprehensive exam, thesis/dissertation. *Entrance requirements:* For master's and doctorate, GRE General Test, 3 letters of recommendation. Additional exam requirements/recommendations for international students: Required—TOEFL (minimum score 550 paper-based; 213 computer-based; 77 iBT). *Application deadline:* For fall admission, 1/15 priority date for domestic students. Applications are processed on a rolling basis. Application fee: $95. Electronic applications accepted. *Financial support:* In 2011–12, 25 students received support, including 7 fellowships with full tuition reimbursements available, 19 research assistantships with full tuition reimbursements available, 8 teaching assistantships with full tuition reimbursements available; institutionally sponsored loans, scholarships/grants, health care benefits, tuition waivers (full and partial), and unspecified assistantships also available. Financial award applicants required to submit FAFSA. *Faculty research:* Geophysics, structural geology, petrology, geochemistry, geodynamics. *Unit head:* Director of Graduate Studies, 607-255-5466, Fax: 607-254-4780. *Application contact:* Graduate Field Assistant, 607-255-5466, Fax: 607-254-4780, E-mail: gradprog@geology.cornell.edu. Web site: http://www.gradschool.cornell.edu/fields.php?id-30&a-2.

Dalhousie University, Faculty of Science, Department of Earth Sciences, Halifax, NS B3H 4R2, Canada. Offers M Sc, PhD. *Degree requirements:* For master's, one foreign language, thesis; for doctorate, one foreign language, thesis/dissertation. *Entrance requirements:* Additional exam requirements/recommendations for international students: Required—TOEFL, IELTS, CANTEST, CAEL, or Michigan English Language Assessment Battery. *Faculty research:* Marine geology and geophysics, Appalachian and Grenville geology, micropaleontology, geodynamics and structural geology, geochronology.

Dartmouth College, Arts and Sciences Graduate Programs, Department of Earth Sciences, Hanover, NH 03755. Offers MS, PhD. Terminal master's awarded for partial completion of doctoral program. *Degree requirements:* For master's, thesis; for doctorate, thesis/dissertation. *Entrance requirements:* For master's and doctorate, GRE General Test, GRE Subject Test. Additional exam requirements/recommendations for international students: Required—TOEFL. *Faculty research:* Geochemistry, remote sensing, geophysics, hydrology, economic geology.

Eastern Michigan University, Graduate School, College of Arts and Sciences, Department of Geography and Geology, Program in Earth Science Education, Ypsilanti, MI 48197. Offers MS. *Students:* 2 full-time (both women), 11 part-time (7 women). Average age 34. 6 applicants, 67% accepted, 4 enrolled. In 2011, 3 degrees awarded. Application fee: $35. *Expenses:* Tuition, state resident: full-time $10,367; part-time $432 per credit hour. Tuition, nonresident: full-time $20,435; part-time $851 per credit hour. *Required fees:* $39 per credit hour. $46 per semester. One-time fee: $100. Tuition and fees vary according to course level, degree level and reciprocity agreements. *Unit head:* Dr. Richard Sambrook, Department Head, 734-487-0218, Fax: 734-487-6979, E-mail: rsambroo@emich.edu. *Application contact:* Dr. Sandra Rutherford, Program Advisor, 734-487-8588, Fax: 734-487-6979, E-mail: srutherf@emich.edu.

East Tennessee State University, School of Graduate Studies, College of Arts and Sciences, Department of Geosciences, Johnson City, TN 37614. Offers geospatial analysis (MS); paleontology (MS). Part-time programs available. *Faculty:* 9 full-time (2 women). *Students:* 6 full-time (4 women), 2 part-time (0 women); includes 1 minority (Two or more races, non-Hispanic/Latino). Average age 28. 8 applicants, 75% accepted, 6 enrolled. *Degree requirements:* For master's, thesis. *Entrance requirements:* For master's, bachelor's degree in

164 facebook.com/petersonspublishing

Peterson's Graduate Programs in the Physical Sciences, Mathematics, Agricultural Sciences, the Environment & Natural Resources 2013

geosciences or related discipline, minimum GPA of 3.0, three letters of recommendation, resume. Additional exam requirements/recommendations for international students: Required—TOEFL (minimum score 550 paper-based; 213 computer-based; 79 iBT). *Application deadline:* For fall admission, 2/1 for domestic and international students. Application fee: $35 ($45 for international students). Electronic applications accepted. *Expenses:* Tuition, state resident: full-time $7312; part-time $350 per credit hour. Tuition, nonresident: full-time $18,490; part-time $621 per credit hour. *Required fees:* $63 per credit hour. Tuition and fees vary according to course load and program. *Financial support:* In 2011–12, 1 research assistantship with full tuition reimbursement (averaging $8,000 per year), 9 teaching assistantships with full tuition reimbursements (averaging $9,500 per year) were awarded; career-related internships or fieldwork, institutionally sponsored loans, scholarships/grants, and unspecified assistantships also available. Financial award application deadline: 7/1; financial award applicants required to submit FAFSA. *Faculty research:* Urban planning, remote sensing, geochemistry of karstic terrains, weather and climate dynamics, social responses to geological hazards, watershed management and geomorphology, soil engineering, Neogene/Quaternary vertebrate evolution and biotic community reconstructions. *Total annual research expenditures:* $140,000. *Unit head:* Dr. Jim Mead, Chair, 423-439-7515, Fax: 423-439-7520, E-mail: mead@etsu.edu. *Application contact:* Gail Powers, Graduate Specialist, 423-439-4703, Fax: 423-439-5624, E-mail: powersg@etsu.edu. Web site: http://www.etsu.edu/cas/geosciences/.

Emporia State University, Graduate School, College of Liberal Arts and Sciences, Department of Physical Sciences, Emporia, KS 66801-5087. Offers earth science (MS); geospatial analysis (Postbaccalaureate Certificate); physical science (MS). Part-time programs available. Postbaccalaureate distance learning degree programs offered (minimal on-campus study). *Faculty:* 14 full-time (3 women). *Students:* 10 full-time (5 women), 24 part-time (9 women); includes 1 minority (American Indian or Alaska Native, non-Hispanic/Latino), 4 international. 12 applicants, 83% accepted, 10 enrolled. In 2011, 8 degrees awarded. *Degree requirements:* For master's, comprehensive exam or thesis. *Entrance requirements:* For master's, physical science qualifying exam, appropriate undergraduate degree. Additional exam requirements/recommendations for international students: Required—TOEFL (minimum score 520 paper-based; 133 computer-based; 68 iBT). *Application deadline:* For fall admission, 8/15 priority date for domestic students. Applications are processed on a rolling basis. Application fee: $30 ($75 for international students). Electronic applications accepted. *Expenses:* Tuition, state resident: full-time $2342; part-time $195 per credit hour. Tuition, nonresident: full-time $7254; part-time $605 per credit hour. *Required fees:* $66 per credit hour. Tuition and fees vary according to campus/location. *Financial support:* In 2011–12, 1 research assistantship with full tuition reimbursement (averaging $8,000 per year), 8 teaching assistantships with full tuition reimbursements (averaging $7,369 per year) were awarded; Federal Work-Study, institutionally sponsored loans, health care benefits, and unspecified assistantships also available. Financial award application deadline: 3/15; financial award applicants required to submit FAFSA. *Faculty research:* Bredigite, larnite, and dicalcium silicates-Marble Canyon. *Unit head:* Dr. James Roach, Interim Chair, 620-341-5330, Fax: 620-341-6055, E-mail: jroach@emporia.edu. *Application contact:* Mary Sewell, Admissions Coordinator, 800-950-GRAD, Fax: 620-341-5909, E-mail: msewell@emporia.edu. Web site: http://www.emporia.edu/physci/.

Florida Atlantic University, Charles E. Schmidt College of Science, Department of Geosciences, Boca Raton, FL 33431-0991. Offers geography (MA); geology (MS); geosciences (PhD). Part-time programs available. *Faculty:* 11 full-time (3 women), 2 part-time/adjunct (0 women). *Students:* 29 full-time (18 women), 11 part-time (5 women); includes 4 minority (1 Asian, non-Hispanic/Latino; 3 Hispanic/Latino), 2 international. Average age 37. 22 applicants, 64% accepted, 8 enrolled. In 2011, 8 master's awarded. *Degree requirements:* For master's, thesis (for some programs). *Entrance requirements:* For master's, GRE General Test, minimum GPA of 3.0. *Application deadline:* For fall admission, 3/15 for domestic and international students; for spring admission, 10/15 for domestic and international students. Applications are processed on a rolling basis. Application fee: $30. Electronic applications accepted. *Expenses: Tuition, area resident:* Part-time $343.02 per credit hour. Tuition, state resident: full-time $8232. Tuition, nonresident: full-time $23,931; part-time $997.14 per credit hour. *Financial support:* Research assistantships with partial tuition reimbursements, teaching assistantships with partial tuition reimbursements, career-related internships or fieldwork, Federal Work-Study, institutionally sponsored loans, and unspecified assistantships available. *Faculty research:* GIS applications, paleontology, hydrogeology, economic development. *Unit head:* Dr. Russell Ivy, Chair, 561-297-3295, Fax: 561-297-2745, E-mail: ivy@fau.edu. *Application contact:* Dr. David Warburton, Graduate Coordinator, 561-297-3312, Fax: 561-297-2745, E-mail: warburto@fau.edu. Web site: http://www.geosciences.fau.edu/.

Florida International University, College of Arts and Sciences, Department of Earth and Environment, Program in Geosciences, Miami, FL 33199. Offers MS, PhD. Part-time and evening/weekend programs available. *Degree requirements:* For master's, thesis optional; for doctorate, comprehensive exam, thesis/dissertation. *Entrance requirements:* For master's, GRE (minimum score of 1000), minimum GPA of 3.0 during last two years of undergraduate study, letter of intent, 3 letters of recommendation, resume; for doctorate, GRE (minimum score of 1120), minimum GPA of 3.0 during last two years of undergraduate study, letter of intent, 3 letters of recommendation, resume. Additional exam requirements/

recommendations for international students: Required—TOEFL (minimum score 550 paper-based; 80 iBT). Electronic applications accepted.

Florida State University, The Graduate School, College of Arts and Sciences, Department of Scientific Computing, Tallahassee, FL 32306-4120. Offers computational science (MS, PSM, PhD), including atmospheric science (PhD), biochemistry (PhD), biological science (PhD), computational molecular biology/bioinformatics (PSM), computational science (PhD), geological science (PhD), materials science (PhD), physics (PhD). Part-time programs available. *Faculty:* 14 full-time (2 women). *Students:* 32 full-time (6 women), 3 part-time (0 women); includes 13 minority (1 Black or African American, non-Hispanic/Latino; 11 Asian, non-Hispanic/Latino; 1 Hispanic/Latino), 13 international. Average age 29. 29 applicants, 41% accepted, 9 enrolled. In 2011, 14 master's, 3 doctorates awarded. Terminal master's awarded for partial completion of doctoral program. *Degree requirements:* For master's, thesis (for some programs); for doctorate, comprehensive exam, thesis/dissertation. *Entrance requirements:* For master's and doctorate, GRE General Test, knowledge of at least one object-oriented computing language, 3 letters of recommendations. Additional exam requirements/recommendations for international students: Required—TOEFL (minimum score 550 paper-based; 80 iBT). *Application deadline:* For fall admission, 1/15 for domestic and international students. Application fee: $30. Electronic applications accepted. *Expenses:* Tuition, state resident: full-time $9474; part-time $350.88 per credit hour. Tuition, nonresident: full-time $16,236; part-time $601.34 per credit hour. *Required fees:* $630 per semester. One-time fee: $20. Tuition and fees vary according to course load and campus/location. *Financial support:* In 2011–12, 32 students received support, including 12 research assistantships with full tuition reimbursements available (averaging $20,000 per year), 18 teaching assistantships with full tuition reimbursements available (averaging $20,000 per year); unspecified assistantships also available. Financial award application deadline: 4/15. *Faculty research:* Morphometrics, mathematical and systems biology, mining proteomic and metabolic data, computational materials research at Scientific Computing, advanced 4-D Var Data-Assimilation methods in dynamic meteorology and oceanography, computational fluid dynamics, astrophysics. *Unit head:* Dr. Sam Huckaba, Interim Dean, 850-644-1081. *Application contact:* Maribel Amwake, Graduate Academic Coordinator, 850-644-0143, Fax: 850-644-0098, E-mail: mamwake@fsu.edu. Web site: http://www.sc.fsu.edu.

Fort Hays State University, Graduate School, College of Arts and Sciences, Department of Geosciences, Program in Geosciences, Hays, KS 67601-4099. Offers geography (MS); geology (MS). *Degree requirements:* For master's, comprehensive exam, thesis. *Entrance requirements:* For master's, GRE General Test. Additional exam requirements/recommendations for international students: Required—TOEFL (minimum score 550 paper-based; 213 computer-based). Electronic applications accepted. *Faculty research:* Cretaceous and late Cenozoic stratigraphy, sedimentation, paleontology.

George Mason University, College of Science, Department of Geography and Geoinformation Science, Fairfax, VA 22030. Offers earth system science (MS); earth systems and geoinformation sciences (PhD); geographic and cartographic sciences (MS); geographic information sciences (Certificate); geoinformatics and geospatial intelligence (MS); geospatial intelligence (Certificate); remote sensing and image processing (Certificate). *Faculty:* 30 full-time (7 women), 10 part-time/adjunct (0 women). *Students:* 51 full-time (18 women), 162 part-time (49 women); includes 36 minority (9 Black or African American, non-Hispanic/Latino; 2 American Indian or Alaska Native, non-Hispanic/Latino; 10 Asian, non-Hispanic/Latino; 8 Hispanic/Latino; 7 Two or more races, non-Hispanic/Latino), 25 international. Average age 35. 121 applicants, 74% accepted, 52 enrolled. In 2011, 32 master's, 5 doctorates, 33 other advanced degrees awarded. *Degree requirements:* For master's, thesis optional. *Entrance requirements:* For master's, GRE (waived for those who have earned a master's degree from U.S. institution), bachelor's degree with minimum GPA of 3.0; 2 copies of official transcripts; current resume; expanded goals statement; 3 letters of recommendation; for doctorate, GRE (waived for those who have earned a master's degree from U.S. institution), bachelor's degree with minimum GPA of 3.0; 2 copies of official transcripts; 3 letters of recommendation; resume; expanded goals statement; for Certificate, GRE (waived for those who have earned a master's degree from U.S. institution), baccalaureate degree with minimum GPA of 3.0; 2 official copies of transcripts; expanded goals statement; 3 letters of recommendation; resume. Additional exam requirements/recommendations for international students: Required—TOEFL (minimum score 570 paper-based; 230 computer-based; 88 iBT), IELTS, Pearson Test of English. *Application deadline:* For fall admission, 4/15 priority date for domestic students; for spring admission, 11/15 priority date for domestic students. Application fee: $65 ($80 for international students). Electronic applications accepted. *Expenses:* Tuition, state resident: full-time $8750; part-time $364.58 per credit. Tuition, nonresident: full-time $24,092; part-time $1003.83 per credit. *Required fees:* $2514; $104.75 per credit. *Financial support:* In 2011–12, 20 students received support, including 1 fellowship with full tuition reimbursement available (averaging $18,000 per year), 15 research assistantships with full and partial tuition reimbursements available (averaging $16,844 per year), 5 teaching assistantships with full and partial tuition reimbursements available (averaging $10,886 per year); career-related internships or fieldwork, Federal Work-Study, scholarships/grants, unspecified assistantships, and health care benefits (full-time research or teaching assistantship recipients) also available. Support available to part-time students. Financial award application deadline: 3/1; financial award applicants required to submit FAFSA. *Faculty research:* Gender and earth science, earth science

Peterson's Graduate Programs in the Physical Sciences, Mathematics, Agricultural Sciences, the Environment & Natural Resources 2013

facebook.com/petersonspublishing **165**

Geosciences

education, remote sensing, planetary geology, hydrology. *Total annual research expenditures:* $2 million. *Unit head:* Peggy Agouris, Chair, 703-993-9265, Fax: 703-993-9230, E-mail: pagouris@gmu.edu. *Application contact:* Sheryl Luzzadder-Beach, Associate Chair/Academic Programs Director, 703-993-1213, Fax: 703-993-9299, E-mail: slbeach@gmu.edu. Web site: http://ggs.gmu.edu/.

Georgia Institute of Technology, Graduate Studies and Research, College of Sciences, School of Earth and Atmospheric Sciences, Atlanta, GA 30332-0340. Offers atmospheric chemistry, aerosols and clouds (MS, PhD); dynamics of weather and climate (MS, PhD); geochemistry (MS, PhD); geophysics (MS, PhD); oceanography (MS, PhD); paleoclimate (MS, PhD); planetary science (MS, PhD); remote sensing (MS, PhD). Part-time programs available. Terminal master's awarded for partial completion of doctoral program. *Degree requirements:* For master's, thesis or alternative; for doctorate, comprehensive exam, thesis/dissertation. *Entrance requirements:* For master's, GRE, letters of recommendation; for doctorate, GRE, academic transcripts, letters of recommendation, personal statement. Additional exam requirements/recommendations for international students: Required—TOEFL (minimum score 550 paper-based; 213 computer-based; 79 iBT). *Faculty research:* Geophysics; atmospheric chemistry, aerosols and clouds; dynamics of weather and climate; geochemistry; oceanography; paleoclimate; planetary science; remote sensing.

Georgia State University, College of Arts and Sciences, Department of Geosciences, Atlanta, GA 30302-3083. Offers geographic information systems (Certificate); geography (MA); geology (MA); hydrogeology (Certificate). Part-time and evening/weekend programs available. *Degree requirements:* For master's, one foreign language, comprehensive exam (for some programs), thesis or alternative. *Entrance requirements:* For master's, GRE General Test, minimum GPA of 2.75. Additional exam requirements/recommendations for international students: Required—TOEFL. Electronic applications accepted. *Faculty research:* Clay mineralogy, geoinformatics, fracture analysis, sedimentology, groundwater.

Graduate School and University Center of the City University of New York, Graduate Studies, Program in Earth and Environmental Sciences, New York, NY 10016-4039. Offers PhD. *Degree requirements:* For doctorate, one foreign language, comprehensive exam, thesis/dissertation. *Entrance requirements:* For doctorate, GRE General Test. Additional exam requirements/recommendations for international students: Required—TOEFL. Electronic applications accepted.

Harvard University, Graduate School of Arts and Sciences, Department of Earth and Planetary Sciences, Cambridge, MA 02138. Offers AM, PhD. Terminal master's awarded for partial completion of doctoral program. *Degree requirements:* For doctorate, comprehensive exam, thesis/dissertation. *Entrance requirements:* For doctorate, GRE General Test. Additional exam requirements/recommendations for international students: Required—TOEFL. Electronic applications accepted. *Expenses: Tuition:* Full-time $36,304. *Required fees:* $1186. Full-time tuition and fees vary according to program. *Faculty research:* Economic geography, geochemistry, geophysics, mineralogy, crystallography.

Hofstra University, School of Education, Health, and Human Services, Programs in Teaching Secondary Education, Hempstead, NY 11549. Offers business education (MS Ed); education technology (Advanced Certificate); English education (MA, MS Ed); foreign language and TESOL (MS Ed); foreign language education (MA, MS Ed), including French, German, Russian, Spanish; mathematics education (MA, MS Ed); science education (MA, MS Ed), including biology, chemistry, earth science, geology, physics; secondary education (Advanced Certificate); social studies education (MA, MS Ed). Part-time and evening/weekend programs available. Postbaccalaureate distance learning degree programs offered (minimal on-campus study). *Students:* 72 full-time (47 women), 51 part-time (30 women); includes 21 minority (9 Black or African American, non-Hispanic/Latino; 7 Asian, non-Hispanic/Latino; 5 Hispanic/Latino). Average age 28. 103 applicants, 91% accepted, 41 enrolled. In 2011, 86 master's, 6 other advanced degrees awarded. *Degree requirements:* For master's, one foreign language, comprehensive exam (for some programs), thesis (for some programs), exit project, electronic portfolio, student teaching, fieldwork, curriculum project, minimum GPA of 3.0; for Advanced Certificate, 3 foreign languages, comprehensive exam (for some programs), thesis project, minimum GPA of 3.0. *Entrance requirements:* For master's, 2 letters of recommendation, teacher certification (MA), essay; for Advanced Certificate, 2 letters of recommendation, essay. Additional exam requirements/recommendations for international students: Required—TOEFL (minimum score 550 paper-based; 213 computer-based; 80 iBT). *Application deadline:* Applications are processed on a rolling basis. Application fee: $70 ($75 for international students). Electronic applications accepted. *Expenses: Tuition:* Full-time $18,990; part-time $1055 per credit hour. *Required fees:* $970. Tuition and fees vary according to program. *Financial support:* In 2011–12, 90 students received support, including 13 fellowships with full and partial tuition reimbursements available (averaging $3,202 per year), 1 research assistantship with full and partial tuition reimbursement available (averaging $11,645 per year); career-related internships or fieldwork, Federal Work-Study, institutionally sponsored loans, scholarships/grants, tuition waivers (full and partial), and unspecified assistantships also available. Support available to part-time students. Financial award applicants required to submit FAFSA. *Faculty research:* Appropriate content and pedagogy in secondary school disciplines, appropriate pedagogy in secondary school disciplines, adolescent development, secondary school organization, alternative secondary school programs. *Unit head:* Dr. Esther Fusco, Chairperson, 516-463-7704, Fax: 516-463-6196, E-mail: catezf@hofstra.edu. *Application contact:* Carol Drummer, Dean

of Graduate Admissions, 516-463-4876, Fax: 516-463-4664, E-mail: gradstudent@hofstra.edu. Web site: http://www.hofstra.edu/education/.

Hunter College of the City University of New York, Graduate School, School of Arts and Sciences, Department of Geography, New York, NY 10021-5085. Offers analytical geography (MA); earth system science (MA); environmental and social issues (MA); geographic information science (Certificate); geographic information systems (MA); teaching earth science (MA). Part-time and evening/weekend programs available. *Faculty:* 7 full-time (3 women), 8 part-time/adjunct (1 woman). *Students:* 2 full-time (1 woman), 49 part-time (24 women); includes 11 minority (4 Black or African American, non-Hispanic/Latino; 4 Asian, non-Hispanic/Latino; 3 Hispanic/Latino), 1 international. Average age 35. 27 applicants, 74% accepted, 13 enrolled. In 2011, 12 master's, 3 other advanced degrees awarded. *Degree requirements:* For master's, comprehensive exam or thesis. *Entrance requirements:* For master's, GRE General Test, minimum B average in major, Boverall; 18 credits of course work in geography; 2 letters of recommendation; for Certificate, minimum B average in major, Boverall. Additional exam requirements/recommendations for international students: Required—TOEFL. *Application deadline:* For fall admission, 4/1 for domestic students; for spring admission, 11/1 for domestic students. Applications are processed on a rolling basis. Application fee: $125. *Expenses:* Tuition, state resident: full-time $8210; part-time $345 per credit. Tuition, nonresident: full-time $15,360; part-time $640 per credit. *Required fees:* $280 per semester. One-time fee: $125. Tuition and fees vary according to class time, campus/location and program. *Financial support:* In 2011–12, 1 fellowship (averaging $3,000 per year), 2 research assistantships (averaging $10,000 per year), 10 teaching assistantships (averaging $6,000 per year) were awarded; career-related internships or fieldwork, Federal Work-Study, institutionally sponsored loans, and unspecified assistantships also available. Financial award application deadline: 3/1. *Faculty research:* Urban geography, economic geography, geographic information science, demographic methods, climate change. *Unit head:* Prof. William Solecki, Chair, 212-772-4536, Fax: 212-772-5268, E-mail: wsolecki@hunter.cuny.edu. *Application contact:* Prof. Marianna Pavlovskaya, Graduate Adviser, 212-772-5320, Fax: 212-772-5268, E-mail: mpavlov@geo.hunter.cuny.edu. Web site: http://www.geo.hunter.cuny.edu/.

Hunter College of the City University of New York, Graduate School, School of Education, Programs in Secondary Education, New York, NY 10021-5085. Offers biology education (MA); chemistry education (MA); earth science (MA); English education (MA); French education (MA); Italian education (MA); mathematics education (MA); physics education (MA); social studies education (MA); Spanish education (MA). *Accreditation:* NCATE. *Faculty:* 49 full-time (31 women), 70 part-time/adjunct (55 women). *Students:* 15 full-time (7 women), 206 part-time (140 women); includes 68 minority (15 Black or African American, non-Hispanic/Latino; 1 American Indian or Alaska Native, non-Hispanic/Latino; 28 Asian, non-Hispanic/Latino; 24 Hispanic/Latino), 4 international. Average age 28. 701 applicants, 49% accepted, 182 enrolled. In 2011, 130 master's awarded. *Degree requirements:* For master's, thesis. *Entrance requirements:* Additional exam requirements/recommendations for international students: Required—TOEFL. *Application deadline:* For fall admission, 4/1 for domestic students, 2/1 for international students; for spring admission, 11/1 for domestic students, 9/1 for international students. Applications are processed on a rolling basis. Application fee: $125. *Expenses:* Tuition, state resident: full-time $8210; part-time $345 per credit. Tuition, nonresident: full-time $15,360; part-time $640 per credit. *Required fees:* $280 per semester. One-time fee: $125. Tuition and fees vary according to class time, campus/location and program. *Financial support:* Fellowships and tuition waivers (full and partial) available. Support available to part-time students. *Unit head:* Dr. Kate Garret, Coordinator, 212-772-4700, E-mail: kgarret@hunter.cuny.edu. *Application contact:* Milena Solo, Director for Graduate Admissions, 212-772-4482, Fax: 212-650-3336, E-mail: milena.solo@hunter.cuny.edu. Web site: http://www.hunter.cuny.edu/school-of-education/programs/graduate.

Idaho State University, Office of Graduate Studies, College of Science and Engineering, Department of Geosciences, Pocatello, ID 83209-8072. Offers geographic information science (MS); geology (MNS, MS); geology with emphasis in environmental geoscience (MS); geophysics/hydrology/geology (MS); geotechnology (Postbaccalaureate Certificate). Part-time programs available. *Degree requirements:* For master's, comprehensive exam, thesis, oral colloquium; for Postbaccalaureate Certificate, thesis optional, minimum 19 credits. *Entrance requirements:* For master's, GRE General Test (minimum 50th percentile in 2 sections), 3 letters of recommendation; for Postbaccalaureate Certificate, GRE General Test, 3 letters of recommendation, bachelor's degree, statement of goals. Additional exam requirements/recommendations for international students: Required—TOEFL (minimum score 550 paper-based; 213 computer-based; 80 iBT). Electronic applications accepted. *Faculty research:* Quantitative field mapping and sampling: microscopic, geochemical, and isotopic analysis of rocks, minerals and water; remote sensing, geographic information systems, and global positioning systems: environmental and watershed management; surficial and fluvial processes: landscape change; regional tectonics, structural geology; planetary geology.

Indiana University Bloomington, University Graduate School, College of Arts and Sciences, Department of Geological Sciences, Bloomington, IN 47405-7000. Offers biogeochemistry (MS, PhD); economic geology (MS, PhD); geobiology (MS, PhD); geophysics, structural geology and tectonics (MS, PhD); hydrogeology (MS, PhD); mineralogy (MS, PhD); stratigraphy and sedimentology (MS, PhD). *Faculty:* 17 full-time (1 woman). *Students:* 60 full-time (26 women), 2

166 facebook.com/petersonspublishing

Peterson's Graduate Programs in the Physical Sciences, Mathematics, Agricultural Sciences, the Environment & Natural Resources 2013

part-time (0 women); includes 5 minority (2 Black or African American, non-Hispanic/Latino; 1 Hispanic/Latino; 2 Two or more races, non-Hispanic/Latino), 18 international. Average age 29. 44 applicants, 55% accepted, 18 enrolled. In 2011, 11 master's, 6 doctorates awarded. Terminal master's awarded for partial completion of doctoral program. *Degree requirements:* For master's, thesis or alternative; for doctorate, comprehensive exam, thesis/dissertation. *Entrance requirements:* For master's and doctorate, GRE General Test. Additional exam requirements/recommendations for international students: Required—TOEFL. *Application deadline:* For fall admission, 1/15 priority date for domestic students, 12/15 for international students; for spring admission, 9/1 priority date for domestic students, 9/1 for international students. Applications are processed on a rolling basis. Application fee: $55 ($65 for international students). *Financial support:* In 2011–12, fellowships with full tuition reimbursements (averaging $17,300 per year), research assistantships with full tuition reimbursements (averaging $16,370 per year), teaching assistantships with full tuition reimbursements (averaging $15,150 per year) were awarded; career-related internships or fieldwork, Federal Work-Study, and institutionally sponsored loans also available. *Faculty research:* Geophysics, geochemistry, hydrogeology, geobiology, planetary science. *Total annual research expenditures:* $644,299. *Unit head:* Simon Brassell, Chair, 812-855-5581, Fax: 812-855-7899, E-mail: geochair@indiana.edu. *Application contact:* Mary Iverson, Graduate Secretary, 812-855-7214, Fax: 812-855-7899, E-mail: miverson@indiana.edu. Web site: http://www.indiana.edu/~geosci/.

Indiana University–Purdue University Indianapolis, School of Science, Department of Earth Sciences, Indianapolis, IN 46202-3272. Offers applied earth sciences (PhD); geology (MS). Part-time and evening/weekend programs available. *Faculty:* 8 full-time (2 women). *Students:* 10 full-time (6 women), 11 part-time (5 women); includes 1 minority (American Indian or Alaska Native, non-Hispanic/Latino), 8 international. Average age 29. 31 applicants, 45% accepted, 14 enrolled. In 2011, 7 master's awarded. *Degree requirements:* For master's, thesis (for some programs). *Entrance requirements:* For master's, GRE General Test, minimum GPA of 3.0. Application fee: $55 ($65 for international students). *Financial support:* In 2011–12, fellowships with full tuition reimbursements (averaging $12,000 per year), teaching assistantships with full tuition reimbursements (averaging $12,103 per year) were awarded; research assistantships with full tuition reimbursements and scholarships/grants also available. Financial award application deadline: 3/1. *Faculty research:* Wetland hydrology, groundwater contamination, soils, sedimentology, sediment chemistry. *Unit head:* Gabriel Filippelli, Chair, 317-274-7484, Fax: 317-274-7966. *Application contact:* Lenore P. Tedesco, Associate Professor, 317-274-7484, Fax: 317-274-7966, E-mail: ltedesco@iupui.edu. Web site: http://www.geology.iupui.edu/.

Iowa State University of Science and Technology, Department of Geological and Atmospheric Sciences, Ames, IA 50011-3212. Offers earth science (MS, PhD); environmental science (MS, PhD); geology (MS, PhD); meteorology (MS, PhD). *Degree requirements:* For master's, thesis (for some programs); for doctorate, thesis/dissertation. *Entrance requirements:* For master's and doctorate, GRE General Test. Additional exam requirements/recommendations for international students: Required—TOEFL (minimum score 550 paper-based; 79 iBT), IELTS (minimum score 6.5). *Application deadline:* For fall admission, 1/1 priority date for domestic students. Application fee: $40 ($90 for international students). Electronic applications accepted. *Unit head:* Dr. Carl E. Jacobson, Director of Graduate Education, 515-294-8048, Fax: 515-294-6049, E-mail: geology@iastate.edu. *Application contact:* Neal Iverson, Information Contact, 515-294-8048, Fax: 515-294-6049, E-mail: geology@iastate.edu. Web site: http://www.ge-at.iastate.edu/.

Iowa State University of Science and Technology, Program in Earth Science, Ames, IA 50011-3212. Offers MS, PhD. *Entrance requirements:* For master's and doctorate, GRE. Additional exam requirements/recommendations for international students: Required—TOEFL (minimum score 550 paper-based; 79 iBT), IELTS (minimum score 6.5). *Application deadline:* For fall admission, 1/1 priority date for domestic students. Electronic applications accepted. *Unit head:* Carl Jacobson, Director of Graduate Education, 515-294-8048, Fax: 515-294-6049, E-mail: geology@iastate.edu. *Application contact:* Neal Iverson, Application Contact, 515-294-8048, Fax: 515-294-6049, E-mail: geology@iastate.edu. Web site: http://www.ge-at.iastate.edu.

The Johns Hopkins University, Zanvyl Krieger School of Arts and Sciences, The Morton K. Blaustein Department of Earth and Planetary Sciences, Baltimore, MD 21218-2699. Offers MA, PhD. *Degree requirements:* For doctorate, comprehensive exam, thesis/dissertation. *Entrance requirements:* For master's and doctorate, GRE General Test. Additional exam requirements/recommendations for international students: Required—TOEFL (minimum score 600 paper-based; 250 computer-based; 100 iBT), IELTS. Electronic applications accepted. *Faculty research:* Oceanography, atmospheric sciences, geophysics, geology, geochemistry.

Lehigh University, College of Arts and Sciences, Department of Earth and Environmental Sciences, Bethlehem, PA 18015. Offers MS, PhD. *Faculty:* 15 full-time (2 women). *Students:* 27 full-time (11 women), 3 part-time (1 woman), 3 international. Average age 27. 38 applicants, 18% accepted, 7 enrolled. In 2011, 3 master's, 1 doctorate awarded. Terminal master's awarded for partial completion of doctoral program. *Degree requirements:* For master's, thesis; for doctorate, thesis/dissertation. *Entrance requirements:* For master's and doctorate, GRE General Test, transcripts, recommendation letters, research statement, faculty advocates. Additional exam requirements/recommendations for international students: Required—TOEFL (minimum score 85 iBT). *Application deadline:* For fall admission, 1/1 for domestic and international students. Applications are processed on a rolling basis. Application fee: $75. Electronic applications accepted. *Financial support:* In 2011–12, 13 students received support, including 3 fellowships with full tuition reimbursements available (averaging $24,500 per year), 10 research assistantships with full tuition reimbursements available (averaging $24,500 per year), 10 teaching assistantships with full tuition reimbursements available (averaging $24,500 per year); career-related internships or fieldwork, Federal Work-Study, institutionally sponsored loans, scholarships/grants, tuition waivers (full and partial), and unspecified assistantships also available. Support available to part-time students. Financial award application deadline: 1/1. *Faculty research:* Tectonics, surficial processes, ecology, environmental change. *Total annual research expenditures:* $1 million. *Unit head:* Dr. Frank J. Pazzaglia, Chairman, 610-758-3667, Fax: 610-758-3677, E-mail: fjp3@lehigh.edu. *Application contact:* Dr. Stephen Peters, Graduate Coordinator, 610-758-3957, Fax: 610-758-3677, E-mail: scp2@lehigh.edu. Web site: http://www.ees.lehigh.edu/.

Loma Linda University, School of Science and Technology, Department of Biological and Earth Sciences, Loma Linda, CA 92350. Offers MS, PhD. *Degree requirements:* For master's, comprehensive exam, thesis; for doctorate, comprehensive exam, thesis/dissertation. *Entrance requirements:* For master's, minimum GPA of 3.0. Additional exam requirements/recommendations for international students: Required—TOEFL (minimum score 550 paper-based; 213 computer-based).

Long Island University–C. W. Post Campus, College of Liberal Arts and Sciences, Department of Earth and Environmental Science, Brookville, NY 11548-1300. Offers earth science (MS); earth science education (MS); environmental studies (MS).

Massachusetts Institute of Technology, School of Science, Department of Earth, Atmospheric, and Planetary Sciences, Cambridge, MA 02139. Offers atmospheric chemistry (PhD, Sc D); atmospheric science (SM, PhD, Sc D); chemical oceanography (SM, PhD, Sc D); climate physics and chemistry (SM, PhD, Sc D); earth and planetary sciences (SM); geochemistry (PhD, Sc D); geology (PhD, Sc D); geophysics (PhD, Sc D); marine geology and geophysics (SM, PhD, Sc D); physical oceanography (SM, PhD, Sc D); planetary sciences (PhD, Sc D). *Faculty:* 33 full-time (6 women). *Students:* 175 full-time (81 women); includes 21 minority (3 Black or African American, non-Hispanic/Latino; 1 American Indian or Alaska Native, non-Hispanic/Latino; 8 Asian, non-Hispanic/Latino; 4 Hispanic/Latino; 5 Two or more races, non-Hispanic/Latino), 58 international. Average age 26. 241 applicants, 28% accepted, 43 enrolled. In 2011, 6 master's, 16 doctorates awarded. Terminal master's awarded for partial completion of doctoral program. *Degree requirements:* For master's, thesis; for doctorate, comprehensive exam, thesis/dissertation. *Entrance requirements:* For master's, GRE General Test; for doctorate, GRE General Test, GRE Subject Test (chemistry or physics for planetary science area). Additional exam requirements/recommendations for international students: Required—TOEFL (minimum score 577 paper-based; 233 computer-based; 91 iBT), IELTS (minimum score 7). *Application deadline:* For fall admission, 1/5 for domestic and international students; for spring admission, 11/1 for domestic and international students. Application fee: $75. Electronic applications accepted. *Expenses: Tuition:* Full-time $40,460; part-time $630 per credit hour. *Required fees:* $272. *Financial support:* In 2011–12, 125 students received support, including 68 fellowships (averaging $32,200 per year), 94 research assistantships (averaging $31,900 per year), 10 teaching assistantships (averaging $30,000 per year); Federal Work-Study, institutionally sponsored loans, scholarships/grants, health care benefits, and unspecified assistantships also available. *Faculty research:* Formation, dynamics and evolution of planetary systems; origin, composition, structure and dynamics of the atmospheres, oceans, surfaces and interiors of the Earth and other planets; evolution and interaction of the physical, chemical, geological and biological components of the Earth system; characterization of past, present and potential future climates and the causes and consequences of climate change; interplay of energy and the environment. *Total annual research expenditures:* $26.2 million. *Unit head:* Prof. Robert van der Hilst, Head, 617-253-2127, Fax: 617-253-8298, E-mail: eapsinfo@mit.edu. *Application contact:* EAPS Education Office, 617-253-3381, Fax: 617-253-8298, E-mail: eapsinfo@mit.edu. Web site: http://eapsweb.mit.edu/.

McGill University, Faculty of Graduate and Postdoctoral Studies, Faculty of Science, Department of Earth and Planetary Sciences, Montréal, QC H3A 2T5, Canada. Offers M Sc, PhD.

McMaster University, School of Graduate Studies, Faculty of Science, School of Geography and Earth Sciences, Hamilton, ON L8S 4M2, Canada. Offers geochemistry (PhD); geology (M Sc, PhD); human geography (MA, PhD); physical geography (M Sc, PhD). Part-time programs available. Terminal master's awarded for partial completion of doctoral program. *Degree requirements:* For master's, thesis; for doctorate, comprehensive exam, thesis/dissertation. *Entrance requirements:* For master's, minimum B+ average. Additional exam requirements/recommendations for international students: Required—TOEFL (minimum score 550 paper-based; 213 computer-based).

Memorial University of Newfoundland, School of Graduate Studies, Department of Earth Sciences, St. John's, NL A1C 5S7, Canada. Offers geology (M Sc, PhD); geophysics (M Sc, PhD). Part-time programs available. *Degree requirements:* For master's, thesis; for doctorate, comprehensive exam, thesis/

Peterson's Graduate Programs in the Physical Sciences, Mathematics, Agricultural Sciences, the Environment & Natural Resources 2013

facebook.com/petersonspublishing   **167**

Geosciences

dissertation, oral thesis defense, entry evaluation. *Entrance requirements:* For master's, honors B Sc; for doctorate, M Sc. Electronic applications accepted. *Faculty research:* Geochemistry, sedimentology, paleoceanography and global change, mineral deposits, petroleum geology, hydrology.

Michigan State University, The Graduate School, College of Natural Science, Department of Geological Sciences, East Lansing, MI 48824. Offers environmental geosciences (MS, PhD); environmental geosciences-environmental toxicology (PhD); geological sciences (MS, PhD). *Degree requirements:* For master's, thesis (for those without prior thesis work); for doctorate, thesis/dissertation. *Entrance requirements:* For master's, GRE General Test, minimum GPA of 3.0, course work in geoscience, 3 letters of recommendation; for doctorate, GRE General Test, 3 letters of recommendation. Additional exam requirements/recommendations for international students: Required—TOEFL (minimum score 550 paper-based; 213 computer-based), Michigan State University ELT (minimum score 85), Michigan English Language Assessment Battery (minimum score 83). Electronic applications accepted. *Faculty research:* Water in the environment, global and biological change, crystal dynamics.

Middle Tennessee State University, College of Graduate Studies, College of Liberal Arts, Department of Geosciences, Murfreesboro, TN 37132. Offers Graduate Certificate. Part-time and evening/weekend programs available. Postbaccalaureate distance learning degree programs offered. *Entrance requirements:* Additional exam requirements/recommendations for international students: Required—TOEFL (minimum score 525 paper-based; 195 computer-based; 71 iBT) or IELTS (minimum score 6). *Expenses:* Tuition, state resident: full-time $10,008. Tuition, nonresident: full-time $25,056. *Financial support:* Application deadline: 5/1. *Unit head:* Dr. Warner Cribb, Interim Chair, 615-898-2726, Fax: 615-898-5592, E-mail: warner.cribb@mtsu.edu. *Application contact:* Dr. Michael D. Allen, Dean and Vice Provost for Research, 615-898-2840, Fax: 615-904-8020, E-mail: michael.allen@mtsu.edu.

Mississippi State University, College of Arts and Sciences, Department of Geosciences, Mississippi State, MS 39762. Offers applied meteorology (MS); broadcast meteorology (MS); earth and atmospheric science (PhD); environmental geoscience (MS); geography (MS); geology (MS); geospatial sciences (MS); professional meteorology/climatology (MS); teachers in geoscience (MS). Postbaccalaureate distance learning degree programs offered (no on-campus study). *Faculty:* 19 full-time (3 women), 2 part-time/adjunct (0 women). *Students:* 72 full-time (27 women), 279 part-time (127 women); includes 40 minority (12 Black or African American, non-Hispanic/Latino; 4 American Indian or Alaska Native, non-Hispanic/Latino; 6 Asian, non-Hispanic/Latino; 14 Hispanic/Latino; 4 Two or more races, non-Hispanic/Latino), 10 international. Average age 35. 228 applicants, 77% accepted, 144 enrolled. In 2011, 89 master's awarded. *Degree requirements:* For master's, thesis (for some programs), comprehensive oral or written exam. *Entrance requirements:* For master's, GRE (for on-campus applicants), minimum undergraduate GPA of 2.75. Additional exam requirements/recommendations for international students: Required—TOEFL (minimum score 475 paper-based; 153 computer-based; 53 iBT); Recommended—IELTS (minimum score 4.5). *Application deadline:* For fall admission, 7/1 for domestic students, 5/1 for international students; for spring admission, 11/1 for domestic students, 9/1 for international students. Applications are processed on a rolling basis. Application fee: $40. Electronic applications accepted. *Expenses:* Tuition, state resident: full-time $5805; part-time $322.50 per credit hour. Tuition, nonresident: full-time $14,670; part-time $815 per credit hour. *Financial support:* In 2011–12, 13 research assistantships with full tuition reimbursements (averaging $20,746 per year), 31 teaching assistantships with full tuition reimbursements (averaging $14,151 per year) were awarded; Federal Work-Study, institutionally sponsored loans, scholarships/grants, tuition waivers (partial), and unspecified assistantships also available. Financial award application deadline: 4/1; financial award applicants required to submit FAFSA. *Faculty research:* Climatology, hydrogeology, sedimentology, meteorology. *Total annual research expenditures:* $6.2 million. *Unit head:* Dr. Darrel Schmitz, Professor and Head, 662-325-3915, Fax: 662-325-9423, E-mail: schmitz@geosci.msstate.edu. *Application contact:* Dr. Christopher P. Dewey, Associate Professor/Graduate Coordinator, 662-325-2909, Fax: 662-325-9423, E-mail: cpd4@msstate.edu. Web site: http://www.msstate.edu/dept/geosciences/.

Missouri State University, Graduate College, College of Natural and Applied Sciences, Department of Geography, Geology, and Planning, Springfield, MO 65897. Offers geospatial sciences (MS, MS Ed), including earth science (MS Ed), geology (MS), human geography and planning (MS), physical geography (MS Ed); natural and applied science (MNAS), including geography, geology and planning; secondary education (MS Ed), including geography. Part-time and evening/weekend programs available. *Faculty:* 19 full-time (4 women). *Students:* 19 full-time (9 women), 12 part-time (7 women), 2 international. Average age 31. 20 applicants, 80% accepted, 11 enrolled. In 2011, 15 master's awarded. *Degree requirements:* For master's, comprehensive exam, thesis (for some programs). *Entrance requirements:* For master's, GRE General Test (MS, MNAS), minimum undergraduate GPA of 3.0 (MS, MNAS), 9-12 teacher certification (MS Ed). Additional exam requirements/recommendations for international students: Required—TOEFL (minimum score 550 paper-based; 213 computer-based; 79 iBT). *Application deadline:* For fall admission, 7/20 priority date for domestic students, 5/1 for international students; for spring admission, 12/20 priority date for domestic students, 9/1 for international students. Applications are processed on a rolling basis. Application fee: $35 ($50 for international students). Electronic

applications accepted. *Expenses:* Tuition, state resident: full-time $4086; part-time $227 per credit hour. Tuition, nonresident: full-time $8172; part-time $454 per credit hour. *Required fees:* $275 per semester. Tuition and fees vary according to course load, campus/location and program. *Financial support:* In 2011–12, 3 research assistantships with full tuition reimbursements (averaging $8,000 per year), 9 teaching assistantships with full tuition reimbursements (averaging $8,000 per year) were awarded; career-related internships or fieldwork, Federal Work-Study, institutionally sponsored loans, scholarships/grants, and unspecified assistantships also available. Financial award application deadline: 3/31; financial award applicants required to submit FAFSA. *Faculty research:* Stratigraphy and ancient meteorite impacts, environmental geochemistry of karst, hyperspectral image processing, water quality, small town planning. *Unit head:* Dr. Thomas Plymate, Head, 417-836-5800, Fax: 417-836-6934, E-mail: tomplymate@missouristate.edu. *Application contact:* Misty Stewart, Coordinator of Graduate Recruitment, 417-836-6079, Fax: 417-836-6200, E-mail: mistystewart@missouristate.edu. Web site: http://geosciences.missouristate.edu/

Montana State University, College of Graduate Studies, College of Letters and Science, Department of Earth Sciences, Bozeman, MT 59717. Offers MS, PhD. Part-time programs available. *Degree requirements:* For master's, comprehensive exam, thesis (for some programs); for doctorate, comprehensive exam, thesis/dissertation. *Entrance requirements:* For master's and doctorate, GRE General Test, minimum GPA of 3.0. Additional exam requirements/recommendations for international students: Required—TOEFL (minimum score 550 paper-based; 213 computer-based). Electronic applications accepted. *Faculty research:* Dinosaur paleontology, climate history/geomicrobiology, stratigraphy/sedimentology/structure/carbon sequestration, igneous petrology South America, historical/urban economic geography western U. S. and China.

Montana Tech of The University of Montana, Graduate School, Geosciences Programs, Butte, MT 59701-8997. Offers geochemistry (MS); geological engineering (MS); geology (MS); geophysical engineering (MS); hydrogeological engineering (MS); hydrogeology (MS). Part-time programs available. *Faculty:* 16 full-time (4 women), 4 part-time/adjunct (0 women). *Students:* 16 full-time (7 women), 12 part-time (6 women); includes 2 minority (1 Black or African American, non-Hispanic/Latino; 1 American Indian or Alaska Native, non-Hispanic/Latino), 1 international. 23 applicants, 65% accepted, 13 enrolled. In 2011, 9 master's awarded. *Degree requirements:* For master's, comprehensive exam (for some programs), thesis (for some programs). *Entrance requirements:* For master's, GRE General Test, minimum GPA of 3.0. Additional exam requirements/recommendations for international students: Required—TOEFL (minimum score 525 paper-based; 195 computer-based; 71 iBT). *Application deadline:* For fall admission, 4/1 priority date for domestic students, 3/1 for international students; for spring admission, 10/1 priority date for domestic students, 7/1 for international students. Applications are processed on a rolling basis. Application fee: $30. Electronic applications accepted. *Financial support:* In 2011–12, 15 students received support, including 10 teaching assistantships with partial tuition reimbursements available (averaging $5,000 per year); research assistantships with partial tuition reimbursements available, career-related internships or fieldwork, tuition waivers (full and partial), and unspecified assistantships also available. Financial award application deadline: 4/1; financial award applicants required to submit FAFSA. *Faculty research:* Water resource development, seismic processing, petroleum reservoir characterization, environmental geochemistry, geologic mapping. *Unit head:* Dr. Mary MacLaughlin, Department Head, 406-496-4655, Fax: 406-496-4260, E-mail: mmaclaughlin@mtech.edu. *Application contact:* Fred Sullivan, Administrator, Graduate School, 406-496-4304, Fax: 406-496-4710, E-mail: fsullivan@mtech.edu. Web site: http://www.mtech.edu/academics/gradschool/degreeprograms/degrees.htm.

Montclair State University, The Graduate School, College of Science and Mathematics, Department of Earth and Environmental Studies, Program in Geoscience, Montclair, NJ 07043-1624. Offers MS. Part-time and evening/weekend programs available. *Students:* 8 full-time (1 woman), 15 part-time (3 women); includes 5 minority (1 Black or African American, non-Hispanic/Latino; 2 Asian, non-Hispanic/Latino; 2 Hispanic/Latino), 1 international. Average age 34. 16 applicants, 44% accepted, 5 enrolled. In 2011, 6 master's awarded. *Degree requirements:* For master's, thesis. *Entrance requirements:* Additional exam requirements/recommendations for international students: Required—TOEFL (minimum score 83 iBT), IELTS (minimum score 6.5). *Application deadline:* Applications are processed on a rolling basis. Application fee: $60. Electronic applications accepted. *Financial support:* In 2011–12, 3 research assistantships with full tuition reimbursements (averaging $7,000 per year) were awarded; Federal Work-Study, scholarships/grants, and unspecified assistantships also available. Support available to part-time students. Financial award application deadline: 3/1; financial award applicants required to submit FAFSA. *Faculty research:* Environmental geochemistry, flood hydrology, geomorphology and weathering processes, regional climate modeling, remote sensing, Cenozoic marine sediment records from polar regions, igneous and metamorphic petrology. *Unit head:* Dr. Matthew Goring, Chairperson, 973-655-5409. *Application contact:* Amy Aiello, Director of Graduate Admissions and Operations, 973-655-5147, Fax: 973-655-7869, E-mail: graduate.school@montclair.edu. Web site: http://www.montclair.edu/graduate/programs-of-study/geoscience/.

Murray State University, College of Science, Engineering and Technology, Program in Geosciences, Murray, KY 42071. Offers MS. Part-time programs available. *Degree requirements:* For master's, comprehensive exam, thesis optional. *Entrance requirements:* Additional exam requirements/recommendations for international students: Required—TOEFL, IELTS.

New Mexico Institute of Mining and Technology, Graduate Studies, Department of Earth and Environmental Science, Socorro, NM 87801. Offers geochemistry (MS, PhD); geology (MS, PhD); geophysics (MS, PhD); hydrology (MS, PhD). *Faculty:* 21 full-time (2 women), 29 part-time/adjunct (5 women). *Students:* 60 full-time (30 women), 18 part-time (10 women); includes 13 minority (1 Black or African American, non-Hispanic/Latino; 2 American Indian or Alaska Native, non-Hispanic/Latino; 3 Asian, non-Hispanic/Latino; 4 Hispanic/Latino; 3 Two or more races, non-Hispanic/Latino), 5 international. Average age 28. 94 applicants, 54% accepted, 20 enrolled. In 2011, 7 master's, 4 doctorates awarded. *Degree requirements:* For master's, thesis optional; for doctorate, thesis/dissertation. *Entrance requirements:* For master's, GRE General Test; for doctorate, GRE General Test, GRE Subject Test. Additional exam requirements/recommendations for international students: Required—TOEFL. *Application deadline:* For fall admission, 3/1 priority date for domestic students; for spring admission, 6/1 for domestic students. Applications are processed on a rolling basis. Application fee: $16. *Expenses:* Tuition, state resident: full-time $4849; part-time $269.41 per credit hour. Tuition, nonresident: full-time $16,041; part-time $891.15 per credit hour. *Required fees:* $622; $65 per credit hour. $20 per semester. Part-time tuition and fees vary according to course load. *Financial support:* In 2011–12, 4 fellowships (averaging $8,205 per year), 32 research assistantships (averaging $20,620 per year), 14 teaching assistantships with full and partial tuition reimbursements (averaging $12,664 per year) were awarded; Federal Work-Study, institutionally sponsored loans, and unspecified assistantships also available. Financial award application deadline: 3/1; financial award applicants required to submit CSS PROFILE or FAFSA. *Faculty research:* Seismology, geochemistry, caves and karst topography, hydrology, volcanology. *Unit head:* Dr. Gary Axen, Chair, 505-835-5178, Fax: 505-835-6436, E-mail: gaxen@ees.nmt.edu. *Application contact:* Dr. Lorie Liebrock, Dean of Graduate Studies, 505-835-5513, Fax: 505-835-5476, E-mail: graduate@nmt.edu. Web site: http://www.ees.nmt.edu/.

North Carolina Central University, Division of Academic Affairs, College of Science and Technology, Department of Environmental, Earth and Geospatial Sciences, Durham, NC 27707-3129. Offers earth sciences (MS). *Degree requirements:* For master's, one foreign language, comprehensive exam. *Entrance requirements:* For master's, GRE, minimum GPA of 3.0 in major, 2.5 overall. Additional exam requirements/recommendations for international students: Required—TOEFL.

North Carolina State University, Graduate School, College of Physical and Mathematical Sciences, Department of Marine, Earth, and Atmospheric Sciences, Raleigh, NC 27695. Offers marine, earth, and atmospheric sciences (MS, PhD); meteorology (MS, PhD); oceanography (MS, PhD). PhD offered jointly with The University of North Carolina Wilmington. Terminal master's awarded for partial completion of doctoral program. *Degree requirements:* For master's, thesis (for some programs), final oral exam; for doctorate, comprehensive exam, thesis/dissertation, final oral exam, preliminary oral and written exams. *Entrance requirements:* For master's, GRE General Test, minimum GPA of 3.0; for doctorate, GRE General Test, GRE Subject Test (for disciplines in biological oceanography and geology), minimum GPA of 3.0. Additional exam requirements/recommendations for international students: Required—TOEFL (minimum score 550 paper-based). Electronic applications accepted. *Faculty research:* Boundary layer and air quality meteorology; climate and mesoscale dynamics; biological, chemical, geological, and physical oceanography; hard rock, soft rock, environmental, and paleo-geology.

Northwestern University, The Graduate School, Judd A. and Marjorie Weinberg College of Arts and Sciences, Department of Geological Sciences, Evanston, IL 60208. Offers MS, PhD. Admissions and degrees offered through The Graduate School. Part-time programs available. *Degree requirements:* For doctorate, thesis/dissertation. *Entrance requirements:* For master's and doctorate, GRE General Test. Additional exam requirements/recommendations for international students: Required—TOEFL. Electronic applications accepted.

Oregon State University, Graduate School, College of Science, Department of Geosciences, Corvallis, OR 97331. Offers geography (MA, MAIS, MS, PhD); geology (MA, MAIS, MS, PhD). Part-time programs available. Terminal master's awarded for partial completion of doctoral program. *Degree requirements:* For doctorate, one foreign language, thesis/dissertation. *Entrance requirements:* For master's and doctorate, GRE General Test, GRE Subject Test, minimum GPA of 3.0 in last 90 hours. Additional exam requirements/recommendations for international students: Required—TOEFL.

Penn State University Park, Graduate School, College of Earth and Mineral Sciences, Department of Geosciences, State College, University Park, PA 16802-1503. Offers M Ed, MS, PhD. *Unit head:* Dr. William E. Easterling, III, Dean, 814-865-6546, Fax: 814-863-7708, E-mail: wee2@psu.edu. *Application contact:* Cynthia E. Nicosia, Director of Graduate Enrollment Services, 814-865-1834, E-mail: cey1@psu.edu. Web site: http://www.geosc.psu.edu/.

Princeton University, Graduate School, Department of Geosciences, Princeton, NJ 08544-1019. Offers atmospheric and oceanic sciences (PhD); geosciences (PhD); ocean sciences and marine biology (PhD). *Degree requirements:* For doctorate, one foreign language, thesis/dissertation. *Entrance requirements:* For doctorate, GRE General Test. Additional exam requirements/recommendations

for international students: Required—TOEFL (minimum score 600 paper-based; 250 computer-based). Electronic applications accepted. *Faculty research:* Biogeochemistry, climate science, earth history, regional geology and tectonics, solid–earth geophysics.

Purdue University, Graduate School, College of Science, Department of Earth and Atmospheric Sciences, West Lafayette, IN 47907. Offers MS, PhD. *Faculty:* 33 full-time (5 women), 2 part-time/adjunct (0 women). *Students:* 73 full-time (29 women), 6 part-time (3 women); includes 8 minority (1 Black or African American, non-Hispanic/Latino; 2 American Indian or Alaska Native, non-Hispanic/Latino; 1 Asian, non-Hispanic/Latino; 4 Hispanic/Latino), 33 international. Average age 28. 122 applicants, 26% accepted, 16 enrolled. In 2011, 11 master's, 6 doctorates awarded. *Degree requirements:* For master's, comprehensive exam, thesis; for doctorate, one foreign language, comprehensive exam, thesis/dissertation. *Entrance requirements:* For master's, GRE General Test, minimum undergraduate GPA of 3.0 or equivalent; for doctorate, GRE General Test, minimum undergraduate or master's GPA of 3.0 or equivalent. Additional exam requirements/recommendations for international students: Required—TOEFL (minimum score 550 paper-based; 213 computer-based; 77 iBT); Recommended—TWE. *Application deadline:* For fall admission, 1/2 priority date for domestic students, 1/2 for international students; for spring admission, 9/1 for domestic and international students. Applications are processed on a rolling basis. Application fee: $60 ($75 for international students). Electronic applications accepted. *Financial support:* Fellowships with partial tuition reimbursements, research assistantships with partial tuition reimbursements, and teaching assistantships with partial tuition reimbursements available. Support available to part-time students. Financial award application deadline: 3/1; financial award applicants required to submit FAFSA. *Faculty research:* Geology, geophysics, hydrogeology, paleoclimatology, environmental science. *Unit head:* Dr. Jonathan M. Harbor, Head, 765-494-4753. *Application contact:* Kathy S. Kincade, Graduate Secretary, 765-494-5984, Fax: 765-496-1210, E-mail: kkincade@purdue.edu. Web site: http://www.eas.purdue.edu.

Rice University, Graduate Programs, Wiess School of Natural Sciences, Department of Earth Science, Houston, TX 77251-1892. Offers MS, PhD. Terminal master's awarded for partial completion of doctoral program. *Degree requirements:* For master's, comprehensive exam, thesis, annual department report and presentation, qualifying exam, orals, 2 publications; for doctorate, comprehensive exam, thesis/dissertation, annual department report and presentation, qualifying exam, orals, 3 publications. *Entrance requirements:* For master's and doctorate, GRE. Additional exam requirements/recommendations for international students: Required—TOEFL (minimum score 600 paper-based; 90 iBT), IELTS. Electronic applications accepted. *Faculty research:* Seismology, structural geology, tectonics and paleomagnetism, geodynamics, high temperature geochemistry, volcanic processes.

Rice University, Graduate Programs, Wiess School–Professional Science Master's Programs, Professional Master's Program in Subsurface Geosciences, Houston, TX 77251-1892. Offers geophysics (MS). Part-time programs available. *Degree requirements:* For master's, internship. *Entrance requirements:* For master's, GRE, letters of recommendation (4). Additional exam requirements/recommendations for international students: Required—TOEFL (minimum score 600 paper-based; 250 computer-based; 90 iBT). Electronic applications accepted. *Faculty research:* Seismology, geodynamics, wave propagation, bio-geochemistry, remote sensing.

St. Francis Xavier University, Graduate Studies, Department of Earth Sciences, Antigonish, NS B2G 2W5, Canada. Offers M Sc. *Degree requirements:* For master's, thesis. *Entrance requirements:* Additional exam requirements/recommendations for international students: Required—TOEFL (minimum score 580 paper-based; 236 computer-based). *Faculty research:* Environmental earth sciences, global change tectonics, paleoclimatology, crustal fluids.

Saint Louis University, Graduate Education, College of Arts and Sciences, Department of Earth and Atmospheric Sciences, St. Louis, MO 63103-2097. Offers geophysics (PhD); geoscience (MS); meteorology (M Pr Met, MS-R, PhD). Part-time programs available. *Degree requirements:* For master's, thesis (for some programs), comprehensive oral exam; for doctorate, thesis/dissertation, preliminary exams. *Entrance requirements:* For master's, GRE General Test, letters of recommendation, resume; for doctorate, GRE General Test, letters of recommendation, resumé, goal statement, transcripts. Additional exam requirements/recommendations for international students: Required—TOEFL (minimum score 525 paper-based; 194 computer-based). Electronic applications accepted. *Faculty research:* Structural geology, mesoscale meteorology and severe storms, weather and climate change prediction.

St. Thomas University, School of Leadership Studies, Institute for Education, Miami Gardens, FL 33054-6459. Offers earth/space science (Certificate); educational administration (MS, Certificate); educational leadership (Ed D); elementary education (MS); ESOL (Certificate); gifted education (Certificate); instructional technology (MS, Certificate); professional/studies (Certificate); reading (MS, Certificate); special education (MS). Part-time and evening/weekend programs available. *Degree requirements:* For master's, comprehensive exam; for doctorate, comprehensive exam, thesis/dissertation. *Entrance requirements:* For master's, interview, minimum GPA of 3.0 or GRE; for doctorate, GRE or MAT. Additional exam requirements/recommendations for international students: Required—TOEFL (minimum score 550 paper-based; 213 computer-based; 79 iBT). Electronic applications accepted.

Peterson's Graduate Programs in the Physical Sciences, Mathematics, Agricultural Sciences, the Environment & Natural Resources 2013

facebook.com/petersonspublishing **169**

Geosciences

San Francisco State University, Division of Graduate Studies, College of Science and Engineering, Department of Geosciences, San Francisco, CA 94132-1722. Offers MS. *Application deadline:* Applications are processed on a rolling basis. *Unit head:* Dr. Oswaldo Garcia, Chair, 415-338-2061, E-mail: ogarcia@sfsu.edu. *Application contact:* Dr. John Caskey, Graduate Coordinator, 415-405-0353, E-mail: caskey@sfsu.edu. Web site: http://tornado.sfsu.edu.

Simon Fraser University, Graduate Studies, Faculty of Science, Department of Earth Sciences, Burnaby, BC V5A 1S6, Canada. Offers M Sc, PhD. Part-time programs available. *Degree requirements:* For master's, thesis. *Entrance requirements:* For master's, minimum GPA of 3.0. Additional exam requirements/recommendations for international students: Required—TOEFL or IELTS. Electronic applications accepted. *Faculty research:* Earth surface processes, environmental geoscience, surficial and Quaternary geology, sedimentology.

South Dakota State University, Graduate School, College of Engineering, Geospatial Science and Engineering Program, Brookings, SD 57007. Offers PhD. Part-time programs available. *Degree requirements:* For doctorate, comprehensive exam, thesis/dissertation. *Entrance requirements:* For doctorate, GRE. Additional exam requirements/recommendations for international students: Required—TOEFL (minimum score 525 paper-based; 197 computer-based; 71 iBT). *Faculty research:* Deforestation, land use/cover change, GIS spatial modeling.

Stanford University, School of Earth Sciences, Department of Geological and Environmental Sciences, Stanford, CA 94305-9991. Offers MS, PhD, Eng. Terminal master's awarded for partial completion of doctoral program. *Degree requirements:* For master's and Eng, thesis; for doctorate, thesis/dissertation. *Entrance requirements:* For master's, doctorate, and Eng, GRE General Test. Additional exam requirements/recommendations for international students: Required—TOEFL. Electronic applications accepted. *Expenses: Tuition:* Full-time $40,050; part-time $890 per credit.

Stanford University, School of Earth Sciences, Earth Systems Program, Stanford, CA 94305-9991. Offers MS. Students admitted at the undergraduate level. Electronic applications accepted. *Expenses: Tuition:* Full-time $40,050; part-time $890 per credit.

State University of New York at New Paltz, Graduate School, School of Education, Department of Secondary Education, New Paltz, NY 12561. Offers adolescence education: biology (MAT, MS Ed); adolescence education: chemistry (MAT, MS Ed); adolescence education: earth science (MAT, MS Ed); adolescence education: English (MAT, MS Ed); adolescence education: French (MAT, MS Ed); adolescence education: social studies (MAT, MS Ed); adolescence education: Spanish (MAT, MS Ed); second language education (MS Ed). *Accreditation:* NCATE. Part-time and evening/weekend programs available. *Faculty:* 18 full-time (10 women), 2 part-time/adjunct (both women). *Students:* 79 full-time (48 women), 76 part-time (55 women); includes 30 minority (3 Black or African American, non-Hispanic/Latino; 2 Asian, non-Hispanic/Latino; 22 Hispanic/Latino; 3 Two or more races, non-Hispanic/Latino), 1 international. Average age 32. 127 applicants, 69% accepted, 64 enrolled. In 2011, 73 master's awarded. *Degree requirements:* For master's, comprehensive exam (for some programs), portfolio. *Entrance requirements:* For master's, minimum GPA of 3.0, New York state teaching certificate (MS Ed). Additional exam requirements/recommendations for international students: Required—TOEFL (minimum score 550 paper-based; 213 computer-based; 80 iBT), IELTS (minimum score 6.5). *Application deadline:* For fall admission, 3/1 priority date for domestic students, 3/1 for international students; for spring admission, 10/1 priority date for domestic students, 10/1 for international students. Application fee: $50. Electronic applications accepted. *Expenses:* Tuition, state resident: full-time $8870; part-time $370 per credit. Tuition, nonresident: full-time $15,160; part-time $632 per credit. *Required fees:* $1188; $34 per credit. $184 per semester. *Financial support:* In 2011–12, 13 students received support, including 3 fellowships with partial tuition reimbursements available (averaging $7,000 per year); Federal Work-Study, institutionally sponsored loans, and tuition waivers (full) also available. Financial award application deadline: 8/1; financial award applicants required to submit FAFSA. *Unit head:* Dr. Devon Duhaney, Chair, 845-257-2850, E-mail: duhaneyd@newpaltz.edu. *Application contact:* Caroline Murphy, Graduate Admissions Advisor, 845-257-3285, Fax: 845-257-3284, E-mail: gradschool@newpaltz.edu. Web site: http://www.newpaltz.edu/secondaryed/.

State University of New York College at Oneonta, Graduate Education, Department of Earth Sciences, Oneonta, NY 13820-4015. Offers MA. Part-time and evening/weekend programs available. *Degree requirements:* For master's, thesis. *Entrance requirements:* For master's, GRE General Test.

Stony Brook University, State University of New York, Graduate School, College of Arts and Sciences, Department of Geosciences, Stony Brook, NY 11794. Offers earth science (MAT); geosciences (MS, PhD). MAT offered through the School of Professional Development. Terminal master's awarded for partial completion of doctoral program. *Degree requirements:* For master's, thesis or alternative; for doctorate, thesis/dissertation. *Entrance requirements:* For master's and doctorate, GRE General Test, minimum GPA of 3.0. Additional exam requirements/recommendations for international students: Required—TOEFL. *Faculty research:* Astronomy, theoretical and observational astrophysics, paleontology, petrology, crystallography.

Texas Tech University, Graduate School, College of Arts and Sciences, Department of Geosciences, Lubbock, TX 79409. Offers atmospheric science (MS); geography (MS); geosciences (MS, PhD). Part-time programs available. *Faculty:* 27 full-time (5 women), 2 part-time/adjunct (0 women). *Students:* 49 full-time (17 women), 22 part-time (6 women); includes 6 minority (all Hispanic/Latino), 13 international. Average age 28. 109 applicants, 30% accepted, 22 enrolled. In 2011, 10 master's, 1 doctorate awarded. *Degree requirements:* For master's, thesis or alternative; for doctorate, comprehensive exam, thesis/dissertation. *Entrance requirements:* For master's and doctorate, GRE General Test. Additional exam requirements/recommendations for international students: Required—TOEFL (minimum score 550 paper-based; 213 computer-based; 79 iBT). *Application deadline:* For fall admission, 6/1 priority date for domestic students, 1/15 for international students; for spring admission, 9/1 priority date for domestic students, 6/15 for international students. Applications are processed on a rolling basis. Application fee: $50 ($75 for international students). Electronic applications accepted. *Expenses:* Tuition, state resident: full-time $5899; part-time $245.80 per credit hour. Tuition, nonresident: full-time $13,411; part-time $558.80 per credit hour. *Required fees:* $2680.60; $86.50 per credit hour. $920.30 per semester. *Financial support:* In 2011–12, 23 students received support. Application deadline: 4/15; applicants required to submit FAFSA. *Faculty research:* Sedimentology and paleontology, geophysics, geochemistry, geospatial technology, hurricanes and severe storms. *Total annual research expenditures:* $1 million. *Unit head:* Dr. Calvin Barnes, Chairman, 806-742-3102, Fax: 806-742-0100, E-mail: cal.barnes@ttu.edu. *Application contact:* Dr. Seiichi Nagihara, Associate Professor, 806-742-3102, Fax: 806-724-0100, E-mail: seiichi.nagihara@ttu.edu. Web site: http://www.gesc.ttu.edu/.

Université du Québec à Chicoutimi, Graduate Programs, Program in Earth Sciences, Chicoutimi, QC G7H 2B1, Canada. Offers M Sc A. Part-time programs available. *Degree requirements:* For master's, thesis. *Entrance requirements:* For master's, appropriate bachelor's degree, proficiency in French.

Université du Québec à Montréal, Graduate Programs, Program in Earth and Atmospheric Sciences, Montréal, QC H3C 3P8, Canada. Offers atmospheric sciences (M Sc); Earth and atmospheric sciences (PhD); Earth science (M Sc); meteorology (PhD, Diploma). PhD programs offered jointly with McGill University. Part-time programs available. *Degree requirements:* For master's, thesis. *Entrance requirements:* For master's and Diploma, appropriate bachelor's degree or equivalent, proficiency in French; for doctorate, appropriate master's degree or equivalent, proficiency in French.

Université du Québec à Montréal, Graduate Programs, Program in Earth Sciences, Montreal, QC H3C 3P8, Canada. Offers earth sciences (M Sc); mineral resources (PhD); non-renewable resources (DESS). Part-time programs available. Terminal master's awarded for partial completion of doctoral program. *Degree requirements:* For master's, thesis (for some programs); for doctorate, thesis/dissertation. *Entrance requirements:* For master's, appropriate bachelor's degree or equivalent, proficiency in French. *Faculty research:* Economic geology, structural geology, geochemistry, Quaternary geology, isotopic geochemistry.

Université du Québec, Institut National de la Recherche Scientifique, Graduate Programs, Research Center—Water, Earth and Environment, Québec, QC G1K 9A9, Canada. Offers earth sciences (M Sc, PhD); earth sciences-environmental technologies (M Sc); water sciences (M Sc, PhD). Part-time programs available. *Faculty:* 40. *Students:* 204 full-time (88 women), 23 part-time (12 women), 103 international. Average age 30. In 2011, 31 master's, 12 doctorates awarded. *Degree requirements:* For master's, thesis optional; for doctorate, thesis/dissertation. *Entrance requirements:* For master's, appropriate bachelor's degree, proficiency in French; for doctorate, appropriate master's degree, proficiency in French. *Application deadline:* For fall admission, 3/30 for domestic and international students; for winter admission, 11/1 for domestic and international students; for spring admission, 3/1 for domestic and international students. Application fee: $45. Electronic applications accepted. *Financial support:* In 2011–12, 184 students received support, including fellowships (averaging $16,500 per year); research assistantships also available. *Faculty research:* Land use, impacts of climate change, adaptation to climate change, integrated management of resources (mineral and water). *Unit head:* Yves Begin, Director, 418-654-2524, Fax: 418-654-2600, E-mail: yves.begin@ete.inrs.ca. *Application contact:* Yvonne Boisvert, Registrar, 418-654-3861, Fax: 418-654-3858, E-mail: registrariat@adm.inrs.ca. Web site: http://www.ete.inrs.ca/.

Université Laval, Faculty of Sciences and Engineering, Department of Geology and Geological Engineering, Programs in Earth Sciences, Québec, QC G1K 7P4, Canada. Offers earth sciences (M Sc, PhD); environmental technologies (M Sc). Offered jointly with INRS-Géressources. Terminal master's awarded for partial completion of doctoral program. *Degree requirements:* For master's, thesis (for some programs); for doctorate, comprehensive exam, thesis/dissertation. *Entrance requirements:* For master's and doctorate, knowledge of French. Electronic applications accepted.

University at Albany, State University of New York, College of Arts and Sciences, Department of Earth and Atmospheric Sciences, Albany, NY 12222-0001. Offers atmospheric science (MS, PhD); geology (MS, PhD). *Degree requirements:* For master's, one foreign language, comprehensive exam, thesis; for doctorate, 2 foreign languages, comprehensive exam, thesis/dissertation, oral exams. *Entrance requirements:* For master's and doctorate, GRE General Test. Additional exam requirements/recommendations for international students: Required—TOEFL (minimum score 550 paper-based; 213 computer-based). Electronic applications accepted. *Faculty research:* Environmental geochemistry, tectonics, mesoscale meteorology, atmospheric chemistry.

University at Buffalo, the State University of New York, Graduate School, College of Arts and Sciences, Department of Geography, Buffalo, NY 14260. Offers earth systems science (MA); economic geography and international business and world trade (MA); environmental modeling and analysis (MA); geographic information science (MA, Certificate); geography (MA, PhD); transportation and business geographics (MA, Certificate); urban and regional geography (MA); MA/MBA. *Faculty:* 15 full-time (7 women), 1 part-time/adjunct (0 women). *Students:* 102 full-time (38 women), 20 part-time (10 women); includes 61 minority (1 Black or African American, non-Hispanic/Latino; 55 Asian, non-Hispanic/Latino; 5 Hispanic/Latino), 1 international. 167 applicants, 33% accepted, 29 enrolled. In 2011, 21 master's, 5 doctorates awarded. Terminal master's awarded for partial completion of doctoral program. *Degree requirements:* For master's, thesis (for some programs), project or portfolio; for doctorate, thesis/dissertation. *Entrance requirements:* For master's, GRE General Test, minimum GPA of 2.9; for doctorate, GRE General Test, minimum GPA of 3.0. Additional exam requirements/recommendations for international students: Required—TOEFL (minimum score 550 paper-based; 213 computer-based; 79 iBT). *Application deadline:* For fall admission, 7/1 priority date for domestic students, 1/10 for international students; for spring admission, 12/1 priority date for domestic students, 10/1 for international students. Applications are processed on a rolling basis. Application fee: $75. Electronic applications accepted. *Financial support:* In 2011–12, 13 students received support, including 8 fellowships with full tuition reimbursements available (averaging $4,750 per year), 13 teaching assistantships with full tuition reimbursements available (averaging $13,520 per year); research assistantships with full tuition reimbursements available, career-related internships or fieldwork, Federal Work-Study, institutionally sponsored loans, traineeships, health care benefits, and unspecified assistantships also available. Financial award application deadline: 1/10. *Faculty research:* International business and world trade, geographic information systems and cartography, transportation, urban and regional analysis, physical and environmental geography. *Total annual research expenditures:* $630,314. *Unit head:* Dr. Sharmistha Bagchi-Sen, Chairman, 716-645-0473, Fax: 716-645-2329, E-mail: geosbs@buffalo.edu. *Application contact:* Betsy Abraham, Graduate Secretary, 716-645-0471, Fax: 716-645-2329, E-mail: babraham@buffalo.edu. Web site: http://www.geog.buffalo.edu/.

The University of Akron, Graduate School, Buchtel College of Arts and Sciences, Department of Geology and Environmental Science, Program in Earth Science, Akron, OH 44325. Offers MS. *Students:* 1 applicant, 100% accepted, 0 enrolled. *Degree requirements:* For master's, comprehensive exam, thesis, seminar, proficiency exam. *Entrance requirements:* For master's, minimum GPA of 2.75, letters of recommendation, statement of purpose. Additional exam requirements/recommendations for international students: Required—TOEFL (minimum score 550 paper-based; 213 computer-based; 79 iBT). *Application deadline:* Applications are processed on a rolling basis. Application fee: $30 ($40 for international students). Electronic applications accepted. *Expenses:* Tuition, state resident: full-time $7038; part-time $391 per credit hour. Tuition, nonresident: full-time $12,051; part-time $670 per credit hour. *Required fees:* $1274; $34 per credit hour. *Unit head:* Dr. LaVerne Friberg, Director of Graduate Studies, 330-972-8046, E-mail: lfribe1@uakron.edu. *Application contact:* Dr. LaVerne Friberg, Director of Graduate Studies, 330-972-8046, E-mail: lfribe1@uakron.edu.

The University of Alabama in Huntsville, School of Graduate Studies, College of Science, Department of Atmospheric and Environmental Science, Huntsville, AL 35899. Offers atmospheric science (MS, PhD); earth system science (MS). Part-time and evening/weekend programs available. *Faculty:* 10 full-time (0 women), 2 part-time/adjunct (0 women). *Students:* 30 full-time (10 women), 5 part-time (4 women); includes 2 minority (1 Black or African American, non-Hispanic/Latino; 1 Asian, non-Hispanic/Latino), 6 international. Average age 26. 31 applicants, 61% accepted, 11 enrolled. In 2011, 9 master's, 4 doctorates awarded. *Degree requirements:* For master's, comprehensive exam, thesis or alternative, oral and written exams; for doctorate, comprehensive exam, thesis/dissertation, oral and written exams. *Entrance requirements:* For master's, GRE General Test, minimum GPA of 3.0; sequence of courses in calculus (including the calculus of vector-valued functions); courses in linear algebra and ordinary differential equations; two semesters each of chemistry and calculus-based physics; proficiency in at least one high-level computer programming language; for doctorate, GRE General Test, minimum GPA of 3.0. Additional exam requirements/recommendations for international students: Required—TOEFL (minimum score 550 paper-based; 213 computer-based; 62 iBT). *Application deadline:* For fall admission, 7/15 for domestic students, 4/1 for international students; for spring admission, 11/30 for domestic students, 9/1 for international students. Applications are processed on a rolling basis. Application fee: $40 ($50 for international students). Electronic applications accepted. *Expenses:* Tuition, state resident: full-time $7830; part-time $473.50 per credit. Tuition, nonresident: full-time $18,748; part-time $1128.33 per credit. Tuition and fees vary according to course load and program. *Financial support:* In 2011–12, 28 students received support, including 27 research assistantships with full and partial tuition reimbursements available (averaging $14,690 per year), 1 teaching assistantship with full tuition reimbursement available (averaging $13,500 per year); career-related internships or fieldwork, Federal Work-Study, institutionally sponsored loans, scholarships/grants, health care benefits, tuition waivers, and unspecified assistantships also available. Support available to part-time students. Financial award application deadline: 4/1; financial award applicants required to submit FAFSA. *Faculty research:* Satellite remote sensing, severe weather, mesoscale

modeling, atmospheric chemistry, data assimilation. *Total annual research expenditures:* $9.1 million. *Unit head:* Dr. Sundar Christopher, Chair, 256-922-7872, Fax: 256-922-7755, E-mail: sundar@nsstc.uah.edu. *Application contact:* Kim Gray, Graduate Studies Admissions Coordinator, 256-824-6002, Fax: 256-824-6405, E-mail: deangrad@uah.edu. Web site: http://www.nsstc.uah.edu/atmos/index.html.

University of Alberta, Faculty of Graduate Studies and Research, Department of Earth and Atmospheric Sciences, Edmonton, AB T6G 2E1, Canada. Offers M Sc, MA, PhD. *Degree requirements:* For master's, thesis, residency; for doctorate, thesis/dissertation, residency. *Entrance requirements:* For master's, B Sc, minimum GPA of 6.5 on a 9.0 scale; for doctorate, M Sc. Additional exam requirements/recommendations for international students: Required—TOEFL or Michigan English Language Assessment Battery. Electronic applications accepted. *Faculty research:* Geology, human geography, physical geography, meteorology.

The University of Arizona, College of Science, Department of Geosciences, Tucson, AZ 85721. Offers MS, PhD. Part-time programs available. *Faculty:* 20 full-time (4 women), 3 part-time/adjunct (0 women). *Students:* 71 full-time (32 women), 6 part-time (2 women); includes 5 minority (1 Black or African American, non-Hispanic/Latino; 3 Hispanic/Latino; 1 Two or more races, non-Hispanic/Latino), 5 international. Average age 29. 171 applicants, 15% accepted, 13 enrolled. In 2011, 9 master's, 10 doctorates awarded. Terminal master's awarded for partial completion of doctoral program. *Degree requirements:* For master's, thesis or prepublication; for doctorate, comprehensive exam, thesis/dissertation. *Entrance requirements:* For master's, GRE General Test, 3 letters of recommendation, curriculum vitae; for doctorate, GRE General Test, statement of purpose, 3 letters of recommendation, curriculum vitae. Additional exam requirements/recommendations for international students: Required—TOEFL (minimum score 550 paper-based; 213 computer-based; 79 iBT). *Application deadline:* For fall admission, 1/15 for domestic and international students. Applications are processed on a rolling basis. Application fee: $75. Electronic applications accepted. *Expenses:* Tuition, state resident: full-time $10,840. Tuition, nonresident: full-time $25,802. *Financial support:* In 2011–12, 35 research assistantships with full tuition reimbursements (averaging $23,134 per year), 20 teaching assistantships with full tuition reimbursements (averaging $22,822 per year) were awarded; career-related internships or fieldwork, institutionally sponsored loans, scholarships/grants, health care benefits, tuition waivers (partial), and unspecified assistantships also available. Financial award application deadline: 1/15. *Faculty research:* Tectonics, geophysics, geochemistry/petrology, economic geology, Quaternary studies, stratigraphy/paleontology. *Total annual research expenditures:* $3 million. *Unit head:* Dr. Karl Flessa, Head, 520-621-7336, Fax: 520-621-2672, E-mail: kflessa@geo.arizona.edu. *Application contact:* Anne Chase, Graduate Program Office, 520-621-6004, Fax: 520-621-2672, E-mail: gradapps@geo.arizona.edu. Web site: http://www.geo.arizona.edu/.

University of Arkansas at Little Rock, Graduate School, College of Science and Mathematics, Program in Geospatial Technology, Little Rock, AR 72204-1099. Offers Graduate Certificate.

University of California, Irvine, School of Physical Sciences, Department of Earth System Science, Irvine, CA 92697. Offers MS, PhD. *Students:* 43 full-time (28 women); includes 4 minority (1 Black or African American, non-Hispanic/Latino; 1 Hispanic/Latino; 2 Two or more races, non-Hispanic/Latino), 19 international. Average age 29. 59 applicants, 31% accepted, 8 enrolled. In 2011, 10 master's, 4 doctorates awarded. *Degree requirements:* For doctorate, thesis/dissertation. *Entrance requirements:* For master's and doctorate, GRE General Test, GRE Subject Test, minimum GPA of 3.0. Additional exam requirements/recommendations for international students: Required—TOEFL (minimum score 550 paper-based; 213 computer-based). *Application deadline:* For fall admission, 1/15 priority date for domestic students, 1/15 for international students. Applications are processed on a rolling basis. Application fee: $80 ($100 for international students). Electronic applications accepted. *Financial support:* Fellowships, research assistantships with full tuition reimbursements, teaching assistantships, career-related internships or fieldwork, institutionally sponsored loans, traineeships, health care benefits, and unspecified assistantships available. Financial award application deadline: 3/1; financial award applicants required to submit FAFSA. *Faculty research:* Atmospheric chemistry, climate change, isotope biogeochemistry, global environmental chemistry. *Unit head:* Michael L. Goulden, Chair, 949-824-1983, Fax: 949-824-3874, E-mail: mgoulden@uci.edu. *Application contact:* Cynthia A. Dennis, Department Assistant, 949-824-3876, Fax: 949-824-3874, E-mail: cadennis@uci.edu. Web site: http://www.ess.uci.edu/.

University of California, Los Angeles, Graduate Division, College of Letters and Science, Department of Earth and Space Sciences, Los Angeles, CA 90095. Offers geochemistry (MS, PhD); geology (MS, PhD); geophysics and space physics (MS, PhD). *Faculty:* 24 full-time (3 women). *Students:* 70 full-time (34 women); includes 13 minority (3 Black or African American, non-Hispanic/Latino; 1 American Indian or Alaska Native, non-Hispanic/Latino; 6 Asian, non-Hispanic/Latino; 1 Hispanic/Latino; 2 Two or more races, non-Hispanic/Latino), 17 international. Average age 28. 121 applicants, 29% accepted, 20 enrolled. In 2011, 9 master's, 7 doctorates awarded. Terminal master's awarded for partial completion of doctoral program. *Degree requirements:* For master's, comprehensive exams or thesis; for doctorate, thesis/dissertation, oral and written qualifying exams. *Entrance requirements:* For master's, GRE General Test, minimum GPA of 3.0; for doctorate, GRE General Test, minimum undergraduate

Peterson's Graduate Programs in the Physical Sciences, Mathematics, Agricultural Sciences, the Environment & Natural Resources 2013

facebook.com/petersonspublishing **171**

Geosciences

GPA of 3.0. *Application deadline:* For fall admission, 1/15 for domestic and international students. Application fee: $70 ($90 for international students). Electronic applications accepted. *Financial support:* In 2011–12, 58 fellowships with full and partial tuition reimbursements, 51 research assistantships with full and partial tuition reimbursements, 29 teaching assistantships with full and partial tuition reimbursements were awarded; Federal Work-Study, institutionally sponsored loans, scholarships/grants, traineeships, health care benefits, tuition waivers (full and partial), and unspecified assistantships also available. Financial award application deadline: 3/1; financial award applicants required to submit FAFSA. *Unit head:* Dr. Craig E. Manning, Chair, 310-825-1475, E-mail: manning@ess.ucla.edu. *Application contact:* Departmental Office, 310-825-3917, E-mail: holbrook@ess.ucla.edu. Web site: http://www.ess.ucla.edu/.

University of California, San Diego, Office of Graduate Studies, Scripps Institution of Oceanography, La Jolla, CA 92093. Offers earth sciences (PhD); marine biology (PhD); oceanography (PhD). *Degree requirements:* For doctorate, comprehensive exam, thesis/dissertation. *Entrance requirements:* For doctorate, GRE General Test. Additional exam requirements/recommendations for international students: Required—TOEFL (minimum score 550 paper-based; 213 computer-based; 80 iBT). Electronic applications accepted.

University of California, Santa Barbara, Graduate Division, College of Letters and Sciences, Division of Mathematics, Life, and Physical Sciences, Department of Earth Science, Santa Barbara, CA 93106-9620. Offers geological sciences (MS, PhD); geophysics (MS). *Faculty:* 20 full-time (3 women). *Students:* 43 full-time (16 women); includes 8 minority (1 American Indian or Alaska Native, non-Hispanic/Latino; 2 Asian, non-Hispanic/Latino; 5 Hispanic/Latino), 5 international. Average age 27. 83 applicants, 16% accepted, 8 enrolled. In 2011, 10 master's, 3 doctorates awarded. Terminal master's awarded for partial completion of doctoral program. *Median time to degree:* Of those who began their doctoral program in fall 2003, 64% received their degree in 8 years or less. *Degree requirements:* For master's, comprehensive exam, thesis, 30 units; for doctorate, comprehensive exam, thesis/dissertation, 30 units, oral qualifying exam. *Entrance requirements:* For master's and doctorate, GRE General Test. Additional exam requirements/recommendations for international students: Required—TOEFL (minimum score 550 paper-based; 80 iBT), IELTS (minimum score 7). *Application deadline:* For fall admission, 1/1 for domestic and international students. Application fee: $80 ($100 for international students). Electronic applications accepted. *Expenses:* Tuition, state resident: full-time $12,192. Tuition, nonresident: full-time $27,294. *Required fees:* $764.13. *Financial support:* In 2011–12, 38 students received support, including 34 fellowships with full and partial tuition reimbursements available (averaging $12,566 per year), 22 research assistantships with full and partial tuition reimbursements available (averaging $7,362 per year), 28 teaching assistantships with full and partial tuition reimbursements available (averaging $7,234 per year); tuition waivers (full and partial) also available. Financial award application deadline: 1/1; financial award applicants required to submit CSS PROFILE or FAFSA. *Faculty research:* Geology, geomaterials and earth's structure; geomorphology, tectonics; geophysics, seismology; paleoclimate, paleoceanography and geochemistry; paleobiology, evolution and paleontology. *Unit head:* Dr. Douglas Burbank, Chair, 805-893-7858, Fax: 805-893-2314, E-mail: burbank@eri.ucsb.edu. *Application contact:* Hannah Smit, Graduate Program Assistant, 805-893-3329, Fax: 805-893-2314, E-mail: hsmit@geol.ucsb.edu. Web site: http://www.geol.ucsb.edu/.

University of California, Santa Cruz, Division of Graduate Studies, Division of Physical and Biological Sciences, Department of Earth and Planetary Sciences, Santa Cruz, CA 95064. Offers MS, PhD. Terminal master's awarded for partial completion of doctoral program. *Degree requirements:* For master's, thesis; for doctorate, one foreign language, thesis/dissertation, qualifying exam. *Entrance requirements:* For master's and doctorate, GRE General Test. Additional exam requirements/recommendations for international students: Required—TOEFL (minimum score 550 paper-based; 220 computer-based; 83 iBT); Recommended—IELTS (minimum score 8). Electronic applications accepted. *Faculty research:* Evolution of continental margins and orogenic belts, geologic processes occurring at plate boundaries, deep-sea sediment diagenesis, paleoecology, hydrogeology.

University of Chicago, Division of the Physical Sciences, Department of the Geophysical Sciences, Chicago, IL 60637-1513. Offers atmospheric sciences (SM, PhD); cosmochemistry (PhD); earth sciences (SM, PhD); paleobiology (PhD); planetary and space sciences (SM, PhD). *Faculty:* 24 full-time (3 women). *Students:* 38 full-time (16 women); includes 2 minority (both Hispanic/Latino), 16 international. Average age 26. 68 applicants, 28% accepted, 10 enrolled. In 2011, 2 master's, 5 doctorates awarded. Terminal master's awarded for partial completion of doctoral program. *Degree requirements:* For master's, thesis, seminar; for doctorate, variable foreign language requirement, comprehensive exam, thesis/dissertation. *Entrance requirements:* For doctorate, GRE General Test. Additional exam requirements/recommendations for international students: Required—TOEFL (minimum score 600 paper-based; 250 computer-based; 96 iBT), IELTS (minimum score 7). *Application deadline:* For fall admission, 1/9 for domestic students, 1/10 for international students. Application fee: $55. Electronic applications accepted. *Financial support:* In 2011–12, research assistantships with full tuition reimbursements (averaging $26,500 per year), teaching assistantships with full tuition reimbursements (averaging $27,000 per year) were awarded; fellowships, Federal Work-Study, institutionally sponsored loans, scholarships/grants, tuition waivers (partial), and unspecified assistantships also available. Financial award application deadline: 1/9. *Faculty research:*

Climatology, evolutionary paleontology, cosmochemistry, geochemistry, oceanic sciences. *Unit head:* Dr. Michael Foote, Chairman, 773-702-8102, Fax: 773-702-9505. *Application contact:* David J. Taylor, Graduate Student Services Coordinator, 773-702-8180, Fax: 773-702-9505, E-mail: info@geosci.uchicago.edu. Web site: http://geosci.uchicago.edu/.

University of Florida, Graduate School, College of Liberal Arts and Sciences, Department of Geological Sciences, Gainesville, FL 32611. Offers hydrologic sciences (MS, MST, PhD); tropical conservation and development (MS, MST, PhD); wetland sciences (MS, MST, PhD). *Faculty:* 17 full-time (3 women). *Students:* 38 full-time (17 women), 3 part-time (2 women); includes 1 minority (Hispanic/Latino), 11 international. Average age 30. 63 applicants, 32% accepted, 11 enrolled. In 2011, 6 master's, 2 doctorates awarded. Terminal master's awarded for partial completion of doctoral program. *Degree requirements:* For master's, thesis (for some programs); for doctorate, one foreign language, thesis/dissertation. *Entrance requirements:* For master's, GRE General Test (minimum score of 1000), minimum GPA of 3.0; for doctorate, GRE General Test (minimum score of 1100), minimum GPA of 3.0. Additional exam requirements/recommendations for international students: Required—TOEFL (minimum score 550 paper-based; 213 computer-based; 80 iBT), IELTS (minimum score 6). *Application deadline:* For fall admission, 1/15 for domestic students; for spring admission, 10/1 for domestic students. Applications are processed on a rolling basis. Application fee: $30. Electronic applications accepted. *Financial support:* In 2011–12, 4 fellowships with full tuition reimbursements, 19 research assistantships with full tuition reimbursements (averaging $16,810 per year), 16 teaching assistantships with full tuition reimbursements (averaging $15,290 per year) were awarded; career-related internships or fieldwork, Federal Work-Study, institutionally sponsored loans, and scholarships/grants also available. Support available to part-time students. Financial award application deadline: 3/1; financial award applicants required to submit FAFSA. *Faculty research:* Paleoclimatology, tectonophysics, petrochemistry, marine geology, geochemistry, hydrology. *Unit head:* Dr. Michael R. Perfit, Chair, 352-392-2231, Fax: 352-392-9294, E-mail: mperfit@ufl.edu. *Application contact:* Dr. John Jaeger, Graduate Coordinator, 352-392-2231, Fax: 352-392-9294, E-mail: jmjaeger@ufl.edu. Web site: http://web.geology.ufl.edu/.

University of Illinois at Chicago, Graduate College, College of Liberal Arts and Sciences, Department of Earth and Environmental Sciences, Chicago, IL 60607-7128. Offers MS, PhD. *Degree requirements:* For master's, thesis; for doctorate, thesis/dissertation. *Entrance requirements:* For master's and doctorate, GRE General Test, minimum GPA of 2.75. Additional exam requirements/recommendations for international students: Required—TOEFL. Electronic applications accepted.

University of Illinois at Urbana–Champaign, Graduate College, College of Liberal Arts and Sciences, School of Earth, Society and Environment, Department of Geology, Champaign, IL 61820. Offers geology (MS, PhD); teaching of earth sciences (MS). *Faculty:* 12 full-time (3 women). *Students:* 21 full-time (10 women), 4 part-time (all women); includes 1 minority (Asian, non-Hispanic/Latino), 10 international. 53 applicants, 17% accepted, 5 enrolled. In 2011, 6 master's, 1 doctorate awarded. Terminal master's awarded for partial completion of doctoral program. *Entrance requirements:* For master's and doctorate, GRE General Test, minimum GPA of 3.0. Additional exam requirements/recommendations for international students: Required—TOEFL. *Application deadline:* Applications are processed on a rolling basis. Application fee: $75 ($90 for international students). Electronic applications accepted. *Financial support:* In 2011–12, 4 fellowships, 17 research assistantships, 12 teaching assistantships were awarded; Federal Work-Study and tuition waivers (full and partial) also available. *Faculty research:* Hydrogeology, structure/tectonics, mineral science. *Unit head:* Thomas M. Johnson, Head, 217-244-2002, Fax: 217-244-4996, E-mail: tmjohnsn@illinois.edu. *Application contact:* Marilyn K. Whalen, Office Administrator, 217-333-3542, Fax: 217-244-4996, E-mail: mkt@illinois.edu. Web site: http://www.geology.illinois.edu/.

The University of Iowa, Graduate College, College of Liberal Arts and Sciences, Department of Geoscience, Iowa City, IA 52242-1316. Offers MS, PhD. *Degree requirements:* For master's, thesis optional, exam; for doctorate, comprehensive exam, thesis/dissertation. *Entrance requirements:* For master's and doctorate, GRE General Test, minimum GPA of 3.0. Additional exam requirements/recommendations for international students: Required—TOEFL (minimum score 550 paper-based; 213 computer-based; 81 iBT). Electronic applications accepted.

University of Maine, Graduate School, College of Education and Human Development, Interdisciplinary Program in Teaching, Orono, ME 04469. Offers earth sciences (MST); generalist (MST); mathematics (MST); physics and astronomy (MST). *Students:* 8 full-time (6 women), 13 part-time (10 women); includes 1 minority (American Indian or Alaska Native, non-Hispanic/Latino). Average age 40. 2 applicants, 50% accepted, 1 enrolled. In 2011, 6 master's awarded. *Entrance requirements:* For master's, GRE General Test, MAT. Application fee: $65. *Expenses:* Tuition, state resident: full-time $5016. Tuition, nonresident: full-time $14,424. *Unit head:* Dr. Susan McKay, Director, 207-581-1016. *Application contact:* Scott G. Delcourt, Associate Dean of the Graduate School, 207-581-3291, Fax: 207-581-3232, E-mail: graduate@maine.edu. Web site: http://www2.umaine.edu/graduate/.

University of Maine, Graduate School, College of Natural Sciences, Forestry, and Agriculture, Department of Earth Sciences, Orono, ME 04469. Offers water resources (MS, PhD). Part-time programs available. *Faculty:* 9 full-time (2 women), 3 part-time/adjunct (0 women). *Students:* 23 full-time (12 women), 10 part-time (5 women), 3 international. Average age 28. 32 applicants, 66% accepted, 17 enrolled. In 2011, 6 master's, 4 doctorates awarded. *Degree requirements:* For master's, thesis; for doctorate, one foreign language, thesis/dissertation. *Entrance requirements:* For master's and doctorate, GRE General Test. Additional exam requirements/recommendations for international students: Required—TOEFL. *Application deadline:* For fall admission, 2/1 priority date for domestic applications. Applications are processed on a rolling basis. Application fee: $65. Electronic applications accepted. *Expenses:* Tuition, state resident: full-time $5016. Tuition, nonresident: full-time $14,424. *Financial support:* In 2011–12, 5 research assistantships with full tuition reimbursements (averaging $16,950 per year), 6 teaching assistantships with full tuition reimbursements (averaging $13,600 per year) were awarded; Federal Work-Study, institutionally sponsored loans, and tuition waivers (full and partial) also available. Financial award application deadline: 3/1. *Faculty research:* Appalachian bedrock geology, Quaternary studies, marine geology. *Unit head:* Dr. Joseph Kelley, Chair, 207-581-2162, Fax: 207-581-2202. *Application contact:* Scott G. Delcourt, Associate Dean of the Graduate School, 207-581-3291, Fax: 207-581-3232, E-mail: graduate@maine.edu. Web site: http://www2.umaine.edu/graduate/.

The University of Manchester, School of Earth, Atmospheric and Environmental Sciences, Manchester, United Kingdom. Offers atmospheric sciences (M Phil, M Sc, PhD); basin studies and petroleum geosciences (M Phil, M Sc, PhD); earth, atmospheric and environmental sciences (M Phil, M Sc, PhD); environmental geochemistry and cosmochemistry (M Phil, M Sc, PhD); isotope geochemistry and cosmochemistry (M Phil, M Sc, PhD); paleontology (M Phil, M Sc, PhD); physics and chemistry of minerals and fluids (M Phil, M Sc, PhD); structural and petrological geosciences (M Phil, M Sc, PhD).

University of Massachusetts Amherst, Graduate School, College of Natural Sciences, Department of Geosciences, Program in Geosciences, Amherst, MA 01003. Offers MS, PhD. Part-time programs available. *Students:* 29 full-time (13 women), 29 part-time (13 women); includes 7 minority (1 American Indian or Alaska Native, non-Hispanic/Latino; 2 Asian, non-Hispanic/Latino; 1 Hispanic/Latino; 3 Two or more races, non-Hispanic/Latino), 8 international. Average age 34. 65 applicants, 57% accepted, 12 enrolled. In 2011, 6 master's, 4 doctorates awarded. Terminal master's awarded for partial completion of doctoral program. *Degree requirements:* For master's, thesis or alternative; for doctorate, comprehensive exam, thesis/dissertation. *Entrance requirements:* For master's and doctorate, GRE General Test. Additional exam requirements/recommendations for international students: Required—TOEFL (minimum score 550 paper-based; 213 computer-based; 80 iBT), IELTS (minimum score 6.5). *Application deadline:* For fall admission, 1/15 for domestic and international students; for spring admission, 10/1 for domestic and international students. Applications are processed on a rolling basis. Application fee: $50 ($65 for international students). Electronic applications accepted. Tuition and fees vary according to course load, campus/location and program. *Financial support:* Fellowships, research assistantships, teaching assistantships, career-related internships or fieldwork, Federal Work-Study, scholarships/grants, traineeships, health care benefits, tuition waivers (full and partial), and unspecified assistantships available. Support available to part-time students. Financial award application deadline: 1/15. *Unit head:* Dr. Laurie Brown, Graduate Program Director, 413-545-2286, Fax: 413-545-1200. *Application contact:* Lindsay DeSantis, Interim Supervisor of Admissions, 413-545-0722, Fax: 413-577-0010, E-mail: gradadm@grad.umass.edu. Web site: http://www.geo.umass.edu/.

University of Missouri–Kansas City, College of Arts and Sciences, Department of Geosciences, Kansas City, MO 64110-2499. Offers environmental and urban geosciences (MS); geosciences (PhD). PhD (interdisciplinary) offered through the School of Graduate Studies. Part-time programs available. *Faculty:* 10 full-time (3 women), 5 part-time/adjunct (0 women). *Students:* 5 full-time (1 woman), 29 part-time (12 women); includes 1 minority (Hispanic/Latino), 5 international. Average age 34. 19 applicants, 63% accepted, 9 enrolled. In 2011, 3 degrees awarded. *Degree requirements:* For master's, thesis; for doctorate, thesis/dissertation, qualifying exam. *Entrance requirements:* For master's, GRE General Test, minimum GPA of 3.0. Additional exam requirements/recommendations for international students: Required—TOEFL (minimum score 550 paper-based; 213 computer-based; 80 iBT). *Application deadline:* For fall admission, 3/15 priority date for domestic students, 3/15 for international students. Applications are processed on a rolling basis. Application fee: $45 ($50 for international students). Electronic applications accepted. *Expenses:* Tuition, state resident: full-time $5798; part-time $322.10 per credit hour. Tuition, nonresident: full-time $14,969; part-time $831.60 per credit hour. *Required fees:* $93.51 per credit hour. *Financial support:* In 2011–12, 3 research assistantships with partial tuition reimbursements (averaging $10,400 per year), 17 teaching assistantships with partial tuition reimbursements (averaging $12,134 per year) were awarded; Federal Work-Study, institutionally sponsored loans, and tuition waivers (full and partial) also available. Support available to part-time students. Financial award application deadline: 3/1; financial award applicants required to submit FAFSA. *Faculty research:* Neotectonics and applied geophysics, environmental geosciences, urban geoscience, geoinformatics-remote sensing, atmospheric research. *Unit head:* Dr. Jimmy Adegoke, Chair, 816-235-1334, Fax: 816-235-5535, E-mail: adegokej@umkc.edu. *Application contact:* Dr. Jejung Lee, Associate Professor, 816-235-6495, Fax: 816-235-5535, E-mail: leej@umkc.edu. Web site: http://cas.umkc.edu/geo/.

The University of Montana, Graduate School, College of Arts and Sciences, Department of Geology, Missoula, MT 59812-0002. Offers applied geoscience (PhD); geology (MS, PhD). *Degree requirements:* For doctorate, thesis/dissertation. *Entrance requirements:* For master's and doctorate, GRE General Test. Additional exam requirements/recommendations for international students: Required—TOEFL (minimum score 525 paper-based; 197 computer-based). *Faculty research:* Environmental geoscience, regional structure and tectonics, groundwater geology, petrology, mineral deposits.

University of Nebraska–Lincoln, Graduate College, College of Arts and Sciences, Department of Geosciences, Lincoln, NE 68588. Offers MS, PhD. *Degree requirements:* For master's, thesis optional, departmental qualifying exam; for doctorate, comprehensive exam, thesis/dissertation, departmental qualifying exams. *Entrance requirements:* For master's and doctorate, GRE General Test. Additional exam requirements/recommendations for international students: Required—TOEFL (minimum score 550 paper-based; 213 computer-based). Electronic applications accepted. *Faculty research:* Hydrogeology, sedimentology, environmental geology, vertebrate paleontology.

University of Nevada, Las Vegas, Graduate College, College of Science, Department of Geoscience, Las Vegas, NV 89154-4010. Offers MS, PhD. Part-time programs available. *Faculty:* 18 full-time (6 women), 13 part-time/adjunct (3 women). *Students:* 11 full-time (6 women), 43 part-time (20 women); includes 5 minority (1 American Indian or Alaska Native, non-Hispanic/Latino; 4 Hispanic/Latino), 11 international. Average age 30. 39 applicants, 87% accepted, 11 enrolled. In 2011, 7 master's, 3 doctorates awarded. *Degree requirements:* For master's, comprehensive exam, thesis; for doctorate, comprehensive exam, thesis/dissertation. *Entrance requirements:* For master's and doctorate, GRE General Test. Additional exam requirements/recommendations for international students: Required—TOEFL (minimum score 550 paper-based; 213 computer-based; 80 iBT), IELTS (minimum score 7). *Application deadline:* For fall admission, 2/1 priority date for domestic students, 5/1 for international students; for spring admission, 10/1 priority date for domestic students, 10/1 for international students. Applications are processed on a rolling basis. Application fee: $60 ($95 for international students). Electronic applications accepted. *Financial support:* In 2011–12, 36 students received support, including 12 research assistantships with partial tuition reimbursements available (averaging $13,575 per year), 24 teaching assistantships with partial tuition reimbursements available (averaging $12,834 per year); institutionally sponsored loans, scholarships/grants, health care benefits, and unspecified assistantships also available. Financial award application deadline: 3/1. *Faculty research:* Petrology, geochemistry and economic geology; climate and earth surface processes; structural geology and tectonics; sedimentary geology and paleontology; hydrogeologic and environmental science. *Total annual research expenditures:* $1.2 million. *Unit head:* Dr. Michael Wells, Chair/Professor, 702-895-0828, Fax: 702-895-4064, E-mail: michael.wells@unlv.edu. *Application contact:* Graduate College Admissions Evaluator, 702-895-3320, Fax: 702-895-4180, E-mail: gradcollege@unlv.edu. Web site: http://geoscience.unlv.edu/.

University of New Hampshire, Graduate School, College of Engineering and Physical Sciences, Department of Earth Sciences, Durham, NH 03824. Offers geology (MS); hydrology (MS). *Faculty:* 17 full-time (5 women). *Students:* 21 full-time (11 women), 13 part-time (6 women); includes 3 minority (2 Black or African American, non-Hispanic/Latino; 1 Asian, non-Hispanic/Latino), 5 international. Average age 27. 60 applicants, 58% accepted, 12 enrolled. In 2011, 10 master's awarded. *Degree requirements:* For master's, thesis. *Entrance requirements:* For master's, GRE General Test. Additional exam requirements/recommendations for international students: Required—TOEFL (minimum score 550 paper-based; 213 computer-based; 80 iBT). *Application deadline:* For fall admission, 4/1 priority date for domestic students, 4/1 for international students; for spring admission, 12/1 for domestic students. Applications are processed on a rolling basis. Application fee: $65. Electronic applications accepted. *Expenses:* Tuition, state resident: full-time $12,360; part-time $687 per credit hour. Tuition, nonresident: full-time $25,680; part-time $1058 per credit hour. International tuition: $29,550 full-time. *Required fees:* $1666; $833 per course. $416.50 per semester. Tuition and fees vary according to course load and degree level. *Financial support:* In 2011–12, 24 students received support, including 12 research assistantships, 8 teaching assistantships; fellowships, career-related internships or fieldwork, Federal Work-Study, scholarships/grants, and tuition waivers (full and partial) also available. Support available to part-time students. Financial award application deadline: 2/15. *Unit head:* Dr. Will Clyde, Chairperson, 603-862-1718, E-mail: earth.sciences@unh.edu. *Application contact:* Sue Clark, Administrative Assistant, 603-862-1718, E-mail: earth.sciences@unh.edu. Web site: http://www.unh.edu/esci/.

University of New Haven, Graduate School, College of Arts and Sciences, Program in Environmental Sciences, West Haven, CT 06516-1916. Offers environmental geoscience (MS); environmental health and management (MS); environmental science (MS); geographical information systems (Certificate). Part-time and evening/weekend programs available. *Students:* 19 full-time (11 women), 15 part-time (6 women); includes 5 minority (2 Black or African American, non-Hispanic/Latino; 1 Asian, non-Hispanic/Latino; 1 Hispanic/Latino; 1 Two or more races, non-Hispanic/Latino), 7 international. 9 applicants, 100% accepted, 5 enrolled. In 2011, 9 master's awarded. *Degree requirements:* For master's, thesis or alternative. *Application deadline:* For fall admission, 5/31 for international students; for winter admission, 10/15 for international students; for spring admission, 1/15 for international students. Applications are processed on a

Peterson's Graduate Programs in the Physical Sciences, Mathematics, Agricultural Sciences, the Environment & Natural Resources 2013

facebook.com/petersonspublishing **173**

rolling basis. Application fee: $50. Electronic applications accepted. *Expenses: Tuition:* Part-time $750 per credit. *Financial support:* Research assistantships with partial tuition reimbursements, teaching assistantships with partial tuition reimbursements, career-related internships or fieldwork, Federal Work-Study, scholarships/grants, tuition waivers, and unspecified assistantships available. Support available to part-time students. Financial award applicants required to submit FAFSA. *Faculty research:* Mapping and assessing geological and living resources in Long Island Sound, geology, San Salvador Island, Bahamas. *Unit head:* Dr. Roman Zajac, Coordinator, 203-932-7108, E-mail: rzajac@newhaven.edu. *Application contact:* Eloise Gormley, Director of Graduate Admissions, 203-932-7449, Fax: 203-932-7137, E-mail: gradinfo@newhaven.edu. Web site: http://www.newhaven.edu/4728/.

University of New Mexico, Graduate School, College of Arts and Sciences, Department of Earth and Planetary Sciences, Albuquerque, NM 87131-0001. Offers MS, PhD. Part-time programs available. *Faculty:* 32 full-time (5 women), 18 part-time/adjunct (8 women). *Students:* 24 full-time (16 women), 31 part-time (17 women); includes 7 minority (2 American Indian or Alaska Native, non-Hispanic/Latino; 4 Hispanic/Latino; 1 Two or more races, non-Hispanic/Latino). Average age 31. 57 applicants, 19% accepted, 9 enrolled. In 2011, 9 master's, 4 doctorates awarded. Terminal master's awarded for partial completion of doctoral program. *Degree requirements:* For master's, comprehensive exam, thesis; for doctorate, comprehensive exam, thesis/dissertation. *Entrance requirements:* For master's and doctorate, GRE General Test. Additional exam requirements/recommendations for international students: Required—TOEFL. *Application deadline:* For fall admission, 1/15 priority date for domestic students, 1/15 for international students; for spring admission, 11/1 priority date for domestic students, 11/1 for international students. Application fee: $50. Electronic applications accepted. *Financial support:* In 2011–12, 54 students received support, including 23 fellowships with full tuition reimbursements available (averaging $2,714 per year), 46 research assistantships with full tuition reimbursements available (averaging $14,363 per year), 27 teaching assistantships with full tuition reimbursements available (averaging $1,982 per year); scholarships/grants and health care benefits also available. Financial award application deadline: 1/31; financial award applicants required to submit FAFSA. *Faculty research:* Climatology, experimental petrology, geochemistry, geographic information technologies, geomorphology, geophysics, hydrogeology, ingeneous petrology, metamorphic petrology, meteoritics, meteorology, micrometeorites, mineralogy, paleoclimatology, paleonology, pedology, petrology, physical volcanology, planetary sciences, precambrian geology, quantenary geology, sedimentary geochemistry, sedimentology, stable isotope geochemistry, stratigraphy, structural geology, tectonics, volcanology. *Total annual research expenditures:* $2.5 million. *Unit head:* Dr. John W. Geissman, Chair, 505-277-4204, Fax: 505-277-8843, E-mail: jgeiss@unm.edu. *Application contact:* Cindy Jaramillo, Administrative Assistant II, 505-277-1635, Fax: 505-277-8843, E-mail: epsdept@unm.edu. Web site: http://epswww.unm.edu/.

University of New Orleans, Graduate School, College of Sciences, Department of Earth and Environmental Sciences, New Orleans, LA 70148. Offers MS. Evening/weekend programs available. *Degree requirements:* For master's, thesis. *Entrance requirements:* For master's, GRE General Test. Additional exam requirements/recommendations for international students: Required—TOEFL (minimum score 550 paper-based; 213 computer-based; 79 iBT). Electronic applications accepted. *Faculty research:* Continental margin structure and seismology, burial diagenesis of siliciclastic sediments, tectonics at convergent plate margins, continental shelf sediment stability, early diagenesis of carbonates.

The University of North Carolina at Charlotte, Graduate School, College of Liberal Arts and Sciences, Department of Geography and Earth Sciences, Charlotte, NC 28223-0001. Offers earth sciences (MS); geography (MA), including community planning, geographic location science and technologies, location analysis, transportation studies, urban regional analysis; geography and urban regional analysis (PhD). Part-time and evening/weekend programs available. *Faculty:* 29 full-time (10 women), 1 part-time/adjunct (0 women). *Students:* 52 full-time (21 women), 43 part-time (17 women); includes 5 minority (3 Black or African American, non-Hispanic/Latino; 1 Hispanic/Latino; 1 Native Hawaiian or other Pacific Islander, non-Hispanic/Latino), 17 international. Average age 30. 50 applicants, 78% accepted, 25 enrolled. In 2011, 22 master's, 1 doctorate awarded. Terminal master's awarded for partial completion of doctoral program. *Degree requirements:* For master's, comprehensive exam, thesis or alternative, project. *Entrance requirements:* For master's, GRE General Test or MAT, Doppelt Mathematical Reasoning Test, minimum GPA of 3.0 in undergraduate major, 2.75 overall. Additional exam requirements/recommendations for international students: Required—TOEFL (minimum score 557 paper-based; 220 computer-based; 83 iBT). *Application deadline:* For fall admission, 7/1 for domestic students, 5/1 for international students; for spring admission, 11/1 for domestic students, 10/1 for international students. Applications are processed on a rolling basis. Application fee: $65 ($75 for international students). Electronic applications accepted. *Expenses: Tuition,* state resident: full-time $3689. Tuition, nonresident: full-time $15,226. *Required fees:* $2198. Tuition and fees vary according to course load and program. *Financial support:* In 2011–12, 1 fellowship (averaging $23,500 per year), 24 research assistantships (averaging $11,954 per year), 20 teaching assistantships (averaging $10,200 per year) were awarded; career-related internships or fieldwork, institutionally sponsored loans, scholarships/grants, and unspecified assistantships also available. Support available to part-time students. Financial award application deadline: 4/1; financial award applicants required to submit

FAFSA. *Faculty research:* Location analysis, applications of GIS technology, community planning and development, regional economic modeling, retail geography. *Total annual research expenditures:* $1 million. *Unit head:* Dr. Harrison Campbell, Graduate Coordinator, 704-687-5997, Fax: 704-687-3182, E-mail: hscampbe@uncc.edu. *Application contact:* Kathy B. Giddings, Director of Graduate Admissions, 704-687-5503, Fax: 704-687-3279, E-mail: gradadm@uncc.edu. Web site: http://www.geoearch.uncc.edu/.

The University of North Carolina Wilmington, College of Arts and Sciences, Department of Geography and Geology, Wilmington, NC 28403-3297. Offers geology (MS); marine science (MS). *Degree requirements:* For master's, comprehensive exam, thesis. *Entrance requirements:* For master's, GRE General Test, GRE Subject Test, minimum B average in undergraduate major and basic prerequisite geology courses.

University of North Dakota, Graduate School, John D. Odegard School of Aerospace Sciences, Program in Earth System Science and Policy, Grand Forks, ND 58202. Offers MEM, MS, PhD. Part-time programs available. *Degree requirements:* For master's, thesis (for some programs); for doctorate, thesis/dissertation (for some programs). *Entrance requirements:* For master's and doctorate, GRE General Test, minimum GPA of 3.0. Additional exam requirements/recommendations for international students: Required—TOEFL (minimum score 550 paper-based; 213 computer-based; 79 iBT), IELTS (minimum score 6.5). Electronic applications accepted.

University of Northern Colorado, Graduate School, College of Natural and Health Sciences, School of Chemistry, Earth Sciences and Physics, Program in Earth Sciences, Greeley, CO 80639. Offers MA. Part-time programs available. *Degree requirements:* For master's, comprehensive exam. *Entrance requirements:* For master's, GRE General Test, 3 letters of recommendation. Electronic applications accepted.

University of Northern Iowa, Graduate College, College of Humanities, Arts and Sciences, Program in Science Education, Cedar Falls, IA 50614. Offers earth science education (MA); physics education (MA); science education (MA). *Students:* 4 full-time (3 women), 27 part-time (19 women); includes 1 minority (Two or more races, non-Hispanic/Latino). 4 applicants, 50% accepted, 2 enrolled. In 2011, 7 master's awarded. *Degree requirements:* For master's, comprehensive exam (for some programs), thesis or alternative. *Entrance requirements:* For master's, minimum GPA of 3.0. Additional exam requirements/recommendations for international students: Required—TOEFL (minimum score 500 paper-based; 180 computer-based; 61 iBT). *Application deadline:* For fall admission, 8/1 priority date for domestic students. Applications are processed on a rolling basis. Application fee: $50 ($70 for international students). Electronic applications accepted. *Expenses:* Tuition, state resident: full-time $7476. Tuition, nonresident: full-time $16,410. *Required fees:* $942. *Financial support:* Application deadline: 2/1. *Unit head:* Dr. Cherin A. Lee, Director, 319-273-7357, Fax: 319-273-3051, E-mail: cherin.lee@uni.edu. *Application contact:* Laurie S. Russell, Record Analyst, 319-273-2623, Fax: 319-273-2885, E-mail: laurie.russell@uni.edu. Web site: http://www.science-ed.uni.edu/.

University of Notre Dame, Graduate School, College of Engineering, Department of Civil Engineering and Geological Sciences, Notre Dame, IN 46556. Offers bioengineering (MS Bio E); civil engineering (MSCE); civil engineering and geological sciences (PhD); environmental engineering (MS Env E); geological sciences (MS). Terminal master's awarded for partial completion of doctoral program. *Degree requirements:* For master's, comprehensive exam; for doctorate, thesis/dissertation, candidacy exam. *Entrance requirements:* For master's and doctorate, GRE General Test. Additional exam requirements/recommendations for international students: Required—TOEFL (minimum score 600 paper-based; 250 computer-based; 80 iBT). Electronic applications accepted. *Faculty research:* Environmental modeling, biological-waste treatment, petrology, environmental geology, geochemistry.

University of Ottawa, Faculty of Graduate and Postdoctoral Studies, Faculty of Science, Ottawa-Carleton Geoscience Centre, Ottawa, ON K1N 6N5, Canada. Offers earth sciences (M Sc, PhD). M Sc, PhD offered jointly with Carleton University. *Degree requirements:* For master's, thesis, seminar; for doctorate, comprehensive exam, thesis/dissertation, seminar. *Entrance requirements:* For master's, honors B Sc degree or equivalent, minimum B average; for doctorate, honors B Sc with minimum B average or M Sc with minimum B+ average. Electronic applications accepted. *Faculty research:* Environmental geoscience, geochemistry/petrology, geomatics/geomathematics, mineral resource studies.

University of Pennsylvania, School of Arts and Sciences, Graduate Group in Earth and Environmental Science, Philadelphia, PA 19104. Offers MS, PhD. Part-time programs available. *Faculty:* 8 full-time (1 woman), 5 part-time/adjunct (0 women). *Students:* 18 full-time (12 women), 1 (woman) part-time, 6 international. 28 applicants, 11% accepted, 2 enrolled. In 2011, 1 master's, 2 doctorates awarded. *Degree requirements:* For master's, one foreign language, thesis; for doctorate, one foreign language, thesis/dissertation. *Entrance requirements:* For master's and doctorate, GRE General Test. Additional exam requirements/recommendations for international students: Required—TOEFL. *Application deadline:* For fall admission, 12/1 priority date for domestic students. Application fee: $70. Electronic applications accepted. *Expenses: Tuition:* Full-time $26,660; part-time $4944 per course. *Required fees:* $2318; $291 per course. Tuition and fees vary according to course load, degree level and program. *Financial support:* Fellowships, research assistantships, teaching assistantships, institutionally sponsored loans, scholarships/grants, traineeships, health care benefits, and

174 facebook.com/petersonspublishing

Peterson's Graduate Programs in the Physical Sciences, Mathematics, Agricultural Sciences, the Environment & Natural Resources 2013

unspecified assistantships available. Financial award application deadline: 12/15. *Faculty research:* Isotope geochemistry, regional tectonics, environmental geology, metamorphic and igneous petrology, paleontology. *Unit head:* Dr. Ralph M. Rosen, Associate Dean for Graduate Studies, 215-898-7156, Fax: 215-573-8068, E-mail: gdasdmis@sas.upenn.edu. *Application contact:* Patricia Rea, Associate Director for Admissions, 215-573-5816, Fax: 215-573-8068, E-mail: gdasadmis@sas.upenn.edu.

University of Rhode Island, Graduate School, College of the Environment and Life Sciences, Department of Geosciences, Kingston, RI 02881. Offers environmental science and management (MESM); environmental sciences (MS, PhD). Part-time programs available. *Faculty:* 6 full-time (2 women). *Students:* 4 part-time (1 woman). In 2011, 3 master's awarded. *Degree requirements:* For master's, comprehensive exam (for some programs), thesis optional; for doctorate, comprehensive exam, thesis/dissertation. *Entrance requirements:* For master's and doctorate, GRE, 2 letters of recommendation. Additional exam requirements/recommendations for international students: Required—TOEFL (minimum score 550 paper-based; 213 computer-based). *Application deadline:* For fall admission, 7/15 for domestic students, 2/1 for international students; for spring admission, 11/15 for domestic students, 7/15 for international students. Application fee: $65. Electronic applications accepted. *Expenses:* Tuition, state resident: full-time $10,432; part-time $580 per credit hour. Tuition, nonresident: full-time $23,130; part-time $1285 per credit hour. *Required fees:* $1362; $36 per credit hour. $35 per semester. One-time fee: $130. *Financial support:* In 2011–12, 2 research assistantships with partial tuition reimbursements (averaging $9,339 per year) were awarded. Financial award application deadline: 7/15; financial award applicants required to submit FAFSA. *Faculty research:* Hydrology and water resources, interior of the earth, quaternary and modern depositional environments, geobiology of Mesozoic terrestrial ecosystems. *Unit head:* Dr. Daivd Fastovsky, Chair, 401-874-2185, Fax: 401-874-2190, E-mail: defastov@uri.edu. *Application contact:* Dr. Thomas Boving, Director of Graduate Studies, 401-874-7053, Fax: 401-874-2190, E-mail: boving@uri.edu. Web site: http://www.uri.edu/cels/geo/.

University of Rochester, School of Arts and Sciences, Department of Earth and Environmental Sciences, Rochester, NY 14627. Offers MS, PhD. *Faculty:* 7 full-time (2 women). *Students:* 9 full-time (4 women), 4 international. 44 applicants, 16% accepted, 3 enrolled. In 2011, 6 master's, 2 doctorates awarded. *Degree requirements:* For doctorate, thesis/dissertation, qualifying exam. *Entrance requirements:* For master's and doctorate, GRE General Test. Additional exam requirements/recommendations for international students: Required—TOEFL. *Application deadline:* For fall admission, 2/1 priority date for domestic students. Application fee: $0. Electronic applications accepted. *Expenses: Tuition:* Full-time $41,040. *Financial support:* Fellowships, research assistantships, teaching assistantships, career-related internships or fieldwork, and tuition waivers (full and partial) available. Financial award application deadline: 2/1. *Faculty research:* Geochemistry and environmental sciences; paleomagnetism, structure and tectonics. *Unit head:* Carmala Garzione, Chair, 585-275-5713, E-mail: carmala.garzione@rochester.edu. *Application contact:* Kathy Lutz, Secretary, 585-275-5713, E-mail: kathy@ur.rochester.edu. Web site: http://www.ees.rochester.edu/.

University of South Carolina, The Graduate School, College of Arts and Sciences, Department of Geological Sciences, Columbia, SC 29208. Offers MS, PhD. Terminal master's awarded for partial completion of doctoral program. *Degree requirements:* For master's, thesis; for doctorate, comprehensive exam, thesis/dissertation, published paper. *Entrance requirements:* For master's and doctorate, GRE General Test. Additional exam requirements/recommendations for international students: Required—TOEFL (minimum score 570 paper-based; 230 computer-based; 75 iBT). Electronic applications accepted. *Faculty research:* Environmental geology, tectonics, petrology, coastal processes, paleoclimatology.

University of Southern California, Graduate School, Dana and David Dornsife College of Letters, Arts and Sciences, Department of Earth Sciences, Los Angeles, CA 90089. Offers geological sciences (MS, PhD). Only Ph.D. and M.S./Ph.D. students are funded.. Part-time programs available. Terminal master's awarded for partial completion of doctoral program. *Degree requirements:* For master's, thesis; for doctorate, comprehensive exam, thesis/dissertation. *Entrance requirements:* For master's and doctorate, GRE. Additional exam requirements/recommendations for international students: Required—TOEFL. Electronic applications accepted. *Faculty research:* Geophysics, paleoceanography, geochemistry, geobiology, structure, tectonics.

The University of Texas at Austin, Graduate School, Jackson School of Geosciences, Austin, TX 78712-1111. Offers MA, MS, PhD. Part-time programs available. *Degree requirements:* For master's, report (MA), thesis (MS); for doctorate, thesis/dissertation. *Entrance requirements:* For master's and doctorate, GRE General Test. *Application deadline:* For fall admission, 2/1 priority date for domestic students; for spring admission, 10/1 for domestic students. Application fee: $50 ($75 for international students). Electronic applications accepted. *Financial support:* Fellowships with partial tuition reimbursements, research assistantships with partial tuition reimbursements, teaching assistantships with partial tuition reimbursements, career-related internships or fieldwork, Federal Work-Study, and institutionally sponsored loans available. Financial award application deadline: 2/1. *Faculty research:* Sedimentary geology, geophysics, hydrogeology, structure/tectonics, vertebrate paleontology. *Unit head:* Dr. Sharon Mosher, Dean, 512-471-6048, E-mail: smosher@jsg.utexas.edu. Application

contact: Jesus Garcia, Senior Academic Advisor, 512-471-8472, E-mail: jgar5@mail.utexas.edu. Web site: http://www.jsg.utexas.edu/.

The University of Texas at Dallas, School of Natural Sciences and Mathematics, Department of Geosciences, Richardson, TX 75080. Offers geochemistry (MS, PhD); geophysics (MS, PhD); geospatial information sciences (MS, PhD); hydrogeology (MS, PhD); sedimentary, stratigraphy, paleontology (PhD); stratigraphy, paleontology (MS); structural geology and tectonics (MS, PhD). Part-time and evening/weekend programs available. *Faculty:* 10 full-time (1 woman). *Students:* 39 full-time (13 women), 20 part-time (7 women); includes 8 minority (2 Black or African American, non-Hispanic/Latino; 4 Asian, non-Hispanic/Latino; 2 Hispanic/Latino), 18 international. Average age 32. 67 applicants, 39% accepted, 14 enrolled. In 2011, 8 master's, 3 doctorates awarded. *Degree requirements:* For master's, thesis optional; for doctorate, thesis/dissertation. *Entrance requirements:* For master's and doctorate, GRE General Test, minimum GPA of 3.0 in upper-level course work in field. Additional exam requirements/recommendations for international students: Required—TOEFL (minimum score 550 paper-based; 215 computer-based). *Application deadline:* For fall admission, 7/15 for domestic students, 5/1 for international students; for spring admission, 11/15 for domestic students, 9/1 for international students. Applications are processed on a rolling basis. Application fee: $50 ($100 for international students). Electronic applications accepted. *Expenses:* Tuition, state resident: full-time $11,170; part-time $620.56 per credit hour. Tuition, nonresident: full-time $20,212; part-time $1122.89 per credit hour. *Financial support:* In 2011–12, 32 students received support, including 13 research assistantships with partial tuition reimbursements available (averaging $21,462 per year), 15 teaching assistantships with partial tuition reimbursements available (averaging $15,800 per year); career-related internships or fieldwork, Federal Work-Study, institutionally sponsored loans, scholarships/grants, and unspecified assistantships also available. Support available to part-time students. Financial award application deadline: 4/30; financial award applicants required to submit FAFSA. *Faculty research:* Cybermapping, GPS applications for geophysics and geology, seismology and ground-penetrating radar, numerical modeling, signal processing and inverse modeling techniques in seismology. *Unit head:* Dr. John Oldow, Department Head, 972-883-2401, Fax: 972-883-2537, E-mail: geosciences@utdallas.edu. *Application contact:* Dr. John W. Geissman, Graduate Advisor, 972-883-2406, Fax: 972-883-2537, E-mail: geissman@utdallas.edu. Web site: http://www.utdallas.edu/geosciences.

University of Tulsa, Graduate School, College of Engineering and Natural Sciences, Department of Geosciences, Tulsa, OK 74104-3189. Offers MS, PhD, JD/MS. Part-time programs available. *Faculty:* 9 full-time (1 woman), 2 part-time/adjunct (1 woman). *Students:* 27 full-time (11 women), 13 part-time (6 women); includes 2 minority (1 Black or African American, non-Hispanic/Latino; 1 American Indian or Alaska Native, non-Hispanic/Latino), 27 international. Average age 27. 81 applicants, 52% accepted, 17 enrolled. In 2011, 3 master's awarded. Terminal master's awarded for partial completion of doctoral program. *Degree requirements:* For master's, thesis (for some programs); for doctorate, comprehensive exam, thesis/dissertation. *Entrance requirements:* For master's and doctorate, GRE General Test. Additional exam requirements/recommendations for international students: Required—TOEFL (minimum score 550 paper-based; 213 computer-based; 80 iBT), IELTS (minimum score 6). *Application deadline:* Applications are processed on a rolling basis. Application fee: $40. Electronic applications accepted. *Expenses: Tuition:* Full-time $17,748; part-time $986 per hour. *Required fees:* $5 per contact hour. $75 per semester. Tuition and fees vary according to program. *Financial support:* In 2011–12, 6 students received support, including 2 fellowships with full and partial tuition reimbursements available (averaging $3,750 per year), 1 research assistantship with full and partial tuition reimbursement available (averaging $12,303 per year), 6 teaching assistantships with full and partial tuition reimbursements available (averaging $10,250 per year); career-related internships or fieldwork, scholarships/grants, health care benefits, and unspecified assistantships also available. Support available to part-time students. Financial award application deadline: 2/1; financial award applicants required to submit FAFSA. *Faculty research:* Petroleum exploration/production and environmental science, including clastic sedimentology, petroleum seismology, seismic stratigraphy, structural geology, geochemistry, and biogeoscience. *Total annual research expenditures:* $637,539. *Unit head:* Dr. Bryan Tapp, Chairperson, 918-631-3018, Fax: 918-631-2091, E-mail: jbt@utulsa.edu. *Application contact:* Dr. Peter J. Michael, Adviser, 918-631-3017, Fax: 918-631-2156, E-mail: pjm@utulsa.edu. Web site: http://www.geo.utulsa.edu/.

University of Victoria, Faculty of Graduate Studies, Faculty of Science, School of Earth and Ocean Sciences, Victoria, BC V8W 2Y2, Canada. Offers M Sc, PhD. Part-time programs available. *Degree requirements:* For master's, thesis; for doctorate, thesis/dissertation, candidacy exam. *Entrance requirements:* For master's and doctorate, GRE. Additional exam requirements/recommendations for international students: Required—TOEFL (minimum score 575 paper-based; 233 computer-based), IELTS (minimum score 7). Electronic applications accepted. *Faculty research:* Climate modeling, geology.

University of Waterloo, Graduate Studies, Faculty of Science, Department of Earth Sciences, Waterloo, ON N2L 3G1, Canada. Offers M Sc, PhD. Part-time programs available. *Degree requirements:* For master's, research paper or thesis; for doctorate, comprehensive exam, thesis/dissertation. *Entrance requirements:* For master's, GRE, honors degree, minimum B average; for doctorate, GRE, master's degree, minimum B average. Additional exam requirements/

Peterson's Graduate Programs in the Physical Sciences, Mathematics, Agricultural Sciences, the Environment & Natural Resources 2013

facebook.com/petersonspublishing **175**

recommendations for international students: Required—TOEFL, TWE. Electronic applications accepted. *Faculty research:* Environmental geology, soil physics.

The University of Western Ontario, Faculty of Graduate Studies, Physical Sciences Division, Department of Earth Sciences, London, ON N6A 5B8, Canada. Offers environment and sustainability (MES); geology (M Sc, PhD); geology and environmental science (M Sc, PhD); geophysics (M Sc, PhD); geophysics and environmental science (M Sc, PhD). *Degree requirements:* For master's, thesis; for doctorate, thesis/dissertation, qualifying exam. *Entrance requirements:* For master's, honors in B Sc; for doctorate, M Sc. Additional exam requirements/recommendations for international students: Required—TOEFL. *Faculty research:* Geophysics, geochemistry, paleontology, sedimentology/stratigraphy, glaciology/quaternary.

University of Windsor, Faculty of Graduate Studies, Faculty of Science, Department of Earth and Environmental Sciences, Windsor, ON N9B 3P4, Canada. Offers earth sciences (M Sc, PhD). Part-time programs available. *Degree requirements:* For master's, thesis; for doctorate, comprehensive exam, thesis/dissertation. *Entrance requirements:* For master's, minimum B average; for doctorate, minimum B average, copies of publication abstract. Additional exam requirements/recommendations for international students: Required—TOEFL (minimum score 560 paper-based; 220 computer-based). *Faculty research:* Aqueous geochemistry and hydrothermal processes, igneous petrochemistry, radiogenic isotopes, radiometric age-dating, diagenetic and sedimentary geochemistry.

Virginia Polytechnic Institute and State University, Graduate School, College of Science, Department of Geosciences, Blacksburg, VA 24061. Offers MS, PhD. *Degree requirements:* For master's, comprehensive exam (for some programs), thesis (for some programs); for doctorate, comprehensive exam (for some programs), thesis/dissertation (for some programs). *Entrance requirements:* For master's and doctorate, GRE. Additional exam requirements/recommendations for international students: Required—TOEFL (minimum score 550 paper-based; 213 computer-based). *Application deadline:* For fall admission, 7/1 for domestic and international students; for spring admission, 12/1 for domestic and international students. Applications are processed on a rolling basis. Application fee: $65. Electronic applications accepted. *Expenses:* Tuition, state resident: full-time $10,048; part-time $558.25 per credit hour. Tuition, nonresident: full-time $19,497; part-time $1083.25 per credit hour. *Required fees:* $405 per semester. Tuition and fees vary according to course load, campus/location and program. *Financial support:* Fellowships with full tuition reimbursements, research assistantships with full tuition reimbursements, teaching assistantships with full tuition reimbursements, career-related internships or fieldwork, Federal Work-Study, scholarships/grants, health care benefits, and unspecified assistantships available. Financial award application deadline: 1/15. *Faculty research:* Paleontology/geobiology, active tectonics, geomorphology, mineralogy/crystallography, mineral physics. *Unit head:* Dr. Kenneth A. Eriksson, Unit Head, 540-231-6894, Fax: 540-231-3386, E-mail: kaeson@vt.edu. *Application contact:* Madeline Schreiber, Information Contact, 540-231-3377, Fax: 540-231-3386, E-mail: mschreib@vt.edu. Web site: http://www.geos.vt.edu/prospectivestudents/graduate.php.

Washington University in St. Louis, Graduate School of Arts and Sciences, Department of Earth and Planetary Sciences, St. Louis, MO 63130-4899. Offers MA, PhD. Terminal master's awarded for partial completion of doctoral program. *Degree requirements:* For master's, thesis; for doctorate, thesis/dissertation. *Entrance requirements:* For master's and doctorate, GRE General Test. Electronic applications accepted.

Wesleyan University, Graduate Programs, Department of Earth and Environmental Sciences, Middletown, CT 06459. Offers MA. *Degree requirements:* For master's, thesis. *Entrance requirements:* For master's, GRE General Test, GRE Subject Test. Additional exam requirements/recommendations for international students: Required—TOEFL. Electronic applications accepted. *Faculty research:* Tectonics, volcanology, stratigraphy, coastal processes, geochemistry.

West Chester University of Pennsylvania, College of Arts and Sciences, Department of Geology and Astronomy, West Chester, PA 19383. Offers earth-space science (Teaching Certificate); general science (Teaching Certificate); geoscience (MA). Part-time and evening/weekend programs available. *Faculty:* 6 part-time/adjunct (1 woman). *Students:* 6 full-time (3 women), 17 part-time (6 women); includes 1 minority (Black or African American, non-Hispanic/Latino). Average age 32. 8 applicants, 88% accepted, 5 enrolled. In 2011, 4 degrees awarded. *Degree requirements:* For master's, comprehensive exam (for some programs), thesis or alternative. *Entrance requirements:* For master's, minimum GPA of 2.5. Additional exam requirements/recommendations for international students: Required—TOEFL (minimum score 550 paper-based; 213 computer-based; 80 iBT). *Application deadline:* For fall admission, 4/15 priority date for domestic students, 3/15 for international students; for spring admission, 10/15 priority date for domestic students, 9/1 for international students. Applications are processed on a rolling basis. Application fee: $45. Electronic applications accepted. *Expenses:* Tuition, state resident: full-time $7488; part-time $416 per credit. Tuition, nonresident: full-time $11,232; part-time $624 per credit. *Required*

fees: $1784.64; $67.59 per credit. Tuition and fees vary according to program. *Financial support:* Unspecified assistantships available. Support available to part-time students. Financial award application deadline: 2/15; financial award applicants required to submit FAFSA. *Faculty research:* Geoscience education, environmental geology, energy and sustainability, astronomy, meteorology. *Unit head:* Dr. Lee Anne Srogi, Chair, 610-436-2727, Fax: 610-436-3036, E-mail: lsrogi@wcupa.edu. *Application contact:* Dr. Martin Helmke, Graduate Coordinator, 610-436-3565, Fax: 610-436-3036, E-mail: mhelmke@wcupa.edu. Web site: http://www.wcupa.edu/_academics/sch_cas.esc/.

Western Connecticut State University, Division of Graduate Studies, School of Arts and Sciences, Department of Physics, Astronomy and Meteorology, Danbury, CT 06810-6885. Offers earth and planetary sciences (MA). Part-time programs available. *Faculty:* 2 full-time (0 women). *Students:* 3 full-time (0 women), 10 part-time (4 women); includes 3 minority (1 Black or African American, non-Hispanic/Latino; 2 Hispanic/Latino). Average age 28. In 2011, 1 degree awarded. *Degree requirements:* For master's, thesis; completion of program in 6 years. *Entrance requirements:* For master's, minimum GPA of 2.5 or GRE; one year each of calculus-based physics and calculus; semester course in differential equations. Additional exam requirements/recommendations for international students: Recommended—TOEFL (minimum score 550 paper-based; 213 computer-based; 79 iBT), IELTS (minimum score 6). *Application deadline:* For fall admission, 8/5 priority date for domestic students; for spring admission, 1/5 priority date for domestic students. Applications are processed on a rolling basis. Application fee: $50. *Expenses:* Contact institution. *Financial support:* Application deadline: 5/1; applicants required to submit FAFSA. *Faculty research:* Data collection and analysis of Gulf Stream surface temperature and circulation; science for visually impaired students including investigations of a satellite orbit, the Moon's surface, spectra of chemical elements and stars, the rotation of the Sun, and the spiral structure of our galaxy. *Unit head:* Dr. James Boyle, Graduate Coordinator, 203-837-8856. *Application contact:* Chris Shankle, Associate Director of Graduate Admissions, 203-837-9005, Fax: 203-837-8326, E-mail: shanklec@wcsu.edu. Web site: http://www.wcsu.edu/physics/.

Western Kentucky University, Graduate Studies, Ogden College of Science and Engineering, Department of Geography and Geology, Bowling Green, KY 42101. Offers geoscience (MS). *Degree requirements:* For master's, comprehensive exam, thesis or alternative. *Entrance requirements:* For master's, GRE General Test, minimum GPA of 2.75. Additional exam requirements/recommendations for international students: Required—TOEFL (minimum score 555 paper-based; 213 computer-based; 79 iBT). *Faculty research:* Hydroclimatology, electronic data sets, groundwater, sinkhole liquification potential, meteorological analysis.

Western Michigan University, Graduate College, College of Arts and Sciences, Department of Geosciences, Program in Earth Science, Kalamazoo, MI 49008. Offers MA. *Degree requirements:* For master's, thesis or alternative, oral exam. *Entrance requirements:* For master's, GRE General Test.

Western Michigan University, Graduate College, College of Arts and Sciences, Department of Geosciences, Program in Geosciences, Kalamazoo, MI 49008. Offers MS, PhD. *Degree requirements:* For master's, oral exam; for doctorate, thesis/dissertation, oral exam. *Entrance requirements:* For master's and doctorate, GRE General Test.

Western Michigan University, Graduate College, College of Arts and Sciences, Mallinson Institute for Science Education, Kalamazoo, MI 49008. Offers science education (MA, PhD); science education: biological sciences (PhD); science education: chemistry (PhD); science education: geosciences (PhD); science education: physical geography (PhD); science education: physics (PhD). *Degree requirements:* For doctorate, thesis/dissertation, oral and written exams. *Entrance requirements:* For master's, undergraduate degree in a science or science education, teacher certification (or appropriate education courses); for doctorate, GRE General Test, master's degree in a science or science education. Additional exam requirements/recommendations for international students: Recommended—TOEFL. Electronic applications accepted. *Faculty research:* History and philosophy of science, curriculum and instruction, science content learning, college science teaching and learning, social and cultural factors in science education.

Yale University, Graduate School of Arts and Sciences, Department of Geology and Geophysics, New Haven, CT 06520. Offers biogeochemistry (PhD); climate dynamics (PhD); geochemistry (PhD); geophysics (PhD); meteorology (PhD); oceanography (PhD); paleontology (PhD); paleooceanography (PhD); petrology (PhD); tectonics (PhD). *Degree requirements:* For doctorate, thesis/dissertation. *Entrance requirements:* For doctorate, GRE General Test. Additional exam requirements/recommendations for international students: Required—TOEFL.

York University, Faculty of Graduate Studies, Faculty of Science and Engineering, Program in Earth and Space Science, Toronto, ON M3J 1P3, Canada. Offers M Sc, PhD. Part-time and evening/weekend programs available. *Degree requirements:* For master's, thesis or alternative; for doctorate, thesis/dissertation. Electronic applications accepted.

176 facebook.com/petersonspublishing

Peterson's Graduate Programs in the Physical Sciences, Mathematics, Agricultural Sciences, the Environment & Natural Resources 2013

Hydrogeology

California State University, Bakersfield, Division of Graduate Studies, School of Natural Sciences, Mathematics, and Engineering, Program in Geology, Bakersfield, CA 93311. Offers geology (MS); hydrogeology (MS, Postbaccalaureate Certificate); petroleum geology (MS). Part-time and evening/weekend programs available. *Degree requirements:* For master's, thesis. *Entrance requirements:* For master's, GRE General Test, BS in geology. *Application deadline:* Applications are processed on a rolling basis. Application fee: $55. *Expenses: Required fees:* $1302 per unit. Part-time tuition and fees vary according to course load and program. *Financial support:* Teaching assistantships, career-related internships or fieldwork, institutionally sponsored loans, and scholarships/grants available. *Unit head:* Dr. Dirk Baron, Department Chair, 661-664-3044, Fax: 661-664-2040, E-mail: dbaron@csub.edu.

California State University, Chico, Office of Graduate Studies, College of Natural Sciences, Department of Geological and Environmental Sciences, Program in Geosciences, Chico, CA 95929-0722. Offers hydrology/hydrogeology (MS). Part-time programs available. *Students:* 3 full-time (0 women), 5 part-time (1 woman); includes 1 minority (Hispanic/Latino). Average age 31. 9 applicants, 56% accepted, 3 enrolled. In 2011, 1 master's awarded. *Degree requirements:* For master's, thesis, oral exam. *Entrance requirements:* For master's, GRE, faculty mentor, statement of purpose. Additional exam requirements/recommendations for international students: Required—TOEFL (minimum score 550 paper-based; 213 computer-based; 80 iBT), IELTS (minimum score 6.5), Pearson Test of English (minimum score 59). *Application deadline:* For fall admission, 3/1 priority date for domestic students, 3/1 for international students; for spring admission, 9/15 priority date for domestic students, 9/15 for international students. Application fee: $55. Electronic applications accepted. Tuition and fees vary according to class time, course load and degree level. *Financial support:* Fellowships, research assistantships, teaching assistantships, and career-related internships or fieldwork available. *Unit head:* Dr. David L. Brown, Chair, 530-898-5262, Fax: 530-898-5234, E-mail: geos@csuchico.edu. *Application contact:* Judy L. Rice, Graduate Admissions Coordinator, 530-898-5416, Fax: 530-898-3342, E-mail: jlrice@csuchico.edu. Web site: http://catalog.csuchico.edu/viewer/12/GEOS.html.

Clemson University, Graduate School, College of Engineering and Science, Department of Environmental Engineering and Earth Sciences, Program in Hydrogeology, Clemson, SC 29634. Offers MS. Part-time programs available. *Students:* 16 full-time (4 women), 5 part-time (2 women); includes 1 minority (Two or more races, non-Hispanic/Latino), 1 international. Average age 30. 13 applicants, 85% accepted, 7 enrolled. In 2011, 8 master's awarded. *Degree requirements:* For master's, thesis optional. *Entrance requirements:* For master's, GRE General Test, minimum GPA of 3.0 during previous 2 years. Additional exam requirements/recommendations for international students: Required—TOEFL. *Application deadline:* Applications are processed on a rolling basis. Application fee: $70 ($80 for international students). Electronic applications accepted. *Financial support:* In 2011–12, 11 students received support, including 6 research assistantships with partial tuition reimbursements available (averaging $18,034 per year), 5 teaching assistantships with partial tuition reimbursements available (averaging $17,784 per year); fellowships with full and partial tuition reimbursements available, career-related internships or fieldwork, institutionally sponsored loans, scholarships/grants, health care benefits, and unspecified assistantships also available. Support available to part-time students. Financial award application deadline: 6/1; financial award applicants required to submit FAFSA. *Faculty research:* Groundwater, geology, environmental geology, geophysics, geochemistry, remediation, modeling, sedimentology. *Total annual research expenditures:* $670,000. *Unit head:* Dr. Tanju Karanfil, Chair, 864-653-1005, Fax: 864-656-5973, E-mail: tkaranf@clemson.edu. *Application contact:* Dr. Jim W. Castle, Hydrogeology Graduate Program Coordinator, 864-656-5015, Fax: 864-656-1041, E-mail: jcastle@clemson.edu. Web site: http://www.clemson.edu/ces/eees/gradprog/hydro/index.html.

East Carolina University, Graduate School, Thomas Harriot College of Arts and Sciences, Department of Geology, Greenville, NC 27858-4353. Offers geology (MS); hydrogeology and environmental geology (Certificate). Part-time programs available. *Degree requirements:* For master's, one foreign language, comprehensive exam, thesis. *Entrance requirements:* For master's, GRE General Test. Additional exam requirements/recommendations for international students: Required—TOEFL. *Application deadline:* For fall admission, 6/1 priority date for domestic students; for spring admission, 10/15 for domestic students. Applications are processed on a rolling basis. Application fee: $50. *Expenses:* Tuition, state resident: full-time $3557; part-time $444.63 per semester hour. Tuition, nonresident: full-time $14,351; part-time $1793.88 per semester hour. *Required fees:* $2016; $252 per semester hour. Part-time tuition and fees vary according to course load, campus/location and program. *Financial support:* Research assistantships with partial tuition reimbursements and teaching assistantships with partial tuition reimbursements available. Support available to part-time students. Financial award application deadline: 6/1. *Unit head:* Dr. Stephen Culver, Chair, 252-328-6360, Fax: 252-328-4391, E-mail: culvers@ecu.edu. *Application contact:* Dean of Graduate School, 252-328-6012, Fax: 252-328-6071, E-mail: gradschool@ecu.edu. Web site: http://www.ecu.edu/geology/.

Georgia State University, College of Arts and Sciences, Department of Geosciences, Atlanta, GA 30302-3083. Offers geographic information systems (Certificate); geography (MA); geology (MA); hydrogeology (Certificate). Part-time and evening/weekend programs available. *Degree requirements:* For master's, one foreign language, comprehensive exam (for some programs), thesis or alternative. *Entrance requirements:* For master's, GRE General Test, minimum GPA of 2.75. Additional exam requirements/recommendations for international students: Required—TOEFL. Electronic applications accepted. *Faculty research:* Clay mineralogy, geoinformatics, fracture analysis, sedimentology, groundwater.

Illinois State University, Graduate School, College of Arts and Sciences, Department of Geography-Geology, Normal, IL 61790-2200. Offers hydrogeology (MS). *Degree requirements:* For master's, thesis optional. *Entrance requirements:* For master's, GRE General Test. *Faculty research:* Thermal transport within the hyporheic zone, nutrient cycling in watersheds, water quality in karst systems, ground water dating using dissolved helium.

Indiana University Bloomington, University Graduate School, College of Arts and Sciences, Department of Geological Sciences, Bloomington, IN 47405-7000. Offers biogeochemistry (MS, PhD); economic geology (MS, PhD); geobiology (MS, PhD); geophysics, structural geology and tectonics (MS, PhD); hydrogeology (MS, PhD); mineralogy (MS, PhD); stratigraphy and sedimentology (MS, PhD). *Faculty:* 17 full-time (1 woman). *Students:* 60 full-time (26 women), 2 part-time (0 women); includes 5 minority (2 Black or African American, non-Hispanic/Latino; 1 Hispanic/Latino; 2 Two or more races, non-Hispanic/Latino), 18 international. Average age 29. 44 applicants, 55% accepted, 18 enrolled. In 2011, 11 master's, 6 doctorates awarded. Terminal master's awarded for partial completion of doctoral program. *Degree requirements:* For master's, thesis or alternative; for doctorate, comprehensive exam, thesis/dissertation. *Entrance requirements:* For master's and doctorate, GRE General Test. Additional exam requirements/recommendations for international students: Required—TOEFL. *Application deadline:* For fall admission, 1/15 priority date for domestic students, 12/15 for international students; for spring admission, 9/1 priority date for domestic students, 9/1 for international students. Applications are processed on a rolling basis. Application fee: $55 ($65 for international students). *Financial support:* In 2011–12, fellowships with full tuition reimbursements (averaging $17,300 per year), research assistantships with full tuition reimbursements (averaging $16,370 per year), teaching assistantships with full tuition reimbursements (averaging $15,150 per year) were awarded; career-related internships or fieldwork, Federal Work-Study, and institutionally sponsored loans also available. *Faculty research:* Geophysics, geochemistry, hydrogeology, geobiology, planetary science. *Total annual research expenditures:* $644,299. *Unit head:* Simon Brassell, Chair, 812-855-5581, Fax: 812-855-7899, E-mail: geochair@indiana.edu. *Application contact:* Mary Iverson, Graduate Secretary, 812-855-7214, Fax: 812-855-7899, E-mail: miverson@indiana.edu. Web site: http://www.indiana.edu/~geosci/.

Montana Tech of The University of Montana, Graduate School, Geosciences Programs, Butte, MT 59701-8997. Offers geochemistry (MS); geological engineering (MS); geology (MS); geophysical engineering (MS); hydrogeological engineering (MS); hydrogeology (MS). Part-time programs available. *Faculty:* 16 full-time (4 women), 4 part-time/adjunct (0 women). *Students:* 16 full-time (7 women), 12 part-time (6 women); includes 2 minority (1 Black or African American, non-Hispanic/Latino; 1 American Indian or Alaska Native, non-Hispanic/Latino), 1 international. 23 applicants, 65% accepted, 13 enrolled. In 2011, 9 master's awarded. *Degree requirements:* For master's, comprehensive exam (for some programs), thesis (for some programs). *Entrance requirements:* For master's, GRE General Test, minimum GPA of 3.0. Additional exam requirements/recommendations for international students: Required—TOEFL (minimum score 525 paper-based; 195 computer-based; 71 iBT). *Application deadline:* For fall admission, 4/1 priority date for domestic students, 3/1 for international students; for spring admission, 10/1 priority date for domestic students, 7/1 for international students. Applications are processed on a rolling basis. Application fee: $30. Electronic applications accepted. *Financial support:* In 2011–12, 15 students received support, including 10 teaching assistantships with partial tuition reimbursements available (averaging $5,000 per year); research assistantships with partial tuition reimbursements available, career-related internships or fieldwork, tuition waivers (full and partial), and unspecified assistantships also available. Financial award application deadline: 4/1; financial award applicants required to submit FAFSA. *Faculty research:* Water resource development, seismic processing, petroleum reservoir characterization, environmental geochemistry, geologic mapping. *Unit head:* Dr. Mary MacLaughlin, Department Head, 406-496-4655, Fax: 406-496-4260, E-mail: mmaclaughlin@mtech.edu. *Application contact:* Fred Sullivan, Administrator, Graduate School, 406-496-4304, Fax: 406-496-4710, E-mail: fsullivan@mtech.edu. Web site: http://www.mtech.edu/academics/gradschool/degreeprograms/degrees.htm.

Ohio University, Graduate College, College of Arts and Sciences, Department of Geological Sciences, Athens, OH 45701-2979. Offers environmental geochemistry (MS); environmental geology (MS); environmental/hydrology (MS); geology (MS); geology education (MS); geomorphology/surficial processes (MS);

Peterson's Graduate Programs in the Physical Sciences, Mathematics, Agricultural Sciences, the Environment & Natural Resources 2013

facebook.com/petersonspublishing   **177**

geophysics (MS); hydrogeology (MS); sedimentology (MS); structure/tectonics (MS). Part-time programs available. *Students:* 19 full-time (10 women). 14 applicants, 64% accepted, 9 enrolled. In 2011, 8 master's awarded. *Degree requirements:* For master's, thesis. *Entrance requirements:* Additional exam requirements/recommendations for international students: Required—TOEFL (minimum score 550 paper-based; 80 iBT) or IELTS (minimum score 6.5). *Application deadline:* For fall admission, 2/1 priority date for domestic students, 2/1 for international students. Application fee: $50 ($55 for international students). Electronic applications accepted. *Financial support:* Research assistantships with full tuition reimbursements, teaching assistantships with full tuition reimbursements, Federal Work-Study, institutionally sponsored loans, scholarships/grants, tuition waivers (partial), and unspecified assistantships available. Financial award application deadline: 2/1. *Faculty research:* Geoscience education, tectonics, fluvial geomorphology, invertebrate paleontology, mine/hydrology. *Total annual research expenditures:* $649,020. *Unit head:* Dr. Gregory Nadon, Chair, 740-593-4212, Fax: 740-593-0486, E-mail: nadon@ohio.edu. *Application contact:* Dr. Keith Milam, Graduate Chair, 740-593-1106, Fax: 740-593-0486, E-mail: milamk@ohio.edu. Web site: http://www.ohiou.edu/geology/.

University of Hawaii at Manoa, Graduate Division, School of Ocean and Earth Science and Technology, Department of Geology and Geophysics, Honolulu, HI 96822. Offers high-pressure geophysics and geochemistry (MS, PhD); hydrogeology and engineering geology (MS, PhD); marine geology and geophysics (MS, PhD); planetary geosciences and remote sensing (MS, PhD); seismology and solid-earth geophysics (MS, PhD); volcanology, petrology, and geochemistry (MS, PhD). Part-time programs available. Terminal master's awarded for partial completion of doctoral program. *Degree requirements:* For master's, thesis optional; for doctorate, comprehensive exam, thesis/dissertation. *Entrance requirements:* For master's and doctorate, GRE General Test, minimum GPA of 3.0. Additional exam requirements/recommendations for international students: Required—TOEFL (minimum score 580 paper-based; 237 computer-based; 92 iBT), IELTS (minimum score 5).

University of Nevada, Reno, Graduate School, Interdisciplinary Program in Hydrologic Sciences, Reno, NV 89557. Offers hydrogeology (MS, PhD); hydrology (MS, PhD). Offered through the M. C. Fleischmann College of Agriculture, the College of Engineering, the Mackay School of Mines, and the Desert Research Institute. Terminal master's awarded for partial completion of doctoral program. *Degree requirements:* For master's, thesis optional; for doctorate, thesis/dissertation. *Entrance requirements:* For master's and doctorate, GRE General Test, minimum GPA of 3.0. Additional exam requirements/recommendations for international students: Required—TOEFL (minimum score 500 paper-based; 173 computer-based; 61 iBT), IELTS (minimum score 6). Electronic applications accepted. *Faculty research:* Groundwater, water resources, surface water, soil science.

The University of Texas at Dallas, School of Natural Sciences and Mathematics, Department of Geosciences, Richardson, TX 75080. Offers geochemistry (MS, PhD); geophysics (MS, PhD); geospatial information sciences (MS, PhD); hydrogeology (MS, PhD); sedimentary, stratigraphy, paleontology (PhD); stratigraphy, paleontology (MS); structural geology and tectonics (MS, PhD). Part-time and evening/weekend programs available. *Faculty:* 10 full-time (1 woman). *Students:* 39 full-time (13 women), 20 part-time (7 women); includes 8 minority (2 Black or African American, non-Hispanic/Latino; 4 Asian, non-Hispanic/Latino; 2 Hispanic/Latino), 18 international. Average age 32. 67 applicants, 39% accepted, 14 enrolled. In 2011, 8 master's, 3 doctorates awarded. *Degree requirements:* For master's, thesis optional; for doctorate, thesis/dissertation. *Entrance requirements:* For master's and doctorate, GRE General Test, minimum GPA of 3.0 in upper-level course work in field. Additional exam requirements/recommendations for international students: Required—TOEFL (minimum score 550 paper-based; 215 computer-based). *Application deadline:* For fall admission, 7/15 for domestic students, 5/1 for international students; for spring admission, 11/15 for domestic students, 9/1 for international students. Applications are processed on a rolling basis. Application fee: $50 ($100 for international students). Electronic applications accepted. *Expenses:* Tuition, state resident: full-time $11,170; part-time $620.56 per credit hour. Tuition, nonresident: full-time $20,212; part-time $1122.89 per credit hour. *Financial support:* In 2011–12, 32 students received support, including 13 research assistantships with partial tuition reimbursements available (averaging $21,462 per year), 15 teaching assistantships with partial tuition reimbursements available (averaging $15,800 per year); career-related internships or fieldwork, Federal Work-Study, institutionally sponsored loans, scholarships/grants, and unspecified assistantships also available. Support available to part-time students. Financial award application deadline: 4/30; financial award applicants required to submit FAFSA. *Faculty research:* Cybermapping, GPS applications for geophysics and geology, seismology and ground-penetrating radar, numerical modeling, signal processing and inverse modeling techniques in seismology. *Unit head:* Dr. John Oldow, Department Head, 972-883-2401, Fax: 972-883-2537, E-mail: geosciences@utdallas.edu. *Application contact:* Dr. John W. Geissman, Graduate Advisor, 972-883-2406, Fax: 972-883-2537, E-mail: geissman@utdallas.edu. Web site: http://www.utdallas.edu/geosciences.

West Virginia University, Eberly College of Arts and Sciences, Department of Geology and Geography, Program in Geology, Morgantown, WV 26506. Offers geomorphology (MS, PhD); geophysics (MS, PhD); hydrogeology (MS, PhD); paleontology (MS, PhD); petroleum geology (PhD); petrology (MS, PhD); stratigraphy (MS, PhD); structure (MS, PhD). Part-time programs available. Terminal master's awarded for partial completion of doctoral program. *Degree requirements:* For master's, thesis (for some programs); for doctorate, comprehensive exam, thesis/dissertation. *Entrance requirements:* For master's, GRE General Test, minimum GPA of 2.5; for doctorate, GRE General Test, minimum GPA of 3.3. Additional exam requirements/recommendations for international students: Required—TOEFL.

Hydrology

Auburn University, Graduate School, Ginn College of Engineering, Department of Civil Engineering, Auburn University, AL 36849. Offers construction engineering and management (MCE, MS, PhD); environmental engineering (MCE, MS, PhD); geotechnical/materials engineering (MCE, MS, PhD); hydraulics/hydrology (MCE, MS, PhD); structural engineering (MCE, MS, PhD); transportation engineering (MCE, MS, PhD). Part-time programs available. *Faculty:* 21 full-time (2 women), 1 part-time/adjunct (0 women). *Students:* 48 full-time (16 women), 62 part-time (14 women); includes 6 minority (4 Black or African American, non-Hispanic/Latino; 1 Asian, non-Hispanic/Latino; 1 Hispanic/Latino), 37 international. Average age 26. 111 applicants, 59% accepted, 25 enrolled. In 2011, 26 master's, 2 doctorates awarded. *Degree requirements:* For master's, project (MCE), thesis (MS); for doctorate, comprehensive exam, thesis/dissertation. *Entrance requirements:* For master's and doctorate, GRE General Test. *Application deadline:* For fall admission, 7/7 for domestic students; for spring admission, 11/24 for domestic students. Applications are processed on a rolling basis. Application fee: $50 ($60 for international students). Electronic applications accepted. *Expenses:* Tuition, state resident: full-time $7290; part-time $405 per credit hour. Tuition, nonresident: full-time $21,870; part-time $1215 per credit hour. *International tuition:* $22,000 full-time. *Required fees:* $1402. *Financial support:* Fellowships, research assistantships, teaching assistantships, and Federal Work-Study. Support available to part-time students. Financial award application deadline: 3/15; financial award applicants required to submit FAFSA. *Unit head:* Dr. J. Michael Stallings, Head, 334-844-4320. *Application contact:* Dr. George Flowers, Dean of the Graduate School, 334-844-2125.

California State University, Bakersfield, Division of Graduate Studies, School of Natural Sciences, Mathematics, and Engineering, Program in Geology, Bakersfield, CA 93311. Offers geology (MS); hydrogeology (MS, Postbaccalaureate Certificate); petroleum geology (MS). Part-time and evening/weekend programs available. *Degree requirements:* For master's, thesis. *Entrance requirements:* For master's, GRE General Test, BS in geology.

Application deadline: Applications are processed on a rolling basis. Application fee: $55. *Expenses: Required fees:* $1302 per unit. Part-time tuition and fees vary according to course load and program. *Financial support:* Teaching assistantships, career-related internships or fieldwork, institutionally sponsored loans, and scholarships/grants available. *Unit head:* Dr. Dirk Baron, Department Chair, 661-664-3044, Fax: 661-664-2040, E-mail: dbaron@csub.edu.

California State University, Chico, Office of Graduate Studies, College of Natural Sciences, Department of Geological and Environmental Sciences, Program in Geosciences, Chico, CA 95929-0722. Offers hydrology/hydrogeology (MS). Part-time programs available. *Students:* 3 full-time (0 women), 5 part-time (1 woman); includes 1 minority (Hispanic/Latino). Average age 31. 9 applicants, 56% accepted, 3 enrolled. In 2011, 1 master's awarded. *Degree requirements:* For master's, thesis, oral exam. *Entrance requirements:* For master's, GRE, faculty mentor, statement of purpose. Additional exam requirements/recommendations for international students: Required—TOEFL (minimum score 550 paper-based; 213 computer-based; 80 iBT), IELTS (minimum score 6.5), Pearson Test of English (minimum score 59). *Application deadline:* For fall admission, 3/1 priority date for domestic students, 3/1 for international students; for spring admission, 9/15 priority date for domestic students, 9/15 for international students. Application fee: $55. Electronic applications accepted. Tuition and fees vary according to class time, course load and degree level. *Financial support:* Fellowships, research assistantships, teaching assistantships, and career-related internships or fieldwork available. *Unit head:* Dr. David L. Brown, Chair, 530-898-5262, Fax: 530-898-5234, E-mail: geos@csuchico.edu. *Application contact:* Judy L. Rice, Graduate Admissions Coordinator, 530-898-5416, Fax: 530-898-3342, E-mail: jlrice@csuchico.edu. Web site: http://catalog.csuchico.edu/viewer/12/GEOS.html.

Colorado State University, Graduate School, Warner College of Natural Resources, Department of Forest and Rangeland Stewardship, Fort Collins, CO

Peterson's Graduate Programs in the Physical Sciences, Mathematics, Agricultural Sciences, the Environment & Natural Resources 2013

80523-1472. Offers forest sciences (MS, PhD); natural resources stewardship (MNRS); rangeland ecosystem science (MS, PhD); watershed science (MS). Part-time programs available. Postbaccalaureate distance learning degree programs offered (no on-campus study). *Faculty:* 12 full-time (2 women). *Students:* 32 full-time (15 women), 81 part-time (31 women); includes 5 minority (3 American Indian or Alaska Native, non-Hispanic/Latino; 2 Hispanic/Latino), 15 international. Average age 35. 33 applicants, 91% accepted, 27 enrolled. In 2011, 27 master's, 2 doctorates awarded. *Degree requirements:* For master's, thesis (for some programs); for doctorate, comprehensive exam, thesis/dissertation. *Entrance requirements:* For master's, GRE General Test (minimum score 1000 verbal and quantitative), minimum GPA of 3.0, 3 letters of recommendation; for doctorate, GRE General Test (combined minimum score of 1100 on the Verbal and Quantitative sections), minimum GPA of 3.0, 3 letters of recommendation, statement of research interest. Additional exam requirements/recommendations for international students: Required—TOEFL (minimum score 550 paper-based; 213 computer-based; 80 iBT), IELTS (minimum score 6.5). *Application deadline:* For fall admission, 2/15 priority date for domestic students, 2/15 for international students; for spring admission, 7/15 priority date for domestic students, 7/15 for international students. Applications are processed on a rolling basis. Application fee: $50. Electronic applications accepted. *Expenses:* Tuition, state resident: full-time $7992. Tuition, nonresident: full-time $19,592. *Required fees:* $1735; $58 per credit. *Financial support:* In 2011–12, 44 students received support, including 1 fellowship (averaging $19,360 per year), 31 research assistantships with full and partial tuition reimbursements available (averaging $17,090 per year), 12 teaching assistantships with full and partial tuition reimbursements available (averaging $6,607 per year); Federal Work-Study, scholarships/grants, and unspecified assistantships also available. Financial award application deadline: 2/15; financial award applicants required to submit FAFSA. *Faculty research:* Ecology, natural resource management, hydrology, restoration, human dimensions. *Total annual research expenditures:* $2.9 million. *Unit head:* Dr. Frederick Smith, Interim Department Head, 970-491-7505, Fax: 970-491-6754, E-mail: fwsmith@colostate.edu. *Application contact:* Sonya LeFebre, Coordinator, 970-491-1907, Fax: 970-491-6754, E-mail: sonya.lefebre@colostate.edu. Web site: http://warnercnr.colostate.edu/frws-home/.

Cornell University, Graduate School, Graduate Fields of Engineering, Field of Civil and Environmental Engineering, Ithaca, NY 14853-0001. Offers engineering management (M Eng, MS, PhD); environmental engineering (M Eng, MS, PhD); environmental fluid mechanics and hydrology (M Eng, MS, PhD); environmental systems engineering (M Eng, MS, PhD); geotechnical engineering (M Eng, MS, PhD); remote sensing (M Eng, MS, PhD); structural engineering (M Eng, MS, PhD); structural mechanics (M Eng, MS); transportation engineering (MS, PhD); transportation systems engineering (M Eng); water resource systems (M Eng, MS, PhD). *Faculty:* 39 full-time (4 women). *Students:* 143 full-time (49 women); includes 20 minority (6 Black or African American, non-Hispanic/Latino; 1 American Indian or Alaska Native, non-Hispanic/Latino; 9 Asian, non-Hispanic/Latino; 4 Hispanic/Latino), 72 international. Average age 25. 574 applicants, 47% accepted, 100 enrolled. In 2011, 88 master's, 13 doctorates awarded. Terminal master's awarded for partial completion of doctoral program. *Degree requirements:* For master's, thesis (MS); for doctorate, comprehensive exam, thesis/dissertation. *Entrance requirements:* For master's and doctorate, GRE General Test (recommended), 2 letters of recommendation. Additional exam requirements/recommendations for international students: Required—TOEFL (minimum score 600 paper-based; 250 computer-based; 77 iBT). *Application deadline:* For fall admission, 1/15 priority date for domestic students; for spring admission, 10/15 for domestic students. Application fee: $95. Electronic applications accepted. *Financial support:* In 2011–12, 50 students received support, including 20 fellowships with full tuition reimbursements available, 27 research assistantships with full tuition reimbursements available, 17 teaching assistantships with full tuition reimbursements available; institutionally sponsored loans, scholarships/grants, health care benefits, tuition waivers (full and partial), and unspecified assistantships also available. Financial award applicants required to submit FAFSA. *Faculty research:* Environmental engineering, geotechnical engineering, remote sensing, environmental fluid mechanics and hydrology, structural engineering. *Unit head:* Director of Graduate Studies, 607-255-7560, Fax: 607-255-9004. *Application contact:* Graduate Field Assistant, 607-255-7560, Fax: 607-255-9004, E-mail: cee_grad@cornell.edu. Web site: http://www.gradschool.cornell.edu/fields.php?id-27&a-2.

Cornell University, Graduate School, Graduate Fields of Engineering, Field of Geological Sciences, Ithaca, NY 14853. Offers economic geology (M Eng, MS, PhD); engineering geology (M Eng, MS, PhD); environmental geophysics (M Eng, MS, PhD); general geology (M Eng, MS, PhD); geobiology (M Eng, MS, PhD); geochemistry and isotope geology (M Eng, MS, PhD); geohydrology (M Eng, MS, PhD); geomorphology (M Eng, MS, PhD); geophysics (M Eng, MS, PhD); geotectonics (M Eng, MS, PhD); marine geology (MS, PhD); mineralogy (M Eng, MS, PhD); paleontology (M Eng, MS, PhD); petroleum geology (M Eng, MS, PhD); petrology (M Eng, MS, PhD); planetary geology (M Eng, MS, PhD); Precambrian geology (M Eng, MS, PhD); Quaternary geology (M Eng, MS, PhD); rock mechanics (M Eng, MS, PhD); sedimentology (M Eng, MS, PhD); seismology (M Eng, MS, PhD); stratigraphy (M Eng, MS, PhD); structural geology (M Eng, MS, PhD). *Faculty:* 37 full-time (5 women). *Students:* 41 full-time (19 women); includes 5 minority (2 Asian, non-Hispanic/Latino; 3 Hispanic/Latino), 7 international. Average age 27. 74 applicants, 19% accepted, 9 enrolled. In 2011, 3 master's, 3 doctorates awarded. *Degree requirements:* For master's, thesis (MS); for doctorate, comprehensive exam, thesis/dissertation. *Entrance requirements:*

For master's and doctorate, GRE General Test, 3 letters of recommendation. Additional exam requirements/recommendations for international students: Required—TOEFL (minimum score 550 paper-based; 213 computer-based; 77 iBT). *Application deadline:* For fall admission, 1/15 priority date for domestic students. Applications are processed on a rolling basis. Application fee: $95. Electronic applications accepted. *Financial support:* In 2011–12, 25 students received support, including 7 fellowships with full tuition reimbursements available, 19 research assistantships with full tuition reimbursements available, 8 teaching assistantships with full tuition reimbursements available; institutionally sponsored loans, scholarships/grants, health care benefits, tuition waivers (full and partial), and unspecified assistantships also available. Financial award applicants required to submit FAFSA. *Faculty research:* Geophysics, structural geology, petrology, geochemistry, geodynamics. *Unit head:* Director of Graduate Studies, 607-255-5466, Fax: 607-254-4780. *Application contact:* Graduate Field Assistant, 607-255-5466, Fax: 607-254-4780, E-mail: gradprog@geology.cornell.edu. Web site: http://www.gradschool.cornell.edu/fields.php?id-30&a-2.

Drexel University, College of Engineering, Department of Civil, Architectural, and Environmental Engineering, Philadelphia, PA 19104-2875. Offers architectural / building systems engineering (PhD); architectural/building systems engineering (MS); civil engineering (MS, PhD); environmental engineering (MS, PhD); geotechnical, geoenvironmental and geosynthetics engineering (MS, PhD); hydraulics, hydrology and water resources engineering (MS, PhD); structures (MS). Part-time and evening/weekend programs available. *Degree requirements:* For master's, thesis optional; for doctorate, thesis/dissertation. *Entrance requirements:* For master's, minimum GPA of 3.0; for doctorate, minimum GPA of 3.5, MS in civil engineering. Additional exam requirements/recommendations for international students: Required—TOEFL. Electronic applications accepted. *Faculty research:* Structural dynamics, hazardous wastes, water resources, pavement materials, groundwater.

Idaho State University, Office of Graduate Studies, College of Science and Engineering, Department of Geosciences, Pocatello, ID 83209-8072. Offers geographic information science (MS); geology (MNS, MS); geology with emphasis in environmental geoscience (MS); geophysics/hydrology/geology (MS); geotechnology (Postbaccalaureate Certificate). Part-time programs available. *Degree requirements:* For master's, comprehensive exam, thesis, oral colloquium; for Postbaccalaureate Certificate, thesis optional, minimum 19 credits. *Entrance requirements:* For master's, GRE General Test (minimum 50th percentile in 2 sections), 3 letters of recommendation; for Postbaccalaureate Certificate, GRE General Test, 3 letters of recommendation, bachelor's degree, statement of goals. Additional exam requirements/recommendations for international students: Required—TOEFL (minimum score 550 paper-based; 213 computer-based; 80 iBT). Electronic applications accepted. *Faculty research:* Quantitative field mapping and sampling: microscopic, geochemical, and isotopic analysis of rocks, minerals and water; remote sensing, geographic information systems, and global positioning systems: environmental and watershed management; surficial and fluvial processes: landscape change; regional tectonics, structural geology; planetary geology.

Illinois State University, Graduate School, College of Arts and Sciences, Department of Geography-Geology, Normal, IL 61790-2200. Offers hydrogeology (MS). *Degree requirements:* For master's, thesis optional. *Entrance requirements:* For master's, GRE General Test. *Faculty research:* Thermal transport within the hyporheic zone, nutrient cycling in watersheds, water quality in karst systems, ground water dating using dissolved helium.

Massachusetts Institute of Technology, School of Engineering, Department of Civil and Environmental Engineering, Cambridge, MA 02139. Offers biological oceanography (PhD, Sc D); chemical oceanography (PhD, Sc D); civil and environmental engineering (PhD, Sc D); civil and environmental systems (PhD, Sc D); civil engineering (PhD, Sc D, CE); coastal engineering (PhD, Sc D); construction engineering and management (PhD, Sc D); environmental and water quality engineering (M Eng); environmental biology (PhD, Sc D); environmental chemistry (PhD, Sc D); environmental engineering (PhD, Sc D); environmental fluid mechanics (PhD, Sc D); environmental science and engineering (SM); geotechnical and geoenvironmental engineering (PhD, Sc D); geotechnology (M Eng); high-performance structures (M Eng); hydrology (PhD, Sc D); information technology (PhD, Sc D); mechanics (SM); oceanographic engineering (PhD, Sc D); structures and materials (PhD, Sc D); transportation (M Eng, PhD, Sc D); SM/MBA. *Faculty:* 35 full-time (6 women), 1 part-time/adjunct (0 women). *Students:* 216 full-time (80 women); includes 30 minority (4 Black or African American, non-Hispanic/Latino; 13 Asian, non-Hispanic/Latino; 8 Hispanic/Latino; 5 Two or more races, non-Hispanic/Latino), 110 international. Average age 27. 589 applicants, 26% accepted, 91 enrolled. In 2011, 62 master's, 14 doctorates awarded. *Degree requirements:* For master's and CE, thesis; for doctorate, comprehensive exam, thesis/dissertation. *Entrance requirements:* For master's and doctorate, GRE General Test. Additional exam requirements/recommendations for international students: Required—TOEFL (minimum score 577 paper-based; 233 computer-based; 90 iBT), IELTS (minimum score 7). *Application deadline:* For fall admission, 12/15 for domestic and international students. Application fee: $75. Electronic applications accepted. *Expenses:* Tuition: Full-time $40,460; part-time $630 per credit hour. *Required fees:* $272. *Financial support:* In 2011–12, 180 students received support, including 51 fellowships (averaging $30,800 per year), 110 research assistantships (averaging $29,500 per year), 19 teaching assistantships (averaging $29,500 per year);

Peterson's Graduate Programs in the Physical Sciences, Mathematics, Agricultural Sciences, the Environment & Natural Resources 2013

facebook.com/petersonspublishing **179**

career-related internships or fieldwork, Federal Work-Study, institutionally sponsored loans, scholarships/grants, health care benefits, and unspecified assistantships also available. *Faculty research:* Environmental chemistry, environmental fluid mechanics and coastal engineering, environmental microbiology, geotechnical engineering and geomechanics, hydrology and hydroclimatology, infrastructure systems, mechanics of materials and structures, transportation systems. *Total annual research expenditures:* $17.7 million. *Unit head:* Prof. Andrew Whittle, Head, 617-253-7101. *Application contact:* Patricia Glidden, Graduate Admissions Coordinator, 617-253-7119, Fax: 617-258-6775, E-mail: cee-admissions@mit.edu. Web site: http://cee.mit.edu/.

Missouri University of Science and Technology, Graduate School, Department of Civil, Architectural, and Environmental Engineering, Rolla, MO 65409. Offers civil engineering (MS, DE, PhD); construction engineering (MS, DE, PhD); environmental engineering (MS); fluid mechanics (MS, DE, PhD); geotechnical engineering (MS, DE, PhD); hydrology and hydraulic engineering (MS, DE, PhD). Part-time and evening/weekend programs available. Terminal master's awarded for partial completion of doctoral program. *Degree requirements:* For master's, thesis optional; for doctorate, comprehensive exam, thesis/dissertation. *Entrance requirements:* For master's, GRE General Test (minimum combined score 1100), minimum GPA of 3.0; for doctorate, GRE General Test (minimum score: verbal and quantitative 400, writing 3.5), minimum GPA of 3.0. Additional exam requirements/recommendations for international students: Required—TOEFL. Electronic applications accepted. *Faculty research:* Earthquake engineering, structural optimization and control systems, structural health monitoring/damage detection, soil-structure interaction, soil mechanics and foundation engineering.

Murray State University, College of Science, Engineering and Technology, Program in Water Science, Murray, KY 42071. Offers MS. Part-time programs available. *Degree requirements:* For master's, comprehensive exam, thesis. *Entrance requirements:* For master's, GRE General Test. Electronic applications accepted. *Faculty research:* Water chemistry, GIS, amphibian biology, nutrient chemistry, limnology.

New Mexico Institute of Mining and Technology, Graduate Studies, Department of Earth and Environmental Science, Program in Hydrology, Socorro, NM 87801. Offers MS, PhD. *Students:* 18 full-time (10 women), 10 part-time (4 women); includes 6 minority (1 Black or African American, non-Hispanic/Latino; 1 Asian, non-Hispanic/Latino; 2 Hispanic/Latino; 2 Two or more races, non-Hispanic/Latino), 1 international. Average age 29. In 2011, 2 degrees awarded. *Degree requirements:* For master's, thesis; for doctorate, thesis/dissertation. *Entrance requirements:* For master's, GRE General Test; for doctorate, GRE General Test, GRE Subject Test. Additional exam requirements/ recommendations for international students: Required—TOEFL (minimum score 540 paper-based; 207 computer-based). *Application deadline:* For fall admission, 3/1 priority date for domestic students; for spring admission, 6/1 for domestic students. Applications are processed on a rolling basis. Application fee: $16 ($30 for international students). *Expenses:* Tuition, state resident: full-time $4849; part-time $269.41 per credit hour. Tuition, nonresident: full-time $16,041; part-time $891.15 per credit hour. *Required fees:* $622; $65 per credit hour. $20 per semester. Part-time tuition and fees vary according to course load. *Financial support:* Federal Work-Study, institutionally sponsored loans, and unspecified assistantships available. Financial award application deadline: 3/1; financial award applicants required to submit CSS PROFILE or FAFSA. *Faculty research:* Surface and subsurface hydrology, numerical simulation, stochastic hydrology, water quality, modeling. *Unit head:* Dr. Fred Phillips, Coordinator, 575-835-5540, Fax: 575-835-6436, E-mail: phillips@nmt.edu. *Application contact:* Dr. Lorie Liebrock, Dean of Graduate Studies, 575-835-5513, Fax: 575-835-5476, E-mail: graduate@nmt.edu.

New Mexico State University, Graduate School, College of Agricultural, Consumer and Environmental Sciences, Department of Agricultural Economics and Agricultural Business, Las Cruces, NM 88003-8001. Offers agribusiness (M Ag, MBA); agricultural economics (MS); economic development (DED); economics (MA); water science management (MS). Part-time programs available. *Faculty:* 10 full-time (2 women). *Students:* 12 full-time (7 women), 4 part-time (3 women); includes 3 minority (1 Asian, non-Hispanic/Latino; 2 Hispanic/Latino), 3 international. Average age 27. 9 applicants, 44% accepted, 2 enrolled. In 2011, 5 master's awarded. *Degree requirements:* For master's, thesis (for some programs); for doctorate, comprehensive exam, thesis/dissertation. *Entrance requirements:* For master's, previous course work in intermediate microeconomics, intermediate macroeconomics, college-level calculus, statistics; for doctorate, previous course work in intermediate microeconomics, intermediate macroeconomics, college-level calculus, statistics, related MS or equivalent, minimum GPA of 3.0. Additional exam requirements/recommendations for international students: Required—TOEFL (minimum score 550 paper-based; 0 computer-based; 79 iBT), IELTS (minimum score 6.5). *Application deadline:* For fall admission, 7/1 priority date for domestic students, 7/1 for international students; for spring admission, 11/1 priority date for domestic students, 11/1 for international students. Applications are processed on a rolling basis. Application fee: $40 ($50 for international students). Electronic applications accepted. *Expenses:* Tuition, state resident: full-time $5004; part-time $208.50 per credit. Tuition, nonresident: full-time $17,446; part-time $726.90 per credit. *Financial support:* In 2011–12, 4 research assistantships (averaging $22,698 per year), 4 teaching assistantships (averaging $15,108 per year) were awarded; career-related internships or fieldwork, Federal Work-Study, scholarships/grants,

traineeships, health care benefits, and unspecified assistantships also available. Support available to part-time students. Financial award application deadline: 3/1. *Faculty research:* Natural resource policy, production economics and farm/ranch management, agribusiness and marketing, international marketing and trade, agricultural risk management. *Unit head:* Dr. Terry Crawford, Head, 575-646-3215, Fax: 575-646-3808, E-mail: crawford@nmsu.edu. *Application contact:* Dr. L. Allen Torell, Professor, 575-646-4732, Fax: 575-646-3808, E-mail: atorell@nmsu.edu. Web site: http://aces.nmsu.edu/academics/aeab/.

Stevens Institute of Technology, Graduate School, Charles V. Schaefer Jr. School of Engineering, Department of Civil, Environmental, and Ocean Engineering, Program in Civil Engineering, Hoboken, NJ 07030. Offers civil engineering (PhD); geotechnical engineering (Certificate); geotechnical/geoenvironmental engineering (M Eng, Engr); hydrologic modeling (M Eng); stormwater management (M Eng); structural engineering (M Eng, Engr); water resources engineering (M Eng). *Degree requirements:* For master's, thesis optional; for doctorate, variable foreign language requirement, thesis/dissertation; for other advanced degree, project or thesis. *Entrance requirements:* For doctorate, GRE. Additional exam requirements/recommendations for international students: Required—TOEFL. Electronic applications accepted.

Université du Québec, Institut National de la Recherche Scientifique, Graduate Programs, Research Center—Water, Earth and Environment, Québec, QC G1K 9A9, Canada. Offers earth sciences (M Sc, PhD); earth sciences-environmental technologies (M Sc); water sciences (M Sc, PhD). Part-time programs available. *Faculty:* 40. *Students:* 204 full-time (88 women), 23 part-time (12 women), 103 international. Average age 30. In 2011, 31 master's, 12 doctorates awarded. *Degree requirements:* For master's, thesis optional; for doctorate, thesis/dissertation. *Entrance requirements:* For master's, appropriate bachelor's degree, proficiency in French; for doctorate, appropriate master's degree, proficiency in French. *Application deadline:* For fall admission, 3/30 for domestic and international students; for winter admission, 11/1 for domestic and international students; for spring admission, 3/1 for domestic and international students. Application fee: $45. Electronic applications accepted. *Financial support:* In 2011–12, 184 students received support, including fellowships (averaging $16,500 per year); research assistantships also available. *Faculty research:* Land use, impacts of climate change, adaptation to climate change, integrated management of resources (mineral and water). *Unit head:* Yves Begin, Director, 418-654-2524, Fax: 418-654-2600, E-mail: yves.begin@ete.inrs.ca. *Application contact:* Yvonne Boisvert, Registrar, 418-654-3861, Fax: 418-654-3858, E-mail: registrariat@adm.inrs.ca. Web site: http://www.ete.inrs.ca/.

The University of Arizona, College of Science, Department of Hydrology and Water Resources, Tucson, AZ 85721. Offers MS, PhD. Part-time programs available. *Faculty:* 15 full-time (1 woman). *Students:* 45 full-time (12 women), 8 part-time (1 woman); includes 9 minority (1 American Indian or Alaska Native, non-Hispanic/Latino; 1 Asian, non-Hispanic/Latino; 4 Hispanic/Latino; 3 Two or more races, non-Hispanic/Latino), 12 international. Average age 31. 66 applicants, 14% accepted, 9 enrolled. In 2011, 7 master's, 5 doctorates awarded. *Degree requirements:* For master's, thesis; for doctorate, thesis/dissertation. *Entrance requirements:* For master's, GRE General Test, 3 letters of recommendation, bachelor's degree in related field; for doctorate, GRE General Test, minimum undergraduate GPA of 3.2, graduate 3.4; 3 letters of recommendation; master's degree in related field; master's thesis abstract. Additional exam requirements/recommendations for international students: Required—TOEFL (minimum score 550 paper-based; 213 computer-based; 79 iBT). *Application deadline:* For fall admission, 5/1 for domestic students, 12/1 for international students; for spring admission, 10/1 for domestic students, 6/1 for international students. Applications are processed on a rolling basis. Application fee: $75. Electronic applications accepted. *Expenses:* Tuition, state resident: full-time $10,840. Tuition, nonresident: full-time $25,802. *Financial support:* In 2011–12, 21 research assistantships with full tuition reimbursements (averaging $23,223 per year), 5 teaching assistantships with full tuition reimbursements (averaging $23,586 per year) were awarded; institutionally sponsored loans, scholarships/grants, health care benefits, and unspecified assistantships also available. Financial award application deadline: 1/31. *Faculty research:* Subsurface and surface hydrology, hydrometeorology/climatology, applied remote sensing, water resource systems, environmental hydrology and water quality. *Total annual research expenditures:* $1.2 million. *Unit head:* Dr. Kevin Lansey, Department Head, 520-621-7120, E-mail: lansey@email.arizona.edu. *Application contact:* Terrie Thompson, Academic Advising Coordinator, 520-621-3131, Fax: 520-621-1422, E-mail: programs@hwr.arizona.edu. Web site: http://www.hwr.arizona.edu/.

University of California, Davis, Graduate Studies, Graduate Group in Hydrologic Sciences, Davis, CA 95616. Offers MS, PhD. Terminal master's awarded for partial completion of doctoral program. *Degree requirements:* For master's, comprehensive exam (for some programs), thesis (for some programs); for doctorate, thesis/dissertation. *Entrance requirements:* For master's, GRE General Test, minimum GPA of 3.0; for doctorate, GRE. Additional exam requirements/recommendations for international students: Required—TOEFL (minimum score 550 paper-based; 213 computer-based). Electronic applications accepted. *Faculty research:* Pollutant transport in surface and subsurface waters, subsurface heterogeneity, micrometeorology evaporation, biodegradation.

University of Colorado Boulder, Graduate School, College of Engineering and Applied Science, Department of Civil, Environmental, and Architectural Engineering, Boulder, CO 80309. Offers building systems (MS, PhD); construction

180 facebook.com/petersonspublishing

Peterson's Graduate Programs in the Physical Sciences, Mathematics, Agricultural Sciences, the Environment & Natural Resources 2013

engineering management (MS, PhD); environmental engineering (MS, PhD); geotechnical engineering and geomechanics (MS, PhD); hydrology, water resources and environmental fluid mechanics (MS, PhD); structural engineering and structural mechanics (MS, PhD). *Faculty:* 37 full-time (8 women). *Students:* 245 full-time (90 women), 53 part-time (15 women); includes 37 minority (1 Black or African American, non-Hispanic/Latino; 2 American Indian or Alaska Native, non-Hispanic/Latino; 15 Asian, non-Hispanic/Latino; 17 Hispanic/Latino; 2 Two or more races, non-Hispanic/Latino), 56 international. Average age 27. 483 applicants, 58% accepted, 83 enrolled. In 2011, 84 master's, 15 doctorates awarded. Terminal master's awarded for partial completion of doctoral program. *Degree requirements:* For master's, comprehensive exam, thesis or alternative; for doctorate, thesis/dissertation. *Entrance requirements:* For master's, GRE General Test, minimum undergraduate GPA of 3.0. *Application deadline:* For fall admission, 3/1 for domestic students, 12/1 for international students; for spring admission, 10/31 for domestic students, 10/1 for international students. Application fee: $50 ($60 for international students). Electronic applications accepted. *Financial support:* In 2011–12, 167 students received support, including 69 fellowships (averaging $12,440 per year), 62 research assistantships with full and partial tuition reimbursements available (averaging $21,979 per year), 20 teaching assistantships with full and partial tuition reimbursements available (averaging $19,877 per year); institutionally sponsored loans, scholarships/grants, health care benefits, and unspecified assistantships also available. Financial award application deadline: 1/15; financial award applicants required to submit FAFSA. *Faculty research:* Building systems engineering, construction engineering and management, environmental engineering, geoenvironmental engineering, geotechnical engineering, materials and mechanics, structural engineering, water resources engineering, life-cycle engineering. *Total annual research expenditures:* $10.9 million. *Application contact:* E-mail: cvengrad@colorado.edu. Web site: http://ceae.colorado.edu/new/.

University of Colorado Denver, College of Engineering and Applied Science, Department of Civil Engineering, Denver, CO 80217. Offers civil engineering (EASPh D); civil engineering systems (PhD); environmental and sustainability engineering (MS, PhD); geographic information systems (MS); geotechnical engineering (MS, PhD); hydrology and hydraulics (MS, PhD); structural engineering (MS, PhD); transportation engineering (MS, PhD). Part-time and evening/weekend programs available. *Faculty:* 14 full-time (1 woman), 6 part-time/adjunct (0 women). *Students:* 66 full-time (11 women), 65 part-time (14 women); includes 30 minority (10 Black or African American, non-Hispanic/Latino; 8 Asian, non-Hispanic/Latino; 10 Hispanic/Latino; 2 Two or more races, non-Hispanic/Latino), 17 international. Average age 34. 49 applicants, 54% accepted, 24 enrolled. In 2011, 30 master's, 2 doctorates awarded. *Degree requirements:* For master's, comprehensive exam, thesis or alternative, 30 credit hours, project or thesis; for doctorate, comprehensive exam, thesis/dissertation, 60 credit hours (30 of which are dissertation research). *Entrance requirements:* For master's, GRE, statement of purpose, transcripts, three references; for doctorate, GRE, statement of purpose, transcripts, references, letter of support from faculty stating willingness to serve as dissertation advisor and outlining plan for financial support. Additional exam requirements/recommendations for international students: Required—TOEFL (minimum score 525 paper-based; 197 computer-based). *Application deadline:* For fall admission, 7/15 for domestic students, 6/15 for international students; for spring admission, 12/1 for domestic students, 11/1 for international students. Applications are processed on a rolling basis. Application fee: $50 ($75 for international students). Electronic applications accepted. *Expenses:* Contact institution. *Financial support:* Research assistantships, teaching assistantships, career-related internships or fieldwork, and Federal Work-Study available. Financial award application deadline: 4/1; financial award applicants required to submit FAFSA. *Faculty research:* Earthquake source physics, environmental biotechnology, hydrologic and hydraulic engineering, sustainability assessments, transportation energy use and greenhouse gas emissions. *Unit head:* Dr. Kevin Rens, Chair, 303-556-8017, Fax: 303-556-2368, E-mail: kevin.rens@ucdenver.edu. *Application contact:* Maria Rase, Program Assistant, 303-556-6712, Fax: 303-556-2368, E-mail: maria.rase@ucdenver.edu. Web site: http://www.ucdenver.edu/academics/colleges/Engineering/Programs/Civil-Engineering/Pages/CivilEngineering.aspx.

University of Florida, Graduate School, College of Liberal Arts and Sciences, Department of Geological Sciences, Gainesville, FL 32611. Offers hydrologic sciences (MS, MST, PhD); tropical conservation and development (MS, MST, PhD); wetland sciences (MS, MST, PhD). *Faculty:* 17 full-time (3 women). *Students:* 38 full-time (17 women), 3 part-time (2 women); includes 1 minority (Hispanic/Latino), 11 international. Average age 30. 63 applicants, 32% accepted, 11 enrolled. In 2011, 6 master's, 2 doctorates awarded. Terminal master's awarded for partial completion of doctoral program. *Degree requirements:* For master's, thesis (for some programs); for doctorate, one foreign language, thesis/dissertation. *Entrance requirements:* For master's, GRE General Test (minimum score of 1000), minimum GPA of 3.0; for doctorate, GRE General Test (minimum score of 1100), minimum GPA of 3.0. Additional exam requirements/recommendations for international students: Required—TOEFL (minimum score 550 paper-based; 213 computer-based; 80 iBT), IELTS (minimum score 6). *Application deadline:* For fall admission, 1/15 for domestic students; for spring admission, 10/1 for domestic students. Applications are processed on a rolling basis. Application fee: $30. Electronic applications accepted. *Financial support:* In 2011–12, 4 fellowships with full tuition reimbursements, 19 research assistantships with full tuition reimbursements (averaging $16,810 per year), 16

teaching assistantships with full tuition reimbursements (averaging $15,290 per year) were awarded; career-related internships or fieldwork, Federal Work-Study, institutionally sponsored loans, and scholarships/grants also available. Support available to part-time students. Financial award application deadline: 3/1; financial award applicants required to submit FAFSA. *Faculty research:* Paleoclimatology, tectonophysics, petrochemistry, marine geology, geochemistry, hydrology. *Unit head:* Dr. Michael R. Perfit, Chair, 352-392-2231, Fax: 352-392-9294, E-mail: mperfit@ufl.edu. *Application contact:* Dr. John Jaeger, Graduate Coordinator, 352-392-2231, Fax: 352-392-9294, E-mail: jmjaeger@ufl.edu. Web site: http://web.geology.ufl.edu/.

University of Idaho, College of Graduate Studies, College of Science, Department of Geological Sciences, Program in Hydrology, Moscow, ID 83844-2282. Offers MS. *Students:* 1 full-time, 4 part-time. Average age 27. In 2011, 1 master's awarded. *Entrance requirements:* For master's, minimum GPA of 2.8. *Application deadline:* For fall admission, 8/1 for domestic students; for spring admission, 12/15 for domestic students. Applications are processed on a rolling basis. Application fee: $60. Electronic applications accepted. *Expenses:* Tuition, state resident: full-time $3874; part-time $334 per credit hour. Tuition, nonresident: full-time $16,394; part-time $861 per credit hour. *Required fees:* $2808; $99 per credit hour. Tuition and fees vary according to program. *Financial support:* Applicants required to submit FAFSA. *Unit head:* Dr. Mickey Gunter, Head, 208-885-6491. *Application contact:* Erick Larson, Director of Graduate Admissions, 208-885-4723, E-mail: gadms@uidaho.edu. Web site: http://www.uidaho.edu/sci/geology/academics/graduateprogram.

University of Nevada, Reno, Graduate School, Interdisciplinary Program in Hydrologic Sciences, Reno, NV 89557. Offers hydrogeology (MS, PhD); hydrology (MS, PhD). Offered through the M. C. Fleischmann College of Agriculture, the College of Engineering, the Mackay School of Mines, and the Desert Research Institute. Terminal master's awarded for partial completion of doctoral program. *Degree requirements:* For master's, thesis optional; for doctorate, thesis/dissertation. *Entrance requirements:* For master's and doctorate, GRE General Test, minimum GPA of 3.0. Additional exam requirements/recommendations for international students: Required—TOEFL (minimum score 500 paper-based; 173 computer-based; 61 iBT), IELTS (minimum score 6). Electronic applications accepted. *Faculty research:* Groundwater, water resources, surface water, soil science.

University of New Brunswick Fredericton, School of Graduate Studies, Faculty of Engineering, Department of Civil Engineering, Fredericton, NB E3B 5A3, Canada. Offers construction engineering and management (M Eng, M Sc E, PhD); environmental engineering (M Eng, M Sc E, PhD); environmental studies (M Eng); geotechnical engineering (M Eng, M Sc E, PhD); groundwater/hydrology (M Eng, M Sc E, PhD); materials (M Eng, M Sc E, PhD); pavements (M Eng, M Sc E, PhD); structures (M Eng, M Sc E, PhD); transportation (M Eng, M Sc E, PhD). Part-time programs available. *Faculty:* 13 full-time (1 woman), 7 part-time/adjunct (1 woman). *Students:* 31 full-time (7 women), 17 part-time (2 women). In 2011, 11 master's, 2 doctorates awarded. *Degree requirements:* For master's, thesis, proposal; for doctorate, comprehensive exam, thesis/dissertation, qualifying exam; proposal; 27 credit hours of courses. *Entrance requirements:* For master's, minimum GPA of 3.0; B Sc E in civil engineering or related engineering degree; for doctorate, minimum GPA of 3.0; graduate degree in engineering or applied science. Additional exam requirements/recommendations for international students: Required—TWE (minimum score 4), TOEFL (minimum score 580 paper-based; 237 computer-based) or IELTS (minimum score 7.5). *Application deadline:* For fall admission, 5/1 priority date for domestic students; for winter admission, 11/1 priority date for domestic students. Applications are processed on a rolling basis. Application fee: $50 Canadian dollars. *Financial support:* In 2011–12, 14 fellowships, 30 research assistantships (averaging $7,000 per year), 42 teaching assistantships (averaging $2,000 per year) were awarded; career-related internships or fieldwork and scholarships/grants also available. *Faculty research:* Construction engineering and management; materials and infrastructure renewal; highway and pavement research; structures and solid mechanics; geotechnical, soil; structure interaction; transportation and planning; environment, solid waste management. *Unit head:* Dr. Eric Hildebrand, Director of Graduate Studies, 506-453-5113, Fax: 506-453-3568, E-mail: edh@unb.ca. *Application contact:* Joyce Moore, Graduate Secretary, 506-452-6127, Fax: 506-453-3568, E-mail: civil-grad@unb.ca. Web site: http://www.unbf.ca/eng/civil/.

University of New Hampshire, Graduate School, College of Engineering and Physical Sciences, Department of Earth Sciences, Durham, NH 03824. Offers geology (MS); hydrology (MS). *Faculty:* 17 full-time (5 women). *Students:* 21 full-time (11 women), 13 part-time (6 women); includes 3 minority (2 Black or African American, non-Hispanic/Latino; 1 Asian, non-Hispanic/Latino), 5 international. Average age 27. 60 applicants, 58% accepted, 12 enrolled. In 2011, 10 master's awarded. *Degree requirements:* For master's, thesis. *Entrance requirements:* For master's, GRE General Test. Additional exam requirements/recommendations for international students: Required—TOEFL (minimum score 550 paper-based; 213 computer-based; 80 iBT). *Application deadline:* For fall admission, 4/1 priority date for domestic students, 4/1 for international students; for spring admission, 12/1 for domestic students. Applications are processed on a rolling basis. Application fee: $65. Electronic applications accepted. *Expenses:* Tuition, state resident: full-time $12,360; part-time $687 per credit hour. Tuition, nonresident: full-time $25,680; part-time $1058 per credit hour. *International tuition:* $29,550 full-time. *Required fees:* $1666; $833 per course. $416.50 per semester. Tuition and fees vary according to course load and degree level. *Financial support:* In

Peterson's Graduate Programs in the Physical Sciences, Mathematics, Agricultural Sciences, the Environment & Natural Resources 2013

facebook.com/petersonspublishing **181**

Hydrology

2011–12, 24 students received support, including 12 research assistantships, 8 teaching assistantships; fellowships, career-related internships or fieldwork, Federal Work-Study, scholarships/grants, and tuition waivers (full and partial) also available. Support available to part-time students. Financial award application deadline: 2/15. *Unit head:* Dr. Will Clyde, Chairperson, 603-862-1718, E-mail: earth.sciences@unh.edu. *Application contact:* Sue Clark, Administrative Assistant, 603-862-1718, E-mail: earth.sciences@unh.edu. Web site: http://www.unh.edu/esci/.

University of Southern Mississippi, Graduate School, College of Science and Technology, Department of Marine Science, Stennis Space Center, MS 39529. Offers hydrographic science (MS); marine science (MS, PhD). Part-time programs available. *Faculty:* 18 full-time (2 women). *Students:* 38 full-time (15 women), 13 part-time (4 women); includes 20 minority (4 Black or African American, non-Hispanic/Latino; 13 Asian, non-Hispanic/Latino; 3 Hispanic/Latino). Average age 31. 47 applicants, 57% accepted, 19 enrolled. In 2011, 15 master's, 1 doctorate awarded. *Degree requirements:* For master's, comprehensive exam, thesis, oral qualifying exam (marine science); for doctorate, 2 foreign languages, comprehensive exam, thesis/dissertation, oral qualifying exam. *Entrance requirements:* For master's, GRE General Test, minimum GPA of 3.0; for doctorate, GRE General Test, minimum GPA of 3.0 (undergraduate), 3.5 (graduate). Additional exam requirements/recommendations for international students: Required—TOEFL. *Application deadline:* For fall admission, 3/1 priority date for domestic students, 3/1 for international students. Application fee: $50. Electronic applications accepted. *Financial support:* In 2011–12, 4 students received support, including 35 research assistantships with full tuition reimbursements available (averaging $20,400 per year), 2 teaching assistantships with full tuition reimbursements available (averaging $20,400 per year); Federal Work-Study and institutionally sponsored loans also available. Financial award application deadline: 3/15. *Faculty research:* Chemical, biological, physical, and geological marine science; remote sensing; bio-optics; numerical modeling; hydrography. *Total annual research expenditures:* $7.1 million. *Unit head:* Dr. William M. Graham, Chair and Professor, 228-688-3177, Fax: 228-688-1121, E-mail: marine.science@usm.edu. *Application contact:* Linda Downs, Senior Office Support Specialist, 228-688-3177, Fax: 228-688-1121, E-mail: marine.science@usm.edu. Web site: http://www.usm.edu/marine/.

University of Washington, Graduate School, College of Engineering, Department of Civil and Environmental Engineering, Seattle, WA 98195-2700. Offers civil engineering (MS, MSE, PhD); construction engineering (MSCE); environmental engineering (MS, MSCE, MSE, PhD); global trade, transportation and logistics (MS); hydrology, water resources, and environmental fluid mechanics (MS, MSCE, MSE, PhD); structural and geotechnical engineering and mechanics (MS, MSCE, MSE, PhD); transportation and construction engineering (MS, MSE, PhD); transportation engineering (MSCE). Part-time programs available. Postbaccalaureate distance learning degree programs offered (no on-campus study). *Faculty:* 47 full-time (11 women), 9 part-time/adjunct (1 woman). *Students:* 195 full-time (67 women), 72 part-time (19 women); includes 37 minority (4 Black or African American, non-Hispanic/Latino; 27 Asian, non-Hispanic/Latino; 6 Hispanic/Latino), 65 international. 654 applicants, 57% accepted, 100 enrolled. In 2011, 88 master's, 7 doctorates awarded. Terminal master's awarded for partial completion of doctoral program. *Degree requirements:* For master's, thesis (for some programs); for doctorate, comprehensive exam, thesis/dissertation, general, qualifying, and final exams; completion of degree within 10 years. *Entrance requirements:* For master's, GRE General Test, minimum GPA of 3.0, statement of purpose, letters of recommendation, transcripts; for doctorate, GRE General Test, minimum GPA of 3.5, statement of purpose, letters of recommendation, transcripts. Additional exam requirements/recommendations for international students: Required—TOEFL (minimum score 580 paper-based; 237 computer-based; 92 iBT); Recommended—IELTS (minimum score 7). *Application deadline:* For fall admission, 1/10 priority date for domestic students, 1/10 for international students. Applications are processed on a rolling basis. Application fee: $75. Electronic applications accepted. *Expenses:* Contact institution. *Financial support:* In 2011–12, 99 students received support, including 16 fellowships with full and partial tuition reimbursements available (averaging $16,173 per year), 71 research assistantships with full tuition reimbursements available (averaging $16,380 per year), 10 teaching assistantships with full tuition reimbursements available (averaging $16,380 per year); scholarships/grants also available. Financial award application deadline: 1/10; financial award applicants required to submit FAFSA. *Faculty research:* Environmental/water resources, hydrology; construction/transportation; structures/ geotechnical. *Total annual research expenditures:* $13.6 million. *Unit head:* Dr. Gregory R. Miller, Professor/Chair, 206-543-0350, Fax: 206-543-1543, E-mail: gmiller@uw.edu. *Application contact:* Lorna Latal, Graduate Adviser, 206-543-2574, Fax: 206-543-1543, E-mail: llatal@u.washington.edu. Web site: http://www.ce.washington.edu/programs/prospective/grad/applying/gen_admission.html.

Virginia Polytechnic Institute and State University, Graduate School, College of Engineering, Department of Civil and Environmental Engineering, Blacksburg, VA 24061. Offers civil engineering (M Eng, MS, PhD); civil infrastructure systems (Certificate); environmental engineering (MS); environmental sciences and engineering (MS); transportation systems engineering (Certificate); treatment process engineering (Certificate); urban hydrology and stormwater management (Certificate); water quality management (Certificate). *Accreditation:* ABET (one or more programs are accredited). *Degree requirements:* For master's, comprehensive exam (for some programs), thesis (for some programs); for doctorate, comprehensive exam (for some programs), thesis/dissertation (for some programs). *Entrance requirements:* For master's and doctorate, GRE. Additional exam requirements/recommendations for international students: Required—TOEFL (minimum score 550 paper-based; 213 computer-based). *Application deadline:* For fall admission, 7/1 for domestic and international students; for spring admission, 12/1 for domestic and international students. Applications are processed on a rolling basis. Application fee: $65. Electronic applications accepted. *Expenses:* Tuition, state resident: full-time $10,048; part-time $558.25 per credit hour. Tuition, nonresident: full-time $19,497; part-time $1083.25 per credit hour. *Required fees:* $405 per semester. Tuition and fees vary according to course load, campus/location and program. *Financial support:* Fellowships with full tuition reimbursements, research assistantships with full tuition reimbursements, teaching assistantships with full tuition reimbursements, career-related internships or fieldwork, Federal Work-Study, scholarships/grants, health care benefits, and unspecified assistantships available. Financial award application deadline: 1/15. *Faculty research:* Construction, environmental geotechnical hydrosystems, structures and transportation engineering. *Unit head:* Dr. Sam Easterling, Unit Head, 540-231-5143, Fax: 540-231-7532, E-mail: seaster@vt.edu. *Application contact:* Marc Widdowson, Information Contact, 540-231-7153, Fax: 540-231-7532, E-mail: mwiddows@vt.edu. Web site: http://www.cee.vt.edu/.

Limnology

Baylor University, Graduate School, College of Arts and Sciences, Department of Biology, Waco, TX 76798. Offers biology (MA, MS, PhD); environmental biology (MS); limnology (MS). Part-time programs available. *Faculty:* 13 full-time (3 women). *Students:* 37 full-time (19 women), 3 part-time (1 woman); includes 8 minority (3 Asian, non-Hispanic/Latino; 1 Hispanic/Latino; 4 Two or more races, non-Hispanic/Latino), 13 international. In 2011, 5 master's, 3 doctorates awarded. *Degree requirements:* For master's, thesis (for some programs); for doctorate, thesis/dissertation. *Entrance requirements:* For master's and doctorate, GRE General Test. *Application deadline:* For fall admission, 1/31 priority date for domestic students. Applications are processed on a rolling basis. Application fee: $25. *Financial support:* Teaching assistantships, career-related internships or fieldwork, Federal Work-Study, institutionally sponsored loans, and tuition waivers (full and partial) available. Support available to part-time students. Financial award application deadline: 2/28. *Faculty research:* Terrestrial ecology, aquatic ecology, genetics. *Unit head:* Dr. Myeongwoo Lee, Graduate Program Director, 254-710-2141, Fax: 254-710-2969, E-mail: myeongwoo_lee@baylor.edu. *Application contact:* Tamara Lehmann, Administrative Assistant, 254-710-2911, Fax: 254-710-2969, E-mail: tamara_lehmann@baylor.edu. Web site: http://www.baylor.edu/biology/.

Cornell University, Graduate School, Graduate Fields of Agriculture and Life Sciences, Field of Ecology and Evolutionary Biology, Ithaca, NY 14853-0001. Offers ecology (PhD), including animal ecology, applied ecology, biogeochemistry, community and ecosystem ecology, limnology, oceanography, physiological ecology, plant ecology, population ecology, theoretical ecology, vertebrate zoology; evolutionary biology (PhD), including ecological genetics, paleobiology, population biology, systematics. *Faculty:* 51 full-time (14 women). *Students:* 52 full-time (36 women); includes 6 minority (1 Asian, non-Hispanic/Latino; 4 Hispanic/Latino; 1 Two or more races, non-Hispanic/Latino), 10 international. Average age 28. 121 applicants, 9% accepted, 7 enrolled. In 2011, 5 doctorates awarded. *Degree requirements:* For doctorate, comprehensive exam, thesis/dissertation, 2 semesters of teaching experience. *Entrance requirements:* For doctorate, GRE General Test, GRE Subject Test (biology), 2 letters of recommendation. Additional exam requirements/recommendations for international students: Required—TOEFL (minimum score 550 paper-based; 213 computer-based; 77 iBT). *Application deadline:* For fall admission, 12/15 for domestic students. Application fee: $95. Electronic applications accepted. *Financial support:* In 2011–12, 15 fellowships with full tuition reimbursements, 8 research assistantships with full tuition reimbursements, 25 teaching assistantships with full tuition reimbursements were awarded; institutionally sponsored loans, scholarships/grants, health care benefits, tuition waivers (full and partial), and unspecified assistantships also available. Financial award applicants required to submit FAFSA. *Faculty research:* Population and organismal biology, population and evolutionary genetics, systematics and macroevolution, biochemistry, conservation biology. *Unit head:* Director of Graduate Studies, 607-254-4230. *Application contact:* Graduate Field Assistant, 607-254-4230, E-mail: eeb_grad_req@cornell.edu. Web site: http://www.gradschool.cornell.edu/fields.php?id-46&a-2.

182 facebook.com/petersonspublishing

Peterson's Graduate Programs in the Physical Sciences, Mathematics, Agricultural Sciences, the Environment & Natural Resources 2013

University of Alaska Fairbanks, School of Fisheries and Ocean Sciences, Program in Marine Sciences and Limnology, Fairbanks, AK 99775-7220. Offers marine biology (MS, PhD); oceanography (PhD), including biological oceanography, chemical oceanography, fisheries, geological oceanography, physical oceanography. Part-time programs available. *Faculty:* 6 full-time (4 women). *Students:* 40 full-time (29 women), 17 part-time (12 women); includes 7 minority (3 Asian, non-Hispanic/Latino; 4 Hispanic/Latino), 4 international. Average age 30. 61 applicants, 20% accepted, 12 enrolled. In 2011, 3 master's, 3 doctorates awarded. *Degree requirements:* For master's, comprehensive exam, thesis, oral defense; for doctorate, comprehensive exam, thesis/dissertation, oral defense. *Entrance requirements:* For master's and doctorate, GRE General Test. Additional exam requirements/recommendations for international students: Required—TOEFL (minimum score 550 paper-based; 213 computer-based; 80 iBT). *Application deadline:* For fall admission, 6/1 for domestic students, 3/1 for international students; for spring admission, 10/15 for domestic students, 8/1 for international students. Applications are processed on a rolling basis. Application fee: $60. Electronic applications accepted. *Expenses:* Tuition, state resident: full-time $6696; part-time $372 per credit. Tuition, nonresident: full-time $13,680; part-time $760 per credit. Tuition and fees vary according to course load and reciprocity agreements. *Financial support:* In 2011–12, 26 research assistantships with tuition reimbursements (averaging $11,484 per year), 7 teaching assistantships with tuition reimbursements (averaging $14,772 per year) were awarded; fellowships with tuition reimbursements, career-related internships or fieldwork, Federal Work-Study, scholarships/grants, health care benefits, and unspecified assistantships also available. Support available to part-time students. Financial award application deadline: 7/1; financial award applicants required to submit FAFSA. *Unit head:* Katrin Iken, Co-Chair, 907-474-7289, Fax: 907-474-5863, E-mail: academics@sfos.uaf.edu. *Application contact:* Christina Neumann, Academic Manager, 907-474-7289, Fax: 907-474-5863, E-mail: clneumann@alaska.edu. Web site: http://www.sfos.uaf.edu/academics/prospective/graduate.html.

University of Florida, Graduate School, College of Agricultural and Life Sciences, Department of Fisheries and Aquatic Sciences, Gainesville, FL 32611. Offers MFAS, MS, PhD. Part-time programs available. *Students:* 39 full-time (22 women), 16 part-time (4 women); includes 2 minority (1 Asian, non-Hispanic/Latino; 1 Hispanic/Latino), 6 international. Average age 31. 37 applicants, 43% accepted, 12 enrolled. In 2011, 8 master's, 3 doctorates awarded. *Degree requirements:* For master's, thesis (for MS); technical paper (for MFAS); for doctorate, comprehensive exam, thesis/dissertation. *Entrance requirements:* For master's and doctorate, GRE General Test, minimum GPA of 3.0. Additional exam requirements/recommendations for international students: Required—TOEFL (minimum score 550 paper-based; 213 computer-based; 80 iBT), IELTS

(minimum score 6). *Application deadline:* For fall admission, 6/1 for domestic students, 3/1 for international students; for spring admission, 10/1 for domestic students, 8/1 for international students. Applications are processed on a rolling basis. Application fee: $30. Electronic applications accepted. *Financial support:* Fellowships, research assistantships, and unspecified assistantships available. Financial award application deadline: 1/31; financial award applicants required to submit FAFSA. *Faculty research:* Conservation and management of aquatic ecosystems; aquatic animal health; water quality, nutrients, and eutrophication; sustainable and quantitative fisheries; aquaculture or ornamental fish, marine baitfish, and shellfish. *Total annual research expenditures:* $10 million. *Unit head:* Dr. Nancy J. Peterson, Associate Director, 352-846-0848, Fax: 352-846-1277, E-mail: njp@ufl.edu. *Application contact:* Dr. Charles Cichra, Graduate Coordinator, 352-273-3621, Fax: 352-392-3672, E-mail: cecichra@ufl.edu. Web site: http://fishweb.ifas.ufl.edu/.

University of Wisconsin–Madison, Graduate School, College of Engineering, Program in Limnology and Marine Science, Madison, WI 53706. Offers MS, PhD. *Faculty:* 28 full-time (7 women). *Students:* 17 full-time (4 women); includes 1 minority (Hispanic/Latino), 1 international. 41 applicants, 10% accepted, 4 enrolled. In 2011, 1 degree awarded. Terminal master's awarded for partial completion of doctoral program. *Median time to degree:* Of those who began their doctoral program in fall 2003, 100% received their degree in 8 years or less. *Degree requirements:* For master's, thesis; for doctorate, thesis/dissertation. *Entrance requirements:* For master's and doctorate, GRE General Test. Additional exam requirements/recommendations for international students: Required—TOEFL. *Application deadline:* For fall admission, 1/1 priority date for domestic students, 1/1 for international students. Application fee: $45. Electronic applications accepted. *Expenses:* Tuition, state resident: full-time $10,296; part-time $643.51 per credit. Tuition, nonresident: full-time $24,054; part-time $1503.40 per credit. *Required fees:* $70.06 per credit. Tuition and fees vary according to course load, campus/location, program and reciprocity agreements. *Financial support:* In 2011–12, fellowships with full tuition reimbursements (averaging $19,032 per year), 24 research assistantships with full tuition reimbursements (averaging $20,100 per year), 4 teaching assistantships with full tuition reimbursements (averaging $20,100 per year) were awarded; Federal Work-Study and institutionally sponsored loans also available. Financial award application deadline: 1/1. *Faculty research:* Lake ecosystems, ecosystem modeling, geochemistry, physiological ecology, chemical limnology. *Unit head:* Steven Loheide, Chair, 608-263-3264, E-mail: loheide@wisc.edu. *Application contact:* Mary Possin, Student Services Coordinator, 608-263-3264, Fax: 608-265-2340, E-mail: mcpossin@wisc.edu. Web site: http://www.engr.wisc.edu/interd/limnology/.

Marine Geology

Cornell University, Graduate School, Graduate Fields of Engineering, Field of Geological Sciences, Ithaca, NY 14853. Offers economic geology (M Eng, MS, PhD); engineering geology (M Eng, MS, PhD); environmental geophysics (M Eng, MS, PhD); general geology (M Eng, MS, PhD); geobiology (M Eng, MS, PhD); geochemistry and isotope geology (M Eng, MS, PhD); geohydrology (M Eng, MS, PhD); geomorphology (M Eng, MS, PhD); geophysics (M Eng, MS, PhD); geotectonics (M Eng, MS, PhD); marine geology (MS, PhD); mineralogy (M Eng, MS, PhD); paleontology (M Eng, MS, PhD); petroleum geology (M Eng, MS, PhD); petrology (M Eng, MS, PhD); planetary geology (M Eng, MS, PhD); Precambrian geology (M Eng, MS, PhD); Quaternary geology (M Eng, MS, PhD); rock mechanics (M Eng, MS, PhD); sedimentology (M Eng, MS, PhD); seismology (M Eng, MS, PhD); stratigraphy (M Eng, MS, PhD); structural geology (M Eng, MS, PhD). *Faculty:* 37 full-time (5 women). *Students:* 41 full-time (19 women); includes 5 minority (2 Asian, non-Hispanic/Latino; 3 Hispanic/Latino), 7 international. Average age 27. 74 applicants, 19% accepted, 9 enrolled. In 2011, 3 master's, 3 doctorates awarded. *Degree requirements:* For master's, thesis (MS); for doctorate, comprehensive exam, thesis/dissertation. *Entrance requirements:* For master's and doctorate, GRE General Test, 3 letters of recommendation. Additional exam requirements/recommendations for international students: Required—TOEFL (minimum score 550 paper-based; 213 computer-based; 77 iBT). *Application deadline:* For fall admission, 1/15 priority date for domestic students. Applications are processed on a rolling basis. Application fee: $95. Electronic applications accepted. *Financial support:* In 2011–12, 25 students received support, including 7 fellowships with full tuition reimbursements available, 19 research assistantships with full tuition reimbursements available, 8 teaching assistantships with full tuition reimbursements available; institutionally sponsored loans, scholarships/grants, health care benefits, tuition waivers (full and partial), and unspecified assistantships also available. Financial award applicants required to submit FAFSA. *Faculty research:* Geophysics, structural geology, petrology, geochemistry, geodynamics. *Unit head:* Director of Graduate Studies, 607-255-5466, Fax: 607-254-4780. *Application contact:* Graduate Field Assistant, 607-255-5466, Fax: 607-254-4780, E-mail: gradprog@geology.cornell.edu. Web site: http://www.gradschool.cornell.edu/fields.php?id-30&a-2.

Massachusetts Institute of Technology, School of Science, Department of Earth, Atmospheric, and Planetary Sciences, Cambridge, MA 02139. Offers atmospheric chemistry (PhD, Sc D); atmospheric science (SM, PhD, Sc D); chemical oceanography (SM, PhD, Sc D); climate physics and chemistry (SM, PhD, Sc D); earth and planetary sciences (SM); geochemistry (PhD, Sc D); geology (PhD, Sc D); geophysics (PhD, Sc D); marine geology and geophysics (SM, PhD, Sc D); physical oceanography (SM, PhD, Sc D); planetary sciences (PhD, Sc D). *Faculty:* 33 full-time (6 women). *Students:* 175 full-time (81 women); includes 21 minority (3 Black or African American, non-Hispanic/Latino; 1 American Indian or Alaska Native, non-Hispanic/Latino; 8 Asian, non-Hispanic/Latino; 4 Hispanic/Latino; 5 Two or more races, non-Hispanic/Latino), 58 international. Average age 26. 241 applicants, 28% accepted, 43 enrolled. In 2011, 6 master's, 16 doctorates awarded. Terminal master's awarded for partial completion of doctoral program. *Degree requirements:* For master's, thesis; for doctorate, comprehensive exam, thesis/dissertation. *Entrance requirements:* For master's, GRE General Test; for doctorate, GRE General Test, GRE Subject Test (chemistry or physics for planetary science area). Additional exam requirements/recommendations for international students: Required—TOEFL (minimum score 577 paper-based; 233 computer-based; 91 iBT), IELTS (minimum score 7). *Application deadline:* For fall admission, 1/5 for domestic and international students; for spring admission, 11/1 for domestic and international students. Application fee: $75. Electronic applications accepted. *Expenses:* Tuition: Full-time $40,460; part-time $630 per credit hour. *Required fees:* $272. *Financial support:* In 2011–12, 125 students received support, including 68 fellowships (averaging $32,200 per year), 94 research assistantships (averaging $31,900 per year), 10 teaching assistantships (averaging $30,000 per year); Federal Work-Study, institutionally sponsored loans, scholarships/grants, health care benefits, and unspecified assistantships also available. *Faculty research:* Formation, dynamics and evolution of planetary systems; origin, composition, structure and dynamics of the atmospheres, oceans, surfaces and interiors of the Earth and other planets; evolution and interaction of the physical, chemical, geological and biological components of the Earth system; characterization of past, present and potential future climates and the causes and consequences of climate change; interplay of energy and the environment. *Total annual research expenditures:*

Peterson's Graduate Programs in the Physical Sciences, Mathematics, Agricultural Sciences, the Environment & Natural Resources 2013

facebook.com/petersonspublishing **183**

Marine Geology

$26.2 million. *Unit head:* Prof. Robert van der Hilst, Head, 617-253-2127, Fax: 617-253-8298, E-mail: eapsinfo@mit.edu. *Application contact:* EAPS Education Office, 617-253-3381, Fax: 617-253-8298, E-mail: eapsinfo@mit.edu. Web site: http://eapsweb.mit.edu/.

University of Delaware, College of Earth, Ocean, and Environment, Newark, DE 19716. Offers geography (MA, MS, PhD); geology (MS, PhD); marine science and policy (MMP, MS, PhD), including marine policy (MMP), marine studies (MS, PhD), oceanography (PhD); ocean engineering (MS, PhD). *Degree requirements:* For master's, thesis; for doctorate, thesis/dissertation. *Entrance requirements:* For master's and doctorate, GRE General Test. Additional exam requirements/recommendations for international students: Required—TOEFL. Electronic applications accepted. *Faculty research:* Marine biology and biochemistry, oceanography, marine policy, physical ocean science and engineering, ocean engineering.

University of Hawaii at Manoa, Graduate Division, School of Ocean and Earth Science and Technology, Department of Geology and Geophysics, Honolulu, HI 96822. Offers high-pressure geophysics and geochemistry (MS, PhD); hydrogeology and engineering geology (MS, PhD); marine geology and geophysics (MS, PhD); planetary geosciences and remote sensing (MS, PhD); seismology and solid-earth geophysics (MS, PhD); volcanology, petrology, and geochemistry (MS, PhD). Part-time programs available. Terminal master's awarded for partial completion of doctoral program. *Degree requirements:* For master's, thesis optional; for doctorate, comprehensive exam, thesis/dissertation. *Entrance requirements:* For master's and doctorate, GRE General Test, minimum GPA of 3.0. Additional exam requirements/recommendations for international students: Required—TOEFL (minimum score 580 paper-based; 237 computer-based; 92 iBT), IELTS (minimum score 5).

University of Miami, Graduate School, Rosenstiel School of Marine and Atmospheric Science, Division of Marine Geology and Geophysics, Coral Gables, FL 33124. Offers MS, PhD. Terminal master's awarded for partial completion of doctoral program. *Degree requirements:* For master's, comprehensive exam, thesis; for doctorate, comprehensive exam, thesis/dissertation. *Entrance requirements:* For master's and doctorate, GRE General Test. Additional exam requirements/recommendations for international students: Required—TOEFL (minimum score 550 paper-based; 213 computer-based). Electronic applications accepted. *Faculty research:* Carbonate sedimentology, low-temperature geochemistry, paleoceanography, geodesy and tectonics.

University of Washington, Graduate School, College of the Environment, School of Oceanography, Seattle, WA 98195. Offers biological oceanography (MS, PhD); chemical oceanography (MS, PhD); marine geology and geophysics (MS, PhD); physical oceanography (MS, PhD). Terminal master's awarded for partial completion of doctoral program. *Degree requirements:* For master's, research project; for doctorate, thesis/dissertation. *Entrance requirements:* For master's and doctorate, GRE General Test, minimum GPA of 3.0. Additional exam requirements/recommendations for international students: Required—TOEFL. Electronic applications accepted. *Faculty research:* Global climate change, hydrothermal vent systems, marine microbiology, marine and freshwater biogeochemistry, biological-physical interactions.

Woods Hole Oceanographic Institution, MIT/WHOI Joint Program in Oceanography/Applied Ocean Science and Engineering, Woods Hole, MA 02543-1541. Offers applied ocean science and engineering (PhD); biological oceanography (PhD); chemical oceanography (PhD); marine geology and geophysics (PhD); physical oceanography (PhD). Program offered jointly with Massachusetts Institute of Technology. *Degree requirements:* For doctorate, thesis/dissertation. *Entrance requirements:* For doctorate, GRE General Test, GRE Subject Test. Additional exam requirements/recommendations for international students: Required—TOEFL. Electronic applications accepted.

Mineralogy

Cornell University, Graduate School, Graduate Fields of Engineering, Field of Geological Sciences, Ithaca, NY 14853. Offers economic geology (M Eng, MS, PhD); engineering geology (M Eng, MS, PhD); environmental geophysics (M Eng, MS, PhD); general geology (M Eng, MS, PhD); geobiology (M Eng, MS, PhD); geochemistry and isotope geology (M Eng, MS, PhD); geohydrology (M Eng, MS, PhD); geomorphology (M Eng, MS, PhD); geophysics (M Eng, MS, PhD); geotectonics (M Eng, MS, PhD); marine geology (MS, PhD); mineralogy (M Eng, MS, PhD); paleontology (M Eng, MS, PhD); petroleum geology (M Eng, MS, PhD); petrology (M Eng, MS, PhD); planetary geology (M Eng, MS, PhD); Precambrian geology (M Eng, MS, PhD); Quaternary geology (M Eng, MS, PhD); rock mechanics (M Eng, MS, PhD); sedimentology (M Eng, MS, PhD); seismology (M Eng, MS, PhD); stratigraphy (M Eng, MS, PhD); structural geology (M Eng, MS, PhD). *Faculty:* 37 full-time (5 women). *Students:* 41 full-time (19 women); includes 5 minority (2 Asian, non-Hispanic/Latino; 3 Hispanic/Latino), 7 international. Average age 27. 74 applicants, 19% accepted, 9 enrolled. In 2011, 3 master's, 3 doctorates awarded. *Degree requirements:* For master's, thesis (MS); for doctorate, comprehensive exam, thesis/dissertation. *Entrance requirements:* For master's and doctorate, GRE General Test, 3 letters of recommendation. Additional exam requirements/recommendations for international students: Required—TOEFL (minimum score 550 paper-based; 213 computer-based; 77 iBT). *Application deadline:* For fall admission, 1/15 priority date for domestic students. Applications are processed on a rolling basis. Application fee: $95. Electronic applications accepted. *Financial support:* In 2011–12, 25 students received support, including 7 fellowships with full tuition reimbursements available, 19 research assistantships with full tuition reimbursements available, 8 teaching assistantships with full tuition reimbursements available; institutionally sponsored loans, scholarships/grants, health care benefits, tuition waivers (full and partial), and unspecified assistantships also available. Financial award applicants required to submit FAFSA. *Faculty research:* Geophysics, structural geology, petrology, geochemistry, geodynamics. *Unit head:* Director of Graduate Studies, 607-255-5466, Fax: 607-254-4780. *Application contact:* Graduate Field Assistant, 607-255-5466, Fax: 607-254-4780, E-mail: gradprog@geology.cornell.edu. Web site: http://www.gradschool.cornell.edu/fields.php?id-30&a-2.

Indiana University Bloomington, University Graduate School, College of Arts and Sciences, Department of Geological Sciences, Bloomington, IN 47405-7000. Offers biogeochemistry (MS, PhD); economic geology (MS, PhD); geobiology (MS, PhD); geophysics, structural geology and tectonics (MS, PhD); hydrogeology (MS, PhD); mineralogy (MS, PhD); stratigraphy and sedimentology (MS, PhD). *Faculty:* 17 full-time (1 woman). *Students:* 60 full-time (26 women), 2 part-time (0 women); includes 5 minority (2 Black or African American, non-Hispanic/Latino; 1 Hispanic/Latino; 2 Two or more races, non-Hispanic/Latino), 18 international. Average age 29. 44 applicants, 55% accepted, 18 enrolled. In 2011, 11 master's, 6 doctorates awarded. Terminal master's awarded for partial completion of doctoral program. *Degree requirements:* For master's, thesis or alternative; for doctorate, comprehensive exam, thesis/dissertation. *Entrance requirements:* For master's and doctorate, GRE General Test. Additional exam requirements/recommendations for international students: Required—TOEFL. *Application deadline:* For fall admission, 1/15 priority date for domestic students, 12/15 for international students; for spring admission, 9/1 priority date for domestic students, 9/1 for international students. Applications are processed on a rolling basis. Application fee: $55 ($65 for international students). *Financial support:* In 2011–12, fellowships with full tuition reimbursements (averaging $17,300 per year), research assistantships with full tuition reimbursements (averaging $16,370 per year), teaching assistantships with full tuition reimbursements (averaging $15,150 per year) were awarded; career-related internships or fieldwork, Federal Work-Study, and institutionally sponsored loans also available. *Faculty research:* Geophysics, geochemistry, hydrogeology, geobiology, planetary science. *Total annual research expenditures:* $644,299. *Unit head:* Simon Brassell, Chair, 812-855-5581, Fax: 812-855-7899, E-mail: geochair@indiana.edu. *Application contact:* Mary Iverson, Graduate Secretary, 812-855-7214, Fax: 812-855-7899, E-mail: miverson@indiana.edu. Web site: http://www.indiana.edu/~geosci/.

Université du Québec à Chicoutimi, Graduate Programs, Program in Mineral Resources, Chicoutimi, QC G7H 2B1, Canada. Offers PhD. Program offered jointly with Université du Québec à Montréal. Part-time programs available. *Degree requirements:* For doctorate, thesis/dissertation. *Entrance requirements:* For doctorate, appropriate master's degree, proficiency in French.

Université du Québec à Montréal, Graduate Programs, Program in Earth Sciences, Montreal, QC H3C 3P8, Canada. Offers earth sciences (M Sc); mineral resources (PhD); non-renewable resources (DESS). Part-time programs available. Terminal master's awarded for partial completion of doctoral program. *Degree requirements:* For master's, thesis (for some programs); for doctorate, thesis/dissertation. *Entrance requirements:* For master's, appropriate bachelor's degree or equivalent, proficiency in French. *Faculty research:* Economic geology, structural geology, geochemistry, Quaternary geology, isotopic geochemistry.

Université du Québec à Montréal, Graduate Programs, Program in Mineral Resources, Montréal, QC H3C 3P8, Canada. Offers PhD. Program offered jointly with Université du Québec à Chicoutimi. Part-time programs available. *Degree requirements:* For doctorate, thesis/dissertation. *Entrance requirements:* For doctorate, appropriate master's degree or equivalent, proficiency in French.

184 facebook.com/petersonspublishing

Peterson's Graduate Programs in the Physical Sciences, Mathematics, Agricultural Sciences, the Environment & Natural Resources 2013

Paleontology

Cornell University, Graduate School, Graduate Fields of Engineering, Field of Geological Sciences, Ithaca, NY 14853. Offers economic geology (M Eng, MS, PhD); engineering geology (M Eng, MS, PhD); environmental geophysics (M Eng, MS, PhD); general geology (M Eng, MS, PhD); geobiology (M Eng, MS, PhD); geochemistry and isotope geology (M Eng, MS, PhD); geohydrology (M Eng, MS, PhD); geomorphology (M Eng, MS, PhD); geophysics (M Eng, MS, PhD); geotectonics (M Eng, MS, PhD); marine geology (MS, PhD); mineralogy (M Eng, MS, PhD); paleontology (M Eng, MS, PhD); petroleum geology (M Eng, MS, PhD); petrology (M Eng, MS, PhD); planetary geology (M Eng, MS, PhD); Precambrian geology (M Eng, MS, PhD); Quaternary geology (M Eng, MS, PhD); rock mechanics (M Eng, MS, PhD); sedimentology (M Eng, MS, PhD); seismology (M Eng, MS, PhD); stratigraphy (M Eng, MS, PhD); structural geology (M Eng, MS, PhD). *Faculty:* 37 full-time (5 women). *Students:* 41 full-time (19 women); includes 5 minority (2 Asian, non-Hispanic/Latino; 3 Hispanic/Latino), 7 international. Average age 27. 74 applicants, 19% accepted, 9 enrolled. In 2011, 3 master's, 3 doctorates awarded. *Degree requirements:* For master's, thesis (MS); for doctorate, comprehensive exam, thesis/dissertation. *Entrance requirements:* For master's and doctorate, GRE General Test, 3 letters of recommendation. Additional exam requirements/recommendations for international students: Required—TOEFL (minimum score 550 paper-based; 213 computer-based; 77 iBT). *Application deadline:* For fall admission, 1/15 priority date for domestic students. Applications are processed on a rolling basis. Application fee: $95. Electronic applications accepted. *Financial support:* In 2011–12, 25 students received support, including 7 fellowships with full tuition reimbursements available, 19 research assistantships with full tuition reimbursements available, 8 teaching assistantships with full tuition reimbursements available; institutionally sponsored loans, scholarships/grants, health care benefits, tuition waivers (full and partial), and unspecified assistantships also available. Financial award applicants required to submit FAFSA. *Faculty research:* Geophysics, structural geology, petrology, geochemistry, geodynamics. *Unit head:* Director of Graduate Studies, 607-255-5466, Fax: 607-254-4780. *Application contact:* Graduate Field Assistant, 607-255-5466, Fax: 607-254-4780, E-mail: gradprog@geology.cornell.edu. Web site: http://www.gradschool.cornell.edu/fields.php?id-30&a-2.

Duke University, Graduate School, Department of Biological Anthropology and Anatomy, Durham, NC 27710. Offers cellular and molecular biology (PhD); gross anatomy and physical anthropology (PhD), including comparative morphology of human and non-human primates, primate social behavior, vertebrate paleontology; neuroanatomy (PhD). *Faculty:* 9 full-time. *Students:* 16 full-time (10 women); includes 3 minority (1 Black or African American, non-Hispanic/Latino; 2 Hispanic/Latino), 1 international. 71 applicants, 7% accepted, 4 enrolled. In 2011, 2 doctorates awarded. *Degree requirements:* For doctorate, one foreign language, thesis/dissertation. *Entrance requirements:* For doctorate, GRE General Test. Additional exam requirements/recommendations for international students: Required—TOEFL (minimum score 550 paper-based; 213 computer-based; 83 iBT), IELTS (minimum score 7). *Application deadline:* For fall admission, 12/8 priority date for domestic students, 12/8 for international students. Application fee: $75. Electronic applications accepted. *Expenses: Tuition:* Full-time $40,720. *Required fees:* $3107. *Financial support:* Fellowships, teaching assistantships, and Federal Work-Study available. Financial award application deadline: 12/31. *Unit head:* Daniel Schmitt, Director of Graduate Studies, 919-684-4124, Fax: 919-684-8542, E-mail: mlsquire@duke.edu. *Application contact:* Elizabeth Hutton, Director of Admissions, 919-684-3913, Fax: 919-684-2277, E-mail: grad-admissions@duke.edu. Web site: http://www.baa.duke.edu/.

East Tennessee State University, School of Graduate Studies, College of Arts and Sciences, Department of Biological Sciences, Johnson City, TN 37614. Offers biology (MS); biomedical sciences (MS); microbiology (MS); paleontology (MS). *Faculty:* 14 full-time (2 women), 1 part-time/adjunct (0 women). *Students:* 31 full-time (15 women), 5 part-time (3 women); includes 2 minority (1 Asian, non-Hispanic/Latino; 1 Hispanic/Latino), 12 international. Average age 26. 55 applicants, 35% accepted, 10 enrolled. In 2011, 24 master's awarded. *Degree requirements:* For master's, comprehensive exam, thesis. *Entrance requirements:* For master's, GRE General Test or GRE Subject Test, minimum GPA of 3.0, undergraduate degree in life or physical sciences, two letters of recommendation. Additional exam requirements/recommendations for international students: Required—TOEFL (minimum score 550 paper-based; 213 computer-based; 79 iBT). *Application deadline:* For fall admission, 4/1 for domestic students, 2/1 for international students; for spring admission, 9/1 for domestic students, 7/1 for international students. Application fee: $35 ($45 for international students). Electronic applications accepted. *Expenses: Tuition:* state resident: full-time $7312; part-time $350 per credit hour. Tuition, nonresident: full-time $18,490; part-time $621 per credit hour. *Required fees:* $63 per credit hour. Tuition and fees vary according to course load and program. *Financial support:* In 2011–12, 29 students received support, including 13 research assistantships with full tuition reimbursements available (averaging $9,000 per year), 14 teaching assistantships with full tuition reimbursements available (averaging $8,500 per year); institutionally sponsored loans, scholarships/grants, and unspecified assistantships also available. Financial award application deadline: 7/1; financial award applicants required to submit FAFSA. *Faculty research:* Genetics, ecology,

evolutionary biology, quantitative biology and modeling, plant molecular biology, neurobiology, physiology, biomedical sciences, microbiology, paleobiology. *Total annual research expenditures:* $160,000. *Unit head:* Dr. Darrell Moore, Interim Chair, 423-439-4329, Fax: 423-439-5958, E-mail: zavadam@etsu.edu. *Application contact:* Gail Powers, Graduate Specialist, 423-439-4703, Fax: 423-439-5624, E-mail: powersg@etsu.edu.

East Tennessee State University, School of Graduate Studies, College of Arts and Sciences, Department of Geosciences, Johnson City, TN 37614. Offers geospatial analysis (MS); paleontology (MS). Part-time programs available. *Faculty:* 9 full-time (2 women). *Students:* 6 full-time (4 women), 2 part-time (0 women); includes 1 minority (Two or more races, non-Hispanic/Latino). Average age 28. 8 applicants, 75% accepted, 6 enrolled. *Degree requirements:* For master's, thesis. *Entrance requirements:* For master's, bachelor's degree in geosciences or related discipline, minimum GPA of 3.0, three letters of recommendation, resume. Additional exam requirements/recommendations for international students: Required—TOEFL (minimum score 550 paper-based; 213 computer-based; 79 iBT). *Application deadline:* For fall admission, 2/1 for domestic and international students. Application fee: $35 ($45 for international students). Electronic applications accepted. *Expenses:* Tuition, state resident: full-time $7312; part-time $350 per credit hour. Tuition, nonresident: full-time $18,490; part-time $621 per credit hour. *Required fees:* $63 per credit hour. Tuition and fees vary according to course load and program. *Financial support:* In 2011–12, 1 research assistantship with full tuition reimbursement (averaging $8,000 per year), 9 teaching assistantships with full tuition reimbursements (averaging $9,500 per year) were awarded; career-related internships or fieldwork, institutionally sponsored loans, scholarships/grants, and unspecified assistantships also available. Financial award application deadline: 7/1; financial award applicants required to submit FAFSA. *Faculty research:* Urban planning, remote sensing, geochemistry of karstic terrains, weather and climate dynamics, social responses to geological hazards, watershed management and geomorphology, soil engineering, Neogene/Quaternary vertebrate evolution and biotic community reconstructions. *Total annual research expenditures:* $140,000. *Unit head:* Dr. Jim Mead, Chair, 423-439-7515, Fax: 423-439-7520, E-mail: mead@etsu.edu. *Application contact:* Gail Powers, Graduate Specialist, 423-439-4703, Fax: 423-439-5624, E-mail: powersg@etsu.edu. Web site: http://www.etsu.edu/cas/geosciences/.

South Dakota School of Mines and Technology, Graduate Division, Department of Geology and Geological Engineering, Rapid City, SD 57701-3995. Offers geology and geological engineering (MS, PhD); paleontology (MS). Part-time programs available. *Degree requirements:* For master's, thesis; for doctorate, thesis/dissertation. *Entrance requirements:* For master's and doctorate, GRE General Test, GRE Subject Test. Additional exam requirements/recommendations for international students: Required—TOEFL, TWE. Electronic applications accepted. *Faculty research:* Contaminants in soil, nitrate leaching, environmental changes, fracture formations, greenhouse effect.

South Dakota School of Mines and Technology, Graduate Division, Program in Paleontology, Rapid City, SD 57701-3995. Offers MS. Part-time programs available. *Degree requirements:* For master's, thesis. *Entrance requirements:* For master's, GRE General Test, GRE Subject Test. Additional exam requirements/recommendations for international students: Required—TOEFL, TWE. Electronic applications accepted. *Faculty research:* Cretaceous vertebrates, Miocene vertebrates, Oligocene vertebrates.

University of Chicago, Division of the Physical Sciences, Department of the Geophysical Sciences, Chicago, IL 60637-1513. Offers atmospheric sciences (SM, PhD); cosmochemistry (PhD); earth sciences (SM, PhD); paleobiology (PhD); planetary and space sciences (SM, PhD). *Faculty:* 24 full-time (3 women). *Students:* 38 full-time (16 women); includes 2 minority (both Hispanic/Latino), 16 international. Average age 26. 68 applicants, 28% accepted, 10 enrolled. In 2011, 2 master's, 5 doctorates awarded. Terminal master's awarded for partial completion of doctoral program. *Degree requirements:* For master's, thesis, seminar; for doctorate, variable foreign language requirement, comprehensive exam, thesis/dissertation. *Entrance requirements:* For doctorate, GRE General Test. Additional exam requirements/recommendations for international students: Required—TOEFL (minimum score 600 paper-based; 250 computer-based; 96 iBT), IELTS (minimum score 7). *Application deadline:* For fall admission, 1/9 for domestic students, 1/10 for international students. Application fee: $55. Electronic applications accepted. *Financial support:* In 2011–12, research assistantships with full tuition reimbursements (averaging $26,500 per year), teaching assistantships with full tuition reimbursements (averaging $27,000 per year) were awarded; fellowships, Federal Work-Study, institutionally sponsored loans, scholarships/grants, tuition waivers (partial), and unspecified assistantships also available. Financial award application deadline: 1/9. *Faculty research:* Climatology, evolutionary paleontology, cosmochemistry, geochemistry, oceanic sciences. *Unit head:* Dr. Michael Foote, Chairman, 773-702-8102, Fax: 773-702-9505. *Application contact:* David J. Taylor, Graduate Student Services Coordinator, 773-702-8180, Fax: 773-702-9505, E-mail: info@geosci.uchicago.edu. Web site: http://geosci.uchicago.edu/.

Peterson's Graduate Programs in the Physical Sciences, Mathematics, Agricultural Sciences, the Environment & Natural Resources 2013

facebook.com/petersonspublishing **185**

The University of Manchester, School of Earth, Atmospheric and Environmental Sciences, Manchester, United Kingdom. Offers atmospheric sciences (M Phil, M Sc, PhD); basin studies and petroleum geosciences (M Phil, M Sc, PhD); earth, atmospheric and environmental sciences (M Phil, M Sc, PhD); environmental geochemistry and cosmochemistry (M Phil, M Sc, PhD); isotope geochemistry and cosmochemistry (M Phil, M Sc, PhD); paleontology (M Phil, M Sc, PhD); physics and chemistry of minerals and fluids (M Phil, M Sc, PhD); structural and petrological geosciences (M Phil, M Sc, PhD).

The University of Texas at Dallas, School of Natural Sciences and Mathematics, Department of Geosciences, Richardson, TX 75080. Offers geochemistry (MS, PhD); geophysics (MS, PhD); geospatial information sciences (MS, PhD); hydrogeology (MS, PhD); sedimentary, stratigraphy, paleontology (PhD); stratigraphy, paleontology (MS); structural geology and tectonics (MS, PhD). Part-time and evening/weekend programs available. *Faculty:* 10 full-time (1 woman). *Students:* 39 full-time (13 women), 20 part-time (7 women); includes 8 minority (2 Black or African American, non-Hispanic/Latino; 4 Asian, non-Hispanic/Latino; 2 Hispanic/Latino), 18 international. Average age 32. 67 applicants, 39% accepted, 14 enrolled. In 2011, 8 master's, 3 doctorates awarded. *Degree requirements:* For master's, thesis optional; for doctorate, thesis/dissertation. *Entrance requirements:* For master's and doctorate, GRE General Test, minimum GPA of 3.0 in upper-level course work in field. Additional exam requirements/recommendations for international students: Required—TOEFL (minimum score 550 paper-based; 215 computer-based). *Application deadline:* For fall admission, 7/15 for domestic students, 5/1 for international students; for spring admission, 11/15 for domestic students, 9/1 for international students. Applications are processed on a rolling basis. Application fee: $50 ($100 for international students). Electronic applications accepted. *Expenses:* Tuition, state resident: full-time $11,170; part-time $620.56 per credit hour. Tuition, nonresident: full-time $20,212; part-time $1122.89 per credit hour. *Financial support:* In 2011–12, 32 students received support, including 13 research assistantships with partial tuition reimbursements available (averaging $21,462 per year), 15 teaching assistantships with partial tuition reimbursements available (averaging $15,800 per year); career-related internships or fieldwork, Federal Work-Study, institutionally sponsored loans, scholarships/grants, and unspecified assistantships also available. Support available to part-time students. Financial award application deadline: 4/30; financial award applicants required to submit FAFSA. *Faculty research:* Cybermapping, GPS applications for geophysics and geology, seismology and ground-penetrating radar, numerical modeling, signal processing and inverse modeling techniques in seismology. *Unit head:* Dr. John Oldow, Department Head, 972-883-2401, Fax: 972-883-2537, E-mail: geosciences@utdallas.edu. *Application contact:* Dr. John W. Geissman, Graduate Advisor, 972-883-2406, Fax: 972-883-2537, E-mail: geissman@utdallas.edu. Web site: http://www.utdallas.edu/geosciences.

West Virginia University, Eberly College of Arts and Sciences, Department of Geology and Geography, Program in Geology, Morgantown, WV 26506. Offers geomorphology (MS, PhD); geophysics (MS, PhD); hydrogeology (MS, PhD); paleontology (MS, PhD); petroleum geology (PhD); petrology (MS, PhD); stratigraphy (MS, PhD); structure (MS, PhD). Part-time programs available. Terminal master's awarded for partial completion of doctoral program. *Degree requirements:* For master's, thesis (for some programs); for doctorate, comprehensive exam, thesis/dissertation. *Entrance requirements:* For master's, GRE General Test, minimum GPA of 2.5; for doctorate, GRE General Test, minimum GPA of 3.3. Additional exam requirements/recommendations for international students: Required—TOEFL.

Yale University, Graduate School of Arts and Sciences, Department of Geology and Geophysics, New Haven, CT 06520. Offers biogeochemistry (PhD); climate dynamics (PhD); geochemistry (PhD); geophysics (PhD); meteorology (PhD); oceanography (PhD); paleontology (PhD); paleooceanography (PhD); petrology (PhD); tectonics (PhD). *Degree requirements:* For doctorate, thesis/dissertation. *Entrance requirements:* For doctorate, GRE General Test. Additional exam requirements/recommendations for international students: Required—TOEFL.

Planetary and Space Sciences

Air Force Institute of Technology, Graduate School of Engineering and Management, Department of Operational Sciences, Dayton, OH 45433-7765. Offers logistics management (MS); operations research (MS, PhD); space operations (MS). Part-time programs available. *Degree requirements:* For master's, thesis; for doctorate, thesis/dissertation. *Entrance requirements:* For doctorate, GRE General Test, minimum GPA of 3.0, U.S. citizenship. *Faculty research:* Optimization, simulation, combat modeling and analysis, reliability and maintainability, resource scheduling.

American Public University System, AMU/APU Graduate Programs, Charles Town, WV 25414. Offers accounting (MBA, MS); administration and supervision (M Ed); criminal justice (MA); emergency and disaster management (MA); entrepreneurship (MBA); environmental policy and management (MS), including environmental planning, environmental sustainability, fish and wildlife management, general (MA, MS), global environmental management; finance (MBA); general (MBA); global business management (MBA); guidance and counseling (M Ed); history (MA), including American history, ancient and classical history, European history, global history, military and diplomatic history, public history; homeland security (MA); homeland security resource allocation (MBA); humanities (MA); information technology (MS), including digital forensics, enterprise software development, information assurance and security, IT project management; information technology management (MBA); intelligence studies (MA), including criminal intelligence, general (MA, MS), homeland security, intelligence analysis, intelligence collection, intelligence operations, terrorism studies; international relations and conflict resolution (MA), including comparative and security issues, conflict resolution, international and transnational security issues, peacekeeping; legal studies (MA); management (MA), including defense management, general (MA, MS), human resource management, organizational leadership, public administration, reverse logistics, strategic consulting; marketing (MBA); military history (MA), including American military history, American revolution, civil war, war since 1946, World War II; military studies (MA), including air warfare, asymmetrical warfare, joint warfare, land warfare, naval warfare, strategic leadership; national security studies (MA), including general (MA, MS), homeland security, regional security studies, security and intelligence analysis, terrorism studies; nonprofit management (MBA); political science (MA), including American politics and government, comparative government and development, public policy; psychology (MA); public administration (MA, MPA), including disaster management (MPA), environmental policy (MA), health policy (MPA), human resources (MPA), national security (MPA), organizational management (MPA), security management (MPA); public health (MA, MPH), including emergency management (MPH), environmental health (MPH), public administration (MA); reverse logistics management (MA); security management (MA); space studies (MS), including aerospace science, planetary science; sports and health sciences (MS); sports management (MS), including coaching theory and strategy, sports administration; teaching (M Ed), including curriculum and instruction for elementary teachers, elementary, elementary reading, (2 English language learners, instructional leadership, online learning, secondary social sciences, special education; transportation and logistics management (MA), including maritime engineering management. Programs offered via distance learning only. Part-time and evening/weekend programs available. Postbaccalaureate distance learning degree programs offered (no on-campus study). *Faculty:* 445 full-time (241 women), 1,360 part-time/adjunct (617 women). *Students:* 688 full-time (338 women), 10,168 part-time (3,706 women); includes 3,130 minority (1,007 Black or African American, non-Hispanic/Latino; 103 American Indian or Alaska Native, non-Hispanic/Latino; 825 Asian, non-Hispanic/Latino; 810 Hispanic/Latino; 51 Native Hawaiian or other Pacific Islander, non-Hispanic/Latino; 334 Two or more races, non-Hispanic/Latino), 134 international. Average age 35. In 2011, 2,386 master's awarded. *Degree requirements:* For master's, comprehensive exam or practicum. *Entrance requirements:* For master's, official transcript showing earned bachelor's degree from institution accredited by recognized accrediting body. Additional exam requirements/recommendations for international students: Required—TOEFL (minimum score 550 paper-based; 213 computer-based), IELTS (minimum score 6.5). *Application deadline:* Applications are processed on a rolling basis. Application fee: $0. Electronic applications accepted. *Expenses: Tuition:* Part-time $325 per credit hour. *Financial support:* Applicants required to submit FAFSA. *Faculty research:* Military history, criminal justice, management performance, national security. *Unit head:* Dr. Karan Powell, Executive Vice President and Provost, 877-468-6268, Fax: 304-724-3780. *Application contact:* Terry Grant, Vice President of Enrollment Management, 877-468-6268, Fax: 304-724-3780, E-mail: info@apus.edu. Web site: http://www.apus.edu.

Arizona State University, College of Liberal Arts and Sciences, School of Earth and Space Exploration, Tempe, AZ 85287-1404. Offers astrophysics (MS, PhD); exploration systems design (PhD); geological sciences (MS, PhD). PhD in exploration systems design is offered in collaboration with the Fulton Schools of Engineering. Terminal master's awarded for partial completion of doctoral program. *Degree requirements:* For master's, thesis, interactive Program of Study (iPOS) submitted before completing 50 percent of required credit hours; for doctorate, thesis/dissertation, interactive Program of Study (iPOS) submitted before completing 50 percent of required credit hours. *Entrance requirements:* For master's and doctorate, GRE, minimum GPA of 3.0 or equivalent in last 2 years of work leading to bachelor's degree. Additional exam requirements/recommendations for international students: Required—TOEFL (minimum score 80 iBT), TOEFL, IELTS, or Pearson Test of English. Electronic applications accepted.

California Institute of Technology, Division of Geological and Planetary Sciences, Pasadena, CA 91125-0001. Offers environmental science and engineering (MS, PhD); geobiology (MS, PhD); geochemistry (MS, PhD); geology (MS, PhD); geophysics (MS, PhD); planetary science (MS, PhD). *Faculty:* 42 full-time (8 women). *Students:* 102 full-time (48 women); includes 10 minority (2 Black

186 facebook.com/petersonspublishing

Peterson's Graduate Programs in the Physical Sciences, Mathematics, Agricultural Sciences, the Environment & Natural Resources 2013

or African American, non-Hispanic/Latino; 7 Asian, non-Hispanic/Latino; 1 Hispanic/Latino), 28 international. Average age 26. 188 applicants, 23% accepted, 21 enrolled. In 2011, 11 master's, 12 doctorates awarded. *Degree requirements:* For doctorate, thesis/dissertation. *Entrance requirements:* For doctorate, GRE General Test. Additional exam requirements/recommendations for international students: Required—TOEFL; Recommended—IELTS, TWE. *Application deadline:* For fall admission, 1/1 for domestic and international students. Application fee: $80. Electronic applications accepted. *Financial support:* In 2011–12, 75 students received support, including 16 fellowships with full tuition reimbursements available (averaging $28,000 per year), 86 research assistantships with full tuition reimbursements available (averaging $28,000 per year); teaching assistantships with full tuition reimbursements available, institutionally sponsored loans, scholarships/grants, health care benefits, and unspecified assistantships also available. Financial award applicants required to submit FAFSA. *Faculty research:* Planetary surfaces, evolution of anaerobic respiratory processes, structural geology and tectonics, theoretical and numerical seismology, global biogeochemical cycles. *Unit head:* Dr. Kenneth A. Farley, Chairman, 626-395-6111, Fax: 626-795-6028, E-mail: dianb@gps.caltech.edu. *Application contact:* Dr. Robert W. Clayton, Academic Officer, 626-395-6909, Fax: 626-795-6028, E-mail: dianb@gps.caltech.edu. Web site: http://www.gps.caltech.edu/.

Columbia University, Graduate School of Arts and Sciences, Division of Natural Sciences, Program in Atmospheric and Planetary Science, New York, NY 10027. Offers M Phil, PhD. Offered jointly through the Departments of Geological Sciences, Astronomy, and Physics and in cooperation with NASA Goddard Space Flight Center's Institute for Space Studies. *Degree requirements:* For doctorate, variable foreign language requirement, thesis/dissertation. *Entrance requirements:* For doctorate, GRE General Test, GRE Subject Test, previous course work in mathematics and physics. Additional exam requirements/recommendations for international students: Required—TOEFL. *Faculty research:* Climate, weather prediction.

Cornell University, Graduate School, Graduate Fields of Arts and Sciences, Field of Astronomy and Space Sciences, Ithaca, NY 14853-0001. Offers astronomy (PhD); astrophysics (PhD); general space sciences (PhD); infrared astronomy (PhD); planetary studies (PhD); radio astronomy (PhD); radiophysics (PhD); theoretical astrophysics (PhD). *Faculty:* 27 full-time (2 women). *Students:* 32 full-time (11 women); includes 5 minority (3 Asian, non-Hispanic/Latino; 2 Hispanic/Latino), 9 international. Average age 26. 101 applicants, 30% accepted, 11 enrolled. In 2011, 5 doctorates awarded. *Degree requirements:* For doctorate, comprehensive exam, thesis/dissertation. *Entrance requirements:* For doctorate, GRE General Test, GRE Subject Test (physics), 3 letters of recommendation. Additional exam requirements/recommendations for international students: Required—TOEFL (minimum score 600 paper-based; 250 computer-based; 77 iBT). *Application deadline:* For fall admission, 1/15 for domestic students. Application fee: $95. Electronic applications accepted. *Financial support:* In 2011–12, 5 fellowships with full tuition reimbursements, 15 research assistantships with full tuition reimbursements, 10 teaching assistantships with full tuition reimbursements were awarded; institutionally sponsored loans, scholarships/grants, health care benefits, tuition waivers (full and partial), and unspecified assistantships also available. Financial award applicants required to submit FAFSA. *Faculty research:* Observational astrophysics, planetary sciences, cosmology, instrumentation, gravitational astrophysics. *Unit head:* Director of Graduate Studies, 607-255-4341. *Application contact:* Graduate Field Assistant, 607-255-4341, E-mail: oconnor@astro.cornell.edu. Web site: http://www.gradschool.cornell.edu/fields.php?id-24&a-2.

Florida Institute of Technology, Graduate Programs, College of Science, Department of Physics and Space Sciences, Melbourne, FL 32901-6975. Offers physics (MS, PhD); space sciences (MS, PhD). Part-time programs available. *Faculty:* 8 full-time (0 women). *Students:* 30 full-time (11 women), 12 part-time (4 women); includes 3 minority (2 Asian, non-Hispanic/Latino; 1 Hispanic/Latino), 13 international. Average age 31. 74 applicants, 51% accepted, 14 enrolled. In 2011, 16 master's, 1 doctorate awarded. Terminal master's awarded for partial completion of doctoral program. *Degree requirements:* For master's, comprehensive exam, thesis optional, oral exam, 6 credits of math methodology; for doctorate, one foreign language, comprehensive exam, thesis/dissertation, publication in referred journal, seminar on dissertation research, dissertation published in a major journal. *Entrance requirements:* For master's, minimum GPA of 3.0, resume, 3 letters of recommendation, vector analysis, statement of objectives; for doctorate, GRE General and Subject Tests (recommended), minimum GPA of 3.2, resume, 3 letters of recommendation, statement of objectives. Additional exam requirements/recommendations for international students: Required—TOEFL (minimum score 550 paper-based; 213 computer-based; 79 iBT). *Application deadline:* For fall admission, 4/1 for international students; for spring admission, 9/30 for international students. Applications are processed on a rolling basis. Electronic applications accepted. *Expenses: Tuition:* Full-time $19,620; part-time $1090 per credit hour. Tuition and fees vary according to campus/location. *Financial support:* In 2011–12, 11 research assistantships with full and partial tuition reimbursements (averaging $13,588 per year), 14 teaching assistantships with full and partial tuition reimbursements (averaging $12,955 per year) were awarded; career-related internships or fieldwork, institutionally sponsored loans, tuition waivers (partial), unspecified assistantships, and tuition remissions also available. Support available to part-time students. Financial award application deadline: 3/1; financial award applicants required to submit FAFSA. *Faculty research:* Lasers, semiconductors,

magnetism, quantum devices, high energy physics. *Total annual research expenditures:* $2.1 million. *Unit head:* Dr. Terry D. Oswalt, Department Head, 321-674-7325, Fax: 321-674-7482, E-mail: toswalt@fit.edu. *Application contact:* Cheryl A. Brown, Associate Director of Graduate Admissions, 321-674-7581, Fax: 321-723-9468, E-mail: cbrown@fit.edu. Web site: http://cos.fit.edu/pss/.

Georgia Institute of Technology, Graduate Studies and Research, College of Sciences, School of Earth and Atmospheric Sciences, Atlanta, GA 30332-0340. Offers atmospheric chemistry, aerosols and clouds (MS, PhD); dynamics of weather and climate (MS, PhD); geochemistry (MS, PhD); geophysics (MS, PhD); oceanography (MS, PhD); paleoclimate (MS, PhD); planetary science (MS, PhD); remote sensing (MS, PhD). Part-time programs available. Terminal master's awarded for partial completion of doctoral program. *Degree requirements:* For master's, thesis or alternative; for doctorate, comprehensive exam, thesis/dissertation. *Entrance requirements:* For master's, GRE, letters of recommendation; for doctorate, GRE, academic transcripts, letters of recommendation, personal statement. Additional exam requirements/recommendations for international students: Required—TOEFL (minimum score 550 paper-based; 213 computer-based; 79 iBT). *Faculty research:* Geophysics; atmospheric chemistry, aerosols and clouds; dynamics of weather and climate; geochemistry; oceanography; paleoclimate; planetary science; remote sensing.

Hampton University, Graduate College, Department of Atmospheric and Planetary Sciences, Hampton, VA 23668. Offers atmospheric sciences (MS, PhD); planetary sciences (MS, PhD).

Harvard University, Graduate School of Arts and Sciences, Department of Earth and Planetary Sciences, Cambridge, MA 02138. Offers AM, PhD. Terminal master's awarded for partial completion of doctoral program. *Degree requirements:* For doctorate, comprehensive exam, thesis/dissertation. *Entrance requirements:* For doctorate, GRE General Test. Additional exam requirements/recommendations for international students: Required—TOEFL. Electronic applications accepted. *Expenses: Tuition:* Full-time $36,304. *Required fees:* $1186. Full-time tuition and fees vary according to program. *Faculty research:* Economic geography, geochemistry, geophysics, mineralogy, crystallography.

Massachusetts Institute of Technology, School of Science, Department of Earth, Atmospheric, and Planetary Sciences, Cambridge, MA 02139. Offers atmospheric chemistry (PhD, Sc D); atmospheric science (SM, PhD, Sc D); chemical oceanography (SM, PhD, Sc D); climate physics and chemistry (SM, PhD, Sc D); earth and planetary sciences (SM); geochemistry (PhD, Sc D); geology (PhD, Sc D); geophysics (PhD, Sc D); marine geology and geophysics (SM, PhD, Sc D); physical oceanography (SM, PhD, Sc D); planetary sciences (PhD, Sc D). *Faculty:* 33 full-time (6 women). *Students:* 175 full-time (81 women); includes 21 minority (3 Black or African American, non-Hispanic/Latino; 1 American Indian or Alaska Native, non-Hispanic/Latino; 8 Asian, non-Hispanic/Latino; 4 Hispanic/Latino; 5 Two or more races, non-Hispanic/Latino), 58 international. Average age 26. 241 applicants, 28% accepted, 43 enrolled. In 2011, 6 master's, 16 doctorates awarded. Terminal master's awarded for partial completion of doctoral program. *Degree requirements:* For master's, thesis; for doctorate, comprehensive exam, thesis/dissertation. *Entrance requirements:* For master's, GRE General Test; for doctorate, GRE General Test, GRE Subject Test (chemistry or physics for planetary science area). Additional exam requirements/recommendations for international students: Required—TOEFL (minimum score 577 paper-based; 233 computer-based; 91 iBT), IELTS (minimum score 7). *Application deadline:* For fall admission, 1/5 for domestic and international students; for spring admission, 11/1 for domestic and international students. Application fee: $75. Electronic applications accepted. *Expenses: Tuition:* Full-time $40,460; part-time $630 per credit hour. *Required fees:* $272. *Financial support:* In 2011–12, 125 students received support, including 68 fellowships (averaging $32,200 per year), 94 research assistantships (averaging $31,900 per year), 10 teaching assistantships (averaging $30,000 per year); Federal Work-Study, institutionally sponsored loans, scholarships/grants, health care benefits, and unspecified assistantships also available. *Faculty research:* Formation, dynamics and evolution of planetary systems; origin, composition, structure and dynamics of the atmospheres, oceans, surfaces and interiors of the Earth and other planets; evolution and interaction of the physical, chemical, geological and biological components of the Earth system; characterization of past, present and potential future climates and the causes and consequences of climate change; interplay of energy and the environment. *Total annual research expenditures:* $26.2 million. *Unit head:* Prof. Robert van der Hilst, Head, 617-253-2127, Fax: 617-253-8298, E-mail: eapsinfo@mit.edu. *Application contact:* EAPS Education Office, 617-253-3381, Fax: 617-253-8298, E-mail: eapsinfo@mit.edu. Web site: http://eapsweb.mit.edu/.

McGill University, Faculty of Graduate and Postdoctoral Studies, Faculty of Science, Department of Earth and Planetary Sciences, Montréal, QC H3A 2T5, Canada. Offers M Sc, PhD.

St. Thomas University, School of Leadership Studies, Institute for Education, Miami Gardens, FL 33054-6459. Offers earth/space science (Certificate); educational administration (MS, Certificate); educational leadership (Ed D); elementary education (MS); ESOL (Certificate); gifted education (Certificate); instructional technology (MS, Certificate); professional/studies (Certificate); reading (MS, Certificate); special education (MS). Part-time and evening/weekend programs available. *Degree requirements:* For master's, comprehensive exam; for doctorate, comprehensive exam, thesis/dissertation. *Entrance requirements:* For master's, interview, minimum GPA of 3.0 or GRE; for doctorate, GRE or MAT.

Peterson's Graduate Programs in the Physical Sciences, Mathematics, Agricultural Sciences, the Environment & Natural Resources 2013

facebook.com/petersonspublishing **187**

Planetary and Space Sciences

Additional exam requirements/recommendations for international students: Required—TOEFL (minimum score 550 paper-based; 213 computer-based; 79 iBT). Electronic applications accepted.

The University of Arizona, College of Science, Department of Planetary Sciences, Tucson, AZ 85721. Offers MS, PhD. *Faculty:* 24 full-time (10 women), 2 part-time/adjunct (1 woman). *Students:* 32 full-time (17 women), 1 (woman) part-time; includes 5 minority (1 Hispanic/Latino; 4 Two or more races, non-Hispanic/Latino), 9 international. Average age 27. 51 applicants, 14% accepted, 7 enrolled. In 2011, 2 master's, 9 doctorates awarded. *Degree requirements:* For master's, thesis (for some programs); for doctorate, one foreign language, thesis/dissertation. *Entrance requirements:* For master's and doctorate, 3 letters of recommendation. Additional exam requirements/recommendations for international students: Required—TOEFL (minimum score 550 paper-based; 213 computer-based; 79 iBT). *Application deadline:* For fall admission, 1/15 for domestic and international students. Applications are processed on a rolling basis. Application fee: $75. Electronic applications accepted. *Expenses:* Tuition, state resident: full-time $10,840. Tuition, nonresident: full-time $25,802. *Financial support:* In 2011–12, 10 research assistantships with full tuition reimbursements (averaging $21,652 per year), 19 teaching assistantships with full tuition reimbursements (averaging $20,954 per year) were awarded; scholarships/grants, health care benefits, tuition waivers (partial), and unspecified assistantships also available. Financial award application deadline: 2/15. *Faculty research:* Cosmochemistry, planetary geology, astronomy, space physics, planetary physics. *Total annual research expenditures:* $30.9 million. *Unit head:* Dr. Michael Drake, Professor/Head/Director, 520-621-6962, Fax: 520-621-4933, E-mail: drake@lpl.arizona.edu. *Application contact:* Pam Streett, Information Contact, 520-621-2828, Fax: 520-621-4933, E-mail: admissions@lpl.arizona.edu. Web site: http://www.lpl.arizona.edu/.

University of Arkansas, Graduate School, Interdisciplinary Program in Space and Planetary Sciences, Fayetteville, AR 72701-1201. Offers MS, PhD. *Students:* 6 full-time (2 women), 20 part-time (11 women); includes 2 minority (1 Hispanic/Latino; 1 Two or more races, non-Hispanic/Latino), 8 international. In 2011, 2 degrees awarded. *Application deadline:* For fall admission, 4/1 for international students; for spring admission, 10/1 for international students. Applications are processed on a rolling basis. Application fee: $40 ($50 for international students). Electronic applications accepted. *Financial support:* In 2011–12, 7 research assistantships, 12 teaching assistantships were awarded; fellowships also available. *Unit head:* Dr. Lin Oliver, Director, 479-575-6571, E-mail: woliver@uark.edu. *Application contact:* Graduate Admissions, 479-575-6246, Fax: 479-575-5908, E-mail: gradinfo@uark.edu. Web site: http://spacecenter.uark.edu.

University of California, Los Angeles, Graduate Division, College of Letters and Science, Department of Earth and Space Sciences, Los Angeles, CA 90095. Offers geochemistry (MS, PhD); geology (MS, PhD); geophysics and space physics (MS, PhD). *Faculty:* 24 full-time (34 women). *Students:* 70 full-time (34 women); includes 13 minority (3 Black or African American, non-Hispanic/Latino; 1 American Indian or Alaska Native, non-Hispanic/Latino; 6 Asian, non-Hispanic/Latino; 1 Hispanic/Latino; 2 Two or more races, non-Hispanic/Latino), 17 international. Average age 28. 121 applicants, 29% accepted, 20 enrolled. In 2011, 9 master's, 7 doctorates awarded. Terminal master's awarded for partial completion of doctoral program. *Degree requirements:* For master's, comprehensive exams or thesis; for doctorate, thesis/dissertation, oral and written qualifying exams. *Entrance requirements:* For master's, GRE General Test, minimum GPA of 3.0; for doctorate, GRE General Test, minimum undergraduate GPA of 3.0. *Application deadline:* For fall admission, 1/15 for domestic and international students. Application fee: $70 ($90 for international students). Electronic applications accepted. *Financial support:* In 2011–12, 58 fellowships with full and partial tuition reimbursements, 51 research assistantships with full and partial tuition reimbursements, 29 teaching assistantships with full and partial tuition reimbursements were awarded; Federal Work-Study, institutionally sponsored loans, scholarships/grants, traineeships, health care benefits, tuition waivers (full and partial), and unspecified assistantships also available. Financial award application deadline: 3/1; financial award applicants required to submit FAFSA. *Unit head:* Dr. Craig E. Manning, Chair, 310-825-1475, E-mail: manning@ess.ucla.edu. *Application contact:* Departmental Office, 310-825-3917, E-mail: holbrook@ess.ucla.edu. Web site: http://www.ess.ucla.edu/.

University of California, Santa Cruz, Division of Graduate Studies, Division of Physical and Biological Sciences, Department of Earth and Planetary Sciences, Santa Cruz, CA 95064. Offers MS, PhD. Terminal master's awarded for partial completion of doctoral program. *Degree requirements:* For master's, thesis; for doctorate, one foreign language, thesis/dissertation, qualifying exam. *Entrance requirements:* For master's and doctorate, GRE General Test. Additional exam requirements/recommendations for international students: Required—TOEFL (minimum score 550 paper-based; 220 computer-based; 83 iBT); Recommended—IELTS (minimum score 8). Electronic applications accepted. *Faculty research:* Evolution of continental margins and orogenic belts, geologic processes occurring at plate boundaries, deep-sea sediment diagenesis, paleoecology, hydrogeology.

University of Chicago, Division of the Physical Sciences, Department of the Geophysical Sciences, Chicago, IL 60637-1513. Offers atmospheric sciences (SM, PhD); cosmochemistry (PhD); earth sciences (SM, PhD); paleobiology (PhD); planetary and space sciences (SM, PhD). *Faculty:* 24 full-time (3 women). *Students:* 38 full-time (16 women); includes 2 minority (both Hispanic/Latino), 16 international. Average age 26. 68 applicants, 28% accepted, 10 enrolled. In 2011, 2 master's, 5 doctorates awarded. Terminal master's awarded for partial completion of doctoral program. *Degree requirements:* For master's, thesis, seminar; for doctorate, variable foreign language requirement, comprehensive exam, thesis/dissertation. *Entrance requirements:* For doctorate, GRE General Test. Additional exam requirements/recommendations for international students: Required—TOEFL (minimum score 600 paper-based; 250 computer-based; 96 iBT), IELTS (minimum score 7). *Application deadline:* For fall admission, 1/9 for domestic students, 1/10 for international students. Application fee: $55. Electronic applications accepted. *Financial support:* In 2011–12, research assistantships with full tuition reimbursements (averaging $26,500 per year), teaching assistantships with full tuition reimbursements (averaging $27,000 per year) were awarded; fellowships, Federal Work-Study, institutionally sponsored loans, scholarships/grants, tuition waivers (partial), and unspecified assistantships also available. Financial award application deadline: 1/9. *Faculty research:* Climatology, evolutionary paleontology, cosmochemistry, geochemistry, oceanic sciences. *Unit head:* Dr. Michael Foote, Chairman, 773-702-8102, Fax: 773-702-9505. *Application contact:* David J. Taylor, Graduate Student Services Coordinator, 773-702-8180, Fax: 773-702-9505, E-mail: info@geosci.uchicago.edu. Web site: http://geosci.uchicago.edu/.

University of Hawaii at Manoa, Graduate Division, School of Ocean and Earth Science and Technology, Department of Geology and Geophysics, Honolulu, HI 96822. Offers high-pressure geophysics and geochemistry (MS, PhD); hydrogeology and engineering geology (MS, PhD); marine geology and geophysics (MS, PhD); planetary geosciences and remote sensing (MS, PhD); seismology and solid-earth geophysics (MS, PhD); volcanology, petrology, and geochemistry (MS, PhD). Part-time programs available. Terminal master's awarded for partial completion of doctoral program. *Degree requirements:* For master's, thesis optional; for doctorate, comprehensive exam, thesis/dissertation. *Entrance requirements:* For master's and doctorate, GRE General Test, minimum GPA of 3.0. Additional exam requirements/recommendations for international students: Required—TOEFL (minimum score 580 paper-based; 237 computer-based; 92 iBT), IELTS (minimum score 5).

University of Houston, College of Liberal Arts and Social Sciences, Department of Health and Human Performance, Houston, TX 77204. Offers exercise science (MS); human nutrition (MS); human space exploration sciences (MS); kinesiology (PhD); physical education (M Ed). *Accreditation:* NCATE (one or more programs are accredited). Part-time and evening/weekend programs available. *Degree requirements:* For master's, comprehensive exam (for some programs), thesis (for some programs); for doctorate, comprehensive exam, thesis/dissertation, qualifying exam, candidacy paper. *Entrance requirements:* For master's, GRE (minimum 35th percentile on each section), minimum cumulative GPA of 3.0; for doctorate, GRE (minimum 35th percentile on each section), minimum cumulative GPA of 3.3. Additional exam requirements/recommendations for international students: Required—TOEFL (minimum score 550 paper-based; 79 iBT). Electronic applications accepted. *Faculty research:* Biomechanics, exercise physiology, obesity, nutrition, space exploration science.

University of Maryland, Baltimore County, Graduate School, College of Arts, Humanities and Social Sciences, Department of Education, Program in Teaching, Baltimore, MD 21250. Offers early childhood education (MAT); elementary education (MAT); secondary education (MAT), including social studies; secondary education (MAT), including art, biology, chemistry, dance, earth/space science, English, foreign language, mathematics, music, physics, theatre. Part-time and evening/weekend programs available. *Faculty:* 24 full-time (18 women), 25 part-time/adjunct (19 women). *Students:* 46 full-time (35 women), 64 part-time (39 women); includes 24 minority (8 Black or African American, non-Hispanic/Latino; 7 Asian, non-Hispanic/Latino; 6 Hispanic/Latino; 1 Native Hawaiian or other Pacific Islander, non-Hispanic/Latino; 2 Two or more races, non-Hispanic/Latino), 4 international. Average age 31. 88 applicants, 57% accepted, 39 enrolled. In 2011, 106 master's awarded. *Degree requirements:* For master's, comprehensive exam (for some programs), thesis (for some programs). *Entrance requirements:* For master's, PRAXIS I or GRE (minimum score of 1000), minimum GPA of 3.0. Additional exam requirements/recommendations for international students: Required—TOEFL. *Application deadline:* For fall admission, 6/1 for domestic students; for spring admission, 11/1 for domestic students. Applications are processed on a rolling basis. Application fee: $50. Electronic applications accepted. *Financial support:* In 2011–12, 6 students received support, including teaching assistantships with full and partial tuition reimbursements available (averaging $12,000 per year); career-related internships or fieldwork, Federal Work-Study, scholarships/grants, tuition waivers, and unspecified assistantships also available. Financial award application deadline: 3/1. *Faculty research:* STEM teacher education, culturally sensitive pedagogy, ESOL/bilingual education, early childhood education, language, literacy and culture. *Unit head:* Dr. Susan M. Blunck, Graduate Program Director, 410-455-2869, Fax: 410-455-3986, E-mail: blunck@umbc.edu. *Application contact:* Cheryl Johnson, 410-455-3388, E-mail: blackwel@umbc.edu. Web site: http://www.umbc.edu/education/.

University of Michigan, College of Engineering, Department of Atmospheric, Oceanic, and Space Sciences, Ann Arbor, MI 48109. Offers atmospheric and space sciences (MS, PhD); geoscience and remote sensing (PhD); space and planetary sciences (PhD); space engineering (M Eng). Part-time programs available. *Students:* 104 full-time (35 women), 1 part-time (0 women). 122 applicants, 57% accepted, 37 enrolled. In 2011, 28 master's, 7 doctorates awarded. Terminal master's awarded for partial completion of doctoral program. *Degree requirements:* For master's, thesis (for some programs); for doctorate, thesis/dissertation, oral defense of dissertation, preliminary exams. *Entrance requirements:* For master's and doctorate, GRE General Test. Additional exam requirements/recommendations for international students: Required—TOEFL. *Application deadline:* Applications are processed on a rolling basis. Application fee: $65 ($75 for international students). Electronic applications accepted. *Financial support:* Fellowships, research assistantships, teaching assistantships, career-related internships or fieldwork, Federal Work-Study, institutionally sponsored loans, and health care benefits available. Support available to part-time students. Financial award applicants required to submit FAFSA. *Faculty research:* Planetary environments, space instrumentation, air pollution meteorology, global climate change, sun-earth connection, space weather. *Unit head:* Dr. James Slavin, Chair, 734-764-7221, Fax: 734-615-4645, E-mail: jaslavin@umich.edu. *Application contact:* Margaret Reid, Student Services Associate, 734-936-0482, Fax: 734-763-0437, E-mail: aoss.um@umich.edu. Web site: http://aoss.engin.umich.edu/.

University of New Mexico, Graduate School, College of Arts and Sciences, Department of Earth and Planetary Sciences, Albuquerque, NM 87131-0001. Offers MS, PhD. Part-time programs available. *Faculty:* 32 full-time (5 women), 18 part-time/adjunct (8 women). *Students:* 24 full-time (16 women), 31 part-time (17 women); includes 7 minority (2 American Indian or Alaska Native, non-Hispanic/Latino; 4 Hispanic/Latino; 1 Two or more races, non-Hispanic/Latino). Average age 31. 57 applicants, 19% accepted, 9 enrolled. In 2011, 9 master's, 4 doctorates awarded. Terminal master's awarded for partial completion of doctoral program. *Degree requirements:* For master's, comprehensive exam, thesis; for doctorate, comprehensive exam, thesis/dissertation. *Entrance requirements:* For master's and doctorate, GRE General Test. Additional exam requirements/recommendations for international students: Required—TOEFL. *Application deadline:* For fall admission, 1/15 priority date for domestic students, 1/15 for international students; for spring admission, 11/1 priority date for domestic students, 11/1 for international students. Application fee: $50. Electronic applications accepted. *Financial support:* In 2011–12, 54 students received support, including 23 fellowships with full tuition reimbursements available (averaging $2,714 per year), 46 research assistantships with full tuition reimbursements available (averaging $14,363 per year), 27 teaching assistantships with full tuition reimbursements available (averaging $1,982 per year); scholarships/grants and health care benefits also available. Financial award application deadline: 1/31; financial award applicants required to submit FAFSA. *Faculty research:* Climatology, experimental petrology, geochemistry, geographic information technologies, geomorphology, geophysics, hydrogeology, igneous petrology, metamorphic petrology, meteoritics, meteorology, micrometeorites, mineralogy, paleoclimatology, paleontology, pedology, petrology, physical volcanology, planetary sciences, precambrian geology, quanternary geology, sedimentary geochemistry, sedimentology, stable isotope geochemistry, stratigraphy, structural geology, tectonics, volcanology. *Total annual research expenditures:* $2.5 million. *Unit head:* Dr. John W. Geissman, Chair, 505-277-4204, Fax: 505-277-8843, E-mail: jgeiss@unm.edu. *Application contact:* Cindy Jaramillo, Administrative Assistant II, 505-277-1635, Fax: 505-277-8843, E-mail: epsdept@unm.edu. Web site: http://epswww.unm.edu/.

University of North Dakota, Graduate School, John D. Odegard School of Aerospace Sciences, Space Studies Program, Grand Forks, ND 58202. Offers MS. Part-time programs available. Postbaccalaureate distance learning degree programs offered (minimal on-campus study). *Degree requirements:* For master's, comprehensive exam, thesis or alternative. *Entrance requirements:* For master's, minimum GPA of 3.0. Additional exam requirements/recommendations for international students: Required—TOEFL (minimum score 550 paper-based; 213 computer-based; 79 iBT), IELTS (minimum score 6.5). Electronic applications accepted. *Faculty research:* Earth-approaching asteroids, international remote sensing statutes, Mercury fly-by design, origin of meteorites, craters on Venus.

University of Pittsburgh, Dietrich School of Arts and Sciences, Department of Geology and Planetary Science, Pittsburgh, PA 15260-3332. Offers geographical information systems (Pro-MS); geology and planetary science (MS, PhD). Part-time programs available. *Faculty:* 7 full-time (2 women), 3 part-time/adjunct (1 woman). *Students:* 24 full-time (11 women), 8 part-time (4 women), 1 international. Average age 30. 27 applicants, 48% accepted, 5 enrolled. In 2011, 5 master's, 5 doctorates awarded. *Degree requirements:* For master's, thesis, oral thesis defense; for doctorate, comprehensive exam, thesis/dissertation, oral dissertation defense. *Entrance requirements:* For master's and doctorate, GRE General Test. Additional exam requirements/recommendations for international students: Required—TOEFL (minimum score 550 paper-based; 213 computer-based; 80 iBT). *Application deadline:* For fall admission, 1/15 priority date for domestic students, 1/15 for international students. Applications are processed on a rolling basis. Application fee: $50. Electronic applications accepted. *Expenses:* Tuition, state resident: full-time $18,774; part-time $760 per credit. Tuition, nonresident: full-time $30,736; part-time $1258 per credit. *Required fees:* $740; $200 per term. Tuition and fees vary according to program. *Financial support:* In 2011–12, 21 students received support, including 2 fellowships with full tuition reimbursements available (averaging $19,165 per year), 9 research assistantships with full and partial tuition reimbursements available (averaging

$14,400 per year), 9 teaching assistantships with full and partial tuition reimbursements available (averaging $16,145 per year); career-related internships or fieldwork, Federal Work-Study, institutionally sponsored loans, scholarships/grants, health care benefits, and tuition waivers (full and partial) also available. Support available to part-time students. Financial award application deadline: 1/15; financial award applicants required to submit FAFSA. *Faculty research:* Geographical information systems, hydrology, low temperature geochemistry, volcanology, paleoclimatology. *Total annual research expenditures:* $1.6 million. *Unit head:* Dr. William Harbert, Chair, 412-624-8783, Fax: 412-624-3914, E-mail: harbert@pitt.edu. *Application contact:* Dr. Rosemary Capo, Director of Graduate Studies, 412-624-8873, Fax: 412-624-3914, E-mail: rcapo@pitt.edu. Web site: http://www.geology.pitt.edu/.

Washington University in St. Louis, Graduate School of Arts and Sciences, Department of Earth and Planetary Sciences, St. Louis, MO 63130-4899. Offers MA, PhD. Terminal master's awarded for partial completion of doctoral program. *Degree requirements:* For master's, thesis; for doctorate, thesis/dissertation. *Entrance requirements:* For master's and doctorate, GRE General Test. Electronic applications accepted.

West Chester University of Pennsylvania, College of Arts and Sciences, Department of Geology and Astronomy, West Chester, PA 19383. Offers earth-space science (Teaching Certificate); general science (Teaching Certificate); geoscience (MA). Part-time and evening/weekend programs available. *Faculty:* 6 part-time/adjunct (1 woman). *Students:* 6 full-time (3 women), 17 part-time (6 women); includes 1 minority (Black or African American, non-Hispanic/Latino). Average age 32. 8 applicants, 88% accepted, 5 enrolled. In 2011, 4 degrees awarded. *Degree requirements:* For master's, comprehensive exam (for some programs), thesis or alternative. *Entrance requirements:* For master's, minimum GPA of 2.5. Additional exam requirements/recommendations for international students: Required—TOEFL (minimum score 550 paper-based; 213 computer-based; 80 iBT). *Application deadline:* For fall admission, 4/15 priority date for domestic students, 3/15 for international students; for spring admission, 10/15 priority date for domestic students, 9/1 for international students. Applications are processed on a rolling basis. Application fee: $45. Electronic applications accepted. *Expenses:* Tuition, state resident: full-time $7488; part-time $416 per credit. Tuition, nonresident: full-time $11,232; part-time $624 per credit. *Required fees:* $1784.64; $67.59 per credit. Tuition and fees vary according to program. *Financial support:* Unspecified assistantships available. Support available to part-time students. Financial award application deadline: 2/15; financial award applicants required to submit FAFSA. *Faculty research:* Geoscience education, environmental geology, energy and sustainability, astronomy, meteorology. *Unit head:* Dr. Lee Anne Srogi, Chair, 610-436-2727, Fax: 610-436-3036, E-mail: lsrogi@wcupa.edu. *Application contact:* Dr. Martin Helmke, Graduate Coordinator, 610-436-3565, Fax: 610-436-3036, E-mail: mhelmke@wcupa.edu. Web site: http://www.wcupa.edu/_academics/sch_cas.esc/.

Western Connecticut State University, Division of Graduate Studies, School of Arts and Sciences, Department of Physics, Astronomy and Meteorology, Danbury, CT 06810-6885. Offers earth and planetary sciences (MA). Part-time programs available. *Faculty:* 2 full-time (0 women). *Students:* 3 full-time (0 women), 10 part-time (4 women); includes 3 minority (1 Black or African American, non-Hispanic/Latino; 2 Hispanic/Latino). Average age 28. In 2011, 1 degree awarded. *Degree requirements:* For master's, thesis, completion of program in 6 years. *Entrance requirements:* For master's, minimum GPA of 2.5 or GRE; one year each of calculus-based physics and calculus; semester course in differential equations. Additional exam requirements/recommendations for international students: Recommended—TOEFL (minimum score 550 paper-based; 213 computer-based; 79 iBT), IELTS (minimum score 6). *Application deadline:* For fall admission, 8/5 priority date for domestic students; for spring admission, 1/5 priority date for domestic students. Applications are processed on a rolling basis. Application fee: $50. *Expenses:* Contact institution. *Financial support:* Application deadline: 5/1; applicants required to submit FAFSA. *Faculty research:* Data collection and analysis of Gulf Stream surface temperature and circulation; science for visually impaired students including investigations of a satellite orbit, the Moon's surface, spectra of chemical elements and stars, the rotation of the Sun, and the spiral structure of our galaxy. *Unit head:* Dr. James Boyle, Graduate Coordinator, 203-837-8856. *Application contact:* Chris Shankle, Associate Director of Graduate Admissions, 203-837-9005, Fax: 203-837-8326, E-mail: shanklec@wcsu.edu. Web site: http://www.wcsu.edu/physics/.

Yale University, Graduate School of Arts and Sciences, Department of Astronomy, New Haven, CT 06520. Offers astronomy (PhD); solar and terrestrial physics (PhD). *Degree requirements:* For doctorate, thesis/dissertation. *Entrance requirements:* For doctorate, GRE General Test, GRE Subject Test (physics).

York University, Faculty of Graduate Studies, Faculty of Science and Engineering, Program in Earth and Space Science, Toronto, ON M3J 1P3, Canada. Offers M Sc, PhD. Part-time and evening/weekend programs available. *Degree requirements:* For master's, thesis or alternative; for doctorate, thesis/dissertation. Electronic applications accepted.

Peterson's Graduate Programs in the Physical Sciences, Mathematics, Agricultural Sciences, the Environment & Natural Resources 2013

facebook.com/petersonspublishing   **189**

Section 4
Marine Sciences and Oceanography

This section contains a directory of institutions offering graduate work in marine sciences and oceanography, followed by an in-depth entry submitted by an institution that chose to prepare a detailed program description. Additional information about programs listed in the directory but not augmented by an in-depth entry may be obtained by writing directly to the dean of a graduate school or chair of a department at the address given in the directory.

For programs offering related work, see also in this book *Chemistry, Geosciences, Meteorology and Atmospheric Sciences,* and *Physics.* In the other guides in this series:

Graduate Programs in the Biological/Biomedical Sciences & Health-Related Medical Professions

See *Biological and Biomedical Sciences; Environmental Biology, and Evolutionary Biology;* and *Marine Biology*

Graduate Programs in Engineering & Applied Sciences

See *Civil and Environmental Engineering, Engineering and Applied Sciences,* and *Ocean Engineering*

CONTENTS

Program Directories

Display and Close-Up

Marine Sciences

California State University, East Bay, Office of Academic Programs and Graduate Studies, College of Science, Department of Biological Sciences, Marine Science Program, Moss Landing, CA 95039. Offers MS. *Students:* 4 applicants, 25% accepted, 0 enrolled. *Degree requirements:* For master's, thesis. *Entrance requirements:* For master's, GRE Subject Test, minimum GPA of 3.0 in field, 2.75 overall; 3 letters of reference; statement of purpose. Additional exam requirements/recommendations for international students: Required—TOEFL. *Application deadline:* For fall admission, 3/15 for domestic students. Application fee: $55. *Expenses:* Tuition, state resident: full-time $6738; part-time $1302 per quarter. Tuition, nonresident: full-time $12,690; part-time $2294 per quarter. *Required fees:* $449 per quarter. Tuition and fees vary according to degree level, program and reciprocity agreements. *Financial support:* Federal Work-Study, institutionally sponsored loans, and scholarships/grants available. Support available to part-time students. Financial award application deadline: 3/1; financial award applicants required to submit FAFSA. *Unit head:* Dr. Kenneth H. Coale, Director, 831-771-4400, Fax: 831-632-4403, E-mail: coale@mlml.calstate.edu. Web site: http://www.mlml.calstate.edu.

California State University, Fresno, Division of Graduate Studies, College of Science and Mathematics, Program in Marine Sciences, Fresno, CA 93740-8027. Offers MS. Part-time programs available. Postbaccalaureate distance learning degree programs offered. *Degree requirements:* For master's, thesis. *Entrance requirements:* For master's, GRE General Test, minimum GPA of 3.0. Additional exam requirements/recommendations for international students: Required—TOEFL. Electronic applications accepted. *Faculty research:* Wetlands ecology, land/water conservation, water irrigation.

California State University, Monterey Bay, College of Science, Media Arts and Technology, Moss Landing Marine Laboratories, Seaside, CA 93955-8001. Offers MS. Part-time programs available. *Degree requirements:* For master's, thesis, thesis defense. *Entrance requirements:* For master's, selected MLML faculty member to serve as potential thesis advisor and selected consortium institution to serve as home campus. Additional exam requirements/recommendations for international students: Required—TOEFL (minimum score 525 paper-based; 213 computer-based; 71 iBT). Electronic applications accepted. *Faculty research:* Remote sensing microbiology trace elements, chemistry ecology of birds, mammals, turtles and fish, invasive species, marine phycology.

California State University, Sacramento, Office of Graduate Studies, College of Natural Sciences and Mathematics, Department of Biological Sciences, Sacramento, CA 95819-6077. Offers biological sciences (MA, MS); immunohematology (MS); marine science (MS). Part-time programs available. *Faculty:* 22 full-time (10 women), 24 part-time/adjunct (11 women). *Students:* 13 full-time, 50 part-time; includes 16 minority (7 Asian, non-Hispanic/Latino; 4 Hispanic/Latino; 4 Native Hawaiian or other Pacific Islander, non-Hispanic/Latino; 1 Two or more races, non-Hispanic/Latino), 2 international. Average age 30. 85 applicants, 40% accepted, 25 enrolled. In 2011, 23 master's awarded. *Degree requirements:* For master's, thesis, writing proficiency exam. *Entrance requirements:* For master's, GRE, bachelor's degree in biology or equivalent; minimum GPA of 3.0 in biology, 2.75 overall during last 2 years of course work. Additional exam requirements/recommendations for international students: Required—TOEFL. *Application deadline:* For fall admission, 2/1 for domestic students, 3/1 for international students; for spring admission, 9/30 for international students. Applications are processed on a rolling basis. Application fee: $55. Electronic applications accepted. *Financial support:* Research assistantships, teaching assistantships, career-related internships or fieldwork, and Federal Work-Study available. Support available to part-time students. Financial award application deadline: 3/1; financial award applicants required to submit FAFSA. *Unit head:* Jennifer Lundmark, Chair, 916-278-7676, Fax: 916-278-6993, E-mail: lundmark@csus.edu. *Application contact:* Jose Martinez, Outreach and Graduate Diversity Coordinator, 916-278-6470, Fax: 916-278-5669, E-mail: martinj@skymail.csus.edu. Web site: http://www.csus.edu/bios.

Coastal Carolina University, College of Science, Conway, SC 29528-6054. Offers coastal marine and wetland studies (MS). Part-time and evening/weekend programs available. *Faculty:* 16 full-time (1 woman). *Students:* 13 full-time (8 women), 19 part-time (11 women); includes 2 minority (1 American Indian or Alaska Native, non-Hispanic/Latino; 1 Hispanic/Latino). Average age 26. 37 applicants, 38% accepted, 10 enrolled. In 2011, 5 master's awarded. *Degree requirements:* For master's, thesis. *Entrance requirements:* For master's, GRE, 2 letters of recommendation, resume, official transcripts, essay. Additional exam requirements/recommendations for international students: Required—TOEFL (minimum score 550 paper-based; 213 computer-based; 79 iBT). *Application deadline:* For fall admission, 3/1 priority date for domestic students, 3/1 for international students; for spring admission, 11/1 priority date for domestic students, 11/1 for international students. Applications are processed on a rolling basis. Application fee: $45. Electronic applications accepted. *Expenses:* Tuition, state resident: full-time $11,040; part-time $460 per credit hour. Tuition, nonresident: full-time $16,560; part-time $690 per credit hour. *Required fees:* $80; $40 per term. *Financial support:* Fellowships, research assistantships, and unspecified assistantships available. Support available to part-time students. Financial award application deadline: 3/1; financial award applicants required to

submit FAFSA. *Unit head:* Dr. Michael H. Roberts, Dean, 843-349-2282, Fax: 843-349-2545, E-mail: mroberts@coastal.edu. *Application contact:* Dr. James O. Luken, Associate Provost/Director of Graduate Studies, 843-349-2235, Fax: 843-349-6444, E-mail: joluken@coastal.edu. Web site: http://coastal.edu/academics/science/index.html.

College of Charleston, Graduate School, School of Sciences and Mathematics, Program in Marine Biology, Charleston, SC 29412. Offers MS. *Faculty:* 39 full-time (13 women), 5 part-time/adjunct (4 women). *Students:* 13 full-time (11 women), 32 part-time (22 women); includes 3 minority (2 Asian, non-Hispanic/Latino; 1 Hispanic/Latino). Average age 25. 110 applicants, 15% accepted, 14 enrolled. In 2011, 11 master's awarded. *Degree requirements:* For master's, comprehensive exam, thesis. *Entrance requirements:* For master's, GRE General Test, 3 letters of recommendation. Additional exam requirements/recommendations for international students: Required—TOEFL (minimum score 81 iBT). *Application deadline:* For fall admission, 2/1 for domestic and international students; for spring admission, 11/1 for domestic and international students. Application fee: $45. Electronic applications accepted. *Expenses:* Tuition, state resident: full-time $5455; part-time $455 per credit. Tuition, nonresident: full-time $13,917; part-time $1160 per credit. *Financial support:* In 2011–12, 4 fellowships (averaging $22,000 per year), 22 research assistantships (averaging $19,000 per year), 19 teaching assistantships (averaging $16,000 per year) were awarded; career-related internships or fieldwork, Federal Work-Study, institutionally sponsored loans, scholarships/grants, and unspecified assistantships also available. Support available to part-time students. Financial award application deadline: 4/1; financial award applicants required to submit FAFSA. *Faculty research:* Ecology, environmental physiology, marine genomics, bioinformatics, toxicology, cell biology, population biology, fisheries science, animal physiology, biodiversity, estuarine ecology, evolution and systematics, microbial processes, plant physiology, immunology. *Unit head:* Dr. Craig J. Plante, Director, 843-953-9187, Fax: 843-953-9199, E-mail: plantec@cofc.edu. *Application contact:* Susan Hallatt, Director of Graduate Admissions, 843-953-5614, Fax: 843-953-1434, E-mail: hallatts@cofc.edu. Web site: http://www.cofc.edu/~marine/.

The College of William and Mary, Virginia Institute of Marine Science, Gloucester Point, VA 23062. Offers MS, PhD. *Faculty:* 68 full-time (25 women), 2 part-time/adjunct (1 woman). *Students:* 90 full-time (58 women), 5 part-time (2 women); includes 9 minority (1 Black or African American, non-Hispanic/Latino; 2 Asian, non-Hispanic/Latino; 2 Hispanic/Latino; 3 Native Hawaiian or other Pacific Islander, non-Hispanic/Latino; 1 Two or more races, non-Hispanic/Latino), 14 international. Average age 28. 99 applicants, 21% accepted, 15 enrolled. In 2011, 12 master's, 8 doctorates awarded. *Degree requirements:* For master's, thesis, qualifying exam; for doctorate, comprehensive exam, thesis/dissertation, qualifying exam. *Entrance requirements:* For master's, GRE, appropriate bachelor's degree; for doctorate, GRE, appropriate bachelor's and master's degrees. Additional exam requirements/recommendations for international students: Required—TOEFL. *Application deadline:* For fall admission, 1/15 for domestic and international students. Application fee: $50. Electronic applications accepted. *Expenses:* Tuition, state resident: full-time $6400; part-time $365 per credit hour. Tuition, nonresident: full-time $19,720; part-time $985 per credit hour. *Required fees:* $4562. *Financial support:* In 2011–12, 93 students received support, including 16 fellowships with full tuition reimbursements available (averaging $19,005 per year), 69 research assistantships with full tuition reimbursements available (averaging $19,005 per year), 8 teaching assistantships with partial tuition reimbursements available (averaging $6,500 per year); career-related internships or fieldwork, Federal Work-Study, scholarships/grants, health care benefits, and unspecified assistantships also available. Support available to part-time students. Financial award application deadline: 6/15; financial award applicants required to submit FAFSA. *Faculty research:* Marine science, oceanography, marine ecology, fisheries, environmental science and ecotoxicology. *Total annual research expenditures:* $17.7 million. *Unit head:* Dr. John T. Wells, Dean/Director, 804-684-7102, Fax: 804-684-7009, E-mail: wells@vims.edu. *Application contact:* Fonda J. Powell, Admissions Coordinator, 804-684-7105, Fax: 804-684-7881, E-mail: fonda@vims.edu. Web site: http://www.vims.edu/.

Cornell University, Graduate School, Graduate Fields of Agriculture and Life Sciences, Field of Natural Resources, Ithaca, NY 14853-0001. Offers aquatic science (MPS, MS, PhD); environmental management (MPS); fishery science (MPS, MS, PhD); forest science (MPS, MS, PhD); resource policy and management (MPS, MS, PhD); wildlife science (MPS, MS, PhD). *Faculty:* 39 full-time (7 women). *Students:* 52 full-time (21 women); includes 4 minority (1 American Indian or Alaska Native, non-Hispanic/Latino; 1 Asian, non-Hispanic/Latino; 1 Hispanic/Latino; 1 Two or more races, non-Hispanic/Latino), 15 international. Average age 32. 72 applicants, 21% accepted, 11 enrolled. In 2011, 2 master's, 5 doctorates awarded. *Degree requirements:* For master's, thesis (MS), project paper (MPS); for doctorate, comprehensive exam, thesis/dissertation. *Entrance requirements:* For master's and doctorate, GRE General Test, 2 letters of recommendation. Additional exam requirements/recommendations for international students: Required—TOEFL (minimum score

550 paper-based; 213 computer-based; 77 iBT). *Application deadline:* For spring admission, 10/30 for domestic students. Applications are processed on a rolling basis. Application fee: $95. Electronic applications accepted. *Financial support:* In 2011–12, 10 fellowships with full tuition reimbursements, 14 research assistantships with full tuition reimbursements, 28 teaching assistantships with full tuition reimbursements were awarded; institutionally sponsored loans, scholarships/grants, health care benefits, tuition waivers (full and partial), and unspecified assistantships also available. Financial award applicants required to submit FAFSA. *Faculty research:* Ecosystem-level dynamics, systems modeling, conservation biology/management, resource management's human dimensions, biogeochemistry. *Unit head:* Director of Graduate Studies, 607-255-2807, Fax: 607-255-0349. *Application contact:* Graduate Field Assistant, 607-255-2807, Fax: 607-255-0349, E-mail: nrgrad@cornell.edu. Web site: http://www.gradschool.cornell.edu/fields.php?id-54&a-2.

Duke University, Graduate School, Program in Marine Science and Conservation, Beaufort, NC 28516. Offers MS. *Faculty:* 18 full-time. *Students:* 33 full-time (24 women); includes 2 minority (1 American Indian or Alaska Native, non-Hispanic/Latino; 1 Asian, non-Hispanic/Latino), 7 international. 65 applicants, 18% accepted, 9 enrolled. *Entrance requirements:* Additional exam requirements/recommendations for international students: Required—TOEFL (minimum score 550 paper-based; 213 computer-based; 83 iBT), IELTS. *Application deadline:* For fall admission, 12/8 priority date for domestic students. Application fee: $75. *Expenses: Tuition:* Full-time $40,720. *Required fees:* $3107. *Financial support:* Fellowships, research assistantships, and teaching assistantships available. *Unit head:* Lisa Campbell, Director of Graduate Studies, 252-504-7585, Fax: 252-504-7648, E-mail: rachel.lopiccolo@duke.edu. *Application contact:* Elizabeth Hutton, Director of Admissions, 919-684-3913, Fax: 919-684-2277, E-mail: grad-admissions@duke.edu. Web site: http://www.env.duke.edu/marinelab.

Duke University, Nicholas School of the Environment, Durham, NC 27708-0328. Offers coastal environmental management (MEM); DEL-environmental leadership (MEM); energy and environment (MEM); environmental economics and policy (MEM); environmental health and security (MEM); forest resource management (MF); global environmental change (MEM); resource ecology (MEM); water and air resources (MEM); JD/AM; JD/MEM; JD/MF; MAT/MEM; MBA/MEM; MBA/MF; MEM/MPP; MF/MPP. *Accreditation:* SAF (one or more programs are accredited). Part-time programs available. *Degree requirements:* For master's, thesis. *Entrance requirements:* For master's, GRE General Test, previous course work in biology or ecology, calculus, statistics, and microeconomics; computer familiarity with word processing and data analysis. Additional exam requirements/recommendations for international students: Required—TOEFL (minimum score 550 paper-based; 213 computer-based). Electronic applications accepted. *Expenses:* Contact institution. *Faculty research:* Ecosystem management, conservation ecology, earth systems, risk assessment.

Florida Institute of Technology, Graduate Programs, College of Engineering, Department of Marine and Environmental Systems, Program in Oceanography, Melbourne, FL 32901-6975. Offers biological oceanography (MS); chemical oceanography (MS); coastal management (MS); geological oceanography (MS); oceanography (PhD); physical oceanography (MS). Part-time programs available. *Faculty:* 11 full-time (0 women), 3 part-time/adjunct (0 women). *Students:* 14 full-time (6 women), 1 (woman) part-time; includes 1 minority (Two or more races, non-Hispanic/Latino), 3 international. Average age 30. 14 applicants, 50% accepted, 2 enrolled. In 2011, 1 degree awarded. *Degree requirements:* For master's, comprehensive exam (for some programs), thesis (for some programs), seminar, field project, written final exam, internship, technical paper, oral presentation; for doctorate, comprehensive exam, thesis/dissertation, seminar, internships, publications. *Entrance requirements:* For master's, GRE General Test, minimum GPA of 3.0, 3 letters of recommendation, resume, transcripts, statement of objectives; for doctorate, GRE General Test, minimum GPA of 3.3, resume, 3 letters of recommendation, statement of objectives, on-campus interview (highly recommended). Additional exam requirements/recommendations for international students: Required—TOEFL (minimum score 550 paper-based; 213 computer-based; 79 iBT). *Application deadline:* Applications are processed on a rolling basis. Electronic applications accepted. *Expenses: Tuition:* Full-time $19,620; part-time $1090 per credit hour. Tuition and fees vary according to campus/location. *Financial support:* Career-related internships or fieldwork, institutionally sponsored loans, tuition waivers (partial), unspecified assistantships, and tuition remissions available. Support available to part-time students. Financial award application deadline: 3/1; financial award applicants required to submit FAFSA. *Faculty research:* Marine geochemistry, ecosystem dynamics, coastal processes, marine pollution, environmental modeling. *Total annual research expenditures:* $1.6 million. *Unit head:* Dr. George Maul, Department Head, 321-674-7453, Fax: 321-674-7212, E-mail: gmaul@fit.edu. *Application contact:* Cheryl A. Brown, Associate Director of Graduate Admission, 321-674-7581, Fax: 321-723-9468, E-mail: cbrown@fit.edu. Web site: http://www.coe.fit.edu/dmes.

Florida State University, The Graduate School, College of Arts and Sciences, Department of Earth, Ocean and Atmospheric Science, Program in Oceanography, Tallahassee, FL 32306-4320. Offers aquatic environmental science (MS, PMS); oceanography (MS, PhD). *Faculty:* 12 full-time (1 woman). *Students:* 59 full-time (32 women); includes 4 minority (1 Black or African American, non-Hispanic/Latino; 3 Asian, non-Hispanic/Latino), 16 international. Average age 27. 55 applicants, 31% accepted, 15 enrolled. In 2011, 3 master's, 3 doctorates awarded. *Degree requirements:* For master's, thesis; for doctorate, comprehensive exam, thesis/dissertation. *Entrance requirements:* For master's and doctorate, GRE General Test, minimum upper-division GPA of 3.0. Additional exam requirements/recommendations for international students: Required—TOEFL (minimum score 550 paper-based; 213 computer-based; 80 iBT). *Application deadline:* For fall admission, 2/15 priority date for domestic students, 2/15 for international students; for spring admission, 7/15 priority date for domestic students, 7/15 for international students. Applications are processed on a rolling basis. Application fee: $30. Electronic applications accepted. *Expenses:* Tuition, state resident: full-time $9474; part-time $350.88 per credit hour. Tuition, nonresident: full-time $16,236; part-time $601.34 per credit hour. *Required fees:* $630 per semester. One-time fee: $20. Tuition and fees vary according to course load and campus/location. *Financial support:* In 2011–12, 47 students received support, including 1 fellowship with full tuition reimbursement available, 31 research assistantships with full tuition reimbursements available, 15 teaching assistantships with full tuition reimbursements available. Financial award application deadline: 2/15; financial award applicants required to submit FAFSA. *Faculty research:* Trace metals in seawater, currents and waves, modeling, benthic ecology, marine biogeochemistry. *Unit head:* Dr. Jeffrey Chanton, Area Coordinator, 850-644-6700, Fax: 850-644-2581, E-mail: chanton@ocean.fsu.edu. *Application contact:* Michaela Lupiani, Academic Coordinator, 850-644-6700, Fax: 850-644-2581, E-mail: admissions@ocean.fsu.edu.

Georgia Institute of Technology, Graduate Studies and Research, College of Sciences, School of Earth and Atmospheric Sciences, Atlanta, GA 30332-0340. Offers atmospheric chemistry, aerosols and clouds (MS, PhD); dynamics of weather and climate (MS, PhD); geochemistry (MS, PhD); geophysics (MS, PhD); oceanography (MS, PhD); paleoclimate (MS, PhD); planetary science (MS, PhD); remote sensing (MS, PhD). Part-time programs available. Terminal master's awarded for partial completion of doctoral program. *Degree requirements:* For master's, thesis or alternative; for doctorate, comprehensive exam, thesis/dissertation. *Entrance requirements:* For master's, GRE, letters of recommendation; for doctorate, GRE, academic transcripts, letters of recommendation, personal statement. Additional exam requirements/recommendations for international students: Required—TOEFL (minimum score 550 paper-based; 213 computer-based; 79 iBT). *Faculty research:* Geophysics; atmospheric chemistry, aerosols and clouds; dynamics of weather and climate; geochemistry; oceanography; paleoclimate; planetary science; remote sensing.

Hawai`i Pacific University, College of Natural and Computational Sciences, Honolulu, HI 96813. Offers global leadership and sustainable development (MA); marine science (MS). Part-time and evening/weekend programs available. *Faculty:* 15 full-time (5 women), 5 part-time/adjunct (1 woman). *Students:* 19 full-time (13 women), 20 part-time (12 women); includes 13 minority (2 Black or African American, non-Hispanic/Latino; 4 Asian, non-Hispanic/Latino; 3 Hispanic/Latino; 1 Native Hawaiian or other Pacific Islander, non-Hispanic/Latino; 3 Two or more races, non-Hispanic/Latino). Average age 25. 55 applicants, 53% accepted, 15 enrolled. In 2011, 3 master's awarded. *Degree requirements:* For master's, thesis. *Entrance requirements:* For master's, GRE, bachelor's degree in science or marine science, minimum GPA of 3.0. Additional exam requirements/recommendations for international students: Recommended—TOEFL (minimum score 550 paper-based; 213 computer-based; 80 iBT), TWE (minimum score 5). *Application deadline:* For fall admission, 2/15 priority date for domestic students; for spring admission, 10/15 priority date for domestic students. Applications are processed on a rolling basis. Application fee: $50. Electronic applications accepted. *Expenses: Tuition:* Full-time $13,230; part-time $735 per credit. Tuition and fees vary according to course load and program. *Financial support:* In 2011–12, 30 students received support. Career-related internships or fieldwork, Federal Work-Study, scholarships/grants, tuition waivers, and unspecified assistantships available. *Unit head:* Dr. Andrew Brittain, Vice President, Research/Dean, 808-236-3553, Fax: 808-236-5880, E-mail: abrittain@hpu.edu. *Application contact:* Chad Schempp, Director of Graduate Admissions, 808-543-8035, Fax: 808-544-0280, E-mail: graduate@hpu.edu. Web site: http://www.hpu.edu/MSMS/.

See Display on next page and Close-Up on page 205.

Instituto Tecnologico de Santo Domingo, Graduate School, Area of Basic And Environmental Sciences, Santo Domingo, Dominican Republic. Offers environmental science (M En S), including environmental education, environmental management, marine resources, natural resources management; mathematics (MS, PhD); renewable energy technology (MS, Certificate).

Jacksonville University, Marine Science Research Institute, Jacksonville, FL 32211. Offers MA, MS. *Degree requirements:* For master's, thesis (for MS).

Medical University of South Carolina, College of Graduate Studies, Program in Molecular and Cellular Biology and Pathobiology, Charleston, SC 29425. Offers cancer biology (PhD); cardiovascular biology (PhD); cardiovascular imaging (PhD); cell regulation (PhD); craniofacial biology (PhD); genetics and development (PhD); marine biomedicine (PhD); DMD/PhD; MD/PhD. *Faculty:* 137 full-time (33 women). *Students:* 28 full-time (23 women); includes 5 minority (4 Black or African American, non-Hispanic/Latino; 1 Hispanic/Latino), 5 international. Average age 30. In 2011, 16 doctorates awarded. *Degree requirements:* For doctorate, thesis/dissertation, oral and written exams. *Entrance requirements:* For doctorate, GRE General Test, interview, minimum GPA of 3.0. Additional exam requirements/recommendations for international students: Required—TOEFL (minimum score 600 paper-based; 250 computer-based; 100 iBT). *Application deadline:* For fall admission, 1/15 priority date for domestic

Peterson's Graduate Programs in the Physical Sciences, Mathematics, Agricultural Sciences, the Environment & Natural Resources 2013

facebook.com/petersonspublishing   **193**

Marine Sciences

students, 1/15 for international students. Applications are processed on a rolling basis. Application fee: $0 ($85 for international students). Electronic applications accepted. *Financial support:* In 2011–12, 39 research assistantships with partial tuition reimbursements (averaging $23,000 per year) were awarded; Federal Work-Study and scholarships/grants also available. Support available to part-time students. Financial award application deadline: 3/10; financial award applicants required to submit FAFSA. *Unit head:* Dr. Donald R. Menick, Director, 843-876-5045, Fax: 843-792-6590, E-mail: menickd@musc.edu. *Application contact:* Dr. Cynthia F. Wright, Associate Dean for Admissions and Career Development, 843-792-2564, Fax: 843-792-6590, E-mail: wrightcf@musc.edu. Web site: http://www.musc.edu/mcbp/.

Memorial University of Newfoundland, School of Graduate Studies, Interdisciplinary Program in Marine Studies, St. John's, NL A1C 5S7, Canada. Offers fisheries resource management (MMS, Advanced Diploma). Part-time programs available. *Degree requirements:* For master's, report. *Entrance requirements:* For master's and Advanced Diploma, high 2nd class degree from a recognized university. *Faculty research:* Biological, ecological and oceanographic aspects of world fisheries; economics; political science; sociology.

North Carolina State University, Graduate School, College of Physical and Mathematical Sciences, Department of Marine, Earth, and Atmospheric Sciences, Raleigh, NC 27695. Offers marine, earth, and atmospheric sciences (MS, PhD); meteorology (MS, PhD); oceanography (MS, PhD). PhD offered jointly with The University of North Carolina Wilmington. Terminal master's awarded for partial completion of doctoral program. *Degree requirements:* For master's, thesis (for some programs), final oral exam; for doctorate, comprehensive exam, thesis/dissertation, final oral exam, preliminary oral and written exams. *Entrance requirements:* For master's, GRE General Test, minimum GPA of 3.0; for doctorate, GRE General Test, GRE Subject Test (for disciplines in biological oceanography and geology), minimum GPA of 3.0. Additional exam requirements/recommendations for international students: Required—TOEFL (minimum score 550 paper-based). Electronic applications accepted. *Faculty research:* Boundary layer and air quality meteorology; climate and mesoscale dynamics; biological, chemical, geological, and physical oceanography; hard rock, soft rock, environmental, and paleo-geology.

Nova Southeastern University, Oceanographic Center, Fort Lauderdale, FL 33314-7796. Offers biological sciences (MS); coastal zone management (MS); marine and coastal studies (MA); marine biology (MS); marine biology and oceanography (PhD), including marine biology, oceanography; marine environmental science (MS). Part-time and evening/weekend programs available. *Faculty:* 15 full-time (1 woman), 5 part-time/adjunct (0 women). *Students:* 130 full-time (86 women), 135 part-time (87 women); includes 34 minority (5 Black or African American, non-Hispanic/Latino; 5 Asian, non-Hispanic/Latino; 22 Hispanic/Latino; 2 Two or more races, non-Hispanic/Latino), 7 international.

Average age 29. 98 applicants, 82% accepted, 67 enrolled. In 2011, 30 master's, 1 doctorate awarded. *Degree requirements:* For master's, thesis; for doctorate, comprehensive exam, thesis/dissertation, departmental qualifying exam. *Entrance requirements:* For master's, GRE General Test; for doctorate, GRE General Test, master's degree. Additional exam requirements/recommendations for international students: Required—TOEFL (minimum score 550 paper-based). *Application deadline:* Applications are processed on a rolling basis. Application fee: $50. *Expenses:* Contact institution. *Financial support:* In 2011–12, 25 research assistantships (averaging $4,000 per year), 3 teaching assistantships (averaging $3,500 per year) were awarded; career-related internships or fieldwork, Federal Work-Study, scholarships/grants, tuition waivers (partial), and unspecified assistantships also available. Support available to part-time students. Financial award applicants required to submit FAFSA. *Faculty research:* Physical, geological, chemical, and biological oceanography. *Unit head:* Dr. Richard Dodge, Dean, 954-262-3600, Fax: 954-262-4020, E-mail: dodge@nsu.nova.edu. *Application contact:* Dr. Richard Spieler, Director of Academic Programs, 954-262-3600, Fax: 954-262-4020, E-mail: spieler@nova.edu. Web site: http://www.nova.edu/ocean/.

Oregon State University, Graduate School, College of Oceanic and Atmospheric Sciences, Program in Marine Resource Management, Corvallis, OR 97331. Offers MA, MS. *Degree requirements:* For master's, thesis optional. *Entrance requirements:* For master's, GRE General Test, minimum GPA of 3.0 in last 90 hours of course work. Additional exam requirements/recommendations for international students: Required—TOEFL. *Faculty research:* Ocean and coastal resources, fisheries resources, marine pollution, marine recreation and tourism.

San Francisco State University, Division of Graduate Studies, College of Science and Engineering, Department of Biology, Program in Marine Science, San Francisco, CA 94132-1722. Offers MS. Program offered through the Moss Landing Marine Laboratories. *Application deadline:* Applications are processed on a rolling basis. *Unit head:* Dr. Kenneth Coale, Director, 831-7714400, E-mail: frontdesk@mlml.calstate.edu. *Application contact:* John Machado, Graduate Coordinator, E-mail: jmachado@mlml.calstate.edu. Web site: http://www.sfsu.edu/~bulletin/current/programs/marines.htm#282.

San Jose State University, Graduate Studies and Research, College of Science, Moss Landing Marine Laboratories, San Jose, CA 95192-0001. Offers MS. *Degree requirements:* For master's, thesis, qualifying exam. *Entrance requirements:* For master's, GRE. Electronic applications accepted. *Faculty research:* Physical oceanography, marine geology, ecology, ichthyology, invertebrate zoology.

Savannah State University, Master of Science in Marine Sciences Program, Savannah, GA 31404. Offers MS. Part-time programs available. *Degree requirements:* For master's, comprehensive exam. *Entrance requirements:* For

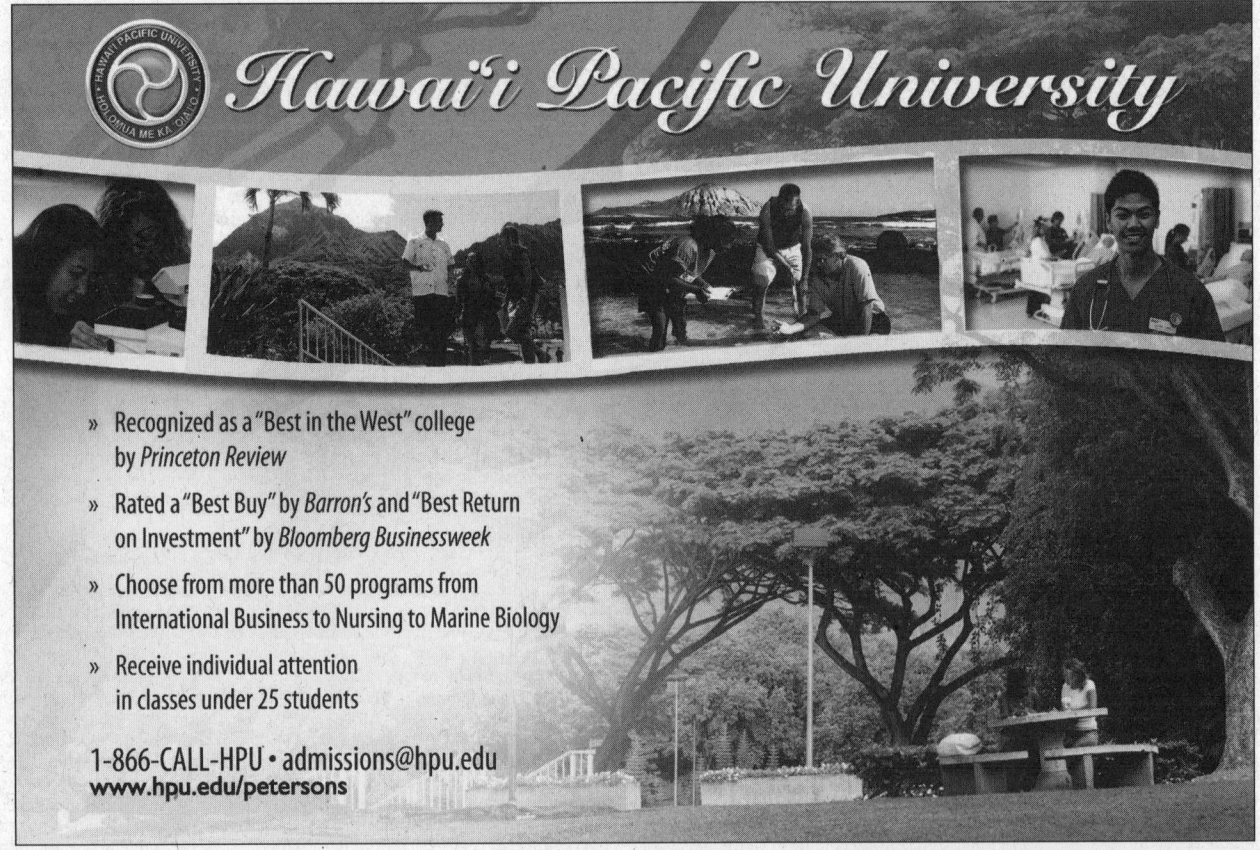
194 facebook.com/petersonspublishing

Peterson's Graduate Programs in the Physical Sciences, Mathematics, Agricultural Sciences, the Environment & Natural Resources 2013

master's, GRE General Test, 3 letters of recommendation, minimum GPA of 3.0, essay. Additional exam requirements/recommendations for international students: Required—TOEFL. Electronic applications accepted.

Stony Brook University, State University of New York, Graduate School, School of Marine and Atmospheric Sciences, Institute for Terrestrial and Planetary Atmospheres, Program in Marine Sciences, Stony Brook, NY 11794. Offers MS, PhD. Evening/weekend programs available. *Degree requirements:* For doctorate, one foreign language, comprehensive exam, thesis/dissertation. *Entrance requirements:* For master's, GRE General Test, official transcripts, minimum GPA of 3.0, 3 letters of recommendation; for doctorate, GRE General Test, minimum GPA of 3.0, 3 letters of recommendation. Additional exam requirements/recommendations for international students: Required—TOEFL (minimum score 600 paper-based; 213 computer-based). Electronic applications accepted.

Texas A&M University at Galveston, Department of Marine Sciences, Galveston, TX 77553-1675. Offers marine resources management (MMRM). Part-time programs available. *Faculty:* 33 full-time (7 women). *Students:* 23 full-time (11 women), 9 part-time (7 women); includes 6 minority (1 American Indian or Alaska Native, non-Hispanic/Latino; 2 Hispanic/Latino; 1 Native Hawaiian or other Pacific Islander, non-Hispanic/Latino; 2 Two or more races, non-Hispanic/Latino). Average age 24. 8 applicants, 88% accepted, 5 enrolled. In 2011, 9 degrees awarded. *Degree requirements:* For master's, thesis (for some programs). *Entrance requirements:* For master's, GRE, course work in economics. Additional exam requirements/recommendations for international students: Required—TOEFL (minimum score 550 paper-based; 213 computer-based; 80 iBT), IELTS (minimum score 6). *Application deadline:* For fall admission, 6/15 for domestic and international students; for spring admission, 10/15 for domestic and international students. Application fee: $50 ($90 for international students). Electronic applications accepted. *Expenses:* Tuition, state resident: full-time $2087; part-time $231.85 per contact hour. Tuition, nonresident: full-time $4904; part-time $545 per contact hour. *Required fees:* $65 per contact hour. $110 per semester. One-time fee: $50. *Financial support:* In 2011–12, 11 students received support, including 2 research assistantships, 9 teaching assistantships; scholarships/grants, health care benefits, and unspecified assistantships also available. Financial award applicants required to submit FAFSA. *Faculty research:* Biogeochemistry, physical oceanography, theoretical chemistry, marine policy. *Unit head:* Dr. Patrick Louchouarn, Professor/Head, 409-740-4710. *Application contact:* Dr. Frederick C. Schlemmer, II, Associate Professor/Graduate Advisor, 409-740-4518, Fax: 409-740-4429, E-mail: schlemme@tamug.edu.

Texas A&M University–Corpus Christi, Graduate Studies and Research, College of Science and Technology, Program in Coastal and Marine System Science, Corpus Christi, TX 78412-5503. Offers PhD.

University of Alaska Fairbanks, School of Fisheries and Ocean Sciences, Program in Marine Sciences and Limnology, Fairbanks, AK 99775-7220. Offers marine biology (MS, PhD); oceanography (PhD), including biological oceanography, chemical oceanography, fisheries, geological oceanography, physical oceanography. Part-time programs available. *Faculty:* 6 full-time (4 women). *Students:* 40 full-time (29 women), 17 part-time (12 women); includes 7 minority (3 Asian, non-Hispanic/Latino; 4 Hispanic/Latino), 4 international. Average age 30. 61 applicants, 20% accepted, 12 enrolled. In 2011, 3 master's, 3 doctorates awarded. *Degree requirements:* For master's, comprehensive exam, thesis, oral defense; for doctorate, comprehensive exam, thesis/dissertation, oral defense. *Entrance requirements:* For master's and doctorate, GRE General Test. Additional exam requirements/recommendations for international students: Required—TOEFL (minimum score 550 paper-based; 213 computer-based; 80 iBT). *Application deadline:* For fall admission, 6/1 for domestic students, 3/1 for international students; for spring admission, 10/15 for domestic students, 8/1 for international students. Applications are processed on a rolling basis. Application fee: $60. Electronic applications accepted. *Expenses:* Tuition, state resident: full-time $6696; part-time $372 per credit. Tuition, nonresident: full-time $13,680; part-time $760 per credit. Tuition and fees vary according to course load and reciprocity agreements. *Financial support:* In 2011–12, 26 research assistantships with tuition reimbursements (averaging $11,484 per year), 7 teaching assistantships with tuition reimbursements (averaging $14,772 per year) were awarded; fellowships with tuition reimbursements, career-related internships or fieldwork, Federal Work-Study, scholarships/grants, health care benefits, and unspecified assistantships also available. Support available to part-time students. Financial award application deadline: 7/1; financial award applicants required to submit FAFSA. *Unit head:* Katrin Iken, Co-Chair, 907-474-7289, Fax: 907-474-5863, E-mail: academics@sfos.uaf.edu. *Application contact:* Christina Neumann, Academic Manager, 907-474-7289, Fax: 907-474-5863, E-mail: clneumann@alaska.edu. Web site: http://www.sfos.uaf.edu/academics/prospective/graduate.html.

The University of British Columbia, Faculty of Science, Department of Earth and Ocean Sciences, Vancouver, BC V6T 1Z4, Canada. Offers atmospheric science (M Sc, PhD); geological engineering (M Eng, MA Sc, PhD); geological sciences (M Sc, PhD); geophysics (M Sc, MA Sc, PhD); oceanography (M Sc, PhD). *Degree requirements:* For master's, thesis (for some programs); for doctorate, comprehensive exam, thesis/dissertation. *Entrance requirements:* Additional exam requirements/recommendations for international students: Required—TOEFL (minimum score 600 paper-based; 250 computer-based; 100 iBT). Electronic applications accepted. *Faculty research:* Oceans and

atmosphere, environmental earth science, hydro geology, mineral deposits, geophysics.

University of California, San Diego, Office of Graduate Studies, Scripps Institution of Oceanography, Program in Marine Biodiversity and Conservation, La Jolla, CA 92093. Offers MAS. *Entrance requirements:* For master's, minimum 3 years post-baccalaureate work experience. Additional exam requirements/recommendations for international students: Required—TOEFL. Electronic applications accepted.

University of California, Santa Barbara, Graduate Division, College of Letters and Sciences, Division of Mathematics, Life, and Physical Sciences, Interdepartmental Program in Marine Science, Santa Barbara, CA 93106-9620. Offers MS, PhD. *Faculty:* 43 full-time (10 women). *Students:* 18 full-time (10 women); includes 1 minority (American Indian or Alaska Native, non-Hispanic/Latino), 3 international. Average age 30. 49 applicants, 16% accepted, 4 enrolled. In 2011, 4 master's, 1 doctorate awarded. *Median time to degree:* Of those who began their doctoral program in fall 2003, 100% received their degree in 8 years or less. *Degree requirements:* For master's, thesis, 39 units; for doctorate, comprehensive exam, thesis/dissertation, 31 units. *Entrance requirements:* For master's and doctorate, GRE. Additional exam requirements/recommendations for international students: Required—TOEFL (minimum score 550 paper-based; 80 iBT), IELTS (minimum score 7). *Application deadline:* For fall admission, 12/15 for domestic and international students. Application fee: $80 ($100 for international students). Electronic applications accepted. *Expenses:* Tuition, state resident: full-time $12,192. Tuition, nonresident: full-time $27,294. *Required fees:* $764.13. *Financial support:* In 2011–12, 18 students received support, including 10 fellowships with full tuition reimbursements available (averaging $11,468 per year), 7 research assistantships with full tuition reimbursements available (averaging $10,895 per year), 3 teaching assistantships with full tuition reimbursements available (averaging $7,908 per year); career-related internships or fieldwork, Federal Work-Study, institutionally sponsored loans, scholarships/grants, health care benefits, tuition waivers (full and partial), and unspecified assistantships also available. Support available to part-time students. Financial award application deadline: 12/15; financial award applicants required to submit FAFSA. *Faculty research:* Ocean carbon cycling, paleooceanography, physiology of marine organisms, bio-optical oceanography, biological oceanography. *Unit head:* Prof. Libe Washburn, Chair/Professor of Geography, 805-893-7367, Fax: 805-893-2578, E-mail: washburn@eri.ucsb.edu. *Application contact:* Melanie Fujii, Graduate Program Assistant, 805-893-2979, Fax: 805-893-5885, E-mail: fujii@lifesci.ucsb.edu. Web site: http://www.igpms.ucsb.edu/.

University of California, Santa Cruz, Division of Graduate Studies, Division of Physical and Biological Sciences, Department of Ocean Sciences, Santa Cruz, CA 95064. Offers MS, PhD. Terminal master's awarded for partial completion of doctoral program. *Degree requirements:* For master's, thesis; for doctorate, comprehensive exam, thesis/dissertation, seminar, qualifying exam. *Entrance requirements:* For master's and doctorate, GRE General Test, GRE Subject Test, 3 letters of recommendation. Additional exam requirements/recommendations for international students: Required—TOEFL (minimum score 550 paper-based; 220 computer-based; 83 iBT); Recommended—IELTS (minimum score 8). Electronic applications accepted. *Faculty research:* Sediment, marine organic and trace metal biogeochemistry; paleoceanography; remote sensing (satellite oceanography); coastal circulation processes; the development of software applications for real-time data acquisition and data visualization; climatology.

University of Connecticut, Graduate School, College of Liberal Arts and Sciences, Department of Marine Sciences, Storrs, CT 06269. Offers MS, PhD. Terminal master's awarded for partial completion of doctoral program. *Degree requirements:* For master's, comprehensive exam; for doctorate, thesis/dissertation. *Entrance requirements:* Additional exam requirements/recommendations for international students: Required—TOEFL (minimum score 550 paper-based; 213 computer-based). Electronic applications accepted.

University of Delaware, College of Earth, Ocean, and Environment, School of Marine Science and Policy, Newark, DE 19716. Offers marine policy (MMP); marine studies (MS, PhD), including marine biosciences, oceanography, physical ocean science and engineering; oceanography (PhD).

University of Florida, Graduate School, College of Agricultural and Life Sciences, Department of Fisheries and Aquatic Sciences, Gainesville, FL 32611. Offers MFAS, MS, PhD. Part-time programs available. *Students:* 39 full-time (22 women), 16 part-time (4 women); includes 2 minority (1 Asian, non-Hispanic/Latino; 1 Hispanic/Latino), 6 international. Average age 31. 37 applicants, 43% accepted, 12 enrolled. In 2011, 8 master's, 3 doctorates awarded. *Degree requirements:* For master's, thesis (for MS); technical paper (for MFAS); for doctorate, comprehensive exam, thesis/dissertation. *Entrance requirements:* For master's and doctorate, GRE General Test, minimum GPA of 3.0. Additional exam requirements/recommendations for international students: Required—TOEFL (minimum score 550 paper-based; 213 computer-based; 80 iBT), IELTS (minimum score 6). *Application deadline:* For fall admission, 6/1 for domestic students, 3/1 for international students; for spring admission, 10/1 for domestic students, 8/1 for international students. Applications are processed on a rolling basis. Application fee: $30. Electronic applications accepted. *Financial support:* Fellowships, research assistantships, and unspecified assistantships available. Financial award application deadline: 1/31; financial award applicants required to submit FAFSA. *Faculty research:* Conservation and management of aquatic ecosystems; aquatic animal health; water quality, nutrients, and eutrophication;

Peterson's Graduate Programs in the Physical Sciences, Mathematics, Agricultural Sciences, the Environment & Natural Resources 2013

facebook.com/petersonspublishing **195**

Marine Sciences

sustainable and quantitative fisheries; aquaculture or ornamental fish, marine baitfish, and shellfish. *Total annual research expenditures:* $10 million. *Unit head:* Dr. Nancy J. Peterson, Associate Director, 352-846-0848, Fax: 352-846-1277, E-mail: njp@ufl.edu. *Application contact:* Dr. Charles Cichra, Graduate Coordinator, 352-273-3621, Fax: 352-392-3672, E-mail: cecichra@ufl.edu. Web site: http://fishweb.ifas.ufl.edu/.

University of Georgia, Franklin College of Arts and Sciences, Department of Marine Sciences, Athens, GA 30602. Offers MS, PhD. *Faculty:* 17 full-time (5 women), 3 part-time/adjunct (0 women). *Students:* 31 full-time (17 women), 1 (woman) part-time; includes 4 minority (1 Asian, non-Hispanic/Latino; 2 Hispanic/Latino; 1 Two or more races, non-Hispanic/Latino), 8 international. Average age 28. 36 applicants, 28% accepted, 6 enrolled. In 2011, 1 master's, 3 doctorates awarded. *Degree requirements:* For master's, thesis; for doctorate, comprehensive exam, thesis/dissertation, teaching experience, field research experience. *Entrance requirements:* For master's and doctorate, GRE General Test. Additional exam requirements/recommendations for international students: Required—TOEFL. *Application deadline:* For fall admission, 2/1 priority date for domestic students, 2/1 for international students; for spring admission, 10/15 priority date for domestic students, 9/1 for international students. Applications are processed on a rolling basis. Application fee: $50. Electronic applications accepted. *Financial support:* In 2011–12, 9 fellowships with full tuition reimbursements (averaging $20,000 per year), 21 research assistantships with full tuition reimbursements (averaging $18,000 per year), 11 teaching assistantships with full tuition reimbursements (averaging $18,000 per year) were awarded. *Faculty research:* Microbial ecology, biogeochemistry, polar biology, coastal ecology, coastal circulation. *Unit head:* Dr. Brian Binder, Director, 706-542-6408, Fax: 706-542-5888, E-mail: bbinder@uga.edu. *Application contact:* Dr. Christof Meile, Graduate Coordinator, 706-542-6549, E-mail: cmeile@uga.edu. Web site: http://www.marsci.uga.edu/.

University of Hawaii at Manoa, Graduate Division, College of Social Sciences, Department of Geography, Graduate Ocean Policy Certificate Program, Honolulu, HI 96822. Offers Graduate Certificate. Part-time programs available. *Entrance requirements:* Additional exam requirements/recommendations for international students: Required—TOEFL (minimum score 500 paper-based; 173 computer-based; 61 iBT), IELTS (minimum score 5).

University of Maine, Graduate School, College of Natural Sciences, Forestry, and Agriculture, School of Marine Sciences, Orono, ME 04469. Offers marine biology (MS, PhD); marine policy (MS); oceanography (MS, PhD). Part-time programs available. *Faculty:* 29 full-time (10 women), 4 part-time/adjunct (2 women). *Students:* 50 full-time (28 women), 21 part-time (10 women), 6 international. Average age 29. 72 applicants, 17% accepted, 8 enrolled. In 2011, 7 master's, 6 doctorates awarded. *Degree requirements:* For master's, thesis; for doctorate, thesis/dissertation. *Entrance requirements:* For master's and doctorate, GRE General Test. Additional exam requirements/recommendations for international students: Required—TOEFL. *Application deadline:* For fall admission, 2/1 priority date for domestic students. Applications are processed on a rolling basis. Application fee: $65. Electronic applications accepted. *Expenses:* Tuition, state resident: full-time $5016. Tuition, nonresident: full-time $14,424. *Financial support:* In 2011–12, 41 research assistantships with tuition reimbursements (averaging $16,713 per year), 6 teaching assistantships with tuition reimbursements (averaging $13,600 per year) were awarded; career-related internships or fieldwork, Federal Work-Study, and tuition waivers (full and partial) also available. Support available to part-time students. Financial award application deadline: 3/1. *Faculty research:* Coastal processes, microbial ecology, crustacean systematics. *Total annual research expenditures:* $2 million. *Unit head:* Dr. Peter Jumars, Director, 207-581-3321, Fax: 207-581-4388. *Application contact:* Scott G. Delcourt, Associate Dean of the Graduate School, 207-581-3291, Fax: 207-581-3232, E-mail: graduate@maine.edu. Web site: http://www2.umaine.edu/graduate/.

University of Maryland, Baltimore, Graduate School, Program in Marine-Estuarine-Environmental Sciences, College Park, MD 20740. Offers MS, PhD. Part-time programs available. *Faculty:* 7. *Students:* 1 applicant, 0% accepted. Terminal master's awarded for partial completion of doctoral program. *Degree requirements:* For master's, thesis, oral defense; for doctorate, comprehensive exam, thesis/dissertation, proposal defense, oral defense. *Entrance requirements:* For master's and doctorate, GRE General Test, minimum GPA of 3.0. Additional exam requirements/recommendations for international students: Required—TOEFL. *Application deadline:* For fall admission, 2/1 for domestic students, 1/1 for international students; for spring admission, 9/1 for domestic students. Applications are processed on a rolling basis. Application fee: $50. Electronic applications accepted. *Financial support:* In 2011–12, 1 research assistantship with tuition reimbursement was awarded; fellowships with tuition reimbursements, teaching assistantships with tuition reimbursements, scholarships/grants, and unspecified assistantships also available. *Unit head:* Dr. Kennedy T. Paynter, Jr., Director, 301-405-6938, Fax: 301-314-4139, E-mail: mees@umd.edu. *Application contact:* Keith T. Brooks, Assistant Dean, 410-706-7131, Fax: 410-706-3473, E-mail: kbrooks@umaryland.edu. Web site: http://www.mees.umd.edu/.

University of Maryland, Baltimore County, Graduate School, College of Natural and Mathematical Sciences, Department of Biological Sciences, Marine-Estuarine-Environmental Sciences Graduate Program, College Park, MD 20742. Offers MS, PhD. Part-time programs available. *Faculty:* 12. *Students:* 4 full-time (2 women), 1 part-time (0 women). 7 applicants, 14% accepted, 1 enrolled. In 2011,

1 master's, 1 doctorate awarded. *Degree requirements:* For master's, thesis, oral defense; for doctorate, comprehensive exam, thesis/dissertation, proposal defense, oral defense. *Entrance requirements:* For master's and doctorate, GRE General Test, minimum GPA of 3.0. Additional exam requirements/recommendations for international students: Required—TOEFL. *Application deadline:* For fall admission, 2/1 for domestic students, 1/1 for international students; for spring admission, 9/1 for domestic students. Applications are processed on a rolling basis. Application fee: $50. Electronic applications accepted. *Financial support:* In 2011–12, 2 fellowships with tuition reimbursements (averaging $22,500 per year), 1 research assistantship with tuition reimbursement (averaging $21,000 per year), 1 teaching assistantship with tuition reimbursement (averaging $20,000 per year) were awarded; career-related internships or fieldwork, scholarships/grants, and unspecified assistantships also available. Financial award application deadline: 12/1. *Unit head:* Dr. Kennedy T. Paynter, Jr., Director, 301-405-6938, Fax: 301-314-4139, E-mail: mees@umd.edu. Web site: http://www.mees.umd.edu.

University of Maryland, College Park, Academic Affairs, College of Computer, Mathematical and Natural Sciences, Program in Marine-Estuarine-Environmental Sciences, College Park, MD 20742. Offers MS, PhD. Part-time programs available. *Faculty:* 130. *Students:* 117 (76 women); includes 10 minority (3 Black or African American, non-Hispanic/Latino; 3 Asian, non-Hispanic/Latino; 4 Hispanic/Latino), 23 international. 93 applicants, 30% accepted, 21 enrolled. In 2011, 12 master's, 10 doctorates awarded. Terminal master's awarded for partial completion of doctoral program. *Degree requirements:* For master's, thesis, oral defense; for doctorate, comprehensive exam, thesis/dissertation, proposal defense, oral defense. *Entrance requirements:* For master's and doctorate, GRE General Test, minimum GPA of 3.0. Additional exam requirements/recommendations for international students: Required—TOEFL. *Application deadline:* For fall admission, 2/1 for domestic and international students; for spring admission, 9/1 for domestic students, 6/1 for international students. Applications are processed on a rolling basis. Application fee: $60. Electronic applications accepted. *Expenses: Tuition, area resident:* Part-time $525 per credit hour. Tuition, state resident: part-time $525 per credit hour. Tuition, nonresident: part-time $1131 per credit hour. *Required fees:* $386.31 per term. Tuition and fees vary according to program. *Financial support:* In 2011–12, 9 teaching assistantships with full tuition reimbursements were awarded; fellowships with full tuition reimbursements, research assistantships with full tuition reimbursements, Federal Work-Study, scholarships/grants, traineeships, health care benefits, and unspecified assistantships also available. Financial award application deadline: 1/1; financial award applicants required to submit FAFSA. *Faculty research:* Marine and estuarine organisms, terrestrial and freshwater ecology, remote environmental sensing, fisheries science, oceanography, environmental chemistry. *Unit head:* Dr. Kennedy T. Paynter, Jr., Director, 301-405-6938, Fax: 301-314-4139, E-mail: mees@umd.edu. *Application contact:* Dr. Charles A. Caramello, Dean of Graduate School, 301-405-0358, Fax: 301-314-9305, E-mail: gradschool@umd.edu. Web site: http://www.mees.umd.edu/.

University of Maryland Eastern Shore, Graduate Programs, Department of Natural Sciences, Program in Marine-Estuarine-Environmental Sciences, College Park, MD 20740. Offers MS, PhD. Part-time programs available. *Faculty:* 28. *Students:* 31 (20 women); includes 16 minority (13 Black or African American, non-Hispanic/Latino; 1 American Indian or Alaska Native, non-Hispanic/Latino; 2 Asian, non-Hispanic/Latino), 8 international. 11 applicants, 91% accepted, 6 enrolled. In 2011, 3 master's, 3 doctorates awarded. *Degree requirements:* For master's, thesis; for doctorate, comprehensive exam, thesis/dissertation, proposal defense. *Entrance requirements:* For master's and doctorate, GRE General Test, minimum GPA of 3.0. Additional exam requirements/recommendations for international students: Required—TOEFL. *Application deadline:* For fall admission, 2/1 for domestic and international students; for spring admission, 9/1 for domestic students, 8/1 for international students. Applications are processed on a rolling basis. Application fee: $30. Electronic applications accepted. *Financial support:* In 2011–12, 30 students received support. Fellowships with tuition reimbursements available, research assistantships with tuition reimbursements available, teaching assistantships with tuition reimbursements available, career-related internships or fieldwork, scholarships/grants, and unspecified assistantships available. Support available to part-time students. Financial award application deadline: 1/1. *Unit head:* Dr. Kennedy T. Paynter, Jr., Director, 301-405-6938, Fax: 301-314-4139, E-mail: mees@umd.edu. *Application contact:* Wayne Smith, Program Assistant, 410-651-6040, Fax: 410-651-7739, E-mail: wesmith@umes.edu. Web site: http://www.mees.umd.edu/.

University of Massachusetts Amherst, Graduate School, Interdisciplinary Programs, Program in Marine Science and Technology, Amherst, MA 01003. Offers MS, PhD. Part-time programs available. *Students:* 2 full-time (both women), 1 (woman) part-time. Average age 27. Terminal master's awarded for partial completion of doctoral program. *Degree requirements:* For master's, thesis or alternative; for doctorate, comprehensive exam, thesis/dissertation. *Entrance requirements:* For master's and doctorate, GRE General Test, 3 letters of recommendation. Additional exam requirements/recommendations for international students: Required—TOEFL (minimum score 550 paper-based; 213 computer-based; 80 iBT), IELTS (minimum score 6.5). *Application deadline:* For fall admission, 12/15 for domestic and international students; for spring admission, 10/1 for domestic and international students. Applications are processed on a rolling basis. Application fee: $50 ($65 for international students). Electronic applications accepted. Tuition and fees vary according to course load, campus/location and program. *Financial support:* Fellowships, research

196 facebook.com/petersonspublishing

Peterson's Graduate Programs in the Physical Sciences, Mathematics, Agricultural Sciences, the Environment & Natural Resources 2013

assistantships, teaching assistantships, career-related internships or fieldwork, Federal Work-Study, scholarships/grants, traineeships, health care benefits, tuition waivers (full), and unspecified assistantships available. Support available to part-time students. Financial award application deadline: 12/15; financial award applicants required to submit FAFSA. *Unit head:* Dr. Francis Juanes, Graduate Program Director, 413-545-2666, Fax: 413-545-4358. *Application contact:* Lindsay DeSantis, Interim Supervisor of Admissions, 413-545-0722, Fax: 413-577-0010, E-mail: gradadm@grad.umass.edu. Web site: http://www.umassmarine.net/.

University of Massachusetts Boston, Office of Graduate Studies, College of Science and Mathematics, Department of Environmental, Earth and Ocean Sciences, Track in Environmental, Earth and Ocean Sciences, Boston, MA 02125-3393. Offers PhD. Part-time and evening/weekend programs available. *Degree requirements:* For doctorate, comprehensive exam, thesis/dissertation, oral exams. *Entrance requirements:* For doctorate, GRE General Test, minimum GPA of 2.75. *Faculty research:* Conservation genetics, anthropogenic and natural influences on community structures of coral reef factors, geographical variation in mitochondrial DNA, protein chemistry and enzymology pertaining to insect cuticle.

University of Miami, Graduate School, Rosenstiel School of Marine and Atmospheric Science, Division of Applied Marine Physics, Coral Gables, FL 33124. Offers applied marine physics (MS, PhD), including coastal ocean dynamics, underwater acoustics and geoacoustics (PhD), wave surface dynamics and air-sea interaction (PhD). Part-time programs available. Terminal master's awarded for partial completion of doctoral program. *Degree requirements:* For master's, comprehensive exam, thesis; for doctorate, comprehensive exam, thesis/dissertation. *Entrance requirements:* For master's and doctorate, GRE General Test. Additional exam requirements/recommendations for international students: Required—TOEFL (minimum score 550 paper-based; 213 computer-based). Electronic applications accepted.

University of Miami, Graduate School, Rosenstiel School of Marine and Atmospheric Science, Division of Marine and Atmospheric Chemistry, Coral Gables, FL 33124. Offers MS, PhD. Terminal master's awarded for partial completion of doctoral program. *Degree requirements:* For master's, comprehensive exam, thesis; for doctorate, comprehensive exam, thesis/dissertation. *Entrance requirements:* For master's and doctorate, GRE General Test. Additional exam requirements/recommendations for international students: Required—TOEFL (minimum score 550 paper-based; 213 computer-based). Electronic applications accepted. *Faculty research:* Global change issues, chemistry of marine waters and marine atmosphere.

University of Michigan, School of Natural Resources and Environment, Program in Natural Resources and Environment, Ann Arbor, MI 48109. Offers aquatic sciences: research and management (MS); behavior, education and communication (MS); conservation biology (MS); conservation ecology (MS); environmental informatics (MS); environmental justice (MS); environmental policy and planning (MS); natural resources and environment (PhD); sustainable systems (MS); terrestrial ecosystems (MS); MS/JD; MS/MBA; MUP/MS. *Faculty:* 45 full-time, 23 part-time/adjunct. *Students:* 450 full-time (254 women); includes 63 minority (7 Black or African American, non-Hispanic/Latino; 2 American Indian or Alaska Native, non-Hispanic/Latino; 35 Asian, non-Hispanic/Latino; 13 Hispanic/Latino; 6 Two or more races, non-Hispanic/Latino; 70 international. Average age 27. 643 applicants. In 2011, 133 master's, 11 doctorates awarded. Terminal master's awarded for partial completion of doctoral program. *Degree requirements:* For master's, practicum or group project; for doctorate, comprehensive exam, thesis/dissertation, oral defense of dissertation, preliminary exam. *Entrance requirements:* For master's, GRE General Test; for doctorate, GRE General Test, master's degree. Additional exam requirements/recommendations for international students: Required—TOEFL (minimum score 560 paper-based; 220 computer-based; 84 iBT). *Application deadline:* For fall admission, 1/5 priority date for domestic students, 1/5 for international students. Applications are processed on a rolling basis. Application fee: $65 ($75 for international students). Electronic applications accepted. *Financial support:* Fellowships with tuition reimbursements, research assistantships with tuition reimbursements, teaching assistantships with tuition reimbursements, career-related internships or fieldwork, Federal Work-Study, institutionally sponsored loans, scholarships/grants, health care benefits, and unspecified assistantships available. Support available to part-time students. Financial award application deadline: 1/5; financial award applicants required to submit FAFSA. *Faculty research:* Stream ecology, plant-insect interactions, fish biology, resource control and reproductive success, remote sensing, conservation ecology. *Unit head:* Dr. Marie Lynn Miranda, Dean, 734-764-2550, Fax: 734-763-8965, E-mail: mlmirand@umich.edu. *Application contact:* Adam D. Ancira, Graduate Admissions Team, 734-764-6453, Fax: 734-936-2195, E-mail: snre.admissions@umich.edu. Web site: http://www.snre.umich.edu/.

University of New England, College of Arts and Sciences, Program in Marine Sciences, Biddeford, ME 04005-9526. Offers MS. *Faculty:* 6 full-time. *Students:* 16 full-time (14 women). In 2011, 3 master's awarded. *Degree requirements:* For master's, thesis. *Application deadline:* For fall admission, 2/15 for domestic students. *Unit head:* Stephan I. Zeeman, Chair, Department of Marine Sciences, 207-602-2410, E-mail: szeeman@une.edu. *Application contact:* Stacy Gato, Assistant Director of Graduate Admissions, 207-221-4225, Fax: 207-221-4898, E-mail: gradadmissions@une.edu.

University of New Hampshire, Graduate School, College of Life Sciences and Agriculture, Department of Natural Resources, Durham, NH 03824. Offers environmental conservation (MS); forestry (MS); integrated coastal ecosystem science, policy, management (MS); natural resources (MS); water resources (MS); wildlife (MS). Part-time programs available. *Faculty:* 40 full-time. *Students:* 32 full-time (15 women), 24 part-time (13 women); includes 2 minority (1 Asian, non-Hispanic/Latino; 1 Hispanic/Latino), 1 international. Average age 29. 79 applicants, 49% accepted, 20 enrolled. In 2011, 10 master's awarded. *Degree requirements:* For master's, thesis or alternative. *Entrance requirements:* For master's, GRE General Test. Additional exam requirements/recommendations for international students: Required—TOEFL (minimum score 550 paper-based; 213 computer-based; 80 iBT). *Application deadline:* For fall admission, 6/1 for domestic students, 4/1 for international students; for spring admission, 12/1 for domestic students. Applications are processed on a rolling basis. Application fee: $65. Electronic applications accepted. *Expenses:* Tuition, state resident: full-time $12,360; part-time $687 per credit hour. Tuition, nonresident: full-time $25,680; part-time $1058 per credit hour. *International tuition:* $29,550 full-time. *Required fees:* $1666; $833 per course. $416.50 per semester. Tuition and fees vary according to course load and degree level. *Financial support:* In 2011–12, 35 students received support, including 3 fellowships, 13 research assistantships, 17 teaching assistantships; career-related internships or fieldwork, Federal Work-Study, scholarships/grants, and tuition waivers (full and partial) also available. Support available to part-time students. Financial award application deadline: 2/15. *Unit head:* Dr. Ted Howard, Chairperson, 603-862-2700, E-mail: natural.resources@unh.edu. *Application contact:* Nancy Brown, Administrative Assistant, 603-862-1022, E-mail: natural.resources@unh.edu. Web site: http://www.nre.unh.edu/academics/.

The University of North Carolina at Chapel Hill, Graduate School, College of Arts and Sciences, Department of Marine Sciences, Chapel Hill, NC 27599. Offers MS, PhD. *Degree requirements:* For master's, comprehensive exam, thesis; for doctorate, comprehensive exam, thesis/dissertation. *Entrance requirements:* For master's and doctorate, GRE General Test, GRE Subject Test, minimum GPA of 3.0.

The University of North Carolina at Chapel Hill, Graduate School, School of Public Health, Department of Environmental Sciences and Engineering, Chapel Hill, NC 27599. Offers air, radiation and industrial hygiene (MPH, MS, MSEE, MSPH, PhD); aquatic and atmospheric sciences (MPH, MS, MSPH, PhD); environmental engineering (MPH, MS, MSEE, MSPH, PhD); environmental health sciences (MPH, MS, MSPH, PhD); environmental management and policy (MPH, MS, MSPH, PhD). Terminal master's awarded for partial completion of doctoral program. *Degree requirements:* For master's, comprehensive exam, thesis (for some programs), research paper; for doctorate, comprehensive exam, thesis/dissertation. *Entrance requirements:* For master's and doctorate, GRE General Test, minimum GPA of 3.0. Additional exam requirements/recommendations for international students: Required—TOEFL. Electronic applications accepted. *Faculty research:* Air, radiation and industrial hygiene, aquatic and atmospheric sciences, environmental health sciences, environmental management and policy, water resources engineering.

The University of North Carolina Wilmington, College of Arts and Sciences, Department of Biology and Marine Biology, Wilmington, NC 28403-3297. Offers biology (MS); marine biology (MS, PhD). Part-time programs available. *Degree requirements:* For master's, comprehensive exam, thesis; for doctorate, comprehensive exam, thesis/dissertation. *Entrance requirements:* For master's, GRE General Test, GRE Subject Test, minimum B average in undergraduate major; for doctorate, GRE General Test, minimum B average in undergraduate major and graduate courses. Additional exam requirements/recommendations for international students: Required—TOEFL (minimum score 550 paper-based; 217 computer-based; 79 iBT), IELTS (minimum score 6.5). Electronic applications accepted. *Faculty research:* Ecology, physiology, cell and molecular biology, systematics, biomechanics.

University of Puerto Rico, Mayagüez Campus, Graduate Studies, College of Arts and Sciences, Department of Marine Sciences, Mayagüez, PR 00681-9000. Offers MS, PhD. Part-time programs available. *Students:* 43 full-time (20 women); includes 34 minority (all Hispanic/Latino), 8 international. 10 applicants, 80% accepted, 6 enrolled. In 2011, 6 master's, 5 doctorates awarded. *Degree requirements:* For master's, one foreign language, thesis, departmental and comprehensive final exams; for doctorate, one foreign language, thesis/dissertation, qualifying, comprehensive, and final exams. *Entrance requirements:* For master's, GRE, minimum GPA of 3.0; for doctorate, GRE, minimum GPA of 3.5. *Application deadline:* For fall admission, 2/15 for domestic and international students; for spring admission, 9/15 for domestic and international students. Applications are processed on a rolling basis. Application fee: $25. Tuition and fees vary according to course level and course load. *Financial support:* In 2011–12, 13 students received support, including 13 research assistantships (averaging $15,000 per year); Federal Work-Study and institutionally sponsored loans also available. *Faculty research:* Marine botany, ecology, chemistry, and parasitology; fisheries; ichthyology; aquaculture. *Unit head:* Dr. John Kubaryk, Director, 787-265-3838, Fax: 787-265-3838, E-mail: john.kubaryk@upr.edu. *Application contact:* Monserrate Casiano, Secretary, 787-832-4040 Ext. 3447, Fax: 787-265-3838, E-mail: monserrate.casiano@upr.edu. Web site: http://cima.uprm.edu.

University of Rhode Island, Graduate School, College of the Environment and Life Sciences, Department of Fisheries, Animal and Veterinary Science, Kingston, RI 02881. Offers animal health and disease (MS); animal science (MS);

Peterson's Graduate Programs in the Physical Sciences, Mathematics, Agricultural Sciences, the Environment & Natural Resources 2013

facebook.com/petersonspublishing **197**

Marine Sciences

aquaculture (MS); aquatic pathology (MS); environmental sciences (PhD), including animal science, aquacultural science, aquatic pathology, fisheries science; fisheries (MS). *Faculty:* 10 full-time (4 women). *Students:* 14 full-time (7 women), 6 part-time (1 woman). In 2011, 5 degrees awarded. *Degree requirements:* For master's, comprehensive exam (for some programs), thesis optional; for doctorate, comprehensive exam, thesis/dissertation. *Entrance requirements:* For master's and doctorate, GRE, 2 letters of recommendation. Additional exam requirements/recommendations for international students: Required—TOEFL (minimum score 550 paper-based; 213 computer-based). *Application deadline:* For fall admission, 7/15 for domestic students, 2/1 for international students; for spring admission, 11/15 for domestic students, 7/15 for international students. Application fee: $65. Electronic applications accepted. *Expenses:* Tuition, state resident: full-time $10,432; part-time $580 per credit hour. Tuition, nonresident: full-time $23,130; part-time $1285 per credit hour. *Required fees:* $1362; $36 per credit hour. $35 per semester. One-time fee: $130. *Financial support:* In 2011–12, 3 research assistantships with full and partial tuition reimbursements (averaging $11,654 per year), 4 teaching assistantships with full and partial tuition reimbursements (averaging $12,214 per year) were awarded. Financial award application deadline: 7/15; financial award applicants required to submit FAFSA. *Unit head:* Dr. David Bengtson, Chair, 401-874-2668, Fax: 401-874-7575, E-mail: bengtson@uri.edu. *Application contact:* Dr. Marta Gomez-Chiarri, Director of Graduate Studies, 401-874-2917, Fax: 401-874-7575, E-mail: gomezchi@uri.edu. Web site: http://www.uri.edu/cels/favs/.

University of San Diego, College of Arts and Sciences, Department of Marine Science and Environmental Studies, San Diego, CA 92110-2492. Offers marine science (MS). Part-time programs available. *Faculty:* 2 full-time (1 woman), 1 part-time/adjunct (0 women). *Students:* 11 full-time (8 women), 9 part-time (7 women); includes 6 minority (1 Black or African American, non-Hispanic/Latino; 2 Hispanic/Latino; 3 Two or more races, non-Hispanic/Latino). Average age 26. 43 applicants, 26% accepted, 6 enrolled. In 2011, 2 master's awarded. *Degree requirements:* For master's, thesis. *Entrance requirements:* For master's, GRE General Test, minimum GPA of 3.0, 1 semester biology w/lab, 1 year chemistry w/lab, 1 year physics w/lab, 1 semester calculus. Additional exam requirements/recommendations for international students: Required—TOEFL (minimum score 580 paper-based; 237 computer-based; 83 iBT), TWE. *Application deadline:* For fall admission, 4/1 for domestic and international students. Applications are processed on a rolling basis. Application fee: $45. Electronic applications accepted. *Expenses: Tuition:* Full-time $22,482; part-time $1249 per unit. *Required fees:* $224. Full-time tuition and fees vary according to course load and degree level. *Financial support:* In 2011–12, 15 students received support. Career-related internships or fieldwork, Federal Work-Study, institutionally sponsored loans, and unspecified assistantships available. Support available to part-time students. Financial award application deadline: 4/1; financial award applicants required to submit FAFSA. *Faculty research:* Marine ecology, environmental geology and geochemistry, climatology, physiological ecology, fisheries and aquaculture. *Unit head:* Dr. Ronald S. Kaufmann, Director, 619-260-5904, Fax: 619-260-6874, E-mail: kaufmann@sandiego.edu. *Application contact:* Monica Mahon, Associate Director of Graduate Admissions, 619-260-4524, Fax: 619-260-4158, E-mail: grads@sandiego.edu. Web site: http://www.sandiego.edu/cas/mars_envi/.

University of South Alabama, Graduate School, College of Arts and Sciences, Department of Marine Sciences, Mobile, AL 36688-0002. Offers MS, PhD. *Faculty:* 6 full-time (1 woman). *Students:* 30 full-time (18 women), 16 part-time (8 women); includes 1 minority (Native Hawaiian or other Pacific Islander, non-Hispanic/Latino), 6 international. 26 applicants, 42% accepted, 6 enrolled. In 2011, 2 master's, 2 doctorates awarded. *Degree requirements:* For master's, comprehensive exam, thesis optional; for doctorate, one foreign language, comprehensive exam, thesis/dissertation, research project. *Entrance requirements:* For master's, GRE, minimum GPA of 3.0, BS in marine sciences or related discipline; for doctorate, GRE, BS or MS in marine sciences or related discipline; minimum undergraduate GPA of 3.0, graduate 3.25. Additional exam requirements/recommendations for international students: Required—TOEFL. *Application deadline:* For fall admission, 4/1 priority date for domestic students, 3/1 for international students. Applications are processed on a rolling basis. Application fee: $35. *Expenses:* Tuition, state resident: full-time $7968; part-time $332 per credit hour. Tuition, nonresident: full-time $15,936; part-time $664 per credit hour. *Financial support:* In 2011–12, fellowships with tuition reimbursements (averaging $13,600 per year), research assistantships (averaging $16,000 per year) were awarded. Financial award application deadline: 4/1. *Unit head:* Dr. Robert Shipp, Chair, 251-460-7136, Fax: 251-460-7136. *Application contact:* Dr. S. L. Varghese, Director of Graduate Studies, 251-460-6280, Fax: 251-460-7928. Web site: http://www.southalabama.edu/marinesciences.

University of South Carolina, The Graduate School, College of Arts and Sciences, Marine Science Program, Columbia, SC 29208. Offers MS, PhD. *Degree requirements:* For master's, thesis; for doctorate, comprehensive exam, thesis/dissertation. *Entrance requirements:* For master's and doctorate, GRE General Test. Additional exam requirements/recommendations for international students: Required—TOEFL (minimum score 570 paper-based; 230 computer-based). Electronic applications accepted. *Faculty research:* Biological, chemical, geological, and physical oceanography; policy.

University of Southern California, Graduate School, Dana and David Dornsife College of Letters, Arts and Sciences, Graduate Program in Ocean Sciences, Los Angeles, CA 90089. Offers MS, PhD. Only Ph.D. and M.S./Ph.D. students are funded.. Part-time programs available. Terminal master's awarded for partial completion of doctoral program. *Degree requirements:* For master's, thesis; for doctorate, comprehensive exam, thesis/dissertation. *Entrance requirements:* For master's and doctorate, GRE. Additional exam requirements/recommendations for international students: Required—TOEFL. Electronic applications accepted. *Faculty research:* Microbial ecology, biogeochemical cycles, marine chemistry, marine biology, global change.

University of Southern Mississippi, Graduate School, College of Science and Technology, Department of Coastal Sciences, Ocean Springs, MS 39566-7000. Offers MS, PhD. Part-time programs available. *Faculty:* 17 full-time (4 women), 2 part-time/adjunct (0 women). *Students:* 82 full-time (36 women), 22 part-time (8 women); includes 8 minority (2 Black or African American, non-Hispanic/Latino; 1 Asian, non-Hispanic/Latino; 4 Hispanic/Latino; 1 Two or more races, non-Hispanic/Latino), 26 international. Average age 31. 67 applicants, 51% accepted, 26 enrolled. In 2011, 22 master's, 1 doctorate awarded. Terminal master's awarded for partial completion of doctoral program. *Degree requirements:* For master's, comprehensive exam, thesis; for doctorate, comprehensive exam, thesis/dissertation. *Entrance requirements:* For master's, GRE General Test, minimum GPA of 3.0 for last 60 hours; for doctorate, GRE General Test, minimum undergraduate GPA of 3.0, graduate 3.5. Additional exam requirements/recommendations for international students: Required—TOEFL, IELTS. *Application deadline:* For fall admission, 3/1 priority date for domestic students, 3/1 for international students. Applications are processed on a rolling basis. Application fee: $50. Electronic applications accepted. *Financial support:* In 2011–12, 1 fellowship with full tuition reimbursement (averaging $10,000 per year), 34 research assistantships with full tuition reimbursements (averaging $16,232 per year) were awarded; Federal Work-Study, scholarships/grants, health care benefits, and unspecified assistantships also available. Financial award application deadline: 3/15; financial award applicants required to submit FAFSA. *Unit head:* Dr. Jeffrey Lotz, Chair, 228-872-4215, Fax: 228-872-4295. *Application contact:* Kalin Buttrich, Administrative Assistant, 228-872-4201, Fax: 228-872-4295. Web site: http://www.usm.edu/graduateschool/table.php.

University of Southern Mississippi, Graduate School, College of Science and Technology, Department of Marine Science, Stennis Space Center, MS 39529. Offers hydrographic science (MS); marine science (MS, PhD). Part-time programs available. *Faculty:* 18 full-time (2 women). *Students:* 38 full-time (15 women), 13 part-time (4 women); includes 20 minority (4 Black or African American, non-Hispanic/Latino; 13 Asian, non-Hispanic/Latino; 3 Hispanic/Latino). Average age 31. 47 applicants, 57% accepted, 19 enrolled. In 2011, 15 master's, 1 doctorate awarded. *Degree requirements:* For master's, comprehensive exam, thesis, oral qualifying exam (marine science); for doctorate, 2 foreign languages, comprehensive exam, thesis/dissertation, oral qualifying exam. *Entrance requirements:* For master's, GRE General Test, minimum GPA of 3.0; for doctorate, GRE General Test, minimum GPA of 3.0 (undergraduate), 3.5 (graduate). Additional exam requirements/recommendations for international students: Required—TOEFL. *Application deadline:* For fall admission, 3/1 priority date for domestic students, 3/1 for international students. Application fee: $50. Electronic applications accepted. *Financial support:* In 2011–12, 4 students received support, including 35 research assistantships with full tuition reimbursements available (averaging $20,400 per year), 2 teaching assistantships with full tuition reimbursements available (averaging $20,400 per year); Federal Work-Study and institutionally sponsored loans also available. Financial award application deadline: 3/15. *Faculty research:* Chemical, biological, physical, and geological marine science; remote sensing; bio-optics; numerical modeling; hydrography. *Total annual research expenditures:* $7.1 million. *Unit head:* Dr. William M. Graham, Chair and Professor, 228-688-3177, Fax: 228-688-1121, E-mail: marine.science@usm.edu. *Application contact:* Linda Downs, Senior Office Support Specialist, 228-688-3177, Fax: 228-688-1121, E-mail: marine.science@usm.edu. Web site: http://www.usm.edu/marine/.

University of South Florida, Graduate School, College of Marine Science, Saint Petersburg, FL 33701. Offers biological oceanography (MS, PhD); chemical oceanography (MS, PhD); geological oceanography (MS, PhD); interdisciplinary (PhD); marine resource assessment (MS, PhD); physical oceanography (MS, PhD). Part-time programs available. *Faculty:* 29 full-time (5 women), 2 part-time/adjunct (1 woman). *Students:* 77 full-time (41 women), 29 part-time (19 women); includes 17 minority (5 Black or African American, non-Hispanic/Latino; 11 Hispanic/Latino; 1 Two or more races, non-Hispanic/Latino), 16 international. Average age 31. 127 applicants, 24% accepted, 25 enrolled. In 2011, 8 master's, 8 doctorates awarded. Terminal master's awarded for partial completion of doctoral program. *Degree requirements:* For master's, comprehensive exam, thesis; for doctorate, comprehensive exam, thesis/dissertation. *Entrance requirements:* For master's and doctorate, GRE, minimum GPA of 3.0 in last 60 hours, three letters of recommendation, research-interest statement, resume. Additional exam requirements/recommendations for international students: Required—TOEFL (minimum score 550 paper-based; 213 computer-based; 79 iBT) or IELTS (minimum score 6.5). *Application deadline:* For fall admission, 1/15 for domestic students, 1/2 for international students; for spring admission, 10/1 for domestic students, 7/1 for international students. Applications are processed on a rolling basis. Application fee: $30. *Financial support:* In 2011–12, 55 students received support, including 45 research assistantships with partial tuition reimbursements available (averaging $14,199 per year), 10 teaching assistantships with partial tuition reimbursements available (averaging $14,196 per year); health care benefits and unspecified assistantships also available.

Financial award application deadline: 1/15. *Faculty research:* Trace metal chemistry, water quality, organic and isotopic geochemistry, physical chemistry, nutrient chemistry. *Total annual research expenditures:* $11.2 million. *Unit head:* Dr. David Naar, Professor and Director of Academic Programs and Student Affairs, 727-553-1637, Fax: 727-553-1189, E-mail: naar@usf.edu. *Application contact:* Dawna L. Ishler, Academic Services Administrator, 727-553-3944, Fax: 727-553-1189, E-mail: advisor@marine.usf.edu. Web site: http://www.marine.usf.edu/.

The University of Texas at Austin, Graduate School, College of Natural Sciences, Department of Marine Science, Austin, TX 78712-1111. Offers MS, PhD. *Degree requirements:* For master's, thesis; for doctorate, thesis/dissertation. *Entrance requirements:* For master's and doctorate, GRE General Test. Additional exam requirements/recommendations for international students: Required—TOEFL. *Application deadline:* For fall admission, 1/1 for domestic and international students. Application fee: $50 ($100 for international students). *Financial support:* Research assistantships with partial tuition reimbursements and teaching assistantships with partial tuition reimbursements available. Financial award application deadline: 1/1. *Unit head:* Dr. Lee A. Fuiman, Associate Director, 361-749-6775, Fax: 361-749-6777, E-mail: lee.fuiman@mail.utexas.edu. *Application contact:* Dr. Gloria Joan Holt, Professor Emeritus, 361-749-6716, Fax: 361-749-6749, E-mail: joanholt@mail.utexas.edu. Web site: http://www.utmsi.utexas.edu/.

University of the Virgin Islands, Graduate Programs, Division of Science and Mathematics, Program in Environmental and Marine Science, Saint Thomas, VI 00802-9990. Offers MS. *Entrance requirements:* For master's, GRE. Additional exam requirements/recommendations for international students: Required—TOEFL (minimum score 550 paper-based; 213 computer-based).

University of Wisconsin–La Crosse, Office of University Graduate Studies, College of Science and Health, Department of Biology, La Crosse, WI 54601-3742. Offers aquatic sciences (MS); biology (MS); cellular and molecular biology (MS); clinical microbiology (MS); microbiology (MS); nurse anesthesia (MS); physiology (MS). Part-time programs available. *Faculty:* 21 full-time (8 women), 3 part-time/adjunct (1 woman). *Students:* 45 full-time (30 women), 47 part-time (22 women); includes 10 minority (1 Black or African American, non-Hispanic/Latino; 5 Asian, non-Hispanic/Latino; 3 Hispanic/Latino; 1 Two or more races, non-Hispanic/Latino), 3 international. Average age 28. 63 applicants, 46% accepted, 24 enrolled. In 2011, 23 master's awarded. *Degree requirements:* For master's, comprehensive exam, thesis. *Entrance requirements:* For master's, GRE General Test, minimum GPA of 2.85. Additional exam requirements/recommendations for international students: Required—TOEFL (minimum score 550 paper-based; 213 computer-based; 79 iBT). *Application deadline:* For fall admission, 2/1 priority date for domestic students, 2/1 for international students; for spring admission, 1/4 priority date for domestic students, 1/4 for international students. Applications are processed on a rolling basis. Application fee: $56. Electronic applications accepted. *Expenses:* Tuition, state resident: full-time $8391; part-time $481.17 per credit. Tuition, nonresident: full-time $17,850; part-time $1006.68 per credit. *Required fees:* $2 per credit. $18.25 per semester. Tuition and fees vary according to course load, program, reciprocity agreements and student level. *Financial support:* In 2011–12, 7 research assistantships with partial tuition reimbursements (averaging $9,712 per year) were awarded; Federal Work-Study, scholarships/grants, health care benefits, and tuition waivers (partial) also available. Support available to part-time students. Financial award application deadline: 3/15; financial award applicants required to submit FAFSA. *Unit head:* Dr. Thomas Volk, Coordinator of Graduate Studies, 608-785-6972, Fax: 608-785-6959, E-mail: volk.thom@uwlax.edu. *Application contact:* Kathryn Kiefer, Director of Admissions, 608-785-8939, E-mail: admissions@uwlax.edu. Web site: http://uwlax.edu/biology/.

University of Wisconsin–Madison, Graduate School, College of Letters and Science, Department of Atmospheric and Oceanic Sciences, Madison, WI 53706-1380. Offers MS, PhD. Part-time programs available. *Degree requirements:* For master's, thesis (for some programs); for doctorate, thesis/dissertation. *Entrance requirements:* For master's and doctorate, GRE General Test, minimum GPA of 3.0; previous course work in chemistry, mathematics, and physics. Electronic applications accepted. *Expenses:* Tuition, state resident: full-time $10,296; part-time $643.51 per credit. Tuition, nonresident: full-time $24,054; part-time $1503.40 per credit. *Required fees:* $70.06 per credit. Tuition and fees vary according to course load, campus/location, program and reciprocity agreements. *Faculty research:* Satellite meteorology, weather systems, global climate change, numerical modeling, atmosphere-ocean interaction.

Western Washington University, Graduate School, Huxley College of the Environment, Department of Environmental Sciences, Bellingham, WA 98225-5996. Offers environmental science (MS); marine and estuarine science (MS). Part-time programs available. *Degree requirements:* For master's, thesis. *Entrance requirements:* For master's, GRE General Test, minimum GPA of 3.0 in last 60 semester hours or last 90 quarter hours. Additional exam requirements/recommendations for international students: Required—TOEFL (minimum score 567 paper-based; 227 computer-based). Electronic applications accepted. *Faculty research:* Landscape ecology, climate change, watershed studies, environmental toxicology and risk assessment, aquatic toxicology, toxic algae, invasive species.

Oceanography

Columbia University, Graduate School of Arts and Sciences, Division of Natural Sciences, Department of Earth and Environmental Sciences, New York, NY 10027. Offers geochemistry (M Phil, MA, PhD); geodetic sciences (M Phil, MA, PhD); geophysics (M Phil, MA, PhD); oceanography (M Phil, MA, PhD). *Degree requirements:* For master's, thesis or alternative, fieldwork, written exam; for doctorate, one foreign language, thesis/dissertation. *Entrance requirements:* For master's and doctorate, GRE General Test, GRE Subject Test, major in natural or physical science. Additional exam requirements/recommendations for international students: Required—TOEFL. *Faculty research:* Structural geology and stratigraphy, petrology, paleontology, rare gas, isotope and aqueous geochemistry.

Cornell University, Graduate School, Graduate Fields of Agriculture and Life Sciences, Field of Ecology and Evolutionary Biology, Ithaca, NY 14853-0001. Offers ecology (PhD), including animal ecology, applied ecology, biogeochemistry, community and ecosystem ecology, limnology, oceanography, physiological ecology, plant ecology, population ecology, theoretical ecology, vertebrate zoology; evolutionary biology (PhD), including ecological genetics, paleobiology, population biology, systematics. *Faculty:* 51 full-time (14 women). *Students:* 52 full-time (36 women); includes 6 minority (1 Asian, non-Hispanic/Latino; 4 Hispanic/Latino; 1 Two or more races, non-Hispanic/Latino), 10 international. Average age 28. 121 applicants, 9% accepted, 7 enrolled. In 2011, 5 doctorates awarded. *Degree requirements:* For doctorate, comprehensive exam, thesis/dissertation, 2 semesters of teaching experience. *Entrance requirements:* For doctorate, GRE General Test, GRE Subject Test (biology), 2 letters of recommendation. Additional exam requirements/recommendations for international students: Required—TOEFL (minimum score 550 paper-based; 213 computer-based; 77 iBT). *Application deadline:* For fall admission, 12/15 for domestic students. Application fee: $95. Electronic applications accepted. *Financial support:* In 2011–12, 15 fellowships with full tuition reimbursements, 8 research assistantships with full tuition reimbursements, 25 teaching assistantships with full tuition reimbursements were awarded; institutionally sponsored loans, scholarships/grants, health care benefits, tuition waivers (full and partial), and unspecified assistantships also available. Financial award applicants required to submit FAFSA. *Faculty research:* Population and organismal biology, population and evolutionary genetics, systematics and macroevolution, biochemistry, conservation biology. *Unit head:* Director of Graduate Studies, 607-254-4230. *Application contact:* Graduate Field Assistant, 607-254-4230, E-mail: eeb_grad_req@cornell.edu. Web site: http://www.gradschool.cornell.edu/fields.php?id-46&a-2.

Dalhousie University, Faculty of Science, Department of Oceanography, Halifax, NS B3H 4R2, Canada. Offers M Sc, PhD. *Degree requirements:* For master's, thesis; for doctorate, thesis/dissertation. *Entrance requirements:* Additional exam requirements/recommendations for international students: Required—TOEFL, IELTS, CANTEST, CAEL, or Michigan English Language Assessment Battery. Electronic applications accepted. *Faculty research:* Biological and physical oceanography, chemical and geological oceanography, atmospheric sciences.

Florida Institute of Technology, Graduate Programs, College of Engineering, Department of Marine and Environmental Systems, Program in Oceanography, Melbourne, FL 32901-6975. Offers biological oceanography (MS); chemical oceanography (MS); coastal management (MS); geological oceanography (MS); oceanography (PhD); physical oceanography (MS). Part-time programs available. *Faculty:* 11 full-time (0 women), 3 part-time/adjunct (0 women). *Students:* 14 full-time (6 women), 1 (woman) part-time; includes 1 minority (Two or more races, non-Hispanic/Latino), 3 international. Average age 30. 14 applicants, 50% accepted, 2 enrolled. In 2011, 1 degree awarded. *Degree requirements:* For master's, comprehensive exam (for some programs), thesis (for some programs), seminar, field project, written final exam, internship, technical paper, oral presentation; for doctorate, comprehensive exam, thesis/dissertation, seminar, internships, publications. *Entrance requirements:* For master's, GRE General Test, minimum GPA of 3.0, 3 letters of recommendation, resume, transcripts, statement of objectives; for doctorate, GRE General Test, minimum GPA of 3.3, resume, 3 letters of recommendation, statement of objectives, on-campus interview (highly recommended). Additional exam requirements/recommendations for international students: Required—TOEFL (minimum score 550 paper-based; 213 computer-based; 79 iBT). *Application deadline:* Applications are processed on a rolling basis. Electronic applications accepted. *Expenses: Tuition:* Full-time $19,620; part-time $1090 per credit hour. Tuition and fees vary according to campus/location. *Financial support:* Career-related internships or fieldwork, institutionally sponsored loans, tuition waivers (partial), unspecified

Peterson's Graduate Programs in the Physical Sciences, Mathematics, Agricultural Sciences, the Environment & Natural Resources 2013

facebook.com/petersonspublishing   **199**

assistantships, and tuition remissions available. Support available to part-time students. Financial award application deadline: 3/1; financial award applicants required to submit FAFSA. *Faculty research:* Marine geochemistry, ecosystem dynamics, coastal processes, marine pollution, environmental modeling. *Total annual research expenditures:* $1.6 million. *Unit head:* Dr. George Maul, Department Head, 321-674-7453, Fax: 321-674-7212, E-mail: gmaul@fit.edu. *Application contact:* Cheryl A. Brown, Associate Director of Graduate Admission, 321-674-7581, Fax: 321-723-9468, E-mail: cbrown@fit.edu. Web site: http://www.coe.fit.edu/dmes.

Florida State University, The Graduate School, College of Arts and Sciences, Department of Earth, Ocean and Atmospheric Science, Program in Oceanography, Tallahassee, FL 32306-4320. Offers aquatic environmental science (MS, PMS); oceanography (MS, PhD). *Faculty:* 12 full-time (1 woman). *Students:* 59 full-time (32 women); includes 4 minority (1 Black or African American, non-Hispanic/Latino; 3 Asian, non-Hispanic/Latino), 16 international. Average age 27. 55 applicants, 31% accepted, 15 enrolled. In 2011, 3 master's, 3 doctorates awarded. *Degree requirements:* For master's, thesis; for doctorate, comprehensive exam, thesis/dissertation. *Entrance requirements:* For master's and doctorate, GRE General Test, minimum upper-division GPA of 3.0. Additional exam requirements/recommendations for international students: Required—TOEFL (minimum score 550 paper-based; 213 computer-based; 80 iBT). *Application deadline:* For fall admission, 2/15 priority date for domestic students, 2/15 for international students; for spring admission, 7/15 priority date for domestic students, 7/15 for international students. Applications are processed on a rolling basis. Application fee: $30. Electronic applications accepted. *Expenses:* Tuition, state resident: full-time $9474; part-time $350.88 per credit hour. Tuition, nonresident: full-time $16,236; part-time $601.34 per credit hour. *Required fees:* $630 per semester. One-time fee: $20. Tuition and fees vary according to course load and campus/location. *Financial support:* In 2011–12, 47 students received support, including 1 fellowship with full tuition reimbursement available, 31 research assistantships with full tuition reimbursements available, 15 teaching assistantships with full tuition reimbursements available. Financial award application deadline: 2/15; financial award applicants required to submit FAFSA. *Faculty research:* Trace metals in seawater, currents and waves, modeling, benthic ecology, marine biogeochemistry. *Unit head:* Dr. Jeffrey Chanton, Area Coordinator, 850-644-6700, Fax: 850-644-2581, E-mail: chanton@ocean.fsu.edu. *Application contact:* Michaela Lupiani, Academic Coordinator, 850-644-6700, Fax: 850-644-2581, E-mail: admissions@ocean.fsu.edu.

Georgia Institute of Technology, Graduate Studies and Research, College of Sciences, School of Earth and Atmospheric Sciences, Atlanta, GA 30332-0340. Offers atmospheric chemistry, aerosols and clouds (MS, PhD); dynamics of weather and climate (MS, PhD); geochemistry (MS, PhD); geophysics (MS, PhD); oceanography (MS, PhD); paleoclimate (MS, PhD); planetary science (MS, PhD); remote sensing (MS, PhD). Part-time programs available. Terminal master's awarded for partial completion of doctoral program. *Degree requirements:* For master's, thesis or alternative; for doctorate, comprehensive exam, thesis/dissertation. *Entrance requirements:* For master's, GRE, letters of recommendation; for doctorate, GRE, academic transcripts, letters of recommendation, personal statement. Additional exam requirements/recommendations for international students: Required—TOEFL (minimum score 550 paper-based; 213 computer-based; 79 iBT). *Faculty research:* Geophysics; atmospheric chemistry, aerosols and clouds; dynamics of weather and climate; geochemistry; oceanography; paleoclimate; planetary science; remote sensing.

Louisiana State University and Agricultural and Mechanical College, Graduate School, School of the Coast and Environment, Department of Oceanography and Coastal Sciences, Baton Rouge, LA 70803. Offers MS, PhD. *Faculty:* 25 full-time (3 women), 2 part-time/adjunct (0 women). *Students:* 55 full-time (26 women), 8 part-time (4 women); includes 1 minority (Hispanic/Latino), 13 international. Average age 29. 41 applicants, 29% accepted, 10 enrolled. In 2011, 4 master's, 5 doctorates awarded. *Degree requirements:* For master's, thesis (for some programs); for doctorate, one foreign language, thesis/dissertation. *Entrance requirements:* For master's, GRE General Test, minimum GPA of 3.0; for doctorate, GRE General Test, MA or MS, minimum GPA of 3.0. Additional exam requirements/recommendations for international students: Required—TOEFL (minimum score 550 paper-based; 213 computer-based; 79 iBT) or IELTS (minimum score 6.5). *Application deadline:* For fall admission, 1/25 priority date for domestic students, 5/15 for international students; for spring admission, 10/15 for international students. Applications are processed on a rolling basis. Application fee: $50 ($70 for international students). *Financial support:* In 2011–12, 61 students received support, including 8 fellowships (averaging $22,270 per year), 47 research assistantships with full and partial tuition reimbursements available (averaging $19,641 per year), 1 teaching assistantship with full and partial tuition reimbursement available (averaging $17,000 per year); Federal Work-Study, institutionally sponsored loans, scholarships/grants, health care benefits, tuition waivers (full and partial), and unspecified assistantships also available. Support available to part-time students. Financial award applicants required to submit FAFSA. *Faculty research:* Physical and geological oceanography, wetland sustainability and restoration fisheries, coastal ecology and biogeochemistry. *Total annual research expenditures:* $7.7 million. *Unit head:* Dr. Donald Baltz, Chair, 225-578-6512, Fax: 225-578-6513, E-mail: dbaltz@lsu.edu. *Application contact:* Dr. Charles Lindau, Graduate Adviser, 225-578-8766, Fax: 225-578-5328, E-mail: clinda1@lsu.edu. Web site: http://www.oceanography.lsu.edu/.

Massachusetts Institute of Technology, School of Engineering, Department of Civil and Environmental Engineering, Cambridge, MA 02139. Offers biological oceanography (PhD, Sc D); chemical oceanography (PhD, Sc D); civil and environmental engineering (PhD, Sc D); civil and environmental systems (PhD, Sc D); civil engineering (PhD, Sc D, CE); coastal engineering (PhD, Sc D); construction engineering and management (PhD, Sc D); environmental and water quality engineering (M Eng); environmental biology (PhD, Sc D); environmental chemistry (PhD, Sc D); environmental engineering (PhD, Sc D); environmental fluid mechanics (PhD, Sc D); environmental science and engineering (SM); geotechnical and geoenvironmental engineering (PhD, Sc D); geotechnology (M Eng); high-performance structures (M Eng); hydrology (PhD, Sc D); information technology (PhD, Sc D); mechanics (SM); oceanographic engineering (PhD, Sc D); structures and materials (PhD, Sc D); transportation (M Eng, PhD, Sc D); SM/MBA. *Faculty:* 35 full-time (6 women), 1 part-time/adjunct (0 women). *Students:* 216 full-time (80 women); includes 30 minority (4 Black or African American, non-Hispanic/Latino; 13 Asian, non-Hispanic/Latino; 8 Hispanic/Latino; 5 Two or more races, non-Hispanic/Latino), 110 international. Average age 27. 589 applicants, 26% accepted, 91 enrolled. In 2011, 62 master's, 14 doctorates awarded. *Degree requirements:* For master's and CE, thesis; for doctorate, comprehensive exam, thesis/dissertation. *Entrance requirements:* For master's and doctorate, GRE General Test. Additional exam requirements/recommendations for international students: Required—TOEFL (minimum score 577 paper-based; 233 computer-based; 90 iBT), IELTS (minimum score 7). *Application deadline:* For fall admission, 12/15 for domestic and international students. Application fee: $75. Electronic applications accepted. *Expenses:* Tuition: Full-time $40,460; part-time $630 per credit hour. *Required fees:* $272. *Financial support:* In 2011–12, 180 students received support, including 51 fellowships (averaging $30,800 per year), 110 research assistantships (averaging $29,500 per year), 19 teaching assistantships (averaging $29,500 per year); career-related internships or fieldwork, Federal Work-Study, institutionally sponsored loans, scholarships/grants, health care benefits, and unspecified assistantships also available. *Faculty research:* Environmental chemistry, environmental fluid mechanics and coastal engineering, environmental microbiology, geotechnical engineering and geomechanics, hydrology and hydroclimatology, infrastructure systems, mechanics of materials and structures, transportation systems. *Total annual research expenditures:* $17.7 million. *Unit head:* Prof. Andrew Whittle, Head, 617-253-7101. *Application contact:* Patricia Glidden, Graduate Admissions Coordinator, 617-253-7119, Fax: 617-258-6775, E-mail: cee-admissions@mit.edu. Web site: http://cee.mit.edu/.

Massachusetts Institute of Technology, School of Science, Department of Biology, Cambridge, MA 02139. Offers biochemistry (PhD); biological oceanography (PhD); biology (PhD); biophysical chemistry and molecular structure (PhD); cell biology (PhD); computational and systems biology (PhD); developmental biology (PhD); genetics (PhD); immunology (PhD); microbiology (PhD); molecular biology (PhD); neurobiology (PhD). *Faculty:* 58 full-time (15 women). *Students:* 248 full-time (129 women); includes 69 minority (5 Black or African American, non-Hispanic/Latino; 1 American Indian or Alaska Native, non-Hispanic/Latino; 25 Asian, non-Hispanic/Latino; 31 Hispanic/Latino; 7 Two or more races, non-Hispanic/Latino), 36 international. Average age 26. 698 applicants, 15% accepted, 44 enrolled. In 2011, 38 doctorates awarded. *Degree requirements:* For doctorate, comprehensive exam, thesis/dissertation. *Entrance requirements:* For doctorate, GRE General Test. Additional exam requirements/recommendations for international students: Required—TOEFL (minimum score 577 paper-based; 233 computer-based), IELTS (minimum score 6.5). *Application deadline:* For fall admission, 12/1 for domestic and international students. Application fee: $75. Electronic applications accepted. *Expenses:* Tuition: Full-time $40,460; part-time $630 per credit hour. *Required fees:* $272. *Financial support:* In 2011–12, 214 students received support, including 129 fellowships (averaging $33,200 per year), 117 research assistantships (averaging $32,900 per year); teaching assistantships, Federal Work-Study, institutionally sponsored loans, scholarships/grants, traineeships, health care benefits, and unspecified assistantships also available. *Faculty research:* Cellular, developmental and molecular (plant and animal) biology; biochemistry, bioengineering, biophysics and structural biology; classical and molecular genetics; immunology and microbiology; cancer biology, molecular medicine, neurobiology and human disease; computational and systems biology. *Total annual research expenditures:* $53.6 million. *Unit head:* Prof. Tania A. Baker, Head, 617-253-4701, E-mail: mitbio@mit.edu. *Application contact:* Biology Education Office, 617-253-3717, Fax: 617-258-9329, E-mail: gradbio@mit.edu. Web site: https://biology.mit.edu/.

Massachusetts Institute of Technology, School of Science, Department of Earth, Atmospheric, and Planetary Sciences, Cambridge, MA 02139. Offers atmospheric chemistry (PhD, Sc D); atmospheric science (SM, PhD, Sc D); chemical oceanography (SM, PhD, Sc D); climate physics and chemistry (SM, PhD, Sc D); earth and planetary sciences (SM); geochemistry (PhD, Sc D); geology (PhD, Sc D); geophysics (PhD, Sc D); marine geology and geophysics (SM, PhD, Sc D); physical oceanography (SM, PhD, Sc D); planetary sciences (PhD, Sc D). *Faculty:* 33 full-time (6 women). *Students:* 175 full-time (81 women); includes 21 minority (3 Black or African American, non-Hispanic/Latino; 1 American Indian or Alaska Native, non-Hispanic/Latino; 8 Asian, non-Hispanic/Latino; 4 Hispanic/Latino; 5 Two or more races, non-Hispanic/Latino), 58 international. Average age 26. 241 applicants, 28% accepted, 43 enrolled. In 2011, 6 master's, 16 doctorates awarded. Terminal master's awarded for partial completion of doctoral program. *Degree requirements:* For master's, thesis; for doctorate, comprehensive exam, thesis/dissertation. *Entrance requirements:* For

200 facebook.com/petersonspublishing

Peterson's Graduate Programs in the Physical Sciences, Mathematics, Agricultural Sciences, the Environment & Natural Resources 2013

master's, GRE General Test; for doctorate, GRE General Test, GRE Subject Test (chemistry or physics for planetary science area). Additional exam requirements/recommendations for international students: Required—TOEFL (minimum score 577 paper-based; 233 computer-based; 91 iBT), IELTS (minimum score 7). *Application deadline:* For fall admission, 1/5 for domestic and international students; for spring admission, 11/1 for domestic and international students. Application fee: $75. Electronic applications accepted. *Expenses: Tuition:* Full-time $40,460; part-time $630 per credit hour. *Required fees:* $272. *Financial support:* In 2011–12, 125 students received support, including 68 fellowships (averaging $32,200 per year), 94 research assistantships (averaging $31,900 per year), 10 teaching assistantships (averaging $30,000 per year); Federal Work-Study, institutionally sponsored loans, scholarships/grants, health care benefits, and unspecified assistantships also available. *Faculty research:* Formation, dynamics and evolution of planetary systems; origin, composition, structure and dynamics of the atmospheres, oceans, surfaces and interiors of the Earth and other planets; evolution and interaction of the physical, chemical, geological and biological components of the Earth system; characterization of past, present and potential future climates and the causes and consequences of climate change; interplay of energy and the environment. *Total annual research expenditures:* $26.2 million. *Unit head:* Prof. Robert van der Hilst, Head, 617-253-2127, Fax: 617-253-8298, E-mail: eapsinfo@mit.edu. *Application contact:* EAPS Education Office, 617-253-3381, Fax: 617-253-8298, E-mail: eapsinfo@mit.edu. Web site: http://eapsweb.mit.edu/.

McGill University, Faculty of Graduate and Postdoctoral Studies, Faculty of Science, Department of Atmospheric and Oceanic Sciences, Montréal, QC H3A 2T5, Canada. Offers atmospheric science (M Sc, PhD); physical oceanography (M Sc, PhD). PhD program in physical oceanography offered jointly with Université Laval.

Memorial University of Newfoundland, School of Graduate Studies, Department of Physics and Physical Oceanography, St. John's, NL A1C 5S7, Canada. Offers atomic and molecular physics (M Sc, PhD); condensed matter physics (M Sc, PhD); physical oceanography (M Sc, PhD); physics (M Sc). Part-time programs available. *Degree requirements:* For master's, thesis, seminar presentation on thesis topic; for doctorate, comprehensive exam, thesis/dissertation, oral defense of thesis. *Entrance requirements:* For master's, honors B Sc or equivalent; for doctorate, M Sc or equivalent. Electronic applications accepted. *Faculty research:* Experiment and theory in atomic and molecular physics, condensed matter physics, physical oceanography, theoretical geophysics and applied nuclear physics.

Naval Postgraduate School, Departments and Academic Groups, Department of Meteorology, Monterey, CA 93943. Offers meteorology (MS, PhD); meteorology and physical oceanography (MS). Program only open to commissioned officers of the United States and friendly nations and selected United States federal civilian employees. Part-time programs available. *Faculty:* 14 full-time (3 women). *Students:* 61 full-time (11 women); includes 11 minority (3 Black or African American, non-Hispanic/Latino; 1 American Indian or Alaska Native, non-Hispanic/Latino; 5 Asian, non-Hispanic/Latino; 2 Hispanic/Latino), 2 international. Average age 35. In 2011, 13 master's, 1 doctorate awarded. *Degree requirements:* For master's, thesis; for doctorate, one foreign language, thesis/dissertation. *Faculty research:* Air-sea interactions, boundary layer meteorology, climate dynamics, numerical weather prediction, tropical cyclones. *Total annual research expenditures:* $3.2 million. *Unit head:* Prof. Wendell Nuss, Department Chair, 831-656-2308, E-mail: nuss@nps.edu. Web site: http://nps.edu/Academics/Schools/GSEAS/Departments/Meteorology/index.html.

Naval Postgraduate School, Departments and Academic Groups, Department of Oceanography, Monterey, CA 93943. Offers physical oceanography (MS, PhD). Program only open to commissioned officers of the United States and friendly nations and selected United States federal civilian employees. Part-time programs available. *Faculty:* 17 full-time (6 women), 2 part-time/adjunct. *Students:* 7 full-time (2 women), 4 international. Average age 35. In 2011, 2 master's, 3 doctorates awarded. *Degree requirements:* For master's, thesis; for doctorate, thesis/dissertation. *Faculty research:* Lagrangian acoustic subsurface technology; naval ocean analysis prediction; nearshore processes; unmanned vehicles; ocean acoustics, turbulence, waves. *Total annual research expenditures:* $9.7 million. *Unit head:* Prof. Jeffrey Paduan, Chairman, 831-656-3350, E-mail: paduan@nps.edu. *Application contact:* Administrative Support Assistant, 831-656-2757. Web site: http://nps.edu/Academics/Schools/GSEAS/Departments/Oceanography/index.html.

Naval Postgraduate School, Departments and Academic Groups, Undersea Warfare Academic Group, Monterey, CA 93943. Offers applied mathematics (MS); applied physics (MS); applied science (MS), including acoustics, operations research, physical oceanography, signal processing; electrical engineering (MS); engineering acoustics (MS, PhD); engineering science (MS), including electrical engineering, mechanical engineering; mechanical engineer (ME); mechanical engineering (MS, MSME); meteorology (MS); operations research (MS); physical oceanography (MS). Program only open to commissioned officers of the United States and friendly nations and selected United States federal civilian employees. Part-time programs available. *Students:* 2 full-time, both international. Average age 36. *Degree requirements:* For master's, thesis. *Faculty research:* Unmanned/autonomous vehicles, sea mines and countermeasures, submarine warfare in the twentieth and twenty-first centuries. *Unit head:* Dr. Clyde Scandrett, Academic Group Chairman, 831-656-2027. Web site: http://www.nps.edu/Academics/Schools/GSEAS/Departments/USW/USW-Index.html.

North Carolina State University, Graduate School, College of Physical and Mathematical Sciences, Department of Marine, Earth, and Atmospheric Sciences, Raleigh, NC 27695. Offers marine, earth, and atmospheric sciences (MS, PhD); meteorology (MS, PhD); oceanography (MS, PhD). PhD offered jointly with The University of North Carolina Wilmington. Terminal master's awarded for partial completion of doctoral program. *Degree requirements:* For master's, thesis (for some programs), final oral exam; for doctorate, comprehensive exam, thesis/dissertation, final oral exam, preliminary oral and written exams. *Entrance requirements:* For master's, GRE General Test, minimum GPA of 3.0; for doctorate, GRE General Test, GRE Subject Test (for disciplines in biological oceanography and geology), minimum GPA of 3.0. Additional exam requirements/recommendations for international students: Required—TOEFL (minimum score 550 paper-based). Electronic applications accepted. *Faculty research:* Boundary layer and air quality meteorology; climate and mesoscale dynamics; biological, chemical, geological, and physical oceanography; hard rock, soft rock, environmental, and paleo-geology.

Nova Southeastern University, Oceanographic Center, Fort Lauderdale, FL 33314-7796. Offers biological sciences (MS); coastal zone management (MS); marine and coastal studies (MA); marine biology (MS); marine biology and oceanography (PhD), including marine biology, oceanography; marine environmental science (MS). Part-time and evening/weekend programs available. *Faculty:* 15 full-time (1 woman), 5 part-time/adjunct (0 women). *Students:* 130 full-time (86 women), 135 part-time (87 women); includes 34 minority (5 Black or African American, non-Hispanic/Latino; 5 Asian, non-Hispanic/Latino; 22 Hispanic/Latino; 2 Two or more races, non-Hispanic/Latino), 7 international. Average age 29. 98 applicants, 82% accepted, 67 enrolled. In 2011, 30 master's, 1 doctorate awarded. *Degree requirements:* For master's, thesis; for doctorate, comprehensive exam, thesis/dissertation, departmental qualifying exam. *Entrance requirements:* For master's, GRE General Test; for doctorate, GRE General Test, master's degree. Additional exam requirements/recommendations for international students: Required—TOEFL (minimum score 550 paper-based). *Application deadline:* Applications are processed on a rolling basis. Application fee: $50. *Expenses:* Contact institution. *Financial support:* In 2011–12, 25 research assistantships (averaging $4,000 per year), 3 teaching assistantships (averaging $3,500 per year) were awarded; career-related internships or fieldwork, Federal Work-Study, scholarships/grants, tuition waivers (partial), and unspecified assistantships also available. Support available to part-time students. Financial award applicants required to submit FAFSA. *Faculty research:* Physical, geological, chemical, and biological oceanography. *Unit head:* Dr. Richard Dodge, Dean, 954-262-3600, Fax: 954-262-4020, E-mail: dodge@nsu.nova.edu. *Application contact:* Dr. Richard Spieler, Director of Academic Programs, 954-262-3600, Fax: 954-262-4020, E-mail: spieler@nova.edu. Web site: http://www.nova.edu/ocean/.

Old Dominion University, College of Sciences, Department of Ocean, Earth and Atmospheric Sciences, Norfolk, VA 23529. Offers ocean and earth sciences (MS); oceanography (PhD). Part-time programs available. *Faculty:* 25 full-time (6 women), 1 part-time/adjunct (0 women). *Students:* 32 full-time (15 women), 8 part-time (3 women); includes 4 minority (1 Black or African American, non-Hispanic/Latino; 1 American Indian or Alaska Native, non-Hispanic/Latino; 1 Asian, non-Hispanic/Latino; 1 Two or more races, non-Hispanic/Latino), 10 international. Average age 30. 32 applicants, 44% accepted, 6 enrolled. In 2011, 7 master's, 5 doctorates awarded. Terminal master's awarded for partial completion of doctoral program. *Degree requirements:* For master's, comprehensive exam (for some programs), thesis (for some programs), 10 days of ship time or fieldwork; for doctorate, comprehensive exam, thesis/dissertation, 10 days of ship time or fieldwork. *Entrance requirements:* For master's, GRE General Test, minimum GPA of 3.0 in major, 2.8 overall; for doctorate, GRE General Test. Additional exam requirements/recommendations for international students: Required—TOEFL (minimum score 550 paper-based; 213 computer-based). *Application deadline:* For fall admission, 2/1 priority date for domestic students, 2/1 for international students. Applications are processed on a rolling basis. Application fee: $40. Electronic applications accepted. *Expenses:* Tuition, state resident: full-time $9096; part-time $379 per credit. Tuition, nonresident: full-time $23,064; part-time $961 per credit. *Required fees:* $127 per semester. One-time fee: $50. *Financial support:* In 2011–12, 16 students received support, including 3 fellowships with full tuition reimbursements available (averaging $22,000 per year), 25 research assistantships with full tuition reimbursements available (averaging $22,000 per year), 14 teaching assistantships with full tuition reimbursements available (averaging $15,500 per year); career-related internships or fieldwork, scholarships/grants, and unspecified assistantships also available. Support available to part-time students. Financial award application deadline: 2/1; financial award applicants required to submit FAFSA. *Faculty research:* Biological, chemical, geological and physical oceanography. *Unit head:* Dr. Rodger Harvey, Department Chair, 757-683-4285, Fax: 757-683-5303, E-mail: rharvey@odu.edu. *Application contact:* William Heffelfinger, Director of Graduate Admissions, 757-683-5554, Fax: 757-683-3255, E-mail: gradadmit@odu.edu. Web site: http://www.odu.edu/sci/oceanography/.

Oregon State University, Graduate School, College of Oceanic and Atmospheric Sciences, Program in Oceanography, Corvallis, OR 97331. Offers MA, MS, PhD. Terminal master's awarded for partial completion of doctoral program. *Degree requirements:* For master's, thesis optional; for doctorate, thesis/dissertation. *Entrance requirements:* For master's and doctorate, GRE General Test, minimum GPA of 3.0 in last 90 hours of course work. Additional exam requirements/

Peterson's Graduate Programs in the Physical Sciences, Mathematics, Agricultural Sciences, the Environment & Natural Resources 2013

facebook.com/petersonspublishing **201**

recommendations for international students: Required—TOEFL. *Faculty research:* Biological, chemical, geological, and physical oceanography.

Princeton University, Graduate School, Department of Geosciences, Program in Atmospheric and Oceanic Sciences, Princeton, NJ 08544-1019. Offers PhD. *Degree requirements:* For doctorate, one foreign language, thesis/dissertation. *Entrance requirements:* For doctorate, GRE General Test, GRE Subject Test. Additional exam requirements/recommendations for international students: Required—TOEFL (minimum score 600 paper-based; 250 computer-based). Electronic applications accepted. *Faculty research:* Climate dynamics, middle atmosphere dynamics and chemistry, oceanic circulation, marine geochemistry, numerical modeling.

Rutgers, The State University of New Jersey, New Brunswick, Graduate School-New Brunswick, Program in Oceanography, Piscataway, NJ 08854-8097. Offers MS, PhD. Terminal master's awarded for partial completion of doctoral program. *Degree requirements:* For master's, thesis; for doctorate, comprehensive exam, thesis/dissertation. *Entrance requirements:* For master's and doctorate, GRE General Test, 1 year course work in calculus, physics, chemistry. Additional exam requirements/recommendations for international students: Required—TOEFL. Electronic applications accepted. *Faculty research:* Coastal observations and modeling, estuarine ecology/fish/benthos, geochemistry, deep sea ecology/hydrothermal vents, molecular biology applications.

Texas A&M University, College of Geosciences, Department of Oceanography, College Station, TX 77843. Offers MS, PhD. *Faculty:* 22. *Students:* 69 full-time (40 women), 16 part-time (7 women); includes 9 minority (1 Black or African American, non-Hispanic/Latino; 1 American Indian or Alaska Native, non-Hispanic/Latino; 3 Asian, non-Hispanic/Latino; 4 Hispanic/Latino), 31 international. Average age 28. In 2011, 9 master's, 8 doctorates awarded. *Degree requirements:* For master's, thesis; for doctorate, thesis/dissertation. *Entrance requirements:* For master's and doctorate, GRE General Test. Additional exam requirements/recommendations for international students: Required—TOEFL. *Application deadline:* For fall admission, 1/15 priority date for domestic students; for spring admission, 10/1 for domestic students. Applications are processed on a rolling basis. Application fee: $50 ($75 for international students). Electronic applications accepted. *Expenses:* Tuition, state resident: full-time $5437; part-time $226.55 per credit hour. Tuition, nonresident: full-time $12,949; part-time $539.55 per credit hour. *Required fees:* $2741. *Financial support:* In 2011–12, fellowships with partial tuition reimbursements (averaging $18,000 per year), research assistantships with partial tuition reimbursements (averaging $18,000 per year), teaching assistantships with partial tuition reimbursements (averaging $18,000 per year) were awarded; Federal Work-Study, scholarships/grants, and tuition waivers (partial) also available. Financial award application deadline: 1/15. *Faculty research:* Ocean circulation, climate studies, coastal and shelf dynamics, marine phytoplankton, stable isotope geochemistry. *Unit head:* Piers Chapman, Head, 979-845-7211, Fax: 979-845-6331. *Application contact:* Christine Arnold, Academic Advisor II, 979-845-7688, Fax: 979-845-6331, E-mail: chrisarnold@tamu.edu. Web site: http://ocean.tamu.edu.

Université du Québec à Rimouski, Graduate Programs, Program in Oceanography, Rimouski, QC G5L 3A1, Canada. Offers M Sc, PhD. Part-time programs available. *Degree requirements:* For master's; for doctorate, thesis/dissertation. *Entrance requirements:* For master's, appropriate bachelor's degree, proficiency in French; for doctorate, appropriate master's degree, proficiency in French.

Université Laval, Faculty of Sciences and Engineering, Program in Oceanography, Québec, QC G1K 7P4, Canada. Offers PhD. Program offered jointly with McGill University and Université du Québec à Rimouski. *Degree requirements:* For doctorate, comprehensive exam, thesis/dissertation. *Entrance requirements:* For doctorate, knowledge of French, knowledge of English. Additional exam requirements/recommendations for international students: Required—TOEFL. Electronic applications accepted.

University of Alaska Fairbanks, School of Fisheries and Ocean Sciences, Program in Marine Sciences and Limnology, Fairbanks, AK 99775-7220. Offers marine biology (MS, PhD); oceanography (PhD), including biological oceanography, chemical oceanography, fisheries, geological oceanography, physical oceanography. Part-time programs available. *Faculty:* 6 full-time (4 women). *Students:* 40 full-time (29 women), 17 part-time (12 women); includes 7 minority (3 Asian, non-Hispanic/Latino; 4 Hispanic/Latino), 4 international. Average age 30. 61 applicants, 20% accepted, 12 enrolled. In 2011, 3 master's, 3 doctorates awarded. *Degree requirements:* For master's, comprehensive exam, thesis, oral defense; for doctorate, comprehensive exam, thesis/dissertation, oral defense. *Entrance requirements:* For master's and doctorate, GRE General Test. Additional exam requirements/recommendations for international students: Required—TOEFL (minimum score 550 paper-based; 213 computer-based; 80 iBT). *Application deadline:* For fall admission, 6/1 for domestic students, 3/1 for international students; for spring admission, 10/15 for domestic students, 8/1 for international students. Applications are processed on a rolling basis. Application fee: $60. Electronic applications accepted. *Expenses:* Tuition, state resident: full-time $6696; part-time $372 per credit. Tuition, nonresident: full-time $13,680; part-time $760 per credit. Tuition and fees vary according to course load and reciprocity agreements. *Financial support:* In 2011–12, 26 research assistantships with tuition reimbursements (averaging $11,484 per year), 7 teaching assistantships with tuition reimbursements (averaging $14,772 per year)

were awarded; fellowships with tuition reimbursements, career-related internships or fieldwork, Federal Work-Study, scholarships/grants, health care benefits, and unspecified assistantships also available. Support available to part-time students. Financial award application deadline: 7/1; financial award applicants required to submit FAFSA. *Unit head:* Katrin Iken, Co-Chair, 907-474-7289, Fax: 907-474-5863, E-mail: academics@sfos.uaf.edu. *Application contact:* Christina Neumann, Academic Manager, 907-474-7289, Fax: 907-474-5863, E-mail: clneumann@alaska.edu. Web site: http://www.sfos.uaf.edu/academics/prospective/graduate.html.

The University of British Columbia, Faculty of Science, Department of Earth and Ocean Sciences, Vancouver, BC V6T 1Z4, Canada. Offers atmospheric science (M Sc, PhD); geological engineering (M Eng, MA Sc, PhD); geological sciences (M Sc, PhD); geophysics (M Sc, MA Sc, PhD); oceanography (M Sc, PhD). *Degree requirements:* For master's, thesis (for some programs); for doctorate, comprehensive exam, thesis/dissertation. *Entrance requirements:* Additional exam requirements/recommendations for international students: Required—TOEFL (minimum score 600 paper-based; 250 computer-based; 100 iBT). Electronic applications accepted. *Faculty research:* Oceans and atmosphere, environmental earth science, hydro geology, mineral deposits, geophysics.

University of California, San Diego, Office of Graduate Studies, Scripps Institution of Oceanography, La Jolla, CA 92093. Offers earth sciences (PhD); marine biology (PhD); oceanography (PhD). *Degree requirements:* For doctorate, comprehensive exam, thesis/dissertation. *Entrance requirements:* For doctorate, GRE General Test. Additional exam requirements/recommendations for international students: Required—TOEFL (minimum score 550 paper-based; 213 computer-based; 80 iBT). Electronic applications accepted.

University of Colorado Boulder, Graduate School, College of Arts and Sciences, Department of Atmospheric and Oceanic Sciences, Boulder, CO 80309. Offers MS, PhD. *Faculty:* 13 full-time (6 women). *Students:* 64 full-time (32 women), 6 part-time (2 women); includes 9 minority (1 Black or African American, non-Hispanic/Latino; 1 American Indian or Alaska Native, non-Hispanic/Latino; 3 Asian, non-Hispanic/Latino; 3 Hispanic/Latino; 1 Two or more races, non-Hispanic/Latino), 17 international. Average age 30. 93 applicants, 33% accepted, 8 enrolled. In 2011, 12 master's, 9 doctorates awarded. *Entrance requirements:* For master's, minimum undergraduate GPA of 3.0. *Application deadline:* For fall admission, 2/1 for domestic students, 12/1 for international students; for spring admission, 10/1 for domestic and international students. Electronic applications accepted. *Financial support:* In 2011–12, 74 students received support, including 31 fellowships (averaging $7,759 per year), 38 research assistantships with full and partial tuition reimbursements available (averaging $25,067 per year), 12 teaching assistantships with full and partial tuition reimbursements available (averaging $20,033 per year); institutionally sponsored loans, scholarships/grants, health care benefits, and unspecified assistantships also available. Financial award applicants required to submit FAFSA. *Faculty research:* Large-scale dynamics of the ocean and the atmosphere, air-sea interaction, radiative transfer and remote sensing of the ocean and the atmosphere, sea ice and its role in climate. *Total annual research expenditures:* $18.4 million. *Application contact:* E-mail: atocasst@colorado.edu. Web site: http://atoc.colorado.edu/.

University of Connecticut, Graduate School, College of Liberal Arts and Sciences, Department of Marine Sciences, Storrs, CT 06269. Offers MS, PhD. Terminal master's awarded for partial completion of doctoral program. *Degree requirements:* For master's, comprehensive exam; for doctorate, thesis/dissertation. *Entrance requirements:* Additional exam requirements/recommendations for international students: Required—TOEFL (minimum score 550 paper-based; 213 computer-based). Electronic applications accepted.

University of Delaware, College of Earth, Ocean, and Environment, School of Marine Science and Policy, Newark, DE 19716. Offers marine policy (MMP); marine studies (MS, PhD), including marine biosciences, oceanography, physical ocean science and engineering; oceanography (PhD).

University of Hawaii at Manoa, Graduate Division, School of Ocean and Earth Science and Technology, Department of Oceanography, Honolulu, HI 96822. Offers MS, PhD. Part-time programs available. Terminal master's awarded for partial completion of doctoral program. *Degree requirements:* For master's, one foreign language, comprehensive exam, thesis, field experience; for doctorate, one foreign language, comprehensive exam, thesis/dissertation, field experience. *Entrance requirements:* For master's and doctorate, GRE General Test. Additional exam requirements/recommendations for international students: Required—TOEFL (minimum score 560 paper-based; 220 computer-based; 83 iBT), IELTS (minimum score 5). *Faculty research:* Physical oceanography, marine chemistry, biological oceanography, atmospheric chemistry, marine geology.

University of Maine, Graduate School, College of Natural Sciences, Forestry, and Agriculture, School of Marine Sciences, Program in Oceanography, Orono, ME 04469. Offers MS, PhD. Part-time programs available. *Students:* 14 full-time (5 women), 5 part-time (1 woman), 3 international. Average age 30. 10 applicants, 50% accepted, 2 enrolled. In 2011, 2 master's, 5 doctorates awarded. *Degree requirements:* For master's, thesis; for doctorate, thesis/dissertation. *Entrance requirements:* For master's and doctorate, GRE General Test. Additional exam requirements/recommendations for international students: Required—TOEFL. *Application deadline:* For fall admission, 2/1 priority date for domestic students. Applications are processed on a rolling basis. Application fee: $65. Electronic applications accepted. *Expenses:* Tuition, state resident: full-time $5016. Tuition,

202 facebook.com/petersonspublishing

Peterson's Graduate Programs in the Physical Sciences, Mathematics, Agricultural Sciences, the Environment & Natural Resources 2013

nonresident: full-time $14,424. *Financial support:* Fellowships with tuition reimbursements, research assistantships with tuition reimbursements, teaching assistantships with tuition reimbursements, career-related internships or fieldwork, Federal Work-Study, and tuition waivers (full and partial) available. Support available to part-time students. Financial award application deadline: 3/1. *Faculty research:* Coastal processes, microbial ecology, crustacean systematics. *Unit head:* Dr. Mary Jane Perry, Coordinator, 207-581-3321. *Application contact:* Scott G. Delcourt, Associate Dean of the Graduate School, 207-581-3291, Fax: 207-581-3232, E-mail: graduate@maine.edu. Web site: http://www2.umaine.edu/graduate/.

University of Maryland, College Park, Academic Affairs, College of Computer, Mathematical and Natural Sciences, Department of Atmospheric and Oceanic Science, College Park, MD 20742. Offers MS, PMS, PhD. Part-time and evening/weekend programs available. Postbaccalaureate distance learning degree programs offered. *Faculty:* 29 full-time (6 women), 7 part-time/adjunct (1 woman). *Students:* 57 full-time (25 women), 8 part-time (6 women); includes 4 minority (2 Asian, non-Hispanic/Latino; 1 Hispanic/Latino; 1 Two or more races, non-Hispanic/Latino), 25 international. 84 applicants, 24% accepted, 17 enrolled. In 2011, 3 master's, 5 doctorates awarded. Terminal master's awarded for partial completion of doctoral program. *Degree requirements:* For master's, comprehensive exam, scholarly paper, written and oral exams; for doctorate, thesis/dissertation, exam. *Entrance requirements:* For master's, GRE General Test, background in mathematics, experience in scientific computer languages, 3 letters of recommendation; for doctorate, GRE General Test. *Application deadline:* For fall admission, 1/15 for domestic and international students. Applications are processed on a rolling basis. Application fee: $75. Electronic applications accepted. *Expenses: Tuition, area resident:* Part-time $525 per credit hour. Tuition, state resident: part-time $525 per credit hour. Tuition, nonresident: part-time $1131 per credit hour. *Required fees:* $386.31 per term. Tuition and fees vary according to program. *Financial support:* In 2011–12, 1 fellowship with partial tuition reimbursement (averaging $10,000 per year), 20 research assistantships (averaging $20,435 per year), 25 teaching assistantships (averaging $20,311 per year) were awarded; Federal Work-Study and scholarships/grants also available. Support available to part-time students. Financial award applicants required to submit FAFSA. *Faculty research:* Weather, atmospheric chemistry, air pollution, global change, radiation. *Total annual research expenditures:* $3.2 million. *Unit head:* James A. Carton, Chair, 301-405-5365, Fax: 301-314-9482, E-mail: carton@umd.edu. *Application contact:* Dr. Charles A. Caramello, Dean of Graduate School, 301-405-0358, Fax: 301-314-9305.

University of Miami, Graduate School, Rosenstiel School of Marine and Atmospheric Science, Division of Meteorology and Physical Oceanography, Coral Gables, FL 33124. Offers meteorology (MS, PhD); physical oceanography (MS, PhD). Terminal master's awarded for partial completion of doctoral program. *Degree requirements:* For master's, comprehensive exam, thesis; for doctorate, comprehensive exam, thesis/dissertation. *Entrance requirements:* For master's and doctorate, GRE General Test. Additional exam requirements/recommendations for international students: Required—TOEFL (minimum score 550 paper-based; 213 computer-based). Electronic applications accepted.

University of New Hampshire, Graduate School, College of Engineering and Physical Sciences, Program in Ocean Engineering, Durham, NH 03824. Offers ocean engineering (MS, PhD); ocean mapping (MS, Postbaccalaureate Certificate). *Faculty:* 13 full-time (1 woman). *Students:* 19 full-time (5 women), 6 part-time (0 women); includes 2 minority (1 Hispanic/Latino; 1 Two or more races, non-Hispanic/Latino), 15 international. Average age 31. 29 applicants, 86% accepted, 13 enrolled. In 2011, 2 master's, 1 doctorate, 6 other advanced degrees awarded. *Degree requirements:* For master's, thesis. *Entrance requirements:* Additional exam requirements/recommendations for international students: Required—TOEFL (minimum score 550 paper-based; 213 computer-based; 80 iBT). *Application deadline:* For fall admission, 4/1 priority date for domestic students; for spring admission, 12/1 for domestic students. Applications are processed on a rolling basis. Application fee: $65. Electronic applications accepted. *Expenses:* Tuition, state resident: full-time $12,360; part-time $687 per credit hour. Tuition, nonresident: full-time $25,680; part-time $1058 per credit hour. *International tuition:* $29,550 full-time. *Required fees:* $1666; $833 per course. $416.50 per semester. Tuition and fees vary according to course load and degree level. *Financial support:* In 2011–12, 18 students received support, including 13 research assistantships, 1 teaching assistantship; fellowships, Federal Work-Study, scholarships/grants, and tuition waivers (full and partial) also available. Support available to part-time students. Financial award application deadline: 2/15. *Unit head:* Dr. Kenneth Baldwin, Chairperson, 603-862-1898. *Application contact:* Jennifer Bedsole, Information Contact, 603-862-0672, E-mail: ocean.engineering@unh.edu. Web site: http://www.unh.edu/oe/.

University of Rhode Island, Graduate School, Graduate School of Oceanography, Narragansett, RI 02882. Offers MO, MS, PhD, MBA/MO, PhD/MA, PhD/MMA. Part-time programs available. *Faculty:* 27 full-time (8 women), 2 part-time/adjunct (0 women). *Students:* 72 full-time (38 women), 16 part-time (10 women); includes 3 minority (all Asian, non-Hispanic/Latino), 8 international. In 2011, 17 master's, 9 doctorates awarded. *Degree requirements:* For master's, comprehensive exam (for some programs), thesis optional; for doctorate, comprehensive exam, thesis/dissertation. *Entrance requirements:* For master's, GRE, 2 letters of recommendation; for doctorate, GRE, 3 letters of recommendation. Additional exam requirements/recommendations for international students: Required—TOEFL (minimum score 600 paper-based; 250 computer-based; 100 iBT). *Application deadline:* For fall admission, 1/15 for domestic and international students; for spring admission, 11/15 for domestic students, 7/15 for international students. Application fee: $65. Electronic applications accepted. *Expenses:* Tuition, state resident: full-time $10,432; part-time $580 per credit hour. Tuition, nonresident: full-time $23,130; part-time $1285 per credit hour. *Required fees:* $1362; $36 per credit hour. $35 per semester. One-time fee: $130. *Financial support:* In 2011–12, 35 research assistantships with full and partial tuition reimbursements (averaging $9,896 per year), 11 teaching assistantships with full and partial tuition reimbursements (averaging $9,802 per year) were awarded. Financial award application deadline: 1/15; financial award applicants required to submit FAFSA. *Faculty research:* The Subduction Factory, life in extreme environments, the marine nitrogen cycle, hurricane prediction, Antarctic ocean circulation. *Unit head:* Dr. David M. Farmer, Dean, 401-874-6222, Fax: 401-874-6889, E-mail: thedean@gso.uri.edu. *Application contact:* Nasser H. Zawia, Dean of the Graduate School, 401-874-5909, Fax: 401-874-5787, E-mail: nzawia@uri.edu. Web site: http://www.gso.uri.edu/.

University of Southern California, Graduate School, Dana and David Dornsife College of Letters, Arts and Sciences, Department of Biological Sciences, Program in Marine Biology and Biological Oceanography, Los Angeles, CA 90089. Offers marine and environmental biology (MS); marine biology and biological oceanography (PhD). Terminal master's awarded for partial completion of doctoral program. *Degree requirements:* For master's, research paper; for doctorate, comprehensive exam, thesis/dissertation, qualifying examination, dissertation defense. *Entrance requirements:* For master's and doctorate, GRE, 3 letters of recommendation, personal statement, resume, minimum GPA of 3.0. Additional exam requirements/recommendations for international students: Required—TOEFL (minimum score 600 paper-based; 250 computer-based; 100 iBT). Electronic applications accepted. *Faculty research:* Microbial ecology, biogeochemistry, and geobiology; biodiversity and molecular ecology; integrative organismal biology; conservation biology; marine genomics.

University of South Florida, Graduate School, College of Marine Science, Saint Petersburg, FL 33701. Offers biological oceanography (MS, PhD); chemical oceanography (MS, PhD); geological oceanography (MS, PhD); interdisciplinary (PhD); marine resource assessment (MS, PhD); physical oceanography (MS, PhD). Part-time programs available. *Faculty:* 29 full-time (5 women), 2 part-time/adjunct (1 woman). *Students:* 77 full-time (41 women), 29 part-time (19 women); includes 17 minority (5 Black or African American, non-Hispanic/Latino; 11 Hispanic/Latino; 1 Two or more races, non-Hispanic/Latino), 16 international. Average age 31. 127 applicants, 24% accepted, 25 enrolled. In 2011, 8 master's, 8 doctorates awarded. Terminal master's awarded for partial completion of doctoral program. *Degree requirements:* For master's, comprehensive exam, thesis; for doctorate, comprehensive exam, thesis/dissertation. *Entrance requirements:* For master's and doctorate, GRE, minimum GPA of 3.0 in last 60 hours, three letters of recommendation, research-interest statement, resume. Additional exam requirements/recommendations for international students: Required—TOEFL (minimum score 550 paper-based; 213 computer-based; 79 iBT) or IELTS (minimum score 6.5). *Application deadline:* For fall admission, 1/15 for domestic students, 1/2 for international students; for spring admission, 10/1 for domestic students, 7/1 for international students. Applications are processed on a rolling basis. Application fee: $30. *Financial support:* In 2011–12, 55 students received support, including 45 research assistantships with partial tuition reimbursements available (averaging $14,199 per year), 10 teaching assistantships with partial tuition reimbursements available (averaging $14,196 per year); health care benefits and unspecified assistantships also available. Financial award application deadline: 1/15. *Faculty research:* Trace metal chemistry, water quality, organic and isotopic geochemistry, physical chemistry, nutrient chemistry. *Total annual research expenditures:* $11.2 million. *Unit head:* Dr. David Naar, Professor and Director of Academic Programs and Student Affairs, 727-553-1637, Fax: 727-553-1189, E-mail: naar@usf.edu. *Application contact:* Dawna L. Ishler, Academic Services Administrator, 727-553-3944, Fax: 727-553-1189, E-mail: advisor@marine.usf.edu. Web site: http://www.marine.usf.edu/.

University of Victoria, Faculty of Graduate Studies, Faculty of Science, School of Earth and Ocean Sciences, Victoria, BC V8W 2Y2, Canada. Offers M Sc, PhD. Part-time programs available. *Degree requirements:* For master's, thesis; for doctorate, thesis/dissertation, candidacy exam. *Entrance requirements:* For master's and doctorate, GRE. Additional exam requirements/recommendations for international students: Required—TOEFL (minimum score 575 paper-based; 233 computer-based), IELTS (minimum score 7). Electronic applications accepted. *Faculty research:* Climate modeling, geology.

University of Washington, Graduate School, College of the Environment, School of Oceanography, Seattle, WA 98195. Offers biological oceanography (MS, PhD); chemical oceanography (MS, PhD); marine geology and geophysics (MS, PhD); physical oceanography (MS, PhD). Terminal master's awarded for partial completion of doctoral program. *Degree requirements:* For master's, research project; for doctorate, thesis/dissertation. *Entrance requirements:* For master's and doctorate, GRE General Test, minimum GPA of 3.0. Additional exam requirements/recommendations for international students: Required—TOEFL. Electronic applications accepted. *Faculty research:* Global climate change, hydrothermal vent systems, marine microbiology, marine and freshwater biogeochemistry, biological-physical interactions.

Peterson's Graduate Programs in the Physical Sciences, Mathematics, Agricultural Sciences, the Environment & Natural Resources 2013

facebook.com/petersonspublishing **203**

Oceanography

University of Wisconsin–Madison, Graduate School, College of Engineering, Program in Limnology and Marine Science, Madison, WI 53706. Offers MS, PhD. *Faculty:* 28 full-time (7 women). *Students:* 17 full-time (4 women); includes 1 minority (Hispanic/Latino), 1 international. 41 applicants, 10% accepted, 4 enrolled. In 2011, 1 degree awarded. Terminal master's awarded for partial completion of doctoral program. *Median time to degree:* Of those who began their doctoral program in fall 2003, 100% received their degree in 8 years or less. *Degree requirements:* For master's, thesis; for doctorate, thesis/dissertation. *Entrance requirements:* For master's and doctorate, GRE General Test. Additional exam requirements/recommendations for international students: Required—TOEFL. *Application deadline:* For fall admission, 1/1 priority date for domestic students, 1/1 for international students. Application fee: $45. Electronic applications accepted. *Expenses:* Tuition, state resident: full-time $10,296; part-time $643.51 per credit. Tuition, nonresident: full-time $24,054; part-time $1503.40 per credit. *Required fees:* $70.06 per credit. Tuition and fees vary according to course load, campus/location, program and reciprocity agreements. *Financial support:* In 2011–12, fellowships with full tuition reimbursements (averaging $19,032 per year), 24 research assistantships with full tuition reimbursements (averaging $20,100 per year), 4 teaching assistantships with full tuition reimbursements (averaging $20,100 per year) were awarded; Federal Work-Study and institutionally sponsored loans also available. Financial award application deadline: 1/1. *Faculty research:* Lake ecosystems, ecosystem modeling, geochemistry, physiological ecology, chemical limnology. *Unit head:* Steven Loheide, Chair, 608-263-3264, E-mail: loheide@wisc.edu. *Application contact:* Mary Possin, Student Services Coordinator, 608-263-3264, Fax: 608-265-2340, E-mail: mcpossin@wisc.edu. Web site: http://www.engr.wisc.edu/interd/limnology/.

University of Wisconsin–Madison, Graduate School, College of Letters and Science, Department of Atmospheric and Oceanic Sciences, Madison, WI 53706-1380. Offers MS, PhD. Part-time programs available. *Degree requirements:* For master's, thesis (for some programs); for doctorate, thesis/dissertation. *Entrance requirements:* For master's and doctorate, GRE General Test, minimum GPA of 3.0; previous course work in chemistry, mathematics, and physics. Electronic applications accepted. *Expenses:* Tuition, state resident: full-time $10,296; part-time $643.51 per credit. Tuition, nonresident: full-time $24,054; part-time $1503.40 per credit. *Required fees:* $70.06 per credit. Tuition and fees vary according to course load, campus/location, program and reciprocity agreements. *Faculty research:* Satellite meteorology, weather systems, global climate change, numerical modeling, atmosphere-ocean interaction.

Woods Hole Oceanographic Institution, MIT/WHOI Joint Program in Oceanography/Applied Ocean Science and Engineering, Woods Hole, MA 02543-1541. Offers applied ocean science and engineering (PhD); biological oceanography (PhD); chemical oceanography (PhD); marine geology and geophysics (PhD); physical oceanography (PhD). Program offered jointly with Massachusetts Institute of Technology. *Degree requirements:* For doctorate, thesis/dissertation. *Entrance requirements:* For doctorate, GRE General Test, GRE Subject Test. Additional exam requirements/recommendations for international students: Required—TOEFL. Electronic applications accepted.

Yale University, Graduate School of Arts and Sciences, Department of Geology and Geophysics, New Haven, CT 06520. Offers biogeochemistry (PhD); climate dynamics (PhD); geochemistry (PhD); geophysics (PhD); meteorology (PhD); oceanography (PhD); paleontology (PhD); paleooceanography (PhD); petrology (PhD); tectonics (PhD). *Degree requirements:* For doctorate, thesis/dissertation. *Entrance requirements:* For doctorate, GRE General Test. Additional exam requirements/recommendations for international students: Required—TOEFL.

204 facebook.com/petersonspublishing

Peterson's Graduate Programs in the Physical Sciences, Mathematics, Agricultural Sciences, the Environment & Natural Resources 2013

HAWAI'I PACIFIC UNIVERSITY

Master of Science in Marine Science

Program of Study

Hawai'i Pacific University's (HPU) Master of Science in Marine Science (MSMS) is a research-based degree program that emphasizes a hands-on approach to learning through the completion of an original thesis project under the mentorship of an experienced marine science researcher. Individualized programs of study ensure that the students have the best possible preparation based on their individual interests, background, and abilities.

Marine science faculty members and researchers in the College of Natural and Computational Sciences work in many fields critical to the understanding and sustainable use of marine resources and systems, including aquaculture, marine biogeochemistry, marine natural product chemistry, benthic ecology, spatial ecology, coral reef ecology, inorganic carbon cycle dynamics, phycology, environmental microbiology, toxicology, marine mammal physiology, and ichthyology.

The MSMS program is designed to be completed in two years of full-time study. In the first year, students take a core course sequence and complete a proposal for their thesis research topic. Thesis research is conducted through the next year, culminating in oral and written presentation of a thesis. Full-time students will take the equivalent of three classes per semester. Graduates have the knowledge and skills to be successful in marine-related technical positions in industry, government, and education or for entry into doctoral marine science programs.

Research Facilities

Research facilities include state-of-the-art laboratories at HPU's Hawai'i Loa campus and the Oceanic Institute, located on the windward side of Oahu. Classes are held at both locations and accessible with a free shuttle.

Located on the windward shores of O'ahu just steps from the Pacific Ocean, the Oceanic Institute is a gateway to the latest science and innovation in marine biology, marine aquaculture, biotechnology, and ocean resource management. Learning and research opportunities abound in this hands-on environment, ranging from new tactics in shrimp production and marine nutrition to fisheries restoration and ecological interactions between cultured fish and wild populations.

On the Hawai'i Loa campus, classroom facilities include wet labs and computer access; indoor and outdoor aquaculture laboratories; maturation and hatchery facilities; biosecure facilities for shrimp and finfish production; large-scale algae, copepod, rotifer, and brine shrimp live-feed production facilities; and analytical laboratories for water quality, physical parameters, and biochemical analyses.

Students in the marine science program also gain field and research experience aboard the *Kaholo*, HPU's 45-foot, double-hulled research vessel.

Financial Aid

Hawai'i Pacific University offers several types of graduate scholarships to new, full-time, degree-seeking students. U.S. citizens, permanent residents, and international students who have a demonstrated financial need may apply.

HPU's graduate scholarships include the Trustee Scholarship of $6000 ($3000 for two semesters), the Dean Scholarship of $4000 ($2000 for two semesters), and the Graduate Kokua Scholarship of $2000 ($1000 for two semesters). New, full-time, degree-seeking students who believe they have a financial need may apply for these graduate scholarships. Other factors that may be considered when evaluating requests are previous academic record, community involvement and service, and professional work experience and achievement.

Priority consideration is given to those students who apply by the deadline. Applications received after the priority deadline will be awarded on a funds-available basis. Applicants will be notified by mail as decisions are made. The type and value of the scholarship will be explained in the award letter.

Cost of Study

Tuition for graduate students enrolled in fall and spring semesters is determined on a per-credit basis; full-time status for a graduate student is 9 credits. Tuition for the optional winter and summer sessions is also determined on a per-credit basis. For the 2012–13 academic year (excluding winter and summer sessions), full-time tuition is $19,080 for the Marine Science program. Other costs include books, personal expenses, fees, and a student bus pass, for an estimated total of $3285.

Living and Housing Costs

The University has off-campus housing for graduate students and an apartment referral service. For the 2012–13 academic year, housing expenses are approximately $12,482. For further graduate housing information, students should visit www.hpu.edu/housing.

Student Group

Students in the program hold undergraduate degrees in marine science, marine biology, environmental science, or other relevant fields, or they have completed sufficient course work in these areas. As the largest private university in Hawai'i, HPU students come from every state in the U.S. and more than 100 other countries. The diversity of the student body stimulates learning about other cultures firsthand, both in and out of the classroom. There is no majority population at HPU. Students are encouraged to examine the values, customs, traditions, and principles of others to gain a clearer understanding of their own perspectives. HPU students develop friendships with students throughout the United States and the world and establish important connections for success in the global economy of the twenty-first century.

Location

Hawai'i Pacific University combines the excitement of an urban, downtown campus with the serenity of a residential campus set in the green foothills of O'ahu's Ko'olau Mountains. The urban campus is located in downtown Honolulu, the business and financial center of the Pacific, within walking distance of shopping and dining. Iolani Palace, the only royal palace in the U.S., is a few blocks away, as are the State Capitol, City Hall, and the Blaisdell Concert Hall. The Honolulu Academy of Arts, Museum of Contemporary Art, Waikiki Aquarium, Honolulu Zoo, and many other cultural attractions are located nearby.

Eight miles away, in Kane'ohe, the Hawai'i Loa campus is situated on 135 acres and is the site of the College of Nursing and Health Sciences and the College of Natural and Computational Sciences. HPU is also affiliated with the Oceanic Institute, an aquaculture research facility located at Makapu'u Point on the windward coast of Oahu. These three distinctive sites are conveniently linked by a free shuttle.

The University

Hawai'i Pacific University is a private, nonprofit university with approximately 8,200 students. Founded in 1965, HPU prides itself on maintaining strong academic programs, small class sizes, individual attention to students, and a diverse faculty and student population. HPU is recognized as a Best in the West college by Princeton Review and *U.S. News & World Report* and a Best Buy by *Barron's* business magazine. HPU offers more than fifty acclaimed undergraduate programs and fourteen distinguished graduate programs. HPU's innovative programs anticipate the changing needs of the community and prepare graduates to live and work as active members of a global society. Students come from all fifty states and from more than 100 countries, making HPU one of the most culturally diverse universities in the world.

Applying

When reviewing an application for admittance into the graduate program, the Graduate Admission Committee considers several factors, including completion of a science baccalaureate degree from an accredited institution, undergraduate grade point average (GPA) of 3.0 or higher, the results of the

Peterson's Graduate Programs in the Physical Sciences, Mathematics, Agricultural Sciences, the Environment & Natural Resources 2013

facebook.com/petersonspublishing **205**

Hawai'i Pacific University

Graduate Record Examinations (GRE) Test, and the outcome of an interview with a graduate program faculty member either in person or by telephone.

Applicants should complete and forward the graduate admissions application, send in the $50 nonrefundable application fee, have official transcripts sent from all colleges or universities previously attended, and forward two letters of recommendation. A resume and personal statement about the applicant's academic and career goals is also required.

Applicants who have not completed a science or marine science baccalaureate may still apply to the graduate program. However, students may be required to complete prerequisite courses. A holistic approach is used, and no one factor will exclude an applicant from consideration. The University is seeking students who have demonstrated the ability and motivation to do graduate level work.

Applicants whose native language is not English must either complete the English Foundations Program (EFP) requirements or have an exemption from EFP through a TOEFL with a score of 550 or above (including a TWE of 5) to demonstrate proficiency in English as a second language.

The University has a rolling admission process and reviews applications throughout the year. In order to ensure adequate time for evaluation and correspondence, it is strongly recommended that applications be submitted early.

Correspondence and Information

Graduate Admissions
Hawai'i Pacific University
1164 Bishop Street, #911
Honolulu, Hawai'i 96813
Phone: 808-544-1135
866-GRAD-HPU (toll-free)
Fax: 808-544-0280
E-mail: graduate@hpu.edu
Web site: www.hpu.edu/hpumsms

THE FACULTY AND THEIR RESEARCH

Andrew Marsh Brittain, Dean/Associate Professor of Microbiology; Ph.D. (microbiology), Hawaii at Manoa. Research interests: Marine and environmental microbiology.

Susan M. Carstenn, Program Chair/Assistant Professor of Environmental Science and Marine and Environmental Science; Ph.D. (systems ecology/environmental science), Florida. Research interests: Finding better ways interface humanity and the environment, with particular emphasis on wetland and coastal ecosystem processes. (scarstenn@hpu.edu)

Yongli Chen, Assistant Professor of Chemistry; Ph.D. (biophysics), Tsinghua (Beijing). Research interests: How abusive drugs like cocaine affect the mammalian central nervous system, finding and designing small organic molecules that can alleviate the drug's effect, screening interesting marine natural products using glutamate receptors as molecular targets, understanding the biochemistry behind the action of marine pharmaceuticals to facilitate drug development and modification for optimization.

Valerie Franck, Assistant Professor of Biology and Marine and Environmental Science; Ph.D. (marine biology), California, Santa Barbara. Research interests: Understanding the complex factors that regulate primary production and phytoplankton species composition, role of iron limitation in regulating the phytoplankton species composition and biogeochemical cycling of silicon and nitrogen.

Varis Grundmanis, Associate Professor of Oceanography and Marine and Environmental Sciences; Ph.D. (chemical oceanography), Washington (Seattle). Research interests: Photographic documentation of marine life in Oahu Marine Life Conservation Districts; physical/chemical oceanography of Kaneohe Bay, Oahu, Hawaii; photographic documentation of marine life in Oahu Marine Life Conservation Districts; physical/chemical oceanography of Kaneohe Bay, Oahu, Hawaii.

John Gutrich, Adjunct Professor of Environmental Studies; Ph.D., Ohio State. Research interests: Ecological economics, ecosystem modeling, wetland ecology and mitigation, invasive species management, risk assessment, sustainable development. (jgutrich@hpu.edu)

Warren Hays, Associate Professor of Biology; Ph.D. (zoology), Hawaii at Manoa. Research interests: Behavioral ecology of small mammals, especially the social systems of mongooses and shrews; cryptic social systems; evolution of sociality; mammalian scent marking and pheromone systems.

F. David Horgen, Associate Professor of Chemistry; Ph.D. (pharmacognosy), Illinois at Chicago. Research interests: Discovery of biologically active secondary metabolites from marine organisms; screening marine bacteria, fungi, algae, and invertebrates for their ability to modulate the function of transient receptor potential (TRP) cation channels; investigating marine cyanobacteria for novel non-ribosomally biosynthesized peptides.

David Hyrenbach, Assistant Professor of Oceanography; Ph.D. (biological oceanography), California, San Diego (Scripps). Research interests: Oceanic habitats of far-ranging pelagic vertebrates (seabirds, turtles, cetaceans, tunas) and the physical mechanisms (upwelling, convergence) that define predictable areas of enhanced biological activity in pelagic systems.

Brenda A. Jensen, Associate Dean/Program Chair of Biology and Marine and Environmental Sciences; Ph.D. (biological oceanography), MIT/Woods Hole Oceanographic Institution. Research interests: Molecular responses to environmental stress, evaluating species-specific susceptibility within tropical marine communities, and developing in vitro and ex vivo (e.g. cell culture) methods to assess susceptibility to environmental contaminants in rare and protected species such as marine mammals, particularly responses of the immune system and those mediated by members of the PER-ARNT-SIM (PAS) family of proteins, which control certain biochemical responses caused by environmental contaminants and hypoxia.

Samuel Kahng, Assistant Professor of Oceanography; Ph.D. (biological oceanography), Hawai'i at Manoa. Research interests: Ecological impacts of *Carijoa riisei* on Black Coral Habitat.

Keith E. Korsmeyer, Program Chair/Professor of Biology and Marine Sciences and Biology; Ph.D. (marine biology), California, San Diego (Scripps). Research interests: Comparative and ecological physiology of fishes, in particular, the metabolic, energetic, and cardio-respiratory specializations of fishes, and the influence of environment on physiological function: cardiac function and oxygen transport to tissues, metabolic compensations to changes in habitat, such as temperature and hypoxia, and bioenergetics of swimming.

Catherine Unabia, Program Chair/Assistant Professor of Biology; Ph.D. (zoology, marine invertebrates), Hawaii at Manoa. Research interests: Larval biology, chemical ecology, sea grass communities, marine microbiology and biotechnology, molluscan evolution and systematics. (cunabia@hpu.edu)

Eric W. Vetter, Associate Professor of Marine Biology; Ph.D. (oceanography), California, San Diego (Scripps). Research interests: Effects of macrophyte detritus on communities in deep submarine canyons, carbon sources for infauna in submarine canyons, impact of submarine canyons on near-shore fisheries, effects of CO_2 sequestration on benthic communities, scavenger communities on the Hawaiian Slope, and influences of hydrothermal venting on benthic animals on Loihi Seamount.

Kristi West, Assistant Professor of Biology; Ph.D. (biomedical science), Hawaii at Manoa; Ph.D. (marine ecology), L'Universite de la Polynesie Francaise. Research interests: Physiology of cetaceans, especially from a nutritional and reproductive perspective; describing life-history traits in cetaceans, in particular those for poorly known species; marine mammal stranding events and information that can be gained by performing thorough necropsies; disease prevalence and environmental influences on Hawaiian cetaceans.

Christopher D. Winn, Associate Professor of Oceanography; Ph.D. (oceanography), Hawai'i at Manoa. Research interests: Marine biogeochemistry and the oceanic carbon cycle.

206 facebook.com/petersonspublishing

Peterson's Graduate Programs in the Physical Sciences, Mathematics, Agricultural Sciences, the Environment & Natural Resources 2013

Section 5
Meteorology and Atmospheric Sciences

This section contains a directory of institutions offering graduate work in meteorology and atmospheric sciences. Additional information about programs listed in the directory may be obtained by writing directly to the dean of a graduate school or chair of a department at the address given in the directory.

For programs offering related work, see also in this book *Astronomy and Astrophysics, Geosciences, Marine Sciences and Oceanography,* and *Physics.* In the other guides in this series:

Graduate Programs in the Biological/Biomedical Sciences & Health-Related Medical Professions

See *Biological and Biomedical Sciences* and *Biophysics*

Graduate Programs in Engineering & Applied Sciences

See *Aerospace/Aeronautical Engineering, Civil and Environmental Engineering, Engineering and Applied Sciences,* and *Mechanical Engineering and Mechanics*

CONTENTS

Program Directories

Atmospheric Sciences

Arizona State University, College of Liberal Arts and Sciences, School of Geographical Sciences, Tempe, AZ 85287-5302. Offers atmospheric science (Graduate Certificate); geographic information (MAS); geographic information systems (MAS); geographical information science (Graduate Certificate); geography (MA, PhD); transportation systems (Graduate Certificate); urban and environmental planning (MUEP). Terminal master's awarded for partial completion of doctoral program. *Degree requirements:* For master's, thesis, interactive Program of Study (iPOS) submitted before completing 50 percent of required credit hours; for doctorate, comprehensive exam, thesis/dissertation, interactive Program of Study (iPOS) submitted before completing 50 percent of required credit hours. *Entrance requirements:* For master's and doctorate, GRE, minimum GPA of 3.0 or equivalent in last 2 years of work leading to bachelor's degree. Additional exam requirements/recommendations for international students: Required—TOEFL (minimum score 80 iBT), TOEFL, IELTS, or Pearson Test of English. Electronic applications accepted. *Expenses:* Contact institution.

Bard College, Bard Center for Environmental Policy, Annandale-on-Hudson, NY 12504. Offers climate science and policy (MS, Professional Certificate), including agriculture (MS), ecosystems (MS); environmental policy (MS, Professional Certificate); sustainability (MBA); MS/JD; MS/MAT. Part-time programs available. *Degree requirements:* For master's, thesis, 4-month, full-time internship. *Entrance requirements:* For master's, GRE, coursework in statistics, chemistry and one other semester of college science; personal statement; curriculum vitae; 3 letters of recommendation; sample of written work. Additional exam requirements/recommendations for international students: Required—TOEFL (minimum score 600 paper-based; 250 computer-based; 100 iBT). Electronic applications accepted. *Expenses:* Contact institution. *Faculty research:* Climate and agriculture, alternative energy, environmental economics, environmental toxicology, EPA law, sustainable development, international relations, literature and composition, human rights, agronomy, advocacy, leadership.

City College of the City University of New York, Graduate School, College of Liberal Arts and Science, Division of Science, Department of Earth and Atmospheric Sciences, New York, NY 10031-9198. Offers earth and environmental science (PhD); earth systems science (MA). PhD program offered jointly with Graduate School and University Center of the City University of New York. *Degree requirements:* For master's, comprehensive exam, thesis. *Entrance requirements:* Additional exam requirements/recommendations for international students: Required—TOEFL (minimum score 500 paper-based; 61 iBT). Electronic applications accepted. *Faculty research:* Water resources, high-temperature geochemistry, sedimentary basin analysis, tectonics.

Clemson University, Graduate School, College of Engineering and Science, Department of Physics and Astronomy, Clemson, SC 29634. Offers physics (MS, PhD), including astronomy and astrophysics, atmospheric physics, biophysics. Part-time programs available. *Faculty:* 27 full-time (3 women). *Students:* 67 full-time (21 women); includes 3 minority (2 Black or African American, non-Hispanic/Latino; 1 Hispanic/Latino), 27 international. Average age 27. 133 applicants, 75% accepted, 31 enrolled. In 2011, 4 master's, 6 doctorates awarded. Terminal master's awarded for partial completion of doctoral program. *Degree requirements:* For master's, thesis or alternative; for doctorate, thesis/dissertation. *Entrance requirements:* For master's and doctorate, GRE General Test. Additional exam requirements/recommendations for international students: Required—TOEFL. *Application deadline:* For fall admission, 1/15 priority date for domestic students; for spring admission, 9/15 priority date for domestic students. Applications are processed on a rolling basis. Application fee: $70 ($80 for international students). Electronic applications accepted. *Financial support:* In 2011–12, 58 students received support, including 1 fellowship with full and partial tuition reimbursement available (averaging $8,000 per year), 24 research assistantships with partial tuition reimbursements available (averaging $13,653 per year), 50 teaching assistantships with partial tuition reimbursements available (averaging $13,265 per year); career-related internships or fieldwork, institutionally sponsored loans, scholarships/grants, health care benefits, and unspecified assistantships also available. Support available to part-time students. Financial award application deadline: 6/1; financial award applicants required to submit FAFSA. *Faculty research:* Radiation physics, solid-state physics, nuclear physics, radar and lidar studies of atmosphere. *Total annual research expenditures:* $2.6 million. *Unit head:* Dr. Peter Barnes, Chair, 864-656-3419, Fax: 864-656-0805, E-mail: peterb@clemson.edu. *Application contact:* Graduate Coordinator, 864-656-6702, Fax: 864-656-0805, E-mail: physgradinfo-l@clemson.edu. Web site: http://physicsnt.clemson.edu/.

Colorado State University, Graduate School, College of Engineering, Department of Atmospheric Science, Fort Collins, CO 80523-1371. Offers MS, PhD. Part-time programs available. *Faculty:* 13 full-time (3 women), 2 part-time/adjunct (0 women). *Students:* 62 full-time (23 women), 33 part-time (13 women); includes 14 minority (3 Black or African American, non-Hispanic/Latino; 8 Hispanic/Latino; 3 Two or more races, non-Hispanic/Latino), 5 international. Average age 27. 121 applicants, 22% accepted, 19 enrolled. In 2011, 13 master's, 7 doctorates awarded. *Degree requirements:* For master's, thesis optional; for doctorate, comprehensive exam, thesis/dissertation. *Entrance requirements:* For master's, GRE General Test, minimum GPA of 3.0; BS in physics, math,

atmospheric science, engineering, chemistry or related major; calculus-based math and differential equations; calculus-based physics; letters of recommendation; for doctorate, GRE General Test, minimum GPA of 3.0; MS with thesis in atmospheric science or related field; statement with interests; curriculum vitae; letters of recommendation. Additional exam requirements/recommendations for international students: Required—TOEFL (minimum score 550 paper-based; 213 computer-based; 80 iBT), IELTS (minimum score 6). *Application deadline:* For fall admission, 1/15 priority date for domestic students, 1/15 for international students; for spring admission, 9/15 priority date for domestic students, 9/15 for international students. Applications are processed on a rolling basis. Application fee: $50. Electronic applications accepted. *Expenses:* Contact institution. *Financial support:* In 2011–12, 77 students received support, including 10 fellowships with full tuition reimbursements available (averaging $30,982 per year), 67 research assistantships with full tuition reimbursements available (averaging $25,683 per year); teaching assistantships with partial tuition reimbursements available, scholarships/grants, health care benefits, and unspecified assistantships also available. Support available to part-time students. Financial award application deadline: 4/15; financial award applicants required to submit FAFSA. *Faculty research:* Global circulation and climate, atmospheric chemistry, radiation and remote sensing, marine meteorology, mesoscale meteorology. *Total annual research expenditures:* $15.9 million. *Unit head:* Dr. Jeffrey Collett, Jr., Head, 970-491-8697, Fax: 970-491-8449, E-mail: jeffrey.collett@colostate.edu. *Application contact:* Jamie Schmidt, Student Counselor, 970-491-8682, Fax: 970-491-8449, E-mail: jamie@atmos.colostate.edu. Web site: http://www.ATMOS.colostate.edu/.

Columbia University, Graduate School of Arts and Sciences, Division of Natural Sciences, Program in Atmospheric and Planetary Science, New York, NY 10027. Offers M Phil, PhD. Offered jointly through the Departments of Geological Sciences, Astronomy, and Physics and in cooperation with NASA Goddard Space Flight Center's Institute for Space Studies. *Degree requirements:* For doctorate, variable foreign language requirement, thesis/dissertation. *Entrance requirements:* For doctorate, GRE General Test, GRE Subject Test, previous course work in mathematics and physics. Additional exam requirements/recommendations for international students: Required—TOEFL. *Faculty research:* Climate, weather prediction.

Columbia University, Graduate School of Arts and Sciences, Program in Climate and Society, New York, NY 10027. Offers MA.

Cornell University, Graduate School, Graduate Fields of Agriculture and Life Sciences, Field of Atmospheric Science, Ithaca, NY 14853-0001. Offers MS, PhD. *Faculty:* 15 full-time (1 woman). *Students:* 7 full-time (2 women); includes 3 minority (all Asian, non-Hispanic/Latino), 2 international. Average age 25. 34 applicants, 12% accepted, 2 enrolled. In 2011, 3 degrees awarded. *Degree requirements:* For master's, thesis; for doctorate, comprehensive exam, thesis/dissertation. *Entrance requirements:* For master's and doctorate, GRE General Test, 2 letters of recommendation. Additional exam requirements/recommendations for international students: Required—TOEFL (minimum score 550 paper-based; 213 computer-based; 77 iBT). *Application deadline:* For fall admission, 2/1 for domestic students; for spring admission, 8/1 priority date for domestic students. Application fee: $95. Electronic applications accepted. *Financial support:* In 2011–12, 6 research assistantships with full tuition reimbursements, 1 teaching assistantship with full tuition reimbursement were awarded; fellowships with full tuition reimbursements, institutionally sponsored loans, traineeships, health care benefits, tuition waivers (full and partial), and unspecified assistantships also available. Financial award applicants required to submit FAFSA. *Faculty research:* Applied climatology, climate dynamics, statistical meteorology/climatology, synoptic meteorology, upper atmospheric science. *Unit head:* Director of Graduate Studies, 607-255-3034, Fax: 607-255-2106, E-mail: atmscigradfield@cornell.edu. *Application contact:* Graduate Field Assistant, 607-255-3034, Fax: 607-255-2106, E-mail: pmv2@cornell.edu. Web site: http://www.gradschool.cornell.edu/fields.php?id-39&a-2.

Creighton University, Graduate School, College of Arts and Sciences, Program in Atmospheric Sciences, Omaha, NE 68178-0001. Offers MS. Part-time programs available. *Faculty:* 4 full-time (0 women). *Students:* 5 full-time (2 women), 1 international. Average age 26. 8 applicants, 88% accepted, 3 enrolled. In 2011, 1 master's awarded. *Degree requirements:* For master's, thesis optional. *Entrance requirements:* For master's, GRE General Test, 3 letters of recommendation. Additional exam requirements/recommendations for international students: Required—TOEFL (minimum score 550 paper-based; 213 computer-based; 80 iBT). *Application deadline:* For fall admission, 3/1 for domestic and international students. Application fee: $50. Electronic applications accepted. *Expenses: Tuition:* Full-time $12,672; part-time $704 per credit hour. *Required fees:* $1410; $136 per semester. Tuition and fees vary according to campus/location and reciprocity agreements. *Financial support:* In 2011–12, 1 research assistantship with full tuition reimbursement (averaging $14,000 per year), 3 teaching assistantships with full tuition reimbursements (averaging $10,913 per year) were awarded. Support available to part-time students. Financial award applicants required to submit FAFSA. *Unit head:* Dr. Joseph Zehnder, Chair, 402-280-2448, E-mail: zehnder@creighton.edu. *Application* *contact:* Taunya Plater, Senior Program Coordinator, 402-280-2870, Fax: 402-280-2423, E-mail: taunyaplater@creighton.edu.

Florida State University, The Graduate School, College of Arts and Sciences, Department of Scientific Computing, Tallahassee, FL 32306-4120. Offers computational science (MS, PSM, PhD), including atmospheric science (PhD); biochemistry (PhD), biological science (PhD), computational molecular biology/bioinformatics (PSM), computational science (PhD), geological science (PhD), materials science (PhD), physics (PhD). Part-time programs available. *Faculty:* 14 full-time (2 women). *Students:* 32 full-time (6 women), 3 part-time (0 women); includes 13 minority (1 Black or African American, non-Hispanic/Latino; 11 Asian, non-Hispanic/Latino; 1 Hispanic/Latino), 13 international. Average age 28. 29 applicants, 41% accepted, 9 enrolled. In 2011, 14 master's, 3 doctorates awarded. Terminal master's awarded for partial completion of doctoral program. *Degree requirements:* For master's, thesis (for some programs); for doctorate, comprehensive exam, thesis/dissertation. *Entrance requirements:* For master's and doctorate, GRE General Test, knowledge of at least one object-oriented computing language, 3 letters of recommendations. Additional exam requirements/recommendations for international students: Required—TOEFL (minimum score 550 paper-based; 80 iBT). *Application deadline:* For fall admission, 1/15 for domestic and international students. Application fee: $30. Electronic applications accepted. *Expenses:* Tuition, state resident: full-time $9474; part-time $350.88 per credit hour. Tuition, nonresident: full-time $16,236; part-time $601.34 per credit hour. *Required fees:* $630 per semester. One-time fee: $20. Tuition and fees vary according to course load and campus/location. *Financial support:* In 2011–12, 32 students received support, including 12 research assistantships with full tuition reimbursements available (averaging $20,000 per year), 18 teaching assistantships with full tuition reimbursements available (averaging $20,000 per year); unspecified assistantships also available. Financial award application deadline: 4/15. *Faculty research:* Morphometrics, mathematical and systems biology, mining proteomic and metabolic data, computational materials research at Scientific Computing, advanced 4-D Var Data-Assimilation methods in dynamic meteorology and oceanography, computational fluid dynamics, astrophysics. *Unit head:* Dr. Sam Huckaba, Interim Dean, 850-644-1081. *Application contact:* Maribel Amwake, Graduate Academic Coordinator, 850-644-0143, Fax: 850-644-0098, E-mail: mamwake@fsu.edu. Web site: http://www.sc.fsu.edu.

George Mason University, College of Science, Program in Climate Dynamics, Fairfax, VA 22030. Offers PhD. *Faculty:* 17 full-time (5 women), 13 part-time/adjunct (4 women). *Students:* 17 full-time (8 women), 1 part-time (0 women), 12 international. Average age 31. 17 applicants, 41% accepted, 3 enrolled. In 2011, 7 doctorates awarded. *Entrance requirements:* For doctorate, GRE (waived for those who have earned a master's degree from U.S. institution), undergraduate degree with minimum GPA of 3.0; 2 copies of official transcripts; current resume; expanded goals statement; 3 letters of recommendation. Additional exam requirements/recommendations for international students: Required—TOEFL (minimum score 570 paper-based; 230 computer-based; 88 iBT), IELTS, Pearson Test of English. *Application deadline:* For fall admission, 4/15 priority date for domestic students, 2/1 for international students; for spring admission, 11/15 priority date for domestic students. Application fee: $65 ($80 for international students). Electronic applications accepted. *Expenses:* Tuition, state resident: full-time $8750; part-time $364.58 per credit. Tuition, nonresident: full-time $24,092; part-time $1003.83 per credit. *Required fees:* $2514; $104.75 per credit. *Financial support:* In 2011–12, 18 students received support, including 3 fellowships with full tuition reimbursements available (averaging $18,000 per year), 14 research assistantships with full and partial tuition reimbursements available (averaging $14,486 per year), 3 teaching assistantships with full and partial tuition reimbursements available (averaging $10,400 per year); career-related internships or fieldwork, Federal Work-Study, scholarships/grants, unspecified assistantships, and health care benefits (full-time research or teaching assistantship recipients) also available. Support available to part-time students. Financial award application deadline: 3/1; financial award applicants required to submit FAFSA. *Total annual research expenditures:* $1.3 million. *Unit head:* Dr. David Straus, Chair, 703-993-9587, Fax: 703-993-9300, E-mail: dstraus@gmu.edu. *Application contact:* Dr. Barry Klinger, Graduate Coordinator, 703-993-9227, Fax: 703-993-9300, E-mail: bklinger@gmu.edu. Web site: http://aoes.gmu.edu/academics/graduate/climate.

Georgia Institute of Technology, Graduate Studies and Research, College of Sciences, School of Earth and Atmospheric Sciences, Atlanta, GA 30332-0340. Offers atmospheric chemistry, aerosols and clouds (MS, PhD); dynamics of weather and climate (MS, PhD); geochemistry (MS, PhD); geophysics (MS, PhD); oceanography (MS, PhD); paleoclimate (MS, PhD); planetary science (MS, PhD); remote sensing (MS, PhD). Part-time programs available. Terminal master's awarded for partial completion of doctoral program. *Degree requirements:* For master's, thesis or alternative; for doctorate, comprehensive exam, thesis/dissertation. *Entrance requirements:* For master's, GRE, letters of recommendation; for doctorate, GRE, academic transcripts, letters of recommendation, personal statement. Additional exam requirements/recommendations for international students: Required—TOEFL (minimum score 550 paper-based; 213 computer-based; 79 iBT). *Faculty research:* Geophysics; atmospheric chemistry, aerosols and clouds; dynamics of weather and climate; geochemistry; oceanography; paleoclimate; planetary science; remote sensing.

Hampton University, Graduate College, Department of Atmospheric and Planetary Sciences, Hampton, VA 23668. Offers atmospheric sciences (MS, PhD); planetary sciences (MS, PhD).

Hampton University, Graduate College, Department of Physics, Hampton, VA 23668. Offers atmospheric physics (MS, PhD); medical physics (MS, PhD); nuclear physics (MS, PhD); optical physics (MS, PhD). Part-time and evening/weekend programs available. Terminal master's awarded for partial completion of doctoral program. *Degree requirements:* For master's, thesis optional; for doctorate, thesis/dissertation, oral defense, qualifying exam. *Entrance requirements:* For master's, GRE General Test; for doctorate, GRE General Test, minimum GPA of 3.0 or master's degree in physics or related field. *Faculty research:* Laser optics, remote sensing.

Howard University, Graduate School and School of Engineering and Computer Science, Department of Atmospheric Sciences, Washington, DC 20059-0002. Offers MS, PhD. Part-time programs available. Terminal master's awarded for partial completion of doctoral program. *Degree requirements:* For master's, thesis; for doctorate, one foreign language; comprehensive exam, thesis/dissertation. *Entrance requirements:* For master's, GRE General Test, minimum GPA of 3.0; for doctorate, GRE General Test, minimum GPA of 3.2. Additional exam requirements/recommendations for international students: Required—TOEFL (minimum score 550 paper-based; 213 computer-based). *Faculty research:* Atmospheric chemistry, climate, atmospheric radiation, gravity waves, aerosols, extraterrestrial atmospheres, turbulence.

Howard University, Graduate School, Department of Chemistry, Washington, DC 20059-0002. Offers analytical chemistry (MS, PhD); atmospheric (MS, PhD); biochemistry (MS, PhD); environmental (MS, PhD); inorganic chemistry (MS, PhD); organic chemistry (MS, PhD); physical chemistry (MS, PhD). Terminal master's awarded for partial completion of doctoral program. *Degree requirements:* For master's, comprehensive exam, thesis, teaching experience; for doctorate, comprehensive exam, thesis/dissertation, teaching experience. *Entrance requirements:* For master's, GRE General Test, minimum GPA of 2.7; for doctorate, GRE General Test, minimum GPA of 3.0. Additional exam requirements/recommendations for international students: Required—TOEFL. Electronic applications accepted. *Faculty research:* Synthetic organics, materials, natural products, mass spectrometry.

Massachusetts Institute of Technology, School of Science, Department of Earth, Atmospheric, and Planetary Sciences, Cambridge, MA 02139. Offers atmospheric chemistry (PhD, Sc D); atmospheric science (SM, PhD, Sc D); chemical oceanography (SM, PhD, Sc D); climate physics and chemistry (SM, PhD, Sc D); earth and planetary sciences (SM); geochemistry (PhD, Sc D); geology (PhD, Sc D); geophysics (PhD, Sc D); marine geology and geophysics (SM, PhD, Sc D); physical oceanography (SM, PhD, Sc D); planetary sciences (PhD, Sc D). *Faculty:* 33 full-time (6 women). *Students:* 175 full-time (81 women); includes 21 minority (3 Black or African American, non-Hispanic/Latino; 1 American Indian or Alaska Native, non-Hispanic/Latino; 8 Asian, non-Hispanic/Latino; 4 Hispanic/Latino; 5 Two or more races, non-Hispanic/Latino), 58 international. Average age 26. 241 applicants, 28% accepted, 43 enrolled. In 2011, 6 master's, 16 doctorates awarded. Terminal master's awarded for partial completion of doctoral program. *Degree requirements:* For master's, thesis; for doctorate, comprehensive exam, thesis/dissertation. *Entrance requirements:* For master's, GRE General Test; for doctorate, GRE General Test, GRE Subject Test (chemistry or physics for planetary science area). Additional exam requirements/recommendations for international students: Required—TOEFL (minimum score 577 paper-based; 233 computer-based; 91 iBT), IELTS (minimum score 7). *Application deadline:* For fall admission, 1/5 for domestic and international students; for spring admission, 11/1 for domestic and international students. Application fee: $75. Electronic applications accepted. *Expenses: Tuition:* Full-time $40,460; part-time $630 per credit hour. *Required fees:* $272. *Financial support:* In 2011–12, 125 students received support, including 68 fellowships (averaging $32,200 per year), 94 research assistantships (averaging $31,900 per year), 10 teaching assistantships (averaging $30,000 per year); Federal Work-Study, institutionally sponsored loans, scholarships/grants, health care benefits, and unspecified assistantships also available. *Faculty research:* Formation, dynamics and evolution of planetary systems; origin, composition, structure and dynamics of the atmospheres, oceans, surfaces and interiors of the Earth and other planets; evolution and interaction of the physical, chemical, geological and biological components of the Earth system; characterization of past, present and potential future climates and the causes and consequences of climate change; interplay of energy and the environment. *Total annual research expenditures:* $26.2 million. *Unit head:* Prof. Robert van der Hilst, Head, 617-253-2127, Fax: 617-253-8298, E-mail: eapsinfo@mit.edu. *Application contact:* EAPS Education Office, 617-253-3381, Fax: 617-253-8298, E-mail: eapsinfo@mit.edu. Web site: http://eapsweb.mit.edu/.

McGill University, Faculty of Graduate and Postdoctoral Studies, Faculty of Science, Department of Atmospheric and Oceanic Sciences, Montréal, QC H3A 2T5, Canada. Offers atmospheric science (M Sc, PhD); physical oceanography (M Sc, PhD). PhD program in physical oceanography offered jointly with Université Laval.

Michigan Technological University, Graduate School, Interdisciplinary Programs, Houghton, MI 49931. Offers atmospheric sciences (PhD); computational sciences and engineering (PhD); engineering environmental (PhD). *Students:* 28 full-time (14 women), 4 part-time (0 women), 20 international.

Peterson's Graduate Programs in the Physical Sciences, Mathematics, Agricultural Sciences, the Environment & Natural Resources 2013

facebook.com/petersonspublishing **209**

Average age 29. 73 applicants, 32% accepted, 10 enrolled. In 2011, 3 doctorates awarded. *Degree requirements:* For doctorate, comprehensive exam, thesis/dissertation. *Entrance requirements:* For doctorate, GRE, statement of purpose, official transcripts, 3 letters of recommendation. Additional exam requirements/recommendations for international students: Required—TOEFL or IELTS. *Expenses:* Tuition, state resident: full-time $12,636; part-time $702 per credit. Tuition, nonresident: full-time $12,636; part-time $702 per credit. *Required fees:* $226; $226 per year. *Financial support:* In 2011–12, 28 students received support, including 3 fellowships with full tuition reimbursements available (averaging $6,065 per year), 17 research assistantships with full tuition reimbursements available (averaging $6,065 per year), 3 teaching assistantships with full tuition reimbursements available (averaging $6,065 per year). *Unit head:* Dr. Jacqueline E. Huntoon, Dean, 906-487-2327, Fax: 906-487-2463, E-mail: jeh@mtu.edu. *Application contact:* Carol T. Wingerson, Senior Staff Assistant, 906-487-2327, Fax: 906-487-2463, E-mail: gradadms@mtu.edu.

Millersville University of Pennsylvania, College of Graduate and Professional Studies, School of Science and Mathematics, Department of Earth Sciences, Millersville, PA 17551-0302. Offers integrated scientific applications (MS), including climate science applications, weather intelligence and risk management. *Degree requirements:* For master's, internship or applied research. *Expenses:* Tuition, state resident: full-time $3744; part-time $416 per credit. Tuition, nonresident: full-time $5616; part-time $624 per credit. *Required fees:* $1130; $125.50 per credit. Tuition and fees vary according to course load. *Unit head:* Dr. Richard D. Clark, Graduate Program Coordinator, 717-872-3930, E-mail: richard.clark@millersville.edu. *Application contact:* Dr. Victor S. DeSantis, Dean of Graduate and Professional Studies, 717-872-3099, Fax: 717-872-3453, E-mail: victor.desantis@millersville.edu.

Mississippi State University, College of Arts and Sciences, Department of Geosciences, Mississippi State, MS 39762. Offers applied meteorology (MS); broadcast meteorology (MS); earth and atmospheric science (PhD); environmental geoscience (MS); geography (MS); geology (MS); geospatial sciences (MS); professional meteorology/climatology (MS); teachers in geoscience (MS). Postbaccalaureate distance learning degree programs offered (no on-campus study). *Faculty:* 19 full-time (5 women), 2 part-time/adjunct (0 women). *Students:* 72 full-time (27 women), 279 part-time (127 women); includes 40 minority (12 Black or African American, non-Hispanic/Latino; 4 American Indian or Alaska Native, non-Hispanic/Latino; 6 Asian, non-Hispanic/Latino; 14 Hispanic/Latino; 4 Two or more races, non-Hispanic/Latino), 10 international. Average age 35. 228 applicants, 77% accepted, 144 enrolled. In 2011, 89 master's awarded. *Degree requirements:* For master's, thesis (for some programs), comprehensive oral or written exam. *Entrance requirements:* For master's, GRE (for on-campus applicants), minimum undergraduate GPA of 2.75. Additional exam requirements/recommendations for international students: Required—TOEFL (minimum score 475 paper-based; 153 computer-based; 53 iBT); Recommended—IELTS (minimum score 4.5). *Application deadline:* For fall admission, 7/1 for domestic students, 5/1 for international students; for spring admission, 11/1 for domestic students, 9/1 for international students. Applications are processed on a rolling basis. Application fee: $40. Electronic applications accepted. *Expenses:* Tuition, state resident: full-time $5805; part-time $322.50 per credit hour. Tuition, nonresident: full-time $14,670; part-time $815 per credit hour. *Financial support:* In 2011–12, 13 research assistantships with full tuition reimbursements (averaging $20,746 per year), 31 teaching assistantships with full tuition reimbursements (averaging $14,151 per year) were awarded; Federal Work-Study, institutionally sponsored loans, scholarships/grants, tuition waivers (partial), and unspecified assistantships also available. Financial award application deadline: 4/1; financial award applicants required to submit FAFSA. *Faculty research:* Climatology, hydrogeology, sedimentology, meteorology. *Total annual research expenditures:* $6.2 million. *Unit head:* Dr. Darrel Schmitz, Professor and Head, 662-325-3915, Fax: 662-325-9423, E-mail: schmitz@geosci.msstate.edu. *Application contact:* Dr. Christopher P. Dewey, Associate Professor/Graduate Coordinator, 662-325-2909, Fax: 662-325-9423, E-mail: cpd4@msstate.edu. Web site: http://www.msstate.edu/dept/geosciences/.

New Mexico Institute of Mining and Technology, Graduate Studies, Department of Physics, Socorro, NM 87801. Offers astrophysics (PhD); atmospheric physics (PhD); instrumentation (MS); mathematical physics (PhD); physics (MS). *Faculty:* 14 full-time (2 women), 19 part-time/adjunct (2 women). *Students:* 30 full-time (12 women), 2 part-time (1 woman); includes 1 minority (Asian, non-Hispanic/Latino), 3 international. Average age 28. 28 applicants, 50% accepted, 5 enrolled. In 2011, 5 master's, 3 doctorates awarded. *Degree requirements:* For master's, thesis optional; for doctorate, thesis/dissertation. *Entrance requirements:* For master's, GRE General Test; for doctorate, GRE General Test, GRE Subject Test. Additional exam requirements/recommendations for international students: Required—TOEFL (minimum score 540 paper-based; 207 computer-based). *Application deadline:* For fall admission, 3/1 priority date for domestic students; for spring admission, 6/1 for domestic students. Applications are processed on a rolling basis. Application fee: $16 ($30 for international students). *Expenses:* Tuition, state resident: full-time $4849; part-time $269.41 per credit hour. Tuition, nonresident: full-time $16,041; part-time $891.15 per credit hour. *Required fees:* $622; $65 per credit hour. $20 per semester. Part-time tuition and fees vary according to course load. *Financial support:* In 2011–12, 18 research assistantships (averaging $38,918 per year), 11 teaching assistantships with full and partial tuition reimbursements (averaging $35,099 per year) were awarded; fellowships, Federal Work-Study, institutionally sponsored loans, and unspecified assistantships also available. Financial award

application deadline: 3/1; financial award applicants required to submit CSS PROFILE or FAFSA. *Faculty research:* Cloud physics, stellar and extragalactic processes. *Unit head:* Dr. Kenneth Eack, Chairman, 575-835-5328, Fax: 575-835-5707, E-mail: dwestpfa@nmt.edu. *Application contact:* Dr. Lorie Liebrock, Dean of Graduate Studies, 575-835-5513, Fax: 575-835-5476, E-mail: graduate@nmt.edu. Web site: http://www.physics.nmt.edu/.

North Carolina State University, Graduate School, College of Physical and Mathematical Sciences, Department of Marine, Earth, and Atmospheric Sciences, Raleigh, NC 27695. Offers marine, earth, and atmospheric sciences (MS, PhD); meteorology (MS, PhD); oceanography (MS, PhD). PhD offered jointly with The University of North Carolina Wilmington. Terminal master's awarded for partial completion of doctoral program. *Degree requirements:* For master's, thesis (for some programs), final oral exam; for doctorate, comprehensive exam, thesis/dissertation, final oral exam, preliminary oral and written exams. *Entrance requirements:* For master's, GRE General Test, minimum GPA of 3.0; for doctorate, GRE General Test, GRE Subject Test (for disciplines in biological oceanography and geology), minimum GPA of 3.0. Additional exam requirements/recommendations for international students: Required—TOEFL (minimum score 550 paper-based). Electronic applications accepted. *Faculty research:* Boundary layer and air quality meteorology; climate and mesoscale dynamics; biological, chemical, geological, and physical oceanography; hard rock, soft rock, environmental, and paleo-geology.

Northern Arizona University, Graduate College, College of Engineering, Forestry and Natural Sciences, School of Earth Sciences and Environmental Sustainability, Flagstaff, AZ 86011. Offers climate science and solutions (MS); earth science (MS); earth sciences and environmental sustainability (PhD); environmental sciences and policy (MS); geology (MS). *Faculty:* 27 full-time (9 women). *Students:* 67 full-time (32 women), 11 part-time (3 women); includes 6 minority (3 American Indian or Alaska Native, non-Hispanic/Latino; 3 Hispanic/Latino), 2 international. 149 applicants, 23% accepted, 30 enrolled. In 2011, 16 degrees awarded. *Degree requirements:* For master's, comprehensive exam (for some programs), thesis (for some programs). *Entrance requirements:* Additional exam requirements/recommendations for international students: Required—TOEFL (minimum score 550 paper-based; 213 computer-based; 80 iBT), IELTS (minimum score 7). *Application deadline:* For fall admission, 2/1 priority date for domestic students, 2/1 for international students. Applications are processed on a rolling basis. Application fee: $65. Electronic applications accepted. *Expenses:* Tuition, state resident: full-time $7190; part-time $355 per credit hour. Tuition, nonresident: full-time $18,092; part-time $1005 per credit hour. *Required fees:* $818; $328 per semester. *Financial support:* In 2011–12, 6 fellowships, 7 research assistantships with partial tuition reimbursements (averaging $12,866 per year), 28 teaching assistantships with partial tuition reimbursements (averaging $12,477 per year) were awarded; career-related internships or fieldwork, Federal Work-Study, scholarships/grants, health care benefits, tuition waivers (full and partial), and unspecified assistantships also available. Financial award applicants required to submit FAFSA. *Unit head:* Dr. Abe Springer, Director, 928-523-7198. *Application contact:* Mark Aasmundstad, Coordinator, 928-523-9333, Fax: 928-523-7432, E-mail: mark.aasmundstad@nau.edu. Web site: http://nau.edu/cefns/natsci/seses/.

The Ohio State University, Graduate School, College of Arts and Sciences, Division of Social and Behavioral Sciences, Department of Geography, Columbus, OH 43210. Offers atmospheric sciences (MS, PhD); geography (MA, PhD). *Faculty:* 24. *Students:* 39 full-time (15 women), 24 part-time (9 women); includes 3 minority (2 Asian, non-Hispanic/Latino; 1 Two or more races, non-Hispanic/Latino), 22 international. Average age 29. In 2011, 6 master's, 7 doctorates awarded. *Degree requirements:* For doctorate, variable foreign language requirement, thesis/dissertation. *Entrance requirements:* Additional exam requirements/recommendations for international students: Required—Michigan English Language Assessment Battery (minimum score 82); Recommended—TOEFL (minimum score 600 paper-based; 250 computer-based). *Application deadline:* For fall admission, 8/15 priority date for domestic students, 7/1 for international students; for winter admission, 12/1 priority date for domestic students, 11/1 for international students; for spring admission, 3/1 priority date for domestic students, 2/1 for international students. Applications are processed on a rolling basis. Application fee: $40 ($50 for international students). Electronic applications accepted. *Expenses:* Tuition, state resident: full-time $11,400. Tuition, nonresident: full-time $28,125. Tuition and fees vary according to course load, degree level, campus/location and program. *Financial support:* Fellowships, research assistantships, teaching assistantships, Federal Work-Study, and institutionally sponsored loans available. Support available to part-time students. *Unit head:* Daniel Sui, Chair, 614-688-5441, Fax: 614-292-6213, E-mail: sui.10@osu.edu. *Application contact:* Graduate Admissions, 614-292-6031, Fax: 614-292-3656, E-mail: gradadmissions@osu.edu. Web site: http://www.geography.osu.edu/.

Oregon State University, Graduate School, College of Oceanic and Atmospheric Sciences, Program in Atmospheric Sciences, Corvallis, OR 97331. Offers MA, MS, PhD. Terminal master's awarded for partial completion of doctoral program. *Degree requirements:* For master's, variable foreign language requirement, thesis, qualifying exams; for doctorate, thesis/dissertation, qualifying exams. *Entrance requirements:* For master's and doctorate, GRE General Test, minimum GPA of 3.0 in last 90 hours of course work. Additional exam requirements/recommendations for international students: Required—TOEFL. *Faculty* *research:* Planetary atmospheres, boundary layer dynamics, climate, statistical meteorology, satellite meteorology, atmospheric chemistry.

Princeton University, Graduate School, Department of Geosciences, Program in Atmospheric and Oceanic Sciences, Princeton, NJ 08544-1019. Offers PhD. *Degree requirements:* For doctorate, one foreign language, thesis/dissertation. *Entrance requirements:* For doctorate, GRE General Test, GRE Subject Test. Additional exam requirements/recommendations for international students: Required—TOEFL (minimum score 600 paper-based; 250 computer-based). Electronic applications accepted. *Faculty research:* Climate dynamics, middle atmosphere dynamics and chemistry, oceanic circulation, marine geochemistry, numerical modeling.

Purdue University, Graduate School, College of Science, Department of Earth and Atmospheric Sciences, West Lafayette, IN 47907. Offers MS, PhD. *Faculty:* 33 full-time (5 women), 2 part-time/adjunct (0 women). *Students:* 73 full-time (29 women), 6 part-time (3 women); includes 8 minority (1 Black or African American, non-Hispanic/Latino; 2 American Indian or Alaska Native, non-Hispanic/Latino; 1 Asian, non-Hispanic/Latino; 4 Hispanic/Latino), 33 international. Average age 28. 122 applicants, 26% accepted, 16 enrolled. In 2011, 11 master's, 6 doctorates awarded. *Degree requirements:* For master's, comprehensive exam, thesis; for doctorate, one foreign language, comprehensive exam, thesis/dissertation. *Entrance requirements:* For master's, GRE General Test, minimum undergraduate GPA of 3.0 or equivalent; for doctorate, GRE General Test, minimum undergraduate or master's GPA of 3.0 or equivalent. Additional exam requirements/recommendations for international students: Required—TOEFL (minimum score 550 paper-based; 213 computer-based; 77 iBT); Recommended—TWE. *Application deadline:* For fall admission, 1/2 priority date for domestic students, 1/2 for international students; for spring admission, 9/1 for domestic and international students. Applications are processed on a rolling basis. Application fee: $60 ($75 for international students). Electronic applications accepted. *Financial support:* Fellowships with partial tuition reimbursements, research assistantships with partial tuition reimbursements, and teaching assistantships with partial tuition reimbursements available. Support available to part-time students. Financial award application deadline: 3/1; financial award applicants required to submit FAFSA. *Faculty research:* Geology, geophysics, hydrogeology, paleoclimatology, environmental science. *Unit head:* Dr. Jonathan M. Harbor, Head, 765-494-4753. *Application contact:* Kathy S. Kincade, Graduate Secretary, 765-494-5984, Fax: 765-496-1210, E-mail: kkincade@purdue.edu. Web site: http://www.eas.purdue.edu.

Rutgers, The State University of New Jersey, New Brunswick, Graduate School-New Brunswick, Department of Environmental Sciences, Piscataway, NJ 08854-8097. Offers air pollution and resources (MS, PhD); aquatic biology (MS, PhD); aquatic chemistry (MS, PhD); atmospheric science (MS, PhD); chemistry and physics of aerosol and hydrosol systems (MS, PhD); environmental chemistry (MS, PhD); environmental microbiology (MS, PhD); environmental toxicology (PhD); exposure assessment (PhD); fate and effects of pollutants (MS, PhD); pollution prevention and control (MS, PhD); water and wastewater treatment (MS, PhD); water resources (MS, PhD). Terminal master's awarded for partial completion of doctoral program. *Degree requirements:* For master's, comprehensive exam, thesis or alternative, oral final exam; for doctorate, comprehensive exam, thesis/dissertation, thesis defense, qualifying exam. *Entrance requirements:* For master's and doctorate, GRE General Test. Additional exam requirements/recommendations for international students: Required—TOEFL. Electronic applications accepted. *Faculty research:* Biological waste treatment; contaminant fate and transport; air, soil and water quality.

South Dakota School of Mines and Technology, Graduate Division, PhD Program in Atmospheric and Environmental Sciences, Rapid City, SD 57701-3995. Offers PhD. Program offered jointly with South Dakota State University. *Degree requirements:* For doctorate, comprehensive exam, thesis/dissertation. *Entrance requirements:* For doctorate, GRE General Test, GRE Subject Test. Additional exam requirements/recommendations for international students: Required—TOEFL, TWE. Electronic applications accepted.

South Dakota School of Mines and Technology, Graduate Division, Program in Atmospheric Sciences, Rapid City, SD 57701-3995. Offers MS. Part-time programs available. *Degree requirements:* For master's, thesis. *Entrance requirements:* Additional exam requirements/recommendations for international students: Required—TOEFL, TWE. Electronic applications accepted. *Faculty research:* Hailstorm observations and numerical modeling, microbursts and lightning, radiative transfer, remote sensing.

Stony Brook University, State University of New York, Graduate School, School of Marine and Atmospheric Sciences, Institute for Terrestrial and Planetary Atmospheres, Program in Atmospheric Sciences, Stony Brook, NY 11794. Offers MS, PhD. Evening/weekend programs available. *Degree requirements:* For doctorate, one foreign language, comprehensive exam, thesis/dissertation. *Entrance requirements:* For master's, GRE, minimum GPA of 3.0, 3 letters of recommendation; for doctorate, GRE, official transcripts, minimum GPA of 3.0, 3 letters of recommendation. Additional exam requirements/recommendations for international students: Required—TOEFL (minimum score 600 paper-based; 213 computer-based). Electronic applications accepted.

Texas Tech University, Graduate School, College of Arts and Sciences, Department of Geosciences, Lubbock, TX 79409. Offers atmospheric science (MS); geography (MS); geosciences (MS, PhD). Part-time programs available. *Faculty:* 27 full-time (5 women), 2 part-time/adjunct (0 women). *Students:* 49 full-

time (17 women), 22 part-time (6 women); includes 6 minority (all Hispanic/Latino), 13 international. Average age 28. 109 applicants, 30% accepted, 22 enrolled. In 2011, 10 master's, 1 doctorate awarded. *Degree requirements:* For master's, thesis or alternative; for doctorate, comprehensive exam, thesis/dissertation. *Entrance requirements:* For master's and doctorate, GRE General Test. Additional exam requirements/recommendations for international students: Required—TOEFL (minimum score 550 paper-based; 213 computer-based; 79 iBT). *Application deadline:* For fall admission, 6/1 priority date for domestic students, 1/15 for international students; for spring admission, 9/1 priority date for domestic students, 6/15 for international students. Applications are processed on a rolling basis. Application fee: $50 ($75 for international students). Electronic applications accepted. *Expenses:* Tuition, state resident: full-time $5899; part-time $245.80 per credit hour. Tuition, nonresident: full-time $13,411; part-time $558.80 per credit hour. Required fees: $2680.60; $86.50 per credit hour. $920.30 per semester. *Financial support:* In 2011–12, 23 students received support. Application deadline: 4/15; applicants required to submit FAFSA. *Faculty research:* Sedimentology and paleontology, geophysics, geochemistry, geospatial technology, hurricanes and severe storms. *Total annual research expenditures:* $1 million. *Unit head:* Dr. Calvin Barnes, Chairman, 806-742-3102, Fax: 806-742-0100, E-mail: cal.barnes@ttu.edu. *Application contact:* Dr. Seiichi Nagihara, Associate Professor, 806-742-3102, Fax: 806-724-0100, E-mail: seiichi.nagihara@ttu.edu. Web site: http://www.gesc.ttu.edu/.

Université du Québec à Montréal, Graduate Programs, Program in Earth and Atmospheric Sciences, Montréal, QC H3C 3P8, Canada. Offers atmospheric sciences (M Sc); Earth and atmospheric sciences (PhD); Earth science (M Sc); meteorology (PhD, Diploma). PhD programs offered jointly with McGill University. Part-time programs available. *Degree requirements:* For master's, thesis. *Entrance requirements:* For master's and Diploma, appropriate bachelor's degree or equivalent, proficiency in French; for doctorate, appropriate master's degree or equivalent, proficiency in French.

University at Albany, State University of New York, College of Arts and Sciences, Department of Earth and Atmospheric Sciences, Albany, NY 12222-0001. Offers atmospheric science (MS, PhD); geology (MS, PhD). *Degree requirements:* For master's, one foreign language, comprehensive exam, thesis; for doctorate, 2 foreign languages, comprehensive exam, thesis/dissertation, oral exams. *Entrance requirements:* For master's and doctorate, GRE General Test. Additional exam requirements/recommendations for international students: Required—TOEFL (minimum score 550 paper-based; 213 computer-based). Electronic applications accepted. *Faculty research:* Environmental geochemistry, tectonics, mesoscale meteorology, atmospheric chemistry.

The University of Alabama in Huntsville, School of Graduate Studies, College of Science, Department of Atmospheric and Environmental Science, Huntsville, AL 35899. Offers atmospheric science (MS, PhD); earth system science (MS). Part-time and evening/weekend programs available. *Faculty:* 10 full-time (0 women), 2 part-time/adjunct (0 women). *Students:* 30 full-time (10 women), 5 part-time (4 women); includes 2 minority (1 Black or African American, non-Hispanic/Latino; 1 Asian, non-Hispanic/Latino), 6 international. Average age 26. 31 applicants, 61% accepted, 11 enrolled. In 2011, 9 master's, 4 doctorates awarded. *Degree requirements:* For master's, comprehensive exam, thesis or alternative, oral and written exams; for doctorate, comprehensive exam, thesis/dissertation, oral and written exams. *Entrance requirements:* For master's, GRE General Test, minimum GPA of 3.0; sequence of courses in calculus (including the calculus of vector-valued functions); courses in linear algebra and ordinary differential equations; two semesters each of chemistry and calculus-based physics; proficiency in at least one high-level computer programming language; for doctorate, GRE General Test, minimum GPA of 3.0. Additional exam requirements/recommendations for international students: Required—TOEFL (minimum score 550 paper-based; 213 computer-based; 62 iBT). *Application deadline:* For fall admission, 7/15 for domestic students, 4/1 for international students; for spring admission, 11/30 for domestic students, 9/1 for international students. Applications are processed on a rolling basis. Application fee: $40 ($50 for international students). Electronic applications accepted. *Expenses:* Tuition, state resident: full-time $7830; part-time $473.50 per credit. Tuition, nonresident: full-time $18,748; part-time $1128.33 per credit. Tuition and fees vary according to course load and program. *Financial support:* In 2011–12, 28 students received support, including 27 research assistantships with full and partial tuition reimbursements available (averaging $14,690 per year), 1 teaching assistantship with full tuition reimbursement available (averaging $13,500 per year); career-related internships or fieldwork, Federal Work-Study, institutionally sponsored loans, scholarships/grants, health care benefits, tuition waivers, and unspecified assistantships also available. Support available to part-time students. Financial award application deadline: 4/1; financial award applicants required to submit FAFSA. *Faculty research:* Satellite remote sensing, severe weather, mesoscale modeling, atmospheric chemistry, data assimilation. *Total annual research expenditures:* $9.1 million. *Unit head:* Dr. Sundar Christopher, Chair, 256-922-7872, Fax: 256-922-7755, E-mail: sundar@nsstc.uah.edu. *Application contact:* Kim Gray, Graduate Studies Admissions Coordinator, 256-824-6002, Fax: 256-824-6405, E-mail: deangrad@uah.edu. Web site: http://www.nsstc.uah.edu/atmos/index.html.

University of Alaska Fairbanks, College of Natural Sciences and Mathematics, Program in Atmospheric Science, Fairbanks, AK 99775-7320. Offers MS, PhD. Part-time programs available. *Students:* 22 full-time (8 women), 1 part-time (0 women); includes 1 minority (Native Hawaiian or other Pacific Islander, non-

Peterson's Graduate Programs in the Physical Sciences, Mathematics, Agricultural Sciences, the Environment & Natural Resources 2013

facebook.com/petersonspublishing **211**

Hispanic/Latino), 9 international. Average age 27. 22 applicants, 45% accepted, 10 enrolled. In 2011, 3 degrees awarded. *Degree requirements:* For master's, comprehensive exam, thesis, oral defense; for doctorate, comprehensive exam, thesis/dissertation, oral defense. *Entrance requirements:* Additional exam requirements/recommendations for international students: Required—TOEFL (minimum score 550 paper-based; 213 computer-based; 80 iBT). *Application deadline:* For fall admission, 6/1 for domestic students, 3/1 for international students; for spring admission, 10/15 for domestic students, 9/1 for international students. Applications are processed on a rolling basis. Application fee: $60. Electronic applications accepted. *Expenses:* Tuition, state resident: full-time $6696; part-time $372 per credit. Tuition, nonresident: full-time $13,680; part-time $760 per credit. Tuition and fees vary according to course load and reciprocity agreements. *Financial support:* In 2011–12, 20 research assistantships with tuition reimbursements (averaging $13,987 per year), 1 teaching assistantship with tuition reimbursement (averaging $17,550 per year) were awarded; fellowships with tuition reimbursements, Federal Work-Study, scholarships/grants, health care benefits, and unspecified assistantships also available. Support available to part-time students. Financial award application deadline: 2/15; financial award applicants required to submit FAFSA. *Faculty research:* Sea ice, climate modeling, atmospheric chemistry, global change, cloud and aerosol physics. *Unit head:* Dr. Nicole Moelders, Program Chair, 907-474-7368, Fax: 907-474-7379, E-mail: atmos@gi.alaska.edu. *Application contact:* Mike Earnest, Director of Admissions, 907-474-7500, Fax: 907-474-5379, E-mail: admissions@uaf.edu. Web site: http://www.uaf.edu/asp/.

The University of Arizona, College of Science, Department of Atmospheric Sciences, Tucson, AZ 85721. Offers MS, PhD. *Faculty:* 6 full-time (2 women). *Students:* 25 full-time (11 women), 2 part-time (0 women); includes 4 minority (2 Hispanic/Latino; 2 Two or more races, non-Hispanic/Latino), 9 international. Average age 29. 34 applicants, 18% accepted, 6 enrolled. In 2011, 6 degrees awarded. *Degree requirements:* For master's, thesis or alternative; for doctorate, comprehensive exam, thesis/dissertation. *Entrance requirements:* For master's, GRE General Test, 3 letters of recommendation; for doctorate, GRE General Test, 3 letters of recommendation, statement of purpose. Additional exam requirements/recommendations for international students: Required—TOEFL (minimum score 550 paper-based; 213 computer-based; 79 iBT). *Application deadline:* For fall admission, 2/1 for domestic students, 12/1 for international students. Applications are processed on a rolling basis. Application fee: $75. Electronic applications accepted. *Expenses:* Tuition, state resident: full-time $10,840. Tuition, nonresident: full-time $25,802. *Financial support:* In 2011–12, 1 research assistantship with full tuition reimbursement (averaging $20,979 per year), 5 teaching assistantships with full tuition reimbursements (averaging $22,137 per year) were awarded; scholarships/grants, health care benefits, tuition waivers (full), and unspecified assistantships also available. *Faculty research:* Climate dynamics, radiative transfer and remote sensing, atmospheric chemistry, atmosphere dynamics, atmospheric electricity. *Total annual research expenditures:* $47,734. *Unit head:* Eric A. Betterton, Head, 520-621-6831, E-mail: betterton@atmo.arizona.edu. *Application contact:* Sonya Flores-Basurto, Information Contact, 520-621-6831, Fax: 520-621-6833, E-mail: sfloresb@email.arizona.edu. Web site: http://www.atmo.arizona.edu.

The University of British Columbia, Faculty of Science, Department of Earth and Ocean Sciences, Vancouver, BC V6T 1Z4, Canada. Offers atmospheric science (M Sc, PhD); geological engineering (M Eng, MA Sc, PhD); geological sciences (M Sc, PhD); geophysics (M Sc, MA Sc, PhD); oceanography (M Sc, PhD). *Degree requirements:* For master's, thesis (for some programs); for doctorate, comprehensive exam, thesis/dissertation. *Entrance requirements:* Additional exam requirements/recommendations for international students: Required—TOEFL (minimum score 600 paper-based; 250 computer-based; 100 iBT). Electronic applications accepted. *Faculty research:* Oceans and atmosphere, environmental earth science, hydro geology, mineral deposits, geophysics.

University of California, Davis, Graduate Studies, Graduate Group in Atmospheric Sciences, Davis, CA 95616. Offers MS, PhD. *Degree requirements:* For master's, comprehensive exam or thesis; for doctorate, thesis/dissertation, 3 part qualifying exam. *Entrance requirements:* For master's and doctorate, GRE General Test, minimum GPA of 3.0. Additional exam requirements/recommendations for international students: Required—TOEFL (minimum score 550 paper-based; 213 computer-based). Electronic applications accepted. *Faculty research:* Air quality, biometeorology, climate dynamics, boundary layer large-scale dynamics.

University of California, Los Angeles, Graduate Division, College of Letters and Science, Department of Atmospheric and Oceanic Sciences, Los Angeles, CA 90095. Offers MS, PhD. *Faculty:* 16 full-time (3 women). *Students:* 40 full-time (22 women); includes 9 minority (7 Asian, non-Hispanic/Latino; 2 Hispanic/Latino), 18 international. Average age 27. 67 applicants, 31% accepted, 4 enrolled. In 2011, 8 master's, 4 doctorates awarded. Terminal master's awarded for partial completion of doctoral program. *Degree requirements:* For master's, comprehensive exam or thesis; for doctorate, thesis/dissertation, oral and written qualifying exams. *Entrance requirements:* For master's, GRE General Test, minimum GPA of 3.0; for doctorate, GRE General Test, minimum undergraduate GPA of 3.0. *Application deadline:* For fall admission, 12/15 for domestic and international students. Application fee: $70 ($90 for international students). Electronic applications accepted. *Financial support:* In 2011–12, 43 fellowships with full and partial tuition reimbursements, 35 research assistantships with full and partial

tuition reimbursements, 18 teaching assistantships with full and partial tuition reimbursements were awarded; Federal Work-Study, institutionally sponsored loans, scholarships/grants, health care benefits, tuition waivers (full and partial), and unspecified assistantships also available. Financial award application deadline: 3/1; financial award applicants required to submit FAFSA. *Unit head:* Dr. David C. Neelin, Chair, 310-206-3734, E-mail: neelin@atmos.ucla.edu. *Application contact:* Departmental Office, 310-825-1217, E-mail: studentinfo@atmos.ucla.edu. Web site: http://www.atmos.ucla.edu.

University of Chicago, Division of the Physical Sciences, Department of the Geophysical Sciences, Chicago, IL 60637-1513. Offers atmospheric sciences (SM, PhD); cosmochemistry (PhD); earth sciences (SM, PhD); paleobiology (PhD); planetary and space sciences (SM, PhD). *Faculty:* 24 full-time (3 women). *Students:* 38 full-time (16 women); includes 2 minority (both Hispanic/Latino), 16 international. Average age 26. 68 applicants, 28% accepted, 10 enrolled. In 2011, 2 master's, 5 doctorates awarded. Terminal master's awarded for partial completion of doctoral program. *Degree requirements:* For master's, thesis, seminar; for doctorate, variable foreign language requirement, comprehensive exam, thesis/dissertation. *Entrance requirements:* For doctorate, GRE General Test. Additional exam requirements/recommendations for international students: Required—TOEFL (minimum score 600 paper-based; 250 computer-based; 96 iBT), IELTS (minimum score 7). *Application deadline:* For fall admission, 1/9 for domestic students, 1/10 for international students. Application fee: $55. Electronic applications accepted. *Financial support:* In 2011–12, research assistantships with full tuition reimbursements (averaging $26,500 per year), teaching assistantships with full tuition reimbursements (averaging $27,000 per year) were awarded; fellowships, Federal Work-Study, institutionally sponsored loans, scholarships/grants, tuition waivers (partial), and unspecified assistantships also available. Financial award application deadline: 1/9. *Faculty research:* Climatology, evolutionary paleontology, cosmochemistry, geochemistry, oceanic sciences. *Unit head:* Dr. Michael Foote, Chairman, 773-702-8102, Fax: 773-702-9505. *Application contact:* David J. Taylor, Graduate Student Services Coordinator, 773-702-8180, Fax: 773-702-9505, E-mail: info@geosci.uchicago.edu. Web site: http://geosci.uchicago.edu/.

University of Colorado Boulder, Graduate School, College of Arts and Sciences, Department of Atmospheric and Oceanic Sciences, Boulder, CO 80309. Offers MS, PhD. *Faculty:* 13 full-time (6 women). *Students:* 64 full-time (32 women), 6 part-time (2 women); includes 9 minority (1 Black or African American, non-Hispanic/Latino; 1 American Indian or Alaska Native, non-Hispanic/Latino; 3 Asian, non-Hispanic/Latino; 3 Hispanic/Latino; 1 Two or more races, non-Hispanic/Latino), 17 international. Average age 30. 93 applicants, 33% accepted, 8 enrolled. In 2011, 12 master's, 9 doctorates awarded. *Entrance requirements:* For master's, minimum undergraduate GPA of 3.0. *Application deadline:* For fall admission, 2/1 for domestic students, 12/1 for international students; for spring admission, 10/1 for domestic and international students. Electronic applications accepted. *Financial support:* In 2011–12, 74 students received support, including 31 fellowships (averaging $7,759 per year), 38 research assistantships with full and partial tuition reimbursements available (averaging $25,067 per year), 12 teaching assistantships with full and partial tuition reimbursements available (averaging $20,033 per year); institutionally sponsored loans, scholarships/grants, health care benefits, and unspecified assistantships also available. Financial award applicants required to submit FAFSA. *Faculty research:* Large-scale dynamics of the ocean and the atmosphere, air-sea interaction, radiative transfer and remote sensing of the ocean and the atmosphere, sea ice and its role in climate. *Total annual research expenditures:* $18.4 million. *Application contact:* E-mail: atocasst@colorado.edu. Web site: http://atoc.colorado.edu/.

University of Guelph, Graduate Studies, Ontario Agricultural College, Department of Land Resource Science, Guelph, ON N1G 2W1, Canada. Offers atmospheric science (M Sc, PhD); environmental and agricultural earth sciences (M Sc, PhD); land resources management (M Sc, PhD); soil science (M Sc, PhD). Part-time programs available. *Degree requirements:* For master's, thesis (for some programs), research project (non-thesis track); for doctorate, comprehensive exam, thesis/dissertation. *Entrance requirements:* For master's, minimum Baverage during previous 2 years of course work; for doctorate, minimum B average during previous 2 years of course work. Additional exam requirements/recommendations for international students: Required—TOEFL (minimum score 550 paper-based; 213 computer-based). Electronic applications accepted. *Faculty research:* Soil science, environmental earth science, land resource management.

University of Houston, College of Natural Sciences and Mathematics, Department of Earth and Atmospheric Sciences, Houston, TX 77204. Offers atmospheric science (PhD); geology (MA, PhD); geophysics (PhD). Part-time programs available. *Degree requirements:* For master's, thesis; for doctorate, comprehensive exam, thesis/dissertation. *Entrance requirements:* For master's and doctorate, GRE General Test. Additional exam requirements/recommendations for international students: Required—TOEFL (minimum score 550 paper-based; 213 computer-based; 79 iBT), IELTS (minimum score 6.5). Electronic applications accepted. *Faculty research:* Atmospherics sciences, seismic and solid earth geophysics, tectonics, environmental hydrochemistry, carbonates, micropaleontology, structure and tectonics, petroleum geology.

University of Illinois at Urbana–Champaign, Graduate College, College of Liberal Arts and Sciences, School of Earth, Society and Environment, Department of Atmospheric Sciences, Champaign, IL 61820. Offers MS, PhD. *Faculty:* 10 full-time (2 women). *Students:* 40 full-time (21 women), 10 part-time (4 women);

includes 2 minority (1 Hispanic/Latino; 1 Two or more races, non-Hispanic/Latino), 15 international. 74 applicants, 15% accepted, 9 enrolled. In 2011, 7 master's, 1 doctorate awarded. *Entrance requirements:* For master's and doctorate, GRE General Test, minimum GPA of 3.0. Additional exam requirements/recommendations for international students: Required—TOEFL. *Application deadline:* Applications are processed on a rolling basis. Application fee: $75 ($90 for international students). Electronic applications accepted. *Financial support:* In 2011–12, 4 fellowships, 38 research assistantships, 21 teaching assistantships were awarded; tuition waivers (full and partial) also available. *Unit head:* Robert Rauber, Head, 217-333-2835, Fax: 217-244-4393, E-mail: r-rauber@illinois.edu. *Application contact:* Shirley Palmisano, Office Administrator, 217-333-2046, Fax: 217-244-4393, E-mail: sjpalm@illinois.edu. Web site: http://www.atmos.illinois.edu/.

The University of Kansas, Graduate Studies, College of Liberal Arts and Sciences, Department of Geography, Lawrence, KS 66045-7613. Offers atmospheric science (MS); geography (MA, PhD); MUP/MA. Part-time programs available. *Faculty:* 22 full-time (4 women). *Students:* 66 full-time (28 women), 20 part-time (6 women); includes 10 minority (1 Black or African American, non-Hispanic/Latino; 7 American Indian or Alaska Native, non-Hispanic/Latino; 1 Hispanic/Latino; 1 Two or more races, non-Hispanic/Latino), 10 international. Average age 33. 49 applicants, 51% accepted, 12 enrolled. In 2011, 9 master's, 2 doctorates awarded. *Degree requirements:* For master's, comprehensive exam, thesis, thesis defense; for doctorate, one foreign language, comprehensive exam, thesis/dissertation, dissertation defense. *Entrance requirements:* For master's and doctorate, GRE General Test, 3 letters of reference, transcripts, statement of interests. Additional exam requirements/recommendations for international students: Required—TOEFL. *Application deadline:* For fall admission, 1/15 priority date for domestic students, 1/15 for international students; for spring admission, 11/1 for domestic students, 10/1 for international students. Applications are processed on a rolling basis. Application fee: $55 ($65 for international students). Electronic applications accepted. Tuition and fees vary according to course load, campus/location, program and reciprocity agreements. *Financial support:* Fellowships with full tuition reimbursements, research assistantships with full tuition reimbursements, teaching assistantships with full and partial tuition reimbursements, and unspecified assistantships available. Financial award application deadline: 1/15. *Faculty research:* Physical geography, techniques (cartography, GIS, remote sensing), cultural/regional geography, atmospheric science. *Unit head:* Johannes Feddema, Chair, 785-864-5534, Fax: 785-864-5378, E-mail: feddema@ku.edu. *Application contact:* Stephen Egbert, Graduate Director, 785-864-4252, Fax: 785-864-5378, E-mail: s-egbert@ku.edu. Web site: http://www.geog.ku.edu/.

The University of Manchester, School of Earth, Atmospheric and Environmental Sciences, Manchester, United Kingdom. Offers atmospheric sciences (M Phil, M Sc, PhD); basin studies and petroleum geosciences (M Phil, M Sc, PhD); earth, atmospheric and environmental sciences (M Phil, M Sc, PhD); environmental geochemistry and cosmochemistry (M Phil, M Sc, PhD); isotope geochemistry and cosmochemistry (M Phil, M Sc, PhD); paleontology (M Phil, M Sc, PhD); physics and chemistry of minerals and fluids (M Phil, M Sc, PhD); structural and petrological geosciences (M Phil, M Sc, PhD).

University of Maryland, Baltimore County, Graduate School, College of Natural and Mathematical Sciences, Department of Physics, Program in Atmospheric Physics, Baltimore, MD 21250. Offers MS, PhD. *Faculty:* 25 full-time (4 women), 20 part-time/adjunct (1 woman). *Students:* 13 full-time (4 women); includes 2 minority (1 Black or African American, non-Hispanic/Latino; 1 Asian, non-Hispanic/Latino), 5 international. Average age 28. 3 applicants, 67% accepted, 1 enrolled. In 2011, 2 degrees awarded. *Degree requirements:* For master's, thesis optional; for doctorate, comprehensive exam, thesis/dissertation. *Entrance requirements:* For master's and doctorate, GRE General Test, minimum GPA of 3.0. Additional exam requirements/recommendations for international students: Required—TOEFL (minimum score 587 paper-based; 240 computer-based; 95 iBT). *Application deadline:* For fall admission, 6/1 for domestic students, 5/1 for international students; for spring admission, 1/1 for domestic students, 11/1 for international students. Applications are processed on a rolling basis. Application fee: $50. Electronic applications accepted. *Financial support:* In 2011–12, 11 students received support, including 1 fellowship with full tuition reimbursement available (averaging $30,000 per year), 7 research assistantships with full tuition reimbursements available (averaging $25,000 per year), 4 teaching assistantships with full tuition reimbursements available (averaging $22,000 per year); career-related internships or fieldwork, scholarships/grants, health care benefits, unspecified assistantships, and NASA Student Fellowship also available. Support available to part-time students. Financial award application deadline: 5/31. *Faculty research:* Lidar, remote sensing, aerosols, satellite remote sensing. *Total annual research expenditures:* $2.7 million. *Unit head:* Dr. Vanderlei Martins, Graduate Program Director, 410-455-2513, Fax: 410-455-1072, E-mail: martins@umbc.edu. *Application contact:* Dr. Vanderlei Martins, 410-455-2513, Fax: 410-455-1072, E-mail: martins@umbc.edu. Web site: http://www.physics.umbc.edu.

University of Massachusetts Lowell, College of Sciences, Department of Environmental, Earth and Atmospheric Sciences, Lowell, MA 01854-2881. Offers atmospheric science (MS, PhD).

University of Michigan, College of Engineering, Department of Atmospheric, Oceanic, and Space Sciences, Ann Arbor, MI 48109. Offers atmospheric and space sciences (MS, PhD); geoscience and remote sensing (PhD); space and planetary sciences (PhD); space engineering (M Eng). Part-time programs available. *Students:* 104 full-time (35 women), 1 part-time (0 women). 122 applicants, 57% accepted, 37 enrolled. In 2011, 28 master's, 7 doctorates awarded. Terminal master's awarded for partial completion of doctoral program. *Degree requirements:* For master's, thesis (for some programs); for doctorate, thesis/dissertation, oral defense of dissertation, preliminary exams. *Entrance requirements:* For master's and doctorate, GRE General Test. Additional exam requirements/recommendations for international students: Required—TOEFL. *Application deadline:* Applications are processed on a rolling basis. Application fee: $65 ($75 for international students). Electronic applications accepted. *Financial support:* Fellowships, research assistantships, teaching assistantships, career-related internships or fieldwork, Federal Work-Study, institutionally sponsored loans, and health care benefits available. Support available to part-time students. Financial award applicants required to submit FAFSA. *Faculty research:* Planetary environments, space instrumentation, air pollution meteorology, global climate change, sun-earth connection, space weather. *Unit head:* Dr. James Slavin, Chair, 734-764-7221, Fax: 734-615-4645, E-mail: jaslavin@umich.edu. *Application contact:* Margaret Reid, Student Services Associate, 734-936-0482, Fax: 734-763-0437, E-mail: aoss.um@umich.edu. Web site: http://aoss.engin.umich.edu/.

University of Missouri, Graduate School, School of Natural Resources, Department of Soil, Environmental, and Atmospheric Sciences, Columbia, MO 65211. Offers atmospheric science (MS, PhD); soil science (MS, PhD). *Faculty:* 9 full-time (0 women). *Students:* 18 full-time (9 women), 15 part-time (7 women); includes 6 minority (3 Black or African American, non-Hispanic/Latino; 1 Asian, non-Hispanic/Latino; 1 Hispanic/Latino; 1 Two or more races, non-Hispanic/Latino), 8 international. Average age 33. 32 applicants, 22% accepted, 7 enrolled. In 2011, 6 master's, 2 doctorates awarded. *Degree requirements:* For doctorate, thesis/dissertation. *Entrance requirements:* For master's and doctorate, GRE General Test, minimum GPA of 3.0. Additional exam requirements/recommendations for international students: Required—TOEFL (minimum score 530 paper-based; 197 computer-based; 71 iBT). *Application deadline:* Applications are processed on a rolling basis. Application fee: $55 ($75 for international students). *Expenses:* Tuition, state resident: full-time $5881. Tuition, nonresident: full-time $15,183. *Required fees:* $952. Tuition and fees vary according to campus/location and program. *Financial support:* Fellowships, research assistantships, teaching assistantships, institutionally sponsored loans, and scholarships/grants available. *Faculty research:* Soil physics; x-ray tomography of soil systems; use of radar in forecasting; soil and water conservation and management and applied soil physics; soil chemical and biogeochemical investigations; fresh water supply regimes (quantity, timing); water quality disturbance mechanisms; best management practices (BMP's); environmental biophysics and ecohydrology; hydrologic scaling, modeling, and change; synoptic and mesoscale dynamics. *Unit head:* Dr. Stephen Anderson, Department Chair, 573-882-6303, E-mail: andersons@missouri.edu. *Application contact:* Leslie Palmer, 573-882-3436, E-mail: palmerl@missouri.edu. Web site: http://www.snr.missouri.edu/seas/academics/graduate-program.php.

University of Nevada, Reno, Graduate School, Interdisciplinary Program in Atmospheric Sciences, Reno, NV 89557. Offers MS, PhD. Terminal master's awarded for partial completion of doctoral program. *Degree requirements:* For master's, thesis optional; for doctorate, thesis/dissertation. *Entrance requirements:* For master's, GRE (recommended), minimum GPA of 2.75; for doctorate, GRE (recommended), minimum GPA of 3.0. Additional exam requirements/recommendations for international students: Required—TOEFL (minimum score 500 paper-based; 173 computer-based; 61 iBT), IELTS (minimum score 6). Electronic applications accepted. *Faculty research:* Atmospheric chemistry, cloud and aerosol physics, atmospheric optics, mesoscale meterology.

The University of North Carolina at Chapel Hill, Graduate School, School of Public Health, Department of Environmental Sciences and Engineering, Chapel Hill, NC 27599. Offers air, radiation and industrial hygiene (MPH, MS, MSEE, MSPH, PhD); aquatic and atmospheric sciences (MPH, MS, MSPH, PhD); environmental engineering (MPH, MS, MSEE, MSPH, PhD); environmental health sciences (MPH, MS, MSPH, PhD); environmental management and policy (MPH, MS, MSPH, PhD). Terminal master's awarded for partial completion of doctoral program. *Degree requirements:* For master's, comprehensive exam, thesis (for some programs), research paper; for doctorate, comprehensive exam, thesis/dissertation. *Entrance requirements:* For master's and doctorate, GRE General Test, minimum GPA of 3.0. Additional exam requirements/recommendations for international students: Required—TOEFL. Electronic applications accepted. *Faculty research:* Air, radiation and industrial hygiene, aquatic and atmospheric sciences, environmental health sciences, environmental management and policy, water resources engineering.

University of North Dakota, Graduate School, John D. Odegard School of Aerospace Sciences, Department of Atmospheric Sciences, Grand Forks, ND 58202. Offers MS, PhD. Part-time programs available. *Degree requirements:* For master's, comprehensive exam, thesis or alternative. *Entrance requirements:* For master's and doctorate, GRE General Test, minimum GPA of 3.0. Additional exam requirements/recommendations for international students: Required—TOEFL (minimum score 550 paper-based; 213 computer-based; 79 iBT), IELTS (minimum score 6.5). Electronic applications accepted.

University of Utah, Graduate School, College of Mines and Earth Sciences, Department of Atmospheric Sciences, Salt Lake City, UT 84112. Offers MS, PhD.

Peterson's Graduate Programs in the Physical Sciences, Mathematics, Agricultural Sciences, the Environment & Natural Resources 2013

facebook.com/petersonspublishing **213**

Atmospheric Sciences

Part-time programs available. *Faculty:* 12 full-time (1 woman), 1 part-time/adjunct (0 women). *Students:* 26 full-time (9 women), 15 part-time (4 women); includes 1 minority (Hispanic/Latino), 7 international. Average age 27. 41 applicants, 34% accepted, 10 enrolled. In 2011, 9 master's, 2 doctorates awarded. Terminal master's awarded for partial completion of doctoral program. *Median time to degree:* Of those who began their doctoral program in fall 2003, 100% received their degree in 8 years or less. *Degree requirements:* For master's, comprehensive exam, thesis optional; for doctorate, comprehensive exam, thesis/dissertation. *Entrance requirements:* For master's and doctorate, GRE General Test, minimum GPA of 3.0, 3 letters of reference. Additional exam requirements/recommendations for international students: Required—TOEFL (minimum score 500 paper-based; 173 computer-based; 61 iBT). *Application deadline:* For fall admission, 1/7 priority date for domestic students, 1/7 for international students. Applications are processed on a rolling basis. Application fee: $55 ($65 for international students). Electronic applications accepted. *Financial support:* In 2011–12, 30 students received support, including 4 fellowships (averaging $30,000 per year), 34 research assistantships (averaging $24,000 per year). Financial award application deadline: 2/15; financial award applicants required to submit FAFSA. *Faculty research:* Clouds, aerosols, and climate; numerical weather prediction; mountain weather and climate; tropical convection and storms; climate variability and change. *Total annual research expenditures:* $3.5 million. *Unit head:* Dr. Kevin D. Perry, Chair, 801-585-9482, Fax: 801-585-3681, E-mail: kevin.perry@utah.edu. *Application contact:* Jessica A. Taylor, Academic Coordinator, 801-581-6136, Fax: 801-585-3681, E-mail: jessica.ann.taylor@utah.edu. Web site: http://www.atmos.utah.edu/.

University of Washington, Graduate School, College of the Environment, Department of Atmospheric Sciences, Seattle, WA 98195. Offers MS, PhD. *Degree requirements:* For master's, thesis; for doctorate, thesis/dissertation, qualifying exam. *Entrance requirements:* For master's and doctorate, GRE General Test, minimum GPA of 3.0. Additional exam requirements/recommendations for international students: Required—TOEFL. *Faculty research:* Climate change, synoptic and mesoscale meteorology, atmospheric chemistry, cloud physics, dynamics of the atmosphere.

University of Wisconsin–Madison, Graduate School, College of Letters and Science, Department of Atmospheric and Oceanic Sciences, Madison, WI 53706-1380. Offers MS, PhD. Part-time programs available. *Degree requirements:* For master's, thesis (for some programs); for doctorate, thesis/dissertation. *Entrance requirements:* For master's and doctorate, GRE General Test, minimum GPA of 3.0; previous course work in chemistry, mathematics, and physics. Electronic applications accepted. *Expenses:* Tuition, state resident: full-time $10,296; part-time $643.51 per credit. Tuition, nonresident: full-time $24,054; part-time $1503.40 per credit. *Required fees:* $70.06 per credit. Tuition and fees vary according to course load, campus/location, program and reciprocity agreements. *Faculty research:* Satellite meteorology, weather systems, global climate change, numerical modeling, atmosphere-ocean interaction.

University of Wyoming, College of Engineering and Applied Sciences, Department of Atmospheric Science, Laramie, WY 82070. Offers MS, PhD. Postbaccalaureate distance learning degree programs offered (minimal on-campus study). Terminal master's awarded for partial completion of doctoral program. *Degree requirements:* For master's, thesis; for doctorate, comprehensive exam, thesis/dissertation. *Entrance requirements:* For master's and doctorate, GRE General Test, minimum GPA of 3.0. Additional exam requirements/recommendations for international students: Required—TOEFL (minimum score 525 paper-based; 250 computer-based). Electronic applications accepted. *Expenses:* Contact institution. *Faculty research:* Cloud physics; aerosols, boundary layer processes; airborne observations; stratospheric aerosols and gases.

Yale University, Graduate School of Arts and Sciences, Department of Geology and Geophysics, New Haven, CT 06520. Offers biogeochemistry (PhD); climate dynamics (PhD); geochemistry (PhD); geophysics (PhD); meteorology (PhD); oceanography (PhD); paleontology (PhD); paleooceanography (PhD); petrology (PhD); tectonics (PhD). *Degree requirements:* For doctorate, thesis/dissertation. *Entrance requirements:* For doctorate, GRE General Test. Additional exam requirements/recommendations for international students: Required—TOEFL.

Meteorology

Columbia University, Graduate School of Arts and Sciences, Program in Climate and Society, New York, NY 10027. Offers MA.

Florida Institute of Technology, Graduate Programs, College of Engineering, Department of Marine and Environmental Systems, Melbourne, FL 32901-6975. Offers earth remote sensing (MS); environmental resource management (MS); environmental science (MS, PhD); meteorology (MS); ocean engineering (MS, PhD); oceanography (MS, PhD), including biological oceanography (MS), chemical oceanography (MS), coastal management (MS), geological oceanography (MS), oceanography (PhD), physical oceanography (MS). Part-time programs available. *Faculty:* 11 full-time (0 women), 3 part-time/adjunct (0 women). *Students:* 52 full-time (18 women), 13 part-time (4 women); includes 4 minority (1 Black or African American, non-Hispanic/Latino; 1 Asian, non-Hispanic/Latino; 1 Hispanic/Latino; 1 Two or more races, non-Hispanic/Latino), 16 international. Average age 28. 117 applicants, 52% accepted, 23 enrolled. In 2011, 13 master's, 1 doctorate awarded. *Degree requirements:* For master's, comprehensive exam (for some programs), thesis (for some programs), seminar, field project, written final exam, technical paper, oral presentation, or internship; for doctorate, comprehensive exam, thesis/dissertation, seminar, internships (oceanography and environmental science), publications. *Entrance requirements:* For master's, GRE General Test (environmental science, oceanography, environmental resource management, meteorology, earth remote sensing), 3 letters of recommendation, minimum GPA of 3.0, resume, transcripts, statement of objectives; for doctorate, GRE General Test (oceanography, environmental science), resume, 3 letters of recommendation, minimum GPA of 3.3, statement of objectives, on-campus interview (highly recommended). Additional exam requirements/recommendations for international students: Required—TOEFL (minimum score 550 paper-based; 213 computer-based; 79 iBT). *Application deadline:* For fall admission, 4/1 for international students; for spring admission, 9/30 for international students. Applications are processed on a rolling basis. Electronic applications accepted. *Expenses: Tuition:* Full-time $19,620; part-time $1090 per credit hour. Tuition and fees vary according to campus/location. *Financial support:* In 2011–12, 5 fellowships with full and partial tuition reimbursements (averaging $7,240 per year), 3 research assistantships with full and partial tuition reimbursements (averaging $7,283 per year), 7 teaching assistantships with full and partial tuition reimbursements (averaging $4,928 per year) were awarded; career-related internships or fieldwork, institutionally sponsored loans, tuition waivers (partial), unspecified assistantships, and tuition remissions also available. Support available to part-time students. Financial award application deadline: 3/1; financial award applicants required to submit FAFSA. *Total annual research expenditures:* $1.6 million. *Unit head:* Dr. George Maul, Department Head, 321-674-7453, Fax: 321-674-7212, E-mail: gmaul@

fit.edu. *Application contact:* Cheryl A. Brown, Associate Director of Graduate Admissions, 321-674-7581, Fax: 321-723-9468, E-mail: cbrown@fit.edu. Web site: http://coe.fit.edu/dmes/.

Florida State University, The Graduate School, College of Arts and Sciences, Department of Earth, Ocean and Atmospheric Science, Program in Meteorology, Tallahassee, FL 32306-4520. Offers MS, PhD. *Faculty:* 14 full-time (2 women). *Students:* 60 full-time (16 women), 14 part-time (4 women); includes 7 minority (2 Black or African American, non-Hispanic/Latino; 4 Hispanic/Latino; 1 Native Hawaiian or other Pacific Islander, non-Hispanic/Latino), 9 international. Average age 25. 113 applicants, 40% accepted, 22 enrolled. In 2011, 14 master's, 7 doctorates awarded. Terminal master's awarded for partial completion of doctoral program. *Degree requirements:* For master's, thesis optional; for doctorate, comprehensive exam, thesis/dissertation. *Entrance requirements:* For master's, GRE General Test (minimum score 1100 verbal and quantitative), minimum GPA of 3.0 in upper-division work; for doctorate, GRE General Test (minimum combined Verbal and Quantitative score: 1100), minimum GPA of 3.0, faculty sponsor. Additional exam requirements/recommendations for international students: Required—TOEFL (minimum score 550 paper-based; 213 computer-based; 80 iBT). *Application deadline:* For fall admission, 1/30 priority date for domestic students, 1/30 for international students; for spring admission, 11/1 for domestic students, 6/30 for international students. Applications are processed on a rolling basis. Application fee: $30. *Expenses:* Tuition, state resident: full-time $9474; part-time $350.88 per credit hour. Tuition, nonresident: full-time $16,236; part-time $601.34 per credit hour. *Required fees:* $630 per semester. One-time fee: $20. Tuition and fees vary according to course load and campus/location. *Financial support:* In 2011–12, 56 students received support, including 2 fellowships with partial tuition reimbursements available (averaging $19,000 per year), 39 research assistantships with partial tuition reimbursements available (averaging $21,500 per year), 15 teaching assistantships with partial tuition reimbursements available (averaging $21,500 per year); career-related internships or fieldwork, scholarships/grants, and unspecified assistantships also available. Financial award applicants required to submit FAFSA. *Faculty research:* Physical, dynamic, and synoptic meteorology; climatology. *Total annual research expenditures:* $600,000. *Unit head:* Dr. Lynn Dudley, Chairman, 850-644-6205, Fax: 850-644-9642, E-mail: ldudley@fsu.edu. *Application contact:* Tim McGann, Academic Program Specialist, 850-644-8580, Fax: 850-644-9642, E-mail: tmcgann@fsu.edu. Web site: http://www.met.fsu.edu/.

Georgia Institute of Technology, Graduate Studies and Research, College of Sciences, School of Earth and Atmospheric Sciences, Atlanta, GA 30332-0340. Offers atmospheric chemistry, aerosols and clouds (MS, PhD); dynamics of weather and climate (MS, PhD); geochemistry (MS, PhD); geophysics (MS, PhD);

214 facebook.com/petersonspublishing

Peterson's Graduate Programs in the Physical Sciences, Mathematics, Agricultural Sciences, the Environment & Natural Resources 2013

oceanography (MS, PhD); paleoclimate (MS, PhD); planetary science (MS, PhD); remote sensing (MS, PhD). Part-time programs available. Terminal master's awarded for partial completion of doctoral program. *Degree requirements:* For master's, thesis or alternative; for doctorate, comprehensive exam, thesis/dissertation. *Entrance requirements:* For master's, GRE, letters of recommendation; for doctorate, GRE, academic transcripts, letters of recommendation, personal statement. Additional exam requirements/recommendations for international students: Required—TOEFL (minimum score 550 paper-based; 213 computer-based; 79 iBT). *Faculty research:* Geophysics; atmospheric chemistry, aerosols and clouds; dynamics of weather and climate; geochemistry; oceanography; paleoclimate; planetary science; remote sensing.

Iowa State University of Science and Technology, Department of Geological and Atmospheric Sciences, Ames, IA 50011-3212. Offers earth science (MS, PhD); environmental science (MS, PhD); geology (MS, PhD); meteorology (MS, PhD). *Degree requirements:* For master's, thesis (for some programs); for doctorate, thesis/dissertation. *Entrance requirements:* For master's and doctorate, GRE General Test. Additional exam requirements/recommendations for international students: Required—TOEFL (minimum score 550 paper-based; 79 iBT), IELTS (minimum score 6.5). *Application deadline:* For fall admission, 1/1 priority date for domestic students. Application fee: $40 ($90 for international students). Electronic applications accepted. *Unit head:* Dr. Carl E. Jacobson, Director of Graduate Education, 515-294-8048, Fax: 515-294-6049, E-mail: geology@iastate.edu. *Application contact:* Neal Iverson, Information Contact, 515-294-8048, Fax: 515-294-6049, E-mail: geology@iastate.edu. Web site: http://www.ge-at.iastate.edu/.

Iowa State University of Science and Technology, Program in Agricultural Meteorology, Ames, IA 50011-1010. Offers MS, PhD. *Entrance requirements:* Additional exam requirements/recommendations for international students: Required—TOEFL (minimum score 550 paper-based; 79 iBT), IELTS (minimum score 6.5). *Application deadline:* Applications are processed on a rolling basis. Electronic applications accepted. *Unit head:* Tom E. Loynachan, Director of Graduate Education, 515-294-1361, Fax: 515-294-8146, E-mail: gradprograms@agron.iastate.edu. *Application contact:* Jaci Severson, Application Contact, 515-294-1361, Fax: 515-294-8146, E-mail: gradprograms@agron.iastate.edu. Web site: http://www.agron.iastate.edu.

Iowa State University of Science and Technology, Program in Meteorology, Ames, IA 50011-1010. Offers MS, PhD. *Entrance requirements:* For master's and doctorate, GRE. Additional exam requirements/recommendations for international students: Required—TOEFL (minimum score 550 paper-based; 79 iBT), IELTS (minimum score 6.5). *Application deadline:* For fall admission, 1/31 priority date for domestic students. Electronic applications accepted. *Unit head:* Mike T. C. Chen, Director of Graduate Education, 515-294-1361, Fax: 515-294-8146, E-mail: meteorologygraduateprograms@iastate.edu. *Application contact:* Jaci Severson, Application Contact, 515-294-1361, Fax: 515-294-8146, E-mail: meteorologygraduateprograms@iastate.edu. Web site: http://www.ge-at.iastate.edu.

McGill University, Faculty of Graduate and Postdoctoral Studies, Faculty of Agricultural and Environmental Sciences, Department of Natural Resource Sciences, Montréal, QC H3A 2T5, Canada. Offers entomology (M Sc, PhD); environmental assessment (M Sc); forest science (M Sc, PhD); microbiology (M Sc, PhD); micrometeorology (M Sc, PhD); neotropical environment (M Sc, PhD); soil science (M Sc, PhD); wildlife biology (M Sc, PhD).

Millersville University of Pennsylvania, College of Graduate and Professional Studies, School of Science and Mathematics, Department of Earth Sciences, Millersville, PA 17551-0302. Offers integrated scientific applications (MS), including climate science applications, weather intelligence and risk management. *Degree requirements:* For master's, internship or applied research. *Expenses:* Tuition, state resident: full-time $3744; part-time $416 per credit. Tuition, nonresident: full-time $5616; part-time $624 per credit. *Required fees:* $1130; $125.50 per credit. Tuition and fees vary according to course load. *Unit head:* Dr. Richard D. Clark, Graduate Program Coordinator, 717-872-3930, E-mail: richard.clark@millersville.edu. *Application contact:* Dr. Victor S. DeSantis, Dean of Graduate and Professional Studies, 717-872-3099, Fax: 717-872-3453, E-mail: victor.desantis@millersville.edu.

Mississippi State University, College of Arts and Sciences, Department of Geosciences, Mississippi State, MS 39762. Offers applied meteorology (MS); broadcast meteorology (MS); earth and atmospheric science (PhD); environmental geoscience (MS); geography (MS); geology (MS); geospatial sciences (MS); professional meteorology/climatology (MS); teachers in geoscience (MS). Postbaccalaureate distance learning degree programs offered (no on-campus study). *Faculty:* 19 full-time (5 women), 2 part-time/adjunct (0 women). *Students:* 72 full-time (27 women), 279 part-time (127 women); includes 40 minority (12 Black or African American, non-Hispanic/Latino; 4 American Indian or Alaska Native, non-Hispanic/Latino; 6 Asian, non-Hispanic/Latino; 14 Hispanic/Latino; 4 Two or more races, non-Hispanic/Latino), 10 international. Average age 35. 228 applicants, 77% accepted, 144 enrolled. In 2011, 89 master's awarded. *Degree requirements:* For master's, thesis (for some programs), comprehensive oral or written exam. *Entrance requirements:* For master's, GRE (for on-campus applicants), minimum undergraduate GPA of 2.75. Additional exam requirements/recommendations for international students: Required—TOEFL (minimum score 475 paper-based; 153 computer-based; 53 iBT); Recommended—IELTS (minimum score 4.5). *Application deadline:* For fall admission, 7/1 for domestic students, 5/1 for international students; for spring admission, 11/1 for domestic students, 9/1 for international students. Applications are processed on a rolling basis. Application fee: $40. Electronic applications accepted. *Expenses:* Tuition, state resident: full-time $5805; part-time $322.50 per credit hour. Tuition, nonresident: full-time $14,670; part-time $815 per credit hour. *Financial support:* In 2011–12, 13 research assistantships with full tuition reimbursements (averaging $20,746 per year), 31 teaching assistantships with full tuition reimbursements (averaging $14,151 per year) were awarded; Federal Work-Study, institutionally sponsored loans, scholarships/grants, tuition waivers (partial), and unspecified assistantships also available. Financial award application deadline: 4/1; financial award applicants required to submit FAFSA. *Faculty research:* Climatology, hydrogeology, sedimentology, meteorology. *Total annual research expenditures:* $6.2 million. *Unit head:* Dr. Darrel Schmitz, Professor and Head, 662-325-3915, Fax: 662-325-9423, E-mail: schmitz@geosci.msstate.edu. *Application contact:* Dr. Christopher P. Dewey, Associate Professor/Graduate Coordinator, 662-325-2909, Fax: 662-325-9423, E-mail: cpd4@msstate.edu. Web site: http://www.msstate.edu/dept/geosciences/.

Naval Postgraduate School, Departments and Academic Groups, Department of Meteorology, Monterey, CA 93943. Offers meteorology (MS, PhD); meteorology and physical oceanography (MS). Program only open to commissioned officers of the United States and friendly nations and selected United States federal civilian employees. Part-time programs available. *Faculty:* 14 full-time (3 women). *Students:* 61 full-time (11 women); includes 11 minority (3 Black or African American, non-Hispanic/Latino; 1 American Indian or Alaska Native, non-Hispanic/Latino; 5 Asian, non-Hispanic/Latino; 2 Hispanic/Latino), 2 international. Average age 35. In 2011, 13 master's, 1 doctorate awarded. *Degree requirements:* For master's, thesis; for doctorate, one foreign language, thesis/dissertation. *Faculty research:* Air-sea interactions, boundary layer meteorology, climate dynamics, numerical weather prediction, tropical cyclones. *Total annual research expenditures:* $3.2 million. *Unit head:* Prof. Wendell Nuss, Department Chair, 831-656-2308, E-mail: nuss@nps.edu. Web site: http://nps.edu/Academics/Schools/GSEAS/Departments/Meteorology/index.html.

Naval Postgraduate School, Departments and Academic Groups, Undersea Warfare Academic Group, Monterey, CA 93943. Offers applied mathematics (MS); applied physics (MS); applied science (MS), including acoustics, operations research, physical oceanography, signal processing; electrical engineering (MS); engineering acoustics (MS, PhD); engineering science (MS), including electrical engineering, mechanical engineering; mechanical engineer (ME); mechanical engineering (MS, MSME); meteorology (MS); operations research (MS); physical oceanography (MS). Program only open to commissioned officers of the United States and friendly nations and selected United States federal civilian employees. Part-time programs available. *Students:* 2 full-time, both international. Average age 36. *Degree requirements:* For master's, thesis. *Faculty research:* Unmanned/autonomous vehicles, sea mines and countermeasures, submarine warfare in the twentieth and twenty-first centuries. *Unit head:* Dr. Clyde Scandrett, Academic Group Chairman, 831-656-2027. Web site: http://www.nps.edu/Academics/Schools/GSEAS/Departments/USW/USW-Index.html.

North Carolina State University, Graduate School, College of Physical and Mathematical Sciences, Department of Marine, Earth, and Atmospheric Sciences, Raleigh, NC 27695. Offers marine, earth, and atmospheric sciences (MS, PhD); meteorology (MS, PhD); oceanography (MS, PhD). PhD offered jointly with The University of North Carolina Wilmington. Terminal master's awarded for partial completion of doctoral program. *Degree requirements:* For master's, thesis (for some programs), final oral exam; for doctorate, comprehensive exam, thesis/dissertation, final oral exam, preliminary oral and written exams. *Entrance requirements:* For master's, GRE General Test, minimum GPA of 3.0; for doctorate, GRE General Test, GRE Subject Test (for disciplines in biological oceanography and geology), minimum GPA of 3.0. Additional exam requirements/recommendations for international students: Required—TOEFL (minimum score 550 paper-based). Electronic applications accepted. *Faculty research:* Boundary layer and air quality meteorology; climate and mesoscale dynamics; biological, chemical, geological, and physical oceanography; hard rock, soft rock, environmental, and paleo-geology.

Northern Arizona University, Graduate College, College of Engineering, Forestry and Natural Sciences, School of Earth Sciences and Environmental Sustainability, Flagstaff, AZ 86011. Offers climate science and solutions (MS); earth science (MS); earth sciences and environmental sustainability (PhD); environmental sciences and policy (MS); geology (MS). *Faculty:* 27 full-time (9 women). *Students:* 67 full-time (32 women), 11 part-time (3 women); includes 6 minority (3 American Indian or Alaska Native, non-Hispanic/Latino; 3 Hispanic/Latino), 2 international. 149 applicants, 23% accepted, 30 enrolled. In 2011, 16 degrees awarded. *Degree requirements:* For master's, comprehensive exam (for some programs), thesis (for some programs). *Entrance requirements:* Additional exam requirements/recommendations for international students: Required—TOEFL (minimum score 550 paper-based; 213 computer-based; 80 iBT), IELTS (minimum score 7). *Application deadline:* For fall admission, 2/1 priority date for domestic students, 2/1 for international students. Applications are processed on a rolling basis. Application fee: $65. Electronic applications accepted. *Expenses:* Tuition, state resident: full-time $7190; part-time $355 per credit hour. Tuition, nonresident: full-time $18,092; part-time $1005 per credit hour. *Required fees:* $818; $328 per semester. *Financial support:* In 2011–12, 6 fellowships, 7

Peterson's Graduate Programs in the Physical Sciences, Mathematics, Agricultural Sciences, the Environment & Natural Resources 2013

facebook.com/petersonspublishing **215**

research assistantships with partial tuition reimbursements (averaging $12,866 per year), 28 teaching assistantships with partial tuition reimbursements (averaging $12,477 per year) were awarded; career-related internships or fieldwork, Federal Work-Study, scholarships/grants, health care benefits, tuition waivers (full and partial), and unspecified assistantships also available. Financial award applicants required to submit FAFSA. *Unit head:* Dr. Abe Springer, Director, 928-523-7198. *Application contact:* Mark Aasmundstad, Coordinator, 928-523-9333, Fax: 928-523-7432, E-mail: mark.aasmundstad@nau.edu. Web site: http://nau.edu/cefns/natsci/seses/.

Penn State University Park, Graduate School, College of Earth and Mineral Sciences, Department of Meteorology, State College, University Park, PA 16802-1503. Offers MS, PhD. *Unit head:* Dr. William E. Easterling, III, Dean, 814-865-6546, Fax: 814-863-7708, E-mail: wee2@psu.edu. *Application contact:* Cynthia E. Nicosia, Director of Graduate Enrollment Services, 814-865-1834, E-mail: cey1@psu.edu. Web site: http://ploneprod.met.psu.edu/.

Plymouth State University, College of Graduate Studies, Graduate Studies in Education, Program in Science, Plymouth, NH 03264-1595. Offers applied meteorology (MS); environmental science and policy (MS); science education (MS).

Saint Louis University, Graduate Education, College of Arts and Sciences, Department of Earth and Atmospheric Sciences, St. Louis, MO 63103-2097. Offers geophysics (PhD); geoscience (MS); meteorology (M Pr Met, MS-R, PhD). Part-time programs available. *Degree requirements:* For master's, thesis (for some programs), comprehensive oral exam; for doctorate, thesis/dissertation, preliminary exams. *Entrance requirements:* For master's, GRE General Test, letters of recommendation, resume; for doctorate, GRE General Test, letters of recommendation, resumé, goal statement, transcripts. Additional exam requirements/recommendations for international students: Required—TOEFL (minimum score 525 paper-based; 194 computer-based). Electronic applications accepted. *Faculty research:* Structural geology, mesoscale meteorology and severe storms, weather and climate change prediction.

San Jose State University, Graduate Studies and Research, College of Science, Department of Meteorology and Climate Science, San Jose, CA 95192-0001. Offers meteorology (MS). *Degree requirements:* For master's, thesis or alternative. *Entrance requirements:* For master's, GRE. Electronic applications accepted.

Texas A&M University, College of Geosciences, Department of Atmospheric Sciences, College Station, TX 77843. Offers MS, PhD. *Faculty:* 17. *Students:* 51 full-time (12 women), 7 part-time (2 women); includes 2 minority (1 Black or African American, non-Hispanic/Latino; 1 Hispanic/Latino), 23 international. Average age 28. In 2011, 8 master's, 4 doctorates awarded. *Degree requirements:* For master's, thesis; for doctorate, thesis/dissertation. *Entrance requirements:* For master's and doctorate, GRE General Test. Additional exam requirements/recommendations for international students: Required—TOEFL. *Application deadline:* For fall admission, 3/1 for domestic students; for spring admission, 10/1 for domestic students. Applications are processed on a rolling basis. Application fee: $50 ($75 for international students). Electronic applications accepted. *Expenses:* Tuition, state resident: full-time $5437; part-time $226.55 per credit hour. Tuition, nonresident: full-time $12,949; part-time $539.55 per credit hour. *Required fees:* $2741. *Financial support:* In 2011–12, fellowships (averaging $16,500 per year), research assistantships with tuition reimbursements (averaging $15,000 per year), teaching assistantships (averaging $15,000 per year) were awarded; career-related internships or fieldwork, institutionally sponsored loans, scholarships/grants, and tuition waivers (partial) also available. Financial award application deadline: 3/1; financial award applicants required to submit FAFSA. *Faculty research:* Radar and satellite rainfall relationships, mesoscale dynamics and numerical modeling, climatology. *Unit head:* Kenneth Bowman, Head, 979-862-7671, E-mail: k-bowman@tamu.edu. *Application contact:* Christine Arnold, Academic Advisor II, 979-845-7688, Fax: 979-862-4466, E-mail: chrisarnold@tamu.edu. Web site: http://atmo.tamu.edu/.

Université du Québec à Montréal, Graduate Programs, Program in Earth and Atmospheric Sciences, Montréal, QC H3C 3P8, Canada. Offers atmospheric sciences (M Sc); Earth and atmospheric sciences (PhD); Earth science (M Sc); meteorology (PhD, Diploma). PhD programs offered jointly with McGill University. Part-time programs available. *Degree requirements:* For master's, thesis. *Entrance requirements:* For master's and Diploma, appropriate bachelor's degree or equivalent, proficiency in French; for doctorate, appropriate master's degree or equivalent, proficiency in French.

University of Hawaii at Manoa, Graduate Division, School of Ocean and Earth Science and Technology, Department of Meteorology, Honolulu, HI 96822. Offers MS, PhD. Part-time programs available. *Degree requirements:* For master's, comprehensive exam, thesis; for doctorate, comprehensive exam, thesis/dissertation. *Entrance requirements:* For master's and doctorate, GRE General Test. Additional exam requirements/recommendations for international students: Required—TOEFL (minimum score 560 paper-based; 220 computer-based; 83 iBT), IELTS (minimum score 5). *Faculty research:* Tropical cyclones, air-sea interactions, mesoscale meteorology, intraseasonal oscillations, tropical climate.

University of Maryland, College Park, Academic Affairs, College of Computer, Mathematical and Natural Sciences, Department of Atmospheric and Oceanic Science, College Park, MD 20742. Offers MS, PMS, PhD. Part-time and evening/weekend programs available. Postbaccalaureate distance learning degree programs offered. *Faculty:* 29 full-time (6 women), 7 part-time/adjunct (1 woman). *Students:* 57 full-time (25 women), 8 part-time (6 women); includes 4 minority (2 Asian, non-Hispanic/Latino; 1 Hispanic/Latino; 1 Two or more races, non-Hispanic/Latino),. 25 international. 84 applicants, 24% accepted, 17 enrolled. In 2011, 3 master's, 5 doctorates awarded. Terminal master's awarded for partial completion of doctoral program. *Degree requirements:* For master's, comprehensive exam, scholarly paper, written and oral exams; for doctorate, thesis/dissertation, exam. *Entrance requirements:* For master's, GRE General Test, background in mathematics, experience in scientific computer languages, 3 letters of recommendation; for doctorate, GRE General Test. *Application deadline:* For fall admission, 1/15 for domestic and international students. Applications are processed on a rolling basis. Application fee: $75. Electronic applications accepted. *Expenses: Tuition, area resident:* Part-time $525 per credit hour. Tuition, state resident: part-time $525 per credit hour. Tuition, nonresident: part-time $1131 per credit hour. *Required fees:* $386.31 per term. Tuition and fees vary according to program. *Financial support:* In 2011–12, 1 fellowship with partial tuition reimbursement (averaging $10,000 per year), 20 research assistantships (averaging $20,435 per year), 25 teaching assistantships (averaging $20,311 per year) were awarded; Federal Work-Study and scholarships/grants also available. Support available to part-time students. Financial award applicants required to submit FAFSA. *Faculty research:* Weather, atmospheric chemistry, air pollution, global change, radiation. *Total annual research expenditures:* $3.2 million. *Unit head:* James A. Carton, Chair, 301-405-5365, Fax: 301-314-9482, E-mail: carton@umd.edu. *Application contact:* Dr. Charles A. Caramello, Dean of Graduate School, 301-405-0358, Fax: 301-314-9305.

University of Miami, Graduate School, Rosenstiel School of Marine and Atmospheric Science, Division of Meteorology and Physical Oceanography, Coral Gables, FL 33124. Offers meteorology (MS, PhD); physical oceanography (MS, PhD). Terminal master's awarded for partial completion of doctoral program. *Degree requirements:* For master's, comprehensive exam, thesis; for doctorate, comprehensive exam, thesis/dissertation. *Entrance requirements:* For master's and doctorate, GRE General Test. Additional exam requirements/recommendations for international students: Required—TOEFL (minimum score 550 paper-based; 213 computer-based). Electronic applications accepted.

University of Oklahoma, College of Atmospheric and Geographic Sciences, School of Meteorology, Norman, OK 73072. Offers meteorology (MS, PhD); professional meteorology (MS). *Faculty:* 33 full-time (5 women), 3 part-time/adjunct (1 woman). *Students:* 60 full-time (17 women), 34 part-time (8 women); includes 3 minority (1 Black or African American, non-Hispanic/Latino; 2 Asian, non-Hispanic/Latino), 12 international. Average age 27. 83 applicants, 34% accepted, 19 enrolled. In 2011, 21 master's, 8 doctorates awarded. Terminal master's awarded for partial completion of doctoral program. *Degree requirements:* For master's, comprehensive exam, thesis or alternative; for doctorate, one foreign language, thesis/dissertation. *Entrance requirements:* For master's, GRE, bachelor's degree in related area; for doctorate, GRE. Additional exam requirements/recommendations for international students: Required—TOEFL (minimum score 600 paper-based; 79 iBT). *Application deadline:* For fall admission, 2/1 priority date for domestic students, 3/1 for international students; for spring admission, 11/1 for domestic students, 9/1 for international students. Applications are processed on a rolling basis. Application fee: $40 ($90 for international students). Electronic applications accepted. *Expenses:* Tuition, state resident: full-time $4087; part-time $170.30 per credit hour. Tuition, nonresident: full-time $14,875; part-time $619.80 per credit hour. *Required fees:* $2659; $100.25 per credit hour. Tuition and fees vary according to course load and degree level. *Financial support:* In 2011–12, 94 students received support, including 6 fellowships with full tuition reimbursements available (averaging $5,000 per year), 59 research assistantships with partial tuition reimbursements available (averaging $17,892 per year), 20 teaching assistantships with partial tuition reimbursements available (averaging $17,443 per year); unspecified assistantships also available. Financial award applicants required to submit FAFSA. *Faculty research:* Clouds, convection and weather system research; instrumentation including surface-based systems and development/application of radar; numerical weather predication and data assimilation; regional climate and climate variation; polar, tropical and boundary-layer/urban meteorology. *Total annual research expenditures:* $8.4 million. *Unit head:* David Parsons, Director, 405-325-8565, Fax: 405-325-7689, E-mail: dparsons@ou.edu. *Application contact:* Celia Jones, Coordinator, Academic Student Services, 405-325-6571, Fax: 405-325-7689, E-mail: cjones@ou.edu. Web site: http://som.ou.edu.

Utah State University, School of Graduate Studies, College of Agriculture, Department of Plants, Soils, and Biometeorology, Logan, UT 84322. Offers biometeorology (MS, PhD); ecology (MS, PhD); plant science (MS, PhD); soil science (MS, PhD). Part-time programs available. Terminal master's awarded for partial completion of doctoral program. *Degree requirements:* For master's, thesis; for doctorate, thesis/dissertation. *Entrance requirements:* For master's, GRE General Test, BS in plant, soil, atmospheric science, or related field; minimum GPA of 3.0; for doctorate, GRE General Test, minimum GPA of 3.0. Additional exam requirements/recommendations for international students: Required—TOEFL. Electronic applications accepted. *Faculty research:* Biotechnology and genomics, plant physiology and biology, nutrient and water efficient landscapes,

216 facebook.com/petersonspublishing

Peterson's Graduate Programs in the Physical Sciences, Mathematics, Agricultural Sciences, the Environment & Natural Resources 2013

physical-chemical-biological processes in soil, environmental biophysics and climate.

Yale University, Graduate School of Arts and Sciences, Department of Geology and Geophysics, New Haven, CT 06520. Offers biogeochemistry (PhD); climate dynamics (PhD); geochemistry (PhD); geophysics (PhD); meteorology (PhD); oceanography (PhD); paleontology (PhD); paleooceanography (PhD); petrology (PhD); tectonics (PhD). *Degree requirements:* For doctorate, thesis/dissertation. *Entrance requirements:* For doctorate, GRE General Test. Additional exam requirements/recommendations for international students: Required—TOEFL.

Peterson's Graduate Programs in the Physical Sciences, Mathematics, Agricultural Sciences, the Environment & Natural Resources 2013

facebook.com/petersonspublishing **217**

Section 6
Physics

This section contains a directory of institutions offering graduate work in physics, followed by in-depth entries submitted by institutions that chose to prepare detailed program descriptions. Additional information about programs listed in the directory but not augmented by an in-depth entry may be obtained by writing directly to the dean of a graduate school or chair of a department at the address given in the directory.

For programs offering related work, see all other areas in this book. In the other guides in this series:

Graduate Programs in the Biological/Biomedical Sciences & Health-Related Medical Professions

See *Allied Health, Biological and Biomedical Sciences, Biophysics,* and *Vision Sciences*

Graduate Programs in Engineering & Applied Sciences

See *Aerospace/Aeronautical Engineering, Electrical and Computer Engineering, Energy and Power Engineering (Nuclear Engineering), Engineering and Applied Sciences, Engineering Physics, Materials Sciences and Engineering,* and *Mechanical Engineering and Mechanics*

CONTENTS

Acoustics

Naval Postgraduate School, Departments and Academic Groups, Undersea Warfare Academic Group, Monterey, CA 93943. Offers applied mathematics (MS); applied physics (MS); applied science (MS), including acoustics, operations research, physical oceanography, signal processing; electrical engineering (MS); engineering acoustics (MS, PhD); engineering science (MS), including electrical engineering, mechanical engineering; mechanical engineer (ME); mechanical engineering (MS, MSME); meteorology (MS); operations research (MS); physical oceanography (MS). Program only open to commissioned officers of the United States and friendly nations and selected United States federal civilian employees. Part-time programs available. *Students:* 2 full-time, both international. Average age 36. *Degree requirements:* For master's, thesis. *Faculty research:* Unmanned/ autonomous vehicles, sea mines and countermeasures, submarine warfare in the twentieth and twenty-first centuries. *Unit head:* Dr. Clyde Scandrett, Academic Group Chairman, 831-656-2027. Web site: http://www.nps.edu/Academics/ Schools/GSEAS/Departments/USW/USW-Index.html.

Penn State University Park, Graduate School, Intercollege Graduate Programs and College of Engineering, Intercollege Graduate Program in Acoustics, State College, University Park, PA 16802-1503. Offers M Eng, MS, PhD. *Unit head:* Dr. Anthony Atchley, Project Chair, 814-865-6364, Fax: 814-865-7595, E-mail: atchley@psu.edu. *Application contact:* Cynthia E. Nicosia, Director, Graduate Enrollment Services, 814-865-1795, Fax: 814-865-4627, E-mail: cey1@psu.edu.

Rensselaer Polytechnic Institute, Graduate School, School of Architecture, PhD Program in Architectural Sciences, Troy, NY 12180-3590. Offers acoustics (PhD); built ecologies (PhD); lighting (PhD). *Degree requirements:* For doctorate, comprehensive exam (for some programs), thesis/dissertation. *Entrance requirements:* For doctorate, GRE General Test, resume, portfolio, research writing sample. Additional exam requirements/recommendations for international students: Required—TOEFL (minimum score 570 paper-based; 230 computer-based; 89 iBT), IELTS (minimum score 6.5). Electronic applications accepted. *Faculty research:* Lighting, acoustics, computation, building systems.

Rensselaer Polytechnic Institute, Graduate School, School of Architecture, Program in Architectural Acoustics, Troy, NY 12180-3590. Offers MS. *Degree requirements:* For master's, thesis. *Entrance requirements:* For master's, GRE General Test. Additional exam requirements/recommendations for international students: Required—TOEFL (minimum score 570 paper-based; 230 computer-based; 89 iBT), IELTS (minimum score 6.5). Electronic applications accepted. *Faculty research:* Acoustics: modeling, auralization, signal processing.

University of Massachusetts Dartmouth, Graduate School, College of Engineering, Department of Electrical and Computer Engineering, North Dartmouth, MA 02747-2300. Offers acoustics (Postbaccalaureate Certificate); communications (Postbaccalaureate Certificate); computer engineering (MS, PhD); computer systems engineering (Postbaccalaureate Certificate); digital signal processing (Postbaccalaureate Certificate); electrical engineering (MS, PhD); electrical engineering systems (Postbaccalaureate Certificate). Part-time programs available. *Faculty:* 15 full-time (3 women), 4 part-time/adjunct (1 woman). *Students:* 37 full-time (5 women), 52 part-time (8 women); includes 9 minority (2 Black or African American, non-Hispanic/Latino; 2 Asian, non-Hispanic/Latino; 1 Hispanic/Latino; 4 Two or more races, non-Hispanic/Latino), 45 international. Average age 29. 83 applicants, 93% accepted, 26 enrolled. In 2011, 17 master's, 1 doctorate awarded. *Degree requirements:* For master's, culminating project or thesis; for doctorate, comprehensive exam, thesis/ dissertation. *Entrance requirements:* For master's, GRE, minimum undergraduate GPA of 3.0, 3 letters of recommendation, statement of intent, resume; for doctorate, GRE, 3 letters of recommendation, resume, statement of intent; for Postbaccalaureate Certificate, 3 letters of recommendation, resume, statement of intent. Additional exam requirements/recommendations for international students: Required—TOEFL (minimum score 533 paper-based; 200 computer-based; 72 iBT). *Application deadline:* For fall admission, 2/15 priority date for domestic students, 1/15 for international students; for spring admission, 11/1 priority date for domestic students, 10/1 for international students. Applications are processed on a rolling basis. Application fee: $40 ($60 for international students). Electronic applications accepted. *Expenses:* Tuition, state resident: full-time $2071; part-time $86.29 per credit. Tuition, nonresident: full-time $8099; part-time $337.46 per credit. *Required fees:* $438.58 per credit. Part-time tuition and fees vary according to class time, course load, degree level and reciprocity agreements. *Financial support:* In 2011–12, 10 research assistantships with full tuition reimbursements (averaging $12,720 per year), 14 teaching assistantships with full tuition reimbursements (averaging $10,385 per year) were awarded; fellowships, Federal Work-Study, and unspecified assistantships also available. Support available to part-time students. Financial award application deadline: 3/1; financial award applicants required to submit FAFSA. *Faculty research:* Speech acoustics, marine applications, signals and systems, applied electromagnetics, intelligent agency. *Total annual research expenditures:* $921,048. *Unit head:* Dr. Karen Payton, Graduate Program Director, 508-999-8434, Fax: 508-999-8489, E-mail: kpayton@umassd.edu. *Application contact:* Elan Turcotte-Shamski, Graduate Admissions Officer, 508-999-8604, Fax: 508-999-8183, E-mail: graduate@ umassd.edu. Web site: http://www.umassd.edu/engineering/ece/graduate/ welcome.cfm.

Applied Physics

Air Force Institute of Technology, Graduate School of Engineering and Management, Department of Engineering Physics, Dayton, OH 45433-7765. Offers applied physics (MS, PhD); electro-optics (MS, PhD); materials science (PhD); nuclear engineering (MS, PhD); space physics (MS). Part-time programs available. *Degree requirements:* For master's, thesis; for doctorate, thesis/ dissertation. *Entrance requirements:* For master's and doctorate, GRE General Test, minimum GPA of 3.0, U.S. citizenship. *Faculty research:* High-energy lasers, space physics, nuclear weapon effects, semiconductor physics.

Alabama Agricultural and Mechanical University, School of Graduate Studies, School of Arts and Sciences, Department of Physics, Huntsville, AL 35811. Offers physics (MS, PhD), including applied physics (PhD), materials science (PhD), optics/lasers (PhD). Part-time and evening/weekend programs available. *Degree requirements:* For doctorate, thesis/dissertation. *Entrance requirements:* For master's and doctorate, GRE General Test. Additional exam requirements/ recommendations for international students: Required—TOEFL (minimum score 500 paper-based; 173 computer-based; 61 iBT). Electronic applications accepted.

California Institute of Technology, Division of Engineering and Applied Science, Option in Applied Physics, Pasadena, CA 91125-0001. Offers MS, PhD. *Degree requirements:* For doctorate, thesis/dissertation. Electronic applications accepted. *Faculty research:* Solid-state electronics, quantum electronics, plasmas, linear and nonlinear laser optics, electromagnetic theory.

Carnegie Mellon University, Mellon College of Science, Department of Physics, Pittsburgh, PA 15213-3891. Offers applied physics (PhD); physics (MS, PhD). *Degree requirements:* For doctorate, thesis/dissertation, qualifying exam. *Entrance requirements:* For doctorate, GRE General Test, GRE Subject Test. Additional exam requirements/recommendations for international students: Required—TOEFL. Electronic applications accepted. *Faculty research:* Astrophysics, condensed matter physics, biological physics, medium energy and nuclear physics, high-energy physics.

Christopher Newport University, Graduate Studies, Department of Physics, Computer Science, and Engineering, Newport News, VA 23606-2998. Offers applied physics and computer science (MS). Part-time and evening/weekend programs available. *Degree requirements:* For master's, comprehensive exam (for some programs), thesis optional. *Entrance requirements:* For master's, GRE General Test, minimum GPA of 3.0. Additional exam requirements/ recommendations for international students: Required—TOEFL (minimum score 580 paper-based; 237 computer-based; 92 iBT). Electronic applications accepted. *Faculty research:* Advanced programming methodologies, experimental nuclear physics, computer architecture, semiconductor nanophysics, laser and optical fiber sensors.

Colorado School of Mines, Graduate School, Department of Physics, Golden, CO 80401-1887. Offers applied physics (MS, PhD). Part-time programs available. *Faculty:* 34 full-time (2 women), 9 part-time/adjunct (3 women). *Students:* 60 full-time (12 women), 7 part-time (2 women); includes 4 minority (1 Asian, non-Hispanic/Latinó; 3 Hispanic/Latino), 10 international. Average age 28. 101 applicants, 35% accepted, 25 enrolled. In 2011, 6 master's, 3 doctorates awarded. *Degree requirements:* For master's, thesis (for some programs); for doctorate, comprehensive exam, thesis/dissertation. *Entrance requirements:* For master's and doctorate, GRE General Test, GRE Subject Test. Additional exam requirements/recommendations for international students: Required—TOEFL (minimum score 550 paper-based; 213 computer-based; 80 iBT). *Application deadline:* For fall admission, 1/15 priority date for domestic students, 1/15 for international students; for spring admission, 10/15 priority date for domestic students, 10/15 for international students. Application fee: $50 ($70 for international students). Electronic applications accepted. *Expenses:* Tuition, state resident: full-time $12,585; part-time $699 per credit. Tuition, nonresident: full-

220 facebook.com/petersonspublishing

Peterson's Graduate Programs in the Physical Sciences, Mathematics, Agricultural Sciences, the Environment & Natural Resources 2013

time $27,270; part-time $1516 per credit. *Required fees:* $1864.20; $670 per semester. *Financial support:* In 2011–12, 48 students received support, including 1 fellowship with full tuition reimbursement available (averaging $20,000 per year), 31 research assistantships with full tuition reimbursements available (averaging $20,000 per year), 16 teaching assistantships with full tuition reimbursements available (averaging $20,000 per year); scholarships/grants, health care benefits, and unspecified assistantships also available. Financial award application deadline: 1/15; financial award applicants required to submit FAFSA. *Faculty research:* Light scattering, low-energy nuclear physics, high fusion plasma diagnostics, laser operations, mathematical physics. *Total annual research expenditures:* $2.4 million. *Unit head:* Dr. Thomas Furtak, Head, 303-273-3843, Fax: 303-273-3919, E-mail: tfurtak@mines.edu. *Application contact:* Dr. David Wood, Professor, 303-273-3853, Fax: 303-273-3919, E-mail: dwood@mines.edu. Web site: http://physics.mines.edu.

Columbia University, The Fu Foundation School of Engineering and Applied Science, Department of Applied Physics and Applied Mathematics, New York, NY 10027. Offers applied physics (Eng Sc D); applied physics and applied mathematics (MS, PhD, Engr); materials science and engineering (MS, Eng Sc D, PhD); medical physics (MS). Part-time programs available. Postbaccalaureate distance learning degree programs offered (no on-campus study). *Faculty:* 32 full-time (2 women), 23 part-time/adjunct (2 women). *Students:* 98 full-time (22 women), 38 part-time (10 women); includes 19 minority (14 Asian, non-Hispanic/Latino; 1 Hispanic/Latino; 4 Two or more races, non-Hispanic/Latino), 50 international. Average age 28. 371 applicants, 18% accepted, 41 enrolled. In 2011, 57 master's, 18 doctorates awarded. Terminal master's awarded for partial completion of doctoral program. *Degree requirements:* For master's, comprehensive exam; for doctorate, thesis/dissertation, qualifying exam. *Entrance requirements:* For master's, GRE General Test, GRE Subject Test (strongly recommended); for doctorate, GRE General Test, GRE Subject Test (applied physics); for Engr, GRE General Test. Additional exam requirements/recommendations for international students: Required—TOEFL, IELTS. *Application deadline:* For fall admission, 12/1 priority date for domestic students, 12/1 for international students; for spring admission, 10/1 priority date for domestic students, 10/1 for international students. Application fee: $95. Electronic applications accepted. *Financial support:* In 2011–12, 71 students received support, including 2 fellowships with full tuition reimbursements available (averaging $31,140 per year), 55 research assistantships with full tuition reimbursements available (averaging $31,133 per year), 16 teaching assistantships with full tuition reimbursements available (averaging $31,133 per year); health care benefits also available. Financial award application deadline: 12/1; financial award applicants required to submit FAFSA. *Faculty research:* Plasma physics and fusion energy; optical and laser physics; atmospheric, oceanic and earth physics; applied mathematics; solid state science and processing of materials, their properties, and their structure; medical physics. *Unit head:* Dr. Ismail C. Noyan, Professor and Department Chairman, 212-854-8919, E-mail: icn2@columbia.edu. *Application contact:* Montserrat Fernandez-Pinkley, Student Services Coordinator, 212-854-4457, Fax: 212-854-8257, E-mail: mf2157@columbia.edu. Web site: http://www.apam.columbia.edu/.

See Display below and Close-Up on page 269.

Cornell University, Graduate School, Graduate Fields of Engineering, Field of Applied Physics, Ithaca, NY 14853-0001. Offers applied physics (PhD); engineering physics (M Eng). *Faculty:* 44 full-time (4 women). *Students:* 93 full-time (16 women); includes 11 minority (6 Asian, non-Hispanic/Latino; 5 Hispanic/Latino), 40 international. Average age 25. 201 applicants, 41% accepted, 30 enrolled. In 2011, 22 master's, 6 doctorates awarded. *Degree requirements:* For doctorate, comprehensive exam, thesis/dissertation, written exams. *Entrance requirements:* For master's, GRE General Test, 3 letters of recommendation; for doctorate, GRE General Test, GRE Subject Test (physics), GRE Writing Assessment, 3 letters of recommendation. Additional exam requirements/recommendations for international students: Required—TOEFL (minimum score 600 paper-based; 250 computer-based; 77 iBT). *Application deadline:* For fall admission, 1/15 for domestic students. Application fee: $95. Electronic applications accepted. *Financial support:* In 2011–12, 70 students received support, including 7 fellowships with full tuition reimbursements available, 49 research assistantships with full tuition reimbursements available, 11 teaching assistantships with full tuition reimbursements available; institutionally sponsored loans, scholarships/grants, health care benefits, tuition waivers (full and partial), and unspecified assistantships also available. *Faculty research:* Quantum and nonlinear optics, plasma physics, solid state physics, condensed matter physics and nanotechnology, electron and x-ray spectroscopy. *Unit head:* Graduate Faculty Representative, 607-255-0638. *Application contact:* Graduate Field Assistant, 607-255-0638, E-mail: aep_info@cornell.edu. Web site: http://www.gradschool.cornell.edu/fields.php?id-23&a-2.

DePaul University, College of Science and Health, Department of Physics, Chicago, IL 60604-2287. Offers applied physics (MS). Part-time and evening/weekend programs available. *Faculty:* 6 full-time (2 women), 3 part-time/adjunct (0 women). *Students:* 7 full-time (2 women), 5 part-time (3 women); includes 1 minority (Black or African American, non-Hispanic/Latino), 3 international. Average age 29. 12 applicants, 42% accepted, 3 enrolled. In 2011, 3 master's awarded. *Degree requirements:* For master's, thesis, oral exams. *Entrance requirements:* For master's, 2 letters of recommendation, BA in physics or closely-related field. Additional exam requirements/recommendations for international students: Required—TOEFL. *Application deadline:* For fall admission, 5/1 priority date for domestic students, 4/1 for international students. Applications are

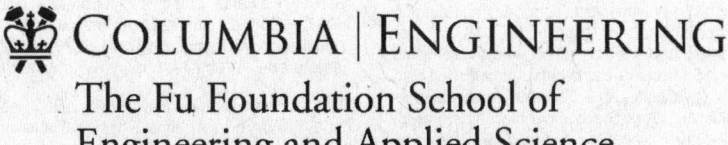

COLUMBIA | ENGINEERING
The Fu Foundation School of
Engineering and Applied Science

Department of Applied Physics and Applied Mathematics

The Department of Applied Physics and Applied Mathematics includes graduate studies in the fields of applied physics, applied mathematics, and materials science and engineering.

The graduate program in applied physics includes plasma physics and controlled fusion; solid state physics; optical and laser physics; medical physics; atmospheric, oceanic, and earth physics, and applied mathematics.

The graduate program in materials science and engineering focuses on understanding, designing, and producing technology-enabling materials by analyzing the relationships amongst the synthesis and processing of materials, their properties, and their detailed structure.

Questions: **seasgradmit@columbia.edu**
Financial Aid Questions: **engradfinaid@columbia.edu**

http://www.engineering.columbia.edu/graduate-2

Peterson's Graduate Programs in the Physical Sciences, Mathematics, Agricultural Sciences, the Environment & Natural Resources 2013

facebook.com/petersonspublishing **221**

processed on a rolling basis. Application fee: $25. Electronic applications accepted. *Financial support:* In 2011–12, teaching assistantships with full tuition reimbursements (averaging $9,000 per year) were awarded; tuition waivers (full) also available. *Faculty research:* Optics, solid-state physics, cosmology, atomic physics, nuclear physics. *Total annual research expenditures:* $54,000. *Unit head:* Dr. Christopher G. Goedde, Chairman, 773-325-7330, Fax: 773-325-7334, E-mail: egoedde@condor.depaul.edu. *Application contact:* Dr. Jesus Pando, Associate Professor, 773-325-7330, Fax: 773-325-7334.

East Carolina University, Graduate School, Thomas Harriot College of Arts and Sciences, Department of Physics, Greenville, NC 27858-4353. Offers applied physics (MS); biomedical physics (PhD); health physics (MS); medical physics (MS). Part-time programs available. *Degree requirements:* For master's, one foreign language, comprehensive exam. *Entrance requirements:* For master's, GRE General Test. Additional exam requirements/recommendations for international students: Required—TOEFL. *Application deadline:* Applications are processed on a rolling basis. Application fee: $50. *Expenses:* Tuition, state resident: full-time $3557; part-time $444.63 per semester hour. Tuition, nonresident: full-time $14,351; part-time $1793.88 per semester hour. *Required fees:* $2016; $252 per semester hour. Part-time tuition and fees vary according to course load, campus/location and program. *Financial support:* Research assistantships with partial tuition reimbursements, teaching assistantships with partial tuition reimbursements, and Federal Work-Study available. Support available to part-time students. Financial award application deadline: 6/1. *Unit head:* Dr. John Sutherland, Chair, 252-328-2023, E-mail: sutherlandj@ecu.edu. *Application contact:* Dean of Graduate School, 252-328-6012, Fax: 252-328-6071, E-mail: gradschool@ecu.edu. Web site: http://www.ecu.edu/cs-cas/physics/Graduate-Program.cfm#.

George Mason University, College of Science, School of Physics, Astronomy and Computational Sciences, Fairfax, VA 22030. Offers applied and engineering physics (MS); computational science (PhD); computational sciences and informatics (MS); physics (PhD). *Faculty:* 55 full-time (11 women), 10 part-time/adjunct (1 woman). *Students:* 49 full-time (12 women), 98 part-time (26 women); includes 23 minority (5 Black or African American, non-Hispanic/Latino; 12 Asian, non-Hispanic/Latino; 6 Hispanic/Latino), 25 international. Average age 35. 79 applicants, 49% accepted, 19 enrolled. In 2011, 12 master's, 17 doctorates, 2 other advanced degrees awarded. *Degree requirements:* For master's, thesis optional. *Entrance requirements:* For master's and doctorate, GRE, baccalaureate degree in related field with minimum GPA of 3.0 in last 60 credit hours; 3 letters of recommendation; expanded goals statement; resume; 2 copies of official transcripts. Additional exam requirements/recommendations for international students: Required—TOEFL (minimum score 570 paper-based; 230 computer-based; 88 iBT), IELTS, Pearson Test of English. *Application deadline:* For fall admission, 4/15 priority date for domestic students; for spring admission, 11/15 priority date for domestic students. Application fee: $65 ($80 for international students). Electronic applications accepted. *Expenses:* Tuition, state resident: full-time $8750; part-time $364.58 per credit. Tuition, nonresident: full-time $24,092; part-time $1003.83 per credit. *Required fees:* $2514; $104.75 per credit. *Financial support:* In 2011–12, 48 students received support, including 5 fellowships with full tuition reimbursements available (averaging $18,000 per year), 33 research assistantships with full and partial tuition reimbursements available (averaging $15,744 per year), 15 teaching assistantships with full and partial tuition reimbursements available (averaging $13,827 per year); career-related internships or fieldwork, Federal Work-Study, scholarships/grants, unspecified assistantships, and health care benefits (full-time research or teaching assistantship recipients) also available. Support available to part-time students. Financial award application deadline: 3/1; financial award applicants required to submit FAFSA. *Faculty research:* Astronomy, astrophysics, and space and planetary science; astronomy and physics education; atomic physics; biophysics and neuroscience. *Total annual research expenditures:* $6.7 million. *Unit head:* Dr. Michael Summers, Chairman, 703-993-3971, Fax: 703-993-1269, E-mail: msummers@gmu.edu. *Application contact:* Dr. Paul So, Information Contact, 703-993-4377, Fax: 703-993-1269, E-mail: paso@gmu.edu. Web site: http://spacs.gmu.edu/.

Harvard University, Graduate School of Arts and Sciences, Department of Physics, Cambridge, MA 02138. Offers experimental physics (PhD); medical engineering/medical physics (PhD), including applied physics, engineering sciences, physics; theoretical physics (PhD). *Degree requirements:* For doctorate, thesis/dissertation, final exams, laboratory experience. *Entrance requirements:* For doctorate, GRE General Test, GRE Subject Test. Additional exam requirements/recommendations for international students: Required—TOEFL. *Expenses: Tuition:* Full-time $36,304. *Required fees:* $1186. Full-time tuition and fees vary according to program. *Faculty research:* Particle physics, condensed matter physics, atomic physics.

Harvard University, Graduate School of Arts and Sciences, School of Engineering and Applied Sciences, Cambridge, MA 02138. Offers applied mathematics (ME, SM, PhD); applied physics (ME, SM, PhD); computer science (ME, SM, PhD); engineering science (ME); engineering sciences (SM, PhD). Part-time programs available. Terminal master's awarded for partial completion of doctoral program. *Degree requirements:* For master's, thesis optional; for doctorate, comprehensive exam, thesis/dissertation. *Entrance requirements:* For master's and doctorate, GRE General Test, GRE Subject Test (recommended); 3 letters of recommendation. Additional exam requirements/recommendations for

international students: Required—TOEFL (minimum score 80 iBT). Electronic applications accepted. *Expenses: Tuition:* Full-time $36,304. *Required fees:* $1186. Full-time tuition and fees vary according to program. *Faculty research:* Applied mathematics, applied physics, computer science and electrical engineering, environmental engineering, mechanical and biomedical engineering.

Idaho State University, Office of Graduate Studies, College of Science and Engineering, Department of Physics, Pocatello, ID 83209-8106. Offers applied physics (PhD); health physics (MS); physics (MNS). Part-time programs available. *Degree requirements:* For master's, comprehensive exam, thesis (for some programs), oral exam (for some programs); for doctorate, comprehensive exam, thesis/dissertation (for some programs), oral exam, written qualifying exam in physics or health physics after 1st year. *Entrance requirements:* For master's, GRE General Test, 3 letters of recommendation, BS or BA in physics, teaching certificate (MNS); for doctorate, GRE General Test (minimum 50th percentile), 3 letters of recommendation, statement of career goals. Additional exam requirements/recommendations for international students: Required—TOEFL (minimum score 550 paper-based; 213 computer-based; 80 iBT). Electronic applications accepted. *Faculty research:* Ion beam applications, low-energy nuclear physics, relativity and cosmology, observational astronomy.

Iowa State University of Science and Technology, Department of Physics and Astronomy, Ames, IA 50011-3160. Offers applied physics (MS, PhD); astrophysics (MS, PhD); condensed matter physics (MS, PhD); high energy physics (MS, PhD); nuclear physics (MS, PhD); physics (MS, PhD). *Degree requirements:* For master's, thesis (for some programs); for doctorate, thesis/dissertation. *Entrance requirements:* For master's and doctorate, GRE General Test, GRE Subject Test (physics). Additional exam requirements/recommendations for international students: Required—TOEFL (minimum score 550 paper-based; 79 iBT), IELTS (minimum score 6.5). *Application deadline:* For fall admission, 2/15 priority date for domestic students, 2/15 for international students; for spring admission, 10/15 for domestic and international students. Applications are processed on a rolling basis. Application fee: $40 ($90 for international students). Electronic applications accepted. *Financial support:* Application deadline: 2/15. *Faculty research:* Condensed-matter physics, including superconductivity and new materials; high-energy and nuclear physics; astronomy and astrophysics; atmospheric and environmental physics. *Total annual research expenditures:* $8.8 million. *Unit head:* Dr. Steve Kawaler, Director of Graduate Education, 515-294-5870, Fax: 515-294-6027, E-mail: physastro@iastate.edu. *Application contact:* Lori Hockett, Application Contact, 515-294-5870, E-mail: phys_astro@iastate.edu. Web site: http://www.physics.iastate.edu/.

Iowa State University of Science and Technology, Program in Applied Physics, Ames, IA 50011-3160. Offers MS, PhD. *Entrance requirements:* For master's and doctorate, GRE. Additional exam requirements/recommendations for international students: Required—TOEFL (minimum score 550 paper-based; 79 iBT), IELTS (minimum score 6.5). *Application deadline:* For fall admission, 2/15 for domestic and international students; for spring admission, 10/15 for domestic and international students. Electronic applications accepted. *Unit head:* Dr. Steven Kawaler, Director of Graduate Education, 515-294-5870, Fax: 515-294-6027, E-mail: physastro@iastate.edu. *Application contact:* Lori Hockett, Application Contact, 515-294-5870, Fax: 515-294-6027, E-mail: physastro@iastate.edu. Web site: http://www.physastro.iastate.edu.

The Johns Hopkins University, Engineering Program for Professionals, Part-time Program in Applied Physics, Baltimore, MD 21218-2699. Offers MS, Post-Master's Certificate. Part-time and evening/weekend programs available. Electronic applications accepted.

Laurentian University, School of Graduate Studies and Research, Programme in Physics, Sudbury, ON P3E 2C6, Canada. Offers M Sc. Part-time programs available. *Degree requirements:* For master's, thesis or alternative. *Entrance requirements:* For master's, honors degree with second class or better. *Faculty research:* Solar neutrino physics and astrophysics, applied acoustics and ultrasonics, powder science and technology, solid state physics, theoretical physics.

Naval Postgraduate School, Departments and Academic Groups, Department of Physics, Monterey, CA 93943. Offers applied physics (MS, PhD); combat systems technology (MS); engineering acoustics (MS, PhD); physics (MS, PhD). Program only open to commissioned officers of the United States and friendly nations and selected United States federal civilian employees. Part-time programs available. *Faculty:* 35 full-time (8 women), 1 part-time/adjunct. *Students:* 117 full-time (18 women); includes 17 minority (3 Black or African American, non-Hispanic/Latino; 1 American Indian or Alaska Native, non-Hispanic/Latino; 6 Asian, non-Hispanic/Latino; 7 Hispanic/Latino), 19 international. Average age 32. In 2011, 24 master's, 2 doctorates awarded. *Degree requirements:* For master's, thesis; for doctorate, thesis/dissertation. *Faculty research:* Acoustics, free electron laser, sensors, weapons and effects. *Total annual research expenditures:* $9.4 million. *Unit head:* Dr. Andres Larraza, Chairman, 831-656-3007, E-mail: larraza@nps.edu. Web site: http://www.nps.edu/Academics/GSEAS/Physics/.

Naval Postgraduate School, Departments and Academic Groups, Space Systems Academic Group, Monterey, CA 93943. Offers applied physics (MS); astronautical engineering (MS); computer science (MS); electrical engineering (MS); mechanical engineering (MS); space systems (Engr); space systems operations (MS). Program only open to commissioned officers of the United

222 facebook.com/petersonspublishing

Peterson's Graduate Programs in the Physical Sciences, Mathematics, Agricultural Sciences, the Environment & Natural Resources 2013

States and friendly nations and selected United States federal civilian employees. Part-time programs available. *Faculty:* 5 full-time, 5 part-time/adjunct (2 women). *Students:* 37 full-time (2 women), 14 part-time; includes 11 minority (5 Black or African American, non-Hispanic/Latino; 2 Asian, non-Hispanic/Latino; 4 Hispanic/Latino), 1 international. Average age 33. In 2011, 20 master's awarded. *Degree requirements:* For master's and Engr, thesis; for doctorate, thesis/dissertation. *Faculty research:* Military applications for space; space reconnaissance and remote sensing; radiation-hardened electronics for space; design, construction and operations of small satellites; satellite communications systems. *Total annual research expenditures:* $2 million. *Unit head:* Dr. Rudy Panholzer, Chairman, 831-656-2154. Web site: http://www.nps.edu/Academics/Schools/GSEAS/Departments/SpaceSystems/.

Naval Postgraduate School, Departments and Academic Groups, Undersea Warfare Academic Group, Monterey, CA 93943. Offers applied mathematics (MS); applied physics (MS); applied science (MS), including acoustics, operations research, physical oceanography, signal processing; electrical engineering (MS); engineering acoustics (MS, PhD); engineering science (MS), including electrical engineering, mechanical engineering; mechanical engineer (ME); mechanical engineering (MS, MSME); meteorology (MS); operations research (MS); physical oceanography (MS). Program only open to commissioned officers of the United States and friendly nations and selected United States federal civilian employees. Part-time programs available. *Students:* 2 full-time, both international. Average age 36. *Degree requirements:* For master's, thesis. *Faculty research:* Unmanned/autonomous vehicles, sea mines and countermeasures, submarine warfare in the twentieth and twenty-first centuries. *Unit head:* Dr. Clyde Scandrett, Academic Group Chairman, 831-656-2027. Web site: http://www.nps.edu/Academics/Schools/GSEAS/Departments/USW/USW-Index.html.

New Jersey Institute of Technology, Office of Graduate Studies, College of Science and Liberal Arts, Department of Physics, Program in Applied Physics, Newark, NJ 07102. Offers MS, PhD. Part-time and evening/weekend programs available. *Students:* 32 full-time (6 women), 5 part-time (1 woman); includes 4 minority (1 Black or African American, non-Hispanic/Latino; 1 Asian, non-Hispanic/Latino; 2 Hispanic/Latino), 30 international. Average age 32. 34 applicants, 62% accepted, 9 enrolled. In 2011, 4 master's, 3 doctorates awarded. Terminal master's awarded for partial completion of doctoral program. *Degree requirements:* For master's, thesis optional; for doctorate, thesis/dissertation, residency. *Entrance requirements:* For master's, GRE General Test; for doctorate, GRE General Test, minimum graduate GPA of 3.5. Additional exam requirements/recommendations for international students: Required—TOEFL (minimum score 550 paper-based; 213 computer-based; 79 iBT). *Application deadline:* For fall admission, 6/1 priority date for domestic students, 5/1 for international students; for spring admission, 11/15 priority date for domestic students, 11/15 for international students. Applications are processed on a rolling basis. Application fee: $65. Electronic applications accepted. *Expenses:* Tuition, state resident: full-time $7980; part-time $867 per credit. Tuition, nonresident: full-time $11,336; part-time $1196 per credit. *Required fees:* $230 per credit. *Financial support:* Fellowships with full and partial tuition reimbursements, research assistantships with full and partial tuition reimbursements, teaching assistantships with full and partial tuition reimbursements, career-related internships or fieldwork, Federal Work-Study, institutionally sponsored loans, and unspecified assistantships available. Financial award application deadline: 1/15. *Unit head:* Dr. N. M. Ravindra, Chair, 973-596-3278, E-mail: n.m.ravindra@njit.edu. *Application contact:* Kathryn Kelly, Director of Admissions, 973-596-3300, Fax: 973-596-3461, E-mail: admissions@njit.edu.

Northern Arizona University, Graduate College, College of Engineering, Forestry and Natural Sciences, Department of Physics and Astronomy, Flagstaff, AZ 86011. Offers applied physics (MS). Part-time programs available. *Faculty:* 12 full-time (2 women). *Students:* 22 full-time (11 women), 3 part-time (1 woman); includes 2 minority (1 Hispanic/Latino; 1 Two or more races, non-Hispanic/Latino), 6 international. Average age 37. 17 applicants, 76% accepted, 11 enrolled. In 2011, 4 degrees awarded. *Degree requirements:* For master's, thesis optional. *Entrance requirements:* Additional exam requirements/recommendations for international students: Required—TOEFL (minimum score 550 paper-based; 213 computer-based; 80 iBT), IELTS (minimum score 7). *Application deadline:* For fall admission, 1/15 priority date for domestic students, 1/15 for international students. Applications are processed on a rolling basis. Application fee: $65. Electronic applications accepted. *Expenses:* Tuition, state resident: full-time $7190; part-time $355 per credit hour. Tuition, nonresident: full-time $18,092; part-time $1005 per credit hour. *Required fees:* $818; $328 per semester. *Financial support:* In 2011–12, 4 research assistantships with partial tuition reimbursements (averaging $12,390 per year), 11 teaching assistantships with partial tuition reimbursements (averaging $12,390 per year) were awarded; Federal Work-Study, scholarships/grants, health care benefits, tuition waivers (full and partial), and unspecified assistantships also available. Financial award applicants required to submit FAFSA. *Unit head:* Dr. Kathy Eastwood, Chair, 928-523-7159, Fax: 928-523-1371, E-mail: kathy.eastwood@nau.edu. *Application contact:* Jamie Housholder, Administrative Assistant, 928-523-8170, Fax: 928-523-1371, E-mail: astro.physics@nau.edu. Web site: http://www.physics.nau.edu/.

Oregon State University, Graduate School, College of Science, Department of Physics, Corvallis, OR 97331. Offers applied physics (MS); physics (MA, MS, PhD). Part-time programs available. Terminal master's awarded for partial completion of doctoral program. *Degree requirements:* For master's, thesis

optional, qualifying exam; for doctorate, thesis/dissertation, qualifying exam. *Entrance requirements:* For master's and doctorate, minimum GPA of 3.0 in last 90 hours. Additional exam requirements/recommendations for international students: Required—TOEFL.

Pittsburg State University, Graduate School, College of Arts and Sciences, Department of Physics, Pittsburg, KS 66762. Offers applied physics (MS); physics (MS); professional physics (MS). *Degree requirements:* For master's, thesis or alternative.

Polytechnic Institute of New York University, Department of Applied Physics, Brooklyn, NY 11201-2990. Offers MS, PhD. Part-time and evening/weekend programs available. *Faculty:* 3 full-time (0 women). *Students:* 1 (woman) full-time, 1 part-time, both international. Average age 29. 7 applicants, 43% accepted, 1 enrolled. *Degree requirements:* For master's, comprehensive exam (for some programs), thesis (for some programs); for doctorate, comprehensive exam, thesis/dissertation. *Entrance requirements:* For master's, BA in physics; for doctorate, departmental qualifying exam, BS in physics. Additional exam requirements/recommendations for international students: Required—TOEFL (minimum score 550 paper-based; 213 computer-based; 80 iBT); Recommended—IELTS (minimum score 6.5). *Application deadline:* For fall admission, 7/31 priority date for domestic students, 4/30 for international students; for spring admission, 12/31 priority date for domestic students, 11/30 for international students. Applications are processed on a rolling basis. Application fee: $75. Electronic applications accepted. *Expenses:* Tuition: Full-time $22,464; part-time $1248 per credit. *Required fees:* $501 per semester. *Financial support:* Fellowships, research assistantships, teaching assistantships, and institutionally sponsored loans available. Support available to part-time students. Financial award applicants required to submit FAFSA. *Faculty research:* Combining microdroplets, UHV cryogenic scanning, tunneling, surface spectroscopy of a single aerosol particle. *Total annual research expenditures:* $1.2 million. *Unit head:* Dr. Lorcan M. Folan, Head, 718-260-3072, E-mail: lfolan@poly.edu. *Application contact:* JeanCarlo Bonilla, Director of Graduate Enrollment Management, 718-260-3182, Fax: 718-260-3624, E-mail: gradinfo@poly.edu.

Rice University, Rice Quantum Institute, Houston, TX 77251-1892. Offers MS, PhD. *Degree requirements:* For master's, thesis; for doctorate, thesis/dissertation. *Entrance requirements:* For master's and doctorate, GRE General Test, GRE Subject Test (physics), minimum GPA of 3.0. Additional exam requirements/recommendations for international students: Required—TOEFL (minimum score 600 paper-based; 250 computer-based; 90 iBT). Electronic applications accepted. *Faculty research:* Nanotechnology, solid state materials, atomic physics, thin films.

Rutgers, The State University of New Jersey, Newark, Graduate School, Program in Applied Physics, Newark, NJ 07102. Offers MS, PhD. MS, PhD offered jointly with New Jersey Institute of Technology. *Entrance requirements:* For master's and doctorate, GRE. Additional exam requirements/recommendations for international students: Required—TOEFL.

Southern Illinois University Carbondale, Graduate School, College of Science, Department of Physics, Carbondale, IL 62901-4701. Offers MS, PhD. *Faculty:* 9 full-time (0 women). *Students:* 5 full-time (1 woman), 26 part-time (4 women); includes 2 minority (1 Asian, non-Hispanic/Latino; 1 Hispanic/Latino), 11 international. 26 applicants, 42% accepted, 9 enrolled. In 2011, 2 master's, 2 doctorates awarded. *Degree requirements:* For master's, one foreign language, thesis. *Entrance requirements:* For master's, minimum GPA of 2.7. Additional exam requirements/recommendations for international students: Required—TOEFL. *Application deadline:* Applications are processed on a rolling basis. Application fee: $20. *Financial support:* In 2011–12, 1 fellowship with full tuition reimbursement, 9 teaching assistantships with full tuition reimbursements were awarded; research assistantships with full tuition reimbursements, career-related internships or fieldwork, Federal Work-Study, institutionally sponsored loans, and tuition waivers (full) also available. Support available to part-time students. Financial award application deadline: 2/15. *Faculty research:* Atomic, molecular, nuclear, and mathematical physics; statistical mechanics; solid-state and low-temperature physics; rheology; material science. *Total annual research expenditures:* $773,352. *Unit head:* Dr. Aldo Migone, Chairperson, 618-453-1054, E-mail: aldo@physics.siu.edu. *Application contact:* Sally Pleasure, Graduate Admissions Committee, 618-453-2643. Web site: http://siuphysics.physics.siu.edu/.

Stanford University, School of Humanities and Sciences, Department of Applied Physics, Stanford, CA 94305-9991. Offers MS, PhD. Terminal master's awarded for partial completion of doctoral program. *Degree requirements:* For doctorate, thesis/dissertation. *Entrance requirements:* For master's and doctorate, GRE General Test, GRE Subject Test. Additional exam requirements/recommendations for international students: Required—TOEFL. Electronic applications accepted. *Expenses:* Tuition: Full-time $40,050; part-time $890 per credit.

State University of New York at Binghamton, Graduate School, School of Arts and Sciences, Department of Physics, Applied Physics, and Astronomy, Binghamton, NY 13902-6000. Offers applied physics (MS); physics (MA, MS, PhD). *Faculty:* 12 full-time (1 woman), 13 part-time/adjunct (6 women). *Students:* 17 full-time (1 woman), 2 part-time (0 women); includes 1 minority (Black or African American, non-Hispanic/Latino), 5 international. Average age 27. 12

Peterson's Graduate Programs in the Physical Sciences, Mathematics, Agricultural Sciences, the Environment & Natural Resources 2013

facebook.com/petersonspublishing **223**

Applied Physics

applicants, 92% accepted, 8 enrolled. In 2011, 1 master's awarded. *Degree requirements:* For master's, thesis or alternative. *Entrance requirements:* For master's, GRE General Test, GRE Subject Test. Additional exam requirements/recommendations for international students: Required—TOEFL (minimum score 550 paper-based; 213 computer-based; 80 iBT). *Application deadline:* For fall admission, 2/15 priority date for domestic students, 2/15 for international students; for spring admission, 10/15 priority date for domestic students, 10/15 for international students. Applications are processed on a rolling basis. Application fee: $60. Electronic applications accepted. *Financial support:* In 2011–12, 19 students received support, including 1 fellowship with full tuition reimbursement available (averaging $11,000 per year), 2 research assistantships with full tuition reimbursements available (averaging $11,000 per year), 15 teaching assistantships with full tuition reimbursements available (averaging $11,000 per year); career-related internships or fieldwork, Federal Work-Study, institutionally sponsored loans, scholarships/grants, health care benefits, and unspecified assistantships also available. Financial award application deadline: 2/15; financial award applicants required to submit FAFSA. *Unit head:* Dr. Eric Cotts, Chairperson, 607-777-4371, E-mail: ecotts@binghamton.edu. *Application contact:* Catherine Smith, Recruiting and Admissions Coordinator, 607-777-2151, Fax: 607-777-2501, E-mail: cmsmith@binghamton.edu.

Texas A&M University, College of Science, Department of Physics and Astronomy, College Station, TX 77843. Offers applied physics (PhD); physics (MS, PhD). *Faculty:* 54. *Students:* 179 full-time (25 women), 8 part-time (0 women); includes 28 minority (3 Black or African American, non-Hispanic/Latino; 1 American Indian or Alaska Native, non-Hispanic/Latino; 4 Asian, non-Hispanic/Latino; 15 Hispanic/Latino; 5 Two or more races, non-Hispanic/Latino), 84 international. In 2011, 16 master's, 17 doctorates awarded. Terminal master's awarded for partial completion of doctoral program. *Degree requirements:* For master's, thesis (for some programs); for doctorate, thesis/dissertation. *Entrance requirements:* For master's and doctorate, GRE General Test, GRE Subject Test. Additional exam requirements/recommendations for international students: Required—TOEFL. *Application deadline:* For fall admission, 3/1 priority date for domestic students; for spring admission, 8/1 for domestic students. Application fee: $50 ($75 for international students). Electronic applications accepted. *Expenses:* Tuition, state resident: full-time $5437; part-time $226.55 per credit hour. Tuition, nonresident: full-time $12,949; part-time $539.55 per credit hour. *Required fees:* $2741. *Financial support:* In 2011–12, research assistantships (averaging $16,200 per year), teaching assistantships (averaging $16,200 per year) were awarded; fellowships also available. Financial award application deadline: 3/1; financial award applicants required to submit FAFSA. *Faculty research:* Condensed-matter, atomic/molecular, high-energy, and nuclear physics; quantum optics. *Unit head:* Dr. Edward S. Fry, Head, 979-845-7717, E-mail: fry@physics.tamu.edu. *Application contact:* Dr. George W. Kattawar, Professor, 979-845-1180, Fax: 979-845-2590, E-mail: kattawar@tamu.edu. Web site: http://physics.tamu.edu/.

Texas Tech University, Graduate School, College of Arts and Sciences, Department of Physics, Lubbock, TX 79409. Offers applied physics (MS); physics (MS, PhD). Part-time programs available. *Faculty:* 18 full-time (2 women), 1 part-time/adjunct (0 women). *Students:* 59 full-time (14 women), 3 part-time (1 woman); includes 7 minority (1 Black or African American, non-Hispanic/Latino; 2 Asian, non-Hispanic/Latino; 3 Hispanic/Latino; 1 Two or more races, non-Hispanic/Latino), 42 international. Average age 29. 40 applicants, 43% accepted, 14 enrolled. In 2011, 7 master's, 5 doctorates awarded. *Degree requirements:* For master's, variable foreign language requirement, thesis or alternative; for doctorate, variable foreign language requirement, thesis/dissertation. *Entrance requirements:* For master's and doctorate, GRE General Test. Additional exam requirements/recommendations for international students: Required—TOEFL (minimum score 550 paper-based; 213 computer-based; 79 iBT). *Application deadline:* For fall admission, 6/1 priority date for domestic students, 1/15 for international students; for spring admission, 9/1 priority date for domestic students, 6/15 for international students. Applications are processed on a rolling basis. Application fee: $50 ($75 for international students). Electronic applications accepted. *Expenses:* Tuition, state resident: full-time $5899; part-time $245.80 per credit hour. Tuition, nonresident: full-time $13,411; part-time $558.80 per credit hour. *Required fees:* $2680.60; $86.50 per credit hour. $920.30 per semester. *Financial support:* In 2011–12, 18 students received support. Application deadline: 4/15; applicants required to submit FAFSA. *Faculty research:* Biophysics, high energy and nuclear physics, condensed matter physics, atomic and molecular physics, physics education. *Total annual research expenditures:* $1.7 million. *Unit head:* Dr. Roger Lichti, Chair, 806-742-3767, Fax: 806-742-1182, E-mail: roger.lichti@ttu.edu. *Application contact:* Dr. Mahdi Sanati, Graduate Recruiter, 806-742-3767, Fax: 806-742-1182, E-mail: m.sanati@ttu.edu. Web site: http://www.phys.ttu.edu/.

Towson University, Program in Applied Physics, Towson, MD 21252-0001. Offers MS. *Students:* 6 full-time (2 women), 1 (woman) part-time; includes 1 minority (Asian, non-Hispanic/Latino), 2 international. *Expenses:* Tuition, state resident: part-time $337 per credit. Tuition, nonresident: part-time $709 per credit. *Required fees:* $99 per credit. *Unit head:* Dr. Raj Kolagani, Dean, 410-704-3134, E-mail: rkolagani@towson.edu.

The University of Arizona, College of Science, Department of Physics, Program in Applied and Industrial Physics, Tucson, AZ 85721. Offers PMS. Part-time programs available. *Students:* 5 full-time (1 woman), 1 part-time (0 women); includes 1 minority (Hispanic/Latino), 2 international. Average age 26. 13 applicants, 38% accepted, 5 enrolled. In 2011, 4 master's awarded. *Degree requirements:* For master's, thesis or alternative, internship, colloquium, business courses. *Entrance requirements:* Additional exam requirements/recommendations for international students: Required—TOEFL (minimum score 550 paper-based; 213 computer-based; 79 iBT). Application fee: $75. Electronic applications accepted. *Expenses:* Tuition, state resident: full-time $10,840. Tuition, nonresident: full-time $25,802. *Financial support:* Career-related internships or fieldwork, Federal Work-Study, and scholarships/grants available. *Faculty research:* Nanotechnology, optics, medical imaging, high energy physics, biophysics. *Unit head:* Dr. Michael Shupe, Department Head, 520-621-2679, E-mail: shupe@physics.arizona.edu. *Application contact:* Lisa Shapouri, Graduate Coordinator, 520-621-2290, Fax: 520-621-4721, E-mail: lisas@physics.arizona.edu. Web site: http://www.physics.arizona.edu/.

University of Arkansas, Graduate School, J. William Fulbright College of Arts and Sciences, Department of Physics, Fayetteville, AR 72701-1201. Offers applied physics (MS); physics (MS, PhD); physics education (MA). *Students:* 11 full-time (3 women), 38 part-time (7 women); includes 3 minority (1 Asian, non-Hispanic/Latino; 1 Hispanic/Latino; 1 Two or more races, non-Hispanic/Latino), 28 international. In 2011, 3 master's, 3 doctorates awarded. *Degree requirements:* For master's, thesis; for doctorate, thesis/dissertation. *Application deadline:* For fall admission, 4/1 for international students; for spring admission, 10/1 for international students. Applications are processed on a rolling basis. Application fee: $40 ($50 for international students). Electronic applications accepted. *Financial support:* In 2011–12, 21 research assistantships, 22 teaching assistantships were awarded; fellowships with tuition reimbursements, career-related internships or fieldwork, and Federal Work-Study also available. Support available to part-time students. Financial award application deadline: 4/1; financial award applicants required to submit FAFSA. *Unit head:* Dr. Julio Gea-Banacloche, Departmental Chairperson, 479-575-2506, Fax: 479-575-4580, E-mail: jgeabana@uark.edu. *Application contact:* Dr. Huaxiang Fu, Graduate Coordinator, 479-575-8606, E-mail: hfu@uark.edu. Web site: http://www.uark.edu/depts/physics/.

University of California, San Diego, Office of Graduate Studies, Department of Electrical and Computer Engineering, La Jolla, CA 92093. Offers applied ocean science (MS, PhD); applied physics (MS, PhD); communication theory and systems (MS, PhD); computer engineering (MS, PhD); electrical engineering (M Eng); electronic circuits and systems (MS, PhD); intelligent systems, robotics and control (MS, PhD); photonics (MS, PhD); signal and image processing (MS, PhD). MS only offered to students who have been admitted to the PhD program. *Entrance requirements:* For master's and doctorate, GRE General Test. Electronic applications accepted.

University of Denver, Faculty of Natural Sciences and Mathematics, Department of Physics and Astronomy, Denver, CO 80208. Offers applied physics (MS); physics (MS, PhD). Part-time programs available. *Faculty:* 10 full-time (3 women), 5 part-time/adjunct (0 women). *Students:* 8 full-time (3 women), 9 part-time (3 women); includes 1 minority (Hispanic/Latino), 2 international. Average age 29. 36 applicants, 19% accepted, 6 enrolled. In 2011, 1 master's, 1 doctorate awarded. Terminal master's awarded for partial completion of doctoral program. *Median time to degree:* Of those who began their doctoral program in fall 2003, 100% received their degree in 8 years or less. *Degree requirements:* For master's, thesis optional; for doctorate, thesis/dissertation. *Entrance requirements:* For master's and doctorate, GRE General Test, GRE Subject Test in physics (strongly preferred), three letters of recommendation, personal statement. Additional exam requirements/recommendations for international students: Required—TOEFL (minimum score 550 paper-based; 80 iBT). *Application deadline:* For fall admission, 3/1 priority date for domestic students. Applications are processed on a rolling basis. Application fee: $60. Electronic applications accepted. *Financial support:* In 2011–12, 15 students received support, including 10 research assistantships with full and partial tuition reimbursements available (averaging $19,300 per year), 10 teaching assistantships with full and partial tuition reimbursements available (averaging $17,370 per year); career-related internships or fieldwork, Federal Work-Study, institutionally sponsored loans, scholarships/grants, and unspecified assistantships also available. Support available to part-time students. Financial award application deadline: 2/15; financial award applicants required to submit FAFSA. *Faculty research:* Atomic and molecular beams and collisions, infrared astronomy, acoustic emission from stressed solids, nano materials. *Unit head:* Dr. Davor Balzar, 303-871-2238, E-mail: davor.balzar@du.edu. *Application contact:* Barbara Stephen, Assistant to the Chair, 303-871-2238, E-mail: barbara.stephen@du.edu. Web site: http://www.physics.du.edu.

University of Maryland, Baltimore County, Graduate School, College of Natural and Mathematical Sciences, Department of Physics, Program in Applied Physics, Baltimore, MD 21250. Offers MS, PhD. Part-time programs available. *Faculty:* 21 full-time (3 women), 16 part-time/adjunct (2 women). *Students:* 30 full-time (9 women), 3 part-time (0 women); includes 4 minority (3 Black or African American, non-Hispanic/Latino; 1 Asian, non-Hispanic/Latino), 12 international. Average age 24. 31 applicants, 52% accepted, 5 enrolled. In 2011, 4 master's, 2 doctorates awarded. Terminal master's awarded for partial completion of doctoral program. *Degree requirements:* For master's, thesis optional; for doctorate, comprehensive exam, thesis/dissertation. *Entrance requirements:* For master's and doctorate, GRE General Test, GRE Subject Test (recommended), minimum GPA of 3.0.

Additional exam requirements/recommendations for international students: Required—TOEFL. *Application deadline:* For fall admission, 1/1 for domestic and international students; for spring admission, 11/30 for domestic students. Applications are processed on a rolling basis. Application fee: $50. Electronic applications accepted. *Financial support:* In 2011–12, 30 students received support, including 4 fellowships with full tuition reimbursements available (averaging $27,000 per year), 14 research assistantships with full tuition reimbursements available (averaging $24,000 per year), 12 teaching assistantships with full tuition reimbursements available (averaging $22,000 per year); career-related internships or fieldwork, scholarships/grants, health care benefits, and unspecified assistantships also available. Support available to part-time students. Financial award application deadline: 5/31. *Faculty research:* Astrophysics, atmospheric physics, nanoscale physics, optics, quantum optics and quantum information. *Total annual research expenditures:* $4.8 million. *Unit head:* Dr. Todd Pittman, Graduate Program Director, 410-455-2513, Fax: 410-455-1072, E-mail: todd.pittman@umbc.edu. *Application contact:* Dr. Lazlo L. Takacs, Graduate Admissions Committee Chair, 410-455-2524, Fax: 410-455-1072, E-mail: takacs@umbc.edu. Web site: http://www.physics.umbc.edu.

University of Massachusetts Boston, Office of Graduate Studies, College of Science and Mathematics, Program in Applied Physics, Boston, MA 02125-3393. Offers MS. Part-time and evening/weekend programs available. *Degree requirements:* For master's, thesis optional. *Entrance requirements:* For master's, minimum GPA of 2.75. *Faculty research:* Experimental laser research, nonlinear optics, experimental and theoretical solid state physics, semiconductor devices, opto-electronics.

University of Massachusetts Lowell, College of Sciences, Department of Physics and Applied Physics, Program in Applied Physics, Lowell, MA 01854-2881. Offers applied mechanics (PhD); applied physics (MS, PhD), including optical sciences (MS). Terminal master's awarded for partial completion of doctoral program. *Degree requirements:* For master's, thesis; for doctorate, 2 foreign languages, thesis/dissertation. *Entrance requirements:* For master's, GRE General Test, 3 letters of reference; for doctorate, GRE General Test, transcripts, 3 letters of reference. Additional exam requirements/recommendations for international students: Required—TOEFL.

University of Michigan, Horace H. Rackham School of Graduate Studies, College of Literature, Science, and the Arts, Applied Physics Program, Ann Arbor, MI 48109. Offers PhD. *Faculty:* 123 full-time (20 women). *Students:* 74 full-time (21 women); includes 22 minority (11 Black or African American, non-Hispanic/Latino; 2 American Indian or Alaska Native, non-Hispanic/Latino; 1 Asian, non-Hispanic/Latino; 5 Hispanic/Latino; 3 Two or more races, non-Hispanic/Latino), 13 international. Average age 23. 118 applicants, 22% accepted, 13 enrolled. In 2011, 11 doctorates awarded. *Degree requirements:* For doctorate, oral defense of dissertation, preliminary and qualifying exams. *Entrance requirements:* For doctorate, GRE General Test. Additional exam requirements/recommendations for international students: Required—TOEFL. *Application deadline:* For fall admission, 1/15 for domestic and international students. Applications are processed on a rolling basis. Application fee: $60 ($75 for international students). Electronic applications accepted. *Financial support:* In 2011–12, 24 students received support, including 33 fellowships with full tuition reimbursements available (averaging $26,500 per year), 37 research assistantships with full tuition reimbursements available (averaging $26,500 per year), 4 teaching assistantships with full tuition reimbursements available (averaging $26,500 per year); traineeships, health care benefits, and unspecified assistantships also available. Financial award application deadline: 1/15; financial award applicants required to submit FAFSA. *Faculty research:* Optical sciences, materials research, quantum structures, medical imaging, environment and science policy. *Total annual research expenditures:* $1.1 million. *Unit head:* Dr. Cagliyan Kurdak, Director, 734-647-4650, Fax: 734-764-2193, E-mail: kurdak@umich.edu. *Application contact:* Charles N. Sutton, Program Assistant, 734-764-4595, Fax: 734-764-2193, E-mail: csutton@umich.edu. Web site: http://applied.physics.lsa.umich.edu/.

University of Missouri–St. Louis, College of Arts and Sciences, Department of Physics and Astronomy, St. Louis, MO 63121. Offers applied physics (MS); physics (PhD). Part-time and evening/weekend programs available. *Faculty:* 11 full-time (2 women), 4 part-time/adjunct (1 woman). *Students:* 19 full-time (7 women), 5 part-time (1 woman), 6 international. Average age 32. 20 applicants, 40% accepted, 4 enrolled. In 2011, 5 master's, 1 doctorate awarded. Terminal master's awarded for partial completion of doctoral program. *Degree requirements:* For master's, thesis optional; for doctorate, thesis/dissertation. *Entrance requirements:* For master's, GRE General Test; for doctorate, GRE General Test, 2 letters of recommendation. Additional exam requirements/recommendations for international students: Required—TOEFL (minimum score 550 paper-based; 213 computer-based). *Application deadline:* For fall admission, 7/1 for domestic and international students; for spring admission, 12/1 for domestic students, 11/1 for international students. Electronic applications accepted. *Expenses:* Tuition, state resident: full-time $6273; part-time $3866 per year. Tuition, nonresident: full-time $14,969; part-time $9980 per year. *Required fees:* $315 per year. *Financial support:* In 2011–12, 7 research assistantships with full and partial tuition reimbursements (averaging $16,200 per year), 10 teaching assistantships with full and partial tuition reimbursements (averaging $14,500 per year) were awarded; fellowships with full tuition reimbursements and career-related internships or fieldwork also available. Financial award applicants required to submit FAFSA. *Faculty research:* Biophysics, atomic physics, nonlinear dynamics, materials science. *Unit head:* Dr. Bruce Wilking, Director of Graduate Studies, 314-516-5931, Fax: 314-516-6152, E-mail: bwilking@umsl.edu. *Application contact:* 314-516-5458, Fax: 314-516-6996, E-mail: gradadm@umsl.edu. Web site: http://www.umsl.edu/~physics/.

The University of North Carolina at Charlotte, Graduate School, College of Liberal Arts and Sciences, Department of Physics and Optical Science, Charlotte, NC 28223-0001. Offers applied physics (MS); optical science and engineering (MS, PhD). *Faculty:* 23 full-time (4 women). *Students:* 3 full-time (2 women), 13 part-time (4 women); includes 2 minority (both Black or African American, non-Hispanic/Latino). Average age 32. 38 applicants, 82% accepted, 13 enrolled. In 2011, 4 master's, 4 doctorates awarded. Terminal master's awarded for partial completion of doctoral program. *Degree requirements:* For master's, thesis optional; for doctorate, thesis/dissertation optional. *Entrance requirements:* For master's, GRE General Test, minimum GPA of 3.0 during previous 2 years, 2.75 overall. Additional exam requirements/recommendations for international students: Required—TOEFL (minimum score 557 paper-based; 220 computer-based; 83 iBT). *Application deadline:* For fall admission, 7/15 for domestic students, 5/1 for international students; for spring admission, 11/15 for domestic students, 10/1 for international students. Applications are processed on a rolling basis. Application fee: $65 ($75 for international students). Electronic applications accepted. *Expenses:* Tuition, state resident: full-time $3689. Tuition, nonresident: full-time $15,226. *Required fees:* $2198. Tuition and fees vary according to course load and program. *Financial support:* In 2011–12, 36 students received support, including 6 fellowships (averaging $41,726 per year), 14 research assistantships (averaging $10,262 per year), 16 teaching assistantships (averaging $7,938 per year); career-related internships or fieldwork, institutionally sponsored loans, scholarships/grants, and unspecified assistantships also available. Support available to part-time students. Financial award application deadline: 4/1; financial award applicants required to submit FAFSA. *Faculty research:* Optics, lasers, microscopy, fibers, astrophysics. *Total annual research expenditures:* $1.4 million. *Unit head:* Dr. Patrick Moyer, Interim Chair, 704-687-8148, Fax: 704-687-3160, E-mail: pjmoyer@uncc.edu. *Application contact:* Kathy B. Giddings, Director of Graduate Admissions, 704-687-5503, Fax: 704-687-3279, E-mail: gradadm@uncc.edu. Web site: http://physics.uncc.edu/.

University of Northern Iowa, Graduate College, College of Humanities, Arts and Sciences, Department of Physics, Cedar Falls, IA 50614. Offers applied physics (PSM). *Students:* 3 full-time (0 women), 5 part-time (1 woman); includes 1 minority (Hispanic/Latino), 1 international. 4 applicants, 75% accepted, 2 enrolled. In 2011, 2 master's awarded. *Degree requirements:* For master's, comprehensive exam (for some programs), thesis or alternative. *Entrance requirements:* For master's, minimum GPA of 3.0. Additional exam requirements/recommendations for international students: Required—TOEFL (minimum score 500 paper-based; 180 computer-based; 61 iBT). *Application deadline:* For fall admission, 8/1 priority date for domestic students. Applications are processed on a rolling basis. Application fee: $50 ($70 for international students). Electronic applications accepted. *Expenses:* Tuition, state resident: full-time $7476. Tuition, nonresident: full-time $16,410. *Required fees:* $942. *Financial support:* Career-related internships or fieldwork, Federal Work-Study, scholarships/grants, and tuition waivers (full and partial) available. Support available to part-time students. Financial award application deadline: 2/1. *Unit head:* Dr. C. Clifton Chancey, Head, 319-273-2420, E-mail: c.chancey@uni.edu. *Application contact:* Laurie S. Russell, Record Analyst, 319-273-2623, Fax: 319-273-2885, E-mail: laurie.russell@uni.edu. Web site: http://www.physics.uni.edu/.

University of South Florida, Graduate School, College of Arts and Sciences, Department of Physics, Tampa, FL 33620-9951. Offers applied physics (PhD); physics (MS). Part-time programs available. *Faculty:* 23 full-time (3 women), 10 part-time/adjunct (2 women). *Students:* 74 full-time (12 women), 13 part-time (0 women); includes 9 minority (3 Black or African American, non-Hispanic/Latino; 2 Asian, non-Hispanic/Latino; 4 Hispanic/Latino), 35 international. Average age 31. 80 applicants, 46% accepted, 20 enrolled. In 2011, 7 master's, 6 doctorates awarded. *Degree requirements:* For master's, comprehensive exam, thesis optional; for doctorate, comprehensive exam, thesis/dissertation. *Entrance requirements:* For master's and doctorate, GRE, minimum GPA of 3.0, three letters of recommendation, statement of purpose. Additional exam requirements/recommendations for international students: Required—TOEFL (minimum score 550 paper-based; 213 computer-based; 79 iBT) or IELTS (minimum score 6.5). *Application deadline:* For fall admission, 2/15 priority date for domestic students, 1/2 for international students; for spring admission, 9/1 for domestic students, 7/1 for international students. Applications are processed on a rolling basis. Application fee: $30. Electronic applications accepted. *Financial support:* In 2011–12, 70 students received support, including 27 research assistantships with tuition reimbursements available (averaging $15,272 per year), 43 teaching assistantships with tuition reimbursements available (averaging $16,267 per year); unspecified assistantships also available. *Faculty research:* Biophysics and biomedical physics, atomic molecular and optical physics, solid state and materials physics, physics education. *Total annual research expenditures:* $2.8 million. *Unit head:* Dr. Pritish Mukherjee, Director of Graduate Studies, 813-974-2871, Fax: 813-974-5813, E-mail: pritish@usf.edu. *Application contact:* Dale Johnson, Program Director, 813-974-5125, Fax: 813-974-5813, E-mail: dejohnso@usf.edu. Web site: http://physics.usf.edu/.

Peterson's Graduate Programs in the Physical Sciences, Mathematics, Agricultural Sciences, the Environment & Natural Resources 2013

facebook.com/petersonspublishing **225**

Applied Physics

The University of Texas at Austin, Graduate School, College of Natural Sciences, Department of Physics, Austin, TX 78712-1111. Offers MA, MS, PhD. *Degree requirements:* For master's, thesis; for doctorate, thesis/dissertation. *Entrance requirements:* For master's and doctorate, GRE General Test, GRE Subject Test (physics). *Application deadline:* For fall admission, 1/15 for domestic students; for spring admission, 10/1 for domestic students. Application fee: $50 ($75 for international students). Electronic applications accepted. *Financial support:* Fellowships, research assistantships, and teaching assistantships available. Financial award application deadline: 1/15. *Unit head:* Dr. Linda Reichl, Associate Dean, 512-471-7253, E-mail: reichl@physics.utexas.edu. *Application contact:* Dr. Takeshi Udagawa, Graduate Adviser, 512-471-1984, Fax: 512-471-9637, E-mail: udagawa@physics.utexas.edu. Web site: http://www.ph.utexas.edu/.

University of Washington, Graduate School, College of Arts and Sciences, Department of Physics, Seattle, WA 98195. Offers MS, PhD. Part-time and evening/weekend programs available. Terminal master's awarded for partial completion of doctoral program. *Degree requirements:* For doctorate, thesis/dissertation. *Entrance requirements:* For master's, GRE; for doctorate, GRE General Test, GRE Subject Test. Additional exam requirements/recommendations for international students: Required—TOEFL. Electronic applications accepted. *Faculty research:* Astro-, atomic, condensed-matter, nuclear, and particle physics; physics education.

Virginia Commonwealth University, Graduate School, College of Humanities and Sciences, Department of Physics, Program in Physics and Applied Physics, Richmond, VA 23284-9005. Offers MS. *Students:* 15 full-time (5 women); includes 1 minority (Hispanic/Latino), 3 international. 13 applicants, 77% accepted, 8 enrolled. In 2011, 5 master's awarded. *Entrance requirements:* For master's, GRE. Additional exam requirements/recommendations for international students: Required—TOEFL (minimum score 600 paper-based; 250 computer-based; 100 iBT); Recommended—IELTS (minimum score 6.5). *Application deadline:* For fall admission, 8/1 for domestic students; for spring admission, 12/1 for domestic

students. Applications are processed on a rolling basis. Application fee: $50. Electronic applications accepted. *Expenses:* Tuition, state resident: full-time $9133; part-time $507 per credit. Tuition, nonresident: full-time $18,777; part-time $1043 per credit. *Required fees:* $77 per credit. Tuition and fees vary according to degree level, campus/location, program and student level. *Financial support:* Federal Work-Study and institutionally sponsored loans available. Support available to part-time students. *Faculty research:* Theoretical and experimental condensed matter physics, general relativity and cosmology, physics education. *Unit head:* Dr. Alison A. Baski, Chair, 804-828-1821, Fax: 804-828-7073, E-mail: aabaski@vcu.edu. *Application contact:* Dr. Shiv N. Khanna, Graduate Program Director, 804-828-1820, Fax: 804-828-7073, E-mail: snkhanna@vcu.edu.

West Virginia University, Eberly College of Arts and Sciences, Department of Physics, Morgantown, WV 26506. Offers applied physics (MS, PhD); astrophysics (MS, PhD); chemical physics (MS, PhD); condensed matter physics (MS, PhD); elementary particle physics (MS, PhD); materials physics (MS, PhD); plasma physics (MS, PhD); solid state physics (MS, PhD); statistical physics (MS, PhD); theoretical physics (MS, PhD). Terminal master's awarded for partial completion of doctoral program. *Degree requirements:* For master's, thesis or alternative, qualifying exam; for doctorate, thesis/dissertation, qualifying exam. *Entrance requirements:* For master's and doctorate, GRE General Test, minimum GPA of 3.0. Additional exam requirements/recommendations for international students: Required—TOEFL. *Faculty research:* Experimental and theoretical condensed-matter, plasma, high-energy theory, nonlinear dynamics, space physics.

Yale University, Graduate School of Arts and Sciences, School of Engineering and Applied Science, Department of Applied Physics, New Haven, CT 06520. Offers MS, PhD. Terminal master's awarded for partial completion of doctoral program. *Degree requirements:* For doctorate, thesis/dissertation, area exam. *Entrance requirements:* For master's and doctorate, GRE General Test. Additional exam requirements/recommendations for international students: Required—TOEFL. *Faculty research:* Condensed-matter physics, optical physics, materials science.

Chemical Physics

Columbia University, Graduate School of Arts and Sciences, Division of Natural Sciences, Department of Chemistry, Program in Chemical Physics, New York, NY 10027. Offers M Phil, PhD. *Entrance requirements:* For master's, GRE General Test, GRE Subject Test. Additional exam requirements/recommendations for international students: Required—TOEFL.

Cornell University, Graduate School, Graduate Fields of Arts and Sciences, Field of Chemistry and Chemical Biology, Ithaca, NY 14853-0001. Offers analytical chemistry (PhD); bio-organic chemistry (PhD); biophysical chemistry (PhD); chemical biology (PhD); chemical physics (PhD); inorganic chemistry (PhD); materials chemistry (PhD); organic chemistry (PhD); organometallic chemistry (PhD); physical chemistry (PhD); polymer chemistry (PhD); theoretical chemistry (PhD). *Faculty:* 46 full-time (3 women). *Students:* 151 full-time (67 women); includes 16 minority (13 Asian, non-Hispanic/Latino; 2 Hispanic/Latino; 1 Two or more races, non-Hispanic/Latino; 48 international. Average age 25. 297 applicants, 35% accepted, 29 enrolled. In 2011, 22 doctorates awarded. *Degree requirements:* For doctorate, comprehensive exam, thesis/dissertation. *Entrance requirements:* For doctorate, GRE General Test, GRE Subject Test (chemistry), 3 letters of recommendation. Additional exam requirements/recommendations for international students: Required—TOEFL (minimum score 600 paper-based; 250 computer-based; 77 iBT). *Application deadline:* For fall admission, 1/10 for domestic students. Application fee: $95. Electronic applications accepted. *Financial support:* In 2011–12, 21 fellowships with full tuition reimbursements, 63 research assistantships with full tuition reimbursements, 59 teaching assistantships with full tuition reimbursements were awarded; institutionally sponsored loans, scholarships/grants, health care benefits, tuition waivers (full and partial), and unspecified assistantships also available. Financial award applicants required to submit FAFSA. *Faculty research:* Analytical, organic, inorganic, physical, materials, chemical biology. *Unit head:* Director of Graduate Studies, 607-255-4139, Fax: 607-255-4137. *Application contact:* Graduate Field Assistant, 607-255-4139, Fax: 607-255-4137, E-mail: chemgrad@cornell.edu. Web site: http://www.gradschool.cornell.edu/fields.php?id-26&a-2.

Harvard University, Graduate School of Arts and Sciences, Committee on Chemical Physics, Cambridge, MA 02138. Offers PhD. *Degree requirements:* For doctorate, one foreign language, thesis/dissertation, cumulative exams. *Entrance requirements:* For doctorate, GRE General Test, GRE Subject Test. Additional exam requirements/recommendations for international students: Required—TOEFL. *Expenses:* Tuition: Full-time $36,304. *Required fees:* $1186. Full-time tuition and fees vary according to program.

Kent State University, College of Arts and Sciences, Chemical Physics Interdisciplinary Program, Kent, OH 44242-0001. Offers MS, PhD. Offered in cooperation with the Departments of Chemistry, Mathematics and Computer Science, and Physics and the Liquid Crystal Institute. Terminal master's awarded

for partial completion of doctoral program. *Degree requirements:* For master's, thesis; for doctorate, thesis/dissertation, candidacy exam. *Entrance requirements:* For master's and doctorate, GRE. Additional exam requirements/recommendations for international students: Required—TOEFL (minimum score 525 paper-based; 197 computer-based). Electronic applications accepted. *Expenses:* Tuition, state resident: full-time $8136; part-time $452 per credit hour. Tuition, nonresident: full-time $14,292; part-time $794 per credit hour.

Marquette University, Graduate School, College of Arts and Sciences, Department of Chemistry, Milwaukee, WI 53201-1881. Offers analytical chemistry (MS, PhD); bioanalytical chemistry (MS, PhD); biophysical chemistry (MS, PhD); chemical physics (MS, PhD); inorganic chemistry (MS, PhD); organic chemistry (MS, PhD); physical chemistry (MS, PhD). Part-time programs available. *Faculty:* 29 full-time (4 women), 1 (woman) part-time/adjunct. *Students:* 42 full-time (11 women), 2 part-time (0 women); includes 5 minority (2 Black or African American, non-Hispanic/Latino; 3 Asian, non-Hispanic/Latino), 31 international. Average age 29. 18 applicants, 100% accepted, 10 enrolled. In 2011, 5 master's, 7 doctorates awarded. Terminal master's awarded for partial completion of doctoral program. *Degree requirements:* For master's, comprehensive exam; for doctorate, thesis/dissertation, cumulative exams. *Entrance requirements:* For master's and doctorate, official transcripts from all current and previous colleges/universities except Marquette, three letters of recommendation from individuals familiar with the applicant's academic work. Additional exam requirements/recommendations for international students: Required—TOEFL (minimum score 530 paper-based; 78 computer-based). *Application deadline:* Applications are processed on a rolling basis. Application fee: $50. Electronic applications accepted. *Expenses: Tuition:* Full-time $17,010; part-time $945 per credit hour. Tuition and fees vary according to program. *Financial support:* In 2011–12, 41 students received support, including 2 fellowships (averaging $17,134 per year), 30 teaching assistantships with full tuition reimbursements available (averaging $20,295 per year); research assistantships, scholarships/grants, health care benefits, tuition waivers (full and partial), and unspecified assistantships also available. Support available to part-time students. Financial award application deadline: 2/15. *Faculty research:* Inorganic complexes, laser Raman spectroscopy, organic synthesis, synthetic bioinorganic chemistry, electro-active organic molecules. *Total annual research expenditures:* $2.1 million. *Unit head:* Dr. Michael Ryan, Chair, 414-288-3537, Fax: 414-288-7066. *Application contact:* Dr. Mark Steinmetz, Director of Graduate Studies, 414-288-7374, Fax: 414-288-7066. Web site: http://www.marquette.edu/chem/graduate.shtml.

McMaster University, School of Graduate Studies, Faculty of Science, Department of Chemistry, Hamilton, ON L8S 4M2, Canada. Offers analytical chemistry (M Sc, PhD); chemical physics (M Sc, PhD); chemistry (M Sc, PhD); inorganic chemistry (M Sc, PhD); organic chemistry (M Sc, PhD); physical chemistry (M Sc, PhD); polymer chemistry (M Sc, PhD). Part-time programs

226 facebook.com/petersonspublishing

Peterson's Graduate Programs in the Physical Sciences, Mathematics, Agricultural Sciences, the Environment & Natural Resources 2013

available. Terminal master's awarded for partial completion of doctoral program. *Degree requirements:* For master's, thesis; for doctorate, comprehensive exam, thesis/dissertation. *Entrance requirements:* For master's, minimum B+ average. Additional exam requirements/recommendations for international students: Required—TOEFL (minimum score 550 paper-based; 213 computer-based).

Michigan State University, The Graduate School, College of Natural Science, Department of Chemistry, East Lansing, MI 48824. Offers chemical physics (PhD); chemistry (MS, PhD); chemistry-environmental toxicology (PhD); computational chemistry (MS). *Entrance requirements:* Additional exam requirements/recommendations for international students: Required—TOEFL. Electronic applications accepted. *Faculty research:* Analytical chemistry, inorganic and organic chemistry, nuclear chemistry, physical chemistry, theoretical and computational chemistry.

The Ohio State University, Graduate School, College of Arts and Sciences, Division of Natural and Mathematical Sciences, Program in Chemical Physics, Columbus, OH 43210. Offers MS, PhD. *Faculty:* 32. *Students:* 3 full-time (1 woman), 5 part-time (1 woman), 3 international. Average age 24. In 2011, 1 master's, 4 doctorates awarded. *Degree requirements:* For master's, thesis optional; for doctorate, thesis/dissertation. *Entrance requirements:* For master's and doctorate, GRE General Test, GRE Subject Test (chemistry or physics). Additional exam requirements/recommendations for international students: Required—Michigan English Language Assessment Battery (minimum score 82); Recommended—TOEFL (minimum score 600 paper-based; 250 computer-based; 79 iBT). *Application deadline:* For fall admission, 8/15 priority date for domestic students, 7/1 for international students; for winter admission, 12/1 priority date for domestic students, 11/1 for international students; for spring admission, 3/1 priority date for domestic students, 2/1 for international students. Applications are processed on a rolling basis. Application fee: $40 ($50 for international students). Electronic applications accepted. *Expenses:* Tuition, state resident: full-time $11,400. Tuition, nonresident: full-time $28,125. Tuition and fees vary according to course load, degree level, campus/location and program. *Financial support:* Fellowships, research assistantships, teaching assistantships, Federal Work-Study, and institutionally sponsored loans available. Support available to part-time students. *Unit head:* Dr. Terry A. Miller, Chair, 614-292-2569, Fax: 614-292-1948, E-mail: miller.104@osu.edu. *Application contact:* Becky Gregory, Program Assistant, 614-292-5195, Fax: 614-292-1948, E-mail: gregory.10@osu.edu. Web site: http://chemphys.chemistry.ohio-state.edu/chemphys/.

Simon Fraser University, Graduate Studies, Faculty of Science, Department of Chemistry, Burnaby, BC V5A 1S6, Canada. Offers chemical physics (PhD); chemistry (PhD). *Degree requirements:* For master's, thesis; for doctorate, thesis/dissertation. *Entrance requirements:* For master's, minimum GPA of 3.0. Additional exam requirements/recommendations for international students: Required—TOEFL (minimum score 600 paper-based; 250 computer-based; 100 iBT). Electronic applications accepted. *Faculty research:* Organic chemistry, nuclear chemistry, physical chemistry, inorganic chemistry, theoretical chemistry.

Simon Fraser University, Graduate Studies, Faculty of Science, Department of Physics, Burnaby, BC V5A 1S6, Canada. Offers biophysics (M Sc, PhD); chemical physics (M Sc, PhD); physics (M Sc, PhD). *Degree requirements:* For master's, thesis; for doctorate, thesis/dissertation. *Entrance requirements:* For master's, minimum GPA of 3.0; for doctorate, minimum GPA of 3.5. Additional exam requirements/recommendations for international students: Required—TOEFL or IELTS. *Faculty research:* Solid-state physics, magnetism, energy research, superconductivity, nuclear physics.

University of Colorado Boulder, Graduate School, College of Arts and Sciences, Department of Physics, Boulder, CO 80309. Offers chemical physics (PhD); geophysics (PhD); liquid crystal science and technology (PhD); mathematical physics (PhD); medical physics (PhD); optical sciences and engineering (PhD); physics (MS, PhD). *Faculty:* 51 full-time (7 women). *Students:* 157 full-time (28 women), 66 part-time (11 women); includes 11 minority (6 Asian, non-Hispanic/Latino; 5 Hispanic/Latino), 75 international. Average age 26. 551 applicants, 25% accepted, 47 enrolled. In 2011, 29 master's, 28 doctorates awarded. Terminal master's awarded for partial completion of doctoral program. *Degree requirements:* For master's, comprehensive exam, thesis or alternative; for doctorate, comprehensive exam, thesis/dissertation. *Entrance requirements:* For master's and doctorate, GRE General Test, GRE Subject Test, minimum undergraduate GPA of 3.0. Additional exam requirements/recommendations for international students: Required—TOEFL. *Application deadline:* For fall admission, 1/15 priority date for domestic students, 1/15 for international students. Applications are processed on a rolling basis. Application fee: $50 ($60 for international students). Electronic applications accepted. *Financial support:* In 2011–12, 216 students received support, including 85 fellowships (averaging $9,233 per year), 131 research assistantships with full and partial tuition reimbursements available (averaging $24,425 per year), 31 teaching assistantships with full and partial tuition reimbursements available (averaging $20,162 per year); institutionally sponsored loans, scholarships/grants, health care benefits, and unspecified assistantships also available. Financial award application deadline: 1/15; financial award applicants required to submit FAFSA. *Faculty research:* Atomic and molecular physics, nuclear physics, condensed matter, elementary particle physics, laser or optical physics, plasma physics, geophysics, OSEP, astrophysics and chemical physics. *Total annual research expenditures:* $26.1 million. *Application contact:* E-mail: physics@colorado.edu. Web site: http://physics.colorado.edu/.

University of Illinois at Urbana–Champaign, Graduate College, College of Liberal Arts and Sciences, School of Chemical Sciences, Department of Chemistry, Champaign, IL 61820. Offers astrochemistry (PhD); chemical physics (PhD); chemistry (MA, MS, PhD); teaching of chemistry (MS); MS/JD; MS/MBA. *Faculty:* 29 full-time (5 women), 1 part-time/adjunct (0 women). *Students:* 279 full-time (95 women), 5 part-time (1 woman); includes 39 minority (4 Black or African American, non-Hispanic/Latino; 1 American Indian or Alaska Native, non-Hispanic/Latino; 19 Asian, non-Hispanic/Latino; 7 Hispanic/Latino; 8 Two or more races, non-Hispanic/Latino), 73 international. 476 applicants, 15% accepted, 71 enrolled. In 2011, 14 master's, 56 doctorates awarded. *Entrance requirements:* For master's and doctorate, GRE General Test, GRE Subject Test, minimum GPA of 3.0. Additional exam requirements/recommendations for international students: Required—TOEFL (minimum score 580 paper-based; 237 computer-based). *Application deadline:* Applications are processed on a rolling basis. Application fee: $75 ($90 for international students). Electronic applications accepted. *Financial support:* In 2011–12, 114 fellowships, 162 research assistantships, 167 teaching assistantships were awarded; tuition waivers (full and partial) also available. *Unit head:* Steven C. Zimmerman, Head, 217-333-6655, Fax: 217-244-5943, E-mail: sczimmer@illinois.edu. *Application contact:* Krista Smith, Program Coordinator, 217-244-4844, Fax: 217-244-5943, E-mail: kristasm@illinois.edu. Web site: http://chemistry.illinois.edu/.

University of Louisville, Graduate School, College of Arts and Sciences, Department of Chemistry, Louisville, KY 40292-0001. Offers analytical chemistry (MS, PhD); biochemistry (MS, PhD); chemical physics (PhD); inorganic chemistry (MS, PhD); organic chemistry (MS, PhD); physical chemistry (MS, PhD). Terminal master's awarded for partial completion of doctoral program. *Degree requirements:* For master's, variable foreign language requirement, comprehensive exam, thesis optional; for doctorate, variable foreign language requirement, comprehensive exam, thesis/dissertation. *Entrance requirements:* For master's and doctorate, BA or BS coursework. Additional exam requirements/recommendations for international students: Required—TOEFL. Electronic applications accepted. *Expenses:* Tuition, state resident: full-time $9692; part-time $539 per credit hour. Tuition, nonresident: full-time $20,168; part-time $1121 per credit hour. Tuition and fees vary according to program and reciprocity agreements. *Faculty research:* Computational chemistry, biophysics nuclear magnetic resonance, synthetic organic chemistry, synthetic inorganic chemistry, medicinal chemistry, protein chemistry, enzymology, nanochemistry, electrochemistry, analytical chemistry, synthetic biology, bioinformatics.

University of Maryland, College Park, Academic Affairs, College of Computer, Mathematical and Natural Sciences, Institute for Physical Science and Technology, Program in Chemical Physics, College Park, MD 20742. Offers MS, PhD. Part-time and evening/weekend programs available. *Students:* 34 full-time (10 women), 1 part-time (0 women); includes 2 minority (both Hispanic/Latino), 16 international. 36 applicants, 33% accepted, 6 enrolled. In 2011, 1 master's, 5 doctorates awarded. Terminal master's awarded for partial completion of doctoral program. *Degree requirements:* For master's, thesis optional, paper, qualifying exam; for doctorate, thesis/dissertation, seminars. *Entrance requirements:* For master's, GRE General Test, GRE Subject Test (chemistry, math or physics), minimum GPA of 3.3, 3 letters of recommendation; for doctorate, GRE Subject Test (chemistry, math, or physics), GRE General Test, minimum GPA of 3.3, 3 letters of recommendation. *Application deadline:* For fall admission, 2/1 for domestic and international students; for spring admission, 6/1 for domestic and international students. Applications are processed on a rolling basis. Application fee: $75. Electronic applications accepted. *Expenses: Tuition, area resident:* Part-time $525 per credit hour. Tuition, state resident: part-time $525 per credit hour. Tuition, nonresident: part-time $1131 per credit hour. *Required fees:* $386.31 per term. Tuition and fees vary according to program. *Financial support:* In 2011–12, 3 fellowships with full and partial tuition reimbursements (averaging $21,289 per year), 25 research assistantships (averaging $20,123 per year), 7 teaching assistantships (averaging $19,581 per year) were awarded; Federal Work-Study and scholarships/grants also available. Financial award applicants required to submit FAFSA. *Faculty research:* Discrete molecules and gases; dynamic phenomena; thermodynamics, statistical mechanical theory and quantum mechanical theory; atmospheric physics; biophysics. *Unit head:* Dr. Michael A. Coplan, Director, 301-405-4858, Fax: 301-314-9396, E-mail: coplan@umd.edu. *Application contact:* Dr. Charles A. Caramello, Dean of Graduate School, 301-405-0358, Fax: 301-314-9305.

University of Nevada, Reno, Graduate School, Interdisciplinary Program in Chemical Physics, Reno, NV 89557. Offers PhD. *Degree requirements:* For doctorate, thesis/dissertation. *Entrance requirements:* For doctorate, GRE, minimum GPA of 3.0. Additional exam requirements/recommendations for international students: Required—TOEFL (minimum score 500 paper-based; 173 computer-based; 61 iBT). Electronic applications accepted. *Faculty research:* Atomic and molecular physics, physical chemistry.

The University of Tennessee, Graduate School, College of Arts and Sciences, Department of Chemistry, Knoxville, TN 37996. Offers analytical chemistry (MS, PhD); chemical physics (PhD); environmental chemistry (MS, PhD); inorganic chemistry (MS, PhD); organic chemistry (MS, PhD); physical chemistry (MS, PhD); polymer chemistry (MS, PhD); theoretical chemistry (PhD). Part-time

Peterson's Graduate Programs in the Physical Sciences, Mathematics, Agricultural Sciences, the Environment & Natural Resources 2013

facebook.com/petersonspublishing **227**

Chemical Physics

programs available. Terminal master's awarded for partial completion of doctoral program. *Degree requirements:* For master's, thesis; for doctorate, thesis/dissertation. *Entrance requirements:* For master's and doctorate, GRE General Test, minimum GPA of 2.7. Additional exam requirements/recommendations for international students: Required—TOEFL. Electronic applications accepted. *Expenses:* Tuition, state resident: full-time $8332; part-time $464 per credit hour. Tuition, nonresident: full-time $25,174; part-time $1400 per credit hour. *Required fees:* $1162; $56 per credit hour. Tuition and fees vary according to program.

University of Utah, Graduate School, College of Science, Department of Chemistry, Salt Lake City, UT 84112-0850. Offers chemical physics (PhD); chemistry (M Phil, MA, MS, PhD); science teacher education (MS). Part-time programs available. Postbaccalaureate distance learning degree programs offered. *Faculty:* 35 full-time (7 women). *Students:* 144 full-time (43 women), 40 part-time (15 women); includes 6 minority (1 Black or African American, non-Hispanic/Latino; 3 Asian, non-Hispanic/Latino; 1 Hispanic/Latino; 1 Two or more races, non-Hispanic/Latino), 54 international. Average age 28. 311 applicants, 28% accepted, 35 enrolled. In 2011, 10 master's, 21 doctorates awarded. Terminal master's awarded for partial completion of doctoral program. *Median time to degree:* Of those who began their doctoral program in fall 2003, 100% received their degree in 8 years or less. *Degree requirements:* For master's, thesis optional, 20 hours course work, 10 hours research; for doctorate, thesis/dissertation, 18 hours course work, 14 hours research. *Entrance requirements:* For master's and doctorate, GRE General Test, minimum GPA of 3.0. Additional exam requirements/recommendations for international students: Required—TOEFL (minimum score 620 paper-based; 260 computer-based; 105 iBT). *Application deadline:* For fall admission, 4/1 for domestic students, 2/1 for international students; for spring admission, 11/1 for domestic and international students. Application fee: $55 ($65 for international students). Electronic applications accepted. *Financial support:* In 2011–12, 1 fellowship with tuition reimbursement (averaging $22,000 per year), 128 research assistantships with tuition reimbursements (averaging $22,500 per year), 55 teaching assistantships with tuition reimbursements (averaging $22,000 per year) were awarded; scholarships/grants and tuition waivers (full) also available. Financial award application deadline: 4/1; financial award applicants required to submit FAFSA. *Faculty research:* Biological, theoretical, inorganic, organic, and physical-analytical chemistry. *Total annual research expenditures:* $13.3 million. *Unit head:* Dr. Henry S. White, Chair, 801-585-6256, Fax: 801-581-8433, E-mail: chair@chemistry.utah.edu. *Application contact:* Jo Hoovey, Graduate Coordinator, 801-581-4393, Fax: 801-581-5408, E-mail: jhoovey@chem.utah.edu. Web site: http://www.chem.utah.edu/.

University of Utah, Graduate School, College of Science, Department of Physics and Astronomy, Salt Lake City, UT 84112. Offers chemical physics (PhD); medical physics (MS, PhD); physics (MA, MS, PhD); physics teaching (MS). Part-time programs available. *Faculty:* 38 full-time (3 women), 1 part-time/adjunct (0 women). *Students:* 77 full-time (22 women), 17 part-time (4 women); includes 3 minority (1 Asian, non-Hispanic/Latino; 2 Hispanic/Latino), 50 international. Average age 29. 68 applicants, 72% accepted, 24 enrolled. In 2011, 7 master's, 9 doctorates awarded. Terminal master's awarded for partial completion of doctoral program. *Median time to degree:* Of those who began their doctoral program in fall 2003, 44% received their degree in 8 years or less. *Degree requirements:* For master's, comprehensive exam (for some programs), thesis or alternative, teaching experience, departmental exam; for doctorate, comprehensive exam, thesis/dissertation, departmental qualifying exam. *Entrance requirements:* For master's and doctorate, GRE General Test, GRE Subject Test, minimum GPA of 3.0. Additional exam requirements/recommendations for international students: Required—TOEFL (minimum score 500 paper-based; 173 computer-based; 69 iBT). *Application deadline:* For fall admission, 4/1 priority date for domestic students, 4/1 for international students. Applications are processed on a rolling basis. Application fee: $55 ($65 for international students). Electronic applications accepted. *Financial support:* In 2011–12, 61 teaching assistantships with full and partial tuition reimbursements (averaging $14,626 per year) were awarded; Federal Work-Study, institutionally sponsored loans, and scholarships/grants also available. Financial award application deadline: 2/15; financial award applicants required to submit FAFSA. *Faculty research:* High-energy, cosmic-ray, astrophysics, medical physics, condensed matter, relativity applied physics, biophysics, astronomy. *Total annual research expenditures:* $6.8 million. *Unit head:* Dr. David Kieda, Chair, 801-581-6901, Fax: 801-581-4801, E-mail: kieda@physics.utah.edu. *Application contact:* Jackie Hadley, Graduate Secretary, 801-581-6861, Fax: 801-581-4801, E-mail: jackie@physics.utah.edu. Web site: http://www.physics.utah.edu/.

University of Utah, Graduate School, College of Science, Interdepartmental Program in Chemical Physics, Salt Lake City, UT 84112-1107. Offers PhD. *Students:* 1 applicant, 100% accepted, 0 enrolled. *Degree requirements:* For doctorate, comprehensive exam, thesis/dissertation. *Entrance requirements:* For doctorate, GRE General Test, GRE Subject Test (physics), minimum undergraduate GPA of 3.0. Additional exam requirements/recommendations for international students: Required—TOEFL (minimum score 500 paper-based; 173 computer-based). *Application deadline:* For fall admission, 4/1 for domestic and international students; for spring admission, 11/1 for domestic and international students. Application fee: $55 ($65 for international students). *Financial support:* Applicants required to submit FAFSA. *Unit head:* Dr. Charles A. Wight, Coordinator of Medical Physics, 801-581-8796, E-mail: wight@chemistry.utah.edu. *Application contact:* Information Contact, 801-581-6958, E-mail: office@science.utah.edu. Web site: http://www.science.utah.edu/.

Virginia Commonwealth University, Graduate School, College of Humanities and Sciences, Department of Chemistry, Richmond, VA 23284-9005. Offers analytical chemistry (MS, PhD); chemical physics (PhD); inorganic chemistry (MS, PhD); organic chemistry (MS, PhD); physical chemistry (MS, PhD). Part-time programs available. *Students:* 49 full-time (20 women), 19 part-time (8 women); includes 10 minority (3 Black or African American, non-Hispanic/Latino; 5 Asian, non-Hispanic/Latino; 1 Hispanic/Latino; 1 Two or more races, non-Hispanic/Latino), 26 international. 56 applicants, 41% accepted, 11 enrolled. In 2011, 3 master's, 8 doctorates awarded. Terminal master's awarded for partial completion of doctoral program. *Degree requirements:* For master's, thesis; for doctorate, thesis/dissertation, comprehensive cumulative exams, research proposal. *Entrance requirements:* For master's, GRE General Test, 30 undergraduate credits in chemistry; for doctorate, GRE General Test. Additional exam requirements/recommendations for international students: Required—TOEFL (minimum score 600 paper-based; 250 computer-based; 100 iBT) or IELTS (minimum score 6.5). *Application deadline:* For fall admission, 3/15 for domestic students; for spring admission, 11/15 for domestic students. Applications are processed on a rolling basis. Application fee: $50. Electronic applications accepted. *Expenses:* Tuition, state resident: full-time $9133; part-time $507 per credit. Tuition, nonresident: full-time $18,777; part-time $1043 per credit. *Required fees:* $77 per credit. Tuition and fees vary according to degree level, campus/location, program and student level. *Financial support:* Fellowships, research assistantships, teaching assistantships, career-related internships or fieldwork, and institutionally sponsored loans available. Support available to part-time students. Financial award application deadline: 7/1; financial award applicants required to submit FAFSA. *Faculty research:* Physical, organic, inorganic, analytical, and polymer chemistry; chemical physics. *Unit head:* Dr. Scott Gronert, Chair, 804-828-1298, Fax: 804-828-8599, E-mail: sgronert@vcu.edu. *Application contact:* Dr. Maryanne M. Collinson, Chair, Graduate Recruiting and Admissions Committee, 804-828-7509, E-mail: mselshal@vcu.edu. Web site: http://www.has.vcu.edu/che/.

Wesleyan University, Graduate Programs, Department of Chemistry and Department of Physics, Program in Chemical Physics, Middletown, CT 06459. Offers MA, PhD. Terminal master's awarded for partial completion of doctoral program. *Degree requirements:* For master's, one foreign language, thesis; for doctorate, one foreign language, thesis/dissertation. *Entrance requirements:* For master's, GRE General Test, GRE Subject Test; for doctorate, GRE Subject Test, BA or BS in chemistry or physics. Additional exam requirements/recommendations for international students: Required—TOEFL. Electronic applications accepted. *Faculty research:* Spectroscopy, photochemistry, reactive collisions, surface physics, quantum theory.

West Virginia University, Eberly College of Arts and Sciences, Department of Physics, Morgantown, WV 26506. Offers applied physics (MS, PhD); astrophysics (MS, PhD); chemical physics (MS, PhD); condensed matter physics (MS, PhD); elementary particle physics (MS, PhD); materials physics (MS, PhD); plasma physics (MS, PhD); solid state physics (MS, PhD); statistical physics (MS, PhD); theoretical physics (MS, PhD). Terminal master's awarded for partial completion of doctoral program. *Degree requirements:* For master's, thesis or alternative, qualifying exam; for doctorate, thesis/dissertation, qualifying exam. *Entrance requirements:* For master's and doctorate, GRE General Test, minimum GPA of 3.0. Additional exam requirements/recommendations for international students: Required—TOEFL. *Faculty research:* Experimental and theoretical condensed-matter, plasma, high-energy theory, nonlinear dynamics, space physics.

Condensed Matter Physics

Cleveland State University, College of Graduate Studies, College of Sciences and Health Professions, Department of Physics, Cleveland, OH 44115. Offers applied optics (MS); condensed matter physics (MS); medical physics (MS); optics and materials (MS); optics and medical imaging (MS). Part-time and evening/weekend programs available. *Faculty:* 4 full-time (0 women), 1 part-time/

adjunct (0 women). *Students:* 2 full-time (0 women), 12 part-time (3 women), 1 international. Average age 36. 29 applicants, 55% accepted, 7 enrolled. In 2011, 7 master's awarded. *Entrance requirements:* For master's, undergraduate degree in engineering, physics, chemistry or mathematics. Additional exam requirements/recommendations for international students: Required—TOEFL (minimum score

228 facebook.com/petersonspublishing

Peterson's Graduate Programs in the Physical Sciences, Mathematics, Agricultural Sciences, the Environment & Natural Resources 2013

525 paper-based; 197 computer-based). *Application deadline:* For fall admission, 7/15 priority date for domestic students, 7/15 for international students. Applications are processed on a rolling basis. Application fee: $30. Electronic applications accepted. *Expenses:* Tuition, state resident: full-time $6416; part-time $494 per credit hour. Tuition, nonresident: full-time $12,074; part-time $929 per credit hour. *Financial support:* In 2011–12, 1 research assistantship with full and partial tuition reimbursement (averaging $5,666 per year) was awarded; fellowships with tuition reimbursements, teaching assistantships, and tuition waivers (full) also available. *Faculty research:* Statistical physics, experimental solid-state physics, theoretical optics, experimental biological physics (macromolecular crystallography), experimental optics. *Total annual research expenditures:* $350,000. *Unit head:* Dr. Miron Kaufman, Chairperson, 216-687-2436, Fax: 216-523-7268, E-mail: m.kaufman@csuohio.edu. *Application contact:* Dr. James A. Lock, Director, 216-687-2420, Fax: 216-523-7268, E-mail: j.lock@csuohio.edu. Web site: http://www.csuohio.edu/sciences/dept/physics/index.html.

Iowa State University of Science and Technology, Department of Physics and Astronomy, Ames, IA 50011-3160. Offers applied physics (MS, PhD); astrophysics (MS, PhD); condensed matter physics (MS, PhD); high energy physics (MS, PhD); nuclear physics (MS, PhD); physics (MS, PhD). *Degree requirements:* For master's, thesis (for some programs); for doctorate, thesis/dissertation. *Entrance requirements:* For master's and doctorate, GRE General Test, GRE Subject Test (physics). Additional exam requirements/recommendations for international students: Required—TOEFL (minimum score 550 paper-based; 79 iBT), IELTS (minimum score 6.5). *Application deadline:* For fall admission, 2/15 priority date for domestic students, 2/15 for international students; for spring admission, 10/15 for domestic and international students. Applications are processed on a rolling basis. Application fee: $40 ($90 for international students). Electronic applications accepted. *Financial support:* Application deadline: 2/15. *Faculty research:* Condensed-matter physics, including superconductivity and new materials; high-energy and nuclear physics; astronomy and astrophysics; atmospheric and environmental physics. *Total annual research expenditures:* $8.8 million. *Unit head:* Dr. Steve Kawaler, Director of Graduate Education, 515-294-5870, Fax: 515-294-6027, E-mail: physastro@iastate.edu. *Application contact:* Lori Hockett, Application Contact, 515-294-5870, E-mail: phys_astro@iastate.edu. Web site: http://www.physics.iastate.edu/.

Iowa State University of Science and Technology, Program in Condensed Matter Physics, Ames, IA 50011-3160. Offers MS, PhD. *Entrance requirements:* For master's and doctorate, GRE. Additional exam requirements/recommendations for international students: Required—TOEFL (minimum score 550 paper-based; 79 iBT), IELTS (minimum score 6.5). *Application deadline:* For fall admission, 2/15 for domestic and international students; for spring admission, 10/15 for domestic and international students. Electronic applications accepted. *Unit head:* Dr. Steven Kawaler, Director of Graduate Education, 515-294-5870, Fax: 515-294-6027, E-mail: physastro@iastate.edu. *Application contact:* Lori Hockett, Information Contact, 515-294-5870, Fax: 515-294-6027, E-mail: physastro@iastate.edu. Web site: http://www.physastro.iastate.edu.

Memorial University of Newfoundland, School of Graduate Studies, Department of Physics and Physical Oceanography, St. John's, NL A1C 5S7, Canada. Offers atomic and molecular physics (M Sc, PhD); condensed matter physics (M Sc, PhD); physical oceanography (M Sc, PhD); physics (M Sc). Part-time programs available. *Degree requirements:* For master's, thesis, seminar presentation on thesis topic; for doctorate, comprehensive exam, thesis/dissertation, oral defense of thesis. *Entrance requirements:* For master's, honors B Sc or equivalent; for doctorate, M Sc or equivalent. Electronic applications accepted. *Faculty research:* Experiment and theory in atomic and molecular

physics, condensed matter physics, physical oceanography, theoretical geophysics and applied nuclear physics.

Rutgers, The State University of New Jersey, New Brunswick, Graduate School-New Brunswick, Department of Physics and Astronomy, Piscataway, NJ 08854-8097. Offers astronomy (MS, PhD); biophysics (PhD); condensed matter physics (MS, PhD); elementary particle physics (MS, PhD); intermediate energy nuclear physics (MS); nuclear physics (MS, PhD); physics (MST); surface science (PhD); theoretical physics (MS, PhD). Part-time programs available. Terminal master's awarded for partial completion of doctoral program. *Degree requirements:* For master's, comprehensive exam, thesis or alternative; for doctorate, comprehensive exam, thesis/dissertation. *Entrance requirements:* For master's and doctorate, GRE General Test, GRE Subject Test. Additional exam requirements/recommendations for international students: Required—TOEFL (minimum score 560 paper-based). Electronic applications accepted. *Faculty research:* Astronomy, high energy, condensed matter, surface, nuclear physics.

University of Alberta, Faculty of Graduate Studies and Research, Department of Physics, Edmonton, AB T6G 2E1, Canada. Offers astrophysics (M Sc, PhD); condensed matter (M Sc, PhD); geophysics (M Sc, PhD); medical physics (M Sc, PhD); subatomic physics (M Sc, PhD). *Degree requirements:* For master's, thesis; for doctorate, thesis/dissertation. *Entrance requirements:* For master's and doctorate, minimum GPA of 7.0 on a 9.0 scale. Additional exam requirements/recommendations for international students: Required—TOEFL. *Faculty research:* Cosmology, astroparticle physics, high-intermediate energy, magnetism, superconductivity.

The University of Manchester, School of Physics and Astronomy, Manchester, United Kingdom. Offers astronomy and astrophysics (M Sc, PhD); biological physics (M Sc, PhD); condensed matter physics (M Sc, PhD); nonlinear and liquid crystals physics (M Sc, PhD); nuclear physics (M Sc, PhD); particle physics (M Sc, PhD); photon physics (M Sc, PhD); physics (M Sc, PhD); theoretical physics (M Sc, PhD).

University of Victoria, Faculty of Graduate Studies, Faculty of Science, Department of Physics and Astronomy, Victoria, BC V8W 2Y2, Canada. Offers astronomy and astrophysics (M Sc, PhD); condensed matter physics (M Sc, PhD); experimental particle physics (M Sc, PhD); medical physics (M Sc, PhD); ocean physics (M Sc, PhD); theoretical physics (M Sc, PhD). *Degree requirements:* For master's, thesis; for doctorate, comprehensive exam, thesis/dissertation, candidacy exam. *Entrance requirements:* For master's and doctorate, GRE. Additional exam requirements/recommendations for international students: Required—TOEFL (minimum score 575 paper-based; 233 computer-based), IELTS (minimum score 7). Electronic applications accepted. *Faculty research:* Old stellar populations; observational cosmology and large scale structure; cp violation; atlas.

West Virginia University, Eberly College of Arts and Sciences, Department of Physics, Morgantown, WV 26506. Offers applied physics (MS, PhD); astrophysics (MS, PhD); chemical physics (MS, PhD); condensed matter physics (MS, PhD); elementary particle physics (MS, PhD); materials physics (MS, PhD); plasma physics (MS, PhD); solid state physics (MS, PhD); statistical physics (MS, PhD); theoretical physics (MS, PhD). Terminal master's awarded for partial completion of doctoral program. *Degree requirements:* For master's, thesis or alternative, qualifying exam; for doctorate, thesis/dissertation, qualifying exam. *Entrance requirements:* For master's and doctorate, GRE General Test, minimum GPA of 3.0. Additional exam requirements/recommendations for international students: Required—TOEFL. *Faculty research:* Experimental and theoretical condensed-matter, plasma, high-energy theory, nonlinear dynamics, space physics.

Mathematical Physics

New Mexico Institute of Mining and Technology, Graduate Studies, Department of Physics, Socorro, NM 87801. Offers astrophysics (PhD); atmospheric physics (PhD); instrumentation (MS); mathematical physics (PhD); physics (MS). *Faculty:* 14 full-time (2 women), 19 part-time/adjunct (2 women). *Students:* 30 full-time (12 women), 2 part-time (1 woman); includes 1 minority (Asian, non-Hispanic/Latino), 3 international. Average age 28. 28 applicants, 50% accepted, 5 enrolled. In 2011, 5 master's, 3 doctorates awarded. *Degree requirements:* For master's, thesis optional; for doctorate, thesis/dissertation. *Entrance requirements:* For master's, GRE General Test; for doctorate, GRE General Test, GRE Subject Test. Additional exam requirements/recommendations for international students: Required—TOEFL (minimum score 540 paper-based; 207 computer-based). *Application deadline:* For fall admission, 3/1 priority date for domestic students; for spring admission, 6/1 for domestic students. Applications are processed on a rolling basis. Application fee: $16 ($30 for international students). *Expenses:* Tuition, state resident: full-time $4849; part-time $269.41 per credit hour. Tuition, nonresident: full-time $16,041; part-time $891.15 per credit hour. *Required fees:* $622; $65 per credit hour. $20 per semester. Part-time tuition and fees vary according to course load. *Financial support:* In 2011–12, 18 research assistantships (averaging $38,918 per year),

11 teaching assistantships with full and partial tuition reimbursements (averaging $35,099 per year) were awarded; fellowships, Federal Work-Study, institutionally sponsored loans, and unspecified assistantships also available. Financial award application deadline: 3/1; financial award applicants required to submit CSS PROFILE or FAFSA. *Faculty research:* Cloud physics, stellar and extragalactic processes. *Unit head:* Dr. Kenneth Eack, Chairman, 575-835-5328, Fax: 575-835-5707, E-mail: dwestpfa@nmt.edu. *Application contact:* Dr. Lorie Liebrock, Dean of Graduate Studies, 575-835-5513, Fax: 575-835-5476, E-mail: graduate@nmt.edu. Web site: http://www.physics.nmt.edu/.

University of Alberta, Faculty of Graduate Studies and Research, Department of Mathematical and Statistical Sciences, Edmonton, AB T6G 2E1, Canada. Offers applied mathematics (M Sc, PhD); biostatistics (M Sc); mathematical finance (M Sc, PhD); mathematical physics (M Sc, PhD); mathematics (M Sc, PhD); statistics (M Sc, PhD, Postgraduate Diploma). Part-time programs available. Terminal master's awarded for partial completion of doctoral program. *Degree requirements:* For master's, thesis (for some programs); for doctorate, comprehensive exam, thesis/dissertation. *Entrance requirements:* Additional exam requirements/recommendations for international students: Required—

Peterson's Graduate Programs in the Physical Sciences, Mathematics, Agricultural Sciences, the Environment & Natural Resources 2013

facebook.com/petersonspublishing **229**

TOEFL (minimum score 580 paper-based; 237 computer-based). Electronic applications accepted. *Faculty research:* Classical and functional analysis, algebra, differential equations, geometry.

University of Colorado Boulder, Graduate School, College of Arts and Sciences, Department of Physics, Boulder, CO 80309. Offers chemical physics (PhD); geophysics (PhD); liquid crystal science and technology (PhD); mathematical physics (PhD); medical physics (PhD); optical sciences and engineering (PhD); physics (MS, PhD). *Faculty:* 51 full-time (7 women). *Students:* 157 full-time (28 women), 66 part-time (11 women); includes 11 minority (6 Asian, non-Hispanic/Latino; 5 Hispanic/Latino), 75 international. Average age 26. 551 applicants, 25% accepted, 47 enrolled. In 2011, 29 master's, 28 doctorates awarded. Terminal master's awarded for partial completion of doctoral program. *Degree requirements:* For master's, comprehensive exam, thesis or alternative; for doctorate, comprehensive exam, thesis/dissertation. *Entrance requirements:* For master's and doctorate, GRE General Test, GRE Subject Test, minimum undergraduate GPA of 3.0. Additional exam requirements/recommendations for international students: Required—TOEFL. *Application deadline:* For fall admission, 1/15 priority date for domestic students, 1/15 for international students. Applications are processed on a rolling basis. Application fee: $50 ($60 for international students). Electronic applications accepted. *Financial support:* In 2011–12, 216 students received support, including 85 fellowships (averaging $9,233 per year), 131 research assistantships with full and partial tuition reimbursements available (averaging $24,425 per year), 31 teaching assistantships with full and partial tuition reimbursements available (averaging $20,162 per year); institutionally sponsored loans, scholarships/grants, health care benefits, and unspecified assistantships also available. Financial award application deadline: 1/15; financial award applicants required to submit FAFSA. *Faculty research:* Atomic and molecular physics, nuclear physics, condensed matter, elementary particle physics, laser or optical physics, plasma physics, geophysics, OSEP, astrophysics and chemical physics. *Total annual research expenditures:* $26.1 million. *Application contact:* E-mail: physics@colorado.edu. Web site: http://physics.colorado.edu/.

Optical Sciences

Air Force Institute of Technology, Graduate School of Engineering and Management, Department of Electrical and Computer Engineering, Dayton, OH 45433-7765. Offers computer engineering (MS, PhD); computer systems/science (MS); electrical engineering (MS, PhD); electro-optics (MS, PhD). *Accreditation:* ABET (one or more programs are accredited). Part-time programs available. *Degree requirements:* For master's, thesis; for doctorate, thesis/dissertation. *Entrance requirements:* For master's and doctorate, GRE General Test, minimum GPA of 3.0, U.S. citizenship. *Faculty research:* Remote sensing, information survivability, microelectronics, computer networks, artificial intelligence.

Air Force Institute of Technology, Graduate School of Engineering and Management, Department of Engineering Physics, Dayton, OH 45433-7765. Offers applied physics (MS, PhD); electro-optics (MS, PhD); materials science (PhD); nuclear engineering (MS, PhD); space physics (MS). Part-time programs available. *Degree requirements:* For master's, thesis; for doctorate, thesis/dissertation. *Entrance requirements:* For master's and doctorate, GRE General Test, minimum GPA of 3.0, U.S. citizenship. *Faculty research:* High-energy lasers, space physics, nuclear weapon effects, semiconductor physics.

Alabama Agricultural and Mechanical University, School of Graduate Studies, School of Arts and Sciences, Department of Physics, Huntsville, AL 35811. Offers physics (MS, PhD), including applied physics (PhD); materials science (PhD); optics/lasers (PhD). Part-time and evening/weekend programs available. *Degree requirements:* For doctorate, thesis/dissertation. *Entrance requirements:* For master's and doctorate, GRE General Test. Additional exam requirements/recommendations for international students: Required—TOEFL (minimum score 500 paper-based; 173 computer-based; 61 iBT). Electronic applications accepted.

Cleveland State University, College of Graduate Studies, College of Sciences and Health Professions, Department of Physics, Cleveland, OH 44115. Offers applied optics (MS); condensed matter physics (MS); medical physics (MS); optics and materials (MS); optics and medical imaging (MS). Part-time and evening/weekend programs available. *Faculty:* 4 full-time (0 women), 1 part-time/adjunct (0 women). *Students:* 2 full-time (0 women), 12 part-time (3 women), 1 international. Average age 36. 29 applicants, 55% accepted, 7 enrolled. In 2011, 7 master's awarded. *Entrance requirements:* For master's, undergraduate degree in engineering, physics, chemistry or mathematics. Additional exam requirements/recommendations for international students: Required—TOEFL (minimum score 525 paper-based; 197 computer-based). *Application deadline:* For fall admission, 7/15 priority date for domestic students, 7/15 for international students. Applications are processed on a rolling basis. Application fee: $30. Electronic applications accepted. *Expenses:* Tuition, state resident: full-time $6416; part-time $494 per credit hour. Tuition, nonresident: full-time $12,074; part-time $929 per credit hour. *Financial support:* In 2011–12, 1 research assistantship with full and partial tuition reimbursement (averaging $5,666 per year) was awarded; fellowships with tuition reimbursements, teaching assistantships, and tuition waivers (full) also available. *Faculty research:* Statistical physics, experimental solid-state physics, theoretical optics, experimental biological physics (macromolecular crystallography), experimental optics. *Total annual research expenditures:* $350,000. *Unit head:* Dr. Miron Kaufman, Chairperson, 216-687-2436, Fax: 216-523-7268, E-mail: m.kaufman@csuohio.edu. *Application contact:* Dr. James A. Lock, Director, 216-687-2420, Fax: 216-523-7268, E-mail: j.lock@csuohio.edu. Web site: http://www.csuohio.edu/sciences/dept/physics/index.html.

Delaware State University, Graduate Programs, Department of Physics, Dover, DE 19901-2277. Offers applied optics (MS); optics (PhD); physics (MS); physics teaching (MS). Part-time and evening/weekend programs available. *Entrance requirements:* For master's, minimum GPA of 3.0 in major, 2.75 overall. Additional exam requirements/recommendations for international students: Required—TOEFL. Electronic applications accepted. *Faculty research:* Thermal properties of solids, nuclear physics, radiation damage in solids.

Duke University, Graduate School, Pratt School of Engineering, Master of Engineering Program, Durham, NC 27708-0271. Offers biomedical engineering (M Eng); civil engineering (M Eng); electrical and computer engineering (M Eng); environmental engineering (M Eng); materials science and engineering (M Eng); mechanical engineering (M Eng); photonics and optical sciences (M Eng). Part-time programs available. *Entrance requirements:* For master's, GRE General Test, resume, 3 letters of recommendation, statement of purpose. Additional exam requirements/recommendations for international students: Required—TOEFL. *Expenses: Tuition:* Full-time $40,720. *Required fees:* $3107.

École Polytechnique de Montréal, Graduate Programs, Department of Engineering Physics, Montréal, QC H3C 3A7, Canada. Offers optical engineering (M Eng, M Sc A, PhD); solid-state physics and engineering (M Eng, M Sc A, PhD). Part-time programs available. *Degree requirements:* For master's, one foreign language, thesis; for doctorate, one foreign language, thesis/dissertation. *Entrance requirements:* For master's, minimum GPA of 2.75; for doctorate, minimum GPA of 3.0. *Faculty research:* Optics, thin-film physics, laser spectroscopy, plasmas, photonic devices.

Norfolk State University, School of Graduate Studies, School of Science and Technology, Program in Optical Engineering, Norfolk, VA 23504. Offers MS.

North Carolina Agricultural and Technical State University, School of Graduate Studies, College of Engineering, Department of Electrical and Computer Engineering, Greensboro, NC 27411. Offers electrical engineering (MSEE, PhD), including communications and signal processing, computer engineering, electronic and optical materials and devices, power systems and control. Part-time programs available. *Degree requirements:* For master's, project, thesis defense; for doctorate, thesis/dissertation. *Entrance requirements:* For master's, GRE General Test, GRE Subject Test, minimum GPA of 2.8; for doctorate, GRE General Test, minimum GPA of 3.0. *Faculty research:* Semiconductor compounds, VLSI design, image processing, optical systems and devices, fault-tolerant computing.

The Ohio State University, College of Optometry, Columbus, OH 43210. Offers optometry (OD); vision science (MS, PhD); OD/MS. *Accreditation:* AOA (one or more programs are accredited). *Faculty:* 22. *Students:* 254 full-time (142 women), 8 part-time (5 women); includes 30 minority (1 Black or African American, non-Hispanic/Latino; 1 American Indian or Alaska Native, non-Hispanic/Latino; 22 Asian, non-Hispanic/Latino; 5 Hispanic/Latino; 1 Two or more races, non-Hispanic/Latino), 2 international. Average age 26. In 2011, 8 master's, 60 doctorates awarded. *Degree requirements:* For master's, thesis; for doctorate, thesis/dissertation. *Entrance requirements:* Additional exam requirements/recommendations for international students: Required—TOEFL (minimum score 600 paper-based; 250 computer-based; 79 iBT), Michigan English Language Assessment Battery (minimum score 82). *Application deadline:* For fall admission, 8/15 priority date for domestic students, 7/1 for international students; for winter admission, 12/1 priority date for domestic students, 11/1 for international students; for spring admission, 3/1 priority date for domestic students, 2/1 for international students. Applications are processed on a rolling basis. Electronic applications accepted. *Expenses:* Contact institution. *Financial support:* Research assistantships with full tuition reimbursements, teaching assistantships with full tuition reimbursements, Federal Work-Study, institutionally sponsored loans, and scholarships/grants available. Financial award application deadline: 2/1; financial award applicants required to submit FAFSA. *Unit head:* Dr. Melvin Shipp, Dean, 614-292-3246, E-mail: shipp.25@osu.edu. *Application contact:* Graduate Admissions, 614-292-9444, Fax: 614-292-3895, E-mail: domestic.grad@osu.edu. Web site: http://www.optometry.ohio-state.edu/.

Rochester Institute of Technology, Graduate Enrollment Services, College of Science, Chester F. Carlson Center for Imaging Science, Rochester, NY 14623-

5603. Offers MS, PhD. Part-time programs available. Postbaccalaureate distance learning degree programs offered (no on-campus study). *Students:* 92 full-time (32 women), 19 part-time (7 women); includes 2 minority (1 Black or African American, non-Hispanic/Latino; 1 Hispanic/Latino), 58 international. Average age 28. 75 applicants, 48% accepted, 30 enrolled. In 2011, 11 master's, 6 doctorates awarded. Terminal master's awarded for partial completion of doctoral program. *Degree requirements:* For master's, thesis; for doctorate, thesis/dissertation. *Entrance requirements:* For master's, GRE, minimum GPA of 3.0. Additional exam requirements/recommendations for international students: Required—TOEFL (minimum score 600 paper-based; 250 computer-based; 100 iBT) or IELTS (minimum score 6.5). *Application deadline:* For fall admission, 1/15 priority date for domestic students, 1/15 for international students. Applications are processed on a rolling basis. Application fee: $50. Electronic applications accepted. *Expenses: Tuition:* Full-time $34,659; part-time $963 per credit hour. *Required fees:* $228; $76 per quarter. *Financial support:* Fellowships with full and partial tuition reimbursements, research assistantships, teaching assistantships, career-related internships or fieldwork, scholarships/grants, unspecified assistantships, and merit-based fellowships covering full tuition, stipends available. Support available to part-time students. Financial award applicants required to submit FAFSA. *Faculty research:* Biomedical imaging, nano-imaging, remote sensing, sensor development, vision and visual perception, astronomy and space weather alert technologies, computational photography, graphical display, emergency response, environmental forecasting, cultural heritage and the application of imaging science to green energy initiatives. *Unit head:* Dr. Stefi Baum, Director, 585-475-6220, Fax: 585-475-5988, E-mail: baum@cis.rit.edu. *Application contact:* Diane Ellison, Assistant Vice President, Graduate Enrollment Services, 585-475-2229, Fax: 585-475-7164, E-mail: gradinfo@rit.edu. Web site: http://www.cis.rit.edu/.

Rose-Hulman Institute of Technology, Faculty of Engineering and Applied Sciences, Department of Physics and Optical Engineering, Terre Haute, IN 47803-3999. Offers optical engineering (MS). Part-time programs available. *Faculty:* 15 full-time (2 women), 3 part-time/adjunct (0 women). *Students:* 4 full-time (1 woman), 2 part-time (0 women), 1 international. Average age 24. 10 applicants, 100% accepted, 3 enrolled. In 2011, 5 master's awarded. *Degree requirements:* For master's, thesis. *Entrance requirements:* For master's, GRE, minimum GPA of 3.0. Additional exam requirements/recommendations for international students: Required—TOEFL (minimum score 580 paper-based; 237 computer-based; 92 iBT). *Application deadline:* For fall admission, 2/1 priority date for domestic students. Applications are processed on a rolling basis. Application fee: $0. *Expenses: Tuition:* Full-time $37,197; part-time $1085 per credit hour. *Financial support:* In 2011–12, 4 students received support. Fellowships with full and partial tuition reimbursements available, research assistantships with full and partial tuition reimbursements available, teaching assistantships, institutionally sponsored loans, scholarships/grants, and tuition waivers (full and partial) available. Financial award application deadline: 2/1. *Faculty research:* Optical design, laser systems, non-linear optics, metrology, optical MEMs, bio-photonics. *Total annual research expenditures:* $413,852. *Unit head:* Dr. Charles Joenathan, Chairman, 812-877-8494, Fax: 812-877-8023, E-mail: charles.joenathan@rose-hulman.edu. *Application contact:* Dr. Daniel J. Moore, Associate Dean of the Faculty, 812-877-8110, Fax: 812-877-8061, E-mail: daniel.j.moore@rose-hulman.edu. Web site: http://www.rose-hulman.edu/phoe/.

The University of Alabama in Huntsville, School of Graduate Studies, College of Engineering, Department of Electrical and Computer Engineering, Huntsville, AL 35899. Offers computer engineering (MSE, PhD), including information assurance (MSE); electrical engineering (MSE, PhD), including optics and photonics technology (MSE), opto-electronics (MSE); optics and photonics (MSE); software engineering (MSSE). Part-time and evening/weekend programs available. *Faculty:* 22 full-time (3 women), 4 part-time/adjunct (0 women). *Students:* 52 full-time (12 women), 138 part-time (22 women); includes 20 minority (7 Black or African American, non-Hispanic/Latino; 2 American Indian or Alaska Native, non-Hispanic/Latino; 8 Asian, non-Hispanic/Latino; 2 Hispanic/Latino; 1 Two or more races, non-Hispanic/Latino), 37 international. Average age 31. 157 applicants, 65% accepted, 48 enrolled. In 2011, 26 master's, 6 doctorates awarded. *Degree requirements:* For master's, comprehensive exam, thesis or alternative, oral and written exams; for doctorate, comprehensive exam, thesis/dissertation, oral and written exams. *Entrance requirements:* For master's, GRE General Test, appropriate bachelor's degree, minimum GPA of 3.0; for doctorate, GRE General Test, minimum GPA of 3.0. Additional exam requirements/recommendations for international students: Required—TOEFL (minimum score 500 paper-based; 173 computer-based; 62 iBT). *Application deadline:* For fall admission, 7/15 for domestic students, 4/1 for international students; for spring admission, 11/30 for domestic students, 9/1 for international students. Applications are processed on a rolling basis. Application fee: $40 ($50 for international students). Electronic applications accepted. *Expenses:* Tuition, state resident: full-time $7830; part-time $473.50 per credit. Tuition, nonresident: full-time $18,748; part-time $1128.33 per credit. Tuition and fees vary according to course load and program. *Financial support:* In 2011–12, 29 students received support, including 2 fellowships (averaging $11,154 per year), 9 research assistantships with full and partial tuition reimbursements available (averaging $10,959 per year), 20 teaching assistantships with full and partial tuition reimbursements available (averaging $11,330 per year); career-related internships or fieldwork, Federal Work-Study, institutionally sponsored loans, scholarships/grants, health care benefits, tuition waivers (full), and unspecified assistantships also available. Support available to part-time students. Financial

award application deadline: 4/1; financial award applicants required to submit FAFSA. *Faculty research:* Optical signal processing, electromagnetics, photonics, nonlinear waves, computer architecture. *Total annual research expenditures:* $16.5 million. *Unit head:* Dr. Robert Lindquist, Chair, 256-824-6316, Fax: 256-824-6803, E-mail: lindquis@ece.uah.edu. *Application contact:* Kim Gray, Graduate Studies Admissions Coordinator, 256-824-6002, Fax: 256-824-6405, E-mail: deangrad@uah.edu. Web site: http://www.ece.uah.edu/.

The University of Alabama in Huntsville, School of Graduate Studies, Interdisciplinary Studies, Interdisciplinary Program in Optical Science and Engineering, Huntsville, AL 35899. Offers PhD. Part-time and evening/weekend programs available. *Faculty:* 12 full-time (0 women), 2 part-time/adjunct (0 women). *Students:* 5 full-time (1 woman), 3 part-time (0 women), 4 international. Average age 31. 14 applicants, 29% accepted, 2 enrolled. In 2011, 4 doctorates awarded. *Degree requirements:* For doctorate, comprehensive exam, thesis/dissertation, written and oral exams. *Entrance requirements:* For doctorate, GRE General Test, minimum GPA of 3.0, BS in physical science or engineering. Additional exam requirements/recommendations for international students: Required—TOEFL (minimum score 550 paper-based; 213 computer-based; 62 iBT). *Application deadline:* For fall admission, 7/15 for domestic students, 4/1 for international students; for spring admission, 11/30 for domestic students, 9/1 for international students. Applications are processed on a rolling basis. Application fee: $40 ($50 for international students). Electronic applications accepted. *Expenses:* Tuition, state resident: full-time $7830; part-time $473.50 per credit. Tuition, nonresident: full-time $18,748; part-time $1128.33 per credit. Tuition and fees vary according to course load and program. *Financial support:* In 2011–12, 4 students received support, including 4 research assistantships with full tuition reimbursements available (averaging $12,156 per year), 1 teaching assistantship with full tuition reimbursement available (averaging $11,600 per year); career-related internships or fieldwork, Federal Work-Study, institutionally sponsored loans, scholarships/grants, health care benefits, and unspecified assistantships also available. Support available to part-time students. Financial award application deadline: 4/1; financial award applicants required to submit FAFSA. *Faculty research:* Laser technology, holography, optical communications, medical image processing, computer design. *Total annual research expenditures:* $1.3 million. *Unit head:* Dr. Robert G. Lindquist, Program Director, 256-824-2882, Fax: 256-824-6618, E-mail: lindquist@ece.uah.edu. *Application contact:* Kim Gray, Graduate Studies Admissions Coordinator, 256-824-6002, Fax: 256-824-6405, E-mail: deangrad@uah.edu. Web site: http://www.uah.edu/OSE/.

The University of Arizona, College of Optical Sciences, Tucson, AZ 85721. Offers MS, PhD. Part-time programs available. *Faculty:* 29 full-time (3 women), 2 part-time/adjunct (0 women). *Students:* 191 full-time (46 women), 89 part-time (11 women); includes 47 minority (7 Black or African American, non-Hispanic/Latino; 1 American Indian or Alaska Native, non-Hispanic/Latino; 13 Asian, non-Hispanic/Latino; 14 Hispanic/Latino; 1 Native Hawaiian or other Pacific Islander, non-Hispanic/Latino; 11 Two or more races, non-Hispanic/Latino), 69 international. Average age 31. 261 applicants, 29% accepted, 53 enrolled. In 2011, 44 master's, 20 doctorates awarded. *Degree requirements:* For master's, thesis (for some programs), exam; for doctorate, thesis/dissertation, oral and written exams. *Entrance requirements:* For master's, GRE General Test, GRE Subject Test (recommended), minimum GPA of 3.0, 2 letters of recommendation, resume; for doctorate, GRE General Test, GRE Subject Test (recommended), minimum GPA of 3.0, 2 letters of recommendation, statement of purpose, resume. Additional exam requirements/recommendations for international students: Required—TOEFL. *Application deadline:* For fall admission, 1/1 for domestic students, 12/1 for international students. Applications are processed on a rolling basis. Application fee: $75. Electronic applications accepted. *Expenses:* Tuition, state resident: full-time $10,840. Tuition, nonresident: full-time $25,802. *Financial support:* In 2011–12, 99 research assistantships with full tuition reimbursements (averaging $23,145 per year), 24 teaching assistantships with full tuition reimbursements (averaging $17,656 per year) were awarded; fellowships and scholarships/grants also available. Financial award application deadline: 1/1. *Faculty research:* Medical optics, medical imaging, optical data storage, optical bistability, nonlinear optical effects. *Total annual research expenditures:* $25.2 million. *Unit head:* Dr. Thomas L. Koch, Dean, 520-621-6997, Fax: 520-621-9613, E-mail: jcwyant@optics.arizona.edu. *Application contact:* Gail Varin, Coordinator, Graduate Academic Progress, 520-626-0888, E-mail: gail@optics.arizona.edu. Web site: http://www.optics.arizona.edu.

University of Central Florida, College of Optics and Photonics, Orlando, FL 32816. Offers optics (MS, PhD). Part-time and evening/weekend programs available. *Faculty:* 34 full-time (4 women), 8 part-time/adjunct (3 women). *Students:* 102 full-time (17 women), 20 part-time (3 women); includes 6 minority (1 Black or African American, non-Hispanic/Latino; 2 Asian, non-Hispanic/Latino; 3 Hispanic/Latino), 67 international. Average age 28. 197 applicants, 18% accepted, 24 enrolled. In 2011, 22 master's, 19 doctorates awarded. *Degree requirements:* For master's, thesis or alternative; for doctorate, thesis/dissertation, departmental qualifying exam, candidacy exam. *Entrance requirements:* For master's, GRE General Test, minimum GPA of 3.0 in last 60 hours; for doctorate, GRE General Test, minimum GPA of 3.5 in last 60 hours. Additional exam requirements/recommendations for international students: Required—TOEFL. *Application deadline:* For fall admission, 2/1 priority date for domestic students; for spring admission, 12/1 for domestic students. Application fee: $30. Electronic applications accepted. *Expenses:* Tuition, state resident: part-time $277.08 per credit hour. Tuition, nonresident: part-time $277.08 per credit hour. Part-time

Peterson's Graduate Programs in the Physical Sciences, Mathematics, Agricultural Sciences, the Environment & Natural Resources 2013

facebook.com/petersonspublishing **231**

Optical Sciences

tuition and fees vary according to degree level and program. *Financial support:* In 2011–12, 63 students received support, including 14 fellowships with partial tuition reimbursements available (averaging $5,600 per year), 80 research assistantships with partial tuition reimbursements available (averaging $11,000 per year); career-related internships or fieldwork, Federal Work-Study, institutionally sponsored loans, tuition waivers (partial), and unspecified assistantships also available. Financial award application deadline: 3/1; financial award applicants required to submit FAFSA. *Unit head:* Dr. Bahaa E. Saleh, Dean and Director, 407-823-6817, E-mail: besaleh@creol.ucf.edu. *Application contact:* Barbara Rodriguez, Director, Admissions and Registration, 407-823-2766, Fax: 407-823-6442, E-mail: gradadmissions@ucf.edu. Web site: http://www.creol.ucf.edu/.

University of Colorado Boulder, Graduate School, College of Arts and Sciences, Department of Physics, Boulder, CO 80309. Offers chemical physics (PhD); geophysics (PhD); liquid crystal science and technology (PhD); mathematical physics (PhD); medical physics (PhD); optical sciences and engineering (PhD); physics (MS, PhD). *Faculty:* 51 full-time (7 women). *Students:* 157 full-time (28 women), 66 part-time (11 women); includes 11 minority (6 Asian, non-Hispanic/Latino; 5 Hispanic/Latino), 75 international. Average age 26. 551 applicants, 25% accepted, 47 enrolled. In 2011, 29 master's, 28 doctorates awarded. Terminal master's awarded for partial completion of doctoral program. *Degree requirements:* For master's, comprehensive exam, thesis or alternative; for doctorate, comprehensive exam, thesis/dissertation. *Entrance requirements:* For master's and doctorate, GRE General Test, GRE Subject Test, minimum undergraduate GPA of 3.0. Additional exam requirements/recommendations for international students: Required—TOEFL. *Application deadline:* For fall admission, 1/15 priority date for domestic students, 1/15 for international students. Applications are processed on a rolling basis. Application fee: $50 ($60 for international students). Electronic applications accepted. *Financial support:* In 2011–12, 216 students received support, including 85 fellowships (averaging $9,233 per year), 131 research assistantships with full and partial tuition reimbursements available (averaging $24,425 per year), 31 teaching assistantships with full and partial tuition reimbursements available (averaging $20,162 per year); institutionally sponsored loans, scholarships/grants, health care benefits, and unspecified assistantships also available. Financial award application deadline: 1/15; financial award applicants required to submit FAFSA. *Faculty research:* Atomic and molecular physics, nuclear physics, condensed matter, elementary particle physics, laser or optical physics, plasma physics, geophysics, OSEP, astrophysics and chemical physics. *Total annual research expenditures:* $26.1 million. *Application contact:* E-mail: physics@colorado.edu. Web site: http://physics.colorado.edu/.

University of Dayton, Program in Electro-Optics, Dayton, OH 45469-1300. Offers MSEO, PhD. Part-time and evening/weekend programs available. *Faculty:* 6 full-time (0 women), 8 part-time/adjunct (0 women). *Students:* 34 full-time (5 women), 4 part-time (0 women); includes 1 minority (Asian, non-Hispanic/Latino), 16 international. Average age 26. 98 applicants, 37% accepted, 17 enrolled. In 2011, 11 master's, 2 doctorates awarded. *Degree requirements:* For master's, comprehensive exam (for some programs), thesis (for some programs); for doctorate, comprehensive exam, thesis/dissertation, departmental qualifying exam. *Entrance requirements:* For master's, BS; for doctorate, MS. Additional exam requirements/recommendations for international students: Required—TOEFL (minimum score 550 paper-based; 213 computer-based; 80 iBT). *Application deadline:* For fall admission, 8/1 for domestic students, 3/1 for international students; for winter admission, 11/1 for domestic students, 9/1 for international students; for spring admission, 11/1 for domestic students, 9/1 for international students. Applications are processed on a rolling basis. Application fee: $0 ($50 for international students). Electronic applications accepted. *Expenses: Tuition:* Full-time $8400; part-time $700 per credit hour. *Required fees:* $25 per semester. Tuition and fees vary according to degree level. *Financial support:* In 2011–12, 23 research assistantships with full tuition reimbursements (averaging $18,000 per year), 4 teaching assistantships with full tuition reimbursements (averaging $14,000 per year) were awarded; institutionally sponsored loans, health care benefits, and unspecified assistantships also available. Financial award applicants required to submit FAFSA. *Faculty research:* Spatial and spatiotemporal solitary waves and their stabilization in nonlinear negative index materials, stimulated photorefractive backscatter leading to six-wave mixing and phase conjugation in iron doped lithium niobate, modeling and characterization of PLZT adaptive microlenses, experimental investigation of self-starting operation in a F8L based on a symmetrical NOLM, negative refraction and sub-wavelength focusing in the visible range using transparent metallo-dielectric stacks. *Total annual research expenditures:* $1.8 million. *Unit head:* Dr. Joseph W. Haus, Director, 937-229-2797, Fax: 937-229-2097, E-mail: jhaus1@udayton.edu. *Application contact:* Dr. Joseph W. Haus, Director, 937-229-2797, Fax: 937-229-2097, E-mail: jhaus1@udayton.edu. Web site: http://www.udayton.edu/learn/graduate/engineering/major_electro_optics.php.

University of Massachusetts Lowell, College of Sciences, Department of Physics and Applied Physics, Program in Applied Physics, Lowell, MA 01854-2881. Offers applied mechanics (PhD); applied physics (MS, PhD), including optical sciences (MS). Terminal master's awarded for partial completion of doctoral program. *Degree requirements:* For master's, thesis; for doctorate, 2 foreign languages, thesis/dissertation. *Entrance requirements:* For master's, GRE General Test, 3 letters of reference; for doctorate, GRE General Test, transcripts, 3 letters of reference. Additional exam requirements/recommendations for international students: Required—TOEFL.

University of New Mexico, Graduate School, College of Arts and Sciences, Optical Science and Engineering Program, Albuquerque, NM 87131. Offers imaging science (MS, PhD); optical science and engineering (MS, PhD); photonics (MS, PhD). Part-time programs available. *Faculty:* 34 full-time (2 women). *Students:* 21 full-time (4 women), 31 part-time (6 women); includes 2 minority (1 American Indian or Alaska Native, non-Hispanic/Latino; 1 Hispanic/Latino), 36 international. Average age 30. 48 applicants, 21% accepted, 8 enrolled. In 2011, 10 master's, 5 doctorates awarded. Terminal master's awarded for partial completion of doctoral program. *Median time to degree:* Of those who began their doctoral program in fall 2003, 55% received their degree in 8 years or less. *Degree requirements:* For master's, comprehensive exam (for some programs), thesis (for some programs); for doctorate, comprehensive exam, thesis/dissertation. *Entrance requirements:* For master's, GRE General Test, GRE Subject Test in physics (preferred), relevant undergraduate coursework, curriculum vitae, letters of recommendation, letter of intent/personal statement; for doctorate, GRE General Test, GRE Subject Test in physics (preferred), relevant undergraduate coursework, curriculum vitae, letters of recommendation. Additional exam requirements/recommendations for international students: Required—TOEFL (minimum score 575 paper-based; 213 computer-based; 79 iBT), IELTS (minimum score 7). *Application deadline:* For fall admission, 1/15 priority date for domestic students, 1/15 for international students; for spring admission, 8/1 priority date for domestic students, 8/1 for international students. Application fee: $50. Electronic applications accepted. *Financial support:* In 2011–12, 34 students received support, including 29 research assistantships with full tuition reimbursements available (averaging $16,097 per year), 10 teaching assistantships with full tuition reimbursements available (averaging $14,400 per year); fellowships with full tuition reimbursements available, career-related internships or fieldwork, scholarships/grants, health care benefits, and unspecified assistantships also available. Support available to part-time students. Financial award application deadline: 2/1; financial award applicants required to submit FAFSA. *Faculty research:* Advanced materials, atom optics, biomedical optics, fiber optics, laser cooling, high intensity interactions, lithography, nano photonics, nonlinear optics, optical imaging, optical sensors, optoelectronics, quantum optics, spectroscopy, ultrafast phenomena. *Unit head:* Dr. Majeed Hayat, General Chair, 505-272-7095, Fax: 505-277-7801, E-mail: hayat@ece.unm.edu. *Application contact:* Doris Williams, Advisor, 505-277-7764, Fax: 505-277-7801, E-mail: dorisw@chtm.unm.edu. Web site: http://www.optics.unm.edu/.

The University of North Carolina at Charlotte, Graduate School, College of Liberal Arts and Sciences, Department of Physics and Optical Science, Charlotte, NC 28223-0001. Offers applied physics (MS); optical science and engineering (MS, PhD). *Faculty:* 23 full-time (4 women). *Students:* 3 full-time (2 women), 13 part-time (4 women); includes 2 minority (both Black or African American, non-Hispanic/Latino). Average age 32. 38 applicants, 82% accepted, 13 enrolled. In 2011, 4 master's, 4 doctorates awarded. Terminal master's awarded for partial completion of doctoral program. *Degree requirements:* For master's, thesis optional; for doctorate, thesis/dissertation optional. *Entrance requirements:* For master's, GRE General Test, minimum GPA of 3.0 during previous 2 years, 2.75 overall. Additional exam requirements/recommendations for international students: Required—TOEFL (minimum score 557 paper-based; 220 computer-based; 83 iBT). *Application deadline:* For fall admission, 7/15 for domestic students, 5/1 for international students; for spring admission, 11/15 for domestic students, 10/1 for international students. Applications are processed on a rolling basis. Application fee: $65 ($75 for international students). Electronic applications accepted. *Expenses: Tuition:* state resident: full-time $3689. Tuition, nonresident: full-time $15,226. *Required fees:* $2198. Tuition and fees vary according to course load and program. *Financial support:* In 2011–12, 36 students received support, including 6 fellowships (averaging $41,726 per year), 14 research assistantships (averaging $10,262 per year), 16 teaching assistantships (averaging $7,938 per year); career-related internships or fieldwork, institutionally sponsored loans, scholarships/grants, and unspecified assistantships also available. Support available to part-time students. Financial award application deadline: 4/1; financial award applicants required to submit FAFSA. *Faculty research:* Optics, lasers, microscopy, fibers, astrophysics. *Total annual research expenditures:* $1.4 million. *Unit head:* Dr. Patrick Moyer, Interim Chair, 704-687-8148, Fax: 704-687-3160, E-mail: pjmoyer@uncc.edu. *Application contact:* Kathy B. Giddings, Director of Graduate Admissions, 704-687-5503, Fax: 704-687-3279, E-mail: gradadm@uncc.edu. Web site: http://physics.uncc.edu/.

University of Rochester, Hajim School of Engineering and Applied Sciences, Center for Entrepreneurship, Rochester, NY 14627-0360. Offers technical entrepreneurship and management (TEAM) (MS), including biomedical engineering, chemical engineering, computer science, electrical and computer engineering, energy and the environment, materials science, mechanical engineering, optics. *Faculty:* 61 full-time (8 women), 5 part-time/adjunct (1 woman). *Students:* 18 full-time (5 women), 3 part-time (1 woman); includes 4 minority (1 Asian, non-Hispanic/Latino; 3 Hispanic/Latino), 12 international. Average age 23. 134 applicants, 48% accepted, 21 enrolled. *Degree requirements:* For master's, comprehensive exam. *Entrance requirements:* For master's, GRE or GMAT, technical concentration of interest, 3 letters of recommendation, personal statement, official transcript. Additional exam requirements/recommendations for international students: Required—TOEFL or IELTS. *Application deadline:* For fall admission, 2/1 for domestic and international students. Applications are processed on a rolling basis. Application fee: $60. Electronic applications accepted. *Expenses: Tuition:* Full-time $41,040. *Financial support:* Career-related internships or fieldwork and scholarships/grants available. Financial award application deadline: 2/1. *Faculty research:* High efficiency solar cells, macromolecular self-assembly, digital signal processing, memory hierarchy management, molecular and physical mechanisms in cell migration. *Unit head:* Duncan T. Moore, Vice Provost for Entrepreneurship, 585-275-5248, Fax: 585-473-6745, E-mail: moore@optics.rochester.edu. *Application contact:* Andrea M. Galati, Executive Director, 585-276-3407, Fax: 585-276-2357, E-mail: andrea.galati@rochester.edu. Web site: http://www.rochester.edu/team.

University of Rochester, Hajim School of Engineering and Applied Sciences, Institute of Optics, Rochester, NY 14627. Offers MS, PhD. *Faculty:* 19 full-time (1 woman). *Students:* 100 full-time (18 women), 10 part-time (3 women); includes 4 minority (1 Black or African American, non-Hispanic/Latino; 2 Asian, non-Hispanic/Latino; 1 Hispanic/Latino), 32 international. 167 applicants, 34% accepted, 30 enrolled. In 2011, 8 master's, 8 doctorates awarded. Terminal master's awarded for partial completion of doctoral program. *Degree requirements:* For master's, comprehensive exam; for doctorate, thesis/ dissertation, preliminary and qualifying exams. *Entrance requirements:* For master's and doctorate, GRE. Additional exam requirements/recommendations for international students: Required—TOEFL. *Application deadline:* For fall admission, 2/1 priority date for domestic students. Application fee: $60. *Expenses: Tuition:* Full-time $41,040. *Financial support:* Fellowships, research assistantships, teaching assistantships, and tuition waivers (full and partial) available. Financial award application deadline: 2/1. *Faculty research:* Biomedical, fiber and optical communication; image science and systems; ultrafast optics and highfield sciences. *Unit head:* Gary W. Wicks, Interim Director, 585-275-4867. *Application contact:* Lissa Cotter, Administrative Assistant, 585-275-7764. Web site: http://www.optics.rochester.edu/.

University of Rochester, School of Nursing, Rochester, NY 14642. Offers acute care nurse practitioner (MS); adult nurse practitioner (MS); adult/geriatric nurse practitioner (MS); care of children and families/pediatric nurse practitioner (MS); care of children and families/pediatric nurse practitioner/neonatal nurse practitioner (MS); clinical nurse leader (MS); clinical research coordinator (MS); family nurse practitioner (MS); family psychiatric mental health nurse practitioner (MS); health care organization management and leadership (MS); health practice research (PhD); nursing (DNP). *Accreditation:* AACN; NLN (one or more programs are accredited). Part-time programs available. Postbaccalaureate distance learning degree programs offered (minimal on-campus study). *Faculty:* 49 full-time (42 women), 72 part-time/adjunct (60 women). *Students:* 38 full-time (32 women), 196 part-time (181 women); includes 37 minority (20 Black or African American, non-Hispanic/Latino; 9 Asian, non-Hispanic/Latino; 8 Hispanic/Latino), 5 international. Average age 36. 68 applicants, 56% accepted, 26 enrolled. In 2011, 49 master's, 7 doctorates awarded. Terminal master's awarded for partial completion of doctoral program. *Median time to degree:* Of those who began their doctoral program in fall 2003, 40% received their degree in 8 years or less. *Degree requirements:* For doctorate, thesis/dissertation. *Entrance requirements:* For master's, BS in nursing, minimum GPA of 3.0, course work in statistics; for doctorate, GRE General Test, MS in nursing, minimum GPA of 3.5. Additional exam requirements/recommendations for international students: Required—or IELTS (minimum score 6.5); Recommended—TOEFL (minimum score 560 paper-based; 230 computer-based; 88 iBT). *Application deadline:* For fall admission, 4/1 priority date for domestic students, 4/1 for international students; for spring admission, 9/1 for domestic and international students. Application fee: $50. Electronic applications accepted. *Expenses: Tuition:* Full-time $41,040. *Financial support:* In 2011–12, 49 students received support, including 1 fellowship with full and partial tuition reimbursement available (averaging $18,700 per year); scholarships/grants, traineeships, health care benefits, tuition waivers (partial), and unspecified assistantships also available. Support available to part-time students. Financial award application deadline: 6/30. *Faculty research:* Clinical research in aging, managing asthma in children, interventions to improve outcomes in critically ill children and their mothers, nurse home visitation studies, medical device evaluation, critical care clinical studies, high risk behavior and prevention, palliative care, pregnancy-related weight gain. *Total annual research expenditures:* $4.3 million. *Unit head:* Dr. Kathy H. Rideout, Interim Dean, 585-273-8902, Fax: 585-273-1268, E-mail: kathy_rideout@urmc.rochester.edu. *Application contact:* Elaine Andolina, Director of Admissions, 585-275-2375, Fax: 585-756-8299, E-mail: elaine_andolina@urmc.rochester.edu. Web site: http://www.son.rochester.edu.

Photonics

Boston University, College of Engineering, Department of Electrical and Computer Engineering, Boston, MA 02215. Offers computer engineering (M Eng, MS, PhD); electrical engineering (M Eng, MS, PhD); photonics (M Eng, MS). Part-time programs available. *Faculty:* 40 full-time (3 women), 5 part-time/adjunct (0 women). *Students:* 221 full-time (43 women), 23 part-time (0 women); includes 21 minority (1 Black or African American, non-Hispanic/Latino; 1 American Indian or Alaska Native, non-Hispanic/Latino; 15 Asian, non-Hispanic/Latino; 2 Hispanic/ Latino; 2 Two or more races, non-Hispanic/Latino), 165 international. Average age 25. 810 applicants, 25% accepted, 112 enrolled. In 2011, 56 master's, 21 doctorates awarded. Terminal master's awarded for partial completion of doctoral program. *Degree requirements:* For master's, thesis (for some programs); for doctorate, comprehensive exam, thesis/dissertation. *Entrance requirements:* For master's and doctorate, GRE General Test. Additional exam requirements/ recommendations for international students: Required—TOEFL (minimum score 550 paper-based; 213 computer-based; 84 iBT), IELTS (minimum score 6.5). *Application deadline:* For fall admission, 3/15 for domestic and international students; for spring admission, 10/1 for domestic and international students. Applications are processed on a rolling basis. Application fee: $70. Electronic applications accepted. *Expenses: Tuition:* Full-time $40,848; part-time $1276 per credit hour. *Required fees:* $572; $286 per semester. *Financial support:* In 2011–12, 126 students received support, including 8 fellowships with full tuition reimbursements available (averaging $28,950 per year), 82 research assistantships with full tuition reimbursements available (averaging $19,300 per year), 18 teaching assistantships with full tuition reimbursements available (averaging $19,300 per year); career-related internships or fieldwork, Federal Work-Study, institutionally sponsored loans, scholarships/grants, traineeships, and health care benefits also available. Financial award application deadline: 1/ 15; financial award applicants required to submit FAFSA. *Faculty research:* Communications and computer networks; signal, image, video, and multimedia processing; solid-state materials, devices, and photonics; systems, control, and reliable computing; VLSI, computer engineering and high-performance computing. *Unit head:* Dr. David Castanon, Interim Chairman, 617-353-9880, Fax: 617-353-6440, E-mail: dac@bu.edu. *Application contact:* Stephen Doherty, Director of Graduate Programs, 617-353-9760, Fax: 617-353-0259, E-mail: enggrad@bu.edu. Web site: http://www.bu.edu/ece/.

Duke University, Graduate School, Pratt School of Engineering, Master of Engineering Program, Durham, NC 27708-0271. Offers biomedical engineering (M Eng); civil engineering (M Eng); electrical and computer engineering (M Eng); environmental engineering (M Eng); materials science and engineering (M Eng); mechanical engineering (M Eng); photonics and optical sciences (M Eng). Part-time programs available. *Entrance requirements:* For master's, GRE General Test, resume, 3 letters of recommendation, statement of purpose. Additional exam requirements/recommendations for international students: Required— TOEFL. *Expenses: Tuition:* Full-time $40,720. *Required fees:* $3107.

Lehigh University, College of Arts and Sciences, Department of Physics, Bethlehem, PA 18015. Offers photonics (MS); physics (MS, PhD); polymer science (MS, PhD). Part-time programs available. *Faculty:* 17 full-time (1 woman). *Students:* 42 full-time (14 women), 1 part-time (0 women), 21 international. Average age 26. 84 applicants, 10% accepted, 8 enrolled. In 2011, 9 master's, 9 doctorates awarded. *Degree requirements:* For doctorate, comprehensive exam, thesis/dissertation. *Entrance requirements:* For master's and doctorate, GRE General Test. Additional exam requirements/recommendations for international students: Required—TOEFL (minimum score 213 computer-based; 79 iBT). *Application deadline:* For fall admission, 2/15 priority date for domestic students, 2/15 for international students. Applications are processed on a rolling basis. Application fee: $75. Electronic applications accepted. *Financial support:* In 2011–12, 42 students received support, including 3 fellowships with full tuition reimbursements available (averaging $26,000 per year), 14 research assistantships with full tuition reimbursements available (averaging $24,770 per year), 25 teaching assistantships with full tuition reimbursements available (averaging $24,770 per year); career-related internships or fieldwork, Federal Work-Study, institutionally sponsored loans, scholarships/grants, tuition waivers (full and partial), and unspecified assistantships also available. Support available to part-time students. Financial award application deadline: 1/15. *Faculty research:* Condensed matter physics; atomic, molecular and optical physics; plasma physics; nonlinear optics and photonics; astronomy and astrophysics. *Total annual research expenditures:* $2.5 million. *Unit head:* Dr. Volkmar Dierolf, Chair, 610-758-3915, Fax: 610-758-5730, E-mail: vod2@lehigh.edu. *Application contact:* Dr. Dimitrios Vavylonis, Graduate Admissions Officer, 610-758-3724, Fax: 610-758-5730, E-mail: div206@lehigh.edu. Web site: http:// www.physics.lehigh.edu/.

Lehigh University, P.C. Rossin College of Engineering and Applied Science, Department of Electrical and Computer Engineering, Bethlehem, PA 18015. Offers electrical engineering (M Eng, MS, PhD); photonics (MS); wireless network engineering (MS). Part-time programs available. *Faculty:* 19 full-time (4 women). *Students:* 43 full-time (7 women), 14 part-time (4 women); includes 2 minority (1 Asian, non-Hispanic/Latino; 1 Hispanic/Latino), 49 international. Average age 26. 383 applicants, 5% accepted, 12 enrolled. In 2011, 15 master's, 14 doctorates awarded. Terminal master's awarded for partial completion of doctoral program. *Degree requirements:* For master's, thesis optional; for doctorate, thesis/ dissertation, qualifying or comprehensive exam for all 1st year PhD's; general

Peterson's Graduate Programs in the Physical Sciences, Mathematics, Agricultural Sciences, the Environment & Natural Resources 2013

facebook.com/petersonspublishing **233**

Photonics

exam 7 months or more prior to completion/dissertation defense. *Entrance requirements:* For master's and doctorate, GRE General Test, BS in field or related field. Additional exam requirements/recommendations for international students: Required—TOEFL (minimum score 79 iBT). *Application deadline:* For fall admission, 1/15 priority date for domestic students, 1/15 for international students; for spring admission, 11/1 for domestic and international students. Application fee: $75. Electronic applications accepted. *Financial support:* In 2011–12, 48 students received support, including 4 fellowships with full tuition reimbursements available (averaging $18,360 per year), 42 research assistantships with full tuition reimbursements available (averaging $21,600 per year), 5 teaching assistantships with full tuition reimbursements available (averaging $18,819 per year); career-related internships or fieldwork, Federal Work-Study, institutionally sponsored loans, scholarships/grants, tuition waivers (full and partial), and unspecified assistantships also available. Support available to part-time students. Financial award application deadline: 1/15. *Faculty research:* Nanostructures/nanodevices, terahertz generation, analog devices, mixed mode design and signal circuits, optoelectronic sensors, micro-fabrication technology and design, packaging/reliability of microsensors, coding and networking information theory, radio frequency, wireless and optical wireless communication, wireless networks. *Total annual research expenditures:* $3.2 million. *Unit head:* Dr. Filbert J. Bartoli, Chair, 610-758-4069, Fax: 610-758-6279, E-mail: fjb205@lehigh.edu. *Application contact:* Coley B. Burke, Graduate Coordinator, 610-758-4072, Fax: 610-758-6279, E-mail: cbb310@lehigh.edu. Web site: http://www.ece.lehigh.edu/.

Lehigh University, P.C. Rossin College of Engineering and Applied Science, Department of Materials Science and Engineering, Bethlehem, PA 18015. Offers materials science and engineering (M Eng, MS, PhD); photonics (MS); polymer science/engineering (M Eng, MS, PhD); MBA/E. Part-time programs available. *Faculty:* 13 full-time (3 women), 1 part-time/adjunct (0 women). *Students:* 28 full-time (6 women), 6 part-time (1 woman); includes 2 minority (both Asian, non-Hispanic/Latino), 14 international. Average age 26. 321 applicants, 2% accepted, 6 enrolled. In 2011, 2 master's, 2 doctorates awarded. *Degree requirements:* For master's, thesis; for doctorate, comprehensive exam, thesis/dissertation. *Entrance requirements:* For master's and doctorate, GRE General Test, minimum GPA of 3.0. Additional exam requirements/recommendations for international students: Required—TOEFL (minimum score 487 paper-based; 216 computer-based; 85 iBT). *Application deadline:* For fall admission, 1/15 priority date for domestic students, 1/15 for international students; for spring admission, 12/1 priority date for domestic students, 12/1 for international students. Applications are processed on a rolling basis. Application fee: $75. Electronic applications accepted. *Financial support:* In 2011–12, 29 students received support, including 3 fellowships with full and partial tuition reimbursements available (averaging $22,400 per year), 25 research assistantships with full tuition reimbursements available (averaging $22,449 per year), 13 teaching assistantships with partial tuition reimbursements available (averaging $17,512 per year); career-related internships or fieldwork, Federal Work-Study, institutionally sponsored loans, scholarships/grants, and unspecified assistantships also available. Support available to part-time students. Financial award application deadline: 1/15. *Faculty research:* Metals, ceramics, crystals, polymers, fatigue crack propagation. *Total annual research expenditures:* $4.1 million. *Unit head:* Dr. Helen Chan, Chairperson, 610-758-5554, Fax: 610-758-4244, E-mail: hmc0@lehigh.edu. *Application contact:* Anne Marie Lobley, Graduate Administrative Coordinator, 610-758-4222, Fax: 610-758-4244, E-mail: amme@lehigh.edu. Web site: http://www.lehigh.edu/~inmatsci/.

Oklahoma State University, College of Arts and Sciences, Department of Physics, Stillwater, OK 74078. Offers photonics (MS, PhD); physics (MS, PhD). *Faculty:* 30 full-time (6 women), 2 part-time/adjunct (1 woman). *Students:* 3 full-time (0 women), 37 part-time (5 women); includes 2 minority (1 Hispanic/Latino; 1 Two or more races, non-Hispanic/Latino), 29 international. Average age 29. 37 applicants, 43% accepted, 6 enrolled. In 2011, 3 master's, 6 doctorates awarded. *Degree requirements:* For master's, thesis; for doctorate, comprehensive exam, thesis/dissertation, oral defense of dissertation, preliminary exam, qualifying exam. *Entrance requirements:* For master's and doctorate, GRE. Additional exam requirements/recommendations for international students: Required—TOEFL (minimum score 550 paper-based; 79 iBT). *Application deadline:* For fall admission, 3/1 for international students; for spring admission, 8/1 for international students. Applications are processed on a rolling basis. Application fee: $40 ($75 for international students). Electronic applications accepted. *Expenses:* Tuition, state resident: full-time $4044; part-time $168.50 per credit hour. Tuition, nonresident: full-time $16,008; part-time $667 per credit hour. *Required fees:* $2122; $88.45 per credit hour. One-time fee: $50. Tuition and fees vary according to course load and campus/location. *Financial support:* In 2011–12, 18 research assistantships (averaging $17,967 per year), 36 teaching assistantships (averaging $16,802 per year) were awarded; career-related internships or fieldwork, Federal Work-Study, scholarships/grants, health care benefits, tuition waivers (partial), and unspecified assistantships also available. Support available to part-time students. Financial award application deadline: 3/1; financial award applicants required to submit FAFSA. *Faculty research:* Lasers and photonics, non-linear optical materials, turbulence, structure and function of biological membranes, particle theory. *Unit head:* Dr. James Wicksted, Head, 405-744-5796, Fax: 405-744-6811. *Application contact:* Dr. Sheryl Tucker, Dean, 405-744-7099, Fax: 405-744-0355, E-mail: grad-i@okstate.edu. Web site: http://physics.okstate.edu.

Oklahoma State University, Graduate College, Stillwater, OK 74078. Offers aerospace security (Graduate Certificate); biobased products and bioenergy (Graduate Certificate); bioinformatics (Graduate Certificate); business data mining (Graduate Certificate); engineering and technology management (Graduate Certificate); environmental science (MS); global issues (Graduate Certificate); information assurance (Graduate Certificate); international studies (MS); natural and applied science (MS); photonics (PhD); plant science (PhD); teaching English to speakers of other languages (Graduate Certificate). Programs are interdisciplinary. *Faculty:* 2 full-time (both women), 3 part-time/adjunct (0 women). *Students:* 86 full-time (50 women), 149 part-time (76 women); includes 55 minority (14 Black or African American, non-Hispanic/Latino; 11 American Indian or Alaska Native, non-Hispanic/Latino; 8 Asian, non-Hispanic/Latino; 7 Hispanic/Latino; 1 Native Hawaiian or other Pacific Islander, non-Hispanic/Latino; 14 Two or more races, non-Hispanic/Latino), 57 international. Average age 31. 597 applicants, 68% accepted, 78 enrolled. In 2011, 98 master's, 8 doctorates awarded. *Degree requirements:* For master's, thesis (for some programs); for doctorate, comprehensive exam, thesis/dissertation. *Entrance requirements:* For master's and doctorate, GRE or GMAT. Additional exam requirements/recommendations for international students: Required—TOEFL (minimum score 550 paper-based; 79 iBT). *Application deadline:* For fall admission, 3/1 for international students; for spring admission, 8/1 for international students. Applications are processed on a rolling basis. Application fee: $40 ($75 for international students). Electronic applications accepted. *Expenses:* Tuition, state resident: full-time $4044; part-time $168.50 per credit hour. Tuition, nonresident: full-time $16,008; part-time $667 per credit hour. *Required fees:* $2122; $88.45 per credit hour. One-time fee: $50. Tuition and fees vary according to course load and campus/location. *Financial support:* In 2011–12, 2 research assistantships (averaging $10,302 per year) were awarded; career-related internships or fieldwork, Federal Work-Study, scholarships/grants, health care benefits, tuition waivers (partial), and unspecified assistantships also available. Support available to part-time students. Financial award application deadline: 3/1; financial award applicants required to submit FAFSA. *Unit head:* Dr. Sheryl Tucker, Dean, 405-744-7099, Fax: 405-744-0355, E-mail: grad-i@okstate.edu. *Application contact:* Dr. Susan Mathew, Coordinator of Admissions, 405-744-6368, Fax: 405-744-0355, E-mail: grad-i@okstate.edu. Web site: http://gradcollege.okstate.edu/.

Princeton University, Princeton Institute for the Science and Technology of Materials (PRISM), Princeton, NJ 08544-1019. Offers materials (PhD).

Stevens Institute of Technology, Graduate School, Charles V. Schaefer Jr. School of Engineering, Department of Electrical and Computer Engineering, Program in Electrical Engineering, Hoboken, NJ 07030. Offers computer architecture and digital systems (M Eng); electrical engineering (PhD); microelectronics and photonics science and technology (M Eng); signal processing for communications (M Eng); telecommunications systems engineering (M Eng); wireless communications (M Eng, Certificate). *Degree requirements:* For master's, thesis optional; for doctorate, variable foreign language requirement, thesis/dissertation. *Entrance requirements:* For master's, doctorate, and Certificate, GRE. Additional exam requirements/recommendations for international students: Required—TOEFL. Electronic applications accepted.

Stevens Institute of Technology, Graduate School, Charles V. Schaefer Jr. School of Engineering, Interdisciplinary Program in Microelectronics and Photonics, Hoboken, NJ 07030. Offers Certificate.

The University of Alabama in Huntsville, School of Graduate Studies, College of Engineering, Department of Electrical and Computer Engineering, Huntsville, AL 35899. Offers computer engineering (MSE, PhD), including information assurance (MSE); electrical engineering (MSE, PhD), including optics and phontonics technology (MSE), opto-electronics (MSE); optics and photonics (MSE); software engineering (MSSE). Part-time and evening/weekend programs available. *Faculty:* 22 full-time (3 women), 4 part-time/adjunct (0 women). *Students:* 52 full-time (12 women), 138 part-time (22 women); includes 20 minority (7 Black or African American, non-Hispanic/Latino; 2 American Indian or Alaska Native, non-Hispanic/Latino; 8 Asian, non-Hispanic/Latino; 2 Hispanic/Latino; 1 Two or more races, non-Hispanic/Latino), 37 international. Average age 31. 157 applicants, 65% accepted, 48 enrolled. In 2011, 26 master's, 6 doctorates awarded. *Degree requirements:* For master's, comprehensive exam, thesis or alternative, oral and written exams; for doctorate, comprehensive exam, thesis/dissertation, oral and written exams. *Entrance requirements:* For master's, GRE General Test, appropriate bachelor's degree, minimum GPA of 3.0; for doctorate, GRE General Test, minimum GPA of 3.0. Additional exam requirements/recommendations for international students: Required—TOEFL (minimum score 500 paper-based; 173 computer-based; 62 iBT). *Application deadline:* For fall admission, 7/15 for domestic students, 4/1 for international students; for spring admission, 11/30 for domestic students, 9/1 for international students. Applications are processed on a rolling basis. Application fee: $40 ($50 for international students). Electronic applications accepted. *Expenses:* Tuition, state resident: full-time $7830; part-time $473.50 per credit. Tuition, nonresident: full-time $18,748; part-time $1128.33 per credit. Tuition and fees vary according to course load and program. *Financial support:* In 2011–12, 29 students received support, including 2 fellowships (averaging $11,154 per year), 9 research assistantships with full and partial tuition reimbursements available (averaging $10,959 per year), 20 teaching assistantships with full and partial tuition reimbursements available (averaging $11,330 per year); career-related internships or fieldwork, Federal Work-Study, institutionally sponsored loans, scholarships/grants, health care benefits, tuition waivers (full), and unspecified assistantships also available. Support available to part-time students. Financial award application deadline: 4/1; financial award applicants required to submit FAFSA. *Faculty research:* Optical signal processing, electromagnetics, photonics, nonlinear waves, computer architecture. *Total annual research expenditures:* $16.5 million. *Unit head:* Dr. Robert Lindquist, Chair, 256-824-6316, Fax: 256-824-6803, E-mail: lindquis@ece.uah.edu. *Application contact:* Kim Gray, Graduate Studies Admissions Coordinator, 256-824-6002, Fax: 256-824-6405, E-mail: deangrad@uah.edu. Web site: http://www.ece.uah.edu/.

The University of Alabama in Huntsville, School of Graduate Studies, College of Science, Department of Physics, Huntsville, AL 35899. Offers education (MS); optics and photonics technology (MS); physics (MS, PhD). Part-time and evening/weekend programs available. *Faculty:* 18 full-time (0 women), 4 part-time/adjunct (1 woman). *Students:* 34 full-time (7 women), 22 part-time (9 women); includes 2 minority (both Asian, non-Hispanic/Latino), 12 international. Average age 29. 48 applicants, 60% accepted, 15 enrolled. In 2011, 10 master's, 3 doctorates awarded. *Degree requirements:* For master's, comprehensive exam, thesis or alternative, oral and written exams; for doctorate, comprehensive exam, thesis/dissertation, oral and written exams. *Entrance requirements:* For master's and doctorate, GRE General Test, minimum GPA of 3.0. Additional exam requirements/recommendations for international students: Required—TOEFL (minimum score 550 paper-based; 213 computer-based; 62 iBT). *Application deadline:* For fall admission, 7/15 for domestic students, 4/1 for international students; for spring admission, 11/30 for domestic students, 9/1 for international students. Applications are processed on a rolling basis. Application fee: $40 ($50 for international students). Electronic applications accepted. *Expenses:* Tuition, state resident: full-time $7830; part-time $473.50 per credit. Tuition, nonresident: full-time $18,748; part-time $1128.33 per credit. Tuition and fees vary according to course load and program. *Financial support:* In 2011–12, 30 students received support, including 18 research assistantships with full and partial tuition reimbursements available (averaging $15,553 per year), 12 teaching assistantships with full and partial tuition reimbursements available (averaging $16,500 per year); career-related internships or fieldwork, Federal Work-Study, institutionally sponsored loans, scholarships/grants, health care benefits, and unspecified assistantships also available. Support available to part-time students. Financial award application deadline: 4/1; financial award applicants required to submit FAFSA. *Faculty research:* Space physics, cosmology/general relativity, optics/quantum optics, astrophysics/gamma-ray astronomy, strophysical instrumentation. *Total annual research expenditures:* $6.2 million. *Unit head:* Dr. Gary Zank, Chair, 256-824-2481, Fax: 256-824-6873, E-mail: gary.zank@uah.edu. *Application contact:* Kim Gray, Graduate Studies Admissions Coordinator, 256-824-6002, Fax: 256-824-6405, E-mail: deangrad@uah.edu. Web site: http://physics.uah.edu/.

University of Arkansas, Graduate School, Interdisciplinary Program in Microelectronics and Photonics, Fayetteville, AR 72701-1201. Offers MS, PhD. *Students:* 7 full-time (0 women), 39 part-time (5 women); includes 6 minority (4 Black or African American, non-Hispanic/Latino; 2 Asian, non-Hispanic/Latino), 19 international. In 2011, 4 master's, 4 doctorates awarded. *Degree requirements:* For doctorate, thesis/dissertation. *Application deadline:* For fall admission, 4/1 for international students; for spring admission, 10/1 for international students. Applications are processed on a rolling basis. Application fee: $40 ($50 for international students). Electronic applications accepted. *Financial support:* In 2011–12, 25 research assistantships, 4 teaching assistantships were awarded; fellowships with tuition reimbursements also available. Financial award application deadline: 4/1; financial award applicants required to submit FAFSA. *Unit head:* Dr. Ken Vickers, Head, 479-575-2875, Fax: 479-575-4580, E-mail: vickers@uark.edu. *Application contact:* Graduate Admissions, 479-575-6246, Fax: 479-575-5908, E-mail: gradinfo@uark.edu. Web site: http://microep.uark.edu.

University of California, San Diego, Office of Graduate Studies, Department of Electrical and Computer Engineering, La Jolla, CA 92093. Offers applied ocean science (MS, PhD); applied physics (MS, PhD); communication theory and systems (MS, PhD); computer engineering (MS, PhD); electrical engineering (M Eng); electronic circuits and systems (MS, PhD); intelligent systems, robotics and control (MS, PhD); photonics (MS, PhD); signal and image processing (MS, PhD). MS only offered to students who have been admitted to the PhD program. *Entrance requirements:* For master's and doctorate, GRE General Test. Electronic applications accepted.

University of California, Santa Barbara, Graduate Division, College of Engineering, Department of Electrical and Computer Engineering, Santa Barbara, CA 93106-2014. Offers communications, control and signal processing (MS, PhD); computer engineering (MS, PhD); electronics and photonics (MS, PhD); MS/PhD. *Faculty:* 37 full-time (3 women), 1 part-time/adjunct (0 women). *Students:* 272 full-time (52 women); includes 40 minority (2 American Indian or Alaska Native, non-Hispanic/Latino; 30 Asian, non-Hispanic/Latino; 6 Hispanic/Latino; 1 Native Hawaiian or other Pacific Islander, non-Hispanic/Latino; 1 Two or more races, non-Hispanic/Latino), 159 international. Average age 26. 1,252 applicants, 27% accepted, 95 enrolled. In 2011, 49 master's, 33 doctorates awarded. Terminal master's awarded for partial completion of doctoral program. *Median time to degree:* Of those who began their doctoral program in fall 2003, 44% received their degree in 8 years or less. *Degree requirements:* For master's,

comprehensive exam, thesis; for doctorate, thesis/dissertation. *Entrance requirements:* For master's and doctorate, GRE General Test. Additional exam requirements/recommendations for international students: Required—TOEFL (minimum score 550 paper-based; 80 iBT), IELTS (minimum score 7). *Application deadline:* For fall admission, 12/15 for domestic and international students; for winter admission, 11/1 for domestic and international students; for spring admission, 1/1 for domestic and international students. Application fee: $80 ($100 for international students). Electronic applications accepted. *Expenses:* Tuition, state resident: full-time $12,192. Tuition, nonresident: full-time $27,294. *Required fees:* $764.13. *Financial support:* In 2011–12, 196 students received support, including 70 fellowships with full and partial tuition reimbursements available (averaging $7,181 per year), 155 research assistantships with full and partial tuition reimbursements available (averaging $15,235 per year), 54 teaching assistantships with full and partial tuition reimbursements available (averaging $9,910 per year); tuition waivers (full and partial) also available. Financial award application deadline: 12/15; financial award applicants required to submit FAFSA. *Faculty research:* Communications, signal processing, computer engineering, control, electronics and photonics. *Total annual research expenditures:* $25.5 million. *Unit head:* Prof. Jerry Gibson, Chair, 805-893-3821, Fax: 805-893-6262, E-mail: gibson@ece.ucsb.edu. *Application contact:* Erika Raquel Klukovich, Graduate Admissions Coordinator, 805-893-3114, Fax: 805-893-5402, E-mail: erika@ece.ucsb.edu. Web site: http://www.ece.ucsb.edu/.

University of Central Florida, College of Optics and Photonics, Orlando, FL 32816. Offers optics (MS, PhD). Part-time and evening/weekend programs available. *Faculty:* 34 full-time (4 women), 8 part-time/adjunct (3 women). *Students:* 102 full-time (17 women), 20 part-time (3 women); includes 6 minority (1 Black or African American, non-Hispanic/Latino; 2 Asian, non-Hispanic/Latino; 3 Hispanic/Latino), 67 international. Average age 28. 197 applicants, 18% accepted, 24 enrolled. In 2011, 22 master's, 19 doctorates awarded. *Degree requirements:* For master's, thesis or alternative; for doctorate, thesis/dissertation, departmental qualifying exam, candidacy exam. *Entrance requirements:* For master's, GRE General Test, minimum GPA of 3.0 in last 60 hours; for doctorate, GRE General Test, minimum GPA of 3.5 in last 60 hours. Additional exam requirements/recommendations for international students: Required—TOEFL. *Application deadline:* For fall admission, 2/1 priority date for domestic students; for spring admission, 12/1 for domestic students. Application fee: $30. Electronic applications accepted. *Expenses:* Tuition, state resident: part-time $277.08 per credit hour. Tuition, nonresident: part-time $277.08 per credit hour. Part-time tuition and fees vary according to degree level and program. *Financial support:* In 2011–12, 63 students received support, including 14 fellowships with partial tuition reimbursements available (averaging $5,600 per year), 80 research assistantships with partial tuition reimbursements available (averaging $11,000 per year); career-related internships or fieldwork, Federal Work-Study, institutionally sponsored loans, tuition waivers (partial), and unspecified assistantships also available. Financial award application deadline: 3/1; financial award applicants required to submit FAFSA. *Unit head:* Dr. Bahaa E. Saleh, Dean and Director, 407-823-6817, E-mail: besaleh@creol.ucf.edu. *Application contact:* Barbara Rodriguez, Director, Admissions and Registration, 407-823-2766, Fax: 407-823-6442, E-mail: gradadmissions@ucf.edu. Web site: http://www.creol.ucf.edu/.

University of New Mexico, Graduate School, College of Arts and Sciences, Optical Science and Engineering Program, Albuquerque, NM 87131. Offers imaging science (MS, PhD); optical science and engineering (MS, PhD); photonics (MS, PhD). Part-time programs available. *Faculty:* 34 full-time (2 women). *Students:* 21 full-time (4 women), 31 part-time (6 women); includes 2 minority (1 American Indian or Alaska Native, non-Hispanic/Latino; 1 Hispanic/Latino), 36 international. Average age 30. 48 applicants, 21% accepted, 8 enrolled. In 2011, 10 master's, 5 doctorates awarded. Terminal master's awarded for partial completion of doctoral program. *Median time to degree:* Of those who began their doctoral program in fall 2003, 55% received their degree in 8 years or less. *Degree requirements:* For master's, comprehensive exam (for some programs), thesis (for some programs); for doctorate, comprehensive exam, thesis/dissertation. *Entrance requirements:* For master's, GRE General Test, GRE Subject Test in physics (preferred), relevant undergraduate coursework, curriculum vitae, letters of recommendation, letter of intent/personal statement; for doctorate, GRE General Test, GRE Subject Test in physics (preferred), relevant undergraduate coursework, curriculum vitae, letters of recommendation. Additional exam requirements/recommendations for international students: Required—TOEFL (minimum score 575 paper-based; 213 computer-based; 79 iBT), IELTS (minimum score 7). *Application deadline:* For fall admission, 1/15 priority date for domestic students, 1/15 for international students; for spring admission, 8/1 priority date for domestic students, 8/1 for international students. Application fee: $50. Electronic applications accepted. *Financial support:* In 2011–12, 34 students received support, including 29 research assistantships with full tuition reimbursements available (averaging $16,097 per year), 10 teaching assistantships with full tuition reimbursements available (averaging $14,400 per year); fellowships with full tuition reimbursements available, career-related internships or fieldwork, scholarships/grants, health care benefits, and unspecified assistantships also available. Support available to part-time students. Financial award application deadline: 2/1; financial award applicants required to submit FAFSA. *Faculty research:* Advanced materials, atom optics, biomedical optics, fiber optics, laser cooling, high intensity interactions, lithography, nano photonics, nonlinear optics, optical imaging, optical sensors, optoelectronics, quantum

Peterson's Graduate Programs in the Physical Sciences, Mathematics, Agricultural Sciences, the Environment & Natural Resources 2013

facebook.com/petersonspublishing **235**

optics, spectroscopy, ultrafast phenomena. *Unit head:* Dr. Majeed Hayat, General Chair, 505-272-7095, Fax: 505-277-7801, E-mail: hayat@ece.unm.edu.

Application contact: Doris Williams, Advisor, 505-277-7764, Fax: 505-277-7801, E-mail: dorisw@chtm.unm.edu. Web site: http://www.optics.unm.edu/.

Physics

Alabama Agricultural and Mechanical University, School of Graduate Studies, School of Arts and Sciences, Department of Physics, Huntsville, AL 35811. Offers physics (MS, PhD), including applied physics (PhD), materials science (PhD), optics/lasers (PhD). Part-time and evening/weekend programs available. *Degree requirements:* For doctorate, thesis/dissertation. *Entrance requirements:* For master's and doctorate, GRE General Test. Additional exam requirements/recommendations for international students: Required—TOEFL (minimum score 500 paper-based; 173 computer-based; 61 iBT). Electronic applications accepted.

American University of Beirut, Graduate Programs, Faculty of Arts and Sciences, Beirut, Lebanon. Offers anthropology (MA); Arabic language and literature (MA); archaeology (MA); biology (MS); chemistry (MS); computational science (MS); computer science (MS); economics (MA); education (MA); English language (MA); English literature (MA); environmental policy planning (MSES); financial economics (MAFE); geology (MS); history (MA); mathematics (MA, MS); Middle Eastern studies (MA); philosophy (MA); physics (MS); political studies (MA); psychology (MA); public administration (MA); sociology (MA); statistics (MA, MS). Part-time programs available. *Faculty:* 154 full-time (44 women), 12 part-time/adjunct (2 women). *Students:* 180 full-time (122 women), 240 part-time (158 women). Average age 25. 336 applicants, 47% accepted, 86 enrolled. In 2011, 57 master's awarded. *Degree requirements:* For master's, one foreign language, comprehensive exam, thesis (for some programs). *Entrance requirements:* For master's, GRE, letter of recommendation. Additional exam requirements/recommendations for international students: Required—TOEFL (minimum score 600 paper-based; 250 computer-based; 97 iBT), IELTS (minimum score 7). *Application deadline:* For fall admission, 4/30 for domestic and international students; for spring admission, 11/1 for domestic and international students. Application fee: $50. *Expenses: Tuition:* Full-time $12,780; part-time $710 per credit. *Required fees:* $528; $528 per credit. Tuition and fees vary according to course load and program. *Financial support:* In 2011–12, 33 students received support. Career-related internships or fieldwork, institutionally sponsored loans, scholarships/grants, health care benefits, and unspecified assistantships available. Financial award application deadline: 2/4; financial award applicants required to submit FAFSA. *Faculty research:* History of composition studies, syntax of Arabic dialects, Oscar Wilde, decadence, Middle Eastern and international politics, neural mechanisms of creativity and consciousness, personality and psycho-socio-cultural-spiritual correlates of negative and positive mental health, philosophy of mind, metaphysics, micropaleontology and stratigraphy, geochemistry, mineralogy and petrology, tectonophysics, Abbasid, Ottoman and Russian history, landscape, Bronze and Iron Age archaeology. *Unit head:* Dr. Patrick McGreevy, Dean, 961-1374374 Ext. 3800, Fax: 961-1744461, E-mail: pm07@aub.edu.lb. *Application contact:* Dr. Salim Kanaan, Director, Admissions Office, 961-1350000 Ext. 2594, Fax: 961-1750775, E-mail: sk00@aub.edu.lb. Web site: http://staff.aub.edu.lb/~webfas.

Arizona State University, College of Liberal Arts and Sciences, Department of Physics, Tempe, AZ 85287-1504. Offers nanoscience (PSM); physics (MNS, PhD). Part-time programs available. Terminal master's awarded for partial completion of doctoral program. *Degree requirements:* For master's, comprehensive exam, thesis or alternative, interactive Program of Study (iPOS) submitted before completing 50 percent of required credit hours; for doctorate, comprehensive exam, thesis/dissertation, interactive Program of Study (iPOS) submitted before completing 50 percent of required credit hours. *Entrance requirements:* For master's and doctorate, GRE, minimum GPA of 3.0 or equivalent in last 2 years of work leading to bachelor's degree. Additional exam requirements/recommendations for international students: Required—TOEFL (minimum score 80 iBT), TOEFL, IELTS, or Pearson Test of English. Electronic applications accepted. *Expenses:* Contact institution.

Auburn University, Graduate School, College of Sciences and Mathematics, Department of Physics, Auburn University, AL 36849. Offers MS, PhD. Part-time programs available. *Faculty:* 22 full-time (1 woman), 3 part-time/adjunct (0 women). *Students:* 17 full-time (3 women), 38 part-time (9 women); includes 3 minority (1 Black or African American, non-Hispanic/Latino; 1 Asian, non-Hispanic/Latino; 1 Hispanic/Latino), 19 international. Average age 28. 20 applicants, 70% accepted, 13 enrolled. In 2011, 5 master's, 7 doctorates awarded. *Degree requirements:* For doctorate, thesis/dissertation, oral and written exams. *Entrance requirements:* For master's and doctorate, GRE General Test. *Application deadline:* For fall admission, 7/7 for domestic students; for spring admission, 11/24 for domestic students. Applications are processed on a rolling basis. Application fee: $50 ($60 for international students). Electronic applications accepted. *Expenses:* Tuition, state resident: full-time $7290; part-time $405 per credit hour. Tuition, nonresident: full-time $21,870; part-time $1215 per credit hour. *International tuition:* $22,000 full-time. *Required fees:* $1402. *Financial support:* Research assistantships, teaching assistantships, career-related internships or fieldwork, and Federal Work-Study available. Support available to part-time students. Financial award application deadline: 3/15; financial award applicants required to submit FAFSA. *Faculty research:* Atomic/radiative physics, plasma physics, condensed matter physics, space physics, nonlinear dynamics. *Unit head:* Dr. Joe D. Perez, Head, 334-844-4264. *Application contact:* Dr. George Flowers, Dean of the Graduate School, 334-844-2125. Web site: http://www.physics.auburn.edu/.

Ball State University, Graduate School, College of Sciences and Humanities, Department of Physics and Astronomy, Program in Physics, Muncie, IN 47306-1099. Offers MA, MAE, MS. *Faculty:* 13. *Students:* 15 full-time (5 women), 7 part-time (3 women), 3 international. Average age 26. 17 applicants, 71% accepted, 6 enrolled. In 2011, 8 master's awarded. *Entrance requirements:* For master's, GRE General Test. Application fee: $50. Tuition and fees vary according to program and reciprocity agreements. *Financial support:* In 2011–12, 16 students received support, including 15 teaching assistantships with full tuition reimbursements available (averaging $8,811 per year); research assistantships with full tuition reimbursements available also available. Financial award application deadline: 3/1. *Faculty research:* Solar energy, particle physics, atomic spectroscopy. *Unit head:* Dr. Thomas Robertson. *Application contact:* Dr. Robert Morris, Associate Provost for Research and Dean of the Graduate School, 765-285-1300, E-mail: rmorris@bsu.edu. Web site: http://www.bsu.edu/physics/.

Baylor University, Graduate School, College of Arts and Sciences, Department of Physics, Waco, TX 76798. Offers MA, MS, PhD. *Students:* 27 full-time (8 women), 2 part-time (0 women); includes 1 minority (Hispanic/Latino), 18 international. In 2011, 2 master's, 6 doctorates awarded. *Degree requirements:* For master's, thesis or alternative; for doctorate, one foreign language, thesis/dissertation. *Entrance requirements:* For master's and doctorate, GRE General Test. *Application deadline:* Applications are processed on a rolling basis. Application fee: $25. *Financial support:* Fellowships, teaching assistantships, Federal Work-Study, and institutionally sponsored loans available. *Unit head:* Dr. Walter Wilcox, Graduate Program Director, 254-710-2510, Fax: 254-710-5083, E-mail: walter_wilcox@baylor.edu. *Application contact:* Marian Nunn-Graves, Administrative Assistant, 254-710-2511, Fax: 254-710-3870, E-mail: marian_nunn-graves@baylor.edu. Web site: http://www.baylor.edu/physics/.

Boston College, Graduate School of Arts and Sciences, Department of Physics, Chestnut Hill, MA 02467-3800. Offers MS, PhD. Terminal master's awarded for partial completion of doctoral program. *Degree requirements:* For master's, thesis (for some programs); for doctorate, thesis/dissertation. *Entrance requirements:* For master's and doctorate, GRE General Test, GRE Subject Test. Additional exam requirements/recommendations for international students: Required—TOEFL (minimum score 600 paper-based; 250 computer-based; 100 iBT). Electronic applications accepted. *Faculty research:* Atmospheric/space physics, astrophysics, atomic and molecular physics, fusion and plasmas, solid-state physics.

Boston University, Graduate School of Arts and Sciences, Department of Physics, Boston, MA 02215. Offers MA, PhD. *Students:* 110 full-time (16 women); includes 7 minority (4 Asian, non-Hispanic/Latino; 3 Hispanic/Latino), 49 international. Average age 26. 313 applicants, 20% accepted, 17 enrolled. In 2011, 4 master's, 13 doctorates awarded. Terminal master's awarded for partial completion of doctoral program. *Degree requirements:* For master's, one foreign language, comprehensive exam, thesis or alternative; for doctorate, one foreign language, comprehensive exam, thesis/dissertation. *Entrance requirements:* For master's and doctorate, GRE General Test, GRE Subject Test. Additional exam requirements/recommendations for international students: Required—TOEFL (minimum score 600 paper-based; 250 computer-based). *Application deadline:* For fall admission, 12/15 for domestic and international students. Application fee: $70. Electronic applications accepted. *Expenses: Tuition:* Full-time $40,848; part-time $1276 per credit hour. *Required fees:* $572; $286 per semester. *Financial support:* In 2011–12, 2 fellowships with full tuition reimbursements (averaging $19,800 per year), 66 research assistantships (averaging $19,300 per year), 29 teaching assistantships with full tuition reimbursements (averaging $19,300 per year) were awarded; Federal Work-Study and scholarships/grants also available. Support available to part-time students. Financial award application deadline: 12/15; financial award applicants required to submit FAFSA. *Unit head:* Dr. Sid Redner, Chairman, 617-353-2618, Fax: 617-353-9393, E-mail: redner@bu.edu. *Application contact:* Mirtha M. Cabello, Administrative Coordinator, 617-353-2623, Fax: 617-353-9393, E-mail: cabello@bu.edu. Web site: http://buphy.bu.edu/.

Bowling Green State University, Graduate College, College of Arts and Sciences, Department of Physics and Astronomy, Bowling Green, OH 43403. Offers geophysics (MS); physics (MAT, MS). *Degree requirements:* For master's, thesis or alternative. *Entrance requirements:* For master's, GRE General Test. Additional exam requirements/recommendations for international students:

236 facebook.com/petersonspublishing

Peterson's Graduate Programs in the Physical Sciences, Mathematics, Agricultural Sciences, the Environment & Natural Resources 2013

Required—TOEFL. Electronic applications accepted. *Faculty research:* Computational physics, solid-state physics, materials science, theoretical physics.

Brandeis University, Graduate School of Arts and Sciences, Department of Physics, Waltham, MA 02454-9110. Offers MS, PhD. Part-time programs available. Terminal master's awarded for partial completion of doctoral program. *Degree requirements:* For master's, qualifying exam, 1-year residency; for doctorate, thesis/dissertation, advanced exam. *Entrance requirements:* For master's, GRE General Test, GRE Subject Test, resume, letters of recommendation; for doctorate, GRE General Test, GRE Subject Test, resume, 2 letters of recommendation. Additional exam requirements/recommendations for international students: Required—TOEFL (minimum score 600 paper-based; 250 computer-based; 100 iBT); Recommended—IELTS (minimum score 7). Electronic applications accepted. *Faculty research:* Astrophysics, condensed-matter and biophysics, high energy and gravitational theory, particle physics, microfluidics, radio astronomy, string theory.

Brigham Young University, Graduate Studies, College of Physical and Mathematical Sciences, Department of Physics and Astronomy, Provo, UT 84602-1001. Offers physics (MS, PhD); physics and astronomy (PhD). Part-time programs available. *Faculty:* 29 full-time (2 women). *Students:* 36 full-time (4 women); includes 5 minority (3 Asian, non-Hispanic/Latino; 2 Hispanic/Latino). Average age 29. 22 applicants, 55% accepted, 8 enrolled. In 2011, 7 master's, 4 doctorates awarded. Terminal master's awarded for partial completion of doctoral program. *Degree requirements:* For master's, thesis; for doctorate, thesis/dissertation, qualifying exam. *Entrance requirements:* For master's and doctorate, GRE Subject Test (physics), GRE General Test, minimum GPA of 3.0 in last 60 hours, ecclesiastical endorsement. Additional exam requirements/recommendations for international students: Required—TOEFL (minimum score 580 paper-based; 85 iBT), IELTS (minimum score 7). *Application deadline:* For fall admission, 1/15 priority date for domestic students, 1/15 for international students. Application fee: $50. Electronic applications accepted. Full-time tuition for non-LDS students: $11,520 per year; $640 per credit. *Expenses: Tuition:* Full-time $5760; part-time $320 per credit. Tuition and fees vary according to student's religious affiliation. *Financial support:* In 2011–12, 35 students received support, including 18 research assistantships with full tuition reimbursements available (averaging $20,490 per year), 17 teaching assistantships with full tuition reimbursements available (averaging $19,485 per year); fellowships with full tuition reimbursements available, institutionally sponsored loans, and tuition waivers (full) also available. Support available to part-time students. Financial award application deadline: 1/15. *Faculty research:* Acoustics; atomic, molecular, and optical physics; theoretical and mathematical physics; condensed matter; astrophysics and plasma. *Total annual research expenditures:* $1.7 million. *Unit head:* Dr. Ross L. Spencer, Chair, 801-422-2341, Fax: 801-422-0553, E-mail: ross_spencer@byu.edu. *Application contact:* Dr. J. Ward Moody, Graduate Coordinator, 801-422-4347, Fax: 801-422-0553, E-mail: jmoody@byu.edu. Web site: http://physics.byu.edu/.

Brock University, Faculty of Graduate Studies, Faculty of Mathematics and Science, Program in Physics, St. Catharines, ON L2S 3A1, Canada. Offers M Sc. Part-time programs available. *Degree requirements:* For master's, thesis. *Entrance requirements:* For master's, honors B Sc in physics. Additional exam requirements/recommendations for international students: Required—TOEFL (minimum score 550 paper-based; 213 computer-based; 80 iBT), IELTS (minimum score 6.5), TWE (minimum score 4). Electronic applications accepted. *Faculty research:* Quantum physics, optical properties, non-crystalline materials, condensed matter physics, biophysics.

Brooklyn College of the City University of New York, Division of Graduate Studies, Department of Physics, Brooklyn, NY 11210-2889. Offers MA, PhD. Part-time programs available. Terminal master's awarded for partial completion of doctoral program. *Degree requirements:* For master's, comprehensive exam, thesis or alternative, 30 credits. *Entrance requirements:* For master's, 2 letters of recommendation, 12 credits in advanced physics; for doctorate, GRE. Additional exam requirements/recommendations for international students: Required—TOEFL (minimum score 500 paper-based; 173 computer-based; 61 iBT). Electronic applications accepted.

Brooklyn College of the City University of New York, Division of Graduate Studies, School of Education, Program in Middle Childhood Education (Science), Brooklyn, NY 11210-2889. Offers biology (MA); chemistry (MA); earth science (MA); general science (MA); physics (MA). Part-time and evening/weekend programs available. *Entrance requirements:* For master's, LAST, interview, previous course work in education and mathematics, resume, 2 letters of recommendation, essay. Additional exam requirements/recommendations for international students: Required—TOEFL (minimum score 500 paper-based; 173 computer-based; 61 iBT). Electronic applications accepted. *Faculty research:* Geometric thinking, mastery of basic facts, problem-solving strategies, history of mathematics.

Brown University, Graduate School, Department of Physics, Providence, RI 02912. Offers Sc M, PhD. *Degree requirements:* For doctorate, thesis/dissertation, qualifying and oral exams.

Bryn Mawr College, Graduate School of Arts and Sciences, Department of Physics, Bryn Mawr, PA 19010-2899. Offers MA, PhD. *Faculty:* 2 full-time (0 women), 2 part-time/adjunct (0 women). *Students:* 2 full-time (0 women), 4 part-time (2 women). Average age 27. 7 applicants, 71% accepted, 3 enrolled. In 2011, 1 master's awarded. *Degree requirements:* For master's, one foreign language, thesis; for doctorate, one foreign language, thesis/dissertation. *Entrance requirements:* For master's and doctorate, GRE General Test, GRE Subject Test. Additional exam requirements/recommendations for international students: Required—TOEFL (minimum score 600 paper-based; 250 computer-based). *Application deadline:* For fall admission, 1/3 for domestic and international students. Application fee: $50. *Expenses: Tuition:* Full-time $34,110; part-time $4500 per unit. *Financial support:* In 2011–12, 1 research assistantship with full tuition reimbursement (averaging $4,750 per year), 2 teaching assistantships with partial tuition reimbursements (averaging $14,000 per year) were awarded; Federal Work-Study, scholarships/grants, tuition waivers (partial), and tuition awards also available. Support available to part-time students. Financial award application deadline: 1/3. *Unit head:* Dr. Peter Beckmann, Chair/Professor of Physics, 610-526-5634. *Application contact:* Teri Lobo, Administrative Assistant to the Graduate School of Arts and Sciences Dean, 610-526-5074.

California Institute of Technology, Division of Physics, Mathematics and Astronomy, Department of Physics, Pasadena, CA 91125-0001. Offers PhD. *Degree requirements:* For doctorate, thesis/dissertation, candidacy and final exams. *Entrance requirements:* For doctorate, GRE General Test, GRE Subject Test. Additional exam requirements/recommendations for international students: Required—TOEFL. *Faculty research:* High-energy physics, nuclear physics, condensed-matter physics, theoretical physics and astrophysics, gravity physics.

California State University, Fresno, Division of Graduate Studies, College of Science and Mathematics, Department of Physics, Fresno, CA 93740-8027. Offers MS. Part-time programs available. *Degree requirements:* For master's, thesis or alternative. *Entrance requirements:* For master's, GRE General Test, minimum GPA of 2.5. Additional exam requirements/recommendations for international students: Required—TOEFL. Electronic applications accepted. *Faculty research:* Energy, astronomy, silicon vertex detector, neuroimaging, particle physics.

California State University, Fullerton, Graduate Studies, College of Natural Science and Mathematics, Department of Physics, Fullerton, CA 92834-9480. Offers MA. Part-time programs available. *Students:* 2 full-time (0 women), 9 part-time (0 women); includes 3 minority (2 Asian, non-Hispanic/Latino; 1 Hispanic/Latino), 1 international. Average age 27. 18 applicants, 50% accepted, 1 enrolled. In 2011, 5 master's awarded. Application fee: $55. *Financial support:* Research assistantships, teaching assistantships, career-related internships or fieldwork, Federal Work-Study, institutionally sponsored loans, and scholarships/grants available. Support available to part-time students. Financial award application deadline: 3/1; financial award applicants required to submit FAFSA. *Unit head:* Dr. Morty Khakoo, Chair, 657-278-3366. *Application contact:* Admissions/Applications, 657-278-2371.

California State University, Long Beach, Graduate Studies, College of Natural Sciences and Mathematics, Department of Physics and Astronomy, Long Beach, CA 90840. Offers physics (MS). Part-time programs available. *Faculty:* 8 full-time (2 women). *Students:* 12 full-time (0 women), 20 part-time (3 women); includes 7 minority (5 Asian, non-Hispanic/Latino; 1 Hispanic/Latino; 1 Two or more races, non-Hispanic/Latino), 2 international. Average age 29. 38 applicants, 61% accepted, 8 enrolled. In 2011, 6 master's awarded. *Degree requirements:* For master's, comprehensive exam or thesis. *Application deadline:* For fall admission, 7/1 for domestic students. Applications are processed on a rolling basis. Application fee: $55. Electronic applications accepted. *Financial support:* Federal Work-Study, institutionally sponsored loans, and scholarships/grants available. Financial award application deadline: 3/2. *Faculty research:* Musical acoustics, modern optics, neutrino physics, quantum gravity, atomic physics. *Unit head:* Dr. Patrick Kenealy, Chair, 562-985-8745, Fax: 562-985-7924, E-mail: kenealyp@csulb.edu. *Application contact:* Dr. Chuhee Kwon, Graduate Advisor, 562-985-4855, Fax: 562-985-7924, E-mail: ckwon@csulb.edu.

California State University, Los Angeles, Graduate Studies, College of Natural and Social Sciences, Department of Physics and Astronomy, Los Angeles, CA 90032-8530. Offers physics (MS). Part-time and evening/weekend programs available. *Faculty:* 2 full-time (0 women), 1 (woman) part-time/adjunct. *Students:* 10 full-time (3 women), 12 part-time (3 women); includes 15 minority (4 Asian, non-Hispanic/Latino; 11 Hispanic/Latino), 1 international. Average age 31. 22 applicants, 73% accepted, 7 enrolled. In 2011, 4 master's awarded. *Degree requirements:* For master's, comprehensive exam or thesis. *Entrance requirements:* Additional exam requirements/recommendations for international students: Required—TOEFL (minimum score 500 paper-based; 173 computer-based). *Application deadline:* For fall admission, 5/1 for domestic and international students. Applications are processed on a rolling basis. Application fee: $55. Electronic applications accepted. *Expenses:* Tuition, state resident: full-time $8225. *Financial support:* Federal Work-Study available. Support available to part-time students. Financial award application deadline: 3/1. *Faculty research:* Intermediate energy, nuclear physics, condensed-matter physics, biophysics. *Unit head:* Dr. Susan Terebey, Chair, 323-343-2100, Fax: 323-343-2497, E-mail: sterebe@calstatela.edu. *Application contact:* Dr. Karin Brown, Acting Associate Dean of Graduate Studies, 323-343-3820, Fax: 323-343-5653, E-mail: kbrown5@calstatela.edu. Web site: http://www.calstatela.edu/dept/physics/.

California State University, Northridge, Graduate Studies, College of Science and Mathematics, Department of Physics and Astronomy, Northridge, CA 91330.

Peterson's Graduate Programs in the Physical Sciences, Mathematics, Agricultural Sciences, the Environment & Natural Resources 2013

facebook.com/petersonspublishing **237**

Physics

Offers physics (MS). Part-time and evening/weekend programs available. *Degree requirements:* For master's, thesis or comprehensive exam. *Entrance requirements:* For master's, GRE General Test or minimum GPA of 3.0. Additional exam requirements/recommendations for international students: Required—TOEFL.

Carleton University, Faculty of Graduate Studies, Faculty of Science, Department of Physics, Ottawa, ON K1S 5B6, Canada. Offers M Sc, PhD. Programs offered jointly with University of Ottawa. *Degree requirements:* For master's, thesis optional, seminar; for doctorate, comprehensive exam, thesis/dissertation, seminar. *Entrance requirements:* For master's, honors degree in science; for doctorate, M Sc. Additional exam requirements/recommendations for international students: Required—TOEFL. *Faculty research:* Experimental and theoretical elementary particle physics, medical physics.

Carnegie Mellon University, Mellon College of Science, Department of Physics, Pittsburgh, PA 15213-3891. Offers applied physics (PhD); physics (MS, PhD). *Degree requirements:* For doctorate, thesis/dissertation, qualifying exam. *Entrance requirements:* For doctorate, GRE General Test, GRE Subject Test. Additional exam requirements/recommendations for international students: Required—TOEFL. Electronic applications accepted. *Faculty research:* Astrophysics, condensed matter physics, biological physics, medium energy and nuclear physics, high-energy physics.

Case Western Reserve University, School of Graduate Studies, Department of Physics, Cleveland, OH 44106. Offers MS, PhD. Part-time programs available. *Faculty:* 23 full-time (4 women), 5 part-time/adjunct (1 woman). *Students:* 50 full-time (5 women), 7 part-time (2 women); includes 4 minority (1 Asian, non-Hispanic/Latino; 1 Hispanic/Latino; 2 Two or more races, non-Hispanic/Latino), 20 international. Average age 26. 150 applicants, 30% accepted, 15 enrolled. In 2011, 2 master's, 4 doctorates awarded. Terminal master's awarded for partial completion of doctoral program. *Degree requirements:* For master's, comprehensive exam, exam; for doctorate, thesis/dissertation, qualifying exam, topical exam. *Entrance requirements:* For master's and doctorate, GRE General Test, GRE Subject Test (physics). Additional exam requirements/recommendations for international students: Required—TOEFL (minimum score 577 paper-based; 213 computer-based; 90 iBT); Recommended—IELTS (minimum score 7). *Application deadline:* For fall admission, 1/15 priority date for domestic students. Applications are processed on a rolling basis. Application fee: $8. Electronic applications accepted. *Financial support:* Fellowships, research assistantships, teaching assistantships, tuition waivers, and unspecified assistantships available. Financial award application deadline: 1/15. *Faculty research:* Condensed-matter physics, imaging physics, nonlinear optics, high-energy physics, cosmology and astrophysics. *Unit head:* Prof. Kathleen Kash, Chair, 216-368-4000, E-mail: kathleen.kash@case.edu. *Application contact:* Patricia Bacevice, Admissions, 216-368-4000, Fax: 216-368-4671, E-mail: pab6@case.edu. Web site: http://www.phys.cwru.edu/.

The Catholic University of America, School of Arts and Sciences, Department of Physics, Washington, DC 20064. Offers MS, PhD. Part-time programs available. *Faculty:* 13 full-time (2 women). *Students:* 16 full-time (5 women), 18 part-time (8 women); includes 4 minority (1 Asian, non-Hispanic/Latino; 3 Hispanic/Latino), 10 international. Average age 28. 23 applicants, 74% accepted, 8 enrolled. In 2011, 2 master's, 4 doctorates awarded. *Degree requirements:* For master's, comprehensive exam, thesis or alternative; for doctorate, comprehensive exam, thesis/dissertation, oral exam. *Entrance requirements:* For master's and doctorate, GRE General Test, statement of purpose, official copies of academic transcripts, three letters of recommendation. Additional exam requirements/recommendations for international students: Required—TOEFL (minimum score 580 paper-based; 237 computer-based). *Application deadline:* For fall admission, 8/1 priority date for domestic students, 7/15 for international students; for spring admission, 12/1 priority date for domestic students, 10/15 for international students. Applications are processed on a rolling basis. Application fee: $55. Electronic applications accepted. *Expenses:* Tuition: Full-time $35,260; part-time $1380 per credit. *Required fees:* $80; $40 per semester hour. One-time fee: $425. *Financial support:* Fellowships, research assistantships, teaching assistantships, Federal Work-Study, scholarships/grants, tuition waivers (full and partial), and unspecified assistantships available. Financial award application deadline: 2/1; financial award applicants required to submit FAFSA. *Faculty research:* Glass and ceramics technologies, astrophysics and computational sciences, the role of evolution in galaxy properties, nuclear physics, biophysics. Total annual research expenditures: $11.6 million. *Unit head:* Dr. Steve Kraemer, Chair, 202-319-5856, Fax: 202-319-4448, E-mail: kraemer@cua.edu. *Application contact:* Andrew Woodall, Director of Graduate Admissions, 202-319-5057, Fax: 202-319-6533, E-mail: cua-admissions@cua.edu. Web site: http://physics.cua.edu/.

Central Connecticut State University, School of Graduate Studies, School of Arts and Sciences, Department of Physics and Earth Science, New Britain, CT 06050-4010. Offers natural sciences (MS); science education (Certificate). Part-time and evening/weekend programs available. *Faculty:* 11 full-time (4 women), 17 part-time/adjunct (3 women). *Students:* 1 full-time (0 women), 9 part-time (6 women); includes 1 minority (Asian, non-Hispanic/Latino). Average age 38. 5 applicants, 80% accepted, 2 enrolled. In 2011, 7 master's awarded. *Degree requirements:* For master's, comprehensive exam, thesis or alternative; for Certificate, qualifying exam. *Entrance requirements:* For master's, minimum

undergraduate GPA of 2.7. Additional exam requirements/recommendations for international students: Required—TOEFL (minimum score 550 paper-based; 213 computer-based). *Application deadline:* For fall admission, 6/1 for domestic students, 5/1 for international students; for spring admission, 11/1 for domestic and international students. Applications are processed on a rolling basis. Application fee: $50. Electronic applications accepted. *Expenses: Tuition, area resident:* Full-time $5137; part-time $482 per credit. Tuition, state resident: full-time $7707; part-time $494 per credit. Tuition, nonresident: full-time $14,311; part-time $494 per credit. *Required fees:* $3865. One-time fee: $62 part-time. *Financial support:* In 2011–12, 1 student received support. Career-related internships or fieldwork, Federal Work-Study, scholarships/grants, and unspecified assistantships available. Support available to part-time students. Financial award application deadline: 4/15; financial award applicants required to submit FAFSA. *Faculty research:* Elementary/secondary science education, particle and solid states, weather patterns, planetary studies. *Unit head:* Dr. Steven Newman, Chair, 860-832-2930, E-mail: newman@ccsu.edu. *Application contact:* Patricia Gardner, Associate Director of Graduate Studies, 860-832-2350, Fax: 860-832-2352, E-mail: graduateadmissions@ccsu.edu. Web site: http://www.physics.ccsu.edu/.

Central Michigan University, College of Graduate Studies, College of Science and Technology, Department of Physics, Mount Pleasant, MI 48859. Offers physics (MS); science of advanced materials (PhD). PhD is an interdisciplinary program. Part-time programs available. *Degree requirements:* For master's, thesis or alternative; for doctorate, comprehensive exam, thesis/dissertation. *Entrance requirements:* For doctorate, GRE, bachelor's degree in physics, chemistry, biochemistry, biology, geology, engineering, mathematics, or other relevant area. Electronic applications accepted. *Faculty research:* Science of advanced materials, polymer physics, laser spectroscopy, observational astronomy, nuclear physics.

Christopher Newport University, Graduate Studies, Department of Physics, Computer Science, and Engineering, Newport News, VA 23606-2998. Offers applied physics and computer science (MS). Part-time and evening/weekend programs available. *Degree requirements:* For master's, comprehensive exam (for some programs), thesis optional. *Entrance requirements:* For master's, GRE General Test, minimum GPA of 3.0. Additional exam requirements/recommendations for international students: Required—TOEFL (minimum score 580 paper-based; 237 computer-based; 92 iBT). Electronic applications accepted. *Faculty research:* Advanced programming methodologies, experimental nuclear physics, computer architecture, semiconductor nanophysics, laser and optical fiber sensors.

City College of the City University of New York, Graduate School, College of Liberal Arts and Science, Division of Science, Department of Physics, New York, NY 10031-9198. Offers MA, PhD. PhD program offered jointly with Graduate School and University Center of the City University of New York. Terminal master's awarded for partial completion of doctoral program. *Degree requirements:* For master's, comprehensive exam; for doctorate, thesis/dissertation. *Entrance requirements:* For doctorate, GRE. Additional exam requirements/recommendations for international students: Required—TOEFL (minimum score 500 paper-based; 61 iBT). Electronic applications accepted.

Clark Atlanta University, School of Arts and Sciences, Department of Physics, Atlanta, GA 30314. Offers MS. Part-time programs available. *Faculty:* 6 full-time (0 women). *Students:* 2 full-time (1 woman), 3 part-time (1 woman); includes 2 minority (both Black or African American, non-Hispanic/Latino), 3 international. Average age 30. 3 applicants, 100% accepted, 2 enrolled. In 2011, 1 master's awarded. *Degree requirements:* For master's, one foreign language, comprehensive exam, thesis optional. *Entrance requirements:* For master's, GRE General Test, minimum GPA of 2.5. Additional exam requirements/recommendations for international students: Required—TOEFL (minimum score 500 paper-based; 173 computer-based; 61 iBT). *Application deadline:* For fall admission, 4/1 for domestic and international students; for spring admission, 11/1 for domestic and international students. Applications are processed on a rolling basis. Application fee: $40 ($55 for international students). *Expenses: Tuition:* Full-time $13,572; part-time $754 per credit hour. *Required fees:* $806; $403 per semester. *Financial support:* Scholarships/grants and unspecified assistantships available. Financial award application deadline: 4/30; financial award applicants required to submit FAFSA. *Faculty research:* Fusion energy, investigations of nonlinear differential equations, difference schemes, collisions in dense plasma. *Unit head:* Dr. Swaraj Tayal, Chairperson, 404-880-6877, E-mail: stayal@cau.edu. *Application contact:* Michelle Clark-Davis, Graduate Program Admissions, 404-880-6605, E-mail: cauadmissions@cau.edu.

Clarkson University, Graduate School, School of Arts and Sciences, Department of Physics, Potsdam, NY 13699. Offers MS, PhD. Part-time programs available. *Faculty:* 13 full-time (1 woman). *Students:* 11 full-time (2 women), 5 international. Average age 26. 23 applicants, 61% accepted, 3 enrolled. In 2011, 4 master's, 3 doctorates awarded. Terminal master's awarded for partial completion of doctoral program. *Degree requirements:* For doctorate, thesis/dissertation, departmental qualifying exam. *Entrance requirements:* For master's and doctorate, GRE, transcripts of all college coursework, three letters of recommendation; resume and personal statement (recommended). Additional exam requirements/recommendations for international students: Required—TOEFL, TSE recommended. *Application deadline:* For fall admission, 1/30 priority

238 facebook.com/petersonspublishing

Peterson's Graduate Programs in the Physical Sciences, Mathematics, Agricultural Sciences, the Environment & Natural Resources 2013

date for domestic students, 1/30 for international students; for spring admission, 9/1 priority date for domestic students, 9/1 for international students. Applications are processed on a rolling basis. Application fee: $25 ($35 for international students). Electronic applications accepted. *Expenses: Tuition:* Full-time $14,376; part-time $1198 per credit hour. *Required fees:* $295 per semester. *Financial support:* In 2011–12, 11 students received support, including fellowships with full tuition reimbursements available (averaging $21,999 per year), 2 research assistantships with full tuition reimbursements available (averaging $21,999 per year), 10 teaching assistantships with full tuition reimbursements available (averaging $21,999 per year); scholarships/grants, tuition waivers (partial), and unspecified assistantships also available. *Faculty research:* Biochemical computing, microthermometers, theoretical and mathematical topics, novel particle tracers. *Total annual research expenditures:* $532,872. *Unit head:* Dr. Dipankar Roy, Chair, 315-268-2396, Fax: 315-268-7754, E-mail: samoy@clarkson.edu. *Application contact:* Jennifer Reed, Graduate School Coordinator, School of Arts and Sciences, 315-268-3802, Fax: 315-268-3989, E-mail: sciencegrad@clarkson.edu. Web site: http://www.clarkson.edu/physics/.

Clark University, Graduate School, Department of Physics, Worcester, MA 01610-1477. Offers MA, PhD. Part-time programs available. *Faculty:* 6 full-time (0 women). *Students:* 8 full-time (4 women), 7 international. Average age 27. 14 applicants, 29% accepted, 2 enrolled. In 2011, 2 master's, 3 doctorates awarded. Terminal master's awarded for partial completion of doctoral program. *Degree requirements:* For master's, thesis or alternative; for doctorate, one foreign language, thesis/dissertation. *Entrance requirements:* Additional exam requirements/recommendations for international students: Required—TOEFL. *Application deadline:* For fall admission, 2/1 for domestic students. Application fee: $50. *Expenses: Tuition:* Full-time $37,000; part-time $1156 per credit hour. *Financial support:* In 2011–12, 2 research assistantships with full tuition reimbursements (averaging $18,280 per year), 5 teaching assistantships with full tuition reimbursements (averaging $18,280 per year) were awarded; fellowships with full and partial tuition reimbursements, Federal Work-Study, and tuition waivers (full and partial) also available. Financial award application deadline: 4/1. *Faculty research:* Statistical and thermal physics, magnetic properties of materials, computer simulation, particle diffusion. *Total annual research expenditures:* $280,000. *Unit head:* Dr. Charles Agosta, Chair, 508-793-7169, Fax: 508-793-8861, E-mail: cagosta@clarku.edu. *Application contact:* Sujata Davis, Department Secretary, 508-793-7169, Fax: 508-793-8861, E-mail: sdavis1@clarku.edu. Web site: http://www.clarku.edu/departments/physics/graduate/index.cfm.

Clemson University, Graduate School, College of Engineering and Science, Department of Physics and Astronomy, Clemson, SC 29634. Offers physics (MS, PhD), including astronomy and astrophysics, atmospheric physics, biophysics. Part-time programs available. *Faculty:* 27 full-time (3 women). *Students:* 67 full-time (21 women); includes 3 minority (2 Black or African American, non-Hispanic/Latino; 1 Hispanic/Latino), 27 international. Average age 27. 133 applicants, 75% accepted, 31 enrolled. In 2011, 4 master's, 6 doctorates awarded. Terminal master's awarded for partial completion of doctoral program. *Degree requirements:* For master's, thesis or alternative; for doctorate, thesis/dissertation. *Entrance requirements:* For master's and doctorate, GRE General Test. Additional exam requirements/recommendations for international students: Required—TOEFL. *Application deadline:* For fall admission, 1/15 priority date for domestic students; for spring admission, 9/15 priority date for domestic students. Applications are processed on a rolling basis. Application fee: $70 ($80 for international students). Electronic applications accepted. *Financial support:* In 2011–12, 58 students received support, including 1 fellowship with full and partial tuition reimbursement available (averaging $8,000 per year), 24 research assistantships with partial tuition reimbursements available (averaging $13,653 per year), 50 teaching assistantships with partial tuition reimbursements available (averaging $13,265 per year); career-related internships or fieldwork, institutionally sponsored loans, scholarships/grants, health care benefits, and unspecified assistantships also available. Support available to part-time students. Financial award application deadline: 6/1; financial award applicants required to submit FAFSA. *Faculty research:* Radiation physics, solid-state physics, nuclear physics, radar and lidar studies of atmosphere. *Total annual research expenditures:* $2.6 million. *Unit head:* Dr. Peter Barnes, Chair, 864-656-3419, Fax: 864-656-0805, E-mail: peterb@clemson.edu. *Application contact:* Graduate Coordinator, 864-656-6702, Fax: 864-656-0805, E-mail: physgradinfo-l@clemson.edu. Web site: http://physicsnt.clemson.edu/.

Cleveland State University, College of Graduate Studies, College of Sciences and Health Professions, Department of Physics, Cleveland, OH 44115. Offers applied optics (MS); condensed matter physics (MS); medical physics (MS); optics and materials (MS); optics and medical imaging (MS). Part-time and evening/weekend programs available. *Faculty:* 4 full-time (0 women), 1 part-time/adjunct (0 women). *Students:* 2 full-time (0 women), 12 part-time (3 women), 1 international. Average age 36. 29 applicants, 55% accepted, 7 enrolled. In 2011, 7 master's awarded. *Entrance requirements:* For master's, undergraduate degree in engineering, physics, chemistry or mathematics. Additional exam requirements/recommendations for international students: Required—TOEFL (minimum score 525 paper-based; 197 computer-based). *Application deadline:* For fall admission, 7/15 priority date for domestic students, 7/15 for international students. Applications are processed on a rolling basis. Application fee: $30. Electronic applications accepted. *Expenses: Tuition,* state resident: full-time $6416; part-time $494 per credit hour. Tuition, nonresident: full-time $12,074; part-time $929

per credit hour. *Financial support:* In 2011–12, 1 research assistantship with full and partial tuition reimbursement (averaging $5,666 per year) was awarded; fellowships with tuition reimbursements, teaching assistantships, and tuition waivers (full) also available. *Faculty research:* Statistical physics, experimental solid-state physics, theoretical optics, experimental biological physics (macromolecular crystallography); experimental optics. *Total annual research expenditures:* $350,000. *Unit head:* Dr. Miron Kaufman, Chairperson, 216-687-2436, Fax: 216-523-7268, E-mail: m.kaufman@csuohio.edu. *Application contact:* Dr. James A. Lock, Director, 216-687-2420, Fax: 216-523-7268, E-mail: j.lock@csuohio.edu. Web site: http://www.csuohio.edu/sciences/dept/physics/index.html.

The College of William and Mary, Faculty of Arts and Sciences, Department of Physics, Williamsburg, VA 23187-8795. Offers MS, PhD. *Faculty:* 37 full-time (4 women). *Students:* 65 full-time (19 women), 1 (woman) part-time; includes 1 minority (Hispanic/Latino), 27 international. Average age 26. 118 applicants, 27% accepted, 14 enrolled. In 2011, 1 master's, 11 doctorates awarded. Terminal master's awarded for partial completion of doctoral program. *Degree requirements:* For master's, minimum GPA of 3.0, 32 credit hours; for doctorate, comprehensive exam, thesis/dissertation, 1-year residency, 2 semesters of physics teaching. *Entrance requirements:* For doctorate, GRE General Test, GRE Subject Test, minimum GPA of 2.5. Additional exam requirements/recommendations for international students: Required—TOEFL. *Application deadline:* For fall admission, 1/15 priority date for domestic students, 1/15 for international students. Applications are processed on a rolling basis. Application fee: $45. Electronic applications accepted. *Expenses:* Tuition, state resident: full-time $6400; part-time $365 per credit hour. Tuition, nonresident: full-time $19,720; part-time $985 per credit hour. *Required fees:* $4562. *Financial support:* In 2011–12, 65 students received support, including 34 research assistantships with full tuition reimbursements available, 31 teaching assistantships with full tuition reimbursements available; career-related internships or fieldwork, health care benefits, tuition waivers (full), and unspecified assistantships also available. *Faculty research:* Nuclear/particle, condensed-matter, atomic, and plasma physics; accelerator physics; molecular/optical physics; computational/nonlinear physics. *Total annual research expenditures:* $4.5 million. *Unit head:* Dr. David Armstrong, Chair, 757-221-3500, Fax: 757-221-3540, E-mail: chair@physics.wm.edu. *Application contact:* Dr. Marc Sher, Chair of Admissions, 757-221-3538, Fax: 757-221-3540, E-mail: grad@physics.wm.edu. Web site: http://www.wm.edu/physics/.

Colorado School of Mines, Graduate School, Department of Physics, Golden, CO 80401-1887. Offers applied physics (MS, PhD). Part-time programs available. *Faculty:* 34 full-time (2 women), 9 part-time/adjunct (3 women). *Students:* 60 full-time (12 women), 7 part-time (2 women); includes 4 minority (1 Asian, non-Hispanic/Latino; 3 Hispanic/Latino), 10 international. Average age 28. 101 applicants, 35% accepted, 25 enrolled. In 2011, 6 master's, 3 doctorates awarded. *Degree requirements:* For master's, thesis (for some programs); for doctorate, comprehensive exam, thesis/dissertation. *Entrance requirements:* For master's and doctorate, GRE General Test, GRE Subject Test. Additional exam requirements/recommendations for international students: Required—TOEFL (minimum score 550 paper-based; 213 computer-based; 80 iBT). *Application deadline:* For fall admission, 1/15 priority date for domestic students, 1/15 for international students; for spring admission, 10/15 priority date for domestic students, 10/15 for international students. Application fee: $50 ($70 for international students). Electronic applications accepted. *Expenses:* Tuition, state resident: full-time $12,585; part-time $699 per credit. Tuition, nonresident: full-time $27,270; part-time $1516 per credit. *Required fees:* $1864.20; $670 per semester. *Financial support:* In 2011–12, 48 students received support, including 1 fellowship with full tuition reimbursement available (averaging $20,000 per year), 31 research assistantships with full tuition reimbursements available (averaging $20,000 per year), 16 teaching assistantships with full tuition reimbursements available (averaging $20,000 per year); scholarships/grants, health care benefits, and unspecified assistantships also available. Financial award application deadline: 1/15; financial award applicants required to submit FAFSA. *Faculty research:* Light scattering, low-energy nuclear physics, high fusion plasma diagnostics, laser operations, mathematical physics. *Total annual research expenditures:* $2.4 million. *Unit head:* Dr. Thomas Furtak, Head, 303-273-3843, Fax: 303-273-3919, E-mail: tfurtak@mines.edu. *Application contact:* Dr. David Wood, Professor, 303-273-3853, Fax: 303-273-3919, E-mail: dwood@mines.edu. Web site: http://physics.mines.edu.

Colorado State University, Graduate School, College of Natural Sciences, Department of Physics, Fort Collins, CO 80523-1875. Offers MS, PhD. Postbaccalaureate distance learning degree programs offered (no on-campus study). *Faculty:* 20 full-time (2 women), 1 part-time/adjunct (0 women). *Students:* 34 full-time (8 women), 37 part-time (5 women); includes 8 minority (1 Black or African American, non-Hispanic/Latino; 2 Asian, non-Hispanic/Latino; 2 Hispanic/Latino; 3 Two or more races, non-Hispanic/Latino), 17 international. Average age 26. 49 applicants, 78% accepted, 20 enrolled. In 2011, 9 master's, 5 doctorates awarded. Terminal master's awarded for partial completion of doctoral program. *Degree requirements:* For master's, comprehensive exam (for some programs), thesis (for some programs); for doctorate, comprehensive exam, thesis/dissertation. *Entrance requirements:* For master's, GRE General Test or GRE Subject Test (physics), minimum GPA of 3.0; 3 letters of recommendation; for doctorate, GRE General Test or GRE Subject Test (physics), minimum GPA of 3.0; transcripts; 3 letters of recommendation; BA (for domestic students); statement of purpose. Additional exam requirements/recommendations for

Peterson's Graduate Programs in the Physical Sciences, Mathematics, Agricultural Sciences, the Environment & Natural Resources 2013

facebook.com/petersonspublishing **239**

international students: Required—TOEFL (minimum score 550 paper-based; 213 computer-based; 80 iBT). *Application deadline:* For fall admission, 2/15 priority date for domestic students, 2/15 for international students; for spring admission, 7/15 priority date for domestic students, 7/15 for international students. Applications are processed on a rolling basis. Application fee: $50. Electronic applications accepted. *Expenses:* Tuition, state resident: full-time $7992. Tuition, nonresident: full-time $19,592. *Required fees:* $1735; $58 per credit. *Financial support:* In 2011–12, 65 students received support, including 6 fellowships (averaging $42,427 per year), 26 research assistantships with full tuition reimbursements available (averaging $15,558 per year), 33 teaching assistantships with full tuition reimbursements available (averaging $14,885 per year); health care benefits also available. Financial award application deadline: 1/15; financial award applicants required to submit FAFSA. *Faculty research:* Experimental condensed-matter physics, laser spectroscopy, optics, theoretical condensed-matter physics, particle physics. *Total annual research expenditures:* $3.2 million. *Unit head:* Dr. John Harton, Chair, 970-491-6246, Fax: 970-491-7947, E-mail: john.harton@colostate.edu. *Application contact:* Bonnie Gillmore, Graduate Contact, 970-491-6207, Fax: 970-491-7947, E-mail: bonnie.gillmore@colostate.edu. Web site: http://www.physics.colostate.edu/.

Columbia University, Graduate School of Arts and Sciences, Division of Natural Sciences, Department of Physics, New York, NY 10027. Offers philosophical foundations of physics (MA); physics (M Phil, PhD). *Degree requirements:* For doctorate, thesis/dissertation. *Entrance requirements:* For master's and doctorate, GRE General Test, GRE Subject Test, 3 years of course work in physics. Additional exam requirements/recommendations for international students: Required—TOEFL. *Faculty research:* Theoretical physics; astrophysics; low-, medium-, and high-energy physics.

Concordia University, School of Graduate Studies, Faculty of Arts and Science, Department of Physics, Montréal, QC H3G 1M8, Canada. Offers M Sc, PhD.

Cornell University, Graduate School, Graduate Fields of Arts and Sciences, Field of Physics, Ithaca, NY 14853-0001. Offers experimental physics (MS, PhD); physics (MS, PhD); theoretical physics (MS, PhD). *Faculty:* 55 full-time (5 women). *Students:* 159 full-time (29 women); includes 11 minority (1 Black or African American, non-Hispanic/Latino; 5 Asian, non-Hispanic/Latino; 4 Hispanic/Latino; 1 Two or more races, non-Hispanic/Latino), 70 international. Average age 26. 455 applicants, 22% accepted, 36 enrolled. In 2011, 29 master's, 24 doctorates awarded. *Degree requirements:* For doctorate, comprehensive exam, thesis/dissertation. *Entrance requirements:* For doctorate, GRE General Test, GRE Subject Test (physics), 3 letters of recommendation. Additional exam requirements/recommendations for international students: Required—TOEFL (minimum score 620 paper-based; 260 computer-based; 105 iBT). *Application deadline:* For fall admission, 1/3 for domestic students. Application fee: $95. Electronic applications accepted. *Financial support:* In 2011–12, 18 fellowships with full tuition reimbursements, 78 research assistantships with full tuition reimbursements, 50 teaching assistantships with full tuition reimbursements were awarded; institutionally sponsored loans, scholarships/grants, health care benefits, tuition waivers (full and partial), and unspecified assistantships also available. Financial award applicants required to submit FAFSA. *Faculty research:* Experimental condensed matter physics, theoretical condensed matter physics, experimental high energy particle physics, theoretical particle physics and field theory, theoretical astrophysics. *Unit head:* Director of Graduate Studies, 607-255-7561. *Application contact:* Graduate Field Assistant, 607-255-7561, E-mail: physics-grad-adm@cornell.edu. Web site: http://www.gradschool.cornell.edu/fields.php?id-36&a-2.

Creighton University, Graduate School, College of Arts and Sciences, Program in Physics, Omaha, NE 68178-0001. Offers MS. Part-time programs available. *Faculty:* 11 full-time (2 women). *Students:* 12 full-time (3 women); includes 2 minority (1 Asian, non-Hispanic/Latino; 1 Hispanic/Latino), 1 international. Average age 24. 16 applicants, 31% accepted, 5 enrolled. In 2011, 5 master's awarded. *Degree requirements:* For master's, comprehensive exam, thesis (for some programs). *Entrance requirements:* For master's, GRE General Test, 3 letters of recommendation. Additional exam requirements/recommendations for international students: Required—TOEFL (minimum score 550 paper-based; 213 computer-based; 80 iBT). *Application deadline:* For fall admission, 3/1 for domestic and international students. Applications are processed on a rolling basis. Application fee: $50. Electronic applications accepted. *Expenses: Tuition:* Full-time $12,672; part-time $704 per credit hour. *Required fees:* $1410; $136 per semester. Tuition and fees vary according to campus/location and reciprocity agreements. *Financial support:* In 2011–12, 8 students received support, including 8 teaching assistantships with full tuition reimbursements available (averaging $11,294 per year). Financial award applicants required to submit FAFSA. *Unit head:* Dr. Michael Nichols, Chair, 402-280-2159, E-mail: mnichols@creighton.edu. *Application contact:* Taunya Plater, Senior Program Coordinator, 402-280-2870, Fax: 402-280-2423, E-mail: taunyaplater@creighton.edu.

Dalhousie University, Faculty of Science, Department of Physics and Atmospheric Science, Halifax, NS B3H 4R2, Canada. Offers M Sc, PhD. *Degree requirements:* For master's, thesis; for doctorate, thesis/dissertation. *Entrance requirements:* Additional exam requirements/recommendations for international students: Required—TOEFL, IELTS, CANTEST, CAEL, or Michigan English Language Assessment Battery. Electronic applications accepted. *Faculty research:* Applied, experimental, and solid-state physics.

Dartmouth College, Arts and Sciences Graduate Programs, Department of Physics and Astronomy, Hanover, NH 03755. Offers MS, PhD. Terminal master's awarded for partial completion of doctoral program. *Degree requirements:* For master's, thesis; for doctorate, thesis/dissertation. *Entrance requirements:* For master's and doctorate, GRE General Test, GRE Subject Test. Additional exam requirements/recommendations for international students: Required—TOEFL. *Faculty research:* Matter physics, plasma and beam physics, space physics, astronomy, cosmology.

Delaware State University, Graduate Programs, Department of Physics, Dover, DE 19901-2277. Offers applied optics (MS); optics (PhD); physics (MS); physics teaching (MS). Part-time and evening/weekend programs available. *Entrance requirements:* For master's, minimum GPA of 3.0 in major, 2.75 overall. Additional exam requirements/recommendations for international students: Required—TOEFL. Electronic applications accepted. *Faculty research:* Thermal properties of solids, nuclear physics, radiation damage in solids.

DePaul University, College of Science and Health, Department of Physics, Chicago, IL 60604-2287. Offers applied physics (MS). Part-time and evening/weekend programs available. *Faculty:* 6 full-time (2 women), 3 part-time/adjunct (0 women). *Students:* 7 full-time (2 women), 5 part-time (3 women); includes 1 minority (Black or African American, non-Hispanic/Latino), 3 international. Average age 29. 12 applicants, 42% accepted, 3 enrolled. In 2011, 3 master's awarded. *Degree requirements:* For master's, thesis, oral exams. *Entrance requirements:* For master's, 2 letters of recommendation, BA in physics or closely-related field. Additional exam requirements/recommendations for international students: Required—TOEFL. *Application deadline:* For fall admission, 5/1 priority date for domestic students, 4/1 for international students. Applications are processed on a rolling basis. Application fee: $25. Electronic applications accepted. *Financial support:* In 2011–12, teaching assistantships with full tuition reimbursements (averaging $9,000 per year) were awarded; tuition waivers (full) also available. *Faculty research:* Optics, solid-state physics, cosmology, atomic physics, nuclear physics. *Total annual research expenditures:* $54,000. *Unit head:* Dr. Christopher G. Goedde, Chairman, 773-325-7330, Fax: 773-325-7334, E-mail: egoedde@condor.depaul.edu. *Application contact:* Dr. Jesus Pando, Associate Professor, 773-325-7330, Fax: 773-325-7334.

Drew University, Caspersen School of Graduate Studies, Program in Education, Madison, NJ 07940-1493. Offers biology (MAT); chemistry (MAT); English (MAT); French (MAT); Italian (MAT); math (MAT); physics (MAT); social studies (MAT); Spanish (MAT); theatre arts (MAT). Part-time programs available. *Entrance requirements:* For master's, transcripts, personal statement, recommendations. Additional exam requirements/recommendations for international students: Required—TOEFL, TWE. *Expenses:* Contact institution.

Drexel University, College of Arts and Sciences, Department of Physics, Philadelphia, PA 19104-2875. Offers MS, PhD. Terminal master's awarded for partial completion of doctoral program. *Degree requirements:* For doctorate, thesis/dissertation. *Entrance requirements:* For master's and doctorate, GRE. Additional exam requirements/recommendations for international students: Required—TOEFL. Electronic applications accepted. *Faculty research:* Nuclear structure, mesoscale meteorology, numerical astrophysics, numerical weather prediction, earth energy radiation budget.

Duke University, Graduate School, Department of Medical Physics, Durham, NC 27708-0586. Offers MS, PhD. *Faculty:* 54 full-time. *Students:* 64 full-time (27 women); includes 5 minority (2 Black or African American, non-Hispanic/Latino; 3 Asian, non-Hispanic/Latino), 27 international. 142 applicants, 34% accepted, 19 enrolled. In 2011, 9 master's, 7 doctorates awarded. *Entrance requirements:* For master's and doctorate, GRE General Test. Additional exam requirements/recommendations for international students: Required—TOEFL (minimum score 550 paper-based; 213 computer-based; 83 iBT), IELTS (minimum score 7). *Application deadline:* For fall admission, 12/8 priority date for domestic students, 12/8 for international students. Application fee: $75. Electronic applications accepted. *Expenses: Tuition:* Full-time $40,720. *Required fees:* $3107. *Financial support:* Fellowships, research assistantships, and teaching assistantships available. Financial award application deadline: 12/15. *Unit head:* Ehsan Samei, Director, 919-684-1400, Fax: 919-684-1490, E-mail: olga.baranova@duke.edu. *Application contact:* Elizabeth Hutton, Director of Admissions, 919-684-3913, Fax: 919-684-2277, E-mail: grad-admissions@duke.edu. Web site: http://www.medicalphysics.duke.edu/.

Duke University, Graduate School, Department of Physics, Durham, NC 27708. Offers PhD. *Faculty:* 36 full-time. *Students:* 85 full-time (22 women); includes 4 minority (all Asian, non-Hispanic/Latino), 66 international. 211 applicants, 23% accepted, 18 enrolled. In 2011, 6 doctorates awarded. *Degree requirements:* For doctorate, thesis/dissertation. *Entrance requirements:* For doctorate, GRE General Test, GRE Subject Test. Additional exam requirements/recommendations for international students: Required—TOEFL (minimum score 550 paper-based; 213 computer-based; 83 iBT), IELTS (minimum score 7). *Application deadline:* For fall admission, 12/8 priority date for domestic students, 12/8 for international students. Application fee: $75. *Expenses: Tuition:* Full-time $40,720. *Required fees:* $3107. *Financial support:* Fellowships, research assistantships, teaching assistantships, and Federal Work-Study available. Financial award application deadline: 12/8. *Unit head:* Dr. Shailesh Chandrasekharan, Director of Graduate Studies, 919-660-2502, Fax: 919-606-2525, E-mail: donna@phy.duke.edu. *Application contact:* Elizabeth Hutton,

240 facebook.com/petersonspublishing

Peterson's Graduate Programs in the Physical Sciences, Mathematics, Agricultural Sciences, the Environment & Natural Resources 2013

Director of Admissions, 919-684-3913, Fax: 919-684-2277, E-mail: grad-admissions@duke.edu. Web site: http://www.phy.duke.edu/graduate/.

East Carolina University, Graduate School, Thomas Harriot College of Arts and Sciences, Department of Physics, Greenville, NC 27858-4353. Offers applied physics (MS); biomedical physics (PhD); health physics (MS); medical physics (MS). Part-time programs available. *Degree requirements:* For master's, one foreign language, comprehensive exam. *Entrance requirements:* For master's, GRE General Test. Additional exam requirements/recommendations for international students: Required—TOEFL. *Application deadline:* Applications are processed on a rolling basis. Application fee: $50. *Expenses:* Tuition, state resident: full-time $3557; part-time $444.63 per semester hour. Tuition, nonresident: full-time $14,351; part-time $1793.88 per semester hour. *Required fees:* $2016; $252 per semester hour. Part-time tuition and fees vary according to course load, campus/location and program. *Financial support:* Research assistantships with partial tuition reimbursements, teaching assistantships with partial tuition reimbursements, and Federal Work-Study available. Support available to part-time students. Financial award application deadline: 6/1. *Unit head:* Dr. John Sutherland, Chair, 252-328-2023, E-mail: sutherlandj@ecu.edu. *Application contact:* Dean of Graduate School, 252-328-6012, Fax: 252-328-6071, E-mail: gradschool@ecu.edu. Web site: http://www.ecu.edu/cs-cas/physics/Graduate-Program.cfm#.

Eastern Michigan University, Graduate School, College of Arts and Sciences, Department of Physics and Astronomy, Ypsilanti, MI 48197. Offers general science (MS); physics (MS); physics education (MS). Part-time and evening/weekend programs available. Postbaccalaureate distance learning degree programs offered (minimal on-campus study). *Faculty:* 10 full-time (3 women). *Students:* 3 full-time (0 women), 12 part-time (3 women); includes 1 minority (Black or African American, non-Hispanic/Latino), 1 international. Average age 27. 19 applicants, 74% accepted, 7 enrolled. In 2011, 4 master's awarded. *Entrance requirements:* Additional exam requirements/recommendations for international students: Required—TOEFL. *Application deadline:* Applications are processed on a rolling basis. Application fee: $35. *Expenses:* Tuition, state resident: full-time $10,367; part-time $432 per credit hour. Tuition, nonresident: full-time $20,435; part-time $851 per credit hour. *Required fees:* $39 per credit hour. $46 per semester. One-time fee: $100. Tuition and fees vary according to course level, degree level and reciprocity agreements. *Financial support:* Fellowships, research assistantships with full tuition reimbursements, teaching assistantships with full tuition reimbursements, career-related internships or fieldwork, Federal Work-Study, institutionally sponsored loans, scholarships/grants, tuition waivers, and unspecified assistantships available. Support available to part-time students. Financial award applicants required to submit FAFSA. *Unit head:* Dr. Alexandria Oakes, Interim Department Head, 734-487-4144, Fax: 734-487-0989, E-mail: aoakes@emich.edu. *Application contact:* Graduate Admissions, 734-487-2400, Fax: 734-487-6559, E-mail: graduate.admissions@emich.edu. Web site: http://www.emich.edu/physics/.

Emory University, Laney Graduate School, Department of Physics, Atlanta, GA 30322-1100. Offers biophysics (PhD); experimental condensed matter physics (PhD); theoretical and computational statistical physics (PhD); MS/PhD. *Faculty:* 19 full-time (2 women). *Students:* 17 full-time (4 women); includes 2 minority (1 Black or African American, non-Hispanic/Latino; 1 Hispanic/Latino), 13 international. Average age 24. 48 applicants, 27% accepted, 10 enrolled. *Degree requirements:* For doctorate, thesis/dissertation, qualifier proposal. *Entrance requirements:* For doctorate, GRE General Test, minimum GPA of 3.0. Additional exam requirements/recommendations for international students: Required—TOEFL (minimum score 600 paper-based). *Application deadline:* For fall admission, 1/3 priority date for domestic students, 1/3 for international students. Application fee: $50. Electronic applications accepted. *Expenses:* Tuition: Full-time $34,800. *Required fees:* $1300. *Financial support:* In 2011–12, 17 students received support. Fellowships, teaching assistantships, institutionally sponsored loans, scholarships/grants, health care benefits, and tuition waivers (full) available. Financial award application deadline: 1/3; financial award applicants required to submit FAFSA. *Faculty research:* Experimental studies of the structure and function of metalloproteins, soft condensed matter, granular materials, biophotonics and fluorescence correlation spectroscopy, single molecule studies of DNA-protein systems. *Total annual research expenditures:* $1.5 million. *Unit head:* Kurt Warncke, Chair, 404-727-4296, Fax: 404-727-0873, E-mail: kwarncke@physics.emory.edu. *Application contact:* Stefan Boettcher, Director of Graduate Studies, 404-727-4298, Fax: 404-727-0873, E-mail: sboettc@emory.edu. Web site: http://www.physics.emory.edu.

Fisk University, Division of Graduate Studies, Department of Physics, Nashville, TN 37208-3051. Offers MA. *Degree requirements:* For master's, thesis. *Entrance requirements:* For master's, GRE General Test, GRE Subject Test, minimum GPA of 3.0. Electronic applications accepted. *Faculty research:* Molecular physics, astrophysics, surface physics, nanobase materials, optical processing.

Florida Agricultural and Mechanical University, Division of Graduate Studies, Research, and Continuing Education, College of Arts and Sciences, Department of Physics, Tallahassee, FL 32307-3200. Offers MS, PhD. *Degree requirements:* For master's, comprehensive exam, thesis optional; for doctorate, comprehensive exam, thesis/dissertation. *Entrance requirements:* For master's, GRE General Test, minimum GPA of 3.0; for doctorate, GRE General Test, minimum GPA of 3.0, letters of recommendation (2). Additional exam requirements/

recommendations for international students: Required—TOEFL (minimum score 550 paper-based). *Faculty research:* Plasma physics, quantum mechanics, condensed matter physics, astrophysics, laser ablation.

Florida Atlantic University, Charles E. Schmidt College of Science, Department of Physics, Boca Raton, FL 33431-0991. Offers MS, PhD. Part-time programs available. *Faculty:* 13 full-time (3 women), 4 part-time/adjunct (1 woman). *Students:* 26 full-time (2 women), 4 part-time (3 women); includes 3 minority (1 Black or African American, non-Hispanic/Latino; 2 Hispanic/Latino), 18 international. Average age 30. 40 applicants, 58% accepted, 10 enrolled. In 2011, 8 degrees awarded. *Degree requirements:* For master's, thesis; for doctorate, thesis/dissertation. *Entrance requirements:* For master's, GRE General Test, minimum GPA of 3.0; for doctorate, GRE General Test. Additional exam requirements/recommendations for international students: Required—TOEFL (minimum score 500 paper-based; 173 computer-based). *Application deadline:* For fall admission, 7/1 for domestic students, 2/15 for international students; for spring admission, 11/1 for domestic students, 7/15 for international students. Applications are processed on a rolling basis. Application fee: $30. *Expenses:* Tuition, area resident: Part-time $343.02 per credit hour. Tuition, state resident: full-time $8232. Tuition, nonresident: full-time $23,931; part-time $997.14 per credit hour. *Financial support:* Fellowships, research assistantships with tuition reimbursements, teaching assistantships with tuition reimbursements, Federal Work-Study, and unspecified assistantships available. *Faculty research:* Astrophysics, spectroscopy, mathematical physics, theory of metals, superconductivity. *Unit head:* Dr. Warner A. Miller, Chair, 561-297-3382, Fax: 561-297-2662, E-mail: wam@physics.fau.edu. *Application contact:* Dr. Leslie Terry, Associate Dean of External Affairs and Community Relations, 561-297-0347, Fax: 561-297-3388. Web site: http://physics.fau.edu/.

Florida Institute of Technology, Graduate Programs, College of Science, Department of Physics and Space Sciences, Melbourne, FL 32901-6975. Offers physics (MS, PhD); space sciences (MS, PhD). Part-time programs available. *Faculty:* 8 full-time (0 women). *Students:* 30 full-time (11 women), 12 part-time (4 women); includes 3 minority (2 Asian, non-Hispanic/Latino; 1 Hispanic/Latino), 13 international. Average age 31. 74 applicants, 51% accepted, 14 enrolled. In 2011, 16 master's, 1 doctorate awarded. Terminal master's awarded for partial completion of doctoral program. *Degree requirements:* For master's, comprehensive exam, thesis optional, oral exam, 6 credits of math methodology; for doctorate, one foreign language, comprehensive exam, thesis/dissertation, publication in referred journal, seminar on dissertation research, dissertation published in a major journal. *Entrance requirements:* For master's, minimum GPA of 3.0, resume, 3 letters of recommendation, vector analysis, statement of objectives; for doctorate, GRE General and Subject Tests (recommended), minimum GPA of 3.2, resume, 3 letters of recommendation, statement of objectives. Additional exam requirements/recommendations for international students: Required—TOEFL (minimum score 550 paper-based; 213 computer-based; 79 iBT). *Application deadline:* For fall admission, 4/1 for international students; for spring admission, 9/30 for international students. Applications are processed on a rolling basis. Electronic applications accepted. *Expenses:* Tuition: Full-time $19,620; part-time $1090 per credit hour. Tuition and fees vary according to campus/location. *Financial support:* In 2011–12, 11 research assistantships with full and partial tuition reimbursements (averaging $13,588 per year), 14 teaching assistantships with full and partial tuition reimbursements (averaging $12,955 per year) were awarded; career-related internships or fieldwork, institutionally sponsored loans, tuition waivers (partial), unspecified assistantships, and tuition remissions also available. Support available to part-time students. Financial award application deadline: 3/1; financial award applicants required to submit FAFSA. *Faculty research:* Lasers, semiconductors, magnetism, quantum devices, high energy physics. *Total annual research expenditures:* $2.1 million. *Unit head:* Dr. Terry D. Oswalt, Department Head, 321-674-7325, Fax: 321-674-7482, E-mail: toswalt@fit.edu. *Application contact:* Cheryl A. Brown, Associate Director of Graduate Admissions, 321-674-7581, Fax: 321-723-9468, E-mail: cbrown@fit.edu. Web site: http://cos.fit.edu/pss/.

Florida International University, College of Arts and Sciences, Department of Physics, Miami, FL 33199. Offers MS, PhD. Part-time and evening/weekend programs available. *Degree requirements:* For master's, one foreign language, thesis; for doctorate, one foreign language, comprehensive exam, thesis/dissertation. *Entrance requirements:* For master's and doctorate, GRE General Test, 2 letters of recommendation. Additional exam requirements/recommendations for international students: Required—TOEFL (minimum score 550 paper-based; 80 iBT). Electronic applications accepted. *Faculty research:* Molecular collision processes (molecular beams), biophysical optics.

Florida State University, The Graduate School, College of Arts and Sciences, Department of Physics, Tallahassee, FL 32306. Offers MS, PhD. *Faculty:* 44 full-time (2 women), 3 part-time/adjunct (1 woman). *Students:* 140 full-time (22 women); includes 58 minority (1 Black or African American, non-Hispanic/Latino; 1 American Indian or Alaska Native, non-Hispanic/Latino; 53 Asian, non-Hispanic/Latino; 3 Hispanic/Latino). Average age 28. 240 applicants, 23% accepted, 31 enrolled. In 2011, 9 master's, 18 doctorates awarded. *Degree requirements:* For doctorate, comprehensive exam, thesis/dissertation. *Entrance requirements:* For master's and doctorate, GRE General Test, minimum GPA of 3.0. Additional exam requirements/recommendations for international students: Required—TOEFL (minimum score 550 paper-based; 213 computer-based; 80 iBT). *Application deadline:* For fall admission, 4/15 for domestic and international

Peterson's Graduate Programs in the Physical Sciences, Mathematics, Agricultural Sciences, the Environment & Natural Resources 2013

facebook.com/petersonspublishing **241**

Physics

students. Application fee: $30. Electronic applications accepted. *Expenses:* Tuition, state resident: full-time $9474; part-time $350.88 per credit hour. Tuition, nonresident: full-time $16,236; part-time $601.34 per credit hour. *Required fees:* $630 per semester. One-time fee: $20. Tuition and fees vary according to course load and campus/location. *Financial support:* In 2011–12, 112 students received support, including 86 research assistantships with full tuition reimbursements available (averaging $18,000 per year), 44 teaching assistantships with full tuition reimbursements available (averaging $18,000 per year); fellowships, career-related internships or fieldwork, and Federal Work-Study also available. Financial award application deadline: 2/15; financial award applicants required to submit FAFSA. *Faculty research:* High energy physics, computational physics, biophysics, condensed matter physics, nuclear physics, astrophysics. *Unit head:* Dr. Mark A. Riley, Chairman, 850-644-2867, Fax: 850-644-8630, E-mail: chair@physics.fsu.edu. *Application contact:* Eleanor C. Speirs, Academic Support Assistant, 850-644-3245, Fax: 850-644-8630, E-mail: graduate@phy.fsu.edu. Web site: http://www.physics.fsu.edu/.

Florida State University, The Graduate School, College of Arts and Sciences, Department of Scientific Computing, Tallahassee, FL 32306-4120. Offers computational science (MS, PSM, PhD), including atmospheric science (PhD), biochemistry (PhD), biological science (PhD), computational molecular biology/bioinformatics (PSM), computational science (PhD), geological science (PhD), materials science (PhD), physics (PhD). Part-time programs available. *Faculty:* 14 full-time (2 women). *Students:* 32 full-time (6 women), 3 part-time (0 women); includes 13 minority (1 Black or African American, non-Hispanic/Latino; 11 Asian, non-Hispanic/Latino; 1 Hispanic/Latino), 13 international. Average age 28. 29 applicants, 41% accepted, 9 enrolled. In 2011, 14 master's, 3 doctorates awarded. Terminal master's awarded for partial completion of doctoral program. *Degree requirements:* For master's, thesis (for some programs); for doctorate, comprehensive exam, thesis/dissertation. *Entrance requirements:* For master's and doctorate, GRE General Test, knowledge of at least one object-oriented computing language, 3 letters of recommendations. Additional exam requirements/recommendations for international students: Required—TOEFL (minimum score 550 paper-based; 80 iBT). *Application deadline:* For fall admission, 1/15 for domestic and international students. Application fee: $30. Electronic applications accepted. *Expenses:* Tuition, state resident: full-time $9474; part-time $350.88 per credit hour. Tuition, nonresident: full-time $16,236; part-time $601.34 per credit hour. *Required fees:* $630 per semester. One-time fee: $20. Tuition and fees vary according to course load and campus/location. *Financial support:* In 2011–12, 32 students received support, including 12 research assistantships with full tuition reimbursements available (averaging $20,000 per year), 18 teaching assistantships with full tuition reimbursements available (averaging $20,000 per year); unspecified assistantships also available. Financial award application deadline: 4/15. *Faculty research:* Morphometrics, mathematical and systems biology, mining proteomic and metabolic data, computational materials research at Scientific Computing, advanced 4-D Var Data-Assimilation methods in dynamic meteorology and oceanography, computational fluid dynamics, astrophysics. *Unit head:* Dr. Sam Huckaba, Interim Dean, 850-644-1081. *Application contact:* Maribel Amwake, Graduate Academic Coordinator, 850-644-0143, Fax: 850-644-0098, E-mail: mamwake@fsu.edu. Web site: http://www.sc.fsu.edu.

George Mason University, College of Science, School of Physics, Astronomy and Computational Sciences, Fairfax, VA 22030. Offers applied and engineering physics (MS); computational science (PhD); computational sciences and informatics (MS); physics (PhD). *Faculty:* 55 full-time (11 women), 10 part-time/adjunct (1 woman). *Students:* 49 full-time (12 women), 98 part-time (26 women); includes 23 minority (5 Black or African American, non-Hispanic/Latino; 12 Asian, non-Hispanic/Latino; 6 Hispanic/Latino), 25 international. Average age 35. 79 applicants, 49% accepted, 19 enrolled. In 2011, 12 master's, 17 doctorates, 2 other advanced degrees awarded. *Degree requirements:* For master's, thesis optional. *Entrance requirements:* For master's and doctorate, GRE, baccalaureate degree in related field with minimum GPA of 3.0 in last 60 credit hours; 3 letters of recommendation; expanded goals statement; resume; 2 copies of official transcripts. Additional exam requirements/recommendations for international students: Required—TOEFL (minimum score 570 paper-based; 230 computer-based; 88 iBT), IELTS, Pearson Test of English. *Application deadline:* For fall admission, 4/15 priority date for domestic students; for spring admission, 11/15 priority date for domestic students. Application fee: $65 ($80 for international students). Electronic applications accepted. *Expenses:* Tuition, state resident: full-time $8750; part-time $364.58 per credit. Tuition, nonresident: full-time $24,092; part-time $1003.83 per credit. *Required fees:* $2514; $104.75 per credit. *Financial support:* In 2011–12, 48 students received support, including 5 fellowships with full tuition reimbursements available (averaging $18,000 per year), 33 research assistantships with full and partial tuition reimbursements available (averaging $15,744 per year), 15 teaching assistantships with full and partial tuition reimbursements available (averaging $13,827 per year); career-related internships or fieldwork, Federal Work-Study, scholarships/grants, unspecified assistantships, and health care benefits (full-time research or teaching assistantship recipients) also available. Support available to part-time students. Financial award application deadline: 3/1; financial award applicants required to submit FAFSA. *Faculty research:* Astronomy, astrophysics, and space and planetary science; astronomy and physics education; atomic physics; biophysics and neuroscience. *Total annual research expenditures:* $6.7 million. *Unit head:* Dr. Michael Summers, Chairman, 703-993-3971, Fax: 703-993-1269, E-mail: msummers@gmu.edu. *Application contact:* Dr. Paul So, Information

Contact, 703-993-4377, Fax: 703-993-1269, E-mail: paso@gmu.edu. Web site: http://spacs.gmu.edu/.

The George Washington University, Columbian College of Arts and Sciences, Department of Physics, Washington, DC 20052. Offers MA, PhD. Part-time and evening/weekend programs available. *Faculty:* 20 full-time (3 women), 9 part-time/adjunct (3 women). *Students:* 16 full-time (3 women), 14 part-time (5 women); includes 4 minority (1 Black or African American, non-Hispanic/Latino; 2 Asian, non-Hispanic/Latino; 1 Native Hawaiian or other Pacific Islander, non-Hispanic/Latino), 16 international. Average age 28. 49 applicants, 37% accepted, 5 enrolled. In 2011, 6 master's, 5 doctorates awarded. *Degree requirements:* For doctorate, thesis/dissertation, general exam. *Entrance requirements:* For master's and doctorate, GRE General Test, minimum GPA of 3.0. Additional exam requirements/recommendations for international students: Required—TOEFL (minimum score 550 paper-based; 213 computer-based; 80 iBT). *Application deadline:* For fall admission, 1/15 priority date for domestic students, 1/15 for international students; for spring admission, 10/1 priority date for domestic students, 9/1 for international students. Applications are processed on a rolling basis. Application fee: $75. Electronic applications accepted. *Financial support:* In 2011–12, 24 students received support. Fellowships with full tuition reimbursements available, research assistantships, teaching assistantships with tuition reimbursements available, Federal Work-Study, and tuition waivers available. Financial award application deadline: 1/15. *Unit head:* Dr. Cornelius Bennhold, Chair, 202-994-6274. *Application contact:* Dr. Mark Reeves, Director, 202-994-6279, Fax: 202-994-3001, E-mail: reevesme@gwu.edu. Web site: http://www.gwu.edu/~physics/.

Georgia Institute of Technology, Graduate Studies and Research, College of Sciences, School of Physics, Atlanta, GA 30332-0001. Offers MS, PhD. Part-time programs available. Terminal master's awarded for partial completion of doctoral program. *Degree requirements:* For doctorate, comprehensive exam, thesis/dissertation. *Entrance requirements:* For master's, GRE General Test, GRE Subject Test, minimum GPA of 3.0; for doctorate, GRE General Test, GRE Subject Test, minimum GPA of 3.4. Additional exam requirements/recommendations for international students: Required—TOEFL. Electronic applications accepted. *Faculty research:* Atomic and molecular physics, chemical physics, condensed matter, optics, nonlinear physics and chaos.

Georgia State University, College of Arts and Sciences, Department of Physics and Astronomy, Program in Physics, Atlanta, GA 30302-3083. Offers MS, PhD. Part-time and evening/weekend programs available. Terminal master's awarded for partial completion of doctoral program. *Degree requirements:* For master's, one foreign language, thesis or alternative, exam; for doctorate, 2 foreign languages, thesis/dissertation, exam. *Entrance requirements:* For master's, GRE General Test; for doctorate, GRE General Test, GRE Subject Test. Additional exam requirements/recommendations for international students: Required—TOEFL. Electronic applications accepted. *Faculty research:* Biophysics; nuclear, condensed-matter, and atomic physics; astrophysics.

Graduate School and University Center of the City University of New York, Graduate Studies, Program in Physics, New York, NY 10016-4039. Offers PhD. *Degree requirements:* For doctorate, thesis/dissertation. *Entrance requirements:* For doctorate, GRE General Test. Additional exam requirements/recommendations for international students: Required—TOEFL. Electronic applications accepted. *Faculty research:* Condensed-matter, particle, nuclear, and atomic physics.

Hampton University, Graduate College, Department of Physics, Hampton, VA 23668. Offers atmospheric physics (MS, PhD); medical physics (MS, PhD); nuclear physics (MS, PhD); optical physics (MS, PhD). Part-time and evening/weekend programs available. Terminal master's awarded for partial completion of doctoral program. *Degree requirements:* For master's, thesis optional; for doctorate, thesis/dissertation, oral defense, qualifying exam. *Entrance requirements:* For master's, GRE General Test; for doctorate, GRE General Test, minimum GPA of 3.0 or master's degree in physics or related field. *Faculty research:* Laser optics, remote sensing.

Harvard University, Graduate School of Arts and Sciences, Department of Physics, Cambridge, MA 02138. Offers experimental physics (PhD); medical engineering/medical physics (PhD), including applied physics, engineering sciences, physics; theoretical physics (PhD). *Degree requirements:* For doctorate, thesis/dissertation, final exams, laboratory experience. *Entrance requirements:* For doctorate, GRE General Test, GRE Subject Test. Additional exam requirements/recommendations for international students: Required—TOEFL. *Expenses: Tuition:* Full-time $36,304. *Required fees:* $1186. Full-time tuition and fees vary according to program. *Faculty research:* Particle physics, condensed matter physics, atomic physics.

Hofstra University, School of Education, Health, and Human Services, Programs in Teaching Secondary Education, Hempstead, NY 11549. Offers business education (MS Ed); education technology (Advanced Certificate); English education (MA, MS Ed); foreign language and TESOL (MS Ed); foreign language education (MA, MS Ed), including French, German, Russian, Spanish; mathematics education (MA, MS Ed); science education (MA, MS Ed), including biology, chemistry, earth science, geology, physics; secondary education (Advanced Certificate); social studies education (MA, MS Ed). Part-time and evening/weekend programs available. Postbaccalaureate distance learning degree programs offered (minimal on-campus study). *Students:* 72 full-time (47 women), 51 part-time (30 women); includes 21 minority (9 Black or African American, non-Hispanic/Latino; 7 Asian, non-Hispanic/Latino; 5 Hispanic/Latino). Average age 28. 103 applicants, 91% accepted, 41 enrolled. In 2011, 86 master's, 6 other advanced degrees awarded. *Degree requirements:* For master's, one foreign language, comprehensive exam (for some programs), thesis (for some programs), exit project, electronic portfolio, student teaching, fieldwork, curriculum project, minimum GPA of 3.0; for Advanced Certificate, 3 foreign languages, comprehensive exam (for some programs), thesis project, minimum GPA of 3.0. *Entrance requirements:* For master's, 2 letters of recommendation, teacher certification (MA), essay; for Advanced Certificate, 2 letters of recommendation, essay. Additional exam requirements/recommendations for international students: Required—TOEFL (minimum score 550 paper-based; 213 computer-based; 80 iBT). *Application deadline:* Applications are processed on a rolling basis. Application fee: $70 ($75 for international students). Electronic applications accepted. *Expenses: Tuition:* Full-time $18,990; part-time $1055 per credit hour. *Required fees:* $970. Tuition and fees vary according to program. *Financial support:* In 2011–12, 90 students received support, including 13 fellowships with full and partial tuition reimbursements available (averaging $3,202 per year), 1 research assistantship with full and partial tuition reimbursement available (averaging $11,645 per year); career-related internships or fieldwork, Federal Work-Study, institutionally sponsored loans, scholarships/grants, tuition waivers (full and partial), and unspecified assistantships also available. Support available to part-time students. Financial award applicants required to submit FAFSA. *Faculty research:* Appropriate content and pedagogy in secondary school disciplines, appropriate pedagogy in secondary school disciplines, adolescent development, secondary school organization, alternative secondary school programs. *Unit head:* Dr. Esther Fusco, Chairperson, 516-463-7704, Fax: 516-463-6196, E-mail: catezf@hofstra.edu. *Application contact:* Carol Drummer, Dean of Graduate Admissions, 516-463-4876, Fax: 516-463-4664, E-mail: gradstudent@hofstra.edu. Web site: http://www.hofstra.edu/education/.

Howard University, Graduate School, Department of Physics and Astronomy, Washington, DC 20059-0002. Offers physics (MS, PhD). *Degree requirements:* For master's, comprehensive exam (for some programs), thesis (for some programs); for doctorate, comprehensive exam, thesis/dissertation, departmental qualifying exam. *Entrance requirements:* For master's, GRE General Test, bachelor's degree in physics or related field, minimum GPA of 3.0; for doctorate, GRE General Test, bachelor's or master's degree in physics or related field, minimum GPA of 3.0. Additional exam requirements/recommendations for international students: Required—TOEFL (minimum score 550 paper-based; 213 computer-based). Electronic applications accepted. *Faculty research:* Atmospheric physics, spectroscopy and optical physics, high energy physics, condensed matter.

Hunter College of the City University of New York, Graduate School, School of Arts and Sciences, Department of Physics, New York, NY 10021-5085. Offers MA, PhD. PhD offered jointly with Graduate School and University Center of the City University of New York. *Faculty:* 12 full-time (3 women). *Students:* 4 full-time (0 women), 4 part-time (0 women); includes 5 minority (4 Black or African American, non-Hispanic/Latino; 1 Asian, non-Hispanic/Latino). Average age 31. 5 applicants, 80% accepted, 0 enrolled. In 2011, 4 master's awarded. Terminal master's awarded for partial completion of doctoral program. *Degree requirements:* For master's, comprehensive exam or thesis. *Entrance requirements:* For master's, minimum 36 credits of course work in mathematics and physics. Additional exam requirements/recommendations for international students: Required—TOEFL. *Application deadline:* For fall admission, 4/1 for domestic students, 2/1 for international students; for spring admission, 11/1 for domestic students, 9/1 for international students. Application fee: $125. *Expenses:* Tuition, state resident: full-time $8210; part-time $345 per credit. Tuition, nonresident: full-time $15,360; part-time $640 per credit. *Required fees:* $280 per semester. One-time fee: $125. Tuition and fees vary according to class time, campus/location and program. *Financial support:* In 2011–12, research assistantships (averaging $20,000 per year), teaching assistantships (averaging $9,000 per year) were awarded; Federal Work-Study, scholarships/grants, and tuition waivers (partial) also available. Support available to part-time students. *Faculty research:* Experimental and theoretical quantum optics, experimental and theoretical condensed matter, mathematical physics. *Unit head:* Ying-Chin Chen, Chairperson, 212-772-5248, Fax: 212-772-5390, E-mail: y.c.chen@hunter.cuny.edu. *Application contact:* William Zlata, Director for Graduate Admissions, 212-772-4482, Fax: 212-650-3336, E-mail: admissions@hunter.cuny.edu. Web site: http://www.hunter.cuny.edu/physics/.

Idaho State University, Office of Graduate Studies, College of Science and Engineering, Department of Physics, Pocatello, ID 83209-8106. Offers applied physics (PhD); health physics (MS); physics (MNS). Part-time programs available. *Degree requirements:* For master's, comprehensive exam, thesis (for some programs), oral exam (for some programs); for doctorate, comprehensive exam, thesis/dissertation (for some programs), oral exam, written qualifying exam in physics or health physics after 1st year. *Entrance requirements:* For master's, GRE General Test, 3 letters of recommendation, BS or BA in physics, teaching certificate (MNS); for doctorate, GRE General Test (minimum 50th percentile), 3 letters of recommendation, statement of career goals. Additional exam requirements/recommendations for international students: Required—TOEFL (minimum score 550 paper-based; 213 computer-based; 80 iBT). Electronic

applications accepted. *Faculty research:* Ion beam applications, low-energy nuclear physics, relativity and cosmology, observational astronomy.

Illinois Institute of Technology, Graduate College, College of Science and Letters, Department of Biological, Chemical and Physical Sciences, Physics Division, Chicago, IL 60616. Offers health physics (MHP); physics (MS, PhD). Part-time and evening/weekend programs available. Postbaccalaureate distance learning degree programs offered (minimal on-campus study). Terminal master's awarded for partial completion of doctoral program. *Degree requirements:* For master's, comprehensive exam (for some programs), thesis (for some programs); for doctorate, comprehensive exam, thesis/dissertation. *Entrance requirements:* For master's, GRE General Test (minimum score 1000 Quantitative and Verbal, 2.5 Analytical Writing), minimum undergraduate GPA of 3.0; for doctorate, GRE General Test (minimum score 1100 Quantitative and Verbal, 3.0 Analytical Writing), minimum undergraduate GPA of 3.0. Additional exam requirements/recommendations for international students: Required—TOEFL (minimum score 523 paper-based; 213 computer-based; 70 iBT); Recommended—IELTS (minimum score 5.5). Electronic applications accepted. *Faculty research:* Experimental, condensed-matter physics; experimental elementary particle physics; membrane biophysics; synchroton radiation techniques; experimental high energy physics, especially symmetry violation and rare decays of hyperons and charm and beauty hadrons.

Indiana University Bloomington, University Graduate School, College of Arts and Sciences, Department of Physics, Bloomington, IN 47405-4201. Offers medical physics (MS); physics (MAT, MS, PhD). Part-time programs available. Postbaccalaureate distance learning degree programs offered (no on-campus study). *Faculty:* 36 full-time (5 women), 11 part-time/adjunct (0 women). *Students:* 88 full-time (19 women), 1 part-time (0 women); includes 7 minority (2 Asian, non-Hispanic/Latino; 5 Hispanic/Latino), 42 international. Average age 27. 197 applicants, 18% accepted, 8 enrolled. In 2011, 11 master's, 6 doctorates awarded. Terminal master's awarded for partial completion of doctoral program. *Degree requirements:* For master's, comprehensive exam (for some programs), thesis (for some programs), qualifying exam; for doctorate, comprehensive exam, thesis/dissertation, qualifying exam. *Entrance requirements:* For master's and doctorate, GRE General Test, GRE Subject Test (physics), minimum GPA of 3.0. Additional exam requirements/recommendations for international students: Required—TOEFL (minimum score 550 paper-based; 213 computer-based; 80 iBT). *Application deadline:* For fall admission, 1/15 priority date for domestic students, 12/1 for international students; for spring admission, 10/1 priority date for domestic students, 9/1 for international students. Applications are processed on a rolling basis. Application fee: $55 ($65 for international students). Electronic applications accepted. *Financial support:* In 2011–12, 1 fellowship with full and partial tuition reimbursement (averaging $18,000 per year), 48 research assistantships with partial tuition reimbursements (averaging $18,800 per year), 30 teaching assistantships with partial tuition reimbursements (averaging $15,530 per year) were awarded; health care benefits also available. *Faculty research:* Accelerator physics, astrophysics and cosmology, biophysics (biocomplexity, neural networks, visual systems, chemical signaling), condensed matter physics (neutron scattering, low-dim. highly correlated systems, complex fluids, quantum computing), particle physics (collider physics, hybrid mesons, lattice gauge, symmetries, collider phenomenology), neutrino physics, nuclear physics (proton and neutron physics, neutrinos, symmetries, nuclear astrophysics, QCD, hadron structure). *Total annual research expenditures:* $13.2 million. *Unit head:* Prof. Rick Van Kooten, Department Chair, 812-855-1247, Fax: 812-855-5533, E-mail: iubphys@indiana.edu. *Application contact:* June Dizer, Director of Academic Support, 812-856-7059, Fax: 812-855-5533, E-mail: gradphys@indiana.edu. Web site: http://physics.indiana.edu/.

Indiana University of Pennsylvania, School of Graduate Studies and Research, College of Natural Sciences and Mathematics, Department of Physics, MA Program in Physics, Indiana, PA 15705-1087. Offers MA. *Faculty:* 4 full-time (0 women). *Students:* 1 full-time (0 women). Average age 37. *Degree requirements:* For master's, thesis optional. *Entrance requirements:* Additional exam requirements/recommendations for international students: Required—TOEFL (minimum score 540 paper-based; 207 computer-based). *Application deadline:* Applications are processed on a rolling basis. Application fee: $50. Electronic applications accepted. *Expenses:* Tuition, state resident: full-time $7488; part-time $416 per credit. Tuition, nonresident: full-time $11,232; part-time $624 per credit. *Required fees:* $2070; $192.20 per credit. $90 per semester. *Financial support:* Application deadline: 4/15; applicants required to submit FAFSA. *Unit head:* Ken Hershman, Chairperson, 724-357-2370, E-mail: hershman@iup.edu. *Application contact:* Dr. Muhammad Numan, Graduate Coordinator, 724-357-2318, E-mail: mznuman@iup.edu. Web site: http://www.iup.edu/upper.aspx?id=49407.

Indiana University of Pennsylvania, School of Graduate Studies and Research, College of Natural Sciences and Mathematics, Department of Physics, MS Program in Physics, Indiana, PA 15705-1087. Offers MS. Part-time programs available. *Faculty:* 4 full-time (0 women). *Students:* 4 full-time (0 women), 1 (woman) part-time, 2 international. Average age 25. 16 applicants, 56% accepted, 1 enrolled. *Degree requirements:* For master's, comprehensive exam (for some programs), thesis (for some programs). *Entrance requirements:* Additional exam requirements/recommendations for international students: Required—TOEFL (minimum score 540 paper-based; 207 computer-based). *Application deadline:* Applications are processed on a rolling basis. Application fee: $50. Electronic

Peterson's Graduate Programs in the Physical Sciences, Mathematics, Agricultural Sciences, the Environment & Natural Resources 2013

facebook.com/petersonspublishing **243**

Physics

applications accepted. *Expenses:* Tuition, state resident: full-time $7488; part-time $416 per credit. Tuition, nonresident: full-time $11,232; part-time $624 per credit. *Required fees:* $2070; $192.20 per credit. $90 per semester. *Financial support:* In 2011–12, 4 research assistantships with full and partial tuition reimbursements (averaging $3,180 per year) were awarded; Federal Work-Study also available. Support available to part-time students. Financial award application deadline: 4/15; financial award applicants required to submit FAFSA. *Unit head:* Dr. Greg Kenning, Graduate Coordinator, 724-357-2318, E-mail: greg.kenning@iup.edu. *Application contact:* Dr. Muhammad Numan, Graduate Coordinator, 724-357-2318, E-mail: mznuman@iup.edu. Web site: http://www.iup.edu/upper.aspx?id=93742.

Indiana University–Purdue University Indianapolis, School of Science, Department of Physics, Indianapolis, IN 46202. Offers MS, PhD. PhD offered jointly with Purdue University. Part-time programs available. *Faculty:* 13 full-time (1 woman), 3 part-time/adjunct (0 women). *Students:* 18 full-time (3 women); includes 6 minority (4 Asian, non-Hispanic/Latino; 2 Hispanic/Latino), 3 international. Average age 29. 21 applicants, 19% accepted, 4 enrolled. In 2011, 4 master's, 3 doctorates awarded. Terminal master's awarded for partial completion of doctoral program. *Degree requirements:* For master's, thesis optional; for doctorate, thesis/dissertation. *Entrance requirements:* For master's and doctorate, GRE. Additional exam requirements/recommendations for international students: Required—TOEFL (minimum score 213 computer-based; 79 iBT). *Application deadline:* For fall admission, 2/1 priority date for domestic students, 3/1 for international students. Applications are processed on a rolling basis. Application fee: $55 ($65 for international students). *Financial support:* In 2011–12, 6 fellowships with full tuition reimbursements (averaging $14,204 per year), 6 teaching assistantships with full tuition reimbursements (averaging $6,245 per year) were awarded; research assistantships with full tuition reimbursements, Federal Work-Study, institutionally sponsored loans, and tuition waivers (full and partial) also available. Support available to part-time students. Financial award application deadline: 2/1. *Faculty research:* Magnetic resonance, photosynthesis, optical physics, biophysics, physics of materials. *Unit head:* Dr. Andrew Gavrin, Chair, 317-274-6900, E-mail: agavrin@iupui.edu. *Application contact:* Dr. Sherry Queener, Director, Graduate Studies and Associate Dean, 317-274-1577, Fax: 317-278-2380. Web site: http://physics.iupui.edu/.

Iowa State University of Science and Technology, Department of Physics and Astronomy, Ames, IA 50011-3160. Offers applied physics (MS, PhD); astrophysics (MS, PhD); condensed matter physics (MS, PhD); high energy physics (MS, PhD); nuclear physics (MS, PhD); physics (MS, PhD). *Degree requirements:* For master's, thesis (for some programs); for doctorate, thesis/dissertation. *Entrance requirements:* For master's and doctorate, GRE General Test, GRE Subject Test (physics). Additional exam requirements/recommendations for international students: Required—TOEFL (minimum score 550 paper-based; 79 iBT), IELTS (minimum score 6.5). *Application deadline:* For fall admission, 2/15 priority date for domestic students, 2/15 for international students; for spring admission, 10/15 for domestic and international students. Applications are processed on a rolling basis. Application fee: $40 ($90 for international students). Electronic applications accepted. *Financial support:* Application deadline: 2/15. *Faculty research:* Condensed-matter physics, including superconductivity and new materials; high-energy and nuclear physics; astronomy and astrophysics; atmospheric and environmental physics. *Total annual research expenditures:* $8.8 million. *Unit head:* Dr. Steve Kawaler, Director of Graduate Education, 515-294-5870, Fax: 515-294-6027, E-mail: physastro@iastate.edu. *Application contact:* Lori Hockett, Application Contact, 515-294-5870, E-mail: phys_astro@iastate.edu. Web site: http://www.physics.iastate.edu/.

Iowa State University of Science and Technology, Program in High Energy Physics, Ames, IA 50011-3160. Offers MS, PhD. *Entrance requirements:* For master's and doctorate, GRE. Additional exam requirements/recommendations for international students: Required—TOEFL (minimum score 550 paper-based; 79 iBT), IELTS (minimum score 6.5). *Application deadline:* For fall admission, 2/15 for domestic students; for spring admission, 10/15 for domestic students. Electronic applications accepted. *Unit head:* Dr. Steven Kawaler, Director of Graduate Education, 515-294-5870, Fax: 515-294-6027, E-mail: physastro@iastate.edu. *Application contact:* Lori Hockett, Application Contact, 515-294-5870, Fax: 515-294-6027, E-mail: physastro@iastate.edu. Web site: http://www.physastro.iastate.edu.

Iowa State University of Science and Technology, Program in Nuclear Physics, Ames, IA 50011-3160. Offers MS, PhD. *Entrance requirements:* For master's and doctorate, GRE. Additional exam requirements/recommendations for international students: Required—TOEFL (minimum score 550 paper-based; 79 iBT), IELTS (minimum score 6.5). *Application deadline:* For fall admission, 2/15 for domestic students; for spring admission, 10/15 for domestic students. Electronic applications accepted. *Unit head:* Dr. Steven Kawaler, Director of Graduate Education, 515-294-5870, Fax: 515-294-6027, E-mail: physastro@iastate.edu. *Application contact:* Lori Hockett, Application Contact, 515-294-5870, Fax: 515-294-6027, E-mail: grad_admissions@iastate.edu. Web site: http://www.physastro.iastate.edu.

The Johns Hopkins University, Zanvyl Krieger School of Arts and Sciences, Henry A. Rowland Department of Physics and Astronomy, Baltimore, MD 21218-2699. Offers astronomy (PhD); physics (PhD). *Degree requirements:* For doctorate, comprehensive exam, thesis/dissertation, minimum B average on

required coursework. *Entrance requirements:* For doctorate, GRE General Test, GRE Subject Test. Additional exam requirements/recommendations for international students: Required—TOEFL (minimum score 600 paper-based; 250 computer-based; 100 iBT), IELTS. Electronic applications accepted. *Faculty research:* High-energy physics, condensed-matter, astrophysics, particle and experimental physics, plasma physics.

Kent State University, College of Arts and Sciences, Department of Physics, Kent, OH 44242-0001. Offers MA, MS, PhD. Terminal master's awarded for partial completion of doctoral program. *Degree requirements:* For master's, thesis; for doctorate, comprehensive exam, thesis/dissertation. *Entrance requirements:* For master's and doctorate, GRE, minimum GPA of 3.0. Additional exam requirements/recommendations for international students: Required—TOEFL. Electronic applications accepted. *Expenses:* Tuition, state resident: full-time $8136; part-time $452 per credit hour. Tuition, nonresident: full-time $14,292; part-time $794 per credit hour. *Faculty research:* Correlated electron materials physics, liquid crystals, complex fluids, computational biophysics, QCD-Hadranphysics.

Lakehead University, Graduate Studies, Department of Physics, Thunder Bay, ON P7B 5E1, Canada. Offers M Sc. *Degree requirements:* For master's, thesis or alternative. *Entrance requirements:* For master's, minimum B average. Additional exam requirements/recommendations for international students: Required—TOEFL. *Faculty research:* Absorbed water, radiation reaction, superlattices and quantum well structures, polaron interactions.

Lehigh University, College of Arts and Sciences, Department of Physics, Bethlehem, PA 18015. Offers photonics (MS); physics (MS, PhD); polymer science (MS, PhD). Part-time programs available. *Faculty:* 17 full-time (1 woman). *Students:* 42 full-time (14 women), 1 part-time (0 women), 21 international. Average age 26. 84 applicants, 10% accepted, 8 enrolled. In 2011, 9 master's, 9 doctorates awarded. *Degree requirements:* For doctorate, comprehensive exam, thesis/dissertation. *Entrance requirements:* For master's and doctorate, GRE General Test. Additional exam requirements/recommendations for international students: Required—TOEFL (minimum score 213 computer-based; 79 iBT). *Application deadline:* For fall admission, 2/15 priority date for domestic students, 2/15 for international students. Applications are processed on a rolling basis. Application fee: $75. Electronic applications accepted. *Financial support:* In 2011–12, 42 students received support, including 3 fellowships with full tuition reimbursements available (averaging $26,000 per year), 14 research assistantships with full tuition reimbursements available (averaging $24,770 per year), 25 teaching assistantships with full tuition reimbursements available (averaging $24,770 per year); career-related internships or fieldwork, Federal Work-Study, institutionally sponsored loans, scholarships/grants, tuition waivers (full and partial), and unspecified assistantships also available. Support available to part-time students. Financial award application deadline: 1/15. *Faculty research:* Condensed matter physics; atomic, molecular and optical physics; plasma physics; nonlinear optics and photonics; astronomy and astrophysics. *Total annual research expenditures:* $2.5 million. *Unit head:* Dr. Volkmar Dierolf, Chair, 610-758-3915, Fax: 610-758-5730, E-mail: vod2@lehigh.edu. *Application contact:* Dr. Dimitrios Vavylonis, Graduate Admissions Officer, 610-758-3724, Fax: 610-758-5730, E-mail: div206@lehigh.edu. Web site: http://www.physics.lehigh.edu/.

Louisiana State University and Agricultural and Mechanical College, Graduate School, College of Science, Department of Physics and Astronomy, Baton Rouge, LA 70803. Offers astronomy (PhD); astrophysics (PhD); medical physics (MS); physics (MS, PhD). *Faculty:* 47 full-time (5 women), 2 part-time/adjunct (0 women). *Students:* 106 full-time (23 women), 1 part-time (0 women); includes 5 minority (3 Black or African American, non-Hispanic/Latino; 2 Hispanic/Latino), 49 international. Average age 27. 166 applicants, 14% accepted, 21 enrolled. In 2011, 5 master's, 11 doctorates awarded. Terminal master's awarded for partial completion of doctoral program. *Degree requirements:* For master's, thesis or alternative; for doctorate, thesis/dissertation. *Entrance requirements:* For master's and doctorate, GRE General Test, minimum GPA of 3.0. Additional exam requirements/recommendations for international students: Required—TOEFL (minimum score 550 paper-based; 213 computer-based; 79 iBT) or IELTS (minimum score 6.5). *Application deadline:* For fall admission, 1/25 priority date for domestic students, 5/15 for international students; for spring admission, 10/15 for international students. Applications are processed on a rolling basis. Application fee: $50 ($70 for international students). Electronic applications accepted. *Financial support:* In 2011–12, 107 students received support, including 8 fellowships with full tuition reimbursements available (averaging $19,566 per year), 57 research assistantships with full and partial tuition reimbursements available (averaging $22,634 per year), 39 teaching assistantships with full and partial tuition reimbursements available (averaging $19,774 per year); Federal Work-Study, institutionally sponsored loans, health care benefits, tuition waivers (full and partial), and unspecified assistantships also available. Financial award application deadline: 3/15; financial award applicants required to submit FAFSA. *Faculty research:* Experimentation and numerical relativity, condensed matter astrophysics, quantum computing, medical physics. *Total annual research expenditures:* $8.1 million. *Unit head:* Dr. Michael Cherry, Chair, 225-578-2262, Fax: 225-578-5855, E-mail: cherry@phys.lsu.edu. *Application contact:* Arnell Dangerfield, Administrative Coordinator, 225-578-1193, Fax: 225-578-5855, E-mail: adanger@lsu.edu. Web site: http://www.phys.lsu.edu/.

Peterson's Graduate Programs in the Physical Sciences, Mathematics, Agricultural Sciences, the Environment & Natural Resources 2013

Louisiana Tech University, Graduate School, College of Engineering and Science, Department of Physics, Ruston, LA 71272. Offers applied computational analysis and modeling (PhD); physics (MS). Part-time programs available. *Degree requirements:* For master's, thesis or alternative; for doctorate, thesis/dissertation. *Entrance requirements:* For master's, GRE General Test, minimum GPA of 3.0 in last 60 hours. Additional exam requirements/recommendations for international students: Required—TOEFL. *Faculty research:* Experimental high energy physics, laser/optics, computational physics, quantum gravity.

Marshall University, Academic Affairs Division, College of Science, Department of Physical Science and Physics, Huntington, WV 25755. Offers physical science (MS). *Faculty:* 9 full-time (2 women). *Students:* 9 full-time (2 women), 8 part-time (1 woman); includes 3 minority (2 Black or African American, non-Hispanic/Latino; 1 Asian, non-Hispanic/Latino), 4 international. Average age 32. In 2011, 3 master's awarded. *Degree requirements:* For master's, thesis optional. Application fee: $40. *Unit head:* Dr. Nicola Orsini, Chairperson, 304-696-2756, E-mail: orsini@marshall.edu. *Application contact:* Dr. Ralph Oberly, Information Contact, 304-696-2757, Fax: 304-746-1902, E-mail: oberly@marshall.edu.

Massachusetts Institute of Technology, School of Science, Department of Physics, Cambridge, MA 02139. Offers SM, PhD. *Faculty:* 68 full-time (5 women), 2 part-time/adjunct (0 women). *Students:* 242 full-time (42 women); includes 26 minority (2 Black or African American, non-Hispanic/Latino; 13 Asian, non-Hispanic/Latino; 10 Hispanic/Latino; 1 Two or more races, non-Hispanic/Latino), 123 international. Average age 26. 686 applicants, 13% accepted, 44 enrolled. In 2011, 1 master's, 33 doctorates awarded. Terminal master's awarded for partial completion of doctoral program. *Degree requirements:* For master's, thesis; for doctorate, comprehensive exam, thesis/dissertation. *Entrance requirements:* For master's and doctorate, GRE General Test, GRE Subject Test (physics). Additional exam requirements/recommendations for international students: Required—IELTS (minimum score 6.5). *Application deadline:* For fall admission, 12/15 for domestic and international students; for spring admission, 11/1 for domestic and international students. Application fee: $75. Electronic applications accepted. *Expenses: Tuition:* Full-time $40,460; part-time $630 per credit hour. *Required fees:* $272. *Financial support:* In 2011–12, 237 students received support, including 65 fellowships (averaging $34,600 per year), 137 research assistantships (averaging $32,400 per year), 34 teaching assistantships (averaging $32,300 per year); Federal Work-Study, institutionally sponsored loans, scholarships/grants, traineeships, health care benefits, and unspecified assistantships also available. *Faculty research:* High-energy and nuclear physics, condensed matter physics, astrophysics, atomic physics, biophysics, plasma physics. *Total annual research expenditures:* $105.5 million. *Unit head:* Prof. Edmund Bertschinger, Head, 617-253-4800, Fax: 617-253-8554, E-mail: physics@mit.edu. *Application contact:* Graduate Admissions, 617-253-4841, Fax: 617-258-8319, E-mail: physics-grad@mit.edu. Web site: http://web.mit.edu/physics/.

McGill University, Faculty of Graduate and Postdoctoral Studies, Faculty of Science, Department of Physics, Montréal, QC H3A 2T5, Canada. Offers M Sc, PhD.

McMaster University, School of Graduate Studies, Faculty of Science, Department of Physics and Astronomy, Hamilton, ON L8S 4M2, Canada. Offers astrophysics (PhD); physics (PhD). Part-time programs available. *Degree requirements:* For doctorate, comprehensive exam, thesis/dissertation. *Entrance requirements:* For doctorate, minimum B+ average. Additional exam requirements/recommendations for international students: Required—TOEFL (minimum score 550 paper-based; 213 computer-based). *Faculty research:* Condensed matter, astrophysics, nuclear, medical, nonlinear dynamics.

Memorial University of Newfoundland, School of Graduate Studies, Department of Physics and Physical Oceanography, St. John's, NL A1C 5S7, Canada. Offers atomic and molecular physics (M Sc, PhD); condensed matter physics (M Sc, PhD); physical oceanography (M Sc, PhD); physics (M Sc). Part-time programs available. *Degree requirements:* For master's, thesis, seminar presentation on thesis topic; for doctorate, comprehensive exam, thesis/dissertation, oral defense of thesis. *Entrance requirements:* For master's, honors B Sc or equivalent; for doctorate, M Sc or equivalent. Electronic applications accepted. *Faculty research:* Experiment and theory in atomic and molecular physics, condensed matter physics, physical oceanography, theoretical geophysics and applied nuclear physics.

Miami University, College of Arts and Science, Department of Physics, Oxford, OH 45056. Offers MAT. Part-time programs available. *Students:* 20 full-time (4 women); includes 1 minority (Two or more races, non-Hispanic/Latino), 4 international. Average age 26. In 2011, 5 master's awarded. *Entrance requirements:* For master's, GRE (recommended), minimum undergraduate cumulative GPA of 2.75. Additional exam requirements/recommendations for international students: Required—TOEFL. *Application deadline:* For fall admission, 3/15 for domestic and international students. Application fee: $50. Electronic applications accepted. *Expenses:* Tuition, state resident: full-time $12,023; part-time $501 per credit hour. Tuition, nonresident: full-time $26,554; part-time $1107 per credit hour. *Required fees:* $528. *Financial support:* Fellowships with full tuition reimbursements, research assistantships, teaching assistantships, Federal Work-Study, institutionally sponsored loans, health care benefits, tuition waivers (full), and unspecified assistantships available. Financial award application deadline: 2/15; financial award applicants required to submit

FAFSA. *Unit head:* Dr. Michael Pechan, Chair, 513-529-4518, Fax: 513-529-5629, E-mail: pechanmj@muohio.edu. *Application contact:* Dr. Samir Bali, Graduate Director, 513-529-5635, E-mail: balis@muohio.edu. Web site: http://www.muphysics.org/.

Michigan State University, The Graduate School, College of Natural Science, Department of Physics and Astronomy, East Lansing, MI 48824. Offers astrophysics and astronomy (MS, PhD); physics (MS, PhD). *Entrance requirements:* Additional exam requirements/recommendations for international students: Required—TOEFL (minimum score 550 paper-based; 213 computer-based), Michigan State University ELT (minimum score 85), Michigan English Language Assessment Battery (minimum score 83). Electronic applications accepted. *Faculty research:* Nuclear and accelerator physics, high energy physics, condensed matter physics, biophysics, astrophysics and astronomy.

Michigan State University, National Superconducting Cyclotron Laboratory, East Lansing, MI 48824. Offers chemistry (PhD); physics (PhD).

Michigan Technological University, Graduate School, College of Sciences and Arts, Department of Physics, Houghton, MI 49931. Offers engineering physics (PhD); physics (MS, PhD). Part-time programs available. *Faculty:* 24 full-time (2 women), 3 part-time/adjunct (0 women). *Students:* 28 full-time (5 women), 3 part-time (1 woman), 23 international. Average age 29. 94 applicants, 13% accepted, 3 enrolled. In 2011, 4 master's, 7 doctorates awarded. Terminal master's awarded for partial completion of doctoral program. *Degree requirements:* For master's, comprehensive exam (for some programs), thesis (for some programs); for doctorate, comprehensive exam, thesis/dissertation, preliminary exam, research proposal. *Entrance requirements:* For master's and doctorate, GRE (recommended minimum quantitative score of 156 [720 old version] and analytical score of 3.0), statement of purpose, official transcripts, 3 letters of recommendation. Additional exam requirements/recommendations for international students: Required—TOEFL (minimum score 88 iBT) or IELTS. *Application deadline:* For fall admission, 3/1 for domestic students, 1/15 for international students. Applications are processed on a rolling basis. Electronic applications accepted. *Expenses:* Tuition, state resident: full-time $12,636; part-time $702 per credit. Tuition, nonresident: full-time $12,636; part-time $702 per credit. *Required fees:* $226; $226 per year. *Financial support:* In 2011–12, 31 students received support, including 1 fellowship with full tuition reimbursement available (averaging $6,065 per year), 12 research assistantships with full tuition reimbursements available (averaging $6,065 per year), 15 teaching assistantships with full tuition reimbursements available (averaging $6,065 per year); career-related internships or fieldwork, Federal Work-Study, scholarships/grants, health care benefits, tuition waivers (partial), unspecified assistantships, and cooperative program also available. Financial award applicants required to submit FAFSA. *Faculty research:* Atmospheric physics, astrophysics, biophysics, materials physics, atomic/molecular physics. *Total annual research expenditures:* $2 million. *Unit head:* Dr. Ravindra Pandey, Chair, 906-487-2831, Fax: 906-487-2933, E-mail: pandey@mtu.edu. *Application contact:* Kathleen S. Wollan, Secretary, 906-487-2086, Fax: 906-487-2933, E-mail: kswollan@mtu.edu. Web site: http://www.phy.mtu.edu/.

Minnesota State University Mankato, College of Graduate Studies, College of Science, Engineering and Technology, Department of Physics and Astronomy, Mankato, MN 56001. Offers MS. *Students:* 7 full-time (0 women), 3 part-time (0 women). *Degree requirements:* For master's, one foreign language, comprehensive exam, thesis or alternative. *Entrance requirements:* For master's, minimum GPA of 3.0 during previous 2 years, recommendation letters. Additional exam requirements/recommendations for international students: Required—TOEFL. *Application deadline:* For fall admission, 7/1 priority date for domestic students; for spring admission, 11/1 for domestic students. Applications are processed on a rolling basis. Application fee: $40. Electronic applications accepted. *Financial support:* Research assistantships, teaching assistantships with full tuition reimbursements, Federal Work-Study, and unspecified assistantships available. Support available to part-time students. Financial award application deadline: 3/15; financial award applicants required to submit FAFSA. *Unit head:* Dr. Youwen Xu, Chairperson, 507-389-5742. *Application contact:* 507-389-2321, E-mail: grad@mnsu.edu. Web site: http://cset.mnsu.edu/pa/.

Mississippi State University, College of Arts and Sciences, Department of Physics and Astronomy, Mississippi State, MS 39762. Offers MS, PhD. Part-time programs available. *Faculty:* 11 full-time (0 women), 1 part-time/adjunct (0 women). *Students:* 37 full-time (9 women), 4 part-time (0 women); includes 2 minority (both Hispanic/Latino), 32 international. Average age 30. 62 applicants, 29% accepted, 10 enrolled. In 2011, 9 master's, 6 doctorates awarded. *Degree requirements:* For master's, thesis optional, comprehensive oral or written exam; for doctorate, thesis/dissertation, comprehensive oral or written exam. *Entrance requirements:* For master's, GRE, minimum GPA of 2.75 on last two years of undergraduate courses; for doctorate, GRE. Additional exam requirements/recommendations for international students: Required—TOEFL (minimum score 475 paper-based; 153 computer-based; 53 iBT); Recommended—IELTS (minimum score 4.5). *Application deadline:* For fall admission, 7/1 priority date for domestic students, 5/1 for international students; for spring admission, 11/1 priority date for domestic students, 9/1 for international students. Applications are processed on a rolling basis. Application fee: $40. Electronic applications accepted. *Expenses:* Tuition, state resident: full-time $5805; part-time $322.50 per credit hour. Tuition, nonresident: full-time $14,670; part-time $815 per credit

Peterson's Graduate Programs in the Physical Sciences, Mathematics, Agricultural Sciences, the Environment & Natural Resources 2013

facebook.com/petersonspublishing **245**

Physics

hour. *Financial support:* In 2011–12, 12 research assistantships with full tuition reimbursements (averaging $13,100 per year), 22 teaching assistantships with full tuition reimbursements (averaging $13,345 per year) were awarded; Federal Work-Study, institutionally sponsored loans, and unspecified assistantships also available. Financial award application deadline: 3/15; financial award applicants required to submit FAFSA. *Faculty research:* Atomic/molecular spectroscopy, theoretical optics, gamma-ray astronomy, experimental nuclear physics, computational physics. *Total annual research expenditures:* $2.2 million. *Unit head:* Dr. Mark A. Novotny, Department Head and Professor, 662-325-2806, Fax: 662-325-8898, E-mail: man40@ra.msstate.edu. *Application contact:* Dr. David Monts, Professor and Graduate Coordinator, 662-325-2931, Fax: 662-325-8898, E-mail: physics@msstate.edu. Web site: http://www.msstate.edu/dept/physics/.

Missouri University of Science and Technology, Graduate School, Department of Physics, Rolla, MO 65409. Offers MS, MST, PhD. *Entrance requirements:* For master's, GRE (minimum score 600 quantitative, 3 writing); for doctorate, GRE (minimum score: 600 quantitative, 3.5 writing). Additional exam requirements/recommendations for international students: Required—TOEFL (minimum score 550 paper-based; 213 computer-based).

Montana State University, College of Graduate Studies, College of Letters and Science, Department of Physics, Bozeman, MT 59717. Offers MS, PhD. Part-time programs available. *Degree requirements:* For master's, comprehensive exam, thesis (for some programs); for doctorate, comprehensive exam, thesis/dissertation. *Entrance requirements:* For master's and doctorate, GRE General Test, GRE Subject Test (physics). Additional exam requirements/recommendations for international students: Required—TOEFL (minimum score 550 paper-based; 213 computer-based). Electronic applications accepted. *Faculty research:* Nanotechnology, gravitational wave, astronomy, photodynamic theory, diode laser development, solar radiation transfer.

Naval Postgraduate School, Departments and Academic Groups, Department of Physics, Monterey, CA 93943. Offers applied physics (MS, PhD); combat systems technology (MS); engineering acoustics (MS, PhD); physics (MS, PhD). Program only open to commissioned officers of the United States and friendly nations and selected United States federal civilian employees. Part-time programs available. *Faculty:* 35 full-time (8 women), 1 part-time/adjunct. *Students:* 117 full-time (18 women); includes 17 minority (3 Black or African American, non-Hispanic/Latino; 1 American Indian or Alaska Native, non-Hispanic/Latino; 6 Asian, non-Hispanic/Latino; 7 Hispanic/Latino; 19 international. Average age 32. In 2011, 24 master's, 2 doctorates awarded. *Degree requirements:* For master's, thesis; for doctorate, thesis/dissertation. *Faculty research:* Acoustics, free electron laser, sensors, weapons and effects. *Total annual research expenditures:* $9.4 million. *Unit head:* Dr. Andres Larraza, Chairman, 831-656-3007, E-mail: larraza@nps.edu. Web site: http://www.nps.edu/Academics/GSEAS/Physics/.

New Mexico Institute of Mining and Technology, Graduate Studies, Department of Physics, Socorro, NM 87801. Offers astrophysics (PhD); atmospheric physics (PhD); instrumentation (MS); mathematical physics (PhD); physics (MS). *Faculty:* 14 full-time (2 women), 19 part-time/adjunct (2 women). *Students:* 30 full-time (12 women), 2 part-time (1 woman); includes 1 minority (Asian, non-Hispanic/Latino), 3 international. Average age 28. 28 applicants, 50% accepted, 5 enrolled. In 2011, 5 master's, 3 doctorates awarded. *Degree requirements:* For master's, thesis optional; for doctorate, thesis/dissertation. *Entrance requirements:* For master's, GRE General Test; for doctorate, GRE General Test, GRE Subject Test. Additional exam requirements/recommendations for international students: Required—TOEFL (minimum score 540 paper-based; 207 computer-based). *Application deadline:* For fall admission, 3/1 priority date for domestic students; for spring admission, 6/1 for domestic students. Applications are processed on a rolling basis. Application fee: $16 ($30 for international students). *Expenses:* Tuition, state resident: full-time $4849; part-time $269.41 per credit hour. Tuition, nonresident: full-time $16,041; part-time $891.15 per credit hour. *Required fees:* $622; $65 per credit hour. $20 per semester. Part-time tuition and fees vary according to course load. *Financial support:* In 2011–12, 18 research assistantships (averaging $38,918 per year), 11 teaching assistantships with full and partial tuition reimbursements (averaging $35,099 per year) were awarded; fellowships, Federal Work-Study, institutionally sponsored loans, and unspecified assistantships also available. Financial award application deadline: 3/1; financial award applicants required to submit CSS PROFILE or FAFSA. *Faculty research:* Cloud physics, stellar and extragalactic processes. *Unit head:* Dr. Kenneth Eack, Chairman, 575-835-5328, Fax: 575-835-5707, E-mail: dwestpfa@nmt.edu. *Application contact:* Dr. Lorie Liebrock, Dean of Graduate Studies, 575-835-5513, Fax: 575-835-5476, E-mail: graduate@nmt.edu. Web site: http://www.physics.nmt.edu/.

New Mexico State University, Graduate School, College of Arts and Sciences, Department of Physics, Las Cruces, NM 88003-8001. Offers physics (MS, PhD); space physics (MS). Part-time programs available. *Faculty:* 14 full-time (1 woman), 3 part-time/adjunct (0 women). *Students:* 34 full-time (7 women), 3 part-time (0 women); includes 3 minority (all Hispanic/Latino), 26 international. Average age 30. 20 applicants, 55% accepted, 8 enrolled. In 2011, 4 master's, 3 doctorates awarded. Terminal master's awarded for partial completion of doctoral program. *Degree requirements:* For master's, comprehensive exam, thesis optional, written qualifying exam; for doctorate, comprehensive exam, thesis/dissertation. *Entrance requirements:* For master's and doctorate, GRE General Test, GRE Subject Test. Additional exam requirements/recommendations for

international students: Required—TOEFL (minimum score 550 paper-based; 79 iBT), IELTS (minimum score 6.5). *Application deadline:* For fall admission, 2/15 priority date for domestic students, 2/15 for international students; for spring admission, 9/1 priority date for domestic students, 9/1 for international students. Applications are processed on a rolling basis. Application fee: $40 ($50 for international students). Electronic applications accepted. *Expenses:* Tuition, state resident: full-time $5004; part-time $208.50 per credit. Tuition, nonresident: full-time $17,446; part-time $726.90 per credit. *Financial support:* In 2011–12, 2 fellowships with partial tuition reimbursements (averaging $16,800 per year), 13 research assistantships (averaging $25,125 per year), 17 teaching assistantships (averaging $26,670 per year) were awarded; scholarships/grants, health care benefits, tuition waivers (partial), and unspecified assistantships also available. Financial award application deadline: 2/15; financial award applicants required to submit FAFSA. *Faculty research:* Nuclear and particle physics, optics, materials science, geophysics, physics education, atmospheric physics. *Total annual research expenditures:* $1.5 million. *Unit head:* Dr. Stefan Zollner, Head, 575-646-7627, Fax: 575-646-1934, E-mail: zollner@nmsu.edu. *Application contact:* Dr. Vassilios Papavassiliou, 575-646-3831, Fax: 575-646-1934, E-mail: graduate_advisor@physics.nmsu.edu. Web site: http://physics.nmsu.edu.

New York University, Graduate School of Arts and Science, Department of Physics, New York, NY 10012-1019. Offers MS, PhD. Part-time programs available. *Faculty:* 25 full-time (1 woman), 5 part-time/adjunct (0 women). *Students:* 72 full-time (7 women), 7 part-time (1 woman), 58 international. Average age 27. 215 applicants, 23% accepted, 19 enrolled. In 2011, 3 master's, 9 doctorates awarded. Terminal master's awarded for partial completion of doctoral program. *Degree requirements:* For master's, thesis (for some programs); for doctorate, one foreign language, thesis/dissertation, research seminar, teaching experience. *Entrance requirements:* For master's, GRE General Test, GRE Subject Test, bachelor's degree in physics; for doctorate, GRE General Test, GRE Subject Test. Additional exam requirements/recommendations for international students: Required—TOEFL. *Application deadline:* For fall admission, 12/12 for domestic and international students. Application fee: $90. *Financial support:* Fellowships with tuition reimbursements, research assistantships with tuition reimbursements, teaching assistantships with tuition reimbursements, Federal Work-Study, institutionally sponsored loans, scholarships/grants, health care benefits, and unspecified assistantships available. Financial award application deadline: 12/12; financial award applicants required to submit FAFSA. *Faculty research:* Atomic physics, elementary particles and fields, astrophysics, condensed-matter physics, neuromagnetism. *Unit head:* David Grier, Chairman, 212-998-7700, Fax: 212-995-4016, E-mail: dgphys@nyu.edu. *Application contact:* Evette Ma, Graduate Program Administrator, 212-998-7700, Fax: 212-995-4016, E-mail: dgsphys@nyu.edu. Web site: http://www.physics.nyu.edu/.

North Carolina Agricultural and Technical State University, School of Graduate Studies, College of Arts and Sciences, Department of Physics, Greensboro, NC 27411. Offers computational sciences (MS); physics (MS).

North Carolina Central University, Division of Academic Affairs, College of Science and Technology, Department of Physics, Durham, NC 27707-3129. Offers MS.

North Carolina State University, Graduate School, College of Physical and Mathematical Sciences, Department of Physics, Raleigh, NC 27695. Offers MS, PhD. Part-time programs available. Terminal master's awarded for partial completion of doctoral program. *Degree requirements:* For master's, thesis (for some programs); for doctorate, thesis/dissertation. *Entrance requirements:* For master's and doctorate, GRE General Test, GRE Subject Test. Electronic applications accepted. *Faculty research:* Astrophysics, optics, physics education, biophysics, geophysics.

North Dakota State University, College of Graduate and Interdisciplinary Studies, College of Science and Mathematics, Department of Physics, Fargo, ND 58108. Offers MS, PhD. Part-time programs available. *Faculty:* 7 full-time (0 women), 1 part-time/adjunct (0 women). *Students:* 8 full-time (0 women), 2 part-time (0 women), 6 international. Average age 25. 5 applicants, 20% accepted, 1 enrolled. Terminal master's awarded for partial completion of doctoral program. *Degree requirements:* For master's, thesis; for doctorate, comprehensive exam, thesis/dissertation. *Entrance requirements:* Additional exam requirements/recommendations for international students: Required—TOEFL (minimum score 550 paper-based; 215 computer-based; 79 iBT). *Application deadline:* For fall admission, 5/1 for international students; for spring admission, 8/1 for international students. Applications are processed on a rolling basis. Application fee: $35. Electronic applications accepted. *Financial support:* In 2011–12, 2 students received support, including 2 research assistantships with tuition reimbursements available (averaging $16,000 per year), teaching assistantships with tuition reimbursements available (averaging $12,000 per year); career-related internships or fieldwork, scholarships/grants, and unspecified assistantships also available. Support available to part-time students. Financial award application deadline: 4/15; financial award applicants required to submit FAFSA. *Faculty research:* Biophysics; condensed matter; surface physics; general relativity, gravitation, and space physics; nonlinear physics. *Unit head:* Dr. Daniel Kroll, Director, 701-231-8968, Fax: 701-231-7088, E-mail: daniel.kroll@ndsu.edu. *Application contact:* Dr. Alexander Wagner, Graduate Advisory Committee Chair,

246 facebook.com/petersonspublishing

Peterson's Graduate Programs in the Physical Sciences, Mathematics, Agricultural Sciences, the Environment & Natural Resources 2013

701-231-9582, Fax: 701-231-7088, E-mail: alexander.wagner@ndsu.edu. Web site: http://www.physics.ndsu.nodak.edu/.

Northeastern University, College of Science, Department of Physics, Boston, MA 02115-5096. Offers MS, PhD. Part-time programs available. *Faculty:* 27 full-time, 9 part-time/adjunct. *Students:* 52 full-time (10 women). Average age 30. 143 applicants, 41% accepted, 14 enrolled. In 2011, 9 master's, 5 doctorates awarded. Terminal master's awarded for partial completion of doctoral program. *Degree requirements:* For master's, thesis optional; for doctorate, thesis/dissertation, qualifying exam. *Entrance requirements:* For master's and doctorate, GRE General Test, GRE Subject Test. *Application deadline:* For fall admission, 2/1 priority date for domestic students, 2/1 for international students. Application fee: $50. *Financial support:* In 2011–12, 20 research assistantships with tuition reimbursements (averaging $18,285 per year), 34 teaching assistantships with tuition reimbursements (averaging $18,285 per year) were awarded; Federal Work-Study, tuition waivers (full and partial), and unspecified assistantships also available. Financial award application deadline: 3/1; financial award applicants required to submit FAFSA. *Faculty research:* Elementary particles and astroparticle physics, nanophysics and condensed matter physics, biological and biomedical physics. *Unit head:* Dr. George Alverson, Graduate Coordinator, 617-373-2938, Fax: 617-373-2943, E-mail: gradphysics@neu.edu. *Application contact:* Jo-Anne Dickinson, Admissions Contact, 617-363-5990, Fax: 617-373-7281, E-mail: gsas@neu.edu. Web site: http://www.physics.neu.edu/.

Northern Arizona University, Graduate College, College of Engineering, Forestry and Natural Sciences, Department of Physics and Astronomy, Flagstaff, AZ 86011. Offers applied physics (MS). Part-time programs available. *Faculty:* 12 full-time (2 women). *Students:* 22 full-time (11 women), 3 part-time (1 woman); includes 2 minority (1 Hispanic/Latino; 1 Two or more races, non-Hispanic/Latino), 6 international. Average age 37. 17 applicants, 76% accepted, 11 enrolled. In 2011, 4 degrees awarded. *Degree requirements:* For master's, thesis optional. *Entrance requirements:* Additional exam requirements/recommendations for international students: Required—TOEFL (minimum score 550 paper-based; 213 computer-based; 80 iBT), IELTS (minimum score 7). *Application deadline:* For fall admission, 1/15 priority date for domestic students, 1/15 for international students. Applications are processed on a rolling basis. Application fee: $65. Electronic applications accepted. *Expenses:* Tuition, state resident: full-time $7190; part-time $355 per credit hour. Tuition, nonresident: full-time $18,092; part-time $1005 per credit hour. *Required fees:* $818; $328 per semester. *Financial support:* In 2011–12, 4 research assistantships with partial tuition reimbursements (averaging $12,390 per year), 11 teaching assistantships with partial tuition reimbursements (averaging $12,390 per year) were awarded; Federal Work-Study, scholarships/grants, health care benefits, tuition waivers (full and partial), and unspecified assistantships also available. Financial award applicants required to submit FAFSA. *Unit head:* Dr. Kathy Eastwood, Chair, 928-523-7159, Fax: 928-523-1371, E-mail: kathy.eastwood@nau.edu. *Application contact:* Jamie Housholder, Administrative Assistant, 928-523-8170, Fax: 928-523-1371, E-mail: astro.physics@nau.edu. Web site: http://www.physics.nau.edu/.

Northern Illinois University, Graduate School, College of Liberal Arts and Sciences, Department of Physics, De Kalb, IL 60115-2854. Offers MS, PhD. Part-time programs available. *Faculty:* 18 full-time (3 women), 3 part-time/adjunct (0 women). *Students:* 29 full-time (5 women), 13 part-time (1 woman); includes 5 minority (1 Black or African American, non-Hispanic/Latino; 1 Asian, non-Hispanic/Latino; 3 Hispanic/Latino), 15 international. Average age 30. 50 applicants, 38% accepted, 7 enrolled. In 2011, 6 master's, 1 doctorate awarded. Terminal master's awarded for partial completion of doctoral program. *Degree requirements:* For master's, comprehensive exam, thesis or alternative, research seminar; for doctorate, thesis/dissertation, candidacy exam, dissertation defense, research seminar. *Entrance requirements:* For master's, GRE General Test, minimum GPA of 2.75; for doctorate, GRE General Test, GRE Subject Test (physics), bachelor's degree in physics or related field; minimum undergraduate GPA of 2.75, graduate 3.2. Additional exam requirements/recommendations for international students: Required—TOEFL (minimum score 550 paper-based; 213 computer-based). *Application deadline:* For fall admission, 6/1 for domestic students, 5/1 for international students; for spring admission, 11/1 for domestic students, 10/1 for international students. Applications are processed on a rolling basis. Application fee: $40. Electronic applications accepted. *Financial support:* In 2011–12, 18 research assistantships with full tuition reimbursements, 20 teaching assistantships with full tuition reimbursements were awarded; fellowships with full tuition reimbursements, career-related internships or fieldwork, Federal Work-Study, scholarships/grants, and unspecified assistantships also available. Support available to part-time students. Financial award applicants required to submit FAFSA. *Faculty research:* Band-structure interpolation schemes, nonlinear procession beams, Mossbauer spectroscopy, beam physics. *Unit head:* Dr. Laurence Lurio, Chair, 815-753-6470, Fax: 815-753-8565, E-mail: lluio@niu.edu. *Application contact:* Graduate School Office, 815-753-0395, E-mail: gradsch@niu.edu. Web site: http://www.physics.niu.edu/.

Northwestern University, The Graduate School, Judd A. and Marjorie Weinberg College of Arts and Sciences, Department of Physics and Astronomy, Evanston, IL 60208. Offers astrophysics (PhD); physics (MS, PhD). Admissions and degrees offered through The Graduate School. *Degree requirements:* For doctorate, thesis/dissertation, qualifying exam. *Entrance requirements:* For doctorate, GRE General Test, GRE Subject Test. Additional exam requirements/recommendations for international students: Required—TOEFL. *Faculty*

research: Nuclear and particle physics, condensed-matter physics, nonlinear physics, astrophysics.

Oakland University, Graduate Study and Lifelong Learning, College of Arts and Sciences, Department of Physics, Rochester, MI 48309-4401. Offers medical physics (PhD); physics (MS). *Degree requirements:* For doctorate, thesis/dissertation. *Entrance requirements:* For master's, minimum GPA of 3.0 for unconditional admission; for doctorate, GRE Subject Test, GRE General Test, minimum GPA of 3.0 for unconditional admission. Additional exam requirements/recommendations for international students: Required—TOEFL (minimum score 550 paper-based; 213 computer-based). Electronic applications accepted. *Expenses:* Contact institution. *Faculty research:* Quantitative molecular imagings of articular cartilage, multifunctional ferrite-ferroelectric layered structures for microwave and millimeter wave devices, magnoelectric materials for antenna structures.

The Ohio State University, Graduate School, College of Arts and Sciences, Division of Natural and Mathematical Sciences, Department of Physics, Columbus, OH 43210. Offers MS, PhD. *Faculty:* 52. *Students:* 81 full-time (13 women), 105 part-time (18 women); includes 11 minority (1 American Indian or Alaska Native, non-Hispanic/Latino; 6 Asian, non-Hispanic/Latino; 4 Hispanic/Latino), 38 international. Average age 26. In 2011, 12 master's, 26 doctorates awarded. *Degree requirements:* For master's, thesis optional; for doctorate, thesis/dissertation. *Entrance requirements:* For master's and doctorate, GRE General Test, GRE Subject Test (physics). Additional exam requirements/recommendations for international students: Required—TOEFL (minimum score 600 paper-based; 250 computer-based), Michigan English Language Assessment Battery (minimum score 82). *Application deadline:* For fall admission, 8/15 priority date for domestic students, 7/1 for international students; for winter admission, 12/1 priority date for domestic students, 11/1 for international students; for spring admission, 3/1 priority date for domestic students, 2/1 for international students. Applications are processed on a rolling basis. Application fee: $40 ($50 for international students). Electronic applications accepted. *Expenses:* Tuition, state resident: full-time $11,400. Tuition, nonresident: full-time $28,125. Tuition and fees vary according to course load, degree level, campus/location and program. *Financial support:* Fellowships, research assistantships, teaching assistantships, Federal Work-Study, and institutionally sponsored loans available. Support available to part-time students. *Unit head:* James J. Beatty, Chair, 614-292-2653, E-mail: beatty@mps.ohio-state.edu. *Application contact:* Graduate Admissions, 614-292-6031, Fax: 614-292-3656, E-mail: gradadmissions@osu.edu. Web site: http://www.physics.ohio-state.edu/.

Ohio University, Graduate College, College of Arts and Sciences, Department of Physics and Astronomy, Athens, OH 45701. Offers astronomy (MS, PhD); physics (MS, PhD). *Faculty:* 27 full-time (3 women), 5 part-time/adjunct (1 woman). *Students:* 81 full-time (27 women); includes 1 minority (Hispanic/Latino), 66 international. Average age 27. 114 applicants, 29% accepted, 14 enrolled. In 2011, 5 master's, 13 doctorates awarded. Terminal master's awarded for partial completion of doctoral program. *Degree requirements:* For master's, thesis or alternative; for doctorate, comprehensive exam, thesis/dissertation. *Entrance requirements:* For master's and doctorate, minimum GPA of 3.0. Additional exam requirements/recommendations for international students: Required—TOEFL (minimum score 600 paper-based; 250 computer-based; 100 iBT), IELTS (minimum score 7), TWE (minimum score 4). *Application deadline:* For fall admission, 2/1 priority date for domestic students, 2/1 for international students. Applications are processed on a rolling basis. Electronic applications accepted. Application fee is waived when completed online. *Financial support:* In 2011–12, 1 fellowship with full tuition reimbursement (averaging $24,007 per year), 51 research assistantships with full tuition reimbursements (averaging $24,007 per year), 29 teaching assistantships with full tuition reimbursements (averaging $21,825 per year) were awarded; scholarships/grants and unspecified assistantships also available. Financial award application deadline: 4/1. *Faculty research:* Nuclear physics, condensed-matter physics, nonlinear systems, astrophysics, biophysics. *Total annual research expenditures:* $3.2 million. *Unit head:* Dr. David Ingram, Chair, 740-593-0336, Fax: 740-593-0433, E-mail: ingram@ohio.edu. *Application contact:* Dr. Marcus Boettcher, Graduate Admissions Chair, 740-593-1714, Fax: 740-593-0433, E-mail: gradapp@phy.ohiou.edu. Web site: http://www.phy.ohiou.edu/.

See Display on next page and Close-Up on page 273.

Oklahoma State University, College of Arts and Sciences, Department of Physics, Stillwater, OK 74078. Offers photonics (MS, PhD); physics (MS, PhD). *Faculty:* 30 full-time (6 women), 2 part-time/adjunct (1 woman). *Students:* 3 full-time (0 women), 37 part-time (5 women); includes 2 minority (1 Hispanic/Latino; 1 Two or more races, non-Hispanic/Latino), 29 international. Average age 29. 37 applicants, 43% accepted, 6 enrolled. In 2011, 3 master's, 6 doctorates awarded. *Degree requirements:* For master's, thesis; for doctorate, comprehensive exam, thesis/dissertation, oral defense of dissertation, preliminary exam, qualifying exam. *Entrance requirements:* For master's and doctorate, GRE. Additional exam requirements/recommendations for international students: Required—TOEFL (minimum score 550 paper-based; 79 iBT). *Application deadline:* For fall admission, 3/1 for international students; for spring admission, 8/1 for international students. Applications are processed on a rolling basis. Application fee: $40 ($75 for international students). Electronic applications accepted. *Expenses:* Tuition, state resident: full-time $4044; part-time $168.50 per credit hour. Tuition,

Peterson's Graduate Programs in the Physical Sciences, Mathematics, Agricultural Sciences, the Environment & Natural Resources 2013

facebook.com/petersonspublishing **247**

Department of

physics + astronomy

Expand your view.

undergraduate programs in :

:: Astronomy: Discover the Cosmos

:: Physics: Prepare for Advanced Research

:: Applied Physics: Get Jobs in R&D

:: Meteorology: Model and Predict Weather

:: our portfolio

Do undergraduate research one-on-one with professors

Learn skills that make you employable

Discover the mathematical laws of nature

Get personal attention in small classes

:: research projects

Kitt Peak: take pictures with our 2.4 meter reflector telescope

Accelerator Lab: measure the same reactions that take place in a supernova

Nanoscience: make state-of-the-art measurements of atomic-scale structures

Biophysics: use new techniques from physics to help understand diseases

Theory: explore new horizons with computational physics

Find us on YouTube
www.youtube.com/OhioUPhysics

Apply online
www.phy.ohiou.edu

OHIO UNIVERSITY
1804

Department of Physics and Astronomy
Athens, Ohio
tel: 740.593.1718
email: physics@ohiou.edu

nonresident: full-time $16,008; part-time $667 per credit hour. *Required fees:* $2122; $88.45 per credit hour. One-time fee: $50. Tuition and fees vary according to course load and campus/location. *Financial support:* In 2011–12, 18 research assistantships (averaging $17,967 per year), 36 teaching assistantships (averaging $16,802 per year) were awarded; career-related internships or fieldwork, Federal Work-Study, scholarships/grants, health care benefits, tuition waivers (partial), and unspecified assistantships also available. Support available to part-time students. Financial award application deadline: 3/1; financial award applicants required to submit FAFSA. *Faculty research:* Lasers and photonics, non-linear optical materials, turbulence, structure and function of biological membranes, particle theory. *Unit head:* Dr. James Wicksted, Head, 405-744-5796, Fax: 405-744-6811. *Application contact:* Dr. Sheryl Tucker, Dean, 405-744-7099, Fax: 405-744-0355, E-mail: grad-i@okstate.edu. Web site: http://physics.okstate.edu.

Old Dominion University, College of Sciences, Program in Physics, Norfolk, VA 23529. Offers MS, PhD. *Faculty:* 22 full-time (2 women), 10 part-time/adjunct (3 women). *Students:* 47 full-time (14 women), 5 part-time (1 woman); includes 1 minority (Asian, non-Hispanic/Latino), 28 international. Average age 32. 77 applicants, 34% accepted, 13 enrolled. In 2011, 7 master's, 5 doctorates awarded. Terminal master's awarded for partial completion of doctoral program. *Degree requirements:* For master's, comprehensive exam, thesis optional; for doctorate, comprehensive exam, thesis/dissertation. *Entrance requirements:* For master's, BS in physics or related field, minimum GPA of 3.0 in major; for doctorate, GRE General Test; GRE Subject Test (strongly recommended), minimum GPA of 3.0; two reference letters. Additional exam requirements/recommendations for international students: Required—TOEFL (minimum score 550 paper-based; 213 computer-based; 79 iBT). *Application deadline:* For fall admission, 2/15 for domestic and international students. Applications are processed on a rolling basis. Application fee: $50. Electronic applications accepted. *Expenses:* Tuition, state resident: full-time $9096; part-time $379 per credit. Tuition, nonresident: full-time $23,064; part-time $961 per credit. *Required fees:* $127 per semester. One-time fee: $50. *Financial support:* In 2011–12, 42 students received support, including 2 fellowships with full tuition reimbursements available (averaging $15,000 per year), 33 research assistantships with full and partial tuition reimbursements available (averaging $24,500 per year), 16 teaching assistantships with full tuition reimbursements available (averaging $22,500 per year); career-related internships or fieldwork, scholarships/grants, tuition waivers (full), and unspecified assistantships also available. Support available to part-time students. Financial award application deadline: 2/15; financial award applicants required to submit FAFSA. *Faculty research:* Nuclear and particle physics, atomic physics, condensed-matter physics, plasma physics, accelerator physics. *Unit head:* Dr. Lepsha Vuskovic, Graduate Program Director, 757-683-4611, Fax: 757-683-3038, E-mail: vuskovic@odu.edu. *Application contact:* Dr. Mark Havey, Graduate Recruitment and Admissions Director, 757-683-4612, Fax: 757-683-3038, E-mail: mhavey@odu.edu. Web site: http://sci.odu.edu/physics/graduate/graduate_overview.shtml.

Oregon State University, Graduate School, College of Science, Department of Physics, Corvallis, OR 97331. Offers applied physics (MS); physics (MA, MS, PhD). Part-time programs available. Terminal master's awarded for partial completion of doctoral program. *Degree requirements:* For master's, thesis optional, qualifying exam; for doctorate, thesis/dissertation, qualifying exam. *Entrance requirements:* For master's and doctorate, minimum GPA of 3.0 in last 90 hours. Additional exam requirements/recommendations for international students: Required—TOEFL.

Penn State University Park, Graduate School, Eberly College of Science, Department of Physics, State College, University Park, PA 16802-1503. Offers M Ed, MS, PhD. *Unit head:* Dr. Nitin Samarth, Head, 814-865-7533, Fax: 814-865-0978. *Application contact:* Rick Robinett, Director of Graduate Studies, 814-863-0965, E-mail: rq9@psu.edu. Web site: http://www.phys.psu.edu.

Pittsburg State University, Graduate School, College of Arts and Sciences, Department of Physics, Pittsburg, KS 66762. Offers applied physics (MS); physics (MS); professional physics (MS). *Degree requirements:* For master's, thesis or alternative.

Portland State University, Graduate Studies, College of Liberal Arts and Sciences, Department of Physics, Portland, OR 97207-0751. Offers MA, MS, PhD. Part-time programs available. *Degree requirements:* For master's, variable foreign language requirement, thesis, oral exam, written report; for doctorate, thesis/dissertation. *Entrance requirements:* For master's, GRE General Test, minimum GPA of 3.0 in upper-division course work or 2.75 overall, 2 letters of recommendation. Additional exam requirements/recommendations for international students: Required—TOEFL (minimum score 550 paper-based; 213 computer-based). *Faculty research:* Statistical physics, membrane biophysics, low-temperature physics, electron microscopy, atmospheric physics.

Princeton University, Graduate School, Department of Physics, Princeton, NJ 08544-1019. Offers PhD. *Degree requirements:* For doctorate, thesis/dissertation, qualifying exam. *Entrance requirements:* For doctorate, GRE General Test, GRE Subject Test. Additional exam requirements/recommendations for international students: Required—TOEFL (minimum score 600 paper-based; 250 computer-based). Electronic applications accepted.

248 facebook.com/petersonspublishing

Peterson's Graduate Programs in the Physical Sciences, Mathematics, Agricultural Sciences, the Environment & Natural Resources 2013

Purdue University, Graduate School, College of Science, Department of Physics, West Lafayette, IN 47907. Offers MS, PhD. Part-time programs available. *Faculty:* 51 full-time (5 women), 3 part-time/adjunct (0 women). *Students:* 126 full-time (18 women), 22 part-time (4 women); includes 7 minority (2 Black or African American, non-Hispanic/Latino; 2 Asian, non-Hispanic/Latino; 2 Hispanic/Latino; 1 Two or more races, non-Hispanic/Latino), 72 international. Average age 27. 305 applicants, 23% accepted, 25 enrolled. In 2011, 12 master's, 32 doctorates awarded. Terminal master's awarded for partial completion of doctoral program. *Degree requirements:* For master's, thesis optional, qualifying exam; for doctorate, thesis/dissertation, qualifying exam. *Entrance requirements:* For master's and doctorate, GRE General Test, GRE Subject Test (physics), minimum undergraduate GPA of 3.0 or equivalent. Additional exam requirements/recommendations for international students: Required—TOEFL (minimum score 550 paper-based; 77 iBT). *Application deadline:* For fall admission, 1/15 for domestic and international students; for spring admission, 8/1 for domestic and international students. Applications are processed on a rolling basis. Application fee: $60 ($75 for international students). Electronic applications accepted. *Financial support:* Fellowships with partial tuition reimbursements, research assistantships with partial tuition reimbursements, and teaching assistantships with partial tuition reimbursements available. Support available to part-time students. Financial award application deadline: 2/1; financial award applicants required to submit FAFSA. *Faculty research:* Solid-state, elementary particle, and nuclear physics; biological physics; acoustics; astrophysics. *Unit head:* Dr. Nicholas J. Giordano, Head, 765-494-3000, Fax: 765-494-0706, E-mail: giordano@purdue.edu. *Application contact:* Sandy J. Formica, Graduate Coordinator, 765-494-3099, E-mail: physcontacts@purdue.edu. Web site: http://www.physics.purdue.edu/.

Queens College of the City University of New York, Division of Graduate Studies, Mathematics and Natural Sciences Division, Department of Physics, Flushing, NY 11367-1597. Offers MA, PhD. Part-time and evening/weekend programs available. *Faculty:* 11 full-time (1 woman). *Students:* 5 part-time (2 women); includes 3 minority (2 Asian, non-Hispanic/Latino; 1 Hispanic/Latino). 11 applicants, 36% accepted, 2 enrolled. In 2011, 2 master's awarded. *Degree requirements:* For master's, comprehensive exam. *Entrance requirements:* For master's, previous course work in calculus, minimum GPA of 3.0. Additional exam requirements/recommendations for international students: Required—TOEFL. *Application deadline:* For fall admission, 4/1 for domestic students; for spring admission, 11/1 for domestic students. Applications are processed on a rolling basis. Application fee: $125. *Expenses:* Tuition, state resident: part-time $345 per credit. Tuition, nonresident: part-time $640 per credit. *Required fees:* $145.25 per semester. *Financial support:* Career-related internships or fieldwork, Federal Work-Study, institutionally sponsored loans, and tuition waivers (partial) available. Support available to part-time students. Financial award application deadline: 4/1; financial award applicants required to submit FAFSA. *Faculty research:* Solid-state physics, low temperature physics, elementary particles and fields. *Unit head:* Dr. Alexander Lisyansky, Chairperson, 718-997-3350, E-mail: alexander_lisyansky@qc.edu. *Application contact:* Dr. J. Marion Dickey, Graduate Adviser, 718-997-3350.

Queen's University at Kingston, School of Graduate Studies and Research, Faculty of Arts and Sciences, Department of Physics, Kingston, ON K7L 3N6, Canada. Offers M Sc, M Sc Eng, PhD. Part-time programs available. *Degree requirements:* For master's, thesis; for doctorate, comprehensive exam, thesis/dissertation. *Entrance requirements:* For master's, first or upper second class honours in Physics; for doctorate, M Sc or M Sc Eng. Additional exam requirements/recommendations for international students: Required—TOEFL (minimum score 550 paper-based; 213 computer-based). *Faculty research:* Theoretical physics, astronomy and astrophysics, subatomic, condensed matter, applied and engineering.

Rensselaer Polytechnic Institute, Graduate School, School of Science, Department of Physics, Applied Physics, and Astronomy, Troy, NY 12180-3590. Offers MS, PhD. Part-time programs available. *Degree requirements:* For doctorate, thesis/dissertation. *Entrance requirements:* For master's and doctorate, GRE General Test, GRE Subject Test. Additional exam requirements/recommendations for international students: Required—TOEFL (minimum score 600 paper-based; 250 computer-based; 100 iBT). Electronic applications accepted. *Faculty research:* Astrophysics, condensed matter, particle physics, optical and biological physics.

Rice University, Graduate Programs, Wiess School of Natural Sciences, Department of Physics and Astronomy, Houston, TX 77251-1892. Offers nanoscale physics (MS); physics and astronomy (PhD); science teaching (MST). Part-time programs available. *Degree requirements:* For master's, thesis (for some programs); for doctorate, thesis/dissertation, minimum B average. *Entrance requirements:* For master's, GRE General Test; for doctorate, GRE General Test, GRE Subject Test. Additional exam requirements/recommendations for international students: Required—TOEFL (minimum score 600 paper-based; 250 computer-based; 90 iBT). Electronic applications accepted. *Faculty research:* Optical physics; ultra cold atoms; membrane electr-statics, peptides, proteins and lipids; solar astrophysics; stellar activity; magnetic fields; young stars.

Rice University, Graduate Programs, Wiess School–Professional Science Master's Programs, Professional Master's Program in Nanoscale Physics, Houston, TX 77251-1892. Offers MS. *Degree requirements:* For master's,

internship. *Entrance requirements:* For master's, GRE General Test, bachelor's degree in physics and related field, 4 letters of recommendation. Additional exam requirements/recommendations for international students: Required—TOEFL (minimum score 600 paper-based; 250 computer-based; 90 iBT). Electronic applications accepted. *Faculty research:* Atomic, molecular, and applied physics, surface and condensed matter physics.

Royal Military College of Canada, Division of Graduate Studies and Research, Science Division, Department of Physics, Kingston, ON K7K 7B4, Canada. Offers M Sc. *Degree requirements:* For master's, thesis. *Entrance requirements:* For master's, honour's degree with second-class standing. Electronic applications accepted.

Rutgers, The State University of New Jersey, New Brunswick, Graduate School-New Brunswick, Department of Physics and Astronomy, Piscataway, NJ 08854-8097. Offers astronomy (MS, PhD); biophysics (PhD); condensed matter physics (MS, PhD); elementary particle physics (MS, PhD); intermediate energy nuclear physics (MS); nuclear physics (MS, PhD); physics (MST); surface science (PhD); theoretical physics (MS, PhD). Part-time programs available. Terminal master's awarded for partial completion of doctoral program. *Degree requirements:* For master's, comprehensive exam, thesis or alternative; for doctorate, comprehensive exam, thesis/dissertation. *Entrance requirements:* For master's and doctorate, GRE General Test, GRE Subject Test. Additional exam requirements/recommendations for international students: Required—TOEFL (minimum score 560 paper-based). Electronic applications accepted. *Faculty research:* Astronomy, high energy, condensed matter, surface, nuclear physics.

St. Francis Xavier University, Graduate Studies, Department of Physics, Antigonish, NS B2G 2W5, Canada. Offers M Sc. *Degree requirements:* For master's, thesis. *Entrance requirements:* For master's, minimum B average in undergraduate course work, honors degree in physics or related area. Additional exam requirements/recommendations for international students: Required—TOEFL (minimum score 580 paper-based; 236 computer-based). *Faculty research:* Atomic and molecular spectroscopy, quantum theory, many body theory, mathematical physics, phase transitions.

San Diego State University, Graduate and Research Affairs, College of Sciences, Department of Physics, Program in Physics, San Diego, CA 92182. Offers MA, MS. Part-time programs available. *Degree requirements:* For master's, thesis, oral exam. *Entrance requirements:* For master's, GRE General Test, GRE Subject Test (physics), 2 letters of recommendation. Additional exam requirements/recommendations for international students: Required—TOEFL. Electronic applications accepted.

San Francisco State University, Division of Graduate Studies, College of Science and Engineering, Department of Physics and Astronomy, San Francisco, CA 94132-1722. Offers physics (MS). Part-time programs available. *Application deadline:* Applications are processed on a rolling basis. Electronic applications accepted. *Unit head:* Dr. Susan Lea, Chair, 415-338-1659, E-mail: physics@stars.sfsu.edu. *Application contact:* Maarten Golterman, Graduate Coordinator, 415-338-1659, E-mail: maarten@stars.sfsu.edu. Web site: http://www.physics.sfsu.edu/.

San Jose State University, Graduate Studies and Research, College of Science, Department of Physics and Astronomy, San Jose, CA 95192-0001. Offers computational physics (MS); physics (MS). Part-time and evening/weekend programs available. *Degree requirements:* For master's, thesis optional. *Entrance requirements:* For master's, GRE. Electronic applications accepted. *Faculty research:* Astrophysics, atmospheric physics, elementary particles, dislocation theory, general relativity.

Simon Fraser University, Graduate Studies, Faculty of Science, Department of Physics, Burnaby, BC V5A 1S6, Canada. Offers biophysics (M Sc, PhD); chemical physics (M Sc, PhD); physics (M Sc, PhD). *Degree requirements:* For master's, thesis; for doctorate, thesis/dissertation. *Entrance requirements:* For master's, minimum GPA of 3.0; for doctorate, minimum GPA of 3.5. Additional exam requirements/recommendations for international students: Required—TOEFL or IELTS. *Faculty research:* Solid-state physics, magnetism, energy research, superconductivity, nuclear physics.

South Dakota School of Mines and Technology, Graduate Division, Program in Physics, Rapid City, SD 57701-3995. Offers MS, PhD.

South Dakota State University, Graduate School, College of Engineering, Department of Physics, Brookings, SD 57007. Offers engineering (MS). Part-time programs available. *Degree requirements:* For master's, comprehensive exam (for some programs), thesis (for some programs), oral exam. *Entrance requirements:* Additional exam requirements/recommendations for international students: Required—TOEFL (minimum score 580 paper-based; 237 computer-based). *Faculty research:* Materials science, astrophysics, remote sensing and atmospheric corrections, theoretical and computational physics, applied physics.

Southern Illinois University Carbondale, Graduate School, College of Science, Department of Physics, Carbondale, IL 62901-4701. Offers MS, PhD. *Faculty:* 9 full-time (0 women). *Students:* 5 full-time (1 woman), 26 part-time (4 women); includes 2 minority (1 Asian, non-Hispanic/Latino; 1 Hispanic/Latino), 11 international. 26 applicants, 42% accepted, 9 enrolled. In 2011, 2 master's, 2 doctorates awarded. *Degree requirements:* For master's, one foreign language,

Peterson's Graduate Programs in the Physical Sciences, Mathematics, Agricultural Sciences, the Environment & Natural Resources 2013

facebook.com/petersonspublishing **249**

Physics

thesis. *Entrance requirements:* For master's, minimum GPA of 2.7. Additional exam requirements/recommendations for international students: Required—TOEFL. *Application deadline:* Applications are processed on a rolling basis. Application fee: $20. *Financial support:* In 2011–12, 1 fellowship with full tuition reimbursement, 9 teaching assistantships with full tuition reimbursements were awarded; research assistantships with full tuition reimbursements, career-related internships or fieldwork, Federal Work-Study, institutionally sponsored loans, and tuition waivers (full) also available. Support available to part-time students. Financial award application deadline: 2/15. *Faculty research:* Atomic, molecular, nuclear, and mathematical physics; statistical mechanics; solid-state and low-temperature physics; rheology; material science. *Total annual research expenditures:* $773,352. *Unit head:* Dr. Aldo Migone, Chairperson, 618-453-1054, E-mail: aldo@physics.siu.edu. *Application contact:* Sally Pleasure, Graduate Admissions Committee, 618-453-2643. Web site: http://siuphysics.physics.siu.edu/.

Southern Methodist University, Dedman College, Department of Physics, Dallas, TX 75275. Offers MS, PhD. Part-time programs available. Terminal master's awarded for partial completion of doctoral program. *Degree requirements:* For master's, thesis optional, oral exam; for doctorate, thesis/dissertation, written exam. *Entrance requirements:* For master's and doctorate, GRE General Test, GRE Subject Test (physics), minimum GPA of 3.0. Additional exam requirements/recommendations for international students: Required—TOEFL. Electronic applications accepted. *Faculty research:* Particle physics, cosmology, astrophysics, mathematics physics, computational physics.

Southern University and Agricultural and Mechanical College, Graduate School, College of Sciences, Department of Physics, Baton Rouge, LA 70813. Offers MS. *Degree requirements:* For master's, thesis. *Entrance requirements:* For master's, GMAT or GRE General Test. Additional exam requirements/recommendations for international students: Required—TOEFL (minimum score 525 paper-based; 193 computer-based). *Faculty research:* Piezoelectric materials and devices, predictive ab-instio calculations, high energy physics, surface growth studies, semiconductor and intermetallics.

Stanford University, School of Humanities and Sciences, Department of Physics, Stanford, CA 94305-9991. Offers PhD. *Degree requirements:* For doctorate, thesis/dissertation, oral exam, qualifying exam. *Entrance requirements:* For doctorate, GRE General Test, GRE Subject Test. Additional exam requirements/recommendations for international students: Required—TOEFL. Electronic applications accepted. *Expenses: Tuition:* Full-time $40,050; part-time $890 per credit.

State University of New York at Binghamton, Graduate School, School of Arts and Sciences, Department of Physics, Applied Physics, and Astronomy, Binghamton, NY 13902-6000. Offers applied physics (MS); physics (MA, MS, PhD). *Faculty:* 12 full-time (1 woman), 13 part-time/adjunct (6 women). *Students:* 17 full-time (1 woman), 2 part-time (0 women); includes 1 minority (Black or African American, non-Hispanic/Latino), 5 international. Average age 27. 12 applicants, 92% accepted, 8 enrolled. In 2011, 1 master's awarded. *Degree requirements:* For master's, thesis or alternative. *Entrance requirements:* For master's, GRE General Test, GRE Subject Test. Additional exam requirements/recommendations for international students: Required—TOEFL (minimum score 550 paper-based; 213 computer-based; 80 iBT). *Application deadline:* For fall admission, 2/15 priority date for domestic students, 2/15 for international students; for spring admission, 10/15 priority date for domestic students, 10/15 for international students. Applications are processed on a rolling basis. Application fee: $60. Electronic applications accepted. *Financial support:* In 2011–12, 19 students received support, including 1 fellowship with full tuition reimbursement available (averaging $11,000 per year), 2 research assistantships with full tuition reimbursements available (averaging $11,000 per year), 15 teaching assistantships with full tuition reimbursements available (averaging $11,000 per year); career-related internships or fieldwork, Federal Work-Study, institutionally sponsored loans, scholarships/grants, health care benefits, and unspecified assistantships also available. Financial award application deadline: 2/15; financial award applicants required to submit FAFSA. *Unit head:* Dr. Eric Cotts, Chairperson, 607-777-4371, E-mail: ecotts@binghamton.edu. *Application contact:* Catherine Smith, Recruiting and Admissions Coordinator, 607-777-2151, Fax: 607-777-2501, E-mail: cmsmith@binghamton.edu.

Stephen F. Austin State University, Graduate School, College of Sciences and Mathematics, Department of Physics and Astronomy, Nacogdoches, TX 75962. Offers physics (MS). Part-time programs available. *Degree requirements:* For master's, comprehensive exam. *Entrance requirements:* For master's, GRE General Test, minimum GPA of 2.8 in last 60 hours, 2.5 overall. Additional exam requirements/recommendations for international students: Required—TOEFL. *Faculty research:* Low-temperature physics, x-ray spectroscopy and metallic glasses, infrared spectroscopy.

Stevens Institute of Technology, Graduate School, Charles V. Schaefer Jr. School of Engineering, Department of Physics and Engineering Physics, Hoboken, NJ 07030. Offers applied optics (Certificate); engineering physics (M Eng); microdevices and microsystems (Certificate); physics (MS, PhD); plasma and surface physics (Certificate). Part-time and evening/weekend programs available. Terminal master's awarded for partial completion of doctoral program. *Degree requirements:* For master's, thesis optional; for doctorate, thesis/dissertation. *Entrance requirements:* For master's and doctorate, GRE.

Additional exam requirements/recommendations for international students: Required—TOEFL. Electronic applications accepted. *Faculty research:* Laser spectroscopy, physical kinetics, semiconductor-device physics, condensed-matter theory.

Stony Brook University, State University of New York, Graduate School, College of Arts and Sciences, Department of Physics and Astronomy, Program in Physics, Stony Brook, NY 11794. Offers modern research instrumentation (MS); physics (MA, PhD); physics education (MAT). *Degree requirements:* For doctorate, one foreign language, thesis/dissertation. *Entrance requirements:* For master's and doctorate, GRE General Test. Additional exam requirements/recommendations for international students: Required—TOEFL.

Syracuse University, College of Arts and Sciences, Program in Physics, Syracuse, NY 13244. Offers MS, PhD. Part-time programs available. *Students:* 74 full-time (11 women); includes 2 minority (1 Asian, non-Hispanic/Latino; 1 Hispanic/Latino), 49 international. Average age 27. 140 applicants, 26% accepted, 11 enrolled. In 2011, 3 master's, 4 doctorates awarded. Terminal master's awarded for partial completion of doctoral program. *Degree requirements:* For master's, thesis or alternative; for doctorate, comprehensive exam, thesis/dissertation. *Entrance requirements:* For master's and doctorate, GRE General Test, GRE Subject Test. Additional exam requirements/recommendations for international students: Required—TOEFL (minimum score 100 iBT). *Application deadline:* For fall admission, 2/1 priority date for domestic students, 2/1 for international students. Application fee: $75. Electronic applications accepted. *Expenses: Tuition:* Part-time $1206 per credit. *Financial support:* Fellowships with full tuition reimbursements, research assistantships with full and partial tuition reimbursements, teaching assistantships with full and partial tuition reimbursements, and tuition waivers (partial) available. Financial award application deadline: 1/1; financial award applicants required to submit FAFSA. *Unit head:* Dr. Simon Catterall, Director, Graduate Studies, 315-443-5978, E-mail: smc@phy.syr.edu. *Application contact:* Diane Sanderson, 315-443-5958, E-mail: graduate@phy.syr.edu. Web site: http://www.physics.syr.edu/.

Temple University, College of Science and Technology, Department of Physics, Philadelphia, PA 19122-6096. Offers MA, PhD. *Faculty:* 17 full-time (4 women). *Students:* 41 full-time (9 women), 2 part-time (0 women); includes 6 minority (1 Black or African American, non-Hispanic/Latino; 3 Asian, non-Hispanic/Latino; 1 Hispanic/Latino; 1 Two or more races, non-Hispanic/Latino), 16 international. Average age 29. 18 applicants, 100% accepted, 6 enrolled. In 2011, 4 master's, 1 doctorate awarded. Terminal master's awarded for partial completion of doctoral program. *Degree requirements:* For master's, comprehensive exam, thesis or alternative; for doctorate, thesis/dissertation, 2 comprehensive exams. *Entrance requirements:* For master's and doctorate, GRE General Test, minimum GPA of 3.0. Additional exam requirements/recommendations for international students: Required—TOEFL (minimum score 550 paper-based; 213 computer-based; 79 iBT). *Application deadline:* For fall admission, 7/15 for domestic students, 12/15 for international students; for spring admission, 11/15 for domestic students, 8/1 for international students. Applications are processed on a rolling basis. Application fee: $50. Electronic applications accepted. *Expenses: Tuition,* state resident: full-time $12,366; part-time $687 per credit hour. Tuition, nonresident: full-time $17,298; part-time $961 per credit hour. *Required fees:* $590; $213 per year. *Financial support:* Fellowships, research assistantships, teaching assistantships, and tuition waivers (full and partial) available. Financial award application deadline: 1/15; financial award applicants required to submit FAFSA. *Faculty research:* Laser-based molecular spectroscopy, elementary particle physics, statistical mechanics, solid-state physics. *Unit head:* Dr. Rongjia Tao, Chair, 215-204-7634, Fax: 215-204-5652, E-mail: physics@temple.edu. *Application contact:* Tara Schumacher, Coordinator of Outreach, 215-204-6575, Fax: 215-204-8781, E-mail: tara.schumacher@temple.edu. Web site: http://www.temple.edu/physics/.

Texas A&M University, College of Science, Department of Physics and Astronomy, College Station, TX 77843. Offers applied physics (PhD); physics (MS, PhD). *Faculty:* 54. *Students:* 179 full-time (25 women), 8 part-time (0 women); includes 28 minority (3 Black or African American, non-Hispanic/Latino; 1 American Indian or Alaska Native, non-Hispanic/Latino; 4 Asian, non-Hispanic/Latino; 15 Hispanic/Latino; 5 Two or more races, non-Hispanic/Latino), 84 international. In 2011, 16 master's, 17 doctorates awarded. Terminal master's awarded for partial completion of doctoral program. *Degree requirements:* For master's, thesis (for some programs); for doctorate, thesis/dissertation. *Entrance requirements:* For master's and doctorate, GRE General Test, GRE Subject Test. Additional exam requirements/recommendations for international students: Required—TOEFL. *Application deadline:* For fall admission, 3/1 priority date for domestic students; for spring admission, 8/1 for domestic students. Application fee: $50 ($75 for international students). Electronic applications accepted. *Expenses: Tuition,* state resident: full-time $5437; part-time $226.55 per credit hour. Tuition, nonresident: full-time $12,949; part-time $539.55 per credit hour. *Required fees:* $2741. *Financial support:* In 2011–12, research assistantships (averaging $16,200 per year), teaching assistantships (averaging $16,200 per year) were awarded; fellowships also available. Financial award application deadline: 3/1; financial award applicants required to submit FAFSA. *Faculty research:* Condensed-matter, atomic/molecular, high-energy, and nuclear physics; quantum optics. *Unit head:* Dr. Edward S. Fry, Head, 979-845-7717, E-mail: fry@physics.tamu.edu. *Application contact:* Dr. George W. Kattawar,

250 facebook.com/petersonspublishing

Peterson's Graduate Programs in the Physical Sciences, Mathematics, Agricultural Sciences, the Environment & Natural Resources 2013

Professor, 979-845-1180, Fax: 979-845-2590, E-mail: kattawar@tamu.edu. Web site: http://physics.tamu.edu/.

Texas A&M University–Commerce, Graduate School, College of Science, Engineering and Agriculture, Department of Physics and Astronomy, Commerce, TX 75429-3011. Offers M Ed, MS. Part-time programs available. *Degree requirements:* For master's, comprehensive exam, thesis (for some programs). *Entrance requirements:* For master's, GRE General Test. Electronic applications accepted.

Texas Christian University, College of Science and Engineering, Department of Physics and Astronomy, Fort Worth, TX 76129-0002. Offers physics (MA, MS, PhD), including astrophysics (PhD), business (PhD), physics (PhD); PhD/MBA. *Faculty:* 7 full-time, 1 part-time/adjunct. *Students:* 3 full-time (1 woman), 13 part-time (4 women); includes 2 minority (1 Asian, non-Hispanic/Latino; 1 Hispanic/Latino), 7 international. Average age 27. 7 applicants, 71% accepted, 5 enrolled. In 2011, 1 master's, 2 doctorates awarded. Terminal master's awarded for partial completion of doctoral program. *Degree requirements:* For master's, comprehensive exam, thesis; for doctorate, comprehensive exam, thesis/dissertation, paper submitted to scientific journal. *Entrance requirements:* For master's and doctorate, GRE General Test, minimum GPA of 3.0. Additional exam requirements/recommendations for international students: Required—TOEFL (minimum score 600 paper-based). *Application deadline:* For fall admission, 2/1 for domestic and international students; for spring admission, 10/1 for domestic and international students. Applications are processed on a rolling basis. Application fee: $60. Electronic applications accepted. *Expenses: Tuition:* Full-time $20,250; part-time $1125 per credit hour. Part-time tuition and fees vary according to course load and program. *Financial support:* In 2011–12, 11 teaching assistantships with full tuition reimbursements (averaging $19,500 per year) were awarded; tuition waivers also available. Financial award application deadline: 2/1. *Unit head:* Dr. William R. Graham, Chairperson, 817-257-7375 Ext. 6383, Fax: 817-257-7742, E-mail: w.graham@tcu.edu. *Application contact:* Dr. Yuri Strzhemechny, Associate Professor, 817-257-7375 Ext. 5793, Fax: 817-257-7742, E-mail: y.strzhemechny@tcu.edu. Web site: http://www.phys.tcu.edu/grad_program.asp.

Texas State University–San Marcos, Graduate School, College of Science and Engineering, Department of Physics, San Marcos, TX 78666. Offers material physics (MS); physics (MS). Part-time programs available. *Faculty:* 7 full-time (0 women), 2 part-time/adjunct (1 woman). *Students:* 11 full-time (0 women), 7 part-time (1 woman); includes 2 minority (both Hispanic/Latino), 2 international. Average age 28. 14 applicants, 50% accepted, 5 enrolled. In 2011, 3 master's awarded. *Degree requirements:* For master's, comprehensive exam, thesis (for some programs). *Entrance requirements:* For master's, minimum GPA of 2.75 in juniorand senior-level physics courses or 2.5 with GRE (minimum combined score of 900 Verbal and Quantitative). Additional exam requirements/recommendations for international students: Required—TOEFL (minimum score 550 paper-based; 213 computer-based; 78 iBT). *Application deadline:* For fall admission, 6/15 priority date for domestic students, 6/1 for international students; for spring admission, 10/15 priority date for domestic students, 10/1 for international students. Applications are processed on a rolling basis. Application fee: $40 ($90 for international students). Electronic applications accepted. *Expenses:* Tuition, state resident: full-time $6408; part-time $3204 per semester. Tuition, nonresident: full-time $14,832; part-time $7416 per semester. *Required fees:* $1824; $912 per semester. Tuition and fees vary according to course load. *Financial support:* In 2011–12, 7 students received support, including 5 research assistantships (averaging $8,397 per year), 7 teaching assistantships (averaging $8,703 per year); career-related internships or fieldwork, Federal Work-Study, and institutionally sponsored loans also available. Support available to part-time students. Financial award application deadline: 4/1; financial award applicants required to submit FAFSA. *Faculty research:* IGERT: new math tools, redesign and development, Novel Hemt-Based Gan, HETERO-Functional. *Total annual research expenditures:* $329,875. *Unit head:* Dr. David Donnelly, Chair, 512-245-2131, Fax: 512-245-2131, E-mail: dd14@txstate.edu. *Application contact:* Dr. J. Michael Willoughby, Dean of Graduate School, 512-245-2581, Fax: 512-245-8365, E-mail: gradcollege@txstate.edu. Web site: http://www.txstate.edu/physics/.

Texas Tech University, Graduate School, College of Arts and Sciences, Department of Physics, Lubbock, TX 79409. Offers applied physics (MS); physics (MS, PhD). Part-time programs available. *Faculty:* 18 full-time (2 women), 1 part-time/adjunct (0 women). *Students:* 59 full-time (14 women), 3 part-time (1 woman); includes 7 minority (1 Black or African American, non-Hispanic/Latino; 2 Asian, non-Hispanic/Latino; 3 Hispanic/Latino; 1 Two or more races, non-Hispanic/Latino), 42 international. Average age 29. 40 applicants, 43% accepted, 14 enrolled. In 2011, 7 master's, 5 doctorates awarded. *Degree requirements:* For master's, variable foreign language requirement, thesis or alternative; for doctorate, variable foreign language requirement, thesis/dissertation. *Entrance requirements:* For master's and doctorate, GRE General Test. Additional exam requirements/recommendations for international students: Required—TOEFL (minimum score 550 paper-based; 213 computer-based; 79 iBT). *Application deadline:* For fall admission, 6/1 priority date for domestic students, 1/15 for international students; for spring admission, 9/1 priority date for domestic students, 6/15 for international students. Applications are processed on a rolling basis. Application fee: $50 ($75 for international students). Electronic applications accepted. *Expenses:* Tuition, state resident: full-time $5899; part-time $245.80

per credit hour. Tuition, nonresident: full-time $13,411; part-time $558.80 per credit hour. *Required fees:* $2680.60; $86.50 per credit hour. $920.30 per semester. *Financial support:* In 2011–12, 18 students received support. Application deadline: 4/15; applicants required to submit FAFSA. *Faculty research:* Biophysics, high energy and nuclear physics, condensed matter physics, atomic and molecular physics, physics education. *Total annual research expenditures:* $1.7 million. *Unit head:* Dr. Roger Lichti, Chair, 806-742-3767, Fax: 806-742-1182, E-mail: roger.lichti@ttu.edu. *Application contact:* Dr. Mahdi Sanati, Graduate Recruiter, 806-742-3767, Fax: 806-742-1182, E-mail: m.sanati@ttu.edu. Web site: http://www.phys.ttu.edu/.

Trent University, Graduate Studies, Program in Applications of Modeling in the Natural and Social Sciences, Department of Physics, Peterborough, ON K9J 7B8, Canada. Offers M Sc. Part-time programs available. *Degree requirements:* For master's, thesis. *Entrance requirements:* For master's, honours degree. *Faculty research:* Radiation physics, chemical physics.

Tufts University, Graduate School of Arts and Sciences, Department of Physics and Astronomy, Medford, MA 02155. Offers physics (MS, PhD). *Faculty:* 17 full-time, 2 part-time/adjunct. *Students:* 26 full-time (10 women), 11 international. Average age 27. 100 applicants, 20% accepted, 6 enrolled. In 2011, 7 master's, 5 doctorates awarded. Terminal master's awarded for partial completion of doctoral program. *Degree requirements:* For master's, thesis optional; for doctorate, thesis/dissertation. *Entrance requirements:* For master's and doctorate, GRE General Test. Additional exam requirements/recommendations for international students: Required—TOEFL (minimum score 550 paper-based; 213 computer-based; 80 iBT). *Application deadline:* For fall admission, 2/15 for domestic students, 12/15 for international students; for spring admission, 10/15 for domestic students, 9/15 for international students. Applications are processed on a rolling basis. Application fee: $75. Electronic applications accepted. *Expenses: Tuition:* Full-time $41,208; part-time $1030 per credit hour. Full-time tuition and fees vary according to degree level, program and student level. Part-time tuition and fees vary according to course load. *Financial support:* Fellowships, research assistantships with full tuition reimbursements, teaching assistantships with full tuition reimbursements, Federal Work-Study, scholarships/grants, tuition waivers (partial), and unspecified assistantships available. Financial award application deadline: 1/15; financial award applicants required to submit FAFSA. *Unit head:* Roger Tobin, Chair, 617-627-3029. *Application contact:* Dr. William Oliver, Graduate Advisor, 617-627-3029. Web site: http://www.tufts.edu/as/physics/.

Tulane University, School of Science and Engineering, Department of Physics and Engineering Physics, New Orleans, LA 70118-5669. Offers physics (PhD). *Degree requirements:* For doctorate, thesis/dissertation. *Entrance requirements:* For doctorate, GRE General Test. Additional exam requirements/recommendations for international students: Required—TOEFL. Electronic applications accepted. *Faculty research:* Surface physics, condensed-matter experiment, condensed-matter theory, nuclear theory, polymers.

Université de Moncton, Faculty of Sciences, Department of Physics and Astronomy, Moncton, NB E1A 3E9, Canada. Offers M Sc. Part-time programs available. *Degree requirements:* For master's, thesis. *Entrance requirements:* For master's, proficiency in French. Electronic applications accepted. *Faculty research:* Thin films, optical properties, solar selective surfaces, microgravity and photonic materials.

Université de Montréal, Faculty of Arts and Sciences, Department of Physics, Montréal, QC H3C 3J7, Canada. Offers M Sc, PhD. *Degree requirements:* For doctorate, thesis/dissertation, general exam. Electronic applications accepted. *Faculty research:* Astronomy; biophysics; solid-state, plasma, and nuclear physics.

Université de Sherbrooke, Faculty of Sciences, Department of Physics, Sherbrooke, QC J1K 2R1, Canada. Offers M Sc, PhD. *Degree requirements:* For master's, thesis; for doctorate, comprehensive exam, thesis/dissertation. *Entrance requirements:* For doctorate, master's degree. Electronic applications accepted. *Faculty research:* Solid-state physics, quantum computing.

Université du Québec à Trois-Rivières, Graduate Programs, Program in Physics, Trois-Rivières, QC G9A 5H7, Canada. Offers matter and energy (MS, PhD).

Université Laval, Faculty of Sciences and Engineering, Department of Physics, Physical Engineering, and Optics, Programs in Physics, Québec, QC G1K 7P4, Canada. Offers M Sc, PhD. Terminal master's awarded for partial completion of doctoral program. *Degree requirements:* For master's, thesis; for doctorate, comprehensive exam, thesis/dissertation. *Entrance requirements:* For master's and doctorate, knowledge of French, comprehension of written English. Electronic applications accepted.

University at Albany, State University of New York, College of Arts and Sciences, Department of Physics, Albany, NY 12222-0001. Offers MS, PhD. *Degree requirements:* For master's, one foreign language; for doctorate, one foreign language, thesis/dissertation. *Entrance requirements:* Additional exam requirements/recommendations for international students: Required—TOEFL (minimum score 550 paper-based; 213 computer-based). Electronic applications accepted. *Faculty research:* Condensed-matter physics, high-energy physics, applied physics, electronic materials, theoretical particle physics.

Peterson's Graduate Programs in the Physical Sciences, Mathematics, Agricultural Sciences, the Environment & Natural Resources 2013

facebook.com/petersonspublishing **251**

University at Buffalo, the State University of New York, Graduate School, College of Arts and Sciences, Department of Physics, Buffalo, NY 14260. Offers MS, PhD. Part-time programs available. *Faculty:* 27 full-time (3 women), 5 part-time/adjunct (0 women). *Students:* 85 full-time (9 women); includes 3 minority (1 Black or African American, non-Hispanic/Latino; 2 American Indian or Alaska Native, non-Hispanic/Latino), 32 international. Average age 29. 190 applicants, 20% accepted, 30 enrolled. In 2011, 5 master's, 11 doctorates awarded. Terminal master's awarded for partial completion of doctoral program. *Degree requirements:* For master's, thesis optional; for doctorate, comprehensive exam, thesis/dissertation. *Entrance requirements:* For master's, letters of recommendation; for doctorate, GRE General Test, letters of recommendation. Additional exam requirements/recommendations for international students: Required—TOEFL (minimum score 550 paper-based; 213 computer-based; 79 iBT). *Application deadline:* For fall admission, 2/1 priority date for domestic students, 2/1 for international students. Application fee: $75. Electronic applications accepted. *Financial support:* In 2011–12, 3 fellowships with full tuition reimbursements (averaging $6,000 per year), 23 research assistantships with full tuition reimbursements (averaging $17,000 per year), 39 teaching assistantships with full tuition reimbursements (averaging $16,500 per year) were awarded; Federal Work-Study, institutionally sponsored loans, scholarships/grants, health care benefits, and unspecified assistantships also available. Financial award application deadline: 3/1; financial award applicants required to submit FAFSA. *Faculty research:* Condensed-matter physics (experimental and theoretical), cosmology (theoretical), high energy and particle physics (experimental and theoretical), computational physics, biophysics (experimental and theoretical), materials physics. *Total annual research expenditures:* $2.6 million. *Unit head:* Dr. Hong Luo, Chairman, 716-645-3421, Fax: 716-645-2507, E-mail: luo@buffalo.edu. *Application contact:* Dr. Xuedong Hu, Director of Graduate Studies, 716-645-5444, Fax: 716-645-2507, E-mail: xhu@buffalo.edu. Web site: http://www.physics.buffalo.edu/.

The University of Akron, Graduate School, Buchtel College of Arts and Sciences, Department of Physics, Akron, OH 44325. Offers MS. Part-time and evening/weekend programs available. *Faculty:* 8 full-time (1 woman), 2 part-time/adjunct (1 woman). *Students:* 10 full-time (2 women), 1 part-time (0 women); includes 1 minority (Asian, non-Hispanic/Latino), 5 international. Average age 26. 22 applicants, 50% accepted, 8 enrolled. In 2011, 5 master's awarded. *Degree requirements:* For master's, thesis, written exam or formal report. *Entrance requirements:* For master's, baccalaureate degree in physics or related field, letters of recommendation, resume, statement of purpose. Additional exam requirements/recommendations for international students: Required—TOEFL (minimum score 550 paper-based; 213 computer-based; 79 iBT). *Application deadline:* For fall admission, 3/15 for domestic students. Applications are processed on a rolling basis. Application fee: $30 ($40 for international students). Electronic applications accepted. *Expenses:* Tuition, state resident: full-time $7038; part-time $391 per credit hour. Tuition, nonresident: full-time $12,051; part-time $670 per credit hour. *Required fees:* $1274; $34 per credit hour. *Financial support:* In 2011–12, 12 teaching assistantships with full tuition reimbursements were awarded. *Faculty research:* Materials physics, surface physics, nanotechnology, polymer physics, condensed matter physics. *Total annual research expenditures:* $31,674. *Unit head:* Dr. Robert Mallik, Chair, 330-972-7145, E-mail: rmallik@uakron.edu. *Application contact:* Dr. Ben Hu, Graduate Director, 330-972-8093, E-mail: byhu@uakron.edu. Web site: http://www.uakron.edu/physics/.

The University of Alabama, Graduate School, College of Arts and Sciences, Department of Physics and Astronomy, Tuscaloosa, AL 35487-0324. Offers physics (MS, PhD). *Faculty:* 24 full-time (1 woman). *Students:* 46 full-time (9 women), 3 part-time (1 woman); includes 1 minority (Hispanic/Latino), 29 international. Average age 28. 39 applicants, 36% accepted, 7 enrolled. In 2011, 7 master's, 3 doctorates awarded. Terminal master's awarded for partial completion of doctoral program. *Median time to degree:* Of those who began their doctoral program in fall 2003, 63% received their degree in 8 years or less. *Degree requirements:* For master's, thesis optional, oral exam; for doctorate, thesis/dissertation, oral and written exams. *Entrance requirements:* For master's and doctorate, GRE General or Subject Test, minimum GPA of 3.0. Additional exam requirements/recommendations for international students: Required—TOEFL (minimum score 550 paper-based; 213 computer-based; 79 iBT). *Application deadline:* For fall admission, 2/15 priority date for domestic students, 2/15 for international students; for spring admission, 11/1 for domestic students, 6/1 for international students. Applications are processed on a rolling basis. Application fee: $50 ($60 for international students). Electronic applications accepted. *Expenses:* Tuition, state resident: full-time $8600. Tuition, nonresident: full-time $21,900. *Financial support:* In 2011–12, 39 students received support, including fellowships with full tuition reimbursements available (averaging $18,000 per year), 14 research assistantships with full tuition reimbursements available (averaging $22,370 per year), 27 teaching assistantships with full tuition reimbursements available (averaging $18,400 per year); career-related internships or fieldwork and institutionally sponsored loans also available. Financial award application deadline: 2/1. *Faculty research:* Condensed matter, high-energy physics, molecular spectroscopy, astrophysics, particle astrophysics. *Total annual research expenditures:* $2.6 million. *Unit head:* Dr. Raymond E. White, III, Chairman and Professor, 205-348-5050, Fax: 205-348-5051, E-mail: rwhite@ua.edu. Web site: http://physics.ua.edu/.

The University of Alabama at Birmingham, College of Arts and Sciences, Program in Physics, Birmingham, AL 35294. Offers MS, PhD. Terminal master's awarded for partial completion of doctoral program. *Degree requirements:* For master's, thesis optional; for doctorate, thesis/dissertation. *Entrance requirements:* For master's and doctorate, GRE General Test, minimum GPA of 3.0. Additional exam requirements/recommendations for international students: Required—TOEFL. *Application deadline:* Applications are processed on a rolling basis. Electronic applications accepted. *Expenses:* Tuition, state resident: full-time $5922; part-time $309 per hour. Tuition, nonresident: full-time $13,428; part-time $726 per hour. Tuition and fees vary according to program. *Financial support:* Fellowships with full tuition reimbursements, research assistantships with full tuition reimbursements, teaching assistantships with full tuition reimbursements, career-related internships or fieldwork, Federal Work-Study, institutionally sponsored loans, scholarships/grants, traineeships, health care benefits, and unspecified assistantships available. Support available to part-time students. Financial award application deadline: 4/15; financial award applicants required to submit FAFSA. *Faculty research:* Laser physics, space physics, optics, biophysics, material physics. *Unit head:* Dr. David L. Shealy, Chair, 205-934-4736, Fax: 205-934-8042. Web site: http://www.phy.uab.edu/.

The University of Alabama in Huntsville, School of Graduate Studies, College of Science, Department of Physics, Huntsville, AL 35899. Offers education (MS); optics and photonics technology (MS); physics (MS, PhD). Part-time and evening/weekend programs available. *Faculty:* 18 full-time (0 women), 4 part-time/adjunct (1 woman). *Students:* 34 full-time (7 women), 22 part-time (9 women); includes 2 minority (both Asian, non-Hispanic/Latino), 12 international. Average age 29. 48 applicants, 60% accepted, 15 enrolled. In 2011, 10 master's, 3 doctorates awarded. *Degree requirements:* For master's, comprehensive exam, thesis or alternative, oral and written exams; for doctorate, comprehensive exam, thesis/dissertation, oral and written exams. *Entrance requirements:* For master's and doctorate, GRE General Test, minimum GPA of 3.0. Additional exam requirements/recommendations for international students: Required—TOEFL (minimum score 550 paper-based; 213 computer-based; 62 iBT). *Application deadline:* For fall admission, 7/15 for domestic students, 4/1 for international students; for spring admission, 11/30 for domestic students, 9/1 for international students. Applications are processed on a rolling basis. Application fee: $40 ($50 for international students). Electronic applications accepted. *Expenses:* Tuition, state resident: full-time $7830; part-time $473.50 per credit. Tuition, nonresident: full-time $18,748; part-time $1128.33 per credit. Tuition and fees vary according to course load and program. *Financial support:* In 2011–12, 30 students received support, including 18 research assistantships with full and partial tuition reimbursements available (averaging $15,553 per year), 12 teaching assistantships with full and partial tuition reimbursements available (averaging $16,500 per year); career-related internships or fieldwork, Federal Work-Study, institutionally sponsored loans, scholarships/grants, health care benefits, and unspecified assistantships also available. Support available to part-time students. Financial award application deadline: 4/1; financial award applicants required to submit FAFSA. *Faculty research:* Space physics, cosmology/general relativity, optics/quantum optics, astrophysics/gamma-ray astronomy, strophysical instrumentation. *Total annual research expenditures:* $6.2 million. *Unit head:* Dr. Gary Zank, Chair, 256-824-2481, Fax: 256-824-6873, E-mail: gary.zank@uah.edu. *Application contact:* Kim Gray, Graduate Studies Admissions Coordinator, 256-824-6002, Fax: 256-824-6405, E-mail: deangrad@uah.edu. Web site: http://physics.uah.edu/.

University of Alaska Fairbanks, College of Natural Sciences and Mathematics, Department of Physics, Fairbanks, AK 99775-5920. Offers computational physics (MS); physics (MAT, MS, PhD); space physics (MS, PhD). Part-time programs available. *Faculty:* 9 full-time (2 women). *Students:* 27 full-time (7 women), 3 part-time (0 women); includes 3 minority (1 American Indian or Alaska Native, non-Hispanic/Latino; 1 Asian, non-Hispanic/Latino; 1 Hispanic/Latino), 8 international. Average age 29. 18 applicants, 28% accepted, 5 enrolled. In 2011, 1 master's, 2 doctorates awarded. Terminal master's awarded for partial completion of doctoral program. *Degree requirements:* For master's, comprehensive exam, thesis or alternative; for doctorate, comprehensive exam, thesis/dissertation, oral defense. *Entrance requirements:* Additional exam requirements/recommendations for international students: Required—TOEFL (minimum score 550 paper-based; 213 computer-based; 80 iBT). *Application deadline:* For fall admission, 6/1 for domestic students, 3/1 for international students; for spring admission, 10/15 for domestic students, 9/1 for international students. Applications are processed on a rolling basis. Application fee: $60. Electronic applications accepted. *Expenses:* Tuition, state resident: full-time $6696; part-time $372 per credit. Tuition, nonresident: full-time $13,680; part-time $760 per credit. Tuition and fees vary according to course load and reciprocity agreements. *Financial support:* In 2011–12, 17 research assistantships with tuition reimbursements (averaging $14,039 per year), 8 teaching assistantships with tuition reimbursements (averaging $7,927 per year) were awarded; fellowships with tuition reimbursements, Federal Work-Study, scholarships/grants, health care benefits, and unspecified assistantships also available. Support available to part-time students. Financial award application deadline: 2/15; financial award applicants required to submit FAFSA. *Faculty research:* Atmospheric and ionospheric radar studies, space plasma theory, magnetospheric dynamics, space weather and auroral studies, turbulence and complex systems. *Unit head:* Ataur Chowdhury, Chair, 907-474-7339, Fax: 907-474-6130, E-mail: physics@uaf.edu. *Application contact:* Mike Earnest, Director of Admissions, 907-474-7500, Fax: 907-474-5379, E-mail: admissions@uaf.edu. Web site: http://www.uaf.edu/physics/.

252 facebook.com/petersonspublishing

Peterson's Graduate Programs in the Physical Sciences, Mathematics, Agricultural Sciences, the Environment & Natural Resources 2013

University of Alberta, Faculty of Graduate Studies and Research, Department of Physics, Edmonton, AB T6G 2E1, Canada. Offers astrophysics (M Sc, PhD); condensed matter (M Sc, PhD); geophysics (M Sc, PhD); medical physics (M Sc, PhD); subatomic physics (M Sc, PhD). *Degree requirements:* For master's, thesis; for doctorate, thesis/dissertation. *Entrance requirements:* For master's and doctorate, minimum GPA of 7.0 on a 9.0 scale. Additional exam requirements/recommendations for international students: Required—TOEFL. *Faculty research:* Cosmology, astroparticle physics, high-intermediate energy, magnetism, superconductivity.

The University of Arizona, College of Science, Department of Physics, Tucson, AZ 85721. Offers applied and industrial physics (PMS); physics (MS, PhD). Part-time programs available. *Faculty:* 23 full-time (2 women), 1 part-time/adjunct (0 women). *Students:* 68 full-time (14 women), 5 part-time (0 women); includes 1 minority (Hispanic/Latino), 33 international. Average age 28. 154 applicants. In 2011, 7 master's, 11 doctorates awarded. Terminal master's awarded for partial completion of doctoral program. *Degree requirements:* For master's, comprehensive exam (for some programs), thesis optional; for doctorate, comprehensive exam, thesis/dissertation. *Entrance requirements:* For master's and doctorate, GRE General Test, GRE Subject Test, minimum GPA of 3.2, 3 letters of recommendation. Additional exam requirements/recommendations for international students: Required—TOEFL (minimum score 550 paper-based; 213 computer-based; 79 iBT). *Application deadline:* For fall admission, 2/1 for domestic students, 12/1 for international students. Applications are processed on a rolling basis. Application fee: $75. Electronic applications accepted. *Expenses:* Tuition, state resident: full-time $10,840. Tuition, nonresident: full-time $25,802. *Financial support:* In 2011–12, 25 research assistantships with full tuition reimbursements (averaging $21,722 per year), 35 teaching assistantships with full tuition reimbursements (averaging $22,599 per year) were awarded; career-related internships or fieldwork, scholarships/grants, health care benefits, tuition waivers (full and partial), and unspecified assistantships also available. Financial award application deadline: 5/1. *Faculty research:* Astrophysics; high-energy, condensed-matter, atomic and molecular physics; optics. *Total annual research expenditures:* $4.2 million. *Unit head:* Dr. Sumit Mazumdar, Head, 520-621-6803, E-mail: sumit@physics.arizona.edu. *Application contact:* Lisa Shapouri, Graduate Coordinator, 520-621-2290, Fax: 520-621-4721, E-mail: lisas@physics.arizona.edu. Web site: http://www.physics.arizona.edu.

University of Arkansas, Graduate School, J. William Fulbright College of Arts and Sciences, Department of Physics, Fayetteville, AR 72701-1201. Offers applied physics (MS); physics (MS, PhD); physics education (MA). *Students:* 11 full-time (3 women), 38 part-time (7 women); includes 3 minority (1 Asian, non-Hispanic/Latino; 1 Hispanic/Latino; 1 Two or more races, non-Hispanic/Latino), 28 international. In 2011, 3 master's, 3 doctorates awarded. *Degree requirements:* For master's, thesis; for doctorate, thesis/dissertation. *Application deadline:* For fall admission, 4/1 for international students; for spring admission, 10/1 for international students. Applications are processed on a rolling basis. Application fee: $40 ($50 for international students). Electronic applications accepted. *Financial support:* In 2011–12, 21 research assistantships, 22 teaching assistantships were awarded; fellowships with tuition reimbursements, career-related internships or fieldwork, and Federal Work-Study also available. Support available to part-time students. Financial award application deadline: 4/1; financial award applicants required to submit FAFSA. *Unit head:* Dr. Julio Gea-Banacloche, Departmental Chairperson, 479-575-2506, Fax: 479-575-4580, E-mail: jgeabana@uark.edu. *Application contact:* Dr. Huaxiang Fu, Graduate Coordinator, 479-575-8606, E-mail: hfu@uark.edu. Web site: http://www.uark.edu/depts/physics/.

The University of British Columbia, Faculty of Science, Program in Physics, Vancouver, BC V6T 1Z1, Canada. Offers M Sc, PhD. *Degree requirements:* For master's, thesis; for doctorate, comprehensive exam, thesis/dissertation. *Entrance requirements:* For master's, GRE General Test, honors degree; for doctorate, GRE General Test, master's degree. Additional exam requirements/recommendations for international students: Required—TOEFL. *Faculty research:* Applied physics, astrophysics, condensed matter, plasma physics, subatomic physics, astronomy.

University of Calgary, Faculty of Graduate Studies, Faculty of Science, Department of Physics and Astronomy, Calgary, AB T2N 1N4, Canada. Offers M Sc, PhD. Part-time programs available. *Degree requirements:* For master's, thesis; for doctorate, thesis/dissertation, oral candidacy exam, written qualifying exam. *Entrance requirements:* For master's and doctorate, GRE General Test, GRE Subject Test. Additional exam requirements/recommendations for international students: Required—TOEFL (minimum score 550 paper-based; 213 computer-based). Electronic applications accepted. *Faculty research:* Astronomy and astrophysics, mass spectrometry, atmospheric physics, space physics, medical physics.

University of California, Berkeley, Graduate Division, College of Letters and Science, Department of Physics, Berkeley, CA 94720-1500. Offers PhD. *Degree requirements:* For doctorate, thesis/dissertation, qualifying exam. *Entrance requirements:* For doctorate, GRE General Test, GRE Subject Test, minimum GPA of 3.0, 3 letters of recommendation. Additional exam requirements/recommendations for international students: Required—TOEFL (minimum score 570 paper-based; 230 computer-based). *Faculty research:* Astrophysics (experimental and theoretical), condensed matter physics (experimental and theoretical), particle physics (experimental and theoretical), atomic/molecular physics, biophysics and complex systems.

University of California, Davis, Graduate Studies, Program in Physics, Davis, CA 95616. Offers MS, PhD. Terminal master's awarded for partial completion of doctoral program. *Degree requirements:* For master's, comprehensive exam (for some programs), thesis (for some programs); for doctorate, thesis/dissertation. *Entrance requirements:* For master's and doctorate, GRE General Test, GRE Subject Test, minimum GPA of 3.0. Additional exam requirements/recommendations for international students: Required—TOEFL (minimum score 550 paper-based; 213 computer-based). Electronic applications accepted. *Faculty research:* Astrophysics, condensed-matter physics, nuclear physics, particle physics, quantum optics.

University of California, Irvine, School of Physical Sciences, Department of Physics and Astronomy, Irvine, CA 92697. Offers physics (MS, PhD); MD/PhD. *Students:* 107 full-time (13 women); includes 22 minority (2 Black or African American, non-Hispanic/Latino; 15 Asian, non-Hispanic/Latino; 3 Hispanic/Latino; 2 Two or more races, non-Hispanic/Latino), 23 international. Average age 27. 276 applicants, 21% accepted, 23 enrolled. In 2011, 24 master's, 15 doctorates awarded. Terminal master's awarded for partial completion of doctoral program. *Degree requirements:* For doctorate, thesis/dissertation. *Entrance requirements:* For master's and doctorate, GRE General Test, GRE Subject Test, minimum GPA of 3.0. Additional exam requirements/recommendations for international students: Required—TOEFL (minimum score 550 paper-based; 213 computer-based). *Application deadline:* For fall admission, 1/15 priority date for domestic students, 1/15 for international students. Application fee: $80 ($100 for international students). Electronic applications accepted. *Financial support:* Fellowships with full tuition reimbursements, research assistantships with full tuition reimbursements, teaching assistantships with partial tuition reimbursements, institutionally sponsored loans, traineeships, health care benefits, and unspecified assistantships available. Financial award application deadline: 3/1; financial award applicants required to submit FAFSA. *Faculty research:* Condensed-matter physics, plasma physics, astrophysics, particle physics, chemical and materials physics, biophysics. *Unit head:* William H. Parker, Chair, 949-824-5948, Fax: 949-824-2174, E-mail: william.parker@uci.edu. *Application contact:* My Banh, Graduate Student Affairs Officer, 949-824-3496, Fax: 949-824-7988, E-mail: mbanh@uci.edu. Web site: http://www.ps.uci.edu/physics/.

University of California, Los Angeles, Graduate Division, College of Letters and Science, Department of Physics and Astronomy, Program in Physics, Los Angeles, CA 90095. Offers physics (MS, PhD). *Students:* 135 full-time (15 women); includes 27 minority (2 Black or African American, non-Hispanic/Latino; 16 Asian, non-Hispanic/Latino; 5 Hispanic/Latino; 1 Native Hawaiian or other Pacific Islander, non-Hispanic/Latino; 3 Two or more races, non-Hispanic/Latino), 34 international. Average age 26. 353 applicants, 18% accepted, 23 enrolled. In 2011, 10 master's, 20 doctorates awarded. Terminal master's awarded for partial completion of doctoral program. *Median time to degree:* Of those who began their doctoral program in fall 2003, 78% received their degree in 8 years or less. *Degree requirements:* For master's, comprehensive exam; for doctorate, thesis/dissertation, oral and written qualifying exams. *Entrance requirements:* For master's, GRE General Test, GRE Subject Test (physics), minimum GPA of 3.0, BS in related field; for doctorate, GRE General Test, GRE Subject Test (physics), minimum undergraduate GPA of 3.0, BS in related field. *Application deadline:* For fall admission, 12/15 for domestic and international students. Application fee: $70 ($90 for international students). Electronic applications accepted. *Financial support:* In 2011–12, 107 fellowships with full and partial tuition reimbursements, 95 research assistantships with full and partial tuition reimbursements, 80 teaching assistantships with full and partial tuition reimbursements were awarded; Federal Work-Study, institutionally sponsored loans, scholarships/grants, health care benefits, tuition waivers (full and partial), and unspecified assistantships also available. Financial award application deadline: 3/1; financial award applicants required to submit FAFSA. *Unit head:* Dr. James Rosenzweig, Chair, 310-825-3440, E-mail: rosenzweig@physics.ucla.edu. *Application contact:* Carol Finn, Graduate Counselor, 310-825-2307, E-mail: apply@physics.ucla.edu. Web site: http://www.physics.ucla.edu.

University of California, Merced, Division of Graduate Studies, School of Natural Sciences, Merced, CA 95343. Offers applied mathematics (MS, PhD); biological engineering and small-scale technologies (MS, PhD); environmental systems (MS, PhD); mechanical engineering and applied mechanics (MS, PhD); physics and chemistry (PhD); quantitative and systems biology (MS, PhD). *Unit head:* Dr. Samuel J. Traina, Dean, 209-228-4723, Fax: 209-228-6906, E-mail: grad.dean@ucmerced.edu. *Application contact:* Tsu Ya, Graduate Admissions and Academic Services Manager, 209-228-4723, Fax: 209-228-6906, E-mail: tya@ucmerced.edu.

University of California, Riverside, Graduate Division, Department of Physics and Astronomy, Riverside, CA 92521-0102. Offers physics (MS, PhD). Part-time programs available. Terminal master's awarded for partial completion of doctoral program. *Degree requirements:* For master's, comprehensive exams or thesis; for doctorate, thesis/dissertation, qualifying exams. *Entrance requirements:* For master's and doctorate, GRE General Test, GRE Subject Test, minimum GPA of 3.2. Additional exam requirements/recommendations for international students: Required—TOEFL (minimum score 550 paper-based; 213 computer-based; 80 iBT). Electronic applications accepted. *Faculty research:* Laser physics and

Peterson's Graduate Programs in the Physical Sciences, Mathematics, Agricultural Sciences, the Environment & Natural Resources 2013

facebook.com/petersonspublishing **253**

Physics

surface science, elementary particle and heavy ion physics, plasma physics, optical physics, astrophysics.

University of California, San Diego, Office of Graduate Studies, Department of Physics, La Jolla, CA 92093. Offers biophysics (MS, PhD); physics (MS, PhD); physics/materials physics (MS). *Degree requirements:* For doctorate, thesis/dissertation. *Entrance requirements:* For master's and doctorate, GRE General Test, GRE Subject Test. Additional exam requirements/recommendations for international students: Required—TOEFL. Electronic applications accepted.

University of California, Santa Barbara, Graduate Division, College of Letters and Sciences, Division of Mathematics, Life, and Physical Sciences, Department of Physics, Santa Barbara, CA 93106-9530. Offers PhD. *Faculty:* 51 full-time (6 women), 2 part-time/adjunct (0 women). *Students:* 129 full-time (22 women); includes 19 minority (13 Asian, non-Hispanic/Latino; 5 Hispanic/Latino; 1 Two or more races, non-Hispanic/Latino), 15 international. Average age 26. 524 applicants, 19% accepted, 22 enrolled. In 2011, 31 doctorates awarded. Terminal master's awarded for partial completion of doctoral program. *Median time to degree:* Of those who began their doctoral program in fall 2003, 70% received their degree in 8 years or less. *Degree requirements:* For doctorate, comprehensive exam, thesis/dissertation. *Entrance requirements:* For doctorate, GRE General Test, GRE Subject Test (physics). Additional exam requirements/recommendations for international students: Required—TOEFL (minimum score 550 paper-based; 80 iBT), IELTS (minimum score 7). *Application deadline:* For fall admission, 12/15 priority date for domestic students, 12/15 for international students. Application fee: $80 ($100 for international students). Electronic applications accepted. *Expenses:* Tuition, state resident: full-time $12,192. Tuition, nonresident: full-time $27,294. *Required fees:* $764.13. *Financial support:* In 2011–12, 128 students received support, including 5 fellowships with full tuition reimbursements available (averaging $30,440 per year), 73 research assistantships with full tuition reimbursements available (averaging $16,218 per year), 39 teaching assistantships with partial tuition reimbursements available (averaging $17,309 per year); Federal Work-Study, scholarships/grants, health care benefits, and unspecified assistantships also available. Financial award application deadline: 12/15; financial award applicants required to submit FAFSA. *Faculty research:* High energy theoretical/experimental physics, condensed matter theoretical/experimental physics, astrophysics and cosmology, biophysics, gravity and relativity. *Total annual research expenditures:* $19 million. *Unit head:* Prof. Omer Blaes, Chair/Professor, 805-893-7239, Fax: 805-893-7239, E-mail: blaes@physics.ucsb.edu. *Application contact:* Prof. Mark Srednicki, Admissions Chair, 805-893-2165, Fax: 805-893-2165, E-mail: mark@physics.ucsb.edu. Web site: http://www.physics.ucsb.edu.

University of California, Santa Cruz, Division of Graduate Studies, Division of Physical and Biological Sciences, Department of Physics, Santa Cruz, CA 95064. Offers MS, PhD. Terminal master's awarded for partial completion of doctoral program. *Degree requirements:* For master's, thesis; for doctorate, one foreign language, thesis/dissertation, qualifying exam. *Entrance requirements:* For master's and doctorate, GRE General Test, GRE Subject Test. Additional exam requirements/recommendations for international students: Required—TOEFL (minimum score 550 paper-based; 220 computer-based; 83 iBT); Recommended—IELTS (minimum score 8). Electronic applications accepted. *Faculty research:* Theoretical and experimental particle physics, astrophysics and cosmology, condensed matter physics.

University of Central Florida, College of Sciences, Department of Physics, Orlando, FL 32816. Offers MS, PhD. Part-time and evening/weekend programs available. *Faculty:* 41 full-time (7 women), 1 part-time/adjunct (0 women). *Students:* 85 full-time (21 women), 2 part-time (0 women); includes 8 minority (2 Asian, non-Hispanic/Latino; 5 Hispanic/Latino; 1 Two or more races, non-Hispanic/Latino), 56 international. Average age 29. 134 applicants, 37% accepted, 17 enrolled. In 2011, 20 master's, 8 doctorates awarded. *Degree requirements:* For master's, thesis or alternative; for doctorate, thesis/dissertation, candidacy and qualifying exams. *Entrance requirements:* For master's, GRE General Test, minimum GPA of 3.0 in last 60 hours of course work; for doctorate, GRE General Test, GRE Subject Test, minimum GPA of 3.0 in last 60 hours or master's qualifying exam. Additional exam requirements/recommendations for international students: Required—TOEFL. *Application deadline:* For fall admission, 2/15 priority date for domestic students. Application fee: $30. Electronic applications accepted. *Expenses:* Tuition, state resident: part-time $277.08 per credit hour. Tuition, nonresident: part-time $277.08 per credit hour. Part-time tuition and fees vary according to degree level and program. *Financial support:* In 2011–12, 68 students received support, including 18 fellowships with partial tuition reimbursements available (averaging $2,500 per year), 45 research assistantships with partial tuition reimbursements available (averaging $11,300 per year), 38 teaching assistantships with partial tuition reimbursements available (averaging $10,800 per year); career-related internships or fieldwork, Federal Work-Study, institutionally sponsored loans, tuition waivers (partial), and unspecified assistantships also available. Financial award application deadline: 3/1; financial award applicants required to submit FAFSA. *Faculty research:* Atomic-molecular physics, condensed-matter physics, biophysics of proteins, laser physics. *Unit head:* Dr. Talat Rahman, Chair, 407-823-2325, E-mail: talat.rahman@ucf.edu. *Application contact:* Barbara Rodriguez, Director, Admissions and Registration, 407-823-2766, Fax: 407-823-6442, E-mail: gradadmissions@ucf.edu. Web site: http://www.physics.ucf.edu/.

University of Central Oklahoma, College of Graduate Studies and Research, College of Mathematics and Science, Department of Engineering and Physics, Edmond, OK 73034-5209. Offers MS. Part-time programs available. *Faculty:* 6 full-time (0 women), 3 part-time/adjunct (0 women). *Students:* 5 full-time (0 women), 9 part-time (3 women); includes 2 minority (1 American Indian or Alaska Native, non-Hispanic/Latino; 1 Asian, non-Hispanic/Latino), 7 international. Average age 27. In 2011, 4 master's awarded. *Degree requirements:* For master's, thesis optional. *Entrance requirements:* For master's, GRE, 24 hours of course work in physics, minimum GPA of 2.75 overall and 3.0 in last 60 hours attempted. Additional exam requirements/recommendations for international students: Required—TOEFL (minimum score 550 paper-based; 213 computer-based). *Application deadline:* Applications are processed on a rolling basis. Application fee: $50. Electronic applications accepted. *Expenses:* Tuition, state resident: full-time $3901; part-time $218.30 per credit hour. Tuition, nonresident: full-time $9198; part-time $511.20 per credit hour. Tuition and fees vary according to program. *Financial support:* Unspecified assistantships available. Financial award application deadline: 3/31; financial award applicants required to submit FAFSA. *Faculty research:* Laser tissue interactions for soft and hard tissues, microfluidics, quantum optics, design of scaffold for tissue engineering applications, micro and nano devices and sensors. *Unit head:* Dr. Baha Jassemnejad, Chairperson, 405-974-5461, Fax: 405-974-3812, E-mail: bjassemnejad@uco.edu. *Application contact:* Dr. Richard Bernard, Dean, Graduate College, 405-974-3493, Fax: 405-974-3852, E-mail: gradcoll@uco.edu. Web site: http://www.uco.edu/cms/engineering/Graduate%20Programs/index.asp.

University of Chicago, Division of the Physical Sciences, Department of Physics, Chicago, IL 60637-1513. Offers PhD. *Degree requirements:* For doctorate, comprehensive exam, thesis/dissertation. *Entrance requirements:* For doctorate, bachelor's degree in physics or related area. Additional exam requirements/recommendations for international students: Required—TOEFL (minimum score 102 iBT).

University of Chicago, Division of the Physical Sciences, Program in the Physical Sciences, Chicago, IL 60637-1513. Offers MS. Part-time programs available. *Degree requirements:* For master's, thesis. *Entrance requirements:* For master's, GRE. Additional exam requirements/recommendations for international students: Required—TOEFL.

University of Cincinnati, Graduate School, McMicken College of Arts and Sciences, Department of Physics, Cincinnati, OH 45221. Offers MS, PhD. Terminal master's awarded for partial completion of doctoral program. *Degree requirements:* For master's, thesis optional; for doctorate, thesis/dissertation. *Entrance requirements:* For master's and doctorate, GRE General Test, GRE Subject Test. Additional exam requirements/recommendations for international students: Required—TOEFL (minimum score 540 paper-based; 207 computer-based). Electronic applications accepted. *Faculty research:* Condensed matter physics, experimental particle physics, theoretical high energy physics, astronomy and astrophysics, computational physics.

University of Colorado at Colorado Springs, College of Letters, Arts and Sciences, Master of Sciences Program, Colorado Springs, CO 80933-7150. Offers applied science bioscience (M Sc); applied science physics (M Sc); biology (M Sc); chemistry (M Sc); health promotion (M Sc); mathematics (M Sc); physics (M Sc); sports medicine (M Sc); sports nutrition (M Sc). Part-time programs available. *Students:* 13 full-time (5 women), 11 part-time (6 women); includes 3 minority (2 Asian, non-Hispanic/Latino; 1 Hispanic/Latino). Average age 33. 15 applicants, 53% accepted, 3 enrolled. In 2011, 39 degrees awarded. *Degree requirements:* For master's, thesis or alternative. *Entrance requirements:* For master's, minimum GPA of 2.75. Additional exam requirements/recommendations for international students: Recommended—TOEFL. *Application deadline:* For fall admission, 6/1 priority date for domestic students; for spring admission, 12/1 for domestic students. Application fee: $60 ($75 for international students). *Expenses:* Contact institution. *Financial support:* In 2011–12, 5 students received support. Fellowships, research assistantships, teaching assistantships, career-related internships or fieldwork, Federal Work-Study, and scholarships/grants available. Support available to part-time students. Financial award application deadline: 3/1; financial award applicants required to submit FAFSA. *Faculty research:* Biomechanics and physiology of elite athletic training, genetic engineering in yeast and bacteria including phage display and DNA repair, immunology and cell biology, synthetic organic chemistry. *Unit head:* Dr. Tom Christensen, Dean, 719-255-4550, Fax: 719-255-4200, E-mail: tchriste@uccs.edu. *Application contact:* Taryn Bailey, Information Contact, 719-255-3702, Fax: 719-255-3037, E-mail: gradinfo@uccs.edu.

University of Colorado Boulder, Graduate School, College of Arts and Sciences, Department of Physics, Boulder, CO 80309. Offers chemical physics (PhD); geophysics (PhD); liquid crystal science and technology (PhD); mathematical physics (PhD); medical physics (PhD); optical sciences and engineering (PhD); physics (MS, PhD). *Faculty:* 51 full-time (7 women). *Students:* 157 full-time (28 women), 66 part-time (11 women); includes 11 minority (6 Asian, non-Hispanic/Latino; 5 Hispanic/Latino), 75 international. Average age 26. 551 applicants, 25% accepted, 47 enrolled. In 2011, 29 master's, 28 doctorates awarded. Terminal master's awarded for partial completion of doctoral program. *Degree requirements:* For master's, comprehensive exam, thesis or alternative; for doctorate, comprehensive exam, thesis/dissertation. *Entrance requirements:*

254 facebook.com/petersonspublishing

Peterson's Graduate Programs in the Physical Sciences, Mathematics, Agricultural Sciences, the Environment & Natural Resources 2013

For master's and doctorate, GRE General Test, GRE Subject Test, minimum undergraduate GPA of 3.0. Additional exam requirements/recommendations for international students: Required—TOEFL. *Application deadline:* For fall admission, 1/15 priority date for domestic students, 1/15 for international students. Applications are processed on a rolling basis. Application fee: $50 ($60 for international students). Electronic applications accepted. *Financial support:* In 2011–12, 216 students received support, including 85 fellowships (averaging $9,233 per year), 131 research assistantships with full and partial tuition reimbursements available (averaging $24,425 per year), 31 teaching assistantships with full and partial tuition reimbursements available (averaging $20,162 per year); institutionally sponsored loans, scholarships/grants, health care benefits, and unspecified assistantships also available. Financial award application deadline: 1/15; financial award applicants required to submit FAFSA. *Faculty research:* Atomic and molecular physics, nuclear physics, condensed matter, elementary particle physics, laser or optical physics, plasma physics, geophysics, OSEP, astrophysics and chemical physics. *Total annual research expenditures:* $26.1 million. *Application contact:* E-mail: physics@colorado.edu. Web site: http://physics.colorado.edu/.

University of Connecticut, Graduate School, College of Liberal Arts and Sciences, Department of Physics, Storrs, CT 06269. Offers MS, PhD. *Degree requirements:* For master's, comprehensive exam; for doctorate, thesis/dissertation. *Entrance requirements:* For master's and doctorate, GRE General Test, GRE Subject Test. Additional exam requirements/recommendations for international students: Required—TOEFL (minimum score 550 paper-based; 213 computer-based). Electronic applications accepted.

University of Delaware, College of Arts and Sciences, Department of Physics and Astronomy, Newark, DE 19716. Offers MS, PhD. Part-time programs available. Terminal master's awarded for partial completion of doctoral program. *Degree requirements:* For master's, thesis; for doctorate, thesis/dissertation. *Entrance requirements:* For master's and doctorate, GRE General Test, GRE Subject Test. Additional exam requirements/recommendations for international students: Required—TOEFL (minimum score 600 paper-based; 250 computer-based). Electronic applications accepted. *Faculty research:* Magnetoresistance and magnetic materials, ultrafast optical phenomena, superfluidity, elementary particle physics, stellar atmospheres and interiors.

University of Denver, Faculty of Natural Sciences and Mathematics, Department of Physics and Astronomy, Denver, CO 80208. Offers applied physics (MS); physics (MS, PhD). Part-time programs available. *Faculty:* 10 full-time (3 women), 5 part-time/adjunct (0 women). *Students:* 8 full-time (3 women), 9 part-time (3 women); includes 1 minority (Hispanic/Latino), 2 international. Average age 29. 36 applicants, 19% accepted, 6 enrolled. In 2011, 1 master's, 1 doctorate awarded. Terminal master's awarded for partial completion of doctoral program. *Median time to degree:* Of those who began their doctoral program in fall 2003, 100% received their degree in 8 years or less. *Degree requirements:* For master's, thesis optional; for doctorate, thesis/dissertation. *Entrance requirements:* For master's and doctorate, GRE General Test, GRE Subject Test in physics (strongly preferred), three letters of recommendation, personal statement. Additional exam requirements/recommendations for international students: Required—TOEFL (minimum score 550 paper-based; 80 iBT). *Application deadline:* For fall admission, 3/1 priority date for domestic students. Applications are processed on a rolling basis. Application fee: $60. Electronic applications accepted. *Financial support:* In 2011–12, 15 students received support, including 10 research assistantships with full and partial tuition reimbursements available (averaging $19,300 per year), 10 teaching assistantships with full and partial tuition reimbursements available (averaging $17,370 per year); career-related internships or fieldwork, Federal Work-Study, institutionally sponsored loans, scholarships/grants, and unspecified assistantships also available. Support available to part-time students. Financial award application deadline: 2/15; financial award applicants required to submit FAFSA. *Faculty research:* Atomic and molecular beams and collisions, infrared astronomy, acoustic emission from stressed solids, nano materials. *Unit head:* Dr. Davor Balzar, Chair, 303-871-2238, E-mail: davor.balzar@du.edu. *Application contact:* Barbara Stephen, Assistant to the Chair, 303-871-2238, E-mail: barbara.stephen@du.edu. Web site: http://www.physics.du.edu.

University of Florida, Graduate School, College of Liberal Arts and Sciences, Department of Physics, Gainesville, FL 32611. Offers MS, MST, PhD. *Faculty:* 45 full-time (4 women), 2 part-time/adjunct (0 women). *Students:* 148 full-time (28 women); includes 12 minority (6 Asian, non-Hispanic/Latino; 6 Hispanic/Latino), 75 international. Average age 28. 293 applicants, 18% accepted, 16 enrolled. In 2011, 16 master's, 27 doctorates awarded. Terminal master's awarded for partial completion of doctoral program. *Degree requirements:* For doctorate, comprehensive exam, thesis/dissertation. *Entrance requirements:* For master's and doctorate, GRE General Test, minimum GPA of 3.0. Additional exam requirements/recommendations for international students: Required—TOEFL (minimum score 550 paper-based; 213 computer-based; 80 iBT), IELTS (minimum score 6). *Application deadline:* For spring admission, 2/1 for domestic students, 1/1 for international students. Applications are processed on a rolling basis. Application fee: $30. Electronic applications accepted. *Financial support:* Fellowships with tuition reimbursements, research assistantships with tuition reimbursements, teaching assistantships with tuition reimbursements, and unspecified assistantships available. Financial award applicants required to submit FAFSA. *Faculty research:* Astrophysics, biological physics (molecular,

magnetic resonance imaging, spectroscopy, biomagnetism), chemical physics (molecular, nano-scale physics, solid state, surface physics, quantum chemistry, quantum electron dynamics, molecular biology), experimental and theory condensed matter physics, low temperature physics (theory and experimental, mathematical physics. *Total annual research expenditures:* $8.4 million. *Unit head:* Dr. John M. Yelton, Chair, 352-392-8475, Fax: 352-392-0524, E-mail: yelton@phys.ufl.edu. *Application contact:* Dr. James N. Fry, Graduate Coordinator, 352-392-6692, Fax: 352-392-0524, E-mail: fry@ufl.edu. Web site: http://www.phys.ufl.edu/.

University of Georgia, Franklin College of Arts and Sciences, Department of Physics and Astronomy, Athens, GA 30602. Offers physics (MS, PhD). *Faculty:* 22 full-time (2 women). *Students:* 46 full-time (15 women), 1 part-time; includes 2 minority (1 Black or African American, non-Hispanic/Latino; 1 Asian, non-Hispanic/Latino), 26 international. Average age 28. 105 applicants, 30% accepted, 11 enrolled. In 2011, 2 master's, 8 doctorates awarded. *Degree requirements:* For master's, thesis; for doctorate, one foreign language, thesis/dissertation. *Entrance requirements:* For master's and doctorate, GRE General Test. *Application deadline:* For fall admission, 7/1 priority date for domestic students; for spring admission, 11/15 for domestic students. Application fee: $50. Electronic applications accepted. *Financial support:* Fellowships, research assistantships, teaching assistantships, and unspecified assistantships available. *Unit head:* Dr. Heinz-Bernd Schuttler, Acting Head, 706-542-2882, E-mail: hbs@uga.edu. *Application contact:* Dr. Loris Magnani, Graduate Coordinator, 706-542-2476, Fax: 706-542-2492, E-mail: loris@physast.uga.edu. Web site: http://www.physast.uga.edu/.

University of Guelph, Graduate Studies, College of Physical and Engineering Science, Guelph-Waterloo Physics Institute, Guelph, ON N1G 2W1, Canada. Offers M Sc, PhD. M Sc, PhD offered jointly with University of Waterloo. Part-time programs available. *Degree requirements:* For master's, project or thesis; for doctorate, comprehensive exam, thesis/dissertation. *Entrance requirements:* For master's, GRE Subject Test, minimum B average for honors degree; for doctorate, GRE Subject Test, minimum B average. Additional exam requirements/recommendations for international students: Required—TOEFL (minimum score 550 paper-based; 213 computer-based), TWE (minimum score 4). *Faculty research:* Condensed matter and material physics, quantum computing, astrophysics and gravitation, industrial and applied physics, subatomic physics.

University of Hawaii at Manoa, Graduate Division, College of Natural Sciences, Department of Physics and Astronomy, Program in Physics, Honolulu, HI 96822. Offers MS, PhD. Part-time programs available. *Degree requirements:* For master's, thesis optional; for doctorate, comprehensive exam, thesis/dissertation. *Entrance requirements:* For master's and doctorate, GRE General Test. Additional exam requirements/recommendations for international students: Required—TOEFL (minimum score 560 paper-based; 220 computer-based; 83 iBT), IELTS (minimum score 5).

University of Houston, College of Natural Sciences and Mathematics, Department of Physics, Houston, TX 77204. Offers MA, PhD. Part-time programs available. Terminal master's awarded for partial completion of doctoral program. *Entrance requirements:* For master's and doctorate, GRE General Test. Electronic applications accepted. *Faculty research:* Condensed-matter, particle physics; high-temperature superconductivity; material/space physics; chaos.

University of Houston–Clear Lake, School of Science and Computer Engineering, Program in Physics, Houston, TX 77058-1098. Offers MS. Part-time and evening/weekend programs available. *Entrance requirements:* For master's, GRE General Test. Additional exam requirements/recommendations for international students: Required—TOEFL (minimum score 550 paper-based; 213 computer-based).

University of Idaho, College of Graduate Studies, College of Science, Department of Physics, Moscow, ID 83844-0903. Offers MS, PhD. *Faculty:* 4 full-time. *Students:* 24 full-time, 5 part-time. Average age 33. In 2011, 7 master's, 1 doctorate awarded. *Degree requirements:* For master's, thesis; for doctorate, thesis/dissertation. *Entrance requirements:* For master's, GRE, minimum GPA of 2.8; for doctorate, GRE, minimum undergraduate GPA of 2.8, 3.0 graduate. *Application deadline:* For fall admission, 8/1 for domestic students; for spring admission, 12/15 for domestic students. Applications are processed on a rolling basis. Application fee: $60. Electronic applications accepted. *Expenses:* Tuition, state resident: full-time $3874; part-time $334 per credit hour. Tuition, nonresident: full-time $16,394; part-time $861 per credit hour. *Required fees:* $2808; $99 per credit hour. Tuition and fees vary according to program. *Financial support:* Research assistantships and teaching assistantships available. Financial award applicants required to submit FAFSA. *Faculty research:* Condensed matter physics, nuclear physics, biological physics, astronomy/planetary science. *Unit head:* Dr. David McIlroy, Chair, 208-885-6380, E-mail: physics@uidaho.edu. *Application contact:* Erick Larson, Director of Graduate Admissions, 208-885-4723, E-mail: gadms@uidaho.edu. Web site: http://www.uidaho.edu/sci/physics.

University of Illinois at Chicago, Graduate College, College of Liberal Arts and Sciences, Department of Physics, Chicago, IL 60607-7128. Offers MS, PhD. Terminal master's awarded for partial completion of doctoral program. *Degree requirements:* For doctorate, thesis/dissertation. *Entrance requirements:* For master's and doctorate, GRE General Test, minimum GPA of 3.0. Additional

Peterson's Graduate Programs in the Physical Sciences, Mathematics, Agricultural Sciences, the Environment & Natural Resources 2013

facebook.com/petersonspublishing **255**

Physics

exam requirements/recommendations for international students: Required—TOEFL. Electronic applications accepted. *Faculty research:* High-energy, laser, and solid-state physics.

University of Illinois at Urbana–Champaign, Graduate College, College of Engineering, Department of Physics, Champaign, IL 61820. Offers physics (MS, PhD); teaching of physics (MS). *Faculty:* 49 full-time (6 women), 2 part-time/adjunct (0 women). *Students:* 183 full-time (28 women), 86 part-time (11 women); includes 22 minority (1 Black or African American, non-Hispanic/Latino; 17 Asian, non-Hispanic/Latino; 3 Hispanic/Latino; 1 Two or more races, non-Hispanic/Latino; 133 international. 445 applicants, 12% accepted, 52 enrolled. In 2011, 11 master's, 39 doctorates awarded. *Entrance requirements:* For master's, GRE, minimum GPA of 3.0; for doctorate, GRE, minimum GPA of 3.5. Additional exam requirements/recommendations for international students: Required—TOEFL (minimum score 550 paper-based; 213 computer-based; 79 iBT) or IELTS (minimum score 6.5). *Application deadline:* Applications are processed on a rolling basis. Application fee: $75 ($90 for international students). Electronic applications accepted. *Financial support:* In 2011–12, 17 fellowships, 173 research assistantships, 131 teaching assistantships were awarded; tuition waivers (full and partial) also available. *Unit head:* Dale J. VanHarlingen, Head, 217-333-3760, Fax: 217-244-4293, E-mail: dvh@illinois.edu. *Application contact:* Melodee Jo Schweighart, Office Manager, 217-333-3645, Fax: 217-244-5073, E-mail: mschweig@illinois.edu. Web site: http://www.physics.illinois.edu/.

The University of Iowa, Graduate College, College of Liberal Arts and Sciences, Department of Physics and Astronomy, Program in Physics, Iowa City, IA 52242-1316. Offers MS, PhD. *Degree requirements:* For master's, thesis optional, exam; for doctorate, comprehensive exam, thesis/dissertation. *Entrance requirements:* For master's and doctorate, GRE General Test, minimum GPA of 3.0. Additional exam requirements/recommendations for international students: Required—TOEFL (minimum score 550 paper-based; 213 computer-based; 81 iBT). Electronic applications accepted.

The University of Kansas, Graduate Studies, College of Liberal Arts and Sciences, Department of Physics and Astronomy, Lawrence, KS 66045. Offers computational physics and astronomy (MS); physics (MS, PhD). *Faculty:* 25 full-time (4 women). *Students:* 42 full-time (9 women), 4 part-time (1 woman); includes 3 minority (1 Black or African American, non-Hispanic/Latino; 1 Hispanic/Latino; 1 Two or more races, non-Hispanic/Latino), 11 international. Average age 29. 59 applicants, 41% accepted, 12 enrolled. In 2011, 3 master's, 4 doctorates awarded. Terminal master's awarded for partial completion of doctoral program. *Degree requirements:* For master's, thesis (for some programs); for doctorate, comprehensive exam, thesis/dissertation, computer skills, communication skills. *Entrance requirements:* For master's and doctorate, GRE Subject Test (physics), undergraduate degree. Additional exam requirements/recommendations for international students: Required—TOEFL (minimum score 53 paper-based; 20 computer-based; 20 iBT). *Application deadline:* For fall admission, 4/1 priority date for domestic students, 4/1 for international students; for spring admission, 11/15 for domestic and international students. Applications are processed on a rolling basis. Application fee: $55 ($65 for international students). Electronic applications accepted. Tuition and fees vary according to course load, campus/location, program and reciprocity agreements. *Financial support:* Fellowships with full and partial tuition reimbursements, research assistantships with full and partial tuition reimbursements, teaching assistantships with full and partial tuition reimbursements, health care benefits, and unspecified assistantships available. Financial award application deadline: 4/1; financial award applicants required to submit FAFSA. *Faculty research:* Condensed-matter, cosmology, elementary particles, nuclear physics, space physics, astrophysics, astrobiology, biophysics, high energy. *Unit head:* Dr. Stephen J. Sanders, Chair, 785-864-4626, Fax: 785-864-5262. *Application contact:* Teri Leahy, Graduate Coordinator, 785-864-1225, Fax: 785-864-5262, E-mail: tleahy@ku.edu. Web site: http://www.physics.ku.edu.

University of Kentucky, Graduate School, College of Arts and Sciences, Program in Physics and Astronomy, Lexington, KY 40506-0032. Offers physics (MS, PhD). *Degree requirements:* For master's, comprehensive exam, thesis optional; for doctorate, comprehensive exam, thesis/dissertation. *Entrance requirements:* For master's, GRE General Test, minimum undergraduate GPA of 2.75; for doctorate, GRE General Test, minimum graduate GPA of 3.0. Additional exam requirements/recommendations for international students: Required—TOEFL (minimum score 550 paper-based; 213 computer-based). Electronic applications accepted. *Faculty research:* Astrophysics, active galactic nuclei, and radio astronomy; Rydbert atoms, and electron scattering; TOF spectroscopy, hyperon interactions and muons; particle theory, lattice gauge theory, quark, and skyrmion models.

University of Lethbridge, School of Graduate Studies, Lethbridge, AB T1K 3M4, Canada. Offers accounting (MScM); addictions counseling (M Sc); agricultural biotechnology (M Sc); agricultural studies (M Sc, MA); anthropology (MA); archaeology (MA); art (MA, MFA); biochemistry (M Sc); biological sciences (M Sc); biomolecular science (PhD); biosystems and biodiversity (PhD); Canadian studies (MA); chemistry (M Sc); computer science (M Sc); computer science and geographical information science (M Sc); counseling psychology (M Ed); dramatic arts (MA); earth, space, and physical science (PhD); economics (MA); educational leadership (M Ed); English (MA); environmental science (M Sc); evolution and behavior (PhD); exercise science (M Sc); finance (MScM); French (MA); French/German (MA); French/Spanish (MA); general education (M Ed); general

management (MScM); geography (M Sc, MA); German (MA); health science (M Sc); history (MA); human resource management and labour relations (MScM); individualized multidisciplinary (M Sc, MA); information systems (MScM); international management (MScM); kinesiology (M Sc, MA); management (M Sc, MA); marketing (MScM); mathematics (M Sc); music (M Mus, MA); Native American studies (MA); neuroscience (M Sc, PhD); new media (MA); nursing (M Sc); philosophy (MA); physics (M Sc); policy and strategy (MScM); political science (MA); psychology (M Sc, MA); religious studies (MA); social sciences (MA); sociology (MA); theatre and dramatic arts (MFA); theoretical and computational science (PhD); urban and regional studies (MA); women's studies (MA). Part-time and evening/weekend programs available. *Degree requirements:* For doctorate, comprehensive exam, thesis/dissertation. *Entrance requirements:* For master's, GMAT (M Sc in management), bachelor's degree in related field, minimum GPA of 3.0 during previous 20 graded semester courses, 2 years teaching or related experience (M Ed); for doctorate, master's degree, minimum graduate GPA of 3.5. Additional exam requirements/recommendations for international students: Required—TOEFL. *Faculty research:* Movement and brain plasticity, gibberellin physiology, photosynthesis, carbon cycling, molecular properties of main-group ring components.

University of Louisiana at Lafayette, College of Sciences, Department of Physics, Lafayette, LA 70504. Offers MS. Part-time programs available. *Degree requirements:* For master's, thesis. *Entrance requirements:* For master's, GRE General Test, minimum GPA of 2.75. Additional exam requirements/recommendations for international students: Required—TOEFL (minimum score 550 paper-based; 213 computer-based). Electronic applications accepted. *Faculty research:* Environmental physics, geophysics, astrophysics, acoustics, atomic physics.

University of Louisville, Graduate School, College of Arts and Sciences, Department of Physics and Astronomy, Louisville, KY 40292. Offers physics (MS, PhD). Part-time programs available. Terminal master's awarded for partial completion of doctoral program. *Degree requirements:* For master's, thesis optional; for doctorate, comprehensive exam, thesis/dissertation. *Entrance requirements:* For master's, GRE General Test. Additional exam requirements/recommendations for international students: Required—TOEFL (minimum score 550 paper-based; 213 computer-based; 80 iBT). Electronic applications accepted. *Expenses:* Tuition, state resident: full-time $9692; part-time $539 per credit hour. Tuition, nonresident: full-time $20,168; part-time $1121 per credit hour. Tuition and fees vary according to program and reciprocity agreements. *Faculty research:* Condensed matter physics; atmospheric science; high energy physics; astrophysics; atomic, molecular, and optical physics.

University of Maine, Graduate School, College of Education and Human Development, Interdisciplinary Program in Teaching, Orono, ME 04469. Offers earth sciences (MST); generalist (MST); mathematics (MST); physics and astronomy (MST). *Students:* 8 full-time (6 women), 13 part-time (10 women); includes 1 minority (American Indian or Alaska Native, non-Hispanic/Latino). Average age 40. 2 applicants, 50% accepted, 1 enrolled. In 2011, 6 master's awarded. *Entrance requirements:* For master's, GRE General Test, MAT. Application fee: $65. *Expenses:* Tuition, state resident: full-time $5016. Tuition, nonresident: full-time $14,424. *Unit head:* Dr. Susan McKay, Director, 207-581-1016. *Application contact:* Scott G. Delcourt, Associate Dean of the Graduate School, 207-581-3291, Fax: 207-581-3232, E-mail: graduate@maine.edu. Web site: http://www2.umaine.edu/graduate/.

University of Maine, Graduate School, College of Liberal Arts and Sciences, Department of Physics and Astronomy, Orono, ME 04469. Offers engineering physics (M Eng); physics (MS, PhD). *Faculty:* 14 full-time (1 woman), 5 part-time/adjunct (2 women). *Students:* 22 full-time (7 women), 15 part-time (2 women), 5 international. Average age 28. 36 applicants, 28% accepted, 10 enrolled. In 2011, 5 master's, 6 doctorates awarded. Terminal master's awarded for partial completion of doctoral program. *Degree requirements:* For doctorate, thesis/dissertation. *Entrance requirements:* For master's, GRE General Test, GRE Subject Test; for doctorate, GRE General Test. Additional exam requirements/recommendations for international students: Required—TOEFL. *Application deadline:* For fall admission, 2/1 priority date for domestic students. Applications are processed on a rolling basis. Application fee: $65. Electronic applications accepted. *Expenses:* Tuition, state resident: full-time $5016. Tuition, nonresident: full-time $14,424. *Financial support:* In 2011–12, 4 research assistantships with full tuition reimbursements (averaging $18,220 per year), 15 teaching assistantships with full tuition reimbursements (averaging $15,300 per year) were awarded; tuition waivers (full and partial) also available. Financial award application deadline: 3/1. *Faculty research:* Solid-state physics, fluids, biophysics, plasma physics, surface physics. *Total annual research expenditures:* $592,151. *Unit head:* Dr. Susan McKay, Chair, 207-581-1015, Fax: 207-581-3410. *Application contact:* Scott G. Delcourt, Associate Dean of the Graduate School, 207-581-3291, Fax: 207-581-3232, E-mail: graduate@maine.edu. Web site: http://www2.umaine.edu/graduate/.

The University of Manchester, School of Earth, Atmospheric and Environmental Sciences, Manchester, United Kingdom. Offers atmospheric sciences (M Phil, M Sc, PhD); basin studies and petroleum geosciences (M Phil, M Sc, PhD); earth, atmospheric and environmental sciences (M Phil, M Sc, PhD); environmental geochemistry and cosmochemistry (M Phil, M Sc, PhD); isotope geochemistry and cosmochemistry (M Phil, M Sc, PhD); paleontology (M Phil, M Sc, PhD);

256 facebook.com/petersonspublishing

Peterson's Graduate Programs in the Physical Sciences, Mathematics, Agricultural Sciences, the Environment & Natural Resources 2013

physics and chemistry of minerals and fluids (M Phil, M Sc, PhD); structural and petrological geosciences (M Phil, M Sc, PhD).

The University of Manchester, School of Physics and Astronomy, Manchester, United Kingdom. Offers astronomy and astrophysics (M Sc, PhD); biological physics (M Sc, PhD); condensed matter physics (M Sc, PhD); nonlinear and liquid crystals physics (M Sc, PhD); nuclear physics (M Sc, PhD); particle physics (M Sc, PhD); photon physics (M Sc, PhD); physics (M Sc, PhD); theoretical physics (M Sc, PhD).

University of Manitoba, Faculty of Graduate Studies, Faculty of Science, Department of Physics and Astronomy, Winnipeg, MB R3T 2N2, Canada. Offers M Sc, PhD. *Degree requirements:* For master's, thesis; for doctorate, one foreign language, thesis/dissertation.

University of Maryland, Baltimore County, Graduate School, College of Arts, Humanities and Social Sciences, Department of Education, Program in Teaching, Baltimore, MD 21250. Offers early childhood education (MAT); elementary education (MAT); secondary education (MAT), including social studies; secondary education (MAT), including art, biology, chemistry, dance, earth/space science, English, foreign language, mathematics, music, physics, theatre. Part-time and evening/weekend programs available. *Faculty:* 24 full-time (18 women), 25 part-time/adjunct (19 women). *Students:* 46 full-time (35 women), 64 part-time (39 women); includes 24 minority (8 Black or African American, non-Hispanic/Latino; 7 Asian, non-Hispanic/Latino; 6 Hispanic/Latino; 1 Native Hawaiian or other Pacific Islander, non-Hispanic/Latino; 2 Two or more races, non-Hispanic/Latino), 4 international. Average age 31. 88 applicants, 57% accepted, 39 enrolled. In 2011, 106 master's awarded. *Degree requirements:* For master's, comprehensive exam (for some programs), thesis (for some programs). *Entrance requirements:* For master's, PRAXIS I or GRE (minimum score of 1000), minimum GPA of 3.0. Additional exam requirements/recommendations for international students: Required—TOEFL. *Application deadline:* For fall admission, 6/1 for domestic students; for spring admission, 11/1 for domestic students. Applications are processed on a rolling basis. Application fee: $50. Electronic applications accepted. *Financial support:* In 2011–12, 6 students received support, including teaching assistantships with full and partial tuition reimbursements available (averaging $12,000 per year); career-related internships or fieldwork, Federal Work-Study, scholarships/grants, tuition waivers, and unspecified assistantships also available. Financial award application deadline: 3/1. *Faculty research:* STEM teacher education, culturally sensitive pedagogy, ESOL/bilingual education, early childhood education, language, literacy and culture. *Unit head:* Dr. Susan M. Blunck, Graduate Program Director, 410-455-2869, Fax: 410-455-3986, E-mail: blunck@umbc.edu. *Application contact:* Cheryl Johnson, 410-455-3388, E-mail: blackwel@umbc.edu. Web site: http://www.umbc.edu/education/.

University of Maryland, Baltimore County, Graduate School, College of Natural and Mathematical Sciences, Department of Physics, Baltimore, MD 21250. Offers applied physics (MS, PhD); atmospheric physics (MS, PhD). Part-time programs available. *Faculty:* 21 full-time (3 women), 16 part-time/adjunct (2 women). *Students:* 45 full-time (13 women), 3 part-time (0 women); includes 4 minority (3 Black or African American, non-Hispanic/Latino; 1 Asian, non-Hispanic/Latino), 19 international. Average age 24. 35 applicants, 54% accepted, 8 enrolled. In 2011, 4 master's, 6 doctorates awarded. Terminal master's awarded for partial completion of doctoral program. *Degree requirements:* For master's, thesis optional; for doctorate, comprehensive exam, thesis/dissertation. *Entrance requirements:* For master's and doctorate, GRE General Test, GRE Subject Test (recommended), minimum GPA of 3.0. Additional exam requirements/recommendations for international students: Required—TOEFL. *Application deadline:* For fall admission, 1/1 for domestic and international students; for spring admission, 11/30 for domestic students. Applications are processed on a rolling basis. Application fee: $50. Electronic applications accepted. *Financial support:* In 2011–12, 42 students received support, including 5 fellowships with full tuition reimbursements available (averaging $30,000 per year), 21 research assistantships with full tuition reimbursements available (averaging $26,000 per year), 16 teaching assistantships with full tuition reimbursements available (averaging $22,000 per year); career-related internships or fieldwork, scholarships/grants, health care benefits, and unspecified assistantships also available. Support available to part-time students. Financial award application deadline: 5/31. *Faculty research:* Quantum optics and quantum computing, astrophysics, atmospheric physics, nanoscale physics. *Total annual research expenditures:* $7.5 million. *Unit head:* Dr. L. Michael Hayden, Chairman, 410-455-2513, Fax: 410-455-1072, E-mail: hayden@umbc.edu. *Application contact:* Dr. Lazlo Takacs, Graduate Admissions Director, 410-455-2524, Fax: 410-455-1072, E-mail: takacs@umbc.edu. Web site: http://www.physics.umbc.edu/.

University of Maryland, College Park, Academic Affairs, College of Computer, Mathematical and Natural Sciences, Department of Physics, College Park, MD 20742. Offers MS, PhD. Part-time and evening/weekend programs available. *Faculty:* 183 full-time (24 women), 44 part-time/adjunct (9 women). *Students:* 220 full-time (28 women), 8 part-time (1 woman); includes 18 minority (4 Black or African American, non-Hispanic/Latino; 10 Asian, non-Hispanic/Latino; 3 Hispanic/Latino; 1 Two or more races, non-Hispanic/Latino), 78 international. 735 applicants, 17% accepted, 39 enrolled. In 2011, 15 master's, 39 doctorates awarded. Terminal master's awarded for partial completion of doctoral program. *Degree requirements:* For master's, thesis optional; for doctorate, thesis/dissertation. *Entrance requirements:* For master's, GRE General Test, GRE

Subject Test (physics), minimum GPA of 3.0, 3 letters of recommendation; for doctorate, GRE General Test, GRE Subject Test (physics), 3 letters of recommendation. *Application deadline:* For fall admission, 1/15 for domestic and international students. Applications are processed on a rolling basis. Application fee: $75. Electronic applications accepted. *Expenses: Tuition, area resident:* Part-time $525 per credit hour. Tuition, state resident: part-time $525 per credit hour. Tuition, nonresident: part-time $1131 per credit hour. *Required fees:* $386.31 per term. Tuition and fees vary according to program. *Financial support:* In 2011–12, 10 fellowships with full and partial tuition reimbursements (averaging $14,820 per year), 168 research assistantships (averaging $20,041 per year), 56 teaching assistantships (averaging $17,683 per year) were awarded; Federal Work-Study and scholarships/grants also available. Support available to part-time students. Financial award applicants required to submit FAFSA. *Faculty research:* Astrometeorology, superconductivity, particle astrophysics, plasma physics, elementary particle theory. *Total annual research expenditures:* $35.1 million. *Unit head:* Dr. Drew Baden, Chair, 301-405-5946, Fax: 301-405-0327, E-mail: drew@umd.edu. *Application contact:* Dr. Charles A. Caramello, Dean of the Graduate School, 301-401-0358, Fax: 301-314-9305.

University of Massachusetts Amherst, Graduate School, College of Natural Sciences, Department of Physics, Amherst, MA 01003. Offers MS, PhD. Part-time programs available. *Faculty:* 40 full-time (5 women). *Students:* 86 full-time (17 women), 1 part-time (0 women); includes 4 minority (3 Hispanic/Latino; 1 Two or more races, non-Hispanic/Latino), 50 international. Average age 28. 199 applicants, 37% accepted, 17 enrolled. In 2011, 7 doctorates awarded. Terminal master's awarded for partial completion of doctoral program. *Degree requirements:* For master's, thesis or alternative; for doctorate, comprehensive exam, thesis/dissertation. *Entrance requirements:* For master's and doctorate, GRE General Test, GRE Subject Test (physics). Additional exam requirements/recommendations for international students: Required—TOEFL (minimum score 550 paper-based; 213 computer-based; 80 iBT), IELTS (minimum score 6.5). *Application deadline:* For fall admission, 2/1 for domestic and international students. Applications are processed on a rolling basis. Application fee: $50 ($65 for international students). Electronic applications accepted. Tuition and fees vary according to course load, campus/location and program. *Financial support:* Fellowships with full and partial tuition reimbursements, research assistantships with full and partial tuition reimbursements, teaching assistantships with full and partial tuition reimbursements, career-related internships or fieldwork, Federal Work-Study, scholarships/grants, traineeships, health care benefits, tuition waivers (full and partial), and unspecified assistantships available. Support available to part-time students. Financial award application deadline: 2/1. *Unit head:* Dr. Krishna S. Kumar, Graduate Program Director, 413-545-2548, Fax: 413-545-0648. *Application contact:* Lindsay DeSantis, Interim Supervisor of Admissions, 413-545-0722, Fax: 413-577-0010, E-mail: gradadm@grad.umass.edu. Web site: http://www.physics.umass.edu/.

University of Massachusetts Dartmouth, Graduate School, College of Engineering, Department of Physics, North Dartmouth, MA 02747-2300. Offers MS. Part-time programs available. *Faculty:* 10 full-time (1 woman), 1 part-time/adjunct (0 women). *Students:* 13 full-time (0 women), 2 part-time (1 woman); includes 1 minority (Asian, non-Hispanic/Latino), 5 international. Average age 26. 15 applicants, 87% accepted, 6 enrolled. In 2011, 5 degrees awarded. *Degree requirements:* For master's, thesis or alternative. *Entrance requirements:* For master's, GRE (for financial consideration), 3 letters of recommendation, resume, statement of intent. Additional exam requirements/recommendations for international students: Required—TOEFL (minimum score 533 paper-based; 200 computer-based; 72 iBT). *Application deadline:* For fall admission, 3/31 priority date for domestic students, 2/28 for international students; for spring admission, 11/15 priority date for domestic students, 10/15 for international students. Applications are processed on a rolling basis. Application fee: $40 ($60 for international students). Electronic applications accepted. *Expenses:* Tuition, state resident: full-time $2071; part-time $86.29 per credit. Tuition, nonresident: full-time $8099; part-time $337.46 per credit. *Required fees:* $438.58 per credit. Part-time tuition and fees vary according to class time, course load, degree level and reciprocity agreements. *Financial support:* In 2011–12, 4 research assistantships with full tuition reimbursements (averaging $8,188 per year), 11 teaching assistantships with full tuition reimbursements (averaging $9,539 per year) were awarded; Federal Work-Study also available. Support available to part-time students. Financial award application deadline: 3/1; financial award applicants required to submit FAFSA. *Faculty research:* AMO physics, ocean physics, experimental nuclear physics, theoretical particle physics, astrophysics. *Total annual research expenditures:* $597,435. *Unit head:* Dr. Gaurav Khanna, Graduate Program Director, 508-910-6605, Fax: 508-999-9115, E-mail: gkhanna@umassd.edu. *Application contact:* Elan Turcotte-Shamski, Graduate Admissions Officer, 508-999-8604, Fax: 508-999-8183, E-mail: graduate@umassd.edu. Web site: http://www.umassd.edu/engineering/phy/graduate/welcome.cfm.

University of Massachusetts Lowell, College of Sciences, Department of Physics and Applied Physics, Program in Physics, Lowell, MA 01854-2881. Offers MS, PhD. *Degree requirements:* For master's, thesis; for doctorate, 2 foreign languages, thesis/dissertation. *Entrance requirements:* For master's, GRE General Test, 3 letters of reference; for doctorate, GRE General Test, transcripts, 3 letters of reference. Additional exam requirements/recommendations for international students: Required—TOEFL.

Peterson's Graduate Programs in the Physical Sciences, Mathematics, Agricultural Sciences, the Environment & Natural Resources 2013

facebook.com/petersonspublishing **257**

Physics

University of Memphis, Graduate School, College of Arts and Sciences, Department of Physics, Memphis, TN 38152. Offers MS. Part-time programs available. *Degree requirements:* For master's, comprehensive exam, thesis or alternative. *Entrance requirements:* For master's, GRE General Test or MAT, 20 undergraduate hours of course work in physics. Electronic applications accepted. *Faculty research:* Solid-state physics, materials science, biophysics, astrophysics, physics education.

University of Miami, Graduate School, College of Arts and Sciences, Department of Physics, Coral Gables, FL 33124. Offers MS, PhD. Terminal master's awarded for partial completion of doctoral program. *Degree requirements:* For master's, comprehensive exam; for doctorate, comprehensive exam, thesis/dissertation. *Entrance requirements:* For master's and doctorate, GRE General Test, GRE Subject Test. Additional exam requirements/recommendations for international students: Required—TOEFL (minimum score 550 paper-based; 213 computer-based; 80 iBT). Electronic applications accepted. *Faculty research:* High-energy theory, marine and atmospheric optics, plasma physics, solid-state physics.

University of Michigan, Horace H. Rackham School of Graduate Studies, College of Literature, Science, and the Arts, Department of Physics, Ann Arbor, MI 48109. Offers MS, PhD. *Faculty:* 64 full-time (13 women). *Students:* 118 full-time (26 women); includes 21 minority (2 Black or African American, non-Hispanic/Latino; 1 American Indian or Alaska Native, non-Hispanic/Latino; 12 Asian, non-Hispanic/Latino; 5 Hispanic/Latino; 1 Native Hawaiian or other Pacific Islander, non-Hispanic/Latino), 51 international. Average age 27. 450 applicants, 22% accepted, 35 enrolled. In 2011, 10 master's, 19 doctorates awarded. Terminal master's awarded for partial completion of doctoral program. *Degree requirements:* For doctorate, thesis/dissertation, oral defense of dissertation, preliminary exam. *Entrance requirements:* For master's, GRE General Test; for doctorate, GRE General Test, GRE Subject Test in physics (recommended). Additional exam requirements/recommendations for international students: Required—TOEFL (minimum score 600 paper-based; 250 computer-based; 100 iBT). *Application deadline:* For fall admission, 12/14 for domestic and international students. Application fee: $65 ($75 for international students). Electronic applications accepted. *Financial support:* In 2011–12, fellowships with full tuition reimbursements (averaging $26,500 per year), research assistantships with full tuition reimbursements (averaging $26,000 per year), teaching assistantships with full tuition reimbursements (averaging $23,000 per year) were awarded. *Faculty research:* Elementary particle, solid-state, atomic, and molecular physics (theoretical and experimental). *Total annual research expenditures:* $14 million. *Unit head:* Dr. Bradford Orr, Chair, 734-764-4437. *Application contact:* Christina A. Zigulis, Graduate Coordinator, 734-936-0658, Fax: 734-763-9694, E-mail: physics.inquiries@umich.edu. Web site: http://www.lsa.umich.edu/physics/.

University of Minnesota, Duluth, Graduate School, Swenson College of Science and Engineering, Department of Physics, Duluth, MN 55812-2496. Offers MS. Part-time programs available. *Degree requirements:* For master's, thesis optional, final oral exam. *Entrance requirements:* For master's, minimum GPA of 3.0 (preferred). Additional exam requirements/recommendations for international students: Required—TOEFL (minimum score 550 paper-based; 213 computer-based; 79 iBT), IELTS (minimum score 6.5), or Michigan English Language Assessment Battery (minimum score 80). Electronic applications accepted. *Faculty research:* Computational physics, neutrino physics, oceanography, computational particle physics, optics, condensed matter.

University of Minnesota, Twin Cities Campus, College of Science and Engineering, School of Physics and Astronomy, Program in Physics, Minneapolis, MN 55455-0213. Offers MS, PhD. Part-time programs available. *Students:* 143 (28 women); includes 6 minority (1 Black or African American, non-Hispanic/Latino; 4 Asian, non-Hispanic/Latino; 1 Hispanic/Latino), 62 international. *Degree requirements:* For master's, thesis; for doctorate, thesis/dissertation. *Entrance requirements:* For master's and doctorate, GRE General Test, GRE Subject Test. Additional exam requirements/recommendations for international students: Required—TOEFL. *Application deadline:* For fall admission, 12/15 for domestic and international students. Applications are processed on a rolling basis. Application fee: $75 ($95 for international students). Electronic applications accepted. *Financial support:* Fellowships, research assistantships, and teaching assistantships available. *Faculty research:* Elementary particles, condensed matter, cosmology, nuclear physics, space physics, biological physics, physics education. *Application contact:* Director of Graduate Studies in Physics, E-mail: grad@physics.umn.edu.

University of Mississippi, Graduate School, College of Liberal Arts, Department of Physics and Astronomy, Oxford, University, MS 38677. Offers physics (MA, MS, PhD). *Students:* 31 full-time (6 women), 2 part-time (1 woman); includes 3 minority (2 Black or African American, non-Hispanic/Latino; 2 Asian, non-Hispanic/Latino; 2 Hispanic/Latino; 1 Native Hawaiian or other Pacific Islander, non-Hispanic/Latino), 17 international. In 2011, 4 master's, 5 doctorates awarded. *Degree requirements:* For master's, thesis (for some programs); for doctorate, thesis/dissertation. *Entrance requirements:* For master's, GRE General Test, minimum GPA of 3.0; for doctorate, GRE General Test. Additional exam requirements/recommendations for international students: Required—TOEFL. *Application deadline:* For fall admission, 4/1 for domestic students; for spring admission, 10/1 for domestic students. Applications are processed on a rolling basis. Application fee: $25. Electronic applications accepted. *Financial support:*

Scholarships/grants available. Financial award application deadline: 3/1; financial award applicants required to submit FAFSA. *Unit head:* Dr. Lucien M. Cremaldi, Chairman, 662-915-7046, Fax: 662-915-5045, E-mail: physics@phy.olemiss.edu. *Application contact:* Dr. Christy M. Wyandt, Associate Dean, 662-915-7474, Fax: 662-915-7577, E-mail: cwyandt@olemiss.edu.

University of Missouri, Graduate School, College of Arts and Sciences, Department of Physics and Astronomy, Columbia, MO 65211. Offers MS, PhD. *Faculty:* 27 full-time (8 women), 1 (woman) part-time/adjunct. *Students:* 32 full-time (3 women), 21 part-time (5 women); includes 4 minority (1 Asian, non-Hispanic/Latino; 1 Hispanic/Latino; 2 Two or more races, non-Hispanic/Latino), 29 international. Average age 28. 85 applicants, 13% accepted, 10 enrolled. In 2011, 6 master's, 8 doctorates awarded. Terminal master's awarded for partial completion of doctoral program. *Degree requirements:* For doctorate, one foreign language, comprehensive exam, thesis/dissertation. *Entrance requirements:* For master's and doctorate, GRE General Test, minimum GPA of 3.0. Additional exam requirements/recommendations for international students: Required—TOEFL (minimum score 550 paper-based; 213 computer-based; 80 iBT). *Application deadline:* For fall admission, 3/15 priority date for domestic students. Applications are processed on a rolling basis. Application fee: $55 ($75 for international students). Electronic applications accepted. *Expenses:* Tuition, state resident: full-time $5881. Tuition, nonresident: full-time $15,183. *Required fees:* $952. Tuition and fees vary according to campus/location and program. *Financial support:* In 2011–12, 35 research assistantships with full tuition reimbursements, 10 teaching assistantships with full tuition reimbursements were awarded; institutionally sponsored loans, health care benefits, and unspecified assistantships also available. *Faculty research:* Experimental and theoretical condensed-matter physics, biological physics, astronomy/astrophysics. *Unit head:* Dr. Peter Pfeifer, Department Chair, 573-882-2335, E-mail: pfeiferp@missouri.edu. *Application contact:* Dr. Carsten Ullrich, Director of Graduate Studies, 573-882-3335, E-mail: ullrichc@missouri.edu. Web site: http://physics.missouri.edu/graduate/.

University of Missouri–Kansas City, College of Arts and Sciences, Department of Physics, Kansas City, MO 64110-2499. Offers MS, PhD. PhD (interdisciplinary) offered through the School of Graduate Studies. Part-time and evening/weekend programs available. *Faculty:* 11 full-time (1 woman), 1 part-time/adjunct (0 women). *Students:* 13 full-time (1 woman), 9 part-time (1 woman); includes 1 minority (Asian, non-Hispanic/Latino), 6 international. Average age 29. 14 applicants, 79% accepted, 7 enrolled. In 2011, 9 master's awarded. Terminal master's awarded for partial completion of doctoral program. *Degree requirements:* For master's, comprehensive exam, thesis optional; for doctorate, comprehensive exam, thesis/dissertation. *Entrance requirements:* For master's and doctorate, GRE General Test. Additional exam requirements/recommendations for international students: Required—TOEFL (minimum score 550 paper-based; 213 computer-based; 80 iBT). *Application deadline:* For fall admission, 4/1 priority date for domestic students, 4/1 for international students; for spring admission, 11/1 priority date for domestic students, 11/1 for international students. Applications are processed on a rolling basis. Application fee: $45 ($50 for international students). Electronic applications accepted. *Expenses:* Tuition, state resident: full-time $5798; part-time $322.10 per credit hour. Tuition, nonresident: full-time $14,969; part-time $831.60 per credit hour. *Required fees:* $93.51 per credit hour. *Financial support:* In 2011–12, 8 research assistantships with full and partial tuition reimbursements (averaging $16,389 per year), 16 teaching assistantships with full and partial tuition reimbursements (averaging $16,275 per year) were awarded; Federal Work-Study, institutionally sponsored loans, and tuition waivers (full and partial) also available. Support available to part-time students. Financial award application deadline: 3/1; financial award applicants required to submit FAFSA. *Faculty research:* Surface physics, material science, statistical mechanics, computational physics, relativity and quantum theory. *Unit head:* Dr. Michael Kruger, Chair, 816-235-5441, E-mail: krugerm@umkc.edu. *Application contact:* Dr. Da Ming Zhu, Principal Graduate Advisor, 816-235-5326, Fax: 816-235-5221, E-mail: zhud@umkc.edu. Web site: http://cas.umkc.edu/physics/.

University of Missouri–St. Louis, College of Arts and Sciences, Department of Physics and Astronomy, St. Louis, MO 63121. Offers applied physics (MS); physics (PhD). Part-time and evening/weekend programs available. *Faculty:* 11 full-time (2 women), 4 part-time/adjunct (1 woman). *Students:* 19 full-time (7 women), 5 part-time (1 woman), 6 international. Average age 32. 20 applicants, 40% accepted, 4 enrolled. In 2011, 5 master's, 1 doctorate awarded. Terminal master's awarded for partial completion of doctoral program. *Degree requirements:* For master's, thesis optional; for doctorate, thesis/dissertation. *Entrance requirements:* For master's, GRE General Test; for doctorate, GRE General Test, 2 letters of recommendation. Additional exam requirements/recommendations for international students: Required—TOEFL (minimum score 550 paper-based; 213 computer-based). *Application deadline:* For fall admission, 7/1 for domestic and international students; for spring admission, 12/1 for domestic students, 11/1 for international students. Application fee: $35 ($40 for international students). Electronic applications accepted. *Expenses:* Tuition, state resident: full-time $6273; part-time $3866 per year. Tuition, nonresident: full-time $14,969; part-time $9980 per year. *Required fees:* $315 per year. *Financial support:* In 2011–12, 7 research assistantships with full and partial tuition reimbursements (averaging $16,200 per year), 10 teaching assistantships with full and partial tuition reimbursements (averaging $14,500 per year) were awarded; fellowships with full tuition reimbursements and career-related internships or

258 facebook.com/petersonspublishing

Peterson's Graduate Programs in the Physical Sciences, Mathematics, Agricultural Sciences, the Environment & Natural Resources 2013

fieldwork also available. Financial award applicants required to submit FAFSA. *Faculty research:* Biophysics, atomic physics, nonlinear dynamics, materials science. *Unit head:* Dr. Bruce Wilking, Director of Graduate Studies, 314-516-5931, Fax: 314-516-6152, E-mail: bwilking@umsl.edu. *Application contact:* 314-516-5458, Fax: 314-516-6996, E-mail: gradadm@umsl.edu. Web site: http://www.umsl.edu/~physics/.

University of Nebraska–Lincoln, Graduate College, College of Arts and Sciences, Department of Physics and Astronomy, Lincoln, NE 68588. Offers astronomy (MS, PhD); physics (MS, PhD). *Degree requirements:* For master's, thesis optional; for doctorate, comprehensive exam, thesis/dissertation. *Entrance requirements:* For master's and doctorate, GRE General Test. Additional exam requirements/recommendations for international students: Required—TOEFL (minimum score 550 paper-based; 213 computer-based). Electronic applications accepted. *Faculty research:* Electromagnetics of solids and thin films, photoionization, ion collisions with atoms, molecules and surfaces, nanostructures.

University of Nevada, Las Vegas, Graduate College, College of Science, Department of Physics, Las Vegas, NV 89154-4002. Offers astronomy (MS, PhD); physics (MS, PhD). Part-time programs available. *Faculty:* 20 full-time (3 women), 7 part-time/adjunct (3 women). *Students:* 2 full-time (0 women), 13 part-time (1 woman), 4 international. Average age 29. 10 applicants, 20% accepted, 0 enrolled. In 2011, 3 master's, 5 doctorates awarded. *Degree requirements:* For master's, thesis, oral exam; for doctorate, comprehensive exam, thesis/dissertation. *Entrance requirements:* For master's and doctorate, GRE General Test. Additional exam requirements/recommendations for international students: Required—TOEFL (minimum score 550 paper-based; 213 computer-based; 80 iBT), IELTS (minimum score 7). *Application deadline:* For fall admission, 8/1 priority date for domestic students, 5/1 for international students; for spring admission, 10/1 priority date for domestic students, 10/1 for international students. Applications are processed on a rolling basis. Application fee: $60 ($95 for international students). Electronic applications accepted. *Financial support:* In 2011–12, 15 students received support, including 1 research assistantship with partial tuition reimbursement available (averaging $33,892 per year), 14 teaching assistantships with partial tuition reimbursements available (averaging $14,882 per year); institutionally sponsored loans, scholarships/grants, health care benefits, and unspecified assistantships also available. Financial award application deadline: 3/1. *Faculty research:* Gamma-ray bursters astrophysics, cosmology and dark matter astrophysics, experimental high pressure physics, theoretical condensed matter physics, laser-plasma atomic physics. *Total annual research expenditures:* $4.4 million. *Unit head:* Dr. Tao Pang, Chair/Professor, 702-895-4454, Fax: 702-895-0804, E-mail: pang@physics.unlv.edu. *Application contact:* Graduate College Admissions Evaluator, 702-895-3320, Fax: 702-895-4180, E-mail: gradcollege@unlv.edu. Web site: http://www.physics.unlv.edu/graduate.html.

University of Nevada, Reno, Graduate School, College of Science, Department of Physics, Reno, NV 89557. Offers MS, PhD. Terminal master's awarded for partial completion of doctoral program. *Degree requirements:* For master's, thesis optional; for doctorate, thesis/dissertation. *Entrance requirements:* For master's, GRE General Test, GRE Subject Test, minimum GPA of 2.75; for doctorate, GRE General Test, GRE Subject Test, minimum GPA of 3.0. Additional exam requirements/recommendations for international students: Required—TOEFL (minimum score 500 paper-based; 173 computer-based; 61 iBT), IELTS (minimum score 6). Electronic applications accepted. *Faculty research:* Atomic and molecular physics.

University of New Brunswick Fredericton, School of Graduate Studies, Faculty of Science, Department of Physics, Fredericton, NB E3B 5A3, Canada. Offers M Sc, PhD. Part-time programs available. *Faculty:* 8 full-time (0 women), 1 (woman) part-time/adjunct. *Students:* 14 full-time (3 women). In 2011, 1 master's, 1 doctorate awarded. *Degree requirements:* For master's, thesis; for doctorate, comprehensive exam, thesis/dissertation. *Entrance requirements:* For master's, B Sc with minimum B average; for doctorate, M Sc, minimum GPA of 3.0. Additional exam requirements/recommendations for international students: Required—TOEFL, TWE. *Application deadline:* For fall admission, 3/1 priority date for domestic students. Applications are processed on a rolling basis. Application fee: $50 Canadian dollars. Electronic applications accepted. *Financial support:* In 2011–12, 3 fellowships with tuition reimbursements (averaging $17,500 per year), 10 research assistantships (averaging $12,000 per year), 22 teaching assistantships (averaging $4,200 per year) were awarded. *Faculty research:* Optical and laser spectroscopy, infrared and microwave spectroscopy, magnetic resonance and magnetic resonance imaging, space and atmospheric physics, theoretical atomic and molecular physics, space plasma theory, theoretical molecular spectroscopy. *Unit head:* Dr. Igor Mastikhin, Director of Graduate Studies, 506-458-7927, Fax: 506-453-4581, E-mail: mast@unb.ca. *Application contact:* Elinor MacFarlane, Graduate Secretary, 506-453-4723, Fax: 506-453-4581, E-mail: elinor@unb.ca. Web site: http://www.unb.ca/fredericton/science/physics/.

University of New Hampshire, Graduate School, College of Engineering and Physical Sciences, Department of Physics, Durham, NH 03824. Offers MS, PhD. *Faculty:* 32 full-time (4 women). *Students:* 33 full-time (7 women), 29 part-time (5 women); includes 5 minority (2 American Indian or Alaska Native, non-Hispanic/Latino; 3 Asian, non-Hispanic/Latino), 22 international. Average age 27. 116

applicants, 33% accepted, 14 enrolled. In 2011, 2 master's, 6 doctorates awarded. Terminal master's awarded for partial completion of doctoral program. *Degree requirements:* For master's, thesis or alternative; for doctorate, thesis/dissertation. *Entrance requirements:* For master's and doctorate, GRE General Test. Additional exam requirements/recommendations for international students: Required—TOEFL (minimum score 550 paper-based; 213 computer-based; 80 iBT). *Application deadline:* For fall admission, 4/1 priority date for domestic students, 4/1 for international students; for spring admission, 12/1 for domestic students. Applications are processed on a rolling basis. Application fee: $65. Electronic applications accepted. *Expenses:* Tuition, state resident: full-time $12,360; part-time $687 per credit hour. Tuition, nonresident: full-time $25,680; part-time $1058 per credit hour. *International tuition:* $29,550 full-time. *Required fees:* $1666; $833 per course. $416.50 per semester. Tuition and fees vary according to course load and degree level. *Financial support:* In 2011–12, 60 students received support, including 42 research assistantships, 18 teaching assistantships; fellowships, Federal Work-Study, scholarships/grants, and tuition waivers (full and partial) also available. Support available to part-time students. Financial award application deadline: 2/15. *Faculty research:* Astrophysics and space physics, nuclear physics, atomic and molecular physics, nonlinear dynamical systems. *Unit head:* Mark McConnell, Chairperson, 603-862-2047. *Application contact:* Katie Makem-Boucher, Administrative Assistant, 603-862-2669, E-mail: physics.grad.info@unh.edu. Web site: http://www.physics.unh.edu/

University of New Mexico, Graduate School, College of Arts and Sciences, Department of Physics and Astronomy, Albuquerque, NM 87131-0001. Offers physics (MS, PhD). Part-time programs available. *Faculty:* 31 full-time (5 women), 6 part-time/adjunct (0 women). *Students:* 55 full-time (13 women), 37 part-time (34 women); includes 9 minority (1 American Indian or Alaska Native, non-Hispanic/Latino; 4 Asian, non-Hispanic/Latino; 3 Hispanic/Latino; 1 Native Hawaiian or other Pacific Islander, non-Hispanic/Latino), 29 international. Average age 30. 124 applicants, 20% accepted, 22 enrolled. In 2011, 11 master's, 8 doctorates awarded. Terminal master's awarded for partial completion of doctoral program. *Median time to degree:* Of those who began their doctoral program in fall 2003, 58% received their degree in 8 years or less. *Degree requirements:* For master's, comprehensive exam (for some programs), thesis optional, preliminary exams (for non-thesis option); for doctorate, comprehensive exam, thesis/dissertation. *Entrance requirements:* For master's and doctorate, GRE General Test; GRE Subject Test (physics). Additional exam requirements/recommendations for international students: Required—TOEFL (minimum score 550 paper-based; 213 computer-based; 80 iBT), IELTS (minimum score 7). *Application deadline:* For fall admission, 1/15 for domestic and international students; for spring admission, 8/1 for domestic and international students. Application fee: $50. Electronic applications accepted. *Financial support:* In 2011–12, 90 students received support, including 4 fellowships with full tuition reimbursements available (averaging $17,000 per year), 58 research assistantships with full tuition reimbursements available (averaging $17,490 per year), 37 teaching assistantships with full tuition reimbursements available (averaging $15,196 per year); career-related internships or fieldwork, scholarships/grants, traineeships, health care benefits, and unspecified assistantships also available. Support available to part-time students. Financial award application deadline: 2/1; financial award applicants required to submit FAFSA. *Faculty research:* Astronomy and astrophysics, biological physics, condensed-matter physics, nonlinear science and complexity, optics and photonics, quantum information, subatomic physics. *Total annual research expenditures:* $6 million. *Unit head:* Dr. Wolfgang Rudolph, Chair, 505-277-1517, Fax: 505-277-1520, E-mail: wrudolph@unm.edu. *Application contact:* Alisa Gibson, Coordinator, Academic Programs, 505-277-1514, Fax: 505-277-1520, E-mail: agibson@unm.edu. Web site: http://panda.unm.edu.

University of New Orleans, Graduate School, College of Sciences, Department of Physics, New Orleans, LA 70148. Offers MS, PhD. Part-time and evening/weekend programs available. *Degree requirements:* For master's, thesis (for some programs). *Entrance requirements:* For master's, GRE General Test. Additional exam requirements/recommendations for international students: Required—TOEFL (minimum score 550 paper-based; 213 computer-based; 79 iBT). Electronic applications accepted. *Faculty research:* Underwater acoustics, applied electromagnetics, experimental atomic beams, digital signal processing, astrophysics.

The University of North Carolina at Chapel Hill, Graduate School, College of Arts and Sciences, Department of Physics and Astronomy, Chapel Hill, NC 27599. Offers physics (MS, PhD). Terminal master's awarded for partial completion of doctoral program. *Degree requirements:* For master's, comprehensive exam; for doctorate, comprehensive exam, thesis/dissertation. *Entrance requirements:* For master's and doctorate, GRE General Test, minimum GPA of 3.0. Electronic applications accepted. *Faculty research:* Observational astronomy, fullerenes, polarized beams, nanotubes, nucleosynthesis in stars and supernovae, superstring theory, ballistic transport in semiconductors, gravitation.

University of North Dakota, Graduate School, College of Arts and Sciences, Department of Physics, Grand Forks, ND 58202. Offers MS, PhD. *Degree requirements:* For master's, thesis, final exam; for doctorate, comprehensive exam, thesis/dissertation, final exam. *Entrance requirements:* For master's, minimum GPA of 3.0; for doctorate, minimum GPA of 3.5. Additional exam requirements/recommendations for international students: Required—TOEFL

Peterson's Graduate Programs in the Physical Sciences, Mathematics, Agricultural Sciences, the Environment & Natural Resources 2013

facebook.com/petersonspublishing **259**

Physics

(minimum score 550 paper-based; 213 computer-based; 79 iBT), IELTS (minimum score 6.5). Electronic applications accepted. *Faculty research:* Solid state physics, atomic and molecular physics, astrophysics, health physics.

University of Northern Iowa, Graduate College, College of Humanities, Arts and Sciences, Department of Physics, Cedar Falls, IA 50614. Offers applied physics (PSM). *Students:* 3 full-time (0 women), 5 part-time (1 woman); includes 1 minority (Hispanic/Latino), 1 international. 4 applicants, 75% accepted, 2 enrolled. In 2011, 2 master's awarded. *Degree requirements:* For master's, comprehensive exam (for some programs), thesis or alternative. *Entrance requirements:* For master's, minimum GPA of 3.0. Additional exam requirements/recommendations for international students: Required—TOEFL (minimum score 500 paper-based; 180 computer-based; 61 iBT). *Application deadline:* For fall admission, 8/1 priority date for domestic students. Applications are processed on a rolling basis. Application fee: $50 ($70 for international students). Electronic applications accepted. *Expenses:* Tuition, state resident: full-time $7476. Tuition, nonresident: full-time $16,410. *Required fees:* $942. *Financial support:* Career-related internships or fieldwork, Federal Work-Study, scholarships/grants, and tuition waivers (full and partial) available. Support available to part-time students. Financial award application deadline: 2/1. *Unit head:* Dr. C. Clifton Chancey, Head, 319-273-2420, E-mail: c.chancey@uni.edu. *Application contact:* Laurie S. Russell, Record Analyst, 319-273-2623, Fax: 319-273-2885, E-mail: laurie.russell@uni.edu. Web site: http://www.physics.uni.edu/.

University of Northern Iowa, Graduate College, College of Humanities, Arts and Sciences, Program in Science Education, Cedar Falls, IA 50614. Offers earth science education (MA); physics education (MA); science education (MA). *Students:* 4 full-time (3 women), 27 part-time (19 women); includes 1 minority (Two or more races, non-Hispanic/Latino). 4 applicants, 50% accepted, 2 enrolled. In 2011, 7 master's awarded. *Degree requirements:* For master's, comprehensive exam (for some programs), thesis or alternative. *Entrance requirements:* For master's, minimum GPA of 3.0. Additional exam requirements/ recommendations for international students: Required—TOEFL (minimum score 500 paper-based; 180 computer-based; 61 iBT). *Application deadline:* For fall admission, 8/1 priority date for domestic students. Applications are processed on a rolling basis. Application fee: $50 ($70 for international students). Electronic applications accepted. *Expenses:* Tuition, state resident: full-time $7476. Tuition, nonresident: full-time $16,410. *Required fees:* $942. *Financial support:* Application deadline: 2/1. *Unit head:* Dr. Cherin A. Lee, Director, 319-273-7357, Fax: 319-273-3051, E-mail: cherin.lee@uni.edu. *Application contact:* Laurie S. Russell, Record Analyst, 319-273-2623, Fax: 319-273-2885, E-mail: laurie.russell@uni.edu. Web site: http://www.science-ed.uni.edu/.

University of North Texas, Toulouse Graduate School, College of Arts and Sciences, Department of Physics, Denton, TX 76203. Offers MA, MS, PhD. Terminal master's awarded for partial completion of doctoral program. *Degree requirements:* For master's, comprehensive exam (for some programs), thesis or problems; for doctorate, one foreign language, comprehensive exam (for some programs), thesis/dissertation. *Entrance requirements:* For master's and doctorate, GRE General Test, 2 letters of recommendation. Additional exam requirements/recommendations for international students: Recommended— TOEFL (minimum score 550 paper-based; 213 computer-based; 79 iBT). Electronic applications accepted. *Expenses:* Tuition, state resident: part-time $100 per credit hour. Tuition, nonresident: part-time $413 per credit hour. *Faculty research:* Atomic, molecular optical; condensed matter, experimental microwave, theoretical, semiconductor.

University of Notre Dame, Graduate School, College of Science, Department of Physics, Notre Dame, IN 46556. Offers MS, PhD. *Degree requirements:* For doctorate, thesis/dissertation, candidacy exam. *Entrance requirements:* For doctorate, GRE General Test, GRE Subject Test. Additional exam requirements/ recommendations for international students: Required—TOEFL (minimum score 600 paper-based; 250 computer-based; 80 iBT). Electronic applications accepted. *Faculty research:* High energy, nuclear, atomic, condensed-matter physics; astrophysics; biophysics.

University of Oklahoma, College of Arts and Sciences, Department of Physics and Astronomy, Norman, OK 73019. Offers physics (MS, PhD). Part-time programs available. *Faculty:* 31 full-time (4 women). *Students:* 41 full-time (9 women), 24 part-time (10 women); includes 1 minority (Asian, non-Hispanic/ Latino), 29 international. Average age 29. 20 applicants, 40% accepted, 7 enrolled. In 2011, 4 master's, 4 doctorates awarded. Terminal master's awarded for partial completion of doctoral program. *Degree requirements:* For master's, thesis or alternative, departmental qualifying exam; for doctorate, thesis/ dissertation, comprehensive, departmental qualifying, oral, and written exams. *Entrance requirements:* For master's and doctorate, GRE General Test, GRE Subject Test, 3 letters of recommendation. Additional exam requirements/ recommendations for international students: Required—TOEFL (minimum score 600 paper-based; 79 iBT). *Application deadline:* For fall admission, 3/1 for domestic and international students; for spring admission, 11/1 for domestic students, 9/1 for international students. Application fee: $40 ($90 for international students). Electronic applications accepted. *Expenses:* Tuition, state resident: full-time $4087; part-time $170.30 per credit hour. Tuition, nonresident: full-time $14,875; part-time $619.80 per credit hour. *Required fees:* $2659; $100.25 per credit hour. Tuition and fees vary according to course load and degree level. *Financial support:* In 2011–12, 65 students received support, including 31

research assistantships with partial tuition reimbursements available (averaging $16,598 per year), 30 teaching assistantships with partial tuition reimbursements available (averaging $14,959 per year); health care benefits and unspecified assistantships also available. Financial award applicants required to submit FAFSA. *Faculty research:* Astronomy and astrophysics, condensed matter physics, atomic molecular and optical physics, high energy physics. *Total annual research expenditures:* $4.6 million. *Unit head:* Greg Parker, Chair, 405-325-3961, Fax: 405-325-7557, E-mail: parker@nhn.ou.edu. *Application contact:* Debbie Barnhill, University Student Services Assistant, 405-325-3961 Ext. 36101, Fax: 405-325-7557, E-mail: dbarnhill@ou.edu. Web site: http://www.nhn.ou.edu.

University of Oregon, Graduate School, College of Arts and Sciences, Department of Physics, Eugene, OR 97403. Offers MA, MS, PhD. Terminal master's awarded for partial completion of doctoral program. *Degree requirements:* For doctorate, thesis/dissertation. *Entrance requirements:* For master's and doctorate, GRE General Test, GRE Subject Test, minimum GPA of 3.0. Additional exam requirements/recommendations for international students: Required—TOEFL. *Faculty research:* Solid-state and chemical physics, optical physics, elementary particle physics, astrophysics, atomic and molecular physics.

University of Ottawa, Faculty of Graduate and Postdoctoral Studies, Faculty of Science, Ottawa-Carleton Institute for Physics, Ottawa, ON K1N 6N5, Canada. Offers M Sc, PhD. M Sc, PhD offered jointly with Carleton University. *Degree requirements:* For master's, thesis or alternative; for doctorate, comprehensive exam, thesis/dissertation, seminar. *Entrance requirements:* For master's, honors B Sc degree or equivalent, minimum B average; for doctorate, M Sc, minimum B+ average. Electronic applications accepted. *Faculty research:* Condensed matter physics and statistical physics (CMS), subatomic physics (SAP), medical physics (Med).

University of Pennsylvania, School of Arts and Sciences, Graduate Group in Physics and Astronomy, Philadelphia, PA 19104. Offers medical physics (MS); physics (PhD). Part-time programs available. *Faculty:* 43 full-time (5 women), 17 part-time/adjunct (1 woman). *Students:* 101 full-time (23 women), 1 part-time (0 women); includes 12 minority (11 Asian, non-Hispanic/Latino; 1 Hispanic/Latino), 17 international. 401 applicants, 9% accepted, 11 enrolled. In 2011, 18 master's, 13 doctorates awarded. *Degree requirements:* For doctorate, thesis/dissertation, oral, preliminary, and final exams. *Entrance requirements:* For doctorate, GRE General Test, GRE Subject Test (recommended). Additional exam requirements/ recommendations for international students: Required—TOEFL. *Application deadline:* For fall admission, 12/1 priority date for domestic students. Application fee: $70. Electronic applications accepted. *Expenses:* Tuition: Full-time $26,660; part-time $4944 per course. *Required fees:* $2318; $291 per course. Tuition and fees vary according to course load, degree level and program. *Financial support:* Fellowships, research assistantships, teaching assistantships, institutionally sponsored loans, scholarships/grants, traineeships, health care benefits, and unspecified assistantships available. Financial award application deadline: 12/15. *Faculty research:* Astrophysics, condensed matter experiment, condensed matter theory, particle experiment, particle theory. *Total annual research expenditures:* $7.3 million. *Unit head:* Larry Gladney, Department Chair, 215-898-8152, E-mail: gladney@sas.upenn.edu. *Application contact:* Millicent Minnick, Academic Coordinator, 215-898-3125, E-mail: admiss@physics.upenn.edu.

University of Pittsburgh, Dietrich School of Arts and Sciences, Department of Physics and Astronomy, Pittsburgh, PA 15260. Offers physics (MS, PhD). *Faculty:* 41 full-time (6 women). *Students:* 90 full-time (20 women); includes 1 minority (Asian, non-Hispanic/Latino), 54 international. Average age 25. 336 applicants, 22% accepted, 16 enrolled. In 2011, 14 master's, 9 doctorates awarded. Terminal master's awarded for partial completion of doctoral program. *Degree requirements:* For master's, comprehensive exam, thesis optional; for doctorate, preliminary and comprehensive exams, 2 terms of student teaching, seminar and/or professional talk presentations, annual committee review meeting, oral/written dissertation. *Entrance requirements:* For master's and doctorate, GRE General Test, GRE Subject Test, minimum GPA of 3.0. Additional exam requirements/recommendations for international students: Required—TOEFL (minimum score 577 paper-based; 233 computer-based; 90 iBT) or IELTS (minimum score 6.5). *Application deadline:* For fall admission, 1/31 priority date for domestic students, 1/31 for international students. Applications are processed on a rolling basis. Application fee: $0 ($50 for international students). Electronic applications accepted. *Expenses:* Tuition, state resident: full-time $18,774; part-time $760 per credit. Tuition, nonresident: full-time $30,736; part-time $1258 per credit. *Required fees:* $740; $200 per term. Tuition and fees vary according to program. *Financial support:* In 2011–12, 10 fellowships with full tuition reimbursements (averaging $28,470 per year), 45 research assistantships with full tuition reimbursements (averaging $23,745 per year), 35 teaching assistantships with full tuition reimbursements (averaging $23,745 per year) were awarded; scholarships/grants, health care benefits, tuition waivers, and unspecified assistantships also available. Financial award application deadline: 1/ 31. *Faculty research:* Astrophysics and cosmology, particle and astroparticle physics, condensed matter and solid-state physics, quantum information, biological physics, nanoscience. *Total annual research expenditures:* $6.4 million. *Unit head:* Dr. David Turnshek, Department Chair, 412-624-6381, Fax: 412-624-9163, E-mail: davidt@pitt.edu. *Application contact:* Dr. Andrew R. Zentner, Graduate Admissions Committee Chair, 412-624-9000, Fax: 412-624-9163, E-mail: zentner@pitt.edu. Web site: http://www.physicsandastronomy.pitt.edu/.

University of Puerto Rico, Mayagüez Campus, Graduate Studies, College of Arts and Sciences, Department of Physics, Mayagüez, PR 00681-9000. Offers MS. Part-time programs available. *Students:* 28 full-time (8 women), 1 (woman) part-time; includes 6 minority (all Hispanic/Latino), 23 international. 10 applicants, 60% accepted, 4 enrolled. In 2011, 2 master's awarded. *Degree requirements:* For master's, comprehensive exam, thesis. *Entrance requirements:* For master's, bachelor's degree in physics or its equivalent. *Application deadline:* For fall admission, 2/15 for domestic and international students; for spring admission, 9/15 for domestic and international students. Applications are processed on a rolling basis. Application fee: $25. Tuition and fees vary according to course level and course load. *Financial support:* In 2011–12, 13 students received support, including 13 teaching assistantships (averaging $8,500 per year); Federal Work-Study and institutionally sponsored loans also available. *Faculty research:* Atomic and molecular physics, nuclear physics, nonlinear thermostatics, fluid dynamics, molecular spectroscopy. *Total annual research expenditures:* $1.8 million. *Unit head:* Dr. Dorial Castellanos, Interim Director, 787-265-3844, Fax: 787-832-1135, E-mail: dorial.castellanos@upr.edu. *Application contact:* Vanessa Gonzalez, Secretary, 787-832-4040 Ext. 3073, Fax: 787-832-1135, E-mail: vanessa@uprm.edu. Web site: http://www.uprm.edu/fisica/.

University of Puerto Rico, Río Piedras, College of Natural Sciences, Department of Physics, San Juan, PR 00931-3300. Offers chemical physics (PhD); physics (MS). Part-time programs available. *Degree requirements:* For master's, comprehensive exam, thesis; for doctorate, comprehensive exam, thesis/dissertation. *Entrance requirements:* For master's, GRE General Test, GRE Subject Test, interview, minimum GPA of 3.0, letter of recommendation (3); for doctorate, GRE, master's degree, minimum GPA of 3.0, letter of recommendation (3). Additional exam requirements/recommendations for international students: Required—TOEFL. *Faculty research:* Energy transfer process through Van der Vacqs interactions, study of the photodissociation of ketene.

University of Regina, Faculty of Graduate Studies and Research, Faculty of Science, Department of Physics, Regina, SK S4S 0A2, Canada. Offers M Sc, PhD. *Faculty:* 9 full-time (0 women). *Students:* 7 full-time (2 women). 13 applicants, 23% accepted. In 2011, 1 master's awarded. *Degree requirements:* For master's, thesis; for doctorate, thesis/dissertation. *Entrance requirements:* For master's, honors degree in physics or engineering physics; for doctorate, M Sc or equivalent. Additional exam requirements/recommendations for international students: Required—TOEFL (minimum score 580 paper-based; 80 iBT), IELTS (minimum score 6.5). *Application deadline:* For fall admission, 5/15 for domestic and international students; for winter admission, 8/15 for domestic and international students. Application fee: $100. Electronic applications accepted. *Financial support:* In 2011–12, 2 fellowships (averaging $6,500 per year), 6 teaching assistantships (averaging $2,298 per year) were awarded; research assistantships, career-related internships or fieldwork, and scholarships/grants also available. Financial award application deadline: 6/15. *Faculty research:* Quantum mechanics, theoretical nuclear physics, quantum field theory, relativistic astrophysics and cosmology, classical electrodynamics. *Unit head:* Dr. Neil Ashton, Head, 306-585-4252, Fax: 306-585-5659, E-mail: neil.ashton@uregina.ca. *Application contact:* Dr. Zisis Papandreaou, Graduate Program Coordinator, 306-585-5379, Fax: 306-585-5659, E-mail: grad@phys.uregina.ca. Web site: http://www.phys.uregina.ca.

University of Rhode Island, Graduate School, College of Arts and Sciences, Department of Physics, Kingston, RI 02881. Offers MS, PhD. Part-time and evening/weekend programs available. *Faculty:* 17 full-time (3 women). *Students:* 16 full-time (7 women), 1 part-time (0 women); includes 2 minority (both Asian, non-Hispanic/Latino), 6 international. In 2011, 1 master's awarded. *Degree requirements:* For master's, comprehensive exam (for some programs), thesis optional; for doctorate, comprehensive exam, thesis/dissertation. *Entrance requirements:* For master's and doctorate, 2 letters of recommendation. Additional exam requirements/recommendations for international students: Required—TOEFL (minimum score 550 paper-based; 213 computer-based). *Application deadline:* For fall admission, 4/15 for domestic students, 2/1 for international students. Application fee: $65. Electronic applications accepted. *Expenses:* Tuition, state resident: full-time $10,432; part-time $580 per credit hour. Tuition, nonresident: full-time $23,130; part-time $1285 per credit hour. *Required fees:* $1362; $36 per credit hour. $35 per semester. One-time fee: $130. *Financial support:* In 2011–12, 1 research assistantship (averaging $13,894 per year), 15 teaching assistantships with full and partial tuition reimbursements (averaging $12,811 per year) were awarded. Financial award application deadline: 3/1; financial award applicants required to submit FAFSA. *Total annual research expenditures:* $910,861. *Unit head:* Dr. Jan Northby, Chair, 401-874-2042, Fax: 401-874-2380, E-mail: jnorthby@uri.edu. *Application contact:* Nasser H. Zawia, Dean of the Graduate School, 401-874-5909, Fax: 401-874-5787, E-mail: nzawia@uri.edu. Web site: http://www.uri.edu/index.html.

University of Rochester, School of Arts and Sciences, Department of Physics and Astronomy, Rochester, NY 14627. Offers physics (MA, MS, PhD); physics and astronomy (PhD). Part-time programs available. *Faculty:* 26 full-time (3 women). *Students:* 105 full-time (23 women), 2 part-time (0 women); includes 8 minority (4 Asian, non-Hispanic/Latino; 4 Hispanic/Latino), 43 international. 354 applicants, 15% accepted, 10 enrolled. In 2011, 22 master's, 4 doctorates awarded. Terminal master's awarded for partial completion of doctoral program. *Degree requirements:* For master's, comprehensive exam, thesis (for some

programs); for doctorate, comprehensive exam, thesis/dissertation, qualifying exam. *Entrance requirements:* For master's and doctorate, GRE General Test. Additional exam requirements/recommendations for international students: Required—TOEFL. *Application deadline:* For fall admission, 1/15 priority date for domestic students. Application fee: $0. *Expenses: Tuition:* Full-time $41,040. *Financial support:* Fellowships, research assistantships, teaching assistantships, and tuition waivers (full and partial) available. Financial award application deadline: 2/1. *Faculty research:* Astronomy and astrophysics, biological physics, condensed matter physics, high energy/nuclear physics, quantum optics. *Unit head:* Nicholas P. Bigelow, Chair, 585-275-4344. *Application contact:* Laura Blumkin, Graduate Coordinator, 585-275-4356, E-mail: laurablumkin@pas.rochester.edu. Web site: http://www.pas.rochester.edu/urpas/pages/graduate/gradprograms.

University of Saskatchewan, College of Graduate Studies and Research, College of Arts and Science, Department of Physics and Engineering Physics, Saskatoon, SK S7N 5A2, Canada. Offers M Sc, PhD. *Degree requirements:* For master's, thesis; for doctorate, comprehensive exam (for some programs), thesis/dissertation. *Entrance requirements:* Additional exam requirements/recommendations for international students: Required—TOEFL (minimum score 80 iBT); Recommended—IELTS (minimum score 6.5). Electronic applications accepted.

University of South Carolina, The Graduate School, College of Arts and Sciences, Department of Physics and Astronomy, Columbia, SC 29208. Offers IMA, MAT, MS, PSM, PhD. IMA and MAT offered in cooperation with the College of Education. Part-time programs available. Terminal master's awarded for partial completion of doctoral program. *Degree requirements:* For master's, comprehensive exam, thesis; for doctorate, one foreign language, comprehensive exam, thesis/dissertation. *Entrance requirements:* For master's and doctorate, GRE General Test, GRE Subject Test. Additional exam requirements/recommendations for international students: Required—TOEFL (minimum score 570 paper-based; 230 computer-based; 75 iBT). Electronic applications accepted. *Faculty research:* Condensed matter, intermediate-energy nuclear physics, foundations of quantum mechanics, astronomy/astrophysics.

The University of South Dakota, Graduate School, College of Arts and Sciences, Department of Earth Sciences and Physics, Vermillion, SD 57069-2390. Offers physics (MS, PhD). PhD program offered jointly with South Dakota School of Mines and Technology and South Dakota State University. *Entrance requirements:* For master's and doctorate, GRE. *Expenses:* Tuition, state resident: full-time $3118.50; part-time $173.25 per credit hour. Tuition, nonresident: full-time $6601; part-time $366.70 per credit hour. *Required fees:* $2268; $126 per credit hour. Tuition and fees vary according to program.

University of Southern California, Graduate School, Dana and David Dornsife College of Letters, Arts and Sciences, Department of Physics and Astronomy, Los Angeles, CA 90089. Offers physics (MA, MS, PhD). Part-time programs available. Terminal master's awarded for partial completion of doctoral program. *Degree requirements:* For master's, comprehensive exam, thesis (for some programs); for doctorate, comprehensive exam, thesis/dissertation. *Entrance requirements:* For doctorate, GRE General Test, GRE Subject Test (physics), 3 letters of recommendation, statement of purpose. Additional exam requirements/recommendations for international students: Required—TOEFL (minimum score 550 paper-based; 213 computer-based; 80 iBT). Electronic applications accepted. *Faculty research:* High-energy particle theory, condensed matter physics, astrophysics, solar and cosmology, biophysics, computational physics.

University of Southern Mississippi, Graduate School, College of Science and Technology, Department of Physics and Astronomy, Hattiesburg, MS 39406-0001. Offers computational science (PhD); physics (MS). *Faculty:* 10 full-time (1 woman). *Students:* 11 full-time (1 woman), 3 part-time (1 woman), 7 international. Average age 31. 20 applicants, 60% accepted, 5 enrolled. In 2011, 5 master's, 2 doctorates awarded. *Degree requirements:* For master's, comprehensive exam, thesis; for doctorate, comprehensive exam, thesis/dissertation. *Entrance requirements:* For master's, GRE General Test, minimum GPA of 2.75 in last 60 hours; for doctorate, GRE General Test, minimum GPA of 3.5. Additional exam requirements/recommendations for international students: Required—TOEFL, IELTS. *Application deadline:* For fall admission, 3/1 priority date for domestic students, 3/1 for international students; for spring admission, 1/10 priority date for domestic students, 1/10 for international students. Applications are processed on a rolling basis. Application fee: $50. *Financial support:* In 2011–12, research assistantships with full tuition reimbursements (averaging $11,800 per year), 15 teaching assistantships with full tuition reimbursements (averaging $11,800 per year) were awarded; Federal Work-Study, scholarships/grants, health care benefits, and unspecified assistantships also available. Financial award application deadline: 3/15; financial award applicants required to submit FAFSA. *Faculty research:* Polymers, atomic physics, fluid mechanics, liquid crystals, refractory materials. *Unit head:* Dr. Khin Maung, Chair, 601-266-4934, Fax: 601-266-5149. *Application contact:* Dr. Khin Maung, Chair, 601-266-4934, Fax: 601-266-5149. Web site: http://www.usm.edu/graduateschool/table.php.

University of South Florida, Graduate School, College of Arts and Sciences, Department of Physics, Tampa, FL 33620-9951. Offers applied physics (PhD); physics (MS). Part-time programs available. *Faculty:* 23 full-time (3 women), 10 part-time/adjunct (2 women). *Students:* 74 full-time (12 women), 13 part-time (0 women); includes 9 minority (3 Black or African American, non-Hispanic/Latino; 2

Peterson's Graduate Programs in the Physical Sciences, Mathematics, Agricultural Sciences, the Environment & Natural Resources 2013

facebook.com/petersonspublishing **261**

Physics

Asian, non-Hispanic/Latino; 4 Hispanic/Latino), 35 international. Average age 31. 80 applicants, 46% accepted, 20 enrolled. In 2011, 7 master's, 6 doctorates awarded. *Degree requirements:* For master's, comprehensive exam, thesis optional; for doctorate, comprehensive exam, thesis/dissertation. *Entrance requirements:* For master's and doctorate, GRE, minimum GPA 3.0, three letters of recommendation, statement of purpose. Additional exam requirements/recommendations for international students: Required—TOEFL (minimum score 550 paper-based; 213 computer-based; 79 iBT) or IELTS (minimum score 6.5). *Application deadline:* For fall admission, 2/15 priority date for domestic students, 1/2 for international students; for spring admission, 9/1 for domestic students, 7/1 for international students. Applications are processed on a rolling basis. Application fee: $30. Electronic applications accepted. *Financial support:* In 2011–12, 70 students received support, including 27 research assistantships with tuition reimbursements available (averaging $15,272 per year), 43 teaching assistantships with tuition reimbursements available (averaging $16,267 per year); unspecified assistantships also available. *Faculty research:* Biophysics and biomedical physics, atomic molecular and optical physics, solid state and materials physics, physics education. *Total annual research expenditures:* $2.8 million. *Unit head:* Dr. Pritish Mukherjee, Director of Graduate Studies, 813-974-2871, Fax: 813-974-5813, E-mail: pritish@usf.edu. *Application contact:* Dale Johnson, Program Director, 813-974-5125, Fax: 813-974-5813, E-mail: dejohnso@usf.edu. Web site: http://physics.usf.edu/.

The University of Tennessee, Graduate School, College of Arts and Sciences, Department of Physics and Astronomy, Knoxville, TN 37996. Offers physics (MS, PhD). Part-time programs available. *Degree requirements:* For master's, thesis or alternative; for doctorate, thesis/dissertation. *Entrance requirements:* For master's and doctorate, minimum GPA of 2.7. Additional exam requirements/recommendations for international students: Required—TOEFL. Electronic applications accepted. *Expenses:* Tuition, state resident: full-time $8332; part-time $464 per credit hour. Tuition, nonresident: full-time $25,174; part-time $1400 per credit hour. *Required fees:* $1162; $56 per credit hour. Tuition and fees vary according to program.

The University of Tennessee Space Institute, Graduate Programs, Program in Physics, Tullahoma, TN 37388-9700. Offers MS, PhD. *Faculty:* 4 full-time (1 woman). *Students:* 5 full-time (0 women), 2 part-time (0 women); includes 1 minority (Asian, non-Hispanic/Latino). 6 applicants, 33% accepted, 1 enrolled. In 2011, 1 master's, 1 doctorate awarded. *Degree requirements:* For master's, thesis (for some programs); for doctorate, one foreign language, thesis/dissertation. *Entrance requirements:* For master's and doctorate, GRE General Test, GRE Subject Test. Additional exam requirements/recommendations for international students: Required—TOEFL (minimum score 550 paper-based; 213 computer-based; 80 iBT), IELTS (minimum score 6.5). *Application deadline:* For fall admission, 2/1 for international students; for spring admission, 6/15 for international students. Applications are processed on a rolling basis. Application fee: $35. Electronic applications accepted. *Financial support:* In 2011–12, 1 fellowship, 5 research assistantships with full tuition reimbursements (averaging $17,791 per year) were awarded; career-related internships or fieldwork, Federal Work-Study, institutionally sponsored loans, health care benefits, tuition waivers (full and partial), and unspecified assistantships also available. Financial award applicants required to submit FAFSA. *Unit head:* Dr. Horace Crater, Degree Program Chairman, 931-393-7469, Fax: 931-393-7444, E-mail: hcrater@utsi.edu. *Application contact:* Dee Merriman, Coordinator III, 931-393-7213, Fax: 931-393-7211, E-mail: dmerrima@utsi.edu. Web site: http://www.utsi.edu/academics/physics/.

The University of Texas at Arlington, Graduate School, College of Science, Department of Physics, Arlington, TX 76019-0059. Offers physics (MS); physics and applied physics (PhD). Part-time programs available. *Faculty:* 21 full-time (1 woman), 1 part-time/adjunct (0 women). *Students:* 46 full-time (11 women), 3 part-time (0 women); includes 9 minority (2 Black or African American, non-Hispanic/Latino; 3 Asian, non-Hispanic/Latino; 3 Hispanic/Latino; 1 Two or more races, non-Hispanic/Latino), 27 international. 42 applicants, 14% accepted, 5 enrolled. In 2011, 8 master's, 8 doctorates awarded. Terminal master's awarded for partial completion of doctoral program. *Degree requirements:* For master's, thesis optional; for doctorate, comprehensive exam, thesis/dissertation, internship or substitute. *Entrance requirements:* For master's, GRE General Test, minimum GPA of 3.0 in last 60 hours of course work; for doctorate, GRE General Test, minimum GPA of 3.0 in last 60 hours of course work, 30 hours graduate course work in physics. Additional exam requirements/recommendations for international students: Required—TOEFL (minimum score 550 paper-based; 213 computer-based; 79 iBT). *Application deadline:* For fall admission, 2/1 for domestic students. Applications are processed on a rolling basis. Application fee: $40 ($70 for international students). *Financial support:* In 2011–12, 7 students received support, including 5 fellowships with full tuition reimbursements available (averaging $2,400 per year), 16 research assistantships with partial tuition reimbursements available (averaging $21,000 per year), 21 teaching assistantships with partial tuition reimbursements available (averaging $24,000 per year); career-related internships or fieldwork, Federal Work-Study, institutionally sponsored loans, scholarships/grants, health care benefits, tuition waivers, and unspecified assistantships also available. Support available to part-time students. Financial award application deadline: 2/1. *Faculty research:* Particle physics, astrophysics, condensed matter theory and experiment. *Unit head:* Dr. Alex Weiss, Chair, 817-272-2266, Fax: 817-272-3637, E-mail: weiss@

uta.edu. *Application contact:* Dr. Asok Ray, Graduate Advisor, 817-272-2266, Fax: 817-272-3637, E-mail: akr@uta.edu.

The University of Texas at Austin, Graduate School, College of Natural Sciences, Department of Physics, Austin, TX 78712-1111. Offers MA, MS, PhD. *Degree requirements:* For master's, thesis; for doctorate, thesis/dissertation. *Entrance requirements:* For master's and doctorate, GRE General Test, GRE Subject Test (physics). *Application deadline:* For fall admission, 1/15 for domestic students; for spring admission, 10/1 for domestic students. Application fee: $50 ($75 for international students). Electronic applications accepted. *Financial support:* Fellowships, research assistantships, and teaching assistantships available. Financial award application deadline: 1/15. *Unit head:* Dr. Linda Reichl, Associate Dean, 512-471-7253, E-mail: reichl@physics.utexas.edu. *Application contact:* Dr. Takeshi Udagawa, Graduate Adviser, 512-471-1984, Fax: 512-471-9637, E-mail: udagawa@physics.utexas.edu. Web site: http://www.ph.utexas.edu/.

The University of Texas at Brownsville, Graduate Studies, College of Science, Mathematics and Technology, Brownsville, TX 78520-4991. Offers biological sciences (MS, MSIS); mathematics (MS); physics (MS). Part-time and evening/weekend programs available. *Degree requirements:* For master's, comprehensive exam, thesis optional. *Entrance requirements:* For master's, GRE General Test. Additional exam requirements/recommendations for international students: Required—TOEFL. *Faculty research:* Fish, insects, barrier islands, algae, curlits.

The University of Texas at Dallas, School of Natural Sciences and Mathematics, Department of Physics, Richardson, TX 75080. Offers applied physics (MS); physics (MS, PhD). Part-time and evening/weekend programs available. *Faculty:* 20 full-time (2 women). *Students:* 49 full-time (6 women), 13 part-time (4 women); includes 5 minority (1 Black or African American, non-Hispanic/Latino; 2 Hispanic/Latino; 1 Native Hawaiian or other Pacific Islander, non-Hispanic/Latino; 1 Two or more races, non-Hispanic/Latino), 18 international. Average age 30. 86 applicants, 22% accepted, 16 enrolled. In 2011, 11 master's, 4 doctorates awarded. *Degree requirements:* For master's, thesis optional, industrial internship; for doctorate, thesis/dissertation, publishable paper. *Entrance requirements:* For master's and doctorate, GRE General Test, minimum GPA of 3.0 in upper-level coursework in field. Additional exam requirements/recommendations for international students: Required—TOEFL (minimum score 550 paper-based; 215 computer-based). *Application deadline:* For fall admission, 7/15 for domestic students, 5/1 for international students; for spring admission, 11/15 for domestic students, 9/1 for international students. Applications are processed on a rolling basis. Application fee: $50 ($100 for international students). Electronic applications accepted. *Expenses:* Tuition, state resident: full-time $11,170; part-time $620.56 per credit hour. Tuition, nonresident: full-time $20,212; part-time $1122.89 per credit hour. *Financial support:* In 2011–12, 46 students received support, including 25 research assistantships with partial tuition reimbursements available (averaging $21,616 per year), 20 teaching assistantships with partial tuition reimbursements available (averaging $15,300 per year); career-related internships or fieldwork, Federal Work-Study, institutionally sponsored loans, scholarships/grants, and unspecified assistantships also available. Support available to part-time students. Financial award application deadline: 4/30; financial award applicants required to submit FAFSA. *Faculty research:* Ionospheric and magnetospheric electrodynamics; high-energy proton collisions and muon detector design and construction (CERN Research); condensed matter physics with emphasis on nanoscience; optical properties of solids including semiconductors, thermoelectric materials and nanomaterials; gravitational lensing and applications to cosmology. *Unit head:* Dr. Robert Glosser, Department Head, 972-883-2876, Fax: 972-883-2848, E-mail: physweb@utdallas.edu. *Application contact:* Barbara Burbey, Graduate Advisor, 972-883-2902, Fax: 972-883-2848, E-mail: bburbey@utdallas.edu. Web site: http://www.utdallas.edu/physics/.

The University of Texas at El Paso, Graduate School, College of Science, Department of Physics, El Paso, TX 79968-0001. Offers MS. Part-time and evening/weekend programs available. *Students:* 7 (5 women); includes 2 minority (1 Asian, non-Hispanic/Latino; 1 Hispanic/Latino), 4 international. Average age 34. 8 applicants, 100% accepted, 4 enrolled. In 2011, 2 master's awarded. *Degree requirements:* For master's, thesis optional. *Entrance requirements:* For master's, GRE, minimum GPA of 3.0. Additional exam requirements/recommendations for international students: Required—TOEFL; Recommended—IELTS. *Application deadline:* For fall admission, 8/1 priority date for domestic students, 3/1 for international students; for spring admission, 11/1 priority date for domestic students, 9/1 for international students. Applications are processed on a rolling basis. Application fee: $45 ($80 for international students). Electronic applications accepted. *Financial support:* In 2011–12, research assistantships with partial tuition reimbursements (averaging $20,250 per year), teaching assistantships (averaging $16,200 per year) were awarded; fellowships with partial tuition reimbursements, institutionally sponsored loans, scholarships/grants, health care benefits, tuition waivers (partial), and unspecified assistantships also available. Support available to part-time students. Financial award application deadline: 3/15; financial award applicants required to submit FAFSA. *Unit head:* Dr. Vivian Incera, Chair, 915-747-5715, Fax: 915-747-5447, E-mail: vincera@utep.edu. *Application contact:* Dr. Benjamin Flores, Interim Dean of the Graduate School, 915-747-5491, Fax: 915-747-5788, E-mail: bflores@utep.edu.

262 facebook.com/petersonspublishing

Peterson's Graduate Programs in the Physical Sciences, Mathematics, Agricultural Sciences, the Environment & Natural Resources 2013

The University of Texas at San Antonio, College of Sciences, Department of Physics and Astronomy, San Antonio, TX 78249-0617. Offers physics (MS, PhD). Part-time programs available. *Faculty:* 13 full-time (4 women), 15 part-time/adjunct (2 women). *Students:* 57 full-time (7 women), 11 part-time (3 women); includes 15 minority (1 Black or African American, non-Hispanic/Latino; 3 Asian, non-Hispanic/Latino; 10 Hispanic/Latino; 1 Two or more races, non-Hispanic/Latino), 21 international. Average age 31. 28 applicants, 50% accepted, 14 enrolled. In 2011, 4 master's, 3 doctorates awarded. Terminal master's awarded for partial completion of doctoral program. *Degree requirements:* For master's, comprehensive exam, thesis or alternative; for doctorate, comprehensive exam, thesis/dissertation or alternative. *Entrance requirements:* For master's, GRE, resume, two letters of recommendation, statement of purpose; for doctorate, GRE, minimum GPA of 3.0 on last 60 hours of undergraduate or graduate coursework, resume, two letters of recommendation, statement of purpose. Additional exam requirements/recommendations for international students: Required—TOEFL (minimum score 500 paper-based; 61 iBT), IELTS (minimum score 6.5). *Application deadline:* For fall admission, 7/1 for domestic students, 4/1 for international students; for spring admission, 11/1 for domestic students, 9/1 for international students. Application fee: $45 ($85 for international students). *Expenses:* Tuition, state resident: full-time $3148; part-time $2176 per semester. Tuition, nonresident: full-time $8782; part-time $5932 per semester. *Required fees:* $719 per semester. *Financial support:* In 2011–12, 32 students received support, including 20 fellowships with full and partial tuition reimbursements available (averaging $25,000 per year), 5 research assistantships with full and partial tuition reimbursements available (averaging $27,000 per year), 7 teaching assistantships with full tuition reimbursements available (averaging $27,000 per year); institutionally sponsored loans, scholarships/grants, and unspecified assistantships also available. *Faculty research:* Ultramicroscopy, computational physics, terahertz spectroscopy, space physics, biophysics, nanotechnology materials physics, astrophysics and cosmology, theoretical condensed matter and experimental condensed matter. *Total annual research expenditures:* $1.9 million. *Unit head:* Dr. Miguel Yacaman, Chair, 210-458-5451, Fax: 210-458-4919, E-mail: miguel.yacaman@utsa.edu. *Application contact:* Dr. Lorenzo Brancaleon, Graduate Advisor of Record, 210-458-5694, Fax: 210-458-5694, E-mail: lorenzo.brancaleon@utsa.edu.

The University of Toledo, College of Graduate Studies, College of Natural Sciences and Mathematics, Department of Physics and Astronomy, Toledo, OH 43606-3390. Offers physics (MS, PhD), including astrophysics (PhD), materials science (PhD), medical physics (PhD). *Faculty:* 26. *Students:* 65 full-time (13 women), 3 part-time (0 women); includes 1 minority (Asian, non-Hispanic/Latino), 24 international. Average age 29. 94 applicants, 15% accepted, 13 enrolled. In 2011, 2 master's, 8 doctorates awarded. *Degree requirements:* For master's, thesis; for doctorate, thesis/dissertation, departmental qualifying exam. *Entrance requirements:* For master's and doctorate, GRE General Test, GRE Subject Test, minimum cumulative point-hour ratio of 2.7 for all previous academic work, three letters of recommendation, statement of purpose, transcripts from all prior institutions attended. Additional exam requirements/recommendations for international students: Required—TOEFL (minimum score 550 paper-based; 213 computer-based; 80 iBT), IELTS (minimum score 6.5). *Application deadline:* For fall admission, 1/15 priority date for domestic students, 1/15 for international students. Applications are processed on a rolling basis. Application fee: $45 ($75 for international students). Electronic applications accepted. *Financial support:* In 2011–12, 47 research assistantships with full and partial tuition reimbursements (averaging $17,484 per year), 22 teaching assistantships with full and partial tuition reimbursements (averaging $19,131 per year) were awarded; Federal Work-Study, institutionally sponsored loans, scholarships/grants, tuition waivers (full), and unspecified assistantships also available. Support available to part-time students. *Faculty research:* Atomic physics, solid-state physics, materials science, astrophysics. *Unit head:* Dr. Lawrence Anderson-Huang, Chair, 419-530-7257, E-mail: lawrence.anderson@utoledo.edu. *Application contact:* Graduate School Office, 419-530-4723, Fax: 419-537-4724, E-mail: grdsch@utnet.utoledo.edu. Web site: http://www.utoledo.edu/nsm/.

University of Toronto, School of Graduate Studies, Faculty of Arts and Science, Department of Physics, Toronto, ON M5S 1A1, Canada. Offers M Sc, PhD. *Degree requirements:* For master's, thesis optional; for doctorate, thesis/dissertation. *Entrance requirements:* For master's, minimum B+ average in an honors physics program or equivalent, 2 letters of reference; for doctorate, M Sc in physics or related field, 2 letters of reference. Additional exam requirements/recommendations for international students: Required—TOEFL (minimum score 580 paper-based; 93 iBT), TWE (minimum score 4). Electronic applications accepted.

University of Tulsa, Graduate School, College of Engineering and Natural Sciences, Department of Physics and Engineering Physics, Program in Physics, Tulsa, OK 74104-3189. Offers MS. Part-time programs available. *Faculty:* 7 full-time (0 women). *Students:* 6 full-time (3 women); includes 1 minority (American Indian or Alaska Native, non-Hispanic/Latino), 4 international. Average age 26. 23 applicants, 39% accepted, 6 enrolled. In 2011, 3 master's awarded. *Degree requirements:* For master's, thesis. *Entrance requirements:* For master's, GRE General Test. Additional exam requirements/recommendations for international students: Required—TOEFL (minimum score 550 paper-based; 213 computer-based; 80 iBT), IELTS (minimum score 6). *Application deadline:* Applications are processed on a rolling basis. Application fee: $40. Electronic applications accepted. *Expenses: Tuition:* Full-time $17,748; part-time $986 per hour.

Required fees: $5 per contact hour. $75 per semester. Tuition and fees vary according to program. *Financial support:* In 2011–12, 2 fellowships (averaging $1,125 per year), 5 research assistantships (averaging $10,827 per year), 4 teaching assistantships (averaging $7,807 per year) were awarded; career-related internships or fieldwork, Federal Work-Study, scholarships/grants, health care benefits, tuition waivers, and unspecified assistantships also available. Support available to part-time students. Financial award application deadline: 2/1. *Faculty research:* Nanotechnology, theoretical plasma physics, theoretical and experimental condensed matter, optics, applications of laser spectroscopy to environmental applications. *Total annual research expenditures:* $2 million. *Unit head:* Dr. George Miller, Program Chair, 918-631-3021, Fax: 918-631-2995, E-mail: george-miller@utulsa.edu. *Application contact:* Dr. Scott Holmstrom, Advisor, 918-631-3031, Fax: 918-631-2995, E-mail: scott-holmstrom@utulsa.edu.

University of Utah, Graduate School, College of Science, Department of Physics and Astronomy, Salt Lake City, UT 84112. Offers chemical physics (PhD); medical physics (MS, PhD); physics (MA, MS, PhD); physics teaching (PhD). Part-time programs available. *Faculty:* 38 full-time (3 women), 1 part-time/adjunct (0 women). *Students:* 77 full-time (22 women), 17 part-time (4 women); includes 3 minority (1 Asian, non-Hispanic/Latino; 2 Hispanic/Latino), 50 international. Average age 29. 68 applicants, 72% accepted, 24 enrolled. In 2011, 7 master's, 9 doctorates awarded. Terminal master's awarded for partial completion of doctoral program. *Median time to degree:* Of those who began their doctoral program in fall 2003, 44% received their degree in 8 years or less. *Degree requirements:* For master's, comprehensive exam (for some programs), thesis or alternative, teaching experience, departmental exam; for doctorate, comprehensive exam, thesis/dissertation, departmental qualifying exam. *Entrance requirements:* For master's and doctorate, GRE General Test, GRE Subject Test, minimum GPA of 3.0. Additional exam requirements/recommendations for international students: Required—TOEFL (minimum score 500 paper-based; 173 computer-based; 69 iBT). *Application deadline:* For fall admission, 4/1 priority date for domestic students, 4/1 for international students. Applications are processed on a rolling basis. Application fee: $55 ($65 for international students). Electronic applications accepted. *Financial support:* In 2011–12, 61 teaching assistantships with full and partial tuition reimbursements (averaging $14,626 per year) were awarded; Federal Work-Study, institutionally sponsored loans, and scholarships/grants also available. Financial award application deadline: 2/15; financial award applicants required to submit FAFSA. *Faculty research:* High-energy, cosmic-ray, astrophysics, medical physics, condensed matter, relativity applied physics, biophysics, astronomy. *Total annual research expenditures:* $6.8 million. *Unit head:* Dr. David Kieda, Chair, 801-581-6901, Fax: 801-581-4801, E-mail: kieda@physics.utah.edu. *Application contact:* Jackie Hadley, Graduate Secretary, 801-581-6861, Fax: 801-581-4801, E-mail: jackie@physics.utah.edu. Web site: http://www.physics.utah.edu/.

University of Vermont, Graduate College, College of Arts and Sciences, Department of Physics, Burlington, VT 05405. Offers MS. *Students:* 4 (2 women). 7 applicants, 43% accepted, 1 enrolled. In 2011, 2 master's awarded. *Entrance requirements:* For master's, GRE General Test. Additional exam requirements/recommendations for international students: Required—TOEFL (minimum score 550 paper-based; 213 computer-based; 80 iBT). *Application deadline:* For fall admission, 4/1 priority date for domestic students, 4/1 for international students. Applications are processed on a rolling basis. Application fee: $40. Electronic applications accepted. *Financial support:* Fellowships, research assistantships, and teaching assistantships available. Financial award application deadline: 3/1. *Unit head:* Dr. Dennis Clougherty, Chairperson, 802-656-2644. *Application contact:* Prof. Kevork Spartalian, Coordinator, 802-656-2644.

University of Victoria, Faculty of Graduate Studies, Faculty of Science, Department of Physics and Astronomy, Victoria, BC V8W 2Y2, Canada. Offers astronomy and astrophysics (M Sc, PhD); condensed matter physics (M Sc, PhD); experimental particle physics (M Sc, PhD); medical physics (M Sc, PhD); ocean physics (M Sc, PhD); theoretical physics (M Sc, PhD). *Degree requirements:* For master's, thesis; for doctorate, comprehensive exam, thesis/dissertation, candidacy exam. *Entrance requirements:* For master's and doctorate, GRE. Additional exam requirements/recommendations for international students: Required—TOEFL (minimum score 575 paper-based; 233 computer-based), IELTS (minimum score 7). Electronic applications accepted. *Faculty research:* Old stellar populations; observational cosmology and large scale structure; cp violation; atlas.

University of Virginia, College and Graduate School of Arts and Sciences, Department of Physics, Charlottesville, VA 22903. Offers physics (MA, MS, PhD); physics education (MA). *Faculty:* 32 full-time (4 women). *Students:* 82 full-time (20 women); includes 3 minority (2 Asian, non-Hispanic/Latino; 1 Hispanic/Latino), 59 international. Average age 26. 192 applicants, 31% accepted, 15 enrolled. In 2011, 19 master's, 18 doctorates awarded. *Degree requirements:* For master's, thesis (for some programs); for doctorate, comprehensive exam, thesis/dissertation. *Entrance requirements:* For master's and doctorate, GRE General Test, GRE Subject Test, 2 or more letters of recommendation. Additional exam requirements/recommendations for international students: Required—TOEFL (minimum score 600 paper-based; 250 computer-based; 90 iBT), IELTS. *Application deadline:* For fall admission, 1/7 for domestic and international students. Applications are processed on a rolling basis. Application fee: $60. Electronic applications accepted. *Financial support:* Fellowships, research assistantships, and teaching assistantships available. Financial award applicants

Peterson's Graduate Programs in the Physical Sciences, Mathematics, Agricultural Sciences, the Environment & Natural Resources 2013

facebook.com/petersonspublishing **263**

Physics

required to submit FAFSA. *Unit head:* Joe Poon, Chair, 434-924-3781, Fax: 434-924-4576, E-mail: phys-chair@physics.virginia.edu. *Application contact:* Despina Louca, Associate Chair for Graduate Studies, 434-924-3781, Fax: 434-924-4576, E-mail: grad-info-request@physics.virginia.edu. Web site: http://www.phys.virginia.edu/.

University of Washington, Graduate School, College of Arts and Sciences, Department of Physics, Seattle, WA 98195. Offers MS, PhD. Part-time and evening/weekend programs available. Terminal master's awarded for partial completion of doctoral program. *Degree requirements:* For doctorate, thesis/dissertation. *Entrance requirements:* For master's, GRE; for doctorate, GRE General Test, GRE Subject Test. Additional exam requirements/recommendations for international students: Required—TOEFL. Electronic applications accepted. *Faculty research:* Astro-, atomic, condensed-matter, nuclear, and particle physics; physics education.

University of Waterloo, Graduate Studies, Faculty of Science, Guelph-Waterloo Physics Institute, Waterloo, ON N2L 3G1, Canada. Offers M Sc, PhD. M Sc, PhD offered jointly with University of Guelph. Part-time programs available. *Degree requirements:* For master's, project or thesis; for doctorate, thesis/dissertation. *Entrance requirements:* For master's, GRE Subject Test, honors degree, minimum B average; for doctorate, GRE Subject Test, master's degree, minimum B average. Additional exam requirements/recommendations for international students: Required—TOEFL, TWE. Electronic applications accepted. *Faculty research:* Condensed-matter and materials physics; industrial and applied physics; subatomic physics; astrophysics and gravitation; atomic, molecular, and optical physics.

The University of Western Ontario, Faculty of Graduate Studies, Physical Sciences Division, Department of Applied Mathematics, London, ON N6A 5B8, Canada. Offers applied mathematics (M Sc, PhD); theoretical physics (PhD). *Degree requirements:* For master's, thesis or alternative; for doctorate, comprehensive exam, thesis/dissertation. *Entrance requirements:* For master's and doctorate, minimum B average. Additional exam requirements/recommendations for international students: Required—TOEFL. *Faculty research:* Fluid dynamics, mathematical and computational methods, theoretical physics.

The University of Western Ontario, Faculty of Graduate Studies, Physical Sciences Division, Department of Physics and Astronomy, Program in Physics, London, ON N6A 5B8, Canada. Offers M Sc, PhD. Terminal master's awarded for partial completion of doctoral program. *Degree requirements:* For master's, thesis; for doctorate, comprehensive exam, thesis/dissertation. *Entrance requirements:* For master's, GRE Subject Test (physics), honors B Sc degree, minimum B average (Canadian), A(international); for doctorate, minimum B average (Canadian), A(international). Additional exam requirements/recommendations for international students: Required—TOEFL (minimum score 580 paper-based; 237 computer-based). *Faculty research:* Condensed-matter and surface science, space and atmospheric physics, atomic and molecular physics, medical physics, theoretical physics.

University of Windsor, Faculty of Graduate Studies, Faculty of Science, Department of Physics, Windsor, ON N9B 3P4, Canada. Offers M Sc, PhD. Part-time programs available. *Degree requirements:* For master's, thesis or alternative; for doctorate, thesis/dissertation. *Entrance requirements:* For master's, GRE General Test, minimum B average; for doctorate, GRE General Test, master's degree. Additional exam requirements/recommendations for international students: Required—TOEFL (minimum score 560 paper-based; 220 computer-based). Electronic applications accepted. *Faculty research:* Electrodynamics, plasma physics, atomic structure/particles, spectroscopy, quantum mechanics.

University of Wisconsin–Madison, Graduate School, College of Letters and Science, Department of Physics, Madison, WI 53706-1380. Offers MA, MS, PhD. Terminal master's awarded for partial completion of doctoral program. *Degree requirements:* For master's, qualifying exam, thesis (MS); for doctorate, thesis/dissertation, preliminary and qualifying exams. *Entrance requirements:* For master's and doctorate, GRE, minimum GPA of 3.0. Additional exam requirements/recommendations for international students: Required—TOEFL. Electronic applications accepted. *Expenses:* Tuition, state resident: full-time $10,296; part-time $643.51 per credit. Tuition, nonresident: full-time $24,054; part-time $1503.40 per credit. *Required fees:* $70.06 per credit. Tuition and fees vary according to course load, campus/location, program and reciprocity agreements. *Faculty research:* Atomic, physics, condensed matter, astrophysics, particles and fields.

University of Wisconsin–Milwaukee, Graduate School, College of Letters and Sciences, Department of Physics, Milwaukee, WI 53201-0413. Offers MS, PhD. *Faculty:* 19 full-time (2 women), 1 (woman) part-time/adjunct. *Students:* 35 full-time (12 women), 8 part-time (2 women); includes 2 minority (1 Asian, non-Hispanic/Latino; 1 Two or more races, non-Hispanic/Latino), 23 international. Average age 29. 59 applicants, 32% accepted, 13 enrolled. In 2011, 1 master's, 6 doctorates awarded. *Degree requirements:* For master's, thesis or alternative; for doctorate, one foreign language, thesis/dissertation. *Entrance requirements:* For master's, GRE General Test, curriculum vitae; for doctorate, GRE General Test. Additional exam requirements/recommendations for international students: Required—TOEFL (minimum score 550 paper-based; 79 iBT), IELTS (minimum score 6.5). *Application deadline:* For fall admission, 1/1 priority date for domestic

students; for spring admission, 9/1 for domestic students. Applications are processed on a rolling basis. Application fee: $56 ($96 for international students). Electronic applications accepted. One-time fee: $506.10 full-time. Tuition and fees vary according to course load and reciprocity agreements. *Financial support:* In 2011–12, 1 fellowship, 14 research assistantships, 20 teaching assistantships were awarded; career-related internships or fieldwork and unspecified assistantships also available. Support available to part-time students. Financial award application deadline: 4/15; financial award applicants required to submit FAFSA. *Faculty research:* Gravitation, biophysics, condensed matter, optics, medical. *Total annual research expenditures:* $6.4 million. *Unit head:* Alan Wiseman, Department Chair, 414-229-4079, E-mail: agw@uwm.edu. *Application contact:* General Information Contact, 414-229-4982, Fax: 414-229-6967, E-mail: gradschool@uwm.edu. Web site: http://www.uwm.edu/dept/physics/.

Utah State University, School of Graduate Studies, College of Science, Department of Physics, Logan, UT 84322. Offers MS, PhD. Part-time programs available. Terminal master's awarded for partial completion of doctoral program. *Degree requirements:* For master's, thesis; for doctorate, comprehensive exam, thesis/dissertation. *Entrance requirements:* For master's and doctorate, GRE General Test, minimum GPA of 3.0. Additional exam requirements/recommendations for international students: Required—TOEFL (minimum score 550 paper-based; 213 computer-based). Electronic applications accepted. *Faculty research:* Upper-atmosphere physics, relativity, gravitational magnetism, particle physics, nanotechnology.

Vanderbilt University, Graduate School, Department of Physics and Astronomy, Nashville, TN 37240-1001. Offers astronomy (MS); physics (MA, MAT, MS, PhD). *Faculty:* 34 full-time (4 women), 2 part-time/adjunct (0 women). *Students:* 78 full-time (20 women), 3 part-time (0 women); includes 13 minority (6 Black or African American, non-Hispanic/Latino; 1 Asian, non-Hispanic/Latino; 4 Hispanic/Latino; 2 Two or more races, non-Hispanic/Latino), 22 international. Average age 28. 171 applicants, 25% accepted, 15 enrolled. In 2011, 8 master's, 4 doctorates awarded. *Degree requirements:* For master's, thesis; for doctorate, comprehensive exam, thesis/dissertation, final and qualifying exams. *Entrance requirements:* For master's, GRE General Test; for doctorate, GRE General Test, GRE Subject Test. Additional exam requirements/recommendations for international students: Required—TOEFL (minimum score 570 paper-based; 230 computer-based; 88 iBT). *Application deadline:* For fall admission, 1/15 for domestic and international students. Application fee: $0. Electronic applications accepted. *Financial support:* Fellowships with full and partial tuition reimbursements, research assistantships with full tuition reimbursements, teaching assistantships with full tuition reimbursements, career-related internships or fieldwork, Federal Work-Study, and institutionally sponsored loans available. Financial award application deadline: 1/15; financial award applicants required to submit CSS PROFILE or FAFSA. *Faculty research:* Experimental and theoretical physics, free electron laser, living-state physics, heavy-ion physics, nuclear structure. *Unit head:* Dr. Robert J. Scherrer, Chair, 615-322-2828, Fax: 615-343-7263, E-mail: robert.scherrer@vanderbilt.edu. *Application contact:* Dr. Julia Velkovska, Director of Graduate Studies, 615-322-0656, Fax: 615-343-7263, E-mail: julia.velkovska@vanderbilt.edu. Web site: http://www.vanderbilt.edu/physics/.

Virginia Commonwealth University, Graduate School, College of Humanities and Sciences, Department of Physics, Program in Physics and Applied Physics, Richmond, VA 23284-9005. Offers MS. *Students:* 15 full-time (5 women); includes 1 minority (Hispanic/Latino), 3 international. 13 applicants, 77% accepted, 8 enrolled. In 2011, 5 master's awarded. *Entrance requirements:* For master's, GRE. Additional exam requirements/recommendations for international students: Required—TOEFL (minimum score 600 paper-based; 250 computer-based; 100 iBT); Recommended—IELTS (minimum score 6.5). *Application deadline:* For fall admission, 8/1 for domestic students; for spring admission, 12/1 for domestic students. Applications are processed on a rolling basis. Application fee: $50. Electronic applications accepted. *Expenses:* Tuition, state resident: full-time $9133; part-time $507 per credit. Tuition, nonresident: full-time $18,777; part-time $1043 per credit. *Required fees:* $77 per credit. Tuition and fees vary according to degree level, campus/location, program and student level. *Financial support:* Federal Work-Study and institutionally sponsored loans available. Support available to part-time students. *Faculty research:* Theoretical and experimental condensed matter physics, general relativity and cosmology, physics education. *Unit head:* Dr. Alison A. Baski, Chair, 804-828-1821, Fax: 804-828-7073, E-mail: aabaski@vcu.edu. *Application contact:* Dr. Shiv N. Khanna, Graduate Program Director, 804-828-1820, Fax: 804-828-7073, E-mail: snkhanna@vcu.edu.

Virginia Polytechnic Institute and State University, Graduate School, College of Science, Department of Physics, Blacksburg, VA 24061. Offers MS, PhD. *Degree requirements:* For master's, comprehensive exam (for some programs), thesis (for some programs); for doctorate, comprehensive exam (for some programs), thesis/dissertation (for some programs). *Entrance requirements:* For master's and doctorate, GRE. Additional exam requirements/recommendations for international students: Required—TOEFL (minimum score 550 paper-based; 213 computer-based). *Application deadline:* For fall admission, 7/1 for domestic and international students; for spring admission, 12/1 for domestic and international students. Applications are processed on a rolling basis. Application fee: $65. Electronic applications accepted. *Expenses:* Tuition, state resident: full-time $10,048; part-time $558.25 per credit hour. Tuition, nonresident: full-time $19,497; part-time $1083.25 per credit hour. *Required fees:* $405 per semester.

264 facebook.com/petersonspublishing

Peterson's Graduate Programs in the Physical Sciences, Mathematics, Agricultural Sciences, the Environment & Natural Resources 2013

Tuition and fees vary according to course load, campus/location and program. *Financial support:* Research assistantships with full tuition reimbursements, teaching assistantships with full tuition reimbursements, career-related internships or fieldwork, Federal Work-Study, scholarships/grants, health care benefits, and unspecified assistantships available. Financial award application deadline: 1/15. *Faculty research:* Condensed matter, particle physics, theoretical and experimental astrophysics, biophysics, mathematical physics. *Unit head:* Dr. Beate Schmittmann, Unit Head, 540-231-5767, Fax: 540-231-7511, E-mail: physics.chair@vt.edu. *Application contact:* Uwe Tauber, Information Contact, 540-231-8998, Fax: 540-231-7511, E-mail: tauber@vt.edu. Web site: http://www.phys.vt.edu/students/grads.shtml.

Virginia State University, School of Graduate Studies, Research, and Outreach, School of Engineering, Science and Technology, Department of Chemistry and Physics, Petersburg, VA 23806-0001. Offers physics (MS). *Degree requirements:* For master's, one foreign language, thesis. *Entrance requirements:* For master's, GRE General Test.

Wake Forest University, Graduate School of Arts and Sciences, Department of Physics, Winston-Salem, NC 27109. Offers MS, PhD. Part-time programs available. *Degree requirements:* For master's, thesis; for doctorate, comprehensive exam, thesis/dissertation. *Entrance requirements:* For master's and doctorate, GRE General Test. Additional exam requirements/recommendations for international students: Required—TOEFL (minimum score 213 computer-based; 79 iBT). Electronic applications accepted.

Washington State University, Graduate School, College of Sciences, Department of Physics and Astronomy, Pullman, WA 99164. Offers physics (MS, PhD). *Faculty:* 20. *Students:* 77 full-time (18 women), 5 part-time (0 women); includes 2 minority (1 Hispanic/Latino; 1 Two or more races, non-Hispanic/Latino), 45 international. Average age 29. 100 applicants, 12% accepted, 9 enrolled. In 2011, 6 master's, 6 doctorates awarded. Terminal master's awarded for partial completion of doctoral program. *Degree requirements:* For master's, comprehensive exam (for some programs), thesis (for some programs), oral exam; for doctorate, comprehensive exam, thesis/dissertation, oral exam, written exam. *Entrance requirements:* For master's and doctorate, GRE General Test, GRE Subject Test, minimum GPA of 3.0 in last half of undergraduate work completed. Additional exam requirements/recommendations for international students: Required—TOEFL (minimum score 550 paper-based; 214 computer-based; 80 iBT), IELTS. *Application deadline:* For fall admission, 1/10 priority date for domestic students, 1/10 for international students; for spring admission, 7/1 priority date for domestic students, 7/1 for international students. Applications are processed on a rolling basis. Application fee: $75. Electronic applications accepted. *Financial support:* In 2011–12, 41 students received support, including 1 fellowship with full and partial tuition reimbursement available (averaging $5,000 per year), 15 research assistantships with full and partial tuition reimbursements available (averaging $13,917 per year), 25 teaching assistantships with full and partial tuition reimbursements available (averaging $13,056 per year); Federal Work-Study and institutionally sponsored loans also available. Financial award application deadline: 3/1; financial award applicants required to submit FAFSA. *Faculty research:* Linear and nonlinear acoustics and optics, shock wave dynamics, solid-state physics, surface physics, high-pressure and semiconductor physics. *Total annual research expenditures:* $2.5 million. *Unit head:* Steve L. Tomsovic, Chair, 509-335-7207, Fax: 509-335-7816, E-mail: tomsovic@wsu.edu. *Application contact:* Graduate School Admissions, 800-GRADWSU, Fax: 509-335-1949, E-mail: gradsch@wsu.edu. Web site: http://www.physics.wsu.edu/.

Washington University in St. Louis, Graduate School of Arts and Sciences, Department of Physics, St. Louis, MO 63130-4899. Offers PhD. Terminal master's awarded for partial completion of doctoral program. *Degree requirements:* For doctorate, thesis/dissertation. *Entrance requirements:* For doctorate, GRE General Test. Electronic applications accepted.

Wayne State University, College of Liberal Arts and Sciences, Department of Physics and Astronomy, Detroit, MI 48202. Offers physics (MA, MS, PhD). *Students:* 57 full-time (15 women), 4 part-time (1 woman); includes 6 minority (2 Black or African American, non-Hispanic/Latino; 1 American Indian or Alaska Native, non-Hispanic/Latino; 2 Asian, non-Hispanic/Latino; 1 Hispanic/Latino), 35 international. Average age 29. 78 applicants, 22% accepted, 14 enrolled. In 2011, 9 master's, 10 doctorates awarded. *Degree requirements:* For master's, thesis (for some programs); for doctorate, thesis/dissertation. *Entrance requirements:* For master's, GRE, 3 letters of recommendation; for doctorate, GRE, 3 letters of recommendation; personal statement. Additional exam requirements/recommendations for international students: Required—TOEFL (minimum score 550 paper-based; 213 computer-based); Recommended—TWE (minimum score 5.5). *Application deadline:* For fall admission, 6/1 priority date for domestic students, 5/1 for international students; for winter admission, 10/1 priority date for domestic students, 9/1 for international students; for spring admission, 2/1 priority date for domestic students, 1/1 for international students. Applications are processed on a rolling basis. Application fee: $50. Electronic applications accepted. *Expenses:* Tuition, state resident: part-time $512.85 per credit. Tuition, nonresident: part-time $1132.65 per credit. *Required fees:* $26.60 per credit. $199.65 per semester. Tuition and fees vary according to course load and program. *Financial support:* In 2011–12, 47 students received support, including 5 fellowships with tuition reimbursements available (averaging $18,700 per year), 25 research assistantships with tuition reimbursements available (averaging

$17,742 per year), 24 teaching assistantships with tuition reimbursements available (averaging $17,391 per year); Federal Work-Study, scholarships/grants, health care benefits, and unspecified assistantships also available. Financial award application deadline: 1/15. *Faculty research:* High energy particle physics, relativistic heavy ion physics, theoretical physics, positron and atomic physics, condensed matter and nano-scale physics. *Total annual research expenditures:* $4.9 million. *Unit head:* Dr. Ratna Naik, Chair, 313-577-2721, Fax: 313-577-3932, E-mail: naik@physics.wayne.edu. *Application contact:* Ashis Mukhopadhay, Chair of the Physics Graduate Admissions Committee, 313-577-2775, Fax: 313-577-3932, E-mail: gradadm@physics.wayne.edu. Web site: http://physics.clas.wayne.edu/.

Wesleyan University, Graduate Programs, Department of Physics, Middletown, CT 06459. Offers MA, PhD. Terminal master's awarded for partial completion of doctoral program. *Degree requirements:* For master's, thesis; for doctorate, thesis/dissertation. *Entrance requirements:* For master's, GRE General Test, GRE Subject Test; for doctorate, GRE Subject Test. Additional exam requirements/recommendations for international students: Required—TOEFL. Electronic applications accepted. *Faculty research:* Biophysics, computational soft matter physics, mesoscopic transport, semiclassical methods and quantum chaos, disordered systems, theoretical atomic physics, low-temperature physics, magnetic resonance, atomic collisions, laser spectroscopy, surface physics, turbulence, granular media.

Western Illinois University, School of Graduate Studies, College of Arts and Sciences, Department of Physics, Macomb, IL 61455-1390. Offers MS. Part-time programs available. *Students:* 16 full-time (1 woman); includes 1 minority (Asian, non-Hispanic/Latino), 12 international. Average age 30. 8 applicants, 88% accepted. In 2011, 10 master's awarded. *Degree requirements:* For master's, thesis or alternative. *Entrance requirements:* Additional exam requirements/recommendations for international students: Required—TOEFL (minimum score 550 paper-based; 213 computer-based; 80 iBT). *Application deadline:* Applications are processed on a rolling basis. Application fee: $30. Electronic applications accepted. *Expenses:* Tuition, state resident: part-time $281.16 per credit hour. Tuition, nonresident: part-time $562.32 per credit hour. Part-time tuition and fees vary according to campus/location and reciprocity agreements. *Financial support:* In 2011–12, 9 students received support, including 9 research assistantships with full tuition reimbursements available (averaging $7,360 per year); health care benefits also available. Financial award applicants required to submit FAFSA. *Unit head:* Dr. Mark Boley, Interim Chairperson, 309-298-1538. *Application contact:* Nancy Parsons, Interim Associate Provost and Director of Graduate Studies, 309-298-1806, Fax: 309-298-2345, E-mail: grad-office@wiu.edu. Web site: http://wiu.edu/physics.

Western Kentucky University, Graduate Studies, Ogden College of Science and Engineering, Department of Physics and Astronomy, Bowling Green, KY 42101. Offers homeland security sciences (MS); physics (MA Ed).

Western Michigan University, Graduate College, College of Arts and Sciences, Department of Physics, Kalamazoo, MI 49008. Offers MA, PhD. *Degree requirements:* For master's, thesis; for doctorate, thesis/dissertation, oral exam. *Entrance requirements:* For doctorate, GRE General Test.

Western Michigan University, Graduate College, College of Arts and Sciences, Mallinson Institute for Science Education, Kalamazoo, MI 49008. Offers science education (MA, PhD); science education: biological sciences (PhD); science education: chemistry (PhD); science education: geosciences (PhD); science education: physical geography (PhD); science education: physics (PhD). *Degree requirements:* For doctorate, thesis/dissertation, oral and written exams. *Entrance requirements:* For master's, undergraduate degree in a science or science education, teacher certification (or appropriate education courses); for doctorate, GRE General Test, master's degree in a science or science education. Additional exam requirements/recommendations for international students: Recommended—TOEFL. Electronic applications accepted. *Faculty research:* History and philosophy of science, curriculum and instruction, science content learning, college science teaching and learning, social and cultural factors in science education.

West Virginia University, Eberly College of Arts and Sciences, Department of Physics, Morgantown, WV 26506. Offers applied physics (MS, PhD); astrophysics (MS, PhD); chemical physics (MS, PhD); condensed matter physics (MS, PhD); elementary particle physics (MS, PhD); materials physics (MS, PhD); plasma physics (MS, PhD); solid state physics (MS, PhD); statistical physics (MS, PhD); theoretical physics (MS, PhD). Terminal master's awarded for partial completion of doctoral program. *Degree requirements:* For master's, thesis or alternative, qualifying exam; for doctorate, thesis/dissertation, qualifying exam. *Entrance requirements:* For master's and doctorate, GRE General Test, minimum GPA of 3.0. Additional exam requirements/recommendations for international students: Required—TOEFL. *Faculty research:* Experimental and theoretical condensed-matter, plasma, high-energy theory, nonlinear dynamics, space physics.

Worcester Polytechnic Institute, Graduate Studies and Research, Department of Physics, Worcester, MA 01609-2280. Offers MS, PhD. *Faculty:* 9 full-time (2 women). *Students:* 11 full-time (3 women), 6 part-time (1 woman); includes 1 minority (Black or African American, non-Hispanic/Latino), 6 international. 42 applicants, 19% accepted, 6 enrolled. In 2011, 1 master's, 2 doctorates awarded. *Degree requirements:* For master's, thesis; for doctorate, comprehensive exam,

Peterson's Graduate Programs in the Physical Sciences, Mathematics, Agricultural Sciences, the Environment & Natural Resources 2013

facebook.com/petersonspublishing **265**

thesis/dissertation. *Entrance requirements:* For master's, GRE (recommended), 3 letters of recommendation; for doctorate, GRE (recommended), 3 letters of recommendation, statement of purpose (recommended). Additional exam requirements/recommendations for international students: Required—TOEFL (minimum score 563 paper-based; 223 computer-based; 84 iBT), IELTS (minimum score 7). *Application deadline:* For fall admission, 1/1 priority date for domestic students, 1/1 for international students; for spring admission, 10/1 priority date for domestic students, 10/1 for international students. Applications are processed on a rolling basis. Application fee: $70. Electronic applications accepted. *Financial support:* Research assistantships, teaching assistantships, career-related internships or fieldwork, institutionally sponsored loans, scholarships/grants, and unspecified assistantships available. Financial award application deadline: 1/1; financial award applicants required to submit FAFSA. *Faculty research:* Soft-condensed matter, complex fluids, bioand medicalphysics, quantum and atom optics, wave function engineering. *Unit head:* Dr. Germano S. Iannacchione, Head, 508-831-5258, Fax: 508-831-5886, E-mail: gsiannac@wpi.edu. *Application contact:* Dr. L. R. Ram-Mohan, Graduate Coordinator, 508-831-5258, Fax: 508-831-5886, E-mail: lrram@wpi.edu. Web site: http://www.wpi.edu/Academics/Depts/Physics/.

Wright State University, School of Graduate Studies, College of Science and Mathematics, Department of Physics, Program in Physics, Dayton, OH 45435. Offers geophysics (MS); medical physics (MS). Part-time and evening/weekend programs available. *Degree requirements:* For master's, thesis. *Entrance requirements:* Additional exam requirements/recommendations for international students: Required—TOEFL. *Faculty research:* Solid-state physics, optics, geophysics.

Yale University, Graduate School of Arts and Sciences, Department of Physics, New Haven, CT 06520. Offers PhD. *Degree requirements:* For doctorate, thesis/dissertation. *Entrance requirements:* For doctorate, GRE General Test, GRE Subject Test.

York University, Faculty of Graduate Studies, Faculty of Science and Engineering, Program in Physics and Astronomy, Toronto, ON M3J 1P3, Canada. Offers M Sc, PhD. Part-time and evening/weekend programs available. *Degree requirements:* For master's, thesis or alternative; for doctorate, comprehensive exam, thesis/dissertation. Electronic applications accepted.

Plasma Physics

Princeton University, Graduate School, Department of Astrophysical Sciences, Program in Plasma Physics, Princeton, NJ 08544-1019. Offers PhD. *Degree requirements:* For doctorate, thesis/dissertation. *Entrance requirements:* For doctorate, GRE General Test, GRE Subject Test. Additional exam requirements/recommendations for international students: Required—TOEFL (minimum score 600 paper-based; 250 computer-based). *Faculty research:* Magnetic fusion energy research, plasma physics, x-ray laser studies.

University of Colorado Boulder, Graduate School, College of Arts and Sciences, Department of Astrophysical and Planetary Sciences, Boulder, CO 80309. Offers astrophysics (MS, PhD); planetary science (MS, PhD). *Faculty:* 22 full-time (3 women). *Students:* 52 full-time (15 women), 2 part-time (1 woman); includes 4 minority (1 Black or African American, non-Hispanic/Latino; 1 American Indian or Alaska Native, non-Hispanic/Latino; 2 Asian, non-Hispanic/Latino), 7 international. Average age 26. 185 applicants, 18% accepted, 14 enrolled. In 2011, 5 master's, 7 doctorates awarded. Terminal master's awarded for partial completion of doctoral program. *Degree requirements:* For master's, comprehensive exam, thesis or alternative; for doctorate, one foreign language, thesis/dissertation. *Entrance requirements:* For master's, GRE General Test, GRE Subject Test, minimum undergraduate GPA of 3.0; for doctorate, GRE General Test, GRE Subject Test. *Application deadline:* For fall admission, 1/15 priority date for domestic students, 12/1 for international students. Applications are processed on a rolling basis. Application fee: $50 ($60 for international students). Electronic applications accepted. *Financial support:* In 2011–12, 55

students received support, including 34 fellowships (averaging $12,309 per year), 27 research assistantships with full and partial tuition reimbursements available (averaging $25,858 per year), 8 teaching assistantships with full and partial tuition reimbursements available (averaging $22,262 per year); institutionally sponsored loans, scholarships/grants, health care benefits, and unspecified assistantships also available. Financial award application deadline: 1/15; financial award applicants required to submit FAFSA. *Faculty research:* Stellar and extragalactic astrophysics cosmology, space astronomy, planetary science. *Total annual research expenditures:* $41.3 million. *Application contact:* E-mail: apsgradsec@colorado.edu. Web site: http://aps.colorado.edu/.

West Virginia University, Eberly College of Arts and Sciences, Department of Physics, Morgantown, WV 26506. Offers applied physics (MS, PhD); astrophysics (MS, PhD); chemical physics (MS, PhD); condensed matter physics (MS, PhD); elementary particle physics (MS, PhD); materials physics (MS, PhD); plasma physics (MS, PhD); solid state physics (MS, PhD); statistical physics (MS, PhD); theoretical physics (MS, PhD). Terminal master's awarded for partial completion of doctoral program. *Degree requirements:* For master's, thesis or alternative, qualifying exam; for doctorate, thesis/dissertation, qualifying exam. *Entrance requirements:* For master's and doctorate, GRE General Test, minimum GPA of 3.0. Additional exam requirements/recommendations for international students: Required—TOEFL. *Faculty research:* Experimental and theoretical condensed-matter, plasma, high-energy theory, nonlinear dynamics, space physics.

Theoretical Physics

Cornell University, Graduate School, Graduate Fields of Arts and Sciences, Field of Physics, Ithaca, NY 14853-0001. Offers experimental physics (MS, PhD); physics (MS, PhD); theoretical physics (MS, PhD). *Faculty:* 55 full-time (5 women). *Students:* 159 full-time (29 women); includes 11 minority (1 Black or African American, non-Hispanic/Latino; 5 Asian, non-Hispanic/Latino; 4 Hispanic/Latino; 1 Two or more races, non-Hispanic/Latino), 70 international. Average age 26. 455 applicants, 22% accepted, 36 enrolled. In 2011, 29 master's, 24 doctorates awarded. *Degree requirements:* For doctorate, comprehensive exam, thesis/dissertation. *Entrance requirements:* For doctorate, GRE General Test, GRE Subject Test (physics), 3 letters of recommendation. Additional exam requirements/recommendations for international students: Required—TOEFL (minimum score 620 paper-based; 260 computer-based; 105 iBT). *Application deadline:* For fall admission, 1/3 for domestic students. Application fee: $95. Electronic applications accepted. *Financial support:* In 2011–12, 18 fellowships with full tuition reimbursements, 78 research assistantships with full tuition reimbursements, 50 teaching assistantships with full tuition reimbursements were awarded; institutionally sponsored loans, scholarships/grants, health care benefits, tuition waivers (full and partial), and unspecified assistantships also available. Financial award applicants required to submit FAFSA. *Faculty research:* Experimental condensed matter physics, theoretical condensed matter physics, experimental high energy particle physics, theoretical particle physics and field theory, theoretical astrophysics. *Unit head:* Director of Graduate Studies, 607-255-7561. *Application contact:* Graduate Field Assistant, 607-255-7561, E-mail: physics-grad-adm@cornell.edu. Web site: http://www.gradschool.cornell.edu/fields.php?id-36&a-2.

Delaware State University, Graduate Programs, Department of Mathematics, Interdisciplinary Program in Applied Mathematics and Theoretical Physics, Dover, DE 19901-2277. Offers PhD. *Degree requirements:* For doctorate, one foreign language, thesis defense. *Entrance requirements:* For doctorate, GRE General Test, MS degree in physics or mathematics. Additional exam requirements/recommendations for international students: Required—TOEFL (minimum score 550 paper-based).

Emory University, Laney Graduate School, Department of Physics, Atlanta, GA 30322-1100. Offers biophysics (PhD); experimental condensed matter physics (PhD); theoretical and computational statistical physics (PhD); MS/PhD. *Faculty:* 19 full-time (2 women). *Students:* 17 full-time (4 women); includes 2 minority (1 Black or African American, non-Hispanic/Latino; 1 Hispanic/Latino), 13 international. Average age 24. 48 applicants, 27% accepted, 10 enrolled. *Degree requirements:* For doctorate, thesis/dissertation, qualifier proposal. *Entrance requirements:* For doctorate, GRE General Test, minimum GPA of 3.0. Additional exam requirements/recommendations for international students: Required—TOEFL (minimum score 600 paper-based). *Application deadline:* For fall admission, 1/3 priority date for domestic students, 1/3 for international students. Application fee: $50. Electronic applications accepted. *Expenses: Tuition:* Full-time $34,800. *Required fees:* $1300. *Financial support:* In 2011–12, 17 students received support. Fellowships, teaching assistantships, institutionally sponsored loans, scholarships/grants, health care benefits, and tuition waivers (full) available. Financial award application deadline: 1/3; financial award applicants required to submit FAFSA. *Faculty research:* Experimental studies of the structure and function of metalloproteins, soft condensed matter, granular materials,

266 facebook.com/petersonspublishing

Peterson's Graduate Programs in the Physical Sciences, Mathematics, Agricultural Sciences, the Environment & Natural Resources 2013

biophotonics and fluorescence correlation spectroscopy, single molecule studies of DNA-protein systems. *Total annual research expenditures:* $1.5 million. *Unit head:* Kurt Warncke, Chair, 404-727-4296, Fax: 404-727-0873, E-mail: kwarncke@physics.emory.edu. *Application contact:* Stefan Boettcher, Director of Graduate Studies, 404-727-4298, Fax: 404-727-0873, E-mail: sboettc@emory.edu. Web site: http://www.physics.emory.edu.

Harvard University, Graduate School of Arts and Sciences, Department of Physics, Cambridge, MA 02138. Offers experimental physics (PhD); medical engineering/medical physics (PhD), including applied physics, engineering sciences, physics; theoretical physics (PhD). *Degree requirements:* For doctorate, thesis/dissertation, final exams, laboratory experience. *Entrance requirements:* For doctorate, GRE General Test, GRE Subject Test. Additional exam requirements/recommendations for international students: Required—TOEFL. *Expenses: Tuition:* Full-time $36,304. *Required fees:* $1186. Full-time tuition and fees vary according to program. *Faculty research:* Particle physics, condensed matter physics, atomic physics.

Rutgers, The State University of New Jersey, New Brunswick, Graduate School-New Brunswick, Department of Physics and Astronomy, Piscataway, NJ 08854-8097. Offers astronomy (MS, PhD); biophysics (PhD); condensed matter physics (MS, PhD); elementary particle physics (MS, PhD); intermediate energy nuclear physics (MS); nuclear physics (MS, PhD); physics (MST); surface science (PhD); theoretical physics (MS, PhD). Part-time programs available. Terminal master's awarded for partial completion of doctoral program. *Degree requirements:* For master's, comprehensive exam, thesis or alternative; for doctorate, comprehensive exam, thesis/dissertation. *Entrance requirements:* For master's and doctorate, GRE General Test, GRE Subject Test. Additional exam requirements/recommendations for international students: Required—TOEFL (minimum score 560 paper-based). Electronic applications accepted. *Faculty research:* Astronomy, high energy, condensed matter, surface, nuclear physics.

The University of Manchester, School of Physics and Astronomy, Manchester, United Kingdom. Offers astronomy and astrophysics (M Sc, PhD); biological physics (M Sc, PhD); condensed matter physics (M Sc, PhD); nonlinear and liquid crystals physics (M Sc, PhD); nuclear physics (M Sc, PhD); particle physics (M Sc, PhD); photon physics (M Sc, PhD); physics (M Sc, PhD); theoretical physics (M Sc, PhD).

University of Victoria, Faculty of Graduate Studies, Faculty of Science, Department of Physics and Astronomy, Victoria, BC V8W 2Y2, Canada. Offers astronomy and astrophysics (M Sc, PhD); condensed matter physics (M Sc, PhD); experimental particle physics (M Sc, PhD); medical physics (M Sc, PhD); ocean physics (M Sc, PhD); theoretical physics (M Sc, PhD). *Degree requirements:* For doctorate, thesis; for doctorate, comprehensive exam, thesis/dissertation, candidacy exam. *Entrance requirements:* For master's and doctorate, GRE. Additional exam requirements/recommendations for international students: Required—TOEFL (minimum score 575 paper-based; 233 computer-based), IELTS (minimum score 7). Electronic applications accepted. *Faculty research:* Old stellar populations; observational cosmology and large scale structure; cp violation; atlas.

West Virginia University, Eberly College of Arts and Sciences, Department of Physics, Morgantown, WV 26506. Offers applied physics (MS, PhD); astrophysics (MS, PhD); chemical physics (MS, PhD); condensed matter physics (MS, PhD); elementary particle physics (MS, PhD); materials physics (MS, PhD); plasma physics (MS, PhD); solid state physics (MS, PhD); statistical physics (MS, PhD); theoretical physics (MS, PhD). Terminal master's awarded for partial completion of doctoral program. *Degree requirements:* For master's, thesis or alternative, qualifying exam; for doctorate, thesis/dissertation, qualifying exam. *Entrance requirements:* For master's and doctorate, GRE General Test, minimum GPA of 3.0. Additional exam requirements/recommendations for international students: Required—TOEFL. *Faculty research:* Experimental and theoretical condensed-matter, plasma, high-energy theory, nonlinear dynamics, space physics.

Peterson's Graduate Programs in the Physical Sciences, Mathematics, Agricultural Sciences, the Environment & Natural Resources 2013

facebook.com/petersonspublishing **267**

COLUMBIA UNIVERSITY
Department of Applied Physics and Applied Mathematics

Programs of Study

The Department of Applied Physics and Applied Mathematics offers graduate study leading to the degrees of Master of Science (M.S.), Doctor of Engineering Science (Eng.Sc.D.), and Doctor of Philosophy (Ph.D.).

The following fields of research (topics of emphasis in parentheses) are available for doctoral study: theoretical and experimental plasma physics (fusion and space plasmas), applied mathematics (analysis of partial differential equations, large-scale scientific computing, nonlinear dynamics, inverse problems, medical imaging, geophysical/geological fluid dynamics, and biomathematics), solid-state physics (semiconductor, surface, low-dimensional physics, and molecular electronics), optical and laser physics (laser interactions with matter and quantum optics), nuclear science (medical applications), earth science (atmosphere, ocean, and climate science and geophysics), and materials science and engineering (thin films; nanomaterials; electronic, optical, and magnetic materials; and mechanical response of materials). Successful completion of 30 points (semester hours) or more of approved graduate course work beyond the master's degree is required for the doctoral degree. In addition, all doctoral candidates must pass written and oral qualifying exams and successfully defend an approved dissertation based on original research. For the M.S. degree, candidates must successfully complete a minimum of 30 points of credit of approved graduate course work at Columbia. A 36-point CAMPEP-approved M.S. degree in medical physics is offered in collaboration with faculty members from the College of Physicians and Surgeons and the Mailman School of Public Health. It prepares students for professional careers in medical physics and provides preparation for the ABR certification exam.

Research Facilities

Research equipment in the Plasma Physics Laboratory includes a toroidal high-beta tokamak for basic and applied research, a steady-state plasma experiment using a linear magnetic mirror, a large laboratory collisionless terrella used to investigate space plasma physics, and the CNT stellarator for nonneutral and antimatter plasma research. The plasma physics group is jointly operating a plasma confinement experiment, LDX, with MIT, incorporating a levitated superconducting ring. The plasma physics group is also actively involved in the NSTX experiment at the Princeton Plasma Physics Laboratory and on the DIII-D Tokamak at General Atomics in San Diego and is part of the U.S. national effort on the ITER project. Research equipment in the solid-state physics and laser physics laboratories includes extensive laser and spectroscopy facilities, a clean room that includes photolithography and thin-film fabrication systems, ultrahigh-vacuum surface preparation and analysis chambers, direct laser writing stations, a molecular-beam epitaxy machine, picosecond and femtosecond lasers, and diamond anvil cells. Research is also conducted in the shared characterization laboratories operated by the NSF Nanoscale Science and Engineering Center, and the DOE Energy Frontier Research Center, which focuses on conversion of sunlight into electricity in nanometer-sized thin films. Materials science and engineering facilities include transmission and scanning electron microscopes, scanning tunneling microscopes and atomic-force microscopes, X-ray diffractometers, an ellipsometer, an X-ray photoelectron spectrometer, laser processing equipment, and mechanical testing equipment. Magnetic and electrical measurement characterization equipment is also available.

There are research opportunities in medical physics at the Columbia–Presbyterian Medical Center, as well as at other medical institutes, employing state-of-the-art medical diagnostic imaging and treatment equipment.

The Applied Mathematics Division is closely linked with the Lamont Doherty Earth Observatory (LDEO), with 5 faculty members sharing appointments in the Department of Earth and Environmental Sciences and with the NASA Goddard Institute for Space Studies (GISS). There are also close ties with Columbia's Center for Computational Biology and Bioinformatics (C2B2) and Columbia's Center for the Multiscale Analysis of Genomic and Cellular Networks (MAGNet).

The Department maintains an extensive network of workstations and desktop computers. It has recently acquired a SiCortex supercomputer with 1,458 cores, which is used for a wide range of departmental computational activities. The research of the plasma physics group is supported by a dedicated data acquisition/data analysis system. Computational researchers have local access to Columbia's 256-processor Linux cluster and to supercomputer systems at the National Center for Atmospheric Research and the Lawrence Berkeley, Brookhaven, and Oak Ridge National Laboratories.

Financial Aid

Financial support is awarded to doctoral candidates only on a competitive basis in the form of assistantships that provide a stipend, a tuition allowance, and medical fees. For 2012–13, the stipend for teaching assistants is $23,750 for nine months; for research assistants, the stipend is $31,667 for twelve months.

Cost of Study

For 2011–12, full-time tuition (RU) for the academic year was $38,678; for master's degree and for part-time study, the cost was $1578 per credit. In addition to medical fees (approximately $1400 for basic coverage), annual fees range from $698–$1000.

Living and Housing Costs

The cost of on-campus, single-student housing (dormitories, suites, and apartments) ranges from $3000 to $6700 per term; married student accommodations range from $1300 to $2550 per month. For the single student, a minimum of $23,500 should be allowed for board, room, and personal expenses for the academic year.

Student Group

Approximately 28,200 students attend the fifteen schools and colleges of Columbia University; more than half are graduate students. On average, the Department has 120 graduate and 110 undergraduate students. The student population has a diverse and international character. Admission is highly competitive; in 2011–12, 40 master's- and Ph.D.-track students matriculated out of 360 applicants, with all doctoral program students being fully supported.

Student Outcomes

Recent Ph.D. recipients have found employment as postdoctoral research scientists at universities in the United States and abroad and as staff members in advanced technology industries and at national laboratories. Some have secured college-level faculty positions. Most M.S. graduates continue studying for the doctorate; a few go on to medical school or law school. M.S. graduates from the program in medical physics have secured positions in hospital departments of radiology and nuclear medicine or have entered doctoral programs.

Location

The 32-acre campus is situated in Morningside Heights on the Upper West Side of Manhattan. This location, 15 minutes from the heart of New York City, allows Columbia to be an integral part of the city while maintaining the character of a unique neighborhood. Cultural, recreational, and athletic opportunities abound at city museums, libraries, concert halls, theaters, restaurants, stadiums, parks, and beaches.

The University and The Department

With extensive resources and an outstanding faculty, Columbia University has played an eminent role in American education since its founding in 1754. The Department of Applied Physics and Applied Mathematics, a department at the forefront of interdisciplinary research and teaching, was established in 1978 as part of the Graduate School of Arts and Sciences and the Fu Foundation School of Engineering and Applied Sciences. The Graduate Program in Materials Science and Engineering joined the Department in fall 2000.

Applying

For fall admission, applications should be submitted online as follows: December 15 for doctoral, doctoral-track, and all financial aid applicants; applications for Master of Science, part-time, and nondegree candidates are reviewed on a rolling basis. Scores from the GRE General Test are required. The GRE Subject Test is required for applicants to the applied physics doctoral program. The GRE Subject Test is strongly urged for doctoral applicants in applied mathematics and materials science and engineering. TOEFL scores are required for students from non-English-speaking countries.

Admissions information and application forms can be found online at http://www.engineering.columbia.edu/graduate-2.

Correspondence and Information

Chairman, Graduate Admissions Committee
Department of Applied Physics and Applied Mathematics
200 S. W. Mudd Building, MC 4701
Columbia University
New York, New York 10027
Phone: 212-854-4457
       212-854-6438 (admissions)
E-mail: seasinfo.apam@columbia.edu
      seasgradmit@columbia.edu (admissions)
Web site: http://www.apam.columbia.edu
      http://www.engineering.columbia.edu/

THE FACULTY AND THEIR RESEARCH

In the Department of Applied Physics and Applied Mathematics, theoretical and experimental research is conducted by 34 full-time faculty members, 18 adjunct professors, and 53 research scientists. Areas of research include applied mathematics, earth/atmosphere/ocean/climate science, biomathematics, biophysics, numerical analysis, inverse problems, medical imaging, space physics, surface physics, condensed-matter physics, electromagnetism, materials science, nanoscience, medical physics, optical and laser physics, plasma physics, and fusion energy science.

William E. Bailey, Associate Professor; Ph.D., Stanford, 1999. Nanoscale magnetic films and heterostructures, materials issues in spin-polarized transport, materials engineering of magnetic dynamics.

Guillaume Bal, Professor; Ph.D., Paris, 1997. Applied mathematics, partial differential equations with random coefficients, high-frequency waves in random media and application to time reversal, inverse problems and imaging with applications to medical imaging and geophysical imaging.

Peterson's Graduate Programs in the Physical Sciences, Mathematics, Agricultural Sciences, the Environment & Natural Resources 2013

facebook.com/petersonspublishing **269**

Columbia University

Katayun Barmak, Professor; Ph.D., MIT, 1989. Processing and structure (crystal structure and microstructure) relationships to electrical and magnetic properties of metal films, developing transmission electron microscopy automated orientation imaging techniques that can be applied to the study of nanostructured materials, use of differential scanning calorimetry for the study solid-state reactions and phase transformations in thin films.

Daniel Bienstock, Professor (joint with Industrial Engineering and Operations Research); Ph.D., MIT, 1985. Applied mathematics, methodology and high-performance implementation of optimization algorithms, applications of optimization: preventing national-scale blackouts, emergency management, approximate solution of massively large optimization problems, higher-dimensional reformulation techniques for integer programming, robust optimization.

Simon J. L. Billinge, Professor; Ph.D., Pennsylvania, 1992. Nanoscale structure-property relationships in functional nanomaterials studied using novel X-ray and neutron scattering techniques coupled with advanced computing, solving the nanostructure problem.

Allen H. Boozer, Professor; Ph.D., Cornell, 1970. Plasma theory, theory of magnetic confinement for fusion energy, nonlinear dynamics.

Mark A. Cane, Professor (joint with Earth and Environmental Sciences); Ph.D., MIT, 1975. Climate dynamics, impacts of climate on society, climate forecasting, physical oceanography, geophysical fluid dynamics, computational fluid dynamics.

Siu-Wai Chan, Professor; Sc.D., MIT, 1985. Nanoparticles, electronic ceramics, grain boundaries and interfaces, oxide thin films.

C. K. Chu, Professor Emeritus; Ph.D., NYU (Courant), 1959. Applied mathematics.

Andrew J. Cole, Assistant Professor; Ph.D., Texas at Austin. Plasma physics and nuclear fusion; particular focus on symmetry-breaking magnetic perturbations and their effect on plasma rotation in magnetically-confined fusion plasmas.

Vincent Duchene, Assistant Professor, Ph.D., Paris, 2011. Partial differential equations, fluid mechanics, hyperbolic equations, Schrödinger operator, mathematical physics, numerical simulations.

Dirk R. Englund, Assistant Professor (joint with Electrical Engineering); Ph.D., Stanford, 2008. Quantum optics in photonic nanostructures, photonic crystal optoelectronic devices and networks, quantum information and metrology, nonlinear optics, electron and nuclear spin-dynamics in solid state systems.

Morton B. Friedman, Professor (joint with Civil Engineering); D.Sc., NYU, 1953. Applied mathematics and mechanics, numerical analysis, parallel computing.

Irving P. Herman, Professor; Ph.D., MIT, 1977. Nanocrystals, optical spectroscopy of nanostructured materials, laser diagnostics of thin-film processing, mechanical properties of nanomaterials.

James Im, Professor; Ph.D., MIT, 1985. Laser-induced crystallization of thin films, phase transformations and nucleation in condensed systems.

Philip Kim, Professor (joint with Physics); Harvard, 1999. Experimental condensed matter physics, physical properties and applications of nanoscale low-dimensional materials, quantum thermal transport phenomena in 1-dimensional nanoscaled materials, mesoscopic thermoelectricity and thermoelectric applications of nanoscale materials, quantum transport in novel 2-dimensional materials, mesoscopic electron transport, thermodynamic processes for sensors and electric devices.

Chris A. Marianetti, Assistant Professor; Ph.D., MIT, 2004. Predicting materials properties from first-principles computations, density-functional theory, dynamical mean-field theory, transition-metal oxides, actinides, energy storage and conversion materials.

Thomas C. Marshall, Professor Emeritus; Ph.D., Illinois, 1960. Accelerator concepts, relativistic beams and radiation, free-electron lasers.

Michael E. Mauel, Professor; Sc.D., MIT, 1983. Plasma physics, waves and instabilities, fusion and equilibrium control, space physics, plasma processing, international energy policy.

Gerald A. Navratil, Professor; Ph.D., Wisconsin–Madison, 1976. Plasma physics, plasma diagnostics, fusion energy science.

I. Cevdet Noyan, Professor; Ph.D., Northwestern, 1984. Characterization and modeling of mechanical and micromechanical deformation, residual stress analysis and nondestructive testing, X-ray and neutron diffraction, microdiffriction analysis.

Richard M. Osgood, Professor (joint with Electrical Engineering); Ph.D., MIT, 1973. Nanoscale optical and electronic phenomena (experimental and computational), femtosecond lasers and laser probing, low-dimensional physics, integrated optics, nanofabrication and materials growth.

Aron Pinczuk, Professor; Ph.D., Pennsylvania, 1969. Spectroscopy of semiconductors and insulators, quantum structures, systems of reduced dimensions, atomic layers of graphene, electron quantum fluids.

Lorenzo M. Polvani, Professor; Ph.D., MIT, 1988. Atmospheric and climate dynamics, geophysical fluid dynamics, numerical methods for weather and climate modeling, planetary atmospheres.

Malvin A. Ruderman, Professor (joint with Physics); Ph.D., Caltech, 1951. Theoretical astrophysics, neutron stars, pulsars, early universe, cosmic gamma rays.

Christopher H. Scholz, Professor (joint with Earth and Environmental Sciences); Ph.D., MIT, 1967. Experimental and theoretical rock mechanics, especially friction, fracture, and hydraulic transport properties; nonlinear systems; mechanics of earthquakes and faulting.

Tiffany A. Shaw, Assistant Professor (joint with Earth and Environmental Sciences), Ph.D., Toronto, 2009. Atmospheric science, advection-diffusion of a passive scalar, Hamiltonian geophysical fluid dynamics, multiple scale asymptotics, wave-mean flow interaction.

Amiya K. Sen, Professor (joint with Electrical Engineering); Ph.D., Columbia, 1963. Plasma physics, fluctuations and anomalous transport in plasmas, control of plasma instabilities, plasma transport.

Adam H. Sobel, Professor; Ph.D., MIT, 1998. Atmospheric science, geophysical fluid dynamics, tropical meteorology, climate dynamics.

Marc W. Spiegelman, Professor; Ph.D., Cambridge, 1989. Coupled fluid/solid mechanics, reactive fluid flow, solid earth and magma dynamics, scientific computation/modeling.

Horst L. Stormer, Professor Emeritus; Ph.D., Stuttgart, 1977. Semiconductors, electronic transport, lower-dimensional physics, transport in nanostructures.

Latha Venkataraman, Associate Professor; Ph.D., Harvard, 1999. Single-molecule transport, single-molecule-force spectroscopy, electron transport in nanowires, scanning tunneling microscopy and spectroscopy.

Francesco A. Volpe, Assistant Professor; Ph.D., Greifswald (Germany), 2003. Plasma physics and magnetic confinement fusion (tokamaks and stellarators) both experimentally and via numerical modelling, with emphasis on: (1) microwave heating, current drive and diagnostics and (2) magnetohydrodynamic instabilities and their control.

Wen I. Wang, Professor (joint with Electrical Engineering); Ph.D., Cornell, 1981. Heterostructure devices and physics, materials properties, molecular-beam epitaxy.

Michael I. Weinstein, Professor; Ph.D., NYU (Courant), 1982. Applied mathematics; partial differential equations and analysis; waves in nonlinear, inhomogeneous, and random media; dynamical systems; multiscale phenomena; applications to nonlinear optics; mathematical physics; fluid dynamics; geosciences.

Chris H. Wiggins, Associate Professor; Ph.D., Princeton, 1998. Applied mathematics, mathematical biology, biopolymer dynamics, soft condensed matter, genetic networks and network inference, machine learning.

Cheng-Shie Wuu, Professor (Public Health, Environmental Health Sciences, and Applied Physics); Ph.D., Kansas, 1985. Microdosimetry, biophysical modeling, dosimetry of brachytherapy, gel dosimetry, second cancers induced by radiotherapy, medical physics.

The Schapiro Center for Engineering and Physical Science Research; to the right, the Seeley W. Mudd Building, home of the Fu Foundation School of Engineering and Applied Science.

Low Memorial Library and grounds.

SELECTED PUBLICATIONS

William E. Bailey

Interface-related damping in polycrystalline Ni81Fe19/Cu/Co93Zr7 tri-layers. *J. Appl. Phys.* 105:07D309, 2009.

Weakly coupled motion of individual layers in ferromagnetic resonance. *Phys. Rev. B: Condens. Matter* 74(6):064409, 2006.

Low relaxation rate in epitaxial vanadium-doped ultrathin iron films. *Phys. Rev. Lett.* 98(11):117601, 2007.

Dopants for independent control of precessional frequency and damping in Ni0.8Fe 0.2(50 nm) thin films. *Appl. Phys. Lett.* 77(6), 2006.

Guillaume Bal

Inverse of transport theory and applications. *Inverse Probl.* 25:053001, 2009.

Convergence to SPDEs Stratonovich form. *Comm. Math. Phys.* 292(2):457–77, 2009.

Time reversal and refocusing in random media. *SIAM J. Appl. Math.* 63(5):1475–98, 2003.

Radiative transport limit for the random Schroedinger equation. *Nonlinearity* 15:513–29, 2002.

Daniel Bienstock

The $N - k$ problem in power grids: New models, formulations and computation. *SIAM J. Optim.* 20(5):2352–80, 2010.

Faster approximation algorithms for covering and packing problems. *SIAM J. Comput.* 35:825–54, 2006.

270 facebook.com/petersonspublishing

Peterson's Graduate Programs in the Physical Sciences, Mathematics, Agricultural Sciences, the Environment & Natural Resources 2013

Subset algebra lift operators for 0-1 integer programming. *SIAM J. Optim.* 15:63–95, 2004.

Potential function methods for approximately solving linear programming problems, theory and practice. *Kluwer Academic Publishers.* Boston, 2002.

Simon J. L. Billinge

The problem with determining atomic structure at the nanoscale. *Science* 316:561–5, 2007.

Ab initio determination of solid-state nanostructure. *Nature* 440:655–8, 2006.

Underneath the Bragg Peaks: Structural Analysis of Complex Materials. Elsevier Science: Oxford, 2004.

Beyond crystallography: The study of disorder nanocrystallinity and crystallographically challenged materials. *Chem. Commun.* 7:749–60, 2004.

Allen H. Boozer

Use of non-axisymmetric shaping in magnetic fusion. *Phys. Plasmas* 16:058102, 2009.

Stellarators and the path from ITER to DEMO. *Plasma Phys. Contr. Fusion* 50:124005, 2008.

Control of asymmetric magnetic perturbations in tokamaks. *Phys. Rev. Lett.* 99:195003, 2007.

Physics of magnetically confined plasmas. *Rev. Modern Phys.* 76:1071–141, 2004.

Mark A. Cane

The El Niño–Southern Oscillation Phenomenon. London: Cambridge University Press, 2010.

The evolution of El Niño, past and future. *Earth Planet. Sci. Lett.* 104:1–10, 2005.

Mapping tropical Pacific sea level: Data assimilation via a reduced state space Kalman filter. *J. Geophys. Res.* 101:22,599–617, 1996.

Experimental forecasts of El Niño. *Nature* 322:827–32, 1986.

Siu-Wai Chan

Controlled synthesis of Co_3O_4 nanopolyhedrons and nanosheets at low temperature. *Chem. Comm.* 48:7569–71, 2009.

In situ ultra-small-angle X-ray scattering study of solution-mediated formation and growth of nanocrystalline ceria. *J. Appl. Crystallogr.* 41(5):918–29, 2008.

Cubic phase stabilization in nanoparticles of hafnia-zirconia oxides: Particle-size and annealing environment effects. *J. Appl. Phys.* 103(12):124303–7, 2008.

Synthesis and redox behavior of nanocrystalline hausmannite. *Chem. Mater.* 19:5609–16, 2007.

C. K. Chu

Domain decomposition for shallow water equations. In *Contemporary Mathematics, Proceedings of the 7th International Conference on Domain Decomposition Methods in Science and Engineering,* October 1993.

Equilibrium response of ocean deep-water circulation to variations in Ekman pumping and deep-water sources. *J. Phys. Oceanogr.* 22:1129, 1992.

Lagrangian turbulence in Stokes flow. *Phys. Fluids* 30:687, 1987.

Solitary waves generated by boundary motion. *Comm. Pure Appl. Math.* 36:495, 1983.

Dirk R. Englund

Resonant excitation of a quantum dot strongly coupled to a photonic crystal nanocavity. *Phys. Rev. Lett.* 104(7):073904, 2010.

Controlled phase shifts with a single quantum dot. *Science* 320(5877):769–72, 2008.

Controlling cavity reflectivity with a single quantum dot. *Nature* 450(7171):857–61, 2007.

Controlling the spontaneous emission rate of single quantum dots in a 2D photonic crystal. *Phys. Rev. Lett.* 95(1):013904, 2005.

Irving P. Herman

Formation of thick, large-area nanoparticle superlattices in lithographically defined geometries. *Nano Lett.* 10(4):1517–21, 2010.

Viscoplastic and granular behavior in films of colloidal nanocrystals. *Phys. Rev. Lett.* 98:026103, 2007.

Physics of the Human Body. Berlin/Heidelberg/New York: Springer, 2007.

Raman microprobe analysis of elastic strain and fracture in electrophoretically deposited CdSe nanocrystal films. *Nano Lett.* 6:175–80, 2006.

James Im

Stochastic modeling of solid nucleation in supercooled liquids. *Appl. Phys. Lett.* 78:3454–6, 2001.

On determining the relevance of athermal nucleation in rapidly quenched liquids. *Appl. Phys. Lett.* 72:662, 1998.

Sequential lateral solidification of thin silicon films on SiO_2. *Appl. Phys. Lett.* 69:2864, 1996.

Phase transformation mechanisms involved in excimer laser crystallization of amorphous silicon films. *Appl. Phys. Lett.* 63:1969–71, 1993.

Philip Kim

Symmetry breaking of the zero energy Landau level in bilayer graphene. *Phys. Rev. Lett.* 104(6):066801, 2010.

Observation of the fractional quantum hall effect in graphene. *Nature* 462(7270):196–9, 2009.

Thermoelectric and magnetothermoelectric transport measurements of graphene. *Phys. Rev. Lett.* 102(9):096807, 2009.

Quantum interference and carrier collimation in grapheneheterojunctions. *Nat. Phys.* 5:222–6, 2009.

Chris A. Marianetti

Electronic coherence in delta-Pu: A DMFT study. *Phys. Rev. Lett.* 101:056403, 2008.

Quasiparticle dispersion and heat capacity of Na0.3CoO2: A DMFT study. *Phys. Rev. Lett.* 99:246404, 2007.

Na induced correlations in the cobaltates. *Phys. Rev. Lett.* 98:176405, 2007.

Electronic structure calculations with dynamical mean-field theory. *Rev. Mod. Phys.* 78:865, 2006.

Thomas C. Marshall

Experimental observation of constructive superposition of wake fields generated by electron bunches in a dielectric-lined waveguide. *Phys. Rev. Sci. Tech.* 9:011301, 2006.

Rectangular dielectric-lined two-beam accelerator structure. In *Particle Accelerator Conference Proceedings,* May 2005.

Nondestructive diagnostic for electron bunch length in accelerators using the wake field radiation spectrum. *Phys. Rev. Sci. Tech.* 8:062801, 2005.

Strong wake fields generated by a train of femtosecond bunches in a planar dielectric microstructure. *Phys. Rev. Special Top.–Accelerators Beams* 7:05130, 2004.

Michael E. Mauel

Turbulent inward pinch of plasma confined by a levitated dipole magnet. *Nat. Phys.* 6:207–12, 2010.

Global and local characterization of turbulent and chaotic structures in a dipole-confined plasma. *Phys. Plasmas* 16:055902, 2009.

Confinement improvement with magnetic levitation of a superconducting dipole. *Nucl. Fusion* 49:055023, 2009.

A Kalman filter for feedback control of rotating external kink instabilities in the presence of noise. *Phys. Plasmas* 16:056112, 2009.

Helium-catalyzed D-D fusion in a levitated dipole. *Nucl. Fusion* 44:193–203, 2004.

Gerald A. Navratil

Measurement of resistive wall mode stability in rotating high-beta DIII-D plasmas. *Nucl. Fusion* 45:368, 2005.

Scaling of the critical plasma rotation for stabilization of the n+1 RWM in DIII-D. *Nucl. Fusion* 44:1197, 2004.

Sustained rotational stabilization of DIII-D plasmas above the no-wall beta limit. *Phys. Plasmas* 9:1997, 2002.

Modeling of active control of external MHD instabilities. *Phys. Plasmas* 8:2170, 2001.

I. Cevdet Noyan

Measurement of strain/load transfer in parallel seven-wire strands with neutron diffraction. *Exp. Mech.* 50(2):265–72, 2010.

A rigorous comparison of X-ray diffraction thickness measurement techniques using silicon-on-insulator thin films. *J. Appl. Cryst.* 42(3):401–10, 2009.

Strain measured in a silicon-on-insulator, complementary metal-oxide-semiconductor device channel induced by embedded silicon-carbon source/drain regions. *Appl. Phys. Lett.* 94(6):063502, 2009.

Applicability of real-space methods to diffraction strain measurements in single crystals. *J. Appl. Cryst.* 41(5):944–9, 2008.

Richard M. Osgood Jr.

Spectro-microscopy of single- and multi-layer graphene supported by a weakly interacting substrate. *Phys. Rev. B (Rapid Comms)* 78:201408.

Engineering nonlinearities in nanoscale optical systems: physics and applications in dispersion-engineered Si nanophotonic wires. *Adv. Opt. Photon.* 1:162–235, 2009.

Experimental demonstration of near-infrared negative-index metamaterials. *Phys. Rev. Lett.* 95:137404, 2005.

Image-state electron scattering on flat Ag/Pt(111) and stepped Ag/Pt(997) surfaces. *Phys. Rev. B* 71:165424, 2004.

Aron Pinczuk

Electric field effect tuning of electron-phonon coupling in graphene. *Phys. Rev. Lett.* 98(16):166802, 2007.

Transition from free to interacting composite fermions away from nu=1/3. *Phys. Rev. Lett.* 97:036804, 2006.

Extrinsic optical recombination in pentacene single crystals: Evidence of gap states. *Appl. Phys. Lett.* 87(21):211117, 2005.

Peterson's Graduate Programs in the Physical Sciences, Mathematics, Agricultural Sciences, the Environment & Natural Resources 2013

facebook.com/petersonspublishing **271**

Columbia University

Splitting of long-wavelength modes of the fractional quantum hall liquid at nu=1/3. *Phys. Rev. Lett.* 95(6):066803, 2005.

Lorenzo M. Polvani

The impact of stratospheric ozone recovery on the Southern Hemisphere westerly jet. *Science* 320(5882):1486–9, 2008.

Transport and mixing of chemical airmasses in idealized baroclinic life cycles. *J. Geophys. Res. Atmos.* 112:D23102, 2007.

Numerically converged solutions of the global primitive equations for testing the dynamical core of atmospheric GCMs. *Monthly Weather Rev.* 11:2539–52, 2004.

Tropospheric response to stratospheric perturbations in a relatively simple general circulation model. *Geophys. Res. Lett.* 29(7):1114, 2002.

The morphogenesis of bands and zonal winds with the atmospheres of the giant outer planets. *Science* 273:335–7, 1996.

Malvin A. Ruderman

A central engine for cosmic gamma-ray burst sources. *Astrophys. J.* 542:243, 2000.

Millisecond pulsar alignment: PSR 0437–47. *Astrophys. J.* 493:397, 1998.

Neutron star magnetic field evolution, crust movement and glitches. *Astrophys. J.* 492:267, 1998.

Models for X-ray emission from isolated pulsars. *Astrophys. J.* 498:373, 1998.

Christopher H. Scholz.

Transition regimes for growing crack populations. *Phys. Rev. E* 65:056105, 2002.

Slip-length scaling for earthquakes: Observations and theory and implications for earthquake physics. *Geophys. Res. Lett.* 28:2995–8, 2001.

Evidence of a strong San Andreas fault. *Geology* 28:163–6, 2000.

Experimental evidence for different strain regimes of crack populations in a clay model. *Geophys. Res. Lett.* 26:1081–4, 1999.

Amiya K. Sen

Radial plasma transport in axisymmetricmagneticfields. *Trans.Fusion& Technology* 48:51111, 2006.

Observation and identification of zonal flows in a basic experiment. *Plasma Phys. Controlled Fusion* 48:51111, 2006.

A new paradigm of plasma transport. *Phys. Plasmas* 13, 2006.

Adaptive optimal stochastic state feedback control of resistive wall modes in tokamaks. *Phys. Plasmas* 13:012512, 2006.

Adam H. Sobel

Poleward-propagating intraseasonal monsoon disturbances in an intermediate-complexity axisymmetric model. *J. Atmos. Sci.* 65:470–89, 2008.

Instability of the axisymmetric monsoon flow and intraseasonal oscillation. *J. Geophys. Res.* 113: D07108, 2008. doi:10.1029/2007JD009291

On the wavelength of the Rossby waves radiated by tropical cyclones. *J. Atmos. Sci.* 65:644–54, 2008.

The role of surface fluxes in tropical intraseasonal oscillations. *Nature Geoscience* 1:653–7, 2008.

Marc W. Spiegelman

A semi-Lagrangian Crank-Nicolson algorithm for the numerical solution of advection-diffusion problems. *Geochem. Geophys. Geosyst.* 7(4):Q04014, 2006.

Linear analysis of melt band formation by simple shear. *Geochem. Geophys. Geosyst.* 4(9):8615, 2003.

Extreme chemical variability as a consequence of channelized melt transport. *Geochem. Geophys. Geosyst.* 4(7):1055, 2003.

Causes and consequences of flow organization during melt transport: The reaction infiltration instability in compactible media. *J. Geophys. Res.* 106(B2):2061–77, 2001.

Horst L. Stormer

High frequency magneto oscillations in GaAs/AlGaAs quantum wells. *Phys. Rev. Lett.* 98:036804, 2007.

Experimental observation of the quantum Hall effect and Berry's phase in graphene. *Nature* 438:201, 2005.

Quantization of the diagonal resistance: Density gradients and the empirical resistance rule in a 2D system. *Phys. Rev. Lett.* 95:066808, 2005.

Evidence for skyrmion crystallization from NMR relaxation experiments. *Phys. Rev. Lett.* 94:196803, 2005.

Latha Venkataraman

Mechanically-controlled binary conductance switching of a single-molecule junction. *Nature Nanotechnology* 4:230, 2009.

Formation and evolution of single molecule junctions. *Phys. Rev. Lett.* 102:126803, 2009.

Single molecule conductance and link chemistry: A comparison of phosphines, methyl thiols and amines. *J. Am. Chem. Soc.* 129:15768–9, 2007.

Single molecule conductance and link chemistry: A comparison of phosphines, methyl thiols and amines. *J. Am. Chem. Soc.* 129:15768–9, 2007.

Electronics and chemistry: Varying single molecule junction conductance with chemical substituent. *Nano Letters* 7:502–6, 2007.

Dependence of single molecule junction conductance on molecular conformation. *Nature* 442:904–7, 2006.

Single-molecule circuits with well-defined molecular conductance. *Nano Letters* 6:458–62, 2006.

Wen I. Wang

Normal incidence intervalence subband absorption in GaSb quantum well enhanced by coupling to InAs conduction band. *Appl. Phys. Lett.* 62:609–11, 1993.

Normal incidence infrared absorption in AlAs/AlGaAs x-valley multiquantum wells. *Appl. Phys. Lett.* 61:1697–9, 1992.

High breakdown voltage AlSbAs/InAs n-channel field effect transistors. *IEEE Electron Device Lett.* 13:192–4, 1992.

Michael I. Weinstein

Cloaking via change of variables for the Helmholtz equation. *Comm. Pure Appl. Math.* 63(8):973–1016, 2010.

A multiscale model of partial melts: 1. Effective equations. *J. Geophys. Res.* 115:B04410, 2010.

A multiscale model of partial melts: 2. Computational studies. *J. Geophys. Res.* 115:B04411, 2010.

Band-edge solitons, nonlinear Schrodinger/Gross–Pitaevskii equations, and effective media. *SIAM J. Multiscale Modeling and Simulation* 8(4):1055–101, 2010.

Chris H. Wiggins

A stochastic spectral analysis of transcriptional regulatory cascades. *Proc. Natl. Acad. Sci. U.S.A.* 106:6529–34, 2009. http://www.ncbi.nlm.nih.gov/pubmed/19351901?dopt=Abstract

A Bayesian approach to network modularity. *Phys. Rev. Lett.* 100:258701, 2008. http://link.aps.org/doi/10.1103/PhysRevLett.100.258701

Multiple events on single molecules: Unbiased estimation in single-molecule biophysics. *Proc. Natl. Acad. Sci. U.S.A.* 104:1750–5, 2006.

Information-theoretic approach to network modularity. *Physical Review E* 71:046117, 2005.

Inferring network mechanisms: The *Drosophila melanogaster* protein interaction network. *Proc. Natl. Acad. Sci. U.S.A.* 102(9):3192–7, 2005.

Cheng-Shie Wuu

3-D dose verification for IMRT using optical CT based polymer gel dosimetry. *Med. Phys.* 33(5):1412–9, 2006.

Radiation-induced second cancers: The impact of 3D-CRT and IMRT. *Int. J. Radiat. Oncol. Biol. Phys.* 56(1):83–8, 2003.

Dosimetry study of Re-188 liquid balloon for intravascular brachytherapy using polymer gel dosimeters and laser-beam optical CT scanner. *Med. Phys.* 30(2):132–7, 2003.

Dosimetric and volumetric criteria for selecting a source activity and/or a source type (I-125 or Pd-103) in the presence of irregular seed placement in permanent prostate implants. *Int. J. Radiat. Oncol. Biol. Phys.* 47:815–20, 2000.

272 facebook.com/petersonspublishing

Peterson's Graduate Programs in the Physical Sciences, Mathematics, Agricultural Sciences, the Environment & Natural Resources 2013

OHIO UNIVERSITY
Department of Physics and Astronomy

Programs of Study

The Department of Physics and Astronomy offers graduate study and research programs leading to the Master of Arts, Master of Science, and Doctor of Philosophy degrees. The program of study emphasizes individual needs and interests in addition to essential general requirements of the discipline. Major areas of current research are experimental and theoretical condensed-matter and surface physics, nanoscience, mathematical and computational physics, biological physics, astronomy and astrophysics.

At the end of a student's first year of graduate study, his or her suitability to continue toward the Ph.D. is evaluated by the full faculty. This evaluation is based primarily on the student's GPA in the core courses. The courses in the second year cover more advanced topics. Master's degrees require completion of 45 graduate credits in physics and have both thesis and nonthesis options.

Prospective students can listen to what current students have to say about the program on the Department of Physics and Astronomy's YouTube page at http://www.youtube.com/OhioUPhysics.

Research Facilities

The physics department occupies two wings of Clippinger Laboratories, a modern, well-equipped research building; the Edwards Accelerator Building, which contains Ohio University's 4.5-MV high-intensity tandem Van de Graaff accelerator; and the Surface Science Research Laboratory, which is isolated from mechanical and electrical disturbances. Specialized facilities for measuring structural, thermal, transport, optical, and magnetic properties of condensed matter are available. In addition to research computers in laboratories, students have access to a Beowulf cluster and the Ohio Supercomputer Center, where massively parallel systems are located. Ohio University is a partner in the MDM Observatory at Kitt Peak, Arizona, which provides guaranteed access to major research telescopes.

Financial Aid

Financial aid is available in the form of teaching assistantships (TAs) and research assistantships (RAs). All cover the full cost of tuition plus a stipend from which a semester fee of $684 must be paid by the student. The current stipend level for TAs and RAs is $22,086 per year. TAs require approximately 15 to 20 hours per week of laboratory and/ or teaching duties.

Cost of Study

Tuition and fees are $4722 per semester for Ohio residents and $8718 per semester for out-of-state students. Students on TA or RA support receive full tuition waivers. Students not otherwise covered by health insurance must pay a $1425 annual premium for student health insurance.

Living and Housing Costs

On-campus rooms for single students start at $2807 per semester. A number of off-campus apartments and rooms are available at various costs.

Student Group

About 20,042 students study on the main campus of the University, and 3,353 of these are graduate students. The graduate student enrollment in the physics department ranges from 70 to 80 students.

Location

Athens is a city of about 25,000, situated in the rolling Appalachian foothills of southeastern Ohio. The surrounding landscape consists of wooded hills rising about the Hocking River valley, and the area offers many outdoor recreational opportunities. Eight state parks lie within easy driving distance of the campus and are popular spots for relaxation. The outstanding intellectual and cultural activities sponsored by this diverse university community are pleasantly blended in Athens with a vibrant tradition in the visual and performing arts.

The University and The Department

Ohio University, founded in 1804 and the oldest institution of higher education in the Northwest Territory, is a comprehensive university with a wide range of graduate and undergraduate programs. The Ph.D. program in physics began in 1959, and more than 250 doctoral degrees have been awarded. Currently, the Department has 25 regular faculty members and additional part-time faculty and postdoctoral fellows. Sponsored research in the Department amounts to approximately $5.85 million per year and comes from NSF, DOE, DOD, NASA, and the state of Ohio. Further information can be found at the Department's home page (http://www.phy.ohiou.edu).

Applying

Online application procedures and downloadable forms can be found at http://www.ohio.edu/graduate/apply.cfm. Information can also be obtained by e-mailing the Department of Physics and Astronomy at gradapp@helios.phy.ohiou.edu.

Correspondence and Information

Graduate Admissions Chair
Department of Physics and Astronomy
Ohio University
Athens, Ohio 45701
Phone: 740-593-1718
E-mail: gradapp@helios.phy.ohio.edu
Web site: http://www.phy.ohiou.edu

THE FACULTY AND THEIR RESEARCH

Professors

Carl R. Brune, Ph.D., Caltech, 1994. Experimental nuclear astrophysics.

David A. Drabold, Distinguished Professor; Ph.D., Washington (St. Louis), 1989. Theoretical condensed matter, computational methodology for electronic structure, theory of topologically disordered materials.

Charlotte Elster, Dr.rer.nat., Bonn, 1986. Nuclear and intermediate-energy theory.

Peterson's Graduate Programs in the Physical Sciences, Mathematics, Agricultural Sciences, the Environment & Natural Resources 2013

facebook.com/petersonspublishing **273**

Ohio University

Alexander O. Govorov, Ph.D., Novosibirsk (Russia), 1991. Theoretical condensed-matter physics, nanoscience.

Steven M. Grimes, Distinguished Professor, Emeritus; Ph.D., Wisconsin–Madison, 1968. Nuclear physics.

Kenneth H. Hicks, Ph.D., Colorado, 1984. Nuclear and intermediate-energy physics.

Saw-Wai Hla, Ph.D., Ljubljana (Slovenia), 1997. Experimental condensed-matter and surface physics, nanoscience.

David C. Ingram, Ph.D., Chair of the Department (interim); Salford (England), 1980. Atomic collisions in solids, thin films, deposition and analysis, surface physics.

Peter Jung, Distinguished Professor; Ph.D., Ulm (Germany), 1985. Nonequilibrium statistical physics, nonlinear stochastic processes, pattern formation, biophysics.

Martin E. Kordesch, Ph.D., Case Western Reserve, 1984. Surface physics, wide-gap materials.

Daniel Phillips, Ph.D., Flinders (Australia), 1995. Theoretical nuclear and particle physics.

M. Prakash, Ph.D., Bombay, 1979. Theoretical nuclear and particle astrophysics.

Joseph C. Shields, Ph.D., Berkeley, 1991. Astrophysics, interstellar medium, active galactic nuclei.

Arthur Smith, Ph.D., Texas at Austin, 1995. Experimental semiconductors, thin film.

Thomas S. Statler, Ph.D., Princeton, 1986. Astrophysics, galactic structure and dynamics.

Sergio E. Ulloa, Ph.D., SUNY at Buffalo, 1984. Theoretical condensed-matter physics.

Associate Professors

Markus Böttcher, Ph.D., Bonn, 1997. High-energy astrophysics.

Horacio E. Castillo, Ph.D., Illinois, 1998. Theoretical condensed-matter physics.

Douglas Clowe, Ph.D., Hawaii, 1998. Observational astrophysics.

Mark Lucas, Ph.D., Illinois, 1994. Experimental nuclear physics., physics education.

Alexander Neiman, Ph.D., Saratov State (Russia), 1991. Biophysics, nonlinear dynamics, stochastic processes.

Julie Roche, Ph.D., Un. B. Pascal (France), 1998. Nuclear and intermediate-energy physics.

Nancy Sandler, Ph.D., Illinois, 1998. Theoretical condensed-matter physics.

Eric Stinaff, Ph.D., Iowa State, 2002. Experimental nanoscience.

David F. J. Tees, Ph.D., McGill, 1996. Experimental biophysics, nanoscience.

Assistant Professors

Gang Chen, Ph.D., Lehigh, 2004. Experimental condensed-matter physics.

Justin Frantz, Ph.D., Columbia, 2004. Experimental nuclear physics.

THEORETICAL RESEARCH ACTIVITIES

Astrophysics. Studies of galaxies and galaxy clusters, with emphasis on galaxy structure, dynamics, and interactions; dark matter and dark energy; quasars and supermassive black holes in galaxy nuclei; high-energy astrophysics related to accretion onto compact objects, relativistic jets, and gamma-ray bursts; asteroids and solar system dynamics. Investigations into these topics employ multiwavelength observations with major facilities (Hubble Space Telescope, Chandra X-ray Observatory, MDM Observatory at Kitt Peak, Arizona) as well as theoretical efforts, including analytic calculations and large-scale numerical simulations.

Biophysics. Computational modeling of complex cellular signaling networks, especially intracellular and intercellular calcium signaling, modeling of neural and glial functions in healthy and epileptic tissue, stochastic modeling of electroreceptors in paddle fish, modeling of the neuronal circuitry of the cat's retina, stochastic and coherence resonance in excitable biologic systems, nanoscale ion channel and receptor clusters, and modeling slow axonal transport.

Condensed-Matter Theory. Statistical mechanics and nonequilibrium dynamics of disordered systems and glassy materials. Some areas of interest include nanoscale-sized dynamical heterogeneities in glassy materials, slow activation-controlled motion of topological defects (e.g., vortices, dislocations), and disordered electronic systems; methodology of first principles simulation: development of local basis density functional methods, time-dependent density functional theory and efficient computation of Wannier functions, and the single-particle-density matrix; theory of disordered insulators: Anderson transition, photo-structural response, novel schemes for structural modeling of glasses, and studies of pressure-induced polyamorphism; and optical and transport phenomena in nanoscale systems, including quantum dots, rings, and channels. Recent activity covers excitons in quantum rings, spin transport in nanocrystals, and quantum acoustoelectric interactions on nanoscale. Other nanoscience problems of interest include electronic transport in complex molecule systems, the role of controlled disorder on the metallic or insulating nature of one- and two-dimensional systems, and the role of collective effects on the optical and transport properties of quantum dot arrays and studies of low-dimensional strongly correlated electron systems, disordered electronic systems, and quantum-Hall-effect physics.

Mathematical and Computational Physics. Quantum simulation, ab initio calculations, and visualization of many-body and few-body systems in condensed-matter and nuclear physics; numerical methods and algorithmic development for high-performance vector and parallel computers; analytical and algorithmic studies in differential and integral equations, probability theory, and series expansions.

Nuclear/Particle Physics and Astrophysics. Research in theoretical nuclear/particle physics at Ohio University focuses on the dynamics of the matter that makes up the atomic nucleus, and examines manifestations of these dynamics in systems ranging in size from a single proton to a neutron star. Researchers combine data from laboratory experiments, astronomical observations, and theoretical studies in order to examine the role of the fundamental forces of nature within these systems. Current topics of interest include models of the nucleon-nucleon force; structure of light nuclei, especially as probed in proton, electron, and photon scattering; proton and neutron structure; reactions on exotic nuclei; relativistic heavy-ion collisions; physics and astrophysics of neutron stars and supernovae; and gravitational waves.

EXPERIMENTAL RESEARCH ACTIVITIES

Astrophysics. Spectroscopic observations of stellar motions and stellar populations in elliptical galaxies and evidence for dark matter, ionized gas in galaxies, gravitational lensing studies of galaxy clusters, nuclear physics applied to astrophysics.

Biological Physics. Stochastic resonance in psychophysics and animal behavior, studies of stochastic nonlinear dynamics in paddlefish electroreceptors, experimental determination of the response of single-cell-adhesion molecules to applied forces using a microcantilever device, lipid bilayer tether pulling on leukocytes and platelets using micropipette aspiration, studies of cell adhesion in pressure gradients in micropipettes, determination of cell membrane mechanical properties, optical studies of biomolecules at the single-molecule level using total internal reflection fluorescence microscopy and fluorescence resonance energy transfer, biomineralization, studies of ice-modifying antifreeze proteins, studies of DNA-protein interactions using optical methods.

Condensed-Matter and Surface Science. Current projects encompass various areas in nanoscale science; scanning-probe techniques; and synthesis and characterization of photonic, composite, and electronic materials. Relevant projects are illustrated by the following list: thin-film growth (by molecular-beam epitaxy) and characterization (using scanning-probe microscopy techniques, including spin-polarized) of the structural, electronic, and magnetic properties of transition-metal nitride layers and magnetic-doped nitride semiconductors; single-atom/molecule manipulation using ultrahigh-vacuum, low-temperature scanning-tunneling microscopy; development of single-molecule electronics; molecular and metal thin films; surface science; electron microscopy of nanoscale structures; amorphous semiconductors and their photonics and electronic properties; MeV ion-beam analysis of materials and measurement of relevant cross-sections; ion-beam and plasma deposition of materials and their characterization; effect of hydrogen and nitrogen to the properties of amorphous carbon; optical spectroscopy and ultrafast laser studies of semiconductor nanostructures and nanostructure-based devices; optical spin manipulation and nanophotonics of individual and coupled nanostructures; growth of semiconducting chalcogenide nanowires for nonvolatile electric memory; synthesis of periodic mesoporous materials through a self-assembly approach; atomic and nanoscale structure characterization by X-ray absorption, fine structure, and small/wide angle X-ray scattering; and study of transparent conductive oxides, low work function surfaces, and thermionic cathodes.

Nuclear and Intermediate-Energy Physics. Contemporary research in experimental nuclear physics involves collaboration with scientists from many different institutions and heavy use of specialized accelerator facilities around the world. Ohio University nuclear physicists are recognized leaders in a variety of experimental programs spanning a broad energy domain. At higher energies, Ohio University's faculty members are leading research programs at Jefferson Laboratory in Virginia. These include the study of electromagnetic production of strange baryons and the search for new exotic baryons in Hall B, precision measurements of the weak charge of the proton in Hall C, and the study of the nature of the gluonic flux tube in Hall D; an active program studying the photoexcitation of the nucleon is also ongoing at the SPring-8 experiment in Japan. At lower energies, faculty members are directing research programs in several distinct areas, including fundamental symmetries in nuclear reactions via precision tests of charge symmetry breaking at TRIUMF in Canada, exotic nuclei far from the line of stability at GANIL and the Hahn-Meitner Institute in Europe, measurements of neutron cross sections at Los Alamos in New Mexico, studies of nuclear level densities at the Holifield Radioactive Ion Beam Facility in Tennessee, and studies of pion photoproduction and QCD sum rules with the LEGS facility at Brookhaven National Laboratory in New York. The Department also operates the high-intensity Ohio University Tandem Van de Graaff accelerator with its unique beam swinger magnet and long flight path for high-precision measurements of various nuclear cross sections and projects in medical physics. The research program is supported by the Ohio University Institute for Nuclear and Particle Physics. Grants are provided by the U.S. National Science Foundation and the U.S. Department of Energy.

SELECTED PUBLICATIONS

Arshakian, T. G., et al. **(M. Böttcher)** Radio-optical-gamma-ray properties of MOJAVE AGN detected by *Fermi*/LAT. *Astron. Astrophys.* 537:A32, 2012.

Kara, E., et al. **(M. Böttcher).** Gamma-ray emission from two blazars behind the galactic plane: B2013+370 and B2023+336. *Astrophys. J.* 746(2):159, 2012.

Roustazadeh, P., and **M. Böttcher.** Synchrotron emission from VHE gamma-ray induced pair cascades in AGN environments. *Astrophys. J.* 750:26, 2012.

Azuma, R. E., et al. **(C. R. Brune).** AZURE: An *R*-matrix code for nuclear astrophysics. *Phys. Rev. C* 81(4):045805, 2010.

Tang, X. D., et al. **(C. R. Brune).** Determination of the $E1$ component of the low-energy $^{12}C(\alpha,\gamma)^{16}O$ cross section. *Phys. Rev. C* 81(4):045809, 2010.

Boyd, Richard, Lee Bernstein, and **C. R. Brune.** Studying nuclear astrophysics at NIF. *Phys. Today* 62(6):60–61, 2009.

Parsaeian, A., and **H. E. Castillo.** Equilibrium and nonequilibrium fluctuations in a glass-forming liquid. *Phys. Rev. Lett.* 102(5):055704, 2009.

Castillo, H. E. Time reparametrization symmetry in spin-glass models. *Phys. Rev. B.* 78(21):214430, 2008.

Castillo, H. E., and A. Parsaeian. Local fluctuations in the ageing of a simple structural glass. *Nat. Phys.* 3(1):26–28, 2007.

Yan, Y., **G. Chen,** and P. G. Van Patten. Ultrafast exciton dynamics in CdTe nanocrystals and CdTe/CdS core/shell nanocrystals, *J. Phys. Chem. C.* 115(46):22717–28, 2011.

Chen, G. in *X-ray Scattering.* New York: Nova Science Publishers, 2011.

Hall, N., et al. **(D. Clowe).** Using the bullet cluster as a gravitational telescope to study z >~ 7 Lyman break galaxies. *Astrophys. J.* 745(2):id155, 2012.

Ragozzine, B., et al. **(D. Clowe).** Weak-lensing results for the merging cluster A1758. *Astrophys. J.* 744(2):id94, 2012.

Gennou, L., et al. **(D. Clowe).** Intracluster light in clusters of galaxies at redshifts 0.4 < z < 0.8. *Astron. Astrophys.* 537:idA64, 2012.

Zhang, M., and **D. A. Drabold.** Approximate theory of temperature coefficient of resistivity and conductivity for amorphous semiconductors. *Phys. Rev. B* 85:125135, 2012.

Prasai, B., and **D. A. Drabold.** Ab initio simulation of solid electrolyte materials in liquid and glassy phases. *Phys. Rev. B* 83(9):094202, 2011.

Cliffe, M., M. T. Dove, **D. A. Drabold,** and **A. L. Goodwin.** Structure determination of disordered materials from diffraction data. *Phys. Rev. Lett.* 104:125501, 2010.

Weppner, S. P. and **Ch. Elster.** Elastic Scattering of 6He based on a cluster description. *Phys. Rev. C* 85:044617, 2012.

Skibinski, R., et al. **(Ch. Elster).** Recent developments of a three-dimensional description of the NN system. *Few Body Syst.* 50:279–81, 2011.

Polyzou, W. et al. **(Ch. Elster).** Mini review of Poincaré invariant quantum theory. *Few Body Syst.* 49:129–47, 2011.

Kuzyk, A., et al. **(A. O. Govorov).** DNA-based self-assembly of chiral plasmonic nanostructures with tailored optical response. *Nature* 483:311–14, 2012.

Türeci H., et al. **(A. Govorov).** Many-body dynamics of exciton creation in a quantum dot by optical absorption: A quantum quench towards Kondo correlations. *Phys. Rev. Lett.* 106:107402, 2011.

Hicks, K. H. On the conundrum of the pentaquark. *Eur. Phys. J. H* February, 2012.

Hwang, S. H., and **K. Hicks** et al. Spin-density matrix elements for $\gamma p \rightarrow K^*0\Sigma+$ at $E\gamma$=1.85–3.0 GeV with evidence for the $\kappa(800)$ meson exchange. *Phys. Rev. Lett.* 108:092001, 2012.

Daniel, A., and **K. Hicks** et al. Measurement of the nuclear multiplicity ratio for K0 hadronization at CLAS. *Phys. Lett. B* 706:26–31, 2011.

Serrate, D., et al. **(S.-W. Hla).** Imaging and manipulating the spin direction of individual atoms. *Nature Nanotechnology* 5(5):350–3, 2010.

Clark, K., et al. **(S.-W. Hla).** Superconductivity in just four pairs of (BETS)$_2$-GaCl$_4$ molecules. *Nature Nanotechnology* 5(4):261–5, 2010.

Newkome, G., et al. **(S.-W. Hla).** Nanoassembly of a fractal polymer: A molecular "Sierpinski hexagonal gasket". *Science* 312:1782–85, 2006.

Pak, J., et al. **(D. C. Ingram).** Growth of expitaxial iron nitride ultrathin film on zinc-blende gallium nitride. *J. Vac. Sci. Tech.* 28(4):536, 2010.

Jadwisienczak, W., et al. **(D. C. Ingram).** Optical properties, luminescence quenching mechanism and radiation hardness of Eu-doped GaN red powder phosphor. *Radiat. Meas.* 45(3-6):500–02, 2010.

Kayani, A., et al. **(D. C. Ingram).** Effect of bias and hydrogenation on the elemental concentration and the thermal stability of amorphous thin carbon films, deposited on Si substrate. *Diam. Relat. Mater.* 18(11):1333–37, 2009.

Lunderberg, E., et.al. **(S. M. Grimes).** Evidence for the ground-state resonance of 26O. *Phys. Rev. Lett.* 108(14):2503, 2012.

Grimes, S. M., and T. N. Massey. Novel investigation of iron cross sections via spherical shell transmission measurements and particle transport calculations for material embrittlement studies. *Nucl. Sci. Eng.* 170:207–33, 2012.

Voinovl, A., et al. **(S. M. Grimes).** g-strength functions in 60Ni from two-step cascades following proton capture. *Phys. Rev. C* 81:024319, 2011.

Li, Y., **P. Jung** and A. Brown. Axonal transport of neurofilaments: A single population of intermittently moving polymers. *J. Neurosci.* 32(2):746–58, 2012.

Sun, L., et al. **(P. Jung).** Endoplasmic reticulum remodeling tunes IP3-dependent Ca²+ release sensitivity. *PLoS One* 6(11):e27928, 2011.

Swaminathan, D., and **P. Jung.** The role of agonist-independent conformational transformation (AICT) in IP3 cluster behavior. *Cell Calcium* 49(3):145–52, 2011.

Masson, E., et al. **(M. Kordesch).** "Supramolecular circuitry": Three chemiluminescent, cucurbit[7]uril-controlled on/off switches. *Org. Lett.* 13(15):3872–5, 2011.

Vaughn, J. M., et al. **(M. Kordesch).** Thermionic electron emission microscopy of metal-oxide multilayers on tungsten. *IBM Journal of Research and Development* 55(4):421–6, 2011.

Kordesch, M. E., et al. Model scandate cathodes investigated by thermionic-emission microscopy. *J. Vac. Sci. Tech. B,* 29(4):04E102–7, 2011.

Blanpied, G., et al. **(M. Lucas).** The N $\rightarrow \Delta$ transition from simultaneous measurements of p(γ,π^+) and p(γ,γ). *Phys. Rev. Lett.* 79:4337, 1997.

Feldman, G., et al. **(M. Lucas).** Compton scattering, meson-exchange, and the polarizabilities of bound nucleons. *Phys. Rev. C: Nucl. Phys.* 54:2124, 1996.

Neiman, A. B., and D. F. Russell. Sensory coding in oscillatory electroreceptors of paddlefish. *Chaos* 21:047505, 2011.

Neiman, A. B., et al. Spontaneous voltage oscillations and response dynamics of a Hodgkin-Huxley type model of sensory hair cells. *J. Math. Neurosci.* 1:11, 2011.

Neiman, A. B., D. F. Russell, and M. H. Rowe. Identifying temporal codes in spontaneously active sensory neurons. *PLoS One* 6(11):e27380, 2011.

Griesshammer, H. W., J. A. McGovern, **D. R. Phillips,** and G. Feldman. Using effective field theory to analyse low-energy Compton scattering data from protons and light nuclei. *Prog. Part. Nucl. Phys.* doi.org/10.1016/j.ppnp.2012.04.003, 2012.

Ji, C., **D. R. Phillips,** and L. Platter. The three-boson system at next-to-leading order in an effective field theory for systems with a large scattering length. *Ann. Phys.* 327(7):1803–24, 2012.

Baru, V., et al. **(D. R. Phillips).** Precision calculation of threshold pi^-d scattering, pi N scattering lengths, and the GMO sum rule. *Nucl. Phys. A872:69–116, 2012.

Androic, D., et al. **(J. Roche)** (G0 Collaboration). The G0 experiment: Apparatus for parity-violating electron scattering measurements at forward and backward angles. *Nuclear Instruments and Methods in Physics Research*

Peterson's Graduate Programs in the Physical Sciences, Mathematics, Agricultural Sciences, the Environment & Natural Resources 2013

facebook.com/petersonspublishing **275**

Section A: Accelerators, Spectrometers, Detectors and Associated Equipment 646(1):59–86, 2011.

Fuchey, E., et al. **(J. Roche)** Exclusive neutral pion electroproduction in the deeply virtual regime. *Phys. Rev. C* 83(2):025201, 2011.

Androic, D., et al. **(J. Roche)** (G0 Collaboration). Strange quark contributions to parity-violating asymmetries in the backward angle G0 electron scattering experiment. *Phys. Rev. Lett.* 104(1):012001, 2010.

Wong, A., et. Al. **(N. Sandler).** Signatures of quantum phase transitions in parallel quantum dots: Crossover from local moment to underscreened spin-1 Kondo physics. *Phys. Rev. B* 85:115316–22, 2012.

Zarea, M., **S. E. Ulloa**, and **N. Sandler.** Enhancement of Kondo effect through Rashba spin-orbit interactions. *Phys. Rev. Lett.* 108:04660–4, 2012.

Zarea, M. and **N. Sandler.** Graphene zigzag ribbons, square lattice models and quantum spin chains. *New J. Phys.* 11:095014, 2009.

Schmidt, K. B., et al. **(J. C. Shields).** The color variability of quasars. *Astrophys. J.* 744:147, 2012.

Capellupo, D. M., et al. **(J. C. Shields).** Variability in quasar broad absorption line outflows - I. Trends in the short-term versus long-term data. *Mon. Not. Roy. Astron. Soc.* 413:908, 2012.

Wang, K., and **A. R. Smith.** Three-dimensional spin mapping of antiferromagnetic nanopyramids having spatially alternating surface anisotropy at room temperature. *Nano Letters*, 2012. doi.org/10.1021/nl204192n.

Chinchore, A., et al. **(A. R. Smith).** Spontaneous formation of quantum height manganese gallium islands and atomic chains on N-polar gallium nitride(000-1). *Appl. Phys. Lett.* 100:061602, 2012.

Wang, K., et al. **(A. R. Smith).** A modular designed ultra-high-vacuum spin-polarized scanning tunneling microscope with controllable magnetic fields for investigating epitaxial thin films. *Rev. Sci. Instrum.* 82(5):053703, 2011.

Statler, T. S. Extreme sensitivity of the YORP effect to small-scale topography. *Icarus* 202(2):502–13, 2009.

Diehl, S., and **T. S. Statler.** The hot interstellar medium in normal elliptical galaxies. III. The thermal structure of the gas. *Astrophys. J.* 687(2):986–96, 2008.

Diehl, S., and **T. S. Statler.** The hot interstellar medium in normal elliptical galaxies. II. Morphological evidence for AGN feedback. *Astrophys. J.* 680(2):897–910, 2008.

Rolon, J. E., et al. **(S. E. Ulloa** and **E. A. Stinaff).** Oscillatory acoustic phonon relaxation of excitons in quantum dot molecules. *J. Opt. Soc. Am. B* 29(2):A146–53, 2012.

Wijesundara, K. C., et al. **(E. A. Stinaff).** Tunable exciton relaxation in vertically coupled semiconductor InAs quantum dots. *Phys. Rev. B* 84(8):081404(R), 2011.

Garrido, M., et al. **(E. A. Stinaff).** Electric field control of a quantum dot molecule through optical excitation. *Appl. Phys. Lett.* 96(21):211115, 2010.

Pai, A., P. Sundd, and **D. F. J. Tees.** In situ microrheological determination of neutrophil stiffening following adhesion in a model capillary. *Ann. Biomed. Eng.* 36:596–603, 2008.

Sundd, P., X. Zou, D.J. Goetz, and **D. F. J. Tees.** Leukocyte adhesion in capillary-sized, P-selectin-coated micropipettes. *Microcirculation* 15:109–22, 2008.

Tees, D. F. J., R. E. Waugh, and D. A. Hammer. A microcantilever device to assess the effect of force on the lifetime of selectin-carbohydrate bonds. *Biophys. J.* 80:668–82, 2001.

Diniz, G. S., A. Latgé, and **S. E. Ulloa.** Helicoidal fields and spin polarized currents in carbon nanotube–DNA hybrids. *Phys. Rev. Lett.* 108:126601, 2012.

Wong, A., et al. **(N. Sandler** and **S. E. Ulloa).** Signatures of quantum phase transitions in parallel quantum dots: Crossover from local moment to underscreened spin-1 Kondo physics. *Phys. Rev. B* 85:115316, 2012.

Ngo, A. T., J. Rodriguez-Laguna, **S. E. Ulloa,** and E. H. Kim, Quantum manipulation via atomic-scale magnetoelectric effects. *Nano Letters* 12:13–16, 2012.

276 facebook.com/petersonspublishing

Peterson's Graduate Programs in the Physical Sciences, Mathematics, Agricultural Sciences, the Environment & Natural Resources 2013

ACADEMIC AND PROFESSIONAL PROGRAMS IN MATHEMATICS

Section 7
Mathematical Sciences

This section contains a directory of institutions offering graduate work in mathematical sciences, followed by in-depth entries submitted by institutions that chose to prepare detailed program descriptions. Additional information about programs listed in the directory but not augmented by an in-depth entry may be obtained by writing directly to the dean of a graduate school or chair of a department at the address given in the directory.

For programs offering work in related fields, see all other areas in this book. In the other guides in this series:

Graduate Programs in the Humanities, Arts & Social Sciences

See *Economics* and *Psychology and Counseling*

Graduate Programs in the Biological/Biomedical Sciences & Health-Related Medical Professions

See *Biological and Biomedical Sciences; Biophysics; Genetics, Developmental Biology, and Reproductive Biology; Pharmacology and Toxicology* and *Public Health*

Graduate Programs in Engineering & Applied Sciences

See *Biomedical Engineering and Biotechnology; Chemical Engineering (Biochemical Engineering); Computer Science and Information Technology; Electrical and Computer Engineering; Engineering and Applied Sciences;* and *Industrial Engineering.*

Graduate Programs in Business, Education, Information Studies, Law & Social Work

See *Business Administration and Management* and *Library and Information Studies*

CONTENTS

Program Directories

Displays and Close-Ups

Applied Mathematics

Acadia University, Faculty of Pure and Applied Science, Department of Mathematics and Statistics, Wolfville, NS B4P 2R6, Canada. Offers applied mathematics and statistics (M Sc). *Degree requirements:* For master's, thesis. *Entrance requirements:* For master's, honors degree in mathematics, statistics or equivalent. Additional exam requirements/recommendations for international students: Required—TOEFL (minimum score 580 paper-based; 237 computer-based; 93 iBT), IELTS (minimum score 6.5). *Faculty research:* Geophysical fluid dynamics, machine scheduling problems, control theory, stochastic optimization, survival analysis.

Air Force Institute of Technology, Graduate School of Engineering and Management, Department of Mathematics and Statistics, Dayton, OH 45433-7765. Offers applied mathematics (MS, PhD). Part-time programs available. *Degree requirements:* For master's, thesis; for doctorate, thesis/dissertation. *Entrance requirements:* For master's, GRE General Test, minimum GPA of 3.0, U.S. citizenship or permanent U.S. residency; for doctorate, GRE General Test, minimum GPA of 3.5, U.S. citizenship or permanent U.S. residency. *Faculty research:* Electromagnetics, groundwater modeling, nonlinear diffusion, goodness of fit, finite element analysis.

Arizona State University, College of Liberal Arts and Sciences, Department of Mathematics and Statistics, Tempe, AZ 85287-1804. Offers applied mathematics (PhD); computational biosciences (PhD); mathematics (MA, MNS, PhD); mathematics education (PhD); statistics (PhD). Part-time programs available. Terminal master's awarded for partial completion of doctoral program. *Degree requirements:* For master's, thesis or alternative, interactive Program of Study (iPOS) submitted before completing 50 percent of required credit hours; for doctorate, comprehensive exam, thesis/dissertation, interactive Program of Study (iPOS) submitted before completing 50 percent of required credit hours. *Entrance requirements:* For master's and doctorate, GRE General Test, minimum GPA of 3.0 or equivalent in last 2 years of work leading to bachelor's degree. Additional exam requirements/recommendations for international students: Required—TOEFL (minimum score 80 iBT), TOEFL, IELTS, or Pearson Test of English. Electronic applications accepted. *Expenses:* Contact institution.

Arizona State University, College of Liberal Arts and Sciences, School of Human Evolution and Social Change, Tempe, AZ 85287-2402. Offers anthropology (PhD); anthropology (archaeology) (PhD); anthropology (bioarchaeology) (PhD); anthropology (museum studies) (MA); anthropology (physical) (PhD); applied mathematics for the life and social sciences (PhD); environmental social science (PhD); environmental social science (urbanism) (PhD); global health (MA); global health (health and culture) (PhD); global health (urbanism) (PhD); immigration studies (Graduate Certificate). Terminal master's awarded for partial completion of doctoral program. *Degree requirements:* For master's, thesis or alternative, interactive Program of Study (iPOS) submitted before completing 50 percent of required credit hours; for doctorate, comprehensive exam, thesis/dissertation, interactive Program of Study (iPOS) submitted before completing 50 percent of required credit hours. *Entrance requirements:* For master's and doctorate, GRE, minimum GPA of 3.0 or equivalent in last 2 years of work leading to bachelor's degree. Additional exam requirements/recommendations for international students: Required—TOEFL (minimum score 80 iBT), TOEFL, IELTS, or Pearson Test of English. Electronic applications accepted.

Auburn University, Graduate School, College of Sciences and Mathematics, Department of Mathematics and Statistics, Auburn University, AL 36849. Offers applied mathematics (MAM, MS); mathematics (MS, PhD); probability and statistics (M Prob S); statistics (MS). *Faculty:* 50 full-time (7 women), 6 part-time/adjunct (4 women). *Students:* 56 full-time (14 women), 52 part-time (14 women); includes 4 minority (3 Black or African American, non-Hispanic/Latino; 1 Hispanic/Latino), 43 international. Average age 28. 160 applicants, 59% accepted, 37 enrolled. In 2011, 17 master's, 9 doctorates awarded. *Degree requirements:* For doctorate, thesis/dissertation. *Entrance requirements:* For master's, GRE General Test, undergraduate mathematics background; for doctorate, GRE General Test, GRE Subject Test. *Application deadline:* For fall admission, 7/7 priority date for domestic students; for spring admission, 11/24 for domestic students. Applications are processed on a rolling basis. Application fee: $50 ($60 for international students). Electronic applications accepted. *Expenses:* Tuition, state resident: full-time $7290; part-time $405 per credit hour. Tuition, nonresident: full-time $21,870; part-time $1215 per credit hour. *International tuition:* $22,000 full-time. *Required fees:* $1402. *Financial support:* Fellowships and teaching assistantships available. Financial award applicants required to submit FAFSA. *Faculty research:* Pure and applied mathematics. *Unit head:* Dr. Michel Smith, Chair, 334-844-4290, Fax: 334-844-6655. *Application contact:* Dr. George Flowers, Dean of the Graduate School, 334-844-2125. Web site: http://www.auburn.edu/~math/.

Bowie State University, Graduate Programs, Program in Applied and Computational Mathematics, Bowie, MD 20715-9465. Offers MS. Part-time and evening/weekend programs available. *Students:* 2 full-time (1 woman), 8 part-time (2 women); includes 9 minority (all Black or African American, non-Hispanic/Latino). Average age 38. 10 applicants, 80% accepted, 5 enrolled. In 2011, 1

master's awarded. *Degree requirements:* For master's, comprehensive exam. *Entrance requirements:* For master's, calculus sequence, differential equations, linear algebra, mathematical probability and statistics. *Application deadline:* For fall admission, 4/1 priority date for domestic students, 4/1 for international students; for spring admission, 11/1 priority date for domestic students, 11/1 for international students. Applications are processed on a rolling basis. Application fee: $40. Electronic applications accepted. *Expenses:* Tuition, state resident: full-time $4140; part-time $3105 per semester. Tuition, nonresident: full-time $7836; part-time $5877 per semester. *Required fees:* $1715; $648 per semester. *Unit head:* Dr. Roman Sznajder, Graduate Program Coordinator, 301-860-3360. *Application contact:* Angela Issac, Information Contact, 301-860-4000.

Brown University, Graduate School, Division of Applied Mathematics, Providence, RI 02912. Offers Sc M, PhD. *Degree requirements:* For master's, thesis or alternative; for doctorate, one foreign language, thesis/dissertation, oral exam. *Entrance requirements:* For master's and doctorate, GRE General Test.

California Institute of Technology, Division of Engineering and Applied Science, Option in Applied and Computational Mathematics, Pasadena, CA 91125-0001. Offers MS, PhD. *Degree requirements:* For doctorate, thesis/dissertation. *Entrance requirements:* For doctorate, GRE Subject Test. Electronic applications accepted. *Faculty research:* Theoretical and computational fluid mechanics, numerical analysis, ordinary and partial differential equations, linear and nonlinear wave propagation, perturbation and asymptotic methods.

California State Polytechnic University, Pomona, Academic Affairs, College of Science, Program in Mathematics, Pomona, CA 91768-2557. Offers applied mathematics (MS); pure mathematics (MS). Part-time programs available. *Students:* 13 full-time (5 women), 32 part-time (15 women); includes 21 minority (12 Asian, non-Hispanic/Latino; 8 Hispanic/Latino; 1 Two or more races, non-Hispanic/Latino), 3 international. Average age 32. 53 applicants, 57% accepted, 14 enrolled. In 2011, 27 master's awarded. *Degree requirements:* For master's, thesis or alternative. *Entrance requirements:* For master's, GRE General Test. *Application deadline:* For fall admission, 5/1 priority date for domestic students; for winter admission, 10/15 priority date for domestic students; for spring admission, 1/20 priority date for domestic students. Applications are processed on a rolling basis. Application fee: $55. Electronic applications accepted. *Expenses:* Tuition, state resident: full-time $6738. Tuition, nonresident: full-time $12,300. *Required fees:* $657. Tuition and fees vary according to course load and program. *Financial support:* Career-related internships or fieldwork, Federal Work-Study, and institutionally sponsored loans available. Support available to part-time students. Financial award application deadline: 3/2; financial award applicants required to submit FAFSA. *Unit head:* Dr. Amber Rosin, Graduate Coordinator, 909-869-2426, Fax: 909-869-4904, E-mail: arrosin@csupomona.edu. *Application contact:* Deborah L. Brandon, Executive Director, Admissions and Outreach, 909-869-3427, Fax: 909-869-5315, E-mail: dlbrandon@csupomona.edu. Web site: http://www.csupomona.edu/~math/.

California State University, East Bay, Office of Academic Programs and Graduate Studies, College of Science, Department of Mathematics and Computer Science, Mathematics Program, Hayward, CA 94542-3000. Offers applied math (MS); mathematics (MS); mathematics teaching (MS). Part-time and evening/weekend programs available. *Faculty:* 3 full-time (1 woman). *Students:* 22 full-time (9 women), 52 part-time (20 women); includes 22 minority (17 Asian, non-Hispanic/Latino; 3 Hispanic/Latino; 1 Native Hawaiian or other Pacific Islander, non-Hispanic/Latino; 1 Two or more races, non-Hispanic/Latino), 6 international. Average age 38. 37 applicants, 81% accepted, 16 enrolled. In 2011, 19 master's awarded. *Degree requirements:* For master's, comprehensive exam or thesis. *Entrance requirements:* For master's, minimum GPA of 3.0 in field. Additional exam requirements/recommendations for international students: Required—TOEFL (minimum score 550 paper-based; 213 computer-based). *Application deadline:* For fall admission, 6/30 for domestic and international students. Application fee: $55. Electronic applications accepted. *Expenses:* Tuition, state resident: full-time $6738; part-time $1302 per quarter. Tuition, nonresident: full-time $12,690; part-time $2294 per quarter. *Required fees:* $449 per quarter. Tuition and fees vary according to degree level, program and reciprocity agreements. *Financial support:* Fellowships, teaching assistantships, Federal Work-Study, institutionally sponsored loans, and scholarships/grants available. Support available to part-time students. Financial award application deadline: 3/1; financial award applicants required to submit FAFSA. *Unit head:* Prof. Edna Reiter, Chair, 510-885-3414, Fax: 510-885-4169, E-mail: eddie.reiter@csueastbay.edu. *Application contact:* Dr. Donald Wolitzer, Math Graduate Advisor, 510-885-3414, Fax: 510-885-4169, E-mail: donald.wolitzer@csueastbay.edu. Web site: http://www20.csueastbay.edu/csci/departments/math-cs/.

California State University, Fullerton, Graduate Studies, College of Natural Science and Mathematics, Department of Mathematics, Fullerton, CA 92834-9480. Offers applied mathematics (MA); mathematics (MA); mathematics for secondary school teachers (MA). Part-time programs available. *Students:* 17 full-time (7 women), 55 part-time (21 women); includes 33 minority (23 Asian, non-Hispanic/Latino; 9 Hispanic/Latino; 1 Two or more races, non-Hispanic/Latino), 4

280 facebook.com/petersonspublishing

Peterson's Graduate Programs in the Physical Sciences, Mathematics, Agricultural Sciences, the Environment & Natural Resources 2013

international. Average age 31. 83 applicants, 60% accepted, 27 enrolled. In 2011, 25 master's awarded. *Degree requirements:* For master's, comprehensive exam or project. *Entrance requirements:* For master's, minimum GPA of 2.5 in last 60 units of course work, major in mathematics or related field. Application fee: $55. *Financial support:* Research assistantships, teaching assistantships, career-related internships or fieldwork, Federal Work-Study, institutionally sponsored loans, and scholarships/grants available. Support available to part-time students. Financial award application deadline: 3/1; financial award applicants required to submit FAFSA. *Unit head:* Dr. Paul Deland, Chair, 657-278-3631. *Application contact:* Admissions/Applications, 657-278-2371.

California State University, Long Beach, Graduate Studies, College of Engineering, Department of Mechanical and Aerospace Engineering, Long Beach, CA 90840. Offers aerospace engineering (MSAE); engineering and industrial applied mathematics (PhD); interdisciplinary engineering (MSE); management engineering (MSE); mechanical engineering (MSME). Part-time programs available. *Faculty:* 11 full-time (3 women), 6 part-time/adjunct (0 women). *Students:* 35 full-time (3 women), 54 part-time (4 women); includes 45 minority (1 Black or African American, non-Hispanic/Latino; 2 American Indian or Alaska Native, non-Hispanic/Latino; 17 Asian, non-Hispanic/Latino; 22 Hispanic/Latino; 3 Two or more races, non-Hispanic/Latino), 9 international. Average age 28. 142 applicants, 51% accepted, 26 enrolled. In 2011, 38 master's awarded. *Entrance requirements:* Additional exam requirements/recommendations for international students: Required—TOEFL. *Application deadline:* For fall admission, 7/1 for domestic students. Application fee: $55. Electronic applications accepted. *Financial support:* Career-related internships or fieldwork, Federal Work-Study, institutionally sponsored loans, scholarships/grants, and unspecified assistantships available. Financial award application deadline: 3/2. *Faculty research:* Unsteady turbulent flows, solar energy, energy conversion, CAD/CAM, computer-assisted instruction. *Unit head:* Dr. Hamid Hefazi, Chair, 562-985-1502, Fax: 562-985-1564, E-mail: hefazi@csulb.edu. *Application contact:* Dr. Hamid Rahai, Graduate Advisor, 562-985-5132, Fax: 562-985-4408, E-mail: rahai@csulb.edu.

California State University, Long Beach, Graduate Studies, College of Natural Sciences and Mathematics, Department of Mathematics and Statistics, Long Beach, CA 90840. Offers mathematics (MS), including applied mathematics, applied statistics, mathematics education for secondary school teachers. Part-time programs available. *Faculty:* 21 full-time (5 women), 1 (woman) part-time/adjunct. *Students:* 67 full-time (31 women), 115 part-time (47 women); includes 95 minority (5 Black or African American, non-Hispanic/Latino; 1 American Indian or Alaska Native, non-Hispanic/Latino; 53 Asian, non-Hispanic/Latino; 29 Hispanic/Latino; 2 Native Hawaiian or other Pacific Islander, non-Hispanic/Latino; 5 Two or more races, non-Hispanic/Latino), 14 international. Average age 31. 162 applicants, 69% accepted, 58 enrolled. In 2011, 41 master's awarded. *Degree requirements:* For master's, comprehensive exam or thesis. *Application deadline:* For fall admission, 7/1 for domestic students; for spring admission, 12/1 for domestic students. Applications are processed on a rolling basis. Application fee: $55. Electronic applications accepted. *Financial support:* Teaching assistantships, Federal Work-Study, institutionally sponsored loans, scholarships/grants, and traineeships available. Financial award application deadline: 3/2. *Faculty research:* Algebra, functional analysis, partial differential equations, operator theory, numerical analysis. *Unit head:* Dr. Robert Mena, Chair, 562-985-4721, Fax: 562-985-8227, E-mail: rmena@csulb.edu. *Application contact:* Dr. Ngo Viet, Graduate Associate Chair, 562-985-4721, Fax: 562-985-8227, E-mail: viet@csulb.edu.

California State University, Los Angeles, Graduate Studies, College of Natural and Social Sciences, Department of Mathematics, Los Angeles, CA 90032-8530. Offers mathematics (MS), including applied mathematics, mathematics. Part-time and evening/weekend programs available. *Faculty:* 4 full-time (0 women), 2 part-time/adjunct (0 women). *Students:* 27 full-time (10 women), 37 part-time (13 women); includes 43 minority (3 Black or African American, non-Hispanic/Latino; 19 Asian, non-Hispanic/Latino; 18 Hispanic/Latino; 3 Two or more races, non-Hispanic/Latino), 5 international. Average age 33. 59 applicants, 68% accepted, 20 enrolled. In 2011, 22 master's awarded. *Degree requirements:* For master's, comprehensive exam or thesis. *Entrance requirements:* For master's, previous course work in mathematics. Additional exam requirements/recommendations for international students: Required—TOEFL (minimum score 500 paper-based; 173 computer-based). *Application deadline:* For fall admission, 5/1 for domestic and international students. Applications are processed on a rolling basis. Application fee: $55. Electronic applications accepted. *Expenses:* Tuition, state resident: full-time $8225. *Financial support:* Teaching assistantships and Federal Work-Study available. Support available to part-time students. Financial award application deadline: 3/1. *Faculty research:* Group theory, functional analysis, convexity theory, ordered geometry. *Unit head:* Dr. Grant Fraser, Chair, 323-343-2150, Fax: 323-343-5071, E-mail: gfraser@calstatela.edu. *Application contact:* Dr. Karin Brown, Acting Associate Dean of Graduate Studies, 323-343-3820, Fax: 323-343-5653, E-mail: kbrown5@calstatela.edu. Web site: http://www.calstatela.edu/academic/math/.

California State University, Northridge, Graduate Studies, College of Science and Mathematics, Department of Mathematics, Northridge, CA 91330. Offers applied mathematics (MS); mathematics (MS); mathematics for educational careers (MS). Part-time and evening/weekend programs available. *Degree requirements:* For master's, thesis (for some programs). *Entrance requirements:* For master's, GRE (if cumulative undergraduate GPA less than 3.0). Additional

exam requirements/recommendations for international students: Required—TOEFL.

Carnegie Mellon University, Mellon College of Science, Department of Mathematical Sciences, Pittsburgh, PA 15213-3891. Offers algorithms, combinatorics, and optimization (PhD); applied mathematics (PhD); computational finance (MS); mathematical finance (PhD); mathematical sciences (MS, DA, PhD); pure and applied logic (PhD). Part-time programs available. Terminal master's awarded for partial completion of doctoral program. *Degree requirements:* For doctorate, thesis/dissertation. *Entrance requirements:* For master's and doctorate, GRE General Test, GRE Subject Test. Additional exam requirements/recommendations for international students: Required—TOEFL. Electronic applications accepted. *Faculty research:* Continuum mechanics, discrete mathematics, applied and computational mathematics.

Case Western Reserve University, School of Graduate Studies, Department of Mathematics, Cleveland, OH 44106. Offers applied mathematics (MS, PhD); mathematics (MS, PhD). Part-time programs available. *Faculty:* 19 full-time (4 women), 1 part-time/adjunct (0 women). *Students:* 22 full-time (11 women), 1 part-time (0 women); includes 1 minority (Two or more races, non-Hispanic/Latino), 11 international. Average age 27. 105 applicants, 14% accepted, 6 enrolled. In 2011, 2 degrees awarded. Terminal master's awarded for partial completion of doctoral program. *Degree requirements:* For master's, thesis or alternative, thesis (applied mathematics); for doctorate, comprehensive exam, thesis/dissertation. *Entrance requirements:* For master's and doctorate, GRE General Test. Additional exam requirements/recommendations for international students: Required—TOEFL (minimum score 577 paper-based; 213 computer-based; 90 iBT); Recommended—IELTS (minimum score 7). *Application deadline:* For fall admission, 1/15 priority date for domestic students; for spring admission, 11/12 for domestic students. Applications are processed on a rolling basis. Application fee: $50. Electronic applications accepted. *Financial support:* Research assistantships, teaching assistantships, institutionally sponsored loans, and unspecified assistantships available. Financial award application deadline: 1/15. *Faculty research:* Probability theory, convexity and high-dimensional phenomena, imaging, geometric evaluation of curves, dynamical systems, large scale scientific computing, life sciences. *Unit head:* Daniela Calvetti, Chair, 216-368-2880, Fax: 216-368-5163, E-mail: daniela.calvetti@case.edu. *Application contact:* Gaythresa Lewis, Admissions, 216-368-5014, Fax: 216-368-5163, E-mail: gxl34@case.edu. Web site: http://www.case.edu/artsci/math/.

Central European University, Graduate Studies, Department of Mathematics and its Applications, Budapest, Hungary. Offers applied mathematics (MS); mathematics and its applications (PhD). *Faculty:* 2 full-time (0 women), 12 part-time/adjunct (1 woman). *Students:* 40 full-time (4 women). Average age 27. 89 applicants, 18% accepted, 14 enrolled. In 2011, 6 master's, 4 doctorates awarded. *Entrance requirements:* For master's and doctorate, entrance exam or GRE, statement of purpose. Additional exam requirements/recommendations for international students: Required—TOEFL (minimum score 570 paper-based; 230 computer-based); Recommended—IELTS (minimum score 6.5). *Application deadline:* For fall admission, 1/24 for domestic and international students. Electronic applications accepted. Tuition charges are reported in euros. *Expenses: Tuition:* Full-time 11,000 euros. *Financial support:* In 2011–12, 39 students received support, including 39 fellowships (averaging $6,100 per year); career-related internships or fieldwork, scholarships/grants, health care benefits, and tuition waivers (full and partial) also available. *Faculty research:* Applied mathematics, such as; algebra, algebraic geometry, bioinformatics, calculus of variations, computational biology, cryptography, discrete mathematics, evolutions equations, fluid mechanics, geometry, number theory, numerical analysis, optimization, ordinary and partial differential equations, probability theory, quantum mechanics, statistics, stochastic processes.. *Unit head:* Gheorghe Morosanu, Head, 36 1 327-3000 Ext. 2430. *Application contact:* Zsuzsanna Jaszberenyi, Admissions Officer, 361-324-3009, Fax: 367-327-3211, E-mail: admissions@ceu.hu. Web site: http://mathematics.ceu.hu/.

Claremont Graduate University, Graduate Programs, School of Mathematical Sciences, Claremont, CA 91711-6160. Offers computational and systems biology (PhD); computational mathematics and numerical analysis (MA, MS); computational science (PhD); engineering and industrial applied mathematics (PhD); mathematics (PhD); operations research and statistics (MA, MS); physical applied mathematics (MA, MS); pure mathematics (MA, MS); scientific computing (MA, MS); systems and control theory (MA, MS). Part-time programs available. *Faculty:* 6 full-time (0 women), 1 part-time/adjunct (0 women). *Students:* 52 full-time (16 women), 24 part-time (9 women); includes 25 minority (3 Black or African American, non-Hispanic/Latino; 10 Asian, non-Hispanic/Latino; 11 Hispanic/Latino; 1 Two or more races, non-Hispanic/Latino), 17 international. Average age 33. In 2011, 15 master's, 3 doctorates awarded. Terminal master's awarded for partial completion of doctoral program. *Entrance requirements:* For master's and doctorate, GRE General Test. Additional exam requirements/recommendations for international students: Required—TOEFL (minimum score 550 paper-based; 213 computer-based; 80 iBT). *Application deadline:* For fall admission, 2/1 priority date for domestic students. Applications are processed on a rolling basis. Application fee: $60. Electronic applications accepted. *Expenses: Tuition:* Full-time $36,374; part-time $1581 per unit. *Required fees:* $165 per semester. *Financial support:* Fellowships, research assistantships, Federal Work-Study, institutionally sponsored loans, scholarships/grants, and tuition waivers (full and partial) available. Support available to part-time students. Financial award application deadline: 2/15; financial award applicants required to submit FAFSA.

Peterson's Graduate Programs in the Physical Sciences, Mathematics, Agricultural Sciences, the Environment & Natural Resources 2013

facebook.com/petersonspublishing **281**

Applied Mathematics

Unit head: Ellis Cumberbatch, Dean, 909-607-3369; Fax: 909-607-8261, E-mail: ellis.cumberbatch@cgu.edu. *Application contact:* Susan Townzen, Program Coordinator, 909-621-8080, Fax: 909-607-8261, E-Mail: susan.n.townzen@cgu.edu. Web site: http://www.cgu.edu/pages/168.asp.

Clemson University, Graduate School, College of Engineering and Science, Department of Mathematical Sciences, Clemson, SC 29634. Offers applied and pure mathematics (MS, PhD); computational mathematics (MS, PhD); operations research (MS, PhD); statistics (MS, PhD). Part-time programs available. *Faculty:* 46 full-time (13 women), 10 part-time/adjunct (5 women). *Students:* 119 full-time (50 women), 6 part-time (4 women); includes 5 minority (2 Black or African American, non-Hispanic/Latino; 2 American Indian or Alaska Native, non-Hispanic/Latino; 1 Two or more races, non-Hispanic/Latino), 40 international. Average age 27. 133 applicants, 75% accepted, 31 enrolled. In 2011, 23 master's, 6 doctorates awarded. *Degree requirements:* For master's, thesis optional, final project; for doctorate, thesis/dissertation, qualifying exams. *Entrance requirements:* For master's and doctorate, GRE General Test. Additional exam requirements/recommendations for international students: Required—TOEFL. *Application deadline:* For fall admission, 1/15 priority date for domestic students, 1/15 for international students; for spring admission, 10/1 priority date for domestic students, 9/15 for international students. Applications are processed on a rolling basis. Application fee: $70 ($80 for international students). Electronic applications accepted. *Financial support:* In 2011–12, 113 students received support, including 1 fellowship with full and partial tuition reimbursement available (averaging $10,000 per year), 9 research assistantships with partial tuition reimbursements available (averaging $18,373 per year), 104 teaching assistantships with partial tuition reimbursements available (averaging $17,869 per year); career-related internships or fieldwork, institutionally sponsored loans, scholarships/grants, health care benefits, and unspecified assistantships also available. Support available to part-time students. Financial award application deadline: 4/15. *Faculty research:* Applied and computational analysis, cryptography, discrete mathematics, optimization, statistics. *Total annual research expenditures:* $780,865. *Unit head:* Dr. Robert L. Taylor, Chair, 864-656-5240, Fax: 864-656-5230, E-mail: rtaylo2@clemson.edu. *Application contact:* Dr. K. B. Kulasekera, Graduate Coordinator, 864-656-5231, Fax: 864-656-5230, E-mail: kk@clemson.edu. Web site: http://www.clemson.edu/ces/departments/math/index.html.

Columbia University, The Fu Foundation School of Engineering and Applied Science, Department of Applied Physics and Applied Mathematics, New York, NY 10027. Offers applied physics (Eng Sc D); applied physics and applied mathematics (MS, PhD, Engr); materials science and engineering (MS, Eng Sc D, PhD); medical physics (MS). Part-time programs available. Postbaccalaureate distance learning degree programs offered (no on-campus study). *Faculty:* 32 full-time (2 women), 23 part-time/adjunct (2 women). *Students:* 98 full-time (22 women), 38 part-time (10 women); includes 19 minority (14 Asian, non-Hispanic/Latino; 1 Hispanic/Latino; 4 Two or more races, non-Hispanic/Latino), 50 international. Average age 28. 371 applicants, 18% accepted, 41 enrolled. In 2011, 57 master's, 18 doctorates awarded. Terminal master's awarded for partial completion of doctoral program. *Degree requirements:* For master's, comprehensive exam; for doctorate, thesis/dissertation, qualifying exam. *Entrance requirements:* For master's, GRE General Test, GRE Subject Test (strongly recommended); for doctorate, GRE General Test, GRE Subject Test (applied physics); for Engr, GRE General Test. Additional exam requirements/recommendations for international students: Required—TOEFL, IELTS. *Application deadline:* For fall admission, 12/1 priority date for domestic students, 12/1 for international students; for spring admission, 10/1 priority date for domestic students, 10/1 for international students. Application fee: $95. Electronic applications accepted. *Financial support:* In 2011–12, 71 students received support, including 2 fellowships with full tuition reimbursements available (averaging $31,140 per year), 55 research assistantships with full tuition reimbursements available (averaging $31,133 per year), 16 teaching assistantships with full tuition reimbursements available (averaging $31,133 per year); health care benefits also available. Financial award application deadline: 12/1; financial award applicants required to submit FAFSA. *Faculty research:* Plasma physics and fusion energy; optical and laser physics; atmospheric, oceanic and earth physics; applied mathematics; solid state science and processing of materials, their properties, and their structure; medical physics. *Unit head:* Dr. Ismail C. Noyan, Professor and Department Chairman, 212-854-8919, E-mail: icn2@columbia.edu. *Application contact:* Montserrat Fernandez-Pinkley, Student Services Coordinator, 212-854-4457, Fax: 212-854-8257, E-mail: mf2157@columbia.edu. Web site: http://www.apam.columbia.edu/.

See Display on page 221 and Close-Up on page 269.

Cornell University, Graduate School, Graduate Fields of Arts and Sciences, Center for Applied Mathematics, Ithaca, NY 14853-0001. Offers PhD. *Faculty:* 95 full-time (6 women). *Students:* 37 full-time (14 women); includes 8 minority (2 Black or African American, non-Hispanic/Latino; 1 Asian, non-Hispanic/Latino; 4 Hispanic/Latino; 1 Two or more races, non-Hispanic/Latino), 11 international. Average age 26. 209 applicants, 10% accepted, 11 enrolled. In 2011, 8 doctorates awarded. *Degree requirements:* For doctorate, one foreign language, comprehensive exam, thesis/dissertation. *Entrance requirements:* For doctorate, GRE General Test, GRE Subject Test (mathematics recommended), 3 letters of recommendation. Additional exam requirements/recommendations for international students: Required—TOEFL (minimum score 550 paper-based; 213 computer-based; 77 iBT). *Application deadline:* For fall admission, 1/15 for domestic students. Application fee: $95. Electronic applications accepted. *Financial support:* In 2011–12, 8 fellowships with full tuition reimbursements, 14 research assistantships with full tuition reimbursements, 15 teaching assistantships with full tuition reimbursements were awarded; institutionally sponsored loans, scholarships/grants, health care benefits, tuition waivers (full and partial), and unspecified assistantships also available. Financial award applicants required to submit FAFSA. *Faculty research:* Nonlinear systems and PDEs, numerical methods, signal and image processing, mathematical biology, discrete mathematics and optimization. *Unit head:* Director of Graduate Studies, 607-255-9860, Fax: 607-255-9860. *Application contact:* Graduate Field Assistant, 607-255-4756, Fax: 607-255-9860, E-mail: appliedmath@cornell.edu. Web site: http://www.gradschool.cornell.edu/academics/fields-study/catalog/?fid=22#tabs-1.

Cornell University, Graduate School, Graduate Fields of Engineering, Field of Chemical Engineering, Ithaca, NY 14853-0001. Offers advanced materials processing (M Eng, MS, PhD); applied mathematics and computational methods (M Eng, MS, PhD); biochemical engineering (M Eng, MS, PhD); chemical reaction engineering (M Eng, MS, PhD); classical and statistical thermodynamics (M Eng, MS, PhD); fluid dynamics, rheology and biorheology (M Eng, MS, PhD); heat and mass transfer (M Eng, MS, PhD); kinetics and catalysis (M Eng, MS, PhD); polymers (M Eng, MS, PhD); surface science (M Eng, MS, PhD). *Faculty:* 29 full-time (2 women). *Students:* 106 full-time (30 women); includes 21 minority (3 Black or African American, non-Hispanic/Latino; 14 Asian, non-Hispanic/Latino; 4 Hispanic/Latino, 46 international. Average age 25. 379 applicants, 35% accepted, 53 enrolled. In 2011, 50 master's, 8 doctorates awarded. *Degree requirements:* For master's, thesis (MS); for doctorate, comprehensive exam, thesis/dissertation. *Entrance requirements:* For master's and doctorate, GRE General Test, 2 letters of recommendation. Additional exam requirements/recommendations for international students: Required—TOEFL (minimum score 600 paper-based; 237 computer-based; 77 iBT). *Application deadline:* For fall admission, 1/15 priority date for domestic students. Application fee: $95. Electronic applications accepted. *Financial support:* In 2011–12, 67 students received support, including 24 fellowships with full tuition reimbursements available, 44 research assistantships with full tuition reimbursements available, 5 teaching assistantships with full tuition reimbursements available; institutionally sponsored loans, scholarships/grants, health care benefits, tuition waivers (full and partial), and unspecified assistantships also available. Financial award applicants required to submit FAFSA. *Faculty research:* Biochemical, biomedical and metabolic engineering; fluid and polymer dynamics; surface science and chemical kinetics; electronics materials; microchemical systems and nanotechnology. *Unit head:* Director of Graduate Studies, 607-255-4550. *Application contact:* Graduate Field Assistant, 607-255-4550, E-mail: dgs@cheme.cornell.edu. Web site: http://www.gradschool.cornell.edu/fields.php?id-25&a-2.

Cornell University, Graduate School, Graduate Fields of Engineering, Field of Operations Research and Information Engineering, Ithaca, NY 14853. Offers applied probability and statistics (PhD); manufacturing systems engineering (PhD); mathematical programming (PhD); operations research and industrial engineering (M Eng). *Faculty:* 38 full-time (6 women). *Students:* 172 full-time (47 women); includes 25 minority (2 Black or African American, non-Hispanic/Latino; 19 Asian, non-Hispanic/Latino; 4 Hispanic/Latino) 120 international. Average age 24. 1,070 applicants, 24% accepted, 106 enrolled. In 2011, 93 master's, 6 doctorates awarded. *Degree requirements:* For doctorate, comprehensive exam, thesis/dissertation. *Entrance requirements:* For master's and doctorate, GRE General Test, 3 letters of recommendation. Additional exam requirements/recommendations for international students: Required—TOEFL (minimum score 600 paper-based; 250 computer-based; 100 iBT). *Application deadline:* For fall admission, 12/15 for domestic students. Application fee: $95. Electronic applications accepted. *Financial support:* In 2011–12, 44 students received support, including 11 fellowships with full tuition reimbursements available, 13 research assistantships with full tuition reimbursements available, 19 teaching assistantships with full tuition reimbursements available; institutionally sponsored loans, scholarships/grants, health care benefits, tuition waivers (full and partial), and unspecified assistantships also available. Financial award applicants required to submit FAFSA. *Faculty research:* Mathematical programming and combinatorial optimization, statistics, stochastic processes, mathematical finance, simulation, manufacturing, e-commerce. *Unit head:* Director of Graduate Studies, 607-255-9128, Fax: 607-255-9129. *Application contact:* Graduate Field Assistant, 607-255-9128, Fax: 607-255-9129, E-mail: orie@cornell.edu. Web site: http://www.gradschool.cornell.edu/fields.php?id-35&a-2.

Dalhousie University, Faculty of Engineering, Department of Engineering Mathematics, Halifax, NS B3J 2X4, Canada. Offers M Sc, PhD. *Degree requirements:* For master's, thesis; for doctorate, thesis/dissertation. *Entrance requirements:* Additional exam requirements/recommendations for international students: Required—TOEFL, IELTS, CANTEST, CAEL, or Michigan English Language Assessment Battery. Electronic applications accepted. *Faculty research:* Piecewise regression and robust statistics, random field theory, dynamical systems, wave loads on offshore structures, digital signal processing.

Delaware State University, Graduate Programs, Department of Mathematics, Interdisciplinary Program in Applied Mathematics and Theoretical Physics, Dover, DE 19901-2277. Offers PhD. *Degree requirements:* For doctorate, one foreign language, thesis defense. *Entrance requirements:* For doctorate, GRE General Test, MS degree in physics or mathematics. Additional exam requirements/

282 facebook.com/petersonspublishing

Peterson's Graduate Programs in the Physical Sciences, Mathematics, Agricultural Sciences, the Environment & Natural Resources 2013

recommendations for international students: Required—TOEFL (minimum score 550 paper-based).

Delaware State University, Graduate Programs, Department of Mathematics, Program in Applied Mathematics, Dover, DE 19901-2277. Offers MS. *Entrance requirements:* Additional exam requirements/recommendations for international students: Required—TOEFL (minimum score 550 paper-based). Electronic applications accepted.

DePaul University, College of Science and Health, Department of Mathematical Sciences, Chicago, IL 60614. Offers applied mathematics (MS), including actuarial science or statistics; applied statistics (MS, Certificate); mathematics education (MA). Part-time and evening/weekend programs available. *Faculty:* 23 full-time (6 women), 18 part-time/adjunct (5 women). *Students:* 122 full-time (57 women), 63 part-time (23 women); includes 52 minority (19 Black or African American, non-Hispanic/Latino; 5 Asian, non-Hispanic/Latino; 10 Hispanic/Latino; 1 Native Hawaiian or other Pacific Islander, non-Hispanic/Latino; 4 Two or more races, non-Hispanic/Latino), 15 international. Average age 30. 40 applicants, 100% accepted. In 2011, 30 master's awarded. *Degree requirements:* For master's, comprehensive exam. *Entrance requirements:* Additional exam requirements/recommendations for international students: Required—TOEFL. *Application deadline:* For fall admission, 7/30 for domestic students, 6/30 for international students; for winter admission, 11/30 for domestic students, 10/31 for international students; for spring admission, 2/15 for domestic students. Applications are processed on a rolling basis. Application fee: $25. *Financial support:* In 2011–12, 12 students received support, including research assistantships with partial tuition reimbursements available (averaging $6,000 per year); teaching assistantships and tuition waivers (full) also available. Financial award application deadline: 4/30. *Faculty research:* Verbally prime algebras, enveloping algebras of Lie, superalgebras and related rings, harmonic analysis, estimation theory. *Unit head:* Dr. Ahmed I. Zayed, Chairperson, 773-325-7806, Fax: 773-325-7807, E-mail: azayed@depaul.edu. *Application contact:* Ann Spittle, Director of Graduate Admissions, 312-362-8300, Fax: 312-362-5749, E-mail: admitdpu@depaul.edu. Web site: http://depaul.edu/~math.

École Polytechnique de Montréal, Graduate Programs, Department of Mathematics and Industrial Engineering, Montréal, QC H3C 3A7, Canada. Offers ergonomy (M Eng, M Sc A, DESS); mathematical method in CA engineering (M Eng, M Sc A, PhD); operational research (M Eng, M Sc A, PhD); production (M Eng, M Sc A); technology management (M Eng, M Sc A). DESS program offered jointly with HEC Montreal and Université de Montréal. Part-time programs available. *Degree requirements:* For master's, one foreign language, thesis. *Entrance requirements:* For master's, minimum GPA of 2.75. *Faculty research:* Use of computers in organizations.

Florida Atlantic University, Charles E. Schmidt College of Science, Department of Mathematical Sciences, Boca Raton, FL 33431-0991. Offers applied mathematics and statistics (MS); mathematical sciences (MS, MST, PhD). Part-time programs available. *Faculty:* 42 full-time (6 women), 38 part-time/adjunct (11 women). *Students:* 42 full-time (6 women), 38 part-time (11 women); includes 18 minority (9 Black or African American, non-Hispanic/Latino; 5 Asian, non-Hispanic/Latino; 3 Hispanic/Latino; 1 Two or more races, non-Hispanic/Latino), 27 international. Average age 32. 76 applicants, 41% accepted, 14 enrolled. In 2011, 24 master's, 6 doctorates awarded. Terminal master's awarded for partial completion of doctoral program. *Degree requirements:* For master's, comprehensive exam (for some programs), thesis (for some programs); for doctorate, comprehensive exam, thesis/dissertation. *Entrance requirements:* For master's and doctorate, GRE General Test, minimum GPA of 3.0. Additional exam requirements/recommendations for international students: Required—TOEFL (minimum score 500 paper-based; 173 computer-based). *Application deadline:* For fall admission, 7/1 priority date for domestic students, 2/15 for international students; for spring admission, 11/1 priority date for domestic students, 7/15 for international students. Applications are processed on a rolling basis. Application fee: $30. Electronic applications accepted. *Expenses: Tuition, area resident:* Part-time $343.02 per credit hour. Tuition, state resident: full-time $8232. Tuition, nonresident: full-time $23,931; part-time $997.14 per credit hour. *Financial support:* In 2011–12, fellowships with partial tuition reimbursements (averaging $20,000 per year), teaching assistantships with partial tuition reimbursements (averaging $20,000 per year) were awarded; Federal Work-Study also available. Financial award application deadline: 4/1. *Faculty research:* Cryptography, statistics, algebra, analysis, combinatorics. *Unit head:* Dr. Lee Klingler, Chair, 561-297-0274, Fax: 561-297-2436, E-mail: klingler@fau.edu. *Application contact:* Dr. Heinrich Niederhausen, Graduate Director, 561-297-3237, Fax: 561-297-2436, E-mail: niederha@fau.edu. Web site: http://www.math.fau.edu/.

Florida Institute of Technology, Graduate Programs, College of Science, Department of Mathematical Sciences, Melbourne, FL 32901-6975. Offers applied mathematics (MS, PhD); operations research (MS, PhD). Part-time and evening/weekend programs available. *Faculty:* 11 full-time (2 women). *Students:* 31 full-time (12 women), 10 part-time (2 women); includes 5 minority (3 Black or African American, non-Hispanic/Latino; 1 Asian, non-Hispanic/Latino; 1 Hispanic/Latino), 20 international. Average age 32. 82 applicants, 61% accepted, 17 enrolled. In 2011, 8 master's, 5 doctorates awarded. *Degree requirements:* For master's, comprehensive exam (for some programs), thesis optional; for doctorate, comprehensive exam, thesis/dissertation, preliminary exam. *Entrance requirements:* For master's, minimum GPA of 3.0, computer programming literacy; for doctorate, minimum GPA of 3.2, resume, 3 letters of recommendation,

statement of objectives. Additional exam requirements/recommendations for international students: Required—TOEFL (minimum score 550 paper-based; 213 computer-based; 79 iBT). *Application deadline:* For fall admission, 4/1 for international students; for spring admission, 9/30 for international students. Applications are processed on a rolling basis. Application fee: $0. Electronic applications accepted. *Expenses: Tuition:* Full-time $19,620; part-time $1090 per credit hour. Tuition and fees vary according to campus/location. *Financial support:* In 2011–12, 17 teaching assistantships with full and partial tuition reimbursements (averaging $7,586 per year) were awarded; research assistantships, career-related internships or fieldwork, institutionally sponsored loans, tuition waivers (partial), unspecified assistantships, and tuition remissions also available. Support available to part-time students. Financial award application deadline: 3/1; financial award applicants required to submit FAFSA. *Faculty research:* Real analysis, numerical analysis, statistics, data analysis, combinatorics, artificial intelligence, simulation. *Total annual research expenditures:* $58,346. *Unit head:* Dr. Semen Koksal, Department Head, 321-674-8765, Fax: 321-674-7412, E-mail: skoksal@fit.edu. *Application contact:* Cheryl A. Brown, Associate Director of Graduate Admissions, 321-674-7581, Fax: 321-723-9468, E-mail: cbrown@fit.edu. Web site: http://cos.fit.edu/math/.

Florida State University, The Graduate School, College of Arts and Sciences, Department of Mathematics, Tallahassee, FL 32306-4510. Offers applied computational mathematics (MS, PhD); biomathematics (MS, PhD); financial mathematics (MS, PhD); pure mathematics (MS, PhD). Part-time programs available. *Faculty:* 52 full-time (13 women), 1 (woman) part-time/adjunct. *Students:* 139 full-time (36 women), 7 part-time (1 woman); includes 15 minority (6 Black or African American, non-Hispanic/Latino; 4 Asian, non-Hispanic/Latino; 5 Hispanic/Latino), 99 international. Average age 27. 336 applicants, 41% accepted, 41 enrolled. In 2011, 43 master's, 14 doctorates awarded. Terminal master's awarded for partial completion of doctoral program. *Degree requirements:* For master's, comprehensive exam (for some programs), thesis optional; for doctorate, comprehensive exam, thesis/dissertation, candidacy exam including written qualifying examinations which differ by degree concentrations. *Entrance requirements:* For master's and doctorate, GRE General Test, minimum upper-division GPA of 3.0, 4-year bachelor's degree. Additional exam requirements/recommendations for international students: Required—TOEFL (minimum score 550 paper-based; 213 computer-bases; 80 iBT) or IELTS (minimum score 6.5). *Application deadline:* For fall admission, 1/1 priority date for domestic students, 1/1 for international students; for spring admission, 10/1 priority date for domestic students, 11/1 for international students. Applications are processed on a rolling basis. Application fee: $30. Electronic applications accepted. *Expenses:* Tuition, state resident: full-time $9474; part-time $350.88 per credit hour. Tuition, nonresident: full-time $16,236; part-time $601.34 per credit hour. *Required fees:* $630 per semester. One-time fee: $20. Tuition and fees vary according to course load and campus/location. *Financial support:* In 2011–12, 106 students received support, including 7 fellowships with full tuition reimbursements available (averaging $22,600 per year), 12 research assistantships with full tuition reimbursements available (averaging $22,000 per year), 78 teaching assistantships with full tuition reimbursements available (averaging $19,300 per year); career-related internships or fieldwork, institutionally sponsored loans, scholarships/grants, health care benefits, and unspecified assistantships also available. *Faculty research:* Algebra and algebraic geometry; applied, financial, numerical, and classical analysis; biomathematics, including shape analysis and anatomical imaging; computational mathematics and numerical algorithms; geometric topology. *Unit head:* Dr. Philip L. Bowers, Chairperson, 850-645-3338, Fax: 850-644-4053, E-mail: bowers@math.fsu.edu. *Application contact:* Dr. Bettye Anne Case, Associate Chair for Graduate Studies, 850-644-1586, Fax: 850-644-4053, E-mail: case@math.fsu.edu. Web site: http://www.math.fsu.edu/.

The George Washington University, Columbian College of Arts and Sciences, Department of Mathematics, Washington, DC 20052. Offers applied mathematics (MA, MS, PhD); pure mathematics (MA, MS, PhD). Part-time and evening/weekend programs available. *Faculty:* 16 full-time (3 women), 5 part-time/adjunct (2 women). *Students:* 16 full-time (2 women), 9 part-time (4 women); includes 3 minority (1 Black or African American, non-Hispanic/Latino; 1 American Indian or Alaska Native, non-Hispanic/Latino; 1 Asian, non-Hispanic/Latino), 12 international. Average age 28. 101 applicants, 80% accepted, 5 enrolled. In 2011, 2 master's awarded. Terminal master's awarded for partial completion of doctoral program. *Degree requirements:* For master's, comprehensive exam; for doctorate, one foreign language, thesis/dissertation, general exam. *Entrance requirements:* For master's and doctorate, GRE General Test, minimum GPA of 3.0, interview. Additional exam requirements/recommendations for international students: Required—TOEFL (minimum score 550 paper-based; 213 computer-based; 80 iBT). *Application deadline:* For fall admission, 1/15 priority date for domestic students, 1/15 for international students; for spring admission, 10/1 priority date for domestic students, 9/1 for international students. Applications are processed on a rolling basis. Application fee: $75. Electronic applications accepted. *Financial support:* In 2011–12, 17 students received support. Fellowships with full tuition reimbursements available, teaching assistantships with tuition reimbursements available, Federal Work-Study, and tuition waivers available. Financial award application deadline: 1/15. *Unit head:* John B. Conway, Chair, 202-994-0553, E-mail: conway@gwu.edu. *Application contact:* 202-994-6210, Fax: 202-994-6213, E-mail: askccas@gwu.edu. Web site: http://www.gwu.edu/~math/.

Peterson's Graduate Programs in the Physical Sciences, Mathematics, Agricultural Sciences, the Environment & Natural Resources 2013

facebook.com/petersonspublishing **283**

Applied Mathematics

Georgia Institute of Technology, Graduate Studies and Research, College of Sciences, School of Mathematics, Atlanta, GA 30332-0001. Offers algorithms, combinatorics, and optimization (PhD); applied mathematics (MS); bioinformatics (PhD); mathematics (PhD); quantitative and computational finance (MS); statistics (MS Stat). Terminal master's awarded for partial completion of doctoral program. *Degree requirements:* For master's, thesis or alternative; for doctorate, one foreign language, thesis/dissertation. *Entrance requirements:* For master's, GRE General Test, minimum GPA of 3.0; for doctorate, GRE General Test, GRE Subject Test, minimum GPA of 3.0. Additional exam requirements/ recommendations for international students: Required—TOEFL. Electronic applications accepted. *Faculty research:* Dynamical systems, discrete mathematics, probability and statistics, mathematical physics.

Hampton University, Graduate College, Program in Applied Mathematics, Hampton, VA 23668. Offers computational mathematics (MS); nonlinear science (MS); statistics and probability (MS). *Degree requirements:* For master's, thesis optional. *Entrance requirements:* For master's, GRE General Test.

Harvard University, Graduate School of Arts and Sciences, School of Engineering and Applied Sciences, Cambridge, MA 02138. Offers applied mathematics (ME, SM, PhD); applied physics (ME, SM, PhD); computer science (ME, SM, PhD); engineering science (ME); engineering sciences (SM, PhD). Part-time programs available. Terminal master's awarded for partial completion of doctoral program. *Degree requirements:* For master's, thesis optional; for doctorate, comprehensive exam, thesis/dissertation. *Entrance requirements:* For master's and doctorate, GRE General Test, GRE Subject Test (recommended), 3 letters of recommendation. Additional exam requirements/recommendations for international students: Required—TOEFL (minimum score 80 iBT). Electronic applications accepted. *Expenses: Tuition:* Full-time $36,304. *Required fees:* $1186. Full-time tuition and fees vary according to program. *Faculty research:* Applied mathematics, applied physics, computer science and electrical engineering, environmental engineering, mechanical and biomedical engineering.

Howard University, Graduate School, Department of Mathematics, Washington, DC 20059-0002. Offers applied mathematics (MS, PhD); mathematics (MS, PhD). Part-time programs available. Terminal master's awarded for partial completion of doctoral program. *Degree requirements:* For master's, comprehensive exam, thesis or alternative, qualifying exam; for doctorate, 2 foreign languages, comprehensive exam, thesis/dissertation, qualifying exams. *Entrance requirements:* For master's, GRE General Test, minimum GPA of 3.0; for doctorate, GRE General Test. Additional exam requirements/recommendations for international students: Required—TOEFL. Electronic applications accepted.

Hunter College of the City University of New York, Graduate School, School of Arts and Sciences, Department of Mathematics and Statistics, New York, NY 10021-5085. Offers applied mathematics (MA); mathematics for secondary education (MA); pure mathematics (MA). Part-time and evening/weekend programs available. *Faculty:* 8 full-time (1 woman), 2 part-time/adjunct (0 women). *Students:* 9 full-time (7 women), 71 part-time (34 women); includes 25 minority (7 Black or African American, non-Hispanic/Latino; 16 Asian, non-Hispanic/Latino; 2 Hispanic/Latino), 11 international. Average age 28. 54 applicants, 56% accepted, 15 enrolled. In 2011, 30 master's awarded. *Degree requirements:* For master's, one foreign language, comprehensive exam, thesis (for some programs). *Entrance requirements:* For master's, GRE General Test, 24 credits in mathematics. Additional exam requirements/recommendations for international students: Required—TOEFL. *Application deadline:* For fall admission, 4/1 for domestic students, 2/1 for international students; for spring admission, 11/1 for domestic students, 9/1 for international students. Application fee: $125. *Expenses:* Tuition, state resident: full-time $8210; part-time $345 per credit. Tuition, nonresident: full-time $15,360; part-time $640 per credit. *Required fees:* $280 per semester. One-time fee: $125. Tuition and fees vary according to class time, campus/location and program. *Financial support:* Federal Work-Study, institutionally sponsored loans, scholarships/grants, and tuition waivers (partial) available. Support available to part-time students. *Faculty research:* Data analysis, dynamical systems, computer graphics, topology, statistical decision theory. *Unit head:* Ada Peluso, Chairperson, 212-772-5300, Fax: 212-772-4858, E-mail: peluso@math.hunter.cuny.edu. *Application contact:* William Zlata, Director for Graduate Admissions, 212-772-4482, Fax: 212-650-3336, E-mail: admissions@hunter.cuny.edu. Web site: http://math.hunter.cuny.edu/.

Illinois Institute of Technology, Graduate College, College of Science and Letters, Department of Applied Mathematics, Chicago, IL 60616-3793. Offers applied mathematics (MS, PhD); collegiate mathematics (PhD); mathematical finance (MMF). MMF program held jointly with Stuart School of Business, PhD (collegiate mathematics) with Department of Math and Science Education. Terminal master's awarded for partial completion of doctoral program. *Degree requirements:* For master's, comprehensive exam, thesis; for doctorate, comprehensive exam, thesis/dissertation. *Entrance requirements:* For master's, GRE General Test (minimum scores: 1100 Quantitative and Verbal, 2.5 Analytical Writing), minimum undergraduate GPA of 3.0; for doctorate, GRE General Test (minimum scores: 1100 Quantitative and Verbal, 3.0 Analytical Writing), minimum undergraduate GPA of 3.5. Additional exam requirements/recommendations for international students: Required—TOEFL (minimum score 523 paper-based; 70 iBT); Recommended—IELTS (minimum score 5.5). Electronic applications accepted. *Faculty research:* Applied analysis, computational mathematics, discrete applied mathematics, stochastics, mathematical finance.

Indiana University Bloomington, University Graduate School, College of Arts and Sciences, Department of Mathematics, Bloomington, IN 47405-7000. Offers applied mathematics-numerical analysis (MA, PhD); mathematics education (MAT); pure mathematics (MA, PhD). *Faculty:* 49 full-time (3 women). *Students:* 124 full-time (23 women), 1 part-time (0 women); includes 13 minority (2 Black or African American, non-Hispanic/Latino; 10 Asian, non-Hispanic/Latino; 1 Hispanic/Latino), 68 international. Average age 27. 242 applicants, 19% accepted, 17 enrolled. In 2011, 20 master's, 12 doctorates awarded. Terminal master's awarded for partial completion of doctoral program. *Degree requirements:* For doctorate, one foreign language, thesis/dissertation. *Entrance requirements:* For master's and doctorate, GRE General Test, GRE Subject Test. Additional exam requirements/recommendations for international students: Required—TOEFL. *Application deadline:* For fall admission, 1/15 priority date for domestic students, 1/15 for international students. Applications are processed on a rolling basis. Application fee: $55 ($65 for international students). Electronic applications accepted. *Financial support:* In 2011–12, 2 students received support, including 9 fellowships with full tuition reimbursements available (averaging $21,450 per year), 11 research assistantships with full tuition reimbursements available (averaging $16,045 per year), 96 teaching assistantships with full tuition reimbursements available (averaging $15,870 per year); scholarships/grants, health care benefits, and unspecified assistantships also available. Financial award application deadline: 1/15. *Faculty research:* Topology, geometry, algebra, applied, analysis. *Unit head:* Kevin Zumbrun, Chair, 812-855-2200. *Application contact:* Kate Bowman, Graduate Secretary, 812-855-2645, Fax: 812-855-0046, E-mail: gradmath@indiana.edu. Web site: http://www.math.indiana.edu/.

Indiana University of Pennsylvania, School of Graduate Studies and Research, College of Natural Sciences and Mathematics, Department of Mathematics, Program in Applied Mathematics, Indiana, PA 15705-1087. Offers MS. *Faculty:* 9 full-time (2 women). *Students:* 17 full-time (3 women), 5 part-time (1 woman); includes 3 minority (1 Black or African American, non-Hispanic/Latino; 1 Asian, non-Hispanic/Latino; 1 Two or more races, non-Hispanic/Latino), 3 international. Average age 27. 31 applicants, 74% accepted, 8 enrolled. In 2011, 8 master's awarded. *Degree requirements:* For master's, thesis optional. *Entrance requirements:* For master's, 2 letters of recommendation. Additional exam requirements/recommendations for international students: Required—TOEFL (minimum score 540 paper-based; 207 computer-based). *Application deadline:* Applications are processed on a rolling basis. Application fee: $50. Electronic applications accepted. *Expenses:* Tuition, state resident: full-time $7488; part-time $416 per credit. Tuition, nonresident: full-time $11,232; part-time $624 per credit. *Required fees:* $2070; $192.20 per credit. $90 per semester. *Financial support:* In 2011–12, 11 research assistantships with full and partial tuition reimbursements (averaging $2,890 per year) were awarded; Federal Work-Study also available. Support available to part-time students. Financial award application deadline: 4/15; financial award applicants required to submit FAFSA. *Unit head:* Dr. Yu-Ju Kuo, Graduate Coordinator, 724-357-4765, E-mail: yuju.kuo@iup.edu. *Application contact:* Dr. Jacqueline Gorman, Dean's Associate, 724-357-2609, E-mail: jgorman@iup.edu. Web site: http://www.iup.edu/math/programs/msappliedmath/default.aspx.

Indiana University–Purdue University Fort Wayne, College of Arts and Sciences, Department of Mathematical Sciences, Fort Wayne, IN 46805-1499. Offers applied mathematics (MS); applied statistics (Certificate); mathematics (MS); operations research (MS); teaching (MAT). Part-time and evening/weekend programs available. *Faculty:* 20 full-time (5 women). *Students:* 1 full-time (0 women), 16 part-time (3 women). Average age 32. 6 applicants, 100% accepted, 3 enrolled. In 2011, 8 master's, 2 other advanced degrees awarded. *Entrance requirements:* For master's, minimum GPA of 3.0, major or minor in mathematics, three letters of recommendation. Additional exam requirements/recommendations for international students: Required—TOEFL (minimum score 550 paper-based; 213 computer-based; 77 iBT); Recommended—TWE. *Application deadline:* For fall admission, 8/1 priority date for domestic students, 7/1 for international students; for spring admission, 12/1 for domestic students, 10/1 for international students. Applications are processed on a rolling basis. Application fee: $55 ($60 for international students). Electronic applications accepted. *Financial support:* In 2011–12, 6 teaching assistantships with partial tuition reimbursements (averaging $12,930 per year) were awarded; scholarships/grants and unspecified assistantships also available. Support available to part-time students. Financial award application deadline: 3/1; financial award applicants required to submit FAFSA. *Faculty research:* Brick factory problem, CR singularities, carleman orthogonal polynomials. *Unit head:* Dr. David A. Legg, Chair, 260-481-6222, Fax: 260-481-0155, E-mail: legg@ipfw.edu. *Application contact:* Dr. W. Douglas Weakley, Director of Graduate Studies, 260-481-6233, Fax: 260-481-0155, E-mail: weakley@ipfw.edu. Web site: http://www.ipfw.edu/math/.

Indiana University–Purdue University Indianapolis, School of Science, Department of Mathematical Sciences, Doctoral Program in Mathematics, Indianapolis, IN 46202-3216. Offers applied mathematics (PhD); mathematical statistics (PhD); mathematics (PhD). *Students:* 17 full-time (7 women), 5 part-time (0 women); includes 2 minority (1 Black or African American, non-Hispanic/Latino; 1 Hispanic/Latino), 10 international. Average age 29. 25 applicants, 44% accepted, 3 enrolled. *Degree requirements:* For doctorate, one foreign language, thesis/dissertation. *Entrance requirements:* For doctorate, GRE General Test. Additional exam requirements/recommendations for international students: Required—TOEFL. *Application deadline:* For fall admission, 2/1 priority date for domestic students. Application fee: $55 ($65 for international students). *Unit* head: Dr. Evgeny Mukhin, Director of Graduate Programs, 317-274-6918, E-mail: grad-program@math.iupui.edu. *Application contact:* Dr. Sherry Queener, Director, Graduate Studies and Associate Dean, 317-274-1577, Fax: 317-278-2380. Web site: http://www.math.iupui.edu/.

Indiana University–Purdue University Indianapolis, School of Science, Department of Mathematical Sciences, Master's Program in Mathematics, Indianapolis, IN 46202-3216. Offers applied mathematics (MS); applied statistics (MS); mathematics (MS); mathematics education (MS). *Students:* 13 full-time (3 women), 30 part-time (12 women); includes 14 minority (1 Black or African American, non-Hispanic/Latino; 9 Asian, non-Hispanic/Latino; 3 Hispanic/Latino; 1 Two or more races, non-Hispanic/Latino), 14 international. Average age 36. 49 applicants, 73% accepted, 15 enrolled. In 2011, 17 master's awarded. *Degree requirements:* For master's, comprehensive exam (for some programs), thesis optional. *Entrance requirements:* Additional exam requirements/ recommendations for international students: Required—TOEFL. Application fee: $55 ($65 for international students). *Unit head:* Dr. Evgeny Mukhin, Director of Graduate Programs, 317-274-6918, E-mail: grad-program@math.iupui.edu. *Application contact:* Dr. Sherry Queener, Director, Graduate Studies and Associate Dean, 317-274-1577, Fax: 317-278-2380. Web site: http://www.math.iupui.edu/.

Indiana University South Bend, College of Liberal Arts and Sciences, South Bend, IN 46634-7111. Offers applied mathematics and computer science (MS); applied psychology (MA); English (MA); liberal studies (MLS). Part-time and evening/weekend programs available. *Faculty:* 79 full-time (33 women). *Students:* 56 full-time (32 women), 115 part-time (80 women); includes 22 minority (18 Black or African American, non-Hispanic/Latino; 2 American Indian or Alaska Native, non-Hispanic/Latino; 2 Hispanic/Latino), 17 international. Average age 37. 67 applicants, 70% accepted, 35 enrolled. In 2011, 49 master's awarded. *Degree requirements:* For master's, thesis (for some programs). *Entrance requirements:* For master's, minimum GPA of 3.0. Additional exam requirements/ recommendations for international students: Required—TOEFL. *Application deadline:* For fall admission, 7/31 priority date for domestic students, 7/1 for international students; for spring admission, 3/31 priority date for domestic students, 11/1 for international students. Applications are processed on a rolling basis. Application fee: $50 ($60 for international students). *Financial support:* In 2011–12, 5 teaching assistantships were awarded; Federal Work-Study also available. Support available to part-time students. *Faculty research:* Artificial intelligence, bioinformatics, English language and literature, creative writing, computer networks. *Total annual research expenditures:* $127,000. *Unit head:* Dr. Lynn R. Williams, Dean, 574-520-4322, Fax: 574-520-4528, E-mail: lwilliam@iusb.edu. *Application contact:* Admissions Counselor, 574-520-4839, Fax: 574-520-4834, E-mail: graduate@iusb.edu. Web site: https://www.iusb.edu/clas/index.php.

Iowa State University of Science and Technology, Department of Mathematics, Ames, IA 50011. Offers applied mathematics (MS, PhD); mathematics (MS, PhD); school mathematics (MSM). *Degree requirements:* For master's, thesis or alternative; for doctorate, thesis/dissertation. *Entrance requirements:* For master's and doctorate, GRE General Test. Additional exam requirements/recommendations for international students: Required—TOEFL (minimum score 550 paper-based; 79 iBT), IELTS (minimum score 6.5). *Application deadline:* For fall admission, 2/1 priority date for domestic students, 2/1 for international students. Application fee: $40 ($90 for international students). Electronic applications accepted. *Financial support:* Scholarships/grants, health care benefits, and unspecified assistantships available. *Unit head:* Dr. Clifford Bergman, Director of Graduate Education, 515-294-0393, Fax: 515-294-5454, E-mail: gradmath@iastate.edu. *Application contact:* Melanie Erickson, Director of Graduate Education, 515-294-0393, Fax: 515-294-5454, E-mail: gradmath@iastate.edu. Web site: http://http://www.math.iastate.edu/Graduate/Prospective.html.

Iowa State University of Science and Technology, Program in Applied Mathematics, Ames, IA 50011-2064. Offers MS, PhD. *Entrance requirements:* For master's and doctorate, GRE. Additional exam requirements/recommendations for international students: Required—TOEFL (minimum score 550 paper-based; 79 iBT), IELTS (minimum score 6.5). *Application deadline:* For fall admission, 2/1 for domestic and international students. Electronic applications accepted. *Unit head:* Dr. Clifford Bergman, Director of Graduate Education, 515-294-0393, Fax: 515-294-5454, E-mail: gradmath@iastate.edu. *Application contact:* Melanie Erickson, Application Contact, 515-294-0393, Fax: 515-294-5454, E-mail: gradmath@iastate.edu. Web site: http://math.iastate.edu/Graduate/Prospective.html.

The Johns Hopkins University, Engineering Program for Professionals, Part-time Program in Applied and Computational Mathematics, Baltimore, MD 21218-2699. Offers MS; Post-Master's Certificate. Part-time and evening/weekend programs available. Electronic applications accepted.

The Johns Hopkins University, Whiting School of Engineering, Department of Applied Mathematics and Statistics, Baltimore, MD 21218-2699. Offers computational medicine (PhD); discrete mathematics (MA, MSE, PhD); financial mathematics (MSE); operations research/optimization/decision science (MA, MSE, PhD); statistics/probability/stochastic processes (MA, MSE, PhD). Terminal master's awarded for partial completion of doctoral program. *Degree requirements:* For master's, thesis (for some programs); for doctorate, thesis/dissertation, oral exam, introductory exam. *Entrance requirements:* For master's

and doctorate, GRE General Test, GRE Subject Test. Additional exam requirements/recommendations for international students: Required—TOEFL (minimum score 600 paper-based; 250 computer-based; 100 iBT). Electronic applications accepted. *Faculty research:* Discrete mathematics, probability, statistics, optimization and operations research, scientific computation, financial mathematics.

Kent State University, College of Arts and Sciences, Department of Mathematical Sciences, Kent, OH 44242-0001. Offers applied mathematics (MA, MS, PhD); pure mathematics (MA, MS, PhD). Part-time programs available. *Degree requirements:* For master's, thesis optional; for doctorate, one foreign language, thesis/dissertation. Electronic applications accepted. *Expenses:* Tuition, state resident: full-time $8136; part-time $452 per credit hour. Tuition, nonresident: full-time $14,292; part-time $794 per credit hour. *Faculty research:* Approximation theory, measure theory, ring theory, functional analysis, complex analysis.

Lehigh University, College of Arts and Sciences, Department of Mathematics, Bethlehem, PA 18015. Offers applied mathematics (MS, PhD); mathematics (MS, PhD); statistics (MS). Part-time programs available. *Faculty:* 23 full-time (1 woman), 2 part-time/adjunct (0 women). *Students:* 31 full-time (16 women), 6 part-time (2 women); includes 1 minority (Asian, non-Hispanic/Latino), 13 international. Average age 26. 140 applicants, 9% accepted, 5 enrolled. In 2011, 11 master's, 2 doctorates awarded. Terminal master's awarded for partial completion of doctoral program. *Degree requirements:* For master's, comprehensive exam, thesis optional; for doctorate, comprehensive exam, thesis/dissertation, qualifying exams, general exam, advanced topic exam. *Entrance requirements:* For master's and doctorate, GRE General Test (strongly recommended), minimum undergraduate GPA of 2.75, 3.0 for last two semesters; adequate background in math. Additional exam requirements/recommendations for international students: Required—TOEFL (minimum score 85 iBT). *Application deadline:* For fall admission, 1/1 priority date for domestic students, 1/1 for international students; for spring admission, 12/1 priority date for domestic students, 12/1 for international students. Applications are processed on a rolling basis. Application fee: $75. Electronic applications accepted. *Financial support:* In 2011–12, 35 students received support, including 2 fellowships with full tuition reimbursements available (averaging $25,000 per year), 23 teaching assistantships with full tuition reimbursements available (averaging $17,500 per year); research assistantships with full tuition reimbursements available, scholarships/grants, and tuition waivers (partial) also available. Financial award application deadline: 1/1. *Faculty research:* Probability and statistics, geometry and topology, number theory, algebra, discrete mathematics, differential equations. *Total annual research expenditures:* $155,033. *Unit head:* Dr. Wei-Min Huang, Chairman, 610-758-3730, Fax: 610-758-3767, E-mail: wh02@lehigh.edu. *Application contact:* Dr. Terry Napier, Graduate Coordinator, 610-758-3755, E-mail: mathgrad@lehigh.edu. Web site: http://www.lehigh.edu/~math/grad.html.

Long Island University–C. W. Post Campus, College of Liberal Arts and Sciences, Department of Mathematics, Brookville, NY 11548-1300. Offers applied mathematics (MS); mathematics education (MS); mathematics for secondary school teachers (MS). Part-time and evening/weekend programs available. *Degree requirements:* For master's, thesis or alternative, oral presentation. *Entrance requirements:* Additional exam requirements/recommendations for international students: Required—TOEFL. Electronic applications accepted. *Faculty research:* Differential geometry, topological groups, general topology, number theory, analysis and statistics, numerical analysis.

McGill University, Faculty of Graduate and Postdoctoral Studies, Faculty of Science, Department of Mathematics and Statistics, Montréal, QC H3A 2T5, Canada. Offers computational science and engineering (M Sc); mathematics and statistics (M Sc, MA, PhD), including applied mathematics (M Sc, MA), pure mathematics (M Sc, MA), statistics (M Sc, MA).

Michigan State University, The Graduate School, College of Natural Science, Department of Mathematics, East Lansing, MI 48824. Offers applied mathematics (MS, PhD); industrial mathematics (MS); mathematics (MAT, MS, PhD). *Entrance requirements:* Additional exam requirements/recommendations for international students: Required—TOEFL. Electronic applications accepted.

Missouri University of Science and Technology, Graduate School, Department of Mathematics and Statistics, Rolla, MO 65409. Offers applied mathematics (MS); mathematics (MST, PhD), including mathematics (PhD); mathematics education (MST), statistics (PhD). Terminal master's awarded for partial completion of doctoral program. *Degree requirements:* For master's, thesis or alternative; for doctorate, one foreign language, thesis/dissertation. *Entrance requirements:* For master's and doctorate, GRE General Test, GRE Subject Test. Electronic applications accepted. *Faculty research:* Analysis, differential equations, topology, statistics.

Montclair State University, The Graduate School, College of Science and Mathematics, Department of Mathematical Sciences, Program in Mathematics, Montclair, NJ 07043-1624. Offers mathematics education (MS); pure and applied mathematics (MS). Part-time and evening/weekend programs available. *Students:* 17 full-time (4 women), 53 part-time (30 women); includes 14 minority (3 Black or African American, non-Hispanic/Latino; 3 Asian, non-Hispanic/Latino; 6 Hispanic/Latino; 2 Two or more races, non-Hispanic/Latino), 1 international. Average age 34. 38 applicants, 50% accepted, 16 enrolled. In 2011, 11 master's awarded. *Degree requirements:* For master's, comprehensive exam. *Entrance requirements:* For master's, GRE General Test, 2 letters of recommendation,

Peterson's Graduate Programs in the Physical Sciences, Mathematics, Agricultural Sciences, the Environment & Natural Resources 2013

facebook.com/petersonspublishing   **285**

essay. Additional exam requirements/recommendations for international students: Required—TOEFL (minimum score 83 iBT), IELTS (minimum score 6.5). *Application deadline:* Applications are processed on a rolling basis. Application fee: $60. Electronic applications accepted. *Financial support:* In 2011–12, 9 research assistantships with full tuition reimbursements (averaging $7,000 per year) were awarded; Federal Work-Study, scholarships/grants, and unspecified assistantships also available. Support available to part-time students. Financial award application deadline: 3/1; financial award applicants required to submit FAFSA. *Faculty research:* Computation, applied analysis. *Unit head:* Dr. Helen Roberts, Chairperson, 973-655-5132. *Application contact:* Amy Aiello, Director of Graduate Admissions and Operations, 973-655-5147, Fax: 973-655-7869, E-mail: graduate.school@montclair.edu.

Naval Postgraduate School, Departments and Academic Groups, Department of Applied Mathematics, Monterey, CA 93943. Offers MS, PhD. Program only open to commissioned officers of the United States and friendly nations and selected United States federal civilian employees. Part-time programs available. *Faculty:* 16 full-time (2 women), 1 part-time/adjunct. *Students:* 11 full-time (1 woman), 1 part-time; includes 2 minority (1 Black or African American, non-Hispanic/Latino; 1 Asian, non-Hispanic/Latino), 1 international. Average age 36. In 2011, 8 master's awarded. *Degree requirements:* For master's, thesis; for doctorate, one foreign language, thesis/dissertation. *Faculty research:* Compact S-box for AES2. rotation symmetric Boolean functions count and crytograhic propertie, pseudospectral method for the optimal control of constrained feedback linearizable systems, nodal triangle-based spectral element method for the shallow water equations on the sphere, axisymmetric equilibria of three-dimensional Smoluchowski equation. *Total annual research expenditures:* $752,000. *Unit head:* Prof. Carlos Borges, Department Chair, 831-656-2124, E-mail: borges@nps.edu. Web site: http://nps.edu/Academics/Schools/GSEAS/Departments/Math/index.html.

Naval Postgraduate School, Departments and Academic Groups, Undersea Warfare Academic Group, Monterey, CA 93943. Offers applied mathematics (MS); applied physics (MS); applied science (MS), including acoustics, operations research, physical oceanography, signal processing; electrical engineering (MS); engineering acoustics (MS, PhD); engineering science (MS), including electrical engineering, mechanical engineering; mechanical engineer (ME); mechanical engineering (MS, MSME); meteorology (MS); operations research (MS); physical oceanography (MS). Program only open to commissioned officers of the United States and friendly nations and selected United States federal civilian employees. Part-time programs available. *Students:* 2 full-time, both international. Average age 36. *Degree requirements:* For master's, thesis. *Faculty research:* Unmanned/autonomous vehicles, sea mines and countermeasures, submarine warfare in the twentieth and twenty-first centuries. *Unit head:* Dr. Clyde Scandrett, Academic Group Chairman, 831-656-2027. Web site: http://www.nps.edu/Academics/Schools/GSEAS/Departments/USW/USW-Index.html.

New Jersey Institute of Technology, Office of Graduate Studies, College of Science and Liberal Arts, Department of Mathematical Science, Program in Applied Mathematics, Newark, NJ 07102. Offers MS. Part-time and evening/weekend programs available. *Students:* 9 full-time (3 women), 5 part-time (3 women); includes 7 minority (2 Black or African American, non-Hispanic/Latino; 1 Asian, non-Hispanic/Latino; 4 Hispanic/Latino), 1 international. Average age 27. 29 applicants, 79% accepted, 7 enrolled. In 2011, 6 master's awarded. *Entrance requirements:* For master's, GRE General Test. Additional exam requirements/recommendations for international students: Required—TOEFL (minimum score 550 paper-based; 213 computer-based; 79 iBT). *Application deadline:* For fall admission, 6/1 priority date for domestic students, 5/1 for international students; for spring admission, 11/15 priority date for domestic students, 11/15 for international students. Applications are processed on a rolling basis. Application fee: $65. Electronic applications accepted. *Expenses:* Tuition, state resident: full-time $7980; part-time $867 per credit. Tuition, nonresident: full-time $11,336; part-time $1196 per credit. *Required fees:* $230 per credit. *Financial support:* Fellowships with full and partial tuition reimbursements, research assistantships with full and partial tuition reimbursements, teaching assistantships with full and partial tuition reimbursements, career-related internships or fieldwork, Federal Work-Study, institutionally sponsored loans, and unspecified assistantships available. Financial award application deadline: 1/15. *Unit head:* Dr. Daljit S. Ahluwalia, Chair, 973-596-8465, E-mail: daljit.ahluwalia@njit.edu. *Application contact:* Kathryn Kelly, Director of Admissions, 973-596-3300, Fax: 973-596-3461, E-mail: admissions@njit.edu. Web site: http://math.njit.edu/academics/graduate/ms-appliedmath/index.php.

New Mexico Institute of Mining and Technology, Graduate Studies, Department of Mathematics, Socorro, NM 87801. Offers applied and industrial mathematics (PhD); industrial mathematics (MS); mathematics (MS); operations research and statistics (MS). *Faculty:* 11 full-time (0 women), 2 part-time/adjunct (1 woman). *Students:* 15 full-time (3 women), 1 part-time (0 women); includes 6 minority (1 Black or African American, non-Hispanic/Latino; 4 Asian, non-Hispanic/Latino; 1 Two or more races, non-Hispanic/Latino), 1 international. Average age 32. 13 applicants, 77% accepted, 6 enrolled. In 2011, 6 degrees awarded. *Degree requirements:* For master's, thesis optional; for doctorate, thesis/dissertation. *Entrance requirements:* For master's, GRE General Test. Additional exam requirements/recommendations for international students: Required—TOEFL (minimum score 540 paper-based; 207 computer-based). *Application deadline:* For fall admission, 3/1 priority date for domestic students; for spring admission, 6/1 for domestic students. Applications are processed on a

rolling basis. Application fee: $16 ($30 for international students). *Expenses:* Tuition, state resident: full-time $4849; part-time $269.41 per credit hour. Tuition, nonresident: full-time $16,041; part-time $891.15 per credit hour. *Required fees:* $622; $65 per credit hour. $20 per semester. Part-time tuition and fees vary according to course load. *Financial support:* In 2011–12, 2 research assistantships (averaging $19,516 per year), 13 teaching assistantships with full and partial tuition reimbursements (averaging $34,112 per year) were awarded; fellowships, Federal Work-Study, and institutionally sponsored loans also available. Financial award application deadline: 3/1; financial award applicants required to submit CSS PROFILE or FAFSA. *Faculty research:* Applied mathematics, differential equations, industrial mathematics, numerical analysis, stochastic processes. *Unit head:* Dr. Anwar Hossain, Chairman, 575-835-5135, Fax: 575-835-5366, E-mail: hossain@nmt.edu. *Application contact:* Dr. Lorie Liebrock, Dean of Graduate Studies, 575-835-5513, Fax: 575-835-5476, E-mail: graduate@nmt.edu. Web site: http://www.nmt.edu/~math/.

North Carolina Agricultural and Technical State University, School of Graduate Studies, College of Arts and Sciences, Department of Mathematics, Greensboro, NC 27411. Offers applied mathematics (MS), including secondary education. *Accreditation:* NCATE. Part-time and evening/weekend programs available. *Degree requirements:* For master's, comprehensive exam, thesis or alternative, qualifying exam. *Entrance requirements:* For master's, GRE General Test, minimum GPA of 3.0.

North Carolina Central University, Division of Academic Affairs, College of Science and Technology, Department of Mathematics and Computer Science, Durham, NC 27707-3129. Offers applied mathematics (MS); mathematics education (MS); pure mathematics (MS). Part-time and evening/weekend programs available. *Degree requirements:* For master's, one foreign language, comprehensive exam, thesis. *Entrance requirements:* For master's, minimum GPA of 3.0 in major, 2.5 overall. Additional exam requirements/recommendations for international students: Required—TOEFL. *Faculty research:* Structure theorems for Lie algebra, Kleene monoids and semi-groups, theoretical computer science, mathematics education.

North Carolina State University, Graduate School, College of Physical and Mathematical Sciences, Department of Mathematics, Program in Applied Mathematics, Raleigh, NC 27695. Offers MS, PhD. *Degree requirements:* For master's, thesis (for some programs); for doctorate, thesis/dissertation. *Entrance requirements:* For master's and doctorate, GRE, GRE Subject Test. Electronic applications accepted. *Faculty research:* Biological and physical modeling, numerical analysis, control, stochastic processes, industrial mathematics.

North Dakota State University, College of Graduate and Interdisciplinary Studies, College of Science and Mathematics, Department of Mathematics, Fargo, ND 58108. Offers applied mathematics (MS, PhD); mathematics (MS, PhD). *Faculty:* 11 full-time (1 woman), 1 part-time/adjunct (0 women). *Students:* 23 full-time (7 women), 2 part-time (0 women); includes 1 minority (Two or more races, non-Hispanic/Latino), 5 international. Average age 28. 28 applicants, 29% accepted, 4 enrolled. In 2011, 1 master's, 3 doctorates awarded. *Degree requirements:* For master's, comprehensive exam, thesis; for doctorate, one foreign language, comprehensive exam, thesis/dissertation, computer proficiency. *Entrance requirements:* For master's and doctorate, GRE General Test. Additional exam requirements/recommendations for international students: Required—TOEFL (minimum score 525 paper-based; 197 computer-based; 71 iBT), IELTS. *Application deadline:* For fall admission, 3/1 priority date for domestic students. Applications are processed on a rolling basis. Application fee: $35. Electronic applications accepted. *Financial support:* In 2011–12, 5 fellowships with full tuition reimbursements (averaging $18,000 per year), 1 research assistantship with tuition reimbursement (averaging $14,000 per year), 17 teaching assistantships with full tuition reimbursements (averaging $9,300 per year) were awarded; Federal Work-Study, institutionally sponsored loans, and tuition waivers (full) also available. Support available to part-time students. Financial award application deadline: 3/31. *Faculty research:* Discrete mathematics, number theory, analysis theory, algebra, applied math. *Unit head:* Dr. Dogan Comez, Chair, 701-231-8171, Fax: 701-231-7598, E-mail: dogan.comez@ndsu.edu. *Application contact:* Dr. Sean Sather-Wagstaff, Graduate Program Director, 701-231-8105, Fax: 701-231-7598, E-mail: sean.sather-wagstaff@ndsu.edu. Web site: http://www.math.ndsu.nodak.edu/.

Northeastern University, College of Science, Department of Mathematics, Boston, MA 02115-5096. Offers applied mathematics (MS); mathematics (MS, PhD); operations research (MSOR). Part-time and evening/weekend programs available. *Faculty:* 39 full-time, 15 part-time/adjunct. *Students:* 52 full-time, 3 part-time. 164 applicants, 58% accepted, 14 enrolled. In 2011, 6 master's, 7 doctorates awarded. *Degree requirements:* For master's, thesis (for some programs); for doctorate, thesis/dissertation, qualifying exams. *Entrance requirements:* For master's and doctorate, GRE Subject Test, GRE General Test. Additional exam requirements/recommendations for international students: Required—TOEFL. *Application deadline:* For fall admission, 2/1 priority date for domestic students, 2/1 for international students. Applications are processed on a rolling basis. Application fee: $50. Electronic applications accepted. *Financial support:* In 2011–12, 26 teaching assistantships with tuition reimbursements (averaging $17,345 per year) were awarded; research assistantships with tuition reimbursements, Federal Work-Study, institutionally sponsored loans, tuition waivers (full and partial), and unspecified assistantships also available. Financial award application deadline: 3/1; financial award applicants required to submit FAFSA. *Faculty research:* Algebra and singularities, combinatorics, topology,

286 facebook.com/petersonspublishing

Peterson's Graduate Programs in the Physical Sciences, Mathematics, Agricultural Sciences, the Environment & Natural Resources 2013

probability and statistics, geometric analysis and partial differential equations. *Unit head:* Dr. Jerzy Weyman, Graduate Coordinator, 617-373-5513, Fax: 617-373-5658, E-mail: j.weyman@neu.edu. *Application contact:* Jo-Anne Dickinson, Admissions Contact, 617-373-5990, Fax: 617-373-7281, E-mail: gsas@neu.edu. Web site: http://www.math.neu.edu/.

Northwestern University, The Graduate School, Interdepartmental Programs, Program in Mathematical Methods in Social Science, Evanston, IL 60208. Offers MS.

Northwestern University, McCormick School of Engineering and Applied Science, Department of Engineering Sciences and Applied Mathematics, Evanston, IL 60208. Offers MS, PhD. Admissions and degrees offered through The Graduate School. Part-time programs available. *Faculty:* 13 full-time (1 woman). *Students:* 48 full-time (11 women), 2 part-time (1 woman); includes 10 minority (6 Asian, non-Hispanic/Latino; 3 Hispanic/Latino; 1 Two or more races, non-Hispanic/Latino), 7 international. Average age 26. 160 applicants, 23% accepted, 16 enrolled. In 2011, 10 master's, 5 doctorates awarded. Terminal master's awarded for partial completion of doctoral program. *Degree requirements:* For master's, comprehensive exam; for doctorate, comprehensive exam, thesis/dissertation. *Entrance requirements:* For master's and doctorate, GRE General Test. Additional exam requirements/recommendations for international students: Required—TOEFL (minimum score 577 paper-based, 233 computer-based, 90 iBT) or IELTS (minimum score 7). *Application deadline:* For fall admission, 1/12 for domestic and international students. Application fee: $75. Electronic applications accepted. *Financial support:* Fellowships with full tuition reimbursements, research assistantships with full tuition reimbursements, teaching assistantships with full tuition reimbursements, career-related internships or fieldwork, institutionally sponsored loans, health care benefits, and unspecified assistantships available. Financial award application deadline: 1/15; financial award applicants required to submit FAFSA. *Faculty research:* Acoustics, asymptotic analysis, bifurcation theory, combustion theory, fluid dynamics, information technology, math biology, microfluidics, moving boundary problems, nonlinear dynamics, pattern formation, waves. *Total annual research expenditures:* $1.9 million. *Unit head:* Dr. Vladimir Volpert, Chair, 847-491-8095, Fax: 847-491-2178, E-mail: v-volpert@northwestern.edu. *Application contact:* Dr. Ed Olmstead, Admission Officer, 847-491-5865, Fax: 847-491-2178, E-mail: weo@northwestern.edu. Web site: http://www.esam.northwestern.edu/index.html.

Oakland University, Graduate Study and Lifelong Learning, College of Arts and Sciences, Department of Mathematics and Statistics, Program in Applied Mathematical Sciences, Rochester, MI 48309-4401. Offers PhD.

Oakland University, Graduate Study and Lifelong Learning, College of Arts and Sciences, Department of Mathematics and Statistics, Program in Industrial Applied Mathematics, Rochester, MI 48309-4401. Offers MS. Part-time and evening/weekend programs available. *Entrance requirements:* For master's, minimum GPA of 3.0 for unconditional admission. Additional exam requirements/recommendations for international students: Required—TOEFL (minimum score 550 paper-based; 213 computer-based). Electronic applications accepted. *Expenses:* Contact institution.

Oklahoma State University, College of Arts and Sciences, Department of Mathematics, Stillwater, OK 74078. Offers applied mathematics (MS, PhD); mathematics education (MS, PhD); pure mathematics (MS, PhD). *Faculty:* 33 full-time (6 women), 8 part-time/adjunct (5 women). *Students:* 5 full-time (2 women), 27 part-time (8 women); includes 2 minority (1 Asian, non-Hispanic/Latino; 1 Two or more races, non-Hispanic/Latino), 21 international. Average age 31. 66 applicants, 14% accepted, 3 enrolled. In 2011, 2 master's, 1 doctorate awarded. *Degree requirements:* For master's, thesis, creative component, or report; for doctorate, comprehensive exam, thesis/dissertation. *Entrance requirements:* For master's and doctorate, GRE (recommended). Additional exam requirements/recommendations for international students: Required—TOEFL (minimum score 550 paper-based; 79 iBT). *Application deadline:* For fall admission, 3/1 for domestic and international students; for spring admission, 10/15 for domestic and international students. Applications are processed on a rolling basis. Application fee: $40 ($75 for international students). Electronic applications accepted. *Expenses:* Tuition, state resident: full-time $4044; part-time $168.50 per credit hour. Tuition, nonresident: full-time $16,008; part-time $667 per credit hour. *Required fees:* $2122; $88.45 per credit hour. One-time fee: $50. Tuition and fees vary according to course load and campus/location. *Financial support:* In 2011–12, 32 teaching assistantships (averaging $18,748 per year) were awarded; health care benefits and tuition waivers (partial) also available. Financial award application deadline: 3/1; financial award applicants required to submit FAFSA. *Unit head:* Dr. Dale Alspach, Head, 405-744-5688, Fax: 405-744-8275. *Application contact:* Dr. Sheryl Tucker, Dean, 405-744-7099, Fax: 405-744-0355, E-mail: grad-i@okstate.edu. Web site: http://www.math.okstate.edu/.

Penn State University Park, Graduate School, Eberly College of Science, Department of Mathematics, State College, University Park, PA 16802-1503. Offers mathematics (M Ed, MA, D Ed, PhD), including applied mathematics (MA). *Unit head:* Dr. John Roe, Head, 814-865-7527, Fax: 814-865-3735, E-mail: roe@math.psu.edu. *Application contact:* Dr. Dimitri Burago, Associate Head of Graduate Studies, 814-865-7741, E-mail: burago@math.psu.edu. Web site: http://www.math.psu.edu.

Princeton University, Graduate School, Program in Applied and Computational Mathematics, Princeton, NJ 08544-1019. Offers PhD. *Degree requirements:* For

doctorate, thesis/dissertation. *Entrance requirements:* For doctorate, GRE General Test, GRE Subject Test. Additional exam requirements/recommendations for international students: Required—TOEFL (minimum score 600 paper-based; 250 computer-based). Electronic applications accepted.

Rensselaer Polytechnic Institute, Graduate School, School of Science, Program in Applied Mathematics, Troy, NY 12180-3590. Offers MS. Part-time programs available. *Entrance requirements:* For master's, GRE General Test. Additional exam requirements/recommendations for international students: Required—TOEFL. Electronic applications accepted. *Faculty research:* Mathematical modeling, differential equations, applications of mathematics in science and engineering, operations research, analysis.

Rice University, Graduate Programs, George R. Brown School of Engineering, Department of Computational and Applied Mathematics, Houston, TX 77251-1892. Offers computational and applied mathematics (MA, MCAM, PhD); computational science and engineering (PhD). *Degree requirements:* For master's, comprehensive exam (for some programs), thesis (for some programs); for doctorate, comprehensive exam, thesis/dissertation. *Entrance requirements:* For master's and doctorate, GRE General Test, minimum GPA of 3.0. Additional exam requirements/recommendations for international students: Required—TOEFL (minimum score 600 paper-based; 250 computer-based; 90 iBT). Electronic applications accepted. *Faculty research:* Inverse problems, partial differential equations, computer algorithms, computational modeling, optimization theory.

Rochester Institute of Technology, Graduate Enrollment Services, College of Science, School of Mathematical Sciences, Rochester, NY 14623-5603. Offers industrial and applied mathematics (MS). Part-time and evening/weekend programs available. *Students:* 12 full-time (4 women), 4 part-time (all women); includes 1 minority (American Indian or Alaska Native, non-Hispanic/Latino), 4 international. Average age 25. 22 applicants, 73% accepted, 10 enrolled. In 2011, 14 master's awarded. *Degree requirements:* For master's, thesis. *Entrance requirements:* For master's, GRE General Test (recommended), minimum GPA of 3.0. Additional exam requirements/recommendations for international students: Required—TOEFL (minimum score 550 paper-based; 213 computer-based; 79 iBT) or IELTS (minimum score 6.5). *Application deadline:* For fall admission, 2/15 priority date for domestic students, 2/15 for international students. Applications are processed on a rolling basis. Application fee: $50. Electronic applications accepted. *Expenses: Tuition:* Full-time $34,659; part-time $963 per credit hour. *Required fees:* $228; $76 per quarter. *Financial support:* Research assistantships with partial tuition reimbursements, teaching assistantships with partial tuition reimbursements, career-related internships or fieldwork, scholarships/grants, and unspecified assistantships available. Support available to part-time students. Financial award applicants required to submit FAFSA. *Faculty research:* Abstract algebra, bioinformatics, combinatorics and graph theory, complex variables, cryptography, dynamical systems and chaos, statistics, topology. *Unit head:* Dr. Douglas Meadows, Head, 585-475-5129, E-mail: dsmsma@rit.edu. *Application contact:* Diane Ellison, Assistant Vice President, Graduate Enrollment Services, 585-475-2229, Fax: 585-475-7164, E-mail: gradinfo@rit.edu.

Rutgers, The State University of New Jersey, Camden, Graduate School of Arts and Sciences, Program in Mathematical Sciences, Camden, NJ 08102. Offers industrial mathematics (MBS); industrial/applied mathematics (MS); mathematical computer science (MS); pure mathematics (MS); teaching in mathematical sciences (MS). Part-time and evening/weekend programs available. *Degree requirements:* For master's, comprehensive exam, thesis optional, survey paper, 30 credits. *Entrance requirements:* For master's, GRE, BS/BA in math or related subject, 2 letters of recommendation. Additional exam requirements/recommendations for international students: Required—TOEFL (minimum score 550 paper-based; 213 computer-based), IELTS. Electronic applications accepted. *Faculty research:* Differential geometry, dynamical systems, vertex operator algebra, automorphic forms, CR-structures.

Rutgers, The State University of New Jersey, New Brunswick, Graduate School-New Brunswick, Department of Mathematics, Piscataway, NJ 08854-8097. Offers applied mathematics (MS, PhD); mathematics (MS, PhD). Part-time programs available. *Degree requirements:* For doctorate, one foreign language, comprehensive exam, thesis/dissertation. *Entrance requirements:* For master's and doctorate, GRE General Test, GRE Subject Test. Additional exam requirements/recommendations for international students: Required—TOEFL. *Faculty research:* Logic and set theory, number theory, mathematical physics, control theory, partial differential equations.

San Diego State University, Graduate and Research Affairs, College of Sciences, Department of Mathematics and Statistics, Program in Applied Mathematics, San Diego, CA 92182. Offers MS. Part-time programs available. *Degree requirements:* For master's, comprehensive exam. *Entrance requirements:* For master's, GRE General Test. Additional exam requirements/recommendations for international students: Required—TOEFL. Electronic applications accepted. *Faculty research:* Modeling, computational fluid dynamics, biomathematics, thermodynamics.

San Jose State University, Graduate Studies and Research, College of Science, Department of Mathematics, San Jose, CA 95192-0001. Offers applied mathematics (MS); mathematics (MA, MS); mathematics education (MA); statistics (MA). Part-time and evening/weekend programs available. *Degree requirements:* For master's, comprehensive exam, thesis (for some programs). *Entrance requirements:* For master's, GRE Subject Test. Electronic applications

Peterson's Graduate Programs in the Physical Sciences, Mathematics, Agricultural Sciences, the Environment & Natural Resources 2013

facebook.com/petersonspublishing **287**

SECTION 7: MATHEMATICAL SCIENCES

Applied Mathematics

accepted. *Faculty research:* Artificial intelligence, algorithms, numerical analysis, software database, number theory.

Santa Clara University, School of Engineering, Program in Applied Mathematics, Santa Clara, CA 95053. Offers MS. Part-time and evening/weekend programs available. *Students:* 9 full-time (2 women), 16 part-time (7 women); includes 6 minority (all Asian, non-Hispanic/Latino), 3 international. Average age 31. 9 applicants, 78% accepted, 4 enrolled. In 2011, 4 degrees awarded. *Degree requirements:* For master's, thesis (for some programs). *Entrance requirements:* For master's, GRE, transcript. Additional exam requirements/recommendations for international students: Required—TOEFL (minimum score 550 paper-based; 213 computer-based; 79 iBT). *Application deadline:* For fall admission, 8/12 for domestic students, 7/15 for international students; for winter admission, 10/28 for domestic students, 9/23 for international students; for spring admission, 2/25 for domestic students, 1/21 for international students. Applications are processed on a rolling basis. Application fee: $60. Electronic applications accepted. *Expenses:* Contact institution. *Financial support:* Research assistantships and teaching assistantships available. Financial award application deadline: 3/2; financial award applicants required to submit FAFSA. *Unit head:* Dr. Alex Zecevic, Associate Dean for Graduate Studies, 408-554-2394, E-mail: azecevic@scu.edu. *Application contact:* Stacey Tinker, Director of Admissions, Graduate Engineering, 408-554-4748, Fax: 408-554-4323, E-mail: stinker@scu.edu.

Simon Fraser University, Graduate Studies, Faculty of Science, Department of Mathematics, Burnaby, BC V5A 1S6, Canada. Offers applied and computational mathematics (M Sc, PhD); mathematics (M Sc, PhD). *Degree requirements:* For master's, thesis; for doctorate, thesis/dissertation. *Entrance requirements:* For master's, GRE General Test, minimum GPA of 3.0, 3 letters of reference; for doctorate, GRE General Test, minimum GPA of 3.5, 3 letters of reference. Additional exam requirements/recommendations for international students: Required—TWE or IELTS. Electronic applications accepted. *Faculty research:* Semi-groups, number theory, optimization, combinations.

Southern Methodist University, Dedman College, Department of Mathematics, Dallas, TX 75275. Offers computational and applied mathematics (MS, PhD). *Degree requirements:* For master's, oral exams; for doctorate, thesis/dissertation, oral and written exams. *Entrance requirements:* For master's and doctorate, GRE General Test, minimum GPA of 3.0, 18 undergraduate hours in mathematics beyond first and second year calculus. Additional exam requirements/recommendations for international students: Required—TOEFL. Electronic applications accepted. *Faculty research:* Numerical analysis and scientific computation, fluid dynamics, optics, wave propagation, mathematical biology.

Southern Oregon University, Graduate Studies, College of Arts and Sciences, Department of Mathematics, Ashland, OR 97520. Offers applied mathematics (PSM). *Expenses:* Tuition, state resident: full-time $12,600; part-time $350 per credit. Tuition, nonresident: full-time $16,200; part-time $450 per credit. *Required fees:* $1590. *Unit head:* Sherry Ettlich, Chair, 541-552-6576, E-mail: ettlich@sou.edu. *Application contact:* Dr. Kemble Yates, Coordinator, 541-552-6578, E-mail: kyates@sou.edu.

Stevens Institute of Technology, Graduate School, Charles V. Schaefer Jr. School of Engineering, Department of Mathematical Sciences, Program in Applied Mathematics, Hoboken, NJ 07030. Offers MS. *Degree requirements:* For master's, thesis optional. *Entrance requirements:* For master's, GRE. Additional exam requirements/recommendations for international students: Required—TOEFL. Electronic applications accepted.

Stony Brook University, State University of New York, Graduate School, College of Engineering and Applied Sciences, Department of Applied Mathematics and Statistics, Stony Brook, NY 11794. Offers MS, PhD. *Degree requirements:* For master's, thesis or alternative; for doctorate, one foreign language, comprehensive exam, thesis/dissertation. *Entrance requirements:* For master's and doctorate, GRE General Test. Additional exam requirements/recommendations for international students: Required—TOEFL. *Faculty research:* Biostatistics, combinatorial analysis, differential equations, modeling.

Temple University, College of Science and Technology, Department of Mathematics, Philadelphia, PA 19122-6096. Offers applied mathematics (MA); mathematics (PhD); pure mathematics (MA). Part-time and evening/weekend programs available. *Faculty:* 14 full-time (1 woman). *Students:* 28 full-time (4 women), 1 (woman) part-time, 4 international. Average age 27. 75 applicants, 29% accepted, 6 enrolled. In 2011, 1 master's, 3 doctorates awarded. Terminal master's awarded for partial completion of doctoral program. *Degree requirements:* For master's, thesis optional, written exam; for doctorate, 2 foreign languages, thesis/dissertation, oral and written exams. *Entrance requirements:* For master's, GRE General Test, minimum GPA of 3.0; for doctorate, GRE General Test, GRE Subject Test, minimum GPA of 3.0. Additional exam requirements/recommendations for international students: Required—TOEFL (minimum score 550 paper-based; 213 computer-based; 79 iBT). *Application deadline:* For fall admission, 2/15 priority date for domestic students, 12/15 for international students; for spring admission, 11/15 priority date for domestic students, 8/1 for international students. Applications are processed on a rolling basis. Application fee: $50. Electronic applications accepted. *Expenses:* Tuition, state resident: full-time $12,366; part-time $687 per credit hour. Tuition, nonresident: full-time $17,298; part-time $961 per credit hour. *Required fees:* $590; $213 per year. *Financial support:* Fellowships, research assistantships, teaching assistantships, Federal Work-Study, and institutionally sponsored loans available. Financial award application deadline: 1/15; financial award applicants

required to submit FAFSA. *Faculty research:* Differential geometry, numerical analysis. *Unit head:* Dr. Gerardo Mendoza, Graduate Chair, 215-204-5053, Fax: 215-204-6433, E-mail: mathematics@temple.edu. *Application contact:* Tara Schumacher, Coordinator of Outreach, 215-204-6575, Fax: 215-204-8781, E-mail: tara.schumacher@temple.edu. Web site: http://math.temple.edu/.

Texas A&M University–Corpus Christi, Graduate Studies and Research, College of Science and Technology, Program in Mathematics, Corpus Christi, TX 78412-5503. Offers applied and computational mathematics (MS); curriculum content (MS). Part-time programs available. *Degree requirements:* For master's, thesis (for some programs). *Entrance requirements:* For master's, 2 letters of recommendation.

Texas Christian University, College of Science and Engineering, Department of Mathematics, Fort Worth, TX 76129-0002. Offers applied mathematics (MS); mathematics (MAT); pure mathematics (MS, PhD). Part-time and evening/weekend programs available. *Faculty:* 12 full-time (2 women). *Students:* 8 full-time (4 women), 5 part-time (1 woman); includes 1 minority (Asian, non-Hispanic/Latino), 2 international. Average age 27. 11 applicants, 36% accepted, 4 enrolled. In 2011, 2 master's awarded. Terminal master's awarded for partial completion of doctoral program. *Degree requirements:* For master's, thesis optional; for doctorate, comprehensive exam, thesis/dissertation. *Entrance requirements:* For master's and doctorate, GRE, 24 hours of math, including courses in elementary calculus of one and several variables, linear algebra, abstract algebra and real analysis. Additional exam requirements/recommendations for international students: Required—TOEFL. *Application deadline:* For fall admission, 3/1 priority date for domestic students, 3/1 for international students; for spring admission, 10/15 priority date for domestic students, 10/15 for international students. Applications are processed on a rolling basis. Application fee: $60. Electronic applications accepted. *Expenses:* Tuition: Full-time $20,250; part-time $1125 per credit hour. Part-time tuition and fees vary according to course load and program. *Financial support:* In 2011–12, 6 research assistantships with full tuition reimbursements (averaging $17,000 per year), 4 teaching assistantships with full tuition reimbursements (averaging $10,000 per year) were awarded; tuition waivers (full) also available. Support available to part-time students. Financial award application deadline: 3/1. *Faculty research:* Differential geometry, topology, analysis, number theory, algebraic geometry. *Unit head:* Dr. George Gilbert, Associate Professor and Chair, 817-257-7335, E-mail: g.gilbert@tcu.edu. *Application contact:* Dr. Ken Richardson, Professor/Director, Mathematics Graduate Program, 817-257-6128, E-mail: k.richardson@tcu.edu. Web site: http://www.math.tcu.edu/.

Texas State University–San Marcos, Graduate School, College of Science and Engineering, Department of Mathematics, Program in Applied Mathematics, San Marcos, TX 78666. Offers MS. Part-time programs available. *Faculty:* 15 full-time (6 women), 1 part-time/adjunct. *Students:* 1 full-time (0 women). Average age 30. 2 applicants, 50% accepted, 0 enrolled. *Degree requirements:* For master's, comprehensive exam, thesis. *Entrance requirements:* For master's, GRE, minimum GPA of 2.75 in last 60 hours of undergraduate work. Additional exam requirements/recommendations for international students: Required—TOEFL (minimum score 550 paper-based; 213 computer-based; 78 iBT). *Application deadline:* For fall admission, 6/15 priority date for domestic students, 6/1 for international students; for spring admission, 10/15 priority date for domestic students, 10/1 for international students. Applications are processed on a rolling basis. Application fee: $40 ($90 for international students). Electronic applications accepted. *Expenses:* Tuition, state resident: full-time $6408; part-time $3204 per semester. Tuition, nonresident: full-time $14,832; part-time $7416 per semester. *Required fees:* $1824; $912 per semester. Tuition and fees vary according to course load. *Financial support:* In 2011–12, 1 student received support. Research assistantships, teaching assistantships, Federal Work-Study, institutionally sponsored loans, scholarships/grants, health care benefits, and unspecified assistantships available. Support available to part-time students. Financial award application deadline: 4/1; financial award applicants required to submit FAFSA. *Unit head:* Dr. Nathaniel Dean, Graduate Advisor, 512-245-2551, Fax: 512-245-3425, E-mail: nd17@txstate.edu. *Application contact:* Dr. Gregory Passty, Graduate Adviser, 512-245-3446, Fax: 512-245-3425, E-mail: gp02@txstate.edu. Web site: http://www.math.txstate.edu/degrees-programs/masters/applied-math.html.

Texas State University–San Marcos, Graduate School, College of Science and Engineering, Department of Mathematics, Program in Mathematics, San Marcos, TX 78666. Offers MS. *Faculty:* 15 full-time (6 women), 1 part-time/adjunct (0 women). *Students:* 21 full-time (13 women), 15 part-time (6 women); includes 13 minority (2 Black or African American, non-Hispanic/Latino; 2 Asian, non-Hispanic/Latino; 7 Hispanic/Latino; 2 Two or more races, non-Hispanic/Latino), 1 international. Average age 30. 22 applicants, 59% accepted, 5 enrolled. In 2011, 5 master's awarded. *Degree requirements:* For master's, comprehensive exam, thesis (for some programs). *Entrance requirements:* For master's, GRE, minimum GPA of 2.75 in last 60 hours of undergraduate course work. Additional exam requirements/recommendations for international students: Required—TOEFL (minimum score 550 paper-based; 213 computer-based; 78 iBT). *Application deadline:* For fall admission, 6/15 priority date for domestic students, 6/1 for international students; for spring admission, 10/15 priority date for domestic students, 10/1 for international students. Applications are processed on a rolling basis. Application fee: $40 ($90 for international students). Electronic applications accepted. *Expenses:* Tuition, state resident: full-time $6408; part-time $3204 per semester. Tuition, nonresident: full-time $14,832; part-time $7416 per semester.

288 facebook.com/petersonspublishing

Peterson's Graduate Programs in the Physical Sciences, Mathematics, Agricultural Sciences, the Environment & Natural Resources 2013

Required fees: $1824; $912 per semester. Tuition and fees vary according to course load. *Financial support:* In 2011–12, 13 students received support, including 7 teaching assistantships (averaging $12,510 per year); research assistantships, Federal Work-Study, institutionally sponsored loans, scholarships/grants, health care benefits, and unspecified assistantships also available. Support available to part-time students. Financial award application deadline: 4/1; financial award applicants required to submit FAFSA. *Unit head:* Dr. Nathaniel Dean, Graduate Advisor, 512-245-3555, Fax: 512-245-3425, E-mail: nd17@txstate.edu. *Application contact:* Dr. Gregory Passty, Graduate Adviser, 512-245-3446, Fax: 512-245-3425, E-mail: gp02@txstate.edu. Web site: http://www.math.txstate.edu/degrees-programs/masters/master-math.html.

Towson University, Program in Applied and Industrial Mathematics, Towson, MD 21252-0001. Offers MS. Part-time and evening/weekend programs available. *Students:* 12 full-time (3 women), 27 part-time (9 women); includes 6 minority (2 Black or African American, non-Hispanic/Latino; 3 Asian, non-Hispanic/Latino; 1 Hispanic/Latino), 7 international. *Entrance requirements:* For master's, bachelor's degree in mathematics or related field; minimum GPA of 3.0, including 3 terms of calculus, one in linear algebra. Additional exam requirements/recommendations for international students: Required—TOEFL (minimum score 550 paper-based). *Application deadline:* Applications are processed on a rolling basis. Application fee: $50. Electronic applications accepted. *Expenses:* Tuition, state resident: part-time $337 per credit. Tuition, nonresident: part-time $709 per credit. *Required fees:* $99 per credit. *Financial support:* Application deadline: 4/1; applicants required to submit FAFSA. *Unit head:* Xuezhang Hou, Graduate Program Director, 410-704-2578, Fax: 410-704-4149, E-mail: xhou@towson.edu.

Tulane University, School of Science and Engineering, Department of Mathematics, New Orleans, LA 70118-5669. Offers applied mathematics (MS); mathematics (MS, PhD); statistics (MS). *Degree requirements:* For master's, thesis (for some programs); for doctorate, thesis/dissertation. *Entrance requirements:* For master's, GRE General Test, minimum B average in undergraduate course work; for doctorate, GRE General Test. Additional exam requirements/recommendations for international students: Required—TOEFL. Electronic applications accepted.

The University of Akron, Graduate School, Buchtel College of Arts and Sciences, Department of Mathematics, Program in Applied Mathematics, Akron, OH 44325. Offers MS. *Students:* 24 full-time (5 women), 3 part-time (2 women), 3 international. Average age 23. 28 applicants, 71% accepted, 7 enrolled. In 2011, 12 master's awarded. *Degree requirements:* For master's, thesis optional, seminar and comprehensive exam or thesis. *Entrance requirements:* For master's, minimum GPA of 2.75, three letters of recommendation, statement of purpose. Additional exam requirements/recommendations for international students: Required—TOEFL (minimum score 550 paper-based; 213 computer-based; 79 iBT). *Application deadline:* Applications are processed on a rolling basis. Application fee: $30 ($40 for international students). Electronic applications accepted. *Expenses:* Tuition, state resident: full-time $7038; part-time $391 per credit hour. Tuition, nonresident: full-time $12,051; part-time $670 per credit hour. *Required fees:* $1274; $34 per credit hour. *Faculty research:* Analysis of nonlinear partial differential equations, finite groups and character theory, mathematics education, modeling and simulation of continuum and nanoscale systems, numerical analysis and scientific computation. *Unit head:* Dr. Gerald Young, Coordinator, 330-972-5731, Fax: 330-972-8630, E-mail: gyoung1@uakron.edu. *Application contact:* Dr. Mark Tausig, Associate Dean, 330-972-6266, Fax: 330-972-6475, E-mail: mtausig@uakron.edu. Web site: http://www.uakron.edu/math/academics/graduate/applied-mathematics-program.dot.

The University of Akron, Graduate School, College of Engineering, Program in Engineering Applied Mathematics, Akron, OH 44325. Offers PhD. *Students:* 1 full-time, 1 (woman) part-time. Average age 35. 2 applicants, 100% accepted, 2 enrolled. In 2011, 2 doctorates awarded. *Degree requirements:* For doctorate, one foreign language, thesis/dissertation, candidacy exam, qualifying exam. *Entrance requirements:* For doctorate, GRE, minimum GPA of 3.0 with bachelor's or master's degree; two letters of recommendation, statement of purpose. Additional exam requirements/recommendations for international students: Required—TOEFL (minimum score 550 paper-based; 213 computer-based; 79 iBT). *Application deadline:* Applications are processed on a rolling basis. Application fee: $30 ($40 for international students). Electronic applications accepted. *Expenses:* Tuition, state resident: full-time $7038; part-time $391 per credit hour. Tuition, nonresident: full-time $12,051; part-time $670 per credit hour. *Required fees:* $1274; $34 per credit hour. *Unit head:* Dr. Gerald Young, Coordinator, 330-972-5731, E-mail: jerry@math.uakron.edu. *Application contact:* Dr. Craig Menzemer, Director of Graduate Studies, College of Engineering, 330-972-5536, E-mail: ccmenze@uakron.edu. Web site: http://www.uakron.edu/math/academics/graduate/engineering-applied-mathematics-ph.-d.-program.dot.

The University of Alabama, Graduate School, College of Arts and Sciences, Department of Mathematics, Tuscaloosa, AL 35487. Offers applied mathematics (PhD); mathematics (MA, PhD); pure mathematics (PhD). *Faculty:* 27 full-time (0 women). *Students:* 52 full-time (21 women), 9 part-time (4 women); includes 3 minority (all Black or African American, non-Hispanic/Latino), 24 international. Average age 28. 47 applicants, 66% accepted, 12 enrolled. In 2011, 15 master's, 4 doctorates awarded. Terminal master's awarded for partial completion of doctoral program. *Median time to degree:* Of those who began their doctoral program in fall 2003, 85% received their degree in 8 years or less. *Degree requirements:* For master's, thesis or alternative; for doctorate, thesis/dissertation. *Entrance requirements:* For master's and doctorate, GRE General Test, minimum

GPA of 3.0. Additional exam requirements/recommendations for international students: Required—TOEFL (minimum score 550 paper-based; 79 iBT). *Application deadline:* For fall admission, 7/1 for domestic students, 5/31 for international students; for spring admission, 11/30 for domestic students, 10/31 for international students. Applications are processed on a rolling basis. Application fee: $50 ($60 for international students). Electronic applications accepted. *Expenses:* Tuition, state resident: full-time $8600. Tuition, nonresident: full-time $21,900. *Financial support:* In 2011–12, 1 fellowship with full tuition reimbursement (averaging $30,000 per year), 35 teaching assistantships with full tuition reimbursements (averaging $12,258 per year) were awarded; research assistantships with full tuition reimbursements, Federal Work-Study, institutionally sponsored loans, scholarships/grants, and unspecified assistantships also available. Support available to part-time students. Financial award application deadline: 7/1. *Faculty research:* Analysis, topology, algebra, fluid mechanics and system control theory, optimization, stochastic processes, numerical analysis. *Total annual research expenditures:* $135,802. *Unit head:* Dr. Zhijian Wu, Chairperson and Professor, 205-348-5080, Fax: 205-348-7067, E-mail: zwu@as.ua.edu. *Application contact:* Dr. Vo Liem, Director, 205-348-4898, Fax: 205-348-7067, E-mail: vliem@as.ua.edu.

The University of Alabama at Birmingham, College of Arts and Sciences, Program in Applied Mathematics, Birmingham, AL 35294. Offers PhD. Program offered jointly with The University of Alabama (Tuscaloosa), The University of Alabama in Huntsville. *Expenses:* Tuition, state resident: full-time $5922; part-time $309 per hour. Tuition, nonresident: full-time $13,428; part-time $726 per hour. Tuition and fees vary according to program. *Unit head:* Dr. Rudi Weikard, 205-934-2154. Web site: http://www.uab.edu/mathematics/ph-d-program.

The University of Alabama in Huntsville, School of Graduate Studies, College of Science, Department of Mathematical Sciences, Huntsville, AL 35899. Offers applied mathematics (PhD); education (MA, MS); mathematics (MA, MS). PhD offered jointly with The University of Alabama (Tuscaloosa) and The University of Alabama at Birmingham. Part-time and evening/weekend programs available. *Faculty:* 15 full-time (1 woman), 1 part-time/adjunct (0 women). *Students:* 17 full-time (8 women), 10 part-time (6 women); includes 5 minority (3 Black or African American, non-Hispanic/Latino; 1 Asian, non-Hispanic/Latino; 1 Hispanic/Latino), 5 international. Average age 28. 21 applicants, 62% accepted, 6 enrolled. In 2011, 5 master's, 1 doctorate awarded. *Degree requirements:* For master's, comprehensive exam, thesis or alternative, oral and written exams; for doctorate, comprehensive exam, thesis/dissertation, oral and written exams. *Entrance requirements:* For master's and doctorate, GRE General Test, minimum GPA of 3.0. Additional exam requirements/recommendations for international students: Required—TOEFL (minimum score 550 paper-based; 213 computer-based; 62 iBT). *Application deadline:* For fall admission, 7/15 for domestic students, 4/1 for international students; for spring admission, 11/30 for domestic students, 9/1 for international students. Applications are processed on a rolling basis. Application fee: $40 ($50 for international students). Electronic applications accepted. *Expenses:* Tuition, state resident: full-time $7830; part-time $473.50 per credit. Tuition, nonresident: full-time $18,748; part-time $1128.33 per credit. Tuition and fees vary according to course load and program. *Financial support:* In 2011–12, 14 students received support, including 1 fellowship with full tuition reimbursement available (averaging $10,000 per year), 1 research assistantship with full tuition reimbursement available (averaging $10,000 per year), 13 teaching assistantships with full tuition reimbursements available (averaging $10,314 per year); career-related internships or fieldwork, Federal Work-Study, institutionally sponsored loans, scholarships/grants, health care benefits, and unspecified assistantships also available. Support available to part-time students. Financial award application deadline: 4/1; financial award applicants required to submit FAFSA. *Faculty research:* Dynamical systems, mathematical biology, stochastic processes, numerical analysis, combinatorics. *Total annual research expenditures:* $222,669. *Unit head:* Dr. Jia Li, Chair, 256-824-6470, Fax: 256-824-6173, E-mail: li@math.uah.edu. *Application contact:* Kim Gray, Graduate Studies Admissions Coordinator, 256-824-6002, Fax: 256-824-6405, E-mail: deangrad@uah.edu. Web site: http://www.math.uah.edu/.

University of Alberta, Faculty of Graduate Studies and Research, Department of Mathematical and Statistical Sciences, Edmonton, AB T6G 2E1, Canada. Offers applied mathematics (M Sc, PhD); biostatistics (M Sc); mathematical finance (M Sc, PhD); mathematical physics (M Sc, PhD); mathematics (M Sc, PhD); statistics (M Sc, PhD, Postgraduate Diploma). Part-time programs available. Terminal master's awarded for partial completion of doctoral program. *Degree requirements:* For master's, thesis (for some programs); for doctorate, comprehensive exam, thesis/dissertation. *Entrance requirements:* Additional exam requirements/recommendations for international students: Required—TOEFL (minimum score 580 paper-based; 237 computer-based). Electronic applications accepted. *Faculty research:* Classical and functional analysis, algebra, differential equations, geometry.

The University of Arizona, College of Science, Department of Mathematics, Program in Mathematical Sciences, Tucson, AZ 85721. Offers applied science and business (PMS). Part-time programs available. *Students:* 51 full-time (13 women), 46 part-time (31 women); includes 7 minority (2 Black or African American, non-Hispanic/Latino; 1 American Indian or Alaska Native, non-Hispanic/Latino; 2 Asian, non-Hispanic/Latino; 2 Hispanic/Latino), 15 international. Average age 33. *Degree requirements:* For master's, thesis, internships, colloquium, business courses. *Entrance requirements:* For master's, GRE, minimum GPA of 3.0, statement of purpose. Additional exam requirements/

Peterson's Graduate Programs in the Physical Sciences, Mathematics, Agricultural Sciences, the Environment & Natural Resources 2013

facebook.com/petersonspublishing **289**

recommendations for international students: Required—TOEFL (minimum score 550 paper-based). Application fee: $75. *Expenses:* Tuition, state resident: full-time $10,840. Tuition, nonresident: full-time $25,802. *Financial support:* Research assistantships, teaching assistantships, career-related internships or fieldwork, Federal Work-Study, scholarships/grants, health care benefits, and unspecified assistantships available. *Faculty research:* Algebra, coding theory, graph theory, combinatorics, probability. *Unit head:* Dr. Michael Tabor, Head, 520-621-4664, Fax: 520-626-5048, E-mail: tabor@math.arizona.edu. *Application contact:* Alaina G. Levine, Director of Special Projects, College of Science, 520-621-3374, Fax: 520-621-8389, E-mail: alaina@u.arizona.edu. Web site: http://psm.arizona.edu.

The University of Arizona, Graduate Interdisciplinary Programs, Graduate Interdisciplinary Program in Applied Mathematics, Tucson, AZ 85721. Offers applied mathematics (MS, PhD); mathematical sciences (PMS). *Students:* 49 full-time (14 women), 2 part-time; includes 6 minority (2 Asian, non-Hispanic/Latino; 3 Hispanic/Latino; 1 Two or more races, non-Hispanic/Latino), 3 international. Average age 27. 108 applicants, 10% accepted, 11 enrolled. In 2011, 5 master's, 3 doctorates awarded. Terminal master's awarded for partial completion of doctoral program. *Degree requirements:* For master's, thesis (for some programs); for doctorate, comprehensive exam, thesis/dissertation. *Entrance requirements:* For master's, GRE, 3 letters of recommendation; for doctorate, GRE, 3 letters of recommendation, statement of purpose. Additional exam requirements/recommendations for international students: Required—TOEFL (minimum score 575 paper-based; 230 computer-based; 80 iBT). *Application deadline:* For fall admission, 1/15 for domestic students, 1/30 for international students. Applications are processed on a rolling basis. Application fee: $75. Electronic applications accepted. *Expenses:* Tuition, state resident: full-time $10,840. Tuition, nonresident: full-time $25,802. *Financial support:* In 2011–12, 1 research assistantship with full tuition reimbursement (averaging $17,120 per year) was awarded; institutionally sponsored loans, scholarships/grants, health care benefits, tuition waivers (full), and unspecified assistantships also available. Financial award application deadline: 3/1; financial award applicants required to submit FAFSA. *Faculty research:* Dynamical systems and chaos, partial differential equations, pattern formation, fluid dynamics and turbulence, scientific computation, mathematical physics, mathematical biology, medical imaging, applied probability and stochastic processes. *Unit head:* Dr. Michael Tabor, Head, 520-621-4664, Fax: 520-626-5048, E-mail: tabor@math.arizona.edu. *Application contact:* Graduate Coordinator, 520-621-2016, Fax: 520-626-5048, E-mail: applmath@u.arizona.edu. Web site: http://appliedmath.arizona.edu/.

University of Arkansas at Little Rock, Graduate School, College of Science and Mathematics, Department of Mathematics and Statistics, Little Rock, AR 72204-1099. Offers applied statistics (Graduate Certificate); mathematical sciences (MS). Part-time and evening/weekend programs available. *Degree requirements:* For master's, comprehensive exam. *Entrance requirements:* For master's, GRE General Test, GRE Subject Test, minimum GPA of 2.7, previous course work in advanced mathematics.

The University of British Columbia, Institute of Applied Mathematics, Vancouver, BC V6T 1Z1, Canada. Offers M Sc, PhD. *Degree requirements:* For master's, thesis (for some programs); for doctorate, comprehensive exam, thesis/dissertation. *Entrance requirements:* For doctorate, master's degree. Additional exam requirements/recommendations for international students: Required—TOEFL. *Faculty research:* Applied analysis, optimization, mathematical biology, numerical analysis, fluid mechanics.

University of California, Berkeley, Graduate Division, College of Letters and Science, Department of Mathematics, Program in Applied Mathematics, Berkeley, CA 94720-1500. Offers PhD. *Degree requirements:* For doctorate, 2 foreign languages, thesis/dissertation, qualifying exam. *Entrance requirements:* For doctorate, GRE General Test, GRE Subject Test, minimum GPA of 3.0, 3 letters of recommendation.

University of California, Davis, Graduate Studies, Graduate Group in Applied Mathematics, Davis, CA 95616. Offers MS, PhD. Terminal master's awarded for partial completion of doctoral program. *Degree requirements:* For master's, thesis; for doctorate, one foreign language, thesis/dissertation. *Entrance requirements:* For master's, GRE General Test, GRE Subject Test, minimum GPA of 3.0; for doctorate, GRE General Test, GRE Subject Test, master's degree, minimum GPA of 3.0. Additional exam requirements/recommendations for international students: Required—TOEFL (minimum score 550 paper-based; 213 computer-based). Electronic applications accepted. *Faculty research:* Mathematical biology, control and optimization, atmospheric sciences, theoretical chemistry, mathematical physics.

University of California, Merced, Division of Graduate Studies, School of Natural Sciences, Merced, CA 95343. Offers applied mathematics (MS, PhD); biological engineering and small-scale technologies (MS, PhD); environmental systems (MS, PhD); mechanical engineering and applied mechanics (MS, PhD); physics and chemistry (PhD); quantitative and systems biology (MS, PhD). *Unit head:* Dr. Samuel J. Traina, Dean, 209-228-4723, Fax: 209-228-6906, E-mail: grad.dean@ucmerced.edu. *Application contact:* Tsu Ya, Graduate Admissions and Academic Services Manager, 209-228-4723, Fax: 209-228-6906, E-mail: tya@ucmerced.edu.

University of California, San Diego, Office of Graduate Studies, Department of Mathematics, La Jolla, CA 92093. Offers applied mathematics (MA); mathematics (MA, PhD); statistics (MS). *Degree requirements:* For doctorate, thesis/dissertation. *Entrance requirements:* For master's and doctorate, GRE General Test, GRE Subject Test. Electronic applications accepted.

University of California, Santa Barbara, Graduate Division, College of Letters and Sciences, Division of Mathematics, Life, and Physical Sciences, Department of Mathematics, Santa Barbara, CA 93106-3080. Offers applied mathematics (MA), including computational science and engineering; mathematics (MA, PhD), including computational science and engineering ; MA/PhD. *Faculty:* 26 full-time (2 women). *Students:* 53 full-time (13 women); includes 5 minority (1 Black or African American, non-Hispanic/Latino; 3 Asian, non-Hispanic/Latino; 5 Hispanic/Latino), 7 international. Average age 26. 186 applicants, 17% accepted, 10 enrolled. In 2011, 7 master's, 3 doctorates awarded. Terminal master's awarded for partial completion of doctoral program. *Median time to degree:* Of those who began their doctoral program in fall 2003, 100% received their degree in 8 years or less. *Degree requirements:* For master's, comprehensive exam (for some programs), thesis (for some programs); for doctorate, comprehensive exam, thesis/dissertation. *Entrance requirements:* For master's and doctorate, GRE General Test, GRE Subject Test (math). Additional exam requirements/recommendations for international students: Required—TOEFL (minimum score 575 paper-based; 80 iBT), IELTS (minimum score 7). *Application deadline:* For fall admission, 1/1 priority date for domestic students, 1/1 for international students. Application fee: $80 ($100 for international students). Electronic applications accepted. *Expenses:* Tuition, state resident: full-time $12,192. Tuition, nonresident: full-time $27,294. *Required fees:* $764.13. *Financial support:* In 2011–12, 50 students received support, including 15 fellowships with full tuition reimbursements available (averaging $12,740 per year), 12 research assistantships with full tuition reimbursements available (averaging $6,000 per year), 48 teaching assistantships with partial tuition reimbursements available (averaging $17,308 per year); Federal Work-Study, institutionally sponsored loans, health care benefits, and tuition waivers (full and partial) also available. Financial award application deadline: 3/2; financial award applicants required to submit FAFSA. *Faculty research:* Topology, differential geometry, algebra, applied mathematics, partial differential equations. *Total annual research expenditures:* $205,000. *Unit head:* Prof. David R. Morrison, Chair, 805-893-3340, Fax: 805-893-2385, E-mail: chair@math.ucsb.edu. *Application contact:* Medina Price, Graduate Advisor, 805-893-8192, Fax: 805-893-2385, E-mail: price@math.ucsb.edu. Web site: http://www.math.ucsb.edu/.

University of California, Santa Cruz, Division of Graduate Studies, Jack Baskin School of Engineering, Program in Statistics and Applied Mathematics, Santa Cruz, CA 95064. Offers MS, PhD. Terminal master's awarded for partial completion of doctoral program. *Degree requirements:* For master's, seminar, qualifying exam, capstone project; for doctorate, thesis/dissertation, seminar, qualifying exam. *Entrance requirements:* For master's and doctorate, GRE General Test; GRE Subject Test in math (recommended). Additional exam requirements/recommendations for international students: Required—TOEFL (minimum score 570 paper-based; 230 computer-based; 89 iBT); Recommended—IELTS (minimum score 8). Electronic applications accepted. *Faculty research:* Bayesian nonparametric methods; computationally intensive Bayesian inference, prediction, and decision-making; envirometrics; fluid mechanics; mathematical biology.

University of Central Arkansas, Graduate School, College of Natural Sciences and Math, Department of Mathematics, Conway, AR 72035-0001. Offers applied mathematics (MS); math education (MA). Part-time programs available. *Faculty:* 16 full-time (4 women). *Students:* 13 full-time (7 women), 8 part-time (4 women); includes 2 minority (1 Asian, non-Hispanic/Latino; 1 Two or more races, non-Hispanic/Latino), 3 international. Average age 29. 12 applicants, 92% accepted, 8 enrolled. In 2011, 7 master's awarded. *Degree requirements:* For master's, comprehensive exam, thesis optional. *Entrance requirements:* For master's, GRE General Test, minimum GPA of 2.7. Additional exam requirements/recommendations for international students: Required—TOEFL (minimum score 550 paper-based; 213 computer-based). *Application deadline:* For fall admission, 3/1 priority date for domestic students; for spring admission, 10/1 priority date for domestic students. Applications are processed on a rolling basis. Application fee: $25 ($50 for international students). *Expenses:* Tuition, state resident: full-time $4834; part-time $398.35 per credit hour. Tuition, nonresident: full-time $8686. *Financial support:* In 2011–12, 11 teaching assistantships with partial tuition reimbursements (averaging $8,500 per year) were awarded; Federal Work-Study, scholarships/grants, and unspecified assistantships also available. Financial award application deadline: 2/15; financial award applicants required to submit FAFSA. *Unit head:* Dr. Ramesh Garimella, Chair, 501-450-3147, Fax: 501-450-5662, E-mail: rameshg@uca.edu. *Application contact:* Susan Wood, Admissions Assistant, 501-450-3124, Fax: 501-450-5678, E-mail: swood@uca.edu. Web site: http://uca.edu/math/.

University of Central Florida, College of Sciences, Department of Mathematics, Orlando, FL 32816. Offers applied mathematics (Certificate); mathematical science (MS); mathematics (PhD). Part-time and evening/weekend programs available. *Faculty:* 43 full-time (7 women), 5 part-time/adjunct (0 women). *Students:* 50 full-time (17 women), 25 part-time (11 women); includes 13 minority (2 Black or African American, non-Hispanic/Latino; 2 Asian, non-Hispanic/Latino; 9 Hispanic/Latino), 18 international. Average age 32. 89 applicants, 55% accepted, 23 enrolled. In 2011, 9 master's, 2 doctorates awarded. *Degree requirements:* For master's, thesis or alternative; for doctorate, thesis/dissertation, candidacy exam. *Entrance requirements:* For master's, GRE General Test, minimum GPA of 3.0 in last 60 hours; for doctorate, GRE Subject Test, minimum

290 facebook.com/petersonspublishing

Peterson's Graduate Programs in the Physical Sciences, Mathematics, Agricultural Sciences, the Environment & Natural Resources 2013

GPA of 3.0 in last 60 hours or master's qualifying exam. Additional exam requirements/recommendations for international students: Required—TOEFL. *Application deadline:* For fall admission, 7/15 for domestic students; for spring admission, 12/1 for domestic students. Application fee: $30. Electronic applications accepted. *Expenses:* Tuition, state resident: part-time $277.08 per credit hour. Tuition, nonresident: part-time $277.08 per credit hour. Part-time tuition and fees vary according to degree level and program. *Financial support:* In 2011–12, 39 students received support, including 5 fellowships with partial tuition reimbursements available (averaging $11,000 per year), 1 research assistantship with partial tuition reimbursement available (averaging $15,800 per year), 40 teaching assistantships with partial tuition reimbursements available (averaging $11,600 per year); career-related internships or fieldwork, Federal Work-Study, institutionally sponsored loans, tuition waivers (partial), and unspecified assistantships also available. Financial award application deadline: 3/1; financial award applicants required to submit FAFSA. *Faculty research:* Applied mathematics, analysis, approximation theory, graph theory, mathematical statistics. *Unit head:* Dr. Piotr Mikusinski, Chair, 407-823-6284, Fax: 407-823-6253, E-mail: piotr.mikusinski@mail.ucf.edu. *Application contact:* Barbara Rodriguez, Director, Admissions and Registration, 407-823-2766, Fax: 407-823-6442, E-mail: gradadmissions@ucf.edu. Web site: http://www.math.ucf.edu/.

University of Central Missouri, The Graduate School, College of Science and Technology, Warrensburg, MO 64093. Offers applied mathematics (MS); aviation safety (MS); biology (MS); computer science (MS); environmental studies (MA); industrial management (MS); mathematics (MS); technology (MS); technology management (PhD). PhD is offered jointly with Indiana State University. Part-time programs available. Postbaccalaureate distance learning degree programs offered. *Entrance requirements:* Additional exam requirements/recommendations for international students: Required—TOEFL (minimum score 550 paper-based; 79 computer-based). Electronic applications accepted.

University of Central Oklahoma, College of Graduate Studies and Research, College of Mathematics and Science, Department of Mathematics and Statistics, Edmond, OK 73034-5209. Offers applied mathematical sciences (MS), including computer science, mathematics, mathematics/computer science teaching, statistics. Part-time programs available. *Faculty:* 7 full-time (4 women), 3 part-time/adjunct (0 women). *Students:* 20 full-time (7 women), 11 part-time (8 women); includes 5 minority (3 Black or African American, non-Hispanic/Latino; 2 Two or more races, non-Hispanic/Latino), 11 international. Average age 29. In 2011, 5 master's awarded. *Degree requirements:* For master's, thesis. *Entrance requirements:* Additional exam requirements/recommendations for international students: Required—TOEFL (minimum score 550 paper-based; 213 computer-based). *Application deadline:* Applications are processed on a rolling basis. Application fee: $50. Electronic applications accepted. *Expenses:* Tuition, state resident: full-time $3901; part-time $218.30 per credit hour. Tuition, nonresident: full-time $9198; part-time $511.20 per credit hour. Tuition and fees vary according to program. *Financial support:* Federal Work-Study and unspecified assistantships available. Financial award application deadline: 3/31; financial award applicants required to submit FAFSA. *Faculty research:* Curvature, FAA, math education. *Unit head:* Dr. Michael Fulkerson, 405-974-5575, E-mail: mfulkerson@uco.edu. *Application contact:* Dr. Richard Bernard, Adviser, 405-974-3493, Fax: 405-974-3824, E-mail: jyates@aix1.uco.edu. Web site: http://www.ucok.edu/graduate.applied.htm.

University of Chicago, Division of the Physical Sciences, Department of Mathematics, Program in Applied Mathematics, Chicago, IL 60637-1513. Offers SM, PhD. *Degree requirements:* For master's, one foreign language, oral exams; for doctorate, one foreign language, thesis/dissertation, 2 qualifying exams. *Entrance requirements:* For master's and doctorate, GRE General Test, GRE Subject Test. Additional exam requirements/recommendations for international students: Required—TOEFL (minimum score 600 paper-based; 250 computer-based). Electronic applications accepted. *Faculty research:* Applied analysis, dynamical systems, theoretical biology, math-physics.

University of Cincinnati, Graduate School, McMicken College of Arts and Sciences, Department of Mathematical Sciences, Cincinnati, OH 45221. Offers applied mathematics (MS, PhD); mathematics education (MAT); pure mathematics (MS, PhD); statistics (MS, PhD). Part-time programs available. Terminal master's awarded for partial completion of doctoral program. *Degree requirements:* For master's, comprehensive exam, thesis or alternative; for doctorate, one foreign language, comprehensive exam, thesis/dissertation. *Entrance requirements:* For master's, GRE, teacher certification (MAT); for doctorate, GRE. Additional exam requirements/recommendations for international students: Required—TOEFL. Electronic applications accepted. *Faculty research:* Algebra, analysis, differential equations, numerical analysis, statistics.

University of Colorado at Colorado Springs, College of Letters, Arts and Sciences, Department of Mathematics, Colorado Springs, CO 80933-7150. Offers applied mathematics (MS); applied science (PhD); mathematics (M Sc). Part-time and evening/weekend programs available. *Faculty:* 10 full-time (1 woman), 1 (woman) part-time/adjunct. *Students:* 9 full-time (2 women), 8 part-time (3 women); includes 1 minority (Black or African American, non-Hispanic/Latino), 1 international. Average age 34. 2 applicants, 100% accepted, 1 enrolled. In 2011, 4 master's awarded. *Degree requirements:* For master's, thesis, qualifying exam. *Entrance requirements:* For master's, GRE General Test, minimum GPA of 3.0. Additional exam requirements/recommendations for international students: Required—TOEFL (minimum score 550 paper-based; 213 computer-based). *Application deadline:* For fall admission, 6/1 for domestic and international

students; for spring admission, 11/1 for domestic and international students. Applications are processed on a rolling basis. Application fee: $60 ($75 for international students). Electronic applications accepted. *Expenses:* Tuition, state resident: part-time $660 per credit hour. Tuition, nonresident: part-time $1133 per credit hour. Tuition and fees vary according to degree level, program and student level. *Financial support:* In 2011–12, 3 students received support. Teaching assistantships, Federal Work-Study, and scholarships/grants available. Support available to part-time students. Financial award application deadline: 3/1; financial award applicants required to submit FAFSA. *Faculty research:* Abelian groups and noncommutative rings, hormone analysis and computer vision, probability and mathematical physics, stochastic dynamics, probability models. *Total annual research expenditures:* $110,911. *Unit head:* Dr. Sarbarish Chakravarty, Chair, 719-255-3549, Fax: 719-255-3605, E-mail: schakrav@uccs.edu. *Application contact:* Josh Goldman, Graduate Assistant, 719-255-3554, Fax: 719-255-3605, E-mail: jgoldman@uccs.edu. Web site: http://www.uccs.edu/math.

University of Colorado Boulder, Graduate School, College of Arts and Sciences, Department of Applied Mathematics, Boulder, CO 80309. Offers MS, PhD. *Faculty:* 16 full-time (2 women). *Students:* 68 full-time (13 women), 8 part-time (1 woman); includes 9 minority (5 Asian, non-Hispanic/Latino; 4 Hispanic/Latino), 11 international. Average age 28. 118 applicants, 14% accepted, 15 enrolled. In 2011, 24 master's, 6 doctorates awarded. Terminal master's awarded for partial completion of doctoral program. *Degree requirements:* For master's, comprehensive exam, thesis or alternative; for doctorate, one foreign language, comprehensive exam, thesis/dissertation. *Entrance requirements:* For master's, GRE General Test, minimum undergraduate GPA of 2.75; for doctorate, GRE General Test. Additional exam requirements/recommendations for international students: Required—TOEFL. *Application deadline:* For fall admission, 2/1 priority date for domestic students, 12/1 for international students. Applications are processed on a rolling basis. Application fee: $50 ($60 for international students). Electronic applications accepted. *Financial support:* In 2011–12, 86 students received support, including 42 fellowships (averaging $8,720 per year), 21 research assistantships with full and partial tuition reimbursements available (averaging $22,938 per year), 42 teaching assistantships with full and partial tuition reimbursements available (averaging $17,663 per year); institutionally sponsored loans, scholarships/grants, health care benefits, and unspecified assistantships also available. Financial award applicants required to submit FAFSA. *Faculty research:* Non-linear phenomena, computational mathematics, physical applied mathematics, statistics. *Total annual research expenditures:* $3.3 million. *Application contact:* E-mail: appm_app@cboulder.colorado.edu. Web site: http://amath.colorado.edu/.

University of Colorado Denver, College of Liberal Arts and Sciences, Department of Mathematical and Statistical Sciences, Denver, CO 80217. Offers applied mathematics (MS, PhD), including applied mathematics, applied probability (MS), applied statistics (MS), computational biology, computational mathematics (PhD), discrete mathematics, finite geometry (PhD), mathematics education (PhD), mathematics of engineering and science (MS), numerical analysis, operations research (MS), optimization and operations research (PhD), probability (PhD), statistics (PhD). Part-time programs available. *Faculty:* 26 full-time (4 women), 2 part-time/adjunct (1 woman). *Students:* 44 full-time (14 women), 14 part-time (5 women); includes 6 minority (4 Asian, non-Hispanic/Latino; 2 Hispanic/Latino), 10 international. Average age 33. 66 applicants, 79% accepted, 17 enrolled. In 2011, 6 master's, 6 doctorates awarded. *Degree requirements:* For master's, comprehensive exam, thesis optional, 30 hours of course work with minimum GPA of 3.0; for doctorate, comprehensive exam, thesis/dissertation. *Entrance requirements:* For master's and doctorate, GRE General Test; GRE Subject Test in math (recommended), 30 hours of course work in mathematics (24 of which must be upper-division mathematics), minimum GPA of 3.0. Additional exam requirements/recommendations for international students: Required—TOEFL (minimum score 525 paper-based; 192 computer-based; 71 iBT). *Application deadline:* For fall admission, 4/1 for domestic students, 3/1 for international students; for spring admission, 11/1 for domestic students, 10/1 for international students. Application fee: $50 ($75 for international students). Electronic applications accepted. *Financial support:* Fellowships with partial tuition reimbursements, research assistantships with full tuition reimbursements, teaching assistantships with full tuition reimbursements, Federal Work-Study, scholarships/grants, and unspecified assistantships available. Financial award application deadline: 4/1; financial award applicants required to submit FAFSA. *Faculty research:* Computational mathematics, computational biology, discrete mathematics and geometry, probability and statistics, optimization. *Unit head:* Dr. Stephen Billups, Graduate Chair, 303-556-4814, E-mail: stephen.billups@ucdenver.edu. *Application contact:* Lisa Herbert, Graduate Program Assistant, 303-556-2341, E-mail: lisa.herbert@ucdenver.edu. Web site: http://www.ucdenver.edu/academics/colleges/CLAS/Departments/math/Pages/MathStats.aspx.

University of Connecticut, Graduate School, College of Liberal Arts and Sciences, Department of Mathematics, Field of Applied Financial Mathematics, Storrs, CT 06269. Offers MS. *Degree requirements:* For master's, comprehensive exam. *Entrance requirements:* Additional exam requirements/recommendations for international students: Required—TOEFL (minimum score 550 paper-based; 213 computer-based). Electronic applications accepted.

University of Dayton, Department of Mathematics, Dayton, OH 45469-1300. Offers applied mathematics (MAS); financial mathematics (MFM); mathematics education (MME). Part-time and evening/weekend programs available. *Faculty:*

Peterson's Graduate Programs in the Physical Sciences, Mathematics, Agricultural Sciences, the Environment & Natural Resources 2013

facebook.com/petersonspublishing **291**

Applied Mathematics

15 full-time (5 women). *Students:* 37 full-time (20 women), 12 part-time (5 women); includes 4 minority (3 Black or African American, non-Hispanic/Latino; 1 Asian, non-Hispanic/Latino), 31 international. Average age 26. 110 applicants, 62% accepted, 25 enrolled. In 2011, 14 master's awarded. *Entrance requirements:* For master's, minimum undergraduate GPA of 2.8 (MAS), 3.0 (MFM, MME). Additional exam requirements/recommendations for international students: Required—TOEFL (minimum score 550 paper-based; 213 computer-based; 80 iBT). *Application deadline:* For fall admission, 3/1 priority date for domestic students, 7/1 for international students; for winter admission, 7/1 for international students; for spring admission, 1/1 for international students. Application fee: $0 ($50 for international students). Electronic applications accepted. *Expenses: Tuition:* Full-time $8400; part-time $700 per credit hour. *Required fees:* $25 per semester. Tuition and fees vary according to degree level. *Financial support:* In 2011–12, 6 teaching assistantships with full tuition reimbursements (averaging $13,400 per year) were awarded; institutionally sponsored loans, health care benefits, and unspecified assistantships also available. Financial award applicants required to submit FAFSA. *Faculty research:* Differential equations, integral equations, general topology, measure theory, graph theory, financial math, math education, numerical analysis. *Unit head:* Dr. Joe D. Mashburn, Chair, 937-229-2511, Fax: 937-229-2566, E-mail: joe.mashburn@notes.udayton.edu. *Application contact:* Alexander Popovski, Associate Director of Graduate and International Admissions, 937-229-2357, Fax: 937-229-4729, E-mail: alex.popovski@notes.udayton.edu.

University of Delaware, College of Arts and Sciences, Department of Mathematical Sciences, Newark, DE 19716. Offers applied mathematics (MS, PhD); mathematics (MS, PhD). Part-time programs available. Terminal master's awarded for partial completion of doctoral program. *Degree requirements:* For master's, thesis (for some programs); for doctorate, one foreign language, thesis/dissertation, qualifying exam. *Entrance requirements:* For master's and doctorate, GRE General Test. Additional exam requirements/recommendations for international students: Required—TOEFL. Electronic applications accepted. *Faculty research:* Scattering theory, inverse problems, fluid dynamics, numerical analysis, combinatorics.

University of Georgia, Franklin College of Arts and Sciences, Department of Mathematics, Athens, GA 30602. Offers applied mathematical science (MAMS); mathematics (MA, PhD). *Faculty:* 31 full-time (4 women). *Students:* 56 full-time (17 women); includes 6 minority (1 Black or African American, non-Hispanic/Latino; 3 Asian, non-Hispanic/Latino; 2 Hispanic/Latino), 13 international. Average age 27. 126 applicants, 24% accepted, 14 enrolled. In 2011, 11 master's, 3 doctorates awarded. *Degree requirements:* For master's, one foreign language, thesis (for some programs); for doctorate, 2 foreign languages, thesis/dissertation. *Entrance requirements:* For master's and doctorate, GRE General Test. *Application deadline:* For fall admission, 7/1 priority date for domestic students; for spring admission, 11/15 for domestic students. Application fee: $50. Electronic applications accepted. *Financial support:* Fellowships, research assistantships, teaching assistantships, and unspecified assistantships available. *Unit head:* Dr. Malcolm Adams, Head, 706-542-2564, E-mail: fu@math.uga.edu. *Application contact:* Dr. Brian D. Boe, Graduate Coordinator, 706-542-2547, Fax: 706-542-2573, E-mail: grad@math.uga.edu. Web site: http://www.math.uga.edu/.

University of Guelph, Graduate Studies, College of Physical and Engineering Science, Department of Mathematics and Statistics, Guelph, ON N1G 2W1, Canada. Offers applied mathematics (PhD); applied statistics (PhD); mathematics and statistics (M Sc). Part-time programs available. *Degree requirements:* For master's, thesis (for some programs); for doctorate, thesis/dissertation. *Entrance requirements:* For master's, minimum B average during previous 2 years of course work; for doctorate, minimum B average. Additional exam requirements/recommendations for international students: Required—TOEFL (minimum score 550 paper-based; 213 computer-based; 89 iBT), IELTS (minimum score 6.5). *Faculty research:* Dynamical systems, mathematical biology, numerical analysis, linear and nonlinear models, reliability and bioassay.

University of Houston, College of Natural Sciences and Mathematics, Department of Mathematics, Houston, TX 77204. Offers applied mathematics (MS); mathematics (MA, PhD). Part-time programs available. *Degree requirements:* For master's, thesis optional. *Entrance requirements:* For master's and doctorate, GRE (Verbal and Quantitative). Additional exam requirements/recommendations for international students: Required—TOEFL (minimum score 550 paper-based; 79 iBT), IELTS (minimum score 6.5). Electronic applications accepted. *Faculty research:* Applied mathematics, modern analysis, computational science, geometry, dynamical systems.

University of Illinois at Chicago, Graduate College, College of Liberal Arts and Sciences, Department of Mathematics, Statistics, and Computer Science, Chicago, IL 60607-7128. Offers applied mathematics (MS, PhD); computational finance (MS, PhD); computer science (MS, PhD); mathematics (DA); mathematics and information sciences for industry (MS); probability and statistics (PhD); pure mathematics (MS, PhD); statistics (MS); teaching of mathematics (MST), including elementary, secondary. Part-time programs available. *Degree requirements:* For master's, comprehensive exam; for doctorate, one foreign language, thesis/dissertation. *Entrance requirements:* For master's and doctorate, GRE General Test, minimum GPA of 3.0. Additional exam requirements/recommendations for international students: Required—TOEFL (minimum score 100 iBT). Electronic applications accepted.

University of Illinois at Urbana–Champaign, Graduate College, College of Liberal Arts and Sciences, Department of Mathematics, Champaign, IL 61820. Offers applied mathematics (MS); applied mathematics: actuarial science (MS); mathematics (MS, PhD); teaching of mathematics (MS). *Faculty:* 64 full-time (6 women), 9 part-time/adjunct (0 women). *Students:* 166 full-time (52 women), 36 part-time (13 women); includes 16 minority (7 Asian, non-Hispanic/Latino; 5 Hispanic/Latino; 4 Two or more races, non-Hispanic/Latino), 111 international. 455 applicants, 23% accepted, 48 enrolled. In 2011, 32 master's, 26 doctorates awarded. *Entrance requirements:* For master's and doctorate, GRE General Test, GRE Subject Test (math), minimum GPA of 3.0. Additional exam requirements/recommendations for international students: Required—TOEFL (minimum score 550 paper-based; 213 computer-based). *Application deadline:* Applications are processed on a rolling basis. Application fee: $75 ($90 for international students). Electronic applications accepted. *Financial support:* In 2011–12, 26 fellowships, 44 research assistantships, 152 teaching assistantships were awarded; tuition waivers (full and partial) also available. *Unit head:* Matthew Ando, Chair, 217-244-2846, Fax: 217-333-9576, E-mail: mando@illinois.edu. *Application contact:* Marci Blocher, Office Support Specialist, 217-333-5749, Fax: 217-333-9576, E-mail: mblocher@illinois.edu. Web site: http://math.illinois.edu/.

The University of Iowa, Graduate College, Program in Applied Mathematical and Computational Sciences, Iowa City, IA 52242-1316. Offers PhD. *Degree requirements:* For doctorate, comprehensive exam, thesis/dissertation. *Entrance requirements:* For doctorate, GRE General Test, minimum GPA of 3.0. Additional exam requirements/recommendations for international students: Required—TOEFL (minimum score 620 paper-based; 260 computer-based; 105 iBT). Electronic applications accepted.

University of Kentucky, Graduate School, College of Arts and Sciences, Program in Mathematics, Lexington, KY 40506-0032. Offers applied mathematics (MS); mathematics (MA, MS, PhD). *Degree requirements:* For master's, comprehensive exam, thesis optional; for doctorate, one foreign language, comprehensive exam, thesis/dissertation. *Entrance requirements:* For master's, GRE General Test, minimum undergraduate GPA of 2.75; for doctorate, GRE General Test, minimum graduate GPA of 3.0. Additional exam requirements/recommendations for international students: Required—TOEFL (minimum score 550 paper-based; 213 computer-based). Electronic applications accepted. *Faculty research:* Numerical analysis, combinatorics, partial differential equations, algebra and number theory, real and complex analysis.

University of Louisville, Graduate School, College of Arts and Sciences, Department of Mathematics, Louisville, KY 40292. Offers applied and industrial mathematics (PhD); mathematics (MA). Part-time programs available. Terminal master's awarded for partial completion of doctoral program. *Degree requirements:* For master's, comprehensive exam (for some programs), thesis optional; for doctorate, comprehensive exam, thesis/dissertation, internship, project. *Entrance requirements:* For master's and doctorate, GRE General Test. Additional exam requirements/recommendations for international students: Required—TOEFL (minimum score 550 paper-based; 215 computer-based; 79 iBT). Electronic applications accepted. *Expenses:* Tuition, state resident: full-time $9692; part-time $539 per credit hour. Tuition, nonresident: full-time $20,168; part-time $1121 per credit hour. Tuition and fees vary according to program and reciprocity agreements. *Faculty research:* Algebra, analysis, bio-mathematics, combinatorics and graph theory, coding theory, consesus theory, financial mathematics, functional equations, partial differential equations.

The University of Manchester, School of Mathematics, Manchester, United Kingdom. Offers actuarial science (PhD); applied mathematics (M Phil, PhD); applied numerical computing (M Phil, PhD); financial mathematics (M Phil, PhD); mathematical logic (M Phil); probability (M Phil, PhD); pure mathematics (M Phil, PhD); statistics (M Phil, PhD).

University of Maryland, Baltimore County, Graduate School, College of Natural and Mathematical Sciences, Department of Mathematics and Statistics, Program in Applied Mathematics, Baltimore, MD 21250. Offers MS, PhD. Part-time and evening/weekend programs available. *Faculty:* 23 full-time (4 women). *Students:* 24 full-time (10 women), 5 part-time (0 women); includes 4 minority (2 Black or African American, non-Hispanic/Latino; 1 Asian, non-Hispanic/Latino; 1 Two or more races, non-Hispanic/Latino), 11 international. Average age 28. 41 applicants, 80% accepted, 18 enrolled. In 2011, 9 master's, 2 doctorates awarded. Terminal master's awarded for partial completion of doctoral program. *Degree requirements:* For master's, comprehensive exam (for some programs), thesis (for some programs); for doctorate, comprehensive exam, thesis/dissertation. *Entrance requirements:* For master's and doctorate, GRE General Test, minimum GPA of 3.0. Additional exam requirements/recommendations for international students: Required—TOEFL (minimum score 600 paper-based; 250 computer-based; 100 iBT). *Application deadline:* For fall admission, 2/15 priority date for domestic students, 1/1 for international students; for spring admission, 10/15 priority date for domestic students, 5/1 for international students. Applications are processed on a rolling basis. Application fee: $50. Electronic applications accepted. *Financial support:* In 2011–12, 17 students received support, including 3 research assistantships with full tuition reimbursements available (averaging $15,500 per year), 14 teaching assistantships with full and partial tuition reimbursements available (averaging $15,500 per year); fellowships with full tuition reimbursements available, career-related internships or fieldwork, scholarships/grants, health care benefits, tuition waivers (full and partial), and unspecified assistantships also available. Support available to part-time students. Financial award application deadline: 2/15. *Faculty research:* Numerical analysis

292 facebook.com/petersonspublishing

Peterson's Graduate Programs in the Physical Sciences, Mathematics, Agricultural Sciences, the Environment & Natural Resources 2013

and scientific computation, optimization theory and algorithms, differential equations and mathematical modeling, mathematical biology and bioinformatics. *Total annual research expenditures:* $401,423. *Unit head:* Dr. Kathleen Hoffman, Director, 410-455-2434, Fax: 410-455-1066, E-mail: khoffman@math.umbc.edu. Web site: http://www.math.umbc.edu.

University of Maryland, College Park, Academic Affairs, College of Computer, Mathematical and Natural Sciences, Department of Mathematics, Applied Mathematics Program, College Park, MD 20742. Offers MS, PhD. Part-time and evening/weekend programs available. *Students:* 88 full-time (27 women), 8 part-time (2 women); includes 19 minority (4 Black or African American, non-Hispanic/Latino; 1 American Indian or Alaska Native, non-Hispanic/Latino; 9 Asian, non-Hispanic/Latino; 2 Hispanic/Latino; 3 Two or more races, non-Hispanic/Latino), 38 international. 306 applicants, 10% accepted, 15 enrolled. In 2011, 7 master's, 9 doctorates awarded. Terminal master's awarded for partial completion of doctoral program. *Degree requirements:* For master's, thesis optional, seminar, scholarly paper; for doctorate, comprehensive exam, thesis/dissertation, exams, seminars. *Entrance requirements:* For master's and doctorate, GRE General Test, GRE Subject Test, minimum GPA of 3.0, 3 letters of recommendation. *Application deadline:* For fall admission, 1/10 priority date for domestic students, 1/10 for international students. Applications are processed on a rolling basis. Application fee: $75. Electronic applications accepted. *Expenses: Tuition, area resident:* Part-time $525 per credit hour. Tuition, state resident: part-time $525 per credit hour. Tuition, nonresident: part-time $1131 per credit hour. *Required fees:* $386.31 per term. Tuition and fees vary according to program. *Financial support:* In 2011–12, 4 fellowships with full and partial tuition reimbursements (averaging $16,867 per year), 22 research assistantships (averaging $19,231 per year), 49 teaching assistantships (averaging $17,075 per year) were awarded. Financial award applicants required to submit FAFSA. *Unit head:* Konstantina Travisa, Director, 301-405-4489, E-mail: trivisa@umd.edu. *Application contact:* Dr. Charles A. Caramello, Dean of Graduate School, 301-405-0358, Fax: 301-314-9305.

University of Massachusetts Amherst, Graduate School, College of Natural Sciences, Department of Mathematics and Statistics, Amherst, MA 01003. Offers applied mathematics (MS); mathematics (MS, PhD); statistics (MS, PhD). *Faculty:* 44 full-time (6 women). *Students:* 64 full-time (17 women), 1 (woman) part-time; includes 7 minority (2 Black or African American, non-Hispanic/Latino; 4 Asian, non-Hispanic/Latino; 1 Two or more races, non-Hispanic/Latino), 26 international. Average age 27. 254 applicants, 20% accepted, 24 enrolled. In 2011, 17 master's, 6 doctorates awarded. Terminal master's awarded for partial completion of doctoral program. *Degree requirements:* For master's, thesis or alternative; for doctorate, comprehensive exam, thesis/dissertation. *Entrance requirements:* For master's and doctorate, GRE General Test, GRE Subject Test (mathematics). Additional exam requirements/recommendations for international students: Required—TOEFL (minimum score 550 paper-based; 213 computer-based; 80 iBT), IELTS (minimum score 6.5). *Application deadline:* For fall admission, 2/1 for domestic and international students. Applications are processed on a rolling basis. Application fee: $50 ($65 for international students). Electronic applications accepted. Tuition and fees vary according to course load, campus/location and program. *Financial support:* Fellowships with full and partial tuition reimbursements, research assistantships with full and partial tuition reimbursements, teaching assistantships with full and partial tuition reimbursements, career-related internships or fieldwork, Federal Work-Study, scholarships/grants, traineeships, health care benefits, tuition waivers (full and partial), and unspecified assistantships available. Support available to part-time students. Financial award application deadline: 2/1. *Unit head:* Dr. Michael Lavine, Department Head, 413-545-2282, Fax: 413-545-1801. *Application contact:* Lindsay DeSantis, Supervisor of Admissions, 413-545-0722, Fax: 413-577-0010, E-mail: gradadm@grad.umass.edu. Web site: http://www.math.umass.edu/.

University of Massachusetts Lowell, College of Sciences, Department of Mathematical Sciences, Lowell, MA 01854-2881. Offers applied mathematics (MS); computational mathematics (PhD); mathematics (MS). Part-time programs available. *Entrance requirements:* For master's, GRE General Test.

University of Memphis, Graduate School, College of Arts and Sciences, Department of Mathematical Sciences, Memphis, TN 38152. Offers applied mathematics (MS); applied statistics (PhD); bioinformatics (MS); computer science (PhD); computer sciences (MS); mathematics (MS, PhD); statistics (MS, PhD). Part-time programs available. Terminal master's awarded for partial completion of doctoral program. *Degree requirements:* For master's, comprehensive exam; for doctorate, one foreign language, thesis/dissertation, oral exams. *Entrance requirements:* For master's and doctorate, GRE General Test, minimum GPA of 2.5. Additional exam requirements/recommendations for international students: Required—TOEFL (minimum score 550 paper-based; 210 computer-based). Electronic applications accepted. *Faculty research:* Combinatorics, ergodic theory, graph theory, Ramsey theory, applied statistics.

University of Michigan–Dearborn, College of Arts, Sciences, and Letters, Master of Science in Applied and Computational Mathematics Program, Dearborn, MI 48128. Offers MS. Part-time and evening/weekend programs available. *Faculty:* 8 full-time (2 women). *Students:* 11 part-time (4 women); includes 1 minority (Black or African American, non-Hispanic/Latino). Average age 36. 6 applicants, 83% accepted, 2 enrolled. In 2011, 5 master's awarded. *Degree requirements:* For master's, thesis or alternative, project. *Entrance requirements:* For master's, 3 letters of recommendation, minimum GPA of 3.0, 2 years course work in math. Additional exam requirements/recommendations for

international students: Required—TOEFL (minimum score 560 paper-based; 220 computer-based). *Application deadline:* For fall admission, 8/1 priority date for domestic students, 4/1 for international students; for winter admission, 12/1 priority date for domestic students, 11/1 for international students; for spring admission, 4/1 for domestic students, 3/1 for international students. Applications are processed on a rolling basis. Application fee: $60. Electronic applications accepted. *Financial support:* Federal Work-Study and scholarships/grants available. Support available to part-time students. Financial award application deadline: 4/1; financial award applicants required to submit FAFSA. *Faculty research:* Partial differential equations, statistics, mathematical biology, approximation theory, stochastic processes. *Unit head:* Dr. Thomas Snabb, Director, 313-593-5162, E-mail: tsnabb@umd.umich.edu. *Application contact:* Carol Ligienza, Coordinator, CASL Graduate Programs, 313-593-1183, Fax: 313-583-6700, E-mail: caslgrad@umd.umich.edu. Web site: http://www.casl.umd.umich.edu/563801/.

University of Minnesota, Duluth, Graduate School, Swenson College of Science and Engineering, Department of Mathematics and Statistics, Duluth, MN 55812-2496. Offers applied and computational mathematics (MS). Part-time programs available. *Degree requirements:* For master's, thesis or alternative. *Entrance requirements:* For master's, GRE General Test, minimum GPA of 3.0. Additional exam requirements/recommendations for international students: Required—TOEFL (minimum score 550 paper-based; 213 computer-based; 79 iBT); Recommended—TWE. Electronic applications accepted. *Faculty research:* Discrete mathematics, diagnostic markers, combinatorics, biostatistics, mathematical modeling and scientific computation.

University of Missouri, Graduate School, College of Arts and Sciences, Department of Mathematics, Program in Applied Mathematics, Columbia, MO 65211. Offers MS. *Students:* 4 full-time (3 women), 1 international. Average age 22. 17 applicants, 18% accepted, 2 enrolled. In 2011, 6 degrees awarded. *Degree requirements:* For master's, thesis. *Entrance requirements:* For master's, GRE General Test, minimum GPA of 3.0. Additional exam requirements/recommendations for international students: Required—TOEFL (minimum score 500 paper-based; 173 computer-based; 61 iBT). *Application deadline:* For fall admission, 1/15 for domestic and international students. Applications are processed on a rolling basis. Application fee: $55 ($75 for international students). Electronic applications accepted. *Expenses:* Tuition, state resident: full-time $5881. Tuition, nonresident: full-time $15,183. *Required fees:* $952. Tuition and fees vary according to campus/location and program. *Financial support:* Fellowships, research assistantships, teaching assistantships, institutionally sponsored loans, health care benefits, and unspecified assistantships available. *Faculty research:* areas of mathematics used frequently in applications. *Unit head:* Dr. Glen Himmelberg, Department Chair, 573-882-6222, E-mail: himmelbergg@missouri.edu. *Application contact:* Amy Crews, Administrative Assistant, 573-882-6222, E-mail: crewsae@missouri.edu.

University of Missouri–St. Louis, College of Arts and Sciences, Department of Mathematics and Computer Science, St. Louis, MO 63121. Offers applied mathematics (PhD), including computer science, mathematics; computer science (MS); mathematics (MA). Part-time and evening/weekend programs available. *Faculty:* 16 full-time (2 women). *Students:* 28 full-time (16 women), 41 part-time (11 women); includes 6 minority (4 Black or African American, non-Hispanic/Latino; 1 American Indian or Alaska Native, non-Hispanic/Latino; 1 Asian, non-Hispanic/Latino), 18 international. Average age 32. 82 applicants, 57% accepted, 18 enrolled. In 2011, 20 master's, 2 doctorates awarded. *Degree requirements:* For master's, thesis optional; for doctorate, thesis/dissertation. *Entrance requirements:* For master's, GRE (for teaching assistantships), 2 letters of recommendation; C programming, C++ or Java (for computer science); for doctorate, GRE General Test, 3 letters of recommendation. Additional exam requirements/recommendations for international students: Required—TOEFL (minimum score 550 paper-based; 213 computer-based). *Application deadline:* For fall admission, 7/1 priority date for domestic students, 7/1 for international students; for spring admission, 12/1 priority date for domestic students, 12/1 for international students. Applications are processed on a rolling basis. Application fee: $35 ($40 for international students). Electronic applications accepted. *Expenses:* Tuition, state resident: full-time $6273; part-time $3866 per year. Tuition, nonresident: full-time $14,969; part-time $9980 per year. *Required fees:* $315 per year. *Financial support:* In 2011–12, 3 research assistantships with full and partial tuition reimbursements (averaging $14,250 per year), 10 teaching assistantships with full and partial tuition reimbursements (averaging $12,400 per year) were awarded; fellowships with full tuition reimbursements also available. Financial award applicants required to submit FAFSA. *Faculty research:* Statistics, algebra, analysis. *Unit head:* Dr. Shiying Zhao, Director of Graduate Studies, 314-516-5741, Fax: 314-516-5400, E-mail: zhao@arch.cs.umsl.edu. *Application contact:* 314-516-5458, Fax: 314-516-6996, E-mail: gradadm@umsl.edu.

University of New Hampshire, Graduate School, College of Engineering and Physical Sciences, Department of Mathematics and Statistics, Durham, NH 03824. Offers applied mathematics (MS); industrial statistics (Postbaccalaureate Certificate); mathematics (MS, MST, PhD); mathematics education (PhD); statistics (MS). *Faculty:* 21 full-time (5 women). *Students:* 26 full-time (12 women), 30 part-time (12 women); includes 4 minority (1 American Indian or Alaska Native, non-Hispanic/Latino; 2 Asian, non-Hispanic/Latino; 1 Two or more races, non-Hispanic/Latino), 13 international. Average age 29. 86 applicants, 47% accepted, 16 enrolled. In 2011, 1,217 master's, 2 doctorates, 4 other advanced degrees

Peterson's Graduate Programs in the Physical Sciences, Mathematics, Agricultural Sciences, the Environment & Natural Resources 2013

facebook.com/petersonspublishing **293**

Applied Mathematics

awarded. Terminal master's awarded for partial completion of doctoral program. *Degree requirements:* For doctorate, 2 foreign languages, thesis/dissertation. *Entrance requirements:* Additional exam requirements/recommendations for international students: Required—TOEFL (minimum score 550 paper-based; 213 computer-based; 80 iBT). *Application deadline:* For fall admission, 4/1 priority date for domestic students, 4/1 for international students; for spring admission, 12/1 for domestic students. Applications are processed on a rolling basis. Application fee: $65. Electronic applications accepted. *Expenses:* Tuition, state resident: full-time $12,360; part-time $687 per credit hour. Tuition, nonresident: full-time $25,680; part-time $1058 per credit hour. *International tuition:* $29,550 full-time. *Required fees:* $1666; $833 per course. $416.50 per semester. Tuition and fees vary according to course load and degree level. *Financial support:* In 2011–12, 41 students received support, including 6 research assistantships, 34 teaching assistantships; fellowships, Federal Work-Study, scholarships/grants, and tuition waivers (full and partial) also available. Support available to part-time students. Financial award application deadline: 2/15. *Faculty research:* Operator theory, complex analysis, algebra, nonlinear dynamics, statistics. *Unit head:* Dr. Edward Hinson, Chairperson, 603-862-2688. *Application contact:* Jan Jankowski, Administrative Assistant, 603-862-2320, E-mail: jan.jankowski@unh.edu. Web site: http://www.math.unh.edu/.

The University of North Carolina at Charlotte, Graduate School, College of Liberal Arts and Sciences, Department of Mathematics and Statistics, Charlotte, NC 28223-0001. Offers applied mathematics (MS, PhD); mathematics (MS); mathematics education (MA). Part-time and evening/weekend programs available. *Faculty:* 48 full-time (7 women). *Students:* 43 full-time (17 women), 27 part-time (10 women); includes 12 minority (7 Black or African American, non-Hispanic/Latino; 3 Asian, non-Hispanic/Latino; 2 Hispanic/Latino), 33 international. Average age 30. 52 applicants, 98% accepted, 16 enrolled. In 2011, 14 master's, 6 doctorates awarded. *Degree requirements:* For master's, comprehensive exam, thesis or alternative; for doctorate, thesis/dissertation. *Entrance requirements:* For master's, GRE General Test, minimum GPA of 3.0 in undergraduate major, 2.75 overall; for doctorate, GRE General Test, minimum overall GPA of 3.0. Additional exam requirements/recommendations for international students: Required—TOEFL (minimum score 557 paper-based; 220 computer-based; 83 iBT), Michigan English Language Assessment Battery (minimum score 78) or IELTS (minimum score 6.5). *Application deadline:* For fall admission, 7/1 for domestic students, 5/1 for international students; for spring admission, 11/1 for domestic students, 10/1 for international students. Applications are processed on a rolling basis. Application fee: $65 ($75 for international students). Electronic applications accepted. *Expenses:* Tuition, state resident: full-time $3689. Tuition, nonresident: full-time $15,226. *Required fees:* $2198. Tuition and fees vary according to course load and program. *Financial support:* In 2011–12, 37 students received support, including 4 fellowships (averaging $22,321 per year), 4 research assistantships (averaging $19,325 per year), 29 teaching assistantships (averaging $11,988 per year); career-related internships or fieldwork, Federal Work-Study, institutionally sponsored loans, scholarships/grants, and unspecified assistantships also available. Support available to part-time students. Financial award application deadline: 4/1; financial award applicants required to submit FAFSA. *Faculty research:* Numerical analysis, differential equations, probability, algebra, analysis, mathematics education, statistics. *Total annual research expenditures:* $1.2 million. *Unit head:* Dr. Alan S. Dow, Chair, 704-687-4560, Fax: 704-687-6415, E-mail: adow@uncc.edu. *Application contact:* Kathy B. Giddings, Director of Graduate Admissions, 704-687-5503, Fax: 704-687-3279, E-mail: gradadm@uncc.edu. Web site: http://www.math.uncc.edu/.

University of Northern Iowa, Graduate College, College of Humanities, Arts and Sciences, Department of Mathematics, Cedar Falls, IA 50614. Offers industrial mathematics (PSM), including actuarial science, continuous quality improvement, mathematical computing and modeling; mathematics (MA), including mathematics, secondary; mathematics for middle grades 4-8 (MA). Part-time programs available. *Students:* 13 full-time (6 women), 23 part-time (17 women); includes 2 minority (1 Black or African American, non-Hispanic/Latino; 1 Asian, non-Hispanic/Latino), 6 international. 35 applicants, 74% accepted, 11 enrolled. In 2011, 19 master's awarded. *Degree requirements:* For master's, comprehensive exam (for some programs), thesis or alternative. *Entrance requirements:* For master's, minimum GPA of 3.0. Additional exam requirements/recommendations for international students: Required—TOEFL (minimum score 600 paper-based; 250 computer-based; 100 iBT). *Application deadline:* For fall admission, 8/1 priority date for domestic students. Applications are processed on a rolling basis. Application fee: $50 ($70 for international students). Electronic applications accepted. *Expenses:* Tuition, state resident: full-time $7476. Tuition, nonresident: full-time $16,410. *Required fees:* $942. *Financial support:* Career-related internships or fieldwork, Federal Work-Study, scholarships/grants, and tuition waivers (full and partial) available. Support available to part-time students. Financial award application deadline: 2/1. *Unit head:* Dr. Douglas Mupasiri, Interim Head, 319-273-2012, E-mail: douglas.mupasiri@uni.edu. *Application contact:* Laurie S. Russell, Record Analyst, 319-273-2623, Fax: 319-273-2885, E-mail: laurie.russell@uni.edu. Web site: http://www.math.uni.edu/.

University of Notre Dame, Graduate School, College of Science, Department of Mathematics, Notre Dame, IN 46556. Offers algebra (PhD); algebraic geometry (PhD); applied mathematics (MSAM); complex analysis (PhD); differential geometry (PhD); logic (PhD); partial differential equations (PhD); topology (PhD). Terminal master's awarded for partial completion of doctoral program. *Degree*

requirements: For doctorate, one foreign language, thesis/dissertation, qualifying exam. *Entrance requirements:* For master's and doctorate, GRE General Test, GRE Subject Test. Additional exam requirements/recommendations for international students: Required—TOEFL (minimum score 600 paper-based; 250 computer-based; 80 iBT). Electronic applications accepted. *Faculty research:* Algebra, analysis, geometry/topology, logic, applied math.

University of Pennsylvania, School of Arts and Sciences, Graduate Group in Applied Mathematics and Computational Science, Philadelphia, PA 19104. Offers PhD. *Faculty:* 26 full-time (2 women). *Students:* 22 full-time (6 women), all international. 116 applicants, 21% accepted, 9 enrolled. *Application deadline:* For fall admission, 1/15 for domestic students. *Expenses:* Tuition: Full-time $26,660; part-time $4944 per course. *Required fees:* $2318; $291 per course. Tuition and fees vary according to course load, degree level and program. *Financial support:* Institutionally sponsored loans, scholarships/grants, traineeships, health care benefits, and unspecified assistantships available. *Unit head:* Dr. C. L. Epstein, Graduate Chair, 215-898-8476, E-mail: cle@math.upenn.edu. *Application contact:* Patricia Rea, Associate Director for Admissions, 215-573-5816, Fax: 215-573-8068, E-mail: gdasadmis@sas.upenn.edu. Web site: http://www.amcs.upenn.edu/.

University of Pittsburgh, Dietrich School of Arts and Sciences, Department of Mathematics, Pittsburgh, PA 15260. Offers applied mathematics (MA, MS); mathematics (MA, MS, PhD). Part-time programs available. *Faculty:* 36 full-time (2 women), 16 part-time/adjunct (2 women). *Students:* 75 full-time (23 women), 4 part-time (2 women); includes 2 minority (1 Black or African American, non-Hispanic/Latino; 1 Native Hawaiian or other Pacific Islander, non-Hispanic/Latino), 43 international. 288 applicants, 17% accepted, 25 enrolled. In 2011, 9 master's, 13 doctorates awarded. Terminal master's awarded for partial completion of doctoral program. *Degree requirements:* For master's, comprehensive exam, thesis (for some programs); for doctorate, comprehensive exam, thesis/dissertation, preliminary exams, defense of dissertation. *Entrance requirements:* For master's, GRE General Test, GRE Subject Test (recommended), minimum GPA of 3.0; for doctorate, GRE General Test, GRE Subject Test (recommended), minimum GPA of 3.0, minimum QPA of 3.25 in math curriculum. Additional exam requirements/recommendations for international students: Required—TOEFL (minimum score 550 paper-based; 213 computer-based; 80 iBT), IELTS (minimum score 6.5). *Application deadline:* For fall admission, 1/15 priority date for domestic students, 1/15 for international students; for spring admission, 9/1 priority date for domestic students, 9/1 for international students. Applications are processed on a rolling basis. Application fee: $50. Electronic applications accepted. *Expenses:* Tuition, state resident: full-time $18,774; part-time $760 per credit. Tuition, nonresident: full-time $30,736; part-time $1258 per credit. *Required fees:* $740; $200 per term. Tuition and fees vary according to program. *Financial support:* In 2011–12, 72 students received support, including 8 fellowships with full and partial tuition reimbursements available (averaging $19,610 per year), 16 research assistantships with full and partial tuition reimbursements available (averaging $16,000 per year), 53 teaching assistantships with full and partial tuition reimbursements available (averaging $16,460 per year); institutionally sponsored loans, scholarships/grants, traineeships, health care benefits, tuition waivers (partial), and unspecified assistantships also available. Financial award application deadline: 1/15. *Faculty research:* Algebra, analysis, computational math, geometry/topology, math biology. *Total annual research expenditures:* $1.8 million. *Unit head:* Ivan Yotov, Chair, 412-624-8361, Fax: 412-624-8397, E-mail: yotov@math.pitt.edu. *Application contact:* Molly Williams, Administrator, 412-624-1175, Fax: 412-624-8397, E-mail: mollyw@pitt.edu. Web site: http://www.mathematics.pitt.edu.

University of Puerto Rico, Mayagüez Campus, Graduate Studies, College of Arts and Sciences, Department of Mathematical Sciences, Mayagüez, PR 00681-9000. Offers applied mathematics (MS); pure mathematics (MS); scientific computation (MS); statistics (MS). Part-time programs available. *Students:* 32 full-time (9 women), 1 (woman) part-time; includes 7 minority (all Hispanic/Latino), 26 international. 23 applicants, 43% accepted, 7 enrolled. In 2011, 10 master's awarded. *Degree requirements:* For master's, one foreign language, comprehensive exam, thesis optional. *Entrance requirements:* For master's, undergraduate degree in mathematics or its equivalent. *Application deadline:* For fall admission, 2/15 for domestic and international students; for spring admission, 9/15 for domestic and international students. Applications are processed on a rolling basis. Application fee: $25. Tuition and fees vary according to course level and course load. *Financial support:* In 2011–12, 31 students received support, including 3 research assistantships (averaging $15,000 per year), 28 teaching assistantships (averaging $8,500 per year); Federal Work-Study and institutionally sponsored loans also available. *Faculty research:* Automata theory, linear algebra, logic. *Unit head:* Prof. Omar Colon, Director, 787-832-4040 Ext. 3848, Fax: 787-265-5454, E-mail: omar.colon.reyes@gmail.com. Web site: http://math.uprm.edu/.

University of Rhode Island, Graduate School, College of Arts and Sciences, Department of Computer Science and Statistics, Kingston, RI 02881. Offers applied mathematics (PhD), including computer science, statistics; computer science (MS, PhD); digital forensics (Graduate Certificate); statistics (MS). Part-time programs available. *Faculty:* 10 full-time (4 women), 1 (woman) part-time/adjunct. *Students:* 16 full-time (3 women), 41 part-time (10 women); includes 8 minority (2 Black or African American, non-Hispanic/Latino; 1 Asian, non-Hispanic/Latino; 5 Hispanic/Latino), 7 international. In 2011, 9 master's, 1 doctorate awarded. *Degree requirements:* For master's, comprehensive exam (for some programs), thesis optional; for doctorate, comprehensive exam, thesis/dissertation. *Entrance requirements:* For master's and doctorate, GRE, 2 letters of recommendation. Additional exam requirements/recommendations for international students: Required—TOEFL (minimum score 550 paper-based; 213 computer-based). *Application deadline:* For fall admission, 7/15 for domestic students, 2/1 for international students; for spring admission, 11/15 for domestic students, 7/15 for international students. Application fee: $65. Electronic applications accepted. *Expenses:* Tuition, state resident: full-time $10,432; part-time $580 per credit hour. Tuition, nonresident: full-time $23,130; part-time $1285 per credit hour. *Required fees:* $1362; $36 per credit hour. $35 per semester. One-time fee: $130. *Financial support:* In 2011–12, 2 research assistantships (averaging $7,004 per year), 9 teaching assistantships with full and partial tuition reimbursements (averaging $9,759 per year) were awarded. Financial award application deadline: 2/1; financial award applicants required to submit FAFSA. *Faculty research:* Bioinformatics, computer and digital forensics, behavioral model of pedestrian dynamics, real-time distributed object computing, cryptography. *Unit head:* Dr. James G. Kowalski, Chair, 401-874-2510, Fax: 401-874-4617, E-mail: kowalski@cs.uri.edu. *Application contact:* Dr. Victor Fay-Wolfe, Director of Graduate Studies, 401-874-2701, Fax: 401-874-4617, E-mail: wolfe@cs.uri.edu. Web site: http://www.cs.uri.edu/.

University of Rhode Island, Graduate School, College of Arts and Sciences, Department of Mathematics, Kingston, RI 02881. Offers applied mathematical sciences (MS, PhD); mathematics (MS, PhD). Part-time programs available. *Faculty:* 21 full-time (6 women). *Students:* 20 full-time (8 women), 9 part-time (4 women), 2 international. In 2011, 6 master's, 1 doctorate awarded. *Degree requirements:* For master's, comprehensive exam (for some programs), thesis optional; for doctorate, one foreign language, comprehensive exam, thesis/dissertation optional. *Entrance requirements:* For master's and doctorate, 2 letters of recommendation. Additional exam requirements/recommendations for international students: Required—TOEFL (minimum score 550 paper-based; 213 computer-based). *Application deadline:* For fall admission, 7/15 for domestic students, 2/1 for international students; for spring admission, 11/15 for domestic students, 7/15 for international students. Application fee: $65. Electronic applications accepted. *Expenses:* Tuition, state resident: full-time $10,432; part-time $580 per credit hour. Tuition, nonresident: full-time $23,130; part-time $1285 per credit hour. *Required fees:* $1362; $36 per credit hour. $35 per semester. One-time fee: $130. *Financial support:* In 2011–12, 13 teaching assistantships with full and partial tuition reimbursements (averaging $14,358 per year) were awarded. Financial award application deadline: 7/15; financial award applicants required to submit FAFSA. *Unit head:* Dr. Nancy Eaton, Chairman, 401-874-2709, Fax: 401-874-4454, E-mail: eaton@math.uri.edu. *Application contact:* Dr. Woong Kook, Director of Graduate Studies, 401-874-4421, Fax: 401-874-4454, E-mail: andrewk@math.uri.edu. Web site: http://www.math.uri.edu/.

University of Southern California, Graduate School, Dana and David Dornsife College of Letters, Arts and Sciences, Department of Mathematics, Los Angeles, CA 90089. Offers applied mathematics (MA, MS, PhD); mathematical finance (MS); mathematics (MA, PhD); statistics (MS). Part-time programs available. Terminal master's awarded for partial completion of doctoral program. *Degree requirements:* For master's, comprehensive exam (for some programs), thesis (for some programs); for doctorate, one foreign language, comprehensive exam, thesis/dissertation. *Entrance requirements:* For master's, GRE General Test, GMAT; for doctorate, GRE General Test, GRE Subject Test (mathematics). Additional exam requirements/recommendations for international students: Required—TOEFL (minimum score 100 iBT). Electronic applications accepted. *Faculty research:* Algebra, algebraic geometry and number theory, analysis/partial differential equations, applied mathematics, financial mathematics, probability, combinatorics and statistics.

The University of Tennessee, Graduate School, College of Arts and Sciences, Department of Mathematics, Knoxville, TN 37996. Offers applied mathematics (MS); mathematical ecology (PhD); mathematics (M Math, MS, PhD). Part-time programs available. *Degree requirements:* For master's, thesis or alternative; for doctorate, one foreign language, thesis/dissertation. *Entrance requirements:* For master's and doctorate, minimum GPA of 2.7. Additional exam requirements/recommendations for international students: Required—TOEFL. Electronic applications accepted. *Expenses:* Tuition, state resident: full-time $8332; part-time $464 per credit hour. Tuition, nonresident: full-time $25,174; part-time $1400 per credit hour. *Required fees:* $1162; $56 per credit hour. Tuition and fees vary according to program.

The University of Texas at Arlington, Graduate School, College of Science, Department of Mathematics, Arlington, TX 76019. Offers applied math (MS); mathematics (PhD); mathematics education (MA). Part-time and evening/weekend programs available. *Faculty:* 24 full-time (8 women), 2 part-time/adjunct (0 women). *Students:* 63 full-time (21 women), 78 part-time (33 women); includes 40 minority (15 Black or African American, non-Hispanic/Latino; 8 Asian, non-Hispanic/Latino; 16 Hispanic/Latino; 1 Two or more races, non-Hispanic/Latino), 36 international. 72 applicants, 92% accepted, 32 enrolled. In 2011, 13 master's, 4 doctorates awarded. *Degree requirements:* For master's, comprehensive exam, thesis or alternative; for doctorate, comprehensive exam, thesis/dissertation, preliminary examinations. *Entrance requirements:* For master's, GRE General Test (minimum score 350 verbal, 650 quantitative); for doctorate, GRE General Test (minimum score 350 verbal, 700 quantitative), 30 hours of graduate course work in mathematics, minimum GPA of 3.0 in last 60 hours of course work. Additional exam requirements/recommendations for international students:

Required—TOEFL (minimum score 550 paper-based; 213 computer-based; 79 iBT). *Application deadline:* For fall admission, 6/1 priority date for domestic students, 4/1 for international students; for winter admission, 10/15 priority date for domestic students, 9/15 for international students. Applications are processed on a rolling basis. Application fee: $35 ($50 for international students). Electronic applications accepted. *Financial support:* In 2011–12, 36 students received support, including 17 fellowships with full tuition reimbursements available (averaging $27,500 per year), 2 research assistantships with partial tuition reimbursements available, 23 teaching assistantships with partial tuition reimbursements available (averaging $20,750 per year); Federal Work-Study, institutionally sponsored loans, scholarships/grants, health care benefits, and unspecified assistantships also available. Financial award application deadline: 2/1; financial award applicants required to submit FAFSA. *Faculty research:* Algebra, combinatorics and geometry, applied mathematics and mathematical biology, computational mathematics, mathematics education, probability and statistics. *Unit head:* Dr. Zhu Jiaping, Chair, 817-272-1114, E-mail: jpzhu@uta.edu. *Application contact:* Dr. Jianzhong Su, Graduate Advisor, 817-272-5684, Fax: 817-272-5802, E-mail: su@uta.edu. Web site: http://www.uta.edu/math.

The University of Texas at Austin, Graduate School, Program in Computational Science, Engineering, and Mathematics, Austin, TX 78712-1111. Offers MS, PhD. Terminal master's awarded for partial completion of doctoral program. *Degree requirements:* For master's, thesis optional; for doctorate, thesis/dissertation, 3 area qualifying exams. *Application deadline:* For fall admission, 2/1 for domestic students. Application fee: $50 ($75 for international students). Electronic applications accepted. *Financial support:* Fellowships with full and partial tuition reimbursements, research assistantships with full and partial tuition reimbursements, and teaching assistantships with full and partial tuition reimbursements available. Financial award application deadline: 2/1. *Unit head:* Clint Dawson, Graduate Adviser, 512-475-8627, E-mail: clint@ices.utexas.edu. *Application contact:* Stephanie Rodriguez, 512-232-3356, E-mail: slr@ices.utexas.edu. Web site: http://www.ices.utexas.edu/graduate-studies/.

The University of Texas at Dallas, School of Natural Sciences and Mathematics, Department of Mathematical Sciences, Richardson, TX 75080. Offers applied mathematics (MS, PhD); bioinformatics and computational biology (MS); engineering mathematics (MS); mathematics (MS); statistics (MS, PhD). Part-time and evening/weekend programs available. *Faculty:* 15 full-time (2 women). *Students:* 53 full-time (21 women), 17 part-time (3 women); includes 21 minority (5 Black or African American, non-Hispanic/Latino; 12 Asian, non-Hispanic/Latino; 4 Hispanic/Latino), 31 international. Average age 31. 127 applicants, 32% accepted, 28 enrolled. In 2011, 16 master's, 7 doctorates awarded. *Degree requirements:* For master's, thesis optional; for doctorate, thesis/dissertation. *Entrance requirements:* For master's, GRE General Test, minimum GPA of 3.0 in upper-level course work in field; for doctorate, GRE General Test, minimum GPA of 3.5 in upper-level course work in field. Additional exam requirements/recommendations for international students: Required—TOEFL (minimum score 550 paper-based; 215 computer-based). *Application deadline:* For fall admission, 7/15 for domestic students, 5/1 for international students; for spring admission, 11/15 for domestic students, 9/1 for international students. Applications are processed on a rolling basis. Application fee: $50 ($100 for international students). Electronic applications accepted. *Expenses:* Tuition, state resident: full-time $11,170; part-time $620.56 per credit hour. Tuition, nonresident: full-time $20,212; part-time $1122.89 per credit hour. *Financial support:* In 2011–12, 39 students received support, including 2 research assistantships (averaging $20,700 per year), 31 teaching assistantships with partial tuition reimbursements available (averaging $15,503 per year); career-related internships or fieldwork, Federal Work-Study, institutionally sponsored loans, scholarships/grants, and unspecified assistantships also available. Support available to part-time students. Financial award application deadline: 4/30; financial award applicants required to submit FAFSA. *Faculty research:* Sequential analysis, applications in semiconductor manufacturing, medical image analysis, computational anatomy, information theory, probability theory. *Unit head:* Dr. Matthew Goeckner, Department Head, 972-883-4292, Fax: 972-883-6622, E-mail: goeckner@utdallas.edu. *Application contact:* Claire C. Troy, Graduate Support Assistant, 972-883-2163, Fax: 972-883-6622, E-mail: utdmath@utdallas.edu. Web site: http://www.utdallas.edu/math.

The University of Texas at San Antonio, College of Sciences, Department of Mathematics, San Antonio, TX 78249-0617. Offers applied mathematics (MS), including industrial mathematics; mathematics (MS); mathematics education (MS). Part-time and evening/weekend programs available. *Faculty:* 10 full-time (1 woman), 1 (woman) part-time/adjunct. *Students:* 33 full-time (14 women), 36 part-time (18 women); includes 32 minority (3 Black or African American, non-Hispanic/Latino; 2 Asian, non-Hispanic/Latino; 27 Hispanic/Latino), 10 international. Average age 30. 56 applicants, 80% accepted, 22 enrolled. In 2011, 15 master's awarded. *Degree requirements:* For master's, comprehensive exam (for some programs), thesis or alternative. *Entrance requirements:* For master's, GRE General Test, minimum GPA of 3.0 in last 60 hours. Additional exam requirements/recommendations for international students: Required—TOEFL (minimum score 500 paper-based; 61 iBT), IELTS (minimum score 5). *Application deadline:* For fall admission, 7/1 for domestic students, 4/1 for international students; for spring admission, 11/1 for domestic students, 9/1 for international students. Application fee: $45 ($85 for international students). *Expenses:* Tuition, state resident: full-time $3148; part-time $2176 per semester. Tuition, nonresident: full-time $8782; part-time $5932 per semester. *Required fees:* $719 per semester. *Financial support:* In 2011–12, 15 teaching assistantships

Peterson's Graduate Programs in the Physical Sciences, Mathematics, Agricultural Sciences, the Environment & Natural Resources 2013

facebook.com/petersonspublishing **295**

(averaging $13,000 per year) were awarded. *Faculty research:* Differential equations, functional analysis, numerical analysis, number theory, logic. *Unit head:* Dr. F. Alexander Norman, Department Chair, 210-458-7254, Fax: 210-458-4439, E-mail: sandy.norman@utsa.edu.

The University of Toledo, College of Graduate Studies, College of Natural Sciences and Mathematics, Department of Mathematics, Toledo, OH 43606-3390. Offers applied mathematics (MS); mathematics (MA, PhD); statistics (MS, PhD). Part-time programs available. *Students:* 33 full-time (10 women), 20 part-time (6 women); includes 2 minority (both Asian, non-Hispanic/Latino), 37 international. Average age 29. 84 applicants, 43% accepted, 19 enrolled. In 2011, 11 master's, 3 doctorates awarded. *Degree requirements:* For master's, comprehensive exam (for some programs), thesis (for some programs); for doctorate, 2 foreign languages, thesis/dissertation. *Entrance requirements:* For master's and doctorate, GRE General Test, GRE Subject Test, minimum cumulative point-hour ratio of 2.7 for all previous academic work, three letters of recommendation, statement of purpose, transcripts from all prior institutions attended. Additional exam requirements/recommendations for international students: Required—TOEFL (minimum score 550 paper-based; 213 computer-based; 80 iBT), IELTS (minimum score 6.5). *Application deadline:* For fall admission, 1/15 priority date for domestic students, 1/15 for international students. Applications are processed on a rolling basis. Application fee: $45 ($75 for international students). Electronic applications accepted. *Financial support:* In 2011–12, 3 research assistantships with full and partial tuition reimbursements (averaging $12,618 per year), 46 teaching assistantships with full and partial tuition reimbursements (averaging $12,860 per year) were awarded; Federal Work-Study, institutionally sponsored loans, scholarships/grants, and unspecified assistantships also available. Support available to part-time students. *Faculty research:* Topology. *Unit head:* Dr. Paul Hewitt, Chair, 419-530-2568, E-mail: paul.hewitt@utoledo.edu. *Application contact:* Graduate School Office, 419-530-4723, Fax: 419-530-4723, E-mail: grdsch@utnet.utoledo.edu. Web site: http://www.utoledo.edu/nsm/.

University of Tulsa, Graduate School, Collins College of Business, Finance/Applied Mathematics Program, Tulsa, OK 74104-3189. Offers MS/MS. Part-time and evening/weekend programs available. *Students:* 1 (woman) full-time. Average age 26. 3 applicants, 67% accepted, 0 enrolled. *Entrance requirements:* Additional exam requirements/recommendations for international students: Required—TOEFL (minimum score 577 paper-based; 233 computer-based; 91 iBT), IELTS (minimum score 6.5). *Application deadline:* Applications are processed on a rolling basis. Application fee: $40. Electronic applications accepted. *Expenses: Tuition:* Full-time $17,748; part-time $986 per hour. *Required fees:* $5 per contact hour. $75 per semester. Tuition and fees vary according to program. *Financial support:* In 2011–12, 1 student received support, including 1 teaching assistantship (averaging $6,061 per year); fellowships, career-related internships or fieldwork, Federal Work-Study, institutionally sponsored loans, scholarships/grants, health care benefits, tuition waivers (full and partial), and unspecified assistantships also available. Support available to part-time students. Financial award application deadline: 2/1; financial award applicants required to submit FAFSA. *Unit head:* Linda Nichols, Associate Dean, 918-631-2242, Fax: 918-631-2142, E-mail: linda-nichols@utulsa.edu. *Application contact:* Information Contact, 918-631-2242, E-mail: graduate-business@utulsa.edu.

University of Washington, Graduate School, College of Arts and Sciences, Department of Applied Mathematics, Seattle, WA 98195. Offers MS, PhD. Terminal master's awarded for partial completion of doctoral program. *Degree requirements:* For master's, thesis optional; for doctorate, thesis/dissertation. *Entrance requirements:* For master's and doctorate, GRE, minimum GPA of 3.0. Additional exam requirements/recommendations for international students: Required—TOEFL. Electronic applications accepted. *Faculty research:* Mathematical modeling for physical, biological, social, and engineering sciences; development of mathematical methods for analysis, including perturbation, asymptotic, transform, vocational, and numerical methods.

University of Washington, Graduate School, College of Arts and Sciences, Department of Mathematics, Seattle, WA 98195. Offers mathematics (MA, MS, PhD); numerical analysis (MS); optimization (MS). Part-time programs available. Terminal master's awarded for partial completion of doctoral program. *Degree requirements:* For master's, thesis optional; for doctorate, 2 foreign languages, thesis/dissertation. *Entrance requirements:* For master's, GRE, minimum GPA of 3.0; for doctorate, GRE General Test, GRE Subject Test (mathematics), minimum GPA of 3.0. Additional exam requirements/recommendations for international students: Required—TOEFL. Electronic applications accepted. *Faculty research:* Algebra, analysis, probability, combinatorics and geometry.

University of Waterloo, Graduate Studies, Faculty of Mathematics, Department of Applied Mathematics, Waterloo, ON N2L 3G1, Canada. Offers M Math, PhD. Part-time programs available. *Degree requirements:* For master's, research paper or thesis; for doctorate, thesis/dissertation. *Entrance requirements:* For master's, honors degree in field, minimum B+ average; for doctorate, master's degree, minimum B+ average. Additional exam requirements/recommendations for international students: Required—TOEFL (minimum score 600 paper-based; 250 computer-based; 100 iBT), TWE (minimum score 4). Electronic applications accepted. *Faculty research:* Differential equations, quantum theory, statistical mechanics, fluid mechanics, relativity, control theory.

The University of Western Ontario, Faculty of Graduate Studies, Physical Sciences Division, Department of Applied Mathematics, London, ON N6A 5B8, Canada. Offers applied mathematics (M Sc, PhD); theoretical physics (PhD). *Degree requirements:* For master's, thesis or alternative; for doctorate, comprehensive exam, thesis/dissertation. *Entrance requirements:* For master's and doctorate, minimum B average. Additional exam requirements/recommendations for international students: Required—TOEFL. *Faculty research:* Fluid dynamics, mathematical and computational methods, theoretical physics.

University of West Georgia, College of Science and Mathematics, Department of Mathematics, Carrollton, GA 30118. Offers teaching and applied mathematics (MS). *Faculty:* 15 full-time (3 women). *Students:* 6 full-time (1 woman), 11 part-time (3 women); includes 14 minority (11 Black or African American, non-Hispanic/Latino; 1 Asian, non-Hispanic/Latino; 2 Hispanic/Latino), 5 international. Average age 33. 9 applicants, 56% accepted, 1 enrolled. In 2011, 1 master's awarded. *Degree requirements:* For master's, comprehensive exam, thesis optional, 36 credit hours. *Entrance requirements:* For master's, GRE. Additional exam requirements/recommendations for international students: Required—TOEFL (minimum score 523 paper-based; 193 computer-based; 69 iBT); Recommended—IELTS (minimum score 6). *Application deadline:* For fall admission, 6/1 for domestic and international students; for spring admission, 11/15 for domestic students, 10/15 for international students. Applications are processed on a rolling basis. Application fee: $30. Electronic applications accepted. *Expenses:* Tuition, state resident: full-time $4336; part-time $181 per credit hour. Tuition, nonresident: full-time $17,362; part-time $724 per credit hour. Tuition and fees vary according to course load, degree level, campus/location and program. *Financial support:* In 2011–12, 3 students received support, including 3 teaching assistantships (averaging $6,800 per year); unspecified assistantships also available. Financial award application deadline: 7/1; financial award applicants required to submit FAFSA. *Unit head:* Dr. Minh Nguyen, Interim Chair, 678-839-6489, Fax: 678-839-6490, E-mail: vnguyen@westga.edu. *Application contact:* Alice Wesley, Departmental Assistant, 678-839-5192, E-mail: awesley@westga.edu. Web site: http://www.westga.edu/math/.

Utah State University, School of Graduate Studies, College of Science, Department of Mathematics and Statistics, Logan, UT 84322. Offers industrial mathematics (MS); mathematical sciences (PhD); mathematics (M Math, MS); statistics (MS). Part-time programs available. Terminal master's awarded for partial completion of doctoral program. *Degree requirements:* For master's, thesis optional, qualifying exam; for doctorate, one foreign language, comprehensive exam, thesis/dissertation. *Entrance requirements:* For master's and doctorate, GRE General Test, minimum GPA of 3.0. Additional exam requirements/recommendations for international students: Required—TOEFL. *Faculty research:* Differential equations, computational mathematics, dynamical systems, probability and statistics, pure mathematics.

Virginia Commonwealth University, Graduate School, College of Humanities and Sciences, Department of Mathematics and Applied Mathematics, Richmond, VA 23284-9005. Offers applied mathematics (MS); mathematics (MS). *Students:* 27 full-time (16 women), 27 part-time (8 women); includes 5 minority (4 Black or African American, non-Hispanic/Latino; 1 Hispanic/Latino), 7 international. 31 applicants, 71% accepted, 16 enrolled. In 2011, 15 master's awarded. *Degree requirements:* For master's, thesis optional. *Entrance requirements:* For master's, GRE General Test, GRE Subject Test, 30 undergraduate semester credits in the mathematical sciences or closely-related fields. Additional exam requirements/recommendations for international students: Required—TOEFL (minimum score 600 paper-based; 250 computer-based; 100 iBT); Recommended—IELTS (minimum score 6.5). *Application deadline:* For fall admission, 3/1 for domestic students; for spring admission, 10/1 for domestic students. Applications are processed on a rolling basis. Application fee: $50. Electronic applications accepted. *Expenses:* Tuition, state resident: full-time $9133; part-time $507 per credit. Tuition, nonresident: full-time $18,777; part-time $1043 per credit. *Required fees:* $77 per credit. Tuition and fees vary according to degree level, campus/location, program and student level. *Financial support:* Fellowships, research assistantships, teaching assistantships, Federal Work-Study, and institutionally sponsored loans available. Support available to part-time students. Financial award applicants required to submit FAFSA. *Faculty research:* Mathematics, applied mathematics. *Unit head:* Dr. Andrew M. Lewis, Chair, 804-828-1301 Ext. 128, Fax: 804-828-8785, E-mail: amlewis@vcu.edu. *Application contact:* Dr. Dewey T. Taylor, Graduate Program Director, 804-828-1301, E-mail: dttaylor2@vcu.edu. Web site: http://www.math.vcu.edu/.

Washington State University, Graduate School, College of Sciences, Department of Mathematics, Pullman, WA 99164. Offers applied mathematics (MS, PhD); mathematics teaching (MS, PhD). Part-time programs available. *Faculty:* 26. *Students:* 45 full-time (12 women), 5 part-time (4 women); includes 7 minority (1 Black or African American, non-Hispanic/Latino; 3 Asian, non-Hispanic/Latino; 2 Hispanic/Latino; 1 Two or more races, non-Hispanic/Latino), 14 international. Average age 30. 71 applicants, 54% accepted, 13 enrolled. In 2011, 2 master's, 4 doctorates awarded. *Degree requirements:* For master's, comprehensive exam (for some programs), thesis (for some programs), oral exam, project; for doctorate, 2 foreign languages, comprehensive exam, thesis/dissertation, oral exam, written exam. *Entrance requirements:* For master's and doctorate, minimum GPA of 3.0, 3 letters of recommendation. Additional exam requirements/recommendations for international students: Required—TOEFL (minimum score 600 paper-based; 250 computer-based), IELTS. *Application*

296 facebook.com/petersonspublishing

Peterson's Graduate Programs in the Physical Sciences, Mathematics, Agricultural Sciences, the Environment & Natural Resources 2013

deadline: For fall admission, 1/10 for domestic and international students; for spring admission, 7/1 for domestic and international students. Applications are processed on a rolling basis. Application fee: $75. Electronic applications accepted. *Financial support:* In 2011–12, 33 students received support, including 2 fellowships with tuition reimbursements available (averaging $2,500 per year), 3 research assistantships with full and partial tuition reimbursements available (averaging $14,634 per year), 27 teaching assistantships with full and partial tuition reimbursements available (averaging $13,383 per year); career-related internships or fieldwork, Federal Work-Study, institutionally sponsored loans, health care benefits, and tuition waivers (partial) also available. Financial award application deadline: 2/15; financial award applicants required to submit FAFSA. *Faculty research:* Computational mathematics, operations research, modeling in the natural sciences, applied statistics. *Unit head:* Dr. K. A. Ariyawansa, Chair, 509-335-4918, Fax: 509-335-1188, E-mail: ari@wsu.edu. *Application contact:* Graduate School Admissions, 800-GRADWSU, Fax: 509-335-1949, E-mail: gradsch@wsu.edu. Web site: http://www.sci.wsu.edu/math/.

Wayne State University, College of Liberal Arts and Sciences, Department of Mathematics, Detroit, MI 48202. Offers applied mathematics (MA); mathematical statistics (MA); mathematics (MA, PhD). *Students:* 50 full-time (16 women), 34 part-time (14 women); includes 13 minority (8 Black or African American, non-Hispanic/Latino; 4 Asian, non-Hispanic/Latino; 1 Two or more races, non-Hispanic/Latino), 32 international. Average age 30. 103 applicants, 50% accepted, 18 enrolled. In 2011, 12 master's, 5 doctorates awarded. *Degree requirements:* For master's, thesis (for some programs), essays, oral exams; for doctorate, one foreign language, thesis/dissertation, oral exams. *Entrance requirements:* For doctorate, master's degree in mathematics or equivalent level of advancement. Additional exam requirements/recommendations for international students: Required—TOEFL (minimum score 550 paper-based; 213 computer-based); Recommended—TWE (minimum score 5.5). *Application deadline:* For fall admission, 6/1 priority date for domestic students, 5/1 for international students; for winter admission, 10/1 priority date for domestic students, 9/1 for international students; for spring admission, 2/1 priority date for domestic students, 1/1 for international students. Applications are processed on a rolling basis. Application fee: $50. Electronic applications accepted. *Expenses:* Tuition, state resident: part-time $512.85 per credit. Tuition, nonresident: part-time $1132.65 per credit. *Required fees:* $26.60 per credit. $199.65 per semester. Tuition and fees vary according to course load and program. *Financial support:* In 2011–12, 43 students received support, including 4 fellowships with tuition reimbursements available (averaging $17,938 per year), 3 research assistantships with tuition reimbursements available (averaging $18,894 per year), 27 teaching assistantships with tuition reimbursements available (averaging $17,391 per year); institutionally sponsored loans, scholarships/grants, health care benefits, tuition waivers (full), and unspecified assistantships also available. Support available to part-time students. *Faculty research:* Harmonic analysis and partial differential equations, group theory and non-commutative ring theory, homotopy theory and applications to topology and geometry, numerical analysis, control and optimization, statistical estimation theory. *Total annual research expenditures:* $708,703. *Unit head:* Daniel Frohardt, Professor and Chair, 313-577-2479, E-mail: danf@math.wayne.edu. *Application contact:* Tiana Fluker, Graduate Secretary, E-mail: tiana@math.wayne.edu. Web site: http://www.math.wayne.edu/.

Western Illinois University, School of Graduate Studies, College of Arts and Sciences, Department of Mathematics, Macomb, IL 61455-1390. Offers applied math (Certificate); mathematics (MS). Part-time programs available. *Students:* 9 full-time (1 woman), 3 part-time (1 woman), 6 international. Average age 27. 11 applicants, 55% accepted. In 2011, 6 master's, 1 other advanced degree awarded. *Degree requirements:* For master's, thesis or alternative. *Entrance requirements:* Additional exam requirements/recommendations for international students: Required—TOEFL (minimum score 500 paper-based; 173 computer-based; 61 iBT). *Application deadline:* Applications are processed on a rolling basis. Application fee: $30. Electronic applications accepted. *Expenses:* Tuition, state resident: part-time $281.16 per credit hour. Tuition, nonresident: part-time $562.32 per credit hour. Part-time tuition and fees vary according to campus/location and reciprocity agreements. *Financial support:* In 2011–12, 11 students received support, including 5 research assistantships with full tuition reimbursements available (averaging $7,360 per year), 6 teaching assistantships with full tuition reimbursements available (averaging $8,480 per year). Financial award applicants required to submit FAFSA. *Unit head:* Dr. Iraj Kalantari, Chairperson, 309-298-1054. *Application contact:* Nancy Parsons, Interim Associate Provost and Director of Graduate Studies, 309-298-1806, Fax: 309-298-2345, E-mail: grad-office@wiu.edu. Web site: http://wiu.edu/mathematics.

Western Michigan University, Graduate College, College of Arts and Sciences, Department of Mathematics, Program in Applied and Computational Mathematics, Kalamazoo, MI 49008. Offers MS.

West Virginia University, Eberly College of Arts and Sciences, Department of Mathematics, Morgantown, WV 26506. Offers applied mathematics (MS, PhD); discrete mathematics (PhD); interdisciplinary mathematics (MS); mathematics for

secondary education (MS); pure mathematics (MS). Part-time programs available. Terminal master's awarded for partial completion of doctoral program. *Degree requirements:* For master's, comprehensive exam (for some programs), thesis optional; for doctorate, one foreign language, comprehensive exam, thesis/dissertation. *Entrance requirements:* For master's, GRE Subject Test (recommended), minimum GPA of 2.5; for doctorate, GRE Subject Test (recommended), master's degree in mathematics. Additional exam requirements/recommendations for international students: Required—TOEFL (paper-based 550; computer-based 213) or IELTS (paper-based 6). *Faculty research:* Combinatorics and graph theory, differential equations, applied and computational mathematics.

Wichita State University, Graduate School, Fairmount College of Liberal Arts and Sciences, Department of Mathematics, Statistics and Physics, Wichita, KS 67260. Offers applied mathematics (PhD); mathematics (PhD). Part-time programs available. *Expenses:* Tuition, state resident: full-time $4746; part-time $263.65 per credit. Tuition, nonresident: full-time $11,669; part-time $648.30 per credit. *Unit head:* Dr. Buma Fridman, Chair, 316-978-3160, Fax: 316-978-3748, E-mail: buma.fridman@wichita.edu. *Application contact:* Dr. Kenneth Miller, Graduate Coordinator, 316-978-3160, Fax: 316-978-3748, E-mail: kenneth.miller@wichita.edu. Web site: http://www.wichita.edu/.

Worcester Polytechnic Institute, Graduate Studies and Research, Department of Mathematical Sciences, Worcester, MA 01609-2280. Offers applied mathematics (MS); applied statistics (MS); financial mathematics (MS); industrial mathematics (MS); mathematical sciences (PhD, Graduate Certificate); mathematics (MME). Part-time and evening/weekend programs available. *Faculty:* 16 full-time (1 woman), 6 part-time/adjunct (2 women). *Students:* 52 full-time (23 women), 32 part-time (18 women); includes 4 minority (1 Black or African American, non-Hispanic/Latino; 3 Hispanic/Latino), 52 international. 326 applicants, 52% accepted, 53 enrolled. In 2011, 25 master's, 1 doctorate awarded. *Degree requirements:* For master's, thesis (for some programs); for doctorate, comprehensive exam, thesis/dissertation. *Entrance requirements:* For master's and doctorate, GRE General Test, GRE Subject Test in math (recommended), 3 letters of recommendation. Additional exam requirements/recommendations for international students: Required—TOEFL (minimum score 563 paper-based; 223 computer-based; 84 iBT), IELTS (minimum score 7). *Application deadline:* For fall admission, 1/1 priority date for domestic students, 1/1 for international students; for spring admission, 10/1 priority date for domestic students, 10/1 for international students. Applications are processed on a rolling basis. Application fee: $70. Electronic applications accepted. *Financial support:* Research assistantships, teaching assistantships, career-related internships or fieldwork, institutionally sponsored loans, scholarships/grants, and unspecified assistantships available. Financial award application deadline: 1/1; financial award applicants required to submit FAFSA. *Faculty research:* Applied analysis and differential equations, computational mathematics, discrete mathematics, applied and computational statistics, industrial and financial mathematics, mathematical biology. *Unit head:* Dr. Bogdan Vernescu, Head, 508-831-5241, Fax: 508-831-5824, E-mail: vernescu@wpi.edu. *Application contact:* Dr. Joseph Petruccelli, Graduate Coordinator, 508-831-5241, Fax: 508-831-5824, E-mail: jdp@wpi.edu. Web site: http://www.wpi.edu/Academics/Depts/Math/.

Wright State University, School of Graduate Studies, College of Science and Mathematics, Department of Mathematics and Statistics, Program in Applied Mathematics, Dayton, OH 45435. Offers MS. *Degree requirements:* For master's, comprehensive exam. *Entrance requirements:* For master's, bachelor's degree in mathematics or related field. Additional exam requirements/recommendations for international students: Required—TOEFL. *Faculty research:* Control theory, ordinary differential equations, partial differential equations, numerical analysis, mathematical modeling.

Yale University, Graduate School of Arts and Sciences, Program in Applied Mathematics, New Haven, CT 06520. Offers M Phil, MS, PhD. *Entrance requirements:* For doctorate, GRE General Test.

York University, Faculty of Graduate Studies, Faculty of Science and Engineering, Program in Mathematics and Statistics, Toronto, ON M3J 1P3, Canada. Offers industrial and applied mathematics (M Sc); mathematics and statistics (MA, PhD). Part-time programs available. *Degree requirements:* For master's, thesis optional; for doctorate, one foreign language, comprehensive exam, thesis/dissertation. Electronic applications accepted.

Youngstown State University, Graduate School, College of Science, Technology, Engineering and Mathematics, Department of Mathematics and Statistics, Youngstown, OH 44555-0001. Offers applied mathematics (MS); computer science (MS); secondary mathematics (MS); statistics (MS). Part-time programs available. *Degree requirements:* For master's, comprehensive exam, thesis optional. *Entrance requirements:* For master's, minimum GPA of 2.7 in computer science and mathematics. Additional exam requirements/recommendations for international students: Required—TOEFL. *Faculty research:* Regression analysis, numerical analysis, statistics, Markov chain, topology and fuzzy sets.

Peterson's Graduate Programs in the Physical Sciences, Mathematics, Agricultural Sciences, the Environment & Natural Resources 2013

facebook.com/petersonspublishing   **297**

Applied Statistics

American University, College of Arts and Sciences, Department of Mathematics and Statistics, Washington, DC 22016-8050. Offers applied statistics (Certificate); mathematics (MA); statistics (MS). Part-time and evening/weekend programs available. *Faculty:* 26 full-time (8 women), 10 part-time/adjunct (0 women). *Students:* 11 full-time (5 women), 8 part-time (4 women); includes 4 minority (3 Black or African American, non-Hispanic/Latino; 1 Hispanic/Latino), 2 international. Average age 29. 44 applicants, 77% accepted, 10 enrolled. In 2011, 11 master's awarded. *Degree requirements:* For master's, comprehensive exam, thesis or alternative, tools of research in foreign language or computer language. *Entrance requirements:* For master's, GRE; for Certificate, bachelor's degree. Additional exam requirements/recommendations for international students: Required—TOEFL. *Application deadline:* For fall admission, 2/1 for domestic students; for spring admission, 10/1 for domestic students. Application fee: $80. *Expenses: Tuition:* Full-time $24,264; part-time $1348 per credit hour. *Required fees:* $430. Tuition and fees vary according to course load and program. *Financial support:* Fellowships, research assistantships, teaching assistantships, career-related internships or fieldwork, Federal Work-Study, institutionally sponsored loans, and unspecified assistantships available. Support available to part-time students. Financial award application deadline: 2/1. *Faculty research:* Logic, random processes, probability analysis, biostatistics, statistical computing. *Unit head:* Dr. Jeffrey D. Adler, Chair, 202-885-3171, Fax: 202-885-3155, E-mail: jadler@american.edu. *Application contact:* Kathleen Clowery, Director, Graduate Admissions, 202-885-3621, Fax: 202-885-1505, E-mail: clowery@american.edu. Web site: http://www.american.edu/cas/mathstat/.

Bowling Green State University, Graduate College, College of Arts and Sciences, Department of Mathematics and Statistics, Bowling Green, OH 43403. Offers applied statistics (MS); mathematics (MA, MAT, PhD); statistics (PhD). Part-time programs available. *Degree requirements:* For master's, thesis or alternative; for doctorate, comprehensive exam, thesis/dissertation. *Entrance requirements:* For master's and doctorate, GRE General Test. Additional exam requirements/recommendations for international students: Required—TOEFL. Electronic applications accepted. *Faculty research:* Statistics and probability, algebra, analysis.

Bowling Green State University, Graduate College, College of Business Administration, Department of Applied Statistics and Operations Research, Bowling Green, OH 43403. Offers applied statistics (MS). Part-time programs available. *Degree requirements:* For master's, thesis or alternative. *Entrance requirements:* For master's, GRE General Test. Additional exam requirements/recommendations for international students: Required—TOEFL. Electronic applications accepted. *Faculty research:* Reliability, linear models, time series, statistical quality control.

Brigham Young University, Graduate Studies, College of Physical and Mathematical Sciences, Department of Statistics, Provo, UT 84602-1001. Offers applied statistics (MS). *Faculty:* 16 full-time (3 women). *Students:* 30 full-time (14 women); includes 1 minority (Asian, non-Hispanic/Latino). Average age 26. 26 applicants, 69% accepted, 14 enrolled. In 2011, 10 master's awarded. *Degree requirements:* For master's, comprehensive exam, thesis (for some programs). *Entrance requirements:* For master's, GRE General Test, minimum undergraduate GPA of 3.3; course work in statistical methods, theory, multivariable calculus and linear algebra with minimum Baverage. Additional exam requirements/recommendations for international students: Required—TOEFL (minimum score 580 paper-based; 237 computer-based; 85 iBT). *Application deadline:* For fall admission, 2/1 for domestic and international students. Application fee: $50. Electronic applications accepted. Full-time tuition for non-LDS students: $11,520 per year; $640 per credit. *Expenses: Tuition:* Full-time $5760; part-time $320 per credit. Tuition and fees vary according to student's religious affiliation. *Financial support:* In 2011–12, 18 students received support, including 4 research assistantships with full and partial tuition reimbursements available (averaging $10,000 per year), 16 teaching assistantships with full and partial tuition reimbursements available (averaging $10,000 per year); scholarships/grants and unspecified assistantships also available. Financial award application deadline: 2/1. *Faculty research:* Statistical genetics, reliability and pollution monitoring, Bayesian methods. Total annual research expenditures: $324,000. *Unit head:* Dr. Del T. Scott, Chair, 801-422-7054, Fax: 801-422-0635, E-mail: scottd@byu.edu. *Application contact:* Dr. Christopher Shane Reese, Graduate Coordinator, 801-422-9250, Fax: 801-422-0635, E-mail: reese@stat.byu.edu. Web site: http://statistics.byu.edu/.

California State University, East Bay, Office of Academic Programs and Graduate Studies, College of Science, Department of Statistics and Biostatistics, Statistics Program, Hayward, CA 94542-3000. Offers actuarial science (MS); applied statistics (MS); computational statistics (MS); mathematical statistics (MS). Part-time and evening/weekend programs available. *Faculty:* 4 full-time (1 woman), 1 part-time/adjunct. *Students:* 19 full-time (6 women), 74 part-time (31 women); includes 32 minority (1 Black or African American, non-Hispanic/Latino; 24 Asian, non-Hispanic/Latino; 6 Hispanic/Latino; 1 Two or more races, non-Hispanic/Latino), 30 international. Average age 30. 82 applicants, 72% accepted, 30 enrolled. In 2011, 49 master's awarded. *Degree requirements:* For master's, comprehensive exam. *Entrance requirements:* For master's, letters of recommendation, minimum GPA of 3.0, math through lower-division calculus. Additional exam requirements/recommendations for international students: Required—TOEFL (minimum score 550 paper-based; 213 computer-based). *Application deadline:* For fall admission, 6/30 for domestic and international students. Application fee: $55. Electronic applications accepted. *Expenses:* Tuition, state resident: full-time $6738; part-time $1302 per quarter. Tuition, nonresident: full-time $12,690; part-time $2294 per quarter. *Required fees:* $449 per quarter. Tuition and fees vary according to degree level, program and reciprocity agreements. *Financial support:* Fellowships, career-related internships or fieldwork, Federal Work-Study, institutionally sponsored loans, scholarships/grants, and unspecified assistantships available. Support available to part-time students. Financial award application deadline: 3/2; financial award applicants required to submit FAFSA. *Unit head:* Dr. Eric Suess, Chair, 510-885-3435, Fax: 510-885-4714, E-mail: eric.suess@csueastbay.edu. *Application contact:* Prof. Mitchell Watnik, Statistics Graduate Coordinator, 510-885-4130, Fax: 510-885-4714, E-mail: mitchell.watnik@csueastbay.edu. Web site: http://www.sci.csueastbay.edu/statistics/.

California State University, Long Beach, Graduate Studies, College of Natural Sciences and Mathematics, Department of Mathematics and Statistics, Long Beach, CA 90840. Offers mathematics (MS), including applied mathematics, applied statistics, mathematics education for secondary school teachers. Part-time programs available. *Faculty:* 21 full-time (5 women), 1 (woman) part-time/adjunct. *Students:* 67 full-time (31 women), 115 part-time (47 women); includes 95 minority (5 Black or African American, non-Hispanic/Latino; 1 American Indian or Alaska Native, non-Hispanic/Latino; 53 Asian, non-Hispanic/Latino; 29 Hispanic/Latino; 2 Native Hawaiian or other Pacific Islander, non-Hispanic/Latino; 5 Two or more races, non-Hispanic/Latino), 14 international. Average age 31. 162 applicants, 69% accepted, 58 enrolled. In 2011, 41 master's awarded. *Degree requirements:* For master's, comprehensive exam or thesis. *Application deadline:* For fall admission, 7/1 for domestic students; for spring admission, 12/1 for domestic students. Applications are processed on a rolling basis. Application fee: $55. Electronic applications accepted. *Financial support:* Teaching assistantships, Federal Work-Study, institutionally sponsored loans, scholarships/grants, and traineeships available. Financial award application deadline: 3/2. *Faculty research:* Algebra, functional analysis, partial differential equations, operator theory, numerical analysis. *Unit head:* Dr. Robert Mena, Chair, 562-985-4721, Fax: 562-985-8227, E-mail: rmena@csulb.edu. *Application contact:* Dr. Ngo Viet, Graduate Associate Chair, 562-985-4721, Fax: 562-985-8227, E-mail: viet@csulb.edu.

Cornell University, Graduate School, Graduate Fields of Engineering, Field of Statistics, Ithaca, NY 14853-0001. Offers applied statistics (MPS); biometry (MS, PhD); decision theory (MS, PhD); economic and social statistics (MS, PhD); engineering statistics (MS, PhD); experimental design (MS, PhD); mathematical statistics (MS, PhD); probability (MS, PhD); sampling (MS, PhD); statistical computing (MS, PhD); stochastic processes (MS, PhD). *Faculty:* 24 full-time (3 women). *Students:* 67 full-time (37 women); includes 7 minority (1 Black or African American, non-Hispanic/Latino; 5 Asian, non-Hispanic/Latino; 1 Hispanic/Latino), 46 international. Average age 25. 594 applicants, 16% accepted, 42 enrolled. In 2011, 44 master's, 4 doctorates awarded. Terminal master's awarded for partial completion of doctoral program. *Degree requirements:* For master's, project (MPS), thesis (MS); for doctorate, one foreign language, thesis/dissertation. *Entrance requirements:* For master's, GRE General Test (MS), 2 letters of recommendation (MS, MPS); for doctorate, GRE General Test, 2 letters of recommendation. Additional exam requirements/recommendations for international students: Required—TOEFL (minimum score 550 paper-based; 213 computer-based; 77 iBT). *Application deadline:* For fall admission, 1/15 for domestic students. Applications are processed on a rolling basis. Application fee: $95. Electronic applications accepted. *Financial support:* In 2011–12, 26 students received support, including 3 fellowships with full tuition reimbursements available, 8 research assistantships with full tuition reimbursements available, 14 teaching assistantships with full tuition reimbursements available; institutionally sponsored loans, scholarships/grants, tuition waivers (full and partial), and unspecified assistantships also available. Financial award applicants required to submit FAFSA. *Faculty research:* Bayesian analysis, survival analysis, nonparametric statistics, stochastic processes, mathematical statistics. *Unit head:* Director of Graduate Studies, 607-255-8066. *Application contact:* Graduate Field Assistant, 607-255-8066, E-mail: csc@cornell.edu. Web site: http://www.gradschool.cornell.edu/fields.php?id-94&a-2.

DePaul University, College of Science and Health, Department of Mathematical Sciences, Chicago, IL 60614. Offers applied mathematics (MS), including actuarial science or statistics; applied statistics (MS, Certificate); mathematics education (MA). Part-time and evening/weekend programs available. *Faculty:* 23 full-time (6 women), 18 part-time/adjunct (5 women). *Students:* 122 full-time (57 women), 63 part-time (23 women); includes 52 minority (19 Black or African American, non-Hispanic/Latino; 18 Asian, non-Hispanic/Latino; 10 Hispanic/Latino; 1 Native Hawaiian or other Pacific Islander, non-Hispanic/Latino; 4 Two or more races, non-Hispanic/Latino), 15 international. Average age 30. 40 applicants, 100% accepted. In 2011, 30 master's awarded. *Degree requirements:*

Peterson's Graduate Programs in the Physical Sciences, Mathematics, Agricultural Sciences, the Environment & Natural Resources 2013

For master's, comprehensive exam. *Entrance requirements:* Additional exam requirements/recommendations for international students: Required—TOEFL. *Application deadline:* For fall admission, 7/30 for domestic students, 6/30 for international students; for winter admission, 11/30 for domestic students, 10/31 for international students; for spring admission, 2/15 for domestic students. Applications are processed on a rolling basis. Application fee: $25. *Financial support:* In 2011–12, 12 students received support, including research assistantships with partial tuition reimbursements available (averaging $6,000 per year); teaching assistantships and tuition waivers (full) also available. Financial award application deadline: 4/30. *Faculty research:* Verbally prime algebras, enveloping algebras of Lie, superalgebras and related rings, harmonic analysis, estimation theory. *Unit head:* Dr. Ahmed I. Zayed, Chairperson, 773-325-7806, Fax: 773-325-7807, E-mail: azayed@depaul.edu. *Application contact:* Ann Spittle, Director of Graduate Admissions, 312-362-8300, Fax: 312-362-5749, E-mail: admitdpu@depaul.edu. Web site: http://depaul.edu/~math.

Eastern Michigan University, Graduate School, College of Arts and Sciences, Department of Mathematics, Ypsilanti, MI 48197. Offers applied statistics (MA); computer science (MA); mathematics (MA); mathematics education (MA). Part-time and evening/weekend programs available. Postbaccalaureate distance learning degree programs offered (minimal on-campus study). *Faculty:* 25 full-time (11 women). *Students:* 16 full-time (9 women), 36 part-time (14 women); includes 9 minority (4 Black or African American, non-Hispanic/Latino; 5 Asian, non-Hispanic/Latino), 6 international. Average age 30. 39 applicants, 82% accepted, 18 enrolled. In 2011, 17 degrees awarded. *Degree requirements:* For master's, thesis optional. *Entrance requirements:* Additional exam requirements/recommendations for international students: Required—TOEFL. *Application deadline:* Applications are processed on a rolling basis. Application fee: $35. *Expenses:* Tuition, state resident: full-time $10,367; part-time $432 per credit hour. Tuition, nonresident: full-time $20,435; part-time $851 per credit hour. *Required fees:* $39 per credit hour. $46 per semester. One-time fee: $100. Tuition and fees vary according to course level, degree level and reciprocity agreements. *Financial support:* Fellowships, research assistantships with full tuition reimbursements, teaching assistantships with full tuition reimbursements, career-related internships or fieldwork, Federal Work-Study, institutionally sponsored loans, scholarships/grants, tuition waivers (partial), and unspecified assistantships available. Support available to part-time students. Financial award applicants required to submit FAFSA. *Unit head:* Dr. Christopher Gardiner, Department Head, 734-487-1444, Fax: 734-487-2489, E-mail: cgardiner@emich.edu. *Application contact:* Dr. Bingwu Wang, Graduate Coordinator, 734-487-5044, Fax: 734-487-2489, E-mail: bwang@emich.edu. Web site: http://www.math.emich.edu.

Florida State University, The Graduate School, College of Arts and Sciences, Department of Statistics, Tallahassee, FL 32306-4330. Offers applied statistics (MS); biostatistics (MS, PhD); mathematical statistics (MS, PhD). Part-time programs available. *Faculty:* 15 full-time (2 women). *Students:* 55 full-time (21 women), 16 part-time (4 women); includes 21 minority (8 Black or African American, non-Hispanic/Latino; 5 Asian, non-Hispanic/Latino; 8 Hispanic/Latino), 24 international. Average age 30. 193 applicants, 15% accepted, 16 enrolled. In 2011, 14 master's, 12 doctorates awarded. Terminal master's awarded for partial completion of doctoral program. *Degree requirements:* For doctorate, thesis/dissertation, departmental qualifying exam. *Entrance requirements:* For master's, GRE General Test, previous course work in calculus, minimum GPA of 3.0; for doctorate, GRE General Test, minimum GPA of 3.0, 1 course in linear algebra (preferred), calculus I-III, real analysis. Additional exam requirements/recommendations for international students: Required—TOEFL (minimum score 100 iBT). *Application deadline:* For fall admission, 7/1 for domestic and international students; for spring admission, 11/1 for domestic and international students. Applications are processed on a rolling basis. Application fee: $30. Electronic applications accepted. *Expenses:* Tuition, state resident: full-time $9474; part-time $350.88 per credit hour. Tuition, nonresident: full-time $16,236; part-time $601.34 per credit hour. *Required fees:* $630 per semester. One-time fee: $20. Tuition and fees vary according to course load and campus/location. *Financial support:* In 2011–12, 1 fellowship with full tuition reimbursement (averaging $5,000 per year), 6 research assistantships with full tuition reimbursements (averaging $15,847 per year), 45 teaching assistantships with full tuition reimbursements (averaging $15,362 per year) were awarded; Federal Work-Study, institutionally sponsored loans, scholarships/grants, health care benefits, and unspecified assistantships also available. Financial award application deadline: 2/15; financial award applicants required to submit FAFSA. *Faculty research:* Statistical inference, probability theory, biostatistics, nonparametric estimation, automatic target recognition. *Total annual research expenditures:* $791,621. *Unit head:* Dr. Xufeng Niu, Chairman, 850-644-4008, Fax: 850-644-5271, E-mail: niu@stat.fsu.edu. *Application contact:* Chauncey Richburg, Academic Support Assistant, 850-644-3514, Fax: 850-644-5271, E-mail: richburg@stat.fsu.edu. Web site: http://stat.fsu.edu/.

Indiana University Bloomington, University Graduate School, College of Arts and Sciences, Department of Statistics, Bloomington, IN 47405-7000. Offers applied statistics (MS); statistical science (MS, PhD). *Students:* 9 full-time (4 women), 1 (woman) part-time; includes 1 minority (Asian, non-Hispanic/Latino), 8 international. 39 applicants, 49% accepted, 10 enrolled. Application fee: $55 ($65 for international students). *Unit head:* Dr. Bennett Bertenthal, Dean, 812-855-2392, E-mail: bbertent@indiana.edu. *Application contact:* Katie Bowman, Department Secretary, 812-855-7828, E-mail: katibowm@indiana.edu. Web site: http://stat.indiana.edu/.

Indiana University–Purdue University Fort Wayne, College of Arts and Sciences, Department of Mathematical Sciences, Fort Wayne, IN 46805-1499. Offers applied mathematics (MS); applied statistics (Certificate); mathematics (MS); operations research (MS); teaching (MAT). Part-time and evening/weekend programs available. *Faculty:* 20 full-time (5 women). *Students:* 1 full-time (0 women), 16 part-time (3 women). Average age 32. 6 applicants, 100% accepted, 3 enrolled. In 2011, 8 master's, 2 other advanced degrees awarded. *Entrance requirements:* For master's, minimum GPA of 3.0, major or minor in mathematics, three letters of recommendation. Additional exam requirements/recommendations for international students: Required—TOEFL (minimum score 550 paper-based; 213 computer-based; 77 iBT); Recommended—TWE. *Application deadline:* For fall admission, 8/1 priority date for domestic students, 7/1 for international students; for spring admission, 12/1 for domestic students, 10/1 for international students. Applications are processed on a rolling basis. Application fee: $55 ($60 for international students). Electronic applications accepted. *Financial support:* In 2011–12, 6 teaching assistantships with partial tuition reimbursements (averaging $12,930 per year) were awarded; scholarships/grants and unspecified assistantships also available. Support available to part-time students. Financial award application deadline: 3/1; financial award applicants required to submit FAFSA. *Faculty research:* Brick factory problem, CR singularities, carleman orthogonal polynomials. *Unit head:* Dr. David A. Legg, Chair, 260-481-6222, Fax: 260-481-0155, E-mail: legg@ipfw.edu. *Application contact:* Dr. W. Douglas Weakley, Director of Graduate Studies, 260-481-6233, Fax: 260-481-0155, E-mail: weakley@ipfw.edu. Web site: http://www.ipfw.edu/math/.

Indiana University–Purdue University Indianapolis, School of Science, Department of Mathematical Sciences, Master's Program in Mathematics, Indianapolis, IN 46202-3216. Offers applied mathematics (MS); applied statistics (MS); mathematics (MS); mathematics education (MS). *Students:* 13 full-time (3 women), 30 part-time (12 women); includes 14 minority (1 Black or African American, non-Hispanic/Latino; 9 Asian, non-Hispanic/Latino; 3 Hispanic/Latino; 1 Two or more races, non-Hispanic/Latino), 14 international. Average age 36. 49 applicants, 73% accepted, 15 enrolled. In 2011, 17 master's awarded. *Degree requirements:* For master's, comprehensive exam (for some programs), thesis optional. *Entrance requirements:* Additional exam requirements/recommendations for international students: Required—TOEFL. Application fee: $55 ($65 for international students). *Unit head:* Dr. Evgeny Mukhin, Director of Graduate Programs, 317-274-6918, E-mail: grad-program@math.iupui.edu. *Application contact:* Dr. Sherry Queener, Director, Graduate Studies and Associate Dean, 317-274-1577, Fax: 317-278-2380. Web site: http://www.math.iupui.edu/.

Instituto Tecnológico y de Estudios Superiores de Monterrey, Campus Monterrey, Graduate and Research Division, Programs in Engineering, Monterrey, Mexico. Offers applied statistics (M Eng); artificial intelligence (PhD); automation engineering (M Eng); chemical engineering (M Eng); civil engineering (M Eng); electrical engineering (M Eng); electronic engineering (M Eng); environmental engineering (M Eng); industrial engineering (M Eng, PhD); manufacturing engineering (M Eng); mechanical engineering (M Eng); systems and quality engineering (M Eng). M Eng program offered jointly with University of Waterloo; PhD in industrial engineering with Texas A&M University. Part-time and evening/weekend programs available. Terminal master's awarded for partial completion of doctoral program. *Degree requirements:* For master's, one foreign language, thesis; for doctorate, one foreign language, thesis/dissertation. *Entrance requirements:* For master's, EXADEP; for doctorate, GRE, master's degree in related field. Additional exam requirements/recommendations for international students: Required—TOEFL. *Faculty research:* Flexible manufacturing cells, materials, statistical methods, environmental prevention, control and evaluation.

Kennesaw State University, College of Science and Mathematics, Program in Applied Statistics, Kennesaw, GA 30144-5591. Offers MSAS. Part-time and evening/weekend programs available. *Students:* 26 full-time (12 women), 57 part-time (19 women); includes 31 minority (21 Black or African American, non-Hispanic/Latino; 1 American Indian or Alaska Native, non-Hispanic/Latino; 4 Asian, non-Hispanic/Latino; 3 Hispanic/Latino; 2 Two or more races, non-Hispanic/Latino), 4 international. Average age 34. 32 applicants, 69% accepted, 14 enrolled. In 2011, 31 master's awarded. *Entrance requirements:* For master's, GRE, minimum GPA of 2.75, resume. Additional exam requirements/recommendations for international students: Required—TOEFL (minimum score 550 paper-based; 213 computer-based; 80 iBT), IELTS (minimum score 6). *Application deadline:* For fall admission, 6/1 for domestic and international students; for spring admission, 11/1 for domestic and international students. Applications are processed on a rolling basis. Application fee: $60. Electronic applications accepted. *Expenses:* Tuition, state resident: full-time $3000; part-time $250 per semester hour. Tuition, nonresident: full-time $10,836; part-time $903 per semester hour. *Required fees:* $774 per semester. *Financial support:* In 2011–12, 2 research assistantships (averaging $4,000 per year) were awarded; unspecified assistantships also available. Financial award application deadline: 4/1; financial award applicants required to submit FAFSA. *Unit head:* Dr. Lewis Van Brackle, Director, 678-797-2409, E-mail: lvanbrac@kennesaw.edu. *Application contact:* Tamara Hutto, Admissions Counselor, 770-420-4377, Fax: 770-423-6885, E-mail: vmarquez@kennesaw.edu. Web site: http://www.kennesaw.edu.

Louisiana State University and Agricultural and Mechanical College, Graduate School, College of Agriculture, Department of Experimental Statistics, Baton Rouge, LA 70803. Offers applied statistics (M App St). Part-time programs

Peterson's Graduate Programs in the Physical Sciences, Mathematics, Agricultural Sciences, the Environment & Natural Resources 2013

facebook.com/petersonspublishing **299**

available. *Faculty:* 8 full-time (0 women). *Students:* 13 full-time (11 women), 3 part-time (1 woman); includes 1 minority (Asian, non-Hispanic/Latino), 11 international. Average age 27. 12 applicants, 42% accepted, 1 enrolled. In 2011, 8 master's awarded. *Degree requirements:* For master's, project. *Entrance requirements:* For master's, GRE General Test, minimum GPA of 3.0. Additional exam requirements/recommendations for international students: Required—TOEFL (minimum score 550 paper-based; 213 computer-based; 79 iBT) or IELTS (minimum score 6.5). *Application deadline:* For fall admission, 1/25 priority date for domestic students, 5/15 for international students; for spring admission, 10/15 priority date for domestic students, 10/15 for international students. Applications are processed on a rolling basis. Application fee: $50 ($70 for international students). Electronic applications accepted. *Financial support:* In 2011–12, 12 students received support, including 2 research assistantships with partial tuition reimbursements available (averaging $15,060 per year), 9 teaching assistantships with partial tuition reimbursements available (averaging $9,422 per year); fellowships, career-related internships or fieldwork, Federal Work-Study, institutionally sponsored loans, tuition waivers (full and partial), and unspecified assistantships also available. Financial award application deadline: 4/1; financial award applicants required to submit FAFSA. *Faculty research:* Linear models, statistical computing, ecological statistics. *Unit head:* Dr. James Geaghan, Head, 225-578-8303, Fax: 225-578-8344, E-mail: jgeaghan@lsu.edu. *Application contact:* Dr. Brian Marx, Graduate Adviser, 225-578-8366, E-mail: bmarx@lsu.edu. Web site: http://www.stat.lsu.edu/.

Loyola University Chicago, Graduate School, Department of Mathematical Sciences and Statistics, Chicago, IL 60660. Offers applied statistics (MS); mathematics and statistics (MS), including pure mathematics. Part-time programs available. *Faculty:* 19 full-time (4 women). *Students:* 38 full-time (25 women), 8 part-time (5 women); includes 14 minority (4 Black or African American, non-Hispanic/Latino; 7 Asian, non-Hispanic/Latino; 2 Hispanic/Latino; 1 Two or more races, non-Hispanic/Latino), 6 international. Average age 28. 75 applicants, 61% accepted, 26 enrolled. In 2011, 18 master's awarded. *Entrance requirements:* For master's, GRE General Test. Additional exam requirements/recommendations for international students: Required—TOEFL. *Application deadline:* For fall admission, 8/1 for domestic students; for spring admission, 12/1 for domestic students. Applications are processed on a rolling basis. Application fee: $0. Electronic applications accepted. *Expenses: Tuition:* Full-time $15,660; part-time $870 per credit hour. *Required fees:* $125 per semester. Tuition and fees vary according to course load and program. *Financial support:* In 2011–12, 13 students received support, including 6 teaching assistantships with tuition reimbursements available (averaging $10,000 per year); career-related internships or fieldwork, Federal Work-Study, institutionally sponsored loans, and tuition waivers (partial) also available. Financial award application deadline: 3/15. *Faculty research:* Probability and statistics, differential equations, algebra, combinations. *Total annual research expenditures:* $10,000. *Unit head:* Dr. Robert Jensen, Chair, 773-508-3578, Fax: 773-508-2123, E-mail: rjensen@luc.edu. *Application contact:* Dr. W. Cary Huffman, Graduate Program Director, 773-508-3563, Fax: 773-508-2123, E-mail: whuffma@luc.edu. Web site: http://math.luc.edu/.

McMaster University, School of Graduate Studies, Faculty of Science, Department of Mathematics and Statistics, Program in Statistics, Hamilton, ON L8S 4M2, Canada. Offers applied statistics (M Sc); medical statistics (M Sc); statistical theory (M Sc). *Degree requirements:* For master's, thesis or alternative. *Entrance requirements:* For master's, honors degree background in mathematics and statistics. Additional exam requirements/recommendations for international students: Required—TOEFL (minimum score 550 paper-based; 213 computer-based). *Faculty research:* Development of polymer production technology, quality of life in patients who use pharmaceutical agents, mathematical modeling, order statistics from progressively censored samples, nonlinear stochastic model in genetics.

Michigan State University, The Graduate School, College of Natural Science, Department of Statistics and Probability, East Lansing, MI 48824. Offers applied statistics (MS); statistics (MS, PhD). *Entrance requirements:* Additional exam requirements/recommendations for international students: Required—TOEFL. Electronic applications accepted.

New Jersey Institute of Technology, Office of Graduate Studies, College of Science and Liberal Arts, Department of Mathematical Science, Program in Applied Statistics, Newark, NJ 07102. Offers MS. Part-time and evening/weekend programs available. *Students:* 18 full-time (12 women), 17 part-time (4 women); includes 11 minority (4 Black or African American, non-Hispanic/Latino; 5 Asian, non-Hispanic/Latino; 2 Hispanic/Latino), 17 international. Average age 32. 95 applicants, 60% accepted, 14 enrolled. In 2011, 11 master's awarded. *Entrance requirements:* For master's, GRE General Test. Additional exam requirements/recommendations for international students: Required—TOEFL (minimum score 550 paper-based; 213 computer-based; 79 iBT). *Application deadline:* For fall admission, 6/1 priority date for domestic students, 5/1 for international students; for spring admission, 11/15 priority date for domestic students, 11/15 for international students. Applications are processed on a rolling basis. Application fee: $65. Electronic applications accepted. *Expenses:* Tuition, state resident: full-time $7980; part-time $867 per credit. Tuition, nonresident: full-time $11,336; part-time $1196 per credit. *Required fees:* $230 per credit. *Financial support:* Fellowships with full and partial tuition reimbursements, research assistantships with full and partial tuition reimbursements, teaching assistantships with full and partial tuition reimbursements, career-related internships or fieldwork, Federal Work-Study, institutionally sponsored loans, and unspecified assistantships available. Financial award application deadline: 1/15. *Unit head:* Dr. Manish Bhattacharjee, Director, 973-596-2949, Fax: 973-596-5591, E-mail: manish.bhattacharjee@njit.edu. *Application contact:* Kathryn Kelly, Director of Admissions, 973-596-3300, Fax: 973-596-3461, E-mail: admissions@njit.edu. Web site: http://math.njit.edu/academics/graduate/ms-appliedstatistics/index.php.

New Mexico State University, Graduate School, College of Business, Department of Economics, Applied Statistics and International Business, Las Cruces, NM 88003. Offers applied statistics (MS); economic development (DED); economics (MA). Part-time programs available. *Faculty:* 16 full-time (3 women), 1 (woman) part-time/adjunct. *Students:* 53 full-time (20 women), 21 part-time (7 women); includes 19 minority (3 Black or African American, non-Hispanic/Latino; 1 Asian, non-Hispanic/Latino; 15 Hispanic/Latino), 37 international. Average age 32. 38 applicants, 58% accepted, 9 enrolled. In 2011, 22 master's, 4 doctorates awarded. Terminal master's awarded for partial completion of doctoral program. *Degree requirements:* For master's, comprehensive exam, thesis or alternative; for doctorate, comprehensive exam, thesis/dissertation, internship, written project. *Entrance requirements:* For master's, minimum GPA of 3.0; for doctorate, appropriate master's degree, minimum GPA of 3.0. Additional exam requirements/recommendations for international students: Required—TOEFL (minimum score 550 paper-based; 0 computer-based; 79 iBT), IELTS (minimum score 6.5). *Application deadline:* For fall admission, 3/1 priority date for domestic students, 3/1 for international students. Applications are processed on a rolling basis. Application fee: $40 ($50 for international students). Electronic applications accepted. *Expenses:* Tuition, state resident: full-time $5004; part-time $208.50 per credit. Tuition, nonresident: full-time $17,446; part-time $726.90 per credit. *Financial support:* In 2011–12, 29 students received support, including 1 fellowship (averaging $5,019 per year), 8 research assistantships (averaging $24,247 per year), 25 teaching assistantships (averaging $17,955 per year); career-related internships or fieldwork, Federal Work-Study, and health care benefits also available. Support available to part-time students. Financial award application deadline: 3/1. *Faculty research:* Public utilities, environment, linear models, biological sampling, public policy, economic development, energy. *Unit head:* Dr. Richard V. Adkisson, Head, 575-646-4988, Fax: 575-646-1915, E-mail: radkisso@nmsu.edu. *Application contact:* Coordinator, 575-646-2736, Fax: 575-646-7721, E-mail: gradinfo@nmsu.edu. Web site: http://business.nmsu.edu/academics/economics-ib/.

North Dakota State University, College of Graduate and Interdisciplinary Studies, College of Science and Mathematics, Department of Statistics, Fargo, ND 58108. Offers applied statistics (MS, Certificate); statistics (PhD); MS/MS. *Faculty:* 5 full-time (1 woman). *Students:* 28 full-time (12 women), 4 part-time (3 women); includes 1 minority (Two or more races, non-Hispanic/Latino), 16 international. Average age 24. 46 applicants, 83% accepted, 15 enrolled. In 2011, 10 master's, 3 doctorates, 4 other advanced degrees awarded. *Degree requirements:* For master's, comprehensive exam, thesis; for doctorate, comprehensive exam, thesis/dissertation. *Entrance requirements:* For master's and doctorate, minimum GPA of 3.0. Additional exam requirements/recommendations for international students: Required—TOEFL (minimum score 550 paper-based; 213 computer-based; 79 iBT). *Application deadline:* For fall admission, 3/15 for international students. Applications are processed on a rolling basis. Application fee: $35. Electronic applications accepted. *Financial support:* In 2011–12, 2 fellowships with full tuition reimbursements, 7 research assistantships with full tuition reimbursements, 9 teaching assistantships with full tuition reimbursements were awarded; career-related internships or fieldwork, Federal Work-Study, institutionally sponsored loans, and tuition waivers (full) also available. Financial award application deadline: 4/15. *Faculty research:* Nonparametric statistics, survival analysis, multivariate analysis, distribution theory, inference modeling, biostatistics. *Unit head:* Dr. Rhonda Magel, Chair, 701-231-7532, Fax: 701-231-8734, E-mail: ndsu.stats@ndsu.edu. *Application contact:* Dawn Halle, Academic Assistant, 701-231-7532, Fax: 702-231-8734, E-mail: ndsu.stats@ndsu.edu. Web site: http://www.ndsu.edu/statistics/.

Northern Arizona University, Graduate College, College of Engineering, Forestry and Natural Sciences, Department of Mathematics and Statistics, Flagstaff, AZ 86011. Offers applied statistics (Certificate); mathematics (MAT, MS); statistics (MS). Part-time programs available. *Faculty:* 38 full-time (12 women). *Students:* 23 full-time (9 women), 18 part-time (12 women); includes 11 minority (2 Black or African American, non-Hispanic/Latino; 2 Asian, non-Hispanic/Latino; 7 Hispanic/Latino), 1 international. Average age 28. 25 applicants, 68% accepted, 9 enrolled. In 2011, 15 master's, 7 other advanced degrees awarded. *Degree requirements:* For master's, comprehensive exam (for some programs), thesis (for some programs). *Entrance requirements:* For master's, minimum GPA of 3.0. Additional exam requirements/recommendations for international students: Required—TOEFL (minimum score 550 paper-based; 213 computer-based; 80 iBT), IELTS (minimum score 7). *Application deadline:* For fall admission, 3/15 priority date for domestic students, 3/15 for international students; for spring admission, 10/15 priority date for domestic students, 10/15 for international students. Applications are processed on a rolling basis. Application fee: $65. Electronic applications accepted. *Expenses:* Tuition, state resident: full-time $7190; part-time $355 per credit hour. Tuition, nonresident: full-time $18,092; part-time $1005 per credit hour. *Required fees:* $818; $328 per semester. *Financial support:* In 2011–12, 22 teaching assistantships with partial tuition reimbursements (averaging $14,051 per year) were awarded; Federal Work-Study, scholarships/grants, health care benefits, tuition waivers (full and partial), and unspecified assistantships also available. Financial award applicants

300 facebook.com/petersonspublishing

Peterson's Graduate Programs in the Physical Sciences, Mathematics, Agricultural Sciences, the Environment & Natural Resources 2013

required to submit FAFSA. *Faculty research:* Topology, statistics, groups, ring theory, number theory. *Unit head:* Dr. Janet M. McShane, Chair, 928-523-1252, Fax: 928-523-5847, E-mail: janet.mcshane@nau.edu. *Application contact:* Sharon O'Connor, Chair, 928-523-3481, Fax: 928-523-5847, E-mail: math.grad@nau.edu. Web site: http://nau.edu/CEFNS/NatSci/Math/Degrees-Programs/.

Oakland University, Graduate Study and Lifelong Learning, College of Arts and Sciences, Department of Mathematics and Statistics, Program in Applied Statistics, Rochester, MI 48309-4401. Offers MS. Part-time and evening/weekend programs available. *Entrance requirements:* For master's, minimum GPA of 3.0 for unconditional admission. Additional exam requirements/recommendations for international students: Required—TOEFL (minimum score 550 paper-based; 213 computer-based). Electronic applications accepted. *Expenses:* Contact institution.

Rochester Institute of Technology, Graduate Enrollment Services, Kate Gleason College of Engineering, Center of Quality and Applied Statistics, Rochester, NY 14623-5603. Offers applied statistics (MS); statistical quality (AC). Part-time and evening/weekend programs available. Postbaccalaureate distance learning degree programs offered (no on-campus study). *Students:* 26 full-time (15 women), 41 part-time (9 women); includes 10 minority (1 Black or African American, non-Hispanic/Latino; 7 Asian, non-Hispanic/Latino; 2 Hispanic/Latino), 13 international. Average age 33. 60 applicants, 58% accepted, 20 enrolled. In 2011, 11 master's, 2 other advanced degrees awarded. *Degree requirements:* For master's, oral exam. *Entrance requirements:* For master's, course work in calculus, minimum GPA of 3.0. Additional exam requirements/recommendations for international students: Required—TOEFL (minimum score 570 paper-based; 230 computer-based; 88 iBT) or IELTS (minimum score 6.5). *Application deadline:* For fall admission, 2/15 priority date for domestic students, 2/15 for international students; for winter admission, 10/15 for domestic students; for spring admission, 2/1 for domestic students. Applications are processed on a rolling basis. Application fee: $50. *Expenses: Tuition:* Full-time $34,659; part-time $963 per credit hour. *Required fees:* $228; $76 per quarter. *Financial support:* Research assistantships with partial tuition reimbursements, career-related internships or fieldwork, institutionally sponsored loans, scholarships/grants, and unspecified assistantships available. Support available to part-time students. Financial award applicants required to submit FAFSA. *Faculty research:* Industrial statistics, quality control; experimental design; reliability; regression techniques; multivariate analysis; nonparametric methods. *Unit head:* Dr. Donald Baker, Director, 585-475-6990, Fax: 585-475-5959, E-mail: cqas@rit.edu. *Application contact:* Diane Ellison, Assistant Vice President, Graduate Enrollment Services, 585-475-2229, Fax: 585-475-7164, E-mail: gradinfo@rit.edu. Web site: http://www.rit.edu/kgcoe/cqas/index.htm.

Rutgers, The State University of New Jersey, New Brunswick, Graduate School-New Brunswick, Program in Statistics, Piscataway, NJ 08854-8097. Offers applied statistics (MS); biostatistics (MS); data mining (MS); quality and productivity management (MS); statistics (MS, PhD). Part-time programs available. Terminal master's awarded for partial completion of doctoral program. *Degree requirements:* For master's, comprehensive exam, essay, exam, non-thesis essay paper; for doctorate, one foreign language, thesis/dissertation, qualifying oral and written exams. *Entrance requirements:* For master's, GRE General Test; for doctorate, GRE General Test, GRE Subject Test (recommended). Additional exam requirements/recommendations for international students: Required—TOEFL (minimum score 550 paper-based; 213 computer-based). Electronic applications accepted. *Faculty research:* Probability, decision theory, linear models, multivariate statistics, statistical computing.

St. Cloud State University, School of Graduate Studies, College of Science and Engineering, Program in Applied Statistics, St. Cloud, MN 56301-4498. Offers MS.

Stevens Institute of Technology, Graduate School, Charles V. Schaefer Jr. School of Engineering, Department of Mathematical Sciences, Program in Applied Statistics, Hoboken, NJ 07030. Offers Certificate. *Entrance requirements:* Additional exam requirements/recommendations for international students: Required—TOEFL. Electronic applications accepted.

Syracuse University, College of Arts and Sciences, Program in Applied Statistics, Syracuse, NY 13244. Offers MS. Part-time programs available. *Students:* 13 full-time (6 women), 1 part-time (0 women), 13 international. Average age 24. 86 applicants, 45% accepted, 7 enrolled. In 2011, 8 master's awarded. *Entrance requirements:* For master's, GRE General Test. Additional exam requirements/recommendations for international students: Required— TOEFL (minimum score 100 iBT). *Application deadline:* For fall admission, 2/1 priority date for domestic students, 2/1 for international students. Application fee: $75. Electronic applications accepted. *Expenses: Tuition:* Part-time $1206 per credit. *Financial support:* Fellowships with full and partial tuition reimbursements, teaching assistantships with full and partial tuition reimbursements, and tuition waivers available. Financial award application deadline: 1/1; financial award applicants required to submit FAFSA. *Unit head:* Dr. Pinyuen Chen, Graduate Contact, 315-443-1577, E-mail: pinchen@syr.edu. *Application contact:* Diana Hahn, Associate Director, Graduate Recruitment and Retention, 315-443-4492; Fax: 315-443-3423, E-mail: grad@syr.edu. Web site: http://thecollege.syr.edu/students/undergraduate/interdisciplinary/applied-statistics/graduate_study.html.

The University of Alabama, Graduate School, Manderson Graduate School of Business, Department of Information Systems, Statistics, and Management Science, Program in Applied Statistics, Tuscaloosa, AL 35487. Offers MS, PhD. Part-time programs available. *Faculty:* 8 full-time (0 women). *Students:* 18 full-

time (5 women), 3 part-time (2 women); includes 1 minority (Black or African American, non-Hispanic/Latino), 11 international. Average age 29. 35 applicants, 46% accepted, 7 enrolled. In 2011, 5 master's, 2 doctorates awarded. Terminal master's awarded for partial completion of doctoral program. *Degree requirements:* For master's, comprehensive exam; for doctorate, comprehensive exam, thesis/dissertation. *Entrance requirements:* For master's and doctorate, GMAT or GRE, 3 semesters of calculus and linear algebra. Additional exam requirements/recommendations for international students: Required—TOEFL (minimum score 550 paper-based; 213 computer-based), IELTS (minimum score 6.5). *Application deadline:* For spring admission, 3/1 priority date for domestic students, 3/1 for international students. Applications are processed on a rolling basis. Application fee: $50 ($60 for international students). Electronic applications accepted. *Expenses: Tuition,* state resident: full-time $8600. Tuition, nonresident: full-time $21,900. *Financial support:* In 2011–12, 9 students received support, including 7 teaching assistantships with tuition reimbursements available (averaging $13,500 per year); scholarships/grants and health care benefits also available. Financial award application deadline: 3/1. *Faculty research:* Data mining, regression analysis, statistical quality control, nonparametric statistics, design of experiments. *Unit head:* Dr. Charles R. Sox, Professor and Department Head, 205-348-8992, E-mail: csox@cba.ua.edu. *Application contact:* Dana Merchant, Administrative Secretary, 205-348-8904, E-mail: dmerchan@cba.ua.edu. Web site: http://www.cba.ua.edu/stats.

University of Arkansas at Little Rock, Graduate School, College of Science and Mathematics, Department of Mathematics and Statistics, Little Rock, AR 72204-1099. Offers applied statistics (Graduate Certificate); mathematical sciences (MS). Part-time and evening/weekend programs available. *Degree requirements:* For master's, comprehensive exam. *Entrance requirements:* For master's, GRE General Test, GRE Subject Test, minimum GPA of 2.7, previous course work in advanced mathematics.

University of California, Riverside, Graduate Division, Department of Statistics, Riverside, CA 92521-0102. Offers applied statistics (PhD); statistics (MS). Terminal master's awarded for partial completion of doctoral program. *Degree requirements:* For master's, comprehensive exam; for doctorate, comprehensive exam, thesis/dissertation. *Entrance requirements:* For master's and doctorate, GRE General Test. Additional exam requirements/recommendations for international students: Required—TOEFL (minimum score 550 paper-based; 213 computer-based; 80 iBT). Electronic applications accepted. *Faculty research:* Design and analysis of gene expression experiments using DNA microarrays, statistical design and analysis of experiments, linear models, probability models and statistical inference, SNP/SFP discovery using DNA microarray, genetic mapping.

University of California, Santa Barbara, Graduate Division, College of Letters and Sciences, Division of Mathematics, Life, and Physical Sciences, Department of Statistics and Applied Probability, Santa Barbara, CA 93106-3110. Offers financial mathematics and statistics (PhD); quantitative methods in the social sciences (PhD); statistics (MA), including applied statistics, mathematical statistics; statistics and applied probability (PhD); MA/PhD. *Faculty:* 11 full-time (3 women). *Students:* 49 full-time (20 women); includes 9 minority (7 Asian, non-Hispanic/Latino; 1 Hispanic/Latino; 1 Two or more races, non-Hispanic/Latino), 31 international. Average age 29. 272 applicants, 19% accepted, 12 enrolled. In 2011, 14 master's, 5 doctorates awarded. Terminal master's awarded for partial completion of doctoral program. *Median time to degree:* Of those who began their doctoral program in fall 2003, 57% received their degree in 8 years or less. *Degree requirements:* For master's, comprehensive exam, thesis optional; for doctorate, comprehensive exam, thesis/dissertation. *Entrance requirements:* For master's and doctorate, GRE General Test. Additional exam requirements/recommendations for international students: Required—TOEFL (minimum score 550 paper-based; 80 iBT), IELTS (minimum score 7). *Application deadline:* For fall admission, 1/1 priority date for domestic students, 1/1 for international students; for winter admission, 11/1 priority date for domestic students, 11/1 for international students; for spring admission, 2/1 priority date for domestic students, 2/1 for international students. Application fee: $80 ($100 for international students). Electronic applications accepted. *Expenses:* Tuition, state resident: full-time $12,192. Tuition, nonresident: full-time $27,294. *Required fees:* $764.13. *Financial support:* In 2011–12, 23 students received support, including 6 fellowships with full tuition reimbursements available (averaging $11,285 per year), 1 research assistantship with full and partial tuition reimbursement available (averaging $2,790 per year), 28 teaching assistantships with partial tuition reimbursements available (averaging $14,557 per year); Federal Work-Study, scholarships/grants, and health care benefits also available. Financial award application deadline: 1/1; financial award applicants required to submit FAFSA. *Faculty research:* Bayesian inference, financial mathematics, stochastic processes, environmental statistics, biostatistical modeling. *Total annual research expenditures:* $139,480. *Unit head:* Dr. Yuedong Wang, Chair, 805-893-4870, E-mail: yeudong@pstat.ucsb.edu. *Application contact:* Dolly J. Cook, Graduate Program Assistant, 805-893-2129, Fax: 805-893-2334, E-mail: cook@pstat.ucsb.edu. Web site: http://www.pstat.ucsb.edu/.

University of Colorado Denver, College of Liberal Arts and Sciences, Department of Mathematical and Statistical Sciences, Denver, CO 80217. Offers applied mathematics (MS, PhD), including applied mathematics, applied probability (MS), applied statistics (MS), computational biology, computational mathematics (PhD), discrete mathematics, finite geometry (PhD), mathematics education (PhD), mathematics of engineering and science (MS), numerical

Peterson's Graduate Programs in the Physical Sciences, Mathematics, Agricultural Sciences, the Environment & Natural Resources 2013

facebook.com/petersonspublishing **301**

analysis, operations research (MS), optimization and operations research (PhD), probability (PhD), statistics (PhD). Part-time programs available. *Faculty:* 26 full-time (4 women), 2 part-time/adjunct (1 woman). *Students:* 44 full-time (14 women), 14 part-time (5 women); includes 6 minority (4 Asian, non-Hispanic/Latino; 2 Hispanic/Latino), 10 international. Average age 33. 66 applicants, 79% accepted, 17 enrolled. In 2011, 6 master's, 6 doctorates awarded. *Degree requirements:* For master's, comprehensive exam, thesis optional, 30 hours of course work with minimum GPA of 3.0; for doctorate, comprehensive exam, thesis/dissertation. *Entrance requirements:* For master's and doctorate, GRE General Test; GRE Subject Test in math (recommended), 30 hours of course work in mathematics (24 of which must be upper-division mathematics), minimum GPA of 3.0. Additional exam requirements/recommendations for international students: Required—TOEFL (minimum score 525 paper-based; 192 computer-based; 71 iBT). *Application deadline:* For fall admission, 4/1 for domestic students, 3/1 for international students; for spring admission, 11/1 for domestic students, 10/1 for international students. Application fee: $50 ($75 for international students). Electronic applications accepted. *Financial support:* Fellowships with partial tuition reimbursements, research assistantships with full tuition reimbursements, teaching assistantships with full tuition reimbursements, Federal Work-Study, scholarships/grants, and unspecified assistantships available. Financial award application deadline: 4/1; financial award applicants required to submit FAFSA. *Faculty research:* Computational mathematics, computational biology, discrete mathematics and geometry, probability and statistics, optimization. *Unit head:* Dr. Stephen Billups, Graduate Chair, 303-556-4814, E-mail: stephen.billups@ucdenver.edu. *Application contact:* Lisa Herbert, Graduate Program Assistant, 303-556-2341, E-mail: lisa.herbert@ucdenver.edu. Web site: http://www.ucdenver.edu/academics/colleges/CLAS/Departments/math/Pages/MathStats.aspx.

University of Guelph, Graduate Studies, College of Physical and Engineering Science, Department of Mathematics and Statistics, Guelph, ON N1G 2W1, Canada. Offers applied mathematics (PhD); applied statistics (PhD); mathematics and statistics (M Sc). Part-time programs available. *Degree requirements:* For master's, thesis (for some programs); for doctorate, thesis/dissertation. *Entrance requirements:* For master's, minimum Baverage during previous 2 years of course work; for doctorate, minimum B average. Additional exam requirements/recommendations for international students: Required—TOEFL (minimum score 550 paper-based; 213 computer-based; 89 iBT), IELTS (minimum score 6.5). *Faculty research:* Dynamical systems, mathematical biology, numerical analysis, linear and nonlinear models, reliability and bioassay.

University of Illinois at Urbana–Champaign, Graduate College, College of Liberal Arts and Sciences, Department of Statistics, Champaign, IL 61820. Offers applied statistics (MS); statistics (PhD). *Faculty:* 10 full-time (4 women), 1 (woman) part-time/adjunct. *Students:* 68 full-time (35 women), 15 part-time (6 women); includes 9 minority (2 Black or African American, non-Hispanic/Latino; 6 Asian, non-Hispanic/Latino; 1 Hispanic/Latino), 56 international. 402 applicants, 33% accepted, 40 enrolled. In 2011, 46 master's, 8 doctorates awarded. *Entrance requirements:* For master's and doctorate, GRE, minimum GPA of 3.0. Additional exam requirements/recommendations for international students: Required—TOEFL (minimum score 590 paper-based; 243 computer-based). *Application deadline:* Applications are processed on a rolling basis. Application fee: $75 ($90 for international students). Electronic applications accepted. *Financial support:* In 2011–12, 2 fellowships, 22 research assistantships, 28 teaching assistantships were awarded; tuition waivers (full and partial) also available. *Faculty research:* Statistical decision theory, sequential analysis, computer-aided stochastic modeling. *Unit head:* Douglas G. Simpson, Chair, 217-244-0885, Fax: 217-244-7190, E-mail: dgs@illinois.edu. *Application contact:* Melissa Banks, Office Support Specialist, 217-333-2167, Fax: 217-244-7190, E-mail: mdbanks@illinois.edu. Web site: http://www.stat.illinois.edu/.

University of Memphis, Graduate School, College of Arts and Sciences, Department of Mathematical Sciences, Memphis, TN 38152. Offers applied mathematics (MS); applied statistics (PhD); bioinformatics (MS); computer science (PhD); computer sciences (MS); mathematics (MS, PhD); statistics (MS, PhD). Part-time programs available. Terminal master's awarded for partial completion of doctoral program. *Degree requirements:* For master's, comprehensive exam; for doctorate, one foreign language, thesis/dissertation, oral exams. *Entrance requirements:* For master's and doctorate, GRE General Test, minimum GPA of 2.5. Additional exam requirements/recommendations for international students: Required—TOEFL (minimum score 550 paper-based; 210 computer-based). Electronic applications accepted. *Faculty research:* Combinatorics, ergodic theory, graph theory, Ramsey theory, applied statistics.

University of Michigan, Horace H. Rackham School of Graduate Studies, College of Literature, Science, and the Arts, Department of Statistics, Ann Arbor, MI 48109. Offers applied statistics (AM); statistics (AM, PhD). *Faculty:* 19 full-time (4 women). *Students:* 130 full-time (60 women); includes 95 minority (92 Asian, non-Hispanic/Latino; 2 Hispanic/Latino; 1 Two or more races, non-Hispanic/Latino), 88 international. Average age 27. 622 applicants, 19% accepted, 54 enrolled. In 2011, 35 master's, 13 doctorates awarded. Terminal master's awarded for partial completion of doctoral program. *Degree requirements:* For master's, thesis; for doctorate, thesis/dissertation, oral defense of dissertation, preliminary exam. *Entrance requirements:* For master's and doctorate, GRE General Test. Additional exam requirements/recommendations for international students: Required—TOEFL (minimum score 560 paper-based; 220 computer-based; 84 iBT), IELTS (minimum score 6.5). *Application deadline:* For fall

admission, 1/15 priority date for domestic students, 1/15 for international students. Applications are processed on a rolling basis. Application fee: $65 ($75 for international students). Electronic applications accepted. *Financial support:* In 2011–12, 64 students received support, including 7 fellowships with full and partial tuition reimbursements available (averaging $25,000 per year), 12 research assistantships with full and partial tuition reimbursements available (averaging $17,270 per year), 45 teaching assistantships with full and partial tuition reimbursements available (averaging $17,270 per year); career-related internships or fieldwork, Federal Work-Study, institutionally sponsored loans, scholarships/grants, health care benefits, and unspecified assistantships also available. Financial award application deadline: 1/15. *Faculty research:* Reliability and degradation modeling, biological and legal applications, bioinformatics, statistical computing, covariance estimation. *Unit head:* Prof. Tailen Hsing, Chair, 734-763-3519, Fax: 734-763-4676, E-mail: statchair@umich.edu. *Application contact:* Judy McDonald, Graduate Program Coordinator, 734-763-3520, Fax: 734-763-4676, E-mail: stat-grad-coordinator@umich.edu. Web site: http://www.stat.lsa.umich.edu/.

University of Northern Colorado, Graduate School, College of Education and Behavioral Sciences, Program in Applied Statistics and Research Methods, Greeley, CO 80639. Offers MS, PhD. Part-time programs available. *Degree requirements:* For master's, comprehensive exam; for doctorate, comprehensive exam, thesis/dissertation. *Entrance requirements:* For master's, 3 letters of reference; for doctorate, GRE General Test, 3 letters of reference. Electronic applications accepted.

University of Notre Dame, Graduate School, College of Science, Department of Applied and Computational Mathematics and Statistics, Notre Dame, IN 46556. Offers applied and computational mathematics and statistics (PhD); applied statistics (MS); computational finance (MS).

University of Pittsburgh, Dietrich School of Arts and Sciences, Department of Statistics, Pittsburgh, PA 15260. Offers applied statistics (MA, MS); statistics (MA, MS, PhD). Part-time programs available. *Faculty:* 8 full-time (1 woman). *Students:* 35 full-time (20 women), 4 part-time (2 women); includes 1 minority (Black or African American, non-Hispanic/Latino), 26 international. Average age 26. 425 applicants, 11% accepted, 12 enrolled. In 2011, 5 master's, 6 doctorates awarded. Terminal master's awarded for partial completion of doctoral program. *Median time to degree:* Of those who began their doctoral program in fall 2003, 100% received their degree in 8 years or less. *Degree requirements:* For master's, comprehensive exam, thesis (for some programs); for doctorate, comprehensive exam, thesis/dissertation. *Entrance requirements:* For master's, 3 semesters of calculus, 1 semester of linear algebra, 1 year of mathematical statistics; for doctorate, 3 semesters of calculus, 1 semester each of linear algebra and advanced calculus, 1 year of mathematical statistics. Additional exam requirements/recommendations for international students: Required—TOEFL (minimum score 550 paper-based; 213 computer-based; 80 iBT). *Application deadline:* For fall admission, 1/15 priority date for domestic students, 1/15 for international students; for spring admission, 10/1 priority date for domestic students, 9/1 for international students. Application fee: $50. Electronic applications accepted. *Expenses:* Tuition, state resident: full-time $18,774; part-time $760 per credit. Tuition, nonresident: full-time $30,736; part-time $1258 per credit. *Required fees:* $740; $200 per term. Tuition and fees vary according to program. *Financial support:* In 2011–12, 1 fellowship with full tuition reimbursement (averaging $19,610 per year), 9 research assistantships with full tuition reimbursements (averaging $16,460 per year), 16 teaching assistantships with full tuition reimbursements (averaging $15,830 per year) were awarded; career-related internships or fieldwork, Federal Work-Study, institutionally sponsored loans, scholarships/grants, health care benefits, and unspecified assistantships also available. Financial award application deadline: 1/15. *Faculty research:* Multivariate statistics, time series, reliability, meta-analysis, linear and nonlinear regression modeling. *Unit head:* Dr. Satish Iyengar, Chair, 412-624-8341, Fax: 412-648-8814, E-mail: sii@pitt.edu. *Application contact:* Dr. Leon J. Gleser, Director of Graduate Studies, 412-624-3925, Fax: 412-648-8814, E-mail: gleser@pitt.edu. Web site: http://www.stat.pitt.edu/.

University of South Carolina, The Graduate School, College of Arts and Sciences, Department of Statistics, Columbia, SC 29208. Offers applied statistics (CAS); industrial statistics (MIS); statistics (MS, PhD). Part-time and evening/weekend programs available. Postbaccalaureate distance learning degree programs offered (minimal on-campus study). Terminal master's awarded for partial completion of doctoral program. *Degree requirements:* For master's, thesis; for doctorate, comprehensive exam, thesis/dissertation. *Entrance requirements:* For master's, GRE General Test or GMAT, 2 years of work experience (MIS); for doctorate, GRE General Test; for CAS, GRE General Test or GMAT. Additional exam requirements/recommendations for international students: Required—TOEFL (minimum score 600 paper-based; 250 computer-based; 100 iBT). Electronic applications accepted. *Expenses:* Contact institution. *Faculty research:* Reliability, environmentrics, statistics computing, psychometrics, bioinformatics.

The University of Texas at San Antonio, College of Business, Department of Management Science and Statistics, San Antonio, TX 78249-0617. Offers applied statistics (MS, PhD); management science (MBA). *Accreditation:* AACSB. Part-time and evening/weekend programs available. *Faculty:* 11 full-time (2 women), 4 part-time/adjunct (3 women). *Students:* 36 full-time (12 women), 23 part-time (8 women); includes 16 minority (3 Black or African American, non-Hispanic/Latino; 5 Asian, non-Hispanic/Latino; 8 Hispanic/Latino), 21 international. Average age 31. 47 applicants, 60% accepted, 21 enrolled. In 2011, 8 master's, 4 doctorates

302 facebook.com/petersonspublishing

Peterson's Graduate Programs in the Physical Sciences, Mathematics, Agricultural Sciences, the Environment & Natural Resources 2013

awarded. *Degree requirements:* For master's, comprehensive exam (for some programs), thesis or alternative; for doctorate, comprehensive exam, thesis/dissertation. *Entrance requirements:* For master's, GMAT, minimum of 36 semester credit hours of coursework beyond any hours acquired in the MBA-leveling courses; statement of purpose; for doctorate, GRE, minimum cumulative GPA of 3.3 in the last 60 hours of coursework; transcripts from all colleges and universities attended; curriculum vitae; statement of academic work experiences, interests, and goals; three letters of recommendation; BA, BS, or MS in mathematics, statistics, or closely-related field. Additional exam requirements/recommendations for international students: Required—TOEFL (minimum score 500 paper-based; 61 iBT), IELTS (minimum score 5). *Application deadline:* For fall admission, 7/1 for domestic students, 4/1 for international students; for spring admission, 11/1 for domestic students, 9/1 for international students. Applications are processed on a rolling basis. Application fee: $45 ($85 for international students). Electronic applications accepted. *Expenses:* Tuition, state resident: full-time $3148; part-time $2176 per semester. Tuition, nonresident: full-time $8782; part-time $5932 per semester. *Required fees:* $719 per semester. *Financial support:* In 2011–12, fellowships (averaging $22,000 per year), research assistantships (averaging $10,000 per year), teaching assistantships (averaging $10,000 per year) were awarded; scholarships/grants, health care benefits, and unspecified assistantships also available. *Faculty research:* Statistical signal processing, reliability and life-testing experiments, modeling decompression sickness using survival analysis. *Unit head:* Dr. Raydel Tullous, Chair, 210-458-6345, Fax: 210-458-6350, E-mail: raydel.tullous@utsa.edu. *Application contact:* Katherine Pope, Graduate Assistant of Record, 210-458-7316, Fax: 210-458-4398, E-mail: katherine.pope@utsa.edu.

University of the District of Columbia, College of Arts and Sciences, Department of Mathematics, Program in Applied Statistics, Washington, DC 20008-1175. Offers MS. *Degree requirements:* For master's, internship or thesis. *Expenses: Tuition, area resident:* Full-time $7580; part-time $421 per credit hour. Tuition, state resident: full-time $8580; part-time $477 per credit hour. Tuition, nonresident: full-time $14,580; part-time $810 per credit hour. *Required fees:* $620; $30 per credit hour. $310 per semester.

University of West Florida, College of Arts and Sciences: Sciences, Department of Mathematics and Statistics, Pensacola, FL 32514-5750. Offers applied statistics (MS); mathematical sciences (MS). Part-time and evening/weekend programs available. *Faculty:* 8 full-time (0 women). *Students:* 10 full-time (2 women), 75 part-time (37 women); includes 23 minority (12 Black or African American, non-Hispanic/Latino; 4 Asian, non-Hispanic/Latino; 5 Hispanic/Latino; 2 Two or more races, non-Hispanic/Latino), 5 international. Average age 34. 57 applicants, 77% accepted, 29 enrolled. In 2011, 13 master's awarded. *Degree requirements:* For master's, thesis optional. *Entrance requirements:* For master's, GRE (minimum score: verbal 420; quantitative 580), minimum GPA of 3.0; official transcripts. Additional exam requirements/recommendations for international students: Required—TOEFL (minimum score 550 paper-based; 213 computer-based). *Application deadline:* For fall admission, 6/1 for domestic and international students; for spring admission, 10/1 for domestic and international students. Applications are processed on a rolling basis. Application fee: $30. *Expenses:* Tuition, state resident: full-time $5729; part-time $302 per credit hour. Tuition, nonresident: full-time $20,059; part-time $961 per credit hour. *Required fees:* $1509; $63 per credit hour. *Financial support:* In 2011–12, 11 fellowships with partial tuition reimbursements (averaging $418 per year), 8 research assistantships with partial tuition reimbursements (averaging $3,280 per year), 15 teaching assistantships with partial tuition reimbursements (averaging $6,656 per year) were awarded; unspecified assistantships also available. Financial award application deadline: 4/15; financial award applicants required to submit FAFSA. *Unit head:* Dr. Kuiyuan Li, Chairperson, 850-474-2287, E-mail: mathstat@uwf.edu. *Application contact:* Terry McCray, Assistant Director of Graduate Admissions, 850-473-7718, Fax: 850-473-7714, E-mail: gradadmissions@uwf.edu. Web site: http://uwf.edu/mathstat/.

Villanova University, Graduate School of Liberal Arts and Sciences, Department of Mathematical Sciences, Program in Applied Statistics, Villanova, PA 19085-1699. Offers MS. Part-time and evening/weekend programs available. *Students:* 22 full-time (10 women), 8 part-time (1 woman); includes 2 minority (both Asian, non-Hispanic/Latino), 2 international. Average age 29. 27 applicants, 93% accepted, 11 enrolled. In 2011, 13 master's awarded. *Degree requirements:* For master's, comprehensive exam. *Entrance requirements:* For master's, GRE, minimum GPA of 3.0. Additional exam requirements/recommendations for international students: Required—TOEFL. *Application deadline:* For fall admission, 5/1 for international students; for spring admission, 10/15 for international students. Applications are processed on a rolling basis. Application fee: $50. Electronic applications accepted. *Expenses: Tuition:* Part-time $675 per credit. Part-time tuition and fees vary according to degree level and program. *Financial support:* Research assistantships, teaching assistantships, scholarships/grants, and unspecified assistantships available. Financial award applicants required to submit FAFSA. *Unit head:* Dr. Michael Levitan, Director, 610-519-4818. *Application contact:* Dr. Adele Lindenmeyr, Dean, Graduate School of Liberal Arts and Sciences, 610-519-7093, Fax: 610-519-7096. Web site: http://www.villanova.edu/artsci/mathematics/graduate/msapplied/.

Washington State University, Graduate School, College of Sciences, Department of Statistics, Pullman, WA 99164. Offers applied statistics (MS); theoretical statistics (MS). *Faculty:* 7. *Students:* 25 full-time (13 women), 2 part-time (0 women); includes 3 minority (1 Asian, non-Hispanic/Latino; 2 Hispanic/Latino), 20 international. Average age 28. 45 applicants, 36% accepted, 9 enrolled. In 2011, 15 master's awarded. *Degree requirements:* For master's, comprehensive exam (for some programs), thesis (for some programs), project. *Entrance requirements:* For master's, GRE, three letters of reference; official copies of all college transcripts. Additional exam requirements/recommendations for international students: Required—TOEFL (minimum score 560 paper-based; 220 computer-based), IELTS. *Application deadline:* For fall admission, 1/10 for domestic and international students; for spring admission, 7/1 for domestic and international students. Application fee: $75. *Financial support:* In 2011–12, 10 students received support, including 4 teaching assistantships with tuition reimbursements available (averaging $18,204 per year). *Faculty research:* Environmental statistics, logistic regression, statistical methods for ecology and wildlife, spatial data analysis, linear and non-linear models. *Total annual research expenditures:* $9,000. *Unit head:* Dr. Michael A. Jacroux, Professor/Chair, 509-335-8645, Fax: 509-335-8369, E-mail: jacroux@wsu.edu. *Application contact:* Graduate School Admissions, 800-GRADWSU, Fax: 509-335-1949, E-mail: gradsch@wsu.edu. Web site: http://www.stat.wsu.edu/.

West Chester University of Pennsylvania, College of Arts and Sciences, Department of Mathematics, West Chester, PA 19383. Offers applied statistics (MS, Certificate); mathematics (MA, Teaching Certificate). Part-time and evening/weekend programs available. *Faculty:* 7 part-time/adjunct (1 woman). *Students:* 24 full-time (8 women), 69 part-time (28 women); includes 19 minority (8 Black or African American, non-Hispanic/Latino; 10 Asian, non-Hispanic/Latino; 1 Hispanic/Latino), 5 international. Average age 31. 73 applicants, 68% accepted, 42 enrolled. In 2011, 13 degrees awarded. *Degree requirements:* For master's, thesis optional. *Entrance requirements:* For master's, GMAT, GRE General Test, or MAT (for MA), interview; for other advanced degree, GMAT, GRE General Test, or MAT (for Teaching Certificate). Additional exam requirements/recommendations for international students: Required—TOEFL (minimum score 550 paper-based; 213 computer-based; 80 iBT). *Application deadline:* For fall admission, 4/15 priority date for domestic students, 3/15 for international students; for spring admission, 10/15 priority date for domestic students, 9/1 for international students. Applications are processed on a rolling basis. Application fee: $45. Electronic applications accepted. *Expenses:* Tuition, state resident: full-time $7488; part-time $416 per credit. Tuition, nonresident: full-time $11,232; part-time $624 per credit. *Required fees:* $1784.64; $67.59 per credit. Tuition and fees vary according to program. *Financial support:* Unspecified assistantships available. Support available to part-time students. Financial award application deadline: 2/15; financial award applicants required to submit FAFSA. *Faculty research:* Teachers teaching with technology in service training program, biostatistics, hierarchical linear models, clustered bionary outcome date. *Unit head:* Dr. Kathleen Jackson, Chair, 610-436-2537, Fax: 610-738-0578, E-mail: kjackson@wcupa.edu. *Application contact:* Dr. Gail Gallitano, Graduate Coordinator, 610-436-2452, Fax: 610-738-0578, E-mail: ggallitano@wcupa.edu. Web site: http://www.wcupa.edu/_academics/sch_cas.mat/.

Worcester Polytechnic Institute, Graduate Studies and Research, Department of Mathematical Sciences, Worcester, MA 01609-2280. Offers applied mathematics (MS); applied statistics (MS); financial mathematics (MS); industrial mathematics (MS); mathematical sciences (PhD, Graduate Certificate); mathematics (MME). Part-time and evening/weekend programs available. *Faculty:* 16 full-time (1 woman), 6 part-time/adjunct (2 women). *Students:* 52 full-time (23 women), 32 part-time (18 women); includes 4 minority (1 Black or African American, non-Hispanic/Latino; 3 Hispanic/Latino), 52 international. 326 applicants, 52% accepted, 53 enrolled. In 2011, 25 master's, 1 doctorate awarded. *Degree requirements:* For master's, thesis (for some programs); for doctorate, comprehensive exam, thesis/dissertation. *Entrance requirements:* For master's and doctorate, GRE General Test, GRE Subject Test in math (recommended), 3 letters of recommendation. Additional exam requirements/recommendations for international students: Required—TOEFL (minimum score 563 paper-based; 223 computer-based; 84 iBT), IELTS (minimum score 7). *Application deadline:* For fall admission, 1/1 priority date for domestic students, 1/1 for international students; for spring admission, 10/1 priority date for domestic students, 10/1 for international students. Applications are processed on a rolling basis. Application fee: $70. Electronic applications accepted. *Financial support:* Research assistantships, teaching assistantships, career-related internships or fieldwork, institutionally sponsored loans, scholarships/grants, and unspecified assistantships available. Financial award application deadline: 1/1; financial award applicants required to submit FAFSA. *Faculty research:* Applied analysis and differential equations, computational mathematics, discrete mathematics, applied and computational statistics, industrial and financial mathematics, mathematical biology. *Unit head:* Dr. Bogdan Vernescu, Head, 508-831-5241, Fax: 508-831-5824, E-mail: vernescu@wpi.edu. *Application contact:* Dr. Joseph Petruccelli, Graduate Coordinator, 508-831-5241, Fax: 508-831-5824, E-mail: jdp@wpi.edu. Web site: http://www.wpi.edu/Academics/Depts/Math/.

Wright State University, School of Graduate Studies, College of Science and Mathematics, Department of Mathematics and Statistics, Program in Applied Statistics, Dayton, OH 45435. Offers MS. *Degree requirements:* For master's, comprehensive exam. *Entrance requirements:* For master's, 1 year of course work in calculus and matrix algebra, previous course work in computer programming and statistics. Additional exam requirements/recommendations for international students: Required—TOEFL. *Faculty research:* Reliability theory, stochastic process, nonparametric statistics, design of experiments, multivariate statistics.

Peterson's Graduate Programs in the Physical Sciences, Mathematics, Agricultural Sciences, the Environment & Natural Resources 2013

facebook.com/petersonspublishing **303**

Biomathematics

North Carolina State University, Graduate School, College of Physical and Mathematical Sciences, Program in Biomathematics, Raleigh, NC 27695. Offers M Biomath, MS, PhD. Part-time programs available. Terminal master's awarded for partial completion of doctoral program. *Degree requirements:* For master's, thesis (for some programs); for doctorate, thesis/dissertation. *Entrance requirements:* For master's and doctorate, GRE General Test. Additional exam requirements/recommendations for international students: Required—TOEFL. Electronic applications accepted. *Faculty research:* Theory and methods of biological modeling, theoretical biology (genetics, ecology, neurobiology), applied biology (wildlife).

University of California, Los Angeles, David Geffen School of Medicine and Graduate Division, Graduate Programs in Medicine, Department of Biomathematics, Program in Biomathematics, Los Angeles, CA 90095. Offers MS, PhD. *Faculty:* 5 full-time (0 women). *Students:* 10 full-time (1 woman); includes 6 minority (5 Asian, non-Hispanic/Latino; 1 Hispanic/Latino), 1 international. Average age 28. 32 applicants, 22% accepted, 3 enrolled. In 2011, 1 master's, 2 doctorates awarded. *Median time to degree:* Of those who began their doctoral program in fall 2003, 100% received their degree in 8 years or less. Application fee: $70 ($90 for international students). Electronic applications accepted. *Financial support:* In 2011–12, 9 fellowships, 9 research assistantships, 5 teaching assistantships were awarded. *Unit head:* Dr. Elliot Landaw, Chair, 310-825-6743, E-mail: elandaw@biomath.ucla.edu. *Application contact:* Departmental Office, 310-825-5554, E-mail: gradprog@biomath.ucla.edu. Web site: http://www.biomath.ucla.edu.

The University of Texas Health Science Center at Houston, Graduate School of Biomedical Sciences, Program in Biomathematics and Biostatistics, Houston, TX 77225-0036. Offers MS, PhD, MD/PhD. Terminal master's awarded for partial completion of doctoral program. *Degree requirements:* For master's, thesis; for doctorate, thesis/dissertation. *Entrance requirements:* For master's and doctorate, GRE General Test. Additional exam requirements/recommendations for international students: Required—TOEFL. Electronic applications accepted. *Faculty research:* Biostatistics, biomarkers, epidemiology, bioinformatics, computational biology.

Biometry

Cornell University, Graduate School, Graduate Fields of Agriculture and Life Sciences, Field of Biometry, Ithaca, NY 14853-0001. Offers MS, PhD. *Faculty:* 11 full-time (0 women). *Students:* 1 full-time (0 women). 15 applicants, 0% accepted, 0 enrolled. In 2011, 1 master's, 1 doctorate awarded. Terminal master's awarded for partial completion of doctoral program. *Degree requirements:* For master's, thesis; for doctorate, comprehensive exam, thesis/dissertation. *Entrance requirements:* For master's and doctorate, GRE General Test, 2 letters of recommendation. Additional exam requirements/recommendations for international students: Required—TOEFL (minimum score 550 paper-based; 213 computer-based; 77 iBT). *Application deadline:* For fall admission, 1/15 for domestic students. Application fee: $95. Electronic applications accepted. *Financial support:* Fellowships with full tuition reimbursements, research assistantships with full tuition reimbursements, teaching assistantships with full tuition reimbursements, institutionally sponsored loans, scholarships/grants, health care benefits, tuition waivers (full and partial), and unspecified assistantships available. Financial award applicants required to submit FAFSA. *Faculty research:* Environmental, agricultural, and biological statistics; biomathematics; modern nonparametric statistics; statistical genetics; computational statistics. *Unit head:* Director of Graduate Studies, 607-255-8066. *Application contact:* Graduate Field Assistant, 607-255-8066, E-mail: bscb@cornell.edu. Web site: http://www.gradschool.cornell.edu/fields.php?id-44&a-2.

Cornell University, Graduate School, Graduate Fields of Engineering, Field of Statistics, Ithaca, NY 14853-0001. Offers applied statistics (MPS); biometry (MS, PhD); decision theory (MS, PhD); economic and social statistics (MS, PhD); engineering statistics (MS, PhD); experimental design (MS, PhD); mathematical statistics (MS, PhD); probability (MS, PhD); sampling (MS, PhD); statistical computing (MS, PhD); stochastic processes (MS, PhD). *Faculty:* 24 full-time (3 women). *Students:* 67 full-time (37 women); includes 7 minority (1 Black or African American, non-Hispanic/Latino; 5 Asian, non-Hispanic/Latino; 1 Hispanic/Latino), 46 international. Average age 25. 594 applicants, 16% accepted, 42 enrolled. In 2011, 44 master's, 4 doctorates awarded. Terminal master's awarded for partial completion of doctoral program. *Degree requirements:* For master's, project (MPS), thesis (MS); for doctorate, one foreign language, thesis/dissertation. *Entrance requirements:* For master's, GRE General Test (MS), 2 letters of recommendation (MS, MPS); for doctorate, GRE General Test, 2 letters of recommendation. Additional exam requirements/recommendations for international students: Required—TOEFL (minimum score 550 paper-based; 213 computer-based; 77 iBT). *Application deadline:* For fall admission, 1/15 for domestic students. Applications are processed on a rolling basis. Application fee: $95. Electronic applications accepted. *Financial support:* In 2011–12, 26 students received support, including 3 fellowships with full tuition reimbursements available, 8 research assistantships with full tuition reimbursements available, 14 teaching assistantships with full tuition reimbursements available; institutionally sponsored loans, scholarships/grants, tuition waivers (full and partial), and unspecified assistantships also available. Financial award applicants required to submit FAFSA. *Faculty research:* Bayesian analysis, survival analysis, nonparametric statistics, stochastic processes, mathematical statistics. *Unit head:* Director of Graduate Studies, 607-255-8066. *Application contact:* Graduate Field Assistant, 607-255-8066, E-mail: csc@cornell.edu. Web site: http://www.gradschool.cornell.edu/fields.php?id-94&a-2.

San Diego State University, Graduate and Research Affairs, College of Health and Human Services, Program in Biostatistics and Biometry, San Diego, CA 92182. Offers biometry (MPH). Electronic applications accepted.

University of Wisconsin–Madison, Graduate School, College of Letters and Science, Department of Statistics, Biometry Program, Madison, WI 53706-1380. Offers MS. *Expenses:* Tuition, state resident: full-time $10,296; part-time $643.51 per credit. Tuition, nonresident: full-time $24,054; part-time $1503.40 per credit. *Required fees:* $70.06 per credit. Tuition and fees vary according to course load, campus/location, program and reciprocity agreements.

Biostatistics

American University of Beirut, Graduate Programs, Faculty of Health Sciences, Beirut, Lebanon. Offers environmental sciences (MSES), including environmental health; epidemiology (MS); epidemiology and biostatistics (MPH); health management and policy (MPH); health promotion and community health (MPH); population health (MS). Part-time programs available. *Faculty:* 29 full-time (19 women), 5 part-time/adjunct (2 women). *Students:* 63 full-time (52 women), 103 part-time (87 women). Average age 27. 156 applicants, 71% accepted, 56 enrolled. In 2011, 69 master's awarded. *Degree requirements:* For master's, one foreign language, comprehensive exam, thesis (for some programs). *Entrance requirements:* For master's, 2 letters of recommendation, personal statement, transcripts. Additional exam requirements/recommendations for international students: Required—TOEFL (minimum score 600 paper-based; 250 computer-based; 97 iBT), IELTS (minimum score 7). *Application deadline:* For fall admission, 2/20 for domestic and international students; for spring admission, 11/1 for domestic and international students. Application fee: $50. Electronic applications accepted. *Expenses: Tuition:* Full-time $12,780; part-time $710 per credit. *Required fees:* $528; $528 per credit. Tuition and fees vary according to course load and program. *Financial support:* In 2011–12, 62 students received support. Scholarships/grants, health care benefits, and unspecified assistantships available. Financial award application deadline: 2/20. *Faculty research:* Tobacco control; health of the elderly; youth health; mental health; women's health; reproductive and sexual health, including HIV/AIDS; water quality; health systems; quality in health care delivery; health human resources; health policy; occupational and environmental health; social inequality; social determinants of health; chronic diseases. *Total annual research expenditures:* $722,649. *Unit head:* Iman Adel Nuwayhid, Dean, 961-1340119, Fax: 961-1744470, E-mail: nuwayhid@aub.edu.lb. *Application contact:* Mitra Tauk, Administrative Coordinator, 961-1350000 Ext. 4687, Fax: 961-1744470, E-mail: mt12@aub.edu.lb. Web site: http://fhs.aub.edu.lb.

304 facebook.com/petersonspublishing

Peterson's Graduate Programs in the Physical Sciences, Mathematics, Agricultural Sciences, the Environment & Natural Resources 2013

Boston University, Graduate School of Arts and Sciences, Intercollegiate Program in Biostatistics, Boston, MA 02215. Offers MA, PhD. *Students:* 55 full-time (32 women), 31 part-time (21 women); includes 18 minority (2 Black or African American, non-Hispanic/Latino; 16 Asian, non-Hispanic/Latino), 25 international. Average age 29. 170 applicants, 22% accepted, 14 enrolled. In 2011, 24 master's, 8 doctorates awarded. Terminal master's awarded for partial completion of doctoral program. *Degree requirements:* For master's, one foreign language, comprehensive exam; for doctorate, one foreign language, comprehensive exam, thesis/dissertation. *Entrance requirements:* For master's and doctorate, GRE General Test, 2 letters of recommendation. Additional exam requirements/recommendations for international students: Required—TOEFL (minimum score 550 paper-based; 213 computer-based). *Application deadline:* For fall admission, 12/15 for domestic and international students. Application fee: $70. Electronic applications accepted. *Expenses: Tuition:* Full-time $40,848; part-time $1276 per credit hour. *Required fees:* $572; $286 per semester. *Financial support:* In 2011–12, 34 students received support, including 29 research assistantships with full tuition reimbursements available (averaging $19,300 per year); fellowships and teaching assistantships also available. Support available to part-time students. Financial award application deadline: 12/15; financial award applicants required to submit FAFSA. *Unit head:* Lisa Sullivan, Chairman, 617-638-5047, Fax: 617-638-4458, E-mail: lsull@bu.edu. *Application contact:* MyHanh Tran, Curriculum Coordinator, 617-638-5207, Fax: 617-638-6484, E-mail: mhtran@bu.edu. Web site: http://sph.bu.edu/Biostatistics/department-of-biostatistics/menu-id-617603.html.

Boston University, School of Public Health, Biostatistics Department, Boston, MA 02118. Offers MA, MPH, PhD. Part-time and evening/weekend programs available. *Faculty:* 26 full-time, 18 part-time/adjunct. *Students:* 10 full-time (6 women), 11 part-time (9 women); includes 4 minority (all Asian, non-Hispanic/Latino), 3 international. Average age 27. 79 applicants, 46% accepted, 14 enrolled. In 2011, 15 master's, 5 doctorates awarded. *Entrance requirements:* For master's, GRE, GMAT, LSAT, DAT, or MCAT; for doctorate, GRE. Additional exam requirements/recommendations for international students: Required—TOEFL (minimum score 600 paper-based; 250 computer-based; 100 iBT), IELTS (minimum score 6). *Application deadline:* For fall admission, 2/1 priority date for domestic students, 2/1 for international students; for spring admission, 10/15 priority date for domestic students, 10/15 for international students. Applications are processed on a rolling basis. Application fee: $115. Electronic applications accepted. *Expenses: Tuition:* Full-time $40,848; part-time $1276 per credit hour. *Required fees:* $572; $286 per semester. *Financial support:* Career-related internships or fieldwork, Federal Work-Study, institutionally sponsored loans, scholarships/grants, traineeships, health care benefits, and unspecified assistantships available. Support available to part-time students. Financial award application deadline: 3/1; financial award applicants required to submit FAFSA. *Unit head:* Dr. Lisa Sullivan, Chair, 617-638-5176, Fax: 617-638-4458, E-mail: biostat@bu.edu. *Application contact:* LePhan Quan, Associate Director of Admissions, 617-638-4640, Fax: 617-638-5299, E-mail: asksph@bu.edu. Web site: http://sph.bu.edu/bio.

Brown University, Graduate School, Division of Biology and Medicine, Department of Community Health, Providence, RI 02912. Offers health services research (MS, PhD); public health (MPH); statistical science (MS, PhD), including biostatistics, epidemiology; MD/PhD. *Accreditation:* CEPH. *Degree requirements:* For doctorate, thesis/dissertation, preliminary exam. *Entrance requirements:* For master's and doctorate, GRE General Test. Additional exam requirements/recommendations for international students: Required—TOEFL.

Brown University, Graduate School, Division of Biology and Medicine, Department of Community Health, Center for Statistical Sciences, Program in Biostatistics, Providence, RI 02912. Offers MS, PhD, MD/PhD. *Degree requirements:* For doctorate, thesis/dissertation, preliminary exam. *Entrance requirements:* For master's and doctorate, GRE General Test.

California State University, East Bay, Office of Academic Programs and Graduate Studies, College of Science, Department of Statistics and Biostatistics, Biostatistics Program, Hayward, CA 94542-3000. Offers MS. Part-time and evening/weekend programs available. *Faculty:* 5 full-time (2 women), 1 part-time/adjunct. *Students:* 2 full-time (both women), 35 part-time (19 women); includes 12 minority (3 Black or African American, non-Hispanic/Latino; 8 Asian, non-Hispanic/Latino; 1 Hispanic/Latino), 14 international. Average age 30. 32 applicants, 78% accepted, 17 enrolled. In 2011, 11 master's awarded. *Degree requirements:* For master's, comprehensive exam. *Entrance requirements:* For master's, minimum GPA of 3.0; math through lower-division calculus; statement of purpose; 2-3 letters of recommendation or GRE. Additional exam requirements/recommendations for international students: Required—TOEFL (minimum score 550 paper-based; 213 computer-based). *Application deadline:* For fall admission, 6/30 for domestic and international students. Application fee: $55. Electronic applications accepted. *Expenses:* Tuition, state resident: full-time $6738; part-time $1302 per quarter. Tuition, nonresident: full-time $12,690; part-time $2294 per quarter. *Required fees:* $449 per quarter. Tuition and fees vary according to degree level, program and reciprocity agreements. *Financial support:* Fellowships, career-related internships or fieldwork, Federal Work-Study, scholarships/grants, and unspecified assistantships available. Support available to part-time students. Financial award application deadline: 3/1; financial award applicants required to submit FAFSA. *Unit head:* Dr. Eric Suess, Chair, 510-885-3435, Fax: 510-885-4714, E-mail: eric.suess@csueastbay.edu. *Application contact:* Prof. Lynn Eudey, Biostatics Graduate Advisor, 510-885-3617, Fax: 510-

885-4714, E-mail: lynn.eudey@csueastbay.edu. Web site: http://www.sci.csueastbay.edu/statistics/.

Case Western Reserve University, School of Medicine and School of Graduate Studies, Graduate Programs in Medicine, Department of Epidemiology and Biostatistics, Program in Biostatistics, Cleveland, OH 44106. Offers MS, PhD. Part-time programs available. Terminal master's awarded for partial completion of doctoral program. *Degree requirements:* For master's, comprehensive exam, thesis, exam/practicum; for doctorate, comprehensive exam, thesis/dissertation. *Entrance requirements:* For master's, GRE General Test or MCAT, 3 recommendations; for doctorate, GRE General Test, 3 recommendations. Additional exam requirements/recommendations for international students: Required—TOEFL (minimum score 550 paper-based; 213 computer-based). Electronic applications accepted. *Faculty research:* Survey sampling and statistical computing, generalized linear models, statistical modeling, models in breast cancer survival.

Columbia University, Columbia University Mailman School of Public Health, Department of Biostatistics, New York, NY 10032. Offers MPH, MS, Dr PH, PhD. PhD offered in cooperation with the Graduate School of Arts and Sciences. Part-time programs available. *Students:* 29 full-time (17 women), 82 part-time (47 women); includes 31 minority (5 Black or African American, non-Hispanic/Latino; 20 Asian, non-Hispanic/Latino; 3 Hispanic/Latino; 3 Two or more races, non-Hispanic/Latino), 36 international. Average age 29. 194 applicants, 57% accepted, 46 enrolled. In 2011, 31 master's, 3 doctorates awarded. *Degree requirements:* For doctorate, thesis/dissertation. *Entrance requirements:* For master's, GRE General Test; for doctorate, GRE General Test, MPH or equivalent (Dr PH). Additional exam requirements/recommendations for international students: Required—TOEFL (minimum score 600 paper-based; 250 computer-based; 100 iBT). *Application deadline:* For fall admission, 1/5 for domestic students. Applications are processed on a rolling basis. Application fee: $60. Electronic applications accepted. *Financial support:* Research assistantships, teaching assistantships, career-related internships or fieldwork, and Federal Work-Study available. Financial award application deadline: 2/1; financial award applicants required to submit FAFSA. *Faculty research:* Statistical methods and public health implications of biomedical experiments, clinical trials, functional data analysis, statistical genetics, and observational studies. *Unit head:* Dr. Roger Vaughan, Chairperson, 212-342-2271, Fax: 212-305-9408. *Application contact:* Dr. Joseph Korevec, Director of Admissions and Financial Aid, 212-305-8698, Fax: 212-342-1861, E-mail: ph-admit@columbia.edu. Web site: http://mailman.columbia.edu/biostat/index.html.

Drexel University, School of Biomedical Engineering, Science and Health Systems, Philadelphia, PA 19104-2875. Offers biomedical engineering (MS, PhD); biomedical science (MS, PhD); biostatistics (MS); clinical/rehabilitation engineering (MS); MD/PhD. *Degree requirements:* For doctorate, thesis/dissertation, 1 year of residency, qualifying exam. *Entrance requirements:* For master's, minimum GPA of 3.0; for doctorate, minimum GPA of 3.0, MS. Additional exam requirements/recommendations for international students: Required—TOEFL. Electronic applications accepted. *Faculty research:* Cardiovascular dynamics, diagnostic and therapeutic ultrasound.

Drexel University, School of Public Health, Department of Epidemiology and Biostatistics, Philadelphia, PA 19104-2875. Offers biostatistics (MS); epidemiology (PhD); epidemiology and biostatistics (Certificate).

Duke University, School of Medicine, Program in Biostatistics, Durham, NC 27710. Offers MS. Part-time programs available. *Faculty:* 6 full-time (0 women). *Students:* 16 part-time (9 women); includes 3 minority (1 Black or African American, non-Hispanic/Latino; 2 Asian, non-Hispanic/Latino), 8 international. 36 applicants, 86% accepted, 16 enrolled. *Degree requirements:* For master's, project. *Application deadline:* For fall admission, 8/15 priority date for domestic students. Application fee: $75. *Expenses: Tuition:* Full-time $40,720. *Required fees:* $3107. *Financial support:* Scholarships/grants available. Financial award application deadline: 5/1; financial award applicants required to submit FAFSA. *Unit head:* Dr. Gregory P. Samsa, Associate Professor, 919-613-5212, Fax: 919-660-7040, E-mail: buckl002@mc.duke.edu. *Application contact:* Dr. Brenda E. Armstrong, Director of Admissions, 919-684-2985, E-mail: samsa001@mc.duke.edu. Web site: http://biostat.duke.edu/master-biostatistics-program/program-overview.

East Tennessee State University, School of Graduate Studies, College of Public Health, Master of Public Health Programs, Johnson City, TN 37614. Offers biostatistics (MPH); community health (MPH); environmental health (MPH); epidemiology (MPH); public health administration (MPH). Part-time programs available. Postbaccalaureate distance learning degree programs offered (no on-campus study). *Students:* 45 full-time (27 women), 31 part-time (21 women); includes 14 minority (8 Black or African American, non-Hispanic/Latino; 3 Asian, non-Hispanic/Latino; 2 Hispanic/Latino; 1 Two or more races, non-Hispanic/Latino), 11 international. 92 applicants, 45% accepted, 40 enrolled. In 2011, 24 master's awarded. *Degree requirements:* For master's, comprehensive exam, field experience. *Entrance requirements:* For master's, GRE General Test, SOPHAS application, minimum GPA of 2.75, letters of recommendation. Additional exam requirements/recommendations for international students: Required—TOEFL (minimum score 550 paper-based; 213 computer-based; 79 iBT). *Application deadline:* For fall admission, 3/1 for domestic and international students. Application fee: $35 ($45 for international students). Electronic applications accepted. *Expenses:* Tuition, state resident: full-time $7312; part-

Peterson's Graduate Programs in the Physical Sciences, Mathematics, Agricultural Sciences, the Environment & Natural Resources 2013

facebook.com/petersonspublishing **305**

time $350 per credit hour. Tuition, nonresident: full-time $18,490; part-time $621 per credit hour. *Required fees:* $63 per credit hour. Tuition and fees vary according to course load and program. *Financial support:* In 2011–12, 31 students received support, including 14 research assistantships with full tuition reimbursements available (averaging $6,000 per year), 2 teaching assistantships with full tuition reimbursements available (averaging $6,000 per year); career-related internships or fieldwork, institutionally sponsored loans, scholarships/grants, and unspecified assistantships also available. Financial award application deadline: 7/1; financial award applicants required to submit FAFSA. *Faculty research:* Rural health issues, youth and adolescent health, health of the elderly, environmental epidemiology, spatial analysis of data. *Unit head:* Dr. Brian Martin, Graduate Program Coordinator, 423-439-4429, Fax: 423-439-6491, E-mail: martinb@etsu.edu. *Application contact:* Mary Duncan, Graduate Specialist, 423-439-4302, Fax: 423-439-5624, E-mail: duncanm@etsu.edu. Web site: http://www.etsu.edu/cph/academics/graduate/MPHHome.aspx.

East Tennessee State University, School of Graduate Studies, College of Public Health, Public Health Certificate Programs, Johnson City, TN 37614. Offers biostatistics (Postbaccalaureate Certificate); epidemiology (Postbaccalaureate Certificate); gerontology (Postbaccalaureate Certificate); health care management (Postbaccalaureate Certificate); rural health (Postbaccalaureate Certificate). Part-time programs available. *Students:* 2 full-time (both women), 5 part-time (all women); includes 4 minority (all Black or African American, non-Hispanic/Latino). 18 applicants, 28% accepted, 5 enrolled. In 2011, 7 Postbaccalaureate Certificates awarded. *Degree requirements:* For Postbaccalaureate Certificate, culminating experience or community-based project. *Entrance requirements:* For degree, minimum GPA of 2.5, 3 letters of recommendation, resume (gerontology). Additional exam requirements/recommendations for international students: Required—TOEFL (minimum score 550 paper-based; 213 computer-based; 79 iBT). *Application deadline:* For fall admission, 6/1 for domestic students, 4/29 for international students; for spring admission, 11/1 for domestic students, 9/30 for international students. Application fee: $35 ($45 for international students). Electronic applications accepted. *Expenses:* Tuition, state resident: full-time $7312; part-time $350 per credit hour. Tuition, nonresident: full-time $18,490; part-time $621 per credit hour. *Required fees:* $63 per credit hour. Tuition and fees vary according to course load and program. *Financial support:* Institutionally sponsored loans and scholarships/grants available. Financial award application deadline: 7/1; financial award applicants required to submit FAFSA. *Faculty research:* Rural health issues, youth and adolescent health, health of the elderly, environmental epidemiology, spatial analysis of data. *Unit head:* Dr. Randy Wykoff, Dean, 423-439-4243, Fax: 423-439-5238, E-mail: wykoff@etsu.edu. *Application contact:* Mary Duncan, Graduate Specialist, 423-439-4302, Fax: 423-439-5624, E-mail: duncanm@etsu.edu.

Emory University, Rollins School of Public Health, Department of Biostatistics and Bioinformatics, Atlanta, GA 30322-1100. Offers bioinformatics (PhD); biostatistics (MSPH); public health informatics (MSPH). PhD offered through the Graduate School of Arts and Sciences. Part-time programs available. *Students:* 7 full-time. Average age 27. 106 applicants, 18% accepted, 7 enrolled. *Degree requirements:* For master's, thesis, practicum. *Entrance requirements:* For master's, GRE General Test. Additional exam requirements/recommendations for international students: Required—TOEFL (minimum score 550 paper-based; 213 computer-based; 80 iBT). *Application deadline:* For fall admission, 12/15 priority date for domestic students, 12/15 for international students. Application fee: $95. Electronic applications accepted. *Expenses:* Tuition: Full-time $34,800. *Required fees:* $1300. *Financial support:* Fellowships with full and partial tuition reimbursements, career-related internships or fieldwork, Federal Work-Study, institutionally sponsored loans, scholarships/grants, traineeships, health care benefits, and unspecified assistantships available. Support available to part-time students. Financial award application deadline: 1/5; financial award applicants required to submit FAFSA. *Unit head:* Lance A. Waller, Chair, 404-727-1057, Fax: 404-727-1370, E-mail: lwaller@emory.edu.

Florida International University, Robert Stempel College of Public Health and Social Work, Programs in Public Health, Miami, FL 33199. Offers biostatistics (MPH); environmental and occupational health (MPH, PhD); epidemiology (MPH, PhD); health policy and management (MPH); health promotion and disease prevention (PhD); health promotion and diseases prevention (MPH). Ph D is fall admission only; MPH offered jointly with University of Miami. *Accreditation:* CEPH. Part-time and evening/weekend programs available. Postbaccalaureate distance learning degree programs offered (no on-campus study). *Degree requirements:* For master's, thesis optional; for doctorate, comprehensive exam, thesis/dissertation. *Entrance requirements:* For master's, minimum GPA of 3.0, letters of recommendation; for doctorate, GRE, resume, minimum GPA of 3.0, letters of recommendation, letter of intent. Additional exam requirements/recommendations for international students: Required—TOEFL (minimum score 550 paper-based; 80 iBT). Electronic applications accepted. *Expenses:* Contact institution. *Faculty research:* Drugs/AIDS intervention among migrant workers, provision of services for active/recovering drug users with HIV.

Florida State University, The Graduate School, College of Arts and Sciences, Department of Statistics, Tallahassee, FL 32306-4330. Offers applied statistics (MS); biostatistics (MS, PhD); mathematical statistics (MS, PhD). Part-time programs available. *Faculty:* 15 full-time (2 women). *Students:* 55 full-time (21 women), 16 part-time (4 women); includes 21 minority (8 Black or African American, non-Hispanic/Latino; 5 Asian, non-Hispanic/Latino; 8 Hispanic/Latino), 24 international. Average age 30. 193 applicants, 15% accepted, 16 enrolled. In

2011, 14 master's, 12 doctorates awarded. Terminal master's awarded for partial completion of doctoral program. *Degree requirements:* For doctorate, thesis/dissertation, departmental qualifying exam. *Entrance requirements:* For master's, GRE General Test, previous course work in calculus, minimum GPA of 3.0; for doctorate, GRE General Test, minimum GPA of 3.0, 1 course in linear algebra (preferred), calculus I-III, real analysis. Additional exam requirements/recommendations for international students: Required—TOEFL (minimum score 100 iBT). *Application deadline:* For fall admission, 7/1 for domestic and international students; for spring admission, 11/1 for domestic and international students. Applications are processed on a rolling basis. Application fee: $30. Electronic applications accepted. *Expenses:* Tuition, state resident: full-time $9474; part-time $350.88 per credit hour. Tuition, nonresident: full-time $16,236; part-time $601.34 per credit hour. *Required fees:* $630 per semester. One-time fee: $20. Tuition and fees vary according to course load and campus/location. *Financial support:* In 2011–12, 1 fellowship with full tuition reimbursement (averaging $5,000 per year), 6 research assistantships with full tuition reimbursements (averaging $15,847 per year), 45 teaching assistantships with full tuition reimbursements (averaging $15,362 per year) were awarded; Federal Work-Study, institutionally sponsored loans, scholarships/grants, health care benefits, and unspecified assistantships also available. Financial award application deadline: 2/15; financial award applicants required to submit FAFSA. *Faculty research:* Statistical inference, probability theory, biostatistics, nonparametric estimation, automatic target recognition. *Total annual research expenditures:* $791,621. *Unit head:* Dr. Xufeng Niu, Chairman, 850-644-4008, Fax: 850-644-5271, E-mail: niu@stat.fsu.edu. *Application contact:* Chauncey Richburg, Academic Support Assistant, 850-644-3514, Fax: 850-644-5271, E-mail: richburg@stat.fsu.edu. Web site: http://stat.fsu.edu/.

George Mason University, College of Health and Human Services, Department of Global and Community Health, Fairfax, VA 22030. Offers biostatistics (Certificate); epidemiology (Certificate); epidemiology and biostatistics (MS); gerontology (Certificate); global health (MS, Certificate); nutrition (Certificate); public health (MPH, Certificate). *Faculty:* 11 full-time (5 women), 16 part-time/adjunct (12 women). *Students:* 101 full-time (84 women), 114 part-time (92 women); includes 85 minority (43 Black or African American, non-Hispanic/Latino; 30 Asian, non-Hispanic/Latino; 11 Hispanic/Latino; 1 Two or more races, non-Hispanic/Latino), 14 international. Average age 32. 162 applicants, 61% accepted, 53 enrolled. In 2011, 80 master's, 15 other advanced degrees awarded. *Degree requirements:* For master's, comprehensive exam (for some programs), thesis or practicum. *Entrance requirements:* For master's, GRE, 2 official transcripts; expanded goals statement; 3 letters of recommendation; resume; 1 completed course in health science, statistics, natural sciences and social science (for MPH); 6 credits of foreign language if not fluent (for MS in global health); for Certificate, 2 official transcripts; expanded goals statement; 3 letters of recommendation; resume; bachelor's degree from regionally-accredited institution with minimum GPA of 3.0; statistics and college-level algebra with minimum B grade (for Certificate in biostatistics). Additional exam requirements/recommendations for international students: Required—TOEFL (minimum score 575 paper-based; 230 computer-based; 88 iBT), IELTS, Pearson Test of English. *Application deadline:* For fall admission, 4/1 priority date for domestic students; for spring admission, 11/1 priority date for domestic students. Applications are processed on a rolling basis. Application fee: $65 ($80 for international students). Electronic applications accepted. *Expenses:* Tuition, state resident: full-time $8750; part-time $364.58 per credit. Tuition, nonresident: full-time $24,092; part-time $1003.83 per credit. *Required fees:* $2514; $104.75 per credit. *Financial support:* In 2011–12, 14 students received support, including 12 research assistantships with full and partial tuition reimbursements available (averaging $15,000 per year), 2 teaching assistantships with full and partial tuition reimbursements (averaging $11,781 per year); career-related internships or fieldwork, Federal Work-Study, scholarships/grants, unspecified assistantships, and health care benefits (full-time research and teaching assistantship recipients) also available. Financial award application deadline: 3/1; financial award applicants required to submit FAFSA. *Faculty research:* Providing introductory and advanced degrees in health-related disciplines centered in global and community issues, health issues and the needs of affected populations at the regional and global level. *Total annual research expenditures:* $64,518. *Unit head:* Dr. Carlos Sluzki, Dean, 703-993-1920, Fax: 703-993-1943, E-mail: csluzki@gmu.edu. *Application contact:* Allan Weiss, Office Manager, 703-993-3126, Fax: 703-993-1908, E-mail: aweiss2@gmu.edu. Web site: http://chhs.gmu.edu/gch/index.

Georgetown University, Graduate School of Arts and Sciences, Programs in Biomedical Sciences, Department of Biostatistics, Bioinformatics and Biomathematics, Washington, DC 20057-1484. Offers biostatistics (MS), including bioinformatics, epidemiology. *Entrance requirements:* For master's, GRE General Test. Additional exam requirements/recommendations for international students: Required—TOEFL. *Faculty research:* Occupation epidemiology, cancer.

The George Washington University, Columbian College of Arts and Sciences, Program in Biostatistics, Washington, DC 20052. Offers MS, PhD. *Students:* 5 full-time (4 women), 14 part-time (10 women); includes 3 minority (all Asian, non-Hispanic/Latino), 7 international. Average age 31. 76 applicants, 75% accepted. In 2011, 2 master's, 2 doctorates awarded. *Degree requirements:* For master's, comprehensive exam; for doctorate, thesis/dissertation, general exam. *Entrance requirements:* For master's and doctorate, GRE General Test, minimum GPA of 3.0. Additional exam requirements/recommendations for international students: Required—TOEFL (minimum score 550 paper-based; 213 computer-based; 80

306 facebook.com/petersonspublishing

Peterson's Graduate Programs in the Physical Sciences, Mathematics, Agricultural Sciences, the Environment & Natural Resources 2013

iBT). *Application deadline:* For fall admission, 1/15 priority date for domestic students, 1/15 for international students; for spring admission, 10/1 priority date for domestic students, 9/1 for international students. Applications are processed on a rolling basis. Application fee: $75. Electronic applications accepted. *Financial support:* In 2011–12, 1 student received support. Fellowships with full tuition reimbursements available, teaching assistantships, and tuition waivers available. *Unit head:* Dr. Zhaohai Li, Director, 202-994-7844, Fax: 202-994-6917, E-mail: zli@gwu.edu. *Application contact:* 202-994-6210, Fax: 202-994-6213, E-mail: askccas@gwu.edu.

The George Washington University, School of Public Health and Health Services, Department of Epidemiology and Biostatistics, Washington, DC 20052. Offers biostatistics (MPH); epidemiology (MPH); microbiology and emerging infectious diseases (MSPH). *Faculty:* 23 full-time (15 women), 26 part-time/adjunct (15 women). *Students:* 62 full-time (54 women), 41 part-time (30 women); includes 37 minority (16 Black or African American, non-Hispanic/Latino; 16 Asian, non-Hispanic/Latino; 3 Hispanic/Latino; 2 Two or more races, non-Hispanic/Latino), 8 international. Average age 27. 298 applicants, 69% accepted, 35 enrolled. In 2011, 49 master's awarded. *Degree requirements:* For master's, case study or special project. *Entrance requirements:* For master's, GMAT, GRE General Test, or MCAT. Additional exam requirements/recommendations for international students: Required—TOEFL. *Application deadline:* For fall admission, 4/15 priority date for domestic students, 4/15 for international students; for spring admission, 11/1 for domestic and international students. Applications are processed on a rolling basis. Application fee: $75. *Financial support:* In 2011–12, 6 students received support. Tuition waivers available. Financial award application deadline: 2/15. *Unit head:* Dr. Alan E. Greenberg, Chair, 202-994-0612, E-mail: aeg1@gwu.edu. *Application contact:* Jane Smith, Director of Admissions, 202-994-0248, Fax: 202-994-1860, E-mail: sphhsinfo@gwumc.edu.

Georgia Health Sciences University, College of Graduate Studies, Program in Biostatistics, Augusta, GA 30912. Offers MS, PhD. *Faculty:* 10 full-time (4 women). *Students:* 10 full-time (5 women), 1 (woman) part-time; includes 2 minority (1 Black or African American, non-Hispanic/Latino; 1 Asian, non-Hispanic/Latino), 4 international. Average age 28. 15 applicants, 53% accepted, 2 enrolled. In 2011, 3 master's awarded. *Degree requirements:* For master's, thesis or alternative. *Entrance requirements:* For master's, GRE General Test, substantial mathematics background, computer literacy. Additional exam requirements/recommendations for international students: Required—TOEFL (minimum score 550 paper-based; 213 computer-based; 79 iBT). *Application deadline:* For fall admission, 2/1 for domestic students. Application fee: $50. Electronic applications accepted. *Financial support:* In 2011–12, 10 research assistantships with full tuition reimbursements (averaging $14,000 per year) were awarded; unspecified assistantships also available. *Faculty research:* Computational biology, clinical trials, statistical genetics, statistical epidemiology, survival analysis. *Total annual research expenditures:* $331,986. *Unit head:* Dr. Varghese George, Chair, 706-721-3785, E-mail: vgeorge@georgiahealth.edu. *Application contact:* Dr. Jennifer Waller, Graduate Program Director and Associate Professor, 706-721-0814, E-mail: jwaller@georgiahealth.edu. Web site: http://biostat.mcg.edu/.

Georgia Southern University, Jack N. Averitt College of Graduate Studies, Jiann-Ping Hsu College of Public Health, Program in Public Health, Statesboro, GA 30460. Offers biostatistics (MPH, Dr PH); community health behavior and education (Dr PH); community health education (MPH); environmental health sciences (MPH); epidemiology (MPH); health services policy management (MPH); public health leadership (Dr PH). *Accreditation:* CEPH. Part-time programs available. *Students:* 87 full-time (60 women), 39 part-time (25 women); includes 68 minority (58 Black or African American, non-Hispanic/Latino; 6 Asian, non-Hispanic/Latino; 4 Hispanic/Latino), 20 international. Average age 30. 73 applicants, 84% accepted, 42 enrolled. In 2011, 22 master's, 4 doctorates awarded. *Degree requirements:* For master's, thesis optional, practicum; for doctorate, comprehensive exam, thesis/dissertation, practicum. *Entrance requirements:* For master's, GRE General Test, minimum GPA of 2.75, resume, 3 letters of reference; for doctorate, GRE, GMAT, MCAT, LSAT, 3 letters of reference, statement of purpose, resume or curriculum vitae. Additional exam requirements/recommendations for international students: Required—TOEFL (minimum score 550 paper-based; 213 computer-based; 80 iBT). *Application deadline:* For fall admission, 3/1 priority date for domestic students, 3/1 for international students; for spring admission, 10/1 priority date for domestic students, 10/1 for international students. Applications are processed on a rolling basis. Application fee: $50. Electronic applications accepted. *Expenses:* Contact institution. *Financial support:* In 2011–12, 59 students received support, including research assistantships with partial tuition reimbursements available (averaging $7,200 per year), teaching assistantships with partial tuition reimbursements available (averaging $7,200 per year); career-related internships or fieldwork, Federal Work-Study, scholarships/grants, tuition waivers (partial), and unspecified assistantships also available. Support available to part-time students. Financial award application deadline: 4/15; financial award applicants required to submit FAFSA. *Faculty research:* Rural public health best practices, health disparity elimination, community initiatives to enhance public health, cost effectiveness analysis, epidemiology of rural public health, environmental health issues, health care system assessment, rural health care, health policy and healthcare financing. *Unit head:* Dr. Charles Hardy, Dean, 912-478-2674, Fax: 912-478-5811, E-mail: chardy@georgiasouthern.edu. *Application contact:* Amanda Gilliland, Coordinator for Graduate Student Recruitment, 912-478-5384, Fax: 912-

478-0740, E-mail: gradadmissions@georgiasouthern.edu. Web site: http://chhs.georgiasouthern.edu/health/.

Grand Valley State University, College of Liberal Arts and Sciences, Program in Biostatistics, Allendale, MI 49401-9403. Offers MS. *Entrance requirements:* For master's, minimum GPA of 3.0. *Faculty research:* Biometrical models, spatial methods, medical statistics, design of experiments.

Harvard University, Cyprus International Institute for the Environment and Public Health in Association with Harvard School of Public Health, Cambridge, MA 02138. Offers environmental health (MS); environmental/public health (PhD); epidemiology and biostatistics (MS). *Entrance requirements:* For master's and doctorate, GRE, resume/curriculum vitae, 3 letters of recommendation, BA or BS (including diploma and official transcripts). Additional exam requirements/recommendations for international students: Required—TOEFL (minimum score 220 computer-based), IELTS (minimum score 7). Electronic applications accepted. *Expenses: Tuition:* Full-time $36,304. *Required fees:* $1186. Full-time tuition and fees vary according to program. *Faculty research:* Air pollution, climate change, biostatistics, sustainable development, environmental management.

Harvard University, Graduate School of Arts and Sciences, Department of Biostatistics, Cambridge, MA 02138. Offers PhD. *Expenses: Tuition:* Full-time $36,304. *Required fees:* $1186. Full-time tuition and fees vary according to program.

Harvard University, Harvard School of Public Health, Department of Biostatistics, Boston, MA 02115-6096. Offers SM, PhD. Part-time programs available. *Faculty:* 53 full-time (16 women), 5 part-time/adjunct (2 women). *Students:* 90 full-time, 1 part-time; includes 25 minority (5 Black or African American, non-Hispanic/Latino; 14 Asian, non-Hispanic/Latino; 4 Hispanic/Latino; 2 Two or more races, non-Hispanic/Latino), 31 international. Average age 26. 203 applicants, 19% accepted, 24 enrolled. In 2011, 11 master's, 1 doctorate awarded. *Degree requirements:* For doctorate, thesis/dissertation, oral and written qualifying exams. *Entrance requirements:* For master's and doctorate, GRE, prior training in mathematics and/or statistics. Additional exam requirements/recommendations for international students: Required—TOEFL (minimum score 590 paper-based; 240 computer-based; 95 iBT); Recommended—IELTS (minimum score 7). *Application deadline:* For fall admission, 12/15 for domestic and international students. Application fee: $115. Electronic applications accepted. *Expenses: Tuition:* Full-time $36,304. *Required fees:* $1186. Full-time tuition and fees vary according to program. *Financial support:* Fellowships, research assistantships, teaching assistantships, Federal Work-Study, scholarships/grants, traineeships, and unspecified assistantships available. Support available to part-time students. Financial award application deadline: 2/17; financial award applicants required to submit FAFSA. *Faculty research:* Statistical genetics, clinical trials, cancer and AIDS research, environmental and mental health, dose response modeling. *Unit head:* Dr. Victor DeGruttola, Chair, 617-432-1056, Fax: 617-432-5619, E-mail: degrut@hsph.harvard.edu. *Application contact:* Vincent W. James, Director of Admissions, 617-432-1031, Fax: 617-432-7080, E-mail: admissions@hsph.harvard.edu. Web site: http://www.hsph.harvard.edu/departments/biostatistics/.

Hunter College of the City University of New York, Graduate School, Schools of the Health Professions, School of Health Sciences, Programs in Urban Public Health, Program in Epidemiology and Biostatistics, New York, NY 10021-5085. Offers MPH. *Accreditation:* CEPH. Part-time and evening/weekend programs available. *Faculty:* 6 full-time (4 women), 1 (woman) part-time/adjunct. *Students:* 6 full-time (1 woman), 48 part-time (29 women); includes 22 minority (9 Black or African American, non-Hispanic/Latino; 11 Asian, non-Hispanic/Latino; 2 Hispanic/Latino), 5 international. Average age 32. 47 applicants, 49% accepted, 12 enrolled. In 2011, 15 master's awarded. *Degree requirements:* For master's, comprehensive exam, thesis optional, internship. *Entrance requirements:* For master's, GRE General Test, previous course work in calculus and statistics. Additional exam requirements/recommendations for international students: Required—TOEFL. *Application deadline:* For fall admission, 4/1 for domestic students; for spring admission, 11/1 for domestic students. Application fee: $125. *Expenses:* Tuition, state resident: full-time $8210; part-time $345 per credit. Tuition, nonresident: full-time $15,360; part-time $640 per credit. *Required fees:* $280 per semester. One-time fee: $125. Tuition and fees vary according to class time, campus/location and program. *Financial support:* In 2011–12, 6 fellowships were awarded; career-related internships or fieldwork, Federal Work-Study, institutionally sponsored loans, and tuition waivers (partial) also available. Support available to part-time students. Financial award application deadline: 3/1. *Unit head:* Victoria Frye, Coordinator, 212-481-7580, Fax: 212-481-5260, E-mail: vfrye@hunter.cuny.edu. *Application contact:* Milena Solo, Director for Graduate Admissions, 212-772-4288, Fax: 212-650-3336, E-mail: milena.solo@hunter.cuny.edu. Web site: http://www.hunter.cuny.edu/uph/grad-test/epidemiology-biostatistics.

Indiana University Bloomington, School of Health, Physical Education and Recreation, Department of Applied Health Science, Bloomington, IN 47405-7000. Offers biostatistics (MPH); environmental health (MPH, PhD); epidemiology (MPH, PhD); health behavior (PhD); health promotion (MS); human development/family studies (MS); nutrition science (MS); public health administration (MPH); safety management (MS); school and college health programs (MS); social, behavioral and community health (MPH). *Accreditation:* CEPH (one or more programs are accredited). *Faculty:* 24 full-time (12 women). *Students:* 169 full-time (126 women), 25 part-time (17 women); includes 56 minority (39 Black or

Peterson's Graduate Programs in the Physical Sciences, Mathematics, Agricultural Sciences, the Environment & Natural Resources 2013

facebook.com/petersonspublishing **307**

Biostatistics

African American, non-Hispanic/Latino; 2 American Indian or Alaska Native, non-Hispanic/Latino; 4 Asian, non-Hispanic/Latino; 9 Hispanic/Latino; 2 Two or more races, non-Hispanic/Latino), 29 international. Average age 30. 170 applicants, 74% accepted, 79 enrolled. In 2011, 52 master's, 9 doctorates awarded. *Degree requirements:* For master's, thesis optional; for doctorate, thesis/dissertation. *Entrance requirements:* For master's, GRE (MS in nutrition science), 3 recommendations; for doctorate, GRE, 3 recommendations. Additional exam requirements/recommendations for international students: Required—TOEFL (minimum score 550 paper-based; 213 computer-based; 79 iBT). *Application deadline:* For fall admission, 4/30 priority date for domestic students, 12/1 for international students; for spring admission, 11/15 priority date for domestic students, 9/1 for international students. Application fee: $55 ($65 for international students). *Financial support:* Fellowships, research assistantships with full and partial tuition reimbursements, teaching assistantships with full and partial tuition reimbursements, career-related internships or fieldwork, Federal Work-Study, institutionally sponsored loans, scholarships/grants, tuition waivers (partial), and fee remissions available. Financial award application deadline: 3/1. *Faculty research:* Cancer education, HIV/AIDS and drug education, public health, parent-child interactions, safety education. *Total annual research expenditures:* $2.8 million. *Unit head:* Dr. David K. Lohrmann, Chair, 812-856-5101, Fax: 812-855-3936, E-mail: dlohrman@indiana.edu. *Application contact:* Dr. Susan Middlestadt, Associate Professor and Graduate Coordinator, 812-856-5768, Fax: 812-855-3936, E-mail: semiddle@indiana.edu. Web site: http://www.indiana.edu/~aphealth/.

Indiana University–Purdue University Indianapolis, Indiana University School of Medicine, Department of Biostatistics, Indianapolis, IN 46202-2896. Offers PhD. Program offered jointly with Purdue University Department of Mathematical Sciences. *Students:* 16 full-time (9 women), 7 part-time (3 women); includes 4 minority (all Asian, non-Hispanic/Latino), 18 international. 30 applicants, 47% accepted, 8 enrolled. *Degree requirements:* For doctorate, thesis/dissertation. *Entrance requirements:* For doctorate, GRE General Test. Additional exam requirements/recommendations for international students: Required—TOEFL. *Application deadline:* For fall admission, 1/15 for domestic and international students. Application fee: $55 ($65 for international students). Electronic applications accepted. *Unit head:* Barry Katz, Chair, 317-274-2674, E-mail: bkatz@iupui.edu. *Application contact:* Benzion Boukai, Co-Director, 317-274-2661, E-mail: bboukai@iupui.edu. Web site: http://biostatgradprograms.iupui.edu/.

Iowa State University of Science and Technology, Bioinformatics and Computational Biology Program, Ames, IA 50011-3260. Offers MS, PhD. *Degree requirements:* For doctorate, thesis/dissertation. *Entrance requirements:* For master's and doctorate, GRE General Test. Additional exam requirements/recommendations for international students: Recommended—TOEFL, IELTS. *Application deadline:* For fall admission, 1/15 priority date for domestic students, 1/15 for international students; for spring admission, 10/15 for domestic and international students. Application fee: $40 ($90 for international students). Electronic applications accepted. *Faculty research:* Functional and structural genomics, genome evolution, macromolecular structure and function, mathematical biology and biological statistics, metabolic and developmental networks. *Unit head:* Dr. Julie Dickerson, Chair, Supervising Committee, 515-294-5122, Fax: 515-294-6790, E-mail: bcb@iastate.edu. *Application contact:* Information Contact, 515-294-5836, Fax: 515-294-2592, E-mail: grad_admissions@iastate.edu. Web site: http://www.bcb.iastate.edu/.

The Johns Hopkins University, Bloomberg School of Public Health, Department of Biostatistics, Baltimore, MD 21205-2179. Offers bioinformatics (MHS); biostatistics (MHS, Sc M, PhD). Part-time programs available. *Degree requirements:* For master's, comprehensive exam (for some programs), thesis (for some programs), written exam, final project; for doctorate, comprehensive exam, thesis/dissertation, 1 year full-time residency, oral and written exams. *Entrance requirements:* For master's and doctorate, GRE General Test, course work in calculus and matrix algebra, 3 letters of recommendation, curriculum vitae. Additional exam requirements/recommendations for international students: Required—TOEFL (minimum score 600 paper-based; 250 computer-based). Electronic applications accepted. *Faculty research:* Statistical genetics, bioinformatics, statistical computing, statistical methods, environmental statistics.

Loma Linda University, School of Public Health, Programs in Epidemiology and Biostatistics, Loma Linda, CA 92350. Offers MPH, MSPH, Dr PH, Postbaccalaureate Certificate. *Entrance requirements:* Additional exam requirements/recommendations for international students: Required—Michigan English Language Assessment Battery or TOEFL.

Louisiana State University Health Sciences Center, School of Public Health, New Orleans, LA 70112. Offers behavioral and community health sciences (MPH); biostatistics (MPH, MS, PhD); community health sciences (PhD); environmental and occupational health sciences (MPH); epidemiology (MPH, PhD); health policy and systems management (MPH). Part-time programs available. *Entrance requirements:* For master's, GRE General Test.

McGill University, Faculty of Graduate and Postdoctoral Studies, Faculty of Medicine, Department of Epidemiology and Biostatistics, Montréal, QC H3A 2T5, Canada. Offers community health (M Sc); environmental health (M Sc); epidemiology and biostatistics (M Sc, PhD, Diploma); health care evaluation (M Sc); medical statistics (M Sc). *Accreditation:* CEPH (one or more programs are accredited).

Medical College of Wisconsin, Graduate School of Biomedical Sciences, Department of Population Health, Division of Biostatistics, Milwaukee, WI 53226-0509. Offers PhD. Part-time programs available. *Degree requirements:* For doctorate, comprehensive exam, thesis/dissertation. *Entrance requirements:* For doctorate, GRE, official transcripts, three letters of recommendation. Additional exam requirements/recommendations for international students: Required—TOEFL. Electronic applications accepted. *Faculty research:* Survival analysis, spatial statistics, time series, genetic statistics, Bayesian statistics.

Medical University of South Carolina, College of Graduate Studies, Division of Biostatistics and Epidemiology, Charleston, SC 29425. Offers biostatistics (MS, PhD); epidemiology (MS, PhD); DMD/PhD; MD/PhD. *Faculty:* 21 full-time (14 women), 1 part-time/adjunct (0 women). *Students:* 14 full-time (11 women), 2 part-time (both women); includes 4 minority (3 Black or African American, non-Hispanic/Latino; 1 Hispanic/Latino), 5 international. Average age 29. 36 applicants, 31% accepted, 5 enrolled. In 2011, 4 degrees awarded. Terminal master's awarded for partial completion of doctoral program. *Median time to degree:* Of those who began their doctoral program in fall 2003, 80% received their degree in 8 years or less. *Degree requirements:* For master's, comprehensive exam, thesis (for some programs); for doctorate, comprehensive exam, oral and written exams. *Entrance requirements:* For master's, GRE General Test, two semesters of college-level calculus; for doctorate, GRE General Test, interview, minimum GPA of 3.0, two semesters of college-level calculus. Additional exam requirements/recommendations for international students: Required—TOEFL (minimum score 600 paper-based; 250 computer-based; 100 iBT). *Application deadline:* For fall admission, 1/15 priority date for domestic students, 1/15 for international students. Applications are processed on a rolling basis. Application fee: $0 ($85 for international students). Electronic applications accepted. *Financial support:* In 2011–12, 18 research assistantships with partial tuition reimbursements (averaging $23,000 per year) were awarded; Federal Work-Study and scholarships/grants also available. Support available to part-time students. Financial award application deadline: 3/10; financial award applicants required to submit FAFSA. *Faculty research:* Health disparities, central nervous system injuries, radiation exposure, analysis of clinical trial data, biomedical information. *Unit head:* Dr. Yuko Y. Palesch, Professor/Director, 843-876-1917, Fax: 843-792-6590, E-mail: paleschy@musc.edu. *Application contact:* Dr. Ramesh Ramakrishnan, Associate Professor, 843-876-1140, Fax: 843-876-1126, E-mail: ramakris@musc.edu. Web site: http://www.musc.edu/dbbe/.

Middle Tennessee State University, College of Graduate Studies, College of Basic and Applied Sciences, Program in Professional Science, Murfreesboro, TN 37132. Offers biostatistics (MS); health care informatics (MS). Part-time and evening/weekend programs available. Postbaccalaureate distance learning degree programs offered. *Students:* 4 full-time (1 woman), 72 part-time (43 women); includes 34 minority (15 Black or African American, non-Hispanic/Latino; 17 Asian, non-Hispanic/Latino; 2 Two or more races, non-Hispanic/Latino). Average age 28. In 2011, 22 master's awarded. *Degree requirements:* For master's, comprehensive exam. *Entrance requirements:* For master's, GRE. Additional exam requirements/recommendations for international students: Required—TOEFL (minimum score 525 paper-based; 195 computer-based; 71 iBT) or IELTS (minimum score 6). *Application deadline:* For fall admission, 6/1 for domestic and international students. Applications are processed on a rolling basis. Application fee: $25 ($30 for international students). *Expenses:* Tuition, state resident: full-time $10,008. Tuition, nonresident: full-time $25,056. *Financial support:* In 2011–12, 7 students received support. Tuition waivers available. Support available to part-time students. Financial award application deadline: 5/1. *Faculty research:* Biotechnology, biostatistics, informatics. *Unit head:* Dr. Robert W. Fischer, Jr., Dean, 615-898-2613, Fax: 615-898-2615. *Application contact:* Dr. Michael D. Allen, Dean and Vice Provost for Research, 615-898-2840, Fax: 615-904-8020, E-mail: michael.allen@mtsu.edu.

New Jersey Institute of Technology, Office of Graduate Studies, College of Science and Liberal Arts, Department of Mathematical Science, Program in Biostatistics, Newark, NJ 07102. Offers MS. Part-time and evening/weekend programs available. Postbaccalaureate distance learning degree programs offered. *Students:* 2 full-time (1 woman), 10 part-time (5 women); includes 7 minority (2 Black or African American, non-Hispanic/Latino; 4 Asian, non-Hispanic/Latino; 1 Hispanic/Latino), 2 international. Average age 31. 30 applicants, 67% accepted, 4 enrolled. In 2011, 7 master's awarded. Terminal master's awarded for partial completion of doctoral program. *Degree requirements:* For master's, thesis optional. *Entrance requirements:* For master's, GRE General Test. Additional exam requirements/recommendations for international students: Required—TOEFL (minimum score 550 paper-based; 213 computer-based; 79 iBT). *Application deadline:* For fall admission, 6/1 priority date for domestic students, 5/1 for international students; for spring admission, 11/15 priority date for domestic students, 11/15 for international students. Applications are processed on a rolling basis. Application fee: $65. Electronic applications accepted. *Expenses:* Tuition, state resident: full-time $7980; part-time $867 per credit. Tuition, nonresident: full-time $11,336; part-time $1196 per credit. *Required fees:* $230 per credit. *Financial support:* Career-related internships or fieldwork, Federal Work-Study, institutionally sponsored loans, and unspecified assistantships available. Financial award application deadline: 1/15. *Unit head:* Dr. Daljit S. Ahluwalia, Chair, 973-596-8465, Fax: 973-596-5591, E-mail: daljit.ahluwalia@njit.edu. *Application contact:* Kathryn Kelly, Director of Admissions, 973-596-3300, Fax: 973-596-3461, E-mail: admissions@njit.edu. Web site: http://math.njit.edu/academics/graduate/ms-biostatistics.php.

308 facebook.com/petersonspublishing

Peterson's Graduate Programs in the Physical Sciences, Mathematics, Agricultural Sciences, the Environment & Natural Resources 2013

The Ohio State University, Graduate School, College of Arts and Sciences, Division of Natural and Mathematical Sciences, Department of Statistics, Columbus, OH 43210. Offers biostatistics (PhD); statistics (M Appl Stat, MS, PhD). *Faculty:* 22. *Students:* 71 full-time (39 women), 49 part-time (19 women); includes 5 minority (1 Black or African American, non-Hispanic/Latino; 4 Asian, non-Hispanic/Latino), 65 international. Average age 27. In 2011, 33 master's, 6 doctorates awarded. *Degree requirements:* For master's, thesis optional; for doctorate, thesis/dissertation. *Entrance requirements:* For master's and doctorate, GRE General Test. Additional exam requirements/recommendations for international students: Required—TOEFL (minimum score 550 paper-based; 250 computer-based; 79 iBT), Michigan English Language Assessment Battery (minimum score 82). *Application deadline:* For fall admission, 8/15 priority date for domestic students, 7/1 for international students; for winter admission, 12/1 priority date for domestic students, 11/1 for international students; for spring admission, 3/1 priority date for domestic students, 2/1 for international students. Applications are processed on a rolling basis. Application fee: $40 ($50 for international students). Electronic applications accepted. *Expenses:* Tuition, state resident: full-time $11,400. Tuition, nonresident: full-time $28,125. Tuition and fees vary according to course load, degree level, campus/location and program. *Financial support:* Fellowships, research assistantships, teaching assistantships, Federal Work-Study, and institutionally sponsored loans available. Support available to part-time students. *Unit head:* L . Mark Berliner, Chair, 614-247-4075, Fax: 614-292-2096, E-mail: berliner.1@osu.edu. *Application contact:* Graduate Admissions, 614-292-6031, Fax: 614-292-3656, E-mail: gradadmissions@osu.edu. Web site: http://www.stat.osu.edu/.

Oregon Health & Science University, School of Medicine, Graduate Programs in Medicine, Department of Public Health and Preventive Medicine, Portland, OR 97239-3098. Offers biostatistics (Certificate); epidemiology and biostatistics (MPH). *Accreditation:* CEPH. Part-time programs available. *Faculty:* 17 full-time (13 women). *Students:* 18 full-time (12 women), 59 part-time (44 women); includes 19 minority (3 Black or African American, non-Hispanic/Latino; 2 American Indian or Alaska Native, non-Hispanic/Latino; 13 Asian, non-Hispanic/Latino; 1 Two or more races, non-Hispanic/Latino), 1 international. Average age 33. 45 applicants, 64% accepted, 28 enrolled. In 2011, 20 master's awarded. *Degree requirements:* For master's, thesis, fieldwork/internship. *Entrance requirements:* For master's, GRE General Test (minimum scores: 153 Verbal/148 Quantitative/4.5 Analytical), previous undergraduate course work in statistics. Additional exam requirements/recommendations for international students: Required—TOEFL (minimum score 550 paper-based; 213 computer-based; 87 iBT). *Application deadline:* For fall admission, 2/1 for domestic students. Application fee: $70. Electronic applications accepted. *Financial support:* Health care benefits available. *Faculty research:* Epidemiologic research, biostatistics, health services research, community-based research, health disparities. *Unit head:* Dr. Thomas M. Becker, Professor/Chair, 503-494-8257, Fax: 503-494-4981, E-mail: pmph@ohsu.edu. *Application contact:* Tree Triano, Education Manager, 503-494-2012, Fax: 503-494-4981, E-mail: pmph@ohsu.edu. Web site: http://www.ohsu.edu/public-health.

Oregon State University, Graduate School, College of Public Health and Human Sciences, Programs in Public Health, Program in Biostatistics, Corvallis, OR 97331. Offers MPH.

Rice University, Graduate Programs, George R. Brown School of Engineering, Department of Statistics, Houston, TX 77251-1892. Offers bioinformatics (PhD); biostatistics (PhD); computational finance (PhD); general statistics (PhD); statistics (M Stat, MA); MBA/M Stat. Part-time programs available. *Degree requirements:* For master's, comprehensive exam; for doctorate, comprehensive exam, thesis/dissertation. *Entrance requirements:* For master's and doctorate, GRE General Test, minimum GPA of 3.0. Additional exam requirements/recommendations for international students: Required—TOEFL (minimum score 630 paper-based; 250 computer-based; 90 iBT). Electronic applications accepted. *Faculty research:* Statistical genetics, non parametric function estimation, computational statistics and visualization, stochastic processes.

Rutgers, The State University of New Jersey, New Brunswick, Graduate School-New Brunswick, BioMaPS Institute for Quantitative Biology, Piscataway, NJ 08854-8097. Offers computational biology and molecular biophysics (PhD). *Degree requirements:* For doctorate, comprehensive exam, thesis/dissertation. *Entrance requirements:* For doctorate, GRE. Additional exam requirements/recommendations for international students: Required—TOEFL. Electronic applications accepted. *Faculty research:* Structural biology, systems biology, bioinformatics, translational medicine, genomics.

Rutgers, The State University of New Jersey, New Brunswick, Graduate School-New Brunswick, Program in Statistics, Piscataway, NJ 08854-8097. Offers applied statistics (MS); biostatistics (MS); data mining (MS); quality and productivity management (MS); statistics (MS, PhD). Part-time programs available. Terminal master's awarded for partial completion of doctoral program. *Degree requirements:* For master's, comprehensive exam, essay, exam, non-thesis essay paper; for doctorate, one foreign language, thesis/dissertation, qualifying oral and written exams. *Entrance requirements:* For master's, GRE General Test; for doctorate, GRE General Test, GRE Subject Test (recommended). Additional exam requirements/recommendations for international students: Required—TOEFL (minimum score 550 paper-based; 213 computer-based). Electronic applications accepted. *Faculty research:* Probability, decision theory, linear models, multivariate statistics, statistical computing.

San Diego State University, Graduate and Research Affairs, College of Health and Human Services, Graduate School of Public Health, San Diego, CA 92182. Offers environmental health (MPH); epidemiology (MPH, PhD), including biostatistics (MPH); global emergency preparedness and response (MS); global health (PhD); health behavior (PhD); health promotion (MPH); health services administration (MPH); toxicology (MS); MPH/MA; MSW/MPH. *Accreditation:* ABET (one or more programs are accredited); CAHME (one or more programs are accredited); CEPH (one or more programs are accredited). Part-time programs available. *Degree requirements:* For master's, comprehensive exam (for some programs), thesis (for some programs); for doctorate, thesis/dissertation. *Entrance requirements:* For master's, GMAT (MPH in health services administration), GRE General Test; for doctorate, GRE General Test. Additional exam requirements/recommendations for international students: Required—TOEFL. *Faculty research:* Evaluation of tobacco, AIDS prevalence and prevention, mammography, infant death project, Alzheimer's in elderly Chinese.

Tufts University, Sackler School of Graduate Biomedical Sciences, Clinical and Translational Science Program, Medford, MA 02155. Offers MS, PhD. *Faculty:* 33 full-time (9 women). *Students:* 31 full-time (16 women); includes 6 minority (4 Asian, non-Hispanic/Latino; 1 Hispanic/Latino; 1 Two or more races, non-Hispanic/Latino), 13 international. Average age 33. In 2011, 11 degrees awarded. Terminal master's awarded for partial completion of doctoral program. *Degree requirements:* For master's, thesis; for doctorate, thesis/dissertation. *Entrance requirements:* For master's and doctorate, MD or PhD, strong clinical research background. Additional exam requirements/recommendations for international students: Required—TOEFL (minimum score 600 paper-based; 250 computer-based; 100 iBT). *Application deadline:* For fall admission, 12/15 for domestic and international students. Application fee: $70. Electronic applications accepted. *Expenses: Tuition:* Full-time $41,208; part-time $1030 per credit hour. Full-time tuition and fees vary according to degree level, program and student level. Part-time tuition and fees vary according to course load. *Financial support:* Application deadline: 12/15. *Faculty research:* Clinical study design, mathematical modeling, meta analysis, epidemiologic research, coronary heart disease. *Unit head:* Dr. David Kent, Program Director, 617-636-3234, Fax: 617-636-8023, E-mail: dkent@tuftsmedicalcenter.edu. *Application contact:* Kellie Melchin, Associate Director of Admissions, 617-636-6767, Fax: 617-636-0375, E-mail: sackler-school@tufts.edu. Web site: http://sackler.tufts.edu/Academics/Degree-Programs/PhD-Programs/Clinical-and-Translational-Science.

Tulane University, School of Public Health and Tropical Medicine, Department of Biostatistics, New Orleans, LA 70118-5669. Offers MS, MSPH, PhD, Sc D. MS and PhD offered through the Graduate School. Part-time programs available. *Degree requirements:* For doctorate, comprehensive exam, thesis/dissertation. *Entrance requirements:* For master's and doctorate, GRE General Test. Additional exam requirements/recommendations for international students: Required—TOEFL. Electronic applications accepted. *Faculty research:* Clinical trials, measurement, longitudinal analyses.

University at Albany, State University of New York, School of Public Health, Department of Epidemiology and Biostatistics, Albany, NY 12222-0001. Offers MS, PhD. *Degree requirements:* For master's, thesis; for doctorate, thesis/dissertation. *Entrance requirements:* For master's and doctorate, GRE General Test. Additional exam requirements/recommendations for international students: Required—TOEFL (minimum score 550 paper-based; 213 computer-based). Electronic applications accepted.

University at Buffalo, the State University of New York, Graduate School, School of Public Health and Health Professions, Department of Biostatistics, Buffalo, NY 14260. Offers MA, MPH, PhD. *Faculty:* 10 full-time (3 women), 2 part-time/adjunct (0 women). *Students:* 41 full-time (24 women), 8 part-time (1 woman); includes 9 minority (3 Black or African American, non-Hispanic/Latino; 3 Asian, non-Hispanic/Latino; 1 Hispanic/Latino; 2 Native Hawaiian or other Pacific Islander, non-Hispanic/Latino), 26 international. Average age 31. 50 applicants, 62% accepted, 17 enrolled. In 2011, 6 master's, 3 doctorates awarded. Terminal master's awarded for partial completion of doctoral program. *Degree requirements:* For master's, comprehensive exam, thesis optional, final oral exam, practical data analysis experience; for doctorate, comprehensive exam, thesis/dissertation, final oral exam. *Entrance requirements:* For master's, GRE, 3 semesters of course work in calculus (mathematics), course work in real analysis (preferred), course work in linear algebra; for doctorate, GRE, master's degree in statistics, biostatistics or equivalent. Additional exam requirements/recommendations for international students: Required—TOEFL (minimum score 640 paper-based; 250 computer-based; 79 iBT). *Application deadline:* For fall admission, 4/1 priority date for domestic students, 4/1 for international students. Application fee: $50. Electronic applications accepted. *Financial support:* In 2011–12, 12 students received support, including 2 fellowships with full tuition reimbursements available (averaging $4,000 per year), 6 research assistantships with full tuition reimbursements available (averaging $24,000 per year), 5 teaching assistantships with full tuition reimbursements available (averaging $20,000 per year); institutionally sponsored loans, scholarships/grants, and tuition waivers (partial) also available. Financial award application deadline: 2/1; financial award applicants required to submit FAFSA. *Faculty research:* Biostatistics, longitudinal data analysis, nonparametrics, statistical genetics, epidemiology. *Unit head:* Dr. Alan D. Hutson, Chair and Associate Professor, 716-829-2594, Fax: 716-829-2200, E-mail: ahutson@buffalo.edu. *Application contact:* Dr. Lili Tian, Director of Graduate Studies and Professor, 716-829-2715, Fax: 716-829-2200, E-mail: ltian@buffalo.edu. Web site: http://sphhp.buffalo.edu/biostat/index.php.

Peterson's Graduate Programs in the Physical Sciences, Mathematics, Agricultural Sciences, the Environment & Natural Resources 2013

facebook.com/petersonspublishing **309**

Biostatistics

The University of Alabama at Birmingham, School of Public Health, Program in Biostatistics, Birmingham, AL 35294. Offers MS, PhD. *Degree requirements:* For master's, variable foreign language requirement, thesis, fieldwork, research project; for doctorate, variable foreign language requirement, comprehensive exam, thesis/dissertation. *Entrance requirements:* For master's, GRE General Test or MAT, minimum GPA of 3.0; for doctorate, GRE General Test or MAT, MPH or MSPH, minimum GPA of 3.0, interview. *Expenses:* Contact institution. *Financial support:* Fellowships and career-related internships or fieldwork available. *Unit head:* Dr. Naomi Fineberg, Chair, 205-934-5971, Fax: 205-975-2540. Web site: http://www.uab.edu/PublicHealth/.

University of Alberta, Faculty of Graduate Studies and Research, Department of Mathematical and Statistical Sciences, Edmonton, AB T6G 2E1, Canada. Offers applied mathematics (M Sc, PhD); biostatistics (M Sc); mathematical finance (M Sc, PhD); mathematical physics (M Sc, PhD); mathematics (M Sc, PhD); statistics (M Sc, PhD, Postgraduate Diploma). Part-time programs available. Terminal master's awarded for partial completion of doctoral program. *Degree requirements:* For master's, thesis (for some programs); for doctorate, comprehensive exam, thesis/dissertation. *Entrance requirements:* Additional exam requirements/recommendations for international students: Required—TOEFL (minimum score 580 paper-based; 237 computer-based). Electronic applications accepted. *Faculty research:* Classical and functional analysis, algebra, differential equations, geometry.

The University of Arizona, Mel and Enid Zuckerman College of Public Health, Program in Biostatistics, Tucson, AZ 85721. Offers PhD. *Faculty:* 9 full-time (6 women), 1 (woman) part-time/adjunct. *Students:* 14 full-time (7 women), 2 part-time (both women); includes 5 minority (2 Black or African American, non-Hispanic/Latino; 1 Asian, non-Hispanic/Latino; 2 Hispanic/Latino), 4 international. Average age 31. 29 applicants, 34% accepted, 3 enrolled. *Entrance requirements:* Additional exam requirements/recommendations for international students: Required—TOEFL (minimum score 550 paper-based; 213 computer-based; 79 iBT). *Application deadline:* For fall admission, 1/1 for domestic and international students. Applications are processed on a rolling basis. Application fee: $75. Electronic applications accepted. *Expenses:* Tuition, state resident: full-time $10,840. Tuition, nonresident: full-time $25,802. *Financial support:* In 2011–12, 4 research assistantships (averaging $18,151 per year), 14 teaching assistantships (averaging $18,469 per year) were awarded. *Total annual research expenditures:* $4.2 million. *Unit head:* Dr. Iman Hakim, Interim Dean, 520-626-7083, E-mail: ihakim@email.arizona.edu. *Application contact:* Lorraine Varela, Special Assistant to the Dean, 520-626-3201, E-mail: varela1@coph.arizona.edu.

University of California, Berkeley, Graduate Division, School of Public Health, Group in Biostatistics, Berkeley, CA 94720-1500. Offers MA, PhD. *Accreditation:* CEPH (one or more programs are accredited). *Degree requirements:* For master's, oral exam; for doctorate, thesis/dissertation, oral exam. *Entrance requirements:* For master's and doctorate, GRE General Test, minimum GPA of 3.0, 3 letters of recommendation. Additional exam requirements/recommendations for international students: Required—TOEFL.

University of California, Davis, Graduate Studies, Graduate Group in Biostatistics, Davis, CA 95616. Offers MS, PhD. *Degree requirements:* For master's, comprehensive exam; for doctorate, thesis/dissertation. *Entrance requirements:* Additional exam requirements/recommendations for international students: Required—TOEFL (minimum score 550 paper-based; 213 computer-based). Electronic applications accepted.

University of California, Los Angeles, Graduate Division, School of Public Health, Department of Biostatistics, Los Angeles, CA 90095. Offers MPH, MS, Dr PH, PhD. *Degree requirements:* For master's, comprehensive exam; for doctorate, thesis/dissertation, oral and written qualifying exams. *Entrance requirements:* For master's, GRE General Test, minimum GPA of 3.0; for doctorate, GRE General Test, minimum undergraduate GPA of 3.0. Electronic applications accepted.

University of Cincinnati, Graduate School, College of Medicine, Graduate Programs in Biomedical Sciences, Department of Environmental Health, Cincinnati, OH 45221. Offers environmental and industrial hygiene (MS, PhD); environmental and occupational medicine (MS); environmental genetics and molecular toxicology (MS, PhD); epidemiology and biostatistics (MS, PhD); occupational safety and ergonomics (MS, PhD). *Accreditation:* ABET (one or more programs are accredited). Terminal master's awarded for partial completion of doctoral program. *Degree requirements:* For master's, thesis; for doctorate, thesis/dissertation, qualifying exam. *Entrance requirements:* For master's, GRE General Test, bachelor's degree in science; for doctorate, GRE General Test. Additional exam requirements/recommendations for international students: Required—TOEFL (minimum score 600 paper-based; 250 computer-based; 100 iBT). Electronic applications accepted. *Faculty research:* Carcinogens and mutagenesis, pulmonary studies, reproduction and development.

University of Colorado Denver, Colorado School of Public Health, Department of Biostatistics and Informatics, Aurora, CO 80045. Offers MS, PhD. Part-time programs available. *Students:* 18 full-time (8 women), 14 part-time (8 women); includes 7 minority (1 American Indian or Alaska Native, non-Hispanic/Latino; 3 Asian, non-Hispanic/Latino; 2 Hispanic/Latino; 1 Two or more races, non-Hispanic/Latino), 3 international. Average age 32. 68 applicants, 24% accepted, 14 enrolled. In 2011, 5 master's awarded. Terminal master's awarded for partial completion of doctoral program. *Degree requirements:* For master's, thesis or alternative, 34 credit hours, project or thesis; for doctorate, comprehensive exam, thesis/dissertation, 78 credit hours (25 of which can be completed while completing a master's degree). *Entrance requirements:* For master's, GRE General Test, baccalaureate degree in scientific field, minimum GPA of 3.0, math course work through integral calculus, two official copies of all academic transcripts, four letters of recommendation/reference, essays describing the applicant's career goals and reasons for applying to the program, resume; for doctorate, GRE General Test, baccalaureate degree in scientific field; master's degree in biostatistics, statistics or equivalent; minimum GPA of 3.0; math course work through integral calculus; two official copies of all academic transcripts; four letters of recommendation/reference; essays; resume. Additional exam requirements/recommendations for international students: Required—TOEFL (minimum score 550 paper-based; 213 computer-based; 80 iBT). *Application deadline:* For fall admission, 2/1 for domestic students. Application fee: $65. Electronic applications accepted. *Expenses:* Contact institution. *Financial support:* Fellowships, research assistantships, Federal Work-Study, scholarships/grants, and unspecified assistantships available. Financial award application deadline: 3/1; financial award applicants required to submit FAFSA. *Faculty research:* Health policy research, nonlinear mixed effects models for longitudinal data, statistical methods in nutrition, clinical trials. *Unit head:* Dr. Gary Grunwald, Director, 303-724-4360, Fax: 303-724-4620, E-mail: gary.grunwald@ucdenver.edu. *Application contact:* Fayette Augillard, Program Coordinator, 303-724-4442, Fax: 303-724-4620, E-mail: fayette.augillard@ucdenver.edu. Web site: http://www.ucdenver.edu/academics/colleges/PublicHealth/departments/Biostatistics/Pages/welcome.aspx.

University of Florida, Graduate School, College of Public Health and Health Professions, Programs in Public Health, Gainesville, FL 32611. Offers biostatistics (MPH); environmental health (MPH); epidemiology (MPH); public health management and policy (MPH); public health practice (MPH); social and behavioral sciences (MPH). *Accreditation:* CEPH. Postbaccalaureate distance learning degree programs offered. *Students:* 76 full-time (57 women), 21 part-time (13 women); includes 33 minority (15 Black or African American, non-Hispanic/Latino; 12 Asian, non-Hispanic/Latino; 6 Hispanic/Latino), 7 international. Average age 30. 313 applicants, 49% accepted, 63 enrolled. In 2011, 66 master's awarded. *Degree requirements:* For master's, internship. *Entrance requirements:* For master's, GRE General Test, minimum GPA of 3.0. Additional exam requirements/recommendations for international students: Required—TOEFL (minimum score 550 paper-based; 213 computer-based; 80 iBT), IELTS (minimum score 6). Application fee: $30. *Financial support:* In 2011–12, 14 students received support, including 1 fellowship, 11 research assistantships, 2 teaching assistantships. Financial award applicants required to submit FAFSA. *Unit head:* Mary Peoples Sheps, Senior Associate Dean for Public Health, 352-273-6084, Fax: 352-273-6448, E-mail: mpeoplessheps@phhp.ufl.edu. Web site: http://www.mph.ufl.edu/.

University of Illinois at Chicago, Graduate College, School of Public Health, Biostatistics Section, Chicago, IL 60607-7128. Offers biostatistics (MS, PhD); quantitative methods (MPH). Part-time programs available. Terminal master's awarded for partial completion of doctoral program. *Degree requirements:* For master's, thesis, field practicum; for doctorate, thesis/dissertation, independent research, internship. *Entrance requirements:* For master's and doctorate, GRE General Test, minimum GPA of 2.75. Additional exam requirements/recommendations for international students: Required—TOEFL. Electronic applications accepted.

The University of Iowa, Graduate College, College of Public Health, Department of Biostatistics, Iowa City, IA 52242-1316. Offers MS, PhD. *Degree requirements:* For master's, thesis optional, exam; for doctorate, comprehensive exam, thesis/dissertation. *Entrance requirements:* For master's and doctorate, GRE General Test, minimum GPA of 3.0. Additional exam requirements/recommendations for international students: Required—TOEFL (minimum score 600 paper-based; 250 computer-based; 100 iBT). Electronic applications accepted.

The University of Kansas, University of Kansas Medical Center, School of Medicine, Department of Biostatistics, Kansas City, KS 66160. Offers MS, PhD. *Faculty:* 14 full-time (2 women), 4 part-time/adjunct. *Students:* 9 full-time (7 women), 1 (woman) part-time, 6 international. Average age 28. 17 applicants, 53% accepted, 6 enrolled. *Degree requirements:* For master's, comprehensive exam; for doctorate, comprehensive exam, thesis/dissertation. *Entrance requirements:* For master's, GRE, coursework in calculus, computer programming, linear algebra, differential equations, and numerical analysis; for doctorate, master's degree. Additional exam requirements/recommendations for international students: Required—TOEFL. *Application deadline:* For fall admission, 3/1 for domestic and international students. Application fee: $60. Electronic applications accepted. Tuition and fees vary according to course load, campus/location, program and reciprocity agreements. *Financial support:* Research assistantships with full tuition reimbursements, scholarships/grants, traineeships, and unspecified assistantships available. Financial award application deadline: 2/14; financial award applicants required to submit FAFSA. *Faculty research:* Biostatistics, clinical trials. *Total annual research expenditures:* $280,581. *Unit head:* Dr. Matthew Mayo, Chair and Professor, 913-588-4735 Ext. 913, Fax: 913-588-0252, E-mail: mmayo@kumc.edu. *Application contact:* Tamela Loos, Graduate Education Coordinator, 913-588-2757, Fax: 913-945-7977, E-mail: tloos@kumc.edu. Web site: http://biostatistics.kumc.edu/.

The University of Kansas, University of Kansas Medical Center, School of Medicine, Department of Preventive Medicine and Public Health, Kansas City, KS 66160. Offers biostatistics (MPH); clinical research (MS); environmental health sciences (MPH); epidemiology (MPH); public health management (MPH); social and behavioral health (MPH); MD/MPH; MPH/MSN; PhD/MPH. Part-time programs available. *Faculty:* 76. *Students:* 51 full-time (32 women), 74 part-time (53 women); includes 35 minority (10 Black or African American, non-Hispanic/Latino; 4 American Indian or Alaska Native, non-Hispanic/Latino; 9 Asian, non-Hispanic/Latino; 8 Hispanic/Latino; 4 Two or more races, non-Hispanic/Latino), 6 international. Average age 33. 77 applicants, 69% accepted, 45 enrolled. In 2011, 25 master's awarded. *Degree requirements:* For master's, thesis, capstone practicum defense. *Entrance requirements:* For master's, GRE, MCAT, LSAT, GMAT or other equivalent graduate professional exam. Additional exam requirements/recommendations for international students: Required—TOEFL. *Application deadline:* For fall admission, 3/1 for domestic and international students. Applications are processed on a rolling basis. Application fee: $60. Tuition and fees vary according to course load, campus/location, program and reciprocity agreements. *Financial support:* In 2011–12, 21 research assistantships (averaging $10,200 per year) were awarded; career-related internships or fieldwork, Federal Work-Study, scholarships/grants, and unspecified assistantships also available. Financial award application deadline: 2/14; financial award applicants required to submit FAFSA. *Faculty research:* Cancer screening and prevention, smoking cessation, obesity and physical activity, health services/outcomes research. *Total annual research expenditures:* $8 million. *Unit head:* Dr. Edward F. Ellerbeck, Chairman, 913-588-2774, Fax: 913-588-2780, E-mail: eellerbe@kumc.edu. *Application contact:* Tanya Honderick, Assistant Director, KU-MPH, 913-588-2720, Fax: 913-588-8505, E-mail: thonderick@kumc.edu. Web site: http://ph.kumc.edu/.

University of Louisville, Graduate School, School of Public Health and Information Sciences, Department of Bioinformatics and Biostatistics, Louisville, KY 40292-0001. Offers biostatistics (MS, PhD); decision science (MS). Part-time programs available. *Degree requirements:* For master's, thesis; for doctorate, comprehensive exam, thesis/dissertation. *Entrance requirements:* For master's and doctorate, GRE, official transcripts, statement of purpose, resume/curriculum vitae, letters of recommendation. Additional exam requirements/recommendations for international students: Required—TOEFL (minimum score 600 paper-based; 250 computer-based; 100 iBT). Electronic applications accepted. *Expenses:* Tuition, state resident: full-time $9692; part-time $539 per credit hour. Tuition, nonresident: full-time $20,168; part-time $1121 per credit hour. Tuition and fees vary according to program and reciprocity agreements. *Faculty research:* Bioinformatics, compound decision problems, infectious disease modeling, inference, statistical genetics, genomics, clinical trials, information theory, utility theory and measurement.

University of Maryland, Baltimore, School of Medicine, Department of Epidemiology and Public Health, Baltimore, MD 21201. Offers biostatistics (MS); clinical research (MS); epidemiology and preventative medicine (PhD); epidemiology and preventive medicine (MPH, MS); gerontology (PhD); human genetics and genomic (PhD); human genetics and genomic medicine (MS); molecular epidemiology (MS, PhD); toxicology (MS, PhD); JD/MS; MD/PhD; MS/PhD. *Accreditation:* CEPH. Part-time programs available. *Students:* 94 full-time (68 women), 61 part-time (46 women); includes 51 minority (18 Black or African American, non-Hispanic/Latino; 25 Asian, non-Hispanic/Latino; 7 Hispanic/Latino; 1 Two or more races, non-Hispanic/Latino), 21 international. Average age 32. 109 applicants, 32% accepted, 19 enrolled. In 2011, 13 master's, 9 doctorates awarded. *Degree requirements:* For doctorate, comprehensive exam, thesis/dissertation. *Entrance requirements:* For master's and doctorate, GRE General Test. Additional exam requirements/recommendations for international students: Required—TOEFL (minimum score 550 paper-based; 213 computer-based; 80 iBT); Recommended—IELTS (minimum score 7). *Application deadline:* For fall admission, 2/1 for domestic students, 1/15 for international students. Application fee: $50. Electronic applications accepted. *Expenses:* Contact institution. *Financial support:* In 2011–12, research assistantships with partial tuition reimbursements (averaging $25,000 per year) were awarded; fellowships, Federal Work-Study, scholarships/grants, and unspecified assistantships also available. Financial award application deadline: 3/1; financial award applicants required to submit FAFSA. *Unit head:* Dr. Laura Hungerford, Program Director, 410-706-8492, Fax: 410-706-4225. *Application contact:* Danielle Fitzpatrick, Program Coordinator, 410-706-8492, Fax: 410-706-4225, E-mail: dfitzpatrick@epi.umaryland.edu. Web site: http://epidemiology.umaryland.edu/Pages/Home.aspx.

University of Maryland, Baltimore County, Graduate School, College of Natural and Mathematical Sciences, Department of Mathematics and Statistics, Program in Statistics, Baltimore, MD 21250. Offers biostatistics (PhD); environmental statistics (MS); statistics (MS, PhD). Part-time and evening/weekend programs available. *Faculty:* 8 full-time (3 women). *Students:* 32 full-time (14 women), 24 part-time (12 women); includes 13 minority (5 Black or African American, non-Hispanic/Latino; 8 Asian, non-Hispanic/Latino), 22 international. Average age 30. 42 applicants, 86% accepted, 14 enrolled. In 2011, 13 master's, 4 doctorates awarded. Terminal master's awarded for partial completion of doctoral program. *Degree requirements:* For master's, comprehensive exam (for some programs), thesis (for some programs); for doctorate, comprehensive exam, thesis/dissertation. *Entrance requirements:* For master's and doctorate, GRE General Test, minimum GPA of 3.0. Additional exam requirements/recommendations for international students: Required—TOEFL (minimum score 600 paper-based; 250 computer-based; 100 iBT). *Application deadline:* For fall admission, 2/15 priority date for domestic students, 1/1 for international students; for spring admission, 10/15 priority date for domestic students, 5/1 for international students.

Applications are processed on a rolling basis. Application fee: $50. Electronic applications accepted. *Financial support:* In 2011–12, 23 students received support, including 4 research assistantships with full tuition reimbursements available (averaging $15,500 per year), 19 teaching assistantships with full tuition reimbursements available (averaging $15,500 per year); fellowships with full tuition reimbursements available, career-related internships or fieldwork, scholarships/grants, health care benefits, tuition waivers (full and partial), and unspecified assistantships also available. Support available to part-time students. Financial award application deadline: 2/15. *Faculty research:* Design of experiments, statistical decision theory and inference, time series analysis, biostatistics and environmental statistics, bioinformatics. *Total annual research expenditures:* $402,833. *Unit head:* Dr. Junyong Park, Director, 410-455-2407, Fax: 410-455-1066, E-mail: junpark@umbc.edu. Web site: http://www.math.umbc.edu.

University of Maryland, College Park, Academic Affairs, School of Public Health, Department of Epidemiology and Biostatistics, College Park, MD 20742. Offers biostatistics (MPH); epidemiology (MPH, PhD). *Faculty:* 13 full-time (9 women), 6 part-time/adjunct (3 women). *Students:* 18 full-time (12 women), 13 part-time (9 women); includes 11 minority (1 Black or African American, non-Hispanic/Latino; 7 Asian, non-Hispanic/Latino; 1 Hispanic/Latino; 2 Two or more races, non-Hispanic/Latino), 3 international. 173 applicants, 10% accepted, 13 enrolled. In 2011, 6 master's, 1 doctorate awarded. *Application deadline:* For fall admission, 1/15 for domestic and international students. Application fee: $75. *Expenses: Tuition, area resident:* Part-time $525 per credit hour. Tuition, state resident: part-time $525 per credit hour. Tuition, nonresident: part-time $1131 per credit hour. *Required fees:* $386.31 per term. Tuition and fees vary according to program. *Financial support:* In 2011–12, 4 fellowships with full and partial tuition reimbursements (averaging $18,850 per year), 7 research assistantships (averaging $16,015 per year), 5 teaching assistantships (averaging $15,969 per year) were awarded. *Total annual research expenditures:* $1.2 million. *Unit head:* Dr. Mei-Ling Lee, Chair, 301-405-4581, E-mail: mltlee@umd.edu. *Application contact:* Dr. Charles A. Caramello, Dean of Graduate School, 301-405-0358, Fax: 301-314-9305. Web site: http://www.sph.umd.edu/epib/.

University of Massachusetts Amherst, Graduate School, School of Public Health and Health Sciences, Department of Public Health, Amherst, MA 01003. Offers biostatistics (MPH, MS, PhD); community health education (MPH, MS, PhD); environmental health sciences (MPH, MS, PhD); epidemiology (MPH, MS, PhD); health policy and management (MPH, MS, PhD); nutrition (MPH, PhD); public health practice (MPH); MPH/MPPA. *Accreditation:* CEPH (one or more programs are accredited). Part-time and evening/weekend programs available. Postbaccalaureate distance learning degree programs offered (no on-campus study). *Faculty:* 46 full-time (26 women). *Students:* 118 full-time (88 women), 249 part-time (183 women); includes 75 minority (28 Black or African American, non-Hispanic/Latino; 21 Asian, non-Hispanic/Latino; 20 Hispanic/Latino; 6 Two or more races, non-Hispanic/Latino), 55 international. Average age 36. 377 applicants, 67% accepted, 91 enrolled. In 2011, 83 master's, 4 doctorates awarded. Terminal master's awarded for partial completion of doctoral program. *Degree requirements:* For master's, thesis (for some programs); for doctorate, comprehensive exam, thesis/dissertation. *Entrance requirements:* For master's and doctorate, GRE General Test. Additional exam requirements/recommendations for international students: Required—TOEFL (minimum score 550 paper-based; 213 computer-based; 80 iBT), IELTS (minimum score 6.5). *Application deadline:* For fall admission, 2/1 for domestic and international students. Applications are processed on a rolling basis. Application fee: $40 ($65 for international students). Electronic applications accepted. Tuition and fees vary according to course load, campus/location and program. *Financial support:* Fellowships with full and partial tuition reimbursements, research assistantships with full and partial tuition reimbursements, teaching assistantships with full and partial tuition reimbursements, career-related internships or fieldwork, Federal Work-Study, scholarships/grants, traineeships, health care benefits, tuition waivers (full and partial), and unspecified assistantships available. Support available to part-time students. Financial award application deadline: 2/1. *Unit head:* Dr. Paula Stamps, Graduate Program Director, 413-545-2861, Fax: 413-545-1645. *Application contact:* Lindsay DeSantis, Interim Supervisor of Admissions, 413-545-0722, Fax: 413-577-0010, E-mail: gradadm@grad.umass.edu. Web site: http://www.umass.edu/sphhs/public_health/.

University of Medicine and Dentistry of New Jersey, UMDNJ–School of Public Health (UMDNJ, Rutgers, NJIT) Piscataway/New Brunswick Campus, Piscataway, NJ 08854. Offers biostatistics (MPH, MS, Dr PH, PhD); clinical epidemiology (Certificate); environmental and occupational health (MPH, Dr PH, PhD, Certificate); epidemiology (MPH, Dr PH, PhD); general public health (Certificate); health education and behavioral science (MPH, Dr PH, PhD); health systems and policy (MPH, PhD); public health preparedness (Certificate); DO/MPH; JD/MPH; MD/MPH; MPH/MBA; MPH/MSPA; MS/MPH; Psy D/MPH. *Accreditation:* CEPH. Part-time and evening/weekend programs available. *Degree requirements:* For master's, thesis, internship; for doctorate, comprehensive exam, thesis/dissertation. *Entrance requirements:* For master's, GRE General Test; for doctorate, GRE General Test, MPH (Dr PH); MA, MPH, or MS (PhD). Additional exam requirements/recommendations for international students: Required—TOEFL. Electronic applications accepted.

University of Memphis, Graduate School, School of Public Health, Memphis, TN 38152. Offers biostatistics (MPH); environmental health (MPH); epidemiology (MPH); health systems management (MPH); public health (MHA); social and

Peterson's Graduate Programs in the Physical Sciences, Mathematics, Agricultural Sciences, the Environment & Natural Resources 2013

facebook.com/petersonspublishing **311**

Biostatistics

behavioral sciences (MPH). Part-time and evening/weekend programs available. Postbaccalaureate distance learning degree programs offered. *Degree requirements:* For master's, comprehensive exam, thesis. *Entrance requirements:* For master's, GRE, letters of recommendation. Additional exam requirements/recommendations for international students: Required—TOEFL. Electronic applications accepted. *Faculty research:* Health and medical savings accounts, adoption rates, health informatics, Telehealth technologies, biostatistics, environmental health, epidemiology, health systems management, social and behavioral sciences.

University of Michigan, School of Public Health, Department of Biostatistics, Ann Arbor, MI 48109. Offers MPH, MS, PhD. MS and PhD offered through the Horace H. Rackham School of Graduate Studies. Terminal master's awarded for partial completion of doctoral program. *Degree requirements:* For doctorate, oral defense of dissertation, qualifying exam. *Entrance requirements:* For master's, GRE General Test; for doctorate, GRE General Test, master's degree. Additional exam requirements/recommendations for international students: Required—TOEFL (minimum score 560 paper-based; 220 computer-based; 100 iBT). Electronic applications accepted. *Faculty research:* Statistical genetics, categorical data analysis, incomplete data, survival analysis, modeling.

University of Michigan, School of Public Health, Program in Clinical Research Design and Statistical Analysis, Ann Arbor, MI 48109. Offers MS. Offered through the Horace H. Rackham School of Graduate Studies; program admits applicants in odd-numbered calendar years only. Evening/weekend programs available. *Degree requirements:* For master's, comprehensive exam. *Entrance requirements:* For master's, GRE General Test or MCAT. Additional exam requirements/recommendations for international students: Recommended—TOEFL (minimum score 560 paper-based; 220 computer-based; 100 iBT). Electronic applications accepted. *Expenses:* Contact institution. *Faculty research:* Survival analysis, missing data, Bayesian inference, health economics, quality of life.

University of Minnesota, Twin Cities Campus, School of Public Health, Major in Biostatistics, Minneapolis, MN 55455-0213. Offers MPH, MS, PhD. Part-time programs available. Terminal master's awarded for partial completion of doctoral program. *Degree requirements:* For master's, comprehensive exam; for doctorate, comprehensive exam, thesis/dissertation. *Entrance requirements:* For master's, GRE General Test, course work in applied statistics, computer programming, multivariable calculus, linear algebra; for doctorate, GRE General Test, bachelor's or master's degree in statistics, biostatistics or mathematics. Additional exam requirements/recommendations for international students: Required—TOEFL (minimum score 600 paper-based; 250 computer-based; 90 iBT). Electronic applications accepted. *Faculty research:* Analysis of spatial and longitudinal data, Bayes/Empirical Bayes methods, survival analysis, longitudinal models, generalized linear models.

The University of North Carolina at Chapel Hill, Graduate School, School of Public Health, Department of Biostatistics, Chapel Hill, NC 27599. Offers MPH, MS, Dr PH, PhD. Part-time programs available. *Degree requirements:* For master's, comprehensive exam, thesis, major paper; for doctorate, comprehensive exam, thesis/dissertation. *Entrance requirements:* For master's and doctorate, GRE General Test, minimum GPA of 3.0. Additional exam requirements/recommendations for international students: Required—TOEFL. Electronic applications accepted. *Faculty research:* Cancer, cardiovascular, environmental biostatistics; AIDS and other infectious diseases; statistical genetics; demography and population studies.

University of North Texas Health Science Center at Fort Worth, School of Public Health, Fort Worth, TX 76107-2699. Offers biostatistics (MPH); community health (MPH); disease control and prevention (Dr PH); environmental and occupational health sciences (MPH); epidemiology (MPH); health administration (MHA); health policy and management (MPH, Dr PH); DO/MPH; MS/MPH; MSN/MPH. MPH offered jointly with University of North Texas; DO/MPH with Texas College of Osteopathic Medicine. *Accreditation:* CEPH. Part-time and evening/weekend programs available. *Degree requirements:* For master's, thesis or alternative, supervised internship; for doctorate, thesis/dissertation, supervised internship. *Entrance requirements:* For master's, GRE General Test. Additional exam requirements/recommendations for international students: Required—TOEFL. Electronic applications accepted.

University of Oklahoma Health Sciences Center, Graduate College, College of Public Health, Program in Biostatistics and Epidemiology, Oklahoma City, OK 73190. Offers biostatistics (MPH, MS, Dr PH, PhD); epidemiology (MPH, MS, Dr PH, PhD). *Accreditation:* CEPH (one or more programs are accredited). Part-time programs available. *Degree requirements:* For master's, comprehensive exam, thesis (for some programs); for doctorate, comprehensive exam, thesis/dissertation. *Entrance requirements:* For master's, 3 letters of recommendation, resume; for doctorate, GRE General Test, letters of recommendation. Additional exam requirements/recommendations for international students: Required—TOEFL (minimum score 570 paper-based; 230 computer-based), TWE. *Faculty research:* Statistical methodology, applied statistics, acute and chronic disease epidemiology.

University of Pennsylvania, Perelman School of Medicine, Biomedical Graduate Studies, Graduate Group in Epidemiology and Biostatistics, Philadelphia, PA 19104. Offers biostatistics (MS, PhD). Part-time programs available. *Faculty:* 108 full-time (40 women). *Students:* 26 full-time (14 women), 7 part-time (2 women); includes 17 minority (all Asian, non-Hispanic/Latino). Average age 25. 84 applicants, 21% accepted, 7 enrolled. In 2011, 6 master's, 4 doctorates awarded. Terminal master's awarded for partial completion of doctoral program. *Degree requirements:* For master's, thesis, evaluations examination; for doctorate, thesis/dissertation, evaluations exam, preliminary exam. *Entrance requirements:* For master's and doctorate, GRE, 1 year of course work in calculus, 1 semester of course work in linear algebra, working knowledge of programming language. Additional exam requirements/recommendations for international students: Required—TOEFL. *Application deadline:* For fall admission, 12/1 for domestic and international students. Application fee: $70. *Expenses: Tuition:* Full-time $26,660; part-time $4944 per course. *Required fees:* $2318; $291 per course. Tuition and fees vary according to course load, degree level and program. *Financial support:* In 2011–12, 28 students received support, including 12 fellowships with full and partial tuition reimbursements available (averaging $24,500 per year), 6 research assistantships with full and partial tuition reimbursements available (averaging $24,500 per year), 1 teaching assistantship with full and partial tuition reimbursement available (averaging $24,500 per year); career-related internships or fieldwork, institutionally sponsored loans, scholarships/grants, traineeships, health care benefits, and unspecified assistantships also available. Financial award application deadline: 12/1. *Faculty research:* Randomized clinical trials, data coordinating centers, methodological approaches to non-experimental epidemiologic studies, theoretical research in biostatistics. *Total annual research expenditures:* $43 million. *Unit head:* Dr. Mary Putt, Director, 215-573-7020, Fax: 215-573-4865, E-mail: mputt@mail.med.upenn.edu. *Application contact:* Catherine Vallejo, Coordinator, Educational Programs in Biostatistics, 215-573-3881, Fax: 215-573-4865, E-mail: vallejo@mail.med.upenn.edu. Web site: http://www.cceb.upenn.edu/.

University of Pittsburgh, Graduate School of Public Health, Department of Biostatistics, Pittsburgh, PA 15260. Offers MPH, MS, PhD. Part-time programs available. *Faculty:* 26 full-time (10 women), 20 part-time/adjunct (8 women). *Students:* 85 full-time (50 women), 12 part-time (9 women); includes 17 minority (4 Black or African American, non-Hispanic/Latino; 11 Asian, non-Hispanic/Latino; 1 Hispanic/Latino; 1 Two or more races, non-Hispanic/Latino), 56 international. Average age 31. 176 applicants, 72% accepted, 22 enrolled. In 2011, 9 master's, 8 doctorates awarded. Terminal master's awarded for partial completion of doctoral program. *Degree requirements:* For master's, thesis; for doctorate, one foreign language, thesis/dissertation. *Entrance requirements:* For master's and doctorate, GRE General Test, previous course work in biology, calculus, and Fortran. Additional exam requirements/recommendations for international students: Required—TOEFL (minimum score 550 paper-based; 80 iBT) or IELTS (minimum score 6.5). *Application deadline:* For fall admission, 3/30 priority date for domestic students, 3/1 for international students; for spring admission, 11/30 for domestic students, 4/5 for international students. Applications are processed on a rolling basis. Application fee: $115. Electronic applications accepted. *Expenses:* Tuition, state resident: full-time $18,774; part-time $760 per credit. Tuition, nonresident: full-time $30,736; part-time $1258 per credit. *Required fees:* $740; $200 per term. Tuition and fees vary according to program. *Financial support:* In 2011–12, 64 students received support, including 2 fellowships with partial tuition reimbursements available (averaging $981 per year), 53 research assistantships with full and partial tuition reimbursements available (averaging $11,732 per year), 9 teaching assistantships with full and partial tuition reimbursements available (averaging $11,891 per year); traineeships and tuition waivers (full and partial) also available. Financial award application deadline: 4/15; financial award applicants required to submit FAFSA. *Faculty research:* Survival analysis, environmental risk assessment, statistical computing, longitudinal data analysis, experimental design. *Total annual research expenditures:* $3.6 million. *Unit head:* Dr. Sally C. Morton, Chair, 412-624-3022, Fax: 412-624-2183, E-mail: scmorton@pitt.edu. *Application contact:* Jessalynn M. Oliver, Department Registrar/Liaison, 412-624-3023, Fax: 412-624-0184, E-mail: jmo39@pitt.edu. Web site: http://www.biostat.pitt.edu/.

University of Puerto Rico, Medical Sciences Campus, Graduate School of Public Health, Department of Social Sciences, Program in Biostatistics, San Juan, PR 00936-5067. Offers MPH. Part-time programs available. *Entrance requirements:* For master's, GRE, previous course work in algebra. *Expenses:* Contact institution.

University of Rochester, School of Medicine and Dentistry, Graduate Programs in Medicine and Dentistry, Department of Biostatistics and Computational Biology, Program in Medical Statistics, Rochester, NY 14627. Offers MS. *Degree requirements:* For master's, internship/applied project. *Expenses: Tuition:* Full-time $41,040.

University of South Carolina, The Graduate School, Arnold School of Public Health, Department of Epidemiology and Biostatistics, Program in Biostatistics, Columbia, SC 29208. Offers MPH, MSPH, Dr PH, PhD. Part-time programs available. *Degree requirements:* For master's, comprehensive exam, thesis (for some programs), practicum (MPH); for doctorate, comprehensive exam, thesis/dissertation (for some programs), practicum (Dr PH). *Entrance requirements:* For master's, GRE General Test; for doctorate, GRE General Test, master's degree. Additional exam requirements/recommendations for international students: Required—TOEFL (minimum score 570 paper-based; 230 computer-based; 88 iBT). Electronic applications accepted. *Faculty research:* Bayesian methods, biometric modeling, nonlinear regression, health survey methodology, measurement of health status.

University of Southern California, Keck School of Medicine and Graduate School, Graduate Programs in Medicine, Department of Preventive Medicine,

Division of Biostatistics, Los Angeles, CA 90089. Offers applied biostatistics/epidemiology (MS); biostatistics (MS, PhD); epidemiology (PhD); genetic epidemiology and statistical genetics (PhD); molecular epidemiology (MS, PhD). *Faculty:* 71 full-time (30 women). *Students:* 97 full-time (51 women); includes 24 minority (18 Asian, non-Hispanic/Latino; 3 Hispanic/Latino; 3 Two or more races, non-Hispanic/Latino), 56 international. Average age 29. 68 applicants, 62% accepted, 17 enrolled. In 2011, 7 master's, 8 doctorates awarded. Terminal master's awarded for partial completion of doctoral program. *Degree requirements:* For master's, thesis; for doctorate, thesis/dissertation. *Entrance requirements:* For master's and doctorate, GRE General Test, GRE Subject Test, minimum GPA of 3.0. Additional exam requirements/recommendations for international students: Required—TOEFL (minimum score 600 paper-based; 300 computer-based; 100 iBT). *Application deadline:* For fall admission, 12/1 priority date for domestic students, 12/1 for international students. Application fee: $85. Electronic applications accepted. *Financial support:* In 2011–12, 3 fellowships with full tuition reimbursements (averaging $29,100 per year), 43 research assistantships with full tuition reimbursements (averaging $29,100 per year), 22 teaching assistantships with full and partial tuition reimbursements (averaging $14,550 per year) were awarded; career-related internships or fieldwork, Federal Work-Study, institutionally sponsored loans, scholarships/grants, traineeships, health care benefits, and unspecified assistantships also available. Financial award application deadline: 5/4; financial award applicants required to submit CSS PROFILE or FAFSA. *Faculty research:* Clinical trials in ophthalmology and cancer research, methods of analysis for epidemiological studies, genetic epidemiology. *Total annual research expenditures:* $1.3 million. *Unit head:* Dr. William Gauderman, Director, 323-442-2633, Fax: 323-442-2993, E-mail: mtrujill@usc.edu. *Application contact:* Mary L. Trujillo, Student Adviser, 323-442-2633, Fax: 323-442-2993, E-mail: mtrujill@usc.edu. Web site: http://keck.usc.edu/Education/Academic_Department_and_Divisions/Department_of_Preventive_Medicine/Divisions/Biostatistics.aspx.

See Display below and Close-Up on page 391.

University of Southern California, Keck School of Medicine and Graduate School, Graduate Programs in Medicine, Department of Preventive Medicine, Master of Public Health Program, Los Angeles, CA 90032-3628. Offers biostatistics/epidemiology (MPH); child and family health (MPH); environmental health (MPH); global health leadership (MPH); health communication (MPH); health education and promotion (MPH); public health policy (MPH). *Accreditation:* CEPH. Part-time programs available. *Faculty:* 22 full-time (12 women), 3 part-time/adjunct (0 women). *Students:* 148 full-time (115 women), 35 part-time (23 women); includes 100 minority (8 Black or African American, non-Hispanic/Latino; 66 Asian, non-Hispanic/Latino; 26 Hispanic/Latino), 26 international. Average age 24. 218 applicants, 73% accepted, 88 enrolled. In 2011, 91 master's awarded. *Degree requirements:* For master's, practicum, final report, oral presentation.

Entrance requirements: For master's, GRE General Test, MCAT, GMAT, minimum GPA of 3.0. Additional exam requirements/recommendations for international students: Required—TOEFL (minimum score 600 paper-based; 250 computer-based; 100 iBT). *Application deadline:* For fall admission, 6/1 priority date for domestic students, 6/1 for international students; for spring admission, 11/1 priority date for domestic students, 10/1 for international students. Applications are processed on a rolling basis. Application fee: $85. Electronic applications accepted. *Financial support:* In 2011–12, 148 students received support. Career-related internships or fieldwork, Federal Work-Study, institutionally sponsored loans, and scholarships/grants available. Support available to part-time students. Financial award application deadline: 5/4; financial award applicants required to submit CSS PROFILE or FAFSA. *Faculty research:* Substance abuse prevention, cancer and heart disease prevention, mass media and health communication research, health promotion, treatment compliance. *Unit head:* Dr. Louise A. Rohrbach, Director, 323-442-8237, Fax: 323-442-8297, E-mail: rohrbac@usc.edu. *Application contact:* Chrystal Romero, Admissions Counselor, 323-442-7257, Fax: 323-442-8297, E-mail: ccromero@usc.edu. Web site: http://mph.usc.edu/main.php.

University of Southern Mississippi, Graduate School, College of Health, Department of Community Health Sciences, Hattiesburg, MS 39406-0001. Offers epidemiology and biostatistics (MPH); health education (MPH); health policy/administration (MPH); occupational/environmental health (MPH); public health nutrition (MPH). *Accreditation:* CEPH. Part-time and evening/weekend programs available. *Faculty:* 8 full-time (4 women), 1 part-time/adjunct (0 women). *Students:* 81 full-time (66 women), 17 part-time (13 women); includes 49 minority (43 Black or African American, non-Hispanic/Latino; 1 Asian, non-Hispanic/Latino; 2 Hispanic/Latino; 3 Two or more races, non-Hispanic/Latino), 7 international. Average age 32. 70 applicants, 94% accepted, 43 enrolled. In 2011, 45 degrees awarded. *Degree requirements:* For master's, comprehensive exam, thesis (for some programs). *Entrance requirements:* For master's, GRE General Test, minimum GPA of 2.75 in last 60 hours. Additional exam requirements/recommendations for international students: Required—TOEFL, IELTS. *Application deadline:* For fall admission, 3/1 priority date for domestic students, 3/1 for international students; for spring admission, 1/10 priority date for domestic students, 1/10 for international students. Applications are processed on a rolling basis. Application fee: $50. Electronic applications accepted. *Financial support:* In 2011–12, 5 research assistantships with full tuition reimbursements (averaging $7,000 per year), 1 teaching assistantship with full tuition reimbursement (averaging $8,263 per year) were awarded; career-related internships or fieldwork, Federal Work-Study, institutionally sponsored loans, scholarships/grants, health care benefits, and unspecified assistantships also available. Financial award application deadline: 3/15; financial award applicants required to submit FAFSA. *Faculty research:* Rural health care delivery, school health, nutrition of pregnant teens, risk factor reduction, sexually transmitted diseases.

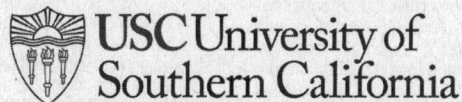
Peterson's Graduate Programs in the Physical Sciences, Mathematics, Agricultural Sciences, the Environment & Natural Resources 2013

facebook.com/petersonspublishing   **313**

Unit head: Dr. Emanual Ahua, Interim Chair, 601-266-5437, Fax: 601-266-5043. *Application contact:* Shonna Breland, Manager of Graduate Admissions, 601-266-6563, Fax: 601-266-5138. Web site: http://www.usm.edu/chs.

University of South Florida, Graduate School, College of Public Health, Department of Epidemiology and Biostatistics, Tampa, FL 33620-9951. Offers MPH, MSPH, PhD. *Accreditation:* CEPH (one or more programs are accredited). Part-time and evening/weekend programs available. *Degree requirements:* For master's, comprehensive exam, thesis (for some programs); for doctorate, comprehensive exam, thesis/dissertation. *Entrance requirements:* For master's, GRE General Test, minimum GPA of 3.0 in upper-level course work, goal statement letter, two professional letters of recommendation, resume/curriculum vitae; for doctorate, GRE General Test, minimum GPA of 3.0 in upper-level course work, 3 professional letters of recommendation, resume/curriculum vitae, writing sample. Additional exam requirements/recommendations for international students: Required—TOEFL (minimum score 550 paper-based; 213 computer-based; 79 iBT). Electronic applications accepted. *Faculty research:* Dementia, mental illness, mental health preventative trails, rural health outreach, clinical and administrative studies.

The University of Texas Health Science Center at Houston, Graduate School of Biomedical Sciences, Program in Biomathematics and Biostatistics, Houston, TX 77225-0036. Offers MS, PhD, MD/PhD. Terminal master's awarded for partial completion of doctoral program. *Degree requirements:* For master's, thesis; for doctorate, thesis/dissertation. *Entrance requirements:* For master's and doctorate, GRE General Test. Additional exam requirements/recommendations for international students: Required—TOEFL. Electronic applications accepted. *Faculty research:* Biostatistics, biomarkers, epidemiology, bioinformatics, computational biology.

The University of Toledo, College of Graduate Studies, College of Medicine and Life Sciences, Department of Public Health and Preventative Medicine, Toledo, OH 43606-3390. Offers biostatistics and epidemiology (Certificate); contemporary gerontological practice (Certificate); environmental and occupational health and safety (MPH); epidemiology (MPH, Certificate); global public health (Certificate); health administration (MPH); health promotion (MPH); medical health and science education (Certificate); nutrition (MPH); occupational health (MSOH, Certificate); public health and emergency response (Certificate); MD/MPH. Part-time and evening/weekend programs available. *Faculty:* 6. *Students:* 95 full-time (74 women), 66 part-time (45 women); includes 37 minority (21 Black or African American, non-Hispanic/Latino; 11 Asian, non-Hispanic/Latino; 3 Hispanic/Latino; 2 Two or more races, non-Hispanic/Latino), 6 international. Average age 29. 132 applicants, 75% accepted, 70 enrolled. In 2011, 60 master's, 26 other advanced degrees awarded. *Degree requirements:* For master's, thesis or alternative. *Entrance requirements:* For master's, GRE, minimum undergraduate GPA of 3.0, three letters of recommendation, statement of purpose, transcripts from all prior institutions attended, resume; for Certificate, minimum undergraduate GPA of 3.0, three letters of recommendation, statement of purpose, transcripts from all prior institutions attended, resume. Additional exam requirements/recommendations for international students: Required—TOEFL (minimum score 550 paper-based; 213 computer-based; 80 iBT), IELTS (minimum score 6.5). *Application deadline:* For fall admission, 3/15 for domestic and international students. Applications are processed on a rolling basis. Application fee: $45 ($75 for international students). Electronic applications accepted. *Financial support:* In 2011–12, 15 research assistantships with full tuition reimbursements (averaging $10,000 per year) were awarded; Federal Work-Study, institutionally sponsored loans, scholarships/grants, tuition waivers (full and partial), and unspecified assistantships also available. *Unit head:* Dr. Sheryl A. Milz, Chair, 419-383-3976, Fax: 419-383-6140, E-mail: sheryl.milz@utoledo.edu. *Application contact:* Joan Mulligan, Admissions Analyst, 419-383-4186, Fax: 419-383-6140, E-mail: joan.mulligan@utoledo.edu. Web site: http://nocphmph.org/.

University of Toronto, School of Graduate Studies, Dalla Lana School of Public Health, Toronto, ON M5S 1A1, Canada. Offers biostatistics (M Sc, PhD); community health (M Sc); epidemiology (MPH, PhD); health and behavioral science (PhD); health promotion (MPH); social science and health (PhD). *Accreditation:* CAHME (one or more programs are accredited); CEPH (one or more programs are accredited). Part-time programs available. *Degree requirements:* For master's, thesis (for some programs), practicum; for doctorate, comprehensive exam, thesis/dissertation, oral thesis defense. *Entrance requirements:* For master's, 2 letters of reference, relevant professional/research experience, minimum B average in final year; for doctorate, 2 letters of reference, relevant professional/research experience, minimum B+ average. Additional exam requirements/recommendations for international students: Required—TOEFL (minimum score 580 paper-based; 93 iBT), TWE (minimum score 5). Electronic applications accepted. *Expenses:* Contact institution.

University of Utah, Graduate School, Interdepartmental Program in Statistics, Salt Lake City, UT 84112-1107. Offers biostatistics (M Stat); econometrics (M Stat); educational psychology (M Stat); mathematics (M Stat); sociology (M Stat); statistics (M Stat). Part-time programs available. *Students:* 25 full-time (10 women), 28 part-time (8 women); includes 8 minority (2 Black or African American, non-Hispanic/Latino; 3 Asian, non-Hispanic/Latino; 3 Hispanic/Latino), 15 international. Average age 33. 59 applicants, 44% accepted, 12 enrolled. In 2011, 18 master's awarded. *Degree requirements:* For master's, comprehensive exam, projects. *Entrance requirements:* For master's, GRE General Test (sociology and educational psychology), minimum GPA of 3.0; course work in

calculus, matrix theory, statistics. Additional exam requirements/recommendations for international students: Required—TOEFL (minimum score 500 paper-based; 173 computer-based; 61 iBT). *Application deadline:* For fall admission, 7/1 for domestic students, 4/1 for international students. Applications are processed on a rolling basis. Application fee: $55 ($65 for international students). *Financial support:* Career-related internships or fieldwork available. *Faculty research:* Biostatistics, management, economics, educational psychology, mathematics. *Unit head:* Richard Fowles, Chair, University Statistics Committee, 801-581-4577, E-mail: fowles@economics.utah.edu. *Application contact:* Laura Egbert, Coordinator, 801-585-6853, E-mail: laura.egbert@utah.edu. Web site: http://www.math.utah.edu/mstat/.

University of Utah, School of Medicine and Graduate School, Graduate Programs in Medicine, Programs in Public Health, Salt Lake City, UT 84112-1107. Offers biostatistics (M Stat); public health (MPH, MSPH, PhD). *Accreditation:* CEPH (one or more programs are accredited). Part-time programs available. *Degree requirements:* For master's, comprehensive exam, thesis or project (MSPH); for doctorate, comprehensive exam, thesis/dissertation. *Entrance requirements:* For master's and doctorate, GRE General Test, 3 letters of reference, in-person interviews, minimum GPA of 3.0. Additional exam requirements/recommendations for international students: Required—TOEFL (minimum score 550 paper-based; 175 computer-based). Electronic applications accepted. *Faculty research:* Health services, health policy, epidemiology of chronic disease, infectious disease epidemiology, cancer epidemiology.

University of Vermont, Graduate College, College of Engineering and Mathematics, Department of Mathematics and Statistics, Program in Biostatistics, Burlington, VT 05405. Offers MS. *Students:* 9 (3 women); includes 2 minority (1 Black or African American, non-Hispanic/Latino; 1 Asian, non-Hispanic/Latino), 1 international. 23 applicants, 91% accepted, 6 enrolled. *Degree requirements:* For master's, thesis or alternative. *Entrance requirements:* Additional exam requirements/recommendations for international students: Required—TOEFL (minimum score 550 paper-based; 213 computer-based; 80 iBT). *Application deadline:* For fall admission, 4/1 priority date for domestic students, 4/1 for international students. Applications are processed on a rolling basis. Application fee: $40. Electronic applications accepted. *Financial support:* Fellowships, research assistantships, and teaching assistantships available. Financial award application deadline: 3/1. *Unit head:* Prof. James Burgmeier, Chair, 802-656-2940. *Application contact:* Prof. Ruth Mickey, Coordinator, 802-656-2940.

University of Washington, Graduate School, Interdisciplinary Graduate Program in Quantitative Ecology and Resource Management, Seattle, WA 98195. Offers MS, PhD. *Degree requirements:* For master's, thesis; for doctorate, thesis/dissertation. *Entrance requirements:* For master's and doctorate, GRE General Test, minimum GPA of 3.0. Additional exam requirements/recommendations for international students: Required—TOEFL. Electronic applications accepted. *Faculty research:* Population dynamics, statistical analysis, ecological modeling and systems analysis of aquatic and terrestrial ecosystems.

University of Washington, Graduate School, School of Public Health, Department of Biostatistics, Seattle, WA 98195. Offers biostatistics (MPH, MS, PhD); clinical research (MS), including biostatistics; statistical genetics (PhD). Part-time programs available. *Faculty:* 39 full-time (18 women), 6 part-time/adjunct (2 women). *Students:* 73 full-time (36 women), 7 part-time (2 women); includes 12 minority (10 Asian, non-Hispanic/Latino; 2 Hispanic/Latino), 23 international. Average age 28. 251 applicants, 14% accepted, 17 enrolled. In 2011, 9 master's, 7 doctorates awarded. Terminal master's awarded for partial completion of doctoral program. *Degree requirements:* For master's, comprehensive exam, thesis, practicum (MPH); for doctorate, comprehensive exam, thesis/dissertation. *Entrance requirements:* For master's and doctorate, GRE General Test, coursework on multivariate calculus, linear algebra and probability; minimum GPA of 3.0. Additional exam requirements/recommendations for international students: Required—TOEFL. *Application deadline:* For fall admission, 1/2 for domestic students. Application fee: $75. Electronic applications accepted. *Financial support:* In 2011–12, 73 research assistantships with full tuition reimbursements (averaging $21,000 per year), 19 teaching assistantships with full tuition reimbursements (averaging $21,000 per year) were awarded; scholarships/grants, traineeships, health care benefits, and tuition waivers (partial) also available. *Faculty research:* Statistical methods for survival data analysis, clinical trials, epidemiological case control and cohort studies, statistical genetics. *Unit head:* Dr. Bruce Weir, Department Chair, 206-543-1044. *Application contact:* Alex MacKenzie, Counseling Services Coordinator, 206-543-1044, Fax: 206-543-3286, E-mail: alexam@u.washington.edu. Web site: http://www.biostat.washington.edu/.

University of Waterloo, Graduate Studies, Faculty of Mathematics, Department of Statistics and Actuarial Science, Waterloo, ON N2L 3G1, Canada. Offers actuarial science (M Math, PhD); biostatistics (PhD); statistics (M Math, PhD); statistics-biostatistics (M Math); statistics-computing (M Math); statistics-finance (M Math). *Degree requirements:* For master's, research paper or thesis; for doctorate, comprehensive exam, thesis/dissertation. *Entrance requirements:* For master's, honors degree in field, minimum B+ average; for doctorate, master's degree, minimum B+ average. Additional exam requirements/recommendations for international students: Required—TOEFL (minimum score 600 paper-based; 250 computer-based; 90 iBT), TWE (minimum score 4.5). Electronic applications accepted. *Faculty research:* Data analysis, risk theory, inference, stochastic processes, quantitative finance.

314 facebook.com/petersonspublishing

Peterson's Graduate Programs in the Physical Sciences, Mathematics, Agricultural Sciences, the Environment & Natural Resources 2013

The University of Western Ontario, Faculty of Graduate Studies, Biosciences Division, Department of Epidemiology and Biostatistics, London, ON N6A 5B8, Canada. Offers M Sc, PhD. *Accreditation:* CEPH (one or more programs are accredited). Part-time programs available. *Degree requirements:* For master's, thesis; for doctorate, comprehensive exam, thesis proposal defense. *Entrance requirements:* For master's, BA or B Sc honors degree, minimum B+ average in last 10 courses; for doctorate, M Sc or equivalent, minimum B+ average in last 10 courses. *Faculty research:* Chronic disease epidemiology, clinical epidemiology.

Virginia Commonwealth University, Medical College of Virginia-Professional Programs, School of Medicine, School of Medicine Graduate Programs, Department of Biostatistics, Richmond, VA 23284-9005. Offers MS, PhD, MD/PhD. Part-time programs available. Terminal master's awarded for partial completion of doctoral program. *Degree requirements:* For master's, thesis; for doctorate, thesis/dissertation, comprehensive oral and written exams. *Entrance requirements:* For master's and doctorate, GRE, MCAT or DAT. Additional exam requirements/recommendations for international students: Required—TOEFL (minimum score 600 paper-based; 250 computer-based; 100 iBT). Electronic applications accepted. *Expenses:* Tuition, state resident: full-time $9133; part-time $507 per credit. Tuition, nonresident: full-time $18,777; part-time $1043 per credit. *Required fees:* $77 per credit. Tuition and fees vary according to degree level, campus/location, program and student level. *Faculty research:* Health services, linear models, response surfaces, design and analysis of drug/chemical combinations, clinical trials.

Washington University in St. Louis, School of Medicine, Division of Biostatistics, St. Louis, MO 63110. Offers biostatistics (MS); genetic epidemiology (Certificate). Part-time programs available. *Faculty:* 15 full-time (4 women), 9 part-time/adjunct (6 women). *Students:* 8 full-time (5 women), 3 part-time (1 woman); includes 6 minority (1 Black or African American, non-Hispanic/Latino; 5 Asian, non-Hispanic/Latino), 2 international. Average age 30. 20 applicants, 60% accepted, 8 enrolled. In 2011, 8 master's awarded. *Entrance requirements:* For master's, GRE, proficiency in computer programming, statistics and biology/genetics. Additional exam requirements/recommendations for international students: Required—TOEFL (minimum score 600 paper-based; 250 computer-based; 100 iBT), TWE. *Application deadline:* For fall admission, 1/31 for domestic

and international students. Applications are processed on a rolling basis. Application fee: $50. Electronic applications accepted. *Expenses:* Contact institution. *Financial support:* In 2011–12, 8 students received support, including 2 research assistantships (averaging $16,000 per year); Federal Work-Study, scholarships/grants, health care benefits, tuition waivers (partial), and unspecified assistantships also available. Financial award application deadline: 1/31; financial award applicants required to submit FAFSA. *Faculty research:* Biostatistics, clinical trials, cardiovascular diseases, genetics, genetic epidemiology. *Unit head:* Dr. Dabeeru C. Rao, Professor/Director of Biostatistics, 314-362-3608, Fax: 314-362-2693, E-mail: rao@wubios.wustl.edu. *Application contact:* Elaine Halley, Program Manager, 314-362-1384, Fax: 314-362-2693, E-mail: elaine@wubios.wustl.edu. Web site: http://www.biostatistics.wustl.edu.

Yale University, School of Medicine, Yale School of Public Health, New Haven, CT 06520. Offers applied biostatistics and epidemiology (APMPH); biostatistics (MPH, MS, PhD), including global health (MPH); chronic disease epidemiology (MPH, PhD), including global health (MPH); environmental health sciences (MPH, PhD), including global health (MPH); epidemiology of microbial diseases (MPH, PhD), including global health (MPH); global health (APMPH); health management (MPH), including global health; health policy (MPH), including global health; health policy and administration (APMPH, PhD); occupational and environmental medicine (APMPH); preventive medicine (APMPH); social and behavioral sciences (APMPH, MPH), including global health (MPH); JD/MPH; M Div/MPH; MBA/MPH; MD/MPH; MEM/MPH; MFS/MPH; MM Sc/MPH; MPH/MA; MSN/MPH. MS and PhD offered through the Graduate School. *Accreditation:* CEPH. Part-time programs available. Terminal master's awarded for partial completion of doctoral program. *Degree requirements:* For master's, thesis, summer internship; for doctorate, comprehensive exam, thesis/dissertation, residency. *Entrance requirements:* For master's, GMAT, GRE, or MCAT, two years of undergraduate coursework in math and science; for doctorate, GRE General Test. Additional exam requirements/recommendations for international students: Required—TOEFL (minimum score 100 iBT). Electronic applications accepted. *Expenses:* Contact institution. *Faculty research:* Genetic and emerging infections epidemiology, virology, cost/quality, vector biology, quantitative methods, aging, asthma, cancer.

Computational Sciences

American University of Beirut, Graduate Programs, Faculty of Arts and Sciences, Beirut, Lebanon. Offers anthropology (MA); Arabic language and literature (MA); archaeology (MA); biology (MS); chemistry (MS); computational science (MS); computer science (MS); economics (MA); education (MA); English language (MA); English literature (MA); environmental policy planning (MSES); financial economics (MAFE); geology (MS); history (MA); mathematics (MA, MS); Middle Eastern studies (MA); philosophy (MA); physics (MS); political studies (MA); psychology (MA); public administration (MA); sociology (MA); statistics (MA, MS). Part-time programs available. *Faculty:* 154 full-time (44 women), 12 part-time/adjunct (2 women). *Students:* 180 full-time (122 women), 240 part-time (158 women). Average age 25. 336 applicants, 47% accepted, 86 enrolled. In 2011, 57 master's awarded. *Degree requirements:* For master's, one foreign language, comprehensive exam, thesis (for some programs). *Entrance requirements:* For master's, GRE, letter of recommendation. Additional exam requirements/recommendations for international students: Required—TOEFL (minimum score 600 paper-based; 250 computer-based; 97 iBT), IELTS (minimum score 7). *Application deadline:* For fall admission, 4/30 for domestic and international students; for spring admission, 11/1 for domestic and international students. Application fee: $50. *Expenses: Tuition:* Full-time $12,780; part-time $710 per credit. *Required fees:* $528; $528 per credit. Tuition and fees vary according to course load and program. *Financial support:* In 2011–12, 33 students received support. Career-related internships or fieldwork, institutionally sponsored loans, scholarships/grants, health care benefits, and unspecified assistantships available. Financial award application deadline: 2/4; financial award applicants required to submit FAFSA. *Faculty research:* History of composition studies, syntax of Arabic dialects, Oscar Wilde, decadence, Middle Eastern and international politics, neural mechanisms of creativity and consciousness, personality and psycho-socio-cultural-spiritual correlates of negative and positive mental health, philosophy of mind, metaphysics, micropaleontology and stratigraphy, geochemistry, mineralogy and petrology, tectonophysics, Abbasid, Ottoman and Russian history, landscape, Bronze and Iron Age archaeology. *Unit head:* Dr. Patrick McGreevy, Dean, 961-1374374 Ext. 3800, Fax: 961-1744461, E-mail: pm07@aub.edu.lb. *Application contact:* Dr. Salim Kanaan, Director, Admissions Office, 961-1350000 Ext. 2594, Fax: 961-1750775, E-mail: sk00@aub.edu.lb. Web site: http://staff.aub.edu.lb/~webfas.

California Institute of Technology, Division of Engineering and Applied Science, Option in Computation and Neural Systems, Pasadena, CA 91125-0001. Offers MS, PhD. Terminal master's awarded for partial completion of doctoral program. *Degree requirements:* For doctorate, thesis/dissertation, qualifying exam. *Entrance requirements:* For doctorate, GRE General Test. *Faculty*

research: Biological and artificial computational devices, modeling of sensory processes and learning, theory of collective computation.

Carnegie Mellon University, Tepper School of Business, Program in Algorithms, Combinatorics, and Optimization, Pittsburgh, PA 15213-3891. Offers PhD. *Degree requirements:* For doctorate, thesis/dissertation. *Entrance requirements:* For doctorate, GRE General Test.

Chapman University, Schmid College of Science and Technology, Computational Sciences Program, Orange, CA 92866. Offers MS. *Faculty:* 14 full-time (3 women), 14 part-time/adjunct (2 women). *Entrance requirements:* Additional exam requirements/recommendations for international students: Required—TOEFL (minimum score 550 paper-based; 213 computer-based; 80 iBT). Application fee: $60. Tuition and fees vary according to degree level and program. *Financial support:* Fellowships, Federal Work-Study, and scholarships/grants available. Financial award applicants required to submit FAFSA. *Unit head:* Dr. Menas Kafatos, Dean, 714-628-7223, E-mail: jhill@chapman.edu. *Application contact:* Saundra Hoover, Director of Graduate Admissions, 714-997-6786, Fax: 714-997-6713, E-mail: shoover@chapman.edu. Web site: http://www.chapman.edu/SCS/CS/MSCS.asp.

Claremont Graduate University, Graduate Programs, School of Mathematical Sciences, Claremont, CA 91711-6160. Offers computational and systems biology (PhD); computational mathematics and numerical analysis (MA, MS); computational science (PhD); engineering and industrial applied mathematics (PhD); mathematics (PhD); operations research and statistics (MA, MS); physical applied mathematics (MA, MS); pure mathematics (MA, MS); scientific computing (MA, MS); systems and control theory (MA, MS). Part-time programs available. *Faculty:* 6 full-time (0 women), 1 part-time/adjunct (0 women). *Students:* 52 full-time (16 women), 24 part-time (9 women); includes 25 minority (3 Black or African American, non-Hispanic/Latino; 10 Asian, non-Hispanic/Latino; 11 Hispanic/Latino; 1 Two or more races, non-Hispanic/Latino), 17 international. Average age 33. In 2011, 15 master's, 3 doctorates awarded. Terminal master's awarded for partial completion of doctoral program. *Entrance requirements:* For master's and doctorate, GRE General Test. Additional exam requirements/recommendations for international students: Required—TOEFL (minimum score 550 paper-based; 213 computer-based; 80 iBT). *Application deadline:* For fall admission, 2/1 priority date for domestic students. Applications are processed on a rolling basis. Application fee: $60. Electronic applications accepted. *Expenses: Tuition:* Full-time $36,374; part-time $1581 per unit. *Required fees:* $165 per semester. *Financial support:* Fellowships, research assistantships, Federal Work-Study, institutionally sponsored loans, scholarships/grants, and tuition waivers (full and partial) available. Support available to part-time students. Financial award

Peterson's Graduate Programs in the Physical Sciences, Mathematics, Agricultural Sciences, the Environment & Natural Resources 2013

facebook.com/petersonspublishing **315**

application deadline: 2/15; financial award applicants required to submit FAFSA. *Unit head:* Ellis Cumberbatch, Dean, 909-607-3369, Fax: 909-607-8261, E-mail: ellis.cumberbatch@cgu.edu. *Application contact:* Susan Townzen, Program Coordinator, 909-621-8080, Fax: 909-607-8261, E-mail: susan.n.townzen@cgu.edu. Web site: http://www.cgu.edu/pages/168.asp.

Clemson University, Graduate School, College of Engineering and Science, Department of Mathematical Sciences, Clemson, SC 29634. Offers applied and pure mathematics (MS, PhD); computational mathematics (MS, PhD); operations research (MS, PhD); statistics (MS, PhD). Part-time programs available. *Faculty:* 46 full-time (13 women), 10 part-time/adjunct (5 women). *Students:* 119 full-time (50 women), 6 part-time (4 women); includes 5 minority (2 Black or African American, non-Hispanic/Latino; 2 American Indian or Alaska Native, non-Hispanic/Latino; 1 Two or more races, non-Hispanic/Latino), 40 international. Average age 27. 133 applicants, 75% accepted, 31 enrolled. In 2011, 23 master's, 6 doctorates awarded. *Degree requirements:* For master's, thesis optional, final project; for doctorate, thesis/dissertation, qualifying exams. *Entrance requirements:* For master's and doctorate, GRE General Test. Additional exam requirements/recommendations for international students: Required—TOEFL. *Application deadline:* For fall admission, 1/15 priority date for domestic students, 1/15 for international students; for spring admission, 10/1 priority date for domestic students, 9/15 for international students. Applications are processed on a rolling basis. Application fee: $70 ($80 for international students). Electronic applications accepted. *Financial support:* In 2011–12, 113 students received support, including 1 fellowship with full and partial tuition reimbursement available (averaging $10,000 per year), 9 research assistantships with partial tuition reimbursements available (averaging $18,373 per year), 104 teaching assistantships with partial tuition reimbursements available (averaging $17,869 per year); career-related internships or fieldwork, institutionally sponsored loans, scholarships/grants, health care benefits, and unspecified assistantships also available. Support available to part-time students. Financial award application deadline: 4/15. *Faculty research:* Applied and computational analysis, cryptography, discrete mathematics, optimization, statistics. *Total annual research expenditures:* $780,865. *Unit head:* Dr. Robert L. Taylor, Chair, 864-656-5240, Fax: 864-656-5230, E-mail: rtaylo2@clemson.edu. *Application contact:* Dr. K. B. Kulasekera, Graduate Coordinator, 864-656-5231, Fax: 864-656-5230, E-mail: kk@clemson.edu. Web site: http://www.clemson.edu/ces/departments/math/index.html.

The College of William and Mary, Faculty of Arts and Sciences, Department of Computer Science, Program in Computational Operations Research, Williamsburg, VA 23187-8795. Offers computer science (MS), including operations research. Part-time programs available. *Faculty:* 9 full-time (2 women), 2 part-time/adjunct (1 woman). *Students:* 20 full-time (5 women); includes 2 minority (both Black or African American, non-Hispanic/Latino), 4 international. Average age 26. *Degree requirements:* For master's, research project. *Entrance requirements:* For master's, GRE General Test, minimum GPA of 2.5. Additional exam requirements/recommendations for international students: Required—TOEFL. *Application deadline:* For fall admission, 3/1 priority date for domestic students, 3/15 for international students; for spring admission, 11/1 for domestic and international students. Applications are processed on a rolling basis. Application fee: $45. Electronic applications accepted. *Expenses:* Tuition, state resident: full-time $6400; part-time $365 per credit hour. Tuition, nonresident: full-time $19,720; part-time $985 per credit hour. *Required fees:* $4562. *Financial support:* In 2011–12, 13 students received support, including 6 fellowships (averaging $9,000 per year), 7 teaching assistantships with full tuition reimbursements available (averaging $11,500 per year); scholarships/grants, tuition waivers (full), and unspecified assistantships also available. Financial award application deadline: 3/1; financial award applicants required to submit FAFSA. *Faculty research:* Metaheuristics, reliability, optimization, statistics, networks. *Unit head:* Dr. Rex Kincaid, Professor, 757-221-2038, Fax: 757-221-1717, E-mail: rrkinc@math.wm.edu. *Application contact:* Vanessa Godwin, Administrative Director, 757-221-3455, Fax: 757-221-1717, E-mail: cor@cs.wm.edu. Web site: http://www.wm.edu/computerscience/grad/.

Cornell University, Graduate School, Graduate Fields of Engineering, Field of Chemical Engineering, Ithaca, NY 14853-0001. Offers advanced materials processing (M Eng, MS, PhD); applied mathematics and computational methods (M Eng, MS, PhD); biochemical engineering (M Eng, MS, PhD); chemical reaction engineering (M Eng, MS, PhD); classical and statistical thermodynamics (M Eng, MS, PhD); fluid dynamics, rheology and biorheology (M Eng, MS, PhD); heat and mass transfer (M Eng, MS, PhD); kinetics and catalysis (M Eng, MS, PhD); polymers (M Eng, MS, PhD); surface science (M Eng, MS, PhD). *Faculty:* 29 full-time (2 women). *Students:* 106 full-time (30 women); includes 21 minority (3 Black or African American, non-Hispanic/Latino; 14 Asian, non-Hispanic/Latino; 4 Hispanic/Latino), 46 international. Average age 25. 379 applicants, 35% accepted, 53 enrolled. In 2011, 50 master's, 8 doctorates awarded. *Degree requirements:* For master's, thesis (MS); for doctorate, comprehensive exam, thesis/dissertation. *Entrance requirements:* For master's and doctorate, GRE General Test, 2 letters of recommendation. Additional exam requirements/recommendations for international students: Required—TOEFL (minimum score 600 paper-based; 237 computer-based; 77 iBT). *Application deadline:* For fall admission, 1/15 priority date for domestic students. Application fee: $95. Electronic applications accepted. *Financial support:* In 2011–12, 67 students received support, including 24 fellowships with full tuition reimbursements available, 44 research assistantships with full tuition reimbursements available, 5 teaching assistantships with full tuition reimbursements available; institutionally

sponsored loans, scholarships/grants, health care benefits, tuition waivers (full and partial), and unspecified assistantships also available. Financial award applicants required to submit FAFSA. *Faculty research:* Biochemical, biomedical and metabolic engineering; fluid and polymer dynamics; surface science and chemical kinetics; electronics materials; microchemical systems and nanotechnology. *Unit head:* Director of Graduate Studies, 607-255-4550. *Application contact:* Graduate Field Assistant, 607-255-4550, E-mail: dgs@cheme.cornell.edu. Web site: http://www.gradschool.cornell.edu/fields.php?id-25&a-2.

Emory University, Laney Graduate School, Department of Physics, Atlanta, GA 30322-1100. Offers biophysics (PhD); experimental condensed matter physics (PhD); theoretical and computational statistical physics (PhD); MS/PhD. *Faculty:* 19 full-time (2 women). *Students:* 17 full-time (4 women); includes 2 minority (1 Black or African American, non-Hispanic/Latino; 1 Hispanic/Latino), 13 international. Average age 24. 48 applicants, 27% accepted, 10 enrolled. *Degree requirements:* For doctorate, thesis/dissertation, qualifier proposal. *Entrance requirements:* For doctorate, GRE General Test, minimum GPA of 3.0. Additional exam requirements/recommendations for international students: Required—TOEFL (minimum score 600 paper-based). *Application deadline:* For fall admission, 1/3 priority date for domestic students, 1/3 for international students. Application fee: $50. Electronic applications accepted. *Expenses:* Tuition: Full-time $34,800. *Required fees:* $1300. *Financial support:* In 2011–12, 17 students received support. Fellowships, teaching assistantships, institutionally sponsored loans, scholarships/grants, health care benefits, and tuition waivers (full) available. Financial award application deadline: 1/3; financial award applicants required to submit FAFSA. *Faculty research:* Experimental studies of the structure and function of metalloproteins, soft condensed matter, granular materials, biophotonics and fluorescence correlation spectroscopy, single molecule studies of DNA-protein systems. *Total annual research expenditures:* $1.5 million. *Unit head:* Kurt Warncke, Chair, 404-727-4296, Fax: 404-727-0873, E-mail: kwarncke@physics.emory.edu. *Application contact:* Stefan Boettcher, Director of Graduate Studies, 404-727-4298, Fax: 404-727-0873, E-mail: sboettc@emory.edu. Web site: http://www.physics.emory.edu.

Florida State University, The Graduate School, College of Arts and Sciences, Department of Scientific Computing, Tallahassee, FL 32306-4120. Offers computational science (MS, PSM, PhD), including atmospheric science (PhD), biochemistry (PhD), biological science (PhD), computational molecular biology/bioinformatics (PSM), computational science (PhD), geological science (PhD), materials science (PhD), physics (PhD). Part-time programs available. *Faculty:* 14 full-time (2 women). *Students:* 32 full-time (6 women), 3 part-time (0 women); includes 13 minority (1 Black or African American, non-Hispanic/Latino; 11 Asian, non-Hispanic/Latino; 1 Hispanic/Latino), 13 international. Average age 28. 29 applicants, 41% accepted, 9 enrolled. In 2011, 14 master's, 3 doctorates awarded. Terminal master's awarded for partial completion of doctoral program. *Degree requirements:* For master's, thesis (for some programs); for doctorate, comprehensive exam, thesis/dissertation. *Entrance requirements:* For master's and doctorate, GRE General Test, knowledge of at least one object-oriented computing language, 3 letters of recommendations. Additional exam requirements/recommendations for international students: Required—TOEFL (minimum score 550 paper-based; 80 iBT). *Application deadline:* For fall admission, 1/15 for domestic and international students. Application fee: $30. Electronic applications accepted. *Expenses:* Tuition, state resident: full-time $9474; part-time $350.88 per credit hour. Tuition, nonresident: full-time $16,236; part-time $601.34 per credit hour. *Required fees:* $630 per semester. One-time fee: $20. Tuition and fees vary according to course load and campus/location. *Financial support:* In 2011–12, 32 students received support, including 12 research assistantships with full tuition reimbursements available (averaging $20,000 per year), 18 teaching assistantships with full tuition reimbursements available (averaging $20,000 per year); unspecified assistantships also available. Financial award application deadline: 4/15. *Faculty research:* Morphometrics, mathematical and systems biology, mining proteomic and metabolic data, computational materials research at Scientific Computing, advanced 4-D Var Data-Assimilation methods in dynamic meteorology and oceanography, computational fluid dynamics, astrophysics. *Unit head:* Dr. Sam Huckaba, Interim Dean, 850-644-1081. *Application contact:* Maribel Amwake, Graduate Academic Coordinator, 850-644-0143, Fax: 850-644-0098, E-mail: mamwake@fsu.edu. Web site: http://www.sc.fsu.edu.

George Mason University, College of Science, School of Physics, Astronomy and Computational Sciences, Fairfax, VA 22030. Offers applied and engineering physics (MS); computational science (PhD); computational sciences and informatics (MS); physics (PhD). *Faculty:* 55 full-time (11 women), 10 part-time/adjunct (1 woman). *Students:* 49 full-time (12 women), 98 part-time (26 women); includes 23 minority (5 Black or African American, non-Hispanic/Latino; 12 Asian, non-Hispanic/Latino; 6 Hispanic/Latino), 25 international. Average age 35. 79 applicants, 49% accepted, 19 enrolled. In 2011, 12 master's, 17 doctorates, 2 other advanced degrees awarded. *Degree requirements:* For master's, thesis optional. *Entrance requirements:* For master's and doctorate, GRE, baccalaureate degree in related field with minimum GPA of 3.0 in last 60 credit hours; 3 letters of recommendation; expanded goals statement; resume; 2 copies of official transcripts. Additional exam requirements/recommendations for international students: Required—TOEFL (minimum score 570 paper-based; 230 computer-based; 88 iBT), IELTS, Pearson Test of English. *Application deadline:* For fall admission, 4/15 priority date for domestic students; for spring admission, 11/15 priority date for domestic students. Application fee: $65 ($80 for international

316 facebook.com/petersonspublishing

Peterson's Graduate Programs in the Physical Sciences, Mathematics, Agricultural Sciences, the Environment & Natural Resources 2013

students). Electronic applications accepted. *Expenses:* Tuition, state resident: full-time $8750; part-time $364.58 per credit. Tuition, nonresident: full-time $24,092; part-time $1003.83 per credit. *Required fees:* $2514; $104.75 per credit. *Financial support:* In 2011–12, 48 students received support, including 5 fellowships with full tuition reimbursements available (averaging $18,000 per year), 33 research assistantships with full and partial tuition reimbursements available (averaging $15,744 per year), 15 teaching assistantships with full and partial tuition reimbursements available (averaging $13,827 per year); career-related internships or fieldwork, Federal Work-Study, scholarships/grants, unspecified assistantships, and health care benefits (full-time research or teaching assistantship recipients) also available. Support available to part-time students. Financial award application deadline: 3/1; financial award applicants required to submit FAFSA. *Faculty research:* Astronomy, astrophysics, and space and planetary science; astronomy and physics education; atomic physics; biophysics and neuroscience. *Total annual research expenditures:* $6.7 million. *Unit head:* Dr. Michael Summers, Chairman, 703-993-3971, Fax: 703-993-1269, E-mail: msummers@gmu.edu. *Application contact:* Dr. Paul So, Information Contact, 703-993-4377, Fax: 703-993-1269, E-mail: paso@gmu.edu. Web site: http://spacs.gmu.edu/.

Hampton University, Graduate College, Program in Applied Mathematics, Hampton, VA 23668. Offers computational mathematics (MS); nonlinear science (MS); statistics and probability (MS). *Degree requirements:* For master's, thesis optional. *Entrance requirements:* For master's, GRE General Test.

Lehigh University, P.C. Rossin College of Engineering and Applied Science, Department of Mechanical Engineering and Mechanics, Bethlehem, PA 18015. Offers computational engineering and mechanics (MS, PhD); mechanical engineering (M Eng, MS, PhD, MBA/E); polymer science/engineering (M Eng, MS, PhD, MBA/E); MBA/E. Part-time and evening/weekend programs available. Postbaccalaureate distance learning degree programs offered. *Faculty:* 24 full-time (0 women). *Students:* 113 full-time (12 women), 30 part-time (3 women); includes 6 minority (3 Black or African American, non-Hispanic/Latino; 2 Asian, non-Hispanic/Latino; 1 Hispanic/Latino), 79 international. Average age 26. 298 applicants, 50% accepted, 37 enrolled. In 2011, 35 master's, 6 doctorates awarded. Terminal master's awarded for partial completion of doctoral program. *Degree requirements:* For master's, thesis; for doctorate, thesis/dissertation, general exam. *Entrance requirements:* Additional exam requirements/recommendations for international students: Required—TOEFL (minimum score 550 paper-based; 213 computer-based; 79 iBT). *Application deadline:* For fall admission, 7/15 for domestic and international students; for spring admission, 12/1 for domestic and international students. Applications are processed on a rolling basis. Application fee: $75. Electronic applications accepted. *Financial support:* In 2011–12, 47 students received support, including 5 fellowships with full and partial tuition reimbursements available (averaging $24,480 per year), 24 research assistantships with full and partial tuition reimbursements available (averaging $20,700 per year), 12 teaching assistantships with full and partial tuition reimbursements available (averaging $25,092 per year); unspecified assistantships and dean's doctoral assistantships also available. Financial award application deadline: 1/15. *Faculty research:* Thermofluids, dynamic systems, CAD/CAM, computational mechanics, solid mechanics. *Total annual research expenditures:* $3.5 million. *Unit head:* Dr. D. Gary Harlow, Chairman, 610-758-4102, Fax: 610-758-6224, E-mail: dgh0@lehigh.edu. *Application contact:* Jo Ann M. Casciano, Graduate Coordinator, 610-758-4107, Fax: 610-758-6224, E-mail: jmc4@lehigh.edu. Web site: http://www.lehigh.edu/~inmem/.

Marquette University, Graduate School, College of Arts and Sciences, Department of Mathematics, Statistics, and Computer Science, Milwaukee, WI 53201-1881. Offers bioinformatics (MS); computational sciences (MS, PhD); computing (MS); mathematics education (MS). Part-time and evening/weekend programs available. Postbaccalaureate distance learning degree programs offered (minimal on-campus study). *Faculty:* 28 full-time (9 women), 10 part-time/adjunct (5 women). *Students:* 14 full-time (3 women), 77 part-time (18 women); includes 9 minority (2 Black or African American, non-Hispanic/Latino; 7 Asian, non-Hispanic/Latino), 24 international. Average age 30. 86 applicants, 65% accepted, 24 enrolled. In 2011, 15 master's, 1 doctorate awarded. Terminal master's awarded for partial completion of doctoral program. *Degree requirements:* For master's, thesis (for some programs), essay with oral presentation; for doctorate, comprehensive exam, thesis/dissertation, qualifying examination. *Entrance requirements:* For master's, official transcripts from all current and previous colleges/universities except Marquette, three letters of recommendation; for doctorate, GRE General Test, official transcripts from all current and previous colleges/universities except Marquette, three letters of recommendation. Additional exam requirements/recommendations for international students: Required—TOEFL (minimum score 530 paper-based; 78 computer-based). *Application deadline:* For fall admission, 1/15 for domestic and international students. Applications are processed on a rolling basis. Application fee: $50. Electronic applications accepted. *Expenses: Tuition:* Full-time $17,010; part-time $945 per credit hour. Tuition and fees vary according to program. *Financial support:* In 2011–12, 23 students received support, including 4 fellowships (averaging $1,375 per year), 5 research assistantships with full tuition reimbursements available (averaging $17,000 per year), 15 teaching assistantships with full tuition reimbursements available (averaging $17,000 per year); scholarships/grants, health care benefits, tuition waivers (full and partial), and unspecified assistantships also available. Support available to part-time students. Financial award application deadline: 2/15. *Faculty research:* Models of physiological systems, mathematical immunology, computational group theory,

mathematical logic, computational science. *Total annual research expenditures:* $621,359. *Unit head:* Dr. Gary Krenz, Chair, 414-288-7573, Fax: 414-288-1578. *Application contact:* Dr. Francis Pastijn, Director of Graduate Studies, 414-288-5229. Web site: http://www.marquette.edu/mscs/grad.shtml.

Massachusetts Institute of Technology, School of Engineering and School of Science and MIT Sloan School of Management, Program in Computation for Design and Optimization, Cambridge, MA 02139. Offers SM. *Faculty:* 39 full-time (5 women). *Students:* 16 full-time (5 women); includes 1 minority (Hispanic/Latino), 11 international. Average age 25. 72 applicants, 24% accepted, 9 enrolled. In 2011, 23 master's awarded. *Degree requirements:* For master's, thesis. *Entrance requirements:* For master's, GRE General Test. Additional exam requirements/recommendations for international students: Required—IELTS. *Application deadline:* For fall admission, 1/10 for domestic and international students. Application fee: $75. Electronic applications accepted. *Expenses: Tuition:* Full-time $40,460; part-time $630 per credit hour. *Required fees:* $272. *Financial support:* In 2011–12, 11 students received support, including 3 fellowships, 10 research assistantships (averaging $29,000 per year), 1 teaching assistantship (averaging $30,600 per year); institutionally sponsored loans, scholarships/grants, health care benefits, and unspecified assistantships also available. *Faculty research:* Computational methods, partial differential equations, optimization, uncertainty quantification, computational mechanics and materials. *Unit head:* Prof. Nicolas Hadjiconstantinou, Co-Director, 617-253-3725, E-mail: cdo_info@mit.edu. Web site: http://computationalengineering.mit.edu/education/.

McGill University, Faculty of Graduate and Postdoctoral Studies, Faculty of Science, Department of Mathematics and Statistics, Montréal, QC H3A 2T5, Canada. Offers computational science and engineering (M Sc); mathematics and statistics (M Sc, MA, PhD), including applied mathematics (M Sc, MA), pure mathematics (M Sc, MA), statistics (M Sc, MA).

Memorial University of Newfoundland, School of Graduate Studies, Interdisciplinary Program in Computational Science, St. John's, NL A1C 5S7, Canada. Offers computational science (M Sc); computational science (cooperative) (M Sc). *Degree requirements:* For master's, thesis optional. *Entrance requirements:* For master's, honors B Sc or significant background in the field. Electronic applications accepted. *Faculty research:* Scientific computing, modeling and simulation, computational fluid dynamics, polymer physics, computational chemistry.

Miami University, School of Engineering and Applied Science, Computational Science and Engineering Program, Oxford, OH 45056. Offers MS. *Students:* 23 full-time (4 women); includes 2 minority (1 Asian, non-Hispanic/Latino; 1 Hispanic/Latino), 8 international. Average age 24. In 2011, 3 degrees awarded. *Entrance requirements:* For master's, GRE. Additional exam requirements/recommendations for international students: Required—TOEFL. *Application deadline:* For fall admission, 2/1 for domestic and international students. Application fee: $50. *Expenses:* Tuition, state resident: full-time $12,023; part-time $501 per credit hour. Tuition, nonresident: full-time $26,554; part-time $1107 per credit hour. *Required fees:* $528. *Financial support:* Fellowships, research assistantships, teaching assistantships, health care benefits, and unspecified assistantships available. Financial award application deadline: 2/15; financial award applicants required to submit FAFSA. *Unit head:* Dr. Marek Dollar, Dean, 513-529-0700, E-mail: seasfyi@muohio.edu. *Application contact:* School of Engineering and Applied Science, 513-529-0700, E-mail: seasgrad@muohio.edu. Web site: http://www.eas.muohio.edu/graduate-degrees/cse.

Michigan Technological University, Graduate School, Interdisciplinary Programs, Houghton, MI 49931. Offers atmospheric sciences (PhD); computational sciences and engineering (PhD); engineering environmental (PhD). *Students:* 28 full-time (14 women), 4 part-time (0 women), 20 international. Average age 29. 73 applicants, 32% accepted, 10 enrolled. In 2011, 3 doctorates awarded. *Degree requirements:* For doctorate, comprehensive exam, thesis/dissertation. *Entrance requirements:* For doctorate, GRE, statement of purpose, official transcripts, 3 letters of recommendation. Additional exam requirements/recommendations for international students: Required—TOEFL or IELTS. *Expenses:* Tuition, state resident: full-time $12,636; part-time $702 per credit. Tuition, nonresident: full-time $12,636; part-time $702 per credit. *Required fees:* $226; $226 per year. *Financial support:* In 2011–12, 28 students received support, including 3 fellowships with full tuition reimbursements available (averaging $6,065 per year), 17 research assistantships with full tuition reimbursements available (averaging $6,065 per year), 3 teaching assistantships with full tuition reimbursements available (averaging $6,065 per year). *Unit head:* Dr. Jacqueline E. Huntoon, Dean, 906-487-2327, Fax: 906-487-2463, E-mail: jeh@mtu.edu. *Application contact:* Carol T. Wingerson, Senior Staff Assistant, 906-487-2327, Fax: 906-487-2463, E-mail: gradadms@mtu.edu.

North Carolina Agricultural and Technical State University, School of Graduate Studies, College of Arts and Sciences, Department of Physics, Greensboro, NC 27411. Offers computational sciences (MS); physics (MS).

Princeton University, Graduate School, Program in Applied and Computational Mathematics, Princeton, NJ 08544-1019. Offers PhD. *Degree requirements:* For doctorate, thesis/dissertation. *Entrance requirements:* For doctorate, GRE General Test, GRE Subject Test. Additional exam requirements/recommendations for international students: Required—TOEFL (minimum score 600 paper-based; 250 computer-based). Electronic applications accepted.

Peterson's Graduate Programs in the Physical Sciences, Mathematics, Agricultural Sciences, the Environment & Natural Resources 2013

facebook.com/petersonspublishing **317**

SECTION 7: MATHEMATICAL SCIENCES

Computational Sciences

Purdue University, Graduate School, College of Health and Human Sciences, Department of Psychological Sciences, West Lafayette, IN 47907. Offers behavioral neuroscience (PhD); clinical psychology (PhD); cognitive psychology (PhD); industrial/organizational psychology (PhD); mathematical and computational cognitive science (PhD). *Accreditation:* APA. *Faculty:* 43 full-time (14 women), 16 part-time/adjunct (8 women). *Students:* 69 full-time (48 women), 6 part-time (5 women); includes 7 minority (2 Black or African American, non-Hispanic/Latino; 1 American Indian or Alaska Native, non-Hispanic/Latino; 1 Asian, non-Hispanic/Latino; 2 Hispanic/Latino; 1 Two or more races, non-Hispanic/Latino), 19 international. Average age 27. 323 applicants, 11% accepted, 21 enrolled. In 2011, 16 doctorates awarded. Terminal master's awarded for partial completion of doctoral program. *Degree requirements:* For doctorate, thesis/dissertation. *Entrance requirements:* For doctorate, GRE General Test, minimum undergraduate GPA of 3.0 or equivalent. Additional exam requirements/recommendations for international students: Required—TOEFL (minimum score 550 paper-based; 77 iBT); Recommended—TWE. *Application deadline:* For fall admission, 12/3 for domestic and international students. Applications are processed on a rolling basis. Application fee: $60 ($75 for international students). Electronic applications accepted. *Financial support:* Fellowships with partial tuition reimbursements, research assistantships with partial tuition reimbursements, teaching assistantships with partial tuition reimbursements, and career-related internships or fieldwork available. Support available to part-time students. Financial award applicants required to submit FAFSA. *Faculty research:* Career development of women in science, development of friendships during childhood and adolescence, social competence, human information processing. *Unit head:* Dr. Christopher R. Agnew, Head, 765-494-6061, Fax: 765-496-1264, E-mail: agnew@psych.purdue.edu. *Application contact:* Nancy A. O'Brien, Graduate Contact, 765-494-6067, Fax: 765-496-1264, E-mail: nobrien@psych.pardue.edu. Web site: http://www.psych.purdue.edu/.

Rice University, Graduate Programs, George R. Brown School of Engineering, Department of Computational and Applied Mathematics, Houston, TX 77251-1892. Offers computational and applied mathematics (MA, MCAM, PhD); computational science and engineering (PhD). *Degree requirements:* For master's, comprehensive exam (for some programs), thesis (for some programs); for doctorate, comprehensive exam, thesis/dissertation. *Entrance requirements:* For master's and doctorate, GRE General Test, minimum GPA of 3.0. Additional exam requirements/recommendations for international students: Required—TOEFL (minimum score 600 paper-based; 250 computer-based; 90 iBT). Electronic applications accepted. *Faculty research:* Inverse problems, partial differential equations, computer algorithms, computational modeling, optimization theory.

Rice University, Graduate Programs, George R. Brown School of Engineering, Program in Computational Science and Engineering, Houston, TX 77251-1892. Offers MCSE.

The Richard Stockton College of New Jersey, School of Graduate and Continuing Studies, Program in Computational Science, Pomona, NJ 08240-0195. Offers MS. Part-time and evening/weekend programs available. *Faculty:* 3 full-time (0 women), 1 part-time/adjunct (0 women). *Students:* 11 full-time (2 women), 15 part-time (5 women); includes 2 minority (both Asian, non-Hispanic/Latino), 1 international. Average age 29. 17 applicants, 76% accepted, 11 enrolled. *Degree requirements:* For master's, thesis optional. *Entrance requirements:* For master's, GRE. Additional exam requirements/recommendations for international students: Required—TOEFL. *Application deadline:* For fall admission, 7/1 for domestic and international students; for spring admission, 12/1 for domestic and international students. Applications are processed on a rolling basis. Application fee: $50. Electronic applications accepted. *Expenses:* Tuition, state resident: full-time $13,035; part-time $543 per credit. Tuition, nonresident: full-time $20,065; part-time $836 per credit. *Required fees:* $3920; $163 per credit. Tuition and fees vary according to degree level. *Financial support:* In 2011–12, 3 students received support, including 9 research assistantships with partial tuition reimbursements available; fellowships, Federal Work-Study, scholarships/grants, and unspecified assistantships also available. Financial award application deadline: 3/1; financial award applicants required to submit FAFSA. *Unit head:* Dr. J. Russell Manson, Program Director, 609-626-3640, E-mail: gradschool@stockton.edu. *Application contact:* Tara Williams, Assistant Director of Enrollment Management, 609-626-3640, Fax: 609-626-6050, E-mail: gradschool@stockton.edu. Web site: http://www.stockton.edu/grad.

Sam Houston State University, College of Sciences, Department of Computer Science, Huntsville, TX 77341. Offers computing and information science (MS); digital forensics (MS); information assurance and security (MS). Part-time programs available. *Faculty:* 11 full-time (2 women), 26 part-time (2 women). *Students:* 38 full-time (8 women), 26 part-time (2 women); includes 14 minority (7 Black or African American, non-Hispanic/Latino; 1 American Indian or Alaska Native, non-Hispanic/Latino; 6 Hispanic/Latino), 34 international. Average age 28. 29 applicants, 83% accepted, 24 enrolled. In 2011, 20 master's awarded. *Entrance requirements:* For master's, GRE General Test. Additional exam requirements/recommendations for international students: Required—TOEFL (minimum score 550 paper-based; 213 computer-based; 79 iBT). *Application deadline:* For fall admission, 8/1 for domestic and international students; for spring admission, 12/1 for domestic and international students. Application fee: $20. *Expenses:* Tuition, state resident: full-time $4420; part-time $221 per credit hour. Tuition, nonresident: full-time $10,680; part-time $534 per credit hour. *Required fees:*

$329 per credit hour. *Financial support:* Research assistantships, teaching assistantships, Federal Work-Study, institutionally sponsored loans, and tuition waivers (partial) available. Financial award application deadline: 5/31; financial award applicants required to submit FAFSA. *Unit head:* Dr. Peter Cooper, Chair, 936-294-1569, Fax: 936-294-4312, E-mail: css_pac@shsu.edu. *Application contact:* Dr. Jiuhung Ji, Advisor, 936-294-1579, E-mail: csc_jxj@shsu.edu. Web site: http://cs.shsu.edu/.

San Diego State University, Graduate and Research Affairs, College of Sciences, Program in Computational Science, San Diego, CA 92182. Offers MS, PhD. *Degree requirements:* For master's, thesis; for doctorate, thesis/dissertation. *Entrance requirements:* For master's, GRE General Test, 3 letters of recommendation; for doctorate, GRE, 3 letters of recommendation. Additional exam requirements/recommendations for international students: Required—TOEFL. Electronic applications accepted.

Simon Fraser University, Graduate Studies, Faculty of Science, Department of Mathematics, Burnaby, BC V5A 1S6, Canada. Offers applied and computational mathematics (M Sc; PhD); mathematics (M Sc, PhD). *Degree requirements:* For master's, thesis; for doctorate, thesis/dissertation. *Entrance requirements:* For master's, GRE General Test, minimum GPA of 3.0, 3 letters of reference; for doctorate, GRE General Test, minimum GPA of 3.5, 3 letters of reference. Additional exam requirements/recommendations for international students: Required—TWE or IELTS. Electronic applications accepted. *Faculty research:* Semi-groups, number theory, optimization, combinations.

South Dakota State University, Graduate School, College of Engineering, Department of Mathematics and Statistics, Brookings, SD 57007. Offers computational science and statistics (PhD); mathematics (MS); statistics (MS). Part-time programs available. Terminal master's awarded for partial completion of doctoral program. *Degree requirements:* For master's, thesis (for some programs), oral exam; for doctorate, comprehensive exam, thesis/dissertation, oral and written exams. *Entrance requirements:* Additional exam requirements/recommendations for international students: Required—TOEFL (minimum score 550 paper-based; 213 computer-based; 80 iBT); Recommended—IELTS. *Faculty research:* Financial mathematics, predictive analytics, operations research, bioinformatics, biostatistics, computational science, statistics, number theory, abstract algebra.

Southern Illinois University Edwardsville, Graduate School, College of Arts and Sciences, Department of Mathematics and Statistics, Edwardsville, IL 62026. Offers mathematics (MS), including computational mathematics, postsecondary mathematics education, pure math, statistics and operations research. Part-time programs available. *Faculty:* 19 full-time (5 women). *Students:* 13 full-time (2 women), 30 part-time (17 women); includes 2 minority (both Black or African American, non-Hispanic/Latino), 12 international. 34 applicants, 47% accepted. In 2011, 14 master's awarded. *Degree requirements:* For master's, thesis (for some programs), research paper/project. *Entrance requirements:* Additional exam requirements/recommendations for international students: Required—TOEFL (minimum score 550 paper-based; 213 computer-based; 79 iBT), IELTS (minimum score 6.5). *Application deadline:* For fall admission, 7/22 for domestic students, 6/1 for international students; for spring admission, 12/9 for domestic students, 10/1 for international students. Applications are processed on a rolling basis. Application fee: $30. Electronic applications accepted. Tuition and fees vary according to course load and program. *Financial support:* In 2011–12, 3 research assistantships with full tuition reimbursements (averaging $9,927 per year), 22 teaching assistantships with full tuition reimbursements (averaging $9,927 per year) were awarded; fellowships with full tuition reimbursements, institutionally sponsored loans, scholarships/grants, and unspecified assistantships also available. Financial award application deadline: 3/1; financial award applicants required to submit FAFSA. *Unit head:* Dr. Krzysztof Jarosz, Chair, 618-650-2354, E-mail: kjarosz@siue.edu. *Application contact:* Dr. Adam Weyhaupt, Director, 618-650-2220, E-mail: aweyhau@siue.edu. Web site: http://www.siue.edu/artsandsciences/math/.

Southern Methodist University, Dedman College, Department of Mathematics, Dallas, TX 75275. Offers computational and applied mathematics (MS, PhD). *Degree requirements:* For master's, oral exams; for doctorate, thesis/dissertation, oral and written exams. *Entrance requirements:* For master's and doctorate, GRE General Test, minimum GPA of 3.0, 18 undergraduate hours in mathematics beyond first and second year calculus. Additional exam requirements/recommendations for international students: Required—TOEFL. Electronic applications accepted. *Faculty research:* Numerical analysis and scientific computation, fluid dynamics, optics, wave propagation, mathematical biology.

Stanford University, School of Engineering, Program in Scientific Computing and Computational Mathematics, Stanford, CA 94305-9991. Offers MS, PhD. Terminal master's awarded for partial completion of doctoral program. *Degree requirements:* For doctorate, thesis/dissertation, qualifying exam. *Entrance requirements:* For master's, GRE General Test; for doctorate, GRE General Test, GRE Subject Test. Additional exam requirements/recommendations for international students: Required—TOEFL. Electronic applications accepted. *Expenses: Tuition:* Full-time $40,050; part-time $890 per credit.

Temple University, College of Science and Technology, Department of Mathematics, Philadelphia, PA 19122-6096. Offers applied mathematics (MA); mathematics (PhD); pure mathematics (MA). Part-time and evening/weekend programs available. *Faculty:* 14 full-time (1 woman). *Students:* 24 full-time (4 women), 1 (woman) part-time, 4 international. Average age 27. 75 applicants,

29% accepted, 6 enrolled. In 2011, 1 master's, 3 doctorates awarded. Terminal master's awarded for partial completion of doctoral program. *Degree requirements:* For master's, thesis optional, written exam; for doctorate, 2 foreign languages, thesis/dissertation, oral and written exams. *Entrance requirements:* For master's, GRE General Test, minimum GPA of 3.0; for doctorate, GRE General Test, GRE Subject Test, minimum GPA of 3.0. Additional exam requirements/recommendations for international students: Required—TOEFL (minimum score 550 paper-based; 213 computer-based; 79 iBT). *Application deadline:* For fall admission, 2/15 priority date for domestic students, 12/15 for international students; for spring admission, 11/15 priority date for domestic students, 8/1 for international students. Applications are processed on a rolling basis. Application fee: $50. Electronic applications accepted. *Expenses:* Tuition, state resident: full-time $12,366; part-time $687 per credit hour. Tuition, nonresident: full-time $17,298; part-time $961 per credit hour. *Required fees:* $590; $213 per year. *Financial support:* Fellowships, research assistantships, teaching assistantships, Federal Work-Study, and institutionally sponsored loans available. Financial award application deadline: 1/15; financial award applicants required to submit FAFSA. *Faculty research:* Differential geometry, numerical analysis. *Unit head:* Dr. Gerardo Mendoza, Graduate Chair, 215-204-5053, Fax: 215-204-6433, E-mail: mathematics@temple.edu. *Application contact:* Tara Schumacher, Coordinator of Outreach, 215-204-6575, Fax: 215-204-8781, E-mail: tara.schumacher@temple.edu. Web site: http://math.temple.edu/.

University at Buffalo, the State University of New York, Graduate School, College of Arts and Sciences, Center for Computational Research, Buffalo, NY 14260. Offers computational science (Advanced Certificate). *Unit head:* Bruce Pitman, Program Coordinator, 716-881-8966, Fax: 716-881-6656, E-mail: pitman@buffalo.edu. *Application contact:* Joseph C. Syracuse, Graduate Enrollment Manager, 716-645-2711, Fax: 716-645-3888, E-mail: jcs32@buffalo.edu. Web site: http://www.ccr.buffalo.edu/display/WEB/Contact.

University of Alaska Fairbanks, College of Natural Sciences and Mathematics, Department of Physics, Fairbanks, AK 99775-5920. Offers computational physics (MS); physics (MAT, MS, PhD); space physics (MS, PhD). Part-time programs available. *Faculty:* 9 full-time (2 women). *Students:* 27 full-time (7 women), 3 part-time (0 women); includes 3 minority (1 American Indian or Alaska Native, non-Hispanic/Latino; 1 Asian, non-Hispanic/Latino; 1 Hispanic/Latino), 8 international. Average age 29. 18 applicants, 28% accepted, 5 enrolled. In 2011, 1 master's, 2 doctorates awarded. Terminal master's awarded for partial completion of doctoral program. *Degree requirements:* For master's, comprehensive exam, thesis or alternative; for doctorate, comprehensive exam, thesis/dissertation, oral defense. *Entrance requirements:* Additional exam requirements/recommendations for international students: Required—TOEFL (minimum score 550 paper-based; 213 computer-based; 80 iBT). *Application deadline:* For fall admission, 6/1 for domestic students, 3/1 for international students; for spring admission, 10/15 for domestic students, 9/1 for international students. Applications are processed on a rolling basis. Application fee: $60. Electronic applications accepted. *Expenses:* Tuition, state resident: full-time $6696; part-time $372 per credit. Tuition, nonresident: full-time $13,680; part-time $760 per credit. Tuition and fees vary according to course load and reciprocity agreements. *Financial support:* In 2011–12, 17 research assistantships with tuition reimbursements (averaging $14,039 per year), 8 teaching assistantships with tuition reimbursements (averaging $7,927 per year) were awarded; fellowships with tuition reimbursements, Federal Work-Study, scholarships/grants, health care benefits, and unspecified assistantships also available. Support available to part-time students. Financial award application deadline: 2/15; financial award applicants required to submit FAFSA. *Faculty research:* Atmospheric and ionospheric radar studies, space plasma theory, magnetospheric dynamics, space weather and auroral studies, turbulence and complex systems. *Unit head:* Ataur Chowdhury, Chair, 907-474-7339, Fax: 907-474-6130, E-mail: physics@uaf.edu. *Application contact:* Mike Earnest, Director of Admissions, 907-474-7500, Fax: 907-474-5379, E-mail: admissions@uaf.edu. Web site: http://www.uaf.edu/physics/.

University of California, Santa Barbara, Graduate Division, College of Engineering, Department of Computer Science, Santa Barbara, CA 93106-5110. Offers cognitive science (PhD); computational science and engineering (PhD); computer science (MS, PhD); technology and society (PhD). *Faculty:* 32 full-time (5 women), 5 part-time/adjunct (0 women). *Students:* 151 full-time (37 women); includes 9 minority (1 American Indian or Alaska Native, non-Hispanic/Latino; 7 Asian, non-Hispanic/Latino; 1 Two or more races, non-Hispanic/Latino), 101 international. Average age 27. 640 applicants, 20% accepted, 51 enrolled. In 2011, 27 master's, 14 doctorates awarded. Terminal master's awarded for partial completion of doctoral program. *Median time to degree:* Of those who began their doctoral program in fall 2003, 80% received their degree in 8 years or less. *Degree requirements:* For master's, comprehensive exam (for some programs), thesis (for some programs), project (for some programs); for doctorate, thesis/dissertation. *Entrance requirements:* For master's and doctorate, GRE. Additional exam requirements/recommendations for international students: Required—TOEFL (minimum score 600 paper-based; 100 iBT), IELTS (minimum score 7). *Application deadline:* For fall admission, 12/15 for domestic and international students. Application fee: $80 ($100 for international students). Electronic applications accepted. *Expenses:* Tuition, state resident: full-time $12,192. Tuition, nonresident: full-time $27,294. *Required fees:* $764.13. *Financial support:* In 2011–12, 116 students received support, including 36 fellowships with full and partial tuition reimbursements available (averaging $12,330 per year), 63 research assistantships with full and partial tuition reimbursements available (averaging $14,876 per year), 44 teaching assistantships with partial tuition reimbursements available (averaging $17,309 per year); career-related internships or fieldwork, Federal Work-Study, institutionally sponsored loans, scholarships/grants, health care benefits, tuition waivers (full and partial), and unspecified assistantships also available. Financial award application deadline: 12/15; financial award applicants required to submit FAFSA. *Faculty research:* Networking and security, database systems, computational science and engineering, programming languages and software engineering, human-computer interaction. *Unit head:* Subhash Suri, Chair, 805-893-5334, Fax: 805-893-8553, E-mail: suri@cs.ucsb.edu. *Application contact:* Katie Ellis, Graduate Advisor, 805-893-4322, Fax: 805-893-8553, E-mail: kellis@cs.ucsb.edu. Web site: http://www.cs.ucsb.edu/.

University of California, Santa Barbara, Graduate Division, College of Engineering, Department of Mechanical Engineering, Santa Barbara, CA 93106-5070. Offers computational science and engineering (MS, PhD); mechanical engineering (MS, PhD); MS/PhD. *Faculty:* 28 full-time (4 women), 8 part-time/adjunct (3 women). *Students:* 80 full-time (9 women); includes 10 minority (1 Black or African American, non-Hispanic/Latino; 7 Asian, non-Hispanic/Latino; 2 Hispanic/Latino), 28 international. Average age 27. 279 applicants, 19% accepted, 19 enrolled. In 2011, 7 master's, 8 doctorates awarded. *Median time to degree:* Of those who began their doctoral program in fall 2003, 100% received their degree in 8 years or less. *Degree requirements:* For master's, thesis; for doctorate, comprehensive exam, thesis/dissertation. *Entrance requirements:* For master's and doctorate, GRE. Additional exam requirements/recommendations for international students: Required—TOEFL (minimum score 550 paper-based; 213 computer-based; 80 iBT), IELTS (minimum score 7). *Application deadline:* For fall admission, 12/15 for domestic and international students. Application fee: $80 ($100 for international students). Electronic applications accepted. *Expenses:* Tuition, state resident: full-time $12,192. Tuition, nonresident: full-time $27,294. *Required fees:* $764.13. *Financial support:* In 2011–12, 72 students received support, including 7 fellowships with full and partial tuition reimbursements available (averaging $22,000 per year), 27 research assistantships with full and partial tuition reimbursements available (averaging $19,099 per year), 24 teaching assistantships with full and partial tuition reimbursements available (averaging $17,308 per year); scholarships/grants, health care benefits, tuition waivers (full and partial), and unspecified assistantships also available. Financial award application deadline: 12/15; financial award applicants required to submit FAFSA. *Faculty research:* Micro/nanoscale technology; computational science and engineering; dynamics systems, controls and robotics; thermofluid sciences; solid mechanics, materials, and structures. *Total annual research expenditures:* $5.7 million. *Unit head:* Dr. Kimberly Turner, Chair, 805-893-8080, Fax: 805-893-8651, E-mail: turner@engineering.ucsb.edu. *Application contact:* Laura L. Reynolds, Staff Graduate Program Advisor, 805-893-2239, Fax: 805-893-8651, E-mail: megrad@engineering.ucsb.edu. Web site: http://www.me.ucsb.edu/.

University of California, Santa Barbara, Graduate Division, College of Letters and Sciences, Division of Mathematics, Life, and Physical Sciences, Department of Ecology, Evolution, and Marine Biology, Santa Barbara, CA 93106-9620. Offers computational science and engineering (MA); computational sciences and engineering (PhD); ecology, evolution, and marine biology (MA, PhD); MA/PhD. *Faculty:* 27 full-time (7 women). *Students:* 58 full-time (39 women); includes 9 minority (1 Black or African American, non-Hispanic/Latino; 5 Asian, non-Hispanic/Latino; 1 Two or more races, non-Hispanic/Latino), 4 international. Average age 30. 131 applicants, 15% accepted, 8 enrolled. In 2011, 4 master's, 4 doctorates awarded. *Median time to degree:* Of those who began their doctoral program in fall 2003, 100% received their degree in 8 years or less. *Degree requirements:* For master's, comprehensive exam (for some programs), thesis (for some programs); for doctorate, comprehensive exam, thesis/dissertation. *Entrance requirements:* For master's and doctorate, GRE General Test. Additional exam requirements/recommendations for international students: Required—TOEFL (minimum score 550 paper-based; 80 iBT), IELTS. *Application deadline:* For fall admission, 12/15 for domestic and international students. Application fee: $80 ($100 for international students). Electronic applications accepted. *Expenses:* Tuition, state resident: full-time $12,192. Tuition, nonresident: full-time $27,294. *Required fees:* $764.13. *Financial support:* In 2011–12, 54 students received support, including 44 fellowships with full and partial tuition reimbursements available (averaging $10,812 per year), 13 research assistantships with full and partial tuition reimbursements available (averaging $8,441 per year), 22 teaching assistantships with partial tuition reimbursements available (averaging $9,346 per year); Federal Work-Study, scholarships/grants, traineeships, health care benefits, and tuition waivers (full and partial) also available. Financial award application deadline: 12/15; financial award applicants required to submit FAFSA. *Faculty research:* Community ecology, evolution, marine biology, population genetics, stream ecology. *Unit head:* Dr. Cheryl Briggs, Chair, 805-893-2415, Fax: 805-893-5885. *Application contact:* Melanie Fujii, Staff Graduate Advisor, 805-893-2979, Fax: 805-893-5885, E-mail: eemb-info@lifesci.ucsb.edu. Web site: http://www.lifesci.ucsb.edu/EEMB/index.html.

University of California, Santa Barbara, Graduate Division, College of Letters and Sciences, Division of Mathematics, Life, and Physical Sciences, Department of Mathematics, Santa Barbara, CA 93106-3080. Offers applied mathematics (MA), including computational science and engineering; mathematics (MA, PhD), including computational science and engineering ; MA/PhD. *Faculty:* 26 full-time (2 women). *Students:* 53 full-time (13 women); includes 9 minority (1 Black or African American, non-Hispanic/Latino; 3 Asian, non-Hispanic/Latino; 5 Hispanic/Latino), 7 international. Average age 26. 186 applicants, 17% accepted, 10

Peterson's Graduate Programs in the Physical Sciences, Mathematics, Agricultural Sciences, the Environment & Natural Resources 2013

facebook.com/petersonspublishing **319**

enrolled. In 2011, 7 master's, 3 doctorates awarded. Terminal master's awarded for partial completion of doctoral program. *Median time to degree:* Of those who began their doctoral program in fall 2003, 100% received their degree in 8 years or less. *Degree requirements:* For master's, comprehensive exam (for some programs), thesis (for some programs); for doctorate, comprehensive exam, thesis/dissertation. *Entrance requirements:* For master's and doctorate, GRE General Test, GRE Subject Test (math). Additional exam requirements/recommendations for international students: Required—TOEFL (minimum score 575 paper-based; 80 iBT), IELTS (minimum score 7). *Application deadline:* For fall admission, 1/1 priority date for domestic students, 1/1 for international students. Application fee: $80 ($100 for international students). Electronic applications accepted. *Expenses:* Tuition, state resident: full-time $12,192. Tuition, nonresident: full-time $27,294. *Required fees:* $764.13. *Financial support:* In 2011–12, 50 students received support, including 15 fellowships with full tuition reimbursements available (averaging $12,740 per year), 12 research assistantships with full tuition reimbursements available (averaging $6,000 per year), 48 teaching assistantships with partial tuition reimbursements available (averaging $17,308 per year); Federal Work-Study, institutionally sponsored loans, health care benefits, and tuition waivers (full and partial) also available. Financial award application deadline: 3/2; financial award applicants required to submit FAFSA. *Faculty research:* Topology, differential geometry, algebra, applied mathematics, partial differential equations. *Total annual research expenditures:* $205,000. *Unit head:* Prof. David R. Morrison, Chair, 805-893-8340, Fax: 805-893-2385, E-mail: chair@math.ucsb.edu. *Application contact:* Medina Price, Graduate Advisor, 805-893-8192, Fax: 805-893-2385, E-mail: price@math.ucsb.edu. Web site: http://www.math.ucsb.edu/.

University of Colorado Denver, College of Liberal Arts and Sciences, Department of Mathematical and Statistical Sciences, Denver, CO 80217. Offers applied mathematics (MS, PhD), including applied mathematics, applied probability (MS), applied statistics (MS), computational biology, computational mathematics (PhD), discrete mathematics, finite geometry (PhD), mathematics education (PhD), mathematics of engineering and science (MS), numerical analysis, operations research (MS), optimization and operations research (PhD), probability (PhD), statistics (PhD). Part-time programs available. *Faculty:* 26 full-time (4 women), 2 part-time/adjunct (1 woman). *Students:* 44 full-time (14 women), 14 part-time (5 women); includes 6 minority (4 Asian, non-Hispanic/Latino; 2 Hispanic/Latino), 10 international. Average age 33. 66 applicants, 79% accepted, 17 enrolled. In 2011, 6 master's, 6 doctorates awarded. *Degree requirements:* For master's, comprehensive exam, thesis optional, 30 hours of course work with minimum GPA of 3.0; for doctorate, comprehensive exam, thesis/dissertation. *Entrance requirements:* For master's and doctorate, GRE General Test; GRE Subject Test in math (recommended), 30 hours of course work in mathematics (24 of which must be upper-division mathematics), minimum GPA of 3.0. Additional exam requirements/recommendations for international students: Required—TOEFL (minimum score 525 paper-based; 192 computer-based; 71 iBT). *Application deadline:* For fall admission, 4/1 for domestic students, 3/1 for international students; for spring admission, 11/1 for domestic students, 10/1 for international students. Application fee: $50 ($75 for international students). Electronic applications accepted. *Financial support:* Fellowships with partial tuition reimbursements, research assistantships with full tuition reimbursements, teaching assistantships with full tuition reimbursements, Federal Work-Study, scholarships/grants, and unspecified assistantships available. Financial award application deadline: 4/1; financial award applicants required to submit FAFSA. *Faculty research:* Computational mathematics, computational biology, discrete mathematics and geometry, probability and statistics, optimization. *Unit head:* Dr. Stephen Billups, Graduate Chair, 303-556-4814, E-mail: stephen.billups@ucdenver.edu. *Application contact:* Lisa Herbert, Graduate Program Assistant, 303-556-2341, E-mail: lisa.herbert@ucdenver.edu. Web site: http://www.ucdenver.edu/academics/colleges/CLAS/Departments/math/Pages/MathStats.aspx.

The University of Iowa, Graduate College, Program in Applied Mathematical and Computational Sciences, Iowa City, IA 52242-1316. Offers PhD. *Degree requirements:* For doctorate, comprehensive exam, thesis/dissertation. *Entrance requirements:* For doctorate, GRE General Test, minimum GPA of 3.0. Additional exam requirements/recommendations for international students: Required—TOEFL (minimum score 620 paper-based; 260 computer-based; 105 iBT). Electronic applications accepted.

The University of Kansas, Graduate Studies, College of Liberal Arts and Sciences, Department of Physics and Astronomy, Lawrence, KS 66045. Offers computational physics and astronomy (MS); physics (MS, PhD). *Faculty:* 25 full-time (4 women). *Students:* 42 full-time (9 women), 4 part-time (1 woman); includes 3 minority (1 Black or African American, non-Hispanic/Latino; 1 Hispanic/Latino; 1 Two or more races, non-Hispanic/Latino), 11 international. Average age 29. 59 applicants, 41% accepted, 12 enrolled. In 2011, 3 master's, 4 doctorates awarded. Terminal master's awarded for partial completion of doctoral program. *Degree requirements:* For master's, thesis (for some programs); for doctorate, comprehensive exam, thesis/dissertation, computer skills, communication skills. *Entrance requirements:* For master's and doctorate, GRE Subject Test (physics), undergraduate degree. Additional exam requirements/recommendations for international students: Required—TOEFL (minimum score 53 paper-based; 20 computer-based; 20 iBT). *Application deadline:* For fall admission, 4/1 priority date for domestic students, 4/1 for international students; for spring admission, 11/15 for domestic and international students. Applications are processed on a rolling basis. Application fee: $55 ($65 for international students). Electronic

applications accepted. Tuition and fees vary according to course load, campus/location, program and reciprocity agreements. *Financial support:* Fellowships with full and partial tuition reimbursements, research assistantships with full and partial tuition reimbursements, teaching assistantships with full and partial tuition reimbursements, health care benefits, and unspecified assistantships available. Financial award application deadline: 4/1; financial award applicants required to submit FAFSA. *Faculty research:* Condensed-matter, cosmology, elementary particles, nuclear physics, space physics, astrophysics, astrobiology, biophysics, high energy. *Unit head:* Dr. Stephen J. Sanders, Chair, 785-864-4626, Fax: 785-864-5262. *Application contact:* Teri Leahy, Graduate Coordinator, 785-864-1225, Fax: 785-864-5262, E-mail: tleahy@ku.edu. Web site: http://www.physics.ku.edu.

University of Lethbridge, School of Graduate Studies, Lethbridge, AB T1K 3M4, Canada. Offers accounting (MScM); addictions counseling (M Sc); agricultural biotechnology (M Sc); agricultural studies (M Sc, MA); anthropology (MA); archaeology (MA); art (MA, MFA); biochemistry (M Sc); biological sciences (M Sc); biomolecular science (PhD); biosystems and biodiversity (PhD); Canadian studies (MA); chemistry (M Sc); computer science (M Sc); computer science and geographical information science (M Sc); counseling psychology (M Ed); dramatic arts (MA); earth, space, and physical science (PhD); economics (MA); educational leadership (M Ed); English (MA); environmental science (M Sc); evolution and behavior (PhD); exercise science (M Sc); finance (MScM); French (MA); French/German (MA); French/Spanish (MA); general education (M Ed); general management (MScM); geography (M Sc, MA); German (MA); health science (M Sc); history (MA); human resource management and labour relations (MScM); individualized multidisciplinary (M Sc, MA); information systems (MScM); international management (MScM); kinesiology (M Sc, MA); management (M Sc, MA); marketing (MScM); mathematics (M Sc); music (M Mus, MA); Native American studies (MA); neuroscience (M Sc, PhD); new media (MA); nursing (M Sc); philosophy (MA); physics (M Sc); policy and strategy (MScM); political science (MA); psychology (M Sc, MA); religious studies (MA); social sciences (MA); sociology (MA); theatre and dramatic arts (MFA); theoretical and computational science (PhD); urban and regional studies (MA); women's studies (MA). Part-time and evening/weekend programs available. *Degree requirements:* For doctorate, comprehensive exam, thesis/dissertation. *Entrance requirements:* For master's, GMAT (M Sc in management), bachelor's degree in related field, minimum GPA of 3.0 during previous 20 graded semester courses, 2 years teaching or related experience (M Ed); for doctorate, master's degree, minimum graduate GPA of 3.5. Additional exam requirements/recommendations for international students: Required—TOEFL. *Faculty research:* Movement and brain plasticity, gibberellin physiology, photosynthesis, carbon cycling, molecular properties of main-group ring components.

University of Manitoba, Faculty of Graduate Studies, Faculty of Science, Program in Mathematical, Computational and Statistical Sciences, Winnipeg, MB R3T 2N2, Canada. Offers MMCSS.

University of Massachusetts Lowell, College of Sciences, Department of Mathematical Sciences, Lowell, MA 01854-2881. Offers applied mathematics (MS); computational mathematics (PhD); mathematics (MS). Part-time programs available. *Entrance requirements:* For master's, GRE General Test.

University of Michigan–Dearborn, College of Arts, Sciences, and Letters, Master of Science in Applied and Computational Mathematics Program, Dearborn, MI 48128. Offers MS. Part-time and evening/weekend programs available. *Faculty:* 8 full-time (2 women). *Students:* 11 part-time (4 women); includes 1 minority (Black or African American, non-Hispanic/Latino). Average age 36. 6 applicants, 83% accepted, 2 enrolled. In 2011, 5 master's awarded. *Degree requirements:* For master's, thesis or alternative, project. *Entrance requirements:* For master's, 3 letters of recommendation, minimum GPA of 3.0, 2 years course work in math. Additional exam requirements/recommendations for international students: Required—TOEFL (minimum score 560 paper-based; 220 computer-based). *Application deadline:* For fall admission, 8/1 priority date for domestic students, 4/1 for international students; for winter admission, 12/1 priority date for domestic students, 11/1 for international students; for spring admission, 4/1 for domestic students, 3/1 for international students. Applications are processed on a rolling basis. Application fee: $60. Electronic applications accepted. *Financial support:* Federal Work-Study and scholarships/grants available. Support available to part-time students. Financial award application deadline: 4/1; financial award applicants required to submit FAFSA. *Faculty research:* Partial differential equations, statistics, mathematical biology, approximation theory, stochastic processes. *Unit head:* Dr. Thomas Snabb, Director, 313-593-5162, E-mail: tsnabb@umd.umich.edu. *Application contact:* Carol Ligienza, Coordinator, CASL Graduate Programs, 313-593-1183, Fax: 313-583-6700, E-mail: caslgrad@umd.umich.edu. Web site: http://www.casl.umd.umich.edu/563801/.

University of Minnesota, Duluth, Graduate School, Swenson College of Science and Engineering, Department of Mathematics and Statistics, Duluth, MN 55812-2496. Offers applied and computational mathematics (MS). Part-time programs available. *Degree requirements:* For master's, thesis or alternative. *Entrance requirements:* For master's, GRE General Test, minimum GPA of 3.0. Additional exam requirements/recommendations for international students: Required—TOEFL (minimum score 550 paper-based; 213 computer-based; 79 iBT); Recommended—TWE. Electronic applications accepted. *Faculty research:* Discrete mathematics, diagnostic markers, combinatorics, biostatistics, mathematical modeling and scientific computation.

320 facebook.com/petersonspublishing

Peterson's Graduate Programs in the Physical Sciences, Mathematics, Agricultural Sciences, the Environment & Natural Resources 2013

University of Minnesota, Twin Cities Campus, Graduate School, Scientific Computation Program, Minneapolis, MN 55455-0213. Offers MS, PhD. Part-time programs available. *Degree requirements:* For master's, thesis; for doctorate, thesis/dissertation. *Entrance requirements:* For doctorate, GRE General Test. Additional exam requirements/recommendations for international students: Required—TOEFL (minimum score 550 paper-based; 213 computer-based; 79 iBT), IELTS (minimum score 6.5). Electronic applications accepted. *Faculty research:* Parallel computations, quantum mechanical dynamics, computational materials science, computational fluid dynamics, computational neuroscience.

University of New Mexico, Graduate School, School of Engineering, Program in Computational Science and Engineering, Albuquerque, NM 87131-2039. Offers Post-Doctoral Certificate. In 2011, 1 degree awarded. *Application deadline:* For fall admission, 6/30 for domestic students; for spring admission, 11/15 for domestic students. Application fee: $50. Electronic applications accepted. *Financial support:* Application deadline: 3/1; applicants required to submit FAFSA. *Faculty research:* Arts technology, biophysics and nanoscale systems, chemistry and chemical biology, civil engineering, climate and weather modeling, computational biology and bioinformatics, cyberinfrastructure, digital arts and humanities, electromagnetics, energy grid modeling, high performance computing and scalable systems, image processing, materials physics, visualization and virtual environments, observational astronomy, open science grid, particle physics, quantum materials and devices, systems biology. *Unit head:* Dr. Susan Rachel Atlas, Unit Administrator, 505-277-0727, Fax: 505-277-8235, E-mail: director@hpc.unm.edu. *Application contact:* Stephanie Grant, Associate Director, Admissions, 505-277-0727, Fax: 505-277-8235, E-mail: slgrant@unm.edu. Web site: http://www.hpc.unm.edu/education/cse-program.

University of Notre Dame, Graduate School, College of Science, Department of Applied and Computational Mathematics and Statistics, Notre Dame, IN 46556. Offers applied and computational mathematics and statistics (PhD); applied statistics (MS); computational finance (MS).

University of Pennsylvania, School of Arts and Sciences, Graduate Group in Applied Mathematics and Computational Science, Philadelphia, PA 19104. Offers PhD. *Faculty:* 26 full-time (2 women). *Students:* 22 full-time (6 women), all international. 116 applicants, 21% accepted, 9 enrolled. *Application deadline:* For fall admission, 1/15 for domestic students. *Expenses: Tuition:* Full-time $26,660; part-time $4944 per course. *Required fees:* $2318; $291 per course. Tuition and fees vary according to course load, degree level and program. *Financial support:* Institutionally sponsored loans, scholarships/grants, traineeships, health care benefits, and unspecified assistantships available. *Unit head:* Dr. C. L. Epstein, Graduate Chair, 215-898-8476, E-mail: cle@math.upenn.edu. *Application contact:* Patricia Rea, Associate Director for Admissions, 215-573-5816, Fax: 215-573-8068, E-mail: gdasadmis@sas.upenn.edu. Web site: http://www.amcs.upenn.edu/.

University of Puerto Rico, Mayagüez Campus, Graduate Studies, College of Arts and Sciences, Department of Mathematical Sciences, Mayagüez, PR 00681-9000. Offers applied mathematics (MS); pure mathematics (MS); scientific computation (MS); statistics (MS). Part-time programs available. *Students:* 32 full-time (9 women), 1 (woman) part-time; includes 7 minority (all Hispanic/Latino), 26 international. 23 applicants, 43% accepted, 7 enrolled. In 2011, 10 master's awarded. *Degree requirements:* For master's, one foreign language, comprehensive exam, thesis optional. *Entrance requirements:* For master's, undergraduate degree in mathematics or its equivalent. *Application deadline:* For fall admission, 2/15 for domestic and international students; for spring admission, 9/15 for domestic and international students. Applications are processed on a rolling basis. Application fee: $25. Tuition and fees vary according to course level and course load. *Financial support:* In 2011–12, 31 students received support, including 3 research assistantships (averaging $15,000 per year), 28 teaching assistantships (averaging $8,500 per year); Federal Work-Study and institutionally sponsored loans also available. *Faculty research:* Automata theory, linear algebra, logic. *Unit head:* Prof. Omar Colon, Director, 787-832-4040 Ext. 3848, Fax: 787-265-5454, E-mail: omar.colon.reyes@gmail.com. Web site: http://math.uprm.edu/.

The University of South Dakota, Graduate School, College of Arts and Sciences, Department of Computer Science, Vermillion, SD 57069-2390. Offers computational sciences and statistics (PhD); computer science (MS). Part-time programs available. *Degree requirements:* For master's, thesis optional. *Entrance requirements:* For master's, GRE General Test, GRE Subject Test (recommended), minimum GPA of 2.7. Additional exam requirements/ recommendations for international students: Required—TOEFL (minimum score 550 paper-based; 213 computer-based; 79 iBT). Electronic applications accepted. *Expenses:* Tuition, state resident: full-time $3118.50; part-time $173.25 per credit hour. Tuition, nonresident: full-time $6601; part-time $366.70 per credit hour. *Required fees:* $2268; $126 per credit hour. Tuition and fees vary according to program.

University of Southern Mississippi, Graduate School, College of Science and Technology, Department of Mathematics, Hattiesburg, MS 39406-0001. Offers computational science (PhD); mathematics (MS). Part-time programs available. *Faculty:* 11 full-time (3 women), 1 part-time/adjunct (0 women). *Students:* 11 full-time (5 women), 3 part-time (1 woman); includes 3 minority (2 Black or African American, non-Hispanic/Latino; 1 Asian, non-Hispanic/Latino), 5 international. Average age 29. 10 applicants, 40% accepted, 4 enrolled. In 2011, 4 master's, 1 doctorate awarded. *Degree requirements:* For master's, comprehensive exam,

thesis or alternative; for doctorate, comprehensive exam, thesis/dissertation. *Entrance requirements:* For master's, GRE General Test, minimum GPA of 2.75 in last 60 hours; for doctorate, GRE General Test, minimum GPA of 3.5. Additional exam requirements/recommendations for international students: Required—TOEFL, IELTS. *Application deadline:* For fall admission, 3/15 priority date for domestic students, 3/15 for international students; for spring admission, 1/10 priority date for domestic students, 1/10 for international students. Applications are processed on a rolling basis. Application fee: $50. Electronic applications accepted. *Financial support:* In 2011–12, fellowships (averaging $18,000 per year), research assistantships with full tuition reimbursements (averaging $11,500 per year), teaching assistantships with full tuition reimbursements (averaging $11,408 per year) were awarded; Federal Work-Study, scholarships/grants, health care benefits, and unspecified assistantships also available. Financial award application deadline: 3/15; financial award applicants required to submit FAFSA. *Faculty research:* Dynamical systems, numerical analysis and multigrid methods, random number generation, matrix theory, group theory. *Unit head:* Dr. Joseph Kolibal, Interim Chair, 601-266-4289, Fax: 601-266-5818. *Application contact:* Dr. James Lambers, Director, Graduate Admissions, 601-266-4289, Fax: 601-266-5818. Web site: http://www.usm.edu/graduateschool/table.php.

University of Southern Mississippi, Graduate School, College of Science and Technology, Department of Physics and Astronomy, Hattiesburg, MS 39406-0001. Offers computational science (PhD); physics (MS). *Faculty:* 10 full-time (1 woman). *Students:* 11 full-time (1 woman), 3 part-time (1 woman), 7 international. Average age 31. 20 applicants, 60% accepted, 5 enrolled. In 2011, 5 master's, 2 doctorates awarded. *Degree requirements:* For master's, comprehensive exam, thesis; for doctorate, comprehensive exam, thesis/dissertation. *Entrance requirements:* For master's, GRE General Test, minimum GPA of 2.75 in last 60 hours; for doctorate, GRE General Test, minimum GPA of 3.5. Additional exam requirements/recommendations for international students: Required—TOEFL, IELTS. *Application deadline:* For fall admission, 3/1 priority date for domestic students, 3/1 for international students; for spring admission, 1/10 priority date for domestic students, 1/10 for international students. Applications are processed on a rolling basis. Application fee: $50. *Financial support:* In 2011–12, research assistantships with full tuition reimbursements (averaging $11,800 per year), 15 teaching assistantships with full tuition reimbursements (averaging $11,800 per year) were awarded; Federal Work-Study, scholarships/grants, health care benefits, and unspecified assistantships also available. Financial award application deadline: 3/15; financial award applicants required to submit FAFSA. *Faculty research:* Polymers, atomic physics, fluid mechanics, liquid crystals, refractory materials. *Unit head:* Dr. Khin Maung, Chair, 601-266-4934, Fax: 601-266-5149. *Application contact:* Dr. Khin Maung, Chair, 601-266-4934, Fax: 601-266-5149. Web site: http://www.usm.edu/graduateschool/table.php.

University of Southern Mississippi, Graduate School, College of Science and Technology, School of Computing, Hattiesburg, MS 39406-0001. Offers computational science (MS, PhD); computer science (MS). *Faculty:* 18 full-time (3 women), 1 (woman) part-time/adjunct. *Students:* 47 full-time (9 women), 20 part-time (4 women); includes 6 minority (2 Black or African American, non-Hispanic/Latino; 2 Asian, non-Hispanic/Latino; 2 Hispanic/Latino), 43 international. Average age 29. 104 applicants, 56% accepted, 21 enrolled. In 2011, 31 master's, 6 doctorates awarded. *Degree requirements:* For master's, comprehensive exam, thesis; for doctorate, comprehensive exam, thesis/dissertation. *Entrance requirements:* For master's, GRE General Test, minimum GPA of 2.75 in last 60 hours; for doctorate, GRE General Test, minimum GPA of 3.5. Additional exam requirements/recommendations for international students: Required—TOEFL, IELTS. *Application deadline:* For fall admission, 3/15 priority date for domestic students, 3/15 for international students; for spring admission, 1/10 priority date for domestic students, 1/10 for international students. Applications are processed on a rolling basis. Application fee: $50. Electronic applications accepted. *Financial support:* In 2011–12, 29 research assistantships with full tuition reimbursements (averaging $8,800 per year), 7 teaching assistantships with full tuition reimbursements (averaging $10,000 per year) were awarded; Federal Work-Study, institutionally sponsored loans, scholarships/grants, health care benefits, and unspecified assistantships also available. Financial award application deadline: 3/15; financial award applicants required to submit FAFSA. *Faculty research:* Satellite telecommunications, advanced life-support systems, artificial intelligence. *Unit head:* Dr. Chaoyang Zhang, Chair, 601-266-4949, Fax: 601-266-6452. *Application contact:* Dr. Chaoyang Zhang, Manager of Graduate Admissions, 601-266-4949, Fax: 601-266-6452. Web site: http://www.usm.edu/graduateschool/table.php.

The University of Tennessee at Chattanooga, Graduate School, College of Engineering and Computer Science, Program in Computational Engineering, Chattanooga, TN 37403. Offers PhD. *Faculty:* 3 full-time (0 women). *Students:* 13 full-time (2 women), 7 part-time (0 women); includes 1 minority (Asian, non-Hispanic/Latino), 10 international. Average age 30. 19 applicants, 53% accepted, 8 enrolled. In 2011, 3 doctorates awarded. *Degree requirements:* For doctorate, comprehensive exam, thesis/dissertation. *Entrance requirements:* For doctorate, GRE General Test. Additional exam requirements/recommendations for international students: Required—TOEFL (minimum score 550 paper-based; 213 computer-based; 79 iBT), IELTS (minimum score 6). *Application deadline:* For fall admission, 8/1 priority date for domestic students, 6/1 for international students; for spring admission, 12/1 priority date for domestic students, 10/1 for international students. Applications are processed on a rolling basis. Application fee: $35. Electronic applications accepted. *Expenses:* Tuition, state resident: full-

Peterson's Graduate Programs in the Physical Sciences, Mathematics, Agricultural Sciences, the Environment & Natural Resources 2013

facebook.com/petersonspublishing   **321**

time $6472; part-time $359 per credit hour. Tuition, nonresident: full-time $20,006; part-time $1111 per credit hour. *Required fees:* $1320; $160 per credit hour. *Financial support:* Career-related internships or fieldwork, scholarships/grants, and unspecified assistantships available. Support available to part-time students. *Faculty research:* Computational fluid dynamics, design optimization, solution algorithms, hydronamics and propulsion. *Total annual research expenditures:* $460,000. *Unit head:* Dr. Tim Swafford, Director, 423-425-5497, Fax: 423-425-5517, E-mail: tim-swafford@utc.edu. *Application contact:* Dr. Jerald Ainsworth, Dean of Graduate Studies, 423-425-4478, Fax: 423-425-5223, E-mail: jerald-ainsworth@utc.edu. Web site: http://www.utc.edu/Academic/EngineeringAndComputerScience/grad/.

The University of Tennessee at Chattanooga, Graduate School, College of Engineering and Computer Science, Program in Engineering, Chattanooga, TN 37403. Offers chemical engineering (MS Engr); civil engineering (MS Engr); computational engineering (MS Engr); electrical engineering (MS Engr); industrial engineering (MS Engr); mechanical engineering (MS Engr). Part-time and evening/weekend programs available. *Faculty:* 27 full-time (3 women), 3 part-time/adjunct (1 woman). *Students:* 40 full-time (7 women), 41 part-time (11 women); includes 23 minority (10 Black or African American, non-Hispanic/Latino; 1 American Indian or Alaska Native, non-Hispanic/Latino; 6 Asian, non-Hispanic/Latino; 4 Hispanic/Latino; 2 Two or more races, non-Hispanic/Latino), 20 international. Average age 28. 89 applicants, 53% accepted, 29 enrolled. In 2011, 8 master's awarded. *Degree requirements:* For master's, comprehensive exam, thesis or alternative, engineering project. *Entrance requirements:* For master's, GRE General Test, minimum undergraduate GPA of 2.5 or 3.0 in last 30 hours of coursework. Additional exam requirements/recommendations for international students: Required—TOEFL (minimum score 550 paper-based; 213 computer-based; 79 iBT), IELTS (minimum score 6). *Application deadline:* For fall admission, 8/1 priority date for domestic students, 6/1 for international students; for spring admission, 12/1 priority date for domestic students, 10/1 for international students. Applications are processed on a rolling basis. Application fee: $35. Electronic applications accepted. *Expenses:* Tuition, state resident: full-time $6472; part-time $359 per credit hour. Tuition, nonresident: full-time $20,006; part-time $1111 per credit hour. *Required fees:* $1320; $160 per credit hour. *Financial support:* Career-related internships or fieldwork, scholarships/grants, and unspecified assistantships available. Support available to part-time students. *Faculty research:* Quality control and reliability engineering, financial management, thermal science, energy conservation, structural analysis. *Total annual research expenditures:* $3.5 million. *Unit head:* Dr. Neslihan Alp, Director, 423-425-4032, Fax: 423-425-5229, E-mail: neslihan-alp@utc.edu. *Application contact:* Dr. Jerald Ainsworth, Dean of Graduate Studies, 423-425-4478, Fax: 423-425-5223, E-mail: jerald-ainsworth@utc.edu. Web site: http://www.utc.edu/Departments/engrcs/ms_engr.php.

The University of Texas at Austin, Graduate School, Program in Computational Science, Engineering, and Mathematics, Austin, TX 78712-1111. Offers MS, PhD. Terminal master's awarded for partial completion of doctoral program. *Degree requirements:* For master's, thesis optional; for doctorate, thesis/dissertation, 3 area qualifying exams. *Application deadline:* For fall admission, 2/1 for domestic students. Application fee: $50 ($75 for international students). Electronic applications accepted. *Financial support:* Fellowships with full and partial tuition reimbursements, research assistantships with full and partial tuition reimbursements, and teaching assistantships with full and partial tuition reimbursements available. Financial award application deadline: 2/1. *Unit head:* Clint Dawson, Graduate Adviser, 512-475-8627, E-mail: clint@ices.utexas.edu. *Application contact:* Stephanie Rodriguez, 512-232-3356, E-mail: slr@ices.utexas.edu. Web site: http://www.ices.utexas.edu/graduate-studies/.

The University of Texas at El Paso, Graduate School, College of Science, Computational Science Program, El Paso, TX 79968-0001. Offers MS, PhD. *Students:* 27 (5 women); includes 12 minority (1 Black or African American, non-Hispanic/Latino; 1 Asian, non-Hispanic/Latino; 10 Hispanic/Latino), 14 international. In 2011, 5 master's awarded. *Degree requirements:* For master's, thesis or internship; for doctorate, thesis/dissertation. *Entrance requirements:* For doctorate, GRE, statement of purpose, letters of recommendation. Additional exam requirements/recommendations for international students: Required—TOEFL; Recommended—IELTS. *Application deadline:* For fall admission, 8/1 for domestic students, 3/1 for international students; for spring admission, 11/1 for domestic students, 9/3 for international students. Applications are processed on a rolling basis. Application fee: $45 ($80 for international students). Electronic applications accepted. *Financial support:* Fellowships with partial tuition reimbursements, research assistantships with partial tuition reimbursements, teaching assistantships with partial tuition reimbursements, institutionally sponsored loans, scholarships/grants, health care benefits, tuition waivers (partial), and unspecified assistantships available. Support available to part-time students. Financial award application deadline: 3/15; financial award applicants required to submit FAFSA. *Unit head:* Dr. Leticia Velazquez, Director, 915-747-6768, Fax: 915-747-6502, E-mail: leti@utep.edu. *Application contact:* Dr.

Benjamin Flores, Interim Dean of the Graduate School, 915-747-5491, Fax: 915-747-5788, E-mail: bflores@utep.edu.

University of Utah, Graduate School, College of Engineering, School of Computing, Computational Engineering and Science Program, Salt Lake City, UT 84112. Offers MS. *Students:* 17 full-time (1 woman), 7 part-time (2 women); includes 5 minority (1 American Indian or Alaska Native, non-Hispanic/Latino; 3 Asian, non-Hispanic/Latino; 1 Two or more races, non-Hispanic/Latino), 12 international. Average age 29. 12 applicants, 83% accepted, 8 enrolled. *Degree requirements:* For master's, comprehensive exam, thesis (for some programs). *Entrance requirements:* For master's, minimum GPA of 3.0. Additional exam requirements/recommendations for international students: Required—TOEFL (minimum score 500 paper-based; 173 computer-based; 61 iBT), IELTS (minimum score 6). *Application deadline:* For fall admission, 1/15 priority date for domestic students, 1/15 for international students. Application fee: $55 ($65 for international students). Electronic applications accepted. *Expenses:* Contact institution. *Financial support:* In 2011–12, 1 student received support, including 1 fellowship (averaging $15,000 per year), 2 research assistantships with full tuition reimbursements available (averaging $12,000 per year), 1 teaching assistantship with full tuition reimbursement available (averaging $12,000 per year); health care benefits and unspecified assistantships also available. Financial award application deadline: 12/15; financial award applicants required to submit FAFSA. *Faculty research:* Mathematical modeling, the formulation of the numerical methodology for solving the problem, the selection of the appropriate computer architecture and algorithms, and the effective interpretation of the results through visualization and/or statistical reduction. *Unit head:* Dr. Kris Sikorski, Director, 801-581-8579, Fax: 801-581-5843, E-mail: sikorski@cs.utah.edu. *Application contact:* Ann Carlstrom, Graduate Advisor, 801-581-7631, Fax: 801-581-5843, E-mail: annc@cs.utah.edu. Web site: http://www.ces.utah.edu.

University of Utah, Graduate School, Professional Master of Science and Technology Program, Salt Lake City, UT 84112-1107. Offers biotechnology (PSM); computational science (PSM); environmental science (PSM); science instrumentation (PSM). Part-time programs available. *Students:* 15 full-time (10 women), 42 part-time (12 women); includes 7 minority (2 Black or African American, non-Hispanic/Latino; 2 Asian, non-Hispanic/Latino; 2 Hispanic/Latino; 1 Native Hawaiian or other Pacific Islander, non-Hispanic/Latino), 2 international. Average age 33. 66 applicants, 48% accepted, 16 enrolled. In 2011, 18 master's awarded. *Degree requirements:* For master's, internship. *Entrance requirements:* For master's, GRE (recommended), minimum undergraduate GPA of 3.0, bachelor's degree from accredited university or college. Additional exam requirements/recommendations for international students: Required—TOEFL (minimum score 500 paper-based; 173 computer-based; 61 iBT), IELTS (minimum score 6). *Application deadline:* For fall admission, 3/1 for domestic and international students. Application fee: $55 ($65 for international students). Electronic applications accepted. *Financial support:* In 2011–12, 8 students received support, including 5 fellowships with full and partial tuition reimbursements available (averaging $16,800 per year), 2 research assistantships (averaging $6,200 per year); unspecified assistantships also available. Financial award applicants required to submit FAFSA. *Faculty research:* Drug delivery systems, in vitro erythroid expansion and HRE (Hypoxia responsive element). *Unit head:* Jennifer Schmidt, Program Director, 801-585-5630, E-mail: jennifer.schmidt@gradschool.utah.edu. *Application contact:* Amy Kimball, Project Coordinator, 801-585-3650, Fax: 801-585-6749, E-mail: amy.kimball@gradschool.utah.edu. Web site: http://www.utah.edu/pmst/.

University of Washington, Graduate School, College of Arts and Sciences, Department of Mathematics, Seattle, WA 98195. Offers mathematics (MA, MS, PhD); numerical analysis (MS); optimization (MS). Part-time programs available. Terminal master's awarded for partial completion of doctoral program. *Degree requirements:* For master's, thesis optional; for doctorate, 2 foreign languages, thesis/dissertation. *Entrance requirements:* For master's, GRE, minimum GPA of 3.0; for doctorate, GRE General Test, GRE Subject Test (mathematics), minimum GPA 3.0. Additional exam requirements/recommendations for international students: Required—TOEFL. Electronic applications accepted. *Faculty research:* Algebra, analysis, probability, combinatorics and geometry.

Western Kentucky University, Graduate Studies, Ogden College of Science and Engineering, Department of Mathematics and Computer Science, Bowling Green, KY 42101. Offers computational mathematics (MS); computer science (MS); mathematics (MA, MS). *Degree requirements:* For master's, comprehensive exam, thesis optional, written exam. *Entrance requirements:* For master's, GRE General Test, minimum GPA of 2.75. Additional exam requirements/recommendations for international students: Required—TOEFL (minimum score 555 paper-based; 213 computer-based; 79 iBT). *Faculty research:* Differential equations numerical analysis, probability statistics, algebra, typology, knot theory.

Western Michigan University, Graduate College, College of Arts and Sciences, Department of Mathematics, Program in Applied and Computational Mathematics, Kalamazoo, MI 49008. Offers MS.

Mathematical and Computational Finance

Bernard M. Baruch College of the City University of New York, Weissman School of Arts and Sciences, Program in Financial Engineering, New York, NY 10010-5585. Offers MS. *Entrance requirements:* For master's, GRE General Test or GMAT, 3 recommendations. Additional exam requirements/recommendations for international students: Required—TOEFL, TWE.

Boston University, School of Management, Boston, MA 02215. Offers business administration (MBA); executive business administration (EMBA); investment management (MS); management (PhD); mathematical finance (MS, PhD); JD/MBA; MBA/MA; MBA/MPH; MBA/MS; MBA/MSIS; MD/MBA; MS/MBA. *Accreditation:* AACSB. Part-time and evening/weekend programs available. *Faculty:* 185 full-time (49 women), 60 part-time/adjunct (15 women). *Students:* 510 full-time (177 women), 736 part-time (263 women); includes 176 minority (20 Black or African American, non-Hispanic/Latino; 121 Asian, non-Hispanic/Latino; 22 Hispanic/Latino; 13 Two or more races, non-Hispanic/Latino), 250 international. Average age 30. 1,387 applicants, 28% accepted, 160 enrolled. In 2011, 557 master's, 8 doctorates awarded. *Degree requirements:* For doctorate, comprehensive exam, thesis/dissertation. *Entrance requirements:* For master's, GMAT (for MBA and MS in investment management); GMAT or GRE General Test (for MS in mathematical finance), resume, 2 letters of recommendation; for doctorate, GMAT or GRE General Test, resume, personal statement, 3 letters of recommendation, 3 essays, official transcripts. *Application deadline:* For fall admission, 1/5 for domestic and international students; for spring admission, 11/1 for domestic students. Application fee: $125. Electronic applications accepted. *Expenses: Tuition:* Full-time $40,848; part-time $1276 per credit hour. *Required fees:* $572; $286 per semester. *Financial support:* Career-related internships or fieldwork, Federal Work-Study, institutionally sponsored loans, scholarships/grants, and tuition waivers (partial) available. Financial award applicants required to submit FAFSA. *Faculty research:* Innovation policy and productivity, corporate social responsibility, risk management, information systems, entrepreneurship, clean energy, sustainability. *Unit head:* Kenneth W. Freeman, Professor/Dean, 617-353-9720, Fax: 617-353-5581, E-mail: kfreeman@bu.edu. *Application contact:* Patti Cudney, Assistant Dean, Graduate Admissions, 617-353-2670, Fax: 617-353-7368, E-mail: mba@bu.edu. Web site: http://management.bu.edu/.

Carnegie Mellon University, Mellon College of Science, Department of Mathematical Sciences, Pittsburgh, PA 15213-3891. Offers algorithms, combinatorics, and optimization (PhD); applied mathematics (PhD); computational finance (MS); mathematical finance (PhD); mathematical sciences (MS, DA, PhD); pure and applied logic (PhD). Part-time programs available. Terminal master's awarded for partial completion of doctoral program. *Degree requirements:* For doctorate, thesis/dissertation. *Entrance requirements:* For master's and doctorate, GRE General Test, GRE Subject Test. Additional exam requirements/recommendations for international students: Required—TOEFL. Electronic applications accepted. *Faculty research:* Continuum mechanics, discrete mathematics, applied and computational mathematics.

Carnegie Mellon University, Tepper School of Business, Pittsburgh, PA 15213-3891. Offers accounting (PhD); algorithms, combinatorics, and optimization (MS, PhD); business management and software engineering (MBMSE); civil engineering and industrial management (MS); computational finance (MSCF); economics (MS, PhD); electronic commerce (MS); environmental engineering and management (MEEM); finance (PhD); financial economics (PhD); industrial administration (MBA), including administration and public management; information systems (PhD); management of manufacturing and automation (PhD); marketing (PhD); mathematical finance (PhD); operations research (PhD); organizational behavior and theory (PhD); political economy (PhD); production and operations management (PhD); public policy and management (MS, MSED); software engineering and business management (MS); JD/MS; JD/MSIA; M Div/MS; MOM/MSIA; MSCF/MSIA. JD/MSIA offered jointly with University of Pittsburgh. Part-time programs available. Terminal master's awarded for partial completion of doctoral program. *Degree requirements:* For doctorate, thesis/dissertation. *Entrance requirements:* For master's, GMAT. Additional exam requirements/recommendations for international students: Required—TOEFL. *Expenses:* Contact institution.

DePaul University, Charles H. Kellstadt Graduate School of Business, Department of Finance, Chicago, IL 60604-2287. Offers behavioral finance (MBA); computational finance (MS); finance (MBA, MSF); financial analysis (MBA); financial management and control (MBA); international marketing and finance (MBA); managerial finance (MBA); real estate (MS); real estate finance and investment (MBA); strategy, execution and valuation (MBA). Part-time and evening/weekend programs available. *Faculty:* 26 full-time (5 women), 31 part-time/adjunct (4 women). *Students:* 454 full-time (138 women), 190 part-time (41 women); includes 85 minority (13 Black or African American, non-Hispanic/Latino; 53 Asian, non-Hispanic/Latino; 17 Hispanic/Latino; 2 Two or more races, non-Hispanic/Latino), 129 international. In 2011, 239 master's awarded. *Entrance requirements:* For master's, GMAT, 2 letters of recommendation, resume. Additional exam requirements/recommendations for international students: Required—TOEFL (minimum score 550 paper-based; 213 computer-based; 80 iBT). *Application deadline:* For fall admission, 7/1 for domestic students, 6/1 for international students; for winter admission, 10/1 for domestic students, 9/1 for

international students; for spring admission, 2/1 for domestic students, 1/1 for international students. Applications are processed on a rolling basis. Application fee: $60. Electronic applications accepted. *Financial support:* In 2011–12, 10 students received support, including 10 research assistantships (averaging $15,120 per year); scholarships/grants and unspecified assistantships also available. Financial award application deadline: 6/1; financial award applicants required to submit FAFSA. *Faculty research:* Derivatives, valuation, international finance, real estate, corporate finance, behavioral finance. *Unit head:* Ali M. Fatemi, Professor and Chair, 312-362-8826, Fax: 312-362-6566, E-mail: afatemi@depaul.edu. *Application contact:* Melissa Booth, Director of Admission and Recruitment, 312-362-6353, Fax: 312-362-6677, E-mail: kgsb@depaul.edu. Web site: http://www.fin.depaul.edu/.

DePaul University, College of Computing and Digital Media, Chicago, IL 60604. Offers animation (MA, MFA); applied technology (MS); business information technology (MS); cinema (MFA); cinema production (MS); computational finance (MS); computer and information sciences (PhD); computer game development (MS); computer graphics and motion technology (MS); computer information and network security (MS); computer science (MS); e-commerce technology (MS); human-computer interaction (MS); information systems (MS); information technology (MA); information technology project management (MS); network engineering and management (MS); predictive analytics (MS); screenwriting (MFA); software engineering (MS); JD/MA; JD/MS. Part-time and evening/weekend programs available. Postbaccalaureate distance learning degree programs offered (no on-campus study). *Faculty:* 64 full-time (16 women), 44 part-time/adjunct (5 women). *Students:* 969 full-time (250 women), 936 part-time (231 women); includes 566 minority (204 Black or African American, non-Hispanic/Latino; 3 American Indian or Alaska Native, non-Hispanic/Latino; 166 Asian, non-Hispanic/Latino; 135 Hispanic/Latino; 7 Native Hawaiian or other Pacific Islander, non-Hispanic/Latino; 51 Two or more races, non-Hispanic/Latino), 282 international. Average age 32. 1,040 applicants, 65% accepted, 324 enrolled. In 2011, 478 master's, 4 doctorates awarded. *Degree requirements:* For master's, thesis (for some programs); for doctorate, comprehensive exam, thesis/dissertation. *Entrance requirements:* For master's, GRE or GMAT (MS in computational finance only), bachelor's degree, resume (MS in predictive analytics only), IT experience (MS in information technology project management only), portfolio review (all MFA programs and MA in animation); for doctorate, GRE, master's degree in computer science. Additional exam requirements/recommendations for international students: Required—TOEFL (minimum score 550 paper-based; 213 computer-based; 80 iBT), IELTS (minimum score 6.5), Pearson Test of English (minimum score 53). *Application deadline:* For fall admission, 8/1 priority date for domestic students, 6/1 for international students; for winter admission, 12/1 priority date for domestic students, 10/1 for international students; for spring admission, 3/1 priority date for domestic students, 1/1 for international students. Applications are processed on a rolling basis. Application fee: $25. Electronic applications accepted. *Expenses:* Contact institution. *Financial support:* In 2011–12, 56 students received support, including 3 fellowships with full tuition reimbursements available (averaging $30,000 per year), 3 research assistantships with full and partial tuition reimbursements available (averaging $22,833 per year), 50 teaching assistantships (averaging $6,194 per year); Federal Work-Study, scholarships/grants, tuition waivers (full and partial), and unspecified assistantships also available. Support available to part-time students. Financial award application deadline: 4/30. *Faculty research:* Data mining, theoretical computer science, gaming, security, animation and film. *Total annual research expenditures:* $3.9 million. *Unit head:* Elly Kafritsas-Wessels, Senior Administrative Assistant, 312-362-5816, Fax: 312-362-5185, E-mail: ekafrits@cdm.depaul.edu. *Application contact:* James Parker, Director of Graduate Admission, 312-362-8714, Fax: 312-362-5179, E-mail: jparke29@cdm.depaul.edu. Web site: http://cdm.depaul.edu.

Florida State University, The Graduate School, College of Arts and Sciences, Department of Mathematics, Tallahassee, FL 32306-4510. Offers applied computational mathematics (MS); biomathematics (MS, PhD); financial mathematics (MS, PhD); pure mathematics (MS, PhD). Part-time programs available. *Faculty:* 52 full-time (13 women), 1 (woman) part-time/adjunct. *Students:* 139 full-time (36 women), 7 part-time (1 woman); includes 15 minority (6 Black or African American, non-Hispanic/Latino; 4 Asian, non-Hispanic/Latino; 5 Hispanic/Latino), 99 international. Average age 27. 336 applicants, 41% accepted, 41 enrolled. In 2011, 43 master's, 14 doctorates awarded. Terminal master's awarded for partial completion of doctoral program. *Degree requirements:* For master's, comprehensive exam (for some programs), thesis optional; for doctorate, comprehensive exam, thesis/dissertation, candidacy exam including written qualifying examinations which differ by degree concentrations. *Entrance requirements:* For master's and doctorate, GRE General Test, minimum upper-division GPA of 3.0, 4-year bachelor's degree. Additional exam requirements/recommendations for international students: Required—TOEFL (minimum score 550 paper-based; 213 computer-bases; 80 iBT) or IELTS (minimum score 6.5). *Application deadline:* For fall admission, 1/1 priority date for domestic students, 1/1 for international students; for spring admission, 10/1 priority date for domestic students, 11/1 for international students. Applications are processed on a rolling basis. Application fee: $30. Electronic applications

Peterson's Graduate Programs in the Physical Sciences, Mathematics, Agricultural Sciences, the Environment & Natural Resources 2013

facebook.com/petersonspublishing **323**

Mathematical and Computational Finance

accepted. *Expenses:* Tuition, state resident: full-time $9474; part-time $350.88 per credit hour. Tuition, nonresident: full-time $16,236; part-time $601.34 per credit hour. *Required fees:* $630 per semester. One-time fee: $20. Tuition and fees vary according to course load and campus/location. *Financial support:* In 2011–12, 106 students received support, including 7 fellowships with full tuition reimbursements available (averaging $22,600 per year), 12 research assistantships with full tuition reimbursements available (averaging $22,000 per year), 78 teaching assistantships with full tuition reimbursements available (averaging $19,300 per year); career-related internships or fieldwork, institutionally sponsored loans, scholarships/grants, health care benefits, and unspecified assistantships also available. *Faculty research:* Algebra and algebraic geometry; applied, financial, numerical, and classical analysis; biomathematics, including shape analysis and anatomical imaging; computational mathematics and numerical algorithms; geometric topology. *Unit head:* Dr. Philip L. Bowers, Chairperson, 850-645-3338, Fax: 850-644-4053, E-mail: bowers@math.fsu.edu. *Application contact:* Dr. Bettye Anne Case, Associate Chair for Graduate Studies, 850-644-1586, Fax: 850-644-4053, E-mail: case@math.fsu.edu. Web site: http://www.math.fsu.edu/.

Georgia Institute of Technology, Graduate Studies and Research, College of Management, Program in Management, Atlanta, GA 30332-0001. Offers accounting (PhD); finance (PhD); information technology management (PhD); marketing (PhD); operations management (PhD); organizational behavior (PhD); quantitative and computational finance (MS); strategic management (PhD). *Accreditation:* AACSB. *Degree requirements:* For doctorate, comprehensive exam, thesis/dissertation, oral exams. *Entrance requirements:* For master's and doctorate, GMAT. Additional exam requirements/recommendations for international students: Required—TOEFL. *Faculty research:* MIS, management of technology, international business, entrepreneurship, operations management.

Georgia Institute of Technology, Graduate Studies and Research, College of Sciences, School of Mathematics, Atlanta, GA 30332-0001. Offers algorithms, combinatorics, and optimization (PhD); applied mathematics (MS); bioinformatics (PhD); mathematics (PhD); quantitative and computational finance (MS); statistics (MS Stat). Terminal master's awarded for partial completion of doctoral program. *Degree requirements:* For master's, thesis or alternative; for doctorate, one foreign language, thesis/dissertation. *Entrance requirements:* For master's, GRE General Test, minimum GPA of 3.0; for doctorate, GRE General Test, GRE Subject Test, minimum GPA of 3.0. Additional exam requirements/recommendations for international students: Required—TOEFL. Electronic applications accepted. *Faculty research:* Dynamical systems, discrete mathematics, probability and statistics, mathematical physics.

Illinois Institute of Technology, Stuart School of Business, Program in Mathematical Finance, Chicago, IL 60616-3793. Offers MMF. Part-time and evening/weekend programs available. *Entrance requirements:* For master's, GRE (minimum score 1200). Additional exam requirements/recommendations for international students: Required—TOEFL (minimum score 600 paper-based; 85 iBT); Recommended—IELTS (minimum score 7). Electronic applications accepted. *Expenses:* Contact institution. *Faculty research:* Factor models for investment management, credit rating and credit risk management, hedge fund performance analysis, option trading and risk management, global asset allocation strategies.

The Johns Hopkins University, Whiting School of Engineering, Department of Applied Mathematics and Statistics, Baltimore, MD 21218-2699. Offers computational medicine (PhD); discrete mathematics (MA, MSE, PhD); financial mathematics (MSE); operations research/optimization/decision science (MA, MSE, PhD); statistics/probability/stochastic processes (MA, MSE, PhD). Terminal master's awarded for partial completion of doctoral program. *Degree requirements:* For master's, thesis (for some programs); for doctorate, thesis/dissertation, oral exam, introductory exam. *Entrance requirements:* For master's and doctorate, GRE General Test, GRE Subject Test. Additional exam requirements/recommendations for international students: Required—TOEFL (minimum score 600 paper-based; 250 computer-based; 100 iBT). Electronic applications accepted. *Faculty research:* Discrete mathematics, probability, statistics, optimization and operations research, scientific computation, financial mathematics.

Monmouth University, The Graduate School, Department of Mathematics, West Long Branch, NJ 07764-1898. Offers financial mathematics (MS). Part-time and evening/weekend programs available. *Faculty:* 2 full-time (0 women). *Students:* 5 full-time (0 women), 4 part-time (3 women); includes 2 minority (1 Black or African American, non-Hispanic/Latino; 1 Hispanic/Latino), 4 international. Average age 30. 12 applicants, 75% accepted, 5 enrolled. In 2011, 1 master's awarded. *Degree requirements:* For master's, 6 credits of financial mathematics practicum. *Entrance requirements:* For master's, minimum GPA of 3.0 in major, 2.5 overall; undergraduate degree in mathematics or related field with substantial component of math; coursework in calculus, linear algebra, differential equations (with some exposure to partial differential equations), and a course in calculus-based statistics. Additional exam requirements/recommendations for international students: Required—TOEFL (minimum score 550 paper-based; 213 computer-based; 79 iBT), IELTS (minimum score 5) or Michigan English Language Assessment Battery (minimum score 77), Cambridge A, B, C. *Application deadline:* For fall admission, 7/15 priority date for domestic students, 6/1 for international students; for spring admission, 10/15 priority date for domestic students, 11/1 for international students. Application fee: $50. *Financial support:* In 2011–12, 2 students received support, including 2 fellowships (averaging $650

per year); research assistantships, career-related internships or fieldwork, scholarships/grants, and unspecified assistantships also available. Support available to part-time students. Financial award applicants required to submit FAFSA. *Faculty research:* Mathematics and computational finance, economics, Monte Carlo methods. *Unit head:* Dr. Joseph Coyle, Program Director, 732-263-5306, E-mail: jcoyle@monmouth.edu. *Application contact:* Kevin Roane, Director, Office of Graduate Admission, 732-571-3452, Fax: 732-263-5123, E-mail: gradadm@monmouth.edu. Web site: http://www.monmouth.edu/academics/schools/science/graduate_programs/mathematics/msfm.asp.

New Jersey Institute of Technology, Office of Graduate Studies, College of Science and Liberal Arts, Department of Mathematical Science, Program in Mathematical and Computational Finance, Newark, NJ 07102. Offers MS. *Students:* 9 full-time (2 women), 1 part-time; includes 2 minority (1 Black or African American, non-Hispanic/Latino; 1 Asian, non-Hispanic/Latino), 8 international. Average age 28. 53 applicants, 64% accepted. *Degree requirements:* For master's, project. *Entrance requirements:* Additional exam requirements/recommendations for international students: Required—TOEFL (minimum score 550 paper-based; 213 computer-based; 79 iBT). *Application deadline:* For fall admission, 6/1 priority date for domestic students, 5/1 for international students; for spring admission, 11/15 priority date for domestic students, 11/15 for international students. Applications are processed on a rolling basis. Application fee: $65. Electronic applications accepted. *Expenses:* Tuition, state resident: full-time $7980; part-time $867 per credit. Tuition, nonresident: full-time $11,336; part-time $1196 per credit. *Required fees:* $230 per credit. *Financial support:* Application deadline: 1/15. *Unit head:* Dr. Daljit S. Ahluwalia, Chair, 973-596-8465, Fax: 973-596-5591, E-mail: daljit.ahluwalia@njit.edu. *Application contact:* Kathryn Kelly, Director of Admissions, 973-596-3300, Fax: 973-596-3461, E-mail: admissions@njit.edu. Web site: http://math.njit.edu/academics/graduate/ms-computationalfinance/index.php.

New York University, Graduate School of Arts and Science, Courant Institute of Mathematical Sciences, Department of Mathematics, New York, NY 10012-1019. Offers atmosphere ocean science and mathematics (PhD); mathematics (MS, PhD); mathematics and statistics/operations research (MS); mathematics in finance (MS); scientific computing (MS). Part-time and evening/weekend programs available. *Faculty:* 46 full-time (0 women). *Students:* 215 full-time (39 women), 116 part-time (20 women); includes 53 minority (3 Black or African American, non-Hispanic/Latino; 1 American Indian or Alaska Native, non-Hispanic/Latino; 41 Asian, non-Hispanic/Latino; 6 Hispanic/Latino; 2 Two or more races, non-Hispanic/Latino), 183 international. Average age 28. 1,619 applicants, 25% accepted, 104 enrolled. In 2011, 71 master's, 18 doctorates awarded. *Degree requirements:* For master's, thesis optional; for doctorate, one foreign language, thesis/dissertation, oral and written exams. *Entrance requirements:* For master's and doctorate, GRE General Test, GRE Subject Test. Additional exam requirements/recommendations for international students: Required—TOEFL. *Application deadline:* For fall admission, 1/4 for domestic students; for spring admission, 11/1 for domestic students. Application fee: $90. *Financial support:* Fellowships with tuition reimbursements, research assistantships with tuition reimbursements, teaching assistantships with tuition reimbursements, Federal Work-Study, institutionally sponsored loans, scholarships/grants, health care benefits, and unspecified assistantships available. Financial award application deadline: 1/4; financial award applicants required to submit FAFSA. *Faculty research:* Partial differential equations, computational science, applied mathematics, geometry and topology, probability and stochastic processes. *Unit head:* Fedor Bogomolov, Director of Graduate Studies, 212-998-3238, Fax: 212-995-4121, E-mail: admissions@math.nyu.edu. *Application contact:* Tamar Arnon, Graduate Program Administrator, 212-998-3238, Fax: 212-995-4121, E-mail: admissions@math.nyu.edu. Web site: http://www.math.nyu.edu/.

North Carolina State University, Graduate School, College of Agriculture and Life Sciences and College of Engineering and College of Physical and Mathematical Sciences, Program in Financial Mathematics, Raleigh, NC 27695. Offers MFM. Part-time programs available. *Degree requirements:* For master's, thesis optional, project/internship. *Entrance requirements:* For master's, GRE General Test. Additional exam requirements/recommendations for international students: Required—TOEFL (minimum score 550 paper-based; 213 computer-based). Electronic applications accepted. *Faculty research:* Financial mathematics modeling and computation, futures, options and commodities markets, real options, credit risk, portfolio optimization.

Polytechnic Institute of New York University, Department of Finance and Risk Engineering, Brooklyn, NY 11201-2990. Offers financial engineering (MS, Advanced Certificate), including capital markets (MS), computational finance (MS), financial technology (MS); financial technology management (Advanced Certificate); organizational behavior (Advanced Certificate); risk management (Advanced Certificate); technology management (Advanced Certificate). Part-time and evening/weekend programs available. *Faculty:* 6 full-time (2 women), 23 part-time/adjunct (5 women). *Students:* 149 full-time (49 women), 44 part-time (8 women); includes 30 minority (6 Black or African American, non-Hispanic/Latino; 22 Asian, non-Hispanic/Latino; 2 Hispanic/Latino), 135 international. Average age 27. 515 applicants, 36% accepted, 102 enrolled. In 2011, 95 degrees awarded. *Degree requirements:* For master's, comprehensive exam (for some programs), thesis (for some programs). *Entrance requirements:* For master's, GMAT, minimum B average in undergraduate course work. Additional exam requirements/recommendations for international students: Required—TOEFL (minimum score 550 paper-based; 213 computer-based; 80 iBT);

324 facebook.com/petersonspublishing

Peterson's Graduate Programs in the Physical Sciences, Mathematics, Agricultural Sciences, the Environment & Natural Resources 2013

Recommended—IELTS (minimum score 6.5). *Application deadline:* For fall admission, 7/31 priority date for domestic students, 4/30 for international students; for spring admission, 12/31 priority date for domestic students, 11/30 for international students. Applications are processed on a rolling basis. Application fee: $75. Electronic applications accepted. *Expenses: Tuition:* Full-time $22,464; part-time $1248 per credit. *Required fees:* $501 per semester. *Financial support:* Institutionally sponsored loans, scholarships/grants, and unspecified assistantships available. Support available to part-time students. Financial award applicants required to submit FAFSA. *Unit head:* Prof. Charles S. Tapiero, Academic Director, 718-260-3653, Fax: 718-260-3874, E-mail: ctapiero@ poly.edu. *Application contact:* JeanCarlo Bonilla, Director, Graduate Enrollment Management, 718-260-3182, Fax: 718-260-3624.

Rice University, Graduate Programs, George R. Brown School of Engineering, Department of Statistics, Houston, TX 77251-1892. Offers bioinformatics (PhD); biostatistics (PhD); computational finance (PhD); general statistics (PhD); statistics (M Stat, MA); MBA/M Stat. Part-time programs available. *Degree requirements:* For master's, comprehensive exam; for doctorate, comprehensive exam, thesis/dissertation. *Entrance requirements:* For master's and doctorate, GRE General Test, minimum GPA of 3.0. Additional exam requirements/ recommendations for international students: Required—TOEFL (minimum score 630 paper-based; 250 computer-based; 90 iBT). Electronic applications accepted. *Faculty research:* Statistical genetics, non parametric function estimation, computational statistics and visualization, stochastic processes.

Stanford University, School of Humanities and Sciences, Department of Mathematics, Stanford, CA 94305-9991. Offers financial mathematics (MS); mathematics (MS, PhD). Terminal master's awarded for partial completion of doctoral program. *Degree requirements:* For doctorate, 2 foreign languages, thesis/dissertation, oral exam. *Entrance requirements:* For master's, GRE General Test; for doctorate, GRE General Test, GRE Subject Test. Additional exam requirements/recommendations for international students: Required— TOEFL. Electronic applications accepted. *Expenses: Tuition:* Full-time $40,050; part-time $890 per credit.

Université de Montréal, Faculty of Arts and Sciences, Department of Economic Sciences, Montréal, QC H3C 3J7, Canada. Offers economics (M Sc, PhD); mathematical and computational finance (M Sc). *Degree requirements:* For master's, one foreign language, thesis; for doctorate, one foreign language, thesis/dissertation, general exam. Electronic applications accepted. *Faculty research:* Applied and economic theory, public choice, international trade, labor economics, industrial organization.

Université de Montréal, Faculty of Arts and Sciences, Department of Mathematics and Statistics, Montréal, QC H3C 3J7, Canada. Offers mathematical and computational finance (M Sc, DESS); mathematics (M Sc, PhD); statistics (M Sc, PhD). *Degree requirements:* For master's, thesis; for doctorate, thesis/ dissertation, general exam. *Entrance requirements:* For master's and doctorate, proficiency in French. Electronic applications accepted. *Faculty research:* Pure and applied mathematics, actuarial mathematics.

University of Alberta, Faculty of Graduate Studies and Research, Department of Mathematical and Statistical Sciences, Edmonton, AB T6G 2E1, Canada. Offers applied mathematics (M Sc, PhD); biostatistics (M Sc); mathematical finance (M Sc, PhD); mathematical physics (M Sc, PhD); mathematics (M Sc, PhD); statistics (M Sc, PhD, Postgraduate Diploma). Part-time programs available. Terminal master's awarded for partial completion of doctoral program. *Degree requirements:* For master's, thesis (for some programs); for doctorate, comprehensive exam, thesis/dissertation. *Entrance requirements:* Additional exam requirements/recommendations for international students: Required— TOEFL (minimum score 580 paper-based; 237 computer-based). Electronic applications accepted. *Faculty research:* Classical and functional analysis, algebra, differential equations, geometry.

University of California, Santa Barbara, Graduate Division, College of Letters and Sciences, Division of Mathematics, Life, and Physical Sciences, Department of Statistics and Applied Probability, Santa Barbara, CA 93106-3110. Offers financial mathematics and statistics (PhD); quantitative methods in the social sciences (PhD); statistics (MA), including applied statistics, mathematical statistics; statistics and applied probability (PhD); MA/PhD. *Faculty:* 11 full-time (3 women). *Students:* 49 full-time (20 women); includes 9 minority (7 Asian, non-Hispanic/Latino; 1 Hispanic/Latino; 1 Two or more races, non-Hispanic/Latino), 31 international. Average age 29. 272 applicants, 19% accepted, 12 enrolled. In 2011, 14 master's, 5 doctorates awarded. Terminal master's awarded for partial completion of doctoral program. *Median time to degree:* Of those who began their doctoral program in fall 2003, 57% received their degree in 8 years or less. *Degree requirements:* For master's, comprehensive exam, thesis optional; for doctorate, comprehensive exam, thesis/dissertation. *Entrance requirements:* For master's and doctorate, GRE General Test. Additional exam requirements/ recommendations for international students: Required—TOEFL (minimum score 550 paper-based; 80 iBT), IELTS (minimum score 7). *Application deadline:* For fall admission, 1/1 priority date for domestic students, 1/1 for international students; for winter admission, 11/1 priority date for domestic students, 11/1 for international students; for spring admission, 2/1 priority date for domestic students, 2/1 for international students. Application fee: $80 ($100 for international students). Electronic applications accepted. *Expenses: Tuition:* state resident: full-time $12,192. Tuition, nonresident: full-time $27,294. *Required fees:* $764.13. *Financial support:* In 2011–12, 23 students received support, including 6

fellowships with full tuition reimbursements available (averaging $11,285 per year), 1 research assistantship with full and partial tuition reimbursement available (averaging $2,790 per year), 28 teaching assistantships with partial tuition reimbursements available (averaging $14,557 per year); Federal Work-Study, scholarships/grants, and health care benefits also available. Financial award application deadline: 1/1; financial award applicants required to submit FAFSA. *Faculty research:* Bayesian inference, financial mathematics, stochastic processes, environmental statistics, biostatistical modeling. *Total annual research expenditures:* $139,480. *Unit head:* Dr. Yuedong Wang, Chair, 805-893-4870, E-mail: yeudong@pstat.ucsb.edu. *Application contact:* Dolly J. Cook, Graduate Program Assistant, 805-893-2129, Fax: 805-893-2334, E-mail: cook@ pstat.ucsb.edu. Web site: http://www.pstat.ucsb.edu/.

University of Chicago, Division of the Physical Sciences, Department of Mathematics, Master of Science in Financial Mathematics Program, Chicago, IL 60637. Offers MS. Part-time and evening/weekend programs available. *Faculty:* 1 full-time (0 women), 13 part-time/adjunct (1 woman). *Students:* 71 full-time (27 women), 74 part-time (10 women); includes 64 minority (all Asian, non-Hispanic/ Latino). Average age 30. 540 applicants, 36% accepted, 90 enrolled. In 2011, 103 master's awarded. *Entrance requirements:* For master's, GRE General Test, GRE Subject Test (math). Additional exam requirements/recommendations for international students: Required—TOEFL (minimum score 600 paper-based; 250 computer-based). *Application deadline:* For fall admission, 12/16 priority date for domestic students, 12/16 for international students. Applications are processed on a rolling basis. Application fee: $55. Electronic applications accepted. *Financial support:* Fellowships, research assistantships, teaching assistantships, and institutionally sponsored loans available. Financial award applicants required to submit FAFSA. *Unit head:* Dr. William DeRonne, Executive Director, 773-702-1458, E-mail: bderonne@uchicago.edu. *Application contact:* Ashley Doss, Program Administrator, 773-834-0785, Fax: 773-834-4386, E-mail: adoss@ uchicago.edu. Web site: http://www-finmath.uchicago.edu/.

University of Connecticut, Graduate School, College of Liberal Arts and Sciences, Department of Mathematics, Field of Applied Financial Mathematics, Storrs, CT 06269. Offers MS. *Degree requirements:* For master's, comprehensive exam. *Entrance requirements:* Additional exam requirements/recommendations for international students: Required—TOEFL (minimum score 550 paper-based; 213 computer-based). Electronic applications accepted.

University of Dayton, Department of Mathematics, Dayton, OH 45469-1300. Offers applied mathematics (MAS); financial mathematics (MFM); mathematics education (MME). Part-time and evening/weekend programs available. *Faculty:* 15 full-time (5 women). *Students:* 37 full-time (20 women), 12 part-time (5 women); includes 4 minority (3 Black or African American, non-Hispanic/Latino; 1 Asian, non-Hispanic/Latino), 31 international. Average age 26. 110 applicants, 62% accepted, 25 enrolled. In 2011, 14 master's awarded. *Entrance requirements:* For master's, minimum undergraduate GPA of 2.8 (MAS), 3.0 (MFM, MME). Additional exam requirements/recommendations for international students: Required—TOEFL (minimum score 550 paper-based; 213 computer-based; 80 iBT). *Application deadline:* For fall admission, 3/1 priority date for domestic students, 7/1 for international students; for winter admission, 7/1 for international students; for spring admission, 1/1 for international students. Application fee: $0 ($50 for international students). Electronic applications accepted. *Expenses: Tuition:* Full-time $8400; part-time $700 per credit hour. *Required fees:* $25 per semester. Tuition and fees vary according to degree level. *Financial support:* In 2011–12, 6 teaching assistantships with full tuition reimbursements (averaging $13,400 per year) were awarded; institutionally sponsored loans, health care benefits, and unspecified assistantships also available. Financial award applicants required to submit FAFSA. *Faculty research:* Differential equations, integral equations, general topology, measure theory, graph theory, financial math, math education, numerical analysis. *Unit head:* Dr. Joe D. Mashburn, Chair, 937-229-2511, Fax: 937-229-2566, E-mail: joe.mashburn@notes.udayton.edu. *Application contact:* Alexander Popovski, Associate Director of Graduate and International Admissions, 937-229-2357, Fax: 937-229-4729, E-mail: alex.popovski@notes.udayton.edu.

University of Illinois at Chicago, Graduate College, College of Liberal Arts and Sciences, Department of Mathematics, Statistics, and Computer Science, Chicago, IL 60607-7128. Offers applied mathematics (MS, PhD); computational finance (MS, PhD); computer science (MS, PhD); mathematics (DA); mathematics and information sciences for industry (MS); probability and statistics (PhD); pure mathematics (MS, PhD); statistics (MS); teaching of mathematics (MST), including elementary, secondary. Part-time programs available. *Degree requirements:* For master's, comprehensive exam; for doctorate, one foreign language, thesis/dissertation. *Entrance requirements:* For master's and doctorate, GRE General Test, minimum GPA of 3.0. Additional exam requirements/ recommendations for international students: Required—TOEFL (minimum score 100 iBT). Electronic applications accepted.

The University of Manchester, School of Mathematics, Manchester, United Kingdom. Offers actuarial science (PhD); applied mathematics (M Phil, PhD); applied numerical computing (M Phil, PhD); financial mathematics (M Phil, PhD); mathematical logic (M Phil); probability (M Phil, PhD); pure mathematics (M Phil, PhD); statistics (M Phil, PhD).

The University of North Carolina at Charlotte, Graduate School, Belk College of Business, Department of Finance, Charlotte, NC 28223-0001. Offers mathematical finance (MS). *Faculty:* 13 full-time (1 woman), 1 part-time/adjunct (0

Peterson's Graduate Programs in the Physical Sciences, Mathematics, Agricultural Sciences, the Environment & Natural Resources 2013

facebook.com/petersonspublishing **325**

women). *Students:* 54 full-time (18 women), 37 part-time (7 women); includes 14 minority (8 Black or African American, non-Hispanic/Latino; 6 Asian, non-Hispanic/Latino), 49 international. Average age 27. 149 applicants, 86% accepted, 50 enrolled. In 2011, 23 master's awarded. *Degree requirements:* For master's, thesis or alternative. *Entrance requirements:* Additional exam requirements/recommendations for international students: Required—TOEFL (minimum score 557 paper-based; 220 computer-based; 87 iBT). Application fee: $65 ($75 for international students). *Expenses:* Tuition, state resident: full-time $3689. Tuition, nonresident: full-time $15,226. *Required fees:* $2198. Tuition and fees vary according to course load and program. *Unit head:* Dr. Joe Mazzola, Interim Dean, 704-687-7577, Fax: 704-687-4014, E-mail: jmazzola@uncc.edu. *Application contact:* Kathy B. Giddings, Director of Graduate Admissions, 704-687-5503, Fax: 704-687-3279, E-mail: gradadm@uncc.edu. Web site: http://belkcollege.uncc.edu/about-college/departments/finance.

University of Notre Dame, Graduate School, College of Science, Department of Applied and Computational Mathematics and Statistics, Notre Dame, IN 46556. Offers applied and computational mathematics and statistics (PhD); applied statistics (MS); computational finance (MS).

University of Southern California, Graduate School, Dana and David Dornsife College of Letters, Arts and Sciences, Department of Economics, Los Angeles, CA 90089. Offers economic development programming (MA, PhD); mathematical finance (MS); M PI/MA; MA/JD. Terminal master's awarded for partial completion of doctoral program. *Degree requirements:* For master's, comprehensive exam; for doctorate, comprehensive exam, thesis/dissertation. *Entrance requirements:* For master's and doctorate, GRE. Additional exam requirements/recommendations for international students: Required—TOEFL (minimum score 93 iBT). Electronic applications accepted. *Faculty research:* Macro theory, development economics, econometrics.

University of Southern California, Graduate School, Dana and David Dornsife College of Letters, Arts and Sciences, Department of Mathematics, Los Angeles, CA 90089. Offers applied mathematics (MA, MS, PhD); mathematical finance (MS); mathematics (MA, PhD); statistics (MS). Part-time programs available. Terminal master's awarded for partial completion of doctoral program. *Degree requirements:* For master's, comprehensive exam (for some programs), thesis (for some programs); for doctorate, one foreign language, comprehensive exam, thesis/dissertation. *Entrance requirements:* For master's, GRE General Test, GMAT; for doctorate, GRE General Test, GRE Subject Test (mathematics). Additional exam requirements/recommendations for international students: Required—TOEFL (minimum score 100 iBT). Electronic applications accepted. *Faculty research:* Algebra, algebraic geometry and number theory, analysis/partial differential equations, applied mathematics, financial mathematics, probability, combinatorics and statistics.

University of Toronto, School of Graduate Studies, Program in Mathematical/Finance, Toronto, ON M5S 1A1, Canada. Offers MMF. *Entrance requirements:* For master's, four-year bachelor's degree in a quantitative, technical discipline from recognized university with minimum of the equivalent of the University of Toronto mid-B (75%) standing in final two years of program or equivalent number of most senior courses. Additional exam requirements/recommendations for international students: Required—TOEFL (minimum score 580 paper-based; 93 iBT), TWE (minimum score 5). Electronic applications accepted.

Mathematics

Alabama State University, Department of Mathematics and Computer Science, Montgomery, AL 36101-0271. Offers mathematics (M Ed, MS, Ed S). Part-time programs available. *Faculty:* 5 full-time (0 women). *Students:* 1 (woman) full-time; minority (Black or African American, non-Hispanic/Latino). Average age 23. 4 applicants, 25% accepted, 0 enrolled. *Degree requirements:* For Ed S, thesis. *Entrance requirements:* For master's, GRE General Test, GRE Subject Test, graduate writing competence test; for Ed S, GRE General Test, MAT, graduate writing competency test. Additional exam requirements/recommendations for international students: Required—TOEFL (minimum score 500 paper-based; 173 computer-based). *Application deadline:* For fall admission, 7/15 for domestic students; for spring admission, 12/15 for domestic students. Applications are processed on a rolling basis. Application fee: $10. *Financial support:* In 2011–12, 1 research assistantship (averaging $9,450 per year) was awarded. *Faculty research:* Discrete mathematics, symbolic dynamics, mathematical social sciences. *Total annual research expenditures:* $25,000. *Unit head:* Dr. Wallace Maryland, Chair, 334-229-4464, Fax: 334-229-4902, E-mail: wmaryl@asunet.alasu.edu. *Application contact:* Dr. Doris Screws, Dean of Graduate Studies, 334-229-4274, Fax: 334-229-4928, E-mail: dscrews@alasu.edu. Web site: http://www.alasu.edu/academics/colleges—departments/science-mathematics—technology/mathematics—computer-science/index.aspx.

American University, College of Arts and Sciences, Department of Mathematics and Statistics, Washington, DC 22016-8050. Offers applied statistics (Certificate); mathematics (MA); statistics (MS). Part-time and evening/weekend programs available. *Faculty:* 26 full-time (8 women), 10 part-time/adjunct (0 women). *Students:* 11 full-time (5 women), 8 part-time (4 women); includes 4 minority (3 Black or African American, non-Hispanic/Latino; 1 Hispanic/Latino), 2 international. Average age 29. 44 applicants, 77% accepted, 10 enrolled. In 2011, 11 master's awarded. *Degree requirements:* For master's, comprehensive exam, thesis or alternative, tools of research in foreign language or computer language. *Entrance requirements:* For master's, GRE; for Certificate, bachelor's degree. Additional exam requirements/recommendations for international students: Required—TOEFL. *Application deadline:* For fall admission, 2/1 for domestic students; for spring admission, 10/1 for domestic students. Application fee: $80. *Expenses:* Tuition: Full-time $24,264; part-time $1348 per credit hour. *Required fees:* $430. Tuition and fees vary according to course load and program. *Financial support:* Fellowships, research assistantships, teaching assistantships, career-related internships or fieldwork, Federal Work-Study, institutionally sponsored loans, and unspecified assistantships available. Support available to part-time students. Financial award application deadline: 2/1. *Faculty research:* Logic, random processes, probability analysis, biostatistics, statistical computing. *Unit head:* Dr. Jeffrey D. Adler, Chair, 202-885-3171, Fax: 202-885-3155, E-mail: jadler@american.edu. *Application contact:* Kathleen Clowery, Director, Graduate Admissions, 202-885-3621, Fax: 202-885-1505, E-mail: clowery@american.edu. Web site: http://www.american.edu/cas/mathstat/.

American University of Beirut, Graduate Programs, Faculty of Arts and Sciences, Beirut, Lebanon. Offers anthropology (MA); Arabic language and literature (MA); archaeology (MA); biology (MS); chemistry (MS); computational science (MS); computer science (MS); economics (MA); education (MA); English language (MA); English literature (MA); environmental policy planning (MSES); financial economics (MAFE); geology (MS); history (MA); mathematics (MA, MS); Middle Eastern studies (MA); philosophy (MA); physics (MS); political studies (MA); psychology (MA); public administration (MA); sociology (MA); statistics (MA, MS). Part-time programs available. *Faculty:* 154 full-time (44 women), 12 part-time/adjunct (2 women). *Students:* 180 full-time (122 women), 240 part-time (158 women). Average age 25. 336 applicants, 47% accepted, 86 enrolled. In 2011, 57 master's awarded. *Degree requirements:* For master's, one foreign language, comprehensive exam, thesis (for some programs). *Entrance requirements:* For master's, GRE, letter of recommendation. Additional exam requirements/recommendations for international students: Required—TOEFL (minimum score 600 paper-based; 250 computer-based; 97 iBT), IELTS (minimum score 7). *Application deadline:* For fall admission, 4/30 for domestic and international students; for spring admission, 11/1 for domestic and international students. Application fee: $50. *Expenses: Tuition:* Full-time $12,780; part-time $710 per credit. *Required fees:* $528; $528 per credit. Tuition and fees vary according to course load and program. *Financial support:* In 2011–12, 33 students received support. Career-related internships or fieldwork, institutionally sponsored loans, scholarships/grants, health care benefits, and unspecified assistantships available. Financial award application deadline: 2/4; financial award applicants required to submit FAFSA. *Faculty research:* History of composition studies, syntax of Arabic dialects, Oscar Wilde, decadence, Middle Eastern and international politics, neural mechanisms of creativity and consciousness, personality and psycho-socio-cultural-spiritual correlates of negative and positive mental health, philosophy of mind, metaphysics, micropaleontology and stratigraphy, geochemistry, mineralogy and petrology, tectonophysics, Abbasid, Ottoman and Russian history, landscape, Bronze and Iron Age archaeology. *Unit head:* Dr. Patrick McGreevy, Dean, 961-1374374 Ext. 3800, Fax: 961-1744461, E-mail: pm07@aub.edu.lb. *Application contact:* Dr. Salim Kanaan, Director, Admissions Office, 961-1350000 Ext. 2594, Fax: 961-1750775, E-mail: sk00@aub.edu.lb. Web site: http://staff.aub.edu.lb/~webfas.

Andrews University, School of Graduate Studies, College of Arts and Sciences, Interdisciplinary Studies in Mathematics and Physical Science Program, Berrien Springs, MI 49104. Offers MS. *Students:* 1 (woman) full-time, 2 part-time (0 women), 1 international. Average age 26. 4 applicants, 25% accepted, 1 enrolled. *Application deadline:* Applications are processed on a rolling basis. Application fee: $40. *Unit head:* Dr. Margarita Mattingly, Chairman, 269-471-3431. *Application contact:* Carolyn Hurst, Supervisor of Graduate Admission, 800-253-3430, Fax: 269-471-3228, E-mail: enroll@andrews.edu.

Appalachian State University, Cratis D. Williams Graduate School, Department of Mathematical Sciences, Boone, NC 28608. Offers mathematics (MA); mathematics education (MA). Part-time programs available. Postbaccalaureate distance learning degree programs offered (no on-campus study). *Faculty:* 24 full-time (9 women), 2 part-time/adjunct (1 woman). *Students:* 12 full-time (5 women), 7 part-time (6 women); includes 1 minority (Hispanic/Latino). 8 applicants, 100% accepted, 5 enrolled. In 2011, 5 master's awarded. *Degree requirements:* For master's, comprehensive exam, thesis optional. *Entrance requirements:* For master's, GRE General Test, 3 letters of recommendation. Additional exam requirements/recommendations for international students: Required—TOEFL (minimum score 570 paper-based; 230 computer-based; 79 iBT), IELTS (minimum score 6.5). *Application deadline:* For fall admission, 3/15 priority date for domestic students, 2/1 for international students; for spring admission, 11/1 for

326 facebook.com/petersonspublishing

Peterson's Graduate Programs in the Physical Sciences, Mathematics, Agricultural Sciences, the Environment & Natural Resources 2013

domestic students, 7/1 for international students. Applications are processed on a rolling basis. Application fee: $55. Electronic applications accepted. *Expenses:* Tuition, state resident: full-time $4040; part-time $180 per semester hour. Tuition, nonresident: full-time $15,900; part-time $760 per semester hour. *Required fees:* $2500; $20 per semester hour. Tuition and fees vary according to campus/location. *Financial support:* In 2011–12, 14 teaching assistantships (averaging $9,500 per year) were awarded; fellowships, research assistantships, career-related internships or fieldwork, Federal Work-Study, scholarships/grants, and unspecified assistantships also available. Financial award application deadline: 4/1; financial award applicants required to submit FAFSA. *Faculty research:* Graph theory, differential equations, logic, geometry, complex analysis, topology, algebra, mathematics education. *Total annual research expenditures:* $80,000. *Unit head:* Dr. Mark Ginn, Chair, 828-262-3050, Fax: 828-265-8617, E-mail: ginnmc@appstate.edu. *Application contact:* Dr. Trina Palmer, Graduate Director, 828-262-3050, E-mail: palmerk@appstate.edu. Web site: http://www.mathsci.appstate.edu/.

Arizona State University, College of Liberal Arts and Sciences, Department of Mathematics and Statistics, Tempe, AZ 85287-1804. Offers applied mathematics (PhD); computational biosciences (PhD); mathematics (MA, MNS, PhD); mathematics education (PhD); statistics (PhD). Part-time programs available. Terminal master's awarded for partial completion of doctoral program. *Degree requirements:* For master's, thesis or alternative, interactive Program of Study (iPOS) submitted before completing 50 percent of required credit hours; for doctorate, comprehensive exam, thesis/dissertation, interactive Program of Study (iPOS) submitted before completing 50 percent of required credit hours. *Entrance requirements:* For master's and doctorate, GRE General Test, minimum GPA of 3.0 or equivalent in last 2 years of work leading to bachelor's degree. Additional exam requirements/recommendations for international students: Required—TOEFL (minimum score 80 iBT), TOEFL, IELTS, or Pearson Test of English. Electronic applications accepted. *Expenses:* Contact institution.

Arkansas State University, Graduate School, College of Sciences and Mathematics, Department of Mathematics and Statistics, Jonesboro, State University, AR 72467. Offers mathematics (MS); mathematics education (MSE). Part-time programs available. *Faculty:* 11 full-time (5 women). *Students:* 12 full-time (7 women), 12 part-time (7 women); includes 2 minority (1 Black or African American, non-Hispanic/Latino; 1 Hispanic/Latino), 4 international. Average age 32. 14 applicants, 93% accepted, 10 enrolled. In 2011, 8 master's awarded. *Degree requirements:* For master's, comprehensive exam, thesis and alternative. *Entrance requirements:* For master's, GRE General Test or MAT, appropriate bachelor's degree, official transcripts, immunization records, valid teaching certificate (for MSE). Additional exam requirements/recommendations for international students: Required—TOEFL (minimum score 550 paper-based; 213 computer-based; 79 iBT), IELTS (minimum score 6), PTE: Pearson Test of English Academic (minimum score 56). *Application deadline:* For fall admission, 7/1 for domestic and international students; for spring admission, 11/15 for domestic students, 11/14 for international students. Applications are processed on a rolling basis. Application fee: $30 ($40 for international students). Electronic applications accepted. *Expenses:* Tuition, state resident: full-time $4044; part-time $225 per credit hour. Tuition, nonresident: full-time $8087; part-time $449 per credit hour. *Required fees:* $936; $52 per credit hour. $25 per term. One-time fee: $30. Tuition and fees vary according to course load and program. *Financial support:* In 2011–12, 10 students received support. Teaching assistantships, career-related internships or fieldwork, scholarships/grants, and unspecified assistantships available. Financial award application deadline: 7/1; financial award applicants required to submit FAFSA. *Unit head:* Dr. Debra Ingram, Chair, 870-972-3090, Fax: 870-972-3950, E-mail: dingram@astate.edu. *Application contact:* Dr. Andrew Sustich, Dean of the Graduate School, 870-972-3029, Fax: 870-972-3857, E-mail: sustich@astate.edu. Web site: http://www.mathstat.astate.edu.

Auburn University, Graduate School, College of Sciences and Mathematics, Department of Mathematics and Statistics, Auburn University, AL 36849. Offers applied mathematics (MAM, MS); mathematics (MS, PhD); probability and statistics (M Prob S); statistics (MS). *Faculty:* 50 full-time (7 women), 6 part-time/adjunct (4 women). *Students:* 56 full-time (14 women), 52 part-time (14 women); includes 4 minority (3 Black or African American, non-Hispanic/Latino; 1 Hispanic/Latino), 43 international. Average age 28. 160 applicants, 59% accepted, 37 enrolled. In 2011, 17 master's, 9 doctorates awarded. *Degree requirements:* For doctorate, thesis/dissertation. *Entrance requirements:* For master's, GRE General Test, undergraduate mathematics background; for doctorate, GRE General Test, GRE Subject Test. *Application deadline:* For fall admission, 7/7 priority date for domestic students; for spring admission, 11/24 for domestic students. Applications are processed on a rolling basis. Application fee: $50 ($60 for international students). Electronic applications accepted. *Expenses:* Tuition, state resident: full-time $7290; part-time $405 per credit hour. Tuition, nonresident: full-time $21,870; part-time $1215 per credit hour. *International tuition:* $22,000 full-time. *Required fees:* $1402. *Financial support:* Fellowships and teaching assistantships available. Financial award applicants required to submit FAFSA. *Faculty research:* Pure and applied mathematics. *Unit head:* Dr. Michel Smith, Chair, 334-844-4290, Fax: 334-844-6655. *Application contact:* Dr. George Flowers, Dean of the Graduate School, 334-844-2125. Web site: http://www.auburn.edu/~math/.

Aurora University, College of Arts and Sciences, Aurora, IL 60506-4892. Offers elementary math and science (MATL); life science (MATL); mathematics (MATL,

MS). Part-time and evening/weekend programs available. *Entrance requirements:* Additional exam requirements/recommendations for international students: Required—TOEFL (minimum score 550 paper-based; 213 computer-based). Electronic applications accepted. *Expenses:* Contact institution.

Ball State University, Graduate School, College of Sciences and Humanities, Department of Mathematical Sciences, Program in Mathematics, Muncie, IN 47306-1099. Offers mathematics (MA, MS); mathematics education (MA). *Faculty:* 20. *Students:* 6 full-time (3 women), 35 part-time (27 women); includes 2 minority (1 Black or African American, non-Hispanic/Latino; 1 Two or more races, non-Hispanic/Latino), 1 international. Average age 39. 23 applicants, 74% accepted, 11 enrolled. In 2011, 7 master's awarded. Application fee: $50. Tuition and fees vary according to program and reciprocity agreements. *Financial support:* In 2011–12, 5 students received support, including 5 teaching assistantships with tuition reimbursements available (averaging $4,246 per year). Financial award application deadline: 3/1. *Unit head:* Dr. Sheryl Stump, Director, 765-285-8662, Fax: 765-285-1721. *Application contact:* Dr. Hanspeter Fischer, Director, 765-285-8640, Fax: 765-285-1721, E-mail: mali@bsu.edu. Web site: http://cms.bsu.edu/Academics/CollegesandDepartments/Math/AcademicsAdmissions/Programs/Masters/MAorMSinMath.aspx.

Baylor University, Graduate School, College of Arts and Sciences, Department of Mathematics, Waco, TX 76798. Offers MS, PhD. *Faculty:* 23 full-time (1 woman). *Students:* 25 full-time (5 women), 1 part-time (0 women); includes 3 minority (1 Asian, non-Hispanic/Latino; 2 Hispanic/Latino), 3 international. 39 applicants, 18% accepted, 5 enrolled. In 2011, 4 master's, 3 doctorates awarded. *Degree requirements:* For master's, final oral exam. *Entrance requirements:* For master's and doctorate, GRE General Test. *Application deadline:* For fall admission, 2/15 for domestic students. Applications are processed on a rolling basis. Application fee: $50. Electronic applications accepted. *Financial support:* Teaching assistantships, career-related internships or fieldwork, Federal Work-Study, and institutionally sponsored loans available. Support available to part-time students. Financial award application deadline: 5/1. *Faculty research:* Algebra, statistics, probability, applied mathematics, numerical analysis. *Unit head:* Dr. Mark Spenski, Graduate Program Director, 254-710-6577, Fax: 254-710-3569, E-mail: ronald_stanke@baylor.edu. *Application contact:* Rita Massey, Graduate Associate, 254-710-3146, Fax: 254-710-3870, E-mail: rita_massey@baylor.edu. Web site: http://www.baylor.edu/math/.

Bemidji State University, School of Graduate Studies, Bemidji, MN 56601-2699. Offers biology (MS); counseling psychology (MS); education (M Ed, MS); English (MA, MS); environmental studies (MS); mathematics (MS); mathematics (elementary and middle level education) (MS); special education (M Sp Ed, MS). Part-time programs available. Postbaccalaureate distance learning degree programs offered (no on-campus study). *Faculty:* 114 full-time (47 women), 22 part-time/adjunct (16 women). *Students:* 68 full-time (45 women), 311 part-time (198 women); includes 21 minority (4 Black or African American, non-Hispanic/Latino; 2 American Indian or Alaska Native, non-Hispanic/Latino; 5 Asian, non-Hispanic/Latino; 5 Hispanic/Latino; 5 Two or more races, non-Hispanic/Latino), 5 international. Average age 34. 82 applicants, 98% accepted, 37 enrolled. In 2011, 72 master's awarded. *Degree requirements:* For master's, comprehensive exam, thesis (for some programs). *Entrance requirements:* For master's, GRE, letters of recommendation, letters of interest. Additional exam requirements/recommendations for international students: Required—TOEFL (minimum score 550 paper-based; 213 computer-based; 80 iBT). *Application deadline:* Applications are processed on a rolling basis. Application fee: $20. Electronic applications accepted. *Expenses:* Tuition, state resident: full-time $6182; part-time $343.45 per credit. Tuition, nonresident: full-time $6182; part-time $343.45 per credit. *Required fees:* $954. *Financial support:* In 2011–12, 253 students received support, including 36 research assistantships with partial tuition reimbursements available (averaging $7,441 per year), 36 teaching assistantships with partial tuition reimbursements available (averaging $7,441 per year); career-related internships or fieldwork, scholarships/grants, health care benefits, and unspecified assistantships also available. Support available to part-time students. Financial award application deadline: 4/15; financial award applicants required to submit FAFSA. *Unit head:* Dr. Patricia Rogers, Dean of Health Sciences and Human Ecology, 218-755-2027, Fax: 218-755-2258, E-mail: progers@bemidjistate.edu. *Application contact:* Joan Miller, Senior Office and Administrative Specialist, 218-755-2027, Fax: 218-755-2258, E-mail: jmiller@bemidjistate.edu. Web site: http://www.bemidjistate.edu/academics/graduate_studies/.

Boston College, Graduate School of Arts and Sciences, Department of Mathematics, Chestnut Hill, MA 02467-3800. Offers PhD, MBA/MA. *Entrance requirements:* Additional exam requirements/recommendations for international students: Required—TOEFL (minimum score 600 paper-based; 250 computer-based; 100 iBT). Electronic applications accepted. *Faculty research:* Abstract algebra and number theory, topology, probability and statistics, computer science, analysis.

Boston University, Graduate School of Arts and Sciences, Department of Mathematics and Statistics, Boston, MA 02215. Offers mathematics (MA, PhD). *Students:* 56 full-time (18 women), 2 part-time (0 women); includes 5 minority (1 Black or African American, non-Hispanic/Latino; 3 Asian, non-Hispanic/Latino; 1 Hispanic/Latino), 25 international. Average age 27. 348 applicants, 16% accepted, 19 enrolled. In 2011, 71 master's, 8 doctorates awarded. Terminal master's awarded for partial completion of doctoral program. *Degree requirements:* For master's, one foreign language, comprehensive exam; for

Peterson's Graduate Programs in the Physical Sciences, Mathematics, Agricultural Sciences, the Environment & Natural Resources 2013

facebook.com/petersonspublishing **327**

Mathematics

doctorate, one foreign language, comprehensive exam, thesis/dissertation. *Entrance requirements:* For master's and doctorate, GRE General Test, GRE Subject Test, 3 letters of recommendation. Additional exam requirements/recommendations for international students: Required—TOEFL (minimum score 600 paper-based; 250 computer-based). *Application deadline:* For fall admission, 1/15 for domestic and international students; for spring admission, 10/15 for domestic and international students. Application fee: $70. Electronic applications accepted. *Expenses: Tuition:* Full-time $40,848; part-time $1276 per credit hour. *Required fees:* $572; $286 per semester. *Financial support:* In 2011–12, 2 fellowships with full tuition reimbursements (averaging $19,800 per year), 17 research assistantships with full tuition reimbursements (averaging $19,300 per year), 34 teaching assistantships with full tuition reimbursements (averaging $19,300 per year) were awarded; Federal Work-Study and scholarships/grants also available. Support available to part-time students. Financial award application deadline: 1/15; financial award applicants required to submit FAFSA. *Unit head:* Tasso Kaper, Chairman, 617-353-9552, Fax: 617-353-8100, E-mail: tasso@bu.edu. *Application contact:* Kathleen Heavey, Staff Coordinator, 617-353-2560, Fax: 617-353-8100, E-mail: kheavey@bu.edu. Web site: http://math.bu.edu/.

Bowling Green State University, Graduate College, College of Arts and Sciences, Department of Mathematics and Statistics, Bowling Green, OH 43403. Offers applied statistics (MS); mathematics (MA, MAT, PhD); statistics (PhD). Part-time programs available. *Degree requirements:* For master's, thesis or alternative; for doctorate, comprehensive exam, thesis/dissertation. *Entrance requirements:* For master's and doctorate, GRE General Test. Additional exam requirements/recommendations for international students: Required—TOEFL. Electronic applications accepted. *Faculty research:* Statistics and probability, algebra, analysis.

Brandeis University, Graduate School of Arts and Sciences, Department of Mathematics, Waltham, MA 02454-9110. Offers MA, PhD, Postbaccalaureate Certificate. Part-time programs available. *Degree requirements:* For doctorate, 2 foreign languages, thesis/dissertation. *Entrance requirements:* For master's, GRE General Test and GRE Subject Test (recommended), resume, letters of recommendation; for doctorate, GRE General Test, GRE Subject Test, resume, letters of recommendation. Additional exam requirements/recommendations for international students: Required—TOEFL (minimum score 600 paper-based; 250 computer-based; 100 iBT); Recommended—IELTS (minimum score 7). Electronic applications accepted. *Faculty research:* Algebra, analysis, number theory, combinatorics, topology.

Brigham Young University, Graduate Studies, College of Physical and Mathematical Sciences, Department of Mathematics, Provo, UT 84602-1001. Offers MS, PhD. Part-time programs available. *Faculty:* 32 full-time (2 women). *Students:* 16 full-time (2 women), 19 part-time (2 women); includes 4 minority (all Asian, non-Hispanic/Latino), 1 international. Average age 23. 24 applicants, 71% accepted, 14 enrolled. In 2011, 13 degrees awarded. Terminal master's awarded for partial completion of doctoral program. *Degree requirements:* For master's, comprehensive exam, thesis (for some programs), project; written exams; for doctorate, comprehensive exam, thesis/dissertation, qualifying exams. *Entrance requirements:* For master's, GRE General Test, GRE Subject Test (math; minimum score of 600), minimum GPA of 3.0 in last 60 hours, bachelor's degree in mathematics; for doctorate, GRE General Test, GRE Subject Test (math; minimum score of 600), master's degree in mathematics or related field. Additional exam requirements/recommendations for international students: Required—TOEFL (minimum score 600 paper-based; 240 computer-based; 85 iBT). *Application deadline:* For fall admission, 3/1 priority date for domestic students, 3/1 for international students; for winter admission, 9/15 for domestic students, 3/1 for international students; for spring admission, 2/15 for domestic and international students. Applications are processed on a rolling basis. Application fee: $50. Electronic applications accepted. Full-time tuition for non-LDS students: $11,520 per year; $640 per credit. *Expenses: Tuition:* Full-time $5760; part-time $320 per credit. Tuition and fees vary according to student's religious affiliation. *Financial support:* In 2011–12, 30 students received support, including 20 research assistantships (averaging $17,400 per year), 30 teaching assistantships with full tuition reimbursements available (averaging $17,400 per year); institutionally sponsored loans also available. Support available to part-time students. Financial award application deadline: 3/1. *Faculty research:* Algebraic geometry/number theory, applied math/nonlinear PDEs, combinatorics/matrix theory, geometric group theory/topology. *Total annual research expenditures:* $653,000. *Unit head:* Dr. Tyler J. Jarvis, Chairperson, 801-422-5925, Fax: 801-422-0504, E-mail: jarvis@math.byu.edu. *Application contact:* Lonette Stoddard, Graduate Secretary, 801-422-2062, Fax: 801-422-0504, E-mail: gradschool@math.byu.edu. Web site: http://www.math.byu.edu/.

Brock University, Faculty of Graduate Studies, Faculty of Mathematics and Science, Program in Mathematics and Statistics, St. Catharines, ON L2S 3A1, Canada. Offers M Sc. Part-time programs available. *Degree requirements:* For master's, thesis or project. *Entrance requirements:* For master's, honors degree. Additional exam requirements/recommendations for international students: Required—TOEFL (minimum score 550 paper-based; 213 computer-based; 80 iBT), IELTS (minimum score 6.5), TWE (minimum score 4). Electronic applications accepted.

Brooklyn College of the City University of New York, Division of Graduate Studies, Department of Mathematics, Brooklyn, NY 11210-2889. Offers mathematics (MA, PhD). Part-time and evening/weekend programs available.

Degree requirements: For master's, comprehensive exam (mathematics). *Entrance requirements:* For master's, minimum GPA of 3.0, 2 letters of recommendation. Additional exam requirements/recommendations for international students: Required—TOEFL (minimum score 500 paper-based; 173 computer-based; 61 iBT). Electronic applications accepted. *Faculty research:* Differential geometry, gauge theory, complex analysis, orthogonal functions.

Brown University, Graduate School, Department of Mathematics, Providence, RI 02912. Offers M Sc, MA, PhD. *Faculty:* 26 full-time (6 women). *Students:* 43 full-time (10 women); includes 3 minority (1 American Indian or Alaska Native, non-Hispanic/Latino; 2 Asian, non-Hispanic/Latino), 24 international. Average age 25. 257 applicants, 10% accepted, 6 enrolled. In 2011, 12 degrees awarded. *Median time to degree:* Of those who began their doctoral program in fall 2003, 100% received their degree in 8 years or less. *Degree requirements:* For doctorate, one foreign language, thesis/dissertation. *Entrance requirements:* For doctorate, GRE. Additional exam requirements/recommendations for international students: Required—TOEFL (minimum score 900 paper-based; 100 iBT) or IELTS (minimum score 7). *Application deadline:* For fall admission, 1/10 priority date for domestic students, 1/10 for international students. Application fee: $75. Electronic applications accepted. *Financial support:* In 2011–12, 43 students received support, including 15 fellowships with full tuition reimbursements available (averaging $21,000 per year), 7 research assistantships with full tuition reimbursements available (averaging $20,500 per year), 21 teaching assistantships with full tuition reimbursements available (averaging $20,500 per year); Federal Work-Study, institutionally sponsored loans, and tuition waivers (full and partial) also available. Financial award application deadline: 1/10; financial award applicants required to submit FAFSA. *Faculty research:* Algebraic geometry, number theory, functional analysis, geometry, topology, theoretical PDE. *Total annual research expenditures:* $1.1 million. *Unit head:* Prof. Jeffrey Hoffstein, Chair, 401-863-3319, Fax: 401-863-9471, E-mail: jhoff@math.brown.edu. *Application contact:* Prof. Justin Holmer, Director of Graduate Studies, 401-863-1123, Fax: 401-863-9471, E-mail: holmer@math.brown.edu. Web site: http://www.math.brown.edu/.

Bryn Mawr College, Graduate School of Arts and Sciences, Department of Mathematics, Bryn Mawr, PA 19010-2899. Offers MA, PhD. Part-time programs available. *Faculty:* 6. *Students:* 4 full-time (all women), 3 part-time (2 women). Average age 30. 11 applicants, 18% accepted, 2 enrolled. In 2011, 1 degree awarded. *Degree requirements:* For master's, one foreign language, thesis; for doctorate, 2 foreign languages, comprehensive exam, thesis/dissertation. *Entrance requirements:* For master's and doctorate, GRE General Test. Additional exam requirements/recommendations for international students: Required—TOEFL (minimum score 600 paper-based; 200 computer-based). *Application deadline:* For fall admission, 1/3 for domestic and international students. Application fee: $50. *Expenses: Tuition:* Full-time $34,110; part-time $4500 per unit. *Financial support:* In 2011–12, 1 research assistantship with full tuition reimbursement (averaging $15,000 per year), 4 teaching assistantships with partial tuition reimbursements (averaging $14,000 per year) were awarded; Federal Work-Study, scholarships/grants, tuition waivers (full and partial), unspecified assistantships, and tuition awards also available. Support available to part-time students. Financial award application deadline: 1/3. *Unit head:* Dr. Leslie C. Cheng, Chair, 610-526-5349, E-mail: lcheng@brynmawr.edu. *Application contact:* Teri R. Lobo, Administrative Assistant to the Graduate School of Arts and Sciences Dean, 610-526-5074, Fax: 610-526-5076, E-mail: lrmiller@brynmawr.edu.

Bucknell University, Graduate Studies, College of Arts and Sciences, Department of Mathematics, Lewisburg, PA 17837. Offers MA, MS. *Faculty:* 21 full-time (8 women). *Students:* 1 full-time (0 women). 3 applicants, 33% accepted, 1 enrolled. *Degree requirements:* For master's, comprehensive exam, thesis or alternative. *Entrance requirements:* For master's, GRE General Test, GRE Subject Test, minimum GPA of 3.0. Additional exam requirements/recommendations for international students: Required—TOEFL (minimum score 600 paper-based). *Application deadline:* For fall admission, 2/1 priority date for domestic students, 1/1 for international students. Application fee: $25. *Financial support:* In 2011–12, 1 student received support, including 1 research assistantship with full tuition reimbursement available (averaging $28,000 per year); unspecified assistantships also available. Financial award application deadline: 2/1. *Unit head:* Dr. Gregory Adams, Chair, 570-577-1343. *Application contact:* Gretchen H. Fegley, Coordinator, 570-577-3655, Fax: 570-577-3760, E-mail: gfegley@bucknell.edu. Web site: http://www.bucknell.edu/.

California Institute of Technology, Division of Physics, Mathematics and Astronomy, Department of Mathematics, Pasadena, CA 91125-0001. Offers PhD. *Degree requirements:* For doctorate, one foreign language, thesis/dissertation, candidacy and final exams. *Entrance requirements:* For doctorate, GRE General Test, GRE Subject Test. Additional exam requirements/recommendations for international students: Required—TOEFL. *Faculty research:* Number theory, combinatorics, differential geometry, dynamical systems, finite groups.

California Polytechnic State University, San Luis Obispo, College of Science and Mathematics, Department of Mathematics, San Luis Obispo, CA 93407. Offers MS. Part-time programs available. *Faculty:* 1 full-time (0 women). *Students:* 9 full-time (4 women), 7 part-time (3 women); includes 4 minority (all Hispanic/Latino). Average age 25. 19 applicants, 32% accepted, 5 enrolled. In 2011, 6 master's awarded. *Degree requirements:* For master's, comprehensive exam, qualifying exams. *Entrance requirements:* For master's, minimum GPA of 2.5 in last 90 quarter units of course work. Additional exam requirements/

recommendations for international students: Required—TOEFL (minimum score 550 paper-based; 213 computer-based) or IELTS (minimum score 6). *Application deadline:* For fall admission, 7/1 for domestic students, 11/30 for international students; for winter admission, 11/1 for domestic students, 6/30 for international students; for spring admission, 2/1 for domestic students. Applications are processed on a rolling basis. Application fee: $55. *Expenses:* Tuition, state resident: full-time $6738. Tuition, nonresident: full-time $17,898. *Required fees:* $2449. *Financial support:* Fellowships, teaching assistantships, career-related internships or fieldwork, Federal Work-Study, and scholarships/grants available. Support available to part-time students. Financial award application deadline: 3/2; financial award applicants required to submit FAFSA. *Faculty research:* Combinatorics, dynamical systems, ordinary and partial differential equations, operator theory, topology. *Unit head:* Dr. Dylan Retsek, Graduate Coordinator, 805-756-2072, Fax: 805-756-6537, E-mail: dretsek@calpoly.edu. *Application contact:* Dr. James Maraviglia, Associate Vice Provost for Marketing and Enrollment Development, 805-756-2311, Fax: 805-756-5400, E-mail: admissions@calpoly.edu. Web site: http://math.calpoly.edu/mathematicsms.html.

California State Polytechnic University, Pomona, Academic Affairs, College of Science, Program in Mathematics, Pomona, CA 91768-2557. Offers applied mathematics (MS); pure mathematics (MS). Part-time programs available. *Students:* 13 full-time (5 women), 32 part-time (15 women); includes 21 minority (12 Asian, non-Hispanic/Latino; 8 Hispanic/Latino; 1 Two or more races, non-Hispanic/Latino), 3 international. Average age 32. 53 applicants, 57% accepted, 14 enrolled. In 2011, 27 master's awarded. *Degree requirements:* For master's, thesis or alternative. *Entrance requirements:* For master's, GRE General Test. *Application deadline:* For fall admission, 5/1 priority date for domestic students; for winter admission, 10/15 priority date for domestic students; for spring admission, 1/20 priority date for domestic students. Applications are processed on a rolling basis. Application fee: $55. Electronic applications accepted. *Expenses:* Tuition, state resident: full-time $6738. Tuition, nonresident: full-time $12,300. *Required fees:* $657. Tuition and fees vary according to course load and program. *Financial support:* Career-related internships or fieldwork, Federal Work-Study, and institutionally sponsored loans available. Support available to part-time students. Financial award application deadline: 3/2; financial award applicants required to submit FAFSA. *Unit head:* Dr. Amber Rosin, Graduate Coordinator, 909-869-2426, Fax: 909-869-4904, E-mail: arrosin@csupomona.edu. *Application contact:* Deborah L. Brandon, Executive Director, Admissions and Outreach, 909-869-3427, Fax: 909-869-5315, E-mail: dlbrandon@csupomona.edu. Web site: http://www.csupomona.edu/~math/.

California State University Channel Islands, Extended Education, Program in Mathematics, Camarillo, CA 93012. Offers MS. Part-time and evening/weekend programs available. *Degree requirements:* For master's, thesis. *Entrance requirements:* For master's, BA in math. Additional exam requirements/recommendations for international students: Required—TOEFL (minimum score 550 paper-based).

California State University, East Bay, Office of Academic Programs and Graduate Studies, College of Science, Department of Mathematics and Computer Science, Mathematics Program, Hayward, CA 94542-3000. Offers applied math (MS); mathematics (MS); mathematics teaching (MS). Part-time and evening/weekend programs available. *Faculty:* 3 full-time (1 woman). *Students:* 22 full-time (9 women), 52 part-time (20 women); includes 22 minority (17 Asian, non-Hispanic/Latino; 3 Hispanic/Latino; 1 Native Hawaiian or other Pacific Islander, non-Hispanic/Latino; 1 Two or more races, non-Hispanic/Latino), 6 international. Average age 38. 37 applicants, 81% accepted, 16 enrolled. In 2011, 19 master's awarded. *Degree requirements:* For master's, comprehensive exam or thesis. *Entrance requirements:* For master's, minimum GPA of 3.0 in field. Additional exam requirements/recommendations for international students: Required—TOEFL (minimum score 550 paper-based; 213 computer-based). *Application deadline:* For fall admission, 6/30 for domestic and international students. Application fee: $55. Electronic applications accepted. *Expenses:* Tuition, state resident: full-time $6738; part-time $1302 per quarter. Tuition, nonresident: full-time $12,690; part-time $2294 per quarter. *Required fees:* $449 per quarter. Tuition and fees vary according to degree level, program and reciprocity agreements. *Financial support:* Fellowships, teaching assistantships, Federal Work-Study, institutionally sponsored loans, and scholarships/grants available. Support available to part-time students. Financial award application deadline: 3/1; financial award applicants required to submit FAFSA. *Unit head:* Prof. Edna Reiter, Chair, 510-885-3414, Fax: 510-885-4169, E-mail: eddie.reiter@csueastbay.edu. *Application contact:* Dr. Donald Wolitzer, Math Graduate Advisor, 510-885-3414, Fax: 510-885-4169, E-mail: donald.wolitzer@csueastbay.edu. Web site: http://www20.csueastbay.edu/csci/departments/math-cs/.

California State University, Fresno, Division of Graduate Studies, College of Science and Mathematics, Department of Mathematics, Fresno, CA 93740-8027. Offers mathematics (MA); teaching (MA). Part-time programs available. *Degree requirements:* For master's, thesis or alternative. *Entrance requirements:* For master's, GRE General Test. Additional exam requirements/recommendations for international students: Required—TOEFL. Electronic applications accepted. *Faculty research:* Diagnostic testing project.

California State University, Fullerton, Graduate Studies, College of Natural Science and Mathematics, Department of Mathematics, Fullerton, CA 92834-9480. Offers applied mathematics (MA); mathematics (MA); mathematics for secondary school teachers (MA). Part-time programs available. *Students:* 17 full-

time (7 women), 55 part-time (21 women); includes 33 minority (23 Asian, non-Hispanic/Latino; 9 Hispanic/Latino; 1 Two or more races, non-Hispanic/Latino), 4 international. Average age 31. 83 applicants, 60% accepted, 27 enrolled. In 2011, 25 master's awarded. *Degree requirements:* For master's, comprehensive exam or project. *Entrance requirements:* For master's, minimum GPA of 2.5 in last 60 units of course work, major in mathematics or related field. Application fee: $55. *Financial support:* Research assistantships, teaching assistantships, career-related internships or fieldwork, Federal Work-Study, institutionally sponsored loans, and scholarships/grants available. Support available to part-time students. Financial award application deadline: 3/1; financial award applicants required to submit FAFSA. *Unit head:* Dr. Paul Deland, Chair, 657-278-3631. *Application contact:* Admissions/Applications, 657-278-2371.

California State University, Long Beach, Graduate Studies, College of Natural Sciences and Mathematics, Department of Mathematics and Statistics, Long Beach, CA 90840. Offers mathematics (MS), including applied mathematics, applied statistics, mathematics education for secondary school teachers. Part-time programs available. *Faculty:* 21 full-time (5 women), 1 (woman) part-time/adjunct. *Students:* 67 full-time (31 women), 115 part-time (47 women); includes 95 minority (5 Black or African American, non-Hispanic/Latino; 1 American Indian or Alaska Native, non-Hispanic/Latino; 53 Asian, non-Hispanic/Latino; 29 Hispanic/Latino; 2 Native Hawaiian or other Pacific Islander, non-Hispanic/Latino; 5 Two or more races, non-Hispanic/Latino), 14 international. Average age 31. 162 applicants, 69% accepted, 58 enrolled. In 2011, 41 master's awarded. *Degree requirements:* For master's, comprehensive exam or thesis. *Application deadline:* For fall admission, 7/1 for domestic students; for spring admission, 12/1 for domestic students. Applications are processed on a rolling basis. Application fee: $55. Electronic applications accepted. *Financial support:* Teaching assistantships, Federal Work-Study, institutionally sponsored loans, scholarships/grants, and traineeships available. Financial award application deadline: 3/2. *Faculty research:* Algebra, functional analysis, partial differential equations, operator theory, numerical analysis. *Unit head:* Dr. Robert Mena, Chair, 562-985-4721, Fax: 562-985-8227, E-mail: rmena@csulb.edu. *Application contact:* Dr. Ngo Viet, Graduate Associate Chair, 562-985-4721, Fax: 562-985-8227, E-mail: viet@csulb.edu.

California State University, Los Angeles, Graduate Studies, College of Natural and Social Sciences, Department of Mathematics, Los Angeles, CA 90032-8530. Offers mathematics (MS), including applied mathematics, mathematics. Part-time and evening/weekend programs available. *Faculty:* 4 full-time (0 women), 2 part-time/adjunct (0 women). *Students:* 27 full-time (10 women), 37 part-time (13 women); includes 43 minority (3 Black or African American, non-Hispanic/Latino; 19 Asian, non-Hispanic/Latino; 18 Hispanic/Latino; 3 Two or more races, non-Hispanic/Latino), 5 international. Average age 33. 59 applicants, 68% accepted, 20 enrolled. In 2011, 22 master's awarded. *Degree requirements:* For master's, comprehensive exam or thesis. *Entrance requirements:* For master's, previous course work in mathematics. Additional exam requirements/recommendations for international students: Required—TOEFL (minimum score 500 paper-based; 173 computer-based). *Application deadline:* For fall admission, 5/1 for domestic and international students. Applications are processed on a rolling basis. Application fee: $55. Electronic applications accepted. *Expenses:* Tuition, state resident: full-time $8225. *Financial support:* Teaching assistantships and Federal Work-Study available. Support available to part-time students. Financial award application deadline: 3/1. *Faculty research:* Group theory, functional analysis, convexity theory, ordered geometry. *Unit head:* Dr. Grant Fraser, Chair, 323-343-2150, Fax: 323-343-5071, E-mail: gfraser@calstatela.edu. *Application contact:* Dr. Karin Brown, Acting Associate Dean of Graduate Studies, 323-343-3820, Fax: 323-343-5653, E-mail: kbrown5@calstatela.edu. Web site: http://www.calstatela.edu/academic/math/.

California State University, Northridge, Graduate Studies, College of Science and Mathematics, Department of Mathematics, Northridge, CA 91330. Offers applied mathematics (MS); mathematics (MS); mathematics for educational careers (MS). Part-time and evening/weekend programs available. *Degree requirements:* For master's, thesis (for some programs). *Entrance requirements:* For master's, GRE (if cumulative undergraduate GPA less than 3.0). Additional exam requirements/recommendations for international students: Required—TOEFL.

California State University, Sacramento, Office of Graduate Studies, College of Natural Sciences and Mathematics, Department of Mathematics and Statistics, Sacramento, CA 95819-6051. Offers MA. Part-time programs available. *Faculty:* 27 full-time (10 women), 10 part-time/adjunct (4 women). *Students:* 6 full-time, 23 part-time; includes 10 minority (1 American Indian or Alaska Native, non-Hispanic/Latino; 3 Asian, non-Hispanic/Latino; 2 Hispanic/Latino; 1 Native Hawaiian or other Pacific Islander, non-Hispanic/Latino; 3 Two or more races, non-Hispanic/Latino). Average age 30. 45 applicants, 53% accepted, 16 enrolled. In 2011, 12 master's awarded. *Degree requirements:* For master's, thesis or alternative, directed reading program preparing for written proficiency exam. *Entrance requirements:* For master's, minimum GPA of 3.0 in mathematics, 2.5 overall during previous 2 years; BA in mathematics or equivalent. Additional exam requirements/recommendations for international students: Required—TOEFL. *Application deadline:* For fall admission, 3/1 for domestic and international students; for spring admission, 9/30 for international students. Applications are processed on a rolling basis. Application fee: $55. Electronic applications accepted. *Financial support:* Research assistantships, teaching assistantships, career-related internships or fieldwork, and Federal Work-Study available.

Peterson's Graduate Programs in the Physical Sciences, Mathematics, Agricultural Sciences, the Environment & Natural Resources 2013

facebook.com/petersonpublishing **329**

Mathematics

Support available to part-time students. Financial award application deadline: 3/1; financial award applicants required to submit FAFSA. *Faculty research:* Algebra, applied mathematics, methods in mathematical finance, subelliptic analysis, topology. *Unit head:* Edward Shea, Chair, 916-278-6534, Fax: 916-278-5586, E-mail: sheaec@csus.edu. *Application contact:* Jose Martinez, Outreach and Graduate Diversity Coordinator, 916-278-6470, Fax: 916-278-5669, E-mail: martinj@skymail.csus.edu. Web site: http://www.csus.edu/math.

California State University, San Bernardino, Graduate Studies, College of Natural Sciences, Department of Mathematics, San Bernardino, CA 92407-2397. Offers mathematics (MA); teaching mathematics (MAT). Part-time programs available. *Students:* 46 full-time (23 women), 8 part-time (1 woman); includes 26 minority (3 Black or African American, non-Hispanic/Latino; 5 Asian, non-Hispanic/Latino; 16 Hispanic/Latino; 2 Two or more races, non-Hispanic/Latino). Average age 30. 23 applicants, 48% accepted, 10 enrolled. In 2011, 13 master's awarded. *Degree requirements:* For master's, advancement to candidacy. *Entrance requirements:* For master's, writing exam, minimum GPA of 3.0 in math courses. Application fee: $55. *Expenses:* Tuition, state resident: full-time $7356. Tuition, nonresident: full-time $7356. *Required fees:* $1077. Tuition and fees vary according to program. *Financial support:* Teaching assistantships available. *Faculty research:* Mathematics education, technology in education, algebra, combinatorics, real analysis. *Unit head:* Dr. Peter D. Williams, Chair, 909-537-5361, Fax: 909-537-7119, E-mail: pwilliam@csusb.edu. *Application contact:* Sandra Kamusikiri, Associate Vice-President/Dean of Graduate Studies, 909-537-5058, E-mail: skamusik@csusb.edu.

California State University, San Marcos, College of Arts and Sciences, Program in Mathematics, San Marcos, CA 92096-0001. Offers MS. Part-time and evening/weekend programs available. *Degree requirements:* For master's, thesis optional. *Entrance requirements:* Additional exam requirements/recommendations for international students: Required—TOEFL, TWE. *Faculty research:* Combinatorics, graph theory, partial differential equations, numerical analysis, computational linear algebra.

Carleton University, Faculty of Graduate Studies, Faculty of Science, School of Mathematics and Statistics, Ottawa, ON K1S 5B6, Canada. Offers mathematics (M Sc, PhD). Programs offered jointly with University of Ottawa. *Degree requirements:* For master's, thesis optional; for doctorate, one foreign language, comprehensive exam, thesis/dissertation. *Entrance requirements:* For master's, honors degree; for doctorate, master's degree. Additional exam requirements/recommendations for international students: Required—TOEFL. *Faculty research:* Pure mathematics, applied mathematics, probability and statistics.

Carnegie Mellon University, Mellon College of Science, Department of Mathematical Sciences, Pittsburgh, PA 15213-3891. Offers algorithms, combinatorics, and optimization (PhD); applied mathematics (PhD); computational finance (MS); mathematical finance (PhD); mathematical sciences (MS, DA, PhD); pure and applied logic (PhD). Part-time programs available. Terminal master's awarded for partial completion of doctoral program. *Degree requirements:* For doctorate, thesis/dissertation. *Entrance requirements:* For master's and doctorate, GRE General Test, GRE Subject Test. Additional exam requirements/recommendations for international students: Required—TOEFL. Electronic applications accepted. *Faculty research:* Continuum mechanics, discrete mathematics, applied and computational mathematics.

Case Western Reserve University, School of Graduate Studies, Department of Mathematics, Cleveland, OH 44106. Offers applied mathematics (MS, PhD); mathematics (MS, PhD). Part-time programs available. *Faculty:* 19 full-time (4 women), 1 part-time/adjunct (0 women). *Students:* 22 full-time (11 women), 1 part-time (0 women); includes 1 minority (Two or more races, non-Hispanic/Latino), 11 international. Average age 27. 105 applicants, 14% accepted, 6 enrolled. In 2011, 2 degrees awarded. Terminal master's awarded for partial completion of doctoral program. *Degree requirements:* For master's, thesis or alternative, thesis (applied mathematics); for doctorate, comprehensive exam, thesis/dissertation. *Entrance requirements:* For master's and doctorate, GRE General Test. Additional exam requirements/recommendations for international students: Required—TOEFL (minimum score 577 paper-based; 213 computer-based; 90 iBT); Recommended—IELTS (minimum score 7). *Application deadline:* For fall admission, 1/15 priority date for domestic students; for spring admission, 11/12 for domestic students. Applications are processed on a rolling basis. Application fee: $50. Electronic applications accepted. *Financial support:* Research assistantships, teaching assistantships, institutionally sponsored loans, and unspecified assistantships available. Financial award application deadline: 1/15. *Faculty research:* Probability theory, convexity and high-dimensional phenomena, imaging, geometric evaluation of curves, dynamical systems, large scale scientific computing, life sciences. *Unit head:* Daniela Calvetti, Chair, 216-368-2880, Fax: 216-368-5163, E-mail: daniela.calvetti@case.edu. *Application contact:* Gaythresa Lewis, Admissions, 216-368-5014, Fax: 216-368-5163, E-mail: gxl34@case.edu. Web site: http://www.case.edu/artsci/math/.

Central Connecticut State University, School of Graduate Studies, School of Arts and Sciences, Department of Mathematical Sciences, New Britain, CT 06050-4010. Offers data mining (MS, Certificate); mathematics (MA, MS, Certificate, Sixth Year Certificate), including actuarial science (MA), computer science (MA), statistics (MA). Part-time and evening/weekend programs available. *Faculty:* 33 full-time (10 women), 66 part-time/adjunct (26 women). *Students:* 19 full-time (9 women), 119 part-time (68 women); includes 23 minority (5 Black or African American, non-Hispanic/Latino; 8 Asian, non-Hispanic/Latino;

8 Hispanic/Latino; 2 Two or more races, non-Hispanic/Latino), 4 international. Average age 37. 65 applicants, 57% accepted, 24 enrolled. In 2011, 24 master's awarded. *Degree requirements:* For master's, comprehensive exam, thesis or alternative; for other advanced degree, qualifying exam. *Entrance requirements:* For master's, minimum undergraduate GPA of 2.7. Additional exam requirements/recommendations for international students: Required—TOEFL (minimum score 550 paper-based; 213 computer-based). *Application deadline:* For fall admission, 5/1 for domestic and international students; for spring admission, 11/1 for domestic and international students. Applications are processed on a rolling basis. Application fee: $50. Electronic applications accepted. *Expenses: Tuition, area resident:* Full-time $5137; part-time $482 per credit. Tuition, state resident: full-time $7707; part-time $494 per credit. Tuition, nonresident: full-time $14,311; part-time $494 per credit. *Required fees:* $3865. One-time fee: $62 part-time. *Financial support:* In 2011–12, 5 students received support. Career-related internships or fieldwork, Federal Work-Study, scholarships/grants, and unspecified assistantships available. Support available to part-time students. Financial award application deadline: 4/15; financial award applicants required to submit FAFSA. *Faculty research:* Statistics, actuarial mathematics, computer systems and engineering, computer programming techniques, operations research. *Unit head:* Dr. Jeffrey McGowan, Chair, 860-832-2835, E-mail: mcgowan@ccsu.edu. *Application contact:* Patricia Gardner, Associate Director of Graduate Studies, 860-832-2350, Fax: 860-832-2352, E-mail: graduateadmissions@ccsu.edu. Web site: http://www.math.ccsu.edu/.

Central European University, Graduate Studies, Department of Mathematics and its Applications, Budapest, Hungary. Offers applied mathematics (MS); mathematics and its applications (PhD). *Faculty:* 2 full-time (0 women), 12 part-time/adjunct (1 woman). *Students:* 40 full-time (4 women). Average age 27. 89 applicants, 18% accepted, 14 enrolled. In 2011, 6 master's, 4 doctorates awarded. *Entrance requirements:* For master's and doctorate, entrance exam or GRE, statement of purpose. Additional exam requirements/recommendations for international students: Required—TOEFL (minimum score 570 paper-based; 230 computer-based); Recommended—IELTS (minimum score 6.5). *Application deadline:* For fall admission, 1/24 for domestic and international students. Electronic applications accepted. Tuition charges are reported in euros. *Expenses: Tuition:* Full-time 11,000 euros. *Financial support:* In 2011–12, 39 students received support, including 39 fellowships (averaging $6,100 per year); career-related internships or fieldwork, scholarships/grants, health care benefits, and tuition waivers (full and partial) also available. *Faculty research:* Applied mathematics, such as: algebra, algebraic geometry, bioinformatics, calculus of variations, computational biology, cryptography, discrete mathematics, evolutions equations, fluid mechanics, geometry, number theory, numerical analysis, optimization, ordinary and partial differential equations, probability theory, quantum mechanics, statistics, stochastic processes.. *Unit head:* Gheorghe Morosanu, Head, 36 1 327-3000 Ext. 2430. *Application contact:* Zsuzsanna Jaszberenyi, Admissions Officer, 361-324-3009, Fax: 367-327-3211, E-mail: admissions@ceu.hu. Web site: http://mathematics.ceu.hu/.

Central Michigan University, College of Graduate Studies, College of Science and Technology, Department of Mathematics, Mount Pleasant, MI 48859. Offers mathematics (MA, PhD), including teaching of college mathematics (PhD). Part-time programs available. *Degree requirements:* For master's, thesis or alternative; for doctorate, thesis/dissertation. *Entrance requirements:* For master's, minimum GPA of 2.7, 20 hours of course work in mathematics; for doctorate, GRE, minimum GPA of 3.0, 20 hours of course work in mathematics. Electronic applications accepted. *Faculty research:* Combinatorics, approximation theory, applied mathematics, statistics, functional analysis and operator theory.

Central Washington University, Graduate Studies and Research, College of the Sciences, Department of Mathematics, Ellensburg, WA 98926. Offers MAT. Program offered during summer only. *Faculty:* 15 full-time (4 women). *Students:* 2 full-time (both women). In 2011, 3 master's awarded. *Degree requirements:* For master's, thesis or alternative. *Entrance requirements:* For master's, minimum GPA of 3.0. Additional exam requirements/recommendations for international students: Required—TOEFL (minimum score 550 paper-based; 213 computer-based; 79 iBT). *Application deadline:* For fall admission, 2/1 priority date for domestic students; for winter admission, 10/1 for domestic students; for spring admission, 1/1 for domestic students. Applications are processed on a rolling basis. Application fee: $50. Electronic applications accepted. *Expenses:* Tuition, state resident: full-time $8112; part-time $270 per credit. Tuition, nonresident: full-time $18,069; part-time $602 per credit. *Required fees:* $924. *Financial support:* Federal Work-Study and health care benefits available. Financial award application deadline: 3/1; financial award applicants required to submit FAFSA. *Unit head:* Dr. Michael Lundin, Professor, 509-963-1398, E-mail: lundin@cwu.edu. *Application contact:* Justine Eason, Admissions Program Coordinator, 509-963-3103, Fax: 509-963-1799, E-mail: masters@cwu.edu.

Chicago State University, School of Graduate and Professional Studies, College of Arts and Sciences, Department of Mathematics and Computer Science, Chicago, IL 60628. Offers computer science (MS); mathematics (MS). *Degree requirements:* For master's, thesis optional, oral exam. *Entrance requirements:* For master's, minimum GPA of 2.75.

City College of the City University of New York, Graduate School, College of Liberal Arts and Science, Division of Science, Department of Mathematics, New York, NY 10031-9198. Offers MA. Part-time programs available. *Degree requirements:* For master's, one foreign language. *Entrance requirements:* Additional exam requirements/recommendations for international students:

Peterson's Graduate Programs in the Physical Sciences, Mathematics, Agricultural Sciences, the Environment & Natural Resources 2013.

Required—TOEFL (minimum score 500 paper-based; 61 iBT). Electronic applications accepted. *Faculty research:* Group theory, number theory, logic, statistics, computational geometry.

Claremont Graduate University, Graduate Programs, School of Mathematical Sciences, Claremont, CA 91711-6160. Offers computational and systems biology (PhD); computational mathematics and numerical analysis (MA, MS); computational science (PhD); engineering and industrial applied mathematics (PhD); mathematics (PhD); operations research and statistics (MA, MS); physical applied mathematics (MA, MS); pure mathematics (MA, MS); scientific computing (MA, MS); systems and control theory (MA, MS). Part-time programs available. *Faculty:* 6 full-time (0 women), 1 part-time/adjunct (0 women). *Students:* 52 full-time (16 women), 24 part-time (9 women); includes 25 minority (3 Black or African American, non-Hispanic/Latino; 10 Asian, non-Hispanic/Latino; 11 Hispanic/Latino; 1 Two or more races, non-Hispanic/Latino), 17 international. Average age 33. In 2011, 15 master's, 3 doctorates awarded. Terminal master's awarded for partial completion of doctoral program. *Entrance requirements:* For master's and doctorate, GRE General Test. Additional exam requirements/recommendations for international students: Required—TOEFL (minimum score 550 paper-based; 213 computer-based; 80 iBT). *Application deadline:* For fall admission, 2/1 priority date for domestic students. Applications are processed on a rolling basis. Application fee: $60. Electronic applications accepted. *Expenses: Tuition:* Full-time $36,374; part-time $1581 per unit. *Required fees:* $165 per semester. *Financial support:* Fellowships, research assistantships, Federal Work-Study, institutionally sponsored loans, scholarships/grants, and tuition waivers (full and partial) available. Support available to part-time students. Financial award application deadline: 2/15; financial award applicants required to submit FAFSA. *Unit head:* Ellis Cumberbatch, Dean, 909-607-3369, Fax: 909-607-8261, E-mail: ellis.cumberbatch@cgu.edu. *Application contact:* Susan Townzen, Program Coordinator, 909-621-8080, Fax: 909-607-8261, E-mail: susan.n.townzen@cgu.edu. Web site: http://www.cgu.edu/pages/168.asp.

Clark Atlanta University, School of Arts and Sciences, Department of Mathematical Sciences, Atlanta, GA 30314. Offers MS. Part-time programs available. *Faculty:* 3 full-time (1 woman), 1 part-time/adjunct (0 women). *Students:* 1 (woman) full-time, 1 (woman) part-time; both minorities (both Black or African American, non-Hispanic/Latino). Average age 26. 1 applicant, 100% accepted, 1 enrolled. In 2011, 3 master's awarded. *Degree requirements:* For master's, one foreign language, thesis optional. *Entrance requirements:* For master's, GRE General Test, minimum GPA of 2.5. Additional exam requirements/recommendations for international students: Required—TOEFL (minimum score 500 paper-based; 173 computer-based; 61 iBT). *Application deadline:* For fall admission, 4/1 for domestic and international students; for spring admission, 11/1 for domestic and international students. Applications are processed on a rolling basis. Application fee: $40 ($55 for international students). *Expenses: Tuition:* Full-time $13,572; part-time $754 per credit hour. *Required fees:* $806; $403 per semester. *Financial support:* In 2011–12, 3 fellowships were awarded; scholarships/grants and unspecified assistantships also available. Financial award application deadline: 4/30; financial award applicants required to submit FAFSA. *Faculty research:* Numerical methods for operator equations, Ada language development. *Unit head:* Dr. Charles Pierre, Chairperson, 404-880-8195, E-mail: cpierre@cau.edu. *Application contact:* Michelle Clark-Davis, Graduate Program Admissions, 404-880-6605, E-mail: cauadmissions@cau.edu.

Clarkson University, Graduate School, School of Arts and Sciences, Department of Mathematics, Potsdam, NY 13699. Offers MS, PhD. Part-time programs available. *Faculty:* 15 full-time (4 women), 2 part-time/adjunct (0 women). *Students:* 23 full-time (4 women), 14 international. Average age 27. 25 applicants, 72% accepted, 3 enrolled. In 2011, 6 degrees awarded. Terminal master's awarded for partial completion of doctoral program. *Degree requirements:* For doctorate, thesis/dissertation, departmental qualifying exam. *Entrance requirements:* For master's and doctorate, GRE, transcripts of all college coursework, three letters of recommendation; resume and personal statement (recommended). Additional exam requirements/recommendations for international students: Required—TOEFL, TSE recommended. *Application deadline:* For fall admission, 1/30 priority date for domestic students, 1/30 for international students; for spring admission, 9/1 priority date for domestic students, 9/1 for international students. Applications are processed on a rolling basis. Application fee: $25 ($35 for international students). Electronic applications accepted. *Expenses: Tuition:* Full-time $14,376; part-time $1198 per credit hour. *Required fees:* $295 per semester. *Financial support:* In 2011–12, 22 students received support, including fellowships with full tuition reimbursements available (averaging $21,999 per year), 6 research assistantships with full tuition reimbursements available (averaging $21,999 per year), 17 teaching assistantships with full tuition reimbursements available (averaging $21,999 per year); scholarships/grants, tuition waivers (partial), and unspecified assistantships also available. *Faculty research:* Theoretical development, solution and application, thermal conductivity, plankton dynamics. *Total annual research expenditures:* $896,083. *Unit head:* Dr. Christopher Lynch, Chair, 315-268-2395, Fax: 315-268-2371, E-mail: clynch@clarkson.edu. *Application contact:* Jennifer Reed, Graduate School Coordinator, School of Arts and Sciences, 315-268-3802, Fax: 315-268-3989, E-mail: sciencegrad@clarkson.edu. Web site: http://www.clarkson.edu/math/.

Clemson University, Graduate School, College of Engineering and Science, Department of Mathematical Sciences, Clemson, SC 29634. Offers applied and pure mathematics (MS, PhD); computational mathematics (MS, PhD); operations research (MS, PhD); statistics (MS, PhD). Part-time programs available. *Faculty:* 46 full-time (13 women), 10 part-time/adjunct (5 women). *Students:* 119 full-time (50 women), 6 part-time (4 women); includes 5 minority (2 Black or African American, non-Hispanic/Latino; 2 American Indian or Alaska Native, non-Hispanic/Latino; 1 Two or more races, non-Hispanic/Latino), 40 international. Average age 27. 133 applicants, 75% accepted, 31 enrolled. In 2011, 23 master's, 6 doctorates awarded. *Degree requirements:* For master's, thesis optional, final project; for doctorate, thesis/dissertation, qualifying exams. *Entrance requirements:* For master's and doctorate, GRE General Test. Additional exam requirements/recommendations for international students: Required—TOEFL. *Application deadline:* For fall admission, 1/15 priority date for domestic students, 1/15 for international students; for spring admission, 10/1 priority date for domestic students, 9/15 for international students. Applications are processed on a rolling basis. Application fee: $70 ($80 for international students). Electronic applications accepted. *Financial support:* In 2011–12, 113 students received support, including 1 fellowship with full and partial tuition reimbursement available (averaging $10,000 per year), 9 research assistantships with partial tuition reimbursements available (averaging $18,373 per year), 104 teaching assistantships with partial tuition reimbursements available (averaging $17,869 per year); career-related internships or fieldwork, institutionally sponsored loans, scholarships/grants, health care benefits, and unspecified assistantships also available. Support available to part-time students. Financial award application deadline: 4/15. *Faculty research:* Applied and computational analysis, cryptography, discrete mathematics, optimization, statistics. *Total annual research expenditures:* $780,865. *Unit head:* Dr. Robert L. Taylor, Chair, 864-656-5240, Fax: 864-656-5230, E-mail: rtaylo2@clemson.edu. *Application contact:* Dr. K. B. Kulasekera, Graduate Coordinator, 864-656-5231, Fax: 864-656-5230, E-mail: kk@clemson.edu. Web site: http://www.clemson.edu/ces/departments/math/index.html.

Cleveland State University, College of Graduate Studies, College of Sciences and Health Professions, Department of Mathematics, Cleveland, OH 44115. Offers MA, MS. Part-time programs available. *Faculty:* 11 full-time (4 women), 1 part-time/adjunct (0 women). *Students:* 8 full-time (4 women), 27 part-time (11 women); includes 3 minority (1 Black or African American, non-Hispanic/Latino; 1 Asian, non-Hispanic/Latino; 1 Hispanic/Latino), 9 international. Average age 32. 59 applicants, 80% accepted, 23 enrolled. In 2011, 16 master's awarded. *Degree requirements:* For master's, exit project. *Entrance requirements:* For master's, GRE. Additional exam requirements/recommendations for international students: Required—TOEFL (minimum score 515 paper-based; 197 computer-based). *Application deadline:* For fall admission, 6/15 priority date for domestic students, 6/15 for international students. Applications are processed on a rolling basis. Application fee: $30. Electronic applications accepted. *Expenses:* Tuition, state resident: full-time $6416; part-time $494 per credit hour. Tuition, nonresident: full-time $12,074; part-time $929 per credit hour. *Financial support:* In 2011–12, 6 students received support, including 3 teaching assistantships with full tuition reimbursements available (averaging $9,000 per year); Federal Work-Study, institutionally sponsored loans, scholarships/grants, and tuition waivers (full and partial) also available. Financial award application deadline: 3/15. *Faculty research:* Algebraic topology, probability and statistics, differential equations, geometry. *Unit head:* Dr. John Peter Holcomb, Jr., Chairperson, 216-687-4681, Fax: 216-523-7340, E-mail: j.p.holcomb@csuohio.edu. *Application contact:* Dr. John F. Oprea, Graduate Program Director, 216-687-4702, Fax: 216-523-7340, E-mail: j.oprea@csuohio.edu. Web site: http://www.csuohio.edu/math/.

The College at Brockport, State University of New York, School of Science and Mathematics, Department of Mathematics, Brockport, NY 14420-2997. Offers MA. Part-time programs available. *Students:* 8 full-time (4 women), 5 part-time (4 women); includes 2 minority (both Asian, non-Hispanic/Latino). 19 applicants, 74% accepted, 7 enrolled. In 2011, 11 master's awarded. *Degree requirements:* For master's, comprehensive exam. *Entrance requirements:* For master's, minimum GPA of 3.0, letters of recommendation; statement of objectives. Additional exam requirements/recommendations for international students: Required—TOEFL (minimum score 550 paper-based; 213 computer-based; 79 iBT). *Application deadline:* For fall admission, 7/15 priority date for domestic students, 7/15 for international students; for spring admission, 11/15 priority date for domestic students, 11/15 for international students. Application fee: $50. Electronic applications accepted. *Financial support:* In 2011–12, 3 teaching assistantships with full tuition reimbursements (averaging $6,000 per year) were awarded; Federal Work-Study, scholarships/grants, and unspecified assistantships also available. Support available to part-time students. Financial award application deadline: 3/15; financial award applicants required to submit FAFSA. *Faculty research:* Mathematical modeling, dynamical systems, complex/functional analysis, graph theory and combinations, algebra and number theory. *Unit head:* Dr. Sanford Miller, Chairperson, 585-395-5178, Fax: 585-395-2304, E-mail: smiller@brockport.edu. *Application contact:* Dr. Howard Skogman, Graduate Director, 585-395-2046, Fax: 585-395-2304, E-mail: hskogman@brockport.edu. Web site: http://www.brockport.edu/graduate/.

College of Charleston, Graduate School, School of Sciences and Mathematics, Program in Mathematics, Charleston, SC 29424-0001. Offers mathematics (MS). Part-time and evening/weekend programs available. *Faculty:* 32 full-time (11 women). *Students:* 13 full-time (4 women), 10 part-time (5 women); includes 3 minority (2 Asian, non-Hispanic/Latino; 1 Two or more races, non-Hispanic/Latino), 3 international. Average age 28. 17 applicants, 76% accepted, 7 enrolled. In 2011, 2 master's, 2 other advanced degrees awarded. *Degree requirements:* For master's, thesis optional. *Entrance requirements:* For master's, GRE, BS in

Peterson's Graduate Programs in the Physical Sciences, Mathematics, Agricultural Sciences, the Environment & Natural Resources 2013

facebook.com/petersonspublishing **331**

Mathematics

mathematics or equivalent, 2 letters of recommendation. Additional exam requirements/recommendations for international students: Required—TOEFL (minimum score 81 iBT). *Application deadline:* For fall admission, 7/1 priority date for domestic students; for spring admission, 11/1 priority date for domestic students. Applications are processed on a rolling basis. Application fee: $45. Electronic applications accepted. *Expenses:* Tuition, state resident: full-time $5455; part-time $455 per credit. Tuition, nonresident: full-time $13,917; part-time $1160 per credit. *Financial support:* In 2011–12, research assistantships (averaging $12,400 per year), teaching assistantships (averaging $13,300 per year) were awarded; Federal Work-Study, scholarships/grants, and unspecified assistantships also available. Support available to part-time students. Financial award application deadline: 4/1; financial award applicants required to submit FAFSA. *Faculty research:* Algebra, dynamical systems, probability, analysis and topology, combinatorics. *Unit head:* Dr. Ben Cox, Director, 843-953-5715, Fax: 843-953-1410, E-mail: coxbl@cofc.edu. *Application contact:* Susan Hallatt, Director of Graduate Admissions, 843-953-5614, Fax: 843-953-1434, E-mail: hallatts@cofc.edu. Web site: http://math.cofc.edu/grad-progs/index.php.

Colorado School of Mines, Graduate School, Department of Mathematical and Computer Sciences, Golden, CO 80401-1887. Offers MS, PhD. Part-time programs available. *Faculty:* 34 full-time (15 women), 3 part-time/adjunct (0 women). *Students:* 68 full-time (22 women), 9 part-time (2 women); includes 7 minority (1 Black or African American, non-Hispanic/Latino; 1 American Indian or Alaska Native, non-Hispanic/Latino; 3 Asian, non-Hispanic/Latino; 2 Hispanic/Latino), 13 international. Average age 26. 129 applicants, 62% accepted, 36 enrolled. In 2011, 8 master's awarded. *Degree requirements:* For master's, thesis (for some programs); for doctorate, comprehensive exam, thesis/dissertation. *Entrance requirements:* For master's and doctorate, GRE General Test. Additional exam requirements/recommendations for international students: Required—TOEFL (minimum score 550 paper-based; 213 computer-based; 80 iBT). *Application deadline:* For fall admission, 1/15 priority date for domestic students, 1/15 for international students; for spring admission, 10/15 priority date for domestic students, 10/15 for international students. Application fee: $50 ($70 for international students). Electronic applications accepted. *Expenses:* Tuition, state resident: full-time $12,585; part-time $699 per credit. Tuition, nonresident: full-time $27,270; part-time $1516 per credit. *Required fees:* $1864.20; $670 per semester. *Financial support:* In 2011–12, 49 students received support, including 3 fellowships with full tuition reimbursements available (averaging $20,000 per year), 25 research assistantships with full tuition reimbursements available (averaging $20,000 per year), 21 teaching assistantships with full tuition reimbursements available (averaging $20,000 per year); scholarships/grants, health care benefits, and unspecified assistantships also available. Financial award application deadline: 1/15; financial award applicants required to submit FAFSA. *Faculty research:* Applied statistics, numerical computation, artificial intelligence, linear optimization. *Total annual research expenditures:* $949,540. *Unit head:* Dr. Willy Hereman, Interim Head, 303-273-3881, Fax: 303-273-3875, E-mail: whereman@mines.edu. *Application contact:* William Navidi, Professor, 303-273-3489, Fax: 303-273-3875, E-mail: wnavidi@mines.edu. Web site: http://mcs.mines.edu.

Colorado State University, Graduate School, College of Natural Sciences, Department of Mathematics, Fort Collins, CO 80523-1874. Offers MAT, MS, PhD. Postbaccalaureate distance learning degree programs offered (no on-campus study). *Faculty:* 24 full-time (5 women). *Students:* 22 full-time (9 women), 29 part-time (11 women); includes 4 minority (1 Black or African American, non-Hispanic/Latino; 1 Asian, non-Hispanic/Latino; 2 Hispanic/Latino), 6 international. Average age 27. 114 applicants, 41% accepted, 10 enrolled. In 2011, 5 master's, 9 doctorates awarded. Terminal master's awarded for partial completion of doctoral program. *Degree requirements:* For master's, comprehensive exam (for some programs), thesis (for some programs); for doctorate, comprehensive exam, thesis/dissertation. *Entrance requirements:* For master's and doctorate, GRE General Test or GMAT, minimum GPA of 3.0, 3 letters of recommendation. Additional exam requirements/recommendations for international students: Required—TOEFL (minimum score 550 paper-based; 213 computer-based; 80 iBT). *Application deadline:* For fall admission, 2/15 priority date for domestic students, 2/15 for international students; for spring admission, 7/15 priority date for domestic students, 7/15 for international students. Applications are processed on a rolling basis. Application fee: $50. Electronic applications accepted. *Expenses:* Tuition, state resident: full-time $7992. Tuition, nonresident: full-time $19,592. *Required fees:* $1735; $58 per credit. *Financial support:* In 2011–12, 6 fellowships (averaging $42,754 per year), 13 research assistantships with full tuition reimbursements (averaging $12,333 per year), 41 teaching assistantships with full tuition reimbursements (averaging $14,535 per year) were awarded; health care benefits also available. Financial award application deadline: 1/15; financial award applicants required to submit FAFSA. *Faculty research:* Numerical analysis, algebraic geometry, combinatorics, number theory, computational mathematics. *Total annual research expenditures:* $1.2 million. *Unit head:* Dr. Gerhard Dangelmayr, Chair, 970-491-6452, Fax: 970-491-2161, E-mail: gerhard@math.colostate.edu. *Application contact:* Bryan Elder, Graduate Coordinator, 970-491-7925, Fax: 970-491-2161, E-mail: elder@math.colostate.edu. Web site: http://www.math.colostate.edu/.

Columbia University, Graduate School of Arts and Sciences, Division of Natural Sciences, Department of Mathematics, New York, NY 10027. Offers M Phil, MA, PhD. *Degree requirements:* For master's, written exam; for doctorate, 2 foreign languages, thesis/dissertation. *Entrance requirements:* For master's and doctorate, GRE General Test, major in mathematics. Additional exam

requirements/recommendations for international students: Required—TOEFL. *Faculty research:* Algebra, topology, analysis.

Concordia University, School of Graduate Studies, Faculty of Arts and Science, Department of Mathematics and Statistics, Montréal, QC H3G 1M8, Canada. Offers mathematics (M Sc, MA, PhD); teaching of mathematics (MTM). *Degree requirements:* For master's, thesis optional; for doctorate, comprehensive exam, thesis/dissertation. *Entrance requirements:* For master's, honors degree in mathematics or equivalent. *Faculty research:* Number theory, computational algebra, mathematical physics, differential geometry, dynamical systems and statistics.

Cornell University, Graduate School, Graduate Fields of Arts and Sciences, Field of Mathematics, Ithaca, NY 14853-0001. Offers PhD. *Faculty:* 49 full-time (4 women). *Students:* 55 full-time (22 women); includes 4 minority (3 Asian, non-Hispanic/Latino; 1 Hispanic/Latino), 34 international. Average age 26. 266 applicants, 14% accepted, 10 enrolled. In 2011, 15 doctorates awarded. *Degree requirements:* For doctorate, one foreign language, comprehensive exam, thesis/dissertation, teaching experience. *Entrance requirements:* For doctorate, GRE General Test, GRE Subject Test (mathematics), 3 letters of recommendation. Additional exam requirements/recommendations for international students: Required—TOEFL (minimum score 600 paper-based; 250 computer-based; 95 iBT). *Application deadline:* For fall admission, 1/15 for domestic students. Application fee: $95. Electronic applications accepted. *Financial support:* In 2011–12, 5 fellowships with full tuition reimbursements, 6 research assistantships with full tuition reimbursements, 42 teaching assistantships with full tuition reimbursements were awarded; institutionally sponsored loans, scholarships/grants, health care benefits, tuition waivers (full and partial), and unspecified assistantships also available. Financial award applicants required to submit FAFSA. *Faculty research:* Analysis, dynamical systems, Lie theory, logic, topology and geometry. *Unit head:* Director of Graduate Studies, 607-255-6757, Fax: 607-255-7149. *Application contact:* Graduate Field Assistant, 607-255-6757, Fax: 607-255-7149, E-mail: gradinfo@math.cornell.edu. Web site: http://www.gradschool.cornell.edu/fields.php?id-32&a-2.

Dalhousie University, Faculty of Science, Department of Mathematics and Statistics, Program in Mathematics, Halifax, NS B3H 4R2, Canada. Offers M Sc, PhD. *Degree requirements:* For master's, thesis; for doctorate, thesis/dissertation. *Entrance requirements:* Additional exam requirements/recommendations for international students: Required—TOEFL, IELTS, CANTEST, CAEL, or Michigan English Language Assessment Battery. Electronic applications accepted. *Faculty research:* Applied mathematics, category theory, algebra, analysis, graph theory.

Dartmouth College, Arts and Sciences Graduate Programs, Department of Mathematics, Hanover, NH 03755. Offers PhD. *Degree requirements:* For doctorate, 2 foreign languages, thesis/dissertation. *Entrance requirements:* For doctorate, GRE General Test, GRE Subject Test. Additional exam requirements/recommendations for international students: Required—TOEFL. *Faculty research:* Mathematical logic, set theory, combinations, number theory.

Delaware State University, Graduate Programs, Department of Mathematics, Program in Mathematics, Dover, DE 19901-2277. Offers MS. *Entrance requirements:* Additional exam requirements/recommendations for international students: Required—TOEFL (minimum score 550 paper-based). Electronic applications accepted.

DePaul University, College of Science and Health, Department of Mathematical Sciences, Chicago, IL 60614. Offers applied mathematics (MS), including actuarial science or statistics; applied statistics (MS, Certificate); mathematics education (MA). Part-time and evening/weekend programs available. *Faculty:* 23 full-time (6 women), 18 part-time/adjunct (5 women). *Students:* 122 full-time (57 women), 63 part-time (23 women); includes 52 minority (19 Black or African American, non-Hispanic/Latino; 18 Asian, non-Hispanic/Latino; 10 Hispanic/Latino; 1 Native Hawaiian or other Pacific Islander, non-Hispanic/Latino; 4 Two or more races, non-Hispanic/Latino), 15 international. Average age 30. 40 applicants, 100% accepted. In 2011, 30 master's awarded. *Degree requirements:* For master's, comprehensive exam. *Entrance requirements:* Additional exam requirements/recommendations for international students: Required—TOEFL. *Application deadline:* For fall admission, 7/30 for domestic students, 6/30 for international students; for winter admission, 11/30 for domestic students, 10/31 for international students; for spring admission, 2/15 for domestic students. Applications are processed on a rolling basis. Application fee: $25. *Financial support:* In 2011–12, 12 students received support, including research assistantships with partial tuition reimbursements available (averaging $6,000 per year); teaching assistantships and tuition waivers (full) also available. Financial award application deadline: 4/30. *Faculty research:* Verbally prime algebras, enveloping algebras of Lie, superalgebras and related rings, harmonic analysis, estimation theory. *Unit head:* Dr. Ahmed I. Zayed, Chairperson, 773-325-7806, Fax: 773-325-7807, E-mail: azayed@depaul.edu. *Application contact:* Ann Spittle, Director of Graduate Admissions, 312-362-8300, Fax: 312-362-5749, E-mail: admitdpu@depaul.edu. Web site: http://depaul.edu/~math.

Dowling College, Programs in Arts and Sciences, Oakdale, NY 11769-1999. Offers integrated math and science (MS); liberal studies (MA). Part-time and evening/weekend programs available. *Faculty:* 7 full-time (1 woman). *Students:* 5 full-time (3 women), 6 part-time (2 women); includes 2 minority (1 Black or African American, non-Hispanic/Latino; 1 Hispanic/Latino). Average age 30. 17 applicants, 76% accepted, 5 enrolled. In 2011, 1 master's awarded. *Degree requirements:* For master's, comprehensive exam, thesis. *Entrance requirements:*

Peterson's Graduate Programs in the Physical Sciences, Mathematics, Agricultural Sciences, the Environment & Natural Resources 2013

For master's, minimum undergraduate GPA of 3.0, 2 letters of recommendation. Additional exam requirements/recommendations for international students: Required—TOEFL (minimum score 550 paper-based). *Application deadline:* For fall admission, 9/1 priority date for domestic students; for winter admission, 1/1 priority date for domestic students; for spring admission, 2/1 priority date for domestic students. Applications are processed on a rolling basis. Application fee: $50. Electronic applications accepted. *Expenses: Tuition:* Full-time $19,162; part-time $933 per credit. *Required fees:* $1330; $700 per year. Tuition and fees vary according to course load. *Financial support:* Federal Work-Study available. Support available to part-time students. Financial award application deadline: 6/30; financial award applicants required to submit FAFSA. *Unit head:* Patricia Sandilands, Director of Operations, School of Arts and Sciences, 631-244-3237, E-mail: sandilap@dowling.edu. *Application contact:* Ronnie S. Macdonald, Assistant Vice President for Enrollment Services/Dean of Admissions, 631-244-3357, Fax: 631-244-1059, E-mail: macdonar@dowling.edu.

Drexel University, College of Arts and Sciences, Department of Mathematics, Program in Mathematics, Philadelphia, PA 19104-2875. Offers MS, PhD. *Degree requirements:* For doctorate, one foreign language, thesis/dissertation. *Entrance requirements:* For master's and doctorate, GRE. Additional exam requirements/recommendations for international students: Required—TOEFL. Electronic applications accepted.

Duke University, Graduate School, Department of Mathematics, Durham, NC 27708. Offers PhD. *Faculty:* 27 full-time. *Students:* 46 full-time (11 women); includes 4 minority (2 Asian, non-Hispanic/Latino; 2 Hispanic/Latino), 19 international. 238 applicants, 15% accepted, 10 enrolled. In 2011, 11 doctorates awarded. *Degree requirements:* For doctorate, 2 foreign languages, thesis/dissertation. *Entrance requirements:* For doctorate, GRE General Test, GRE Subject Test. Additional exam requirements/recommendations for international students: Required—TOEFL (minimum score 550 paper-based; 213 computer-based; 83 iBT), IELTS (minimum score 7). *Application deadline:* For fall admission, 12/8 priority date for domestic students, 12/8 for international students. Application fee: $75. Electronic applications accepted. *Expenses: Tuition:* Full-time $40,720. *Required fees:* $3107. *Financial support:* Fellowships, research assistantships, teaching assistantships, and Federal Work-Study available. Financial award application deadline: 12/8. *Unit head:* Thomas Witelski, Director of Graduate Studies, 919-660-2801, Fax: 919-660-2821, E-mail: sholder@math.duke.edu. *Application contact:* Elizabeth Hutton, Director of Admissions, 919-684-3913, Fax: 919-684-2277, E-mail: grad-admissions@duke.edu. Web site: http://www.math.duke.edu/graduate.

Duquesne University, Graduate School of Liberal Arts, Program in Computational Mathematics, Pittsburgh, PA 15282-0001. Offers MA, MS. *Faculty:* 21 full-time (5 women), 11 part-time/adjunct (5 women). *Students:* 14 full-time (4 women), 3 part-time (1 woman); includes 2 minority (1 Black or African American, non-Hispanic/Latino; 1 Asian, non-Hispanic/Latino), 4 international. Average age 28. 11 applicants, 82% accepted, 5 enrolled. In 2011, 3 degrees awarded. *Degree requirements:* For master's, thesis. *Entrance requirements:* For master's, GRE General Test. Additional exam requirements/recommendations for international students: Required—TOEFL. *Application deadline:* For fall admission, 8/1 for domestic students, 5/1 for international students. Applications are processed on a rolling basis. Electronic applications accepted. *Expenses: Tuition:* Full-time $16,596; part-time $922 per credit. *Required fees:* $1584; $88 per credit. Tuition and fees vary according to program. *Financial support:* In 2011–12, 3 research assistantships with full tuition reimbursements (averaging $10,000 per year), 2 teaching assistantships with full tuition reimbursements (averaging $10,000 per year) were awarded; Federal Work-Study, institutionally sponsored loans, scholarships/grants, and unspecified assistantships also available. Financial award application deadline: 5/1. *Unit head:* Dr. Jeff Jackson, Chair, 412-396-6467. *Application contact:* Linda Rendulic, Assistant to the Dean, 412-396-6400, E-mail: rendulic@duq.edu.

East Carolina University, Graduate School, Thomas Harriot College of Arts and Sciences, Department of Mathematics, Greenville, NC 27858-4353. Offers mathematics (MA); mathematics in the community college (MA); statistics (MA, Certificate). Part-time and evening/weekend programs available. *Degree requirements:* For master's, comprehensive exam. *Entrance requirements:* For master's, GRE General Test, MAT. Additional exam requirements/recommendations for international students: Required—TOEFL. *Application deadline:* For fall admission, 6/1 for domestic students; for spring admission, 10/15 for domestic students. Applications are processed on a rolling basis. Application fee: $50. *Expenses: Tuition,* state resident: full-time $3557; part-time $444.63 per semester hour. Tuition, nonresident: full-time $14,351; part-time $1793.88 per semester hour. *Required fees:* $2016; $252 per semester hour. Part-time tuition and fees vary according to course load, campus/location and program. *Financial support:* Research assistantships with partial tuition reimbursements and teaching assistantships with partial tuition reimbursements available. Financial award application deadline: 6/1. *Unit head:* Dr. Johannes H. Hattingh, Chair, 252-328-6461, E-mail: hattinghj@ecu.edu. *Application contact:* Dean of Graduate School, 252-328-6012, Fax: 252-328-6071, E-mail: gradschool@ecu.edu. Web site: http://www.ecu.edu/cs-cas/math/graduateprogram.cfm.

Eastern Illinois University, Graduate School, College of Sciences, Department of Mathematics and Computer Science, Charleston, IL 61920-3099. Offers mathematics (MA); mathematics education (MA). *Entrance requirements:* For master's, GRE General Test. *Expenses:* Tuition, state resident: part-time $279 per credit hour. Tuition, nonresident: part-time $670 per credit hour. *Required fees:* $179.07 per credit hour. $1253 per semester.

Eastern Kentucky University, The Graduate School, College of Arts and Sciences, Department of Mathematics and Statistics, Richmond, KY 40475-3102. Offers mathematical sciences (MS). Part-time programs available. *Degree requirements:* For master's, comprehensive exam. *Entrance requirements:* For master's, GRE General Test, minimum GPA of 2.5. *Faculty research:* Graph theory, number theory, ring theory, topology, statistics, Abstract Algebra.

Eastern Michigan University, Graduate School, College of Arts and Sciences, Department of Mathematics, Ypsilanti, MI 48197. Offers applied statistics (MA); computer science (MA); mathematics (MA); mathematics education (MA). Part-time and evening/weekend programs available. Postbaccalaureate distance learning degree programs offered (minimal on-campus study). *Faculty:* 25 full-time (11 women). *Students:* 16 full-time (9 women), 36 part-time (14 women); includes 9 minority (4 Black or African American, non-Hispanic/Latino; 5 Asian, non-Hispanic/Latino), 6 international. Average age 30. 39 applicants, 82% accepted, 18 enrolled. In 2011, 17 degrees awarded. *Degree requirements:* For master's, thesis optional. *Entrance requirements:* Additional exam requirements/recommendations for international students: Required—TOEFL. *Application deadline:* Applications are processed on a rolling basis. Application fee: $35. *Expenses:* Tuition, state resident: full-time $10,367; part-time $432 per credit hour. Tuition, nonresident: full-time $20,435; part-time $851 per credit hour. *Required fees:* $39 per credit hour. $46 per semester. One-time fee: $100. Tuition and fees vary according to course level, degree level and reciprocity agreements. *Financial support:* Fellowships, research assistantships with full tuition reimbursements, teaching assistantships with full tuition reimbursements, career-related internships or fieldwork, Federal Work-Study, institutionally sponsored loans, scholarships/grants, tuition waivers (partial), and unspecified assistantships available. Support available to part-time students. Financial award applicants required to submit FAFSA. *Unit head:* Dr. Christopher Gardiner, Department Head, 734-487-1444, Fax: 734-487-2489, E-mail: cgardiner@emich.edu. *Application contact:* Dr. Bingwu Wang, Graduate Coordinator, 734-487-5044, Fax: 734-487-2489, E-mail: bwang@emich.edu. Web site: http://www.math.emich.edu.

Eastern New Mexico University, Graduate School, College of Liberal Arts and Sciences, Department of Mathematical Sciences, Portales, NM 88130. Offers MA. Part-time programs available. *Faculty:* 6 full-time (3 women). *Students:* 1 (woman) part-time; minority (Two or more races, non-Hispanic/Latino). 2 applicants, 50% accepted, 1 enrolled. In 2011, 1 master's awarded. *Degree requirements:* For master's, thesis optional, 3 comprehensive exams, one course in analysis, one sequence of algebra or partial differential equations. *Entrance requirements:* For master's, minimum GPA of 3.0, completion of standard calculus sequence and courses in linear algebra, differential equations, and abstract algebra. Additional exam requirements/recommendations for international students: Required—TOEFL (minimum score 550 paper-based; 213 computer-based; 79 iBT), IELTS (minimum score 6). *Application deadline:* For fall admission, 7/20 priority date for domestic students, 6/20 for international students; for spring admission, 12/15 priority date for domestic students, 11/15 for international students. Applications are processed on a rolling basis. Application fee: $10. Electronic applications accepted. *Financial support:* In 2011–12, 1 teaching assistantship with partial tuition reimbursement (averaging $8,500 per year) was awarded; career-related internships or fieldwork, scholarships/grants, tuition waivers (partial), and unspecified assistantships also available. Support available to part-time students. Financial award applicants required to submit FAFSA. *Unit head:* Dr. Kristi Jarman, Graduate Coordinator, 575-562-2336, Fax: 575-562-2555, E-mail: kristi.jarman@enmu.edu. *Application contact:* Christina Parmer, Department Secretary, 575-562-2309, Fax: 575-562-4091, E-mail: christina.parmer@enmu.edu. Web site: http://liberal-arts.enmu.edu/math/.

Eastern Washington University, Graduate Studies, College of Science, Health and Engineering, Department of Mathematics, Cheney, WA 99004-2431. Offers mathematics (MS); teaching mathematics (MA). Part-time programs available. *Faculty:* 11 full-time (4 women). *Students:* 7 full-time (4 women), 12 part-time (6 women); includes 1 minority (Asian, non-Hispanic/Latino). Average age 32. 22 applicants, 45% accepted, 8 enrolled. In 2011, 3 master's awarded. *Degree requirements:* For master's, comprehensive exam, thesis (for some programs). *Entrance requirements:* For master's, GRE General Test, departmental qualifying exam, minimum GPA of 3.0. *Application deadline:* For fall admission, 4/1 priority date for domestic students; for spring admission, 1/15 for domestic students. Applications are processed on a rolling basis. Application fee: $50. *Financial support:* In 2011–12, 12 teaching assistantships with partial tuition reimbursements (averaging $12,000 per year) were awarded; career-related internships or fieldwork, Federal Work-Study, institutionally sponsored loans, scholarships/grants, health care benefits, tuition waivers (partial), and unspecified assistantships also available. Support available to part-time students. Financial award application deadline: 2/1; financial award applicants required to submit FAFSA. *Unit head:* Dr. Christian Hansen, Chair, 509-359-6225, Fax: 509-359-4700. *Application contact:* Dr. Yves Nievergelt, Adviser, 509-359-2219.

East Tennessee State University, School of Graduate Studies, College of Arts and Sciences, Department of Mathematics and Statistics, Johnson City, TN 37614. Offers mathematics (MS); precollegiate mathematics (MS). Part-time and evening/weekend programs available. *Faculty:* 16 full-time (5 women). *Students:* 14 full-time (5 women), 1 part-time (0 women); includes 1 minority (Black or African American, non-Hispanic/Latino), 3 international. Average age 29. 28

Peterson's Graduate Programs in the Physical Sciences, Mathematics, Agricultural Sciences, the Environment & Natural Resources 2013

facebook.com/petersonspublishing **333**

Mathematics

applicants, 43% accepted, 8 enrolled. In 2011, 10 master's awarded. *Degree requirements:* For master's, comprehensive exam, thesis. *Entrance requirements:* For master's, GRE General Test, bachelor's degree in math or related area, three letters of recommendation. Additional exam requirements/recommendations for international students: Required—TOEFL (minimum score 550 paper-based; 213 computer-based; 79 iBT). *Application deadline:* For fall admission, 6/1 for domestic students, 4/30 for international students; for spring admission, 11/1 for domestic students, 11/30 for international students. Application fee: $35 ($45 for international students). Electronic applications accepted. *Expenses:* Tuition, state resident: full-time $7312; part-time $350 per credit hour. Tuition, nonresident: full-time $18,490; part-time $621 per credit hour. *Required fees:* $63 per credit hour. Tuition and fees vary according to course load and program. *Financial support:* In 2011–12, 14 students received support, including 14 teaching assistantships with full tuition reimbursements available (averaging $9,500 per year); career-related internships or fieldwork, institutionally sponsored loans, scholarships/grants, unspecified assistantships, and laboratory assistantships also available. Financial award application deadline: 7/1; financial award applicants required to submit FAFSA. *Faculty research:* Graph theory and combinatorics, probability and statistics, analysis, numerical and applied math, computational biology, mathematics education, knot theory, mathematical epidemiology, social network analysis. *Total annual research expenditures:* $200,000. *Unit head:* Dr. Robert Price, Chair, 423-439-4349, Fax: 423-439-8361, E-mail: pricejr@etsu.edu. *Application contact:* Bethany Glassbrenner, Graduate Specialist, 423-439-6165, Fax: 423-439-5624, E-mail: glassbrenner@etsu.edu.

Elizabeth City State University, School of Mathematics, Science and Technology, Program in Mathematics, Elizabeth City, NC 27909-7806. Offers MS. Part-time and evening/weekend programs available. *Degree requirements:* For master's, thesis. *Entrance requirements:* For master's, MAT and/or GRE. Additional exam requirements/recommendations for international students: Required—TOEFL. Electronic applications accepted. *Faculty research:* Oceanic temperature effects, mathematics strategies in elementary schools, multimedia, Antarctic temperature mapping, computer networks, water quality, remote sensing, polar ice, satellite imagery.

Emory University, Laney Graduate School, Department of Mathematics and Computer Science, Atlanta, GA 30322-1100. Offers computer science (MS); computer science and informatics (PhD); mathematics (MS, PhD). *Faculty:* 27 full-time (4 women), 2 part-time/adjunct (0 women). *Students:* 44 full-time (12 women); includes 10 minority (9 Asian, non-Hispanic/Latino; 1 Hispanic/Latino), 15 international. Average age 24. 171 applicants, 23% accepted, 25 enrolled. In 2011, 1 master's, 3 doctorates awarded. Terminal master's awarded for partial completion of doctoral program. *Degree requirements:* For master's, thesis; for doctorate, one foreign language, comprehensive exam, thesis/dissertation. *Entrance requirements:* For master's and doctorate, GRE General Test. *Application deadline:* For fall admission, 1/3 priority date for domestic students, 1/3 for international students. Application fee: $50. Electronic applications accepted. *Expenses: Tuition:* Full-time $34,800. *Required fees:* $1300. *Financial support:* In 2011–12, fellowships (averaging $12,550 per year), teaching assistantships (averaging $16,480 per year) were awarded; scholarships/grants and tuition waivers also available. Financial award application deadline: 1/3. *Total annual research expenditures:* $1.1 million. *Unit head:* Dr. Vaidy Sunderam, Chairman, 404-727-5926, Fax: 404-727-5611, E-mail: vss@emory.edu. *Application contact:* Prof. James Lu, Director of Graduate Studies, 404-712-8638, Fax: 404-727-5611, E-mail: jlu@mathcs.emory.edu. Web site: http://www.mathcs.emory.edu/.

Emporia State University, Graduate School, College of Liberal Arts and Sciences, Department of Mathematics, Computer Science and Economics, Emporia, KS 66801-5087. Offers mathematics (MS). Part-time programs available. *Faculty:* 14 full-time (2 women), 1 (woman) part-time/adjunct. *Students:* 7 full-time (2 women), 22 part-time (12 women); includes 1 minority (Asian, non-Hispanic/Latino), 7 international. 19 applicants, 79% accepted, 8 enrolled. In 2011, 4 master's awarded. *Degree requirements:* For master's, comprehensive exam or thesis. *Entrance requirements:* For master's, appropriate undergraduate degree. Additional exam requirements/recommendations for international students: Required—TOEFL (minimum score 520 paper-based; 133 computer-based; 68 iBT). *Application deadline:* For fall admission, 8/15 priority date for domestic students. Applications are processed on a rolling basis. Application fee: $30 ($75 for international students). Electronic applications accepted. *Expenses:* Tuition, state resident: full-time $2342; part-time $195 per credit hour. Tuition, nonresident: full-time $7254; part-time $605 per credit hour. *Required fees:* $66 per credit hour. Tuition and fees vary according to campus/location. *Financial support:* In 2011–12, 1 research assistantship with full tuition reimbursement (averaging $7,059 per year), 3 teaching assistantships with full tuition reimbursements (averaging $7,809 per year) were awarded; career-related internships or fieldwork, Federal Work-Study, institutionally sponsored loans, health care benefits, and unspecified assistantships also available. Financial award application deadline: 3/15; financial award applicants required to submit FAFSA. *Unit head:* Dr. H. Joe Yanik, Chair, 620-341-5281, Fax: 620-341-6055, E-mail: hyanik@emporia.edu. *Application contact:* Dr. H. Joe Yanik, Graduate Coordinator, 620-341-5639, E-mail: hyanik@emporia.edu. Web site: http://www.emporia.edu/math-cs/home.htm.

Fairfield University, College of Arts and Sciences, Fairfield, CT 06824-5195. Offers American studies (MA); communication (MA); creative writing (MFA); mathematics (MS). Part-time and evening/weekend programs available. Postbaccalaureate distance learning degree programs offered (minimal on-campus study). *Faculty:* 15 full-time (5 women), 1 (woman) part-time/adjunct. *Students:* 88 full-time (50 women), 95 part-time (56 women); includes 16 minority (6 Black or African American, non-Hispanic/Latino; 2 American Indian or Alaska Native, non-Hispanic/Latino; 1 Asian, non-Hispanic/Latino; 7 Hispanic/Latino), 6 international. Average age 38. 93 applicants, 66% accepted, 33 enrolled. In 2011, 48 master's awarded. *Degree requirements:* For master's, capstone research course. *Entrance requirements:* For master's, minimum GPA of 3.0, 2 letters of recommendation, resume. Additional exam requirements/recommendations for international students: Required—TOEFL (minimum score 550 paper-based; 213 computer-based; 80 iBT) or IELTS (minimum score 6.5). *Application deadline:* For fall admission, 5/14 for international students; for spring admission, 10/15 for international students. Applications are processed on a rolling basis. Application fee: $60. Electronic applications accepted. *Expenses: Tuition:* Part-time $600 per credit hour. *Required fees:* $25 per term. *Financial support:* In 2011–12, 27 students received support. Scholarships/grants and unspecified assistantships available. Financial award applicants required to submit FAFSA. *Faculty research:* Non-commutative algebra, partial differential equations, writing (fiction, non-fiction and poetry), communication for social change, comparative media systems, negotiation and management. *Unit head:* Dr. Robbin Crabtree, Dean, 203-254-4000 Ext. 3263, Fax: 203-254-4119, E-mail: rcrabtree@fairfield.edu. *Application contact:* Marianne Gumpper, Director of Graduate and Continuing Studies Admission, 203-254-4184, Fax: 203-254-4073, E-mail: gradadmis@fairfield.edu. Web site: http://www.fairfield.edu/cas/cas_grad_1.html.

Fairleigh Dickinson University, Metropolitan Campus, University College: Arts, Sciences, and Professional Studies, School of Computer Sciences and Engineering, Program in Mathematical Foundation, Teaneck, NJ 07666-1914. Offers MS.

Fayetteville State University, Graduate School, Department of Mathematics and Computer Science, Fayetteville, NC 28301-4298. Offers mathematics (MS). Part-time and evening/weekend programs available. *Faculty:* 9 full-time (3 women). *Students:* 3 full-time (1 woman), 3 part-time (0 women); includes 5 minority (all Black or African American, non-Hispanic/Latino). Average age 35. 1 applicant, 100% accepted, 1 enrolled. *Degree requirements:* For master's, comprehensive exam, thesis or alternative, internship. *Entrance requirements:* For master's, GRE General Test. *Application deadline:* For fall admission, 4/15 for domestic students; for spring admission, 10/15 for domestic students. Applications are processed on a rolling basis. Application fee: $35. Electronic applications accepted. *Faculty research:* Mathematical modeling in medicine: derivation of mathematical criteria for cure of cancer, AIDS, diabetes; error correcting codes and cryptography; qualitative properties of dynamical systems: ODE, FDE, PDE; homeomorphisms: ring, group; mathematical modeling of military strategy and outcomes for symmetrical warfare. *Unit head:* Dr. Dwight House, Chairperson, 910-672-1664, E-mail: dhouse@uncfsu.edu. *Application contact:* Katrina Hoffman, Graduate Admissions Officer, 910-672-1374, Fax: 910-672-1470, E-mail: khoffma1@uncfsu.edu.

Florida Atlantic University, Charles E. Schmidt College of Science, Department of Mathematical Sciences, Boca Raton, FL 33431-0991. Offers applied mathematics and statistics (MS); mathematical sciences (MS, MST, PhD). Part-time programs available. *Faculty:* 42 full-time (6 women), 38 part-time/adjunct (11 women). *Students:* 42 full-time (6 women), 38 part-time (11 women); includes 18 minority (9 Black or African American, non-Hispanic/Latino; 5 Asian, non-Hispanic/Latino; 3 Hispanic/Latino; 1 Two or more races, non-Hispanic/Latino), 27 international. Average age 32. 76 applicants, 41% accepted, 14 enrolled. In 2011, 24 master's, 6 doctorates awarded. Terminal master's awarded for partial completion of doctoral program. *Degree requirements:* For master's, comprehensive exam (for some programs), thesis (for some programs); for doctorate, comprehensive exam, thesis/dissertation. *Entrance requirements:* For master's and doctorate, GRE General Test, minimum GPA of 3.0. Additional exam requirements/recommendations for international students: Required—TOEFL (minimum score 500 paper-based; 173 computer-based). *Application deadline:* For fall admission, 7/1 priority date for domestic students, 2/15 for international students; for spring admission, 11/1 priority date for domestic students, 7/15 for international students. Applications are processed on a rolling basis. Application fee: $30. Electronic applications accepted. *Expenses: Tuition, area resident:* Part-time $343.02 per credit hour. Tuition, state resident: full-time $8232. Tuition, nonresident: full-time $23,931; part-time $997.14 per credit hour. *Financial support:* In 2011–12, fellowships with partial tuition reimbursements (averaging $20,000 per year), teaching assistantships with partial tuition reimbursements (averaging $20,000 per year) were awarded; Federal Work-Study also available. Financial award application deadline: 4/1. *Faculty research:* Cryptography, statistics, algebra, analysis, combinatorics. *Unit head:* Dr. Lee Klingler, Chair, 561-297-0274, Fax: 561-297-2436, E-mail: klingler@fau.edu. *Application contact:* Dr. Heinrich Niederhausen, Graduate Director, 561-297-3237, Fax: 561-297-2436, E-mail: niederha@fau.edu. Web site: http://www.math.fau.edu/.

Florida International University, College of Arts and Sciences, Department of Mathematics and Statistics, Program in Mathematical Sciences, Miami, FL 33199. Offers MS. Part-time and evening/weekend programs available. *Entrance requirements:* For master's, GRE, letter of intent; three letters of recommendation; minimum GPA of 3.0 in upper-division mathematics courses. Additional exam requirements/recommendations for international students: Required—TOEFL (minimum score 550 paper-based; 80 iBT). Electronic applications accepted.

334 facebook.com/petersonspublishing

Peterson's Graduate Programs in the Physical Sciences, Mathematics, Agricultural Sciences, the Environment & Natural Resources 2013

Florida State University, The Graduate School, College of Arts and Sciences, Department of Mathematics, Tallahassee, FL 32306-4510. Offers applied computational mathematics (MS, PhD); biomathematics (MS, PhD); financial mathematics (MS, PhD); pure mathematics (MS, PhD). Part-time programs available. *Faculty:* 52 full-time (13 women), 1 (woman) part-time/adjunct. *Students:* 139 full-time (36 women), 7 part-time (1 woman); includes 15 minority (6 Black or African American, non-Hispanic/Latino; 4 Asian, non-Hispanic/Latino; 5 Hispanic/Latino), 99 international. Average age 27. 336 applicants, 41% accepted, 41 enrolled. In 2011, 43 master's, 14 doctorates awarded. Terminal master's awarded for partial completion of doctoral program. *Degree requirements:* For master's, comprehensive exam (for some programs), thesis optional; for doctorate, comprehensive exam, thesis/dissertation, candidacy exam including written qualifying examinations which differ by degree concentrations. *Entrance requirements:* For master's and doctorate, GRE General Test, minimum upper-division GPA of 3.0, 4-year bachelor's degree. Additional exam requirements/recommendations for international students: Required—TOEFL (minimum score 550 paper-based; 213 computer-bases; 80 iBT) or IELTS (minimum score 6.5). *Application deadline:* For fall admission, 1/1 priority date for domestic students, 1/1 for international students; for spring admission, 10/1 priority date for domestic students, 11/1 for international students. Applications are processed on a rolling basis. Application fee: $30. Electronic applications accepted. *Expenses:* Tuition, state resident: full-time $9474; part-time $350.88 per credit hour. Tuition, nonresident: full-time $16,236; part-time $601.34 per credit hour. Required fees: $630 per semester. One-time fee: $20. Tuition and fees vary according to course load and campus/location. *Financial support:* In 2011–12, 106 students received support, including 7 fellowships with full tuition reimbursements available (averaging $22,600 per year), 12 research assistantships with full tuition reimbursements available (averaging $22,000 per year), 78 teaching assistantships with full tuition reimbursements available (averaging $19,300 per year); career-related internships or fieldwork, institutionally sponsored loans, scholarships/grants, health care benefits, and unspecified assistantships also available. *Faculty research:* Algebra and algebraic geometry; applied, financial, numerical, and classical analysis; biomathematics, including shape analysis and anatomical imaging; computational mathematics and numerical algorithms; geometric topology. *Unit head:* Dr. Philip L. Bowers, Chairperson, 850-645-3338, Fax: 850-644-4053, E-mail: bowers@math.fsu.edu. *Application contact:* Dr. Bettye Anne Case, Associate Chair for Graduate Studies, 850-644-1586, Fax: 850-644-4053, E-mail: case@math.fsu.edu. Web site: http://www.math.fsu.edu/.

George Mason University, College of Science, Department of Mathematical Sciences, Fairfax, VA 22030. Offers actuarial sciences (Certificate); mathematics (MS, PhD). *Faculty:* 32 full-time (8 women), 11 part-time/adjunct (4 women). *Students:* 19 full-time (6 women), 38 part-time (14 women); includes 9 minority (2 Black or African American, non-Hispanic/Latino; 4 Asian, non-Hispanic/Latino; 3 Hispanic/Latino), 5 international. Average age 32. 82 applicants, 49% accepted, 20 enrolled. In 2011, 3 master's, 1 doctorate, 3 other advanced degrees awarded. *Degree requirements:* For master's, comprehensive exam, thesis optional. *Entrance requirements:* For master's, GRE, 3 letters of recommendation; official college transcripts; expanded goals statement; resume; for doctorate, GRE (recommended), master's degree in math or undergraduate coursework with math preparation with minimum GPA of 3.0 in last 60 credits; 2 copies of official transcripts; 3 letters of recommendation; expanded goals statement; for Certificate, 3 letters of recommendation; official transcripts. Additional exam requirements/recommendations for international students: Required—TOEFL (minimum score 570 paper-based; 230 computer-based; 88 iBT), IELTS, Pearson Test of English. *Application deadline:* For fall admission, 4/15 priority date for domestic students; for spring admission, 11/1 priority date for domestic students. Application fee: $65 ($80 for international students). Electronic applications accepted. *Expenses:* Tuition, state resident: full-time $8750; part-time $364.58 per credit. Tuition, nonresident: full-time $24,092; part-time $1003.83 per credit. Required fees: $2514; $104.75 per credit. *Financial support:* In 2011–12, 20 students received support, including 3 fellowships with full tuition reimbursements available (averaging $18,000 per year), 6 research assistantships with full and partial tuition reimbursements available (averaging $15,794 per year), 11 teaching assistantships with full and partial tuition reimbursements available (averaging $20,249 per year); career-related internships or fieldwork, Federal Work-Study, scholarships/grants, unspecified assistantships, and health care benefits (full-time research or teaching assistantship recipients) also available. Support available to part-time students. Financial award application deadline: 3/1; financial award applicants required to submit FAFSA. *Faculty research:* Nonlinear dynamics and topology, with an emphasis on global bifurcations and chaos; numerical and theoretical methods of dynamical systems. *Total annual research expenditures:* $922,388. *Unit head:* Stephen H. Sapperstone, Acting Chair, 703-993-1462, Fax: 703-993-1491, E-mail: sap@gmu.edu. *Application contact:* Walter D. Morris, Jr., Graduate Coordinator, 703-993-1481, Fax: 703-993-1491, E-mail: wmorris@gmu.edu. Web site: http://math.gmu.edu/.

Georgetown University, Graduate School of Arts and Sciences, Department of Mathematics, Washington, DC 20057. Offers mathematics and statistics (MS).

The George Washington University, Columbian College of Arts and Sciences, Department of Mathematics, Washington, DC 20052. Offers applied mathematics (MA, MS, PhD); pure mathematics (MA, MS, PhD). Part-time and evening/weekend programs available. *Faculty:* 16 full-time (3 women), 5 part-time/adjunct (2 women). *Students:* 16 full-time (2 women), 9 part-time (4 women); includes 3 minority (1 Black or African American, non-Hispanic/Latino; 1 American Indian or Alaska Native, non-Hispanic/Latino; 1 Asian, non-Hispanic/Latino), 12 international. Average age 28. 101 applicants, 80% accepted, 5 enrolled. In 2011, 2 master's awarded. Terminal master's awarded for partial completion of doctoral program. *Degree requirements:* For master's, comprehensive exam; for doctorate, one foreign language, thesis/dissertation, general exam. *Entrance requirements:* For master's and doctorate, GRE General Test, minimum GPA of 3.0, interview. Additional exam requirements/recommendations for international students: Required—TOEFL (minimum score 550 paper-based; 213 computer-based; 80 iBT). *Application deadline:* For fall admission, 1/15 priority date for domestic students, 1/15 for international students; for spring admission, 10/1 priority date for domestic students, 9/1 for international students. Applications are processed on a rolling basis. Application fee: $75. Electronic applications accepted. *Financial support:* In 2011–12, 17 students received support. Fellowships with full tuition reimbursements available, teaching assistantships with tuition reimbursements available, Federal Work-Study, and tuition waivers available. Financial award application deadline: 1/15. *Unit head:* John B. Conway, Chair, 202-994-0553, E-mail: conway@gwu.edu. *Application contact:* 202-994-6210, Fax: 202-994-6213, E-mail: askccas@gwu.edu. Web site: http://www.gwu.edu/~math/.

Georgia Institute of Technology, Graduate Studies and Research, College of Sciences, School of Mathematics, Atlanta, GA 30332-0001. Offers algorithms, combinatorics, and optimization (PhD); applied mathematics (MS); bioinformatics (PhD); mathematics (PhD); quantitative and computational finance (MS); statistics (MS Stat). Terminal master's awarded for partial completion of doctoral program. *Degree requirements:* For master's, thesis or alternative; for doctorate, one foreign language, thesis/dissertation. *Entrance requirements:* For master's, GRE General Test, minimum GPA of 3.0; for doctorate, GRE General Test, GRE Subject Test, minimum GPA of 3.0. Additional exam requirements/recommendations for international students: Required—TOEFL. Electronic applications accepted. *Faculty research:* Dynamical systems, discrete mathematics, probability and statistics, mathematical physics.

Georgia Institute of Technology, Graduate Studies and Research, Multidisciplinary Program in Algorithms, Combinatorics, and Optimization, Atlanta, GA 30332-0001. Offers PhD. *Degree requirements:* For doctorate, thesis/dissertation. *Entrance requirements:* For doctorate, GRE General Test, GRE Subject Test (computer science or mathematics). Additional exam requirements/recommendations for international students: Required—TOEFL. Electronic applications accepted. *Faculty research:* Complexity, graph minors, combinatorial optimization, mathematical programming, probabilistic methods.

Georgian Court University, School of Arts and Sciences, Lakewood, NJ 08701-2697. Offers biology (MA); Catholic school leadership (Certificate); clinical mental health counseling (MA); holistic health studies (MA); mathematics (MA); pastoral ministry (Certificate); religious education (Certificate); school psychology (Certificate); theology (MA, Certificate). Part-time and evening/weekend programs available. *Faculty:* 21 full-time (10 women), 6 part-time/adjunct (5 women). *Students:* 88 full-time (84 women), 126 part-time (107 women); includes 29 minority (11 Black or African American, non-Hispanic/Latino; 5 Asian, non-Hispanic/Latino; 12 Hispanic/Latino; 1 Two or more races, non-Hispanic/Latino), 1 international. Average age 39. 210 applicants, 54% accepted, 79 enrolled. In 2011, 5 master's awarded. *Degree requirements:* For master's, comprehensive exam (for some programs), thesis (for some programs). *Entrance requirements:* For master's, GRE, MAT, or NTE/PRAXIS, 3 letters of recommendation. Additional exam requirements/recommendations for international students: Required—TOEFL (minimum score 550 paper-based; 213 computer-based). *Application deadline:* For fall admission, 8/1 priority date for domestic students, 4/1 for international students; for spring admission, 1/1 priority date for domestic students, 7/1 for international students. Applications are processed on a rolling basis. Application fee: $40. Electronic applications accepted. *Expenses: Tuition:* Full-time $13,410; part-time $745 per credit. *Required fees:* $450 per year. Tuition and fees vary according to campus/location and program. *Financial support:* Scholarships/grants, health care benefits, and unspecified assistantships available. Financial award application deadline: 4/15; financial award applicants required to submit FAFSA. *Unit head:* Dr. Rita Kipp, Dean, 732-987-2493, Fax: 732-987-2007. *Application contact:* Patrick Givens, Assistant Director of Graduate Admissions, 732-987-2736, Fax: 732-987-2084, E-mail: graduateadmissions@georgian.edu. Web site: http://www.georgian.edu/arts_sciences/index.htm.

Georgia Southern University, Jack N. Averitt College of Graduate Studies, Allen E. Paulson College of Science and Technology, Department of Mathematical Sciences, Statesboro, GA 30460. Offers mathematics (MS). Part-time programs available. *Students:* 36 full-time (7 women), 1 (woman) part-time; includes 6 minority (5 Black or African American, non-Hispanic/Latino; 1 Asian, non-Hispanic/Latino), 14 international. Average age 28. 22 applicants, 100% accepted, 15 enrolled. In 2011, 7 master's awarded. *Degree requirements:* For master's, comprehensive exam, thesis, terminal exam, project. *Entrance requirements:* For master's, GRE, BS in engineering, science, or mathematics; course work in calculus, probability, linear algebra; proficiency in a computer programming language. Additional exam requirements/recommendations for international students: Required—TOEFL (minimum score 550 paper-based; 213 computer-based; 80 iBT). *Application deadline:* For fall admission, 3/1 priority date for domestic students, 3/1 for international students; for spring admission, 10/1 priority date for domestic students, 10/1 for international students. Applications are processed on a rolling basis. Application fee: $50. Electronic applications accepted. *Expenses:* Tuition, state resident: full-time $6300; part-

Peterson's Graduate Programs in the Physical Sciences, Mathematics, Agricultural Sciences, the Environment & Natural Resources 2013

facebook.com/petersonspublishing **335**

Mathematics

time $263 per semester hour. Tuition, nonresident: full-time $25,174; part-time $1049 per semester hour. *Required fees:* $1872. *Financial support:* In 2011–12, 34 students received support, including research assistantships with partial tuition reimbursements available (averaging $7,200 per year), teaching assistantships with partial tuition reimbursements available (averaging $7,200 per year); career-related internships or fieldwork, Federal Work-Study, scholarships/grants, tuition waivers (partial), and unspecified assistantships also available. Support available to part-time students. Financial award application deadline: 4/15; financial award applicants required to submit FAFSA. *Faculty research:* Optimization, approximation theory, computed tomography, harmonic analysis, applied statistics. *Total annual research expenditures:* $2,200. *Unit head:* Dr. Martha Abell, Chair, 912-478-5132, Fax: 912-478-0654, E-mail: martha@georgiasouthern.edu. *Application contact:* Amanda Gilliland, Coordinator for Graduate Student Recruitment, 912-478-5384, Fax: 912-478-0740, E-mail: gradadmissions@georgiasouthern.edu. Web site: http://cost.georgiasouthern.edu/math.

Georgia State University, College of Arts and Sciences, Department of Mathematics and Statistics, Atlanta, GA 30302-3083. Offers mathematics (MA, MS); mathematics and statistics (PhD). Part-time and evening/weekend programs available. *Degree requirements:* For master's, comprehensive exam (for some programs), thesis (for some programs), exam; for doctorate, comprehensive exam, thesis/dissertation. *Entrance requirements:* For master's and doctorate, GRE. Additional exam requirements/recommendations for international students: Required—TOEFL. Electronic applications accepted. *Faculty research:* Analysis, biostatistics, discrete mathematics, linear algebra, statistics.

Graduate School and University Center of the City University of New York, Graduate Studies, Program in Mathematics, New York, NY 10016-4039. Offers PhD. *Degree requirements:* For doctorate, 2 foreign languages, thesis/dissertation. *Entrance requirements:* For doctorate, GRE General Test. Additional exam requirements/recommendations for international students: Required—TOEFL. Electronic applications accepted.

Hardin-Simmons University, Graduate School, Holland School of Sciences and Mathematics, Abilene, TX 79698-0001. Offers MS, DPT. Part-time programs available. *Faculty:* 5 full-time (0 women). *Students:* 4 full-time (2 women), 1 part-time (0 women). Average age 25. 4 applicants, 100% accepted, 4 enrolled. In 2011, 8 master's awarded. *Degree requirements:* For master's, comprehensive exam, thesis or alternative, internship; for doctorate, comprehensive exam, thesis/dissertation or alternative. *Entrance requirements:* For master's, minimum undergraduate GPA of 3.0 in major, 2.7 overall; 2 semesters of course work each in biology, chemistry and geology; interview; writing sample; occupational experience; for doctorate, letters of recommendation, interview, writing sample. Additional exam requirements/recommendations for international students: Required—TOEFL (minimum score 550 paper-based; 213 computer-based; 75 iBT). *Application deadline:* For fall admission, 8/15 priority date for domestic students, 4/1 for international students; for spring admission, 1/5 priority date for domestic students, 9/1 for international students. Applications are processed on a rolling basis. Application fee: $50. *Expenses: Tuition:* Full-time $12,870; part-time $715 per credit hour. *Required fees:* $650; $110 per semester. Tuition and fees vary according to degree level. *Financial support:* In 2011–12, 1 fellowship (averaging $300 per year) was awarded; career-related internships or fieldwork and scholarships/grants also available. Support available to part-time students. Financial award application deadline: 6/30; financial award applicants required to submit FAFSA. *Unit head:* Dr. Christopher McNair, Dean, 325-670-1401, Fax: 325-670-1385, E-mail: cmcnair@hsutx.edu. *Application contact:* Dr. Nancy Kucinski, Dean of Graduate Studies, 325-670-1298, Fax: 325-670-1564, E-mail: gradoff@hsutx.edu. Web site: http://www.hsutx.edu/academics/holland.

Harvard University, Graduate School of Arts and Sciences, Department of Mathematics, Cambridge, MA 02138. Offers PhD. *Degree requirements:* For doctorate, 2 foreign languages, thesis/dissertation, qualifying exam. *Entrance requirements:* For doctorate, GRE General Test, GRE Subject Test. Additional exam requirements/recommendations for international students: Required—TOEFL. *Expenses: Tuition:* Full-time $36,304. *Required fees:* $1186. Full-time tuition and fees vary according to program.

Howard University, Graduate School, Department of Mathematics, Washington, DC 20059-0002. Offers applied mathematics (MS, PhD); mathematics (MS, PhD). Part-time programs available. Terminal master's awarded for partial completion of doctoral program. *Degree requirements:* For master's, comprehensive exam, thesis or alternative, qualifying exam; for doctorate, 2 foreign languages, comprehensive exam, thesis/dissertation, qualifying exams. *Entrance requirements:* For master's, GRE General Test, minimum GPA of 3.0; for doctorate, GRE General Test. Additional exam requirements/recommendations for international students: Required—TOEFL. Electronic applications accepted.

Hunter College of the City University of New York, Graduate School, School of Arts and Sciences, Department of Mathematics and Statistics, New York, NY 10021-5085. Offers applied mathematics (MA); mathematics for secondary education (MA); pure mathematics (MA). Part-time and evening/weekend programs available. *Faculty:* 8 full-time (1 woman), 2 part-time/adjunct (0 women). *Students:* 9 full-time (7 women), 71 part-time (34 women); includes 25 minority (7 Black or African American, non-Hispanic/Latino; 16 Asian, non-Hispanic/Latino; 2 Hispanic/Latino), 11 international. Average age 28. 54 applicants, 56% accepted, 15 enrolled. In 2011, 30 master's awarded. *Degree requirements:* For master's, one foreign language, comprehensive exam, thesis (for some programs).

Entrance requirements: For master's, GRE General Test, 24 credits in mathematics. Additional exam requirements/recommendations for international students: Required—TOEFL. *Application deadline:* For fall admission, 4/1 for domestic students, 2/1 for international students; for spring admission, 11/1 for domestic students, 9/1 for international students. Application fee: $125. *Expenses:* Tuition, state resident: full-time $8210; part-time $345 per credit. Tuition, nonresident: full-time $15,360; part-time $640 per credit. *Required fees:* $280 per semester. One-time fee: $125. Tuition and fees vary according to class time, campus/location and program. *Financial support:* Federal Work-Study, institutionally sponsored loans, scholarships/grants, and tuition waivers (partial) available. Support available to part-time students. *Faculty research:* Data analysis, dynamical systems, computer graphics, topology, statistical decision theory. *Unit head:* Ada Peluso, Chairperson, 212-772-5300, Fax: 212-772-4858, E-mail: peluso@math.hunter.cuny.edu. *Application contact:* William Zlata, Director for Graduate Admissions, 212-772-4482, Fax: 212-650-3336, E-mail: admissions@hunter.cuny.edu. Web site: http://math.hunter.cuny.edu/.

Idaho State University, Office of Graduate Studies, College of Science and Engineering, Department of Mathematics, Pocatello, ID 83209-8085. Offers mathematics (MS, DA); mathematics for secondary teachers (MA). Part-time programs available. *Degree requirements:* For master's, comprehensive exam, thesis (for some programs), oral and written exams; for doctorate, comprehensive exam, thesis/dissertation, teaching internships. *Entrance requirements:* For master's, GRE General Test, GRE Subject Test, course work in modern algebra, differential equations, advanced calculus, introductory analysis; for doctorate, GRE General Test, GRE Subject Test, minimum graduate GPA of 3.5, MS in mathematics, teaching experience, 3 letters of recommendation. Additional exam requirements/recommendations for international students: Required—TOEFL (minimum score 550 paper-based; 213 computer-based; 80 iBT). Electronic applications accepted. *Faculty research:* Algebra, analysis geometry, statistics, applied mathematics.

Illinois State University, Graduate School, College of Arts and Sciences, Department of Mathematics, Program in Mathematics, Normal, IL 61790-2200. Offers MA, MS. *Degree requirements:* For master's, thesis or alternative. *Entrance requirements:* For master's, GRE General Test, minimum GPA of 2.8 in last 60 hours of course work.

Indiana State University, College of Graduate and Professional Studies, College of Arts and Sciences, Department of Mathematics and Computer Science, Terre Haute, IN 47809. Offers math teaching (MA, MS); mathematics and computer science (MA); mathematics and computer sciences (MS). Part-time programs available. *Degree requirements:* For master's, thesis or alternative. *Entrance requirements:* For master's, 24 semester hours of course work in undergraduate mathematics. Electronic applications accepted.

Indiana University Bloomington, University Graduate School, College of Arts and Sciences, Department of Mathematics, Bloomington, IN 47405-7000. Offers applied mathematics-numerical analysis (MA, PhD); mathematics education (MAT); pure mathematics (MA, PhD). *Faculty:* 49 full-time (3 women). *Students:* 124 full-time (23 women), 1 part-time (0 women); includes 13 minority (2 Black or African American, non-Hispanic/Latino; 10 Asian, non-Hispanic/Latino; 1 Hispanic/Latino), 68 international. Average age 27. 242 applicants, 19% accepted, 17 enrolled. In 2011, 20 master's, 12 doctorates awarded. Terminal master's awarded for partial completion of doctoral program. *Degree requirements:* For doctorate, one foreign language, thesis/dissertation. *Entrance requirements:* For master's and doctorate, GRE General Test, GRE Subject Test. Additional exam requirements/recommendations for international students: Required—TOEFL. *Application deadline:* For fall admission, 1/15 priority date for domestic students, 1/15 for international students. Applications are processed on a rolling basis. Application fee: $55 ($65 for international students). Electronic applications accepted. *Financial support:* In 2011–12, 2 students received support, including 9 fellowships with full tuition reimbursements available (averaging $21,450 per year), 11 research assistantships with full tuition reimbursements available (averaging $16,045 per year), 96 teaching assistantships with full tuition reimbursements available (averaging $15,870 per year); scholarships/grants, health care benefits, and unspecified assistantships also available. Financial award application deadline: 1/15. *Faculty research:* Topology, geometry, algebra, applied, analysis. *Unit head:* Kevin Zumbrun, Chair, 812-855-2200. *Application contact:* Kate Bowman, Graduate Secretary, 812-855-2645, Fax: 812-855-0046, E-mail: gradmath@indiana.edu. Web site: http://www.math.indiana.edu/.

Indiana University of Pennsylvania, School of Graduate Studies and Research, College of Natural Sciences and Mathematics, Department of Mathematics, Indiana, PA 15705-1087. Offers applied mathematics (MS); elementary and middle school mathematics education (M Ed); mathematics education (M Ed). Part-time programs available. *Faculty:* 9 full-time (2 women). *Students:* 21 full-time (7 women), 15 part-time (11 women); includes 5 minority (1 Black or African American, non-Hispanic/Latino; 3 Asian, non-Hispanic/Latino; 1 Two or more races, non-Hispanic/Latino), 3 international. Average age 28. 42 applicants, 64% accepted, 13 enrolled. In 2011, 14 master's awarded. *Degree requirements:* For master's, thesis optional. *Entrance requirements:* For master's, 2 letters of recommendation. Additional exam requirements/recommendations for international students: Required—TOEFL (minimum score 540 paper-based; 207 computer-based). *Application deadline:* Applications are processed on a rolling basis. Application fee: $50. Electronic applications accepted. *Expenses:* Tuition, state resident: full-time $7488; part-time $416 per credit. Tuition, nonresident:

336 facebook.com/petersonspublishing

Peterson's Graduate Programs in the Physical Sciences, Mathematics, Agricultural Sciences, the Environment & Natural Resources 2013

full-time $11,232; part-time $624 per credit. *Required fees:* $2070; $192.20 per credit. $90 per semester. *Financial support:* In 2011–12, 13 research assistantships with full and partial tuition reimbursements (averaging $3,073 per year) were awarded; career-related internships or fieldwork and Federal Work-Study also available. Support available to part-time students. Financial award application deadline: 4/15; financial award applicants required to submit FAFSA. *Unit head:* Dr. Franciso E. Alarcon, Chairperson, 724-357-2608, E-mail: falarcon@iup.edu. *Application contact:* Dr. Yu-Ju Kuo, Program Coordinator, 724-357-3797, E-mail: yjkuo@iup.edu. Web site: http://www.iup.edu/upper.aspx?id=216.

Indiana University–Purdue University Fort Wayne, College of Arts and Sciences, Department of Mathematical Sciences, Fort Wayne, IN 46805-1499. Offers applied mathematics (MS); applied statistics (Certificate); mathematics (MS); operations research (MS); teaching (MAT). Part-time and evening/weekend programs available. *Faculty:* 20 full-time (5 women). *Students:* 1 full-time (0 women), 16 part-time (3 women). Average age 32. 6 applicants, 100% accepted, 3 enrolled. In 2011, 8 master's, 2 other advanced degrees awarded. *Entrance requirements:* For master's, minimum GPA of 3.0, major or minor in mathematics, three letters of recommendation. Additional exam requirements/recommendations for international students: Required—TOEFL (minimum score 550 paper-based; 213 computer-based; 77 iBT); Recommended—TWE. *Application deadline:* For fall admission, 8/1 priority date for domestic students, 7/1 for international students; for spring admission, 12/1 for domestic students, 10/1 for international students. Applications are processed on a rolling basis. Application fee: $55 ($60 for international students). Electronic applications accepted. *Financial support:* In 2011–12, 6 teaching assistantships with partial tuition reimbursements (averaging $12,930 per year) were awarded; scholarships/grants and unspecified assistantships also available. Support available to part-time students. Financial award application deadline: 3/1; financial award applicants required to submit FAFSA. *Faculty research:* Brick factory problem, CR singularities, carleman orthogonal polynomials. *Unit head:* Dr. David A. Legg, Chair, 260-481-6222, Fax: 260-481-0155, E-mail: legg@ipfw.edu. *Application contact:* Dr. W. Douglas Weakley, Director of Graduate Studies, 260-481-6233, Fax: 260-481-0155, E-mail: weakley@ipfw.edu. Web site: http://www.ipfw.edu/math/.

Indiana University–Purdue University Indianapolis, School of Science, Department of Mathematical Sciences, Doctoral Program in Mathematics, Indianapolis, IN 46202-3216. Offers applied mathematics (PhD); mathematical statistics (PhD); mathematics (PhD). *Students:* 17 full-time (7 women), 5 part-time (0 women); includes 2 minority (1 Black or African American, non-Hispanic/Latino; 1 Hispanic/Latino), 10 international. Average age 29. 25 applicants, 44% accepted, 3 enrolled. *Degree requirements:* For doctorate, one foreign language, thesis/dissertation. *Entrance requirements:* For doctorate, GRE General Test. Additional exam requirements/recommendations for international students: Required—TOEFL. *Application deadline:* For fall admission, 2/1 priority date for domestic students. Application fee: $55 ($65 for international students). *Unit head:* Dr. Evgeny Mukhin, Director of Graduate Programs, 317-274-6918, E-mail: grad-program@math.iupui.edu. *Application contact:* Dr. Sherry Queener, Director, Graduate Studies and Associate Dean, 317-274-1577, Fax: 317-278-2380. Web site: http://www.math.iupui.edu/.

Indiana University–Purdue University Indianapolis, School of Science, Department of Mathematical Sciences, Master's Program in Mathematics, Indianapolis, IN 46202-3216. Offers applied mathematics (MS); applied statistics (MS); mathematics (MS); mathematics education (MS). *Students:* 13 full-time (3 women), 30 part-time (12 women); includes 14 minority (1 Black or African American, non-Hispanic/Latino; 9 Asian, non-Hispanic/Latino; 3 Hispanic/Latino; 1 Two or more races, non-Hispanic/Latino), 14 international. Average age 36. 49 applicants, 73% accepted, 15 enrolled. In 2011, 17 master's awarded. *Degree requirements:* For master's, comprehensive exam (for some programs), thesis optional. *Entrance requirements:* Additional exam requirements/recommendations for international students: Required—TOEFL. Application fee: $55 ($65 for international students). *Unit head:* Dr. Evgeny Mukhin, Director of Graduate Programs, 317-274-6918, E-mail: grad-program@math.iupui.edu. *Application contact:* Dr. Sherry Queener, Director, Graduate Studies and Associate Dean, 317-274-1577, Fax: 317-278-2380. Web site: http://www.math.iupui.edu/.

Instituto Tecnologico de Santo Domingo, Graduate School, Area of Basic And Environmental Sciences, Santo Domingo, Dominican Republic. Offers environmental science (M En S), including environmental education, environmental management, marine resources, natural resources management; mathematics (MS, PhD); renewable energy technology (MS, Certificate).

Iowa State University of Science and Technology, Department of Mathematics, Ames, IA 50011. Offers applied mathematics (MS, PhD); mathematics (MS, PhD); school mathematics (MSM). *Degree requirements:* For master's, thesis or alternative; for doctorate, thesis/dissertation. *Entrance requirements:* For master's and doctorate, GRE General Test. Additional exam requirements/recommendations for international students: Required—TOEFL (minimum score 550 paper-based; 79 iBT), IELTS (minimum score 6.5). *Application deadline:* For fall admission, 2/1 priority date for domestic students, 2/1 for international students. Application fee: $40 ($90 for international students). Electronic applications accepted. *Financial support:* Scholarships/grants, health care benefits, and unspecified assistantships available. *Unit head:* Dr. Clifford Bergman, Director of Graduate Education, 515-294-0393, Fax: 515-294-5454, E-mail: gradmath@iastate.edu. *Application contact:* Melanie Erickson, Director of

Graduate Education, 515-294-0393, Fax: 515-294-5454, E-mail: gradmath@iastate.edu. Web site: http://http://www.math.iastate.edu/Graduate/Prospective.html.

Jackson State University, Graduate School, College of Science, Engineering and Technology, Department of Mathematics, Jackson, MS 39217. Offers mathematics (MS). Part-time and evening/weekend programs available. *Degree requirements:* For master's, comprehensive exam, thesis (for some programs). *Entrance requirements:* For master's, GRE General Test. Additional exam requirements/recommendations for international students: Required—TOEFL (minimum score 520 paper-based; 195 computer-based; 67 iBT).

Jacksonville State University, College of Graduate Studies and Continuing Education, College of Arts and Sciences, Department of Mathematics, Jacksonville, AL 36265-1602. Offers MS. Part-time and evening/weekend programs available. *Degree requirements:* For master's, comprehensive exam, thesis (for some programs). *Entrance requirements:* For master's, GRE General Test or MAT. Electronic applications accepted. *Expenses:* Tuition, state resident: part-time $336 per hour. Tuition, nonresident: part-time $672 per hour. Part-time tuition and fees vary according to degree level.

James Madison University, The Graduate School, College of Science and Mathematics, Department of Mathematics and Statistics, Harrisonburg, VA 22807. Offers M Ed. Part-time programs available. *Faculty:* 2 full-time (1 woman), 1 (woman) part-time/adjunct. *Students:* 3 part-time (1 woman). Average age 27. In 2011, 2 master's awarded. *Degree requirements:* For master's, comprehensive exam. *Entrance requirements:* For master's, undergraduate major in mathematics. *Application deadline:* For fall admission, 5/1 priority date for domestic students; for spring admission, 9/1 priority date for domestic students. Application fee: $55. *Expenses:* Tuition, state resident: full-time $8016; part-time $334 per credit hour. Tuition, nonresident: full-time $22,656; part-time $944 per credit hour. *Financial support:* Application deadline: 3/1; applicants required to submit FAFSA. *Unit head:* Dr. David C. Carothers, Academic Unit Head, 540-568-6184, E-mail: carothdc@jmu.edu. *Application contact:* Lynette M. Bible, Director of Graduate Admissions, 540-568-6395, Fax: 540-568-7860, E-mail: biblelm@jmu.edu.

John Carroll University, Graduate School, Department of Mathematics, University Heights, OH 44118-4581. Offers MA, MS. Part-time and evening/weekend programs available. *Degree requirements:* For master's, comprehensive exam, thesis (for some programs), research essay. *Entrance requirements:* For master's, minimum GPA of 2.5, teaching certificate (MA). Electronic applications accepted. *Faculty research:* Algebraic topology, algebra, differential geometry, combinatorics, Lie groups.

The Johns Hopkins University, Zanvyl Krieger School of Arts and Sciences, Department of Mathematics, Baltimore, MD 21218-2699. Offers PhD. *Degree requirements:* For doctorate, one foreign language, thesis/dissertation, 3 qualifying exams. *Entrance requirements:* For doctorate, GRE General Test, GRE Subject Test. Additional exam requirements/recommendations for international students: Required—TOEFL (minimum score 600 paper-based; 250 computer-based; 100 iBT), IELTS. Electronic applications accepted. *Faculty research:* Algebraic geometry, number theory, algebraic topology, differential geometry, partial differential equations.

Kansas State University, Graduate School, College of Arts and Sciences, Department of Mathematics, Manhattan, KS 66506. Offers MS, PhD. Part-time programs available. *Faculty:* 31 full-time (4 women), 2 part-time/adjunct (0 women). *Students:* 43 full-time (10 women); includes 5 minority (2 Black or African American, non-Hispanic/Latino; 1 Asian, non-Hispanic/Latino; 2 Hispanic/Latino), 22 international. Average age 28. 52 applicants, 54% accepted, 12 enrolled. In 2011, 3 master's, 7 doctorates awarded. Terminal master's awarded for partial completion of doctoral program. *Degree requirements:* For master's, thesis or alternative; for doctorate, one foreign language, thesis/dissertation. *Entrance requirements:* For master's, GRE, bachelor's degree in mathematics; for doctorate, master's degree in mathematics. Additional exam requirements/recommendations for international students: Required—TOEFL (minimum score 600 paper-based; 250 computer-based). *Application deadline:* For fall admission, 2/1 priority date for domestic students, 2/1 for international students; for spring admission, 8/1 priority date for domestic students, 8/1 for international students. Applications are processed on a rolling basis. Application fee: $40 ($55 for international students). Electronic applications accepted. *Financial support:* In 2011–12, 38 teaching assistantships with full tuition reimbursements (averaging $15,928 per year) were awarded; research assistantships, Federal Work-Study, institutionally sponsored loans, and scholarships/grants also available. Support available to part-time students. Financial award application deadline: 3/1; financial award applicants required to submit FAFSA. *Faculty research:* Low-dimensional topology, geometry, complex and harmonic analysis, group and representation theory, noncommunicative spaces. *Total annual research expenditures:* $419,016. *Unit head:* Louis Pigno, Department Head, 785-532-6750, Fax: 785-532-0546, E-mail: lpigno@ksu.edu. *Application contact:* Diego Maldonado, Graduate Studies Director, 785-532-0581, Fax: 785-532-0546, E-mail: dmaldona@math.ksu.edu. Web site: http://www.math.ksu.edu/.

Kent State University, College of Arts and Sciences, Department of Mathematical Sciences, Kent, OH 44242-0001. Offers applied mathematics (MA, MS, PhD); pure mathematics (MA, MS, PhD). Part-time programs available. *Degree requirements:* For master's, thesis optional; for doctorate, one foreign language, thesis/dissertation. Electronic applications accepted. *Expenses:*

Peterson's Graduate Programs in the Physical Sciences, Mathematics, Agricultural Sciences, the Environment & Natural Resources 2013

facebook.com/petersonspublishing **337**

Mathematics

Tuition, state resident: full-time $8136; part-time $452 per credit hour. Tuition, nonresident: full-time $14,292; part-time $794 per credit hour. *Faculty research:* Approximation theory, measure theory, ring theory, functional analysis, complex analysis.

Kent State University, Graduate School of Education, Health, and Human Services, School of Teaching, Learning and Curriculum Studies, Program in Math Specialization, Kent, OH 44242-0001. Offers M Ed, MA. Part-time programs available. *Faculty:* 3 full-time (2 women). *Students:* 1 (woman) full-time, 4 part-time (all women); includes 1 minority (Asian, non-Hispanic/Latino). 3 applicants, 100% accepted. In 2011, 2 master's awarded. *Entrance requirements:* For master's, 2 letters of reference, goals statement. Additional exam requirements/recommendations for international students: Required—TOEFL (minimum score 550 paper-based; 213 computer-based; 80 iBT). *Application deadline:* Applications are processed on a rolling basis. Application fee: $30 ($60 for international students). Electronic applications accepted. *Expenses:* Tuition, state resident: full-time $8136; part-time $452 per credit hour. Tuition, nonresident: full-time $14,292; part-time $794 per credit hour. *Financial support:* In 2011–12, 1 research assistantship (averaging $9,000 per year) was awarded. *Unit head:* Dr. Mike Mikusa, Coordinator, 330-672-0647, E-mail: mmikusa@kent.edu. *Application contact:* Nancy Miller, Academic Program Coordinator, Office of Graduate Student Services, 330-672-2576, Fax: 330-672-9162, E-mail: ogs@kent.edu.

Lakehead University, Graduate Studies, School of Mathematical Sciences, Thunder Bay, ON P7B 5E1, Canada. Offers computer science (M Sc); mathematical science (MA). Part-time and evening/weekend programs available. *Degree requirements:* For master's, thesis optional. *Entrance requirements:* For master's, minimum B average, honours degree in mathematics or computer science. Additional exam requirements/recommendations for international students: Required—TOEFL. *Faculty research:* Numerical analysis, classical analysis, theoretical computer science, abstract harmonic analysis, functional analysis.

Lamar University, College of Graduate Studies, College of Arts and Sciences, Department of Mathematics, Beaumont, TX 77710. Offers MS. *Faculty:* 6 full-time (2 women). *Students:* 10 full-time (5 women), 2 part-time (1 woman); includes 3 minority (1 Black or African American, non-Hispanic/Latino; 1 Asian, non-Hispanic/Latino; 1 Hispanic/Latino), 4 international. Average age 27. 8 applicants, 88% accepted, 2 enrolled. In 2011, 3 master's awarded. *Degree requirements:* For master's, comprehensive exam (for some programs), thesis optional. *Entrance requirements:* For master's, GRE General Test, minimum GPA of 2.5 in last 60 hours of undergraduate course work. Additional exam requirements/recommendations for international students: Required—TOEFL. *Application deadline:* For fall admission, 5/15 priority date for domestic students; for spring admission, 10/1 priority date for domestic students. Applications are processed on a rolling basis. Application fee: $25 ($50 for international students). *Expenses:* Tuition, state resident: full-time $5430; part-time $272 per credit hour. Tuition, nonresident: full-time $11,540; part-time $577 per credit hour. *Required fees:* $1916. *Financial support:* In 2011–12, 4 teaching assistantships (averaging $12,000 per year) were awarded; fellowships and research assistantships also available. Financial award application deadline: 4/1. *Faculty research:* Complex analysis, differential equations, algebra, topology statistics. *Total annual research expenditures:* $43,585. *Unit head:* Charles F. Coppin, Chair, 409-880-8792, Fax: 409-880-8794, E-mail: chair@math.lamar.edu. *Application contact:* Dr. Paul Chiou, Professor, 409-880-8800, Fax: 409-880-8794, E-mail: chiou@math.lamar.edu.

Lehigh University, College of Arts and Sciences, Department of Mathematics, Bethlehem, PA 18015. Offers applied mathematics (MS, PhD); mathematics (MS, PhD); statistics (MS). Part-time programs available. *Faculty:* 23 full-time (1 woman), 2 part-time/adjunct (0 women). *Students:* 31 full-time (16 women), 6 part-time (2 women); includes 1 minority (Asian, non-Hispanic/Latino), 13 international. Average age 26. 140 applicants, 9% accepted, 5 enrolled. In 2011, 11 master's, 2 doctorates awarded. Terminal master's awarded for partial completion of doctoral program. *Degree requirements:* For master's, comprehensive exam, thesis optional; for doctorate, comprehensive exam, thesis/dissertation, qualifying exams, general exam, advanced topic exam. *Entrance requirements:* For master's and doctorate, GRE General Test (strongly recommended), minimum undergraduate GPA of 2.75, 3.0 for last two semesters; adequate background in math. Additional exam requirements/recommendations for international students: Required—TOEFL (minimum score 85 iBT). *Application deadline:* For fall admission, 1/1 priority date for domestic students, 1/1 for international students; for spring admission, 12/1 priority date for domestic students, 12/1 for international students. Applications are processed on a rolling basis. Application fee: $75. Electronic applications accepted. *Financial support:* In 2011–12, 35 students received support, including 2 fellowships with full tuition reimbursements available (averaging $25,000 per year), 23 teaching assistantships with full tuition reimbursements available (averaging $17,500 per year); research assistantships with full tuition reimbursements available, scholarships/grants, and tuition waivers (partial) also available. Financial award application deadline: 1/1. *Faculty research:* Probability and statistics, geometry and topology, number theory, algebra, discrete mathematics, differential equations. *Total annual research expenditures:* $155,033. *Unit head:* Dr. Wei-Min Huang, Chairman, 610-758-3730, Fax: 610-758-3767, E-mail: wh02@lehigh.edu. *Application contact:* Dr. Terry Napier, Graduate Coordinator, 610-758-3755, E-mail: mathgrad@lehigh.edu. Web site: http://www.lehigh.edu/~math/grad.html.

Lehman College of the City University of New York, Division of Natural and Social Sciences, Department of Mathematics and Computer Science, Program in Mathematics, Bronx, NY 10468-1589. Offers MA. Part-time and evening/weekend programs available. *Degree requirements:* For master's, one foreign language, thesis or alternative.

Long Island University–C. W. Post Campus, College of Liberal Arts and Sciences, Department of Mathematics, Brookville, NY 11548-1300. Offers applied mathematics (MS); mathematics education (MS); mathematics for secondary school teachers (MS). Part-time and evening/weekend programs available. *Degree requirements:* For master's, thesis or alternative, oral presentation. *Entrance requirements:* Additional exam requirements/recommendations for international students: Required—TOEFL. Electronic applications accepted. *Faculty research:* Differential geometry, topological groups, general topology, number theory, analysis and statistics, numerical analysis.

Louisiana State University and Agricultural and Mechanical College, Graduate School, College of Science, Department of Mathematics, Baton Rouge, LA 70803. Offers MS, PhD. *Faculty:* 56 full-time (5 women), 2 part-time/adjunct (0 women). *Students:* 90 full-time (26 women), 3 part-time (1 woman); includes 6 minority (1 Black or African American, non-Hispanic/Latino; 1 American Indian or Alaska Native, non-Hispanic/Latino; 4 Hispanic/Latino), 41 international. Average age 27. 142 applicants, 56% accepted, 13 enrolled. In 2011, 15 master's, 10 doctorates awarded. Terminal master's awarded for partial completion of doctoral program. *Degree requirements:* For doctorate, 2 foreign languages, thesis/dissertation. *Entrance requirements:* For master's and doctorate, GRE General Test, minimum GPA of 3.0. Additional exam requirements/recommendations for international students: Required—TOEFL (minimum score 550 paper-based; 213 computer-based; 79 iBT) or IELTS (minimum score 6.5). *Application deadline:* For fall admission, 1/25 priority date for domestic students, 5/15 for international students; for spring admission, 10/15 for international students. Applications are processed on a rolling basis. Application fee: $50 ($70 for international students). Electronic applications accepted. *Financial support:* In 2011–12, 87 students received support, including 20 fellowships with full and partial tuition reimbursements available (averaging $19,457 per year), 10 research assistantships with full and partial tuition reimbursements available (averaging $18,180 per year), 51 teaching assistantships with full and partial tuition reimbursements available (averaging $18,506 per year); Federal Work-Study, institutionally sponsored loans, scholarships/grants, health care benefits, tuition waivers (full), and unspecified assistantships also available. Financial award application deadline: 3/1; financial award applicants required to submit FAFSA. *Faculty research:* Algebra, graph theory and combinatorics, algebraic topology, analysis and probability, topological algebra. *Total annual research expenditures:* $1.7 million. *Unit head:* Dr. Robert Perlis, Chair, 225-578-1618, Fax: 225-578-4276, E-mail: perlis@math.lsu.edu. *Application contact:* Dr. William Adkins, Graduate Adviser, 225-578-1568, Fax: 225-578-4276, E-mail: mmadki@lsu.edu. Web site: http://www.math.lsu.edu/.

Louisiana Tech University, Graduate School, College of Engineering and Science, Department of Mathematics and Statistics, Ruston, LA 71272. Offers MS. Part-time programs available. *Degree requirements:* For master's, thesis or alternative. *Entrance requirements:* For master's, GRE General Test, minimum GPA of 3.0 in last 60 hours. Additional exam requirements/recommendations for international students: Required—TOEFL.

Loyola University Chicago, Graduate School, Department of Mathematical Sciences and Statistics, Chicago, IL 60660. Offers applied statistics (MS); mathematics and statistics (MS), including pure mathematics. Part-time programs available. *Faculty:* 19 full-time (4 women). *Students:* 38 full-time (25 women), 8 part-time (5 women); includes 14 minority (4 Black or African American, non-Hispanic/Latino; 7 Asian, non-Hispanic/Latino; 2 Hispanic/Latino; 1 Two or more races, non-Hispanic/Latino), 6 international. Average age 28. 75 applicants, 61% accepted, 26 enrolled. In 2011, 18 master's awarded. *Entrance requirements:* For master's, GRE General Test. Additional exam requirements/recommendations for international students: Required—TOEFL. *Application deadline:* For fall admission, 8/1 for domestic students; for spring admission, 12/1 for domestic students. Applications are processed on a rolling basis. Application fee: $0. Electronic applications accepted. *Expenses: Tuition:* Full-time $15,660; part-time $870 per credit hour. *Required fees:* $125 per semester. Tuition and fees vary according to course load and program. *Financial support:* In 2011–12, 13 students received support, including 6 teaching assistantships with tuition reimbursements available (averaging $10,000 per year); career-related internships or fieldwork, Federal Work-Study, institutionally sponsored loans, and tuition waivers (partial) also available. Financial award application deadline: 3/15. *Faculty research:* Probability and statistics, differential equations, algebra, combinations. *Total annual research expenditures:* $10,000. *Unit head:* Dr. Robert Jensen, Chair, 773-508-3578, Fax: 773-508-2123, E-mail: rjensen@luc.edu. *Application contact:* Dr. W. Cary Huffman, Graduate Program Director, 773-508-3563, Fax: 773-508-2123, E-mail: whuffma@luc.edu. Web site: http://math.luc.edu/.

Marquette University, Graduate School, College of Arts and Sciences, Department of Mathematics, Statistics, and Computer Science, Milwaukee, WI 53201-1881. Offers bioinformatics (MS); computational sciences (MS, PhD); computing (MS); mathematics education (MS). Part-time and evening/weekend programs available. Postbaccalaureate distance learning degree programs offered (minimal on-campus study). *Faculty:* 28 full-time (9 women), 10 part-time/adjunct (5 women). *Students:* 14 full-time (3 women), 77 part-time (18 women);

includes 9 minority (2 Black or African American, non-Hispanic/Latino; 7 Asian, non-Hispanic/Latino), 24 international. Average age 30. 86 applicants, 65% accepted, 24 enrolled. In 2011, 15 master's, 1 doctorate awarded. Terminal master's awarded for partial completion of doctoral program. *Degree requirements:* For master's, thesis (for some programs), essay with oral presentation; for doctorate, comprehensive exam, thesis/dissertation, qualifying examination. *Entrance requirements:* For master's, official transcripts from all current and previous colleges/universities except Marquette, three letters of recommendation; for doctorate, GRE General Test, official transcripts from all current and previous colleges/universities except Marquette, three letters of recommendation. Additional exam requirements/recommendations for international students: Required—TOEFL (minimum score 530 paper-based; 78 computer-based). *Application deadline:* For fall admission, 1/15 for domestic and international students. Applications are processed on a rolling basis. Application fee: $50. Electronic applications accepted. *Expenses: Tuition:* Full-time $17,010; part-time $945 per credit hour. Tuition and fees vary according to program. *Financial support:* In 2011–12, 23 students received support, including 4 fellowships (averaging $1,375 per year), 5 research assistantships with full tuition reimbursements available (averaging $17,000 per year), 15 teaching assistantships with full tuition reimbursements available (averaging $17,000 per year); scholarships/grants, health care benefits, tuition waivers (full and partial), and unspecified assistantships also available. Support available to part-time students. Financial award application deadline: 2/15. *Faculty research:* Models of physiological systems, mathematical immunology, computational group theory, mathematical logic, computational science. *Total annual research expenditures:* $621,359. *Unit head:* Dr. Gary Krenz, Chair, 414-288-7573, Fax: 414-288-1578. *Application contact:* Dr. Francis Pastijn, Director of Graduate Studies, 414-288-5229. Web site: http://www.marquette.edu/mscs/grad.shtml.

Marshall University, Academic Affairs Division, College of Science, Department of Mathematics, Huntington, WV 25755. Offers MA. *Faculty:* 24 full-time (7 women), 1 (woman) part-time/adjunct. *Students:* 14 full-time (3 women), 3 part-time (1 woman); includes 3 minority (1 Black or African American, non-Hispanic/Latino; 1 Hispanic/Latino; 1 Two or more races, non-Hispanic/Latino), 8 international. Average age 28. In 2011, 9 master's awarded. *Degree requirements:* For master's, thesis (for some programs). *Entrance requirements:* For master's, GRE General Test. Application fee: $40. *Unit head:* Dr. Alfred Akinsete, Chairperson, 304-6963285, E-mail: akinsete@marshall.edu. *Application contact:* Dr. Bonnie Lawrence, Information Contact, 304-696-3040, Fax: 304-746-1902, E-mail: lawrence@marshall.edu.

Massachusetts Institute of Technology, School of Science, Department of Mathematics, Cambridge, MA 02139. Offers PhD. *Faculty:* 48 full-time (4 women), 1 part-time/adjunct (0 women). *Students:* 102 full-time (18 women); includes 9 minority (6 Asian, non-Hispanic/Latino; 1 Hispanic/Latino; 2 Two or more races, non-Hispanic/Latino), 55 international. Average age 25. 452 applicants, 12% accepted, 22 enrolled. In 2011, 34 doctorates awarded. *Degree requirements:* For doctorate, one foreign language, comprehensive exam, thesis/dissertation, language exam in one of the following languages: Chinese, French, German, or Russian. *Entrance requirements:* For doctorate, GRE General Test, GRE Subject Test (mathematics). Additional exam requirements/recommendations for international students: Required—IELTS (minimum score 6). *Application deadline:* For fall admission, 12/15 for domestic and international students. Application fee: $75. Electronic applications accepted. *Expenses: Tuition:* Full-time $40,460; part-time $630 per credit hour. *Required fees:* $272. *Financial support:* In 2011–12, 96 students received support, including 52 fellowships (averaging $29,100 per year), 17 research assistantships (averaging $31,200 per year), 33 teaching assistantships (averaging $34,300 per year); Federal Work-Study, institutionally sponsored loans, scholarships/grants, health care benefits, and unspecified assistantships also available. *Faculty research:* Analysis, geometry and topology; algebra and number theory; representation theory; combinatorics, theoretical computer science and computational biology; physical applied mathematics and computational science. *Total annual research expenditures:* $6 million. *Unit head:* Prof. Michael Sipser, Head, 617-253-4381, Fax: 617-253-4358, E-mail: math@mit.edu. *Application contact:* Graduate Education, 617-253-2689, Fax: 617-253-4358, E-mail: gradofc@math.mit.edu. Web site: http://math.mit.edu.

McGill University, Faculty of Graduate and Postdoctoral Studies, Faculty of Science, Department of Mathematics and Statistics, Montréal, QC H3A 2T5, Canada. Offers computational science and engineering (M Sc); mathematics and statistics (M Sc, MA, PhD), including applied mathematics (M Sc, MA), pure mathematics (M Sc, MA), statistics (M Sc, MA).

McMaster University, School of Graduate Studies, Faculty of Science, Department of Mathematics and Statistics, Hamilton, ON L8S 4M2, Canada. Offers mathematics (M Sc, PhD); statistics (M Sc), including applied statistics, medical statistics, statistical theory. Part-time programs available. *Degree requirements:* For master's, thesis or alternative, oral exam; for doctorate, comprehensive exam, thesis/dissertation. *Entrance requirements:* For master's, minimum B+ average in last year of honors degree; for doctorate, minimum B+ average, M Sc in mathematics or statistics. Additional exam requirements/recommendations for international students: Required—TOEFL (minimum score 550 paper-based; 213 computer-based). *Faculty research:* Algebra, analysis, applied mathematics, geometry and topology, probability and statistics.

McNeese State University, Doré School of Graduate Studies, College of Science, Department of Mathematics, Computer Science, and Statistics, Lake Charles, LA 70609. Offers computer science (MS); mathematics (MS); statistics

(MS). Evening/weekend programs available. *Faculty:* 13 full-time (4 women). *Students:* 17 full-time (7 women), 6 part-time (2 women); includes 1 minority (Black or African American, non-Hispanic/Latino), 9 international. In 2011, 17 master's awarded. *Degree requirements:* For master's, comprehensive exam, thesis or alternative, written exam. *Entrance requirements:* For master's, GRE. *Application deadline:* For fall admission, 5/15 priority date for domestic students, 5/15 for international students; for spring admission, 10/15 priority date for domestic students, 10/15 for international students. Applications are processed on a rolling basis. Application fee: $20 ($30 for international students). *Expenses:* Tuition, state resident: part-time $519 per credit hour. Tuition and fees vary according to course load. *Financial support:* Teaching assistantships available. Financial award application deadline: 5/1. *Unit head:* Sid Bradley, Head, 337-475-5788, Fax: 337-475-5799, E-mail: sbradley@mcneese.edu. *Application contact:* Dr. George F. Mead, Jr., Interim Dean of Dore' School of Graduate Studies, 337-475-5396, Fax: 337-475-5397, E-mail: admissions@mcneese.edu.

Memorial University of Newfoundland, School of Graduate Studies, Department of Mathematics and Statistics, St. John's, NL A1C 5S7, Canada. Offers mathematics (M Sc, PhD); statistics (M Sc, MAS, PhD). Part-time programs available. *Degree requirements:* For master's, thesis, practicum and report (MAS); for doctorate, comprehensive exam, thesis/dissertation, oral defense of thesis. *Entrance requirements:* For master's, 2nd class honors degree (MAS); for doctorate, MAS or M Sc in mathematics and statistics. Electronic applications accepted. *Faculty research:* Algebra, topology, applied mathematics, mathematical statistics, applied statistics and probability.

Miami University, College of Arts and Science, Department of Mathematics, Oxford, OH 45056. Offers MA, MAT, MS. *Students:* 22 full-time (6 women), 2 part-time (0 women); includes 1 minority (Black or African American, non-Hispanic/Latino), 2 international. Average age 24. In 2011, 13 master's awarded. *Entrance requirements:* For master's, minimum undergraduate GPA of 3.0 during previous 2 years or 2.75 overall. Additional exam requirements/recommendations for international students: Required—TOEFL. *Application deadline:* For fall admission, 2/1 for domestic and international students. Application fee: $50. Electronic applications accepted. *Expenses:* Tuition, state resident: full-time $12,023; part-time $501 per credit hour. Tuition, nonresident: full-time $26,554; part-time $1107 per credit hour. *Required fees:* $528. *Financial support:* Research assistantships, teaching assistantships, health care benefits, and unspecified assistantships available. Financial award application deadline: 2/1; financial award applicants required to submit FAFSA. *Unit head:* Dr. Patrick Dowling, Department Chair, 513-529-5818, E-mail: dowlinpn@muohio.edu. *Application contact:* Dr. Doug Ward, Director of Graduate Studies, 513-529-3534, E-mail: wardde@muohio.edu. Web site: http://unixgen1.mcs.muohio.edu/~mathematics/.

Michigan State University, The Graduate School, College of Natural Science, Department of Mathematics, East Lansing, MI 48824. Offers applied mathematics (MS, PhD); industrial mathematics (MS); mathematics (MAT, MS, PhD). *Entrance requirements:* Additional exam requirements/recommendations for international students: Required—TOEFL. Electronic applications accepted.

Michigan Technological University, Graduate School, College of Sciences and Arts, Department of Mathematical Sciences, Houghton, MI 49931. Offers MS, PhD. Part-time programs available. *Faculty:* 33 full-time (8 women), 5 part-time/adjunct (0 women). *Students:* 37 full-time (11 women), 7 part-time (5 women), 28 international. Average age 29. 78 applicants, 45% accepted, 12 enrolled. In 2011, 9 master's, 1 doctorate awarded. Terminal master's awarded for partial completion of doctoral program. *Degree requirements:* For master's, comprehensive exam (for some programs), thesis (for some programs); for doctorate, comprehensive exam, thesis/dissertation, proficiency exam. *Entrance requirements:* For master's and doctorate, GRE, statement of purpose, official transcripts, 3 letters of recommendation. Additional exam requirements/recommendations for international students: Required—TOEFL (minimum score 79 iBT). *Application deadline:* Applications are processed on a rolling basis. Electronic applications accepted. *Expenses:* Tuition, state resident: full-time $12,636; part-time $702 per credit. Tuition, nonresident: full-time $12,636; part-time $702 per credit. *Required fees:* $226; $226 per year. *Financial support:* In 2011–12, 37 students received support, including 1 fellowship with full tuition reimbursement available (averaging $6,065 per year), 3 research assistantships with full tuition reimbursements available (averaging $6,065 per year), 25 teaching assistantships with full tuition reimbursements available (averaging $6,065 per year); career-related internships or fieldwork, Federal Work-Study, scholarships/grants, health care benefits, tuition waivers (partial), unspecified assistantships, and cooperative program also available. Financial award applicants required to submit FAFSA. *Faculty research:* Fluid dynamics, mathematical modeling, design theory, coding theory, statistical genetics. *Total annual research expenditures:* $118,207. *Unit head:* Dr. Mark S. Gockenbach, Chair, 906-487-2068, Fax: 906-487-3133, E-mail: msgocken@mtu.edu. *Application contact:* Dr. Jianping Dong, Director of Graduate Studies, 906-487-2928, Fax: 906-487-3133, E-mail: jdong@mtu.edu. Web site: http://www.mtu.edu/math/.

Middle Tennessee State University, College of Graduate Studies, College of Basic and Applied Sciences, Department of Mathematical Sciences, Murfreesboro, TN 37132. Offers mathematics (MS, MST, PhD). Part-time and evening/weekend programs available. Postbaccalaureate distance learning degree programs offered. *Faculty:* 26 full-time (12 women). *Students:* 2 full-time (1 woman), 34 part-time (16 women); includes 13 minority (6 Black or African American, non-Hispanic/Latino; 5 Asian, non-Hispanic/Latino; 2 Hispanic/Latino).

Peterson's Graduate Programs in the Physical Sciences, Mathematics, Agricultural Sciences, the Environment & Natural Resources 2013

facebook.com/petersonspublishing **339**

Mathematics

Average age 32. 47 applicants, 62% accepted. In 2011, 12 master's awarded. *Degree requirements:* For master's, comprehensive exam, thesis optional; for doctorate, comprehensive exam, thesis/dissertation. *Entrance requirements:* For master's, GRE General Test or MAT. Additional exam requirements/recommendations for international students: Required—TOEFL (minimum score 525 paper-based; 195 computer-based; 71 iBT) or IELTS (minimum score 6). *Application deadline:* For fall admission, 6/1 for domestic and international students. Applications are processed on a rolling basis. Application fee: $25 ($30 for international students). Electronic applications accepted. *Expenses:* Tuition, state resident: full-time $10,008. Tuition, nonresident: full-time $25,056. *Financial support:* In 2011–12, 11 students received support. Tuition waivers available. Support available to part-time students. Financial award application deadline: 5/1; financial award applicants required to submit FAFSA. *Faculty research:* Graph theory, computational science. *Unit head:* Dr. Donald A. Nelson, Interim Chair, 615-898-2669, Fax: 615-898-5422, E-mail: donald.nelson@mtsu.edu. *Application contact:* Dr. Michael D. Allen, Dean and Vice Provost for Research, 615-898-2840, Fax: 615-904-8020, E-mail: michael.allen@mtsu.edu.

Minnesota State University Mankato, College of Graduate Studies, College of Science, Engineering and Technology, Department of Mathematics and Statistics, Program in Mathematics, Mankato, MN 56001. Offers MA, MS. *Students:* 11 full-time (6 women), 10 part-time (5 women). *Degree requirements:* For master's, one foreign language, comprehensive exam, thesis or alternative. *Entrance requirements:* For master's, GRE General Test, minimum GPA of 3.0 during previous 2 years. Additional exam requirements/recommendations for international students: Required—TOEFL. *Application deadline:* For fall admission, 7/1 priority date for domestic students; for spring admission, 11/1 for domestic students. Applications are processed on a rolling basis. Application fee: $40. Electronic applications accepted. *Financial support:* Research assistantships with partial tuition reimbursements, teaching assistantships with partial tuition reimbursements, and unspecified assistantships available. Financial award application deadline: 3/15; financial award applicants required to submit FAFSA. *Unit head:* Dr. Deepak Sanjel, Graduate Coordinator, 507-389-2319. *Application contact:* 507-389-2321, E-mail: grad@mnsu.edu. Web site: http://cset.mnsu.edu/mathstat/program/grad.html.

Mississippi College, Graduate School, College of Arts and Sciences, School of Science and Mathematics, Department of Mathematics, Clinton, MS 39058. Offers M Ed, MCS, MS. Part-time programs available. *Degree requirements:* For master's, comprehensive exam, thesis optional. *Entrance requirements:* For master's, GRE or NTE, minimum GPA of 2.5. Additional exam requirements/recommendations for international students: Recommended—TOEFL, IELTS. Electronic applications accepted.

Mississippi State University, College of Arts and Sciences, Department of Mathematics and Statistics, Mississippi State, MS 39762. Offers mathematical sciences (PhD); mathematics (MS); statistics (MS). Part-time programs available. *Faculty:* 19 full-time (4 women). *Students:* 41 full-time (23 women), 6 part-time (2 women); includes 7 minority (4 Black or African American, non-Hispanic/Latino; 2 Asian, non-Hispanic/Latino; 1 Two or more races, non-Hispanic/Latino), 23 international. Average age 29. 58 applicants, 41% accepted, 11 enrolled. In 2011, 10 master's, 1 doctorate awarded. Terminal master's awarded for partial completion of doctoral program. *Degree requirements:* For master's, thesis optional, comprehensive oral or written exam; for doctorate, one foreign language, thesis/dissertation, comprehensive oral and written exam. *Entrance requirements:* For master's, minimum GPA of 2.75 on last two years of undergraduate courses; for doctorate, GRE. Additional exam requirements/recommendations for international students: Required—TOEFL (minimum score 475 paper-based; 153 computer-based; 53 iBT); Recommended—IELTS (minimum score 4.5). *Application deadline:* For fall admission, 3/15 priority date for domestic students, 5/1 for international students; for spring admission, 11/1 for domestic students, 9/1 for international students. Applications are processed on a rolling basis. Application fee: $40. Electronic applications accepted. *Expenses:* Tuition, state resident: full-time $5805; part-time $322.50 per credit hour. Tuition, nonresident: full-time $14,670; part-time $815 per credit hour. *Financial support:* In 2011–12, 30 teaching assistantships with full tuition reimbursements (averaging $13,693 per year) were awarded; Federal Work-Study, institutionally sponsored loans, tuition waivers (partial), and unspecified assistantships also available. Financial award application deadline: 4/1; financial award applicants required to submit FAFSA. *Faculty research:* Differential equations, algebra, numerical analysis, functional analysis, applied statistics. *Total annual research expenditures:* $1.1 million. *Unit head:* Dr. Mohsen Razzaghi, Interim Head, 662-325-3414, Fax: 662-325-0005, E-mail: razzaghi@math.msstate.edu. *Application contact:* Dr. Corlis Johnson, Associate Department Head/Graduate Coordinator, 662-325-3414, Fax: 662-325-0005, E-mail: cjohnson@math.msstate.edu. Web site: http://www.msstate.edu/dept/math/.

Missouri State University, Graduate College, College of Natural and Applied Sciences, Department of Mathematics, Springfield, MO 65897. Offers mathematics (MS); natural and applied science (MNAS), including mathematics (MNAS, MS Ed); secondary education (MNAS), including mathematics (MNAS, MS Ed). Part-time programs available. *Faculty:* 21 full-time (6 women). *Students:* 18 full-time (8 women), 7 part-time (3 women); includes 2 minority (1 Black or African American, non-Hispanic/Latino; 1 Hispanic/Latino), 4 international. Average age 27. 11 applicants, 100% accepted, 8 enrolled. In 2011, 4 master's awarded. *Degree requirements:* For master's, comprehensive exam, thesis or alternative. *Entrance requirements:* For master's, GRE (MS, MNAS), minimum

undergraduate GPA of 3.0 (MS, MNAS), 9-12 teacher certification (MS Ed). Additional exam requirements/recommendations for international students: Required—TOEFL (minimum score 550 paper-based; 213 computer-based; 79 iBT). *Application deadline:* For fall admission, 7/20 priority date for domestic students, 5/1 for international students; for spring admission, 12/20 priority date for domestic students, 9/1 for international students. Applications are processed on a rolling basis. Application fee: $35 ($50 for international students). Electronic applications accepted. *Expenses:* Tuition, state resident: full-time $4086; part-time $227 per credit hour. Tuition, nonresident: full-time $8172; part-time $454 per credit hour. *Required fees:* $275 per semester. Tuition and fees vary according to course load, campus/location and program. *Financial support:* In 2011–12, 4 teaching assistantships with full tuition reimbursements (averaging $9,730 per year) were awarded; Federal Work-Study, institutionally sponsored loans, scholarships/grants, and unspecified assistantships also available. Financial award application deadline: 3/31; financial award applicants required to submit FAFSA. *Faculty research:* Harmonic analysis, commutative algebra, number theory, K-theory, probability. *Unit head:* Dr. Kenneth Vollmar, Interim Head, 417-836-5112, Fax: 417-836-6966, E-mail: mathematics@missouristate.edu. *Application contact:* Misty Stewart, Coordinator of Graduate Recruitment, 417-836-6079, Fax: 417-836-6200, E-mail: mistystewart@missouristate.edu. Web site: http://math.missouristate.edu/.

Missouri University of Science and Technology, Graduate School, Department of Mathematics and Statistics, Rolla, MO 65409. Offers applied mathematics (MS); mathematics (MST, PhD), including mathematics (PhD), mathematics education (MST), statistics (PhD). Terminal master's awarded for partial completion of doctoral program. *Degree requirements:* For master's, thesis or alternative; for doctorate, one foreign language, thesis/dissertation. *Entrance requirements:* For master's and doctorate, GRE General Test, GRE Subject Test. Electronic applications accepted. *Faculty research:* Analysis, differential equations, topology, statistics.

Montana State University, College of Graduate Studies, College of Letters and Science, Department of Mathematical Sciences, Bozeman, MT 59717. Offers mathematics (MS, PhD), including mathematics education option (MS); statistics (MS, PhD). Part-time programs available. Postbaccalaureate distance learning degree programs offered (minimal on-campus study). *Degree requirements:* For master's, comprehensive exam, thesis (for some programs); for doctorate, comprehensive exam, thesis/dissertation. *Entrance requirements:* For master's and doctorate, GRE General Test. Additional exam requirements/recommendations for international students: Required—TOEFL (minimum score 550 paper-based; 213 computer-based). Electronic applications accepted. *Faculty research:* Applied mathematics, dynamical systems, statistics, mathematics education, mathematical and computational biology.

Montclair State University, The Graduate School, College of Science and Mathematics, Department of Mathematical Sciences, Program in Mathematics, Montclair, NJ 07043-1624. Offers mathematics education (MS); pure and applied mathematics (MS). Part-time and evening/weekend programs available. *Students:* 17 full-time (4 women), 53 part-time (30 women); includes 14 minority (3 Black or African American, non-Hispanic/Latino; 3 Asian, non-Hispanic/Latino; 6 Hispanic/Latino; 2 Two or more races, non-Hispanic/Latino), 1 international. Average age 34. 38 applicants, 50% accepted, 16 enrolled. In 2011, 11 master's awarded. *Degree requirements:* For master's, comprehensive exam. *Entrance requirements:* For master's, GRE General Test, 2 letters of recommendation, essay. Additional exam requirements/recommendations for international students: Required—TOEFL (minimum score 83 iBT), IELTS (minimum score 6.5). *Application deadline:* Applications are processed on a rolling basis. Application fee: $60. Electronic applications accepted. *Financial support:* In 2011–12, 9 research assistantships with full tuition reimbursements (averaging $7,000 per year) were awarded; Federal Work-Study, scholarships/grants, and unspecified assistantships also available. Support available to part-time students. Financial award application deadline: 3/1; financial award applicants required to submit FAFSA. *Faculty research:* Computation, applied analysis. *Unit head:* Dr. Helen Roberts, Chairperson, 973-655-5132. *Application contact:* Amy Aiello, Director of Graduate Admissions and Operations, 973-655-5147, Fax: 973-655-7869, E-mail: graduate.school@montclair.edu.

Morgan State University, School of Graduate Studies, School of Computer, Mathematical, and Natural Sciences, Department of Mathematics, Baltimore, MD 21251. Offers MA. Part-time and evening/weekend programs available. *Degree requirements:* For master's, comprehensive exam, thesis. *Entrance requirements:* For master's, GRE. Additional exam requirements/recommendations for international students: Required—TOEFL (minimum score 550 paper-based; 213 computer-based). *Faculty research:* Number theory, semigroups, analysis, operations research.

Murray State University, College of Science, Engineering and Technology, Program in Mathematics and Statistics, Murray, KY 42071. Offers MA, MAT, MS. Part-time programs available. *Degree requirements:* For master's, comprehensive exam, thesis optional. *Entrance requirements:* For master's, GRE General Test. Additional exam requirements/recommendations for international students: Required—TOEFL. *Faculty research:* Algebraic structures, mathematical biology, topology.

New Jersey Institute of Technology, Office of Graduate Studies, College of Science and Liberal Arts, Department of Mathematical Science, Program in Mathematics Science, Newark, NJ 07102. Offers PhD. Part-time and evening/

340 facebook.com/petersonspublishing

Peterson's Graduate Programs in the Physical Sciences, Mathematics, Agricultural Sciences, the Environment & Natural Resources 2013

weekend programs available. *Students:* 35 full-time (10 women), 3 part-time (2 women); includes 8 minority (4 Asian, non-Hispanic/Latino; 2 Hispanic/Latino; 2 Two or more races, non-Hispanic/Latino), 23 international. Average age 24. 64 applicants, 52% accepted. *Entrance requirements:* For doctorate, GRE General Test, minimum graduate GPA of 3.5. Additional exam requirements/recommendations for international students: Required—TOEFL (minimum score 550 paper-based; 213 computer-based; 79 iBT). *Application deadline:* For fall admission, 6/1 priority date for domestic students, 5/1 for international students; for spring admission, 11/15 priority date for domestic students, 11/15 for international students. Applications are processed on a rolling basis. Application fee: $65. Electronic applications accepted. *Expenses:* Tuition, state resident: full-time $7980; part-time $867 per credit. Tuition, nonresident: full-time $11,336; part-time $1196 per credit. *Required fees:* $230 per credit. *Financial support:* Fellowships with full and partial tuition reimbursements, research assistantships with full and partial tuition reimbursements, teaching assistantships with full and partial tuition reimbursements, career-related internships or fieldwork, Federal Work-Study, institutionally sponsored loans, and unspecified assistantships available. Financial award application deadline: 1/15. *Unit head:* Dr. Daljit S. Ahluwalia, Chair, 973-596-8465, E-mail: daljit.ahluwalia@njit.edu. *Application contact:* Kathryn Kelly, Director of Admissions, 973-596-3300, Fax: 973-596-3461, E-mail: admissions@njit.edu.

New Mexico Institute of Mining and Technology, Graduate Studies, Department of Mathematics, Socorro, NM 87801. Offers applied and industrial mathematics (PhD); industrial mathematics (MS); mathematics (MS); operations research and statistics (MS). *Faculty:* 11 full-time (0 women), 2 part-time/adjunct (1 woman). *Students:* 15 full-time (3 women), 1 part-time (0 women); includes 6 minority (1 Black or African American, non-Hispanic/Latino; 4 Asian, non-Hispanic/Latino; 1 Two or more races, non-Hispanic/Latino), 1 international. Average age 32. 13 applicants, 77% accepted, 6 enrolled. In 2011, 6 degrees awarded. *Degree requirements:* For master's, thesis optional; for doctorate, thesis/dissertation. *Entrance requirements:* For master's, GRE General Test. Additional exam requirements/recommendations for international students: Required—TOEFL (minimum score 540 paper-based; 207 computer-based). *Application deadline:* For fall admission, 3/1 priority date for domestic students; for spring admission, 6/1 for domestic students. Applications are processed on a rolling basis. Application fee: $16 ($30 for international students). *Expenses:* Tuition, state resident: full-time $4849; part-time $269.41 per credit hour. Tuition, nonresident: full-time $16,041; part-time $891.15 per credit hour. *Required fees:* $622; $65 per credit hour. $20 per semester. Part-time tuition and fees vary according to course load. *Financial support:* In 2011–12, 2 research assistantships (averaging $19,516 per year), 13 teaching assistantships with full and partial tuition reimbursements (averaging $34,112 per year) were awarded; fellowships, Federal Work-Study, and institutionally sponsored loans also available. Financial award application deadline: 3/1; financial award applicants required to submit CSS PROFILE or FAFSA. *Faculty research:* Applied mathematics, differential equations, industrial mathematics, numerical analysis, stochastic processes. *Unit head:* Dr. Anwar Hossain, Chairman, 575-835-5135, Fax: 575-835-5366, E-mail: hossain@nmt.edu. *Application contact:* Dr. Lorie Liebrock, Dean of Graduate Studies, 575-835-5513, Fax: 575-835-5476, E-mail: graduate@nmt.edu. Web site: http://www.nmt.edu/~math/.

New Mexico State University, Graduate School, College of Arts and Sciences, Department of Mathematical Sciences, Las Cruces, NM 88003-8001. Offers MS, PhD. Part-time programs available. *Faculty:* 22 full-time (5 women). *Students:* 39 full-time (10 women), 7 part-time (1 woman); includes 8 minority (1 Black or African American, non-Hispanic/Latino; 1 American Indian or Alaska Native, non-Hispanic/Latino; 1 Asian, non-Hispanic/Latino; 5 Hispanic/Latino), 25 international. Average age 32. 39 applicants, 87% accepted, 13 enrolled. In 2011, 8 master's, 5 doctorates awarded. *Degree requirements:* For master's, thesis optional, final oral exam; for doctorate, one foreign language, comprehensive exam, thesis/dissertation, final oral exam. *Entrance requirements:* For master's, GRE Subject Test (preferred), 24 credits of upper-division math/statistics, including real analysis and modern algebra. Additional exam requirements/recommendations for international students: Required—TOEFL (minimum score 550 paper-based; 0 computer-based; 79 iBT), IELTS (minimum score 6.5). *Application deadline:* For fall admission, 2/1 priority date for domestic students, 2/1 for international students; for spring admission, 10/1 for domestic and international students. Applications are processed on a rolling basis. Application fee: $40 ($50 for international students). Electronic applications accepted. *Expenses:* Tuition, state resident: full-time $5004; part-time $208.50 per credit. Tuition, nonresident: full-time $17,446; part-time $726.90 per credit. *Financial support:* In 2011–12, 2 fellowships (averaging $2,816 per year), 2 research assistantships (averaging $20,806 per year), 33 teaching assistantships (averaging $24,691 per year) were awarded; scholarships/grants, health care benefits, and unspecified assistantships also available. Financial award application deadline: 2/1. *Faculty research:* Commutative algebra, dynamical systems, harmonic analysis and applications, partial differential equations, algebraic topology, probability and statistics. *Total annual research expenditures:* $1.1 million. *Unit head:* Dr. Joseph Lakey, Head, 575-646-3901, Fax: 575-646-1064, E-mail: jlakey@nmsu.edu. *Application contact:* Dr. John Harding, Professor, 575-646-4315, Fax: 575-646-1064, E-mail: jharding@nmsu.edu. Web site: http://www.math.nmsu.edu/.

New York University, Graduate School of Arts and Science, Courant Institute of Mathematical Sciences, Department of Mathematics, New York, NY 10012-1019. Offers atmosphere ocean science and mathematics (PhD); mathematics (MS, PhD); mathematics and statistics/operations research (MS); mathematics in finance (MS); scientific computing (MS). Part-time and evening/weekend programs available. *Faculty:* 46 full-time (0 women). *Students:* 215 full-time (39 women), 116 part-time (20 women); includes 53 minority (3 Black or African American, non-Hispanic/Latino; 1 American Indian or Alaska Native, non-Hispanic/Latino; 41 Asian, non-Hispanic/Latino; 6 Hispanic/Latino; 2 Two or more races, non-Hispanic/Latino), 183 international. Average age 28. 1,619 applicants, 25% accepted, 104 enrolled. In 2011, 71 master's, 18 doctorates awarded. *Degree requirements:* For master's, thesis optional; for doctorate, one foreign language, thesis/dissertation, oral and written exams. *Entrance requirements:* For master's and doctorate, GRE General Test, GRE Subject Test. Additional exam requirements/recommendations for international students: Required—TOEFL. *Application deadline:* For fall admission, 1/4 for domestic students; for spring admission, 11/1 for domestic students. Application fee: $90. *Financial support:* Fellowships with tuition reimbursements, research assistantships with tuition reimbursements, teaching assistantships with tuition reimbursements, Federal Work-Study, institutionally sponsored loans, scholarships/grants, health care benefits, and unspecified assistantships available. Financial award application deadline: 1/4; financial award applicants required to submit FAFSA. *Faculty research:* Partial differential equations, computational science, applied mathematics, geometry and topology, probability and stochastic processes. *Unit head:* Fedor Bogomolov, Director of Graduate Studies, 212-998-3238, Fax: 212-995-4121, E-mail: admissions@math.nyu.edu. *Application contact:* Tamar Arnon, Graduate Program Administrator, 212-998-3238, Fax: 212-995-4121, E-mail: admissions@math.nyu.edu. Web site: http://www.math.nyu.edu/.

Nicholls State University, Graduate Studies, College of Arts and Sciences, Department of Mathematics and Computer Science, Thibodaux, LA 70310. Offers community/technical college mathematics (MS). Part-time and evening/weekend programs available. *Degree requirements:* For master's, comprehensive exam. *Entrance requirements:* For master's, GRE General Test. Electronic applications accepted. *Faculty research:* Operations research, statistics, numerical analysis, algebra, topology.

North Carolina Agricultural and Technical State University, School of Graduate Studies, College of Arts and Sciences, Department of Mathematics, Greensboro, NC 27411. Offers applied mathematics (MS), including secondary education. *Accreditation:* NCATE. Part-time and evening/weekend programs available. *Degree requirements:* For master's, comprehensive exam, thesis or alternative, qualifying exam. *Entrance requirements:* For master's, GRE General Test, minimum GPA of 3.0.

North Carolina Central University, Division of Academic Affairs, College of Science and Technology, Department of Mathematics and Computer Science, Durham, NC 27707-3129. Offers applied mathematics (MS); mathematics education (MS); pure mathematics (MS). Part-time and evening/weekend programs available. *Degree requirements:* For master's, one foreign language, comprehensive exam, thesis. *Entrance requirements:* For master's, minimum GPA of 3.0 in major, 2.5 overall. Additional exam requirements/recommendations for international students: Required—TOEFL. *Faculty research:* Structure theorems for Lie algebra, Kleene monoids and semi-groups, theoretical computer science, mathematics education.

North Carolina State University, Graduate School, College of Agriculture and Life Sciences and College of Engineering and College of Physical and Mathematical Sciences, Program in Financial Mathematics, Raleigh, NC 27695. Offers MFM. Part-time programs available. *Degree requirements:* For master's, thesis optional, project/internship. *Entrance requirements:* For master's, GRE General Test. Additional exam requirements/recommendations for international students: Required—TOEFL (minimum score 550 paper-based; 213 computer-based). Electronic applications accepted. *Faculty research:* Financial mathematics modeling and computation, futures, options and commodities markets, real options, credit risk, portfolio optimization.

North Carolina State University, Graduate School, College of Physical and Mathematical Sciences, Department of Mathematics, Program in Mathematics, Raleigh, NC 27695. Offers MS, PhD. *Degree requirements:* For master's, thesis (for some programs); for doctorate, thesis/dissertation. *Entrance requirements:* For master's and doctorate, GRE, GRE Subject Test (recommended). Electronic applications accepted.

North Dakota State University, College of Graduate and Interdisciplinary Studies, College of Science and Mathematics, Department of Mathematics, Fargo, ND 58108. Offers applied mathematics (MS, PhD); mathematics (MS, PhD). *Faculty:* 11 full-time (1 woman), 1 part-time/adjunct (0 women). *Students:* 23 full-time (7 women), 2 part-time (0 women); includes 1 minority (Two or more races, non-Hispanic/Latino), 5 international. Average age 28. 28 applicants, 29% accepted, 4 enrolled. In 2011, 1 master's, 3 doctorates awarded. *Degree requirements:* For master's, comprehensive exam, thesis; for doctorate, one foreign language, comprehensive exam, thesis/dissertation, computer proficiency. *Entrance requirements:* For master's and doctorate, GRE General Test. Additional exam requirements/recommendations for international students: Required—TOEFL (minimum score 525 paper-based; 197 computer-based; 71 iBT), IELTS. *Application deadline:* For fall admission, 3/1 priority date for domestic students. Applications are processed on a rolling basis. Application fee: $35. Electronic applications accepted. *Financial support:* In 2011–12, 5 fellowships with full tuition reimbursements (averaging $18,000 per year), 1 research assistantship with tuition reimbursement (averaging $14,000 per year), 17

Peterson's Graduate Programs in the Physical Sciences, Mathematics, Agricultural Sciences, the Environment & Natural Resources 2013

facebook.com/petersonspublishing **341**

teaching assistantships with full tuition reimbursements (averaging $9,300 per year) were awarded; Federal Work-Study, institutionally sponsored loans, and tuition waivers (full) also available. Support available to part-time students. Financial award application deadline: 3/31. *Faculty research:* Discrete mathematics, number theory, analysis theory, algebra, applied math. *Unit head:* Dr. Dogan Comez, Chair, 701-231-8171, Fax: 701-231-7598, E-mail: dogan.comez@ndsu.edu. *Application contact:* Dr. Sean Sather-Wagstaff, Graduate Program Director, 701-231-8105, Fax: 701-231-7598, E-mail: sean.sather-wagstaff@ndsu.edu. Web site: http://www.math.ndsu.nodak.edu/.

Northeastern Illinois University, Graduate College, College of Arts and Sciences, Department of Mathematics, Programs in Mathematics, Chicago, IL 60625-4699. Offers mathematics (MS); mathematics for elementary school teachers (MA). Part-time and evening/weekend programs available. *Degree requirements:* For master's, comprehensive exam, thesis optional, project. *Entrance requirements:* For master's, minimum GPA of 2.75, 6 undergraduate courses in mathematics. Additional exam requirements/recommendations for international students: Required—TOEFL (minimum score 550 paper-based; 213 computer-based; 79 iBT). Electronic applications accepted. *Faculty research:* Numerical analysis, mathematical biology, operations research, statistics, geometry and mathematics of finance.

Northeastern University, College of Science, Department of Mathematics, Boston, MA 02115-5096. Offers applied mathematics (MS); mathematics (MS, PhD); operations research (MSOR). Part-time and evening/weekend programs available. *Faculty:* 39 full-time, 15 part-time/adjunct. *Students:* 52 full-time, 3 part-time. 164 applicants, 58% accepted, 14 enrolled. In 2011, 6 master's, 7 doctorates awarded. *Degree requirements:* For master's, thesis (for some programs); for doctorate, thesis/dissertation, qualifying exams. *Entrance requirements:* For master's and doctorate, GRE Subject Test, GRE General Test. Additional exam requirements/recommendations for international students: Required—TOEFL. *Application deadline:* For fall admission, 2/1 priority date for domestic students, 2/1 for international students. Applications are processed on a rolling basis. Application fee: $50. Electronic applications accepted. *Financial support:* In 2011–12, 26 teaching assistantships with tuition reimbursements (averaging $17,345 per year) were awarded; research assistantships with tuition reimbursements, Federal Work-Study, institutionally sponsored loans, tuition waivers (full and partial), and unspecified assistantships also available. Financial award application deadline: 3/1; financial award applicants required to submit FAFSA. *Faculty research:* Algebra and singularities, combinatorics, topology, probability and statistics, geometric analysis and partial differential equations. *Unit head:* Dr. Jerzy Weyman, Graduate Coordinator, 617-373-5513, Fax: 617-373-5658, E-mail: j.weyman@neu.edu. *Application contact:* Jo-Anne Dickinson, Admissions Contact, 617-373-5990, Fax: 617-373-7281, E-mail: gsas@neu.edu. Web site: http://www.math.neu.edu/.

Northern Arizona University, Graduate College, College of Engineering, Forestry and Natural Sciences, Department of Mathematics and Statistics, Flagstaff, AZ 86011. Offers applied statistics (Certificate); mathematics (MAT, MS); statistics (MS). Part-time programs available. *Faculty:* 38 full-time (12 women). *Students:* 23 full-time (9 women), 18 part-time (12 women); includes 11 minority (2 Black or African American, non-Hispanic/Latino; 2 Asian, non-Hispanic/Latino; 7 Hispanic/Latino), 1 international. Average age 28. 25 applicants, 68% accepted, 9 enrolled. In 2011, 15 master's, 7 other advanced degrees awarded. *Degree requirements:* For master's, comprehensive exam (for some programs), thesis (for some programs). *Entrance requirements:* For master's, minimum GPA of 3.0. Additional exam requirements/recommendations for international students: Required—TOEFL (minimum score 550 paper-based; 213 computer-based; 80 iBT), IELTS (minimum score 7). *Application deadline:* For fall admission, 3/15 priority date for domestic students, 3/15 for international students; for spring admission, 10/15 priority date for domestic students, 10/15 for international students. Applications are processed on a rolling basis. Application fee: $65. Electronic applications accepted. *Expenses:* Tuition, state resident: full-time $7190; part-time $355 per credit hour. Tuition, nonresident: full-time $18,092; part-time $1005 per credit hour. *Required fees:* $818; $328 per semester. *Financial support:* In 2011–12, 22 teaching assistantships with partial tuition reimbursements (averaging $14,051 per year) were awarded; Federal Work-Study, scholarships/grants, health care benefits, tuition waivers (full and partial), and unspecified assistantships also available. Financial award applicants required to submit FAFSA. *Faculty research:* Topology, statistics, groups, ring theory, number theory. *Unit head:* Dr. Janet M. McShane, Chair, 928-523-1252, Fax: 928-523-5847, E-mail: janet.mcshane@nau.edu. *Application contact:* Sharon O'Connor, Chair, 928-523-3481, Fax: 928-523-5847, E-mail: math.grad@nau.edu. Web site: http://nau.edu/CEFNS/NatSci/Math/Degrees-Programs/.

Northern Illinois University, Graduate School, College of Liberal Arts and Sciences, Department of Mathematical Sciences, De Kalb, IL 60115-2854. Offers mathematical sciences (PhD); mathematics (MS); statistics (MS). Part-time programs available. *Faculty:* 43 full-time (10 women), 4 part-time/adjunct (0 women). *Students:* 61 full-time (25 women), 39 part-time (16 women); includes 10 minority (3 Black or African American, non-Hispanic/Latino; 5 Asian, non-Hispanic/Latino; 1 Native Hawaiian or other Pacific Islander, non-Hispanic/Latino; 1 Two or more races, non-Hispanic/Latino), 19 international. Average age 31. 71 applicants, 69% accepted, 21 enrolled. In 2011, 40 master's, 5 doctorates awarded. Terminal master's awarded for partial completion of doctoral program. *Degree requirements:* For master's, comprehensive exam, thesis optional; for doctorate, one foreign language, thesis/dissertation, candidacy exam, dissertation

defense, internship. *Entrance requirements:* For master's, GRE General Test, minimum GPA of 2.75; for doctorate, GRE General Test, minimum GPA of 2.75 (undergraduate), 3.2 (graduate). Additional exam requirements/recommendations for international students: Required—TOEFL (minimum score 550 paper-based; 213 computer-based). *Application deadline:* For fall admission, 6/1 for domestic students, 5/1 for international students; for spring admission, 11/1 for domestic students, 10/1 for international students. Applications are processed on a rolling basis. Application fee: $40. Electronic applications accepted. *Financial support:* In 2011–12, 1 research assistantship with full tuition reimbursement, 40 teaching assistantships with full tuition reimbursements were awarded; fellowships with full tuition reimbursements, career-related internships or fieldwork, Federal Work-Study, scholarships/grants, tuition waivers (full), and unspecified assistantships also available. Support available to part-time students. Financial award applicants required to submit FAFSA. *Faculty research:* Numerical linear algebra, noncommutative rings, nonlineal partial differential equations, finite group theory, abstract harmonic analysis. *Unit head:* Dr. Bernie Harris, Chair, 815-753-0566, Fax: 815-753-1112, E-mail: harris@math.niu.edu. *Application contact:* Dr. John Ye, Director, Graduate Studies, 815-753-0568, E-mail: ye@math.niu.edu. Web site: http://www.math.niu.edu/.

Northwestern University, The Graduate School, Judd A. and Marjorie Weinberg College of Arts and Sciences, Department of Mathematics, Evanston, IL 60208. Offers PhD. Admissions and degrees offered through The Graduate School. Part-time programs available. *Degree requirements:* For doctorate, thesis/dissertation, preliminary exam. *Entrance requirements:* For doctorate, GRE General Test, GRE Subject Test. Additional exam requirements/recommendations for international students: Required—TOEFL. *Faculty research:* Algebra, algebraic topology, analysis dynamical systems, partial differential equations.

Oakland University, Graduate Study and Lifelong Learning, College of Arts and Sciences, Department of Mathematics and Statistics, Program in Mathematics, Rochester, MI 48309-4401. Offers MA. *Entrance requirements:* Additional exam requirements/recommendations for international students: Required—TOEFL (minimum score 550 paper-based; 213 computer-based). Electronic applications accepted. *Expenses:* Contact institution.

The Ohio State University, Graduate School, College of Arts and Sciences, Division of Natural and Mathematical Sciences, Department of Mathematics, Columbus, OH 43210. Offers MA, MS, PhD. *Faculty:* 62. *Students:* 53 full-time (9 women), 80 part-time (22 women); includes 6 minority (2 Black or African American, non-Hispanic/Latino; 1 Asian, non-Hispanic/Latino; 3 Hispanic/Latino), 54 international. Average age 27. In 2011, 7 master's, 22 doctorates awarded. *Degree requirements:* For master's, thesis optional; for doctorate, 2 foreign languages, thesis/dissertation. *Entrance requirements:* For master's and doctorate, GRE General Test, GRE Subject Test (mathematics). Additional exam requirements/recommendations for international students: Required—TOEFL, Michigan English Language Assessment Battery (minimum score 82). *Application deadline:* For fall admission, 8/15 priority date for domestic students, 7/1 for international students; for winter admission, 12/1 priority date for domestic students, 11/1 for international students; for spring admission, 3/1 priority date for domestic students, 2/1 for international students. Applications are processed on a rolling basis. Application fee: $40 ($50 for international students). Electronic applications accepted. *Expenses:* Tuition, state resident: full-time $11,400. Tuition, nonresident: full-time $28,125. Tuition and fees vary according to course load, degree level, campus/location and program. *Financial support:* Fellowships, research assistantships, teaching assistantships, Federal Work-Study, institutionally sponsored loans, and unspecified assistantships available. Support available to part-time students. *Unit head:* Luis Casian, Chair, 614-292-7173, E-mail: casian@math.ohio-state.edu. *Application contact:* Denise Witcher, Graduate Studies Secretary, 614-292-6274, Fax: 614-292-1479, E-mail: dwitcher@math.ohio-state.edu. Web site: http://www.math.osu.edu/.

Ohio University, Graduate College, College of Arts and Sciences, Department of Mathematics, Athens, OH 45701-2979. Offers MS, PhD. Part-time and evening/weekend programs available. *Students:* 46 full-time (14 women), 2 part-time (0 women); includes 3 minority (1 American Indian or Alaska Native, non-Hispanic/Latino; 2 Asian, non-Hispanic/Latino), 19 international. 103 applicants, 47% accepted, 24 enrolled. In 2011, 19 master's, 3 doctorates awarded. Terminal master's awarded for partial completion of doctoral program. *Degree requirements:* For master's, thesis optional; for doctorate, comprehensive exam, thesis/dissertation. *Entrance requirements:* For master's and doctorate, minimum GPA of 3.0. Additional exam requirements/recommendations for international students: Required—TOEFL (minimum score 550 paper-based; 80 iBT) or IELTS (minimum score 6.5). *Application deadline:* For fall admission, 2/1 priority date for domestic students, 2/1 for international students. Applications are processed on a rolling basis. Application fee: $50 ($55 for international students). Electronic applications accepted. *Financial support:* Fellowships with full tuition reimbursements, teaching assistantships with full tuition reimbursements, Federal Work-Study, and institutionally sponsored loans available. Financial award application deadline: 2/1. *Faculty research:* Algebra (group and ring theory), functional analysis, topology, differential equations, computational math. *Unit head:* Dr. Jeff Connor, Chair, 740-593-1254, Fax: 740-593-9805, E-mail: connor@math.ohiou.edu. *Application contact:* Dr. Winfried Just, Graduate Chair, 740-593-1260, Fax: 740-593-9805, E-mail: just@ohio.edu. Web site: http://www.math.ohiou.edu/.

Oklahoma State University, College of Arts and Sciences, Department of Mathematics, Stillwater, OK 74078. Offers applied mathematics (MS, PhD);

Peterson's Graduate Programs in the Physical Sciences, Mathematics, Agricultural Sciences, the Environment & Natural Resources 2013

mathematics education (MS, PhD); pure mathematics (MS, PhD). *Faculty:* 33 full-time (6 women), 8 part-time/adjunct (5 women). *Students:* 5 full-time (2 women), 27 part-time (8 women); includes 2 minority (1 Asian, non-Hispanic/Latino; 1 Two or more races, non-Hispanic/Latino), 21 international. Average age 31. 66 applicants, 14% accepted, 3 enrolled. In 2011, 2 master's, 1 doctorate awarded. *Degree requirements:* For master's, thesis, creative component, or report; for doctorate, comprehensive exam, thesis/dissertation. *Entrance requirements:* For master's and doctorate, GRE (recommended). Additional exam requirements/recommendations for international students: Required—TOEFL (minimum score 550 paper-based; 79 iBT). *Application deadline:* For fall admission, 3/1 for domestic and international students; for spring admission, 10/15 for domestic and international students. Applications are processed on a rolling basis. Application fee: $40 ($75 for international students). Electronic applications accepted. *Expenses:* Tuition, state resident: full-time $4044; part-time $168.50 per credit hour. Tuition, nonresident: full-time $16,008; part-time $667 per credit hour. *Required fees:* $2122; $88.45 per credit hour. One-time fee: $50. Tuition and fees vary according to course load and campus/location. *Financial support:* In 2011–12, 32 teaching assistantships (averaging $18,748 per year) were awarded; health care benefits and tuition waivers (partial) also available. Financial award application deadline: 3/1; financial award applicants required to submit FAFSA. *Unit head:* Dr. Dale Alspach, Head, 405-744-5688, Fax: 405-744-8275. *Application contact:* Dr. Sheryl Tucker, Dean, 405-744-7099, Fax: 405-744-0355, E-mail: grad-i@okstate.edu. Web site: http://www.math.okstate.edu/.

Old Dominion University, College of Sciences, Programs in Computational and Applied Mathematics, Norfolk, VA 23529. Offers MS, PhD. Part-time programs available. *Faculty:* 22 full-time (0 women), 2 part-time/adjunct (0 women). *Students:* 25 full-time (9 women), 11 part-time (7 women); includes 7 minority (4 Black or African American, non-Hispanic/Latino; 2 Asian, non-Hispanic/Latino; 1 Hispanic/Latino), 16 international. Average age 28. 31 applicants, 55% accepted, 8 enrolled. In 2011, 7 master's, 10 doctorates awarded. Terminal master's awarded for partial completion of doctoral program. *Degree requirements:* For master's, project; for doctorate, comprehensive exam, thesis/dissertation, candidacy exam. *Entrance requirements:* For master's, minimum GPA of 3.0 in major, 2.5 overall; for doctorate, GRE General Test, 3 recommendation letters, transcripts, essay. Additional exam requirements/recommendations for international students: Required—TOEFL. *Application deadline:* For fall admission, 6/1 for domestic students, 5/15 for international students; for winter admission, 11/1 for domestic students, 10/1 for international students; for spring admission, 3/1 for domestic students, 2/1 for international students. Applications are processed on a rolling basis. Application fee: $40. Electronic applications accepted. *Expenses:* Tuition, state resident: full-time $9096; part-time $379 per credit. Tuition, nonresident: full-time $23,064; part-time $961 per credit. *Required fees:* $127 per semester. One-time fee: $50. *Financial support:* In 2011–12, 4 fellowships with full tuition reimbursements (averaging $17,000 per year), 4 research assistantships with full tuition reimbursements (averaging $16,000 per year), 12 teaching assistantships with full tuition reimbursements (averaging $15,000 per year) were awarded; scholarships/grants also available. Financial award application deadline: 2/15; financial award applicants required to submit FAFSA. *Faculty research:* Numerical analysis, integral equations, continuum mechanics. *Total annual research expenditures:* $506,890. *Unit head:* Dr. Richard Noren, Graduate Program Director, 757-683-3882, Fax: 757-683-3885, E-mail: rnoren@odu.edu. *Application contact:* William Heffelfinger, Director of Graduate Admissions, 757-683-5554, Fax: 757-683-3255, E-mail: gradadmit@odu.edu. Web site: http://sci.odu.edu/math/academics/grad.shtml.

Oregon State University, Graduate School, College of Science, Department of Mathematics, Corvallis, OR 97331. Offers MA, MAIS, MS, PhD. Terminal master's awarded for partial completion of doctoral program. *Degree requirements:* For master's, variable foreign language requirement, thesis or alternative; for doctorate, one foreign language, thesis/dissertation, qualifying exams. *Entrance requirements:* For master's and doctorate, minimum GPA of 3.0 in last 90 hours. Additional exam requirements/recommendations for international students: Required—TOEFL.

Penn State University Park, Graduate School, Eberly College of Science, Department of Mathematics, State College, University Park, PA 16802-1503. Offers mathematics (M Ed, MA, D Ed, PhD), including applied mathematics (MA). *Unit head:* Dr. John Roe, Head, 814-865-7527, Fax: 814-865-3735, E-mail: roe@math.psu.edu. *Application contact:* Dr. Dimitri Burago, Associate Head of Graduate Studies, 814-865-7741, E-mail: burago@math.psu.edu. Web site: http://www.math.psu.edu.

Pittsburg State University, Graduate School, College of Arts and Sciences, Department of Mathematics, Pittsburg, KS 66762. Offers MS. *Degree requirements:* For master's, thesis or alternative. *Faculty research:* Operations research, numerical analysis, applied analysis, applied algebra.

Polytechnic Institute of New York University, Department of Mathematics, Brooklyn, NY 11201-2990. Offers MS, PhD. Part-time and evening/weekend programs available. *Faculty:* 2 full-time (0 women). *Students:* 12 full-time (4 women), 7 part-time (1 woman); includes 5 minority (2 Black or African American, non-Hispanic/Latino; 1 Asian, non-Hispanic/Latino; 2 Hispanic/Latino), 10 international. Average age 32. 54 applicants, 41% accepted, 8 enrolled. In 2011, 10 master's, 1 doctorate awarded. *Degree requirements:* For master's, comprehensive exam (for some programs), thesis (for some programs); for doctorate, comprehensive exam, thesis/dissertation. *Entrance requirements:*

Additional exam requirements/recommendations for international students: Required—TOEFL (minimum score 550 paper-based; 213 computer-based; 80 iBT); Recommended—IELTS (minimum score 6.5). *Application deadline:* For fall admission, 7/31 priority date for domestic students, 4/30 for international students; for spring admission, 12/31 priority date for domestic students, 11/30 for international students. Applications are processed on a rolling basis. Application fee: $75. Electronic applications accepted. *Expenses: Tuition:* Full-time $22,464; part-time $1248 per credit. *Required fees:* $501 per semester. *Financial support:* In 2011–12, 5 fellowships (averaging $35,280 per year), 5 teaching assistantships (averaging $47,554 per year) were awarded; research assistantships, institutionally sponsored loans, scholarships/grants, and unspecified assistantships also available. Support available to part-time students. Financial award applicants required to submit FAFSA. *Total annual research expenditures:* $263,503. *Unit head:* Dr. Erwin Lutwak, Head, 718-260-3366, Fax: 718-260-3139, E-mail: lutwak@magnus.poly.edu. *Application contact:* JeanCarlo Bonilla, Director of Graduate Enrollment Management, 718-260-3182, Fax: 718-260-3624, E-mail: gradinfo@poly.edu.

Portland State University, Graduate Studies, College of Liberal Arts and Sciences, Department of Mathematics and Statistics, Portland, OR 97207-0751. Offers mathematical sciences (PhD); mathematics education (PhD); statistics (MS); MA/MS. *Degree requirements:* For master's, thesis or alternative, exams; for doctorate, 2 foreign languages, thesis/dissertation, exams. *Entrance requirements:* For master's, GRE General Test, GRE Subject Test, minimum GPA of 3.0 in upper-division course work or 2.75 overall; for doctorate, GRE General Test. Additional exam requirements/recommendations for international students: Required—TOEFL (minimum score 550 paper-based; 213 computer-based). *Faculty research:* Algebra, topology, statistical distribution theory, control theory, statistical robustness.

Portland State University, Graduate Studies, Systems Science Program, Portland, OR 97207-0751. Offers computational intelligence (Certificate); computer modeling and simulation (Certificate); systems science (MS); systems science/anthropology (PhD); systems science/business administration (PhD); systems science/civil engineering (PhD); systems science/economics (PhD); systems science/engineering management (PhD); systems science/general (PhD); systems science/mathematical sciences (PhD); systems science/mechanical engineering (PhD); systems science/psychology (PhD); systems science/sociology (PhD). *Degree requirements:* For doctorate, variable foreign language requirement, thesis/dissertation. *Entrance requirements:* For master's, 2 letters of recommendation; for doctorate, GMAT, GRE General Test, minimum undergraduate GPA of 3.0. Additional exam requirements/recommendations for international students: Required—TOEFL. *Faculty research:* Systems theory and methodology, artificial intelligence neural networks, information theory, nonlinear dynamics/chaos, modeling and simulation.

Prairie View A&M University, College of Arts and Sciences, Department of Mathematics, Prairie View, TX 77446-0519. Offers MS. Part-time and evening/weekend programs available. *Degree requirements:* For master's, comprehensive exam, thesis. *Entrance requirements:* For master's, GRE General Test, bachelor's degree in mathematics. *Faculty research:* Stochastic processor, queuing theory, waveler numeric analyses, delay systems mathematic modeling.

Princeton University, Graduate School, Department of Mathematics, Princeton, NJ 08544-1019. Offers PhD. *Degree requirements:* For doctorate, 2 foreign languages, thesis/dissertation. *Entrance requirements:* For doctorate, GRE General Test, GRE Subject Test, 3 letters of recommendation. Additional exam requirements/recommendations for international students: Required—TOEFL (minimum score 600 paper-based; 250 computer-based). Electronic applications accepted.

Purdue University, Graduate School, College of Science, Department of Mathematics, West Lafayette, IN 47907. Offers MS, PhD. *Faculty:* 69 full-time (10 women), 1 (woman) part-time/adjunct. *Students:* 151 full-time (32 women), 11 part-time (1 woman); includes 13 minority (3 Black or African American, non-Hispanic/Latino; 3 Asian, non-Hispanic/Latino; 5 Hispanic/Latino; 2 Two or more races, non-Hispanic/Latino), 87 international. Average age 27. 564 applicants, 8% accepted, 23 enrolled. In 2011, 17 master's, 12 doctorates awarded. Terminal master's awarded for partial completion of doctoral program. *Degree requirements:* For doctorate, one foreign language, thesis/dissertation, oral and written exams. *Entrance requirements:* For master's and doctorate, GRE General Test, GRE Subject Test in advanced mathematics (strongly recommended), minimum undergraduate GPA of 3.0 or equivalent. Additional exam requirements/recommendations for international students: Required—TOEFL (minimum score 570 paper-based; 77 iBT). *Application deadline:* For fall admission, 1/15 for domestic and international students; for spring admission, 12/1 for domestic students, 10/15 for international students. Application fee: $60 ($75 for international students). Electronic applications accepted. *Financial support:* In 2011–12, fellowships with full and partial tuition reimbursements (averaging $16,000 per year), teaching assistantships with partial tuition reimbursements (averaging $16,020 per year) were awarded. Support available to part-time students. Financial award application deadline: 3/1; financial award applicants required to submit FAFSA. *Faculty research:* Algebra, analysis, topology, differential equations, applied mathematics. *Unit head:* Dr. Laszlo Lempert, Head, 765-494-1908, Fax: 765-494-0548, E-mail: lempert@purdue.edu. *Application contact:* Rebecca A. Lank, Graduate Contact, 765-494-1961, Fax: 765-494-0548, E-mail: lankr@purdue.edu. Web site: http://www.math.purdue.edu/.

Peterson's Graduate Programs in the Physical Sciences, Mathematics, Agricultural Sciences, the Environment & Natural Resources 2013

facebook.com/petersonspublishing **343**

SECTION 7: MATHEMATICAL SCIENCES

Mathematics

Purdue University Calumet, Graduate Studies Office, School of Engineering, Mathematics, and Science, Department of Mathematics, Computer Science, and Statistics, Hammond, IN 46323-2094. Offers computer science (MS); mathematics (MAT, MS). Part-time programs available. *Entrance requirements:* Additional exam requirements/recommendations for international students: Required—TOEFL. *Faculty research:* Topology, analysis, algebra, mathematics education.

Queens College of the City University of New York, Division of Graduate Studies, Mathematics and Natural Sciences Division, Department of Mathematics, Flushing, NY 11367-1597. Offers MA. Part-time and evening/weekend programs available. *Faculty:* 31 full-time (6 women). *Students:* 7 full-time (3 women), 47 part-time (22 women); includes 28 minority (4 Black or African American, non-Hispanic/Latino; 17 Asian, non-Hispanic/Latino; 7 Hispanic/Latino), 6 international. 49 applicants, 47% accepted, 16 enrolled. In 2011, 9 master's awarded. *Degree requirements:* For master's, comprehensive exam. *Entrance requirements:* For master's, minimum GPA of 3.0. Additional exam requirements/recommendations for international students: Required—TOEFL. *Application deadline:* For fall admission, 4/1 for domestic students; for spring admission, 11/1 for domestic students. Applications are processed on a rolling basis. Application fee: $125. *Expenses:* Tuition, state resident: part-time $345 per credit. Tuition, nonresident: part-time $640 per credit. *Required fees:* $145.25 per semester. *Financial support:* Career-related internships or fieldwork, Federal Work-Study, institutionally sponsored loans, and tuition waivers (partial) available. Support available to part-time students. Financial award application deadline: 4/1; financial award applicants required to submit FAFSA. *Faculty research:* Topology, differential equations, combinatorics. *Unit head:* Dr. Wallace Goldberg, Chairperson, 718-997-5800, E-mail: wallace_goldberg@qc.edu. *Application contact:* Dr. Nick Metas, Graduate Adviser, 718-997-5800, E-mail: nick_metas@qc.edu.

Queen's University at Kingston, School of Graduate Studies and Research, Faculty of Arts and Sciences, Department of Mathematics and Statistics, Kingston, ON K7L 3N6, Canada. Offers mathematics (M Sc, M Sc Eng, PhD); statistics (M Sc, M Sc Eng, PhD). Part-time programs available. *Degree requirements:* For master's, thesis; for doctorate, comprehensive exam, thesis/dissertation. *Entrance requirements:* Additional exam requirements/recommendations for international students: Required—TOEFL. *Faculty research:* Algebra, analysis, applied mathematics, statistics.

Rensselaer Polytechnic Institute, Graduate School, School of Science, Program in Mathematics, Troy, NY 12180-3590. Offers MS, PhD. Part-time programs available. Terminal master's awarded for partial completion of doctoral program. *Degree requirements:* For doctorate, comprehensive exam, thesis/dissertation, preliminary exam, candidacy presentation. *Entrance requirements:* For master's and doctorate, GRE General Test. Additional exam requirements/recommendations for international students: Required—TOEFL. Electronic applications accepted. *Faculty research:* Inverse problems, biomathematics, operations research, applied mathematics, mathematical modeling.

Rhode Island College, School of Graduate Studies, Faculty of Arts and Sciences, Department of Mathematics and Computer Science, Providence, RI 02908-1991. Offers mathematics (MA); mathematics content specialist (CGS). Part-time and evening/weekend programs available. *Faculty:* 3 full-time (2 women). *Students:* 1 full-time (0 women), 4 part-time (1 woman). Average age 31. In 2011, 1 master's awarded. *Degree requirements:* For master's, comprehensive exam. *Entrance requirements:* For master's, GRE General Test or MAT, minimum of 30 hours beyond pre-calculus math, 3 letters of recommendation, interview. Additional exam requirements/recommendations for international students: Recommended—TOEFL (minimum score 550 paper-based; 213 computer-based; 79 iBT). *Application deadline:* For fall admission, 3/1 for domestic students; for spring admission, 11/1 for domestic students. Applications are processed on a rolling basis. Application fee: $50. *Expenses:* Tuition, state resident: full-time $8592; part-time $358 per credit hour. Tuition, nonresident: full-time $16,800; part-time $700 per credit hour. *Required fees:* $602; $22 per credit. $72 per term. *Financial support:* In 2011–12, 3 teaching assistantships with full tuition reimbursements (averaging $4,550 per year) were awarded; Federal Work-Study, scholarships/grants, health care benefits, and unspecified assistantships also available. Support available to part-time students. Financial award application deadline: 5/15; financial award applicants required to submit FAFSA. *Unit head:* Dr. Raimundo Kovac, Chair, 401-456-8038. *Application contact:* Graduate Studies, 401-456-8700. Web site: http://www.ric.edu/mathComputerScience/index.php.

Rice University, Graduate Programs, Wiess School of Natural Sciences, Department of Mathematics, Houston, TX 77251-1892. Offers PhD. Terminal master's awarded for partial completion of doctoral program. *Degree requirements:* For doctorate, one foreign language, comprehensive exam, thesis/dissertation. *Entrance requirements:* For doctorate, GRE Subject Test, GRE General Test. Additional exam requirements/recommendations for international students: Required—TOEFL (minimum score 600 paper-based; 90 iBT). Electronic applications accepted. *Faculty research:* Algebraic geometry/algebra, complex analysis and Teichmuller theory, dynamical systems and Ergodic theory, topology, differential geometry and geometric analysis.

Rivier University, School of Graduate Studies, Department of Computer Science and Mathematics, Nashua, NH 03060. Offers computer science (MS); mathematics (MAT). Part-time and evening/weekend programs available.

Entrance requirements: For master's, GRE Subject Test. Electronic applications accepted.

Roosevelt University, Graduate Division, College of Arts and Sciences, Department of Mathematics and Actuarial Science, Program in Mathematics, Chicago, IL 60605. Offers mathematical sciences (MS), including actuarial science. Part-time and evening/weekend programs available. *Faculty research:* Statistics, mathematics education, finite groups, computers in mathematics.

Rowan University, Graduate School, College of Liberal Arts and Sciences, Department of Mathematics, Glassboro, NJ 08028-1701. Offers MA. Part-time and evening/weekend programs available. *Degree requirements:* For master's, thesis. *Entrance requirements:* For master's, GRE General Test. Additional exam requirements/recommendations for international students: Required—TOEFL. Electronic applications accepted.

Royal Military College of Canada, Division of Graduate Studies and Research, Science Division, Department of Mathematics and Computer Science, Kingston, ON K7K 7B4, Canada. Offers computer science (M Sc); mathematics (M Sc). *Degree requirements:* For master's, thesis. *Entrance requirements:* For master's, honours degree with second-class standing. Electronic applications accepted.

Rutgers, The State University of New Jersey, Camden, Graduate School of Arts and Sciences, Program in Mathematical Sciences, Camden, NJ 08102. Offers industrial mathematics (MBS); industrial/applied mathematics (MS); mathematical computer science (MS); pure mathematics (MS); teaching in mathematical sciences (MS). Part-time and evening/weekend programs available. *Degree requirements:* For master's, comprehensive exam, thesis optional, survey paper, 30 credits. *Entrance requirements:* For master's, GRE, BS/BA in math or related subject, 2 letters of recommendation. Additional exam requirements/recommendations for international students: Required—TOEFL (minimum score 550 paper-based; 213 computer-based), IELTS. Electronic applications accepted. *Faculty research:* Differential geometry, dynamical systems, vertex operator algebra, automorphic forms, CR-structures.

Rutgers, The State University of New Jersey, Newark, Graduate School, Program in Mathematical Sciences, Newark, NJ 07102. Offers PhD. *Degree requirements:* For doctorate, thesis/dissertation, written qualifying exam. *Entrance requirements:* For doctorate, GRE General Test, minimum B average. Additional exam requirements/recommendations for international students: Required—TOEFL. Electronic applications accepted. *Faculty research:* Number theory, automorphic form, low-dimensional topology, Kleinian groups, representation theory.

Rutgers, The State University of New Jersey, New Brunswick, Graduate School-New Brunswick, Department of Mathematics, Piscataway, NJ 08854-8097. Offers applied mathematics (MS, PhD); mathematics (MS, PhD). Part-time programs available. *Degree requirements:* For doctorate, one foreign language, comprehensive exam, thesis/dissertation. *Entrance requirements:* For master's and doctorate, GRE General Test, GRE Subject Test. Additional exam requirements/recommendations for international students: Required—TOEFL. *Faculty research:* Logic and set theory, number theory, mathematical physics, control theory, partial differential equations.

St. Cloud State University, School of Graduate Studies, College of Science and Engineering, Department of Mathematics, St. Cloud, MN 56301-4498. Offers MS. *Degree requirements:* For master's, comprehensive exam (for some programs), thesis or alternative. *Entrance requirements:* For master's, GRE General Test, minimum GPA of 2.75. Additional exam requirements/recommendations for international students: Required—Michigan English Language Assessment Battery; Recommended—TOEFL (minimum score 550 paper-based; 213 computer-based), IELTS (minimum score 6.5). Electronic applications accepted.

Saint Joseph's University, College of Arts and Sciences, Department of Mathematics and Computer Science, Philadelphia, PA 19131-1395. Offers computer science (MS); mathematics and computer science (Post-Master's Certificate). Part-time and evening/weekend programs available. *Faculty:* 5 full-time (2 women). *Students:* 47 full-time (11 women), 20 part-time (10 women); includes 6 minority (2 Black or African American, non-Hispanic/Latino; 3 Asian, non-Hispanic/Latino; 1 Two or more races, non-Hispanic/Latino), 54 international. Average age 27. 49 applicants, 61% accepted, 23 enrolled. In 2011, 31 master's awarded. *Entrance requirements:* For master's, 2 letters of recommendation. *Application deadline:* For fall admission, 7/15 priority date for domestic students, 4/15 for international students; for winter admission, 4/15 for domestic students, 1/15 for international students; for spring admission, 11/15 priority date for domestic students, 10/15 for international students. Applications are processed on a rolling basis. Application fee: $35. Electronic applications accepted. *Expenses:* Tuition: Part-time $735 per credit hour. Tuition and fees vary according to degree level and program. *Financial support:* Teaching assistantships with partial tuition reimbursements and unspecified assistantships available. Financial award applicants required to submit FAFSA. *Faculty research:* Computer vision, pathways to careers. *Unit head:* Dr. George Grevera, Director, Graduate Computer Science, 610-660-1535, Fax: 610-660-3082, E-mail: ggrevera@sju.edu. *Application contact:* Kate McConnell, Director, Graduate College of Arts and Sciences Admissions and Retention, 610-660-3184, Fax: 610-660-3230, E-mail: kate.mcconnell@sju.edu. Web site: http://macs.sju.edu/cscmsprog/index.html.

Saint Louis University, Graduate Education, College of Arts and Sciences and Graduate Education, Department of Mathematics and Computer Science, St.

344 facebook.com/petersonspublishing

Peterson's Graduate Programs in the Physical Sciences, Mathematics, Agricultural Sciences, the Environment & Natural Resources 2013

Louis, MO 63103-2097. Offers mathematics (MA, MA-R, PhD). Part-time programs available. *Degree requirements:* For master's, comprehensive exam, thesis (for some programs); for doctorate, one foreign language, thesis/dissertation, preliminary exams. *Entrance requirements:* For master's, GRE General Test, letters of recommendation, resume, interview; for doctorate, GRE General Test, letters of recommendation, resumé, interview, transcripts, goal statement. Additional exam requirements/recommendations for international students: Required—TOEFL (minimum score 525 paper-based; 194 computer-based). Electronic applications accepted. *Faculty research:* Algebra, groups and rings, analysis, differential geometry, topology.

Salem State University, School of Graduate Studies, Program in Mathematics, Salem, MA 01970-5353. Offers MAT, MS. Part-time and evening/weekend programs available. *Entrance requirements:* For master's, GRE or MAT. Additional exam requirements/recommendations for international students: Required—TOEFL (minimum score 550 paper-based; 80 iBT) or IELTS (minimum score 5.5).

Sam Houston State University, College of Sciences, Department of Mathematics and Statistics, Huntsville, TX 77341. Offers mathematics (MA, MS); statistics (MS). Part-time programs available. *Faculty:* 23 full-time (6 women). *Students:* 29 full-time (11 women), 12 part-time (8 women); includes 11 minority (1 Black or African American, non-Hispanic/Latino; 4 Asian, non-Hispanic/Latino; 6 Hispanic/Latino), 16 international. Average age 32. 32 applicants, 66% accepted, 19 enrolled. In 2011, 9 master's awarded. *Entrance requirements:* For master's, GRE General Test. Additional exam requirements/recommendations for international students: Required—TOEFL (minimum score 550 paper-based; 213 computer-based; 79 iBT). *Application deadline:* For fall admission, 8/1 for domestic students, 6/25 for international students; for spring admission, 12/1 for domestic students, 11/12 for international students. Applications are processed on a rolling basis. Application fee: $45 ($75 for international students). Electronic applications accepted. *Expenses:* Tuition, state resident: full-time $4420; part-time $221 per credit hour. Tuition, nonresident: full-time $10,680; part-time $534 per credit hour. *Required fees:* $329 per credit hour. *Financial support:* Teaching assistantships and institutionally sponsored loans available. Support available to part-time students. Financial award application deadline: 5/31; financial award applicants required to submit FAFSA. *Unit head:* Dr. Mark Klespis, Chair, 936-294-1577, Fax: 936-294-1882, E-mail: klespis@shsu.edu. *Application contact:* Dr. Jianzhong Wang, Advisor, 936-294-3521, Fax: 936-294-1882, E-mail: mth_jxw@shsu.edu. Web site: http://www.shsu.edu/~mcss_www/.

San Diego State University, Graduate and Research Affairs, College of Sciences, Department of Mathematics and Statistics, San Diego, CA 92182. Offers applied mathematics (MS); mathematics (MA); mathematics and science education (PhD); statistics (MS). PhD offered jointly wtih University of California, San Diego. Part-time programs available. *Degree requirements:* For doctorate, thesis/dissertation. *Entrance requirements:* For master's, GRE General Test; for doctorate, GRE, minimum GPA of 3.25 in last 30 undergraduate semester units, minimum graduate GPA of 3.5, MSE recommendation form, 3 letters of recommendation. Additional exam requirements/recommendations for international students: Required—TOEFL. Electronic applications accepted. *Faculty research:* Teacher education in mathematics.

San Francisco State University, Division of Graduate Studies, College of Science and Engineering, Department of Mathematics, San Francisco, CA 94132-1722. Offers MA. *Application deadline:* Applications are processed on a rolling basis. *Unit head:* Dr. David Bao, Chair, 415-338-2251, E-mail: statmath@math.sfsu.edu. *Application contact:* Dr. Eric Hayashi, Graduate Coordinator, 415-338-2251, E-mail: hayashi@math.sfsu.edu. Web site: http://math.sfsu.edu.

San Jose State University, Graduate Studies and Research, College of Science, Department of Mathematics, San Jose, CA 95192-0001. Offers applied mathematics (MS); mathematics (MA, MS); mathematics education (MA); statistics (MA). Part-time and evening/weekend programs available. *Degree requirements:* For master's, comprehensive exam, thesis (for some programs). *Entrance requirements:* For master's, GRE Subject Test. Electronic applications accepted. *Faculty research:* Artificial intelligence, algorithms, numerical analysis, software database, number theory.

Simon Fraser University, Graduate Studies, Faculty of Science, Department of Mathematics, Burnaby, BC V5A 1S6, Canada. Offers applied and computational mathematics (M Sc, PhD); mathematics (M Sc, PhD). *Degree requirements:* For master's, thesis; for doctorate, thesis/dissertation. *Entrance requirements:* For master's, GRE General Test, minimum GPA of 3.0, 3 letters of reference; for doctorate, GRE General Test, minimum GPA of 3.5, 3 letters of reference. Additional exam requirements/recommendations for international students: Required—TWE or IELTS. Electronic applications accepted. *Faculty research:* Semi-groups, number theory, optimization, combinations.

Smith College, Graduate and Special Programs, Center for Women in Mathematics Post-Baccalaureate Program, Northampton, MA 01063. Offers Postbaccalaureate Certificate. Part-time programs available. *Faculty:* 12 full-time (5 women). *Students:* 14 full-time (all women); includes 4 minority (3 Black or African American, non-Hispanic/Latino; 1 Asian, non-Hispanic/Latino). Average age 26. 30 applicants, 40% accepted, 10 enrolled. In 2011, 12 Postbaccalaureate Certificates awarded. *Entrance requirements:* Additional exam requirements/recommendations for international students: Required—TOEFL. *Application deadline:* For fall admission, 7/1 for domestic students; for spring admission, 12/15 for domestic students. Applications are processed on a rolling basis.

Application fee: $60. *Expenses: Tuition:* Full-time $14,925; part-time $1245 per credit. *Financial support:* In 2011–12, 14 students received support. Scholarships/grants and tuition waivers (full) available. Support available to part-time students. *Unit head:* Ruth Haas, Director, 413-585-3872, E-mail: rhaas@smith.edu. *Application contact:* Jim Henle, Director, 413-585-3867, E-mail: jhenle@smith.edu.

South Dakota State University, Graduate School, College of Engineering, Department of Mathematics and Statistics, Brookings, SD 57007. Offers computational science and statistics (PhD); mathematics (MS); statistics (MS). Part-time programs available. Terminal master's awarded for partial completion of doctoral program. *Degree requirements:* For master's, thesis (for some programs), oral exam; for doctorate, comprehensive exam, thesis/dissertation, oral and written exams. *Entrance requirements:* Additional exam requirements/recommendations for international students: Required—TOEFL (minimum score 550 paper-based; 213 computer-based; 80 iBT); Recommended—IELTS. *Faculty research:* Financial mathematics, predictive analytics, operations research, bioinformatics, biostatistics, computational science, statistics, number theory, abstract algebra.

Southeast Missouri State University, School of Graduate Studies, Department of Mathematics, Cape Girardeau, MO 63701-4799. Offers MNS. Part-time and evening/weekend programs available. Postbaccalaureate distance learning degree programs offered (minimal on-campus study). *Faculty:* 13 full-time (5 women). *Students:* 5 full-time (2 women), 11 part-time (6 women); includes 1 minority (Asian, non-Hispanic/Latino), 3 international. Average age 32. 5 applicants, 80% accepted, 4 enrolled. In 2011, 4 master's awarded. *Degree requirements:* For master's, research paper and comprehensive exam or thesis and oral defense. *Entrance requirements:* For master's, minimum undergraduate GPA of 2.5, 2.75 in last 30 hours of undergraduate course work in mathematics and science; major in mathematics or minimum C grade in prerequisite courses; 2 letters of recommendation. Additional exam requirements/recommendations for international students: Required—TOEFL (minimum score 550 paper-based; 213 computer-based; 79 iBT); Recommended—IELTS (minimum score 6). *Application deadline:* For fall admission, 8/1 for domestic students, 7/1 for international students; for spring admission, 11/21 for domestic students, 11/1 for international students. Applications are processed on a rolling basis. Application fee: $30 ($40 for international students). Electronic applications accepted. *Expenses:* Tuition, state resident: full-time $4896; part-time $272 per credit hour. Tuition, nonresident: full-time $8649; part-time $480.50 per credit hour. *Financial support:* In 2011–12, 7 students received support, including 8 teaching assistantships with full tuition reimbursements available (averaging $7,600 per year); career-related internships or fieldwork, Federal Work-Study, scholarships/grants, tuition waivers (full), and unspecified assistantships also available. Financial award application deadline: 6/30; financial award applicants required to submit FAFSA. *Faculty research:* Algebraic geometry, combinatorics, differential equations, mathematics education, statistics. *Unit head:* Dr. Craig Roberts, Interim Chairperson, 573-651-2164, Fax: 573-986-6811, E-mail: croberts@semo.edu. *Application contact:* Alisa Aleen McFerron, Assistant Director of Admissions for Operations, 573-651-5937, Fax: 573-651-5936, E-mail: amcferron@semo.edu. Web site: http://www5.semo.edu/math/.

Southern Connecticut State University, School of Graduate Studies, School of Arts and Sciences, Department of Mathematics, New Haven, CT 06515-1355. Offers MS. Part-time and evening/weekend programs available. *Faculty:* 3 full-time (0 women). *Students:* 8 full-time (6 women), 13 part-time (10 women); includes 2 minority (1 Black or African American, non-Hispanic/Latino; 1 Asian, non-Hispanic/Latino). 55 applicants, 16% accepted, 8 enrolled. In 2011, 3 master's awarded. *Degree requirements:* For master's, thesis or alternative. *Entrance requirements:* For master's, interview. *Application deadline:* For fall admission, 7/15 priority date for domestic students. Applications are processed on a rolling basis. Application fee: $50. Electronic applications accepted. *Expenses:* Tuition, state resident: full-time $5137; part-time $413 per credit. *Required fees:* $4008; $55 per term. *Financial support:* Application deadline: 4/15; applicants required to submit FAFSA. *Unit head:* Dr. Alain D'Amour, Chairperson, 203-392-5579, Fax: 203-392-6805, E-mail: damoura1@southernct.edu. *Application contact:* Dr. Therese Bennett, Graduate Coordinator, 203-392-6997, Fax: 203-392-6805, E-mail: bennettt1@southernct.edu.

Southern Illinois University Carbondale, Graduate School, College of Science, Department of Mathematics, Carbondale, IL 62901-4701. Offers mathematics (MA, MS, PhD); statistics (MS). PhD offered jointly with Southeast Missouri State University. Part-time programs available. *Faculty:* 32 full-time (2 women), 1 part-time/adjunct (0 women). *Students:* 33 full-time (14 women), 5 part-time (1 woman); includes 2 minority (1 Black or African American, non-Hispanic/Latino; 1 Hispanic/Latino), 25 international. Average age 26. 43 applicants, 37% accepted, 9 enrolled. In 2011, 11 master's, 4 doctorates awarded. *Degree requirements:* For master's, thesis; for doctorate, 2 foreign languages, thesis/dissertation. *Entrance requirements:* For master's, minimum GPA of 2.7; for doctorate, minimum GPA of 3.25. Additional exam requirements/recommendations for international students: Required—TOEFL. *Application deadline:* Applications are processed on a rolling basis. Application fee: $0. *Financial support:* In 2011–12, 28 students received support, including 24 teaching assistantships with full tuition reimbursements available; fellowships with full tuition reimbursements available, research assistantships with full tuition reimbursements available, Federal Work-Study, institutionally sponsored loans, and tuition waivers (full) also available. Support available to part-time students. *Faculty research:* Differential equations,

Peterson's Graduate Programs in the Physical Sciences, Mathematics, Agricultural Sciences, the Environment & Natural Resources 2013

facebook.com/petersonspublishing **345**

Mathematics

combinatorics, probability, algebra, numerical analysis. *Unit head:* Dr. Andrew Earnest, Chairperson, 618-453-6522, Fax: 618-453-5300, E-mail: aearnest@math.siu.edu. *Application contact:* Linda Gibson, Graduate Studies Office Specialist, 618-453-6597, Fax: 618-453-5300, E-mail: lgibson@math.siu.edu. Web site: http://www.math.siu.edu/.

Southern Illinois University Edwardsville, Graduate School, College of Arts and Sciences, Department of Mathematics and Statistics, Edwardsville, IL 62026. Offers mathematics (MS), including computational mathematics, postsecondary mathematics education, pure math, statistics and operations research. Part-time programs available. *Faculty:* 19 full-time (5 women). *Students:* 13 full-time (2 women), 30 part-time (17 women); includes 2 minority (both Black or African American, non-Hispanic/Latino), 12 international. 34 applicants, 47% accepted. In 2011, 14 master's awarded. *Degree requirements:* For master's, thesis (for some programs), research paper/project. *Entrance requirements:* Additional exam requirements/recommendations for international students: Required—TOEFL (minimum score 550 paper-based; 213 computer-based; 79 iBT), IELTS (minimum score 6.5). *Application deadline:* For fall admission, 7/22 for domestic students, 6/1 for international students; for spring admission, 12/9 for domestic students, 10/1 for international students. Applications are processed on a rolling basis. Application fee: $30. Electronic applications accepted. Tuition and fees vary according to course load and program. *Financial support:* In 2011–12, 3 research assistantships with full tuition reimbursements (averaging $9,927 per year), 22 teaching assistantships with full tuition reimbursements (averaging $9,927 per year) were awarded; fellowships with full tuition reimbursements, institutionally sponsored loans, scholarships/grants, and unspecified assistantships also available. Financial award application deadline: 3/1; financial award applicants required to submit FAFSA. *Unit head:* Dr. Krzysztof Jarosz, Chair, 618-650-2354, E-mail: kjarosz@siue.edu. *Application contact:* Dr. Adam Weyhaupt, Director, 618-650-2220, E-mail: aweyhau@siue.edu. Web site: http://www.siue.edu/artsandsciences/math/.

Southern Methodist University, Dedman College, Department of Mathematics, Dallas, TX 75275. Offers computational and applied mathematics (MS, PhD). *Degree requirements:* For master's, oral exams; for doctorate, thesis/dissertation, oral and written exams. *Entrance requirements:* For master's and doctorate, GRE General Test, minimum GPA of 3.0, 18 undergraduate hours in mathematics beyond first and second year calculus. Additional exam requirements/recommendations for international students: Required—TOEFL. Electronic applications accepted. *Faculty research:* Numerical analysis and scientific computation, fluid dynamics, optics, wave propagation, mathematical biology.

Southern University and Agricultural and Mechanical College, Graduate School, College of Sciences, Department of Mathematics, Baton Rouge, LA 70813. Offers MS. *Degree requirements:* For master's, comprehensive exam, thesis optional. *Entrance requirements:* For master's, GMAT, GRE General Test. Additional exam requirements/recommendations for international students: Required—TOEFL. *Faculty research:* Algebraic number theory, abstract algebra, computer analysis, probability, mathematics education.

Stanford University, School of Engineering, Program in Scientific Computing and Computational Mathematics, Stanford, CA 94305-9991. Offers MS, PhD. Terminal master's awarded for partial completion of doctoral program. *Degree requirements:* For doctorate, thesis/dissertation, qualifying exam. *Entrance requirements:* For master's, GRE General Test; for doctorate, GRE General Test, GRE Subject Test. Additional exam requirements/recommendations for international students: Required—TOEFL. Electronic applications accepted. *Expenses: Tuition:* Full-time $40,050; part-time $890 per credit.

Stanford University, School of Humanities and Sciences, Department of Mathematics, Stanford, CA 94305-9991. Offers financial mathematics (MS); mathematics (MS, PhD). Terminal master's awarded for partial completion of doctoral program. *Degree requirements:* For doctorate, 2 foreign languages, thesis/dissertation, oral exam. *Entrance requirements:* For master's, GRE General Test; for doctorate, GRE General Test, GRE Subject Test. Additional exam requirements/recommendations for international students: Required—TOEFL. Electronic applications accepted. *Expenses: Tuition:* Full-time $40,050; part-time $890 per credit.

State University of New York at Binghamton, Graduate School, School of Arts and Sciences, Department of Mathematical Sciences, Binghamton, NY 13902-6000. Offers computer science (MA, PhD); probability and statistics (MA, PhD). Part-time programs available. *Faculty:* 27 full-time (4 women), 18 part-time/adjunct (7 women). *Students:* 45 full-time (11 women), 27 part-time (9 women); includes 5 minority (2 Black or African American, non-Hispanic/Latino; 2 Hispanic/Latino; 1 Native Hawaiian or other Pacific Islander, non-Hispanic/Latino), 31 international. Average age 28. 86 applicants, 45% accepted, 22 enrolled. In 2011, 12 master's, 3 doctorates awarded. Terminal master's awarded for partial completion of doctoral program. *Degree requirements:* For master's, thesis or alternative; for doctorate, 2 foreign languages, thesis/dissertation. *Entrance requirements:* For master's and doctorate, GRE General Test, GRE Subject Test. Additional exam requirements/recommendations for international students: Required—TOEFL (minimum score 550 paper-based; 213 computer-based; 80 iBT). *Application deadline:* For fall admission, 4/15 priority date for domestic students, 4/15 for international students; for spring admission, 11/30 priority date for domestic students, 11/30 for international students. Applications are processed on a rolling basis. Application fee: $60. Electronic applications accepted. *Financial support:* In 2011–12, 58 students received support, including

5 fellowships with full tuition reimbursements available (averaging $16,500 per year), research assistantships with full tuition reimbursements available (averaging $16,500 per year), 51 teaching assistantships with full tuition reimbursements available (averaging $16,500 per year); career-related internships or fieldwork, Federal Work-Study, institutionally sponsored loans, scholarships/grants, health care benefits, tuition waivers (full and partial), and unspecified assistantships also available. Financial award application deadline: 2/15; financial award applicants required to submit FAFSA. *Unit head:* Dr. Fernando Guzman, Chairperson, 607-777-2148, E-mail: fer@math.binghamton.edu. *Application contact:* Catherine Smith, Recruiting and Admissions Coordinator, 607-777-2151, Fax: 607-777-2501, E-mail: cmsmith@binghamton.edu.

State University of New York at Fredonia, Graduate Studies, Department of Mathematical Sciences, Fredonia, NY 14063-1136. Offers MS Ed. Part-time and evening/weekend programs available. *Expenses: Tuition,* state resident: full-time $6666; part-time $370 per credit hour. Tuition, nonresident: full-time $11,376; part-time $632 per credit hour. *Required fees:* $1059.30; $58.85 per credit hour. Tuition and fees vary according to course load.

State University of New York College at Cortland, Graduate Studies, School of Arts and Sciences, Department of Mathematics, Cortland, NY 13045. Offers MAT, MS Ed.

State University of New York College at Potsdam, School of Arts and Sciences, Department of Mathematics, Potsdam, NY 13676. Offers MA. Part-time and evening/weekend programs available. *Faculty:* 6 full-time (2 women). *Students:* 2 full-time (0 women); includes 1 minority (Two or more races, non-Hispanic/Latino). 2 applicants, 100% accepted, 2 enrolled. In 2011, 8 master's awarded. *Entrance requirements:* For master's, minimum GPA of 3.0 in all undergraduate math courses, 2.75 in last 60 hours of undergraduate coursework. Additional exam requirements/recommendations for international students: Required—TOEFL (minimum score 550 paper-based; 213 computer-based; 80 iBT), IELTS (minimum score 6). *Application deadline:* For fall admission, 4/1 priority date for domestic students, 4/1 for international students; for winter admission, 10/15 for domestic and international students; for spring admission, 3/1 priority date for domestic students, 3/1 for international students. Applications are processed on a rolling basis. Application fee: $50. *Expenses:* Tuition, state resident: full-time $8870; part-time $370 per credit hour. Tuition, nonresident: full-time $15,160; part-time $632 per credit hour. *Required fees:* $1066; $44.10 per credit hour. One-time fee: $3. *Financial support:* In 2011–12, 1 student received support. Teaching assistantships with full tuition reimbursements available, Federal Work-Study, and unspecified assistantships available. Support available to part-time students. Financial award application deadline: 3/1; financial award applicants required to submit FAFSA. *Unit head:* Dr. Joel Foisy, Chairperson, 315-267-2084, Fax: 315-267-3176, E-mail: foisyjs@potsdam.edu. *Application contact:* Peter Cutler, Graduate Admissions Counselor, 315-267-2165, Fax: 315-267-4802, E-mail: graduate@potsdam.edu.

Stephen F. Austin State University, Graduate School, College of Sciences and Mathematics, Department of Mathematics and Statistics, Nacogdoches, TX 75962. Offers mathematics (MS); mathematics education (MS); statistics (MS). *Degree requirements:* For master's, comprehensive exam, thesis optional. *Entrance requirements:* For master's, GRE General Test, minimum GPA of 2.8 in last 60 hours, 2.5 overall. Additional exam requirements/recommendations for international students: Required—TOEFL. *Faculty research:* Kernel type estimators, fractal mappings, spline curve fitting, robust regression continua theory.

Stevens Institute of Technology, Graduate School, Charles V. Schaefer Jr. School of Engineering, Department of Mathematical Sciences, Program in Mathematics, Hoboken, NJ 07030. Offers MS, PhD. *Degree requirements:* For master's, thesis optional; for doctorate, one foreign language, thesis/dissertation. *Entrance requirements:* For master's and doctorate, GRE. Additional exam requirements/recommendations for international students: Required—TOEFL. Electronic applications accepted.

Stony Brook University, State University of New York, Graduate School, College of Arts and Sciences, Department of Mathematics, Stony Brook, NY 11794. Offers MA, MAT, PhD. *Degree requirements:* For doctorate, 2 foreign languages, thesis/dissertation. *Entrance requirements:* For master's and doctorate, GRE General Test. Additional exam requirements/recommendations for international students: Required—TOEFL. *Faculty research:* Real analysis, relativity and mathematical physics, complex analysis, topology, combinatorics.

Syracuse University, College of Arts and Sciences, Program in Mathematics, Syracuse, NY 13244. Offers MS, PhD. Part-time programs available. *Students:* 43 full-time (10 women); includes 3 minority (1 Asian, non-Hispanic/Latino; 1 Hispanic/Latino; 1 Two or more races, non-Hispanic/Latino), 12 international. Average age 26. 73 applicants, 22% accepted, 11 enrolled. In 2011, 12 master's, 5 doctorates awarded. Terminal master's awarded for partial completion of doctoral program. *Degree requirements:* For doctorate, 2 foreign languages, thesis/dissertation, qualifying exam. *Entrance requirements:* For master's and doctorate, GRE General Test, GRE Subject Test (recommended). Additional exam requirements/recommendations for international students: Required—TOEFL (minimum score 100 iBT). *Application deadline:* For fall admission, 2/1 priority date for domestic students, 2/1 for international students. Application fee: $75. Electronic applications accepted. *Expenses: Tuition:* Part-time $1206 per credit. *Financial support:* Fellowships with full tuition reimbursements, research

Peterson's Graduate Programs in the Physical Sciences, Mathematics, Agricultural Sciences, the Environment & Natural Resources 2013

assistantships with full tuition reimbursements, and teaching assistantships with full and partial tuition reimbursements available. Financial award application deadline: 1/1; financial award applicants required to submit FAFSA. *Faculty research:* Pure mathematics, numerical mathematics, computing statistics. *Unit head:* Dr. Mark Kleiner, Associate Chair for Graduate Studies, 315-443-1499, Fax: 315-443-1475, E-mail: mkleiner@syr.edu. *Application contact:* Christine Gillmore, Associate Director, Graduate Recruitment and Retention, 315-443-1471, E-mail: cgilmore@syr.edu. Web site: http://math.syr.edu.

Tarleton State University, College of Graduate Studies, College of Science and Technology, Department of Mathematics, Stephenville, TX 76402. Offers mathematics (MS). Part-time and evening/weekend programs available. *Faculty:* 3 full-time (1 woman). *Students:* 3 full-time (all women), 1 (woman) part-time, 1 international. Average age 30. 4 applicants, 100% accepted, 2 enrolled. In 2011, 5 master's awarded. *Degree requirements:* For master's, comprehensive exam, thesis (for some programs). *Entrance requirements:* For master's, GRE General Test, minimum GPA of 3.0. Additional exam requirements/recommendations for international students: Required—TOEFL (minimum score 550 paper-based; 213 computer-based; 80 iBT). *Application deadline:* For fall admission, 8/5 priority date for domestic students; for spring admission, 12/1 for domestic students. Applications are processed on a rolling basis. Application fee: $30 ($130 for international students). Electronic applications accepted. *Expenses:* Tuition, state resident: full-time $3131.46; part-time $174 per credit hour. Tuition, nonresident: full-time $8225; part-time $457 per credit hour. *Required fees:* $1446. Tuition and fees vary according to course load and campus/location. *Financial support:* Research assistantships, teaching assistantships, career-related internships or fieldwork, and Federal Work-Study available. Support available to part-time students. Financial award application deadline: 5/1; financial award applicants required to submit FAFSA. *Unit head:* Dr. Bryant Wyatt, Department Head, 254-968-9168, Fax: 254-968-9534, E-mail: wyatt@tarleton.edu. *Application contact:* Information Contact, 254-968-9104, Fax: 254-968-9670, E-mail: gradoffice@tarleton.edu. Web site: http://www.tarleton.edu/~math/index.html.

Temple University, College of Science and Technology, Department of Mathematics, Philadelphia, PA 19122-6096. Offers applied mathematics (MA); mathematics (PhD); pure mathematics (MA). Part-time and evening/weekend programs available. *Faculty:* 14 full-time (1 woman). *Students:* 24 full-time (4 women), 1 (woman) part-time, 4 international. Average age 27. 75 applicants, 29% accepted, 6 enrolled. In 2011, 1 master's, 3 doctorates awarded. Terminal master's awarded for partial completion of doctoral program. *Degree requirements:* For master's, thesis optional, written exam; for doctorate, 2 foreign languages, thesis/dissertation, oral and written exams. *Entrance requirements:* For master's, GRE General Test, minimum GPA of 3.0; for doctorate, GRE General Test, GRE Subject Test, minimum GPA of 3.0. Additional exam requirements/recommendations for international students: Required—TOEFL (minimum score 550 paper-based; 213 computer-based; 79 iBT). *Application deadline:* For fall admission, 2/15 priority date for domestic students, 12/15 for international students; for spring admission, 11/15 priority date for domestic students, 8/1 for international students. Applications are processed on a rolling basis. Application fee: $50. Electronic applications accepted. *Expenses:* Tuition, state resident: full-time $12,366; part-time $687 per credit hour. Tuition, nonresident: full-time $17,298; part-time $961 per credit hour. *Required fees:* $590; $213 per year. *Financial support:* Fellowships, research assistantships, teaching assistantships, Federal Work-Study, and institutionally sponsored loans available. Financial award application deadline: 1/15; financial award applicants required to submit FAFSA. *Faculty research:* Differential geometry, numerical analysis. *Unit head:* Dr. Gerardo Mendoza, Graduate Chair, 215-204-5053, Fax: 215-204-6433, E-mail: mathematics@temple.edu. *Application contact:* Tara Schumacher, Coordinator of Outreach, 215-204-6575, Fax: 215-204-8781, E-mail: tara.schumacher@temple.edu. Web site: http://math.temple.edu/.

Tennessee State University, The School of Graduate Studies and Research, College of Arts and Sciences, Department of Physics and Mathematics, Nashville, TN 37209-1561. Offers mathematical sciences (MS). *Entrance requirements:* For master's, GRE General Test. Electronic applications accepted.

Tennessee Technological University, Graduate School, College of Arts and Sciences, Department of Mathematics, Cookeville, TN 38505. Offers MS. Part-time programs available. *Faculty:* 17 full-time (4 women). *Students:* 10 full-time (0 women), 1 part-time (0 women); includes 2 minority (1 Black or African American, non-Hispanic/Latino; 1 American Indian or Alaska Native, non-Hispanic/Latino), 2 international. Average age 27. 11 applicants, 55% accepted, 5 enrolled. In 2011, 2 master's awarded. *Degree requirements:* For master's, thesis or alternative. *Entrance requirements:* For master's, GRE General Test. Additional exam requirements/recommendations for international students: Required—TOEFL (minimum score 550 paper-based; 79 iBT), IELTS (minimum score 5.5), PTE Academic. *Application deadline:* For fall admission, 8/1 for domestic students, 5/1 for international students; for spring admission, 12/1 for domestic students, 10/1 for international students. Application fee: $25 ($30 for international students). Electronic applications accepted. *Expenses:* Tuition, state resident: full-time $8094; part-time $422 per credit hour. Tuition, nonresident: full-time $20,574; part-time $1046 per credit hour. *Financial support:* In 2011–12, 3 research assistantships (averaging $7,500 per year), 7 teaching assistantships (averaging $7,500 per year) were awarded. Financial award application deadline: 4/1. *Unit head:* Dr. Allan Mills, Interim Chairperson, 931-372-3441, Fax: 931-372-6353, E-mail: amills@tntech.edu. *Application contact:* Shelia K. Kendrick, Coordinator of Graduate Admissions, 931-372-3808, Fax: 931-372-3497, E-mail: skendrick@tntech.edu.

Texas A&M International University, Office of Graduate Studies and Research, College of Arts and Sciences, Department of Engineering, Mathematics, and Physics, Laredo, TX 78041-1900. Offers mathematics (MS). *Faculty:* 4 full-time (0 women). *Students:* 5 full-time (1 woman), 7 part-time (1 woman); includes 11 minority (all Hispanic/Latino), 1 international. Average age 28. 9 applicants, 56% accepted, 1 enrolled. In 2011, 2 master's awarded. *Degree requirements:* For master's, comprehensive exam, thesis (for some programs). *Entrance requirements:* For master's, GRE General Test. Additional exam requirements/recommendations for international students: Required—TOEFL (minimum score 550 paper-based; 213 computer-based; 79 iBT). *Application deadline:* For fall admission, 4/30 priority date for domestic students, 4/30 for international students; for spring admission, 11/30 for domestic students, 10/1 for international students. Applications are processed on a rolling basis. Application fee: $35 ($50 for international students). *Expenses:* Tuition, state resident: full-time $5063. *Financial support:* In 2011–12, 6 students received support, including 4 research assistantships (averaging $9,100 per year), 2 teaching assistantships; Federal Work-Study, scholarships/grants, and unspecified assistantships also available. Financial award application deadline: 4/1. *Unit head:* Dr. Rafic Bachnak, Chair, 956-326-2408, Fax: 956-326-2439, E-mail: rbachnak@tamiu.edu. *Application contact:* Suzanne Hansen-Alford, Director of Graduate Recruiting, 956-326-3023, Fax: 956-326-3021, E-mail: graduateschool@tamiu.edu. Web site: http://www.tamiu.edu/coas/depts/dmps/.

Texas A&M University, College of Science, Department of Mathematics, College Station, TX 77843. Offers MS, PhD. Part-time programs available. Postbaccalaureate distance learning degree programs offered (minimal on-campus study). *Faculty:* 55. *Students:* 128 full-time (40 women), 30 part-time (16 women); includes 9 minority (1 Black or African American, non-Hispanic/Latino; 4 Asian, non-Hispanic/Latino; 3 Hispanic/Latino; 1 Two or more races, non-Hispanic/Latino), 82 international. Average age 27. In 2011, 25 master's, 2 doctorates awarded. Terminal master's awarded for partial completion of doctoral program. *Degree requirements:* For master's, comprehensive exam, thesis optional; for doctorate, one foreign language, comprehensive exam, thesis/dissertation. *Entrance requirements:* For master's and doctorate, GRE General Test. Additional exam requirements/recommendations for international students: Required—TOEFL (minimum score 550 paper-based; 213 computer-based). *Application deadline:* For fall admission, 3/1 for domestic and international students; for spring admission, 8/1 for domestic and international students. Applications are processed on a rolling basis. Application fee: $50 ($75 for international students). Electronic applications accepted. *Expenses:* Tuition, state resident: full-time $5437; part-time $226.55 per credit hour. Tuition, nonresident: full-time $12,949; part-time $539.55 per credit hour. *Required fees:* $2741. *Financial support:* In 2011–12, fellowships with partial tuition reimbursements (averaging $17,850 per year), research assistantships with partial tuition reimbursements (averaging $17,850 per year), teaching assistantships with partial tuition reimbursements (averaging $17,850 per year) were awarded; career-related internships or fieldwork, institutionally sponsored loans, scholarships/grants, and unspecified assistantships also available. Financial award application deadline: 3/1; financial award applicants required to submit FAFSA. *Faculty research:* Functional analysis, numerical analysis, algebra, geometry/topology, applied mathematics. *Unit head:* Dr. Emil Straube, Head, 979-845-9424, Fax: 979-845-6028, E-mail: e-straube@tamu.edu. *Application contact:* Monique Stewart, Academic Advisor I, 979-862-4137, Fax: 979-862-4190, E-mail: stewart@math.tamu.edu. Web site: http://www.math.tamu.edu/.

Texas A&M University–Commerce, Graduate School, College of Science, Engineering and Agriculture, Department of Mathematics, Commerce, TX 75429-3011. Offers MA, MS. Part-time programs available. *Degree requirements:* For master's, comprehensive exam, thesis (for some programs). *Entrance requirements:* For master's, GRE General Test. Electronic applications accepted.

Texas A&M University–Corpus Christi, Graduate Studies and Research, College of Science and Technology, Program in Mathematics, Corpus Christi, TX 78412-5503. Offers applied and computational mathematics (MS); curriculum content (MS). Part-time programs available. *Degree requirements:* For master's, thesis (for some programs). *Entrance requirements:* For master's, 2 letters of recommendation.

Texas A&M University–Kingsville, College of Graduate Studies, College of Arts and Sciences, Department of Mathematics, Kingsville, TX 78363. Offers MS. Part-time programs available. *Degree requirements:* For master's, comprehensive exam, thesis or alternative. *Entrance requirements:* For master's, GRE General Test. Additional exam requirements/recommendations for international students: Required—TOEFL. *Faculty research:* Complex analysis, multivariate analysis, algebra, numerical analysis, applied statistics.

Texas Christian University, College of Science and Engineering, Department of Mathematics, Fort Worth, TX 76129-0002. Offers applied mathematics (MS); mathematics (MAT); pure mathematics (MS, PhD). Part-time and evening/weekend programs available. *Faculty:* 12 full-time (2 women). *Students:* 8 full-time (4 women), 5 part-time (1 woman); includes 1 minority (Asian, non-Hispanic/Latino), 2 international. Average age 27. 11 applicants, 36% accepted, 4 enrolled. In 2011, 2 master's awarded. Terminal master's awarded for partial completion of doctoral program. *Degree requirements:* For master's, thesis optional; for doctorate, comprehensive exam, thesis/dissertation. *Entrance requirements:* For

Peterson's Graduate Programs in the Physical Sciences, Mathematics, Agricultural Sciences, the Environment & Natural Resources 2013

facebook.com/petersonspublishing **347**

master's and doctorate, GRE, 24 hours of math, including courses in elementary calculus of one and several variables, linear algebra, abstract algebra and real analysis. Additional exam requirements/recommendations for international students: Required—TOEFL. *Application deadline:* For fall admission, 3/1 priority date for domestic students, 3/1 for international students; for spring admission, 10/15 priority date for domestic students, 10/15 for international students. Applications are processed on a rolling basis. Application fee: $60. Electronic applications accepted. *Expenses: Tuition:* Full-time $20,250; part-time $1125 per credit hour. Part-time tuition and fees vary according to course load and program. *Financial support:* In 2011–12, 6 research assistantships with full tuition reimbursements (averaging $17,000 per year), 4 teaching assistantships with full tuition reimbursements (averaging $10,000 per year) were awarded; tuition waivers (full) also available. Support available to part-time students. Financial award application deadline: 3/1. *Faculty research:* Differential geometry, topology, analysis, number theory, algebraic geometry. *Unit head:* Dr. George Gilbert, Associate Professor and Chair, 817-257-7335, E-mail: g.gilbert@tcu.edu. *Application contact:* Dr. Ken Richardson, Professor/Director, Mathematics Graduate Program, 817-257-6128, E-mail: k.richardson@tcu.edu. Web site: http://www.math.tcu.edu/.

Texas Southern University, School of Science and Technology, Department of Mathematics, Houston, TX 77004-4584. Offers MS. Part-time and evening/weekend programs available. *Degree requirements:* For master's, comprehensive exam, thesis. *Entrance requirements:* For master's, GRE General Test, minimum GPA of 2.5. Additional exam requirements/recommendations for international students: Required—TOEFL. Electronic applications accepted. *Faculty research:* Statistics, number theory, topology, differential equations, numerical analysis.

Texas State University–San Marcos, Graduate School, College of Science and Engineering, Department of Mathematics, San Marcos, TX 78666. Offers applied mathematics (MS); mathematics (MS); mathematics education (PhD); middle school mathematics teaching (M Ed). Part-time programs available. *Faculty:* 17 full-time (7 women), 1 part-time/adjunct (0 women). *Students:* 42 full-time (28 women), 28 part-time (16 women); includes 17 minority (3 Black or African American, non-Hispanic/Latino; 2 Asian, non-Hispanic/Latino; 10 Hispanic/Latino; 2 Two or more races, non-Hispanic/Latino), 5 international. Average age 33. 27 applicants, 56% accepted, 11 enrolled. In 2011, 17 master's awarded. *Degree requirements:* For master's, comprehensive exam, thesis (for some programs). *Entrance requirements:* For master's, GRE General Test, minimum GPA of 2.75 in last 60 hours of course work. Additional exam requirements/recommendations for international students: Required—TOEFL (minimum score 550 paper-based; 213 computer-based; 78 iBT). *Application deadline:* For fall admission, 6/15 priority date for domestic students, 6/1 for international students; for spring admission, 10/15 priority date for domestic students, 10/1 for international students. Applications are processed on a rolling basis. Application fee: $40 ($90 for international students). Electronic applications accepted. *Expenses:* Tuition, state resident: full-time $6408; part-time $3204 per semester. Tuition, nonresident: full-time $14,832; part-time $7416 per semester. *Required fees:* $1824; $912 per semester. Tuition and fees vary according to course load. *Financial support:* In 2011–12, 26 students received support, including 6 research assistantships (averaging $20,592 per year), 26 teaching assistantships (averaging $21,258 per year); Federal Work-Study and institutionally sponsored loans also available. Support available to part-time students. Financial award application deadline: 4/1; financial award applicants required to submit FAFSA. *Faculty research:* Dynamic geometry, mathematics education, Route Protocos, Mathworks 3m podcast, math initiative, MST Teacher Prep. *Total annual research expenditures:* $1.2 million. *Unit head:* Dr. Nathaniel Dean, Jr., Chair, 512-245-3555, Fax: 512-245-3425, E-mail: nd17@txstate.edu. *Application contact:* Dr. Gregory Passty, Graduate Adviser, 512-245-3446, Fax: 512-245-3425, E-mail: passty@txstate.edu. Web site: http://www.math.txstate.edu/.

Texas Tech University, Graduate School, College of Arts and Sciences, Department of Mathematics and Statistics, Lubbock, TX 79409. Offers mathematics (MA, MS, PhD); statistics (MS). Part-time programs available. Postbaccalaureate distance learning degree programs offered (minimal on-campus study). *Faculty:* 45 full-time (8 women). *Students:* 107 full-time (48 women), 10 part-time (3 women); includes 9 minority (1 Black or African American, non-Hispanic/Latino; 2 Asian, non-Hispanic/Latino; 4 Hispanic/Latino; 2 Two or more races, non-Hispanic/Latino), 62 international. Average age 28. 92 applicants, 71% accepted, 29 enrolled. In 2011, 35 master's, 8 doctorates awarded. *Degree requirements:* For master's, thesis or alternative; for doctorate, comprehensive exam, thesis/dissertation. *Entrance requirements:* For master's and doctorate, GRE General Test. Additional exam requirements/recommendations for international students: Required—TOEFL (minimum score 550 paper-based; 213 computer-based; 79 iBT). *Application deadline:* For fall admission, 6/1 priority date for domestic students, 1/15 for international students; for spring admission, 9/1 priority date for domestic students, 6/15 for international students. Applications are processed on a rolling basis. Application fee: $50 ($75 for international students). Electronic applications accepted. *Expenses:* Tuition, state resident: full-time $5899; part-time $245.80 per credit hour. Tuition, nonresident: full-time $13,411; part-time $558.80 per credit hour. *Required fees:* $2680.60; $86.50 per credit hour. $920.30 per semester. *Financial support:* In 2011–12, 41 students received support. Application deadline: 4/15; applicants required to submit FAFSA. *Faculty research:* Numerical analysis, mathematical biology, complex analysis, algebra and geometry, ordinary and partial differential equations. *Total annual research expenditures:* $2.2 million. *Unit head:* Dr. Kent Pearce, Chair, 806-742-2566, Fax: 806-742-1112, E-mail: kent.pearce@ttu.edu.

Application contact: Dr. Ram Iyer, Graduate Adviser, 806-742-2566, Fax: 806-742-1112, E-mail: ram.iyer@ttu.edu. Web site: http://www.math.ttu.edu/.

Texas Woman's University, Graduate School, College of Arts and Sciences, Department of Mathematics and Computer Science, Denton, TX 76201. Offers mathematics (MA, MS); mathematics teaching (MS). Part-time and evening/weekend programs available. *Faculty:* 11 full-time (9 women), 1 part-time/adjunct (0 women). *Students:* 9 full-time (7 women), 37 part-time (30 women); includes 13 minority (1 Black or African American, non-Hispanic/Latino; 4 Asian, non-Hispanic/Latino; 8 Hispanic/Latino), 1 international. Average age 35. 10 applicants, 90% accepted, 8 enrolled. In 2011, 6 master's awarded. *Degree requirements:* For master's, comprehensive exam, thesis. *Entrance requirements:* For master's, 2 letters of reference. Additional exam requirements/recommendations for international students: Required—TOEFL (minimum score 550 paper-based; 213 computer-based; 79 iBT). *Application deadline:* For fall admission, 7/1 priority date for domestic students, 3/1 for international students; for spring admission, 12/1 priority date for domestic students, 7/1 for international students. Applications are processed on a rolling basis. Application fee: $50 ($75 for international students). Electronic applications accepted. *Expenses:* Tuition, state resident: full-time $3834; part-time $213 per credit hour. Tuition, nonresident: full-time $9468; part-time $526 per credit hour. *Required fees:* $213 per credit hour. Tuition and fees vary according to course load. *Financial support:* In 2011–12, 13 students received support, including 4 research assistantships (averaging $13,248 per year), 7 teaching assistantships (averaging $13,248 per year); career-related internships or fieldwork, Federal Work-Study, institutionally sponsored loans, scholarships/grants, traineeships, health care benefits, and unspecified assistantships also available. Support available to part-time students. Financial award application deadline: 3/1; financial award applicants required to submit FAFSA. *Faculty research:* Biopharmaceutical statistics, dynamic systems and control theory, Bayesian inference, math and computer science curriculum innovation, computer modeling of physical phehomenon. *Unit head:* Dr. Don E. Edwards, Chair, 940-898-2166, Fax: 940-898-2179, E-mail: mathcs@twu.edu. *Application contact:* Dr. Samuel Wheeler, Assistant Director of Admissions, 940-898-3188, Fax: 940-898-3081, E-mail: wheelersr@twu.edu. Web site: http://www.twu.edu/math-computer-science/.

Tufts University, Graduate School of Arts and Sciences, Department of Mathematics, Medford, MA 02155. Offers MA, MS, PhD. *Faculty:* 20 full-time, 5 part-time/adjunct. *Students:* 38 full-time (18 women); includes 3 minority (1 Black or African American, non-Hispanic/Latino; 2 Asian, non-Hispanic/Latino), 9 international. Average age 27. 71 applicants, 37% accepted, 13 enrolled. In 2011, 7 master's, 3 doctorates awarded. Terminal master's awarded for partial completion of doctoral program. *Degree requirements:* For master's, one foreign language, thesis; for doctorate, 2 foreign languages, thesis/dissertation. *Entrance requirements:* For master's, GRE General Test; for doctorate, GRE General Test, GRE Subject Tests. Additional exam requirements/recommendations for international students: Required—TOEFL (minimum score 550 paper-based; 213 computer-based; 80 iBT). *Application deadline:* For fall admission, 1/15 for domestic students, 12/15 for international students. Applications are processed on a rolling basis. Application fee: $75. Electronic applications accepted. *Expenses: Tuition:* Full-time $41,208; part-time $1030 per credit hour. Full-time tuition and fees vary according to degree level, program and student level. Part-time tuition and fees vary according to course load. *Financial support:* Fellowships, research assistantships, teaching assistantships with full tuition reimbursements, Federal Work-Study, scholarships/grants, tuition waivers (partial), and unspecified assistantships available. Financial award application deadline: 1/15; financial award applicants required to submit FAFSA. *Unit head:* Boris Hasselblatt, Chair, 617-627-3234, E-mail: mathgrad@tufts.edu. *Application contact:* Kim Ruane, Graduate Advisor, 617-627-3234, E-mail: mathgrad@tufts.edu. Web site: http://www.tufts.edu/as/math/.

Tulane University, School of Science and Engineering, Department of Mathematics, New Orleans, LA 70118-5669. Offers applied mathematics (MS); mathematics (MS, PhD); statistics (MS). *Degree requirements:* For master's, thesis (for some programs); for doctorate, thesis/dissertation. *Entrance requirements:* For master's, GRE General Test, minimum B average in undergraduate course work; for doctorate, GRE General Test. Additional exam requirements/recommendations for international students: Required—TOEFL. Electronic applications accepted.

Université de Moncton, Faculty of Sciences, Department of Mathematics and Statistics, Moncton, NB E1A 3E9, Canada. Offers mathematics (M Sc). *Degree requirements:* For master's, one foreign language, thesis. *Entrance requirements:* For master's, minimum GPA of 3.0. Electronic applications accepted. *Faculty research:* Statistics, numerical analysis, fixed point theory, mathematical physics.

Université de Montréal, Faculty of Arts and Sciences, Department of Mathematics and Statistics, Montréal, QC H3C 3J7, Canada. Offers mathematical and computational finance (M Sc, DESS); mathematics (M Sc, PhD); statistics (M Sc, PhD). *Degree requirements:* For master's, thesis; for doctorate, thesis/dissertation, general exam. *Entrance requirements:* For master's and doctorate, proficiency in French. Electronic applications accepted. *Faculty research:* Pure and applied mathematics, actuarial mathematics.

Université de Sherbrooke, Faculty of Sciences, Department of Mathematics, Sherbrooke, QC J1K 2R1, Canada. Offers M Sc, PhD. *Degree requirements:* For master's, thesis; for doctorate, comprehensive exam, thesis/dissertation. *Entrance requirements:* For doctorate, master's degree. Electronic applications

Peterson's Graduate Programs in the Physical Sciences, Mathematics, Agricultural Sciences, the Environment & Natural Resources 2013

accepted. *Faculty research:* Measure theory, differential equations, probability, statistics, error control codes.

Université du Québec à Montréal, Graduate Programs, Program in Mathematics, Montréal, QC H3C 3P8, Canada. Offers M Sc, PhD. Part-time programs available. *Degree requirements:* For master's, thesis; for doctorate, thesis/dissertation. *Entrance requirements:* For master's, appropriate bachelor's degree or equivalent, proficiency in French; for doctorate, appropriate master's degree or equivalent, proficiency in French.

Université du Québec à Trois-Rivières, Graduate Programs, Program in Mathematics and Computer Science, Trois-Rivières, QC G9A 5H7, Canada. Offers M Sc. *Faculty research:* Probability, statistics.

Université Laval, Faculty of Sciences and Engineering, Department of Mathematics and Statistics, Programs in Mathematics, Québec, QC G1K 7P4, Canada. Offers M Sc, PhD. Terminal master's awarded for partial completion of doctoral program. *Degree requirements:* For master's, thesis (for some programs); for doctorate, comprehensive exam, thesis/dissertation. *Entrance requirements:* For master's and doctorate, knowledge of French and English. Electronic applications accepted.

University at Albany, State University of New York, College of Arts and Sciences, Department of Mathematics and Statistics, Albany, NY 12222-0001. Offers mathematics (PhD); secondary teaching (MA); statistics (MA). *Degree requirements:* For doctorate, one foreign language, thesis/dissertation. *Entrance requirements:* For doctorate, GRE General Test. Additional exam requirements/recommendations for international students: Required—TOEFL (minimum score 550 paper-based; 213 computer-based). Electronic applications accepted.

University at Buffalo, the State University of New York, Graduate School, College of Arts and Sciences, Department of Mathematics, Buffalo, NY 14260. Offers MA, PhD. *Faculty:* 34 full-time (3 women), 17 part-time/adjunct (7 women). *Students:* 74 full-time (24 women); includes 24 minority (23 Asian, non-Hispanic/Latino; 1 Hispanic/Latino). Average age 29. 81 applicants, 33% accepted, 24 enrolled. In 2011, 16 master's, 9 doctorates awarded. Terminal master's awarded for partial completion of doctoral program. *Degree requirements:* For master's, comprehensive exam (for some programs), thesis (for some programs), project (for some programs); for doctorate, comprehensive exam, thesis/dissertation. *Entrance requirements:* Additional exam requirements/recommendations for international students: Required—TOEFL (minimum score 550 paper-based; 213 computer-based; 79 iBT). *Application deadline:* For fall admission, 1/15 priority date for domestic students, 1/15 for international students; for spring admission, 9/15 priority date for domestic students, 9/15 for international students. Applications are processed on a rolling basis. Application fee: $75. Electronic applications accepted. *Financial support:* In 2011–12, 33 students received support, including fellowships with full tuition reimbursements available (averaging $4,000 per year), 50 teaching assistantships with full tuition reimbursements available (averaging $16,188 per year); research assistantships, Federal Work-Study, institutionally sponsored loans, and unspecified assistantships also available. Financial award application deadline: 1/15; financial award applicants required to submit FAFSA. *Faculty research:* Algebra, analysis, applied mathematics, logic, number theory, topology. *Total annual research expenditures:* $354,932. *Unit head:* Dr. Brian D. Hassard, Chairman, 716-645-8780, Fax: 716-645-5039, E-mail: chair@math.buffalo.edu. *Application contact:* Dr. Gino Biondini, Director of Graduate Studies, 716-645-8783, Fax: 716-645-5039, E-mail: graduatedirector@math.buffalo.edu. Web site: http://www.math.buffalo.edu/.

The University of Akron, Graduate School, Buchtel College of Arts and Sciences, Department of Mathematics, Program in Mathematics, Akron, OH 44325. Offers MS. Part-time and evening/weekend programs available. *Students:* 18 full-time (2 women), 3 part-time (2 women); includes 3 minority (2 Black or African American, non-Hispanic/Latino; 1 Two or more races, non-Hispanic/Latino). Average age 26. 7 applicants, 86% accepted, 3 enrolled. In 2011, 1 master's awarded. *Degree requirements:* For master's, thesis optional, seminar and comprehensive exam or thesis. *Entrance requirements:* For master's, minimum GPA of 2.75, three letters of recommendation, statement of purpose. Additional exam requirements/recommendations for international students: Required—TOEFL (minimum score 550 paper-based; 213 computer-based; 79 iBT). *Application deadline:* Applications are processed on a rolling basis. Application fee: $30 ($40 for international students). Electronic applications accepted. *Expenses:* Tuition, state resident: full-time $7038; part-time $391 per credit hour. Tuition, nonresident: full-time $12,051; part-time $670 per credit hour. *Required fees:* $1274; $34 per credit hour. *Unit head:* Dr. Gerald Young, Coordinator, 330-972-5731, E-mail: gyoung1@uakron.edu. *Application contact:* Associate Dean. Web site: http://www.uakron.edu/math/academics/graduate/index.dot.

The University of Alabama, Graduate School, College of Arts and Sciences, Department of Mathematics, Tuscaloosa, AL 35487. Offers applied mathematics (PhD); mathematics (MA, PhD); pure mathematics (PhD). *Faculty:* 27 full-time (0 women). *Students:* 52 full-time (21 women), 9 part-time (4 women); includes 3 minority (all Black or African American, non-Hispanic/Latino), 24 international. Average age 28. 47 applicants, 66% accepted, 12 enrolled. In 2011, 15 master's, 4 doctorates awarded. Terminal master's awarded for partial completion of doctoral program. *Median time to degree:* Of those who began their doctoral program in fall 2003, 85% received their degree in 8 years or less. *Degree requirements:* For master's, thesis or alternative; for doctorate, thesis/dissertation. *Entrance requirements:* For master's and doctorate, GRE General Test, minimum

GPA of 3.0. Additional exam requirements/recommendations for international students: Required—TOEFL (minimum score 550 paper-based; 79 iBT). *Application deadline:* For fall admission, 7/1 for domestic students, 5/31 for international students; for spring admission, 11/30 for domestic students, 10/31 for international students. Applications are processed on a rolling basis. Application fee: $50 ($60 for international students). Electronic applications accepted. *Expenses:* Tuition, state resident: full-time $8600. Tuition, nonresident: full-time $21,900. *Financial support:* In 2011–12, 1 fellowship with full tuition reimbursement (averaging $30,000 per year), 35 teaching assistantships with full tuition reimbursements (averaging $12,258 per year) were awarded; research assistantships with full tuition reimbursements, Federal Work-Study, institutionally sponsored loans, scholarships/grants, and unspecified assistantships also available. Support available to part-time students. Financial award application deadline: 7/1. *Faculty research:* Analysis, topology, algebra, fluid mechanics and system control theory, optimization, stochastic processes, numerical analysis. *Total annual research expenditures:* $135,802. *Unit head:* Dr. Zhijian Wu, Chairperson and Professor, 205-348-5080, Fax: 205-348-7067, E-mail: zwu@as.ua.edu. *Application contact:* Dr. Vo Liem, Director, 205-348-4898, Fax: 205-348-7067, E-mail: vliem@as.ua.edu.

The University of Alabama at Birmingham, College of Arts and Sciences, Program in Mathematics, Birmingham, AL 35294. Offers MS. Terminal master's awarded for partial completion of doctoral program. *Degree requirements:* For master's, thesis optional. *Entrance requirements:* For master's, GRE General Test. *Application deadline:* Applications are processed on a rolling basis. Electronic applications accepted. *Expenses:* Tuition, state resident: full-time $5922; part-time $309 per hour. Tuition, nonresident: full-time $13,428; part-time $726 per hour. Tuition and fees vary according to program. *Financial support:* Fellowships with full tuition reimbursements, research assistantships, teaching assistantships with full tuition reimbursements, career-related internships or fieldwork, Federal Work-Study, institutionally sponsored loans, scholarships/grants, traineeships, health care benefits, tuition waivers (full and partial), and unspecified assistantships available. Support available to part-time students. Financial award application deadline: 8/1; financial award applicants required to submit FAFSA. *Faculty research:* Differential equations, topology, mathematical physics, dynamic systems. *Unit head:* Dr. Rudi Weikard, Chair, 205-934-2154, Fax: 205-934-9025, E-mail: weikard@uab.edu. *Application contact:* Dr. Gunter Stolz, Graduate Recruitment Coordinator/Professor, 205-934-2154, Fax: 205-934-9025, E-mail: stolz@math.uab.edu. Web site: http://www.uab.edu/mathematics/masters-program.

The University of Alabama in Huntsville, School of Graduate Studies, College of Science, Department of Mathematical Sciences, Huntsville, AL 35899. Offers applied mathematics (PhD); education (MA, MS); mathematics (MA, MS). PhD offered jointly with The University of Alabama (Tuscaloosa) and The University of Alabama at Birmingham. Part-time and evening/weekend programs available. *Faculty:* 15 full-time (1 woman), 1 part-time/adjunct (0 women). *Students:* 17 full-time (8 women), 10 part-time (6 women); includes 5 minority (3 Black or African American, non-Hispanic/Latino; 1 Asian, non-Hispanic/Latino; 1 Hispanic/Latino), 5 international. Average age 28. 21 applicants, 62% accepted, 6 enrolled. In 2011, 5 master's, 1 doctorate awarded. *Degree requirements:* For master's, comprehensive exam, thesis or alternative, oral and written exams; for doctorate, comprehensive exam, thesis/dissertation, oral and written exams. *Entrance requirements:* For master's and doctorate, GRE General Test, minimum GPA of 3.0. Additional exam requirements/recommendations for international students: Required—TOEFL (minimum score 550 paper-based; 213 computer-based; 62 iBT). *Application deadline:* For fall admission, 7/15 for domestic students, 4/1 for international students; for spring admission, 11/30 for domestic students, 9/1 for international students. Applications are processed on a rolling basis. Application fee: $40 ($50 for international students). Electronic applications accepted. *Expenses:* Tuition, state resident: full-time $7830; part-time $473.50 per credit. Tuition, nonresident: full-time $18,748; part-time $1128.33 per credit. Tuition and fees vary according to course load and program. *Financial support:* In 2011–12, 14 students received support, including 1 fellowship with full tuition reimbursement available (averaging $10,000 per year), 1 research assistantship with full tuition reimbursement available (averaging $10,000 per year), 13 teaching assistantships with full tuition reimbursements available (averaging $10,314 per year); career-related internships or fieldwork, Federal Work-Study, institutionally sponsored loans, scholarships/grants, health care benefits, and unspecified assistantships also available. Support available to part-time students. Financial award application deadline: 4/1; financial award applicants required to submit FAFSA. *Faculty research:* Dynamical systems, mathematical biology, stochastic processes, numerical analysis, combinatorics. *Total annual research expenditures:* $222,669. *Unit head:* Dr. Jia Li, Chair, 256-824-6470, Fax: 256-824-6173, E-mail: li@math.uah.edu. *Application contact:* Kim Gray, Graduate Studies Admissions Coordinator, 256-824-6002, Fax: 256-824-6405, E-mail: deangrad@uah.edu. Web site: http://www.math.uah.edu/.

University of Alaska Fairbanks, College of Natural Sciences and Mathematics, Department of Mathematics and Statistics, Fairbanks, AK 99775-6660. Offers mathematics (MAT, PhD); statistics (MS, Graduate Certificate). Part-time programs available. *Faculty:* 14 full-time (6 women), 1 (woman) part-time/adjunct. *Students:* 7 full-time (2 women), 3 part-time (2 women), 4 international. Average age 27. 18 applicants, 39% accepted, 5 enrolled. In 2011, 1 master's, 4 doctorates awarded. Terminal master's awarded for partial completion of doctoral program. *Degree requirements:* For master's, comprehensive exam, thesis or alternative; for doctorate, comprehensive exam, thesis/dissertation, oral defense.

Peterson's Graduate Programs in the Physical Sciences, Mathematics, Agricultural Sciences, the Environment & Natural Resources 2013

facebook.com/petersonspublishing **349**

Entrance requirements: Additional exam requirements/recommendations for international students: Required—TOEFL (minimum score 550 paper-based; 213 computer-based; 80 iBT). *Application deadline:* For fall admission, 6/1 for domestic students, 3/1 for international students; for spring admission, 10/15 for domestic students, 9/1 for international students. Applications are processed on a rolling basis. Application fee: $60. Electronic applications accepted. *Expenses:* Tuition, state resident: full-time $6696; part-time $372 per credit. Tuition, nonresident: full-time $13,680; part-time $760 per credit. Tuition and fees vary according to course load and reciprocity agreements. *Financial support:* In 2011–12, 1 research assistantship with tuition reimbursement (averaging $8,313 per year), 5 teaching assistantships with tuition reimbursements (averaging $17,550 per year) were awarded; fellowships with tuition reimbursements, career-related internships or fieldwork, Federal Work-Study, scholarships/grants, health care benefits, and unspecified assistantships also available. Support available to part-time students. Financial award application deadline: 2/15; financial award applicants required to submit FAFSA. *Faculty research:* Kriging, arrangements of hyperplanes, bifurcation analysis of time-periodic differential-delay equations, inverse problems, phylogenic tree construction. *Total annual research expenditures:* $22,000. *Unit head:* Dr. John Rhodes, Department Chair, 907-474-7332, Fax: 907-474-5394, E-mail: fymath@uaf.edu. *Application contact:* Mike Earnest, Director of Admissions, 907-474-7500, Fax: 907-474-5379, E-mail: admissions@uaf.edu. Web site: http://www.dms.uaf.edu/.

University of Alberta, Faculty of Graduate Studies and Research, Department of Mathematical and Statistical Sciences, Edmonton, AB T6G 2E1, Canada. Offers applied mathematics (M Sc, PhD); biostatistics (M Sc); mathematical finance (M Sc, PhD); mathematical physics (M Sc, PhD); mathematics (M Sc, PhD); statistics (M Sc, PhD, Postgraduate Diploma). Part-time programs available. Terminal master's awarded for partial completion of doctoral program. *Degree requirements:* For master's, thesis (for some programs); for doctorate, comprehensive exam, thesis/dissertation. *Entrance requirements:* Additional exam requirements/recommendations for international students: Required—TOEFL (minimum score 580 paper-based; 237 computer-based). Electronic applications accepted. *Faculty research:* Classical and functional analysis, algebra, differential equations, geometry.

The University of Arizona, College of Science, Department of Mathematics, Tucson, AZ 85721. Offers mathematical sciences (PMS), including applied science and business; mathematics (MA, MS, PhD). Part-time programs available. *Faculty:* 52 full-time (7 women), 6 part-time/adjunct (1 woman). *Students:* 60 full-time (16 women), 7 part-time (3 women); includes 6 minority (1 Asian, non-Hispanic/Latino; 2 Hispanic/Latino; 3 Two or more races, non-Hispanic/Latino), 18 international. Average age 30. 98 applicants, 31% accepted, 13 enrolled. In 2011, 15 master's, 3 doctorates awarded. *Degree requirements:* For master's, thesis; for doctorate, 2 foreign languages, thesis/dissertation. *Entrance requirements:* For master's, GRE; for doctorate, GRE, statement of purpose. Additional exam requirements/recommendations for international students: Required—TOEFL (minimum score 550 paper-based; 213 computer-based; 79 iBT). *Application deadline:* For fall admission, 2/1 for domestic students, 12/1 for international students; for spring admission, 10/1 for domestic students, 6/1 for international students. Applications are processed on a rolling basis. Application fee: $75. Electronic applications accepted. *Expenses:* Tuition, state resident: full-time $10,840. Tuition, nonresident: full-time $25,802. *Financial support:* In 2011–12, 37 research assistantships (averaging $21,837 per year), 44 teaching assistantships (averaging $21,556 per year) were awarded; scholarships/grants, health care benefits, tuition waivers (full and partial), and unspecified assistantships also available. Financial award application deadline: 3/5. *Faculty research:* Algebra/number theory, computational science, dynamical systems, geometry, analysis. *Total annual research expenditures:* $4.2 million. *Unit head:* Department Head's Office, 520-621-2713. *Application contact:* Sandy Sutton, Graduate Coordinator, 520-621-2068, Fax: 520-621-8322, E-mail: gradoffice@math.arizona.edu. Web site: http://math.arizona.edu/.

The University of Arizona, Graduate Interdisciplinary Programs, Graduate Interdisciplinary Program in Applied Mathematics, Tucson, AZ 85721. Offers applied mathematics (MS, PhD); mathematical sciences (PMS). *Students:* 49 full-time (14 women), 2 part-time; includes 6 minority (2 Asian, non-Hispanic/Latino; 3 Hispanic/Latino; 1 Two or more races, non-Hispanic/Latino), 3 international. Average age 27. 108 applicants, 10% accepted, 11 enrolled. In 2011, 5 master's, 3 doctorates awarded. Terminal master's awarded for partial completion of doctoral program. *Degree requirements:* For master's, thesis (for some programs); for doctorate, comprehensive exam, thesis/dissertation. *Entrance requirements:* For master's, GRE, 3 letters of recommendation; for doctorate, GRE, 3 letters of recommendation, statement of purpose. Additional exam requirements/recommendations for international students: Required—TOEFL (minimum score 575 paper-based; 230 computer-based; 80 iBT). *Application deadline:* For fall admission, 1/15 for domestic students, 1/30 for international students. Applications are processed on a rolling basis. Application fee: $75. Electronic applications accepted. *Expenses:* Tuition, state resident: full-time $10,840. Tuition, nonresident: full-time $25,802. *Financial support:* In 2011–12, 1 research assistantship with full tuition reimbursement (averaging $17,120 per year) was awarded; institutionally sponsored loans, scholarships/grants, health care benefits, tuition waivers (full), and unspecified assistantships also available. Financial award application deadline: 3/1; financial award applicants required to submit FAFSA. *Faculty research:* Dynamical systems and chaos, partial differential equations, pattern formation, fluid dynamics and turbulence, scientific computation, mathematical physics, mathematical biology, medical imaging,

applied probability and stochastic processes. *Unit head:* Dr. Michael Tabor, Head, 520-621-4664, Fax: 520-626-5048, E-mail: tabor@math.arizona.edu. *Application contact:* Graduate Coordinator, 520-621-2016, Fax: 520-626-5048, E-mail: applmath@u.arizona.edu. Web site: http://appliedmath.arizona.edu/.

University of Arkansas, Graduate School, J. William Fulbright College of Arts and Sciences, Department of Mathematical Sciences, Program in Mathematics, Fayetteville, AR 72701-1201. Offers MS, PhD. *Students:* 24 full-time (11 women), 27 part-time (11 women); includes 6 minority (3 Black or African American, non-Hispanic/Latino; 2 Hispanic/Latino; 1 Two or more races, non-Hispanic/Latino), 14 international. In 2011, 2 master's, 3 doctorates awarded. *Degree requirements:* For master's, thesis or alternative; for doctorate, 2 foreign languages, thesis/dissertation. *Application deadline:* For fall admission, 4/1 for international students; for spring admission, 10/1 for international students. Applications are processed on a rolling basis. Application fee: $40 ($50 for international students). Electronic applications accepted. *Financial support:* In 2011–12, 2 research assistantships, 44 teaching assistantships were awarded; fellowships with tuition reimbursements, career-related internships or fieldwork, and Federal Work-Study also available. Support available to part-time students. Financial award application deadline: 4/1; financial award applicants required to submit FAFSA. *Unit head:* Dr. Chaim Goodman-Strauss, Chair, 479-575-3351, Fax: 479-575-8630, E-mail: strauss@uark.edu. *Application contact:* Dr. John Ryan, Graduate Coordinator, 479-575-3351, Fax: 479-575-8630, E-mail: jryan@uark.edu. Web site: http://math.uark.edu/.

University of Arkansas at Little Rock, Graduate School, College of Science and Mathematics, Department of Mathematics and Statistics, Little Rock, AR 72204-1099. Offers applied statistics (Graduate Certificate); mathematical sciences (MS). Part-time and evening/weekend programs available. *Degree requirements:* For master's, comprehensive exam. *Entrance requirements:* For master's, GRE General Test, GRE Subject Test, minimum GPA of 2.7, previous course work in advanced mathematics.

University of Arkansas at Little Rock, Graduate School, College of Science and Mathematics, Program in Integrated Science and Mathematics, Little Rock, AR 72204-1099. Offers MS.

The University of British Columbia, Faculty of Science, Program in Mathematics, Vancouver, BC V6T 1Z2, Canada. Offers M Sc, MA, PhD. Part-time programs available. *Degree requirements:* For master's, thesis or alternative, essay, qualifying exam; for doctorate, comprehensive exam, thesis/dissertation, qualifying exam, thesis proposal. *Entrance requirements:* Additional exam requirements/recommendations for international students: Required—TOEFL (minimum score 600 paper-based; 250 computer-based; 100 iBT). Electronic applications accepted. *Faculty research:* Applied mathematics, financial mathematics, pure mathematics.

University of Calgary, Faculty of Graduate Studies, Faculty of Science, Department of Mathematics and Statistics, Calgary, AB T2N 1N4, Canada. Offers M Sc, PhD. *Degree requirements:* For master's, comprehensive exam, thesis; for doctorate, thesis/dissertation, candidacy exam, preliminary exams. *Entrance requirements:* For master's, honors degree in applied math, pure math, or statistics; for doctorate, MA or M Sc. Additional exam requirements/recommendations for international students: Required—TOEFL (minimum score 600 paper-based; 250 computer-based) or IELTS (minimum score 7). *Faculty research:* Combinatorics, applied mathematics, statistics, probability, analysis.

University of California, Berkeley, Graduate Division, College of Letters and Science, Department of Mathematics, Berkeley, CA 94720-1500. Offers applied mathematics (PhD); mathematics (MA, PhD). Terminal master's awarded for partial completion of doctoral program. *Degree requirements:* For master's, exam or thesis; for doctorate, 2 foreign languages, thesis/dissertation, qualifying exam. *Entrance requirements:* For master's and doctorate, GRE General Test, GRE Subject Test, minimum GPA of 3.0, 3 letters of recommendation. *Faculty research:* Algebra, analysis, logic, geometry/topology.

University of California, Davis, Graduate Studies, Program in Mathematics, Davis, CA 95616. Offers MA, MAT, PhD. Terminal master's awarded for partial completion of doctoral program. *Degree requirements:* For master's, comprehensive exam; for doctorate, one foreign language, thesis/dissertation. *Entrance requirements:* For master's and doctorate, GRE General Test, GRE Subject Test, minimum GPA of 3.0. Additional exam requirements/recommendations for international students: Required—TOEFL (minimum score 550 paper-based; 213 computer-based). Electronic applications accepted. *Faculty research:* Mathematical physics, geometric topology, probability, partial differential equations, applied mathematics.

University of California, Irvine, School of Physical Sciences, Department of Mathematics, Irvine, CA 92697. Offers MS, PhD. *Students:* 111 full-time (29 women), 1 part-time (0 women); includes 23 minority (2 Black or African American, non-Hispanic/Latino; 16 Asian, non-Hispanic/Latino; 3 Hispanic/Latino; 2 Two or more races, non-Hispanic/Latino), 48 international. Average age 27. 263 applicants, 21% accepted, 25 enrolled. In 2011, 13 master's, 14 doctorates awarded. *Degree requirements:* For doctorate, thesis/dissertation. *Entrance requirements:* For master's and doctorate, GRE General Test, GRE Subject Test, minimum GPA of 3.0. Additional exam requirements/recommendations for international students: Required—TOEFL (minimum score 550 paper-based; 213 computer-based). *Application deadline:* For fall admission, 1/15 priority date for domestic students, 1/15 for international students. Applications are processed on

350 facebook.com/petersonspublishing

Peterson's Graduate Programs in the Physical Sciences, Mathematics, Agricultural Sciences, the Environment & Natural Resources 2013

a rolling basis. Application fee: $80 ($100 for international students). Electronic applications accepted. *Financial support:* Fellowships, research assistantships with full tuition reimbursements, teaching assistantships, institutionally sponsored loans, traineeships, health care benefits, and unspecified assistantships available. Financial award application deadline: 3/1; financial award applicants required to submit FAFSA. *Faculty research:* Algebra and logic, geometry and topology, probability, mathematical physics. *Unit head:* Prof. Frederic Yui-Ming Wan, Professor, 949-824-5529, Fax: 949-824-7993, E-mail: fwan@uci.edu. *Application contact:* Donna M. McConnell, Graduate Affairs Officer, 949-824-5544, Fax: 949-824-7993, E-mail: dmcconne@uci.edu. Web site: http://www.math.uci.edu/.

University of California, Los Angeles, Graduate Division, College of Letters and Science, Department of Mathematics, Los Angeles, CA 90095. Offers MA, MAT, PhD. *Faculty:* 49 full-time (4 women). *Students:* 144 full-time (20 women); includes 17 minority (14 Asian, non-Hispanic/Latino; 3 Hispanic/Latino), 43 international. Average age 26. 445 applicants, 15% accepted, 18 enrolled. In 2011, 36 master's, 30 doctorates awarded. Terminal master's awarded for partial completion of doctoral program. *Degree requirements:* For master's, comprehensive exam or thesis; for doctorate, one foreign language, thesis/dissertation, oral and written qualifying exams. *Entrance requirements:* For master's, GRE General Test, GRE Subject Test, minimum GPA of 3.2 in mathematics, 12 quarter courses of upper-division math; for doctorate, GRE General Test, GRE Subject Test, minimum GPA of 3.5 in mathematics, 12 quarter courses of upper-division math. *Application deadline:* For fall admission, 12/15 for domestic students, 11/15 for international students. Application fee: $70 ($90 for international students). Electronic applications accepted. *Financial support:* In 2011–12, 122 fellowships with full and partial tuition reimbursements, 76 research assistantships with full and partial tuition reimbursements, 119 teaching assistantships with full and partial tuition reimbursements were awarded; Federal Work-Study, institutionally sponsored loans, scholarships/grants, health care benefits, tuition waivers (full and partial), and unspecified assistantships also available. Financial award application deadline: 3/1; financial award applicants required to submit FAFSA. *Unit head:* Dr. Sorin Popa, Chair, 310-825-8502, E-mail: popa@math.ucla.edu. *Application contact:* Department Office, 310-825-4971, E-mail: gradapps@math.ucla.edu. Web site: http://www.math.ucla.edu.

University of California, Riverside, Graduate Division, Department of Mathematics, Riverside, CA 92521-0102. Offers MA, MS, PhD. Part-time programs available. *Faculty:* 30 full-time (5 women), 15 part-time/adjunct (4 women). *Students:* 71 full-time (13 women); includes 21 minority (1 Black or African American, non-Hispanic/Latino; 10 Asian, non-Hispanic/Latino; 10 Hispanic/Latino), 2 international. Average age 28. 101 applicants, 12% accepted, 1 enrolled. In 2011, 2 master's, 8 doctorates awarded. Terminal master's awarded for partial completion of doctoral program. *Degree requirements:* For master's, comprehensive exam; for doctorate, thesis/dissertation, qualifying exams. *Entrance requirements:* For master's and doctorate, GRE General Test, minimum GPA of 3.2. Additional exam requirements/recommendations for international students: Required—TOEFL (minimum score 550 paper-based; 213 computer-based; 80 iBT). *Application deadline:* For fall admission, 5/1 for domestic students, 2/1 for international students; for winter admission, 9/1 for domestic students, 7/1 for international students; for spring admission, 12/1 for domestic students, 10/1 for international students. Applications are processed on a rolling basis. Application fee: $80 ($100 for international students). Electronic applications accepted. *Financial support:* In 2011–12, fellowships with tuition reimbursements (averaging $12,000 per year), teaching assistantships with full and partial tuition reimbursements (averaging $16,500 per year) were awarded; research assistantships, career-related internships or fieldwork, Federal Work-Study, institutionally sponsored loans, health care benefits, and tuition waivers (full and partial) also available. Financial award application deadline: 1/5; financial award applicants required to submit FAFSA. *Faculty research:* Algebraic geometry, commutative algebra, Lie algebra, differential equations, differential geometry. *Unit head:* Dr. Vyjayanthi Chari, Chair, 951-827-6463, Fax: 951-827-7314, E-mail: chari@math.ucr.edu. *Application contact:* Krista Anderson, Graduate Program Assistant, 951-827-7378, Fax: 951-827-7314, E-mail: krista@math.ucr.edu. Web site: http://www.math.ucr.edu/.

University of California, San Diego, Office of Graduate Studies, Department of Mathematics, La Jolla, CA 92093. Offers applied mathematics (MA); mathematics (MA, PhD); statistics (MS). *Degree requirements:* For doctorate, thesis/dissertation. *Entrance requirements:* For master's and doctorate, GRE General Test, GRE Subject Test. Electronic applications accepted.

University of California, Santa Barbara, Graduate Division, College of Letters and Sciences, Division of Mathematics, Life, and Physical Sciences, Department of Mathematics, Santa Barbara, CA 93106-3080. Offers applied mathematics (MA), including computational science and engineering; mathematics (MA, PhD), including computational science and engineering; MA/PhD. *Faculty:* 26 full-time (2 women). *Students:* 53 full-time (13 women); includes 9 minority (1 Black or African American, non-Hispanic/Latino; 3 Asian, non-Hispanic/Latino; 5 Hispanic/Latino), 7 international. Average age 26. 186 applicants, 17% accepted, 10 enrolled. In 2011, 7 master's, 3 doctorates awarded. Terminal master's awarded for partial completion of doctoral program. *Median time to degree:* Of those who began their doctoral program in fall 2003, 100% received their degree in 8 years or less. *Degree requirements:* For master's, comprehensive exam (for some programs), thesis (for some programs); for doctorate, comprehensive exam, thesis/dissertation. *Entrance requirements:* For master's and doctorate, GRE General Test, GRE Subject Test (math). Additional exam requirements/

recommendations for international students: Required—TOEFL (minimum score 575 paper-based; 80 iBT), IELTS (minimum score 7). *Application deadline:* For fall admission, 1/1 priority date for domestic students, 1/1 for international students. Application fee: $80 ($100 for international students). Electronic applications accepted. *Expenses:* Tuition, state resident: full-time $12,192. Tuition, nonresident: full-time $27,294. *Required fees:* $764.13. *Financial support:* In 2011–12, 50 students received support, including 15 fellowships with full tuition reimbursements available (averaging $12,740 per year), 12 research assistantships with full tuition reimbursements available (averaging $6,000 per year), 48 teaching assistantships with partial tuition reimbursements available (averaging $17,308 per year); Federal Work-Study, institutionally sponsored loans, health care benefits, and tuition waivers (full and partial) also available. Financial award application deadline: 3/2; financial award applicants required to submit FAFSA. *Faculty research:* Topology, differential geometry, algebra, applied mathematics, partial differential equations. *Total annual research expenditures:* $205,000. *Unit head:* Prof. David R. Morrison, Chair, 805-893-8340, Fax: 805-893-2385, E-mail: chair@math.ucsb.edu. *Application contact:* Medina Price, Graduate Advisor, 805-893-8192, Fax: 805-893-2385, E-mail: price@math.ucsb.edu. Web site: http://www.math.ucsb.edu/.

University of California, Santa Cruz, Division of Graduate Studies, Division of Physical and Biological Sciences, Department of Mathematics, Santa Cruz, CA 95064. Offers MA, PhD. Terminal master's awarded for partial completion of doctoral program. *Degree requirements:* For master's, thesis; for doctorate, one foreign language, thesis/dissertation, qualifying exam. *Entrance requirements:* For doctorate, GRE General Test, GRE Subject Test. Additional exam requirements/recommendations for international students: Required—TOEFL (minimum score 550 paper-based; 220 computer-based; 83 iBT); Recommended—IELTS (minimum score 8). Electronic applications accepted. *Faculty research:* Vertex operator algebras, algebraic topology, elliptic cohomology, quantum field theory, automorphic forms, dynamical systems, celestial mechanics, geometric mechanics, bifurcation theory, control theory, representations of Lie and p-adic groups, applications to number theory, Bessel functions, Rankin-Selberg integrals, Gelfand-Graev models, differential geometry, nonlinear analysis, harmonic maps, Ginzburg-Landau problem.

University of Central Arkansas, Graduate School, College of Natural Sciences and Math, Department of Mathematics, Conway, AR 72035-0001. Offers applied mathematics (MS); math education (MA). Part-time programs available. *Faculty:* 16 full-time (4 women). *Students:* 13 full-time (7 women), 8 part-time (4 women); includes 2 minority (1 Asian, non-Hispanic/Latino; 1 Two or more races, non-Hispanic/Latino), 3 international. Average age 29. 12 applicants, 92% accepted, 8 enrolled. In 2011, 7 master's awarded. *Degree requirements:* For master's, comprehensive exam, thesis optional. *Entrance requirements:* For master's, GRE General Test, minimum GPA of 2.7. Additional exam requirements/recommendations for international students: Required—TOEFL (minimum score 550 paper-based; 213 computer-based). *Application deadline:* For fall admission, 3/1 priority date for domestic students; for spring admission, 10/1 priority date for domestic students. Applications are processed on a rolling basis. Application fee: $25 ($50 for international students). *Expenses:* Tuition, state resident: full-time $4834; part-time $398.35 per credit hour. Tuition, nonresident: full-time $8686. *Financial support:* In 2011–12, 11 teaching assistantships with partial tuition reimbursements (averaging $8,500 per year) were awarded; Federal Work-Study, scholarships/grants, and unspecified assistantships also available. Financial award application deadline: 2/15; financial award applicants required to submit FAFSA. *Unit head:* Dr. Ramesh Garimella, Chair, 501-450-3147, Fax: 501-450-5662, E-mail: rameshg@uca.edu. *Application contact:* Susan Wood, Admissions Assistant, 501-450-3124, Fax: 501-450-5678, E-mail: swood@uca.edu. Web site: http://uca.edu/math/.

University of Central Florida, College of Sciences, Department of Mathematics, Orlando, FL 32816. Offers applied mathematics (Certificate); mathematical science (MS); mathematics (PhD). Part-time and evening/weekend programs available. *Faculty:* 43 full-time (7 women), 5 part-time/adjunct (0 women). *Students:* 50 full-time (17 women), 25 part-time (11 women); includes 13 minority (2 Black or African American, non-Hispanic/Latino; 2 Asian, non-Hispanic/Latino; 9 Hispanic/Latino), 18 international. Average age 32. 89 applicants, 55% accepted, 23 enrolled. In 2011, 9 master's, 2 doctorates awarded. *Degree requirements:* For master's, thesis or alternative; for doctorate, thesis/dissertation, candidacy exam. *Entrance requirements:* For master's, GRE General Test, minimum GPA of 3.0 in last 60 hours; for doctorate, GRE Subject Test, minimum GPA of 3.0 in last 60 hours or master's qualifying exam. Additional exam requirements/recommendations for international students: Required—TOEFL. *Application deadline:* For fall admission, 7/15 for domestic students; for spring admission, 12/1 for domestic students. Application fee: $30. Electronic applications accepted. *Expenses:* Tuition, state resident: part-time $277.08 per credit hour. Tuition, nonresident: part-time $277.08 per credit hour. Part-time tuition and fees vary according to degree level and program. *Financial support:* In 2011–12, 39 students received support, including 5 fellowships with partial tuition reimbursements available (averaging $11,000 per year), 1 research assistantship with partial tuition reimbursement available (averaging $15,800 per year), 40 teaching assistantships with partial tuition reimbursements available (averaging $11,600 per year); career-related internships or fieldwork, Federal Work-Study, institutionally sponsored loans, tuition waivers (partial), and unspecified assistantships also available. Financial award application deadline: 3/1; financial award applicants required to submit FAFSA. *Faculty research:* Applied mathematics, analysis, approximation theory, graph theory, mathematical

Peterson's Graduate Programs in the Physical Sciences, Mathematics, Agricultural Sciences, the Environment & Natural Resources 2013

facebook.com/petersonspublishing **351**

Mathematics

statistics. *Unit head:* Dr. Piotr Mikusinski, Chair, 407-823-6284, Fax: 407-823-6253, E-mail: piotr.mikusinski@mail.ucf.edu. *Application contact:* Barbara Rodriguez, Director, Admissions and Registration, 407-823-2766, Fax: 407-823-6442, E-mail: gradadmissions@ucf.edu. Web site: http://www.math.ucf.edu/.

University of Central Missouri, The Graduate School, College of Science and Technology, Warrensburg, MO 64093. Offers applied mathematics (MS); aviation safety (MS); biology (MS); computer science (MS); environmental studies (MA); industrial management (MS); mathematics (MS); technology (MS); technology management (PhD). PhD is offered jointly with Indiana State University. Part-time programs available. Postbaccalaureate distance learning degree programs offered. *Entrance requirements:* Additional exam requirements/recommendations for international students: Required—TOEFL (minimum score 550 paper-based; 79 computer-based). Electronic applications accepted.

University of Central Oklahoma, College of Graduate Studies and Research, College of Mathematics and Science, Department of Mathematics and Statistics, Edmond, OK 73034-5209. Offers applied mathematical sciences (MS), including computer science, mathematics, mathematics/computer science teaching, statistics. Part-time programs available. *Faculty:* 7 full-time (4 women), 3 part-time/adjunct (0 women). *Students:* 20 full-time (7 women), 11 part-time (8 women); includes 5 minority (3 Black or African American, non-Hispanic/Latino; 2 Two or more races, non-Hispanic/Latino), 11 international. Average age 29. In 2011, 5 master's awarded. *Degree requirements:* For master's, thesis. *Entrance requirements:* Additional exam requirements/recommendations for international students: Required—TOEFL (minimum score 550 paper-based; 213 computer-based). *Application deadline:* Applications are processed on a rolling basis. Application fee: $50. Electronic applications accepted. *Expenses:* Tuition, state resident: full-time $3901; part-time $218.30 per credit hour. Tuition, nonresident: full-time $9198; part-time $511.20 per credit hour. Tuition and fees vary according to program. *Financial support:* Federal Work-Study and unspecified assistantships available. Financial award application deadline: 3/31; financial award applicants required to submit FAFSA. *Faculty research:* Curvature, FAA, math education. *Unit head:* Dr. Michael Fulkerson, 405-974-5575, E-mail: mfulkerson@uco.edu. *Application contact:* Dr. Richard Bernard, Adviser, 405-974-3493, Fax: 405-974-3824, E-mail: jyates@aix1.uco.edu. Web site: http://www.ucok.edu/graduate.applied.htm.

University of Chicago, Division of the Physical Sciences, Department of Mathematics, Chicago, IL 60637-1513. Offers applied mathematics (SM, PhD); financial mathematics (MS); mathematics (SM, PhD). *Faculty:* 58 full-time (9 women). *Students:* 88 full-time (22 women), 40 international. 423 applicants, 13% accepted, 17 enrolled. In 2011, 15 master's, 17 doctorates awarded. *Degree requirements:* For master's, one foreign language; for doctorate, one foreign language, thesis/dissertation, 2 qualifying exams, oral topic presentation. *Entrance requirements:* For master's and doctorate, GRE General Test, GRE Subject Test. Additional exam requirements/recommendations for international students: Required—TOEFL (minimum score 600 paper-based; 250 computer-based). *Application deadline:* For fall admission, 1/5 for domestic and international students. Application fee: $55. Electronic applications accepted. *Financial support:* In 2011–12, 40 fellowships, 48 teaching assistantships were awarded; research assistantships, career-related internships or fieldwork, institutionally sponsored loans, and scholarships/grants also available. Financial award application deadline: 1/5; financial award applicants required to submit CSS PROFILE or FAFSA. *Faculty research:* Analysis, differential geometry, algebra number theory, topology, algebraic geometry. *Unit head:* Dr. Shmuel Weinberger, Chair, 773-702-7349, Fax: 773-702-9787. *Application contact:* Laurie Wail, Graduate Studies Administrator, 773-702-7358, Fax: 773-702-9787, E-mail: lwail@math.uchicago.edu. Web site: http://www.math.uchicago.edu/.

University of Cincinnati, Graduate School, McMicken College of Arts and Sciences, Department of Mathematical Sciences, Cincinnati, OH 45221. Offers applied mathematics (MS, PhD); mathematics education (MAT); pure mathematics (MS, PhD); statistics (MS, PhD). Part-time programs available. Terminal master's awarded for partial completion of doctoral program. *Degree requirements:* For master's, comprehensive exam, thesis or alternative; for doctorate, one foreign language, comprehensive exam, thesis/dissertation. *Entrance requirements:* For master's, GRE, teacher certification (MAT); for doctorate, GRE. Additional exam requirements/recommendations for international students: Required—TOEFL. Electronic applications accepted. *Faculty research:* Algebra, analysis, differential equations, numerical analysis, statistics.

University of Colorado at Colorado Springs, College of Letters, Arts and Sciences, Department of Mathematics, Colorado Springs, CO 80933-7150. Offers applied mathematics (MS); applied science (PhD); mathematics (M Sc). Part-time and evening/weekend programs available. *Faculty:* 10 full-time (1 woman), 1 (woman) part-time/adjunct. *Students:* 9 full-time (2 women), 8 part-time (3 women); includes 1 minority (Black or African American, non-Hispanic/Latino), 1 international. Average age 34. 2 applicants, 100% accepted, 1 enrolled. In 2011, 4 master's awarded. *Degree requirements:* For master's, thesis, qualifying exam. *Entrance requirements:* For master's, GRE General Test, minimum GPA of 3.0. Additional exam requirements/recommendations for international students: Required—TOEFL (minimum score 550 paper-based; 213 computer-based). *Application deadline:* For fall admission, 6/1 for domestic and international students; for spring admission, 11/1 for domestic and international students. Applications are processed on a rolling basis. Application fee: $60 ($75 for international students). Electronic applications accepted. *Expenses:* Tuition, state resident: part-time $660 per credit hour. Tuition, nonresident: part-time $1133 per

credit hour. Tuition and fees vary according to degree level, program and student level. *Financial support:* In 2011–12, 3 students received support. Teaching assistantships, Federal Work-Study, and scholarships/grants available. Support available to part-time students. Financial award application deadline: 3/1; financial award applicants required to submit FAFSA. *Faculty research:* Abelian groups and noncommutative rings, hormone analysis and computer vision, probability and mathematical physics, stochastic dynamics, probability models. *Total annual research expenditures:* $110,911. *Unit head:* Dr. Sarbarish Chakravarty, Chair, 719-255-3549, Fax: 719-255-3605, E-mail: schakrav@uccs.edu. *Application contact:* Josh Goldman, Graduate Assistant, 719-255-3554, Fax: 719-255-3605, E-mail: jgoldman@uccs.edu. Web site: http://www.uccs.edu/math.

University of Colorado at Colorado Springs, College of Letters, Arts and Sciences, Master of Sciences Program, Colorado Springs, CO 80933-7150. Offers applied science bioscience (M Sc); applied science physics (M Sc); biology (M Sc); chemistry (M Sc); health promotion (M Sc); mathematics (M Sc); physics (M Sc); sports medicine (M Sc); sports nutrition (M Sc). Part-time programs available. *Students:* 13 full-time (5 women), 11 part-time (6 women); includes 3 minority (2 Asian, non-Hispanic/Latino; 1 Hispanic/Latino). Average age 33. 15 applicants, 53% accepted, 3 enrolled. In 2011, 39 degrees awarded. *Degree requirements:* For master's, thesis or alternative. *Entrance requirements:* For master's, minimum GPA of 2.75. Additional exam requirements/recommendations for international students: Recommended—TOEFL. *Application deadline:* For fall admission, 6/1 priority date for domestic students; for spring admission, 12/1 for domestic students. Application fee: $60 ($75 for international students). *Expenses:* Contact institution. *Financial support:* In 2011–12, 5 students received support. Fellowships, research assistantships, teaching assistantships, career-related internships or fieldwork, Federal Work-Study, and scholarships/grants available. Support available to part-time students. Financial award application deadline: 3/1; financial award applicants required to submit FAFSA. *Faculty research:* Biomechanics and physiology of elite athletic training, genetic engineering in yeast and bacteria including phage display and DNA repair, immunology and cell biology, synthetic organic chemistry. *Unit head:* Dr. Tom Christensen, Dean, 719-255-4550, Fax: 719-255-4200, E-mail: tchriste@uccs.edu. *Application contact:* Taryn Bailey, Information Contact, 719-255-3702, Fax: 719-255-3037, E-mail: gradinfo@uccs.edu.

University of Colorado Boulder, Graduate School, College of Arts and Sciences, Department of Mathematics, Boulder, CO 80309. Offers MA, MS, PhD. *Faculty:* 25 full-time (4 women). *Students:* 63 full-time (15 women), 2 part-time (0 women); includes 8 minority (1 Black or African American, non-Hispanic/Latino; 1 American Indian or Alaska Native, non-Hispanic/Latino; 2 Asian, non-Hispanic/Latino; 4 Hispanic/Latino), 8 international. Average age 27. 148 applicants, 21% accepted, 9 enrolled. In 2011, 13 master's, 8 doctorates awarded. Terminal master's awarded for partial completion of doctoral program. *Degree requirements:* For master's, comprehensive exam, thesis or alternative; for doctorate, one foreign language, comprehensive exam, thesis/dissertation, 2 preliminary exams. *Entrance requirements:* For master's, minimum undergraduate GPA of 3.0. *Application deadline:* For fall admission, 1/15 priority date for domestic students, 1/15 for international students; for spring admission, 11/1 for domestic and international students. Applications are processed on a rolling basis. Application fee: $50 ($60 for international students). Electronic applications accepted. *Financial support:* In 2011–12, 76 students received support, including 17 fellowships (averaging $2,124 per year), 1 research assistantship with full and partial tuition reimbursement available (averaging $21,053 per year), 56 teaching assistantships with full and partial tuition reimbursements available (averaging $23,482 per year); institutionally sponsored loans, scholarships/grants, health care benefits, and unspecified assistantships also available. Financial award application deadline: 2/1; financial award applicants required to submit FAFSA. *Faculty research:* Pure mathematics, applied mathematics and mathematical physics (including algebra, algebraic geometry, differential equations, differential geometry, logic and foundations). *Total annual research expenditures:* $307,615. *Application contact:* E-mail: gradmath@colorado.edu. Web site: http://math.colorado.edu/.

University of Colorado Denver, College of Liberal Arts and Sciences, Department of Mathematical and Statistical Sciences, Denver, CO 80217. Offers applied mathematics (MS, PhD), including applied mathematics, applied probability (MS), applied statistics (MS), computational biology, computational mathematics (PhD), discrete mathematics, finite geometry (PhD), mathematics education (PhD), mathematics of engineering and science (MS), numerical analysis, operations research (MS), optimization and operations research (PhD), probability (PhD), statistics (PhD). Part-time programs available. *Faculty:* 26 full-time (4 women), 2 part-time/adjunct (1 woman). *Students:* 44 full-time (14 women), 14 part-time (5 women); includes 6 minority (4 Asian, non-Hispanic/Latino; 2 Hispanic/Latino), 10 international. Average age 33. 66 applicants, 79% accepted, 17 enrolled. In 2011, 6 master's, 6 doctorates awarded. *Degree requirements:* For master's, comprehensive exam, thesis optional, 30 hours of course work with minimum GPA of 3.0; for doctorate, comprehensive exam, thesis/dissertation. *Entrance requirements:* For master's and doctorate, GRE General Test; GRE Subject Test in math (recommended), 30 hours of course work in mathematics (24 of which must be upper-division mathematics), minimum GPA of 3.0. Additional exam requirements/recommendations for international students: Required—TOEFL (minimum score 525 paper-based; 192 computer-based; 71 iBT). *Application deadline:* For fall admission, 4/1 for domestic students, 3/1 for international students; for spring admission, 11/1 for domestic students, 10/1 for international students. Application fee: $50 ($75 for international students). Electronic applications accepted. *Financial support:* Fellowships with partial tuition reimbursements, research assistantships with full tuition reimbursements, teaching assistantships with full tuition reimbursements, Federal Work-Study, scholarships/grants, and unspecified assistantships available. Financial award application deadline: 4/1; financial award applicants required to submit FAFSA. *Faculty research:* Computational mathematics, computational biology, discrete mathematics and geometry, probability and statistics, optimization. *Unit head:* Dr. Stephen Billups, Graduate Chair, 303-556-4814, E-mail: stephen.billups@ucdenver.edu. *Application contact:* Lisa Herbert, Graduate Program Assistant, 303-556-2341, E-mail: lisa.herbert@ucdenver.edu. Web site: http://www.ucdenver.edu/academics/colleges/CLAS/Departments/math/Pages/MathStats.aspx.

University of Colorado Denver, College of Liberal Arts and Sciences, Program in Integrated Sciences, Denver, CO 80217. Offers applied science (MIS); computer science (MIS); mathematics (MIS). Part-time and evening/weekend programs available. *Students:* 5 full-time (3 women), 2 part-time; includes 3 minority (2 Hispanic/Latino; 1 Two or more races, non-Hispanic/Latino). Average age 38. 4 applicants, 25% accepted, 1 enrolled. In 2011, 1 master's awarded. *Degree requirements:* For master's, thesis or alternative, 30 credit hours; thesis or project. *Entrance requirements:* For master's, GRE if undergraduate GPA is 3.0 or less, minimum of 40 semester hours in mathematics, computer science, physics, biology, chemistry and/or geology; essay; three letters of recommendation. Additional exam requirements/recommendations for international students: Required—TOEFL (minimum score 525 paper-based; 197 computer-based; 71 iBT). *Application deadline:* For fall admission, 4/15 for domestic and international students; for spring admission, 10/15 for domestic and international students. Application fee: $50 ($75 for international students). Electronic applications accepted. *Financial support:* Application deadline: 4/1; applicants required to submit FAFSA. *Faculty research:* Computer science, applied science, mathematics. *Unit head:* Dr. Daniel Howard, Professor and Dean, 303-556-2624, Fax: 303-556-4861, E-mail: dan.howard@ucdenver.edu. *Application contact:* 303-556-2557, Fax: 303-556-4861, E-mail: clas@ucdenver.edu. Web site: http://thunder1.cudenver.edu/clas/mis/index.html.

University of Connecticut, Graduate School, College of Liberal Arts and Sciences, Department of Mathematics, Field of Mathematics, Storrs, CT 06269. Offers actuarial science (MS, PhD); mathematics (MS, PhD). Terminal master's awarded for partial completion of doctoral program. *Degree requirements:* For master's, comprehensive exam; for doctorate, thesis/dissertation. *Entrance requirements:* For master's and doctorate, GRE General Test. Additional exam requirements/recommendations for international students: Required—TOEFL (minimum score 550 paper-based; 213 computer-based). Electronic applications accepted.

University of Delaware, College of Arts and Sciences, Department of Mathematical Sciences, Newark, DE 19716. Offers applied mathematics (MS, PhD); mathematics (MS, PhD). Part-time programs available. Terminal master's awarded for partial completion of doctoral program. *Degree requirements:* For master's, thesis (for some programs); for doctorate, one foreign language, thesis/dissertation, qualifying exam. *Entrance requirements:* For master's and doctorate, GRE General Test. Additional exam requirements/recommendations for international students: Required—TOEFL. Electronic applications accepted. *Faculty research:* Scattering theory, inverse problems, fluid dynamics, numerical analysis, combinatorics.

University of Denver, Faculty of Natural Sciences and Mathematics, Department of Mathematics, Denver, CO 80208. Offers MA, MS, PhD. Part-time programs available. *Faculty:* 16 full-time (4 women), 3 part-time/adjunct (2 women). *Students:* 19 part-time (6 women); includes 1 minority (Hispanic/Latino), 7 international. Average age 28. 39 applicants, 87% accepted, 9 enrolled. In 2011, 5 master's, 1 doctorate awarded. Terminal master's awarded for partial completion of doctoral program. *Median time to degree:* Of those who began their doctoral program in fall 2003, 100% received their degree in 8 years or less. *Degree requirements:* For master's, computer language, foreign language, or laboratory experience; for doctorate, one foreign language, comprehensive exam, thesis/dissertation, oral and written exams. *Entrance requirements:* For master's, GRE General Test, BA or BS in mathematics or related field; for doctorate, GRE General Test. Additional exam requirements/recommendations for international students: Required—TOEFL (minimum score 550 paper-based; 80 iBT). *Application deadline:* Applications are processed on a rolling basis. Application fee: $60. Electronic applications accepted. *Financial support:* In 2011–12, 15 students received support, including 14 teaching assistantships with full and partial tuition reimbursements available (averaging $18,300 per year); career-related internships or fieldwork, Federal Work-Study, institutionally sponsored loans, scholarships/grants, and unspecified assistantships also available. Support available to part-time students. Financial award application deadline: 2/15; financial award applicants required to submit FAFSA. *Faculty research:* Real-time software, convex bodies, multidimensional data, parallel computer clusters. *Unit head:* Dr. Nicholas Ormes, Chair, 303-871-3325, Fax: 303-871-3173, E-mail: normes@math.du.edu. *Application contact:* Information Contact, 303-871-2911, Fax: 303-871-3173, E-mail: math-info@math.du.edu. Web site: http://www.du.edu/nsm/departments/mathematics/.

University of Florida, Graduate School, College of Liberal Arts and Sciences, Department of Mathematics, Gainesville, FL 32611. Offers MA, MAT, MS, MST, PhD. Part-time programs available. *Faculty:* 42 full-time (3 women), 1 part-time/adjunct (0 women). *Students:* 106 full-time (36 women), 7 part-time (1 woman);

includes 14 minority (3 Black or African American, non-Hispanic/Latino; 6 Asian, non-Hispanic/Latino; 5 Hispanic/Latino), 40 international. Average age 27. 221 applicants, 14% accepted, 13 enrolled. In 2011, 10 master's, 8 doctorates awarded. Terminal master's awarded for partial completion of doctoral program. *Degree requirements:* For master's, comprehensive exam, thesis optional, first-year exam; for doctorate, one foreign language, comprehensive exam, thesis/dissertation. *Entrance requirements:* For master's and doctorate, GRE General Test, minimum GPA of 3.0. Additional exam requirements/recommendations for international students: Required—TOEFL (minimum score 550 paper-based; 213 computer-based; 80 iBT), IELTS (minimum score 6). *Application deadline:* For fall admission, 6/1 priority date for domestic students. Applications are processed on a rolling basis. Application fee: $30. Electronic applications accepted. *Financial support:* Fellowships, research assistantships, teaching assistantships, career-related internships or fieldwork, and unspecified assistantships available. Financial award applicants required to submit FAFSA. *Faculty research:* Combinatorics and number theory, group theory, probability theory, logic, differential geometry and mathematical physics. *Unit head:* Dr. James E. Keesling, Chairman, 352-392-0281 Ext. 224, Fax: 352-392-8357, E-mail: kees@ufl.edu. *Application contact:* Dr. Paul L. Robinson, Graduate Coordinator, 352-392-0281 Ext. 223, Fax: 352-392-8357, E-mail: paulr@ufl.edu. Web site: http://www.math.ufl.edu/gradprog/.

University of Georgia, Franklin College of Arts and Sciences, Department of Mathematics, Athens, GA 30602. Offers applied mathematical science (MAMS); mathematics (MA, PhD). *Faculty:* 31 full-time (4 women). *Students:* 56 full-time (17 women); includes 6 minority (1 Black or African American, non-Hispanic/Latino; 3 Asian, non-Hispanic/Latino; 2 Hispanic/Latino), 13 international. Average age 27. 126 applicants, 24% accepted, 14 enrolled. In 2011, 11 master's, 3 doctorates awarded. *Degree requirements:* For master's, one foreign language, thesis (for some programs); for doctorate, 2 foreign languages, thesis/dissertation. *Entrance requirements:* For master's and doctorate, GRE General Test. *Application deadline:* For fall admission, 7/1 priority date for domestic students; for spring admission, 11/15 for domestic students. Application fee: $50. Electronic applications accepted. *Financial support:* Fellowships, research assistantships, teaching assistantships, and unspecified assistantships available. *Unit head:* Dr. Malcolm Adams, Head, 706-542-2564, E-mail: fu@math.uga.edu. *Application contact:* Dr. Brian D. Boe, Graduate Coordinator, 706-542-2547, Fax: 706-542-2573, E-mail: grad@math.uga.edu. Web site: http://www.math.uga.edu/.

University of Guelph, Graduate Studies, College of Physical and Engineering Science, Department of Mathematics and Statistics, Guelph, ON N1G 2W1, Canada. Offers applied mathematics (PhD); applied statistics (PhD); mathematics and statistics (M Sc). Part-time programs available. *Degree requirements:* For master's, thesis (for some programs); for doctorate, thesis/dissertation. *Entrance requirements:* For master's, minimum B average during previous 2 years of course work; for doctorate, minimum B average. Additional exam requirements/recommendations for international students: Required—TOEFL (minimum score 550 paper-based; 213 computer-based; 89 iBT), IELTS (minimum score 6.5). *Faculty research:* Dynamical systems, mathematical biology, numerical analysis, linear and nonlinear models, reliability and bioassay.

University of Hawaii at Manoa, Graduate Division, College of Natural Sciences, Department of Mathematics, Honolulu, HI 96822. Offers MA, PhD. Part-time programs available. *Degree requirements:* For doctorate, one foreign language, comprehensive exam, thesis/dissertation. *Entrance requirements:* For master's and doctorate, GRE General Test, minimum GPA of 3.0. Additional exam requirements/recommendations for international students: Required—TOEFL (minimum score 500 paper-based; 173 computer-based; 61 iBT), IELTS (minimum score 5). *Faculty research:* Analysis, algebra, lattice theory, logic topology, differential geometry.

University of Houston, College of Natural Sciences and Mathematics, Department of Mathematics, Houston, TX 77204. Offers applied mathematics (MS); mathematics (MA, PhD). Part-time programs available. *Degree requirements:* For master's, thesis optional. *Entrance requirements:* For master's and doctorate, GRE (Verbal and Quantitative). Additional exam requirements/recommendations for international students: Required—TOEFL (minimum score 550 paper-based; 79 iBT), IELTS (minimum score 6.5). Electronic applications accepted. *Faculty research:* Applied mathematics, modern analysis, computational science, geometry, dynamical systems.

University of Houston–Clear Lake, School of Science and Computer Engineering, Program in Mathematical Sciences, Houston, TX 77058-1098. Offers MS. Part-time and evening/weekend programs available. *Entrance requirements:* For master's, GRE General Test. Additional exam requirements/recommendations for international students: Required—TOEFL (minimum score 550 paper-based; 213 computer-based).

University of Idaho, College of Graduate Studies, College of Science, Department of Mathematics, Moscow, ID 83844-1103. Offers MAT, MS, PhD. *Faculty:* 6 full-time, 1 part-time/adjunct. *Students:* 20 full-time, 8 part-time. Average age 35. In 2011, 15 master's, 1 doctorate awarded. *Degree requirements:* For doctorate, 2 foreign languages, thesis/dissertation. *Entrance requirements:* For master's, minimum GPA of 2.8; for doctorate, minimum undergraduate GPA of 2.8, 3.0 graduate. *Application deadline:* For fall admission, 8/1 for domestic students; for spring admission, 12/15 for domestic students. Applications are processed on a rolling basis. Application fee: $60. Electronic applications accepted. *Expenses:* Tuition, state resident: full-time $3874; part-

Peterson's Graduate Programs in the Physical Sciences, Mathematics, Agricultural Sciences, the Environment & Natural Resources 2013

facebook.com/petersonspublishing **353**

Mathematics

time $334 per credit hour. Tuition, nonresident: full-time $16,394; part-time $861 per credit hour. *Required fees:* $2808; $99 per credit hour. Tuition and fees vary according to program. *Financial support:* Research assistantships and teaching assistantships available. Financial award applicants required to submit FAFSA. *Faculty research:* Bioinformatics and mathematical biology, analysis and differential equations, combinatorics, probability and stochastic processes, discrete geometry. *Unit head:* Dr. Monte Boisen, Chair, 208-885-6742, E-mail: math@uidaho.edu. *Application contact:* Erick Larson, Director of Graduate Admissions, 208-885-4723, E-mail: gadms@uidaho.edu. Web site: http://www.uidaho.edu/sci/math.

University of Illinois at Chicago, Graduate College, College of Liberal Arts and Sciences, Department of Mathematics, Statistics, and Computer Science, Chicago, IL 60607-7128. Offers applied mathematics (MS, PhD); computational finance (MS, PhD); computer science (MS, PhD); mathematics (DA); mathematics and information sciences for industry (MS); probability and statistics (PhD); pure mathematics (MS, PhD); statistics (MS); teaching of mathematics (MST), including elementary, secondary. Part-time programs available. *Degree requirements:* For master's, comprehensive exam; for doctorate, one foreign language, thesis/dissertation. *Entrance requirements:* For master's and doctorate, GRE General Test, minimum GPA of 3.0. Additional exam requirements/recommendations for international students: Required—TOEFL (minimum score 100 iBT). Electronic applications accepted.

University of Illinois at Urbana–Champaign, Graduate College, College of Liberal Arts and Sciences, Department of Mathematics, Champaign, IL 61820. Offers applied mathematics (MS); applied mathematics: actuarial science (MS); mathematics (MS, PhD); teaching of mathematics (MS). *Faculty:* 64 full-time (6 women), 9 part-time/adjunct (0 women). *Students:* 166 full-time (52 women), 36 part-time (13 women); includes 16 minority (7 Asian, non-Hispanic/Latino; 5 Hispanic/Latino; 4 Two or more races, non-Hispanic/Latino), 111 international. 455 applicants, 23% accepted, 48 enrolled. In 2011, 32 master's, 26 doctorates awarded. *Entrance requirements:* For master's and doctorate, GRE General Test, GRE Subject Test (math), minimum GPA of 3.0. Additional exam requirements/recommendations for international students: Required—TOEFL (minimum score 550 paper-based; 213 computer-based). *Application deadline:* Applications are processed on a rolling basis. Application fee: $75 ($90 for international students). Electronic applications accepted. *Financial support:* In 2011–12, 26 fellowships, 44 research assistantships, 152 teaching assistantships were awarded; tuition waivers (full and partial) also available. *Unit head:* Matthew Ando, Chair, 217-244-2846, Fax: 217-333-9576, E-mail: mando@illinois.edu. *Application contact:* Marci Blocher, Office Support Specialist, 217-333-5749, Fax: 217-333-9576, E-mail: mblocher@illinois.edu. Web site: http://math.illinois.edu/.

The University of Iowa, Graduate College, College of Liberal Arts and Sciences, Department of Mathematics, Iowa City, IA 52242-1316. Offers MS, PhD. *Degree requirements:* For master's, thesis optional, exam; for doctorate, comprehensive exam, thesis/dissertation. *Entrance requirements:* For master's and doctorate, GRE General Test, minimum GPA of 3.0. Additional exam requirements/recommendations for international students: Required—TOEFL (minimum score 620 paper-based; 260 computer-based; 105 iBT). Electronic applications accepted.

The University of Kansas, Graduate Studies, College of Liberal Arts and Sciences, Department of Mathematics, Lawrence, KS 66045. Offers mathematics (MA, PhD). *Faculty:* 38 full-time (8 women). *Students:* 72 full-time (10 women), 4 part-time (0 women); includes 3 minority (2 Asian, non-Hispanic/Latino; 1 Two or more races, non-Hispanic/Latino), 37 international. Average age 28. 110 applicants, 43% accepted, 19 enrolled. In 2011, 15 master's, 6 doctorates awarded. Terminal master's awarded for partial completion of doctoral program. *Degree requirements:* For master's, comprehensive exam, thesis or alternative; for doctorate, one foreign language, comprehensive exam, thesis/dissertation, 1 computer language. *Entrance requirements:* For master's and doctorate, GRE. Additional exam requirements/recommendations for international students: Required—TOEFL. *Application deadline:* For fall admission, 1/31 priority date for domestic students, 1/31 for international students. Applications are processed on a rolling basis. Application fee: $55 ($65 for international students). Electronic applications accepted. Tuition and fees vary according to course load, campus/location, program and reciprocity agreements. *Financial support:* Fellowships with full tuition reimbursements, research assistantships with full and partial tuition reimbursements, teaching assistantships with full tuition reimbursements, institutionally sponsored loans, scholarships/grants, health care benefits, and unspecified assistantships available. Support available to part-time students. Financial award application deadline: 1/31. *Faculty research:* Commutative algebra, algebraic geometry, combinatorics, stochastic adaptive control, probability analysis, operator algebras, harmonic analysis, PDES, numerical analysis, dynamical systems, topology, set theory. *Unit head:* Prof. Satya Mandal, Chair, 785-864-3651, Fax: 785-864-5255, E-mail: mandal@math.ku.edu. *Application contact:* Prof. Milena Stanislavova, Admissions Director of Graduate Studies, 785-864-3651, E-mail: stanis@math.ku.edu. Web site: http://www.math.ku.edu/.

University of Kentucky, Graduate School, College of Arts and Sciences, Program in Mathematics, Lexington, KY 40506-0032. Offers applied mathematics (MS); mathematics (MA, MS, PhD). *Degree requirements:* For master's, comprehensive exam, thesis optional; for doctorate, one foreign language, comprehensive exam, thesis/dissertation. *Entrance requirements:* For master's, GRE General Test, minimum undergraduate GPA of 2.75; for doctorate, GRE

General Test, minimum graduate GPA of 3.0. Additional exam requirements/recommendations for international students: Required—TOEFL (minimum score 550 paper-based; 213 computer-based). Electronic applications accepted. *Faculty research:* Numerical analysis, combinatorics, partial differential equations, algebra and number theory, real and complex analysis.

University of Lethbridge, School of Graduate Studies, Lethbridge, AB T1K 3M4, Canada. Offers accounting (MScM); addictions counseling (M Sc); agricultural biotechnology (M Sc); agricultural studies (M Sc, MA); anthropology (MA); archaeology (MA); art (MA, MFA); biochemistry (M Sc); biological sciences (M Sc); biomolecular science (PhD); biosystems and biodiversity (PhD); Canadian studies (MA); chemistry (M Sc); computer science (M Sc); computer science and geographical information science (M Sc); counseling psychology (M Ed); dramatic arts (MA); earth, space, and physical science (PhD); economics (MA); educational leadership (M Ed); English (MA); environmental science (M Sc); evolution and behavior (PhD); exercise science (M Sc); finance (MScM); French (MA); French/German (MA); French/Spanish (MA); general education (M Ed); general management (MScM); geography (M Sc, MA); German (MA); health science (M Sc); history (MA); human resource management and labour relations (MScM); individualized multidisciplinary (M Sc, MA); information systems (MScM); international management (MScM); kinesiology (M Sc, MA); management (M Sc, MA); marketing (MScM); mathematics (M Sc); music (M Mus, MA); Native American studies (MA); neuroscience (M Sc, PhD); new media (MA); nursing (M Sc); philosophy (MA); physics (M Sc); policy and strategy (MScM); political science (MA); psychology (M Sc, MA); religious studies (MA); social sciences (MA); sociology (MA); theatre and dramatic arts (MFA); theoretical and computational science (PhD); urban and regional studies (MA); women's studies (MA). Part-time and evening/weekend programs available. *Degree requirements:* For doctorate, comprehensive exam, thesis/dissertation. *Entrance requirements:* For master's, GMAT (M Sc in management), bachelor's degree in related field, minimum GPA of 3.0 during previous 20 graded semester courses, 2 years teaching or related experience (M Ed); for doctorate, master's degree, minimum graduate GPA of 3.5. Additional exam requirements/recommendations for international students: Required—TOEFL. *Faculty research:* Movement and brain plasticity, gibberellin physiology, photosynthesis, carbon cycling, molecular properties of main-group ring components.

University of Louisiana at Lafayette, College of Sciences, Department of Mathematics, Lafayette, LA 70504. Offers MS, PhD. Terminal master's awarded for partial completion of doctoral program. *Degree requirements:* For master's, thesis or alternative; for doctorate, 2 foreign languages, comprehensive exam, thesis/dissertation. *Entrance requirements:* For master's, GRE General Test, minimum GPA of 2.75; for doctorate, GRE General Test, minimum GPA of 3.0. Additional exam requirements/recommendations for international students: Required—TOEFL (minimum score 550 paper-based; 213 computer-based). Electronic applications accepted. *Faculty research:* Topology, algebra, applied mathematics, analysis.

University of Louisville, Graduate School, College of Arts and Sciences, Department of Mathematics, Louisville, KY 40292. Offers applied and industrial mathematics (PhD); mathematics (MA). Part-time programs available. Terminal master's awarded for partial completion of doctoral program. *Degree requirements:* For master's, comprehensive exam (for some programs), thesis optional; for doctorate, comprehensive exam, thesis/dissertation, internship, project. *Entrance requirements:* For master's and doctorate, GRE General Test. Additional exam requirements/recommendations for international students: Required—TOEFL (minimum score 550 paper-based; 215 computer-based; 79 iBT). Electronic applications accepted. *Expenses:* Tuition, state resident: full-time $9692; part-time $539 per credit hour. Tuition, nonresident: full-time $20,168; part-time $1121 per credit hour. Tuition and fees vary according to program and reciprocity agreements. *Faculty research:* Algebra, analysis, bio-mathematics, combinatorics and graph theory, coding theory, consesus theory, financial mathematics, functional equations, partial differential equations.

University of Maine, Graduate School, College of Liberal Arts and Sciences, Department of Mathematics and Statistics, Orono, ME 04469. Offers mathematics (MA). *Faculty:* 18 full-time (3 women), 10 part-time/adjunct (5 women). *Students:* 11 full-time (4 women), 3 part-time (1 woman); includes 1 minority (Hispanic/Latino), 2 international. Average age 28. 15 applicants, 80% accepted, 11 enrolled. In 2011, 3 master's awarded. *Degree requirements:* For master's, thesis optional. *Entrance requirements:* For master's, GRE General Test. Additional exam requirements/recommendations for international students: Required—TOEFL. *Application deadline:* For fall admission, 2/1 priority date for domestic students. Applications are processed on a rolling basis. Application fee: $65. Electronic applications accepted. *Expenses:* Tuition, state resident: full-time $5016. Tuition, nonresident: full-time $14,424. *Financial support:* In 2011–12, 7 teaching assistantships with full tuition reimbursements (averaging $13,600 per year) were awarded; tuition waivers (full and partial) also available. Financial award application deadline: 3/1. *Total annual research expenditures:* $144,295. *Unit head:* Dr. David Bradley, Chair, 207-581-3920, Fax: 207-581-4977. *Application contact:* Scott G. Delcourt, Associate Dean of the Graduate School, 207-581-3291, Fax: 207-581-3232, E-mail: graduate@maine.edu. Web site: http://www2.umaine.edu/graduate/.

The University of Manchester, School of Mathematics, Manchester, United Kingdom. Offers actuarial science (PhD); applied mathematics (M Phil, PhD); applied numerical computing (M Phil, PhD); financial mathematics (M Phil, PhD);

Peterson's Graduate Programs in the Physical Sciences, Mathematics, Agricultural Sciences, the Environment & Natural Resources 2013

mathematical logic (M Phil); probability (M Phil, PhD); pure mathematics (M Phil, PhD); statistics (M Phil, PhD).

University of Manitoba, Faculty of Graduate Studies, Faculty of Science, Department of Mathematics, Winnipeg, MB R3T 2N2, Canada. Offers M Sc, PhD. *Degree requirements:* For master's, one foreign language, thesis or alternative; for doctorate, one foreign language, thesis/dissertation.

University of Manitoba, Faculty of Graduate Studies, Faculty of Science, Program in Mathematical, Computational and Statistical Sciences, Winnipeg, MB R3T 2N2, Canada. Offers MMCSS.

University of Maryland, College Park, Academic Affairs, College of Computer, Mathematical and Natural Sciences, Department of Mathematics, Program in Mathematics, College Park, MD 20742. Offers MA, PhD. Part-time and evening/weekend programs available. *Students:* 71 full-time (13 women), 13 part-time (2 women); includes 8 minority (4 Asian, non-Hispanic/Latino; 4 Hispanic/Latino), 23 international. 254 applicants, 11% accepted, 15 enrolled. In 2011, 7 master's, 12 doctorates awarded. Terminal master's awarded for partial completion of doctoral program. *Degree requirements:* For master's, thesis or alternative; for doctorate, one foreign language, thesis/dissertation, written exam, oral exam. *Entrance requirements:* For master's, GRE General Test, GRE Subject Test, minimum GPA of 3.0, 3 letters of recommendation; for doctorate, GRE General Test, GRE Subject Test, 3 letters of recommendation. *Application deadline:* For fall admission, 1/15 priority date for domestic students, 1/15 for international students; for spring admission, 10/1 for domestic students, 6/1 for international students. Applications are processed on a rolling basis. Application fee: $75. Electronic applications accepted. *Expenses: Tuition, area resident:* Part-time $525 per credit hour. Tuition, state resident: part-time $525 per credit hour. Tuition, nonresident: part-time $1131 per credit hour. *Required fees:* $386.31 per term. Tuition and fees vary according to program. *Financial support:* In 2011–12, 6 fellowships with partial tuition reimbursements (averaging $11,380 per year), 8 research assistantships (averaging $18,863 per year), 47 teaching assistantships (averaging $17,224 per year) were awarded. Financial award applicants required to submit FAFSA. *Unit head:* James Yorke, 301-405-5048, E-mail: yorke@umd.edu. *Application contact:* Dr. Charles A. Caramello, Dean of Graduate School, 301-405-0358, Fax: 301-314-9305.

University of Massachusetts Amherst, Graduate School, College of Natural Sciences, Department of Mathematics and Statistics, Amherst, MA 01003. Offers applied mathematics (MS); mathematics (MS, PhD); statistics (MS, PhD). *Faculty:* 44 full-time (6 women). *Students:* 64 full-time (17 women), 1 (woman) part-time; includes 7 minority (2 Black or African American, non-Hispanic/Latino; 4 Asian, non-Hispanic/Latino; 1 Two or more races, non-Hispanic/Latino), 26 international. Average age 27. 254 applicants, 20% accepted, 24 enrolled. In 2011, 17 master's, 6 doctorates awarded. Terminal master's awarded for partial completion of doctoral program. *Degree requirements:* For master's, thesis or alternative; for doctorate, comprehensive exam, thesis/dissertation. *Entrance requirements:* For master's and doctorate, GRE General Test, GRE Subject Test (mathematics). Additional exam requirements/recommendations for international students: Required—TOEFL (minimum score 550 paper-based; 213 computer-based; 80 iBT), IELTS (minimum score 6.5). *Application deadline:* For fall admission, 2/1 for domestic and international students. Applications are processed on a rolling basis. Application fee: $50 ($65 for international students). Electronic applications accepted. Tuition and fees vary according to course load, campus/location and program. *Financial support:* Fellowships with full and partial tuition reimbursements, research assistantships with full and partial tuition reimbursements, teaching assistantships with full and partial tuition reimbursements, career-related internships or fieldwork, Federal Work-Study, scholarships/grants, traineeships, health care benefits, tuition waivers (full and partial), and unspecified assistantships available. Support available to part-time students. Financial award application deadline: 2/1. *Unit head:* Dr. Michael Lavine, Department Head, 413-545-2282, Fax: 413-545-1801. *Application contact:* Lindsay DeSantis, Supervisor of Admissions, 413-545-0722, Fax: 413-577-0010, E-mail: gradadm@grad.umass.edu. Web site: http://www.math.umass.edu/.

University of Massachusetts Lowell, College of Sciences, Department of Mathematical Sciences, Lowell, MA 01854-2881. Offers applied mathematics (MS); computational mathematics (PhD); mathematics (MS). Part-time programs available. *Entrance requirements:* For master's, GRE General Test.

University of Memphis, Graduate School, College of Arts and Sciences, Department of Mathematical Sciences, Memphis, TN 38152. Offers applied mathematics (MS); applied statistics (PhD); bioinformatics (MS); computer science (PhD); computer sciences (MS); mathematics (MS, PhD); statistics (MS, PhD). Part-time programs available. Terminal master's awarded for partial completion of doctoral program. *Degree requirements:* For master's, comprehensive exam; for doctorate, one foreign language, thesis/dissertation, oral exams. *Entrance requirements:* For master's and doctorate, GRE General Test, minimum GPA of 2.5. Additional exam requirements/recommendations for international students: Required—TOEFL (minimum score 550 paper-based; 210 computer-based). Electronic applications accepted. *Faculty research:* Combinatorics, ergodic theory, graph theory, Ramsey theory, applied statistics.

University of Miami, Graduate School, College of Arts and Sciences, Department of Mathematics, Coral Gables, FL 33124. Offers MA, MS, PhD. Part-time and evening/weekend programs available. Terminal master's awarded for partial completion of doctoral program. *Degree requirements:* For master's,

comprehensive exam, qualifying exams; for doctorate, one foreign language, thesis/dissertation, qualifying exams. *Entrance requirements:* For master's and doctorate, GRE General Test, minimum GPA of 3.0. Additional exam requirements/recommendations for international students: Required—TOEFL (minimum score 550 paper-based; 213 computer-based; 59 iBT). Electronic applications accepted. *Faculty research:* Applied mathematics, probability, geometric analysis, differential equations, algebraic combinatorics.

University of Michigan, Horace H. Rackham School of Graduate Studies, College of Literature, Science, and the Arts, Department of Mathematics, Ann Arbor, MI 48109. Offers applied and interdisciplinary mathematics (AM, MS, PhD); mathematics (AM, MS, PhD). Part-time programs available. *Faculty:* 65 full-time (10 women). *Students:* 141 full-time (35 women); includes 15 minority (1 Black or African American, non-Hispanic/Latino; 6 Asian, non-Hispanic/Latino; 5 Hispanic/Latino; 1 Native Hawaiian or other Pacific Islander, non-Hispanic/Latino; 2 Two or more races, non-Hispanic/Latino), 56 international. Average age 26. 604 applicants, 15% accepted, 34 enrolled. In 2011, 32 master's, 22 doctorates awarded. *Degree requirements:* For doctorate, one foreign language, comprehensive exam, thesis/dissertation, oral defense of dissertation, preliminary exam. *Entrance requirements:* For master's and doctorate, GRE General Test, GRE Subject Test. Additional exam requirements/recommendations for international students: Required—TOEFL (minimum score 560 paper-based; 220 computer-based; 84 iBT). *Application deadline:* For fall admission, 1/22 for domestic students, 1/15 for international students. Applications are processed on a rolling basis. Application fee: $65 ($75 for international students). Electronic applications accepted. *Financial support:* In 2011–12, 129 students received support, including 25 fellowships with full tuition reimbursements available (averaging $25,000 per year), 13 research assistantships with full tuition reimbursements available (averaging $17,702 per year), 91 teaching assistantships with full tuition reimbursements available (averaging $17,702 per year). Financial award application deadline: 3/15. *Faculty research:* Algebra, analysis, topology, applied mathematics, geometry. *Unit head:* Prof. Mel Hochster, Chair, 734-936-1310, Fax: 734-763-0937, E-mail: math-chair@umich.edu. *Application contact:* Prof. Sergey Fomin, Admissions Director, 734-764-7436, Fax: 734-763-0937, E-mail: math-admissionsdir@umich.edu. Web site: http://www.math.lsa.umich.edu/.

University of Minnesota, Twin Cities Campus, College of Science and Engineering, School of Mathematics, Minneapolis, MN 55455-0213. Offers mathematics (MS, PhD); quantitative finance (Certificate). Part-time programs available. *Faculty:* 63 full-time (3 women). *Students:* 224 (65 women); includes 23 minority (7 Black or African American, non-Hispanic/Latino; 1 American Indian or Alaska Native, non-Hispanic/Latino; 13 Asian, non-Hispanic/Latino; 2 Hispanic/Latino), 108 international. Terminal master's awarded for partial completion of doctoral program. *Degree requirements:* For master's, thesis (for some programs); for doctorate, 2 foreign languages, thesis/dissertation. *Entrance requirements:* For master's, GRE Subject Test (recommended); for doctorate, GRE Subject Test. Additional exam requirements/recommendations for international students: Required—TOEFL. *Application deadline:* For fall admission, 12/15 for domestic and international students. Applications are processed on a rolling basis. Application fee: $75 ($95 for international students). Electronic applications accepted. *Financial support:* Fellowships and teaching assistantships available. *Faculty research:* Partial and ordinary differential equations, algebra and number theory, geometry, combinatorics, numerical analysis, probability. *Application contact:* Mathematics Graduate Program, E-mail: gradprog@math.umn.edu. Web site: http://www.math.umn.edu.

University of Mississippi, Graduate School, College of Liberal Arts, Department of Mathematics, Oxford, University, MS 38677. Offers MA, MS, PhD. *Students:* 29 full-time (13 women), 4 part-time (2 women); includes 5 minority (all Black or African American, non-Hispanic/Latino), 6 international. In 2011, 1 master's, 1 doctorate awarded. *Degree requirements:* For master's, thesis (for some programs); for doctorate, thesis/dissertation. *Entrance requirements:* For master's, GRE General Test, minimum GPA of 3.0; for doctorate, GRE General Test. Additional exam requirements/recommendations for international students: Required—TOEFL. *Application deadline:* For fall admission, 4/1 for domestic students; for spring admission, 10/1 for domestic students. Applications are processed on a rolling basis. Application fee: $25. Electronic applications accepted. *Financial support:* Scholarships/grants available. Financial award application deadline: 3/1; financial award applicants required to submit FAFSA. *Unit head:* Dr. Iwo M. Labuda, Interim Chairman, 662-915-7071, Fax: 662-915-5491, E-mail: mdepart@olemiss.edu. *Application contact:* Dr. Christy M. Wyandt, Associate Dean, 662-915-7474, Fax: 662-915-7577, E-mail: cwyandt@olemiss.edu.

University of Missouri, Graduate School, College of Arts and Sciences, Department of Mathematics, Columbia, MO 65211. Offers applied mathematics (MS); mathematics (MA, MST, PhD). *Faculty:* 40 full-time (6 women), 1 (woman) part-time/adjunct. *Students:* 60 full-time (7 women), 12 part-time (2 women); includes 2 minority (1 Hispanic/Latino; 1 Two or more races, non-Hispanic/Latino), 27 international. Average age 28. 119 applicants, 27% accepted, 22 enrolled. In 2011, 14 master's, 10 doctorates awarded. *Degree requirements:* For doctorate, 2 foreign languages, comprehensive exam, thesis/dissertation. *Entrance requirements:* For master's and doctorate, GRE General Test, minimum GPA of 3.0; bachelor's degree from accredited institution. Additional exam requirements/recommendations for international students: Required—TOEFL (minimum score 500 paper-based; 173 computer-based; 61 iBT). *Application deadline:* For fall

Peterson's Graduate Programs in the Physical Sciences, Mathematics, Agricultural Sciences, the Environment & Natural Resources 2013

facebook.com/petersonspublishing **355**

Mathematics

admission, 1/15 for domestic students. Applications are processed on a rolling basis. Application fee: $55 ($75 for international students). Electronic applications accepted. *Expenses:* Tuition, state resident: full-time $5881. Tuition, nonresident: full-time $15,183. *Required fees:* $952. Tuition and fees vary according to campus/location and program. *Financial support:* In 2011–12, 7 fellowships with full tuition reimbursements, 4 research assistantships with full tuition reimbursements, 64 teaching assistantships with full tuition reimbursements were awarded; institutionally sponsored loans, health care benefits, and unspecified assistantships also available. Financial award applicants required to submit FAFSA. *Faculty research:* Algebraic geometry, analysis (real, complex, functional and harmonic), analytic functions, applied mathematics, financial mathematics and mathematics of insurance, commutative rings, scattering theory, differential equations (ordinary and partial), differential geometry, dynamical systems, general relativity, mathematical physics, number theory, probabilistic analysis and topology. *Unit head:* Dr. Glen Himmelberg, Department Chair, 573-882-6222, E-mail: himmelbergg@missouri.edu. *Application contact:* Amy Crews, Administrative Assistant, 573-882-6222, E-mail: crewsae@missouri.edu. Web site: http://www.math.missouri.edu/.

University of Missouri–Kansas City, College of Arts and Sciences, Department of Mathematics and Statistics, Kansas City, MO 64110-2499. Offers MA, MS, PhD. PhD (interdisciplinary) offered through the School of Graduate Studies. Part-time programs available. *Faculty:* 14 full-time (5 women), 2 part-time/adjunct (0 women). *Students:* 8 full-time (4 women), 22 part-time (9 women); includes 3 minority (all Asian, non-Hispanic/Latino), 5 international. Average age 31. 28 applicants, 64% accepted, 6 enrolled. In 2011, 13 master's awarded. Terminal master's awarded for partial completion of doctoral program. *Degree requirements:* For master's, written exam; for doctorate, 2 foreign languages, thesis/dissertation, oral and written exams. *Entrance requirements:* For master's, bachelor's degree in mathematics, minimum GPA of 3.0; for doctorate, GMAT or GRE General Test. Additional exam requirements/recommendations for international students: Required—TOEFL (minimum score 550 paper-based; 213 computer-based; 80 iBT). *Application deadline:* For fall admission, 3/15 for domestic and international students; for spring admission, 10/15 for domestic and international students. Applications are processed on a rolling basis. Application fee: $45 ($50 for international students). Electronic applications accepted. *Expenses:* Tuition, state resident: full-time $5798; part-time $322.10 per credit hour. Tuition, nonresident: full-time $14,969; part-time $831.60 per credit hour. *Required fees:* $93.51 per credit hour. *Financial support:* In 2011–12, 2 research assistantships (averaging $16,275 per year), 9 teaching assistantships with full tuition reimbursements (averaging $17,150 per year) were awarded; Federal Work-Study, institutionally sponsored loans, and tuition waivers (full and partial) also available. Support available to part-time students. Financial award application deadline: 3/1; financial award applicants required to submit FAFSA. *Faculty research:* Numerical analysis, statistics, biostatistics commutative algebra, differential equations. *Unit head:* Dr. Jie Chen, Chair/Professor, 816-235-1641, Fax: 816-235-5517, E-mail: umkcmathdept@umkc.edu. *Application contact:* Dr. Hristo Voulov, Associate Professor, 816-235-1641, Fax: 816-235-5517, E-mail: umkcmathdept@umkc.edu. Web site: http://cas.umkc.edu/math/.

University of Missouri–St. Louis, College of Arts and Sciences, Department of Mathematics and Computer Science, St. Louis, MO 63121. Offers applied mathematics (PhD), including computer science, mathematics; computer science (MS); mathematics (MA). Part-time and evening/weekend programs available. *Faculty:* 16 full-time (2 women). *Students:* 28 full-time (16 women), 41 part-time (11 women); includes 6 minority (4 Black or African American, non-Hispanic/Latino; 1 American Indian or Alaska Native, non-Hispanic/Latino; 1 Asian, non-Hispanic/Latino), 18 international. Average age 32. 82 applicants, 57% accepted, 18 enrolled. In 2011, 20 master's, 2 doctorates awarded. *Degree requirements:* For master's, thesis optional; for doctorate, thesis/dissertation. *Entrance requirements:* For master's, GRE (for teaching assistantships), 2 letters of recommendation; C programming, C++ or Java (for computer science); for doctorate, GRE General Test, 3 letters of recommendation. Additional exam requirements/recommendations for international students: Required—TOEFL (minimum score 550 paper-based; 213 computer-based). *Application deadline:* For fall admission, 7/1 priority date for domestic students, 7/1 for international students; for spring admission, 12/1 priority date for domestic students, 12/1 for international students. Applications are processed on a rolling basis. Application fee: $35 ($40 for international students). Electronic applications accepted. *Expenses:* Tuition, state resident: full-time $6273; part-time $3866 per year. Tuition, nonresident: full-time $14,969; part-time $9980 per year. *Required fees:* $315 per year. *Financial support:* In 2011–12, 3 research assistantships with full and partial tuition reimbursements (averaging $14,250 per year), 10 teaching assistantships with full and partial tuition reimbursements (averaging $12,400 per year) were awarded; fellowships with full tuition reimbursements also available. Financial award applicants required to submit FAFSA. *Faculty research:* Statistics, algebra, analysis. *Unit head:* Dr. Shiying Zhao, Director of Graduate Studies, 314-516-5741, Fax: 314-516-5400, E-mail: zhao@arch.cs.umsl.edu. *Application contact:* 314-516-5458, Fax: 314-516-6996, E-mail: gradadm@umsl.edu.

The University of Montana, Graduate School, College of Arts and Sciences, Department of Mathematical Sciences, Missoula, MT 59812-0002. Offers mathematics (MA, PhD), including college teaching (PhD), traditional mathematics research (PhD); mathematics education (MA). Part-time programs available. Terminal master's awarded for partial completion of doctoral program. *Degree requirements:* For doctorate, thesis/dissertation. *Entrance requirements:*

For master's and doctorate, GRE General Test. Additional exam requirements/recommendations for international students: Required—TOEFL (minimum score 525 paper-based; 195 computer-based).

University of Nebraska at Omaha, Graduate Studies, College of Arts and Sciences, Department of Mathematics, Omaha, NE 68182. Offers MA, MAT, MS. Part-time programs available. *Faculty:* 18 full-time (4 women). *Students:* 11 full-time (3 women), 31 part-time (9 women); includes 5 minority (1 Black or African American, non-Hispanic/Latino; 2 Asian, non-Hispanic/Latino; 2 Hispanic/Latino), 3 international. Average age 31. 18 applicants, 50% accepted, 8 enrolled. In 2011, 15 master's awarded. *Degree requirements:* For master's, comprehensive exam, thesis (for some programs). *Entrance requirements:* For master's, minimum GPA of 3.0, 15 undergraduate math hours. Additional exam requirements/recommendations for international students: Required—TOEFL (minimum score 500 paper-based; 173 computer-based; 61 iBT). *Application deadline:* For fall admission, 7/31 priority date for domestic students; for spring admission, 11/30 priority date for domestic students. Applications are processed on a rolling basis. Application fee: $45. Electronic applications accepted. *Financial support:* In 2011–12, 19 students received support, including 1 research assistantship with tuition reimbursement available, 13 teaching assistantships with tuition reimbursements available; Federal Work-Study, institutionally sponsored loans, traineeships, tuition waivers (partial), and unspecified assistantships also available. Support available to part-time students. Financial award application deadline: 3/1; financial award applicants required to submit FAFSA. *Unit head:* Dr. Jack W. Heidel, Chairperson, 402-554-3430. *Application contact:* Dr. Steve From, 402-554-2341, Fax: 402-554-3143, E-mail: graduate@unomaha.edu.

University of Nebraska–Lincoln, Graduate College, College of Arts and Sciences, Department of Mathematics, Lincoln, NE 68588. Offers mathematics (MA, MAT, MS, PhD); mathematics and computer science (PhD). *Degree requirements:* For master's, thesis optional; for doctorate, variable foreign language requirement, comprehensive exam, thesis/dissertation. *Entrance requirements:* Additional exam requirements/recommendations for international students: Required—TOEFL (minimum score 550 paper-based; 213 computer-based). Electronic applications accepted. *Faculty research:* Applied mathematics, commutative algebra, algebraic geometry, Bayesian statistics, biostatistics.

University of Nevada, Las Vegas, Graduate College, College of Science, Department of Mathematical Sciences, Las Vegas, NV 89154-4020. Offers MS, PhD. Part-time programs available. *Faculty:* 31 full-time (6 women), 3 part-time/adjunct (0 women). *Students:* 11 full-time (4 women), 39 part-time (9 women); includes 8 minority (3 Asian, non-Hispanic/Latino; 4 Hispanic/Latino; 1 Two or more races, non-Hispanic/Latino), 18 international. Average age 31. 51 applicants, 45% accepted, 13 enrolled. In 2011, 13 master's, 1 doctorate awarded. *Degree requirements:* For master's, comprehensive exam (for some programs), thesis (for some programs), oral exam. *Entrance requirements:* For master's and doctorate, GRE General Test. Additional exam requirements/recommendations for international students: Required—TOEFL (minimum score 550 paper-based; 213 computer-based; 80 iBT), IELTS (minimum score 7). *Application deadline:* For fall admission, 2/1 priority date for domestic students, 5/1 for international students; for spring admission, 10/1 for domestic and international students. Applications are processed on a rolling basis. Application fee: $60 ($75 for international students). Electronic applications accepted. *Financial support:* In 2011–12, 44 students received support, including 44 teaching assistantships with partial tuition reimbursements available (averaging $10,940 per year); institutionally sponsored loans, scholarships/grants, health care benefits, and unspecified assistantships also available. Financial award application deadline: 3/1. *Faculty research:* Statistics and biostatistics, numerical analysis and scientific computing, partial differential equations, number theory, mathematical logic. *Total annual research expenditures:* $169,373. *Unit head:* Dr. Derrick Dubose, Chair/Professor, 702-895-0382, Fax: 702-895-4343, E-mail: dubose@unlv.nevada.edu. *Application contact:* Graduate College Admissions Evaluator, 702-895-3320, Fax: 702-895-4180, E-mail: gradcollege@unlv.edu. Web site: http://sciences.unlv.edu/Mathematics/study_grad.html.

University of Nevada, Reno, Graduate School, College of Science, Department of Mathematics and Statistics, Reno, NV 89557. Offers mathematics (MS); teaching mathematics (MATM). *Degree requirements:* For master's, thesis optional. *Entrance requirements:* For master's, GRE General Test, minimum GPA of 2.75. Additional exam requirements/recommendations for international students: Required—TOEFL (minimum score 500 paper-based; 173 computer-based; 61 iBT), IELTS (minimum score 6). Electronic applications accepted. *Faculty research:* Operator algebra, nonlinear systems, differential equations.

University of New Brunswick Fredericton, School of Graduate Studies, Faculty of Science, Department of Mathematics and Statistics, Fredericton, NB E3B 5A3, Canada. Offers M Sc, PhD. *Faculty:* 10 full-time (0 women), 1 part-time/adjunct (0 women). *Students:* 19 full-time (5 women), 1 (woman) part-time. In 2011, 4 master's, 3 doctorates awarded. *Degree requirements:* For master's, thesis; for doctorate, comprehensive exam, thesis/dissertation. *Entrance requirements:* For master's and doctorate, minimum GPA of 3.0. Additional exam requirements/recommendations for international students: Required—TOEFL (minimum score 550 paper-based; 80 computer-based), TWE (minimum score 4); Recommended—IELTS (minimum score 7). *Application deadline:* For fall admission, 3/1 priority date for domestic students. Applications are processed on a rolling basis. Application fee: $50 Canadian dollars. *Financial support:* In 2011–12, 12 fellowships, 39 research assistantships, 19 teaching assistantships were awarded. *Faculty research:* Algebra, general relativity, mathematical biology, quantum field theory, pure math, data analysis, experimental design. *Unit head:* Dr. James Watmough, Director of Graduate Studies, 506-458-7363, Fax: 506-453-4705, E-mail: watmough@unb.ca. *Application contact:* Marilyn Hetherington, Graduate Secretary, 506-458-7373, Fax: 506-453-4705, E-mail: mhetheri@unb.ca. Web site: http://www.unb.ca/fredericton/science/math/.

University of New Hampshire, Graduate School, College of Engineering and Physical Sciences, Department of Mathematics and Statistics, Durham, NH 03824. Offers applied mathematics (MS); industrial statistics (Postbaccalaureate Certificate); mathematics (MS, MST, PhD); mathematics education (PhD); statistics (MS). *Faculty:* 21 full-time (5 women). *Students:* 26 full-time (12 women), 30 part-time (12 women); includes 4 minority (1 American Indian or Alaska Native, non-Hispanic/Latino; 2 Asian, non-Hispanic/Latino; 1 Two or more races, non-Hispanic/Latino), 13 international. Average age 29. 86 applicants, 47% accepted, 16 enrolled. In 2011, 1,217 master's, 2 doctorates, 4 other advanced degrees awarded. Terminal master's awarded for partial completion of doctoral program. *Degree requirements:* For doctorate, 2 foreign languages, thesis/dissertation. *Entrance requirements:* Additional exam requirements/recommendations for international students: Required—TOEFL (minimum score 550 paper-based; 213 computer-based; 80 iBT). *Application deadline:* For fall admission, 4/1 priority date for domestic students, 4/1 for international students; for spring admission, 12/1 for domestic students. Applications are processed on a rolling basis. Application fee: $65. Electronic applications accepted. *Expenses:* Tuition, state resident: full-time $12,360; part-time $687 per credit hour. Tuition, nonresident: full-time $25,680; part-time $1058 per credit hour. *International tuition:* $29,550 full-time. *Required fees:* $1666; $833 per course. $416.50 per semester. Tuition and fees vary according to course load and degree level. *Financial support:* In 2011–12, 41 students received support, including 6 research assistantships, 34 teaching assistantships; fellowships, Federal Work-Study, scholarships/grants, and tuition waivers (full and partial) also available. Support available to part-time students. Financial award application deadline: 2/15. *Faculty research:* Operator theory, complex analysis, algebra, nonlinear dynamics, statistics. *Unit head:* Dr. Edward Hinson, Chairperson, 603-862-2688. *Application contact:* Jan Jankowski, Administrative Assistant, 603-862-2320, E-mail: jan.jankowski@unh.edu. Web site: http://www.math.unh.edu/.

University of New Mexico, Graduate School, College of Arts and Sciences, Department of Mathematics and Statistics, Albuquerque, NM 87131-2039. Offers mathematics (MS, PhD); statistics (MS, PhD). Part-time programs available. *Faculty:* 87 full-time (33 women), 59 part-time/adjunct (22 women). *Students:* 51 full-time (12 women), 34 part-time (10 women); includes 15 minority (all Hispanic/Latino), 28 international. Average age 32. 82 applicants, 68% accepted, 25 enrolled. In 2011, 20 master's, 7 doctorates awarded. Terminal master's awarded for partial completion of doctoral program. *Degree requirements:* For master's, comprehensive exam (for some programs), thesis or alternative; for doctorate, one foreign language, comprehensive exam, thesis/dissertation, 4 department seminars. *Entrance requirements:* For master's and doctorate, minimum GPA of 3.0, 3 letters of recommendation, letter of intent. Additional exam requirements/recommendations for international students: Required—TOEFL (minimum score 550 paper-based; 213 computer-based). *Application deadline:* For fall admission, 2/15 priority date for domestic students; for spring admission, 11/1 priority date for domestic students. Application fee: $50. Electronic applications accepted. *Financial support:* In 2011–12, 59 students received support, including 15 research assistantships with tuition reimbursements available (averaging $8,419 per year), 46 teaching assistantships with tuition reimbursements available (averaging $14,812 per year); health care benefits and unspecified assistantships also available. Financial award application deadline: 2/15; financial award applicants required to submit FAFSA. *Faculty research:* Pure and applied mathematics, applied statistics, numerical analysis, biostatistics, differential geometry, fluid dynamics, nonparametric curve estimation. *Total annual research expenditures:* $1.5 million. *Unit head:* Dr. Terry Loring, Chair, 505-277-4613, Fax: 505-277-5505, E-mail: loring@math.unm.edu. *Application contact:* Ana Parra Lombard, Coordinator, Program Advisement, 505-277-5250, Fax: 505-277-5505, E-mail: aparra@math.unm.edu. Web site: http://math.unm.edu/.

University of New Orleans, Graduate School, College of Sciences, Department of Mathematics, New Orleans, LA 70148. Offers MS. Part-time programs available. *Entrance requirements:* For master's, BA or BS in mathematics. Additional exam requirements/recommendations for international students: Required—TOEFL (minimum score 550 paper-based; 213 computer-based; 79 iBT). Electronic applications accepted. *Faculty research:* Differential equations, combinatorics, statistics, complex analysis, algebra.

The University of North Carolina at Chapel Hill, Graduate School, College of Arts and Sciences, Department of Mathematics, Chapel Hill, NC 27599. Offers MA, MS, PhD. *Degree requirements:* For master's, comprehensive exam, thesis or alternative, computer proficiency; for doctorate, 2 foreign languages, thesis/dissertation, 3 comprehensive exams, computer proficiency. *Entrance requirements:* For master's and doctorate, GRE General Test, minimum GPA of 3.0. Additional exam requirements/recommendations for international students: Required—TOEFL. Electronic applications accepted. *Faculty research:* Algebraic geometry, topology, analysis, lie theory, applied math.

The University of North Carolina at Charlotte, Graduate School, College of Liberal Arts and Sciences, Department of Mathematics and Statistics, Charlotte, NC 28223-0001. Offers applied mathematics (MS, PhD); mathematics (MS); mathematics education (MA). Part-time and evening/weekend programs available. *Faculty:* 48 full-time (7 women). *Students:* 43 full-time (17 women), 27 part-time (10 women); includes 12 minority (7 Black or African American, non-Hispanic/Latino; 3 Asian, non-Hispanic/Latino; 2 Hispanic/Latino), 33 international. Average age 30. 52 applicants, 98% accepted, 16 enrolled. In 2011, 14 master's, 6 doctorates awarded. *Degree requirements:* For master's, comprehensive exam, thesis or alternative; for doctorate, thesis/dissertation. *Entrance requirements:* For master's, GRE General Test, minimum GPA of 3.0 in undergraduate major, 2.75 overall; for doctorate, GRE General Test, minimum overall GPA of 3.0. Additional exam requirements/recommendations for international students: Required—TOEFL (minimum score 557 paper-based; 220 computer-based; 83 iBT), Michigan English Language Assessment Battery (minimum score 78) or IELTS (minimum score 6.5). *Application deadline:* For fall admission, 7/1 for domestic students, 5/1 for international students; for spring admission, 11/1 for domestic students, 10/1 for international students. Applications are processed on a rolling basis. Application fee: $65 ($75 for international students). Electronic applications accepted. *Expenses:* Tuition, state resident: full-time $3689. Tuition, nonresident: full-time $15,226. *Required fees:* $2198. Tuition and fees vary according to course load and program. *Financial support:* In 2011–12, 37 students received support, including 4 fellowships (averaging $22,321 per year), 4 research assistantships (averaging $19,325 per year), 29 teaching assistantships (averaging $11,988 per year); career-related internships or fieldwork, Federal Work-Study, institutionally sponsored loans, scholarships/grants, and unspecified assistantships also available. Support available to part-time students. Financial award application deadline: 4/1; financial award applicants required to submit FAFSA. *Faculty research:* Numerical analysis, differential equations, probability, algebra, analysis, mathematics education, statistics. *Total annual research expenditures:* $1.2 million. *Unit head:* Dr. Alan S. Dow, Chair, 704-687-4560, Fax: 704-687-6415, E-mail: adow@uncc.edu. *Application contact:* Kathy B. Giddings, Director of Graduate Admissions, 704-687-5503, Fax: 704-687-3279, E-mail: gradadm@uncc.edu. Web site: http://www.math.uncc.edu/.

The University of North Carolina at Charlotte, Graduate School, College of Liberal Arts and Sciences, Department of Sociology, Charlotte, NC 28223-0001. Offers health research (MA); mathematical sociology and quantitative methods (MA); organizations, occupations, and work (MA); political sociology (MA); race and gender (MA); social psychology (MA); social theory (MA); sociology of education (MA); stratification (MA). Part-time and evening/weekend programs available. *Faculty:* 17 full-time (10 women). *Students:* 14 full-time (8 women), 12 part-time (5 women); includes 5 minority (2 Black or African American, non-Hispanic/Latino; 3 Asian, non-Hispanic/Latino). Average age 30. 13 applicants, 85% accepted, 8 enrolled. In 2011, 4 master's awarded. *Degree requirements:* For master's, thesis or comprehensive exam. *Entrance requirements:* For master's, GRE or MAT, minimum GPA of 3.0 in last 2 years, 2.75 overall. Additional exam requirements/recommendations for international students: Required—TOEFL (minimum score 557 paper-based; 220 computer-based; 83 iBT). *Application deadline:* For fall admission, 7/1 for domestic students, 5/1 for international students; for spring admission, 11/1 for domestic students, 10/1 for international students. Applications are processed on a rolling basis. Application fee: $65 ($75 for international students). Electronic applications accepted. *Expenses:* Tuition, state resident: full-time $3689. Tuition, nonresident: full-time $15,226. *Required fees:* $2198. Tuition and fees vary according to course load and program. *Financial support:* In 2011–12, 11 students received support, including 6 research assistantships (averaging $13,125 per year), 5 teaching assistantships (averaging $10,800 per year); career-related internships or fieldwork, institutionally sponsored loans, scholarships/grants, and unspecified assistantships also available. Support available to part-time students. Financial award application deadline: 4/1; financial award applicants required to submit FAFSA. *Faculty research:* Social psychology, sociology of education, social gerontology, quantitative methodology, medical sociology. *Total annual research expenditures:* $448,481. *Unit head:* Dr. Lisa Rachotte, Chair, 704-687-2288, Fax: 704-687-3091, E-mail: lrashott@uncc.edu. *Application contact:* Kathy B. Giddings, Director of Graduate Admissions, 704-687-5503, Fax: 704-687-3279, E-mail: gradadm@uncc.edu. Web site: http://sociology.uncc.edu/.

The University of North Carolina at Greensboro, Graduate School, College of Arts and Sciences, Department of Mathematics and Statistics, Greensboro, NC 27412-5001. Offers mathematics (MA, PhD). Part-time programs available. *Degree requirements:* For master's, comprehensive exam, thesis (for some programs). *Entrance requirements:* For master's, GRE General Test. Additional exam requirements/recommendations for international students: Required—TOEFL. Electronic applications accepted. *Faculty research:* General and geometric topology, statistics, computer networks, symbolic logic, mathematics education.

The University of North Carolina Wilmington, College of Arts and Sciences, Department of Mathematics and Statistics, Wilmington, NC 28403-3297. Offers MS. *Degree requirements:* For master's, comprehensive exam, thesis. *Entrance requirements:* For master's, GRE General Test, GRE Subject Test, minimum B average in undergraduate major. Additional exam requirements/recommendations for international students: Required—TOEFL (minimum score 550 paper-based; 217 computer-based; 79 iBT), IELTS (minimum score 6.5).

University of North Dakota, Graduate School, College of Arts and Sciences, Department of Mathematics, Grand Forks, ND 58202. Offers M Ed, MS. Part-time programs available. *Degree requirements:* For master's, thesis or alternative, final exam. *Entrance requirements:* For master's, minimum GPA of 3.0. Additional exam requirements/recommendations for international students: Required—

Peterson's Graduate Programs in the Physical Sciences, Mathematics, Agricultural Sciences, the Environment & Natural Resources 2013

facebook.com/petersonspublishing **357**

TOEFL (minimum score 550 paper-based; 213 computer-based; 79 iBT), IELTS (minimum score 6.5). Electronic applications accepted. *Faculty research:* Statistics, measure theory, topological vector spaces, algebra, applied math.

University of Northern British Columbia, Office of Graduate Studies, Prince George, BC V2N 4Z9, Canada. Offers business administration (Diploma); community health science (M Sc); disability management (MA); education (M Ed); first nations studies (MA); gender studies (MA); history (MA); interdisciplinary studies (MA); international studies (MA); mathematical, computer and physical sciences (M Sc); natural resources and environmental studies (M Sc, MA, MNRES, PhD); political science (MA); psychology (M Sc, PhD); social work (MSW). Part-time and evening/weekend programs available. Postbaccalaureate distance learning degree programs offered (no on-campus study). *Degree requirements:* For master's, thesis; for doctorate, thesis/dissertation. *Entrance requirements:* For master's, GRE, minimum B average in undergraduate course work; for doctorate, candidacy exam, minimum A average in graduate course work.

University of Northern Colorado, Graduate School, College of Natural and Health Sciences, School of Mathematical Sciences, Greeley, CO 80639. Offers mathematical teaching (MA); mathematics (MA, PhD); mathematics education (PhD); mathematics: liberal arts (MA). Part-time programs available. *Degree requirements:* For master's, comprehensive exam, thesis or alternative; for doctorate, comprehensive exam, thesis/dissertation. *Entrance requirements:* For master's, GRE General Test (liberal arts), 3 letters of recommendation; for doctorate, GRE General Test, 3 letters of recommendation. Electronic applications accepted.

University of Northern Iowa, Graduate College, College of Humanities, Arts and Sciences, Department of Mathematics, Cedar Falls, IA 50614. Offers industrial mathematics (PSM), including actuarial science, continuous quality improvement, mathematical computing and modeling; mathematics (MA), including mathematics, secondary; mathematics for middle grades 4-8 (MA). Part-time programs available. *Students:* 13 full-time (6 women), 23 part-time (17 women); includes 2 minority (1 Black or African American, non-Hispanic/Latino; 1 Asian, non-Hispanic/Latino), 6 international. 35 applicants, 74% accepted, 11 enrolled. In 2011, 19 master's awarded. *Degree requirements:* For master's, comprehensive exam (for some programs), thesis or alternative. *Entrance requirements:* For master's, minimum GPA of 3.0. Additional exam requirements/recommendations for international students: Required—TOEFL (minimum score 600 paper-based; 250 computer-based; 100 iBT). *Application deadline:* For fall admission, 8/1 priority date for domestic students. Applications are processed on a rolling basis. Application fee: $50 ($70 for international students). Electronic applications accepted. *Expenses:* Tuition, state resident: full-time $7476. Tuition, nonresident: full-time $16,410. *Required fees:* $942. *Financial support:* Career-related internships or fieldwork, Federal Work-Study, scholarships/grants, and tuition waivers (full and partial) available. Support available to part-time students. Financial award application deadline: 2/1. *Unit head:* Dr. Douglas Mupasiri, Interim Head, 319-273-2012, Fax: 319-273-2546, E-mail: douglas.mupasiri@uni.edu. *Application contact:* Laurie S. Russell, Record Analyst, 319-273-2623, Fax: 319-273-2885, E-mail: laurie.russell@uni.edu. Web site: http://www.math.uni.edu/.

University of North Florida, College of Arts and Sciences, Department of Mathematics and Statistics, Jacksonville, FL 32224. Offers mathematical sciences (MS); statistics (MS). Part-time and evening/weekend programs available. *Faculty:* 5 full-time (3 women). *Students:* 15 full-time (2 women), 5 part-time (2 women); includes 1 minority (Black or African American, non-Hispanic/Latino), 7 international. Average age 29. 23 applicants, 70% accepted, 11 enrolled. In 2011, 6 master's awarded. *Degree requirements:* For master's, comprehensive exam, thesis optional. *Entrance requirements:* For master's, GRE General Test, minimum GPA of 3.0 in last 60 hours of course work. Additional exam requirements/recommendations for international students: Required—TOEFL (minimum score 500 paper-based; 173 computer-based; 61 iBT). *Application deadline:* For fall admission, 7/1 priority date for domestic students, 6/1 for international students; for spring admission, 11/1 priority date for domestic students, 10/1 for international students. Applications are processed on a rolling basis. Application fee: $30. Electronic applications accepted. *Expenses:* Tuition, state resident: full-time $8793; part-time $366.38 per credit hour. Tuition, nonresident: full-time $23,502; part-time $979.24 per credit hour. *Required fees:* $1384; $57.66 per credit hour. Tuition and fees vary according to course load and program. *Financial support:* In 2011–12, 13 students received support, including 6 teaching assistantships (averaging $5,499 per year); Federal Work-Study, scholarships/grants, tuition waivers (partial), and unspecified assistantships also available. Support available to part-time students. Financial award application deadline: 4/1; financial award applicants required to submit FAFSA. *Faculty research:* Real analysis, number theory, Euclidean geometry. *Total annual research expenditures:* $11,341. *Unit head:* Dr. Scott H. Hochwald, Chair, 904-620-2653, Fax: 904-620-2818, E-mail: shochwal@unf.edu. *Application contact:* Lillith Richardson, Assistant Director, The Graduate School, 904-620-1360, Fax: 904-620-1362, E-mail: graduateschool@unf.edu. Web site: http://www.unf.edu/coas/math-stat/.

University of North Texas, Toulouse Graduate School, College of Arts and Sciences, Department of Mathematics, Denton, TX 76203. Offers MA, MS, PhD. Part-time programs available. Terminal master's awarded for partial completion of doctoral program. *Degree requirements:* For master's, thesis (for some programs); for doctorate, one foreign language, comprehensive exam, thesis/

dissertation. *Entrance requirements:* For master's and doctorate, GRE General Test. Additional exam requirements/recommendations for international students: Recommended—TOEFL (minimum score 550 paper-based; 213 computer-based). *Expenses:* Tuition, state resident: part-time $100 per credit hour. Tuition, nonresident: part-time $413 per credit hour. *Faculty research:* Differential equations, descriptive set theory, combinatorics, functional analysis, algebra.

University of Notre Dame, Graduate School, College of Science, Department of Mathematics, Notre Dame, IN 46556. Offers algebra (PhD); algebraic geometry (PhD); applied mathematics (MSAM); complex analysis (PhD); differential geometry (PhD); logic (PhD); partial differential equations (PhD); topology (PhD). Terminal master's awarded for partial completion of doctoral program. *Degree requirements:* For doctorate, one foreign language, thesis/dissertation, qualifying exam. *Entrance requirements:* For master's and doctorate, GRE General Test, GRE Subject Test. Additional exam requirements/recommendations for international students: Required—TOEFL (minimum score 600 paper-based; 250 computer-based; 80 iBT). Electronic applications accepted. *Faculty research:* Algebra, analysis, geometry/topology, logic, applied math.

University of Oklahoma, College of Arts and Sciences, Department of Mathematics, Norman, OK 73019. Offers MA, MS, PhD, MBA/MS. Part-time programs available. *Faculty:* 33 full-time (3 women). *Students:* 56 full-time (26 women), 9 part-time (2 women); includes 4 minority (1 American Indian or Alaska Native, non-Hispanic/Latino; 2 Asian, non-Hispanic/Latino; 1 Two or more races, non-Hispanic/Latino), 27 international. Average age 30. 32 applicants, 66% accepted, 12 enrolled. In 2011, 13 master's, 7 doctorates awarded. Terminal master's awarded for partial completion of doctoral program. *Degree requirements:* For master's, comprehensive exam, thesis optional; for doctorate, 2 foreign languages, thesis/dissertation, qualifying exam. *Entrance requirements:* Additional exam requirements/recommendations for international students: Required—TOEFL (minimum score 550 paper-based; 79 iBT). *Application deadline:* For fall admission, 4/1 priority date for domestic students, 3/1 for international students; for spring admission, 11/1 for domestic students, 9/1 for international students. Applications are processed on a rolling basis. Application fee: $40 ($90 for international students). Electronic applications accepted. *Expenses:* Tuition, state resident: full-time $4087; part-time $170.30 per credit hour. Tuition, nonresident: full-time $14,875; part-time $619.80 per credit hour. *Required fees:* $2659; $100.25 per credit hour. Tuition and fees vary according to course load and degree level. *Financial support:* In 2011–12, 6 fellowships with full tuition reimbursements (averaging $3,455 per year), 57 teaching assistantships with partial tuition reimbursements (averaging $15,139 per year) were awarded; scholarships/grants, health care benefits, and unspecified assistantships also available. Financial award applicants required to submit FAFSA. *Faculty research:* Algebra, analysis, geometry, mathematics pedagogy, topology. *Total annual research expenditures:* $396,756. *Unit head:* Paul Goodey, Chair, 405-325-6711, Fax: 405-325-7484, E-mail: pgoodey@ou.edu. *Application contact:* Cristin Sloan, Assistant to the Graduate Director, 405-325-6711, Fax: 405-325-7484, E-mail: csloan@ou.edu. Web site: http://www.math.ou.edu.

See Display on next page and Close-Up on page 389.

University of Oregon, Graduate School, College of Arts and Sciences, Department of Mathematics, Eugene, OR 97403. Offers MA, MS, PhD. Part-time programs available. Terminal master's awarded for partial completion of doctoral program. *Degree requirements:* For doctorate, 2 foreign languages, thesis/dissertation. *Entrance requirements:* For master's and doctorate, GRE General Test, GRE Subject Test. Additional exam requirements/recommendations for international students: Required—TOEFL. *Faculty research:* Algebra, topology, analytic geometry, numerical analysis, statistics.

University of Ottawa, Faculty of Graduate and Postdoctoral Studies, Faculty of Science, Ottawa-Carleton Institute of Mathematics and Statistics, Ottawa, ON K1N 6N5, Canada. Offers M Sc, PhD. M Sc, PhD offered jointly with Carleton University. Part-time programs available. *Degree requirements:* For master's, thesis optional; for doctorate, one foreign language, comprehensive exam, thesis/dissertation. *Entrance requirements:* For master's, honors B Sc degree or equivalent, minimum B average; for doctorate, M Sc, minimum B+ average. Electronic applications accepted. *Faculty research:* Pure mathematics, applied mathematics, probability and statistics.

University of Pennsylvania, School of Arts and Sciences, Graduate Group in Mathematics, Philadelphia, PA 19104. Offers AM, PhD. *Faculty:* 29 full-time (2 women), 6 part-time/adjunct (0 women). *Students:* 61 full-time (10 women), 1 part-time (0 women); includes 4 minority (all Asian, non-Hispanic/Latino), 33 international. 246 applicants, 14% accepted, 15 enrolled. In 2011, 7 master's, 10 doctorates awarded. Terminal master's awarded for partial completion of doctoral program. *Degree requirements:* For master's, one foreign language, thesis or alternative; for doctorate, 2 foreign languages, thesis/dissertation. *Entrance requirements:* For master's and doctorate, GRE General Test, GRE Subject Test. Additional exam requirements/recommendations for international students: Required—TOEFL. *Application deadline:* For fall admission, 12/1 priority date for domestic students. Application fee: $70. Electronic applications accepted. *Expenses: Tuition:* Full-time $26,660; part-time $4944 per course. *Required fees:* $2318; $291 per course. Tuition and fees vary according to course load, degree level and program. *Financial support:* In 2011–12, 13 fellowships, 27 teaching assistantships were awarded; institutionally sponsored loans, scholarships/grants, traineeships, health care benefits, and unspecified assistantships also available. Financial award application deadline: 12/15. *Faculty research:* Geometry-

358 facebook.com/petersonspublishing

Peterson's Graduate Programs in the Physical Sciences, Mathematics, Agricultural Sciences, the Environment & Natural Resources 2013

topology, analysis, algebra, logic, combinatorics. *Unit head:* Jonathan Block, Department Chair, 215-898-8468, E-mail: blockj@math.upenn.edu. *Application contact:* 215-898-8178.

University of Pittsburgh, Dietrich School of Arts and Sciences, Department of Mathematics, Pittsburgh, PA 15260. Offers applied mathematics (MA, MS); mathematics (MA, MS, PhD). Part-time programs available. *Faculty:* 36 full-time (2 women), 16 part-time/adjunct (2 women). *Students:* 75 full-time (23 women), 4 part-time (2 women); includes 2 minority (1 Black or African American, non-Hispanic/Latino; 1 Native Hawaiian or other Pacific Islander, non-Hispanic/Latino), 43 international. 288 applicants, 17% accepted, 25 enrolled. In 2011, 9 master's, 13 doctorates awarded. Terminal master's awarded for partial completion of doctoral program. *Degree requirements:* For master's, comprehensive exam, thesis (for some programs); for doctorate, comprehensive exam, thesis/dissertation, preliminary exams, defense of dissertation. *Entrance requirements:* For master's, GRE General Test, GRE Subject Test (recommended), minimum GPA of 3.0; for doctorate, GRE General Test, GRE Subject Test (recommended), minimum GPA of 3.0, minimum QPA of 3.25 in math curriculum. Additional exam requirements/recommendations for international students: Required—TOEFL (minimum score 550 paper-based; 213 computer-based; 80 iBT), IELTS (minimum score 6.5). *Application deadline:* For fall admission, 1/15 priority date for domestic students, 1/15 for international students; for spring admission, 9/1 priority date for domestic students, 9/1 for international students. Applications are processed on a rolling basis. Application fee: $50. Electronic applications accepted. *Expenses:* Tuition, state resident: full-time $18,774; part-time $760 per credit. Tuition, nonresident: full-time $30,736; part-time $1258 per credit. *Required fees:* $740; $200 per term. Tuition and fees vary according to program. *Financial support:* In 2011–12, 72 students received support, including 8 fellowships with full and partial tuition reimbursements available (averaging $19,610 per year), 16 research assistantships with full and partial tuition reimbursements available (averaging $16,000 per year), 53 teaching assistantships with full and partial tuition reimbursements available (averaging $16,460 per year); institutionally sponsored loans, scholarships/grants, traineeships, health care benefits, tuition waivers (partial), and unspecified assistantships also available. Financial award application deadline: 1/15. *Faculty research:* Algebra, analysis, computational math, geometry/topology, math biology. *Total annual research expenditures:* $1.8 million. *Unit head:* Ivan Yotov, Chair, 412-624-8361, Fax: 412-624-8397, E-mail: yotov@math.pitt.edu. *Application contact:* Molly Williams, Administrator, 412-624-1175, Fax: 412-624-8397, E-mail: mollyw@pitt.edu. Web site: http://www.mathematics.pitt.edu.

University of Puerto Rico, Mayagüez Campus, Graduate Studies, College of Arts and Sciences, Department of Mathematical Sciences, Mayagüez, PR 00681-9000. Offers applied mathematics (MS); pure mathematics (MS); scientific computation (MS); statistics (MS). Part-time programs available. *Students:* 32 full-time (9 women), 1 (woman) part-time; includes 7 minority (all Hispanic/Latino), 26 international. 23 applicants, 43% accepted, 7 enrolled. In 2011, 10 master's awarded. *Degree requirements:* For master's, one foreign language, comprehensive exam, thesis optional. *Entrance requirements:* For master's, undergraduate degree in mathematics or its equivalent. *Application deadline:* For fall admission, 2/15 for domestic and international students; for spring admission, 9/15 for domestic and international students. Applications are processed on a rolling basis. Application fee: $25. Tuition and fees vary according to course level and course load. *Financial support:* In 2011–12, 31 students received support, including 3 research assistantships (averaging $15,000 per year), 28 teaching assistantships (averaging $8,500 per year); Federal Work-Study and institutionally sponsored loans also available. *Faculty research:* Automata theory, linear algebra, logic. *Unit head:* Prof. Omar Colon, Director, 787-832-4040 Ext. 3848, Fax: 787-265-5454, E-mail: omar.colon.reyes@gmail.com. Web site: http://math.uprm.edu/.

University of Puerto Rico, Río Piedras, College of Natural Sciences, Department of Mathematics, San Juan, PR 00931-3300. Offers MS, PhD. Part-time programs available. *Degree requirements:* For master's, comprehensive exam, thesis; for doctorate, comprehensive exam, thesis/dissertation. *Entrance requirements:* For master's and doctorate, GRE General Test and GRE Subject Test, interview, minimum GPA of 3.0, 3 letters of recommendation. *Faculty research:* Investigation of database logistics, cryptograph systems, distribution and spectral theory, Boolean function, differential equations.

University of Regina, Faculty of Graduate Studies and Research, Faculty of Science, Department of Mathematics and Statistics, Regina, SK S4S 0A2, Canada. Offers mathematics (M Sc, MA, PhD); statistics (M Sc, MA, PhD). *Faculty:* 21 full-time (2 women). *Students:* 25 full-time (8 women). 24 applicants, 75% accepted. In 2011, 5 master's, 2 doctorates awarded. *Degree requirements:* For master's, thesis; for doctorate, comprehensive exam, thesis/dissertation. *Entrance requirements:* Additional exam requirements/recommendations for international students: Required—TOEFL (minimum score 580 paper-based; 80 iBT), IELTS (minimum score 6.5). *Application deadline:* Applications are processed on a rolling basis. Application fee: $100. Electronic applications accepted. *Financial support:* In 2011–12, 2 fellowships (averaging $6,500 per year), 3 teaching assistantships (averaging $2,298 per year) were awarded; research assistantships and scholarships/grants also available. Financial award application deadline: 6/15. *Faculty research:* Discrete mathematics, actuarial science and statistics, matrix theory, mathematical science, numerical analysis. *Unit head:* Dr. Allen Herman, Head, 306-585-4487, Fax: 306-585-4020, E-mail: allen.herman@uregina.ca. *Application contact:* Dr. Martin Argerami, Graduate Program Coordinator, 306-585-4340, Fax: 306-585-4020, E-mail: martin.argerami@math.uregina.ca. Web site: http://www.math.uregina.ca.

Peterson's Graduate Programs in the Physical Sciences, Mathematics, Agricultural Sciences, the Environment & Natural Resources 2013

facebook.com/petersonspublishing **359**

Mathematics

University of Rhode Island, Graduate School, College of Arts and Sciences, Department of Mathematics, Kingston, RI 02881. Offers applied mathematical sciences (MS, PhD); mathematics (MS, PhD). Part-time programs available. *Faculty:* 21 full-time (6 women). *Students:* 20 full-time (8 women), 9 part-time (4 women), 2 international. In 2011, 6 master's, 1 doctorate awarded. *Degree requirements:* For master's, comprehensive exam (for some programs), thesis optional; for doctorate, one foreign language, comprehensive exam, thesis/dissertation optional. *Entrance requirements:* For master's and doctorate, 2 letters of recommendation. Additional exam requirements/recommendations for international students: Required—TOEFL (minimum score 550 paper-based; 213 computer-based). *Application deadline:* For fall admission, 7/15 for domestic students, 2/1 for international students; for spring admission, 11/15 for domestic students, 7/15 for international students. Application fee: $65. Electronic applications accepted. *Expenses:* Tuition, state resident: full-time $10,432; part-time $580 per credit hour. Tuition, nonresident: full-time $23,130; part-time $1285 per credit hour. *Required fees:* $1362; $36 per credit hour. $35 per semester. One-time fee: $130. *Financial support:* In 2011–12, 13 teaching assistantships with full and partial tuition reimbursements (averaging $14,358 per year) were awarded. Financial award application deadline: 7/15; financial award applicants required to submit FAFSA. *Unit head:* Dr. Nancy Eaton, Chairman, 401-874-2709, Fax: 401-874-4454, E-mail: eaton@math.uri.edu. *Application contact:* Dr. Woong Kook, Director of Graduate Studies, 401-874-4421, Fax: 401-874-4454, E-mail: andrewk@math.uri.edu. Web site: http://www.math.uri.edu/.

University of Rochester, School of Arts and Sciences, Department of Mathematics, Rochester, NY 14627. Offers PhD. *Faculty:* 18 full-time (2 women). *Students:* 29 full-time (8 women); includes 1 minority (Hispanic/Latino), 12 international. 87 applicants, 20% accepted, 5 enrolled. In 2011, 4 doctorates awarded. Terminal master's awarded for partial completion of doctoral program. *Degree requirements:* For doctorate, thesis/dissertation, qualifying exam. *Entrance requirements:* For doctorate, GRE General Test. Additional exam requirements/recommendations for international students: Required—TOEFL. *Application deadline:* For fall admission, 1/15 priority date for domestic students. Electronic applications accepted. *Expenses: Tuition:* Full-time $41,040. *Financial support:* Fellowships, research assistantships, teaching assistantships, and tuition waivers (full and partial) available. Financial award application deadline: 1/15. *Faculty research:* Algebra and number theory, analysis, geometry, mathematical physics and probability, topology. *Unit head:* Allan Greenleaf, Chair, 585-275-9421. *Application contact:* Joan Robinson, Administrative Assistant, Graduate Program, 585-275-9422. Web site: http://www.math.rochester.edu/.

University of Saskatchewan, College of Graduate Studies and Research, College of Arts and Science, Department of Mathematics and Statistics, Saskatoon, SK S7N 5A2, Canada. Offers M Math, MA, PhD. *Degree requirements:* For master's, thesis (for some programs); for doctorate, comprehensive exam (for some programs), thesis/dissertation. *Entrance requirements:* Additional exam requirements/recommendations for international students: Required—TOEFL (minimum score 80 iBT); Recommended—IELTS (minimum score 6.5). Electronic applications accepted.

University of South Alabama, Graduate School, College of Arts and Sciences, Department of Mathematics and Statistics, Mobile, AL 36688. Offers mathematics (MS). Part-time and evening/weekend programs available. *Faculty:* 17 full-time (4 women). *Students:* 8 full-time (3 women), 2 part-time (0 women); includes 1 minority (Two or more races, non-Hispanic/Latino), 2 international. 16 applicants, 69% accepted, 5 enrolled. *Degree requirements:* For master's, comprehensive exam, thesis optional. *Entrance requirements:* For master's, GRE, BS in mathematics or a mathematics-related field. Additional exam requirements/recommendations for international students: Required—TOEFL. *Application deadline:* For fall admission, 7/15 priority date for domestic students, 6/15 for international students; for spring admission, 12/1 priority date for domestic students, 11/1 for international students. Applications are processed on a rolling basis. Application fee: $35. *Expenses:* Tuition, state resident: full-time $7968; part-time $332 per credit hour. Tuition, nonresident: full-time $15,936; part-time $664 per credit hour. *Financial support:* Fellowships and research assistantships available. Support available to part-time students. Financial award application deadline: 4/1. *Faculty research:* Knot theory, chaos theory. *Unit head:* Dr. Scott Carter, Chair, 251-460-6264, Fax: 251-460-7969. *Application contact:* Dr. Dan Silver, Graduate Coordinator, 251-460-6264. Web site: http://www.southalabama.edu/mathstat.

University of South Carolina, The Graduate School, College of Arts and Sciences, Department of Mathematics, Columbia, SC 29208. Offers mathematics (MA, MS, PhD); mathematics education (M Math, MAT). MAT offered in cooperation with the College of Education. Part-time programs available. Terminal master's awarded for partial completion of doctoral program. *Degree requirements:* For master's, comprehensive exam, thesis (for some programs); for doctorate, one foreign language, comprehensive exam, thesis/dissertation, admission to candidacy exam, residency. *Entrance requirements:* For master's and doctorate, GRE General Test. Additional exam requirements/recommendations for international students: Required—TOEFL (minimum score 600 paper-based; 250 computer-based; 100 iBT). Electronic applications accepted. *Faculty research:* Computational mathematics, analysis (classical/modern), discrete mathematics, algebra, number theory.

The University of South Dakota, Graduate School, College of Arts and Sciences, Department of Mathematics, Vermillion, SD 57069-2390. Offers MA, MNS, MS. Part-time programs available. *Degree requirements:* For master's,

thesis (for some programs). *Entrance requirements:* For master's, GRE, minimum GPA of 2.7. Additional exam requirements/recommendations for international students: Required—TOEFL (minimum score 550 paper-based; 213 computer-based; 79 iBT). Electronic applications accepted. *Expenses:* Tuition, state resident: full-time $3118.50; part-time $173.25 per credit hour. Tuition, nonresident: full-time $6601; part-time $366.70 per credit hour. *Required fees:* $2268; $126 per credit hour. Tuition and fees vary according to program.

University of Southern California, Graduate School, Dana and David Dornsife College of Letters, Arts and Sciences, Department of Mathematics, Los Angeles, CA 90089. Offers applied mathematics (MA, MS, PhD); mathematical finance (MS); mathematics (MA, PhD); statistics (MS). Part-time programs available. Terminal master's awarded for partial completion of doctoral program. *Degree requirements:* For master's, comprehensive exam (for some programs), thesis (for some programs); for doctorate, one foreign language, comprehensive exam, thesis/dissertation. *Entrance requirements:* For master's, GRE General Test, GMAT; for doctorate, GRE General Test, GRE Subject Test (mathematics). Additional exam requirements/recommendations for international students: Required—TOEFL (minimum score 100 iBT). Electronic applications accepted. *Faculty research:* Algebra, algebraic geometry and number theory, analysis/partial differential equations, applied mathematics, financial mathematics, probability, combinatorics and statistics.

University of Southern Mississippi, Graduate School, College of Science and Technology, Department of Mathematics, Hattiesburg, MS 39406-0001. Offers computational science (PhD); mathematics (MS). Part-time programs available. *Faculty:* 11 full-time (3 women), 1 part-time/adjunct (0 women). *Students:* 11 full-time (5 women), 3 part-time (1 woman); includes 3 minority (2 Black or African American, non-Hispanic/Latino; 1 Asian, non-Hispanic/Latino), 5 international. Average age 29. 10 applicants, 40% accepted, 4 enrolled. In 2011, 4 master's, 1 doctorate awarded. *Degree requirements:* For master's, comprehensive exam, thesis or alternative; for doctorate, comprehensive exam, thesis/dissertation. *Entrance requirements:* For master's, GRE General Test, minimum GPA of 2.75 in last 60 hours; for doctorate, GRE General Test, minimum GPA of 3.5. Additional exam requirements/recommendations for international students: Required—TOEFL, IELTS. *Application deadline:* For fall admission, 3/15 priority date for domestic students, 3/15 for international students; for spring admission, 1/10 priority date for domestic students, 1/10 for international students. Applications are processed on a rolling basis. Application fee: $50. Electronic applications accepted. *Financial support:* In 2011–12, fellowships (averaging $18,000 per year), research assistantships with full tuition reimbursements (averaging $11,500 per year), teaching assistantships with full tuition reimbursements (averaging $11,408 per year) were awarded; Federal Work-Study, scholarships/grants, health care benefits, and unspecified assistantships also available. Financial award application deadline: 3/15; financial award applicants required to submit FAFSA. *Faculty research:* Dynamical systems, numerical analysis and multigrid methods, random number generation, matrix theory, group theory. *Unit head:* Dr. Joseph Kolibal, Interim Chair, 601-266-4289, Fax: 601-266-5818. *Application contact:* Dr. James Lambers, Director, Graduate Admissions, 601-266-4289, Fax: 601-266-5818. Web site: http://www.usm.edu/graduateschool/table.php.

University of South Florida, Graduate School, College of Arts and Sciences, Department of Mathematics and Statistics, Tampa, FL 33620-9951. Offers mathematics (MA, PhD); statistics (MA). Part-time and evening/weekend programs available. *Faculty:* 27 full-time (2 women), 12 part-time/adjunct (3 women). *Students:* 80 full-time (28 women), 17 part-time (4 women); includes 14 minority (3 Black or African American, non-Hispanic/Latino; 7 Asian, non-Hispanic/Latino; 3 Hispanic/Latino; 1 Two or more races, non-Hispanic/Latino), 37 international. Average age 32. 108 applicants, 66% accepted, 31 enrolled. In 2011, 22 master's, 3 doctorates awarded. Terminal master's awarded for partial completion of doctoral program. *Degree requirements:* For master's, comprehensive exam, thesis optional; for doctorate, comprehensive exam, thesis/dissertation. *Entrance requirements:* For master's, GRE, minimum GPA of 3.0; for doctorate, GRE, minimum GPA of 3.5, three letters of recommendation, personal statement of goals. Additional exam requirements/recommendations for international students: Required—TOEFL (minimum score 550 paper-based; 213 computer-based; 79 iBT) or IELTS (minimum score 6.5). *Application deadline:* For fall admission, 2/1 for domestic students, 1/2 for international students; for spring admission, 8/1 for domestic students, 6/1 for international students. Application fee: $30. Electronic applications accepted. *Financial support:* In 2011–12, 61 students received support, including 6 research assistantships (averaging $16,990 per year), 55 teaching assistantships with partial tuition reimbursements available (averaging $13,742 per year); unspecified assistantships also available. Financial award application deadline: 2/1. *Faculty research:* Approximation theory, differential equations, discrete mathematics, functional analysis topology. *Total annual research expenditures:* $615,749. *Unit head:* Dr. Marcus McWaters, Chairperson, 813-974-3838, Fax: 813-974-2700, E-mail: mmm@usf.edu. *Application contact:* Dr. Xiang-Dong Hou, Graduate Admissions Director, 813-974-2561, Fax: 813-974-2700, E-mail: xhou@cas.usf.edu. Web site: http://www.math.usf.edu/.

The University of Tennessee, Graduate School, College of Arts and Sciences, Department of Mathematics, Knoxville, TN 37996. Offers applied mathematics (MS); mathematical ecology (PhD); mathematics (M Math, MS, PhD). Part-time programs available. *Degree requirements:* For master's, thesis or alternative; for doctorate, one foreign language, thesis/dissertation. *Entrance requirements:* For master's and doctorate, minimum GPA of 2.7. Additional exam requirements/recommendations for international students: Required—TOEFL. Electronic applications accepted. *Expenses:* Tuition, state resident: full-time $8332; part-time $464 per credit hour. Tuition, nonresident: full-time $25,174; part-time $1400 per credit hour. *Required fees:* $1162; $56 per credit hour. Tuition and fees vary according to program.

The University of Texas at Arlington, Graduate School, College of Engineering, Department of Computer Science and Engineering, Arlington, TX 76019. Offers computer engineering (MS, PhD); computer science (MS, PhD); mathematical sciences, computer science (PhD); software engineering (MS). Part-time programs available. Postbaccalaureate distance learning degree programs offered (minimal on-campus study). *Faculty:* 31 full-time (3 women). *Students:* 206 full-time (46 women), 98 part-time (21 women); includes 7 minority (1 Black or African American, non-Hispanic/Latino; 4 Asian, non-Hispanic/Latino; 1 Hispanic/Latino; 1 Two or more races, non-Hispanic/Latino), 247 international. 752 applicants, 60% accepted, 89 enrolled. In 2011, 60 master's, 12 doctorates awarded. Terminal master's awarded for partial completion of doctoral program. *Degree requirements:* For master's, comprehensive exam (for some programs), thesis; for doctorate, comprehensive exam, thesis/dissertation. *Entrance requirements:* For master's, GRE General Test, minimum GPA of 3.0 (3.2 in computer science-related classes); for doctorate, GRE General Test, minimum GPA of 3.5. Additional exam requirements/recommendations for international students: Required—TOEFL (minimum score 550 paper-based; 230 computer-based; 92 iBT), IELTS (minimum score 6.5). *Application deadline:* For fall admission, 6/1 for domestic students, 5/1 for international students; for spring admission, 12/1 for domestic students, 10/1 for international students. Applications are processed on a rolling basis. Application fee: $35 ($50 for international students). *Financial support:* In 2011–12, 8 fellowships with full tuition reimbursements (averaging $24,000 per year), 48 research assistantships with partial tuition reimbursements (averaging $19,200 per year), 43 teaching assistantships with partial tuition reimbursements (averaging $18,000 per year) were awarded; career-related internships or fieldwork and scholarships/grants also available. Financial award application deadline: 6/1; financial award applicants required to submit FAFSA. *Faculty research:* Algorithms, homeland security, mobile pervasive computing, high performance computing bioinformation. *Unit head:* Dr. Fillia Makedon, Chairman, 817-272-3605, E-mail: makedon@uta.edu. *Application contact:* Dr. Bahram Khalili, Graduate Advisor, 817-272-5407, Fax: 817-272-3784, E-mail: khalili@uta.edu. Web site: http://www.cse.uta.edu/.

The University of Texas at Arlington, Graduate School, College of Science, Department of Mathematics, Arlington, TX 76019. Offers applied math (MS); mathematics (PhD); mathematics education (MA). Part-time and evening/weekend programs available. *Faculty:* 24 full-time (8 women), 2 part-time/adjunct (0 women). *Students:* 63 full-time (21 women), 78 part-time (33 women); includes 40 minority (15 Black or African American, non-Hispanic/Latino; 8 Asian, non-Hispanic/Latino; 16 Hispanic/Latino; 1 Two or more races, non-Hispanic/Latino), 36 international. 72 applicants, 92% accepted, 32 enrolled. In 2011, 13 master's, 4 doctorates awarded. *Degree requirements:* For master's, comprehensive exam, thesis or alternative; for doctorate, comprehensive exam, thesis/dissertation, preliminary examinations. *Entrance requirements:* For master's, GRE General Test (minimum score 350 verbal, 650 quantitative); for doctorate, GRE General Test (minimum score 350 verbal, 700 quantitative), 30 hours of graduate course work in mathematics, minimum GPA of 3.0 in last 60 hours of course work. Additional exam requirements/recommendations for international students: Required—TOEFL (minimum score 550 paper-based; 213 computer-based; 79 iBT). *Application deadline:* For fall admission, 6/1 priority date for domestic students, 4/1 for international students; for winter admission, 10/15 priority date for domestic students, 9/15 for international students. Applications are processed on a rolling basis. Application fee: $35 ($50 for international students). Electronic applications accepted. *Financial support:* In 2011–12, 36 students received support, including 17 fellowships with full tuition reimbursements available (averaging $27,500 per year), 2 research assistantships with partial tuition reimbursements available, 23 teaching assistantships with partial tuition reimbursements available (averaging $20,750 per year); Federal Work-Study, institutionally sponsored loans, scholarships/grants, health care benefits, and unspecified assistantships also available. Financial award application deadline: 2/1; financial award applicants required to submit FAFSA. *Faculty research:* Algebra, combinatorics and geometry, applied mathematics and mathematical biology, computational mathematics, mathematics education, probability and statistics. *Unit head:* Dr. Zhu Jiaping, Chair, 817-272-1114, E-mail: jpzhu@uta.edu. *Application contact:* Dr. Jianzhong Su, Graduate Advisor, 817-272-5684, Fax: 817-272-5802, E-mail: su@uta.edu. Web site: http://www.uta.edu/math.

The University of Texas at Austin, Graduate School, College of Natural Sciences, Department of Mathematics, Austin, TX 78712-1111. Offers MA, PhD. *Entrance requirements:* For master's and doctorate, GRE General Test. *Application deadline:* For fall admission, 2/1 priority date for domestic students. Application fee: $50 ($75 for international students). Electronic applications accepted. *Financial support:* Fellowships and teaching assistantships with partial tuition reimbursements available. Financial award application deadline: 2/1. *Unit head:* Dr. Alan Reid, Chair, 512-471-3153, E-mail: areid@math.utexas.edu. *Application contact:* Dr. Dan Knopf, Graduate Adviser, 512-471-8131, E-mail: danknopf@math.utexas.edu. Web site: http://www.ma.utexas.edu/academics/graduate/.

The University of Texas at Brownsville, Graduate Studies, College of Science, Mathematics and Technology, Brownsville, TX 78520-4991. Offers biological sciences (MS, MSIS); mathematics (MS); physics (MS). Part-time and evening/weekend programs available. *Degree requirements:* For master's, comprehensive exam, thesis optional. *Entrance requirements:* For master's, GRE General Test. Additional exam requirements/recommendations for international students: Required—TOEFL. *Faculty research:* Fish, insects, barrier islands, algae, curlits.

The University of Texas at Dallas, School of Natural Sciences and Mathematics, Department of Mathematical Sciences, Richardson, TX 75080. Offers applied mathematics (MS, PhD); bioinformatics and computational biology (MS); engineering mathematics (MS); mathematics (MS, PhD); statistics (MS, PhD). Part-time and evening/weekend programs available. *Faculty:* 15 full-time (2 women). *Students:* 53 full-time (21 women), 17 part-time (3 women); includes 21 minority (5 Black or African American, non-Hispanic/Latino; 12 Asian, non-Hispanic/Latino; 4 Hispanic/Latino), 31 international. Average age 31. 127 applicants, 32% accepted, 28 enrolled. In 2011, 16 master's, 7 doctorates awarded. *Degree requirements:* For master's, thesis optional; for doctorate, thesis/dissertation. *Entrance requirements:* For master's, GRE General Test, minimum GPA of 3.0 in upper-level course work in field; for doctorate, GRE General Test, minimum GPA of 3.5 in upper-level course work in field. Additional exam requirements/recommendations for international students: Required—TOEFL (minimum score 550 paper-based; 215 computer-based). *Application deadline:* For fall admission, 7/15 for domestic students, 5/1 for international students; for spring admission, 11/15 for domestic students, 9/1 for international students. Applications are processed on a rolling basis. Application fee: $50 ($100 for international students). Electronic applications accepted. *Expenses:* Tuition, state resident: full-time $11,170; part-time $620.56 per credit hour. Tuition, nonresident: full-time $20,212; part-time $1122.89 per credit hour. *Financial support:* In 2011–12, 39 students received support, including 2 research assistantships (averaging $20,700 per year), 31 teaching assistantships with partial tuition reimbursements available (averaging $15,503 per year); career-related internships or fieldwork, Federal Work-Study, institutionally sponsored loans, scholarships/grants, and unspecified assistantships also available. Support available to part-time students. Financial award application deadline: 4/30; financial award applicants required to submit FAFSA. *Faculty research:* Sequential analysis, applications in semiconductor manufacturing, medical image analysis, computational anatomy, information theory, probability theory. *Unit head:* Dr. Matthew Goeckner, Department Head, 972-883-4292, Fax: 972-883-6622, E-mail: goeckner@utdallas.edu. *Application contact:* Claire C. Troy, Graduate Support Assistant, 972-883-2163, Fax: 972-883-6622, E-mail: utdmath@utdallas.edu. Web site: http://www.utdallas.edu/math.

The University of Texas at El Paso, Graduate School, College of Science, Department of Mathematical Sciences, El Paso, TX 79968-0001. Offers mathematical sciences (MS); mathematics (teaching) (MAT); statistics (MS). Part-time and evening/weekend programs available. *Students:* 46 (16 women); includes 26 minority (2 Black or African American, non-Hispanic/Latino; 1 Asian, non-Hispanic/Latino; 23 Hispanic/Latino), 16 international. Average age 34. 24 applicants, 83% accepted, 12 enrolled. In 2011, 3 master's awarded. *Degree requirements:* For master's, thesis optional. *Entrance requirements:* For master's, minimum GPA of 3.0, letters of recommendation. Additional exam requirements/recommendations for international students: Required—TOEFL; Recommended—IELTS. *Application deadline:* For fall admission, 8/1 priority date for domestic students, 3/1 for international students; for spring admission, 11/1 priority date for domestic students, 9/1 for international students. Applications are processed on a rolling basis. Application fee: $45 ($80 for international students). Electronic applications accepted. *Financial support:* In 2011–12, research assistantships with partial tuition reimbursements (averaging $21,812 per year), teaching assistantships with partial tuition reimbursements (averaging $17,450 per year) were awarded; fellowships with tuition reimbursements, institutionally sponsored loans, scholarships/grants, health care benefits, tuition waivers (partial), and unspecified assistantships also available. Support available to part-time students. Financial award application deadline: 3/15; financial award applicants required to submit FAFSA. *Unit head:* Dr. Maria C. Mariani, Chair, 915-747-5761, Fax: 915-747-6502, E-mail: mcmariani@utep.edu. *Application contact:* Dr. Benjamin Flores, Interim Dean of the Graduate School, 915-747-5491, Fax: 915-747-5788, E-mail: bflores@utep.edu.

The University of Texas at San Antonio, College of Sciences, Department of Mathematics, San Antonio, TX 78249-0617. Offers applied mathematics (MS), including industrial mathematics; mathematics (MS); mathematics education (MS). Part-time and evening/weekend programs available. *Faculty:* 10 full-time (1 woman), 1 (woman) part-time/adjunct. *Students:* 33 full-time (14 women), 36 part-time (18 women); includes 32 minority (3 Black or African American, non-Hispanic/Latino; 2 Asian, non-Hispanic/Latino; 27 Hispanic/Latino), 10 international. Average age 30. 56 applicants, 80% accepted, 22 enrolled. In 2011, 15 master's awarded. *Degree requirements:* For master's, comprehensive exam (for some programs), thesis or alternative. *Entrance requirements:* For master's, GRE General Test, minimum GPA of 3.0 in last 60 hours. Additional exam requirements/recommendations for international students: Required—TOEFL (minimum score 500 paper-based; 61 iBT), IELTS (minimum score 5). *Application deadline:* For fall admission, 7/1 for domestic students, 4/1 for international students; for spring admission, 11/1 for domestic students, 9/1 for international students. Application fee: $45 ($85 for international students). *Expenses:* Tuition, state resident: full-time $3148; part-time $2176 per semester. Tuition, nonresident: full-time $8782; part-time $5932 per semester. *Required fees:* $719

Peterson's Graduate Programs in the Physical Sciences, Mathematics, Agricultural Sciences, the Environment & Natural Resources 2013

facebook.com/petersonspublishing **361**

Mathematics

per semester. *Financial support:* In 2011–12, 15 teaching assistantships (averaging $13,000 per year) were awarded. *Faculty research:* Differential equations, functional analysis, numerical analysis, number theory, logic. *Unit head:* Dr. F. Alexander Norman, Department Chair, 210-458-7254, Fax: 210-458-4439, E-mail: sandy.norman@utsa.edu.

The University of Texas at Tyler, College of Arts and Sciences, Department of Mathematics, Tyler, TX 75799-0001. Offers MS, MSIS. *Degree requirements:* For master's, comprehensive exam, thesis optional. *Entrance requirements:* For master's, GRE General Test. Additional exam requirements/recommendations for international students: Required—TOEFL (minimum score 79 computer-based). *Faculty research:* Discrete geometry, knot theory, commutative algebra, noncommutative rings, group theory, mathematical biology, mathematical physics.

The University of Texas–Pan American, College of Science and Mathematics, Department of Mathematics, Edinburg, TX 78539. Offers mathematical sciences (MS); mathematics teaching (MS). Part-time and evening/weekend programs available. *Degree requirements:* For master's, comprehensive exam. *Entrance requirements:* For master's, GRE General Test, minimum GPA of 3.0. *Application deadline:* For fall admission, 7/12 priority date for domestic students; for spring admission, 11/9 priority date for domestic students. Applications are processed on a rolling basis. Application fee: $0. Tuition and fees vary according to course load, program and student level. *Financial support:* Teaching assistantships, Federal Work-Study, institutionally sponsored loans, scholarships/grants, and tuition waivers (partial) available. Support available to part-time students. Financial award application deadline: 6/1. *Faculty research:* Boundary value problems in differential equations, training of public school teachers in methods of presenting mathematics, harmonic analysis, inverse problems, commutative algebra. *Unit head:* Dr. Andras Balogh, Interim Chair, 956-665-3452, E-mail: abalogh@utpa.edu. *Application contact:* Dr. Monty Taylor, Graduate Program Coordinator, 956-665-3557, E-mail: taylor@utpa.edu. Web site: http://www.math.utpa.edu/gradmath.html.

University of the Incarnate Word, School of Graduate Studies and Research, School of Mathematics, Science, and Engineering, Program in Mathematics, San Antonio, TX 78209-6397. Offers mathematics teaching (MA); research statistics (MS). Part-time and evening/weekend programs available. *Faculty:* 1 full-time (0 women), 1 (woman) part-time/adjunct. *Students:* 1 (woman) full-time, 1 (woman) part-time; includes 1 minority (Hispanic/Latino). Average age 23. 4 applicants, 100% accepted, 1 enrolled. *Degree requirements:* For master's, capstone or prerequisite knowledge (for research statistics). *Entrance requirements:* For master's, GRE (minimum score 800 verbal and quantitative), 18 hours of undergraduate mathematics with minimum GPA of 3.0; letter of recommendation by a professional in the field, writing sample, teaching experience at the precollege level. Additional exam requirements/recommendations for international students: Required—TOEFL (minimum score 560 paper-based; 220 computer-based; 83 iBT). *Application deadline:* Applications are processed on a rolling basis. Application fee: $20. Electronic applications accepted. *Expenses: Tuition:* Part-time $725 per credit hour. Tuition and fees vary according to degree level. *Financial support:* Federal Work-Study and scholarships/grants available. Financial award applicants required to submit FAFSA. *Faculty research:* Scholarship and career development for undergraduate mathematics majors. *Total annual research expenditures:* $140,844. *Unit head:* Dr. Paul Messina, Mathematics Graduate Program Coordinator, 210-832-5665, Fax: 210-829-3153, E-mail: messina@uiwtx.edu. *Application contact:* Andrea Cyterski-Acosta, Dean of Enrollment, 210-829-6005, Fax: 210-829-3921, E-mail: admis@uiwtx.edu. Web site: http://www.uiw.edu/math/mathprogramsgrad.html and.

The University of Toledo, College of Graduate Studies, College of Natural Sciences and Mathematics, Department of Mathematics, Toledo, OH 43606-3390. Offers applied mathematics (MS); mathematics (MA, PhD); statistics (MS, PhD). Part-time programs available. *Faculty:* 18. *Students:* 33 full-time (10 women), 20 part-time (6 women); includes 2 minority (both Asian, non-Hispanic/Latino), 37 international. Average age 29. 84 applicants, 43% accepted, 19 enrolled. In 2011, 11 master's, 3 doctorates awarded. *Degree requirements:* For master's, comprehensive exam (for some programs), thesis (for some programs); for doctorate, 2 foreign languages, thesis/dissertation. *Entrance requirements:* For master's and doctorate, GRE General Test, GRE Subject Test, minimum cumulative point-hour ratio of 2.7 for all previous academic work, three letters of recommendation, statement of purpose, transcripts from all prior institutions attended. Additional exam requirements/recommendations for international students: Required—TOEFL (minimum score 550 paper-based; 213 computer-based; 80 iBT), IELTS (minimum score 6.5). *Application deadline:* For fall admission, 1/15 priority date for domestic students, 1/15 for international students. Applications are processed on a rolling basis. Application fee: $45 ($75 for international students). Electronic applications accepted. *Financial support:* In 2011–12, 3 research assistantships with full and partial tuition reimbursements (averaging $12,618 per year), 46 teaching assistantships with full and partial tuition reimbursements (averaging $12,860 per year) were awarded; Federal Work-Study, institutionally sponsored loans, scholarships/grants, and unspecified assistantships also available. Support available to part-time students. *Faculty research:* Topology. *Unit head:* Dr. Paul Hewitt, Chair, 419-530-2568, E-mail: paul.hewitt@utoledo.edu. *Application contact:* Graduate School Office, 419-530-4723, Fax: 419-530-4723, E-mail: grdsch@utnet.utoledo.edu. Web site: http://www.utoledo.edu/nsm/.

University of Toronto, School of Graduate Studies, Faculty of Arts and Science, Department of Mathematics, Toronto, ON M5S 1A1, Canada. Offers M Sc, MMF, PhD. Part-time programs available. *Degree requirements:* For master's, thesis optional, research project; for doctorate, thesis/dissertation. *Entrance requirements:* For master's, minimum B average in final year, bachelor's degree in mathematics or a related area, 3 letters of reference; for doctorate, master's degree in mathematics or a related area, minimum A average, 3 letters of reference. Additional exam requirements/recommendations for international students: Required—TOEFL (minimum score 580 paper-based; 93 iBT), TWE (minimum score 4). Electronic applications accepted.

University of Tulsa, Graduate School, College of Arts and Sciences, School of Education, Program in Teaching Arts, Tulsa, OK 74104-3189. Offers art (MTA); biology (MTA); English (MTA); history (MTA); mathematics (MTA); theatre (MTA). Part-time programs available. *Students:* 2 applicants, 0% accepted, 0 enrolled. In 2011, 1 master's awarded. *Entrance requirements:* For master's, GRE General Test. Additional exam requirements/recommendations for international students: Required—TOEFL (minimum score 577 paper-based; 233 computer-based), IELTS (minimum score 6.5). *Application deadline:* Applications are processed on a rolling basis. Application fee: $40. Electronic applications accepted. *Expenses: Tuition:* Full-time $17,748; part-time $986 per hour. *Required fees:* $5 per contact hour. $75 per semester. Tuition and fees vary according to program. *Financial support:* Fellowships with full and partial tuition reimbursements, research assistantships with full and partial tuition reimbursements, teaching assistantships with full and partial tuition reimbursements, career-related internships or fieldwork, Federal Work-Study, scholarships/grants, health care benefits, tuition waivers (full and partial), and unspecified assistantships available. Support available to part-time students. Financial award application deadline: 2/1; financial award applicants required to submit FAFSA. *Unit head:* Dr. David Brown, Advisor, 918-631-2719, Fax: 918-631-2133, E-mail: david-brown@utulsa.edu. *Application contact:* Dr. David Brown, Advisor, 918-631-2719, Fax: 918-631-2133, E-mail: david-brown@utulsa.edu.

University of Tulsa, Graduate School, College of Engineering and Natural Sciences, Department of Mathematics, Tulsa, OK 74104-3189. Offers MS, MTA, MSF/MSAM. Part-time programs available. *Faculty:* 10 full-time (1 woman). *Students:* 6 full-time (2 women), 3 part-time (1 woman); includes 1 minority (Hispanic/Latino), 2 international. Average age 25. 10 applicants, 90% accepted, 6 enrolled. In 2011, 3 master's awarded. *Degree requirements:* For master's, thesis (for some programs). *Entrance requirements:* For master's, GRE General Test. Additional exam requirements/recommendations for international students: Required—TOEFL (minimum score 550 paper-based; 213 computer-based; 80 iBT), IELTS (minimum score 6). *Application deadline:* Applications are processed on a rolling basis. Application fee: $40. Electronic applications accepted. *Expenses: Tuition:* Full-time $17,748; part-time $986 per hour. *Required fees:* $5 per contact hour. $75 per semester. Tuition and fees vary according to program. *Financial support:* In 2011–12, 5 students received support, including 5 teaching assistantships with full and partial tuition reimbursements available (averaging $11,585 per year); fellowships with full and partial tuition reimbursements available, research assistantships with full and partial tuition reimbursements available, career-related internships or fieldwork, Federal Work-Study, scholarships/grants, health care benefits, tuition waivers (full and partial), and unspecified assistantships also available. Support available to part-time students. Financial award application deadline: 2/1; financial award applicants required to submit FAFSA. *Faculty research:* Optimization theory, numerical analysis, mathematical physics, modeling, Bayesian statistical inference. *Unit head:* Dr. Bill Coberly, Department Chair, 918-631-3119, Fax: 918-631-3077, E-mail: coberly@utulsa.edu. *Application contact:* Dr. Shirley Pomeranz, Advisor, 918-631-2990, Fax: 918-631-3077, E-mail: shirley-pomeranz@utulsa.edu. Web site: http://www.utulsa.edu/academics/colleges/college-of-engineering-and-natural-sciences/departments-and-schools/department-of-mathematics.aspx.

University of Utah, Graduate School, College of Science, Department of Mathematics, Salt Lake City, UT 84112-0090. Offers M Stat, MA, MS, PhD. Part-time programs available. *Faculty:* 46 full-time (6 women), 1 part-time/adjunct (0 women). *Students:* 85 full-time (22 women), 46 part-time (27 women); includes 8 minority (1 Black or African American, non-Hispanic/Latino; 2 Asian, non-Hispanic/Latino; 3 Hispanic/Latino; 2 Two or more races, non-Hispanic/Latino), 26 international. Average age 30. 144 applicants, 24% accepted, 16 enrolled. In 2011, 28 master's, 13 doctorates awarded. *Median time to degree:* Of those who began their doctoral program in fall 2003, 100% received their degree in 8 years or less. *Degree requirements:* For master's, thesis or alternative, written or oral exam; for doctorate, comprehensive exam, thesis/dissertation, written and oral exams. *Entrance requirements:* For master's and doctorate, GRE Subject Test (math), minimum undergraduate GPA of 3.0. Additional exam requirements/recommendations for international students: Required—TOEFL (minimum score 500 paper-based; 173 computer-based; 61 iBT). *Application deadline:* For fall admission, 1/15 for domestic and international students; for spring admission, 11/1 for domestic and international students. Application fee: $55 ($65 for international students). Electronic applications accepted. *Financial support:* In 2011–12, 71 students received support, including 19 research assistantships with full tuition reimbursements available (averaging $15,800 per year), 52 teaching assistantships with full tuition reimbursements available (averaging $15,300 per year); fellowships also available. Financial award application deadline: 1/15. *Faculty research:* Algebraic geometry, geometry and topology materials and microstructure, mathematical biology, probability and statistics. *Total annual research expenditures:* $3.4 million. *Unit head:* Dr. Aaron Bertram, Chairman,

362 facebook.com/petersonspublishing

Peterson's Graduate Programs in the Physical Sciences, Mathematics, Agricultural Sciences, the Environment & Natural Resources 2013

801-581-6851, Fax: 801-581-4148, E-mail: bertram@math.utah.edu. *Application contact:* Dr. Andrejs Treibergs, Graduate Advisor, 801-581-8350, Fax: 801-581-4148, E-mail: treiberg@math.utah.edu. Web site: http://www.math.utah.edu/.

University of Utah, Graduate School, Interdepartmental Program in Statistics, Salt Lake City, UT 84112-1107. Offers biostatistics (M Stat); econometrics (M Stat); educational psychology (M Stat); mathematics (M Stat); sociology (M Stat); statistics (M Stat). Part-time programs available. *Students:* 25 full-time (10 women), 28 part-time (8 women); includes 8 minority (2 Black or African American, non-Hispanic/Latino; 3 Asian, non-Hispanic/Latino; 3 Hispanic/Latino), 15 international. Average age 33. 59 applicants, 44% accepted, 12 enrolled. In 2011, 18 master's awarded. *Degree requirements:* For master's, comprehensive exam, projects. *Entrance requirements:* For master's, GRE General Test (sociology and educational psychology), minimum GPA of 3.0; course work in calculus, matrix theory, statistics. Additional exam requirements/recommendations for international students: Required—TOEFL (minimum score 500 paper-based; 173 computer-based; 61 iBT). *Application deadline:* For fall admission, 7/1 for domestic students, 4/1 for international students. Applications are processed on a rolling basis. Application fee: $55 ($65 for international students). *Financial support:* Career-related internships or fieldwork available. *Faculty research:* Biostatistics, management, economics, educational psychology, mathematics. *Unit head:* Richard Fowles, Chair, University Statistics Committee, 801-581-4577, E-mail: fowles@economics.utah.edu. *Application contact:* Laura Egbert, Coordinator, 801-585-6853, E-mail: laura.egbert@utah.edu. Web site: http://www.math.utah.edu/mstat/.

University of Vermont, Graduate College, College of Engineering and Mathematics, Department of Mathematics and Statistics, Program in Mathematics, Burlington, VT 05405. Offers mathematics (MS, PhD); mathematics education (MST). *Students:* 23 (6 women), 3 international. 53 applicants, 45% accepted, 5 enrolled. In 2011, 7 degrees awarded. *Degree requirements:* For doctorate, thesis/dissertation. *Entrance requirements:* For master's and doctorate, GRE General Test. Additional exam requirements/recommendations for international students: Required—TOEFL (minimum score 550 paper-based; 213 computer-based; 80 iBT). *Application deadline:* For fall admission, 1/15 priority date for domestic students, 1/15 for international students. Applications are processed on a rolling basis. Application fee: $40. Electronic applications accepted. *Financial support:* Fellowships, research assistantships, and teaching assistantships available. Financial award application deadline: 3/1. *Unit head:* Dr. James Burgmeier, Chair, 802-656-2940. *Application contact:* Prof. Jun Yu, Coordinator, 802-656-2940.

University of Victoria, Faculty of Graduate Studies, Faculty of Science, Department of Mathematics and Statistics, Victoria, BC V8W 2Y2, Canada. Offers M Sc, MA, PhD. Part-time programs available. *Degree requirements:* For master's, thesis; for doctorate, one foreign language, thesis/dissertation, 3 qualifying exams, candidacy exam. *Entrance requirements:* Additional exam requirements/recommendations for international students: Required—TOEFL (minimum score 575 paper-based; 233 computer-based), IELTS (minimum score 7). Electronic applications accepted. *Faculty research:* Functional analysis and operator theory, applied ordinary and partial differential equations, discrete mathematics and graph theory.

University of Virginia, College and Graduate School of Arts and Sciences, Department of Mathematics, Charlottesville, VA 22903. Offers math education (MA); mathematics (MA, MS, PhD). *Faculty:* 26 full-time (4 women). *Students:* 54 full-time (13 women); includes 4 minority (2 Asian, non-Hispanic/Latino; 1 Hispanic/Latino; 1 Two or more races, non-Hispanic/Latino), 8 international. Average age 26. 143 applicants, 16% accepted, 8 enrolled. In 2011, 6 master's, 8 doctorates awarded. *Degree requirements:* For master's, one foreign language, comprehensive exam, thesis optional; for doctorate, one foreign language, comprehensive exam, thesis/dissertation. *Entrance requirements:* For master's and doctorate, GRE General Test, GRE Subject Test, 2-3 letters of recommendation. Additional exam requirements/recommendations for international students: Required—TOEFL (minimum score 600 paper-based; 250 computer-based; 90 iBT), IELTS. *Application deadline:* For fall admission, 1/15 for domestic and international students. Applications are processed on a rolling basis. Application fee: $60. Electronic applications accepted. *Financial support:* Fellowships, teaching assistantships, and unspecified assistantships available. Financial award application deadline: 1/15; financial award applicants required to submit FAFSA. *Unit head:* Brian Parshall, Chair, 434-924-4919, Fax: 434-982-3084, E-mail: bjp8w@virginia.edu. *Application contact:* Barbara MacCluer, Director of Graduate Studies, 434-924-4919, Fax: 434-924-3084, E-mail: bdm3f@virginia.edu. Web site: http://www.math.virginia.edu/.

University of Washington, Graduate School, College of Arts and Sciences, Department of Mathematics, Seattle, WA 98195. Offers mathematics (MA, MS, PhD); numerical analysis (MS); optimization (MS). Part-time programs available. Terminal master's awarded for partial completion of doctoral program. *Degree requirements:* For master's, thesis optional; for doctorate, 2 foreign languages, thesis/dissertation. *Entrance requirements:* For master's, GRE, minimum GPA of 3.0; for doctorate, GRE General Test, GRE Subject Test (mathematics), minimum GPA of 3.0. Additional exam requirements/recommendations for international students: Required—TOEFL. Electronic applications accepted. *Faculty research:* Algebra, analysis, probability, combinatorics and geometry.

University of Washington, Graduate School, Interdisciplinary Graduate Program in Quantitative Ecology and Resource Management, Seattle, WA 98195. Offers

MS, PhD. *Degree requirements:* For master's, thesis; for doctorate, thesis/dissertation. *Entrance requirements:* For master's and doctorate, GRE General Test, minimum GPA of 3.0. Additional exam requirements/recommendations for international students: Required—TOEFL. Electronic applications accepted. *Faculty research:* Population dynamics, statistical analysis, ecological modeling and systems analysis of aquatic and terrestrial ecosystems.

University of Waterloo, Graduate Studies, Faculty of Mathematics, Department of Combinatorics and Optimization, Waterloo, ON N2L 3G1, Canada. Offers M Math, PhD. *Degree requirements:* For master's, research paper or thesis; for doctorate, comprehensive exam, thesis/dissertation. *Entrance requirements:* For master's, GRE General Test, honors degree in field, minimum B+ average; for doctorate, GRE General Test, master's degree, minimum A average. Additional exam requirements/recommendations for international students: Required—TOEFL, TWE. Electronic applications accepted. *Faculty research:* Algebraic and enumerative combinatorics, continuous optimization, cryptography, discrete optimization and graph theory.

University of Waterloo, Graduate Studies, Faculty of Mathematics, Department of Pure Mathematics, Waterloo, ON N2L 3G1, Canada. Offers M Math, PhD. Part-time programs available. Terminal master's awarded for partial completion of doctoral program. *Degree requirements:* For master's, thesis optional; for doctorate, comprehensive exam, thesis/dissertation. *Entrance requirements:* For master's, honors degree in field, minimum B+ average; for doctorate, master's degree, minimum B+ average. Additional exam requirements/recommendations for international students: Required—TOEFL (minimum score 580 paper-based; 237 computer-based; 92 iBT), TWE (minimum score 4). Electronic applications accepted. *Faculty research:* Algebra, algebraic and differential geometry, functional and harmonic analysis, logic and universal algebra, number theory.

The University of Western Ontario, Faculty of Graduate Studies, Physical Sciences Division, Department of Mathematics, London, ON N6A 5B8, Canada. Offers M Sc, PhD. Terminal master's awarded for partial completion of doctoral program. *Degree requirements:* For master's, thesis or alternative; for doctorate, one foreign language, comprehensive exam, thesis/dissertation, qualifying exam. *Entrance requirements:* For master's, minimum B average, honors degree; for doctorate, master's degree. Additional exam requirements/recommendations for international students: Required—TOEFL (minimum score 550 paper-based; 213 computer-based). *Faculty research:* Algebra and number theory, analysis, geometry and topology.

University of West Florida, College of Arts and Sciences: Sciences, Department of Mathematics and Statistics, Pensacola, FL 32514-5750. Offers applied statistics (MS); mathematical sciences (MS). Part-time and evening/weekend programs available. *Faculty:* 8 full-time (0 women). *Students:* 10 full-time (2 women), 75 part-time (37 women); includes 23 minority (12 Black or African American, non-Hispanic/Latino; 4 Asian, non-Hispanic/Latino; 5 Hispanic/Latino; 2 Two or more races, non-Hispanic/Latino), 5 international. Average age 34. 57 applicants, 77% accepted, 29 enrolled. In 2011, 13 master's awarded. *Degree requirements:* For master's, thesis optional. *Entrance requirements:* For master's, GRE (minimum score: verbal 420; quantitative 580), minimum GPA of 3.0; official transcripts. Additional exam requirements/recommendations for international students: Required—TOEFL (minimum score 550 paper-based; 213 computer-based). *Application deadline:* For fall admission, 6/1 for domestic and international students; for spring admission, 10/1 for domestic and international students. Applications are processed on a rolling basis. Application fee: $30. *Expenses:* Tuition, state resident: full-time $5729; part-time $302 per credit hour. Tuition, nonresident: full-time $20,059; part-time $961 per credit hour. *Required fees:* $1509; $63 per credit hour. *Financial support:* In 2011–12, 11 fellowships with partial tuition reimbursements (averaging $418 per year), 8 research assistantships with partial tuition reimbursements (averaging $3,280 per year), 15 teaching assistantships with partial tuition reimbursements (averaging $6,656 per year) were awarded; unspecified assistantships also available. Financial award application deadline: 4/15; financial award applicants required to submit FAFSA. *Unit head:* Dr. Kuiyuan Li, Chairperson, 850-474-2287, E-mail: mathstat@uwf.edu. *Application contact:* Terry McCray, Assistant Director of Graduate Admissions, 850-473-7718, Fax: 850-473-7714, E-mail: gradadmissions@uwf.edu. Web site: http://uwf.edu/mathstat/.

University of West Georgia, College of Science and Mathematics, Department of Mathematics, Carrollton, GA 30118. Offers teaching and applied mathematics (MS). *Faculty:* 15 full-time (3 women). *Students:* 6 full-time (1 woman), 11 part-time (3 women); includes 14 minority (11 Black or African American, non-Hispanic/Latino; 1 Asian, non-Hispanic/Latino; 2 Hispanic/Latino), 5 international. Average age 33. 9 applicants, 56% accepted, 1 enrolled. In 2011, 1 master's awarded. *Degree requirements:* For master's, comprehensive exam, thesis optional, 36 credit hours. *Entrance requirements:* For master's, GRE. Additional exam requirements/recommendations for international students: Required—TOEFL (minimum score 523 paper-based; 193 computer-based; 69 iBT); Recommended—IELTS (minimum score 6). *Application deadline:* For fall admission, 6/1 for domestic and international students; for spring admission, 11/15 for domestic students, 10/15 for international students. Applications are processed on a rolling basis. Application fee: $30. Electronic applications accepted. *Expenses:* Tuition, state resident: full-time $4336; part-time $181 per credit hour. Tuition, nonresident: full-time $17,362; part-time $724 per credit hour. Tuition and fees vary according to course load, degree level, campus/location and program. *Financial support:* In 2011–12, 3 students received support, including 3 teaching assistantships (averaging $6,800 per year); unspecified assistantships

Peterson's Graduate Programs in the Physical Sciences, Mathematics, Agricultural Sciences, the Environment & Natural Resources 2013

facebook.com/petersonspublishing **363**

Mathematics

also available. Financial award application deadline: 7/1; financial award applicants required to submit FAFSA. *Unit head:* Dr. Minh Nguyen, Interim Chair, 678-839-6489, Fax: 678-839-6490, E-mail: vnguyen@westga.edu. *Application contact:* Alice Wesley, Departmental Assistant, 678-839-5192, E-mail: awesley@westga.edu. Web site: http://www.westga.edu/math/.

University of Windsor, Faculty of Graduate Studies, Faculty of Science, Department of Mathematics and Statistics, Windsor, ON N9B 3P4, Canada. Offers mathematics (M Sc); statistics (M Sc, PhD). *Degree requirements:* For master's, thesis or alternative; for doctorate, comprehensive exam, thesis/dissertation. *Entrance requirements:* For master's, minimum B average; for doctorate, minimum A average. Additional exam requirements/recommendations for international students: Required—TOEFL (minimum score 560 paper-based; 220 computer-based). Electronic applications accepted. *Faculty research:* Applied mathematics, operational research, fluid dynamics.

University of Wisconsin–Madison, Graduate School, College of Letters and Science, Department of Mathematics, Madison, WI 53706. Offers PhD. *Degree requirements:* For doctorate, comprehensive exam, thesis/dissertation, classes in a minor field; minimum GPA of 3.3. *Entrance requirements:* For doctorate, GRE General Test, GRE Subject Test (math). Additional exam requirements/recommendations for international students: Required—TOEFL (minimum score 580 paper-based; 237 computer-based; 92 iBT), IELTS. Electronic applications accepted. *Expenses:* Tuition, state resident: full-time $10,296; part-time $643.51 per credit. Tuition, nonresident: full-time $24,054; part-time $1503.40 per credit. *Required fees:* $70.06 per credit. Tuition and fees vary according to course load, campus/location, program and reciprocity agreements. *Faculty research:* Analysis, applied/computational mathematics, geometry/topology, logic, algebra/number theory, probability.

University of Wisconsin–Milwaukee, Graduate School, College of Letters and Sciences, Department of Mathematical Sciences, Milwaukee, WI 53201-0413. Offers mathematics (MS, PhD). *Faculty:* 32 full-time (3 women), 2 part-time/adjunct (1 woman). *Students:* 70 full-time (20 women), 18 part-time (5 women); includes 7 minority (1 Black or African American, non-Hispanic/Latino; 1 American Indian or Alaska Native, non-Hispanic/Latino; 3 Asian, non-Hispanic/Latino; 1 Hispanic/Latino; 1 Two or more races, non-Hispanic/Latino), 24 international. Average age 30. 123 applicants, 33% accepted, 28 enrolled. In 2011, 22 master's, 2 doctorates awarded. *Degree requirements:* For master's, comprehensive exam, thesis optional; for doctorate, 2 foreign languages, thesis/dissertation. *Entrance requirements:* Additional exam requirements/recommendations for international students: Required—TOEFL (minimum score 550 paper-based; 79 iBT), IELTS (minimum score 6.5). *Application deadline:* For fall admission, 1/1 priority date for domestic students; for spring admission, 9/1 for domestic students. Applications are processed on a rolling basis. Application fee: $56 ($96 for international students). Electronic applications accepted. One-time fee: $506.10 full-time. Tuition and fees vary according to course load and reciprocity agreements. *Financial support:* In 2011–12, 23 fellowships, 9 research assistantships, 56 teaching assistantships were awarded; career-related internships or fieldwork, health care benefits, and unspecified assistantships also available. Support available to part-time students. Financial award application deadline: 4/15; financial award applicants required to submit FAFSA. *Faculty research:* Algebra, applied mathematics, atmospheric science, probability and statistics, topology. *Total annual research expenditures:* $1.3 million. *Unit head:* Richard Stockbridge, Department Chair, 414-229-4568, E-mail: stockbri@uwm.edu. *Application contact:* General Information Contact, 414-229-4982, Fax: 414-229-6967, E-mail: gradschool@uwm.edu. Web site: http://www.uwm.edu/dept/math/.

University of Wyoming, College of Arts and Sciences, Department of Mathematics, Laramie, WY 82071. Offers mathematics (MA, MAT, MS, MST, PhD); mathematics/computer science (PhD). Part-time programs available. Terminal master's awarded for partial completion of doctoral program. *Degree requirements:* For master's, comprehensive exam, thesis, qualifying exam; for doctorate, comprehensive exam, thesis/dissertation, preliminary exam. *Entrance requirements:* For master's and doctorate, GRE General Test, minimum GPA of 3.0. Additional exam requirements/recommendations for international students: Required—TOEFL (minimum score 540 paper-based; 76 iBT). *Faculty research:* Numerical analysis, classical analysis, mathematical modeling, algebraic combinations.

Utah State University, School of Graduate Studies, College of Science, Department of Mathematics and Statistics, Logan, UT 84322. Offers industrial mathematics (MS); mathematical sciences (PhD); mathematics (M Math, MS); statistics (MS). Part-time programs available. Terminal master's awarded for partial completion of doctoral program. *Degree requirements:* For master's, thesis optional, qualifying exam; for doctorate, one foreign language, comprehensive exam, thesis/dissertation. *Entrance requirements:* For master's and doctorate, GRE General Test, minimum GPA of 3.0. Additional exam requirements/recommendations for international students: Required—TOEFL. *Faculty research:* Differential equations, computational mathematics, dynamical systems, probability and statistics, pure mathematics.

Vanderbilt University, Graduate School, Department of Mathematics, Nashville, TN 37240-1001. Offers MA, MAT, MS, PhD. *Faculty:* 32 full-time (2 women). *Students:* 40 full-time (8 women), 1 (woman) part-time; includes 2 minority (1 Hispanic/Latino; 1 Two or more races, non-Hispanic/Latino), 22 international. Average age 27. 153 applicants, 13% accepted, 12 enrolled. In 2011, 6 master's, 4 doctorates awarded. *Degree requirements:* For master's, one foreign language,

thesis or alternative; for doctorate, one foreign language, comprehensive exam, thesis/dissertation. *Entrance requirements:* For master's and doctorate, GRE General Test, GRE Subject Test. Additional exam requirements/recommendations for international students: Required—TOEFL (minimum score 570 paper-based; 230 computer-based; 88 iBT). *Application deadline:* For fall admission, 1/15 for domestic and international students. Application fee: $0. Electronic applications accepted. *Financial support:* Fellowships with full and partial tuition reimbursements, research assistantships with full tuition reimbursements, teaching assistantships with full tuition reimbursements, Federal Work-Study, institutionally sponsored loans, scholarships/grants, and health care benefits available. Financial award application deadline: 1/15; financial award applicants required to submit CSS PROFILE or FAFSA. *Faculty research:* Algebra, topology, applied mathematics, graph theory, analytical mathematics. *Unit head:* Dr. Dietmar Bisch, Chair, 615-322-1999, Fax: 615-343-0215, E-mail: dietmar.bisch@vanderbilt.edu. *Application contact:* Dr. Mike Neamtu, Director of Graduate Studies, 615-322-6655, Fax: 315-343-0215, E-mail: marian.neamtu@vanderbilt.edu. Web site: http://www.math.vanderbilt.edu/.

Villanova University, Graduate School of Liberal Arts and Sciences, Department of Mathematical Sciences, Program in Mathematical Sciences, Villanova, PA 19085-1699. Offers MA. Part-time and evening/weekend programs available. *Students:* 15 full-time (8 women), 12 part-time (4 women); includes 2 minority (both Black or African American, non-Hispanic/Latino). Average age 31. 20 applicants, 95% accepted, 12 enrolled. In 2011, 15 master's awarded. *Degree requirements:* For master's, comprehensive exam. *Entrance requirements:* For master's, GRE, minimum GPA of 3.0. Additional exam requirements/recommendations for international students: Required—TOEFL. *Application deadline:* For fall admission, 5/1 for international students; for spring admission, 10/15 for international students. Applications are processed on a rolling basis. Application fee: $50. Electronic applications accepted. *Expenses:* Tuition: Part-time $675 per credit. Part-time tuition and fees vary according to degree level and program. *Financial support:* Research assistantships and Federal Work-Study available. Financial award applicants required to submit FAFSA. *Unit head:* Dr. Douglas Norton, Chair, 610-519-4850. *Application contact:* Dr. Adele Lindenmeyr, Dean, Graduate School of Liberal Arts and Sciences, 610-519-7093, Fax: 610-519-7096. Web site: http://www.villanova.edu/artsci/mathematics/graduate/mamath.htm.

Virginia Commonwealth University, Graduate School, College of Humanities and Sciences, Department of Mathematics and Applied Mathematics, Richmond, VA 23284-9005. Offers applied mathematics (MS); mathematics (MS). *Students:* 27 full-time (16 women), 27 part-time (8 women); includes 5 minority (4 Black or African American, non-Hispanic/Latino; 1 Hispanic/Latino), 7 international. 31 applicants, 71% accepted, 16 enrolled. In 2011, 15 master's awarded. *Degree requirements:* For master's, thesis optional. *Entrance requirements:* For master's, GRE General Test, GRE Subject Test, 30 undergraduate semester credits in the mathematical sciences or closely-related fields. Additional exam requirements/recommendations for international students: Required—TOEFL (minimum score 600 paper-based; 250 computer-based; 100 iBT); Recommended—IELTS (minimum score 6.5). *Application deadline:* For fall admission, 3/1 for domestic students; for spring admission, 10/1 for domestic students. Applications are processed on a rolling basis. Application fee: $50. Electronic applications accepted. *Expenses:* Tuition, state resident: full-time $9133; part-time $507 per credit. Tuition, nonresident: full-time $18,777; part-time $1043 per credit. *Required fees:* $77 per credit. Tuition and fees vary according to degree level, campus/location, program and student level. *Financial support:* Fellowships, research assistantships, teaching assistantships, Federal Work-Study, and institutionally sponsored loans available. Support available to part-time students. Financial award applicants required to submit FAFSA. *Faculty research:* Mathematics, applied mathematics. *Unit head:* Dr. Andrew M. Lewis, Chair, 804-828-1301 Ext. 128, Fax: 804-828-8785, E-mail: amlewis@vcu.edu. *Application contact:* Dr. Dewey T. Taylor, Graduate Program Director, 804-828-1301, E-mail: dttaylor2@vcu.edu. Web site: http://www.math.vcu.edu/.

Virginia Polytechnic Institute and State University, Graduate School, College of Science, Department of Mathematics, Blacksburg, VA 24061. Offers MS, PhD. *Degree requirements:* For master's, comprehensive exam (for some programs), thesis (for some programs); for doctorate, comprehensive exam (for some programs), thesis/dissertation (for some programs). *Entrance requirements:* For master's and doctorate, GRE. Additional exam requirements/recommendations for international students: Required—TOEFL (minimum score 550 paper-based; 213 computer-based). *Application deadline:* For fall admission, 7/1 for domestic and international students; for spring admission, 12/1 for domestic and international students. Applications are processed on a rolling basis. Application fee: $65. Electronic applications accepted. *Expenses:* Tuition, state resident: full-time $10,048; part-time $558.25 per credit hour. Tuition, nonresident: full-time $19,497; part-time $1083.25 per credit hour. *Required fees:* $405 per semester. Tuition and fees vary according to course load, campus/location and program. *Financial support:* Fellowships with full tuition reimbursements, research assistantships with full tuition reimbursements, teaching assistantships with full tuition reimbursements, career-related internships or fieldwork, Federal Work-Study, scholarships/grants, health care benefits, and unspecified assistantships available. Financial award application deadline: 1/15. *Faculty research:* Differential equations, operator theory, numerical analysis, algebra, control theory. *Unit head:* Dr. Peter E. Haskell, Unit Head, 540-231-8282, Fax: 540-231-5960, E-mail: phaskell@vt.edu. *Application contact:* Jeff Borggaard, Information

364 facebook.com/petersonspublishing

Peterson's Graduate Programs in the Physical Sciences, Mathematics, Agricultural Sciences, the Environment & Natural Resources 2013

Contact, 540-231-7667, Fax: 540-231-5960, E-mail: jborggaard@vt.edu. Web site: http://www.math.vt.edu/grGeneralInfo.php.

Virginia State University, School of Graduate Studies, Research, and Outreach, School of Engineering, Science and Technology, Department of Mathematics and Computer Science, Petersburg, VA 23806-0001. Offers computer science (MS); mathematics (MS); mathematics education (M Ed). *Degree requirements:* For master's, thesis (for some programs).

Wake Forest University, Graduate School of Arts and Sciences, Department of Mathematics, Winston-Salem, NC 27109. Offers MA. Part-time programs available. *Degree requirements:* For master's, one foreign language, thesis optional. *Entrance requirements:* For master's, GRE General Test. Additional exam requirements/recommendations for international students: Required—TOEFL (minimum score 213 computer-based; 79 iBT). Electronic applications accepted. *Faculty research:* Algebra, ring theory, topology, differential equations.

Washington State University, Graduate School, College of Sciences, Department of Mathematics, Pullman, WA 99164. Offers applied mathematics (MS, PhD); mathematics teaching (MS, PhD). Part-time programs available. *Faculty:* 26. *Students:* 45 full-time (12 women), 5 part-time (4 women); includes 7 minority (1 Black or African American, non-Hispanic/Latino; 3 Asian, non-Hispanic/Latino; 2 Hispanic/Latino; 1 Two or more races, non-Hispanic/Latino), 14 international. Average age 30. 71 applicants, 54% accepted, 13 enrolled. In 2011, 2 master's, 4 doctorates awarded. *Degree requirements:* For master's, comprehensive exam (for some programs), thesis (for some programs), oral exam, project; for doctorate, 2 foreign languages, comprehensive exam, thesis/dissertation, oral exam, written exam. *Entrance requirements:* For master's and doctorate, minimum GPA of 3.0, 3 letters of recommendation. Additional exam requirements/recommendations for international students: Required—TOEFL (minimum score 600 paper-based; 250 computer-based), IELTS. *Application deadline:* For fall admission, 1/10 for domestic and international students; for spring admission, 7/1 for domestic and international students. Applications are processed on a rolling basis. Application fee: $75. Electronic applications accepted. *Financial support:* In 2011–12, 33 students received support, including 2 fellowships with tuition reimbursements available (averaging $2,500 per year), 3 research assistantships with full and partial tuition reimbursements available (averaging $14,634 per year), 27 teaching assistantships with full and partial tuition reimbursements available (averaging $13,383 per year); career-related internships or fieldwork, Federal Work-Study, institutionally sponsored loans, health care benefits, and tuition waivers (partial) also available. Financial award application deadline: 2/15; financial award applicants required to submit FAFSA. *Faculty research:* Computational mathematics, operations research, modeling in the natural sciences, applied statistics. *Unit head:* Dr. K. A. Ariyawansa, Chair, 509-335-4918, Fax: 509-335-1188, E-mail: ari@wsu.edu. *Application contact:* Graduate School Admissions, 800-GRADWSU, Fax: 509-335-1949, E-mail: gradsch@wsu.edu. Web site: http://www.sci.wsu.edu/math/.

Washington University in St. Louis, Graduate School of Arts and Sciences, Department of Mathematics, St. Louis, MO 63130-4899. Offers mathematics (MA, PhD); statistics (MA). Terminal master's awarded for partial completion of doctoral program. *Degree requirements:* For master's, thesis or alternative; for doctorate, thesis/dissertation. *Entrance requirements:* For master's and doctorate, GRE General Test. Electronic applications accepted.

Washington University in St. Louis, School of Engineering and Applied Science, Department of Electrical and Systems Engineering, St. Louis, MO 63130-4899. Offers electrical engineering (MS, D Sc, PhD); systems science and mathematics (MS, D Sc, PhD). Part-time programs available. Terminal master's awarded for partial completion of doctoral program. *Degree requirements:* For master's, thesis or alternative; for doctorate, comprehensive exam, thesis/dissertation. *Entrance requirements:* For master's, minimum GPA of 3.0 in the last 2 years of undergraduate course work; for doctorate, GRE. Additional exam requirements/recommendations for international students: Required—TOEFL (minimum score 550 paper-based; 213 computer-based; 80 iBT). Electronic applications accepted. *Faculty research:* Applied physics and electronics, signal and image processing, systems analysis, biomedicine, and energy.

Wayne State University, College of Liberal Arts and Sciences, Department of Mathematics, Detroit, MI 48202. Offers applied mathematics (MA); mathematical statistics (MA); mathematics (MA, PhD). *Students:* 50 full-time (16 women), 34 part-time (14 women); includes 13 minority (8 Black or African American, non-Hispanic/Latino; 4 Asian, non-Hispanic/Latino; 1 Two or more races, non-Hispanic/Latino), 32 international. Average age 30. 103 applicants, 50% accepted, 18 enrolled. In 2011, 12 master's, 5 doctorates awarded. *Degree requirements:* For master's, thesis (for some programs), essays, oral exams; for doctorate, one foreign language, thesis/dissertation, oral exams. *Entrance requirements:* For doctorate, master's degree in mathematics or equivalent level of advancement. Additional exam requirements/recommendations for international students: Required—TOEFL (minimum score 550 paper-based; 213 computer-based); Recommended—TWE (minimum score 5.5). *Application deadline:* For fall admission, 6/1 priority date for domestic students, 5/1 for international students; for winter admission, 10/1 priority date for domestic students, 9/1 for international students; for spring admission, 2/1 priority date for domestic students, 1/1 for international students. Applications are processed on a rolling basis. Application fee: $50. Electronic applications accepted. *Expenses:* Tuition, state resident: part-time $512.85 per credit. Tuition, nonresident: part-time $1132.65 per credit. *Required fees:* $26.60 per credit. $199.65 per semester.

Tuition and fees vary according to course load and program. *Financial support:* In 2011–12, 43 students received support, including 4 fellowships with tuition reimbursements available (averaging $17,938 per year), 3 research assistantships with tuition reimbursements available (averaging $18,894 per year), 27 teaching assistantships with tuition reimbursements available (averaging $17,391 per year); institutionally sponsored loans, scholarships/grants, health care benefits, tuition waivers (full), and unspecified assistantships also available. Support available to part-time students. *Faculty research:* Harmonic analysis and partial differential equations, group theory and non-commutative ring theory, homotopy theory and applications to topology and geometry, numerical analysis, control and optimization, statistical estimation theory. *Total annual research expenditures:* $708,703. *Unit head:* Daniel Frohardt, Professor and Chair, 313-577-2479, E-mail: danf@math.wayne.edu. *Application contact:* Tiana Fluker, Graduate Secretary, E-mail: tiana@math.wayne.edu. Web site: http://www.math.wayne.edu/.

Wesleyan University, Graduate Programs, Department of Mathematics and Computer Science, Middletown, CT 06459. Offers MA, PhD. Terminal master's awarded for partial completion of doctoral program. *Degree requirements:* For master's, one foreign language, thesis; for doctorate, 2 foreign languages, thesis/dissertation. *Entrance requirements:* For master's, GRE General Test, GRE Subject Test; for doctorate, GRE Subject Test. Additional exam requirements/recommendations for international students: Required—TOEFL. Electronic applications accepted. *Faculty research:* Topology, analysis.

See Display on next page and Close-Up on page 393.

West Chester University of Pennsylvania, College of Arts and Sciences, Department of Mathematics, West Chester, PA 19383. Offers applied statistics (MS, Certificate); mathematics (MA, Teaching Certificate). Part-time and evening/weekend programs available. *Faculty:* 7 part-time/adjunct (1 woman). *Students:* 24 full-time (8 women), 69 part-time (28 women); includes 19 minority (8 Black or African American, non-Hispanic/Latino; 10 Asian, non-Hispanic/Latino; 1 Hispanic/Latino), 5 international. Average age 31. 73 applicants, 68% accepted, 42 enrolled. In 2011, 13 degrees awarded. *Degree requirements:* For master's, thesis optional. *Entrance requirements:* For master's, GMAT, GRE General Test, or MAT (for MA), interview; for other advanced degree, GMAT, GRE General Test, or MAT (for Teaching Certificate). Additional exam requirements/recommendations for international students: Required—TOEFL (minimum score 550 paper-based; 213 computer-based; 80 iBT). *Application deadline:* For fall admission, 4/15 priority date for domestic students, 3/15 for international students; for spring admission, 10/15 priority date for domestic students, 9/1 for international students. Applications are processed on a rolling basis. Application fee: $45. Electronic applications accepted. *Expenses:* Tuition, state resident: full-time $7488; part-time $416 per credit. Tuition, nonresident: full-time $11,232; part-time $624 per credit. *Required fees:* $1784.64; $67.59 per credit. Tuition and fees vary according to program. *Financial support:* Unspecified assistantships available. Support available to part-time students. Financial award application deadline: 2/15; financial award applicants required to submit FAFSA. *Faculty research:* Teachers teaching with technology in service training program, biostatistics, hierarchical linear models, clustered binary outcome model. *Unit head:* Dr. Kathleen Jackson, Chair, 610-436-2537, Fax: 610-738-0578, E-mail: kjackson@wcupa.edu. *Application contact:* Dr. Gail Gallitano, Graduate Coordinator, 610-436-2452, Fax: 610-738-0578, E-mail: ggallitano@wcupa.edu. Web site: http://www.wcupa.edu/_academics/sch_cas.mat/.

Western Carolina University, Graduate School, College of Arts and Sciences, Department of Mathematics and Computer Science, Cullowhee, NC 28723. Offers applied mathematics (MS). Part-time and evening/weekend programs available. *Students:* 11 full-time (6 women), 7 part-time (2 women); includes 1 minority (Two or more races, non-Hispanic/Latino). Average age 27. 16 applicants, 88% accepted, 9 enrolled. In 2011, 7 master's awarded. *Degree requirements:* For master's, thesis or alternative. *Entrance requirements:* For master's, GRE General Test, appropriate undergraduate degree, 3 letters of recommendation. Additional exam requirements/recommendations for international students: Required—TOEFL (minimum score 550 paper-based; 270 computer-based; 79 iBT). *Application deadline:* For fall admission, 5/1 priority date for domestic students; for spring admission, 9/1 priority date for domestic students. Applications are processed on a rolling basis. Application fee: $50. *Expenses:* Tuition, state resident: full-time $3348. Tuition, nonresident: full-time $12,933. *Required fees:* $3155. *Financial support:* Fellowships, research assistantships with full and partial tuition reimbursements, teaching assistantships with full and partial tuition reimbursements, career-related internships or fieldwork, institutionally sponsored loans, scholarships/grants, and unspecified assistantships available. Financial award application deadline: 3/31; financial award applicants required to submit FAFSA. *Unit head:* Dr. Tuval Foguel, Department Head, 828-227-3831, Fax: 828-227-7240, E-mail: tsfoguel@email.wcu.edu. *Application contact:* Admissions Specialist for Applied Mathematics, 828-227-7398, Fax: 828-227-7480, E-mail: gradsch@email.wcu.edu. Web site: http://www.cs.wcu.edu/.

Western Connecticut State University, Division of Graduate Studies, School of Arts and Sciences, Department of Mathematics, Danbury, CT 06810-6885. Offers mathematics (MA); theoretical mathematics (MA). Part-time programs available. *Faculty:* 3 full-time (2 women). *Students:* 8 part-time (4 women). Average age 30. In 2011, 1 degree awarded. *Degree requirements:* For master's, thesis or research project, completion of program in 6 years. *Entrance requirements:* For master's, minimum GPA of 2.5. Additional exam requirements/recommendations

Peterson's Graduate Programs in the Physical Sciences, Mathematics, Agricultural Sciences, the Environment & Natural Resources 2013

facebook.com/petersonspublishing **365**

for international students: Recommended—TOEFL (minimum score 550 paper-based; 213 computer-based; 79 iBT), IELTS (minimum score 6). *Application deadline:* For fall admission, 8/5 priority date for domestic students; for spring admission, 1/5 priority date for domestic students. Applications are processed on a rolling basis. Application fee: $50. Tuition and fees vary according to course level, course load, degree level and program. *Financial support:* Application deadline: 5/1; applicants required to submit FAFSA. *Faculty research:* Eulerian mathematical principles. *Unit head:* Dr. Sam Lightwood, Graduate Coordinator, 203-837-9369, Fax: 203-837-8525, E-mail: lightwoods@wcsu.edu. *Application contact:* Chris Shankle, Associate Director of Graduate Studies, 203-837-9005, Fax: 203-837-8326, E-mail: shanklec@wcsu.edu. Web site: http://www.wcsu.edu/math/.

Western Illinois University, School of Graduate Studies, College of Arts and Sciences, Department of Mathematics, Macomb, IL 61455-1390. Offers applied math (Certificate); mathematics (MS). Part-time programs available. *Students:* 9 full-time (1 woman), 3 part-time (1 woman), 6 international. Average age 27. 11 applicants, 55% accepted. In 2011, 6 master's, 1 other advanced degree awarded. *Degree requirements:* For master's, thesis or alternative. *Entrance requirements:* Additional exam requirements/recommendations for international students: Required—TOEFL (minimum score 500 paper-based; 173 computer-based; 61 iBT). *Application deadline:* Applications are processed on a rolling basis. Application fee: $30. Electronic applications accepted. *Expenses:* Tuition, state resident: part-time $281.16 per credit hour. Tuition, nonresident: part-time $562.32 per credit hour. Part-time tuition and fees vary according to campus/location and reciprocity agreements. *Financial support:* In 2011–12, 11 students received support, including 5 research assistantships with full tuition reimbursements available (averaging $7,360 per year), 6 teaching assistantships with full tuition reimbursements available (averaging $8,480 per year). Financial award applicants required to submit FAFSA. *Unit head:* Dr. Iraj Kalantari, Chairperson, 309-298-1054. *Application contact:* Nancy Parsons, Interim Associate Provost and Director of Graduate Studies, 309-298-1806, Fax: 309-298-2345, E-mail: grad-office@wiu.edu. Web site: http://wiu.edu/mathematics.

Western Kentucky University, Graduate Studies, Ogden College of Science and Engineering, Department of Mathematics and Computer Science, Bowling Green, KY 42101. Offers computational mathematics (MS); computer science (MS); mathematics (MA, MS). *Degree requirements:* For master's, comprehensive exam, thesis optional, written exam. *Entrance requirements:* For master's, GRE General Test, minimum GPA of 2.75. Additional exam requirements/recommendations for international students: Required—TOEFL (minimum score 555 paper-based; 213 computer-based; 79 iBT). *Faculty research:* Differential equations numerical analysis, probability statistics, algebra, typology, knot theory.

Western Michigan University, Graduate College, College of Arts and Sciences, Department of Mathematics, Programs in Mathematics, Kalamazoo, MI 49008. Offers mathematics (MA, PhD); mathematics education (MA, PhD). *Degree requirements:* For master's, oral exams; for doctorate, one foreign language, thesis/dissertation, oral exams, 3 comprehensive exams, internship. *Entrance requirements:* For doctorate, GRE General Test.

Western Washington University, Graduate School, College of Sciences and Technology, Department of Mathematics, Bellingham, WA 98225-5996. Offers MS. Part-time programs available. *Degree requirements:* For master's, thesis (for some programs), project, qualifying examination. *Entrance requirements:* For master's, GRE General Test, minimum GPA of 3.0 in last 60 semester hours or last 90 quarter hours. Additional exam requirements/recommendations for international students: Required—TOEFL (minimum score 567 paper-based; 227 computer-based). Electronic applications accepted. *Faculty research:* Numerical analysis, combinatorics, harmonic analysis, inverse problems, reliability testing.

West Texas A&M University, College of Agriculture, Nursing, and Natural Sciences, Department of Mathematics, Physical Sciences and Engineering Technology, Program in Mathematics, Canyon, TX 79016-0001. Offers MS. Part-time programs available. *Degree requirements:* For master's, comprehensive exam, thesis optional. *Entrance requirements:* For master's, GRE General Test. Additional exam requirements/recommendations for international students: Required—TOEFL (minimum score 550 paper-based). Electronic applications accepted.

West Virginia University, Eberly College of Arts and Sciences, Department of Mathematics, Morgantown, WV 26506. Offers applied mathematics (MS, PhD); discrete mathematics (PhD); interdisciplinary mathematics (MS); mathematics for secondary education (MS); pure mathematics (MS). Part-time programs available. Terminal master's awarded for partial completion of doctoral program. *Degree requirements:* For master's, comprehensive exam (for some programs), thesis optional; for doctorate, one foreign language, comprehensive exam, thesis/dissertation. *Entrance requirements:* For master's, GRE Subject Test (recommended), minimum GPA of 2.5; for doctorate, GRE Subject Test (recommended), master's degree in mathematics. Additional exam requirements/recommendations for international students: Required—TOEFL (paper-based 550; computer-based 213) or IELTS (paper-based 6). *Faculty research:* Combinatorics and graph theory, differential equations, applied and computational mathematics.

Wichita State University, Graduate School, Fairmount College of Liberal Arts and Sciences, Department of Mathematics, Statistics and Physics, Wichita, KS 67260. Offers applied mathematics (PhD); mathematics (MS). Part-time programs available. *Expenses:* Tuition, state resident: full-time $4746; part-time $263.65 per credit. Tuition, nonresident: full-time $11,669; part-time $648.30 per credit.

366 facebook.com/petersonspublishing

Peterson's Graduate Programs in the Physical Sciences, Mathematics, Agricultural Sciences, the Environment & Natural Resources 2013

Unit head: Dr. Buma Fridman, Chair, 316-978-3160, Fax: 316-978-3748, E-mail: buma.fridman@wichita.edu. *Application contact:* Dr. Kenneth Miller, Graduate Coordinator, 316-978-3160, Fax: 316-978-3748, E-mail: kenneth.miller@wichita.edu. Web site: http://www.wichita.edu/.

Wilfrid Laurier University, Faculty of Graduate and Postdoctoral Studies, Faculty of Science, Department of Mathematics, Waterloo, ON N2L 3C5, Canada. Offers mathematics for science and finance (M Sc). Part-time programs available. *Degree requirements:* For master's, thesis optional. *Entrance requirements:* For master's, 4-year honors degree in mathematics, minimum B+ average. Additional exam requirements/recommendations for international students: Required—TOEFL (minimum score 89 iBT). Electronic applications accepted. *Faculty research:* Modeling, analysis, resolution, and generalization of financial and scientific problems.

Wilkes University, College of Graduate and Professional Studies, College of Science and Engineering, Department of Mathematics and Computer Science, Wilkes-Barre, PA 18766-0002. Offers mathematics (MS, MS Ed). Part-time programs available. *Students:* 4 part-time (1 woman). Average age 34. In 2011, 1 master's awarded. *Degree requirements:* For master's, thesis or alternative. *Entrance requirements:* For master's, GRE General Test. Additional exam requirements/recommendations for international students: Required—TOEFL (minimum score 550 paper-based; 213 computer-based; 79 iBT). *Application deadline:* Applications are processed on a rolling basis. Application fee: $45 ($65 for international students). Electronic applications accepted. *Financial support:* Federal Work-Study and unspecified assistantships available. Financial award application deadline: 3/1; financial award applicants required to submit FAFSA. *Unit head:* Dr. Barbara Bracken, Chair, 570-408-4836, Fax: 570-408-7883, E-mail: barbara.bracken@wilkes.edu. *Application contact:* Erin Sutzko, Director of Extended Learning, 570-408-4253, Fax: 570-408-7846, E-mail: erin.sutzko@wilkes.edu. Web site: http://www.wilkes.edu/pages/389.asp.

Worcester Polytechnic Institute, Graduate Studies and Research, Department of Mathematical Sciences, Worcester, MA 01609-2280. Offers applied mathematics (MS); applied statistics (MS); financial mathematics (MS); industrial mathematics (MS); mathematical sciences (PhD, Graduate Certificate); mathematics (MME). Part-time and evening/weekend programs available. *Faculty:* 16 full-time (1 woman), 6 part-time/adjunct (2 women). *Students:* 52 full-time (23 women), 32 part-time (18 women); includes 4 minority (1 Black or African American, non-Hispanic/Latino; 3 Hispanic/Latino), 52 international. 326 applicants, 52% accepted, 53 enrolled. In 2011, 25 master's, 1 doctorate awarded. *Degree requirements:* For master's, thesis (for some programs); for doctorate, comprehensive exam, thesis/dissertation. *Entrance requirements:* For master's and doctorate, GRE General Test, GRE Subject Test in math (recommended), 3 letters of recommendation. Additional exam requirements/recommendations for international students: Required—TOEFL (minimum score

563 paper-based; 223 computer-based; 84 iBT), IELTS (minimum score 7). *Application deadline:* For fall admission, 1/1 priority date for domestic students, 1/1 for international students; for spring admission, 10/1 priority date for domestic students, 10/1 for international students. Applications are processed on a rolling basis. Application fee: $70. Electronic applications accepted. *Financial support:* Research assistantships, teaching assistantships, career-related internships or fieldwork, institutionally sponsored loans, scholarships/grants, and unspecified assistantships available. Financial award application deadline: 1/1; financial award applicants required to submit FAFSA. *Faculty research:* Applied analysis and differential equations, computational mathematics, discrete mathematics, applied and computational statistics, industrial and financial mathematics, mathematical biology. *Unit head:* Dr. Bogdan Vernescu, Head, 508-831-5241, Fax: 508-831-5824, E-mail: vernescu@wpi.edu. *Application contact:* Dr. Joseph Petruccelli, Graduate Coordinator, 508-831-5241, Fax: 508-831-5824, E-mail: jdp@wpi.edu. Web site: http://www.wpi.edu/Academics/Depts/Math/.

Wright State University, School of Graduate Studies, College of Science and Mathematics, Department of Mathematics and Statistics, Program in Mathematics, Dayton, OH 45435. Offers MS. *Degree requirements:* For master's, comprehensive exam. *Entrance requirements:* For master's, previous course work in mathematics beyond calculus. Additional exam requirements/recommendations for international students: Required—TOEFL. *Faculty research:* Analysis, algebraic combinatorics, graph theory, operator theory.

Yale University, Graduate School of Arts and Sciences, Department of Mathematics, New Haven, CT 06520. Offers M Phil, MS, PhD. *Degree requirements:* For doctorate, 2 foreign languages, thesis/dissertation. *Entrance requirements:* For doctorate, GRE General Test, GRE Subject Test.

York University, Faculty of Graduate Studies, Faculty of Science and Engineering, Program in Mathematics and Statistics, Toronto, ON M3J 1P3, Canada. Offers industrial and applied mathematics (M Sc); mathematics and statistics (MA, PhD). Part-time programs available. *Degree requirements:* For master's, thesis optional; for doctorate, one foreign language, comprehensive exam, thesis/dissertation. Electronic applications accepted.

Youngstown State University, Graduate School, College of Science, Technology, Engineering and Mathematics, Department of Mathematics and Statistics, Youngstown, OH 44555-0001. Offers applied mathematics (MS); computer science (MS); secondary mathematics (MS); statistics (MS). Part-time programs available. *Degree requirements:* For master's, comprehensive exam, thesis optional. *Entrance requirements:* For master's, minimum GPA of 2.7 in computer science and mathematics. Additional exam requirements/recommendations for international students: Required—TOEFL. *Faculty research:* Regression analysis, numerical analysis, statistics, Markov chain, topology and fuzzy sets.

Statistics

Acadia University, Faculty of Pure and Applied Science, Department of Mathematics and Statistics, Wolfville, NS B4P 2R6, Canada. Offers applied mathematics and statistics (M Sc). *Degree requirements:* For master's, thesis. *Entrance requirements:* For master's, honors degree in mathematics, statistics or equivalent. Additional exam requirements/recommendations for international students: Required—TOEFL (minimum score 580 paper-based; 237 computer-based; 93 iBT), IELTS (minimum score 6.5). *Faculty research:* Geophysical fluid dynamics, machine scheduling problems, control theory, stochastic optimization, survival analysis.

American University, College of Arts and Sciences, Department of Mathematics and Statistics, Washington, DC 22016-8050. Offers applied statistics (Certificate); mathematics (MA); statistics (MS). Part-time and evening/weekend programs available. *Faculty:* 26 full-time (8 women), 10 part-time/adjunct (0 women). *Students:* 11 full-time (5 women), 8 part-time (4 women); includes 4 minority (3 Black or African American, non-Hispanic/Latino; 1 Hispanic/Latino), 2 international. Average age 29. 44 applicants, 77% accepted, 10 enrolled. In 2011, 11 master's awarded. *Degree requirements:* For master's, comprehensive exam, thesis or alternative, tools of research in foreign language or computer language. *Entrance requirements:* For master's, GRE; for Certificate, bachelor's degree. Additional exam requirements/recommendations for international students: Required—TOEFL. *Application deadline:* For fall admission, 2/1 for domestic students; for spring admission, 10/1 for domestic students. Application fee: $80. *Expenses: Tuition:* Full-time $24,264; part-time $1348 per credit hour. *Required fees:* $430. Tuition and fees vary according to course load and program. *Financial support:* Fellowships, research assistantships, teaching assistantships, career-related internships or fieldwork, Federal Work-Study, institutionally sponsored loans, and unspecified assistantships available. Support available to part-time students. Financial award application deadline: 2/1. *Faculty research:* Logic, random processes, probability analysis, biostatistics, statistical computing. *Unit head:* Dr. Jeffrey D. Adler, Chair, 202-885-3171, Fax: 202-885-3155, E-mail: jadler@american.edu. *Application contact:* Kathleen Clowery, Director, Graduate

Admissions, 202-885-3621, Fax: 202-885-1505, E-mail: clowery@american.edu. Web site: http://www.american.edu/cas/mathstat/.

American University of Beirut, Graduate Programs, Faculty of Arts and Sciences, Beirut, Lebanon. Offers anthropology (MA); Arabic language and literature (MA); archaeology (MA); biology (MS); chemistry (MS); computational science (MS); computer science (MS); economics (MA); education (MA); English language (MA); English literature (MA); environmental policy planning (MSES); financial economics (MAFE); geology (MS); history (MA); mathematics (MA, MS); Middle Eastern studies (MA); philosophy (MA); physics (MS); political studies (MA); psychology (MA); public administration (MA); sociology (MA); statistics (MA, MS). Part-time programs available. *Faculty:* 154 full-time (44 women), 12 part-time/adjunct (2 women). *Students:* 180 full-time (122 women), 240 part-time (158 women). Average age 25. 336 applicants, 47% accepted, 86 enrolled. In 2011, 57 master's awarded. *Degree requirements:* For master's, one foreign language, comprehensive exam, thesis (for some programs). *Entrance requirements:* For master's, GRE, letter of recommendation. Additional exam requirements/recommendations for international students: Required—TOEFL (minimum score 600 paper-based; 250 computer-based; 97 iBT), IELTS (minimum score 7). *Application deadline:* For fall admission, 4/30 for domestic and international students; for spring admission, 11/1 for domestic and international students. Application fee: $50. *Expenses: Tuition:* Full-time $12,780; part-time $710 per credit. *Required fees:* $528; $528 per credit. Tuition and fees vary according to course load and program. *Financial support:* In 2011–12, 33 students received support. Career-related internships or fieldwork, institutionally sponsored loans, scholarships/grants, health care benefits, and unspecified assistantships available. Financial award application deadline: 2/4; financial award applicants required to submit FAFSA. *Faculty research:* History of composition studies, syntax of Arabic dialects, Oscar Wilde, decadence, Middle Eastern and international politics, neural mechanisms of creativity and consciousness, personality and psycho-socio-cultural-spiritual correlates of negative and positive mental health, philosophy of mind, metaphysics, micropaleontology and stratigraphy, geochemistry, mineralogy and petrology, tectonophysics, Abbasid,

Peterson's Graduate Programs in the Physical Sciences, Mathematics, Agricultural Sciences, the Environment & Natural Resources 2013

facebook.com/petersonspublishing **367**

Statistics

Ottoman and Russian history, landscape, Bronze and Iron Age archaeology. *Unit head:* Dr. Patrick McGreevy, Dean, 961-1374374 Ext. 3800, Fax: 961-1744461, E-mail: pm07@aub.edu.lb. *Application contact:* Dr. Salim Kanaan, Director, Admissions Office, 961-1350000 Ext. 2594, Fax: 961-1750775, E-mail: sk00@aub.edu.lb. Web site: http://staff.aub.edu.lb/~webfas.

Arizona State University, College of Liberal Arts and Sciences, Department of Mathematics and Statistics, Tempe, AZ 85287-1804. Offers applied mathematics (PhD); computational biosciences (PhD); mathematics (MA, MNS, PhD); mathematics education (PhD); statistics (PhD). Part-time programs available. Terminal master's awarded for partial completion of doctoral program. *Degree requirements:* For master's, thesis or alternative, interactive Program of Study (iPOS) submitted before completing 50 percent of required credit hours; for doctorate, comprehensive exam, thesis/dissertation, interactive Program of Study (iPOS) submitted before completing 50 percent of required credit hours. *Entrance requirements:* For master's and doctorate, GRE General Test, minimum GPA of 3.0 or equivalent in last 2 years of work leading to bachelor's degree. Additional exam requirements/recommendations for international students: Required—TOEFL (minimum score 80 iBT), TOEFL, IELTS, or Pearson Test of English. Electronic applications accepted. *Expenses:* Contact institution.

Arizona State University, Graduate College, Interdisciplinary Program in Statistics, Tempe, AZ 85287-1003. Offers MS, Graduate Certificate. Part-time and evening/weekend programs available. Postbaccalaureate distance learning degree programs offered (minimal on-campus study). *Degree requirements:* For master's, thesis and oral defense/examination or applied project with oral defense/examination; interactive Program of Study (iPOS) submitted before completing 50 percent of required credit hours. *Entrance requirements:* For master's, minimum GPA of 3.0 in the last 2 years of work leading to the bachelor's degree, 3 letters of recommendation, statement of goals; for Graduate Certificate, bachelor's degree, completion of intro to applied statistics, 1 semester of calculus. Additional exam requirements/recommendations for international students: Required—TOEFL (minimum score 550 paper-based; 213 computer-based; 80 iBT), IELTS (minimum score 6.5). Electronic applications accepted.

Auburn University, Graduate School, College of Sciences and Mathematics, Department of Mathematics and Statistics, Auburn University, AL 36849. Offers applied mathematics (MAM, MS); mathematics (MS, PhD); probability and statistics (M Prob S); statistics (MS). *Faculty:* 50 full-time (7 women), 6 part-time/adjunct (4 women). *Students:* 56 full-time (14 women), 52 part-time (14 women); includes 4 minority (3 Black or African American, non-Hispanic/Latino; 1 Hispanic/Latino), 43 international. Average age 28. 160 applicants, 59% accepted, 37 enrolled. In 2011, 17 master's, 9 doctorates awarded. *Degree requirements:* For doctorate, thesis/dissertation. *Entrance requirements:* For master's, GRE General Test, undergraduate mathematics background; for doctorate, GRE General Test, GRE Subject Test. *Application deadline:* For fall admission, 7/7 priority date for domestic students; for spring admission, 11/24 for domestic students. Applications are processed on a rolling basis. Application fee: $50 ($60 for international students). Electronic applications accepted. *Expenses:* Tuition, state resident: full-time $7290; part-time $405 per credit hour. Tuition, nonresident: full-time $21,870; part-time $1215 per credit hour. *International tuition:* $22,000 full-time. *Required fees:* $1402. *Financial support:* Fellowships and teaching assistantships available. Financial award applicants required to submit FAFSA. *Faculty research:* Pure and applied mathematics. *Unit head:* Dr. Michel Smith, Chair, 334-844-4290, Fax: 334-844-6655. *Application contact:* Dr. George Flowers, Dean of the Graduate School, 334-844-2125. Web site: http://www.auburn.edu/~math/.

Ball State University, Graduate School, College of Sciences and Humanities, Department of Mathematical Sciences, Program in Statistics, Muncie, IN 47306-1099. Offers MA. *Faculty:* 20. *Students:* 9 full-time (2 women), 9 part-time (2 women); includes 1 minority (Black or African American, non-Hispanic/Latino), 6 international. Average age 27. 16 applicants, 69% accepted, 5 enrolled. In 2011, 8 master's awarded. Application fee: $50. Tuition and fees vary according to program and reciprocity agreements. *Financial support:* In 2011–12, 12 students received support, including 11 teaching assistantships with tuition reimbursements available (averaging $9,915 per year). Financial award application deadline: 3/1. *Faculty research:* Robust methods. *Unit head:* Dr. Sheryl Stump, Director, 765-285-8662, Fax: 765-285-1721. *Application contact:* Dr. Hanspeter Fischer, Director, 765-285-8640, Fax: 765-285-1721, E-mail: mali@bsu.edu. Web site: http://cms.bsu.edu/Academics/CollegesandDepartments/Math/AcademicsAdmissions/Programs/Masters/MAorMSinStatistics.aspx.

Baylor University, Graduate School, College of Arts and Sciences, Department of Statistics, Waco, TX 76798. Offers MA, PhD. *Faculty:* 7 full-time (1 woman), 4 part-time/adjunct (1 woman). *Students:* 26 full-time (15 women), 1 part-time (0 women); includes 1 minority (Asian, non-Hispanic/Latino), 6 international. Average age 24. 38 applicants, 16% accepted. In 2011, 2 master's, 7 doctorates awarded. *Degree requirements:* For doctorate, thesis/dissertation. *Entrance requirements:* For master's, GRE General Test, 3 semesters of course work in calculus; for doctorate, GRE General Test. *Application deadline:* Applications are processed on a rolling basis. Application fee: $25. *Financial support:* In 2011–12, 1 fellowship, 5 research assistantships, 7 teaching assistantships were awarded; institutionally sponsored loans also available. *Faculty research:* Mathematical statistics, probability theory, biostatistics, linear models, time series. *Unit head:* Dr. James Stamey, Graduate Program Director, 254-710-7405, E-mail: james_stamey@baylor.edu. *Application contact:* Dr. James Stamey, Graduate Program Director, 254-710-7405, E-mail: james_stamey@baylor.edu. Web site: http://www.baylor.edu/statistics/.

Bernard M. Baruch College of the City University of New York, Zicklin School of Business, Department of Statistics and Computer Information Systems, Program in Statistics, New York, NY 10010-5585. Offers MBA, MS. Part-time and evening/weekend programs available. *Entrance requirements:* For master's, GMAT, 2 letters of recommendation, resume, 2 years of work experience. Additional exam requirements/recommendations for international students: Required—TOEFL (minimum score 590 paper-based; 243 computer-based), TWE.

Bowling Green State University, Graduate College, College of Arts and Sciences, Department of Mathematics and Statistics, Bowling Green, OH 43403. Offers applied statistics (MS); mathematics (MA, MAT, PhD); statistics (PhD). Part-time programs available. *Degree requirements:* For master's, thesis or alternative; for doctorate, comprehensive exam, thesis/dissertation. *Entrance requirements:* For master's and doctorate, GRE General Test. Additional exam requirements/recommendations for international students: Required—TOEFL. Electronic applications accepted. *Faculty research:* Statistics and probability, algebra, analysis.

Brigham Young University, Graduate Studies, College of Physical and Mathematical Sciences, Department of Statistics, Provo, UT 84602-1001. Offers applied statistics (MS). *Faculty:* 16 full-time (3 women). *Students:* 30 full-time (14 women); includes 1 minority (Asian, non-Hispanic/Latino). Average age 26. 26 applicants, 69% accepted, 14 enrolled. In 2011, 10 master's awarded. *Degree requirements:* For master's, comprehensive exam, thesis (for some programs). *Entrance requirements:* For master's, GRE General Test, minimum undergraduate GPA of 3.3; course work in statistical methods, theory, multivariable calculus and linear algebra with minimum Baverage. Additional exam requirements/recommendations for international students: Required—TOEFL (minimum score 580 paper-based; 237 computer-based; 85 iBT). *Application deadline:* For fall admission, 2/1 for domestic and international students. Application fee: $50. Electronic applications accepted. Full-time tuition for non-LDS students: $11,520 per year; $640 per credit. *Expenses: Tuition:* Full-time $5760; part-time $320 per credit. Tuition and fees vary according to student's religious affiliation. *Financial support:* In 2011–12, 18 students received support, including 4 research assistantships with full and partial tuition reimbursements available (averaging $10,000 per year), 16 teaching assistantships with full and partial tuition reimbursements available (averaging $10,000 per year); scholarships/grants and unspecified assistantships also available. Financial award application deadline: 2/1. *Faculty research:* Statistical genetics, reliability and pollution monitoring, Bayesian methods. *Total annual research expenditures:* $324,000. *Unit head:* Dr. Del T. Scott, Chair, 801-422-7054, Fax: 801-422-0635, E-mail: scottd@byu.edu. *Application contact:* Dr. Christopher Shane Reese, Graduate Coordinator, 801-422-9250, Fax: 801-422-0635, E-mail: reese@stat.byu.edu. Web site: http://statistics.byu.edu/.

Brock University, Faculty of Graduate Studies, Faculty of Mathematics and Science, Program in Mathematics and Statistics, St. Catharines, ON L2S 3A1, Canada. Offers M Sc. Part-time programs available. *Degree requirements:* For master's, thesis or project. *Entrance requirements:* For master's, honors degree. Additional exam requirements/recommendations for international students: Required—TOEFL (minimum score 550 paper-based; 213 computer-based; 80 iBT), IELTS (minimum score 6.5), TWE (minimum score 4). Electronic applications accepted.

California State University, East Bay, Office of Academic Programs and Graduate Studies, College of Science, Department of Statistics and Biostatistics, Statistics Program, Hayward, CA 94542-3000. Offers actuarial science (MS); applied statistics (MS); computational statistics (MS); mathematical statistics (MS). Part-time and evening/weekend programs available. *Faculty:* 4 full-time (1 woman), 1 part-time/adjunct. *Students:* 19 full-time (6 women), 74 part-time (31 women); includes 32 minority (1 Black or African American, non-Hispanic/Latino; 24 Asian, non-Hispanic/Latino; 6 Hispanic/Latino; 1 Two or more races, non-Hispanic/Latino), 30 international. Average age 30. 82 applicants, 72% accepted, 30 enrolled. In 2011, 49 master's awarded. *Degree requirements:* For master's, comprehensive exam. *Entrance requirements:* For master's, letters of recommendation, minimum GPA of 3.0, math through lower-division calculus. Additional exam requirements/recommendations for international students: Required—TOEFL (minimum score 550 paper-based; 213 computer-based). *Application deadline:* For fall admission, 6/30 for domestic and international students. Application fee: $55. Electronic applications accepted. *Expenses:* Tuition, state resident: full-time $6738; part-time $1302 per quarter. Tuition, nonresident: full-time $12,690; part-time $2294 per quarter. *Required fees:* $449 per quarter. Tuition and fees vary according to degree level, program and reciprocity agreements. *Financial support:* Fellowships, career-related internships or fieldwork, Federal Work-Study, institutionally sponsored loans, scholarships/grants, and unspecified assistantships available. Support available to part-time students. Financial award application deadline: 3/2; financial award applicants required to submit FAFSA. *Unit head:* Dr. Eric Suess, Chair, 510-885-3435, Fax: 510-885-4714, E-mail: eric.suess@csueastbay.edu. *Application contact:* Prof. Mitchell Watnik, Statistics Graduate Coordinator, 510-885-4130, Fax: 510-885-4714, E-mail: mitchell.watnik@csueastbay.edu. Web site: http://www.sci.csueastbay.edu/statistics/.

Peterson's Graduate Programs in the Physical Sciences, Mathematics, Agricultural Sciences, the Environment & Natural Resources 2013

California State University, Sacramento, Office of Graduate Studies, College of Natural Sciences and Mathematics, Department of Mathematics and Statistics, Sacramento, CA 95819-6051. Offers MA. Part-time programs available. *Faculty:* 27 full-time (10 women), 10 part-time/adjunct (4 women). *Students:* 6 full-time, 23 part-time; includes 10 minority (1 American Indian or Alaska Native, non-Hispanic/Latino; 3 Asian, non-Hispanic/Latino; 2 Hispanic/Latino; 1 Native Hawaiian or other Pacific Islander, non-Hispanic/Latino; 3 Two or more races, non-Hispanic/Latino). Average age 30. 45 applicants, 53% accepted, 16 enrolled. In 2011, 12 master's awarded. *Degree requirements:* For master's, thesis or alternative, directed reading program preparing for written proficiency exam. *Entrance requirements:* For master's, minimum GPA of 3.0 in mathematics, 2.5 overall during previous 2 years; BA in mathematics or equivalent. Additional exam requirements/recommendations for international students: Required—TOEFL. *Application deadline:* For fall admission, 3/1 for domestic and international students; for spring admission, 9/30 for international students. Applications are processed on a rolling basis. Application fee: $55. Electronic applications accepted. *Financial support:* Research assistantships, teaching assistantships, career-related internships or fieldwork, and Federal Work-Study available. Support available to part-time students. Financial award application deadline: 3/1; financial award applicants required to submit FAFSA. *Faculty research:* Algebra, applied mathematics, methods in mathematical finance, subelliptic analysis, topology. *Unit head:* Edward Shea, Chair, 916-278-6534, Fax: 916-278-5586, E-mail: sheaec@csus.edu. *Application contact:* Jose Martinez, Outreach and Graduate Diversity Coordinator, 916-278-6470, Fax: 916-278-5669, E-mail: martinj@skymail.csus.edu. Web site: http://www.csus.edu/math.

Carnegie Mellon University, College of Humanities and Social Sciences, Department of Statistics, Pittsburgh, PA 15213-3891. Offers machine learning and statistics (PhD); mathematical finance (PhD); statistics (MS, PhD), including applied statistics (PhD), computational statistics (PhD), theoretical statistics (PhD); statistics and public policy (PhD). Terminal master's awarded for partial completion of doctoral program. *Degree requirements:* For doctorate, comprehensive exam, thesis/dissertation. *Entrance requirements:* For master's and doctorate, GRE General Test. Additional exam requirements/recommendations for international students: Required—TOEFL. *Faculty research:* Stochastic processes, Bayesian statistics, statistical computing, decision theory, psychiatric statistics.

Case Western Reserve University, School of Graduate Studies, Department of Statistics, Cleveland, OH 44106. Offers MS, PhD. *Faculty:* 4 full-time (2 women), 6 part-time/adjunct (1 woman). *Students:* 17 full-time (7 women), 6 part-time (2 women); includes 3 minority (all Asian, non-Hispanic/Latino), 14 international. Average age 33. 20 applicants, 0% accepted. In 2011, 1 master's, 3 doctorates awarded. *Degree requirements:* For master's, thesis (for some programs); for doctorate, thesis/dissertation. *Entrance requirements:* Additional exam requirements/recommendations for international students: Required—TOEFL (minimum score 550 paper-based; 213 computer-based; 79 iBT). *Application deadline:* For fall admission, 3/1 priority date for domestic students. Application fee: $50. Electronic applications accepted. *Financial support:* Teaching assistantships and career-related internships or fieldwork available. Support available to part-time students. Financial award application deadline: 3/1. *Faculty research:* Generalized linear models, asymptotics for restricted MLE Bayesian inference, sample survey theory, statistical computing, nonparametric inference, projection pursuit, stochastic processes, dynamical systems and chaotic behavior. *Unit head:* Jill Korbin, Interim Chair, 216-368-6942, Fax: 216-368-0252, E-mail: jill.korbin@case.edu. *Application contact:* Sharon Dingess, Admissions, 216-368-6941, Fax: 216-368-0252, E-mail: skd@case.edu. Web site: http://stat.cwru.edu/.

Central Connecticut State University, School of Graduate Studies, School of Arts and Sciences, Department of Mathematical Sciences, New Britain, CT 06050-4010. Offers data mining (MS, Certificate); mathematics (MA, MS, Certificate, Sixth Year Certificate), including actuarial science (MA), computer science (MA), statistics (MA). Part-time and evening/weekend programs available. *Faculty:* 33 full-time (10 women), 66 part-time/adjunct (26 women). *Students:* 19 full-time (9 women), 119 part-time (68 women); includes 23 minority (5 Black or African American, non-Hispanic/Latino; 8 Asian, non-Hispanic/Latino; 8 Hispanic/Latino; 2 Two or more races, non-Hispanic/Latino), 4 international. Average age 37. 65 applicants, 57% accepted, 24 enrolled. In 2011, 24 master's awarded. *Degree requirements:* For master's, comprehensive exam, thesis or alternative; for other advanced degree, qualifying exam. *Entrance requirements:* For master's, minimum undergraduate GPA of 2.7. Additional exam requirements/recommendations for international students: Required—TOEFL (minimum score 550 paper-based; 213 computer-based). *Application deadline:* For fall admission, 5/1 for domestic and international students; for spring admission, 11/1 for domestic and international students. Applications are processed on a rolling basis. Application fee: $50. Electronic applications accepted. *Expenses: Tuition, area resident:* Full-time $5137; part-time $482 per credit. Tuition, state resident: full-time $7707; part-time $494 per credit. Tuition, nonresident: full-time $14,311; part-time $494 per credit. *Required fees:* $3865. One-time fee: $62 part-time. *Financial support:* In 2011–12, 5 students received support. Career-related internships or fieldwork, Federal Work-Study, scholarships/grants, and unspecified assistantships available. Support available to part-time students. Financial award application deadline: 4/15; financial award applicants required to submit FAFSA. *Faculty research:* Statistics, actuarial mathematics, computer systems and engineering, computer programming techniques, operations research. *Unit head:* Dr. Jeffrey McGowan, Chair, 860-832-2835, E-mail: mcgowan@ccsu.edu. *Application contact:* Patricia Gardner, Associate Director of Graduate Studies, 860-832-2350, Fax: 860-832-2352, E-mail: graduateadmissions@ccsu.edu. Web site: http://www.math.ccsu.edu/.

Claremont Graduate University, Graduate Programs, School of Mathematical Sciences, Claremont, CA 91711-6160. Offers computational and systems biology (PhD); computational mathematics and numerical analysis (MA, MS); computational science (PhD); engineering and industrial applied mathematics (PhD); mathematics (PhD); operations research and statistics (MA, MS); physical applied mathematics (MA, MS); pure mathematics (MA, MS); scientific computing (MA, MS); systems and control theory (MA, MS). Part-time programs available. *Faculty:* 6 full-time (0 women), 1 part-time/adjunct (0 women). *Students:* 52 full-time (16 women), 24 part-time (9 women); includes 25 minority (3 Black or African American, non-Hispanic/Latino; 10 Asian, non-Hispanic/Latino; 11 Hispanic/Latino; 1 Two or more races, non-Hispanic/Latino), 17 international. Average age 33. In 2011, 15 master's, 3 doctorates awarded. Terminal master's awarded for partial completion of doctoral program. *Entrance requirements:* For master's and doctorate, GRE General Test. Additional exam requirements/recommendations for international students: Required—TOEFL (minimum score 550 paper-based; 213 computer-based; 80 iBT). *Application deadline:* For fall admission, 2/1 priority date for domestic students. Applications are processed on a rolling basis. Application fee: $60. Electronic applications accepted. *Expenses: Tuition:* Full-time $36,374; part-time $1581 per unit. *Required fees:* $165 per semester. *Financial support:* Fellowships, research assistantships, Federal Work-Study, institutionally sponsored loans, scholarships/grants, and tuition waivers (full and partial) available. Support available to part-time students. Financial award application deadline: 2/15; financial award applicants required to submit FAFSA. *Unit head:* Ellis Cumberbatch, Dean, 909-607-3369, Fax: 909-607-8261, E-mail: ellis.cumberbatch@cgu.edu. *Application contact:* Susan Townzen, Program Coordinator, 909-621-8080, Fax: 909-607-8261, E-mail: susan.n.townzen@cgu.edu. Web site: http://www.cgu.edu/pages/168.asp.

Clemson University, Graduate School, College of Business and Behavioral Science, Department of Economics, Clemson, SC 29634. Offers applied economics (PhD), including applied economics, applied economics and statistics; applied economics and statistics (MS, PhD); economics (MA, PhD). Part-time programs available. *Faculty:* 19 full-time (0 women), 5 part-time/adjunct (0 women). *Students:* 85 full-time (32 women), 11 part-time (5 women); includes 9 minority (5 Black or African American, non-Hispanic/Latino; 1 Asian, non-Hispanic/Latino; 3 Hispanic/Latino), 48 international. Average age 27. 145 applicants, 74% accepted, 35 enrolled. In 2011, 20 master's, 5 doctorates awarded. Terminal master's awarded for partial completion of doctoral program. *Degree requirements:* For master's, thesis (for some programs); for doctorate, comprehensive exam, thesis/dissertation. *Entrance requirements:* For master's, GRE General Test or GMAT; for doctorate, GRE General Test. Additional exam requirements/recommendations for international students: Required—TOEFL. *Application deadline:* For fall admission, 4/15 for international students; for spring admission, 9/15 for international students. Application fee: $70 ($80 for international students). Electronic applications accepted. *Expenses:* Contact institution. *Financial support:* In 2011–12, 53 students received support, including 12 fellowships (averaging $9,361 per year), 1 research assistantship with partial tuition reimbursement available (averaging $18,000 per year), 48 teaching assistantships with partial tuition reimbursements available (averaging $13,433 per year); career-related internships or fieldwork, institutionally sponsored loans, scholarships/grants, health care benefits, and unspecified assistantships also available. Support available to part-time students. Financial award applicants required to submit FAFSA. *Faculty research:* Applied price theory, industrial organization, international economics, labor economics, public economics. *Total annual research expenditures:* $153,240. *Unit head:* Dr. Raymond Sauer, Interim Chair, 864-656-3969, Fax: 864-656-4192, E-mail: sauerr@clemson.edu. *Application contact:* Dr. Curtis J . Simon, Director of Graduate Programs, 864-656-3966, Fax: 864-656-4192, E-mail: cjsmn@clemson.edu. Web site: http://www.clemson.edu/econ.

Clemson University, Graduate School, College of Engineering and Science, Department of Mathematical Sciences, Clemson, SC 29634. Offers applied and pure mathematics (MS, PhD); computational mathematics (MS, PhD); operations research (MS, PhD); statistics (MS, PhD). Part-time programs available. *Faculty:* 46 full-time (13 women), 10 part-time/adjunct (5 women). *Students:* 119 full-time (50 women), 6 part-time (4 women); includes 5 minority (2 Black or African American, non-Hispanic/Latino; 2 American Indian or Alaska Native, non-Hispanic/Latino; 1 Two or more races, non-Hispanic/Latino), 40 international. Average age 27. 133 applicants, 75% accepted, 31 enrolled. In 2011, 23 master's, 6 doctorates awarded. *Degree requirements:* For master's, thesis optional, final project; for doctorate, thesis/dissertation, qualifying exams. *Entrance requirements:* For master's and doctorate, GRE General Test. Additional exam requirements/recommendations for international students: Required—TOEFL. *Application deadline:* For fall admission, 1/15 priority date for domestic students, 1/15 for international students; for spring admission, 10/1 priority date for domestic students, 9/15 for international students. Applications are processed on a rolling basis. Application fee: $70 ($80 for international students). Electronic applications accepted. *Financial support:* In 2011–12, 113 students received support, including 1 fellowship with full and partial tuition reimbursement available (averaging $10,000 per year), 9 research assistantships with partial tuition reimbursements available (averaging $18,373 per year), 104 teaching assistantships with partial tuition reimbursements available (averaging $17,869 per year); career-related internships or fieldwork, institutionally sponsored loans, scholarships/grants, health care benefits, and unspecified assistantships also

Peterson's Graduate Programs in the Physical Sciences, Mathematics, Agricultural Sciences, the Environment & Natural Resources 2013

facebook.com/petersonspublishing **369**

available. Support available to part-time students. Financial award application deadline: 4/15. *Faculty research:* Applied and computational analysis, cryptography, discrete mathematics, optimization, statistics. *Total annual research expenditures:* $780,865. *Unit head:* Dr. Robert L. Taylor, Chair, 864-656-5240, Fax: 864-656-5230, E-mail: rtaylo2@clemson.edu. *Application contact:* Dr. K. B. Kulasekera, Graduate Coordinator, 864-656-5231, Fax: 864-656-5230, E-mail: kk@clemson.edu. Web site: http://www.clemson.edu/ces/departments/math/index.html.

Colorado State University, Graduate School, College of Natural Sciences, Department of Statistics, Fort Collins, CO 80523-1877. Offers MS, PhD. Postbaccalaureate distance learning degree programs offered (no on-campus study). *Faculty:* 12 full-time (4 women), 1 part-time/adjunct (0 women). *Students:* 20 full-time (9 women), 69 part-time (26 women); includes 12 minority (1 Black or African American, non-Hispanic/Latino; 4 Asian, non-Hispanic/Latino; 6 Hispanic/Latino; 1 Two or more races, non-Hispanic/Latino), 20 international. Average age 33. 148 applicants, 22% accepted, 14 enrolled. In 2011, 15 master's, 1 doctorate awarded. Terminal master's awarded for partial completion of doctoral program. *Degree requirements:* For master's, comprehensive exam (for some programs), thesis (for some programs), project, seminar; for doctorate, comprehensive exam, thesis/dissertation, candidacy exam, preliminary exam, seminar. *Entrance requirements:* For master's and doctorate, GRE General Test, minimum GPA of 3.0, background in math and statistics. Additional exam requirements/recommendations for international students: Required—TOEFL (minimum score 550 paper-based; 213 computer-based; 80 iBT). *Application deadline:* For fall admission, 2/1 priority date for domestic students, 2/1 for international students. Application fee: $50. Electronic applications accepted. *Expenses:* Tuition, state resident: full-time $7992. Tuition, nonresident: full-time $19,592. *Required fees:* $1735; $58 per credit. *Financial support:* In 2011–12, 32 students received support, including 6 research assistantships with full tuition reimbursements available (averaging $11,550 per year), 26 teaching assistantships with full tuition reimbursements available (averaging $14,666 per year); fellowships and health care benefits also available. Financial award application deadline: 1/15; financial award applicants required to submit FAFSA. *Faculty research:* Applied probability, linear models and experimental design, time-series analysis, non-parametric statistical inference, statistical consulting. *Total annual research expenditures:* $1.1 million. *Unit head:* Dr. Jean Opsomer, Professor and Chair, 970-491-3841, Fax: 970-491-7895, E-mail: jean.opsomer@colostate.edu. *Application contact:* Kristin Stephens, Graduate Admissions Coordinator, 970-491-6546, Fax: 970-491-7895, E-mail: kristin.stephens@colostate.edu. Web site: http://www.stat.colostate.edu/.

Columbia University, Graduate School of Arts and Sciences, Division of Natural Sciences, Department of Statistics, New York, NY 10027. Offers M Phil, MA, PhD, MD/PhD. Part-time programs available. *Degree requirements:* For doctorate, thesis/dissertation. *Entrance requirements:* For master's and doctorate, GRE General Test, GRE Subject Test. Additional exam requirements/recommendations for international students: Required—TOEFL.

Columbia University, Graduate School of Arts and Sciences, Program in Quantitative Methods in the Social Sciences, New York, NY 10027. Offers MA. Part-time programs available.

Cornell University, Graduate School, Graduate Fields of Engineering, Field of Operations Research and Information Engineering, Ithaca, NY 14853. Offers applied probability and statistics (PhD); manufacturing systems engineering (PhD); mathematical programming (PhD); operations research and industrial engineering (M Eng). *Faculty:* 38 full-time (6 women). *Students:* 172 full-time (47 women); includes 25 minority (2 Black or African American, non-Hispanic/Latino; 19 Asian, non-Hispanic/Latino; 4 Hispanic/Latino), 120 international. Average age 24. 1,070 applicants, 24% accepted, 106 enrolled. In 2011, 93 master's, 6 doctorates awarded. *Degree requirements:* For doctorate, comprehensive exam, thesis/dissertation. *Entrance requirements:* For master's and doctorate, GRE General Test, 3 letters of recommendation. Additional exam requirements/recommendations for international students: Required—TOEFL (minimum score 600 paper-based; 250 computer-based; 100 iBT). *Application deadline:* For fall admission, 12/15 for domestic students. Application fee: $95. Electronic applications accepted. *Financial support:* In 2011–12, 44 students received support, including 11 fellowships with full tuition reimbursements available, 13 research assistantships with full tuition reimbursements available, 19 teaching assistantships with full tuition reimbursements available; institutionally sponsored loans, scholarships/grants, health care benefits, tuition waivers (full and partial), and unspecified assistantships also available. Financial award applicants required to submit FAFSA. *Faculty research:* Mathematical programming and combinatorial optimization, statistics, stochastic processes, mathematical finance, simulation, manufacturing, e-commerce. *Unit head:* Director of Graduate Studies, 607-255-9128, Fax: 607-255-9129. *Application contact:* Graduate Field Assistant, 607-255-9128, Fax: 607-255-9129, E-mail: orie@cornell.edu. Web site: http://www.gradschool.cornell.edu/fields.php?id-35&a-2.

Cornell University, Graduate School, Graduate Fields of Engineering, Field of Statistics, Ithaca, NY 14853-0001. Offers applied statistics (MPS); biometry (MS, PhD); decision theory (MS, PhD); economic and social statistics (MS, PhD); engineering statistics (MS, PhD); experimental design (MS, PhD); mathematical statistics (MS, PhD); probability (MS, PhD); sampling (MS, PhD); statistical computing (MS, PhD); stochastic processes (MS, PhD). *Faculty:* 24 full-time (3 women). *Students:* 67 full-time (37 women); includes 7 minority (1 Black or African American, non-Hispanic/Latino; 5 Asian, non-Hispanic/Latino; 1 Hispanic/Latino),

46 international. Average age 25. 594 applicants, 16% accepted, 42 enrolled. In 2011, 44 master's, 4 doctorates awarded. Terminal master's awarded for partial completion of doctoral program. *Degree requirements:* For master's, project (MPS), thesis (MS); for doctorate, one foreign language, thesis/dissertation. *Entrance requirements:* For master's, GRE General Test (MS), 2 letters of recommendation (MS, MPS); for doctorate, GRE General Test, 2 letters of recommendation. Additional exam requirements/recommendations for international students: Required—TOEFL (minimum score 550 paper-based; 213 computer-based; 77 iBT). *Application deadline:* For fall admission, 1/15 for domestic students. Applications are processed on a rolling basis. Application fee: $95. Electronic applications accepted. *Financial support:* In 2011–12, 26 students received support, including 3 fellowships with full tuition reimbursements available, 8 research assistantships with full tuition reimbursements available, 14 teaching assistantships with full tuition reimbursements available; institutionally sponsored loans, scholarships/grants, tuition waivers (full and partial), and unspecified assistantships also available. Financial award applicants required to submit FAFSA. *Faculty research:* Bayesian analysis, survival analysis, nonparametric statistics, stochastic processes, mathematical statistics. *Unit head:* Director of Graduate Studies, 607-255-8066. *Application contact:* Graduate Field Assistant, 607-255-8066, E-mail: csc@cornell.edu. Web site: http://www.gradschool.cornell.edu/fields.php?id-94&a-2.

Dalhousie University, Faculty of Science, Department of Mathematics and Statistics, Program in Statistics, Halifax, NS B3H 4R2, Canada. Offers M Sc, PhD. *Degree requirements:* For master's, thesis, 50 hours of consulting; for doctorate, thesis/dissertation, 50 hours of consulting. *Entrance requirements:* Additional exam requirements/recommendations for international students: Required—TOEFL, IELTS, CANTEST, CAEL, or Michigan English Language Assessment Battery. Electronic applications accepted. *Faculty research:* Data analysis, multivariate analysis, robustness, time series, statistical genetics.

Duke University, Graduate School, Department of Statistical Science, Durham, NC 27708. Offers PhD. Part-time programs available. *Faculty:* 20 full-time. *Students:* 34 full-time (13 women); includes 4 minority (1 Black or African American, non-Hispanic/Latino; 1 American Indian or Alaska Native, non-Hispanic/Latino; 2 Asian, non-Hispanic/Latino), 21 international. 184 applicants, 9% accepted, 8 enrolled. In 2011, 8 doctorates awarded. *Degree requirements:* For doctorate, thesis/dissertation. *Entrance requirements:* For doctorate, GRE General Test. Additional exam requirements/recommendations for international students: Required—TOEFL (minimum score 550 paper-based; 213 computer-based; 83 iBT), IELTS (minimum score 7). *Application deadline:* For fall admission, 12/8 priority date for domestic students, 12/8 for international students. Application fee: $75. Electronic applications accepted. *Expenses: Tuition:* Full-time $40,720. *Required fees:* $3107. *Financial support:* Fellowships, research assistantships, teaching assistantships available. Financial award application deadline: 12/8. *Unit head:* Mike West, Director of Graduate Studies, 919-684-8029, Fax: 919-684-8594, E-mail: karen@stat.duke.edu. *Application contact:* Elizabeth Hutton, 919-684-3913, Fax: 919-684-2277, E-mail: grad-admissions@duke.edu. Web site: http://www.stat.duke.edu/.

East Carolina University, Graduate School, Thomas Harriot College of Arts and Sciences, Department of Mathematics, Greenville, NC 27858-4353. Offers mathematics (MA); mathematics in the community college (MA); statistics (MA, Certificate). Part-time and evening/weekend programs available. *Degree requirements:* For master's, comprehensive exam. *Entrance requirements:* For master's, GRE General Test, MAT. Additional exam requirements/recommendations for international students: Required—TOEFL. *Application deadline:* For fall admission, 6/1 for domestic students; for spring admission, 10/15 for domestic students. Applications are processed on a rolling basis. Application fee: $50. *Expenses:* Tuition, state resident: full-time $3557; part-time $444.63 per semester hour. Tuition, nonresident: full-time $14,351; part-time $1793.88 per semester hour. *Required fees:* $2016; $252 per semester hour. Part-time tuition and fees vary according to course load, campus/location and program. *Financial support:* Research assistantships with partial tuition reimbursements and teaching assistantships with partial tuition reimbursements available. Financial award application deadline: 6/1. *Unit head:* Dr. Johannes H. Hattingh, Chair, 252-328-6461, E-mail: hattinghj@ecu.edu. *Application contact:* Dean of Graduate School, 252-328-6012, Fax: 252-328-6071, E-mail: gradschool@ecu.edu. Web site: http://www.ecu.edu/cs-cas/math/graduateprogram.cfm.

Florida Atlantic University, Charles E. Schmidt College of Science, Department of Mathematical Sciences, Boca Raton, FL 33431-0991. Offers applied mathematics and statistics (MS); mathematical sciences (MS, MST, PhD). Part-time programs available. *Faculty:* 42 full-time (6 women), 38 part-time/adjunct (11 women). *Students:* 42 full-time (6 women), 38 part-time (11 women); includes 18 minority (9 Black or African American, non-Hispanic/Latino; 5 Asian, non-Hispanic/Latino; 3 Hispanic/Latino; 1 Two or more races, non-Hispanic/Latino), 27 international. Average age 32. 76 applicants, 41% accepted, 14 enrolled. In 2011, 24 master's, 6 doctorates awarded. Terminal master's awarded for partial completion of doctoral program. *Degree requirements:* For master's, comprehensive exam (for some programs), thesis (for some programs); for doctorate, comprehensive exam, thesis/dissertation. *Entrance requirements:* For master's and doctorate, GRE General Test, minimum GPA of 3.0. Additional exam requirements/recommendations for international students: Required—TOEFL (minimum score 500 paper-based; 173 computer-based). *Application deadline:* For fall admission, 7/1 priority date for domestic students, 2/15 for

370 facebook.com/petersonspublishing

Peterson's Graduate Programs in the Physical Sciences, Mathematics, Agricultural Sciences, the Environment & Natural Resources 2013

international students; for spring admission, 11/1 priority date for domestic students, 7/15 for international students. Applications are processed on a rolling basis. Application fee: $30. Electronic applications accepted. *Expenses: Tuition, area resident:* Part-time $343.02 per credit hour. Tuition, state resident: full-time $8232. Tuition, nonresident: full-time $23,931; part-time $997.14 per credit hour. *Financial support:* In 2011–12, fellowships with partial tuition reimbursements (averaging $20,000 per year), teaching assistantships with partial tuition reimbursements (averaging $20,000 per year) were awarded; Federal Work-Study also available. Financial award application deadline: 4/1. *Faculty research:* Cryptography, statistics, algebra, analysis, combinatorics. *Unit head:* Dr. Lee Klingler, Chair, 561-297-0274, Fax: 561-297-2436, E-mail: klingler@fau.edu. *Application contact:* Dr. Heinrich Niederhausen, Graduate Director, 561-297-3237, Fax: 561-297-2436, E-mail: niederha@fau.edu. Web site: http://www.math.fau.edu/.

Florida International University, College of Arts and Sciences, Department of Mathematics and Statistics, Program in Statistics, Miami, FL 33199. Offers MS. Part-time and evening/weekend programs available. *Degree requirements:* For master's, thesis optional. *Entrance requirements:* For master's, GRE General Test, minimum GPA of 3.0, 3 letters of recommendation, resume. Additional exam requirements/recommendations for international students: Required—TOEFL (minimum score 550 paper-based; 80 iBT). Electronic applications accepted.

Florida State University, The Graduate School, College of Arts and Sciences, Department of Statistics, Tallahassee, FL 32306-4330. Offers applied statistics (MS); biostatistics (MS, PhD); mathematical statistics (MS, PhD). Part-time programs available. *Faculty:* 15 full-time (2 women). *Students:* 55 full-time (21 women), 16 part-time (4 women); includes 21 minority (8 Black or African American, non-Hispanic/Latino; 5 Asian, non-Hispanic/Latino; 8 Hispanic/Latino), 24 international. Average age 30. 193 applicants, 15% accepted, 16 enrolled. In 2011, 14 master's, 12 doctorates awarded. Terminal master's awarded for partial completion of doctoral program. *Degree requirements:* For doctorate, thesis/dissertation, departmental qualifying exam. *Entrance requirements:* For master's, GRE General Test, previous course work in calculus, minimum GPA of 3.0; for doctorate, GRE General Test, minimum GPA of 3.0, 1 course in linear algebra (preferred), calculus I-III, real analysis. Additional exam requirements/recommendations for international students: Required—TOEFL (minimum score 100 iBT). *Application deadline:* For fall admission, 7/1 for domestic and international students; for spring admission, 11/1 for domestic and international students. Applications are processed on a rolling basis. Application fee: $30. Electronic applications accepted. *Expenses:* Tuition, state resident: full-time $9474; part-time $350.88 per credit hour. Tuition, nonresident: full-time $16,236; part-time $601.34 per credit hour. *Required fees:* $630 per semester. One-time fee: $20. Tuition and fees vary according to course load and campus/location. *Financial support:* In 2011–12, 1 fellowship with full tuition reimbursement (averaging $5,000 per year), 6 research assistantships with full tuition reimbursements (averaging $15,847 per year), 45 teaching assistantships with full tuition reimbursements (averaging $15,362 per year) were awarded; Federal Work-Study, institutionally sponsored loans, scholarships/grants, health care benefits, and unspecified assistantships also available. Financial award application deadline: 2/15; financial award applicants required to submit FAFSA. *Faculty research:* Statistical inference, probability theory, biostatistics, nonparametric estimation, automatic target recognition. *Total annual research expenditures:* $791,621. *Unit head:* Dr. Xufeng Niu, Chairman, 850-644-4008, Fax: 850-644-5271, E-mail: niu@stat.fsu.edu. *Application contact:* Chauncey Richburg, Academic Support Assistant, 850-644-3514, Fax: 850-644-5271, E-mail: richburg@stat.fsu.edu. Web site: http://stat.fsu.edu/.

Florida State University, The Graduate School, College of Education, Department of Educational Psychology and Learning Systems, Program in Measurement and Statistics, Tallahassee, FL 32306. Offers MS, PhD, Ed S. *Faculty:* 4 full-time (2 women). *Students:* 28 full-time (17 women), 6 part-time (0 women); includes 3 minority (2 Black or African American, non-Hispanic/Latino; 1 Asian, non-Hispanic/Latino), 23 international. Average age 33. 15 applicants, 67% accepted, 2 enrolled. In 2011, 2 master's, 4 doctorates awarded. *Median time to degree:* Of those who began their doctoral program in fall 2003, 67% received their degree in 8 years or less. *Degree requirements:* For master's, comprehensive exam; for doctorate, comprehensive exam, thesis/dissertation, preliminary exam, prospectus. *Entrance requirements:* Additional exam requirements/recommendations for international students: Required—TOEFL (minimum score 550 paper-based; 213 computer-based; 80 iBT). *Application deadline:* For fall admission, 7/1 for domestic and international students; for winter admission, 11/1 for domestic and international students; for spring admission, 3/1 for domestic and international students. Application fee: $30. Electronic applications accepted. *Expenses:* Tuition, state resident: full-time $9474; part-time $350.88 per credit hour. Tuition, nonresident: full-time $16,236; part-time $601.34 per credit hour. *Required fees:* $630 per semester. One-time fee: $20. Tuition and fees vary according to course load and campus/location. *Financial support:* Fellowships with full and partial tuition reimbursements, research assistantships with full and partial tuition reimbursements, teaching assistantships with full and partial tuition reimbursements, Federal Work-Study, scholarships/grants, health care benefits, and unspecified assistantships available. *Faculty research:* Methods for meta analysis; IRT/mixIRT; CBT; modeling, especially of large data sets. *Unit head:* Dr. Betsy Becker, Program Leader, 850-645-2371, Fax: 850-644-8776, E-mail: bbecker@fsu.edu. *Application contact:* Peggy Lollie, Program Assistant, 850-644-8786, Fax: 850-644-8776, E-mail: plollie@fsu.edu.

George Mason University, Volgenau School of Engineering, Department of Statistics, Fairfax, VA 22030. Offers federal statistics (Certificate); statistical science (MS, PhD). *Faculty:* 13 full-time (3 women), 4 part-time/adjunct (0 women). *Students:* 27 full-time (13 women), 41 part-time (16 women); includes 16 minority (3 Black or African American, non-Hispanic/Latino; 11 Asian, non-Hispanic/Latino; 2 Hispanic/Latino), 15 international. Average age 32. 72 applicants, 57% accepted, 18 enrolled. In 2011, 17 master's, 1 doctorate, 3 other advanced degrees awarded. *Degree requirements:* For master's, comprehensive exam, thesis optional, qualifying exams; for doctorate, comprehensive exam, thesis/dissertation, qualifying exams. *Entrance requirements:* For master's, GRE/GMAT, bachelor's degree from accredited institution with minimum of GPA of 3.0 in a major that includes calculus, matrix algebra, calculus-based probability and statistics; personal goal statement; 2 official copies of transcripts; 3 letters of recommendation; resume; official bank statement; proof of financial support; photocopy of passport; for doctorate, GRE, MS in math intensive discipline with minimum GPA of 3.5, personal goals statement, 2 official copies of transcripts, 3 letters of recommendation, resume, official bank statement, proof of financial support, photocopy of passport; for Certificate, bachelor's degree with 2 courses in calculus and probability or statistics, personal goals statement, 2 official copies of transcripts, 1-3 letters of recommendation (depending on program) resume, official bank statement, proof of financial support, photocopy of passport. Additional exam requirements/recommendations for international students: Required—TOEFL (minimum score 575 paper-based; 230 computer-based; 88 iBT), IELTS, Pearson Test of English. *Application deadline:* For fall admission, 1/15 priority date for domestic students; for spring admission, 8/1 for domestic students. Applications are processed on a rolling basis. Application fee: $65 ($80 for international students). Electronic applications accepted. *Expenses:* Tuition, state resident: full-time $8750; part-time $364.58 per credit. Tuition, nonresident: full-time $24,092; part-time $1003.83 per credit. *Required fees:* $2514; $104.75 per credit. *Financial support:* In 2011–12, 23 students received support, including 3 fellowships with full tuition reimbursements available (averaging $18,000 per year), 7 research assistantships with full and partial tuition reimbursements available (averaging $16,992 per year), 13 teaching assistantships with full and partial tuition reimbursements available (averaging $10,983 per year); career-related internships or fieldwork, Federal Work-Study, scholarships/grants, unspecified assistantships, and health care benefits (full-time research or teaching assistantship recipients) also available. Support available to part-time students. Financial award application deadline: 3/1; financial award applicants required to submit FAFSA. *Faculty research:* Computational statistics, nonparametric function estimation, scientific and statistical visualization, statistical applications to engineering, survey research. *Total annual research expenditures:* $248,416. *Unit head:* Dr. William Rosenberger, Chair, 703-993-3645, Fax: 703-993-1700, E-mail: wrosenbe@gmu.edu. *Application contact:* Elizabeth Quigley, Administrative Assistant, 703-993-9107, Fax: 703-993-1700, E-mail: equigley@gmu.edu. Web site: http://statistics.gmu.edu/.

Georgetown University, Graduate School of Arts and Sciences, Department of Mathematics, Washington, DC 20057. Offers mathematics and statistics (MS).

The George Washington University, Columbian College of Arts and Sciences, Department of Statistics, Washington, DC 20052. Offers statistics (MS, PhD); survey design and data analysis (Graduate Certificate). Part-time and evening/weekend programs available. *Faculty:* 16 full-time (3 women), 17 part-time/adjunct (3 women). *Students:* 94 full-time (48 women), 76 part-time (31 women); includes 20 minority (5 Black or African American, non-Hispanic/Latino; 1 American Indian or Alaska Native, non-Hispanic/Latino; 11 Asian, non-Hispanic/Latino; 2 Hispanic/Latino; 1 Two or more races, non-Hispanic/Latino), 93 international. Average age 27. 387 applicants, 83% accepted, 93 enrolled. In 2011, 26 master's, 7 doctorates, 21 other advanced degrees awarded. Terminal master's awarded for partial completion of doctoral program. *Degree requirements:* For master's, comprehensive exam; for doctorate, thesis/dissertation, general exam. *Entrance requirements:* For master's and doctorate, GRE General Test, interview, minimum GPA of 3.0. Additional exam requirements/recommendations for international students: Required—TOEFL (minimum score 550 paper-based; 213 computer-based; 80 iBT). *Application deadline:* For fall admission, 1/15 priority date for domestic students, 1/15 for international students; for spring admission, 10/1 priority date for domestic students, 9/1 for international students. Applications are processed on a rolling basis. Application fee: $75. Electronic applications accepted. *Financial support:* In 2011–12, 13 students received support. Fellowships with tuition reimbursements available, teaching assistantships with tuition reimbursements available, Federal Work-Study, and tuition waivers available. Financial award application deadline: 1/15. *Unit head:* Dr. Reza Modarres, Chair, 202-994-6888, E-mail: reza@gwu.edu. *Application contact:* Information Contact, 202-994-6356, Fax: 202-994-6917. Web site: http://www.gwu.edu/~stat/.

Georgia Institute of Technology, Graduate Studies and Research, College of Sciences, School of Mathematics, Atlanta, GA 30332-0001. Offers algorithms, combinatorics, and optimization (PhD); applied mathematics (MS); bioinformatics (PhD); mathematics (PhD); quantitative and computational finance (MS); statistics (MS Stat). Terminal master's awarded for partial completion of doctoral program. *Degree requirements:* For master's, thesis or alternative; for doctorate, one foreign language, thesis/dissertation. *Entrance requirements:* For master's, GRE General Test, minimum GPA of 3.0; for doctorate, GRE General Test, GRE Subject Test, minimum GPA of 3.0. Additional exam requirements/recommendations for international students: Required—TOEFL. Electronic

Peterson's Graduate Programs in the Physical Sciences, Mathematics, Agricultural Sciences, the Environment & Natural Resources 2013

facebook.com/petersonspublishing **371**

applications accepted. *Faculty research:* Dynamical systems, discrete mathematics, probability and statistics, mathematical physics.

Georgia Institute of Technology, Graduate Studies and Research, Multidisciplinary Program in Statistics, Atlanta, GA 30332-0001. Offers MS Stat. Part-time programs available. *Degree requirements:* For master's, thesis optional. *Entrance requirements:* For master's, GRE General Test, minimum GPA of 3.0. Additional exam requirements/recommendations for international students: Required—TOEFL. *Faculty research:* Statistical control procedures, statistical modeling of transportation systems.

Georgia State University, College of Arts and Sciences, Department of Mathematics and Statistics, Atlanta, GA 30302-3083. Offers mathematics (MA, MS); mathematics and statistics (PhD). Part-time and evening/weekend programs available. *Degree requirements:* For master's, comprehensive exam (for some programs), thesis (for some programs), exam; for doctorate, comprehensive exam, thesis/dissertation. *Entrance requirements:* For master's and doctorate, GRE. Additional exam requirements/recommendations for international students: Required—TOEFL. Electronic applications accepted. *Faculty research:* Analysis, biostatistics, discrete mathematics, linear algebra, statistics.

Hampton University, Graduate College, Program in Applied Mathematics, Hampton, VA 23668. Offers computational mathematics (MS); nonlinear science (MS); statistics and probability (MS). *Degree requirements:* For master's, thesis optional. *Entrance requirements:* For master's, GRE General Test.

Harvard University, Graduate School of Arts and Sciences, Department of Statistics, Cambridge, MA 02138. Offers AM, PhD. Terminal master's awarded for partial completion of doctoral program. *Degree requirements:* For master's, one foreign language; for doctorate, one foreign language, thesis/dissertation, exam, qualifying paper. *Entrance requirements:* For master's and doctorate, GRE General Test, GRE Subject Test (recommended). Additional exam requirements/recommendations for international students: Required—TOEFL. *Expenses:* Tuition: Full-time $36,304. *Required fees:* $1186. Full-time tuition and fees vary according to program. *Faculty research:* Interactive graphic analysis of multidimensional data, data analysis, modeling and inference, statistical modeling of U.S. economic time series.

Indiana University Bloomington, University Graduate School, College of Arts and Sciences, Department of Statistics, Bloomington, IN 47405-7000. Offers applied statistics (MS); statistical science (MS, PhD). *Students:* 9 full-time (4 women), 1 (woman) part-time; includes 1 minority (Asian, non-Hispanic/Latino), 8 international. 39 applicants, 49% accepted, 10 enrolled. Application fee: $55 ($65 for international students). *Unit head:* Dr. Bennett Bertenthal, Dean, 812-855-2392, E-mail: bbertent@indiana.edu. *Application contact:* Katie Bowman, Department Secretary, 812-855-7828, E-mail: katibowm@indiana.edu. Web site: http://stat.indiana.edu/.

Indiana University–Purdue University Indianapolis, School of Science, Department of Mathematical Sciences, Doctoral Program in Mathematics, Indianapolis, IN 46202-3216. Offers applied mathematics (PhD); mathematical statistics (PhD); mathematics (PhD). *Students:* 17 full-time (7 women), 5 part-time (0 women); includes 2 minority (1 Black or African American, non-Hispanic/Latino; 1 Hispanic/Latino), 10 international. Average age 29. 25 applicants, 44% accepted, 3 enrolled. *Degree requirements:* For doctorate, one foreign language, thesis/dissertation. *Entrance requirements:* For doctorate, GRE General Test. Additional exam requirements/recommendations for international students: Required—TOEFL. *Application deadline:* For fall admission, 2/1 priority date for domestic students. Application fee: $55 ($65 for international students). *Unit head:* Dr. Evgeny Mukhin, Director of Graduate Programs, 317-274-6918, E-mail: grad-program@math.iupui.edu. *Application contact:* Dr. Sherry Queener, Director, Graduate Studies and Associate Dean, 317-274-1577, Fax: 317-278-2380. Web site: http://www.math.iupui.edu/.

Iowa State University of Science and Technology, Department of Statistics, Ames, IA 50011-1210. Offers MS, PhD, MBA/MS. *Entrance requirements:* For master's and doctorate, GRE General Test. Additional exam requirements/recommendations for international students: Required—TOEFL (minimum score 550 paper-based; 79 iBT), IELTS (minimum score 6.5). *Application deadline:* For fall admission, 1/15 priority date for domestic students, 1/15 for international students; for spring admission, 9/15 priority date for domestic students, 9/15 for international students. Application fee: $40 ($90 for international students). *Unit head:* Dr. Alicia Carriquiry, Director of Graduate Education, 515-294-3440, Fax: 515-294-4040, E-mail: statistics@iastate.edu. *Application contact:* Sharon Shepard, Secretary II, 515-294-3440, Fax: 515-294-4040, E-mail: statistics@iastate.edu. Web site: http://www.stat.iastate.edu/.

James Madison University, The Graduate School, College of Science and Mathematics, Department of Mathematics and Statistics, Harrisonburg, VA 22807. Offers M Ed. Part-time programs available. *Faculty:* 2 full-time (1 woman), 1 (woman) part-time/adjunct. *Students:* 3 part-time (1 woman). Average age 27. In 2011, 2 master's awarded. *Degree requirements:* For master's, comprehensive exam. *Entrance requirements:* For master's, undergraduate major in mathematics. *Application deadline:* For fall admission, 5/1 priority date for domestic students; for spring admission, 9/1 priority date for domestic students. Application fee: $55. *Expenses:* Tuition, state resident: full-time $8016; part-time $334 per credit hour. Tuition, nonresident: full-time $22,656; part-time $944 per credit hour. *Financial support:* Application deadline: 3/1; applicants required to submit FAFSA. *Unit head:* Dr. David C. Carothers, Academic Unit Head, 540-568-

6184, E-mail: carothdc@jmu.edu. *Application contact:* Lynette M. Bible, Director of Graduate Admissions, 540-568-6395, Fax: 540-568-7860, E-mail: biblelm@jmu.edu.

The Johns Hopkins University, Whiting School of Engineering, Department of Applied Mathematics and Statistics, Baltimore, MD 21218-2699. Offers computational medicine (PhD); discrete mathematics (MA, MSE, PhD); financial mathematics (MSE); operations research/optimization/decision science (MA, MSE, PhD); statistics/probability/stochastic processes (MA, MSE, PhD). Terminal master's awarded for partial completion of doctoral program. *Degree requirements:* For master's, thesis (for some programs); for doctorate, thesis/dissertation, oral exam, introductory exam. *Entrance requirements:* For master's and doctorate, GRE General Test, GRE Subject Test. Additional exam requirements/recommendations for international students: Required—TOEFL (minimum score 600 paper-based; 250 computer-based; 100 iBT). Electronic applications accepted. *Faculty research:* Discrete mathematics, probability, statistics, optimization and operations research, scientific computation, financial mathematics.

The Johns Hopkins University, Whiting School of Engineering, Program in Engineering Management, Baltimore, MD 21218-2699. Offers biomaterials (MSEM); communications science (MSEM); computer science (MSEM); fluid mechanics (MSEM); materials science and engineering (MSEM); mechanical engineering (MSEM); mechanics and materials (MSEM); nano-biotechnology (MSEM); nanomaterials and nanotechnology (MSEM); probability and statistics (MSEM); smart product and device design (MSEM); systems analysis, management and environmental policy (MSEM). *Entrance requirements:* For master's, GRE, 3 letters of recommendation, resume. Additional exam requirements/recommendations for international students: Required—TOEFL (minimum score 600 paper-based; 250 computer-based; 100 iBT) or IELTS (minimum score 7). Electronic applications accepted.

Kansas State University, Graduate School, College of Arts and Sciences, Department of Statistics, Manhattan, KS 66506. Offers MS, PhD. *Faculty:* 12 full-time (6 women), 4 part-time/adjunct (0 women). *Students:* 47 full-time (29 women), 16 part-time (6 women); includes 7 minority (6 Asian, non-Hispanic/Latino; 1 Hispanic/Latino), 34 international. Average age 32. 93 applicants, 42% accepted, 9 enrolled. In 2011, 15 master's, 2 doctorates awarded. Terminal master's awarded for partial completion of doctoral program. *Degree requirements:* For master's, thesis optional; for doctorate, thesis/dissertation, qualifying and preliminary exams. *Entrance requirements:* For master's, GRE; for doctorate, GRE, previous course work in statistics and mathematics. Additional exam requirements/recommendations for international students: Required—TOEFL (minimum score 550 paper-based; 213 computer-based). *Application deadline:* For fall admission, 2/1 priority date for domestic students, 2/1 for international students; for spring admission, 7/1 priority date for domestic students, 8/1 for international students. Applications are processed on a rolling basis. Application fee: $40 ($55 for international students). Electronic applications accepted. *Financial support:* In 2011–12, 3 research assistantships (averaging $16,439 per year), 34 teaching assistantships with full tuition reimbursements (averaging $14,030 per year) were awarded; Federal Work-Study, institutionally sponsored loans, and scholarships/grants also available. Support available to part-time students. Financial award application deadline: 3/1; financial award applicants required to submit FAFSA. *Faculty research:* Linear and nonlinear statistical models, design analysis of experiments, nonparametric methods for reliability and survival data, resampling methods and their application, categorical data analysis. *Total annual research expenditures:* $17,594. *Unit head:* James Neill, Head, 785-532-6883, Fax: 785-532-7336, E-mail: jwneill@ksu.edu. *Application contact:* Teresa Zerbe, Coordinator, 785-532-0511, Fax: 785-532-7336, E-mail: tzerbe@ksu.edu. Web site: http://www.k-state.edu/stats/.

Lehigh University, College of Arts and Sciences, Department of Mathematics, Bethlehem, PA 18015. Offers applied mathematics (MS, PhD); mathematics (MS, PhD); statistics (MS). Part-time programs available. *Faculty:* 23 full-time (1 woman), 2 part-time/adjunct (0 women). *Students:* 31 full-time (16 women), 6 part-time (2 women); includes 1 minority (Asian, non-Hispanic/Latino), 13 international. Average age 26. 140 applicants, 9% accepted, 5 enrolled. In 2011, 11 master's, 2 doctorates awarded. Terminal master's awarded for partial completion of doctoral program. *Degree requirements:* For master's, comprehensive exam, thesis optional; for doctorate, comprehensive exam, thesis/dissertation, qualifying exams, general exam, advanced topic exam. *Entrance requirements:* For master's and doctorate, GRE General Test (strongly recommended), minimum undergraduate GPA of 2.75, 3.0 for last two semesters; adequate background in math. Additional exam requirements/recommendations for international students: Required—TOEFL (minimum score 85 iBT). *Application deadline:* For fall admission, 1/1 priority date for domestic students, 1/1 for international students; for spring admission, 12/1 priority date for domestic students, 12/1 for international students. Applications are processed on a rolling basis. Application fee: $75. Electronic applications accepted. *Financial support:* In 2011–12, 35 students received support, including 2 fellowships with full tuition reimbursements available (averaging $25,000 per year), 23 teaching assistantships with full tuition reimbursements available (averaging $17,500 per year); research assistantships with full tuition reimbursements available, scholarships/grants, and tuition waivers (partial) also available. Financial award application deadline: 1/1. *Faculty research:* Probability and statistics, geometry and topology, number theory, algebra, discrete mathematics, differential equations. *Total annual research expenditures:* $155,033. *Unit head:* Dr. Wei-Min Huang, Chairman, 610-758-

372 facebook.com/petersonspublishing

Peterson's Graduate Programs in the Physical Sciences, Mathematics, Agricultural Sciences, the Environment & Natural Resources 2013

3730, Fax: 610-758-3767, E-mail: wh02@lehigh.edu. *Application contact:* Dr. Terry Napier, Graduate Coordinator, 610-758-3755, E-mail: mathgrad@lehigh.edu. Web site: http://www.lehigh.edu/~math/grad.html.

Louisiana State University and Agricultural and Mechanical College, Graduate School, College of Agriculture, Department of Experimental Statistics, Baton Rouge, LA 70803. Offers applied statistics (M App St). Part-time programs available. *Faculty:* 8 full-time (0 women). *Students:* 13 full-time (11 women), 3 part-time (1 woman); includes 1 minority (Asian, non-Hispanic/Latino), 11 international. Average age 27. 12 applicants, 42% accepted, 1 enrolled. In 2011, 8 master's awarded. *Degree requirements:* For master's, project. *Entrance requirements:* For master's, GRE General Test, minimum GPA of 3.0. Additional exam requirements/recommendations for international students: Required—TOEFL (minimum score 550 paper-based; 213 computer-based; 79 iBT) or IELTS (minimum score 6.5). *Application deadline:* For fall admission, 1/25 priority date for domestic students, 5/15 for international students; for spring admission, 10/15 priority date for domestic students, 10/15 for international students. Applications are processed on a rolling basis. Application fee: $50 ($70 for international students). Electronic applications accepted. *Financial support:* In 2011–12, 12 students received support, including 2 research assistantships with partial tuition reimbursements available (averaging $15,060 per year), 9 teaching assistantships with partial tuition reimbursements available (averaging $9,422 per year); fellowships, career-related internships or fieldwork, Federal Work-Study, institutionally sponsored loans, tuition waivers (full and partial), and unspecified assistantships also available. Financial award application deadline: 4/1; financial award applicants required to submit FAFSA. *Faculty research:* Linear models, statistical computing, ecological statistics. *Unit head:* Dr. James Geaghan, Head, 225-578-8303, Fax: 225-578-8344, E-mail: jgeaghan@lsu.edu. *Application contact:* Dr. Brian Marx, Graduate Adviser, 225-578-8366, E-mail: bmarx@lsu.edu. Web site: http://www.stat.lsu.edu/.

Louisiana Tech University, Graduate School, College of Engineering and Science, Department of Mathematics and Statistics, Ruston, LA 71272. Offers MS. Part-time programs available. *Degree requirements:* For master's, thesis or alternative. *Entrance requirements:* For master's, GRE General Test, minimum GPA of 3.0 in last 60 hours. Additional exam requirements/recommendations for international students: Required—TOEFL.

Loyola University Chicago, Graduate School, Department of Mathematical Sciences and Statistics, Chicago, IL 60660. Offers applied statistics (MS); mathematics and statistics (MS), including pure mathematics. Part-time programs available. *Faculty:* 19 full-time (4 women). *Students:* 38 full-time (25 women), 8 part-time (5 women); includes 14 minority (4 Black or African American, non-Hispanic/Latino; 7 Asian, non-Hispanic/Latino; 2 Hispanic/Latino; 1 Two or more races, non-Hispanic/Latino), 6 international. Average age 28. 75 applicants, 61% accepted, 26 enrolled. In 2011, 18 master's awarded. *Entrance requirements:* For master's, GRE General Test. Additional exam requirements/recommendations for international students: Required—TOEFL. *Application deadline:* For fall admission, 8/1 for domestic students; for spring admission, 12/1 for domestic students. Applications are processed on a rolling basis. Application fee: $0. Electronic applications accepted. *Expenses: Tuition:* Full-time $15,660; part-time $870 per credit hour. *Required fees:* $125 per semester. Tuition and fees vary according to course load and program. *Financial support:* In 2011–12, 13 students received support, including 6 teaching assistantships with tuition reimbursements available (averaging $10,000 per year); career-related internships or fieldwork, Federal Work-Study, institutionally sponsored loans, and tuition waivers (partial) also available. Financial award application deadline: 3/15. *Faculty research:* Probability and statistics, differential equations, algebra, combinations. *Total annual research expenditures:* $10,000. *Unit head:* Dr. Robert Jensen, Chair, 773-508-3578, Fax: 773-508-2123, E-mail: rjensen@luc.edu. *Application contact:* Dr. W. Cary Huffman, Graduate Program Director, 773-508-3563, Fax: 773-508-2123, E-mail: whuffma@luc.edu. Web site: http://math.luc.edu/.

McGill University, Faculty of Graduate and Postdoctoral Studies, Faculty of Arts, Department of Economics, Montréal, QC H3A 2T5, Canada. Offers economics (MA, PhD); social statistics (MA).

McGill University, Faculty of Graduate and Postdoctoral Studies, Faculty of Arts, Department of Sociology, Montréal, QC H3A 2T5, Canada. Offers medical sociology (MA); neo-tropical environment (MA); social statistics (MA); sociology (MA, PhD, Diploma).

McGill University, Faculty of Graduate and Postdoctoral Studies, Faculty of Science, Department of Mathematics and Statistics, Montréal, QC H3A 2T5, Canada. Offers computational science and engineering (M Sc); mathematics and statistics (M Sc, MA, PhD), including applied mathematics (M Sc, MA), pure mathematics (M Sc, MA), statistics (M Sc, MA).

McMaster University, School of Graduate Studies, Faculty of Science, Department of Mathematics and Statistics, Program in Statistics, Hamilton, ON L8S 4M2, Canada. Offers applied statistics (M Sc); medical statistics (M Sc); statistical theory (M Sc). *Degree requirements:* For master's, thesis or alternative. *Entrance requirements:* For master's, honors degree background in mathematics and statistics. Additional exam requirements/recommendations for international students: Required—TOEFL (minimum score 550 paper-based; 213 computer-based). *Faculty research:* Development of polymer production technology, quality of life in patients who use pharmaceutical agents, mathematical modeling, order

statistics from progressively censored samples, nonlinear stochastic model in genetics.

McNeese State University, Doré School of Graduate Studies, College of Science, Department of Mathematics, Computer Science, and Statistics, Lake Charles, LA 70609. Offers computer science (MS); mathematics (MS); statistics (MS). Evening/weekend programs available. *Faculty:* 13 full-time (4 women). *Students:* 17 full-time (7 women), 6 part-time (2 women); includes 1 minority (Black or African American, non-Hispanic/Latino), 9 international. In 2011, 17 master's awarded. *Degree requirements:* For master's, comprehensive exam, thesis or alternative, written exam. *Entrance requirements:* For master's, GRE. *Application deadline:* For fall admission, 5/15 priority date for domestic students, 5/15 for international students; for spring admission, 10/15 priority date for domestic students, 10/15 for international students. Applications are processed on a rolling basis. Application fee: $20 ($30 for international students). *Expenses:* Tuition, state resident: part-time $519 per credit hour. Tuition and fees vary according to course load. *Financial support:* Teaching assistantships available. Financial award application deadline: 5/1. *Unit head:* Sid Bradley, Head, 337-475-5788, Fax: 337-475-5799, E-mail: sbradley@mcneese.edu. *Application contact:* Dr. George F. Mead, Jr., Interim Dean of Dore' School of Graduate Studies, 337-475-5396, Fax: 337-475-5397, E-mail: admissions@mcneese.edu.

Memorial University of Newfoundland, School of Graduate Studies, Department of Mathematics and Statistics, St. John's, NL A1C 5S7, Canada. Offers mathematics (M Sc, PhD); statistics (M Sc, MAS, PhD). Part-time programs available. *Degree requirements:* For master's, thesis, practicum and report (MAS); for doctorate, comprehensive exam, thesis/dissertation, oral defense of thesis. *Entrance requirements:* For master's, 2nd class honors degree (MAS); for doctorate, MAS or M Sc in mathematics and statistics. Electronic applications accepted. *Faculty research:* Algebra, topology, applied mathematics, mathematical statistics, applied statistics and probability.

Miami University, College of Arts and Science, Department of Statistics, Oxford, OH 45056. Offers MS. *Students:* 12 full-time (8 women), 4 part-time (2 women); includes 4 minority (all Asian, non-Hispanic/Latino), 4 international. Average age 27. In 2011, 5 master's awarded. *Entrance requirements:* For master's, minimum GPA of 2.75 overall or 3.0 for last four semesters. Additional exam requirements/recommendations for international students: Required—TOEFL. *Application deadline:* For fall admission, 2/1 for domestic and international students. Application fee: $50. Electronic applications accepted. *Expenses:* Tuition, state resident: full-time $12,023; part-time $501 per credit hour. Tuition, nonresident: full-time $26,554; part-time $1107 per credit hour. *Required fees:* $528. *Financial support:* Research assistantships, teaching assistantships, health care benefits, and unspecified assistantships available. Financial award application deadline: 2/15; financial award applicants required to submit FAFSA. *Unit head:* Dr. A. John Bailer, Professor/Chair, 513-529-3538, E-mail: baileraj@muohio.edu. *Application contact:* Dr. David J. Groggel, Associate Professor and Director of Graduate Studies, 513-529-6087, E-mail: groggedj@muohio.edu. Web site: http://www.units.muohio.edu/sta/.

Michigan State University, The Graduate School, College of Natural Science, Department of Statistics and Probability, East Lansing, MI 48824. Offers applied statistics (MS); statistics (MS, PhD). *Entrance requirements:* Additional exam requirements/recommendations for international students: Required—TOEFL. Electronic applications accepted.

Minnesota State University Mankato, College of Graduate Studies, College of Science, Engineering and Technology, Department of Mathematics and Statistics, Program in Statistics, Mankato, MN 56001. Offers MS. *Students:* 8 full-time (2 women), 4 part-time (1 woman). *Degree requirements:* For master's, one foreign language, comprehensive exam, thesis or alternative. *Entrance requirements:* For master's, GRE General Test, minimum GPA of 3.0 during previous 2 years. Additional exam requirements/recommendations for international students: Required—TOEFL. *Application deadline:* For fall admission, 7/1 priority date for domestic students; for spring admission, 11/1 for domestic students. Applications are processed on a rolling basis. Application fee: $40. Electronic applications accepted. *Financial support:* Research assistantships with partial tuition reimbursements, teaching assistantships with partial tuition reimbursements, and unspecified assistantships available. Financial award application deadline: 3/15; financial award applicants required to submit FAFSA. *Unit head:* Dr. Brian Martensen, Chairperson, 507-389-1453. *Application contact:* 507-389-2321, E-mail: grad@mnsu.edu. Web site: http://cset.mnsu.edu/mathstat/program/grad.html.

Mississippi State University, College of Arts and Sciences, Department of Mathematics and Statistics, Mississippi State, MS 39762. Offers mathematical sciences (PhD); mathematics (MS); statistics (MS). Part-time programs available. *Faculty:* 19 full-time (4 women), 6 part-time (2 women); includes 7 minority (4 Black or African American, non-Hispanic/Latino; 2 Asian, non-Hispanic/Latino; 1 Two or more races, non-Hispanic/Latino), 23 international. Average age 29. 58 applicants, 41% accepted, 11 enrolled. In 2011, 10 master's, 1 doctorate awarded. Terminal master's awarded for partial completion of doctoral program. *Degree requirements:* For master's, thesis optional, comprehensive oral or written exam; for doctorate, one foreign language, thesis/dissertation, comprehensive oral and written exam. *Entrance requirements:* For master's, minimum GPA of 2.75 on last two years of undergraduate courses; for doctorate, GRE. Additional exam requirements/recommendations for international students: Required—TOEFL (minimum score 475 paper-based; 153

Peterson's Graduate Programs in the Physical Sciences, Mathematics, Agricultural Sciences, the Environment & Natural Resources 2013

facebook.com/petersonspublishing **373**

computer-based; 53 iBT); Recommended—IELTS (minimum score 4.5). *Application deadline:* For fall admission, 3/15 priority date for domestic students, 5/1 for international students; for spring admission, 11/1 for domestic students, 9/1 for international students. Applications are processed on a rolling basis. *Application fee:* $40. Electronic applications accepted. *Expenses:* Tuition, state resident: full-time $5805; part-time $322.50 per credit hour. Tuition, nonresident: full-time $14,670; part-time $815 per credit hour. *Financial support:* In 2011–12, 30 teaching assistantships with full tuition reimbursements (averaging $13,693 per year) were awarded; Federal Work-Study, institutionally sponsored loans, tuition waivers (partial), and unspecified assistantships also available. Financial award application deadline: 4/1; financial award applicants required to submit FAFSA. *Faculty research:* Differential equations, algebra, numerical analysis, functional analysis, applied statistics. *Total annual research expenditures:* $1.1 million. *Unit head:* Dr. Mohsen Razzaghi, Interim Head, 662-325-3414, Fax: 662-325-0005, E-mail: razzaghi@math.msstate.edu. *Application contact:* Dr. Corlis Johnson, Associate Department Head/Graduate Coordinator, 662-325-3414, Fax: 662-325-0005, E-mail: cjohnson@math.msstate.edu. Web site: http://www.msstate.edu/dept/math/.

Missouri University of Science and Technology, Graduate School, Department of Mathematics and Statistics, Rolla, MO 65409. Offers applied mathematics (MS); mathematics (MST, PhD), including mathematics (PhD), mathematics education (MST); statistics (PhD). Terminal master's awarded for partial completion of doctoral program. *Degree requirements:* For master's, thesis or alternative; for doctorate, one foreign language, thesis/dissertation. *Entrance requirements:* For master's and doctorate, GRE General Test, GRE Subject Test. Electronic applications accepted. *Faculty research:* Analysis, differential equations, topology, statistics.

Montana State University, College of Graduate Studies, College of Letters and Science, Department of Ecology, Bozeman, MT 59717. Offers ecological and environmental statistics (MS); ecology and environmental sciences (PhD); fish and wildlife biology (PhD); fish and wildlife management (MS). Part-time programs available. *Degree requirements:* For master's, comprehensive exam, thesis (for some programs); for doctorate, comprehensive exam, thesis/dissertation. *Entrance requirements:* For master's and doctorate, GRE, minimum GPA of 3.0, letters of recommendation, essay. Additional exam requirements/recommendations for international students: Required—TOEFL (minimum score 550 paper-based; 213 computer-based). Electronic applications accepted. *Faculty research:* Community ecology, population ecology, land-use effects, management and conservation, environmental modeling.

Montana State University, College of Graduate Studies, College of Letters and Science, Department of Mathematical Sciences, Bozeman, MT 59717. Offers mathematics (MS, PhD), including mathematics education option (MS); statistics (MS, PhD). Part-time programs available. Postbaccalaureate distance learning degree programs offered (minimal on-campus study). *Degree requirements:* For master's, comprehensive exam, thesis (for some programs); for doctorate, comprehensive exam, thesis/dissertation. *Entrance requirements:* For master's and doctorate, GRE General Test. Additional exam requirements/recommendations for international students: Required—TOEFL (minimum score 550 paper-based; 213 computer-based). Electronic applications accepted. *Faculty research:* Applied mathematics, dynamical systems, statistics, mathematics education, mathematical and computational biology.

Montclair State University, The Graduate School, College of Science and Mathematics, Department of Mathematical Sciences, Program in Statistics, Montclair, NJ 07043-1624. Offers MS. Part-time and evening/weekend programs available. *Students:* 3 full-time (1 woman), 12 part-time (8 women); includes 5 minority (1 Black or African American, non-Hispanic/Latino; 2 Asian, non-Hispanic/Latino; 2 Hispanic/Latino), 1 international. Average age 34. 9 applicants, 33% accepted, 0 enrolled. In 2011, 1 master's awarded. *Degree requirements:* For master's, comprehensive exam, thesis or alternative. *Entrance requirements:* For master's, GRE General Test, 2 letters of recommendation, essay. Additional exam requirements/recommendations for international students: Required—TOEFL (minimum score 83 iBT), IELTS (minimum score 6.5). *Application deadline:* Applications are processed on a rolling basis. Application fee: $60. Electronic applications accepted. *Financial support:* Federal Work-Study, scholarships/grants, and unspecified assistantships available. Support available to part-time students. Financial award application deadline: 3/1; financial award applicants required to submit FAFSA. *Faculty research:* Biostatisics, time series. *Unit head:* Dr. Helen Roberts, Chairperson, 973-655-5132. *Application contact:* Amy Aiello, Executive Director of The Graduate School, 973-655-5147, Fax: 973-655-7869, E-mail: graduate.school@montclair.edu. Web site: http://www.montclair.edu/csam/mathematical-sciences/graduate-programs/statistics/.

Murray State University, College of Science, Engineering and Technology, Program in Mathematics and Statistics, Murray, KY 42071. Offers MA, MAT, MS. Part-time programs available. *Degree requirements:* For master's, comprehensive exam, thesis optional. *Entrance requirements:* For master's, GRE General Test. Additional exam requirements/recommendations for international students: Required—TOEFL. *Faculty research:* Algebraic structures, mathematical biology, topolgy.

New Mexico Institute of Mining and Technology, Graduate Studies, Department of Mathematics, Socorro, NM 87801. Offers applied and industrial mathematics (PhD); industrial mathematics (MS); mathematics (MS); operations research and statistics (MS). *Faculty:* 11 full-time (0 women), 2 part-time/adjunct (1 woman). *Students:* 15 full-time (3 women), 1 part-time (0 women); includes 6 minority (1 Black or African American, non-Hispanic/Latino; 4 Asian, non-Hispanic/Latino; 1 Two or more races, non-Hispanic/Latino), 1 international. Average age 32. 13 applicants, 77% accepted, 6 enrolled. In 2011, 6 degrees awarded. *Degree requirements:* For master's, thesis optional; for doctorate, thesis/dissertation. *Entrance requirements:* For master's, GRE General Test. Additional exam requirements/recommendations for international students: Required—TOEFL (minimum score 540 paper-based; 207 computer-based). *Application deadline:* For fall admission, 3/1 priority date for domestic students; for spring admission, 6/1 for domestic students. Applications are processed on a rolling basis. Application fee: $16 ($30 for international students). *Expenses:* Tuition, state resident: full-time $4849; part-time $269.41 per credit hour. Tuition, nonresident: full-time $16,041; part-time $891.15 per credit hour. *Required fees:* $622; $65 per credit hour. $20 per semester. Part-time tuition and fees vary according to course load. *Financial support:* In 2011–12, 2 research assistantships (averaging $19,516 per year), 13 teaching assistantships with full and partial tuition reimbursements (averaging $34,112 per year) were awarded; fellowships, Federal Work-Study, and institutionally sponsored loans also available. Financial award application deadline: 3/1; financial award applicants required to submit CSS PROFILE or FAFSA. *Faculty research:* Applied mathematics, differential equations, industrial mathematics, numerical analysis, stochastic processes. *Unit head:* Dr. Anwar Hossain, Chairman, 575-835-5135, Fax: 575-835-5366, E-mail: hossain@nmt.edu. *Application contact:* Dr. Lorie Liebrock, Dean of Graduate Studies, 575-835-5513, Fax: 575-835-5476, E-mail: graduate@nmt.edu. Web site: http://www.nmt.edu/~math/.

New York University, Leonard N. Stern School of Business, Department of Information, Operations and Management Sciences, New York, NY 10012-1019. Offers information systems (MBA, PhD); operations management (MBA, PhD); statistics (MBA, PhD). *Faculty research:* Knowledge management, economics of information, computer-supported groups and communities financial information systems, data mining and business intelligence.

North Carolina State University, Graduate School, College of Physical and Mathematical Sciences, Department of Statistics, Raleigh, NC 27695. Offers M Stat, MS, PhD. Part-time programs available. *Degree requirements:* For master's, comprehensive exam, thesis (for some programs), final oral exam; for doctorate, thesis/dissertation, final oral and written exams, written and oral preliminary exams. *Entrance requirements:* For master's and doctorate, GRE General Test. Additional exam requirements/recommendations for international students: Required—TOEFL. Electronic applications accepted. *Faculty research:* Biostatistics; time series; spatial, inference, environmental, industrial, genetics applications; nonlinear models; DOE.

North Dakota State University, College of Graduate and Interdisciplinary Studies, College of Science and Mathematics, Department of Statistics, Fargo, ND 58108. Offers applied statistics (MS, Certificate); statistics (PhD); MS/MS. *Faculty:* 5 full-time (1 woman). *Students:* 28 full-time (12 women), 4 part-time (3 women); includes 1 minority (Two or more races, non-Hispanic/Latino), 16 international. Average age 24. 46 applicants, 83% accepted, 15 enrolled. In 2011, 10 master's, 3 doctorates, 4 other advanced degrees awarded. *Degree requirements:* For master's, comprehensive exam, thesis; for doctorate, comprehensive exam, thesis/dissertation. *Entrance requirements:* For master's and doctorate, minimum GPA of 3.0. Additional exam requirements/recommendations for international students: Required—TOEFL (minimum score 550 paper-based; 213 computer-based; 79 iBT). *Application deadline:* For fall admission, 3/15 for international students. Applications are processed on a rolling basis. Application fee: $35. Electronic applications accepted. *Financial support:* In 2011–12, 2 fellowships with full tuition reimbursements, 7 research assistantships with full tuition reimbursements, 9 teaching assistantships with full tuition reimbursements were awarded; career-related internships or fieldwork, Federal Work-Study, institutionally sponsored loans, and tuition waivers (full) also available. Financial award application deadline: 4/15. *Faculty research:* Nonparametric statistics, survival analysis, multivariate analysis, distribution theory, inference modeling, biostatistics. *Unit head:* Dr. Rhonda Magel, Chair, 701-231-7532, Fax: 701-231-8734, E-mail: ndsu.stats@ndsu.edu. *Application contact:* Dawn Halle, Academic Assistant, 701-231-7532, Fax: 702-231-8734, E-mail: ndsu.stats@ndsu.edu. Web site: http://www.ndsu.edu/statistics/.

Northern Arizona University, Graduate College, College of Engineering, Forestry and Natural Sciences, Department of Mathematics and Statistics, Flagstaff, AZ 86011. Offers applied statistics (Certificate); mathematics (MAT, MS); statistics (MS). Part-time programs available. *Faculty:* 38 full-time (12 women). *Students:* 23 full-time (9 women), 18 part-time (12 women); includes 11 minority (2 Black or African American, non-Hispanic/Latino; 2 Asian, non-Hispanic/Latino; 7 Hispanic/Latino), 1 international. Average age 28. 25 applicants, 68% accepted, 9 enrolled. In 2011, 15 master's, 7 other advanced degrees awarded. *Degree requirements:* For master's, comprehensive exam (for some programs), thesis (for some programs). *Entrance requirements:* For master's, minimum GPA of 3.0. Additional exam requirements/recommendations for international students: Required—TOEFL (minimum score 550 paper-based; 213 computer-based; 80 iBT), IELTS (minimum score 7). *Application deadline:* For fall admission, 3/15 priority date for domestic students, 3/15 for international students; for spring admission, 10/15 priority date for domestic students, 10/15 for international students. Applications are processed on a rolling basis. Application fee: $65. Electronic applications accepted. *Expenses:* Tuition, state resident: full-time $7190; part-time $355 per credit hour. Tuition, nonresident: full-

374 facebook.com/petersonspublishing

Peterson's Graduate Programs in the Physical Sciences, Mathematics, Agricultural Sciences, the Environment & Natural Resources 2013

$18,092; part-time $1005 per credit hour. *Required fees:* $818; $328 per semester. *Financial support:* In 2011–12, 22 teaching assistantships with partial tuition reimbursements (averaging $14,051 per year) were awarded; Federal Work-Study, scholarships/grants, health care benefits, tuition waivers (full and partial), and unspecified assistantships also available. Financial award applicants required to submit FAFSA. *Faculty research:* Topology, statistics, groups, ring theory, number theory. *Unit head:* Dr. Janet M. McShane, Chair, 928-523-1252, Fax: 928-523-5847, E-mail: janet.mcshane@nau.edu. *Application contact:* Sharon O'Connor, Chair, 928-523-3481, Fax: 928-523-5847, E-mail: math.grad@nau.edu. Web site: http://nau.edu/CEFNS/NatSci/Math/Degrees-Programs/.

Northern Illinois University, Graduate School, College of Liberal Arts and Sciences, Department of Mathematical Sciences, Division of Statistics, De Kalb, IL 60115-2854. Offers MS. Part-time programs available. *Faculty:* 8 full-time (1 woman), 1 part-time/adjunct (0 women). *Students:* 14 full-time (9 women), 5 part-time (2 women); includes 2 minority (1 Black or African American, non-Hispanic/Latino; 1 Asian, non-Hispanic/Latino), 7 international. Average age 30. 28 applicants, 68% accepted, 9 enrolled. In 2011, 11 master's awarded. *Degree requirements:* For master's, comprehensive exam, thesis optional. *Entrance requirements:* For master's, GRE General Test, minimum GPA of 2.75, course work in statistics, calculus, linear algebra. Additional exam requirements/recommendations for international students: Required—TOEFL (minimum score 550 paper-based; 213 computer-based). *Application deadline:* For fall admission, 6/1 for domestic students, 5/1 for international students; for spring admission, 11/1 for domestic students, 10/1 for international students. Applications are processed on a rolling basis. Application fee: $40. Electronic applications accepted. *Financial support:* In 2011–12, 2 research assistantships with full tuition reimbursements, 20 teaching assistantships with full tuition reimbursements were awarded; fellowships with full tuition reimbursements, career-related internships or fieldwork, Federal Work-Study, scholarships/grants, tuition waivers (full), and unspecified assistantships also available. Support available to part-time students. Financial award applicants required to submit FAFSA. *Faculty research:* Reality and life testing, quality control, statistical inference from stochastic process, nonparametric statistics. *Unit head:* Dr. Rama T. Lingham, Director, 815-753-6773, Fax: 815-753-6776. *Application contact:* Dr. Sanjib Basu, Director, Graduate Studies, 815-753-6799, E-mail: basu@math.niu.edu. Web site: http://www.niu.edu/stat/.

Northwestern University, The Graduate School, Judd A. and Marjorie Weinberg College of Arts and Sciences, Department of Statistics, Evanston, IL 60208. Offers MS, PhD. Admissions and degrees offered through The Graduate School. Part-time programs available. Terminal master's awarded for partial completion of doctoral program. *Degree requirements:* For master's, final exam; for doctorate, thesis/dissertation, preliminary exam, final exam. *Entrance requirements:* For master's and doctorate, GRE General Test. Additional exam requirements/recommendations for international students: Required—TOEFL. *Faculty research:* Theoretical statistics, applied statistics, computational methods, statistical designs, complex models.

Northwestern University, McCormick School of Engineering and Applied Science, Department of Industrial Engineering and Management Sciences, Program in Analytics, Evanston, IL 60208. Offers MS.

Oakland University, Graduate Study and Lifelong Learning, College of Arts and Sciences, Department of Mathematics and Statistics, Program in Statistical Methods, Rochester, MI 48309-4401. Offers Certificate. *Entrance requirements:* Additional exam requirements/recommendations for international students: Required—TOEFL (minimum score 550 paper-based; 213 computer-based). *Expenses:* Contact institution.

The Ohio State University, Graduate School, College of Arts and Sciences, Division of Natural and Mathematical Sciences, Department of Statistics, Columbus, OH 43210. Offers biostatistics (PhD); statistics (M Appl Stat, MS, PhD). *Faculty:* 22. *Students:* 71 full-time (39 women), 49 part-time (19 women); includes 5 minority (1 Black or African American, non-Hispanic/Latino; 4 Asian, non-Hispanic/Latino), 65 international. Average age 27. In 2011, 33 master's, 6 doctorates awarded. *Degree requirements:* For master's, thesis optional; for doctorate, thesis/dissertation. *Entrance requirements:* For master's and doctorate, GRE General Test. Additional exam requirements/recommendations for international students: Required—TOEFL (minimum score 550 paper-based; 250 computer-based; 79 iBT), Michigan English Language Assessment Battery (minimum score 82). *Application deadline:* For fall admission, 8/15 priority date for domestic students, 7/1 for international students; for winter admission, 12/1 priority date for domestic students, 11/1 for international students; for spring admission, 3/1 priority date for domestic students, 2/1 for international students. Applications are processed on a rolling basis. Application fee: $40 ($50 for international students). Electronic applications accepted. *Expenses:* Tuition, state resident: full-time $11,400. Tuition, nonresident: full-time $28,125. Tuition and fees vary according to course load, degree level, campus/location and program. *Financial support:* Fellowships, research assistantships, teaching assistantships, Federal Work-Study, and institutionally sponsored loans available. Support available to part-time students. *Unit head:* L . Mark Berliner, Chair, 614-247-4075, Fax: 614-292-2096, E-mail: berliner.1@osu.edu. *Application contact:* Graduate Admissions, 614-292-6031, Fax: 614-292-3656, E-mail: gradadmissions@osu.edu. Web site: http://www.stat.osu.edu/.

Oklahoma State University, College of Arts and Sciences, Department of Statistics, Stillwater, OK 74078. Offers MS, PhD. *Faculty:* 8 full-time (3 women), 2 part-time/adjunct (1 woman). *Students:* 21 full-time (6 women), 4 part-time (3 women); includes 3 minority (all Asian, non-Hispanic/Latino), 12 international. Average age 31. 75 applicants, 21% accepted, 6 enrolled. In 2011, 5 master's, 1 doctorate awarded. *Degree requirements:* For master's, comprehensive exam, thesis optional; for doctorate, comprehensive exam, thesis/dissertation. *Entrance requirements:* For master's and doctorate, GRE. Additional exam requirements/recommendations for international students: Required—TOEFL (minimum score 550 paper-based), IELTS (minimum score 7). *Application deadline:* For fall admission, 3/1 for international students; for spring admission, 8/1 for international students. Applications are processed on a rolling basis. Application fee: $40 ($75 for international students). Electronic applications accepted. *Expenses:* Tuition, state resident: full-time $4044; part-time $168.50 per credit hour. Tuition, nonresident: full-time $16,008; part-time $667 per credit hour. *Required fees:* $2122; $88.45 per credit hour. One-time fee: $50. Tuition and fees vary according to course load and campus/location. *Financial support:* In 2011–12, 19 teaching assistantships (averaging $15,603 per year) were awarded; research assistantships, career-related internships or fieldwork, Federal Work-Study, scholarships/grants, health care benefits, tuition waivers (partial), and unspecified assistantships also available. Support available to part-time students. Financial award application deadline: 3/1; financial award applicants required to submit FAFSA. *Faculty research:* Linear models, sampling methods, ranking and selections procedures, categorical data, multiple comparisons. *Unit head:* Dr. Ibrahim Ahmad, Head, 405-744-5684, Fax: 405-744-3533. *Application contact:* Dr. Sheryl Tucker, Dean, 405-744-7099, Fax: 405-744-0355, E-mail: grad-i@okstate.edu. Web site: http://statistics.okstate.edu.

Oregon State University, Graduate School, College of Science, Department of Statistics, Corvallis, OR 97331. Offers operations research (MA, MS); statistics (MA, MS, PhD). Part-time programs available. *Degree requirements:* For master's, consulting experience; for doctorate, thesis/dissertation, consulting experience. *Entrance requirements:* For master's and doctorate, minimum GPA of 3.0 in last 90 hours. Additional exam requirements/recommendations for international students: Required—TOEFL. *Faculty research:* Analysis of enumerative data, nonparametric statistics, asymptotics, experimental design, generalized regression models, linear model theory, reliability theory, survival analysis, wildlife and general survey methodology.

Penn State University Park, Graduate School, Eberly College of Science, Department of Statistics, State College, University Park, PA 16802-1503. Offers MA, MAS, MS, PhD. *Unit head:* Dr. Bruce G. Lindsay, Head, 814-865-1348, Fax: 814-863-7114, E-mail: bgl@psu.edu. *Application contact:* Information Contact, 814-865-8630, E-mail: b2a@psu.edu. Web site: http://stat.psu.edu/.

Portland State University, Graduate Studies, College of Liberal Arts and Sciences, Department of Mathematics and Statistics, Portland, OR 97207-0751. Offers mathematical sciences (PhD); mathematics education (PhD); statistics (MS); MA/MS. *Degree requirements:* For master's, thesis or alternative, exams; for doctorate, 2 foreign languages, thesis/dissertation, exams. *Entrance requirements:* For master's, GRE General Test, GRE Subject Test, minimum GPA of 3.0 in upper-division course work or 2.75 overall; for doctorate, GRE General Test. Additional exam requirements/recommendations for international students: Required—TOEFL (minimum score 550 paper-based; 213 computer-based). *Faculty research:* Algebra, topology, statistical distribution theory, control theory, statistical robustness.

Purdue University, Graduate School, College of Science, Department of Statistics, West Lafayette, IN 47909. Offers MS, PhD. Part-time programs available. *Faculty:* 51 full-time (20 women). *Students:* 91 full-time (38 women); includes 85 minority (5 Black or African American, non-Hispanic/Latino; 1 American Indian or Alaska Native, non-Hispanic/Latino; 76 Asian, non-Hispanic/Latino; 1 Hispanic/Latino; 2 Native Hawaiian or other Pacific Islander, non-Hispanic/Latino). Average age 27. 535 applicants, 7% accepted, 32 enrolled. In 2011, 33 master's, 9 doctorates awarded. Terminal master's awarded for partial completion of doctoral program. *Degree requirements:* For master's, comprehensive exam; for doctorate, thesis/dissertation, qualifying exams. *Entrance requirements:* For master's and doctorate, GRE General Test. Additional exam requirements/recommendations for international students: Required—TOEFL (minimum score 100 computer-based; 7 iBT); Recommended—IELTS. *Application deadline:* For fall admission, 1/15 for domestic and international students; for spring admission, 10/15 for domestic students, 9/15 for international students. Application fee: $65. Electronic applications accepted. *Financial support:* In 2011–12, 4 students received support, including 4 fellowships with full tuition reimbursements available (averaging $20,000 per year), 2 research assistantships with full tuition reimbursements available (averaging $20,000 per year), 5 teaching assistantships with full tuition reimbursements available (averaging $20,000 per year); career-related internships or fieldwork and unspecified assistantships also available. Support available to part-time students. Financial award application deadline: 1/15; financial award applicants required to submit FAFSA. *Faculty research:* Nonparametric models, computational finance, design of experiments, probability theory, bioinformatics. *Unit head:* Dr. Rebecca W. Doerge, Head, 765-494-3141, Fax: 765-494-0558, E-mail: doerge@purdue.edu. *Application contact:* Becca Miller, Graduate Secretary, 765-494-5794, Fax: 765-494-0558, E-mail: rlmitche@purdue.edu. Web site: http://www.stat.purdue.edu/.

Queen's University at Kingston, School of Graduate Studies and Research, Faculty of Arts and Sciences, Department of Mathematics and Statistics, Kingston, ON K7L 3N6, Canada. Offers mathematics (M Sc, M Sc Eng, PhD);

Peterson's Graduate Programs in the Physical Sciences, Mathematics, Agricultural Sciences, the Environment & Natural Resources 2013

facebook.com/petersonspublishing **375**

statistics (M Sc, M Sc Eng, PhD). Part-time programs available. *Degree requirements:* For master's, thesis; for doctorate, comprehensive exam, thesis/dissertation. *Entrance requirements:* Additional exam requirements/recommendations for international students: Required—TOEFL. *Faculty research:* Algebra, analysis, applied mathematics, statistics.

Rice University, Graduate Programs, George R. Brown School of Engineering, Department of Statistics, Houston, TX 77251-1892. Offers bioinformatics (PhD); biostatistics (PhD); computational finance (PhD); general statistics (PhD); statistics (M Stat, MA); MBA/M Stat. Part-time programs available. *Degree requirements:* For master's, comprehensive exam; for doctorate, comprehensive exam, thesis/dissertation. *Entrance requirements:* For master's and doctorate, GRE General Test, minimum GPA of 3.0. Additional exam requirements/recommendations for international students: Required—TOEFL (minimum score 630 paper-based; 250 computer-based; 90 iBT). Electronic applications accepted. *Faculty research:* Statistical genetics, non parametric function estimation, computational statistics and visualization, stochastic processes.

Rochester Institute of Technology, Graduate Enrollment Services, Kate Gleason College of Engineering, Center of Quality and Applied Statistics, Rochester, NY 14623-5603. Offers applied statistics (MS); statistical quality (AC). Part-time and evening/weekend programs available. Postbaccalaureate distance learning degree programs offered (no on-campus study). *Students:* 26 full-time (15 women), 41 part-time (9 women); includes 10 minority (1 Black or African American, non-Hispanic/Latino; 7 Asian, non-Hispanic/Latino; 2 Hispanic/Latino), 13 international. Average age 33. 60 applicants, 58% accepted, 20 enrolled. In 2011, 11 master's, 2 other advanced degrees awarded. *Degree requirements:* For master's, oral exam. *Entrance requirements:* For master's, course work in calculus, minimum GPA of 3.0. Additional exam requirements/recommendations for international students: Required—TOEFL (minimum score 570 paper-based; 230 computer-based; 88 iBT) or IELTS (minimum score 6.5). *Application deadline:* For fall admission, 2/15 priority date for domestic students, 2/15 for international students; for winter admission, 10/15 for domestic students; for spring admission, 2/1 for domestic students. Applications are processed on a rolling basis. Application fee: $50. *Expenses: Tuition:* Full-time $34,659; part-time $963 per credit hour. *Required fees:* $228; $76 per quarter. *Financial support:* Research assistantships with partial tuition reimbursements, career-related internships or fieldwork, institutionally sponsored loans, scholarships/grants, and unspecified assistantships available. Support available to part-time students. Financial award applicants required to submit FAFSA. *Faculty research:* Industrial statistics, quality control; experimental design; reliability; regression techniques; multivariate analysis; nonparametric methods. *Unit head:* Dr. Donald Baker, Director, 585-475-6990, Fax: 585-475-5959, E-mail: cqas@rit.edu. *Application contact:* Diane Ellison, Assistant Vice President, Graduate Enrollment Services, 585-475-2229, Fax: 585-475-7164, E-mail: gradinfo@rit.edu. Web site: http://www.rit.edu/kgcoe/cqas/index.htm.

Rutgers, The State University of New Jersey, New Brunswick, Graduate School-New Brunswick, Program in Statistics, Piscataway, NJ 08854-8097. Offers applied statistics (MS); biostatistics (MS); data mining (MS); quality and productivity management (MS); statistics (MS, PhD). Part-time programs available. Terminal master's awarded for partial completion of doctoral program. *Degree requirements:* For master's, comprehensive exam, essay, exam, non-thesis essay paper; for doctorate, one foreign language, thesis/dissertation, qualifying oral and written exams. *Entrance requirements:* For master's, GRE General Test; for doctorate, GRE General Test, GRE Subject Test (recommended). Additional exam requirements/recommendations for international students: Required—TOEFL (minimum score 550 paper-based; 213 computer-based). Electronic applications accepted. *Faculty research:* Probability, decision theory, linear models, multivariate statistics, statistical computing.

Sam Houston State University, College of Sciences, Department of Mathematics and Statistics, Huntsville, TX 77341. Offers mathematics (MA, MS); statistics (MS). Part-time programs available. *Faculty:* 23 full-time (6 women). *Students:* 29 full-time (11 women), 12 part-time (8 women); includes 11 minority (1 Black or African American, non-Hispanic/Latino; 4 Asian, non-Hispanic/Latino; 6 Hispanic/Latino), 16 international. Average age 32. 32 applicants, 66% accepted, 19 enrolled. In 2011, 9 master's awarded. *Entrance requirements:* For master's, GRE General Test. Additional exam requirements/recommendations for international students: Required—TOEFL (minimum score 550 paper-based; 213 computer-based; 79 iBT). *Application deadline:* For fall admission, 8/1 for domestic students, 6/25 for international students; for spring admission, 12/1 for domestic students, 11/12 for international students. Applications are processed on a rolling basis. Application fee: $45 ($75 for international students). Electronic applications accepted. *Expenses:* Tuition, state resident: full-time $4420; part-time $221 per credit hour. Tuition, nonresident: full-time $10,680; part-time $534 per credit hour. *Required fees:* $329 per credit hour. *Financial support:* Teaching assistantships and institutionally sponsored loans available. Support available to part-time students. Financial award application deadline: 5/31; financial award applicants required to submit FAFSA. *Unit head:* Dr. Mark Klespis, Chair, 936-294-1577, Fax: 936-294-1882, E-mail: klespis@shsu.edu. *Application contact:* Dr. Jianzhong Wang, Advisor, 936-294-3521, Fax: 936-294-1882, E-mail: mth_jxw@shsu.edu. Web site: http://www.shsu.edu/~mcss_www/.

San Diego State University, Graduate and Research Affairs, College of Sciences, Department of Mathematics and Statistics, Program in Statistics, San Diego, CA 92182. Offers MS. Part-time programs available. *Degree requirements:* For master's, comprehensive exam. *Entrance requirements:* For master's, GRE General Test. Additional exam requirements/recommendations for international students: Required—TOEFL. Electronic applications accepted.

San Jose State University, Graduate Studies and Research, College of Science, Department of Mathematics, San Jose, CA 95192-0001. Offers applied mathematics (MS); mathematics (MA, MS); mathematics education (MA); statistics (MA). Part-time and evening/weekend programs available. *Degree requirements:* For master's, comprehensive exam, thesis (for some programs). *Entrance requirements:* For master's, GRE Subject Test. Electronic applications accepted. *Faculty research:* Artificial intelligence, algorithms, numerical analysis, software database, number theory.

Simon Fraser University, Graduate Studies, Faculty of Science, Department of Statistics and Actuarial Science, Burnaby, BC V5A 1S6, Canada. Offers M Sc, PhD. Part-time programs available. *Degree requirements:* For master's, participation in consulting, project; for doctorate, comprehensive exam, thesis/dissertation. *Entrance requirements:* For master's, minimum GPA of 3.0; for doctorate, minimum GPA of 3.5. Additional exam requirements/recommendations for international students: Required—TOEFL. Electronic applications accepted. *Faculty research:* Biostatistics, experimental design, envirometrics, statistical computing, statistical theory.

South Dakota State University, Graduate School, College of Engineering, Department of Mathematics and Statistics, Brookings, SD 57007. Offers computational science and statistics (PhD); mathematics (MS); statistics (MS). Part-time programs available. Terminal master's awarded for partial completion of doctoral program. *Degree requirements:* For master's, thesis (for some programs), oral exam; for doctorate, comprehensive exam, thesis/dissertation, oral and written exams. *Entrance requirements:* Additional exam requirements/recommendations for international students: Required—TOEFL (minimum score 550 paper-based; 213 computer-based; 80 iBT); Recommended—IELTS. *Faculty research:* Financial mathematics, predictive analytics, operations research, bioinformatics, biostatistics, computational science, statistics, number theory, abstract algebra.

Southern Illinois University Carbondale, Graduate School, College of Science, Department of Mathematics, Carbondale, IL 62901-4701. Offers mathematics (MA, MS, PhD); statistics (MS). PhD offered jointly with Southeast Missouri State University. Part-time programs available. *Faculty:* 32 full-time (2 women), 1 part-time/adjunct (0 women). *Students:* 33 full-time (14 women), 5 part-time (1 woman); includes 2 minority (1 Black or African American, non-Hispanic/Latino; 1 Hispanic/Latino), 25 international. Average age 26. 43 applicants, 37% accepted, 9 enrolled. In 2011, 11 master's, 4 doctorates awarded. *Degree requirements:* For master's, thesis; for doctorate, 2 foreign languages, thesis/dissertation. *Entrance requirements:* For master's, minimum GPA of 2.7; for doctorate, minimum GPA of 3.25. Additional exam requirements/recommendations for international students: Required—TOEFL. *Application deadline:* Applications are processed on a rolling basis. Application fee: $0. *Financial support:* In 2011–12, 28 students received support, including 24 teaching assistantships with full tuition reimbursements available; fellowships with full tuition reimbursements available, research assistantships with full tuition reimbursements available, Federal Work-Study, institutionally sponsored loans, and tuition waivers (full) also available. Support available to part-time students. *Faculty research:* Differential equations, combinatorics, probability, algebra, numerical analysis. *Unit head:* Dr. Andrew Earnest, Chairperson, 618-453-6522, Fax: 618-453-5300, E-mail: aearnest@math.siu.edu. *Application contact:* Linda Gibson, Graduate Studies Office Specialist, 618-453-6597, Fax: 618-453-5300, E-mail: lgibson@math.siu.edu. Web site: http://www.math.siu.edu/.

Southern Illinois University Edwardsville, Graduate School, College of Arts and Sciences, Department of Mathematics and Statistics, Edwardsville, IL 62026. Offers mathematics (MS), including computational mathematics, postsecondary mathematics education, pure math, statistics and operations research. Part-time programs available. *Faculty:* 19 full-time (5 women). *Students:* 13 full-time (2 women), 30 part-time (17 women); includes 2 minority (both Black or African American, non-Hispanic/Latino), 12 international. 34 applicants, 47% accepted. In 2011, 14 master's awarded. *Degree requirements:* For master's, thesis (for some programs), research paper/project. *Entrance requirements:* Additional exam requirements/recommendations for international students: Required—TOEFL (minimum score 550 paper-based; 213 computer-based; 79 iBT), IELTS (minimum score 6.5). *Application deadline:* For fall admission, 7/22 for domestic students, 6/1 for international students; for spring admission, 12/9 for domestic students, 10/1 for international students. Applications are processed on a rolling basis. Application fee: $30. Electronic applications accepted. Tuition and fees vary according to course load and program. *Financial support:* In 2011–12, 3 research assistantships with full tuition reimbursements (averaging $9,927 per year), 22 teaching assistantships with full tuition reimbursements (averaging $9,927 per year) were awarded; fellowships with full tuition reimbursements, institutionally sponsored loans, scholarships/grants, and unspecified assistantships also available. Financial award application deadline: 3/1; financial award applicants required to submit FAFSA. *Unit head:* Dr. Krzysztof Jarosz, Chair, 618-650-2354, E-mail: kjarosz@siue.edu. *Application contact:* Dr. Adam Weyhaupt, Director, 618-650-2220, E-mail: aweyhau@siue.edu. Web site: http://www.siue.edu/artsandsciences/math/.

Southern Methodist University, Dedman College, Department of Statistical Science, Dallas, TX 75275-0332. Offers MS, PhD. Part-time programs available. *Degree requirements:* For master's, thesis, oral and written exams; for doctorate,

376 facebook.com/petersonspublishing

Peterson's Graduate Programs in the Physical Sciences, Mathematics, Agricultural Sciences, the Environment & Natural Resources 2013

thesis/dissertation, oral and written exams. *Entrance requirements:* For master's, GRE General Test, 12 hours of advanced math courses; for doctorate, GRE General Test, minimum GPA of 3.0. Additional exam requirements/recommendations for international students: Required—TOEFL. Electronic applications accepted. *Faculty research:* Regression, time series, linear models sampling, nonparametrics, biostatistics.

Stanford University, School of Humanities and Sciences, Department of Statistics, Stanford, CA 94305-9991. Offers MS, PhD. Terminal master's awarded for partial completion of doctoral program. *Degree requirements:* For doctorate, thesis/dissertation, oral exam, qualifying exams. *Entrance requirements:* For master's, GRE General Test; for doctorate, GRE General Test, GRE Subject Test. Additional exam requirements/recommendations for international students: Required—TOEFL. Electronic applications accepted. *Expenses: Tuition:* Full-time $40,050; part-time $890 per credit.

State University of New York at Binghamton, Graduate School, School of Arts and Sciences, Department of Mathematical Sciences, Binghamton, NY 13902-6000. Offers computer science (MA, PhD); probability and statistics (MA, PhD). Part-time programs available. *Faculty:* 27 full-time (4 women), 18 part-time/adjunct (7 women). *Students:* 45 full-time (11 women), 27 part-time (9 women); includes 5 minority (2 Black or African American, non-Hispanic/Latino; 2 Hispanic/Latino; 1 Native Hawaiian or other Pacific Islander, non-Hispanic/Latino), 31 international. Average age 28. 86 applicants, 45% accepted, 22 enrolled. In 2011, 12 master's, 3 doctorates awarded. Terminal master's awarded for partial completion of doctoral program. *Degree requirements:* For master's, thesis or alternative; for doctorate, 2 foreign languages, thesis/dissertation. *Entrance requirements:* For master's and doctorate, GRE General Test, GRE Subject Test. Additional exam requirements/recommendations for international students: Required—TOEFL (minimum score 550 paper-based; 213 computer-based; 80 iBT). *Application deadline:* For fall admission, 4/15 priority date for domestic students, 4/15 for international students; for spring admission, 11/30 priority date for domestic students, 11/30 for international students. Applications are processed on a rolling basis. Application fee: $60. Electronic applications accepted. *Financial support:* In 2011–12, 58 students received support, including 5 fellowships with full tuition reimbursements available (averaging $16,500 per year), research assistantships with full tuition reimbursements available (averaging $16,500 per year), 51 teaching assistantships with full tuition reimbursements available (averaging $16,500 per year); career-related internships or fieldwork, Federal Work-Study, institutionally sponsored loans, scholarships/grants, health care benefits, tuition waivers (full and partial), and unspecified assistantships also available. Financial award application deadline: 2/15; financial award applicants required to submit FAFSA. *Unit head:* Dr. Fernando Guzman, Chairperson, 607-777-2148, E-mail: fer@math.binghamton.edu. *Application contact:* Catherine Smith, Recruiting and Admissions Coordinator, 607-777-2151, Fax: 607-777-2501, E-mail: cmsmith@binghamton.edu.

Stephen F. Austin State University, Graduate School, College of Sciences and Mathematics, Department of Mathematics and Statistics, Nacogdoches, TX 75962. Offers mathematics (MS); mathematics education (MS); statistics (MS). *Degree requirements:* For master's, comprehensive exam, thesis optional. *Entrance requirements:* For master's, GRE General Test, minimum GPA of 2.8 in last 60 hours, 2.5 overall. Additional exam requirements/recommendations for international students: Required—TOEFL. *Faculty research:* Kernel type estimators, fractal mappings, spline curve fitting, robust regression continua theory.

Stevens Institute of Technology, Graduate School, Charles V. Schaefer Jr. School of Engineering, Department of Mathematical Sciences, Program in Stochastic Systems, Hoboken, NJ 07030. Offers MS, Certificate.

Stony Brook University, State University of New York, Graduate School, College of Engineering and Applied Sciences, Department of Applied Mathematics and Statistics, Stony Brook, NY 11794. Offers MS, PhD. *Degree requirements:* For master's, thesis or alternative; for doctorate, one foreign language, comprehensive exam, thesis/dissertation. *Entrance requirements:* For master's and doctorate, GRE General Test. Additional exam requirements/recommendations for international students: Required—TOEFL. *Faculty research:* Biostatistics, combinatorial analysis, differential equations, modeling.

Temple University, Fox School of Business, Doctoral Programs in Business, Philadelphia, PA 19122-6096. Offers accounting (PhD); entrepreneurship (PhD); finance (PhD); international business (PhD); management information systems (PhD); marketing (PhD); risk management and insurance (PhD); statistics (PhD); strategic management (PhD); tourism and sport (PhD). *Accreditation:* AACSB. *Degree requirements:* For doctorate, thesis/dissertation. *Entrance requirements:* For doctorate, GRE General Test, GMAT, minimum GPA of 3.0, master's degree. Additional exam requirements/recommendations for international students: Required—TOEFL (minimum score 600 paper-based; 250 computer-based; 100 iBT), IELTS (minimum score 7.5). Electronic applications accepted. *Expenses:* Tuition, state resident: full-time $12,366; part-time $687 per credit hour. Tuition, nonresident: full-time $17,298; part-time $961 per credit hour. *Required fees:* $590; $213 per year.

Temple University, Fox School of Business, Specialized Master's Programs, Philadelphia, PA 19122-6096. Offers accountancy (MS); actuarial science (MS); finance (MS); financial engineering (MS); human resource management (MS); marketing (MS); statistics (MS). *Accreditation:* AACSB. Part-time programs available. *Entrance requirements:* For master's, GRE General Test or GMAT, minimum undergraduate GPA of 3.0. Additional exam requirements/recommendations for international students: Required—TOEFL (minimum score 600 paper-based; 250 computer-based; 100 iBT), IELTS (minimum score 7.5). *Expenses:* Tuition, state resident: full-time $12,366; part-time $687 per credit hour. Tuition, nonresident: full-time $17,298; part-time $961 per credit hour. *Required fees:* $590; $213 per year.

Texas A&M University, College of Science, Department of Statistics, College Station, TX 77843. Offers MS, PhD. Part-time programs available. *Faculty:* 30. *Students:* 71 full-time (33 women), 113 part-time (43 women); includes 36 minority (5 Black or African American, non-Hispanic/Latino; 1 American Indian or Alaska Native, non-Hispanic/Latino; 21 Asian, non-Hispanic/Latino; 6 Hispanic/Latino; 3 Two or more races, non-Hispanic/Latino), 55 international. Average age 29. In 2011, 24 master's, 16 doctorates awarded. Terminal master's awarded for partial completion of doctoral program. *Degree requirements:* For doctorate, thesis/dissertation. *Entrance requirements:* For master's and doctorate, GRE General Test. Additional exam requirements/recommendations for international students: Required—TOEFL. *Application deadline:* For fall admission, 3/1 priority date for domestic students; for spring admission, 8/1 for domestic students. Applications are processed on a rolling basis. Application fee: $50 ($75 for international students). *Expenses:* Tuition, state resident: full-time $5437; part-time $226.55 per credit hour. Tuition, nonresident: full-time $12,949; part-time $539.55 per credit hour. *Required fees:* $2741. *Financial support:* Fellowships, research assistantships, teaching assistantships, and career-related internships or fieldwork available. Financial award application deadline: 3/1. *Faculty research:* Time series, chemometrics, biometrics, smoothing, linear models. *Unit head:* Dr. Simon Sheather, Head, 979-845-3141, Fax: 979-845-3144, E-mail: sheather@stat.tamu.edu. *Application contact:* P. Fred Dahm, Graduate Director, 979-845-7251, Fax: 979-845-3144, E-mail: fdahm@stat.tamu.edu. Web site: http://www.stat.tamu.edu/.

Texas Tech University, Graduate School, College of Arts and Sciences, Department of Mathematics and Statistics, Lubbock, TX 79409. Offers mathematics (MA, MS, PhD); statistics (MS). Part-time programs available. Postbaccalaureate distance learning degree programs offered (minimal on-campus study). *Faculty:* 45 full-time (8 women). *Students:* 107 full-time (48 women), 10 part-time (3 women); includes 9 minority (1 Black or African American, non-Hispanic/Latino; 2 Asian, non-Hispanic/Latino; 4 Hispanic/Latino; 2 Two or more races, non-Hispanic/Latino), 62 international. Average age 28. 92 applicants, 71% accepted, 29 enrolled. In 2011, 35 master's, 8 doctorates awarded. *Degree requirements:* For master's, thesis or alternative; for doctorate, comprehensive exam, thesis/dissertation. *Entrance requirements:* For master's and doctorate, GRE General Test. Additional exam requirements/recommendations for international students: Required—TOEFL (minimum score 550 paper-based; 213 computer-based; 79 iBT). *Application deadline:* For fall admission, 6/1 priority date for domestic students, 1/15 for international students; for spring admission, 9/1 priority date for domestic students, 6/15 for international students. Applications are processed on a rolling basis. Application fee: $50 ($75 for international students). Electronic applications accepted. *Expenses:* Tuition, state resident: full-time $5899; part-time $245.80 per credit hour. Tuition, nonresident: full-time $13,411; part-time $558.80 per credit hour. *Required fees:* $2680.60; $86.50 per credit hour. $920.30 per semester. *Financial support:* In 2011–12, 41 students received support. Application deadline: 4/15; applicants required to submit FAFSA. *Faculty research:* Numerical analysis, mathematical biology, complex analysis, algebra and geometry, ordinary and partial differential equations. *Total annual research expenditures:* $2.2 million. *Unit head:* Dr. Kent Pearce, Chair, 806-742-2566, Fax: 806-742-1112, E-mail: kent.pearce@ttu.edu. *Application contact:* Dr. Ram Iyer, Graduate Adviser, 806-742-2566, Fax: 806-742-1112, E-mail: ram.iyer@ttu.edu. Web site: http://www.math.ttu.edu/.

Texas Tech University, Graduate School, Rawls College of Business Administration, Programs in Business Administration, Lubbock, TX 79409. Offers agricultural business (MBA); business administration (IMBA); business statistics (MBA); entrepreneurship and innovation (MBA); general business (MBA); health organization management (MBA); international business (MBA); management and leadership skills (MBA); management information systems (MBA); marketing (MBA); real estate (MBA); JD/MBA; MBA/M Arch; MBA/MA; MBA/MD; MBA/MS; MBA/Pharm D. Part-time and evening/weekend programs available. *Faculty:* 49 full-time (8 women), 2 part-time/adjunct (0 women). *Students:* 195 full-time (55 women), 397 part-time (101 women); includes 123 minority (27 Black or African American, non-Hispanic/Latino; 4 American Indian or Alaska Native, non-Hispanic/Latino; 31 Asian, non-Hispanic/Latino; 61 Hispanic/Latino), 38 international. Average age 31. 374 applicants, 83% accepted, 255 enrolled. In 2011, 256 degrees awarded. *Degree requirements:* For master's, capstone course. *Entrance requirements:* For master's, GMAT, holistic review of academic credentials. Additional exam requirements/recommendations for international students: Required—TOEFL (minimum score 550 paper-based; 213 computer-based; 79 iBT). *Application deadline:* For fall admission, 4/1 priority date for domestic students, 1/15 for international students; for spring admission, 9/1 priority date for domestic students, 6/15 for international students. Applications are processed on a rolling basis. Application fee: $50 ($75 for international students). Electronic applications accepted. *Expenses:* Tuition, state resident: full-time $5899; part-time $245.80 per credit hour. Tuition, nonresident: full-time $13,411; part-time $558.80 per credit hour. *Required fees:* $2680.60; $86.50 per credit hour. $920.30 per semester. *Financial support:* In 2011–12, 22 research assistantships (averaging $8,800 per year) were awarded; teaching assistantships, career-related internships or fieldwork, Federal Work-Study,

Peterson's Graduate Programs in the Physical Sciences, Mathematics, Agricultural Sciences, the Environment & Natural Resources 2013

facebook.com/petersonspublishing **377**

scholarships/grants, health care benefits, and unspecified assistantships also available. Support available to part-time students. Financial award applicants required to submit FAFSA. *Unit head:* Dr. W. Jay Conover, Director, 806-742-1546, Fax: 806-742-3958, E-mail: jay.conover@ttu.edu. *Application contact:* Elizabeth Stuart, Director, Graduate Services Center, 806-742-3184, Fax: 806-742-3958, E-mail: ba_grad@ttu.edu. Web site: http://mba.ba.ttu.edu/.

Tulane University, School of Science and Engineering, Department of Mathematics, New Orleans, LA 70118-5669. Offers applied mathematics (MS); mathematics (MS, PhD); statistics (MS). *Degree requirements:* For master's, thesis (for some programs); for doctorate, thesis/dissertation. *Entrance requirements:* For master's, GRE General Test, minimum B average in undergraduate course work; for doctorate, GRE General Test. Additional exam requirements/recommendations for international students: Required—TOEFL. Electronic applications accepted.

Université de Montréal, Faculty of Arts and Sciences, Department of Mathematics and Statistics, Montréal, QC H3C 3J7, Canada. Offers mathematical and computational finance (M Sc, DESS); mathematics (M Sc, PhD); statistics (M Sc, PhD). *Degree requirements:* For master's, thesis; for doctorate, thesis/dissertation, general exam. *Entrance requirements:* For master's and doctorate, proficiency in French. Electronic applications accepted. *Faculty research:* Pure and applied mathematics, actuarial mathematics.

Université Laval, Faculty of Sciences and Engineering, Department of Mathematics and Statistics, Program in Statistics, Québec, QC G1K 7P4, Canada. Offers M Sc. *Degree requirements:* For master's, thesis (for some programs). *Entrance requirements:* For master's, knowledge of French and English. Electronic applications accepted.

University at Albany, State University of New York, College of Arts and Sciences, Department of Mathematics and Statistics, Albany, NY 12222-0001. Offers mathematics (PhD); secondary teaching (MA); statistics (MA). *Degree requirements:* For doctorate, one foreign language, thesis/dissertation. *Entrance requirements:* For doctorate, GRE General Test. Additional exam requirements/recommendations for international students: Required—TOEFL (minimum score 550 paper-based; 213 computer-based). Electronic applications accepted.

University at Albany, State University of New York, School of Education, Department of Educational and Counseling Psychology, Albany, NY 12222-0001. Offers counseling psychology (MS, PhD, CAS); educational psychology (Ed D); educational psychology and statistics (MS); measurements and evaluation (Ed D); rehabilitation counseling (MS), including counseling psychology; school counselor (CAS); school psychology (Psy D, CAS); special education (MS); statistics and research design (Ed D). *Accreditation:* APA (one or more programs are accredited). Evening/weekend programs available. *Degree requirements:* For doctorate, thesis/dissertation. *Entrance requirements:* For doctorate, GRE General Test. Additional exam requirements/recommendations for international students: Required—TOEFL (minimum score 550 paper-based; 213 computer-based). Electronic applications accepted.

The University of Akron, Graduate School, Buchtel College of Arts and Sciences, Department of Statistics, Akron, OH 44325. Offers MS. Part-time and evening/weekend programs available. *Faculty:* 8 full-time (1 woman), 2 part-time/adjunct (0 women). *Students:* 20 full-time (6 women), 4 part-time (2 women); includes 2 minority (both Black or African American, non-Hispanic/Latino), 13 international. Average age 30. 23 applicants, 78% accepted, 8 enrolled. In 2011, 15 master's awarded. *Degree requirements:* For master's, comprehensive exam, thesis optional. *Entrance requirements:* For master's, minimum GPA of 2.75; baccalaureate degree in statistics, mathematics, or related area; three letters of recommendation; one semester of applied statistics; three semesters of calculus, linear algebra, or equivalent. Additional exam requirements/recommendations for international students: Required—TOEFL (minimum score 550 paper-based; 213 computer-based; 79 iBT). *Application deadline:* Applications are processed on a rolling basis. Application fee: $30 ($40 for international students). Electronic applications accepted. *Expenses:* Tuition, state resident: full-time $7038; part-time $391 per credit hour. Tuition, nonresident: full-time $12,051; part-time $670 per credit hour. *Required fees:* $1274; $34 per credit hour. *Financial support:* In 2011–12, 1 research assistantship, 15 teaching assistantships with full tuition reimbursements were awarded. *Faculty research:* Experimental design, sampling, actuarial science, biostatistics. *Total annual research expenditures:* $495. *Unit head:* Dr. Richard Steiner, Associate Chair, 330-972-8010, E-mail: rps@uakron.edu. Web site: http://www.uakron.edu/stat/.

University of Alaska Fairbanks, College of Natural Sciences and Mathematics, Department of Mathematics and Statistics, Fairbanks, AK 99775-6660. Offers mathematics (MAT, PhD); statistics (MS, Graduate Certificate). Part-time programs available. *Faculty:* 14 full-time (6 women), 1 (woman) part-time/adjunct. *Students:* 7 full-time (2 women), 3 part-time (2 women), 4 international. Average age 27. 18 applicants, 39% accepted, 5 enrolled. In 2011, 1 master's, 4 doctorates awarded. Terminal master's awarded for partial completion of doctoral program. *Degree requirements:* For master's, comprehensive exam, thesis or alternative; for doctorate, comprehensive exam, thesis/dissertation, oral defense. *Entrance requirements:* Additional exam requirements/recommendations for international students: Required—TOEFL (minimum score 550 paper-based; 213 computer-based; 80 iBT). *Application deadline:* For fall admission, 6/1 for domestic students, 3/1 for international students; for spring admission, 10/15 for domestic students, 9/1 for international students. Applications are processed on a rolling basis. Application fee: $60. Electronic applications accepted. *Expenses:*

Tuition, state resident: full-time $6696; part-time $372 per credit. Tuition, nonresident: full-time $13,680; part-time $760 per credit. Tuition and fees vary according to course load and reciprocity agreements. *Financial support:* In 2011–12, 1 research assistantship with tuition reimbursement (averaging $8,313 per year), 5 teaching assistantships with tuition reimbursements (averaging $17,550 per year) were awarded; fellowships with tuition reimbursements, career-related internships or fieldwork, Federal Work-Study, scholarships/grants, health care benefits, and unspecified assistantships also available. Support available to part-time students. Financial award application deadline: 2/15; financial award applicants required to submit FAFSA. *Faculty research:* Kriging, arrangements of hyperplanes, bifurcation analysis of time-periodic differential-delay equations, inverse problems, phylogenic tree construction. *Total annual research expenditures:* $22,000. *Unit head:* Dr. John Rhodes, Department Chair, 907-474-7332, Fax: 907-474-5394, E-mail: fymath@uaf.edu. *Application contact:* Mike Earnest, Director of Admissions, 907-474-7500, Fax: 907-474-5379, E-mail: admissions@uaf.edu. Web site: http://www.dms.uaf.edu/.

University of Alberta, Faculty of Graduate Studies and Research, Department of Mathematical and Statistical Sciences, Edmonton, AB T6G 2E1, Canada. Offers applied mathematics (M Sc, PhD); biostatistics (M Sc); mathematical finance (M Sc, PhD); mathematical physics (M Sc, PhD); mathematics (M Sc, PhD); statistics (M Sc, PhD, Postgraduate Diploma). Part-time programs available. Terminal master's awarded for partial completion of doctoral program. *Degree requirements:* For master's, thesis (for some programs); for doctorate, comprehensive exam, thesis/dissertation. *Entrance requirements:* Additional exam requirements/recommendations for international students: Required—TOEFL (minimum score 580 paper-based; 237 computer-based). Electronic applications accepted. *Faculty research:* Classical and functional analysis, algebra, differential equations, geometry.

The University of Arizona, Graduate Interdisciplinary Programs, Graduate Interdisciplinary Program in Statistics, Tucson, AZ 85721. Offers MS, PhD. *Students:* 15 full-time (5 women), 4 part-time (1 woman); includes 3 minority (2 Asian, non-Hispanic/Latino; 1 Hispanic/Latino), 7 international. Average age 33. 19 applicants, 63% accepted, 5 enrolled. *Application deadline:* For fall admission, 2/1 for domestic and international students; for spring admission, 8/1 for domestic and international students. Application fee: $75. *Expenses:* Tuition, state resident: full-time $10,840. Tuition, nonresident: full-time $25,802. *Unit head:* Dr. Andrew Comrie, Dean, 520-621-3512, Fax: 520-621-4101, E-mail: gradadm@grad.arizona.edu. *Application contact:* Dr. Andrew Carnie, Faculty Director, 520-621-8368, E-mail: gidp@email.arizona.edu. Web site: http://stat.bio5.org/.

University of Arkansas, Graduate School, J. William Fulbright College of Arts and Sciences, Department of Mathematical Sciences, Program in Statistics, Fayetteville, AR 72701-1201. Offers MS. *Students:* 14 full-time (3 women), 1 part-time (0 women), 11 international. In 2011, 8 master's awarded. *Degree requirements:* For master's, thesis. *Application deadline:* For fall admission, 4/1 for international students; for spring admission, 10/1 for international students. Applications are processed on a rolling basis. Application fee: $40 ($50 for international students). Electronic applications accepted. *Financial support:* In 2011–12, 4 research assistantships, 65 teaching assistantships were awarded; fellowships, career-related internships or fieldwork, and Federal Work-Study also available. Support available to part-time students. Financial award application deadline: 4/1; financial award applicants required to submit FAFSA. *Unit head:* Dr. Laurie Meaux, Chair of Studies, 479-575-3352, Fax: 479-575-8630, E-mail: lmeaux@uark.edu. *Application contact:* Dr. John Ryan, Graduate Coordinator, 479-575-3351, Fax: 479-575-8630, E-mail: jryan@uark.edu. Web site: http://stat.uark.edu/.

The University of British Columbia, Faculty of Science, Department of Statistics, Vancouver, BC V6T 1Z2, Canada. Offers M Sc, PhD. *Degree requirements:* For master's, thesis or alternative, seminar; for doctorate, comprehensive exam, thesis/dissertation. *Entrance requirements:* Additional exam requirements/recommendations for international students: Required—TOEFL (minimum score 600 paper-based; 250 computer-based; 100 iBT), IELTS (minimum score 7.5). Electronic applications accepted. *Faculty research:* Theoretical, applied, biostatistical, and computational statistics.

University of Calgary, Faculty of Graduate Studies, Faculty of Science, Department of Mathematics and Statistics, Calgary, AB T2N 1N4, Canada. Offers M Sc, PhD. *Degree requirements:* For master's, comprehensive exam, thesis; for doctorate, thesis/dissertation, candidacy exam, preliminary exams. *Entrance requirements:* For master's, honors degree in applied math, pure math, or statistics; for doctorate, MA or M Sc. Additional exam requirements/recommendations for international students: Required—TOEFL (minimum score 600 paper-based; 250 computer-based) or IELTS (minimum score 7). *Faculty research:* Combinatorics, applied mathematics, statistics, probability, analysis.

University of California, Berkeley, Graduate Division, College of Letters and Science, Department of Statistics, Berkeley, CA 94720-1500. Offers MA, PhD. *Degree requirements:* For doctorate, thesis/dissertation, qualifying exam, written preliminary exam. *Entrance requirements:* For master's and doctorate, GRE General Test, minimum GPA of 3.0, 3 letters of recommendation.

University of California, Davis, Graduate Studies, Program in Statistics, Davis, CA 95616. Offers MS, PhD. Terminal master's awarded for partial completion of doctoral program. *Degree requirements:* For master's, comprehensive exam; for doctorate, thesis/dissertation. *Entrance requirements:* For master's and doctorate, GRE General Test, minimum GPA of 3.0. Additional exam requirements/

378 facebook.com/petersonspublishing

Peterson's Graduate Programs in the Physical Sciences, Mathematics, Agricultural Sciences, the Environment & Natural Resources 2013

recommendations for international students: Required—TOEFL (minimum score 550 paper-based; 213 computer-based). Electronic applications accepted. *Faculty research:* Nonparametric analysis, time series analysis, biostatistics, curve estimation, reliability.

University of California, Irvine, Donald Bren School of Information and Computer Sciences, Department of Statistics, Irvine, CA 92697. Offers MS, PhD. *Students:* 36 full-time (18 women), 2 part-time (1 woman); includes 5 minority (all Asian, non-Hispanic/Latino), 20 international. Average age 26. 127 applicants, 32% accepted, 17 enrolled. In 2011, 11 master's, 1 doctorate awarded. Application fee: $80 ($100 for international students). *Unit head:* Jessica M. Utts, Chair, 949-824-0649, Fax: 949-824-9863, E-mail: jutts@uci.edu. *Application contact:* Kris Bolcer, Assistant Director, Graduate Affairs, 949-824-5156, Fax: 949-824-4163, E-mail: kbolcer@uci.edu. Web site: http://www.stat.uci.edu/.

University of California, Los Angeles, Graduate Division, College of Letters and Science, Department of Statistics, Los Angeles, CA 90095. Offers MS, PhD. *Faculty:* 11 full-time (0 women). *Students:* 86 full-time (26 women); includes 21 minority (14 Asian, non-Hispanic/Latino; 4 Hispanic/Latino; 1 Native Hawaiian or other Pacific Islander, non-Hispanic/Latino; 2 Two or more races, non-Hispanic/Latino), 34 international. Average age 28. 417 applicants, 19% accepted, 31 enrolled. In 2011, 16 master's, 7 doctorates awarded. Terminal master's awarded for partial completion of doctoral program. *Degree requirements:* For master's, comprehensive exam or thesis; for doctorate, thesis/dissertation, oral and written exams, student teaching. *Entrance requirements:* For master's, GRE General Test, minimum GPA of 3.2, 12 quarter or 8 semester courses in upper-division quantitative work; for doctorate, GRE General Test, minimum GPA of 3.5, 12 quarter or 8 semester courses in upper-division quantitative work. Application fee: $70 ($90 for international students). Electronic applications accepted. *Financial support:* In 2011–12, 29 fellowships with full and partial tuition reimbursements, 34 research assistantships with full and partial tuition reimbursements, 45 teaching assistantships with full and partial tuition reimbursements were awarded; Federal Work-Study, institutionally sponsored loans, scholarships/grants, health care benefits, tuition waivers (full and partial), and unspecified assistantships also available. Financial award application deadline: 3/1; financial award applicants required to submit FAFSA. *Unit head:* Dr. Jan DeLeeuw, Chair, 310-825-9550, E-mail: deleeuw@stat.ucla.edu. *Application contact:* Glenda Jones, Student Affairs Officer, 310-206-3742, E-mail: glenda@stat.ucla.edu. Web site: http://www.stat.ucla.edu.

University of California, Riverside, Graduate Division, Department of Statistics, Riverside, CA 92521-0102. Offers applied statistics (PhD); statistics (MS). Terminal master's awarded for partial completion of doctoral program. *Degree requirements:* For master's, comprehensive exam; for doctorate, comprehensive exam, thesis/dissertation. *Entrance requirements:* For master's and doctorate, GRE General Test. Additional exam requirements/recommendations for international students: Required—TOEFL (minimum score 550 paper-based; 213 computer-based; 80 iBT). Electronic applications accepted. *Faculty research:* Design and analysis of gene expression experiments using DNA microarrays, statistical design and analysis of experiments, linear models, probability models and statistical inference, SNP/SFP discovery using DNA microarray, genetic mapping.

University of California, San Diego, Office of Graduate Studies, Department of Mathematics, La Jolla, CA 92093. Offers applied mathematics (MA); mathematics (MA, PhD); statistics (MS). *Degree requirements:* For doctorate, thesis/dissertation. *Entrance requirements:* For master's and doctorate, GRE General Test, GRE Subject Test. Electronic applications accepted.

University of California, Santa Barbara, Graduate Division, College of Letters and Sciences, Division of Mathematics, Life, and Physical Sciences, Department of Statistics and Applied Probability, Santa Barbara, CA 93106-3110. Offers financial mathematics and statistics (PhD); quantitative methods in the social sciences (PhD); statistics (MA), including applied statistics, mathematical statistics; statistics and applied probability (PhD); MA/PhD. *Faculty:* 11 full-time (3 women). *Students:* 49 full-time (20 women); includes 9 minority (7 Asian, non-Hispanic/Latino; 1 Hispanic/Latino; 1 Two or more races, non-Hispanic/Latino), 31 international. Average age 29. 272 applicants, 19% accepted, 12 enrolled. In 2011, 14 master's, 5 doctorates awarded. Terminal master's awarded for partial completion of doctoral program. *Median time to degree:* Of those who began their doctoral program in fall 2003, 57% received their degree in 8 years or less. *Degree requirements:* For master's, comprehensive exam, thesis optional; for doctorate, comprehensive exam, thesis/dissertation. *Entrance requirements:* For master's and doctorate, GRE General Test. Additional exam requirements/recommendations for international students: Required—TOEFL (minimum score 550 paper-based; 80 iBT), IELTS (minimum score 7). *Application deadline:* For fall admission, 1/1 priority date for domestic students, 1/1 for international students; for winter admission, 11/1 priority date for domestic students, 11/1 for international students; for spring admission, 2/1 priority date for domestic students, 2/1 for international students. Application fee: $80 ($100 for international students). Electronic applications accepted. *Expenses:* Tuition, state resident: full-time $12,192. Tuition, nonresident: full-time $27,294. *Required fees:* $764.13. *Financial support:* In 2011–12, 23 students received support, including 6 fellowships with full tuition reimbursements available (averaging $11,285 per year), 1 research assistantship with full and partial tuition reimbursement available (averaging $2,790 per year), 28 teaching assistantships with partial tuition reimbursements available (averaging $14,557 per year); Federal Work-Study, scholarships/grants, and health care benefits also available. Financial award

application deadline: 1/1; financial award applicants required to submit FAFSA. *Faculty research:* Bayesian inference, financial mathematics, stochastic processes, environmental statistics, biostatistical modeling. *Total annual research expenditures:* $139,480. *Unit head:* Dr. Yuedong Wang, Chair, 805-893-4870, E-mail: yeudong@pstat.ucsb.edu. *Application contact:* Dolly J. Cook, Graduate Program Assistant, 805-893-2129, Fax: 805-893-2334, E-mail: cook@pstat.ucsb.edu. Web site: http://www.pstat.ucsb.edu/.

University of California, Santa Cruz, Division of Graduate Studies, Jack Baskin School of Engineering, Program in Statistics and Applied Mathematics, Santa Cruz, CA 95064. Offers MS, PhD. Terminal master's awarded for partial completion of doctoral program. *Degree requirements:* For master's, seminar, qualifying exam, capstone project; for doctorate, thesis/dissertation, seminar, qualifying exam. *Entrance requirements:* For master's and doctorate, GRE General Test; GRE Subject Test in math (recommended). Additional exam requirements/recommendations for international students: Required—TOEFL (minimum score 570 paper-based; 230 computer-based; 89 iBT); Recommended—IELTS (minimum score 8). Electronic applications accepted. *Faculty research:* Bayesian nonparametric methods; computationally intensive Bayesian inference, prediction, and decision-making; envirometrics; fluid mechanics; mathematical biology.

University of Central Florida, College of Sciences, Department of Statistics and Actuarial Science, Orlando, FL 32816. Offers SAS data mining (Certificate); statistical computing (MS). Part-time and evening/weekend programs available. *Faculty:* 11 full-time (2 women), 2 part-time/adjunct (0 women). *Students:* 38 full-time (17 women), 25 part-time (9 women); includes 17 minority (7 Black or African American, non-Hispanic/Latino; 6 Asian, non-Hispanic/Latino; 4 Hispanic/Latino), 18 international. Average age 30. 60 applicants, 82% accepted, 32 enrolled. In 2011, 16 master's, 10 other advanced degrees awarded. *Degree requirements:* For master's, comprehensive exam. *Entrance requirements:* For master's, GRE General Test, minimum GPA of 3.0 in last 60 hours. Additional exam requirements/recommendations for international students: Required—TOEFL. *Application deadline:* For fall admission, 7/15 for domestic students; for spring admission, 12/1 for domestic students. Application fee: $30. Electronic applications accepted. *Expenses:* Tuition, state resident: part-time $277.08 per credit hour. Tuition, nonresident: part-time $277.08 per credit hour. Part-time tuition and fees vary according to degree level and program. *Financial support:* In 2011–12, 19 students received support, including 2 fellowships with partial tuition reimbursements available (averaging $7,000 per year), 1 research assistantship with partial tuition reimbursement available (averaging $5,300 per year), 16 teaching assistantships with partial tuition reimbursements available (averaging $11,600 per year); career-related internships or fieldwork, Federal Work-Study, institutionally sponsored loans, tuition waivers (partial), and unspecified assistantships also available. Financial award application deadline: 3/1; financial award applicants required to submit FAFSA. *Faculty research:* Multivariate analysis, quality control, shrinkage estimation. *Unit head:* Dr. David Nickerson, Chair, 407-823-2289, Fax: 407-823-5419, E-mail: david.nickerson@ucf.edu. *Application contact:* Barbara Rodriguez, Director, Admissions and Registration, 407-823-2766, Fax: 407-823-6442, E-mail: gradadmissions@ucf.edu. Web site: http://statistics.cos.ucf.edu/.

University of Central Oklahoma, College of Graduate Studies and Research, College of Mathematics and Science, Department of Mathematics and Statistics, Edmond, OK 73034-5209. Offers applied mathematical sciences (MS), including computer science, mathematics, mathematics/computer science teaching, statistics. Part-time programs available. *Faculty:* 7 full-time (4 women), 3 part-time/adjunct (0 women). *Students:* 20 full-time (7 women), 11 part-time (8 women); includes 5 minority (3 Black or African American, non-Hispanic/Latino; 2 Two or more races, non-Hispanic/Latino), 11 international. Average age 29. In 2011, 5 master's awarded. *Degree requirements:* For master's, thesis. *Entrance requirements:* Additional exam requirements/recommendations for international students: Required—TOEFL (minimum score 550 paper-based; 213 computer-based). *Application deadline:* Applications are processed on a rolling basis. Application fee: $50. Electronic applications accepted. *Expenses:* Tuition, state resident: full-time $3901; part-time $218.30 per credit hour. Tuition, nonresident: full-time $9198; part-time $511.20 per credit hour. Tuition and fees vary according to program. *Financial support:* Federal Work-Study and unspecified assistantships available. Financial award application deadline: 3/31; financial award applicants required to submit FAFSA. *Faculty research:* Curvature, FAA, math education. *Unit head:* Dr. Michael Fulkerson, 405-974-5575, E-mail: mfulkerson@uco.edu. *Application contact:* Dr. Richard Bernard, Adviser, 405-974-3493, Fax: 405-974-3824, E-mail: jyates@aix1.uco.edu. Web site: http://www.ucok.edu/graduate.applied.htm.

University of Chicago, Booth School of Business, Full-Time MBA Program, Chicago, IL 60637. Offers accounting (MBA); analytic finance (MBA); analytic management (MBA); business administration (PhD); econometrics and statistics (MBA); economics (MBA); entrepreneurship (MBA); finance (MBA); general management (MBA); health administration and policy (Certificate); human resource management (MBA); international business (IMBA, MBA); managerial and organizational behavior (MBA); marketing management (MBA); operations management (MBA); strategic management (MBA); MBA/AM; MBA/JD; MBA/MA; MBA/MD; MBA/MPP. *Accreditation:* AACSB. Part-time and evening/weekend programs available. *Faculty:* 166 full-time, 32 part-time/adjunct. *Students:* 1,160 full-time (412 women); includes 316 minority (61 Black or African American, non-Hispanic/Latino; 173 Asian, non-Hispanic/Latino; 63 Hispanic/Latino; 19 Two or

Peterson's Graduate Programs in the Physical Sciences, Mathematics, Agricultural Sciences, the Environment & Natural Resources 2013

facebook.com/petersonspublishing **379**

more races, non-Hispanic/Latino), 378 international. Average age 28. 4,169 applicants, 575 enrolled. In 2011, 1,423 master's, 19 doctorates awarded. Terminal master's awarded for partial completion of doctoral program. *Entrance requirements:* For master's, GMAT, 2 letters of recommendation, 3 essays, resume, interview, transcripts. Additional exam requirements/recommendations for international students: Required—TOEFL (minimum score 600 paper-based; 250 computer-based; 104 iBT), IELTS. *Application deadline:* For fall admission, 10/12 priority date for domestic students, 10/12 for international students; for winter admission, 1/4 for domestic and international students; for spring admission, 4/4 for domestic and international students. Application fee: $200. Electronic applications accepted. *Expenses:* Contact institution. *Financial support:* Fellowships available. Financial award applicants required to submit FAFSA. *Faculty research:* Finance, marketing, economics, entrepreneurship, strategy, management. *Unit head:* Stacey Kole, Deputy Dean, 773-702-7121. *Application contact:* Kurt Ahlm, Associate Dean of Student Recruitment and Admissions, 773-702-7369, Fax: 773-702-9085, E-mail: admissions@chicagobooth.edu. Web site: http://chicagobooth.edu/.

University of Chicago, Division of the Physical Sciences, Department of Statistics, Chicago, IL 60637. Offers SM, PhD. Part-time programs available. *Faculty:* 23 full-time (4 women), 4 part-time/adjunct (0 women). *Students:* 88 full-time (39 women), 2 part-time (0 women); includes 6 minority (all Asian, non-Hispanic/Latino), 68 international. Average age 25. 563 applicants, 16% accepted, 39 enrolled. In 2011, 47 master's, 5 doctorates awarded. Terminal master's awarded for partial completion of doctoral program. *Degree requirements:* For master's, thesis; for doctorate, thesis/dissertation. *Entrance requirements:* For master's and doctorate, GRE General Test. Additional exam requirements/recommendations for international students: Required—TOEFL. *Application deadline:* For fall admission, 12/31 for domestic and international students. Application fee: $55. Electronic applications accepted. *Financial support:* In 2011–12, fellowships with full tuition reimbursements (averaging $21,150 per year), research assistantships with full tuition reimbursements (averaging $21,150 per year), teaching assistantships with full tuition reimbursements (averaging $21,150 per year) were awarded; tuition waivers (full) also available. Financial award application deadline: 12/31. *Faculty research:* Genetics, econometrics, generalized linear models, history of statistics, probability theory. *Total annual research expenditures:* $953,626. *Unit head:* Kathryn Kraynik, Department Administrator, 773-702-8335, E-mail: kraynik@galton.uchicago.edu. *Application contact:* Matt Johnston, Admissions Specialist, 773-702-0541, E-mail: mhj@galton.uchicago.edu. Web site: http://www.stat.uchicago.edu/.

University of Cincinnati, Graduate School, McMicken College of Arts and Sciences, Department of Mathematical Sciences, Cincinnati, OH 45221. Offers applied mathematics (MS, PhD); mathematics education (MAT); pure mathematics (MS, PhD); statistics (MS, PhD). Part-time programs available. Terminal master's awarded for partial completion of doctoral program. *Degree requirements:* For master's, comprehensive exam, thesis or alternative; for doctorate, one foreign language, comprehensive exam, thesis/dissertation. *Entrance requirements:* For master's, GRE, teacher certification (MAT); for doctorate, GRE. Additional exam requirements/recommendations for international students: Required—TOEFL. Electronic applications accepted. *Faculty research:* Algebra, analysis, differential equations, numerical analysis, statistics.

University of Colorado Denver, College of Liberal Arts and Sciences, Department of Mathematical and Statistical Sciences, Denver, CO 80217. Offers applied mathematics (MS, PhD), including applied mathematics, applied probability (MS), applied statistics (MS), computational biology, computational mathematics (PhD), discrete mathematics, finite geometry (PhD), mathematics education (PhD), mathematics of engineering and science (MS), numerical analysis, operations research (MS), optimization and operations research (PhD), probability (PhD), statistics (PhD). Part-time programs available. *Faculty:* 26 full-time (4 women), 2 part-time/adjunct (1 woman). *Students:* 44 full-time (14 women), 14 part-time (5 women); includes 6 minority (4 Asian, non-Hispanic/Latino; 2 Hispanic/Latino), 10 international. Average age 33. 66 applicants, 79% accepted, 17 enrolled. In 2011, 6 master's, 6 doctorates awarded. *Degree requirements:* For master's, comprehensive exam, thesis optional, 30 hours of course work with minimum GPA of 3.0; for doctorate, comprehensive exam, thesis/dissertation. *Entrance requirements:* For master's and doctorate, GRE General Test; GRE Subject Test in math (recommended), 30 hours of course work in mathematics (24 of which must be upper-division mathematics), minimum GPA of 3.0. Additional exam requirements/recommendations for international students: Required—TOEFL (minimum score 525 paper-based; 192 computer-based; 71 iBT). *Application deadline:* For fall admission, 4/1 for domestic students, 3/1 for international students; for spring admission, 11/1 for domestic students, 10/1 for international students. Application fee: $50 ($75 for international students). Electronic applications accepted. *Financial support:* Fellowships with partial tuition reimbursements, research assistantships with full tuition reimbursements, teaching assistantships with full tuition reimbursements, Federal Work-Study, scholarships/grants, and unspecified assistantships available. Financial award application deadline: 4/1; financial award applicants required to submit FAFSA. *Faculty research:* Computational mathematics, computational biology, discrete mathematics and geometry, probability and statistics, optimization. *Unit head:* Dr. Stephen Billups, Graduate Chair, 303-556-4814, E-mail: stephen.billups@ucdenver.edu. *Application contact:* Lisa Herbert, Graduate Program Assistant, 303-556-2341, E-mail: lisa.herbert@ucdenver.edu. Web site:

http://www.ucdenver.edu/academics/colleges/CLAS/Departments/math/Pages/MathStats.aspx.

University of Connecticut, Graduate School, College of Liberal Arts and Sciences, Department of Statistics, Storrs, CT 06269. Offers MS, PhD. Terminal master's awarded for partial completion of doctoral program. *Degree requirements:* For master's, comprehensive exam; for doctorate, thesis/dissertation. *Entrance requirements:* For master's and doctorate, GRE General Test. Additional exam requirements/recommendations for international students: Required—TOEFL (minimum score 550 paper-based; 213 computer-based). Electronic applications accepted.

University of Delaware, College of Agriculture and Natural Resources, Department of Food and Resource Economics, Program in Statistics, Newark, DE 19716. Offers MS. Part-time programs available. *Entrance requirements:* For master's, GRE General Test, 3 letters of recommendation. Additional exam requirements/recommendations for international students: Required—TOEFL (minimum score 550 paper-based; 213 computer-based). Electronic applications accepted.

University of Denver, Daniels College of Business, Department of Business Information and Analytics, Denver, CO 80208. Offers business intelligence (MS); data mining (MS). *Faculty:* 12 full-time (2 women), 2 part-time/adjunct (0 women). *Entrance requirements:* Additional exam requirements/recommendations for international students: Required—TOEFL (minimum score 570 paper-based; 88 iBT). *Application deadline:* For fall admission, 1/15 priority date for domestic students. Applications are processed on a rolling basis. Application fee: $60. Electronic applications accepted. *Financial support:* Career-related internships or fieldwork, Federal Work-Study, institutionally sponsored loans, and scholarships/grants available. Support available to part-time students. Financial award application deadline: 2/15; financial award applicants required to submit FAFSA. *Unit head:* Dr. Anthony Hayter, Professor, 303-871-4341, E-mail: anthony.hayter@du.edu. *Application contact:* Information Contact, 303-871-3416. Web site: http://daniels.du.edu/schoolsdepartments/dbia/index.html.

University of Denver, Morgridge College of Education, Denver, CO 80208. Offers advanced study in law librarianship (Certificate); child and family studies (MA, PhD); counseling psychology (MA, PhD); curriculum and instruction (MA, PhD, Certificate); educational leadership (Ed D, PhD); educational leadership and policy studies (MA, Certificate); higher education (MA, PhD); library and information science (MLIS); research methods and statistics (MA, PhD); school administration (PhD); school psychology (Ed S). *Accreditation:* ALA; APA (one or more programs are accredited). Part-time and evening/weekend programs available. Postbaccalaureate distance learning degree programs offered (no on-campus study). *Faculty:* 34 full-time (25 women), 70 part-time/adjunct (54 women). *Students:* 385 full-time (289 women), 386 part-time (303 women); includes 168 minority (49 Black or African American, non-Hispanic/Latino; 8 American Indian or Alaska Native, non-Hispanic/Latino; 25 Asian, non-Hispanic/Latino; 71 Hispanic/Latino; 1 Native Hawaiian or other Pacific Islander, non-Hispanic/Latino; 14 Two or more races, non-Hispanic/Latino), 17 international. Average age 33. 668 applicants, 72% accepted, 256 enrolled. In 2011, 308 master's, 43 doctorates, 55 other advanced degrees awarded. Terminal master's awarded for partial completion of doctoral program. *Degree requirements:* For master's, comprehensive exam; for doctorate, 2 foreign languages, comprehensive exam, thesis/dissertation. *Entrance requirements:* For master's and doctorate, GRE General Test or GMAT. Additional exam requirements/recommendations for international students: Required—TOEFL (minimum score 550 paper-based; 80 iBT). *Application deadline:* Applications are processed on a rolling basis. Application fee: $60. Electronic applications accepted. *Financial support:* In 2011–12, 72 teaching assistantships with full and partial tuition reimbursements (averaging $9,049 per year) were awarded; career-related internships or fieldwork, Federal Work-Study, institutionally sponsored loans, scholarships/grants, and unspecified assistantships also available. Support available to part-time students. Financial award application deadline: 2/15; financial award applicants required to submit FAFSA. *Faculty research:* Parkinson's disease, personnel training, development and assessments, gifted education, service-learning, transportation, public schools. *Unit head:* Dr. Gregory M. Anderson, Dean, 303-871-3665, E-mail: gregory.m.anderson@du.edu. *Application contact:* Chris Dowen, Director, MCE Admission Office, 303-871-2783, E-mail: chris.dowen@du.edu. Web site: http://www.du.edu/education/.

University of Florida, Graduate School, College of Liberal Arts and Sciences, Department of Statistics, Gainesville, FL 32611. Offers M Stat, MS Stat, PhD. Part-time programs available. *Faculty:* 10 full-time (0 women). *Students:* 74 full-time (22 women), 1 part-time (0 women); includes 4 minority (3 Asian, non-Hispanic/Latino; 1 Hispanic/Latino), 55 international. Average age 29. 395 applicants, 3% accepted, 12 enrolled. In 2011, 8 master's, 3 doctorates awarded. Terminal master's awarded for partial completion of doctoral program. *Degree requirements:* For master's, variable foreign language requirement, comprehensive exam, final oral exam; thesis (for MS Stat); for doctorate, comprehensive exam, thesis/dissertation. *Entrance requirements:* For master's and doctorate, GRE General Test, minimum GPA of 3.0. Additional exam requirements/recommendations for international students: Required—TOEFL (minimum score 550 paper-based; 213 computer-based; 80 iBT), IELTS (minimum score 6). *Application deadline:* For fall admission, 2/1 priority date for domestic students, 2/1 for international students. Applications are processed on a rolling basis. Application fee: $30. Electronic applications accepted. *Financial support:* Fellowships, research assistantships, teaching assistantships, and

380 facebook.com/petersonspublishing

Peterson's Graduate Programs in the Physical Sciences, Mathematics, Agricultural Sciences, the Environment & Natural Resources 2013

unspecified assistantships available. Financial award application deadline: 2/1; financial award applicants required to submit FAFSA. *Faculty research:* Bayesian statistics, biostatistics, Markov Chain Monte Carlo (MCMC), nonparametric statistics, statistical genetics/genomics. *Total annual research expenditures:* $701,961. *Unit head:* Dr. Michael J. Daniels, Chair, 352-273-1845, Fax: 352-392-5175, E-mail: mdaniels@stat.ufl.edu. *Application contact:* Dr. James P. Hobert, Coordinator, 352-392-1941, Fax: 352-392-5175, E-mail: jhobert@stat.ufl.edu. Web site: http://www.stat.ufl.edu/.

University of Georgia, Franklin College of Arts and Sciences, Department of Statistics, Athens, GA 30602. Offers MS, PhD. *Faculty:* 18 full-time (6 women). *Students:* 65 full-time (23 women), 5 part-time (3 women); includes 5 minority (1 Black or African American, non-Hispanic/Latino; 4 Asian, non-Hispanic/Latino), 38 international. Average age 28. 203 applicants, 20% accepted, 17 enrolled. In 2011, 19 master's awarded. *Degree requirements:* For master's, thesis (for some programs); for doctorate, one foreign language, thesis/dissertation. *Entrance requirements:* For master's and doctorate, GRE General Test. *Application deadline:* For fall admission, 7/1 priority date for domestic students; for spring admission, 11/15 for domestic students. Application fee: $50. Electronic applications accepted. *Financial support:* Fellowships, research assistantships, teaching assistantships, and unspecified assistantships available. *Unit head:* Dr. John Stufken, Head, 706-542-8218, Fax: 706-542-3391, E-mail: jstufken@stat.uga.edu. *Application contact:* Dr. Lynn Seymour, Graduate Coordinator, 706-542-3307, Fax: 706-542-3391, E-mail: seymour@stat.uga.edu. Web site: http://www.stat.uga.edu/.

University of Guelph, Graduate Studies, College of Physical and Engineering Science, Department of Mathematics and Statistics, Guelph, ON N1G 2W1, Canada. Offers applied mathematics (PhD); applied statistics (PhD); mathematics and statistics (M Sc). Part-time programs available. *Degree requirements:* For master's, thesis (for some programs); for doctorate, thesis/dissertation. *Entrance requirements:* For master's, minimum B average during previous 2 years of course work; for doctorate, minimum B average. Additional exam requirements/recommendations for international students: Required—TOEFL (minimum score 550 paper-based; 213 computer-based; 89 iBT), IELTS (minimum score 6.5). *Faculty research:* Dynamical systems, mathematical biology, numerical analysis, linear and nonlinear models, reliability and bioassay.

University of Houston–Clear Lake, School of Science and Computer Engineering, Program in Statistics, Houston, TX 77058-1098. Offers MS. *Entrance requirements:* For master's, GRE General Test. Additional exam requirements/recommendations for international students: Required—TOEFL (minimum score 550 paper-based; 213 computer-based).

University of Idaho, College of Graduate Studies, College of Science, Department of Statistics, Moscow, ID 83844-1104. Offers MS. *Faculty:* 6 full-time, 1 part-time/adjunct. *Students:* 16 full-time, 4 part-time. Average age 34. In 2011, 5 master's awarded. *Degree requirements:* For master's, thesis or alternative. *Entrance requirements:* For master's, minimum GPA of 2.8. *Application deadline:* For fall admission, 8/1 for domestic students; for spring admission, 12/15 for domestic students. Applications are processed on a rolling basis. Application fee: $60. Electronic applications accepted. *Expenses:* Tuition, state resident: full-time $3874; part-time $334 per credit hour. Tuition, nonresident: full-time $16,394; part-time $861 per credit hour. *Required fees:* $2808; $99 per credit hour. Tuition and fees vary according to program. *Financial support:* Research assistantships and teaching assistantships available. Financial award applicants required to submit FAFSA. *Faculty research:* Statistical genetics, biostatistics, nonlinear population dynamics, multivariate and computational statistics, Six Sigma innovation and design. *Unit head:* Dr. Christopher J. Williams, Chair, 208-885-2929, E-mail: stat@uidaho.edu. *Application contact:* Erick Larson, Director of Graduate Admissions, 208-885-4723, E-mail: gadms@uidaho.edu. Web site: http://www.uidaho.edu/sci/stat/.

University of Illinois at Chicago, Graduate College, College of Liberal Arts and Sciences, Department of Mathematics, Statistics, and Computer Science, Chicago, IL 60607-7128. Offers applied mathematics (MS, PhD); computational finance (MS, PhD); computer science (MS, PhD); mathematics (DA); mathematics and information sciences for industry (MS); probability and statistics (PhD); pure mathematics (MS, PhD); statistics (MS); teaching of mathematics (MST), including elementary, secondary. Part-time programs available. *Degree requirements:* For master's, comprehensive exam; for doctorate, one foreign language, thesis/dissertation. *Entrance requirements:* For master's and doctorate, GRE General Test, minimum GPA of 3.0. Additional exam requirements/recommendations for international students: Required—TOEFL (minimum score 100 iBT). Electronic applications accepted.

University of Illinois at Urbana–Champaign, Graduate College, College of Liberal Arts and Sciences, Department of Statistics, Champaign, IL 61820. Offers applied statistics (MS); statistics (PhD). *Faculty:* 10 full-time (4 women), 1 (woman) part-time/adjunct. *Students:* 68 full-time (35 women), 15 part-time (6 women); includes 9 minority (2 Black or African American, non-Hispanic/Latino; 6 Asian, non-Hispanic/Latino; 1 Hispanic/Latino), 56 international. 402 applicants, 33% accepted, 40 enrolled. In 2011, 46 master's, 8 doctorates awarded. *Entrance requirements:* For master's and doctorate, GRE, minimum GPA of 3.0. Additional exam requirements/recommendations for international students: Required—TOEFL (minimum score 590 paper-based; 243 computer-based). *Application deadline:* Applications are processed on a rolling basis. Application fee: $75 ($90 for international students). Electronic applications accepted. *Financial support:* In

2011–12, 2 fellowships, 22 research assistantships, 28 teaching assistantships were awarded; tuition waivers (full and partial) also available. *Faculty research:* Statistical decision theory, sequential analysis, computer-aided stochastic modeling. *Unit head:* Douglas G. Simpson, Chair, 217-244-0885, Fax: 217-244-7190, E-mail: dgs@illinois.edu. *Application contact:* Melissa Banks, Office Support Specialist, 217-333-2167, Fax: 217-244-7190, E-mail: mdbanks@illinois.edu. Web site: http://www.stat.illinois.edu/.

The University of Iowa, Graduate College, College of Education, Department of Psychological and Quantitative Foundations, Iowa City, IA 52242-1316. Offers counseling psychology (PhD); educational measurement and statistics (MA, PhD); educational psychology (MA, PhD); school psychology (PhD, Ed S); JD/PhD. *Accreditation:* APA. *Degree requirements:* For master's, thesis optional, exam; for doctorate, comprehensive exam, thesis/dissertation; for Ed S, exam. *Entrance requirements:* For master's, doctorate, and Ed S, GRE General Test, minimum GPA of 3.0. Additional exam requirements/recommendations for international students: Required—TOEFL (minimum score 550 paper-based; 213 computer-based; 81 iBT). Electronic applications accepted.

The University of Iowa, Graduate College, College of Liberal Arts and Sciences, Department of Statistics and Actuarial Science, Iowa City, IA 52242-1316. Offers MS, PhD. *Degree requirements:* For master's, thesis optional, exam; for doctorate, comprehensive exam, thesis/dissertation. *Entrance requirements:* For master's and doctorate, GRE General Test, minimum GPA of 3.0. Additional exam requirements/recommendations for international students: Required—TOEFL (minimum score 550 paper-based; 213 computer-based; 81 iBT). Electronic applications accepted.

University of Kentucky, Graduate School, College of Arts and Sciences, Program in Statistics, Lexington, KY 40506-0032. Offers MS, PhD. *Degree requirements:* For master's, comprehensive exam, thesis optional; for doctorate, comprehensive exam, thesis/dissertation. *Entrance requirements:* For master's, GRE General Test, minimum undergraduate GPA of 2.75; for doctorate, GRE General Test, minimum graduate GPA of 3.0. Additional exam requirements/recommendations for international students: Required—TOEFL (minimum score 550 paper-based; 213 computer-based). Electronic applications accepted. *Faculty research:* Computer intensive statistical inference, biostatistics, mathematical and applied statistics, applied probability.

The University of Manchester, School of Mathematics, Manchester, United Kingdom. Offers actuarial science (PhD); applied mathematics (M Phil, PhD); applied numerical computing (M Phil, PhD); financial mathematics (M Phil, PhD); mathematical logic (M Phil); probability (M Phil, PhD); pure mathematics (M Phil, PhD); statistics (M Phil, PhD).

The University of Manchester, School of Social Sciences, Manchester, United Kingdom. Offers ethnographic documentary (M Phil); interdisciplinary study of culture (PhD); philosophy (PhD); politics (PhD); social anthropology (PhD); social anthropology with visual media (PhD); social change (PhD); social statistics (PhD); sociology (PhD); visual anthropology (M Phil).

University of Manitoba, Faculty of Graduate Studies, Faculty of Science, Department of Statistics, Winnipeg, MB R3T 2N2, Canada. Offers M Sc, PhD. *Degree requirements:* For master's, thesis or alternative; for doctorate, one foreign language, thesis/dissertation.

University of Manitoba, Faculty of Graduate Studies, Faculty of Science, Program in Mathematical, Computational and Statistical Sciences, Winnipeg, MB R3T 2N2, Canada. Offers MMCSS.

University of Maryland, Baltimore County, Graduate School, College of Natural and Mathematical Sciences, Department of Mathematics and Statistics, Program in Statistics, Baltimore, MD 21250. Offers biostatistics (PhD); environmental statistics (MS); statistics (MS, PhD). Part-time and evening/weekend programs available. *Faculty:* 8 full-time (3 women). *Students:* 32 full-time (14 women), 24 part-time (12 women); includes 13 minority (5 Black or African American, non-Hispanic/Latino; 8 Asian, non-Hispanic/Latino), 22 international. Average age 30. 42 applicants, 86% accepted, 14 enrolled. In 2011, 13 master's, 4 doctorates awarded. Terminal master's awarded for partial completion of doctoral program. *Degree requirements:* For master's, comprehensive exam (for some programs), thesis (for some programs); for doctorate, comprehensive exam, thesis/dissertation. *Entrance requirements:* For master's and doctorate, GRE General Test, minimum GPA of 3.0. Additional exam requirements/recommendations for international students: Required—TOEFL (minimum score 600 paper-based; 250 computer-based; 100 iBT). *Application deadline:* For fall admission, 2/15 priority date for domestic students, 1/1 for international students; for spring admission, 10/15 priority date for domestic students, 5/1 for international students. Applications are processed on a rolling basis. Application fee: $50. Electronic applications accepted. *Financial support:* In 2011–12, 23 students received support, including 4 research assistantships with full tuition reimbursements available (averaging $15,500 per year), 19 teaching assistantships with full tuition reimbursements available (averaging $15,500 per year); fellowships with full tuition reimbursements available, career-related internships or fieldwork, scholarships/grants, health care benefits, tuition waivers (full and partial), and unspecified assistantships also available. Support available to part-time students. Financial award application deadline: 2/15. *Faculty research:* Design of experiments, statistical decision theory and inference, time series analysis, biostatistics and environmental statistics, bioinformatics. *Total annual research expenditures:* $402,833. *Unit head:* Dr. Junyong Park, Director, 410-455-2407,

Peterson's Graduate Programs in the Physical Sciences, Mathematics, Agricultural Sciences, the Environment & Natural Resources 2013

facebook.com/petersonspublishing **381**

Fax: 410-455-1066, E-mail: junpark@umbc.edu. Web site: http://www.math.umbc.edu.

University of Maryland, College Park, Academic Affairs, College of Computer, Mathematical and Natural Sciences, Department of Mathematics, Program in Mathematical Statistics, College Park, MD 20742. Offers MA, PhD. Part-time and evening/weekend programs available. *Students:* 20 full-time (8 women), 7 part-time (4 women); includes 6 minority (1 Black or African American, non-Hispanic/Latino; 5 Asian, non-Hispanic/Latino, 15 international. 102 applicants, 6% accepted, 3 enrolled. In 2011, 7 master's, 3 doctorates awarded. Terminal master's awarded for partial completion of doctoral program. *Degree requirements:* For master's, thesis or comprehensive exams, scholarly paper; for doctorate, one foreign language, thesis/dissertation, written and oral exams. *Entrance requirements:* For master's and doctorate, GRE General Test, GRE Subject Test (mathematics), minimum GPA of 3.0, 3 letters of recommendation. *Application deadline:* For fall admission, 5/1 for domestic students, 2/1 for international students; for spring admission, 10/1 for domestic students, 6/1 for international students. Applications are processed on a rolling basis. Application fee: $75. Electronic applications accepted. *Expenses: Tuition, area resident:* Part-time $525 per credit hour. Tuition, state resident: part-time $525 per credit hour. Tuition, nonresident: part-time $1131 per credit hour. *Required fees:* $386.31 per term. Tuition and fees vary according to program. *Financial support:* In 2011–12, 1 fellowship with partial tuition reimbursement (averaging $8,000 per year), 1 research assistantship (averaging $18,302 per year), 13 teaching assistantships (averaging $16,986 per year) were awarded. Financial award applicants required to submit FAFSA. *Faculty research:* Statistics and probability, stochastic processes, nonparametric statistics, space-time statistics. *Unit head:* Dr. Abram M. Kagan, Director, 301-405-5061, Fax: 301-314-0827, E-mail: amk@math.umd.edu. *Application contact:* Dr. Charles A. Caramello, Dean of Graduate School, 301-405-0358, Fax: 301-314-9305.

University of Massachusetts Amherst, Graduate School, College of Natural Sciences, Department of Mathematics and Statistics, Amherst, MA 01003. Offers applied mathematics (MS); mathematics (MS, PhD); statistics (MS, PhD). *Faculty:* 44 full-time (6 women). *Students:* 64 full-time (17 women), 1 (woman) part-time; includes 7 minority (2 Black or African American, non-Hispanic/Latino; 4 Asian, non-Hispanic/Latino; 1 Two or more races, non-Hispanic/Latino), 26 international. Average age 27. 254 applicants, 20% accepted, 24 enrolled. In 2011, 17 master's, 6 doctorates awarded. Terminal master's awarded for partial completion of doctoral program. *Degree requirements:* For master's, thesis or alternative; for doctorate, comprehensive exam, thesis/dissertation. *Entrance requirements:* For master's and doctorate, GRE General Test, GRE Subject Test (mathematics). Additional exam requirements/recommendations for international students: Required—TOEFL (minimum score 550 paper-based; 213 computer-based; 80 iBT), IELTS (minimum score 6.5). *Application deadline:* For fall admission, 2/1 for domestic and international students. Applications are processed on a rolling basis. Application fee: $50 ($65 for international students). Electronic applications accepted. Tuition and fees vary according to course load, campus/location and program. *Financial support:* Fellowships with full and partial tuition reimbursements, research assistantships with full and partial tuition reimbursements, teaching assistantships with full and partial tuition reimbursements, career-related internships or fieldwork, Federal Work-Study, scholarships/grants, traineeships, health care benefits, tuition waivers (full and partial), and unspecified assistantships available. Support available to part-time students. Financial award application deadline: 2/1. *Unit head:* Dr. Michael Lavine, Department Head, 413-545-2282, Fax: 413-545-1801. *Application contact:* Lindsay DeSantis, Supervisor of Admissions, 413-545-0722, Fax: 413-577-0010, E-mail: gradadm@grad.umass.edu. Web site: http://www.math.umass.edu/.

University of Memphis, Graduate School, College of Arts and Sciences, Department of Mathematical Sciences, Memphis, TN 38152. Offers applied mathematics (MS); applied statistics (PhD); bioinformatics (MS); computer science (PhD); computer sciences (MS); mathematics (MS, PhD); statistics (MS, PhD). Part-time programs available. Terminal master's awarded for partial completion of doctoral program. *Degree requirements:* For master's, comprehensive exam; for doctorate, one foreign language, thesis/dissertation, oral exams. *Entrance requirements:* For master's and doctorate, GRE General Test, minimum GPA of 2.5. Additional exam requirements/recommendations for international students: Required—TOEFL (minimum score 550 paper-based; 210 computer-based). Electronic applications accepted. *Faculty research:* Combinatorics, ergodic theory, graph theory, Ramsey theory, applied statistics.

University of Michigan, Horace H. Rackham School of Graduate Studies, College of Literature, Science, and the Arts, Department of Statistics, Ann Arbor, MI 48109. Offers applied statistics (AM); statistics (AM, PhD). *Faculty:* 19 full-time (4 women). *Students:* 130 full-time (60 women); includes 95 minority (92 Asian, non-Hispanic/Latino; 2 Hispanic/Latino; 1 Two or more races, non-Hispanic/Latino), 88 international. Average age 27. 622 applicants, 19% accepted, 54 enrolled. In 2011, 35 master's, 13 doctorates awarded. Terminal master's awarded for partial completion of doctoral program. *Degree requirements:* For master's, thesis; for doctorate, thesis/dissertation, oral defense of dissertation, preliminary exam. *Entrance requirements:* For master's and doctorate, GRE General Test. Additional exam requirements/recommendations for international students: Required—TOEFL (minimum score 560 paper-based; 220 computer-based; 84 iBT), IELTS (minimum score 6.5). *Application deadline:* For fall admission, 1/15 priority date for domestic students, 1/15 for international students.

Applications are processed on a rolling basis. Application fee: $65 ($75 for international students). Electronic applications accepted. *Financial support:* In 2011–12, 64 students received support, including 7 fellowships with full and partial tuition reimbursements available (averaging $25,000 per year), 12 research assistantships with full and partial tuition reimbursements available (averaging $17,270 per year), 45 teaching assistantships with full and partial tuition reimbursements available (averaging $17,270 per year); career-related internships or fieldwork, Federal Work-Study, institutionally sponsored loans, scholarships/grants, health care benefits, and unspecified assistantships also available. Financial award application deadline: 1/15. *Faculty research:* Reliability and degradation modeling, biological and legal applications, bioinformatics, statistical computing, covariance estimation. *Unit head:* Prof. Tailen Hsing, Chair, 734-763-3519, Fax: 734-763-4676, E-mail: statchair@umich.edu. *Application contact:* Judy McDonald, Graduate Program Coordinator, 734-763-3520, Fax: 734-763-4676, E-mail: stat-grad-coordinator@umich.edu. Web site: http://www.stat.lsa.umich.edu/.

University of Minnesota, Twin Cities Campus, Graduate School, College of Liberal Arts, School of Statistics, Minneapolis, MN 55455-0213. Offers MS, PhD. Part-time programs available. *Faculty:* 18 full-time (2 women), 3 part-time/adjunct (0 women). *Students:* 71 full-time (30 women), 3 part-time (all women); includes 2 minority (1 Asian, non-Hispanic/Latino; 1 Two or more races, non-Hispanic/Latino), 44 international. Average age 24. 275 applicants, 20% accepted, 24 enrolled. In 2011, 13 master's, 6 doctorates awarded. Terminal master's awarded for partial completion of doctoral program. *Degree requirements:* For doctorate, comprehensive exam, thesis/dissertation. *Entrance requirements:* For master's and doctorate, GRE General Test. Additional exam requirements/recommendations for international students: Required—TOEFL (minimum score 100 iBT). *Application deadline:* For fall admission, 12/15 priority date for domestic students, 12/15 for international students. Applications are processed on a rolling basis. Application fee: $75 ($95 for international students). Electronic applications accepted. *Financial support:* In 2011–12, 48 students received support, including 2 fellowships with full tuition reimbursements available (averaging $14,633 per year), 8 research assistantships with full tuition reimbursements available (averaging $14,633 per year), 38 teaching assistantships with full tuition reimbursements available (averaging $14,633 per year); scholarships/grants and health care benefits also available. Financial award application deadline: 12/15. *Faculty research:* Data analysis, statistical computing, experimental design, probability theory, Bayesian inference, risk analysis. *Total annual research expenditures:* $923,741. *Unit head:* Prof. Glen Meeden, Director, 612-625-8321, Fax: 612-624-8868, E-mail: glen@stat.umn.edu. *Application contact:* Mary Hildre, Executive Administrative Specialist, 612-625-7300, Fax: 612-624-8868, E-mail: mary@stat.umn.edu. Web site: http://www.stat.umn.edu/.

University of Missouri, Graduate School, College of Arts and Sciences, Department of Statistics, Columbia, MO 65211. Offers MA, PhD. *Faculty:* 15 full-time (4 women), 1 part-time/adjunct (0 women). *Students:* 54 full-time (14 women), 5 part-time (2 women); includes 2 minority (both Black or African American, non-Hispanic/Latino), 38 international. Average age 27. 169 applicants, 11% accepted, 17 enrolled. In 2011, 12 master's, 3 doctorates awarded. *Degree requirements:* For doctorate, comprehensive exam, thesis/dissertation. *Entrance requirements:* For master's, GRE General Test, minimum GPA of 3.0 in math and statistics courses; bachelor's degree from accredited college/university in related area; for doctorate, GRE General Test, minimum GPA of 3.0, 3.5 in math/statistics. Additional exam requirements/recommendations for international students: Required—TOEFL (minimum score 535 paper-based; 200 computer-based; 73 iBT). *Application deadline:* For fall admission, 1/15 priority date for domestic students; for winter admission, 10/15 priority date for domestic students. Applications are processed on a rolling basis. Application fee: $55 ($75 for international students). Electronic applications accepted. *Expenses:* Tuition, state resident: full-time $5881. Tuition, nonresident: full-time $15,183. *Required fees:* $952. Tuition and fees vary according to campus/location and program. *Financial support:* In 2011–12, 7 fellowships with full tuition reimbursements, 8 research assistantships with full tuition reimbursements, 26 teaching assistantships with full tuition reimbursements were awarded; institutionally sponsored loans, health care benefits, and tuition waivers (full and partial) also available. *Faculty research:* Statistical problems in the fields of ecology, genetics, economics, meteorology, wildlife management, epidemiology, AIDS research, geophysics, climatology. *Unit head:* Dr. Nancy Flournoy, Department Chair, E-mail: flournoyn@missouri.edu. *Application contact:* Tracy Pickens, Office Support Staff IV, 573-882-6377, E-mail: pickenst@missouri.edu. Web site: http://www.stat.missouri.edu/.

University of Missouri–Kansas City, College of Arts and Sciences, Department of Mathematics and Statistics, Kansas City, MO 64110-2499. Offers MA, MS, PhD. PhD (interdisciplinary) offered through the School of Graduate Studies. Part-time programs available. *Faculty:* 14 full-time (5 women), 2 part-time/adjunct (0 women). *Students:* 8 full-time (4 women), 22 part-time (9 women); includes 3 minority (all Asian, non-Hispanic/Latino), 5 international. Average age 31. 28 applicants, 64% accepted, 6 enrolled. In 2011, 13 master's awarded. Terminal master's awarded for partial completion of doctoral program. *Degree requirements:* For master's, written exam; for doctorate, 2 foreign languages, thesis/dissertation, oral and written exams. *Entrance requirements:* For master's, bachelor's degree in mathematics, minimum GPA of 3.0; for doctorate, GMAT or GRE General Test. Additional exam requirements/recommendations for international students: Required—TOEFL (minimum score 550 paper-based; 213 computer-based; 80 iBT). *Application deadline:* For fall admission, 3/15 for domestic and international students; for spring admission, 10/15 for domestic and

382 facebook.com/petersonspublishing

Peterson's Graduate Programs in the Physical Sciences, Mathematics, Agricultural Sciences, the Environment & Natural Resources 2013

international students. Applications are processed on a rolling basis. Application fee: $45 ($50 for international students). Electronic applications accepted. *Expenses:* Tuition, state resident: full-time $5798; part-time $322.10 per credit hour. Tuition, nonresident: full-time $14,969; part-time $831.60 per credit hour. *Required fees:* $93.51 per credit hour. *Financial support:* In 2011–12, 2 research assistantships (averaging $16,275 per year), 9 teaching assistantships with full tuition reimbursements (averaging $17,150 per year) were awarded; Federal Work-Study, institutionally sponsored loans, and tuition waivers (full and partial) also available. Support available to part-time students. Financial award application deadline: 3/1; financial award applicants required to submit FAFSA. *Faculty research:* Numerical analysis, statistics, biostatistics commutative algebra, differential equations. *Unit head:* Dr. Jie Chen, Chair/Professor, 816-235-1641, Fax: 816-235-5517, E-mail: umkcmathdept@umkc.edu. *Application contact:* Dr. Hristo Voulov, Associate Professor, 816-235-1641, Fax: 816-235-5517, E-mail: umkcmathdept@umkc.edu. Web site: http://cas.umkc.edu/math/.

University of Nebraska–Lincoln, Graduate College, College of Agricultural Sciences and Natural Resources, Department of Statistics, Lincoln, NE 68588. Offers MS, PhD. *Degree requirements:* For master's, thesis optional. *Entrance requirements:* For master's, GRE General Test. Additional exam requirements/recommendations for international students: Required—TOEFL (minimum score 550 paper-based; 213 computer-based). Electronic applications accepted. *Faculty research:* Design of experiments, linear models, spatial variability, statistical modeling and inference, sampling.

University of New Brunswick Fredericton, School of Graduate Studies, Faculty of Science, Department of Mathematics and Statistics, Fredericton, NB E3B 5A3, Canada. Offers M Sc, PhD. *Faculty:* 10 full-time (0 women), 1 part-time/adjunct (0 women). *Students:* 19 full-time (5 women), 1 (woman) part-time. In 2011, 4 master's, 3 doctorates awarded. *Degree requirements:* For master's, thesis; for doctorate, comprehensive exam, thesis/dissertation. *Entrance requirements:* For master's and doctorate, minimum GPA of 3.0. Additional exam requirements/recommendations for international students: Required—TOEFL (minimum score 550 paper-based; 80 computer-based), TWE (minimum score 4); Recommended—IELTS (minimum score 7). *Application deadline:* For fall admission, 3/1 priority date for domestic students. Applications are processed on a rolling basis. Application fee: $50 Canadian dollars. *Financial support:* In 2011–12, 12 fellowships, 39 research assistantships, 19 teaching assistantships were awarded. *Faculty research:* Algebra, general relativity, mathematical biology, quantum field theory, pure math, data analysis, experimental design. *Unit head:* Dr. James Watmough, Director of Graduate Studies, 506-458-7363, Fax: 506-453-4705, E-mail: watmough@unb.ca. *Application contact:* Marilyn Hetherington, Graduate Secretary, 506-458-7373, Fax: 506-453-4705, E-mail: mhetheri@unb.ca. Web site: http://www.unb.ca/fredericton/science/math/.

University of New Hampshire, Graduate School, College of Engineering and Physical Sciences, Department of Mathematics and Statistics, Durham, NH 03824. Offers applied mathematics (MS); industrial statistics (Postbaccalaureate Certificate); mathematics (MS, MST, PhD); mathematics education (PhD); statistics (MS). *Faculty:* 21 full-time (5 women). *Students:* 26 full-time (12 women), 30 part-time (12 women); includes 4 minority (1 American Indian or Alaska Native, non-Hispanic/Latino; 2 Asian, non-Hispanic/Latino; 1 Two or more races, non-Hispanic/Latino), 13 international. Average age 29. 86 applicants, 47% accepted, 16 enrolled. In 2011, 1,217 master's, 2 doctorates, 4 other advanced degrees awarded. Terminal master's awarded for partial completion of doctoral program. *Degree requirements:* For doctorate, 2 foreign languages, thesis/dissertation. *Entrance requirements:* Additional exam requirements/recommendations for international students: Required—TOEFL (minimum score 550 paper-based; 213 computer-based; 80 iBT). *Application deadline:* For fall admission, 4/1 priority date for domestic students, 4/1 for international students; for spring admission, 12/1 for domestic students. Applications are processed on a rolling basis. Application fee: $65. Electronic applications accepted. *Expenses:* Tuition, state resident: full-time $12,360; part-time $687 per credit hour. Tuition, nonresident: full-time $25,680; part-time $1058 per credit hour. *International tuition:* $29,550 full-time. *Required fees:* $1666; $833 per course. $416.50 per semester. Tuition and fees vary according to course load and degree level. *Financial support:* In 2011–12, 41 students received support, including 6 research assistantships, 34 teaching assistantships; fellowships, Federal Work-Study, scholarships/grants, and tuition waivers (full and partial) also available. Support available to part-time students. Financial award application deadline: 2/15. *Faculty research:* Operator theory, complex analysis, algebra, nonlinear dynamics, statistics. *Unit head:* Dr. Edward Hinson, Chairperson, 603-862-2688. *Application contact:* Jan Jankowski, Administrative Assistant, 603-862-2320, E-mail: jan.jankowski@unh.edu. Web site: http://www.math.unh.edu/.

University of New Mexico, Graduate School, College of Arts and Sciences, Department of Mathematics and Statistics, Albuquerque, NM 87131-2039. Offers mathematics (MS, PhD); statistics (MS, PhD). Part-time programs available. *Faculty:* 87 full-time (33 women), 59 part-time/adjunct (22 women). *Students:* 51 full-time (12 women), 34 part-time (10 women); includes 15 minority (all Hispanic/Latino), 28 international. Average age 32. 82 applicants, 68% accepted, 25 enrolled. In 2011, 20 master's, 7 doctorates awarded. Terminal master's awarded for partial completion of doctoral program. *Degree requirements:* For master's, comprehensive exam (for some programs), thesis or alternative; for doctorate, one foreign language, comprehensive exam, thesis/dissertation, 4 department seminars. *Entrance requirements:* For master's and doctorate, minimum GPA of 3.0, 3 letters of recommendation, letter of intent. Additional exam requirements/

recommendations for international students: Required—TOEFL (minimum score 550 paper-based; 213 computer-based). *Application deadline:* For fall admission, 2/15 priority date for domestic students; for spring admission, 11/1 priority date for domestic students. Application fee: $50. Electronic applications accepted. *Financial support:* In 2011–12, 59 students received support, including 15 research assistantships with tuition reimbursements available (averaging $8,419 per year), 46 teaching assistantships with tuition reimbursements available (averaging $14,812 per year); health care benefits and unspecified assistantships also available. Financial award application deadline: 2/15; financial award applicants required to submit FAFSA. *Faculty research:* Pure and applied mathematics, applied statistics, numerical analysis, biostatistics, differential geometry, fluid dynamics, nonparametric curve estimation. *Total annual research expenditures:* $1.5 million. *Unit head:* Dr. Terry Loring, Chair, 505-277-4613, Fax: 505-277-5505, E-mail: loring@math.unm.edu. *Application contact:* Ana Parra Lombard, Coordinator, Program Advisement, 505-277-5250, Fax: 505-277-5505, E-mail: aparra@math.unm.edu. Web site: http://math.unm.edu/.

The University of North Carolina at Chapel Hill, Graduate School, College of Arts and Sciences, Department of Statistics, Chapel Hill, NC 27599. Offers MS, PhD. *Degree requirements:* For master's, comprehensive exam, essay or thesis; for doctorate, comprehensive exam, thesis/dissertation. *Entrance requirements:* For master's and doctorate, GRE General Test, GRE Subject Test, minimum GPA of 3.0. Additional exam requirements/recommendations for international students: Required—TOEFL.

The University of North Carolina Wilmington, College of Arts and Sciences, Department of Mathematics and Statistics, Wilmington, NC 28403-3297. Offers MS. *Degree requirements:* For master's, comprehensive exam, thesis. *Entrance requirements:* For master's, GRE General Test, GRE Subject Test, minimum B average in undergraduate major. Additional exam requirements/recommendations for international students: Required—TOEFL (minimum score 550 paper-based; 217 computer-based; 79 iBT), IELTS (minimum score 6.5).

University of North Florida, College of Arts and Sciences, Department of Mathematics and Statistics, Jacksonville, FL 32224. Offers mathematical sciences (MS); statistics (MS). Part-time and evening/weekend programs available. *Faculty:* 5 full-time (3 women). *Students:* 15 full-time (2 women), 5 part-time (2 women); includes 1 minority (Black or African American, non-Hispanic/Latino), 7 international. Average age 29. 23 applicants, 70% accepted, 11 enrolled. In 2011, 6 master's awarded. *Degree requirements:* For master's, comprehensive exam, thesis optional. *Entrance requirements:* For master's, GRE General Test, minimum GPA of 3.0 in last 60 hours of course work. Additional exam requirements/recommendations for international students: Required—TOEFL (minimum score 500 paper-based; 173 computer-based; 61 iBT). *Application deadline:* For fall admission, 7/1 priority date for domestic students, 6/1 for international students; for spring admission, 11/1 priority date for domestic students, 10/1 for international students. Applications are processed on a rolling basis. Application fee: $30. Electronic applications accepted. *Expenses:* Tuition, state resident: full-time $8793; part-time $366.38 per credit hour. Tuition, nonresident: full-time $23,502; part-time $979.24 per credit hour. *Required fees:* $1384; $57.66 per credit hour. Tuition and fees vary according to course load and program. *Financial support:* In 2011–12, 13 students received support, including 6 teaching assistantships (averaging $5,499 per year); Federal Work-Study, scholarships/grants, tuition waivers (partial), and unspecified assistantships also available. Support available to part-time students. Financial award application deadline: 4/1; financial award applicants required to submit FAFSA. *Faculty research:* Real analysis, number theory, Euclidean geometry. *Total annual research expenditures:* $11,341. *Unit head:* Dr. Scott H. Hochwald, Chair, 904-620-2653, Fax: 904-620-2818, E-mail: shochwal@unf.edu. *Application contact:* Lillith Richardson, Assistant Director, The Graduate School, 904-620-1360, Fax: 904-620-1362, E-mail: graduateschool@unf.edu. Web site: http://www.unf.edu/coas/math-stat/.

University of Notre Dame, Graduate School, College of Science, Department of Applied and Computational Mathematics and Statistics, Notre Dame, IN 46556. Offers applied and computational mathematics (PhD); applied statistics (MS); computational finance (MS).

University of Ottawa, Faculty of Graduate and Postdoctoral Studies, Faculty of Science, Ottawa-Carleton Institute of Mathematics and Statistics, Ottawa, ON K1N 6N5, Canada. Offers M Sc, PhD. M Sc, PhD offered jointly with Carleton University. Part-time programs available. *Degree requirements:* For master's, thesis optional; for doctorate, one foreign language, comprehensive exam, thesis/dissertation. *Entrance requirements:* For master's, honors B Sc degree or equivalent, minimum B average; for doctorate, M Sc, minimum B+ average. Electronic applications accepted. *Faculty research:* Pure mathematics, applied mathematics, probability and statistics.

University of Pennsylvania, Wharton School, Department of Statistics, Philadelphia, PA 19104. Offers MBA, PhD. *Degree requirements:* For doctorate, comprehensive exam, thesis/dissertation. *Entrance requirements:* For master's and doctorate, GRE. Additional exam requirements/recommendations for international students: Required—TOEFL, TWE. *Expenses: Tuition:* Full-time $26,660; part-time $4944 per course. *Required fees:* $2318; $291 per course. Tuition and fees vary according to course load, degree level and program. *Faculty research:* Nonparametric function estimation, analysis of algorithms, time series analysis, observational studies, inference.

Peterson's Graduate Programs in the Physical Sciences, Mathematics, Agricultural Sciences, the Environment & Natural Resources 2013

facebook.com/petersonspublishing **383**

University of Pittsburgh, Dietrich School of Arts and Sciences, Department of Statistics, Pittsburgh, PA 15260. Offers applied statistics (MA, MS); statistics (MA, MS, PhD). Part-time programs available. *Faculty:* 8 full-time (1 woman). *Students:* 35 full-time (20 women), 4 part-time (2 women); includes 1 minority (Black or African American, non-Hispanic/Latino), 26 international. Average age 26. 425 applicants, 11% accepted, 12 enrolled. In 2011, 5 master's, 6 doctorates awarded. Terminal master's awarded for partial completion of doctoral program. *Median time to degree:* Of those who began their doctoral program in fall 2003, 100% received their degree in 8 years or less. *Degree requirements:* For master's, comprehensive exam, thesis (for some programs); for doctorate, comprehensive exam, thesis/dissertation. *Entrance requirements:* For master's, 3 semesters of calculus, 1 semester of linear algebra, 1 year of mathematical statistics; for doctorate, 3 semesters of calculus, 1 semester each of linear algebra and advanced calculus, 1 year of mathematical statistics. Additional exam requirements/recommendations for international students: Required—TOEFL (minimum score 550 paper-based; 213 computer-based; 80 iBT). *Application deadline:* For fall admission, 1/15 priority date for domestic students, 1/15 for international students; for spring admission, 10/1 priority date for domestic students, 9/1 for international students. Application fee: $50. Electronic applications accepted. *Expenses:* Tuition, state resident: full-time $18,774; part-time $760 per credit. Tuition, nonresident: full-time $30,736; part-time $1258 per credit. *Required fees:* $740; $200 per term. Tuition and fees vary according to program. *Financial support:* In 2011–12, 1 fellowship with full tuition reimbursement (averaging $19,610 per year), 9 research assistantships with full tuition reimbursements (averaging $16,460 per year), 16 teaching assistantships with full tuition reimbursements (averaging $15,830 per year) were awarded; career-related internships or fieldwork, Federal Work-Study, institutionally sponsored loans, scholarships/grants, health care benefits, and unspecified assistantships also available. Financial award application deadline: 1/15. *Faculty research:* Multivariate statistics, time series, reliability, meta-analysis, linear and nonlinear regression modeling. *Unit head:* Dr. Satish Iyengar, Chair, 412-624-8341, Fax: 412-648-8814, E-mail: sii@pitt.edu. *Application contact:* Dr. Leon J. Gleser, Director of Graduate Studies, 412-624-3925, Fax: 412-648-8814, E-mail: gleser@pitt.edu. Web site: http://www.stat.pitt.edu/.

University of Puerto Rico, Mayagüez Campus, Graduate Studies, College of Arts and Sciences, Department of Mathematical Sciences, Mayagüez, PR 00681-9000. Offers applied mathematics (MS); pure mathematics (MS); scientific computation (MS); statistics (MS). Part-time programs available. *Students:* 32 full-time (9 women), 1 (woman) part-time; includes 7 minority (all Hispanic/Latino), 26 international. 23 applicants, 43% accepted, 7 enrolled. In 2011, 10 master's awarded. *Degree requirements:* For master's, one foreign language, comprehensive exam, thesis optional. *Entrance requirements:* For master's, undergraduate degree in mathematics or its equivalent. *Application deadline:* For fall admission, 2/15 for domestic and international students; for spring admission, 9/15 for domestic and international students. Applications are processed on a rolling basis. Application fee: $25. Tuition and fees vary according to course level and course load. *Financial support:* In 2011–12, 31 students received support, including 3 research assistantships (averaging $15,000 per year), 28 teaching assistantships (averaging $8,500 per year); Federal Work-Study and institutionally sponsored loans also available. *Faculty research:* Automata theory, linear algebra, logic. *Unit head:* Prof. Omar Colon, Director, 787-832-4040 Ext. 3848, Fax: 787-265-5454, E-mail: omar.colon.reyes@gmail.com. Web site: http://math.uprm.edu/.

University of Regina, Faculty of Graduate Studies and Research, Faculty of Science, Department of Mathematics and Statistics, Regina, SK S4S 0A2, Canada. Offers mathematics (M Sc, MA, PhD); statistics (M Sc, MA, PhD). *Faculty:* 21 full-time (2 women). *Students:* 25 full-time (8 women). 24 applicants, 75% accepted. In 2011, 5 master's, 2 doctorates awarded. *Degree requirements:* For master's, thesis; for doctorate, comprehensive exam, thesis/dissertation. *Entrance requirements:* Additional exam requirements/recommendations for international students: Required—TOEFL (minimum score 580 paper-based; 80 iBT), IELTS (minimum score 6.5). *Application deadline:* Applications are processed on a rolling basis. Application fee: $100. Electronic applications accepted. *Financial support:* In 2011–12, 2 fellowships (averaging $6,500 per year), 3 teaching assistantships (averaging $2,298 per year) were awarded; research assistantships and scholarships/grants also available. Financial award application deadline: 6/15. *Faculty research:* Discrete mathematics, actuarial science and statistics, matrix theory, mathematical science, numerical analysis. *Unit head:* Dr. Allen Herman, Head, 306-585-4487, Fax: 306-585-4020, E-mail: allen.herman@uregina.ca. *Application contact:* Dr. Martin Argerami, Graduate Program Coordinator, 306-585-4340, Fax: 306-585-4020, E-mail: martin.argerami@math.uregina.ca. Web site: http://www.math.uregina.ca.

University of Rhode Island, Graduate School, College of Arts and Sciences, Department of Computer Science and Statistics, Kingston, RI 02881. Offers applied mathematics (PhD), including computer science, statistics; computer science (MS, PhD); digital forensics (Graduate Certificate); statistics (MS). Part-time programs available. *Faculty:* 10 full-time (4 women), 1 (woman) part-time/adjunct. *Students:* 16 full-time (3 women), 41 part-time (10 women); includes 8 minority (2 Black or African American, non-Hispanic/Latino; 1 Asian, non-Hispanic/Latino; 5 Hispanic/Latino), 7 international. In 2011, 9 master's, 1 doctorate awarded. *Degree requirements:* For master's, comprehensive exam (for some programs), thesis optional; for doctorate, comprehensive exam, thesis/dissertation. *Entrance requirements:* For master's and doctorate, GRE, 2 letters of recommendation. Additional exam requirements/recommendations for international students: Required—TOEFL (minimum score 550 paper-based; 213 computer-based). *Application deadline:* For fall admission, 7/15 for domestic students, 2/1 for international students; for spring admission, 11/15 for domestic students, 7/15 for international students. Application fee: $65. Electronic applications accepted. *Expenses:* Tuition, state resident: full-time $10,432; part-time $580 per credit hour. Tuition, nonresident: full-time $23,130; part-time $1285 per credit hour. *Required fees:* $1362; $36 per credit hour. $35 per semester. One-time fee: $130. *Financial support:* In 2011–12, 2 research assistantships (averaging $7,004 per year), 9 teaching assistantships with full and partial tuition reimbursements (averaging $9,759 per year) were awarded. Financial award application deadline: 2/1; financial award applicants required to submit FAFSA. *Faculty research:* Bioinformatics, computer and digital forensics, behavioral model of pedestrian dynamics, real-time distributed object computing, cryptography. *Unit head:* Dr. James G. Kowalski, Chair, 401-874-2510, Fax: 401-874-4617, E-mail: kowalski@cs.uri.edu. *Application contact:* Dr. Victor Fay-Wolfe, Director of Graduate Studies, 401-874-2701, Fax: 401-874-4617, E-mail: wolfe@cs.uri.edu. Web site: http://www.cs.uri.edu/.

University of Rochester, School of Medicine and Dentistry, Graduate Programs in Medicine and Dentistry, Department of Biostatistics and Computational Biology, Programs in Statistics, Rochester, NY 14627. Offers MA, PhD. *Expenses: Tuition:* Full-time $41,040.

University of Saskatchewan, College of Graduate Studies and Research, College of Arts and Science, Department of Mathematics and Statistics, Saskatoon, SK S7N 5A2, Canada. Offers M Math, MA, PhD. *Degree requirements:* For master's, thesis (for some programs); for doctorate, comprehensive exam (for some programs), thesis/dissertation. *Entrance requirements:* Additional exam requirements/recommendations for international students: Required—TOEFL (minimum score 80 iBT); Recommended—IELTS (minimum score 6.5). Electronic applications accepted.

University of South Africa, College of Economic and Management Sciences, Pretoria, South Africa. Offers accounting (D Admin, D Com); accounting science (DA); auditing (D Admin, D Com); business administration (M Tech); business economics (D Admin); business leadership (DBL); business management (D Admin, D Com); economic management analysis (M Tech); economics (D Admin, D Com, PhD); human resource development (M Tech); industrial psychology (D Admin, D Com, PhD); logistics (D Com); marketing (M Tech); public administration (D Admin, D Com, DPA, PhD); public management (M Tech); quantitative management (D Admin, D Com); real estate (M Tech); statistics (D Admin, PhD); tourism management (D Admin, D Com); transport economics (D Admin, D Com).

University of South Carolina, The Graduate School, College of Arts and Sciences, Department of Statistics, Columbia, SC 29208. Offers applied statistics (CAS); industrial statistics (MIS); statistics (MS, PhD). Part-time and evening/weekend programs available. Postbaccalaureate distance learning degree programs offered (minimal on-campus study). Terminal master's awarded for partial completion of doctoral program. *Degree requirements:* For master's, thesis; for doctorate, comprehensive exam, thesis/dissertation. *Entrance requirements:* For master's, GRE General Test or GMAT, 2 years of work experience (MIS); for doctorate, GRE General Test; for CAS, GRE General Test or GMAT. Additional exam requirements/recommendations for international students: Required—TOEFL (minimum score 600 paper-based; 250 computer-based; 100 iBT). Electronic applications accepted. *Expenses:* Contact institution. *Faculty research:* Reliability, environmetrics, statistics computing, psychometrics, bioinformatics.

The University of South Dakota, Graduate School, College of Arts and Sciences, Department of Computer Science, Vermillion, SD 57069-2390. Offers computational sciences and statistics (PhD); computer science (MS). Part-time programs available. *Degree requirements:* For master's, thesis optional. *Entrance requirements:* For master's, GRE General Test, GRE Subject Test (recommended), minimum GPA of 2.7. Additional exam requirements/recommendations for international students: Required—TOEFL (minimum score 550 paper-based; 213 computer-based; 79 iBT). Electronic applications accepted. *Expenses:* Tuition, state resident: full-time $3118.50; part-time $173.25 per credit hour. Tuition, nonresident: full-time $6601; part-time $366.70 per credit hour. *Required fees:* $2268; $126 per credit hour. Tuition and fees vary according to program.

University of Southern California, Graduate School, Dana and David Dornsife College of Letters, Arts and Sciences, Department of Mathematics, Los Angeles, CA 90089. Offers applied mathematics (MA, MS, PhD); mathematical finance (MS); mathematics (MA, PhD); statistics (MS). Part-time programs available. Terminal master's awarded for partial completion of doctoral program. *Degree requirements:* For master's, comprehensive exam (for some programs), thesis (for some programs); for doctorate, one foreign language, comprehensive exam, thesis/dissertation. *Entrance requirements:* For master's, GRE General Test, GMAT; for doctorate, GRE General Test, GRE Subject Test (mathematics). Additional exam requirements/recommendations for international students: Required—TOEFL (minimum score 100 iBT). Electronic applications accepted. *Faculty research:* Algebra, algebraic geometry and number theory, analysis/partial differential equations, applied mathematics, financial mathematics, probability, combinatorics and statistics.

University of Southern Maine, College of Arts and Sciences, Program in Statistics, Portland, ME 04104-9300. Offers MS.

384 facebook.com/petersonspublishing

Peterson's Graduate Programs in the Physical Sciences, Mathematics, Agricultural Sciences, the Environment & Natural Resources 2013

University of South Florida, Graduate School, College of Arts and Sciences, Department of Mathematics and Statistics, Tampa, FL 33620-9951. Offers mathematics (MA, PhD); statistics (MA). Part-time and evening/weekend programs available. *Faculty:* 27 full-time (2 women), 12 part-time/adjunct (3 women). *Students:* 80 full-time (28 women), 17 part-time (4 women); includes 14 minority (3 Black or African American, non-Hispanic/Latino; 7 Asian, non-Hispanic/Latino; 3 Hispanic/Latino; 1 Two or more races, non-Hispanic/Latino), 37 international. Average age 32. 108 applicants, 66% accepted, 31 enrolled. In 2011, 22 master's, 3 doctorates awarded. Terminal master's awarded for partial completion of doctoral program. *Degree requirements:* For master's, comprehensive exam, thesis optional; for doctorate, comprehensive exam, thesis/dissertation. *Entrance requirements:* For master's, GRE, minimum GPA of 3.0; for doctorate, GRE, minimum GPA of 3.5, three letters of recommendation, personal statement of goals. Additional exam requirements/recommendations for international students: Required—TOEFL (minimum score 550 paper-based; 213 computer-based; 79 iBT) or IELTS (minimum score 6.5). *Application deadline:* For fall admission, 2/1 for domestic students, 1/2 for international students; for spring admission, 8/1 for domestic students, 6/1 for international students. Application fee: $30. Electronic applications accepted. *Financial support:* In 2011–12, 61 students received support, including 6 research assistantships (averaging $16,990 per year), 55 teaching assistantships with partial tuition reimbursements available (averaging $13,742 per year); unspecified assistantships also available. Financial award application deadline: 2/1. *Faculty research:* Approximation theory, differential equations, discrete mathematics, functional analysis topology. *Total annual research expenditures:* $615,749. *Unit head:* Dr. Marcus McWaters, Chairperson, 813-974-3838, Fax: 813-974-2700, E-mail: mmm@usf.edu. *Application contact:* Dr. Xiang-Dong Hou, Graduate Admissions Director, 813-974-2561, Fax: 813-974-2700, E-mail: xhou@cas.usf.edu. Web site: http://www.math.usf.edu/.

The University of Tennessee, Graduate School, College of Business Administration, Department of Statistics, Knoxville, TN 37996. Offers industrial statistics (MS); statistics (MS). Part-time programs available. *Degree requirements:* For master's, thesis or alternative. *Entrance requirements:* For master's, GMAT or GRE General Test, minimum GPA of 2.7. Additional exam requirements/recommendations for international students: Required—TOEFL. Electronic applications accepted. *Expenses:* Tuition, state resident: full-time $8332; part-time $464 per credit hour. Tuition, nonresident: full-time $25,174; part-time $1400 per credit hour. *Required fees:* $1162; $56 per credit hour. Tuition and fees vary according to program.

The University of Tennessee, Graduate School, College of Business Administration, Program in Business Administration, Knoxville, TN 37996. Offers accounting (PhD); finance (MBA, PhD); logistics and transportation (MBA, PhD); management (PhD); marketing (MBA, PhD); operations management (MBA); professional business administration (MBA); statistics (PhD); JD/MBA; MS/MBA; Pharm D/MBA. Pharm D/MBA offered jointly with The University of Tennessee Health Science Center. *Accreditation:* AACSB. Postbaccalaureate distance learning degree programs offered. *Degree requirements:* For master's, thesis or alternative; for doctorate, thesis/dissertation. *Entrance requirements:* For master's and doctorate, GMAT, minimum GPA of 2.7. Additional exam requirements/recommendations for international students: Required—TOEFL. Electronic applications accepted. *Expenses:* Tuition, state resident: full-time $8332; part-time $464 per credit hour. Tuition, nonresident: full-time $25,174; part-time $1400 per credit hour. *Required fees:* $1162; $56 per credit hour. Tuition and fees vary according to program.

The University of Texas at Austin, Graduate School, College of Natural Sciences, Department of Statistics and Scientific Computation, Austin, TX 78712-1111. Offers MS Stat. *Entrance requirements:* For master's, GRE General Test. *Application deadline:* For fall admission, 2/1 priority date for domestic students. Application fee: $50 ($75 for international students). *Financial support:* Teaching assistantships with partial tuition reimbursements available. Financial award application deadline: 2/1. *Unit head:* Lauren Ancel Meyers, Director, 512-232-0693, E-mail: director@ssc.utexas.edu.

The University of Texas at Dallas, School of Natural Sciences and Mathematics, Department of Mathematical Sciences, Richardson, TX 75080. Offers applied mathematics (MS, PhD); bioinformatics and computational biology (MS); engineering mathematics (MS); mathematics (MS); statistics (MS, PhD). Part-time and evening/weekend programs available. *Faculty:* 15 full-time (2 women). *Students:* 53 full-time (21 women), 17 part-time (3 women); includes 21 minority (5 Black or African American, non-Hispanic/Latino; 12 Asian, non-Hispanic/Latino; 4 Hispanic/Latino), 31 international. Average age 31. 127 applicants, 32% accepted, 28 enrolled. In 2011, 16 master's, 7 doctorates awarded. *Degree requirements:* For master's, thesis optional; for doctorate, thesis/dissertation. *Entrance requirements:* For master's, GRE General Test, minimum GPA of 3.0 in upper-level course work in field; for doctorate, GRE General Test, minimum GPA of 3.5 in upper-level course work in field. Additional exam requirements/recommendations for international students: Required—TOEFL (minimum score 550 paper-based; 215 computer-based). *Application deadline:* For fall admission, 7/15 for domestic students, 5/1 for international students; for spring admission, 11/15 for domestic students, 9/1 for international students. Applications are processed on a rolling basis. Application fee: $50 ($100 for international students). Electronic applications accepted. *Expenses:* Tuition, state resident: full-time $11,170; part-time $620.56 per credit hour. Tuition, nonresident: full-time $20,212; part-time $1122.89 per credit hour. *Financial*

support: In 2011–12, 39 students received support, including 2 research assistantships (averaging $20,700 per year), 31 teaching assistantships with partial tuition reimbursements available (averaging $15,503 per year); career-related internships or fieldwork, Federal Work-Study, institutionally sponsored loans, scholarships/grants, and unspecified assistantships also available. Support available to part-time students. Financial award application deadline: 4/30; financial award applicants required to submit FAFSA. *Faculty research:* Sequential analysis, applications in semiconductor manufacturing, medical image analysis, computational anatomy, information theory, probability theory. *Unit head:* Dr. Matthew Goeckner, Department Head, 972-883-4292, Fax: 972-883-6622, E-mail: goeckner@utdallas.edu. *Application contact:* Claire C. Troy, Graduate Support Assistant, 972-883-2163, Fax: 972-883-6622, E-mail: utdmath@utdallas.edu. Web site: http://www.utdallas.edu/math.

The University of Texas at El Paso, Graduate School, College of Science, Department of Mathematical Sciences, El Paso, TX 79968-0001. Offers mathematical sciences (MS); mathematics (teaching) (MAT); statistics (MS). Part-time and evening/weekend programs available. *Students:* 46 (16 women); includes 26 minority (2 Black or African American, non-Hispanic/Latino; 1 Asian, non-Hispanic/Latino; 23 Hispanic/Latino), 16 international. Average age 34. 24 applicants, 83% accepted, 12 enrolled. In 2011, 3 master's awarded. *Degree requirements:* For master's, thesis optional. *Entrance requirements:* For master's, minimum GPA of 3.0, letters of recommendation. Additional exam requirements/recommendations for international students: Required—TOEFL; Recommended—IELTS. *Application deadline:* For fall admission, 8/1 priority date for domestic students, 3/1 for international students; for spring admission, 11/1 priority date for domestic students, 9/1 for international students. Applications are processed on a rolling basis. Application fee: $45 ($80 for international students). Electronic applications accepted. *Financial support:* In 2011–12, research assistantships with partial tuition reimbursements (averaging $21,812 per year), teaching assistantships with partial tuition reimbursements (averaging $17,450 per year) were awarded; fellowships with tuition reimbursements, institutionally sponsored loans, scholarships/grants, health care benefits, tuition waivers (partial), and unspecified assistantships also available. Support available to part-time students. Financial award application deadline: 3/15; financial award applicants required to submit FAFSA. *Unit head:* Dr. Maria C. Mariani, Chair, 915-747-5761, Fax: 915-747-6502, E-mail: mcmariani@utep.edu. *Application contact:* Dr. Benjamin Flores, Interim Dean of the Graduate School, 915-747-5491, Fax: 915-747-5788, E-mail: bflores@utep.edu.

The University of Texas at San Antonio, College of Business, Department of Management Science and Statistics, San Antonio, TX 78249-0617. Offers applied statistics (MS, PhD); management science (MBA). *Accreditation:* AACSB. Part-time and evening/weekend programs available. *Faculty:* 11 full-time (2 women), 4 part-time/adjunct (3 women). *Students:* 36 full-time (12 women), 23 part-time (8 women); includes 16 minority (3 Black or African American, non-Hispanic/Latino; 5 Asian, non-Hispanic/Latino; 8 Hispanic/Latino), 21 international. Average age 31. 47 applicants, 60% accepted, 21 enrolled. In 2011, 8 master's, 4 doctorates awarded. *Degree requirements:* For master's, comprehensive exam (for some programs), thesis or alternative; for doctorate, comprehensive exam, thesis/dissertation. *Entrance requirements:* For master's, GMAT, minimum of 36 semester credit hours of coursework beyond any hours acquired in the MBA-leveling courses; statement of purpose; for doctorate, GRE, minimum cumulative GPA of 3.3 in the last 60 hours of coursework; transcripts from all colleges and universities attended; curriculum vitae; statement of academic work experiences, interests, and goals; three letters of recommendation; BA, BS, or MS in mathematics, statistics, or closely-related field. Additional exam requirements/recommendations for international students: Required—TOEFL (minimum score 500 paper-based; 61 iBT), IELTS (minimum score 5). *Application deadline:* For fall admission, 7/1 for domestic students, 4/1 for international students; for spring admission, 11/1 for domestic students, 9/1 for international students. Applications are processed on a rolling basis. Application fee: $45 ($85 for international students). Electronic applications accepted. *Expenses:* Tuition, state resident: full-time $3148; part-time $2176 per semester. Tuition, nonresident: full-time $8782; part-time $5932 per semester. *Required fees:* $719 per semester. *Financial support:* In 2011–12, fellowships (averaging $22,000 per year), research assistantships (averaging $10,000 per year), teaching assistantships (averaging $10,000 per year) were awarded; scholarships/grants, health care benefits, and unspecified assistantships also available. *Faculty research:* Statistical signal processing, reliability and life-testing experiments, modeling decompression sickness using survival analysis. *Unit head:* Dr. Raydel Tullous, Chair, 210-458-6345, Fax: 210-458-6350, E-mail: raydel.tullous@utsa.edu. *Application contact:* Katherine Pope, Graduate Assistant of Record, 210-458-7316, Fax: 210-458-4398, E-mail: katherine.pope@utsa.edu.

University of the Incarnate Word, School of Graduate Studies and Research, School of Mathematics, Science, and Engineering, Program in Mathematics, San Antonio, TX 78209-6397. Offers mathematics teaching (MA); research statistics (MS). Part-time and evening/weekend programs available. *Faculty:* 1 full-time (0 women), 1 (woman) part-time/adjunct. *Students:* 1 (woman) full-time, 1 (woman) part-time; includes 1 minority (Hispanic/Latino). Average age 23. 4 applicants, 100% accepted, 1 enrolled. *Degree requirements:* For master's, capstone or prerequisite knowledge (for research statistics). *Entrance requirements:* For master's, GRE (minimum score 800 verbal and quantitative), 18 hours of undergraduate mathematics with minimum GPA of 3.0; letter of recommendation by a professional in the field, writing sample, teaching experience at the precollege level. Additional exam requirements/recommendations for international

Peterson's Graduate Programs in the Physical Sciences, Mathematics, Agricultural Sciences, the Environment & Natural Resources 2013

facebook.com/petersonspublishing **385**

students: Required—TOEFL (minimum score 560 paper-based; 220 computer-based; 83 iBT). *Application deadline:* Applications are processed on a rolling basis. Application fee: $20. Electronic applications accepted. *Expenses: Tuition:* Part-time $725 per credit hour. Tuition and fees vary according to degree level. *Financial support:* Federal Work-Study and scholarships/grants available. Financial award applicants required to submit FAFSA. *Faculty research:* Scholarship and career development for undergraduate mathematics majors. *Total annual research expenditures:* $140,844. *Unit head:* Dr. Paul Messina, Mathematics Graduate Program Coordinator, 210-832-5665, Fax: 210-829-3153, E-mail: messina@uiwtx.edu. *Application contact:* Andrea Cyterski-Acosta, Dean of Enrollment, 210-829-6005, Fax: 210-829-3921, E-mail: admis@uiwtx.edu. Web site: http://www.uiw.edu/math/mathprogramsgrad.html and.

University of the Incarnate Word, School of Graduate Studies and Research, School of Mathematics, Science, and Engineering, Program in Research Statistics, San Antonio, TX 78209-6397. Offers MS. *Faculty:* 5 full-time (2 women). *Students:* 2 full-time (both women), 10 part-time (5 women); includes 9 minority (2 Black or African American, non-Hispanic/Latino; 1 Asian, non-Hispanic/Latino; 6 Hispanic/Latino). Average age 31. 5 applicants, 80% accepted, 2 enrolled. In 2011, 8 master's awarded. *Expenses: Tuition:* Part-time $725 per credit hour. Tuition and fees vary according to degree level. *Faculty research:* Statistical methods applied to commercial analysis problems, research in national food policy. *Total annual research expenditures:* $30,000. *Unit head:* Dr. Paul Edward Messina, Mathematics Graduate Program Coordinator, 210-832-5665, Fax: 210-829-3153, E-mail: messina@uiwtx.edu. *Application contact:* Andrea Cyterski-Acosta, Dean of Enrollment, 210-829-6005, Fax: 210-829-3921, E-mail: admis@uiwtx.edu. Web site: http://www.uiw.edu/gradstudies/graduatestudiesprograms.html#researchstatistics.

The University of Toledo, College of Graduate Studies, College of Natural Sciences and Mathematics, Department of Mathematics, Toledo, OH 43606-3390. Offers applied mathematics (MS); mathematics (MA, PhD); statistics (MS, PhD). Part-time programs available. *Faculty:* 18. *Students:* 33 full-time (10 women), 20 part-time (6 women); includes 2 minority (both Asian, non-Hispanic/Latino), 37 international. Average age 29. 84 applicants, 43% accepted, 19 enrolled. In 2011, 11 master's, 3 doctorates awarded. *Degree requirements:* For master's, comprehensive exam (for some programs), thesis (for some programs); for doctorate, 2 foreign languages, thesis/dissertation. *Entrance requirements:* For master's and doctorate, GRE General Test, GRE Subject Test, minimum cumulative point-hour ratio of 2.7 for all previous academic work, three letters of recommendation, statement of purpose, transcripts from all prior institutions attended. Additional exam requirements/recommendations for international students: Required—TOEFL (minimum score 550 paper-based; 213 computer-based; 80 iBT), IELTS (minimum score 6.5). *Application deadline:* For fall admission, 1/15 priority date for domestic students, 1/15 for international students. Applications are processed on a rolling basis. Application fee: $45 ($75 for international students). Electronic applications accepted. *Financial support:* In 2011–12, 3 research assistantships with full and partial tuition reimbursements (averaging $12,618 per year), 46 teaching assistantships with full and partial tuition reimbursements (averaging $12,860 per year) were awarded; Federal Work-Study, institutionally sponsored loans, scholarships/grants, and unspecified assistantships also available. Support available to part-time students. *Faculty research:* Topology. *Unit head:* Dr. Paul Hewitt, Chair, 419-530-2568, E-mail: paul.hewitt@utoledo.edu. *Application contact:* Graduate School Office, 419-530-4723, Fax: 419-530-4723, E-mail: grdsch@utnet.utoledo.edu. Web site: http://www.utoledo.edu/nsm/.

University of Toronto, School of Graduate Studies, Faculty of Arts and Science, Department of Statistics, Toronto, ON M5S 1A1, Canada. Offers M Sc, PhD. Part-time programs available. *Degree requirements:* For doctorate, comprehensive exam, thesis/dissertation. *Entrance requirements:* For master's, GRE (recommended for students educated outside of Canada), 3 letters of reference; for doctorate, GRE (recommended for students educated outside of Canada), 3 letters of reference, M Stat or equivalent, minimum B+ average. Additional exam requirements/recommendations for international students: Required—TOEFL (minimum score 580 paper-based; 93 iBT), TWE (minimum score 4). Electronic applications accepted.

University of Utah, Graduate School, College of Education, Department of Educational Psychology, Salt Lake City, UT 84112. Offers counseling psychology (PhD); educational psychology (MA); elementary education (M Ed); instructional design and educational technology (M Ed); instructional design and technology (M Ed, MS); learning and cognition (MS, PhD); learning sciences (MA); professional counseling (MS); professional psychology (M Ed); reading and literacy (M Ed, PhD); school counseling (M Ed, MS); school psychology (M Ed, MS, PhD); statistics (M Stat). *Accreditation:* APA (one or more programs are accredited). Evening/weekend programs available. Postbaccalaureate distance learning degree programs offered (minimal on-campus study). *Faculty:* 23 full-time (12 women), 9 part-time/adjunct (7 women). *Students:* 104 full-time (85 women), 107 part-time (78 women); includes 26 minority (1 American Indian or Alaska Native, non-Hispanic/Latino; 4 Asian, non-Hispanic/Latino; 17 Hispanic/Latino; 1 Native Hawaiian or other Pacific Islander, non-Hispanic/Latino; 3 Two or more races, non-Hispanic/Latino), 4 international. Average age 32. 213 applicants, 27% accepted, 48 enrolled. In 2011, 39 master's, 9 doctorates awarded. *Median time to degree:* Of those who began their doctoral program in fall 2003, 50% received their degree in 8 years or less. *Degree requirements:* For master's, variable foreign language requirement, comprehensive exam, thesis (for

some programs); for doctorate, variable foreign language requirement, thesis/dissertation, oral exam. *Entrance requirements:* For master's and doctorate, GRE General Test, minimum GPA of 3.0. Additional exam requirements/recommendations for international students: Required—TOEFL (minimum score 500 paper-based; 173 computer-based). *Application deadline:* For fall admission, 4/1 for domestic and international students; for spring admission, 11/1 for domestic and international students. Application fee: $55 ($65 for international students). *Expenses:* Contact institution. *Financial support:* In 2011–12, 59 students received support, including 25 fellowships with full and partial tuition reimbursements available (averaging $12,000 per year), 7 research assistantships with full and partial tuition reimbursements available (averaging $12,000 per year), 27 teaching assistantships with full and partial tuition reimbursements available (averaging $12,000 per year); career-related internships or fieldwork, Federal Work-Study, institutionally sponsored loans, scholarships/grants, and unspecified assistantships also available. Financial award application deadline: 2/1; financial award applicants required to submit FAFSA. *Faculty research:* Autism, computer technology and instruction, cognitive behavior, aging, group counseling. *Total annual research expenditures:* $371,256. *Unit head:* Dr. Elaine Clark, Chair, 801-581-7148, Fax: 801-581-5566, E-mail: clark@ed.utah.edu. *Application contact:* Kendra Lee Wiebke, Academic Program Specialist, 801-581-7148, Fax: 801-581-5566, E-mail: kendra.wiebke@utah.edu. Web site: http://www.ed.utah.edu/edps/.

University of Utah, Graduate School, David Eccles School of Business, Business Administration Program, Salt Lake City, UT 84112. Offers business administration (EMBA, MBA, PMBA); statistics (M Stat). Part-time and evening/weekend programs available. *Entrance requirements:* For master's, GMAT, statistics course with minimum B grade, minimum undergraduate GPA of 3.0. Additional exam requirements/recommendations for international students: Required—TOEFL (minimum score 600 paper-based; 250 computer-based; 100 iBT), IELTS (minimum score 7). Electronic applications accepted. *Expenses:* Contact institution. *Faculty research:* Corporate finance, strategy services, consumer behavior, financial disclosures, operations.

University of Utah, Graduate School, Interdepartmental Program in Statistics, Salt Lake City, UT 84112-1107. Offers biostatistics (M Stat); econometrics (M Stat); educational psychology (M Stat); mathematics (M Stat); sociology (M Stat); statistics (M Stat). Part-time programs available. *Students:* 25 full-time (10 women), 28 part-time (8 women); includes 8 minority (2 Black or African American, non-Hispanic/Latino; 3 Asian, non-Hispanic/Latino; 3 Hispanic/Latino), 15 international. Average age 33. 59 applicants, 44% accepted, 12 enrolled. In 2011, 18 master's awarded. *Degree requirements:* For master's, comprehensive exam, projects. *Entrance requirements:* For master's, GRE General Test (sociology and educational psychology), minimum GPA of 3.0; course work in calculus, matrix theory, statistics. Additional exam requirements/recommendations for international students: Required—TOEFL (minimum score 500 paper-based; 173 computer-based; 61 iBT). *Application deadline:* For fall admission, 7/1 for domestic students, 4/1 for international students. Applications are processed on a rolling basis. Application fee: $55 ($65 for international students). *Financial support:* Career-related internships or fieldwork available. *Faculty research:* Biostatistics, management, economics, educational psychology, mathematics. *Unit head:* Richard Fowles, Chair, University Statistics Committee, 801-581-4577, E-mail: fowles@economics.utah.edu. *Application contact:* Laura Egbert, Coordinator, 801-585-6853, E-mail: laura.egbert@utah.edu. Web site: http://www.math.utah.edu/mstat/.

University of Utah, Graduate School, Professional Master of Science and Technology Program, Salt Lake City, UT 84112-1107. Offers biotechnology (PSM); computational science (PSM); environmental science (PSM); science instrumentation (PSM). Part-time programs available. *Students:* 15 full-time (10 women), 42 part-time (12 women); includes 7 minority (2 Black or African American, non-Hispanic/Latino; 2 Asian, non-Hispanic/Latino; 2 Hispanic/Latino; 1 Native Hawaiian or other Pacific Islander, non-Hispanic/Latino), 2 international. Average age 33. 66 applicants, 48% accepted, 16 enrolled. In 2011, 18 master's awarded. *Degree requirements:* For master's, internship. *Entrance requirements:* For master's, GRE (recommended), minimum undergraduate GPA of 3.0, bachelor's degree from accredited university or college. Additional exam requirements/recommendations for international students: Required—TOEFL (minimum score 500 paper-based; 173 computer-based; 61 iBT), IELTS (minimum score 6). *Application deadline:* For fall admission, 3/1 for domestic and international students. Application fee: $55 ($65 for international students). Electronic applications accepted. *Financial support:* In 2011–12, 8 students received support, including 5 fellowships with full and partial tuition reimbursements available (averaging $16,800 per year), 2 research assistantships (averaging $6,200 per year); unspecified assistantships also available. Financial award applicants required to submit FAFSA. *Faculty research:* Drug delivery systems, in vitro erythroid expansion and HRE (Hypoxia responsive element). *Unit head:* Jennifer Schmidt, Program Director, 801-585-5630, E-mail: jennifer.schmidt@gradschool.utah.edu. *Application contact:* Amy Kimball, Project Coordinator, 801-585-3650, Fax: 801-585-6749, E-mail: amy.kimball@gradschool.utah.edu. Web site: http://www.utah.edu/pmst/.

University of Vermont, Graduate College, College of Engineering and Mathematics, Department of Mathematics and Statistics, Program in Statistics, Burlington, VT 05405. Offers MS. *Students:* 12 (3 women); includes 1 minority (Black or African American, non-Hispanic/Latino), 4 international. 41 applicants, 85% accepted, 10 enrolled. In 2011, 4 master's awarded. *Entrance requirements:*

386 facebook.com/petersonspublishing

Peterson's Graduate Programs in the Physical Sciences, Mathematics, Agricultural Sciences, the Environment & Natural Resources 2013

Additional exam requirements/recommendations for international students: Required—TOEFL (minimum score 550 paper-based; 213 computer-based). *Application deadline:* For fall admission, 4/1 priority date for domestic students, 4/1 for international students. Applications are processed on a rolling basis. Application fee: $40. Electronic applications accepted. *Financial support:* Fellowships, research assistantships, and teaching assistantships available. Financial award application deadline: 3/1. *Faculty research:* Applied statistics. *Unit head:* James Burgmeier, Chair, 802-656-2940. *Application contact:* Prof. Ruth Mickey, Coordinator, 802-656-2940.

University of Victoria, Faculty of Graduate Studies, Faculty of Science, Department of Mathematics and Statistics, Victoria, BC V8W 2Y2, Canada. Offers M Sc, MA, PhD. Part-time programs available. *Degree requirements:* For master's, thesis; for doctorate, one foreign language, thesis/dissertation, 3 qualifying exams, candidacy exam. *Entrance requirements:* Additional exam requirements/recommendations for international students: Required—TOEFL (minimum score 575 paper-based; 233 computer-based), IELTS (minimum score 7). Electronic applications accepted. *Faculty research:* Functional analysis and operator theory, applied ordinary and partial differential equations, discrete mathematics and graph theory.

University of Virginia, College and Graduate School of Arts and Sciences, Department of Statistics, Charlottesville, VA 22903. Offers MS, PhD. *Faculty:* 7 full-time (2 women). *Students:* 43 full-time (17 women), 2 part-time (0 women); includes 6 minority (all Asian, non-Hispanic/Latino), 29 international. Average age 27. 236 applicants, 25% accepted, 22 enrolled. In 2011, 19 master's, 1 doctorate awarded. *Degree requirements:* For master's, exam; for doctorate, comprehensive exam, thesis/dissertation. *Entrance requirements:* For master's and doctorate, GRE General Test, 3 letters of recommendation. Additional exam requirements/recommendations for international students: Required—TOEFL (minimum score 600 paper-based; 250 computer-based; 90 iBT), IELTS (minimum score 7). *Application deadline:* For fall admission, 2/1 for domestic and international students. Applications are processed on a rolling basis. Application fee: $60. Electronic applications accepted. *Financial support:* Fellowships and teaching assistantships available. Financial award applicants required to submit FAFSA. *Unit head:* Ted Chang, Chairman, 434-924-3222, Fax: 434-924-3076, E-mail: tcc8v@virginia.edu. *Application contact:* Dan Spitzner, Director of Graduate Studies, 434-924-3222, Fax: 434-924-3076, E-mail: spitzner@virginia.edu. Web site: http://www.stat.virginia.edu/.

University of Washington, Graduate School, College of Arts and Sciences, Department of Statistics, Seattle, WA 98195. Offers MS, PhD. Terminal master's awarded for partial completion of doctoral program. *Degree requirements:* For master's, thesis optional; for doctorate, one foreign language, thesis/dissertation. *Entrance requirements:* For master's and doctorate, GRE General Test, minimum GPA of 3.0. Additional exam requirements/recommendations for international students: Required—TOEFL. *Faculty research:* Mathematical statistics, stochastic modeling, spatial statistics, statistical computing.

University of Washington, Graduate School, School of Public Health, Department of Biostatistics, Seattle, WA 98195. Offers biostatistics (MPH, MS, PhD); clinical research (MS), including biostatistics; statistical genetics (PhD). Part-time programs available. *Faculty:* 39 full-time (18 women), 6 part-time/adjunct (2 women). *Students:* 73 full-time (36 women), 7 part-time (2 women); includes 12 minority (10 Asian, non-Hispanic/Latino; 2 Hispanic/Latino), 23 international. Average age 28. 251 applicants, 14% accepted, 17 enrolled. In 2011, 9 master's, 7 doctorates awarded. Terminal master's awarded for partial completion of doctoral program. *Degree requirements:* For master's, comprehensive exam, thesis, practicum (MPH); for doctorate, comprehensive exam, thesis/dissertation. *Entrance requirements:* For master's and doctorate, GRE General Test, coursework on multivariate calculus, linear algebra and probability; minimum GPA of 3.0. Additional exam requirements/recommendations for international students: Required—TOEFL. *Application deadline:* For fall admission, 1/2 for domestic students. Application fee: $75. Electronic applications accepted. *Financial support:* In 2011–12, 73 research assistantships with full tuition reimbursements (averaging $21,000 per year), 19 teaching assistantships with full tuition reimbursements (averaging $21,000 per year) were awarded; scholarships/grants, traineeships, health care benefits, and tuition waivers (partial) also available. *Faculty research:* Statistical methods for survival data analysis, clinical trials, epidemiological case control and cohort studies, statistical genetics. *Unit head:* Dr. Bruce Weir, Department Chair, 206-543-1044. *Application contact:* Alex MacKenzie, Counseling Services Coordinator, 206-543-1044, Fax: 206-543-3286, E-mail: alexam@u.washington.edu. Web site: http://www.biostat.washington.edu/.

University of Waterloo, Graduate Studies, Faculty of Mathematics, Department of Statistics and Actuarial Science, Waterloo, ON N2L 3G1, Canada. Offers actuarial science (M Math, PhD); biostatistics (PhD); statistics (M Math, PhD); statistics-biostatistics (M Math); statistics-computing (M Math); statistics-finance (M Math). *Degree requirements:* For master's, research paper or thesis; for doctorate, comprehensive exam, thesis/dissertation. *Entrance requirements:* For master's, honors degree in field, minimum B+ average; for doctorate, master's degree, minimum B+ average. Additional exam requirements/recommendations for international students: Required—TOEFL (minimum score 600 paper-based; 250 computer-based; 90 iBT), TWE (minimum score 4.5). Electronic applications accepted. *Faculty research:* Data analysis, risk theory, inference, stochastic processes, quantitative finance.

The University of Western Ontario, Faculty of Graduate Studies, Physical Sciences Division, Department of Statistical and Actuarial Sciences, London, ON N6A 5B8, Canada. Offers M Sc, PhD. *Degree requirements:* For master's, thesis (for some programs); for doctorate, comprehensive exam, thesis/dissertation. *Entrance requirements:* For master's, honours BA with B+ average. Additional exam requirements/recommendations for international students: Required—TOEFL. *Faculty research:* Statistical theory, statistical applications, probability, actuarial science.

University of Windsor, Faculty of Graduate Studies, Faculty of Science, Department of Mathematics and Statistics, Windsor, ON N9B 3P4, Canada. Offers mathematics (M Sc); statistics (M Sc, PhD). *Degree requirements:* For master's, thesis or alternative; for doctorate, comprehensive exam, thesis/dissertation. *Entrance requirements:* For master's, minimum B average; for doctorate, minimum A average. Additional exam requirements/recommendations for international students: Required—TOEFL (minimum score 560 paper-based; 220 computer-based). Electronic applications accepted. *Faculty research:* Applied mathematics, operational research, fluid dynamics.

University of Wisconsin–Madison, Graduate School, College of Letters and Science, Department of Statistics, Madison, WI 53706-1380. Offers biometry (MS); statistics (MS, PhD). Part-time programs available. *Degree requirements:* For master's, exam; for doctorate, thesis/dissertation. *Entrance requirements:* For master's and doctorate, GRE. Additional exam requirements/recommendations for international students: Required—TOEFL. Electronic applications accepted. *Expenses:* Tuition, state resident: full-time $10,296; part-time $643.51 per credit. Tuition, nonresident: full-time $24,054; part-time $1503.40 per credit. *Required fees:* $70.06 per credit. Tuition and fees vary according to course load, campus/location, program and reciprocity agreements. *Faculty research:* Biostatistics, bootstrap and other resampling theory and methods, linear and nonlinear models, nonparametrics, time series and stochastic processes.

University of Wyoming, College of Arts and Sciences, Department of Statistics, Laramie, WY 82070. Offers MS, PhD. Terminal master's awarded for partial completion of doctoral program. *Degree requirements:* For master's, comprehensive exam (for some programs), thesis (for some programs); for doctorate, comprehensive exam, thesis/dissertation. *Entrance requirements:* For master's, GMAT, GRE General Test, minimum GPA of 3.0; for doctorate, GRE General Test, minimum GPA of 3.0. Additional exam requirements/recommendations for international students: Required—TOEFL; Recommended—TWE. Electronic applications accepted. *Faculty research:* Linear models categorical, Baysain, spatial biological sciences and engineering, multivariate.

Utah State University, School of Graduate Studies, College of Science, Department of Mathematics and Statistics, Logan, UT 84322. Offers industrial mathematics (MS); mathematical sciences (PhD); mathematics (M Math, MS); statistics (MS). Part-time programs available. Terminal master's awarded for partial completion of doctoral program. *Degree requirements:* For master's, thesis optional, qualifying exam; for doctorate, one foreign language, comprehensive exam, thesis/dissertation. *Entrance requirements:* For master's and doctorate, GRE General Test, minimum GPA of 3.0. Additional exam requirements/recommendations for international students: Required—TOEFL. *Faculty research:* Differential equations, computational mathematics, dynamical systems, probability and statistics, pure mathematics.

Virginia Commonwealth University, Graduate School, College of Humanities and Sciences, Department of Statistical Sciences and Operations Research, Richmond, VA 23284-9005. Offers operations research (MS); statistics (MS); systems modeling and analysis (PhD). *Students:* 20 applicants, 70% accepted, 11 enrolled. *Entrance requirements:* For master's, GRE General Test, 30 undergraduate credits in mathematics, statistics, or operations research, including calculus I and II, multivariate calculus, linear algebra, probability and statistics. Additional exam requirements/recommendations for international students: Required—TOEFL (minimum score 600 paper-based; 250 computer-based; 100 iBT); Recommended—IELTS (minimum score 6.5). *Application deadline:* For fall admission, 3/1 for domestic students; for spring admission, 10/15 for domestic students. Applications are processed on a rolling basis. Application fee: $50. Electronic applications accepted. *Expenses:* Tuition, state resident: full-time $9133; part-time $507 per credit. Tuition, nonresident: full-time $18,777; part-time $1043 per credit. *Required fees:* $77 per credit. Tuition and fees vary according to degree level, campus/location, program and student level. *Unit head:* Dr. D'Arcy P. Mays, Chair, 804-828-1301 Ext. 151, E-mail: jemays@vcu.edu. *Application contact:* Dr. Edward L. Boone, Director, 804-828-4637, E-mail: elboone@VCU.edu. Web site: http://www.stat.vcu.edu/.

Virginia Polytechnic Institute and State University, Graduate School, College of Science, Department of Statistics, Blacksburg, VA 24061. Offers MS, PhD. *Degree requirements:* For master's, comprehensive exam (for some programs), thesis (for some programs); for doctorate, comprehensive exam (for some programs), thesis/dissertation (for some programs). *Entrance requirements:* For master's and doctorate, GRE. Additional exam requirements/recommendations for international students: Required—TOEFL (minimum score 550 paper-based; 213 computer-based). *Application deadline:* For fall admission, 7/1 for domestic and international students; for spring admission, 12/1 for domestic and international students. Applications are processed on a rolling basis. Application fee: $65. Electronic applications accepted. *Expenses:* Tuition, state resident: full-time $10,048; part-time $558.25 per credit hour. Tuition, nonresident: full-time

Peterson's Graduate Programs in the Physical Sciences, Mathematics, Agricultural Sciences, the Environment & Natural Resources 2013

facebook.com/petersonspublishing **387**

Statistics

$19,497; part-time $1083.25 per credit hour. *Required fees:* $405 per semester. Tuition and fees vary according to course load, campus/location and program. *Financial support:* Research assistantships with full tuition reimbursements, teaching assistantships with full tuition reimbursements, career-related internships or fieldwork, Federal Work-Study, scholarships/grants, health care benefits, and unspecified assistantships available. Financial award application deadline: 1/15. *Faculty research:* Design and sampling theory, computing and simulation, nonparametric statistics, robust and multivariate methods, biostatistics quality. *Unit head:* Dr. Eric P. Smith, Unit Head, 540-231-5657, Fax: 540-231-3863, E-mail: epsmith@vt.edu. *Application contact:* Jeffrey Birch, Information Contact, 540-231-7934, Fax: 540-231-3863, E-mail: jbbirch@vt.edu. Web site: http://www.stat.vt.edu/students/gradprog.html.

Washington State University, Graduate School, College of Sciences, Department of Statistics, Pullman, WA 99164. Offers applied statistics (MS); theoretical statistics (MS). *Faculty:* 7. *Students:* 25 full-time (13 women), 2 part-time (0 women); includes 3 minority (1 Asian, non-Hispanic/Latino; 2 Hispanic/Latino), 20 international. Average age 28. 45 applicants, 36% accepted, 9 enrolled. In 2011, 15 master's awarded. *Degree requirements:* For master's, comprehensive exam (for some programs), thesis (for some programs), project. *Entrance requirements:* For master's, GRE, three letters of reference; official copies of all college transcripts. Additional exam requirements/recommendations for international students: Required—TOEFL (minimum score 560 paper-based; 220 computer-based), IELTS. *Application deadline:* For fall admission, 1/10 for domestic and international students; for spring admission, 7/1 for domestic and international students. Application fee: $75. *Financial support:* In 2011–12, 10 students received support, including 4 teaching assistantships with tuition reimbursements available (averaging $18,204 per year). *Faculty research:* Environmental statistics, logistic regression, statistical methods for ecology and wildlife, spatial data analysis, linear and non-linear models. *Total annual research expenditures:* $9,000. *Unit head:* Dr. Michael A. Jacroux, Professor/Chair, 509-335-8645, Fax: 509-335-8369, E-mail: jacroux@wsu.edu. *Application contact:* Graduate School Admissions, 800-GRADWSU, Fax: 509-335-1949, E-mail: gradsch@wsu.edu. Web site: http://www.stat.wsu.edu/.

Washington University in St. Louis, Graduate School of Arts and Sciences, Department of Mathematics, St. Louis, MO 63130-4899. Offers mathematics (MA, PhD); statistics (MA). Terminal master's awarded for partial completion of doctoral program. *Degree requirements:* For master's, thesis or alternative; for doctorate, thesis/dissertation. *Entrance requirements:* For master's and doctorate, GRE General Test. Electronic applications accepted.

Wayne State University, College of Liberal Arts and Sciences, Department of Mathematics, Detroit, MI 48202. Offers applied mathematics (MA); mathematical statistics (MA); mathematics (MA, PhD). *Students:* 50 full-time (16 women), 34 part-time (14 women); includes 13 minority (8 Black or African American, non-Hispanic/Latino; 4 Asian, non-Hispanic/Latino; 1 Two or more races, non-Hispanic/Latino), 32 international. Average age 30. 103 applicants, 50% accepted, 18 enrolled. In 2011, 12 master's, 5 doctorates awarded. *Degree requirements:* For master's, thesis (for some programs), essays, oral exams; for doctorate, one foreign language, thesis/dissertation, oral exams. *Entrance requirements:* For doctorate, master's degree in mathematics or equivalent level of advancement. Additional exam requirements/recommendations for international students: Required—TOEFL (minimum score 550 paper-based; 213 computer-based); Recommended—TWE (minimum score 5.5). *Application deadline:* For fall admission, 6/1 priority date for domestic students, 5/1 for international students; for winter admission, 10/1 priority date for domestic students, 9/1 for international students; for spring admission, 2/1 priority date for domestic students, 1/1 for international students. Applications are processed on a rolling basis. Application fee: $50. Electronic applications accepted. *Expenses:* Tuition, state resident: part-time $512.85 per credit. Tuition, nonresident: part-time $1132.65 per credit. *Required fees:* $26.60 per credit. $199.65 per semester. Tuition and fees vary according to course load and program. *Financial support:* In 2011–12, 43 students received support, including 4 fellowships with tuition

reimbursements available (averaging $17,938 per year), 3 research assistantships with tuition reimbursements available (averaging $18,894 per year), 27 teaching assistantships with tuition reimbursements available (averaging $17,391 per year); institutionally sponsored loans, scholarships/grants, health care benefits, tuition waivers (full), and unspecified assistantships also available. Support available to part-time students. *Faculty research:* Harmonic analysis and partial differential equations, group theory and non-commutative ring theory, homotopy theory and applications to topology and geometry, numerical analysis, control and optimization, statistical estimation theory. *Total annual research expenditures:* $708,703. *Unit head:* Daniel Frohardt, Professor and Chair, 313-577-2479, E-mail: danf@math.wayne.edu. *Application contact:* Tiana Fluker, Graduate Secretary, E-mail: tiana@math.wayne.edu. Web site: http://www.math.wayne.edu/.

Western Michigan University, Graduate College, College of Arts and Sciences, Department of Statistics, Kalamazoo, MI 49008. Offers MS, PhD.

West Virginia University, College of Business and Economics, Division of Economics and Finance, Morgantown, WV 26506. Offers business analysis (MA); developmental financial economics (PhD); environmental and resource economics (PhD); international economics (PhD); mathematical economics (MA); monetary economics (PhD); public finance (PhD); public policy (MA); regional and urban economics (PhD); statistics and economics (MA). Terminal master's awarded for partial completion of doctoral program. *Degree requirements:* For master's, thesis optional; for doctorate, comprehensive exam, thesis/dissertation. *Entrance requirements:* For master's and doctorate, GRE General Test, minimum GPA of 3.0; course work in intermediate microeconomics, intermediate macroeconomics, calculus, and statistics. Additional exam requirements/recommendations for international students: Required—TOEFL. Electronic applications accepted. *Faculty research:* Financial economics, regional/urban development, public economics, international trade/international finance/development economics, monetary economics.

West Virginia University, Eberly College of Arts and Sciences, Department of Statistics, Morgantown, WV 26506. Offers MS. *Degree requirements:* For master's, comprehensive exam, thesis. *Entrance requirements:* For master's, minimum GPA of 3.0, course work in linear algebra and multivariable calculus. Additional exam requirements/recommendations for international students: Required—TOEFL. *Faculty research:* Linear models, categorical data analysis, statistical computing, experimental design, non parametric analysis.

Yale University, Graduate School of Arts and Sciences, Department of Statistics, New Haven, CT 06520. Offers MA, PhD. Terminal master's awarded for partial completion of doctoral program. *Degree requirements:* For doctorate, thesis/dissertation. *Entrance requirements:* For doctorate, GRE General Test, GRE Subject Test.

York University, Faculty of Graduate Studies, Faculty of Science and Engineering, Program in Mathematics and Statistics, Toronto, ON M3J 1P3, Canada. Offers industrial and applied mathematics (M Sc); mathematics and statistics (MA, PhD). Part-time programs available. *Degree requirements:* For master's, thesis optional; for doctorate, one foreign language, comprehensive exam, thesis/dissertation. Electronic applications accepted.

Youngstown State University, Graduate School, College of Science, Technology, Engineering and Mathematics, Department of Mathematics and Statistics, Youngstown, OH 44555-0001. Offers applied mathematics (MS); computer science (MS); secondary mathematics (MS); statistics (MS). Part-time programs available. *Degree requirements:* For master's, comprehensive exam, thesis optional. *Entrance requirements:* For master's, minimum GPA of 2.7 in computer science and mathematics. Additional exam requirements/recommendations for international students: Required—TOEFL. *Faculty research:* Regression analysis, numerical analysis, statistics, Markov chain, topology and fuzzy sets.

388 facebook.com/petersonspublishing

Peterson's Graduate Programs in the Physical Sciences, Mathematics, Agricultural Sciences, the Environment & Natural Resources 2013

UNIVERSITY OF OKLAHOMA
Department of Mathematics

Programs of Study

While the Mathematics Department at the University of Oklahoma (OU) offers three different graduate degrees—M.S., M.A., and Ph.D.—students are considered to be on either two tracks, the M.S. track or the M.A./Ph.D. track.

The M.A./Ph.D track is the standard program for most students seeking a Ph.D. in mathematics. All students in the program (regardless of their future specialization) need to pass the three Ph.D. qualifying examinations in algebra, analysis, and topology. Each of these exams is associated with a two-semester graduate course sequence that forms the core of the M.A. degree and also count toward the Ph.D. degree. Students who pass all three qualifying examinations can go into the Ph.D. program in one of the following two options.

Ph.D. program (traditional option): This is essentially the same as the M.A./Ph.D. program above. The main difference is that students who already have a master's degree in mathematics may apply directly to this program. Students with a baccalaureate degree apply to the M.A./Ph.D. program and move into to the Ph.D. program on successful completion of the Ph.D. qualifying examinations. The student's ultimate goal in this program is to write and defend a dissertation representing an original contribution to research in mathematics.

Ph.D. program (RUME—research in undergraduate mathematics—option): As is the case with the traditional option, students who already have a master's degree in mathematics may apply to this program, while students with a baccalaureate degree apply to the M.A./Ph.D. program. The student's ultimate goal in this program is to write and defend a dissertation representing an original contribution to research in undergraduate mathematics education.

Students with strong mathematical backgrounds are encouraged to take "free shot" attempts at the Ph.D. qualifying examinations, usually held in August, the week before classes start. These attempts are only offered to students when they first enter the program, and results do not go on the student's record unless they pass.

The M.S. track (Master of Science program) is offered by the Mathematics Department for students who want to pursue studies in mathematics beyond the undergraduate level, but who do not plan to obtain a doctorate in mathematics. Recent graduates of the M.S. program have gone on to careers as actuaries, statistical analysts, and software engineers. Some become mathematics teachers in settings ranging from middle school to two- and four-year colleges. Still others have gone on to obtain doctorates and academic positions in fields other than mathematics, such as economics, mathematics education, and computer science.

Students will be able to select from a broad range of options in pure and applied mathematics and in research in undergraduate mathematics education as they pursue their graduate degree, including: (1) Algebra and Number Theory: algebraic geometry, algebraic groups, combinatorics, modular forms, representation theory (real, p-adic, Lie, automorphic); (2) Analysis: global analysis, harmonic analysis, integrable systems, PDEs, signal processing, spectral theory, wavelets and frames; (3) Applied Mathematics and Mathematical Physics: control theory, dynamical systems, modeling; (4) Geometry: convexity, harmonic maps, Riemannian geometry, group actions, non-negative curvature; (5) RUME: research in undergraduate mathematics education, diversity and equity, international comparative education; (6) Topology: algebraic and geometric topology, dimension theory, geometric group theory, hyperbolic geometry, low-dimensional topology, Teichmuller theory.

Additional information about the University's graduate programs in mathematics can be found at http://math.ou.edu/grad/programs.html.

Research Facilities

Students in the Department have a wide range of facilities and resources to support their study and research efforts. The department maintains two servers, Aftermath and Zeus, both of which run the Linux operating system. The Aftermath server hosts login shells and some software, while Zeus is the primary file server and provides NFS service to workstations throughout the department. The file system is protected by a RAID backup system. The systems manager should be able to recover a user's lost data for up to three or four weeks. There are two workstation clusters for graduate students in the department.

The library's LORA system gives students access to MathSciNet, the definitive database of mathematics literature reviews and bibliographical information (available in BibTeX format); JSTOR, and numerous other online databases and resources from off-campus locations.

Financial Aid

Most students are employed as graduate teaching assistants while earning their degrees. The students' transition into their new roles as educators is facilitated by a lighter course load in the first year and participation in the Department's graduate teaching seminar. Other graduate teaching assistant duties include grading, working in the Mathematics Help Center, and assisting in multisection courses.

During the 2009–10 academic year, stipends for graduate teaching assistants who were fully English-language qualified to teach ranged from $15,038 to $16,187. Stipends for graduate teaching assistants who were not fully English-language qualified started at $14,030.

Other opportunities include graduate assistantships. A variable number of teaching assistantships are available for the summer semester in June and July each year, with a stipend of approximately $2500. Several faculty members also provide support for research assistants using funds from research grants. Research assistants usually participate in research-related projects under the supervision of the faculty member. Further details regarding financial support for graduate students can be found at http://math.ou.edu/grad/finance.html.

Cost of Study

In the 2011–12 academic year, tuition and fees for graduate students totaled $310.55 per credit hour for Oklahoma students and $760.05 per credit hour for nonresident students.

Peterson's Graduate Programs in the Physical Sciences, Mathematics, Agricultural Sciences, the Environment & Natural Resources 2013

facebook.com/petersonspublishing **389**

University of Oklahoma

Living and Housing Costs

The University offers several on-campus apartment choices. In addition, there are a large number of privately owned apartments, duplexes, and houses available in Norman. Many off-campus housing locations are served by CART, the Cleveland Area Rapid Transit system, which is free for OU students.

Student Group

The OU mathematics graduate program is comprised of about 70 students, representing over a dozen different countries from around the globe. There is an active Mathematics Graduate Student Association which provides guidance and mentoring and organizes various events for graduate students. Additional details about the association can be found online at http://math.ou.edu/~mgsa/.

Location

As part of the dynamic Southwest, Oklahoma benefits from both its rich historic heritage and the vital and modern growth of its metropolitan areas. Although by location a suburb of Oklahoma City, Norman is an independent community with a permanent population of more than 95,000. Norman residents enjoy extensive parks and recreation programs and a 10,000-acre lake and park area. *Money* magazine named Norman as the nation's sixth best place to live in the 2008 edition of its annual rankings.

The University and The Department

The Mathematics Department at the University of Oklahoma has a long and rich academic tradition dating back to the mid-1890s. Students who pursue a graduate degree in mathematics at OU become part of a team that is responsible for the instruction of 10,000–12,000 OU undergraduate students annually. The Department's faculty members strive to maintain a vibrant and collegial research atmosphere and also serve as sources of inspiration, mentoring, and advice. The strong sense of community is enhanced by having faculty, postdoctoral, and student offices, as well as a common room and instructional classrooms, all housed in the same building. Prospective graduate students can experience the Mathematics Department in person during OU MathFest, an annual two-day open house for prospective graduate students. Dates, schedules, and a registration form for MathFest are available at http://www.math.ou.edu/grad/mathfest/2010/ou_mathfest_2010.html.

Applying

Prospective students should submit the Mathematics Department graduate application form online, or may also download, print, and mail the form with the required materials listed below to the Mathematics Department. To ensure full consideration, the complete application and all supporting material needs to be received by the Department by January 31. The Department will forward everything to the Office of Admissions. Applications after this date will be considered, but those received after May 31 are rarely considered. International applicants are subject to the University's April 1 deadline.

In addition to the application form, students must submit official transcripts from all colleges and universities attended, GRE scores, TOEFL scores (if English is not the student's native language), and letters of reference from 3 people familiar with the student's work in mathematics (using the form found at http://math.ou.edu/grad/gradapp/Reference_Request.pdf). While the University's forms indicate an application fee is necessary, the Mathematics Department prescreens all applications and makes qualified applicants an offer; the application fee can be submitted then.

Correspondence and Information

Director of Graduate Studies
University of Oklahoma
Department of Mathematics
601 Elm Street, PHSC 423
Norman, Oklahoma 73019
Phone: 800-522-0772 (toll-free)
E-mail: mathgraddir@ou.edu
Web site: http://www.math.ou.edu

THE FACULTY

The Mathematics Department at the University of Oklahoma has 34 permanent faculty members, 8 visiting faculty members, and a support staff of 6 (including a full-time undergraduate adviser). Virtually all of the department's faculty have active research programs (many externally funded) and regularly publish articles in mathematical journals and participate in conferences around the world.

Additional details regarding the Mathematics Department faculty can be found at http://www.math.ou.edu/people/faculty_research.html.

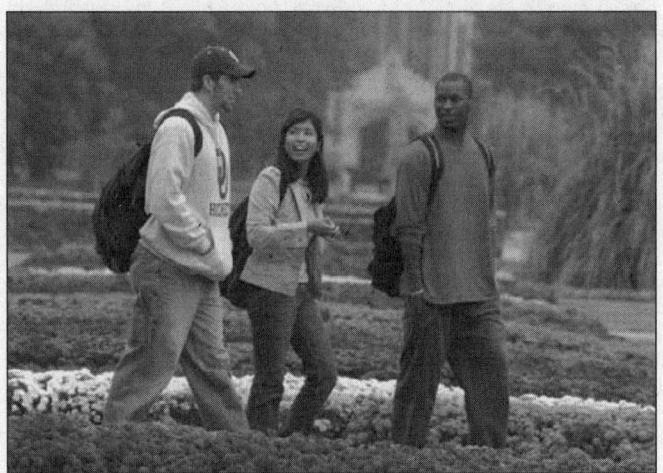

Students walk to class on the Norman campus.

390 facebook.com/petersonspublishing

Peterson's Graduate Programs in the Physical Sciences, Mathematics, Agricultural Sciences, the Environment & Natural Resources 2013

UNIVERSITY OF SOUTHERN CALIFORNIA
Division of Biostatistics

Programs of Study

Graduate education at the University of Southern California (USC) prepares students for leadership in research, teaching, or professional practice in the private or public sector. Rigorous individually tailored course work and research forms the basis for the graduate programs.

Graduate studies in biostatistics, epidemiology, molecular epidemiology, and statistical genetics and genetic epidemiology are contained within USC's Keck School of Medicine. The University offers the Master of Science (M.S.) and Doctor of Philosophy (Ph.D.) degrees. The Ph.D. in biostatistics is designed to produce a biostatistician with a deep knowledge of statistical theory and methodology. The Ph.D. in statistical genetics and genetic epidemiology is a joint effort to combine biostatistics, epidemiology, statistical and molecular genetics, and computational methods in order to develop new and cutting-edge statistical methodology that is appropriate for human genomic studies.

Master's degree studies in biostatistics focus on the theory of biostatistics, data analytic methods, experimental design (including clinical trials), statistical methods in human genetics, biomedical informatics, and statistical computing methods. The master's degree in applied biostatistics and epidemiology includes applied biostatistics, epidemiological research methods, and research applications, including cancer, infectious disease, chronic disease, and environmental epidemiology. Doctoral studies cover the areas of biostatistics and data analysis; descriptive, genetic, and molecular epidemiology; computational methods; clinical trial methodology; and related fields of field research, such as population disease and treatment trials.

The Division of Biostatistics also offers a joint-degree program in either the M.S. or Ph.D. in molecular epidemiology in conjunction with the Department of Biochemistry and Molecular Biology. The objective of the M.S. degree is to train students in the application of statistical methods to the design of biomedical research. The objective of the doctoral degree is to produce a molecular epidemiologist with in-depth laboratory, statistical, and analytical skills in both epidemiology and the molecular biosciences.

Research Facilities

Hands-on research alongside a faculty mentor is the norm at USC. Graduate students work alongside colleagues as coinvestigators on epidemiological, clinical trial, and environmental research projects. Graduate students have myriad opportunities to participate in the latest clinical and biomedical research projects. Research teams gain expertise on study design as well as statistical methodology, data analysis, and manuscript preparation. The University's Health Sciences Campus contains the Norris Cancer Center, the General Clinical Research Center, the Zilkha Neurogenetic Research Institute, and the Doheny Eye Institute Vision Research Center.

USC has a dozen libraries to serve all the varied needs of its graduate students. Primary source materials include ongoing research projects and recent faculty and staff members' publications. In addition, electronic resources in hundreds of subjects plus online archives and Internet access are available for students through the library system.

Financial Aid

Most graduate students who demonstrate financial need qualify for low-interest loans or assistantships. Graduate assistantships are awarded to Ph.D. students only on the basis of scholastic accomplishment and competence. Students exchange teaching and laboratory assistant time for tuition waivers and stipends.

The Sponsored Projects Information Network (SPIN) is a computerized database of funding opportunities—federal, private, and corporate—created to help faculty members identify external financial support for research and education. SPIN funds that are directed toward USC programs in biostatistics result in research funds and fellowships for graduate students.

Cost of Study

Estimated costs for 2012–13 are as follows: tuition, $45,000; books and supplies, $3000; and other miscellaneous expenses, $7000.

Living and Housing Costs

Estimated housing costs for the Los Angeles area are approximately $20,000 per year. Housing costs vary greatly, depending on the location and type of accommodation. There are ample housing facilities in the many communities surrounding the medical school.

Student Group

There are approximately 3,000 graduate students at USC and 115 in the biostatistics, epidemiology, and genetics programs. The relatively small size of the programs facilitates student–faculty member interchange and good accessibility for students to their professors and mentors.

Location

University of Southern California campuses are mostly centered around Los Angeles, with other facilities in nearby Alhambra, Pasadena, and Marina del Rey; on Catalina Island; and further away in Orange County to the south and Sacramento to the north. Los Angeles is the second-largest city in the U.S. and the nucleus of southern California. The scenic, sunny, and culturally diverse area of Los Angeles offers miles of beaches, acres of recreational and park areas, and some of the finest arts and cultural opportunities in the nation.

The University

USC is the oldest and largest independent coeducational university in the West. The campus is composed of 169 buildings located in a 150-acre parklike setting near downtown Los Angeles. USC is among the ten most successful private universities in the country in attracting research support from external sources (more than $100 million annually). Graduate students in the Division of Biostatistics take the majority of their courses at the Health Sciences Campus, 3 miles northeast of downtown Los Angeles and 7 miles from the USC University Park Campus. The Health Sciences Campus is adjacent to the Los Angeles County–USC Medical Center, one of the nation's largest teaching hospitals. The surrounding neighborhoods are among the most historically significant in the city, with rich educational resources.

Applying

For the M.S. degree, an undergraduate degree in mathematics, statistics, biostatistics, or computer science is most helpful. Undergraduate preparation should include differential and integral calculus, mathematical statistics, and basic computer programming. The Ph.D. requires successful scores on a screening examination (the M.S. prepares students for this exam). Applicants must apply online through USC's general Web site. They must also get the department's preapplication via the graduate program's direct Web site at http://www.usc.edu/medicine/biostats.

Correspondence and Information

Graduate Programs in Biostatistics, Epidemiology, Molecular Epidemiology, and Statistical Genetics and Genetic Epidemiology
Division of Biostatistics
Department of Preventive Medicine
Keck School of Medicine
Soto Street Building
University of Southern California
2001 North Soto Street, Suite 201A
Los Angeles, California 90032-9234
Phone: 323-442-1810
Fax: 323-442-2993
E-mail: mtrujill@usc.edu
Web site: http://www.usc.edu/medicine/biostats

THE FACULTY AND THEIR RESEARCH

Hooman Allayee, Associate Professor; Ph.D., UCLA, 1999. Genetic approaches to cardiovascular and metabolic disorders.

Todd Alonzo, Professor of Research; Ph.D., Washington (Seattle), 2000. Design and analysis of clinical trials, pediatric oncology, statistical methodology, and missing data methodology.

Edward Avol, Professor; M.S., Caltech, 1974. Chronic respiratory effects of airborne pollutants in populations.

Stanley Azen, Professor; Ph.D., UCLA, 1969. Biostatistical methodology.

Lourdes Baezconde-Garbanati, Associate Professor; Ph.D., UCLA, 1994. Cancer control research.

Kiros Berhane, Professor; Ph.D., Toronto, 1994. Analysis of health effects of environmental exposures.

Jonathan Buckley, Professor of Research (also with Pediatrics, CHLA); Ph.D., Melbourne, 1981. Epidemiology of childhood cancer, clinical trials, molecular epidemiology.

John Casagrande, Clinical Associate Professor; D.Ph., UCLA, 1978. Computer applications in research.

Jiu-Chiuan Chen, Visiting Associate Professor; Sc.D., Harvard, 2002. Cardiovascular and neurological effects of air pollution, characterization of individual susceptibility to health effects of air pollution.

Peterson's Graduate Programs in the Physical Sciences, Mathematics, Agricultural Sciences, the Environment & Natural Resources 2013

facebook.com/petersonspublishing **391**

University of Southern California

Lu Chen, Assistant Professor of Research; Ph.D., USC, 1998. Statistical design and analysis of clinical trials for pediatric cancer.

Chih-Ping Chou, Professor; Ph.D., UCLA, 1983. Evaluation of approaches to substance-abuse prevention among adolescents, statistical methods in prevention research.

Myles Cockburn, Visiting Associate Professor of Research; Ph.D., Otago (New Zealand), 1998. Epidemiology of melanoma, gastric cancer, and *Helicobacter pylori;* computational methods; geographical information systems (GIS).

David Conti, Associate Professor; Ph.D., Case Western Reserve, 2002. Statistical methods in genetic association studies, use of hierarchical models in epidemiology.

Victoria Cortessis, Assistant Professor; Ph.D., UCLA, 1993. Genetic-epidemiologic and molecular genetic studies of congenital disorders, adult-onset cancers and etiologic relationships among these entities.

Wendy Cozen, Associate Professor of Research; M.P.H., UCLA, 1989. Epidemiology of hematologic neoplasms, Hodgkin's disease, non-Hodgkin's lymphoma.

N. Tess Cruz, Assistant Professor of Clinical; Ph.D., Massachusetts, 1993. Public health communications research, anti-tobacco media and pro-tobacco marketing effects.

Dennis Deapen, Professor; Dr.Ph., UCLA, 1982. Cancer outcomes among breast implant patients; lupus erythematosus, diabetes, multiple sclerosis, and Alzheimer's disease.

Sandrah Eckel, Assistant Professor; Ph.D., Johns Hopkins, 2009. Health effects of air pollution in vulnerable populations.

Meridith Franklin, Assistant Professor; Ph.D., Harvard, 2007. Developing and applying spatio-temporal statistical methods for environmental data.

Manuela Gago, Assistant Professor of Research.

W. James Gauderman, Professor and Director of Biostatistics division; Ph.D., USC, 1992. Biostatistical methodology, genetic-epidemiological analysis of pedigree data, health outcomes to environmental exposure.

Frank Gilliland, Professor; M.D., Minnesota, 1992. Environmental exposures on air pollution.

Michael I. Goran, Professor (also with Physiology and Biophysics); Ph.D., Manchester (England), 1986. Biophysics etiology prevention of obesity, type 2 diabetes in children.

Susan Groshen, Professor of Research; Ph.D., Rutgers, 1980. New drugs and treating cancer.

Robert Haile, Professor; Ph.D., UCLA, 1979. Genetic epidemiology of breast, colon, and prostate cancers.

Christopher Haiman, Associate Professor; Sc.D. Genetics and molecular epidemiology.

Ann Hamilton, Associate Professor; Ph.D., UCLA, 1987. Breast, prostate, and testicular cancer; Kaposi's sarcoma; cancers in twins.

Brian Henderson, Professor; M.D., Chicago, 1962. Cancers of the breast, prostate, ovary, testes, and endometrium in different ethnic groups.

Andrea Hricko, Professor; M.P.H., North Carolina, 1971. Outreach and education techniques, translational and community-based participatory research.

Sue A. Ingles, Associate Professor; D.P.H., UCLA, 1993. Nutritional genetics and breast, prostate, and colorectal cancer.

Carol Koprowski, Assistant Professor; Ph.D., USC, 1998. Diet and physical activity.

Mark Krailo, Professor of Research; Ph.D., Waterloo, 1981. Clinical trials on cancer treatment.

Christianne Lane, Assistant Professor of Research; Ph.D., USC, 2009. Geriatric populations and adolescence transdisciplinary research on energetic and cancer.

Peter W. Laird, Associate Professor; Ph.D., Amsterdam (Netherlands Cancer Institute), 1988. Biochemistry and molecular biology, cancer genetics, gene regulation.

Bryan Langholz, Professor of Research; Ph.D., Washington (Seattle), 1984. Cancer and other chronic diseases, cohort studies.

Juan Pablo Lewinger, Assistant Professor.

Thomas Mack, Professor (also with Pathology); M.P.H., Harvard, 1969. Chronic disease in twins.

Wendy Mack, Professor (also with Pathology); Ph.D., USC, 1989. Biostatistical methodology in cardiovascular research, clinical trials using angiographic and ultrasound endpoints.

Paul Marjoram, Associate Professor of Research; Ph.D., University College (London), 1992. Computational biology; the coalescent, probabilistic models; microarray data.

Rob McConnell, Professor; M.D., California, San Francisco, 1980. Environmental exposures, air pollution.

Roberta McKean-Cowdin, Assistant Professor of Research; Ph.D., 1996. Breast, brain, and endometrial cancer.

Joel Milam, Assistant Professor of Research; Ph.D., USC, 2002.

Josh Millstein, Assistant Professor; Ph.D., UCS, 2005. Statistical methods for casual inference, permutation-based false discovery rates, and methods for identifying genes involved in epistatic interactions.

Elaine Nezami, Associate Professor and M.S. Dean; Ph.D., USC, 1994. Chronic disease, cancer, cardiovascular.

Cecilia Patino-Sutton, Assistant Professor; Ph.D., USC, 2010. Promoting scientific discoveries and their applications to patients, improving public health and health care.

Celeste Pearce, Assistant Professor of Research; Ph.D.

Mary Ann Pentz, Professor; Ph.D., Syracuse, 1978. Development and testing of school/community-based prevention intervention for adolescents.

Jean Richardson, Professor; M.P.H., UCLA, 1971. Cancer control, behavioral and epidemiological research methods,

Louise Rohrbach, Associate Professor of Research; Ph.D., USC, 1989. Community-based interventions for disease prevention and health promotion; prevention of tobacco, alcohol, and other drug abuse.

Towhid Salam, Assistant Professor of Research; Ph. D., USC, 2009. Environmental exposures, genetic and epigenetic influences on asthma and related conditions.

Jonathan Samet, Professor and Chair of Preventive Medicine; M.D., M.S., Harvard School of Public Health.

Fredrick Schumacher, Assistant Professor; Ph.D., Case Western Reserve, 2006. Genetic epidemiology (cancer, obesity); cancer genetics; gene-environment interactions; biostatistics.

Kimberly Siegmund, Associate Professor; Ph.D., Washington (Seattle), 1995. Statistical methods for genetics.

Richard Sposto, Professor of Research; Ph.D., UCLA, 1981. Biostatistics, clinical trials in pediatric oncology, Bayesian analysis of survival data.

Donna Spruijt-Metz, Associate Professor of Research; Ph.D., Amsterdam Vrije, 1996. Obesity and type 2 diabetes, smoking prevention.

Mariana Stern, Associate Professor; Ph.D., Texas Health Science Center, 1997. Colorectal and breast cancer, genes–diet, genes–smoking.

Daniel Stram, Professor; Ph.D., Temple, 1983. Modern statistical methods, measurement error methods in cancer epidemiology, repeated measures data, human genetics data.

Ping Sun, Assistant Professor of Research; Ph.D., USC, 1999. Cardiovascular disease and cancer.

Steven Sussman, Professor; Ph.D., Illinois at Chicago, 1984. Drug abuse, cessation, school-based alcohol, tobacco.

Duncan Thomas, Professor; Ph.D., McGill, 1976. Statistical methods, occupational and environmental health.

Paul D. Thomas, Associate Professor and Director of Bioinformatics; Ph.D., Development and application of computational methods for reconstructing gene evolution to understand the function of human genes.

Jennifer Unger, Professor; Ph.D., USC, 1996. Psychosocial and cultural factors in adolescent.

Thomas Valente, Professor; Ph.D., USC, 1991. Health promotion, substance abuse.

Heather Volk, Assistant Professor of Research; Ph.D., Saint Louis, 2006. Environmental and genetic epidemiology of autism and other neurodevelopmental disorders, gene-environment interaction in complex disease.

Richard Watanabe, Associate Professor; Ph.D., USC, 1995. Type 2 diabetes, biologic systems, positional cloning and gene characterization in complex disease.

Anna Wu, Professor; Ph.D., UCLA, 1983. Various cancers among Asian migrants to the U.S.

392 facebook.com/petersonspublishing

Peterson's Graduate Programs in the Physical Sciences, Mathematics, Agricultural Sciences, the Environment & Natural Resources 2013

WESLEYAN UNIVERSITY
Department of Mathematics and Computer Science

Programs of Study

The Department of Mathematics and Computer Science offers a program of courses and research leading to the degrees of Master of Arts and Doctor of Philosophy.

The Ph.D. degree demands breadth of knowledge, intensive specialization in one field, original contribution to that field, and expository skill. First-year courses are designed to provide a strong foundation in algebra, analysis, and topology. Students have the option to substitute computer science for one of these three. Written preliminary examinations are taken after the first year. During the second year, the student continues with a variety of courses, sampling areas of possible concentration. The student must choose a thesis adviser by the end of the second year and pass the special preliminary examination, which is an oral exam managed by the student's adviser and examination committee, by the end of the third year. Also required is the ability to read mathematics in at least one of the following languages: French, German, and Russian. The usual time required for completion of all requirements for a Ph.D., including the dissertation, is five years.

During their time in the program, most Ph.D. candidates teach one course per year, typically small sections (fewer than 20 students) of calculus.

The M.A. degree is designed to ensure basic knowledge and the capacity for sustained scholarly study; requirements are six semester courses at the graduate level and the writing and oral presentation of a thesis. The thesis requires (at least) independent search and study of the literature.

Students are also involved in a variety of Departmental activities, including seminars and colloquiums. The small size of the program contributes to an atmosphere of informality and accessibility.

The emphasis at Wesleyan is in pure mathematics and theoretical computer science, and most Wesleyan Ph.D.'s have chosen academic careers.

Research Facilities

The Department is housed in the Science Center, where all graduate students and faculty members have offices. Computer facilities are available for both learning and research purposes. The Science Library collection has about 120,000 volumes, with extensive mathematics holdings; there are more than 200 subscriptions to mathematics journals, and approximately sixty new mathematics books arrive each month. The proximity of students and faculty and the daily gatherings at teatime are also key elements of the research environment.

Financial Aid

Each applicant for admission is automatically considered for appointment to an assistantship. For the 2012–13 academic year, a nine-month stipend is $18,375, plus a dependency allowance when appropriate, and an additional three-month stipend of $6125 is usually available for the student who wishes to remain on campus to study during the summer. Costs of tuition and health fees are borne by the University. All students in good standing are given financial support for the duration of their studies.

Cost of Study

The only academic costs to the student are books and other educational materials.

Living and Housing Costs

The University provides some subsidized housing and assists in finding private housing. The monthly rent of a single student's housing (a private room in a 2- or 4-person house, with common kitchen and living area) is about $640.

Student Group

The number of graduate students in mathematics ranges from 18 to 22, with an entering class of 3 to 5 each year. There have always been both male and female students, graduates of small colleges and large universities, and U.S. and international students, including, in recent years, students from Bulgaria, Chile, China, Germany, India, Iran, and Sri Lanka.

Location

Middletown, Connecticut, is a small city of 40,000 by the Connecticut River, about 19 miles southeast of Hartford and 25 miles northeast of New Haven, midway between New York and Boston. The University provides many cultural and recreational opportunities, supplemented by those in the countryside and in larger cities nearby.

The University

Founded in 1831, Wesleyan is an independent coeducational institution of liberal arts and sciences, with Ph.D. programs in biology, chemistry, ethnomusicology, mathematics, and physics and master's programs in a number of departments. Current enrollments show about 2,800 undergraduates and 145 graduate students.

Peterson's Graduate Programs in the Physical Sciences, Mathematics, Agricultural Sciences, the Environment & Natural Resources 2013

facebook.com/petersonspublishing   **393**

Wesleyan University

Applying

No specific courses are required for admission, but it is expected that the equivalent of an undergraduate major in mathematics will have been completed. The complete application consists of the application form, transcripts of all previous academic work at or beyond the college level, letters of recommendation from 3 college instructors familiar with the applicant's mathematical ability and performance, and GRE scores (if available). Applications should be submitted by February 15 in order to receive adequate consideration, but requests for admission from outstanding candidates are welcome at any time. Preference is given to Ph.D. candidates.

Correspondence and Information

Department of Mathematics and Computer Science
Graduate Education Committee
Wesleyan University
Middletown, Connecticut 06459-0128
United States
Phone: 860-685-2620
E-mail: ccanalia@wesleyan.edu
Web site: http://www.math.wesleyan.edu

THE FACULTY AND THEIR RESEARCH

Professors

Petra Bonfert-Taylor, Ph.D., Berlin Technical. Complex analysis, complex dynamics, geometric function theory, discrete groups.

Wai Kiu Chan, Ph.D., Ohio State. Number theory, quadratic forms.

Karen L. Collins, Ph.D., MIT. Combinatorics.

Adam Fieldsteel, Ph.D., Berkeley. Ergodic theory.

Mark Hovey, Ph.D., MIT. Algebraic topology and homological algebra.

Michael S. Keane, Dr.rer.nat., Erlangen-Nuremberg. Ergodic theory, random walks, statistical physics.

Philip H. Scowcroft, Ph.D., Cornell. Foundations of mathematics, model-theoretic algebra.

Edward C. Taylor, Ph.D., SUNY at Stony Brook. Analysis, low-dimensional geometry and topology.

Carol Wood, Ph.D., Yale. Mathematical logic, applications of model theory to algebra.

Associate Professor

David Pollack, Ph.D., Harvard. Number theory, automorphic forms, representation of p-adic groups.

Assistant Professors

Ilesanmi Adeboye, Ph.D., Michigan. Topology and geometry, Hyperbolic geometry.

David Constantine, Ph.D., Michigan. Riemannian geometry, dynamics, rigidity, homogeneous dynamics, Lie groups, symmetric spaces.

Constance Leidy, Ph.D., Rice. Knot theory, low-dimensional topology.

Christopher Rasmussen, Ph.D., Arizona. Algebraic geometry.

Professors of Computer Science

Danny Krizanc, Ph.D., Harvard. Theoretical computer science.

Associate Professors of Computer Science

James Lipton, Ph.D., Cornell. Logic and computation, logic programming, type theory, linear logic.

Norman Danner, Ph.D., Indiana Bloomington. Logic, theoretical computer science.

Assistant Professor of Computer Science

Eric Aaron, Ph.D., Cornell. Intelligent virtual agents, reasoning about navigation, hybrid systems, game artificial intelligence, behavioral animation/robotics, applied logic, cognitive modeling, attention, automated verification, tumor modeling.

Professors Emeriti

W. Wistar Comfort, Ph.D., Washington (Seattle). Point-set topology, ultrafilters, set theory, topological groups.

Ethan M. Coven, Ph.D., Yale. Dynamical systems.

Anthony W. Hager, Ph.D., Penn State. Lattice-ordered algebraic structures, general and categorical topology.

F. E. J. Linton, Ph.D., Columbia. Categorical algebra, functorial semantics, topoi.

James D. Reid, Ph.D., Washington (Seattle). Abelian groups, module theory.

Michael Rice, Ph.D., Wesleyan. Parallel computing, formal specification methods.

Lewis C. Robertson, Ph.D., UCLA. Lie groups, topological groups, representation theory.

Robert A. Rosenbaum, Ph.D., Yale. Geometry, mathematics and science education.

394 facebook.com/petersonspublishing

Peterson's Graduate Programs in the Physical Sciences, Mathematics, Agricultural Sciences, the Environment & Natural Resources 2013

ACADEMIC AND PROFESSIONAL PROGRAMS IN THE AGRICULTURAL SCIENCES

Section 8
Agricultural and Food Sciences

This section contains a directory of institutions offering graduate work in agricultural and food sciences. Additional information about programs listed in the directory may be obtained by writing directly to the dean of a graduate school or chair of a department at the address given in the directory.

For programs offering related work, see also in this book *Natural Resources*. In the other guides in this series:

Graduate Programs in the Humanities, Arts & Social Sciences

See *Architecture (Landscape Architecture)* and *Economics (Agricultural Economics and Agribusiness)*

Graduate Programs in the Biological/Biomedical Sciences & Health-Related Medical Professions

See *Biological and Biomedical Sciences; Botany and Plant Biology; Ecology, Environmental Biology, and Evolutionary Biology; Entomology; Genetics, Developmental Biology, and Reproductive Biology; Nutrition; Pathology and Pathobiology; Physiology; Veterinary Medicine and Sciences;* and *Zoology*

Graduate Programs in Engineering & Applied Sciences

See *Agricultural Engineering and Bioengineering* and *Biomedical Engineering and Biotechnology*

Graduate Programs in Business, Education, Information Studies, Law & Social Work

See *Education (Agricultural Education)*

CONTENTS

Program Directories

Agricultural Sciences—General

Alabama Agricultural and Mechanical University, School of Graduate Studies, College of Agricultural, Life and Natural Sciences, Huntsville, AL 35811. Offers MS, MURP, PhD. Part-time and evening/weekend programs available. Terminal master's awarded for partial completion of doctoral program. *Degree requirements:* For doctorate, one foreign language, thesis/dissertation. *Entrance requirements:* For master's, GRE General Test; for doctorate, GRE General Test, MS. Additional exam requirements/recommendations for international students: Required—TOEFL (minimum score 500 paper-based; 173 computer-based; 61 iBT). Electronic applications accepted. *Faculty research:* Remote sensing, environmental pollutants, food biotechnology, plant growth.

Alcorn State University, School of Graduate Studies, School of Agriculture and Applied Science, Alcorn State, MS 39096-7500. Offers agricultural economics (MS Ag); agronomy (MS Ag); animal science (MS Ag). *Degree requirements:* For master's, thesis optional. *Faculty research:* Aquatic systems, dairy herd improvement, fruit production, alternative farming practices.

Angelo State University, College of Graduate Studies, College of Arts and Sciences, Department of Agriculture, San Angelo, TX 76909. Offers animal science (MS). Part-time and evening/weekend programs available. *Faculty:* 4 full-time (0 women). *Students:* 17 full-time (7 women), 6 part-time (3 women); includes 1 minority (Asian, non-Hispanic/Latino). Average age 23. 15 applicants, 73% accepted, 8 enrolled. In 2011, 11 master's awarded. *Degree requirements:* For master's, comprehensive exam, thesis optional. *Entrance requirements:* For master's, GRE General Test, essay. Additional exam requirements/recommendations for international students: Required—TOEFL or IELTS. *Application deadline:* For fall admission, 7/15 priority date for domestic students, 6/10 for international students; for spring admission, 12/1 priority date for domestic students, 11/1 for international students. Applications are processed on a rolling basis. Application fee: $40 ($50 for international students). Electronic applications accepted. *Financial support:* In 2011–12, 10 students received support, including 9 research assistantships (averaging $9,887 per year); Federal Work-Study, scholarships/grants, and unspecified assistantships also available. Support available to part-time students. Financial award application deadline: 3/1. *Faculty research:* Effect of protein and energy on feedlot performance, bitterweed toxicosis in sheep, meat laboratory, North Concho watershed project, baseline vegetation. *Unit head:* Dr. Gilbert R. Engdahl, Department Head, 325-942-2027 Ext. 227, E-mail: gil.engdahl@angelo.edu. *Application contact:* Dr. Cody B. Scott, Graduate Advisor, 325-942-2027 Ext. 284, E-mail: cody.scott@angelo.edu. Web site: http://www.angelo.edu/dept/agriculture/.

Arkansas State University, Graduate School, College of Agriculture and Technology, Jonesboro, State University, AR 72467. Offers agricultural education (SCCT); agriculture (MSA); vocational-technical administration (SCCT). Part-time programs available. *Faculty:* 15 full-time (3 women). *Students:* 12 full-time (6 women), 23 part-time (9 women); includes 5 minority (all Black or African American, non-Hispanic/Latino), 7 international. Average age 33. 12 applicants, 83% accepted, 7 enrolled. In 2011, 12 master's awarded. *Degree requirements:* For master's, comprehensive exam, thesis or alternative; for SCCT, comprehensive exam. *Entrance requirements:* For master's, GRE General Test or MAT, appropriate bachelor's degree, official transcripts, immunization records; for SCCT, GRE General Test or MAT, interview, master's degree, official transcript, immunization records. Additional exam requirements/recommendations for international students: Required—TOEFL (minimum score 550 paper-based; 213 computer-based; 79 iBT), IELTS (minimum score 6), PTE: Pearson Test of English Academic (minimum score 56). *Application deadline:* For fall admission, 7/1 for domestic and international students; for spring admission, 11/15 for domestic students, 11/14 for international students. Applications are processed on a rolling basis. Application fee: $30 ($40 for international students). Electronic applications accepted. *Expenses:* Tuition, state resident: full-time $4044; part-time $225 per credit hour. Tuition, nonresident: full-time $8087; part-time $449 per credit hour. *Required fees:* $936; $52 per credit hour. $25 per term. One-time fee: $30. Tuition and fees vary according to course load and program. *Financial support:* In 2011–12, 5 students received support. Teaching assistantships, career-related internships or fieldwork, scholarships/grants, and unspecified assistantships available. Financial award application deadline: 7/1; financial award applicants required to submit FAFSA. *Unit head:* Dr. David Beasley, Interim Dean, 870-972-2085, Fax: 870-972-3885, E-mail: dbbeasley@astate.edu. *Application contact:* Dr. Andrew Sustich, Dean of the Graduate School, 870-972-3029, Fax: 870-972-3857, E-mail: sustich@astate.edu. Web site: http://www.astate.edu/agri/.

Auburn University, Graduate School, College of Agriculture, Auburn University, AL 36849. Offers M Ag, M Aq, MS, PhD. Part-time programs available. *Faculty:* 109 full-time (24 women), 10 part-time/adjunct (1 woman). *Students:* 134 full-time (57 women), 147 part-time (62 women); includes 22 minority (11 Black or African American, non-Hispanic/Latino; 7 Asian, non-Hispanic/Latino; 4 Hispanic/Latino), 122 international. Average age 29. 232 applicants, 51% accepted, 72 enrolled. In 2011, 38 master's, 20 doctorates awarded. *Degree requirements:* For doctorate, thesis/dissertation. *Entrance requirements:* For master's and doctorate, GRE General Test. *Application deadline:* For fall admission, 7/7 for domestic students; for spring admission, 11/24 for domestic students. Applications are processed on a rolling basis. Application fee: $50 ($60 for international students). Electronic applications accepted. *Expenses:* Tuition, state resident: full-time $7290; part-time $405 per credit hour. Tuition, nonresident: full-time $21,870; part-time $1215 per credit hour. *International tuition:* $22,000 full-time. *Required fees:* $1402. *Financial support:* Fellowships, research assistantships, teaching assistantships, and Federal Work-Study. Support available to part-time students. Financial award application deadline: 3/15; financial award applicants required to submit FAFSA. *Unit head:* William Batchelor, Dean, 334-844-2345. *Application contact:* Dr. George Flowers, Dean of the Graduate School, 334-844-2125. Web site: http://www.ag.auburn.edu/.

Brigham Young University, Graduate Studies, College of Life Sciences, Provo, UT 84602-1001. Offers MPH, MS, PhD. *Faculty:* 126 full-time (16 women), 4 part-time/adjunct (1 woman). *Students:* 186 full-time (72 women), 54 part-time (21 women); includes 36 minority (2 American Indian or Alaska Native, non-Hispanic/Latino; 13 Asian, non-Hispanic/Latino; 18 Hispanic/Latino; 3 Native Hawaiian or other Pacific Islander, non-Hispanic/Latino), 10 international. Average age 27. 157 applicants, 50% accepted, 62 enrolled. In 2011, 52 master's, 6 doctorates awarded. *Degree requirements:* For master's, comprehensive exam, thesis; for doctorate, comprehensive exam, thesis/dissertation. *Entrance requirements:* For master's and doctorate, GRE General Test, minimum GPA of 3.0 for last 60 hours of course work. Additional exam requirements/recommendations for international students: Required—TOEFL (minimum score 530 paper-based; 237 computer-based; 85 iBT), IELTS. *Application deadline:* For fall admission, 2/1 for domestic and international students. Application fee: $50. Electronic applications accepted. Full-time tuition for non-LDS students: $11,520 per year; $640 per credit. *Expenses: Tuition:* Full-time $5760; part-time $320 per credit. Tuition and fees vary according to student's religious affiliation. *Financial support:* In 2011–12, 201 students received support, including 29 fellowships with full and partial tuition reimbursements available (averaging $8,250 per year), 68 research assistantships with full and partial tuition reimbursements available (averaging $12,860 per year), 99 teaching assistantships with full and partial tuition reimbursements available (averaging $16,012 per year); scholarships/grants and tuition waivers (partial) also available. Financial award application deadline: 2/1. *Total annual research expenditures:* $4.7 million. *Unit head:* Dr. Rodney J. Brown, Dean, 801-422-3963, Fax: 801-422-0050. *Application contact:* Sue Pratley, Application Contact, 801-422-3963, Fax: 801-422-0050, E-mail: sue_pratley@byu.edu. Web site: http://lifesciences.byu.edu/home/.

California Polytechnic State University, San Luis Obispo, College of Agriculture, Food and Environmental Sciences, Program in Agriculture, San Luis Obispo, CA 93407. Offers MS. Part-time programs available. *Faculty:* 3 full-time (1 woman). *Students:* 37 full-time (27 women), 29 part-time (19 women); includes 13 minority (1 Black or African American, non-Hispanic/Latino; 2 American Indian or Alaska Native, non-Hispanic/Latino; 4 Asian, non-Hispanic/Latino; 4 Hispanic/Latino; 1 Native Hawaiian or other Pacific Islander, non-Hispanic/Latino; 1 Two or more races, non-Hispanic/Latino), 2 international. Average age 27. 54 applicants, 44% accepted, 18 enrolled. In 2011, 46 master's awarded. *Degree requirements:* For master's, comprehensive exam, thesis. *Entrance requirements:* For master's, GRE, minimum GPA of 2.75 in last 90 quarter units of course work. Additional exam requirements/recommendations for international students: Required—TOEFL (minimum score 550 paper-based; 213 computer-based) or IELTS (minimum score 6). *Application deadline:* For fall admission, 4/1 for domestic students, 11/30 for international students; for winter admission, 10/1 for domestic students, 6/30 for international students; for spring admission, 10/1 for domestic students. Applications are processed on a rolling basis. Application fee: $55. Electronic applications accepted. *Expenses:* Tuition, state resident: full-time $6738. Tuition, nonresident: full-time $17,898. *Required fees:* $2449. *Financial support:* Fellowships, research assistantships, teaching assistantships, career-related internships or fieldwork, Federal Work-Study, institutionally sponsored loans, scholarships/grants, and unspecified assistantships available. Support available to part-time students. Financial award application deadline: 3/2; financial award applicants required to submit FAFSA. *Faculty research:* Sustainability, specialty crops, dairy products technology, irrigation training, recreation, parks, and tourism management. *Unit head:* Dr. Mark Shelton, Associate Dean/Graduate Coordinator, 805-756-2161, Fax: 805-756-6577, E-mail: mshelton@calpoly.edu.

California State Polytechnic University, Pomona, Academic Affairs, College of Agriculture, Pomona, CA 91768-2557. Offers MS. Part-time programs available. *Faculty:* 33 full-time (14 women), 20 part-time/adjunct (16 women). *Students:* 10 full-time (all women), 39 part-time (36 women); includes 20 minority (2 Black or African American, non-Hispanic/Latino; 10 Asian, non-Hispanic/Latino; 6 Hispanic/Latino; 2 Two or more races, non-Hispanic/Latino), 3 international. Average age 29. 46 applicants, 54% accepted, 20 enrolled. In 2011, 11 master's awarded. *Degree requirements:* For master's, thesis or alternative. *Application deadline:* For fall admission, 5/1 priority date for domestic students; for winter admission, 10/15 priority date for domestic students; for spring admission, 1/2 priority date for domestic students. Applications are processed on a rolling basis. Application fee: $55. Electronic applications accepted. *Expenses:* Tuition, state resident: full-time $6738. Tuition, nonresident: full-time $12,300. *Required fees:* $657. Tuition and fees vary according to course load and program. *Financial*

398 facebook.com/petersonspublishing

Peterson's Graduate Programs in the Physical Sciences, Mathematics, Agricultural Sciences, the Environment & Natural Resources 2013

support: Career-related internships or fieldwork, Federal Work-Study, and institutionally sponsored loans available. Support available to part-time students. Financial award application deadline: 3/2; financial award applicants required to submit FAFSA. *Faculty research:* Equine nutrition, physiology, and reproduction; leadership development; bioartificial pancreas; plant science; ruminant and human nutrition. *Unit head:* Dr. Lester C. Young, Dean, 909-869-2203, E-mail: lcyoung@csupomona.edu. *Application contact:* Dan Hostetler, Chair/Professor, 909-869-2189, Fax: 909-869-5036, E-mail: dghostetler@csupomona.edu. Web site: http://www.csupomona.edu/~agri/.

Clemson University, Graduate School, College of Agriculture, Forestry and Life Sciences, Clemson, SC 29634. Offers M Ag Ed, MFR, MS, PhD. Part-time programs available. *Faculty:* 83 full-time (34 women), 16 part-time/adjunct (5 women). *Students:* 293 full-time (156 women), 83 part-time (46 women); includes 27 minority (9 Black or African American, non-Hispanic/Latino; 5 Asian, non-Hispanic/Latino; 9 Hispanic/Latino; 4 Two or more races, non-Hispanic/Latino), 86 international. Average age 31. 441 applicants, 31% accepted, 97 enrolled. In 2011, 56 master's, 29 doctorates awarded. Terminal master's awarded for partial completion of doctoral program. *Degree requirements:* For master's, thesis (for some programs); for doctorate, thesis/dissertation. *Entrance requirements:* For master's and doctorate, GRE General Test. Additional exam requirements/recommendations for international students: Required—TOEFL. *Application deadline:* For fall admission, 4/15 for domestic and international students; for spring admission, 10/1 for domestic students, 9/15 for international students. Applications are processed on a rolling basis. Application fee: $70 ($80 for international students). Electronic applications accepted. *Expenses:* Contact institution. *Financial support:* In 2011–12, 236 students received support, including 19 fellowships with full and partial tuition reimbursements available (averaging $2,500 per year), 141 research assistantships with partial tuition reimbursements available (averaging $1,359 per year), 121 teaching assistantships with partial tuition reimbursements available (averaging $1,570 per year); career-related internships or fieldwork, Federal Work-Study, institutionally sponsored loans, scholarships/grants, and unspecified assistantships also available. Financial award applicants required to submit FAFSA. *Total annual research expenditures:* $10.9 million. *Unit head:* Dr. Thomas Scott, Dean, 864-656-7592, Fax: 864-656-1286. *Application contact:* Dr. Joseph Culin, Associate Dean for Research and Graduate Studies, 864-656-2810, E-mail: jculin@clemson.edu. Web site: http://www.clemson.edu/cafls/.

Colorado State University, Graduate School, College of Agricultural Sciences, Fort Collins, CO 80523-1101. Offers M Agr, MLA, MS, PhD. Part-time and evening/weekend programs available. Postbaccalaureate distance learning degree programs offered (no on-campus study). *Faculty:* 102 full-time (19 women), 1 part-time/adjunct (0 women). *Students:* 156 full-time (73 women), 170 part-time (89 women); includes 23 minority (6 Black or African American, non-Hispanic/Latino; 3 American Indian or Alaska Native, non-Hispanic/Latino; 1 Asian, non-Hispanic/Latino; 10 Hispanic/Latino; 3 Two or more races, non-Hispanic/Latino), 54 international. Average age 31. 241 applicants, 69% accepted, 78 enrolled. In 2011, 75 master's, 12 doctorates awarded. *Degree requirements:* For master's, thesis (for some programs); for doctorate, comprehensive exam (for some programs), thesis/dissertation. *Entrance requirements:* For master's and doctorate, GRE General Test, minimum GPA of 3.0, 3 letters of recommendation, bachelor's degree. Additional exam requirements/recommendations for international students: Recommended—TOEFL (minimum score 550 paper-based; 150 computer-based). *Application deadline:* For fall admission, 7/1 for domestic and international students; for spring admission, 1/1 for domestic and international students. Applications are processed on a rolling basis. Application fee: $50. Electronic applications accepted. *Expenses:* Tuition, state resident: full-time $7992. Tuition, nonresident: full-time $19,592. *Required fees:* $1735; $58 per credit. *Financial support:* In 2011–12, 140 students received support, including 21 fellowships (averaging $29,337 per year), 86 research assistantships (averaging $14,540 per year), 27 teaching assistantships (averaging $11,072 per year); scholarships/grants and unspecified assistantships also available. Financial award applicants required to submit FAFSA. *Faculty research:* Systems methodology, biotechnology, plant and animal breeding, water management, plant protection. *Total annual research expenditures:* $13.8 million. *Unit head:* Dr. Craig Beyrouty, Dean, 970-491-6274, Fax: 970-491-4895, E-mail: craig.beyrouty@colostate.edu. *Application contact:* Pam Schell, Administrative Assistant, 970-491-2410, Fax: 970-491-4895, E-mail: pam.schell@colostate.edu. Web site: http://www.agsci.colostate.edu/.

Dalhousie University, Faculty of Graduate Studies, Nova Scotia Agricultural College, Truro, NS B2N 5E3, Canada. Offers M Sc. Part-time programs available. *Degree requirements:* For master's, thesis, candidacy exam. *Entrance requirements:* For master's, minimum GPA of 3.0. Additional exam requirements/recommendations for international students: Required—1 of 5 approved tests: TOEFL, IELTS, CANTEST, CAEL, Michigan English Language Assessment Battery. Electronic applications accepted. *Faculty research:* Agribiology, soil science, animal science, plant science, and agricultural chemistry.

Illinois State University, Graduate School, College of Applied Science and Technology, Department of Agriculture, Normal, IL 61790-2200. Offers agribusiness (MS). *Degree requirements:* For master's, thesis optional. *Entrance requirements:* For master's, GRE General Test, minimum GPA of 3.0 in last 60 hours. *Faculty research:* Engineering-economic system models for rural ethanol production facilities, development and evaluation of a propane-fueled, production

scale, on-site thermal destruction system C-FAR 2007; field scale evaluation and technology transfer of economically, ecologically systems; sound liquid swine manure treatment and application.

Instituto Tecnológico y de Estudios Superiores de Monterrey, Campus Monterrey, Graduate and Research Division, Program in Agriculture, Monterrey, Mexico. Offers agricultural parasitology (PhD); agricultural sciences (MS); farming productivity (MS); food processing engineering (MS); phytopathology (MS). Part-time programs available. *Degree requirements:* For master's, one foreign language, thesis; for doctorate, one foreign language, thesis/dissertation. *Entrance requirements:* For master's, EXADEP; for doctorate, GMAT or GRE, master's degree in related field. Additional exam requirements/recommendations for international students: Required—TOEFL. *Faculty research:* Animal embryos and reproduction, crop entomology, tropical agriculture, agricultural productivity, induced mutation in oleaginous plants.

Iowa State University of Science and Technology, Program in Sustainable Agriculture, Ames, IA 50011-1020. Offers MS, PhD. *Entrance requirements:* For master's and doctorate, GRE General Test. Additional exam requirements/recommendations for international students: Required—TOEFL (minimum score 570 paper-based; 80 iBT), IELTS (minimum score 6.5). *Application deadline:* For fall admission, 2/1 for domestic and international students; for spring admission, 6/1 priority date for domestic students, 6/1 for international students. Application fee: $40 ($90 for international students). Electronic applications accepted. *Unit head:* Dr. Mike Duffy, Director of Graduate Education, 515-294-6518, Fax: 515-294-1337, E-mail: gpsa@iastate.edu. *Application contact:* Charles Sauer, Information Contact, 515-294-6518, Fax: 515-294-1337, E-mail: gpsa@iastate.edu. Web site: http://www.sust.ag.iastate.edu/gpsa/application.html.

Kansas State University, Graduate School, College of Agriculture, Manhattan, KS 66506. Offers MAB, MS, PhD. Part-time programs available. Postbaccalaureate distance learning degree programs offered (minimal on-campus study). *Faculty:* 172 full-time (33 women), 44 part-time/adjunct (5 women). *Students:* 359 full-time (145 women), 135 part-time (74 women); includes 41 minority (14 Black or African American, non-Hispanic/Latino; 2 American Indian or Alaska Native, non-Hispanic/Latino; 10 Asian, non-Hispanic/Latino; 14 Hispanic/Latino; 1 Two or more races, non-Hispanic/Latino), 147 international. Average age 30. 275 applicants, 50% accepted, 73 enrolled. In 2011, 103 master's, 32 doctorates awarded. Terminal master's awarded for partial completion of doctoral program. *Degree requirements:* For doctorate, thesis/dissertation. *Entrance requirements:* For master's, GRE, minimum undergraduate GPA of 3.0; for doctorate, GRE, minimum undergraduate GPA of 3.5. Additional exam requirements/recommendations for international students: Required—TOEFL (minimum score 550 paper-based; 213 computer-based). *Application deadline:* For fall admission, 2/1 priority date for domestic students, 2/1 for international students; for spring admission, 8/1 priority date for domestic students, 8/1 for international students. Applications are processed on a rolling basis. Application fee: $40 ($55 for international students). Electronic applications accepted. *Financial support:* In 2011–12, 258 research assistantships (averaging $20,435 per year), 29 teaching assistantships (averaging $18,437 per year) were awarded; career-related internships or fieldwork, Federal Work-Study, institutionally sponsored loans, scholarships/grants, and tuition waivers (partial) also available. Support available to part-time students. Financial award application deadline: 3/1; financial award applicants required to submit FAFSA. *Total annual research expenditures:* $24.2 million. *Unit head:* Gary M. Pierzynski, Interim Dean, 785-532-6101, Fax: 785-532-6563, E-mail: gmp@ksu.edu. *Application contact:* Shannon Fox, Administrative Assistant, 785-532-6191, Fax: 785-532-2983, E-mail: grad@ksu.edu. Web site: http://www.ag.k-state.edu.

Louisiana State University and Agricultural and Mechanical College, Graduate School, College of Agriculture, Baton Rouge, LA 70803. Offers M App St, MS, MSBAE, PhD. Part-time programs available. *Students:* 347 full-time (175 women), 150 part-time (82 women); includes 53 minority (34 Black or African American, non-Hispanic/Latino; 5 Asian, non-Hispanic/Latino; 13 Hispanic/Latino; 1 Two or more races, non-Hispanic/Latino), 156 international. Average age 32. 243 applicants, 44% accepted, 74 enrolled. In 2011, 84 master's, 51 doctorates awarded. Terminal master's awarded for partial completion of doctoral program. *Degree requirements:* For doctorate, thesis/dissertation. *Entrance requirements:* For master's and doctorate, GRE General Test, minimum GPA of 3.0. Additional exam requirements/recommendations for international students: Required—TOEFL (minimum score 550 paper-based; 213 computer-based; 79 iBT) or IELTS (minimum score 6.5). *Application deadline:* For fall admission, 5/15 for domestic and international students; for spring admission, 10/15 for domestic and international students. Applications are processed on a rolling basis. Application fee: $50 ($70 for international students). Electronic applications accepted. *Financial support:* In 2011–12, 411 students received support, including 4 fellowships with full tuition reimbursements available (averaging $15,996 per year), 226 research assistantships with partial tuition reimbursements available (averaging $17,738 per year), 51 teaching assistantships with partial tuition reimbursements available (averaging $12,923 per year); career-related internships or fieldwork, Federal Work-Study, institutionally sponsored loans, health care benefits, tuition waivers (full), and unspecified assistantships also available. Support available to part-time students. Financial award applicants required to submit FAFSA. *Faculty research:* Biotechnology, resource economics and marketing, aquaculture, food science and technology. *Total annual research expenditures:* $391,005. *Unit head:* Dr. Kenneth Koonce, Dean, 225-578-2362, Fax: 225-578-2526, E-mail: kkoonce@lsu.edu. *Application contact:* Paula

Peterson's Graduate Programs in the Physical Sciences, Mathematics, Agricultural Sciences, the Environment & Natural Resources 2013

facebook.com/petersonspublishing **399**

SECTION 8: AGRICULTURAL AND FOOD SCIENCES

Agricultural Sciences—General

Beecher, Recruiting Coordinator, 225-578-2468, E-mail: pbeeche@lsu.edu. Web site: http://www.coa.lsu.edu/.

McGill University, Faculty of Graduate and Postdoctoral Studies, Faculty of Agricultural and Environmental Sciences, Montréal, QC H3A 2T5, Canada. Offers M Sc, M Sc A, PhD, Certificate, Graduate Diploma.

McNeese State University, Doré School of Graduate Studies, College of Science, Department of Agricultural Sciences, Program in Environmental and Chemical Sciences, Lake Charles, LA 70609. Offers agricultural sciences (MS); environmental science (MS). Evening/weekend programs available. *Faculty:* 12 full-time (1 woman). *Students:* 23 full-time (13 women), 10 part-time (5 women); includes 6 minority (4 Black or African American, non-Hispanic/Latino; 1 American Indian or Alaska Native, non-Hispanic/Latino; 1 Hispanic/Latino), 1 international. In 2011, 13 master's awarded. *Degree requirements:* For master's, comprehensive exam, thesis or alternative. *Entrance requirements:* For master's, GRE. *Application deadline:* For fall admission, 5/15 priority date for domestic students, 5/15 for international students; for spring admission, 10/15 priority date for domestic students, 10/15 for international students. Applications are processed on a rolling basis. Application fee: $20 ($30 for international students). *Expenses:* Tuition, state resident: part-time $519 per credit hour. Tuition and fees vary according to course load. *Financial support:* Application deadline: 5/1. *Unit head:* Dr. Bruce C. Wyman, Coordinator, 337-475-5669, Fax: 337-475-5677, E-mail: wyman@mcneese.edu. *Application contact:* Dr. Bruce C. Wyman, Coordinator, 337-475-5669, Fax: 337-475-5677, E-mail: wyman@mcneese.edu.

Michigan State University, The Graduate School, College of Agriculture and Natural Resources, East Lansing, MI 48824. Offers MA, MIPS, MS, MURP, PhD. *Faculty research:* Plant science, animal sciences, forestry, fisheries and wildlife, recreation and tourism.

Mississippi State University, College of Agriculture and Life Sciences, Department of Biochemistry, Molecular Biology, Entomology and Plant Pathology, Mississippi State, MS 39762. Offers agriculture life sciences (MS), including entomology and plant pathology; molecular biology (PhD). *Faculty:* 25 full-time (1 woman). *Students:* 46 full-time (17 women), 14 part-time (6 women); includes 4 minority (2 Black or African American, non-Hispanic/Latino; 2 Two or more races, non-Hispanic/Latino), 18 international. Average age 30. 43 applicants, 33% accepted, 13 enrolled. In 2011, 7 master's, 5 doctorates awarded. Terminal master's awarded for partial completion of doctoral program. *Degree requirements:* For master's, thesis (for some programs), comprehensive oral or written exam; for doctorate, thesis/dissertation, comprehensive oral and written exam. *Entrance requirements:* For master's, GRE General Test, minimum GPA of 2.75; for doctorate, GRE. Additional exam requirements/recommendations for international students: Required—TOEFL (minimum score 550 paper-based; 213 computer-based; 79 iBT); Recommended—IELTS (minimum score 6.5). *Application deadline:* For fall admission, 7/1 for domestic students, 5/1 for international students; for spring admission, 11/1 for domestic students, 9/1 for international students. Applications are processed on a rolling basis. Application fee: $40. Electronic applications accepted. *Expenses:* Tuition, state resident: full-time $5805; part-time $322.50 per credit hour. Tuition, nonresident: full-time $14,670; part-time $815 per credit hour. *Financial support:* In 2011–12, 41 research assistantships with full tuition reimbursements (averaging $15,714 per year) were awarded; Federal Work-Study, institutionally sponsored loans, and unspecified assistantships also available. Financial award application deadline: 4/1; financial award applicants required to submit FAFSA. *Faculty research:* Fish nutrition, plant and animal molecular biology, plant biochemistry, enzymology, lipid metabolism, chromatin, cell wall synthesis in rice, a model grass bioenergy species and the source of rice stover residues, using reverse genetic and functional genomic and proteomic approaches. *Unit head:* Dr. Scott T. Willard, Professor and Department Head, 662-325-2640, Fax: 662-325-8664, E-mail: swilliard@ads.msstate.edu. *Application contact:* Dr. Din-Pow Ma, Professor/ Graduate Coordinator, 662-325-7739, Fax: 662-325-8664, E-mail: dm1@ ra.msstate.edu.

Mississippi State University, College of Agriculture and Life Sciences, Department of Plant and Soil Sciences, Mississippi State, MS 39762. Offers agriculture (MS), including agronomy, horticulture, weed science. *Faculty:* 30 full-time (1 woman), 1 part-time/adjunct (0 women). *Students:* 34 full-time (11 women), 21 part-time (5 women); includes 5 minority (3 Black or African American, non-Hispanic/Latino; 2 American Indian or Alaska Native, non-Hispanic/Latino), 13 international. Average age 30. 33 applicants, 42% accepted, 12 enrolled. In 2011, 6 master's awarded. *Degree requirements:* For master's, thesis, exit seminar describing thesis research. *Entrance requirements:* For master's, GRE (weed science), minimum GPA of 2.75 (agronomy/horticulture), 3.0 (weed science). Additional exam requirements/recommendations for international students: Required—TOEFL (minimum score 550 paper-based; 213 computer-based; 79 iBT); Recommended—IELTS (minimum score 6.5). *Application deadline:* For fall admission, 7/1 for domestic students, 5/1 for international students; for spring admission, 10/1 for domestic students, 9/1 for international students. Applications are processed on a rolling basis. Application fee: $40. Electronic applications accepted. *Expenses:* Tuition, state resident: full-time $5805; part-time $322.50 per credit hour. Tuition, nonresident: full-time $14,670; part-time $815 per credit hour. *Financial support:* In 2011–12, 30 research assistantships (averaging $14,692 per year), 3 teaching assistantships (averaging $15,133 per year) were awarded; Federal Work-Study, institutionally sponsored loans, scholarships/grants, and unspecified assistantships also available. Financial award application deadline: 4/1; financial award applicants

required to submit FAFSA. *Unit head:* Dr. J. Mike Phillips, Professor and Head, 662-325-2311, Fax: 662-325-8742, E-mail: jmp657@msstate.edu. *Application contact:* Dr. William Kingery, Graduate Coordinator, 662-325-2748, Fax: 662-325-8742, E-mail: wkingery@pss.msstate.edu. Web site: http://www.pss.msstate.edu/

Mississippi State University, College of Agriculture and Life Sciences, School of Human Sciences, Mississippi State, MS 39762. Offers agricultural sciences (PhD), including agriculture and extension education; agriculture and extension education (MS). *Accreditation:* NCATE (one or more programs are accredited). Part-time programs available. *Faculty:* 14 full-time (7 women). *Students:* 7 full-time (3 women), 48 part-time (34 women); includes 12 minority (all Black or African American, non-Hispanic/Latino), 2 international. Average age 37. 14 applicants, 79% accepted, 10 enrolled. In 2011, 13 master's, 1 doctorate awarded. *Degree requirements:* For master's, thesis optional, comprehensive oral or written exam. *Entrance requirements:* For master's, GRE, minimum GPA of 2.75 in last 4 semesters of course work; for doctorate, minimum GPA of 3.0 on prior graduate work. Additional exam requirements/recommendations for international students: Required—TOEFL (minimum score 475 paper-based; 153 computer-based; 53 iBT); Recommended—IELTS (minimum score 4.5). *Application deadline:* For fall admission, 7/1 for domestic students, 5/1 for international students; for spring admission, 11/1 for domestic students, 9/1 for international students. Applications are processed on a rolling basis. Application fee: $40. Electronic applications accepted. *Expenses:* Tuition, state resident: full-time $5805; part-time $322.50 per credit hour. Tuition, nonresident: full-time $14,670; part-time $815 per credit hour. *Financial support:* In 2011–12, 3 research assistantships (averaging $12,543 per year), 3 teaching assistantships with full tuition reimbursements (averaging $12,536 per year) were awarded; Federal Work-Study, institutionally sponsored loans, and unspecified assistantships also available. Financial award application deadline: 4/1; financial award applicants required to submit FAFSA. *Faculty research:* Animal welfare, agroscience, information technology, learning styles, problem solving. *Unit head:* Dr. Michael Newman, Director and Professor, 662-325-2950, E-mail: mnewman@ humansci.msstate.edu. *Application contact:* Dr. Jacquelyn Deeds, Professor and Graduate Coordinator, 662-325-7834, E-mail: jdeeds@ais.msstate.edu. Web site: http://www.humansci.msstate.edu.

Missouri State University, Graduate College, William H. Darr School of Agriculture, Springfield, MO 65897. Offers plant science (MS); secondary education (MS Ed), including agriculture. Part-time programs available. *Faculty:* 14 full-time (3 women), 1 part-time/adjunct (0 women). *Students:* 15 full-time (9 women), 15 part-time (8 women), 4 international. Average age 29. 19 applicants, 100% accepted, 14 enrolled. In 2011, 9 master's awarded. *Degree requirements:* For master's, comprehensive exam, thesis or alternative. *Entrance requirements:* For master's, GRE (MS in plant science, MNAS), 9-12 teacher certification (MS Ed), minimum GPA of 3.0 (MS plant science, MNAS). Additional exam requirements/recommendations for international students: Required—TOEFL (minimum score 550 paper-based; 213 computer-based; 79 iBT). *Application deadline:* For fall admission, 7/20 priority date for domestic students, 5/1 for international students; for spring admission, 12/20 priority date for domestic students, 9/1 for international students. Applications are processed on a rolling basis. Application fee: $35 ($50 for international students). Electronic applications accepted. *Expenses:* Tuition, state resident: full-time $4086; part-time $227 per credit hour. Tuition, nonresident: full-time $8172; part-time $454 per credit hour. *Required fees:* $275 per semester. Tuition and fees vary according to course load, campus/location and program. *Financial support:* In 2011–12, 6 research assistantships with full tuition reimbursements (averaging $8,288 per year), 3 teaching assistantships with full tuition reimbursements (averaging $8,576 per year) were awarded; Federal Work-Study, institutionally sponsored loans, scholarships/grants, and unspecified assistantships also available. Financial award application deadline: 3/31; financial award applicants required to submit FAFSA. *Faculty research:* Grapevine biotechnology, agricultural marketing, Asian elephant reproduction, poultry science, integrated pest management. *Unit head:* Dr. W. Anson Elliott, Head, 417-836-5638, E-mail: ansonelliot@ missouristate.edu. *Application contact:* Misty Stewart, Coordinator of Graduate Recruitment, 417-836-6079, Fax: 417-836-6200, E-mail: mistystewart@ missouristate.edu. Web site: http://ag.missouristate.edu/.

Montana State University, College of Graduate Studies, College of Agriculture, Bozeman, MT 59717. Offers MS, PhD. Part-time programs available. Postbaccalaureate distance learning degree programs offered (minimal on-campus study). *Degree requirements:* For master's, comprehensive exam; for doctorate, comprehensive exam, thesis/dissertation. *Entrance requirements:* For master's and doctorate, GRE General Test. Additional exam requirements/recommendations for international students: Required—TOEFL (minimum score 550 paper-based; 213 computer-based). Electronic applications accepted.

Morehead State University, Graduate Programs, College of Science and Technology, Department of Agricultural Sciences, Morehead, KY 40351. Offers career and technical agricultural education (MS). Part-time and evening/weekend programs available. *Degree requirements:* For master's, comprehensive exam, thesis or alternative, exit exam. *Entrance requirements:* For master's, GRE, minimum GPA of 3.0 for undergraduate major. Additional exam requirements/recommendations for international students: Required—TOEFL (minimum score 500 paper-based; 173 computer-based). Electronic applications accepted.

Murray State University, School of Agriculture, Murray, KY 42071. Offers agriculture (MS); agriculture education (MS). Evening/weekend programs

400 facebook.com/petersonspublishing

Peterson's Graduate Programs in the Physical Sciences, Mathematics, Agricultural Sciences, the Environment & Natural Resources 2013

available. Postbaccalaureate distance learning degree programs offered (minimal on-campus study). *Degree requirements:* For master's, comprehensive exam, thesis (for some programs). *Entrance requirements:* Additional exam requirements/recommendations for international students: Required—TOEFL. *Faculty research:* Ultrasound in beef, corn and soybean research, tobacco research.

New Mexico State University, Graduate School, College of Agricultural, Consumer and Environmental Sciences, Department of Entomology, Plant Pathology and Weed Science, Las Cruces, NM 88003-8001. Offers agricultural biology (MS). Part-time programs available. *Faculty:* 6 full-time (2 women), 2 part-time/adjunct (0 women). *Students:* 11 full-time (3 women), 5 part-time (2 women); includes 5 minority (4 Hispanic/Latino; 1 Two or more races, non-Hispanic/Latino), 3 international. Average age 26. 6 applicants, 67% accepted, 4 enrolled. In 2011, 5 master's awarded. *Degree requirements:* For master's, comprehensive exam, thesis. *Entrance requirements:* For master's, GRE General Test. Additional exam requirements/recommendations for international students: Required—TOEFL (minimum score 550 paper-based; 0 computer-based; 79 iBT), IELTS (minimum score 6.5). *Application deadline:* For fall admission, 7/1 priority date for domestic students; for spring admission, 11/1 priority date for domestic students. Applications are processed on a rolling basis. Application fee: $40 ($50 for international students). Electronic applications accepted. *Expenses:* Tuition, state resident: full-time $5004; part-time $208.50 per credit. Tuition, nonresident: full-time $17,446; part-time $726.90 per credit. *Financial support:* In 2011–12, 9 students received support, including 2 fellowships (averaging $4,304 per year), 9 research assistantships with full tuition reimbursements available (averaging $20,235 per year); teaching assistantships with partial tuition reimbursements available, career-related internships or fieldwork, and health care benefits also available. Financial award application deadline: 3/1. *Faculty research:* Integrated pest management, pesticide application and safety, livestock ectoparasite research, biotechnology, nematology. *Unit head:* Dr. Jill Schroeder, Interim Head, 575-646-3225, Fax: 575-646-8087, E-mail: jischroe@nmsu.edu. *Application contact:* Cindy Bullard, Intermediate Administrative Assistant, 575-646-1145, Fax: 575-646-8087, E-mail: cbullard@nmsu.edu. Web site: http://eppws.nmsu.edu/.

North Carolina Agricultural and Technical State University, School of Graduate Studies, School of Agriculture and Environmental Sciences, Greensboro, NC 27411. Offers MAT, MS. Part-time and evening/weekend programs available. *Degree requirements:* For master's, comprehensive exam, qualifying exam. *Entrance requirements:* For master's, GRE General Test. *Faculty research:* Aid for small farmers, agricultural technology, housing, food science, nutrition.

North Carolina State University, Graduate School, College of Agriculture and Life Sciences, Raleigh, NC 27695. Offers M Tox, MAE, MB, MBAE, MFG, MFM, MFS, MG, MMB, MN, MP, MS, MZS, Ed D, PhD, Certificate. Part-time programs available. Electronic applications accepted.

North Dakota State University, College of Graduate and Interdisciplinary Studies, College of Agriculture, Food Systems, and Natural Resources, Fargo, ND 58108. Offers MS, PhD. Part-time programs available. *Faculty:* 87 full-time (21 women), 1 part-time/adjunct (0 women). *Students:* 159 full-time (77 women), 57 part-time (26 women); includes 4 minority (2 Hispanic/Latino; 2 Two or more races, non-Hispanic/Latino), 109 international. 108 applicants, 59% accepted, 34 enrolled. *Degree requirements:* For doctorate, thesis/dissertation. *Entrance requirements:* Additional exam requirements/recommendations for international students: Required—TOEFL. *Application deadline:* Applications are processed on a rolling basis. Application fee: $35. Electronic applications accepted. *Financial support:* Fellowships with full tuition reimbursements, research assistantships with full tuition reimbursements, teaching assistantships with full tuition reimbursements, career-related internships or fieldwork, Federal Work-Study, and institutionally sponsored loans available. Support available to part-time students. *Faculty research:* Horticulture and forestry, plant and wheat breeding, diseases of insects, animal and range sciences, soil science, veterinary medicine. *Unit head:* Dr. Kenneth F. Grafton, Dean, 701-231-8790, Fax: 701-231-8520, E-mail: k.grafton@ndsu.edu. *Application contact:* Sonya Goergen, Marketing, Recruitment, and Public Relations Coordinator, 701-231-7033, Fax: 701-231-6524. Web site: http://www.ag.ndsu.nodak.edu/.

Northwest Missouri State University, Graduate School, Melvin and Valorie Booth College of Business and Professional Studies, Department of Agriculture, Maryville, MO 64468-6001. Offers agricultural economics (MBA); agriculture (MS); teaching agriculture (MS Ed). Part-time programs available. *Faculty:* 7 full-time (2 women). *Students:* 10 full-time (5 women), 4 part-time (1 woman). 10 applicants, 100% accepted, 6 enrolled. In 2011, 6 master's awarded. *Degree requirements:* For master's, comprehensive exam, thesis (for some programs). *Entrance requirements:* For master's, GRE General Test, minimum undergraduate GPA of 2.5, writing sample. Additional exam requirements/recommendations for international students: Required—TOEFL (minimum score 550 paper-based; 213 computer-based). *Application deadline:* For fall admission, 7/1 for domestic and international students; for spring admission, 11/15 for domestic and international students. Applications are processed on a rolling basis. Application fee: $0 ($50 for international students). *Financial support:* In 2011–12, 4 research assistantships with full tuition reimbursements (averaging $6,000 per year), 2 teaching assistantships with full tuition reimbursements (averaging $6,000 per year) were awarded; unspecified assistantships also available. Financial award application deadline: 4/1; financial award applicants required to submit FAFSA. *Unit head:* Dr. Arley Larson, Chairperson, 660-562-

1161. *Application contact:* Dr. Gregory Haddock, Dean of Graduate School, 660-562-1145, Fax: 660-562-1096, E-mail: gradsch@nwmissouri.edu.

Nova Scotia Agricultural College, Research and Graduate Studies, Truro, NS B2N 5E3, Canada. Offers agriculture (M Sc), including air quality, animal behavior, animal molecular genetics, animal nutrition, animal technology, aquaculture, botany, crop management, crop physiology, ecology, environmental microbiology, food science, horticulture, nutrient management, pest management, physiology, plant biotechnology, plant pathology, soil chemistry, soil fertility, waste management and composting, water quality. Program offered jointly with Dalhousie University. Part-time programs available. *Degree requirements:* For master's, thesis, ATC Exam Teaching Assistantship. *Entrance requirements:* For master's, honors B Sc, minimum GPA of 3.0. Additional exam requirements/recommendations for international students: Required—TOEFL (minimum score 580 paper-based; 237 computer-based; 92 iBT), IELTS, Michigan English Language Assessment Battery, CanTEST, CAEL. *Faculty research:* Bio-product development, organic agriculture, nutrient management, air and water quality, agricultural biotechnology.

The Ohio State University, Graduate School, College of Food, Agricultural, and Environmental Sciences, Columbus, OH 43210. Offers M Ed, MS, PhD. Part-time programs available. *Faculty:* 320. *Students:* 394 full-time (214 women), 157 part-time (91 women); includes 47 minority (13 Black or African American, non-Hispanic/Latino; 17 Asian, non-Hispanic/Latino; 14 Hispanic/Latino; 3 Two or more races, non-Hispanic/Latino), 195 international. Average age 29. In 2011, 53 master's, 51 doctorates awarded. *Degree requirements:* For doctorate, thesis/dissertation. *Entrance requirements:* Additional exam requirements/recommendations for international students: Required—TOEFL (minimum score 550 paper-based; 213 computer-based), IELTS (minimum score 6.5), or Michigan English Language Assessment Battery (minimum score 82). *Application deadline:* For fall admission, 8/15 priority date for domestic students, 7/1 for international students; for winter admission, 12/1 priority date for domestic students, 11/1 for international students; for spring admission, 3/1 priority date for domestic students, 2/1 for international students. Applications are processed on a rolling basis. Application fee: $40 ($50 for international students). Electronic applications accepted. *Expenses:* Tuition, state resident: full-time $11,400. Tuition, nonresident: full-time $28,125. Tuition and fees vary according to course load, degree level, campus/location and program. *Financial support:* Fellowships, research assistantships, teaching assistantships, career-related internships or fieldwork, Federal Work-Study, institutionally sponsored loans, and unspecified assistantships available. Support available to part-time students. *Unit head:* Bobby D. Moser, Dean, 614-292-4218, Fax: 614-292-0452, E-mail: moser.2@osu.edu. *Application contact:* Graduate Admissions, 614-292-6031, Fax: 614-292-3656, E-mail: gradadmissions@osu.edu. Web site: http://cfaes.osu.edu/.

Oklahoma State University, College of Agricultural Science and Natural Resources, Stillwater, OK 74078. Offers M Ag, MS, PhD. Postbaccalaureate distance learning degree programs offered. *Faculty:* 238 full-time (54 women), 14 part-time/adjunct (2 women). *Students:* 163 full-time (79 women), 331 part-time (164 women); includes 53 minority (9 Black or African American, non-Hispanic/Latino; 15 American Indian or Alaska Native, non-Hispanic/Latino; 6 Asian, non-Hispanic/Latino; 10 Hispanic/Latino; 13 Two or more races, non-Hispanic/Latino), 178 international. Average age 29. 499 applicants, 29% accepted, 83 enrolled. In 2011, 120 master's, 33 doctorates awarded. *Degree requirements:* For master's, thesis (for some programs); for doctorate, comprehensive exam, thesis/dissertation. *Entrance requirements:* For master's and doctorate, GRE or GMAT. Additional exam requirements/recommendations for international students: Required—TOEFL (minimum score 550 paper-based; 79 iBT). *Application deadline:* For fall admission, 3/1 for international students; for spring admission, 8/1 for international students. Applications are processed on a rolling basis. Application fee: $40 ($75 for international students). Electronic applications accepted. *Expenses:* Tuition, state resident: full-time $4044; part-time $168.50 per credit hour. Tuition, nonresident: full-time $16,008; part-time $667 per credit hour. *Required fees:* $2122; $88.45 per credit hour. One-time fee: $50. Tuition and fees vary according to course load and campus/location. *Financial support:* In 2011–12, 281 research assistantships (averaging $16,006 per year), 23 teaching assistantships (averaging $14,476 per year) were awarded; fellowships, career-related internships or fieldwork, Federal Work-Study, scholarships/grants, health care benefits, tuition waivers (partial), and unspecified assistantships also available. Support available to part-time students. Financial award application deadline: 3/1; financial award applicants required to submit FAFSA. *Unit head:* Dr. Robert E. Whitson, Dean, 405-744-5398, Fax: 405-744-2480. *Application contact:* Dr. Sheryl Tucker, Dean, 405-744-7099, Fax: 405-744-0355, E-mail: grad-i@okstate.edu. Web site: http://www.dasnr.okstate.edu.

Oregon State University, Graduate School, College of Agricultural Sciences, Corvallis, OR 97331. Offers M Ag, M Agr, MA, MAIS, MAT, MS, PhD. Part-time programs available. Terminal master's awarded for partial completion of doctoral program. *Degree requirements:* For doctorate, thesis/dissertation. *Entrance requirements:* For master's and doctorate, GRE, minimum GPA of 3.0 in last 90 hours of course work. Additional exam requirements/recommendations for international students: Required—TOEFL. *Faculty research:* Fish and wildlife biology, food science, soil/water/plant relationships, natural resources, animal biochemistry.

Penn State University Park, Graduate School, College of Agricultural Sciences, State College, University Park, PA 16802-1503. Offers M Agr, M Ed, MFR, MPS, MS, PhD, Certificate. *Students:* 337 full-time (199 women), 44 part-time (20

Peterson's Graduate Programs in the Physical Sciences, Mathematics, Agricultural Sciences, the Environment & Natural Resources 2013

facebook.com/petersonspublishing **401**

Agricultural Sciences—General

women). Average age 28. 610 applicants, 27% accepted, 112 enrolled. In 2011, 74 master's, 44 doctorates awarded. *Entrance requirements:* Additional exam requirements/recommendations for international students: Required—TOEFL (minimum score 550 paper-based; 213 computer-based; 80 iBT). *Application deadline:* Applications are processed on a rolling basis. Application fee: $65. Electronic applications accepted. *Financial support:* Fellowships, research assistantships, and teaching assistantships available. Financial award applicants required to submit FAFSA. *Unit head:* Dr. Bruce A. McPheron, Dean, 814-865-2541, Fax: 814-865-3103, E-mail: bam10@psu.edu. *Application contact:* Cynthia E. Nicosia, Director of Graduate Enrollment Services, 814-865-1834, E-mail: cey1@psu.edu. Web site: http://agsci.psu.edu/.

Prairie View A&M University, College of Agriculture and Human Sciences, Prairie View, TX 77446-0519. Offers agricultural economics (MS); animal sciences (MS); interdisciplinary human sciences (MS); soil science (MS). Part-time and evening/weekend programs available. *Degree requirements:* For master's, comprehensive exam, thesis (for some programs), field placement. *Entrance requirements:* For master's, GRE General Test, minimum GPA of 2.45. Additional exam requirements/recommendations for international students: Required—TOEFL (minimum score 550 paper-based). *Faculty research:* Domestic violence prevention, water quality, food growth regulators, wetland dynamics, biochemistry, obesity and nutrition, family therapy.

Purdue University, Graduate School, College of Agriculture, West Lafayette, IN 47907. Offers EMBA, M Agr, MA, MS, MSF, PhD. Part-time programs available. *Faculty:* 283 full-time (51 women), 67 part-time/adjunct (16 women). *Students:* 470 full-time (234 women), 126 part-time (45 women); includes 48 minority (11 Black or African American, non-Hispanic/Latino; 3 American Indian or Alaska Native, non-Hispanic/Latino; 10 Asian, non-Hispanic/Latino; 16 Hispanic/Latino; 8 Two or more races, non-Hispanic/Latino), 234 international. Average age 29. 840 applicants, 32% accepted, 147 enrolled. In 2011, 138 master's, 68 doctorates awarded. *Degree requirements:* For doctorate, thesis/dissertation. *Entrance requirements:* Additional exam requirements/recommendations for international students: Required—TOEFL. *Application deadline:* Applications are processed on a rolling basis. Application fee: $60 ($75 for international students). Electronic applications accepted. *Financial support:* Fellowships with tuition reimbursements, research assistantships with tuition reimbursements, teaching assistantships with tuition reimbursements, career-related internships or fieldwork, and tuition waivers (partial) available. Support available to part-time students. Financial award applicants required to submit FAFSA. *Unit head:* Dr. Jay W. Akridge, Dean, 765-494-8391, E-mail: akridge@purdue.edu. Web site: http://www.ag.purdue.edu/Pages/default.aspx.

Sam Houston State University, College of Sciences, Department of Agricultural and Industrial Sciences, Huntsville, TX 77341. Offers agriculture (MS). Part-time and evening/weekend programs available. *Faculty:* 15 full-time (2 women). *Students:* 21 full-time (11 women), 9 part-time (4 women); includes 4 minority (1 Asian, non-Hispanic/Latino; 3 Hispanic/Latino), 1 international. Average age 26. 21 applicants, 62% accepted, 8 enrolled. In 2011, 22 master's awarded. *Degree requirements:* For master's, thesis optional. *Entrance requirements:* For master's, GRE General Test, minimum GPA of 2.5. Additional exam requirements/recommendations for international students: Required—TOEFL (minimum score 550 paper-based; 213 computer-based; 79 iBT). *Application deadline:* For fall admission, 8/1 for domestic students, 6/25 for international students; for spring admission, 12/1 for domestic students, 11/12 for international students. Applications are processed on a rolling basis. Application fee: $45 ($75 for international students). Electronic applications accepted. *Expenses:* Tuition, state resident: full-time $4420; part-time $221 per credit hour. Tuition, nonresident: full-time $10,680; part-time $534 per credit hour. *Required fees:* $329 per credit hour. *Financial support:* Research assistantships and teaching assistantships available. Financial award application deadline: 5/31; financial award applicants required to submit FAFSA. *Unit head:* Dr. Stanley F. Kelley, Chair, 936-294-1189, Fax: 936-294-1232, E-mail: sfkelley@shsu.edu. *Application contact:* Tammy Gray, Advisor, 936-294-1230, E-mail: dca_tag@shsu.edu. Web site: http://www.shsu.edu/~agr_www/.

South Dakota State University, Graduate School, College of Agriculture and Biological Sciences, Brookings, SD 57007. Offers MS, PhD. Part-time programs available. *Degree requirements:* For master's, thesis, oral exam; for doctorate, thesis/dissertation, preliminary oral and written exams. *Entrance requirements:* Additional exam requirements/recommendations for international students: Required—TOEFL.

Southern Arkansas University–Magnolia, Graduate Programs, Magnolia, AR 71754. Offers agriculture (MS); business administration (MBA); computer and information sciences (MS); education (M Ed), including counseling and development, curriculum and instruction, educational administration and supervision, elementary education, middle level, reading, secondary education, TESOL; kinesiology (M Ed); library media and information specialist (M Ed); mental health and clinical counseling (MS); public administration (MPA); school counseling (M Ed); teaching (MAT). *Accreditation:* NCATE. Part-time and evening/weekend programs available. Postbaccalaureate distance learning degree programs offered. *Faculty:* 34 full-time (15 women), 8 part-time/adjunct (5 women). *Students:* 87 full-time (62 women), 320 part-time (224 women); includes 116 minority (111 Black or African American, non-Hispanic/Latino; 2 American Indian or Alaska Native, non-Hispanic/Latino; 2 Asian, non-Hispanic/Latino; 1 Hispanic/Latino), 25 international. Average age 33. 201 applicants, 98% accepted, 156 enrolled. In 2011, 162 master's awarded. *Degree requirements:*

For master's, comprehensive exam (for some programs), thesis optional. *Entrance requirements:* For master's, GRE, MAT or GMAT, minimum GPA of 2.5. Additional exam requirements/recommendations for international students: Required—TOEFL (minimum score 173 computer-based). *Application deadline:* For fall admission, 7/15 for domestic and international students; for winter admission, 12/1 for domestic and international students; for spring admission, 12/1 for domestic and international students. Applications are processed on a rolling basis. Application fee: $25 ($35 for international students). Electronic applications accepted. *Expenses:* Tuition, state resident: part-time $232 per credit. Tuition, nonresident: part-time $339 per credit. *Required fees:* $44 per credit. Part-time tuition and fees vary according to course load. *Financial support:* Career-related internships or fieldwork, Federal Work-Study, scholarships/grants, tuition waivers (full), and unspecified assistantships available. Financial award applicants required to submit FAFSA. *Faculty research:* Alternative certification for teachers, supervision of instruction, instructional leadership, counseling. *Unit head:* Dr. Kim Bloss, Dean, School of Graduate Studies, 870-235-4150, Fax: 870-235-5227, E-mail: kkbloss@saumag.edu. *Application contact:* Gaye Calhoun, Admissions Specialist, 870-235-4150, Fax: 870-235-5227, E-mail: glcalhoun@saumag.edu. Web site: http://www.saumag.edu/graduate.

Southern Illinois University Carbondale, Graduate School, College of Agriculture, Carbondale, IL 62901-4701. Offers MS, MBA/MS. Part-time programs available. *Faculty:* 51 full-time (8 women). *Students:* 67 full-time (45 women), 73 part-time (34 women); includes 6 minority (4 Black or African American, non-Hispanic/Latino; 1 American Indian or Alaska Native, non-Hispanic/Latino; 1 Hispanic/Latino), 11 international. 67 applicants, 45% accepted, 22 enrolled. In 2011, 34 master's awarded. *Entrance requirements:* For master's, minimum GPA of 2.7. Additional exam requirements/recommendations for international students: Required—TOEFL. *Application deadline:* Applications are processed on a rolling basis. Application fee: $0. *Financial support:* In 2011–12, 35 students received support, including 31 research assistantships; fellowships, teaching assistantships, career-related internships or fieldwork, Federal Work-Study, institutionally sponsored loans, and tuition waivers (full) also available. Support available to part-time students. *Faculty research:* Production and studies in crops, animal nutrition, agribusiness economics and management, forest biology and ecology, microcomputers in agriculture. *Unit head:* Gary L. Minish, Dean, 618-453-2469. *Application contact:* Lu Lyons, Supervisor, Admissions, 618-453-4512, E-mail: llyons@siu.edu.

Southern University and Agricultural and Mechanical College, Graduate School, College of Agricultural, Family and Consumer Sciences, Baton Rouge, LA 70813. Offers urban forestry (MS). *Degree requirements:* For master's, thesis. *Entrance requirements:* For master's, GRE, minimum GPA of 3.0. Additional exam requirements/recommendations for international students: Required—TOEFL (minimum score 525 paper-based; 193 computer-based). *Faculty research:* Urban forest interactions with environment, social and economic impacts of urban forests, tree biology/pathology, development of urban forest management tools.

Tarleton State University, College of Graduate Studies, College of Agricultural and Environmental Sciences, Department of Agricultural and Consumer Sciences, Stephenville, TX 76402. Offers agriculture education (MS). Part-time and evening/weekend programs available. Postbaccalaureate distance learning degree programs offered (minimal on-campus study). *Faculty:* 4 full-time (1 woman), 3 part-time/adjunct (1 woman). *Students:* 22 full-time (13 women), 11 part-time (4 women); includes 1 minority (Hispanic/Latino), 1 international. Average age 26. 17 applicants, 88% accepted, 12 enrolled. In 2011, 12 master's awarded. *Degree requirements:* For master's, comprehensive exam. *Entrance requirements:* For master's, GRE General Test, minimum GPA of 3.0. Additional exam requirements/recommendations for international students: Required—TOEFL (minimum score 550 paper-based; 213 computer-based; 80 iBT). *Application deadline:* For fall admission, 8/5 priority date for domestic students; for spring admission, 12/1 for domestic students. Applications are processed on a rolling basis. Application fee: $30 ($130 for international students). Electronic applications accepted. *Expenses:* Tuition, state resident: full-time $3131.46; part-time $174 per credit hour. Tuition, nonresident: full-time $8225; part-time $457 per credit hour. *Required fees:* $1446. Tuition and fees vary according to course load and campus/location. *Financial support:* Research assistantships, Federal Work-Study, institutionally sponsored loans, scholarships/grants, and unspecified assistantships available. Financial award application deadline: 5/1; financial award applicants required to submit FAFSA. *Unit head:* Dr. Rudy Tarpley, Head, 254-968-9201, Fax: 254-968-9199, E-mail: tarpley@tarleton.edu. *Application contact:* Information Contact, 254-968-9104, Fax: 254-968-9670, E-mail: gradoffice@tarleton.edu. Web site: http://www.tarleton.edu/~asd.

Tarleton State University, College of Graduate Studies, College of Agricultural and Environmental Sciences, Department of Environmental and Agricultural Management, Stephenville, TX 76402. Offers agriculture (MS). Part-time and evening/weekend programs available. *Faculty:* 10 full-time (1 woman). *Students:* 31 full-time (24 women), 13 part-time (8 women); includes 5 minority (3 Hispanic/Latino; 2 Two or more races, non-Hispanic/Latino), 2 international. Average age 28. 8 applicants, 100% accepted, 7 enrolled. In 2011, 12 master's awarded. *Degree requirements:* For master's, comprehensive exam. *Entrance requirements:* For master's, GRE, minimum GPA of 3.0. Additional exam requirements/recommendations for international students: Required—TOEFL (minimum score 550 paper-based; 213 computer-based; 80 iBT). *Application deadline:* For fall admission, 8/5 priority date for domestic students; for spring

402 facebook.com/petersonspublishing

Peterson's Graduate Programs in the Physical Sciences, Mathematics, Agricultural Sciences, the Environment & Natural Resources 2013

admission, 12/1 for domestic students. Applications are processed on a rolling basis. Application fee: $30 ($130 for international students). Electronic applications accepted. *Expenses:* Tuition, state resident: full-time $3131.46; part-time $174 per credit hour. Tuition, nonresident: full-time $8225; part-time $457 per credit hour. *Required fees:* $1446. Tuition and fees vary according to course load and campus/location. *Financial support:* Research assistantships available. Financial award application deadline: 5/1; financial award applicants required to submit FAFSA. *Unit head:* Dr. Roger Wittie, Head, 254-968-9931, Fax: 254-968-9228, E-mail: wittie@tarleton.edu. *Application contact:* Information Contact, 254-968-9104, Fax: 254-968-9670, E-mail: gradoffice@tarleton.edu. Web site: http://www.tarleton.edu/~aahrm.

Tennessee State University, The School of Graduate Studies and Research, School of Agriculture and Consumer Sciences, Nashville, TN 37209-1561. Offers agricultural sciences (MS), including agribusiness, agricultural education, animal science, plant science. Part-time and evening/weekend programs available. *Degree requirements:* For master's, thesis. *Entrance requirements:* For master's, GRE General Test, GRE Subject Test, MAT. *Faculty research:* Small farm economics, ornamental horticulture, beef cattle production, rural elderly.

Texas A&M University, College of Agriculture and Life Sciences, College Station, TX 77843. Offers M Agr, M Ed, M Eng, MAB, MS, DE, Ed D, PhD. Part-time programs available. Postbaccalaureate distance learning degree programs offered (minimal on-campus study). *Faculty:* 323. *Students:* 1,004 full-time (506 women), 349 part-time (152 women); includes 204 minority (45 Black or African American, non-Hispanic/Latino; 3 American Indian or Alaska Native, non-Hispanic/Latino; 25 Asian, non-Hispanic/Latino; 120 Hispanic/Latino; 1 Native Hawaiian or other Pacific Islander, non-Hispanic/Latino; 10 Two or more races, non-Hispanic/Latino), 415 international. Average age 29. In 2011, 171 master's, 82 doctorates awarded. *Entrance requirements:* Additional exam requirements/recommendations for international students: Required—TOEFL (minimum score 550 paper-based; 213 computer-based). *Application deadline:* For fall admission, 7/21 priority date for domestic students, 6/1 for international students; for spring admission, 12/1 priority date for domestic students, 10/1 for international students. Applications are processed on a rolling basis. Application fee: $50 ($75 for international students). Electronic applications accepted. *Expenses:* Tuition, state resident: full-time $5437; part-time $226.55 per credit hour. Tuition, nonresident: full-time $12,949; part-time $539.55 per credit hour. *Required fees:* $2741. *Financial support:* Fellowships, research assistantships, teaching assistantships, career-related internships or fieldwork, Federal Work-Study, institutionally sponsored loans, scholarships/grants, tuition waivers (partial), and unspecified assistantships available. Support available to part-time students. Financial award applicants required to submit FAFSA. *Faculty research:* Plant sciences, animal sciences, environmental natural resources, biological and agricultural engineering, agricultural economics. *Unit head:* Dr. Mark Hussey, Vice Chancellor/Dean, 979-845-4747, Fax: 979-845-9938, E-mail: mhussey@tamu.edu. *Application contact:* Graduate Admissions, 979-845-1044, E-mail: admissions@tamu.edu. Web site: http://aglifesciences.tamu.edu/.

Texas A&M University–Commerce, Graduate School, College of Science, Engineering and Agriculture, Department of Agricultural Sciences, Commerce, TX 75429-3011. Offers agricultural education (M Ed, MS); agricultural sciences (M Ed, MS). Part-time programs available. *Degree requirements:* For master's, comprehensive exam, thesis (for some programs). *Entrance requirements:* For master's, GRE General Test. Electronic applications accepted. *Faculty research:* Soil conservation, retention.

Texas A&M University–Kingsville, College of Graduate Studies, College of Agriculture and Home Economics, Kingsville, TX 78363. Offers MS, PhD. Part-time and evening/weekend programs available. *Degree requirements:* For master's, comprehensive exam, thesis or alternative; for doctorate, one foreign language, comprehensive exam, thesis/dissertation. *Entrance requirements:* For master's, GRE General Test, minimum GPA of 3.0; for doctorate, GRE General Test, minimum GPA of 3.5. Additional exam requirements/recommendations for international students: Required—TOEFL. *Faculty research:* Mesquite cloning; genesis of soil salinity; dove management; bone development; egg, meat, and milk consumption versus price.

Texas Tech University, Graduate School, College of Agricultural Sciences and Natural Resources, Lubbock, TX 79409. Offers M Agr, MAB, MLA, MS, Ed D, PhD, JD/MS. Part-time programs available. Postbaccalaureate distance learning degree programs offered (minimal on-campus study). *Faculty:* 67 full-time (16 women), 13 part-time/adjunct (1 woman). *Students:* 265 full-time (118 women), 100 part-time (42 women); includes 25 minority (5 Black or African American, non-Hispanic/Latino; 2 American Indian or Alaska Native, non-Hispanic/Latino; 2 Asian, non-Hispanic/Latino; 11 Hispanic/Latino; 5 Two or more races, non-Hispanic/Latino), 84 international. Average age 29. 273 applicants, 48% accepted, 84 enrolled. In 2011, 64 master's, 27 doctorates awarded. *Degree requirements:* For master's, thesis or alternative; for doctorate, thesis/dissertation. *Entrance requirements:* For master's and doctorate, GRE General Test, formal approval from departmental committee. Additional exam requirements/recommendations for international students: Required—TOEFL (minimum score 550 paper-based; 213 computer-based; 79 iBT). *Application deadline:* For fall admission, 6/1 priority date for domestic students, 1/15 for international students; for spring admission, 9/1 priority date for domestic students, 6/15 for international students. Applications are processed on a rolling basis. Application fee: $50 ($75 for international students). Electronic applications accepted. *Expenses:* Contact institution. *Financial support:* In 2011–12, 179 students received support. Career-related internships or fieldwork, Federal Work-Study, institutionally sponsored loans, scholarships/grants, traineeships, health care benefits, and unspecified assistantships available. Support available to part-time students. Financial award application deadline: 4/15; financial award applicants required to submit FAFSA. *Faculty research:* Biotechnology and genomics, water management, food safety, policy, ecology. *Total annual research expenditures:* $13.7 million. *Unit head:* Dr. Michael L. Galyean, Dean, 806-742-2810, E-mail: michael.galyean@ttu.edu. *Application contact:* Dr. Cindy Akers, Assistant Dean for Academic and Student Programs, 806-742-2808, Fax: 806-742-2836, E-mail: cindy.akers@ttu.edu. Web site: http://www.depts.ttu.edu/agriculturalsciences/.

Tropical Agriculture Research and Higher Education Center, Graduate School, Turrialba, Costa Rica. Offers agribusiness management (MS); agroforestry systems (PhD); development practices (MS); ecological agriculture (MS); environmental socioeconomics (MS); forestry in tropical and subtropical zones (PhD); integrated watershed management (MS); international sustainable tourism (MS); management and conservation of tropical rainforests and biodiversity (MS); tropical agriculture (PhD); tropical agroforestry (MS). *Entrance requirements:* For master's, GRE, 2 years of related professional experience, letters of recommendation; for doctorate, GRE, 4 letters of recommendation, letter of support from employing organization, master's degree in agronomy, biological sciences, forestry, natural resources or related field. Additional exam requirements/recommendations for international students: Required—TOEFL (minimum score 550 paper-based; 213 computer-based). Electronic applications accepted. *Faculty research:* Biodiversity in fragmented landscapes, ecosystem management, integrated pest management, environmental livestock production, biotechnology carbon balances in diverse land uses.

Universidad Nacional Pedro Henriquez Urena, Graduate School, Santo Domingo, Dominican Republic. Offers agricultural diversity (MS), including horticultural/fruit production, tropical animal production; conservation of monuments and cultural assets (M Arch); ecology and environment (MS); environmental engineering (MEE); international relations (MA); natural resource management (MS); political science (MA); project optimization (MPM); project feasibility (MPM); project management (MPM); sanitation engineering (ME); science for teachers (MS); tropical Caribbean architecture (M Arch).

Université Laval, Faculty of Agricultural and Food Sciences, Québec, QC G1K 7P4, Canada. Offers M Sc, PhD, Diploma. Part-time programs available. *Degree requirements:* For doctorate, comprehensive exam, thesis/dissertation. Electronic applications accepted.

University of Alberta, Faculty of Graduate Studies and Research, Department of Agricultural, Food and Nutritional Science, Edmonton, AB T6G 2E1, Canada. Offers M Ag, M Eng, M Sc, PhD, MBA/M Ag. *Degree requirements:* For master's, thesis; for doctorate, comprehensive exam, thesis/dissertation. *Entrance requirements:* For master's, minimum GPA of 3.3; for doctorate, minimum GPA of 3.5. Additional exam requirements/recommendations for international students: Required—IELTS (minimum score 6.5), TOEFL (minimum score of 550 paper-based or a total iBT score of 88 with a score of at least 20 on each of the individual skill areas), Michigan English Language Assessment Battery (minimum score 85); CAEL (overall minimum score 60). *Faculty research:* Animal science, food science, nutrition and metabolism, bioresource engineering, plant science and range management.

The University of Arizona, College of Agriculture and Life Sciences, Tucson, AZ 85721. Offers M Ag Ed, M Ed, MHE Ed, MS, PhD. Part-time programs available. *Faculty:* 116 full-time (36 women), 12 part-time/adjunct (4 women). *Students:* 264 full-time (144 women), 61 part-time (35 women); includes 68 minority (5 Black or African American, non-Hispanic/Latino; 2 American Indian or Alaska Native, non-Hispanic/Latino; 5 Asian, non-Hispanic/Latino; 32 Hispanic/Latino; 24 Two or more races, non-Hispanic/Latino), 76 international. Average age 31. 358 applicants, 37% accepted, 66 enrolled. In 2011, 71 master's, 35 doctorates awarded. *Degree requirements:* For doctorate, thesis/dissertation. *Entrance requirements:* For master's, GRE, GMAT, or MAT, bachelor's degree or equivalent, minimum GPA of 3.0. Additional exam requirements/recommendations for international students: Required—TOEFL. *Application deadline:* For fall admission, 1/1 for domestic students, 12/1 for international students. Applications are processed on a rolling basis. Application fee: $75. Electronic applications accepted. *Expenses:* Tuition, state resident: full-time $10,840. Tuition, nonresident: full-time $25,802. *Financial support:* In 2011–12, 128 research assistantships with full and partial tuition reimbursements (averaging $18,577 per year), 66 teaching assistantships with full and partial tuition reimbursements (averaging $17,553 per year) were awarded; fellowships with full and partial tuition reimbursements, career-related internships or fieldwork, Federal Work-Study, institutionally sponsored loans, scholarships/grants, traineeships, health care benefits, tuition waivers (full and partial), and unspecified assistantships also available. *Faculty research:* Regulation of skeletal muscle mass during growth, bone health and osteoporosis prevention, regulation of gene expression, development of new crops for arid and semi-arid lands, molecular genetics and pathogenesis of the opportunistic pathogen. *Total annual research expenditures:* $52.7 million. *Unit head:* Dr. Shane Burgess, Dean, 520-621-7621, Fax: 520-621-7196, E-mail: dean@cals.arizona.edu. *Application contact:* 520-621-3612, Fax: 520-621-8662. Web site: http://www.ag.arizona.edu/.

University of Arkansas, Graduate School, Dale Bumpers College of Agricultural, Food and Life Sciences, Fayetteville, AR 72701-1201. Offers MS, PhD. *Students:* 101 full-time (41 women), 217 part-time (112 women); includes 31 minority (11

Peterson's Graduate Programs in the Physical Sciences, Mathematics, Agricultural Sciences, the Environment & Natural Resources 2013

facebook.com/petersonspublishing **403**

Black or African American, non-Hispanic/Latino; 2 American Indian or Alaska Native, non-Hispanic/Latino; 3 Asian, non-Hispanic/Latino; 9 Hispanic/Latino; 6 Two or more races, non-Hispanic/Latino), 86 international. 164 applicants, 59% accepted. In 2011, 72 master's, 22 doctorates awarded. *Degree requirements:* For doctorate, thesis/dissertation. *Application deadline:* For fall admission, 4/1 for international students; for spring admission, 10/1 for international students. Applications are processed on a rolling basis. Application fee: $40 ($50 for international students). Electronic applications accepted. *Financial support:* In 2011–12, 167 research assistantships, 7 teaching assistantships were awarded; fellowships with tuition reimbursements, career-related internships or fieldwork, Federal Work-Study, scholarships/grants, and unspecified assistantships also available. Support available to part-time students. Financial award application deadline: 4/1; financial award applicants required to submit FAFSA. *Unit head:* Dr. Michael E. Vayda, Dean, 479-575-2034, Fax: 479-575-7273, E-mail: mvayda@uark.edu. *Application contact:* Graduate Admissions, 479-575-6246, Fax: 479-575-5908, E-mail: gradinfo@uark.edu. Web site: http://bumperscollege.uark.edu/.

The University of British Columbia, Faculty of Land and Food Systems, Vancouver, BC V6T 1Z1, Canada. Offers M Sc, MFS, PhD. *Degree requirements:* For master's, thesis; for doctorate, comprehensive exam, thesis/dissertation. *Entrance requirements:* Additional exam requirements/recommendations for international students: Required—TOEFL (minimum score 577 paper-based; 233 computer-based; 90 iBT), IELTS (minimum score 6.5). Electronic applications accepted.

University of California, Davis, Graduate Studies, Graduate Group in International Agricultural Development, Davis, CA 95616. Offers MS. *Degree requirements:* For master's, comprehensive exam (for some programs), thesis (for some programs). *Entrance requirements:* For master's, GRE General Test, minimum GPA of 3.0. Additional exam requirements/recommendations for international students: Required—TOEFL (minimum score 550 paper-based; 213 computer-based). Electronic applications accepted. *Faculty research:* Aspects of agricultural, environmental and social sciences on agriculture and related issues in developing countries.

University of Connecticut, Graduate School, College of Agriculture and Natural Resources, Storrs, CT 06269. Offers MS, PhD. Terminal master's awarded for partial completion of doctoral program. *Degree requirements:* For master's, comprehensive exam; for doctorate, comprehensive exam, thesis/dissertation. *Entrance requirements:* For master's and doctorate, GRE General Test. Additional exam requirements/recommendations for international students: Required—TOEFL (minimum score 550 paper-based; 213 computer-based). Electronic applications accepted.

University of Delaware, College of Agriculture and Natural Resources, Newark, DE 19716. Offers MA, MS, PhD. Part-time programs available. *Degree requirements:* For master's, thesis; for doctorate, thesis/dissertation. *Entrance requirements:* For master's and doctorate, GRE General Test. Electronic applications accepted.

University of Florida, Graduate School, College of Agricultural and Life Sciences, Gainesville, FL 32611. Offers M Ag, MAB, MFAS, MFRC, MFYCS, MS, DPM, PhD, JD/MFRC, JD/MS, JD/PhD. Part-time programs available. *Faculty:* 346 full-time (93 women), 12 part-time/adjunct (4 women). *Students:* 893 full-time (456 women), 272 part-time (140 women); includes 140 minority (31 Black or African American, non-Hispanic/Latino; 6 American Indian or Alaska Native, non-Hispanic/Latino; 43 Asian, non-Hispanic/Latino; 59 Hispanic/Latino; 1 Native Hawaiian or other Pacific Islander, non-Hispanic/Latino), 417 international. Average age 30. 921 applicants, 34% accepted, 229 enrolled. In 2011, 217 master's, 109 doctorates awarded. *Degree requirements:* For master's, comprehensive exam (for some programs), thesis (for some programs); for doctorate, comprehensive exam, thesis/dissertation. *Entrance requirements:* For master's and doctorate, GRE General Test, minimum GPA of 3.0. Additional exam requirements/recommendations for international students: Required—TOEFL (minimum score 550 paper-based; 213 computer-based; 80 iBT), IELTS (minimum score 6). *Application deadline:* Applications are processed on a rolling basis. Application fee: $30. Electronic applications accepted. *Financial support:* In 2011–12, 461 students received support, including 85 fellowships with tuition reimbursements available, 312 research assistantships with tuition reimbursements available, 64 teaching assistantships with tuition reimbursements available; career-related internships or fieldwork, Federal Work-Study, institutionally sponsored loans, and unspecified assistantships also available. Support available to part-time students. Financial award application deadline: 2/1; financial award applicants required to submit FAFSA. *Faculty research:* Institute of Food and Agricultural Science: agriculture, human and natural resources, and the life sciences to enhance and sustain the quality of human life. *Total annual research expenditures:* $145.9 million. *Unit head:* Dr. Teresa Balser, Dean, 352-392-1961, E-mail: tcbalser@ufl.edu. Web site: http://www.cals.ufl.edu/.

University of Georgia, College of Agricultural and Environmental Sciences, Athens, GA 30602. Offers MA Ext, MADS, MAE, MAL, MCCS, MFT, MPPPM, MS, PhD. *Faculty:* 210 full-time (34 women), 22 part-time/adjunct (4 women). *Students:* 338 full-time (171 women), 81 part-time (30 women); includes 38 minority (22 Black or African American, non-Hispanic/Latino; 9 Asian, non-Hispanic/Latino; 5 Hispanic/Latino; 2 Two or more races, non-Hispanic/Latino), 156 international. Average age 29. 450 applicants, 39% accepted, 95 enrolled. In 2011, 98 master's, 35 doctorates awarded. *Degree requirements:* For doctorate,

thesis/dissertation. *Entrance requirements:* For master's and doctorate, GRE General Test. *Application deadline:* For fall admission, 7/1 priority date for domestic students; for spring admission, 11/15 for domestic students. Application fee: $50. Electronic applications accepted. *Financial support:* Fellowships, research assistantships, teaching assistantships, career-related internships or fieldwork, and unspecified assistantships available. *Unit head:* Dr. J. Scott Angle, Dean, 706-542-3924, Fax: 706-542-0803, E-mail: caesdean@uga.edu. *Application contact:* Krista Haynes, Director of Enrolled Student Services, 706-425-1789, Fax: 706-425-3094, E-mail: gradoff@uga.edu. Web site: http://www.caes.uga.edu/.

University of Guelph, Graduate Studies, Ontario Agricultural College, Guelph, ON N1G 2W1, Canada. Offers M Sc, MLA, PhD, Diploma, MA/M Sc. Part-time programs available. Postbaccalaureate distance learning degree programs offered (minimal on-campus study). *Degree requirements:* For doctorate, thesis/dissertation.

University of Hawaii at Manoa, Graduate Division, College of Tropical Agriculture and Human Resources, Honolulu, HI 96822. Offers MS, PhD. Part-time programs available. *Entrance requirements:* Additional exam requirements/recommendations for international students: Required—TOEFL or IELTS.

University of Illinois at Urbana–Champaign, Graduate College, College of Agricultural, Consumer and Environmental Sciences, Program in Agricultural Production, Champaign, IL 61820. Offers MS. Applications are only accepted for the fall semester. Part-time programs available. *Students:* 8 full-time (4 women); includes 1 minority (Hispanic/Latino), 1 international. 7 applicants, 100% accepted, 4 enrolled. In 2011, 3 master's awarded. *Degree requirements:* For master's, internship. *Entrance requirements:* For master's, GRE, minimum GPA of 3.0 for last 60 hours of undergraduate work and any graduate study. Additional exam requirements/recommendations for international students: Required—TOEFL (minimum score 590 paper-based; 243 computer-based). Application fee: $75 ($90 for international students). *Unit head:* Bryan White, Director, 217-333-1044. *Application contact:* Gregory S. Harman, Admissions Support Staff, 217-244-4637.

University of Kentucky, Graduate School, College of Agriculture, Lexington, KY 40506-0032. Offers MS, MSFAM, MSFOR, PhD. Part-time programs available. Terminal master's awarded for partial completion of doctoral program. *Degree requirements:* For master's, comprehensive exam, thesis (for some programs); for doctorate, comprehensive exam, thesis/dissertation. *Entrance requirements:* For master's, GRE General Test, minimum undergraduate GPA of 2.75; for doctorate, GRE General Test, minimum undergraduate GPA of 2.75, graduate 3.0. Additional exam requirements/recommendations for international students: Required—TOEFL (minimum score 550 paper-based; 213 computer-based). Electronic applications accepted.

University of Lethbridge, School of Graduate Studies, Lethbridge, AB T1K 3M4, Canada. Offers accounting (MScM); addictions counseling (M Sc); agricultural biotechnology (M Sc); agricultural studies (M Sc, MA); anthropology (MA); archaeology (MA); art (MA, MFA); biochemistry (M Sc); biological sciences (M Sc); biomolecular science (PhD); biosystems and biodiversity (PhD); Canadian studies (MA); chemistry (M Sc); computer science (M Sc); computer science and geographical information science (M Sc); counseling psychology (M Ed); dramatic arts (MA); earth, space, and physical science (PhD); economics (MA); educational leadership (M Ed); English (MA); environmental science (M Sc); evolution and behavior (PhD); exercise science (M Sc); finance (MScM); French (MA); French/German (MA); French/Spanish (MA); general education (M Ed); general management (MScM); geography (M Sc, MA); German (MA); health science (M Sc); history (MA); human resource management and labour relations (MScM); individualized multidisciplinary (M Sc, MA); information systems (MScM); international management (MScM); kinesiology (M Sc, MA); management (M Sc, MA); marketing (MScM); mathematics (M Sc); music (M Mus, MA); Native American studies (MA); neuroscience (M Sc, PhD); new media (MA); nursing (M Sc); philosophy (MA); physics (M Sc); policy and strategy (MScM); political science (MA); psychology (M Sc, MA); religious studies (MA); social sciences (MA); sociology (MA); theatre and dramatic arts (MFA); theoretical and computational science (PhD); urban and regional studies (MA); women's studies (MA). Part-time and evening/weekend programs available. *Degree requirements:* For doctorate, comprehensive exam, thesis/dissertation. *Entrance requirements:* For master's, GMAT (M Sc in management), bachelor's degree in related field, minimum GPA of 3.0 during previous 20 graded semester courses, 2 years teaching or related experience (M Ed); for doctorate, master's degree, minimum graduate GPA of 3.5. Additional exam requirements/recommendations for international students: Required—TOEFL. *Faculty research:* Movement and brain plasticity, gibberellin physiology, photosynthesis, carbon cycling, molecular properties of main-group ring components.

University of Maine, Graduate School, College of Natural Sciences, Forestry, and Agriculture, Orono, ME 04469. Offers MF, MPS, MS, MWC, PhD, CAS. *Accreditation:* SAF (one or more programs are accredited). Part-time and evening/weekend programs available. *Faculty:* 165 full-time (65 women), 79 part-time/adjunct (54 women). *Students:* 423 full-time (280 women), 153 part-time (98 women); includes 23 minority (1 Black or African American, non-Hispanic/Latino; 10 American Indian or Alaska Native, non-Hispanic/Latino; 9 Asian, non-Hispanic/Latino; 2 Hispanic/Latino; 1 Two or more races, non-Hispanic/Latino), 59 international. Average age 31. 523 applicants, 40% accepted, 161 enrolled. In 2011, 93 master's, 28 doctorates, 1 other advanced degree awarded. *Degree*

404 facebook.com/petersonspublishing

Peterson's Graduate Programs in the Physical Sciences, Mathematics, Agricultural Sciences, the Environment & Natural Resources 2013

requirements: For doctorate, thesis/dissertation. *Entrance requirements:* For master's and doctorate, GRE General Test. Additional exam requirements/recommendations for international students: Required—TOEFL. *Application deadline:* For fall admission, 2/1 priority date for domestic students. Applications are processed on a rolling basis. Application fee: $65. Electronic applications accepted. *Expenses:* Tuition, state resident: full-time $5016. Tuition, nonresident: full-time $14,424. *Financial support:* Career-related internships or fieldwork, Federal Work-Study, institutionally sponsored loans, scholarships/grants, tuition waivers (full and partial), and unspecified assistantships available. Support available to part-time students. Financial award application deadline: 3/1. *Total annual research expenditures:* $5,510. *Unit head:* Dr. Edward Ashworth, Dean, 207-581-3206, Fax: 207-581-3207. *Application contact:* Scott G. Delcourt, Associate Dean of the Graduate School, 207-581-3291, Fax: 207-581-3232, E-mail: graduate@maine.edu. Web site: http://www2.umaine.edu/graduate/.

University of Manitoba, Faculty of Graduate Studies, Faculty of Agricultural and Food Sciences, Winnipeg, MB R3T 2N2, Canada. Offers M Sc, PhD. *Degree requirements:* For master's, thesis or alternative; for doctorate, variable foreign language requirement, thesis/dissertation.

University of Maryland, College Park, Academic Affairs, College of Agriculture and Natural Resources, College Park, MD 20742. Offers MS, DVM, PhD. Part-time and evening/weekend programs available. *Faculty:* 332 full-time (148 women), 37 part-time/adjunct (20 women). *Students:* 338 full-time (219 women), 27 part-time (20 women); includes 53 minority (8 Black or African American, non-Hispanic/Latino; 23 Asian, non-Hispanic/Latino; 17 Hispanic/Latino; 1 Native Hawaiian or other Pacific Islander, non-Hispanic/Latino; 4 Two or more races, non-Hispanic/Latino), 97 international. 511 applicants, 22% accepted, 81 enrolled. In 2011, 32 master's, 48 doctorates awarded. *Degree requirements:* For doctorate, thesis/dissertation. *Entrance requirements:* For master's, minimum GPA of 3.0. Additional exam requirements/recommendations for international students: Required—TOEFL. *Application deadline:* For fall admission, 2/1 priority date for domestic students, 2/1 for international students; for spring admission, 6/1 for domestic and international students. Applications are processed on a rolling basis. Application fee: $75. Electronic applications accepted. *Expenses:* Tuition, area resident: Part-time $525 per credit hour. Tuition, state resident: part-time $525 per credit hour. Tuition, nonresident: part-time $1131 per credit hour. *Required fees:* $386.31 per term. Tuition and fees vary according to program. *Financial support:* In 2011–12, 6 fellowships with full and partial tuition reimbursements (averaging $14,063 per year), 81 research assistantships with tuition reimbursements (averaging $17,176 per year), 96 teaching assistantships with tuition reimbursements (averaging $16,882 per year) were awarded; career-related internships or fieldwork, Federal Work-Study, and scholarships/grants also available. Support available to part-time students. Financial award applicants required to submit FAFSA. *Total annual research expenditures:* $36.6 million. *Unit head:* Dr. Cheng-i Wei, Dean, 301-405-2072, Fax: 301-314-9146, E-mail: wei@umd.edu. *Application contact:* Dr. Charles A. Caramello, Dean of Graduate School, 301-405-0358, Fax: 301-314-9305.

University of Maryland Eastern Shore, Graduate Programs, Department of Agriculture, Princess Anne, MD 21853-1299. Offers food and agricultural sciences (MS); food science and technology (PhD). *Degree requirements:* For master's, comprehensive exam, thesis (for some programs), oral exam; for doctorate, comprehensive exam, thesis/dissertation. *Entrance requirements:* For master's, GRE, minimum GPA of 3.0. Additional exam requirements/recommendations for international students: Required—TOEFL (minimum score 213 computer-based; 80 iBT). Electronic applications accepted. *Faculty research:* Poultry and swine nutrition and management, soybean specialty products, farm management practices, aquaculture technology.

University of Minnesota, Twin Cities Campus, Graduate School, College of Food, Agricultural and Natural Resource Sciences, Saint Paul, MN 55108. Offers MS, PhD. Part-time programs available. *Faculty:* 741 full-time (180 women). *Students:* 515 full-time (277 women), 44 part-time (18 women); includes 34 minority (2 Black or African American, non-Hispanic/Latino; 11 Asian, non-Hispanic/Latino; 12 Hispanic/Latino; 1 Native Hawaiian or other Pacific Islander, non-Hispanic/Latino; 8 Two or more races, non-Hispanic/Latino), 164 international. Average age 30. 820 applicants, 41% accepted, 180 enrolled. In 2011, 66 master's, 59 doctorates awarded. Terminal master's awarded for partial completion of doctoral program. *Degree requirements:* For master's, comprehensive exam, thesis; for doctorate, comprehensive exam, thesis/dissertation. *Entrance requirements:* For master's and doctorate, GRE General Test. Additional exam requirements/recommendations for international students: Required—TOEFL (minimum score 550 paper-based; 213 computer-based; 79 iBT), IELTS (minimum score 6.5), TOEFL preferred. *Application deadline:* For fall admission, 12/15 priority date for domestic students, 12/15 for international students; for spring admission, 10/15 for domestic and international students. Applications are processed on a rolling basis. Application fee: $75 ($95 for international students). Electronic applications accepted. *Financial support:* In 2011–12, fellowships with full tuition reimbursements (averaging $23,500 per year), research assistantships with full and partial tuition reimbursements (averaging $18,000 per year), teaching assistantships with full and partial tuition reimbursements (averaging $18,000 per year) were awarded; career-related internships or fieldwork, institutionally sponsored loans, scholarships/grants, health care benefits, tuition waivers (full), and unspecified assistantships also available. Support available to part-time students. Financial award application deadline: 12/15. *Total annual research expenditures:* $38.9 million. *Unit head:* Dr.

F. Abel Ponce de Leon, Senior Associate Dean, 612-625-4772, Fax: 612-625-1260, E-mail: apl@umn.edu. *Application contact:* Lisa Wiley, Graduate Programs Coordinator, 612-624-2748, Fax: 612-625-1260, E-mail: lwiley@umn.edu. Web site: http://www.cfans.umn.edu/GraduateStudents/index.htm.

University of Missouri, Graduate School, College of Agriculture, Food and Natural Resources, Columbia, MO 65211. Offers MS, PhD, Graduate Certificate, MD/PhD. Part-time programs available. *Faculty:* 431 full-time (121 women), 40 part-time/adjunct (11 women). *Students:* 272 full-time (136 women), 52 part-time (21 women); includes 18 minority (4 Black or African American, non-Hispanic/Latino; 1 American Indian or Alaska Native, non-Hispanic/Latino; 4 Asian, non-Hispanic/Latino; 7 Hispanic/Latino; 2 Two or more races, non-Hispanic/Latino), 114 international. Average age 29. 268 applicants, 37% accepted, 70 enrolled. In 2011, 45 master's, 27 doctorates awarded. Terminal master's awarded for partial completion of doctoral program. *Degree requirements:* For master's, thesis (for some programs); for doctorate, variable foreign language requirement, comprehensive exam (for some programs), thesis/dissertation. *Entrance requirements:* For master's and doctorate, GRE General Test, minimum GPA of 3.0. Additional exam requirements/recommendations for international students: Required—TOEFL (minimum score 500 paper-based; 173 computer-based; 61 iBT), IELTS (minimum score 5.5). *Application deadline:* Applications are processed on a rolling basis. Application fee: $55 ($75 for international students). Electronic applications accepted. *Expenses:* Tuition, state resident: full-time $5881. Tuition, nonresident: full-time $15,183. *Required fees:* $952. Tuition and fees vary according to campus/location and program. *Financial support:* Fellowships with tuition reimbursements, research assistantships with tuition reimbursements, teaching assistantships with tuition reimbursements, and institutionally sponsored loans available. *Unit head:* Dr. Thomas L. Payne, Dean, 573-882-3846, E-mail: paynet@missouri.edu. *Application contact:* Dr. Bryan L. Garton, Associate Dean, E-mail: gartonb@missouri.edu. Web site: http://cafnr.missouri.edu/.

University of Nebraska–Lincoln, Graduate College, College of Agricultural Sciences and Natural Resources, Lincoln, NE 68588. Offers M Ag, MA, MBA, MS, PhD. *Degree requirements:* For doctorate, comprehensive exam, thesis/dissertation. *Entrance requirements:* Additional exam requirements/recommendations for international students: Required—TOEFL. Electronic applications accepted. *Faculty research:* Environmental sciences, animal sciences, human resources and family sciences, plant breeding and genetics, food and nutrition.

University of Nevada, Reno, Graduate School, College of Agriculture, Biotechnology and Natural Resources, Reno, NV 89557. Offers MS, PhD. Terminal master's awarded for partial completion of doctoral program. *Degree requirements:* For master's, thesis optional; for doctorate, thesis/dissertation. *Entrance requirements:* For master's, GRE General Test, minimum GPA of 2.75; for doctorate, GRE General Test, minimum GPA of 3.0. Additional exam requirements/recommendations for international students: Required—TOEFL (minimum score 500 paper-based; 173 computer-based; 61 iBT), IELTS (minimum score 6). Electronic applications accepted.

University of Puerto Rico, Mayagüez Campus, Graduate Studies, College of Agricultural Sciences, Mayagüez, PR 00681-9000. Offers MS. Part-time programs available. *Students:* 127 full-time (68 women), 6 part-time (2 women); includes 105 minority (all Hispanic/Latino), 25 international. 98 applicants, 55% accepted, 43 enrolled. In 2011, 24 master's awarded. *Degree requirements:* For master's, comprehensive exam, thesis. *Application deadline:* For fall admission, 2/15 for domestic and international students; for spring admission, 9/15 for domestic and international students. Applications are processed on a rolling basis. Application fee: $25. Tuition and fees vary according to course level and course load. *Financial support:* In 2011–12, 64 students received support, including 45 research assistantships with tuition reimbursements available (averaging $15,000 per year), 19 teaching assistantships with tuition reimbursements available (averaging $8,500 per year); career-related internships or fieldwork, Federal Work-Study, and institutionally sponsored loans also available. *Total annual research expenditures:* $459,210. *Unit head:* Prof. Aristides Armstrong, Associate Dean, 787-832-4040 Ext. 2181, E-mail: aristides.armstrong@upr.edu. *Application contact:* Carmen Figueroa, Student Affairs Official, 787-265-3809, Fax: 787-265-5489, E-mail: carmen.figueroa11@upr.edu. Web site: http://www.uprm.edu/agricultura.

University of Saskatchewan, College of Graduate Studies and Research, College of Agriculture, Saskatoon, SK S7N 5A2, Canada. Offers M Ag, M Sc, MA, PhD, Diploma, PGD. Part-time programs available. *Degree requirements:* For master's, thesis (for some programs); for doctorate, comprehensive exam (for some programs), thesis/dissertation. *Entrance requirements:* Additional exam requirements/recommendations for international students: Required—TOEFL (minimum score 80 iBT); Recommended—IELTS (minimum score 6.5).

University of South Africa, College of Agriculture and Environmental Sciences, Pretoria, South Africa. Offers agriculture (MS); consumer science (MCS); environmental management (MA, MS, PhD); environmental science (MA, MS, PhD); geography (MA, MS, PhD); horticulture (M Tech); human ecology (MHE); life sciences (MS); nature conservation (M Tech).

The University of Tennessee, Graduate School, College of Agricultural Sciences and Natural Resources, Knoxville, TN 37996. Offers MS, PhD. Part-time programs available. Postbaccalaureate distance learning degree programs offered (minimal on-campus study). *Degree requirements:* For master's, thesis

Peterson's Graduate Programs in the Physical Sciences, Mathematics, Agricultural Sciences, the Environment & Natural Resources 2013

facebook.com/petersonspublishing **405**

Agricultural Sciences—General

(for some programs); for doctorate, thesis/dissertation. *Entrance requirements:* For master's and doctorate, minimum GPA of 2.7. Additional exam requirements/recommendations for international students: Required—TOEFL. Electronic applications accepted. *Expenses:* Tuition, state resident: full-time $8332; part-time $464 per credit hour. Tuition, nonresident: full-time $25,174; part-time $1400 per credit hour. *Required fees:* $1162; $56 per credit hour. Tuition and fees vary according to program.

The University of Tennessee at Martin, Graduate Programs, College of Agriculture and Applied Sciences, Program in Agricultural and Natural Resources Management, Martin, TN 38238-1000. Offers MSANR. Part-time programs available. Postbaccalaureate distance learning degree programs offered (no on-campus study). *Faculty:* 22. *Students:* 40 (15 women); includes 2 minority (both Black or African American, non-Hispanic/Latino), 1 international. 25 applicants, 84% accepted, 18 enrolled. In 2011, 6 master's awarded. *Degree requirements:* For master's, comprehensive exam, thesis optional. *Entrance requirements:* For master's, GRE General Test, minimum GPA of 2.5. Additional exam requirements/recommendations for international students: Required—TOEFL (minimum score 525 paper-based; 197 computer-based; 71 iBT). *Application deadline:* For fall admission, 8/1 priority date for domestic students, 7/15 for international students; for spring admission, 12/15 priority date for domestic students, 12/1 for international students. Applications are processed on a rolling basis. Application fee: $30 ($130 for international students). Electronic applications accepted. *Expenses:* Tuition, state resident: full-time $6726; part-time $374 per credit hour. Tuition, nonresident: full-time $19,136; part-time $1064 per credit hour. *Required fees:* $61 per credit hour. *Financial support:* In 2011–12, 4 students received support, including 4 research assistantships with full tuition reimbursements available (averaging $7,470 per year); scholarships/grants and unspecified assistantships also available. Support available to part-time students. Financial award application deadline: 2/15; financial award applicants required to submit FAFSA. *Unit head:* Dr. Joey Melhorn, Interim Coordinator, 731-881-7275, Fax: 731-881-7968, E-mail: melhorn@utm.edu. *Application contact:* Linda S. Arant, Student Services Specialist, 731-881-7012, Fax: 731-881-7499, E-mail: larant@utm.edu. Web site: http://www.utm.edu/departments/caas/msanr.

University of Vermont, Graduate College, College of Agriculture and Life Sciences, Burlington, VT 05405. Offers MPA, MS, MSD, PhD, MD/MS, MD/PhD. Part-time programs available. *Students:* 147 (93 women); includes 8 minority (1 Black or African American, non-Hispanic/Latino; 5 Asian, non-Hispanic/Latino; 2 Hispanic/Latino), 20 international. 212 applicants, 41% accepted, 35 enrolled. In 2011, 43 master's, 2 doctorates awarded. *Degree requirements:* For doctorate, one foreign language, thesis/dissertation. *Entrance requirements:* For master's and doctorate, GRE General Test. Additional exam requirements/recommendations for international students: Required—TOEFL (minimum score 550 paper-based; 213 computer-based; 80 iBT). Application fee: $40. Electronic applications accepted. *Financial support:* Fellowships, research assistantships, teaching assistantships, career-related internships or fieldwork, Federal Work-Study, and tuition waivers (full and partial) available. Financial award application deadline: 3/1. *Unit head:* Dr. Thomas C. Vogelmann, Dean, 802-656-2980. *Application contact:* Ralph Swenson, Director of Graduate Admissions, 802-656-2699, Fax: 802-656-0519, E-mail: graduate.admissions@uvm.edu.

University of Wisconsin–Madison, Graduate School, College of Agricultural and Life Sciences, Madison, WI 53706-1380. Offers MA, MPS, MS, PhD. Part-time programs available. *Entrance requirements:* For master's and doctorate, GRE. Additional exam requirements/recommendations for international students: Required—TOEFL. Electronic applications accepted. *Expenses:* Tuition, state resident: full-time $10,296; part-time $643.51 per credit. Tuition, nonresident: full-time $24,054; part-time $1503.40 per credit. *Required fees:* $70.06 per credit. Tuition and fees vary according to course load, campus/location, program and reciprocity agreements.

University of Wisconsin–River Falls, Outreach and Graduate Studies, College of Agriculture, Food, and Environmental Sciences, River Falls, WI 54022. Offers MS. Part-time programs available. *Degree requirements:* For master's, comprehensive exam, thesis (for some programs). *Entrance requirements:* For master's, minimum GPA of 2.75. Additional exam requirements/recommendations for international students: Required—TOEFL (minimum score 500 paper-based; 65 iBT), IELTS (minimum score 5.4). Electronic applications accepted.

University of Wyoming, College of Agriculture and Natural Resources, Laramie, WY 82070. Offers MA, MS, PhD. Part-time programs available. Terminal master's awarded for partial completion of doctoral program. *Degree requirements:* For doctorate, thesis/dissertation. *Entrance requirements:* For master's and doctorate, GRE General Test, minimum GPA of 3.0. Electronic applications accepted. *Faculty research:* Nutrition, molecular biology, animal science, plant science, entomology.

Utah State University, School of Graduate Studies, College of Agriculture, Logan, UT 84322. Offers MDA, MFMS, MS, PhD. Part-time programs available. Postbaccalaureate distance learning degree programs offered (minimal on-campus study). Terminal master's awarded for partial completion of doctoral program. *Degree requirements:* For doctorate, thesis/dissertation. *Entrance requirements:* For master's and doctorate, GRE General Test, minimum GPA of 3.0. Additional exam requirements/recommendations for international students: Required—TOEFL. *Faculty research:* Low-input agriculture, anti-viral chemotherapy, lactic culture, environmental biophysics and climate.

Virginia Polytechnic Institute and State University, Graduate School, College of Agriculture and Life Sciences, Blacksburg, VA 24061. Offers MS, MSLFS, PhD, Certificate. *Faculty:* 218 full-time (63 women), 2 part-time/adjunct (both women). *Students:* 321 full-time (179 women), 94 part-time (59 women); includes 51 minority (25 Black or African American, non-Hispanic/Latino; 2 American Indian or Alaska Native, non-Hispanic/Latino; 13 Asian, non-Hispanic/Latino; 9 Hispanic/Latino; 2 Two or more races, non-Hispanic/Latino), 99 international. Average age 29. 377 applicants, 37% accepted, 96 enrolled. In 2011, 61 master's, 44 doctorates awarded. *Degree requirements:* For master's, comprehensive exam (for some programs), thesis (for some programs); for doctorate, comprehensive exam (for some programs), thesis/dissertation (for some programs). *Entrance requirements:* For master's and doctorate, GRE. Additional exam requirements/recommendations for international students: Required—TOEFL (minimum score 550 paper-based; 213 computer-based). *Application deadline:* For fall admission, 7/1 for domestic students, 4/1 for international students; for spring admission, 12/1 for domestic students, 9/1 for international students. Applications are processed on a rolling basis. Application fee: $65. Electronic applications accepted. *Expenses:* Tuition, state resident: full-time $10,048; part-time $558.25 per credit hour. Tuition, nonresident: full-time $19,497; part-time $1083.25 per credit hour. *Required fees:* $405 per semester. Tuition and fees vary according to course load, campus/location and program. *Financial support:* In 2011–12, 1 fellowship with full tuition reimbursement (averaging $17,000 per year), 204 research assistantships with full tuition reimbursements (averaging $20,592 per year), 70 teaching assistantships with full tuition reimbursements (averaging $20,725 per year) were awarded. Financial award application deadline: 3/1; financial award applicants required to submit FAFSA. *Total annual research expenditures:* $38.7 million. *Unit head:* Dr. Alan L. Grant, Dean, 540-231-4152, Fax: 540-231-4163, E-mail: algrant@vt.edu. *Application contact:* Sheila Norman, Contact, 540-231-4152, Fax: 540-231-4163, E-mail: snorman@vt.edu. Web site: http://www.cals.vt.edu/.

Virginia Polytechnic Institute and State University, VT Online, Blacksburg, VA 24061. Offers advanced transportation systems (Certificate); aerospace engineering (MS); agricultural and life sciences (MSLFS); business information systems (Graduate Certificate); career and technical education (MS); civil engineering (MS); computer engineering (M Eng, MS); decision support systems (Graduate Certificate); eLearning leadership (MA); electrical engineering (M Eng, MS); engineering administration (MEA); environmental engineering (Certificate); environmental politics and policy (Graduate Certificate); environmental sciences and engineering (MS); foundations of political analysis (Graduate Certificate); health product risk management (Graduate Certificate); industrial and systems engineering (MS); information policy and society (Graduate Certificate); information security (Graduate Certificate); information technology (MIT); instructional technology (MA); integrative STEM education (MA Ed); liberal arts (Graduate Certificate); life sciences: health product risk management (MS); natural resources (MNR, Graduate Certificate); networking (Graduate Certificate); nonprofit and nongovernmental organization management (Graduate Certificate); ocean engineering (MS); political science (MA); security studies (Graduate Certificate); software development (Graduate Certificate). *Expenses:* Tuition, state resident: full-time $10,048; part-time $558.25 per credit hour. Tuition, nonresident: full-time $19,497; part-time $1083.25 per credit hour. *Required fees:* $405 per semester. Tuition and fees vary according to course load, campus/location and program. *Application contact:* Graduate School Applications General Assistance, 540-231-8636, Fax: 540-231-2039, E-mail: gradappl@vt.edu. Web site: http://www.vto.vt.edu/.

Virginia State University, School of Graduate Studies, Research, and Outreach, School of Agriculture, Petersburg, VA 23806-0001. Offers MS.

Washington State University, Graduate School, College of Agricultural, Human, and Natural Resource Sciences, Department of Crop and Soil Sciences, Program in Agriculture, Pullman, WA 99164. Offers MS. *Faculty:* 25. *Students:* 6 full-time (4 women), 13 part-time (7 women); includes 2 minority (1 American Indian or Alaska Native, non-Hispanic/Latino; 1 Hispanic/Latino), 20 international. Average age 27. 22 applicants, 50% accepted, 8 enrolled. In 2011, 3 master's awarded. *Degree requirements:* For master's, comprehensive exam (for some programs), thesis (for some programs), oral defense. *Entrance requirements:* For master's, transcripts of all college course work, three letters of reference, personal statement describing intent and interest area(s). Additional exam requirements/recommendations for international students: Required—TOEFL, IELTS. *Application deadline:* For fall admission, 1/10 for domestic and international students; for spring admission, 7/1 for domestic and international students. Application fee: $75. *Financial support:* In 2011–12, 1 fellowship (averaging $2,850 per year), research assistantships (averaging $18,204 per year), teaching assistantships (averaging $18,204 per year) were awarded. *Total annual research expenditures:* $6.2 million. *Unit head:* Dr. Richard Koenig, Interim Director, 509-335-2726, Fax: 509-335-8674, E-mail: richk@wsu.edu. *Application contact:* Graduate School Admissions, 800-GRADWSU, Fax: 509-335-1949, E-mail: gradsch@wsu.edu. Web site: http://msag.wsu.edu.

Western Kentucky University, Graduate Studies, Ogden College of Science and Engineering, Department of Agriculture, Bowling Green, KY 42101. Offers MA Ed, MS. Part-time and evening/weekend programs available. *Degree requirements:* For master's, comprehensive exam, thesis optional. *Entrance requirements:* For master's, GRE General Test, minimum GPA of 2.75. Additional exam requirements/recommendations for international students: Required—TOEFL (minimum score 555 paper-based; 213 computer-based; 79 iBT). *Faculty*

406 facebook.com/petersonspublishing

Peterson's Graduate Programs in the Physical Sciences, Mathematics, Agricultural Sciences, the Environment & Natural Resources 2013

research: Establishment of warm season grasses, heat composting, enrichment activities in agricultural education.

West Texas A&M University, College of Agriculture, Nursing, and Natural Sciences, Division of Agriculture, Canyon, TX 79016-0001. Offers agricultural business and economics (MS); agriculture (PhD); animal science (MS); plant science (MS). Part-time programs available. *Degree requirements:* For master's, comprehensive exam, thesis optional. *Entrance requirements:* For master's, GRE General Test. Additional exam requirements/recommendations for international

students: Required—TOEFL (minimum score 550 paper-based). Electronic applications accepted.

West Virginia University, Davis College of Agriculture, Forestry and Consumer Sciences, Morgantown, WV 26506. Offers M Agr, MS, MSF, PhD. Part-time programs available. *Degree requirements:* For master's, thesis; for doctorate, thesis/dissertation. *Entrance requirements:* Additional exam requirements/recommendations for international students: Required—TOEFL. Electronic applications accepted. *Faculty research:* Reproductive physiology, soil and water quality, human nutrition, aquaculture, wildlife management.

Agronomy and Soil Sciences

Alabama Agricultural and Mechanical University, School of Graduate Studies, College of Agricultural, Life and Natural Sciences, Department of Biological and Environmental Sciences, Huntsville, AL 35811. Offers plant and soil science (MS, PhD). Evening/weekend programs available. Terminal master's awarded for partial completion of doctoral program. *Degree requirements:* For master's, thesis; for doctorate, one foreign language, thesis/dissertation. *Entrance requirements:* For master's, GRE General Test, BS in agriculture; for doctorate, GRE General Test, master's degree. Additional exam requirements/recommendations for international students: Required—TOEFL (minimum score 500 paper-based; 173 computer-based; 61 iBT). Electronic applications accepted. *Faculty research:* Plant breeding, cytogenetics, crop production, soil chemistry and fertility, remote sensing.

Alcorn State University, School of Graduate Studies, School of Agriculture and Applied Science, Alcorn State, MS 39096-7500. Offers agricultural economics (MS Ag); agronomy (MS Ag); animal science (MS Ag). *Degree requirements:* For master's, thesis optional. *Faculty research:* Aquatic systems, dairy herd improvement, fruit production, alternative farming practices.

American University of Beirut, Graduate Programs, Faculty of Agricultural and Food Sciences, Beirut, Lebanon. Offers agricultural economics (MS); animal sciences (MS); ecosystem management (MSES); food technology (MS); irrigation (MS); mechanization (MS); nutrition (MS); plant protection (MS); plant science (MS); poultry science (MS); soils (MS). Part-time programs available. *Faculty:* 21 full-time (6 women), 2 part-time/adjunct (0 women). *Students:* 12 full-time (all women), 93 part-time (77 women). Average age 24. 96 applicants, 67% accepted, 21 enrolled. In 2011, 25 master's awarded. *Degree requirements:* For master's, one foreign language, comprehensive exam, thesis (for some programs). *Entrance requirements:* Additional exam requirements/recommendations for international students: Required—TOEFL (minimum score 600 paper-based; 250 computer-based; 100 iBT), IELTS (minimum score 7.5). *Application deadline:* For fall admission, 2/20 for domestic and international students; for spring admission, 11/15 for domestic and international students. Applications are processed on a rolling basis. Application fee: $50. Electronic applications accepted. *Expenses:* Tuition: Full-time $12,780; part-time $710 per credit. *Required fees:* $528; $528 per credit. Tuition and fees vary according to course load and program. *Financial support:* In 2011–12, 22 research assistantships with partial tuition reimbursements (averaging $15,000 per year), 40 teaching assistantships with full and partial tuition reimbursements (averaging $1,000 per year) were awarded; scholarships/grants, health care benefits, and unspecified assistantships also available. Financial award application deadline: 2/2. *Faculty research:* Nutritional food-based dietary guidelines, community and therapeutic nutrition, food safety and food microbiology, landscape planning, nature and rural heritage conservation, pathology, immunology and control of poultry and animal diseases, agricultural economics and development, production of biodiesel from algae, national study on living conditions of refugees. *Unit head:* Prof. Nahla Hwalla, Dean, 961-1343002 Ext. 4400, Fax: 961-1744460, E-mail: nahla@aub.edu.lb. *Application contact:* Dr. Salim Kanaan, Director, Admissions Office, 961-1350000 Ext. 2594, Fax: 961-1750775, E-mail: sk00@aub.edu.lb. Web site: http://www.aub.edu.lb/fafs/Pages/index.aspx.

Auburn University, Graduate School, College of Agriculture, Department of Agronomy and Soils, Auburn University, AL 36849. Offers M Ag, MS, PhD. Part-time programs available. *Faculty:* 26 full-time (6 women). *Students:* 16 full-time (7 women), 27 part-time (8 women); includes 3 minority (2 Asian, non-Hispanic/Latino; 1 Hispanic/Latino), 17 international. Average age 28. 28 applicants, 54% accepted, 12 enrolled. In 2011, 6 master's, 2 doctorates awarded. *Degree requirements:* For master's, thesis (for some programs); for doctorate, thesis/dissertation. *Entrance requirements:* For master's and doctorate, GRE General Test. *Application deadline:* For fall admission, 7/7 for domestic students; for spring admission, 11/24 for domestic students. Applications are processed on a rolling basis. Application fee: $50 ($60 for international students). Electronic applications accepted. *Expenses:* Tuition, state resident: full-time $7290; part-time $405 per credit hour. Tuition, nonresident: full-time $21,870; part-time $1215 per credit hour. *International tuition:* $22,000 full-time. *Required fees:* $1402. *Financial support:* Research assistantships, teaching assistantships, and Federal Work-Study available. Support available to part-time students. Financial award application deadline: 3/15; financial award applicants required to submit FAFSA. *Faculty research:* Plant breeding and genetics; weed science; crop production;

soil fertility and plant nutrition; soil genesis, morphology, and classification. *Unit head:* Dr. Joseph T. Touchton, Head, 334-844-4100, E-mail: jtouchto@ag.auburn.edu. *Application contact:* Dr. George Flowers, Dean of the Graduate School, 334-844-2125.

Colorado State University, Graduate School, College of Agricultural Sciences, Department of Soil and Crop Sciences, Fort Collins, CO 80523-1170. Offers MS, PhD. Part-time programs available. *Faculty:* 19 full-time (4 women), 1 part-time/adjunct (0 women). *Students:* 23 full-time (8 women), 18 part-time (6 women); includes 3 minority (2 Black or African American, non-Hispanic/Latino; 1 Asian, non-Hispanic/Latino), 11 international. Average age 33. 28 applicants, 36% accepted, 9 enrolled. In 2011, 6 master's, 5 doctorates awarded. Terminal master's awarded for partial completion of doctoral program. *Degree requirements:* For master's, thesis; for doctorate, comprehensive exam, thesis/dissertation, student teaching. *Entrance requirements:* For master's, GRE, minimum GPA of 3.0, appropriate bachelor's degree, letters of recommendation, statement of purpose; for doctorate, GRE, minimum GPA of 3.0, appropriate master's degree, letters of recommendation. Additional exam requirements/recommendations for international students: Required—TOEFL (minimum score 550 paper-based; 213 computer-based; 80 iBT). *Application deadline:* For fall admission, 4/1 priority date for domestic students, 5/1 for international students; for spring admission, 9/1 priority date for domestic students, 10/1 for international students. Application fee: $50. Electronic applications accepted. *Expenses:* Tuition, state resident: full-time $7992. Tuition, nonresident: full-time $19,592. *Required fees:* $1735; $58 per credit. *Financial support:* In 2011–12, 20 students received support, including 4 fellowships with full tuition reimbursements available (averaging $35,814 per year), 15 research assistantships with full tuition reimbursements available (averaging $19,994 per year), 1 teaching assistantship with full tuition reimbursement available (averaging $7,721 per year); scholarships/grants and unspecified assistantships also available. Financial award application deadline: 2/15; financial award applicants required to submit FAFSA. *Faculty research:* Water quality, soil fertility, soil/plant ecosystems, plant breeding and genetics, cropping systems . *Total annual research expenditures:* $4.5 million. *Unit head:* Dr. Eugene Kelly, Head, 970-491-6881, Fax: 970-491-0564, E-mail: eugene.kelly@colostate.edu. *Application contact:* Karen Allison, Graduate Contact, 970-491-6295, Fax: 970-491-0564, E-mail: karen.allison@colostate.edu. Web site: http://www.soilcrop.colostate.edu/.

Cornell University, Graduate School, Graduate Fields of Agriculture and Life Sciences, Field of Soil and Crop Sciences, Ithaca, NY 14853-0001. Offers agronomy (MS, PhD); environmental information science (MS, PhD); environmental management (MPS); field crop science (MS, PhD); soil science (MS, PhD). *Faculty:* 39 full-time (9 women). *Students:* 19 full-time (11 women); includes 5 minority (all Hispanic/Latino), 4 international. Average age 28. 39 applicants, 18% accepted, 6 enrolled. In 2011, 5 master's, 5 doctorates awarded. *Degree requirements:* For master's, thesis (MS); for doctorate, comprehensive exam, thesis/dissertation. *Entrance requirements:* For master's and doctorate, GRE General Test, 2 letters of recommendation. Additional exam requirements/recommendations for international students: Required—TOEFL (minimum score 550 paper-based; 213 computer-based; 77 iBT). *Application deadline:* For fall admission, 2/1 priority date for domestic students. Applications are processed on a rolling basis. Application fee: $95. Electronic applications accepted. *Financial support:* In 2011–12, 5 fellowships with full tuition reimbursements, 2 research assistantships with full tuition reimbursements, 7 teaching assistantships with full tuition reimbursements were awarded; institutionally sponsored loans, traineeships, health care benefits, tuition waivers (full and partial), and unspecified assistantships also available. *Faculty research:* Soil chemistry, physics and biology; crop physiology and management; environmental information science and modeling; international agriculture; weed science. *Unit head:* Director of Graduate Studies, 607-255-3267, Fax: 607-255-8615. *Application contact:* Graduate Field Assistant, 607-255-3267, Fax: 607-255-8615, E-mail: ljh4@cornell.edu. Web site: http://www.gradschool.cornell.edu/fields.php?id-5A&a-2.

Iowa State University of Science and Technology, Department of Agronomy, Ames, IA 50011-1010. Offers agricultural meteorology (MS, PhD); agronomy (MS); crop production and physiology (MS, PhD); plant breeding (MS, PhD); soil science (MS, PhD). *Degree requirements:* For master's, thesis or alternative. *Entrance requirements:* Additional exam requirements/recommendations for international students: Recommended—TQEFL (minimum score 550 paper-

Peterson's Graduate Programs in the Physical Sciences, Mathematics, Agricultural Sciences, the Environment & Natural Resources 2013

facebook.com/petersonspublishing **407**

Agronomy and Soil Sciences

based; 79 iBT), IELTS (minimum score 6.5). *Application deadline:* For fall admission, 4/15 priority date for domestic students, 4/15 for international students; for spring admission, 10/1 priority date for domestic students, 10/1 for international students. Applications are processed on a rolling basis. Application fee: $40 ($90 for international students). Electronic applications accepted. *Unit head:* Dr. Tom Loynachan, Director of Graduate Education, 515-294-2999, Fax: 515-294-5506, E-mail: msagron@iastate.edu. *Application contact:* Dawn Miller, Application Contact, 515-294-2999, Fax: 515-294-5506, E-mail: msagron@iastate.edu. Web site: http://www.agron.iastate.edu/.

Iowa State University of Science and Technology, Program in Crop Production and Physiology, Ames, IA 50011-1010. Offers MS, PhD. *Entrance requirements:* Additional exam requirements/recommendations for international students: Required—TOEFL (minimum score 550 paper-based; 79 iBT), IELTS (minimum score 6.5). *Application deadline:* Applications are processed on a rolling basis. Electronic applications accepted. *Unit head:* Tom E. Loynachan, Director of Graduate Education, 515-294-1361, Fax: 515-294-8146, E-mail: gradprograms@agron.iastate.edu. *Application contact:* Jaci Severson, Application Contact, 515-294-1361, Fax: 515-294-8146, E-mail: gradprograms@agron.iastate.edu. Web site: http://www.agron.iastate.edu.

Iowa State University of Science and Technology, Program in Soil Science, Ames, IA 50011-1010. Offers MS, PhD. *Entrance requirements:* Additional exam requirements/recommendations for international students: Required—TOEFL (minimum score 550 paper-based; 79 iBT), IELTS (minimum score 6.5). *Application deadline:* Applications are processed on a rolling basis. Electronic applications accepted. *Unit head:* Tom E. Loynachan, Director of Graduate Education, 515-294-1361, Fax: 515-294-8146, E-mail: gradprograms@agron.iastate.edu. *Application contact:* Jaci Severson, Application Contact, 515-294-1361, Fax: 515-294-8146, E-mail: grad_admissions@iastate.edu. Web site: http://www.agron.iastate.edu.

Kansas State University, Graduate School, College of Agriculture, Department of Agronomy, Manhattan, KS 66506. Offers crop science (MS, PhD); plant breeding and genetics (MS, PhD); range management (MS, PhD); soil science (MS, PhD); weed science (MS, PhD). Part-time programs available. *Faculty:* 28 full-time (4 women), 11 part-time/adjunct (1 woman). *Students:* 62 full-time (18 women), 10 part-time (4 women); includes 4 minority (2 Black or African American, non-Hispanic/Latino; 1 Asian, non-Hispanic/Latino; 1 Hispanic/Latino), 34 international. Average age 31. 31 applicants, 42% accepted, 9 enrolled. In 2011, 8 master's, 4 doctorates awarded. Terminal master's awarded for partial completion of doctoral program. *Degree requirements:* For master's, thesis or alternative, oral exam; for doctorate, thesis/dissertation, preliminary exams. *Entrance requirements:* For master's, minimum GPA of 3.0 in BS; for doctorate, minimum GPA of 3.5 in master's program. Additional exam requirements/recommendations for international students: Required—TOEFL (minimum score 500 paper-based; 250 computer-based). *Application deadline:* For fall admission, 2/1 priority date for domestic students, 2/1 for international students; for spring admission, 8/1 priority date for domestic students, 8/1 for international students. Applications are processed on a rolling basis. Application fee: $40 ($55 for international students). Electronic applications accepted. *Financial support:* In 2011–12, 64 research assistantships (averaging $21,705 per year), 7 teaching assistantships with partial tuition reimbursements (averaging $18,200 per year) were awarded; institutionally sponsored loans and scholarships/grants also available. Support available to part-time students. Financial award application deadline: 3/1; financial award applicants required to submit FAFSA. *Faculty research:* Range and forage science, soil and environmental science, crop physiology, weed science, plant breeding and genetics. *Total annual research expenditures:* $5.5 million. *Unit head:* Dr. William Schapaugh, Head, 785-532-6101, Fax: 785-532-6094, E-mail: wts@ksu.edu. *Application contact:* Dr. Scott Staggenborg, Graduate Coordinator, 785-532-7214, Fax: 785-532-6094, E-mail: sstaggen@ksu.edu. Web site: http://www.agronomy.k-state.edu/DesktopDefault.aspx.

Louisiana State University and Agricultural and Mechanical College, Graduate School, College of Agriculture, School of Plant, Environmental and Soil Sciences, Department of Agronomy and Environmental Management, Baton Rouge, LA 70803. Offers agronomy (MS, PhD). Part-time programs available. *Faculty:* 32 full-time (4 women). *Students:* 39 full-time (11 women), 5 part-time (1 woman); includes 4 minority (1 Asian, non-Hispanic/Latino; 2 Hispanic/Latino; 1 Two or more races, non-Hispanic/Latino), 19 international. Average age 29. 27 applicants, 37% accepted, 4 enrolled. In 2011, 3 master's, 5 doctorates awarded. *Degree requirements:* For master's, thesis or alternative; for doctorate, thesis/dissertation. *Entrance requirements:* For master's and doctorate, GRE General Test, minimum GPA of 3.0. Additional exam requirements/recommendations for international students: Required—TOEFL (minimum score 550 paper-based; 213 computer-based; 79 iBT) or IELTS (minimum score 6.5). *Application deadline:* For fall admission, 1/25 priority date for domestic students, 5/15 for international students; for spring admission, 10/15 for international students. Applications are processed on a rolling basis. Application fee: $50 ($70 for international students). Electronic applications accepted. *Financial support:* In 2011–12, 41 students received support, including 34 research assistantships with partial tuition reimbursements available (averaging $19,212 per year), 1 teaching assistantship with partial tuition reimbursement available (averaging $16,000 per year); fellowships, Federal Work-Study, scholarships/grants, tuition waivers (full), and unspecified assistantships also available. Support available to part-time students. Financial award applicants required to submit FAFSA. *Faculty research:* Crop

production, resource management, environmental studies, soil science, plant genetics. *Total annual research expenditures:* $54,474. *Unit head:* Dr. Don LaBonte, Director, 225-578-2110, Fax: 225-578-1403, E-mail: dlabonte@lsu.edu. *Application contact:* Dr. David Weindofr, Graduate Coordinator, 225-578-0396, Fax: 225-578-1403, E-mail: dweindorf@agcenter.lsu.edu. Web site: http://www.agronomy.lsu.edu/.

McGill University, Faculty of Graduate and Postdoctoral Studies, Faculty of Agricultural and Environmental Sciences, Department of Bioresource Engineering, Montréal, QC H3A 2T5, Canada. Offers computer applications (M Sc, M Sc A, PhD); food engineering (M Sc, M Sc A, PhD); grain drying (M Sc, M Sc A, PhD); irrigation and drainage (M Sc, M Sc A, PhD); machinery (M Sc, M Sc A, PhD); pollution control (M Sc, M Sc A, PhD); post-harvest technology (M Sc, M Sc A, PhD); soil dynamics (M Sc, M Sc A, PhD); structure and environment (M Sc, M Sc A, PhD); vegetable and fruit storage (M Sc, M Sc A, PhD).

McGill University, Faculty of Graduate and Postdoctoral Studies, Faculty of Agricultural and Environmental Sciences, Department of Natural Resource Sciences, Montréal, QC H3A 2T5, Canada. Offers entomology (M Sc, PhD); environmental assessment (M Sc); forest science (M Sc, PhD); microbiology (M Sc, PhD); micrometeorology (M Sc, PhD); neotropical environment (M Sc, PhD); soil science (M Sc, PhD); wildlife biology (M Sc, PhD).

Michigan State University, The Graduate School, College of Agriculture and Natural Resources, Department of Crop and Soil Sciences, East Lansing, MI 48824. Offers crop and soil sciences (MS, PhD); crop and soil sciences-environmental toxicology (PhD); plant breeding and genetics-crop and soil sciences (MS); plant breeding, genetics and biotechnology-crop and soil sciences (PhD). *Entrance requirements:* Additional exam requirements/recommendations for international students: Required—TOEFL (minimum score 550 paper-based; 213 computer-based), Michigan State University ELT (minimum score 85), Michigan Michigan English Language Assessment Battery (minimum score 83). Electronic applications accepted.

Michigan State University, The Graduate School, College of Agriculture and Natural Resources, MSU-DOE Plant Research Laboratory, East Lansing, MI 48824. Offers biochemistry and molecular biology (PhD); cellular and molecular biology (PhD); crop and soil sciences (PhD); genetics (PhD); microbiology and molecular genetics (PhD); plant biology (PhD); plant physiology (PhD). Offered jointly with the Department of Energy. *Degree requirements:* For doctorate, comprehensive exam, thesis/dissertation, laboratory rotation, defense of dissertation. *Entrance requirements:* For doctorate, GRE General Test, acceptance into one of the affiliated department programs; 3 letters of recommendation; bachelor's degree or equivalent in life sciences, chemistry, biochemistry, or biophysics; research experience. Electronic applications accepted. *Faculty research:* Role of hormones in the regulation of plant development and physiology, molecular mechanisms associated with signal recognition, development and application of genetic methods and materials, protein routing and function.

Mississippi State University, College of Agriculture and Life Sciences, Department of Plant and Soil Sciences, Mississippi State, MS 39762. Offers agriculture (MS), including agronomy, horticulture, weed science. *Faculty:* 30 full-time (1 woman), 1 part-time/adjunct (0 women). *Students:* 34 full-time (11 women), 21 part-time (5 women); includes 5 minority (3 Black or African American, non-Hispanic/Latino; 2 American Indian or Alaska Native, non-Hispanic/Latino), 13 international. Average age 30. 33 applicants, 42% accepted, 12 enrolled. In 2011, 6 master's awarded. *Degree requirements:* For master's, thesis, exit seminar describing thesis research. *Entrance requirements:* For master's, GRE (weed science), minimum GPA of 2.75 (agronomy/horticulture), 3.0 (weed science). Additional exam requirements/recommendations for international students: Required—TOEFL (minimum score 550 paper-based; 213 computer-based; 79 iBT); Recommended—IELTS (minimum score 6.5). *Application deadline:* For fall admission, 7/1 for domestic students, 5/1 for international students; for spring admission, 10/1 for domestic students, 9/1 for international students. Applications are processed on a rolling basis. Application fee: $40. Electronic applications accepted. *Expenses:* Tuition, state resident: full-time $5805; part-time $322.50 per credit hour. Tuition, nonresident: full-time $14,670; part-time $815 per credit hour. *Financial support:* In 2011–12, 30 research assistantships (averaging $14,692 per year), 3 teaching assistantships (averaging $15,133 per year) were awarded; Federal Work-Study, institutionally sponsored loans, scholarships/grants, and unspecified assistantships also available. Financial award application deadline: 4/1; financial award applicants required to submit FAFSA. *Unit head:* Dr. J. Mike Phillips, Professor and Head, 662-325-2311, Fax: 662-325-8742, E-mail: jmp657@msstate.edu. *Application contact:* Dr. William Kingery, Graduate Coordinator, 662-325-2748, Fax: 662-325-8742, E-mail: wkingery@pss.msstate.edu. Web site: http://www.pss.msstate.edu/

North Carolina Agricultural and Technical State University, School of Graduate Studies, School of Agriculture and Environmental Sciences, Department of Natural Resources and Environmental Design, Greensboro, NC 27411. Offers plant, soil and environmental science (MS). Part-time and evening/weekend programs available. *Degree requirements:* For master's, comprehensive exam, thesis optional, qualifying exam. *Entrance requirements:* For master's, GRE General Test, minimum GPA of 3.0. *Faculty research:* Soil parameters and

408 facebook.com/petersonspublishing

Peterson's Graduate Programs in the Physical Sciences, Mathematics, Agricultural Sciences, the Environment & Natural Resources 2013

compaction of forest site, controlled traffic effects on soil, improving soybean and vegetable crops.

North Carolina State University, Graduate School, College of Agriculture and Life Sciences, Department of Crop Science, Raleigh, NC 27695. Offers MS, PhD. Part-time programs available. Terminal master's awarded for partial completion of doctoral program. *Degree requirements:* For master's, thesis; for doctorate, thesis/dissertation. *Entrance requirements:* For master's and doctorate, GRE. Electronic applications accepted. *Faculty research:* Crop breeding and genetics, application of biotechnology to crop improvement, plant physiology, crop physiology and management, agroecology.

North Carolina State University, Graduate School, College of Agriculture and Life Sciences, Department of Soil Science, Raleigh, NC 27695. Offers MS, PhD. Part-time programs available. Postbaccalaureate distance learning degree programs offered. *Degree requirements:* For master's, thesis (for some programs); for doctorate, thesis/dissertation. *Entrance requirements:* For master's and doctorate, GRE, minimum GPA of 3.0. Additional exam requirements/ recommendations for international students: Required—TOEFL (minimum score 75 iBT). Electronic applications accepted. *Faculty research:* Soil management, soil-environmental relations, chemical and physical properties of soils, nutrient and water management, land use.

North Dakota State University, College of Graduate and Interdisciplinary Studies, College of Agriculture, Food Systems, and Natural Resources, Department of Soil Science, Fargo, ND 58108. Offers environmental and conservation science (PhD); environmental conservation science (MS); natural resource management (MS, PhD); soil sciences (MS, PhD). Part-time programs available. *Students:* 7 full-time (5 women), 3 part-time (1 woman), 4 international. Average age 23. 4 applicants, 50% accepted, 0 enrolled. In 2011, 4 degrees awarded. *Degree requirements:* For master's, comprehensive exam, thesis, classroom teaching; for doctorate, comprehensive exam, thesis/dissertation, classroom teaching. *Entrance requirements:* Additional exam requirements/ recommendations for international students: Required—TOEFL (minimum score 525 paper-based; 193 computer-based; 71 iBT). *Application deadline:* For fall admission, 5/1 for international students; for winter admission, 8/1 for international students. Applications are processed on a rolling basis. Application fee: $35. Electronic applications accepted. *Financial support:* In 2011–12, 7 research assistantships with full tuition reimbursements (averaging $14,300 per year) were awarded; fellowships, Federal Work-Study, institutionally sponsored loans, and scholarships/grants also available. Financial award application deadline: 3/15. *Faculty research:* Microclimate, nitrogen management, landscape studies, water quality, soil management. *Unit head:* Dr. Donald Kirby, Interim Chair, 701-231-8901, Fax: 701-231-7861. *Application contact:* Sonya Goergen, Marketing, Recruitment, and Public Relations Coordinator, 701-231-7033, Fax: 701-231-6524. Web site: http://www.ndsu.edu/ndsu/academic/factsheets/ag/soilsci.shtml.

Nova Scotia Agricultural College, Research and Graduate Studies, Truro, NS B2N 5E3, Canada. Offers agriculture (M Sc), including air quality, animal behavior, animal molecular genetics, animal nutrition, animal technology, aquaculture, botany, crop management, crop physiology, ecology, environmental microbiology, food science, horticulture, nutrient management, pest management, physiology, plant biotechnology, plant pathology, soil chemistry, soil fertility, waste management and composting, water quality. Program offered jointly with Dalhousie University. Part-time programs available. *Degree requirements:* For master's, thesis, ATC Exam Teaching Assistantship. *Entrance requirements:* For master's, honors B Sc, minimum GPA of 3.0. Additional exam requirements/ recommendations for international students: Required—TOEFL (minimum score 580 paper-based; 237 computer-based; 92 iBT), IELTS, Michigan English Language Assessment Battery, CanTEST, CAEL. *Faculty research:* Bio-product development, organic agriculture, nutrient management, air and water quality, agricultural biotechnology.

The Ohio State University, Graduate School, College of Food, Agricultural, and Environmental Sciences, School of Environment and Natural Resources, Program in Soil Science, Columbus, OH 43210. Offers MS, PhD. *Faculty:* 9. *Students:* 1 (woman) full-time, 1 (woman) part-time, 1 international. Average age 29. In 2011, 3 master's, 4 doctorates awarded. *Degree requirements:* For doctorate, thesis/ dissertation. *Entrance requirements:* For master's and doctorate, GRE General Test. Additional exam requirements/recommendations for international students: Required—TOEFL (minimum score 550 paper-based; 213 computer-based), IELTS (minimum score 6.5), or Michigan English Language Assessment Battery (minimum score 82). *Application deadline:* For fall admission, 8/15 priority date for domestic students, 7/1 for international students; for winter admission, 12/1 priority date for domestic students, 11/1 for international students; for spring admission, 3/1 priority date for domestic students, 2/1 for international students. Applications are processed on a rolling basis. Application fee: $40 ($50 for international students). Electronic applications accepted. *Expenses:* Tuition, state resident: full-time $11,400. Tuition, nonresident: full-time $28,125. Tuition and fees vary according to course load, degree level, campus/location and program. *Unit head:* Ronald Hendrick, Director, 614-292-8522, E-mail: hendrick.15@ osu.edu. *Application contact:* Amy Schmidt, Graduate Program Coordinator, 614-292-9883, Fax: 614-292-7432, E-mail: schmidt.442@osu.edu. Web site: http:// senr.osu.edu/Future_Graduate_Students/Graduate_Areas_of_Specialization/ Soil_Science_.htm.

Oklahoma State University, College of Agricultural Science and Natural Resources, Department of Horticulture and Landscape Architecture, Stillwater,

OK 74078. Offers agriculture (M Ag); crop science (PhD); environmental science (PhD); horticulture (MS); plant science (PhD). *Faculty:* 20 full-time (2 women), 2 part-time/adjunct (1 woman). *Students:* 3 full-time (all women), 12 part-time (8 women); includes 2 minority (1 Black or African American, non-Hispanic/Latino; 1 American Indian or Alaska Native, non-Hispanic/Latino), 7 international. Average age 28. 6 applicants, 67% accepted, 4 enrolled. In 2011, 6 degrees awarded. *Degree requirements:* For master's, thesis (for some programs); for doctorate, comprehensive exam, thesis/dissertation. *Entrance requirements:* For master's and doctorate, GRE or GMAT. Additional exam requirements/recommendations for international students: Required—TOEFL (minimum score 550 paper-based; 79 iBT). *Application deadline:* For fall admission, 3/1 for international students; for spring admission, 8/1 for international students. Applications are processed on a rolling basis. Application fee: $40 ($75 for international students). Electronic applications accepted. *Expenses:* Tuition, state resident: full-time $4044; part-time $168.50 per credit hour. Tuition, nonresident: full-time $16,008; part-time $667 per credit hour. *Required fees:* $2122; $88.45 per credit hour. One-time fee: $50. Tuition and fees vary according to course load and campus/location. *Financial support:* In 2011–12, 13 research assistantships (averaging $14,145 per year) were awarded; career-related internships or fieldwork, Federal Work-Study, scholarships/grants, health care benefits, tuition waivers (partial), and unspecified assistantships also available. Support available to part-time students. Financial award application deadline: 3/1; financial award applicants required to submit FAFSA. *Faculty research:* Stress and postharvest physiology; water utilization and runoff; IPM systems and nursery, turf, floriculture, vegetable, net and fruit produces and natural resources, food extraction, and processing; public garden management. *Unit head:* Dr. Dale Maronek, Head, 405-744-5414, Fax: 405-744-9709. *Application contact:* Dr. Sheryl Tucker, Dean, 405-744-7099, Fax: 405-744-0355, E-mail: grad-i@okstate.edu. Web site: http:// www.hortla.okstate.edu/.

Oklahoma State University, College of Agricultural Science and Natural Resources, Department of Plant and Soil Sciences, Stillwater, OK 74078. Offers crop science (PhD); environmental science (PhD); plant and soil sciences (MS); plant science (PhD); soil science (M Ag, PhD). *Faculty:* 31 full-time (4 women), 1 part-time/adjunct (0 women). *Students:* 19 full-time (5 women), 42 part-time (20 women); includes 5 minority (2 Black or African American, non-Hispanic/Latino; 1 Asian, non-Hispanic/Latino; 2 Two or more races, non-Hispanic/Latino), 33 international. Average age 28. 32 applicants, 22% accepted, 3 enrolled. In 2011, 18 master's, 3 doctorates awarded. *Degree requirements:* For master's, thesis; for doctorate, comprehensive exam, thesis/dissertation. *Entrance requirements:* For master's and doctorate, GRE or GMAT. Additional exam requirements/ recommendations for international students: Required—TOEFL (minimum score 550 paper-based; 79 iBT). *Application deadline:* For fall admission, 3/1 for international students; for spring admission, 8/1 for international students. Applications are processed on a rolling basis. Application fee: $40 ($75 for international students). Electronic applications accepted. *Expenses:* Tuition, state resident: full-time $4044; part-time $168.50 per credit hour. Tuition, nonresident: full-time $16,008; part-time $667 per credit hour. *Required fees:* $2122; $88.45 per credit hour. One-time fee: $50. Tuition and fees vary according to course load and campus/location. *Financial support:* In 2011–12, 49 research assistantships (averaging $14,782 per year), 3 teaching assistantships (averaging $17,080 per year) were awarded; career-related internships or fieldwork, Federal Work-Study, scholarships/grants, health care benefits, tuition waivers (partial), and unspecified assistantships also available. Support available to part-time students. Financial award application deadline: 3/1; financial award applicants required to submit FAFSA. *Faculty research:* Crop science, weed science, rangeland ecology and management, biotechnology, breeding and genetics. *Unit head:* Dr. Don R. Murray, Interim Head, 405-744-6130, Fax: 405-744-5269. *Application contact:* Dr. Sheryl Tucker, Dean, 405-744-7099, Fax: 405-744-0355, E-mail: grad-i@ okstate.edu. Web site: http://www.pss.okstate.edu.

Oregon State University, Graduate School, College of Agricultural Sciences, Department of Crop and Soil Science, Program in Crop Science, Corvallis, OR 97331. Offers M Agr, MAIS, MS, PhD. Part-time programs available. *Degree requirements:* For master's, thesis (for some programs); for doctorate, variable foreign language requirement, thesis/dissertation. *Entrance requirements:* For master's and doctorate, GRE, minimum GPA of 3.0 in last 90 hours of course work. Additional exam requirements/recommendations for international students: Required—TOEFL. *Faculty research:* Cereal and new crops breeding and genetics; weed science; seed technology and production; potato, new crops, and general crop production; plant physiology.

Oregon State University, Graduate School, College of Agricultural Sciences, Department of Crop and Soil Science, Program in Soil Science, Corvallis, OR 97331. Offers M Agr, MAIS, MS, PhD. Part-time programs available. *Degree requirements:* For master's, thesis (for some programs); for doctorate, variable foreign language requirement, thesis/dissertation. *Entrance requirements:* For master's and doctorate, GRE, minimum GPA of 3.0 in last 90 hours of course work. Additional exam requirements/recommendations for international students: Required—TOEFL. *Faculty research:* Soil physics, chemistry, biology, fertility, and genesis.

Penn State University Park, Graduate School, College of Agricultural Sciences, Department of Crop and Soil Sciences, State College, University Park, PA 16802-1503. Offers agronomy (MS, PhD); soil science (MS, PhD); turfgrass management (MPS). *Unit head:* Dr. Bruce A. McPheron, Dean, 814-865-2541, Fax: 814-865-3103, E-mail: bam10@psu.edu. *Application contact:* Cynthia E.

Peterson's Graduate Programs in the Physical Sciences, Mathematics, Agricultural Sciences, the Environment & Natural Resources 2013

facebook.com/petersonspublishing **409**

Agronomy and Soil Sciences

Nicosia, Director of Graduate Enrollment Services, 814-865-1834, E-mail: cey1@psu.edu. Web site: http://cropsoil.psu.edu/.

Prairie View A&M University, College of Agriculture and Human Sciences, Prairie View, TX 77446-0519. Offers agricultural economics (MS); animal sciences (MS); interdisciplinary human sciences (MS); soil science (MS). Part-time and evening/weekend programs available. *Degree requirements:* For master's, comprehensive exam, thesis (for some programs), field placement. *Entrance requirements:* For master's, GRE General Test, minimum GPA of 2.45. Additional exam requirements/recommendations for international students: Required—TOEFL (minimum score 550 paper-based). *Faculty research:* Domestic violence prevention, water quality, food growth regulators, wetland dynamics, biochemistry, obesity and nutrition, family therapy.

Purdue University, Graduate School, College of Agriculture, Department of Agronomy, West Lafayette, IN 47907. Offers MS, PhD. Part-time programs available. *Faculty:* 36 full-time (6 women), 13 part-time/adjunct (3 women). *Students:* 56 full-time (23 women), 10 part-time (2 women); includes 3 minority (1 Black or African American, non-Hispanic/Latino; 1 American Indian or Alaska Native, non-Hispanic/Latino; 1 Hispanic/Latino), 22 international. Average age 29. 71 applicants, 25% accepted, 13 enrolled. In 2011, 6 master's, 7 doctorates awarded. *Degree requirements:* For doctorate, thesis/dissertation. *Entrance requirements:* For master's and doctorate, GRE General Test, minimum undergraduate GPA of 3.0 or equivalent. Additional exam requirements/recommendations for international students: Recommended—TOEFL (minimum score 550 paper-based; 77 iBT), TWE. *Application deadline:* For fall admission, 4/15 for domestic and international students; for spring admission, 10/15 for domestic students, 9/15 for international students. Applications are processed on a rolling basis. Application fee: $60 ($75 for international students). Electronic applications accepted. *Financial support:* Fellowships with tuition reimbursements, research assistantships with tuition reimbursements, and teaching assistantships with tuition reimbursements available. Support available to part-time students. Financial award applicants required to submit FAFSA. *Faculty research:* Plant genetics and breeding, crop physiology and ecology, agricultural meteorology, soil microbiology. *Unit head:* Dr. J. M. Anderson, Head, 765-494-5565, E-mail: janderson@purdue.edu. *Application contact:* Karen N. Clymer, Graduate Coordinator, 765-494-4775, E-mail: kclymer@purdue.edu.

South Dakota State University, Graduate School, College of Agriculture and Biological Sciences, Department of Plant Science, Brookings, SD 57007. Offers agronomy (PhD); biological sciences (PhD); plant science (MS). *Degree requirements:* For master's, thesis (for some programs), oral exam; for doctorate, comprehensive exam, thesis/dissertation, preliminary oral and written exams. *Entrance requirements:* Additional exam requirements/recommendations for international students: Required—TOEFL (minimum score 560 paper-based; 220 computer-based; 83 iBT).

Southern Illinois University Carbondale, Graduate School, College of Agriculture, Department of Plant, Soil, and General Agriculture, Carbondale, IL 62901-4701. Offers horticultural science (MS); plant and soil science (MS). *Faculty:* 12 full-time (1 woman), 8 part-time/adjunct (0 women). *Students:* 13 full-time (5 women), 30 part-time (11 women); includes 4 minority (2 Black or African American, non-Hispanic/Latino; 1 American Indian or Alaska Native, non-Hispanic/Latino; 1 Hispanic/Latino), 6 international. 13 applicants, 69% accepted, 5 enrolled. In 2011, 7 master's awarded. *Degree requirements:* For master's, thesis. *Entrance requirements:* For master's, minimum GPA of 2.7. Additional exam requirements/recommendations for international students: Required—TOEFL. *Application deadline:* Applications are processed on a rolling basis. Application fee: $0. *Financial support:* In 2011–12, 22 students received support, including 15 research assistantships with full tuition reimbursements available, 6 teaching assistantships with full tuition reimbursements available; fellowships with full tuition reimbursements available, Federal Work-Study, institutionally sponsored loans, and tuition waivers (full) also available. Support available to part-time students. *Faculty research:* Herbicides, fertilizers, agriculture education, landscape design, plant breeding. *Total annual research expenditures:* $2 million. *Unit head:* Dr. Brian Klubek, Chair, 618-453-2496, E-mail: bklubek@siu.edu. *Application contact:* Lisa Hartline, Administrative Clerk, 618-453-1770, E-mail: lisah@siu.edu.

Texas A&M University, College of Agriculture and Life Sciences, Department of Soil and Crop Sciences, College Station, TX 77843. Offers agronomy (M Agr, MS, PhD); food science and technology (MS, PhD); genetics (PhD); molecular and environmental plant sciences (MS, PhD); plant breeding (MS, PhD); soil science (MS, PhD). *Faculty:* 37. *Students:* 98 full-time (36 women), 29 part-time (4 women); includes 12 minority (4 Black or African American, non-Hispanic/Latino; 3 Asian, non-Hispanic/Latino; 5 Hispanic/Latino), 42 international. Average age 26. In 2011, 4 master's, 8 doctorates awarded. *Degree requirements:* For master's, thesis; for doctorate, thesis/dissertation. *Entrance requirements:* For master's and doctorate, GRE General Test. Additional exam requirements/recommendations for international students: Required—TOEFL. *Application deadline:* For fall admission, 3/1 priority date for domestic students; for spring admission, 8/1 for domestic students. Applications are processed on a rolling basis. Application fee: $50 ($75 for international students). *Expenses:* Tuition, state resident: full-time $5437; part-time $226.55 per credit hour. Tuition, nonresident: full-time $12,949; part-time $539.55 per credit hour. *Required fees:* $2741. *Financial support:* In 2011–12, fellowships (averaging $16,000 per year), research assistantships with partial tuition reimbursements (averaging $15,000 per year) were awarded; career-related internships or fieldwork, Federal Work-

Study, and institutionally sponsored loans also available. *Faculty research:* Soil and crop management, turfgrass science, weed science, cereal chemistry, food protein chemistry. *Unit head:* Dr. David D. Baltensperger, Department Head, 979-845-3001, E-mail: dbaltensperger@ag.tamu.edu. *Application contact:* Graduate Admissions, 979-845-1044, E-mail: admissions@tamu.edu. Web site: http://soilcrop.tamu.edu.

Texas A&M University–Kingsville, College of Graduate Studies, College of Agriculture and Home Economics, Program in Plant and Soil Sciences, Kingsville, TX 78363. Offers MS, PhD. *Degree requirements:* For master's, comprehensive exam, thesis or alternative. *Entrance requirements:* For master's, GRE General Test, minimum GPA of 3.0. Additional exam requirements/recommendations for international students: Required—TOEFL.

Texas Tech University, Graduate School, College of Agricultural Sciences and Natural Resources, Department of Plant and Soil Science, Lubbock, TX 79409. Offers crop science (MS); horticulture (MS); plant and soil science (PhD); plant protection (MS); soil science (MS); JD/MS. Part-time programs available. Postbaccalaureate distance learning degree programs offered (no on-campus study). *Faculty:* 8 full-time (4 women), 11 part-time/adjunct (1 woman). *Students:* 63 full-time (25 women), 39 part-time (19 women); includes 6 minority (3 Black or African American, non-Hispanic/Latino; 1 Asian, non-Hispanic/Latino; 2 Hispanic/Latino), 30 international. Average age 31. 63 applicants, 32% accepted, 15 enrolled. In 2011, 13 master's, 7 doctorates awarded. *Degree requirements:* For master's, thesis or alternative; for doctorate, thesis/dissertation. *Entrance requirements:* For master's and doctorate, GRE General Test, formal approval from departmental committee. Additional exam requirements/recommendations for international students: Required—TOEFL (minimum score 550 paper-based; 213 computer-based; 79 iBT). *Application deadline:* For fall admission, 6/1 priority date for domestic students, 1/15 for international students; for spring admission, 9/1 priority date for domestic students, 6/15 for international students. Applications are processed on a rolling basis. Application fee: $50 ($75 for international students). Electronic applications accepted. *Expenses:* Tuition, state resident: full-time $5899; part-time $245.80 per credit hour. Tuition, nonresident: full-time $13,411; part-time $558.80 per credit hour. *Required fees:* $2680.60; $86.50 per credit hour. $920.30 per semester. *Financial support:* In 2011–12, 52 students received support. Application deadline: 4/15; applicants required to submit FAFSA. *Faculty research:* Molecular and cellular biology of plant stress, physiology/genetics of crop production in semi-arid conditions, improvement of native plants, soil science and management, fibers and biopolymers. *Total annual research expenditures:* $6 million. *Unit head:* Dr. Richard E. Zartman, Chair, 806-742-2838 Ext. 230, Fax: 806-742-0775, E-mail: richard.zartman@ttu.edu. *Application contact:* Dr. Eric Hequet, Graduate Adviser, 806-742-2838 Ext. 239, Fax: 806-742-0775, E-mail: eric.hequet@ttu.edu. Web site: http://www.pssc.ttu.edu/.

Tuskegee University, Graduate Programs, College of Agricultural, Environmental and Natural Sciences, Department of Agricultural Sciences, Program in Plant and Soil Sciences, Tuskegee, AL 36088. Offers MS. *Faculty:* 13 full-time (1 woman), 2 part-time/adjunct (1 woman). *Students:* 4 full-time (2 women); includes 2 minority (both Black or African American, non-Hispanic/Latino), 1 international. Average age 30. In 2011, 3 master's awarded. *Degree requirements:* For master's, thesis. *Entrance requirements:* For master's, GRE General Test. Additional exam requirements/recommendations for international students: Required—TOEFL (minimum score 500 paper-based; 69 computer-based). *Application deadline:* For fall admission, 7/15 for domestic students. Applications are processed on a rolling basis. Application fee: $25 ($35 for international students). *Expenses: Tuition:* Full-time $17,070; part-time $705 per credit hour. *Financial support:* Application deadline: 4/15. *Unit head:* Dr. P. K. Biswas, Head, 334-727-8446. *Application contact:* Dr. Robert L. Laney, Jr., Vice President/Director of Admissions and Enrollment Management, 334-727-8580, Fax: 334-727-5750, E-mail: planey@tuskegee.edu.

Université Laval, Faculty of Agricultural and Food Sciences, Department of Soils and Agricultural Engineering, Programs in Soils and Environment Science, Québec, QC G1K 7P4, Canada. Offers environmental technology (M Sc); soils and environment science (M Sc, PhD). Terminal master's awarded for partial completion of doctoral program. *Degree requirements:* For master's, thesis (for some programs); for doctorate, comprehensive exam, thesis/dissertation. *Entrance requirements:* For master's and doctorate, knowledge of French and English. Electronic applications accepted.

Université Laval, Faculty of Forestry, Geography and Geomatics, Program in Agroforestry, Québec, QC G1K 7P4, Canada. Offers M Sc. *Degree requirements:* For master's, thesis (for some programs). *Entrance requirements:* For master's, English exam (comprehension of English), knowledge of French, knowledge of a third language. Electronic applications accepted.

University of Alberta, Faculty of Graduate Studies and Research, Department of Renewable Resources, Edmonton, AB T6G 2E1, Canada. Offers agroforestry (M Ag, M Sc, MF); conservation biology (M Sc, PhD); forest biology and management (M Sc, PhD); land reclamation and remediation (M Sc, PhD); protected areas and wildlands management (M Sc, PhD); soil science (M Ag, M Sc, PhD); water and land resources (M Ag, M Sc, PhD); wildlife ecology and management (M Sc, PhD); MBA/M Ag; MBA/MF. Part-time programs available. *Degree requirements:* For master's, thesis (for some programs); for doctorate, comprehensive exam, thesis/dissertation. *Entrance requirements:* For master's, minimum 2 years of relevant professional experiences, minimum GPA of 3.0; for

410 facebook.com/petersonspublishing

Peterson's Graduate Programs in the Physical Sciences, Mathematics, Agricultural Sciences, the Environment & Natural Resources 2013

doctorate, minimum GPA of 3.0. Additional exam requirements/recommendations for international students: Required—TOEFL (minimum score 550 paper-based; 213 computer-based). Electronic applications accepted. *Faculty research:* Natural and managed landscapes.

The University of Arizona, College of Agriculture and Life Sciences, Department of Soil, Water and Environmental Science, Tucson, AZ 85721. Offers MS, PhD. *Faculty:* 10 full-time (3 women), 1 (woman) part-time/adjunct. *Students:* 50 full-time (32 women), 7 part-time (2 women); includes 15 minority (2 Black or African American, non-Hispanic/Latino; 1 American Indian or Alaska Native, non-Hispanic/Latino; 1 Asian, non-Hispanic/Latino; 8 Hispanic/Latino; 3 Two or more races, non-Hispanic/Latino), 15 international. Average age 31. 37 applicants, 54% accepted, 13 enrolled. In 2011, 10 master's, 11 doctorates awarded. *Degree requirements:* For master's, thesis; for doctorate, comprehensive exam, thesis/dissertation. *Entrance requirements:* For master's, GRE (recommended), minimum GPA of 3.0, letter of interest, 3 letters of recommendation; for doctorate, GRE (recommended), MS, minimum GPA of 3.0, letter of interest, 3 letters of recommendation. Additional exam requirements/recommendations for international students: Required—TOEFL (minimum score 550 paper-based; 213 computer-based; 80 iBT). *Application deadline:* For fall admission, 6/1 for domestic students, 12/1 for international students; for spring admission, 10/1 for domestic students, 6/1 for international students. Applications are processed on a rolling basis. Application fee: $75. *Expenses:* Tuition, state resident: full-time $10,840. Tuition, nonresident: full-time $25,802. *Financial support:* In 2011–12, 14 students received support, including 24 research assistantships with full and partial tuition reimbursements available (averaging $18,526 per year), 2 teaching assistantships with full and partial tuition reimbursements available (averaging $18,529 per year); fellowships, Federal Work-Study, institutionally sponsored loans, scholarships/grants, health care benefits, tuition waivers (full and partial), and unspecified assistantships also available. Financial award application deadline: 5/1. *Faculty research:* Plant production, environmental microbiology, contaminant flow and transport, aquaculture. *Total annual research expenditures:* $3.4 million. *Unit head:* Dr. Jeffery C. Silvertooth, Head, 520-621-7228, Fax: 520-621-1647, E-mail: silver@ag.arizona.edu. *Application contact:* Alicia Velasquez, 520-621-1606, Fax: 520-621-1647, E-mail: avelasqu@ag.arizona.edu. Web site: http://ag.arizona.edu/SWES/.

University of Arkansas, Graduate School, Dale Bumpers College of Agricultural, Food and Life Sciences, Department of Crop, Soil and Environmental Sciences, Fayetteville, AR 72701-1201. Offers agronomy (MS, PhD). *Students:* 11 full-time (3 women), 36 part-time (14 women); includes 3 minority (1 Black or African American, non-Hispanic/Latino; 2 Two or more races, non-Hispanic/Latino), 21 international. In 2011, 6 master's, 3 doctorates awarded. *Degree requirements:* For master's, thesis optional; for doctorate, variable foreign language requirement, thesis/dissertation. *Application deadline:* For fall admission, 4/1 for international students; for spring admission, 10/1 for international students. Applications are processed on a rolling basis. Application fee: $40 ($50 for international students). Electronic applications accepted. *Financial support:* In 2011–12, 36 research assistantships were awarded; fellowships with tuition reimbursements, teaching assistantships, career-related internships or fieldwork, and Federal Work-Study also available. Support available to part-time students. Financial award application deadline: 4/1; financial award applicants required to submit FAFSA. *Unit head:* Dr. Robert Bacon, Interim Departmental Chairperson, 479-575-2347, Fax: 479-575-7465, E-mail: rbacon@uark.edu. *Application contact:* Dr. Kristofor Brye, Graduate Coordinator, 479-575-5742, E-mail: kbrye@uark.edu. Web site: http://cses.uark.edu.

The University of British Columbia, Faculty of Land and Food Systems, Program in Soil Science, Vancouver, BC V6T 1Z1, Canada. Offers M Sc, PhD. *Degree requirements:* For master's, thesis; for doctorate, comprehensive exam, thesis/dissertation. *Entrance requirements:* Additional exam requirements/recommendations for international students: Required—TOEFL (minimum score 577 paper-based; 233 computer-based; 90 iBT), IELTS (minimum score 6.5). Electronic applications accepted. *Faculty research:* Soil and water conservation, land use, land use and land classification, soil physics, soil chemistry and mineralogy.

University of California, Davis, Graduate Studies, Graduate Group in Horticulture and Agronomy, Davis, CA 95616. Offers MS. *Degree requirements:* For master's, comprehensive exam (for some programs), thesis (for some programs). *Entrance requirements:* For master's, GRE General Test. Additional exam requirements/recommendations for international students: Required—TOEFL (minimum score 550 paper-based; 213 computer-based). Electronic applications accepted. *Faculty research:* Postharvest physiology, mineral nutrition, crop improvement, plant growth and development.

University of California, Davis, Graduate Studies, Graduate Group in Soils and Biogeochemistry, Davis, CA 95616. Offers MS, PhD. Terminal master's awarded for partial completion of doctoral program. *Degree requirements:* For master's, comprehensive exam (for some programs), thesis (for some programs); for doctorate, thesis/dissertation. *Entrance requirements:* For master's, minimum GPA of 3.3; for doctorate, GRE, minimum GPA of 3.3. Additional exam requirements/recommendations for international students: Required—TOEFL (minimum score 550 paper-based; 213 computer-based). Electronic applications accepted. *Faculty research:* Rhizosphere ecology, soil transport processes, biogeochemical cycling, sustainable agriculture.

University of California, Riverside, Graduate Division, Environmental Sciences Department, Riverside, CA 92521-0102. Offers MS, PhD. *Faculty:* 27 full-time (4 women). *Students:* 27 full-time (12 women); includes 4 minority (1 Asian, non-Hispanic/Latino; 3 Hispanic/Latino), 11 international. Average age 29. In 2011, 5 master's, 1 doctorate awarded. *Degree requirements:* For doctorate, thesis/dissertation. *Entrance requirements:* For master's and doctorate, minimum GPA of 3.2. Additional exam requirements/recommendations for international students: Required—TOEFL (minimum score 550 paper-based; 213 computer-based; 80 iBT). *Application deadline:* For fall admission, 5/1 for domestic students, 2/1 for international students; for winter admission, 9/1 for domestic students, 7/1 for international students; for spring admission, 12/1 for domestic students, 10/1 for international students. Application fee: $80 ($100 for international students). Electronic applications accepted. *Financial support:* Fellowships with tuition reimbursements and research assistantships with tuition reimbursements available. *Faculty research:* Environmental chemistry and ecotoxicology, environmental microbiology, environmental and natural resource economics and policy, soil and water sciences, environmental sciences and management. *Unit head:* Dr. Michael Anderson, Chair, 951-827-3757. *Application contact:* John Herring, Program Assistant, 951-827-2441, E-mail: soilwater@ucr.edu. Web site: http://envisci.ucr.edu/.

University of Connecticut, Graduate School, College of Agriculture and Natural Resources, Department of Plant Science, Storrs, CT 06269. Offers plant and soil sciences (MS, PhD). Terminal master's awarded for partial completion of doctoral program. *Degree requirements:* For master's, comprehensive exam; for doctorate, thesis/dissertation. *Entrance requirements:* For master's and doctorate, GRE General Test, GRE Subject Test. Additional exam requirements/recommendations for international students: Required—TOEFL (minimum score 550 paper-based; 213 computer-based). Electronic applications accepted.

University of Delaware, College of Agriculture and Natural Resources, Department of Plant and Soil Sciences, Newark, DE 19716. Offers MS, PhD. Part-time programs available. Terminal master's awarded for partial completion of doctoral program. *Degree requirements:* For master's, thesis; for doctorate, thesis/dissertation. *Entrance requirements:* For master's and doctorate, GRE General Test. Additional exam requirements/recommendations for international students: Required—TOEFL (minimum score 550 paper-based; 213 computer-based). Electronic applications accepted. *Faculty research:* Soil chemistry, plant and cell tissue culture, plant breeding and genetics, soil physics, soil biochemistry, plant molecular biology, soil microbiology.

University of Florida, Graduate School, College of Agricultural and Life Sciences, Department of Agronomy, Gainesville, FL 32611. Offers M Ag, MS, PhD. Part-time programs available. *Faculty:* 15 full-time (4 women). *Students:* 40 full-time (12 women), 5 part-time (0 women); includes 2 minority (1 Asian, non-Hispanic/Latino; 1 Hispanic/Latino), 24 international. Average age 29. 23 applicants, 35% accepted, 7 enrolled. In 2011, 8 master's, 2 doctorates awarded. Terminal master's awarded for partial completion of doctoral program. *Degree requirements:* For master's, thesis (for some programs); for doctorate, comprehensive exam, thesis/dissertation (for some programs). *Entrance requirements:* For master's and doctorate, GRE General Test, minimum GPA of 3.0. Additional exam requirements/recommendations for international students: Required—TOEFL (minimum score 550 paper-based; 213 computer-based; 80 iBT), IELTS (minimum score 6). *Application deadline:* For fall admission, 6/1 priority date for domestic students, 5/1 for international students; for spring admission, 9/1 for domestic students, 8/1 for international students. Applications are processed on a rolling basis. Application fee: $30. Electronic applications accepted. *Financial support:* Fellowships, research assistantships, career-related internships or fieldwork, institutionally sponsored loans, and unspecified assistantships available. Financial award application deadline: 1/1; financial award applicants required to submit FAFSA. *Faculty research:* Plant breeding and genetics weed science, crop physiology and ecology, crop management and nutrition. *Total annual research expenditures:* $2.3 million. *Unit head:* Dr. Maria Gallo, Chair, 352-392-1811 Ext. 206, Fax: 352-392-1840, E-mail: mgm@ufl.edu. *Application contact:* Dr. Jerry M. Bennett, Graduate Coordinator, 352-273-1811 Ext. 230, Fax: 352-392-1840, E-mail: jmbt@ufl.edu. Web site: http://agronomy.ifas.ufl.edu/.

University of Florida, Graduate School, College of Agricultural and Life Sciences, Department of Soil and Water Science, Gainesville, FL 32611. Offers MS, PhD. Part-time and evening/weekend programs available. Postbaccalaureate distance learning degree programs offered (no on-campus study). *Faculty:* 20 full-time (3 women). *Students:* 68 full-time (35 women), 53 part-time (21 women); includes 9 minority (1 Black or African American, non-Hispanic/Latino; 1 American Indian or Alaska Native, non-Hispanic/Latino; 3 Asian, non-Hispanic/Latino; 4 Hispanic/Latino), 39 international. Average age 33. 71 applicants, 46% accepted, 25 enrolled. In 2011, 22 master's, 8 doctorates awarded. Terminal master's awarded for partial completion of doctoral program. *Degree requirements:* For master's, thesis optional; for doctorate, comprehensive exam, thesis/dissertation. *Entrance requirements:* For master's and doctorate, GRE General Test (minimum score 1000 taken within last 5 years), minimum GPA of 3.0. Additional exam requirements/recommendations for international students: Required—TOEFL (minimum score 550 paper-based; 213 computer-based; 80 iBT), IELTS (minimum score 6). *Application deadline:* For fall admission, 3/1 priority date for domestic students, 3/1 for international students; for spring admission, 10/1 for domestic and international students. Applications are processed on a rolling basis. Application fee: $30. Electronic applications accepted. *Financial support:*

Peterson's Graduate Programs in the Physical Sciences, Mathematics, Agricultural Sciences, the Environment & Natural Resources 2013

facebook.com/petersonspublishing **411**

Agronomy and Soil Sciences

Fellowships, research assistantships, teaching assistantships, career-related internships or fieldwork, Federal Work-Study, institutionally sponsored loans, and unspecified assistantships available. Support available to part-time students. Financial award applicants required to submit FAFSA. *Faculty research:* Nutrient, pesticide, and waste management; soil, water, and aquifer remediation; carbon dynamics and ecosystem services; landscape analysis and modeling; wetlands and aquatic ecosystems. *Unit head:* Dr. K. Ramesh Reddy, Chair, 352-392-1804 Ext. 317, Fax: 352-392-3399, E-mail: krr@ufl.edu. *Application contact:* Dr. Andrew Ogram, Graduate Coordinator, 352-392-1951 Ext. 211, Fax: 352-392-3902, E-mail: aogram@ufl.edu. Web site: http://soils.ifas.ufl.edu/.

University of Georgia, College of Agricultural and Environmental Sciences, Department of Crop and Soil Sciences, Athens, GA 30602. Offers crop and soil science (MS, PhD); crop and soil sciences (MCCS); plant protection and pest management (MPPPM). Part-time programs available. *Faculty:* 28 full-time (2 women), 4 part-time/adjunct (1 woman). *Students:* 35 full-time (10 women), 4 part-time (0 women); includes 2 minority (1 Black or African American, non-Hispanic/Latino; 1 Asian, non-Hispanic/Latino), 15 international. Average age 28. 32 applicants, 41% accepted, 5 enrolled. In 2011, 7 master's, 1 doctorate awarded. *Degree requirements:* For master's, thesis (MS); for doctorate, comprehensive exam, thesis/dissertation. *Entrance requirements:* For master's and doctorate, GRE General Test. Additional exam requirements/recommendations for international students: Required—TOEFL (minimum score 550 paper-based; 213 computer-based). *Application deadline:* For fall admission, 7/1 priority date for domestic students, 4/15 for international students; for spring admission, 11/15 for domestic students, 10/15 for international students. Applications are processed on a rolling basis. Application fee: $50. Electronic applications accepted. *Financial support:* In 2011–12, research assistantships with full tuition reimbursements (averaging $14,600 per year), teaching assistantships with full tuition reimbursements (averaging $15,350 per year) were awarded; fellowships, scholarships/grants, tuition waivers (full), and unspecified assistantships also available. *Faculty research:* Plant breeding, genomics, nutrient management, water quality, soil chemistry. *Unit head:* Dr. Donn Graham Shilling, Head, 706-542-2461, Fax: 706-542-0914, E-mail: dgs@uga.edu. *Application contact:* Dr. Miguel L. Cabrera, Graduate Coordinator, 706-542-1242, Fax: 706-542-0914, E-mail: mcabrera@uga.edu. Web site: http://www.cropsoil.uga.edu/.

University of Guelph, Graduate Studies, Ontario Agricultural College, Department of Land Resource Science, Guelph, ON N1G 2W1, Canada. Offers atmospheric science (M Sc, PhD); environmental and agricultural earth sciences (M Sc, PhD); land resources management (M Sc, PhD); soil science (M Sc, PhD). Part-time programs available. *Degree requirements:* For master's, thesis (for some programs), research project (non-thesis track); for doctorate, comprehensive exam, thesis/dissertation. *Entrance requirements:* For master's, minimum B average during previous 2 years of course work; for doctorate, minimum B average during previous 2 years of course work. Additional exam requirements/recommendations for international students: Required—TOEFL (minimum score 550 paper-based; 213 computer-based). Electronic applications accepted. *Faculty research:* Soil science, environmental earth science, land resource management.

University of Idaho, College of Graduate Studies, College of Agricultural and Life Sciences, Department of Plant, Soil, and Entomological Sciences, Program in Soil and Land Resources, Moscow, ID 83844-2282. Offers MS, PhD. *Students:* 5 full-time, 3 part-time. Average age 30. In 2011, 3 master's awarded. *Degree requirements:* For doctorate, thesis/dissertation. *Entrance requirements:* For master's and doctorate, GRE General Test, minimum GPA of 3.0. *Application deadline:* For fall admission, 8/1 for domestic students; for spring admission, 12/15 for domestic students. Applications are processed on a rolling basis. Application fee: $60. Electronic applications accepted. *Expenses:* Tuition, state resident: full-time $3874; part-time $334 per credit hour. Tuition, nonresident: full-time $16,394; part-time $861 per credit hour. *Required fees:* $2808; $99 per credit hour. Tuition and fees vary according to program. *Financial support:* Applicants required to submit FAFSA. *Faculty research:* Pedology, soil biology and biochemistry, soil chemistry, soil fertility and plant nutrition, soil physics. *Unit head:* Dr. James B. Johnson, Department Head, 208-885-6274, E-mail: nthompson@uidaho.edu. *Application contact:* Erick Larson, Director of Graduate Admissions, 208-885-4723, E-mail: gadms@uidaho.edu.

University of Illinois at Urbana–Champaign, Graduate College, College of Agricultural, Consumer and Environmental Sciences, Department of Crop Sciences, Champaign, IL 61820. Offers bioinformatics: crop sciences (MS); crop sciences (MS, PhD). Postbaccalaureate distance learning degree programs offered (no on-campus study). *Faculty:* 42 full-time (5 women), 1 (woman) part-time/adjunct. *Students:* 101 full-time (30 women), 45 part-time (13 women); includes 8 minority (1 Black or African American, non-Hispanic/Latino; 4 Asian, non-Hispanic/Latino; 3 Hispanic/Latino), 44 international. 121 applicants, 29% accepted, 31 enrolled. In 2011, 26 master's, 5 doctorates awarded. *Entrance requirements:* For master's and doctorate, GRE, minimum GPA of 3.0. Additional exam requirements/recommendations for international students: Required—TOEFL (minimum score 570 paper-based). *Application deadline:* Applications are processed on a rolling basis. Application fee: $75 ($90 for international students). Electronic applications accepted. *Financial support:* In 2011–12, 40 fellowships, 81 research assistantships, 26 teaching assistantships were awarded; tuition waivers (full and partial) also available. *Faculty research:* Plant breeding and genetics, molecular biology, crop production, plant physiology, weed science. *Unit head:* German A. Bollero, Head, 217-333-9475, Fax: 217-333-9817, E-mail: gbollero@illinois.edu. *Application contact:* S. Dianne Carson, Office Support Specialist, 217-244-0396, Fax: 217-333-9817, E-mail: sdcarson@illinois.edu. Web site: http://www.cropsci.illinois.edu.

University of Kentucky, Graduate School, College of Agriculture, Program in Crop Science, Lexington, KY 40506-0032. Offers MS, PhD. *Degree requirements:* For master's, comprehensive exam, thesis optional; for doctorate, comprehensive exam, thesis/dissertation. *Entrance requirements:* For master's, GRE General Test, minimum GPA of 2.75; for doctorate, GRE General Test, minimum GPA of 3.0. Additional exam requirements/recommendations for international students: Required—TOEFL (minimum score 550 paper-based; 213 computer-based). Electronic applications accepted. *Faculty research:* Crop physiology, crop ecology, crop management, crop breeding and genetics, weed science.

University of Kentucky, Graduate School, College of Agriculture, Program in Plant and Soil Science, Lexington, KY 40506-0032. Offers MS. *Degree requirements:* For master's, comprehensive exam, thesis optional. *Entrance requirements:* For master's, GRE General Test, minimum undergraduate GPA of 2.75, graduate 3.0. Additional exam requirements/recommendations for international students: Required—TOEFL (minimum score 550 paper-based; 213 computer-based). Electronic applications accepted.

University of Kentucky, Graduate School, College of Agriculture, Program in Soil Science, Lexington, KY 40506-0032. Offers PhD. *Degree requirements:* For doctorate, comprehensive exam, thesis/dissertation. *Entrance requirements:* For doctorate, GRE General Test, minimum graduate GPA of 3.0, undergraduate 2.75. Additional exam requirements/recommendations for international students: Required—TOEFL (minimum score 550 paper-based; 213 computer-based). Electronic applications accepted. *Faculty research:* Soil fertility and plant nutrition, soil chemistry and physics, soil genesis and morphology, soil management and conservation, water and environmental quality.

University of Maine, Graduate School, College of Natural Sciences, Forestry, and Agriculture, Department of Plant, Soil, and Environmental Sciences, Orono, ME 04469. Offers biological sciences (PhD); ecology and environmental sciences (MS, PhD); forest resources (PhD); horticulture (MS); plant science (PhD); plant, soil, and environmental sciences (MS); resource utilization (MS). *Faculty:* 9 full-time (3 women), 7 part-time/adjunct (3 women). *Students:* 7 full-time (4 women), 2 part-time (0 women), 2 international. Average age 30. 14 applicants, 50% accepted, 5 enrolled. In 2011, 4 degrees awarded. *Entrance requirements:* For master's and doctorate, GRE General Test. Additional exam requirements/recommendations for international students: Required—TOEFL. *Application deadline:* Applications are processed on a rolling basis. Application fee: $65. Electronic applications accepted. *Expenses:* Tuition, state resident: full-time $5016. Tuition, nonresident: full-time $14,424. *Financial support:* In 2011–12, 16 research assistantships with full tuition reimbursements (averaging $17,336 per year), 1 teaching assistantship with full tuition reimbursement (averaging $13,600 per year) were awarded; scholarships/grants, tuition waivers (full and partial), and unspecified assistantships also available. *Total annual research expenditures:* $179,065. *Unit head:* Dr. Gregory Porter, Chair, 207-581-2943, Fax: 207-581-3207. *Application contact:* Scott G. Delcourt, Associate Dean of the Graduate School, 207-581-3291, Fax: 207-581-3232, E-mail: graduate@maine.edu. Web site: http://www2.umaine.edu/graduate/.

University of Manitoba, Faculty of Graduate Studies, Faculty of Agricultural and Food Sciences, Department of Plant Science, Winnipeg, MB R3T 2N2, Canada. Offers agronomy and plant protection (M Sc, PhD); horticulture (M Sc, PhD); plant breeding and genetics (M Sc, PhD); plant physiology-biochemistry (M Sc, PhD). *Degree requirements:* For master's, thesis; for doctorate, one foreign language, thesis/dissertation.

University of Manitoba, Faculty of Graduate Studies, Faculty of Agricultural and Food Sciences, Department of Soil Science, Winnipeg, MB R3T 2N2, Canada. Offers M Sc, PhD. *Degree requirements:* For master's, thesis; for doctorate, one foreign language, thesis/dissertation.

University of Massachusetts Amherst, Graduate School, College of Natural Sciences, Department of Plant, Soil and Insect Sciences, Program in Plant and Soil Sciences, Amherst, MA 01003. Offers plant and soil sciences (MS, PhD); soil science (MS). Postbaccalaureate distance learning degree programs offered (minimal on-campus study). *Students:* 24 full-time (12 women), 21 part-time (13 women); includes 4 minority (1 Black or African American, non-Hispanic/Latino; 1 Asian, non-Hispanic/Latino; 2 Hispanic/Latino), 18 international. Average age 33. 35 applicants, 57% accepted, 17 enrolled. In 2011, 7 master's, 4 doctorates awarded. Terminal master's awarded for partial completion of doctoral program. *Degree requirements:* For master's, thesis or alternative; for doctorate, comprehensive exam, thesis/dissertation. *Entrance requirements:* For master's and doctorate, GRE General Test. Additional exam requirements/recommendations for international students: Required—TOEFL (minimum score 550 paper-based; 213 computer-based; 80 iBT), IELTS (minimum score 6.5). *Application deadline:* For fall admission, 1/7 for domestic and international students; for spring admission, 10/1 for domestic and international students. Applications are processed on a rolling basis. Application fee: $50 ($65 for international students). Electronic applications accepted. Tuition and fees vary according to course load, campus/location and program. *Financial support:* Fellowships with full and partial tuition reimbursements, research assistantships with full and partial tuition reimbursements, teaching assistantships with full and partial tuition reimbursements, career-related internships or fieldwork, Federal Work-Study, scholarships/grants, traineeships, health care benefits, tuition

412 facebook.com/petersonspublishing

Peterson's Graduate Programs in the Physical Sciences, Mathematics, Agricultural Sciences, the Environment & Natural Resources 2013

waivers (full and partial), and unspecified assistantships available. Support available to part-time students. Financial award application deadline: 1/7. *Unit head:* Dr. Geunhwa Jung, Graduate Program Director, 413-545-1059, Fax: 413-545-2115. *Application contact:* Lindsay DeSantis, Interim Supervisor of Admissions, 413-545-0722, Fax: 413-577-0010, E-mail: gradadm@grad.umass.edu. Web site: http://www.umass.edu/psis/.

University of Minnesota, Twin Cities Campus, Graduate School, College of Food, Agricultural and Natural Resource Sciences, Land and Atmospheric Science Graduate Program, Saint Paul, MN 55108. Offers MS, PhD. *Faculty:* 46 full-time (8 women). *Students:* 22 full-time (10 women), 1 (woman) part-time; includes 2 minority (1 Hispanic/Latino; 1 Two or more races, non-Hispanic/Latino), 5 international. Average age 30. 29 applicants, 45% accepted, 8 enrolled. In 2011, 2 degrees awarded. Terminal master's awarded for partial completion of doctoral program. *Degree requirements:* For master's, comprehensive exam, thesis; for doctorate, comprehensive exam, thesis/dissertation. *Entrance requirements:* For master's and doctorate, GRE General Test, minimum GPA of 3.0. Additional exam requirements/recommendations for international students: Required—TOEFL (minimum score 550 paper-based; 213 computer-based; 79 iBT), IELTS (minimum score 6.5), TOEFL preferred. *Application deadline:* For fall admission, 12/15 priority date for domestic students, 12/15 for international students; for spring admission, 10/15 priority date for domestic students, 10/15 for international students. Applications are processed on a rolling basis. Application fee: $75 ($95 for international students). Electronic applications accepted. *Financial support:* In 2011–12, fellowships with full tuition reimbursements (averaging $23,500 per year), research assistantships with full and partial tuition reimbursements (averaging $17,000 per year), teaching assistantships with full and partial tuition reimbursements (averaging $17,000 per year) were awarded; scholarships/grants, health care benefits, tuition waivers (full), and unspecified assistantships also available. Support available to part-time students. *Faculty research:* Soil water and atmospheric resources, soil physical management, agricultural chemicals and their management, plant nutrient management, biological nitrogen fixation. *Unit head:* Dr. Timothy Griffis, Co-Director of Graduate Studies, 612-625-3117, Fax: 612-625-2208, E-mail: tgriffis@umn.edu. *Application contact:* Kari Jarco, Program Coordinator, 612-625-5251, Fax: 612-625-2208, E-mail: kjarcho@umn.edu. Web site: http://www.laas.umn.edu/.

University of Missouri, Graduate School, College of Agriculture, Food and Natural Resources, Division of Plant Sciences, Columbia, MO 65211. Offers crop, soil and pest management (MS, PhD); entomology (MS, PhD); horticulture (MS, PhD); plant biology and genetics (MS, PhD); plant stress biology (MS, PhD). *Faculty:* 40 full-time (11 women). *Students:* 73 full-time (37 women), 8 part-time (4 women); includes 2 minority (1 Black or African American, non-Hispanic/Latino; 1 American Indian or Alaska Native, non-Hispanic/Latino), 29 international. Average age 28. 52 applicants, 42% accepted, 20 enrolled. In 2011, 8 master's, 9 doctorates awarded. Terminal master's awarded for partial completion of doctoral program. *Degree requirements:* For master's, thesis; for doctorate, comprehensive exam, thesis/dissertation. *Entrance requirements:* For master's and doctorate, GRE General Test, minimum GPA of 3.0; bachelor's degree from accredited college. Additional exam requirements/recommendations for international students: Required—TOEFL (minimum score 500 paper-based; 173 computer-based; 61 iBT), IELTS (minimum score 5.5). *Application deadline:* For fall admission, 1/15 priority date for domestic students. Applications are processed on a rolling basis. Application fee: $55 ($75 for international students), Electronic applications accepted. *Expenses:* Tuition, state resident: full-time $5881. Tuition, nonresident: full-time $15,183. *Required fees:* $952. Tuition and fees vary according to campus/location and program. *Financial support:* In 2011–12, 2 fellowships with tuition reimbursements, 59 research assistantships with tuition reimbursements, 1 teaching assistantship with tuition reimbursement were awarded; institutionally sponsored loans, scholarships/grants, health care benefits, and unspecified assistantships also available. Support available to part-time students. *Faculty research:* Crop, soil and pest management; entomology; horticulture; plant biology and genetics; plant microbiology and pathology. *Unit head:* Dr. Michael Collins, Director, 573-882-1957, E-mail: collinsm@missouri.edu. *Application contact:* Dr. James Schoelz, Director of Graduate Studies, 573-882-1185, E-mail: schoelzj@missouri.edu. Web site: http://plantsci.missouri.edu/graduate/.

University of Missouri, Graduate School, School of Natural Resources, Department of Soil, Environmental, and Atmospheric Sciences, Columbia, MO 65211. Offers atmospheric science (MS, PhD); soil science (MS, PhD). *Faculty:* 9 full-time (0 women). *Students:* 18 full-time (9 women), 15 part-time (7 women); includes 6 minority (3 Black or African American, non-Hispanic/Latino; 1 Asian, non-Hispanic/Latino; 1 Hispanic/Latino; 1 Two or more races, non-Hispanic/Latino), 8 international. Average age 33. 32 applicants, 22% accepted, 7 enrolled. In 2011, 6 master's, 2 doctorates awarded. *Degree requirements:* For doctorate, thesis/dissertation. *Entrance requirements:* For master's and doctorate, GRE General Test, minimum GPA of 3.0. Additional exam requirements/recommendations for international students: Required—TOEFL (minimum score 530 paper-based; 197 computer-based; 71 iBT). *Application deadline:* Applications are processed on a rolling basis. Application fee: $55 ($75 for international students). *Expenses:* Tuition, state resident: full-time $5881. Tuition, nonresident: full-time $15,183. *Required fees:* $952. Tuition and fees vary according to campus/location and program. *Financial support:* Fellowships, research assistantships, teaching assistantships, institutionally sponsored loans, and scholarships/grants available. *Faculty research:* Soil physics; x-ray tomography of soil systems; use of radar in forecasting; soil and water

conservation and management and applied soil physics; soil chemical and biogeochemical investigations; fresh water supply regimes (quantity, timing); water quality disturbance mechanisms; best management practices (BMP's); environmental biophysics and ecohydrology; hydrologic scaling, modeling, and change; synoptic and mesoscale dynamics. *Unit head:* Dr. Stephen Anderson, Department Chair, 573-882-6303, E-mail: andersons@missouri.edu. *Application contact:* Leslie Palmer, 573-882-3436, E-mail: palmerl@missouri.edu. Web site: http://www.snr.missouri.edu/seas/academics/graduate-program.php.

University of Nebraska–Lincoln, Graduate College, College of Agricultural Sciences and Natural Resources, Department of Agronomy and Horticulture, Program in Agronomy, Lincoln, NE 68588. Offers MS, PhD. *Degree requirements:* For master's, thesis; for doctorate, comprehensive exam, thesis/dissertation. *Entrance requirements:* Additional exam requirements/recommendations for international students: Required—TOEFL (minimum score 500 paper-based; 173 computer-based). Electronic applications accepted. *Faculty research:* Crop physiology and production, plant breeding and genetics, range and forage management, soil and water science, weed science.

University of Puerto Rico, Mayagüez Campus, Graduate Studies, College of Agricultural Sciences, Department of Agronomy and Soils, Mayagüez, PR 00681-9000. Offers agronomy (MS); soils (MS). Part-time programs available. *Students:* 28 full-time (11 women), 2 part-time (1 woman); includes 25 minority (all Hispanic/Latino), 3 international. 10 applicants, 80% accepted, 6 enrolled. In 2011, 10 degrees awarded. *Degree requirements:* For master's, comprehensive exam, thesis. *Application deadline:* For fall admission, 2/15 for domestic and international students; for spring admission, 9/15 for domestic and international students. Applications are processed on a rolling basis. Application fee: $25. Tuition and fees vary according to course level and course load. *Financial support:* In 2011–12, 30 research assistantships with tuition reimbursements (averaging $15,000 per year), 9 teaching assistantships with tuition reimbursements (averaging $8,500 per year) were awarded; Federal Work-Study and institutionally sponsored loans also available. *Faculty research:* Soil physics and chemistry, soil management, plant physiology, ecology, plant breeding. *Total annual research expenditures:* $330,000. *Unit head:* Dr. Hipolito O'Farrill, Director, 787-265-3851, E-mail: hipolito.ofarrill@upr.edu. *Application contact:* Carmen Figueroa, Student Affairs Official, 787-265-3809, Fax: 787-265-5489, E-mail: carmen.figueroa11@upr.edu. Web site: http://www.uprm.edu/agricultura/agrosuelos/.

University of Puerto Rico, Mayagüez Campus, Graduate Studies, College of Agricultural Sciences, Department of Crop Protection, Mayagüez, PR 00681-9000. Offers MS. Part-time programs available. *Students:* 20 full-time (14 women); includes 14 minority (all Hispanic/Latino), 5 international. 3 applicants, 100% accepted, 1 enrolled. In 2011, 4 master's awarded. *Degree requirements:* For master's, comprehensive exam, thesis. *Entrance requirements:* For master's, minimum GPA of 2.75, BS in agricultural science or its equivalent. *Application deadline:* For fall admission, 2/15 for domestic and international students; for spring admission, 9/15 for domestic and international students. Applications are processed on a rolling basis. Application fee: $25. Tuition and fees vary according to course level and course load. *Financial support:* Career-related internships or fieldwork, Federal Work-Study, and institutionally sponsored loans available. Financial award application deadline: 5/30. *Faculty research:* Nematology, virology, plant pathology, weed control, peas and soybean seed diseases. *Unit head:* Dr. Hipolito O'Farrill, Director, 787-265-3859, Fax: 787-265-5490, E-mail: hipolito.ofarrill@upr.edu. *Application contact:* Prof. Nydia Vicente, Coordinator, 787-832-4040 Ext. 3104, Fax: 787-265-5490, E-mail: nvicente@uprm.edu. Web site: http://www.uprm.edu/agricultura/proteccion.

University of Saskatchewan, College of Graduate Studies and Research, College of Agriculture, Department of Soil Science, Saskatoon, SK S7N 5A2, Canada. Offers M Ag, M Sc, PhD, Diploma. *Degree requirements:* For master's, thesis (for some programs); for doctorate, comprehensive exam (for some programs), thesis/dissertation. *Entrance requirements:* Additional exam requirements/recommendations for international students: Required—TOEFL (minimum score 80 iBT); Recommended—IELTS (minimum score 6.5).

University of Vermont, Graduate College, College of Agriculture and Life Sciences, Department of Plant and Soil Science, Burlington, VT 05405. Offers MS, PhD. *Students:* 26 (16 women), 3 international. 27 applicants, 33% accepted, 6 enrolled. In 2011, 7 degrees awarded. *Degree requirements:* For master's, thesis; for doctorate, one foreign language, thesis/dissertation. *Entrance requirements:* For master's and doctorate, GRE General Test. Additional exam requirements/recommendations for international students: Required—TOEFL (minimum score 550 paper-based; 213 computer-based; 80 iBT). *Application deadline:* For fall admission, 2/15 priority date for domestic students, 2/15 for international students. Applications are processed on a rolling basis. Application fee: $40. Electronic applications accepted. *Financial support:* Fellowships, research assistantships, and teaching assistantships available. Financial award application deadline: 3/1. *Faculty research:* Soil chemistry, plant nutrition. *Unit head:* Dr. Deborah Neher, Chairperson, 802-656-2630. *Application contact:* Dr. Josef Gorres, Coordinator, 802-656-2630. Web site: http://www.uvm.edu/~pss.

University of Wisconsin–Madison, Graduate School, College of Agricultural and Life Sciences, Department of Agronomy, Madison, WI 53706-1380. Offers agronomy (MS, PhD); plant breeding and plant genetics (MS, PhD). *Degree requirements:* For master's, thesis or alternative; for doctorate, thesis/dissertation. *Entrance requirements:* For master's and doctorate, GRE, minimum GPA of 3.0.

Peterson's Graduate Programs in the Physical Sciences, Mathematics, Agricultural Sciences, the Environment & Natural Resources 2013

facebook.com/petersonspublishing   **413**

Agronomy and Soil Sciences

Additional exam requirements/recommendations for international students: Required—TOEFL (minimum score 580 paper-based; 213 computer-based). Electronic applications accepted. *Expenses:* Tuition, state resident: full-time $10,296; part-time $643.51 per credit. Tuition, nonresident: full-time $24,054; part-time $1503.40 per credit. *Required fees:* $70.06 per credit. Tuition and fees vary according to course load, campus/location, program and reciprocity agreements. *Faculty research:* Plant breeding and genetics, plant molecular biology and physiology, cropping systems and management, weed science.

University of Wisconsin–Madison, Graduate School, College of Agricultural and Life Sciences, Department of Soil Science, Madison, WI 53706. Offers MS, PhD. *Degree requirements:* For master's, comprehensive exam, thesis; for doctorate, comprehensive exam, thesis/dissertation. *Entrance requirements:* For master's and doctorate, GRE General Test. Additional exam requirements/ recommendations for international students: Required—TOEFL. Electronic applications accepted. *Expenses:* Tuition, state resident: full-time $10,296; part-time $643.51 per credit. Tuition, nonresident: full-time $24,054; part-time $1503.40 per credit. *Required fees:* $70.06 per credit. Tuition and fees vary according to course load, campus/location, program and reciprocity agreements. *Faculty research:* Soil characterization and mapping, fate of toxicants in the environment, soil microbiology, permafrost, water quality and quantity.

University of Wyoming, College of Agriculture and Natural Resources, Department of Plant Sciences, Laramie, WY 82070. Offers agronomy (MS, PhD). *Degree requirements:* For master's, thesis; for doctorate, thesis/dissertation. *Entrance requirements:* For master's and doctorate, GRE General Test, minimum GPA of 3.0. Additional exam requirements/recommendations for international students: Required—TOEFL (minimum score 525 paper-based; 197 computer-based). Electronic applications accepted. *Faculty research:* Crops, weeds, plant diseases.

University of Wyoming, College of Agriculture and Natural Resources, Department of Renewable Resources, Laramie, WY 82070. Offers agroecology (MS); entomology (MS, PhD); entomology/water resources (MS, PhD); rangeland ecology and watershed management (MS, PhD), including soil sciences (PhD); soil sciences and water resources (MS); rangeland ecology and watershed management/water resources (MS, PhD); soil science (MS); soil science/water resources (PhD). Part-time programs available. *Degree requirements:* For master's, comprehensive exam, thesis, oral examination; for doctorate, comprehensive exam, thesis/dissertation, preliminary oral and written exam, oral final exam. *Entrance requirements:* For master's and doctorate, GRE General Test, minimum GPA of 3.0. Additional exam requirements/recommendations for international students: Required—TOEFL. Electronic applications accepted. *Faculty research:* Plant control, grazing management, riparian restoration, riparian management, reclamation.

Utah State University, School of Graduate Studies, College of Agriculture, Department of Plants, Soils, and Biometeorology, Logan, UT 84322. Offers biometeorology (MS, PhD); ecology (MS, PhD); plant science (MS, PhD); soil science (MS, PhD). Part-time programs available. Terminal master's awarded for partial completion of doctoral program. *Degree requirements:* For master's, thesis; for doctorate, thesis/dissertation. *Entrance requirements:* For master's, GRE General Test, BS in plant, soil, atmospheric science, or related field; minimum GPA of 3.0; for doctorate, GRE General Test, minimum GPA of 3.0. Additional exam requirements/recommendations for international students: Required—TOEFL. Electronic applications accepted. *Faculty research:* Biotechnology and genomics, plant physiology and biology, nutrient and water efficient landscapes, physical-chemical-biological processes in soil, environmental biophysics and climate.

Virginia Polytechnic Institute and State University, Graduate School, College of Agriculture and Life Sciences, Department of Crop and Soil Environmental Sciences, Blacksburg, VA 24061. Offers MS, PhD. *Degree requirements:* For master's, comprehensive exam (for some programs); thesis (for some programs); for doctorate, comprehensive exam (for some programs), thesis/dissertation (for some programs). *Entrance requirements:* For master's and doctorate, GRE. Additional exam requirements/recommendations for international students: Required—TOEFL (minimum score 550 paper-based; 213 computer-based). *Application deadline:* For fall admission, 7/1 for domestic and international students; for spring admission, 12/1 for domestic and international students. Applications are processed on a rolling basis. Application fee: $65. Electronic applications accepted. *Expenses:* Tuition, state resident: full-time $10,048; part-time $558.25 per credit hour. Tuition, nonresident: full-time $19,497; part-time $1083.25 per credit hour. *Required fees:* $405 per semester. Tuition and fees vary according to course load, campus/location and program. *Financial support:* Research assistantships with full tuition reimbursements, teaching assistantships with full tuition reimbursements, career-related internships or fieldwork, Federal Work-Study, scholarships/grants, health care benefits, and unspecified

assistantships available. Financial award application deadline: 1/15. *Faculty research:* Environmental soil chemistry, waste management, soil fertility, plant molecular genetics, turfgrass management. *Unit head:* Tom Thompson, Head, 540-231-9775, Fax: 540-231-3431, E-mail: tlthomps@vt.edu. *Application contact:* Lee Daniels, Information Contact, 540-231-7175, Fax: 540-231-3431, E-mail: wdaniels@vt.edu. Web site: http://www.cses.vt.edu/.

Washington State University, Graduate School, College of Agricultural, Human, and Natural Resource Sciences, Department of Crop and Soil Sciences, Program in Crop Sciences, Pullman, WA 99164. Offers MS, PhD. *Faculty:* 25. *Students:* 34 full-time (16 women), 8 part-time (3 women); includes 2 minority (1 Asian, non-Hispanic/Latino; 1 Hispanic/Latino), 15 international. Average age 29. 63 applicants, 19% accepted, 11 enrolled. In 2011, 4 master's, 2 doctorates awarded. Terminal master's awarded for partial completion of doctoral program. *Degree requirements:* For master's, comprehensive exam (for some programs), thesis (for some programs), oral exam; for doctorate, comprehensive exam, thesis/dissertation, oral exam, written exam. *Entrance requirements:* For master's and doctorate, GRE General Test, personal statement of educational goals and professional expectations. Additional exam requirements/recommendations for international students: Required—TOEFL (minimum score 550 paper-based; 213 computer-based), IELTS. *Application deadline:* For fall admission, 1/10 priority date for domestic students, 1/10 for international students; for spring admission, 7/1 priority date for domestic students, 7/1 for international students. Applications are processed on a rolling basis. Application fee: $75. Electronic applications accepted. *Financial support:* In 2011–12, 5 fellowships (averaging $7,580 per year), 15 research assistantships with full and partial tuition reimbursements (averaging $18,204 per year), 1 teaching assistantship with full and partial tuition reimbursement (averaging $18,204 per year) were awarded; career-related internships or fieldwork, Federal Work-Study, institutionally sponsored loans, tuition waivers (partial), and teaching associateships also available. Financial award application deadline: 2/1; financial award applicants required to submit FAFSA. *Faculty research:* Barley genetics, soil biology, soil fertility, winter wheat breeding, weed science. *Total annual research expenditures:* $6.2 million. *Unit head:* Dr. Richard Koenig, Chair, 509-335-2726, Fax: 509-335-8674, E-mail: richk@wsu.edu. *Application contact:* Graduate School Admissions, 800-GRADWSU, Fax: 509-335-1949, E-mail: gradsch@wsu.edu. Web site: http://www.css.edu/.

Washington State University, Graduate School, College of Agricultural, Human, and Natural Resource Sciences, Department of Crop and Soil Sciences, Program in Soil Sciences, Pullman, WA 99164. Offers MS, PhD. *Faculty:* 25. *Students:* 27 full-time (13 women), 5 part-time (4 women); includes 3 minority (1 Black or African American, non-Hispanic/Latino; 1 American Indian or Alaska Native, non-Hispanic/Latino; 1 Asian, non-Hispanic/Latino), 7 international. Average age 29. 33 applicants, 39% accepted, 10 enrolled. In 2011, 4 master's, 1 doctorate awarded. Terminal master's awarded for partial completion of doctoral program. *Degree requirements:* For master's, comprehensive exam (for some programs), thesis (for some programs), oral exam; for doctorate, comprehensive exam, thesis/dissertation, oral exam, written exam. *Entrance requirements:* For master's and doctorate, GRE. Additional exam requirements/recommendations for international students: Required—TOEFL (minimum score 550 paper-based; 213 computer-based), IELTS. *Application deadline:* For fall admission, 1/10 priority date for domestic students, 1/10 for international students; for spring admission, 7/1 priority date for domestic students, 7/1 for international students. Applications are processed on a rolling basis. Application fee: $75. Electronic applications accepted. *Financial support:* In 2011–12, 1 fellowship (averaging $4,000 per year), 11 research assistantships with full and partial tuition reimbursements (averaging $18,204 per year), 1 teaching assistantship with tuition reimbursement (averaging $18,204 per year) were awarded; career-related internships or fieldwork, Federal Work-Study, institutionally sponsored loans, and tuition waivers (partial) also available. Financial award application deadline: 4/1; financial award applicants required to submit FAFSA. *Faculty research:* Environmental soils, soil/water quality, soil microbiology, soil physics. *Total annual research expenditures:* $6.2 million. *Unit head:* Dr. Richard Koenig, Interim Director, 509-335-2726, Fax: 509-335-8674, E-mail: richk@wsu.edu. *Application contact:* Graduate School Admissions, 800-GRADWSU, Fax: 509-335-1949, E-mail: gradsch@wsu.edu. Web site: http://css.wsu.edu/.

West Virginia University, Davis College of Agriculture, Forestry and Consumer Sciences, Division of Plant and Soil Sciences, Program in Agricultural Sciences, Morgantown, WV 26506. Offers animal and food sciences (PhD); plant and soil sciences (PhD). *Degree requirements:* For doctorate, thesis/dissertation, oral and written exams. *Entrance requirements:* Additional exam requirements/recommendations for international students: Required—TOEFL. *Faculty research:* Ruminant nutrition, metabolism, forage utilization, physiology, reproduction.

414 facebook.com/petersonspublishing

Peterson's Graduate Programs in the Physical Sciences, Mathematics, Agricultural Sciences, the Environment & Natural Resources 2013

Animal Sciences

Alcorn State University, School of Graduate Studies, School of Agriculture and Applied Science, Alcorn State, MS 39096-7500. Offers agricultural economics (MS Ag); agronomy (MS Ag); animal science (MS Ag). *Degree requirements:* For master's, thesis optional. *Faculty research:* Aquatic systems, dairy herd improvement, fruit production, alternative farming practices.

American University of Beirut, Graduate Programs, Faculty of Agricultural and Food Sciences, Beirut, Lebanon. Offers agricultural economics (MS); animal sciences (MS); ecosystem management (MSES); food technology (MS); irrigation (MS); mechanization (MS); nutrition (MS); plant protection (MS); plant science (MS); poultry science (MS); soils (MS). Part-time programs available. *Faculty:* 21 full-time (6 women), 2 part-time/adjunct (0 women). *Students:* 12 full-time (all women), 93 part-time (77 women). Average age 24. 96 applicants, 67% accepted, 21 enrolled. In 2011, 25 master's awarded. *Degree requirements:* For master's, one foreign language, comprehensive exam, thesis (for some programs). *Entrance requirements:* Additional exam requirements/recommendations for international students: Required—TOEFL (minimum score 600 paper-based; 250 computer-based; 100 iBT), IELTS (minimum score 7.5). *Application deadline:* For fall admission, 2/20 for domestic and international students; for spring admission, 11/15 for domestic and international students. Applications are processed on a rolling basis. Application fee: $50. Electronic applications accepted. *Expenses:* Tuition: Full-time $12,780; part-time $710 per credit. *Required fees:* $528; $528 per credit. Tuition and fees vary according to course load and program. *Financial support:* In 2011–12, 22 research assistantships with partial tuition reimbursements (averaging $15,000 per year), 40 teaching assistantships with full and partial tuition reimbursements (averaging $1,000 per year) were awarded; scholarships/grants, health care benefits, and unspecified assistantships also available. Financial award application deadline: 2/2. *Faculty research:* Nutritional food-based dietary guidelines, community and therapeutic nutrition, food safety and food microbiology, landscape planning, nature and rural heritage conservation, pathology, immunology and control of poultry and animal diseases, agricultural economics and development, production of biodiesel from algae, national study on living conditions of refugees. *Unit head:* Prof. Nahla Hwalla, Dean, 961-1343002 Ext. 4400, Fax: 961-1744460, E-mail: nahla@aub.edu.lb. *Application contact:* Dr. Salim Kanaan, Director, Admissions Office, 961-1350000 Ext. 2594, Fax: 961-1750775, E-mail: sk00@aub.edu.lb. Web site: http://www.aub.edu.lb/fafs/Pages/index.aspx.

Angelo State University, College of Graduate Studies, College of Arts and Sciences, Department of Agriculture, San Angelo, TX 76909. Offers animal science (MS). Part-time and evening/weekend programs available. *Faculty:* 4 full-time (0 women). *Students:* 17 full-time (7 women), 6 part-time (3 women); includes 1 minority (Asian; non-Hispanic/Latino). Average age 23. 15 applicants, 73% accepted, 8 enrolled. In 2011, 11 master's awarded. *Degree requirements:* For master's, comprehensive exam, thesis optional. *Entrance requirements:* For master's, GRE General Test, essay. Additional exam requirements/ recommendations for international students: Required—TOEFL or IELTS. *Application deadline:* For fall admission, 7/15 priority date for domestic students, 6/10 for international students; for spring admission, 12/1 priority date for domestic students, 11/1 for international students. Applications are processed on a rolling basis. Application fee: $40 ($50 for international students). Electronic applications accepted. *Financial support:* In 2011–12, 10 students received support, including 9 research assistantships (averaging $9,887 per year); Federal Work-Study, scholarships/grants, and unspecified assistantships also available. Support available to part-time students. Financial award application deadline: 3/1. *Faculty research:* Effect of protein and energy on feedlot performance, bitterweed toxicosis in sheep, meat laboratory, North Concho watershed project, baseline vegetation. *Unit head:* Dr. Gilbert R. Engdahl, Department Head, 325-942-2027 Ext. 227, E-mail: gil.engdahl@angelo.edu. *Application contact:* Dr. Cody B. Scott, Graduate Advisor, 325-942-2027 Ext. 284, E-mail: cody.scott@angelo.edu. Web site: http://www.angelo.edu/dept/agriculture/.

Auburn University, Graduate School, College of Agriculture, Department of Animal Sciences, Auburn University, AL 36849. Offers M Ag, MS, PhD. Part-time programs available. *Faculty:* 23 full-time (5 women), 1 part-time/adjunct (0 women). *Students:* 5 full-time (1 woman), 9 part-time (8 women); includes 3 minority (all Black or African American, non-Hispanic/Latino). Average age 25. 30 applicants, 30% accepted, 6 enrolled. In 2011, 2 master's awarded. *Degree requirements:* For master's, thesis (for some programs); for doctorate, thesis/ dissertation. *Entrance requirements:* For master's and doctorate, GRE General Test. *Application deadline:* For fall admission, 7/7 for domestic students; for spring admission, 11/24 for domestic students. Applications are processed on a rolling basis. Application fee: $50 ($60 for international students). Electronic applications accepted. *Expenses:* Tuition, state resident: full-time $7290; part-time $405 per credit hour. Tuition, nonresident: full-time $21,870; part-time $1215 per credit hour. *International tuition:* $22,000 full-time. *Required fees:* $1402. *Financial support:* Research assistantships, teaching assistantships, and Federal Work-Study available. Support available to part-time students. Financial award application deadline: 3/15; financial award applicants required to submit FAFSA. *Faculty research:* Animal breeding and genetics, animal biochemistry and nutrition, physiology of reproduction, animal production. *Unit head:* Dr. L. Wayne

Greene, Head, 334-844-1528. *Application contact:* Dr. George Flowers, Dean of the Graduate School, 334-844-2125.

Auburn University, Graduate School, College of Agriculture, Department of Poultry Science, Auburn University, AL 36849. Offers M Ag, MS, PhD. Part-time programs available. *Faculty:* 16 full-time (3 women). *Students:* 11 full-time (6 women), 10 part-time (6 women); includes 2 minority (both Asian, non-Hispanic/ Latino), 8 international. Average age 29. 26 applicants, 15% accepted, 2 enrolled. In 2011, 1 degree awarded. *Degree requirements:* For master's, thesis (for some programs); for doctorate, thesis/dissertation. *Entrance requirements:* For master's, GRE General Test; for doctorate, GRE General Test, MS. *Application deadline:* For fall admission, 7/7 for domestic students; for spring admission, 11/ 24 for domestic students. Applications are processed on a rolling basis. Application fee: $50 ($60 for international students). Electronic applications accepted. *Expenses:* Tuition, state resident: full-time $7290; part-time $405 per credit hour. Tuition, nonresident: full-time $21,870; part-time $1215 per credit hour. *International tuition:* $22,000 full-time. *Required fees:* $1402. *Financial support:* Research assistantships and Federal Work-Study available. Support available to part-time students. Financial award application deadline: 3/15; financial award applicants required to submit FAFSA. *Faculty research:* Poultry nutrition, poultry breeding, poultry physiology, poultry diseases and parasites, processing/food science. *Unit head:* Dr. Donald E. Conner, Head, 334-844-4133, E-mail: connede@auburn.edu. *Application contact:* Dr. George Flowers, Dean of the Graduate School, 334-844-2125. Web site: http://www.ag.auburn.edu/poul/.

Boise State University, Graduate College, College of Arts and Sciences, Department of Biology, Program in Raptor Biology, Boise, ID 83725-0399. Offers MS. Part-time programs available. *Degree requirements:* For master's, thesis. *Entrance requirements:* For master's, GRE General Test, minimum GPA of 3.0. Electronic applications accepted. *Faculty research:* Avian ecology.

Brigham Young University, Graduate Studies, College of Life Sciences, Department of Plant and Wildlife Sciences, Provo, UT 84602-1001. Offers environmental science (MS); genetics and biotechnology (MS); wildlife and wildlands conservation (MS, PhD). *Faculty:* 26 full-time (1 woman), 1 (woman) part-time/adjunct. *Students:* 50 full-time (18 women); includes 8 minority (2 Asian, non-Hispanic/Latino; 4 Hispanic/Latino; 2 Native Hawaiian or other Pacific Islander, non-Hispanic/Latino), 4 international. Average age 25. 29 applicants, 41% accepted, 9 enrolled. In 2011, 18 master's, 1 doctorate awarded. *Degree requirements:* For master's, thesis; for doctorate, comprehensive exam, thesis/ dissertation, minimum GPA of 3.2, 54 hours (18 dissertation, 36 coursework). *Entrance requirements:* For master's, GRE General Test, minimum GPA of 3.2 during last 60 hours of course work; for doctorate, GRE, minimum GPA of 3.2. Additional exam requirements/recommendations for international students: Required—TOEFL (minimum score 580 paper-based; 237 computer-based; 85 iBT). *Application deadline:* 2/1 for domestic and international students. Applications are processed on a rolling basis. Electronic applications accepted. Full-time tuition for non-LDS students: $11,520 per year; $640 per credit. *Expenses:* Tuition: Full-time $5760; part-time $320 per credit. Tuition and fees vary according to student's religious affiliation. *Financial support:* In 2011–12, 2 research assistantships with partial tuition reimbursements (averaging $16,650 per year), 37 teaching assistantships with partial tuition reimbursements (averaging $16,650 per year) were awarded; scholarships/grants and tuition waivers (partial) also available. Financial award application deadline: 2/1. *Faculty research:* Environmental science, plant genetics, plant ecology, plant nutrition and pathology, wildlife and wildlands conservation. *Total annual research expenditures:* $2.1 million. *Unit head:* Dr. Val J. Anderson, Chair, 801-422-3527, Fax: 801-422-0008, E-mail: val_anderson@byu.edu. *Application contact:* Dr. Loreen Allphin, Graduate Coordinator, 801-422-5603, Fax: 801-422-0008, E-mail: loreen_allphin@byu.edu. Web site: http://pws.byu.edu/home/.

California State University, Fresno, Division of Graduate Studies, College of Agricultural Sciences and Technology, Department of Animal Science and Agricultural Education, Fresno, CA 93740-8027. Offers animal science (MS). Part-time and evening/weekend programs available. *Degree requirements:* For master's, thesis. *Entrance requirements:* For master's, GRE General Test, minimum GPA of 3.0 in last 60 hours. Additional exam requirements/ recommendations for international students: Required—TOEFL. Electronic applications accepted. *Faculty research:* Horse nutrition, animal health and welfare, electronic monitoring.

Clemson University, Graduate School, College of Agriculture, Forestry and Life Sciences, Department of Animal and Veterinary Sciences, Clemson, SC 29634. Offers animal and veterinary sciences (MS, PhD). *Faculty:* 10 full-time (5 women), 1 part-time/adjunct (0 women). *Students:* 9 full-time (6 women), 1 (woman) part-time; includes 1 minority (Black or African American, non-Hispanic/Latino), 1 international. Average age 29. 11 applicants, 45% accepted, 2 enrolled. In 2011, 3 doctorates awarded. *Degree requirements:* For doctorate, thesis/dissertation. *Entrance requirements:* For master's and doctorate, GRE General Test. Additional exam requirements/recommendations for international students: Required—TOEFL. *Application deadline:* For fall admission, 4/15 for international students; for spring admission, 9/15 for international students. Applications are

Peterson's Graduate Programs in the Physical Sciences, Mathematics, Agricultural Sciences, the Environment & Natural Resources 2013

facebook.com/petersonspublishing **415**

processed on a rolling basis. Application fee: $70 ($80 for international students). Electronic applications accepted. *Expenses:* Contact institution. *Financial support:* In 2011–12, 8 students received support, including 6 research assistantships with partial tuition reimbursements available (averaging $12,667 per year), 4 teaching assistantships with partial tuition reimbursements available (averaging $14,750 per year); fellowships with full and partial tuition reimbursements available, career-related internships or fieldwork, Federal Work-Study, institutionally sponsored loans, scholarships/grants, and unspecified assistantships also available. Financial award applicants required to submit FAFSA. *Total annual research expenditures:* $1.1 million. *Unit head:* Dr. Susan K. Duckett, Chair, 864-656-2570, Fax: 864-656-3131, E-mail: sducket@clemson.edu. *Application contact:* Dr. Denzil Maurice, 864-656-4023, E-mail: dmrc@clemson.edu. Web site: http://www.clemson.edu/avs.

Colorado State University, Graduate School, College of Agricultural Sciences, Department of Animal Sciences, Fort Collins, CO 80523-1171. Offers MS, PhD. *Faculty:* 22 full-time (3 women). *Students:* 25 full-time (13 women), 22 part-time (16 women); includes 4 minority (1 Black or African American, non-Hispanic/Latino; 1 American Indian or Alaska Native, non-Hispanic/Latino; 2 Hispanic/Latino), 9 international. Average age 28. 37 applicants, 24% accepted, 6 enrolled. In 2011, 23 master's, 5 doctorates awarded. *Degree requirements:* For master's, variable foreign language requirement, comprehensive exam, thesis, one article prepared for publication in a refereed scientific journal with degree candidate as senior author and approval of on-campus graduate committee consisting of three faculty members; for doctorate, variable foreign language requirement, comprehensive exam, thesis/dissertation, two articles prepared for publication in refereed scientific publication with degree candidate as senior author and approval of on-campus graduate committee consisting of three faculty members. *Entrance requirements:* For master's, GRE General Test (minimum score 1000 verbal and quantitative), minimum GPA of 3.0; reference letters; for doctorate, GRE General Test (combined minimum score of 1000 on the Verbal and Quantitative sections), minimum GPA of 3.0; reference letters. Additional exam requirements/recommendations for international students: Required—TOEFL (minimum score 525 paper-based; 71 computer-based), IELTS (minimum score 6.5). *Application deadline:* For fall admission, 4/1 for domestic and international students; for spring admission, 10/1 for domestic and international students. Applications are processed on a rolling basis. Application fee: $50. Electronic applications accepted. *Expenses:* Tuition, state resident: full-time $7992. Tuition, nonresident: full-time $19,592. *Required fees:* $1735; $58 per credit. *Financial support:* In 2011–12, 34 students received support, including 1 fellowship with full tuition reimbursement available (averaging $35,000 per year), 30 research assistantships with full tuition reimbursements available (averaging $12,804 per year), 3 teaching assistantships with full tuition reimbursements available (averaging $13,182 per year); scholarships/grants and unspecified assistantships also available. Financial award applicants required to submit FAFSA. *Faculty research:* Meat science, food safety, livestock management systems, equine science, breeding and genetics. *Total annual research expenditures:* $2.9 million. *Unit head:* Dr. Kevin Pond, Department Head, 970-491-7295, Fax: 970-491-5326, E-mail: kevin.pond@colostate.edu. *Application contact:* Melissa Weiss, Administrative Assistant, 970-491-1442, Fax: 970-491-5326, E-mail: m.weiss@colostate.edu. Web site: http://www.ansci.colostate.edu/.

Cornell University, Graduate School, Graduate Fields of Agriculture and Life Sciences, Field of Animal Science, Ithaca, NY 14853-0001. Offers animal breeding (MS, PhD); animal genetics (MS, PhD). *Faculty:* 36 full-time (9 women). *Students:* 31 full-time (18 women); includes 5 minority (3 Asian, non-Hispanic/Latino; 2 Hispanic/Latino), 11 international. Average age 29. 40 applicants, 15% accepted, 6 enrolled. In 2011, 5 master's, 7 doctorates awarded. *Degree requirements:* For master's, thesis, teaching experience; for doctorate, comprehensive exam, thesis/dissertation, teaching experience. *Entrance requirements:* For master's and doctorate, 2 letters of recommendation. Additional exam requirements/recommendations for international students: Required—TOEFL (minimum score 550 paper-based; 213 computer-based; 77 iBT). *Application deadline:* For fall admission, 4/1 for domestic students; for spring admission, 9/1 for domestic students. Application fee: $95. Electronic applications accepted. *Financial support:* In 2011–12, 7 fellowships with full tuition reimbursements, 13 research assistantships with full tuition reimbursements, 8 teaching assistantships with full tuition reimbursements were awarded; institutionally sponsored loans, scholarships/grants, health care benefits, tuition waivers (full and partial), and unspecified assistantships also available. Financial award applicants required to submit FAFSA. *Faculty research:* Quantitative genetics, genetic improvement of animal populations, statistical genetics. *Unit head:* Director of Graduate Studies, 607-255-4416, Fax: 607-254-5413, E-mail: shh4@cornell.edu. *Application contact:* Graduate Field Assistant, 607-255-4416, Fax: 607-254-5413, E-mail: shh4@cornell.edu. Web site: http://www.gradschool.cornell.edu/fields.php?id-41&a-2.

Fort Valley State University, College of Graduate Studies and Extended Education, Program in Animal Science, Fort Valley, GA 31030. Offers MS. *Degree requirements:* For master's, thesis. *Entrance requirements:* For master's, GRE General Test. Additional exam requirements/recommendations for international students: Recommended—TOEFL.

Iowa State University of Science and Technology, Department of Animal Science, Ames, IA 50011-3150. Offers animal breeding and genetics (MS, PhD); animal physiology (MS); animal psychology (PhD); animal science (MS, PhD); meat science (MS, PhD). *Degree requirements:* For master's, thesis or alternative; for doctorate, thesis/dissertation. *Entrance requirements:* For master's and doctorate, GRE General Test. Additional exam requirements/recommendations for international students: Required—TOEFL (minimum score 550 paper-based; 80 iBT), IELTS (minimum score 6.5). *Application deadline:* For fall admission, 2/1 priority date for domestic students, 2/1 for international students; for spring admission, 9/1 priority date for domestic students, 9/1 for international students. Application fee: $40 ($90 for international students). Electronic applications accepted. *Faculty research:* Animal breeding, animal nutrition, meat science, muscle biology, nutritional physiology. *Unit head:* Dr. Joseph Sebranek, Director of Graduate Education, 515-294-2160, Fax: 515-294-6994, E-mail: dlnelson@iastate.edu. *Application contact:* Donna Nelson, Graduate Secretary, 515-294-2160, Fax: 515-294-6994, E-mail: dlnelson@iastate.edu. Web site: http://www.ans.iastate.edu/stud/prosp_grad/.

Iowa State University of Science and Technology, Program in Animal Breeding and Genetics, Ames, IA 50011-3150. Offers animal breeding and genetics (MS); immunogenetics (PhD); molecular genetics (PhD); quantitative genetics (PhD). *Entrance requirements:* For master's and doctorate, GRE. Additional exam requirements/recommendations for international students: Required—TOEFL (minimum score 550 paper-based; 80 iBT), IELTS (minimum score 6.5). *Application deadline:* For fall admission, 2/1 for domestic and international students; for spring admission, 9/1 for domestic and international students. Electronic applications accepted. *Unit head:* Joe Sebranek, Director of Graduate Education, 515-294-2160, Fax: 515-294-6994, E-mail: dlnelson@iastate.edu. *Application contact:* Donna Nelson, Application Contact, 515-294-2160, Fax: 515-294-6994, E-mail: dlnelson@iastate.edu. Web site: http://www.ans.iastate.edu/stud/prosp_grad/.

Iowa State University of Science and Technology, Program in Animal Physiology, Ames, IA 50011-3150. Offers MS, PhD. *Entrance requirements:* For master's and doctorate, GRE. Additional exam requirements/recommendations for international students: Required—TOEFL (minimum score 550 paper-based; 80 iBT), IELTS (minimum score 6.5). *Application deadline:* For fall admission, 2/1 for domestic and international students; for spring admission, 9/1 for domestic and international students. Electronic applications accepted. *Unit head:* Joe Sebranek, Director of Graduate Education, 515-294-2160, Fax: 515-294-6994, E-mail: dlnelson@iastate.edu. *Application contact:* Donna Nelson, Application Contact, 515-294-2160, Fax: 515-294-6994, E-mail: dlnelson@iastate.edu. Web site: http://www.admissions.iastate.edu/apply/index.php.

Iowa State University of Science and Technology, Program in Meat Science, Ames, IA 50011-3150. Offers MS, PhD. *Entrance requirements:* For master's and doctorate, GRE. Additional exam requirements/recommendations for international students: Required—TOEFL (minimum score 550 paper-based; 80 iBT), IELTS (minimum score 6.5). *Application deadline:* For fall admission, 2/1 for domestic students; for spring admission, 9/1 for domestic students. Electronic applications accepted. *Unit head:* Joe Sebranek, Director of Graduate Education, 515-294-2160, Fax: 515-294-6994, E-mail: dlnelson@iastate.edu. *Application contact:* Donna Nelson, Application Contact, 515-294-2160, Fax: 515-294-6994, E-mail: dlnelson@iastate.edu. Web site: http://www.ans.iastate.edu/stud/prosp_grad/.

Kansas State University, Graduate School, College of Agriculture, Department of Animal Sciences and Industry, Manhattan, KS 66506. Offers animal breeding and genetics (MS, PhD); meat science (MS, PhD); monogastric nutrition (MS, PhD); physiology (MS, PhD); ruminant nutrition (MS, PhD). *Faculty:* 38 full-time (9 women), 7 part-time/adjunct (0 women). *Students:* 52 full-time (19 women), 12 part-time (6 women); includes 1 minority (Hispanic/Latino), 11 international. Average age 27. 45 applicants, 36% accepted, 14 enrolled. In 2011, 16 master's, 5 doctorates awarded. *Degree requirements:* For master's, thesis, oral exam; for doctorate, thesis/dissertation, preliminary exams. *Entrance requirements:* Additional exam requirements/recommendations for international students: Required—TOEFL (minimum score 550 paper-based; 213 computer-based). *Application deadline:* For fall admission, 2/1 priority date for domestic students, 2/1 for international students; for spring admission, 8/1 priority date for domestic students, 8/1 for international students. Applications are processed on a rolling basis. Application fee: $40 ($55 for international students). Electronic applications accepted. *Financial support:* In 2011–12, 1 fellowship, 45 research assistantships (averaging $17,652 per year), 5 teaching assistantships with full tuition reimbursements (averaging $13,397 per year) were awarded; health care benefits and unspecified assistantships also available. Financial award application deadline: 3/1; financial award applicants required to submit FAFSA. *Faculty research:* Animal nutrition, animal physiology, meat science, animal genetics. *Total annual research expenditures:* $1.5 million. *Unit head:* Dr. Ken Odde, Head, 785-532-1227, Fax: 785-532-7059, E-mail: kenodde@ksu.edu. *Application contact:* Dr. Evan Titgemeyer, Director, 785-532-1220, Fax: 785-532-7059, E-mail: etitgeme@ksu.edu. Web site: http://www.asi.k-state.edu/DesktopDefault.aspx.

Louisiana State University and Agricultural and Mechanical College, Graduate School, College of Agriculture, School of Animal Sciences, Baton Rouge, LA 70803. Offers MS, PhD. Part-time programs available. *Faculty:* 18 full-time (2 women). *Students:* 37 full-time (25 women), 6 part-time (2 women); includes 3 minority (1 Black or African American, non-Hispanic/Latino; 2 Hispanic/Latino), 10 international. Average age 28. 17 applicants, 65% accepted, 11 enrolled. In 2011, 5 master's, 1 doctorate awarded. Terminal master's awarded for partial completion of doctoral program. *Degree requirements:* For master's, thesis; for doctorate, thesis/dissertation. *Entrance requirements:* For master's and doctorate, GRE General Test, minimum GPA of 3.0. Additional exam

416 facebook.com/petersonspublishing

Peterson's Graduate Programs in the Physical Sciences, Mathematics, Agricultural Sciences, the Environment & Natural Resources 2013

requirements/recommendations for international students: Required—TOEFL (minimum score 550 paper-based; 213 computer-based; 79 iBT) or IELTS (minimum score 6.5). *Application deadline:* For fall admission, 1/25 priority date for domestic students, 5/15 for international students; for spring admission, 10/15 for international students. Applications are processed on a rolling basis. Application fee: $50 ($70 for international students). Electronic applications accepted. *Financial support:* In 2011–12, 34 students received support, including 13 research assistantships with partial tuition reimbursements available (averaging $13,633 per year), 17 teaching assistantships with partial tuition reimbursements available (averaging $14,118 per year); fellowships, Federal Work-Study, institutionally sponsored loans, scholarships/grants, health care benefits, tuition waivers (full and partial), and unspecified assistantships also available. Support available to part-time students. Financial award applicants required to submit FAFSA. *Faculty research:* Reproductive physiology, biotechnology, meats, non-ruminant and ruminant nutrition, daily science. *Total annual research expenditures:* $1.1,124. *Unit head:* Dr. Gary Hay, Head, 225-578-3241, Fax: 225-578-3279, E-mail: ghay@agcenter.lsu.edu. *Application contact:* Dr. Donald L. Thompson, Jr., Graduate Coordinator, 225-578-3445, Fax: 225-578-3279, E-mail: dthomp1@agcenter.lsu.edu. Web site: http://www.lsuagcenter.com/en/our_offices/departments/Animal_Sciences/.

McGill University, Faculty of Graduate and Postdoctoral Studies, Faculty of Agricultural and Environmental Sciences, Department of Animal Science, Montréal, QC H3A 2T5, Canada. Offers M Sc, M Sc A, PhD.

Michigan State University, College of Veterinary Medicine and The Graduate School, Graduate Programs in Veterinary Medicine, Department of Large Animal Clinical Sciences, East Lansing, MI 48824. Offers MS, PhD. *Entrance requirements:* Additional exam requirements/recommendations for international students: Required—TOEFL (minimum score 550 paper-based; 213 computer-based), Michigan State University ELT (minimum score 85), Michigan English Language Assessment Battery (minimum score 83). Electronic applications accepted.

Michigan State University, College of Veterinary Medicine and The Graduate School, Graduate Programs in Veterinary Medicine, Department of Small Animal Clinical Sciences, East Lansing, MI 48824. Offers MS. *Degree requirements:* For master's, thesis. *Entrance requirements:* Additional exam requirements/recommendations for international students: Required—TOEFL, Michigan State University ELT (minimum score 85), Michigan English Language Assessment Battery (minimum score 83).

Michigan State University, The Graduate School, College of Agriculture and Natural Resources, Department of Animal Science, East Lansing, MI 48824. Offers animal science (MS, PhD); animal science-environmental toxicology (PhD). *Entrance requirements:* Additional exam requirements/recommendations for international students: Required—TOEFL (minimum score 550 paper-based; 213 computer-based), Michigan State University ELT (minimum score 85), Michigan English Language Assessment Battery (minimum score 83). Electronic applications accepted.

Mississippi State University, College of Agriculture and Life Sciences, Department of Animal Dairy Sciences, Mississippi State, MS 39762. Offers agricultural life sciences (MS), including animal physiology (MS, PhD), genetics (MS, PhD); agricultural science (PhD), including animal dairy sciences, animal nutrition; life sciences (PhD), including animal physiology (MS, PhD), genetics (MS, PhD). *Faculty:* 12 full-time (5 women). *Students:* 22 full-time (14 women), 14 part-time (7 women); includes 4 minority (2 Black or African American, non-Hispanic/Latino; 2 Hispanic/Latino), 7 international. Average age 30. 35 applicants, 20% accepted, 5 enrolled. In 2011, 5 master's, 4 doctorates awarded. *Degree requirements:* For master's, thesis, comprehensive oral or written exam; for doctorate, thesis/dissertation, comprehensive oral or written exam. *Entrance requirements:* For master's, GRE General Test, minimum GPA of 3.0; for doctorate, GRE General Test. Additional exam requirements/recommendations for international students: Required—TOEFL (minimum score 575 paper-based). *Application deadline:* For fall admission, 7/1 for domestic students, 5/1 for international students; for spring admission, 11/1 for domestic students, 9/1 for international students. Applications are processed on a rolling basis. Application fee: $40. Electronic applications accepted. *Expenses:* Tuition, state resident: full-time $5805; part-time $322.50 per credit hour. Tuition, nonresident: full-time $14,670; part-time $815 per credit hour. *Financial support:* In 2011–12, 16 research assistantships (averaging $12,270 per year), 1 teaching assistantship (averaging $10,014 per year) were awarded; Federal Work-Study, institutionally sponsored loans, and unspecified assistantships also available. Financial award application deadline: 4/1; financial award applicants required to submit FAFSA. *Faculty research:* Ecology and population dynamics, physiology, biochemistry and behavior, systematics. *Total annual research expenditures:* $496,000. *Unit head:* Dr. Scott Willard, Professor and Department Head, 662-325-2802, Fax: 662-325-8873, E-mail: swillard@bch.msstate.edu. *Application contact:* Dr. Brian Rude, Professor and Graduate Coordinator, 662-325-2802, Fax: 662-325-8873, E-mail: brude@ads.msstate.edu. Web site: http://www.ads.msstate.edu/.

Mississippi State University, College of Agriculture and Life Sciences, Department of Poultry Science, Mississippi State, MS 39762. Offers MS, PhD. *Faculty:* 2 full-time (0 women). *Students:* 7 full-time (2 women), 5 international. Average age 29. 4 applicants, 0% accepted, 0 enrolled. In 2011, 4 master's, 1 doctorate awarded. *Degree requirements:* For master's, comprehensive exam, thesis optional; for doctorate, comprehensive exam, thesis/dissertation. *Entrance*

requirements: Additional exam requirements/recommendations for international students: Required—TOEFL (minimum score 475 paper-based; 153 computer-based; 53 iBT); Recommended—IELTS (minimum score 4.5). *Application deadline:* For fall admission, 7/1 for domestic students, 5/1 for international students; for spring admission, 10/1 for domestic students, 11/1 for international students. Applications are processed on a rolling basis. Application fee: $40. Electronic applications accepted. *Expenses:* Tuition, state resident: full-time $5805; part-time $322.50 per credit hour. Tuition, nonresident: full-time $14,670; part-time $815 per credit hour. *Financial support:* In 2011–12, 3 research assistantships with partial tuition reimbursements (averaging $14,179 per year), 1 teaching assistantship with partial tuition reimbursement (averaging $16,360 per year) were awarded; Federal Work-Study, institutionally sponsored loans, scholarships/grants, and unspecified assistantships also available. Financial award application deadline: 4/1; financial award applicants required to submit FAFSA. *Unit head:* Dr. Mary Beck, Professor and Head, 662-325-5430, Fax: 662-325-8292, E-mail: mbeck@poultry.msstate.edu. *Application contact:* Dr. Chris McDaniel, Professor and Graduate Coordinator, 662-325-1839, Fax: 662-325-8292, E-mail: cmcdaniel@poultry.msstate.edu. Web site: http://www.poultry.msstate.edu/.

Montana State University, College of Graduate Studies, College of Agriculture, Department of Animal and Range Sciences, Bozeman, MT 59717. Offers MS, PhD. Part-time programs available. *Degree requirements:* For master's, comprehensive exam; for doctorate, comprehensive exam, thesis/dissertation. *Entrance requirements:* For master's, GRE, minimum GPA of 3.0; undergraduate coursework in animal science, range science or closely-related field; faculty adviser; for doctorate, GRE. Additional exam requirements/recommendations for international students: Required—TOEFL (minimum score 550 paper-based; 213 computer-based; 80 iBT). Electronic applications accepted. *Faculty research:* Rangeland ecology, wildlife habitat management, residual feed intake, post-partum effect of bulls, increasing efficiency of sheep production systems.

New Mexico State University, Graduate School, College of Agricultural, Consumer and Environmental Sciences, Department of Animal and Range Sciences, Las Cruces, NM 88003-8001. Offers animal science (MS, PhD); domestic animal biology (M Ag); range science (M Ag, MS, PhD). Part-time programs available. *Faculty:* 15 full-time (3 women). *Students:* 33 full-time (19 women), 5 part-time (3 women); includes 4 minority (all Hispanic/Latino), 7 international. Average age 28. 23 applicants, 30% accepted, 4 enrolled. In 2011, 7 master's, 3 doctorates awarded. *Degree requirements:* For master's, thesis, seminar, experimental statistics; for doctorate, thesis/dissertation, research tool. *Entrance requirements:* For master's, minimum GPA of 3.0 in last 60 hours of undergraduate course work (MS); for doctorate, minimum graduate GPA of 3.2. Additional exam requirements/recommendations for international students: Required—TOEFL (minimum score 530 paper-based; 0 computer-based; 71 iBT), IELTS (minimum score 6). *Application deadline:* For fall admission, 7/1 priority date for domestic students, 7/1 for international students; for spring admission, 11/1 for domestic and international students. Applications are processed on a rolling basis. Application fee: $40 ($50 for international students). Electronic applications accepted. *Expenses:* Tuition, state resident: full-time $5004; part-time $208.50 per credit. Tuition, nonresident: full-time $17,446; part-time $726.90 per credit. *Financial support:* In 2011–12, 31 students received support, including 1 fellowship (averaging $3,754 per year), 8 research assistantships (averaging $21,980 per year), 19 teaching assistantships (averaging $22,750 per year); career-related internships or fieldwork, Federal Work-Study, scholarships/grants, traineeships, health care benefits, and unspecified assistantships also available. Support available to part-time students. Financial award application deadline: 3/15. *Faculty research:* Reproductive physiology, ruminant nutrition, nutrition toxicology, range ecology, wildland hydrology. *Unit head:* Dr. Tim Ross, Interim Head, 575-646-2514, Fax: 575-646-5441, E-mail: tross@nmsu.edu. *Application contact:* Dr. Tim Ross, Interim Head, 575-646-2514, Fax: 575-646-5441, E-mail: tross@nmsu.edu. Web site: http://aces.nmsu.edu/academics/anrs.

North Carolina Agricultural and Technical State University, School of Graduate Studies, School of Agriculture and Environmental Sciences, Department of Animal Sciences, Greensboro, NC 27411. Offers animal health science (MS).

North Carolina State University, Graduate School, College of Agriculture and Life Sciences, Department of Animal Science, Raleigh, NC 27695. Offers animal and poultry science (PhD); animal science (MS). *Degree requirements:* For master's, thesis optional. *Entrance requirements:* For master's, GRE, minimum GPA of 3.0. Electronic applications accepted. *Faculty research:* Nutrient utilization, mineral nutrition, genomics, endocrinology, reproductive physiology.

North Carolina State University, Graduate School, College of Agriculture and Life Sciences, Department of Poultry Science, Raleigh, NC 27695. Offers MS. Part-time programs available. *Degree requirements:* For master's, thesis. Electronic applications accepted. *Faculty research:* Reproductive physiology, nutrition, toxicology, immunology, molecular biology.

North Dakota State University, College of Graduate and Interdisciplinary Studies, College of Agriculture, Food Systems, and Natural Resources, Department of Animal and Range Sciences, Fargo, ND 58108. Offers animal science (MS, PhD); natural resource management (MS, PhD); range sciences (MS, PhD). *Faculty:* 19 full-time (4 women), 1 part-time/adjunct (0 women). *Students:* 24 full-time (16 women), 9 part-time (5 women), 4 international. Average age 25. 15 applicants, 47% accepted, 4 enrolled. In 2011, 4 master's, 5

Peterson's Graduate Programs in the Physical Sciences, Mathematics, Agricultural Sciences, the Environment & Natural Resources 2013

facebook.com/petersonspublishing **417**

Animal Sciences

doctorates awarded. *Degree requirements:* For master's, thesis; for doctorate, comprehensive exam, thesis/dissertation. *Entrance requirements:* For master's and doctorate, GRE General Test. Additional exam requirements/recommendations for international students: Required—TOEFL (minimum score 71 iBT). *Application deadline:* Applications are processed on a rolling basis. Application fee: $35. *Financial support:* In 2011–12, 1 fellowship with tuition reimbursement (averaging $18,000 per year), 29 research assistantships with tuition reimbursements (averaging $13,000 per year) were awarded; teaching assistantships, Federal Work-Study, institutionally sponsored loans, and tuition waivers (partial) also available. Financial award application deadline: 3/15. *Faculty research:* Reproduction, nutrition, meat and muscle biology, breeding/genetics. *Unit head:* Dr. Gregory Lardy, Chair, 701-231-7641, Fax: 701-231-7590, E-mail: gregory.lardy@ndsu.edu. *Application contact:* Sonya Goergen, Marketing, Recruitment, and Public Relations Coordinator, 701-231-7033, Fax: 701-231-6524.

Nova Scotia Agricultural College, Research and Graduate Studies, Truro, NS B2N 5E3, Canada. Offers agriculture (M Sc), including air quality, animal behavior, animal molecular genetics, animal nutrition, animal technology, aquaculture, botany, crop management, crop physiology, ecology, environmental microbiology, food science, horticulture, nutrient management, pest management, physiology, plant biotechnology, plant pathology, soil chemistry, soil fertility, waste management and composting, water quality. Program offered jointly with Dalhousie University. Part-time programs available. *Degree requirements:* For master's, thesis, ATC Exam Teaching Assistantship. *Entrance requirements:* For master's, honors B Sc, minimum GPA of 3.0. Additional exam requirements/recommendations for international students: Required—TOEFL (minimum score 580 paper-based; 237 computer-based; 92 iBT), IELTS, Michigan English Language Assessment Battery, CanTEST, CAEL. *Faculty research:* Bio-product development, organic agriculture, nutrient management, air and water quality, agricultural biotechnology.

The Ohio State University, Graduate School, College of Food, Agricultural, and Environmental Sciences, Department of Animal Sciences, Columbus, OH 43210. Offers MS, PhD. *Faculty:* 30. *Students:* 31 full-time (19 women), 13 part-time (7 women); includes 6 minority (1 Black or African American, non-Hispanic/Latino; 4 Hispanic/Latino; 1 Two or more races, non-Hispanic/Latino), 15 international. Average age 27. In 2011, 6 master's, 2 doctorates awarded. *Degree requirements:* For master's, thesis; for doctorate, thesis/dissertation. *Entrance requirements:* For master's and doctorate, GRE General Test. Additional exam requirements/recommendations for international students: Required—TOEFL (minimum score 550 paper-based; 213 computer-based), IELTS (minimum score 6.5), or Michigan English Language Assessment Battery (minimum score 82). *Application deadline:* For fall admission, 8/15 priority date for domestic students, 7/1 for international students; for winter admission, 12/1 priority date for domestic students, 11/1 for international students; for spring admission, 3/1 priority date for domestic students, 2/1 for international students. Applications are processed on a rolling basis. Application fee: $40 ($50 for international students). Electronic applications accepted. *Expenses:* Tuition, state resident: full-time $11,400. Tuition, nonresident: full-time $28,125. Tuition and fees vary according to course load, degree level, campus/location and program. *Financial support:* Fellowships, research assistantships, teaching assistantships, Federal Work-Study, and institutionally sponsored loans available. Support available to part-time students. *Unit head:* Ronald Kensinger, Chair, 614-292-6401, E-mail: kensinger.4@osu.edu. *Application contact:* Animal Science Graduate Programs, 614-292-6401, Fax: 614-292-2929, E-mail: gradadmissions@osu.edu. Web site: http://ansci.osu.edu/.

Oklahoma State University, College of Agricultural Science and Natural Resources, Department of Animal Science, Stillwater, OK 74078. Offers animal sciences (M Ag, MS); food science (MS, PhD). *Faculty:* 26 full-time (4 women), 3 part-time/adjunct (0 women). *Students:* 23 full-time (15 women), 39 part-time (21 women); includes 4 minority (3 Hispanic/Latino; 1 Two or more races, non-Hispanic/Latino), 21 international. Average age 27. 106 applicants, 19% accepted, 17 enrolled. In 2011, 23 master's, 7 doctorates awarded. *Degree requirements:* For master's, thesis; for doctorate, comprehensive exam, thesis/dissertation. *Entrance requirements:* For master's and doctorate, GRE or GMAT. Additional exam requirements/recommendations for international students: Required—TOEFL (minimum score 550 paper-based; 79 iBT). *Application deadline:* For fall admission, 3/1 for international students; for spring admission, 8/1 for international students. Applications are processed on a rolling basis. Application fee: $40 ($75 for international students). Electronic applications accepted. *Expenses:* Tuition, state resident: full-time $4044; part-time $168.50 per credit hour. Tuition, nonresident: full-time $16,008; part-time $667 per credit hour. *Required fees:* $2122; $88.45 per credit hour. One-time fee: $50. Tuition and fees vary according to course load and campus/location. *Financial support:* In 2011–12, 32 research assistantships (averaging $14,481 per year), 1 teaching assistantship (averaging $11,064 per year) were awarded; career-related internships or fieldwork, Federal Work-Study, scholarships/grants, health care benefits, tuition waivers (partial), and unspecified assistantships also available. Support available to part-time students. Financial award application deadline: 3/1; financial award applicants required to submit FAFSA. *Faculty research:* Quantitative trait loci identification for economical traits in swing/beef; waste management strategies in livestock; endocrine control of reproductive processes in farm animals; cholesterol synthesis, inhibition, and reduction; food safety research. *Unit head:* Dr. Ronald Kensinger, Head, 405-744-6062, Fax: 405-744-

7390. *Application contact:* Dr. Sheryl Tucker, Dean, 405-744-7099, Fax: 405-744-0355, E-mail: grad-i@okstate.edu. Web site: http://www.ansi.okstate.edu.

Oregon State University, Graduate School, College of Agricultural Sciences, Department of Animal Sciences, Corvallis, OR 97331. Offers M Agr, MAIS, MS, PhD. Terminal master's awarded for partial completion of doctoral program. *Degree requirements:* For master's, thesis (for some programs); for doctorate, thesis/dissertation. *Entrance requirements:* For master's and doctorate, GRE General Test, minimum GPA of 3.0 in last 90 hours. Additional exam requirements/recommendations for international students: Required—TOEFL. *Faculty research:* Reproductive physiology, population genetics, general nutrition of ruminants and nonruminants, embryo physiology, endocrinology.

Penn State University Park, Graduate School, College of Agricultural Sciences, Department of Dairy and Animal Science, State College, University Park, PA 16802-1503. Offers animal science (MPS, MS, PhD). *Unit head:* Dr. Bruce A. McPheron, Dean, 814-865-2541, Fax: 814-865-3103, E-mail: bam10@psu.edu. *Application contact:* Cynthia E. Nicosia, Director of Graduate Enrollment Services, 814-865-1834, E-mail: cey1@psu.edu. Web site: http://www.das.psu.edu.

Prairie View A&M University, College of Agriculture and Human Sciences, Prairie View, TX 77446-0519. Offers agricultural economics (MS); animal sciences (MS); interdisciplinary human sciences (MS); soil science (MS). Part-time and evening/weekend programs available. *Degree requirements:* For master's, comprehensive exam, thesis (for some programs), field placement. *Entrance requirements:* For master's, GRE General Test, minimum GPA of 2.45. Additional exam requirements/recommendations for international students: Required—TOEFL (minimum score 550 paper-based). *Faculty research:* Domestic violence prevention, water quality, food growth regulators, wetland dynamics, biochemistry, obesity and nutrition, family therapy.

Purdue University, Graduate School, College of Agriculture, Department of Animal Sciences, West Lafayette, IN 47907. Offers MS, PhD. Part-time programs available. *Faculty:* 29 full-time (3 women), 6 part-time/adjunct (2 women). *Students:* 49 full-time (34 women), 10 part-time (7 women); includes 5 minority (1 Black or African American, non-Hispanic/Latino; 1 Asian, non-Hispanic/Latino; 2 Hispanic/Latino; 1 Two or more races, non-Hispanic/Latino), 28 international. Average age 28. 65 applicants, 37% accepted, 16 enrolled. In 2011, 14 master's, 4 doctorates awarded. Terminal master's awarded for partial completion of doctoral program. *Degree requirements:* For master's, thesis optional; for doctorate, thesis/dissertation. *Entrance requirements:* For master's, GRE General Test, minimum undergraduate GPA of 3.0 or equivalent; for doctorate, GRE General Test, minimum undergraduate GPA of 3.0 or equivalent; master's degree with minimum GPA of 3.0 or equivalent. Additional exam requirements/recommendations for international students: Required—TOEFL (minimum score 550 paper-based; 77 iBT), TWE. *Application deadline:* For fall admission, 6/1 priority date for domestic students, 3/1 for international students; for spring admission, 10/1 priority date for domestic students, 8/1 for international students. Applications are processed on a rolling basis. Application fee: $60 ($75 for international students). Electronic applications accepted. *Financial support:* In 2011–12, 35 students received support, including fellowships with full tuition reimbursements available (averaging $17,475 per year), 29 research assistantships with full tuition reimbursements available (averaging $18,577 per year). Support available to part-time students. Financial award applicants required to submit FAFSA. *Faculty research:* Genetics, meat science, nutrition, management, ethology. *Unit head:* Dr. Alan G. Mathew, Head, 765-494-4806. *Application contact:* Miller J. Marlene, Graduate Contact, 765-494-4863, E-mail: marlenem@purdue.edu. Web site: http://www.ansc.purdue.edu/.

Purdue University, Graduate School, College of Health and Human Sciences, Department of Nutrition Science, West Lafayette, IN 47907. Offers animal health (MS, PhD); biochemical and molecular nutrition (MS, PhD); growth and development (MS, PhD); human and clinical nutrition (MS, PhD); public health and education (MS, PhD). *Faculty:* 17 full-time (10 women), 14 part-time/adjunct (12 women). *Students:* 35 full-time (33 women), 2 part-time (both women); includes 3 minority (1 Black or African American, non-Hispanic/Latino; 2 Asian, non-Hispanic/Latino), 17 international. Average age 28. 120 applicants, 18% accepted, 11 enrolled. In 2011, 5 master's, 8 doctorates awarded. *Degree requirements:* For master's, thesis; for doctorate, thesis/dissertation. *Entrance requirements:* For master's and doctorate, GRE General Test, scores in verbal and quantitative areas must be greater than 1000 or 300 if the GRE was taken August 1, 2011 or after, minimum undergraduate GPA of 3.0 or equivalent. Additional exam requirements/recommendations for international students: Required—TOEFL (minimum score 600 paper-based; 77 iBT). *Application deadline:* For fall admission, 1/15 for domestic and international students. Applications are processed on a rolling basis. Application fee: $60 ($75 for international students). Electronic applications accepted. *Financial support:* Fellowships, research assistantships, and teaching assistantships available. Support available to part-time students. Financial award applicants required to submit FAFSA. *Faculty research:* Nutrient requirements, nutrient metabolism, nutrition and disease prevention. *Unit head:* Dr. Connie M. Weaver, Head, 765-494-8237, Fax: 765-494-0674, E-mail: weavercm@purdue.edu. *Application contact:* Marilyn McCammack, Graduate Secretary, 765-476-7492, E-mail: mccammac@purdue.edu. Web site: http://www.cfs.purdue.edu/fn/.

Rutgers, The State University of New Jersey, New Brunswick, Graduate School-New Brunswick, Program in Endocrinology and Animal Biosciences, Piscataway, NJ 08854-8097. Offers MS, PhD. Terminal master's awarded for

418 facebook.com/petersonspublishing

Peterson's Graduate Programs in the Physical Sciences, Mathematics, Agricultural Sciences, the Environment & Natural Resources 2013

partial completion of doctoral program. *Degree requirements:* For master's, thesis; for doctorate, comprehensive exam, thesis/dissertation. *Entrance requirements:* For master's and doctorate, GRE General Test. Additional exam requirements/recommendations for international students: Required—TOEFL. Electronic applications accepted. *Faculty research:* Comparative and behavioral endocrinology, epigenetic regulation of the endocrine system, exercise physiology and immunology, fetal and neonatal developmental programming, mammary gland biology and breast cancer, neuroendocrinology and alcohol studies, reproductive and developmental toxicology.

South Dakota State University, Graduate School, College of Agriculture and Biological Sciences, Department of Animal and Range Sciences, Brookings, SD 57007. Offers animal science (MS, PhD); biological sciences (PhD). Part-time programs available. *Degree requirements:* For master's, thesis, oral exam; for doctorate, comprehensive exam, thesis/dissertation, preliminary oral and written exams. *Entrance requirements:* Additional exam requirements/recommendations for international students: Required—TOEFL (minimum score 550 paper-based; 213 computer-based; 79 iBT). *Faculty research:* Ruminant and nonruminant nutrition, meat science, reproductive physiology, range utilization, ecology genetics, muscle biology, animal production.

South Dakota State University, Graduate School, College of Agriculture and Biological Sciences, Department of Dairy Science, Brookings, SD 57007. Offers animal sciences (MS, PhD); biological sciences (MS, PhD). Part-time programs available. *Degree requirements:* For master's, thesis, oral exam; for doctorate, comprehensive exam, thesis/dissertation, preliminary oral and written exams. *Entrance requirements:* Additional exam requirements/recommendations for international students: Required—TOEFL (minimum score 550 paper-based; 213 computer-based). *Faculty research:* Dairy cattle nutrition, energy metabolism, food safety, dairy processing technology.

Southern Illinois University Carbondale, Graduate School, College of Agriculture, Department of Animal Science, Food and Nutrition, Program in Animal Science, Carbondale, IL 62901-4701. Offers MS. *Faculty:* 14 full-time (5 women), 1 (woman) part-time/adjunct. *Students:* 11 full-time (8 women), 3 part-time (all women). Average age 29. 10 applicants, 0% accepted. In 2011, 5 master's awarded. *Degree requirements:* For master's, thesis. *Entrance requirements:* For master's, minimum GPA of 2.7. Additional exam requirements/recommendations for international students: Required—TOEFL. *Application deadline:* Applications are processed on a rolling basis. Application fee: $0. *Financial support:* In 2011–12, 13 research assistantships with full tuition reimbursements, 2 teaching assistantships with full tuition reimbursements were awarded; fellowships with full tuition reimbursements, career-related internships or fieldwork, Federal Work-Study, institutionally sponsored loans, and tuition waivers (full) also available. Support available to part-time students. *Faculty research:* Nutrition, reproductive physiology, animal biotechnology, phytoestrogens and animal reproduction. *Total annual research expenditures:* $300,000. *Unit head:* Dr. Todd A. Winters, Interim Chair, 618-453-1760, Fax: 618-453-5231, E-mail: tw3a@siu.edu. *Application contact:* Ruth Cook, Administrative Clerk, 618-453-1762, E-mail: racook@siu.edu. Web site: http://www.coas.siu.edu/default2.asp?active_page_id=112.

Sul Ross State University, Division of Agricultural and Natural Resource Science, Program in Animal Science, Alpine, TX 79832. Offers M Ag, MS. Part-time programs available. *Degree requirements:* For master's, thesis (for some programs). *Entrance requirements:* For master's, GRE General Test, minimum GPA of 2.5 in last 60 hours of undergraduate work. *Faculty research:* Reproductive physiology, meat processing, animal nutrition, equine foot and motion studies, Spanish goat and Barbido sheep studies.

Texas A&M University, College of Agriculture and Life Sciences, Department of Animal Science, College Station, TX 77843. Offers M Agr, MS, PhD. *Faculty:* 27. *Students:* 81 full-time (55 women), 38 part-time (18 women); includes 13 minority (4 Black or African American, non-Hispanic/Latino; 7 Hispanic/Latino; 1 Native Hawaiian or other Pacific Islander, non-Hispanic/Latino; 1 Two or more races, non-Hispanic/Latino), 11 international. Average age 26. In 2011, 28 master's, 2 doctorates awarded. *Degree requirements:* For master's, thesis; for doctorate, thesis/dissertation. *Entrance requirements:* For master's and doctorate, GRE General Test. Additional exam requirements/recommendations for international students: Required—TOEFL. *Application deadline:* For fall admission, 2/1 priority date for domestic students; for spring admission, 10/1 priority date for domestic students. Applications are processed on a rolling basis. Application fee: $50 ($75 for international students). *Expenses:* Tuition, state resident: full-time $5437; part-time $226.55 per credit hour. Tuition, nonresident: full-time $12,949; part-time $539.55 per credit hour. *Required fees:* $2741. *Financial support:* In 2011–12, fellowships (averaging $15,000 per year), research assistantships (averaging $12,950 per year), teaching assistantships (averaging $11,500 per year) were awarded; career-related internships or fieldwork, Federal Work-Study, institutionally sponsored loans, and scholarships/grants also available. Financial award application deadline: 2/1; financial award applicants required to submit FAFSA. *Faculty research:* Genetic engineering/gene markers, dietary effects on colon cancer, biotechnology. *Unit head:* Dr. H. Russell Cross, Interim Head, 979-845-1543, Fax: 979-845-6433, E-mail: hrcross@tamu.edu. *Application contact:* Graduate Admissions, 979-845-1044, E-mail: admissions@tamu.edu. Web site: http://animalscience.tamu.edu/.

Texas A&M University, College of Agriculture and Life Sciences, Department of Poultry Science, College Station, TX 77843. Offers M Agr, MS, PhD. Part-time

and evening/weekend programs available. Postbaccalaureate distance learning degree programs offered (no on-campus study). *Faculty:* 14. *Students:* 33 full-time (18 women), 9 part-time (5 women); includes 8 minority (2 Black or African American, non-Hispanic/Latino; 1 Asian, non-Hispanic/Latino; 4 Hispanic/Latino; 1 Two or more races, non-Hispanic/Latino), 17 international. Average age 29. In 2011, 8 degrees awarded. Terminal master's awarded for partial completion of doctoral program. *Degree requirements:* For master's, thesis (for some programs); for doctorate, thesis/dissertation. *Entrance requirements:* For master's and doctorate, GRE General Test. Additional exam requirements/recommendations for international students: Required—TOEFL. Application fee: $50 ($75 for international students). Electronic applications accepted. *Expenses:* Tuition, state resident: full-time $5437; part-time $226.55 per credit hour. Tuition, nonresident: full-time $12,949; part-time $539.55 per credit hour. *Required fees:* $2741. *Financial support:* In 2011–12, fellowships with partial tuition reimbursements (averaging $18,000 per year) were awarded; research assistantships with partial tuition reimbursements, teaching assistantships, scholarships/grants, and unspecified assistantships also available. Financial award application deadline: 4/1; financial award applicants required to submit FAFSA. *Faculty research:* Poultry diseases and immunology, avian genetics and physiology, nutrition and metabolism, poultry processing and food safety, waste management. *Unit head:* Dr. John B. Carey, Head, 979-845-1931, E-mail: jcarey@poultry.tamu.edu. *Application contact:* Jennifer Allen, Academic Advisor II, 979-845-1654, E-mail: jallen@poultry.tamu.edu. Web site: http://gallus.tamu.edu/.

Texas A&M University–Kingsville, College of Graduate Studies, College of Agriculture and Home Economics, Program in Animal Sciences, Kingsville, TX 78363. Offers MS. *Degree requirements:* For master's, comprehensive exam, thesis or alternative. *Entrance requirements:* For master's, GRE General Test, minimum GPA of 3.0. Additional exam requirements/recommendations for international students: Required—TOEFL.

Texas Tech University, Graduate School, College of Agricultural Sciences and Natural Resources, Department of Animal and Food Sciences, Lubbock, TX 79409-2141. Offers animal science (MS, PhD); food science (MS). *Faculty:* 16 full-time (5 women). *Students:* 66 full-time (30 women), 10 part-time (2 women); includes 4 minority (1 Asian, non-Hispanic/Latino; 2 Hispanic/Latino; 1 Two or more races, non-Hispanic/Latino), 15 international. Average age 27. 80 applicants, 44% accepted, 27 enrolled. In 2011, 12 master's, 6 doctorates awarded. *Degree requirements:* For master's, thesis or alternative, internship (M Agr); for doctorate, thesis/dissertation. *Entrance requirements:* For master's and doctorate, GRE General Test, formal approval from departmental committee. Additional exam requirements/recommendations for international students: Required—TOEFL (minimum score 550 paper-based; 213 computer-based; 79 iBT). *Application deadline:* For fall admission, 6/1 priority date for domestic students, 1/15 for international students; for spring admission, 9/1 priority date for domestic students, 6/15 for international students. Applications are processed on a rolling basis. Application fee: $50 ($75 for international students). Electronic applications accepted. *Expenses:* Tuition, state resident: full-time $5899; part-time $245.80 per credit hour. Tuition, nonresident: full-time $13,411; part-time $558.80 per credit hour. *Required fees:* $2680.60; $86.50 per credit hour. $920.30 per semester. *Financial support:* In 2011–12, 40 students received support. Application deadline: 4/15; applicants required to submit FAFSA. *Faculty research:* Animal nutrition, health and welfare (species of emphasis: beef cattle, dairy cattle, swine, horse, sheep and goat); animal physiology and reproduction; meat science and muscle biology; food safety, security and public health, food science. *Total annual research expenditures:* $2.9 million. *Unit head:* Dr. Leslie D. Thompson, Chairman, 806-742-2805 Ext. 223, Fax: 806-742-0898, E-mail: leslie.thompson@ttu.edu. *Application contact:* Sandy Gellner, Graduate Secretary, 806-742-2805 Ext. 221, Fax: 806-742-0898, E-mail: sandra.gellner@ttu.edu. Web site: http://www.afs.ttu.edu/.

Tufts University, Cummings School of Veterinary Medicine, Program in Conservation Medicine, Medford, MA 02155. Offers MS. *Faculty:* 39 part-time/adjunct (21 women). *Students:* 9 full-time (8 women); includes 1 minority (Black or African American, non-Hispanic/Latino), 2 international. 15 applicants, 60% accepted, 9 enrolled. *Degree requirements:* For master's, case study, preceptorship. *Entrance requirements:* For master's, GRE, official transcripts, curriculum vitae. Additional exam requirements/recommendations for international students: Required—TOEFL or IELTS. *Application deadline:* For fall admission, 4/1 for domestic and international students. Application fee: $70. Electronic applications accepted. *Expenses: Tuition:* Full-time $41,208; part-time $1030 per credit hour. Full-time tuition and fees vary according to degree level, program and student level. Part-time tuition and fees vary according to course load. *Financial support:* Federal Work-Study available. Financial award application deadline: 5/15; financial award applicants required to submit FAFSA. *Faculty research:* Non-invasive saliva collection techniques for free-ranging mountain gorillas and captive eastern gorillas, animal sentinels for infectious diseases. *Unit head:* Dr. Gretchen Kaufman, Director, 508-839-7918, E-mail: gretchen.kaufman@tufts.edu. *Application contact:* Rebecca Russo, Director of Admissions, 508-839-7920, Fax: 508-887-4820, E-mail: vetadmissions@tufts.edu. Web site: http://www.tufts.edu/vet/mcm/.

Tuskegee University, Graduate Programs, College of Agricultural, Environmental and Natural Sciences, Department of Agricultural Sciences, Program in Animal and Poultry Sciences, Tuskegee, AL 36088. Offers MS. *Faculty:* 13 full-time (1 woman), 2 part-time/adjunct (1 woman). *Students:* 9 full-

Peterson's Graduate Programs in the Physical Sciences, Mathematics, Agricultural Sciences, the Environment & Natural Resources 2013

facebook.com/petersonspublishing **419**

Animal Sciences

time (7 women), 1 (woman) part-time; all minorities (9 Black or African American, non-Hispanic/Latino; 1 Hispanic/Latino). Average age 25. In 2011, 4 master's awarded. *Degree requirements:* For master's, thesis. *Entrance requirements:* For master's, GRE General Test. Additional exam requirements/recommendations for international students: Required—TOEFL (minimum score 500 paper-based; 69 computer-based). *Application deadline:* For fall admission, 7/15 for domestic students. Applications are processed on a rolling basis. Application fee: $25 ($35 for international students). *Expenses: Tuition:* Full-time $17,070; part-time $705 per credit hour. *Financial support:* Application deadline: 4/15. *Unit head:* Dr. P. K. Biswas, Head, 334-727-8446. *Application contact:* Dr. Robert L. Laney, Jr., Vice President/Director of Admissions and Enrollment Management, 334-727-8580, Fax: 334-727-5750, E-mail: planey@tuskegee.edu.

Universidad Nacional Pedro Henriquez Urena, Graduate School, Santo Domingo, Dominican Republic. Offers agricultural diversity (MS), including horticultural/fruit production, tropical animal production; conservation of monuments and cultural assets (M Arch); ecology and environment (MS); environmental engineering (MEE); international relations (MA); natural resource management (MS); political science (MA); project optimization (MPM); project feasibility (MPM); project management (MPM); sanitation engineering (ME); science for teachers (MS); tropical Caribbean architecture (M Arch).

Université Laval, Faculty of Agricultural and Food Sciences, Department of Animal Sciences, Programs in Animal Sciences, Québec, QC G1K 7P4, Canada. Offers M Sc, PhD. Part-time programs available. Terminal master's awarded for partial completion of doctoral program. *Degree requirements:* For master's, thesis; for doctorate, comprehensive exam, thesis/dissertation. *Entrance requirements:* For master's and doctorate, knowledge of French and English. Electronic applications accepted.

The University of Arizona, College of Agriculture and Life Sciences, Department of Animal Sciences, Tucson, AZ 85721. Offers MS, PhD. Part-time programs available. *Faculty:* 6 full-time (0 women), 1 part-time/adjunct (0 women). *Students:* 16 full-time (7 women), 1 (woman) part-time; includes 3 minority (1 Hispanic/Latino; 2 Two or more races, non-Hispanic/Latino). Average age 32. 26 applicants, 65% accepted, 12 enrolled. In 2011, 12 master's, 2 doctorates awarded. *Degree requirements:* For master's, thesis; for doctorate, thesis/dissertation. *Entrance requirements:* For master's, GRE Subject Test, 3 letters of recommendation, minimum GPA of 3.0; for doctorate, GRE Subject Test (biology or chemistry recommended), 3 letters of recommendation, statement of purpose, minimum GPA of 3.0. Additional exam requirements/recommendations for international students: Required—TOEFL (minimum score 550 paper-based; 213 computer-based; 80 iBT). *Application deadline:* Applications are processed on a rolling basis. Application fee: $75. *Expenses:* Tuition, state resident: full-time $10,840. Tuition, nonresident: full-time $25,802. *Financial support:* In 2011–12, 10 students received support, including 9 research assistantships with partial tuition reimbursements available (averaging $19,830 per year), 2 teaching assistantships with partial tuition reimbursements available (averaging $13,315 per year); fellowships, scholarships/grants, health care benefits, and unspecified assistantships also available. Financial award application deadline: 4/1. *Faculty research:* Nutrition of beef and dairy cattle, reproduction and breeding, muscle growth and function, animal stress, meat science. *Total annual research expenditures:* $693,286. *Unit head:* Dr. Ronald E. Allen, Professor and Head, 520-621-7626, Fax: 520-621-9435, E-mail: rallen@ag.arizona.edu. *Application contact:* Dr. Lance Baumgard, Graduate Committee Chair, 520-621-1487, Fax: 520-621-9435, E-mail: baumgard@ag.arizona.edu. Web site: http://animal.cals.arizona.edu/.

University of Arkansas, Graduate School, Dale Bumpers College of Agricultural, Food and Life Sciences, Department of Animal Science, Fayetteville, AR 72701-1201. Offers MS, PhD. *Students:* 9 full-time (6 women), 16 part-time (8 women), 3 international. In 2011, 5 master's, 3 doctorates awarded. *Degree requirements:* For master's, thesis; for doctorate, variable foreign language requirement, thesis/dissertation. *Entrance requirements:* For master's, GRE General Test or minimum GPA of 2.7. *Application deadline:* For fall admission, 4/1 for international students; for spring admission, 10/1 for international students. Applications are processed on a rolling basis. Application fee: $40 ($50 for international students). Electronic applications accepted. *Financial support:* In 2011–12, 11 research assistantships, 2 teaching assistantships were awarded; fellowships with tuition reimbursements, career-related internships or fieldwork, and Federal Work-Study also available. Support available to part-time students. Financial award application deadline: 4/1; financial award applicants required to submit FAFSA. *Unit head:* Dr. Michael Looper, Chair, 479-575-4351, E-mail: looper@uark.edu. *Application contact:* Dr. David Kreider, Graduate Coordinator, 479-575-6323, E-mail: dkreider@uark.edu. Web site: http://animalscience.uark.edu.

University of Arkansas, Graduate School, Dale Bumpers College of Agricultural, Food and Life Sciences, Department of Poultry Science, Fayetteville, AR 72701-1201. Offers MS, PhD. *Students:* 9 full-time (4 women), 29 part-time (14 women); includes 3 minority (all Hispanic/Latino), 15 international. In 2011, 5 master's, 8 doctorates awarded. *Degree requirements:* For master's, thesis; for doctorate, variable foreign language requirement, thesis/dissertation. *Application deadline:* For fall admission, 4/1 for international students; for spring admission, 10/1 for international students. Applications are processed on a rolling basis. Application fee: $40 ($50 for international students). Electronic applications accepted. *Financial support:* In 2011–12, 25 research assistantships were awarded; fellowships with tuition reimbursements, teaching assistantships, career-related internships or fieldwork, and Federal Work-Study also available. Support available

to part-time students. Financial award application deadline: 4/1; financial award applicants required to submit FAFSA. *Unit head:* Dr. Mike Kidd, Department Head, 479-575-4952, E-mail: mkidd@uark.edu. *Application contact:* Dr. Mike Slavik, Graduate Coordinator, 479-575-4952, E-mail: mslavik@uark.edu. Web site: http://www.poultryscience.uark.edu/.

The University of British Columbia, Faculty of Land and Food Systems, Animal Science Graduate Program, Vancouver, BC V6T 1Z1, Canada. Offers M Sc, PhD. *Degree requirements:* For master's, thesis; for doctorate, comprehensive exam, thesis/dissertation. *Entrance requirements:* Additional exam requirements/recommendations for international students: Required—TOEFL (minimum score 577 paper-based; 233 computer-based; 90 iBT), IELTS (minimum score 6.5). Electronic applications accepted. *Faculty research:* Animal production, animal behavior and welfare, reproductive physiology, animal genetics, aquaculture and fish physiology.

University of California, Davis, Graduate Studies, Graduate Group in Animal Biology, Davis, CA 95616. Offers MAM, MS, PhD. Terminal master's awarded for partial completion of doctoral program. *Degree requirements:* For master's, comprehensive exam (for some programs), thesis (for some programs); for doctorate, thesis/dissertation. *Entrance requirements:* For master's, GRE General Test, minimum GPA of 3.0. Additional exam requirements/recommendations for international students: Required—TOEFL (minimum score 550 paper-based; 213 computer-based). Electronic applications accepted. *Faculty research:* Genetics, nutrition, physiology and behavior in domestic and aquatic animals.

University of Connecticut, Graduate School, College of Agriculture and Natural Resources, Department of Animal Science, Storrs, CT 06269. Offers MS, PhD. Terminal master's awarded for partial completion of doctoral program. *Degree requirements:* For master's, comprehensive exam, thesis; for doctorate, comprehensive exam, thesis/dissertation. *Entrance requirements:* For master's and doctorate, GRE General Test, GRE Subject Test. Additional exam requirements/recommendations for international students: Required—TOEFL (minimum score 550 paper-based; 213 computer-based). Electronic applications accepted.

University of Delaware, College of Agriculture and Natural Resources, Department of Animal and Food Sciences, Newark, DE 19716. Offers animal sciences (MS, PhD); food sciences (MS). Part-time programs available. Terminal master's awarded for partial completion of doctoral program. *Degree requirements:* For master's, thesis; for doctorate, comprehensive exam, thesis/dissertation. *Entrance requirements:* For master's and doctorate, GRE General Test. Additional exam requirements/recommendations for international students: Required—TOEFL. Electronic applications accepted. *Faculty research:* Food chemistry, food microbiology, process engineering technology, packaging, food analysis, microbial genetics, molecular endocrinology, growth physiology, avian immunology and virology, monogastric nutrition, avian genomics.

University of Florida, Graduate School, College of Agricultural and Life Sciences, Department of Animal Sciences, Gainesville, FL 32611. Offers MS, PhD. Part-time programs available. *Faculty:* 24 full-time (5 women). *Students:* 34 full-time (18 women), 4 part-time (all women); includes 5 minority (1 Black or African American, non-Hispanic/Latino; 1 American Indian or Alaska Native, non-Hispanic/Latino; 1 Asian, non-Hispanic/Latino; 2 Hispanic/Latino), 12 international. Average age 28. 49 applicants, 35% accepted, 13 enrolled. In 2011, 13 master's, 2 doctorates awarded. *Degree requirements:* For master's, variable foreign language requirement, comprehensive exam (for some programs), thesis optional, one departmental and one exit seminar; for doctorate, comprehensive exam, thesis/dissertation, two departmental seminars, one exit seminar. *Entrance requirements:* For master's and doctorate, GRE General Test, minimum GPA of 3.0. Additional exam requirements/recommendations for international students: Required—TOEFL (minimum score 550 paper-based; 213 computer-based; 80 iBT), IELTS (minimum score 6). *Application deadline:* For fall admission, 3/1 priority date for domestic students, 2/1 for international students; for winter admission, 9/1 for domestic students, 8/1 for international students; for spring admission, 1/1 for domestic students, 12/1 for international students. Applications are processed on a rolling basis. Application fee: $30. Electronic applications accepted. *Financial support:* Fellowships, research assistantships, and teaching assistantships available. Financial award applicants required to submit FAFSA. *Faculty research:* Ruminal metabolism and fermentation, enteric greenhouse gas emissions, beef cattle nutrition; embryonic development, fertility, uterine biology, dairy cattle, heat stress; genetic and genomic evaluation of animals in multibreed populations; prostaglandin and immune response to lipopolysaccharides in dairy cattle, dietary fatty acids and their effects on reproduction, immunity and energy metabolism; metabolic influences of nutrients on reproduction. *Unit head:* Dr. Geoffrey Dahl, Chair, 352-392-1981 Ext. 221, Fax: 352-392-5595, E-mail: gdahl@ufl.edu. *Application contact:* Dr. Joel H. Brendemuhl, Graduate Coordinator, 352-392-8073, Fax: 352-392-1913, E-mail: brendj@ufl.edu. Web site: http://animal.ufl.edu/.

University of Florida, Interdisciplinary Concentration in Animal Molecular and Cellular Biology, Gainesville, FL 32611. Offers MS, PhD. Program offered jointly by College of Agricultural and Life Sciences, College of Liberal Arts and Sciences, College of Medicine, and College of Veterinary Medicine. *Students:* 12 full-time (7 women); includes 1 minority (Hispanic/Latino), 7 international. Average age 30. 7 applicants, 0% accepted, 0 enrolled. In 2011, 1 master's, 1 doctorate awarded. *Entrance requirements:* For master's and doctorate, GRE General Test (minimum score 1000), minimum GPA of 3.0. Additional exam requirements/

420 facebook.com/petersonspublishing

Peterson's Graduate Programs in the Physical Sciences, Mathematics, Agricultural Sciences, the Environment & Natural Resources 2013

recommendations for international students: Required—TOEFL (minimum score 550 paper-based; 213 computer-based; 80 iBT), IELTS (minimum score 6). Application fee: $30. Electronic applications accepted. *Financial support:* Fellowships and research assistantships available. Financial award applicants required to submit FAFSA. *Unit head:* Dr. Alan D. Ealy, Director, 352-392-5590, Fax: 352-392-5595, E-mail: ealy@ufl.edu. *Application contact:* Dr. Joel H. Brendemuhl, Assistant Chair, 352-392-8073, Fax: 352-392-5595, E-mail: brendj@ufl.edu. Web site: http://www.animal.ufl.edu/amcb/.

University of Georgia, College of Agricultural and Environmental Sciences, Department of Animal and Dairy Sciences, Athens, GA 30602. Offers animal and dairy science (PhD); animal and dairy sciences (MADS); animal science (MS); dairy science (MS). *Faculty:* 20 full-time (3 women), 1 part-time/adjunct (0 women). *Students:* 19 full-time (16 women), 4 part-time (2 women); includes 1 minority (Black or African American, non-Hispanic/Latino), 5 international. Average age 27. 27 applicants, 37% accepted, 3 enrolled. In 2011, 13 master's, 2 doctorates awarded. *Degree requirements:* For master's, thesis; for doctorate, one foreign language, thesis/dissertation. *Entrance requirements:* For master's and doctorate, GRE General Test. *Application deadline:* For fall admission, 7/1 priority date for domestic students; for spring admission, 11/15 for domestic students. Application fee: $50. Electronic applications accepted. *Financial support:* Fellowships, research assistantships, teaching assistantships, and unspecified assistantships available. *Unit head:* Dr. J. Keith Bertrand, Interim Head, 706-542-6259, Fax: 706-542-2465, E-mail: adshead@uga.edu. *Application contact:* Dr. Michael J. Azain, Graduate Coordinator, 706-542-0963, Fax: 706-583-0274, E-mail: mazain@uga.edu. Web site: http://www.ads.uga.edu.

University of Georgia, College of Agricultural and Environmental Sciences, Department of Poultry Science, Athens, GA 30602. Offers animal nutrition (PhD); poultry science (MS, PhD). *Faculty:* 13 full-time (2 women), 3 part-time/adjunct (1 woman). *Students:* 16 full-time (7 women), 5 part-time (2 women); includes 2 minority (1 Black or African American, non-Hispanic/Latino; 1 Hispanic/Latino), 5 international. Average age 28. 14 applicants, 36% accepted, 3 enrolled. In 2011, 4 master's, 4 doctorates awarded. *Degree requirements:* For master's, thesis; for doctorate, one foreign language, thesis/dissertation. *Entrance requirements:* For master's and doctorate, GRE General Test. *Application deadline:* For fall admission, 7/1 priority date for domestic students; for spring admission, 11/15 for domestic students. Application fee: $50. Electronic applications accepted. *Financial support:* Fellowships, research assistantships, teaching assistantships, and unspecified assistantships available. *Unit head:* Dr. Michael Lacy, Head, 706-542-1351, E-mail: mlacy@uga.edu. *Application contact:* Dr. Larry R. McDougald, Graduate Coordinator, 706-542-1337, Fax: 706-542-1827, E-mail: lrmcd@uga.edu. Web site: http://www.poultry.uga.edu/.

University of Guelph, Graduate Studies, Ontario Agricultural College, Department of Animal and Poultry Science, Guelph, ON N1G 2W1, Canada. Offers M Sc, PhD. Part-time programs available. *Degree requirements:* For master's, thesis (for some programs); for doctorate, comprehensive exam, thesis/dissertation. *Entrance requirements:* For master's, minimum Baverage during previous 2 years of course work; for doctorate, minimum Baverage. Additional exam requirements/recommendations for international students: Required—TOEFL (minimum score 550 paper-based; 213 computer-based; 89 iBT), IELTS (minimum score 6.5). *Faculty research:* Animal breeding and genetics (quantitative or molecular), animal nutrition (monogastric or ruminant), animal physiology (environmental, reproductive or behavioral), behavior and welfare.

University of Hawaii at Manoa, Graduate Division, College of Tropical Agriculture and Human Resources, Department of Human Nutrition, Food and Animal Sciences, Program in Animal Sciences, Honolulu, HI 96822. Offers MS. Part-time programs available. *Entrance requirements:* For master's, GRE General Test. Additional exam requirements/recommendations for international students: Required—TOEFL (minimum score 580 paper-based; 100 iBT), IELTS (minimum score 5). *Faculty research:* Nutritional biochemistry, food composition, nutrition education, nutritional epidemiology, international nutrition, food toxicology.

University of Idaho, College of Graduate Studies, College of Agricultural and Life Sciences, Department of Animal and Veterinary Science, Moscow, ID 83843-2330. Offers animal physiology (PhD); animal science (MS), including production. *Faculty:* 1 full-time, 1 part-time/adjunct. *Students:* 13 full-time, 17 part-time. Average age 30. In 2011, 8 master's, 1 doctorate awarded. *Degree requirements:* For doctorate, thesis/dissertation. *Entrance requirements:* For master's, GRE General Test, minimum GPA of 2.8; for doctorate, minimum undergraduate GPA of 2.8, graduate 3.0. *Application deadline:* For fall admission, 8/1 for domestic students; for spring admission, 12/15 for domestic students. Applications are processed on a rolling basis. Application fee: $60. Electronic applications accepted. *Expenses:* Tuition, state resident: full-time $3874; part-time $334 per credit hour. Tuition, nonresident: full-time $16,394; part-time $861 per credit hour. *Required fees:* $2808; $99 per credit hour. Tuition and fees vary according to program. *Financial support:* Research assistantships and teaching assistantships available. Financial award applicants required to submit FAFSA. *Faculty research:* Reproductive biology, muscle and growth physiology, meat science, aquaculture, ruminant nutrition. *Unit head:* Dr. Carl W. Hunt, Head, 208-885-6345, E-mail: avs-students@uidaho.edu. *Application contact:* Erick Larson, Director of Graduate Admissions, 208-885-4723, E-mail: gadms@uidaho.edu. Web site: http://www.uidaho.edu/cals/avs.

University of Illinois at Urbana–Champaign, Graduate College, College of Agricultural, Consumer and Environmental Sciences, Department of Animal Sciences, Champaign, IL 61820. Offers animal sciences (MS, PhD); bioinformatics: animal sciences (MS). *Faculty:* 34 full-time (5 women), 2 part-time/adjunct (0 women). *Students:* 92 full-time (40 women), 7 part-time (4 women); includes 5 minority (1 Black or African American, non-Hispanic/Latino; 1 Asian, non-Hispanic/Latino; 2 Hispanic/Latino; 1 Two or more races, non-Hispanic/Latino), 39 international. 69 applicants, 20% accepted, 12 enrolled. In 2011, 12 master's, 15 doctorates awarded. *Entrance requirements:* For master's and doctorate, GRE General Test, GRE Subject Test (biology), minimum GPA of 3.0. Additional exam requirements/recommendations for international students: Required—TOEFL (minimum score 590 paper-based; 243 computer-based), TWE. *Application deadline:* Applications are processed on a rolling basis. Application fee: $75 ($90 for international students). Electronic applications accepted. *Financial support:* In 2011–12, 13 fellowships, 78 research assistantships, 17 teaching assistantships were awarded; tuition waivers (full and partial) also available. *Unit head:* Neal R. Merchen, Head, 217-333-3462, Fax: 217-244-2871, E-mail: nmerchen@illinois.edu. *Application contact:* Lori Kelso, Resource and Policy Analyst, 217-244-0418, Fax: 217-333-5044, E-mail: lkelso@illinois.edu. Web site: http://www.ansci.illinois.edu/.

University of Kentucky, Graduate School, College of Agriculture, Program in Animal Sciences, Lexington, KY 40506-0032. Offers MS, PhD. Terminal master's awarded for partial completion of doctoral program. *Degree requirements:* For master's, comprehensive exam, thesis optional; for doctorate, comprehensive exam, thesis/dissertation. *Entrance requirements:* For master's, GRE General Test, minimum undergraduate GPA of 2.75; for doctorate, GRE General Test, minimum graduate GPA of 3.0. Additional exam requirements/recommendations for international students: Required—TOEFL (minimum score 550 paper-based; 213 computer-based). Electronic applications accepted. *Faculty research:* Nutrition of horses, cattle, swine, poultry, and sheep; physiology of reproduction and lactation; food science; microbiology.

University of Maine, Graduate School, College of Natural Sciences, Forestry, and Agriculture, Department of Animal and Veterinary Sciences, Orono, ME 04469. Offers animal sciences (MPS, MS). Part-time programs available. *Faculty:* 7 full-time (0 women), 2 part-time/adjunct (1 woman). *Students:* 4 full-time (1 woman), 2 part-time (both women), 1 international. Average age 35. 10 applicants, 10% accepted, 1 enrolled. In 2011, 2 degrees awarded. *Entrance requirements:* For master's, GRE General Test. Additional exam requirements/recommendations for international students: Required—TOEFL. *Application deadline:* For fall admission, 2/1 priority date for domestic students. Applications are processed on a rolling basis. Application fee: $65. Electronic applications accepted. *Expenses:* Tuition, state resident: full-time $5016. Tuition, nonresident: full-time $14,424. *Financial support:* In 2011–12, 4 research assistantships with full tuition reimbursements (averaging $16,794 per year), 1 teaching assistantship with full tuition reimbursement (averaging $13,600 per year) were awarded; Federal Work-Study, institutionally sponsored loans, and tuition waivers (full and partial) also available. Financial award application deadline: 3/1. *Faculty research:* Animal nutrition, parasitology, veterinary pathology, reproductive physiology, marine life nutrition and management. *Unit head:* Dr. James Weber, Chair, 207-581-2774, Fax: 207-581-2770. *Application contact:* Scott G. Delcourt, Associate Dean of the Graduate School, 207-581-3291, Fax: 207-581-3232, E-mail: graduate@maine.edu. Web site: http://www2.umaine.edu/graduate/.

University of Manitoba, Faculty of Graduate Studies, Faculty of Agricultural and Food Sciences, Department of Animal Science, Winnipeg, MB R3T 2N2, Canada. Offers M Sc, PhD. *Degree requirements:* For master's, thesis; for doctorate, one foreign language, thesis/dissertation.

University of Maryland, College Park, Academic Affairs, College of Agriculture and Natural Resources, Department of Animal and Avian Sciences, Program in Animal Sciences, College Park, MD 20742. Offers MS, PhD. *Students:* 33 full-time (19 women), 2 part-time (both women); includes 3 minority (2 Asian, non-Hispanic/Latino; 1 Hispanic/Latino), 15 international. 41 applicants, 22% accepted, 8 enrolled. In 2011, 5 master's, 5 doctorates awarded. *Degree requirements:* For master's, thesis, oral exam or written comprehensive exam; for doctorate, thesis/dissertation, journal publication, scientific paper. *Entrance requirements:* For master's, GRE General Test, minimum GPA of 3.0; for doctorate, GRE General Test. Additional exam requirements/recommendations for international students: Required—TOEFL. *Application deadline:* For fall admission, 5/15 for domestic students, 2/1 for international students; for spring admission, 10/1 for domestic students, 6/1 for international students. Applications are processed on a rolling basis. Application fee: $75. Electronic applications accepted. *Expenses:* Tuition, area resident: Part-time $525 per credit hour. Tuition, state resident: part-time $525 per credit hour. Tuition, nonresident: part-time $1131 per credit hour. *Required fees:* $386.31 per term. Tuition and fees vary according to program. *Financial support:* In 2011–12, 1 fellowship (averaging $10,800 per year), 31 teaching assistantships (averaging $16,473 per year) were awarded; research assistantships also available. Financial award applicants required to submit FAFSA. *Faculty research:* Animal physiology, cell biology and biochemistry, reproduction, biometrics, animal behavior. *Unit head:* Dr. Tom Porter, Chairman, 301-405-1366, Fax: 301-314-9059, E-mail: teporter@umd.edu. *Application contact:* Dr. Charles A. Caramello, Dean of Graduate School, 301-405-0358, Fax: 301-314-9305, E-mail: ccaramel@umd.edu.

University of Massachusetts Amherst, Graduate School, College of Natural Sciences, Department of Animal Biotechnology and Biomedical Sciences, Amherst, MA 01003. Offers MS, PhD. Part-time programs available. *Faculty:* 23

Peterson's Graduate Programs in the Physical Sciences, Mathematics, Agricultural Sciences, the Environment & Natural Resources 2013

facebook.com/petersonspublishing **421**

Animal Sciences

full-time (10 women). *Students:* 27 full-time (16 women), 9 international. Average age 30. 51 applicants, 18% accepted, 6 enrolled. In 2011, 6 master's, 2 doctorates awarded. Terminal master's awarded for partial completion of doctoral program. *Degree requirements:* For master's, thesis or alternative; for doctorate, comprehensive exam, thesis/dissertation. *Entrance requirements:* For master's and doctorate, GRE General Test. Additional exam requirements/recommendations for international students: Required—TOEFL (minimum score 550 paper-based; 213 computer-based; 80 iBT), IELTS (minimum score 6.5). *Application deadline:* For fall admission, 2/1 for domestic and international students; for spring admission, 10/1 for domestic and international students. Applications are processed on a rolling basis. Application fee: $50 ($65 for international students). Electronic applications accepted. Tuition and fees vary according to course load, campus/location and program. *Financial support:* Fellowships with full and partial tuition reimbursements, research assistantships with full and partial tuition reimbursements, teaching assistantships with full and partial tuition reimbursements, career-related internships or fieldwork, Federal Work-Study, scholarships/grants, traineeships, health care benefits, tuition waivers (full and partial), and unspecified assistantships available. Support available to part-time students. Financial award application deadline: 2/1. *Unit head:* Dr. Lisa Minter, Graduate Program Director, 413-577-1193, Fax: 413-577-1150. *Application contact:* Lindsay DeSantis, Interim Supervisor of Admissions, 413-545-0722, Fax: 413-577-0010, E-mail: gradadm@grad.umass.edu. Web site: http://www.vasci.umass.edu/graduate-program-overview.

University of Minnesota, Twin Cities Campus, Graduate School, College of Food, Agricultural and Natural Resource Sciences, Program in Animal Science, Minneapolis, MN 55455-0213. Offers MS, PhD. Part-time programs available. *Faculty:* 39 full-time (9 women). *Students:* 29 full-time (18 women), 2 part-time (1 woman); includes 1 minority (Hispanic/Latino), 9 international. Average age 30. 29 applicants, 48% accepted, 10 enrolled. In 2011, 3 degrees awarded. Terminal master's awarded for partial completion of doctoral program. *Degree requirements:* For master's, comprehensive exam, thesis; for doctorate, comprehensive exam, thesis/dissertation. *Entrance requirements:* For master's and doctorate, GRE. Additional exam requirements/recommendations for international students: Required—TOEFL (minimum score 550 paper-based; 213 computer-based; 79 iBT), IELTS (minimum score 6.5), TOEFL preferred. *Application deadline:* For fall admission, 12/15 priority date for domestic students, 12/15 for international students; for spring admission, 10/15 priority date for domestic students, 10/15 for international students. Applications are processed on a rolling basis. Application fee: $75 ($95 for international students). Electronic applications accepted. *Financial support:* In 2011–12, fellowships with full tuition reimbursements (averaging $23,500 per year), research assistantships with full tuition reimbursements (averaging $20,800 per year), teaching assistantships with full tuition reimbursements (averaging $20,800 per year) were awarded; scholarships/grants and unspecified assistantships also available. Support available to part-time students. *Faculty research:* Physiology, growth biology, nutrition, genetics, production systems. *Total annual research expenditures:* $1.1 million. *Unit head:* Dr. William Dayton, Director of Graduate Studies, 612-624-2234, Fax: 612-625-5789, E-mail: wdayton@umn.edu. *Application contact:* Kim Reno, Assistant to the Director of Graduate Studies, 612-624-3491, E-mail: renox001@umn.edu. Web site: http://www.ansci.umn.edu/gradprogram/.

University of Missouri, Graduate School, College of Agriculture, Food and Natural Resources, Department of Animal Sciences, Columbia, MO 65211. Offers MS, PhD. *Faculty:* 28 full-time (3 women), 2 part-time/adjunct (0 women). *Students:* 50 full-time (27 women), 3 part-time (1 woman); includes 4 minority (1 Asian, non-Hispanic/Latino; 2 Hispanic/Latino; 1 Two or more races, non-Hispanic/Latino), 9 international. Average age 26. 43 applicants, 40% accepted, 16 enrolled. In 2011, 10 master's, 6 doctorates awarded. Terminal master's awarded for partial completion of doctoral program. *Degree requirements:* For doctorate, 2 foreign languages, comprehensive exam, thesis/dissertation. *Entrance requirements:* For master's, GRE General Test, minimum GPA of 3.0; for doctorate, GRE General Test (minimum score: Verbal 400, Quantitative 550), minimum GPA of 3.0. Additional exam requirements/recommendations for international students: Required—TOEFL (minimum score 500 paper-based; 173 computer-based; 61 iBT), IELTS (minimum score 5.5). *Application deadline:* Applications are processed on a rolling basis. Application fee: $55 ($75 for international students). Electronic applications accepted. *Expenses:* Tuition, state resident: full-time $5881. Tuition, nonresident: full-time $15,183. *Required fees:* $952. Tuition and fees vary according to campus/location and program. *Financial support:* Fellowships, research assistantships with tuition reimbursements, teaching assistantships with tuition reimbursements, institutionally sponsored loans, scholarships/grants, health care benefits, and unspecified assistantships available. Support available to part-time students. Financial award applicants required to submit FAFSA. *Faculty research:* Reproductive and environmental physiology; ruminant and monogastric nutrition; genetics/genomics; meat science and livestock production across swine, dairy cattle, beef cattle, poultry, companion animals and horses. *Unit head:* Dr. Rod Geisert, Department Chair, 573-884-0934, E-mail: geisertr@missouri.edu. *Application contact:* Cinda Hudlow, Administrative Assistant, 573-882-7446, E-mail: hudlowc@missouri.edu. Web site: http://animalsciences.missouri.edu/academics/graduates.php.

University of Nebraska–Lincoln, Graduate College, College of Agricultural Sciences and Natural Resources, Department of Animal Science, Lincoln, NE 68588. Offers MS, PhD. *Degree requirements:* For master's, thesis; for doctorate, comprehensive exam, thesis/dissertation. *Entrance requirements:* For master's and doctorate, GRE General Test. Additional exam requirements/

recommendations for international students: Required—TOEFL (minimum score 525 paper-based; 195 computer-based). Electronic applications accepted. *Faculty research:* Animal breeding and genetics, meat and poultry products, nonruminant and ruminant nutrition, physiology.

University of Nevada, Reno, Graduate School, College of Agriculture, Biotechnology and Natural Resources, Department of Animal Science, Reno, NV 89557. Offers MS. *Degree requirements:* For master's, thesis optional. *Entrance requirements:* For master's, GRE, minimum GPA of 2.75. Additional exam requirements/recommendations for international students: Required—TOEFL (minimum score 500 paper-based; 173 computer-based; 61 iBT), IELTS (minimum score 6). Electronic applications accepted. *Faculty research:* Sperm fertility, embryo development, ruminant utilization of forages.

University of New Hampshire, Graduate School, College of Life Sciences and Agriculture, Department of Biological Sciences, Program in Animal Science, Durham, NH 03824. Offers MS. Part-time programs available. *Faculty:* 23 full-time. *Students:* 1 (woman) full-time, 5 part-time (4 women). Average age 29. 14 applicants, 21% accepted, 3 enrolled. In 2011, 2 master's awarded. *Entrance requirements:* For master's, GRE General Test. Additional exam requirements/recommendations for international students: Required—TOEFL (minimum score 550 paper-based; 213 computer-based; 80 iBT). *Application deadline:* For fall admission, 6/1 priority date for domestic students, 4/1 for international students; for spring admission, 12/1 for domestic students. Applications are processed on a rolling basis. Application fee: $65. Electronic applications accepted. *Expenses:* Tuition, state resident: full-time $12,360; part-time $687 per credit hour. Tuition, nonresident: full-time $25,680; part-time $1058 per credit hour. *International tuition:* $29,550 full-time. *Required fees:* $1666; $833 per course. $416.50 per semester. Tuition and fees vary according to course load and degree level. *Financial support:* In 2011–12, 5 students received support, including 1 research assistantship, 4 teaching assistantships; fellowships, career-related internships or fieldwork, Federal Work-Study, scholarships/grants, and tuition waivers (full and partial) also available. Support available to part-time students. Financial award application deadline: 2/15. *Unit head:* Dr. Larry Harris, Chair, 603-862-3897. *Application contact:* Diane Lavalliere, Administrative Assistant, 603-862-2100. Web site: http://www.mcbs.unh.edu/.

University of New Hampshire, Graduate School, College of Life Sciences and Agriculture, Department of Molecular, Cellular and Biomedical Sciences, Program in Animal and Nutritional Sciences, Durham, NH 03824. Offers PhD. Part-time programs available. *Faculty:* 23 full-time. *Students:* 3 full-time (2 women), 3 part-time (all women); includes 1 minority (Hispanic/Latino). Average age 39. 5 applicants, 40% accepted, 1 enrolled. *Entrance requirements:* For doctorate, GRE. Additional exam requirements/recommendations for international students: Required—TOEFL (minimum score 550 paper-based; 213 computer-based; 80 iBT). *Application deadline:* For fall admission, 6/1 priority date for domestic students, 4/1 for international students; for spring admission, 12/1 for domestic students. Application fee: $65. Electronic applications accepted. *Expenses:* Tuition, state resident: full-time $12,360; part-time $687 per credit hour. Tuition, nonresident: full-time $25,680; part-time $1058 per credit hour. *International tuition:* $29,550 full-time. *Required fees:* $1666; $833 per course. $416.50 per semester. Tuition and fees vary according to course load and degree level. *Financial support:* In 2011–12, 4 students received support, including 1 research assistantship, 3 teaching assistantships; fellowships, scholarships/grants, traineeships, and unspecified assistantships also available. Support available to part-time students. *Unit head:* Dr. Rick Cote, Chairperson, 603-862-2458. *Application contact:* Flora Joyal, Administrative Assistant, 603-862-4095, E-mail: ansc.grad.program.info@unh.edu. Web site: http://www.biolsci.unh.edu/.

University of Puerto Rico, Mayagüez Campus, Graduate Studies, College of Agricultural Sciences, Department of Animal Industries, Mayagüez, PR 00681-9000. Offers MS. Part-time programs available. *Students:* 18 full-time (10 women); includes 17 minority (all Hispanic/Latino), 1 international. 9 applicants, 67% accepted, 3 enrolled. In 2011, 4 master's awarded. *Degree requirements:* For master's, comprehensive exam, thesis. *Entrance requirements:* For master's, minimum GPA of 2.75, BS in agricultural science or closely-related field. *Application deadline:* For fall admission, 2/15 for domestic and international students; for spring admission, 9/15 for domestic and international students. Applications are processed on a rolling basis. Application fee: $25. Tuition and fees vary according to course level and course load. *Financial support:* In 2011–12, 12 students received support, including 6 research assistantships with tuition reimbursements available (averaging $15,000 per year), 6 teaching assistantships with tuition reimbursements available (averaging $8,500 per year); Federal Work-Study and institutionally sponsored loans also available. *Faculty research:* Swine production and nutrition, poultry production, dairy science and technology, microbiology. *Unit head:* Dr. Jose LaTorre, Director, 787-265-3854, Fax: 787-834-4548, E-mail: jose.latorre1@upr.edu. *Application contact:* Dr. Teodoro Ruiz, Coordinator, 787-832-4040 Ext. 2574, Fax: 787-834-4548, E-mail: truiz@uprm.edu. Web site: http://www.uprm.edu/agricultura/inpe/.

University of Rhode Island, Graduate School, College of the Environment and Life Sciences, Department of Fisheries, Animal and Veterinary Science, Kingston, RI 02881. Offers animal health and disease (MS); animal science (MS); aquaculture (MS); aquatic pathology (MS); environmental sciences (PhD), including animal science, aquacultural science, aquatic pathology, fisheries science; fisheries (MS). *Faculty:* 10 full-time (4 women). *Students:* 14 full-time (7 women), 6 part-time (1 woman). In 2011, 5 degrees awarded. *Degree requirements:* For master's, comprehensive exam (for some programs), thesis

422 facebook.com/petersonspublishing

Peterson's Graduate Programs in the Physical Sciences, Mathematics, Agricultural Sciences, the Environment & Natural Resources 2013

optional; for doctorate, comprehensive exam, thesis/dissertation. *Entrance requirements:* For master's and doctorate, GRE, 2 letters of recommendation. Additional exam requirements/recommendations for international students: Required—TOEFL (minimum score 550 paper-based; 213 computer-based). *Application deadline:* For fall admission, 7/15 for domestic students, 2/1 for international students; for spring admission, 11/15 for domestic students, 7/15 for international students. Application fee: $65. Electronic applications accepted. *Expenses:* Tuition, state resident: full-time $10,432; part-time $580 per credit hour. Tuition, nonresident: full-time $23,130; part-time $1285 per credit hour. *Required fees:* $1362; $36 per credit hour. $35 per semester. One-time fee: $130. *Financial support:* In 2011–12, 3 research assistantships with full and partial tuition reimbursements (averaging $11,654 per year), 4 teaching assistantships with full and partial tuition reimbursements (averaging $12,214 per year) were awarded. Financial award application deadline: 7/15; financial award applicants required to submit FAFSA. *Unit head:* Dr. David Bengtson, Chair, 401-874-2668, Fax: 401-874-7575, E-mail: bengtson@uri.edu. *Application contact:* Dr. Marta Gomez-Chiarri, Director of Graduate Studies, 401-874-2917, Fax: 401-874-7575, E-mail: gomezchi@uri.edu. Web site: http://www.uri.edu/cels/favs/.

University of Saskatchewan, College of Graduate Studies and Research, College of Agriculture, Department of Animal and Poultry Science, Saskatoon, SK S7N 5A2, Canada. Offers M Ag, M Sc, PhD. *Degree requirements:* For master's, thesis; for doctorate, thesis/dissertation. *Entrance requirements:* Additional exam requirements/recommendations for international students: Required—TOEFL.

University of Saskatchewan, Western College of Veterinary Medicine and College of Graduate Studies and Research, Graduate Programs in Veterinary Medicine, Department of Large Animal Clinical Sciences, Saskatoon, SK S7N 5A2, Canada. Offers M Sc, M Vet Sc, PhD. *Degree requirements:* For master's, thesis (for some programs); for doctorate, comprehensive exam (for some programs), thesis/dissertation. *Entrance requirements:* Additional exam requirements/recommendations for international students: Required—TOEFL (minimum score 80 iBT); Recommended—IELTS (minimum score 6.5). Electronic applications accepted. *Faculty research:* Reproduction, infectious diseases, epidemiology, food safety.

University of Saskatchewan, Western College of Veterinary Medicine and College of Graduate Studies and Research, Graduate Programs in Veterinary Medicine, Department of Small Animal Clinical Sciences, Saskatoon, SK S7N 5A2, Canada. Offers small animal clinical sciences (M Sc, PhD); veterinary anesthesiology, radiology and surgery (M Vet Sc); veterinary internal medicine (M Vet Sc). *Degree requirements:* For master's, thesis (for some programs); for doctorate, comprehensive exam (for some programs), thesis/dissertation. *Entrance requirements:* Additional exam requirements/recommendations for international students: Required—TOEFL (minimum score 80 iBT); Recommended—IELTS (minimum score 6.5). Electronic applications accepted. *Faculty research:* Orthopedics, wildlife, cardiovascular exercise/myelopathy, ophthalmology.

The University of Tennessee, Graduate School, College of Agricultural Sciences and Natural Resources, Department of Animal Science, Knoxville, TN 37996. Offers animal anatomy (PhD); breeding (MS, PhD); management (MS, PhD); nutrition (MS, PhD); physiology (MS, PhD). Part-time programs available. *Degree requirements:* For master's, thesis; for doctorate, thesis/dissertation. *Entrance requirements:* For master's and doctorate, GRE General Test, minimum GPA of 2.7. Additional exam requirements/recommendations for international students: Required—TOEFL. Electronic applications accepted. *Expenses:* Tuition, state resident: full-time $8332; part-time $464 per credit hour. Tuition, nonresident: full-time $25,174; part-time $1400 per credit hour. *Required fees:* $1162; $56 per credit hour. Tuition and fees vary according to program.

University of Vermont, Graduate College, College of Agriculture and Life Sciences, Department of Animal Sciences, Burlington, VT 05405. Offers MS, PhD. *Students:* 2 (1 woman). 14 applicants, 7% accepted, 0 enrolled. In 2011, 2 master's awarded. *Degree requirements:* For master's, thesis; for doctorate, one foreign language, thesis/dissertation. *Entrance requirements:* For master's and doctorate, GRE General Test. Additional exam requirements/recommendations for international students: Required—TOEFL (minimum score 550 paper-based; 213 computer-based; 80 iBT). *Application deadline:* For fall admission, 4/1 priority date for domestic students. Applications are processed on a rolling basis. Application fee: $40. Electronic applications accepted. *Financial support:* Fellowships, research assistantships, and teaching assistantships available. Financial award application deadline: 3/1. *Faculty research:* Animal nutrition, dairy production. *Unit head:* Dr. Andre-Denis Wright, Chairperson, 802-656-2070. *Application contact:* Dr. David Kerr, Coordinator, 802-656-2070.

University of Vermont, Graduate College, College of Agriculture and Life Sciences, Program in Animal, Nutrition and Food Sciences, Burlington, VT 05405. Offers PhD. *Students:* 18 (7 women); includes 2 minority (both Asian, non-Hispanic/Latino), 10 international. 10 applicants, 20% accepted, 1 enrolled. In 2011, 2 doctorates awarded. *Degree requirements:* For doctorate, one foreign language, thesis/dissertation. *Entrance requirements:* For doctorate, GRE General Test. Additional exam requirements/recommendations for international students: Required—TOEFL (minimum score 550 paper-based; 213 computer-based; 80 iBT). *Application deadline:* For fall admission, 4/1 priority date for domestic students, 4/1 for international students. Applications are processed on a rolling basis. Application fee: $40. Electronic applications accepted. *Financial support:* Application deadline: 3/1. *Unit head:* Dr. Andre-Denis Wright,

Chairperson, 802-656-2070. *Application contact:* Dr. David Kerr, Coordinator, 802-656-2070.

University of Wisconsin–Madison, Graduate School, College of Agricultural and Life Sciences, Department of Animal Sciences, Madison, WI 53706-1380. Offers MS, PhD. Part-time programs available. Terminal master's awarded for partial completion of doctoral program. *Degree requirements:* For master's, thesis; for doctorate, thesis/dissertation. *Entrance requirements:* For master's and doctorate, GRE General Test. Additional exam requirements/recommendations for international students: Required—TOEFL (minimum score 550 paper-based; 213 computer-based; 80 iBT). Electronic applications accepted. *Expenses:* Tuition, state resident: full-time $10,296; part-time $643.51 per credit. Tuition, nonresident: full-time $24,054; part-time $1503.40 per credit. *Required fees:* $70.06 per credit. Tuition and fees vary according to course load, campus/location, program and reciprocity agreements. *Faculty research:* Animal biology, immunity and toxicology, endocrinology and reproductive physiology, genetics-animal breeding, meat science, muscle biology.

University of Wisconsin–Madison, Graduate School, College of Agricultural and Life Sciences, Department of Dairy Science, Madison, WI 53706-1380. Offers MS, PhD. Part-time programs available. Terminal master's awarded for partial completion of doctoral program. *Degree requirements:* For master's, thesis; for doctorate, thesis/dissertation. *Entrance requirements:* For master's and doctorate, GRE General Test. Additional exam requirements/recommendations for international students: Required—TOEFL (minimum score 550 paper-based; 213 computer-based; 80 iBT). Electronic applications accepted. *Expenses:* Tuition, state resident: full-time $10,296; part-time $643.51 per credit. Tuition, nonresident: full-time $24,054; part-time $1503.40 per credit. *Required fees:* $70.06 per credit. Tuition and fees vary according to course load, campus/location, program and reciprocity agreements. *Faculty research:* Genetics, nutrition, lactation, reproduction, management of dairy cattle.

University of Wyoming, College of Agriculture and Natural Resources, Department of Animal Sciences, Program in Animal Sciences, Laramie, WY 82070. Offers MS, PhD. *Degree requirements:* For master's, comprehensive exam, thesis; for doctorate, comprehensive exam, thesis/dissertation. *Entrance requirements:* For master's, GRE General Test, minimum GPA of 3.0; for doctorate, GRE General Test or MS degree, minimum GPA of 3.0. Additional exam requirements/recommendations for international students: Required—TOEFL (minimum score 525 paper-based). *Faculty research:* Reproductive biology, ruminant nutrition meat science, muscle biology, food microbiology, lipid metabolism.

Utah State University, School of Graduate Studies, College of Agriculture, Department of Animal, Dairy and Veterinary Sciences, Logan, UT 84322. Offers animal science (MS, PhD); bioveterinary science (MS, PhD); dairy science (MS). Part-time programs available. *Degree requirements:* For master's, thesis (for some programs); for doctorate, comprehensive exam, thesis/dissertation. *Entrance requirements:* For master's and doctorate, GRE General Test, minimum GPA of 3.0. Additional exam requirements/recommendations for international students: Required—TOEFL. Electronic applications accepted. *Faculty research:* Monoclonal antibodies, antiviral chemotherapy, management systems, biotechnology, rumen fermentation manipulation.

Virginia Polytechnic Institute and State University, Graduate School, College of Agriculture and Life Sciences, Department of Animal and Poultry Sciences, Blacksburg, VA 24061. Offers MS, PhD. *Degree requirements:* For master's, comprehensive exam (for some programs), thesis (for some programs); for doctorate, comprehensive exam (for some programs), thesis/dissertation (for some programs). *Entrance requirements:* For master's and doctorate, GRE. Additional exam requirements/recommendations for international students: Required—TOEFL (minimum score 550 paper-based; 213 computer-based). *Application deadline:* For fall admission, 7/1 for domestic and international students; for spring admission, 12/1 for domestic and international students. Applications are processed on a rolling basis. Application fee: $65. Electronic applications accepted. *Expenses:* Tuition, state resident: full-time $10,048; part-time $558.25 per credit hour. Tuition, nonresident: full-time $19,497; part-time $1083.25 per credit hour. *Required fees:* $405 per semester. Tuition and fees vary according to course load, campus/location and program. *Financial support:* Fellowships with full tuition reimbursements, research assistantships with full tuition reimbursements, teaching assistantships with full tuition reimbursements, career-related internships or fieldwork, Federal Work-Study, scholarships/grants, health care benefits, and unspecified assistantships available. Financial award application deadline: 1/15. *Faculty research:* Quantitative genetics of cattle and sheep, swine nutrition and management, animal molecular biology, nutrition of grazing livestock. *Unit head:* Dr. David E. Gerrard, Unit Head, 540-231-9157, Fax: 540-231-3010, E-mail: dgerrard@vt.edu. *Application contact:* David Notter, Contact, 540-231-5135, Fax: 540-231-3010, E-mail: drnotter@vt.edu. Web site: http://www.apsc.vt.edu/

Virginia Polytechnic Institute and State University, Graduate School, College of Agriculture and Life Sciences, Department of Dairy Science, Blacksburg, VA 24061. Offers MS, PhD. *Degree requirements:* For master's, comprehensive exam (for some programs), thesis (for some programs); for doctorate, comprehensive exam (for some programs), thesis/dissertation (for some programs). *Entrance requirements:* For master's and doctorate, GRE. Additional exam requirements/recommendations for international students: Required—TOEFL (minimum score 550 paper-based; 213 computer-based). *Application*

Peterson's Graduate Programs in the Physical Sciences, Mathematics, Agricultural Sciences, the Environment & Natural Resources 2013

facebook.com/petersonspublishing **423**

deadline: For fall admission, 7/1 for domestic and international students; for spring admission, 12/1 for domestic and international students. Applications are processed on a rolling basis. Application fee: $65. Electronic applications accepted. *Expenses:* Tuition, state resident: full-time $10,048; part-time $558.25 per credit hour. Tuition, nonresident: full-time $19,497; part-time $1083.25 per credit hour. *Required fees:* $405 per semester. Tuition and fees vary according to course load, campus/location and program. *Financial support:* In 2011–12, 5 fellowships with full tuition reimbursements (averaging $7,424 per year), 10 research assistantships with full tuition reimbursements (averaging $16,972 per year), 2 teaching assistantships with full tuition reimbursements (averaging $13,868 per year) were awarded; career-related internships or fieldwork, Federal Work-Study, scholarships/grants, health care benefits, and unspecified assistantships also available. Financial award application deadline: 1/15. *Faculty research:* Genetics, nutrition, reproduction, lactation. *Unit head:* Dr. Michael Akers, Unit Head, 540-231-6331, Fax: 540-231-3010, E-mail: rma@vt.edu. *Application contact:* Isis Mullarky, Information Contact, 540-231-2410, Fax: 540-231-3010, E-mail: mullarky@vt.edu. Web site: http://www.dasc.vt.edu/.

Washington State University, Graduate School, College of Agricultural, Human, and Natural Resource Sciences, Department of Animal Sciences, Pullman, WA 99164. Offers MS, PhD. Part-time programs available. *Faculty:* 29. *Students:* 18 full-time (12 women), 3 part-time (2 women); includes 3 minority (1 Black or African American, non-Hispanic/Latino; 1 Asian, non-Hispanic/Latino; 1 Hispanic/Latino), 7 international. Average age 26. 47 applicants, 21% accepted, 8 enrolled. In 2011, 3 master's, 2 doctorates awarded. *Degree requirements:* For master's, comprehensive exam (for some programs), thesis (for some programs), oral exam; for doctorate, comprehensive exam, thesis/dissertation, oral and written exam. *Entrance requirements:* For master's, GRE, minimum GPA of 3.0, 3 letters of recommendation, department questionnaire; for doctorate, GRE General Test, minimum GPA of 3.0. Additional exam requirements/recommendations for international students: Required—TOEFL, IELTS. *Application deadline:* For fall admission, 1/10 priority date for domestic students, 1/10 for international students; for spring admission, 7/1 priority date for domestic students, 7/1 for international students. Applications are processed on a rolling basis. Application fee: $75. Electronic applications accepted. *Financial support:* In 2011–12, fellowships (averaging $5,000 per year), research assistantships with full and partial tuition reimbursements (averaging $18,204 per year), teaching assistantships with full and partial tuition reimbursements (averaging $18,204 per year) were awarded;

career-related internships or fieldwork, Federal Work-Study, institutionally sponsored loans, scholarships/grants, health care benefits, tuition waivers (partial), and teaching associateships also available. Financial award application deadline: 4/1; financial award applicants required to submit FAFSA. *Faculty research:* Reproduction, genetics, equine cytokines, fish diseases and vaccines. *Total annual research expenditures:* $682,000. *Unit head:* Dr. Margaret Benson, Professor and Chair, 509-335-5523, Fax: 509-335-1082, E-mail: m_benson@wsu.edu. *Application contact:* Graduate School Admissions, 800-GRADWSU, Fax: 509-335-1949, E-mail: gradsch@wsu.edu. Web site: http://www.asci.wsu.edu/.

West Texas A&M University, College of Agriculture, Nursing, and Natural Sciences, Division of Agriculture, Emphasis in Animal Science, Canyon, TX 79016-0001. Offers MS. Part-time programs available. *Degree requirements:* For master's, comprehensive exam, thesis optional. *Entrance requirements:* For master's, GRE General Test. Additional exam requirements/recommendations for international students: Required—TOEFL (minimum score 550 paper-based). Electronic applications accepted. *Faculty research:* Nutrition, animal breeding, meat science, reproduction physiology, feedlots.

West Virginia University, Davis College of Agriculture, Forestry and Consumer Sciences, Division of Animal and Nutritional Sciences, Program in Animal and Nutritional Sciences, Morgantown, WV 26506. Offers breeding (MS); food sciences (MS); nutrition (MS); physiology (MS); production management (MS); reproduction (MS). Part-time programs available. *Degree requirements:* For master's, thesis, oral and written exams. *Entrance requirements:* For master's, GRE, minimum GPA of 2.5. Additional exam requirements/recommendations for international students: Required—TOEFL. *Faculty research:* Animal nutrition, reproductive physiology, food science.

West Virginia University, Davis College of Agriculture, Forestry and Consumer Sciences, Division of Plant and Soil Sciences, Program in Agricultural Sciences, Morgantown, WV 26506. Offers animal and food sciences (PhD); plant and soil sciences (PhD). *Degree requirements:* For doctorate, thesis/dissertation, oral and written exams. *Entrance requirements:* Additional exam requirements/recommendations for international students: Required—TOEFL. *Faculty research:* Ruminant nutrition, metabolism, forage utilization, physiology, reproduction.

Aquaculture

American University of Beirut, Graduate Programs, Faculty of Agricultural and Food Sciences, Beirut, Lebanon. Offers agricultural economics (MS); animal sciences (MS); ecosystem management (MSES); food technology (MS); irrigation (MS); mechanization (MS); nutrition (MS); plant protection (MS); plant science (MS); poultry science (MS); soils (MS). Part-time programs available. *Faculty:* 21 full-time (6 women), 2 part-time/adjunct (0 women). *Students:* 12 full-time (all women), 93 part-time (77 women). Average age 24. 96 applicants, 67% accepted, 21 enrolled. In 2011, 25 master's awarded. *Degree requirements:* For master's, one foreign language, comprehensive exam, thesis (for some programs). *Entrance requirements:* Additional exam requirements/recommendations for international students: Required—TOEFL (minimum score 600 paper-based; 250 computer-based; 100 iBT), IELTS (minimum score 7.5). *Application deadline:* For fall admission, 2/20 for domestic and international students; for spring admission, 11/15 for domestic and international students. Applications are processed on a rolling basis. Application fee: $50. Electronic applications accepted. *Expenses:* Tuition: Full-time $12,780; part-time $710 per credit. *Required fees:* $528; $528 per credit. Tuition and fees vary according to course load and program. *Financial support:* In 2011–12, 22 research assistantships with partial tuition reimbursements (averaging $15,000 per year), 40 teaching assistantships with full and partial tuition reimbursements (averaging $1,000 per year) were awarded; scholarships/grants, health care benefits, and unspecified assistantships also available. Financial award application deadline: 2/2. *Faculty research:* Nutritional food-based dietary guidelines, community and therapeutic nutrition, food safety and food microbiology, landscape planning, nature and rural heritage conservation, pathology, immunology and control of poultry and animal diseases, agricultural economics and development, production of biodiesel from algae, national study on living conditions of refugees. *Unit head:* Prof. Nahla Hwalla, Dean, 961-1343002 Ext. 4400, Fax: 961-1744460, E-mail: nahla@aub.edu.lb. *Application contact:* Dr. Salim Kanaan, Director, Admissions Office, 961-1350000 Ext. 2594, Fax: 961-1750775, E-mail: sk00@aub.edu.lb. Web site: http://www.aub.edu.lb/fafs/Pages/index.aspx.

Auburn University, Graduate School, College of Agriculture, Department of Fisheries and Allied Aquacultures, Auburn University, AL 36849. Offers M Aq, MS, PhD. Part-time programs available. *Faculty:* 20 full-time (3 women). *Students:* 33 full-time (15 women), 53 part-time (24 women); includes 4 minority (1 Black or African American, non-Hispanic/Latino; 1 Asian, non-Hispanic/Latino; 2 Hispanic/Latino), 49 international. Average age 28. 48 applicants, 48% accepted, 19 enrolled. In 2011, 15 master's, 5 doctorates awarded. *Degree requirements:* For master's, thesis (for some programs); for doctorate, 2 foreign languages, thesis/dissertation. *Entrance requirements:* For master's and doctorate, GRE General Test. *Application deadline:* For fall admission, 7/7 for domestic students; for spring admission, 11/24 for domestic students. Applications are processed on a rolling basis. Application fee: $50 ($60 for international students). Electronic applications accepted. *Expenses:* Tuition, state resident: full-time $7290; part-time $405 per credit hour. Tuition, nonresident: full-time $21,870; part-time $1215 per credit hour. *International tuition:* $22,000 full-time. *Required fees:* $1402. *Financial support:* Fellowships, research assistantships, teaching assistantships, and Federal Work-Study available. Support available to part-time students. Financial award application deadline: 3/15; financial award applicants required to submit FAFSA. *Faculty research:* Channel catfish production; aquatic animal health; community and population ecology; pond management; production hatching, breeding and genetics. *Total annual research expenditures:* $8 million. *Unit head:* Dr. David B. Rouse, Head, 334-844-4786. *Application contact:* Dr. George Flowers, Dean of the Graduate School, 334-844-2125. Web site: http://www.ag.auburn.edu/fish/.

Clemson University, Graduate School, College of Agriculture, Forestry and Life Sciences, Department of Forestry and Natural Resources, Program in Wildlife and Fisheries Biology, Clemson, SC 29634. Offers MS, PhD. *Students:* 14 full-time (9 women), 7 part-time (5 women); includes 2 minority (1 Black or African American, non-Hispanic/Latino; 1 Hispanic/Latino), 1 international. Average age 35. 36 applicants, 47% accepted, 16 enrolled. In 2011, 1 doctorate awarded. *Degree requirements:* For master's, thesis; for doctorate, thesis/dissertation. *Entrance requirements:* For master's, GRE General Test, minimum undergraduate GPA of 3.0; for doctorate, GRE General Test. Additional exam requirements/recommendations for international students: Required—TOEFL, IELTS. *Application deadline:* For fall admission, 6/1 for domestic students, 4/15 for international students; for spring admission, 9/15 for international students. Applications are processed on a rolling basis. Application fee: $70 ($80 for international students). Electronic applications accepted. *Expenses:* Contact institution. *Financial support:* In 2011–12, 12 students received support, including 8 research assistantships with partial tuition reimbursements available (averaging $15,248 per year), 5 teaching assistantships with partial tuition reimbursements available (averaging $13,800 per year); fellowships with full and partial tuition reimbursements available, career-related internships or fieldwork, institutionally sponsored loans, scholarships/grants, health care benefits, and unspecified assistantships also available. Support available to part-time students. Financial award applicants required to submit FAFSA. *Faculty research:* Intensive freshwater culture systems, conservation biology, stream management, applied

424 facebook.com/petersonspublishing

Peterson's Graduate Programs in the Physical Sciences, Mathematics, Agricultural Sciences, the Environment & Natural Resources 2013

wildlife management. *Unit head:* Dr. Patricia Layton, Chair, 864-656-3303, Fax: 864-656-3304, E-mail: playton@clemson.edu. *Application contact:* Dr. David Guynn, Graduate Program Coordinator, 864-656-4830, Fax: 864-656-5344, E-mail: dguynn@clemson.edu. Web site: http://www.clemson.edu/cafls/departments/forestry/.

Kentucky State University, College of Agriculture, Food Science and Sustainable Systems, Frankfort, KY 40601. Offers aquaculture (MS); environmental studies (MS). Part-time and evening/weekend programs available. *Faculty:* 10 full-time (1 woman), 1 part-time/adjunct (0 women). *Students:* 34 full-time (16 women), 32 part-time (6 women); includes 22 minority (15 Black or African American, non-Hispanic/Latino; 3 Asian, non-Hispanic/Latino; 1 Hispanic/Latino; 1 Native Hawaiian or other Pacific Islander, non-Hispanic/Latino; 2 Two or more races, non-Hispanic/Latino), 12 international. Average age 34. 55 applicants, 51% accepted, 18 enrolled. In 2011, 16 master's awarded. *Degree requirements:* For master's, comprehensive exam, thesis optional. *Entrance requirements:* For master's, GRE, GMAT. Additional exam requirements/recommendations for international students: Required—TOEFL (minimum score 525 paper-based; 173 computer-based). *Application deadline:* Applications are processed on a rolling basis. Application fee: $30 ($100 for international students). Electronic applications accepted. *Expenses:* Tuition, state resident: full-time $6192; part-time $344 per credit hour. Tuition, nonresident: full-time $9522; part-time $529 per credit hour. *Required fees:* $450; $25 per credit hour. Tuition and fees vary according to course load. *Financial support:* In 2011–12, 41 students received support, including 18 research assistantships (averaging $11,378 per year); career-related internships or fieldwork, scholarships/grants, tuition waivers (partial), and unspecified assistantships also available. Financial award application deadline: 4/15; financial award applicants required to submit FAFSA. *Unit head:* Dr. Teferi Tsegaye, Dean, 502-597-6310, E-mail: teferi.tsegaye@kysu.edu. *Application contact:* Dr. Titilayo Ufomata, Acting Director of Graduate Studies, 502-597-6443, E-mail: titilayo.ufomata@kysu.edu. Web site: http://www.kysu.edu/academics/collegesAndSchools/CAFSSS/.

Memorial University of Newfoundland, School of Graduate Studies, Interdisciplinary Program in Aquaculture, St. John's, NL A1C 5S7, Canada. Offers M Sc. Part-time programs available. *Degree requirements:* For master's, thesis, seminar or thesis topic. *Entrance requirements:* For master's, honors B Sc or diploma in aquaculture from the Marine Institute of Memorial University of Newfoundland. Electronic applications accepted. *Faculty research:* Marine fish larval biology, fin fish nutrition, shellfish culture, fin fish virology, fin fish reproductive biology.

Nova Scotia Agricultural College, Research and Graduate Studies, Truro, NS B2N 5E3, Canada. Offers agriculture (M Sc), including air quality, animal behavior, animal molecular genetics, animal nutrition, animal technology, aquaculture, botany, crop management, crop physiology, ecology, environmental microbiology, food science, horticulture, nutrient management, pest management, physiology, plant biotechnology, plant pathology, soil chemistry, soil fertility, waste management and composting, water quality. Program offered jointly with Dalhousie University. Part-time programs available. *Degree requirements:* For master's, thesis, ATC Exam Teaching Assistantship. *Entrance requirements:* For master's, honors B Sc, minimum GPA of 3.0. Additional exam requirements/recommendations for international students: Required—TOEFL (minimum score 580 paper-based; 237 computer-based; 92 iBT), IELTS, Michigan English Language Assessment Battery, CanTEST, CAEL. *Faculty research:* Bio-product development, organic agriculture, nutrient management, air and water quality, agricultural biotechnology.

Purdue University, Graduate School, College of Agriculture, Department of Forestry and Natural Resources, West Lafayette, IN 47907. Offers fisheries and aquatic sciences (MS, MSF, PhD); forest biology (MS, MSF, PhD); natural resource social science (MS, PhD); natural resources social science (MSF); quantitative ecology (MS, MSF, PhD); wildlife science (MS, MSF, PhD); wood products and wood products manufacturing (MS, MSF, PhD). *Faculty:* 26 full-time (3 women), 9 part-time/adjunct (1 woman). *Students:* 67 full-time (31 women), 8 part-time (3 women); includes 3 minority (2 Hispanic/Latino; 1 Two or more races, non-Hispanic/Latino), 17 international. Average age 29. 58 applicants, 16% accepted, 8 enrolled. In 2011, 9 master's, 11 doctorates awarded. *Degree requirements:* For master's, thesis; for doctorate, thesis/dissertation. *Entrance requirements:* For master's and doctorate, GRE General Test with minimum score required: verbal >=50th percentile; Quantitative >= 50th percentile; Analytical writing = 4.0 or greater, minimum undergraduate GPA of 3.2 or equivalent. Additional exam requirements/recommendations for international students: Required—TOEFL (minimum score 550 paper-based; 77 iBT). *Application deadline:* For fall admission, 1/5 for domestic students, 1/15 for international students; for spring admission, 9/15 for domestic and international students. Applications are processed on a rolling basis. Application fee: $60 ($75 for international students). Electronic applications accepted. *Financial support:* In

2011–12, 10 research assistantships (averaging $15,259 per year) were awarded; fellowships, teaching assistantships, career-related internships or fieldwork, and scholarships/grants also available. Support available to part-time students. Financial award application deadline: 1/5; financial award applicants required to submit FAFSA. *Faculty research:* Wildlife management, forest management, forest ecology, forest soils, limnology. *Unit head:* Dr. Robert K. Swihart, Interim Head, 765-494-3590, Fax: 765-494-9461, E-mail: rswihart@purdue.edu. *Application contact:* Kelly J. Garrett, Graduate Secretary, 765-494-3572, Fax: 765-494-9461, E-mail: kgarrett@purdue.edu. Web site: http://www.fnr.purdue.edu/.

Texas A&M University–Corpus Christi, Graduate Studies and Research, College of Science and Technology, Program in Mariculture, Corpus Christi, TX 78412-5503. Offers MS.

University of Arkansas at Pine Bluff, School of Agriculture, Fisheries and Human Sciences, Pine Bluff, AR 71601-2799. Offers aquaculture and fisheries (MS).

University of Florida, Graduate School, College of Agricultural and Life Sciences, Department of Fisheries and Aquatic Sciences, Gainesville, FL 32611. Offers MFAS, MS, PhD. Part-time programs available. *Students:* 39 full-time (22 women), 16 part-time (4 women); includes 2 minority (1 Asian, non-Hispanic/Latino; 1 Hispanic/Latino), 6 international. Average age 31. 37 applicants, 43% accepted, 12 enrolled. In 2011, 8 master's, 3 doctorates awarded. *Degree requirements:* For master's, thesis (for MS); technical paper (for MFAS); for doctorate, comprehensive exam, thesis/dissertation. *Entrance requirements:* For master's and doctorate, GRE General Test, minimum GPA of 3.0. Additional exam requirements/recommendations for international students: Required—TOEFL (minimum score 550 paper-based; 213 computer-based; 80 iBT), IELTS (minimum score 6). *Application deadline:* For fall admission, 6/1 for domestic students, 3/1 for international students; for spring admission, 10/1 for domestic students, 8/1 for international students. Applications are processed on a rolling basis. Application fee: $30. Electronic applications accepted. *Financial support:* Fellowships, research assistantships, and unspecified assistantships available. Financial award application deadline: 1/31; financial award applicants required to submit FAFSA. *Faculty research:* Conservation and management of aquatic ecosystems; aquatic animal health; water quality, nutrients, and eutrophication; sustainable and quantitative fisheries; aquaculture or ornamental fish, marine baitfish, and shellfish. *Total annual research expenditures:* $10 million. *Unit head:* Dr. Nancy J. Peterson, Associate Director, 352-846-0848, Fax: 352-846-1277, E-mail: njp@ufl.edu. *Application contact:* Dr. Charles Cichra, Graduate Coordinator, 352-273-3621, Fax: 352-392-3672, E-mail: cecichra@ufl.edu. Web site: http://fishweb.ifas.ufl.edu/.

University of Guelph, Graduate Studies, Ontario Agricultural College, Program in Aquaculture, Guelph, ON N1G 2W1, Canada. Offers M Sc. *Degree requirements:* For master's, practicum, research project. *Entrance requirements:* For master's, minimum B average during previous 2 years of course work. *Faculty research:* Protein and amino acid metabolism, genetics, gamete cryogenics, pathology, epidemiology.

University of Rhode Island, Graduate School, College of the Environment and Life Sciences, Department of Fisheries, Animal and Veterinary Science, Kingston, RI 02881. Offers animal health and disease (MS); animal science (MS); aquaculture (MS); aquatic pathology (MS); environmental sciences (PhD), including animal science, aquacultural science, aquatic pathology, fisheries science; fisheries (MS). *Faculty:* 10 full-time (4 women). *Students:* 14 full-time (7 women), 6 part-time (1 woman). In 2011, 5 degrees awarded. *Degree requirements:* For master's, comprehensive exam (for some programs), thesis optional; for doctorate, comprehensive exam, thesis/dissertation. *Entrance requirements:* For master's and doctorate, GRE, 2 letters of recommendation. Additional exam requirements/recommendations for international students: Required—TOEFL (minimum score 550 paper-based; 213 computer-based). *Application deadline:* For fall admission, 7/15 for domestic students, 2/1 for international students; for spring admission, 11/15 for domestic students, 7/15 for international students. Application fee: $65. Electronic applications accepted. *Expenses:* Tuition, state resident: full-time $10,432; part-time $580 per credit hour. Tuition, nonresident: full-time $23,130; part-time $1285 per credit hour. *Required fees:* $1362; $36 per credit hour. $35 per semester. One-time fee: $130. *Financial support:* In 2011–12, 3 research assistantships with full and partial tuition reimbursements (averaging $11,654 per year), 4 teaching assistantships with full and partial tuition reimbursements (averaging $12,214 per year) were awarded. Financial award application deadline: 7/15; financial award applicants required to submit FAFSA. *Unit head:* Dr. David Bengtson, Chair, 401-874-2668, Fax: 401-874-7575, E-mail: bengtson@uri.edu. *Application contact:* Dr. Marta Gomez-Chiarri, Director of Graduate Studies, 401-874-2917, Fax: 401-874-7575, E-mail: gomezchi@uri.edu. Web site: http://www.uri.edu/cels/favs/.

Peterson's Graduate Programs in the Physical Sciences, Mathematics, Agricultural Sciences, the Environment & Natural Resources 2013

facebook.com/petersonspublishing **425**

Food Science and Technology

Alabama Agricultural and Mechanical University, School of Graduate Studies, College of Agricultural, Life and Natural Sciences, Department of Family and Consumer Sciences, Huntsville, AL 35811. Offers family and consumer sciences (MS); food science (MS, PhD). Part-time and evening/weekend programs available. *Degree requirements:* For master's, comprehensive exam, thesis optional; for doctorate, one foreign language, thesis/dissertation. *Entrance requirements:* For master's, GRE General Test; for doctorate, GRE General Test, MS. Additional exam requirements/recommendations for international students: Required—TOEFL (minimum score 500 paper-based; 173 computer-based; 61 iBT). Electronic applications accepted. *Faculty research:* Food biotechnology, nutrition, food microbiology, food engineering, food chemistry.

Alabama Agricultural and Mechanical University, School of Graduate Studies, College of Agricultural, Life and Natural Sciences, Department of Food and Animal Sciences, Huntsville, AL 35811. Offers food science (MS, PhD). *Entrance requirements:* Additional exam requirements/recommendations for international students: Required—TOEFL (minimum score 500 paper-based; 173 computer-based; 61 iBT).

American University of Beirut, Graduate Programs, Faculty of Agricultural and Food Sciences, Beirut, Lebanon. Offers agricultural economics (MS); animal sciences (MS); ecosystem management (MSES); food technology (MS); irrigation (MS); mechanization (MS); nutrition (MS); plant protection (MS); plant science (MS); poultry science (MS); soils (MS). Part-time programs available. *Faculty:* 21 full-time (6 women), 2 part-time/adjunct (0 women). *Students:* 12 full-time (all women), 93 part-time (77 women). Average age 24. 96 applicants, 67% accepted, 21 enrolled. In 2011, 25 master's awarded. *Degree requirements:* For master's, one foreign language, comprehensive exam, thesis (for some programs). *Entrance requirements:* Additional exam requirements/recommendations for international students: Required—TOEFL (minimum score 600 paper-based; 250 computer-based; 100 iBT), IELTS (minimum score 7.5). *Application deadline:* For fall admission, 2/20 for domestic and international students; for spring admission, 11/15 for domestic and international students. Applications are processed on a rolling basis. Application fee: $50. Electronic applications accepted. *Expenses: Tuition:* Full-time $12,780; part-time $710 per credit. *Required fees:* $528; $528 per credit. Tuition and fees vary according to course load and program. *Financial support:* In 2011–12, 22 research assistantships with partial tuition reimbursements (averaging $15,000 per year), 40 teaching assistantships with full and partial tuition reimbursements (averaging $1,000 per year) were awarded; scholarships/grants, health care benefits, and unspecified assistantships also available. Financial award application deadline: 2/2. *Faculty research:* Nutritional food-based dietary guidelines, community and therapeutic nutrition, food safety and food microbiology, landscape planning, nature and rural heritage conservation, pathology, immunology and control of poultry and animal diseases, agricultural economics and development, production of biodiesel from algae, national study on living conditions of refugees. *Unit head:* Prof. Nahla Hwalla, Dean, 961-1343002 Ext. 4400, Fax: 961-1744460, E-mail: nahla@aub.edu.lb. *Application contact:* Dr. Salim Kanaan, Director, Admissions Office, 961-1350000 Ext. 2594, Fax: 961-1750775, E-mail: sk00@aub.edu.lb. Web site: http://www.aub.edu.lb/fafs/Pages/index.aspx.

Auburn University, Graduate School, College of Human Sciences, Department of Nutrition and Food Science, Auburn University, AL 36849. Offers global hospitality and retailing (Graduate Certificate); nutrition (MS, PhD). Part-time programs available. *Faculty:* 13 full-time (5 women). *Students:* 23 full-time (15 women), 25 part-time (16 women); includes 5 minority (4 Black or African American, non-Hispanic/Latino; 1 Asian, non-Hispanic/Latino), 19 international. Average age 29. 56 applicants, 38% accepted, 11 enrolled. In 2011, 4 master's, 2 doctorates awarded. *Degree requirements:* For master's, thesis (for some programs); for doctorate, thesis/dissertation. *Entrance requirements:* For master's and doctorate, GRE General Test. *Application deadline:* For fall admission, 7/7 for domestic students; for spring admission, 11/24 for domestic students. Applications are processed on a rolling basis. Application fee: $50 ($60 for international students). Electronic applications accepted. *Expenses: Tuition,* state resident: full-time $7290; part-time $405 per credit hour. Tuition, nonresident: full-time $21,870; part-time $1215 per credit hour. *International tuition:* $22,000 full-time. *Required fees:* $1402. *Financial support:* Research assistantships, teaching assistantships, career-related internships or fieldwork, and Federal Work-Study available. Support available to part-time students. Financial award application deadline: 3/15; financial award applicants required to submit FAFSA. *Faculty research:* Food quality and safety, diet, food supply, physical activity in maintenance of health, prevention of selected chronic disease states. *Unit head:* Dr. Martin O'Neill, Head, 334-844-3266. *Application contact:* Dr. George Flowers, Dean of the Graduate School, 334-844-2125. Web site: http://www.humsci.auburn.edu/nufs/.

Boston University, Metropolitan College, Program in Gastronomy, Boston, MA 02215. Offers business (MLA); communications (MLA); food policy (MLA); history and culture (MLA). Part-time and evening/weekend programs available. *Faculty:* 1 (woman) full-time, 13 part-time/adjunct (7 women). *Students:* 11 full-time (10 women), 72 part-time (61 women); includes 11 minority (2 Black or African American, non-Hispanic/Latino; 5 Asian, non-Hispanic/Latino; 3 Hispanic/Latino;

1 Two or more races, non-Hispanic/Latino), 6 international. Average age 28. 59 applicants, 53% accepted, 23 enrolled. In 2011, 9 master's awarded. *Degree requirements:* For master's, thesis optional. *Entrance requirements:* Additional exam requirements/recommendations for international students: Required—TOEFL. *Application deadline:* Applications are processed on a rolling basis. Application fee: $70. Electronic applications accepted. *Expenses: Tuition:* Full-time $40,848; part-time $1276 per credit hour. *Required fees:* $572; $286 per semester. *Financial support:* In 2011–12, 3 research assistantships (averaging $5,000 per year) were awarded; career-related internships or fieldwork, scholarships/grants, and unspecified assistantships also available. Support available to part-time students. Financial award applicants required to submit FAFSA. *Faculty research:* Food studies. *Unit head:* Dr. Rachel Black, Assistant Professor, 617-353-6291, Fax: 617-353-4130, E-mail: rblack@bu.edu. Web site: http://www.bu.edu/met/gastronomy.

Brigham Young University, Graduate Studies, College of Life Sciences, Department of Nutrition, Dietetics and Food Science, Provo, UT 84602-1001. Offers food science (MS); nutrition (MS). *Faculty:* 12 full-time (5 women). *Students:* 10 full-time (7 women), 1 (woman) part-time. Average age 24. 3 applicants, 67% accepted, 2 enrolled. In 2011, 3 master's awarded. *Degree requirements:* For master's, comprehensive exam, thesis. *Entrance requirements:* For master's, GRE General Test. Additional exam requirements/recommendations for international students: Required—TOEFL (minimum score 550 paper-based; 213 computer-based). *Application deadline:* For fall admission, 2/1 for domestic and international students; for winter admission, 6/30 for domestic and international students. Application fee: $50. Electronic applications accepted. Full-time tuition for non-LDS students: $11,520 per year; $640 per credit. *Expenses: Tuition:* Full-time $5760; part-time $320 per credit. Tuition and fees vary according to student's religious affiliation. *Financial support:* In 2011–12, 9 students received support, including 4 research assistantships (averaging $20,325 per year), 3 teaching assistantships (averaging $20,325 per year); career-related internships or fieldwork, institutionally sponsored loans, and scholarships/grants also available. Financial award application deadline: 4/1. *Faculty research:* Dairy foods, lipid oxidation, food processes, magnesium and selenium nutrition, nutrient effect on gene expression. *Total annual research expenditures:* $321,576. *Unit head:* Dr. Michael L. Dunn, Chair, 801-422-6670, Fax: 801-422-0258, E-mail: michael_dunn@byu.edu. *Application contact:* Dr. Susan Fullmer, Graduate Coordinator, 801-422-3349, Fax: 801-422-0258, E-mail: susan_fullmer@byu.edu.

California State University, Fresno, Division of Graduate Studies, College of Agricultural Sciences and Technology, Department of Food Science and Nutritional Sciences, Fresno, CA 93740-8027. Offers MS. Part-time programs available. *Degree requirements:* For master's, thesis. *Entrance requirements:* For master's, GRE General Test, minimum GPA of 3.0 in last 60 units. Additional exam requirements/recommendations for international students: Required—TOEFL. Electronic applications accepted. *Faculty research:* Liquid foods, analysis, mushrooms, gaseous ozone, natamycin.

California State University, Long Beach, Graduate Studies, College of Health and Human Services, Department of Family and Consumer Sciences, Master of Science in Nutritional Science Program, Long Beach, CA 90840. Offers food science (MS); hospitality foodservice and hotel management (MS); nutritional science (MS). Part-time programs available. *Students:* 32 full-time (29 women), 23 part-time (all women); includes 18 minority (2 Black or African American, non-Hispanic/Latino; 6 Asian, non-Hispanic/Latino; 5 Hispanic/Latino; 5 Two or more races, non-Hispanic/Latino). Average age 27. 108 applicants, 32% accepted, 21 enrolled. In 2011, 11 master's awarded. *Degree requirements:* For master's, thesis, oral presentation of thesis or directed project. *Entrance requirements:* For master's, GRE, minimum GPA of 2.5 in last 60 units. *Application deadline:* For fall admission, 5/1 for domestic students. Applications are processed on a rolling basis. Application fee: $55. Electronic applications accepted. *Financial support:* Federal Work-Study, institutionally sponsored loans, and scholarships/grants available. Financial award application deadline: 3/2. *Faculty research:* Protein and water-soluble vitamins, sensory evaluation of foods, mineral deficiencies in humans, child nutrition, minerals and blood pressure. *Unit head:* Dr. M. Sue Stanley, Chair, 562-985-4484, Fax: 562-985-4414, E-mail: stanleym@csulb.edu. *Application contact:* Dr. Mary Jacob, Graduate Coordinator, 562-985-4484, Fax: 562-985-4414, E-mail: marjacob@csulb.edu.

Chapman University, Schmid College of Science and Technology, Food Science Program, Orange, CA 92866. Offers MS, MBA/MS. Part-time and evening/weekend programs available. *Faculty:* 3 full-time (2 women), 4 part-time/adjunct (all women). *Students:* 24 full-time (20 women), 26 part-time (18 women); includes 22 minority (1 Black or African American, non-Hispanic/Latino; 19 Asian, non-Hispanic/Latino; 1 Hispanic/Latino; 1 Native Hawaiian or other Pacific Islander, non-Hispanic/Latino), 16 international. Average age 27. 40 applicants, 80% accepted, 19 enrolled. In 2011, 14 master's awarded. *Degree requirements:* For master's, comprehensive exam, thesis optional. *Entrance requirements:* For master's, GRE or GMAT, minimum undergraduate GPA of 3.0. Additional exam requirements/recommendations for international students: Required—TOEFL (minimum score 550 paper-based; 213 computer-based; 80 iBT). *Application*

426 facebook.com/petersonspublishing

Peterson's Graduate Programs in the Physical Sciences, Mathematics, Agricultural Sciences, the Environment & Natural Resources 2013

deadline: For fall admission, 5/2 priority date for domestic students; for spring admission, 11/1 priority date for domestic students. Application fee: $60. Electronic applications accepted. Tuition and fees vary according to degree level and program. *Financial support:* Fellowships, Federal Work-Study, and scholarships/grants available. Financial award applicants required to submit FAFSA. *Unit head:* Dr. Anuradha Prakash, Program Director, 714-744-7895, E-mail: prakash@chapman.edu. *Application contact:* Gianne Diosomito, Graduate Admission Counselor, 714-997-6711, E-mail: diosomit@chapman.edu.

Clemson University, Graduate School, College of Agriculture, Forestry and Life Sciences, Department of Food, Nutrition and Packaging Sciences, Program in Food, Nutrition, and Culinary Science, Clemson, SC 29634. Offers MS. *Students:* 29 full-time (21 women), 7 part-time (5 women); includes 3 minority (all Hispanic/Latino), 13 international. Average age 28. 82 applicants, 18% accepted, 10 enrolled. In 2011, 7 master's awarded. *Degree requirements:* For master's, thesis. *Entrance requirements:* For master's, GRE General Test. Additional exam requirements/recommendations for international students: Required—TOEFL, IELTS. *Application deadline:* For fall admission, 6/1 for domestic students, 4/15 for international students; for spring admission, 9/15 for international students. Applications are processed on a rolling basis. Application fee: $70 ($80 for international students). Electronic applications accepted. *Expenses:* Contact institution. *Financial support:* In 2011–12, 16 students received support, including 8 research assistantships with partial tuition reimbursements available (averaging $10,189 per year), 10 teaching assistantships with partial tuition reimbursements available (averaging $10,158 per year); fellowships with full and partial tuition reimbursements available, career-related internships or fieldwork, institutionally sponsored loans, scholarships/grants, health care benefits, and unspecified assistantships also available. Support available to part-time students. Financial award applicants required to submit FAFSA. *Unit head:* Dr. Anthony L. Pometto, Chair, 864-656-4382, Fax: 864-656-3131, E-mail: pometto@clemson.edu. *Application contact:* Dr. Paul Dawson, Coordinator, 864-656-1138, Fax: 864-656-3131, E-mail: pdawson@clemson.edu. Web site: http://www.clemson.edu/foodscience.

Clemson University, Graduate School, College of Agriculture, Forestry and Life Sciences, Department of Food, Nutrition and Packaging Sciences and Department of Animal and Veterinary Sciences, Program in Food Technology, Clemson, SC 29634. Offers PhD. *Students:* 10 full-time (7 women), 7 part-time (3 women); includes 4 minority (2 Black or African American, non-Hispanic/Latino; 1 Asian, non-Hispanic/Latino; 1 Hispanic/Latino), 4 international. Average age 39. 23 applicants, 17% accepted, 1 enrolled. In 2011, 2 doctorates awarded. *Degree requirements:* For doctorate, thesis/dissertation. *Entrance requirements:* For doctorate, GRE General Test. Additional exam requirements/recommendations for international students: Required—TOEFL, IELTS. *Application deadline:* For fall admission, 6/1 for domestic students, 4/15 for international students; for spring admission, 9/15 for international students. Applications are processed on a rolling basis. Application fee: $70 ($80 for international students). Electronic applications accepted. *Expenses:* Contact institution. *Financial support:* In 2011–12, 7 students received support, including 4 research assistantships with partial tuition reimbursements available (averaging $19,500 per year), 4 teaching assistantships with partial tuition reimbursements available (averaging $11,875 per year); fellowships with full and partial tuition reimbursements available, career-related internships or fieldwork, institutionally sponsored loans, scholarships/grants, health care benefits, and unspecified assistantships also available. Support available to part-time students. Financial award applicants required to submit FAFSA. *Unit head:* Dr. Anthony Pometto, III, Coordinator, 864-656-4382, Fax: 864-656-3131, E-mail: pometto@clemson.edu. *Application contact:* Dr. Paul Dawson, Coordinator, 864-656-1138, Fax: 864-656-3131, E-mail: pdawson@clemson.edu. Web site: http://www.clemson.edu/foodscience/.

Colorado State University, Graduate School, College of Applied Human Sciences, Department of Food Science and Human Nutrition, Fort Collins, CO 80523-1571. Offers MS, PhD. *Accreditation:* AND. Part-time programs available. *Faculty:* 17 full-time (9 women), 1 (woman) part-time/adjunct. *Students:* 48 full-time (42 women), 39 part-time (28 women); includes 8 minority (1 Black or African American, non-Hispanic/Latino; 2 Asian, non-Hispanic/Latino; 3 Hispanic/Latino; 2 Two or more races, non-Hispanic/Latino), 4 international. Average age 31. 108 applicants, 47% accepted, 23 enrolled. In 2011, 20 master's, 3 doctorates awarded. *Degree requirements:* For master's, thesis; for doctorate, thesis/dissertation. *Entrance requirements:* For master's and doctorate, GRE General Test, minimum GPA of 3.0, resume, 3 letters of recommendation. Additional exam requirements/recommendations for international students: Required—TOEFL (minimum score 550 paper-based; 213 computer-based; 80 iBT). *Application deadline:* For fall admission, 2/15 priority date for domestic students, 2/15 for international students; for spring admission, 7/15 priority date for domestic students, 7/15 for international students. Application fee: $50. Electronic applications accepted. *Expenses:* Tuition, state resident: full-time $7992. Tuition, nonresident: full-time $19,592. *Required fees:* $1735; $58 per credit. *Financial support:* In 2011–12, 17 students received support, including 9 research assistantships with full and partial tuition reimbursements available (averaging $10,616 per year), 8 teaching assistantships with full and partial tuition reimbursements available (averaging $9,033 per year); fellowships, Federal Work-Study, scholarships/grants, and unspecified assistantships also available. Financial award application deadline: 3/1; financial award applicants required to submit FAFSA. *Faculty research:* Metabolic regulation, nutrition education, food safety, obesity and diabetes, metabolism. *Total annual research expenditures:* $2.9 million. *Unit head:* Dr. Christopher Melby, Head, 970-491-6736, Fax: 970-

491-7252, E-mail: christopher.melby@colostate.edu. *Application contact:* Paula Coleman, Graduate Coordinator, 970-491-3819, Fax: 970-491-3875, E-mail: pcoleman@cahs.colostate.edu. Web site: http://www.fshn.cahs.colostate.edu/.

Cornell University, Graduate School, Graduate Fields of Agriculture and Life Sciences, Field of Food Science and Technology, Ithaca, NY 14853-0001. Offers dairy science (MPS, MS, PhD); food chemistry (MPS, MS, PhD); food engineering (MPS, MS, PhD); food microbiology (MPS, MS, PhD); food processing waste technology (MPS, MS, PhD); food science (MFS, MPS, MS, PhD); international food science (MPS, MS, PhD); sensory evaluation (MPS, MS, PhD). *Faculty:* 43 full-time (10 women). *Students:* 91 full-time (61 women); includes 12 minority (3 Black or African American, non-Hispanic/Latino; 4 Asian, non-Hispanic/Latino; 3 Hispanic/Latino; 2 Two or more races, non-Hispanic/Latino), 52 international. Average age 27. 185 applicants, 24% accepted, 32 enrolled. In 2011, 17 master's, 7 doctorates awarded. Terminal master's awarded for partial completion of doctoral program. *Degree requirements:* For master's, thesis (MS), teaching experience; for doctorate, comprehensive exam, thesis/dissertation, teaching experience. *Entrance requirements:* For master's and doctorate, GRE General Test, 3 letters of recommendation. Additional exam requirements/recommendations for international students: Required—TOEFL (minimum score 550 paper-based; 213 computer-based; 77 iBT). *Application deadline:* For fall admission, 1/30 priority date for domestic students. Application fee: $95. Electronic applications accepted. *Financial support:* In 2011–12, 4 fellowships with full tuition reimbursements, 45 research assistantships with full tuition reimbursements, 10 teaching assistantships with full tuition reimbursements were awarded; institutionally sponsored loans, scholarships/grants, health care benefits, tuition waivers (full and partial), and unspecified assistantships also available. Financial award applicants required to submit FAFSA. *Faculty research:* Food microbiology/biotechnology, food engineering/processing, food safety/toxicology, sensory science/flavor chemistry, food packaging. *Unit head:* Director of Graduate Studies, 607-255-7637, Fax: 607-254-4868. *Application contact:* Graduate Field Assistant, 607-255-7637, Fax: 607-254-4868, E-mail: fdscigrad@cornell.edu. Web site: http://www.gradschool.cornell.edu/fields.php?id-50&a-2.

Dalhousie University, Faculty of Engineering, Department of Food Science and Technology, Halifax, NS B3J 1Z1, Canada. Offers M Sc, PhD. *Degree requirements:* For master's, thesis; for doctorate, thesis/dissertation. *Entrance requirements:* Additional exam requirements/recommendations for international students: Required—TOEFL, IELTS, CANTEST, CAEL, or Michigan English Language Assessment Battery. Electronic applications accepted. *Faculty research:* Food microbiology, food safety/HALLP, rheology and rheometry, food processing, seafood processing.

Drexel University, Goodwin College of Professional Studies, School of Technology and Professional Studies, Philadelphia, PA 19104-2875. Offers construction management (MS); engineering technology (MS); food science (MS); hospitality management (MS); professional studies: creativity studies (MS); professional studies: e-learning leadership (MS); professional studies: homeland security management (MS); project management (MS); property management (MS); sport management (MS). Postbaccalaureate distance learning degree programs offered.

Florida State University, The Graduate School, College of Human Sciences, Department of Nutrition, Food and Exercise Sciences, Tallahassee, FL 32306-1493. Offers exercise physiology (PhD); nutrition and food science (MS, PhD), including clinical nutrition (MS), food science, human nutrition (PhD), nutrition education and health promotion (MS), nutrition science (MS), sports nutrition (MS); sports sciences (MS). Part-time programs available. *Faculty:* 18 full-time (10 women). *Students:* 88 full-time (56 women), 15 part-time (5 women); includes 24 minority (9 Black or African American, non-Hispanic/Latino; 4 Asian, non-Hispanic/Latino; 10 Hispanic/Latino; 1 Native Hawaiian or other Pacific Islander, non-Hispanic/Latino), 21 international. Average age 26. 172 applicants, 51% accepted, 32 enrolled. In 2011, 38 master's, 7 doctorates awarded. *Degree requirements:* For master's, comprehensive exam (for some programs), thesis optional; for doctorate, thesis/dissertation. *Entrance requirements:* For master's, GRE General Test, minimum upper-division GPA of 3.0; for doctorate, GRE General Test, minimum upper-division GPA of 3.0, MS. Additional exam requirements/recommendations for international students: Required—TOEFL (minimum score 550 paper-based; 80 iBT). *Application deadline:* For fall admission, 7/1 for domestic students, 3/1 for international students; for spring admission, 11/1 for domestic students, 5/1 for international students. Applications are processed on a rolling basis. Application fee: $30. Electronic applications accepted. *Expenses:* Tuition, state resident: full-time $9474; part-time $350.88 per credit hour. Tuition, nonresident: full-time $16,236; part-time $601.34 per credit hour. *Required fees:* $630 per semester. One-time fee: $20. Tuition and fees vary according to course load and campus/location. *Financial support:* In 2011–12, 59 students received support, including fellowships with partial tuition reimbursements available (averaging $10,000 per year), 17 research assistantships with partial tuition reimbursements available (averaging $8,000 per year), 47 teaching assistantships with partial tuition reimbursements available (averaging $8,000 per year); career-related internships or fieldwork, Federal Work-Study, institutionally sponsored loans, scholarships/grants, and unspecified assistantships also available. Financial award application deadline: 1/15; financial award applicants required to submit FAFSA. *Faculty research:* Body composition, functional food, chronic disease and aging response; food safety, food allergy, and safety/quality detection methods; sports nutrition, energy and human performance; strength training, functional performance, cardiovascular

Peterson's Graduate Programs in the Physical Sciences, Mathematics, Agricultural Sciences, the Environment & Natural Resources 2013

facebook.com/petersonspublishing **427**

Food Science and Technology

physiology, sarcopenia . *Unit head:* Dr. Bahram H. Arjmandi, Professor/Chair, 850-645-1517, Fax: 850-645-5000, E-mail: barjmandi@fsu.edu. *Application contact:* Joseph J. Carroll, Administrative Support Assistant, 850-644-4800, Fax: 850-645-5000, E-mail: jjcarroll@admin.fsu.edu. Web site: http://www.chs.fsu.edu/.

Framingham State University, Division of Graduate and Continuing Education, Programs in Food and Nutrition, Food Science and Nutrition Science Program, Framingham, MA 01701-9101. Offers MS. Part-time and evening/weekend programs available. *Entrance requirements:* For master's, GRE General Test.

Illinois Institute of Technology, Graduate College, College of Science and Letters, Program in Food Safety and Technology, Chicago, IL 60616-3793. Offers MFPE, MFST, MS. Part-time programs available. *Degree requirements:* For master's, comprehensive exam (for some programs), thesis (for some programs). *Entrance requirements:* For master's, GRE General Test, minimum undergraduate GPA of 3.0. Additional exam requirements/recommendations for international students: Required—TOEFL (minimum score 523 paper-based; 213 computer-based; 70 iBT). Electronic applications accepted. *Faculty research:* Microbial food safety and security, food virology, interfacial colloidial phenomena, development of DNA-based methods for detection, differentiation and tracking of foodborne pathogens in food systems and environment, appetite and obesity management and vascular disease.

Iowa State University of Science and Technology, Department of Food Science and Human Nutrition, Ames, IA 50011-1123. Offers food science and technology (MS, PhD); nutrition (MS, PhD). *Degree requirements:* For master's, thesis; for doctorate, thesis/dissertation. *Entrance requirements:* For master's and doctorate, GRE General Test. Additional exam requirements/recommendations for international students: Required—TOEFL (minimum score 550 paper-based; 79 iBT), IELTS (minimum score 6.5). *Application deadline:* For fall admission, 1/15 priority date for domestic students, 1/15 for international students. Applications are processed on a rolling basis. Application fee: $40 ($90 for international students). Electronic applications accepted. *Unit head:* Dr. Pat Murphy, Director of Graduate Education, 515-294-6442, Fax: 515-294-6193, E-mail: gradsecretary@iastate.edu. *Application contact:* Tong Wang, Director of Graduate Education, 515-294-6442, Fax: 515-294-6193, E-mail: gradsecretary@iastate.edu. Web site: http://www.fshn.hs.iastate.edu.

Kansas State University, Graduate School, College of Agriculture, Food Science Institute, Manhattan, KS 66506. Offers MS, PhD. Part-time programs available. Postbaccalaureate distance learning degree programs offered (minimal on-campus study). *Faculty:* 27 full-time (7 women). *Students:* 31 full-time (19 women), 88 part-time (53 women); includes 16 minority (5 Black or African American, non-Hispanic/Latino; 6 Asian, non-Hispanic/Latino; 4 Hispanic/Latino; 1 Two or more races, non-Hispanic/Latino), 18 international. Average age 31. 62 applicants, 56% accepted, 25 enrolled. In 2011, 23 master's, 3 doctorates awarded. *Degree requirements:* For master's, thesis, residency; for doctorate, thesis/dissertation, preliminary exams, residency. *Entrance requirements:* For master's, GRE General Test, minimum GPA of 3.0 in undergraduate course work, course work in mathematics; for doctorate, GRE General Test, minimum GPA of 3.5 in master's course work. Additional exam requirements/recommendations for international students: Required—TOEFL (minimum score 550 paper-based; 213 computer-based). *Application deadline:* For fall admission, 2/1 priority date for domestic students, 2/1 for international students; for spring admission, 8/1 priority date for domestic students, 8/1 for international students. Applications are processed on a rolling basis. Application fee: $40 ($55 for international students). Electronic applications accepted. *Financial support:* Research assistantships with partial tuition reimbursements, teaching assistantships with partial tuition reimbursements, Federal Work-Study, institutionally sponsored loans, and scholarships/grants available. Support available to part-time students. Financial award application deadline: 3/1; financial award applicants required to submit FAFSA. *Faculty research:* Food safety and defense, food chemistry, ingredient technology, food nutrients and bioactive compounds, new product development, meat and dairy technology, sensory evaluation. *Total annual research expenditures:* $399,599. *Unit head:* Curtis Kastner, Head, 785-532-4057, Fax: 785-532-5681, E-mail: ckastner@ksu.edu. *Application contact:* J. Scott Smith, Director, 785-532-1219, Fax: 785-532-5681, E-mail: jsschem@ksu.edu. Web site: http://foodsci.k-state.edu/DesktopDefault.aspx.

Louisiana State University and Agricultural and Mechanical College, Graduate School, College of Agriculture, Department of Food Science, Baton Rouge, LA 70803. Offers MS, PhD. Part-time programs available. *Faculty:* 11 full-time (4 women). *Students:* 39 full-time (20 women), 5 part-time (2 women); includes 2 minority (both Black or African American, non-Hispanic/Latino), 31 international. Average age 28. 61 applicants, 25% accepted, 10 enrolled. In 2011, 10 master's, 3 doctorates awarded. *Degree requirements:* For master's, thesis; for doctorate, thesis/dissertation. *Entrance requirements:* For master's and doctorate, GRE General Test, minimum GPA of 3.0. Additional exam requirements/recommendations for international students: Required—TOEFL (minimum score 550 paper-based; 213 computer-based; 79 iBT), IELTS (minimum score 6.5). *Application deadline:* For fall admission, 1/25 priority date for domestic students, 5/15 for international students; for spring admission, 10/15 for international students. Applications are processed on a rolling basis. Application fee: $50 ($70 for international students). Electronic applications accepted. *Financial support:* In 2011–12, 40 students received support, including 1 fellowship (averaging $19,027 per year), 29 research assistantships with partial tuition reimbursements available (averaging $17,052 per year), 1 teaching assistantship with partial tuition

reimbursement available (averaging $18,000 per year); Federal Work-Study, institutionally sponsored loans, scholarships/grants, health care benefits, tuition waivers (full and partial), and unspecified assistantships also available. Support available to part-time students. Financial award application deadline: 4/1; financial award applicants required to submit FAFSA. *Faculty research:* Food chemistry/analysis, food microbiology, food processing/engineering, sensory science, product development. *Total annual research expenditures:* $18,426. *Unit head:* Dr. John W. Finley, Head, 225-578-5206, Fax: 225-578-5300, E-mail: jfinley@agcenter.lsu.edu. *Application contact:* Dr. Kenneth McMillan, Graduate Coordinator, 225-578-3438, Fax: 225-578-5300, E-mail: kmcmill@lsu.edu. Web site: http://www.lsu.edu/foodscience/.

McGill University, Faculty of Agricultural and Postdoctoral Studies, Faculty of Agricultural and Environmental Sciences, Department of Food Science and Agricultural Chemistry, Montréal, QC H3A 2T5, Canada. Offers M Sc, PhD.

Memorial University of Newfoundland, School of Graduate Studies, Department of Biochemistry, St. John's, NL A1C 5S7, Canada. Offers biochemistry (M Sc, PhD); food science (M Sc, PhD). Part-time programs available. *Degree requirements:* For master's, thesis; for doctorate, comprehensive exam, thesis/dissertation, oral defense of thesis. *Entrance requirements:* For master's, 2nd class degree in related field; for doctorate, M Sc. Electronic applications accepted. *Faculty research:* Toxicology, cell and molecular biology, food engineering, marine biotechnology, lipid biology.

Michigan State University, College of Veterinary Medicine and The Graduate School, Graduate Programs in Veterinary Medicine, National Food Safety and Toxicology Center, East Lansing, MI 48824. Offers food safety (MS). *Entrance requirements:* Additional exam requirements/recommendations for international students: Required—TOEFL, Michigan State University ELT (minimum score 85), Michigan English Language Assessment Battery (minimum score 83). Electronic applications accepted.

Michigan State University, The Graduate School, College of Agriculture and Natural Resources and College of Natural Science, Department of Food Science and Human Nutrition, East Lansing, MI 48824. Offers food science (MS, PhD); food science environmental toxicology (PhD); human nutrition (MS, PhD); human nutrition-environmental toxicology (PhD). *Entrance requirements:* Additional exam requirements/recommendations for international students: Required—TOEFL (minimum score 550 paper-based; 213 computer-based), Michigan State University ELT (minimum score 85), Michigan English Language Assessment Battery (minimum score 83). Electronic applications accepted.

Mississippi State University, College of Agriculture and Life Sciences, Department of Food Science, Nutrition and Health Promotion, Mississippi State, MS 39762. Offers food science and technology (MS, PhD); health promotion (MS); nutrition (MS, PhD). Postbaccalaureate distance learning degree programs offered (no on-campus study). *Faculty:* 9 full-time (3 women), 3 part-time/adjunct (1 woman). *Students:* 45 full-time (33 women), 38 part-time (31 women); includes 15 minority (8 Black or African American, non-Hispanic/Latino; 2 American Indian or Alaska Native, non-Hispanic/Latino; 1 Asian, non-Hispanic/Latino; 2 Hispanic/Latino; 1 Native Hawaiian or other Pacific Islander, non-Hispanic/Latino; 1 Two or more races, non-Hispanic/Latino), 18 international. Average age 30. 132 applicants, 28% accepted, 26 enrolled. In 2011, 27 master's, 3 doctorates awarded. *Degree requirements:* For master's, comprehensive exam, thesis; for doctorate, comprehensive exam, thesis/dissertation. *Entrance requirements:* For master's, GRE General Test, minimum GPA of 2.8; for doctorate, GRE General Test, minimum GPA of 3.0. Additional exam requirements/recommendations for international students: Required—TOEFL (minimum score 475 paper-based; 153 computer-based; 53 iBT); Recommended—IELTS (minimum score 4.5). *Application deadline:* For fall admission, 7/1 for domestic students, 5/1 for international students; for spring admission, 11/1 for domestic students, 9/1 for international students. Applications are processed on a rolling basis. Application fee: $40. Electronic applications accepted. *Expenses:* Tuition, state resident: full-time $5805; part-time $322.50 per credit hour. Tuition, nonresident: full-time $14,670; part-time $815 per credit hour. *Financial support:* In 2011–12, 8 research assistantships with full tuition reimbursements (averaging $13,126 per year), 4 teaching assistantships with full tuition reimbursements (averaging $12,741 per year) were awarded; Federal Work-Study, institutionally sponsored loans, scholarships/grants, and unspecified assistantships also available. Financial award application deadline: 4/1; financial award applicants required to submit FAFSA. *Faculty research:* Food preservation, food chemistry, food safety, food processing, product development. *Unit head:* Dr. Juan Silva, Professor and Interim Head, 662-325-3200, Fax: 662-325-8728, E-mail: jls@ra.msstate.edu. Web site: http://www.fsnhp.msstate.edu.

New Mexico State University, Graduate School, College of Agricultural, Consumer and Environmental Sciences, Department of Family and Consumer Sciences, Las Cruces, NM 88003-8001. Offers family and child science (MS); family and consumer science education (MS); food science and technology (MS); marriage and family therapy (MS); nutrition and dietetic science (MS). Part-time programs available. *Faculty:* 11 full-time (9 women), 1 (woman) part-time/adjunct. *Students:* 30 full-time (29 women), 18 part-time (15 women); includes 22 minority (1 American Indian or Alaska Native, non-Hispanic/Latino; 1 Asian, non-Hispanic/Latino; 20 Hispanic/Latino), 5 international. Average age 31. 21 applicants, 67% accepted, 12 enrolled. In 2011, 21 master's awarded. *Degree requirements:* For master's, comprehensive exam (for some programs), thesis (for some programs), oral exam. *Entrance requirements:* For master's, GRE, 3 letters of reference,

428 facebook.com/petersonspublishing

Peterson's Graduate Programs in the Physical Sciences, Mathematics, Agricultural Sciences, the Environment & Natural Resources 2013

resume. Additional exam requirements/recommendations for international students: Required—TOEFL (minimum score 550 paper-based; 0 computer-based; 79 iBT), IELTS (minimum score 6.5). *Application deadline:* For fall admission, 6/30 priority date for domestic students, 3/1 for international students; for spring admission, 11/30 for domestic and international students. Applications are processed on a rolling basis. Application fee: $40 ($50 for international students). Electronic applications accepted. *Expenses:* Tuition, state resident: full-time $5004; part-time $208.50 per credit. Tuition, nonresident: full-time $17,446; part-time $726.90 per credit. *Financial support:* In 2011–12, 1 fellowship (averaging $3,754 per year), 3 research assistantships (averaging $21,281 per year), 10 teaching assistantships (averaging $11,851 per year) were awarded; career-related internships or fieldwork, Federal Work-Study, scholarships/grants, health care benefits, and unspecified assistantships also available. Support available to part-time students. Financial award application deadline: 3/1; financial award applicants required to submit FAFSA. *Faculty research:* Work, stress, and family functioning; food product analysis; childhood obesity; relationship education. *Total annual research expenditures:* $750,000. *Unit head:* Dr. Esther Devall, Head, 575-646-3936, Fax: 575-646-1889, E-mail: edevall@nmsu.edu. *Application contact:* Dr. Roselyn Smitley, Coordinator, 575-646-1183, Fax: 575-646-1889, E-mail: rosmite@nmsu.edu. Web site: http://fcs.nmsu.edu.

New York University, Steinhardt School of Culture, Education, and Human Development, Department of Nutrition, Food Studies, and Public Health, Program in Food Studies and Food Management, New York, NY 10012-1019. Offers food studies (MA), including food culture, food systems; food studies and food management (PhD). Part-time programs available. *Degree requirements:* For master's, thesis (for some programs); for doctorate, thesis/dissertation. *Entrance requirements:* For doctorate, GRE General Test, interview. Additional exam requirements/recommendations for international students: Required—TOEFL. Electronic applications accepted. *Faculty research:* Cultural and social history of food, food systems and agriculture, food and aesthetics, political economy of food.

North Carolina State University, Graduate School, College of Agriculture and Life Sciences, Department of Food Science, Raleigh, NC 27695. Offers MFS, MS, PhD. *Degree requirements:* For master's, thesis (for some programs); for doctorate, thesis/dissertation. *Entrance requirements:* For master's and doctorate, GRE. Electronic applications accepted. *Faculty research:* Food safety, value-added food products, environmental quality, nutrition and health, biotechnology.

North Dakota State University, College of Graduate and Interdisciplinary Studies, College of Agriculture, Food Systems, and Natural Resources, Department of Cereal and Food Sciences, Fargo, ND 58108. Offers cereal science (MS, PhD). Part-time programs available. *Faculty:* 4 full-time (1 woman). *Students:* 15 full-time (10 women), 5 part-time (4 women), 15 international. 8 applicants, 38% accepted, 2 enrolled. In 2011, 2 master's, 2 doctorates awarded. Terminal master's awarded for partial completion of doctoral program. *Degree requirements:* For master's, comprehensive exam, thesis; for doctorate, comprehensive exam, thesis/dissertation. *Entrance requirements:* Additional exam requirements/recommendations for international students: Required—TOEFL (minimum score 550 paper-based; 213 computer-based; 79 iBT), IELTS (minimum score 6). *Application deadline:* For fall admission, 3/15 priority date for domestic students; for spring admission, 9/30 for domestic students. Application fee: $35. *Financial support:* In 2011–12, 15 research assistantships with full tuition reimbursements (averaging $12,000 per year) were awarded; career-related internships or fieldwork and unspecified assistantships also available. Support available to part-time students. *Faculty research:* Legume food products, cereal proteins and product quality, oilseeds functional components. *Unit head:* Dr. Deland Myers, Chair, 701-231-7711, Fax: 701-231-5171, E-mail: deland.myers@ndsu.edu. *Application contact:* Sonya Goergen, Marketing, Recruitment, and Public Relations Coordinator, 701-231-7033, Fax: 701-231-6524.

North Dakota State University, College of Graduate and Interdisciplinary Studies, Interdisciplinary Program in Food Safety, Fargo, ND 58108. Offers MS, PhD. Part-time programs available. Postbaccalaureate distance learning degree programs offered (minimal on-campus study). *Faculty:* 10 full-time (5 women), 3 part-time/adjunct (2 women). *Students:* 8 full-time (5 women), 4 part-time (3 women), 7 international. Average age 25. 22 applicants, 18% accepted, 4 enrolled. In 2011, 3 master's awarded. Terminal master's awarded for partial completion of doctoral program. *Degree requirements:* For master's, thesis; for doctorate, comprehensive exam, thesis/dissertation. *Entrance requirements:* Additional exam requirements/recommendations for international students: Required—TOEFL (minimum score 525 paper-based; 197 computer-based; 71 iBT), TWE (minimum score 5). *Application deadline:* Applications are processed on a rolling basis. Application fee: $35. Electronic applications accepted. *Financial support:* In 2011–12, 9 research assistantships with full tuition reimbursements (averaging $16,000 per year) were awarded; scholarships/grants also available. *Faculty research:* Mycotoxins in grain, pathogens in meat systems, sensor development for food pathogens. *Unit head:* Dr. Clifford Hall, Associate Director, 701-231-6359, Fax: 701-231-5171, E-mail: clifford.hall@ndsu.edu. *Application contact:* Sonya Goergen, Marketing, Recruitment, and Public Relations Coordinator, 701-231-7033, Fax: 701-231-6524.

Nova Scotia Agricultural College, Research and Graduate Studies, Truro, NS B2N 5E3, Canada. Offers agriculture (M Sc), including air quality, animal behavior, animal molecular genetics, animal nutrition, animal technology, aquaculture, botany, crop management, crop physiology, ecology, environmental microbiology, food science, horticulture, nutrient management, pest management, physiology, plant biotechnology, plant pathology, soil chemistry, soil fertility, waste management and composting, water quality. Program offered jointly with Dalhousie University. Part-time programs available. *Degree requirements:* For master's, thesis, ATC Exam Teaching Assistantship. *Entrance requirements:* For master's, honors B Sc, minimum GPA of 3.0. Additional exam requirements/recommendations for international students: Required—TOEFL (minimum score 580 paper-based; 237 computer-based; 92 iBT), IELTS, Michigan English Language Assessment Battery, CanTEST, CAEL. *Faculty research:* Bio-product development, organic agriculture, nutrient management, air and water quality, agricultural biotechnology.

The Ohio State University, Graduate School, College of Food, Agricultural, and Environmental Sciences, Department of Food Science and Nutrition, Columbus, OH 43210. Offers food science (MS, PhD). *Accreditation:* AND. *Faculty:* 15. *Students:* 48 full-time (31 women), 15 part-time (7 women); includes 11 minority (5 Black or African American, non-Hispanic/Latino; 4 Asian, non-Hispanic/Latino; 2 Hispanic/Latino), 29 international. Average age 28. In 2011, 10 master's, 10 doctorates awarded. *Degree requirements:* For master's, thesis optional; for doctorate, thesis/dissertation. *Entrance requirements:* For master's and doctorate, GRE General Test. Additional exam requirements/recommendations for international students: Required—TOEFL (minimum score 550 paper-based; 213 computer-based), IELTS (minimum score 6.5), or Michigan English Language Assessment Battery (minimum score 82). *Application deadline:* For fall admission, 8/15 priority date for domestic students, 7/1 for international students; for winter admission, 12/1 priority date for domestic students, 11/1 for international students; for spring admission, 3/1 priority date for domestic students, 2/1 for international students. Applications are processed on a rolling basis. Application fee: $40 ($50 for international students). Electronic applications accepted. *Expenses:* Tuition, state resident: full-time $11,400. Tuition, nonresident: full-time $28,125. Tuition and fees vary according to course load, degree level, campus/location and program. *Financial support:* Fellowships, research assistantships, Federal Work-Study, and institutionally sponsored loans available. Support available to part-time students. *Unit head:* Richard Linton, Chair, 614-247-7881, E-mail: linton.60@osu.edu. *Application contact:* Graduate Admissions, 614-292-6031, Fax: 614-292-3656, E-mail: gradadmissions@osu.edu. Web site: http://fst.osu.edu/.

Oklahoma State University, College of Agricultural Science and Natural Resources, Department of Animal Science, Stillwater, OK 74078. Offers animal sciences (M Ag, MS); food science (MS, PhD). *Faculty:* 26 full-time (4 women), 3 part-time/adjunct (0 women). *Students:* 23 full-time (15 women), 39 part-time (21 women); includes 4 minority (3 Hispanic/Latino; 1 Two or more races, non-Hispanic/Latino), 21 international. Average age 27. 106 applicants, 19% accepted, 17 enrolled. In 2011, 23 master's, 7 doctorates awarded. *Degree requirements:* For master's, thesis; for doctorate, comprehensive exam, thesis/dissertation. *Entrance requirements:* For master's and doctorate, GRE or GMAT. Additional exam requirements/recommendations for international students: Required—TOEFL (minimum score 550 paper-based; 79 iBT). *Application deadline:* For fall admission, 3/1 for international students; for spring admission, 8/1 for international students. Applications are processed on a rolling basis. Application fee: $40 ($75 for international students). Electronic applications accepted. *Expenses:* Tuition, state resident: full-time $4044; part-time $168.50 per credit hour. Tuition, nonresident: full-time $16,008; part-time $667 per credit hour. *Required fees:* $2122; $88.45 per credit hour. One-time fee: $50. Tuition and fees vary according to course load and campus/location. *Financial support:* In 2011–12, 32 research assistantships (averaging $14,481 per year), 1 teaching assistantship (averaging $11,064 per year) were awarded; career-related internships or fieldwork, Federal Work-Study, scholarships/grants, health care benefits, tuition waivers (partial), and unspecified assistantships also available. Support available to part-time students. Financial award application deadline: 3/1; financial award applicants required to submit FAFSA. *Faculty research:* Quantitative trait loci identification for economical traits in swine/beef; waste management strategies in livestock; endocrine control of reproductive processes in farm animals; cholesterol synthesis, inhibition, and reduction; food safety research. *Unit head:* Dr. Ronald Kensinger, Head, 405-744-6062, Fax: 405-744-7390. *Application contact:* Dr. Sheryl Tucker, Dean, 405-744-7099, Fax: 405-744-0355, E-mail: grad-i@okstate.edu. Web site: http://www.ansi.okstate.edu.

Oregon State University, Graduate School, College of Agricultural Sciences, Department of Food Science and Technology, Corvallis, OR 97331. Offers M Agr, MAIS, MS, PhD. *Degree requirements:* For master's, thesis (for some programs); for doctorate, thesis/dissertation. *Entrance requirements:* For master's and doctorate, GRE General Test, minimum GPA of 3.0 in last 90 hours. Additional exam requirements/recommendations for international students: Required—TOEFL. *Faculty research:* Diet, cancer, and anticarcinogenesis; sensory analysis; chemistry and biochemistry.

Penn State University Park, Graduate School, College of Agricultural Sciences, Department of Food Science, State College, University Park, PA 16802-1503. Offers MS, PhD. *Unit head:* Dr. Bruce A. McPheron, Dean, 814-865-2541, Fax: 814-865-3103, E-mail: bam10@psu.edu. *Application contact:* Cynthia E. Nicosia, Director of Graduate Enrollment Services, 814-865-1834, E-mail: cey1@psu.edu. Web site: http://foodscience.psu.edu.

Purdue University, Graduate School, College of Agriculture, Department of Food Science, West Lafayette, IN 47907. Offers MS, PhD. *Faculty:* 21 full-time (7 women), 12 part-time/adjunct (0 women). *Students:* 53 full-time (40 women), 4 part-time (3 women); includes 3 minority (1 Black or African American, non-

Peterson's Graduate Programs in the Physical Sciences, Mathematics, Agricultural Sciences, the Environment & Natural Resources 2013

facebook.com/petersonspublishing **429**

Food Science and Technology

Hispanic/Latino; 2 Asian, non-Hispanic/Latino), 33 international. Average age 28. 122 applicants, 11% accepted, 13 enrolled. In 2011, 14 master's, 5 doctorates awarded. *Degree requirements:* For master's, thesis (for some programs); for doctorate, thesis/dissertation, teaching assistantship. *Entrance requirements:* For master's, GRE General Test, minimum score (before 8/2011) Verbal 400, Quantitative 500, Analytical 4.0; (After 8/2011) Verbal 146, Quantitative 144, Analytical 4.0, minimum undergraduate GPA of 3.0 or equivalent; for doctorate, GRE General Test, minimum score (before 8/2011) Verbal 400, Quantitative 500, Analytical 4.0; (After 8/2011) Verbal 146, Quantitative 144, Analytical 4.0, minimum undergraduate GPA of 3.0 or equivalent; master's degree with minimum GPA of 3.0 or equivalent. Additional exam requirements/recommendations for international students: Required—TOEFL (minimum score 575 paper-based; 77 iBT). *Application deadline:* For fall admission, 7/15 priority date for domestic students, 7/15 for international students; for spring admission, 11/15 for domestic and international students. Applications are processed on a rolling basis. Application fee: $60 ($75 for international students). Electronic applications accepted. *Financial support:* In 2011–12, 4 fellowships (averaging $24,500 per year), 38 research assistantships (averaging $13,500 per year), 1 teaching assistantship (averaging $13,500 per year) were awarded; career-related internships or fieldwork also available. Support available to part-time students. Financial award application deadline: 4/1; financial award applicants required to submit FAFSA. *Faculty research:* Processing, technology, microbiology, chemistry of foods, carbohydrate chemistry. *Unit head:* Dr. R. Chandrasekaran, Head/Graduate Committee Chair, 765-494-8328, Fax: 765-494-7953, E-mail: nielsens@foodsci.purdue.edu. *Application contact:* Dr. Mitzi L Barnett, Graduate Contact for Admissions, 765-494-8256, E-mail: mbarnett@purdue.edu.

Rutgers, The State University of New Jersey, New Brunswick, Graduate School-New Brunswick, Program in Food Science, Piscataway, NJ 08854-8097. Offers M Phil, MS, PhD. Part-time and evening/weekend programs available. Postbaccalaureate distance learning degree programs offered (minimal on-campus study). *Degree requirements:* For master's, thesis or alternative; for doctorate, thesis/dissertation. *Entrance requirements:* For master's and doctorate, GRE General Test. *Faculty research:* Nutraceuticals and functional foods, food and flavor analysis, food chemistry and biochemistry, food nanotechnology, food engineering and processing.

South Dakota State University, Graduate School, College of Education and Human Sciences, Department of Nutrition, Food Science and Hospitality, Brookings, SD 57007. Offers dietetics (MS); nutrition, food science and hospitality (MFCS); nutritional sciences (MS, PhD). Part-time programs available. *Degree requirements:* For master's, comprehensive exam (for some programs), thesis (for some programs), oral exam. *Entrance requirements:* Additional exam requirements/recommendations for international students: Required—TOEFL (minimum score 525 paper-based). *Faculty research:* Food chemistry, bone density, functional food, nutrition education, nutrition biochemistry.

Texas A&M University, College of Agriculture and Life Sciences, Department of Nutrition and Food Science, College Station, TX 77843. Offers food science and technology (M Agr); nutrition (MS, PhD). *Faculty:* 15. *Students:* 56 full-time (40 women), 5 part-time (2 women); includes 8 minority (2 Black or African American, non-Hispanic/Latino; 3 Asian, non-Hispanic/Latino; 3 Hispanic/Latino), 25 international. *Degree requirements:* For master's, thesis; for doctorate, thesis/dissertation. *Entrance requirements:* For master's and doctorate, GRE General Test. Additional exam requirements/recommendations for international students: Required—TOEFL. *Application deadline:* For fall admission, 2/1 priority date for domestic students; for spring admission, 10/1 priority date for domestic students. Applications are processed on a rolling basis. Application fee: $50 ($75 for international students). *Expenses:* Tuition, state resident: full-time $5437; part-time $226.55 per credit hour. Tuition, nonresident: full-time $12,949; part-time $539.55 per credit hour. *Required fees:* $2741. *Financial support:* Fellowships, research assistantships, teaching assistantships, career-related internships or fieldwork, and scholarships/grants available. *Faculty research:* Food safety, microbiology, product development. *Unit head:* Dr. Jimmy T. Keeton, Department Head, 979-458-3428, E-mail: jkeeton@tamu.edu. *Application contact:* Graduate Admissions, 979-845-1044, E-mail: admissions@tamu.edu. Web site: http://nfs.tamu.edu.

Texas A&M University, College of Agriculture and Life Sciences, Department of Soil and Crop Sciences, College Station, TX 77843. Offers agronomy (M Agr, MS, PhD); food science and technology (MS, PhD); genetics (PhD); molecular and environmental plant sciences (MS, PhD); plant breeding (MS, PhD); soil science (MS, PhD). *Faculty:* 37. *Students:* 98 full-time (36 women), 29 part-time (4 women); includes 12 minority (4 Black or African American, non-Hispanic/Latino; 3 Asian, non-Hispanic/Latino; 5 Hispanic/Latino), 42 international. Average age 26. In 2011, 4 master's, 8 doctorates awarded. *Degree requirements:* For master's, thesis; for doctorate, thesis/dissertation. *Entrance requirements:* For master's and doctorate, GRE General Test. Additional exam requirements/recommendations for international students: Required—TOEFL. *Application deadline:* For fall admission, 3/1 priority date for domestic students; for spring admission, 8/1 for domestic students. Applications are processed on a rolling basis. Application fee: $50 ($75 for international students). *Expenses:* Tuition, state resident: full-time $5437; part-time $226.55 per credit hour. Tuition, nonresident: full-time $12,949; part-time $539.55 per credit hour. *Required fees:* $2741. *Financial support:* In 2011–12, fellowships (averaging $16,000 per year), research assistantships with partial tuition reimbursements (averaging $15,000 per year) were awarded; career-related internships or fieldwork, Federal Work-

Study, and institutionally sponsored loans also available. *Faculty research:* Soil and crop management, turfgrass science, weed science, cereal chemistry, food protein chemistry. *Unit head:* Dr. David D. Baltensperger, Department Head, 979-845-3001, E-mail: dbaltensperger@ag.tamu.edu. *Application contact:* Graduate Admissions, 979-845-1044, E-mail: admissions@tamu.edu. Web site: http://soilcrop.tamu.edu.

Texas Tech University, Graduate School, College of Agricultural Sciences and Natural Resources, Department of Animal and Food Sciences, Lubbock, TX 79409-2141. Offers animal science (MS, PhD); food science (MS). *Faculty:* 16 full-time (5 women). *Students:* 66 full-time (30 women), 10 part-time (2 women); includes 4 minority (1 Asian, non-Hispanic/Latino; 2 Hispanic/Latino; 1 Two or more races, non-Hispanic/Latino), 15 international. Average age 27. 80 applicants, 44% accepted, 27 enrolled. In 2011, 12 master's, 6 doctorates awarded. *Degree requirements:* For master's, thesis or alternative, internship (M Agr); for doctorate, thesis/dissertation. *Entrance requirements:* For master's and doctorate, GRE General Test, formal approval from departmental committee. Additional exam requirements/recommendations for international students: Required—TOEFL (minimum score 550 paper-based; 213 computer-based; 79 iBT). *Application deadline:* For fall admission, 6/1 priority date for domestic students, 1/15 for international students; for spring admission, 9/1 priority date for domestic students, 6/15 for international students. Applications are processed on a rolling basis. Application fee: $50 ($75 for international students). Electronic applications accepted. *Expenses:* Tuition, state resident: full-time $5899; part-time $245.80 per credit hour. Tuition, nonresident: full-time $13,411; part-time $558.80 per credit hour. *Required fees:* $2680.60; $86.50 per credit hour. $920.30 per semester. *Financial support:* In 2011–12, 40 students received support. Application deadline: 4/15; applicants required to submit FAFSA. *Faculty research:* Animal nutrition, health and welfare (species of emphasis: beef cattle, dairy cattle, swine, horse, sheep and goat); animal physiology and reproduction; meat science and muscle biology; food safety, security and public health, food science. *Total annual research expenditures:* $2.9 million. *Unit head:* Dr. Leslie D. Thompson, Chairman, 806-742-2805 Ext. 223, Fax: 806-742-0898, E-mail: leslie.thompson@ttu.edu. *Application contact:* Sandy Gellner, Graduate Secretary, 806-742-2805 Ext. 221, Fax: 806-742-0898, E-mail: sandra.gellner@ttu.edu. Web site: http://www.afs.ttu.edu/.

Texas Woman's University, Graduate School, College of Health Sciences, Department of Nutrition and Food Sciences, Denton, TX 76201. Offers exercise and sports nutrition (MS); food science (MS); food systems administration (MS); nutrition (MS, PhD). Part-time and evening/weekend programs available. *Faculty:* 14 full-time (7 women). *Students:* 94 full-time (88 women), 79 part-time (73 women); includes 42 minority (10 Black or African American, non-Hispanic/Latino; 15 Asian, non-Hispanic/Latino; 17 Hispanic/Latino), 13 international. Average age 28. 103 applicants, 85% accepted, 51 enrolled. In 2011, 58 master's, 2 doctorates awarded. *Degree requirements:* For master's, comprehensive exam, thesis or alternative; for doctorate, comprehensive exam, thesis/dissertation, qualifying exam. *Entrance requirements:* For master's, GRE General Test (preferred minimum score 143 [350 old version] Verbal, 141 [450 old version] Quantitative), minimum GPA of 3.25, resume; for doctorate, GRE General Test (preferred minimum score 150 [450 old version] Verbal, 141 [550 old version] Quantitative), minimum GPA of 3.5 on last 60 undergraduate hours and graduate course work, 2 letters of reference, resume. Additional exam requirements/recommendations for international students: Required—TOEFL (minimum score 550 paper-based; 213 computer-based; 79 iBT). *Application deadline:* For fall admission, 7/1 priority date for domestic students, 3/1 for international students; for spring admission, 12/1 priority date for domestic students, 7/1 for international students. Applications are processed on a rolling basis. Application fee: $50 ($75 for international students). Electronic applications accepted. *Expenses:* Tuition, state resident: full-time $3834; part-time $213 per credit hour. Tuition, nonresident: full-time $9468; part-time $526 per credit hour. *Required fees:* $213 per credit hour. Tuition and fees vary according to course load. *Financial support:* In 2011–12, 138 students received support, including 23 research assistantships (averaging $12,942 per year), teaching assistantships (averaging $12,942 per year); career-related internships or fieldwork, Federal Work-Study, institutionally sponsored loans, scholarships/grants, traineeships, health care benefits, and unspecified assistantships also available. Support available to part-time students. Financial award application deadline: 3/1; financial award applicants required to submit FAFSA. *Faculty research:* Bioactive food components and cancer, nutraceuticals and functional foods in diabetes, obesity and bone health, food safety, dietary modulation of dyslipidemia, childhood obesity prevention. *Total annual research expenditures:* $612,544. *Unit head:* Dr. Chandan Prasad, Chair, 940-898-2636, Fax: 940-898-2634, E-mail: cprasad@twu.edu. *Application contact:* Dr. Samuel Wheeler, Assistant Director of Admissions, 940-898-3188, Fax: 940-898-3081, E-mail: wheelersr@twu.edu. Web site: http://www.twu.edu/nutrition-food-sciences/.

Tuskegee University, Graduate Programs, College of Agricultural, Environmental and Natural Sciences, Department of Food and Nutritional Sciences, Tuskegee, AL 36088. Offers MS. *Faculty:* 4 full-time (3 women). *Students:* 8 full-time (7 women); includes 6 minority (all Black or African American, non-Hispanic/Latino), 2 international. Average age 28. In 2011, 7 master's awarded. *Degree requirements:* For master's, thesis. *Entrance requirements:* For master's, GRE General Test. Additional exam requirements/recommendations for international students: Required—TOEFL (minimum score 500 paper-based; 69 computer-based). *Application deadline:* For fall admission, 7/15 for domestic students. Applications are processed on a rolling basis. Application fee: $25 ($35 for international students). *Expenses: Tuition:* Full-time $17,070; part-time $705

430 facebook.com/petersonspublishing

Peterson's Graduate Programs in the Physical Sciences, Mathematics, Agricultural Sciences, the Environment & Natural Resources 2013

per credit hour. *Financial support:* Application deadline: 4/15. *Unit head:* Dr. Ralphenia Pace, Head, 334-727-8162. *Application contact:* Dr. Robert L. Laney, Jr., Vice President/Director of Admissions and Enrollment Management, 334-727-8580, Fax: 334-727-5750, E-mail: planey@tuskegee.edu.

Universidad de las Américas–Puebla, Division of Graduate Studies, School of Engineering, Program in Chemical Engineering, Puebla, Mexico. Offers chemical engineering (MS); food technology (MS). Part-time and evening/weekend programs available. *Degree requirements:* For master's, one foreign language, thesis. *Faculty research:* Food science, reactors, oil industry, biotechnology.

Universidad de las Américas–Puebla, Division of Graduate Studies, School of Engineering, Program in Food Sciences, Puebla, Mexico. Offers MS.

Université de Moncton, School of Food Science, Nutrition and Family Studies, Moncton, NB E1A 3E9, Canada. Offers foods/nutrition (M Sc). Part-time programs available. *Degree requirements:* For master's, one foreign language, thesis. *Entrance requirements:* For master's, previous course work in statistics. Electronic applications accepted. *Faculty research:* Clinic nutrition (anemia, elderly, osteoporosis), applied nutrition, metabolic activities of lactic bacteria, solubility of low density lipoproteins, bile acids.

Université Laval, Faculty of Agricultural and Food Sciences, Department of Food Sciences and Nutrition, Programs in Food Sciences and Technology, Québec, QC G1K 7P4, Canada. Offers M Sc, PhD. Terminal master's awarded for partial completion of doctoral program. *Degree requirements:* For master's, thesis (for some programs); for doctorate, comprehensive exam, thesis/dissertation. *Entrance requirements:* For master's and doctorate, knowledge of French and English. Electronic applications accepted.

University of Arkansas, Graduate School, Dale Bumpers College of Agricultural, Food and Life Sciences, Department of Food Science, Fayetteville, AR 72701-1201. Offers MS, PhD. *Students:* 13 full-time (4 women), 27 part-time (16 women); includes 4 minority (3 Black or African American, non-Hispanic/Latino; 1 Hispanic/Latino), 19 international. In 2011, 8 master's, 4 doctorates awarded. *Degree requirements:* For master's, thesis; for doctorate, thesis/dissertation. *Application deadline:* For fall admission, 4/1 for international students; for spring admission, 10/1 for international students. Applications are processed on a rolling basis. Application fee: $40 ($50 for international students). Electronic applications accepted. *Financial support:* In 2011–12, 25 research assistantships were awarded; fellowships with tuition reimbursements, teaching assistantships, career-related internships or fieldwork, Federal Work-Study, scholarships/grants, and unspecified assistantships also available. Support available to part-time students. Financial award application deadline: 4/1; financial award applicants required to submit FAFSA. *Unit head:* Dr. Jean-Francois Meullenet, Department Head, 479-575-4605, E-mail: jfmeull@uark.edu. *Application contact:* Graduate Admissions, 479-575-6246, Fax: 479-575-5908, E-mail: gradinfo@uark.edu. Web site: http://www.foodscience.uark.edu/.

University of Arkansas, Graduate School, Dale Bumpers College of Agricultural, Food and Life Sciences, Program in Agricultural, Food and Life Sciences, Fayetteville, AR 72701-1201. Offers MS. Part-time and evening/weekend programs available. Postbaccalaureate distance learning degree programs offered (minimal on-campus study). *Students:* 1 full-time (0 women), 26 part-time (12 women); includes 3 minority (1 Black or African American, non-Hispanic/Latino; 1 American Indian or Alaska Native, non-Hispanic/Latino; 1 Hispanic/Latino). In 2011, 5 master's awarded. *Degree requirements:* For master's, thesis optional. *Application deadline:* For fall admission, 4/1 for international students; for spring admission, 10/1 for international students. Applications are processed on a rolling basis. Application fee: $40 ($50 for international students). Electronic applications accepted. *Financial support:* Fellowships, research assistantships, teaching assistantships, career-related internships or fieldwork, and Federal Work-Study available. Support available to part-time students. Financial award application deadline: 4/1; financial award applicants required to submit FAFSA. *Unit head:* Dr. Michael E. Vayda, Dean, 479-575-2034, E-mail: mvayda@uark.edu. *Application contact:* Diana Bisbee, Program Coordinator, 479-575-2025, E-mail: dbisbee@uark.edu. Web site: http://bumperscollege.uark.edu/.

The University of British Columbia, Faculty of Land and Food Systems, Program in Food Science, Vancouver, BC V6T 1Z1, Canada. Offers M Sc, MFS, PhD. *Degree requirements:* For master's, thesis; for doctorate, comprehensive exam, thesis/dissertation. *Entrance requirements:* Additional exam requirements/recommendations for international students: Required—TOEFL (minimum score 577 paper-based; 233 computer-based; 90 iBT), IELTS (minimum score 6.5). Electronic applications accepted. *Faculty research:* Food chemistry and biochemistry, food process science, food toxicology and safety, food microbiology, food biotechnology.

University of California, Davis, Graduate Studies, Graduate Group in Food Science, Davis, CA 95616. Offers MS, PhD. Terminal master's awarded for partial completion of doctoral program. *Degree requirements:* For master's, comprehensive exam (for some programs), thesis (for some programs); for doctorate, thesis/dissertation. *Entrance requirements:* For master's and doctorate, GRE General Test, minimum GPA of 3.0. Additional exam requirements/recommendations for international students: Required—TOEFL (minimum score 550 paper-based; 213 computer-based). Electronic applications accepted.

University of Delaware, College of Agriculture and Natural Resources, Department of Animal and Food Sciences, Newark, DE 19716. Offers animal sciences (MS, PhD); food sciences (MS). Part-time programs available. Terminal

master's awarded for partial completion of doctoral program. *Degree requirements:* For master's, thesis; for doctorate, comprehensive exam, thesis/dissertation. *Entrance requirements:* For master's and doctorate, GRE General Test. Additional exam requirements/recommendations for international students: Required—TOEFL. Electronic applications accepted. *Faculty research:* Food chemistry, food microbiology, process engineering technology, packaging, food analysis, microbial genetics, molecular endocrinology, growth physiology, avian immunology and virology, monogastric nutrition, avian genomics.

University of Florida, Graduate School, College of Agricultural and Life Sciences, Department of Food Science and Human Nutrition, Gainesville, FL 32611. Offers nutritional sciences (MS, PhD). *Faculty:* 20 full-time (8 women). *Students:* 75 full-time (48 women), 11 part-time (4 women); includes 16 minority (6 Black or African American, non-Hispanic/Latino; 6 Asian, non-Hispanic/Latino; 4 Hispanic/Latino), 39 international. Average age 28. 215 applicants, 15% accepted, 27 enrolled. In 2011, 27 master's, 3 doctorates awarded. *Degree requirements:* For master's, thesis optional; for doctorate, thesis/dissertation. *Entrance requirements:* For master's and doctorate, GRE General Test, minimum GPA of 3.0. Additional exam requirements/recommendations for international students: Required—TOEFL. *Application deadline:* For fall admission, 6/1 priority date for domestic students. Applications are processed on a rolling basis. Application fee: $30. Electronic applications accepted. *Financial support:* Fellowships, research assistantships, teaching assistantships, and career-related internships or fieldwork available. Financial award applicants required to submit FAFSA. *Faculty research:* Pesticide research, nutritional biochemistry and microbiology, food safety and toxicology assessment and dietetics, food chemistry. *Unit head:* Dr. Neil F. Shay, Chair, 352-392-1991, Fax: 352-392-9467, E-mail: nshay@ufl.edu. *Application contact:* Dr. Harry Sitren, Coordinator, 352-392-1991 Ext. 216, Fax: 352-392-9467, E-mail: hssitren@ifas.ufl.edu. Web site: http://fshn.ifas.ufl.edu/.

University of Georgia, College of Agricultural and Environmental Sciences, Department of Food Science and Technology, Athens, GA 30602. Offers food science (MS, PhD); food technology (MFT). Part-time programs available. *Faculty:* 18 full-time (5 women), 3 part-time/adjunct (0 women). *Students:* 58 full-time (43 women), 18 part-time (10 women); includes 14 minority (6 Black or African American, non-Hispanic/Latino; 6 Asian, non-Hispanic/Latino; 1 Hispanic/Latino; 1 Two or more races, non-Hispanic/Latino), 29 international. Average age 28. 135 applicants, 24% accepted, 17 enrolled. In 2011, 10 master's, 4 doctorates awarded. *Degree requirements:* For master's, thesis; for doctorate, thesis/dissertation. *Entrance requirements:* For master's and doctorate, GRE General Test. Additional exam requirements/recommendations for international students: Required—TOEFL (minimum score 550 paper-based; 213 computer-based). *Application deadline:* For fall admission, 7/1 for domestic students, 5/1 for international students; for spring admission, 11/15 for domestic students, 10/1 for international students. Applications are processed on a rolling basis. Application fee: $50. Electronic applications accepted. *Financial support:* Fellowships, research assistantships, teaching assistantships, and unspecified assistantships available. *Total annual research expenditures:* $1.5 million. *Unit head:* Dr. Rakesh K. Singh, Head, 706-542-2286, E-mail: rsingh@uga.edu. *Application contact:* Dr. Mark A. Harrison, Graduate Coordinator, 706-542-1088, Fax: 706-542-1050, E-mail: mahfst@uga.edu. Web site: http://www.caes.uga.edu/departments/fst/.

University of Guelph, Graduate Studies, Ontario Agricultural College, Department of Food Science, Guelph, ON N1G 2W1, Canada. Offers food safety and quality assurance (M Sc); food science (M Sc, PhD). *Degree requirements:* For master's, thesis; for doctorate, comprehensive exam, thesis/dissertation. *Entrance requirements:* For master's, minimum B average during previous 2 years of honors B Sc degree; for doctorate, minimum B average. Additional exam requirements/recommendations for international students: Required—TOEFL (minimum score 550 paper-based; 213 computer-based), IELTS (minimum score 6.5). Electronic applications accepted. *Faculty research:* Food chemistry, food microbiology, food processing, preservation and utilization.

University of Hawaii at Manoa, Graduate Division, College of Tropical Agriculture and Human Resources, Department of Human Nutrition, Food and Animal Sciences, Program in Food Science, Honolulu, HI 96822. Offers MS. Part-time programs available. *Degree requirements:* For master's, thesis optional. *Entrance requirements:* For master's, GRE General Test. Additional exam requirements/recommendations for international students: Required—TOEFL (minimum score 580 paper-based; 237 computer-based; 92 iBT), IELTS (minimum score 5). *Faculty research:* Biochemistry of natural products, sensory evaluation, food processing, food chemistry, food safety.

University of Idaho, College of Graduate Studies, College of Agricultural and Life Sciences, Bistate School of Food Science, Moscow, ID 83844-2312. Offers MS, PhD. *Faculty:* 3 full-time. *Students:* 6 full-time, 3 part-time. Average age 29. In 2011, 2 master's awarded. *Entrance requirements:* For master's, minimum GPA of 2.8. *Application deadline:* For fall admission, 8/1 for domestic students; for spring admission, 12/15 for domestic students. Applications are processed on a rolling basis. Application fee: $60. Electronic applications accepted. *Expenses:* Tuition, state resident: full-time $3874; part-time $334 per credit hour. Tuition, nonresident: full-time $16,394; part-time $861 per credit hour. *Required fees:* $2808; $99 per credit hour. Tuition and fees vary according to program. *Financial support:* Research assistantships and teaching assistantships available. Financial award applicants required to submit FAFSA. *Faculty research:* Food biotechnology, food and environmental toxicology, bio-preservation of food

Peterson's Graduate Programs in the Physical Sciences, Mathematics, Agricultural Sciences, the Environment & Natural Resources 2013

facebook.com/petersonspublishing **431**

Food Science and Technology

products, conversion of biomass. *Unit head:* Dr. Denise Smith, Director, 208-885-0707, E-mail: foodscience@uidaho.edu. *Application contact:* Erick Larson, Director of Graduate Admissions, 208-885-4723, E-mail: gadms@uidaho.edu. Web site: http://www.cals.uidaho.edu/sfs/.

University of Illinois at Urbana–Champaign, Graduate College, College of Agricultural, Consumer and Environmental Sciences, Department of Food Science and Human Nutrition, Champaign, IL 61820. Offers food science (MS); food science and human nutrition (MS, PhD), including professional science (MS); human nutrition (MS). Part-time programs available. Postbaccalaureate distance learning degree programs offered (minimal on-campus study). *Faculty:* 25 full-time (11 women), 1 (woman) part-time/adjunct. *Students:* 72 full-time (51 women), 28 part-time (20 women); includes 13 minority (2 Black or African American, non-Hispanic/Latino; 9 Asian, non-Hispanic/Latino; 1 Hispanic/Latino; 1 Two or more races, non-Hispanic/Latino), 42 international. 175 applicants, 27% accepted, 37 enrolled. In 2011, 30 master's, 3 doctorates awarded. *Entrance requirements:* For master's and doctorate, GRE, minimum GPA of 3.0. Additional exam requirements/recommendations for international students: Required—TOEFL (minimum score 550 paper-based; 213 computer-based; 79 iBT) or IELTS (minimum score 6.5). *Application deadline:* Applications are processed on a rolling basis. Application fee: $75 ($90 for international students). Electronic applications accepted. *Financial support:* In 2011–12, 14 fellowships, 44 research assistantships, 16 teaching assistantships were awarded; tuition waivers (full and partial) also available. *Unit head:* Faye L. Dong, Head, 217-244-4498, Fax: 217-265-0925, E-mail: fayedong@illinois.edu. *Application contact:* Terri Cummings, Director of Student Services, 217-244-4405, Fax: 217-265-0925, E-mail: tcumming@illinois.edu. Web site: http://fshn.illinois.edu/.

University of Maine, Graduate School, College of Natural Sciences, Forestry, and Agriculture, Department of Food Science and Human Nutrition, Orono, ME 04469. Offers food and nutritional sciences (PhD); food science and human nutrition (MS). Part-time programs available. *Faculty:* 7 full-time (6 women), 5 part-time/adjunct (2 women). *Students:* 33 full-time (26 women), 7 part-time (6 women); includes 5 minority (3 American Indian or Alaska Native, non-Hispanic/Latino; 2 Asian, non-Hispanic/Latino), 5 international. Average age 27. 22 applicants, 59% accepted, 9 enrolled. In 2011, 9 master's, 1 doctorate awarded. *Degree requirements:* For master's, thesis; for doctorate, thesis/dissertation. *Entrance requirements:* For master's, GRE General Test, minimum GPA of 3.0; for doctorate, GRE General Test. Additional exam requirements/recommendations for international students: Required—TOEFL. *Application deadline:* For fall admission, 2/1 priority date for domestic students. Applications are processed on a rolling basis. Application fee: $65. Electronic applications accepted. *Expenses:* Tuition, state resident: full-time $5016. Tuition, nonresident: full-time $14,424. *Financial support:* In 2011–12, 4 research assistantships with full tuition reimbursements (averaging $18,596 per year), 3 teaching assistantships with full tuition reimbursements (averaging $13,600 per year) were awarded; scholarships/grants and tuition waivers (full and partial) also available. Financial award application deadline: 3/1. *Faculty research:* Product development of fruit and vegetables, lipid oxidation in fish and meat, analytical methods development, metabolism of potato glycoalkaloids, seafood quality. *Unit head:* Dr. Rodney Bush, 207-581-1621. *Application contact:* Scott G. Delcourt, Associate Dean of the Graduate School, 207-581-3291, Fax: 207-581-3232, E-mail: graduate@maine.edu. Web site: http://www2.umaine.edu/graduate/.

University of Manitoba, Faculty of Graduate Studies, Faculty of Agricultural and Food Sciences, Department of Food Science, Winnipeg, MB R3T 2N2, Canada. Offers food and nutritional sciences (PhD); food science (M Sc); foods and nutrition (M Sc). *Degree requirements:* For master's, thesis.

University of Maryland, College Park, Academic Affairs, College of Agriculture and Natural Resources, Department of Nutrition and Food Science, Program in Food Science, College Park, MD 20742. Offers MS, PhD. *Students:* 25 full-time (12 women), 1 (woman) part-time; includes 4 minority (2 Black or African American, non-Hispanic/Latino; 1 Asian, non-Hispanic/Latino; 1 Hispanic/Latino), 17 international. 52 applicants, 10% accepted, 4 enrolled. In 2011, 4 master's, 3 doctorates awarded. *Degree requirements:* For master's, comprehensive exam, research-based thesis or equivalent paper; for doctorate, comprehensive exam, thesis/dissertation. *Entrance requirements:* For master's, GRE General Test, minimum GPA of 3.0, professional experience, 3 letters of recommendation; for doctorate, GRE General Test, minimum GPA of 3.0. Additional exam requirements/recommendations for international students: Required—TOEFL. *Application deadline:* For fall admission, 12/15 for domestic and international students; for spring admission, 6/1 for domestic and international students. Applications are processed on a rolling basis. Application fee: $75. Electronic applications accepted. *Expenses:* Tuition, area resident: Part-time $525 per credit hour. Tuition, state resident: part-time $525 per credit hour. Tuition, nonresident: part-time $1131 per credit hour. *Required fees:* $386.31 per term. Tuition and fees vary according to program. *Financial support:* In 2011–12, 9 research assistantships (averaging $15,737 per year), 14 teaching assistantships (averaging $15,907 per year) were awarded; fellowships also available. Financial award applicants required to submit FAFSA. *Faculty research:* Food chemistry, engineering, microbiology, and processing technology; quality assurance; membrane separations, rheology and texture measurement. *Unit head:* Lucy Yu, Acting Chair, 301-405-0773, E-mail: lyu5@umd.edu. *Application contact:* Dr. Charles A. Caramello, Dean of Graduate School, 301-405-0358, Fax: 301-314-9305, E-mail: ccaramel@umd.edu.

University of Maryland Eastern Shore, Graduate Programs, Department of Agriculture, Program in Food and Agricultural Sciences, Princess Anne, MD 21853-1299. Offers MS. *Degree requirements:* For master's, comprehensive exam, thesis or alternative, oral exams. *Entrance requirements:* For master's, GRE General Test, minimum GPA of 3.0. Additional exam requirements/recommendations for international students: Required—TOEFL (minimum score 213 computer-based; 80 iBT). Electronic applications accepted. *Faculty research:* Poultry and swine nutrition and management, soybean specialty products, farm management practices, agriculture technology.

University of Maryland Eastern Shore, Graduate Programs, Department of Agriculture, Program in Food Science and Technology, Princess Anne, MD 21853-1299. Offers PhD. *Degree requirements:* For doctorate, comprehensive exam, thesis/dissertation. *Entrance requirements:* For doctorate, minimum GPA of 3.0, strong background in food science and related fields, intended dissertation research. Additional exam requirements/recommendations for international students: Required—TOEFL (minimum score 213 computer-based; 80 iBT). Electronic applications accepted. *Faculty research:* Prevalence, growth, survival and control of listeria; microbial models of the effect of storage temperature.

University of Massachusetts Amherst, Graduate School, College of Natural Sciences, Department of Food Science, Amherst, MA 01003. Offers MS, PhD. Part-time programs available. *Faculty:* 16 full-time (4 women). *Students:* 34 full-time (24 women), 19 part-time (12 women); includes 4 minority (1 Black or African American, non-Hispanic/Latino; 2 Asian, non-Hispanic/Latino; 1 Hispanic/Latino), 35 international. Average age 27. 156 applicants, 21% accepted, 20 enrolled. In 2011, 4 master's, 1 doctorate awarded. Terminal master's awarded for partial completion of doctoral program. *Degree requirements:* For master's, thesis or alternative; for doctorate, comprehensive exam, thesis/dissertation. *Entrance requirements:* For master's and doctorate, GRE General Test. Additional exam requirements/recommendations for international students: Required—TOEFL (minimum score 550 paper-based; 213 computer-based; 80 iBT), IELTS (minimum score 6.5). *Application deadline:* For fall admission, 2/1 for domestic and international students; for spring admission, 10/1 for domestic and international students. Applications are processed on a rolling basis. Application fee: $50 ($65 for international students). Electronic applications accepted. Tuition and fees vary according to course load, campus/location and program. *Financial support:* Fellowships with full and partial tuition reimbursements, research assistantships with full and partial tuition reimbursements, teaching assistantships with full and partial tuition reimbursements, career-related internships or fieldwork, Federal Work-Study, scholarships/grants, traineeships, health care benefits, tuition waivers (full and partial), and unspecified assistantships available. Support available to part-time students. Financial award application deadline: 2/1. *Unit head:* Dr. Ronald G. Labbe, Graduate Program Director, 413-545-2276, Fax: 413-545-1262. *Application contact:* Lindsay DeSantis, Interim Supervisor of Admissions, 413-545-0721, Fax: 413-577-0010, E-mail: gradadm@grad.umass.edu. Web site: http://www.umass.edu/foodsci/.

University of Minnesota, Twin Cities Campus, Graduate School, College of Food, Agricultural and Natural Resource Sciences, Program in Food Science, Minneapolis, MN 55455-0213. Offers MS, PhD. Part-time programs available. *Faculty:* 24 full-time (7 women). *Students:* 42 full-time (30 women), 8 part-time (2 women); includes 3 minority (1 Black or African American, non-Hispanic/Latino; 2 Hispanic/Latino), 22 international. Average age 30. 135 applicants, 49% accepted, 21 enrolled. In 2011, 6 master's, 4 doctorates awarded. Terminal master's awarded for partial completion of doctoral program. *Degree requirements:* For master's, comprehensive exam, thesis; for doctorate, comprehensive exam, thesis/dissertation. *Entrance requirements:* For master's and doctorate, GRE General Test, previous course work in general chemistry, organic chemistry, calculus, physics, and biology. Additional exam requirements/recommendations for international students: Required—TOEFL (minimum score 550 paper-based; 213 computer-based; 79 iBT), IELTS (minimum score 6.5), TOEFL preferred. *Application deadline:* For fall admission, 12/15 for domestic and international students; for spring admission, 10/15 for domestic and international students. Applications are processed on a rolling basis. Application fee: $75 ($95 for international students). Electronic applications accepted. *Financial support:* In 2011–12, fellowships with full tuition reimbursements (averaging $23,500 per year), research assistantships with full and partial tuition reimbursements (averaging $17,500 per year), teaching assistantships with full and partial tuition reimbursements (averaging $17,500 per year) were awarded; career-related internships or fieldwork, scholarships/grants, traineeships, health care benefits, and unspecified assistantships also available. Support available to part-time students. *Faculty research:* Food chemistry, food microbiology, food technology, grain science, dairy science, food safety. *Total annual research expenditures:* $2.1 million. *Unit head:* Dr. David E. Smith, Director of Graduate Studies, 612-624-3260, Fax: 612-625-5272, E-mail: desmith@umn.edu. *Application contact:* Nancy L. Toedt, Program Coordinator, 612-624-6753, Fax: 612-625-5272, E-mail: ntoedt@umn.edu. Web site: http://fscn.cfans.umn.edu/education/foodsciencegraduate/index.htm.

University of Missouri, Graduate School, College of Agriculture, Food and Natural Resources, Department of Food Science, Columbia, MO 65211. Offers food science (MS, PhD); foods and food systems management (MS); human nutrition (MS). *Faculty:* 12 full-time (4 women), 2 part-time/adjunct (0 women). *Students:* 37 full-time (23 women), 11 part-time (3 women); includes 1 minority (Hispanic/Latino), 31 international. Average age 26. 67 applicants, 37% accepted, 16 enrolled. In 2011, 7 degrees awarded. Terminal master's awarded for partial completion of doctoral program. *Degree requirements:* For doctorate, comprehensive exam, thesis/dissertation. *Entrance requirements:* For master's, GRE General Test (minimum score: Verbal and Quantitative 1000 with neither section below 400, Analytical 3.5), minimum GPA of 3.0; BS in food science from accredited university; for doctorate, GRE General Test (minimum score: Verbal and Quantitative 1000 with neither section below 400, Analytical 3.5), minimum GPA of 3.0; BS and MS in food science from accredited university. Additional exam requirements/recommendations for international students: Required—TOEFL (minimum score 550 paper-based; 79 iBT). *Application deadline:* For fall admission, 4/1 priority date for domestic students; for winter admission, 10/1 priority date for domestic students. Applications are processed on a rolling basis. Application fee: $55 ($75 for international students). Electronic applications accepted. *Expenses:* Tuition, state resident: full-time $5881. Tuition, nonresident: full-time $15,183. *Required fees:* $952. Tuition and fees vary according to campus/location and program. *Financial support:* Fellowships, research assistantships with tuition reimbursements, teaching assistantships with tuition reimbursements, institutionally sponsored loans, scholarships/grants, health care benefits, and unspecified assistantships available. Support available to part-time students. *Faculty research:* Food chemistry, food analysis, food microbiology, food engineering and process control, functional foods, meat science and processing technology.. *Unit head:* Dr. Jinglu Tan, Department Chair, 573-882-2369, E-mail: tanj@missouri.edu. *Application contact:* JoAnn Lewis, 573-882-4113, E-mail: lewisj@missouri.edu. Web site: http://foodscience.missouri.edu/graduate/.

University of Nebraska–Lincoln, Graduate College, College of Agricultural Sciences and Natural Resources, Department of Food Science and Technology, Lincoln, NE 68588. Offers MS, PhD. *Degree requirements:* For master's, thesis optional; for doctorate, comprehensive exam, thesis/dissertation. *Entrance requirements:* For master's and doctorate, GRE General Test. Additional exam requirements/recommendations for international students: Required—TOEFL (minimum score 505 paper-based; 213 computer-based). Electronic applications accepted. *Faculty research:* Food chemistry, microbiology, processing, engineering, and biotechnology.

University of Puerto Rico, Mayagüez Campus, Graduate Studies, College of Agricultural Sciences, Department of Food Science and Technology, Mayagüez, PR 00681-9000. Offers MS. Part-time programs available. *Students:* 30 full-time (9 women); includes 19 minority (all Hispanic/Latino), 11 international. 10 applicants, 70% accepted, 3 enrolled. In 2011, 3 master's awarded. *Degree requirements:* For master's, comprehensive exam, thesis. *Entrance requirements:* For master's, minimum GPA of 2.5. *Application deadline:* For fall admission, 2/15 for domestic and international students; for spring admission, 9/15 for domestic and international students. Applications are processed on a rolling basis. Application fee: $25. Tuition and fees vary according to course level and course load. *Financial support:* Federal Work-Study and institutionally sponsored loans available. *Faculty research:* Food microbiology, food science, seafood technology, food engineering and packaging, fermentation. *Total annual research expenditures:* $128,100. *Unit head:* Dr. Edna Negron, Director, 787-265-5410, Fax: 787-265-5410, E-mail: edna.negron1@upr.edu. *Application contact:* Gloria Aguilar, Administrative Assistant, 787-832-4040 Ext. 3078, Fax: 787-265-5410, E-mail: gloriag.aguilar@upr.edu. Web site: http://www.uprm.edu/agricultura/cita/.

University of Rhode Island, Graduate School, College of the Environment and Life Sciences, Department of Nutrition and Food Sciences, Kingston, RI 02881. Offers food science (MS, PhD); nutrition (MS, PhD). Part-time programs available. *Faculty:* 7 full-time (5 women), 1 (woman) part-time/adjunct. *Students:* 15 full-time (14 women), 13 part-time (10 women); includes 1 minority (Asian, non-Hispanic/Latino), 1 international. In 2011, 9 master's awarded. *Degree requirements:* For master's, comprehensive exam (for some programs), thesis optional; for doctorate, thesis/dissertation. *Entrance requirements:* For master's and doctorate, GRE, 2 letters of recommendation. Additional exam requirements/recommendations for international students: Required—TOEFL (minimum score 550 paper-based; 213 computer-based). *Application deadline:* For fall admission, 7/15 for domestic students, 2/1 for international students; for spring admission, 11/15 for domestic students, 7/15 for international students. Application fee: $65. Electronic applications accepted. *Expenses:* Tuition, state resident: full-time $10,432; part-time $580 per credit hour. Tuition, nonresident: full-time $23,130; part-time $1285 per credit hour. *Required fees:* $1362; $36 per credit hour. $35 per semester. One-time fee: $130. *Financial support:* In 2011–12, 1 research assistantship with full and partial tuition reimbursement (averaging $8,471 per year), 4 teaching assistantships with full and partial tuition reimbursements (averaging $11,298 per year) were awarded. Financial award application deadline: 7/15; financial award applicants required to submit FAFSA. *Faculty research:* Food safety and quality, marine resource utilization, nutrition in underserved populations, eating behavior, lipid metabolism. *Unit head:* Dr. Geoffrey Greene, Chair, 401-874-4028, Fax: 401-874-5974, E-mail: gwg@uri.edu. *Application contact:* Dr. Geoffrey Greene, Director of Graduate Studies, 401-874-4028, E-mail: gwg@uri.edu. Web site: http://cels.uri.edu/nfs/.

University of Saskatchewan, College of Graduate Studies and Research, College of Agriculture, Department of Applied Microbiology and Food Science, Saskatoon, SK S7N 5A2, Canada. Offers M Ag, M Sc, PhD. *Degree requirements:* For master's, thesis; for doctorate, comprehensive exam (for some programs), thesis/dissertation. *Entrance requirements:* Additional exam requirements/recommendations for international students: Required—TOEFL (minimum score 80 iBT); Recommended—IELTS (minimum score 6.5).

University of Southern California, Graduate School, School of Pharmacy, Regulatory Science Programs, Los Angeles, CA 90089. Offers clinical research design and management (Graduate Certificate); food safety (Graduate Certificate); patient and product safety (Graduate Certificate); preclinical drug development (Graduate Certificate); regulatory and clinical affairs (Graduate Certificate); regulatory science (MS, DRSc). Part-time and evening/weekend programs available. Postbaccalaureate distance learning degree programs offered (minimal on-campus study). Terminal master's awarded for partial completion of doctoral program. *Degree requirements:* For master's, thesis optional; for doctorate, comprehensive exam, thesis/dissertation. *Entrance requirements:* For master's, GRE. Additional exam requirements/recommendations for international students: Required—TOEFL (minimum score 603 paper-based; 250 computer-based; 100 iBT). Electronic applications accepted.

The University of Tennessee, Graduate School, College of Agricultural Sciences and Natural Resources, Department of Food Science and Technology, Knoxville, TN 37996. Offers food science and technology (MS, PhD), including food chemistry (PhD), food microbiology (PhD), food processing (PhD), sensory evaluation of foods (PhD). Part-time programs available. *Degree requirements:* For master's, thesis or alternative; for doctorate, thesis/dissertation. *Entrance requirements:* For master's and doctorate, GRE General Test, minimum GPA of 2.7. Additional exam requirements/recommendations for international students: Required—TOEFL. Electronic applications accepted. *Expenses:* Tuition, state resident: full-time $8332; part-time $464 per credit hour. Tuition, nonresident: full-time $25,174; part-time $1400 per credit hour. *Required fees:* $1162; $56 per credit hour. Tuition and fees vary according to program.

The University of Tennessee at Martin, Graduate Programs, College of Agriculture and Applied Sciences, Department of Family and Consumer Sciences, Martin, TN 38238-1000. Offers dietetics (MSFCS); general family and consumer sciences (MSFCS). Part-time programs available. Postbaccalaureate distance learning degree programs offered (minimal on-campus study). *Faculty:* 8. *Students:* 36 (34 women); includes 11 minority (6 Black or African American, non-Hispanic/Latino; 4 Hispanic/Latino; 1 Two or more races, non-Hispanic/Latino), 1 international. 28 applicants, 71% accepted, 15 enrolled. In 2011, 15 master's awarded. *Degree requirements:* For master's, comprehensive exam, thesis optional. *Entrance requirements:* For master's, GRE General Test, minimum GPA of 2.5. Additional exam requirements/recommendations for international students: Required—TOEFL (minimum score 525 paper-based; 197 computer-based; 71 iBT). *Application deadline:* For fall admission, 8/1 priority date for domestic students, 6/15 for international students; for spring admission, 12/15 priority date for domestic students, 12/1 for international students. Applications are processed on a rolling basis. Application fee: $30 ($130 for international students). Electronic applications accepted. *Expenses:* Tuition, state resident: full-time $6726; part-time $374 per credit hour. Tuition, nonresident: full-time $19,136; part-time $1064 per credit hour. *Required fees:* $61 per credit hour. *Financial support:* In 2011–12, 2 students received support, including 2 research assistantships with full tuition reimbursements available (averaging $6,283 per year); scholarships/grants and unspecified assistantships also available. Support available to part-time students. Financial award application deadline: 2/15; financial award applicants required to submit FAFSA. *Faculty research:* Children with developmental disabilities, regional food product development and marketing, parent education. *Unit head:* Dr. Lisa LeBleu, Coordinator, 731-881-7116, Fax: 731-881-7106, E-mail: llebleu@utm.edu. *Application contact:* Linda S. Arant, Student Services Specialist, 731-881-7012, Fax: 731-881-7499, E-mail: larant@utm.edu. Web site: http://www.utm.edu/departments/caas/fcs/index.php.

University of Vermont, Graduate College, College of Agriculture and Life Sciences, Program in Animal, Nutrition and Food Sciences, Burlington, VT 05405. Offers PhD. *Students:* 18 (7 women); includes 2 minority (both Asian, non-Hispanic/Latino), 10 international. 10 applicants, 20% accepted, 1 enrolled. In 2011, 2 doctorates awarded. *Degree requirements:* For doctorate, one foreign language, thesis/dissertation. *Entrance requirements:* For doctorate, GRE General Test. Additional exam requirements/recommendations for international students: Required—TOEFL (minimum score 550 paper-based; 213 computer-based; 80 iBT). *Application deadline:* For fall admission, 4/1 priority date for domestic students, 4/1 for international students. Applications are processed on a rolling basis. Application fee: $40. Electronic applications accepted. *Financial support:* Application deadline: 3/1. *Unit head:* Dr. Andre-Denis Wright, Chairperson, 802-656-2070. *Application contact:* Dr. David Kerr, Coordinator, 802-656-2070.

University of Wisconsin–Madison, Graduate School, College of Agricultural and Life Sciences, Department of Food Science, Madison, WI 53706-1380. Offers MS, PhD. Part-time programs available. *Degree requirements:* For master's, thesis; for doctorate, thesis/dissertation. *Entrance requirements:* For master's and doctorate, GRE General Test. Additional exam requirements/recommendations for international students: Required—TOEFL. Electronic applications accepted. *Expenses:* Tuition, state resident: full-time $10,296; part-time $643.51 per credit. Tuition, nonresident: full-time $24,054; part-time $1503.40 per credit. *Required fees:* $70.06 per credit. Tuition and fees vary according to course load, campus/location, program and reciprocity agreements. *Faculty research:* Food chemistry, food engineering, food microbiology, food processing.

University of Wisconsin–Stout, Graduate School, College of Human Development, Program in Food and Nutritional Sciences, Menomonie , WI 54751. Offers MS. Part-time programs available. *Degree requirements:* For master's,

Peterson's Graduate Programs in the Physical Sciences, Mathematics,
Agricultural Sciences, the Environment & Natural Resources 2013

facebook.com/petersonspublishing **433**

Food Science and Technology

thesis. *Entrance requirements:* For master's, minimum GPA of 3.0. Additional exam requirements/recommendations for international students: Required—TOEFL (minimum score 500 paper-based; 173 computer-based; 61 iBT). Electronic applications accepted. *Faculty research:* Disease states and nutrition, childhood obesity, nutraceuticals, food safety, nanotechnology.

University of Wyoming, College of Agriculture and Natural Resources, Department of Animal Sciences, Program in Food Science and Human Nutrition, Laramie, WY 82070. Offers MS. *Degree requirements:* For master's, thesis. *Entrance requirements:* For master's, GRE General Test, minimum GPA of 3.0. Additional exam requirements/recommendations for international students: Required—TOEFL (minimum score 525 paper-based). Electronic applications accepted. *Faculty research:* Protein and lipid metabolism, food microbiology, food safety, meat science.

Utah State University, School of Graduate Studies, College of Agriculture, Department of Nutrition, Dietetics, and Food Sciences, Logan, UT 84322. Offers dietetic administration (MDA); food microbiology and safety (MFMS); nutrition and food sciences (MS, PhD); nutrition science (MS, PhD), including molecular biology. Postbaccalaureate distance learning degree programs offered. *Degree requirements:* For master's, thesis; for doctorate, comprehensive exam, thesis/dissertation, teaching experience. *Entrance requirements:* For master's, GRE General Test, minimum GPA of 3.0, course work in chemistry, biochemistry, physics, math, bacteriology, physiology; for doctorate, GRE General Test, minimum GPA of 3.2, course work in chemistry, MS or manuscript in referred journal. Additional exam requirements/recommendations for international students: Required—TOEFL (minimum score 550 paper-based). Electronic applications accepted. *Faculty research:* Mineral balance, meat microbiology and nitrate interactions, milk ultrafiltration, lactic culture, milk coagulation.

Virginia Polytechnic Institute and State University, Graduate School, College of Agriculture and Life Sciences, Department of Food Science and Technology, Blacksburg, VA 24061. Offers food science and technology (MSLFS, PhD); health product risk management (Certificate); produce food safety (Certificate). *Degree requirements:* For master's, comprehensive exam (for some programs), thesis (for some programs); for doctorate, comprehensive exam (for some programs), thesis/dissertation (for some programs). *Entrance requirements:* For master's and doctorate, GRE. Additional exam requirements/recommendations for international students: Required—TOEFL (minimum score 550 paper-based; 213 computer-based). *Application deadline:* For fall admission, 7/1 for domestic and international students; for spring admission, 12/1 for domestic and international students. Applications are processed on a rolling basis. Application fee: $65. Electronic applications accepted. *Expenses:* Tuition, state resident: full-time $10,048; part-time $558.25 per credit hour. Tuition, nonresident: full-time $19,497; part-time $1083.25 per credit hour. *Required fees:* $405 per semester. Tuition and fees vary according to course load, campus/location and program. *Financial support:* Research assistantships with full tuition reimbursements, teaching assistantships with full tuition reimbursements, career-related internships or fieldwork, Federal Work-Study, scholarships/grants, health care benefits, and unspecified assistantships available. Financial award application deadline: 1/15. *Faculty research:* Food microbiology, food chemistry, food processing, engineering, muscle foods. *Unit head:* Dr. Joseph E. Marcy, Unit Head, 540-231-6806, Fax: 540-231-9293, E-mail: jmarcy@vt.edu. *Application contact:* Joe Eifert, Information Contact, 540-231-3658, Fax: 540-231-9293, E-mail: jeifert@vt.edu. Web site: http://www.fst.vt.edu/.

Washington State University, Graduate School, College of Agricultural, Human, and Natural Resource Sciences, Department of Food Science and Human Nutrition, Program in Food Science, Pullman, WA 99164. Offers MS, PhD. *Faculty:* 7. *Students:* 21 full-time (11 women), 9 part-time (5 women), 17 international. Average age 30. 131 applicants, 6% accepted, 7 enrolled. In 2011, 6 master's, 2 doctorates awarded. *Degree requirements:* For master's, comprehensive exam (for some programs), thesis (for some programs), oral exam, written exam; for doctorate, comprehensive exam, thesis/dissertation, oral exam, written exam. *Entrance requirements:* For master's, GRE General Test, official transcripts; letter of interest; minimum GPA of 3.0; resume; 3 letters of recommendation, 1 from major advisor; for doctorate, GRE General Test, MS demonstrating ability to conduct and report research; minimum GPA of 3.0; resume; 3 letters of recommendation, 1 from major advisor. Additional exam requirements/recommendations for international students: Required—TOEFL (minimum score 550 paper-based; 213 computer-based; 80 iBT), IELTS. *Application deadline:* For fall admission, 1/10 priority date for domestic students, 1/10 for international students; for spring admission, 7/1 priority date for domestic

students, 7/1 for international students. Applications are processed on a rolling basis. Application fee: $75. Electronic applications accepted. *Financial support:* In 2011–12, 21 students received support, including fellowships with tuition reimbursements available (averaging $4,250 per year), 9 research assistantships with full and partial tuition reimbursements available (averaging $18,204 per year), 1 teaching assistantship with full and partial tuition reimbursement available (averaging $18,204 per year); career-related internships or fieldwork, Federal Work-Study, institutionally sponsored loans, scholarships/grants, tuition waivers (partial), and unspecified assistantships also available. Financial award application deadline: 2/1; financial award applicants required to submit FAFSA. *Faculty research:* Sports anemia, lipid chemistry, malfunction of edible oils and fats, malolactic fermentation, wine microbiology. *Total annual research expenditures:* $570,000. *Unit head:* Dr. Denise Smith, Director, 509-335-2101, Fax: 509-335-4815, E-mail: denise.smith@wsu.edu. *Application contact:* Graduate School Admissions, 800-GRADWSU, Fax: 509-335-1949, E-mail: gradsch@wsu.edu. Web site: http://nrs.wsu.edu/graduate/.

Wayne State University, College of Liberal Arts and Sciences, Department of Nutrition and Food Science, Detroit, MI 48202. Offers MA, MS, PhD. *Students:* 45 full-time (37 women), 18 part-time (17 women); includes 11 minority (3 Black or African American, non-Hispanic/Latino; 7 Asian, non-Hispanic/Latino; 1 Two or more races, non-Hispanic/Latino), 19 international. Average age 30. 91 applicants, 43% accepted, 22 enrolled. In 2011, 8 master's, 4 doctorates awarded. Terminal master's awarded for partial completion of doctoral program. *Degree requirements:* For master's, thesis (for some programs), essay (for MA); for doctorate, thesis/dissertation. *Entrance requirements:* For master's, GRE General Test, minimum GPA of 3.0, basic courses in nutrition and food science; for doctorate, GRE General Test, minimum GPA of 3.0; two letters of recommendation; personal statement. Additional exam requirements/recommendations for international students: Required—TOEFL (minimum score 550 paper-based; 213 computer-based); Recommended—TWE (minimum score 5.5). *Application deadline:* For fall admission, 12/31 for domestic students, 12/1 for international students; for winter admission, 10/1 priority date for domestic students, 9/1 for international students; for spring admission, 2/1 priority date for domestic students, 1/1 for international students. Applications are processed on a rolling basis. Application fee: $50. Electronic applications accepted. *Expenses:* Tuition, state resident: part-time $512.85 per credit. Tuition, nonresident: part-time $1132.65 per credit. *Required fees:* $26.60 per credit. $199.65 per semester. Tuition and fees vary according to course load and program. *Financial support:* In 2011–12, 22 students received support, including 1 fellowship with tuition reimbursement available (averaging $15,750 per year), 3 research assistantships with tuition reimbursements available (averaging $19,332 per year), 8 teaching assistantships with tuition reimbursements available (averaging $17,467 per year); career-related internships or fieldwork, Federal Work-Study, scholarships/grants, health care benefits, and unspecified assistantships also available. Financial award application deadline: 4/1. *Faculty research:* Nutrition, cancer and gene expression, food microbiology and food safety, lipids, lipoprotein and cholesterol metabolism, obesity and diabetes, metabolomics. *Total annual research expenditures:* $261,392. *Unit head:* Dr. K. L. Catherine Jen, Chair, 313-577-2500, E-mail: ac1578@wayne.edu. *Application contact:* Debra Zebrari, Academic Services Officer II, E-mail: ab8207@wayne.edu. Web site: http://www.science.wayne.edu/~nfs/.

West Virginia University, Davis College of Agriculture, Forestry and Consumer Sciences, Division of Animal and Nutritional Sciences, Program in Animal and Nutritional Sciences, Morgantown, WV 26506. Offers breeding (MS); food sciences (MS); nutrition (MS); physiology (MS); production management (MS); reproduction (MS). Part-time programs available. *Degree requirements:* For master's, thesis, oral and written exams. *Entrance requirements:* For master's, GRE, minimum GPA of 2.5. Additional exam requirements/recommendations for international students: Required—TOEFL. *Faculty research:* Animal nutrition, reproductive physiology, food science.

West Virginia University, Davis College of Agriculture, Forestry and Consumer Sciences, Division of Plant and Soil Sciences, Program in Agricultural Sciences, Morgantown, WV 26506. Offers animal and food sciences (PhD); plant and soil sciences (PhD). *Degree requirements:* For doctorate, thesis/dissertation, oral and written exams. *Entrance requirements:* Additional exam requirements/recommendations for international students: Required—TOEFL. *Faculty research:* Ruminant nutrition, metabolism, forage utilization, physiology, reproduction.

Horticulture

Auburn University, Graduate School, College of Agriculture, Department of Horticulture, Auburn University, AL 36849. Offers M Ag, MS, PhD. Part-time programs available. *Faculty:* 19 full-time (4 women). *Students:* 9 full-time (3 women), 20 part-time (6 women); includes 3 minority (1 Black or African American, non-Hispanic/Latino; 1 Asian, non-Hispanic/Latino; 1 Hispanic/Latino), 5 international. Average age 29. 17 applicants, 47% accepted, 4 enrolled. In 2011,

6 master's, 3 doctorates awarded. *Degree requirements:* For master's, thesis (for some programs); for doctorate, thesis/dissertation. *Entrance requirements:* For master's and doctorate, GRE General Test. *Application deadline:* For fall admission, 7/7 for domestic students; for spring admission, 11/24 for domestic students. Applications are processed on a rolling basis. Application fee: $50 ($60 for international students). Electronic applications accepted. *Expenses:* Tuition,

state resident: full-time $7290; part-time $405 per credit hour. Tuition, nonresident: full-time $21,870; part-time $1215 per credit hour. *International tuition:* $22,000 full-time. *Required fees:* $1402. *Financial support:* Research assistantships, teaching assistantships, and Federal Work-Study available. Support available to part-time students. Financial award application deadline: 3/15; financial award applicants required to submit FAFSA. *Faculty research:* Environmental regulators, water quality, weed control, growth regulators, plasticulture. *Unit head:* Dr. J. David Williams, Chair, 334-844-4862. *Application contact:* Dr. George Flowers, Dean of the Graduate School, 334-844-2125. Web site: http://www.ag.auburn.edu/dept/hf/index.html.

Colorado State University, Graduate School, College of Agricultural Sciences, Department of Horticulture and Landscape Architecture, Fort Collins, CO 80523-1173. Offers horticulture (MS, PhD); landscape architecture (MLA). Part-time programs available. *Faculty:* 24 full-time (4 women). *Students:* 25 full-time (14 women), 16 part-time (7 women); includes 7 minority (1 Black or African American, non-Hispanic/Latino; 1 American Indian or Alaska Native, non-Hispanic/Latino; 3 Hispanic/Latino; 2 Two or more races, non-Hispanic/Latino), 8 international. Average age 32. 36 applicants, 83% accepted, 10 enrolled. In 2011, 4 degrees awarded. *Degree requirements:* For master's, thesis (for some programs); for doctorate, comprehensive exam, thesis/dissertation. *Entrance requirements:* For master's, GRE General Test (minimum score in upper 50th percentile, 1100 verbal and quantitative), minimum GPA of 3.0, letters of reference, related bachelor's degree or experience; for doctorate, GRE General Test (upper 50th percentile and combined minimum score of 1100 for the Verbal and Quantitative sections), minimum GPA of 3.0, letters of reference, statement of purpose, related bachelor's degree or experience. Additional exam requirements/recommendations for international students: Required—TOEFL (minimum score 550 paper-based; 213 computer-based; 80 iBT). *Application deadline:* Applications are processed on a rolling basis. Application fee: $50. Electronic applications accepted. *Expenses:* Tuition, state resident: full-time $7992. Tuition, nonresident: full-time $19,592. *Required fees:* $1735; $58 per credit. *Financial support:* In 2011–12, 18 students received support, including 6 fellowships with full tuition reimbursements available (averaging $23,722 per year), 7 research assistantships with partial tuition reimbursements available (averaging $10,041 per year), 5 teaching assistantships with partial tuition reimbursements available (averaging $11,002 per year); scholarships/grants and unspecified assistantships also available. Financial award applicants required to submit FAFSA. *Faculty research:* Antioxidants in food crops, environmental physiology, water conservation, tissue culture, rhizosphere biology, cancer prevention through dietary intervention. *Total annual research expenditures:* $2.4 million. *Unit head:* Dr. Stephen J. Wallner, Head, 970-491-7018, Fax: 970-491-7745, E-mail: stephen.wallner@colostate.edu. *Application contact:* Kathi Nietfeld, Coordinator, 970-491-7018, Fax: 970-491-7745, E-mail: kathi.nietfeld@colostate.edu. Web site: http://hla.agsci.colostate.edu/.

Cornell University, Graduate School, Graduate Fields of Agriculture and Life Sciences, Field of Horticulture, Ithaca, NY 14853-0001. Offers controlled environment agriculture (MPS, PhD); controlled environment horticulture (MS); greenhouse crops (MPS, MS, PhD); horticultural business management (MPS, MS, PhD); horticultural physiology (MPS, MS, PhD); landscape horticulture (MPS, MS, PhD); nursery crops (MPS, MS, PhD); nutrition of horticultural crops (MPS, MS, PhD); plant propagation (MPS, MS, PhD); public garden management (MPS, MS, PhD); restoration ecology (MPS, MS, PhD); taxonomy of ornamental plants (MPS, MS, PhD); turfgrass science (MPS, MS, PhD); urban horticulture (MPS, MS, PhD); weed science (MPS, MS, PhD). *Faculty:* 49 full-time (13 women). *Students:* 36 full-time (19 women); includes 6 minority (3 Hispanic/Latino; 3 Two or more races, non-Hispanic/Latino), 10 international. Average age 30. 44 applicants, 18% accepted, 8 enrolled. In 2011, 9 master's, 7 doctorates awarded. *Degree requirements:* For master's, thesis (MS); for doctorate, comprehensive exam, thesis/dissertation. *Entrance requirements:* For master's and doctorate, GRE General Test, 3 letters of recommendation. Additional exam requirements/recommendations for international students: Required—TOEFL (minimum score 550 paper-based; 213 computer-based; 77 iBT). *Application deadline:* For fall admission, 1/15 for domestic students; for spring admission, 8/15 for domestic students. Application fee: $95. Electronic applications accepted. *Financial support:* In 2011–12, 5 fellowships with full tuition reimbursements, 19 research assistantships with full tuition reimbursements, 8 teaching assistantships with full tuition reimbursements were awarded; institutionally sponsored loans, scholarships/grants, health care benefits, tuition waivers (full and partial), and unspecified assistantships also available. Financial award applicants required to submit FAFSA. *Faculty research:* Plant selection/plant materials, greenhouse management, greenhouse crop production, urban landscape management, turfgrass management. *Unit head:* Director of Graduate Studies, 607-255-4568, Fax: 607-255-0599. *Application contact:* Graduate Field Assistant, 607-255-4568, Fax: 607-255-0599, E-mail: hortgrad@cornell.edu. Web site: http://www.gradschool.cornell.edu/fields.php?id-XX&a-2.

Iowa State University of Science and Technology, Department of Horticulture, Ames, IA 50011-1100. Offers MS, PhD. *Degree requirements:* For master's, thesis; for doctorate, thesis/dissertation. *Entrance requirements:* For master's and doctorate, GRE General Test. Additional exam requirements/recommendations for international students: Required—TOEFL (minimum score 550 paper-based; 79 iBT), IELTS (minimum score 6.5). *Application deadline:* Applications are processed on a rolling basis. Application fee: $40 ($90 for international students). Electronic applications accepted. *Unit head:* Dr. Rajeev Arora, Director of Graduate Education, 515-294-2751, Fax: 515-294-0730, E-mail: rarora@

iastate.edu. *Application contact:* Dr. Rajeev Arora, Director of Graduate Education, 515-294-2751, Fax: 515-294-0730, E-mail: rarora@iastate.edu. Web site: http://www.hort.iastate.edu/.

Kansas State University, Graduate School, College of Agriculture, Department of Horticulture, Forestry and Recreation Resources, Manhattan, KS 66506. Offers horticulture (MS, PhD). *Faculty:* 20 full-time (6 women). *Students:* 26 full-time (14 women), 4 part-time (1 woman), 8 international. Average age 40. 4 applicants, 100% accepted, 4 enrolled. In 2011, 4 master's, 3 doctorates awarded. *Degree requirements:* For master's, thesis, oral exam; for doctorate, thesis/dissertation, preliminary exams. *Entrance requirements:* For master's and doctorate, GRE General Test. Additional exam requirements/recommendations for international students: Required—TOEFL (minimum score 550 paper-based; 213 computer-based). *Application deadline:* For fall admission, 2/1 priority date for domestic students, 2/1 for international students; for spring admission, 8/1 priority date for domestic students, 8/1 for international students. Applications are processed on a rolling basis. Application fee: $40 ($55 for international students). Electronic applications accepted. *Financial support:* In 2011–12, 22 research assistantships (averaging $18,444 per year), 7 teaching assistantships (averaging $20,000 per year) were awarded; career-related internships or fieldwork, institutionally sponsored loans, and scholarships/grants also available. Support available to part-time students. Financial award application deadline: 3/1; financial award applicants required to submit FAFSA. *Faculty research:* Environmental stress, phytochemicals and health, crop nutrition, sustainable horticulture, turfgrass science. *Total annual research expenditures:* $815,455. *Unit head:* Stuart Warren, Head, 785-532-6170, Fax: 785-532-6949, E-mail: slwarren@ksu.edu. *Application contact:* Dr. Stuart Warren, Director, 785-532-6170, Fax: 785-532-6949, E-mail: slwarren@ksu.edu. Web site: http://www.hfrr.k-state.edu/DesktopDefault.aspx.

Louisiana State University and Agricultural and Mechanical College, Graduate School, College of Agriculture, School of Plant, Environmental and Soil Sciences, Department of Horticulture, Baton Rouge, LA 70803. Offers MS, PhD. Part-time programs available. *Faculty:* 10 full-time (1 woman). *Students:* 4 full-time (1 woman), 3 part-time (2 women); includes 1 minority (Black or African American, non-Hispanic/Latino), 2 international. Average age 32. 4 applicants, 25% accepted, 0 enrolled. In 2011, 1 master's, 1 doctorate awarded. Terminal master's awarded for partial completion of doctoral program. *Degree requirements:* For master's, thesis (for some programs); for doctorate, thesis/dissertation. *Entrance requirements:* For master's and doctorate, GRE General Test, minimum GPA of 3.0. Additional exam requirements/recommendations for international students: Required—TOEFL (minimum score 550 paper-based; 213 computer-based; 79 iBT) or IELTS (minimum score 6.5). *Application deadline:* For fall admission, 7/1 priority date for domestic students, 5/15 for international students; for spring admission, 10/15 for international students. Applications are processed on a rolling basis. Application fee: $50 ($70 for international students). Electronic applications accepted. *Financial support:* In 2011–12, 5 students received support, including 3 research assistantships with partial tuition reimbursements available (averaging $19,333 per year); fellowships, Federal Work-Study, health care benefits, tuition waivers (full and partial), and unspecified assistantships also available. Financial award application deadline: 4/15; financial award applicants required to submit FAFSA. *Faculty research:* Plant breeding, stress physiology, postharvest physiology, biotechnology. *Unit head:* Dr. Don LaBonte, Director, 225-578-1043, Fax: 225-578-1403, E-mail: dlabont@lsu.edu. *Application contact:* Dr. David Weindorf, Graduate Coordinator, 225-578-0396, Fax: 225-578-1403, E-mail: dweindorf@agcenter.lsu.edu. Web site: http://www.lsuagcenter.com/en/our_offices/departments/SPESS/Horticulture/.

Michigan State University, The Graduate School, College of Agriculture and Natural Resources, Department of Horticulture, East Lansing, MI 48824. Offers horticulture (MS, PhD); plant breeding, genetics and biotechnology-horticulture (MS, PhD). *Entrance requirements:* Additional exam requirements/recommendations for international students: Required—TOEFL. Electronic applications accepted.

Mississippi State University, College of Agriculture and Life Sciences, Department of Plant and Soil Sciences, Mississippi State, MS 39762. Offers agriculture (MS), including agronomy, horticulture, weed science. *Faculty:* 30 full-time (1 woman), 1 part-time/adjunct (0 women). *Students:* 34 full-time (11 women), 21 part-time (5 women); includes 5 minority (3 Black or African American, non-Hispanic/Latino; 2 American Indian or Alaska Native, non-Hispanic/Latino), 13 international. Average age 30. 33 applicants, 42% accepted, 12 enrolled. In 2011, 6 master's awarded. *Degree requirements:* For master's, thesis, exit seminar describing thesis research. *Entrance requirements:* For master's, GRE (weed science), minimum GPA of 2.75 (agronomy/horticulture), 3.0 (weed science). Additional exam requirements/recommendations for international students: Required—TOEFL (minimum score 550 paper-based; 213 computer-based; 79 iBT); Recommended—IELTS (minimum score 6.5). *Application deadline:* For fall admission, 7/1 for domestic students, 5/1 for international students; for spring admission, 10/1 for domestic students, 9/1 for international students. Applications are processed on a rolling basis. Application fee: $40. Electronic applications accepted. *Expenses:* Tuition, state resident: full-time $5805; part-time $322.50 per credit hour. Tuition, nonresident: full-time $14,670; part-time $815 per credit hour. *Financial support:* In 2011–12, 30 research assistantships (averaging $14,692 per year), 3 teaching assistantships (averaging $15,133 per year) were awarded; Federal Work-Study, institutionally sponsored loans, scholarships/grants, and unspecified assistantships also available. Financial award application deadline: 4/1; financial award applicants

Peterson's Graduate Programs in the Physical Sciences, Mathematics, Agricultural Sciences, the Environment & Natural Resources 2013

facebook.com/petersonspublishing **435**

Horticulture

required to submit FAFSA. *Unit head:* Dr. J. Mike Phillips, Professor and Head, 662-325-2311, Fax: 662-325-8742, E-mail: jmp657@msstate.edu. *Application contact:* Dr. William Kingery, Graduate Coordinator, 662-325-2748, Fax: 662-325-8742, E-mail: wkingery@pss.msstate.edu. Web site: http://www.pss.msstate.edu/

New Mexico State University, Graduate School, College of Agricultural, Consumer and Environmental Sciences, Department of Plant and Environmental Sciences, Las Cruces, NM 88003-8001. Offers horticulture (MS); plant and environmental sciences (MS, PhD). Part-time programs available. *Faculty:* 21 full-time (3 women). *Students:* 45 full-time (17 women), 19 part-time (8 women); includes 9 minority (3 American Indian or Alaska Native, non-Hispanic/Latino; 5 Hispanic/Latino; 1 Two or more races, non-Hispanic/Latino), 20 international. Average age 32. 27 applicants, 52% accepted, 11 enrolled. In 2011, 6 master's, 7 doctorates awarded. Terminal master's awarded for partial completion of doctoral program. *Degree requirements:* For master's, thesis; for doctorate, one foreign language, comprehensive exam, thesis/dissertation, qualifying exam, 2 seminars. *Entrance requirements:* For master's, GRE, minimum GPA of 3.0, 3 letters of reference, letter of purpose or intent; for doctorate, GRE, minimum GPA of 3.3; 3 letters of reference, letter of purpose or intent. Additional exam requirements/recommendations for international students: Required—TOEFL (minimum score 550 paper-based; 0 computer-based; 79 iBT), IELTS (minimum score 6.5). *Application deadline:* Applications are processed on a rolling basis. Application fee: $40 ($50 for international students). Electronic applications accepted. *Expenses:* Tuition, state resident: full-time $5004; part-time $208.50 per credit. Tuition, nonresident: full-time $17,446; part-time $726.90 per credit. *Financial support:* In 2011–12, 8 students received support, including 3 fellowships (averaging $2,892 per year), 28 research assistantships with partial tuition reimbursements available (averaging $22,079 per year), 14 teaching assistantships with partial tuition reimbursements available (averaging $22,188 per year); career-related internships or fieldwork, Federal Work-Study, scholarships/grants, health care benefits, and unspecified assistantships also available. Support available to part-time students. Financial award application deadline: 3/1. *Faculty research:* Plant breeding and genetics, molecular biology, plant physiology, soil science and environmental remediation, urban horticulture and turfgrass management. *Unit head:* Dr. Richard Pratt, Head, 575-646-3406, Fax: 575-646-6041, E-mail: ricpratt@nmsu.edu. *Application contact:* Esther Ramirez, Information Contact, 575-646-3406, Fax: 575-646-6041, E-mail: esramire@nmsu.edu. Web site: http://aces.nmsu.edu/pes.

North Carolina State University, Graduate School, College of Agriculture and Life Sciences, Department of Horticultural Science, Raleigh, NC 27695. Offers MS, PhD, Certificate. Postbaccalaureate distance learning degree programs offered. Terminal master's awarded for partial completion of doctoral program. *Degree requirements:* For master's, thesis (for some programs); for doctorate, thesis/dissertation. *Entrance requirements:* For master's and doctorate, GRE General Test, bachelor's degree in agriculture or biology, minimum GPA of 3.0. Electronic applications accepted. *Faculty research:* Plant physiology, breeding and genetics, tissue culture, herbicide physiology, propagation.

Nova Scotia Agricultural College, Research and Graduate Studies, Truro, NS B2N 5E3, Canada. Offers agriculture (M Sc), including air quality, animal behavior, animal molecular genetics, animal nutrition, animal technology, aquaculture, botany, crop management, crop physiology, ecology, environmental microbiology, food science, horticulture, nutrient management, pest management, physiology, plant biotechnology, plant pathology, soil chemistry, soil fertility, waste management and composting, water quality. Program offered jointly with Dalhousie University. Part-time programs available. *Degree requirements:* For master's, thesis, ATC Exam Teaching Assistantship. *Entrance requirements:* For master's, honors B Sc, minimum GPA of 3.0. Additional exam requirements/recommendations for international students: Required—TOEFL (minimum score 580 paper-based; 237 computer-based; 92 iBT), IELTS, Michigan English Language Assessment Battery, CanTEST, CAEL. *Faculty research:* Bio-product development, organic agriculture, nutrient management, air and water quality, agricultural biotechnology.

The Ohio State University, Graduate School, College of Food, Agricultural, and Environmental Sciences, Department of Horticulture and Crop Science, Columbus, OH 43210. Offers MS, PhD. *Faculty:* 38. *Students:* 48 full-time (24 women), 19 part-time (12 women), 27 international. Average age 29. In 2011, 6 master's, 7 doctorates awarded. *Degree requirements:* For master's, thesis optional; for doctorate, thesis/dissertation. *Entrance requirements:* For master's and doctorate, GRE General Test. Additional exam requirements/recommendations for international students: Required—TOEFL (minimum score 550 paper-based; 213 computer-based), IELTS (minimum score 6.5), or Michigan English Language Assessment Battery (minimum score 82). *Application deadline:* For fall admission, 8/15 priority date for domestic students, 7/1 for international students; for winter admission, 12/1 priority date for domestic students, 11/1 for international students; for spring admission, 3/1 priority date for domestic students, 2/1 for international students. Applications are processed on a rolling basis. Application fee: $40 ($50 for international students). Electronic applications accepted. *Expenses:* Tuition, state resident: full-time $11,400. Tuition, nonresident: full-time $28,125. Tuition and fees vary according to course load, degree level, campus/location and program. *Financial support:* Fellowships, research assistantships, teaching assistantships, Federal Work-Study, and institutionally sponsored loans available. Support available to part-time students. *Unit head:* R. Mark Sulc, Interim Chair, 614-292-9084; E-mail: sulc.2@osu.edu.

Application contact: Graduate Admissions, 614-292-6031, Fax: 614-292-3656, E-mail: gradadmissions@osu.edu. Web site: http://hcs.osu.edu/.

Oklahoma State University, College of Agricultural Science and Natural Resources, Department of Horticulture and Landscape Architecture, Stillwater, OK 74078. Offers agriculture (M Ag); crop science (PhD); environmental science (PhD); horticulture (MS); plant science (PhD). *Faculty:* 20 full-time (2 women), 2 part-time/adjunct (1 woman). *Students:* 3 full-time (all women), 12 part-time (8 women); includes 2 minority (1 Black or African American, non-Hispanic/Latino; 1 American Indian or Alaska Native, non-Hispanic/Latino), 7 international. Average age 28. 6 applicants, 67% accepted, 4 enrolled. In 2011, 6 degrees awarded. *Degree requirements:* For master's, thesis (for some programs); for doctorate, comprehensive exam, thesis/dissertation. *Entrance requirements:* For master's and doctorate, GRE or GMAT. Additional exam requirements/recommendations for international students: Required—TOEFL (minimum score 550 paper-based; 79 iBT). *Application deadline:* For fall admission, 3/1 for international students; for spring admission, 8/1 for international students. Applications are processed on a rolling basis. Application fee: $40 ($75 for international students). Electronic applications accepted. *Expenses:* Tuition, state resident: full-time $4044; part-time $168.50 per credit hour. Tuition, nonresident: full-time $16,008; part-time $667 per credit hour. *Required fees:* $2122; $88.45 per credit hour. One-time fee: $50. Tuition and fees vary according to course load and campus/location. *Financial support:* In 2011–12, 13 research assistantships (averaging $14,145 per year) were awarded; career-related internships or fieldwork, Federal Work-Study, scholarships/grants, health care benefits, tuition waivers (partial), and unspecified assistantships also available. Support available to part-time students. Financial award application deadline: 3/1; financial award applicants required to submit FAFSA. *Faculty research:* Stress and postharvest physiology; water utilization and runoff; IPM systems and nursery, turf, floriculture, vegetable, net and fruit produces and natural resources, food extraction, and processing; public garden management. *Unit head:* Dr. Dale Maronek, Head, 405-744-5414, Fax: 405-744-9709. *Application contact:* Dr. Sheryl Tucker, Dean, 405-744-7099, Fax: 405-744-0355, E-mail: grad-i@okstate.edu. Web site: http://www.hortla.okstate.edu/.

Oregon State University, Graduate School, College of Agricultural Sciences, Department of Horticulture, Corvallis, OR 97331. Offers M Ag, MAIS, MS, PhD. *Degree requirements:* For master's, thesis (for some programs); for doctorate, thesis/dissertation. *Entrance requirements:* For master's and doctorate, GRE General Test, minimum GPA of 3.0 in last 90 hours. Additional exam requirements/recommendations for international students: Required—TOEFL.

Penn State University Park, Graduate School, College of Agricultural Sciences, Department of Horticulture, State College, University Park, PA 16802-1503. Offers MS, PhD. *Unit head:* Dr. Bruce A. McPheron, Dean, 814-865-2541, Fax: 814-865-3103, E-mail: bam10@psu.edu. *Application contact:* Cynthia E. Nicosia, Director of Graduate Enrollment Services, 814-865-1834, E-mail: cey1@psu.edu. Web site: http://horticulture.psu.edu.

Purdue University, Graduate School, College of Agriculture, Department of Horticulture, West Lafayette, IN 47907. Offers M Agr, MS, PhD. Part-time programs available. *Faculty:* 27 full-time (5 women), 4 part-time/adjunct (1 woman). *Students:* 29 full-time (15 women), 3 part-time (1 woman); includes 3 minority (1 Hispanic/Latino; 2 Two or more races, non-Hispanic/Latino), 17 international. Average age 30. 46 applicants, 15% accepted, 5 enrolled. In 2011, 5 master's, 5 doctorates awarded. Terminal master's awarded for partial completion of doctoral program. *Degree requirements:* For master's, thesis optional; for doctorate, thesis/dissertation. *Entrance requirements:* For master's and doctorate, GRE general test, minimum undergraduate GPA of 3.0 or equivalent. Additional exam requirements/recommendations for international students: Required—TOEFL (minimum score 550 paper-based; 77 iBT); Recommended—TWE. *Application deadline:* For fall admission, 5/1 for domestic and international students; for spring admission, 10/1 for domestic and international students. Applications are processed on a rolling basis. Application fee: $60 ($75 for international students). Electronic applications accepted. *Financial support:* Fellowships, research assistantships with tuition reimbursements, and teaching assistantships with tuition reimbursements available. Support available to part-time students. Financial award applicants required to submit FAFSA. *Faculty research:* Floral scent and plant volatile biosynthesis, mineral nutrient utilization from cellular to global scales, hormone signalling and transport, regulation of plant architecture and reproduction, plant cell cycle regulation, water utilization and stress responses, sustainable biofuel production, enhancement of salt tolerance in crop plants, natural genetic variation, plant epigenetics, mechanisms of heterosis; hybridizatiion and species breeding barriers. *Unit head:* Dr. Robert J. Joly, Interim Head, 765-494-1306, Fax: 765-494-0391, E-mail: joly@purdue.edu. *Application contact:* Colleen K. Flynn, Graduate Contact, 765-494-1306, Fax: 765-494-0391, E-mail: martinck@purdue.edu. Web site: http://www.hort.purdue.edu/hort/hort.html.

Rutgers, The State University of New Jersey, New Brunswick, Graduate School-New Brunswick, Program in Plant Biology, Piscataway, NJ 08854-8097. Offers horticulture and plant technology (MS, PhD); molecular and cellular biology (MS, PhD); organismal and population biology (MS, PhD); plant pathology (MS, PhD). Part-time programs available. Terminal master's awarded for partial completion of doctoral program. *Degree requirements:* For master's, comprehensive exam, thesis or alternative; for doctorate, comprehensive exam, thesis/dissertation. *Entrance requirements:* For master's and doctorate, GRE General Test, GRE Subject Test (recommended). Additional exam requirements/

436 facebook.com/petersonspublishing

Peterson's Graduate Programs in the Physical Sciences, Mathematics, Agricultural Sciences, the Environment & Natural Resources 2013

recommendations for international students: Required—TOEFL (minimum score 600 paper-based; 250 computer-based). Electronic applications accepted. *Faculty research:* Molecular biology and biochemistry of plants, plant development and genomics, plant protection, plant improvement, plant management of horticultural and field crops.

Southern Illinois University Carbondale, Graduate School, College of Agriculture, Department of Plant, Soil, and General Agriculture, Carbondale, IL 62901-4701. Offers horticultural science (MS); plant and soil science (MS). *Faculty:* 12 full-time (1 woman), 8 part-time/adjunct (0 women). *Students:* 13 full-time (5 women), 30 part-time (11 women); includes 4 minority (2 Black or African American, non-Hispanic/Latino; 1 American Indian or Alaska Native, non-Hispanic/Latino; 1 Hispanic/Latino), 6 international. 13 applicants, 69% accepted, 5 enrolled. In 2011, 7 master's awarded. *Degree requirements:* For master's, thesis. *Entrance requirements:* For master's, minimum GPA of 2.7. Additional exam requirements/recommendations for international students: Required—TOEFL. *Application deadline:* Applications are processed on a rolling basis. Application fee: $0. *Financial support:* In 2011–12, 22 students received support, including 15 research assistantships with full tuition reimbursements available, 6 teaching assistantships with full tuition reimbursements available; fellowships with full tuition reimbursements available, Federal Work-Study, institutionally sponsored loans, and tuition waivers (full) also available. Support available to part-time students. *Faculty research:* Herbicides, fertilizers, agriculture education, landscape design, plant breeding. *Total annual research expenditures:* $2 million. *Unit head:* Dr. Brian Klubek, Chair, 618-453-2496, E-mail: bklubek@siu.edu. *Application contact:* Lisa Hartline, Administrative Clerk, 618-453-1770, E-mail: lisah@siu.edu.

Texas A&M University, College of Agriculture and Life Sciences, Department of Horticultural Sciences, College Station, TX 77843. Offers M Agr, MS, PhD. *Faculty:* 14. *Students:* 28 full-time (15 women), 10 part-time (5 women); includes 4 minority (2 Asian, non-Hispanic/Latino; 2 Hispanic/Latino), 18 international. Average age 29. In 2011, 5 master's, 3 doctorates awarded. Terminal master's awarded for partial completion of doctoral program. *Degree requirements:* For master's, thesis (for some programs), professional internship; for doctorate, thesis/dissertation. *Entrance requirements:* For master's and doctorate, GRE General Test. Additional exam requirements/recommendations for international students: Required—TOEFL. Application fee: $50 ($75 for international students). Electronic applications accepted. *Expenses:* Tuition, state resident: full-time $5437; part-time $226.55 per credit hour. Tuition, nonresident: full-time $12,949; part-time $539.55 per credit hour. *Required fees:* $2741. *Financial support:* In 2011–12, 30 students received support, including fellowships with full tuition reimbursements available (averaging $15,000 per year), research assistantships with partial tuition reimbursements available (averaging $14,000 per year), teaching assistantships with partial tuition reimbursements available (averaging $14,000 per year); career-related internships or fieldwork and tuition waivers (partial) also available. Financial award application deadline: 4/1. *Faculty research:* Plant breeding, molecular biology, plant nutrition, post-harvest physiology, plant physiology. *Unit head:* Dr. Leland S. Pierson, III, Head, 979-458-2048, Fax: 979-845-0627, E-mail: plpm-head@ag.tamu.edu. *Application contact:* Dr. Michael Arnold, Professor, 979-845-1499, Fax: 979-845-0627, E-mail: ma-arnold@tamu.edu. Web site: http://hortsciences.tamu.edu/.

Texas Tech University, Graduate School, College of Agricultural Sciences and Natural Resources, Department of Plant and Soil Science, Lubbock, TX 79409. Offers crop science (MS); horticulture (MS); plant and soil science (PhD); plant protection (MS); soil science (MS); JD/MS. Part-time programs available. Postbaccalaureate distance learning degree programs offered (no on-campus study). *Faculty:* 8 full-time (4 women), 11 part-time/adjunct (1 woman). *Students:* 63 full-time (25 women), 39 part-time (19 women); includes 6 minority (3 Black or African American, non-Hispanic/Latino; 1 Asian, non-Hispanic/Latino; 2 Hispanic/Latino), 30 international. Average age 31. 63 applicants, 32% accepted, 15 enrolled. In 2011, 13 master's, 7 doctorates awarded. *Degree requirements:* For master's, thesis or alternative; for doctorate, thesis/dissertation. *Entrance requirements:* For master's and doctorate, GRE General Test, formal approval from departmental committee. Additional exam requirements/recommendations for international students: Required—TOEFL (minimum score 550 paper-based; 213 computer-based; 79 iBT). *Application deadline:* For fall admission, 6/1 priority date for domestic students, 1/15 for international students; for spring admission, 9/1 priority date for domestic students, 6/15 for international students. Applications are processed on a rolling basis. Application fee: $50 ($75 for international students). Electronic applications accepted. *Expenses:* Tuition, state resident: full-time $5899; part-time $245.80 per credit hour. Tuition, nonresident: full-time $13,411; part-time $558.80 per credit hour. *Required fees:* $2680.60; $86.50 per credit hour. $920.30 per semester. *Financial support:* In 2011–12, 52 students received support. Application deadline: 4/15; applicants required to submit FAFSA. *Faculty research:* Molecular and cellular biology of plant stress, physiology/genetics of crop production in semi-arid conditions, improvement of native plants, soil science and management, fibers and biopolymers. *Total annual research expenditures:* $6 million. *Unit head:* Dr. Richard E. Zartman, Chair, 806-742-2838 Ext. 230, Fax: 806-742-0775, E-mail: richard.zartman@ttu.edu. *Application contact:* Dr. Eric Hequet, Graduate Adviser, 806-742-2838 Ext. 239, Fax: 806-742-0775, E-mail: eric.hequet@ttu.edu. Web site: http://www.pssc.ttu.edu/.

Universidad Nacional Pedro Henriquez Urena, Graduate School, Santo Domingo, Dominican Republic. Offers agricultural diversity (MS), including

horticultural/fruit production, tropical animal production; conservation of monuments and cultural assets (M Arch); ecology and environment (MS); environmental engineering (MEE); international relations (MA); natural resource management (MS); political science (MA); project optimization (MPM); project feasibility (MPM); project management (MPM); sanitation engineering (ME); science for teachers (MS); tropical Caribbean architecture (M Arch).

University of Arkansas, Graduate School, Dale Bumpers College of Agricultural, Food and Life Sciences, Department of Horticulture, Fayetteville, AR 72701-1201. Offers MS. *Students:* 4 full-time (1 woman), 7 part-time (1 woman), 3 international. In 2011, 3 master's awarded. *Degree requirements:* For master's, thesis. *Application deadline:* For fall admission, 4/1 for international students; for spring admission, 10/1 for international students. Applications are processed on a rolling basis. Application fee: $40 ($50 for international students). Electronic applications accepted. *Financial support:* In 2011–12, 7 research assistantships were awarded; fellowships, teaching assistantships, career-related internships or fieldwork, and Federal Work-Study also available. Support available to part-time students. Financial award application deadline: 4/1; financial award applicants required to submit FAFSA. *Unit head:* Dr. David Hensley, Department Head, 479-575-2603, E-mail: dhensley@uark.edu. *Application contact:* Dr. J. Brad Murphy, Graduate Coordinator, 479-575-2603, E-mail: jbmurph@comp.uark.edu. Web site: http://hort.uark.edu.

University of California, Davis, Graduate Studies, Graduate Group in Horticulture and Agronomy, Davis, CA 95616. Offers MS. *Degree requirements:* For master's, comprehensive exam (for some programs), thesis (for some programs). *Entrance requirements:* For master's, GRE General Test. Additional exam requirements/recommendations for international students: Required—TOEFL (minimum score 550 paper-based; 213 computer-based). Electronic applications accepted. *Faculty research:* Postharvest physiology, mineral nutrition, crop improvement, plant growth and development.

University of Delaware, College of Agriculture and Natural Resources, Longwood Graduate Program in Public Horticulture, Newark, DE 19716. Offers MS. *Degree requirements:* For master's, thesis, internship. *Entrance requirements:* For master's, GRE General Test, introductory taxonomy course. Additional exam requirements/recommendations for international students: Required—TOEFL. Electronic applications accepted. *Faculty research:* Management and development of publicly oriented horticultural institutions.

University of Florida, Graduate School, College of Agricultural and Life Sciences, Department of Environmental Horticulture, Gainesville, FL 32611. Offers MS, PhD. Postbaccalaureate distance learning degree programs offered (no on-campus study). *Faculty:* 17 full-time (3 women), 1 (woman) part-time/adjunct. *Students:* 21 full-time (10 women), 14 part-time (7 women); includes 2 minority (1 Black or African American, non-Hispanic/Latino; 1 Hispanic/Latino), 11 international. Average age 30. 18 applicants, 28% accepted, 5 enrolled. In 2011, 10 master's, 4 doctorates awarded. *Degree requirements:* For master's, comprehensive exam, thesis optional, teaching experience; for doctorate, comprehensive exam, thesis/dissertation, teaching experience. *Entrance requirements:* For master's and doctorate, GRE General Test, minimum GPA of 3.0. Additional exam requirements/recommendations for international students: Required—TOEFL (minimum score 550 paper-based; 213 computer-based; 80 iBT), IELTS (minimum score 6). *Application deadline:* For fall admission, 1/15 priority date for domestic students, 1/15 for international students; for spring admission, 9/1 for domestic and international students. Applications are processed on a rolling basis. Application fee: $30. Electronic applications accepted. *Financial support:* Fellowships, research assistantships, teaching assistantships, and unspecified assistantships available. Financial award application deadline: 2/1; financial award applicants required to submit FAFSA. *Faculty research:* Breeding and genetics, conservation horticulture landscape design and ecology, floriculture, nursery and foliage crop production, turfgrasses, urban horticulture. *Total annual research expenditures:* $1.5 million. *Unit head:* Dr. Terril A. Nell, Chair, 352-273-4583, Fax: 352-392-3870, E-mail: tanell@ufl.edu. *Application contact:* Dr. Charles L. Guy, Graduate Coordinator, 352-392-1831 Ext. 222, Fax: 352-392-3870, E-mail: clguy@ufl.edu. Web site: http://hort.ifas.ufl.edu/.

University of Florida, Graduate School, College of Agricultural and Life Sciences, Department of Horticultural Sciences, Gainesville, FL 32611. Offers MS, PhD. *Faculty:* 29 full-time (9 women), 1 part-time/adjunct (0 women). *Students:* 73 full-time (33 women), 18 part-time (10 women); includes 7 minority (1 Black or African American, non-Hispanic/Latino; 3 Asian, non-Hispanic/Latino; 3 Hispanic/Latino), 46 international. Average age 30. 36 applicants, 42% accepted, 9 enrolled. In 2011, 15 master's, 10 doctorates awarded. *Degree requirements:* For master's, thesis optional; for doctorate, comprehensive exam, thesis/dissertation. *Entrance requirements:* For master's and doctorate, GRE General Test, minimum GPA of 3.0. Additional exam requirements/recommendations for international students: Required—TOEFL (minimum score 550 paper-based; 213 computer-based; 80 iBT), IELTS (minimum score 6). *Application deadline:* For fall admission, 1/1 priority date for domestic students, 1/1 for international students; for spring admission, 8/1 for domestic and international students. Applications are processed on a rolling basis. Application fee: $30. Electronic applications accepted. *Financial support:* Institutionally sponsored loans available. Financial award application deadline: 6/1; financial award applicants required to submit FAFSA. *Faculty research:* Breeding and genetics, crop production, organic/sustainable agriculture and nutrition, physiology and biochemistry, plant molecular and cellular biology, postharvest

Peterson's Graduate Programs in the Physical Sciences, Mathematics, Agricultural Sciences, the Environment & Natural Resources 2013

facebook.com/petersonspublishing **437**

Horticulture

biology. *Total annual research expenditures:* $15.6 million. *Unit head:* Dr. Daniel J. Cantliffe, Chair, 352-273-4766, Fax: 352-392-6479, E-mail: djcant@ufl.edu. *Application contact:* Dr. Steven A. Sargent, Graduate Coordinator, 352-273-4780, E-mail: sasa@ufl.edu. Web site: http://www.hos.ufl.edu/.

University of Georgia, College of Agricultural and Environmental Sciences, Department of Horticulture, Athens, GA 30602. Offers horticulture (MS, PhD); plant protection and pest management (MPPPM). Part-time programs available. *Faculty:* 21 full-time (5 women), 1 (woman) part-time/adjunct. *Students:* 17 full-time (8 women), 4 part-time (1 woman), 9 international. Average age 31. 9 applicants, 22% accepted. In 2011, 2 master's, 1 doctorate awarded. *Degree requirements:* For master's, thesis (MS); for doctorate, one foreign language, thesis/dissertation. *Entrance requirements:* For master's and doctorate, GRE General Test. *Application deadline:* For fall admission, 7/1 priority date for domestic students; for spring admission, 11/15 for domestic students. Application fee: $50. Electronic applications accepted. *Financial support:* In 2011–12, fellowships with partial tuition reimbursements (averaging $1,338 per year), research assistantships with partial tuition reimbursements (averaging $1,338 per year), teaching assistantships with partial tuition reimbursements (averaging $1,338 per year) were awarded; unspecified assistantships also available. *Unit head:* Dr. Douglas A. Bailey, Head, 706-542-2471, Fax: 706-542-0624, E-mail: dabailey@uga.edu. *Application contact:* Dr. Marc Van Iersel, Graduate Coordinator, 706-583-0284, Fax: 706-542-0624, E-mail: mvanier@uga.edu. Web site: http://www.hort.uga.edu/.

University of Guelph, Graduate Studies, Ontario Agricultural College, Department of Plant Agriculture, Guelph, ON N1G 2W1, Canada. Offers M Sc, PhD. Part-time programs available. *Degree requirements:* For master's, thesis; for doctorate, comprehensive exam, thesis/dissertation. *Entrance requirements:* For master's, minimum B average during previous 2 years of course work; for doctorate, minimum B average. Additional exam requirements/recommendations for international students: Required—TOEFL (minimum score 550 paper-based; 213 computer-based; 89 iBT), IELTS (minimum score 6.5), Michigan English Language Assessment Battery (minimum score: 85). Electronic applications accepted. *Faculty research:* Plant physiology, biochemistry, taxonomy, morphology, genetics, production, ecology, breeding and biotechnology.

University of Hawaii at Manoa, Graduate Division, College of Tropical Agriculture and Human Resources, Department of Tropical Plant and Soil Sciences, Honolulu, HI 96822. Offers MS, PhD. Part-time programs available. *Degree requirements:* For master's, thesis optional; for doctorate, comprehensive exam, thesis/dissertation. *Entrance requirements:* For master's and doctorate, GRE General Test. Additional exam requirements/recommendations for international students: Required—TOEFL (minimum score 520 paper-based; 213 computer-based; 79 iBT), IELTS (minimum score 5). *Faculty research:* Genetics and breeding; physiology, culture, and management; weed science; turfgrass and landscape; sensory evaluation.

University of Maine, Graduate School, College of Natural Sciences, Forestry, and Agriculture, Department of Plant, Soil, and Environmental Sciences, Program in Horticulture, Orono, ME 04469. Offers MS. *Students:* 1 (woman) full-time, 1 part-time (0 women), 1 international. Average age 30. 2 applicants, 50% accepted, 1 enrolled. In 2011, 2 degrees awarded. *Entrance requirements:* For master's, GRE General Test. Additional exam requirements/recommendations for international students: Required—TOEFL. *Application deadline:* For fall admission, 2/1 priority date for domestic students. Applications are processed on a rolling basis. Application fee: $65. Electronic applications accepted. *Expenses:* Tuition, state resident: full-time $5016. Tuition, nonresident: full-time $14,424. *Financial support:* Tuition waivers (full and partial) available. Financial award application deadline: 3/1. *Unit head:* Dr. Gregory Porter, Department Chair, 207-584-2938. *Application contact:* Scott G. Delcourt, Associate Dean of the Graduate School, 207-581-3291, Fax: 207-581-3232, E-mail: graduate@maine.edu. Web site: http://www2.umaine.edu/graduate/.

University of Manitoba, Faculty of Graduate Studies, Faculty of Agricultural and Food Sciences, Department of Plant Science, Winnipeg, MB R3T 2N2, Canada. Offers agronomy and plant protection (M Sc, PhD); horticulture (M Sc, PhD); plant breeding and genetics (M Sc, PhD); plant physiology-biochemistry (M Sc, PhD). *Degree requirements:* For master's, thesis; for doctorate, one foreign language, thesis/dissertation.

University of Maryland, College Park, Academic Affairs, College of Agriculture and Natural Resources, Department of Plant Science and Landscape Architecture, Plant Science Program, College Park, MD 20742. Offers MS, PhD. *Students:* 23 full-time (15 women), 4 part-time (2 women); includes 6 minority (2 Black or African American, non-Hispanic/Latino; 4 Hispanic/Latino), 6 international. 35 applicants, 26% accepted, 7 enrolled. In 2011, 4 master's, 2 doctorates awarded. *Entrance requirements:* For doctorate, GRE General Test. Additional exam requirements/recommendations for international students: Required—TOEFL. *Application deadline:* For fall admission, 5/1 for domestic students, 2/1 for international students; for spring admission, 6/1 for domestic and international students. Applications are processed on a rolling basis. Application fee: $75. Electronic applications accepted. *Expenses: Tuition, area resident:* Part-time $525 per credit hour. Tuition, state resident: part-time $525 per credit hour. Tuition, nonresident: part-time $1131 per credit hour. *Required fees:* $386.31 per term. Tuition and fees vary according to program. *Financial support:* In 2011–12, 1 fellowship (averaging $10,000 per year), 19 research assistantships (averaging $16,583 per year), 4 teaching assistantships (averaging $17,275 per year) were

awarded; career-related internships or fieldwork also available. Financial award applicants required to submit FAFSA. *Faculty research:* Mineral nutrition, genetics and breeding, chemical growth, histochemistry, postharvest physiology. *Unit head:* Dr. Gary Coleman, Coordinator, 301-405-4371, Fax: 301-314-9308, E-mail: wkenwort@umd.edu. *Application contact:* Dr. Charles A. Caramello, Dean of Graduate School, 301-405-0358, Fax: 301-314-9305.

University of Missouri, Graduate School, College of Agriculture, Food and Natural Resources, Division of Plant Sciences, Program in Horticulture, Columbia, MO 65211. Offers MS, PhD. *Degree requirements:* For master's, thesis; for doctorate, variable foreign language requirement, thesis/dissertation. *Entrance requirements:* For master's and doctorate, GRE General Test, minimum GPA of 3.0. *Application deadline:* Applications are processed on a rolling basis. Application fee: $55 ($75 for international students). *Expenses:* Tuition, state resident: full-time $5881. Tuition, nonresident: full-time $15,183. *Required fees:* $952. Tuition and fees vary according to campus/location and program. *Financial support:* Research assistantships, teaching assistantships, and institutionally sponsored loans available. *Unit head:* Dr. Michael Collins, Director, 573-882-1957, E-mail: collinsm@missouri.edu. *Application contact:* Dr. Jeanne Mihail, Director of Graduate Studies, 573-882-0574, E-mail: mihailj@missouri.edu.

University of Nebraska–Lincoln, Graduate College, College of Agricultural Sciences and Natural Resources, Department of Agronomy and Horticulture, Program in Horticulture, Lincoln, NE 68588. Offers MS, PhD. *Degree requirements:* For master's, thesis optional. *Entrance requirements:* For master's, GRE General Test. Additional exam requirements/recommendations for international students: Required—TOEFL (minimum score 600 paper-based; 250 computer-based). Electronic applications accepted. *Faculty research:* Horticultural crops: production, management, cultural, and ecological aspects; tissue and cell culture; plant nutrition and anatomy; postharvest physiology and ecology.

University of Puerto Rico, Mayagüez Campus, Graduate Studies, College of Agricultural Sciences, Department of Horticulture, Mayagüez, PR 00681-9000. Offers MS. Part-time programs available. *Students:* 12 full-time (5 women), 1 part-time (0 women); includes 12 minority (all Hispanic/Latino). 5 applicants, 100% accepted, 4 enrolled. In 2011, 1 master's awarded. *Degree requirements:* For master's, comprehensive exam, thesis. *Entrance requirements:* For master's, BS in agricultural science or its equivalent. *Application deadline:* For fall admission, 2/15 for domestic and international students; for spring admission, 9/15 for domestic and international students. Applications are processed on aʲ rolling basis. Application fee: $25. Tuition and fees vary according to course level and course load. *Financial support:* Federal Work-Study and institutionally sponsored loans available. *Faculty research:* Growth regulators, floriculture, starchy crops, coffee and fruit technology. *Unit head:* Prof. Hipolito O'Farrill, Director, 787-265-3852, Fax: 787-265-0860, E-mail: hipolito.ofarrill@upr.edu. *Application contact:* Janice Perez, Secretary, 787-832-4040 Ext. 3511, E-mail: japerez@uprm.edu. Web site: http://www.uprm.edu/agricultura/horticultura/.

University of South Africa, College of Agriculture and Environmental Sciences, Pretoria, South Africa. Offers agriculture (MS); consumer science (MCS); environmental management (MA, MS, PhD); environmental science (MA, MS, PhD); geography (MA, MS, PhD); horticulture (M Tech); human ecology (MHE); life sciences (MS); nature conservation (M Tech).

University of Vermont, Graduate College, College of Agriculture and Life Sciences, Department of Plant and Soil Science, Burlington, VT 05405. Offers MS, PhD. *Students:* 26 (16 women), 3 international. 27 applicants, 33% accepted, 6 enrolled. In 2011, 7 degrees awarded. *Degree requirements:* For master's, thesis; for doctorate, one foreign language, thesis/dissertation. *Entrance requirements:* For master's and doctorate, GRE General Test. Additional exam requirements/recommendations for international students: Required—TOEFL (minimum score 550 paper-based; 213 computer-based; 80 iBT). *Application deadline:* For fall admission, 2/15 priority date for domestic students, 2/15 for international students. Applications are processed on a rolling basis. Application fee: $40. Electronic applications accepted. *Financial support:* Fellowships, research assistantships, and teaching assistantships available. Financial award application deadline: 3/1. *Faculty research:* Soil chemistry, plant nutrition. *Unit head:* Dr. Deborah Neher, Chairperson, 802-656-2630. *Application contact:* Dr. Josef Gorres, Coordinator, 802-656-2630. Web site: http://www.uvm.edu/~pss.

University of Washington, Graduate School, College of the Environment, School of Forest Resources, Seattle, WA 98195. Offers bioresource science and engineering (MS, PhD); environmental horticulture (MEH); environmental horticulture and urban forestry (MS, PhD); forest ecology (MS, PhD); forest management (MFR); forest soils (MS, PhD); forest systems and bioenergy (MS, PhD); restoration ecology (MS, PhD); social sciences (MS, PhD); sustainable resource management (MS, PhD); wildlife science (MS, PhD); MFR/MAIS; MPA/MS. *Accreditation:* SAF. *Degree requirements:* For master's, thesis (for some programs); for doctorate, comprehensive exam (for some programs), thesis/dissertation. *Entrance requirements:* For master's and doctorate, GRE, minimum GPA of 3.0. Additional exam requirements/recommendations for international students: Required—TOEFL. Electronic applications accepted. *Faculty research:* Ecosystem analysis, silviculture and forest protection, paper science and engineering, environmental horticulture and urban forestry, natural resource policy and economics.

University of Wisconsin–Madison, Graduate School, College of Agricultural and Life Sciences, Department of Horticulture, Madison, WI 53706-1380. Offers

Peterson's Graduate Programs in the Physical Sciences, Mathematics, Agricultural Sciences, the Environment & Natural Resources 2013

MS, PhD. Part-time programs available. Terminal master's awarded for partial completion of doctoral program. *Degree requirements:* For master's, comprehensive exam, thesis (for some programs); for doctorate, comprehensive exam, thesis/dissertation. *Entrance requirements:* For master's and doctorate, minimum GPA of 3.0. Additional exam requirements/recommendations for international students: Required—TOEFL (minimum score 580 paper-based; 213 computer-based). Electronic applications accepted. *Expenses:* Tuition, state resident: full-time $10,296; part-time $643.51 per credit. Tuition, nonresident: full-time $24,054; part-time $1503.40 per credit. *Required fees:* $70.06 per credit. Tuition and fees vary according to course load, campus/location, program and reciprocity agreements. *Faculty research:* Biotechnology, crop breeding/genetics, environmental physiology, crop management, cytogenetics.

Virginia Polytechnic Institute and State University, Graduate School, College of Agriculture and Life Sciences, Department of Horticulture, Blacksburg, VA 24061. Offers MS, PhD. *Degree requirements:* For master's, comprehensive exam (for some programs), thesis (for some programs); for doctorate, comprehensive exam (for some programs), thesis/dissertation (for some programs). *Entrance requirements:* For master's and doctorate, GRE. Additional exam requirements/recommendations for international students: Required—TOEFL (minimum score 550 paper-based; 213 computer-based). *Application deadline:* For fall admission, 7/1 for domestic and international students; for spring admission, 12/1 for domestic and international students. Applications are processed on a rolling basis. Application fee: $65. Electronic applications accepted. *Expenses:* Tuition, state resident: full-time $10,048; part-time $558.25 per credit hour. Tuition, nonresident: full-time $19,497; part-time $1083.25 per credit hour. *Required fees:* $405 per semester. Tuition and fees vary according to course load, campus/location and program. *Financial support:* Research assistantships with full tuition reimbursements, teaching assistantships with full tuition reimbursements, career-related internships or fieldwork, Federal Work-Study, scholarships/grants, health care benefits, and unspecified assistantships available. Financial award application deadline: 1/15. *Unit head:* Dr. Jerzy Nowak, Unit Head, 540-231-2663, Fax: 540-231-3083, E-mail: jenowak@vt.edu. *Application contact:* Roger Harris, Information Contact, 540-231-5451, Fax: 540-231-3083, E-mail: rharris@vt.edu. Web site: http://www.hort.vt.edu/.

Washington State University, Graduate School, College of Agricultural, Human, and Natural Resource Sciences, Department of Horticulture and Landscape Architecture, Pullman, WA 99164. Offers horticulture (MS, PhD); landscape architecture (MSLA). Part-time programs available. *Faculty:* 18. *Students:* 31 full-time (15 women), 7 part-time (3 women); includes 1 minority (Hispanic/Latino), 14 international. Average age 30. 58 applicants, 17% accepted, 6 enrolled. In 2011, 8 master's, 1 doctorate awarded. *Degree requirements:* For master's, comprehensive exam (for some programs), thesis (for some programs), oral exam; for doctorate, comprehensive exam, thesis/dissertation, oral exam, written exam. *Entrance requirements:* For master's and doctorate, GRE General Test, GRE Subject Test, minimum GPA of 3.0, 3 letters of recommendation. Additional exam requirements/recommendations for international students: Required—TOEFL (minimum score 550 paper-based). *Application deadline:* For fall admission, 2/1 priority date for domestic students, 3/1 for international students; for spring admission, 9/1 for domestic students, 7/1 for international students. Applications are processed on a rolling basis. Application fee: $75. Electronic applications accepted. *Financial support:* In 2011–12, 16 students received support, including fellowships (averaging $2,275 per year), 10 research assistantships with full and partial tuition reimbursements available (averaging $18,204 per year), 2 teaching assistantships with full and partial tuition reimbursements available (averaging $18,204 per year); career-related internships or fieldwork, Federal Work-Study, institutionally sponsored loans, and health care benefits also available. Financial award application deadline: 4/1; financial award applicants required to submit FAFSA. *Faculty research:* Post-harvest physiology, genetics/plant breeding, molecular biology. *Total annual research expenditures:* $3.9 million. *Unit head:* Dr. N. Richard Knowles, Chair, 509-335-9502, Fax: 509-335-8690, E-mail: rknowles@wsu.edu. *Application contact:* Graduate School Admissions, 800-GRADWSU, Fax: 509-335-1949, E-mail: gradsch@wsu.edu. Web site: http://hortla.wsu.edu/.

West Virginia University, Davis College of Agriculture, Forestry and Consumer Sciences, Division of Plant and Soil Sciences, Morgantown, WV 26506. Offers agricultural sciences (PhD), including animal and food sciences, plant and soil sciences; agronomy (MS); entomology (MS); environmental microbiology (MS); horticulture (MS); plant pathology (MS). *Degree requirements:* For master's, thesis. *Entrance requirements:* For master's, GRE, minimum GPA of 2.5. Additional exam requirements/recommendations for international students: Required—TOEFL. *Faculty research:* Water quality, reclamation of disturbed land, crop production, pest control, environmental protection.

Plant Sciences

Alabama Agricultural and Mechanical University, School of Graduate Studies, College of Agricultural, Life and Natural Sciences, Department of Biological and Environmental Sciences, Huntsville, AL 35811. Offers plant and soil science (MS, PhD). Evening/weekend programs available. Terminal master's awarded for partial completion of doctoral program. *Degree requirements:* For master's, thesis; for doctorate, one foreign language, thesis/dissertation. *Entrance requirements:* For master's, GRE General Test, BS in agriculture; for doctorate, GRE General Test, master's degree. Additional exam requirements/recommendations for international students: Required—TOEFL (minimum score 500 paper-based; 173 computer-based; 61 iBT). Electronic applications accepted. *Faculty research:* Plant breeding, cytogenetics, crop production, soil chemistry and fertility, remote sensing.

American University of Beirut, Graduate Programs, Faculty of Agricultural and Food Sciences, Beirut, Lebanon. Offers agricultural economics (MS); animal sciences (MS); ecosystem management (MSES); food technology (MS); irrigation (MS); mechanization (MS); nutrition (MS); plant protection (MS); plant science (MS); poultry science (MS); soils (MS). Part-time programs available. *Faculty:* 21 full-time (6 women), 2 part-time/adjunct (0 women). *Students:* 12 full-time (all women), 93 part-time (77 women). Average age 24. 96 applicants, 67% accepted, 21 enrolled. In 2011, 25 master's awarded. *Degree requirements:* For master's, one foreign language, comprehensive exam, thesis (for some programs). *Entrance requirements:* Additional exam requirements/recommendations for international students: Required—TOEFL (minimum score 600 paper-based; 250 computer-based; 100 iBT), IELTS (minimum score 7.5). *Application deadline:* For fall admission, 2/20 for domestic and international students; for spring admission, 11/15 for domestic and international students. Applications are processed on a rolling basis. Application fee: $50. Electronic applications accepted. *Expenses: Tuition:* Full-time $12,780; part-time $710 per credit. *Required fees:* $528; $528 per credit. Tuition and fees vary according to course load and program. *Financial support:* In 2011–12, 22 research assistantships with partial tuition reimbursements (averaging $15,000 per year), 40 teaching assistantships with full and partial tuition reimbursements (averaging $1,000 per year) were awarded; scholarships/grants, health care benefits, and unspecified assistantships also available. Financial award application deadline: 2/2. *Faculty research:* Nutritional food-based dietary guidelines, community and therapeutic nutrition, food safety and food microbiology, landscape planning, nature and rural heritage conservation, pathology, immunology and control of poultry and animal diseases, agricultural economics and development, production of biodiesel from algae, national study on living conditions of refugees. *Unit head:* Prof. Nahla Hwalla, Dean, 961-1343002 Ext. 4400, Fax: 961-1744460, E-mail: nahla@aub.edu.lb. *Application contact:* Dr. Salim Kanaan, Director, Admissions Office, 961-1350000 Ext. 2594, Fax: 961-1750775, E-mail: sk00@aub.edu.lb. Web site: http://www.aub.edu.lb/fafs/Pages/index.aspx.

Brigham Young University, Graduate Studies, College of Life Sciences, Department of Plant and Wildlife Sciences, Provo, UT 84602-1001. Offers environmental science (MS); genetics and biotechnology (MS); wildlife and wildlands conservation (MS, PhD). *Faculty:* 26 full-time (1 woman), 1 (woman) part-time/adjunct. *Students:* 50 full-time (18 women); includes 8 minority (2 Asian, non-Hispanic/Latino; 4 Hispanic/Latino; 2 Native Hawaiian or other Pacific Islander, non-Hispanic/Latino), 4 international. Average age 25. 29 applicants, 41% accepted, 9 enrolled. In 2011, 18 master's, 1 doctorate awarded. *Degree requirements:* For master's, thesis; for doctorate, comprehensive exam, thesis/dissertation, minimum GPA of 3.2, 54 hours (18 dissertation, 36 coursework). *Entrance requirements:* For master's, GRE General Test, minimum GPA of 3.2 during last 60 hours of course work; for doctorate, GRE, minimum GPA of 3.2. Additional exam requirements/recommendations for international students: Required—TOEFL (minimum score 580 paper-based; 237 computer-based; 85 iBT). *Application deadline:* 2/1 for domestic and international students. Applications are processed on a rolling basis. Electronic applications accepted. Full-time tuition for non-LDS students: $11,520 per year; $640 per credit. *Expenses: Tuition:* Full-time $5760; part-time $320 per credit. Tuition and fees vary according to student's religious affiliation. *Financial support:* In 2011–12, 2 research assistantships with partial tuition reimbursements (averaging $16,650 per year), 37 teaching assistantships with partial tuition reimbursements (averaging $16,650 per year) were awarded; scholarships/grants and tuition waivers (partial) also available. Financial award application deadline: 2/1. *Faculty research:* Environmental science, plant genetics, plant ecology, plant nutrition and pathology, wildlife and wildlands conservation. *Total annual research expenditures:* $2.1 million. *Unit head:* Dr. Val J. Anderson, Chair, 801-422-3527, Fax: 801-422-0008, E-mail: val_anderson@byu.edu. *Application contact:* Dr. Loreen Allphin, Graduate Coordinator, 801-422-5603, Fax: 801-422-0008, E-mail: loreen_allphin@byu.edu. Web site: http://pws.byu.edu/home/.

California State University, Fresno, Division of Graduate Studies, College of Agricultural Sciences and Technology, Department of Plant Science, Fresno, CA 93740-8027. Offers MS. Part-time programs available. *Degree requirements:* For master's, thesis. *Entrance requirements:* For master's, GRE General Test, minimum GPA of 2.5. Additional exam requirements/recommendations for international students: Required—TOEFL. Electronic applications accepted.

Peterson's Graduate Programs in the Physical Sciences, Mathematics, Agricultural Sciences, the Environment & Natural Resources 2013

facebook.com/petersonspublishing **439**

Plant Sciences

Faculty research: Crop patterns, small watershed management, electronic monitoring of feedlot cattle, disease control, dairy operations.

Clemson University, Graduate School, College of Agriculture, Forestry and Life Sciences, Department of Forestry and Natural Resources, Program in Plant and Environmental Sciences, Clemson, SC 29634. Offers MS, PhD. *Students:* 43 full-time (16 women), 10 part-time (1 woman); includes 2 minority (1 Hispanic/Latino; 1 Two or more races, non-Hispanic/Latino), 16 international. Average age 31. 36 applicants, 47% accepted, 16 enrolled. In 2011, 12 master's, 3 doctorates awarded. *Degree requirements:* For master's, thesis; for doctorate, comprehensive exam, thesis/dissertation. *Entrance requirements:* For master's, GRE General Test, bachelor's degree in biological science or related disciplines; for doctorate, GRE General Test. Additional exam requirements/recommendations for international students: Required—TOEFL, IELTS. *Application deadline:* Applications are processed on a rolling basis. Electronic applications accepted. *Expenses:* Contact institution. *Financial support:* In 2011–12, 37 students received support, including 3 fellowships with full and partial tuition reimbursements available (averaging $9,667 per year), 29 research assistantships with partial tuition reimbursements available (averaging $16,876 per year), 10 teaching assistantships with partial tuition reimbursements available (averaging $12,424 per year); career-related internships or fieldwork, institutionally sponsored loans, scholarships/grants, health care benefits, and unspecified assistantships also available. Support available to part-time students. Financial award application deadline: 3/15; financial award applicants required to submit FAFSA. *Faculty research:* Sustainable agroecology, horticulture and turfgrass, physiology and pathology of plants. *Unit head:* Dr. Patricia Layton, School Director, 864-656-3302, Fax: 864-656-3304, E-mail: playton@clemson.edu. *Application contact:* Dr. Halina Knap, Coordinator, 864-656-3523, Fax: 864-656-3443, E-mail: hskrpsk@clemson.edu. Web site: http://www.clemson.edu/cafls/departments/pes/.

Colorado State University, Graduate School, College of Agricultural Sciences, Department of Bioagricultural Sciences and Pest Management, Fort Collins, CO 80523-1177. Offers entomology (MS, PhD); plant pathology and weed science (MS, PhD). Part-time programs available. *Faculty:* 20 full-time (5 women). *Students:* 8 full-time (5 women), 26 part-time (10 women); includes 2 minority (1 American Indian or Alaska Native, non-Hispanic/Latino; 1 Hispanic/Latino), 4 international. Average age 33. 7 applicants, 43% accepted, 1 enrolled. In 2011, 2 master's, 1 doctorate awarded. *Degree requirements:* For master's, comprehensive exam, thesis; for doctorate, comprehensive exam, thesis/dissertation. *Entrance requirements:* For master's, GRE General Test, minimum GPA of 3.0, letters of recommendation; for doctorate, GRE General Test, minimum GPA of 3.0, letters of recommendation, essay. Additional exam requirements/recommendations for international students: Required—TOEFL (minimum score 550 paper-based; 213 computer-based; 80 iBT). *Application deadline:* For fall admission, 1/15 priority date for domestic students, 1/1 for international students; for spring admission, 9/1 priority date for domestic students, 9/1 for international students. Applications are processed on a rolling basis. Application fee: $50. Electronic applications accepted. *Expenses:* Tuition, state resident: full-time $7992. Tuition, nonresident: full-time $19,592. *Required fees:* $1735; $58 per credit. *Financial support:* In 2011–12, 10 fellowships with partial tuition reimbursements (averaging $29,548 per year), 18 research assistantships with full tuition reimbursements (averaging $15,794 per year), 12 teaching assistantships with full tuition reimbursements (averaging $10,933 per year) were awarded; unspecified assistantships also available. Financial award application deadline: 1/15; financial award applicants required to submit FAFSA. *Faculty research:* Entomology specialization, plant pathology specialization, weed science specialization, ecology and biodiversity, integrated pest management. *Total annual research expenditures:* $3 million. *Unit head:* Dr. Thomas O. Holtzer, Head, 970-491-5261, Fax: 970-491-3862, E-mail: tholtzer@lamar.colostate.edu. *Application contact:* Janet Dill, Education Coordinator, 970-491-0402, Fax: 970-491-3862, E-mail: janet.dill@colostate.edu. Web site: http://www.colostate.edu/Depts/bspm/.

Colorado State University, Graduate School, College of Agricultural Sciences, Department of Soil and Crop Sciences, Fort Collins, CO 80523-1170. Offers MS, PhD. Part-time programs available. *Faculty:* 19 full-time (4 women), 1 part-time/adjunct (0 women). *Students:* 23 full-time (8 women), 18 part-time (6 women); includes 3 minority (2 Black or African American, non-Hispanic/Latino; 1 Asian, non-Hispanic/Latino), 11 international. Average age 33. 28 applicants, 36% accepted, 9 enrolled. In 2011, 6 master's, 5 doctorates awarded. Terminal master's awarded for partial completion of doctoral program. *Degree requirements:* For master's, thesis; for doctorate, comprehensive exam, thesis/dissertation, student teaching. *Entrance requirements:* For master's, GRE, minimum GPA of 3.0, appropriate bachelor's degree, letters of recommendation, statement of purpose; for doctorate, GRE, minimum GPA of 3.0, appropriate master's degree, letters of recommendation. Additional exam requirements/recommendations for international students: Required—TOEFL (minimum score 550 paper-based; 213 computer-based; 80 iBT). *Application deadline:* For fall admission, 4/1 priority date for domestic students, 5/1 for international students; for spring admission, 9/1 priority date for domestic students, 10/1 for international students. Application fee: $50. Electronic applications accepted. *Expenses:* Tuition, state resident: full-time $7992. Tuition, nonresident: full-time $19,592. *Required fees:* $1735; $58 per credit. *Financial support:* In 2011–12, 20 students received support, including 4 fellowships with full tuition reimbursements available (averaging $35,814 per year), 15 research assistantships with full tuition reimbursements available (averaging $19,994 per year), 1 teaching assistantship

with full tuition reimbursement available (averaging $7,721 per year); scholarships/grants and unspecified assistantships also available. Financial award application deadline: 2/15; financial award applicants required to submit FAFSA. *Faculty research:* Water quality, soil fertility, soil/plant ecosystems, plant breeding and genetics, cropping systems . *Total annual research expenditures:* $4.5 million. *Unit head:* Dr. Eugene Kelly, Head, 970-491-6881, Fax: 970-491-0564, E-mail: eugene.kelly@colostate.edu. *Application contact:* Karen Allison, Graduate Contact, 970-491-6295, Fax: 970-491-0564, E-mail: karen.allison@colostate.edu. Web site: http://www.soilcrop.colostate.edu/.

Cornell University, Graduate School, Graduate Fields of Agriculture and Life Sciences, Field of Plant Breeding, Ithaca, NY 14853-0001. Offers plant breeding (MPS, MS, PhD); plant genetics (MPS, MS, PhD). *Faculty:* 30 full-time (7 women). *Students:* 33 full-time (17 women); includes 5 minority (3 Asian, non-Hispanic/Latino; 2 Hispanic/Latino), 14 international. Average age 26. 56 applicants, 30% accepted, 13 enrolled. In 2011, 7 master's, 2 doctorates awarded. Terminal master's awarded for partial completion of doctoral program. *Degree requirements:* For master's, thesis (MS), project paper (MPS); for doctorate, comprehensive exam, thesis/dissertation. *Entrance requirements:* For master's and doctorate, GRE General Test, GRE Subject Test (recommended), 3 letters of recommendation. Additional exam requirements/recommendations for international students: Required—TOEFL (minimum score 550 paper-based; 213 computer-based; 77 iBT). *Application deadline:* For fall admission, 1/15 priority date for domestic students. Application fee: $95. Electronic applications accepted. *Financial support:* In 2011–12, 7 fellowships with full tuition reimbursements, 13 research assistantships with full tuition reimbursements, 2 teaching assistantships with full tuition reimbursements were awarded; institutionally sponsored loans, scholarships/grants, health care benefits, tuition waivers (full and partial), and unspecified assistantships also available. Financial award applicants required to submit FAFSA. *Faculty research:* Crop breeding for improved yield, stress resistance and quality; genetics and genomics of crop plants; applications of molecular biology and bioinformatics to crop improvement; genetic diversity and utilization of wild germplasm; international agriculture. *Unit head:* Director of Graduate Studies, 607-255-2180. *Application contact:* Graduate Field Assistant, 607-255-2180, E-mail: plbrgrad@cornell.edu. Web site: http://www.gradschool.cornell.edu/fields.php?id-58&a-2.

Cornell University, Graduate School, Graduate Fields of Agriculture and Life Sciences, Field of Plant Protection, Ithaca, NY 14853-0001. Offers MPS. *Faculty:* 22 full-time (4 women). *Students:* 1 applicant, 0% accepted. *Degree requirements:* For master's, internship, final exam. *Entrance requirements:* For master's, GRE General Test, 3 letters of recommendation. Additional exam requirements/recommendations for international students: Required—TOEFL (minimum score 550 paper-based; 213 computer-based; 77 iBT). *Application deadline:* For fall admission, 4/1 for domestic students. Application fee: $95. Electronic applications accepted. *Financial support:* Fellowships with full tuition reimbursements, research assistantships with full tuition reimbursements, teaching assistantships with full tuition reimbursements, institutionally sponsored loans, scholarships/grants, health care benefits, tuition waivers (full and partial), and unspecified assistantships available. Financial award applicants required to submit FAFSA. *Faculty research:* Fruit and vegetable crop insects and diseases, systems modeling, biological control, plant protection economics, integrated pest management. *Unit head:* Director of Graduate Studies, 315-787-2323, Fax: 315-787-2326. *Application contact:* Graduate Field Assistant, 315-787-2323, Fax: 315-787-2326, E-mail: plprotection@cornell.edu. Web site: http://www.gradschool.cornell.edu/fields.php?id-60&a-2.

Delaware State University, Graduate Programs, Department of Agriculture and Natural Resources, Program in Plant Science, Dover, DE 19901-2277. Offers MS. *Entrance requirements:* For master's, GRE. Additional exam requirements/recommendations for international students: Required—TOEFL (minimum score 550 paper-based).

Illinois State University, Graduate School, College of Arts and Sciences, Department of Biological Sciences, Normal, IL 61790-2200. Offers animal behavior (MS); bacteriology (MS); biochemistry (MS); biological sciences (MS); biology (PhD); biophysics (MS); biotechnology (MS); botany (MS, PhD); cell biology (MS); conservation biology (MS); developmental biology (MS); ecology (MS, PhD); entomology (MS); evolutionary biology (MS); genetics (MS, PhD); immunology (MS); microbiology (MS, PhD); molecular biology (MS); molecular genetics (MS); neurobiology (MS); neuroscience (MS); parasitology (MS); physiology (MS, PhD); plant biology (MS); plant molecular biology (MS); plant sciences (MS); structural biology (MS); zoology (MS, PhD). Part-time programs available. *Degree requirements:* For master's, thesis or alternative; for doctorate, variable foreign language requirement, thesis/dissertation, 2 terms of residency. *Entrance requirements:* For master's, GRE General Test, minimum GPA of 2.6 in last 60 hours of course work; for doctorate, GRE General Test. *Faculty research:* Redoc balance and drug development in schistosoma mansoni, control of the growth of listeria monocytogenes at low temperature, regulation of cell expansion and microtubule function by SPRI, CRUI: physiology and fitness consequences of different life history phenotypes.

Iowa State University of Science and Technology, Program in Plant Breeding, Ames, IA 50011-1010. Offers MS, PhD. *Degree requirements:* For master's, thesis optional. *Entrance requirements:* For master's and doctorate, GRE. Additional exam requirements/recommendations for international students: Required—TOEFL (minimum score 550 paper-based; 79 iBT), IELTS (minimum score 6.5). *Application deadline:* Applications are processed on a rolling basis.

440 facebook.com/petersonspublishing

Peterson's Graduate Programs in the Physical Sciences, Mathematics, Agricultural Sciences, the Environment & Natural Resources 2013

Electronic applications accepted. *Unit head:* Tom E. Loynachan, Director of Graduate Education, 515-294-1361, Fax: 515-294-8146, E-mail: gradprograms@agron.iastate.edu. *Application contact:* Jaci Severson, Application Contact, 515-294-1361, Fax: 515-294-8146, E-mail: grad_admissions@iastate.edu. Web site: http://www.agron.iastate.edu.

Kansas State University, Graduate School, College of Agriculture, Department of Agronomy, Manhattan, KS 66506. Offers crop science (MS, PhD); plant breeding and genetics (MS, PhD); range management (MS, PhD); soil science (MS, PhD); weed science (MS, PhD). Part-time programs available. *Faculty:* 28 full-time (4 women), 11 part-time/adjunct (1 woman). *Students:* 62 full-time (18 women), 10 part-time (4 women); includes 4 minority (2 Black or African American, non-Hispanic/Latino; 1 Asian, non-Hispanic/Latino; 1 Hispanic/Latino), 34 international. Average age 31. 31 applicants, 42% accepted, 9 enrolled. In 2011, 8 master's, 4 doctorates awarded. Terminal master's awarded for partial completion of doctoral program. *Degree requirements:* For master's, thesis or alternative, oral exam; for doctorate, thesis/dissertation, preliminary exams. *Entrance requirements:* For master's, minimum GPA of 3.0 in BS; for doctorate, minimum GPA of 3.5 in master's program. Additional exam requirements/recommendations for international students: Required—TOEFL (minimum score 500 paper-based; 250 computer-based). *Application deadline:* For fall admission, 2/1 priority date for domestic students, 2/1 for international students; for spring admission, 8/1 priority date for domestic students, 8/1 for international students. Applications are processed on a rolling basis. Application fee: $40 ($55 for international students). Electronic applications accepted. *Financial support:* In 2011–12, 64 research assistantships (averaging $21,705 per year), 7 teaching assistantships with partial tuition reimbursements (averaging $18,200 per year) were awarded; institutionally sponsored loans and scholarships/grants also available. Support available to part-time students. Financial award application deadline: 3/1; financial award applicants required to submit FAFSA. *Faculty research:* Range and forage science, soil and environmental science, crop physiology, weed science, plant breeding and genetics. *Total annual research expenditures:* $5.5 million. *Unit head:* Dr. William Schapaugh, Head, 785-532-6101, Fax: 785-532-6094, E-mail: wts@ksu.edu. *Application contact:* Dr. Scott Staggenborg, Graduate Coordinator, 785-532-7214, Fax: 785-532-6094, E-mail: sstaggen@ksu.edu. Web site: http://www.agronomy.k-state.edu/DesktopDefault.aspx.

Lehman College of the City University of New York, Division of Natural and Social Sciences, Department of Biological Sciences, Program in Plant Sciences, Bronx, NY 10468-1589. Offers PhD. *Degree requirements:* For doctorate, 2 foreign languages, thesis/dissertation. *Entrance requirements:* For doctorate, GRE General Test.

McGill University, Faculty of Graduate and Postdoctoral Studies, Faculty of Agricultural and Environmental Sciences, Department of Plant Science, Montréal, QC H3A 2T5, Canada. Offers M Sc, M Sc A, PhD, Certificate.

Miami University, College of Arts and Science, Department of Botany, Oxford, OH 45056. Offers MA, MAT, MS, PhD. Part-time programs available. *Students:* 59 full-time (30 women), 183 part-time (142 women); includes 15 minority (3 Black or African American, non-Hispanic/Latino; 2 Asian, non-Hispanic/Latino; 5 Hispanic/Latino; 5 Two or more races, non-Hispanic/Latino), 22 international. Average age 34. In 2011, 11 master's, 4 doctorates awarded. *Entrance requirements:* For master's, GRE General Test, minimum undergraduate GPA of 3.0 during previous 2 years or 2.75 overall; for doctorate, GRE General Test, minimum undergraduate GPA of 2.75, 3.0 graduate. Additional exam requirements/recommendations for international students: Required—TOEFL (minimum score 550 paper-based). *Application deadline:* For fall admission, 1/1 for domestic and international students. Applications are processed on a rolling basis. Application fee: $50. Electronic applications accepted. *Expenses:* Tuition, state resident: full-time $12,023; part-time $501 per credit hour. Tuition, nonresident: full-time $26,554; part-time $1107 per credit hour. *Required fees:* $528. *Financial support:* Research assistantships, teaching assistantships with full tuition reimbursements, Federal Work-Study, institutionally sponsored loans, health care benefits, and unspecified assistantships available. Financial award application deadline: 2/15; financial award applicants required to submit FAFSA. *Faculty research:* Evolution of plants, fungi and algae; bioinformatics; molecular biology of plants and cyanobacteria; food web dynamics; plant science education. *Unit head:* Dr. John Kiss, Chair, 513-529-4200, E-mail: kissjz@muohio.edu. *Application contact:* Dr. Richard C. Moore, Graduate Coordinator, 513-529-4278, E-mail: moorerc@muohio.edu. Web site: http://www.muohio.edu/botany/.

Michigan State University, The Graduate School, College of Agriculture and Natural Resources, MSU-DOE Plant Research Laboratory, East Lansing, MI 48824. Offers biochemistry and molecular biology (PhD); cellular and molecular biology (PhD); crop and soil sciences (PhD); genetics (PhD); microbiology and molecular genetics (PhD); plant biology (PhD); plant physiology (PhD). Offered jointly with the Department of Energy. *Degree requirements:* For doctorate, comprehensive exam, thesis/dissertation, laboratory rotation, defense of dissertation. *Entrance requirements:* For doctorate, GRE General Test, acceptance into one of the affiliated department programs; 3 letters of recommendation; bachelor's degree or equivalent in life sciences, chemistry, biochemistry, or biophysics; research experience. Electronic applications accepted. *Faculty research:* Role of hormones in the regulation of plant development and physiology, molecular mechanisms associated with signal recognition, development and application of genetic methods and materials, protein routing and function.

Michigan State University, The Graduate School, College of Agriculture and Natural Resources, Program in Plant Breeding and Genetics, East Lansing, MI 48824. Offers MS, PhD. *Entrance requirements:* Additional exam requirements/recommendations for international students: Required—TOEFL. Electronic applications accepted. *Faculty research:* Applied plant breeding and genetics; disease, insect and herbicide resistances; gene isolation and genomics; abiotic stress factors; molecular mapping.

Mississippi State University, College of Agriculture and Life Sciences, Department of Plant and Soil Sciences, Mississippi State, MS 39762. Offers agriculture (MS), including agronomy, horticulture, weed science. *Faculty:* 30 full-time (1 woman), 1 part-time/adjunct (0 women). *Students:* 34 full-time (11 women), 21 part-time (5 women); includes 5 minority (3 Black or African American, non-Hispanic/Latino; 2 American Indian or Alaska Native, non-Hispanic/Latino), 13 international. Average age 30. 33 applicants, 42% accepted, 12 enrolled. In 2011, 6 master's awarded. *Degree requirements:* For master's, thesis, exit seminar describing thesis research. *Entrance requirements:* For master's, GRE (weed science), minimum GPA of 2.75 (agronomy/horticulture), 3.0 (weed science). Additional exam requirements/recommendations for international students: Required—TOEFL (minimum score 550 paper-based; 213 computer-based; 79 iBT); Recommended—IELTS (minimum score 6.5). *Application deadline:* For fall admission, 7/1 for domestic students, 5/1 for international students; for spring admission, 10/1 for domestic students, 9/1 for international students. Applications are processed on a rolling basis. Application fee: $40. Electronic applications accepted. *Expenses:* Tuition, state resident: full-time $5805; part-time $322.50 per credit hour. Tuition, nonresident: full-time $14,670; part-time $815 per credit hour. *Financial support:* In 2011–12, 30 research assistantships (averaging $14,692 per year), 3 teaching assistantships (averaging $15,133 per year) were awarded; Federal Work-Study, institutionally sponsored loans, scholarships/grants, and unspecified assistantships also available. Financial award application deadline: 4/1; financial award applicants required to submit FAFSA. *Unit head:* Dr. J. Mike Phillips, Professor and Head, 662-325-2311, Fax: 662-325-8742, E-mail: jmp657@msstate.edu. *Application contact:* Dr. William Kingery, Graduate Coordinator, 662-325-2748, Fax: 662-325-8742, E-mail: wkingery@pss.msstate.edu. Web site: http://www.pss.msstate.edu/

Missouri State University, Graduate College, William H. Darr School of Agriculture, Springfield, MO 65897. Offers plant science (MS); secondary education (MS Ed), including agriculture. Part-time programs available. *Faculty:* 14 full-time (3 women), 1 part-time/adjunct (0 women). *Students:* 15 full-time (9 women), 15 part-time (8 women), 4 international. Average age 29. 19 applicants, 100% accepted, 14 enrolled. In 2011, 9 master's awarded. *Degree requirements:* For master's, comprehensive exam, thesis or alternative. *Entrance requirements:* For master's, GRE (MS in plant science, MNAS), 9-12 teacher certification (MS Ed), minimum GPA of 3.0 (MS plant science, MNAS). Additional exam requirements/recommendations for international students: Required—TOEFL (minimum score 550 paper-based; 213 computer-based; 79 iBT). *Application deadline:* For fall admission, 7/20 priority date for domestic students, 5/1 for international students; for spring admission, 12/20 priority date for domestic students, 9/1 for international students. Applications are processed on a rolling basis. Application fee: $35 ($50 for international students). Electronic applications accepted. *Expenses:* Tuition, state resident: full-time $4086; part-time $227 per credit hour. Tuition, nonresident: full-time $8172; part-time $454 per credit hour. *Required fees:* $275 per semester. Tuition and fees vary according to course load, campus/location and program. *Financial support:* In 2011–12, 6 research assistantships with full tuition reimbursements (averaging $8,288 per year), 3 teaching assistantships with full tuition reimbursements (averaging $8,576 per year) were awarded; Federal Work-Study, institutionally sponsored loans, scholarships/grants, and unspecified assistantships also available. Financial award application deadline: 3/31; financial award applicants required to submit FAFSA. *Faculty research:* Grapevine biotechnology, agricultural marketing, Asian elephant reproduction, poultry science, integrated pest management. *Unit head:* Dr. W. Anson Elliott, Head, 417-836-5638, E-mail: ansonelliot@missouristate.edu. *Application contact:* Misty Stewart, Coordinator of Graduate Recruitment, 417-836-6079, Fax: 417-836-6200, E-mail: mistystewart@missouristate.edu. Web site: http://ag.missouristate.edu/.

Montana State University, College of Graduate Studies, College of Agriculture, Department of Plant Sciences and Plant Pathology, Bozeman, MT 59717. Offers plant pathology (MS); plant sciences (MS, PhD), including plant genetics (PhD), plant pathology (PhD). Part-time programs available. *Degree requirements:* For master's, comprehensive exam; for doctorate, comprehensive exam, thesis/dissertation. *Entrance requirements:* For master's, GRE General Test, minimum GPA of 3.0; for doctorate, GRE General Test. Additional exam requirements/recommendations for international students: Required—TOEFL (minimum score 550 paper-based; 213 computer-based). Electronic applications accepted. *Faculty research:* Plant genetics, plant metabolism, plant microbe interactions, plant pathology, entomology research.

New Mexico State University, Graduate School, College of Agricultural, Consumer and Environmental Sciences, Department of Entomology, Plant Pathology and Weed Science, Las Cruces, NM 88003-8001. Offers agricultural biology (MS). Part-time programs available. *Faculty:* 6 full-time (2 women), 2 part-time/adjunct (0 women). *Students:* 11 full-time (3 women), 5 part-time (2 women); includes 5 minority (4 Hispanic/Latino; 1 Two or more races, non-Hispanic/Latino), 3 international. Average age 26. 6 applicants, 67% accepted, 4 enrolled. In 2011,

Peterson's Graduate Programs in the Physical Sciences, Mathematics, Agricultural Sciences, the Environment & Natural Resources 2013

facebook.com/petersonspublishing **441**

Plant Sciences

5 master's awarded. *Degree requirements:* For master's, comprehensive exam, thesis. *Entrance requirements:* For master's, GRE General Test. Additional exam requirements/recommendations for international students: Required—TOEFL (minimum score 550 paper-based; 0 computer-based; 79 iBT), IELTS (minimum score 6.5). *Application deadline:* For fall admission, 7/1 priority date for domestic students; for spring admission, 11/1 priority date for domestic students. Applications are processed on a rolling basis. Application fee: $40 ($50 for international students). Electronic applications accepted. *Expenses:* Tuition, state resident: full-time $5004; part-time $208.50 per credit. Tuition, nonresident: full-time $17,446; part-time $726.90 per credit. *Financial support:* In 2011–12, 9 students received support, including 2 fellowships (averaging $4,304 per year), 9 research assistantships with full tuition reimbursements available (averaging $20,235 per year); teaching assistantships with partial tuition reimbursements available, career-related internships or fieldwork, and health care benefits also available. Financial award application deadline: 3/1. *Faculty research:* Integrated pest management, pesticide application and safety, livestock ectoparasite research, biotechnology, nematology. *Unit head:* Dr. Jill Schroeder, Interim Head, 575-646-3225, Fax: 575-646-8087, E-mail: jischroe@nmsu.edu. *Application contact:* Cindy Bullard, Intermediate Administrative Assistant, 575-646-1145, Fax: 575-646-8087, E-mail: cbullard@nmsu.edu. Web site: http://eppws.nmsu.edu/.

New Mexico State University, Graduate School, College of Agricultural, Consumer and Environmental Sciences, Department of Plant and Environmental Sciences, Las Cruces, NM 88003-8001. Offers horticulture (MS); plant and environmental sciences (MS, PhD). Part-time programs available. *Faculty:* 21 full-time (3 women). *Students:* 45 full-time (17 women), 19 part-time (8 women); includes 9 minority (3 American Indian or Alaska Native, non-Hispanic/Latino; 5 Hispanic/Latino; 1 Two or more races, non-Hispanic/Latino), 20 international. Average age 32. 27 applicants, 52% accepted, 11 enrolled. In 2011, 6 master's, 7 doctorates awarded. Terminal master's awarded for partial completion of doctoral program. *Degree requirements:* For master's, thesis; for doctorate, one foreign language, comprehensive exam, thesis/dissertation, qualifying exam, 2 seminars. *Entrance requirements:* For master's, GRE, minimum GPA of 3.0, 3 letters of reference, letter of purpose or intent; for doctorate, GRE, minimum GPA of 3.3; 3 letters of reference, letter of purpose or intent. Additional exam requirements/recommendations for international students: Required—TOEFL (minimum score 550 paper-based; 0 computer-based; 79 iBT), IELTS (minimum score 6.5). *Application deadline:* Applications are processed on a rolling basis. Application fee: $40 ($50 for international students). Electronic applications accepted. *Expenses:* Tuition, state resident: full-time $5004; part-time $208.50 per credit. Tuition, nonresident: full-time $17,446; part-time $726.90 per credit. *Financial support:* In 2011–12, 8 students received support, including 3 fellowships (averaging $2,892 per year), 28 research assistantships with partial tuition reimbursements available (averaging $22,079 per year), 14 teaching assistantships with partial tuition reimbursements available (averaging $22,188 per year); career-related internships or fieldwork, Federal Work-Study, scholarships/grants, health care benefits, and unspecified assistantships also available. Support available to part-time students. Financial award application deadline: 3/1. *Faculty research:* Plant breeding and genetics, molecular biology, plant physiology, soil science and environmental remediation, urban horticulture and turfgrass management. *Unit head:* Dr. Richard Pratt, Head, 575-646-3406, Fax: 575-646-6041, E-mail: ricpratt@nmsu.edu. *Application contact:* Esther Ramirez, Information Contact, 575-646-3406, Fax: 575-646-6041, E-mail: esramire@nmsu.edu. Web site: http://aces.nmsu.edu/pes.

North Carolina Agricultural and Technical State University, School of Graduate Studies, School of Agriculture and Environmental Sciences, Department of Natural Resources and Environmental Design, Greensboro, NC 27411. Offers plant, soil and environmental science (MS). Part-time and evening/weekend programs available. *Degree requirements:* For master's, comprehensive exam, thesis optional, qualifying exam. *Entrance requirements:* For master's, GRE General Test, minimum GPA of 3.0. *Faculty research:* Soil parameters and compaction of forest site, controlled traffic effects on soil, improving soybean and vegetable crops.

North Dakota State University, College of Graduate and Interdisciplinary Studies, College of Agriculture, Food Systems, and Natural Resources, Department of Plant Sciences, Fargo, ND 58108. Offers crop and weed sciences (MS); horticulture (MS); natural resource management (MS); plant sciences (PhD). Part-time programs available. *Faculty:* 31 full-time (5 women). *Students:* 51 full-time (19 women), 16 part-time (6 women); includes 4 minority (2 Hispanic/Latino; 2 Two or more races, non-Hispanic/Latino), 36 international. Average age 26. 16 applicants, 69% accepted, 6 enrolled. In 2011, 9 master's, 3 doctorates awarded. *Degree requirements:* For master's, thesis; for doctorate, thesis/dissertation. *Entrance requirements:* Additional exam requirements/recommendations for international students: Required—TOEFL (minimum score 525 paper-based; 197 computer-based; 71 iBT). *Application deadline:* For fall admission, 5/1 for international students; for winter admission, 8/1 for international students. Applications are processed on a rolling basis. Application fee: $35. Electronic applications accepted. *Financial support:* In 2011–12, 2 fellowships (averaging $19,950 per year), 64 research assistantships were awarded; teaching assistantships, Federal Work-Study, and institutionally sponsored loans also available. Financial award application deadline: 4/15. *Faculty research:* Biotechnology, weed control science, plant breeding, plant genetics, crop physiology. *Unit head:* Dr. Richard Horsley, Head, 701-231-7971, Fax: 701-231-8474, E-mail: richard.horsley@ndsu.edu. *Application contact:* Sonya Goergen, Marketing, Recruitment, and Public Relations Coordinator, 701-231-7033, Fax: 701-231-6524. Web site: http://www.ndsu.nodak.edu/.

Oklahoma State University, College of Agricultural Science and Natural Resources, Department of Horticulture and Landscape Architecture, Stillwater, OK 74078. Offers agriculture (M Ag); crop science (PhD); environmental science (PhD); horticulture (MS); plant science (PhD). *Faculty:* 20 full-time (2 women), 2 part-time/adjunct (1 woman). *Students:* 3 full-time (all women), 12 part-time (8 women); includes 2 minority (1 Black or African American, non-Hispanic/Latino; 1 American Indian or Alaska Native, non-Hispanic/Latino), 7 international. Average age 28. 6 applicants, 67% accepted, 4 enrolled. In 2011, 6 degrees awarded. *Degree requirements:* For master's, thesis (for some programs); for doctorate, comprehensive exam, thesis/dissertation. *Entrance requirements:* For master's and doctorate, GRE or GMAT. Additional exam requirements/recommendations for international students: Required—TOEFL (minimum score 550 paper-based; 79 iBT). *Application deadline:* For fall admission, 3/1 for international students; for spring admission, 8/1 for international students. Applications are processed on a rolling basis. Application fee: $40 ($75 for international students). Electronic applications accepted. *Expenses:* Tuition, state resident: full-time $4044; part-time $168.50 per credit hour. Tuition, nonresident: full-time $16,008; part-time $667 per credit hour. *Required fees:* $2122; $88.45 per credit hour. One-time fee: $50. Tuition and fees vary according to course load and campus/location. *Financial support:* In 2011–12, 13 research assistantships (averaging $14,145 per year) were awarded; career-related internships or fieldwork, Federal Work-Study, scholarships/grants, health care benefits, tuition waivers (partial), and unspecified assistantships also available. Support available to part-time students. Financial award application deadline: 3/1; financial award applicants required to submit FAFSA. *Faculty research:* Stress and postharvest physiology; water utilization and runoff; IPM systems and nursery, turf, floriculture, vegetable, net and fruit produces and natural resources, food extraction, and processing; public garden management. *Unit head:* Dr. Dale Maronek, Head, 405-744-5414, Fax: 405-744-9709. *Application contact:* Dr. Sheryl Tucker, Dean, 405-744-7099, Fax: 405-744-0355, E-mail: grad-i@okstate.edu. Web site: http://www.hortla.okstate.edu/.

Oklahoma State University, College of Agricultural Science and Natural Resources, Department of Plant and Soil Sciences, Stillwater, OK 74078. Offers crop science (PhD); environmental science (PhD); plant and soil sciences (MS); plant science (PhD); soil science (M Ag, PhD). *Faculty:* 31 full-time (4 women), 1 part-time/adjunct (0 women). *Students:* 19 full-time (5 women), 42 part-time (20 women); includes 5 minority (2 Black or African American, non-Hispanic/Latino; 1 Asian, non-Hispanic/Latino; 2 Two or more races, non-Hispanic/Latino), 33 international. Average age 28. 32 applicants, 22% accepted, 3 enrolled. In 2011, 18 master's, 3 doctorates awarded. *Degree requirements:* For master's, thesis; for doctorate, comprehensive exam, thesis/dissertation. *Entrance requirements:* For master's and doctorate, GRE or GMAT. Additional exam requirements/recommendations for international students: Required—TOEFL (minimum score 550 paper-based; 79 iBT). *Application deadline:* For fall admission, 3/1 for international students; for spring admission, 8/1 for international students. Applications are processed on a rolling basis. Application fee: $40 ($75 for international students). Electronic applications accepted. *Expenses:* Tuition, state resident: full-time $4044; part-time $168.50 per credit hour. Tuition, nonresident: full-time $16,008; part-time $667 per credit hour. *Required fees:* $2122; $88.45 per credit hour. One-time fee: $50. Tuition and fees vary according to course load and campus/location. *Financial support:* In 2011–12, 49 research assistantships (averaging $14,782 per year), 3 teaching assistantships (averaging $17,080 per year) were awarded; career-related internships or fieldwork, Federal Work-Study, scholarships/grants, health care benefits, tuition waivers (partial), and unspecified assistantships also available. Support available to part-time students. Financial award application deadline: 3/1; financial award applicants required to submit FAFSA. *Faculty research:* Crop science, weed science, rangeland ecology and management, biotechnology, breeding and genetics. *Unit head:* Dr. Don R. Murray, Interim Head, 405-744-6130, Fax: 405-744-5269. *Application contact:* Dr. Sheryl Tucker, Dean, 405-744-7099, Fax: 405-744-0355, E-mail: grad-i@okstate.edu. Web site: http://www.pss.okstate.edu.

Oklahoma State University, College of Arts and Sciences, Department of Botany, Stillwater, OK 74078. Offers botany (MS); environmental science (MS, PhD); plant science (PhD). *Faculty:* 15 full-time (6 women), 3 part-time/adjunct (1 woman). *Students:* 1 full-time (0 women), 9 part-time (5 women); includes 3 minority (1 American Indian or Alaska Native, non-Hispanic/Latino; 1 Hispanic/Latino; 1 Two or more races, non-Hispanic/Latino). Average age 28. 9 applicants, 22% accepted, 2 enrolled. In 2011, 1 degree awarded. *Degree requirements:* For master's, thesis; for doctorate, comprehensive exam, thesis/dissertation. *Entrance requirements:* For master's and doctorate, GRE or GMAT. Additional exam requirements/recommendations for international students: Required—TOEFL (minimum score 550 paper-based; 79 iBT). *Application deadline:* For fall admission, 3/1 for international students; for spring admission, 8/1 for international students. Applications are processed on a rolling basis. Application fee: $40 ($75 for international students). Electronic applications accepted. *Expenses:* Tuition, state resident: full-time $4044; part-time $168.50 per credit hour. Tuition, nonresident: full-time $16,008; part-time $667 per credit hour. *Required fees:* $2122; $88.45 per credit hour. One-time fee: $50. Tuition and fees vary according to course load and campus/location. *Financial support:* In 2011–12, 3 research assistantships (averaging $16,004 per year), 9 teaching assistantships (averaging $15,405 per year) were awarded; career-related internships or fieldwork, Federal Work-Study, scholarships/grants, health care benefits, tuition waivers (partial),

442 facebook.com/petersonspublishing

Peterson's Graduate Programs in the Physical Sciences, Mathematics, Agricultural Sciences, the Environment & Natural Resources 2013

and unspecified assistantships also available. Support available to part-time students. Financial award application deadline: 3/1; financial award applicants required to submit FAFSA. *Faculty research:* Ethnobotany, developmental genetics of Arabidopsis, biological roles of Plasmodesmata, community ecology and biodiversity, nutrient cycling in grassland ecosystems. *Unit head:* Dr. Linda Watson, Head, 405-744-5559, Fax: 405-744-7074. *Application contact:* Dr. Sheryl Tucker, Dean, 405-744-7099, Fax: 405-744-0355, E-mail: grad-i@okstate.edu. Web site: http://botany.okstate.edu.

Oklahoma State University, Graduate College, Stillwater, OK 74078. Offers aerospace security (Graduate Certificate); biobased products and bioenergy (Graduate Certificate); bioinformatics (Graduate Certificate); business data mining (Graduate Certificate); engineering and technology management (Graduate Certificate); environmental science (MS); global issues (Graduate Certificate); information assurance (Graduate Certificate); international studies (MS); natural and applied science (MS); photonics (PhD); plant science (PhD); teaching English to speakers of other languages (Graduate Certificate). Programs are interdisciplinary. *Faculty:* 2 full-time (both women), 3 part-time/adjunct (0 women). *Students:* 86 full-time (50 women), 149 part-time (76 women); includes 55 minority (14 Black or African American, non-Hispanic/Latino; 11 American Indian or Alaska Native, non-Hispanic/Latino; 8 Asian, non-Hispanic/Latino; 7 Hispanic/Latino; 1 Native Hawaiian or other Pacific Islander, non-Hispanic/Latino; 14 Two or more races, non-Hispanic/Latino), 57 international. Average age 31. 597 applicants, 68% accepted, 78 enrolled. In 2011, 98 master's, 8 doctorates awarded. *Degree requirements:* For master's, thesis (for some programs); for doctorate, comprehensive exam, thesis/dissertation. *Entrance requirements:* For master's and doctorate, GRE or GMAT. Additional exam requirements/recommendations for international students: Required—TOEFL (minimum score 550 paper-based; 79 iBT). *Application deadline:* For fall admission, 3/1 for international students; for spring admission, 8/1 for international students. Applications are processed on a rolling basis. Application fee: $40 ($75 for international students). Electronic applications accepted. *Expenses:* Tuition, state resident: full-time $4044; part-time $168.50 per credit hour. Tuition, nonresident: full-time $16,008; part-time $667 per credit hour. Required fees: $2122; $88.45 per credit hour. One-time fee: $50. Tuition and fees vary according to course load and campus/location. *Financial support:* In 2011–12, 2 research assistantships (averaging $10,302 per year) were awarded; career-related internships or fieldwork, Federal Work-Study, scholarships/grants, health care benefits, tuition waivers (partial), and unspecified assistantships also available. Support available to part-time students. Financial award application deadline: 3/1; financial award applicants required to submit FAFSA. *Unit head:* Dr. Sheryl Tucker, Dean, 405-744-7099, Fax: 405-744-0355, E-mail: grad-i@okstate.edu. *Application contact:* Dr. Susan Mathew, Coordinator of Admissions, 405-744-6368, Fax: 405-744-0355, E-mail: grad-i@okstate.edu. Web site: http://gradcollege.okstate.edu/.

Purdue University, Graduate School, PULSe Purdue University Life Sciences Program, West Lafayette, IN 47907. Offers biomolecular structure and biophysics (PhD); biotechnology (PhD); chemical biology (PhD); chromatin and regulation of gene expression (PhD); integrative neuroscience (PhD); integrative plant sciences (PhD); membrane biology (PhD); microbiology (PhD); molecular evolutionary and cancer biology (PhD); molecular evolutionary genetics (PhD); molecular virology (PhD). *Students:* 90 full-time (45 women); includes 7 minority (3 Black or African American, non-Hispanic/Latino; 1 Asian, non-Hispanic/Latino; 2 Hispanic/Latino; 1 Two or more races, non-Hispanic/Latino), 40 international. Average age 26. 427 applicants, 24% accepted, 35 enrolled. *Entrance requirements:* For doctorate, GRE test required, minimum undergraduate GPA of 3.0. Additional exam requirements/recommendations for international students: Required—TOEFL (minimum score 550 paper-based; 77 iBT). *Application deadline:* For fall admission, 1/15 priority date for domestic students, 1/15 for international students. Applications are processed on a rolling basis. Application fee: $60 ($75 for international students). Electronic applications accepted. *Financial support:* In 2011–12, research assistantships with tuition reimbursements (averaging $22,500 per year), teaching assistantships with tuition reimbursements (averaging $22,500 per year) were awarded. *Unit head:* Dr. Christine A. Hrycyna, Head, 765-494-7322, E-mail: hrycyna@purdue.edu. *Application contact:* Emily E. Bramson, Graduate Contact, 765-494-5865, E-mail: bramson@purdue.edu. Web site: http://www.gradschool.purdue.edu/pulse.

South Dakota State University, Graduate School, College of Agriculture and Biological Sciences, Department of Plant Science, Brookings, SD 57007. Offers agronomy (PhD); biological sciences (PhD); plant science (MS). *Degree requirements:* For master's, thesis (for some programs), oral exam; for doctorate, comprehensive exam, thesis/dissertation, preliminary oral and written exams. *Entrance requirements:* Additional exam requirements/recommendations for international students: Required—TOEFL (minimum score 560 paper-based; 220 computer-based; 83 iBT).

Southern Illinois University Carbondale, Graduate School, College of Agriculture, Department of Plant, Soil, and General Agriculture, Carbondale, IL 62901-4701. Offers horticultural science (MS); plant and soil science (MS). *Faculty:* 12 full-time (1 woman), 8 part-time/adjunct (0 women). *Students:* 13 full-time (5 women), 30 part-time (11 women); includes 4 minority (2 Black or African American, non-Hispanic/Latino; 1 American Indian or Alaska Native, non-Hispanic/Latino; 1 Hispanic/Latino), 6 international. 13 applicants, 69% accepted, 5 enrolled. In 2011, 7 master's awarded. *Degree requirements:* For master's, thesis. *Entrance requirements:* For master's, minimum GPA of 2.7. Additional exam requirements/recommendations for international students: Required—

TOEFL. *Application deadline:* Applications are processed on a rolling basis. Application fee: $0. *Financial support:* In 2011–12, 22 students received support, including 15 research assistantships with full tuition reimbursements available, 6 teaching assistantships with full tuition reimbursements available; fellowships with full tuition reimbursements available, Federal Work-Study, institutionally sponsored loans, and tuition waivers (full) also available. Support available to part-time students. *Faculty research:* Herbicides, fertilizers, agriculture education, landscape design, plant breeding. *Total annual research expenditures:* $2 million. *Unit head:* Dr. Brian Klubek, Chair, 618-453-2496, E-mail: bklubek@siu.edu. *Application contact:* Lisa Hartline, Administrative Clerk, 618-453-1770, E-mail: lisah@siu.edu.

State University of New York College of Environmental Science and Forestry, Department of Environmental and Forest Biology, Syracuse, NY 13210-2779. Offers applied ecology (MPS); chemical ecology (MPS, MS, PhD); conservation biology (MPS, MS, PhD); ecology (MPS, MS, PhD); entomology (MPS, MS, PhD); environmental interpretation (MPS, MS, PhD); environmental physiology (MPS, MS, PhD); fish and wildlife biology and management (MPS, MS, PhD); forest pathology and mycology (MPS, MS, PhD); plant biotechnology (MPS); plant science and biotechnology (MPS, MS, PhD). *Degree requirements:* For master's, thesis (for some programs); for doctorate, comprehensive exam, thesis/dissertation. *Entrance requirements:* For master's and doctorate, GRE General Test, GRE Subject Test, minimum GPA of 3.0. Additional exam requirements/recommendations for international students: Required—TOEFL (minimum score 550 paper-based; 213 computer-based; 80 iBT), IELTS (minimum score 6). *Application deadline:* For fall admission, 2/1 priority date for domestic students, 2/1 for international students; for spring admission, 11/1 priority date for domestic students, 11/1 for international students. Applications are processed on a rolling basis. Application fee: $60. *Expenses:* Tuition, state resident: full-time $8870; part-time $370 per credit hour. Tuition, nonresident: full-time $15,160; part-time $632 per credit hour. Required fees: $60; $370 per credit hour. $350 per semester. One-time fee: $85. *Financial support:* Fellowships with full and partial tuition reimbursements, research assistantships with full and partial tuition reimbursements, teaching assistantships with full and partial tuition reimbursements, Federal Work-Study, institutionally sponsored loans, scholarships/grants, health care benefits, and unspecified assistantships available. Financial award application deadline: 6/30. *Faculty research:* Ecology, fish and wildlife biology and management, plant science, entomology. *Total annual research expenditures:* $4.1 million. *Unit head:* Dr. Donald J. Leopold, Chair, 315-470-6760, Fax: 315-470-6934. *Application contact:* Dr. Dudley J. Raynal, Dean, Instruction and Graduate Studies, 315-470-6599, Fax: 315-470-6978, E-mail: esfgrad@esf.edu. Web site: http://www.esf.edu/efb/.

Texas A&M University, College of Agriculture and Life Sciences, Department of Soil and Crop Sciences, College Station, TX 77843. Offers agronomy (M Agr, MS, PhD); food science and technology (MS, PhD); genetics (PhD); molecular and environmental plant sciences (MS, PhD); plant breeding (MS, PhD); soil science (MS, PhD). *Faculty:* 37. *Students:* 98 full-time (36 women), 29 part-time (4 women); includes 12 minority (4 Black or African American, non-Hispanic/Latino; 3 Asian, non-Hispanic/Latino; 5 Hispanic/Latino), 42 international. Average age 26. In 2011, 4 master's, 8 doctorates awarded. *Degree requirements:* For master's, thesis; for doctorate, thesis/dissertation. *Entrance requirements:* For master's and doctorate, GRE General Test. Additional exam requirements/recommendations for international students: Required—TOEFL. *Application deadline:* For fall admission, 3/1 priority date for domestic students; for spring admission, 8/1 for domestic students. Applications are processed on a rolling basis. Application fee: $50 ($75 for international students). *Expenses:* Tuition, state resident: full-time $5437; part-time $226.55 per credit hour. Tuition, nonresident: full-time $12,949; part-time $539.55 per credit hour. Required fees: $2741. *Financial support:* In 2011–12, fellowships (averaging $16,000 per year), research assistantships with partial tuition reimbursements (averaging $15,000 per year) were awarded; career-related internships or fieldwork, Federal Work-Study, and institutionally sponsored loans also available. *Faculty research:* Soil and crop management, turfgrass science, weed science, cereal chemistry, food protein chemistry. *Unit head:* Dr. David D. Baltensperger, Department Head, 979-845-3001, E-mail: dbaltensperger@ag.tamu.edu. *Application contact:* Graduate Admissions, 979-845-1044, E-mail: admissions@tamu.edu. Web site: http://soilcrop.tamu.edu.

Texas A&M University–Kingsville, College of Graduate Studies, College of Agriculture and Home Economics, Program in Plant and Soil Sciences, Kingsville, TX 78363. Offers MS, PhD. *Degree requirements:* For master's, comprehensive exam, thesis or alternative. *Entrance requirements:* For master's, GRE General Test, minimum GPA of 3.0. Additional exam requirements/recommendations for international students: Required—TOEFL.

Texas Tech University, Graduate School, College of Agricultural Sciences and Natural Resources, Department of Plant and Soil Science, Lubbock, TX 79409. Offers crop science (MS); horticulture (MS); plant and soil science (PhD); plant protection (MS); soil science (MS); JD/MS. Part-time programs available. Postbaccalaureate distance learning degree programs offered (no on-campus study). *Faculty:* 8 full-time (4 women), 11 part-time/adjunct (1 woman). *Students:* 63 full-time (25 women), 39 part-time (19 women); includes 6 minority (3 Black or African American, non-Hispanic/Latino; 1 Asian, non-Hispanic/Latino; 2 Hispanic/Latino), 30 international. Average age 31. 63 applicants, 32% accepted, 15 enrolled. In 2011, 13 master's, 7 doctorates awarded. *Degree requirements:* For master's, thesis or alternative; for doctorate, thesis/dissertation. *Entrance*

Peterson's Graduate Programs in the Physical Sciences, Mathematics, Agricultural Sciences, the Environment & Natural Resources 2013

facebook.com/petersonspublishing **443**

requirements: For master's and doctorate, GRE General Test, formal approval from departmental committee. Additional exam requirements/recommendations for international students: Required—TOEFL (minimum score 550 paper-based; 213 computer-based; 79 iBT). *Application deadline:* For fall admission, 6/1 priority date for domestic students, 1/15 for international students; for spring admission, 9/1 priority date for domestic students, 6/15 for international students. Applications are processed on a rolling basis. Application fee: $50 ($75 for international students). Electronic applications accepted. *Expenses:* Tuition, state resident: full-time $5899; part-time $245.80 per credit hour. Tuition, nonresident: full-time $13,411; part-time $558.80 per credit hour. *Required fees:* $2680.60; $86.50 per credit hour. $920.30 per semester. *Financial support:* In 2011–12, 52 students received support. Application deadline: 4/15; applicants required to submit FAFSA. *Faculty research:* Molecular and cellular biology of plant stress, physiology/genetics of crop production in semi-arid conditions, improvement of native plants, soil science and management, fibers and biopolymers. *Total annual research expenditures:* $6 million. *Unit head:* Dr. Richard E. Zartman, Chair, 806-742-2838 Ext. 230, Fax: 806-742-0775, E-mail: richard.zartman@ttu.edu. *Application contact:* Dr. Eric Hequet, Graduate Adviser, 806-742-2838 Ext. 239, Fax: 806-742-0775, E-mail: eric.hequet@ttu.edu. Web site: http://www.pssc.ttu.edu/.

Tuskegee University, Graduate Programs, College of Agricultural, Environmental and Natural Sciences, Department of Agricultural Sciences, Program in Plant and Soil Sciences, Tuskegee, AL 36088. Offers MS. *Faculty:* 13 full-time (1 woman), 2 part-time/adjunct (1 woman). *Students:* 4 full-time (2 women); includes 2 minority (both Black or African American, non-Hispanic/Latino), 1 international. Average age 30. In 2011, 3 master's awarded. *Degree requirements:* For master's, thesis. *Entrance requirements:* For master's, GRE General Test. Additional exam requirements/recommendations for international students: Required—TOEFL (minimum score 500 paper-based; 69 computer-based). *Application deadline:* For fall admission, 7/15 for domestic students. Applications are processed on a rolling basis. Application fee: $25 ($35 for international students). *Expenses: Tuition:* Full-time $17,070; part-time $705 per credit hour. *Financial support:* Application deadline: 4/15. *Unit head:* Dr. P. K. Biswas, Head, 334-727-8446. *Application contact:* Dr. Robert L. Laney, Jr., Vice President/Director of Admissions and Enrollment Management, 334-727-8580, Fax: 334-727-5750, E-mail: planey@tuskegee.edu.

The University of Arizona, College of Agriculture and Life Sciences, School of Plant Sciences, Tucson, AZ 85721. Offers plant pathology (PhD); plant sciences (MS, PhD). Part-time programs available. *Faculty:* 19 full-time (6 women), 3 part-time/adjunct (1 woman). *Students:* 26 full-time (11 women), 1 part-time (0 women); includes 4 minority (1 American Indian or Alaska Native, non-Hispanic/Latino; 1 Asian, non-Hispanic/Latino; 2 Two or more races, non-Hispanic/Latino), 10 international. Average age 30. 41 applicants, 22% accepted, 5 enrolled. In 2011, 5 master's, 4 doctorates awarded. *Degree requirements:* For master's, thesis or alternative; for doctorate, thesis/dissertation. *Entrance requirements:* For master's, GRE General Test, GRE Subject Test (biology or chemistry recommended), minimum GPA of 3.0, academic resume, 3 letters of recommendation; for doctorate, GRE General Test, GRE Subject Test (biology or chemistry recommended), minimum GPA of 3.0, academic resume, statement of interest, 3 letters of recommendation. Additional exam requirements/recommendations for international students: Required—TOEFL. *Application deadline:* For fall admission, 12/1 for domestic and international students; for spring admission, 6/1 for domestic and international students. Applications are processed on a rolling basis. Application fee: $75. Electronic applications accepted. *Expenses:* Tuition, state resident: full-time $10,840. Tuition, nonresident: full-time $25,802. *Financial support:* In 2011–12, 10 research assistantships with full tuition reimbursements (averaging $19,951 per year) were awarded; fellowships, teaching assistantships with full tuition reimbursements, career-related internships or fieldwork, Federal Work-Study, scholarships/grants, health care benefits, tuition waivers (partial), and unspecified assistantships also available. *Faculty research:* Molecular/cell biology, plant genetics and physiology, agronomic and horticultural production (including turf and ornamentals). *Total annual research expenditures:* $10.8 million. *Unit head:* Dr. Robert T. Leonard, Head, 520-621-1945. *Application contact:* Dr. Rachel W. Pfister, Graduate Coordinator/Advisor, 520-621-8423, Fax: 520-621-7186, E-mail: pfister@ag.arizona.edu. Web site: http://cals.arizona.edu/spls/.

University of Arkansas, Graduate School, Dale Bumpers College of Agricultural, Food and Life Sciences, Interdepartmental Program in Plant Science, Fayetteville, AR 72701-1201. Offers PhD. *Students:* 1 full-time (0 women), 13 part-time (5 women), 6 international. In 2011, 1 doctorate awarded. *Degree requirements:* For doctorate, thesis/dissertation. *Application deadline:* For fall admission, 4/1 for international students; for spring admission, 10/1 for international students. Applications are processed on a rolling basis. Application fee: $40 ($50 for international students). Electronic applications accepted. *Financial support:* In 2011–12, 9 research assistantships were awarded; fellowships with tuition reimbursements, teaching assistantships, career-related internships or fieldwork, and Federal Work-Study also available. Support available to part-time students. Financial award application deadline: 4/1; financial award applicants required to submit FAFSA. *Unit head:* Dr. A. Rick Bennett, Department Head, 479-575-2445, E-mail: rbennett@uark.edu. *Application contact:* Dr. Ioannis Tzanetakis, Graduate Coordinator, 479-575-3180, E-mail: itzaneta@uark.edu. Web site: http://plantpathology.uark.edu/.

The University of British Columbia, Faculty of Land and Food Systems, Plant Science Program, Vancouver, BC V6T 1Z1, Canada. Offers M Sc, PhD. Part-time programs available. *Degree requirements:* For master's, thesis; for doctorate, comprehensive exam, thesis/dissertation. *Entrance requirements:* Additional exam requirements/recommendations for international students: Required—TOEFL (minimum score 577 paper-based; 233 computer-based; 90 iBT), IELTS (minimum score 6.5). Electronic applications accepted. *Faculty research:* Plant physiology and biochemistry, biotechnology, plant protection (insect, weeds, and diseases), plant breeding, plant-environment interaction.

University of California, Riverside, Graduate Division, Department of Botany and Plant Sciences, Riverside, CA 92521-0102. Offers plant biology (MS, PhD), including plant cell, molecular, and developmental biology (PhD), plant ecology (PhD), plant genetics (PhD). Part-time programs available. *Faculty:* 40 full-time (13 women). *Students:* 66 full-time (40 women); includes 12 minority (5 Asian, non-Hispanic/Latino; 7 Hispanic/Latino), 24 international. Average age 29. In 2011, 3 master's, 3 doctorates awarded. Terminal master's awarded for partial completion of doctoral program. *Degree requirements:* For master's, comprehensive exams or thesis; for doctorate, thesis/dissertation, qualifying exams. *Entrance requirements:* For master's and doctorate, GRE General Test, minimum GPA of 3.2. Additional exam requirements/recommendations for international students: Required—TOEFL (minimum score 550 paper-based; 213 computer-based; 80 iBT). *Application deadline:* For fall admission, 5/1 for domestic students, 2/1 for international students; for winter admission, 2/1 for domestic students, 7/1 for international students; for spring admission, 12/1 for domestic students, 10/1 for international students. Applications are processed on a rolling basis. Application fee: $80 ($100 for international students). Electronic applications accepted. *Financial support:* In 2011–12, fellowships with tuition reimbursements (averaging $12,000 per year), research assistantships with tuition reimbursements (averaging $23,000 per year), teaching assistantships with tuition reimbursements (averaging $16,500 per year) were awarded; career-related internships or fieldwork, Federal Work-Study, institutionally sponsored loans, scholarships/grants, and tuition waivers (full and partial) also available. *Faculty research:* Agricultural plant biology; biochemistry and physiology; cellular, molecular and developmental biology; ecology, evolution, systematics and ethnobotany; genetics, genomics and bioinformatics. *Unit head:* Dr. Mikeal Roose, Chair, 951-827-4413. *Application contact:* Deidra Kornfeld, Graduate Program Assistant, 800-735-0717, Fax: 951-827-5517, E-mail: deidra.kornfeld@ucr.edu. Web site: http://www.plantbiology.ucr.edu/.

University of Connecticut, Graduate School, College of Agriculture and Natural Resources, Department of Plant Science, Storrs, CT 06269. Offers plant and soil sciences (MS, PhD). Terminal master's awarded for partial completion of doctoral program. *Degree requirements:* For master's, comprehensive exam; for doctorate, thesis/dissertation. *Entrance requirements:* For master's and doctorate, GRE General Test, GRE Subject Test. Additional exam requirements/recommendations for international students: Required—TOEFL (minimum score 550 paper-based; 213 computer-based). Electronic applications accepted.

University of Delaware, College of Agriculture and Natural Resources, Department of Plant and Soil Sciences, Newark, DE 19716. Offers MS, PhD. Part-time programs available. Terminal master's awarded for partial completion of doctoral program. *Degree requirements:* For master's, thesis; for doctorate, thesis/dissertation. *Entrance requirements:* For master's and doctorate, GRE General Test. Additional exam requirements/recommendations for international students: Required—TOEFL (minimum score 550 paper-based; 213 computer-based). Electronic applications accepted. *Faculty research:* Soil chemistry, plant and cell tissue culture, plant breeding and genetics, soil physics, soil biochemistry, plant molecular biology, soil microbiology.

University of Florida, Graduate School, College of Agricultural and Life Sciences, Program in Plant Medicine, Gainesville, FL 32611. Offers plant medicine (DPM); tropical conservation and development (DPM). Part-time programs available. *Students:* 26 full-time (11 women); includes 4 minority (1 Asian, non-Hispanic/Latino; 2 Hispanic/Latino; 1 Native Hawaiian or other Pacific Islander, non-Hispanic/Latino), 6 international. Average age 31. 8 applicants, 38% accepted, 3 enrolled. In 2011, 3 doctorates awarded. *Degree requirements:* For doctorate, comprehensive exam, thesis/dissertation. *Entrance requirements:* For doctorate, GRE General Test, minimum GPA of 3.0. Additional exam requirements/recommendations for international students: Required—TOEFL (minimum score 550 paper-based; 213 computer-based; 80 iBT), IELTS (minimum score 6). *Application deadline:* For fall admission, 6/15 for domestic and international students; for spring admission, 9/15 for domestic and international students. Application fee: $30. *Financial support:* Fellowships and research assistantships available. Financial award applicants required to submit FAFSA. *Total annual research expenditures:* $120,571. *Unit head:* Dr. Eric Triplett, Director, 352-392-5430, Fax: 352-392-7348, E-mail: ewt@ufl.edu. *Application contact:* Dr. Robert J. McGovern, Graduate Coordinator, 352-392-3631 Ext. 213, Fax: 352-392-8988, E-mail: rjmcgov@ufl.edu. Web site: http://www.dpm.ifas.ufl.edu/.

University of Georgia, College of Agricultural and Environmental Sciences, Institute of Plant Breeding, Genetics and Genomics, Athens, GA 30602. Offers MS, PhD. *Students:* 19 full-time (6 women), 2 part-time (1 woman), 11 international. Average age 29. 16 applicants, 25% accepted, 1 enrolled. In 2011, 2 master's, 4 doctorates awarded. *Financial support:* Tuition waivers and unspecified assistantships available. *Unit head:* Dr. John H. Dayton, Director, 706-542-5607, Fax: 706-583-8120, E-mail: pbgg@uga.edu. *Application contact:*

444 facebook.com/petersonspublishing

Peterson's Graduate Programs in the Physical Sciences, Mathematics, Agricultural Sciences, the Environment & Natural Resources 2013

Dr. Dayton Wilde, Graduate Coordinator, 706-542-5607, E-mail: pbgg@uga.edu. Web site: http://www.plantbreeding.uga.edu/index.html.

University of Hawaii at Manoa, Graduate Division, College of Tropical Agriculture and Human Resources, Department of Plant and Environmental Protection Sciences, Honolulu, HI 96822. Offers entomology (MS, PhD); tropical plant pathology (MS, PhD). Part-time programs available. Terminal master's awarded for partial completion of doctoral program. *Degree requirements:* For master's, thesis optional; for doctorate, comprehensive exam, thesis/dissertation. *Entrance requirements:* For master's and doctorate, GRE General Test. Additional exam requirements/recommendations for international students: Required—TOEFL (minimum score 500 paper-based; 173 computer-based; 61 iBT), IELTS (minimum score 5). *Faculty research:* Nematology, virology, mycology, bacteriology, epidemiology.

University of Idaho, College of Graduate Studies, College of Agricultural and Life Sciences, Department of Plant, Soil, and Entomological Sciences, Program in Plant Science, Moscow, ID 83844-2282. Offers MS, PhD. *Students:* 18 full-time, 9 part-time. Average age 32. In 2011, 4 master's awarded. *Degree requirements:* For doctorate, thesis/dissertation. *Entrance requirements:* For master's and doctorate, GRE General Test, minimum GPA of 3.0. *Application deadline:* For fall admission, 8/1 for domestic students; for spring admission, 12/15 for domestic students. Application fee: $60. *Expenses:* Tuition, state resident: full-time $3874; part-time $334 per credit hour. Tuition, nonresident: full-time $16,394; part-time $861 per credit hour. *Required fees:* $2808; $99 per credit hour. Tuition and fees vary according to program. *Financial support:* Applicants required to submit FAFSA. *Faculty research:* Controlling root diseases in wheat and barley, sustainable agriculture, horticulture and urban landscape management, reduced herbicide rates control weeds in grain, wheat breeding program. *Unit head:* Dr. James B. Johnson, Chair, 208-885-6274, E-mail: nthompson@uidaho.edu. *Application contact:* Erick Larson, Director of Graduate Admissions, 208-885-4723, E-mail: gadms@uidaho.edu.

University of Kentucky, Graduate School, College of Agriculture, Program in Plant and Soil Science, Lexington, KY 40506-0032. Offers MS. *Degree requirements:* For master's, comprehensive exam, thesis optional. *Entrance requirements:* For master's, GRE General Test, minimum undergraduate GPA of 2.75, graduate 3.0. Additional exam requirements/recommendations for international students: Required—TOEFL (minimum score 550 paper-based; 213 computer-based). Electronic applications accepted.

University of Maine, Graduate School, College of Natural Sciences, Forestry, and Agriculture, Department of Biological Sciences, Orono, ME 04469. Offers biological sciences (PhD); botany and plant pathology (MS); ecology and environmental science (MS, PhD), including water resources; entomology (MS); plant science (PhD); zoology (MS, PhD). Part-time programs available. *Faculty:* 23 full-time (8 women), 7 part-time/adjunct (4 women). *Students:* 28 full-time (19 women), 13 part-time (9 women); includes 1 minority (Asian, non-Hispanic/Latino), 3 international. Average age 29. 38 applicants, 18% accepted, 5 enrolled. In 2011, 2 master's, 2 doctorates awarded. *Degree requirements:* For doctorate, thesis/dissertation. *Entrance requirements:* For master's and doctorate, GRE General Test. Additional exam requirements/recommendations for international students: Required—TOEFL. *Application deadline:* For fall admission, 2/1 priority date for domestic students. Applications are processed on a rolling basis. Application fee: $65. Electronic applications accepted. *Expenses:* Tuition, state resident: full-time $5016. Tuition, nonresident: full-time $14,424. *Financial support:* In 2011–12, 1 fellowship with full tuition reimbursement (averaging $18,000 per year), 5 research assistantships with full tuition reimbursements (averaging $18,000 per year), 19 teaching assistantships with full tuition reimbursements (averaging $13,600 per year) were awarded; career-related internships or fieldwork, Federal Work-Study, institutionally sponsored loans, and tuition waivers (full and partial) also available. Financial award application deadline: 3/1. *Total annual research expenditures:* $569,533. *Unit head:* Dr. Jody Jellison, Chair, 207-581-2551, Fax: 207-581-2537. *Application contact:* Scott G. Delcourt, Associate Dean of the Graduate School, 207-581-3291, Fax: 207-581-3232, E-mail: graduate@maine.edu. Web site: http://www2.umaine.edu/graduate/.

University of Maine, Graduate School, College of Natural Sciences, Forestry, and Agriculture, Department of Plant, Soil, and Environmental Sciences, Orono, ME 04469. Offers biological sciences (PhD); ecology and environmental sciences (MS, PhD); forest resources (PhD); horticulture (MS); plant science (PhD); plant, soil, and environmental sciences (MS); resource utilization (MS). *Faculty:* 9 full-time (3 women), 7 part-time/adjunct (3 women). *Students:* 7 full-time (4 women), 2 part-time (0 women), 2 international. Average age 30. 14 applicants, 50% accepted, 5 enrolled. In 2011, 4 degrees awarded. *Entrance requirements:* For master's and doctorate, GRE General Test. Additional exam requirements/recommendations for international students: Required—TOEFL. *Application deadline:* Applications are processed on a rolling basis. Application fee: $65. Electronic applications accepted. *Expenses:* Tuition, state resident: full-time $5016. Tuition, nonresident: full-time $14,424. *Financial support:* In 2011–12, 16 research assistantships with full tuition reimbursements (averaging $17,336 per year), 1 teaching assistantship with full tuition reimbursement (averaging $13,600 per year) were awarded; scholarships/grants, tuition waivers (full and partial), and unspecified assistantships also available. *Total annual research expenditures:* $179,065. *Unit head:* Dr. Gregory Porter, Chair, 207-581-2943, Fax: 207-581-3207. *Application contact:* Scott G. Delcourt, Associate Dean of the Graduate

School, 207-581-3291, Fax: 207-581-3232, E-mail: graduate@maine.edu. Web site: http://www2.umaine.edu/graduate/.

The University of Manchester, Faculty of Life Sciences, Manchester, United Kingdom. Offers adaptive organismal biology (M Phil, PhD); animal biology (M Phil, PhD); biochemistry (M Phil, PhD); bioinformatics (M Phil, PhD); biomolecular sciences (M Phil, PhD); biotechnology (M Phil, PhD); cell biology (M Phil, PhD); cell matrix research (M Phil, PhD); channels and transporters (M Phil, PhD); developmental biology (M Phil, PhD); Egyptology (M Phil, PhD); environmental biology (M Phil, PhD); evolutionary biology (M Phil, PhD); gene expression (M Phil, PhD); genetics (M Phil, PhD); history of science, technology and medicine (M Phil, PhD); immunology (M Phil, PhD); integrative neurobiology and behavior (M Phil, PhD); membrane trafficking (M Phil, PhD); microbiology (M Phil, PhD); molecular and cellular neuroscience (M Phil, PhD); molecular biology (M Phil, PhD); molecular cancer studies (M Phil, PhD); neuroscience (M Phil, PhD); ophthalmology (M Phil, PhD); optometry (M Phil, PhD); organelle function (M Phil, PhD); pharmacology (M Phil, PhD); physiology (M Phil, PhD); plant sciences (M Phil, PhD); stem cell research (M Phil, PhD); structural biology (M Phil, PhD); systems neuroscience (M Phil, PhD); toxicology (M Phil, PhD).

University of Manitoba, Faculty of Graduate Studies, Faculty of Agricultural and Food Sciences, Department of Plant Science, Winnipeg, MB R3T 2N2, Canada. Offers agronomy and plant protection (M Sc, PhD); horticulture (M Sc, PhD); plant breeding and genetics (M Sc, PhD); plant physiology-biochemistry (M Sc, PhD). *Degree requirements:* For master's, thesis; for doctorate, one foreign language, thesis/dissertation.

University of Massachusetts Amherst, Graduate School, College of Natural Sciences, Department of Plant, Soil and Insect Sciences, Program in Plant and Soil Sciences, Amherst, MA 01003. Offers plant and soil sciences (MS, PhD); soil science (MS). Postbaccalaureate distance learning degree programs offered (minimal on-campus study). *Students:* 24 full-time (12 women), 21 part-time (13 women); includes 4 minority (1 Black or African American, non-Hispanic/Latino; 1 Asian, non-Hispanic/Latino; 2 Hispanic/Latino), 18 international. Average age 33. 35 applicants, 57% accepted, 17 enrolled. In 2011, 7 master's, 4 doctorates awarded. Terminal master's awarded for partial completion of doctoral program. *Degree requirements:* For master's, thesis or alternative; for doctorate, comprehensive exam, thesis/dissertation. *Entrance requirements:* For master's and doctorate, GRE General Test. Additional exam requirements/ recommendations for international students: Required—TOEFL (minimum score 550 paper-based; 213 computer-based; 80 iBT), IELTS (minimum score 6.5). *Application deadline:* For fall admission, 1/7 for domestic and international students; for spring admission, 10/1 for domestic and international students. Applications are processed on a rolling basis. Application fee: $50 ($65 for international students). Electronic applications accepted. Tuition and fees vary according to course load, campus/location and program. *Financial support:* Fellowships with full and partial tuition reimbursements, research assistantships with full and partial tuition reimbursements, teaching assistantships with full and partial tuition reimbursements, career-related internships or fieldwork, Federal Work-Study, scholarships/grants, traineeships, health care benefits, tuition waivers (full and partial), and unspecified assistantships available. Support available to part-time students. Financial award application deadline: 1/7. *Unit head:* Dr. Geunhwa Jung, Graduate Program Director, 413-545-1059, Fax: 413-545-2115. *Application contact:* Lindsay DeSantis, Interim Supervisor of Admissions, 413-545-0722, Fax: 413-577-0010, E-mail: gradadm@grad.umass.edu. Web site: http://www.umass.edu/psis/.

University of Massachusetts Amherst, Graduate School, Interdisciplinary Programs, Program in Plant Biology, Amherst, MA 01003. Offers biochemistry and metabolism (MS, PhD); cell biology and physiology (MS, PhD); environmental, ecological and integrative (PhD); environmental, ecological and integrative biology (MS); genetics and evolution (MS, PhD). *Students:* 16 full-time (7 women), 1 (woman) part-time, 7 international. Average age 27. 22 applicants, 50% accepted, 5 enrolled. In 2011, 3 degrees awarded. *Median time to degree:* Of those who began their doctoral program in fall 2003, 100% received their degree in 8 years or less. *Degree requirements:* For master's, thesis; for doctorate, 2 foreign languages, comprehensive exam, thesis/dissertation. *Entrance requirements:* For master's and doctorate, GRE General Test. Additional exam requirements/recommendations for international students: Required—TOEFL (minimum score 550 paper-based; 213 computer-based; 80 iBT), IELTS (minimum score 6.5). *Application deadline:* For fall admission, 12/15 for domestic and international students; for spring admission, 10/1 for domestic and international students. Applications are processed on a rolling basis. Application fee: $50 ($65 for international students). Electronic applications accepted. Tuition and fees vary according to course load, campus/location and program. *Financial support:* Fellowships with full and partial tuition reimbursements, research assistantships with full and partial tuition reimbursements, teaching assistantships with full and partial tuition reimbursements, career-related internships or fieldwork, Federal Work-Study, scholarships/grants, traineeships, health care benefits, tuition waivers (full and partial), and unspecified assistantships available. Support available to part-time students. Financial award application deadline: 12/15. *Unit head:* Dr. Elsbeth L. Walker, Graduate Program Director, 413-577-3217, Fax: 413-545-3243. *Application contact:* Lindsay DeSantis, Interim Supervisor of Admissions, 413-545—0722, Fax: 413-577-0010, E-mail: gradadm@grad.umass.edu. Web site: http://www.bio.umass.edu/plantbio/.

Peterson's Graduate Programs in the Physical Sciences, Mathematics, Agricultural Sciences, the Environment & Natural Resources 2013

facebook.com/petersonspublishing   **445**

Plant Sciences

University of Minnesota, Twin Cities Campus, Graduate School, College of Food, Agricultural and Natural Resource Sciences, Program in Applied Plant Sciences, Minneapolis, MN 55455-0213. Offers MS, PhD. Part-time programs available. *Faculty:* 59 full-time (13 women). *Students:* 51 full-time (24 women), 6 part-time (2 women); includes 6 minority (3 Asian, non-Hispanic/Latino; 3 Hispanic/Latino), 10 international. Average age 30. 60 applicants, 43% accepted, 17 enrolled. In 2011, 3 master's, 1 doctorate awarded. Terminal master's awarded for partial completion of doctoral program. *Degree requirements:* For master's, comprehensive exam, thesis; for doctorate, comprehensive exam, thesis/dissertation. *Entrance requirements:* For master's and doctorate, GRE General Test. Additional exam requirements/recommendations for international students: Required—TOEFL (minimum score 550 paper-based; 213 computer-based; 79 iBT), IELTS (minimum score 6.5), TOEFL preferred. *Application deadline:* For fall admission, 12/1 priority date for domestic students, 12/1 for international students; for spring admission, 10/15 priority date for domestic students, 10/15 for international students. Applications are processed on a rolling basis. Application fee: $75 ($95 for international students). Electronic applications accepted. *Financial support:* In 2011–12, fellowships with full tuition reimbursements (averaging $24,000 per year), research assistantships with full and partial tuition reimbursements (averaging $21,000 per year) were awarded; teaching assistantships, scholarships/grants, health care benefits, and unspecified assistantships also available. *Faculty research:* Weed science, horticulture, crop management, sustainable agriculture, biotechnology, plant breeding. *Total annual research expenditures:* $5.6 million. *Unit head:* Dr. Jim Anderson, Director of Graduate Studies, 612-625-9763, Fax: 612-625-1268, E-mail: ander319@umn.edu. *Application contact:* Lynne Medgaarden, Assistant to the Director of Graduate Studies, 612-625-4742, Fax: 612-625-1268, E-mail: medga001@umn.edu. Web site: http://www.appliedplantsciences.umn.edu/.

University of Missouri, Graduate School, College of Agriculture, Food and Natural Resources, Division of Plant Sciences, Program in Plant Biology and Genetics, Columbia, MO 65211. Offers MS, PhD. Terminal master's awarded for partial completion of doctoral program. *Degree requirements:* For master's, thesis; for doctorate, thesis/dissertation. *Entrance requirements:* For master's and doctorate, GRE General Test, minimum GPA of 3.0. *Application deadline:* For fall admission, 3/1 priority date for domestic students. Applications are processed on a rolling basis. Application fee: $55 ($75 for international students). *Expenses:* Tuition, state resident: full-time $5881. Tuition, nonresident: full-time $15,183. *Required fees:* $952. Tuition and fees vary according to campus/location and program. *Financial support:* Research assistantships, teaching assistantships, and institutionally sponsored loans available. *Unit head:* Dr. Jeanne Mihail, Director of Graduate Studies, 573-882-0574, E-mail: mihailj@missouri.edu. *Application contact:* Dr. Jeanne Mihail, Director of Graduate Studies, 573-882-0574, E-mail: mihailj@missouri.edu.

University of Rhode Island, Graduate School, College of the Environment and Life Sciences, Department of Plant Sciences, Kingston, RI 02881. Offers entomology (MS, PhD); plant sciences (MS, PhD). Part-time programs available. *Faculty:* 10 full-time (2 women). *Students:* 7 full-time (4 women), 7 part-time (3 women). In 2011, 8 master's awarded. *Degree requirements:* For master's, comprehensive exam (for some programs), thesis optional; for doctorate, comprehensive exam, thesis/dissertation. *Entrance requirements:* For master's and doctorate, GRE, 2 letters of recommendation. Additional exam requirements/recommendations for international students: Required—TOEFL (minimum score 550 paper-based; 213 computer-based). *Application deadline:* For fall admission, 7/15 for domestic students, 2/1 for international students; for spring admission, 11/15 for domestic students, 7/15 for international students. Application fee: $65. Electronic applications accepted. *Expenses:* Tuition, state resident: full-time $10,432; part-time $580 per credit hour. Tuition, nonresident: full-time $23,130; part-time $1285 per credit hour. *Required fees:* $1362; $36 per credit hour. $35 per semester. One-time fee: $130. *Financial support:* In 2011–12, 3 teaching assistantships with full and partial tuition reimbursements (averaging $11,578 per year) were awarded. Financial award application deadline: 7/15; financial award applicants required to submit FAFSA. *Faculty research:* Plant development and management; pest management; tick biology, ecology, and control; identification and replacement of invasive ornamentals. *Unit head:* Dr. David Bengtson, Interim Chair, 401-874-2668, Fax: 401-874-2494, E-mail: bengtson@uri.edu. *Application contact:* Dr. Thomas Mather, Director of Graduate Studies, 401-874-5616, Fax: 401-874-2494, E-mail: tmather@uri.edu. Web site: http://cels.uri.edu/pls/.

University of Saskatchewan, College of Graduate Studies and Research, College of Agriculture, Department of Plant Sciences, Saskatoon, SK S7N 5A2, Canada. Offers M Sc, PhD. *Degree requirements:* For master's, thesis; for doctorate, comprehensive exam (for some programs), thesis/dissertation. *Entrance requirements:* Additional exam requirements/recommendations for international students: Required—TOEFL (minimum score 80 iBT); Recommended—IELTS (minimum score 6.5).

The University of Tennessee, Graduate School, College of Agricultural Sciences and Natural Resources, Department of Plant Sciences, Knoxville, TN 37996. Offers floriculture (MS); landscape design (MS); public horticulture (MS); turfgrass (MS); woody ornamentals (MS). Part-time programs available. *Degree requirements:* For master's, thesis or alternative. *Entrance requirements:* For master's, minimum GPA of 2.7. Additional exam requirements/recommendations for international students: Required—TOEFL. Electronic applications accepted. *Expenses:* Tuition, state resident: full-time $8332; part-time $464 per credit hour.

Tuition, nonresident: full-time $25,174; part-time $1400 per credit hour. *Required fees:* $1162; $56 per credit hour. Tuition and fees vary according to program.

University of Vermont, Graduate College, College of Agriculture and Life Sciences, Department of Plant and Soil Science, Burlington, VT 05405. Offers MS, PhD. *Students:* 26 (16 women), 3 international. 27 applicants, 33% accepted, 6 enrolled. In 2011, 7 degrees awarded. *Degree requirements:* For master's, thesis; for doctorate, one foreign language, thesis/dissertation. *Entrance requirements:* For master's and doctorate, GRE General Test. Additional exam requirements/recommendations for international students: Required—TOEFL (minimum score 550 paper-based; 213 computer-based; 80 iBT). *Application deadline:* For fall admission, 2/15 priority date for domestic students, 2/15 for international students. Applications are processed on a rolling basis. Application fee: $40. Electronic applications accepted. *Financial support:* Fellowships, research assistantships, and teaching assistantships available. Financial award application deadline: 3/1. *Faculty research:* Soil chemistry, plant nutrition. *Unit head:* Dr. Deborah Neher, Chairperson, 802-656-2630. *Application contact:* Dr. Josef Gorres, Coordinator, 802-656-2630. Web site: http://www.uvm.edu/~pss.

The University of Western Ontario, Faculty of Graduate Studies, Biosciences Division, Department of Plant Sciences, London, ON N6A 5B8, Canada. Offers plant and environmental sciences (M Sc); plant sciences (M Sc, PhD); plant sciences and environmental sciences (PhD); plant sciences and molecular biology (M Sc, PhD). *Degree requirements:* For master's, thesis; for doctorate, thesis/dissertation. *Entrance requirements:* For doctorate, M Sc or equivalent. Additional exam requirements/recommendations for international students: Required—TOEFL. *Faculty research:* Ecology systematics, plant biochemistry and physiology, yeast genetics, molecular biology.

University of Wisconsin–Madison, Graduate School, College of Agricultural and Life Sciences, Department of Agronomy, Madison, WI 53706-1380. Offers agronomy (MS, PhD); plant breeding and plant genetics (MS, PhD). *Degree requirements:* For master's, thesis or alternative; for doctorate, thesis/dissertation. *Entrance requirements:* For master's and doctorate, GRE, minimum GPA of 3.0. Additional exam requirements/recommendations for international students: Required—TOEFL (minimum score 580 paper-based; 213 computer-based). Electronic applications accepted. *Expenses:* Tuition, state resident: full-time $10,296; part-time $643.51 per credit. Tuition, nonresident: full-time $24,054; part-time $1503.40 per credit. *Required fees:* $70.06 per credit. Tuition and fees vary according to course load, campus/location, program and reciprocity agreements. *Faculty research:* Plant breeding and genetics, plant molecular biology and physiology; cropping systems and management, weed science.

University of Wisconsin–Madison, Graduate School, College of Agricultural and Life Sciences, Plant Breeding and Plant Genetics Program, Madison, WI 53706-1380. Offers MS, PhD. Part-time programs available. Terminal master's awarded for partial completion of doctoral program. *Degree requirements:* For master's, comprehensive exam, thesis; for doctorate, comprehensive exam, thesis/dissertation, formal exit seminar. *Entrance requirements:* For master's and doctorate, GRE, minimum GPA of 3.0. Additional exam requirements/recommendations for international students: Required—TOEFL (minimum: 550 paper, 213 computer, 80 iBT), IELTS (minimum: 6) or MELAB (minimum: 77). Electronic applications accepted. *Expenses:* Tuition, state resident: full-time $10,296; part-time $643.51 per credit. Tuition, nonresident: full-time $24,054; part-time $1503.40 per credit. *Required fees:* $70.06 per credit. Tuition and fees vary according to course load, campus/location, program and reciprocity agreements. *Faculty research:* Plant improvement, classical and molecular genetics, quantitative and statistical genetics, cytogenetics, stress and pest resistances.

Utah State University, School of Graduate Studies, College of Agriculture, Department of Plants, Soils, and Biometeorology, Logan, UT 84322. Offers biometeorology (MS, PhD); ecology (MS, PhD); plant science (MS, PhD); soil science (MS, PhD). Part-time programs available. Terminal master's awarded for partial completion of doctoral program. *Degree requirements:* For master's, thesis; for doctorate, thesis/dissertation. *Entrance requirements:* For master's, GRE General Test, BS in plant, soil, atmospheric science, or related field; minimum GPA of 3.0; for doctorate, GRE General Test, minimum GPA of 3.0. Additional exam requirements/recommendations for international students: Required—TOEFL. Electronic applications accepted. *Faculty research:* Biotechnology and genomics, plant physiology and biology, nutrient and water efficient landscapes, physical-chemical-biological processes in soil, environmental biophysics and climate.

Virginia State University, School of Graduate Studies, Research, and Outreach, School of Agriculture, Department of Agriculture and Human Ecology, Petersburg, VA 23806-0001. Offers plant science (MS).

West Texas A&M University, College of Agriculture, Nursing, and Natural Sciences, Division of Agriculture, Emphasis in Plant Science, Canyon, TX 79016-0001. Offers MS. Part-time programs available. *Degree requirements:* For master's, comprehensive exam, thesis optional. *Entrance requirements:* For master's, GRE General Test. Additional exam requirements/recommendations for international students: Required—TOEFL (minimum score 550 paper-based). Electronic applications accepted. *Faculty research:* Crop and soil disciplines.

West Virginia University, Davis College of Agriculture, Forestry and Consumer Sciences, Division of Plant and Soil Sciences, Program in Agricultural Sciences,

Morgantown, WV 26506. Offers animal and food sciences (PhD); plant and soil sciences (PhD). *Degree requirements:* For doctorate, thesis/dissertation, oral and written exams. *Entrance requirements:* Additional exam requirements/ recommendations for international students: Required—TOEFL. *Faculty research:* Ruminant nutrition, metabolism, forage utilization, physiology, reproduction.

Viticulture and Enology

California State University, Fresno, Division of Graduate Studies, College of Agricultural Sciences and Technology, Department of Viticulture and Enology, Fresno, CA 93740-8027. Offers MS. Part-time and evening/weekend programs available. *Degree requirements:* For master's, comprehensive exam (for some programs), thesis (for some programs). *Entrance requirements:* For master's, GRE General Test, minimum GPA of 2.5. Additional exam requirements/ recommendations for international students: Required—TOEFL. Electronic applications accepted. *Faculty research:* Ethel carbonate formation, clinical an physiological characterization, grape and wine quality.

University of California, Davis, Graduate Studies, Graduate Group in Viticulture and Enology, Davis, CA 95616. Offers MS, PhD. *Degree requirements:* For master's, comprehensive exam (for some programs), thesis (for some programs). *Entrance requirements:* Additional exam requirements/recommendations for international students: Required—TOEFL (minimum score 550 paper-based; 213 computer-based).

Peterson's Graduate Programs in the Physical Sciences, Mathematics, Agricultural Sciences, the Environment & Natural Resources 2013

facebook.com/petersonspublishing **447**

ACADEMIC AND PROFESSIONAL PROGRAMS IN THE ENVIRONMENT AND NATURAL RESOURCES

Section 9
Environmental Sciences and Management

This section contains a directory of institutions offering graduate work in environmental sciences and management, followed by an in-depth entry submitted by an institution that chose to prepare a detailed program description. Additional information about programs listed in the directory but not augmented by an in-depth entry may be obtained by writing directly to the dean of a graduate school or chair of a department at the address given in the directory.

For programs offering related work, see also in this book *Natural Resources.* In the other guides in this series:

Graduate Programs in the Humanities, Arts & Social Sciences
See *Political Science and International Affairs* and *Public, Regional, and Industrial Affairs*
Graduate Programs in the Biological/Biomedical Sciences & Health-Related Medical Professions
See *Ecology, Environmental Biology, and Evolutionary Biology*
Graduate Programs in Engineering & Applied Sciences
See *Management of Engineering and Technology*

CONTENTS

Program Directories

Display and Close-Up

Environmental Management and Policy

Adelphi University, College of Arts and Sciences, Program in Environmental Studies, Garden City, NY 11530-0701. Offers MS. *Students:* 12 full-time (4 women), 8 part-time (5 women); includes 3 minority (1 Black or African American, non-Hispanic/Latino; 2 Hispanic/Latino), 1 international. Average age 27. In 2011, 8 master's awarded. *Degree requirements:* For master's, thesis optional. *Entrance requirements:* For master's, GRE General Test, 2 letters of recommendation; course work in microeconomics, political science, statistics/calculus, and either chemistry or physics; computer literacy. Additional exam requirements/recommendations for international students: Required—TOEFL (minimum score 550 paper-based; 213 computer-based; 80 iBT). *Application deadline:* For fall admission, 5/1 for international students; for spring admission, 11/1 for international students. Applications are processed on a rolling basis. Application fee: $50. Electronic applications accepted. *Expenses: Tuition:* Full-time $29,600; part-time $930 per credit. *Required fees:* $1100. *Financial support:* Research assistantships with full and partial tuition reimbursements, teaching assistantships, career-related internships or fieldwork, Federal Work-Study, institutionally sponsored loans, and unspecified assistantships available. Financial award application deadline: 2/15; financial award applicants required to submit FAFSA. *Faculty research:* Contaminates sites, workplace exposure level of contaminants, climate change and human health. *Unit head:* Dr. Anagnostis Agelarakis, Director, 516-877-4112, E-mail: agelarak@adelphi.edu. *Application contact:* Christine Murphy, Director of Admissions, 516-877-3050, Fax: 516-877-3039, E-mail: graduateadmissions@adelphi.edu. Web site: http://academics.adelphi.edu/arts-sciences-programs/ms-environmental-study.php.

See Display below and Close-Up on page 509.

Air Force Institute of Technology, Graduate School of Engineering and Management, Department of Systems and Engineering Management, Dayton, OH 45433-7765. Offers cost analysis (MS); environmental and engineering management (MS); environmental engineering science (MS); information resource/systems management (MS). *Accreditation:* ABET. Part-time programs available. *Degree requirements:* For master's, thesis. *Entrance requirements:* For master's, GRE, GMAT, minimum GPA of 3.0.

American Public University System, AMU/APU Graduate Programs, Charles Town, WV 25414. Offers accounting (MBA, MS); administration and supervision (M Ed); criminal justice (MA); emergency and disaster management (MA); entrepreneurship (MBA); environmental policy and management (MS), including environmental planning, environmental sustainability, fish and wildlife management, general (MA, MS), global environmental management; finance (MBA); general (MBA); global business management (MBA); guidance and counseling (M Ed); history (MA), including American history, ancient and classical history, European history, global history, military and diplomatic history, public history; homeland security (MA); homeland security resource allocation (MBA); humanities (MA); information technology (MS), including digital forensics, enterprise software development, information assurance and security, IT project management; information technology management (MBA); intelligence studies (MA), including criminal intelligence, general (MA, MS), homeland security, intelligence analysis, intelligence collection, intelligence operations, terrorism studies; international relations and conflict resolution (MA), including comparative and security issues, conflict resolution, international and transnational security issues, peacekeeping; legal studies (MA); management (MA), including defense management, general (MA, MS), human resource management, organizational leadership, public administration, reverse logistics, strategic consulting; marketing (MBA); military history (MA), including American military history, American revolution, civil war, war since 1946, World War II; military studies (MA), including air warfare, asymmetrical warfare, joint warfare, land warfare, naval warfare, strategic leadership; national security studies (MA), including general (MA, MS), homeland security, regional security studies, security and intelligence analysis, terrorism studies; nonprofit management (MBA); political science (MA), including American politics and government, comparative government and development, public policy; psychology (MA); public administration (MA, MPA), including disaster management (MPA), environmental policy (MA), health policy (MPA), human resources (MPA), national security (MPA), organizational management (MPA), security management (MPA); public health (MA, MPH), including emergency management (MPH), environmental health (MPH), public administration (MA); reverse logistics management (MA); security management (MA); space studies (MS), including aerospace science, planetary science; sports and health sciences (MS); sports management (MS), including coaching theory and strategy, sports administration; teaching (M Ed), including curriculum and instruction for elementary teachers, elementary, elementary reading, English language learners, instructional leadership, online learning, secondary social sciences, special education; transportation and logistics management (MA), including maritime engineering management. Programs offered via distance learning only. Part-time and evening/weekend programs available. Postbaccalaureate distance learning degree programs offered (no on-campus study). *Faculty:* 445 full-time (241 women), 1,360 part-time/adjunct (617 women).

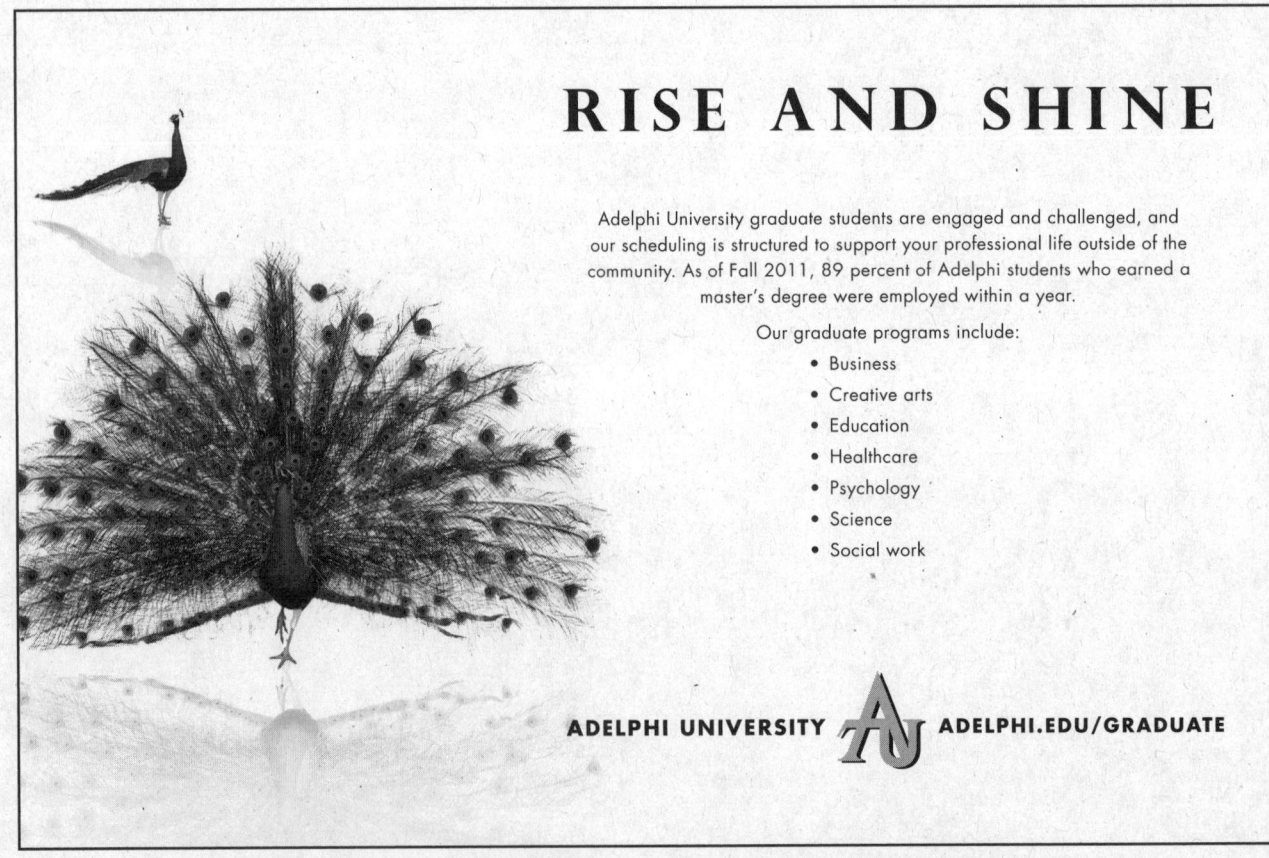
452 facebook.com/petersonspublishing

Peterson's Graduate Programs in the Physical Sciences, Mathematics, Agricultural Sciences, the Environment & Natural Resources 2013

Environmental Management and Policy

Students: 688 full-time (338 women), 10,168 part-time (3,706 women); includes 3,130 minority (1,007 Black or African American, non-Hispanic/Latino; 103 American Indian or Alaska Native, non-Hispanic/Latino; 825 Asian, non-Hispanic/Latino; 810 Hispanic/Latino; 51 Native Hawaiian or other Pacific Islander, non-Hispanic/Latino; 334 Two or more races, non-Hispanic/Latino), 134 international. Average age 35. In 2011, 2,386 master's awarded. *Degree requirements:* For master's, comprehensive exam or practicum. *Entrance requirements:* For master's, official transcript showing earned bachelor's degree from institution accredited by recognized accrediting body. Additional exam requirements/recommendations for international students: Required—TOEFL (minimum score 550 paper-based; 213 computer-based), IELTS (minimum score 6.5). *Application deadline:* Applications are processed on a rolling basis. Application fee: $0. Electronic applications accepted. *Expenses: Tuition:* Part-time $325 per credit hour. *Financial support:* Applicants required to submit FAFSA. *Faculty research:* Military history, criminal justice, management performance, national security. *Unit head:* Dr. Karan Powell, Executive Vice President and Provost, 877-468-6268, Fax: 304-724-3780. *Application contact:* Terry Grant, Vice President of Enrollment Management, 877-468-6268, Fax: 304-724-3780, E-mail: info@apus.edu. Web site: http://www.apus.edu.

American University, College of Arts and Sciences, Department of Environmental Science, Washington, DC 20016. Offers environmental assessment (Graduate Certificate); environmental science (MS). *Faculty:* 4 full-time (0 women), 1 (woman) part-time/adjunct. *Students:* 8 full-time (4 women), 5 part-time (3 women); includes 2 minority (both Asian, non-Hispanic/Latino), 1 international. Average age 28. 19 applicants, 74% accepted, 3 enrolled. In 2011, 9 master's awarded. *Degree requirements:* For master's, comprehensive exam, thesis (for some programs). *Entrance requirements:* For master's, GRE General Test, GRE Subject Test, one year calculus, lab science. Additional exam requirements/recommendations for international students: Required—TOEFL. *Application deadline:* For fall admission, 2/1 for domestic students; for spring admission, 10/1 for domestic students. Application fee: $80. *Expenses: Tuition:* Full-time $24,264; part-time $1348 per credit hour. *Required fees:* $430. Tuition and fees vary according to course load and program. *Financial support:* Research assistantships and teaching assistantships available. Financial award application deadline: 2/1. *Unit head:* Dr. Albert Mei-Chu Cheh, Chair, 202-885-8014, Fax: 202-885-1752, E-mail: acheh@american.edu. *Application contact:* Kathleen Clowery, Director, Graduate Admissions, 202-885-3621, Fax: 202-885-1505, E-mail: clowery@american.edu. Web site: http://www.american.edu/cas/environmental/.

American University, School of International Service, Washington, DC 20016-8071. Offers comparative and international disability policy (MA); comparative and regional studies (Certificate); cross-cultural communication (Certificate); development management (MS); ethics, peace, and global affairs (MA); European studies (Certificate); global environmental policy (MA, Certificate); global information technology (Certificate); international affairs (MA), including comparative and international disability policy, comparative and regional studies, international economic relations, international politics, natural resources and sustainable development, U.S. foreign policy; international communication (MA, Certificate); international development (MA, Certificate); international economic policy (Certificate); international economic relations (Certificate); international media (MA); international peace and conflict resolution (MA, Certificate); international politics (Certificate); international relations (PhD); international service (MIS); peacebuilding (Certificate); social enterprise (MA); the Americas (Certificate); United States foreign policy (Certificate); JD/MA. Part-time and evening/weekend programs available. Postbaccalaureate distance learning degree programs offered (no on-campus study). *Faculty:* 108 full-time (45 women), 51 part-time/adjunct (23 women). *Students:* 595 full-time (375 women), 399 part-time (243 women); includes 201 minority (64 Black or African American, non-Hispanic/Latino; 6 American Indian or Alaska Native, non-Hispanic/Latino; 53 Asian, non-Hispanic/Latino; 66 Hispanic/Latino; 12 Two or more races, non-Hispanic/Latino), 153 international. Average age 27. 2,096 applicants, 63% accepted, 370 enrolled. In 2011, 331 master's, 2 doctorates, 2 other advanced degrees awarded. Terminal master's awarded for partial completion of doctoral program. *Degree requirements:* For master's, one foreign language, comprehensive exam, thesis or alternative; for doctorate, one foreign language, comprehensive exam, thesis/dissertation, research practicum; for Certificate, minimum 15 credit hours related course work. *Entrance requirements:* For master's, GRE, 24 credits of course work in related social sciences, minimum GPA of 3.5, 2 letters of recommendation, bachelor's degree, resume, statement of purpose; for doctorate, GRE, 3 letters of recommendation, 24 credits in related social sciences; for Certificate, bachelor's degree. Additional exam requirements/recommendations for international students: Required—TOEFL (minimum score 600 paper-based; 250 computer-based; 100 iBT). *Application deadline:* For fall admission, 1/15 priority date for domestic students; for spring admission, 10/1 priority date for domestic students. Applications are processed on a rolling basis. Application fee: $50. *Expenses: Tuition:* Full-time $24,264; part-time $1348 per credit hour. *Required fees:* $430. Tuition and fees vary according to course load and program. *Financial support:* Fellowships with partial tuition reimbursements, research assistantships with partial tuition reimbursements, teaching assistantships with partial tuition reimbursements, career-related internships or fieldwork, Federal Work-Study, institutionally sponsored loans, and scholarships/grants available. Financial award application deadline: 1/15. *Faculty research:* International intellectual property, international environmental issues, international law and legal order, international telecommunications/technology, international

sustainable development. *Unit head:* Dr. James Goldgeier, Dean, 202-885-1603, Fax: 202-885-2494, E-mail: goldgeier@american.edu. *Application contact:* Amanda Taylor, Director of Graduate Admissions and Financial Aid, 202-885-2496, Fax: 202-885-1109, E-mail: ataylor@american.edu. Web site: http://www.american.edu/sis/.

American University of Beirut, Graduate Programs, Faculty of Arts and Sciences, Beirut, Lebanon. Offers anthropology (MA); Arabic language and literature (MA); archaeology (MA); biology (MS); chemistry (MS); computational science (MS); computer science (MS); economics (MA); education (MA); English language (MA); English literature (MA); environmental policy planning (MSES); financial economics (MAFE); geology (MS); history (MA); mathematics (MA, MS); Middle Eastern studies (MA); philosophy (MA); physics (MS); political studies (MA); psychology (MA); public administration (MA); sociology (MA); statistics (MA, MS). Part-time programs available. *Faculty:* 154 full-time (44 women), 12 part-time/adjunct (2 women). *Students:* 180 full-time (122 women), 240 part-time (158 women). Average age 25. 336 applicants, 47% accepted, 86 enrolled. In 2011, 57 master's awarded. *Degree requirements:* For master's, one foreign language, comprehensive exam, thesis (for some programs). *Entrance requirements:* For master's, GRE, letter of recommendation. Additional exam requirements/recommendations for international students: Required—TOEFL (minimum score 600 paper-based; 250 computer-based; 97 iBT), IELTS (minimum score 7). *Application deadline:* For fall admission, 4/30 for domestic and international students; for spring admission, 11/1 for domestic and international students. Application fee: $50. *Expenses: Tuition:* Full-time $12,780; part-time $710 per credit. *Required fees:* $528; $528 per credit. Tuition and fees vary according to course load and program. *Financial support:* In 2011–12, 33 students received support. Career-related internships or fieldwork, institutionally sponsored loans, scholarships/grants, health care benefits, and unspecified assistantships available. Financial award application deadline: 2/4; financial award applicants required to submit FAFSA. *Faculty research:* History of composition studies, syntax of Arabic dialects, Oscar Wilde, decadence, Middle Eastern and international politics, neural mechanisms of creativity and consciousness, personality and psycho-socio-cultural-spiritual correlates of negative and positive mental health, philosophy of mind, metaphysics, micropaleontology and stratigraphy, geochemistry, mineralogy and petrology, tectonophysics, Abbasid, Ottoman and Russian history, landscape, Bronze and Iron Age archaeology. *Unit head:* Dr. Patrick McGreevy, Dean, 961-1374374 Ext. 3800, Fax: 961-1744461, E-mail: pm07@aub.edu.lb. *Application contact:* Dr. Salim Kanaan, Director, Admissions Office, 961-1350000 Ext. 2594, Fax: 961-1750775, E-mail: sk00@aub.edu.lb. Web site: http://staff.aub.edu.lb/~webfas.

Antioch University New England, Graduate School, Department of Environmental Studies, Doctoral Program in Environmental Studies, Keene, NH 03431-3552. Offers PhD. *Degree requirements:* For doctorate, thesis/dissertation, practicum. *Entrance requirements:* For doctorate, master's degree and previous experience in the environmental field. Additional exam requirements/recommendations for international students: Required—TOEFL (minimum score 600 paper-based; 250 computer-based). Electronic applications accepted. *Expenses:* Contact institution. *Faculty research:* Environmental history, green politics, ecopsychology.

Antioch University New England, Graduate School, Department of Environmental Studies, Individualized Program, Keene, NH 03431-3552. Offers MS. *Degree requirements:* For master's, practicum, seminar, thesis or project. *Entrance requirements:* For master's, detailed proposal.

Antioch University New England, Graduate School, Department of Environmental Studies, Program in Environmental Advocacy and Organizing, Keene, NH 03431-3552. Offers MS. *Degree requirements:* For master's, practicum, seminar. *Entrance requirements:* For master's, samples of written work, portfolio, letters of recommendation, interview.

Antioch University New England, Graduate School, Department of Environmental Studies, Program in Resource Management and Conservation, Keene, NH 03431-3552. Offers MS. *Degree requirements:* For master's, thesis optional, practicum. *Entrance requirements:* For master's, previous undergraduate course work in science and math. Additional exam requirements/recommendations for international students: Required—TOEFL (minimum score 600 paper-based; 250 computer-based). Electronic applications accepted. *Expenses:* Contact institution. *Faculty research:* Waste management, land use.

Antioch University New England, Graduate School, Department of Organization and Management, Program in Organizational and Environmental Sustainability (Green MBA), Keene, NH 03431-3552. Offers MBA. Part-time programs available. *Entrance requirements:* For master's, GRE, resume, 3 letters of recommendation. Additional exam requirements/recommendations for international students: Required—TOEFL (minimum score 600 paper-based; 250 computer-based).

Antioch University Seattle, Graduate Programs, Center for Creative Change, Seattle, WA 98121-1814. Offers environment and community (MA); management (MS); organizational psychology (MA); strategic communications (MA); whole system design (MA). Evening/weekend programs available. Electronic applications accepted. *Expenses:* Contact institution.

Appalachian State University, Cratis D. Williams Graduate School, Department of Government and Justice Studies, Boone, NC 28608. Offers criminal justice (MS); political science (MA), including American government, environmental

Peterson's Graduate Programs in the Physical Sciences, Mathematics, Agricultural Sciences, the Environment & Natural Resources 2013

facebook.com/petersonspublishing **453**

Environmental Management and Policy

politics and policy analysis, international relations; public administration (MPA), including public management, town, city and county management. Part-time programs available. Postbaccalaureate distance learning degree programs offered (no on-campus study). *Faculty:* 27 full-time (9 women), 4 part-time/adjunct (1 woman). *Students:* 68 full-time (31 women), 56 part-time (26 women); includes 12 minority (8 Black or African American, non-Hispanic/Latino; 4 Hispanic/Latino; 1 international. 85 applicants, 74% accepted, 44 enrolled. In 2011, 34 master's awarded. *Degree requirements:* For master's, variable foreign language requirement, comprehensive exam, thesis optional. *Entrance requirements:* For master's, GRE General Test, 3 letters of recommendation. Additional exam requirements/recommendations for international students: Required—TOEFL (minimum score 570 paper-based; 230 computer-based; 79 iBT), IELTS (minimum score 6.5). *Application deadline:* For fall admission, 3/15 priority date for domestic students, 2/1 for international students; for spring admission, 11/1 for domestic students, 7/1 for international students. Applications are processed on a rolling basis. Application fee: $55. Electronic applications accepted. *Expenses:* Tuition, state resident: full-time $4040; part-time $180 per semester hour. Tuition, nonresident: full-time $15,900; part-time $760 per semester hour. *Required fees:* $2500; $20 per semester hour. Tuition and fees vary according to campus/ location. *Financial support:* In 2011–12, 20 research assistantships (averaging $8,000 per year) were awarded; fellowships, teaching assistantships, career-related internships or fieldwork, Federal Work-Study, scholarships/grants, and unspecified assistantships also available. Financial award application deadline: 4/ 1; financial award applicants required to submit FAFSA. *Faculty research:* Campaign finance, emerging democracies, bureaucratic politics, judicial behavior, administration of justice. *Total annual research expenditures:* $24,000. *Unit head:* Dr. Brian Ellison, Chairperson, 828-262-3085, E-mail: ellisonba@appstate.edu. *Application contact:* Sandy Krause, Director of Admissions and Recruiting, 828-262-2130, Fax: 828-262-2709, E-mail: krausesl@appstate.edu. Web site: http://www.pscj.appstate.edu.

Aquinas College, School of Management, Grand Rapids, MI 49506-1799. Offers health care administration (M Mgt); marketing management (M Mgt); organizational leadership (M Min); sustainable business (M Mgt, MSB). Part-time and evening/weekend programs available. *Faculty:* 11 full-time (3 women), 7 part-time/adjunct (0 women). *Students:* 12 full-time (6 women), 56 part-time (32 women); includes 7 minority (3 Black or African American, non-Hispanic/Latino; 1 Asian, non-Hispanic/Latino; 3 Hispanic/Latino). *Entrance requirements:* For master's, GMAT, minimum undergraduate GPA of 2.75, 2 years of work experience. Additional exam requirements/recommendations for international students: Required—TOEFL (minimum score 550 paper-based; 213 computer-based). *Application deadline:* Applications are processed on a rolling basis. *Expenses:* Contact institution. *Financial support:* Scholarships/grants available. Support available to part-time students. Financial award application deadline: 3/ 15; financial award applicants required to submit FAFSA. *Unit head:* Brian DiVita, Director, 616-632-2922, Fax: 616-732-4489. *Application contact:* Lynn Atkins-Rykert, Administrative Assistant, 616-632-2924, Fax: 616-732-4489, E-mail: atkinlyn@aquinas.edu.

Arizona State University, College of Technology and Innovation, Department of Technology Management, Mesa, AZ 85212. Offers technology (aviation management and human factors) (MS); technology (environmental technology management) (MS); technology (global technology and development) (MS); technology (graphic information technology) (MS); technology (management of technology) (MS). Part-time and evening/weekend programs available. Postbaccalaureate distance learning degree programs offered (minimal on-campus study). *Degree requirements:* For master's, thesis or applied project and oral defense; interactive Program of Study (iPOS) submitted before completing 50 percent of required credit hours. *Entrance requirements:* For master's, GRE, minimum GPA of 3.0 or equivalent in last 2 years of work leading to bachelor's degree. Additional exam requirements/recommendations for international students: Required—TOEFL (minimum score 83 iBT), TOEFL, IELTS, or Pearson Test of English. Electronic applications accepted. *Faculty research:* Digital imaging, digital publishing, Internet development/e-commerce, information aviation human factors, pilot selection, databases, multimedia, commercial digital photography, digital workflow, computer graphics modeling and animation, information design, sociotechnology, visual and technical literacy, environmental management, quality management, project management, industrial ethics, hazardous materials, environmental chemistry.

Arizona State University, W. P. Carey School of Business, Morrison School of Agribusiness and Resource Management, Mesa, AZ 85212. Offers agribusiness (MS). Part-time and evening/weekend programs available. *Degree requirements:* For master's, thesis, oral defense, interactive Program of Study (iPOS) submitted before completing 50 percent of required credit hours. *Entrance requirements:* For master's, GMAT or GRE General Test, minimum GPA of 3.0 in last 2 years of work leading to bachelor's degree, 3 letters of recommendation, resume, official transcripts, statement of intent. Additional exam requirements/recommendations for international students: Required—TOEFL (minimum score 550 paper-based; 213 computer-based; 80 iBT), IELTS (minimum score 6.5); Recommended— TWE. Electronic applications accepted. *Faculty research:* Consumer behavior and marketing strategies in food markets, supply-chain management, derivatives and risk management, and international agricultural trade and policy.

Bard College, Bard Center for Environmental Policy, Annandale-on-Hudson, NY 12504. Offers climate science and policy (MS, Professional Certificate), including agriculture (MS), ecosystems (MS); environmental policy (MS, Professional

Certificate); sustainability (MBA); MS/JD; MS/MAT. Part-time programs available. *Degree requirements:* For master's, thesis, 4-month, full-time internship. *Entrance requirements:* For master's, GRE, coursework in statistics, chemistry and one other semester of college science; personal statement; curriculum vitae; 3 letters of recommendation; sample of written work. Additional exam requirements/ recommendations for international students: Required—TOEFL (minimum score 600 paper-based; 250 computer-based; 100 iBT). Electronic applications accepted. *Expenses:* Contact institution. *Faculty research:* Climate and agriculture, alternative energy, environmental economics, environmental toxicology, EPA law, sustainable development, international relations, literature and composition, human rights, agronomy, advocacy, leadership.

Baylor University, Graduate School, College of Arts and Sciences, Department of Environmental Science, Waco, TX 76798. Offers MES, MS. *Students:* 11 full-time (5 women), 1 part-time (0 women); includes 2 minority (1 Black or African American, non-Hispanic/Latino; 1 Hispanic/Latino), 2 international. In 2011, 5 master's awarded. *Degree requirements:* For master's, thesis. *Entrance requirements:* For master's, GRE General Test. *Application deadline:* For fall admission, 2/14 priority date for domestic students; for spring admission, 8/15 for domestic students. Applications are processed on a rolling basis. Application fee: $25. *Financial support:* Research assistantships, teaching assistantships, career-related internships or fieldwork, Federal Work-Study, and institutionally sponsored loans available. *Faculty research:* Renewable energy/waste management policies, Third World environmental problem solving, ecotourism. *Unit head:* Dr. Joe Yelderman, Graduate Program Director, 254-710-1385, Fax: 254-710-3409, E-mail: joe_yelderman@baylor.edu. *Application contact:* Glenda Plemons, Administrative Assistant, 254-710-3405, Fax: 254-710-3870, E-mail: glenda_plemons@baylor.edu. Web site: http://www.baylor.edu/ environmental%5Fstudies/.

Baylor University, Graduate School, College of Arts and Sciences, Program in Air Science and Environment, Waco, TX 76798. Offers IMES. *Unit head:* Dr. Larry Lyon, Dean, 254-710-3588, Fax: 254-710-3870, E-mail: larry_lyon@baylor.edu. *Application contact:* Suzanne Keener, Administrative Assistant, 254-710-3588, Fax: 254-710-3870.

Bemidji State University, School of Graduate Studies, Bemidji, MN 56601-2699. Offers biology (MS); counseling psychology (MS); education (M Ed, MS); English (MA, MS); environmental studies (MS); mathematics (MS); mathematics (elementary and middle level education) (MS); special education (M Sp Ed, MS). Part-time programs available. Postbaccalaureate distance learning degree programs offered (no on-campus study). *Faculty:* 114 full-time (47 women), 22 part-time/adjunct (16 women). *Students:* 68 full-time (45 women), 311 part-time (198 women); includes 21 minority (4 Black or African American, non-Hispanic/ Latino; 2 American Indian or Alaska Native, non-Hispanic/Latino; 5 Asian, non-Hispanic/Latino; 5 Hispanic/Latino; 5 Two or more races, non-Hispanic/Latino), 5 international. Average age 34. 82 applicants, 98% accepted, 37 enrolled. In 2011, 72 master's awarded. *Degree requirements:* For master's, comprehensive exam, thesis (for some programs). *Entrance requirements:* For master's, GRE, letters of recommendation, letters of interest. Additional exam requirements/ recommendations for international students: Required—TOEFL (minimum score 550 paper-based; 213 computer-based; 80 iBT). *Application deadline:* Applications are processed on a rolling basis. Application fee: $20. Electronic applications accepted. *Expenses:* Tuition, state resident: full-time $6182; part-time $343.45 per credit. Tuition, nonresident: full-time $6182; part-time $343.45 per credit. *Required fees:* $954. *Financial support:* In 2011–12, 253 students received support, including 36 research assistantships with partial tuition reimbursements available (averaging $7,441 per year), 36 teaching assistantships with partial tuition reimbursements available (averaging $7,441 per year); career-related internships or fieldwork, scholarships/grants, health care benefits, and unspecified assistantships also available. Support available to part-time students. Financial award application deadline: 4/15; financial award applicants required to submit FAFSA. *Unit head:* Dr. Patricia Rogers, Dean of Health Sciences and Human Ecology, 218-755-2027, Fax: 218-755-2258, E-mail: progers@bemidjistate.edu. *Application contact:* Joan Miller, Senior Office and Administrative Specialist, 218-755-2027, Fax: 218-755-2258, E-mail: jmiller@ bemidjistate.edu. Web site: http://www.bemidjistate.edu/academics/ graduate_studies/.

Boise State University, Graduate College, College of Social Sciences and Public Affairs, Department of Public Policy and Administration, Boise, ID 83725-0399. Offers environmental and natural resources policy and administration (MPA); general public administration (MPA); state and local government policy and administration (MPA). *Accreditation:* NASPAA. Part-time programs available. *Degree requirements:* For master's, comprehensive exam, directed research project, internship. *Entrance requirements:* For master's, GRE General Test, minimum GPA of 3.0. Additional exam requirements/recommendations for international students: Required—TOEFL. Electronic applications accepted.

Boston University, Graduate School of Arts and Sciences, Department of Geography and Environment, Boston, MA 02215. Offers energy and environmental analysis (MA); environmental remote sensing and GIs (MA); geography (MA); geography and environment (PhD); international relations and environmental policy (MA). *Students:* 60 full-time (21 women), 6 part-time (4 women); includes 7 minority (1 American Indian or Alaska Native, non-Hispanic/ Latino; 2 Asian, non-Hispanic/Latino; 1 Hispanic/Latino; 3 Two or more races, non-Hispanic/Latino), 20 international. Average age 28. 87 applicants, 17% accepted, 13 enrolled. In 2011, 1 master's, 2 doctorates awarded. Terminal

454 facebook.com/petersonspublishing

Peterson's Graduate Programs in the Physical Sciences, Mathematics, Agricultural Sciences, the Environment & Natural Resources 2013

master's awarded for partial completion of doctoral program. *Degree requirements:* For master's, one foreign language, comprehensive exam, thesis; for doctorate, one foreign language, comprehensive exam, thesis/dissertation. *Entrance requirements:* For master's and doctorate, GRE General Test, GRE Subject Test, 3 letters of recommendation. Additional exam requirements/recommendations for international students: Required—TOEFL (minimum score 600 paper-based; 250 computer-based). *Application deadline:* For fall admission, 7/1 for domestic and international students; for spring admission, 11/15 for domestic and international students. Application fee: $70. Electronic applications accepted. *Expenses: Tuition:* Full-time $40,848; part-time $1276 per credit hour. *Required fees:* $572; $286 per semester. *Financial support:* In 2011–12, 4 fellowships with full tuition reimbursements (averaging $19,800 per year), 15 research assistantships with full tuition reimbursements (averaging $19,300 per year), 11 teaching assistantships with full tuition reimbursements (averaging $19,300 per year) were awarded; Federal Work-Study and unspecified assistantships also available. Support available to part-time students. Financial award application deadline: 1/15; financial award applicants required to submit FAFSA. *Total annual research expenditures:* $1.2 million. *Unit head:* Robert Kaufmann, Chairman, 617-353-3940, Fax: 617-353-8399, E-mail: kaufmann@bu.edu. *Application contact:* Christopher DeVits, Graduate Program Coordinator, 617-353-7554, Fax: 617-353-8399, E-mail: cdevits@bu.edu. Web site: http://www.bu.edu/geography.

Boston University, Graduate School of Arts and Sciences, Department of International Relations, Boston, MA 02215. Offers African studies (Certificate); Asian studies (Certificate); global development policy (MA); international affairs (MA); international relations and communication (MA); international relations and environmental policy (MA); international relations and religion (MA); Latin American studies (MA); mid-career international relations (MA); JD/MA; MBA/MA. *Students:* 48 full-time (36 women), 8 part-time (5 women); includes 10 minority (4 Asian, non-Hispanic/Latino; 2 Hispanic/Latino; 1 Native Hawaiian or other Pacific Islander, non-Hispanic/Latino; 3 Two or more races, non-Hispanic/Latino), 14 international. Average age 26. 492 applicants, 59% accepted, 56 enrolled. In 2011, 41 master's awarded. *Degree requirements:* For master's, one foreign language, capstone. *Entrance requirements:* For master's, GRE General Test, 3 letters of recommendation, transcript of all prior college coursework, statement of purpose. Additional exam requirements/recommendations for international students: Required—TOEFL (minimum score 600 paper-based; 94 iBT). *Application deadline:* For fall admission, 4/15 for domestic and international students; for spring admission, 10/15 for domestic and international students. Application fee: $70. Electronic applications accepted. *Expenses: Tuition:* Full-time $40,848; part-time $1276 per credit hour. *Required fees:* $572; $286 per semester. *Financial support:* In 2011–12, 20 students received support. Federal Work-Study and unspecified assistantships available. Financial award application deadline: 1/15; financial award applicants required to submit FAFSA. *Unit head:* William Grimes, Chairman, 617-353-9420, Fax: 617-353-9290, E-mail: wgrimes@bu.edu. *Application contact:* Michael Williams, Graduate Program Administrator, 617-353-9349, Fax: 617-353-9290, E-mail: mawillia@bu.edu. Web site: http://www.bu.edu/IR/.

California State University, Chico, Office of Graduate Studies, College of Behavioral and Social Sciences, Department of Geography and Planning, Program in Geography, Chico, CA 95929-0722. Offers environmental policy and planning (MA); geography (MA). Part-time programs available. *Faculty:* 7 full-time (3 women). *Students:* 4 full-time (0 women), 3 part-time (2 women). Average age 31. 5 applicants, 80% accepted, 3 enrolled. In 2011, 1 master's awarded. *Degree requirements:* For master's, thesis or project. *Entrance requirements:* For master's, GRE General Test, two letters of recommendation, statement of purpose, writing sample. Additional exam requirements/recommendations for international students: Required—TOEFL (minimum score 550 paper-based; 213 computer-based; 80 iBT), IELTS (minimum score 6.5), Pearson Test of English (minimum score 59). *Application deadline:* For fall admission, 3/1 priority date for domestic students, 3/1 for international students; for spring admission, 9/15 priority date for domestic students, 9/15 for international students. Application fee: $55. Electronic applications accepted. Tuition and fees vary according to class time, course load and degree level. *Financial support:* Career-related internships or fieldwork, institutionally sponsored loans, scholarships/grants, and unspecified assistantships available. Financial award application deadline: 3/1; financial award applicants required to submit FAFSA. *Unit head:* Dr. Jacquelyn Chase, Chair, 530-898-5285, Fax: 530-898-6781, E-mail: geop@csuchico.edu. *Application contact:* Judy L. Rice, Graduate Admissions Coordinator, 530-898-6871, E-mail: jlrice@csuchico.edu. Web site: http://catalog.csuchico.edu/viewer/11/GEOG/GEOGNONEPN.html.

California State University, Fullerton, Graduate Studies, College of Humanities and Social Sciences, Program in Environmental Studies, Fullerton, CA 92834-9480. Offers environmental sciences (MS). Part-time programs available. *Students:* 23 full-time (13 women), 51 part-time (25 women); includes 21 minority (2 Black or African American, non-Hispanic/Latino; 10 Asian, non-Hispanic/Latino; 5 Hispanic/Latino; 4 Two or more races, non-Hispanic/Latino), 2 international. Average age 31. 63 applicants, 63% accepted, 29 enrolled. In 2011, 18 master's awarded. *Degree requirements:* For master's, thesis. *Entrance requirements:* For master's, minimum GPA of 2.5 in last 60 units of course work. Application fee: $55. *Financial support:* Career-related internships or fieldwork, Federal Work-Study, institutionally sponsored loans, and scholarships/grants available. Support available to part-time students. Financial award application deadline: 3/1; financial award applicants required to submit FAFSA. *Unit head:* Dr. John Bock,

Coordinator, 657-278-4373. *Application contact:* Admissions/Applications, 657-278-2371.

Central European University, Graduate Studies, Department of Environmental Sciences and Policy, Budapest, Hungary. Offers MS, PhD. Part-time programs available. *Faculty:* 10 full-time (2 women), 4 part-time/adjunct (1 woman). *Students:* 106 full-time (64 women), 14 part-time (8 women). Average age 29. 1,280 applicants, 5% accepted, 50 enrolled. In 2011, 37 master's, 10 doctorates awarded. Terminal master's awarded for partial completion of doctoral program. *Degree requirements:* For master's, one foreign language, thesis; for doctorate, one foreign language, comprehensive exam, thesis/dissertation. *Entrance requirements:* For master's and doctorate, interview. Additional exam requirements/recommendations for international students: Required—TOEFL (minimum score 570 paper-based; 230 computer-based); Recommended—IELTS (minimum score 6.5). *Application deadline:* For fall admission, 1/24 priority date for domestic students, 1/24 for international students. Application fee: $0. Electronic applications accepted. Tuition charges are reported in euros. *Expenses: Tuition:* Full-time 11,000 euros. *Financial support:* In 2011–12, 52 students received support, including 32 fellowships with full and partial tuition reimbursements available (averaging $6,100 per year); career-related internships or fieldwork, institutionally sponsored loans, scholarships/grants, and tuition waivers (full and partial) also available. Financial award application deadline: 1/5. *Faculty research:* Management of ecological systems, environmental impact assessment, energy conservation, climate change policy, forest policy in countries in transition. *Unit head:* Dr. Alan Watt, Head, 36-1-327-3021, Fax: 36-1-327-3031, E-mail: envsci@ceu.hu. *Application contact:* Krisztina Szabados, Department Coordinator, 361-327-3021, Fax: 361-327-3031, E-mail: envsci@ceu.hu. Web site: http://www.ceu.hu/envsci/.

Clarkson University, Graduate School, Institute for a Sustainable Environment, Program in Environmental Politics and Governance, Potsdam, NY 13699. Offers MS. Part-time programs available. Terminal master's awarded for partial completion of doctoral program. *Degree requirements:* For master's, thesis. *Entrance requirements:* For master's, GRE, transcripts of all college coursework, resume, personal statement, three letters of recommendation. Additional exam requirements/recommendations for international students: Required—TOEFL (minimum score 550 paper-based; 213 computer-based; 80 iBT), IELTS (minimum score 6.5). *Application deadline:* For fall admission, 1/30 priority date for domestic students, 1/30 for international students; for spring admission, 9/1 priority date for domestic students, 9/1 for international students. Applications are processed on a rolling basis. Application fee: $25 ($35 for international students). Electronic applications accepted. *Expenses: Tuition:* Full-time $14,376; part-time $1198 per credit hour. *Required fees:* $295 per semester. *Financial support:* In 2011–12, fellowships with full tuition reimbursements (averaging $21,999 per year), research assistantships with full tuition reimbursements (averaging $21,999 per year), teaching assistantships with full tuition reimbursements (averaging $21,999 per year) were awarded; scholarships/grants, tuition waivers (partial), and unspecified assistantships also available. *Unit head:* Dr. Philip Hopke, Director, 315-268-3856, Fax: 315-268-4291, E-mail: hopkepk@clarkson.edu. *Application contact:* Suzann Cheney, Administrative Secretary, 315-268-3856, Fax: 315-268-4291, E-mail: scheney@clarkson.edu. Web site: http://www.clarkson.edu/epg/.

Clark University, Graduate School, Department of International Development, Community, and Environment, Program in Environmental Science and Policy, Worcester, MA 01610-1477. Offers MA, MA/MBA. Part-time programs available. *Students:* 53 full-time (33 women), 7 part-time (2 women); includes 2 minority (1 Black or African American, non-Hispanic/Latino; 1 Asian, non-Hispanic/Latino), 30 international. Average age 29. 105 applicants, 73% accepted, 35 enrolled. In 2011, 23 master's awarded. *Degree requirements:* For master's, thesis. *Entrance requirements:* For master's, 3 references, resume or curriculum vitae. Additional exam requirements/recommendations for international students: Required—TOEFL (minimum score 575 paper-based; 233 computer-based; 90 iBT) or IELTS (minimum score 6.5). *Application deadline:* For fall admission, 1/15 for domestic students. Application fee: $50. *Expenses: Tuition:* Full-time $37,000; part-time $1156 per credit hour. *Financial support:* In 2011–12, research assistantships with partial tuition reimbursements (averaging $5,000 per year), teaching assistantships with partial tuition reimbursements (averaging $5,000 per year) were awarded; fellowships with partial tuition reimbursements, institutionally sponsored loans, and scholarships/grants also available. *Faculty research:* Environmental justice, children's health and risk assessment, smart grids and energy technology transitions, uncertainty-risk analysis, climate variability modeling, . *Unit head:* Dr. David Bell, Director, 508-793-8820, Fax: 508-793-8820, E-mail: dbell@clarku.edu. *Application contact:* Paula Hall, IDCE Graduate Admissions, 508-793-7201, Fax: 508-793-8820, E-mail: idce@clarku.edu. Web site: http://clarku.edu/departments/idce/academicsGradESP.cfm.

Clark University, Graduate School, Department of International Development, Community, and Environment, Program in Geographic Information Science for Development and Environment, Worcester, MA 01610-1477. Offers MA. *Students:* 33 full-time (17 women), 2 part-time (both women); includes 1 minority (Black or African American, non-Hispanic/Latino), 19 international. Average age 26. 70 applicants, 54% accepted, 17 enrolled. In 2011, 22 master's awarded. *Degree requirements:* For master's, thesis. *Entrance requirements:* For master's, 3 references, resume or curriculum vitae. Additional exam requirements/recommendations for international students: Required—TOEFL (minimum score 575 paper-based; 233 computer-based; 90 iBT) or IELTS (minimum score 6.5).

Peterson's Graduate Programs in the Physical Sciences, Mathematics, Agricultural Sciences, the Environment & Natural Resources 2013

facebook.com/petersonspublishing **455**

Environmental Management and Policy

Application deadline: For fall admission, 1/15 for domestic students. Application fee: $50. Expenses: Tuition: Full-time $37,000; part-time $1156 per credit hour. Financial support: In 2011–12, research assistantships with partial tuition reimbursements (averaging $5,000 per year), teaching assistantships with partial tuition reimbursements (averaging $5,000 per year) were awarded; fellowships with partial tuition reimbursements, institutionally sponsored loans, and scholarships/grants also available. Faculty research: Land-use change, the effects of environmental influences on child health and development, quantitative methods, watershed management, brownfields redevelopment, human/environment interactions, biodiversity conservation, climate change. Unit head: Dr. David Bell, IDCE Director, 508-793-8820, Fax: 508-793-8820, E-mail: dbell@clarku.edu. Application contact: Paula Hall, IDCE Graduate Admissions Office, 508-793-7205, E-mail: idce@clarku.edu. Web site: http://clarku.edu/departments/idce/academicsGradGISDE.cfm.

Clemson University, Graduate School, College of Agriculture, Forestry and Life Sciences, Department of Forestry and Natural Resources, Program in Plant and Environmental Sciences, Clemson, SC 29634. Offers MS, PhD. Students: 43 full-time (16 women), 10 part-time (1 woman); includes 2 minority (1 Hispanic/Latino; 1 Two or more races, non-Hispanic/Latino), 16 international. Average age 31. 36 applicants, 47% accepted, 16 enrolled. In 2011, 12 master's, 3 doctorates awarded. Degree requirements: For master's, thesis; for doctorate, comprehensive exam, thesis/dissertation. Entrance requirements: For master's, GRE General Test, bachelor's degree in biological science or related disciplines; for doctorate, GRE General Test. Additional exam requirements/recommendations for international students: Required—TOEFL, IELTS. Application deadline: Applications are processed on a rolling basis. Electronic applications accepted. Expenses: Contact institution. Financial support: In 2011–12, 37 students received support, including 3 fellowships with full and partial tuition reimbursements available (averaging $9,667 per year), 29 research assistantships with partial tuition reimbursements available (averaging $16,876 per year), 10 teaching assistantships with partial tuition reimbursements available (averaging $12,424 per year); career-related internships or fieldwork, institutionally sponsored loans, scholarships/grants, health care benefits, and unspecified assistantships also available. Support available to part-time students. Financial award application deadline: 3/15; financial award applicants required to submit FAFSA. Faculty research: Sustainable agroecology, horticulture and turfgrass, physiology and pathology of plants. Unit head: Dr. Patricia Layton, School Director, 864-656-3302, Fax: 864-656-3304, E-mail: playton@clemson.edu. Application contact: Dr. Halina Knap, Coordinator, 864-656-3523, Fax: 864-656-3443, E-mail: hskrpsk@clemson.edu. Web site: http://www.clemson.edu/cafls/departments/pes/.

Cleveland State University, College of Graduate Studies, Maxine Goodman Levin College of Urban Affairs, Program in Environmental Studies, Cleveland, OH 44115. Offers environmental nonprofit management (MAES); environmental planning (MAES); geographic information systems (Certificate); policy and administration (MAES); sustainable economic development (MAES); urban economic development (Certificate); urban real estate development and finance (Certificate); JD/MAES. Part-time and evening/weekend programs available. Faculty: 26 full-time (10 women), 3 part-time/adjunct (0 women). Students: 12 full-time (5 women), 23 part-time (12 women); includes 1 minority (Asian, non-Hispanic/Latino), 4 international. 18 applicants, 61% accepted, 6 enrolled. In 2011, 9 master's awarded. Degree requirements: For master's, thesis or alternative, exit project. Entrance requirements: For master's, GRE General Test (minimum score: verbal and quantitative in 40th percentile, analytical writing 4.0), minimum GPA of 3.0. Additional exam requirements/recommendations for international students: Required—TOEFL (minimum score 525 paper-based; 197 computer-based; 65 iBT). Application deadline: For fall admission, 7/15 priority date for domestic students, 5/15 for international students; for spring admission, 11/1 for international students. Applications are processed on a rolling basis. Application fee: $30. Electronic applications accepted. Expenses: Tuition, state resident: full-time $6416; part-time $494 per credit hour. Tuition, nonresident: full-time $12,074; part-time $929 per credit hour. Financial support: In 2011–12, 6 students received support, including 2 research assistantships with full and partial tuition reimbursements available (averaging $7,200 per year), 4 teaching assistantships with full and partial tuition reimbursements available (averaging $2,400 per year); career-related internships or fieldwork, scholarships/grants, traineeships, and unspecified assistantships also available. Support available to part-time students. Financial award application deadline: 3/1; financial award applicants required to submit FAFSA. Faculty research: Environmental policy and administration, environmental planning, geographic information systems (GIS), urban sustainability planning and management, energy policy, land re-use. Unit head: Dr. Sanda Kaufman, Director, 216-687-2367, Fax: 216-687-9342, E-mail: s.kaufman@csuohio.edu. Application contact: Joan Demko, Graduate Academic Program Specialist, 216-523-7522, Fax: 216-687-5398, E-mail: urbanprograms@csuohio.edu. Web site: http://urban.csuohio.edu/academics/graduate/maes/.

Cleveland State University, College of Graduate Studies, Maxine Goodman Levin College of Urban Affairs, Program in Urban Planning, Design, and Development, Cleveland, OH 44115. Offers economic development (MUPDD); environmental sustainability (MUPDD); geographic information systems (Certificate); historic preservation (MUPDD); housing and neighborhood development (MUPDD); urban economic development (Certificate); urban real estate development and finance (MUPDD, Certificate); JD/MUPDD. Accreditation: ACSP. Part-time and evening/weekend programs available. Faculty: 32 full-time (19 women), 8 part-time/adjunct (4 women). Students: 30 full-time (10 women), 28

part-time (17 women); includes 9 minority (6 Black or African American, non-Hispanic/Latino; 3 Hispanic/Latino), 5 international. Average age 38. 91 applicants, 45% accepted, 21 enrolled. In 2011, 24 master's awarded. Degree requirements: For master's, thesis or alternative, capstone seminar. Entrance requirements: For master's, GRE General Test (minimum score in 50th percentile verbal and quantitative, 4.0 analytical writing), minimum GPA of 3.0. Additional exam requirements/recommendations for international students: Required—TOEFL (minimum score 525 paper-based; 197 computer-based; 65 iBT). Application deadline: For fall admission, 7/15 priority date for domestic students, 5/15 for international students; for spring admission, 11/1 for international students. Applications are processed on a rolling basis. Application fee: $30. Electronic applications accepted. Expenses: Tuition, state resident: full-time $6416; part-time $494 per credit hour. Tuition, nonresident: full-time $12,074; part-time $929 per credit hour. Financial support: In 2011–12, 15 students received support, including 10 research assistantships with full and partial tuition reimbursements available (averaging $6,960 per year), 5 teaching assistantships with full and partial tuition reimbursements available (averaging $6,960 per year); career-related internships or fieldwork, Federal Work-Study, scholarships/grants, tuition waivers, and unspecified assistantships also available. Support available to part-time students. Financial award application deadline: 3/1; financial award applicants required to submit FAFSA. Faculty research: Housing and neighborhood development, urban housing policy, environmental sustainability, economic development, GIS and planning decision support. Unit head: Dr. William Dennis Keating, Director, 216-687-2298, Fax: 216-687-2013, E-mail: w.keating@csuohio.edu. Application contact: Joan Demko, Graduate Program Coordinator, 216-523-7522, Fax: 216-687-5398, E-mail: urbanprograms@csuohio.edu. Web site: http://urban.csuohio.edu/academics/graduate/mupdd/.

College of the Atlantic, Program in Human Ecology, Bar Harbor, ME 04609-1198. Offers M Phil. Degree requirements: For master's, thesis. Faculty research: Conservation of endangered species, public policy/community planning, environmental education, history, philosophy.

Columbia University, Graduate School of Arts and Sciences, Program in Climate and Society, New York, NY 10027. Offers MA.

Columbia University, School of International and Public Affairs, Program in Environmental Science and Policy, New York, NY 10027. Offers MPA. Program admits applicants for late May/early June start only. Degree requirements: For master's, workshops. Entrance requirements: For master's, GRE (recommended), previous course work in biology and chemistry, earth sciences (recommended), economics (strongly recommended). Additional exam requirements/recommendations for international students: Required—TOEFL. Electronic applications accepted. Faculty research: Ecological management of enclosed ecosystems vegetation dynamics, environmental policy and management, energy policy, nuclear waste policy, environmental and natural resource economics and policy, carbon sequestration, urban planning, environmental risk assessment/toxicology, environmental justice.

Concordia University, School of Graduate Studies, Faculty of Arts and Science, Department of Geography, Planning and Environment, Montréal, QC H3G 1M8, Canada. Offers environmental impact assessment (Diploma); geography, urban and environmental studies (M Sc).

Cornell University, Graduate School, Graduate Fields of Agriculture and Life Sciences, Field of Natural Resources, Ithaca, NY 14853-0001. Offers aquatic science (MPS, MS, PhD); environmental management (MPS); fishery science (MPS, MS, PhD); forest science (MPS, MS, PhD); resource policy and management (MPS, MS, PhD); wildlife science (MPS, MS, PhD). Faculty: 39 full-time (7 women). Students: 52 full-time (21 women); includes 4 minority (1 American Indian or Alaska Native, non-Hispanic/Latino; 1 Asian, non-Hispanic/Latino; 1 Hispanic/Latino; 1 Two or more races, non-Hispanic/Latino), 15 international. Average age 32. 72 applicants, 21% accepted, 11 enrolled. In 2011, 2 master's, 5 doctorates awarded. Degree requirements: For master's, thesis (MS), project paper (MPS); for doctorate, comprehensive exam, thesis/dissertation. Entrance requirements: For master's and doctorate, GRE General Test, 2 letters of recommendation. Additional exam requirements/recommendations for international students: Required—TOEFL (minimum score 550 paper-based; 213 computer-based; 77 iBT). Application deadline: For spring admission, 10/30 for domestic students. Applications are processed on a rolling basis. Application fee: $95. Electronic applications accepted. Financial support: In 2011–12, 10 fellowships with full tuition reimbursements, 14 research assistantships with full tuition reimbursements, 28 teaching assistantships with full tuition reimbursements were awarded; institutionally sponsored loans, scholarships/grants, health care benefits, tuition waivers (full and partial), and unspecified assistantships also available. Financial award applicants required to submit FAFSA. Faculty research: Ecosystem-level dynamics, systems modeling, conservation biology/management, resource management's human dimensions, biogeochemistry. Unit head: Director of Graduate Studies, 607-255-2807, Fax: 607-255-0349. Application contact: Graduate Field Assistant, 607-255-2807, Fax: 607-255-0349, E-mail: nrgrad@cornell.edu. Web site: http://www.gradschool.cornell.edu/fields.php?id-54&a-2.

Cornell University, Graduate School, Graduate Fields of Agriculture and Life Sciences, Field of Soil and Crop Sciences, Ithaca, NY 14853-0001. Offers agronomy (MS, PhD); environmental information science (MS, PhD); environmental management (MPS); field crop science (MS, PhD); soil science (MS, PhD). Faculty: 39 full-time (9 women). Students: 19 full-time (11 women);

includes 5 minority (all Hispanic/Latino), 4 international. Average age 28. 39 applicants, 18% accepted, 6 enrolled. In 2011, 5 master's, 5 doctorates awarded. *Degree requirements:* For master's, thesis (MS); for doctorate, comprehensive exam, thesis/dissertation. *Entrance requirements:* For master's and doctorate, GRE General Test, 2 letters of recommendation. Additional exam requirements/recommendations for international students: Required—TOEFL (minimum score 550 paper-based; 213 computer-based; 77 iBT). *Application deadline:* For fall admission, 2/1 priority date for domestic students. Applications are processed on a rolling basis. Application fee: $95. Electronic applications accepted. *Financial support:* In 2011–12, 5 fellowships with full tuition reimbursements, 2 research assistantships with full tuition reimbursements, 7 teaching assistantships with full tuition reimbursements were awarded; institutionally sponsored loans, traineeships, health care benefits, tuition waivers (full and partial), and unspecified assistantships also available. *Faculty research:* Soil chemistry, physics and biology; crop physiology and management; environmental information science and modeling; international agriculture; weed science. *Unit head:* Director of Graduate Studies, 607-255-3267, Fax: 607-255-8615. *Application contact:* Graduate Field Assistant, 607-255-3267, Fax: 607-255-8615, E-mail: ljh4@cornell.edu. Web site: http://www.gradschool.cornell.edu/fields.php?id=5A&a-2.

Cornell University, Graduate School, Graduate Fields of Architecture, Art and Planning, Field of Regional Science, Ithaca, NY 14853-0001. Offers environmental studies (MA, MS, PhD); international spatial problems (MA, MS, PhD); location theory (MA, MS, PhD); multiregional economic analysis (MA, MS, PhD); peace science (MA, MS, PhD); planning methods (MA, MS, PhD); urban and regional economics (MA, MS, PhD). *Faculty:* 22 full-time (6 women). *Students:* 18 full-time (7 women); includes 1 minority (Black or African American, non-Hispanic/Latino), 16 international. Average age 31. 14 applicants, 29% accepted, 4 enrolled. In 2011, 3 master's, 4 doctorates awarded. Terminal master's awarded for partial completion of doctoral program. *Degree requirements:* For master's, thesis; for doctorate, comprehensive exam, thesis/dissertation. *Entrance requirements:* For master's and doctorate, GRE General Test, 2 letters of recommendation. Additional exam requirements/recommendations for international students: Required—TOEFL (minimum score 600 paper-based; 250 computer-based; 77 iBT). *Application deadline:* For fall admission, 1/15 priority date for domestic students. Application fee: $95. Electronic applications accepted. *Financial support:* In 2011–12, 1 research assistantship with full tuition reimbursement, 4 teaching assistantships with full tuition reimbursements were awarded; fellowships with full tuition reimbursements, institutionally sponsored loans, scholarships/grants, health care benefits, tuition waivers (full and partial), and unspecified assistantships also available. Financial award applicants required to submit FAFSA. *Faculty research:* Urban and regional growth, spatial economics, formation of spatial patterns by socioeconomic systems, non-linear dynamics and complex systems, environmental-economic systems. *Unit head:* Director of Graduate Studies, 607-255-6848, Fax: 607-255-1971. *Application contact:* Graduate Field Assistant, 607-255-6848, Fax: 607-255-1971, E-mail: regsci@cornell.edu. Web site: http://www.gradschool.cornell.edu/fields.php?id=92&a-2.

Cornell University, Graduate School, Graduate Fields of Arts and Sciences, Field of Archaeology, Ithaca, NY 14853-0001. Offers environmental archaeology (MA); historical archaeology (MA); Latin American archaeology (MA); medieval archaeology (MA); Mediterranean and Near Eastern archaeology (MA); Stone Age archaeology (MA). *Faculty:* 21 full-time (7 women). *Students:* 6 full-time (5 women); includes 1 minority (Hispanic/Latino). Average age 25. 20 applicants, 30% accepted, 2 enrolled. In 2011, 2 master's awarded. *Degree requirements:* For master's, one foreign language, thesis. *Entrance requirements:* For master's, GRE General Test, 3 letters of recommendation, sample of written work. Additional exam requirements/recommendations for international students: Required—TOEFL (minimum score 550 paper-based; 213 computer-based; 77 iBT). *Application deadline:* For fall admission, 1/15 for domestic students. Application fee: $95. Electronic applications accepted. *Financial support:* In 2011–12, 1 fellowship with full tuition reimbursement was awarded; research assistantships with full tuition reimbursements, teaching assistantships with full tuition reimbursements, institutionally sponsored loans, scholarships/grants, health care benefits, tuition waivers (full and partial), and unspecified assistantships also available. Financial award applicants required to submit FAFSA. *Faculty research:* Anatolia, Lydia, Sardis, classical and Hellenistic Greece; science in archaeology; North American Indians; Stone Age Africa; Mayan trade. *Unit head:* Director of Graduate Studies, 607-255-6768, E-mail: blj7@cornell.edu. *Application contact:* Graduate Field Assistant, 607-255-6768, E-mail: dsd6@cornell.edu. Web site: http://www.gradschool.cornell.edu/fields.php?id=97&a-2.

Dalhousie University, Faculty of Management, School for Resource and Environmental Studies, Halifax, NS B3H 3J5, Canada. Offers MES, MREM, MLIS/MREM. Part-time programs available. *Degree requirements:* For master's, thesis. *Entrance requirements:* For master's, honors degree. Additional exam requirements/recommendations for international students: Required—TOEFL, IELTS, CANTEST, CAEL, or Michigan English Language Assessment Battery. Electronic applications accepted. *Faculty research:* Resource management and ecology, aboriginal resource rights, management of toxic substances, environmental impact assessment, forest management, policy, coastal zone management.

Drexel University, College of Arts and Sciences, Program in Environmental Policy, Philadelphia, PA 19104-2875. Offers MS. Part-time and evening/weekend programs available. *Degree requirements:* For master's, thesis optional. Electronic applications accepted.

Duke University, Graduate School, Department of Environment, Durham, NC 27708. Offers natural resource economics/policy (PhD); natural resource science/ecology (PhD); natural resource systems science (PhD); JD/AM. Part-time programs available. *Faculty:* 28 full-time. *Students:* 53 full-time (32 women); includes 3 minority (1 Black or African American, non-Hispanic/Latino; 2 Asian, non-Hispanic/Latino), 16 international. 87 applicants, 20% accepted, 9 enrolled. In 2011, 10 doctorates awarded. *Degree requirements:* For doctorate, variable foreign language requirement, thesis/dissertation. *Entrance requirements:* For doctorate, GRE General Test. Additional exam requirements/recommendations for international students: Required—TOEFL (minimum score 550 paper-based; 213 computer-based; 83 iBT), IELTS (minimum score 7). *Application deadline:* For fall admission, 12/8 priority date for domestic students, 12/8 for international students. Application fee: $75. Electronic applications accepted. *Expenses: Tuition:* Full-time $40,720. *Required fees:* $3107. *Financial support:* Fellowships, research assistantships, teaching assistantships, and Federal Work-Study available. Financial award application deadline: 12/8. *Unit head:* Gaby Katul, Director of Graduate Studies, 919-613-8002, Fax: 919-613-8061, E-mail: meg.stephens@duke.edu. *Application contact:* Elizabeth Hutton, Director, Graduate Admissions, 919-684-3913, Fax: 919-684-2277, E-mail: grad-admissions@duke.edu. Web site: http://www.env.duke.edu/.

Duke University, Graduate School, Program in Environmental Policy, Durham, NC 27708. Offers PhD. *Faculty:* 29 full-time. *Students:* 8 full-time (4 women), 3 international. 67 applicants, 10% accepted, 4 enrolled. *Degree requirements:* For doctorate, comprehensive exam, thesis/dissertation. *Entrance requirements:* For doctorate, GRE General Test. Additional exam requirements/recommendations for international students: Required—TOEFL (minimum score 550 paper-based; 213 computer-based; 83 iBT), IELTS (minimum score 7). *Application deadline:* For fall admission, 12/8 priority date for domestic students, 12/8 for international students. Application fee: $75. Electronic applications accepted. *Expenses: Tuition:* Full-time $40,720. *Required fees:* $3107. *Financial support:* Fellowships, research assistantships, and teaching assistantships available. Financial award application deadline: 12/8. *Unit head:* Jeff Vincent, Dean, 919-613-8002, Fax: 919-613-8061, E-mail: meg.stephens@duke.edu. *Application contact:* Elizabeth Hutton, Director of Admissions, 919-684-3913, E-mail: grad-admissions@duke.edu. Web site: http://www.nicholas.duke.edu/programs/doctoral/upep/.

Duke University, Nicholas School of the Environment, Durham, NC 27708-0328. Offers coastal environmental management (MEM); DEL-environmental leadership (MEM); energy and environment (MEM); environmental economics and policy (MEM); environmental health and security (MEM); forest resource management (MF); global environmental change (MEM); resource ecology (MEM); water and air resources (MEM); JD/AM; JD/MEM; JD/MF; MAT/MEM; MBA/MEM; MBA/MF; MEM/MPP; MF/MPP. *Accreditation:* SAF (one or more programs are accredited). Part-time programs available. *Degree requirements:* For master's, thesis. *Entrance requirements:* For master's, GRE General Test, previous course work in biology or ecology, calculus, statistics, and microeconomics; computer familiarity with word processing and data analysis. Additional exam requirements/recommendations for international students: Required—TOEFL (minimum score 550 paper-based; 213 computer-based). Electronic applications accepted. *Expenses:* Contact institution. *Faculty research:* Ecosystem management, conservation ecology, earth systems, risk assessment.

Duquesne University, Bayer School of Natural and Environmental Sciences, Environmental Science and Management Program, Pittsburgh, PA 15282-0001. Offers environmental management (Certificate); environmental science (Certificate); environmental science and management (MS); JD/MS; MBA/MS; MS/MS. Part-time and evening/weekend programs available. Postbaccalaureate distance learning degree programs offered (minimal on-campus study). *Faculty:* 2 full-time (0 women), 8 part-time/adjunct (1 woman). *Students:* 20 full-time (8 women), 19 part-time (11 women); includes 4 minority (1 Black or African American, non-Hispanic/Latino; 2 Asian, non-Hispanic/Latino; 1 Hispanic/Latino), 7 international. Average age 26. 31 applicants, 61% accepted, 10 enrolled. In 2011, 10 degrees awarded. *Degree requirements:* For master's, thesis (for some programs), minimum of 36 credit hours; for Certificate, minimum of 18 credit hours. *Entrance requirements:* For master's, GRE General Test, course work in biology, chemistry, and calculus or statistics; 3 letters of reference, official transcripts, statement of purpose; for Certificate, undergraduate degree, 3 letters of reference, official transcripts, statement of purpose. Additional exam requirements/recommendations for international students: Required—TOEFL (minimum score 80 iBT). *Application deadline:* For fall admission, 4/1 priority date for domestic students, 4/1 for international students; for spring admission, 10/1 priority date for domestic students, 10/1 for international students. Applications are processed on a rolling basis. Application fee: $40. *Expenses:* Contact institution. *Financial support:* In 2011–12, 13 students received support, including 2 fellowships (averaging $17,300 per year), 5 research assistantships (averaging $13,408 per year); career-related internships or fieldwork, scholarships/grants, tuition waivers (partial), and unspecified assistantships also available. Financial award application deadline: 5/31. *Faculty research:* Watershed management systems, environmental analytical chemistry, environmental endocrinology, environmental microbiology, aquatic biology. *Unit head:* Dr. John Stolz, Director, 412-396-4367, Fax: 412-396-4092, E-mail: stolz@duq.edu. *Application contact:* Heather Costello, Graduate Academic Advisor, 412-396-6339, Fax: 412-396-4881, E-mail: costelloh@duq.edu. Web site: http://www.science.duq.edu/.

Peterson's Graduate Programs in the Physical Sciences, Mathematics, Agricultural Sciences, the Environment & Natural Resources 2013

facebook.com/petersonspublishing **457**

Environmental Management and Policy

The Evergreen State College, Graduate Programs, Program in Environmental Studies, Olympia, WA 98505. Offers MES. Part-time and evening/weekend programs available. *Faculty:* 5 full-time (3 women), 5 part-time/adjunct (1 woman). *Students:* 45 full-time (22 women), 51 part-time (26 women); includes 11 minority (2 Black or African American, non-Hispanic/Latino; 2 American Indian or Alaska Native, non-Hispanic/Latino; 3 Asian, non-Hispanic/Latino; 3 Hispanic/Latino; 1 Native Hawaiian or other Pacific Islander, non-Hispanic/Latino). Average age 32. 74 applicants, 93% accepted, 42 enrolled. In 2011, 27 master's awarded. *Degree requirements:* For master's, thesis. *Entrance requirements:* For master's, GRE, BA or BS; minimum GPA of 3.0 in last 90 quarter hours toward BA/BS; 15 quarter hours in social sciences and biological or physical science, 4 in statistics, biology, and microeconomics; 3 letters of recommendation; evidence of writing, analytical and general communication skills of high quality and at level appropriate for graduate study. Additional exam requirements/recommendations for international students: Required—TOEFL (minimum score 600 paper-based; 250 computer-based; 100 iBT). *Application deadline:* For fall admission, 2/15 priority date for domestic students, 2/15 for international students. Applications are processed on a rolling basis. Application fee: $50. Electronic applications accepted. *Expenses:* Contact institution. *Financial support:* In 2011–12, 55 students received support, including 12 fellowships with partial tuition reimbursements available (averaging $1,852 per year); career-related internships or fieldwork, Federal Work-Study, institutionally sponsored loans, scholarships/grants, tuition waivers (partial), and unspecified assistantships also available. Support available to part-time students. Financial award application deadline: 3/1; financial award applicants required to submit FAFSA. *Faculty research:* Phytoplankton, bacterial ecology, computer science, software engineering, scientific database, digital government communities, Riparian forests interaction with streams and energy through leaf litterfall, ethnic identities in cultural landscape, Greek landscape of wildland fire, Native American landscape, Western American public lands and landscapes, public policy/administration, political economy/science, American government, natural resource policy/economics. *Unit head:* Dr. Martha Henderson, Director, 360-867-6225, Fax: 360-867-5430, E-mail: mhenders@evergreen.edu. *Application contact:* Gail Wootan, Assistant Director, 360-867-6225, Fax: 360-867-5430, E-mail: wootang@evergreen.edu. Web site: http://www.evergreen.edu/mes/.

Florida Atlantic University, Dorothy F. Schmidt College of Arts and Letters, Department of History, Boca Raton, FL 33431-0991. Offers environmental studies (Certificate); history (MA). Part-time programs available. *Faculty:* 17 full-time (7 women), 6 part-time/adjunct (1 woman). *Students:* 10 full-time (3 women), 18 part-time (6 women); includes 4 minority (1 Black or African American, non-Hispanic/Latino; 1 Asian, non-Hispanic/Latino; 2 Hispanic/Latino), 2 international. Average age 36. 21 applicants, 48% accepted, 6 enrolled. In 2011, 11 master's awarded. *Degree requirements:* For master's, one foreign language, thesis optional. *Entrance requirements:* For master's, GRE General Test, minimum GPA of 3.0. *Application deadline:* For fall admission, 6/1 priority date for domestic students, 2/15 for international students; for spring admission, 10/15 for domestic students, 8/15 for international students. Applications are processed on a rolling basis. Application fee: $30. Electronic applications accepted. *Expenses: Tuition, area resident:* Part-time $343.02 per credit hour. Tuition, state resident: full-time $8232. Tuition, nonresident: full-time $23,931; part-time $997.14 per credit hour. *Financial support:* Fellowships, research assistantships, teaching assistantships with tuition reimbursements, career-related internships or fieldwork, Federal Work-Study, and tuition waivers (partial) available. Support available to part-time students. Financial award application deadline: 3/1. *Faculty research:* Twentieth century America, U. S. urban history, Florida history, history of socialism, Latin America. *Unit head:* Dr. Patricia Kollander, Chair, 561-297-3841, Fax: 561-297-2704, E-mail: kollande@fau.edu. *Application contact:* Ben Lowe, Director of Graduate Programs, 561-297-3846, Fax: 561-297-2704, E-mail: bplowe@fau.edu. Web site: http://www.fau.edu/history/.

Florida Gulf Coast University, College of Professional Studies, Program in Public Administration, Fort Myers, FL 33965-6565. Offers criminal justice (MPA); environmental policy (MPA); general public administration (MPA); management (MPA). *Accreditation:* NASPAA. Part-time programs available. *Faculty:* 37 full-time (15 women), 38 part-time/adjunct (12 women). *Students:* 67 full-time (41 women), 13 part-time (9 women); includes 17 minority (10 Black or African American, non-Hispanic/Latino; 4 Hispanic/Latino; 3 Two or more races, non-Hispanic/Latino), 1 international. Average age 32. 41 applicants, 63% accepted, 17 enrolled. In 2011, 30 master's awarded. *Entrance requirements:* For master's, GRE General Test, MAT, minimum GPA of 3.0. Additional exam requirements/recommendations for international students: Required—TOEFL (minimum score 550 paper-based; 213 computer-based). *Application deadline:* For fall admission, 7/1 priority date for domestic students; for spring admission, 11/15 for domestic students. Applications are processed on a rolling basis. Application fee: $30. Electronic applications accepted. *Expenses:* Tuition, state resident: full-time $8289. Tuition, nonresident: full-time $28,895. *Required fees:* $1831. One-time fee: $30 full-time. *Financial support:* In 2011–12, 5 research assistantships were awarded; career-related internships or fieldwork and tuition waivers (full and partial) also available. Support available to part-time students. *Faculty research:* Personnel, public policy, public finance, housing policy. *Unit head:* Roger Green, Chair, 239-590-7838, E-mail: tbusson@fgcu.edu. *Application contact:* Howard Smith, Assistant Professor/Director of MPA Program, 239-590-7837, Fax: 239-590-7846, E-mail: hsmith@fgcu.edu.

Florida Institute of Technology, Graduate Programs, College of Engineering, Department of Marine and Environmental Systems, Melbourne, FL 32901-6975.

Offers earth remote sensing (MS); environmental resource management (MS); environmental science (MS, PhD); meteorology (MS); ocean engineering (MS, PhD); oceanography (MS, PhD), including biological oceanography (MS), chemical oceanography (MS), coastal management (MS), geological oceanography (MS), oceanography (PhD), physical oceanography (MS). Part-time programs available. *Faculty:* 11 full-time (0 women), 3 part-time/adjunct (0 women). *Students:* 52 full-time (18 women), 13 part-time (4 women); includes 4 minority (1 Black or African American, non-Hispanic/Latino; 1 Asian, non-Hispanic/Latino; 1 Hispanic/Latino; 1 Two or more races, non-Hispanic/Latino), 16 international. Average age 28. 117 applicants, 52% accepted, 23 enrolled. In 2011, 13 master's, 1 doctorate awarded. *Degree requirements:* For master's, comprehensive exam (for some programs), thesis (for some programs), seminar, field project, written final exam, technical paper, oral presentation, or internship; for doctorate, comprehensive exam, thesis/dissertation, seminar, internships (oceanography and environmental science), publications. *Entrance requirements:* For master's, GRE General Test (environmental science, oceanography, environmental resource management, meteorology, earth remote sensing), 3 letters of recommendation, minimum GPA of 3.0, resume, transcripts, statement of objectives; for doctorate, GRE General Test (oceanography, environmental science), resume, 3 letters of recommendation, minimum GPA of 3.3, statement of objectives, on-campus interview (highly recommended). Additional exam requirements/recommendations for international students: Required—TOEFL (minimum score 550 paper-based; 213 computer-based; 79 iBT). *Application deadline:* For fall admission, 4/1 for international students; for spring admission, 9/30 for international students. Applications are processed on a rolling basis. Electronic applications accepted. *Expenses: Tuition:* Full-time $19,620; part-time $1090 per credit hour. Tuition and fees vary according to campus/location. *Financial support:* In 2011–12, 5 fellowships with full and partial tuition reimbursements (averaging $7,240 per year), 3 research assistantships with full and partial tuition reimbursements (averaging $7,283 per year), 7 teaching assistantships with full and partial tuition reimbursements (averaging $4,928 per year) were awarded; career-related internships or fieldwork, institutionally sponsored loans, tuition waivers (partial), unspecified assistantships, and tuition remissions also available. Support available to part-time students. Financial award application deadline: 3/1; financial award applicants required to submit FAFSA. *Total annual research expenditures:* $1.6 million. *Unit head:* Dr. George Maul, Department Head, 321-674-7453, Fax: 321-674-7212, E-mail: gmaul@fit.edu. *Application contact:* Cheryl A. Brown, Associate Director of Graduate Admissions, 321-674-7581, Fax: 321-723-9468, E-mail: cbrown@fit.edu. Web site: http://coe.fit.edu/dmes/.

Florida International University, College of Arts and Sciences, Department of Earth and Environment, Program in Environmental Studies, Miami, FL 33199. Offers MS. Part-time programs available. *Degree requirements:* For master's, thesis or alternative. *Entrance requirements:* For master's, GRE General Test, minimum GPA of 3.0, 3 letters of recommendation, letter of intent. Additional exam requirements/recommendations for international students: Required—TOEFL (minimum score 550 paper-based; 80 iBT). Electronic applications accepted.

George Mason University, College of Science, Department of Environmental Science and Policy, Fairfax, VA 22030. Offers environmental management (Certificate); environmental science and policy (MS); environmental science and public policy (PhD). *Faculty:* 21 full-time (7 women), 9 part-time/adjunct (4 women). *Students:* 68 full-time (50 women), 106 part-time (59 women); includes 24 minority (6 Black or African American, non-Hispanic/Latino; 8 Asian, non-Hispanic/Latino; 9 Hispanic/Latino; 1 Two or more races, non-Hispanic/Latino), 15 international. Average age 35. 102 applicants, 52% accepted, 40 enrolled. In 2011, 17 master's, 15 doctorates, 3 other advanced degrees awarded. *Degree requirements:* For doctorate, thesis/dissertation, internship. *Entrance requirements:* For master's, GRE, bachelor's degree with minimum GPA of 3.0 in related field; 3 letters of recommendation; expanded goals statement; 2 official copies of transcripts; for doctorate, GRE, bachelor's degree with minimum GPA of 3.0; 3 letters of recommendation; current resume; expanded goals statement; 2 official copies of transcripts; for Certificate, GRE, 3 letters of recommendation; undergraduate degree in related field; expanded goals statement; resume; 2 official copies of transcripts. Additional exam requirements/recommendations for international students: Required—TOEFL (minimum score 570 paper-based; 230 computer-based; 88 iBT), IELTS, Pearson Test of English. *Application deadline:* For fall admission, 2/15 priority date for domestic students; for spring admission, 10/1 priority date for domestic students. Application fee: $65 ($80 for international students). Electronic applications accepted. *Expenses:* Tuition, state resident: full-time $8750; part-time $364.58 per credit. Tuition, nonresident: full-time $24,092; part-time $1003.83 per credit. *Required fees:* $2514; $104.75 per credit. *Financial support:* In 2011–12, 53 students received support, including 2 fellowships with full tuition reimbursements available (averaging $18,000 per year), 6 research assistantships with full and partial tuition reimbursements available (averaging $19,109 per year), 46 teaching assistantships with full and partial tuition reimbursements available (averaging $11,712 per year); career-related internships or fieldwork, Federal Work-Study, scholarships/grants, unspecified assistantships, and health care benefits (full-time research or teaching assistantship recipients) also available. Support available to part-time students. Financial award application deadline: 3/1; financial award applicants required to submit FAFSA. *Total annual research expenditures:* $1.4 million. *Unit head:* Dr. Robert B. Jonas, Chair, 703-993-7590, Fax: 703-993-1066, E-mail: rjonas@gmu.edu. *Application contact:* Sharon Bloomquist, Graduate Program

Coordinator, 703-993-3187, Fax: 703-993-1066, E-mail: sbloomqu@gmu.edu. Web site: http://esp.gmu.edu/.

The George Washington University, Columbian College of Arts and Sciences, Program in Environmental and Resource Policy, Washington, DC 20052. Offers MA. *Students:* 16 full-time (9 women), 9 part-time (5 women); includes 3 minority (1 Black or African American, non-Hispanic/Latino; 1 Asian, non-Hispanic/Latino; 1 Hispanic/Latino), 2 international. Average age 25. 71 applicants, 86% accepted. In 2011, 7 master's awarded. *Degree requirements:* For master's, capstone course. *Entrance requirements:* For master's, GRE General Test, minimum GPA of 3.0, two letters of recommendation. Additional exam requirements/recommendations for international students: Required—TOEFL (minimum score 600 paper-based; 250 computer-based; 100 iBT). *Application deadline:* For fall admission, 4/1 priority date for domestic students, 4/1 for international students; for spring admission, 10/1 priority date for domestic students, 9/1 for international students. Applications are processed on a rolling basis. Application fee: $60. Electronic applications accepted. *Financial support:* In 2011–12, 2 students received support. Fellowships with tuition reimbursements available, institutionally sponsored loans, and tuition waivers available. Financial award application deadline: 1/15. *Unit head:* Prof. Henry Teng, Chair, 202-994-1008. *Application contact:* 202-994-6210, Fax: 202-994-6213, E-mail: askccas@gwu.edu. Web site: http://www.gwu.edu/~tspppa/academics/affiliated_environment_policy.cfm.

Georgia Institute of Technology, Graduate Studies and Research, College of Architecture, City and Regional Planning Program, Atlanta, GA 30332-0001. Offers city and regional planning (PhD); economic development (MCRP); environmental planning and management (MCRP); geographic information systems (MCRP); land and community development (MCRP); land use planning (MCRP); transportation (MCRP); urban design (MCRP); MCP/MSCE. *Accreditation:* ACSP. *Degree requirements:* For master's, thesis, internship. *Entrance requirements:* For master's, GRE General Test, minimum GPA of 2.7. Additional exam requirements/recommendations for international students: Required—TOEFL. Electronic applications accepted.

Goddard College, Graduate Division, Master of Arts in Individualized Studies Program, Plainfield, VT 05667-9432. Offers consciousness studies (MA); environmental studies (MA); transformative language arts (MA). Postbaccalaureate distance learning degree programs offered (minimal on-campus study). *Degree requirements:* For master's, thesis. *Entrance requirements:* For master's, 3 letters of recommendation, study plan, bibliography/resource list, interview. Electronic applications accepted. *Expenses:* Contact institution.

Green Mountain College, Program in Environmental Studies, Poultney, VT 05764-1199. Offers MS. Distance learning only. Part-time and evening/weekend programs available. Postbaccalaureate distance learning degree programs offered (no on-campus study). *Entrance requirements:* For master's, portfolio, curriculum vitae, 3 recommendations. Electronic applications accepted. *Faculty research:* Herbarium specimen, solar electricity's value, environmental politics.

Hardin-Simmons University, Graduate School, Holland School of Sciences and Mathematics, Program in Environmental Management, Abilene, TX 79698-0001. Offers MS. Part-time programs available. *Faculty:* 5 full-time (0 women). *Students:* 4 full-time (2 women), 1 part-time (0 women). Average age 25. 4 applicants, 100% accepted, 4 enrolled. In 2011, 8 master's awarded. *Degree requirements:* For master's, comprehensive exam, thesis or alternative, internship. *Entrance requirements:* For master's, minimum undergraduate GPA of 3.0 in major, 2.7 overall; 2 semesters of course work each in biology, chemistry, and geology; interview; writing sample; occupational experience. Additional exam requirements/recommendations for international students: Required—TOEFL (minimum score 550 paper-based; 213 computer-based; 75 iBT). *Application deadline:* For fall admission, 8/15 priority date for domestic students, 4/1 for international students; for spring admission, 1/5 priority date for domestic students, 9/1 for international students. Applications are processed on a rolling basis. Application fee: $50. *Expenses: Tuition:* Full-time $12,870; part-time $715 per credit hour. *Required fees:* $650; $110 per semester. Tuition and fees vary according to degree level. *Financial support:* In 2011–12, 1 fellowship (averaging $300 per year) was awarded; career-related internships or fieldwork and scholarships/grants also available. Support available to part-time students. Financial award application deadline: 6/30; financial award applicants required to submit FAFSA. *Faculty research:* South American history, herpetology, geology, environmental education, petroleum biodegradation, environmental ecology and microbiology. *Unit head:* Dr. Mark Ouimette, Director, 325-670-1383, Fax: 325-670-1391, E-mail: ouimette@hsutx.edu. *Application contact:* Dr. Nancy Kucinski, Dean of Graduate Studies, 325-670-1298, Fax: 325-670-1564, E-mail: gradoff@hsutx.edu. Web site: http://www.hsutx.edu/academics/holland/graduate/environmental.

Harvard University, Extension School, Cambridge, MA 02138-3722. Offers applied sciences (CAS); biotechnology (ALM); educational technologies (ALM); educational technology (CET); English for graduate and professional studies (DGP); environmental management (ALM, CEM); information technology (ALM); journalism (ALM); liberal arts (ALM); management (ALM, CM); mathematics for teaching (ALM); museum studies (ALM); premedical studies (Diploma); publication and communication (CPC). Part-time and evening/weekend programs available. *Degree requirements:* For master's, thesis. *Entrance requirements:* For master's, 3 completed graduate courses with grade of B or higher. Additional exam requirements/recommendations for international students: Required—

TOEFL (minimum score 600 paper-based; 250 computer-based), TWE (minimum score 5). *Expenses:* Contact institution.

Humboldt State University, Academic Programs, College of Natural Resources and Sciences, Programs in Environmental Systems, Arcata, CA 95521-8299. Offers environmental systems (MS), including energy, environment and society, environmental resources engineering, geology, math modeling. *Students:* 32 full-time (12 women), 4 part-time (2 women); includes 5 minority (1 Black or African American, non-Hispanic/Latino; 1 Asian, non-Hispanic/Latino; 1 Hispanic/Latino; 2 Two or more races, non-Hispanic/Latino), 3 international. Average age 28. 58 applicants, 36% accepted, 13 enrolled. In 2011, 12 master's awarded. *Degree requirements:* For master's, thesis. *Entrance requirements:* For master's, GRE, appropriate bachelor's degree, minimum GPA of 2.5, 3 letters of recommendation. Additional exam requirements/recommendations for international students: Required—TOEFL. *Application deadline:* For fall admission, 2/15 for domestic students; for spring admission, 10/15 for domestic students. Applications are processed on a rolling basis. Application fee: $55. *Expenses:* Tuition, state resident: full-time $6734. Tuition, nonresident: full-time $15,662; part-time $372 per credit. *Required fees:* $903. Tuition and fees vary according to program. *Financial support:* Application deadline: 3/1; applicants required to submit FAFSA. *Faculty research:* Mathematical modeling, international development technology, geology, environmental resources engineering. *Unit head:* Dr. Chris Dugaw, Chair, 707-826-4251, Fax: 707-826-4145, E-mail: dugaw@humboldt.edu. *Application contact:* Dr. Dale Oliver, Coordinator, 707-826-4921, Fax: 707-826-3140, E-mail: dale.oliver@humboldt.edu.

Idaho State University, Office of Graduate Studies, College of Science and Engineering, Civil and Environmental Engineering Department, Pocatello, ID 83209-8060. Offers civil engineering (MS); environmental engineering (MS); environmental science and management (MS). Part-time programs available. *Degree requirements:* For master's, comprehensive exam (for some programs), thesis optional, thesis project, 2 semesters of seminar. *Entrance requirements:* For master's, GRE. Additional exam requirements/recommendations for international students: Required—TOEFL (minimum score 550 paper-based; 213 computer-based; 80 iBT). Electronic applications accepted. *Faculty research:* Floor vibration investigations, earthquake engineering, base isolation systems and seismic risk assessment, infrastructure revitalization (building foundations and damage, bridge structures, highways, and dams), slope stability and soil erosion, pavement rehabilitation, computational fluid dynamics and flood control structures, microbial fuel cells, water treatment and water quality modeling, environmental risk assessment, biotechnology, nanotechnology.

Illinois Institute of Technology, Stuart School of Business, Program in Environmental Management and Sustainability, Chicago, IL 60661. Offers MS, JD/MS, MBA/MS. Part-time and evening/weekend programs available. *Entrance requirements:* For master's, GRE (minimum score 1000) or GMAT (500). Additional exam requirements/recommendations for international students: Required—TOEFL (minimum score 600 paper-based; 85 iBT). Recommended—IELTS (minimum score 7). Electronic applications accepted. *Expenses:* Contact institution. *Faculty research:* Wind energy, carbon footprint reduction, critical asset management, solar energy, water quality management.

Indiana University Bloomington, School of Public and Environmental Affairs, Public Affairs Programs, Bloomington, IN 47405. Offers comparative and international affairs (MPA); economic development (MPA); energy (MPA); environmental policy (PhD); environmental policy and natural resource management (MPA); hazardous materials management (Certificate); information systems (MPA); international development (MPA); local government management (MPA); nonprofit management (MPA, Certificate); policy analysis (MPA); public budgeting and financial management (Certificate); public finance (PhD); public financial administration (MPA); public management (MPA, PhD, Certificate); public policy analysis (PhD); social entrepreneurship (Certificate); specialized public affairs (MPA); sustainability and sustainable development (MPA); JD/MPA; MPA/MA; MPA/MIS; MPA/MLS; MSES/MPA. *Accreditation:* NASPAA (one or more programs are accredited). Part-time programs available. *Faculty:* 80 full-time (30 women), 102 part-time/adjunct (43 women). *Students:* 338 full-time, 30 part-time; includes 27 minority (7 Black or African American, non-Hispanic/Latino; 2 American Indian or Alaska Native, non-Hispanic/Latino; 10 Asian, non-Hispanic/Latino; 8 Hispanic/Latino), 56 international. Average age 24. 501 applicants, 148 enrolled. In 2011, 172 master's, 7 doctorates awarded. *Degree requirements:* For master's, core classes, capstone, internship; for doctorate, comprehensive exam, thesis/dissertation. *Entrance requirements:* For master's, GRE General Test or GMAT, official transcripts, 3 letters of recommendation, resume, personal statement; for doctorate, GRE General Test or LSAT, official transcripts, 3 letters of recommendation, resume or curriculum vitae, statement of purpose. Additional exam requirements/recommendations for international students: Required—TOEFL (minimum score 600 paper-based; 96 iBT); Recommended—IELTS (minimum score 7). *Application deadline:* For fall admission, 2/1 priority date for domestic students, 12/1 for international students. Applications are processed on a rolling basis. Application fee: $55 ($65 for international students). Electronic applications accepted. *Financial support:* Fellowships with partial tuition reimbursements, research assistantships with partial tuition reimbursements, teaching assistantships with partial tuition reimbursements, career-related internships or fieldwork, Federal Work-Study, scholarships/grants, health care benefits, unspecified assistantships, and Service Corps programs available. Financial award application deadline: 2/1; financial award applicants required to submit FAFSA. *Faculty research:* Comparative and international affairs,

Peterson's Graduate Programs in the Physical Sciences, Mathematics, Agricultural Sciences, the Environment & Natural Resources 2013

facebook.com/petersonspublishing **459**

Environmental Management and Policy

environmental policy and resource management, policy analysis, public finance, public management, urban management, nonprofit management, energy policy, social policy, public finance. *Unit head:* Jennifer Forney, Director of Graduate Student Services, 812-855-9485, Fax: 812-856-3665, E-mail: speampo@indiana.edu. *Application contact:* Admissions Assistant, 812-855-2840, E-mail: speaapps@indiana.edu. Web site: http://www.indiana.edu/~spea/prospective_students/masters/.

Indiana University of Pennsylvania, School of Graduate Studies and Research, College of Humanities and Social Sciences, Department of Geography and Regional Planning, Program in Environmental Planning, Indiana, PA 15705-1087. Offers MS. *Faculty:* 8 full-time (0 women). *Students:* 2 full-time (1 woman), 1 part-time (0 women). Average age 32. 5 applicants, 20% accepted, 1 enrolled. In 2011, 2 master's awarded. *Entrance requirements:* Additional exam requirements/recommendations for international students: Required—TOEFL (minimum score 540 paper-based; 207 computer-based). *Application deadline:* Applications are processed on a rolling basis. Application fee: $50. Electronic applications accepted. *Expenses:* Tuition, state resident: full-time $7488; part-time $416 per credit. Tuition, nonresident: full-time $11,232; part-time $624 per credit. *Required fees:* $2070; $192.20 per credit. $90 per semester. *Financial support:* In 2011–12, 2 research assistantships (averaging $3,712 per year) were awarded. Financial award application deadline: 4/15; financial award applicants required to submit FAFSA. *Unit head:* Dr. Kevin Patrick, 724-357-3767, E-mail: kevin.patrick@iup.edu. *Application contact:* Dr. John E. Benhart, Jr., Chairperson, 724-357-2250, E-mail: jbenhart@iup.edu. Web site: http://www.iup.edu/page.aspx?id=41705.

Instituto Tecnologico de Santo Domingo, Graduate School, Area of Basic And Environmental Sciences, Santo Domingo, Dominican Republic. Offers environmental science (M En S), including environmental education, environmental management, marine resources, natural resources management; mathematics (MS, PhD); renewable energy technology (MS, Certificate).

Instituto Tecnológico y de Estudios Superiores de Monterrey, Campus Estado de México, Professional and Graduate Division, Estado de Mexico, Mexico. Offers administration of information technologies (MITA); architecture (M Arch); business administration (GMBA, MBA); computer sciences (MCS, PhD); education (M Ed); educational institution administration (MAD); educational technology and innovation (PhD); electronic commerce (MEC); environmental systems (MS); finance (MAF); humanistic studies (MHS); information sciences and knowledge management (MISKM); information systems (MS); manufacturing systems (MS); marketing (MEM); quality systems and productivity (MS); science and materials engineering (PhD); telecommunications management (MTM). Part-time programs available. Postbaccalaureate distance learning degree programs offered (minimal on-campus study). *Degree requirements:* For master's, one foreign language, thesis (for some programs); for doctorate, one foreign language, thesis/dissertation. *Entrance requirements:* For master's, E-PAEP 500, interview; for doctorate, E-PAEP 500, research proposal. Additional exam requirements/recommendations for international students: Required—TOEFL (minimum score 550 paper-based). *Faculty research:* Surface treatments by plasmas, mechanical properties, robotics, graphical computing, mechatronics security protocols.

Instituto Tecnológico y de Estudios Superiores de Monterrey, Campus Irapuato, Graduate Programs, Irapuato, Mexico. Offers administration (MBA); administration of information technology (MAIT); administration of telecommunications (MAT); architecture (M Arch); computer science (MCS); education (M Ed); educational administration (MEA); educational innovation and technology (DEIT); educational technology (MET); electronic commerce (MBA); environmental administration and planning (MEAP); environmental systems (MES); finances (MBA); humanistic studies (MHS); international management for Latin American executives (MIMLAE); library and information science (MLIS); manufacturing quality management (MMQM); marketing research (MBA).

Inter American University of Puerto Rico, Metropolitan Campus, Graduate Programs, Program in Environmental Evaluation and Protection, San Juan, PR 00919-1293. Offers MS.

The Johns Hopkins University, Engineering Program for Professionals, Part-Time Program in Environmental Planning and Management, Baltimore, MD 21218-2699. Offers MS, Post-Master's Certificate. Part-time and evening/weekend programs available. Postbaccalaureate distance learning degree programs offered (no on-campus study).

The Johns Hopkins University, Whiting School of Engineering, Program in Engineering Management, Baltimore, MD 21218-2699. Offers biomaterials (MSEM); communications science (MSEM); computer science (MSEM); fluid mechanics (MSEM); materials science and engineering (MSEM); mechanical engineering (MSEM); mechanics and materials (MSEM); nano-biotechnology (MSEM); nanomaterials and nanotechnology (MSEM); probability and statistics (MSEM); smart product and device design (MSEM); systems analysis, management and environmental policy (MSEM). *Entrance requirements:* For master's, GRE, 3 letters of recommendation, resume. Additional exam requirements/recommendations for international students: Required—TOEFL (minimum score 600 paper-based; 250 computer-based; 100 iBT) or IELTS (minimum score 7). Electronic applications accepted.

The Johns Hopkins University, Zanvyl Krieger School of Arts and Sciences, Advanced Academic Programs, Program in Environmental Sciences and Policy, Baltimore, MD 21218-2699. Offers MS. Part-time and evening/weekend programs available. Postbaccalaureate distance learning degree programs offered (minimal on-campus study). *Degree requirements:* For master's, thesis (for some programs). *Entrance requirements:* For master's, minimum GPA of 3.0, coursework in chemistry and calculus. Additional exam requirements/recommendations for international students: Required—TOEFL (minimum score 250 computer-based).

Kean University, College of Business and Public Management, Program in Public Administration, Union, NJ 07083. Offers environmental management (MPA); health services administration (MPA); non-profit management (MPA); public administration (MPA). *Accreditation:* NASPAA. *Faculty:* 14 full-time (7 women). *Students:* 65 full-time (34 women), 77 part-time (41 women); includes 92 minority (68 Black or African American, non-Hispanic/Latino; 7 Asian, non-Hispanic/Latino; 17 Hispanic/Latino), 4 international. Average age 32. 69 applicants, 70% accepted, 32 enrolled. In 2011, 48 master's awarded. *Degree requirements:* For master's, thesis, internship, research seminar. *Entrance requirements:* For master's, minimum GPA of 3.0, 2 letters of recommendation, interview, writing sample, transcripts, resume. Additional exam requirements/recommendations for international students: Required—TOEFL (minimum score 79 iBT). *Application deadline:* For fall admission, 6/1 for domestic and international students; for spring admission, 12/1 for domestic and international students. Applications are processed on a rolling basis. Application fee: $75 ($150 for international students). Electronic applications accepted. *Expenses:* Tuition, state resident: full-time $11,302; part-time $550 per credit. Tuition, nonresident: full-time $15,318; part-time $674 per credit. *Required fees:* $2849; $130 per credit. Tuition and fees vary according to degree level. *Financial support:* In 2011–12, 14 research assistantships with full tuition reimbursements (averaging $3,263 per year) were awarded; unspecified assistantships also available. Financial award applicants required to submit FAFSA. *Unit head:* Dr. Patricia Moore, Program Coordinator, 908-737-4314, E-mail: pmoore@kean.edu. *Application contact:* Reenat Hasan, Admissions Counselor, 908-737-5923, Fax: 908-737-5925, E-mail: hasanr@kean.edu. Web site: http://www.kean.edu/KU/Public-Administration.

Kentucky State University, College of Agriculture, Food Science and Sustainable Systems, Frankfort, KY 40601. Offers aquaculture (MS); environmental studies (MS). Part-time and evening/weekend programs available. *Faculty:* 10 full-time (1 woman), 1 part-time/adjunct (0 women). *Students:* 34 full-time (16 women), 32 part-time (6 women); includes 22 minority (15 Black or African American, non-Hispanic/Latino; 3 Asian, non-Hispanic/Latino; 1 Hispanic/Latino; 1 Native Hawaiian or other Pacific Islander, non-Hispanic/Latino; 2 Two or more races, non-Hispanic/Latino), 12 international. Average age 34. 55 applicants, 51% accepted, 18 enrolled. In 2011, 16 master's awarded. *Degree requirements:* For master's, comprehensive exam, thesis optional. *Entrance requirements:* For master's, GRE, GMAT. Additional exam requirements/recommendations for international students: Required—TOEFL (minimum score 525 paper-based; 173 computer-based). *Application deadline:* Applications are processed on a rolling basis. Application fee: $30 ($100 for international students). Electronic applications accepted. *Expenses:* Tuition, state resident: full-time $6192; part-time $344 per credit hour. Tuition, nonresident: full-time $9522; part-time $529 per credit hour. *Required fees:* $450; $25 per credit hour. Tuition and fees vary according to course load. *Financial support:* In 2011–12, 41 students received support, including 18 research assistantships (averaging $11,378 per year); career-related internships or fieldwork, scholarships/grants, tuition waivers (partial), and unspecified assistantships also available. Financial award application deadline: 4/15; financial award applicants required to submit FAFSA. *Unit head:* Dr. Teferi Tsegaye, Dean, 502-597-6310, E-mail: teferi.tsegaye@kysu.edu. *Application contact:* Dr. Titilayo Ufomata, Acting Director of Graduate Studies, 502-597-6443, E-mail: titilayo.ufomata@kysu.edu. Web site: http://www.kysu.edu/academics/collegesAndSchools/CAFSSS/.

Lamar University, College of Graduate Studies, College of Engineering, Department of Civil Engineering, Beaumont, TX 77710. Offers civil engineering (ME, MES, DE); environmental engineering (MS); environmental studies (MS). Part-time programs available. *Faculty:* 7 full-time (1 woman), 1 part-time/adjunct (0 women). *Students:* 34 full-time (6 women), 13 part-time (4 women); includes 5 minority (1 Black or African American, non-Hispanic/Latino; 3 Asian, non-Hispanic/Latino; 1 Hispanic/Latino), 34 international. Average age 28. 43 applicants, 84% accepted, 9 enrolled. In 2011, 30 master's, 3 doctorates awarded. *Degree requirements:* For master's, thesis optional; for doctorate, thesis/dissertation. *Entrance requirements:* For master's and doctorate, GRE General Test. Additional exam requirements/recommendations for international students: Required—TOEFL. *Application deadline:* For fall admission, 5/15 priority date for domestic students; for spring admission, 10/1 priority date for domestic students. Applications are processed on a rolling basis. Application fee: $25 ($50 for international students). *Expenses:* Tuition, state resident: full-time $5430; part-time $272 per credit hour. Tuition, nonresident: full-time $11,540; part-time $577 per credit hour. *Required fees:* $1916. *Financial support:* In 2011–12, 45 fellowships with partial tuition reimbursements (averaging $1,000 per year), 10 research assistantships with partial tuition reimbursements (averaging $7,200 per year), 3 teaching assistantships with partial tuition reimbursements (averaging $7,200 per year) were awarded; scholarships/grants and tuition waivers (partial) also available. Financial award application deadline: 4/1. *Faculty research:* Environmental remediations, construction productivity, geotechnical soil stabilization, lake/reservoir hydrodynamics, air pollution. *Unit head:* Dr. Enno Koehn, Chair, 409-880-8759, Fax: 409-880-8121, E-mail: koehneu@

hal.lamar.edu. *Application contact:* Sandy Drane, Coordinator of Graduate Admissions, 409-880-8356, Fax: 409-880-8414, E-mail: gradmissions@hal.lamar.edu.

Lehigh University, College of Arts and Sciences, Program in Environmental Initiative, Bethlehem, PA 18015. Offers environmental law and policy (Graduate Certificate); environmental policy design (MA). Part-time programs available. *Students:* 4 full-time (all women), 2 part-time (both women). Average age 26. 2 applicants, 100% accepted, 1 enrolled. In 2011, 10 degrees awarded. *Degree requirements:* For master's, thesis optional, thesis or additional course work. *Entrance requirements:* For master's, minimum GPA of 2.75, 3.0 for last two undergraduate semesters. Additional exam requirements/recommendations for international students: Required—TOEFL. *Application deadline:* For fall admission, 1/15 for domestic and international students; for spring admission, 12/1 for domestic and international students. Applications are processed on a rolling basis. Application fee: $75. Electronic applications accepted. *Financial support:* In 2011–12, 1 teaching assistantship with full tuition reimbursement (averaging $17,900 per year) was awarded; scholarships/grants and tuition waivers (partial) also available. Financial award application deadline: 1/15; financial award applicants required to submit FAFSA. *Faculty research:* Environmental law, politics, sustainability, policy (national and local). *Unit head:* Dr. John Gilroy, Director, 610-758-5964, Fax: 610-758-6377, E-mail: ei@lehigh.edu. *Application contact:* Terry Harnett, Academic Coordinator, 610-758-4745, Fax: 610-758-6232, E-mail: mth204@lehigh.edu. Web site: http://www.ei.lehigh.edu.

Long Island University–C. W. Post Campus, College of Liberal Arts and Sciences, Department of Earth and Environmental Science, Brookville, NY 11548-1300. Offers earth science (MS); earth science education (MS); environmental studies (MS).

Louisiana State University and Agricultural and Mechanical College, Graduate School, School of the Coast and Environment, Department of Environmental Sciences, Baton Rouge, LA 70803. Offers environmental planning and management (MS); environmental toxicology (MS). *Faculty:* 9 full-time (3 women). *Students:* 24 full-time (16 women), 9 part-time (4 women); includes 6 minority (3 Black or African American, non-Hispanic/Latino; 2 Asian, non-Hispanic/Latino; 1 Hispanic/Latino), 6 international. Average age 27. 19 applicants, 74% accepted, 7 enrolled. In 2011, 14 master's awarded. *Degree requirements:* For master's, thesis (for some programs). *Entrance requirements:* For master's, GRE General Test, minimum GPA of 3.0. Additional exam requirements/recommendations for international students: Required—TOEFL (minimum score 550 paper-based; 213 computer-based; 79 iBT) or IELTS (minimum score 6.5). *Application deadline:* For fall admission, 1/25 priority date for domestic students, 5/15 for international students; for spring admission, 10/15 for international students. Applications are processed on a rolling basis. Application fee: $50 ($70 for international students). Electronic applications accepted. *Financial support:* In 2011–12, 30 students received support, including 1 fellowship with full and partial tuition reimbursement available (averaging $17,831 per year), 15 research assistantships with full and partial tuition reimbursements available (averaging $15,467 per year), 6 teaching assistantships with full and partial tuition reimbursements available (averaging $10,333 per year); career-related internships or fieldwork, Federal Work-Study, institutionally sponsored loans, scholarships/grants, health care benefits, and unspecified assistantships also available. Support available to part-time students. Financial award applicants required to submit FAFSA. *Faculty research:* Environmental toxicology, environmental policy and law, microbial ecology, bioremediation, genetic toxicology. *Total annual research expenditures:* $1.9 million. *Unit head:* Dr. Ed Laws, Chair, 225-578-8521, Fax: 225-578-4286, E-mail: edlaws@lsu.edu. *Application contact:* Charlotte G. St. Romain, Academic Coordinator, 225-578-8522, Fax: 225-578-4286, E-mail: cstrom4@lsu.edu. Web site: http://info.envs.lsu.edu/.

Marylhurst University, Department of Business Administration, Marylhurst, OR 97036-0261. Offers finance (MBA); general management (MBA); government policy and administration (MBA); green development (MBA); health care management (MBA); marketing (MBA); natural and organic resources (MBA); nonprofit management (MBA); organizational behavior (MBA); real estate (MBA); renewable energy (MBA); sustainable business (MBA). Part-time and evening/weekend programs available. Postbaccalaureate distance learning degree programs offered (no on-campus study). *Faculty:* 3 full-time (0 women), 36 part-time/adjunct (6 women). *Students:* 29 full-time (15 women), 675 part-time (373 women); includes 178 minority (59 Black or African American, non-Hispanic/Latino; 6 American Indian or Alaska Native, non-Hispanic/Latino; 34 Asian, non-Hispanic/Latino; 46 Hispanic/Latino; 4 Native Hawaiian or other Pacific Islander, non-Hispanic/Latino; 29 Two or more races, non-Hispanic/Latino), 14 international. Average age 37. 262 applicants, 91% accepted, 194 enrolled. In 2011, 352 master's awarded. *Degree requirements:* For master's, comprehensive exam, capstone course. *Entrance requirements:* For master's, GMAT (if GPA less than 3.0 and fewer than 5 years of work experience), interview, resume, 2 letters of recommendation. Additional exam requirements/recommendations for international students: Recommended—TOEFL (minimum score 550 paper-based; 213 computer-based; 80 iBT). *Application deadline:* For fall admission, 9/11 priority date for domestic students, 9/11 for international students; for winter admission, 12/15 priority date for domestic students, 12/15 for international students; for spring admission, 3/15 priority date for domestic students, 3/17 for international students. Applications are processed on a rolling basis. Application fee: $50. Electronic applications accepted. *Expenses: Tuition:* Full-time $14,796;

part-time $548 per quarter hour. Tuition and fees vary according to program. *Financial support:* Scholarships/grants available. Support available to part-time students. Financial award applicants required to submit FAFSA. *Unit head:* David McNamee, Interim Chair, 503-636-8141, Fax: 503-697-5597, E-mail: mba@marylhurst.edu. *Application contact:* Maruska Lynch, Graduate Admissions Specialist, 800-634-9982 Ext. 6322, Fax: 503-699-6320, E-mail: admissions@marylhurst.edu. Web site: http://www.marylhurst.edu/.

McGill University, Faculty of Graduate and Postdoctoral Studies, Faculty of Agricultural and Environmental Sciences, Department of Natural Resource Sciences, Montréal, QC H3A 2T5, Canada. Offers entomology (M Sc, PhD); environmental assessment (M Sc); forest science (M Sc, PhD); microbiology (M Sc, PhD); micrometeorology (M Sc, PhD); neotropical environment (M Sc, PhD); soil science (M Sc, PhD); wildlife biology (M Sc, PhD).

Michigan Technological University, Graduate School, College of Sciences and Arts, Department of Social Sciences, Houghton, MI 49931. Offers environmental policy (MS, PhD); industrial archaeology (MS); industrial heritage and archeology (PhD). Part-time programs available. *Faculty:* 22 full-time (7 women), 8 part-time/adjunct (4 women). *Students:* 24 full-time (12 women), 8 part-time (3 women); includes 4 minority (1 American Indian or Alaska Native, non-Hispanic/Latino; 3 Asian, non-Hispanic/Latino, 6 international. Average age 23. 40 applicants, 55% accepted, 11 enrolled. In 2011, 8 degrees awarded. Terminal master's awarded for partial completion of doctoral program. *Degree requirements:* For master's, comprehensive exam (for some programs), thesis (for some programs); for doctorate, comprehensive exam, thesis/dissertation. *Entrance requirements:* For master's and doctorate, GRE, statement of purpose, official transcripts, 3 letters of recommendation, writing sample, resume/curriculum vitae. Additional exam requirements/recommendations for international students: Required—TOEFL (minimum score 79 iBT). *Application deadline:* For fall admission, 2/1 for domestic and international students. Applications are processed on a rolling basis. Electronic applications accepted. *Expenses:* Tuition, state resident: full-time $12,636; part-time $702 per credit. Tuition, nonresident: full-time $12,636; part-time $702 per credit. *Required fees:* $226; $226 per year. *Financial support:* In 2011–12, 26 students received support, including fellowships with full tuition reimbursements available (averaging $6,065 per year), 7 research assistantships with full tuition reimbursements available (averaging $6,065 per year), 13 teaching assistantships with full tuition reimbursements available (averaging $6,065 per year); career-related internships or fieldwork, Federal Work-Study, scholarships/grants, health care benefits, tuition waivers (partial), unspecified assistantships, and cooperative program also available. Financial award applicants required to submit FAFSA. *Faculty research:* Industrial archeology of early American industry, mining history, environmental policy, land-use policy, citizen participation in environmental decision-making. *Total annual research expenditures:* $176,455. *Unit head:* Dr. Patrick E. Martin, Chair, 906-487-2113, Fax: 906-487-2468, E-mail: srmartin@mtu.edu. *Application contact:* Carol T. Wingerson, Senior Staff Assistant, 906-487-2327, Fax: 906-487-2463, E-mail: gradadms@mtu.edu. Web site: http://www.social.mtu.edu/.

Missouri State University, Graduate College, Interdisciplinary Program in Administrative Studies, Springfield, MO 65897. Offers applied communication (MS); criminal justice (MS); environmental management (MS); homeland security (MS); project management (MS); sports management (MS). Part-time and evening/weekend programs available. Postbaccalaureate distance learning degree programs offered (no on-campus study). *Students:* 22 full-time (12 women), 61 part-time (28 women); includes 14 minority (5 Black or African American, non-Hispanic/Latino; 2 Asian, non-Hispanic/Latino; 4 Hispanic/Latino; 3 Two or more races, non-Hispanic/Latino). Average age 32. 31 applicants, 97% accepted, 18 enrolled. In 2011, 31 master's awarded. *Degree requirements:* For master's, comprehensive exam, thesis or alternative. *Entrance requirements:* For master's, GRE, GMAT, 3 years of work experience. Additional exam requirements/recommendations for international students: Required—TOEFL (minimum score 550 paper-based; 213 computer-based; 79 iBT). *Application deadline:* For fall admission, 7/20 priority date for domestic students; for spring admission, 12/20 priority date for domestic students. Applications are processed on a rolling basis. Application fee: $35 ($50 for international students). Electronic applications accepted. *Expenses:* Tuition, state resident: full-time $4086; part-time $227 per credit hour. Tuition, nonresident: full-time $8172; part-time $454 per credit hour. *Required fees:* $275 per semester. Tuition and fees vary according to course load, campus/location and program. *Financial support:* Career-related internships or fieldwork, Federal Work-Study, institutionally sponsored loans, scholarships/grants, and unspecified assistantships available. Support available to part-time students. Financial award application deadline: 3/31; financial award applicants required to submit FAFSA. *Unit head:* Dr. Thomas Tomasi, Interim Program Director, 417-836-5335, Fax: 417-836-6888, E-mail: tomtomasi@missouristate.edu. *Application contact:* Misty Stewart, Coordinator of Graduate Recruitment, 417-836-6079, Fax: 417-836-6200, E-mail: mistystewart@missouristate.edu. Web site: http://msas.missouristate.edu.

Montclair State University, The Graduate School, College of Science and Mathematics, Department of Earth and Environmental Studies, PhD Program in Environmental Management, Montclair, NJ 07043-1624. Offers PhD. *Students:* 22 full-time (14 women), 15 part-time (7 women); includes 6 minority (2 Black or African American, non-Hispanic/Latino; 4 Hispanic/Latino), 15 international. Average age 34. 31 applicants, 48% accepted, 9 enrolled. In 2011, 2 doctorates awarded. *Degree requirements:* For doctorate, thesis/dissertation. *Entrance requirements:* For doctorate, GRE General Test, 3 letters of recommendation,

Peterson's Graduate Programs in the Physical Sciences, Mathematics, Agricultural Sciences, the Environment & Natural Resources 2013

facebook.com/petersonspublishing **461**

essay. Additional exam requirements/recommendations for international students: Required—TOEFL (minimum score 83 iBT) or IELTS (minimum score 6.5). *Application deadline:* For fall admission, 2/1 for domestic students. Application fee: $60. Electronic applications accepted. *Financial support:* In 2011–12, 15 research assistantships with full tuition reimbursements (averaging $15,000 per year) were awarded; tuition waivers (full) and unspecified assistantships also available. Financial award application deadline: 3/1; financial award applicants required to submit FAFSA. *Faculty research:* Environmental geochemisty/remediation/forensics, environmental law and policy, regional climate modeling, remote sensing, Cenozoic marine sediment records from polar regions, sustainability science . *Unit head:* Dr. Michael Kruge, Director, 973-655-5423, Fax: 973-655-6810. *Application contact:* Amy Aiello, Director of Graduate Admissions and Operations, 973-655-5147, Fax: 973-655-7869, E-mail: graduate.school@montclair.edu. Web site: http://www.montclair.edu/csam/doctoral-environment-management/.

Montclair State University, The Graduate School, College of Science and Mathematics, Department of Earth and Environmental Studies, Program in Environmental Studies, Montclair, NJ 07043-1624. Offers environmental education (MA); environmental management (MA); environmental science (MA). Part-time and evening/weekend programs available. *Students:* 14 full-time (8 women), 21 part-time (12 women); includes 4 minority (1 Asian, non-Hispanic/Latino; 3 Hispanic/Latino), 2 international. Average age 34. 40 applicants, 55% accepted, 12 enrolled. In 2011, 16 master's awarded. *Degree requirements:* For master's, thesis. *Entrance requirements:* For master's, GRE General Test, 2 letters of recommendation, essay. Additional exam requirements/recommendations for international students: Required—TOEFL (minimum score 83 iBT), IELTS (minimum score 6.5). *Application deadline:* Applications are processed on a rolling basis. Application fee: $60. Electronic applications accepted. *Financial support:* In 2011–12, 10 research assistantships with full tuition reimbursements (averaging $7,000 per year) were awarded; Federal Work-Study, scholarships/grants, and unspecified assistantships also available. Support available to part-time students. Financial award application deadline: 3/1; financial award applicants required to submit FAFSA. *Faculty research:* Environmental geochemisty/remediation/forensics, environmental law and policy, regional climate modeling, remote sensing, Cenozoic marine sediment records from polar regions, sustainability science. *Unit head:* Dr. Matthew Goring, Chairperson, 973-655-5409. *Application contact:* Amy Aiello, Executive Director of The Graduate School, 973-655-5147, Fax: 973-655-7869, E-mail: graduate.school@montclair.edu. Web site: http://www.montclair.edu/csam/earth-environment-studies/academic-programs/ma-ms-degrees/ma-concentration-environmental-studies/.

Monterey Institute of International Studies, Graduate School of International Policy and Management, Program in International Environmental Policy, Monterey, CA 93940-2691. Offers MA. *Degree requirements:* For master's, one foreign language. *Entrance requirements:* For master's, minimum GPA of 3.0, proficiency in a foreign language. Additional exam requirements/recommendations for international students: Required—TOEFL (minimum score 550 paper-based; 213 computer-based; 80 iBT). Electronic applications accepted. *Expenses: Tuition:* Full-time $32,800; part-time $1560 per credit. *Required fees:* $28 per semester.

Morehead State University, Graduate Programs, College of Science and Technology, Department of Biology and Chemistry, Morehead, KY 40351. Offers biology (MS); biology regional analysis (MS). Part-time programs available. *Degree requirements:* For master's, comprehensive exam, thesis optional, oral and written final exams. *Entrance requirements:* For master's, GRE General Test, minimum GPA of 3.0 in biology, 2.5 overall; undergraduate major/minor in biology, environmental science, or equivalent. Additional exam requirements/recommendations for international students: Required—TOEFL (minimum score 525 paper-based; 173 computer-based). Electronic applications accepted. *Faculty research:* Atherosclerosis, RNA evolution, cancer biology, water quality, ecology, immunoparasitology.

Naropa University, Graduate Programs, Program in Environmental Leadership, Boulder, CO 80302-6697. Offers MA. *Faculty:* 2 full-time (both women), 3 part-time/adjunct (1 woman). *Students:* 28 full-time (19 women), 1 (woman) part-time, 3 international. Average age 30. 30 applicants, 83% accepted, 14 enrolled. In 2011, 15 master's awarded. *Degree requirements:* For master's, comprehensive exam, applied leadership project. *Entrance requirements:* For master's, in-person interview, writing sample, letter of interest, resume, 3 letters of recommendation. Additional exam requirements/recommendations for international students: Required—TOEFL (minimum score 600 paper-based; 250 computer-based). *Application deadline:* For fall admission, 1/15 priority date for domestic students, 1/15 for international students. Applications are processed on a rolling basis. Application fee: $60. Electronic applications accepted. *Expenses: Tuition:* Full-time $20,400; part-time $850 per credit. *Required fees:* $660; $250 per semester. *Financial support:* In 2011–12, 13 students received support, including 4 research assistantships with partial tuition reimbursements available (averaging $2,175 per year), 2 teaching assistantships with partial tuition reimbursements available (averaging $2,175 per year); Federal Work-Study, scholarships/grants, tuition waivers (partial), and unspecified assistantships also available. Support available to part-time students. Financial award application deadline: 3/1; financial award applicants required to submit FAFSA. *Unit head:* Dr. Jeanine Canty, Director, School of Natural and Social Sciences, 303-245-4735, E-mail: jcanty@naropa.edu. *Application contact:* Roslynn Regnery, Graduate Admissions

Counselor, 303-546-3598, Fax: 303-546-3583, E-mail: rregnery@naropa.edu. Web site: http://www.naropa.edu/academics/snss/grad/environmental-leadership-ma/index.php.

New Jersey Institute of Technology, Office of Graduate Studies, College of Science and Liberal Arts, Department of Chemistry and Environmental Science, Program in Environmental Policy Studies, Newark, NJ 07102. Offers MS. Part-time and evening/weekend programs available. *Students:* 5 part-time (4 women); includes 2 minority (1 Black or African American, non-Hispanic/Latino; 1 Hispanic/Latino). Average age 33. 7 applicants, 86% accepted, 2 enrolled. In 2011, 1 master's awarded. Terminal master's awarded for partial completion of doctoral program. *Degree requirements:* For master's, thesis or alternative. *Entrance requirements:* For master's, GRE General Test. Additional exam requirements/recommendations for international students: Required—TOEFL (minimum score 550 paper-based; 213 computer-based; 79 iBT). *Application deadline:* For fall admission, 6/1 priority date for domestic students, 5/1 for international students; for spring admission, 11/15 priority date for domestic students, 11/15 for international students. Applications are processed on a rolling basis. Application fee: $65. Electronic applications accepted. *Expenses: Tuition,* state resident: full-time $7980; part-time $867 per credit. Tuition, nonresident: full-time $11,336; part-time $1196 per credit. *Required fees:* $230 per credit. *Financial support:* Fellowships with full and partial tuition reimbursements, research assistantships with full and partial tuition reimbursements, teaching assistantships with full and partial tuition reimbursements, career-related internships or fieldwork, Federal Work-Study, institutionally sponsored loans, and unspecified assistantships available. Financial award application deadline: 1/15. *Unit head:* Dr. Nancy L. Jackson, Director, 973-596-8467, E-mail: nancy.jackson@njit.edu. *Application contact:* Kathryn Kelly, Director of Admissions, 973-596-3300, Fax: 973-596-3461, E-mail: admissions@njit.edu. Web site: http://chemistry.njit.edu/academics/graduate/env-policy/.

The New School, Milano The New School for Management and Urban Policy, Program in Environmental Policy and Sustainability Management, New York, NY 10011. Offers MS.

New York Institute of Technology, Graduate Division, School of Engineering and Computing Sciences, Program in Energy Management, Old Westbury, NY 11568-8000. Offers energy management (MS); energy technology (Advanced Certificate); environmental management (Advanced Certificate); facilities management (Advanced Certificate). Part-time and evening/weekend programs available. Postbaccalaureate distance learning degree programs offered. *Students:* 48 full-time (8 women), 97 part-time (17 women); includes 32 minority (11 Black or African American, non-Hispanic/Latino; 1 American Indian or Alaska Native, non-Hispanic/Latino; 4 Asian, non-Hispanic/Latino; 15 Hispanic/Latino; 1 Two or more races, non-Hispanic/Latino), 31 international. Average age 32. In 2011, 53 master's, 28 other advanced degrees awarded. *Degree requirements:* For master's, comprehensive exam, thesis or alternative. *Entrance requirements:* For master's, minimum QPA of 2.85. Additional exam requirements/recommendations for international students: Required—TOEFL (minimum score 550 paper-based; 213 computer-based). *Application deadline:* For fall admission, 7/1 priority date for domestic students; for spring admission, 12/1 priority date for domestic students. Applications are processed on a rolling basis. Application fee: $50. Electronic applications accepted. *Expenses: Tuition:* Part-time $930 per credit hour. *Financial support:* Fellowships, research assistantships with partial tuition reimbursements, institutionally sponsored loans, tuition waivers (full and partial), and unspecified assistantships available. Support available to part-time students. Financial award applicants required to submit FAFSA. *Unit head:* Dr. Robert Amundsen, Department Chair, 516-686-7578, E-mail: ramundse@nyit.edu. *Application contact:* Dr. Jacquelyn Nealon, Vice President for Enrollment Services, 516-686-7925, Fax: 516-686-7597, E-mail: jnealon@nyit.edu.

New York University, School of Continuing and Professional Studies, Center for Global Affairs, New York, NY 10012-1019. Offers global affairs (MS), including environment/energy policy, human rights and international law, international development and humanitarian assistance, international relations, peace building, private sector, transnational security. Part-time and evening/weekend programs available. *Faculty:* 10 full-time (3 women), 40 part-time/adjunct (18 women). *Students:* 132 full-time (86 women), 179 part-time (123 women); includes 37 minority (12 Black or African American, non-Hispanic/Latino; 14 Asian, non-Hispanic/Latino; 11 Hispanic/Latino), 39 international. Average age 31. 484 applicants, 49% accepted, 117 enrolled. In 2011, 117 master's awarded. *Degree requirements:* For master's, thesis. *Entrance requirements:* For master's, GRE/GMAT only upon request, relevant professional work, internship or volunteer experience. Additional exam requirements/recommendations for international students: Required—TOEFL (minimum score 600 paper-based; 250 computer-based; 100 iBT), IELTS (minimum score 7). *Application deadline:* For fall admission, 2/1 priority date for domestic students, 2/1 for international students; for spring admission, 10/15 priority date for domestic students, 8/15 for international students. Applications are processed on a rolling basis. Application fee: $150. Electronic applications accepted. *Financial support:* In 2011–12, 34 students received support, including 206 fellowships (averaging $2,702 per year); scholarships/grants also available. Financial award application deadline: 3/1; financial award applicants required to submit FAFSA. *Unit head:* Dr. Vera Jelinek, Divisional Dean and Clinical Associate Professor. *Application contact:* Office of Admissions, 212-998-7100, E-mail: scps.gradadmissions@nyu.edu. Web site: http://www.scps.nyu.edu/academics/departments.html.

462 facebook.com/petersonspublishing

Peterson's Graduate Programs in the Physical Sciences, Mathematics, Agricultural Sciences, the Environment & Natural Resources 2013

Northeastern Illinois University, Graduate College, College of Arts and Sciences, Department of Geography, Environmental Studies and Economics, Program in Geography and Environmental Studies, Chicago, IL 60625-4699. Offers MA. Part-time and evening/weekend programs available. *Degree requirements:* For master's, comprehensive exam, thesis optional. *Entrance requirements:* For master's, undergraduate minor in geography or environmental studies, minimum GPA of 2.75. Additional exam requirements/recommendations for international students: Required—TOEFL (minimum score 550 paper-based; 213 computer-based; 79 iBT). Electronic applications accepted. *Faculty research:* Segregation and urbanization of minority groups in the Chicago area, scale dependence and parameterization in nonpoint source pollution modeling, ecological land classification and mapping, ecosystem restoration, soil-vegetation relationships.

Northern Arizona University, Graduate College, College of Engineering, Forestry and Natural Sciences, School of Earth Sciences and Environmental Sustainability, Flagstaff, AZ 86011. Offers climate science and solutions (MS); earth science (MS); earth sciences and environmental sustainability (PhD); environmental sciences and policy (MS); geology (MS). *Faculty:* 27 full-time (9 women). *Students:* 67 full-time (32 women), 11 part-time (3 women); includes 6 minority (3 American Indian or Alaska Native, non-Hispanic/Latino; 3 Hispanic/Latino), 2 international. 149 applicants, 23% accepted, 30 enrolled. In 2011, 16 degrees awarded. *Degree requirements:* For master's, comprehensive exam (for some programs), thesis (for some programs). *Entrance requirements:* Additional exam requirements/recommendations for international students: Required—TOEFL (minimum score 550 paper-based; 213 computer-based; 80 iBT), IELTS (minimum score 7). *Application deadline:* For fall admission, 2/1 priority date for domestic students, 2/1 for international students. Applications are processed on a rolling basis. Application fee: $65. Electronic applications accepted. *Expenses:* Tuition, state resident: full-time $7190; part-time $355 per credit hour. Tuition, nonresident: full-time $18,092; part-time $1005 per credit hour. *Required fees:* $818; $328 per semester. *Financial support:* In 2011–12, 6 fellowships, 7 research assistantships with partial tuition reimbursements (averaging $12,866 per year), 28 teaching assistantships with partial tuition reimbursements (averaging $12,477 per year) were awarded; career-related internships or fieldwork, Federal Work-Study, scholarships/grants, health care benefits, tuition waivers (full and partial), and unspecified assistantships also available. Financial award applicants required to submit FAFSA. *Unit head:* Dr. Abe Springer, Director, 928-523-7198. *Application contact:* Mark Aasmundstad, Coordinator, 928-523-9333, Fax: 928-523-7432, E-mail: mark.aasmundstad@nau.edu. Web site: http://nau.edu/cefns/natsci/seses/.

Nova Scotia Agricultural College, Research and Graduate Studies, Truro, NS B2N 5E3, Canada. Offers agriculture (M Sc), including air quality, animal behavior, animal molecular genetics, animal nutrition, animal technology, aquaculture, botany, crop management, crop physiology, ecology, environmental microbiology, food science, horticulture, nutrient management, pest management, physiology, plant biotechnology, plant pathology, soil chemistry, soil fertility, waste management and composting, water quality. Program offered jointly with Dalhousie University. Part-time programs available. *Degree requirements:* For master's, thesis, ATC Exam Teaching Assistantship. *Entrance requirements:* For master's, honors B Sc, minimum GPA of 3.0. Additional exam requirements/recommendations for international students: Required—TOEFL (minimum score 580 paper-based; 237 computer-based; 92 iBT), IELTS, Michigan English Language Assessment Battery, CanTEST, CAEL. *Faculty research:* Bio-product development, organic agriculture, nutrient management, air and water quality, agricultural biotechnology.

Ohio University, Graduate College, College of Arts and Sciences, Department of Geological Sciences, Athens, OH 45701-2979. Offers environmental geochemistry (MS); environmental geology (MS); environmental/hydrology (MS); geology (MS); geology education (MS); geomorphology/surficial processes (MS); geophysics (MS); hydrogeology (MS); sedimentology (MS); structure/tectonics (MS). Part-time programs available. *Students:* 19 full-time (10 women). 14 applicants, 64% accepted, 9 enrolled. In 2011, 8 master's awarded. *Degree requirements:* For master's, thesis. *Entrance requirements:* Additional exam requirements/recommendations for international students: Required—TOEFL (minimum score 550 paper-based; 80 iBT) or IELTS (minimum score 6.5). *Application deadline:* For fall admission, 2/1 priority date for domestic students, 2/1 for international students. Application fee: $50 ($55 for international students). Electronic applications accepted. *Financial support:* Research assistantships with full tuition reimbursements, teaching assistantships with full tuition reimbursements, Federal Work-Study, institutionally sponsored loans, scholarships/grants, tuition waivers (partial), and unspecified assistantships available. Financial award application deadline: 2/1. *Faculty research:* Geoscience education, tectonics, fluvial geomorphology, invertebrate paleontology, mine/hydrology. *Total annual research expenditures:* $649,020. *Unit head:* Dr. Gregory Nadon, Chair, 740-593-4212, Fax: 740-593-0486, E-mail: nadon@ohio.edu. *Application contact:* Dr. Keith Milam, Graduate Chair, 740-593-1106, Fax: 740-593-0486, E-mail: milamk@ohio.edu. Web site: http://www.ohiou.edu/geology/.

Ohio University, Graduate College, Voinovich School of Leadership and Public Affairs, Program in Environmental Studies, Athens, OH 45701-2979. Offers MS. Part-time programs available. *Students:* 27 full-time (18 women), 6 part-time (2 women); includes 2 minority (1 Hispanic/Latino; 1 Two or more races, non-Hispanic/Latino), 2 international. 37 applicants, 38% accepted, 13 enrolled. In

2011, 8 master's awarded. *Degree requirements:* For master's, comprehensive exam (for some programs), written exams or thesis, research project. *Entrance requirements:* For master's, minimum GPA of 3.0. Additional exam requirements/recommendations for international students: Required—TOEFL (minimum score 600 paper-based; 100 iBT) or IELTS (minimum score 7). *Application deadline:* For fall admission, 1/1 priority date for domestic students, 1/1 for international students; for winter admission, 10/1 for domestic and international students; for spring admission, 2/1 for domestic and international students. Application fee: $50 ($55 for international students). Electronic applications accepted. *Financial support:* Fellowships with tuition reimbursements, research assistantships with tuition reimbursements, teaching assistantships with tuition reimbursements, career-related internships or fieldwork, Federal Work-Study, institutionally sponsored loans, scholarships/grants, tuition waivers (full and partial), and unspecified assistantships available. Financial award application deadline: 1/1. *Faculty research:* Air quality modeling, conservation biology, environmental policy, geographical information systems, land management and watershed restoration. *Unit head:* Dr. Geoffrey Buckley, Director, 740-593-9846, Fax: 740-593-0924, E-mail: buckleyg@ohio.edu. *Application contact:* Marnie Miller, Graduate Admissions, 740-593-2800, E-mail: graduate@ohio.edu. Web site: http://www.ohio.edu/envstu/.

Pace University, Dyson College of Arts and Sciences, Department of Public Administration, New York, NY 10038. Offers environmental management (MPA); government management (MPA); health care administration (MPA); management for public safety and homeland security (MA); nonprofit management (MPA); JD/MPA. Offered at White Plains, NY location only. Part-time and evening/weekend programs available. *Faculty:* 4 full-time (2 women), 6 part-time/adjunct (1 woman). *Students:* 66 full-time (41 women), 76 part-time (47 women); includes 73 minority (40 Black or African American, non-Hispanic/Latino; 1 American Indian or Alaska Native, non-Hispanic/Latino; 7 Asian, non-Hispanic/Latino; 21 Hispanic/Latino; 4 Two or more races, non-Hispanic/Latino), 10 international. Average age 31. 73 applicants, 89% accepted, 33 enrolled. In 2011, 49 master's awarded. *Degree requirements:* For master's, capstone project. *Entrance requirements:* For master's, GRE General Test. Additional exam requirements/recommendations for international students: Required—TOEFL. *Application deadline:* For fall admission, 8/1 priority date for domestic students; for spring admission, 12/1 priority date for domestic students. Applications are processed on a rolling basis. Application fee: $70. Electronic applications accepted. *Expenses: Tuition:* Part-time $990 per credit. *Required fees:* $168 per semester. Tuition and fees vary according to course load and degree level. *Financial support:* Research assistantships, career-related internships or fieldwork, Federal Work-Study, and tuition waivers (partial) available. Support available to part-time students. Financial award applicants required to submit FAFSA. *Unit head:* Dr. Farrokh Hormozi, Chairperson, 914-422-4285, E-mail: fhormozi@pace.edu. *Application contact:* Susan Ford-Goldschein, Director of Admissions, 914-422-4283, Fax: 914-422-4287, E-mail: gradwp@pace.edu.

Penn State University Park, Graduate School, Intercollege Graduate Programs, Intercollege Program in Environmental Pollution Control, State College, University Park, PA 16802-1503. Offers MEPC, MS. *Unit head:* Dr. Herschel A. Elliott, Chair, 814-865-1417, Fax: 814-863-1031, E-mail: helliott3@psu.edu. *Application contact:* Cynthia E. Nicosia, Director, Graduate Enrollment Services, 814-865-1795, Fax: 814-865-4627, E-mail: cey1@psu.edu.

Plymouth State University, College of Graduate Studies, Graduate Studies in Education, Program in Science, Plymouth, NH 03264-1595. Offers applied meteorology (MS); environmental science and policy (MS); science education (MS).

Point Park University, School of Arts and Sciences, Department of Natural Science and Engineering Technology, Pittsburgh, PA 15222-1984. Offers engineering management (MS); environmental studies (MS). Part-time and evening/weekend programs available. *Faculty:* 4 full-time, 4 part-time/adjunct. *Students:* 14 full-time (7 women), 19 part-time (6 women); includes 4 minority (2 Black or African American, non-Hispanic/Latino; 2 Two or more races, non-Hispanic/Latino), 6 international. Average age 35. 53 applicants, 60% accepted, 14 enrolled. In 2011, 15 master's awarded. *Degree requirements:* For master's, comprehensive exam (for some programs), thesis or alternative. *Entrance requirements:* For master's, minimum QPA of 2.75, 2 letters of recommendation, minimum B average in engineering technology or a related field, official undergraduate transcript, statement of intent, resume. Additional exam requirements/recommendations for international students: Required—TOEFL. *Application deadline:* Applications are processed on a rolling basis. Application fee: $30. Electronic applications accepted. *Expenses: Tuition:* Full-time $13,050; part-time $725 per credit. *Required fees:* $720; $40 per credit. *Financial support:* In 2011–12, 15 students received support, including 2 teaching assistantships with full tuition reimbursements available (averaging $6,400 per year); scholarships/grants also available. Financial award application deadline: 4/15; financial award applicants required to submit FAFSA. *Unit head:* Dr. Mark Farrell, Chair, 412-392-3879, Fax: 421-392-3962, E-mail: mfarrell@pointpark.edu. *Application contact:* Jennifer Sellman, Recruiter/Counselor, 412-392-4794, Fax: 412-392-6164, E-mail: jseelman@pointpark.edu.

Polytechnic University of Puerto Rico, Graduate School, Hato Rey, PR 00919. Offers business administration (MBA), including computer information systems, general management, management of information systems, management of international enterprises; civil engineering (ME, MS); computer engineering (ME, MS); computer science (MCS, MS); electrical engineering (ME, MS); engineering

Peterson's Graduate Programs in the Physical Sciences, Mathematics, Agricultural Sciences, the Environment & Natural Resources 2013

facebook.com/petersonspublishing **463**

Environmental Management and Policy

management (MEM); environmental management (MEM); landscape architecture (M Land Arch); manufacturing competitiveness (MMC, MS); manufacturing engineering (ME, MS); mechanical engineering (M Mech E). Part-time and evening/weekend programs available. *Entrance requirements:* For master's, 3 letters of recommendation.

Polytechnic University of Puerto Rico, Miami Campus, Graduate School, Miami, FL 33166. Offers accounting (MBA); business administration (MBA); construction management (MEM); environmental management (MEM); finance (MBA); human resources management (MBA); logistics and supply chain management (MBA); management of international enterprises (MBA); manufacturing management (MEM); marketing management (MBA); project management (MBA). Part-time and evening/weekend programs available. Postbaccalaureate distance learning degree programs offered (no on-campus study). *Entrance requirements:* For master's, minimum GPA of 3.0. Electronic applications accepted.

Polytechnic University of Puerto Rico, Orlando Campus, Graduate School, Winter Park, FL 32792. Offers accounting (MBA); business administration (MBA); construction management (MEM); engineering management (MEM); environmental management (MEM); finance (MBA); human resources management (MBA); management of international enterprises (MBA); management of technology (MBA); manufacturing management (MEM). Part-time and evening/weekend programs available. Postbaccalaureate distance learning degree programs offered (no on-campus study). *Entrance requirements:* For master's, minimum GPA of 3.0. Additional exam requirements/recommendations for international students: Recommended—TOEFL. Electronic applications accepted.

Portland State University, Graduate Studies, College of Liberal Arts and Sciences, Program in Environmental Sciences and Management, Portland, OR 97207-0751. Offers environmental management (MEM); environmental sciences/biology (PhD); environmental sciences/chemistry (PhD); environmental sciences/civil engineering (PhD); environmental sciences/geography (PhD); environmental sciences/geology (PhD); environmental sciences/physics (PhD); environmental studies (MS); science/environmental science (MST). Part-time programs available. *Degree requirements:* For master's, thesis or alternative; for doctorate, variable foreign language requirement, comprehensive exam, thesis/dissertation, oral and qualifying exams. *Entrance requirements:* For master's, GRE General Test, 3 letters of recommendation; for doctorate, minimum GPA of 3.0 in upper-division course work or 2.75 overall. Additional exam requirements/recommendations for international students: Required—TOEFL (minimum score 550 paper-based; 213 computer-based). *Faculty research:* Environmental aspects of biology, chemistry, civil engineering, geology, physics.

Prescott College, Graduate Programs, Program in Environmental Studies, Prescott, AZ 86301. Offers environmental studies (MA); student-directed independent study (MA). Part-time programs available. Postbaccalaureate distance learning degree programs offered (minimal on-campus study). *Faculty:* 1 full-time (0 women), 24 part-time/adjunct (7 women). *Students:* 9 full-time (5 women), 28 part-time (16 women); includes 5 minority (1 American Indian or Alaska Native, non-Hispanic/Latino; 3 Hispanic/Latino; 1 Two or more races, non-Hispanic/Latino), 1 international. Average age 35. 27 applicants, 81% accepted, 10 enrolled. In 2011, 17 master's awarded. *Degree requirements:* For master's, thesis, fieldwork or internship, practicum. *Entrance requirements:* For master's, 2 letters of recommendation, resume. Additional exam requirements/recommendations for international students: Required—TOEFL (minimum score 500 paper-based; 173 computer-based). *Application deadline:* For fall admission, 4/15 priority date for domestic students, 4/15 for international students; for spring admission, 9/15 priority date for domestic students, 9/15 for international students. Applications are processed on a rolling basis. Application fee: $40. Electronic applications accepted. *Expenses: Tuition:* Full-time $16,440; part-time $685 per credit. *Required fees:* $150 per semester. One-time fee: $350. *Financial support:* Career-related internships or fieldwork, Federal Work-Study, and scholarships/grants available. Financial award applicants required to submit FAFSA. *Unit head:* Peter Sherman, Interim Chair, 928-350-1014, Fax: 928-776-5151, E-mail: psherman@prescott.edu. *Application contact:* Kerstin Alicki, Admissions Counselor, 928-350-2100, Fax: 928-776-5242, E-mail: admissions@prescott.edu.

Purdue University, Graduate School, College of Agriculture, Department of Forestry and Natural Resources, West Lafayette, IN 47907. Offers fisheries and aquatic sciences (MS, MSF, PhD); forest biology (MS, MSF, PhD); natural resource social science (MS, PhD); natural resources social science (MSF); quantitative ecology (MS, MSF, PhD); wildlife science (MS, MSF, PhD); wood products and wood products manufacturing (MS, MSF, PhD). *Faculty:* 26 full-time (3 women), 9 part-time/adjunct (1 woman). *Students:* 67 full-time (31 women), 8 part-time (3 women); includes 3 minority (2 Hispanic/Latino; 1 Two or more races, non-Hispanic/Latino), 17 international. Average age 29. 58 applicants, 16% accepted, 8 enrolled. In 2011, 9 master's, 11 doctorates awarded. *Degree requirements:* For master's, thesis; for doctorate, thesis/dissertation. *Entrance requirements:* For master's and doctorate, GRE General Test with minimum score required: verbal >=50th percentile; Quantitative >= 50th percentile; Analytical writing = 4.0 or greater, minimum undergraduate GPA of 3.2 or equivalent. Additional exam requirements/recommendations for international students: Required—TOEFL (minimum score 550 paper-based; 77 iBT). *Application deadline:* For fall admission, 1/5 for domestic students, 1/15 for international students; for spring admission, 9/15 for domestic and international students. Applications are processed on a rolling basis. Application fee: $60 ($75

for international students). Electronic applications accepted. *Financial support:* In 2011–12, 10 research assistantships (averaging $15,259 per year) were awarded; fellowships, teaching assistantships, career-related internships or fieldwork, and scholarships/grants also available. Support available to part-time students. Financial award application deadline: 1/5; financial award applicants required to submit FAFSA. *Faculty research:* Wildlife management, forest management, forest ecology, forest soils, limnology. *Unit head:* Dr. Robert K. Swihart, Interim Head, 765-494-3590, Fax: 765-494-9461, E-mail: rswihart@purdue.edu. *Application contact:* Kelly J. Garrett, Graduate Secretary, 765-494-3572, Fax: 765-494-9461, E-mail: kgarrett@purdue.edu. Web site: http://www.fnr.purdue.edu/.

Rensselaer Polytechnic Institute, Graduate School, School of Humanities, Arts, and Social Sciences, Program in Ecological Economics, Troy, NY 12180-3590. Offers ecological economics (PhD); ecological economics, values, and policy (PMS). Part-time programs available. *Degree requirements:* For doctorate, comprehensive exam, thesis/dissertation. *Entrance requirements:* For doctorate, GRE General Test or GMAT, writing sample, statement of background goals, 2 recommendation letters, resume or curriculum vitae. Additional exam requirements/recommendations for international students: Required—TOEFL (minimum score 600 paper-based; 250 computer-based; 100 iBT), IELTS. Electronic applications accepted. *Faculty research:* Economic development and trade with a focus on technology, lifestyles, and environment; input-output analysis; pollution policy in the electric power sector; electricity market design; renewable energy integration in the power grid; experimental economics; law and economics; environmental economics; behavioral economics; technology change; applied econometrics.

Rice University, Graduate Programs, Wiess School–Professional Science Master's Programs, Professional Master's Program in Environmental Analysis and Decision Making, Houston, TX 77251-1892. Offers MS. Part-time programs available. *Degree requirements:* For master's, internship. *Entrance requirements:* For master's, GRE General Test, letters of recommendation (4). Additional exam requirements/recommendations for international students: Required—TOEFL (minimum score 600 paper-based; 250 computer-based; 90 iBT). Electronic applications accepted. *Faculty research:* Environmental biotechnology, environmental nanochemistry, environmental statistics, remote sensing.

Rochester Institute of Technology, Graduate Enrollment Services, College of Applied Science and Technology, School of Engineering Technology, Department of Civil Engineering Technology, Environmental Management and Safety, Rochester, NY 14623-5603. Offers environmental health and safety management (MS); facility management (MS). Part-time and evening/weekend programs available. Postbaccalaureate distance learning degree programs offered (minimal on-campus study). *Students:* 18 full-time (3 women), 56 part-time (21 women); includes 12 minority (4 Black or African American, non-Hispanic/Latino; 1 American Indian or Alaska Native, non-Hispanic/Latino; 5 Asian, non-Hispanic/Latino; 2 Hispanic/Latino), 14 international. Average age 34. 64 applicants, 42% accepted, 19 enrolled. In 2011, 26 master's awarded. *Degree requirements:* For master's, thesis or project. *Entrance requirements:* For master's, minimum GPA of 3.0. Additional exam requirements/recommendations for international students: Required—TOEFL (minimum score 550 paper-based; 213 computer-based; 79 iBT) or IELTS (minimum score 6.5). *Application deadline:* For fall admission, 2/15 priority date for domestic students, 2/15 for international students; for winter admission, 11/1 priority date for domestic students; for spring admission, 2/1 priority date for domestic students, 1/1 for international students. Applications are processed on a rolling basis. Application fee: $50. Electronic applications accepted. *Expenses: Tuition:* Full-time $34,659; part-time $963 per credit hour. *Required fees:* $228; $76 per quarter. *Financial support:* Research assistantships with partial tuition reimbursements, teaching assistantships with partial tuition reimbursements, career-related internships or fieldwork, scholarships/grants, and unspecified assistantships available. Support available to part-time students. Financial award applicants required to submit FAFSA. *Faculty research:* Environmental, health and safety (EHS) issues; regulatory, voluntary and business drivers for EHS programs; design and implementation of effective EHS management systems and programs; design and implementation of performance measurement processes. *Unit head:* Dr. Christy Tyler, Graduate Program Director, 585-475-5042, E-mail: actsbi@rit.edu. *Application contact:* Diane Ellison, Assistant Vice President, Graduate Enrollment Services, 585-475-2229, Fax: 585-475-7164, E-mail: gradinfo@rit.edu. Web site: http://www.rit.edu/cast/cetems/.

Royal Roads University, Graduate Studies, Environment and Sustainability Program, Victoria, BC V9B 5Y2, Canada. Offers environment and management (M Sc, MA); environmental education and communication (MA, G Dip, Graduate Certificate); MA/MS. Postbaccalaureate distance learning degree programs offered (minimal on-campus study). *Degree requirements:* For master's, thesis. *Entrance requirements:* For master's, 5-7 years of related work experience. Electronic applications accepted. *Faculty research:* Sustainable development, atmospheric processes, sustainable communities, chemical fate and transport of persistent organic pollutants, educational technology.

Sacred Heart University, Graduate Programs, College of Arts and Sciences, Department of Biology, Fairfield, CT 06825-1000. Offers environmental systems analysis and management (MS).

St. Cloud State University, School of Graduate Studies, College of Science and Engineering, Department of Environmental and Technological Studies, St. Cloud,

464 facebook.com/petersonspublishing

Peterson's Graduate Programs in the Physical Sciences, Mathematics, Agricultural Sciences, the Environment & Natural Resources 2013

MN 56301-4498. Offers MS. *Degree requirements:* For master's, thesis or alternative. *Entrance requirements:* For master's, minimum GPA of 2.75. Additional exam requirements/recommendations for international students: Required—TOEFL (minimum score 550 paper-based; 213 computer-based), Michigan English Language Assessment Battery; Recommended—IELTS (minimum score 6.5). Electronic applications accepted.

St. Edward's University, School of Management and Business, Program in Environmental Management and Sustainability, Austin, TX 78704. Offers PSM. *Degree requirements:* For master's, internship. *Entrance requirements:* For master's, GRE or GMAT, 2 letters of recommendation, minimum GPA of 3.0 in last 60 hours of course work. Additional exam requirements/recommendations for international students: Required—TOEFL (minimum score 550 paper-based; 213 computer-based; 79 iBT) or IELTS (minimum score 6). *Application deadline:* For fall admission, 5/15 for domestic and international students. Applications are processed on a rolling basis. Application fee: $45 ($50 for international students). Electronic applications accepted. *Expenses: Tuition:* Full-time $17,550; part-time $975 per credit hour. *Required fees:* $50 per trimester. Full-time tuition and fees vary according to course load and program. *Unit head:* Dr. William J. Quinn, Director, 512-448-8457, Fax: 512-448-8492, E-mail: billq@stedwards.edu. *Application contact:* Derrick Mueller, Graduate Admission Coordinator, 512-448-8600, Fax: 512-428-1032, E-mail: derrickm@stedwards.edu. Web site: http://www.stedwards.edu.

Samford University, Howard College of Arts and Sciences, Birmingham, AL 35229. Offers MSEM, JD/MSEM. Part-time and evening/weekend programs available. *Faculty:* 5 full-time (0 women), 8 part-time/adjunct (0 women). *Students:* 15 full-time (5 women), 15 part-time (8 women); includes 5 minority (4 Black or African American, non-Hispanic/Latino; 1 Asian, non-Hispanic/Latino), 12 international. Average age 28. 18 applicants, 94% accepted, 15 enrolled. In 2011, 18 master's awarded. *Entrance requirements:* For master's, GRE General Test (minimum score 1000) or MAT (minimum score 50), minimum GPA of 3.0, 3 years of work experience. Additional exam requirements/recommendations for international students: Required—TOEFL (minimum score 550 paper-based; 213 computer-based; 80 iBT). *Application deadline:* For fall admission, 1/1 for domestic students, 8/1 for international students; for winter admission, 2/1 for domestic students; for spring admission, 1/2 for domestic students, 12/14 for international students. Applications are processed on a rolling basis. Application fee: $35. *Expenses:* Contact institution. *Faculty research:* Mosquito fish as an environmental model for pollutants, PCB contamination, environmental epidemiology and toxicology, GIS, geology and natural resource management, energy management. *Unit head:* David W. Chapman, Dean, 205-726-2771, Fax: 205-726-2279. *Application contact:* Dr. Ronald N. Hunsinger, Professor/Chair, 205-726-2944, Fax: 205-726-2479, E-mail: rnhunsin@samford.edu. Web site: http://www.samford.edu/schools/artsci.

San Francisco State University, Division of Graduate Studies, College of Science and Engineering, Department of Geography and Human Environmental Studies, San Francisco, CA 94132-1722. Offers geographic information science (MS); geography (MA), including resource management and environmental planning. *Unit head:* Dr. Jerry Davis, Chair, 415-338-2049, E-mail: jerry@sfsu.edu. *Application contact:* Nancy Wilkinson, Graduate Coordinator, 415-338-2049. Web site: http://www.bss.sfsu.edu/geog.

San Jose State University, Graduate Studies and Research, College of Social Sciences, Department of Environmental Studies, San Jose, CA 95192-0001. Offers MS. Part-time programs available. *Degree requirements:* For master's, comprehensive exam, thesis or alternative. *Entrance requirements:* Additional exam requirements/recommendations for international students: Required—TOEFL (minimum score 580 paper-based). Electronic applications accepted. *Faculty research:* Remote sensing, land use/land cover mapping.

Shippensburg University of Pennsylvania, School of Graduate Studies, College of Arts and Sciences, Department of Geography and Earth Science, Shippensburg, PA 17257-2299. Offers geoenvironmental studies (MS). Part-time and evening/weekend programs available. *Faculty:* 9 full-time (2 women), 1 part-time/adjunct (0 women). *Students:* 27 full-time (9 women), 11 part-time (4 women); includes 2 minority (1 Black or African American, non-Hispanic/Latino; 1 Hispanic/Latino), 1 international. Average age 29. 38 applicants, 45% accepted, 17 enrolled. In 2011, 10 master's awarded. *Degree requirements:* For master's, comprehensive exam, thesis (6 credits) or 1 semester research project (3 credits) and internship (6 credits); practicum exam. *Entrance requirements:* For master's, GRE (if GPA less than 2.75), 12 credit hours in geography or earth sciences or 15 credit hours each in social sciences (including 6 hours in geography) and natural sciences (including 6 in the earth sciences) or a combined total of 18 credits in geography and earth science. Additional exam requirements/recommendations for international students: Required—TOEFL (minimum score 580 paper-based; 237 computer-based); Recommended—IELTS (minimum score 6). *Application deadline:* For fall admission, 3/30 for international students; for spring admission, 9/30 for international students. Applications are processed on a rolling basis. Application fee: $30. Electronic applications accepted. *Expenses: Tuition, area resident:* Part-time $416 per credit. Tuition, state resident: part-time $416 per credit. Tuition, nonresident: part-time $624 per credit. *Required fees:* $119 per credit. *Financial support:* In 2011–12, 10 research assistantships with full tuition reimbursements (averaging $5,000 per year) were awarded; career-related internships or fieldwork, scholarships/grants, unspecified assistantships, and resident hall director and student payroll positions also available. Support available to part-time students. Financial award application deadline: 3/1; financial

award applicants required to submit FAFSA. *Unit head:* Dr. Tim Hawkins, Associate Professor, 717-477-1685, Fax: 717-477-4029, E-mail: twhawk@ship.edu. *Application contact:* Jeremy R. Goshorn, Assistant Dean of Graduate Admissions, 717-477-1231, Fax: 717-477-4016, E-mail: jrgoshorn@ship.edu. Web site: http://www.ship.edu/geo-ess/.

Shippensburg University of Pennsylvania, School of Graduate Studies, College of Arts and Sciences, Department of Sociology and Anthropology, Shippensburg, PA 17257-2299. Offers organizational development and leadership (MS), including business, communications, environmental management, higher education structure and policy, historical administration, individual and organizational development, management information systems, public organizations, social structures and organizations. Part-time and evening/weekend programs available. *Faculty:* 3 full-time (all women). *Students:* 12 full-time (6 women), 40 part-time (34 women); includes 6 minority (3 Black or African American, non-Hispanic/Latino; 2 Asian, non-Hispanic/Latino; 1 Two or more races, non-Hispanic/Latino), 2 international. Average age 33. 52 applicants, 46% accepted, 16 enrolled. In 2011, 34 master's awarded. *Degree requirements:* For master's, capstone experience including internship. *Entrance requirements:* For master's, interview (if GPA less than 2.75), resume, personal goals statement. Additional exam requirements/recommendations for international students: Required—TOEFL (minimum score 580 paper-based; 237 computer-based); Recommended—IELTS (minimum score 6). *Application deadline:* For fall admission, 4/30 for international students; for spring admission, 9/30 for international students. Applications are processed on a rolling basis. Application fee: $30. Electronic applications accepted. *Expenses: Tuition, area resident:* Part-time $416 per credit. Tuition, state resident: part-time $416 per credit. Tuition, nonresident: part-time $624 per credit. *Required fees:* $119 per credit. *Financial support:* In 2011–12, 9 research assistantships with full tuition reimbursements (averaging $5,000 per year) were awarded; career-related internships or fieldwork, scholarships/grants, unspecified assistantships, and resident hall director and student payroll positions also available. Support available to part-time students. Financial award applicants required to submit FAFSA. *Unit head:* Dr. Barbara Denison, Program Coordinator, 717-477-1735, Fax: 717-477-4011, E-mail: bjdeni@ship.edu. *Application contact:* Jeremy R. Goshorn, Assistant Dean of Graduate Admissions, 717-477-1231, Fax: 717-477-4016, E-mail: jrgoshorn@ship.edu. Web site: http://www.ship.edu/odl/.

Simon Fraser University, Graduate Studies, Faculty of Applied Sciences, School of Resource and Environmental Management, Burnaby, BC V5A 1S6, Canada. Offers MRM, PhD. *Degree requirements:* For master's, thesis or alternative, research project; for doctorate, comprehensive exam, thesis/dissertation. *Entrance requirements:* For master's, minimum GPA of 3.0; for doctorate, GRE Writing Assessment, minimum GPA of 3.5. Additional exam requirements/recommendations for international students: Required—TOEFL or IELTS. *Faculty research:* Management of resources, resource economics, regional planning, public policy analysis, tourism and parks.

Slippery Rock University of Pennsylvania, Graduate Studies (Recruitment), College of Health, Environment, and Science, Department of Parks, Recreation, and Environmental Education, Slippery Rock, PA 16057-1383. Offers environmental education (M Ed); park and resource management (MS). Part-time and evening/weekend programs available. Postbaccalaureate distance learning degree programs offered (no on-campus study). *Faculty:* 3 full-time (1 woman), 3 part-time/adjunct (2 women). *Students:* 20 full-time (10 women), 75 part-time (38 women); includes 2 minority (1 Hispanic/Latino; 1 Two or more races, non-Hispanic/Latino), 1 international. Average age 30. 66 applicants, 77% accepted, 32 enrolled. In 2011, 49 degrees awarded. *Degree requirements:* For master's, comprehensive exam (for some programs), thesis (for some programs), internship. *Entrance requirements:* For master's, GRE General Test, MAT, minimum GPA of 2.75. Additional exam requirements/recommendations for international students: Required—TOEFL (minimum score 550 paper-based; 213 computer-based; 80 iBT). *Application deadline:* For fall admission, 3/1 priority date for domestic students, 5/1 for international students; for spring admission, 10/1 priority date for domestic students, 9/1 for international students. Applications are processed on a rolling basis. Application fee: $25 ($30 for international students). Electronic applications accepted. *Expenses:* Contact institution. *Financial support:* Career-related internships or fieldwork, Federal Work-Study, institutionally sponsored loans, scholarships/grants, tuition waivers (partial), and unspecified assistantships available. Support available to part-time students. Financial award application deadline: 5/1; financial award applicants required to submit FAFSA. *Unit head:* Dr. Daniel Dziubek, Graduate Coordinator, 724-738-2958, Fax: 724-738-2938, E-mail: daniel.dziubek@sru.edu. *Application contact:* Angela Barrett, Director of Graduate Admissions, 724-738-2051, Fax: 724-738-2146, E-mail: graduate.admissions@sru.edu.

Southeast Missouri State University, School of Graduate Studies, Department of Human Environmental Studies, Cape Girardeau, MO 63701-4799. Offers human environmental studies (MA). Part-time programs available. *Faculty:* 10 full-time (7 women). *Students:* 10 full-time (9 women), 10 part-time (all women), 1 international. Average age 29. 11 applicants, 100% accepted, 9 enrolled. In 2011, 7 master's awarded. *Degree requirements:* For master's, comprehensive exam, thesis or alternative, internship. *Entrance requirements:* For master's, MAT or GRE General Test, minimum undergraduate GPA of 2.75; 18 credit hours in human environment studies or related field. Additional exam requirements/recommendations for international students: Required—TOEFL (minimum score 550 paper-based; 213 computer-based; 79 iBT); Recommended—IELTS

Peterson's Graduate Programs in the Physical Sciences, Mathematics, Agricultural Sciences, the Environment & Natural Resources 2013

facebook.com/petersonspublishing **465**

(minimum score 6). *Application deadline:* For fall admission, 8/1 for domestic students, 7/1 for international students; for spring admission, 11/21 for domestic students, 11/1 for international students. Applications are processed on a rolling basis. Application fee: $30 ($40 for international students). Electronic applications accepted. *Expenses:* Tuition, state resident: full-time $4896; part-time $272 per credit hour. Tuition, nonresident: full-time $8649; part-time $480.50 per credit hour. *Financial support:* In 2011–12, 7 students received support, including 1 teaching assistantship with full tuition reimbursement available (averaging $7,600 per year); career-related internships or fieldwork, Federal Work-Study, scholarships/grants, tuition waivers (full), and unspecified assistantships also available. Financial award application deadline: 6/30; financial award applicants required to submit FAFSA. *Faculty research:* Gerontology educational models, military families, nutrition education and obesity, interior design and construction, kitchen and bath design, infant stimulation and sensory systems. *Unit head:* Dr. Shelba Y. Branscum, 573-651-2729, Fax: 573-651-2949, E-mail: sybranscum@semo.edu. *Application contact:* Alisa Aleen McFerron, Assistant Director of Admission for Operations, 573-651-5937, Fax: 573-651-5936, E-mail: amcferron@semo.edu. Web site: http://www.semo.edu/hes/.

Southern Illinois University Carbondale, Graduate School, College of Liberal Arts, Department of Geography, Carbondale, IL 62901-4701. Offers environmental resources and policy (PhD); geography and environmental resources (MS). *Faculty:* 7 full-time (1 woman), 1 part-time/adjunct (0 women). *Students:* 16 full-time (4 women), 14 part-time (7 women); includes 2 minority (both Black or African American, non-Hispanic/Latino), 6 international. Average age 27. 21 applicants, 76% accepted, 9 enrolled. In 2011, 5 master's awarded. *Degree requirements:* For master's, thesis; for doctorate, thesis/dissertation. *Entrance requirements:* For master's, minimum GPA of 2.7; for doctorate, minimum GPA of 3.25. Additional exam requirements/recommendations for international students: Required—TOEFL. *Application deadline:* Applications are processed on a rolling basis. Application fee: $20. *Financial support:* In 2011–12, 21 students received support, including 6 research assistantships with full tuition reimbursements available, 11 teaching assistantships with full tuition reimbursements available; fellowships with full tuition reimbursements available, career-related internships or fieldwork, Federal Work-Study, institutionally sponsored loans, and tuition waivers (full) also available. Support available to part-time students. Financial award application deadline: 4/1; *Faculty research:* Natural resources management emphasizing water resources and environmental quality of air, water, and land systems. *Unit head:* Dr. Leslie Duram, Chair, 618-536-3375, Fax: 618-453-2671, E-mail: duram@siu.edu. *Application contact:* Jennie Absher, Administrative Clerk, 618-536-3375, E-mail: jabsher@siu.edu. Web site: http://info.geography.siu.edu/.

Southern Illinois University Edwardsville, Graduate School, College of Arts and Sciences, Program in Environmental Science Management, Edwardsville, IL 62026-0001. Offers MS. Part-time and evening/weekend programs available. *Students:* 5 full-time (4 women), 4 part-time (2 women); includes 4 minority (1 Asian, non-Hispanic/Latino; 1 Hispanic/Latino; 2 Native Hawaiian or other Pacific Islander, non-Hispanic/Latino), 1 international. 16 applicants. In 2011, 4 master's awarded. *Degree requirements:* For master's, thesis, internship. *Entrance requirements:* For master's, GRE. Additional exam requirements/recommendations for international students: Required—TOEFL (minimum score 550 paper-based; 213 computer-based; 79 iBT), IELTS (minimum score 6.5). *Application deadline:* For fall admission, 7/22 for domestic students, 6/1 for international students; for spring admission, 12/9 for domestic students, 10/1 for international students. Applications are processed on a rolling basis. Application fee: $30. Electronic applications accepted. Tuition and fees vary according to course load and program. *Financial support:* Fellowships with full tuition reimbursements, research assistantships with full tuition reimbursements, teaching assistantships with full tuition reimbursements, institutionally sponsored loans, scholarships/grants, and unspecified assistantships available. Financial award application deadline: 3/1; financial award applicants required to submit FAFSA. *Unit head:* Dr. Kevin Johnson, Program Director, 618-650-5934, E-mail: kevjohn@siue.edu. *Application contact:* Michelle Robinson, Coordinator of Graduate Recruitment, 618-650-2811, Fax: 618-650-3523, E-mail: michero@siue.edu. Web site: http://www.siue.edu/artsandsciences/environment/psm.shtml.

Stanford University, School of Earth Sciences, Earth Systems Program, Stanford, CA 94305-9991. Offers MS. Students admitted at the undergraduate level. Electronic applications accepted. *Expenses: Tuition:* Full-time $40,050; part-time $890 per credit.

State University of New York College of Environmental Science and Forestry, Department of Environmental Resources Engineering, Syracuse, NY 13210-2779. Offers ecological engineering (MS, PhD); environmental and resources engineering (MPS, MS, PhD); environmental management (MPS); geospatial information science and engineering (MS, PhD); mapping sciences (MPS); water resources engineering (MS, PhD). *Degree requirements:* For master's, thesis (for some programs); for doctorate, comprehensive exam, thesis/dissertation. *Entrance requirements:* For master's and doctorate, GRE General Test, minimum GPA of 3.0. Additional exam requirements/recommendations for international students: Required—TOEFL (minimum score 550 paper-based; 213 computer-based; 80 iBT), IELTS (minimum score 6). *Application deadline:* For fall admission, 2/1 priority date for domestic students, 2/1 for international students; for spring admission, 11/1 priority date for domestic students, 11/1 for international students. Applications are processed on a rolling basis. Application

fee: $60. *Expenses:* Tuition, state resident: full-time $8870; part-time $370 per credit hour. Tuition, nonresident: full-time $15,160; part-time $632 per credit hour. *Required fees:* $60; $370 per credit hour. $350 per semester. One-time fee: $85. *Financial support:* Fellowships with full and partial tuition reimbursements, research assistantships with full and partial tuition reimbursements, teaching assistantships with full and partial tuition reimbursements, Federal Work-Study, institutionally sponsored loans, scholarships/grants, health care benefits, and unspecified assistantships available. Financial award application deadline: 6/30; financial award applicants required to submit FAFSA. *Faculty research:* Forest engineering, paper science and engineering, wood products engineering. *Total annual research expenditures:* $968,412. *Unit head:* Dr. Theodore Endreny, Chair, 315-470-6565, Fax: 315-470-6958, E-mail: te@esf.edu. *Application contact:* Dr. Dudley J. Raynal, Dean, Instruction and Graduate Studies, 315-470-6599, Fax: 315-470-6978, E-mail: esfgrad@esf.edu. Web site: http://www.esf.edu/ere.

State University of New York College of Environmental Science and Forestry, Department of Environmental Studies, Syracuse, NY 13210-2779. Offers MPS, MS. *Degree requirements:* For master's, thesis (for some programs). *Entrance requirements:* For master's, GRE General Test. Application fee: $60. *Expenses:* Tuition, state resident: full-time $8870; part-time $370 per credit hour. Tuition, nonresident: full-time $15,160; part-time $632 per credit hour. *Required fees:* $60; $370 per credit hour. $350 per semester. One-time fee: $85. *Unit head:* Dr. Valerie Luzadis, Chair, 315-470-6636. *Application contact:* Scott Shannon, Associate Provost for Instruction/Dean of the Graduate School, 315-470-6599, Fax: 315-470-6978, E-mail: sshannon@esf.edu. Web site: http://www.esf.edu/es/

State University of New York College of Environmental Science and Forestry, Department of Forest and Natural Resources Management, Syracuse, NY 13210-2779. Offers ecology and ecosystems (MPS, MS, PhD); economics, governance and human dimensions (MPS, MS, PhD); environmental and natural resources policy (MPS, MS); forest and natural resources management (MPS, MS, PhD); monitoring, analysis and modeling (MPS, MS, PhD). *Accreditation:* SAF. *Degree requirements:* For master's, thesis (for some programs); for doctorate, comprehensive exam, thesis/dissertation. *Entrance requirements:* For master's and doctorate, GRE General Test, minimum GPA of 3.0. Additional exam requirements/recommendations for international students: Required—TOEFL (minimum score 550 paper-based; 213 computer-based; 80 iBT), IELTS (minimum score 6). *Application deadline:* For fall admission, 2/1 priority date for domestic students, 2/1 for international students; for spring admission, 11/1 priority date for domestic students, 11/1 for international students. Applications are processed on a rolling basis. Application fee: $60. *Expenses:* Tuition, state resident: full-time $8870; part-time $370 per credit hour. Tuition, nonresident: full-time $15,160; part-time $632 per credit hour. *Required fees:* $60; $370 per credit hour. $350 per semester. One-time fee: $85. *Financial support:* Fellowships with full and partial tuition reimbursements, research assistantships with full and partial tuition reimbursements, teaching assistantships with full and partial tuition reimbursements, career-related internships or fieldwork, Federal Work-Study, institutionally sponsored loans, scholarships/grants, health care benefits, and unspecified assistantships available. Financial award application deadline: 6/30; financial award applicants required to submit FAFSA. *Faculty research:* Silviculture recreation management, tree improvement, operations management, economics. *Total annual research expenditures:* $2.1 million. *Unit head:* Dr. David Newman, Chair, 315-470-6534, Fax: 315-470-6535. *Application contact:* Dr. Dudley J. Raynal, Dean, Instruction and Graduate Studies, 315-470-6599, Fax: 315-470-6978, E-mail: esfgrad@esf.edu. Web site: http://www.esf.edu/fnrm/.

State University of New York College of Environmental Science and Forestry, Program in Environmental Science, Syracuse, NY 13210-2779. Offers biophysical and ecological economics (MPS); coupled natural and human systems (MPS); ecosystem restoration (MPS); environmental and community land planning (MPS, MS); environmental and natural resources policy (PhD); environmental communication and participatory processes (MPS, MS); environmental monitoring and modeling (MPS); environmental policy and democratic processes (MPS, MS); environmental systems and risk management (MS); water and wetland resource studies (MPS, MS). Part-time programs available. *Degree requirements:* For master's, thesis (for some programs); for doctorate, comprehensive exam, thesis/dissertation. *Entrance requirements:* For master's and doctorate, GRE General Test, minimum GPA of 3.0. Additional exam requirements/recommendations for international students: Required—TOEFL (minimum score 550 paper-based; 213 computer-based; 80 iBT), IELTS (minimum score 6). *Application deadline:* For fall admission, 2/1 priority date for domestic students, 2/1 for international students; for spring admission, 11/1 priority date for domestic students, 11/1 for international students. Applications are processed on a rolling basis. Application fee: $60. *Expenses:* Tuition, state resident: full-time $8870; part-time $370 per credit hour. Tuition, nonresident: full-time $15,160; part-time $632 per credit hour. *Required fees:* $60; $370 per credit hour. $350 per semester. One-time fee: $85. *Financial support:* Fellowships with full and partial tuition reimbursements, research assistantships with full and partial tuition reimbursements, teaching assistantships with full and partial tuition reimbursements, career-related internships or fieldwork, Federal Work-Study, institutionally sponsored loans, scholarships/grants, health care benefits, and unspecified assistantships available. Support available to part-time students. Financial award application deadline: 6/30; financial award applicants required to submit FAFSA. *Faculty research:* Environmental education/communications, water resources, land resources, waste management. *Total annual research*

466 facebook.com/petersonspublishing

Peterson's Graduate Programs in the Physical Sciences, Mathematics, Agricultural Sciences, the Environment & Natural Resources 2013

expenditures: $169,919. *Unit head:* Dr. Ruth Yanai, Coordinator, 315-470-6955, Fax: 315-470-6700, E-mail: rdyanai@esf.edu. *Application contact:* Dr. Dudley J. Raynal, Dean, Instruction and Graduate Studies, 315-470-6599, Fax: 315-470-6978, E-mail: esfgrad@esf.edu. Web site: http://www.esf.edu/environmentalscience/.

Stony Brook University, State University of New York, Graduate School, College of Engineering and Applied Sciences, Department of Technology and Society, Program in Energy and Environmental Systems, Stony Brook, NY 11794. Offers MS, Advanced Certificate. Part-time programs available. *Degree requirements:* For master's, thesis, project. Electronic applications accepted.

Stony Brook University, State University of New York, School of Professional Development, Stony Brook, NY 11794. Offers biology-grade 7-12 (MAT); chemistry-grade 7-12 (MAT); coaching (Graduate Certificate); coaching online (Graduate Certificate); computer integrated engineering (Graduate Certificate); earth science-grade 7-12 (MAT); educational computing (Graduate Certificate); educational leadership (Advanced Certificate); English-grade 7-12 (MAT); environmental management (Graduate Certificate); environmental/occupational health and safety (Graduate Certificate); French-grade 7-12 (MAT); German-grade 7-12 (MAT); human resource management (Graduate Certificate); human resource management online (Graduate Certificate); information systems management (Graduate Certificate); Italian-grade 7-12 (MAT); liberal studies (MA); liberal studies online (MAT); mathematics-grade 7-12 (MAT); operation research (Graduate Certificate); physics-grade 7-12 (MAT); professional studies online (MPS); school administration and supervision (Graduate Certificate); school building leadership (Graduate Certificate); school district administration (Graduate Certificate); school district business leadership (Advanced Certificate); school district leadership (Graduate Certificate); social science and the professions (MPS), including environmental waste management, human resource management; social studies-grade 7-12 (MAT); Spanish-grade 7-12 (MAT); waste management (Graduate Certificate). Part-time and evening/weekend programs available. Postbaccalaureate distance learning degree programs offered. *Degree requirements:* For master's, one foreign language, thesis or alternative.

Texas Christian University, College of Science and Engineering, School of Geology, Energy and the Environment, Fort Worth, TX 76129-0002. Offers environmental management (MEM); environmental science (MA, MS); geology (MS). Part-time programs available. *Faculty:* 6 full-time (1 woman), 1 part-time/adjunct. *Students:* 9 full-time (3 women), 30 part-time (15 women); includes 3 minority (all Hispanic/Latino), 1 international. Average age 27. 24 applicants, 88% accepted, 12 enrolled. In 2011, 15 master's awarded. *Degree requirements:* For master's, comprehensive exam (for some programs), thesis (for some programs). *Entrance requirements:* For master's, GRE. Additional exam requirements/recommendations for international students: Required—TOEFL (minimum score 550 paper-based; 213 computer-based; 80 iBT). *Application deadline:* For fall admission, 2/28 priority date for domestic students, 2/28 for international students. Application fee: $60. *Expenses:* Tuition: Full-time $20,250; part-time $1125 per credit hour. Part-time tuition and fees vary according to course load and program. *Financial support:* In 2011–12, 15 teaching assistantships with full tuition reimbursements (averaging $15,000 per year) were awarded. Financial award application deadline: 2/28. *Unit head:* Dr. Phil Hartman, Dean, 817-257-7727, E-mail: p.hartman@tcu.edu. *Application contact:* Dr. Magnus Rittby, Associate Dean for Administration and Graduate Programs, 817-257-7729, Fax: 817-257-7736, E-mail: m.rittby@tcu.edu.

Texas Southern University, School of Public Affairs, Program in Urban Planning and Environmental Policy, Houston, TX 77004-4584. Offers MS, PhD. *Accreditation:* ACSP. Part-time and evening/weekend programs available. *Degree requirements:* For master's, comprehensive exam, thesis optional. *Entrance requirements:* For master's, GRE General Test, minimum GPA of 2.5. Additional exam requirements/recommendations for international students: Required—TOEFL. Electronic applications accepted.

Texas State University–San Marcos, Graduate School, College of Liberal Arts, Department of Geography, Program in Resource and Environmental Studies, San Marcos, TX 78666. Offers MAG. Part-time and evening/weekend programs available. *Faculty:* 7 full-time (2 women), 1 part-time/adjunct (0 women). *Students:* 7 full-time (3 women), 10 part-time (6 women). Average age 30. 11 applicants, 45% accepted, 2 enrolled. In 2011, 15 master's awarded. *Degree requirements:* For master's, comprehensive exam. *Entrance requirements:* For master's, GRE General Test, minimum GPA of 3.0 in last 60 hours of course work, letter of interest, 2 letters of recommendation, curriculum vitae/resume. Additional exam requirements/recommendations for international students: Required—TOEFL (minimum score 550 paper-based; 213 computer-based; 78 iBT). *Application deadline:* For fall admission, 5/1 priority date for domestic students, 4/15 for international students; for spring admission, 10/15 priority date for domestic students, 10/1 for international students. Applications are processed on a rolling basis. Application fee: $40 ($90 for international students). *Expenses:* Tuition, state resident: full-time $6408; part-time $3204 per semester. Tuition, nonresident: full-time $14,832; part-time $7416 per semester. *Required fees:* $1824; $912 per semester. Tuition and fees vary according to course load. *Financial support:* In 2011–12, 17 students received support, including 1 research assistantship (averaging $9,855 per year), 1 teaching assistantship (averaging $11,097 per year); career-related internships or fieldwork, Federal Work-Study, institutionally sponsored loans, and scholarships/grants also available. Support available to part-time students. Financial award application deadline: 4/1; financial award applicants required to submit FAFSA. *Unit head:* Dr.

David Butler, Graduate Adviser, 512-245-2170, Fax: 512-245-8353, E-mail: db25@txstate.edu. *Application contact:* Dr. J. Michael Willoughby, Dean of Graduate School, 512-245-2581, Fax: 512-245-8365, E-mail: gradcollege@txstate.edu. Web site: http://www.geo.txstate.edu/.

Texas Tech University, Graduate School, College of Architecture, PhD Program in Land-Use Planning, Management, and Design, Lubbock, TX 79409. Offers PhD. *Students:* 4 full-time (2 women), 3 part-time (1 woman); includes 1 minority (Black or African American, non-Hispanic/Latino), 2 international. Average age 36. 9 applicants, 67% accepted, 2 enrolled. In 2011, 1 doctorate awarded. *Degree requirements:* For doctorate, comprehensive exam, thesis/dissertation. *Entrance requirements:* For doctorate, GRE General Test. Additional exam requirements/recommendations for international students: Required—TOEFL (minimum score 550 paper-based; 213 computer-based; 79 iBT). *Application deadline:* For fall admission, 6/1 priority date for domestic students, 1/15 for international students; for spring admission, 9/1 priority date for domestic students, 6/15 for international students. Applications are processed on a rolling basis. Application fee: $50 ($75 for international students). Electronic applications accepted. *Expenses:* Tuition, state resident: full-time $5899; part-time $245.80 per credit hour. Tuition, nonresident: full-time $13,411; part-time $558.80 per credit hour. *Required fees:* $2680.60; $86.50 per credit hour. $920.30 per semester. *Financial support:* Application deadline: 4/15; applicants required to submit FAFSA. *Faculty research:* Architecture, landscape architecture, geography, urban planning, environmental policy. *Unit head:* Dr. Saif Haq, Program Director, 806-742-3136 Ext. 284, Fax: 806-742-4604, E-mail: saif.haq@ttu.edu. *Application contact:* Jess Schwintz, Coordinator of Academic Programs, 806-742-3169 Ext. 228, Fax: 806-742-1400, E-mail: jess.schwintz@ttu.edu. Web site: http://www.arch.ttu.edu/programs/LPMD.

Towson University, Program in Geography and Environmental Planning, Towson, MD 21252-0001. Offers MA. Part-time and evening/weekend programs available. *Students:* 12 full-time (4 women), 20 part-time (10 women); includes 2 minority (1 Black or African American, non-Hispanic/Latino; 1 Hispanic/Latino), 2 international. *Degree requirements:* For master's, thesis optional. *Entrance requirements:* For master's, 9 credits of course work in geography, minimum GPA of 3.0 in geography, 2 narrative letters of recommendation. Additional exam requirements/recommendations for international students: Required—TOEFL. *Application deadline:* Applications are processed on a rolling basis. Application fee: $50. Electronic applications accepted. *Expenses:* Tuition, state resident: part-time $337 per credit. Tuition, nonresident: part-time $709 per credit. *Required fees:* $99 per credit. *Financial support:* Application deadline: 4/1; applicants required to submit FAFSA. *Unit head:* Martin Roberge, Graduate Program Director, 410-704-5011, Fax: 410-704-3880, E-mail: mroberge@towson.edu. Web site: http://www.towson.edu/geography/.

Trent University, Graduate Studies, Program in Environmental and Life Sciences, Environmental and Resource Studies Program, Peterborough, ON K9J 7B8, Canada. Offers M Sc, PhD. *Degree requirements:* For master's, thesis; for doctorate, thesis/dissertation. *Entrance requirements:* For master's, honours degree; for doctorate, master's degree. *Faculty research:* Environmental biogeochemistry, aquatic organic contaminants, fisheries, wetland ecology, renewable resource management.

Tropical Agriculture Research and Higher Education Center, Graduate School, Turrialba, Costa Rica. Offers agribusiness management (MS); agroforestry systems (PhD); development practices (MS); ecological agriculture (MS); environmental socioeconomics (MS); forestry in tropical and subtropical zones (PhD); integrated watershed management (MS); international sustainable tourism (MS); management and conservation of tropical rainforests and biodiversity (MS); tropical agriculture (PhD); tropical agroforestry (MS). *Entrance requirements:* For master's, GRE, 2 years of related professional experience, letters of recommendation; for doctorate, GRE, 4 letters of recommendation, letter of support from employing organization, master's degree in agronomy, biological sciences, forestry, natural resources or related field. Additional exam requirements/recommendations for international students: Required—TOEFL (minimum score 550 paper-based; 213 computer-based). Electronic applications accepted. *Faculty research:* Biodiversity in fragmented landscapes, ecosystem management, integrated pest management, environmental livestock production, biotechnology carbon balances in diverse land uses.

Troy University, Graduate School, College of Arts and Sciences, Program in Environmental and Biological Sciences, Troy, AL 36082. Offers MS. Part-time and evening/weekend programs available. *Faculty:* 6 full-time (1 woman), 1 part-time/adjunct (4 women). *Students:* 11 full-time (6 women), 15 part-time (11 women); includes 8 minority (2 Black or African American, non-Hispanic/Latino; 4 Asian, non-Hispanic/Latino; 2 Hispanic/Latino). Average age 25. 71 applicants, 58% accepted, 9 enrolled. In 2011, 12 master's awarded. *Degree requirements:* For master's, comprehensive exam or thesis, minimum GPA of 3.0, admission to candidacy. *Entrance requirements:* For master's, GRE (minimum score of 850) or MAT (minimum score of 385), minimum undergraduate GPA of 2.5, 2 letters of recommendation. Additional exam requirements/recommendations for international students: Required—TOEFL (minimum score 523 paper-based; 193 computer-based; 70 iBT), IELTS (minimum score 6). *Application deadline:* Applications are processed on a rolling basis. Application fee: $50. Electronic applications accepted. *Expenses:* Tuition, state resident: full-time $6960; part-time $290 per credit hour. Tuition, nonresident: full-time $13,920; part-time $580 per credit hour. *Required fees:* $386 per term. *Unit head:* Dr. Glenn Cohen, Chairman, 334-670-3660, Fax: 334-670-3662, E-mail: gcohen@troy.edu.

Peterson's Graduate Programs in the Physical Sciences, Mathematics, Agricultural Sciences, the Environment & Natural Resources 2013

facebook.com/petersonspublishing **467**

Environmental Management and Policy

Application contact: Brenda K. Campbell, Director of Graduate Admissions, 334-670-3178, Fax: 334-670-3733, E-mail: bcamp@troy.edu.

Troy University, Graduate School, College of Arts and Sciences, Program in Public Administration, Troy, AL 36082. Offers education (MPA); environmental management (MPA); government contracting (MPA); health care administration (MPA); justice administration (MPA); national security affairs (MPA); nonprofit management (MPA); public human resources management (MPA); public management (MPA). *Accreditation:* NASPAA. Part-time and evening/weekend programs available. Postbaccalaureate distance learning degree programs offered (no on-campus study). *Faculty:* 17 full-time (10 women), 10 part-time/adjunct (3 women). *Students:* 97 full-time (71 women), 400 part-time (259 women); includes 298 minority (264 Black or African American, non-Hispanic/Latino; 5 American Indian or Alaska Native, non-Hispanic/Latino; 15 Asian, non-Hispanic/Latino; 11 Hispanic/Latino; 3 Two or more races, non-Hispanic/Latino). Average age 33. 323 applicants, 63% accepted, 97 enrolled. In 2011, 249 master's awarded. *Degree requirements:* For master's, capstone course, minimum GPA of 3.0, admission to candidacy. *Entrance requirements:* For master's, GRE (minimum score of 920), MAT (minimum score of 400) or GMAT (minimum score of 490), minimum undergraduate GPA of 2.5, letter of recommendation, essay. Additional exam requirements/recommendations for international students: Required—TOEFL (minimum score 523 paper-based; 193 computer-based; 70 iBT), IELTS (minimum score 6). *Application deadline:* Applications are processed on a rolling basis. Application fee: $50. Electronic applications accepted. *Expenses:* Tuition, state resident: full-time $6960; part-time $290 per credit hour. Tuition, nonresident: full-time $13,920; part-time $580 per credit hour. *Required fees:* $386 per term. *Financial support:* Available to part-time students. Applicants required to submit FAFSA. *Unit head:* Dr. Charles Kruprick, Chairman, 334-670-5968, Fax: 334-670-5647, E-mail: ckrupnickl@troy.edu. *Application contact:* Brenda K. Campbell, Director of Graduate Admissions, 334-670-3178, Fax: 334-670-3733, E-mail: bcamp@troy.edu.

Tufts University, Graduate School of Arts and Sciences, Department of Urban and Environmental Policy and Planning, Medford, MA 02155. Offers community development (MA); environmental policy (MA); health and human welfare (MA); housing policy (MA); international environment/development policy (MA); public policy (MPP); MA/MS; MALD/MA. *Accreditation:* ACSP (one or more programs are accredited). Part-time programs available. *Faculty:* 14 full-time, 17 part-time/adjunct. *Students:* 120 full-time (84 women); includes 24 minority (8 Black or African American, non-Hispanic/Latino; 3 American Indian or Alaska Native, non-Hispanic/Latino; 5 Asian, non-Hispanic/Latino; 8 Hispanic/Latino), 9 international. Average age 27. 186 applicants, 67% accepted, 51 enrolled. In 2011, 42 master's awarded. *Degree requirements:* For master's, thesis, internship. *Entrance requirements:* For master's, GRE General Test. Additional exam requirements/recommendations for international students: Required—TOEFL (minimum score 550 paper-based; 213 computer-based; 80 iBT). *Application deadline:* For fall admission, 1/15 for domestic students, 12/15 for international students. Applications are processed on a rolling basis. Application fee: $75. Electronic applications accepted. *Expenses:* Contact institution. *Financial support:* Teaching assistantships with partial tuition reimbursements, career-related internships or fieldwork, Federal Work-Study, scholarships/grants, tuition waivers (partial), and unspecified assistantships available. Support available to part-time students. Financial award application deadline: 1/15; financial award applicants required to submit FAFSA. *Unit head:* Julian Agyeman, Chair, 617-627-3394, Fax: 617-627-3377. *Application contact:* Ann Urosevich, Department Administrator, 617-627-3394. Web site: http://ase.tufts.edu/uep/.

Tufts University, Graduate School of Arts and Sciences, Graduate Certificate Programs, Community Environmental Studies Program, Medford, MA 02155. Offers Certificate. Part-time and evening/weekend programs available. Electronic applications accepted. *Expenses:* Contact institution.

Tufts University, Graduate School of Arts and Sciences, Graduate Certificate Programs, Environmental Management Program, Medford, MA 02155. Offers Certificate. Part-time and evening/weekend programs available. Electronic applications accepted. *Expenses: Tuition:* Full-time $41,208; part-time $1030 per credit hour. Full-time tuition and fees vary according to degree level, program and student level. Part-time tuition and fees vary according to course load.

Tufts University, School of Engineering, Department of Civil and Environmental Engineering, Medford, MA 02155. Offers bioengineering (ME, MS), including environmental technology; civil engineering (ME, MS, PhD), including geotechnical engineering, structural engineering, water diplomacy (PhD); environmental engineering (ME, MS, PhD), including environmental engineering and environmental sciences, environmental geotechnology, environmental health, environmental science and management, hazardous materials management, water diplomacy (PhD), water resources engineering. Part-time programs available. *Faculty:* 18 full-time, 5 part-time/adjunct. *Students:* 102 full-time (50 women); includes 8 minority (1 Black or African American, non-Hispanic/Latino; 6 Asian, non-Hispanic/Latino; 1 Hispanic/Latino), 37 international. Average age 27. 162 applicants, 59% accepted, 37 enrolled. In 2011, 18 degrees awarded. Terminal master's awarded for partial completion of doctoral program. *Degree requirements:* For master's, thesis or alternative; for doctorate, thesis/dissertation. *Entrance requirements:* For master's and doctorate, GRE General Test. Additional exam requirements/recommendations for international students: Required—TOEFL (minimum score 550 paper-based; 213 computer-based; 80 iBT). *Application deadline:* For fall admission, 1/15 priority date for domestic students, 12/15 for international students; for spring admission, 10/15 for

domestic students, 9/15 for international students. Applications are processed on a rolling basis. Application fee: $75. Electronic applications accepted. *Expenses: Tuition:* Full-time $41,208; part-time $1030 per credit hour. Full-time tuition and fees vary according to degree level, program and student level. Part-time tuition and fees vary according to course load. *Financial support:* Fellowships with full tuition reimbursements, research assistantships with full and partial tuition reimbursements, teaching assistantships with full and partial tuition reimbursements, Federal Work-Study, scholarships/grants, tuition waivers (partial), and unspecified assistantships available. Financial award application deadline: 1/15; financial award applicants required to submit FAFSA. *Faculty research:* Environmental and water resources engineering, environmental health, geotechnical and geoenvironmental engineering, structural engineering and mechanics, water diplomacy. *Unit head:* Dr. Kurt Penell, Chair, 617-627-3211, Fax: 617-627-3994. *Application contact:* Laura Sacco, Information Contact, 617-627-3211, E-mail: ceeinfo@tufts.edu. Web site: http://www.ase.tufts.edu/cee/.

Universidad Autonoma de Guadalajara, Graduate Programs, Guadalajara, Mexico. Offers administrative law and justice (LL M); advertising and corporate communications (MA); architecture (M Arch); business (MBA); computational science (MCC); education (Ed M, Ed D); English-Spanish translation (MA); entrepreneurship and management (MBA); integrated management of digital animation (MA); international business (MIB); international corporate law (LL M); internet technologies (MS); manufacturing systems (MMS); occupational health (MS); philosophy (MA, PhD); power electronics (MS); quality systems (MQS); renewable energy (MS); social evaluation of projects (MBA); strategic market research (MBA); tax law (MA); teaching mathematics (MA).

Universidad del Turabo, Graduate Programs, Programs in Science and Technology, Gurabo, PR 00778-3030. Offers environmental analysis (MSE), including environmental chemistry; environmental management (MSE), including pollution management; environmental science (D Sc), including environmental biology. *Students:* 8 full-time (4 women), 101 part-time (68 women); includes 101 minority (all Hispanic/Latino). Average age 39. 58 applicants, 76% accepted, 39 enrolled. In 2011, 16 master's, 3 doctorates awarded. *Entrance requirements:* For master's, GRE, EXADEP, interview. *Application deadline:* For fall admission, 8/5 for domestic students. Application fee: $25. *Unit head:* David Mendez, Head, 787-743-7979. *Application contact:* Virginia Gonzalez, Admissions Officer, 787-746-3009.

Universidad Metropolitana, School of Environmental Affairs, Program in Environmental Planning, San Juan, PR 00928-1150. Offers MP. Part-time programs available. *Degree requirements:* For master's, thesis. *Entrance requirements:* For master's, EXADEP, interview. Electronic applications accepted.

Universidad Metropolitana, School of Environmental Affairs, Program in Environmental Studies, San Juan, PR 00928-1150. Offers MAES. Part-time programs available. *Degree requirements:* For master's, thesis or alternative. *Entrance requirements:* For master's, EXADEP, interview. Electronic applications accepted.

Université de Montréal, Faculty of Medicine, Programs in Environment and Prevention, Montréal, QC H3C 3J7, Canada. Offers environment, health and disaster management (DESS). Electronic applications accepted. *Faculty research:* Health, environment, pollutants, protection, waste.

Université du Québec à Chicoutimi, Graduate Programs, Program in Renewable Resources, Chicoutimi, QC G7H 2B1, Canada. Offers M Sc. Part-time programs available. *Degree requirements:* For master's, thesis. *Entrance requirements:* For master's, appropriate bachelor's degree, proficiency in French.

Université du Québec, Institut National de la Recherche Scientifique, Graduate Programs, Research Center—Water, Earth and Environment, Québec, QC G1K 9A9, Canada. Offers earth sciences (M Sc, PhD); earth sciences-environmental technologies (M Sc); water sciences (M Sc, PhD). Part-time programs available. *Faculty:* 40. *Students:* 204 full-time (88 women), 23 part-time (12 women), 103 international. Average age 30. In 2011, 31 master's, 12 doctorates awarded. *Degree requirements:* For master's, thesis optional; for doctorate, thesis/dissertation. *Entrance requirements:* For master's, appropriate bachelor's degree, proficiency in French; for doctorate, appropriate master's degree, proficiency in French. *Application deadline:* For fall admission, 3/30 for domestic and international students; for winter admission, 11/1 for domestic and international students; for spring admission, 3/1 for domestic and international students. Application fee: $45. Electronic applications accepted. *Financial support:* In 2011–12, 184 students received support, including fellowships (averaging $16,500 per year); research assistantships also available. *Faculty research:* Land use, impacts of climate change, adaptation to climate change, integrated management of resources (mineral and water). *Unit head:* Yves Begin, Director, 418-654-2524, Fax: 418-654-2600, E-mail: yves.begin@ete.inrs.ca. *Application contact:* Yvonne Boisvert, Registrar, 418-654-3861, Fax: 418-654-3858, E-mail: registrariat@adm.inrs.ca. Web site: http://www.ete.inrs.ca/.

Université Laval, Faculty of Administrative Sciences, Programs in Business Administration, Québec, QC G1K 7P4, Canada. Offers accounting (MBA); agri-food management (MBA); electronic business (MBA, Diploma); factory management and logistics (MBA); finance (MBA); firm management (MBA); geomatic management (MBA); information technology management (MBA); international management (MBA); management (MBA); management accounting (MBA, Diploma); marketing (MBA); modeling and organizational decision (MBA); occupational health and safety management (MBA); pharmacy management

468 facebook.com/petersonspublishing

Peterson's Graduate Programs in the Physical Sciences, Mathematics, Agricultural Sciences, the Environment & Natural Resources 2013

(MBA); social and environmental responsibility (MBA); technological entrepreneurship (Diploma). *Accreditation:* AACSB. Part-time and evening/weekend programs available. Postbaccalaureate distance learning degree programs offered (no on-campus study). *Entrance requirements:* For master's and Diploma, knowledge of French and English. Electronic applications accepted.

Université Laval, Faculty of Agricultural and Food Sciences, Department of Soils and Agricultural Engineering, Programs in Agri-Food Engineering, Québec, QC G1K 7P4, Canada. Offers agri-food engineering (M Sc); environmental technology (M Sc). *Degree requirements:* For master's, thesis (for some programs). *Entrance requirements:* For master's, knowledge of French. Electronic applications accepted.

Université Laval, Faculty of Agricultural and Food Sciences, Department of Soils and Agricultural Engineering, Programs in Soils and Environment Science, Québec, QC G1K 7P4, Canada. Offers environmental technology (M Sc); soils and environment science (M Sc, PhD). Terminal master's awarded for partial completion of doctoral program. *Degree requirements:* For master's, thesis (for some programs); for doctorate, comprehensive exam, thesis/dissertation. *Entrance requirements:* For master's and doctorate, knowledge of French and English. Electronic applications accepted.

University at Albany, State University of New York, College of Arts and Sciences, Department of Biological Sciences, Program in Biodiversity, Conservation, and Policy, Albany, NY 12222-0001. Offers MS. *Degree requirements:* For master's, one foreign language. *Entrance requirements:* For master's, GRE General Test. *Faculty research:* Aquatic ecology, plant community ecology, biodiversity and public policy, restoration ecology, coastal and estuarine science.

University of Alaska Fairbanks, College of Engineering and Mines, Department of Civil and Environmental Engineering, Program in Environmental Engineering, Fairbanks, AK 99775-5900. Offers engineering (PhD), including environmental engineering; environmental engineering (MS), including environmental contaminants, environmental science and management, water supply and waste treatment. Part-time programs available. *Students:* 3 full-time (0 women), 1 (woman) part-time. Average age 26. 5 applicants, 60% accepted, 1 enrolled. In 2011, 2 degrees awarded. *Degree requirements:* For master's, comprehensive exam, thesis or alternative; for doctorate, comprehensive exam, thesis/dissertation, oral exam, oral defense. *Entrance requirements:* For master's, basic computer techniques; for doctorate, GRE General Test. Additional exam requirements/recommendations for international students: Required—TOEFL (minimum score 575 paper-based; 213 computer-based). *Application deadline:* For fall admission, 6/1 for domestic students, 3/1 for international students; for spring admission, 10/15 for domestic students, 9/1 for international students. Applications are processed on a rolling basis. Application fee: $60. Electronic applications accepted. *Expenses:* Tuition, state resident: full-time $6696; part-time $372 per credit. Tuition, nonresident: full-time $13,680; part-time $760 per credit. Tuition and fees vary according to course load and reciprocity agreements. *Financial support:* In 2011–12, 1 research assistantship (averaging $16,834 per year), 2 teaching assistantships (averaging $6,390 per year) were awarded; fellowships, career-related internships or fieldwork, Federal Work-Study, scholarships/grants, health care benefits, and unspecified assistantships also available. Support available to part-time students. Financial award application deadline: 7/1; financial award applicants required to submit FAFSA. *Unit head:* Dr. David Barnes, Department Chair, 907-474-7241, Fax: 907-474-6087, E-mail: fyeqe@uaf.edu. *Application contact:* Mike Earnest, Director of Admissions, 907-474-7500, Fax: 907-474-5379, E-mail: admissions@uaf.edu. Web site: http://www.alaska.edu/uaf/cem/cee/env/.

University of Alaska Fairbanks, College of Liberal Arts, Department of Northern Studies, Fairbanks, AK 99775-6460. Offers environmental politics and policy (MA); Northern history (MA). Part-time programs available. *Faculty:* 1 (woman) full-time. *Students:* 12 full-time (7 women), 18 part-time (9 women); includes 3 minority (1 American Indian or Alaska Native, non-Hispanic/Latino; 1 Hispanic/Latino; 1 Two or more races, non-Hispanic/Latino), 2 international. Average age 36. 25 applicants, 40% accepted, 7 enrolled. In 2011, 6 degrees awarded. *Degree requirements:* For master's, comprehensive exam, thesis or alternative. *Entrance requirements:* Additional exam requirements/recommendations for international students: Required—TOEFL (minimum score 550 paper-based; 213 computer-based; 80 iBT). *Application deadline:* For fall admission, 6/1 for domestic students, 3/1 for international students; for spring admission, 10/15 for domestic students, 9/1 for international students. Applications are processed on a rolling basis. Application fee: $60. Electronic applications accepted. *Expenses:* Tuition, state resident: full-time $6696; part-time $372 per credit. Tuition, nonresident: full-time $13,680; part-time $760 per credit. Tuition and fees vary according to course load and reciprocity agreements. *Financial support:* In 2011–12, 2 research assistantships with tuition reimbursements (averaging $2,982 per year), 2 teaching assistantships with tuition reimbursements (averaging $8,428 per year) were awarded; fellowships with tuition reimbursements, career-related internships or fieldwork, Federal Work-Study, scholarships/grants, health care benefits, and unspecified assistantships also available. Support available to part-time students. Financial award application deadline: 1/1; financial award applicants required to submit FAFSA. *Faculty research:* Canadian history, environmental history, Native Alaskan history and art, fetal alcohol syndrome. *Unit head:* Mary Ehrlander, Director, 907-474-7126, Fax: 907-474-5817, E-mail: fynors@uaf.edu. *Application contact:* Mike Earnest, Director of Admissions, 907-474-7500, Fax: 907-474-5379, E-mail: admissions@uaf.edu. Web site: http://www.uaf.edu/northern/.

University of Alberta, Faculty of Graduate Studies and Research, Department of Economics, Edmonton, AB T6G 2E1, Canada. Offers economics (MA, PhD); economics and finance (MA); environmental and natural resource economics (PhD). Part-time programs available. *Degree requirements:* For doctorate, thesis/dissertation. *Entrance requirements:* For master's and doctorate, GRE. Additional exam requirements/recommendations for international students: Required—TOEFL. *Faculty research:* Public finance, international trade, industrial organization, Pacific Rim economics, monetary economics.

University of Calgary, Faculty of Graduate Studies, Interdisciplinary Graduate Programs, Calgary, AB T2N 1N4, Canada. Offers interdisciplinary research (M Sc, MA, PhD); resources and the environment (M Sc, MA, PhD). Part-time programs available. *Degree requirements:* For master's, thesis; for doctorate, thesis/dissertation, written and oral candidacy exam. *Entrance requirements:* Additional exam requirements/recommendations for international students: Required—TOEFL (minimum score 600 paper-based; 250 computer-based).

University of Calgary, Faculty of Law, Programs in Natural Resources, Energy and Environmental Law, Calgary, AB T2N 1N4, Canada. Offers LL M, Postbaccalaureate Certificate. Part-time and evening/weekend programs available. *Degree requirements:* For master's, thesis optional. *Entrance requirements:* For master's, JD or LL B. Additional exam requirements/recommendations for international students: Required—TOEFL (minimum score 100 iBT); IELTS (minimum score 7). Electronic applications accepted. *Faculty research:* Natural resources law and regulations; environmental law, ethics and policies; oil and gas and energy law; water and municipal law; Aboriginal law.

University of California, Berkeley, Graduate Division, College of Natural Resources, Department of Environmental Science, Policy, and Management, Berkeley, CA 94720-1500. Offers environmental science, policy, and management (MS, PhD); forestry (MF). Terminal master's awarded for partial completion of doctoral program. *Degree requirements:* For master's, thesis optional; for doctorate, thesis/dissertation, qualifying exam. *Entrance requirements:* For master's and doctorate, GRE General Test, minimum GPA of 3.0, 3 letters of recommendation. Additional exam requirements/recommendations for international students: Required—TOEFL. Electronic applications accepted. *Faculty research:* Biology and ecology of insects; ecosystem function and environmental issues of soils; plant health/interactions from molecular to ecosystem levels; range management and ecology; forest and resource policy, sustainability, and management.

University of California, Berkeley, UC Berkeley Extension, Certificate Programs in Sustainability Studies, Berkeley, CA 94720-1500. Offers leadership in sustainability and environmental management (Professional Certificate); solar energy and green building (Professional Certificate); sustainable design (Professional Certificate).

University of California, Santa Barbara, Graduate Division, College of Letters and Sciences, Division of Social Sciences, Department of Global and International Studies, Santa Barbara, CA 93106-7065. Offers global culture and religion (MA); global government and human rights (MA); political economy, sustainable development, and the environment (MA). *Faculty:* 11 full-time (5 women), 5 part-time/adjunct (2 women). *Students:* 32 full-time (20 women); includes 9 minority (4 Asian, non-Hispanic/Latino; 2 Hispanic/Latino; 2 Native Hawaiian or other Pacific Islander, non-Hispanic/Latino; 1 Two or more races, non-Hispanic/Latino), 1 international. Average age 28. 55 applicants, 38% accepted, 15 enrolled. In 2011, 14 degrees awarded. *Degree requirements:* For master's, one foreign language, thesis or alternative, 2 years of a second language. *Entrance requirements:* For master's, GRE, 2 years of a second language with minimum B grade, 3 letters of recommendation, resume/curriculum vitae. Additional exam requirements/recommendations for international students: Required—TOEFL (minimum score 600 paper-based; 80 iBT), IELTS (minimum score 7). *Application deadline:* For fall admission, 12/15 for domestic and international students. Application fee: $80 ($100 for international students). Electronic applications accepted. *Expenses:* Tuition, state resident: full-time $12,192. Tuition, nonresident: full-time $27,294. *Required fees:* $764.13. *Financial support:* In 2011–12, 37 fellowships with full tuition reimbursements (averaging $8,000 per year), 42 teaching assistantships with partial tuition reimbursements (averaging $10,292 per year) were awarded; career-related internships or fieldwork, Federal Work-Study, and scholarships/grants also available. Financial award application deadline: 12/15; financial award applicants required to submit FAFSA. *Faculty research:* Global culture religion, global governance human rights, political economy, environment, sustainable development. *Total annual research expenditures:* $240,000. *Unit head:* Prof. Giles Gunn, Chair, 805-893-4299, Fax: 805-893-8003, E-mail: ggunn@global.ucsb.edu. *Application contact:* Jessea Gay Marie, Graduate Program Advisor/Internship Assistance Officer, 805-893-4668, Fax: 805-893-8003, E-mail: gd-admissions@global.ucsb.edu. Web site: http://www.globl.ucsb.edu/.

University of California, Santa Barbara, Graduate Division, Donald Bren School of Environmental Science and Management, Santa Barbara, CA 93106-5131. Offers economics and environmental science (PhD); environmental science and management (MESM, PhD); technology and society (PhD). *Faculty:* 18 full-time (3 women), 3 part-time/adjunct (0 women). *Students:* 227 full-time (113 women); includes 33 minority (3 Black or African American, non-Hispanic/Latino; 1 American Indian or Alaska Native, non-Hispanic/Latino; 16 Asian, non-Hispanic/Latino; 9 Hispanic/Latino; 1 Native Hawaiian or other Pacific Islander, non-Hispanic/Latino; 3 Two or more races, non-Hispanic/Latino), 27 international. Average age 28. 447 applicants, 51% accepted, 109 enrolled. In 2011, 93

Peterson's Graduate Programs in the Physical Sciences, Mathematics, Agricultural Sciences, the Environment & Natural Resources 2013

facebook.com/petersonspublishing **469**

master's, 5 doctorates awarded. *Median time to degree:* Of those who began their doctoral program in fall 2003, 90% received their degree in 8 years or less. *Degree requirements:* For master's, thesis; for doctorate, thesis/dissertation. *Entrance requirements:* For master's and doctorate, GRE. Additional exam requirements/recommendations for international students: Required—TOEFL (minimum score 550 paper-based; 80 iBT), IELTS (minimum score 7). *Application deadline:* For fall admission, 12/15 priority date for domestic students, 12/15 for international students. Application fee: $80 ($100 for international students). Electronic applications accepted. *Expenses:* Tuition, state resident: full-time $12,192. Tuition, nonresident: full-time $27,294. *Required fees:* $764.13. *Financial support:* In 2011–12, 34 students received support, including 53 fellowships with full and partial tuition reimbursements available, 10 research assistantships with full and partial tuition reimbursements available, 18 teaching assistantships with full and partial tuition reimbursements available; career-related internships or fieldwork and tuition waivers (full and partial) also available. Financial award application deadline: 12/15; financial award applicants required to submit FAFSA. *Faculty research:* Coastal marine resources management, conservation planning, corporate environmental management, economics and politics of the environment, energy and climate, pollution prevention and remediation, water resources management. *Unit head:* Bryant Wieneke, Assistant Dean, Planning and Administration, 805-893-2212, Fax: 805-893-7612, E-mail: bryant@bren.ucsb.edu. *Application contact:* Dori Molnar, Graduate Advisor, 805-893-7611, Fax: 805-893-7612, E-mail: admissions@bren.ucsb.edu. Web site: http://www.bren.ucsb.edu/.

University of California, Santa Cruz, Division of Graduate Studies, Division of Social Sciences, Program in Environmental Studies, Santa Cruz, CA 95064. Offers PhD. *Degree requirements:* For doctorate, thesis/dissertation, qualifying exam. *Entrance requirements:* For doctorate, GRE General Test. Additional exam requirements/recommendations for international students: Required—TOEFL (minimum score 550 paper-based; 220 computer-based; 83 iBT); Recommended—IELTS (minimum score 8). Electronic applications accepted. *Faculty research:* Political economy and sustainability, conservation biology, agroecology, environmental policy analysis.

University of Central Missouri, The Graduate School, College of Science and Technology, Warrensburg, MO 64093. Offers applied mathematics (MS); aviation safety (MS); biology (MS); computer science (MS); environmental studies (MA); industrial management (MS); mathematics (MS); technology (MS); technology management (PhD). PhD is offered jointly with Indiana State University. Part-time programs available. Postbaccalaureate distance learning degree programs offered. *Entrance requirements:* Additional exam requirements/recommendations for international students: Required—TOEFL (minimum score 550 paper-based; 79 computer-based). Electronic applications accepted.

University of Chicago, Irving B. Harris Graduate School of Public Policy Studies, Chicago, IL 60637-1513. Offers environmental science and policy (MS); public policy studies (AM, MPP, PhD); JD/MPP; MBA/MPP; MPP/M Div; MPP/MA. Part-time programs available. *Degree requirements:* For doctorate, thesis/dissertation. *Entrance requirements:* Additional exam requirements/recommendations for international students: Required—TOEFL. Electronic applications accepted. *Expenses:* Contact institution. *Faculty research:* Family and child policy, international security, health policy, social policy.

University of Colorado Boulder, Graduate School, College of Arts and Sciences, Program in Environmental Studies, Boulder, CO 80309. Offers MS, PhD. *Faculty:* 6 full-time (3 women). *Students:* 37 full-time (24 women), 12 part-time (4 women); includes 8 minority (1 Black or African American, non-Hispanic/Latino; 4 American Indian or Alaska Native, non-Hispanic/Latino; 1 Asian, non-Hispanic/Latino; 1 Hispanic/Latino; 1 Two or more races, non-Hispanic/Latino). Average age 31. 198 applicants, 13% accepted, 11 enrolled. In 2011, 15 master's, 3 doctorates awarded. *Entrance requirements:* For master's, minimum undergraduate GPA of 3.0. *Application deadline:* For fall admission, 1/15 for domestic students, 12/1 for international students. Electronic applications accepted. *Financial support:* In 2011–12, 51 students received support, including 25 fellowships (averaging $6,054 per year), 11 research assistantships with full and partial tuition reimbursements available (averaging $18,839 per year), 14 teaching assistantships with full and partial tuition reimbursements available (averaging $21,037 per year); institutionally sponsored loans, scholarships/grants, health care benefits, and unspecified assistantships also available. Financial award applicants required to submit FAFSA. *Faculty research:* Climate and atmospheric chemistry, water sciences, environmental policy and sustainability, waste management and environmental remediation, biogeochemical cycles. *Total annual research expenditures:* $1.1 million. *Application contact:* E-mail: envsgrad@colorado.edu. Web site: http://www.colorado.edu/envirostudies.

University of Colorado Denver, College of Architecture and Planning, Program in Urban and Regional Planning, Denver, CO 80217-3364. Offers economic and community development planning (MURP); land use and environmental planning (MURP); urban place making (MURP). *Accreditation:* ACSP. Part-time programs available. *Students:* 100 full-time (43 women), 9 part-time (2 women); includes 15 minority (2 Black or African American, non-Hispanic/Latino; 1 American Indian or Alaska Native, non-Hispanic/Latino; 2 Asian, non-Hispanic/Latino; 8 Hispanic/Latino; 2 Two or more races, non-Hispanic/Latino), 7 international. Average age 30. 123 applicants, 66% accepted, 35 enrolled. In 2011, 69 master's awarded. *Degree requirements:* For master's, thesis optional, minimum of 51 semester hours. *Entrance requirements:* For master's, GRE if GPA below 3.0, writing

sample. Additional exam requirements/recommendations for international students: Required—TOEFL (minimum score 550 paper-based; 213 computer-based). *Application deadline:* For fall admission, 2/15 priority date for domestic students; for spring admission, 10/1 for domestic students. Applications are processed on a rolling basis. Application fee: $50 ($75 for international students). Electronic applications accepted. *Expenses:* Contact institution. *Financial support:* Career-related internships or fieldwork, Federal Work-Study, and scholarships/grants available. Financial award application deadline: 4/1; financial award applicants required to submit FAFSA. *Faculty research:* Physical planning, environmental planning, economic development planning. *Unit head:* Brian Muller, Associate Professor and Chair, 303-556-5967, E-mail: brian.muller@ucdenver.edu. *Application contact:* Michael Harper, Administrative Coordinator, Graduate Admissions and PhD Program, 303-556-6042, E-mail: michael.t.harper@ucdenver.edu. Web site: http://www.cudenver.edu/cap.

University of Colorado Denver, College of Liberal Arts and Sciences, Program in Humanities, Denver, CO 80217. Offers community health science (MSS); humanities (MH); international studies (MSS); society and the environment (MSS); women's and gender studies (MSS). Part-time and evening/weekend programs available. *Students:* 41 full-time (28 women), 42 part-time (26 women); includes 13 minority (1 Black or African American, non-Hispanic/Latino; 2 American Indian or Alaska Native, non-Hispanic/Latino; 2 Asian, non-Hispanic/Latino; 8 Hispanic/Latino). Average age 33. 30 applicants, 60% accepted, 10 enrolled. In 2011, 19 master's awarded. *Degree requirements:* For master's, thesis or alternative, 36 credit hours, project or thesis. *Entrance requirements:* For master's, writing sample, statement of purpose/letter of intent. Additional exam requirements/recommendations for international students: Required—TOEFL (minimum score 525 paper-based; 197 computer-based; 71 iBT). *Application deadline:* For fall admission, 5/15 for domestic and international students; for spring admission, 10/15 for domestic and international students. Application fee: $50 ($75 for international students). Electronic applications accepted. *Financial support:* Federal Work-Study and scholarships/grants available. Financial award application deadline: 4/1; financial award applicants required to submit FAFSA. *Faculty research:* Women and gender in the classical Mediterranean, communication theory and democracy, relationship between psychology and philosophy. *Unit head:* Myra Bookman, Associate Director of Humanities and Social Science, 303-556-2496, Fax: 303-556-8100, E-mail: myra.bookman@ucdenver.edu. *Application contact:* Catherine Osmundson, Program Assistant, 303-556-2305, E-mail: catherine.osmundson@ucdenver.edu. Web site: http://www.ucdenver.edu/academics/colleges/CLAS/Programs/HumanitiesSocialSciences/Programs/Pages/Admissions.aspx.

University of Colorado Denver, School of Public Affairs, Program in Public Affairs and Administration, Denver, CO 80127. Offers public administration (MPA), including domestic violence, emergency management and homeland security, environmental policy, management and law, homeland security and defense, local government, nonprofit management, public administration; public affairs (PhD). *Accreditation:* NASPAA. Part-time and evening/weekend programs available. Postbaccalaureate distance learning degree programs offered (no on-campus study). *Faculty:* 19 full-time (9 women), 14 part-time/adjunct (5 women). *Students:* 264 full-time (158 women), 177 part-time (100 women); includes 54 minority (17 Black or African American, non-Hispanic/Latino; 2 American Indian or Alaska Native, non-Hispanic/Latino; 11 Asian, non-Hispanic/Latino; 22 Hispanic/Latino; 2 Two or more races, non-Hispanic/Latino), 31 international. Average age 34. 215 applicants, 67% accepted, 96 enrolled. In 2011, 155 master's, 4 doctorates awarded. *Degree requirements:* For master's, thesis or alternative, 36-39 credit hours; for doctorate, comprehensive exam, thesis/dissertation, minimum of 66 semester hours, including at least 30 hours of doctoral dissertation. *Entrance requirements:* For master's and doctorate, GRE, resume, essay, transcripts, recommendations. Additional exam requirements/recommendations for international students: Required—TOEFL (minimum score 550 paper-based; 223 computer-based). *Application deadline:* For fall admission, 2/1 for domestic students; for spring admission, 10/15 priority date for domestic students. Application fee: $50 ($75 for international students). Electronic applications accepted. *Expenses:* Contact institution. *Financial support:* Fellowships with partial tuition reimbursements, research assistantships with partial tuition reimbursements, teaching assistantships with partial tuition reimbursements, Federal Work-Study, and scholarships/grants available. Support available to part-time students. Financial award application deadline: 4/1; financial award applicants required to submit FAFSA. *Faculty research:* Housing, education and the social and economic issues of vulnerable populations; nonprofit governance and management; education finance, effectiveness and reform; P-20 education initiatives; municipal government accountability. *Unit head:* Dr. Kathleen Beatty, Director of Executive MPA Program, 303-315-2485, Fax: 303-315-2229, E-mail: kathleen.beatty@ucdenver.edu. *Application contact:* Annie Davies, Director of Marketing, Community Outreach and Alumni Affairs, 303-315-2896, Fax: 303-315-2229, E-mail: annie.davies@ucdenver.edu. Web site: http://www.ucdenver.edu/academics/colleges/SPA/Academics/programs/PublicAffairsAdmin/Pages/index.aspx.

University of Dayton, Department of Mechanical and Aerospace Engineering, Dayton, OH 45469-1300. Offers aerospace engineering (MSAE, DE, PhD); mechanical engineering (MSME, DE, PhD); renewable and clean energy (MS). Part-time programs available. Postbaccalaureate distance learning degree programs offered (no on-campus study). *Faculty:* 16 full-time (2 women), 11 part-time/adjunct (1 woman). *Students:* 150 full-time (22 women), 28 part-time (6 women); includes 15 minority (7 Black or African American, non-Hispanic/Latino;

470 facebook.com/petersonspublishing

Peterson's Graduate Programs in the Physical Sciences, Mathematics, Agricultural Sciences, the Environment & Natural Resources 2013

3 Asian, non-Hispanic/Latino; 5 Hispanic/Latino), 77 international. Average age 27. 177 applicants, 63% accepted, 55 enrolled. In 2011, 66 master's, 4 doctorates awarded. Terminal master's awarded for partial completion of doctoral program. *Degree requirements:* For master's, thesis optional; for doctorate, variable foreign language requirement, thesis/dissertation, departmental qualifying exam. *Entrance requirements:* Additional exam requirements/recommendations for international students: Required—TOEFL (minimum score 550 paper-based; 213 computer-based; 80 iBT). *Application deadline:* For fall admission, 8/1 priority date for domestic students, 6/1 for international students; for winter admission, 9/1 for international students; for spring admission, 3/1 for international students. Applications are processed on a rolling basis. Application fee: $0. Electronic applications accepted. *Expenses: Tuition:* Full-time $8400; part-time $700 per credit hour. *Required fees:* $25 per semester. Tuition and fees vary according to degree level. *Financial support:* In 2011–12, 25 students received support, including 29 research assistantships with full tuition reimbursements available (averaging $11,000 per year), 7 teaching assistantships with full tuition reimbursements available (averaging $9,100 per year). Financial award applicants required to submit FAFSA. *Faculty research:* Jet engine combustion, surface coating friction and wear, aircraft thermal management, aerospace fuels, energy efficient buildings, energy efficient manufacturing, renewable energy. *Total annual research expenditures:* $1.2 million. *Unit head:* Dr. Kelly Kissock, Chair, 937-229-2999, Fax: 937-229-4766, E-mail: kelly.kissock@udayton.edu. *Application contact:* Dr. Vinod Jain, Graduate Program Director, 937-229-2992, Fax: 937-229-4766, E-mail: vinod.jain@notes.udayton.edu, Web site: http://www.udayton.edu/engineering/mechanical_and_aerospace/.

University of Delaware, Center for Energy and Environmental Policy, Newark, DE 19716. Offers energy and environmental policy (MA, MEEP, PhD); urban affairs and public policy (PhD), including technology, environment, and society. *Degree requirements:* For master's, analytical paper or thesis; for doctorate, comprehensive exam, thesis/dissertation. *Entrance requirements:* For master's, GRE General Test, minimum GPA of 3.0; for doctorate, GRE General Test, minimum GPA of 3.5. Additional exam requirements/recommendations for international students: Required—TOEFL. Electronic applications accepted. *Faculty research:* Sustainable development, renewable energy, climate change, environmental policy, environmental justice, disaster policy.

University of Denver, University College, Denver, CO 80208. Offers arts and culture (MLS, Certificate), including art, literature, and culture, arts development and program management (Certificate), creative writing; environmental policy and management (MAS, Certificate), including energy and sustainability (Certificate), environmental assessment of nuclear power (Certificate), environmental health and safety (Certificate), environmental management, natural resource management (Certificate); geographic information systems (MAS, Certificate); global affairs (MLS, Certificate), including translation studies, world history and culture; healthcare leadership (MPH, Certificate), including healthcare policy, law, and ethics, medical and healthcare information technologies, strategic management of healthcare; information and communications technology (MCIS, Certificate), including database design and administration (Certificate), geographic information systems (MCIS), information security systems security (Certificate), information systems security (MCIS), project management (MCIS, MPS, Certificate), software design and administration (Certificate), software design and programming (MCIS), technology management, telecommunications technology (MCIS), Web design and development; leadership and organizations (MPS, Certificate), including human capital in organizations, philanthropic leadership, project management (MCIS, MPS, Certificate), strategic innovation and change; organizational and professional communication (MPS, Certificate), including alternative dispute resolution, organizational communication, organizational development and training, public relations and marketing; security management (MAS, Certificate), including emergency planning and response, information security (MAS), organizational security; strategic human resource management (MPS, Certificate), including global human resources (MPS), human resource management and development (MPS). Part-time and evening/weekend programs available. Postbaccalaureate distance learning degree programs offered (no on-campus study). *Faculty:* 204 part-time/adjunct (80 women). *Students:* 56 full-time (26 women), 1,096 part-time (647 women); includes 196 minority (81 Black or African American, non-Hispanic/Latino; 7 American Indian or Alaska Native, non-Hispanic/Latino; 30 Asian, non-Hispanic/Latino; 66 Hispanic/Latino; 3 Native Hawaiian or other Pacific Islander, non-Hispanic/Latino; 9 Two or more races, non-Hispanic/Latino), 76 international. Average age 36. 572 applicants, 95% accepted, 410 enrolled. In 2011, 404 master's, 123 other advanced degrees awarded. *Degree requirements:* For master's, capstone project. *Entrance requirements:* For master's, two letters of recommendation, personal statement, resume. Additional exam requirements/recommendations for international students: Required—TOEFL (minimum score 550 paper-based; 80 iBT). *Application deadline:* For fall admission, 7/20 priority date for domestic students, 6/8 for international students; for winter admission, 10/26 priority date for domestic students, 9/14 for international students; for spring admission, 2/1 priority date for domestic students, 12/14 for international students. Applications are processed on a rolling basis. Application fee: $75. Electronic applications accepted. *Expenses:* Contact institution. *Financial support:* Applicants required to submit FAFSA. *Unit head:* Dr. James Davis, Dean, 303-871-2291, Fax: 303-871-4047, E-mail: jdavis@du.edu. *Application contact:* Information Contact, 303-871-3155, Fax: 303-871-4047, E-mail: ucolinfo@du.edu. Web site: http://www.universitycollege.du.edu/.

The University of Findlay, Graduate and Professional Studies, College of Sciences, Master of Science Program in Environmental, Safety and Health Management, Findlay, OH 45840-3653. Offers MSEM. Part-time and evening/weekend programs available. Postbaccalaureate distance learning degree programs offered (no on-campus study). *Faculty:* 11 full-time (2 women), 3 part-time/adjunct (1 woman). *Students:* 4 full-time (2 women), 68 part-time (23 women); includes 6 minority (2 Black or African American, non-Hispanic/Latino; 3 Asian, non-Hispanic/Latino; 1 Hispanic/Latino), 23 international. Average age 35. 22 applicants, 82% accepted, 15 enrolled. In 2011, 33 master's awarded. *Degree requirements:* For master's, thesis, cumulative project. *Entrance requirements:* For master's, GRE, bachelor's degree from accredited institution, minimum undergraduate GPA of 3.0 in last 64 hours of course work. Additional exam requirements/recommendations for international students: Required—TOEFL (minimum score 550 paper-based; 213 computer-based; 80 iBT). *Application deadline:* Applications are processed on a rolling basis. Application fee: $25. Electronic applications accepted. *Expenses: Tuition:* Full-time $6300; part-time $700 per semester hour. *Required fees:* $35 per semester hour. One-time fee: $25. Tuition and fees vary according to course load, degree level and program. *Financial support:* In 2011–12, 1 research assistantship with full and partial tuition reimbursement (averaging $4,200 per year), 1 teaching assistantship with full and partial tuition reimbursement (averaging $3,600 per year) were awarded; career-related internships or fieldwork, Federal Work-Study, health care benefits, and unspecified assistantships also available. Financial award application deadline: 4/1; financial award applicants required to submit FAFSA. *Unit head:* Dr. William Doyle, Director, 419-434-5747, Fax: 419-434-4822. *Application contact:* Heather Riffle, Assistant Director, Graduate and Professional Studies, 419-434-4640, Fax: 419-434-5517, E-mail: riffle@findlay.edu. Web site: http://www.findlay.edu.

University of Guelph, Graduate Studies, Ontario Agricultural College, Department of Land Resource Science, Guelph, ON N1G 2W1, Canada. Offers atmospheric science (M Sc, PhD); environmental and agricultural earth sciences (M Sc, PhD); land resources management (M Sc, PhD); soil science (M Sc, PhD). Part-time programs available. *Degree requirements:* For master's, thesis (for some programs), research project (non-thesis track); for doctorate, comprehensive exam, thesis/dissertation. *Entrance requirements:* For master's, minimum B average during previous 2 years of course work; for doctorate, minimum B average during previous 2 years of course work. Additional exam requirements/recommendations for international students: Required—TOEFL (minimum score 550 paper-based; 213 computer-based). Electronic applications accepted. *Faculty research:* Soil science, environmental earth science, land resource management.

University of Hawaii at Manoa, Graduate Division, College of Social Sciences, Department of Urban and Regional Planning, Honolulu, HI 96822. Offers community planning and social policy (MURP); disaster preparedness and emergency management (Graduate Certificate); environmental planning and management (MURP); land use and infrastructure planning (MURP); urban and regional planning (PhD, Graduate Certificate); urban and regional planning in Asia and Pacific (MURP). *Accreditation:* ACSP. Part-time programs available. *Entrance requirements:* For master's, GRE General Test, minimum GPA of 3.0; for doctorate, GRE General Test. Additional exam requirements/recommendations for international students: Required—TOEFL (minimum score 500 paper-based; 173 computer-based; 61 iBT), IELTS (minimum score 5).

University of Hawaii at Manoa, Graduate Division, College of Tropical Agriculture and Human Resources, Department of Natural Resources and Environmental Management, Honolulu, HI 96822. Offers MS, PhD. Part-time programs available. Terminal master's awarded for partial completion of doctoral program. *Degree requirements:* For master's, thesis optional; for doctorate, comprehensive exam, thesis/dissertation. *Entrance requirements:* For master's and doctorate, GRE General Test, minimum GPA of 3.0 in last 4 semesters of course work. Additional exam requirements/recommendations for international students: Required—TOEFL (minimum score 600 paper-based; 250 computer-based; 100 iBT), IELTS (minimum score 7). *Faculty research:* Bioeconomics, natural resource management.

University of Houston–Clear Lake, School of Business, Program in Administrative Science, Houston, TX 77058-1098. Offers environmental management (MS); human resource management (MA). *Accreditation:* CAHME (one or more programs are accredited). Part-time and evening/weekend programs available. *Degree requirements:* For master's, thesis optional. *Entrance requirements:* For master's, GMAT. Additional exam requirements/recommendations for international students: Required—TOEFL (minimum score 550 paper-based; 213 computer-based). Electronic applications accepted.

University of Illinois at Springfield, Graduate Programs, College of Public Affairs and Administration, Program in Environmental Studies, Springfield, IL 62703-5407. Offers environmental science (MS); environmental studies (MA). Part-time and evening/weekend programs available. Postbaccalaureate distance learning degree programs offered (no on-campus study). *Faculty:* 5 full-time (1 woman). *Students:* 14 full-time (10 women), 75 part-time (43 women); includes 6 minority (3 Black or African American, non-Hispanic/Latino; 2 Asian, non-Hispanic/Latino; 1 Hispanic/Latino), 5 international. Average age 35. 53 applicants, 57% accepted, 20 enrolled. In 2011, 28 master's awarded. *Degree requirements:* For master's, thesis or project. *Entrance requirements:* For master's, minimum undergraduate GPA of 3.0, 2 letters of recommendation, goals essay. Additional exam requirements/recommendations for international students: Required—TOEFL (minimum score 500 paper-based; 176 computer-based; 61

Peterson's Graduate Programs in the Physical Sciences, Mathematics, Agricultural Sciences, the Environment & Natural Resources 2013

facebook.com/petersonspublishing 471

iBT). *Application deadline:* Applications are processed on a rolling basis. Application fee: $50 ($60 for international students). Electronic applications accepted. *Expenses:* Tuition, state resident: full-time $6978; part-time $290.75 per credit hour. Tuition, nonresident: full-time $15,282; part-time $636.75 per credit hour. *Required fees:* $2106; $87.75 per credit hour. *Financial support:* In 2011–12, fellowships with full tuition reimbursements (averaging $8,550 per year), research assistantships with full tuition reimbursements (averaging $8,550 per year), teaching assistantships with full tuition reimbursements (averaging $8,550 per year) were awarded; career-related internships or fieldwork, Federal Work-Study, scholarships/grants, health care benefits, and unspecified assistantships also available. Support available to part-time students. Financial award application deadline: 11/15; financial award applicants required to submit FAFSA. *Unit head:* Dr. Dennis Ruez, Program Administrator, 217-206-8424, E-mail: druez2@uis.edu. *Application contact:* Dr. Lynn Pardie, Office of Graduate Studies, 800-252-8533, Fax: 217-206-7623, E-mail: lpard1@uis.edu. Web site: http://www.uis.edu/environmentalstudies/.

University of Maine, Graduate School, College of Liberal Arts and Sciences, Department of History, Orono, ME 04469. Offers American studies (MA, PhD); Canadian studies (MA, PhD); East Asian (MA); environmental (MA); European (MA); technology (MA). *Faculty:* 11 full-time (1 woman), 2 part-time/adjunct (1 woman). *Students:* 24 full-time (8 women), 35 part-time (13 women); includes 4 minority (2 American Indian or Alaska Native, non-Hispanic/Latino; 2 Hispanic/Latino). Average age 38. 43 applicants, 40% accepted, 15 enrolled. In 2011, 5 master's, 3 doctorates awarded. Terminal master's awarded for partial completion of doctoral program. *Degree requirements:* For master's, variable foreign language requirement, thesis optional; for doctorate, one foreign language, thesis/dissertation. *Entrance requirements:* For master's and doctorate, GRE General Test. Additional exam requirements/recommendations for international students: Required—TOEFL. *Application deadline:* For fall admission, 2/1 priority date for domestic students. Applications are processed on a rolling basis. Application fee: $65. Electronic applications accepted. *Expenses:* Tuition, state resident: full-time $5016. Tuition, nonresident: full-time $14,424. *Financial support:* In 2011–12, 9 teaching assistantships with tuition reimbursements (averaging $12,790 per year) were awarded; career-related internships or fieldwork, Federal Work-Study, and tuition waivers (full and partial) also available. Support available to part-time students. Financial award application deadline: 3/1. *Faculty research:* Canadian labor and working classes; American social, cultural, and urban history. *Unit head:* Dr. Nathan Godfried, Chair, 207-581-1923, Fax: 207-581-1817. *Application contact:* Scott G. Delcourt, Associate Dean of the Graduate School, 207-581-3291, Fax: 207-581-3232, E-mail: graduate@maine.edu. Web site: http://www2.umaine.edu/graduate/.

The University of Manchester, School of Environment and Development, Manchester, United Kingdom. Offers architecture (M Phil, PhD); development policy and management (M Phil, PhD); human geography (M Phil, PhD); physical geography (M Phil, PhD); planning and landscape (M Phil, PhD).

University of Maryland, Baltimore County, Graduate School, College of Arts, Humanities and Social Sciences, Department of Geography and Environmental Systems, Program in Geography and Environmental Systems, Baltimore, MD 21250. Offers MS, PhD. *Faculty:* 11 full-time (4 women), 6 part-time/adjunct (1 woman). *Students:* 17 full-time (10 women), 15 part-time (12 women); includes 1 minority (Black or African American, non-Hispanic/Latino), 1 international. Average age 30. 30 applicants, 30% accepted, 6 enrolled. In 2011, 3 master's awarded. Terminal master's awarded for partial completion of doctoral program. *Degree requirements:* For master's, thesis optional, annual faculty evaluation, research paper; for doctorate, comprehensive exam, thesis/dissertation, annual faculty evaluation, qualifying exams, proposal and dissertation defense. *Entrance requirements:* For master's and doctorate, GRE, minimum GPA of 3.0 overall, 3.3 in major. Additional exam requirements/recommendations for international students: Required—TOEFL (minimum score 550 paper-based; 213 computer-based; 80 iBT). *Application deadline:* For fall admission, 2/1 for domestic and international students. Application fee: $50. Electronic applications accepted. *Financial support:* In 2011–12, 15 students received support, including 5 research assistantships with full tuition reimbursements available (averaging $18,392 per year), 10 teaching assistantships with full tuition reimbursements available (averaging $18,392 per year); fellowships, scholarships/grants, traineeships, health care benefits, and unspecified assistantships also available. Financial award application deadline: 2/1. *Faculty research:* Watershed processes, climate and weather systems; ecology and biogeography; landscape ecology and land-use change; human geography, urban sustainability and environmental health; environmental policy; geographic information science and remote sensing. *Unit head:* Dr. Christopher M. Swan, Graduate Program Director, 410-455-2002, E-mail: gpd.ges@umbc.edu. *Application contact:* Kathryn Nee, Coordinator of Domestic Admissions, 410-455-2944, E-mail: nee@umbc.edu. Web site: http://www.umbc.edu/ges/GES_graduate_program.html.

University of Maryland University College, Graduate School of Management and Technology, Program in Environmental Management, Adelphi, MD 20783. Offers MS, Certificate. Offered evenings and weekends only. Part-time and evening/weekend programs available. Postbaccalaureate distance learning degree programs offered (no on-campus study). *Students:* 11 full-time (5 women), 399 part-time (204 women); includes 119 minority (74 Black or African American, non-Hispanic/Latino; 4 American Indian or Alaska Native, non-Hispanic/Latino; 10 Asian, non-Hispanic/Latino; 24 Hispanic/Latino; 7 Two or more races, non-Hispanic/Latino), 8 international. Average age 35. 87 applicants, 100% accepted,

55 enrolled. In 2011, 84 master's, 20 other advanced degrees awarded. *Degree requirements:* For master's, thesis or alternative, capstone course. *Application deadline:* Applications are processed on a rolling basis. Application fee: $50. Electronic applications accepted. *Financial support:* Federal Work-Study and scholarships/grants available. Support available to part-time students. Financial award application deadline: 6/1; financial award applicants required to submit FAFSA. *Unit head:* Joyce Shirazi, Chair, Information Technology Management, 240-684-2400, Fax: 240-684-2401, E-mail: joyce.shirazi@umuc.edu. *Application contact:* Coordinator, Graduate Admissions, 800-888-8682, Fax: 240-684-2151, E-mail: newgrad@umuc.edu. Web site: http://www.umuc.edu/grad/envm.shtml.

University of Massachusetts Amherst, Graduate School, College of Natural Sciences, Department of Environmental Conservation, Amherst, MA 01003. Offers building systems (MS, PhD); environmental policy and human dimensions (MS, PhD); forest resources (MS, PhD); sustainability science (MS); water, wetlands and watersheds (MS, PhD); wildlife and fisheries conservation (MS, PhD). Part-time programs available. *Faculty:* 57 full-time (10 women). *Students:* 61 full-time (26 women), 34 part-time (13 women); includes 4 minority (1 Black or African American, non-Hispanic/Latino; 2 Hispanic/Latino; 1 Two or more races, non-Hispanic/Latino), 12 international. Average age 32. 84 applicants, 40% accepted, 22 enrolled. In 2011, 1 master's, 2 doctorates awarded. Terminal master's awarded for partial completion of doctoral program. *Degree requirements:* For master's, thesis or alternative; for doctorate, comprehensive exam, thesis/dissertation. *Entrance requirements:* For master's and doctorate, GRE General Test. Additional exam requirements/recommendations for international students: Required—TOEFL (minimum score 550 paper-based; 213 computer-based; 80 iBT), IELTS (minimum score 6.5). *Application deadline:* For fall admission, 2/1 for domestic and international students; for spring admission, 10/1 for domestic and international students. Applications are processed on a rolling basis. Application fee: $50 ($65 for international students). Electronic applications accepted. Tuition and fees vary according to course load, campus/location and program. *Financial support:* Fellowships with full and partial tuition reimbursements, research assistantships with full and partial tuition reimbursements, teaching assistantships with full and partial tuition reimbursements, career-related internships or fieldwork, Federal Work-Study, scholarships/grants, traineeships, health care benefits, tuition waivers (full and partial), and unspecified assistantships available. Support available to part-time students. Financial award application deadline: 2/1. *Unit head:* Dr. Kevin McGarigal, Graduate Program Director, 413-545-2257, Fax: 413-545-4358. *Application contact:* Lindsay DeSantis, Interim Supervisor of Admissions, 413-545-0721, Fax: 413-577-0100, E-mail: gradadm@grad.umass.edu. Web site: http://eco.umass.edu/.

University of Massachusetts Dartmouth, Graduate School, School of Education, Public Policy, and Civic Engagement, Department of Public Policy, North Dartmouth, MA 02747-2300. Offers educational policy (Postbaccalaureate Certificate); environmental policy (Postbaccalaureate Certificate); public policy (MPP). Part-time programs available. Postbaccalaureate distance learning degree programs offered (minimal on-campus study). *Faculty:* 8 full-time (2 women). *Students:* 12 full-time (10 women), 44 part-time (23 women); includes 12 minority (5 Black or African American, non-Hispanic/Latino; 1 American Indian or Alaska Native, non-Hispanic/Latino; 2 Asian, non-Hispanic/Latino; 3 Hispanic/Latino; 1 Two or more races, non-Hispanic/Latino), 1 international. Average age 34. 52 applicants, 98% accepted, 32 enrolled. In 2011, 6 master's, 11 other advanced degrees awarded. *Entrance requirements:* For master's and Postbaccalaureate Certificate, GRE or GMAT, 2 letters of recommendation, resume, statement of intent. Additional exam requirements/recommendations for international students: Required—TOEFL (minimum score 600 paper-based; 250 computer-based). *Application deadline:* For fall admission, 3/1 for domestic students, 2/1 for international students; for spring admission, 11/15 for domestic students, 10/15 for international students. Applications are processed on a rolling basis. Application fee: $40 ($60 for international students). Electronic applications accepted. *Expenses:* Tuition, state resident: full-time $2071; part-time $86.29 per credit. Tuition, nonresident: full-time $8099; part-time $337.46 per credit. *Required fees:* $438.58 per credit. Part-time tuition and fees vary according to class time, course load, degree level and reciprocity agreements. *Financial support:* In 2011–12, 3 research assistantships with full tuition reimbursements (averaging $6,916 per year), 1 teaching assistantship with full tuition reimbursement (averaging $6,000 per year) were awarded; Federal Work-Study and unspecified assistantships also available. Support available to part-time students. Financial award application deadline: 3/1. *Faculty research:* Demographic analysis, legal and regulatory framework. *Total annual research expenditures:* $123,168. *Unit head:* Dr. Michael Goodman, Graduate Program Director, 508-990-9660, Fax: 508-999-8374, E-mail: mgoodman@umassd.edu. *Application contact:* Elan Turcotte-Shamski, Graduate Admissions Officer, 508-999-8604, Fax: 508-999-8183, E-mail: graduate@umassd.edu. Web site: http://www.umassd.edu/seppce/publicpolicy/index.html.

University of Massachusetts Lowell, School of Health and Environment, Department of Work Environment, Lowell, MA 01854-2881. Offers cleaner production and pollution prevention (MS, Sc D); environmental risk assessment (Certificate); epidemiology (MS, Sc D); ergonomics and safety (MS, Sc D); identification and control of ergonomic hazards (Certificate); job stress and healthy job redesign (Certificate); occupational and environmental hygiene (MS, Sc D); radiological health physics and general work environment protection (Certificate); work environment policy (MS, Sc D). *Accreditation:* ABET (one or more programs are accredited). Part-time programs available. Terminal master's

472 facebook.com/petersonspublishing

Peterson's Graduate Programs in the Physical Sciences, Mathematics, Agricultural Sciences, the Environment & Natural Resources 2013

awarded for partial completion of doctoral program. *Degree requirements:* For master's, thesis optional; for doctorate, thesis/dissertation. *Entrance requirements:* For master's and doctorate, GRE General Test. Additional exam requirements/recommendations for international students: Required—TOEFL.

University of Miami, Graduate School, School of Business Administration, Department of Economics, Coral Gables, FL 33124. Offers economic development (MA, PhD); environmental economics (PhD); human resource economics (MA, PhD); international economics (MA, PhD); macroeconomics (PhD). Students admitted every two years in the fall semester. Terminal master's awarded for partial completion of doctoral program. *Degree requirements:* For master's, comprehensive exam; for doctorate, comprehensive exam, thesis/dissertation. *Entrance requirements:* For master's and doctorate, GRE General Test, minimum GPA of 3.0. Additional exam requirements/recommendations for international students: Required—TOEFL (minimum score 550 paper-based). *Faculty research:* International economics/trade, applied microeconomics, development.

University of Michigan, School of Natural Resources and Environment, Program in Natural Resources and Environment, Ann Arbor, MI 48109. Offers aquatic sciences: research and management (MS); behavior, education and communication (MS); conservation biology (MS); conservation ecology (MS); environmental informatics (MS); environmental justice (MS); environmental policy and planning (MS); natural resources and environment (PhD); sustainable systems (MS); terrestrial ecosystems (MS); MS/JD; MS/MBA; MUP/MS. *Faculty:* 45 full-time, 23 part-time/adjunct. *Students:* 450 full-time (254 women); includes 63 minority (7 Black or African American, non-Hispanic/Latino; 2 American Indian or Alaska Native, non-Hispanic/Latino; 35 Asian, non-Hispanic/Latino; 13 Hispanic/Latino; 6 Two or more races, non-Hispanic/Latino; 70 international. Average age 27. 643 applicants. In 2011, 133 master's, 11 doctorates awarded. Terminal master's awarded for partial completion of doctoral program. *Degree requirements:* For master's, practicum or group project; for doctorate, comprehensive exam, thesis/dissertation, oral defense of dissertation, preliminary exam. *Entrance requirements:* For master's, GRE General Test; for doctorate, GRE General Test, master's degree. Additional exam requirements/recommendations for international students: Required—TOEFL (minimum score 560 paper-based; 220 computer-based; 84 iBT). *Application deadline:* For fall admission, 1/5 priority date for domestic students, 1/5 for international students. Applications are processed on a rolling basis. Application fee: $65 ($75 for international students). Electronic applications accepted. *Financial support:* Fellowships with tuition reimbursements, research assistantships with tuition reimbursements, teaching assistantships with tuition reimbursements, career-related internships or fieldwork, Federal Work-Study, institutionally sponsored loans, scholarships/grants, health care benefits, and unspecified assistantships available. Support available to part-time students. Financial award application deadline: 1/5; financial award applicants required to submit FAFSA. *Faculty research:* Stream ecology, plant-insect interactions, fish biology, resource control and reproductive success, remote sensing, conservation ecology. *Unit head:* Dr. Marie Lynn Miranda, Dean, 734-764-2550, Fax: 734-763-8965, E-mail: mlmirand@umich.edu. *Application contact:* Adam D. Ancira, Graduate Admissions Team, 734-764-6453, Fax: 734-936-2195, E-mail: snre.admissions@umich.edu. Web site: http://www.snre.umich.edu/.

University of Minnesota, Twin Cities Campus, Graduate School, Hubert H. Humphrey School of Public Affairs, Program in Science, Technology, and Environmental Policy, Minneapolis, MN 55455-0213. Offers MS, JD/MS. Part-time programs available. *Degree requirements:* For master's, thesis. *Entrance requirements:* For master's, GRE General Test, undergraduate training in the biological or physical sciences or engineering, minimum undergraduate GPA of 3.0. Additional exam requirements/recommendations for international students: Required—TOEFL (minimum score 600 paper-based; 250 computer-based; 100 iBT). Electronic applications accepted. *Faculty research:* Economics, history, philosophy, and politics of science and technology; organization and management of science and technology.

The University of Montana, Graduate School, College of Arts and Sciences, Program in Environmental Studies (EVST), Missoula, MT 59812-0002. Offers MS, JD/MS. Part-time programs available. *Faculty:* 5 full-time (2 women), 3 part-time/adjunct (1 woman). *Students:* 33 full-time (25 women), 21 part-time (15 women); includes 1 minority (Hispanic/Latino). Average age 30. 60 applicants, 70% accepted, 21 enrolled. In 2011, 19 degrees awarded. *Degree requirements:* For master's, thesis, portfolio or professional paper. *Entrance requirements:* For master's, GRE General Test (minimum score: 500 verbal for tests taken prior to August 2011; 153 verbal for tests taken after August 2011). Additional exam requirements/recommendations for international students: Required—TOEFL (minimum score 580 paper-based; 237 computer-based; 92 iBT). *Application deadline:* For fall admission, 2/1 priority date for domestic students, 2/1 for international students. Application fee: $51. *Financial support:* In 2011–12, 21 students received support, including 3 fellowships with partial tuition reimbursements available (averaging $5,000 per year), 1 research assistantship with full tuition reimbursement available (averaging $2,100 per year), 6 teaching assistantships with full tuition reimbursements available (averaging $9,000 per year). Financial award application deadline: 4/15. *Faculty research:* Pollution ecology, sustainable agriculture, environmental writing, environmental policy, environmental justice, habitat-land management. *Total annual research expenditures:* $119,595. *Unit head:* Dr. Len Broberg, Director, 406-243-5209, Fax: 406-243-6090, E-mail: len.broberg@mso.umt.edu. *Application contact:*

Karen Hurd, Administrative Assistant, 406-243-6273, Fax: 406-243-6090, E-mail: karen.hurd@mso.umt.edu. Web site: http://www.cas.umt.edu/evst.

University of Nevada, Reno, Graduate School, College of Science, Mackay School of Earth Sciences and Engineering, Department of Geography, Program in Land Use Planning, Reno, NV 89557. Offers MS. *Degree requirements:* For master's, thesis. *Entrance requirements:* For master's, GRE General Test, minimum GPA of 3.0. Additional exam requirements/recommendations for international students: Required—TOEFL (minimum score 500 paper-based; 173 computer-based; 61 iBT), IELTS (minimum score 6). Electronic applications accepted. *Faculty research:* Contemporary planning, environmental planning.

University of New Brunswick Fredericton, School of Graduate Studies, Faculty of Engineering, Department of Chemical Engineering, Fredericton, NB E3B 5A3, Canada. Offers chemical engineering (M Eng, M Sc E, PhD); environmental studies (M Eng). Part-time programs available. *Faculty:* 11 full-time (3 women), 1 part-time/adjunct (0 women). *Students:* 63 full-time (25 women), 4 part-time (1 woman). In 2011, 15 master's, 1 doctorate awarded. *Degree requirements:* For master's, thesis; for doctorate, comprehensive exam, thesis/dissertation, qualifying exam. *Entrance requirements:* For master's and doctorate, minimum GPA of 3.0. Additional exam requirements/recommendations for international students: Required—TOEFL (minimum score 580 paper-based), TWE (minimum score 4). *Application deadline:* For fall admission, 3/1 priority date for domestic students. Application fee: $50 Canadian dollars. Electronic applications accepted. *Financial support:* In 2011–12, 60 fellowships, 5 research assistantships with tuition reimbursements (averaging $18,000 per year), 51 teaching assistantships (averaging $1,500 per year) were awarded. *Faculty research:* Processing and characterizing nanoengineered composite materials based on carbon nanotubes, enhanced oil recovery processes and oil sweep strategies for conventional and heavy oils, pulp and paper, waste-water treatment, chemistry and corrosion of high and lower temperature water systems. *Unit head:* Dr. Kecheng Li, Director of Graduate Studies, 506-451-6861, Fax: 506-453-3591, E-mail: kecheng@unb.ca. *Application contact:* Sylvia Demerson, Graduate Secretary, 506-453-4520, Fax: 506-453-3591, E-mail: sdemerso@unb.ca. Web site: http://www.unbf.ca/eng/che/

University of New Brunswick Fredericton, School of Graduate Studies, Faculty of Engineering, Department of Civil Engineering, Fredericton, NB E3B 5A3, Canada. Offers construction engineering and management (M Eng, M Sc E, PhD); environmental engineering (M Eng, M Sc E, PhD); environmental studies (M Eng); geotechnical engineering (M Eng, M Sc E, PhD); groundwater/hydrology (M Eng, M Sc E, PhD); materials (M Eng, M Sc E, PhD); pavements (M Eng, M Sc E, PhD); structures (M Eng, M Sc E, PhD); transportation (M Eng, M Sc E, PhD). Part-time programs available. *Faculty:* 13 full-time (1 woman), 7 part-time/adjunct (1 woman). *Students:* 31 full-time (7 women), 17 part-time (2 women). In 2011, 11 master's, 2 doctorates awarded. *Degree requirements:* For master's, thesis, proposal; for doctorate, comprehensive exam, thesis/dissertation, qualifying exam; proposal; 27 credit hours of courses. *Entrance requirements:* For master's, minimum GPA of 3.0; B Sc E in civil engineering or related engineering degree; for doctorate, minimum GPA of 3.0; graduate degree in engineering or applied science. Additional exam requirements/recommendations for international students: Required—TWE (minimum score 4), TOEFL (minimum score 580 paper-based; 237 computer-based) or IELTS (minimum score 7.5). *Application deadline:* For fall admission, 5/1 priority date for domestic students; for winter admission, 11/1 priority date for domestic students. Applications are processed on a rolling basis. Application fee: $50 Canadian dollars. *Financial support:* In 2011–12, 14 fellowships, 30 research assistantships (averaging $7,000 per year), 42 teaching assistantships (averaging $2,000 per year) were awarded; career-related internships or fieldwork and scholarships/grants also available. *Faculty research:* Construction engineering and management; materials and infrastructure renewal; highway and pavement research; structures and solid mechanics; geotechnical, soil; structure interaction; transportation and planning; environment, solid waste management. *Unit head:* Dr. Eric Hildebrand, Director of Graduate Studies, 506-453-5113, Fax: 506-453-3568, E-mail: edh@unb.ca. *Application contact:* Joyce Moore, Graduate Secretary, 506-452-6127, Fax: 506-453-3568, E-mail: civil-grad@unb.ca. Web site: http://www.unbf.ca/eng/civil/.

University of New Brunswick Fredericton, School of Graduate Studies, Faculty of Forestry and Environmental Management, Fredericton, NB E3B 5A3, Canada. Offers ecological foundations of forest management (PhD); environmental management (MEM); forest engineering (M Sc FE, MFE); forest products marketing (MBA); forest resources (M Sc F, MF, PhD). Part-time programs available. *Faculty:* 22 full-time (3 women), 1 part-time/adjunct (0 women). *Students:* 72 full-time (27 women), 15 part-time (12 women). In 2011, 13 master's, 4 doctorates awarded. *Degree requirements:* For master's, thesis; for doctorate, thesis/dissertation. *Entrance requirements:* For master's and doctorate, minimum GPA of 3.0. Additional exam requirements/recommendations for international students: Required—TWE (minimum score 4), TOEFL (minimum score 580 paper-based) or IELTS. *Application deadline:* For fall admission, 3/1 priority date for domestic students. Application fee: $50 Canadian dollars. Electronic applications accepted. *Financial support:* In 2011–12, 55 fellowships, 34 teaching assistantships were awarded. *Faculty research:* Forest machines, soils, and ecosystems; integrated forest management; forest meteorology; wood engineering; stream ecosystems dynamics; forest and natural resources policy; forest operations planning; wood technology and mechanics; forest road construction and engineering; forest, wildlife, insect, bird, and fire ecology; remote sensing; insect impacts; Silviculture; LiDAR analytics; integrated pest

Peterson's Graduate Programs in the Physical Sciences, Mathematics, Agricultural Sciences, the Environment & Natural Resources 2013

facebook.com/petersonspublishing **473**

management; forest tree genetics; genetic resource conservation and sustainable management. *Unit head:* Dr. John Kershaw, Director of Graduate Studies, 506-453-4933, Fax: 506-453-3538, E-mail: kershaw@unb.ca. *Application contact:* Faith Sharpe, Graduate Secretary, 506-458-7520, Fax: 506-453-3538, E-mail: fsharpe@unb.ca. Web site: http://www.unb.ca/fredericton/forestry/.

University of New Hampshire, Graduate School, College of Life Sciences and Agriculture, Department of Natural Resources, Durham, NH 03824. Offers environmental conservation (MS); forestry (MS); integrated coastal ecosystem science, policy, management (MS); natural resources (MS); water resources (MS); wildlife (MS). Part-time programs available. *Faculty:* 40 full-time. *Students:* 32 full-time (15 women), 24 part-time (13 women); includes 2 minority (1 Asian, non-Hispanic/Latino; 1 Hispanic/Latino), 1 international. Average age 29. 79 applicants, 49% accepted, 20 enrolled. In 2011, 10 master's awarded. *Degree requirements:* For master's, thesis or alternative. *Entrance requirements:* For master's, GRE General Test. Additional exam requirements/recommendations for international students: Required—TOEFL (minimum score 550 paper-based; 213 computer-based; 80 iBT). *Application deadline:* For fall admission, 6/1 for domestic students, 4/1 for international students; for spring admission, 12/1 for domestic students. Applications are processed on a rolling basis. Application fee: $65. Electronic applications accepted. *Expenses:* Tuition, state resident: full-time $12,360; part-time $687 per credit hour. Tuition, nonresident: full-time $25,680; part-time $1058 per credit hour. *International tuition:* $29,550 full-time. *Required fees:* $1666; $833 per course. $416.50 per semester. Tuition and fees vary according to course load and degree level. *Financial support:* In 2011–12, 35 students received support, including 3 fellowships, 13 research assistantships, 17 teaching assistantships; career-related internships or fieldwork, Federal Work-Study, scholarships/grants, and tuition waivers (full and partial) also available. Support available to part-time students. Financial award application deadline: 2/15. *Unit head:* Dr. Ted Howard, Chairperson, 603-862-2700, E-mail: natural.resources@unh.edu. *Application contact:* Nancy Brown, Administrative Assistant, 603-862-1022, E-mail: natural.resources@unh.edu. Web site: http://www.nre.unh.edu/academics/.

University of New Haven, Graduate School, College of Arts and Sciences, Program in Environmental Sciences, West Haven, CT 06516-1916. Offers environmental geoscience (MS); environmental health and management (MS); environmental science (MS); geographical information systems (Certificate). Part-time and evening/weekend programs available. *Students:* 19 full-time (11 women), 15 part-time (6 women); includes 5 minority (2 Black or African American, non-Hispanic/Latino; 1 Asian, non-Hispanic/Latino; 1 Hispanic/Latino; 1 Two or more races, non-Hispanic/Latino), 7 international. 9 applicants, 100% accepted, 5 enrolled. In 2011, 9 master's awarded. *Degree requirements:* For master's, thesis or alternative. *Application deadline:* For fall admission, 5/31 for international students; for winter admission, 10/15 for international students; for spring admission, 1/15 for international students. Applications are processed on a rolling basis. Application fee: $50. Electronic applications accepted. *Expenses:* Tuition: Part-time $750 per credit. *Financial support:* Research assistantships with partial tuition reimbursements, teaching assistantships with partial tuition reimbursements, career-related internships or fieldwork, Federal Work-Study, scholarships/grants, tuition waivers, and unspecified assistantships available. Support available to part-time students. Financial award applicants required to submit FAFSA. *Faculty research:* Mapping and assessing geological and living resources in Long Island Sound, geology, San Salvador Island, Bahamas. *Unit head:* Dr. Roman Zajac, Coordinator, 203-932-7108, E-mail: rzajac@newhaven.edu. *Application contact:* Eloise Gormley, Director of Graduate Admissions, 203-932-7449, Fax: 203-932-7137, E-mail: gradinfo@newhaven.edu. Web site: http://www.newhaven.edu/4728/.

University of New Mexico, Graduate School, Water Resources Program, Albuquerque, NM 87131-2039. Offers hydroscience (MWR); policy management (MWR). Part-time programs available. *Faculty:* 1 full-time (0 women). *Students:* 16 full-time (12 women), 33 part-time (18 women); includes 16 minority (1 Black or African American, non-Hispanic/Latino; 6 American Indian or Alaska Native, non-Hispanic/Latino; 2 Asian, non-Hispanic/Latino; 6 Hispanic/Latino; 1 Two or more races, non-Hispanic/Latino). Average age 36. 29 applicants, 62% accepted, 11 enrolled. In 2011, 8 degrees awarded. *Degree requirements:* For master's, professional project. *Entrance requirements:* For master's, minimum GPA of 3.0 during last 2 years of undergraduate work, 3 letters of reference. Additional exam requirements/recommendations for international students: Required—TOEFL (minimum score 550 paper-based; 213 computer-based). *Application deadline:* For fall admission, 7/15 for domestic students; for spring admission, 11/15 for domestic students. Applications are processed on a rolling basis. Application fee: $50. Electronic applications accepted. *Financial support:* In 2011–12, 24 students received support, including 3 research assistantships with full and partial tuition reimbursements available (averaging $5,791 per year); career-related internships or fieldwork, institutionally sponsored loans, scholarships/grants, and unspecified assistantships also available. Financial award application deadline: 3/1; financial award applicants required to submit FAFSA. *Faculty research:* Sustainable water resources, transboundary water resources, economics, water law, hydrology, developing countries, hydrogeology. *Total annual research expenditures:* $150,557. *Unit head:* Dr. Bruce M. Thomson, Director, 505-277-5249, Fax: 505-277-5226, E-mail: bthomson@unm.edu. *Application contact:* Annamarie Cordova, Administrative Assistant II, 505-277-7759, Fax: 505-277-5226, E-mail: acordova@unm.edu. Web site: http://www.unm.edu/~wrp/.

The University of North Carolina at Chapel Hill, Graduate School, School of Public Health, Department of Environmental Sciences and Engineering, Chapel Hill, NC 27599. Offers air, radiation and industrial hygiene (MPH, MS, MSEE, MSPH, PhD); aquatic and atmospheric sciences (MPH, MS, MSPH, PhD); environmental engineering (MPH, MS, MSEE, MSPH, PhD); environmental health sciences (MPH, MS, MSPH, PhD); environmental management and policy (MPH, MS, MSPH, PhD). Terminal master's awarded for partial completion of doctoral program. *Degree requirements:* For master's, comprehensive exam, thesis (for some programs), research paper; for doctorate, comprehensive exam, thesis/dissertation. *Entrance requirements:* For master's and doctorate, GRE General Test, minimum GPA of 3.0. Additional exam requirements/recommendations for international students: Required—TOEFL. Electronic applications accepted. *Faculty research:* Air, radiation and industrial hygiene, aquatic and atmospheric sciences, environmental health sciences, environmental management and policy, water resources engineering.

The University of North Carolina Wilmington, College of Arts and Sciences, Department of Environmental Studies, Wilmington, NC 28403-3297. Offers coastal management (MA); environmental education and interpretation (MA); environmental management (MA); individualized study (MA). Part-time programs available. *Degree requirements:* For master's, comprehensive exam, thesis or alternative, final project, practicum. *Entrance requirements:* For master's, GRE, 3 letters of recommendation. Additional exam requirements/recommendations for international students: Required—TOEFL (minimum score 550 paper-based; 217 computer-based; 79 iBT), IELTS (minimum score 6.5). Electronic applications accepted. *Faculty research:* Coastal management, environmental management, environmental education, environmental law, natural resource management.

University of Northern British Columbia, Office of Graduate Studies, Prince George, BC V2N 4Z9, Canada. Offers business administration (Diploma); community health science (M Sc); disability management (MA); education (M Ed); first nations studies (MA); gender studies (MA); history (MA); interdisciplinary studies (MA); international studies (MA); mathematical, computer and physical sciences (M Sc); natural resources and environmental studies (M Sc, MA, MNRES, PhD); political science (MA); psychology (M Sc, PhD); social work (MSW). Part-time and evening/weekend programs available. Postbaccalaureate distance learning degree programs offered (no on-campus study). *Degree requirements:* For master's, thesis; for doctorate, thesis/dissertation. *Entrance requirements:* For master's, GRE, minimum B average in undergraduate course work; for doctorate, candidacy exam, minimum A average in graduate course work.

University of Oregon, Graduate School, College of Arts and Sciences, Environmental Studies Program, Eugene, OR 97403. Offers environmental science, studies, and policy (PhD); environmental studies (MA, MS). *Degree requirements:* For master's, one foreign language, thesis; for doctorate, comprehensive exam, thesis/dissertation. *Entrance requirements:* For master's, GRE General Test, minimum GPA of 3.0; for doctorate, GRE General Test. Additional exam requirements/recommendations for international students: Required—TOEFL (minimum score 550 paper-based; 213 computer-based). Electronic applications accepted.

University of Pennsylvania, School of Arts and Sciences, College of Liberal and Professional Studies, Philadelphia, PA 19104. Offers environmental studies (MES); individualized study (MLA). *Students:* 151 full-time (84 women), 353 part-time (222 women); includes 81 minority (30 Black or African American, non-Hispanic/Latino; 1 American Indian or Alaska Native, non-Hispanic/Latino; 24 Asian, non-Hispanic/Latino; 12 Hispanic/Latino; 14 Two or more races, non-Hispanic/Latino), 57 international. 654 applicants, 55% accepted, 278 enrolled. In 2011, 195 degrees awarded. *Application deadline:* For fall admission, 12/1 priority date for domestic students. Application fee: $70. Electronic applications accepted. *Expenses: Tuition:* Full-time $26,660; part-time $4944 per course. *Required fees:* $2318; $291 per course. Tuition and fees vary according to course load, degree level and program. *Unit head:* Dr. Kristine Billmyer, Associate Dean/Director, 215-898-8681, E-mail: gdasdmis@sas.upenn.edu. *Application contact:* Patricia Rea, Coordinator for Admissions, 215-573-5816, Fax: 215-573-8068, E-mail: gdasadmis@sas.upenn.edu.

University of Pittsburgh, Graduate School of Public and International Affairs, Division of International Development, Pittsburgh, PA 15260. Offers development planning and environmental sustainability (MID); human security (MID); nongovernmental organizations and civil society (MID); MID/JD; MID/MBA; MID/MPH; MID/MPIA; MID/MSIS; MID/MSW; MPA/MID. Part-time programs available. *Faculty:* 26 full-time (12 women), 47 part-time/adjunct (19 women). *Students:* 76 full-time (54 women), 10 part-time (7 women); includes 14 minority (1 Black or African American, non-Hispanic/Latino; 2 Asian, non-Hispanic/Latino; 9 Hispanic/Latino; 1 Native Hawaiian or other Pacific Islander, non-Hispanic/Latino; 1 Two or more races, non-Hispanic/Latino), 10 international. Average age 25. 122 applicants, 70% accepted, 31 enrolled. In 2011, 29 master's awarded. *Degree requirements:* For master's, thesis optional, internship, capstone seminar. *Entrance requirements:* For master's, GRE General Test, 3 letters of recommendation; minimum GPA of 3.2 (recommended). Additional exam requirements/recommendations for international students: Required—TOEFL (minimum score 550 paper-based; 213 computer-based; 80 iBT), TWE (minimum score 4); Recommended—IELTS (minimum score 7). *Application deadline:* For fall admission, 2/1 for domestic students, 1/5 for international students; for spring admission, 11/1 for domestic students, 8/1 for international students. Application fee: $50. Electronic applications accepted. *Expenses:* Tuition, state resident: full-

474 facebook.com/petersonspublishing

Peterson's Graduate Programs in the Physical Sciences, Mathematics, Agricultural Sciences, the Environment & Natural Resources 2013

time $18,774; part-time $760 per credit. Tuition, nonresident: full-time $30,736; part-time $1258 per credit. *Required fees:* $740 per term. Tuition and fees vary according to program. *Financial support:* In 2011–12, 28 students received support. Scholarships/grants, tuition waivers (full and partial), unspecified assistantships, and student employment available. Financial award application deadline: 2/1. *Faculty research:* Nongovernmental organizations, religion and civil society, international development, development economics and policy, human rights and development, humanitarian intervention, ethnic conflict and civil war, post-conflict peace-building, corruption and transnational governance, civil society and public affairs, political constraints on rural development. *Total annual research expenditures:* $892,349. *Unit head:* Dr. Paul J. Nelson, Director, 412-648-7645, Fax: 412-648-2605, E-mail: pjnelson@pitt.edu. *Application contact:* Elizabeth Hruby, Graduate Enrollment Counselor, 412-648-7640, Fax: 412-648-7641, E-mail: eah44@pitt.edu. Web site: http://www.gspia.pitt.edu/.

University of Puerto Rico, Río Piedras, Graduate School of Planning, San Juan, PR 00931-3300. Offers economic planning systems (MP); environmental planning (MP); social policy and planning (MP); urban and territorial planning (MP). *Accreditation:* ACSP. Part-time programs available. *Degree requirements:* For master's, comprehensive exam, thesis, planning project defense. *Entrance requirements:* For master's, PAEG, GRE, minimum GPA of 3.0, 2 letters of recommendation. *Faculty research:* Municipalities, historic Atlas, Puerto Rico, economic future.

University of Rhode Island, Graduate School, College of the Environment and Life Sciences, Department of Environmental and Natural Resource Economics, Kingston, RI 02881. Offers MESM, MS, PhD. Part-time programs available. *Faculty:* 7 full-time (2 women). *Students:* 37 full-time (17 women), 4 part-time (2 women); includes 2 minority (1 Asian, non-Hispanic/Latino; 1 Hispanic/Latino), 15 international. In 2011, 3 doctorates awarded. *Degree requirements:* For master's, comprehensive exam (for some programs), thesis optional; for doctorate, comprehensive exam, thesis/dissertation. *Entrance requirements:* For master's, GRE, 2 letters of recommendation; for doctorate, GRE, 3 letters of recommendation. Additional exam requirements/recommendations for international students: Required—TOEFL (minimum score 550 paper-based; 213 computer-based). *Application deadline:* For fall admission, 7/15 for domestic students, 2/1 for international students; for spring admission, 11/15 for domestic students, 7/15 for international students. Application fee: $65. Electronic applications accepted. *Expenses:* Tuition, state resident: full-time $10,432; part-time $580 per credit hour. Tuition, nonresident: full-time $23,130; part-time $1285 per credit hour. *Required fees:* $1362; $36 per credit hour. $35 per semester. One-time fee: $130. *Financial support:* In 2011–12, 2 research assistantships with partial tuition reimbursements (averaging $10,698 per year), 6 teaching assistantships with full and partial tuition reimbursements (averaging $11,113 per year) were awarded. Financial award application deadline: 7/15; financial award applicants required to submit FAFSA. *Faculty research:* Policy Simulation Laboratory: utilizes computer technologies to help understand the consequences of policy actions, experimental economics. *Unit head:* Dr. James Opaluch, Chair, 401-874-4590, Fax: 401-874-4766, E-mail: jimo@uri.edu. *Application contact:* Dr. James Opaluch, Graduate Admission Committee, 401-874-4590, Fax: 401-874-4766, E-mail: jimo@uri.edu. Web site: http://www.uri.edu/cels/enre/.

University of Rochester, Hajim School of Engineering and Applied Sciences, Center for Entrepreneurship, Rochester, NY 14627-0360. Offers technical entrepreneurship and management (TEAM) (MS), including biomedical engineering, chemical engineering, computer science, electrical and computer engineering, energy and the environment, materials science, mechanical engineering, optics. *Faculty:* 61 full-time (8 women), 5 part-time/adjunct (1 woman). *Students:* 18 full-time (5 women), 3 part-time (1 woman); includes 4 minority (1 Asian, non-Hispanic/Latino; 3 Hispanic/Latino), 12 international. Average age 23. 134 applicants, 48% accepted, 21 enrolled. *Degree requirements:* For master's, comprehensive exam. *Entrance requirements:* For master's, GRE or GMAT, technical concentration of interest, 3 letters of recommendation, personal statement, official transcript. Additional exam requirements/recommendations for international students: Required—TOEFL or IELTS. *Application deadline:* For fall admission, 2/1 for domestic and international students. Applications are processed on a rolling basis. Application fee: $60. Electronic applications accepted. *Expenses: Tuition:* Full-time $41,040. *Financial support:* Career-related internships or fieldwork and scholarships/grants available. Financial award application deadline: 2/1. *Faculty research:* High efficiency solar cells, macromolecular self-assembly, digital signal processing, memory hierarchy management, molecular and physical mechanisms in cell migration. *Unit head:* Duncan T. Moore, Vice Provost for Entrepreneurship, 585-275-5248, Fax: 585-473-6745, E-mail: moore@optics.rochester.edu. *Application contact:* Andrea M. Galati, Executive Director, 585-276-3407, Fax: 585-276-2357, E-mail: andrea.galati@rochester.edu. Web site: http://www.rochester.edu/team.

University of South Africa, College of Agriculture and Environmental Sciences, Pretoria, South Africa. Offers agriculture (MS); consumer science (MCS); environmental management (MA, MS, PhD); environmental science (MA, MS, PhD); geography (MA, MS, PhD); horticulture (M Tech); human ecology (MHE); life sciences (MS); nature conservation (M Tech).

University of South Carolina, The Graduate School, School of the Environment, Program in Earth and Environmental Resources Management, Columbia, SC 29208. Offers MEERM, JD/MEERM. Part-time programs available. Postbaccalaureate distance learning degree programs offered (no on-campus study). *Degree requirements:* For master's, thesis optional. *Entrance*

requirements: For master's, GRE General Test. Additional exam requirements/recommendations for international students: Required—TOEFL. Electronic applications accepted. *Faculty research:* Hydrology, sustainable development, environmental geology and engineering, energy/environmental resources management.

University of South Florida, Graduate School, College of Arts and Sciences, Department of Geography, Tampa, FL 33620-9951. Offers environmental science and policy (MS); geography (MA); geography and environmental science and policy (PhD); urban and regional planning (MURP). Part-time and evening/weekend programs available. *Faculty:* 19 full-time (6 women), 7 part-time/adjunct (3 women). *Students:* 20 full-time (7 women), 13 part-time (5 women); includes 10 minority (4 Black or African American, non-Hispanic/Latino; 1 American Indian or Alaska Native, non-Hispanic/Latino; 1 Asian, non-Hispanic/Latino; 3 Hispanic/Latino; 1 Two or more races, non-Hispanic/Latino), 1 international. Average age 31. 37 applicants, 59% accepted, 8 enrolled. In 2011, 5 master's awarded. *Degree requirements:* For master's, comprehensive exam, thesis; for doctorate, comprehensive exam, thesis/dissertation. *Entrance requirements:* For master's, GRE General Test, minimum GPA of 3.0, letter of intent, two letters of recommendation (three for MS); for doctorate, GRE General Test, minimum GPA of 3.2 in last 60 hours, letter of intent, two letters of recommendation. Additional exam requirements/recommendations for international students: Required—TOEFL (minimum score 600 paper-based; 213 computer-based), TOEFL (minimum score 550 paper-based, 213 computer-based, 79 iBT) or IELTS (minimum score 6.5); TOEFL (minimum score 600 paper-based) for ESP MS and PhD. *Application deadline:* For fall admission, 2/15 for domestic students, 1/2 for international students; for spring admission, 10/15 for domestic students, 6/1 for international students. Application fee: $30. *Financial support:* In 2011–12, 28 students received support, including 3 research assistantships (averaging $12,345 per year), 25 teaching assistantships with tuition reimbursements available (averaging $12,807 per year); unspecified assistantships also available. Financial award application deadline: 3/1. *Faculty research:* Natural hazards, geographic information systems models, soil contamination, urban geography and social theory. *Total annual research expenditures:* $143,091. *Unit head:* Dr. Kevin Archer, Chair, 813-974-4843, Fax: 813-974-4808, E-mail: karcher2@usf.edu. *Application contact:* Dr. Jennifer Collins, Program Director, 813-974-4242, Fax: 813-974-4808, E-mail: collinsjm@usf.edu. Web site: http://gep.usf.edu/.

University of South Florida–St. Petersburg Campus, College of Arts and Sciences, St. Petersburg, FL 33701. Offers digital journalism and design (MA); environmental science and policy (MA, MS); Florida studies (MLA); journalism and media studies (MA); liberal studies (MLA); psychology (MA). Part-time programs available. *Students:* 36 full-time (19 women), 76 part-time (47 women); includes 16 minority (9 Black or African American, non-Hispanic/Latino; 1 Asian, non-Hispanic/Latino; 2 Hispanic/Latino; 4 Two or more races, non-Hispanic/Latino), 1 international. Average age 34. 72 applicants, 53% accepted, 28 enrolled. In 2011, 23 master's awarded. *Degree requirements:* For master's, comprehensive exam, thesis or project. *Entrance requirements:* For master's, GRE, LSAT, MCAT (varies by program), letter of intent, 3 letters of recommendation, writing samples, bachelor's degree from regionally-accredited institution with minimum GPA of 3.0 overall or in upper two years. Additional exam requirements/recommendations for international students: Required—TOEFL (minimum score 550 paper-based; 79 iBT); Recommended—IELTS. *Application deadline:* For fall admission, 6/1 priority date for domestic students, 3/15 for international students; for spring admission, 10/15 priority date for domestic students, 6/1 for international students. Applications are processed on a rolling basis. Application fee: $30. Electronic applications accepted. *Expenses:* Tuition, state resident: full-time $8847. Tuition, nonresident: full-time $18,423. One-time fee: $35 full-time. Full-time tuition and fees vary according to course load and program. *Financial support:* Applicants required to submit FAFSA. *Unit head:* Dr. Frank A. Biafora, Dean, 727-873-4156, E-mail: fbiafora@usfsp.edu. *Application contact:* Eric Douthirt, Enrollment Management Specialist, 727-873-4567, Fax: 727-873-4889, E-mail: douthirt@usfsp.edu. Web site: http://www.usfsp.edu/coas/

The University of Tennessee, Graduate School, College of Arts and Sciences, Department of Sociology, Knoxville, TN 37996. Offers criminology (MA, PhD); energy, environment, and resource policy (MA, PhD); political economy (MA, PhD). Part-time programs available. *Degree requirements:* For master's, thesis or alternative; for doctorate, thesis/dissertation. *Entrance requirements:* For master's, GRE General Test, minimum GPA of 3.0; for doctorate, GRE General Test, minimum GPA of 3.5. Additional exam requirements/recommendations for international students: Required—TOEFL. Electronic applications accepted. *Expenses:* Tuition, state resident: full-time $8332; part-time $464 per credit hour. Tuition, nonresident: full-time $25,174; part-time $1400 per credit hour. *Required fees:* $1162; $56 per credit hour. Tuition and fees vary according to program.

The University of Texas at Austin, Graduate School, College of Liberal Arts, Teresa Lozano Long Institute of Latin American Studies, Austin, TX 78712-1111. Offers cultural politics of Afro-Latin and indigenous peoples (MA); development studies (MA); environmental studies (MA); human rights (MA); Latin American and international law (LL M); JD/MA; MA/MA; MBA/MA; MP Aff/MA; MSCRP/MA. LL M offered jointly with The University of Texas School of Law. *Entrance requirements:* For master's, GRE General Test. Application fee: $50 ($75 for international students). *Financial support:* Fellowships available. Financial award application deadline: 2/1. *Unit head:* Charles R. Hale, Director, 512-471-7530, E-mail: crhale@mail.utexas.edu. *Application contact:* Dr. Henry Dietz, Graduate

Peterson's Graduate Programs in the Physical Sciences, Mathematics, Agricultural Sciences, the Environment & Natural Resources 2013

facebook.com/petersonspublishing **475**

Environmental Management and Policy

Adviser, 512-471-8770, E-mail: dietz@mail.utexas.edu. Web site: http://www.utexas.edu/cola/insts/llilas/.

University of Washington, Graduate School, Interdisciplinary Graduate Program in Quantitative Ecology and Resource Management, Seattle, WA 98195. Offers MS, PhD. *Degree requirements:* For master's, thesis; for doctorate, thesis/dissertation. *Entrance requirements:* For master's and doctorate, GRE General Test, minimum GPA of 3.0. Additional exam requirements/recommendations for international students: Required—TOEFL. Electronic applications accepted. *Faculty research:* Population dynamics, statistical analysis, ecological modeling and systems analysis of aquatic and terrestrial ecosystems.

University of Waterloo, Graduate Studies, Faculty of Environment, Department of Environment and Resource Studies, Waterloo, ON N2L 3G1, Canada. Offers MES. Part-time programs available. *Degree requirements:* For master's, thesis. *Entrance requirements:* For master's, honors degree, minimum B average, resume. Additional exam requirements/recommendations for international students: Required—TOEFL, TWE. Electronic applications accepted. *Faculty research:* Applied sustainability; sustainable water policy; food, agriculture, and the environment; biology studies; environment and business; ecological monitoring; soil ecosystem dynamics; urban water demand management; demand response.

University of Waterloo, Graduate Studies, Faculty of Environment, Program in Tourism Policy and Planning, Waterloo, ON N2L 3G1, Canada. Offers MAES. Part-time programs available. *Degree requirements:* For master's, research paper. *Entrance requirements:* For master's, honors degree in related field, minimum B average. Additional exam requirements/recommendations for international students: Required—TOEFL, TWE. Electronic applications accepted. *Faculty research:* Urban and regional economics, regional economic development, strategic planning, environmental economics, economic geography.

University of Wisconsin–Green Bay, Graduate Studies, Program in Environmental Science and Policy, Green Bay, WI 54311-7001. Offers MS. Part-time programs available. *Faculty:* 14 full-time (3 women), 2 part-time/adjunct (0 women). *Students:* 26 full-time (14 women), 19 part-time (11 women); includes 7 minority (1 Black or African American, non-Hispanic/Latino; 2 American Indian or Alaska Native, non-Hispanic/Latino; 2 Hispanic/Latino; 2 Two or more races, non-Hispanic/Latino). Average age 30. 15 applicants, 73% accepted, 7 enrolled. In 2011, 4 master's awarded. *Degree requirements:* For master's, thesis. *Entrance requirements:* For master's, GRE General Test, minimum GPA of 3.0. *Application deadline:* For fall admission, 8/1 for domestic students; for spring admission, 11/1 for domestic students. Applications are processed on a rolling basis. Application fee: $56. Electronic applications accepted. *Expenses:* Tuition, state resident: full-time $7312; part-time $406 per credit. Tuition, nonresident: full-time $16,771; part-time $932 per credit. *Required fees:* $1312; $55 per credit. Tuition and fees vary according to reciprocity agreements. *Financial support:* In 2011–12, 4 teaching assistantships with full tuition reimbursements were awarded; research assistantships with full tuition reimbursements, career-related internships or fieldwork, Federal Work-Study, and institutionally sponsored loans also available. Financial award application deadline: 7/15; financial award applicants required to submit FAFSA. *Faculty research:* Bald eagle, parasitic population of domestic and wild animals, resource recovery, anaerobic digestion of organic waste. *Unit head:* Dr. Kevin Fermanich, Chair, 920-465-2240, E-mail: fermanik@uwgb.edu. *Application contact:* Inga Zile, Graduate Studies Coordinator, 920-465-2123, E-mail: zilei@uwgb.edu. Web site: http://www.uwgb.edu/gradstu/.

Utah State University, School of Graduate Studies, College of Natural Resources, Department of Environment and Society, Logan, UT 84322. Offers bioregional planning (MS); geography (MA, MS); human dimensions of ecosystem science and management (MS, PhD); recreation resource management (MS, PhD). *Degree requirements:* For master's, comprehensive exam, thesis (for some programs). *Entrance requirements:* For master's and doctorate, GRE General Test, minimum GPA of 3.0. Additional exam requirements/recommendations for international students: Required—TOEFL. Electronic applications accepted. *Faculty research:* Geographic information systems/geographic and environmental education, bioregional planning, natural resource and environmental policy, outdoor recreation and tourism, natural resource and environmental management.

Vanderbilt University, School of Engineering, Department of Civil and Environmental Engineering, Program in Environmental Engineering, Nashville, TN 37240-1001. Offers environmental engineering (M Eng); environmental management (MS, PhD). MS and PhD offered through the Graduate School. Part-time programs available. *Faculty:* 9 full-time (0 women), 1 (woman) part-time/adjunct. *Students:* 34 full-time (20 women); includes 4 minority (1 Black or African American, non-Hispanic/Latino; 1 Asian, non-Hispanic/Latino; 1 Hispanic/Latino; 1 Two or more races, non-Hispanic/Latino), 6 international. Average age 30. 111 applicants, 11% accepted, 9 enrolled. In 2011, 5 master's, 2 doctorates awarded. Terminal master's awarded for partial completion of doctoral program. *Degree requirements:* For master's, thesis or alternative; for doctorate, thesis/dissertation. *Entrance requirements:* For master's and doctorate, GRE General Test. Additional exam requirements/recommendations for international students: Required—TOEFL. *Application deadline:* For fall admission, 1/15 for domestic students; for spring admission, 11/1 for domestic students. Applications are processed on a rolling basis. Application fee: $0. Electronic applications accepted. *Financial support:* In 2011–12, 5 fellowships with full tuition reimbursements (averaging $30,000 per year), 12 research assistantships with full tuition reimbursements (averaging $26,400 per year), 7 teaching assistantships with full tuition reimbursements (averaging $25,020 per year) were awarded; career-related internships or fieldwork, institutionally sponsored loans, scholarships/grants, traineeships, and tuition waivers (full and partial) also available. Financial award application deadline: 1/15. *Faculty research:* Waste treatment, hazardous waste management, chemical waste treatment, water quality. *Unit head:* Dr. David S. Kosson, Chair, 615-322-2697, Fax: 615-322-3365, E-mail: david.kosson@vanderbilt.edu. *Application contact:* Dr. James H. Clarke, Administrator, 615-322-3897, Fax: 615-322-3365. Web site: http://www.cee.vanderbilt.edu/.

Vermont Law School, Law School, Environmental Law Center, South Royalton, VT 05068-0096. Offers LL M, MELP, JD/MELP. Part-time programs available. *Faculty:* 15 full-time (6 women), 10 part-time/adjunct (9 women). *Students:* 55 full-time (33 women); includes 12 minority (4 Black or African American, non-Hispanic/Latino; 1 American Indian or Alaska Native, non-Hispanic/Latino; 3 Asian, non-Hispanic/Latino; 1 Hispanic/Latino; 3 Two or more races, non-Hispanic/Latino). Average age 30. 148 applicants, 83% accepted, 41 enrolled. In 2011, 53 master's awarded. *Entrance requirements:* Additional exam requirements/recommendations for international students: Required—TOEFL. *Application deadline:* For fall admission, 3/1 priority date for domestic students. Applications are processed on a rolling basis. Application fee: $60. *Financial support:* In 2011–12, 2 fellowships with full tuition reimbursements (averaging $5,000 per year) were awarded; career-related internships or fieldwork, Federal Work-Study, institutionally sponsored loans, scholarships/grants, and tuition waivers (partial) also available. Support available to part-time students. Financial award application deadline: 3/1; financial award applicants required to submit FAFSA. *Faculty research:* Environment and technology; takings; international environmental law; interaction among science, law, and environmental policy; air pollution. *Total annual research expenditures:* $52,000. *Unit head:* Marc Mihaly, Associate Dean, 802-831-1342, Fax: 802-763-2490, E-mail: admiss@vermontlaw.edu. *Application contact:* Anne Mansfield, Associate Director, 802-831-1338, Fax: 802-763-2940, E-mail: admiss@vermontlaw.edu. Web site: http://www.vermontlaw.edu/.

Virginia Commonwealth University, Graduate School, School of Life Sciences, Center for Environmental Studies, Richmond, VA 23284-9005. Offers M Env Sc, MS. *Degree requirements:* For master's, thesis. *Entrance requirements:* For master's, GRE General Test. Additional exam requirements/recommendations for international students: Required—TOEFL (minimum score 600 paper-based; 250 computer-based; 100 iBT). Electronic applications accepted. *Expenses:* Tuition, state resident: full-time $9133; part-time $507 per credit. Tuition, nonresident: full-time $18,777; part-time $1043 per credit. *Required fees:* $77 per credit. Tuition and fees vary according to degree level, campus/location, program and student level.

Virginia Polytechnic Institute and State University, Graduate School, College of Architecture and Urban Studies, School of Public and International Affairs, Blacksburg, VA 24061. Offers economic development (Certificate); government and international affairs (MPIA); homeland security policy (Certificate); local government management (Certificate); nonprofit and nongovernmental organization management (Certificate); planning, governance and globalization (PhD); public administration and public affairs (MPA, PhD); urban and regional planning (MURPL). *Accreditation:* ACSP. *Degree requirements:* For master's, comprehensive exam (for some programs), thesis (for some programs); for doctorate, comprehensive exam (for some programs), thesis/dissertation (for some programs). *Entrance requirements:* For master's and doctorate, GRE. Additional exam requirements/recommendations for international students: Required—TOEFL (minimum score 550 paper-based; 213 computer-based). *Application deadline:* For fall admission, 7/1 for domestic and international students; for spring admission, 12/1 for domestic and international students. Applications are processed on a rolling basis. Application fee: $65. Electronic applications accepted. *Expenses:* Tuition, state resident: full-time $10,048; part-time $558.25 per credit hour. Tuition, nonresident: full-time $19,497; part-time $1083.25 per credit hour. *Required fees:* $405 per semester. Tuition and fees vary according to course load, campus/location and program. *Financial support:* Teaching assistantships with full tuition reimbursements, career-related internships or fieldwork, Federal Work-Study, scholarships/grants, health care benefits, and unspecified assistantships available. Financial award application deadline: 1/15. *Faculty research:* Design theory, environmental planning, town planning, transportation planning. *Unit head:* Dr. Karen M. Hult, Unit Head, 540-231-5351, Fax: 540-231-9938, E-mail: khult@vt.edu. *Application contact:* Krystal D. Wright, Information Contact, 540-231-2291, Fax: 540-231-9938, E-mail: garch@vt.edu. Web site: http://www.spia.vt.edu/.

Virginia Polytechnic Institute and State University, Graduate School, College of Liberal Arts and Human Sciences, Department of Political Science, Blacksburg, VA 24061. Offers environmental politics and policy (Certificate); foundations of political analysis (Certificate); information policy and society (Certificate); political science (MA); security studies (Certificate). *Degree requirements:* For master's, comprehensive exam (for some programs), thesis (for some programs). *Entrance requirements:* For master's, GRE. Additional exam requirements/recommendations for international students: Required—TOEFL (minimum score 550 paper-based; 213 computer-based). *Application deadline:* For fall admission, 7/1 for domestic and international students; for spring admission, 12/1 for domestic and international students. Applications are processed on a rolling basis. Application fee: $65. Electronic applications accepted. *Expenses:* Tuition,

476 facebook.com/petersonspublishing

Peterson's Graduate Programs in the Physical Sciences, Mathematics, Agricultural Sciences, the Environment & Natural Resources 2013

state resident: full-time $10,048; part-time $558.25 per credit hour. Tuition, nonresident: full-time $19,497; part-time $1083.25 per credit hour. *Required fees:* $405 per semester. Tuition and fees vary according to course load, campus/location and program. *Financial support:* Teaching assistantships with full tuition reimbursements, career-related internships or fieldwork, Federal Work-Study, scholarships/grants, health care benefits, and unspecified assistantships available. Financial award application deadline: 1/15. *Faculty research:* Comparative politics, international relations, American government and politics, research methods. *Unit head:* Dr. Ilja A. Luciak, Unit Head, 540-231-6571, Fax: 540-231-6078, E-mail: iluciak@vt.edu. *Application contact:* Tim Luke, Information Contact, 540-231-6633, Fax: 540-231-6078, E-mail: twluke@vt.edu. Web site: http://www.psci.vt.edu/.

Virginia Polytechnic Institute and State University, VT Online, Blacksburg, VA 24061. Offers advanced transportation systems (Certificate); aerospace engineering (MS); agricultural and life sciences (MSLFS); business information systems (Graduate Certificate); career and technical education (MS); civil engineering (MS); computer engineering (M Eng, MS); decision support systems (Graduate Certificate); eLearning leadership (MA); electrical engineering (M Eng, MS); engineering administration (MEA); environmental engineering (Certificate); environmental politics and policy (Graduate Certificate); environmental sciences and engineering (MS); foundations of political analysis (Graduate Certificate); health product risk management (Graduate Certificate); industrial and systems engineering (MS); information policy and society (Graduate Certificate); information security (Graduate Certificate); information technology (MIT); instructional technology (MA); integrative STEM education (MA Ed); liberal arts (Graduate Certificate); life sciences: health product risk management (MS); natural resources (MNR, Graduate Certificate); networking (Graduate Certificate); nonprofit and nongovernmental organization management (Graduate Certificate); ocean engineering (MS); political science (MA); security studies (Graduate Certificate); software development (Graduate Certificate). *Expenses:* Tuition, state resident: full-time $10,048; part-time $558.25 per credit hour. Tuition, nonresident: full-time $19,497; part-time $1083.25 per credit hour. *Required fees:* $405 per semester. Tuition and fees vary according to course load, campus/location and program. *Application contact:* Graduate School Applications General Assistance, 540-231-8636, Fax: 540-231-2039, E-mail: gradappl@vt.edu. Web site: http://www.vto.vt.edu/.

Webster University, College of Arts and Sciences, Department of Biological Sciences, St. Louis, MO 63119-3194. Offers environmental management (MS); nurse anesthesia (MS); professional science management and leadership (MA). Part-time programs available. Postbaccalaureate distance learning degree programs offered (no on-campus study). *Degree requirements:* For master's, comprehensive exam (for some programs), thesis (for some programs). *Entrance requirements:* Additional exam requirements/recommendations for international students: Required—TOEFL. *Expenses: Tuition:* Full-time $10,890; part-time $605 per credit hour. Tuition and fees vary according to campus/location and program.

Webster University, George Herbert Walker School of Business and Technology, Department of Business, St. Louis, MO 63119-3194. Offers business (MA); business and organizational security management (MBA); computer resources and information management (MBA); environmental management (MBA); finance (MA, MBA); health services management (MBA); human resources development (MBA); human resources management (MBA); international business (MA, MBA); management and leadership (MBA); marketing (MBA); procurement and acquisitions management (MBA); telecommunications management (MBA). *Accreditation:* ACBSP. Part-time and evening/weekend programs available. Postbaccalaureate distance learning degree programs offered (no on-campus study). *Degree requirements:* For master's, comprehensive exam (for some programs), thesis (for some programs). *Entrance requirements:* Additional exam requirements/recommendations for international students: Required—TOEFL. *Expenses: Tuition:* Full-time $10,890; part-time $605 per credit hour. Tuition and fees vary according to campus/location and program.

Webster University, George Herbert Walker School of Business and Technology, Department of Management, St. Louis, MO 63119-3194. Offers business and organizational security management (MA); computer resources and information management (MA); environmental management (MS); government contracting (Certificate); health care management (MA); health services management (MA); human resources development (MA); human resources management (MA); management (DM); management and leadership (MA); marketing (MA); nonprofit management (Certificate); procurement and acquisitions management (MA); public administration (MA); quality management (MA); space systems operations management (MS); telecommunications management (MA). *Accreditation:* ACBSP. Part-time and evening/weekend programs available. Postbaccalaureate distance learning degree programs offered (no on-campus study). *Degree requirements:* For master's, thesis (for some programs); for doctorate, thesis/dissertation, written exam. *Entrance requirements:* For doctorate, GMAT, 3 years of work experience, MBA. Additional exam requirements/recommendations for international students: Required—TOEFL. *Expenses: Tuition:* Full-time $10,890; part-time $605 per credit hour. Tuition and fees vary according to campus/location and program.

Wesley College, Business Program, Dover, DE 19901-3875. Offers environmental management (MBA); executive leadership (MBA); management (MBA). Executive leadership concentration also offered at New Castle, DE

location. Part-time and evening/weekend programs available. *Entrance requirements:* For master's, GMAT or GRE, minimum undergraduate GPA of 2.75.

Wesley College, Environmental Studies Program, Dover, DE 19901-3875. Offers MS. Part-time and evening/weekend programs available. *Entrance requirements:* For master's, BA/BSM in science or engineering field, portfolio.

West Virginia University, Davis College of Agriculture, Forestry and Consumer Sciences, Division of Resource Management and Sustainable Development, Morgantown, WV 26506. Offers agricultural and extension education (MS, PhD), including agricultural and extension education, teaching vocational-agriculture (MS); agricultural and resource economics (MS); human and community development (PhD); natural resource economics (PhD); resource management (PhD); resource management and sustainable development (PhD). Part-time programs available. *Degree requirements:* For master's, thesis; for doctorate, comprehensive exam, thesis/dissertation. *Entrance requirements:* For master's, GRE General Test. Additional exam requirements/recommendations for international students: Required—TOEFL. *Faculty research:* Environmental economics, energy economics, agriculture.

West Virginia University, Eberly College of Arts and Sciences, Department of Geology and Geography, Program in Geography, Morgantown, WV 26506. Offers energy and environmental resources (MA); geographic information systems (PhD); geography-regional development (PhD); GIS/cartographic analysis (MA); regional development (MA). Part-time programs available. *Degree requirements:* For master's, thesis, oral and written exams; for doctorate, comprehensive exam, thesis/dissertation, oral and written exams. *Entrance requirements:* For master's and doctorate, GRE General Test, minimum GPA of 3.0. Additional exam requirements/recommendations for international students: Required—TOEFL. Electronic applications accepted. *Faculty research:* Space, place and development, geographic information science, environmental geography.

Wilfrid Laurier University, Faculty of Graduate and Postdoctoral Studies, Faculty of Arts, Department of Geography and Environmental Studies, Waterloo, ON N2L 3C5, Canada. Offers environmental and resource management (MA, MES, PhD); environmental science (M Sc, MES, PhD); geomatics (M Sc, MES, PhD); human geography (MES, PhD). Part-time programs available. *Degree requirements:* For master's, thesis optional; for doctorate, thesis/dissertation. *Entrance requirements:* For master's, honors BA in geography, minimum B average in undergraduate course work; honors BSc with minimum B+ or honors BES or BA in physical geography, environmental or earth sciences or the equivalent; for doctorate, MA in geography, minimum Aaverage. Additional exam requirements/recommendations for international students: Required—TOEFL (minimum score 89 iBT). Electronic applications accepted. *Faculty research:* Resources management, urban, economic, physical, cultural, earth surfaces, geomatics, historical, regional, spatial data handling.

Wilfrid Laurier University, Faculty of Graduate and Postdoctoral Studies, School of International Policy and Governance, International Public Policy Program, Waterloo, ON N2L 3C5, Canada. Offers global governance (MIPP); human security (MIPP); international economic relations (MIPP); international environmental policy (MIPP). Offered jointly with University of Waterloo. *Entrance requirements:* For master's, honours BA with minimum B average. Additional exam requirements/recommendations for international students: Required—TOEFL (minimum score 89 iBT). Electronic applications accepted. *Faculty research:* International environmental policy, international economic relations, human security, global governance.

Willamette University, Graduate School of Education, Salem, OR 97301-3931. Offers environmental literacy (M Ed); reading (M Ed); special education (M Ed); teaching (MAT). *Accreditation:* NCATE. Evening/weekend programs available. *Degree requirements:* For master's, leadership project (action research). *Entrance requirements:* For master's, California Basic Educational Skills Test, Multiple Subject Assessment for Teachers, PRAXIS, minimum GPA of 3.0, classroom experience, 2 letters of reference. Additional exam requirements/recommendations for international students: Recommended—TOEFL. Electronic applications accepted. *Expenses:* Contact institution. *Faculty research:* Educational leadership, multicultural education, middle school education, clinical supervision, educational technology.

Wilmington University, College of Business, New Castle, DE 19720-6491. Offers accounting (MBA, MS); business administration (MBA, DBA); environmental stewardship (MBA); finance (MBA); health care administration (MBA, MSM); homeland security (MBA, MSM); human resource management (MSM); management information systems (MBA, MSN); marketing (MSM); marketing management (MBA); military leadership (MSM); organizational leadership (MBA, MSM); public administration (MSM). Part-time and evening/weekend programs available. *Faculty:* 4 full-time (0 women). *Students:* 266 full-time (121 women), 700 part-time (505 women). Average age 34. *Entrance requirements:* Additional exam requirements/recommendations for international students: Required—TOEFL (minimum score 500 paper-based; 173 computer-based). *Application deadline:* Applications are processed on a rolling basis. Application fee: $35. Electronic applications accepted. *Expenses: Tuition:* Part-time $534 per credit hour. *Required fees:* $25 per term. *Financial support:* Applicants required to submit FAFSA. *Unit head:* Dr. Donald W. Durandetta, Dean, 302-356-6780, E-mail: donald.w.durandetta@wilmu.edu. *Application contact:* Chris Ferguson, Director of Admissions, 302-356-4636 Ext. 256, Fax:

Peterson's Graduate Programs in the Physical Sciences, Mathematics, Agricultural Sciences, the Environment & Natural Resources 2013

facebook.com/petersonspublishing **477**

302-328-5164, E-mail: inquire@wilmcoll.edu. Web site: http://www.wilmu.edu/business/.

Yale University, Graduate School of Arts and Sciences, Department of Forestry and Environmental Studies, New Haven, CT 06520. Offers environmental sciences (PhD); forestry (PhD). *Degree requirements:* For doctorate, thesis/dissertation. *Entrance requirements:* For doctorate, GRE General Test.

Yale University, School of Forestry and Environmental Studies, New Haven, CT 06511. Offers MEM, MES, MF, MFS, PhD, JD/MEM, MBA/MEM, MBA/MF, MEM/M Arch, MEM/MA, MEM/MPH, MF/MA. *Accreditation:* SAF (one or more programs are accredited). Part-time programs available. Terminal master's awarded for partial completion of doctoral program. *Degree requirements:* For master's, thesis (for some programs); for doctorate, thesis/dissertation. *Entrance requirements:* For master's, GRE General Test, GMAT or LSAT; for doctorate, GRE General Test. Additional exam requirements/recommendations for international students: Required—TOEFL (minimum score 600 paper-based; 250 computer-based; 100 iBT). Electronic applications accepted. *Expenses:* Contact

institution. *Faculty research:* Environmental policy, social ecology, industrial environmental management, forestry, environmental health, urban ecology, water science policy.

York University, Faculty of Graduate Studies, Program in Environmental Studies, Toronto, ON M3J 1P3, Canada. Offers MES, PhD, MES/LL B, MES/MA. Part-time programs available. *Degree requirements:* For master's, thesis optional; for doctorate, comprehensive exam, thesis/dissertation, research seminar. Electronic applications accepted.

Youngstown State University, Graduate School, College of Liberal Arts and Social Sciences, Program in Environmental Studies, Youngstown, OH 44555-0001. Offers environmental studies (MS); industrial/institutional management (Certificate); risk management (Certificate). *Degree requirements:* For master's, comprehensive exam, thesis, oral defense of dissertation. *Entrance requirements:* For master's, GRE General Test or minimum GPA of 2.7. Additional exam requirements/recommendations for international students: Required—TOEFL.

Environmental Sciences

Alabama State University, Department of Earth and Environmental Sciences, Montgomery, AL 36101-0271. Offers MS, PhD. *Faculty:* 9 full-time. *Degree requirements:* For master's, one foreign language, thesis or alternative; for doctorate, one foreign language, thesis/dissertation. *Entrance requirements:* For master's, GRE General Test, minimum B average in undergraduate course work; for doctorate, GRE General Test. Additional exam requirements/recommendations for international students: Required—TOEFL. *Application deadline:* For fall admission, 2/1 for domestic and international students. Application fee: $45. Electronic applications accepted. *Financial support:* Research assistantships with full tuition reimbursements, teaching assistantships with full tuition reimbursements, career-related internships or fieldwork, Federal Work-Study, and institutionally sponsored loans available. Financial award application deadline: 2/1. *Faculty research:* Sedimentation, isotopes, biogeochemistry, marine geology, structural geology. *Unit head:* Dr. Stephen Nelson, Chair, 504-862-3194, Fax: 504-865-5199, E-mail: snelson@tulane.edu. *Application contact:* Dr. Doris Screws, Dean of Graduate Studies, 334-229-4274, Fax: 334-229-4928, E-mail: dscrews@alasu.edu.

Alaska Pacific University, Graduate Programs, Environmental Science Department, Program in Environmental Science, Anchorage, AK 99508-4672. Offers MSES. Part-time programs available. *Degree requirements:* For master's, thesis. *Entrance requirements:* For master's, GRE General Test, minimum GPA of 3.0. Additional exam requirements/recommendations for international students: Required—TOEFL (minimum score 550 paper-based; 213 computer-based).

American University, College of Arts and Sciences, Department of Biology, Washington, DC 20016-8007. Offers applied science (MS), including biotechnology, environmental science assessment; biology (MA, MS). Part-time programs available. *Faculty:* 10 full-time (4 women), 3 part-time/adjunct (2 women). *Students:* 8 full-time (2 women), 4 part-time (1 woman); includes 4 minority (1 Black or African American, non-Hispanic/Latino; 3 Asian, non-Hispanic/Latino), 1 international. Average age 25. 15 applicants, 60% accepted, 6 enrolled. In 2011, 9 master's awarded. *Degree requirements:* For master's, comprehensive exam, thesis (for some programs). *Entrance requirements:* For master's, GRE General Test, GRE Subject Test. Additional exam requirements/recommendations for international students: Required—TOEFL. *Application deadline:* For fall admission, 2/1 for domestic students; for spring admission, 10/1 for domestic students. Application fee: $80. *Expenses: Tuition:* Full-time $24,264; part-time $1348 per credit hour. *Required fees:* $430. Tuition and fees vary according to course load and program. *Financial support:* Fellowships, research assistantships with tuition reimbursements, teaching assistantships with tuition reimbursements, career-related internships or fieldwork, Federal Work-Study, and institutionally sponsored loans available. Financial award application deadline: 2/1. *Faculty research:* Neurobiology, cave biology, population genetics, vertebrate physiology. *Unit head:* Dr. David Carlini, Chair, 202-885-2194, Fax: 202-885-2182, E-mail: carlini@american.edu. *Application contact:* Kathleen Clowery, Director, Graduate Admissions, 202-885-3621, Fax: 202-885-1505, E-mail: clowery@american.edu. Web site: http://www.american.edu/cas/biology/.

American University, College of Arts and Sciences, Department of Environmental Science, Washington, DC 20016. Offers environmental assessment (Graduate Certificate); environmental science (MS). *Faculty:* 4 full-time (0 women), 1 (woman) part-time/adjunct. *Students:* 8 full-time (4 women), 5 part-time (3 women); includes 2 minority (both Asian, non-Hispanic/Latino), 1 international. Average age 28. 19 applicants, 74% accepted, 3 enrolled. In 2011, 9 master's awarded. *Degree requirements:* For master's, comprehensive exam, thesis (for some programs). *Entrance requirements:* For master's, GRE General Test, GRE Subject Test, one year calculus, lab science. Additional exam requirements/recommendations for international students: Required—TOEFL. *Application deadline:* For fall admission, 2/1 for domestic students; for spring admission, 10/1 for domestic students. Application fee: $80. *Expenses: Tuition:*

Full-time $24,264; part-time $1348 per credit hour. *Required fees:* $430. Tuition and fees vary according to course load and program. *Financial support:* Research assistantships and teaching assistantships available. Financial award application deadline: 2/1. *Unit head:* Dr. Albert Mei-Chu Cheh, Chair, 202-885-8014, Fax: 202-885-1752, E-mail: acheh@american.edu. *Application contact:* Kathleen Clowery, Director, Graduate Admissions, 202-885-3621, Fax: 202-885-1505, E-mail: clowery@american.edu. Web site: http://www.american.edu/cas/environmental/.

American University of Beirut, Graduate Programs, Faculty of Agricultural and Food Sciences, Beirut, Lebanon. Offers agricultural economics (MS); animal sciences (MS); ecosystem management (MSES); food technology (MS); irrigation (MS); mechanization (MS); nutrition (MS); plant protection (MS); plant science (MS); poultry science (MS); soils (MS). Part-time programs available. *Faculty:* 21 full-time (6 women), 2 part-time/adjunct (0 women). *Students:* 12 full-time (all women), 93 part-time (77 women). Average age 24. 96 applicants, 67% accepted, 21 enrolled. In 2011, 25 master's awarded. *Degree requirements:* For master's, one foreign language, comprehensive exam, thesis (for some programs). *Entrance requirements:* Additional exam requirements/recommendations for international students: Required—TOEFL (minimum score 600 paper-based; 250 computer-based; 100 iBT), IELTS (minimum score 7.5). *Application deadline:* For fall admission, 2/20 for domestic and international students; for spring admission, 11/15 for domestic and international students. Applications are processed on a rolling basis. Application fee: $50. Electronic applications accepted. *Expenses: Tuition:* Full-time $12,780; part-time $710 per credit. *Required fees:* $528; $528 per credit. Tuition and fees vary according to course load and program. *Financial support:* In 2011–12, 22 research assistantships with partial tuition reimbursements (averaging $15,000 per year), 40 teaching assistantships with full and partial tuition reimbursements (averaging $1,000 per year) were awarded; scholarships/grants, health care benefits, and unspecified assistantships also available. Financial award application deadline: 2/2. *Faculty research:* Nutritional food-based dietary guidelines, community and therapeutic nutrition, food safety and food microbiology, landscape planning, nature and rural heritage conservation, pathology, immunology and control of poultry and animal diseases, agricultural economics and development, production of biodiesel from algae, national study on living conditions of refugees. *Unit head:* Prof. Nahla Hwalla, Dean, 961-1343002 Ext. 4400, Fax: 961-1744460, E-mail: nahla@aub.edu.lb. *Application contact:* Dr. Salim Kanaan, Director, Admissions Office, 961-1350000 Ext. 2594, Fax: 961-1750775, E-mail: sk00@aub.edu.lb. Web site: http://www.aub.edu.lb/fafs/Pages/index.aspx.

American University of Beirut, Graduate Programs, Faculty of Engineering and Architecture, Beirut, Lebanon. Offers applied energy (MME); civil engineering (ME, PhD); electrical and computer engineering (ME, PhD); engineering management (MEM); environmental and water resources (ME); environmental and water resources engineering (PhD); environmental technology (MSES); mechanical engineering (ME, PhD); urban design (MUD); urban planning and policy (MUP). Part-time programs available. *Faculty:* 53 full-time (8 women), 10 part-time/adjunct (2 women). *Students:* 290 full-time (101 women), 59 part-time (18 women). Average age 25. 336 applicants, 80% accepted, 83 enrolled. In 2011, 72 master's, 5 doctorates awarded. *Degree requirements:* For master's, one foreign language, comprehensive exam, thesis (for some programs); for doctorate, one foreign language, comprehensive exam, thesis/dissertation, publications. *Entrance requirements:* For master's, GRE (for electrical and computer engineering), letters of recommendation; for doctorate, GRE, letters of recommendation, master's degree, transcripts, curriculum vitae, interview. Additional exam requirements/recommendations for international students: Required—TOEFL (minimum score 600 paper-based; 250 computer-based; 100 iBT), IELTS (minimum score 7.5). *Application deadline:* For fall admission, 2/5 priority date for domestic students, 2/5 for international students; for spring admission, 11/1 priority date for domestic students, 11/1 for international students.

478 facebook.com/petersonspublishing

Peterson's Graduate Programs in the Physical Sciences, Mathematics, Agricultural Sciences, the Environment & Natural Resources 2013

Applications are processed on a rolling basis. Application fee: $50. Electronic applications accepted. *Expenses: Tuition:* Full-time $12,780; part-time $710 per credit. *Required fees:* $528; $528 per credit. Tuition and fees vary according to course load and program. *Financial support:* In 2011–12, 9 fellowships with full tuition reimbursements (averaging $24,800 per year), 33 research assistantships with full tuition reimbursements (averaging $24,800 per year), 74 teaching assistantships with full tuition reimbursements (averaging $9,800 per year) were awarded; career-related internships or fieldwork, institutionally sponsored loans, scholarships/grants, health care benefits, and unspecified assistantships also available. *Total annual research expenditures:* $1.1 million. *Unit head:* Prof. Makram T. Suidan, Dean, 961-135-0000 Ext. 3400, Fax: 961-174-4462, E-mail: msuidan@aub.edu.lb. *Application contact:* Dr. Salim Kanaan, Director, Admissions Office, 961-135-0000 Ext. 2594, Fax: 961-175-0775, E-mail: sk00@aub.edu.lb. Web site: http://staff.aub.edu.lb/~webfea.

American University of Beirut, Graduate Programs, Faculty of Health Sciences, Beirut, Lebanon. Offers environmental sciences (MSES), including environmental health; epidemiology (MS); epidemiology and biostatistics (MPH); health management and policy (MPH); health promotion and community health (MPH); population health (MS). Part-time programs available. *Faculty:* 29 full-time (19 women), 5 part-time/adjunct (2 women). *Students:* 63 full-time (52 women), 103 part-time (87 women). Average age 27. 156 applicants, 71% accepted, 56 enrolled. In 2011, 69 master's awarded. *Degree requirements:* For master's, one foreign language, comprehensive exam, thesis (for some programs). *Entrance requirements:* For master's, 2 letters of recommendation, personal statement, transcripts. Additional exam requirements/recommendations for international students: Required—TOEFL (minimum score 600 paper-based; 250 computer-based; 97 iBT), IELTS (minimum score 7). *Application deadline:* For fall admission, 2/20 for domestic and international students; for spring admission, 11/1 for domestic and international students. Application fee: $50. Electronic applications accepted. *Expenses: Tuition:* Full-time $12,780; part-time $710 per credit. *Required fees:* $528; $528 per credit. Tuition and fees vary according to course load and program. *Financial support:* In 2011–12, 62 students received support. Scholarships/grants, health care benefits, and unspecified assistantships available. Financial award application deadline: 2/20. *Faculty research:* Tobacco control; health of the elderly; youth health; mental health; women's health; reproductive and sexual health, including HIV/AIDS; water quality; health systems; quality in health care delivery; health human resources; health policy; occupational and environmental health; social inequality; social determinants of health; chronic diseases. *Total annual research expenditures:* $722,649. *Unit head:* Iman Adel Nuwayhid, Dean, 961-1340119, Fax: 961-1744470, E-mail: nuwayhid@aub.edu.lb. *Application contact:* Mitra Tauk, Administrative Coordinator, 961-1350000 Ext. 4687, Fax: 961-1744470, E-mail: mt12@aub.edu.lb. Web site: http://fhs.aub.edu.lb.

Antioch University New England, Graduate School, Department of Environmental Studies, Doctoral Program in Environmental Studies, Keene, NH 03431-3552. Offers PhD. *Degree requirements:* For doctorate, thesis/dissertation, practicum. *Entrance requirements:* For doctorate, master's degree and previous experience in the environmental field. Additional exam requirements/recommendations for international students: Required—TOEFL (minimum score 600 paper-based; 250 computer-based). Electronic applications accepted. *Expenses:* Contact institution. *Faculty research:* Environmental history, green politics, ecopsychology.

Antioch University New England, Graduate School, Department of Environmental Studies, Program in Environmental Education, Keene, NH 03431-3552. Offers MS. *Degree requirements:* For master's, practicum. *Entrance requirements:* For master's, previous undergraduate course work in biology, chemistry, mathematics (environmental biology); resume; 3 letters of recommendation. Additional exam requirements/recommendations for international students: Required—TOEFL (minimum score 550 paper-based; 213 computer-based). Electronic applications accepted. *Expenses:* Contact institution. *Faculty research:* Sustainability, natural resources inventory.

Arizona State University, College of Liberal Arts and Sciences, School of Human Evolution and Social Change, Tempe, AZ 85287-2402. Offers anthropology (PhD); anthropology (archaeology) (PhD); anthropology (bioarchaeology) (PhD); anthropology (museum studies) (MA); anthropology (physical) (PhD); applied mathematics for the life and social sciences (PhD); environmental social science (PhD); environmental social science (urbanism) (PhD); global health (MA); global health (health and culture) (PhD); global health (urbanism) (PhD); immigration studies (Graduate Certificate). Terminal master's awarded for partial completion of doctoral program. *Degree requirements:* For master's, thesis or alternative, interactive Program of Study (iPOS) submitted before completing 50 percent of required credit hours; for doctorate, comprehensive exam, thesis/dissertation, interactive Program of Study (iPOS) submitted before completing 50 percent of required credit hours. *Entrance requirements:* For master's and doctorate, GRE, minimum GPA of 3.0 or equivalent in last 2 years of work leading to bachelor's degree. Additional exam requirements/recommendations for international students: Required—TOEFL (minimum score 80 iBT), TOEFL, IELTS, or Pearson Test of English. Electronic applications accepted.

Arkansas State University, Graduate School, College of Sciences and Mathematics, Program in Environmental Sciences, Jonesboro, State University, AR 72467. Offers MS, PhD. Part-time programs available. *Faculty:* 1 (woman) full-time. *Students:* 21 full-time (8 women), 9 part-time (7 women); includes 3 minority (2 Black or African American, non-Hispanic/Latino; 1 Hispanic/Latino), 6 international. Average age 32. 14 applicants, 57% accepted, 6 enrolled. In 2011, 5 master's, 1 doctorate awarded. *Degree requirements:* For master's, comprehensive exam, thesis (for some programs); for doctorate, comprehensive exam, thesis/dissertation. *Entrance requirements:* For master's, GRE General Test, appropriate bachelor's degree, letters of reference, interview, official transcript, immunization records, letter of intent; for doctorate, GRE, appropriate bachelor's or master's degree, interview, letters of reference, personal statement, official transcript, immunization records. Additional exam requirements/recommendations for international students: Required—TOEFL (minimum score 550 paper-based; 213 computer-based; 79 iBT), IELTS (minimum score 6), PTE: Pearson Test of English Academic (minimum score 56). *Application deadline:* For fall admission, 2/15 for domestic and international students; for spring admission, 8/15 for domestic and international students. Applications are processed on a rolling basis. Application fee: $50. Electronic applications accepted. *Expenses:* Tuition, state resident: full-time $4044; part-time $225 per credit hour. Tuition, nonresident: full-time $8087; part-time $449 per credit hour. *Required fees:* $936; $52 per credit hour. $25 per term. One-time fee: $30. Tuition and fees vary according to course load and program. *Financial support:* In 2011–12, 14 students received support. Fellowships, research assistantships, teaching assistantships, career-related internships or fieldwork, scholarships/grants, and unspecified assistantships available. Financial award application deadline: 7/1; financial award applicants required to submit FAFSA. *Unit head:* Dr. Thomas Risch, Director, 870-972-2007, Fax: 870-972-2008, E-mail: trisch@astate.edu. *Application contact:* Dr. Andrew Sustich, Dean of the Graduate School, 870-972-3029, Fax: 870-972-3857, E-mail: sustich@astate.edu. Web site: http://www.astate.edu/a/scimath/evs/.

Ball State University, Graduate School, College of Sciences and Humanities, Program in Environmental Science, Muncie, IN 47306-1099. Offers PhD. *Students:* 2 full-time (0 women), 4 part-time (2 women), 1 international. 8 applicants, 63% accepted, 5 enrolled. In 2011, 4 doctorates awarded. Tuition and fees vary according to program and reciprocity agreements. *Financial support:* In 2011–12, 4 students received support, including 4 teaching assistantships with full and partial tuition reimbursements available (averaging $9,331 per year). Financial award application deadline: 3/1; financial award applicants required to submit FAFSA. *Unit head:* E. Michael Perdue, Director, 765-285-8096. *Application contact:* Dr. Robert Morris, Associate Provost for Research and Dean of the Graduate School, 765-285-1300, E-mail: rmorris@bsu.edu. Web site: http://cms.bsu.edu/Academics/CollegesandDepartments/EnvironmentalScience.aspx.

Baylor University, Graduate School, College of Arts and Sciences, The Institute of Ecological, Earth and Environmental Sciences, Waco, TX 76798. Offers PhD. *Students:* 8 full-time (3 women); includes 2 minority (1 Hispanic/Latino; 1 Two or more races, non-Hispanic/Latino), 5 international. *Unit head:* Dr. Joseph D. White, Director, 254-710-2911, E-mail: joseph_d_white@baylor.edu. *Application contact:* Suzanne Keener, Administrative Assistant, 254-710-3588, Fax: 254-710-3870. Web site: http://www.baylor.edu/TIEEES/.

Brigham Young University, Graduate Studies, College of Life Sciences, Department of Plant and Wildlife Sciences, Provo, UT 84602-1001. Offers environmental science (MS); genetics and biotechnology (MS); wildlife and wildlands conservation (MS, PhD). *Faculty:* 26 full-time (1 woman), 1 (woman) part-time/adjunct. *Students:* 50 full-time (18 women); includes 8 minority (2 Asian, non-Hispanic/Latino; 4 Hispanic/Latino; 2 Native Hawaiian or other Pacific Islander, non-Hispanic/Latino), 4 international. Average age 25. 29 applicants, 41% accepted, 9 enrolled. In 2011, 18 master's, 1 doctorate awarded. *Degree requirements:* For master's, thesis; for doctorate, comprehensive exam, thesis/dissertation, minimum GPA of 3.2, 54 hours (18 dissertation, 36 coursework). *Entrance requirements:* For master's, GRE General Test, minimum GPA of 3.2 during last 60 hours of course work; for doctorate, GRE, minimum GPA of 3.2. Additional exam requirements/recommendations for international students: Required—TOEFL (minimum score 580 paper-based; 237 computer-based; 85 iBT). *Application deadline:* 2/1 for domestic and international students. Applications are processed on a rolling basis. Electronic applications accepted. Full-time tuition for non-LDS students: $11,520 per year; $640 per credit. *Expenses: Tuition:* Full-time $5760; part-time $320 per credit. Tuition and fees vary according to student's religious affiliation. *Financial support:* In 2011–12, 2 research assistantships with partial tuition reimbursements (averaging $16,650 per year), 37 teaching assistantships with partial tuition reimbursements (averaging $16,650 per year) were awarded; scholarships/grants and tuition waivers (partial) also available. Financial award application deadline: 2/1. *Faculty research:* Environmental science, plant genetics, plant ecology, plant nutrition and pathology, wildlife and wildlands conservation. *Total annual research expenditures:* $2.1 million. *Unit head:* Dr. Val J. Anderson, Chair, 801-422-3527, Fax: 801-422-0008, E-mail: val_anderson@byu.edu. *Application contact:* Dr. Loreen Allphin, Graduate Coordinator, 801-422-5603, Fax: 801-422-0008, E-mail: loreen_allphin@byu.edu. Web site: http://pws.byu.edu/home/.

California Institute of Technology, Division of Geological and Planetary Sciences, Pasadena, CA 91125-0001. Offers environmental science and engineering (MS, PhD); geobiology (MS, PhD); geochemistry (MS, PhD); geology (MS, PhD); geophysics (MS, PhD); planetary science (MS, PhD). *Faculty:* 42 full-time (8 women). *Students:* 102 full-time (48 women); includes 10 minority (2 Black or African American, non-Hispanic/Latino; 7 Asian, non-Hispanic/Latino; 1 Hispanic/Latino), 28 international. Average age 26. 188 applicants, 23% accepted, 21 enrolled. In 2011, 11 master's, 12 doctorates awarded. *Degree*

Peterson's Graduate Programs in the Physical Sciences, Mathematics, Agricultural Sciences, the Environment & Natural Resources 2013

facebook.com/petersonspublishing **479**

requirements: For doctorate, thesis/dissertation. *Entrance requirements:* For doctorate, GRE General Test. Additional exam requirements/recommendations for international students: Required—TOEFL; Recommended—IELTS, TWE. *Application deadline:* For fall admission, 1/1 for domestic and international students. Application fee: $80. Electronic applications accepted. *Financial support:* In 2011–12, 75 students received support, including 16 fellowships with full tuition reimbursements available (averaging $28,000 per year), 86 research assistantships with full tuition reimbursements available (averaging $28,000 per year); teaching assistantships with full tuition reimbursements available, institutionally sponsored loans, scholarships/grants, health care benefits, and unspecified assistantships also available. Financial award applicants required to submit FAFSA. *Faculty research:* Planetary surfaces, evolution of anaerobic respiratory processes, structural geology and tectonics, theoretical and numerical seismology, global biogeochemical cycles. *Unit head:* Dr. Kenneth A. Farley, Chairman, 626-395-6111, Fax: 626-795-6028, E-mail: dianb@gps.caltech.edu. *Application contact:* Dr. Robert W. Clayton, Academic Officer, 626-395-6909, Fax: 626-795-6028, E-mail: dianb@gps.caltech.edu. Web site: http://www.gps.caltech.edu/.

California State Polytechnic University, Pomona, Academic Affairs, College of Environmental Design, John T. Lyle Center for Regenerative Studies, Pomona, CA 91768-2557. Offers MS. Part-time programs available. *Students:* 10 full-time (3 women), 25 part-time (17 women); includes 11 minority (1 Black or African American, non-Hispanic/Latino; 3 Asian, non-Hispanic/Latino; 5 Hispanic/Latino; 2 Two or more races, non-Hispanic/Latino), 1 international. Average age 31. 22 applicants, 73% accepted, 9 enrolled. In 2011, 8 master's awarded. *Application deadline:* For fall admission, 5/1 priority date for domestic students; for winter admission, 10/15 priority date for domestic students; for spring admission, 1/20 priority date for domestic students. Applications are processed on a rolling basis. Application fee: $55. Electronic applications accepted. *Expenses:* Tuition, state resident: full-time $6738. Tuition, nonresident: full-time $12,300. *Required fees:* $657. Tuition and fees vary according to course load and program. *Financial support:* Application deadline: 3/2; applicants required to submit FAFSA. *Unit head:* Dr. Kyle D. Brown, Director, 909-869-5178, E-mail: kdbrown@csupomona.edu. *Application contact:* Deborah L. Brandon, Executive Director, Admissions and Outreach, 909-869-3427, Fax: 909-869-5315, E-mail: dlbrandon@csupomona.edu. Web site: http://www.csupomona.edu/~crs/.

California State University, Chico, Office of Graduate Studies, College of Natural Sciences, Department of Geological and Environmental Sciences, Program in Environmental Science, Chico, CA 95929-0722. Offers MS. Part-time programs available. *Students:* 7 full-time (1 woman), 3 part-time (1 woman); includes 1 minority (Asian, non-Hispanic/Latino), 1 international. Average age 31. 26 applicants, 42% accepted, 4 enrolled. In 2011, 5 master's awarded. *Degree requirements:* For master's, thesis, oral exam. *Entrance requirements:* For master's, GRE, two letters of recommendation, faculty mentor, statement of purpose. Additional exam requirements/recommendations for international students: Required—TOEFL (minimum score 550 paper-based; 213 computer-based; 80 iBT), IELTS (minimum score 6.5), Pearson Test of English (minimum score 59). *Application deadline:* For fall admission, 3/1 priority date for domestic students, 3/1 for international students; for spring admission, 9/15 priority date for domestic students, 9/15 for international students. Application fee: $55. Electronic applications accepted. Tuition and fees vary according to class time, course load and degree level. *Financial support:* Research assistantships, teaching assistantships, and career-related internships or fieldwork available. Financial award application deadline: 3/1; financial award applicants required to submit FAFSA. *Unit head:* Dr. David L. Brown, Chair, 530-898-5262, Fax: 530-898-5234, E-mail: geos@csuchico.edu. *Application contact:* Judy L. Rice, Graduate Admissions Coordinator, 530-898-5416, Fax: 530-898-3342, E-mail: jlrice@csuchico.edu. Web site: http://catalog.csuchico.edu/viewer/12/GEOS.html.

California State University, Dominguez Hills, College of Natural and Behavioral Sciences, Program in Environmental Science, Carson, CA 90747-0001. Offers MS. *Faculty:* 6 full-time (2 women), 3 part-time/adjunct (2 women). *Students:* 6 full-time (2 women), 10 part-time (3 women); includes 6 minority (2 Black or African American, non-Hispanic/Latino; 4 Hispanic/Latino), 3 international. Average age 34. 8 applicants, 50% accepted, 4 enrolled. Application fee: $55. *Unit head:* Dr. John Keyantash, Chair, 310-243-2363, E-mail: jkeyantash@csudh.edu. *Application contact:* Brandy McLelland, Interim Director, Student Information Services, 310-243-3645, E-mail: bmclelland@csudh.edu. Web site: http://www.nbs.csudh.edu/.

California State University, East Bay, Office of Academic Programs and Graduate Studies, College of Science, Department of Earth and Environmental Sciences, Hayward, CA 94542-3000. Offers geology (MS), including environmental geology, geology. Part-time and evening/weekend programs available. *Faculty:* 1 full-time (0 women), 1 part-time/adjunct (0 women). *Students:* 3 full-time (2 women), 12 part-time (5 women); includes 2 minority (1 Asian, non-Hispanic/Latino; 1 Hispanic/Latino). Average age 37. 9 applicants, 56% accepted, 3 enrolled. *Degree requirements:* For master's, thesis or project. *Entrance requirements:* For master's, GRE, minimum GPA of 2.75 in field, 2.5 overall; 2 letters of recommendation. Additional exam requirements/recommendations for international students: Required—TOEFL (minimum score 550 paper-based; 213 computer-based). *Application deadline:* For fall admission, 6/30 for domestic and international students. Application fee: $55. Electronic applications accepted. *Expenses:* Tuition, state resident: full-time $6738; part-time $1302 per quarter. Tuition, nonresident: full-time $12,690; part-time $2294 per quarter. *Required*

fees: $449 per quarter. Tuition and fees vary according to degree level, program and reciprocity agreements. *Financial support:* Career-related internships or fieldwork, Federal Work-Study, and institutionally sponsored loans available. Support available to part-time students. Financial award application deadline: 3/2; financial award applicants required to submit FAFSA. *Faculty research:* Hydrology, seismic activity; origins of life. *Unit head:* Dr. Jeffery Seitz, Chair, 510-885-3486, Fax: 510-885-2526, E-mail: jeff.seitz@csueastbay.edu. *Application contact:* Prof. Mitchell Craig, Geology Graduate Advisor, 510-885-3425, Fax: 510-885-2526, E-mail: mitchell.craig@csueastbay.edu. Web site: http://www20.csueastbay.edu/csci/departments/earth/.

California State University, Fullerton, Graduate Studies, College of Humanities and Social Sciences, Program in Environmental Studies, Fullerton, CA 92834-9480. Offers environmental sciences (MS). Part-time programs available. *Students:* 23 full-time (13 women), 51 part-time (25 women); includes 21 minority (2 Black or African American, non-Hispanic/Latino; 10 Asian, non-Hispanic/Latino; 5 Hispanic/Latino; 4 Two or more races, non-Hispanic/Latino), 2 international. Average age 31. 63 applicants, 63% accepted, 29 enrolled. In 2011, 18 master's awarded. *Degree requirements:* For master's, thesis. *Entrance requirements:* For master's, minimum GPA of 2.5 in last 60 units of course work. Application fee: $55. *Financial support:* Career-related internships or fieldwork, Federal Work-Study, institutionally sponsored loans, and scholarships/grants available. Support available to part-time students. Financial award application deadline: 3/1; financial award applicants required to submit FAFSA. *Unit head:* Dr. John Bock, Coordinator, 657-278-4373. *Application contact:* Admissions/Applications, 657-278-2371.

California State University, Northridge, Graduate Studies, College of Science and Mathematics, Department of Chemistry and Biochemistry, Northridge, CA 91330. Offers biochemistry (MS); chemistry (MS), including chemistry, environmental chemistry. *Degree requirements:* For master's, thesis. *Entrance requirements:* For master's, GRE General Test or minimum GPA of 3.0. Additional exam requirements/recommendations for international students: Required—TOEFL. Electronic applications accepted.

California State University, San Bernardino, Graduate Studies, College of Social and Behavioral Sciences, Program in Environmental Sciences, San Bernardino, CA 92407-2397. Offers MS. *Students:* 15 full-time (7 women), 7 part-time (4 women); includes 8 minority (3 Asian, non-Hispanic/Latino; 4 Hispanic/Latino; 1 Two or more races, non-Hispanic/Latino), 1 international. Average age 27. 10 applicants, 80% accepted, 6 enrolled. In 2011, 5 master's awarded. *Expenses:* Tuition, state resident: full-time $7356. Tuition, nonresident: full-time $7356. *Required fees:* $1077. Tuition and fees vary according to program. *Unit head:* Dr. Brett Stanley, Chair, 909-537-3313, E-mail: bstanley@csusb.edu. *Application contact:* Sandra Kamusikiri, Associate Vice-President/Dean of Graduate Studies, 909-537-5058, E-mail: skamusik@csusb.edu.

Christopher Newport University, Graduate Studies, Department of Biology, Chemistry and Environmental Science, Newport News, VA 23606-2998. Offers environmental science (MS). Part-time and evening/weekend programs available. *Degree requirements:* For master's, comprehensive exam, thesis optional. *Entrance requirements:* For master's, GRE General Test, minimum GPA of 3.0. Additional exam requirements/recommendations for international students: Required—TOEFL (minimum score 580 paper-based; 237 computer-based; 92 iBT). Electronic applications accepted. *Faculty research:* Wetlands ecology and restoration, aquatic ecology, wetlands mitigation, greenhouse gases.

City College of the City University of New York, Graduate School, College of Liberal Arts and Science, Division of Science, Department of Earth and Atmospheric Sciences, New York, NY 10031-9198. Offers earth and environmental science (PhD); earth systems science (MA). PhD program offered jointly with Graduate School and University Center of the City University of New York. *Degree requirements:* For master's, comprehensive exam, thesis. *Entrance requirements:* Additional exam requirements/recommendations for international students: Required—TOEFL (minimum score 500 paper-based; 61 iBT). Electronic applications accepted. *Faculty research:* Water resources, high-temperature geochemistry, sedimentary basin analysis, tectonics.

Clarion University of Pennsylvania, Office of Research and Graduate Studies, Master of Science in Biology Program, Clarion, PA 16214. Offers biological sciences (MS); environmental sciences (MS). Part-time programs available. *Students:* 9 full-time (7 women), 1 international. Average age 25. In 2011, 7 master's awarded. *Degree requirements:* For master's, thesis or alternative. *Entrance requirements:* For master's, GRE General Test, minimum QPA of 2.75. Additional exam requirements/recommendations for international students: Required—TOEFL (minimum score 600 paper-based; 250 computer-based; 100 iBT). *Application deadline:* For fall admission, 4/1 for domestic students, 4/15 for international students; for spring admission, 11/1 for domestic students, 9/15 for international students. Applications are processed on a rolling basis. Application fee: $30. Electronic applications accepted. *Financial support:* Available to part-time students. Application deadline: 3/1. *Unit head:* Dr. William Barnes, Chair, 814-393-2559, Fax: 814-393-2731, E-mail: wbarnes@clarion.edu. *Application contact:* Dr. Andrew Keth, Graduate Coordinator, 814-393-1734, Fax: 814-393-2731, E-mail: aketh@clarion.edu. Web site: http://www.clarion.edu/26395/.

Clarkson University, Graduate School, Institute for a Sustainable Environment, Program in Environmental Science and Engineering, Potsdam, NY 13699. Offers MS, PhD. Part-time programs available. *Faculty:* 8 full-time (4 women). *Students:* 32 full-time (18 women), 1 (woman) part-time; includes 1 minority (Two or more

480 facebook.com/petersonspublishing

Peterson's Graduate Programs in the Physical Sciences, Mathematics, Agricultural Sciences, the Environment & Natural Resources 2013

races, non-Hispanic/Latino), 13 international. Average age 26. 55 applicants, 44% accepted, 8 enrolled. In 2011, 7 master's, 4 doctorates awarded. Terminal master's awarded for partial completion of doctoral program. *Degree requirements:* For master's, thesis; for doctorate, comprehensive exam, thesis/dissertation, departmental qualifying exam. *Entrance requirements:* For master's and doctorate, GRE, transcripts of all college coursework, resume, personal statement, three letters of recommendation. Additional exam requirements/recommendations for international students: Required—TOEFL (minimum score 550 paper-based; 213 computer-based; 80 iBT), IELTS (minimum score 6.5). *Application deadline:* For fall admission, 1/30 priority date for domestic students, 1/30 for international students; for spring admission, 9/1 priority date for domestic students, 9/1 for international students. Applications are processed on a rolling basis. Application fee: $25 ($35 for international students). Electronic applications accepted. *Expenses: Tuition:* Full-time $14,376; part-time $1198 per credit hour. *Required fees:* $295 per semester. *Financial support:* In 2011–12, 30 students received support, including fellowships with full tuition reimbursements available (averaging $21,999 per year), 14 research assistantships with full tuition reimbursements available (averaging $21,999 per year), 6 teaching assistantships with full tuition reimbursements available (averaging $21,999 per year); scholarships/grants, tuition waivers (partial), and unspecified assistantships also available. *Faculty research:* Biological, chemical, physical and social systems, renewable energy, environmental health. *Unit head:* Dr. Philip Hopke, Director, 315-268-3856, Fax: 315-268-4291, E-mail: hopkepk@clarkson.edu. *Application contact:* Suzann Cheney, Administrative Secretary, 315-268-3856, Fax: 315-268-4291, E-mail: scheney@clarkson.edu. Web site: http://www.clarkson.edu/ese/.

Clemson University, Graduate School, College of Agriculture, Forestry and Life Sciences, Program in Environmental Toxicology, Clemson, SC 29634. Offers MS, PhD. *Students:* 25 full-time (12 women), 2 part-time (0 women); includes 2 minority (1 Hispanic/Latino; 1 Two or more races, non-Hispanic/Latino), 6 international. Average age 30. 44 applicants, 16% accepted, 7 enrolled. In 2011, 2 master's, 1 doctorate awarded. *Degree requirements:* For master's, thesis; for doctorate, one foreign language, thesis/dissertation. *Entrance requirements:* For master's and doctorate, GRE General Test. Additional exam requirements/recommendations for international students: Required—TOEFL. *Application deadline:* For fall admission, 2/1 for domestic and international students; for spring admission, 9/15 for domestic and international students. Applications are processed on a rolling basis. Application fee: $70 ($80 for international students). Electronic applications accepted. *Financial support:* In 2011–12, 23 students received support, including 1 fellowship with full and partial tuition reimbursement available, 10 research assistantships with partial tuition reimbursements available (averaging $13,607 per year), 16 teaching assistantships with partial tuition reimbursements available (averaging $15,875 per year); career-related internships or fieldwork, Federal Work-Study, institutionally sponsored loans, scholarships/grants, health care benefits, and unspecified assistantships also available. Financial award applicants required to submit FAFSA. *Faculty research:* Biochemical toxicology, analytical toxicology, ecological risk assessment, aqutic toxicology, environmental engineering. *Total annual research expenditures:* $3 million. *Unit head:* Dr. Lisa J. Bain, Graduate Program Director, 864-656-5050, E-mail: lbain@clemson.edu. *Application contact:* Dr. Lisa J. Bain, Graduate Program Director, 864-656-5050, E-mail: lbain@clemson.edu. Web site: http://www.clemson.edu/entox.

Cleveland State University, College of Graduate Studies, College of Sciences and Health Professions, Department of Biological, Geological, and Environmental Sciences, Cleveland, OH 44115. Offers biology (MS); environmental science (MS); museum studies for natural historians (MS); regulatory biology (PhD); JD/MS. Part-time programs available. *Faculty:* 11 full-time (3 women), 1 part-time/adjunct (0 women). *Students:* 17 full-time (9 women), 83 part-time (50 women); includes 8 minority (4 Black or African American, non-Hispanic/Latino; 2 Asian, non-Hispanic/Latino; 2 Hispanic/Latino), 42 international. Average age 30. 97 applicants, 33% accepted, 18 enrolled. In 2011, 9 master's, 8 doctorates awarded. Terminal master's awarded for partial completion of doctoral program. *Degree requirements:* For master's, comprehensive exam (for some programs), thesis (for some programs); for doctorate, comprehensive exam, thesis/dissertation. *Entrance requirements:* For master's, GRE General Test, 2 letters of recommendation; for doctorate, GRE General Test, 2 letters of recommendation; 1-2 page essay; statement of career goals and research interests. Additional exam requirements/recommendations for international students: Required—TOEFL (minimum score 525 paper-based; 197 computer-based). *Application deadline:* For fall admission, 4/1 priority date for domestic students, 4/1 for international students; for spring admission, 12/1 priority date for domestic students. Applications are processed on a rolling basis. Application fee: $30. Electronic applications accepted. *Expenses:* Tuition, state resident: full-time $6416; part-time $494 per credit hour. Tuition, nonresident: full-time $12,074; part-time $929 per credit hour. *Financial support:* In 2011–12, 29 students received support, including research assistantships with full and partial tuition reimbursements available (averaging $16,500 per year), teaching assistantships with full and partial tuition reimbursements available (averaging $16,500 per year); institutionally sponsored loans and unspecified assistantships also available. *Faculty research:* Molecular and cell biology, immunology, urban ecology. *Unit head:* Dr. Jeffrey Dean, Chair, 216-687-2120, Fax: 216-687-6972, E-mail: j.dean@csuohio.edu. *Application contact:* Dr. Deborah L. Brown, Interim Assistant Director, Graduate Admissions, 216-523-7572, Fax: 216-687-5400, E-

mail: d.l.brown@csuohio.edu. Web site: http://www.csuohio.edu/sciences/dept/biology/index.html.

The College at Brockport, State University of New York, School of Science and Mathematics, Department of Environmental Science and Biology, Brockport, NY 14420-2997. Offers MS. Part-time programs available. *Students:* 11 full-time (4 women), 21 part-time (8 women); includes 2 minority (1 Asian, non-Hispanic/Latino; 1 Hispanic/Latino). 18 applicants, 100% accepted, 7 enrolled. In 2011, 1 master's awarded. *Degree requirements:* For master's, comprehensive exam, thesis. *Entrance requirements:* For master's, minimum GPA of 3.0, letters of recommendation, sample of scientific writing; statement of objectives. Additional exam requirements/recommendations for international students: Required—TOEFL (minimum score 550 paper-based; 213 computer-based; 79 iBT). *Application deadline:* For fall admission, 4/15 priority date for domestic students, 4/15 for international students; for spring admission, 11/15 priority date for domestic students, 11/15 for international students. Application fee: $50. Electronic applications accepted. *Financial support:* In 2011–12, 1 research assistantship with full tuition reimbursement was awarded; Federal Work-Study, scholarships/grants, and unspecified assistantships also available. Support available to part-time students. Financial award application deadline: 3/15; financial award applicants required to submit FAFSA. *Faculty research:* Aquatic and terrestrial ecology/organismal biology, watersheds and wetlands, persistent toxic chemicals, soil-plant interactions, aquaculture. *Unit head:* Dr. James Haynes, Chairperson, 585-395-5975, Fax: 585-395-5969, E-mail: jhaynes@brockport.edu. *Application contact:* Dr. Christopher Norment, Graduate Director, 585-395-5748, Fax: 585-395-5969, E-mail: cnorment@brockport.edu. Web site: http://www.brockport.edu/graduate.

College of Charleston, Graduate School, School of Sciences and Mathematics, Program in Environmental Studies, Charleston, SC 29424-0001. Offers MS. Part-time and evening/weekend programs available. *Faculty:* 21 full-time (8 women), 3 part-time/adjunct (2 women). *Students:* 42 full-time (30 women), 32 part-time (19 women); includes 2 minority (1 Asian, non-Hispanic/Latino; 1 Two or more races, non-Hispanic/Latino). Average age 27. 49 applicants, 61% accepted, 27 enrolled. In 2011, 22 master's awarded. *Degree requirements:* For master's, thesis optional, thesis or research internship. *Entrance requirements:* For master's, GRE, minimum GPA of 3.0, 3 letters of recommendation. Additional exam requirements/recommendations for international students: Required—TOEFL (minimum score 81 iBT). *Application deadline:* For fall admission, 3/1 for domestic students; for spring admission, 11/1 for domestic students. Application fee: $45. Electronic applications accepted. *Expenses:* Contact institution. *Financial support:* In 2011–12, 5 research assistantships (averaging $17,000 per year), 6 teaching assistantships (averaging $16,000 per year) were awarded; fellowships, career-related internships or fieldwork, Federal Work-Study, scholarships/grants, and unspecified assistantships also available. Support available to part-time students. Financial award application deadline: 4/1; financial award applicants required to submit FAFSA. *Unit head:* Dr. Timothy Callahan, Director, 843-953-2000, Fax: 843-953-2001, E-mail: callahant@cofc.edu. *Application contact:* Susan Hallatt, Director of Graduate Admissions, 843-953-5614, Fax: 843-953-1434, E-mail: hallatts@cofc.edu. Web site: http://spinner.cofc.edu/~environ/?referrer-webcluster&.

College of Staten Island of the City University of New York, Graduate Programs, Program in Environmental Science, Staten Island, NY 10314-6600. Offers MS. Part-time and evening/weekend programs available. *Faculty:* 3 full-time (0 women), 4 part-time/adjunct (2 women). *Students:* 39 (22 women). Average age 28. 18 applicants, 94% accepted, 13 enrolled. In 2011, 2 master's awarded. Terminal master's awarded for partial completion of doctoral program. *Degree requirements:* For master's, thesis. *Entrance requirements:* For master's, GRE General Test, 1 year of course work in chemistry, physics, calculus, and ecology; minimum GPA of 3.0 in undergraduate science and engineering; bachelor's degree in a natural science or engineering; interview. Additional exam requirements/recommendations for international students: Required—TOEFL (minimum score 550 paper-based; 213 computer-based; 79 iBT), IELTS (minimum score 6.5). *Application deadline:* For fall admission, 4/18 priority date for domestic students, 4/18 for international students; for spring admission, 11/21 priority date for domestic students, 11/21 for international students. Applications are processed on a rolling basis. Application fee: $125. Electronic applications accepted. *Expenses:* Tuition, state resident: full-time $8210; part-time $345 per credit. Tuition, nonresident: part-time $640 per credit. *Required fees:* $128 per semester. *Financial support:* Career-related internships or fieldwork, Federal Work-Study, and scholarships/grants available. Support available to part-time students. Financial award applicants required to submit FAFSA. *Unit head:* Dr. Alfred Levine, Director, 718-982-2822, Fax: 718-982-3923, E-mail: alfred.levine@mail.csi.cuny.edu. *Application contact:* Sasha Spence, Assistant Director for Graduate Admissions, 718-982-2699, Fax: 718-982-2500, E-mail: sasha.spence@csi.cuny.edu. Web site: http://www.csi.cuny.edu/catalog/graduate/master-of-science-in-environmental-science-ms.htm.

Colorado School of Mines, Graduate School, Division of Environmental Science and Engineering, Golden, CO 80401-1887. Offers MS, PhD. Part-time programs available. *Faculty:* 23 full-time (6 women), 8 part-time/adjunct (3 women). *Students:* 98 full-time (46 women), 21 part-time (10 women); includes 15 minority (2 Black or African American, non-Hispanic/Latino; 4 Asian, non-Hispanic/Latino; 8 Hispanic/Latino; 1 Two or more races, non-Hispanic/Latino), 8 international. Average age 28. 175 applicants, 58% accepted, 50 enrolled. In 2011, 20 master's, 2 doctorates awarded. *Degree requirements:* For master's, thesis (for some

Peterson's Graduate Programs in the Physical Sciences, Mathematics, Agricultural Sciences, the Environment & Natural Resources 2013

facebook.com/petersonspublishing **481**

Environmental Sciences

programs); for doctorate, comprehensive exam, thesis/dissertation. *Entrance requirements:* For master's and doctorate, GRE General Test. Additional exam requirements/recommendations for international students: Required—TOEFL (minimum score 550 paper-based; 213 computer-based; 80 iBT). *Application deadline:* For fall admission, 1/15 priority date for domestic students, 1/15 for international students; for spring admission, 10/15 priority date for domestic students, 10/15 for international students. Application fee: $50 ($70 for international students). Electronic applications accepted. *Expenses:* Tuition, state resident: full-time $12,585; part-time $699 per credit. Tuition, nonresident: full-time $27,270; part-time $1516 per credit. *Required fees:* $1864.20; $670 per semester. *Financial support:* In 2011–12, 49 students received support, including 15 fellowships with full tuition reimbursements available (averaging $20,000 per year), 33 research assistantships with full tuition reimbursements available (averaging $20,000 per year), 1 teaching assistantship with full tuition reimbursement available (averaging $20,000 per year); scholarships/grants, health care benefits, and unspecified assistantships also available. Financial award application deadline: 1/15; financial award applicants required to submit FAFSA. *Faculty research:* Treatment of water and wastes, environmental law: policy and practice, natural environment systems, hazardous waste management, environmental data analysis. *Total annual research expenditures:* $3.3 million. *Unit head:* Dr. John McCray, Director, 303-384-3490, Fax: 303-273-3413, E-mail: jmccray@mines.edu. *Application contact:* Tim VanHaverbeke, Research Faculty, 303-273-3467, Fax: 303-273-3413, E-mail: tvanhave@mines.edu. Web site: http://ese.mines.edu.

Columbia University, Graduate School of Arts and Sciences, Program in Climate and Society, New York, NY 10027. Offers MA.

Columbia University, School of International and Public Affairs, Program in Environmental Science and Policy, New York, NY 10027. Offers MPA. Program admits applicants for late May/early June start only. *Degree requirements:* For master's, workshops. *Entrance requirements:* For master's, GRE (recommended), previous course work in biology and chemistry, earth sciences (recommended), economics (strongly recommended). Additional exam requirements/recommendations for international students: Required—TOEFL. Electronic applications accepted. *Faculty research:* Ecological management of enclosed ecosystems vegetation dynamics, environmental policy and management, energy policy, nuclear waste policy, environmental and natural resource economics and policy, carbon sequestration, urban planning, environmental risk assessment/toxicology, environmental justice.

Columbus State University, Graduate Studies, College of Letters and Sciences, Environmental Science Program, Columbus, GA 31907-5645. Offers MS. Part-time and evening/weekend programs available. *Degree requirements:* For master's, thesis. *Entrance requirements:* For master's, GRE General Test, minimum GPA of 3.0. Additional exam requirements/recommendations for international students: Required—TOEFL (minimum score 550 paper-based; 213 computer-based; 79 iBT). Electronic applications accepted.

Cornell University, Graduate School, Graduate Fields of Agriculture and Life Sciences, Field of Soil and Crop Sciences, Ithaca, NY 14853-0001. Offers agronomy (MS, PhD); environmental information science (MS, PhD); environmental management (MPS); field crop science (MS, PhD); soil science (MS, PhD). *Faculty:* 39 full-time (9 women). *Students:* 19 full-time (11 women); includes 5 minority (all Hispanic/Latino), 4 international. Average age 28. 39 applicants, 18% accepted, 6 enrolled. In 2011, 5 master's, 5 doctorates awarded. *Degree requirements:* For master's, thesis (MS); for doctorate, comprehensive exam, thesis/dissertation. *Entrance requirements:* For master's and doctorate, GRE General Test, 2 letters of recommendation. Additional exam requirements/recommendations for international students: Required—TOEFL (minimum score 550 paper-based; 213 computer-based; 77 iBT). *Application deadline:* For fall admission, 2/1 priority date for domestic students. Applications are processed on a rolling basis. Application fee: $95. Electronic applications accepted. *Financial support:* In 2011–12, 5 fellowships with full tuition reimbursements, 2 research assistantships with full tuition reimbursements, 7 teaching assistantships with full tuition reimbursements were awarded; institutionally sponsored loans, traineeships, health care benefits, tuition waivers (full and partial), and unspecified assistantships also available. *Faculty research:* Soil chemistry, physics and biology; crop physiology and management; environmental information science and modeling; international agriculture; weed science. *Unit head:* Director of Graduate Studies, 607-255-3267, Fax: 607-255-8615. *Application contact:* Graduate Field Assistant, 607-255-3267, Fax: 607-255-8615, E-mail: ljh4@cornell.edu. Web site: http://www.gradschool.cornell.edu/fields.php?id=5A&a-2.

Drexel University, College of Arts and Sciences, Program in Environmental Science, Philadelphia, PA 19104-2875. Offers MS, PhD. Part-time and evening/weekend programs available. Terminal master's awarded for partial completion of doctoral program. *Degree requirements:* For master's, thesis optional; for doctorate, thesis/dissertation. Electronic applications accepted.

Duke University, Graduate School, Department of Environment, Durham, NC 27708. Offers natural resource economics/policy (PhD); natural resource science/ecology (PhD); natural resource systems science (PhD); JD/AM. Part-time programs available. *Faculty:* 28 full-time. *Students:* 53 full-time (32 women); includes 3 minority (1 Black or African American, non-Hispanic/Latino; 2 Asian, non-Hispanic/Latino), 16 international. 87 applicants, 20% accepted, 9 enrolled. In 2011, 10 doctorates awarded. *Degree requirements:* For doctorate, variable foreign language requirement, thesis/dissertation. *Entrance requirements:* For doctorate, GRE General Test. Additional exam requirements/recommendations for international students: Required—TOEFL (minimum score 550 paper-based; 213 computer-based; 83 iBT), IELTS (minimum score 7). *Application deadline:* For fall admission, 12/8 priority date for domestic students, 12/8 for international students. Application fee: $75. Electronic applications accepted. *Expenses: Tuition:* Full-time $40,720. *Required fees:* $3107. *Financial support:* Fellowships, research assistantships, teaching assistantships, and Federal Work-Study available. Financial award application deadline: 12/8. *Unit head:* Gaby Katul, Director of Graduate Studies, 919-613-8002, Fax: 919-613-8061, E-mail: meg.stephens@duke.edu. *Application contact:* Elizabeth Hutton, Director, Graduate Admissions, 919-684-3913, Fax: 919-684-2277, E-mail: grad-admissions@duke.edu. Web site: http://www.env.duke.edu/.

Duke University, Nicholas School of the Environment, Durham, NC 27708-0328. Offers coastal environmental management (MEM); DEL-environmental leadership (MEM); energy and environment (MEM); environmental economics and policy (MEM); environmental health and security (MEM); forest resource management (MF); global environmental change (MEM); resource ecology (MEM); water and air resources (MEM); JD/AM; JD/MEM; JD/MF; MAT/MEM; MBA/MEM; MBA/MF; MEM/MPP; MF/MPP. *Accreditation:* SAF (one or more programs are accredited). Part-time programs available. *Degree requirements:* For master's, thesis. *Entrance requirements:* For master's, GRE General Test, previous course work in biology or ecology, calculus, statistics, and microeconomics; computer familiarity with word processing and data analysis. Additional exam requirements/recommendations for international students: Required—TOEFL (minimum score 550 paper-based; 213 computer-based). Electronic applications accepted. *Expenses:* Contact institution. *Faculty research:* Ecosystem management, conservation ecology, earth systems, risk assessment.

Duquesne University, Bayer School of Natural and Environmental Sciences, Environmental Science and Management Program, Pittsburgh, PA 15282-0001. Offers environmental management (Certificate); environmental science (Certificate); environmental science and management (MS); JD/MS; MBA/MS; MS/MS. Part-time and evening/weekend programs available. Postbaccalaureate distance learning degree programs offered (minimal on-campus study). *Faculty:* 2 full-time (0 women), 8 part-time/adjunct (1 woman). *Students:* 20 full-time (8 women), 19 part-time (11 women); includes 4 minority (1 Black or African American, non-Hispanic/Latino; 2 Asian, non-Hispanic/Latino; 1 Hispanic/Latino), 7 international. Average age 26. 31 applicants, 61% accepted, 10 enrolled. In 2011, 10 degrees awarded. *Degree requirements:* For master's, thesis (for some programs), minimum of 36 credit hours; for Certificate, minimum of 18 credit hours. *Entrance requirements:* For master's, GRE General Test, course work in biology, chemistry, and calculus or statistics; 3 letters of reference, official transcripts, statement of purpose; for Certificate, undergraduate degree, 3 letters of reference, official transcripts, statement of purpose. Additional exam requirements/recommendations for international students: Required—TOEFL (minimum score 80 iBT). *Application deadline:* For fall admission, 4/1 priority date for domestic students, 4/1 for international students; for spring admission, 10/1 priority date for domestic students, 10/1 for international students. Applications are processed on a rolling basis. Application fee: $40. *Expenses:* Contact institution. *Financial support:* In 2011–12, 13 students received support, including 2 fellowships (averaging $17,300 per year), 5 research assistantships (averaging $13,408 per year); career-related internships or fieldwork, scholarships/grants, tuition waivers (partial), and unspecified assistantships also available. Financial award application deadline: 5/31. *Faculty research:* Watershed management systems, environmental analytical chemistry, environmental endocrinology, environmental microbiology, aquatic biology. *Unit head:* Dr. John Stolz, Director, 412-396-4367, Fax: 412-396-4092, E-mail: stolz@duq.edu. *Application contact:* Heather Costello, Graduate Academic Advisor, 412-396-6339, Fax: 412-396-4881, E-mail: costelloh@duq.edu. Web site: http://www.science.duq.edu/.

Florida Agricultural and Mechanical University, School of the Environment, Tallahassee, FL 32307. Offers MS, PhD. *Faculty:* 9 full-time (2 women). *Students:* 30 full-time (22 women), 4 part-time (3 women); includes 32 minority (26 Black or African American, non-Hispanic/Latino; 5 Asian, non-Hispanic/Latino; 1 Hispanic/Latino). Average age 25. 21 applicants, 14% accepted, 3 enrolled. In 2011, 4 master's, 5 doctorates awarded. *Degree requirements:* For master's, thesis; for doctorate, comprehensive exam, thesis/dissertation, oral exam. *Entrance requirements:* For master's and doctorate, GRE General Test, minimum GPA of 3.0. Additional exam requirements/recommendations for international students: Required—TOEFL. *Application deadline:* For fall admission, 7/31 priority date for domestic students, 7/31 for international students; for spring admission, 11/1 priority date for domestic students, 9/1 for international students. Application fee: $30. *Financial support:* In 2011–12, 30 students received support, including 30 research assistantships with full and partial tuition reimbursements available; career-related internships or fieldwork, institutionally sponsored loans, scholarships/grants, and unspecified assistantships also available. Financial award application deadline: 6/10; financial award applicants required to submit FAFSA. *Faculty research:* Environmental chemistry, environmental policy and risk management, aquatic and terrestrial ecology, biomolecular sciences. *Unit head:* Dr. Michael Abazinge, Director, 850-599-3550, Fax: 850-599-8183, E-mail: michael.abazinge@famu.edu. *Application contact:* Hazel Taylor, Specialist, Academic Programs, 850-599-8193, Fax: 850-412-7785, E-mail: hazel.taylor@famu.edu. Web site: http://www.famu.edu/index.cfm?environmentalscience.

482 facebook.com/petersonspublishing

Peterson's Graduate Programs in the Physical Sciences, Mathematics, Agricultural Sciences, the Environment & Natural Resources 2013

Florida Atlantic University, Charles E. Schmidt College of Science, Environmental Sciences Program, Boca Raton, FL 33431-0991. Offers MS. *Students:* 24 full-time (14 women), 5 part-time (3 women); includes 6 minority (1 Black or African American, non-Hispanic/Latino; 5 Hispanic/Latino), 1 international. Average age 26. 22 applicants, 50% accepted, 5 enrolled. In 2011, 3 master's awarded. *Degree requirements:* For master's, thesis. *Entrance requirements:* For master's, GRE General Test, minimum GPA of 3.0. Additional exam requirements/recommendations for international students: Required—TOEFL. *Application deadline:* For fall admission, 3/15 for domestic and international students; for spring admission, 10/1 for domestic and international students. Application fee: $30. *Expenses: Tuition, area resident:* Part-time $343.02 per credit hour. Tuition, state resident: full-time $8232. Tuition, nonresident: full-time $23,931; part-time $997.14 per credit hour. *Financial support:* Teaching assistantships, career-related internships or fieldwork, and Federal Work-Study available. *Faculty research:* Tropical and terrestrial ecology, coastal/marine/wetlands ecology, hydrogeology, tropical botany. *Unit head:* Dr. Dale Gawlik, Director, 561-297-3333, Fax: 561-297-2067, E-mail: dgawlik@fau.edu. *Application contact:* Dr. Leslie Terry, Associate Dean of External Affairs and Community Relations, 561-297-0347, Fax: 561-297-3388. Web site: http://www.ces.fau.edu/.

Florida Gulf Coast University, College of Arts and Sciences, Program in Environmental Science, Fort Myers, FL 33965-6565. Offers MS. Part-time programs available. *Faculty:* 202 full-time (85 women), 165 part-time/adjunct (62 women). *Students:* 31 full-time (21 women), 10 part-time (4 women); includes 2 minority (both Hispanic/Latino), 1 international. Average age 30. 46 applicants, 59% accepted, 16 enrolled. In 2011, 6 master's awarded. *Entrance requirements:* For master's, GRE General Test, minimum GPA of 3.0. Additional exam requirements/recommendations for international students: Required—TOEFL (minimum score 550 paper-based; 213 computer-based). *Application deadline:* For fall admission, 2/15 priority date for domestic students. Applications are processed on a rolling basis. Application fee: $30. Electronic applications accepted. *Expenses:* Tuition, state resident: full-time $8289. Tuition, nonresident: full-time $28,895. *Required fees:* $1831. One-time fee: $30 full-time. *Faculty research:* Political issues in environmental science, recycling, environmentally-friendly buildings, pathophysiology, immunotoxicology of marine organisms. *Unit head:* Dr. Michael Savarese, Chair, 239-590-7165, Fax: 239-590-7200, E-mail: msavares@fgcu.edu. *Application contact:* Patricia Price, Executive Secretary, 239-590-7196, Fax: 239-590-7200, E-mail: price@fgcu.edu.

Florida Institute of Technology, Graduate Programs, College of Engineering, Department of Marine and Environmental Systems, Melbourne, FL 32901-6975. Offers earth remote sensing (MS); environmental resource management (MS); environmental science (MS, PhD); meteorology (MS); ocean engineering (MS, PhD); oceanography (MS, PhD), including biological oceanography (MS), chemical oceanography (MS), coastal management (MS), geological oceanography (MS), oceanography (PhD), physical oceanography (MS). Part-time programs available. *Faculty:* 11 full-time (0 women), 3 part-time/adjunct (0 women). *Students:* 52 full-time (18 women), 13 part-time (4 women); includes 4 minority (1 Black or African American, non-Hispanic/Latino; 1 Asian, non-Hispanic/Latino; 1 Hispanic/Latino; 1 Two or more races, non-Hispanic/Latino), 16 international. Average age 28. 117 applicants, 52% accepted, 23 enrolled. In 2011, 13 master's, 1 doctorate awarded. *Degree requirements:* For master's, comprehensive exam (for some programs), thesis (for some programs), seminar, field project, written final exam, technical paper, oral presentation, or internship; for doctorate, comprehensive exam, thesis/dissertation, seminar, internships (oceanography and environmental science), publications. *Entrance requirements:* For master's, GRE General Test (environmental science, oceanography, environmental resource management, meteorology, earth remote sensing), 3 letters of recommendation, minimum GPA of 3.0, resume, transcripts, statement of objectives; for doctorate, GRE General Test (oceanography, environmental science), resume, 3 letters of recommendation, minimum GPA of 3.3, statement of objectives, on-campus interview (highly recommended). Additional exam requirements/recommendations for international students: Required—TOEFL (minimum score 550 paper-based; 213 computer-based; 79 iBT). *Application deadline:* For fall admission, 4/1 for international students; for spring admission, 9/30 for international students. Applications are processed on a rolling basis. Electronic applications accepted. *Expenses: Tuition:* Full-time $19,620; part-time $1090 per credit hour. Tuition and fees vary according to campus/location. *Financial support:* In 2011–12, 5 fellowships with full and partial tuition reimbursements (averaging $7,240 per year), 3 research assistantships with full and partial tuition reimbursements (averaging $7,283 per year), 7 teaching assistantships with full and partial tuition reimbursements (averaging $4,928 per year) were awarded; career-related internships or fieldwork, institutionally sponsored loans, tuition waivers (partial), unspecified assistantships, and tuition remissions also available. Support available to part-time students. Financial award application deadline: 3/1; financial award applicants required to submit FAFSA. *Total annual research expenditures:* $1.6 million. *Unit head:* Dr. George Maul, Department Head, 321-674-7453, Fax: 321-674-7212, E-mail: gmaul@fit.edu. *Application contact:* Cheryl A. Brown, Associate Director of Graduate Admissions, 321-674-7581, Fax: 321-723-9468, E-mail: cbrown@fit.edu. Web site: http://coe.fit.edu/dmes/.

Florida International University, College of Arts and Sciences, Department of Earth and Environment, Program in Environmental Studies, Miami, FL 33199. Offers MS. Part-time programs available. *Degree requirements:* For master's, thesis or alternative. *Entrance requirements:* For master's, GRE General Test,

minimum GPA of 3.0, 3 letters of recommendation, letter of intent. Additional exam requirements/recommendations for international students: Required—TOEFL (minimum score 550 paper-based; 80 iBT). Electronic applications accepted.

Florida State University, The Graduate School, College of Arts and Sciences, Department of Earth, Ocean and Atmospheric Science, Program in Oceanography, Tallahassee, FL 32306-4320. Offers aquatic environmental science (MS, PMS); oceanography (MS, PhD). *Faculty:* 12 full-time (1 woman). *Students:* 59 full-time (32 women); includes 4 minority (1 Black or African American, non-Hispanic/Latino; 3 Asian, non-Hispanic/Latino), 16 international. Average age 27. 55 applicants, 31% accepted, 15 enrolled. In 2011, 3 master's, 3 doctorates awarded. *Degree requirements:* For master's, thesis; for doctorate, comprehensive exam, thesis/dissertation. *Entrance requirements:* For master's and doctorate, GRE General Test, minimum upper-division GPA of 3.0. Additional exam requirements/recommendations for international students: Required—TOEFL (minimum score 550 paper-based; 213 computer-based; 80 iBT). *Application deadline:* For fall admission, 2/15 priority date for domestic students, 2/15 for international students; for spring admission, 7/15 priority date for domestic students, 7/15 for international students. Applications are processed on a rolling basis. Application fee: $30. Electronic applications accepted. *Expenses:* Tuition, state resident: full-time $9474; part-time $350.88 per credit hour. Tuition, nonresident: full-time $16,236; part-time $601.34 per credit hour. *Required fees:* $630 per semester. One-time fee: $20. Tuition and fees vary according to course load and campus/location. *Financial support:* In 2011–12, 47 students received support, including 1 fellowship with full tuition reimbursement available, 31 research assistantships with full tuition reimbursements available, 15 teaching assistantships with full tuition reimbursements available. Financial award application deadline: 2/15; financial award applicants required to submit FAFSA. *Faculty research:* Trace metals in seawater, currents and waves, modeling, benthic ecology, marine biogeochemistry. *Unit head:* Dr. Jeffrey Chanton, Area Coordinator, 850-644-6700, Fax: 850-644-2581, E-mail: chanton@ocean.fsu.edu. *Application contact:* Michaela Lupiani, Academic Coordinator, 850-644-6700, Fax: 850-644-2581, E-mail: admissions@ocean.fsu.edu.

Friends University, Graduate School, Wichita, KS 67213. Offers accounting (MBA); business administration (MBA); business law (MBL); Christian ministry (MACM); environment science (MSES); family therapy (MSFT); global leadership and management (MA); health care leadership (MHCL); management information systems (MMIS); operations management (MSOM); organization development (MSOD); teaching (MAT). Part-time and evening/weekend programs available. Postbaccalaureate distance learning degree programs offered (no on-campus study). *Faculty:* 14 full-time (5 women), 2 part-time/adjunct (1 woman). *Students:* 158 full-time (114 women), 616 part-time (367 women); includes 159 minority (83 Black or African American, non-Hispanic/Latino; 12 American Indian or Alaska Native, non-Hispanic/Latino; 26 Asian, non-Hispanic/Latino; 22 Hispanic/Latino; 2 Native Hawaiian or other Pacific Islander, non-Hispanic/Latino; 14 Two or more races, non-Hispanic/Latino). Average age 36. 497 applicants, 68% accepted, 256 enrolled. In 2011, 341 degrees awarded. *Degree requirements:* For master's, research project. *Entrance requirements:* For master's, bachelor's degree from accredited institution, official transcripts from institution granting bachelor's degree, interview with program director, letter(s) of recommendation. Additional exam requirements/recommendations for international students: Required—TOEFL (minimum score 560 paper-based; 220 computer-based). *Application deadline:* Applications are processed on a rolling basis. Application fee: $45 ($65 for international students). Electronic applications accepted. *Expenses: Tuition:* Part-time $601 per credit hour. One-time fee: $45 full-time. Tuition and fees vary according to campus/location and program. *Financial support:* Applicants required to submit FAFSA. *Unit head:* Dr. Evelyn Hume, Dean, 800-794-6945 Ext. 5859, Fax: 316-295-5040, E-mail: evelyn_hume@friends.edu. *Application contact:* Jeanette Hanson, Executive Director of Adult Recruitment, 800-794-6945, Fax: 316-295-5050, E-mail: jeanette@friends.edu. Web site: http://www.friends.edu.

Gannon University, School of Graduate Studies, College of Engineering and Business, School of Engineering and Computer Science, Program in Environmental and Occupational Science and Health, Erie, PA 16541-0001. Offers Certificate. Part-time and evening/weekend programs available. *Entrance requirements:* Additional exam requirements/recommendations for international students: Required—TOEFL (minimum score 79 iBT). *Application deadline:* Applications are processed on a rolling basis. Application fee: $25. Electronic applications accepted. *Financial support:* Scholarships/grants available. Financial award application deadline: 7/1; financial award applicants required to submit FAFSA. *Unit head:* Dr. Harry Diz, Chair, 814-871-7633, E-mail: diz001@gannon.edu. *Application contact:* Kara Morgan, Director of Graduate Admissions, 814-871-5831, Fax: 814-871-5827, E-mail: graduate@gannon.edu.

Gannon University, School of Graduate Studies, College of Engineering and Business, School of Engineering and Computer Science, Program in Environmental Science and Engineering, Erie, PA 16541-0001. Offers MS. Part-time and evening/weekend programs available. *Students:* 7 full-time (3 women), 3 part-time (2 women), 2 international. Average age 26. 31 applicants, 65% accepted, 2 enrolled. In 2011, 4 master's awarded. *Degree requirements:* For master's, thesis, internship, research paper or project. *Entrance requirements:* For master's, GRE. Additional exam requirements/recommendations for international students: Required—TOEFL (minimum score 79 iBT). *Application deadline:* Applications are processed on a rolling basis. Application fee: $25. Electronic

Peterson's Graduate Programs in the Physical Sciences, Mathematics, Agricultural Sciences, the Environment & Natural Resources 2013

facebook.com/petersonspublishing **483**

Environmental Sciences

applications accepted. *Financial support:* Scholarships/grants and unspecified assistantships available. Financial award application deadline: 7/1; financial award applicants required to submit FAFSA. *Faculty research:* Water quality, renewable energy, human health risk assessment, solid waste management, soil and groundwater contamination. *Unit head:* Dr. Harry Diz, Chair, 814-871-7633, E-mail: diz001@gannon.edu. *Application contact:* Kara Morgan, Director of Graduate Admissions, 814-871-5831, Fax: 814-871-5827, E-mail: graduate@gannon.edu.

George Mason University, College of Science, Department of Environmental Science and Policy, Fairfax, VA 22030. Offers environmental management (Certificate); environmental science and policy (MS); environmental science and public policy (PhD). *Faculty:* 21 full-time (7 women), 9 part-time/adjunct (4 women). *Students:* 68 full-time (50 women), 106 part-time (59 women); includes 24 minority (6 Black or African American, non-Hispanic/Latino; 8 Asian, non-Hispanic/Latino; 9 Hispanic/Latino; 1 Two or more races, non-Hispanic/Latino), 15 international. Average age 35. 102 applicants, 52% accepted, 40 enrolled. In 2011, 17 master's, 15 doctorates, 3 other advanced degrees awarded. *Degree requirements:* For doctorate, thesis/dissertation, internship. *Entrance requirements:* For master's, GRE, bachelor's degree with minimum GPA of 3.0 in related field; 3 letters of recommendation; expanded goals statement; 2 official copies of transcripts; for doctorate, GRE, bachelor's degree with minimum GPA of 3.0; 3 letters of recommendation; current resume; expanded goals statement; 2 official copies of transcripts; for Certificate, GRE, 3 letters of recommendation; undergraduate degree in related field; expanded goals statement; resume; 2 official copies of transcripts. Additional exam requirements/recommendations for international students: Required—TOEFL (minimum score 570 paper-based; 230 computer-based; 88 iBT), IELTS, Pearson Test of English. *Application deadline:* For fall admission, 2/15 priority date for domestic students; for spring admission, 10/1 priority date for domestic students. Application fee: $65 ($80 for international students). Electronic applications accepted. *Expenses:* Tuition, state resident: full-time $8750; part-time $364.58 per credit. Tuition, nonresident: full-time $24,092; part-time $1003.83 per credit. *Required fees:* $2514; $104.75 per credit. *Financial support:* In 2011–12, 53 students received support, including 2 fellowships with full tuition reimbursements available (averaging $18,000 per year), 6 research assistantships with full and partial tuition reimbursements available (averaging $19,109 per year), 46 teaching assistantships with full and partial tuition reimbursements available (averaging $11,712 per year); career-related internships or fieldwork, Federal Work-Study, scholarships/grants, unspecified assistantships, and health care benefits (full-time research or teaching assistantship recipients) also available. Support available to part-time students. Financial award application deadline: 3/1; financial award applicants required to submit FAFSA. *Total annual research expenditures:* $1.4 million. *Unit head:* Dr. Robert B. Jonas, Chair, 703-993-7590, Fax: 703-993-1066, E-mail: rjonas@gmu.edu. *Application contact:* Sharon Bloomquist, Graduate Program Coordinator, 703-993-3187, Fax: 703-993-1066, E-mail: sbloomqu@gmu.edu. Web site: http://esp.gmu.edu/.

Georgia Institute of Technology, Graduate Studies and Research, College of Sciences, School of Earth and Atmospheric Sciences, Atlanta, GA 30332-0340. Offers atmospheric chemistry, aerosols and clouds (MS, PhD); dynamics of weather and climate (MS, PhD); geochemistry (MS, PhD); geophysics (MS, PhD); oceanography (MS, PhD); paleoclimate (MS, PhD); planetary science (MS, PhD); remote sensing (MS, PhD). Part-time programs available. Terminal master's awarded for partial completion of doctoral program. *Degree requirements:* For master's, thesis or alternative; for doctorate, comprehensive exam, thesis/dissertation. *Entrance requirements:* For master's, GRE, letters of recommendation; for doctorate, GRE, academic transcripts, letters of recommendation, personal statement. Additional exam requirements/recommendations for international students: Required—TOEFL (minimum score 550 paper-based; 213 computer-based; 79 iBT). *Faculty research:* Geophysics; atmospheric chemistry, aerosols and clouds; dynamics of weather and climate; geochemistry; oceanography; paleoclimate; planetary science; remote sensing.

Graduate School and University Center of the City University of New York, Graduate Studies, Program in Earth and Environmental Sciences, New York, NY 10016-4039. Offers PhD. *Degree requirements:* For doctorate, one foreign language, comprehensive exam, thesis/dissertation. *Entrance requirements:* For doctorate, GRE General Test. Additional exam requirements/recommendations for international students: Required—TOEFL. Electronic applications accepted.

Harvard University, Cyprus International Institute for the Environment and Public Health in Association with Harvard School of Public Health, Cambridge, MA 02138. Offers environmental health (MS); environmental/public health (PhD); epidemiology and biostatistics (MS). *Entrance requirements:* For master's and doctorate, GRE, resume/curriculum vitae, 3 letters of recommendation, BA or BS (including diploma and official transcripts). Additional exam requirements/recommendations for international students: Required—TOEFL (minimum score 220 computer-based), IELTS (minimum score 7). Electronic applications accepted. *Expenses: Tuition:* Full-time $36,304. *Required fees:* $1186. Full-time tuition and fees vary according to program. *Faculty research:* Air pollution, climate change, biostatistics, sustainable development, environmental management.

Howard University, Graduate School, Department of Chemistry, Washington, DC 20059-0002. Offers analytical chemistry (MS, PhD); atmospheric (MS, PhD); biochemistry (MS, PhD); environmental (MS, PhD); inorganic chemistry (MS, PhD); organic chemistry (MS, PhD); physical chemistry (MS, PhD). Terminal master's awarded for partial completion of doctoral program. *Degree*

requirements: For master's, comprehensive exam, thesis, teaching experience; for doctorate, comprehensive exam, thesis/dissertation, teaching experience. *Entrance requirements:* For master's, GRE General Test, minimum GPA of 2.7; for doctorate, GRE General Test, minimum GPA of 3.0. Additional exam requirements/recommendations for international students: Required—TOEFL. Electronic applications accepted. *Faculty research:* Synthetic organics, materials, natural products, mass spectrometry.

Humboldt State University, Academic Programs, College of Natural Resources and Sciences, Programs in Environmental Systems, Arcata, CA 95521-8299. Offers environmental systems (MS), including energy, environment and society, environmental resources engineering, geology, math modeling. *Students:* 32 full-time (12 women), 4 part-time (2 women); includes 5 minority (1 Black or African American, non-Hispanic/Latino; 1 Asian, non-Hispanic/Latino; 1 Hispanic/Latino; 2 Two or more races, non-Hispanic/Latino), 3 international. Average age 28. 58 applicants, 36% accepted, 13 enrolled. In 2011, 12 master's awarded. *Degree requirements:* For master's, thesis. *Entrance requirements:* For master's, GRE, appropriate bachelor's degree, minimum GPA of 2.5, 3 letters of recommendation. Additional exam requirements/recommendations for international students: Required—TOEFL. *Application deadline:* For fall admission, 2/15 for domestic students; for spring admission, 10/15 for domestic students. Applications are processed on a rolling basis. Application fee: $55. *Expenses:* Tuition, state resident: full-time $6734. Tuition, nonresident: full-time $15,662; part-time $372 per credit. *Required fees:* $903. Tuition and fees vary according to program. *Financial support:* Application deadline: 3/1; applicants required to submit FAFSA. *Faculty research:* Mathematical modeling, international development technology, geology, environmental resources engineering. *Unit head:* Dr. Chris Dugaw, Chair, 707-826-4251, Fax: 707-826-4145, E-mail: dugaw@humboldt.edu. *Application contact:* Dr. Dale Oliver, Coordinator, 707-826-4921, Fax: 707-826-3140, E-mail: dale.oliver@humboldt.edu.

Hunter College of the City University of New York, Graduate School, School of Arts and Sciences, Department of Geography, New York, NY 10021-5085. Offers analytical geography (MA); earth system science (MA); environmental and social issues (MA); geographic information science (Certificate); geographic information systems (MA); teaching earth science (MA). Part-time and evening/weekend programs available. *Faculty:* 7 full-time (3 women), 8 part-time/adjunct (1 woman). *Students:* 2 full-time (1 woman), 49 part-time (24 women); includes 11 minority (4 Black or African American, non-Hispanic/Latino; 4 Asian, non-Hispanic/Latino; 3 Hispanic/Latino), 1 international. Average age 35. 27 applicants, 74% accepted, 13 enrolled. In 2011, 12 master's, 3 other advanced degrees awarded. *Degree requirements:* For master's, comprehensive exam or thesis. *Entrance requirements:* For master's, GRE General Test, minimum B average in major, Boverall; 18 credits of course work in geography; 2 letters of recommendation; for Certificate, minimum B average in major, Boverall. Additional exam requirements/recommendations for international students: Required—TOEFL. *Application deadline:* For fall admission, 4/1 for domestic students; for spring admission, 11/1 for domestic students. Applications are processed on a rolling basis. Application fee: $125. *Expenses:* Tuition, state resident: full-time $345 per credit. Tuition, nonresident: full-time $15,360; part-time $640 per credit. *Required fees:* $280 per semester. One-time fee: $125. Tuition and fees vary according to class time, campus/location and program. *Financial support:* In 2011–12, 1 fellowship (averaging $3,000 per year), 2 research assistantships (averaging $10,000 per year), 10 teaching assistantships (averaging $6,000 per year) were awarded; career-related internships or fieldwork, Federal Work-Study, institutionally sponsored loans, and unspecified assistantships also available. Financial award application deadline: 3/1. *Faculty research:* Urban geography, economic geography, geographic information science, demographic methods, climate change. *Unit head:* Prof. William Solecki, Chair, 212-772-4536, Fax: 212-772-5268, E-mail: wsolecki@hunter.cuny.edu. *Application contact:* Prof. Marianna Pavlovskaya, Graduate Adviser, 212-772-5320, Fax: 212-772-5268, E-mail: mpavlov@geo.hunter.cuny.edu. Web site: http://www.geo.hunter.cuny.edu/.

Idaho State University, Office of Graduate Studies, College of Science and Engineering, Civil and Environmental Engineering Department, Pocatello, ID 83209-8060. Offers civil engineering (MS); environmental engineering (MS); environmental science and management (MS). Part-time programs available. *Degree requirements:* For master's, comprehensive exam (for some programs), thesis optional, thesis project, 2 semesters of seminar. *Entrance requirements:* For master's, GRE. Additional exam requirements/recommendations for international students: Required—TOEFL (minimum score 550 paper-based; 213 computer-based; 80 iBT). Electronic applications accepted. *Faculty research:* Floor vibration investigations, earthquake engineering, base isolation systems and seismic risk assessment, infrastructure revitalization (building foundations and damage, bridge structures, highways, and dams), slope stability and soil erosion, pavement rehabilitation, computational fluid dynamics and flood control structures, microbial fuel cells, water treatment and water quality modeling, environmental risk assessment, biotechnology, nanotechnology.

Idaho State University, Office of Graduate Studies, College of Science and Engineering, Department of Geosciences, Pocatello, ID 83209-8072. Offers geographic information science (MS); geology (MNS, MS); geology with emphasis in environmental geoscience (MS); geophysics/hydrology/geology (MS); geotechnology (Postbaccalaureate Certificate). Part-time programs available. *Degree requirements:* For master's, comprehensive exam, thesis, oral colloquium; for Postbaccalaureate Certificate, thesis optional; minimum 19 credits. *Entrance requirements:* For master's, GRE General Test (minimum 50th percentile in 2 sections), 3 letters of recommendation; for Postbaccalaureate Certificate, GRE General Test, 3 letters of recommendation, bachelor's degree, statement of goals. Additional exam requirements/recommendations for international students: Required—TOEFL (minimum score 550 paper-based; 213 computer-based; 80 iBT). Electronic applications accepted. *Faculty research:* Quantitative field mapping and sampling: microscopic, geochemical, and isotopic analysis of rocks, minerals and water; remote sensing, geographic information systems, and global positioning systems: environmental and watershed management; surficial and fluvial processes: landscape change; regional tectonics, structural geology; planetary geology.

Idaho State University, Office of Graduate Studies, Department of Interdisciplinary Studies, Pocatello, ID 83209. Offers general interdisciplinary (M Ed, MA, MNS); waste management and environmental science (MS). Part-time programs available. *Degree requirements:* For master's, comprehensive exam, thesis optional. *Entrance requirements:* For master's, GRE General Test or MAT, minimum GPA of 3.0. Additional exam requirements/recommendations for international students: Required—TOEFL (minimum score 550 paper-based; 213 computer-based; 80 iBT).

Indiana University Bloomington, School of Public and Environmental Affairs, Environmental Science Programs, Bloomington, IN 47405. Offers applied ecology (MSES); energy (MSES); environmental chemistry, toxicology, and risk assessment (MSES); environmental science (PhD); specialized environmental science (MSES); water resources (MSES); JD/MSES; MSES/MPA; MSES/MS. Part-time programs available. *Faculty:* 80 full-time (30 women), 102 part-time/adjunct (43 women). *Students:* 142 full-time, 6 part-time; includes 8 minority (2 Black or African American, non-Hispanic/Latino; 5 Asian, non-Hispanic/Latino; 1 Hispanic/Latino), 18 international. Average age 24. 152 applicants, 57 enrolled. In 2011, 58 master's, 2 doctorates awarded. Terminal master's awarded for partial completion of doctoral program. *Degree requirements:* For master's, core classes; capstone or thesis; internship; for doctorate, comprehensive exam, thesis/dissertation. *Entrance requirements:* For master's, GRE General Test or GMAT, official transcripts, 3 letters of recommendation, resume, personal statement; for doctorate, GRE General Test or LSAT, official transcripts, 3 letters of recommendation, resume or curriculum vitae, statement of purpose. Additional exam requirements/recommendations for international students: Required—TOEFL (minimum score 600 paper-based; 96 iBT); Recommended—IELTS (minimum score 7). *Application deadline:* For fall admission, 2/1 priority date for domestic students, 12/1 for international students. Applications are processed on a rolling basis. Application fee: $55 ($65 for international students). Electronic applications accepted. *Financial support:* Fellowships with partial tuition reimbursements, research assistantships with partial tuition reimbursements, teaching assistantships with partial tuition reimbursements, career-related internships or fieldwork, Federal Work-Study, scholarships/grants, health care benefits, unspecified assistantships, and Service Corps programs available. Financial award application deadline: 2/1; financial award applicants required to submit FAFSA. *Faculty research:* Applied ecology, bio-geo chemistry, toxicology, wetlands ecology, environmental microbiology, forest ecology, environmental chemistry. *Unit head:* Jennifer J. Forney, Director, Graduate Student Services, 812-855-9485, Fax: 812-856-3665, E-mail: speampo@indiana.edu. *Application contact:* Admissions Assistant, 812-855-2840, Fax: 812-856-3665, E-mail: speaapps@indiana.edu. Web site: http://www.indiana.edu/~spea/prospective_students/masters/.

Instituto Tecnologico de Santo Domingo, Graduate School, Area of Basic And Environmental Sciences, Santo Domingo, Dominican Republic. Offers environmental science (M En S), including environmental education, environmental management, marine resources, natural resources management; mathematics (MS, PhD); renewable energy technology (MS, Certificate).

Instituto Tecnológico y de Estudios Superiores de Monterrey, Campus Ciudad de México, Virtual University Division, Ciudad de Mexico, Mexico. Offers administration of information technologies (MA); computer sciences (MA); education (MA, PhD); educational technology (MA); environmental engineering (MA); environmental systems (MA); humanistic studies (MA); industrial engineering (MA); international business for Latin America (MA); quality systems (MA); quality systems and productivity (MA). Part-time and evening/weekend programs available. Postbaccalaureate distance learning degree programs offered (minimal on-campus study). *Entrance requirements:* For master's and doctorate, Instituto entrance exam. Additional exam requirements/recommendations for international students: Required—TOEFL.

Inter American University of Puerto Rico, San Germán Campus, Graduate Studies Center, Program in Environmental Sciences, San Germán, PR 00683-5008. Offers MS. Part-time and evening/weekend programs available. *Degree requirements:* For master's, comprehensive exam, thesis. *Entrance requirements:* For master's, GRE General Test or EXADEP, minimum GPA of 3.0. *Application deadline:* For fall admission, 4/30 priority date for domestic students; for spring admission, 11/15 for domestic students. Applications are processed on a rolling basis. Application fee: $31. *Expenses: Required fees:* $213 per semester. *Financial support:* Fellowships, research assistantships, teaching assistantships, Federal Work-Study, and unspecified assistantships available. *Faculty research:* Environmental biology, environmental chemistry, water resources and unit operations. *Unit head:* Dr. Elba T. Irizarry, Director of Graduate Studies Center, 787-264-1912 Ext. 7357, Fax: 787-892-6350, E-mail: elbat@sg.inter.edu.

Iowa State University of Science and Technology, Department of Geological and Atmospheric Sciences, Ames, IA 50011-3212. Offers earth science (MS, PhD); environmental science (MS, PhD); geology (MS, PhD); meteorology (MS, PhD). *Degree requirements:* For master's, thesis (for some programs); for doctorate, thesis/dissertation. *Entrance requirements:* For master's and doctorate, GRE General Test. Additional exam requirements/recommendations for international students: Required—TOEFL (minimum score 550 paper-based; 79 iBT), IELTS (minimum score 6.5). *Application deadline:* For fall admission, 1/1 priority date for domestic students. Application fee: $40 ($90 for international students). Electronic applications accepted. *Unit head:* Dr. Carl E. Jacobson, Director of Graduate Education, 515-294-8048, Fax: 515-294-6049, E-mail: geology@iastate.edu. *Application contact:* Neal Iverson, Information Contact, 515-294-8048, Fax: 515-294-6049, E-mail: geology@iastate.edu. Web site: http://www.ge-at.iastate.edu/.

Iowa State University of Science and Technology, Program in Environmental Sciences, Ames, IA 50011-1020. Offers MS, PhD. *Degree requirements:* For master's, thesis; for doctorate, thesis/dissertation. *Entrance requirements:* For master's and doctorate, GRE General Test. Additional exam requirements/recommendations for international students: Required—TOEFL (minimum score 550 paper-based; 79 iBT), IELTS (minimum score 6.5). *Application deadline:* For fall admission, 2/1 for domestic and international students; for spring admission, 6/1 for domestic and international students. Application fee: $40 ($90 for international students). Electronic applications accepted. *Unit head:* Dr. John Downing, Director of Graduate Education, 515-294-6518, Fax: 515-294-1337, E-mail: enscigradoffice@iastate.edu. *Application contact:* Charles Sauer, Information Contact, 515-294-6518, Fax: 515-294-1337, E-mail: enscigradoffice@iastate.edu. Web site: http://www.ensci.iastate.edu/grad/applying.html.

Jackson State University, Graduate School, College of Science, Engineering and Technology, Department of Biology, Jackson, MS 39217. Offers environmental science (MS, PhD). Part-time and evening/weekend programs available. *Degree requirements:* For master's, comprehensive exam, thesis (alternative accepted for MST); for doctorate, comprehensive exam, thesis/dissertation. *Entrance requirements:* For master's, GRE General Test; for doctorate, MAT. Additional exam requirements/recommendations for international students: Required—TOEFL (minimum score 520 paper-based; 195 computer-based; 67 iBT). *Faculty research:* Comparative studies on the carbohydrate composition of marine macroalgae, host-parasite relationship between the spruce budworm and entomepathogen fungus.

The Johns Hopkins University, Zanvyl Krieger School of Arts and Sciences, Advanced Academic Programs, Program in Environmental Sciences and Policy, Baltimore, MD 21218-2699. Offers MS. Part-time and evening/weekend programs available. Postbaccalaureate distance learning degree programs offered (minimal on-campus study). *Degree requirements:* For master's, thesis (for some programs). *Entrance requirements:* For master's, minimum GPA of 3.0, coursework in chemistry and calculus. Additional exam requirements/recommendations for international students: Required—TOEFL (minimum score 250 computer-based).

Laurentian University, School of Graduate Studies and Research, Programme in Chemistry and Biochemistry, Sudbury, ON P3E 2C6, Canada. Offers analytical chemistry (M Sc); biochemistry (M Sc); environmental chemistry (M Sc); organic chemistry (M Sc); physical/theoretical chemistry (M Sc). Part-time programs available. *Degree requirements:* For master's, thesis or alternative. *Entrance requirements:* For master's, honors degree with minimum second class. *Faculty research:* Cell cycle checkpoints, kinetic modeling, toxicology to metal stress, quantum chemistry, biogeochemistry metal speciation.

Lehigh University, College of Arts and Sciences, Department of Earth and Environmental Sciences, Bethlehem, PA 18015. Offers MS, PhD. *Faculty:* 15 full-time (2 women). *Students:* 27 full-time (11 women), 3 part-time (1 woman), 3 international. Average age 27. 38 applicants, 18% accepted, 7 enrolled. In 2011, 3 master's, 1 doctorate awarded. Terminal master's awarded for partial completion of doctoral program. *Degree requirements:* For master's, thesis; for doctorate, thesis/dissertation. *Entrance requirements:* For master's and doctorate, GRE General Test, transcripts, recommendation letters, research statement, faculty advocates. Additional exam requirements/recommendations for international students: Required—TOEFL (minimum score 85 iBT). *Application deadline:* For fall admission, 1/1 for domestic and international students. Applications are processed on a rolling basis. Application fee: $75. Electronic applications accepted. *Financial support:* In 2011–12, 13 students received support, including 3 fellowships with full tuition reimbursements available (averaging $24,500 per year), 10 research assistantships with full tuition reimbursements available (averaging $24,500 per year), 10 teaching assistantships with full tuition reimbursements available (averaging $24,500 per year); career-related internships or fieldwork, Federal Work-Study, institutionally sponsored loans, scholarships/grants, tuition waivers (full and partial), and unspecified assistantships also available. Support available to part-time students. Financial award application deadline: 1/1. *Faculty research:* Tectonics, surficial processes, ecology, environmental change. *Total annual research expenditures:* $1 million. *Unit head:* Dr. Frank J. Pazzaglia, Chairman, 610-758-3667, Fax: 610-758-3677, E-mail: fjp3@lehigh.edu. *Application contact:* Dr. Stephen Peters, Graduate Coordinator, 610-758-3957, Fax: 610-758-3677, E-mail: scp2@lehigh.edu. Web site: http://www.ees.lehigh.edu/.

Peterson's Graduate Programs in the Physical Sciences, Mathematics, Agricultural Sciences, the Environment & Natural Resources 2013

facebook.com/petersonspublishing **485**

Environmental Sciences

Louisiana State University and Agricultural and Mechanical College, Graduate School, College of Agriculture, School of Renewable Natural Resources, Baton Rouge, LA 70803. Offers fisheries (MS); forestry (MS, PhD); wildlife (MS); wildlife and fisheries science (PhD). *Faculty:* 31 full-time (5 women). *Students:* 53 full-time (13 women), 11 part-time (2 women); includes 2 minority (both Hispanic/Latino), 16 international. Average age 30. 21 applicants, 33% accepted, 7 enrolled. In 2011, 12 master's, 7 doctorates awarded. *Degree requirements:* For master's, thesis; for doctorate, thesis/dissertation. *Entrance requirements:* For master's, GRE General Test, minimum GPA of 3.0; for doctorate, GRE General Test, MS, minimum GPA of 3.0. Additional exam requirements/recommendations for international students: Required—TOEFL (minimum score 550 paper-based; 213 computer-based; 79 iBT), IELTS (minimum score 6.5). *Application deadline:* For fall admission, 1/25 priority date for domestic students, 5/15 for international students; for spring admission, 10/15 for international students. Applications are processed on a rolling basis. Application fee: $50 ($70 for international students). Electronic applications accepted. *Financial support:* In 2011–12, 61 students received support, including 52 research assistantships with partial tuition reimbursements available (averaging $19,938 per year), 1 teaching assistantship (averaging $22,000 per year); fellowships, Federal Work-Study, institutionally sponsored loans, scholarships/grants, health care benefits, tuition waivers (full and partial), and unspecified assistantships also available. Financial award application deadline: 4/15; financial award applicants required to submit FAFSA. *Faculty research:* Forest biology and management, aquaculture, fisheries biology and ecology, upland and wetlands wildlife. *Total annual research expenditures:* $47,156. *Unit head:* Dr. Allen Rutherford, Director, 225-578-4131, Fax: 225-578-4227, E-mail: druther@lsu.edu. *Application contact:* Dr. William Kelso, Coordinator of Graduate Studies, 225-578-4176, Fax: 225-578-4227, E-mail: wkelso@lsu.edu. Web site: http://www.fwf.lsu.edu/.

Louisiana State University and Agricultural and Mechanical College, Graduate School, School of the Coast and Environment, Department of Environmental Sciences, Baton Rouge, LA 70803. Offers environmental planning and management (MS); environmental toxicology (MS). *Faculty:* 9 full-time (3 women). *Students:* 24 full-time (16 women), 9 part-time (4 women); includes 6 minority (3 Black or African American, non-Hispanic/Latino; 2 Asian, non-Hispanic/Latino; 1 Hispanic/Latino), 6 international. Average age 27. 19 applicants, 74% accepted, 7 enrolled. In 2011, 14 master's awarded. *Degree requirements:* For master's, thesis (for some programs). *Entrance requirements:* For master's, GRE General Test, minimum GPA of 3.0. Additional exam requirements/recommendations for international students: Required—TOEFL (minimum score 550 paper-based; 213 computer-based; 79 iBT) or IELTS (minimum score 6.5). *Application deadline:* For fall admission, 1/25 priority date for domestic students, 5/15 for international students; for spring admission, 10/15 for international students. Applications are processed on a rolling basis. Application fee: $50 ($70 for international students). Electronic applications accepted. *Financial support:* In 2011–12, 30 students received support, including 1 fellowship with full and partial tuition reimbursement available (averaging $17,831 per year), 15 research assistantships with full and partial tuition reimbursements available (averaging $15,467 per year), 6 teaching assistantships with full and partial tuition reimbursements available (averaging $10,333 per year); career-related internships or fieldwork, Federal Work-Study, institutionally sponsored loans, scholarships/grants, health care benefits, and unspecified assistantships also available. Support available to part-time students. Financial award applicants required to submit FAFSA. *Faculty research:* Environmental toxicology, environmental policy and law, microbial ecology, bioremediation, genetic toxicology. *Total annual research expenditures:* $1.9 million. *Unit head:* Dr. Ed Laws, Chair, 225-578-8521, Fax: 225-578-4286, E-mail: edlaws@lsu.edu. *Application contact:* Charlotte G. St. Romain, Academic Coordinator, 225-578-8522, Fax: 225-578-4286, E-mail: cstrom4@lsu.edu. Web site: http://info.envs.lsu.edu/.

Loyola Marymount University, College of Science and Engineering, Department of Civil Engineering and Environmental Science, Program in Environmental Science, Los Angeles, CA 90045. Offers MS. Part-time programs available. *Faculty:* 7 full-time (1 woman), 2 part-time/adjunct (0 women). *Students:* 25 full-time (13 women), 10 part-time (7 women); includes 14 minority (2 Black or African American, non-Hispanic/Latino; 8 Asian, non-Hispanic/Latino; 3 Hispanic/Latino; 1 Two or more races, non-Hispanic/Latino), 3 international. Average age 28. 17 applicants, 100% accepted, 12 enrolled. In 2011, 2 master's awarded. *Degree requirements:* For master's, comprehensive exam, thesis or alternative. *Entrance requirements:* For master's, 2 letters of recommendation, personal statement. Additional exam requirements/recommendations for international students: Required—TOEFL (minimum score 550 paper-based; 213 computer-based; 80 iBT). *Application deadline:* Applications are processed on a rolling basis. Application fee: $50. Electronic applications accepted. *Financial support:* In 2011–12, 12 students received support. Scholarships/grants and unspecified assistantships available. Support available to part-time students. Financial award application deadline: 6/1; financial award applicants required to submit FAFSA. *Total annual research expenditures:* $80,391. *Unit head:* Prof. Joe J. Reichenberger, Graduate Director, 310-338-2830, E-mail: jreichenberger@lmu.edu. *Application contact:* Chake H. Kouyoumjian, Associate Dean of Graduate Studies, 310-338-2721, E-mail: ckouyoum@lmu.edu. Web site: http://cse.lmu.edu/departments/civilengineering.htm.

Marshall University, Academic Affairs Division, College of Information Technology and Engineering, Division of Applied Science and Technology, Program in Environmental Science, Huntington, WV 25755. Offers MS. Part-time and evening/weekend programs available. *Students:* 22 full-time (7 women), 14 part-time (5 women); includes 2 minority (both Asian, non-Hispanic/Latino), 4 international. Average age 30. In 2011, 7 master's awarded. *Degree requirements:* For master's, final project, oral exam. *Entrance requirements:* For master's, GRE General Test or MAT, minimum GPA of 2.5, course work in calculus. Application fee: $40. *Financial support:* Tuition waivers (full) available. Support available to part-time students. Financial award application deadline: 8/1; financial award applicants required to submit FAFSA. *Unit head:* Dr. D. Scott Simonton, Associate Professor, 304-746-2045, E-mail: simonton@marshall.edu. *Application contact:* Information Contact, 304-746-1900, Fax: 304-746-1902, E-mail: services@marshall.edu. Web site: http://www.marshall.edu/cite/.

Massachusetts Institute of Technology, School of Engineering, Department of Civil and Environmental Engineering, Cambridge, MA 02139. Offers biological oceanography (PhD, Sc D); chemical oceanography (PhD, Sc D); civil and environmental engineering (PhD, Sc D); civil and environmental systems (PhD, Sc D); civil engineering (PhD, Sc D, CE); coastal engineering (PhD, Sc D); construction engineering and management (PhD, Sc D); environmental and water quality engineering (M Eng); environmental biology (PhD, Sc D); environmental chemistry (PhD, Sc D); environmental engineering (PhD, Sc D); environmental fluid mechanics (PhD, Sc D); environmental science and engineering (SM); geotechnical and geoenvironmental engineering (PhD, Sc D); geotechnology (M Eng); high-performance structures (M Eng); hydrology (PhD, Sc D); information technology (PhD, Sc D); mechanics (SM); oceanographic engineering (PhD, Sc D); structures and materials (PhD, Sc D); transportation (M Eng, PhD, Sc D); SM/MBA. *Faculty:* 35 full-time (6 women), 1 part-time/adjunct (0 women). *Students:* 216 full-time (80 women); includes 30 minority (4 Black or African American, non-Hispanic/Latino; 13 Asian, non-Hispanic/Latino; 8 Hispanic/Latino; 5 Two or more races, non-Hispanic/Latino), 110 international. Average age 27. 589 applicants, 26% accepted, 91 enrolled. In 2011, 62 master's, 14 doctorates awarded. *Degree requirements:* For master's and CE, thesis; for doctorate, comprehensive exam, thesis/dissertation. *Entrance requirements:* For master's and doctorate, GRE General Test. Additional exam requirements/recommendations for international students: Required—TOEFL (minimum score 577 paper-based; 233 computer-based; 90 iBT), IELTS (minimum score 7). *Application deadline:* For fall admission, 12/15 for domestic and international students. Application fee: $75. Electronic applications accepted. *Expenses:* Tuition: Full-time $40,460; part-time $630 per credit hour. *Required fees:* $272. *Financial support:* In 2011–12, 180 students received support, including 51 fellowships (averaging $30,800 per year), 110 research assistantships (averaging $29,500 per year), 19 teaching assistantships (averaging $29,500 per year); career-related internships or fieldwork, Federal Work-Study, institutionally sponsored loans, scholarships/grants, health care benefits, and unspecified assistantships also available. *Faculty research:* Environmental chemistry, environmental fluid mechanics and coastal engineering, environmental microbiology, geotechnical engineering and geomechanics, hydrology and hydroclimatology, infrastructure systems, mechanics of materials and structures, transportation systems. *Total annual research expenditures:* $17.7 million. *Unit head:* Prof. Andrew Whittle, Head, 617-253-7101. *Application contact:* Patricia Glidden, Graduate Admissions Coordinator, 617-253-7119, Fax: 617-258-6775, E-mail: cee-admissions@mit.edu. Web site: http://cee.mit.edu/.

McNeese State University, Doré School of Graduate Studies, College of Science, Department of Agricultural Sciences, Program in Environmental and Chemical Sciences, Lake Charles, LA 70609. Offers agricultural sciences (MS); environmental science (MS). Evening/weekend programs available. *Faculty:* 12 full-time (1 woman). *Students:* 23 full-time (13 women), 10 part-time (5 women); includes 6 minority (4 Black or African American, non-Hispanic/Latino; 1 American Indian or Alaska Native, non-Hispanic/Latino; 1 Hispanic/Latino), 1 international. In 2011, 13 master's awarded. *Degree requirements:* For master's, comprehensive exam, thesis or alternative. *Entrance requirements:* For master's, GRE. *Application deadline:* For fall admission, 5/15 priority date for domestic students, 5/15 for international students; for spring admission, 10/15 priority date for domestic students, 10/15 for international students. Applications are processed on a rolling basis. Application fee: $20 ($30 for international students). *Expenses:* Tuition, state resident: part-time $519 per credit hour. Tuition and fees vary according to course load. *Financial support:* Application deadline: 5/1. *Unit head:* Dr. Bruce C. Wyman, Coordinator, 337-475-5669, Fax: 337-475-5677, E-mail: wyman@mcneese.edu. *Application contact:* Dr. Bruce C. Wyman, Coordinator, 337-475-5669, Fax: 337-475-5677, E-mail: wyman@mcneese.edu.

Memorial University of Newfoundland, School of Graduate Studies, Interdisciplinary Program in Environmental Science, St. John's, NL A1C 5S7, Canada. Offers M Env Sc, M Sc. Part-time programs available. *Degree requirements:* For master's, thesis (M Sc), project (M Env Sci). *Entrance requirements:* For master's, honors B Sc or 2nd class B Eng. Electronic applications accepted. *Faculty research:* Earth and ocean systems, environmental chemistry and toxicology, environmental engineering.

Mercer University, Graduate Studies, Macon Campus, School of Engineering, Macon, GA 31207-0003. Offers biomedical engineering (MSE); computer engineering (MSE); electrical engineering (MSE); engineering management (MSE); environmental engineering (MSE); environmental systems (MS); mechanical engineering (MSE); software engineering (MSE); software systems (MS); technical communications management (MS); technical management (MS). Part-time and evening/weekend programs available. Postbaccalaureate distance learning degree programs offered (no on-campus study). *Faculty:* 17 full-time (3 women), 1 part-time/adjunct (0 women). *Students:* 12 full-time (3 women), 113 part-time (28 women); includes 23 minority (13 Black or African American, non-Hispanic/Latino; 9 Asian, non-Hispanic/Latino; 1 Hispanic/Latino). Average age 31. In 2011, 44 master's awarded. *Degree requirements:* For master's, thesis or alternative. *Entrance requirements:* For master's, minimum undergraduate GPA of 3.0. Additional exam requirements/recommendations for international students: Required—TOEFL. *Application deadline:* For fall admission, 7/1 for domestic students; for spring admission, 11/15 for domestic students. Applications are processed on a rolling basis. Application fee: $35 ($50 for international students). Electronic applications accepted. *Expenses:* Contact institution. *Financial support:* Federal Work-Study available. *Unit head:* Dr. Wade H. Shaw, Dean, 478-301-2459, Fax: 478-301-5593, E-mail: shaw_wh@mercer.edu. *Application contact:* Greg Lofton, Graduate Program Coordinator, 478-301-5480, Fax: 478-301-5434, E-mail: lofton_g@mercer.edu. Web site: http://engineering.mercer.edu/.

Miami University, Institute of Environmental Sciences, Oxford, OH 45056. Offers M En. Part-time programs available. *Students:* 58 full-time (34 women), 2 part-time (1 woman); includes 7 minority (1 Black or African American, non-Hispanic/Latino; 1 American Indian or Alaska Native, non-Hispanic/Latino; 4 Asian, non-Hispanic/Latino; 1 Two or more races, non-Hispanic/Latino), 1 international. Average age 29. In 2011, 16 degrees awarded. *Entrance requirements:* For master's, minimum undergraduate GPA of 3.0 during previous 2 years or 2.75 overall. Additional exam requirements/recommendations for international students: Required—TOEFL. *Application deadline:* For fall admission, 2/1 for domestic and international students. Application fee: $50. *Expenses:* Tuition, state resident: full-time $12,023; part-time $501 per credit hour. Tuition, nonresident: full-time $26,554; part-time $1107 per credit hour. *Required fees:* $528. *Financial support:* Fellowships with tuition reimbursements, research assistantships, teaching assistantships, career-related internships or fieldwork, Federal Work-Study, health care benefits, tuition waivers (full), and unspecified assistantships available. Financial award application deadline: 2/15; financial award applicants required to submit FAFSA. *Unit head:* Dr. Thomas Crist, Director of IES and Professor of Zoology, 513-529-5811, Fax: 513-529-5814, E-mail: ies@muohio.edu. *Application contact:* Dr. Thomas Crist, Director of IES and Professor of Zoology, 513-529-5811, Fax: 513-529-5814, E-mail: ies@muohio.edu. Web site: http://www.cas.muohio.edu/ies/.

Michigan State University, The Graduate School, College of Natural Science, Department of Geological Sciences, East Lansing, MI 48824. Offers environmental geosciences (MS, PhD); environmental geosciences-environmental toxicology (PhD); geological sciences (MS, PhD). *Degree requirements:* For master's, thesis (for those without prior thesis work); for doctorate, thesis/dissertation. *Entrance requirements:* For master's, GRE General Test, minimum GPA of 3.0, course work in geoscience, 3 letters of recommendation; for doctorate, GRE General Test, 3 letters of recommendation. Additional exam requirements/recommendations for international students: Required—TOEFL (minimum score 550 paper-based; 213 computer-based), Michigan State University ELT (minimum score 85), Michigan English Language Assessment Battery (minimum score 83). Electronic applications accepted. *Faculty research:* Water in the environment, global and biological change, crystal dynamics.

Minnesota State University Mankato, College of Graduate Studies, College of Science, Engineering and Technology, Department of Biological Sciences, Program in Environmental Sciences, Mankato, MN 56001. Offers MS. *Students:* 2 full-time (0 women), 10 part-time (3 women). *Degree requirements:* For master's, one foreign language, comprehensive exam, thesis or alternative. *Entrance requirements:* For master's, minimum GPA of 3.0 during previous 2 years. Additional exam requirements/recommendations for international students: Required—TOEFL. *Application deadline:* For fall admission, 7/1 priority date for domestic students; for spring admission, 11/1 for domestic students. Applications are processed on a rolling basis. Application fee: $40. Electronic applications accepted. *Financial support:* Research assistantships with partial tuition reimbursements, teaching assistantships with partial tuition reimbursements, career-related internships or fieldwork, Federal Work-Study, institutionally sponsored loans, and unspecified assistantships available. Financial award application deadline: 3/15; financial award applicants required to submit FAFSA. *Unit head:* Dr. Beth Proctor, Graduate Coordinator, 507-389-5697. *Application contact:* 507-389-2321, E-mail: grad@mnsu.edu.

Montana State University, College of Graduate Studies, College of Agriculture, Department of Land Resources and Environmental Sciences, Bozeman, MT 59717. Offers land rehabilitation (interdisciplinary) (MS); land resources and environmental sciences (MS), including land rehabilitation (interdisciplinary), land resources and environmental sciences. Part-time programs available. *Degree requirements:* For master's, comprehensive exam. *Entrance requirements:* For master's, GRE General Test. Additional exam requirements/recommendations for international students: Required—TOEFL (minimum score 550 paper-based; 213 computer-based). Electronic applications accepted. *Faculty research:* Soil nutrient management and plant nutrition, isotope biogeochemistry of soils, biodegradation of hydrocarbons in soils and natural waters, remote sensing, GIS systems, managed and natural ecosystems, microbial and metabolic diversity in geothermally heated soils, integrated management of weeds, diversified cropping systems, insect behavior and ecology, river ecology, microbial biogeochemistry, weed ecology.

Montana State University, College of Graduate Studies, College of Letters and Science, Department of Ecology, Bozeman, MT 59717. Offers ecological and environmental statistics (MS); ecology and environmental sciences (PhD); fish and wildlife biology (PhD); fish and wildlife management (MS). Part-time programs available. *Degree requirements:* For master's, comprehensive exam, thesis (for some programs); for doctorate, comprehensive exam, thesis/dissertation. *Entrance requirements:* For master's and doctorate, GRE, minimum GPA of 3.0, letters of recommendation, essay. Additional exam requirements/recommendations for international students: Required—TOEFL (minimum score 550 paper-based; 213 computer-based). Electronic applications accepted. *Faculty research:* Community ecology, population ecology, land-use effects, management and conservation, environmental modeling.

Montclair State University, The Graduate School, College of Science and Mathematics, Department of Earth and Environmental Studies, Program in Environmental Studies, Montclair, NJ 07043-1624. Offers environmental education (MA); environmental management (MA); environmental science (MA). Part-time and evening/weekend programs available. *Students:* 14 full-time (8 women), 21 part-time (12 women); includes 4 minority (1 Asian, non-Hispanic/Latino; 3 Hispanic/Latino), 2 international. Average age 34. 40 applicants, 55% accepted, 12 enrolled. In 2011, 16 master's awarded. *Degree requirements:* For master's, thesis. *Entrance requirements:* For master's, GRE General Test, 2 letters of recommendation, essay. Additional exam requirements/recommendations for international students: Required—TOEFL (minimum score 83 iBT), IELTS (minimum score 6.5). *Application deadline:* Applications are processed on a rolling basis. Application fee: $60. Electronic applications accepted. *Financial support:* In 2011–12, 10 research assistantships with full tuition reimbursements (averaging $7,000 per year) were awarded; Federal Work-Study, scholarships/grants, and unspecified assistantships also available. Support available to part-time students. Financial award application deadline: 3/1; financial award applicants required to submit FAFSA. *Faculty research:* Environmental geochemistry/remediation/forensics, environmental law and policy, regional climate modeling, remote sensing, Cenozoic marine sediment records from polar regions, sustainability science. *Unit head:* Dr. Matthew Goring, Chairperson, 973-655-5409. *Application contact:* Amy Aiello, Executive Director of The Graduate School, 973-655-5147, Fax: 973-655-7869, E-mail: graduate.school@montclair.edu. Web site: http://www.montclair.edu/csam/earth-environment-studies/academic-programs/ma-ms-degrees/ma-concentration-environmental-studies/.

Murray State University, College of Health Sciences and Human Services, Program in Occupational Safety and Health, Murray, KY 42071. Offers environmental science (MS); industrial hygiene (MS); safety management (MS). *Accreditation:* ABET. Part-time programs available. *Degree requirements:* For master's, comprehensive exam, thesis optional, professional internship. Electronic applications accepted. *Faculty research:* Light effects on plant growth, ergonomics, toxic effects of pets' pesticides, traffic safety.

New Jersey Institute of Technology, Office of Graduate Studies, College of Science and Liberal Arts, Department of Chemistry and Environmental Science, Program in Environmental Science, Newark, NJ 07102. Offers MS, PhD. Part-time and evening/weekend programs available. *Students:* 20 full-time (13 women), 9 part-time (5 women); includes 3 minority (1 Black or African American, non-Hispanic/Latino; 1 Asian, non-Hispanic/Latino; 1 Hispanic/Latino), 15 international. Average age 32. 45 applicants, 53% accepted, 12 enrolled. In 2011, 14 master's, 1 doctorate awarded. *Degree requirements:* For doctorate, thesis/dissertation. *Entrance requirements:* For master's, GRE General Test; for doctorate, GRE General Test, minimum graduate GPA of 3.5. Additional exam requirements/recommendations for international students: Required—TOEFL (minimum score 550 paper-based; 213 computer-based; 79 iBT). *Application deadline:* For fall admission, 6/1 priority date for domestic students, 5/1 for international students; for spring admission, 11/15 priority date for domestic students, 11/15 for international students. Applications are processed on a rolling basis. Application fee: $65. Electronic applications accepted. *Expenses:* Tuition, state resident: full-time $7980; part-time $867 per credit. Tuition, nonresident: full-time $11,336; part-time $1196 per credit. *Required fees:* $230 per credit. *Financial support:* Fellowships with full and partial tuition reimbursements, research assistantships with full and partial tuition reimbursements, teaching assistantships with full and partial tuition reimbursements, career-related internships or fieldwork, Federal Work-Study, institutionally sponsored loans, and unspecified assistantships available. Financial award application deadline: 3/15. *Unit head:* Dr. Somenath Mitra, Chair, 673-596-5611, E-mail: mitra@njit.edu. *Application contact:* Kathryn Kelly, Director of Admissions, 973-596-3300, Fax: 973-596-3461, E-mail: admissions@njit.edu.

New Mexico State University, Graduate School, College of Agricultural, Consumer and Environmental Sciences, Department of Plant and Environmental Sciences, Las Cruces, NM 88003-8001. Offers horticulture (MS); plant and environmental sciences (MS, PhD). Part-time programs available. *Faculty:* 21 full-time (3 women). *Students:* 45 full-time (17 women), 19 part-time (8 women); includes 9 minority (3 American Indian or Alaska Native, non-Hispanic/Latino; 5 Hispanic/Latino; 1 Two or more races, non-Hispanic/Latino), 20 international. Average age 32. 27 applicants, 52% accepted, 11 enrolled. In 2011, 6 master's, 7 doctorates awarded. Terminal master's awarded for partial completion of doctoral program. *Degree requirements:* For master's, thesis; for doctorate, one foreign language, comprehensive exam, thesis/dissertation, qualifying exam, 2 seminars. *Entrance requirements:* For master's, GRE, minimum GPA of 3.0, 3 letters of

Peterson's Graduate Programs in the Physical Sciences, Mathematics, Agricultural Sciences, the Environment & Natural Resources 2013

facebook.com/petersonspublishing **487**

reference, letter of purpose or intent; for doctorate, GRE, minimum GPA of 3.3; 3 letters of reference, letter of purpose or intent. Additional exam requirements/ recommendations for international students: Required—TOEFL (minimum score 550 paper-based; 0 computer-based; 79 iBT), IELTS (minimum score 6.5). *Application deadline:* Applications are processed on a rolling basis. Application fee: $40 ($50 for international students). Electronic applications accepted. *Expenses:* Tuition, state resident: full-time $5004; part-time $208.50 per credit. Tuition, nonresident: full-time $17,446; part-time $726.90 per credit. *Financial support:* In 2011–12, 8 students received support, including 3 fellowships (averaging $2,892 per year), 28 research assistantships with partial tuition reimbursements available (averaging $22,079 per year), 14 teaching assistantships with partial tuition reimbursements available (averaging $22,188 per year); career-related internships or fieldwork, Federal Work-Study, scholarships/grants, health care benefits, and unspecified assistantships also available. Support available to part-time students. Financial award application deadline: 3/1. *Faculty research:* Plant breeding and genetics, molecular biology, plant physiology, soil science and environmental remediation, urban horticulture and turfgrass management. *Unit head:* Dr. Richard Pratt, Head, 575-646-3406, Fax: 575-646-6041, E-mail: ricpratt@nmsu.edu. *Application contact:* Esther Ramirez, Information Contact, 575-646-3406, Fax: 575-646-6041, E-mail: esramire@nmsu.edu. Web site: http://aces.nmsu.edu/pes.

North Carolina Agricultural and Technical State University, School of Graduate Studies, School of Agriculture and Environmental Sciences, Greensboro, NC 27411. Offers MAT, MS. Part-time and evening/weekend programs available. *Degree requirements:* For master's, comprehensive exam, qualifying exam. *Entrance requirements:* For master's, GRE General Test. *Faculty research:* Aid for small farmers, agricultural technology, housing, food science, nutrition.

North Dakota State University, College of Graduate and Interdisciplinary Studies, College of Agriculture, Food Systems, and Natural Resources, Department of Soil Science, Fargo, ND 58108. Offers environmental and conservation science (PhD); environmental conservation science (MS); natural resource management (MS, PhD); soil sciences (MS, PhD). Part-time programs available. *Students:* 7 full-time (5 women), 3 part-time (1 woman), 4 international. Average age 23. 4 applicants, 50% accepted, 0 enrolled. In 2011, 4 degrees awarded. *Degree requirements:* For master's, comprehensive exam, thesis, classroom teaching; for doctorate, comprehensive exam, thesis/dissertation, classroom teaching. *Entrance requirements:* Additional exam requirements/ recommendations for international students: Required—TOEFL (minimum score 525 paper-based; 193 computer-based; 71 iBT). *Application deadline:* For fall admission, 5/1 for international students; for winter admission, 8/1 for international students. Applications are processed on a rolling basis. Application fee: $35. Electronic applications accepted. *Financial support:* In 2011–12, 7 research assistantships with full tuition reimbursements (averaging $14,300 per year) were awarded; fellowships, Federal Work-Study, institutionally sponsored loans, and scholarships/grants also available. Financial award application deadline: 3/15. *Faculty research:* Microclimate, nitrogen management, landscape studies, water quality, soil management. *Unit head:* Dr. Donald Kirby, Interim Chair, 701-231-8901, Fax: 701-231-7861. *Application contact:* Sonya Goergen, Marketing, Recruitment, and Public Relations Coordinator, 701-231-7033, Fax: 701-231-6524. Web site: http://www.ndsu.edu/ndsu/academic/factsheets/ag/soilsci.shtml.

North Dakota State University, College of Graduate and Interdisciplinary Studies, College of Science and Mathematics, Department of Biological Sciences, Fargo, ND 58108. Offers biology (MS); botany (MS, PhD); cellular and molecular biology (PhD); environmental and conservation sciences (MS, PhD); genomics (PhD); natural resources management (MS, PhD); zoology (MS, PhD). *Faculty:* 13 full-time (7 women), 3 part-time/adjunct (1 woman). *Students:* 20 full-time (10 women), 2 part-time (both women); includes 1 minority (American Indian or Alaska Native, non-Hispanic/Latino), 2 international. 12 applicants, 33% accepted, 4 enrolled. In 2011, 3 degrees awarded. *Degree requirements:* For master's, thesis; for doctorate, thesis/dissertation. *Entrance requirements:* For master's and doctorate, GRE General Test. Additional exam requirements/ recommendations for international students: Required—TOEFL. *Application deadline:* For fall admission, 1/15 for domestic students. Applications are processed on a rolling basis. Application fee: $35. Electronic applications accepted. *Financial support:* Fellowships with full tuition reimbursements, research assistantships with full tuition reimbursements, teaching assistantships with full tuition reimbursements, career-related internships or fieldwork, Federal Work-Study, institutionally sponsored loans, scholarships/grants, tuition waivers (full), and unspecified assistantships available. Support available to part-time students. Financial award application deadline: 4/15; financial award applicants required to submit FAFSA. *Faculty research:* Comparative endocrinology, physiology, behavioral ecology, plant cell biology, aquatic biology. *Unit head:* Dr. Wendy Reed, Head, 701-231-7087, E-mail: wendy.reed@ndsu.edu. *Application contact:* Sonya Goergen, Marketing, Recruitment, and Public Relations Coordinator, 701-231-7033, Fax: 701-231-6524. Web site: http://biology.ndsu.nodak.edu/.

North Dakota State University, College of Graduate and Interdisciplinary Studies, Interdisciplinary Program in Environmental and Conservation Sciences, Fargo, ND 58108. Offers MS, PhD. *Students:* 32 full-time (15 women), 10 part-time (3 women); includes 1 minority (Two or more races, non-Hispanic/Latino), 21 international. 23 applicants, 22% accepted, 5 enrolled. In 2011, 5 master's, 5 doctorates awarded. *Degree requirements:* For master's, comprehensive exam,

thesis. *Entrance requirements:* Additional exam requirements/recommendations for international students: Required—TOEFL (minimum score 550 paper-based; 213 computer-based; 79 iBT). *Application deadline:* For fall admission, 5/1 for international students; for spring admission, 5/1 for international students. Application fee: $35. *Unit head:* Dr. Craig Stockwell, Director, 701-231-8449, Fax: 701-231-7149, E-mail: craig.stockwell@ndsu.edu. *Application contact:* Madonna Fitzgerald, Administrative Assistant, 701-231-6456, E-mail: madonna.fitzgerald@ndsu.edu. Web site: http://www.ndsu.nodak.edu/ecs/.

Northern Arizona University, Graduate College, College of Engineering, Forestry and Natural Sciences, School of Earth Sciences and Environmental Sustainability, Flagstaff, AZ 86011. Offers climate science and solutions (MS); earth science (MS); earth sciences and environmental sustainability (PhD); environmental sciences and policy (MS); geology (MS). *Faculty:* 27 full-time (9 women). *Students:* 67 full-time (32 women), 11 part-time (3 women); includes 6 minority (3 American Indian or Alaska Native, non-Hispanic/Latino; 3 Hispanic/Latino), 2 international. 149 applicants, 23% accepted, 30 enrolled. In 2011, 16 degrees awarded. *Degree requirements:* For master's, comprehensive exam (for some programs), thesis (for some programs). *Entrance requirements:* Additional exam requirements/recommendations for international students: Required—TOEFL (minimum score 550 paper-based; 213 computer-based; 80 iBT), IELTS (minimum score 7). *Application deadline:* For fall admission, 2/1 priority date for domestic students, 2/1 for international students. Applications are processed on a rolling basis. Application fee: $65. Electronic applications accepted. *Expenses:* Tuition, state resident: full-time $7190; part-time $355 per credit hour. Tuition, nonresident: full-time $18,092; part-time $1005 per credit hour. *Required fees:* $818; $328 per semester. *Financial support:* In 2011–12, 6 fellowships, 7 research assistantships with partial tuition reimbursements (averaging $12,866 per year), 28 teaching assistantships with partial tuition reimbursements (averaging $12,477 per year) were awarded; career-related internships or fieldwork, Federal Work-Study, scholarships/grants, health care benefits, tuition waivers (full and partial), and unspecified assistantships also available. Financial award applicants required to submit FAFSA. *Unit head:* Dr. Abe Springer, Director, 928-523-7198. *Application contact:* Mark Aasmundstad, Coordinator, 928-523-9333, Fax: 928-523-7432, E-mail: mark.aasmundstad@nau.edu. Web site: http://nau.edu/cefns/natsci/seses/.

Nova Scotia Agricultural College, Research and Graduate Studies, Truro, NS B2N 5E3, Canada. Offers agriculture (M Sc), including air quality, animal behavior, animal molecular genetics, animal nutrition, animal technology, aquaculture, botany, crop management, crop physiology, ecology, environmental microbiology, food science, horticulture, nutrient management, pest management, physiology, plant biotechnology, plant pathology, soil chemistry, soil fertility, waste management and composting, water quality. Program offered jointly with Dalhousie University. Part-time programs available. *Degree requirements:* For master's, thesis, ATC Exam Teaching Assistantship. *Entrance requirements:* For master's, honors B Sc, minimum GPA of 3.0. Additional exam requirements/ recommendations for international students: Required—TOEFL (minimum score 580 paper-based; 237 computer-based; 92 iBT), IELTS, Michigan English Language Assessment Battery, CanTEST, CAEL. *Faculty research:* Bio-product development, organic agriculture, nutrient management, air and water quality, agricultural biotechnology.

Nova Southeastern University, Oceanographic Center, Fort Lauderdale, FL 33314-7796. Offers biological sciences (MS); coastal zone management (MS); marine and coastal studies (MA); marine biology (MS); marine biology and oceanography (PhD), including marine biology, oceanography; marine environmental science (MS). Part-time and evening/weekend programs available. *Faculty:* 15 full-time (1 woman), 5 part-time/adjunct (0 women). *Students:* 130 full-time (86 women), 135 part-time (87 women); includes 34 minority (5 Black or African American, non-Hispanic/Latino; 5 Asian, non-Hispanic/Latino; 22 Hispanic/Latino; 2 Two or more races, non-Hispanic/Latino), 7 international. Average age 29. 98 applicants, 82% accepted, 67 enrolled. In 2011, 30 master's, 1 doctorate awarded. *Degree requirements:* For master's, thesis; for doctorate, comprehensive exam, thesis/dissertation, departmental qualifying exam. *Entrance requirements:* For master's, GRE General Test; for doctorate, GRE General Test, master's degree. Additional exam requirements/recommendations for international students: Required—TOEFL (minimum score 550 paper-based). *Application deadline:* Applications are processed on a rolling basis. Application fee: $50. *Expenses:* Contact institution. *Financial support:* In 2011–12, 25 research assistantships (averaging $4,000 per year), 3 teaching assistantships (averaging $3,500 per year) were awarded; career-related internships or fieldwork, Federal Work-Study, scholarships/grants, tuition waivers (partial), and unspecified assistantships also available. Support available to part-time students. Financial award applicants required to submit FAFSA. *Faculty research:* Physical, geological, chemical, and biological oceanography. *Unit head:* Dr. Richard Dodge, Dean, 954-262-3600, Fax: 954-262-4020, E-mail: dodge@nsu.nova.edu. *Application contact:* Dr. Richard Spieler, Director of Academic Programs, 954-262-3600, Fax: 954-262-4020, E-mail: spieler@nova.edu. Web site: http://www.nova.edu/ocean/.

Oakland University, Graduate Study and Lifelong Learning, College of Arts and Sciences, Department of Chemistry, Rochester, MI 48309-4401. Offers biological sciences: health and environmental chemistry (PhD); chemistry (MS). *Degree requirements:* For master's, thesis; for doctorate, thesis/dissertation. *Entrance requirements:* For master's, minimum GPA of 3.0 for unconditional admission; for doctorate, GRE Subject Test, minimum GPA of 3.0 for unconditional admission.

Additional exam requirements/recommendations for international students: Required—TOEFL (minimum score 550 paper-based; 213 computer-based). Electronic applications accepted. *Faculty research:* Chemistry of free radical species generated from biological intermediates; fate of toxic organic compounds in the environment; electroanalytical and surface chemistry at solid/liquid interface; computational modeling of intermolecular interactions and surface phenomena; metabolism and biological activity of modified fatty acids and xenobiotic carboxylic acids; physiologic and pathologic mechanisms that modulate immune responses.

The Ohio State University, Graduate School, College of Food, Agricultural, and Environmental Sciences, School of Environment and Natural Resources, Columbus, OH 43210. Offers MS, PhD. *Faculty:* 35. *Students:* 72 full-time (40 women), 20 part-time (13 women); includes 8 minority (1 Black or African American, non-Hispanic/Latino; 2 Asian, non-Hispanic/Latino; 3 Hispanic/Latino; 2 Two or more races, non-Hispanic/Latino), 10 international. Average age 30. In 2011, 12 master's, 3 doctorates awarded. *Degree requirements:* For master's, thesis; for doctorate, thesis/dissertation. *Entrance requirements:* For master's and doctorate, GRE. Additional exam requirements/recommendations for international students: Required—TOEFL (minimum score 550 paper-based; 79 iBT), Michigan English Language Assessment Battery (minimum score 82). *Application deadline:* Applications are processed on a rolling basis. Application fee: $40 ($50 for international students). Electronic applications accepted. *Expenses:* Tuition, state resident: full-time $11,400. Tuition, nonresident: full-time $28,125. Tuition and fees vary according to course load, degree level, campus/location and program. *Unit head:* Ronald Hendrick, Director, 614-292-8522, E-mail: hendrick.15@osu.edu. *Application contact:* Amy Schmidt, Graduate Program Coordinator, 614-292-9883, Fax: 614-292-7432, E-mail: schmidt.442@osu.edu. Web site: http://senr.osu.edu/default.asp.

Oklahoma State University, College of Agricultural Science and Natural Resources, Department of Horticulture and Landscape Architecture, Stillwater, OK 74078. Offers agriculture (M Ag); crop science (PhD); environmental science (PhD); horticulture (MS); plant science (PhD). *Faculty:* 20 full-time (2 women), 2 part-time/adjunct (1 woman). *Students:* 3 full-time (all women), 12 part-time (8 women); includes 2 minority (1 Black or African American, non-Hispanic/Latino; 1 American Indian or Alaska Native, non-Hispanic/Latino), 7 international. Average age 28. 6 applicants, 67% accepted, 4 enrolled. In 2011, 6 degrees awarded. *Degree requirements:* For master's, thesis (for some programs); for doctorate, comprehensive exam, thesis/dissertation. *Entrance requirements:* For master's and doctorate, GRE or GMAT. Additional exam requirements/recommendations for international students: Required—TOEFL (minimum score 550 paper-based; 79 iBT). *Application deadline:* For fall admission, 3/1 for international students; for spring admission, 8/1 for international students. Applications are processed on a rolling basis. Application fee: $40 ($75 for international students). Electronic applications accepted. *Expenses:* Tuition, state resident: full-time $4044; part-time $168.50 per credit hour. Tuition, nonresident: full-time $16,008; part-time $667 per credit hour. *Required fees:* $2122; $88.45 per credit hour. One-time fee: $50. Tuition and fees vary according to course load and campus/location. *Financial support:* In 2011–12, 13 research assistantships (averaging $14,145 per year) were awarded; career-related internships or fieldwork, Federal Work-Study, scholarships/grants, health care benefits, tuition waivers (partial), and unspecified assistantships also available. Support available to part-time students. Financial award application deadline: 3/1; financial award applicants required to submit FAFSA. *Faculty research:* Stress and postharvest physiology; water utilization and runoff; IPM systems and nursery, turf, floriculture, vegetable, net and fruit produces and natural resources, food extraction, and processing; public garden management. *Unit head:* Dr. Dale Maronek, Head, 405-744-5414, Fax: 405-744-9709. *Application contact:* Dr. Sheryl Tucker, Dean, 405-744-7099, Fax: 405-744-0355, E-mail: grad-i@okstate.edu. Web site: http://www.hortla.okstate.edu/.

Oklahoma State University, College of Agricultural Science and Natural Resources, Department of Plant and Soil Sciences, Stillwater, OK 74078. Offers crop science (PhD); environmental science (PhD); plant and soil sciences (MS); plant science (PhD); soil science (M Ag, PhD). *Faculty:* 31 full-time (4 women), 1 part-time/adjunct (0 women). *Students:* 19 full-time (5 women), 42 part-time (20 women); includes 5 minority (2 Black or African American, non-Hispanic/Latino; 1 Asian, non-Hispanic/Latino; 2 Two or more races, non-Hispanic/Latino), 33 international. Average age 28. 32 applicants, 22% accepted, 3 enrolled. In 2011, 18 master's, 3 doctorates awarded. *Degree requirements:* For master's, thesis; for doctorate, comprehensive exam, thesis/dissertation. *Entrance requirements:* For master's and doctorate, GRE or GMAT. Additional exam requirements/recommendations for international students: Required—TOEFL (minimum score 550 paper-based; 79 iBT). *Application deadline:* For fall admission, 3/1 for international students; for spring admission, 8/1 for international students. Applications are processed on a rolling basis. Application fee: $40 ($75 for international students). Electronic applications accepted. *Expenses:* Tuition, state resident: full-time $4044; part-time $168.50 per credit hour. Tuition, nonresident: full-time $16,008; part-time $667 per credit hour. *Required fees:* $2122; $88.45 per credit hour. One-time fee: $50. Tuition and fees vary according to course load and campus/location. *Financial support:* In 2011–12, 49 research assistantships (averaging $14,782 per year), 3 teaching assistantships (averaging $17,080 per year) were awarded; career-related internships or fieldwork, Federal Work-Study, scholarships/grants, health care benefits, tuition waivers (partial), and unspecified assistantships also available. Support available to part-time students. Financial award application deadline: 3/1; financial award applicants required to submit

FAFSA. *Faculty research:* Crop science, weed science, rangeland ecology and management, biotechnology, breeding and genetics. *Unit head:* Dr. Don R. Murray, Interim Head, 405-744-6130, Fax: 405-744-5269. *Application contact:* Dr. Sheryl Tucker, Dean, 405-744-7099, Fax: 405-744-0355, E-mail: grad-i@okstate.edu. Web site: http://www.pss.okstate.edu.

Oklahoma State University, College of Arts and Sciences, Department of Botany, Stillwater, OK 74078. Offers botany (MS); environmental science (MS, PhD); plant science (PhD). *Faculty:* 15 full-time (6 women), 3 part-time/adjunct (1 woman). *Students:* 1 full-time (0 women), 9 part-time (5 women); includes 3 minority (1 American Indian or Alaska Native, non-Hispanic/Latino; 1 Hispanic/Latino; 1 Two or more races, non-Hispanic/Latino). Average age 28. 9 applicants, 22% accepted, 2 enrolled. In 2011, 1 degree awarded. *Degree requirements:* For master's, thesis; for doctorate, comprehensive exam, thesis/dissertation. *Entrance requirements:* For master's and doctorate, GRE or GMAT. Additional exam requirements/recommendations for international students: Required—TOEFL (minimum score 550 paper-based; 79 iBT). *Application deadline:* For fall admission, 3/1 for international students; for spring admission, 8/1 for international students. Applications are processed on a rolling basis. Application fee: $40 ($75 for international students). Electronic applications accepted. *Expenses:* Tuition, state resident: full-time $4044; part-time $168.50 per credit hour. Tuition, nonresident: full-time $16,008; part-time $667 per credit hour. *Required fees:* $2122; $88.45 per credit hour. One-time fee: $50. Tuition and fees vary according to course load and campus/location. *Financial support:* In 2011–12, 3 research assistantships (averaging $16,004 per year), 9 teaching assistantships (averaging $15,405 per year) were awarded; career-related internships or fieldwork, Federal Work-Study, scholarships/grants, health care benefits, tuition waivers (partial), and unspecified assistantships also available. Support available to part-time students. Financial award application deadline: 3/1; financial award applicants required to submit FAFSA. *Faculty research:* Ethnobotany, developmental genetics of Arabidopsis, biological roles of Plasmodesmata, community ecology and biodiversity, nutrient cycling in grassland ecosystems. *Unit head:* Dr. Linda Watson, Head, 405-744-5559, Fax: 405-744-7074. *Application contact:* Dr. Sheryl Tucker, Dean, 405-744-7099, Fax: 405-744-0355, E-mail: grad-i@okstate.edu. Web site: http://botany.okstate.edu.

Oklahoma State University, Graduate College, Stillwater, OK `74078. Offers aerospace security (Graduate Certificate); biobased products and bioenergy (Graduate Certificate); bioinformatics (Graduate Certificate); business data mining (Graduate Certificate); engineering and technology management (Graduate Certificate); environmental science (MS); global issues (Graduate Certificate); information assurance (Graduate Certificate); international studies (MS); natural and applied science (MS); photonics (PhD); plant science (PhD); teaching English to speakers of other languages (Graduate Certificate). Programs are interdisciplinary. *Faculty:* 2 full-time (both women), 3 part-time/adjunct (0 women). *Students:* 86 full-time (50 women), 149 part-time (76 women); includes 55 minority (14 Black or African American, non-Hispanic/Latino; 11 American Indian or Alaska Native, non-Hispanic/Latino; 8 Asian, non-Hispanic/Latino; 7 Hispanic/Latino; 1 Native Hawaiian or other Pacific Islander, non-Hispanic/Latino; 14 Two or more races, non-Hispanic/Latino), 57 international. Average age 31. 597 applicants, 68% accepted, 78 enrolled. In 2011, 98 master's, 8 doctorates awarded. *Degree requirements:* For master's, thesis (for some programs); for doctorate, comprehensive exam, thesis/dissertation. *Entrance requirements:* For master's and doctorate, GRE or GMAT. Additional exam requirements/recommendations for international students: Required—TOEFL (minimum score 550 paper-based; 79 iBT). *Application deadline:* For fall admission, 3/1 for international students; for spring admission, 8/1 for international students. Applications are processed on a rolling basis. Application fee: $40 ($75 for international students). Electronic applications accepted. *Expenses:* Tuition, state resident: full-time $4044; part-time $168.50 per credit hour. Tuition, nonresident: full-time $16,008; part-time $667 per credit hour. *Required fees:* $2122; $88.45 per credit hour. One-time fee: $50. Tuition and fees vary according to course load and campus/location. *Financial support:* In 2011–12, 2 research assistantships (averaging $10,302 per year) were awarded; career-related internships or fieldwork, Federal Work-Study, scholarships/grants, health care benefits, tuition waivers (partial), and unspecified assistantships also available. Support available to part-time students. Financial award application deadline: 3/1; financial award applicants required to submit FAFSA. *Unit head:* Dr. Sheryl Tucker, Dean, 405-744-7099, Fax: 405-744-0355, E-mail: grad-i@okstate.edu. *Application contact:* Dr. Susan Mathew, Coordinator of Admissions, 405-744-6368, Fax: 405-744-0355, E-mail: grad-i@okstate.edu. Web site: http://gradcollege.okstate.edu/.

Oregon Health & Science University, School of Medicine, Graduate Programs in Medicine, Department of Environmental and Biomolecular Systems, Portland, OR 97239-3098. Offers biochemistry and molecular biology (MS, PhD); environmental science and engineering (MS, PhD). Part-time programs available. *Faculty:* 14 full-time (4 women), 1 (woman) part-time/adjunct. *Students:* 28 full-time (20 women), 5 part-time (3 women); includes 11 minority (1 Black or African American, non-Hispanic/Latino; 3 American Indian or Alaska Native, non-Hispanic/Latino; 2 Asian, non-Hispanic/Latino; 4 Hispanic/Latino; 1 Two or more races, non-Hispanic/Latino), 5 international. Average age 30. 36 applicants, 25% accepted, 5 enrolled. In 2011, 9 master's, 2 doctorates awarded. Terminal master's awarded for partial completion of doctoral program. *Degree requirements:* For master's, thesis (for some programs); for doctorate, comprehensive exam, thesis/dissertation, qualifying exam. *Entrance requirements:* For master's and doctorate, GRE General Test (minimum scores: 500 Verbal/600 Quantitative/4.5 Analytical) or MCAT (for some programs).

Peterson's Graduate Programs in the Physical Sciences, Mathematics, Agricultural Sciences, the Environment & Natural Resources 2013

facebook.com/petersonspublishing **489**

Environmental Sciences

Additional exam requirements/recommendations for international students: Required—TOEFL. *Application deadline:* For fall admission, 7/15 for domestic students, 5/15 for international students; for winter admission, 10/15 for domestic students, 9/15 for international students; for spring admission, 1/15 for domestic students, 12/15 for international students. Applications are processed on a rolling basis. Application fee: $70. Electronic applications accepted. *Financial support:* Health care benefits and full tuition and stipends for PhD students available. *Unit head:* Dr. Paul Tratnyek, Program Director, 503-748-1070, E-mail: info@ebs.ogi.edu. *Application contact:* Nancy Christie, Program Coordinator, 503-748-1070, E-mail: info@ebs.ogi.edu.

Oregon State University, Graduate School, College of Agricultural Sciences, Department of Environmental and Molecular Toxicology, Corvallis, OR 97331. Offers toxicology (MS, PhD).

Oregon State University, Graduate School, Program in Environmental Sciences, Corvallis, OR 97331. Offers MA, MS, PhD.

Pace University, Dyson College of Arts and Sciences, Program in Environmental Science, New York, NY 10038. Offers MS. Offered at Pleasantville, NY location only. *Students:* 19 full-time (9 women), 12 part-time (10 women); includes 3 minority (all Asian, non-Hispanic/Latino), 7 international. Average age 31. 22 applicants, 59% accepted, 8 enrolled. In 2011, 7 master's awarded. *Degree requirements:* For master's, research project. *Entrance requirements:* For master's, GRE. Additional exam requirements/recommendations for international students: Required—TOEFL. *Application deadline:* For fall admission, 8/1 priority date for domestic students; for spring admission, 12/1 priority date for domestic students. Applications are processed on a rolling basis. Application fee: $70. Electronic applications accepted. *Expenses: Tuition:* Part-time $990 per credit. *Required fees:* $168 per semester. Tuition and fees vary according to course load and degree level. *Unit head:* Dr. Melissa Grigione, Co-Director, Environmental Science Graduate Program, 914-773-3509, Fax: 914-773-3634, E-mail: mgrigione@pace.edu. *Application contact:* Susan Ford-Goldschein, Director of Graduate Admissions, 914-422-4283, Fax: 914-422-4287, E-mail: gradwp@pace.edu.

Penn State Harrisburg, Graduate School, School of Science, Engineering and Technology, Middletown, PA 17057-4898. Offers computer science (MS); electrical engineering (M Eng, MS); engineering management (MPS); engineering science (M Eng); environmental engineering (M Eng); environmental pollution control (MEPC, MS). Part-time and evening/weekend programs available. *Unit head:* Dr. Jerry F. Shoup, Interim Director, 717-948-6352, E-mail: jfs1@psu.edu. *Application contact:* Robert Coffman, Director of Admissions, 717-948-6250, Fax: 717-948-6325, E-mail: ric1@psu.edu. Web site: http://harrisburg.psu.edu/science-engineering-technology.

Penn State University Park, Graduate School, Intercollege Graduate Programs, Intercollege Program in Environmental Pollution Control, State College, University Park, PA 16802-1503. Offers MEPC, MS. *Unit head:* Dr. Herschel A. Elliott, Chair, 814-865-1417, Fax: 814-863-1031, E-mail: helliott3@psu.edu. *Application contact:* Cynthia E. Nicosia, Director, Graduate Enrollment Services, 814-865-1795, Fax: 814-865-4627, E-mail: cey1@psu.edu.

Polytechnic Institute of New York University, Department of Civil Engineering, Major in Environmental Science, Brooklyn, NY 11201-2990. Offers MS. Part-time and evening/weekend programs available. *Students:* 2 full-time (both women), 3 part-time (all women); includes 3 minority (2 Black or African American, non-Hispanic/Latino; 1 Asian, non-Hispanic/Latino), 1 international. 18 applicants, 33% accepted, 1 enrolled. In 2011, 1 master's awarded. *Degree requirements:* For master's, comprehensive exam (for some programs), thesis (for some programs). *Entrance requirements:* Additional exam requirements/recommendations for international students: Required—TOEFL (minimum score 550 paper-based; 213 computer-based; 80 iBT); Recommended—IELTS (minimum score 6.5). *Application deadline:* For fall admission, 7/31 priority date for domestic students, 4/30 for international students; for spring admission, 12/31 priority date for domestic students, 10/30 for international students. Applications are processed on a rolling basis. Application fee: $75. Electronic applications accepted. *Expenses: Tuition:* Full-time $22,464; part-time $1248 per credit. *Required fees:* $501 per semester. *Financial support:* Fellowships, research assistantships, teaching assistantships, institutionally sponsored loans, scholarships/grants, and unspecified assistantships available. Support available to part-time students. Financial award applicants required to submit FAFSA. *Unit head:* Dr. Lawrence Chiarelli, Head, 718-260-4040, Fax: 718-260-3433, E-mail: lchiarel@poly.edu. *Application contact:* JeanCarlo Bonilla, Director of Graduate Enrollment Management, 718-260-3182, Fax: 718-260-3624, E-mail: gradinfo@poly.edu.

Pontifical Catholic University of Puerto Rico, College of Sciences, Department of Biology, Ponce, PR 00717-0777. Offers environmental sciences (MS). *Degree requirements:* For master's, thesis. *Entrance requirements:* For master's, GRE, 2 letters of recommendation, interview, minimum GPA of 2.75.

Portland State University, Graduate Studies, College of Liberal Arts and Sciences, Department of Geology, Portland, OR 97207-0751. Offers environmental sciences and resources (PhD); geology (MA, MS); science/geology (MAT, MST). Part-time programs available. *Degree requirements:* For master's, comprehensive exam, thesis, field comprehensive; for doctorate, thesis/dissertation, 2 years of residency. *Entrance requirements:* For master's, GRE General Test, GRE Subject Test, BA/BS in geology, minimum GPA of 3.0 in upper-division course work or 2.75 overall. Additional exam requirements/recommendations for international students: Required—TOEFL (minimum score 550 paper-based; 213 computer-based). *Faculty research:* Sediment transport, volcanic environmental geology, coastal and fluvial processes.

Portland State University, Graduate Studies, College of Liberal Arts and Sciences, Program in Environmental Sciences and Management, Portland, OR 97207-0751. Offers environmental management (MEM); environmental sciences/biology (PhD); environmental sciences/chemistry (PhD); environmental sciences/civil engineering (PhD); environmental sciences/geography (PhD); environmental sciences/geology (PhD); environmental sciences/physics (PhD); environmental studies (MS); science/environmental science (MST). Part-time programs available. *Degree requirements:* For master's, thesis or alternative; for doctorate, variable foreign language requirement, comprehensive exam, thesis/dissertation, oral and qualifying exams. *Entrance requirements:* For master's, GRE General Test, 3 letters of recommendation; for doctorate, minimum GPA of 3.0 in upper-division course work or 2.75 overall. Additional exam requirements/recommendations for international students: Required—TOEFL (minimum score 550 paper-based; 213 computer-based). *Faculty research:* Environmental aspects of biology, chemistry, civil engineering, geology, physics.

Queens College of the City University of New York, Division of Graduate Studies, Mathematics and Natural Sciences Division, School of Earth and Environmental Sciences, Flushing, NY 11367-1597. Offers MA. Part-time and evening/weekend programs available. *Faculty:* 14 full-time (4 women). *Students:* 1 full-time (0 women), 19 part-time (9 women); includes 3 minority (1 Asian, non-Hispanic/Latino; 2 Hispanic/Latino), 1 international. 13 applicants, 38% accepted, 3 enrolled. In 2011, 3 master's awarded. *Degree requirements:* For master's, comprehensive exam, thesis. *Entrance requirements:* For master's, GRE, previous course work in calculus, physics, and chemistry; minimum GPA of 3.0. Additional exam requirements/recommendations for international students: Required—TOEFL. *Application deadline:* For fall admission, 4/1 for domestic students; for spring admission, 11/1 for domestic students. Applications are processed on a rolling basis. Application fee: $125. *Expenses:* Tuition, state resident: part-time $345 per credit. Tuition, nonresident: part-time $640 per credit. *Required fees:* $145.25 per semester. *Financial support:* Career-related internships or fieldwork, Federal Work-Study, institutionally sponsored loans, tuition waivers (partial), and unspecified assistantships available. Support available to part-time students. Financial award application deadline: 4/1; financial award applicants required to submit FAFSA. *Faculty research:* Sedimentology/stratigraphy, paleontology, field petrology. *Unit head:* Dr. Yan Zheng, Chairperson, 718-997-3300. *Application contact:* Dr. Hannes Brueckner, Graduate Adviser, 718-997-3300, E-mail: hannes_brueckner@qc.edu.

Rice University, Graduate Programs, George R. Brown School of Engineering, Department of Civil and Environmental Engineering, Houston, TX 77251-1892. Offers civil engineering (MCE, MS, PhD); environmental engineering (MEE, MES, MS, PhD); environmental science (MEE, MES, MS, PhD). Part-time programs available. *Degree requirements:* For master's, thesis (for some programs); for doctorate, thesis/dissertation. *Entrance requirements:* For master's and doctorate, GRE General Test, GRE Subject Test, minimum GPA of 3.25. Additional exam requirements/recommendations for international students: Required—TOEFL (minimum score 600 paper-based; 250 computer-based; 90 iBT). Electronic applications accepted. *Faculty research:* Biology and chemistry of groundwater, pollutant fate in groundwater systems, water quality monitoring, urban storm water runoff, urban air quality.

Rice University, Graduate Programs, Wiess School–Professional Science Master's Programs, Houston, TX 77251-1892. Offers MS.

The Richard Stockton College of New Jersey, School of Graduate and Continuing Studies, Program in Environmental Science, Pomona, NJ 08240-0195. Offers PSM. Part-time and evening/weekend programs available. *Faculty:* 6 full-time (2 women), 2 part-time/adjunct (both women). *Students:* 2 full-time (both women), 12 part-time (3 women). Average age 32. 10 applicants, 60% accepted, 3 enrolled. In 2011, 5 degrees awarded. *Degree requirements:* For master's, thesis optional, project. *Entrance requirements:* For master's, GRE. Additional exam requirements/recommendations for international students: Required—TOEFL. *Application deadline:* For fall admission, 7/1 for domestic and international students; for spring admission, 12/1 for domestic and international students. Applications are processed on a rolling basis. Application fee: $50. Electronic applications accepted. *Expenses:* Tuition, state resident: full-time $13,035; part-time $543 per credit. Tuition, nonresident: full-time $20,065; part-time $836 per credit. *Required fees:* $3920; $163 per credit. Tuition and fees vary according to degree level. *Financial support:* In 2011–12, 5 students received support, including 6 research assistantships; fellowships with partial tuition reimbursements available, Federal Work-Study, scholarships/grants, and unspecified assistantships also available. Financial award application deadline: 3/1; financial award applicants required to submit FAFSA. *Unit head:* Dr. Tait Chirenje, Program Director, 609-626-3640, E-mail: gradschool@stockton.edu. *Application contact:* Tara Williams, Assistant Director of Graduate Enrollment Management, 609-626-3640, Fax: 609-626-6050, E-mail: gradschool@stockton.edu. Web site: http://www.stockton.edu/grad.

Rochester Institute of Technology, Graduate Enrollment Services, College of Science, School of Life Sciences, Program in Environmental Science, Rochester, NY 14623-5603. Offers MS. Part-time and evening/weekend programs available. *Students:* 14 full-time (7 women), 4 part-time (3 women), 2 international. Average

490 facebook.com/petersonspublishing

Peterson's Graduate Programs in the Physical Sciences, Mathematics, Agricultural Sciences, the Environment & Natural Resources 2013

age 25. 26 applicants, 31% accepted, 5 enrolled. In 2011, 5 degrees awarded. *Degree requirements:* For master's, thesis. *Entrance requirements:* For master's, GRE General Test (recommended), minimum GPA of 3.0. Additional exam requirements/recommendations for international students: Required—TOEFL (minimum score 550 paper-based; 213 computer-based; 79 iBT) or IELTS (minimum score 6.5). *Application deadline:* For fall admission, 2/15 priority date for domestic students, 2/15 for international students; for winter admission, 11/1 for domestic students; for spring admission, 2/1 for domestic students. Applications are processed on a rolling basis. Application fee: $50. Electronic applications accepted. *Expenses: Tuition:* Full-time $34,659; part-time $963 per credit hour. *Required fees:* $228; $76 per quarter. *Financial support:* Fellowships with partial tuition reimbursements, research assistantships with partial tuition reimbursements, teaching assistantships with partial tuition reimbursements, career-related internships or fieldwork, scholarships/grants, and unspecified assistantships available. Support available to part-time students. Financial award applicants required to submit FAFSA. *Faculty research:* Environmental chemistry; digital imaging; environmental biology; remote sensing; mathematics and statistics; environmental public policy; environmental economics; feedbacks among benthic fauna, algae and biogeochemical cycling during eutrophication of a shallow estuary. *Unit head:* Dr. Christy Tyler, Graduate Program Director, 585-475-5042, Fax: 585-475-5000, E-mail: actsbi@rit.edu. *Application contact:* Diane Ellison, Assistant Vice President, Graduate Enrollment Services, 585-475-2229, Fax: 585-475-7164, E-mail: gradinfo@rit.edu.

Royal Military College of Canada, Division of Graduate Studies and Research, Engineering Division, Program in Environmental Science, Kingston, ON K7K 7B4, Canada. Offers M Sc, PhD. *Degree requirements:* For master's, thesis; for doctorate, comprehensive exam, thesis/dissertation. *Entrance requirements:* For master's, honours degree with second-class standing; for doctorate, master's degree. Electronic applications accepted.

Rutgers, The State University of New Jersey, Newark, Graduate School, Program in Environmental Science, Newark, NJ 07102. Offers MS, PhD. MS, PhD offered jointly with New Jersey Institute of Technology. *Entrance requirements:* For master's and doctorate, GRE, minimum B average.

Rutgers, The State University of New Jersey, New Brunswick, Graduate School-New Brunswick, Department of Environmental Sciences, Piscataway, NJ 08854-8097. Offers air pollution and resources (MS, PhD); aquatic biology (MS, PhD); aquatic chemistry (MS, PhD); atmospheric science (MS, PhD); chemistry and physics of aerosol and hydrosol systems (MS, PhD); environmental chemistry (MS, PhD); environmental microbiology (MS, PhD); environmental toxicology (PhD); exposure assessment (PhD); fate and effects of pollutants (MS, PhD); pollution prevention and control (MS, PhD); water and wastewater treatment (MS, PhD); water resources (MS, PhD). Terminal master's awarded for partial completion of doctoral program. *Degree requirements:* For master's, comprehensive exam, thesis or alternative, oral final exam; for doctorate, comprehensive exam, thesis/dissertation, thesis defense, qualifying exam. *Entrance requirements:* For master's and doctorate, GRE General Test. Additional exam requirements/recommendations for international students: Required—TOEFL. Electronic applications accepted. *Faculty research:* Biological waste treatment; contaminant fate and transport; air, soil and water quality.

South Dakota School of Mines and Technology, Graduate Division, PhD Program in Atmospheric and Environmental Sciences, Rapid City, SD 57701-3995. Offers PhD. Program offered jointly with South Dakota State University. *Degree requirements:* For doctorate, comprehensive exam, thesis/dissertation. *Entrance requirements:* For doctorate, GRE General Test, GRE Subject Test. Additional exam requirements/recommendations for international students: Required—TOEFL, TWE. Electronic applications accepted.

Southeast Missouri State University, School of Graduate Studies, Program in Environmental Science, Cape Girardeau, MO 63701-4799. Offers MS. *Faculty:* 15 full-time (3 women). *Students:* 3 full-time (1 woman), 5 part-time (3 women), 3 international. Average age 28. 6 applicants, 100% accepted, 4 enrolled. In 2011, 1 master's awarded. *Degree requirements:* For master's, comprehensive exam (for some programs), thesis (for some programs), applied research project. *Entrance requirements:* For master's, GRE, minimum undergraduate GPA of 2.5; letter of intent; 2 letters of recommendation; 20 hours in science with minimum GPA of 3.0. Additional exam requirements/recommendations for international students: Required—TOEFL (minimum score 550 paper-based; 213 computer-based; 79 iBT); Recommended—IELTS (minimum score 6). *Application deadline:* For fall admission, 8/1 for domestic students, 7/1 for international students; for spring admission, 11/21 for domestic students, 11/1 for international students. Applications are processed on a rolling basis. Application fee: $30 ($40 for international students). Electronic applications accepted. *Expenses:* Tuition, state resident: full-time $4896; part-time $272 per credit hour. Tuition, nonresident: full-time $8649; part-time $480.50 per credit hour. *Financial support:* In 2011–12, 5 students received support, including 4 teaching assistantships with full tuition reimbursements available (averaging $7,600 per year); career-related internships or fieldwork, Federal Work-Study, scholarships/grants, tuition waivers (full), and unspecified assistantships also available. Financial award application deadline: 6/30; financial award applicants required to submit FAFSA. *Faculty research:* Contamination of soils and water with environmental chemicals, influence of environmental factors on respiratory health, determination of energy-related pollutants in environmental samples, economic valuation of water resources, impacts of environmental chemicals on wildlife species. *Total annual research expenditures:* $100,000. *Unit head:* Dr. Stephen R. Overmann, Program Director,

573-651-2386, E-mail: sovermann@semo.edu. *Application contact:* Gail Amick, Administrative Secretary, 573-651-2049, Fax: 573-651-2001, E-mail: gamick@semo.edu. Web site: http://www.semo.edu/study/envirosci

Southern Illinois University Carbondale, Graduate School, College of Science, Department of Geology and Department of Geography, Program in Environmental Resources and Policy, Carbondale, IL 62901-4701. Offers PhD. *Students:* 14 full-time (7 women), 19 part-time (3 women); includes 4 minority (3 Black or African American, non-Hispanic/Latino; 1 American Indian or Alaska Native, non-Hispanic/Latino), 8 international. 16 applicants, 31% accepted, 5 enrolled. In 2011, 4 doctorates awarded. *Entrance requirements:* For doctorate, GRE. *Unit head:* Dr. Steven Esling, Chair, 618-453-3351, Fax: 618-453-7393, E-mail: esling@geo.siu.edu. *Application contact:* Dana Wise, Office Specialist, 618-453-7328, E-mail: dwise@siu.edu.

Southern Illinois University Edwardsville, Graduate School, College of Arts and Sciences, Program in Environmental Sciences, Edwardsville, IL 62026-0001. Offers MS. Part-time and evening/weekend programs available. *Students:* 10 full-time (5 women), 28 part-time (15 women); includes 3 minority (1 Hispanic/Latino; 2 Two or more races, non-Hispanic/Latino), 6 international. 27 applicants, 15% accepted, 0 enrolled. In 2011, 7 master's awarded. *Degree requirements:* For master's, thesis (for some programs), final exam, oral exam. *Entrance requirements:* For master's, GRE. Additional exam requirements/recommendations for international students: Required—TOEFL (minimum score 550 paper-based; 213 computer-based; 79 iBT), IELTS (minimum score 6.5). *Application deadline:* For fall admission, 7/22 for domestic students, 6/1 for international students; for spring admission, 12/9 for domestic students, 10/1 for international students. Applications are processed on a rolling basis. Application fee: $30. Electronic applications accepted. Tuition and fees vary according to course load and program. *Financial support:* In 2011–12, 3 research assistantships with full tuition reimbursements (averaging $9,927 per year), 7 teaching assistantships with full tuition reimbursements (averaging $9,927 per year) were awarded; fellowships with full tuition reimbursements, institutionally sponsored loans, scholarships/grants, and unspecified assistantships also available. Financial award application deadline: 3/1; financial award applicants required to submit FAFSA. *Unit head:* Dr. Kevin Johnson, Program Director, 618-650-5934, E-mail: kevjohn@siue.edu. *Application contact:* Michelle Robinson, Coordinator of Graduate Recruitment, 618-650-2811, Fax: 618-650-3523, E-mail: michero@siue.edu. Web site: http://www.siue.edu/artsandsciences/environment/masters.shtml.

Southern Methodist University, Bobby B. Lyle School of Engineering, Department of Environmental and Civil Engineering, Dallas, TX 75275-0340. Offers applied science (MS, PhD); civil and environmental engineering (PhD); civil engineering (MS); environmental engineering (MS); environmental science (MS), including environmental systems management. Part-time and evening/weekend programs available. Postbaccalaureate distance learning degree programs offered (no on-campus study). Terminal master's awarded for partial completion of doctoral program. *Degree requirements:* For master's, thesis optional; for doctorate, thesis/dissertation, oral and written qualifying exams. *Entrance requirements:* For master's, GRE General Test, minimum GPA of 3.0 in last 2 years; bachelor's degree in engineering, mathematics, or sciences; for doctorate, GRE, BS and MS in related field, minimum GPA of 3.3. Additional exam requirements/recommendations for international students: Required—TOEFL. Electronic applications accepted. *Faculty research:* Human and environmental health effects of endocrine disrupters, development of air pollution control systems for diesel engines, structural analysis and design, modeling and design of waste treatment systems.

Southern University and Agricultural and Mechanical College, Graduate School, College of Sciences, Department of Chemistry, Baton Rouge, LA 70813. Offers analytical chemistry (MS); biochemistry (MS); environmental sciences (MS); inorganic chemistry (MS); organic chemistry (MS); physical chemistry (MS). *Degree requirements:* For master's, thesis. *Entrance requirements:* For master's, GMAT or GRE General Test. Additional exam requirements/recommendations for international students: Required—TOEFL (minimum score 525 paper-based; 193 computer-based). *Faculty research:* Synthesis of macrocyclic ligands, latex accelerators, anticancer drugs, biosensors, absorption isotheums, isolation of specific enzymes from plants.

Stanford University, School of Earth Sciences, Department of Geological and Environmental Sciences, Stanford, CA 94305-9991. Offers MS, PhD, Eng. Terminal master's awarded for partial completion of doctoral program. *Degree requirements:* For master's and Eng, thesis; for doctorate, thesis/dissertation. *Entrance requirements:* For master's, doctorate, and Eng, GRE General Test. Additional exam requirements/recommendations for international students: Required—TOEFL. Electronic applications accepted. *Expenses: Tuition:* Full-time $40,050; part-time $890 per credit.

Stanford University, School of Earth Sciences, Earth Systems Program, Stanford, CA 94305-9991. Offers MS. Students admitted at the undergraduate level. Electronic applications accepted. *Expenses: Tuition:* Full-time $40,050; part-time $890 per credit.

State University of New York College of Environmental Science and Forestry, Department of Chemistry, Syracuse, NY 13210-2779. Offers biochemistry (MPS, MS, PhD); environmental chemistry (MPS, MS, PhD); organic chemistry of natural products (MPS, MS, PhD); polymer chemistry (MPS, MS, PhD). *Degree requirements:* For master's, thesis; for doctorate, comprehensive

Peterson's Graduate Programs in the Physical Sciences, Mathematics, Agricultural Sciences, the Environment & Natural Resources 2013

facebook.com/petersonspublishing **491**

exam, thesis/dissertation. *Entrance requirements:* For master's and doctorate, GRE General Test, GRE Subject Test, minimum GPA of 3.0. Additional exam requirements/recommendations for international students: Required—TOEFL (minimum score 550 paper-based; 213 computer-based; 80 iBT), IELTS (minimum score 6). *Application deadline:* For fall admission, 2/1 priority date for domestic students, 2/1 for international students; for spring admission, 11/1 priority date for domestic students, 11/1 for international students. Applications are processed on a rolling basis. Application fee: $60. Electronic applications accepted. *Expenses:* Tuition, state resident: full-time $8870; part-time $370 per credit hour. Tuition, nonresident: full-time $15,160; part-time $632 per credit hour. *Required fees:* $60; $370 per credit hour. $350 per semester. One-time fee: $85. *Financial support:* Fellowships with full tuition reimbursements, research assistantships with full tuition reimbursements, teaching assistantships with full tuition reimbursements, Federal Work-Study, institutionally sponsored loans, scholarships/grants, health care benefits, and unspecified assistantships available. Financial award application deadline: 6/30; financial award applicants required to submit FAFSA. *Faculty research:* Polymer chemistry, biochemistry. *Total annual research expenditures:* $1.8 million. *Unit head:* Prof. Gregory Boyer, Chair, 315-470-6825, Fax: 315-470-6856, E-mail: glboyer@esf.edu. *Application contact:* Scott Shannon, Associate Provost for Instruction/Dean of the Graduate School, 315-470-6599, Fax: 315-470-6978, E-mail: sshannon@esf.edu. Web site: http://www.esf.edu/chemistry.

State University of New York College of Environmental Science and Forestry, Department of Environmental and Forest Biology, Syracuse, NY 13210-2779. Offers applied ecology (MPS); chemical ecology (MPS, MS, PhD); conservation biology (MPS, MS, PhD); ecology (MPS, MS, PhD); entomology (MPS, MS, PhD); environmental interpretation (MPS, MS, PhD); environmental physiology (MPS, MS, PhD); fish and wildlife biology and management (MPS, MS, PhD); forest pathology and mycology (MPS, MS, PhD); plant biotechnology (MPS); plant science and biotechnology (MPS, MS, PhD). *Degree requirements:* For master's, thesis (for some programs); for doctorate, comprehensive exam, thesis/dissertation. *Entrance requirements:* For master's and doctorate, GRE General Test, GRE Subject Test, minimum GPA of 3.0. Additional exam requirements/recommendations for international students: Required—TOEFL (minimum score 550 paper-based; 213 computer-based; 80 iBT), IELTS (minimum score 6). *Application deadline:* For fall admission, 2/1 priority date for domestic students, 2/1 for international students; for spring admission, 11/1 priority date for domestic students, 11/1 for international students. Applications are processed on a rolling basis. Application fee: $60. *Expenses:* Tuition, state resident: full-time $8870; part-time $370 per credit hour. Tuition, nonresident: full-time $15,160; part-time $632 per credit hour. *Required fees:* $60; $370 per credit hour. $350 per semester. One-time fee: $85. *Financial support:* Fellowships with full and partial tuition reimbursements, research assistantships with full and partial tuition reimbursements, teaching assistantships with full and partial tuition reimbursements, Federal Work-Study, institutionally sponsored loans, scholarships/grants, health care benefits, and unspecified assistantships available. Financial award application deadline: 6/30. *Faculty research:* Ecology, fish and wildlife biology and management, plant science, entomology. *Total annual research expenditures:* $4.1 million. *Unit head:* Dr. Donald J. Leopold, Chair, 315-470-6760, Fax: 315-470-6934. *Application contact:* Dr. Dudley J. Raynal, Dean, Instruction and Graduate Studies, 315-470-6599, Fax: 315-470-6978, E-mail: esfgrad@esf.edu. Web site: http://www.esf.edu/efb/.

State University of New York College of Environmental Science and Forestry, Program in Environmental Science, Syracuse, NY 13210-2779. Offers biophysical and ecological economics (MPS); coupled natural and human systems (MPS); ecosystem restoration (MPS); environmental and community land planning (MPS, MS); environmental and natural resources policy (PhD); environmental communication and participatory processes (MPS, MS); environmental monitoring and modeling (MPS); environmental policy and democratic processes (MPS, MS); environmental systems and risk management (MS); water and wetland resource studies (MPS, MS). Part-time programs available. *Degree requirements:* For master's, thesis (for some programs); for doctorate, comprehensive exam, thesis/dissertation. *Entrance requirements:* For master's and doctorate, GRE General Test, minimum GPA of 3.0. Additional exam requirements/recommendations for international students: Required—TOEFL (minimum score 550 paper-based; 213 computer-based; 80 iBT), IELTS (minimum score 6). *Application deadline:* For fall admission, 2/1 priority date for domestic students, 2/1 for international students; for spring admission, 11/1 priority date for domestic students, 11/1 for international students. Applications are processed on a rolling basis. Application fee: $60. *Expenses:* Tuition, state resident: full-time $8870; part-time $370 per credit hour. Tuition, nonresident: full-time $15,160; part-time $632 per credit hour. *Required fees:* $60; $370 per credit hour. $350 per semester. One-time fee: $85. *Financial support:* Fellowships with full and partial tuition reimbursements, research assistantships with full and partial tuition reimbursements, teaching assistantships with full and partial tuition reimbursements, career-related internships or fieldwork, Federal Work-Study, institutionally sponsored loans, scholarships/grants, health care benefits, and unspecified assistantships available. Support available to part-time students. Financial award application deadline: 6/30; financial award applicants required to submit FAFSA. *Faculty research:* Environmental education/communications, water resources, land resources, waste management. *Total annual research expenditures:* $169,919. *Unit head:* Dr. Ruth Yanai, Coordinator, 315-470-6955, Fax: 315-470-6700, E-mail: rdyanai@esf.edu. *Application contact:* Dr. Dudley J. Raynal, Dean, Instruction and Graduate Studies, 315-470-6599, Fax: 315-470-

6978, E-mail: esfgrad@esf.edu. Web site: http://www.esf.edu/environmentalscience/.

Stephen F. Austin State University, Graduate School, College of Sciences and Mathematics, Division of Environmental Science, Nacogdoches, TX 75962. Offers MS. *Degree requirements:* For master's, comprehensive exam. *Entrance requirements:* For master's, GRE General Test, minimum GPA of 2.8 in last 60 hours, 2.5 overall. Additional exam requirements/recommendations for international students: Required—TOEFL.

Tarleton State University, College of Graduate Studies, College of Science and Technology, Department of Chemistry, Geosciences and Environmental Sciences, Stephenville, TX 76402. Offers environmental science (MS). Part-time and evening/weekend programs available. *Faculty:* 3 full-time (2 women), 1 part-time/adjunct (0 women). *Students:* 3 full-time (2 women), 5 part-time (all women); includes 1 minority (Hispanic/Latino). Average age 32. 5 applicants, 100% accepted, 3 enrolled. In 2011, 3 master's awarded. *Degree requirements:* For master's, comprehensive exam, thesis optional. *Entrance requirements:* For master's, GRE General Test, minimum GPA of 3.0. Additional exam requirements/recommendations for international students: Required—TOEFL (minimum score 550 paper-based; 213 computer-based; 80 iBT). *Application deadline:* For fall admission, 8/5 priority date for domestic students; for spring admission, 12/1 for domestic students. Applications are processed on a rolling basis. Application fee: $30 ($130 for international students). Electronic applications accepted. *Expenses:* Tuition, state resident: full-time $3131.46; part-time $174 per credit hour. Tuition, nonresident: full-time $8225; part-time $457 per credit hour. *Required fees:* $1446. Tuition and fees vary according to course load and campus/location. *Financial support:* Research assistantships, teaching assistantships, career-related internships or fieldwork, and Federal Work-Study available. Support available to part-time students. Financial award application deadline: 5/1; financial award applicants required to submit FAFSA. *Unit head:* Dr. Beth Rinard Hinga, Head, 254-968-9894, Fax: 254-968-9953, E-mail: rinard@tarleton.edu. *Application contact:* Information Contact, 254-968-9104, Fax: 254-968-9670, E-mail: gradoffice@tarleton.edu. Web site: http://www.tarleton.edu/~physci.

Taylor University, Master of Environmental Science Program, Upland, IN 46989-1001. Offers MES. *Faculty:* 1 full-time (0 women), 3 part-time/adjunct (0 women). *Students:* 16 full-time (10 women), 2 part-time (1 woman), 2 international. Average age 24. 31 applicants, 35% accepted, 8 enrolled. In 2011, 14 master's awarded. *Degree requirements:* For master's, thesis (for some programs). *Application deadline:* Applications are processed on a rolling basis. Application fee: $0. *Expenses:* Contact institution. *Financial support:* In 2011–12, 16 students received support, including 18 fellowships (averaging $10,000 per year), 5 teaching assistantships (averaging $6,000 per year); scholarships/grants also available. Financial award applicants required to submit FAFSA. *Faculty research:* Environmental assessment. *Unit head:* Dr. Edwin Richard Squiers, Chair, 765-998-5386, Fax: 765-998-4976, E-mail: rcsquiers@taylor.edu. *Application contact:* Becky Taylor, Program Assistant, 765-998-4960, Fax: 765-998-4976, E-mail: mes@taylor.edu. Web site: http://www.taylor.edu/academics/graduate/master-environmental-science/index.shtml.

Tennessee Technological University, Graduate School, College of Arts and Sciences, Department of Environmental Sciences, Cookeville, TN 38505. Offers biology (PhD); chemistry (PhD). Part-time programs available. *Students:* 4 full-time (2 women), 12 part-time (5 women); includes 3 minority (1 Black or African American, non-Hispanic/Latino; 1 American Indian or Alaska Native, non-Hispanic/Latino; 1 Hispanic/Latino), 4 international. 8 applicants, 50% accepted, 2 enrolled. In 2011, 1 doctorate awarded. *Degree requirements:* For doctorate, comprehensive exam, thesis/dissertation. *Entrance requirements:* For doctorate, GRE. Additional exam requirements/recommendations for international students: Required—TOEFL (minimum score 550 paper-based; 79 iBT), IELTS (minimum score 5.5), PTE Academic. *Application deadline:* For fall admission, 8/1 for domestic students, 5/1 for international students; for spring admission, 12/1 for domestic students, 10/2 for international students. Application fee: $25 ($30 for international students). Electronic applications accepted. *Expenses:* Tuition, state resident: full-time $8094; part-time $422 per credit hour. Tuition, nonresident: full-time $20,574; part-time $1046 per credit hour. *Financial support:* In 2011–12, 5 research assistantships (averaging $10,000 per year), 3 teaching assistantships (averaging $10,000 per year) were awarded; fellowships also available. Financial award application deadline: 4/1. *Application contact:* Shelia K. Kendrick, Coordinator of Graduate Admissions, 931-372-3808, Fax: 931-372-3497, E-mail: skendrick@tntech.edu.

Texas A&M University–Commerce, Graduate School, College of Science, Engineering and Agriculture, Department of Biological and Environmental Sciences, Commerce, TX 75429-3011. Offers biological sciences (M Ed, MS); environmental sciences (Certificate). *Degree requirements:* For master's, comprehensive exam, thesis (for some programs). *Entrance requirements:* For master's, GRE General Test. Electronic applications accepted. *Faculty research:* Microbiology, botany, environmental science, birds.

Texas A&M University–Corpus Christi, Graduate Studies and Research, College of Science and Technology, Program in Environmental Science, Corpus Christi, TX 78412-5503. Offers MS. Part-time and evening/weekend programs available. *Degree requirements:* For master's, comprehensive exam, thesis (for some programs). *Entrance requirements:* For master's, GRE General Test.

Additional exam requirements/recommendations for international students: Required—TOEFL. Electronic applications accepted.

Texas Christian University, College of Science and Engineering, School of Geology, Energy and the Environment, Fort Worth, TX 76129-0002. Offers environmental management (MEM); environmental science (MA, MS); geology (MS). Part-time programs available. *Faculty:* 6 full-time (1 woman), 1 part-time/adjunct. *Students:* 9 full-time (3 women), 30 part-time (15 women); includes 3 minority (all Hispanic/Latino), 1 international. Average age 27. 24 applicants, 88% accepted, 12 enrolled. In 2011, 15 master's awarded. *Degree requirements:* For master's, comprehensive exam (for some programs), thesis (for some programs). *Entrance requirements:* For master's, GRE. Additional exam requirements/recommendations for international students: Required—TOEFL (minimum score 550 paper-based; 213 computer-based; 80 iBT). *Application deadline:* For fall admission, 2/28 priority date for domestic students, 2/28 for international students. Application fee: $60. *Expenses: Tuition:* Full-time $20,250; part-time $1125 per credit hour. Part-time tuition and fees vary according to course load and program. *Financial support:* In 2011–12, 15 teaching assistantships with full tuition reimbursements (averaging $15,000 per year) were awarded. Financial award application deadline: 2/28. *Unit head:* Dr. Phil Hartman, Dean, 817-257-7727, E-mail: p.hartman@tcu.edu. *Application contact:* Dr. Magnus Rittby, Associate Dean for Administration and Graduate Programs, 817-257-7729, Fax: 817-257-7736, E-mail: m.rittby@tcu.edu.

Texas Tech University, Graduate School, College of Arts and Sciences, Department of Environmental Toxicology, Lubbock, TX 79409. Offers MS, PhD, JD/MS, MBA/MS, MS/MPA. Part-time programs available. *Faculty:* 13 full-time (2 women), 2 part-time/adjunct (0 women). *Students:* 47 full-time (26 women), 1 (woman) part-time; includes 5 minority (1 Black or African American, non-Hispanic/Latino; 3 Hispanic/Latino; 1 Two or more races, non-Hispanic/Latino), 17 international. Average age 27. 40 applicants, 48% accepted, 8 enrolled. In 2011, 8 master's, 4 doctorates awarded. *Degree requirements:* For master's, thesis; for doctorate, thesis/dissertation. *Entrance requirements:* For master's and doctorate, GRE General Test. Additional exam requirements/recommendations for international students: Required—TOEFL (minimum score 550 paper-based; 213 computer-based; 79 iBT). *Application deadline:* For fall admission, 6/1 priority date for domestic students, 1/15 for international students; for spring admission, 9/1 priority date for domestic students, 6/15 for international students. Applications are processed on a rolling basis. Application fee: $50 ($75 for international students). Electronic applications accepted. *Expenses:* Tuition, state resident: full-time $5899; part-time $245.80 per credit hour. Tuition, nonresident: full-time $13,411; part-time $558.80 per credit hour. *Required fees:* $2680.60; $86.50 per credit hour. $920.30 per semester. *Financial support:* In 2011–12, 25 students received support. Application deadline: 4/15; applicants required to submit FAFSA. *Faculty research:* Terrestrial and aquatic toxicology, biochemical and developmental toxicology, advanced materials, countermeasures to biologic and chemical threats, molecular epidemiology and modeling. *Total annual research expenditures:* $2.1 million. *Unit head:* Dr. Ronald J. Kendall, Director and Chairman, 806-885-4567, Fax: 806-885-2132, E-mail: ron.kendall@tiehh.ttu.edu. *Application contact:* Ryan Bounds, Assistant Managing Director, 806-885-4567, Fax: 806-885-2132, E-mail: ryan.bounds@ttu.edu. Web site: http://www.tiehh.ttu.edu/.

Thompson Rivers University, Program in Environmental Science, Kamloops, BC V2C 5N3, Canada. Offers MS. *Entrance requirements:* For master's, personal resume, 2 letters of recommendation. Additional exam requirements/recommendations for international students: Required—TOEFL.

Towson University, Program in Environmental Science, Towson, MD 21252-0001. Offers MS, Postbaccalaureate Certificate. Part-time and evening/weekend programs available. *Students:* 4 full-time (3 women), 35 part-time (19 women); includes 5 minority (1 Black or African American, non-Hispanic/Latino; 1 American Indian or Alaska Native, non-Hispanic/Latino; 3 Asian, non-Hispanic/Latino), 2 international. *Entrance requirements:* For master's, GRE (recommended), bachelor's degree in related field, minimum GPA of 3.0. *Application deadline:* Applications are processed on a rolling basis. Application fee: $50. Electronic applications accepted. *Expenses:* Tuition, state resident: part-time $337 per credit. Tuition, nonresident: part-time $709 per credit. *Required fees:* $99 per credit. *Financial support:* Application deadline: 4/1; applicants required to submit FAFSA. *Unit head:* Dr. Steven Lev, Graduate Program Director, 410-704-2744, Fax: 410-704-2604, E-mail: slev@towson.edu.

Tufts University, School of Engineering, Department of Civil and Environmental Engineering, Medford, MA 02155. Offers bioengineering (ME, MS), including environmental technology; civil engineering (ME, MS, PhD), including geotechnical engineering, structural engineering, water diplomacy (PhD); environmental engineering (ME, MS, PhD), including environmental engineering and environmental sciences, environmental geotechnology, environmental health, environmental science and management, hazardous materials management, water diplomacy (PhD), water resources engineering. Part-time programs available. *Faculty:* 18 full-time, 5 part-time/adjunct. *Students:* 102 full-time (50 women); includes 8 minority (1 Black or African American, non-Hispanic/Latino; 6 Asian, non-Hispanic/Latino; 1 Hispanic/Latino), 37 international. Average age 27. 162 applicants, 59% accepted, 37 enrolled. In 2011, 18 degrees awarded. Terminal master's awarded for partial completion of doctoral program. *Degree requirements:* For master's, thesis or alternative; for doctorate, thesis/dissertation. *Entrance requirements:* For master's and doctorate, GRE General Test. Additional exam requirements/recommendations for international students:

Required—TOEFL (minimum score 550 paper-based; 213 computer-based; 80 iBT). *Application deadline:* For fall admission, 1/15 priority date for domestic students, 12/15 for international students; for spring admission, 10/15 for domestic students, 9/15 for international students. Applications are processed on a rolling basis. Application fee: $75. Electronic applications accepted. *Expenses: Tuition:* Full-time $41,208; part-time $1030 per credit hour. Full-time tuition and fees vary according to degree level, program and student level. Part-time tuition and fees vary according to course load. *Financial support:* Fellowships with full tuition reimbursements, research assistantships with full and partial tuition reimbursements, teaching assistantships with full and partial tuition reimbursements, Federal Work-Study, scholarships/grants, tuition waivers (partial), and unspecified assistantships available. Financial award application deadline: 1/15; financial award applicants required to submit FAFSA. *Faculty research:* Environmental and water resources engineering, environmental health, geotechnical and geoenvironmental engineering, structural engineering and mechanics, water diplomacy. *Unit head:* Dr. Kurt Penell, Chair, 617-627-3211, Fax: 617-627-3994. *Application contact:* Laura Sacco, Information Contact, 617-627-3211, E-mail: ceeinfo@tufts.edu. Web site: http://www.ase.tufts.edu/cee/.

Tuskegee University, Graduate Programs, College of Agricultural, Environmental and Natural Sciences, Department of Agricultural Sciences, Program in Environmental Sciences, Tuskegee, AL 36088. Offers MS. *Faculty:* 13 full-time (1 woman), 2 part-time/adjunct (1 woman). *Students:* 5 full-time (3 women); includes 4 minority (all Black or African American, non-Hispanic/Latino). In 2011, 2 master's awarded. *Degree requirements:* For master's, thesis. *Entrance requirements:* For master's, GRE General Test. Additional exam requirements/recommendations for international students: Required—TOEFL (minimum score 500 paper-based; 69 computer-based). *Application deadline:* For fall admission, 7/15 for domestic students. Applications are processed on a rolling basis. Application fee: $25 ($35 for international students). *Expenses: Tuition:* Full-time $17,070; part-time $705 per credit hour. *Financial support:* Application deadline: 4/15. *Unit head:* Dr. P. K. Biswas, Head, 334-727-8446. *Application contact:* Dr. Robert L. Laney, Jr., Vice President/Director of Admissions and Enrollment Management, 334-727-8580, Fax: 334-727-5750, E-mail: planey@tuskegee.edu.

Universidad del Turabo, Graduate Programs, Programs in Science and Technology, Gurabo, PR 00778-3030. Offers environmental analysis (MSE), including environmental chemistry; environmental management (MSE), including pollution management; environmental science (D Sc), including environmental biology. *Students:* 8 full-time (4 women), 101 part-time (68 women); includes 101 minority (all Hispanic/Latino). Average age 39. 58 applicants, 76% accepted, 39 enrolled. In 2011, 16 master's, 3 doctorates awarded. *Entrance requirements:* For master's, GRE, EXADEP, interview. *Application deadline:* For fall admission, 8/5 for domestic students. Application fee: $25. *Unit head:* David Mendez, Head, 787-743-7979. *Application contact:* Virginia Gonzalez, Admissions Officer, 787-746-3009.

Universidad Nacional Pedro Henriquez Urena, Graduate School, Santo Domingo, Dominican Republic. Offers agricultural diversity (MS), including horticultural/fruit production, tropical animal production; conservation of monuments and cultural assets (M Arch); ecology and environment (MS); environmental engineering (MEE); international relations (MA); natural resource management (MS); political science (MA); project optimization (MPM); project feasibility (MPM); project management (MPM); sanitation engineering (ME); science for teachers (MS); tropical Caribbean architecture (M Arch).

Université de Sherbrooke, Faculty of Sciences, Centre Universitaire de Formation en Environnement, Sherbrooke, QC J1K 2R1, Canada. Offers M Sc, Diploma. Postbaccalaureate distance learning degree programs offered (no on-campus study). Electronic applications accepted. *Faculty research:* Environmental studies.

Université du Québec à Montréal, Graduate Programs, Program in Environmental Sciences, Montréal, QC H3C 3P8, Canada. Offers M Sc, PhD, Certificate. Part-time programs available. *Degree requirements:* For master's, research report; for doctorate, thesis/dissertation. *Entrance requirements:* For master's, appropriate bachelor's degree or equivalent, proficiency in French; for doctorate, appropriate master's degree or equivalent, proficiency in French.

Université du Québec à Trois-Rivières, Graduate Programs, Program in Environmental Sciences, Trois-Rivières, QC G9A 5H7, Canada. Offers M Sc, PhD. Part-time programs available. *Degree requirements:* For master's, thesis. *Entrance requirements:* For master's, appropriate bachelor's degree, proficiency in French.

Université du Québec en Abitibi-Témiscamingue, Graduate Programs, Program in Environmental Sciences, Rouyn-Noranda, QC J9X 5E4, Canada. Offers biology (MS); environmental sciences (PhD); sustainable forest ecosystem management (MS).

Université Laval, Faculty of Sciences and Engineering, Department of Geology and Geological Engineering, Programs in Earth Sciences, Québec, QC G1K 7P4, Canada. Offers earth sciences (M Sc, PhD); environmental technologies (M Sc). Offered jointly with INRS-Géressources. Terminal master's awarded for partial completion of doctoral program. *Degree requirements:* For master's, thesis (for some programs); for doctorate, comprehensive exam, thesis/dissertation. *Entrance requirements:* For master's and doctorate, knowledge of French. Electronic applications accepted.

Peterson's Graduate Programs in the Physical Sciences, Mathematics, Agricultural Sciences, the Environment & Natural Resources 2013

facebook.com/petersonspublishing **493**

Environmental Sciences

University at Albany, State University of New York, College of Arts and Sciences, Department of Biological Sciences, Program in Biodiversity, Conservation, and Policy, Albany, NY 12222-0001. Offers MS. *Degree requirements:* For master's, one foreign language. *Entrance requirements:* For master's, GRE General Test. *Faculty research:* Aquatic ecology, plant community ecology, biodiversity and public policy, restoration ecology, coastal and estuarine science.

University at Buffalo, the State University of New York, Graduate School, College of Arts and Sciences, Department of Geography, Buffalo, NY 14260. Offers earth systems science (MA); economic geography and international business and world trade (MA); environmental modeling and analysis (MA); geographic information science (MA, Certificate); geography (MA, PhD); transportation and business geographics (MA, Certificate); urban and regional geography (MA); MA/MBA. *Faculty:* 15 full-time (7 women), 1 part-time/adjunct (0 women). *Students:* 102 full-time (38 women), 20 part-time (10 women); includes 61 minority (1 Black or African American, non-Hispanic/Latino; 55 Asian, non-Hispanic/Latino; 5 Hispanic/Latino), 1 international. 167 applicants, 33% accepted, 29 enrolled. In 2011, 21 master's, 5 doctorates awarded. Terminal master's awarded for partial completion of doctoral program. *Degree requirements:* For master's, thesis (for some programs), project or portfolio; for doctorate, thesis/dissertation. *Entrance requirements:* For master's, GRE General Test, minimum GPA of 2.9; for doctorate, GRE General Test, minimum GPA of 3.0. Additional exam requirements/recommendations for international students: Required—TOEFL (minimum score 550 paper-based; 213 computer-based; 79 iBT). *Application deadline:* For fall admission, 7/1 priority date for domestic students, 1/10 for international students; for spring admission, 12/1 priority date for domestic students, 10/1 for international students. Applications are processed on a rolling basis. Application fee: $75. Electronic applications accepted. *Financial support:* In 2011–12, 13 students received support, including 8 fellowships with full tuition reimbursements available (averaging $4,750 per year), 13 teaching assistantships with full tuition reimbursements available (averaging $13,520 per year); research assistantships with full tuition reimbursements available, career-related internships or fieldwork, Federal Work-Study, institutionally sponsored loans, traineeships, health care benefits, and unspecified assistantships also available. Financial award application deadline: 1/10. *Faculty research:* International business and world trade, geographic information systems and cartography, transportation, urban and regional analysis, physical and environmental geography. *Total annual research expenditures:* $630,314. *Unit head:* Dr. Sharmistha Bagchi-Sen, Chairman, 716-645-0473, Fax: 716-645-2329, E-mail: geosbs@buffalo.edu. *Application contact:* Betsy Abraham, Graduate Secretary, 716-645-0471, Fax: 716-645-2329, E-mail: babraham@buffalo.edu. Web site: http://www.geog.buffalo.edu/.

The University of Alabama in Huntsville, School of Graduate Studies, College of Science, Department of Atmospheric and Environmental Science, Huntsville, AL 35899. Offers atmospheric science (MS, PhD); earth system science (MS). Part-time and evening/weekend programs available. *Faculty:* 10 full-time (0 women), 2 part-time/adjunct (0 women). *Students:* 30 full-time (10 women), 5 part-time (4 women); includes 2 minority (1 Black or African American, non-Hispanic/Latino; 1 Asian, non-Hispanic/Latino), 6 international. Average age 26. 31 applicants, 61% accepted, 11 enrolled. In 2011, 9 master's, 4 doctorates awarded. *Degree requirements:* For master's, comprehensive exam, thesis or alternative, oral and written exams; for doctorate, comprehensive exam, thesis/dissertation, oral and written exams. *Entrance requirements:* For master's, GRE General Test, minimum GPA of 3.0; sequence of courses in calculus (including the calculus of vector-valued functions); courses in linear algebra and ordinary differential equations; two semesters each of chemistry and calculus-based physics; proficiency in at least one high-level computer programming language; for doctorate, GRE General Test, minimum GPA of 3.0. Additional exam requirements/recommendations for international students: Required—TOEFL (minimum score 550 paper-based; 213 computer-based; 62 iBT). *Application deadline:* For fall admission, 7/15 for domestic students, 4/1 for international students; for spring admission, 11/30 for domestic students, 9/1 for international students. Applications are processed on a rolling basis. Application fee: $40 ($50 for international students). Electronic applications accepted. *Expenses:* Tuition, state resident: full-time $7830; part-time $473.50 per credit. Tuition, nonresident: full-time $18,748; part-time $1128.33 per credit. Tuition and fees vary according to course load and program. *Financial support:* In 2011–12, 28 students received support, including 27 research assistantships with full and partial tuition reimbursements available (averaging $14,690 per year), 1 teaching assistantship with full tuition reimbursement available (averaging $13,500 per year); career-related internships or fieldwork, Federal Work-Study, institutionally sponsored loans, scholarships/grants, health care benefits, tuition waivers, and unspecified assistantships also available. Support available to part-time students. Financial award application deadline: 4/1; financial award applicants required to submit FAFSA. *Faculty research:* Satellite remote sensing, severe weather, mesoscale modeling, atmospheric chemistry, data assimilation. *Total annual research expenditures:* $9.1 million. *Unit head:* Dr. Sundar Christopher, Chair, 256-922-7872, Fax: 256-922-7755, E-mail: sundar@nsstc.uah.edu. *Application contact:* Kim Gray, Graduate Studies Admissions Coordinator, 256-824-6002, Fax: 256-824-6405, E-mail: deangrad@uah.edu. Web site: http://www.nsstc.uah.edu/atmos/index.html.

University of Alaska Anchorage, School of Engineering, Program in Applied Environmental Science and Technology, Anchorage, AK 99508. Offers M AEST, MS. Part-time and evening/weekend programs available. *Degree requirements:* For master's, comprehensive exam, thesis (for some programs). *Entrance requirements:* For master's, GRE General Test. Additional exam requirements/recommendations for international students: Required—TOEFL (minimum score 550 paper-based; 213 computer-based). *Faculty research:* Wastewater treatment, environmental regulations, water resources management, justification of public facilities, rural sanitation, biological treatment process.

University of Alaska Fairbanks, College of Engineering and Mines, Department of Civil and Environmental Engineering, Program in Environmental Engineering, Fairbanks, AK 99775-5900. Offers engineering (PhD), including environmental engineering; environmental engineering (MS), including environmental contaminants, environmental science and management, water supply and waste treatment. Part-time programs available. *Students:* 3 full-time (0 women), 1 (woman) part-time. Average age 26. 5 applicants, 60% accepted, 1 enrolled. In 2011, 2 degrees awarded. *Degree requirements:* For master's, comprehensive exam, thesis or alternative; for doctorate, comprehensive exam, thesis/dissertation, oral exam, oral defense. *Entrance requirements:* For master's, basic computer techniques; for doctorate, GRE General Test. Additional exam requirements/recommendations for international students: Required—TOEFL (minimum score 575 paper-based; 213 computer-based). *Application deadline:* For fall admission, 6/1 for domestic students, 3/1 for international students; for spring admission, 10/15 for domestic students, 9/1 for international students. Applications are processed on a rolling basis. Application fee: $60. Electronic applications accepted. *Expenses:* Tuition, state resident: full-time $6696; part-time $372 per credit. Tuition, nonresident: full-time $13,680; part-time $760 per credit. Tuition and fees vary according to course load and reciprocity agreements. *Financial support:* In 2011–12, 1 research assistantship (averaging $16,834 per year), 2 teaching assistantships (averaging $6,390 per year) were awarded; fellowships, career-related internships or fieldwork, Federal Work-Study, scholarships/grants, health care benefits, and unspecified assistantships also available. Support available to part-time students. Financial award application deadline: 7/1; financial award applicants required to submit FAFSA. *Unit head:* Dr. David Barnes, Department Chair, 907-474-7241, Fax: 907-474-6087, E-mail: fyeqe@uaf.edu. *Application contact:* Mike Earnest, Director of Admissions, 907-474-7500, Fax: 907-474-5379, E-mail: admissions@uaf.edu. Web site: http://www.alaska.edu/uaf/cem/cee/env/.

University of Alaska Fairbanks, College of Engineering and Mines, Department of Civil and Environmental Engineering, Program in Environmental Quality Science, Fairbanks, AK 99775-5900. Offers MS. Part-time programs available. *Students:* 3 full-time (all women), 1 international. Average age 24. 1 applicant, 100% accepted, 1 enrolled. *Degree requirements:* For master's, comprehensive exam, thesis or alternative. *Entrance requirements:* For master's, calculus, chemistry, basic computer techniques. Additional exam requirements/recommendations for international students: Required—TOEFL (minimum score 575 paper-based; 213 computer-based). *Application deadline:* For fall admission, 6/1 for domestic students, 3/1 for international students; for spring admission, 10/15 for domestic students, 9/1 for international students. Applications are processed on a rolling basis. Application fee: $60. Electronic applications accepted. *Expenses:* Tuition, state resident: full-time $6696; part-time $372 per credit. Tuition, nonresident: full-time $13,680; part-time $760 per credit. Tuition and fees vary according to course load and reciprocity agreements. *Financial support:* In 2011–12, 1 research assistantship, 7,974 teaching assistantships were awarded; fellowships, career-related internships or fieldwork, Federal Work-Study, scholarships/grants, health care benefits, and unspecified assistantships also available. Support available to part-time students. Financial award application deadline: 7/1; financial award applicants required to submit FAFSA. *Unit head:* Dr. David Barnes, Department Chair, 907-474-7241, Fax: 907-474-6087, E-mail: fyeqe@uaf.edu. *Application contact:* Mike Earnest, Director of Admissions, 907-474-7500, Fax: 907-474-5379, E-mail: admissions@uaf.edu. Web site: http://www.alaska.edu/uaf/cem/cee/env/.

University of Alaska Fairbanks, College of Natural Sciences and Mathematics, Department of Chemistry and Biochemistry, Fairbanks, AK 99775-6160. Offers biochemistry and molecular biology (MS, PhD); chemistry (MA, MS); environmental chemistry (MS, PhD). Part-time programs available. *Faculty:* 7 full-time (0 women). *Students:* 26 full-time (11 women), 5 part-time (3 women); includes 4 minority (1 American Indian or Alaska Native, non-Hispanic/Latino; 2 Asian, non-Hispanic/Latino; 1 Hispanic/Latino), 7 international. Average age 27. 28 applicants, 29% accepted, 6 enrolled. In 2011, 4 master's, 3 doctorates awarded. *Degree requirements:* For master's, comprehensive exam, thesis or alternative; for doctorate, comprehensive exam, thesis/dissertation, oral defense. *Entrance requirements:* Additional exam requirements/recommendations for international students: Required—TOEFL (minimum score 550 paper-based; 213 computer-based). *Application deadline:* For fall admission, 6/1 for domestic students, 3/1 for international students; for spring admission, 10/15 for domestic students, 9/1 for international students. Applications are processed on a rolling basis. Application fee: $60. Electronic applications accepted. *Expenses:* Tuition, state resident: full-time $6696; part-time $372 per credit. Tuition, nonresident: full-time $13,680; part-time $760 per credit. Tuition and fees vary according to course load and reciprocity agreements. *Financial support:* In 2011–12, 8 research assistantships with tuition reimbursements (averaging $12,759 per year), 16 teaching assistantships with tuition reimbursements (averaging $17,112 per year) were awarded; fellowships with tuition reimbursements, Federal Work-Study, scholarships/grants, health care benefits, and unspecified assistantships also available. Support available to part-time students. Financial award application deadline: 7/1; financial award applicants required to submit FAFSA.

Faculty research: Atmospheric aerosols, cold adaptation, hibernation and neuroprotection, liganogated ion channels, arctic contaminants. *Unit head:* Bill Simpson, Department Chair, 907-474-5510, Fax: 907-474-5640, E-mail: fychem@uaf.edu. *Application contact:* Mike Earnest, Director of Admissions, 907-474-7500, Fax: 907-474-5379, E-mail: admissions@uaf.edu. Web site: http://www.uaf.edu/chem.

University of Alberta, Faculty of Graduate Studies and Research, Department of Civil and Environmental Engineering, Edmonton, AB T6G 2E1, Canada. Offers construction engineering and management (M Eng, M Sc, PhD); environmental engineering (M Eng, M Sc, PhD); environmental science (M Sc, PhD); geoenvironmental engineering (M Eng, M Sc, PhD); geotechnical engineering (M Eng, M Sc, PhD); mining engineering (M Eng, M Sc, PhD); petroleum engineering (M Eng, M Sc, PhD); structural engineering (M Eng, M Sc, PhD); water resources (M Eng, M Sc, PhD). Part-time programs available. Postbaccalaureate distance learning degree programs offered (minimal on-campus study). *Degree requirements:* For master's, thesis (for some programs); for doctorate, thesis/dissertation. *Entrance requirements:* For master's, minimum GPA of 3.0 in last 2 years of undergraduate studies; for doctorate, minimum GPA of 3.0. Additional exam requirements/recommendations for international students: Required—TOEFL (minimum score 550 paper-based; 213 computer-based). Electronic applications accepted. *Faculty research:* Mining.

The University of Arizona, College of Agriculture and Life Sciences, Department of Soil, Water and Environmental Science, Tucson, AZ 85721. Offers MS, PhD. *Faculty:* 10 full-time (3 women), 1 (woman) part-time/adjunct. *Students:* 50 full-time (32 women), 7 part-time (2 women); includes 15 minority (2 Black or African American, non-Hispanic/Latino; 1 American Indian or Alaska Native, non-Hispanic/Latino; 1 Asian, non-Hispanic/Latino; 8 Hispanic/Latino; 3 Two or more races, non-Hispanic/Latino), 15 international. Average age 31. 37 applicants, 54% accepted, 13 enrolled. In 2011, 10 master's, 11 doctorates awarded. *Degree requirements:* For master's, thesis; for doctorate, comprehensive exam, thesis/dissertation. *Entrance requirements:* For master's, GRE (recommended), minimum GPA of 3.0, letter of interest, 3 letters of recommendation; for doctorate, GRE (recommended), MS, minimum GPA of 3.0, letter of interest, 3 letters of recommendation. Additional exam requirements/recommendations for international students: Required—TOEFL (minimum score 550 paper-based; 213 computer-based; 80 iBT). *Application deadline:* For fall admission, 6/1 for domestic students, 12/1 for international students; for spring admission, 10/1 for domestic students, 6/1 for international students. Applications are processed on a rolling basis. Application fee: $75. *Expenses:* Tuition, state resident: full-time $10,840. Tuition, nonresident: full-time $25,802. *Financial support:* In 2011–12, 14 students received support, including 24 research assistantships with full and partial tuition reimbursements available (averaging $18,526 per year), 2 teaching assistantships with full and partial tuition reimbursements available (averaging $18,529 per year); fellowships, Federal Work-Study, institutionally sponsored loans, scholarships/grants, health care benefits, tuition waivers (full and partial), and unspecified assistantships also available. Financial award application deadline: 5/1. *Faculty research:* Plant production, environmental microbiology, contaminant flow and transport, aquaculture. *Total annual research expenditures:* $3.4 million. *Unit head:* Dr. Jeffery C. Silvertooth, Head, 520-621-7228, Fax: 520-621-1647, E-mail: silver@ag.arizona.edu. *Application contact:* Alicia Velasquez, 520-621-1606, Fax: 520-621-1647, E-mail: avelasqu@ag.arizona.edu. Web site: http://ag.arizona.edu/SWES/.

The University of Arizona, College of Agriculture and Life Sciences, Graduate Interdisciplinary Program in Arid Lands Resource Sciences, Tucson, AZ 85721. Offers PhD. *Faculty:* 5. *Students:* 22 full-time (9 women), 4 part-time (1 woman); includes 6 minority (1 Asian, non-Hispanic/Latino; 5 Two or more races, non-Hispanic/Latino), 10 international. Average age 41. 7 applicants, 57% accepted, 4 enrolled. *Degree requirements:* For doctorate, one foreign language, comprehensive exam, thesis/dissertation. *Entrance requirements:* For doctorate, GRE. Additional exam requirements/recommendations for international students: Required—TOEFL (minimum score 550 paper-based; 213 computer-based). *Application deadline:* For fall admission, 2/15 priority date for domestic students, 2/15 for international students; for spring admission, 8/1 priority date for domestic students, 8/15 for international students. Applications are processed on a rolling basis. Application fee: $75. *Expenses:* Tuition, state resident: full-time $10,840. Tuition, nonresident: full-time $25,802. *Financial support:* In 2011–12, 2 research assistantships with full tuition reimbursements (averaging $14,670 per year), 1 teaching assistantship with full tuition reimbursement (averaging $14,164 per year) were awarded; fellowships, career-related internships or fieldwork, scholarships/grants, health care benefits, and unspecified assistantships also available. Financial award application deadline: 4/1. *Faculty research:* International development; famine, famine early warning systems, and food security; land use, history, change, degradation, desertification, management, and policy; sustainable agriculture and farming systems; remote sensing and spatial analysis; carbon sequestration; political-ecology of natural resources; ethnoecology and other ethno-sciences; economic and agricultural policy and development; economic botany; borderlands issues; globalization; civil conflict; urban development. *Total annual research expenditures:* $2.3 million. *Unit head:* Dr. Stuart E. Marsh, Chair, 520-621-8574, E-mail: smarsh@ag.arizona.edu. *Application contact:* Anita E. Finnell, Graduate Coordinator, 520-621-9111, Fax: 520-621-3816, E-mail: alrsgidp@email.arizona.edu. Web site: http://alrs.arizona.edu/.

University of California, Berkeley, Graduate Division, College of Natural Resources, Department of Environmental Science, Policy, and Management, Berkeley, CA 94720-1500. Offers environmental science, policy, and management (MS, PhD); forestry (MF). Terminal master's awarded for partial completion of doctoral program. *Degree requirements:* For master's, thesis optional; for doctorate, thesis/dissertation, qualifying exam. *Entrance requirements:* For master's and doctorate, GRE General Test, minimum GPA of 3.0, 3 letters of recommendation. Additional exam requirements/recommendations for international students: Required—TOEFL. Electronic applications accepted. *Faculty research:* Biology and ecology of insects; ecosystem function and environmental issues of soils; plant health/interactions from molecular to ecosystem levels; range management and ecology; forest and resource policy, sustainability, and management.

University of California, Davis, Graduate Studies, Graduate Group in Soils and Biogeochemistry, Davis, CA 95616. Offers MS, PhD. Terminal master's awarded for partial completion of doctoral program. *Degree requirements:* For master's, comprehensive exam (for some programs), thesis (for some programs); for doctorate, thesis/dissertation. *Entrance requirements:* For master's, minimum GPA of 3.3; for doctorate, GRE, minimum GPA of 3.3. Additional exam requirements/recommendations for international students: Required—TOEFL (minimum score 550 paper-based; 213 computer-based). Electronic applications accepted. *Faculty research:* Rhizosphere ecology, soil transport processes, biogeochemical cycling, sustainable agriculture.

University of California, Los Angeles, Graduate Division, School of Public Health, Department of Environmental Health Sciences, Los Angeles, CA 90095. Offers environmental health sciences (MS, PhD); environmental science and engineering (D Env); molecular toxicology (PhD); JD/MPH. *Accreditation:* ABET (one or more programs are accredited). *Degree requirements:* For master's, comprehensive exam or thesis; for doctorate, thesis/dissertation, oral and written qualifying exams. *Entrance requirements:* For master's, GRE General Test, minimum GPA of 3.0; for doctorate, GRE General Test, minimum undergraduate GPA of 3.0. Electronic applications accepted.

University of California, Los Angeles, Graduate Division, School of Public Health, Program in Environmental Science and Engineering, Los Angeles, CA 90095. Offers D Env. *Degree requirements:* For doctorate, thesis/dissertation, oral and written qualifying exams. *Entrance requirements:* For doctorate, GRE General Test, minimum undergraduate GPA of 3.0, master's degree or equivalent in a natural science, engineering, or public health. *Faculty research:* Toxic and hazardous substances, air and water pollution, risk assessment/management, water resources, marine science.

University of California, Merced, Division of Graduate Studies, School of Natural Sciences, Merced, CA 95343. Offers applied mathematics (MS, PhD); biological engineering and small-scale technologies (MS, PhD); environmental systems (MS, PhD); mechanical engineering and applied mechanics (MS, PhD); physics and chemistry (PhD); quantitative and systems biology (MS, PhD). *Unit head:* Dr. Samuel J. Traina, Dean, 209-228-4723, Fax: 209-228-6906, E-mail: grad.dean@ucmerced.edu. *Application contact:* Tsu Ya, Graduate Admissions and Academic Services Manager, 209-228-4723, Fax: 209-228-6906, E-mail: tya@ucmerced.edu.

University of California, Riverside, Graduate Division, Graduate Materials Science and Engineering Program, Riverside, CA 92521. Offers MS, PhD. *Entrance requirements:* For master's and doctorate, GRE. Additional exam requirements/recommendations for international students: Required—TOEFL (minimum score 550 paper-based; 213 computer-based; 80 iBT). Electronic applications accepted.

University of California, Santa Barbara, Graduate Division, College of Letters and Sciences, Division of Social Sciences, Department of Economics, Santa Barbara, CA 93106-9210. Offers economics (MA, PhD); economics and environmental science (PhD); MA/PhD. *Faculty:* 27 full-time (4 women), 21 part-time/adjunct (7 women). *Students:* 112 full-time (43 women); includes 23 minority (10 Asian, non-Hispanic/Latino; 12 Hispanic/Latino; 1 Two or more races, non-Hispanic/Latino), 27 international. Average age 26. 376 applicants, 49% accepted, 59 enrolled. In 2011, 52 master's, 4 doctorates awarded. Terminal master's awarded for partial completion of doctoral program. *Degree requirements:* For master's, comprehensive exam; for doctorate, comprehensive exam, thesis/dissertation. *Entrance requirements:* For master's and doctorate, GRE General Test, 3 letters of recommendation, statement of purpose, personal achievements/contributions statement, resume/curriculum vitae, transcripts for post-secondary institutions attended. Additional exam requirements/recommendations for international students: Required—TOEFL (minimum score 550 paper-based; 80 iBT), IELTS (minimum score 7). *Application deadline:* For fall admission, 12/1 priority date for domestic students, 12/1 for international students. Application fee: $80 ($100 for international students). Electronic applications accepted. *Expenses:* Tuition, state resident: full-time $12,192. Tuition, nonresident: full-time $27,294. *Required fees:* $764.13. *Financial support:* In 2011–12, 65 students received support, including 17 fellowships with full and partial tuition reimbursements available (averaging $19,000 per year), 7 research assistantships with full and partial tuition reimbursements available (averaging $19,000 per year), 106 teaching assistantships with partial tuition reimbursements available (averaging $17,000 per year); Federal Work-Study, institutionally sponsored loans, scholarships/grants, health care benefits, tuition waivers (full and partial), and unspecified assistantships also available. Support available to

Peterson's Graduate Programs in the Physical Sciences, Mathematics, Agricultural Sciences, the Environment & Natural Resources 2013

facebook.com/petersonspublishing **495**

Environmental Sciences

part-time students. Financial award application deadline: 12/1; financial award applicants required to submit FAFSA. *Faculty research:* Labor economics, econometrics, macroeconomic theory and policy, environmental and natural resources economics (EES), experimental and behavioral economics. *Unit head:* Prof. Olivier Deschenes, Director of Graduate Studies, 805-893-5617, Fax: 805-893-8830, E-mail: olivier@econ.ucsb.edu. *Application contact:* Mark Patterson, Graduate Advisor, 805-893-2205, Fax: 805-893-8830, E-mail: mark@econ.ucsb.edu. Web site: http://www.econ.ucsb.edu/.

University of California, Santa Barbara, Graduate Division, Donald Bren School of Environmental Science and Management, Santa Barbara, CA 93106-5131. Offers economics and environmental science (PhD); environmental science and management (MESM, PhD); technology and society (PhD). *Faculty:* 18 full-time (3 women), 3 part-time/adjunct (0 women). *Students:* 227 full-time (113 women); includes 33 minority (3 Black or African American, non-Hispanic/Latino; 1 American Indian or Alaska Native, non-Hispanic/Latino; 16 Asian, non-Hispanic/Latino; 9 Hispanic/Latino; 1 Native Hawaiian or other Pacific Islander, non-Hispanic/Latino; 3 Two or more races, non-Hispanic/Latino), 27 international. Average age 28. 447 applicants, 51% accepted, 109 enrolled. In 2011, 93 master's, 5 doctorates awarded. *Median time to degree:* Of those who began their doctoral program in fall 2003, 90% received their degree in 8 years or less. *Degree requirements:* For master's, thesis; for doctorate, thesis/dissertation. *Entrance requirements:* For master's and doctorate, GRE. Additional exam requirements/recommendations for international students: Required—TOEFL (minimum score 550 paper-based; 80 iBT), IELTS (minimum score 7). *Application deadline:* For fall admission, 12/15 priority date for domestic students, 12/15 for international students. Application fee: $80 ($100 for international students). Electronic applications accepted. *Expenses:* Tuition, state resident: full-time $12,192. Tuition, nonresident: full-time $27,294. *Required fees:* $764.13. *Financial support:* In 2011–12, 34 students received support, including 53 fellowships with full and partial tuition reimbursements available, 10 research assistantships with full and partial tuition reimbursements available, 18 teaching assistantships with full and partial tuition reimbursements available; career-related internships or fieldwork and tuition waivers (full and partial) also available. Financial award application deadline: 12/15; financial award applicants required to submit FAFSA. *Faculty research:* Coastal marine resources management, conservation planning, corporate environmental management, economics and politics of the environment, energy and climate, pollution prevention and remediation, water resources management. *Unit head:* Bryant Wieneke, Assistant Dean, Planning and Administration, 805-893-2212, Fax: 805-893-7612, E-mail: bryant@bren.ucsb.edu. *Application contact:* Dori Molnar, Graduate Advisor, 805-893-7611, Fax: 805-893-7612, E-mail: admissions@bren.ucsb.edu. Web site: http://www.bren.ucsb.edu/.

University of Chicago, Irving B. Harris Graduate School of Public Policy Studies, Chicago, IL 60637-1513. Offers environmental science and policy (MS); public policy studies (AM, MPP, PhD); JD/MPP; MBA/MPP; MPP/M Div; MPP/MA. Part-time programs available. *Degree requirements:* For doctorate, thesis/dissertation. *Entrance requirements:* Additional exam requirements/recommendations for international students: Required—TOEFL. Electronic applications accepted. *Expenses:* Contact institution. *Faculty research:* Family and child policy, international security, health policy, social policy.

University of Cincinnati, Graduate School, College of Engineering and Applied Science, Department of Civil and Environmental Engineering, Program in Environmental Sciences, Cincinnati, OH 45221. Offers MS, PhD. Part-time programs available. *Degree requirements:* For master's, thesis or alternative; for doctorate, one foreign language, thesis/dissertation. *Entrance requirements:* For master's and doctorate, GRE General Test. Additional exam requirements/recommendations for international students: Required—TOEFL (minimum score 580 paper-based; 237 computer-based; 92 iBT). Electronic applications accepted. *Faculty research:* Environmental microbiology, solid-waste management, air pollution control, water pollution control, aerosols.

University of Colorado at Colorado Springs, College of Letters, Arts and Sciences, Department of Geography and Environmental Studies, Colorado Springs, CO 80933-7150. Offers MA. Part-time programs available. *Faculty:* 12 full-time (3 women). *Students:* 6 full-time (2 women), 8 part-time (5 women); includes 1 minority (Hispanic/Latino). Average age 36. 7 applicants, 100% accepted, 4 enrolled. In 2011, 5 master's awarded. *Degree requirements:* For master's, comprehensive exam (for some programs), thesis (for some programs). *Entrance requirements:* For master's, GRE (recommended minimum combined score for the verbal and quantitative tests of 1000, plus proficiency on the writing requirement, minimum undergraduate GPA of 3.0, statement of intent (essay). Additional exam requirements/recommendations for international students: Recommended—TOEFL. *Application deadline:* For fall admission, 2/1 priority date for domestic students, 2/1 for international students. Applications are processed on a rolling basis. Application fee: $60 ($75 for international students). *Expenses:* Tuition, state resident: part-time $660 per credit hour. Tuition, nonresident: part-time $1133 per credit hour. Tuition and fees vary according to degree level, program and student level. *Financial support:* In 2011–12, 5 students received support. Federal Work-Study and scholarships/grants available. Support available to part-time students. Financial award application deadline: 3/1; financial award applicants required to submit FAFSA. *Faculty research:* Natural hazard mitigation and policy issues, applied geography, geographic information systems, population geography. *Total annual research expenditures:* $208,755. *Unit head:* Dr. Emily Skop, Associate Professor, 719-

255-3789, Fax: 719-255-4066, E-mail: eskop@uccs.edu. *Application contact:* Mary McGill, Program Assistant, 719-255-3016, E-mail: mmcgill@uccs.edu. Web site: http://www.uccs.edu/geography/.

University of Colorado Denver, College of Liberal Arts and Sciences, Department of Geography and Environmental Sciences, Denver, CO 80217. Offers environmental sciences (MS), including air quality, ecosystems, environmental health, environmental science education, geo-spatial analysis, hazardous waste, water quality. Part-time and evening/weekend programs available. *Students:* 42 full-time (25 women), 6 part-time (5 women); includes 6 minority (2 Black or African American, non-Hispanic/Latino; 1 Asian, non-Hispanic/Latino; 2 Hispanic/Latino; 1 Two or more races, non-Hispanic/Latino), 10 international. Average age 29. 31 applicants, 68% accepted, 13 enrolled. In 2011, 24 master's awarded. *Degree requirements:* For master's, thesis or alternative, 30 credits including 21 of core requirements and 9 of environmental science electives. *Entrance requirements:* For master's, GRE General Test, BA in one of the natural/physical sciences or engineering (or equivalent background); prerequisite coursework in calculus and physics (one semester each), general chemistry with lab and general biology with lab (two semesters each), three letters of recommendation. Additional exam requirements/recommendations for international students: Required—TOEFL (minimum score 525 paper-based; 197 computer-based). *Application deadline:* For fall admission, 4/1 for domestic and international students; for spring admission, 10/1 for domestic and international students. Application fee: $50 ($75 for international students). Electronic applications accepted. *Financial support:* Research assistantships, teaching assistantships, and Federal Work-Study available. Financial award application deadline: 4/1; financial award applicants required to submit FAFSA. *Faculty research:* Air quality, environmental health, ecosystems, hazardous waste, water quality, geo-spatial analysis and environmental science education. *Unit head:* Dr. Brian K. Page, Department Chair, 303-556-8332, Fax: 303-556-6197, E-mail: john.wyckoff@cudenver.edu. *Application contact:* Sue Eddleman, Program Assistant, 303-556-6197, E-mail: sue.eddleman@ucdenver.edu. Web site: http://www.ucdenver.edu/academics/colleges/CLAS/Departments/ges/Pages/Geography.aspx.

University of Guam, Office of Graduate Studies, College of Natural and Applied Sciences, Program in Environmental Science, Mangilao, GU 96923. Offers MS. Part-time programs available. *Degree requirements:* For master's, thesis. *Entrance requirements:* For master's, GRE General Test. Additional exam requirements/recommendations for international students: Required—TOEFL. *Faculty research:* Water resources, ecology, karst formations, hydrogeology, meteorology.

University of Guelph, Graduate Studies, Ontario Agricultural College, Department of Land Resource Science, Guelph, ON N1G 2W1, Canada. Offers atmospheric science (M Sc, PhD); environmental and agricultural earth sciences (M Sc, PhD); land resources management (M Sc, PhD); soil science (M Sc, PhD). Part-time programs available. *Degree requirements:* For master's, thesis (for some programs), research project (non-thesis track); for doctorate, comprehensive exam, thesis/dissertation. *Entrance requirements:* For master's, minimum B average during previous 2 years of course work; for doctorate, minimum B average during previous 2 years of course work. Additional exam requirements/recommendations for international students: Required—TOEFL (minimum score 550 paper-based; 213 computer-based). Electronic applications accepted. *Faculty research:* Soil science, environmental earth science, land resource management.

University of Hawaii at Hilo, Program in Tropical Conservation Biology and Environmental Science, Hilo, HI 96720-4091. Offers MS.

University of Houston–Clear Lake, School of Science and Computer Engineering, Program in Environmental Science, Houston, TX 77058-1098. Offers MS. Part-time and evening/weekend programs available. *Entrance requirements:* For master's, GRE General Test. Additional exam requirements/recommendations for international students: Required—TOEFL (minimum score 550 paper-based; 213 computer-based).

University of Idaho, College of Graduate Studies, Program in Environmental Science, Moscow, ID 83844-3006. Offers environmental science (MS, PhD); natural resources and environmental science (PSM); water resources (MS, PhD). *Faculty:* 19 full-time, 1 part-time/adjunct. *Students:* 87 full-time, 57 part-time. Average age 32. In 2011, 20 master's, 2 doctorates awarded. *Application deadline:* For fall admission, 8/1 for domestic students; for spring admission, 12/15 for domestic students. Applications are processed on a rolling basis. Application fee: $60. Electronic applications accepted. *Expenses:* Tuition, state resident: full-time $3874; part-time $334 per credit hour. Tuition, nonresident: full-time $16,394; part-time $861 per credit hour. *Required fees:* $2808; $99 per credit hour. Tuition and fees vary according to program. *Financial support:* Research assistantships and teaching assistantships available. Financial award applicants required to submit FAFSA. *Unit head:* Dr. Jan Boll, Director, 208-885-6113, Fax: 208-885-4674, E-mail: envs@uidaho.edu. *Application contact:* Erick Larson, Director of Graduate Admissions, 208-885-4723, E-mail: gadms@uidaho.edu. Web site: http://www.uidaho.edu/cogs/envs.

University of Illinois at Springfield, Graduate Programs, College of Public Affairs and Administration, Program in Environmental Studies, Springfield, IL 62703-5407. Offers environmental science (MS); environmental studies (MA). Part-time and evening/weekend programs available. Postbaccalaureate distance learning degree programs offered (no on-campus study). *Faculty:* 5 full-time (1 woman). *Students:* 14 full-time (10 women), 75 part-time (43 women); includes 6 minority (3 Black or African American, non-Hispanic/Latino; 2 Asian, non-Hispanic/Latino; 1 Hispanic/Latino), 5 international. Average age 35. 53 applicants, 57% accepted, 20 enrolled. In 2011, 28 master's awarded. *Degree requirements:* For master's, thesis or project. *Entrance requirements:* For master's, minimum undergraduate GPA of 3.0, 2 letters of recommendation, goals essay. Additional exam requirements/recommendations for international students: Required—TOEFL (minimum score 500 paper-based; 176 computer-based; 61 iBT). *Application deadline:* Applications are processed on a rolling basis. Application fee: $50 ($60 for international students). Electronic applications accepted. *Expenses:* Tuition, state resident: full-time $6978; part-time $290.75 per credit hour. Tuition, nonresident: full-time $15,282; part-time $636.75 per credit hour. *Required fees:* $2106; $87.75 per credit hour. *Financial support:* In 2011–12, fellowships with full tuition reimbursements (averaging $8,550 per year), research assistantships with full tuition reimbursements (averaging $8,550 per year), teaching assistantships with full tuition reimbursements (averaging $8,550 per year) were awarded; career-related internships or fieldwork, Federal Work-Study, scholarships/grants, health care benefits, and unspecified assistantships also available. Support available to part-time students. Financial award application deadline: 11/15; financial award applicants required to submit FAFSA. *Unit head:* Dr. Dennis Ruez, Program Administrator, 217-206-8424, E-mail: druez2@uis.edu. *Application contact:* Dr. Lynn Pardie, Office of Graduate Studies, 800-252-8533, Fax: 217-206-7623, E-mail: lpard1@uis.edu. Web site: http://www.uis.edu/environmentalstudies/.

University of Illinois at Urbana–Champaign, Graduate College, College of Agricultural, Consumer and Environmental Sciences, Department of Natural Resources and Environmental Science, Champaign, IL 61820. Offers MS, PhD, MS/JD. Part-time programs available. Postbaccalaureate distance learning degree programs offered (no on-campus study). *Faculty:* 21 full-time (6 women), 1 part-time/adjunct (0 women). *Students:* 62 full-time (26 women), 81 part-time (38 women); includes 9 minority (1 Black or African American, non-Hispanic/Latino; 1 American Indian or Alaska Native, non-Hispanic/Latino; 1 Asian, non-Hispanic/Latino; 5 Hispanic/Latino; 1 Two or more races, non-Hispanic/Latino), 19 international. 124 applicants, 40% accepted, 42 enrolled. In 2011, 21 master's, 3 doctorates awarded. *Entrance requirements:* For master's and doctorate, GRE, minimum GPA of 3.0. Additional exam requirements/recommendations for international students: Required—TOEFL (minimum score 600 paper-based; 250 computer-based). *Application deadline:* Applications are processed on a rolling basis. Application fee: $75 ($90 for international students). Electronic applications accepted. *Financial support:* In 2011–12, 7 fellowships, 66 research assistantships, 26 teaching assistantships were awarded; tuition waivers (full and partial) also available. *Unit head:* Jeffrey D. Brawn, Head, 217-244-5937, Fax: 217-244-3219, E-mail: jbrawn@illinois.edu. *Application contact:* Karen M. Claus, Secretary, 217-333-5824, Fax: 217-244-3219, E-mail: kclaus@illinois.edu. Web site: http://nres.illinois.edu/.

University of Illinois at Urbana–Champaign, Graduate College, College of Engineering, Department of Civil and Environmental Engineering, Champaign, IL 61820. Offers civil engineering (MS); environmental engineering in civil engineering (MS, PhD); environmental science in civil engineering (MS, PhD); M Arch/MS; MBA/MS. *Faculty:* 46 full-time (7 women). *Students:* 421 full-time (123 women), 76 part-time (22 women); includes 54 minority (2 Black or African American, non-Hispanic/Latino; 1 American Indian or Alaska Native, non-Hispanic/Latino; 31 Asian, non-Hispanic/Latino; 14 Hispanic/Latino; 6 Two or more races, non-Hispanic/Latino), 271 international. 1,112 applicants, 41% accepted, 169 enrolled. In 2011, 154 master's, 29 doctorates awarded. *Entrance requirements:* For master's and doctorate, GRE. Additional exam requirements/recommendations for international students: Required—TOEFL (minimum score 550 paper-based; 213 computer-based; 79 iBT) or IELTS (minimum score 6.5). *Application deadline:* Applications are processed on a rolling basis. Application fee: $75 ($90 for international students). Electronic applications accepted. *Financial support:* In 2011–12, 57 fellowships, 258 research assistantships, 90 teaching assistantships were awarded; tuition waivers (full and partial) also available. *Unit head:* Amr S. Elnashai, Jr., Head, 217-265-5497, Fax: 217-265-8040, E-mail: aelnash@illinois.edu. *Application contact:* Maxine M. Peyton, Office Manager, 217-333-6636, Fax: 217-333-9464, E-mail: mpeyton@illinois.edu. Web site: http://cee.illinois.edu/.

The University of Kansas, Graduate Studies, School of Engineering, Program in Environmental Science, Lawrence, KS 66045. Offers MS, PhD. Part-time programs available. *Faculty:* 9 full-time (1 woman), 1 part-time/adjunct (0 women). *Students:* 7 full-time (3 women), 1 part-time (0 women); includes 3 minority (2 Asian, non-Hispanic/Latino; 1 Hispanic/Latino). Average age 28. 12 applicants, 75% accepted, 1 enrolled. In 2011, 1 master's awarded. *Degree requirements:* For master's, thesis or alternative, exam; for doctorate, comprehensive exam, thesis/dissertation. *Entrance requirements:* For master's, GRE, minimum GPA of 3.0; for doctorate, GRE, minimum GPA of 3.5. Additional exam requirements/recommendations for international students: Required—TOEFL. *Application deadline:* For fall admission, 3/1 priority date for domestic students, 3/1 for international students; for spring admission, 12/1 priority date for domestic students, 8/15 for international students. Applications are processed on a rolling basis. Application fee: $55 ($65 for international students). Electronic applications accepted. Tuition and fees vary according to course load, campus/location, program and reciprocity agreements. *Financial support:* Fellowships with full tuition reimbursements, research assistantships with full tuition reimbursements, teaching assistantships, and career-related internships or fieldwork available.

Financial award application deadline: 2/7. *Faculty research:* Water quality, water treatment, wastewater treatment, air quality, air pollution control, solid waste, hazardous waste, water resources engineering, water resources science. *Unit head:* Craig D. Adams, Professor and Chair, 785-864-2700, Fax: 785-864-5631, E-mail: adamscd@ku.edu. *Application contact:* Bruce M. McEnroe, Professor and Graduate Advisor, 785-864-2925, Fax: 785-864-2925, E-mail: mcenroe@ku.edu. Web site: http://www.ceae.ku.edu/.

University of Lethbridge, School of Graduate Studies, Lethbridge, AB T1K 3M4, Canada. Offers accounting (MScM); addictions counseling (M Sc); agricultural biotechnology (M Sc); agricultural studies (M Sc, MA); anthropology (MA); archaeology (MA); art (MA, MFA); biochemistry (M Sc); biological sciences (M Sc); biomolecular science (PhD); biosystems and biodiversity (PhD); Canadian studies (MA); chemistry (M Sc); computer science (M Sc); computer science and geographical information science (M Sc); counseling psychology (M Ed); dramatic arts (MA); earth, space, and physical science (PhD); economics (MA); educational leadership (M Ed); English (MA); environmental science (M Sc); evolution and behavior (PhD); exercise science (M Sc); finance (MScM); French (MA); French/German (MA); French/Spanish (MA); general education (M Ed); general management (MScM); geography (M Sc, MA); German (MA); health science (M Sc); history (MA); human resource management and labour relations (MScM); individualized multidisciplinary (M Sc, MA); information systems (MScM); international management (MScM); kinesiology (M Sc, MA); management (M Sc, MA); marketing (MScM); mathematics (M Sc); music (M Mus, MA); Native American studies (MA); neuroscience (M Sc, PhD); new media (MA); nursing (M Sc); philosophy (MA); physics (M Sc); policy and strategy (MScM); political science (MA); psychology (M Sc, MA); religious studies (MA); social sciences (MA); sociology (MA); theatre and dramatic arts (MFA); theoretical and computational science (PhD); urban and regional studies (MA); women's studies (MA). Part-time and evening/weekend programs available. *Degree requirements:* For doctorate, comprehensive exam, thesis/dissertation. *Entrance requirements:* For master's, GMAT (M Sc in management), bachelor's degree in related field, minimum GPA of 3.0 during previous 20 graded semester courses, 2 years teaching or related experience (M Ed); for doctorate, master's degree, minimum graduate GPA of 3.5. Additional exam requirements/recommendations for international students: Required—TOEFL. *Faculty research:* Movement and brain plasticity, gibberellin physiology, photosynthesis, carbon cycling, molecular properties of main-group ring components.

University of Maine, Graduate School, College of Natural Sciences, Forestry, and Agriculture, Department of Biological Sciences, Program in Ecology and Environmental Science, Orono, ME 04469. Offers water resources (PhD). Part-time programs available. *Students:* 40 full-time (31 women), 14 part-time (6 women). Average age 31. 72 applicants, 25% accepted, 12 enrolled. In 2011, 7 master's, 5 doctorates awarded. *Degree requirements:* For doctorate, thesis/dissertation. *Entrance requirements:* For master's and doctorate, GRE General Test. Additional exam requirements/recommendations for international students: Required—TOEFL. *Application deadline:* For fall admission, 2/1 priority date for domestic students. Applications are processed on a rolling basis. Application fee: $65. Electronic applications accepted. *Expenses:* Tuition, state resident: full-time $5016. Tuition, nonresident: full-time $14,424. *Financial support:* Career-related internships or fieldwork, Federal Work-Study, institutionally sponsored loans, and tuition waivers (full) available. Financial award application deadline: 3/1. *Unit head:* Dr. Mark Anderson, Coordinator, 207-581-3198. *Application contact:* Scott G. Delcourt, Associate Dean of the Graduate School, 207-581-3291, Fax: 207-581-3232, E-mail: graduate@maine.edu. Web site: http://www2.umaine.edu/graduate/.

University of Maine, Graduate School, College of Natural Sciences, Forestry, and Agriculture, Department of Plant, Soil, and Environmental Sciences, Orono, ME 04469. Offers biological sciences (PhD); ecology and environmental sciences (MS, PhD); forest resources (PhD); horticulture (MS); plant science (PhD); plant, soil, and environmental sciences (MS); resource utilization (MS). *Faculty:* 9 full-time (3 women), 7 part-time/adjunct (3 women). *Students:* 7 full-time (4 women), 2 part-time (0 women), 2 international. Average age 30. 14 applicants, 50% accepted, 5 enrolled. In 2011, 4 degrees awarded. *Entrance requirements:* For master's and doctorate, GRE General Test. Additional exam requirements/recommendations for international students: Required—TOEFL. *Application deadline:* Applications are processed on a rolling basis. Application fee: $65. Electronic applications accepted. *Expenses:* Tuition, state resident: full-time $5016. Tuition, nonresident: full-time $14,424. *Financial support:* In 2011–12, 16 research assistantships with full tuition reimbursements (averaging $17,336 per year), 1 teaching assistantship with full tuition reimbursement (averaging $13,600 per year) were awarded; scholarships/grants, tuition waivers (full and partial), and unspecified assistantships also available. *Total annual research expenditures:* $179,065. *Unit head:* Dr. Gregory Porter, Chair, 207-581-2943, Fax: 207-581-3207. *Application contact:* Scott G. Delcourt, Associate Dean of the Graduate School, 207-581-3291, Fax: 207-581-3232, E-mail: graduate@maine.edu. Web site: http://www2.umaine.edu/graduate/.

The University of Manchester, School of Earth, Atmospheric and Environmental Sciences, Manchester, United Kingdom. Offers atmospheric sciences (M Phil, M Sc, PhD); basin studies and petroleum geosciences (M Phil, M Sc, PhD); earth, atmospheric and environmental sciences (M Phil, M Sc, PhD); environmental geochemistry and cosmochemistry (M Phil, M Sc, PhD); isotope geochemistry and cosmochemistry (M Phil, M Sc, PhD); paleontology (M Phil, M Sc, PhD);

Peterson's Graduate Programs in the Physical Sciences, Mathematics, Agricultural Sciences, the Environment & Natural Resources 2013

facebook.com/petersonspublishing **497**

Environmental Sciences

physics and chemistry of minerals and fluids (M Phil, M Sc, PhD); structural and petrological geosciences (M Phil, M Sc, PhD).

University of Manitoba, Faculty of Graduate Studies, Clayton H. Riddell Faculty of Environment, Earth, and Resources, Department of Environment and Geography, Winnipeg, MB R3T 2N2, Canada. Offers environment (M Env); environment and geography (M Sc); geography (MA, PhD). *Degree requirements:* For master's, thesis; for doctorate, one foreign language, thesis/dissertation.

University of Maryland, Baltimore, Graduate School, Program in Marine-Estuarine-Environmental Sciences, College Park, MD 20740. Offers MS, PhD. Part-time programs available. *Faculty:* 7. *Students:* 1 applicant, 0% accepted. Terminal master's awarded for partial completion of doctoral program. *Degree requirements:* For master's, thesis, oral defense; for doctorate, comprehensive exam, thesis/dissertation, proposal defense, oral defense. *Entrance requirements:* For master's and doctorate, GRE General Test, minimum GPA of 3.0. Additional exam requirements/recommendations for international students: Required—TOEFL. *Application deadline:* For fall admission, 2/1 for domestic students, 1/1 for international students; for spring admission, 9/1 for domestic students. Applications are processed on a rolling basis. Application fee: $50. Electronic applications accepted. *Financial support:* In 2011–12, 1 research assistantship with tuition reimbursement was awarded; fellowships with tuition reimbursements, teaching assistantships with tuition reimbursements, scholarships/grants, and unspecified assistantships also available. *Unit head:* Dr. Kennedy T. Paynter, Jr., Director, 301-405-6938, Fax: 301-314-4139, E-mail: mees@umd.edu. *Application contact:* Keith T. Brooks, Assistant Dean, 410-706-7131, Fax: 410-706-3473, E-mail: kbrooks@umaryland.edu. Web site: http://www.mees.umd.edu/.

University of Maryland, Baltimore County, Graduate School, College of Natural and Mathematical Sciences, Department of Biological Sciences, Marine-Estuarine-Environmental Sciences Graduate Program, College Park, MD 20742. Offers MS, PhD. Part-time programs available. *Faculty:* 12. *Students:* 4 full-time (2 women), 1 part-time (0 women). 7 applicants, 14% accepted, 1 enrolled. In 2011, 1 master's, 1 doctorate awarded. *Degree requirements:* For master's, thesis, oral defense; for doctorate, comprehensive exam, thesis/dissertation, proposal defense, oral defense. *Entrance requirements:* For master's and doctorate, GRE General Test, minimum GPA of 3.0. Additional exam requirements/recommendations for international students: Required—TOEFL. *Application deadline:* For fall admission, 2/1 for domestic students, 1/1 for international students; for spring admission, 9/1 for domestic students. Applications are processed on a rolling basis. Application fee: $50. Electronic applications accepted. *Financial support:* In 2011–12, 2 fellowships with tuition reimbursements (averaging $22,500 per year), 1 research assistantship with tuition reimbursement (averaging $21,000 per year), 1 teaching assistantship with tuition reimbursement (averaging $20,000 per year) were awarded; career-related internships or fieldwork, scholarships/grants, and unspecified assistantships also available. Financial award application deadline: 12/1. *Unit head:* Dr. Kennedy T. Paynter, Jr., Director, 301-405-6938, Fax: 301-314-4139, E-mail: mees@umd.edu. Web site: http://www.mees.umd.edu.

University of Maryland, College Park, Academic Affairs, College of Agriculture and Natural Resources, Department of Environmental Science and Technology, College Park, MD 20742. Offers MS, PhD. *Faculty:* 30 full-time (6 women), 3 part-time/adjunct (1 woman). *Students:* 28 full-time (18 women), 5 part-time (3 women); includes 3 minority (1 Black or African American, non-Hispanic/Latino; 1 Asian, non-Hispanic/Latino; 1 Two or more races, non-Hispanic/Latino), 4 international. 69 applicants, 29% accepted, 8 enrolled. In 2011, 3 master's, 2 doctorates awarded. *Application deadline:* For fall admission, 1/15 for domestic and international students; for spring admission, 8/15 for domestic students, 6/1 for international students. Applications are processed on a rolling basis. Application fee: $75. Electronic applications accepted. *Expenses: Tuition, area resident:* Part-time $525 per credit hour. Tuition, state resident: part-time $525 per credit hour. Tuition, nonresident: part-time $1131 per credit hour. *Required fees:* $386.31 per term. Tuition and fees vary according to program. *Financial support:* In 2011–12, 1 fellowship with full tuition reimbursement (averaging $20,000 per year), 12 research assistantships (averaging $17,215 per year), 14 teaching assistantships (averaging $17,535 per year) were awarded. *Total annual research expenditures:* $4.1 million. *Unit head:* William Bowerman, Chair, 301-405-1306, E-mail: wbowerma@umd.edu. *Application contact:* Dr. Charles A. Caramello, Dean of Graduate School, 301-405-0358, Fax: 301-314-9305, E-mail: ccaramel@umd.edu. Web site: http://www.enst.umd.edu/.

University of Maryland, College Park, Academic Affairs, College of Computer, Mathematical and Natural Sciences, Program in Marine-Estuarine-Environmental Sciences, College Park, MD 20742. Offers MS, PhD. Part-time programs available. *Faculty:* 130. *Students:* 117 (76 women); includes 10 minority (3 Black or African American, non-Hispanic/Latino; 3 Asian, non-Hispanic/Latino; 4 Hispanic/Latino), 23 international. 93 applicants, 30% accepted, 21 enrolled. In 2011, 12 master's, 10 doctorates awarded. Terminal master's awarded for partial completion of doctoral program. *Degree requirements:* For master's, thesis, oral defense; for doctorate, comprehensive exam, thesis/dissertation, proposal defense, oral defense. *Entrance requirements:* For master's and doctorate, GRE General Test, minimum GPA of 3.0. Additional exam requirements/recommendations for international students: Required—TOEFL. *Application deadline:* For fall admission, 2/1 for domestic and international students; for spring admission, 9/1 for domestic students, 6/1 for international students. Applications are processed on a rolling basis. Application fee: $60. Electronic applications

accepted. *Expenses: Tuition, area resident:* Part-time $525 per credit hour. Tuition, state resident: part-time $525 per credit hour. Tuition, nonresident: part-time $1131 per credit hour. *Required fees:* $386.31 per term. Tuition and fees vary according to program. *Financial support:* In 2011–12, 9 teaching assistantships with full tuition reimbursements were awarded; fellowships with full tuition reimbursements, research assistantships with full tuition reimbursements, Federal Work-Study, scholarships/grants, traineeships, health care benefits, and unspecified assistantships also available. Financial award application deadline: 1/1; financial award applicants required to submit FAFSA. *Faculty research:* Marine and estuarine organisms, terrestrial and freshwater ecology, remote environmental sensing, fisheries science, oceanography, environmental chemistry. *Unit head:* Dr. Kennedy T. Paynter, Jr., Director, 301-405-6938, Fax: 301-314-4139, E-mail: mees@umd.edu. *Application contact:* Dr. Charles A. Caramello, Dean of Graduate School, 301-405-0358, Fax: 301-314-9305, E-mail: gradschool@umd.edu. Web site: http://www.mees.umd.edu/.

University of Maryland Eastern Shore, Graduate Programs, Department of Natural Sciences, Program in Marine-Estuarine-Environmental Sciences, College Park, MD 20740. Offers MS, PhD. Part-time programs available. *Faculty:* 28. *Students:* 31 (20 women); includes 16 minority (13 Black or African American, non-Hispanic/Latino; 1 American Indian or Alaska Native, non-Hispanic/Latino; 2 Asian, non-Hispanic/Latino), 8 international. 11 applicants, 91% accepted, 6 enrolled. In 2011, 3 master's, 3 doctorates awarded. *Degree requirements:* For master's, thesis; for doctorate, comprehensive exam, thesis/dissertation, proposal defense. *Entrance requirements:* For master's and doctorate, GRE General Test, minimum GPA of 3.0. Additional exam requirements/recommendations for international students: Required—TOEFL. *Application deadline:* For fall admission, 2/1 for domestic and international students; for spring admission, 9/1 for domestic students, 8/1 for international students. Applications are processed on a rolling basis. Application fee: $30. Electronic applications accepted. *Financial support:* In 2011–12, 30 students received support. Fellowships with tuition reimbursements available, research assistantships with tuition reimbursements available, teaching assistantships with tuition reimbursements available, career-related internships or fieldwork, scholarships/grants, and unspecified assistantships available. Support available to part-time students. Financial award application deadline: 1/1. *Unit head:* Dr. Kennedy T. Paynter, Jr., Director, 301-405-6938, Fax: 301-314-4139, E-mail: mees@umd.edu. *Application contact:* Wayne Smith, Program Assistant, 410-651-6040, Fax: 410-651-7739, E-mail: wesmith@umes.edu. Web site: http://www.mees.umd.edu/.

University of Massachusetts Boston, Office of Graduate Studies, College of Science and Mathematics, Department of Environmental, Earth and Ocean Sciences, Track in Environmental, Earth and Ocean Sciences, Boston, MA 02125-3393. Offers PhD. Part-time and evening/weekend programs available. *Degree requirements:* For doctorate, comprehensive exam, thesis/dissertation, oral exams. *Entrance requirements:* For doctorate, GRE General Test, minimum GPA of 2.75. *Faculty research:* Conservation genetics, anthropogenic and natural influences on community structures of coral reef factors, geographical variation in mitochondrial DNA, protein chemistry and enzymology pertaining to insect cuticle.

University of Massachusetts Lowell, College of Engineering, Department of Civil and Environmental Engineering and College of Sciences, Program in Environmental Studies, Lowell, MA 01854-2881. Offers environmental engineering (MSES); environmental studies (PhD, Certificate). Part-time programs available. *Degree requirements:* For master's, thesis optional. *Entrance requirements:* For master's, GRE General Test. *Faculty research:* Remote sensing of air pollutants, atmospheric deposition of toxic metals, contaminant transport in groundwater, soil remediation.

University of Massachusetts Lowell, College of Sciences, Department of Chemistry, Lowell, MA 01854-2881. Offers analytical chemistry (PhD); biochemistry (PhD); chemistry (MS, PhD); environmental studies (PhD); green chemistry (PhD); inorganic chemistry (PhD); organic chemistry (PhD); polymer science (MS). Terminal master's awarded for partial completion of doctoral program. *Degree requirements:* For master's, thesis; for doctorate, 2 foreign languages, thesis/dissertation. *Entrance requirements:* For master's and doctorate, GRE General Test. Electronic applications accepted.

University of Massachusetts Lowell, School of Health and Environment, Department of Work Environment, Lowell, MA 01854-2881. Offers cleaner production and pollution prevention (MS, Sc D); environmental risk assessment (Certificate); epidemiology (MS, Sc D); ergonomics and safety (MS, Sc D); identification and control of ergonomic hazards (Certificate); job stress and healthy job redesign (Certificate); occupational and environmental hygiene (MS, Sc D); radiological health physics and general work environment protection (Certificate); work environment policy (MS, Sc D). *Accreditation:* ABET (one or more programs are accredited). Part-time programs available. Terminal master's awarded for partial completion of doctoral program. *Degree requirements:* For master's, thesis optional; for doctorate, thesis/dissertation. *Entrance requirements:* For master's and doctorate, GRE General Test. Additional exam requirements/recommendations for international students: Required—TOEFL.

University of Medicine and Dentistry of New Jersey, Graduate School of Biomedical Sciences, Graduate Programs in Biomedical Sciences–Piscataway, Program in Environmental Sciences/Exposure Assessment, Piscataway, NJ 08854-5635. Offers PhD, MD/PhD. PhD offered jointly with Rutgers, The State University of New Jersey, New Brunswick. *Entrance requirements:* Additional exam requirements/recommendations for international students: Required—TOEFL. Electronic applications accepted.

University of Michigan, School of Natural Resources and Environment, Program in Natural Resources and Environment, Ann Arbor, MI 48109. Offers aquatic sciences: research and management (MS); behavior, education and communication (MS); conservation biology (MS); conservation ecology (MS); environmental informatics (MS); environmental justice (MS); environmental policy and planning (MS); natural resources and environment (PhD); sustainable systems (MS); terrestrial ecosystems (MS); MS/JD; MS/MBA; MUP/MS. *Faculty:* 45 full-time, 23 part-time/adjunct. *Students:* 450 full-time (254 women); includes 63 minority (7 Black or African American, non-Hispanic/Latino; 2 American Indian or Alaska Native, non-Hispanic/Latino; 35 Asian, non-Hispanic/Latino; 13 Hispanic/Latino; 6 Two or more races, non-Hispanic/Latino), 70 international. Average age 27. 643 applicants. In 2011, 133 master's, 11 doctorates awarded. Terminal master's awarded for partial completion of doctoral program. *Degree requirements:* For master's, practicum or group project; for doctorate, comprehensive exam, thesis/dissertation, oral defense of dissertation, preliminary exam. *Entrance requirements:* For master's, GRE General Test; for doctorate, GRE General Test, master's degree. Additional exam requirements/recommendations for international students: Required—TOEFL (minimum score 560 paper-based; 220 computer-based; 84 iBT). *Application deadline:* For fall admission, 1/5 priority date for domestic students, 1/5 for international students. Applications are processed on a rolling basis. Application fee: $65 ($75 for international students). Electronic applications accepted. *Financial support:* Fellowships with tuition reimbursements, research assistantships with tuition reimbursements, teaching assistantships with tuition reimbursements, career-related internships or fieldwork, Federal Work-Study, institutionally sponsored loans, scholarships/grants, health care benefits, and unspecified assistantships available. Support available to part-time students. Financial award application deadline: 1/5; financial award applicants required to submit FAFSA. *Faculty research:* Stream ecology, plant-insect interactions, fish biology, resource control and reproductive success, remote sensing, conservation ecology. *Unit head:* Dr. Marie Lynn Miranda, Dean, 734-764-2550, Fax: 734-763-8965, E-mail: mlmirand@umich.edu. *Application contact:* Adam D. Ancira, Graduate Admissions Team, 734-764-6453, Fax: 734-936-2195, E-mail: snre.admissions@umich.edu. Web site: http://www.snre.umich.edu/.

University of Michigan–Dearborn, College of Arts, Sciences, and Letters, Master of Science in Environmental Science Program, Dearborn, MI 48128. Offers MS. Part-time and evening/weekend programs available. *Faculty:* 17 full-time (6 women), 1 part-time/adjunct (0 women). *Students:* 5 full-time (4 women), 25 part-time (13 women); includes 3 minority (1 Black or African American, non-Hispanic/Latino; 1 Asian, non-Hispanic/Latino; 1 Hispanic/Latino). Average age 30. 13 applicants, 100% accepted, 9 enrolled. In 2011, 7 master's awarded. *Degree requirements:* For master's, thesis optional. *Entrance requirements:* For master's, 2 letters of reference, minimum GPA of 3.0. Additional exam requirements/recommendations for international students: Required—TOEFL (minimum score 560 paper-based; 220 computer-based). *Application deadline:* For fall admission, 8/1 priority date for domestic students, 4/1 for international students; for winter admission, 12/1 priority date for domestic students, 11/1 for international students; for spring admission, 4/1 for domestic students, 3/1 for international students. Applications are processed on a rolling basis. Application fee: $60. *Financial support:* In 2011–12, 1 fellowship (averaging $2,500 per year), 2 research assistantships (averaging $2,500 per year) were awarded. Financial award application deadline: 4/1; financial award applicants required to submit FAFSA. *Faculty research:* Fate and transport of heavy metals; land use and impact on ground water and surface water quality; ecosystems and management; natural resources; plant, animal and microbial diversity. *Unit head:* Dr. Sonia Tiquia-Arashiro, Director, 313-593-5148, E-mail: smtiquia@umich.edu. *Application contact:* Carol Ligienza, Administrative Coordinator, CASL Graduate Programs, 313-593-1183, Fax: 313-583-6700, E-mail: caslgrad@umd.umich.edu. Web site: http://www.umd.umich.edu/envsci_ms/.

The University of Montana, Graduate School, College of Arts and Sciences, Program in Environmental Studies (EVST), Missoula, MT 59812-0002. Offers MS, JD/MS. Part-time programs available. *Faculty:* 5 full-time (2 women), 3 part-time/adjunct (1 woman). *Students:* 33 full-time (25 women), 21 part-time (15 women); includes 1 minority (Hispanic/Latino). Average age 30. 60 applicants, 70% accepted, 21 enrolled. In 2011, 19 degrees awarded. *Degree requirements:* For master's, thesis, portfolio or professional paper. *Entrance requirements:* For master's, GRE General Test (minimum score: 500 verbal for tests taken prior to August 2011; 153 verbal for tests taken after August 2011). Additional exam requirements/recommendations for international students: Required—TOEFL (minimum score 580 paper-based; 237 computer-based; 92 iBT). *Application deadline:* For fall admission, 2/1 priority date for domestic students, 2/1 for international students. Application fee: $51. *Financial support:* In 2011–12, 21 students received support, including 3 fellowships with partial tuition reimbursements available (averaging $5,000 per year), 1 research assistantship with full tuition reimbursement available (averaging $2,100 per year), 6 teaching assistantships with full tuition reimbursements available (averaging $9,000 per year). Financial award application deadline: 4/15. *Faculty research:* Pollution ecology, sustainable agriculture, environmental writing, environmental policy, environmental justice, habitat-land management. *Total annual research expenditures:* $119,595. *Unit head:* Dr. Len Broberg, Director, 406-243-5209, Fax: 406-243-6090, E-mail: len.broberg@mso.umt.edu. *Application contact:*

Karen Hurd, Administrative Assistant, 406-243-6273, Fax: 406-243-6090, E-mail: karen.hurd@mso.umt.edu. Web site: http://www.cas.umt.edu/evst.

University of Nevada, Las Vegas, Graduate College, Greenspun College of Urban Affairs, School of Environmental and Public Affairs, Las Vegas, NV 89154-4030. Offers crisis and emergency management (MS); environmental science (MS, PhD); non-profit management (Certificate); public administration (MPA); public affairs (PhD); public management (Certificate); solar and renewabale energy (Certificate); urban leadership (MA); workforce development and organizational leadership (PhD). Part-time programs available. *Faculty:* 28 full-time (10 women), 53 part-time/adjunct (11 women). *Students:* 49 full-time (19 women), 117 part-time (57 women); includes 62 minority (31 Black or African American, non-Hispanic/Latino; 1 American Indian or Alaska Native, non-Hispanic/Latino; 4 Asian, non-Hispanic/Latino; 21 Hispanic/Latino; 5 Two or more races, non-Hispanic/Latino), 5 international. Average age 36. 94 applicants, 66% accepted, 47 enrolled. In 2011, 46 master's, 4 doctorates, 4 other advanced degrees awarded. *Degree requirements:* For master's, comprehensive exam (for some programs), thesis; for doctorate, comprehensive exam (for some programs), thesis/dissertation. *Entrance requirements:* Additional exam requirements/recommendations for international students: Required—TOEFL (minimum score 550 paper-based; 213 computer-based; 80 iBT), IELTS (minimum score 7). *Application deadline:* For fall admission, 2/15 priority date for domestic students, 5/1 for international students; for spring admission, 11/15 priority date for domestic students, 10/1 for international students. Applications are processed on a rolling basis. Application fee: $60 ($95 for international students). Electronic applications accepted. *Financial support:* In 2011–12, 33 students received support, including 20 research assistantships with partial tuition reimbursements available (averaging $11,193 per year), 13 teaching assistantships with partial tuition reimbursements available (averaging $10,928 per year); institutionally sponsored loans, scholarships/grants, health care benefits, and unspecified assistantships also available. Financial award application deadline: 3/1. *Faculty research:* Community and organizational resilience; environmental decision-making and management; budgeting and human resource/workforce management; urban design, sustainability and governance; public and non-profit management. *Total annual research expenditures:* $1.3 million. *Unit head:* Dr. Christopher Stream, Chair/Associate Professor, 702-895-5120, Fax: 702-895-4436, E-mail: chris.stream@unlv.edu. *Application contact:* Graduate College Admissions Evaluator, 702-895-3320, Fax: 702-895-4180, E-mail: gradcollege@unlv.edu. Web site: http://sepa.unlv.edu/.

University of Nevada, Reno, Graduate School, College of Agriculture, Biotechnology and Natural Resources, Department of Natural Resources and Environmental Sciences, Reno, NV 89557. Offers MS. *Degree requirements:* For master's, thesis optional. *Entrance requirements:* For master's, GRE, minimum GPA of 2.75. Additional exam requirements/recommendations for international students: Required—TOEFL (minimum score 500 paper-based; 173 computer-based; 61 iBT), IELTS (minimum score 6). Electronic applications accepted. *Faculty research:* Range management, plant physiology, remote sensing, soils, wildlife.

University of Nevada, Reno, Graduate School, Interdisciplinary Program in Environmental Sciences and Health, Reno, NV 89557. Offers MS, PhD. Terminal master's awarded for partial completion of doctoral program. *Degree requirements:* For master's, thesis; for doctorate, thesis/dissertation. *Entrance requirements:* For master's, GRE General Test, minimum GPA of 2.75; for doctorate, GRE General Test, minimum GPA of 3.0. Additional exam requirements/recommendations for international students: Required—TOEFL (minimum score 500 paper-based; 173 computer-based; 61 iBT), IELTS (minimum score 6). Electronic applications accepted. *Faculty research:* Environmental chemistry, environmental toxicology, ecological toxicology.

University of New Haven, Graduate School, College of Arts and Sciences, Program in Environmental Sciences, West Haven, CT 06516-1916. Offers environmental geoscience (MS); environmental health and management (MS); environmental science (MS); geographical information systems (Certificate). Part-time and evening/weekend programs available. *Students:* 19 full-time (11 women), 15 part-time (6 women); includes 5 minority (2 Black or African American, non-Hispanic/Latino; 1 Asian, non-Hispanic/Latino; 1 Hispanic/Latino; 1 Two or more races, non-Hispanic/Latino), 7 international. 9 applicants, 100% accepted, 5 enrolled. In 2011, 9 master's awarded. *Degree requirements:* For master's, thesis or alternative. *Application deadline:* For fall admission, 5/31 for international students; for winter admission, 10/15 for international students; for spring admission, 1/15 for international students. Applications are processed on a rolling basis. Application fee: $50. Electronic applications accepted. *Expenses: Tuition:* Part-time $750 per credit. *Financial support:* Research assistantships with partial tuition reimbursements, teaching assistantships with partial tuition reimbursements, career-related internships or fieldwork, Federal Work-Study, scholarships/grants, tuition waivers, and unspecified assistantships available. Support available to part-time students. Financial award applicants required to submit FAFSA. *Faculty research:* Mapping and assessing geological and living resources in Long Island Sound, geology, San Salvador Island, Bahamas. *Unit head:* Dr. Roman Zajac, Coordinator, 203-932-7108, E-mail: rzajac@newhaven.edu. *Application contact:* Eloise Gormley, Director of Graduate Admissions, 203-932-7449, Fax: 203-932-7137, E-mail: gradinfo@newhaven.edu. Web site: http://www.newhaven.edu/4728/.

University of New Orleans, Graduate School, College of Sciences, Department of Earth and Environmental Sciences, New Orleans, LA 70148. Offers MS.

Peterson's Graduate Programs in the Physical Sciences, Mathematics, Agricultural Sciences, the Environment & Natural Resources 2013

facebook.com/petersonspublishing **499**

Environmental Sciences

Evening/weekend programs available. *Degree requirements:* For master's, thesis. *Entrance requirements:* For master's, GRE General Test. Additional exam requirements/recommendations for international students: Required—TOEFL (minimum score 550 paper-based; 213 computer-based; 79 iBT). Electronic applications accepted. *Faculty research:* Continental margin structure and seismology, burial diagenesis of siliclastic sediments, tectonics at convergent plate margins, continental shelf sediment stability, early diagenesis of carbonates.

The University of North Carolina at Chapel Hill, Graduate School, School of Public Health, Department of Environmental Sciences and Engineering, Chapel Hill, NC 27599. Offers air, radiation and industrial hygiene (MPH, MS, MSEE, MSPH, PhD); aquatic and atmospheric sciences (MPH, MS, MSPH, PhD); environmental engineering (MPH, MS, MSEE, MSPH, PhD); environmental health sciences (MPH, MS, MSPH, PhD); environmental management and policy (MPH, MS, MSPH, PhD). Terminal master's awarded for partial completion of doctoral program. *Degree requirements:* For master's, comprehensive exam, thesis (for some programs), research paper; for doctorate, comprehensive exam, thesis/ dissertation. *Entrance requirements:* For master's and doctorate, GRE General Test, minimum GPA of 3.0. Additional exam requirements/recommendations for international students: Required—TOEFL. Electronic applications accepted. *Faculty research:* Air, radiation and industrial hygiene, aquatic and atmospheric sciences, environmental health sciences, environmental management and policy, water resources engineering.

University of Northern Iowa, Graduate College, College of Humanities, Arts and Sciences, Environmental Programs, Cedar Falls, IA 50614. Offers environmental health (MS); environmental science (MS). *Students:* 6 full-time (4 women), 5 part-time (4 women), 3 international. 7 applicants, 29% accepted, 2 enrolled. In 2011, 1 master's awarded. *Degree requirements:* For master's, comprehensive exam, thesis or alternative. *Entrance requirements:* For master's, minimum GPA of 3.0; 3 letters of recommendation. Additional exam requirements/recommendations for international students: Required—TOEFL (minimum score 500 paper-based; 180 computer-based; 61 iBT). *Application deadline:* For fall admission, 8/1 priority date for domestic students. Applications are processed on a rolling basis. Application fee: $50 ($70 for international students). Electronic applications accepted. *Expenses:* Tuition, state resident: full-time $7476. Tuition, nonresident: full-time $16,410. *Required fees:* $942. *Financial support:* Application deadline: 2/1. *Unit head:* Dr. Maureen Clayton, Head, 319-273-7147, Fax: 319-273-7125, E-mail: maureen.clayton@uni.edu. *Application contact:* Laurie S. Russell, Record Analyst, 319-273-2623, Fax: 319-273-2885, E-mail: laurie.russell@uni.edu. Web site: http://www.envprogs.uni.edu/.

University of North Texas, Toulouse Graduate School, College of Arts and Sciences, Department of Biological Sciences, Program in Environmental Science, Denton, TX 76203. Offers MS, PhD. *Degree requirements:* For master's, oral defense of thesis; for doctorate, one foreign language, comprehensive exam, thesis/dissertation. *Entrance requirements:* For master's and doctorate, GRE General Test. Additional exam requirements/recommendations for international students: Recommended—TOEFL (minimum score 550 paper-based; 213 computer-based; 79 iBT). *Expenses:* Tuition, state resident: part-time $100 per credit hour. Tuition, nonresident: part-time $413 per credit hour.

University of Oklahoma, College of Engineering, School of Civil Engineering and Environmental Science, Program in Environmental Science, Norman, OK 73013. Offers air (M Env Sc); environmental science (PhD). Part-time programs available. *Students:* 7 full-time (5 women), 8 part-time (7 women); includes 1 minority (Black or African American, non-Hispanic/Latino), 3 international. Average age 29. 5 applicants, 40% accepted, 1 enrolled. In 2011, 4 master's, 1 doctorate awarded. Terminal master's awarded for partial completion of doctoral program. *Degree requirements:* For master's, comprehensive exam, oral exams; for doctorate, comprehensive exam, thesis/dissertation, oral and qualifying exams. *Entrance requirements:* For master's, minimum GPA of 3.0; for doctorate, minimum graduate GPA of 3.5. Additional exam requirements/recommendations for international students: Required—TOEFL (minimum score 600 paper-based; 100 iBT). *Application deadline:* For fall admission, 4/1 priority date for domestic students, 3/1 for international students; for spring admission, 11/1 for domestic students, 9/1 for international students. Applications are processed on a rolling basis. Application fee: $40 ($90 for international students). Electronic applications accepted. *Expenses:* Tuition, state resident: full-time $4087; part-time $170.30 per credit hour. Tuition, nonresident: full-time $14,875; part-time $619.80 per credit hour. *Required fees:* $2659; $100.25 per credit hour. Tuition and fees vary according to course load and degree level. *Financial support:* In 2011–12, 9 students received support. Scholarships/grants available. Financial award applicants required to submit FAFSA. *Faculty research:* Constructed wetlands, sustainable water treatment technologies, subsurface transport and fate of chemicals. *Unit head:* Robert C. Knox, Director, 405-325-5911, Fax: 405-325-4217, E-mail: rknox@ou.edu. *Application contact:* Susan Williams, Graduate Programs Assistant, 405-325-2344, Fax: 405-325-4147, E-mail: srwilliams@ou.edu. Web site: http://cees.ou.edu.

University of Pennsylvania, School of Arts and Sciences, Graduate Group in Earth and Environmental Science, Philadelphia, PA 19104. Offers MS, PhD. Part-time programs available. *Faculty:* 8 full-time (1 woman), 5 part-time/adjunct (0 women). *Students:* 18 full-time (12 women), 1 (woman) part-time, 6 international. 28 applicants, 11% accepted, 2 enrolled. In 2011, 1 master's, 2 doctorates awarded. *Degree requirements:* For master's, one foreign language, thesis; for doctorate, one foreign language, thesis/dissertation. *Entrance requirements:* For master's and doctorate, GRE General Test. Additional exam requirements/

recommendations for international students: Required—TOEFL. *Application deadline:* For fall admission, 12/1 priority date for domestic students. Application fee: $70. Electronic applications accepted. *Expenses: Tuition:* Full-time $26,660; part-time $4944 per course. *Required fees:* $2318; $291 per course. Tuition and fees vary according to course load, degree level and program. *Financial support:* Fellowships, research assistantships, teaching assistantships, institutionally sponsored loans, scholarships/grants, traineeships, health care benefits, and unspecified assistantships available. Financial award application deadline: 12/15. *Faculty research:* Isotope geochemistry, regional tectonics, environmental geology, metamorphic and igneous petrology, paleontology. *Unit head:* Dr. Ralph M. Rosen, Associate Dean for Graduate Studies, 215-898-7156, Fax: 215-573-8068, E-mail: gdasdmis@sas.upenn.edu. *Application contact:* Patricia Rea, Associate Director for Admissions, 215-573-5816, Fax: 215-573-8068, E-mail: gdasadmis@sas.upenn.edu.

University of Puerto Rico, Río Piedras, College of Natural Sciences, Department of Environmental Sciences, San Juan, PR 00931-3300. Offers MS, PhD.

University of Rhode Island, Graduate School, College of the Environment and Life Sciences, Department of Fisheries, Animal and Veterinary Science, Kingston, RI 02881. Offers animal health and disease (MS); animal science (MS); aquaculture (MS); aquatic pathology (MS); environmental sciences (PhD), including animal science, aquacultural science, aquatic pathology, fisheries science; fisheries (MS). *Faculty:* 10 full-time (4 women). *Students:* 14 full-time (7 women), 6 part-time (1 woman). In 2011, 5 degrees awarded. *Degree requirements:* For master's, comprehensive exam (for some programs), thesis optional; for doctorate, comprehensive exam, thesis/dissertation. *Entrance requirements:* For master's and doctorate, GRE, 2 letters of recommendation. Additional exam requirements/recommendations for international students: Required—TOEFL (minimum score 550 paper-based; 213 computer-based). *Application deadline:* For fall admission, 7/15 for domestic students, 2/1 for international students; for spring admission, 11/15 for domestic students, 7/15 for international students. Application fee: $65. Electronic applications accepted. *Expenses:* Tuition, state resident: full-time $10,432; part-time $580 per credit hour. Tuition, nonresident: full-time $23,130; part-time $1285 per credit hour. *Required fees:* $1362; $36 per credit hour. $35 per semester. One-time fee: $130. *Financial support:* In 2011–12, 3 research assistantships with full and partial tuition reimbursements (averaging $11,654 per year), 4 teaching assistantships with full and partial tuition reimbursements (averaging $12,214 per year) were awarded. Financial award application deadline: 7/15; financial award applicants required to submit FAFSA. *Unit head:* Dr. David Bengtson, Chair, 401-874-2668, Fax: 401-874-7575, E-mail: bengtson@uri.edu. *Application contact:* Dr. Marta Gomez-Chiarri, Director of Graduate Studies, 401-874-2917, Fax: 401-874-7575, E-mail: gomezchi@uri.edu. Web site: http://www.uri.edu/cels/favs/.

University of Saint Francis, Graduate School, Department of Biology, Fort Wayne, IN 46808-3994. Offers environmental science (MS). Part-time and evening/weekend programs available. Postbaccalaureate distance learning degree programs offered (minimal on-campus study). *Faculty:* 6 full-time (1 woman), 3 part-time/adjunct (0 women). *Students:* 1 full-time (0 women), 12 part-time (6 women); includes 2 minority (both Black or African American, non-Hispanic/Latino). In 2011, 3 master's awarded. *Degree requirements:* For master's, thesis, internship. *Entrance requirements:* For master's, minimum GPA of 3.2, three letters of recommendation, statement of professional goals, resume. *Application deadline:* For fall admission, 7/1 for domestic students. Applications are processed on a rolling basis. Electronic applications accepted. Application fee is waived when completed online. *Financial support:* Career-related internships or fieldwork, institutionally sponsored loans, tuition waivers (full and partial), and unspecified assistantships available. Support available to part-time students. *Unit head:* Dr. Joe T. Steensma, Chair, 260-399-7700 Ext. 8305, E-mail: jsteensma@sf.edu. *Application contact:* Kyna Steury-Johnson, Admissions Counselor, 260-399-7700 Ext. 6316, E-mail: ksteury@sf.edu. Web site: http://www.sf.edu/sf/arts-sciences/biology.

University of Saskatchewan, College of Graduate Studies and Research, School of Environment and Sustainability, Saskatoon, SK S7N 5A2, Canada. Offers MES.

University of South Africa, College of Agriculture and Environmental Sciences, Pretoria, South Africa. Offers agriculture (MS); consumer science (MCS); environmental management (MA, MS, PhD); environmental science (MA, MS, PhD); geography (MA, MS, PhD); horticulture (M Tech); human ecology (MHE); life sciences (MS); nature conservation (M Tech).

University of South Florida, Graduate School, College of Arts and Sciences, Department of Chemistry, Tampa, FL 33620-9951. Offers analytical chemistry (MS, PhD); biochemistry (MS, PhD); computational chemistry (MS, PhD); environmental chemistry (MS, PhD); inorganic chemistry (MS, PhD); organic chemistry (MS); physical chemistry (MS, PhD); polymer chemistry (PhD). Part-time programs available. *Faculty:* 25 full-time (4 women), 9 part-time/adjunct (1 woman). *Students:* 118 full-time (46 women), 14 part-time (7 women); includes 28 minority (8 Black or African American, non-Hispanic/Latino; 11 Asian, non-Hispanic/Latino; 9 Hispanic/Latino), 58 international. Average age 29. 127 applicants, 31% accepted, 19 enrolled. In 2011, 3 master's, 16 doctorates awarded. Terminal master's awarded for partial completion of doctoral program. *Degree requirements:* For master's, comprehensive exam, thesis (for some programs); for doctorate, comprehensive exam, thesis/dissertation. *Entrance*

500 facebook.com/petersonspublishing

Peterson's Graduate Programs in the Physical Sciences, Mathematics, Agricultural Sciences, the Environment & Natural Resources 2013

requirements: For master's and doctorate, GRE General Test, minimum GPA of 3.0. Additional exam requirements/recommendations for international students: Required—TOEFL (minimum score 550 paper-based; 213 computer-based; 79 iBT) or IELTS (minimum score 6.5). *Application deadline:* For fall admission, 2/15 priority date for domestic students, 1/2 for international students; for spring admission, 10/1 priority date for domestic students, 6/1 for international students. Applications are processed on a rolling basis. Application fee: $30. Electronic applications accepted. *Financial support:* In 2011–12, 136 students received support, including 28 research assistantships with tuition reimbursements available (averaging $15,020 per year), 108 teaching assistantships with tuition reimbursements available (averaging $15,164 per year); unspecified assistantships also available. Financial award application deadline: 6/30. *Faculty research:* Synthesis, bio-organic chemistry, bioinorganic chemistry, environmental chemistry, NMR. *Total annual research expenditures:* $3.1 million. *Unit head:* Dr. Randy Larsen, Chairperson, 813-974-4129, Fax: 813-974-3203, E-mail: rlarsen@cas.usf.edu. *Application contact:* Patricia Muisener, Director, 813-974-1730, Fax: 813-974-3203, E-mail: muisener@cas.usf.edu. Web site: http://chemistry.usf.edu/.

University of South Florida, Graduate School, College of Arts and Sciences, Department of Geography, Tampa, FL 33620-9951. Offers environmental science and policy (MS); geography (MA); geography and environmental science and policy (PhD); urban and regional planning (MURP). Part-time and evening/weekend programs available. *Faculty:* 19 full-time (6 women), 7 part-time/adjunct (3 women). *Students:* 20 full-time (7 women), 13 part-time (5 women); includes 10 minority (4 Black or African American, non-Hispanic/Latino; 1 American Indian or Alaska Native, non-Hispanic/Latino; 1 Asian, non-Hispanic/Latino; 3 Hispanic/Latino; 1 Two or more races, non-Hispanic/Latino), 1 international. Average age 31. 37 applicants, 59% accepted, 8 enrolled. In 2011, 5 master's awarded. *Degree requirements:* For master's, comprehensive exam, thesis; for doctorate, comprehensive exam, thesis/dissertation. *Entrance requirements:* For master's, GRE General Test, minimum GPA of 3.0, letter of intent, two letters of recommendation (three for MS); for doctorate, GRE General Test, minimum GPA of 3.2 in last 60 hours, letter of intent, two letters of recommendation. Additional exam requirements/recommendations for international students: Required—TOEFL (minimum score 600 paper-based; 213 computer-based), TOEFL (minimum score 550 paper-based, 213 computer-based, 79 iBT) or IELTS (minimum score 6.5); TOEFL (minimum score 600 paper-based) for ESP MS and PhD. *Application deadline:* For fall admission, 2/15 for domestic students, 1/2 for international students; for spring admission, 10/15 for domestic students, 6/1 for international students. Application fee: $30. *Financial support:* In 2011–12, 28 students received support, including 3 research assistantships (averaging $12,345 per year), 25 teaching assistantships with tuition reimbursements available (averaging $12,807 per year); unspecified assistantships also available. Financial award application deadline: 3/1. *Faculty research:* Natural hazards, geographic information systems models, soil contamination, urban geography and social theory. *Total annual research expenditures:* $143,091. *Unit head:* Dr. Kevin Archer, Chair, 813-974-4843, Fax: 813-974-4808, E-mail: karcher2@usf.edu. *Application contact:* Dr. Jennifer Collins, Program Director, 813-974-4242, Fax: 813-974-4808, E-mail: collinsjm@usf.edu. Web site: http://gep.usf.edu/.

University of South Florida–St. Petersburg Campus, College of Arts and Sciences, St. Petersburg, FL 33701. Offers digital journalism and design (MA); environmental science and policy (MA, MS); Florida studies (MLA); journalism and media studies (MA); liberal studies (MLA); psychology (MA). Part-time programs available. *Students:* 36 full-time (19 women), 76 part-time (47 women); includes 16 minority (9 Black or African American, non-Hispanic/Latino; 1 Asian, non-Hispanic/Latino; 2 Hispanic/Latino; 4 Two or more races, non-Hispanic/Latino), 1 international. Average age 34. 72 applicants, 53% accepted, 28 enrolled. In 2011, 23 master's awarded. *Degree requirements:* For master's, comprehensive exam, thesis or project. *Entrance requirements:* For master's, GRE, LSAT, MCAT (varies by program), letter of intent, 3 letters of recommendation, writing samples, bachelor's degree from regionally-accredited institution with minimum GPA of 3.0 overall or in upper two years. Additional exam requirements/recommendations for international students: Required—TOEFL (minimum score 550 paper-based; 79 iBT); Recommended—IELTS. *Application deadline:* For fall admission, 6/1 priority date for domestic students, 3/15 for international students; for spring admission, 10/15 priority date for domestic students, 6/1 for international students. Applications are processed on a rolling basis. Application fee: $30. Electronic applications accepted. *Expenses:* Tuition, state resident: full-time $8847. Tuition, nonresident: full-time $18,423. One-time fee: $35 full-time. Full-time tuition and fees vary according to course load and program. *Financial support:* Applicants required to submit FAFSA. *Unit head:* Dr. Frank A. Biafora, Dean, 727-873-4156, E-mail: fbiafora@usfsp.edu. *Application contact:* Eric Douthirt, Enrollment Management Specialist, 727-873-4567, Fax: 727-873-4889, E-mail: douthirt@usfsp.edu. Web site: http://www.usfsp.edu/coas/.

The University of Tennessee at Chattanooga, Graduate School, College of Arts and Sciences, Department of Biological and Environmental Sciences, Chattanooga, TN 37403. Offers environmental science (MS). Part-time and evening/weekend programs available. *Faculty:* 10 full-time (1 woman), 1 (woman) part-time/adjunct. *Students:* 19 full-time (11 women), 16 part-time (10 women); includes 1 minority (Black or African American, non-Hispanic/Latino). Average age 25. In 2011, 5 master's awarded. *Degree requirements:* For master's, thesis optional. *Entrance requirements:* For master's, GRE General Test, minimum undergraduate GPA of 2.75; undergraduate course work in ecology or knowledge

equivalent. Additional exam requirements/recommendations for international students: Required—TOEFL (minimum score 550 paper-based; 213 computer-based; 79 iBT), IELTS (minimum score 6). *Application deadline:* For fall admission, 8/1 priority date for domestic students, 6/1 for international students; for spring admission, 12/1 priority date for domestic students, 10/1 for international students. Applications are processed on a rolling basis. Application fee: $35. Electronic applications accepted. *Expenses:* Tuition, state resident: full-time $6472; part-time $359 per credit hour. Tuition, nonresident: full-time $20,006; part-time $1111 per credit hour. *Required fees:* $1320; $160 per credit hour. *Financial support:* Career-related internships or fieldwork, scholarships/grants, and unspecified assistantships available. Support available to part-time students. Financial award applicants required to submit FAFSA. *Faculty research:* Bioremediation, stream fish ecology and conservation, environmental law and policy, avian conservation and management. *Total annual research expenditures:* $420,228. *Unit head:* Dr. John Tucker, Department Head, 423-425-4341, Fax: 423-425-2285, E-mail: john-tucker@utc.edu. *Application contact:* Dr. Jerald Ainsworth, Dean of Graduate Studies, 423-425-4478, Fax: 423-425-5223, E-mail: jerald-ainsworth@utc.edu. Web site: http://www.utc.edu/Academic/BiologicalAndEnvironmentalSciences/.

The University of Texas at Arlington, Graduate School, College of Science, Department of Earth and Environmental Sciences, Program in Environmental and Earth Sciences, Arlington, TX 76019. Offers environmental science (MS, PhD); geology (MS, PhD). Part-time and evening/weekend programs available. *Faculty:* 5 full-time (0 women), 1 part-time/adjunct (0 women). *Students:* 22 full-time (13 women), 25 part-time (12 women); includes 9 minority (2 Black or African American, non-Hispanic/Latino; 1 American Indian or Alaska Native, non-Hispanic/Latino; 2 Asian, non-Hispanic/Latino; 4 Hispanic/Latino), 11 international. 23 applicants, 74% accepted, 10 enrolled. In 2011, 11 master's, 1 doctorate awarded. Terminal master's awarded for partial completion of doctoral program. *Degree requirements:* For master's, thesis optional; for doctorate, comprehensive exam, thesis/dissertation. *Entrance requirements:* For master's, GRE General Test. Additional exam requirements/recommendations for international students: Required—TOEFL (minimum score 550 paper-based; 213 computer-based). *Application deadline:* Applications are processed on a rolling basis. Application fee: $35 ($50 for international students). Electronic applications accepted. *Financial support:* In 2011–12, 4 fellowships (averaging $1,000 per year), 7 teaching assistantships (averaging $14,700 per year) were awarded; career-related internships or fieldwork, Federal Work-Study, institutionally sponsored loans, scholarships/grants, health care benefits, and unspecified assistantships also available. Financial award applicants required to submit FAFSA. *Unit head:* Dr. John S. Wickham, Chair, 817-272-2987, Fax: 817-272-2628, E-mail: wickham@uta.edu. *Application contact:* Dr. Andrew Hunt, Graduate Advisor, 817-272-2987, Fax: 817-272-2628, E-mail: hunt@uta.edu. Web site: http://www.uta.edu/ees.

The University of Texas at El Paso, Graduate School, College of Science, Environmental Science Program, El Paso, TX 79968-0001. Offers MS. *Students:* 14 (8 women); includes 5 minority (all Hispanic/Latino), 4 international. In 2011, 5 master's awarded. *Degree requirements:* For master's, thesis. *Entrance requirements:* For master's, GRE, bachelor's degree in a science or engineering discipline, 3 letters of recommendation. Additional exam requirements/recommendations for international students: Required—TOEFL. *Application deadline:* For fall admission, 8/1 for domestic students, 3/1 for international students; for spring admission, 11/1 for domestic students, 9/3 for international students. *Unit head:* Dr. Carl Lieb, Program Director, 915-747-5554, Fax: 915-747-5990. *Application contact:* Dr. Benjamin Flores, Interim Dean of the Graduate School, 915-747-5554, Fax: 915-747-5990, E-mail: bflores@utep.edu.

The University of Texas at El Paso, Graduate School, Interdisciplinary Program in Environmental Science and Engineering, El Paso, TX 79968-0001. Offers PhD. Part-time and evening/weekend programs available. *Students:* 61 (20 women); includes 23 minority (1 American Indian or Alaska Native, non-Hispanic/Latino; 2 Asian, non-Hispanic/Latino; 20 Hispanic/Latino), 30 international. Average age 34. In 2011, 2 doctorates awarded. *Degree requirements:* For doctorate, thesis/dissertation. *Entrance requirements:* For doctorate, GRE, letters of recommendation. Additional exam requirements/recommendations for international students: Required—TOEFL; Recommended—IELTS. *Application deadline:* For fall admission, 8/1 for domestic students, 3/1 for international students; for spring admission, 11/1 for domestic students, 9/3 for international students. Applications are processed on a rolling basis. Application fee: $45 ($80 for international students). Electronic applications accepted. *Financial support:* In 2011–12, research assistantships with partial tuition reimbursements (averaging $22,500 per year), teaching assistantships with partial tuition reimbursements (averaging $18,000 per year) were awarded; fellowships with partial tuition reimbursements, institutionally sponsored loans, scholarships/grants, health care benefits, tuition waivers (partial), and unspecified assistantships also available. Support available to part-time students. Financial award application deadline: 3/15; financial award applicants required to submit FAFSA. *Unit head:* Dr. Barry A. Benedict, Director, 915-747-5604, Fax: 915-747-5145, E-mail: babenedict@utep.edu. *Application contact:* Dr. Benjamin Flores, Interim Dean of the Graduate School, 915-747-5491, Fax: 915-747-5788, E-mail: bflores@utep.edu.

The University of Texas at San Antonio, College of Engineering, Department of Civil and Environmental Engineering, San Antonio, TX 78249-0617. Offers civil engineering (MCE, MS, MSCE); environmental science and engineering (PhD). Part-time and evening/weekend programs available. *Faculty:* 13 full-time (2

Peterson's Graduate Programs in the Physical Sciences, Mathematics, Agricultural Sciences, the Environment & Natural Resources 2013

facebook.com/petersonspublishing **501**

Environmental Sciences

women), 5 part-time/adjunct. *Students:* 48 full-time (13 women), 25 part-time (3 women); includes 27 minority (5 Black or African American, non-Hispanic/Latino; 3 Asian, non-Hispanic/Latino; 19 Hispanic/Latino), 27 international. Average age 30. 58 applicants, 67% accepted, 23 enrolled. In 2011, 21 master's, 2 doctorates awarded. *Degree requirements:* For master's, comprehensive exam (for some programs), thesis (for some programs); for doctorate, comprehensive exam, thesis/dissertation. *Entrance requirements:* For master's, GRE General Test, bachelor's degree with 18 credit hours in field of study or in another appropriate field of study, statement of purpose; for doctorate, GRE, BA or BS and MS from accredited university, minimum GPA of 3.0 in upper-division and graduate courses, resume, three letters of recommendation, statement of purpose. Additional exam requirements/recommendations for international students: Required—TOEFL (minimum score 550 paper-based; 79 iBT), IELTS (minimum score 5). *Application deadline:* For fall admission, 7/1 for domestic students, 4/1 for international students; for spring admission, 11/1 for domestic students, 9/1 for international students. Application fee: $45 ($85 for international students). *Expenses:* Tuition, state resident: full-time $3148; part-time $2176 per semester. Tuition, nonresident: full-time $8782; part-time $5932 per semester. *Required fees:* $719 per semester. *Financial support:* In 2011–12, 29 students received support, including 5 fellowships (averaging $4,100 per year), 18 research assistantships with partial tuition reimbursements available (averaging $19,882 per year), 18 teaching assistantships (averaging $4,680 per year); scholarships/grants and unspecified assistantships also available. Financial award application deadline: 3/31. *Faculty research:* Fate, transport and reactivity of chemicals in natural systems/contaminant adsorption/desorption involving nano-particles; transportation infrastructure management and pavement materials; hydrologic analysis; beneficial use of wastes and industrial by-products; pavement-vehicle interaction. *Unit head:* Dr. Athanassio T. Papagiannakis, Chair, 210-458-7517, Fax: 210-458-6475, E-mail: at.papagiannakis@utsa.edu. *Application contact:* Athanassios Papagiannakis, Graduate Advisor of Record, 210-458-7517, Fax: 210-458-7517, E-mail: at.papagiannakis@utsa.edu.

The University of Texas at San Antonio, College of Sciences, Department of Biology, San Antonio, TX 78249-0617. Offers biology (MS); biotechnology (MS), including bioprocessing technician, biotechnology; cell and molecular biology (PhD); environmental science (MS); neurobiology (PhD). *Faculty:* 34 full-time (6 women), 7 part-time/adjunct (1 woman). *Students:* 117 full-time (62 women), 64 part-time (35 women); includes 63 minority (10 Black or African American, non-Hispanic/Latino; 10 Asian, non-Hispanic/Latino; 36 Hispanic/Latino; 7 Two or more races, non-Hispanic/Latino), 54 international. Average age 27. 239 applicants, 45% accepted, 50 enrolled. In 2011, 62 master's, 3 doctorates awarded. Terminal master's awarded for partial completion of doctoral program. *Degree requirements:* For master's, comprehensive exam, thesis or alternative; for doctorate, thesis/dissertation. *Entrance requirements:* For master's, GRE General Test, bachelor's degree with 18 credit hours in field of study or in another appropriate field of study; for doctorate, GRE General Test, 3 letters of recommendation, statement of purpose, resume. Additional exam requirements/recommendations for international students: Required—TOEFL (minimum score 500 paper-based; 100 iBT), IELTS (minimum score 5). *Application deadline:* For fall admission, 7/1 for domestic students, 4/1 for international students; for spring admission, 11/1 for domestic students, 9/1 for international students. Application fee: $45 ($85 for international students). *Expenses:* Tuition, state resident: full-time $3148; part-time $2176 per semester. Tuition, nonresident: full-time $8782; part-time $5932 per semester. *Required fees:* $719 per semester. *Financial support:* In 2011–12, 66 students received support, including 4 fellowships (averaging $22,350 per year), 34 research assistantships (averaging $22,350 per year), 8 teaching assistantships (averaging $22,350 per year). *Faculty research:* Development of human and veterinary vaccines against a fungal disease, mammalian germ cells and stem cells, dopamine neuron physiology and addiction, plant biochemistry, dendritic computation and synaptic plasticity. *Total annual research expenditures:* $2.8 million. *Unit head:* Dr. Edwin J. Barea-Rodriguez, Chair, 210-458-4511, Fax: 210-458-5658, E-mail: edwin.barea@utsa.edu. *Application contact:* Rene Munguia, Program Coordinator, 210-458-4642, Fax: 210-458-5658, E-mail: rene.munguia@utsa.edu.

The University of Texas at San Antonio, College of Sciences, Department of Geological Sciences, San Antonio, TX 78249-0617. Offers MS. Part-time programs available. *Faculty:* 9 full-time (3 women), 4 part-time/adjunct (0 women). *Students:* 16 full-time (9 women), 9 part-time (2 women); includes 4 minority (1 Asian, non-Hispanic/Latino; 2 Hispanic/Latino; 1 Two or more races, non-Hispanic/Latino), 4 international. Average age 30. 22 applicants, 86% accepted, 10 enrolled. In 2011, 2 master's awarded. *Degree requirements:* For master's, comprehensive exam, thesis (for some programs). *Entrance requirements:* For master's, GRE General Test, three letters of recommendation, statement of research interest. Additional exam requirements/recommendations for international students: Required—TOEFL (minimum score 500 paper-based; 61 iBT), IELTS (minimum score 5). *Application deadline:* For fall admission, 7/1 for domestic students, 4/1 for international students; for spring admission, 11/1 for domestic students, 9/1 for international students. Application fee: $45 ($85 for international students). *Expenses:* Tuition, state resident: full-time $3148; part-time $2176 per semester. Tuition, nonresident: full-time $8782; part-time $5932 per semester. *Required fees:* $719 per semester. *Financial support:* Tuition waivers available. *Faculty research:* Low temperature geochemistry, aqueous geochemistry, hydrogeology, groundwater modeling, stratigraphy, carbonate petrology, paleontology, micropaleontology, remote sensing, GIS, geoinformatics, tectonics, structural geology, metamorphic petrology, geochronology, sediment

transports, methodology. *Unit head:* Dr. Alan R. Dutton, Department Chair, 210-458-4455, Fax: 210-458-4469, E-mail: alan.dutton@utsa.edu. *Application contact:* Graduate Advisor of Record, 210-458-4455, Fax: 210-458-4469, E-mail: geosciences@utsa.edu. Web site: http://www.utsa.edu/geosci/.

University of the Virgin Islands, Graduate Programs, Division of Science and Mathematics, Program in Environmental and Marine Science, Saint Thomas, VI 00802-9990. Offers MS. *Entrance requirements:* For master's, GRE. Additional exam requirements/recommendations for international students: Required—TOEFL (minimum score 550 paper-based; 213 computer-based).

The University of Toledo, College of Graduate Studies, College of Natural Sciences and Mathematics, Department of Environmental Sciences, Toledo, OH 43606-3390. Offers biology (MS, PhD), including ecology. Part-time programs available. *Faculty:* 26. *Students:* 9 full-time (4 women), 2 part-time (1 woman); includes 1 minority (Black or African American, non-Hispanic/Latino), 1 international. Average age 30. 9 applicants, 56% accepted, 5 enrolled. In 2011, 3 master's awarded. *Degree requirements:* For master's, thesis (for some programs). *Entrance requirements:* For master's, GRE General Test, minimum cumulative point-hour ratio of 2.7 for all previous academic work, three letters of recommendation, statement of purpose, transcripts from all prior institutions attended. Additional exam requirements/recommendations for international students: Required—TOEFL (minimum score 550 paper-based; 213 computer-based; 80 iBT), IELTS (minimum score 6.5). *Application deadline:* For fall admission, 1/15 priority date for domestic students, 1/15 for international students. Applications are processed on a rolling basis. Application fee: $45 ($75 for international students). Electronic applications accepted. *Financial support:* In 2011–12, 5 research assistantships with full and partial tuition reimbursements (averaging $18,126 per year), 12 teaching assistantships with full and partial tuition reimbursements (averaging $12,850 per year) were awarded; Federal Work-Study, institutionally sponsored loans, scholarships/grants, tuition waivers (full), and unspecified assistantships also available. Support available to part-time students. *Faculty research:* Environmental geochemistry, geophysics, petrology and mineralogy, paleontology, geohydrology. *Unit head:* Dr. Timothy G. Fisher, Chair, 419-530-2883, E-mail: timothy.fisher@utoledo.edu. *Application contact:* Graduate School Office, 419-530-4723, Fax: 419-530-4724, E-mail: grdsch@utnet.utoledo.edu. Web site: http://www.utoledo.edu/nsm/.

University of Toronto, School of Graduate Studies, Department of Physical and Environmental Sciences, Toronto, ON M5S 1A1, Canada. Offers environmental science (M Env Sc, PhD). *Entrance requirements:* For master's, bachelor's degree (B Sc or B Eng), minimum B average in last two years of undergraduate program, two half-courses or one full-course each in chemistry, physics, calculus and biology. Additional exam requirements/recommendations for international students: Required—TOEFL (minimum score 580 paper-based; 93 iBT), TWE (minimum score 4). *Application deadline:* For fall admission, 2/1 for domestic students. Application fee: $110. Electronic applications accepted. *Unit head:* W. A. Gough, Chair, 416-287-7197, Fax: 416-287-7204, E-mail: gough@utsc.utoronto.ca. *Application contact:* 416-978-6614, Fax: 416-946-0992, E-mail: gradschool@utoronto.ca. Web site: http://www.utsc.utoronto.ca/~physsci/.

University of Utah, Graduate School, Professional Master of Science and Technology Program, Salt Lake City, UT 84112-1107. Offers biotechnology (PSM); computational science (PSM); environmental science (PSM); science instrumentation (PSM). Part-time programs available. *Students:* 15 full-time (10 women), 42 part-time (12 women); includes 7 minority (2 Black or African American, non-Hispanic/Latino; 2 Asian, non-Hispanic/Latino; 2 Hispanic/Latino; 1 Native Hawaiian or other Pacific Islander, non-Hispanic/Latino), 2 international. Average age 33. 66 applicants, 48% accepted, 16 enrolled. In 2011, 18 master's awarded. *Degree requirements:* For master's, internship. *Entrance requirements:* For master's, GRE (recommended), minimum undergraduate GPA of 3.0, bachelor's degree from accredited university or college. Additional exam requirements/recommendations for international students: Required—TOEFL (minimum score 500 paper-based; 173 computer-based; 61 iBT), IELTS (minimum score 6). *Application deadline:* For fall admission, 3/1 for domestic and international students. Application fee: $55 ($65 for international students). Electronic applications accepted. *Financial support:* In 2011–12, 8 students received support, including 5 fellowships with full and partial tuition reimbursements available (averaging $16,800 per year), 2 research assistantships (averaging $6,200 per year); unspecified assistantships also available. Financial award applicants required to submit FAFSA. *Faculty research:* Drug delivery systems, in vitro erythroid expansion and HRE (Hypoxia responsive element). *Unit head:* Jennifer Schmidt, Program Director, 801-585-5630, E-mail: jennifer.schmidt@gradschool.utah.edu. *Application contact:* Amy Kimball, Project Coordinator, 801-585-3650, Fax: 801-585-6749, E-mail: amy.kimball@gradschool.utah.edu. Web site: http://www.utah.edu/pmst/.

University of Virginia, College and Graduate School of Arts and Sciences, Department of Environmental Sciences, Charlottesville, VA 22903. Offers MA, MS, PhD. *Faculty:* 29 full-time (5 women), 2 part-time/adjunct (both women). *Students:* 68 full-time (41 women), 1 (woman) part-time; includes 2 minority (1 Black or African American, non-Hispanic/Latino; 1 Asian, non-Hispanic/Latino), 9 international. Average age 28. 93 applicants, 37% accepted, 17 enrolled. In 2011, 8 master's, 8 doctorates awarded. *Degree requirements:* For master's, thesis; for doctorate, comprehensive exam, thesis/dissertation. *Entrance requirements:* For master's and doctorate, GRE General Test, 2 letters of recommendation. Additional exam requirements/recommendations for international students: Required—TOEFL (minimum score 600 paper-based; 250 computer-based; 90

502 facebook.com/petersonspublishing

Peterson's Graduate Programs in the Physical Sciences, Mathematics, Agricultural Sciences, the Environment & Natural Resources 2013

iBT), IELTS (minimum score 7). *Application deadline:* For fall admission, 12/1 for domestic and international students; for winter admission, 10/15 for domestic and international students. Applications are processed on a rolling basis. Application fee: $60. Electronic applications accepted. *Financial support:* Fellowships, research assistantships, and teaching assistantships available. Financial award application deadline: 12/1; financial award applicants required to submit FAFSA. *Unit head:* Patricia Wiberg, Chairman, 434-924-7761, Fax: 434-982-2137, E-mail: pw3z@virginia.edu. *Application contact:* Graduate Admissions Chair, 434-924-7761, Fax: 434-982-2137. Web site: http://www.evsc.virginia.edu/.

The University of Western Ontario, Faculty of Graduate Studies, Biosciences Division, Department of Plant Sciences, London, ON N6A 5B8, Canada. Offers plant and environmental sciences (M Sc); plant sciences (M Sc, PhD); plant sciences and environmental sciences (PhD); plant sciences and molecular biology (M Sc, PhD). *Degree requirements:* For master's, thesis; for doctorate, thesis/dissertation. *Entrance requirements:* For doctorate, M Sc or equivalent. Additional exam requirements/recommendations for international students: Required—TOEFL. *Faculty research:* Ecology systematics, plant biochemistry and physiology, yeast genetics, molecular biology.

The University of Western Ontario, Faculty of Graduate Studies, Physical Sciences Division, Department of Earth Sciences, London, ON N6A 5B8, Canada. Offers environment and sustainability (MES); geology (M Sc, PhD); geology and environmental science (M Sc, PhD); geophysics (M Sc, PhD); geophysics and environmental science (M Sc, PhD). *Degree requirements:* For master's, thesis; for doctorate, thesis/dissertation, qualifying exam. *Entrance requirements:* For master's, honors in B Sc; for doctorate, M Sc. Additional exam requirements/recommendations for international students: Required—TOEFL. *Faculty research:* Geophysics, geochemistry, paleontology, sedimentology/stratigraphy, glaciology/quaternary.

University of West Florida, College of Arts and Sciences: Sciences, Department of Environmental Sciences, Pensacola, FL 32514-5750. Offers MS. Part-time programs available. *Faculty:* 5 full-time (0 women). *Students:* 6 full-time (4 women), 13 part-time (8 women); includes 2 minority (1 Black or African American, non-Hispanic/Latino; 1 Two or more races, non-Hispanic/Latino). Average age 31. 11 applicants, 64% accepted, 4 enrolled. In 2011, 4 master's awarded. *Entrance requirements:* For master's, GRE (minimum score: 450 verbal; 550 quantitative), official transcripts; formal letter of interest, background, and professional goals; three letters of recommendation by individuals in professionally-relevant fields (waived for graduates of UWF Department of Environmental Sciences); current curriculum vitae/resume. Additional exam requirements/recommendations for international students: Required—TOEFL (minimum score 550 paper-based; 213 computer-based). *Application deadline:* For fall admission, 6/1 for domestic and international students; for spring admission, 10/1 for domestic and international students. Application fee: $30. *Expenses:* Tuition, state resident: full-time $5729; part-time $302 per credit hour. Tuition, nonresident: full-time $20,059; part-time $961 per credit hour. *Required fees:* $1509; $63 per credit hour. *Financial support:* In 2011–12, 2 research assistantships with partial tuition reimbursements (averaging $3,500 per year), 6 teaching assistantships with partial tuition reimbursements (averaging $3,760 per year) were awarded; unspecified assistantships also available. Financial award application deadline: 4/15; financial award applicants required to submit FAFSA. *Unit head:* Dr. Matthew C. Schwartz, Chairperson, 850-474-3469. *Application contact:* Terry McCray, Assistant Director of Graduate Admissions, 850-473-7718, Fax: 850-473-7714, E-mail: gradadmissions@uwf.edu. Web site: http://uwf.edu/environmental/.

University of Windsor, Faculty of Graduate Studies, GLIER-Great Lakes Institute for Environmental Research, Windsor, ON N9B 3P4, Canada. Offers environmental science (M Sc, PhD). *Degree requirements:* For master's, thesis; for doctorate, thesis/dissertation. *Entrance requirements:* For master's, minimum B+ average; for doctorate, M Sc degree, minimum B+ average. Additional exam requirements/recommendations for international students: Required—TOEFL (minimum score 560 paper-based; 220 computer-based). Electronic applications accepted. *Faculty research:* Environmental chemistry and toxicology, conservation and resource management, iron formation geochemistry.

University of Wisconsin–Green Bay, Graduate Studies, Program in Environmental Science and Policy, Green Bay, WI 54311-7001. Offers MS. Part-time programs available. *Faculty:* 14 full-time (3 women), 2 part-time/adjunct (0 women). *Students:* 26 full-time (14 women), 19 part-time (11 women); includes 7 minority (1 Black or African American, non-Hispanic/Latino; 2 American Indian or Alaska Native, non-Hispanic/Latino; 2 Hispanic/Latino; 2 Two or more races, non-Hispanic/Latino). Average age 30. 15 applicants, 73% accepted, 7 enrolled. In 2011, 4 master's awarded. *Degree requirements:* For master's, thesis. *Entrance requirements:* For master's, GRE General Test, minimum GPA of 3.0. *Application deadline:* For fall admission, 8/1 for domestic students; for spring admission, 11/1 for domestic students. Applications are processed on a rolling basis. Application fee: $56. Electronic applications accepted. *Expenses:* Tuition, state resident: full-time $7312; part-time $406 per credit. Tuition, nonresident: full-time $16,771; part-time $932 per credit. *Required fees:* $1312; $55 per credit. Tuition and fees vary according to reciprocity agreements. *Financial support:* In 2011–12, 4 teaching assistantships with full tuition reimbursements were awarded; research assistantships with full tuition reimbursements, career-related internships or fieldwork, Federal Work-Study, and institutionally sponsored loans also available. Financial award application deadline: 7/15; financial award applicants required to submit FAFSA. *Faculty research:* Bald eagle, parasitic population of domestic and

wild animals, resource recovery, anaerobic digestion of organic waste. *Unit head:* Dr. Kevin Fermanich, Chair, 920-465-2240, E-mail: fermanik@uwgb.edu. *Application contact:* Inga Zile, Graduate Studies Coordinator, 920-465-2123, E-mail: zilei@uwgb.edu. Web site: http://www.uwgb.edu/gradstu/.

University of Wisconsin–Madison, Graduate School, Gaylord Nelson Institute for Environmental Studies, Environmental Monitoring Program, Madison, WI 53706-1380. Offers MS, PhD. Part-time programs available. *Faculty:* 1 full-time (0 women), 1 part-time/adjunct (0 women). *Students:* 3 (2 women), 1 international. Average age 39. *Degree requirements:* For master's, thesis or alternative; for doctorate, thesis/dissertation. *Expenses:* Tuition, state resident: full-time $10,296; part-time $643.51 per credit. Tuition, nonresident: full-time $24,054; part-time $1503.40 per credit. *Required fees:* $70.06 per credit. Tuition and fees vary according to course load, campus/location, program and reciprocity agreements. *Financial support:* In 2011–12, 1 student received support, including fellowships with full tuition reimbursements available (averaging $18,756 per year), 1 research assistantship with full tuition reimbursement available (averaging $14,960 per year), teaching assistantships with full tuition reimbursements available (averaging $9,392 per year); career-related internships or fieldwork, Federal Work-Study, scholarships/grants, health care benefits, unspecified assistantships, and project assistantships also available. *Faculty research:* Remote sensing, geographic information systems, climate modeling, natural resource management. *Unit head:* Stephen J. Ventura, Chair, 608-262-6416, Fax: 608-262-2273, E-mail: sventura@wisc.edu. *Application contact:* Jim Miller, Student Services Coordinator, 608-263-4373, Fax: 608-262-2273, E-mail: jemiller@wisc.edu. Web site: http://nelson.wisc.edu.

Vanderbilt University, Graduate School, Department of Earth and Environmental Sciences, Nashville, TN 37240-1001. Offers MAT, MS. *Faculty:* 8 full-time (2 women). *Students:* 11 full-time (6 women), 1 part-time; includes 1 minority (Hispanic/Latino). Average age 29. 40 applicants, 25% accepted, 7 enrolled. In 2011, 16 master's awarded. *Degree requirements:* For master's, thesis. *Entrance requirements:* For master's, GRE General Test, GRE Subject Test (recommended). Additional exam requirements/recommendations for international students: Required—TOEFL (minimum score 570 paper-based; 230 computer-based; 88 iBT). *Application deadline:* For fall admission, 1/15 for domestic and international students. Application fee: $0. Electronic applications accepted. *Financial support:* Fellowships with full and partial tuition reimbursements, research assistantships with full and partial tuition reimbursements, teaching assistantships with full tuition reimbursements, career-related internships or fieldwork, Federal Work-Study, institutionally sponsored loans, and health care benefits available. Financial award application deadline: 1/15; financial award applicants required to submit CSS PROFILE or FAFSA. *Faculty research:* Geochemical processes, magmatic processes and crustal evolution, paleoecology and paleoenvironments, sedimentary systems, transport phenomena, environmental policy. *Unit head:* Dr. John C. Ayers, Chair, 615-283-0775, Fax: 615-322-2138, E-mail: john.c.ayers@vanderbilt.edu. *Application contact:* Jewell Beasley-Stanley, Administrative Assistant, 615-322-2976, Fax: 615-322-2138, E-mail: jewell.williams@vanderbilt.edu. Web site: http://www.vanderbilt.edu/ees/.

Virginia Polytechnic Institute and State University, Graduate School, College of Engineering, Department of Civil and Environmental Engineering, Blacksburg, VA 24061. Offers civil engineering (M Eng, MS, PhD); civil infrastructure systems (Certificate); environmental engineering (MS); environmental sciences and engineering (MS); transportation systems engineering (Certificate); treatment process engineering (Certificate); urban hydrology and stormwater management (Certificate); water quality management (Certificate). *Accreditation:* ABET (one or more programs are accredited). *Degree requirements:* For master's, comprehensive exam (for some programs), thesis (for some programs); for doctorate, comprehensive exam (for some programs), thesis/dissertation (for some programs). *Entrance requirements:* For master's and doctorate, GRE. Additional exam requirements/recommendations for international students: Required—TOEFL (minimum score 550 paper-based; 213 computer-based). *Application deadline:* For fall admission, 7/1 for domestic and international students; for spring admission, 12/1 for domestic and international students. Applications are processed on a rolling basis. Application fee: $65. Electronic applications accepted. *Expenses:* Tuition, state resident: full-time $10,048; part-time $558.25 per credit hour. Tuition, nonresident: full-time $19,497; part-time $1083.25 per credit hour. *Required fees:* $405 per semester. Tuition and fees vary according to course load, campus/location and program. *Financial support:* Fellowships with full tuition reimbursements, research assistantships with full tuition reimbursements, teaching assistantships with full tuition reimbursements, career-related internships or fieldwork, Federal Work-Study, scholarships/grants, health care benefits, and unspecified assistantships available. Financial award application deadline: 1/15. *Faculty research:* Construction, environmental geotechnical hydrosystems, structures and transportation engineering. *Unit head:* Dr. Sam Easterling, Unit Head, 540-231-5143, Fax: 540-231-7532, E-mail: seaster@vt.edu. *Application contact:* Marc Widdowson, Information Contact, 540-231-7153, Fax: 540-231-7532, E-mail: mwiddows@vt.edu. Web site: http://www.cee.vt.edu/.

Virginia Polytechnic Institute and State University, Graduate School, College of Natural Resources and Environment, Department of Geography, Program in Geospatial and Environmental Analysis, Blacksburg, VA 24061. Offers PhD. *Expenses:* Tuition, state resident: full-time $10,048; part-time $558.25 per credit hour. Tuition, nonresident: full-time $19,497; part-time $1083.25 per credit hour.

Peterson's Graduate Programs in the Physical Sciences, Mathematics, Agricultural Sciences, the Environment & Natural Resources 2013

facebook.com/petersonspublishing **503**

Environmental Sciences

Required fees: $405 per semester. Tuition and fees vary according to course load, campus/location and program. *Unit head:* Dr. Laurence W. Carstensen, Unit Head, 540-231-2600, Fax: 540-231-7557, E-mail: carstens@vt.edu. *Application contact:* Karen Bland, Information Contact, 540-231-7557, Fax: 540-231-7557, E-mail: kbland@vt.edu.

Virginia Polytechnic Institute and State University, VT Online, Blacksburg, VA 24061. Offers advanced transportation systems (Certificate); aerospace engineering (MS); agricultural and life sciences (MSLFS); business information systems (Graduate Certificate); career and technical education (MS); civil engineering (MS); computer engineering (M Eng, MS); decision support systems (Graduate Certificate); eLearning leadership (MA); electrical engineering (M Eng, MS); engineering administration (MEA); environmental engineering (Certificate); environmental politics and policy (Graduate Certificate); environmental sciences and engineering (MS); foundations of political analysis (Graduate Certificate); health product risk management (Graduate Certificate); industrial and systems engineering (MS); information policy and society (Graduate Certificate); information security (Graduate Certificate); information technology (MIT); instructional technology (MA); integrative STEM education (MA Ed); liberal arts (Graduate Certificate); life sciences: health product risk management (MS); natural resources (MNR, Graduate Certificate); networking (Graduate Certificate); nonprofit and nongovernmental organization management (Graduate Certificate); ocean engineering (MS); political science (MA); security studies (Graduate Certificate); software development (Graduate Certificate). *Expenses:* Tuition, state resident: full-time $10,048; part-time $558.25 per credit hour. Tuition, nonresident: full-time $19,497; part-time $1083.25 per credit hour. *Required fees:* $405 per semester. Tuition and fees vary according to course load, campus/ location and program. *Application contact:* Graduate School Applications General Assistance, 540-231-8636, Fax: 540-231-2039, E-mail: gradappl@vt.edu. Web site: http://www.vto.vt.edu/.

Washington State University, Graduate School, College of Agricultural, Human, and Natural Resource Sciences, Department of Natural Resource Sciences, Pullman, WA 99164. Offers MS. *Faculty:* 15. *Students:* 9 full-time (5 women), 2 part-time (1 woman); includes 1 minority (Hispanic/Latino). Average age 27. 18 applicants, 28% accepted, 5 enrolled. In 2011, 5 master's awarded. *Degree requirements:* For master's, comprehensive exam (for some programs), thesis (for some programs), oral exam. *Entrance requirements:* For master's, GRE General Test, official copies of all college transcripts, three letters of recommendation. Additional exam requirements/recommendations for international students: Required—TOEFL, IELTS. *Application deadline:* For fall admission, 1/10 priority date for domestic students, 1/10 for international students; for spring admission, 7/1 for domestic and international students. Applications are processed on a rolling basis. Application fee: $75. *Financial support:* In 2011–12, fellowships (averaging $2,333 per year), research assistantships with full and partial tuition reimbursements (averaging $13,917 per year), teaching assistantships with full and partial tuition reimbursements (averaging $13,056 per year) were awarded; career-related internships or fieldwork, Federal Work-Study, institutionally sponsored loans, tuition waivers (partial), and unspecified assistantships also available. Financial award application deadline: 2/15; financial award applicants required to submit FAFSA. *Faculty research:* Restoration ecology, landscape ecology, controlled and uncontrolled wild-land fire. *Total annual research expenditures:* $967,000. *Unit head:* Dr. Keith A. Blatner, Chair, 509-335-6166, E-mail: blatner@wsu.edu. *Application contact:* Graduate School Admissions, 800-GRADWSU, Fax: 509-335-1949, E-mail: gradsch@wsu.edu. Web site: http://www.natural-resources.wsu.edu/.

Washington State University, Graduate School, College of Sciences, School of Earth and Environmental Sciences, Program in Environmental and Natural Resource Sciences, Pullman, WA 99164. Offers PhD. *Students:* 13 full-time (9 women), 3 part-time (all women); includes 1 minority (Hispanic/Latino), 4 international. Average age 30. 25 applicants, 48% accepted, 12 enrolled. In 2011, 4 doctorates awarded. Application fee: $75. *Unit head:* Dr. Keith A. Blatner, Chair, 509-335-6166, E-mail: blatner@wsu.edu. *Application contact:* Graduate School Admissions, 800-GRADWSU, Fax: 509-335-1949, E-mail: gradsch@wsu.edu.

Washington State University, Graduate School, College of Sciences, School of Earth and Environmental Sciences, Program in Environmental Science, Pullman, WA 99164. Offers environmental and natural resource sciences (PhD); environmental science (MS). *Faculty:* 7. *Students:* 10 full-time (6 women), 1 part-time (0 women); includes 1 minority (Asian, non-Hispanic/Latino), 1 international. Average age 29. 43 applicants, 47% accepted, 13 enrolled. In 2011, 8 master's awarded. *Degree requirements:* For master's, comprehensive exam (for some programs), thesis (for some programs), oral exam; for doctorate, comprehensive exam, thesis/dissertation, oral exam, written exam. *Entrance requirements:* For master's, 3 undergraduate semester hours each in sociology or cultural anthropology, environmental science, biological sciences, and calculus or statistics; 4 in general ecology; and 6 in general chemistry or general physics; for doctorate, minimum GPA of 3.0. Additional exam requirements/recommendations for international students: Required—TOEFL, IELTS. *Application deadline:* For fall admission, 1/10 priority date for domestic students, 1/10 for international students. Applications are processed on a rolling basis. Application fee: $75. *Financial support:* In 2011–12, 16 students received support, including 1 fellowship (averaging $3,000 per year), 4 research assistantships with full and partial tuition reimbursements available (averaging $13,917 per year), 4 teaching assistantships with full and partial tuition reimbursements available (averaging $13,506 per year); Federal Work-Study, institutionally sponsored loans, and tuition waivers (partial) also available. Financial award application deadline: 2/15; financial award applicants required to submit FAFSA. *Unit head:* Dr. John A. Wolff, Head, 509-335-2825, E-mail: jawolff@mail.wsu.edu. *Application contact:* Graduate School Admissions, 800-GRADWSU, Fax: 509-335-1949, E-mail: gradsch@wsu.edu. Web site: http://esrp.wsu.edu/.

Washington State University Tri-Cities, Graduate Programs, Program in Agricultural, Human, and Natural Resource Science, Richland, WA 99354. Offers MS. *Faculty:* 17. *Students:* 7 full-time (2 women), all international. Average age 29. 3 applicants, 100% accepted, 3 enrolled. *Degree requirements:* For master's, comprehensive exam (for some programs), thesis (for some programs), special project. *Entrance requirements:* For master's, GRE, minimum GPA of 3.0, 3 letters of recommendation. Additional exam requirements/recommendations for international students: Required—TOEFL. *Application deadline:* For fall admission, 1/10 priority date for domestic students, 1/10 for international students; for spring admission, 7/1 priority date for domestic students, 7/1 for international students. Application fee: $75. *Financial support:* Application deadline: 4/1; applicants required to submit FAFSA. *Unit head:* Dr. Kate McAteer, Director, 509-372-7371, E-mail: kmcateer@tricity.wsu.edu. *Application contact:* Bonnie Bates, Academic Coordinator, 509-372-7171, Fax: 509-335-1949, E-mail: bbates@tricity.wsu.edu. Web site: http://www.tricity.wsu.edu/tricity/catalog/biology.htm.

Washington State University Tri-Cities, Graduate Programs, Program in Environmental Science, Richland, WA 99352-1671. Offers environmental and natural resource sciences (PhD); environmental science (MS). Part-time programs available. *Faculty:* 40. *Students:* 9 full-time (2 women), 33 part-time (18 women); includes 4 minority (2 Black or African American, non-Hispanic/Latino; 1 Asian, non-Hispanic/Latino; 1 Hispanic/Latino), 1 international. Average age 30. 8 applicants, 100% accepted, 8 enrolled. In 2011, 10 degrees awarded. *Degree requirements:* For master's, comprehensive exam, thesis (for some programs), oral exam; for doctorate, comprehensive exam, thesis/dissertation. *Entrance requirements:* For master's, GRE General Test, minimum GPA of 3.0, 3 letters of recommendation. Additional exam requirements/recommendations for international students: Required—TOEFL (minimum score 550 paper-based; 213 computer-based). *Application deadline:* For fall admission, 1/10 priority date for domestic students, 1/10 for international students; for spring admission, 7/1 priority date for domestic students, 7/1 for international students. Application fee: $75. *Financial support:* In 2011–12, 8 students received support, including research assistantships with full and partial tuition reimbursements available (averaging $14,634 per year), teaching assistantships with full and partial tuition reimbursements available (averaging $13,383 per year); fellowships, Federal Work-Study, scholarships/grants, health care benefits, and unspecified assistantships also available. Financial award application deadline: 1/15. *Faculty research:* Radiation ecology, cytogenetics. *Unit head:* John Strand, Graduate Advisor, 509-372-7326, E-mail: jstrand@tricity.wsu.edu. *Application contact:* Bonnie Bates, Graduate School Admissions, 800-GRADWSU, Fax: 509-372-7171, E-mail: bbates@tricity.wsu.edu. Web site: http://www.tricity.wsu.edu/science/environmental.html.

Washington State University Vancouver, Graduate Programs, Program in Environmental Science, Vancouver, WA 98686. Offers MS. *Faculty:* 16. *Students:* 18 full-time (10 women), 2 part-time (1 woman); includes 3 minority (1 American Indian or Alaska Native, non-Hispanic/Latino; 1 Asian, non-Hispanic/Latino; 1 Hispanic/Latino). Average age 29. 15 applicants, 20% accepted, 1 enrolled. In 2011, 7 master's awarded. *Degree requirements:* For master's, comprehensive exam, thesis (for some programs). *Entrance requirements:* For master's, GRE General Test, minimum GPA of 3.0, 3 letters of recommendation. Additional exam requirements/recommendations for international students: Required—TOEFL (minimum score 550 paper-based; 213 computer-based). *Application deadline:* For fall admission, 1/10 priority date for domestic students, 1/10 for international students; for spring admission, 7/1 priority date for domestic students, 7/1 for international students. Application fee: $75. *Financial support:* In 2011–12, research assistantships with tuition reimbursements (averaging $14,634 per year), teaching assistantships (averaging $13,383 per year) were awarded. Financial award application deadline: 2/15. *Faculty research:* Conservation biology, environmental chemistry. *Unit head:* Dr. Stephen Bollens, Graduate Program Coordinator, 360-546-9611, Fax: 360-546-9064, E-mail: tissot@vancouver.wsu.edu. *Application contact:* Dawn Banker, Academic Coordinator, 360-546-9478, Fax: 360-546-9064, E-mail: bankerd@vancouver.wsu.edu. Web site: http://www.vancouver.wsu.edu/programs/sci/mses.htm.

Wesleyan University, Graduate Programs, Department of Earth and Environmental Sciences, Middletown, CT 06459. Offers MA. *Degree requirements:* For master's, thesis. *Entrance requirements:* For master's, GRE General Test, GRE Subject Test. Additional exam requirements/recommendations for international students: Required—TOEFL. Electronic applications accepted. *Faculty research:* Tectonics, volcanology, stratigraphy, coastal processes, geochemistry.

Western Connecticut State University, Division of Graduate Studies, School of Arts and Sciences, Department of Biological and Environmental Sciences, Danbury, CT 06810-6885. Offers MA. Part-time programs available. *Faculty:* 3 full-time (1 woman). *Students:* 6 part-time (4 women); includes 1 minority (Black or African American, non-Hispanic/Latino). Average age 27. In 2011, 6 degrees awarded. *Degree requirements:* For master's, comprehensive exam or thesis, completion of program in 6 years. *Entrance requirements:* For master's, minimum GPA of 2.5. Additional exam requirements/recommendations for international students: Recommended—TOEFL (minimum score 550 paper-based; 213

504 facebook.com/petersonspublishing

Peterson's Graduate Programs in the Physical Sciences, Mathematics, Agricultural Sciences, the Environment & Natural Resources 2013

computer-based; 79 iBT), IELTS (minimum score 6). *Application deadline:* For fall admission, 8/5 priority date for domestic students; for spring admission, 1/5 priority date for domestic students. Applications are processed on a rolling basis. Application fee: $50. *Expenses:* Contact institution. *Financial support:* Application deadline: 5/1; applicants required to submit FAFSA. *Faculty research:* Biology, taxonomy and evolution of aquatic flowering plants; aquatic plant reproductive systems, the spread of invasive aquatic plants, aquatic plant structure, and the taxonomy of water starworts (Callitrichaceae) and riverweeds (Podostemaceae). *Unit head:* Dr. Richard Halliburton, Graduate Coordinator, 203-837-8233, Fax: 203-837-8525, E-mail: halliburtonr@wcsu.edu. *Application contact:* Chris Shankle, Associate Director of Graduate Studies, 203-837-9005, Fax: 203-837-8326, E-mail: shanklec@wcsu.edu. Web site: http://www.wcsu.edu/biology/.

Western Washington University, Graduate School, Huxley College of the Environment, Department of Environmental Sciences, Bellingham, WA 98225-5996. Offers environmental science (MS); marine and estuarine science (MS). Part-time programs available. *Degree requirements:* For master's, thesis. *Entrance requirements:* For master's, GRE General Test, minimum GPA of 3.0 in last 60 semester hours or last 90 quarter hours. Additional exam requirements/recommendations for international students: Required—TOEFL (minimum score 567 paper-based; 227 computer-based). Electronic applications accepted. *Faculty research:* Landscape ecology, climate change, watershed studies, environmental toxicology and risk assessment, aquatic toxicology, toxic algae, invasive species.

Western Washington University, Graduate School, Huxley College of the Environment, Department of Environmental Studies, Bellingham, WA 98225-5996. Offers environmental education (M Ed); geography (MS). Part-time programs available. *Degree requirements:* For master's, thesis. *Entrance requirements:* For master's, GRE General Test, minimum GPA of 3.0 in last 60 semester hours or last 90 quarter hours. Additional exam requirements/recommendations for international students: Required—TOEFL (minimum score 567 paper-based; 227 computer-based). Electronic applications accepted. *Faculty research:* Geomorphology; pedogenesis; quaternary studies and climate change in the western U.S. landscape ecology, biogeography, pyrogeography, and spatial analysis.

West Texas A&M University, College of Agriculture, Nursing, and Natural Sciences, Department of Life, Earth, and Environmental Sciences, Program in Environmental Science, Canyon, TX 79016-0001. Offers MS. Part-time programs available. *Degree requirements:* For master's, comprehensive exam, thesis optional. *Entrance requirements:* For master's, GRE General Test. Additional exam requirements/recommendations for international students: Required—TOEFL (minimum score 550 paper-based). Electronic applications accepted. *Faculty research:* Degradation of presistant pesticides in soils and ground water, air quality.

Wichita State University, Graduate School, Fairmount College of Liberal Arts and Sciences, Department of Geology, Wichita, KS 67260. Offers earth, environmental, and physical sciences (MS). Part-time programs available. *Expenses:* Tuition, state resident: full-time $4746; part-time $263.65 per credit. Tuition, nonresident: full-time $11,669; part-time $648.30 per credit. *Unit head:* Dr. William Parcell, Chair, 316-978-3140, E-mail: william.parcell@wichita.edu. *Application contact:* Dr. Collette Burke, Graduate Coordinator for EEPS Program, 316-978-3140, E-mail: collette.burke@wichita.edu. Web site: http://www.wichita.edu/.

Wilfrid Laurier University, Faculty of Graduate and Postdoctoral Studies, Faculty of Arts, Department of Geography and Environmental Studies, Waterloo, ON N2L 3C5, Canada. Offers environmental and resource management (MA, MES, PhD); environmental science (M Sc, MES, PhD); geomatics (M Sc, MES, PhD); human geography (MES, PhD). Part-time programs available. *Degree requirements:* For master's, thesis optional; for doctorate, thesis/dissertation. *Entrance requirements:* For master's, honors BA in geography, minimum B average in undergraduate course work; honors BSc with minimum B+ or honors BES or BA in physical geography, environmental or earth sciences or the equivalent; for doctorate, MA in geography, minimum Aaverage. Additional exam requirements/recommendations for international students: Required—TOEFL (minimum score 89 iBT). Electronic applications accepted. *Faculty research:* Resources management, urban, economic, physical, cultural, earth surfaces, geomatics, historical, regional, spatial data handling.

Wright State University, School of Graduate Studies, College of Science and Mathematics, Department of Biological Sciences, Dayton, OH 45435. Offers biological sciences (MS); environmental sciences (MS). *Degree requirements:* For master's, thesis optional. *Entrance requirements:* Additional exam requirements/recommendations for international students: Required—TOEFL.

Wright State University, School of Graduate Studies, College of Science and Mathematics, Department of Chemistry, Dayton, OH 45435. Offers chemistry (MS); environmental sciences (MS). Part-time and evening/weekend programs available. *Degree requirements:* For master's, oral defense of thesis, seminar. *Entrance requirements:* Additional exam requirements/recommendations for international students: Required—TOEFL. *Faculty research:* Polymer synthesis and characterization, laser kinetics, organic and inorganic synthesis, analytical and environmental chemistry.

Wright State University, School of Graduate Studies, College of Science and Mathematics, Program in Environmental Sciences, Dayton, OH 45435. Offers PhD.

Yale University, Graduate School of Arts and Sciences, Department of Forestry and Environmental Studies, New Haven, CT 06520. Offers environmental sciences (PhD); forestry (PhD). *Degree requirements:* For doctorate, thesis/dissertation. *Entrance requirements:* For doctorate, GRE General Test.

Yale University, School of Forestry and Environmental Studies, New Haven, CT 06511. Offers MEM, MES, MF, MFS, PhD, JD/MEM, MBA/MEM, MBA/MF, MEM/M Arch, MEM/MA, MEM/MPH, MF/MA. *Accreditation:* SAF (one or more programs are accredited). Part-time programs available. Terminal master's awarded for partial completion of doctoral program. *Degree requirements:* For master's, thesis (for some programs); for doctorate, thesis/dissertation. *Entrance requirements:* For master's, GRE General Test, GMAT or LSAT; for doctorate, GRE General Test. Additional exam requirements/recommendations for international students: Required—TOEFL (minimum score 600 paper-based; 250 computer-based; 100 iBT). Electronic applications accepted. *Expenses:* Contact institution. *Faculty research:* Environmental policy, social ecology, industrial environmental management, forestry, environmental health, urban ecology, water science policy.

Marine Affairs

American Public University System, AMU/APU Graduate Programs, Charles Town, WV 25414. Offers accounting (MBA, MS); administration and supervision (M Ed); criminal justice (MA); emergency and disaster management (MA); entrepreneurship (MBA); environmental policy and management (MS), including environmental planning, environmental sustainability, fish and wildlife management, general (MA, MS), global environmental management; finance (MBA); general (MBA); global business management (MBA); guidance and counseling (M Ed); history (MA), including American history, ancient and classical history, European history, global history, military and diplomatic history, public history; homeland security (MA); homeland security resource allocation (MBA); humanities (MA); information technology (MS), including digital forensics, enterprise software development, information assurance and security, IT project management; information technology management (MBA); intelligence studies (MA), including criminal intelligence, general (MA, MS), homeland security, intelligence analysis, intelligence collection, intelligence operations, terrorism studies; international relations and conflict resolution (MA), including comparative and security issues, conflict resolution, international and transnational security issues, peacekeeping; legal studies (MA); management (MA), including defense management, general (MA, MS), human resource management, organizational leadership, public administration, reverse logistics, strategic consulting; marketing (MBA); military history (MA), including American military history, American revolution, civil war, war since 1946, World War II; military studies (MA), including air warfare, asymmetrical warfare, joint warfare, land warfare, naval warfare, strategic leadership; national security studies (MA), including general (MA, MS), homeland security, regional security studies, security and intelligence analysis, terrorism studies; nonprofit management (MBA); political science (MA), including American politics and government, comparative government and development, public policy; psychology (MA); public administration (MA, MPA), including disaster management (MPA), environmental policy (MA), health policy (MPA), human resources (MPA), national security (MPA), organizational management (MPA), security management (MPA); public health (MA, MPH), including emergency management (MPH), environmental health (MPH), public administration (MA); reverse logistics management (MA); security management (MA); space studies (MA), including aerospace science, planetary science; sports and health sciences (MS); sports management (MS), including coaching theory and strategy, sports administration; teaching (M Ed), including curriculum and instruction for elementary teachers, elementary, elementary reading, English language learners, instructional leadership, online learning, secondary social sciences, special education; transportation and logistics management (MA), including maritime engineering management. Programs offered via distance learning only. Part-time and evening/weekend programs available. Postbaccalaureate distance learning degree programs offered (no on-campus study). *Faculty:* 445 full-time (241 women), 1,360 part-time/adjunct (617 women). *Students:* 688 full-time (338 women), 10,168 part-time (3,706 women); includes 3,130 minority (1,007 Black or African American, non-Hispanic/Latino; 103 American Indian or Alaska Native, non-Hispanic/Latino; 825 Asian, non-Hispanic/Latino; 810 Hispanic/Latino; 51 Native Hawaiian or other Pacific Islander, non-Hispanic/Latino; 334 Two or more races, non-Hispanic/Latino), 134 international. Average age 35. In 2011, 2,386 master's awarded. *Degree requirements:* For master's, comprehensive exam or practicum. *Entrance requirements:* For

Peterson's Graduate Programs in the Physical Sciences, Mathematics, Agricultural Sciences, the Environment & Natural Resources 2013

facebook.com/petersonspublishing **505**

master's, official transcript showing earned bachelor's degree from institution accredited by recognized accrediting body. Additional exam requirements/ recommendations for international students: Required—TOEFL (minimum score 550 paper-based; 213 computer-based), IELTS (minimum score 6.5). *Application deadline:* Applications are processed on a rolling basis. Application fee: $0. Electronic applications accepted. *Expenses: Tuition:* Part-time $325 per credit hour. *Financial support:* Applicants required to submit FAFSA. *Faculty research:* Military history, criminal justice, management performance, national security. *Unit head:* Dr. Karan Powell, Executive Vice President and Provost, 877-468-6268, Fax: 304-724-3780. *Application contact:* Terry Grant, Vice President of Enrollment Management, 877-468-6268, Fax: 304-724-3780, E-mail: info@apus.edu. Web site: http://www.apus.edu.

Dalhousie University, Faculty of Management, Marine Affairs Program, Halifax, NS B3H 3J5, Canada. Offers MMM. *Degree requirements:* For master's, project. *Entrance requirements:* For master's, minimum GPA of 3.0. Additional exam requirements/recommendations for international students: Required—TOEFL, IELTS, CANTEST, CAEL, or Michigan English Language Assessment Battery. Electronic applications accepted. *Faculty research:* Coastal zone management, sea use planning, development of non-living resources, protection and preservation of the coastal and marine environment, marine law and policy, fisheries management, maritime transport, conflict management.

Duke University, Nicholas School of the Environment, Durham, NC 27708-0328. Offers coastal environmental management (MEM); DEL-environmental leadership (MEM); energy and environment (MEM); environmental economics and policy (MEM); environmental health and security (MEM); forest resource management (MF); global environmental change (MEM); resource ecology (MEM); water and air resources (MEM); JD/AM; JD/MEM; JD/MF; MAT/MEM; MBA/MEM; MBA/MF; MEM/MPP; MF/MPP. *Accreditation:* SAF (one or more programs are accredited). Part-time programs available. *Degree requirements:* For master's, thesis. *Entrance requirements:* For master's, GRE General Test, previous course work in biology or ecology, calculus, statistics, and microeconomics; computer familiarity with word processing and data analysis. Additional exam requirements/ recommendations for international students: Required—TOEFL (minimum score 550 paper-based; 213 computer-based). Electronic applications accepted. *Expenses:* Contact institution. *Faculty research:* Ecosystem management, conservation ecology, earth systems, risk assessment.

Louisiana State University and Agricultural and Mechanical College, Graduate School, School of the Coast and Environment, Department of Oceanography and Coastal Sciences, Baton Rouge, LA 70803. Offers MS, PhD. *Faculty:* 25 full-time (3 women), 2 part-time/adjunct (0 women). *Students:* 55 full-time (26 women), 8 part-time (4 women); includes 1 minority (Hispanic/Latino), 13 international. Average age 29. 41 applicants, 29% accepted, 10 enrolled. In 2011, 4 master's, 5 doctorates awarded. *Degree requirements:* For master's, thesis (for some programs); for doctorate, one foreign language, thesis/dissertation. *Entrance requirements:* For master's, GRE General Test, minimum GPA of 3.0; for doctorate, GRE General Test, MA or MS, minimum GPA of 3.0. Additional exam requirements/recommendations for international students: Required— TOEFL (minimum score 550 paper-based; 213 computer-based; 79 iBT) or IELTS (minimum score 6.5). *Application deadline:* For fall admission, 1/25 priority date for domestic students, 5/15 for international students; for spring admission, 10/15 for international students. Applications are processed on a rolling basis. Application fee: $50 ($70 for international students). *Financial support:* In 2011– 12, 61 students received support, including 8 fellowships (averaging $22,270 per year), 47 research assistantships with full and partial tuition reimbursements available (averaging $19,641 per year), 1 teaching assistantship with full and partial tuition reimbursement available (averaging $17,000 per year); Federal Work-Study, institutionally sponsored loans, scholarships/grants, health care benefits, tuition waivers (full and partial), and unspecified assistantships also available. Support available to part-time students. Financial award applicants required to submit FAFSA. *Faculty research:* Physical and geological oceanography, wetland sustainability and restoration fisheries, coastal ecology and biogeochemistry. *Total annual research expenditures:* $7.7 million. *Unit head:* Dr. Donald Baltz, Chair, 225-578-6512, Fax: 225-578-6513, E-mail: dbaltz@ lsu.edu. *Application contact:* Dr. Charles Lindau, Graduate Adviser, 225-578- 8766, Fax: 225-578-5328, E-mail: clinda1@lsu.edu. Web site: http:// www.oceanography.lsu.edu/.

Memorial University of Newfoundland, School of Graduate Studies, Department of Sociology, St. John's, NL A1C 5S7, Canada. Offers gender (PhD); maritime sociology (PhD); sociology (M Phil, MA); work and development (PhD). Part-time programs available. *Degree requirements:* For master's, comprehensive exam, thesis optional, program journal (M Phil); for doctorate, one foreign language, comprehensive exam, thesis/dissertation, oral defense of thesis. *Entrance requirements:* For master's, 2nd class degree from university of recognized standing in area of study; for doctorate, MA, M Phil, or equivalent. Electronic applications accepted. *Faculty research:* Work and development, gender, maritime sociology.

Memorial University of Newfoundland, School of Graduate Studies, Interdisciplinary Program in Marine Studies, St. John's, NL A1C 5S7, Canada. Offers fisheries resource management (MMS, Advanced Diploma). Part-time programs available. *Degree requirements:* For master's, report. *Entrance requirements:* For master's and Advanced Diploma, high 2nd class degree from a recognized university. *Faculty research:* Biological, ecological and oceanographic aspects of world fisheries; economics; political science; sociology.

Nova Southeastern University, Oceanographic Center, Fort Lauderdale, FL 33314-7796. Offers biological sciences (MS); coastal zone management (MS); marine and coastal studies (MA); marine biology (MS); marine biology and oceanography (PhD), including marine biology, oceanography; marine environmental science (MS). Part-time and evening/weekend programs available. *Faculty:* 15 full-time (1 woman), 5 part-time/adjunct (0 women). *Students:* 130 full-time (86 women), 135 part-time (87 women); includes 34 minority (5 Black or African American, non-Hispanic/Latino; 5 Asian, non-Hispanic/Latino; 22 Hispanic/Latino; 2 Two or more races, non-Hispanic/Latino), 7 international. Average age 29. 98 applicants, 82% accepted, 67 enrolled. In 2011, 30 master's, 1 doctorate awarded. *Degree requirements:* For master's, thesis; for doctorate, comprehensive exam, thesis/dissertation, departmental qualifying exam. *Entrance requirements:* For master's, GRE General Test; for doctorate, GRE General Test, master's degree. Additional exam requirements/recommendations for international students: Required—TOEFL (minimum score 550 paper-based). *Application deadline:* Applications are processed on a rolling basis. Application fee: $50. *Expenses:* Contact institution. *Financial support:* In 2011–12, 25 research assistantships (averaging $4,000 per year), 3 teaching assistantships (averaging $3,500 per year) were awarded; career-related internships or fieldwork, Federal Work-Study, scholarships/grants, tuition waivers (partial), and unspecified assistantships also available. Support available to part-time students. Financial award applicants required to submit FAFSA. *Faculty research:* Physical, geological, chemical, and biological oceanography. *Unit head:* Dr. Richard Dodge, Dean, 954-262-3600, Fax: 954-262-4020, E-mail: dodge@nsu.nova.edu. *Application contact:* Dr. Richard Spieler, Director of Academic Programs, 954- 262-3600, Fax: 954-262-4020, E-mail: spieler@nova.edu. Web site: http:// www.nova.edu/ocean/.

Old Dominion University, College of Business and Public Administration, MBA Program, Norfolk, VA 23529. Offers business and economic forecasting (MBA); financial analysis and valuation (MBA); information technology and enterprise integration (MBA); international business (MBA); maritime and port management (MBA); public administration (MBA). *Accreditation:* AACSB. Part-time and evening/weekend programs available. *Faculty:* 66 full-time (15 women), 6 part-time/adjunct (1 woman). *Students:* 69 full-time (21 women), 230 part-time (85 women); includes 49 minority (22 Black or African American, non-Hispanic/Latino; 1 American Indian or Alaska Native, non-Hispanic/Latino; 10 Asian, non-Hispanic/ Latino; 3 Hispanic/Latino; 1 Native Hawaiian or other Pacific Islander, non-Hispanic/Latino; 12 Two or more races, non-Hispanic/Latino), 19 international. Average age 31. 177 applicants, 43% accepted, 53 enrolled. In 2011, 115 master's awarded. *Entrance requirements:* For master's, GMAT, GRE, letter of reference, resume, coursework in calculus, essay. Additional exam requirements/ recommendations for international students: Required—TOEFL (minimum score 550 paper-based; 213 computer-based; 80 iBT). *Application deadline:* For fall admission, 6/1 priority date for domestic students, 4/15 for international students; for spring admission, 11/1 priority date for domestic students, 10/1 for international students. Applications are processed on a rolling basis. Application fee: $75. Electronic applications accepted. *Expenses:* Tuition, state resident: full-time $9096; part-time $379 per credit. Tuition, nonresident: full-time $23,064; part-time $961 per credit. *Required fees:* $127 per semester. One-time fee: $50. *Financial support:* In 2011–12, 44 students received support, including 90 research assistantships with partial tuition reimbursements available (averaging $8,900 per year); career-related internships or fieldwork, scholarships/grants, and unspecified assistantships also available. Support available to part-time students. Financial award application deadline: 2/15; financial award applicants required to submit FAFSA. *Faculty research:* International business, buyer behavior, financial markets, strategy, operations research, maritime and transportation economics. *Unit head:* Dr. Larry Filer, Graduate Program Director, 757-683-3585, Fax: 757- 683-5750, E-mail: mbainfo@odu.edu. *Application contact:* Shanna Wood, MBA Program Manager, 757-683-3585, Fax: 757-683-5750, E-mail: mbainfo@ odu.edu. Web site: http://bpa.odu.edu/mba/.

Oregon State University, Graduate School, College of Oceanic and Atmospheric Sciences, Program in Marine Resource Management, Corvallis, OR 97331. Offers MA, MS. *Degree requirements:* For master's, thesis optional. *Entrance requirements:* For master's, GRE General Test, minimum GPA of 3.0 in last 90 hours of course work. Additional exam requirements/recommendations for international students: Required—TOEFL. *Faculty research:* Ocean and coastal resources, fisheries resources, marine pollution, marine recreation and tourism.

Stevens Institute of Technology, Graduate School, Charles V. Schaefer Jr. School of Engineering, Department of Civil, Environmental, and Ocean Engineering, Program in Maritime Systems, Hoboken, NJ 07030. Offers MS.

Stony Brook University, State University of New York, Graduate School, School of Marine and Atmospheric Sciences, Program in Marine Conservation and Policy, Stony Brook, NY 11794. Offers MA. *Degree requirements:* For master's, capstone project or internship. *Entrance requirements:* For master's, minimum GPA of 3.0; one semester of college-level biology and three additional semester courses in college-level math or science; personal statement; 3 letters of reference; official transcripts. Electronic applications accepted.

Université du Québec à Rimouski, Graduate Programs, Program in Management of Marine Resources, Rimouski, QC G5L 3A1, Canada. Offers M Sc, Diploma. Part-time programs available. *Entrance requirements:* For master's, appropriate bachelor's degree, proficiency in French.

506 facebook.com/petersonspublishing

Peterson's Graduate Programs in the Physical Sciences, Mathematics, Agricultural Sciences, the Environment & Natural Resources 2013

University of Delaware, College of Earth, Ocean, and Environment, School of Marine Science and Policy, Newark, DE 19716. Offers marine policy (MMP); marine studies (MS, PhD), including marine biosciences, oceanography, physical ocean science and engineering; oceanography (PhD).

University of Maine, Graduate School, College of Natural Sciences, Forestry, and Agriculture, School of Marine Sciences, Program in Marine Policy, Orono, ME 04469. Offers MS. *Students:* 9 full-time (6 women), 2 part-time (1 woman). Average age 27. 8 applicants, 13% accepted, 1 enrolled. In 2011, 1 degree awarded. *Degree requirements:* For master's, thesis. *Entrance requirements:* For master's, GRE General Test. Additional exam requirements/recommendations for international students: Required—TOEFL. *Application deadline:* For fall admission, 2/1 priority date for domestic students. Applications are processed on a rolling basis. Application fee: $65. Electronic applications accepted. *Expenses:* Tuition, state resident: full-time $5016. Tuition, nonresident: full-time $14,424. *Financial support:* Fellowships with tuition reimbursements, research assistantships with tuition reimbursements, teaching assistantships with tuition reimbursements, career-related internships or fieldwork, Federal Work-Study, and tuition waivers (full and partial) available. Support available to part-time students. Financial award application deadline: 3/1. *Unit head:* Dr. Yong Chen, Coordinator, 207-581-4303. *Application contact:* Scott G. Delcourt, Associate Dean of the Graduate School, 207-581-3291, Fax: 207-581-3232, E-mail: graduate@maine.edu. Web site: http://www2.umaine.edu/graduate/.

University of Miami, Graduate School, Rosenstiel School of Marine and Atmospheric Science, Division of Marine Affairs and Policy, Coral Gables, FL 33124. Offers MA, MS, JD/MA. Part-time programs available. *Degree requirements:* For master's, comprehensive exam, thesis (for some programs), internship, paper. *Entrance requirements:* For master's, GRE General Test. Additional exam requirements/recommendations for international students: Required—TOEFL (minimum score 550 paper-based; 213 computer-based). Electronic applications accepted.

University of Rhode Island, Graduate School, College of the Environment and Life Sciences, Department of Marine Affairs, Kingston, RI 02881. Offers MA, MESM, MMA, PhD, JD/MMA. Part-time programs available. *Faculty:* 6 full-time (1 woman). *Students:* 19 full-time (11 women), 6 part-time (5 women); includes 1 minority (Asian, non-Hispanic/Latino), 3 international. In 2011, 10 master's, 2 doctorates awarded. *Degree requirements:* For master's, comprehensive exam (for some programs), thesis optional; for doctorate, comprehensive exam, thesis/dissertation. *Entrance requirements:* For master's, GRE (for MA), 2 letters of recommendation (for MMA); for doctorate, GRE, 2 letters of recommendation, writing sample. Additional exam requirements/recommendations for international students: Required—TOEFL (minimum score 550 paper-based; 213 computer-based). *Application deadline:* For fall admission, 4/7 for domestic students, 2/1 for international students. Application fee: $65. Electronic applications accepted. *Expenses:* Tuition, state resident: full-time $10,432; part-time $580 per credit hour. Tuition, nonresident: full-time $23,130; part-time $1285 per credit hour. *Required fees:* $1362; $36 per credit hour. $35 per semester. One-time fee: $130. *Financial support:* In 2011–12, 1 research assistantship with full tuition reimbursement (averaging $7,403 per year) was awarded. Financial award application deadline: 2/1; financial award applicants required to submit FAFSA. *Faculty research:* Assessing change in coastal ecosystems and its impact to society. *Unit head:* Dr. Robert Thompson, Chair, 401-874-4485, Fax: 401-874-2156, E-mail: rob@uri.edu. *Application contact:* Dr. Richard Burroughs, Director of Master's Studies, 401-874-4045, Fax: 401-874-2156, E-mail: rburroughs@uri.edu. Web site: http://cels.uri.edu/maf/.

University of San Diego, College of Arts and Sciences, Department of Marine Science and Environmental Studies, San Diego, CA 92110-2492. Offers marine science (MS). Part-time programs available. *Faculty:* 2 full-time (1 woman), 1 part-time/adjunct (0 women). *Students:* 11 full-time (8 women), 9 part-time (7 women); includes 6 minority (1 Black or African American, non-Hispanic/Latino; 2 Hispanic/Latino; 3 Two or more races, non-Hispanic/Latino). Average age 26. 43 applicants, 26% accepted, 6 enrolled. In 2011, 2 master's awarded. *Degree requirements:* For master's, thesis. *Entrance requirements:* For master's, GRE General Test, minimum GPA of 3.0, 1 semester biology w/lab, 1 year chemistry w/lab, 1 year physics w/lab, 1 semester calculus. Additional exam requirements/recommendations for international students: Required—TOEFL (minimum score 580 paper-based; 237 computer-based; 83 iBT), TWE. *Application deadline:* For fall admission, 4/1 for domestic and international students. Applications are processed on a rolling basis. Application fee: $45. Electronic applications accepted. *Expenses:* Tuition: Full-time $22,482; part-time $1249 per unit. *Required fees:* $224. Full-time tuition and fees vary according to course load and degree level. *Financial support:* In 2011–12, 15 students received support. Career-related internships or fieldwork, Federal Work-Study, institutionally sponsored loans, and unspecified assistantships available. Support available to part-time students. Financial award application deadline: 4/1; financial award applicants required to submit FAFSA. *Faculty research:* Marine ecology, environmental geology and geochemistry, climatology, physiological ecology, fisheries and aquaculture. *Unit head:* Dr. Ronald S. Kaufmann, Director, 619-260-5904, Fax: 619-260-6874, E-mail: kaufmann@sandiego.edu. *Application contact:* Monica Mahon, Associate Director of Graduate Admissions, 619-260-4524, Fax: 619-260-4158, E-mail: grads@sandiego.edu. Web site: http://www.sandiego.edu/cas/mars_envi/.

University of Washington, Graduate School, College of the Environment, School of Marine and Environmental Affairs, Seattle, WA 98195. Offers MMA, Graduate Certificate. *Degree requirements:* For master's, thesis. *Entrance requirements:* For master's, GRE General Test, minimum GPA of 3.0. Additional exam requirements/recommendations for international students: Required—TOEFL. Electronic applications accepted. *Faculty research:* Marine pollution, port authorities, fisheries management, global climate change, marine environmental protection.

University of West Florida, College of Arts and Sciences: Sciences, School of Allied Health and Life Sciences, Department of Biology, Pensacola, FL 32514-5750. Offers biological chemistry (MS); biology (MS); biology education (MST); biotechnology (MS); coastal zone studies (MS); environmental biology (MS). *Faculty:* 12 full-time (3 women), 1 part-time/adjunct (0 women). *Students:* 9 full-time (7 women), 30 part-time (16 women); includes 2 minority (both Hispanic/Latino), 3 international. Average age 29. 21 applicants, 48% accepted, 5 enrolled. In 2011, 4 master's awarded. *Degree requirements:* For master's, thesis. *Entrance requirements:* For master's, GRE (minimum score: verbal 450, quantitative 550), official transcripts, BS in biology or related field; letter of interest; relevant past experience; three letters of recommendation from individuals who can evaluate applicant's academic ability. Additional exam requirements/recommendations for international students: Required—TOEFL (minimum score 550 paper-based; 213 computer-based). *Application deadline:* For fall admission, 6/1 for domestic and international students; for spring admission, 10/1 for domestic and international students. Applications are processed on a rolling basis. Application fee: $30. *Expenses:* Tuition, state resident: full-time $5729; part-time $302 per credit hour. Tuition, nonresident: full-time $20,059; part-time $961 per credit hour. *Required fees:* $1509; $63 per credit hour. *Financial support:* In 2011–12, 18 fellowships with partial tuition reimbursements (averaging $126 per year), 14 research assistantships with partial tuition reimbursements (averaging $5,980 per year), 4 teaching assistantships with partial tuition reimbursements (averaging $7,858 per year) were awarded; unspecified assistantships also available. Financial award application deadline: 4/15; financial award applicants required to submit FAFSA. *Unit head:* Dr. George L. Stewart, Chairperson, 850-474-2748. *Application contact:* Terry McCray, Assistant Director of Graduate Admissions, 850-473-7718, Fax: 850-473-7714, E-mail: gradadmissions@uwf.edu.

Peterson's Graduate Programs in the Physical Sciences, Mathematics, Agricultural Sciences, the Environment & Natural Resources 2013

facebook.com/petersonspublishing **507**

ADELPHI UNIVERSITY
College of the Arts and Sciences
Program in Environmental Studies

Program of Study

The Master of Science in environmental studies program comprises 36 credits of course work, incorporating classroom, laboratory, and field opportunities, and an optional thesis or internship. The thesis provides additional flexibility for the student with more specific career or educational goals. Full-time students can anticipate three semesters of 12 credits each. Field classes, internships, and research are also offered during the summer months.

The program is organized into a common course area and two areas of concentration—the global human environment and the global physical environment—and one area of integration, environmental education. In recognition of the context of both areas of concentration in the contemporary world, courses are required from the common area for all students. These offerings are fundamental to both concentrations and provide insights into the social, political, institutional, economic, and physical applications of environmental issues. Within each concentration, opportunities exist for the student to make program selections that reflect areas of faculty and student interest. For example, such selections could focus on the physical, chemical, biological, and biochemical aspects of pollutant detection; the cultural, societal, epidemiological, public health, paleontological, and paleopathological effects of environmental perturbations; or the economic, governmental, and social interactions consequent to environmental concerns. It is also possible for a student to elect sufficient courses from all areas to achieve a broader focus on environmental studies, leading to certification for teaching purposes. Additional opportunities are provided for the student in the form of technical field and laboratory experiences, as well as special topic courses that might not be available on a regular basis.

The faculty members draw their expertise from a wide spectrum of disciplines. Instructors are committed to involving participants fully in the multidisciplinary nature of environmental problems and the search for solutions. The environmental studies program provides firm, integrated foundations in both the social-political-cultural and the scientific-technical areas. This preparation makes students environmentally aware members of society in many professions, in graduate study in environmental studies/sciences, or in both.

Research Facilities

The University's primary research holdings are at Swirbul Library and include 600,000 volumes (including bound periodicals and government publications), 806,000 items in microformats, 33,000 audiovisual items, and online access to more than 61,000 electronic journal titles and 221 research databases.

Financial Aid

The program offers a number of stipends and financial assistance awards to teaching and research assistants on a yearly basis. Further opportunities for financial support over the course of every academic year, including the summers, are offered through the research projects and activities of faculty members.

Cost of Study

For the 2012–13 academic year, the tuition rate is $965 per credit. University fees range from $315 to $550 per semester.

Living and Housing Costs

The University assists single and married students in finding suitable accommodations whenever possible. The cost of living is dependent on location and number of rooms rented.

Location

Located in historic Garden City, New York, 45 minutes from Manhattan and 20 minutes from Queens, Adelphi's 75-acre suburban campus is known for the beauty of its landscape and architecture. The campus is a short walk from the Long Island Railroad and is convenient to New York's major airports and several major highways. Off-campus centers are located in Manhattan, Hauppauge, and Poughkeepsie.

The University and The College

Founded in 1896, Adelphi is a fully accredited, private university with nearly 8,000 undergraduate, graduate, and returning-adult students in the arts and sciences, business, clinical psychology, education, nursing, and social work. Students come from forty-three states and forty-five countries. The *Fiske Guide to Colleges* recognized Adelphi as a Best Buy in higher education for the sixth year in a row. The University is one of only twenty-five private institutions in the nation to earn this recognition.

Mindful of the cultural inheritance of the past, the College of Arts and Sciences encompasses those realms of inquiry that have characterized the modern pursuit of knowledge. The faculty members of the College place a high priority on students' intellectual development in and out of the classroom and structure programs to foster that growth. Students analyze original research and other creative work, develop firsthand facility with creative and research methodologies, undertake

Peterson's Graduate Programs in the Physical Sciences, Mathematics,
Agricultural Sciences, the Environment & Natural Resources 2013

facebook.com/petersonspublishing **509**

collaborative work with peers and mentors, engage in serious internships, and hone communicative skills.

Applying

Students should have a bachelor's degree in environmental studies or a related field and a demonstrated promise of successful achievement in the field. A student must submit a completed application, a $50 application fee, and official college transcripts. For more information, students should contact the graduate coordinator.

Correspondence and Information

Beth Christensen, Director of Environmental Studies Program
College of Arts and Sciences
Science Building, Room 118
One South Avenue
Adelphi University
Garden City, New York 11530
United States
Phone: 516-877-4174
Fax: 516-877-4485
E-mail: christensen@adelphi.edu
Web site: http://academics.adelphi.edu/artsci/env/graduate-environmental-studies.php

THE FACULTY AND THEIR RESEARCH

Anagnostis Agelarakis, Ph.D., Columbia. Physical anthropology, anthropological archaeology, ethnohistory, environmental studies.

Beth Christensen, Ph.D., South Carolina. Cenozoic climate and sea-level change, influence of African climate on hominid evolution, New Jersey margin geology, reef sediments, southern ocean paleoceanography.

Anthony Cok, Ph.D., Dalhousie. Environmental geology, marine resources, meteorology, earth science, hydrogeology.

Jonna Coombs, Ph.D., Penn State. Biology, bioremediation.

John Dooher, Ph.D., Stevens. Energy utilization, physics, electromagnetic theory, biomass gasification, engineering thermodynamics and kinetic theory.

Bryan Wygal, Ph.D., Nevada, Reno. Human ecology, New World and subarctic archaeology, peopling of the Americas, prehistoric technology, field methods.

Adelphi's campus is located in historic Garden City, Long Island, New York.

A registered arboretum, Adelphi is truly a green campus.

510 facebook.com/petersonspublishing

Peterson's Graduate Programs in the Physical Sciences, Mathematics, Agricultural Sciences, the Environment & Natural Resources 2013

Section 10
Natural Resources

This section contains a directory of institutions offering graduate work in natural resources. Additional information about programs listed in the directory may be obtained by writing directly to the dean of a graduate school or chair of a department at the address given in the directory.

For programs offering related work, see also in this book *Environmental Sciences and Management* and *Meteorology and Atmospheric Sciences.* In the other guides in this series:

Graduate Programs in the Humanities, Arts & Social Sciences

See *Architecture (Landscape Architecture)* and *Public, Regional, and Industrial Affairs*

Graduate Programs in the Biological/Biomedical Sciences & Health-Related Medical Professions

See *Biological and Biomedical Sciences; Botany and Plant Biology; Ecology, Environmental Biology, and Evolutionary Biology; Entomology; Genetics, Developmental Biology, and Reproductive Biology; Nutrition; Pathology and Pathobiology; Pharmacology and Toxicology; Physiology; Veterinary Medicine and Sciences;* and *Zoology*

Graduate Programs in Engineering & Applied Sciences

See *Agricultural Engineering and Bioengineering; Civil and Environmental Engineering; Geological, Mineral/Mining, and Petroleum Engineering; Management of Engineering and Technology;* and *Ocean Engineering*

CONTENTS

Program Directories

Fish, Game, and Wildlife Management

American Public University System, AMU/APU Graduate Programs, Charles Town, WV 25414. Offers accounting (MBA, MS); administration and supervision (M Ed); criminal justice (MA); emergency and disaster management (MA); entrepreneurship (MBA); environmental policy and management (MS), including environmental planning, environmental sustainability, fish and wildlife management, general (MA, MS), global environmental management; finance (MBA); general (MBA); global business management (MBA); guidance and counseling (M Ed); history (MA), including American history, ancient and classical history, European history, global history, military and diplomatic history, public history; homeland security (MA); homeland security resource allocation (MBA); humanities (MA); information technology (MS), including digital forensics, enterprise software development, information assurance and security, IT project management; information technology management (MBA); intelligence studies (MA), including criminal intelligence, general (MA, MS), homeland security, intelligence analysis, intelligence collection, intelligence operations, terrorism studies; international relations and conflict resolution (MA), including comparative and security issues, conflict resolution, international and transnational security issues, peacekeeping; legal studies (MA); management (MA), including defense management, general (MA, MS), human resource management, organizational leadership, public administration, reverse logistics, strategic consulting; marketing (MBA); military history (MA), including American military history, American revolution, civil war, war since 1946, World War II; military studies (MA), including air warfare, asymmetrical warfare, joint warfare, land warfare, naval warfare, strategic leadership; national security studies (MA), including general (MA, MS), homeland security, regional security studies, security and intelligence analysis, terrorism studies; nonprofit management (MBA); political science (MA), including American politics and government, comparative government and development, public policy; psychology (MA); public administration (MA, MPA), including disaster management (MPA), environmental policy (MA), health policy (MPA), human resources (MPA), national security (MPA), organizational management (MPA), security management (MPA); public health (MA, MPH), including emergency management (MPH), environmental health (MPH), public administration (MA); reverse logistics management (MA); security management (MA); space studies (MS), including aerospace science, planetary science; sports and health sciences (MS); sports management (MS), including coaching theory and strategy, sports administration; teaching (M Ed), including curriculum and instruction for elementary teachers, elementary, elementary reading, English language learners, instructional leadership, online learning, secondary social sciences, special education; transportation and logistics management (MA), including maritime engineering management. Programs offered via distance learning only. Part-time and evening/weekend programs available. Postbaccalaureate distance learning degree programs offered (no on-campus study). *Faculty:* 445 full-time (241 women), 1,360 part-time/adjunct (617 women). *Students:* 688 full-time (338 women), 10,168 part-time (3,706 women); includes 3,130 minority (1,007 Black or African American, non-Hispanic/Latino; 103 American Indian or Alaska Native, non-Hispanic/Latino; 825 Asian, non-Hispanic/Latino; 810 Hispanic/Latino; 51 Native Hawaiian or other Pacific Islander, non-Hispanic/Latino; 334 Two or more races, non-Hispanic/Latino), 134 international. Average age 35. In 2011, 2,386 master's awarded. *Degree requirements:* For master's, comprehensive exam or practicum. *Entrance requirements:* For master's, official transcript showing earned bachelor's degree from institution accredited by recognized accrediting body. Additional exam requirements/recommendations for international students: Required—TOEFL (minimum score 550 paper-based; 213 computer-based), IELTS (minimum score 6.5). *Application deadline:* Applications are processed on a rolling basis. Application fee: $0. Electronic applications accepted. *Expenses: Tuition:* Part-time $325 per credit hour. *Financial support:* Applicants required to submit FAFSA. *Faculty research:* Military history, criminal justice, management performance, national security. *Unit head:* Dr. Karan Powell, Executive Vice President and Provost, 877-468-6268, Fax: 304-724-3780. *Application contact:* Terry Grant, Vice President of Enrollment Management, 877-468-6268, Fax: 304-724-3780, E-mail: info@apus.edu. Web site: http://www.apus.edu.

Arkansas Tech University, Center for Leadership and Learning, College of Natural and Health Sciences, Russellville, AR 72801. Offers fisheries and wildlife biology (MS); health informatics (MS); nursing (MSN). Part-time programs available. *Students:* 6 full-time (4 women), 45 part-time (34 women); includes 2 minority (1 Black or African American, non-Hispanic/Latino; 1 American Indian or Alaska Native, non-Hispanic/Latino), 1 international. Average age 40. In 2011, 9 master's awarded. *Degree requirements:* For master's, thesis (for some programs), project. *Entrance requirements:* For master's, GRE General Test. Additional exam requirements/recommendations for international students: Required—TOEFL (minimum score 550 paper-based; 213 computer-based; 79 iBT), IELTS (minimum score 6). *Application deadline:* For fall admission, 3/1 priority date for domestic students, 5/1 for international students; for spring admission, 10/1 priority date for domestic students, 10/1 for international students. Applications are processed on a rolling basis. Application fee: $25 ($75 for international students). Electronic applications accepted. *Expenses:* Tuition, state resident: full-time $4968; part-time $207 per credit hour. Tuition, nonresident: full-time $9936; part-time $414 per credit hour. *Required fees:* $375 per semester.

Tuition and fees vary according to course load. *Financial support:* In 2011–12, teaching assistantships with full tuition reimbursements (averaging $4,800 per year) were awarded; research assistantships with full tuition reimbursements, career-related internships or fieldwork, Federal Work-Study, scholarships/grants, health care benefits, and unspecified assistantships also available. Support available to part-time students. Financial award application deadline: 4/15; financial award applicants required to submit FAFSA. *Unit head:* Dr. Jeff Robertson, Dean, 479-968-0498, E-mail: jrobertson@atu.edu. *Application contact:* Dr. Mary B. Gunter, Dean of Graduate College, 479-968-0398, Fax: 479-964-0542, E-mail: gradcollege@atu.edu. Web site: http://www.atu.edu/nhs/.

Auburn University, Graduate School, College of Agriculture, Department of Fisheries and Allied Aquacultures, Auburn University, AL 36849. Offers M Aq, MS, PhD. Part-time programs available. *Faculty:* 20 full-time (3 women). *Students:* 33 full-time (15 women), 53 part-time (24 women); includes 4 minority (1 Black or African American, non-Hispanic/Latino; 1 Asian, non-Hispanic/Latino; 2 Hispanic/Latino), 49 international. Average age 28. 48 applicants, 48% accepted, 19 enrolled. In 2011, 15 master's, 5 doctorates awarded. *Degree requirements:* For master's, thesis (for some programs); for doctorate, 2 foreign languages, thesis/dissertation. *Entrance requirements:* For master's and doctorate, GRE General Test. *Application deadline:* For fall admission, 7/7 for domestic students; for spring admission, 11/24 for domestic students. Applications are processed on a rolling basis. Application fee: $50 ($60 for international students). Electronic applications accepted. *Expenses:* Tuition, state resident: full-time $7290; part-time $405 per credit hour. Tuition, nonresident: full-time $21,870; part-time $1215 per credit hour. *International tuition:* $22,000 full-time. *Required fees:* $1402. *Financial support:* Fellowships, research assistantships, teaching assistantships, and Federal Work-Study available. Support available to part-time students. Financial award application deadline: 3/15; financial award applicants required to submit FAFSA. *Faculty research:* Channel catfish production; aquatic animal health; community and population ecology; pond management; production hatching, breeding and genetics. *Total annual research expenditures:* $8 million. *Unit head:* Dr. David B. Rouse, Head, 334-844-4786. *Application contact:* Dr. George Flowers, Dean of the Graduate School, 334-844-2125. Web site: http://www.ag.auburn.edu/fish/.

Auburn University, Graduate School, School of Forestry and Wildlife Sciences, Auburn University, AL 36849. Offers forest economics (PhD); forestry (MS, PhD); natural resource conservation (MNR); wildlife sciences (MS, PhD). *Accreditation:* SAF. Part-time programs available. *Faculty:* 32 full-time (6 women), 2 part-time/adjunct (0 women). *Students:* 28 full-time (12 women), 36 part-time (15 women), 18 international. Average age 28. 28 applicants, 43% accepted, 10 enrolled. In 2011, 22 master's, 5 doctorates awarded. *Degree requirements:* For master's, thesis (MS); for doctorate, thesis/dissertation. *Entrance requirements:* For master's and doctorate, GRE General Test. *Application deadline:* For fall admission, 7/7 for domestic students; for spring admission, 11/24 for domestic students. Applications are processed on a rolling basis. Application fee: $50 ($60 for international students). Electronic applications accepted. *Expenses:* Tuition, state resident: full-time $7290; part-time $405 per credit hour. Tuition, nonresident: full-time $21,870; part-time $1215 per credit hour. *International tuition:* $22,000 full-time. *Required fees:* $1402. *Financial support:* Fellowships, research assistantships, teaching assistantships, and Federal Work-Study available. Support available to part-time students. Financial award application deadline: 3/15; financial award applicants required to submit FAFSA. *Faculty research:* Forest nursery management, silviculture and vegetation management, biological processes and ecological relationships, growth and yield of plantations and natural stands, urban forestry, forest taxation, law and policy. *Unit head:* Dr. James P. Shepard, Dean, 334-844-4000, Fax: 334-844-1084, E-mail: brinker@forestry.auburn.edu. *Application contact:* Dr. George Flowers, Dean of the Graduate School, 334-844-2125. Web site: http://www.forestry.auburn.edu/.

Brigham Young University, Graduate Studies, College of Life Sciences, Department of Plant and Wildlife Sciences, Provo, UT 84602-1001. Offers environmental science (MS); genetics and biotechnology (MS); wildlife and wildlands conservation (MS, PhD). *Faculty:* 26 full-time (1 woman), 1 (woman) part-time/adjunct. *Students:* 50 full-time (18 women); includes 8 minority (2 Asian, non-Hispanic/Latino; 4 Hispanic/Latino; 2 Native Hawaiian or other Pacific Islander, non-Hispanic/Latino), 4 international. Average age 25. 29 applicants, 41% accepted, 9 enrolled. In 2011, 18 master's, 1 doctorate awarded. *Degree requirements:* For master's, thesis; for doctorate, comprehensive exam, thesis/dissertation, minimum GPA of 3.2, 54 hours (18 dissertation, 36 coursework). *Entrance requirements:* For master's, GRE General Test, minimum GPA of 3.2 during last 60 hours of course work; for doctorate, GRE, minimum GPA of 3.2. Additional exam requirements/recommendations for international students: Required—TOEFL (minimum score 580 paper-based; 237 computer-based; 85 iBT). *Application deadline:* 2/1 for domestic and international students. Applications are processed on a rolling basis. Electronic applications accepted. Full-time tuition for non-LDS students: $11,520 per year; $640 per credit. *Expenses: Tuition:* Full-time $5760; part-time $320 per credit. Tuition and fees vary according to student's religious affiliation. *Financial support:* In 2011–12, 2 research assistantships with partial tuition reimbursements (averaging $16,650

512 facebook.com/petersonspublishing

Peterson's Graduate Programs in the Physical Sciences, Mathematics, Agricultural Sciences, the Environment & Natural Resources 2013

per year), 37 teaching assistantships with partial tuition reimbursements (averaging $16,650 per year) were awarded; scholarships/grants and tuition waivers (partial) also available. Financial award application deadline: 2/1. *Faculty research:* Environmental science, plant genetics, plant ecology, plant nutrition and pathology, wildlife and wildlands conservation. *Total annual research expenditures:* $2.1 million. *Unit head:* Dr. Val J. Anderson, Chair, 801-422-3527, Fax: 801-422-0008, E-mail: val_anderson@byu.edu. *Application contact:* Dr. Loreen Allphin, Graduate Coordinator, 801-422-5603, Fax: 801-422-0008, E-mail: loreen_allphin@byu.edu. Web site: http://pws.byu.edu/home/.

Clemson University, Graduate School, College of Agriculture, Forestry and Life Sciences, Department of Forestry and Natural Resources, Program in Wildlife and Fisheries Biology, Clemson, SC 29634. Offers MS, PhD. *Students:* 14 full-time (9 women), 7 part-time (5 women); includes 2 minority (1 Black or African American, non-Hispanic/Latino; 1 Hispanic/Latino), 1 international. Average age 35. 36 applicants, 47% accepted, 16 enrolled. In 2011, 1 doctorate awarded. *Degree requirements:* For master's, thesis; for doctorate, thesis/dissertation. *Entrance requirements:* For master's, GRE General Test, minimum undergraduate GPA of 3.0; for doctorate, GRE General Test. Additional exam requirements/ recommendations for international students: Required—TOEFL, IELTS. *Application deadline:* For fall admission, 6/1 for domestic students, 4/15 for international students; for spring admission, 9/15 for international students. Applications are processed on a rolling basis. Application fee: $70 ($80 for international students). Electronic applications accepted. *Expenses:* Contact institution. *Financial support:* In 2011–12, 12 students received support, including 8 research assistantships with partial tuition reimbursements available (averaging $15,248 per year), 5 teaching assistantships with partial tuition reimbursements available (averaging $13,800 per year); fellowships with full and partial tuition reimbursements available, career-related internships or fieldwork, institutionally sponsored loans, scholarships/grants, health care benefits, and unspecified assistantships also available. Support available to part-time students. Financial award applicants required to submit FAFSA. *Faculty research:* Intensive freshwater culture systems, conservation biology, stream management, applied wildlife management. *Unit head:* Dr. Patricia Layton, Chair, 864-656-3303, Fax: 864-656-3304, E-mail: playton@clemson.edu. *Application contact:* Dr. David Guynn, Graduate Program Coordinator, 864-656-4830, Fax: 864-656-5344, E-mail: dguynn@clemson.edu. Web site: http://www.clemson.edu/cafls/departments/forestry/.

Colorado State University, Graduate School, Warner College of Natural Resources, Department of Fishery and Wildlife Biology, Fort Collins, CO 80523-1474. Offers fish, wildlife and conservation biology (MFWCB); fishery and wildlife biology (MFWB, MS, PhD). *Faculty:* 15 full-time (4 women). *Students:* 11 full-time (3 women), 19 part-time (8 women); includes 2 minority (both Hispanic/Latino). Average age 31. 11 applicants, 55% accepted, 6 enrolled. In 2011, 5 master's, 2 doctorates awarded. Terminal master's awarded for partial completion of doctoral program. *Degree requirements:* For master's, comprehensive exam, thesis (for some programs); for doctorate, comprehensive exam, thesis/dissertation. *Entrance requirements:* For master's, GRE General Test (combined minimum score of 1200 on the Verbal and Quantitative sections), minimum GPA of 3.0, BA or BS in related field, letters of recommendation, resume, transcripts; for doctorate, GRE General Test (minimum score 1000 verbal and quantitative), minimum GPA of 3.0, MS in related field. Additional exam requirements/ recommendations for international students: Required—TOEFL (minimum score 550 paper-based; 213 computer-based; 80 iBT). *Application deadline:* For fall admission, 2/15 priority date for domestic students, 2/15 for international students. Applications are processed on a rolling basis. Application fee: $50. Electronic applications accepted. *Expenses:* Tuition, state resident: full-time $7992. Tuition, nonresident: full-time $19,592. *Required fees:* $1735; $58 per credit. *Financial support:* In 2011–12, 4 fellowships with full and partial tuition reimbursements (averaging $25,954 per year), 19 research assistantships with full and partial tuition reimbursements (averaging $14,721 per year), 11 teaching assistantships with full and partial tuition reimbursements (averaging $7,502 per year) were awarded; career-related internships or fieldwork, scholarships/grants, tuition waivers (full and partial), and unspecified assistantships also available. Financial award application deadline: 2/15; financial award applicants required to submit FAFSA. *Faculty research:* Conservation biology, aquatic ecology, animal behavior, population modeling, habitat evaluation and management. *Total annual research expenditures:* $3.2 million. *Unit head:* Dr. Kenneth R. Wilson, Head, 970-491-7755, Fax: 970-491-5091, E-mail: kenneth.wilson@colostate.edu. *Application contact:* Joyce Pratt, Graduate Contact, 970-491-5020, Fax: 970-491-5091, E-mail: joyce.pratt@colostate.edu. Web site: http://warnercnr.colostate.edu/fwcb-home/.

Cornell University, Graduate School, Graduate Fields of Agriculture and Life Sciences, Field of Natural Resources, Ithaca, NY 14853-0001. Offers aquatic science (MPS, MS, PhD); environmental management (MPS); fishery science (MPS, MS, PhD); forest science (MPS, MS, PhD); resource policy and management (MPS, MS, PhD); wildlife science (MPS, MS, PhD). *Faculty:* 39 full-time (7 women). *Students:* 52 full-time (21 women); includes 4 minority (1 American Indian or Alaska Native, non-Hispanic/Latino; 1 Asian, non-Hispanic/ Latino; 1 Hispanic/Latino; 1 Two or more races, non-Hispanic/Latino), 15 international. Average age 32. 72 applicants, 21% accepted, 11 enrolled. In 2011, 2 master's, 5 doctorates awarded. *Degree requirements:* For master's, thesis (MS), project paper (MPS); for doctorate, comprehensive exam, thesis/ dissertation. *Entrance requirements:* For master's and doctorate, GRE General Test, 2 letters of recommendation. Additional exam requirements/

recommendations for international students: Required—TOEFL (minimum score 550 paper-based; 213 computer-based; 77 iBT). *Application deadline:* For spring admission, 10/30 for domestic students. Applications are processed on a rolling basis. Application fee: $95. Electronic applications accepted. *Financial support:* In 2011–12, 10 fellowships with full tuition reimbursements, 14 research assistantships with full tuition reimbursements, 28 teaching assistantships with full tuition reimbursements were awarded; institutionally sponsored loans, scholarships/grants, health care benefits, tuition waivers (full and partial), and unspecified assistantships also available. Financial award applicants required to submit FAFSA. *Faculty research:* Ecosystem-level dynamics, systems modeling, conservation biology/management, resource management's human dimensions, biogeochemistry. *Unit head:* Director of Graduate Studies, 607-255-2807, Fax: 607-255-0349. *Application contact:* Graduate Field Assistant, 607-255-2807, Fax: 607-255-0349, E-mail: nrgrad@cornell.edu. Web site: http://www.gradschool.cornell.edu/fields.php?id-54&a-2.

Frostburg State University, Graduate School, College of Liberal Arts and Sciences, Department of Biology, Program in Fisheries and Wildlife Management, Frostburg, MD 21532-1099. Offers MS. Part-time and evening/weekend programs available. *Degree requirements:* For master's, thesis. *Entrance requirements:* For master's, GRE General Test, resume. Additional exam requirements/ recommendations for international students: Required—TOEFL. Electronic applications accepted. *Faculty research:* Evolution and systematics of freshwater fishes, biochemical mechanisms of temperature adaptation in freshwater fishes, wildlife and fish parasitology, biology of freshwater invertebrates, remote sensing.

Humboldt State University, Academic Programs, College of Natural Resources and Sciences, Programs in Natural Resources, Arcata, CA 95521-8299. Offers natural resources (MS), including fisheries, forestry, natural resources planning and interpretation, rangeland resources and wildland soils, wastewater utilization, watershed management, wildlife. *Students:* 45 full-time (26 women), 28 part-time (11 women); includes 4 minority (2 Asian, non-Hispanic/Latino; 1 Hispanic/Latino; 1 Two or more races, non-Hispanic/Latino), 1 international. Average age 30. 100 applicants, 22% accepted, 11 enrolled. In 2011, 25 master's awarded. *Degree requirements:* For master's, thesis or alternative. *Entrance requirements:* For master's, GRE, appropriate bachelor's degree, minimum GPA of 2.5, 3 letters of recommendation, resume. Additional exam requirements/recommendations for international students: Required—TOEFL (minimum score 500 paper-based; 173 computer-based). *Application deadline:* For fall admission, 2/1 for domestic and international students; for spring admission, 9/30 for domestic and international students. Applications are processed on a rolling basis. Application fee: $55. *Expenses:* Tuition, state resident: full-time $6734. Tuition, nonresident: full-time $15,662; part-time $372 per credit. *Required fees:* $903. Tuition and fees vary according to program. *Financial support:* Fellowships, career-related internships or fieldwork, and Federal Work-Study available. Support available to part-time students. Financial award application deadline: 3/1; financial award applicants required to submit FAFSA. *Faculty research:* Spotted owl habitat, pre-settlement vegetation, hardwood utilization, tree physiology, fisheries. *Unit head:* Dr. Robert Van Kirk, Coordinator, 707-826-3744, E-mail: rob.vankirk@humboldt.edu. *Application contact:* Julie Tucker, Administrative Support Coordinator, 707-826-3256, E-mail: jlt7002@humboldt.edu. Web site: http://www.humboldt.edu/cnrs/graduate_programs.

Iowa State University of Science and Technology, Department of Natural Resource Ecology and Management, Ames, IA 50011-3140. Offers forestry (MS, PhD); wildlife ecology (MS). *Entrance requirements:* For master's and doctorate, GRE General Test. Additional exam requirements/recommendations for international students: Required—TOEFL (minimum score 550 paper-based; 79 iBT), IELTS (minimum score 6.5). *Application deadline:* For fall admission, 4/1 priority date for domestic students, 4/1 for international students; for spring admission, 10/1 priority date for domestic students, 10/1 for international students. Application fee: $40 ($90 for international students). Electronic applications accepted. *Unit head:* Dr. Janette Thompson, Director of Graduate Education, 515-294-7400, Fax: 515-294-7406, E-mail: nremgradinfo@iastate.edu. *Application contact:* Kelly Kyle, Director of Graduate Education, 515-294-7400, Fax: 515-294-7406, E-mail: nremgradinfo@iastate.edu. Web site: http://www.nrem.iastate.edu/.

Iowa State University of Science and Technology, Program in Fisheries Biology, Ames, IA 50011-3140. Offers MS, PhD. *Entrance requirements:* For master's and doctorate, GRE. Additional exam requirements/recommendations for international students: Required—TOEFL (minimum score 550 paper-based; 79 iBT), IELTS (minimum score 6.5). *Application deadline:* For fall admission, 4/1 for domestic students; for spring admission, 10/1 for domestic students. Electronic applications accepted. *Unit head:* Janette Thompson, Director of Graduate Education, 515-294-7400, Fax: 515-294-7406, E-mail: nremgradinfo@iastate.edu. *Application contact:* Kelly Kyle, Information Contact, 515-294-7400, Fax: 515-294-7406, E-mail: nremgradinfo@iastate.edu. Web site: http://www.nrem.iastate.edu.

Louisiana State University and Agricultural and Mechanical College, Graduate School, College of Agriculture, School of Renewable Natural Resources, Baton Rouge, LA 70803. Offers fisheries (MS); forestry (MS, PhD); wildlife (MS); wildlife and fisheries science (PhD). *Faculty:* 31 full-time (5 women). *Students:* 53 full-time (13 women), 11 part-time (2 women); includes 2 minority (both Hispanic/Latino), 16 international. Average age 30. 21 applicants, 33% accepted, 7 enrolled. In 2011, 12 master's, 7 doctorates awarded. *Degree requirements:* For master's, thesis; for doctorate, thesis/dissertation. *Entrance requirements:* For master's, GRE General Test, minimum GPA of 3.0; for

Peterson's Graduate Programs in the Physical Sciences, Mathematics, Agricultural Sciences, the Environment & Natural Resources 2013

facebook.com/petersonspublishing **513**

Fish, Game, and Wildlife Management

doctorate, GRE General Test, MS, minimum GPA of 3.0. Additional exam requirements/recommendations for international students: Required—TOEFL (minimum score 550 paper-based; 213 computer-based; 79 iBT), IELTS (minimum score 6.5). *Application deadline:* For fall admission, 1/25 priority date for domestic students, 5/15 for international students; for spring admission, 10/15 for international students. Applications are processed on a rolling basis. Application fee: $50 ($70 for international students). Electronic applications accepted. *Financial support:* In 2011–12, 61 students received support, including 52 research assistantships with partial tuition reimbursements available (averaging $19,938 per year), 1 teaching assistantship (averaging $22,000 per year); fellowships, Federal Work-Study, institutionally sponsored loans, scholarships/grants, health care benefits, tuition waivers (full and partial), and unspecified assistantships also available. Financial award application deadline: 4/15; financial award applicants required to submit FAFSA. *Faculty research:* Forest biology and management, aquaculture, fisheries biology and ecology, upland and wetlands wildlife. *Total annual research expenditures:* $47,156. *Unit head:* Dr. Allen Rutherford, Director, 225-578-4131, Fax: 225-578-4227, E-mail: druther@lsu.edu. *Application contact:* Dr. William Kelso, Coordinator of Graduate Studies, 225-578-4176, Fax: 225-578-4227, E-mail: wkelso@lsu.edu. Web site: http://www.fwf.lsu.edu/.

McGill University, Faculty of Graduate and Postdoctoral Studies, Faculty of Agricultural and Environmental Sciences, Department of Natural Resource Sciences, Montréal, QC H3A 2T5, Canada. Offers entomology (M Sc, PhD); environmental assessment (M Sc); forest science (M Sc, PhD); microbiology (M Sc, PhD); micrometeorology (M Sc, PhD); neotropical environment (M Sc, PhD); soil science (M Sc, PhD); wildlife biology (M Sc, PhD).

Memorial University of Newfoundland, School of Graduate Studies, Interdisciplinary Program in Marine Studies, St. John's, NL A1C 5S7, Canada. Offers fisheries resource management (MMS, Advanced Diploma). Part-time programs available. *Degree requirements:* For master's, report. *Entrance requirements:* For master's and Advanced Diploma, high 2nd class degree from a recognized university. *Faculty research:* Biological, ecological and oceanographic aspects of world fisheries; economics; political science; sociology.

Michigan State University, The Graduate School, College of Agriculture and Natural Resources, Department of Fisheries and Wildlife, East Lansing, MI 48824. Offers fisheries and wildlife (MS, PhD); fisheries and wildlife environmental toxicology (PhD). *Entrance requirements:* Additional exam requirements/recommendations for international students: Required—TOEFL (minimum score 550 paper-based; 213 computer-based), Michigan State University ELT (minimum score 85), Michigan English Language Assessment Battery (minimum score 83). Electronic applications accepted.

Mississippi State University, College of Forest Resources, Department of Wildlife, Fisheries and Aquaculture, Mississippi State, MS 39762. Offers forest resources (PhD); including wildlife and fisheries; wildlife and fisheries science (MS). Part-time programs available. *Faculty:* 20 full-time (1 woman), 1 part-time/adjunct (0 women). *Students:* 64 full-time (19 women), 17 part-time (7 women); includes 4 minority (1 Black or African American, non-Hispanic/Latino; 2 Hispanic/Latino; 1 Two or more races, non-Hispanic/Latino), 8 international. Average age 28. 33 applicants, 45% accepted, 15 enrolled. In 2011, 16 master's, 3 doctorates awarded. *Degree requirements:* For master's, thesis, comprehensive oral or written exam; for doctorate, comprehensive exam, thesis/dissertation. *Entrance requirements:* For master's, GRE or minimum GPA of 3.0 on last 60 hours of undergraduate courses, bachelor's degree; for doctorate, GRE or minimum GPA of 3.2 on prior graduate studies, master's degree. Additional exam requirements/recommendations for international students: Required—TOEFL (minimum score 550 paper-based; 213 computer-based; 79 iBT); Recommended—IELTS (minimum score 6.5). *Application deadline:* For fall admission, 7/1 for domestic students, 5/1 for international students; for spring admission, 11/1 for domestic students, 9/1 for international students. Applications are processed on a rolling basis. Application fee: $40. Electronic applications accepted. *Expenses:* Tuition, state resident: full-time $5805; part-time $322.50 per credit hour. Tuition, nonresident: full-time $14,670; part-time $815 per credit hour. *Financial support:* In 2011–12, 56 research assistantships with partial tuition reimbursements (averaging $14,621 per year) were awarded; Federal Work-Study, institutionally sponsored loans, and unspecified assistantships also available. Financial award application deadline: 4/1; financial award applicants required to submit FAFSA. *Faculty research:* Spatial technology, habitat restoration, aquaculture, fisheries, wildlife management. *Unit head:* Dr. Bruce D. Leopold, Department Head and Graduate Coordinator, 662-325-2615, Fax: 662-325-8726, E-mail: bleopold@cfr.msstate.edu. *Application contact:* Dr. Eric Dibble, Professor and Coordinator of Graduate Studies, 662-325-7494, Fax: 662-325-8726, E-mail: edibble@cfr.msstate.edu. Web site: http://www.cfr.msstate.edu/wildlife/index.asp.

Montana State University, College of Graduate Studies, College of Letters and Science, Department of Ecology, Bozeman, MT 59717. Offers ecological and environmental statistics (MS); ecology and environmental sciences (PhD); fish and wildlife biology (PhD); fish and wildlife management (MS). Part-time programs available. *Degree requirements:* For master's, comprehensive exam, thesis (for some programs); for doctorate, comprehensive exam, thesis/dissertation. *Entrance requirements:* For master's and doctorate, GRE, minimum GPA of 3.0, letters of recommendation, essay. Additional exam requirements/recommendations for international students: Required—TOEFL (minimum score 550 paper-based; 213 computer-based). Electronic applications accepted.

Faculty research: Community ecology, population ecology, land-use effects, management and conservation, environmental modeling.

New Mexico Highlands University, Graduate Studies, College of Arts and Sciences, Department of Biology, Chemistry, Natural Resource Management, Las Vegas, NM 87701. Offers chemistry (MS); life science (MS). Part-time programs available. *Faculty:* 14 full-time (6 women). *Students:* 21 full-time (7 women), 8 part-time (2 women); includes 16 minority (1 American Indian or Alaska Native, non-Hispanic/Latino; 15 Hispanic/Latino), 11 international. Average age 29. 30 applicants, 80% accepted, 10 enrolled. In 2011, 10 master's awarded. *Degree requirements:* For master's, comprehensive exam, thesis. *Entrance requirements:* For master's, minimum undergrad GPA of 3.0. Additional exam requirements/recommendations for international students: Required—TOEFL (minimum score 540 paper-based; 207 computer-based). *Application deadline:* For fall admission, 8/1 priority date for domestic students. Applications are processed on a rolling basis. Application fee: $15. *Expenses:* Tuition, state resident: full-time $2767; part-time $146 per credit hour. Tuition, nonresident: full-time $4879; part-time $234 per credit hour. *International tuition:* $5436 full-time. *Required fees:* $737. *Financial support:* In 2011–12, 17 students received support. Career-related internships or fieldwork, Federal Work-Study, institutionally sponsored loans, scholarships/grants, tuition waivers (full and partial), and unspecified assistantships available. Support available to part-time students. Financial award application deadline: 3/1. *Faculty research:* Invasive organisms in managed and wildland ecosystems, juniper and pinyon ecology and management, vegetation and community structure, big game management, quantitative forestry. *Unit head:* Dr. Mary Shaw, Department Head, 505-454-3407, E-mail: shaw_mary@nmhu.edu. *Application contact:* Diane Trujillo, Administrative Assistant, Graduate Studies, 505-454-3266, Fax: 505-426-2117, E-mail: dtrujillo@nmhu.edu.

New Mexico State University, Graduate School, College of Agricultural, Consumer and Environmental Sciences, Department of Fish, Wildlife and Conservation Ecology, Las Cruces, NM 88003. Offers wildlife science (MS). *Faculty:* 7 full-time (2 women), 1 (woman) part-time/adjunct. *Students:* 20 full-time (5 women), 6 part-time (3 women); includes 4 minority (all Hispanic/Latino), 1 international. Average age 27. 18 applicants, 33% accepted, 6 enrolled. In 2011, 9 master's awarded. *Degree requirements:* For master's, thesis (for some programs). *Entrance requirements:* For master's, GRE General Test, minimum GPA of 3.0. Additional exam requirements/recommendations for international students: Required—TOEFL (minimum score 550 paper-based; 0 computer-based; 79 iBT), IELTS (minimum score 6.5). *Application deadline:* For fall admission, 4/1 priority date for domestic students; for spring admission, 11/1 priority date for domestic students. Applications are processed on a rolling basis. Application fee: $40 ($50 for international students). Electronic applications accepted. *Expenses:* Tuition, state resident: full-time $5004; part-time $208.50 per credit. Tuition, nonresident: full-time $17,446; part-time $726.90 per credit. *Financial support:* In 2011–12, 1 fellowship (averaging $2,718 per year), 12 research assistantships with partial tuition reimbursements (averaging $19,196 per year), 5 teaching assistantships with partial tuition reimbursements (averaging $7,900 per year) were awarded; career-related internships or fieldwork, Federal Work-Study, scholarships/grants, health care benefits, and unspecified assistantships also available. Support available to part-time students. Financial award application deadline: 4/1. *Faculty research:* Ecosystems analyses, landscape and wildlife ecology, wildlife and fish population dynamics, management models, wildlife and fish habitat relationships. *Unit head:* Dr. Martha J. Desmond, Interim Head, 575-646-1217, Fax: 575-646-1281, E-mail: mdesmond@nmsu.edu. *Application contact:* Doris J. Morgan, Intermediate Administrative Assistant, 575-646-7051, Fax: 575-646-1281, E-mail: domorgan@nmsu.edu. Web site: http://aces.nmsu.edu/academics/FWS.

North Carolina State University, Graduate School, College of Natural Resources, Program in Fisheries and Wildlife Sciences, Raleigh, NC 27695. Offers MFWS, MS, PhD. *Degree requirements:* For master's, thesis optional. *Entrance requirements:* For master's, GRE General Test. Additional exam requirements/recommendations for international students: Required—TOEFL. Electronic applications accepted. *Faculty research:* Fisheries biology; ecology of marine, estuarine, and anadromous fishes; aquaculture pond water quality; larviculture of freshwater and marine finfish; predator/prey interactions.

Oregon State University, Graduate School, College of Agricultural Sciences, Department of Fisheries and Wildlife, Program in Fisheries Science, Corvallis, OR 97331. Offers M Agr, MAIS, MS, PhD. Part-time programs available. *Degree requirements:* For master's, thesis (for some programs); for doctorate, thesis/dissertation. *Entrance requirements:* For master's and doctorate, GRE, minimum GPA of 3.0 in last 90 hours. Additional exam requirements/recommendations for international students: Required—TOEFL. *Faculty research:* Fisheries ecology, fish toxicology, stream ecology, quantitative analyses of marine and freshwater fish populations.

Oregon State University, Graduate School, College of Agricultural Sciences, Department of Fisheries and Wildlife, Program in Wildlife Science, Corvallis, OR 97331. Offers MAIS, MS, PhD. *Degree requirements:* For master's, thesis (for some programs); for doctorate, thesis/dissertation. *Entrance requirements:* For master's and doctorate, GRE, minimum GPA of 3.0 in last 90 hours. Additional exam requirements/recommendations for international students: Required—TOEFL.

Penn State University Park, Graduate School, College of Agricultural Sciences, School of Forest Resources, State College, University Park, PA 16802-1503.

Peterson's Graduate Programs in the Physical Sciences, Mathematics, Agricultural Sciences, the Environment & Natural Resources 2013

Offers forest resources (M Agr, MFR, MS, PhD); wildlife and fisheries science (M Agr, MFR, MS, PhD). *Unit head:* Dr. Bruce A. McPheron, Dean, 814-865-2541, Fax: 814-865-3103, E-mail: bam10@psu.edu. *Application contact:* Cynthia E. Nicosia, Director of Graduate Enrollment Services, 814-865-1834, E-mail: cey1@psu.edu. Web site: http://sfr.psu.edu/.

Purdue University, Graduate School, College of Agriculture, Department of Forestry and Natural Resources, West Lafayette, IN 47907. Offers fisheries and aquatic sciences (MS, MSF, PhD); forest biology (MS, MSF, PhD); natural resource social science (MS, PhD); natural resources social science (MSF); quantitative ecology (MS, MSF, PhD); wildlife science (MS, MSF, PhD); wood products and wood products manufacturing (MS, MSF, PhD). *Faculty:* 26 full-time (3 women), 9 part-time/adjunct (1 woman). *Students:* 67 full-time (31 women), 8 part-time (3 women); includes 3 minority (2 Hispanic/Latino; 1 Two or more races, non-Hispanic/Latino), 17 international. Average age 29. 58 applicants, 16% accepted, 8 enrolled. In 2011, 9 master's, 11 doctorates awarded. *Degree requirements:* For master's, thesis; for doctorate, thesis/dissertation. *Entrance requirements:* For master's and doctorate, GRE General Test with minimum score required: verbal >=50th percentile; Quantitative >= 50th percentile; Analytical writing = 4.0 or greater, minimum undergraduate GPA of 3.2 or equivalent. Additional exam requirements/recommendations for international students: Required—TOEFL (minimum score 550 paper-based; 77 iBT). *Application deadline:* For fall admission, 1/5 for domestic students, 1/15 for international students; for spring admission, 9/15 for domestic and international students. Applications are processed on a rolling basis. Application fee: $60 ($75 for international students). Electronic applications accepted. *Financial support:* In 2011–12, 10 research assistantships (averaging $15,259 per year) were awarded; fellowships, teaching assistantships, career-related internships or fieldwork, and scholarships/grants also available. Support available to part-time students. Financial award application deadline: 1/5; financial award applicants required to submit FAFSA. *Faculty research:* Wildlife management, forest management, forest ecology, forest soils, limnology. *Unit head:* Dr. Robert K. Swihart, Interim Head, 765-494-3590, Fax: 765-494-9461, E-mail: rswihart@purdue.edu. *Application contact:* Kelly J. Garrett, Graduate Secretary, 765-494-3572, Fax: 765-494-9461, E-mail: kgarrett@purdue.edu. Web site: http://www.fnr.purdue.edu/.

South Dakota State University, Graduate School, College of Agriculture and Biological Sciences, Department of Wildlife and Fisheries Sciences, Brookings, SD 57007. Offers MS, PhD. Part-time programs available. *Degree requirements:* For master's, thesis, oral exam; for doctorate, comprehensive exam, thesis/dissertation, interim exam, oral and written comprehensive exams. *Entrance requirements:* For master's and doctorate, GRE. Additional exam requirements/recommendations for international students: Required—TOEFL (minimum score 525 paper-based; 197 computer-based; 71 iBT). *Faculty research:* Agriculture interactions, wetland conservation, biostress, wildlife and fisheries ecology and techniques.

State University of New York College of Environmental Science and Forestry, Department of Environmental and Forest Biology, Syracuse, NY 13210-2779. Offers applied ecology (MPS); chemical ecology (MPS, MS, PhD); conservation biology (MPS, MS, PhD); ecology (MPS, MS, PhD); entomology (MPS, MS, PhD); environmental interpretation (MPS, MS, PhD); environmental physiology (MPS, MS, PhD); fish and wildlife biology and management (MPS, MS, PhD); forest pathology and mycology (MPS, MS, PhD); plant biotechnology (MPS); plant science and biotechnology (MPS, MS, PhD). *Degree requirements:* For master's, thesis (for some programs); for doctorate, comprehensive exam, thesis/dissertation. *Entrance requirements:* For master's and doctorate, GRE General Test, GRE Subject Test, minimum GPA of 3.0. Additional exam requirements/recommendations for international students: Required—TOEFL (minimum score 550 paper-based; 213 computer-based; 80 iBT), IELTS (minimum score 6). *Application deadline:* For fall admission, 2/1 priority date for domestic students, 2/1 for international students; for spring admission, 11/1 priority date for domestic students, 11/1 for international students. Applications are processed on a rolling basis. Application fee: $60. *Expenses:* Tuition, state resident: full-time $8870; part-time $370 per credit hour. Tuition, nonresident: full-time $15,160; part-time $632 per credit hour. *Required fees:* $60; $370 per credit hour. $350 per semester. One-time fee: $85. *Financial support:* Fellowships with full and partial tuition reimbursements, research assistantships with full and partial tuition reimbursements, teaching assistantships with full and partial tuition reimbursements, Federal Work-Study, institutionally sponsored loans, scholarships/grants, health care benefits, and unspecified assistantships available. Financial award application deadline: 6/30. *Faculty research:* Ecology, fish and wildlife biology and management, plant science, entomology. *Total annual research expenditures:* $4.1 million. *Unit head:* Dr. Donald J. Leopold, Chair, 315-470-6760, Fax: 315-470-6934. *Application contact:* Dr. Dudley J. Raynal, Dean, Instruction and Graduate Studies, 315-470-6599, Fax: 315-470-6978, E-mail: esfgrad@esf.edu. Web site: http://www.esf.edu/efb/.

Sul Ross State University, Division of Agricultural and Natural Resource Science, Program in Range and Wildlife Management, Alpine, TX 79832. Offers M Ag, MS. Part-time programs available. *Degree requirements:* For master's, thesis (for some programs). *Entrance requirements:* For master's, GRE General Test, minimum undergraduate GPA of 2.5 in last 60 hours.

Tennessee Technological University, Graduate School, College of Arts and Sciences, Department of Biology, Cookeville, TN 38505. Offers fish, game, and wildlife management (MS). Part-time programs available. *Faculty:* 22 full-time (2 women). *Students:* 4 full-time (3 women), 12 part-time (8 women), 1 international. Average age 25. 12 applicants, 42% accepted, 5 enrolled. In 2011, 12 master's awarded. *Degree requirements:* For master's, thesis. *Entrance requirements:* For master's, GRE. Additional exam requirements/recommendations for international students: Required—TOEFL (minimum score 550 paper-based; 79 iBT), IELTS (minimum score 5.5), PTE Academic. *Application deadline:* For fall admission, 8/1 for domestic students, 5/1 for international students; for spring admission, 12/1 for domestic students, 10/1 for international students. Application fee: $25 ($30 for international students). Electronic applications accepted. *Expenses:* Tuition, state resident: full-time $8094; part-time $422 per credit hour. Tuition, nonresident: full-time $20,574; part-time $1046 per credit hour. *Financial support:* In 2011–12, 17 research assistantships (averaging $9,000 per year), 8 teaching assistantships (averaging $7,500 per year) were awarded. Financial award application deadline: 4/1. *Faculty research:* Aquatics, environmental studies. *Unit head:* Dr. Daniel Combs, Interim Chairperson, 931-372-3134, Fax: 931-372-6257, E-mail: dlcombs@tntech.edu. *Application contact:* Shelia K. Kendrick, Coordinator of Graduate Admissions, 931-372-3808, Fax: 931-372-3497, E-mail: skendrick@tntech.edu.

Texas A&M University, College of Agriculture and Life Sciences, Department of Wildlife and Fisheries Sciences, College Station, TX 77843. Offers MS, PhD. Part-time programs available. Postbaccalaureate distance learning degree programs offered (no on-campus study). *Faculty:* 29. *Students:* 88 full-time (49 women), 57 part-time (28 women); includes 44 minority (4 Black or African American, non-Hispanic/Latino; 2 American Indian or Alaska Native, non-Hispanic/Latino; 1 Asian, non-Hispanic/Latino; 37 Hispanic/Latino), 20 international. Average age 26. In 2011, 18 master's, 9 doctorates awarded. Terminal master's awarded for partial completion of doctoral program. *Degree requirements:* For master's, thesis, final oral defense; for doctorate, thesis/dissertation, final oral defense. *Entrance requirements:* For master's and doctorate, GRE General Test, minimum GPA of 3.0. Additional exam requirements/recommendations for international students: Required—TOEFL (minimum score 550 paper-based; 213 computer-based). *Application deadline:* For fall admission, 3/1 for international students; for spring admission, 8/1 for international students. Applications are processed on a rolling basis. Application fee: $50 ($75 for international students). Electronic applications accepted. *Expenses:* Tuition, state resident: full-time $5437; part-time $226.55 per credit hour. Tuition, nonresident: full-time $12,949; part-time $539.55 per credit hour. *Required fees:* $2741. *Financial support:* In 2011–12, fellowships with partial tuition reimbursements (averaging $22,000 per year), research assistantships (averaging $14,400 per year), teaching assistantships (averaging $14,400 per year) were awarded; career-related internships or fieldwork, institutionally sponsored loans, and scholarships/grants also available. Financial award application deadline: 3/1; financial award applicants required to submit FAFSA. *Faculty research:* Wildlife ecology and management, fisheries ecology and management, aquaculture, biological inventories and museum collections, biosystematics and genome analysis. *Unit head:* Dr. John Carey, Interim Department Head, 979-845-5777, Fax: 979-845-3786, E-mail: jcarey@poultry.tamu.edu. *Application contact:* Felix Arnold, Academic Advisor II, 979-845-5768, Fax: 979-845-3786, E-mail: fwarnold@tamu.edu. Web site: http://wfscnet.tamu.edu/.

Texas A&M University–Kingsville, College of Graduate Studies, College of Agriculture and Home Economics, Program in Range and Wildlife Management, Kingsville, TX 78363. Offers MS. *Degree requirements:* For master's, comprehensive exam, thesis or alternative. *Entrance requirements:* For master's, GRE General Test, minimum GPA of 3.0. Additional exam requirements/recommendations for international students: Required—TOEFL.

Texas A&M University–Kingsville, College of Graduate Studies, College of Agriculture and Home Economics, Program in Wildlife Science, Kingsville, TX 78363. Offers PhD. *Degree requirements:* For doctorate, one foreign language, comprehensive exam, thesis/dissertation. *Entrance requirements:* For doctorate, GRE General Test, minimum GPA of 3.5.

Texas State University–San Marcos, Graduate School, College of Science and Engineering, Department of Biology, Program in Wildlife Ecology, San Marcos, TX 78666. Offers MS. *Faculty:* 5 full-time (0 women). *Students:* 22 full-time (17 women), 6 part-time (2 women); includes 8 minority (1 Black or African American, non-Hispanic/Latino; 1 Asian, non-Hispanic/Latino; 6 Hispanic/Latino), 1 international. Average age 28. 10 applicants, 70% accepted, 5 enrolled. In 2011, 14 master's awarded. *Degree requirements:* For master's, thesis. *Entrance requirements:* For master's, GRE General Test (preferred minimum combined score of 1000 Verbal and Quantitative), bachelor's degree in biology or related discipline, minimum GPA of 3.0 in last 60 hours of undergraduate work. Additional exam requirements/recommendations for international students: Required—TOEFL (minimum score 550 paper-based; 213 computer-based; 78 iBT). *Application deadline:* For fall admission, 6/15 priority date for domestic students, 6/1 for international students; for spring admission, 10/15 priority date for domestic students, 10/1 for international students. Applications are processed on a rolling basis. Application fee: $40 ($90 for international students). Electronic applications accepted. *Expenses:* Tuition, state resident: full-time $6408; part-time $3204 per semester. Tuition, nonresident: full-time $14,832; part-time $7416 per semester. *Required fees:* $1824; $912 per semester. Tuition and fees vary according to course load. *Financial support:* In 2011–12, 7 students received support, including 3 research assistantships (averaging $7,650 per year), 22 teaching assistantships (averaging $12,681 per year); Federal Work-Study and institutionally sponsored loans also available. Support available to part-time

Peterson's Graduate Programs in the Physical Sciences, Mathematics, Agricultural Sciences, the Environment & Natural Resources 2013

facebook.com/petersonspublishing **515**

students. Financial award application deadline: 4/1; financial award applicants required to submit FAFSA. *Unit head:* Dr. Thomas Randy Simpson, Graduate Advisor, 512-245-2178, Fax: 512-245-8713, E-mail: r_simpson@txstate.edu. *Application contact:* Dr. J. Michael Willoughby, Dean of the Graduate School, 512-245-2581, Fax: 512-245-8365, E-mail: jw02@swt.edu. Web site: http://www.gradcollege.txstate.edu/Prospect_Students/Pgms_Apps/Masters/Science/Wild_Eco.html.

Texas Tech University, Graduate School, College of Agricultural Sciences and Natural Resources, Department of Natural Resources Management, Lubbock, TX 79409. Offers fisheries science (MS, PhD); range science (MS, PhD); wildlife, aquatic, and wildlands science and management (MS, PhD). Part-time programs available. *Faculty:* 11 full-time (1 woman). *Students:* 50 full-time (13 women), 3 part-time (0 women); includes 7 minority (1 American Indian or Alaska Native, non-Hispanic/Latino; 3 Hispanic/Latino; 3 Two or more races, non-Hispanic/Latino), 7 international. Average age 27. 20 applicants, 45% accepted, 8 enrolled. In 2011, 4 master's, 2 doctorates awarded. *Degree requirements:* For master's, thesis; for doctorate, thesis/dissertation. *Entrance requirements:* For master's and doctorate, GRE General Test, formal approval from departmental committee. Additional exam requirements/recommendations for international students: Required—TOEFL (minimum score 550 paper-based; 213 computer-based; 79 iBT). *Application deadline:* For fall admission, 6/1 priority date for domestic students, 1/15 for international students; for spring admission, 9/1 priority date for domestic students, 6/15 for international students. Applications are processed on a rolling basis. Application fee: $50 ($75 for international students). Electronic applications accepted. *Expenses:* Tuition, state resident: full-time $5899; part-time $245.80 per credit hour. Tuition, nonresident: full-time $13,411; part-time $558.80 per credit hour. *Required fees:* $2680.60; $86.50 per credit hour. $920.30 per semester. *Financial support:* In 2011–12, 17 students received support. Application deadline: 4/15; applicants required to submit FAFSA. *Faculty research:* Use of fire on range lands; big game, upland game, and waterfowl; playa lakes in the southern Great Plains; conservation biology; fish ecology and physiology. *Total annual research expenditures:* $2.1 million. *Unit head:* Dr. Mark Wallace, Interim Chairman, 806-742-2841, Fax: 806-742-2280, E-mail: mark.wallace@ttu.edu. *Application contact:* Renee Dillon, Senior Business Assistant, 806-742-2841, E-mail: renee.dillon@ttu.edu. Web site: http://www.rw.ttu.edu/dept/.

Université du Québec à Rimouski, Graduate Programs, Program in Wildlife Resources Management, Rimouski, QC G5L 3A1, Canada. Offers biology (PhD); wildlife resources management (M Sc, Diploma). PhD offered jointly with Université du Québec à Montréal, Université du Québec à Trois-Rivières, and Université du Québec en Abitibi-Témiscamingue. *Entrance requirements:* For degree, appropriate bachelor's degree, proficiency in French.

University of Alaska Fairbanks, College of Natural Sciences and Mathematics, Department of Biology and Wildlife, Fairbanks, AK 99775-6100. Offers biological sciences (MS, PhD), including biology, botany, wildlife biology (PhD), zoology; biology (MAT, MS); wildlife biology (MS). Part-time programs available. *Faculty:* 20 full-time (10 women). *Students:* 74 full-time (43 women), 29 part-time (18 women); includes 12 minority (1 Asian, non-Hispanic/Latino; 6 Hispanic/Latino; 5 Two or more races, non-Hispanic/Latino), 4 international. Average age 29. 45 applicants, 40% accepted, 15 enrolled. In 2011, 12 master's, 11 doctorates awarded. *Degree requirements:* For master's, comprehensive exam, thesis, oral exam, oral defense; for doctorate, comprehensive exam, thesis/dissertation, oral exam, oral defense. *Entrance requirements:* For master's and doctorate, GRE General Test, GRE Subject Test (biology). Additional exam requirements/recommendations for international students: Required—TOEFL (minimum score 550 paper-based; 213 computer-based; 80 iBT), TWE. *Application deadline:* For fall admission, 6/1 for domestic students, 3/1 for international students; for spring admission, 10/15 for domestic students, 9/1 for international students. Applications are processed on a rolling basis. Application fee: $60. Electronic applications accepted. *Expenses:* Tuition, state resident: full-time $6696; part-time $372 per credit. Tuition, nonresident: full-time $13,680; part-time $760 per credit. Tuition and fees vary according to course load and reciprocity agreements. *Financial support:* In 2011–12, 26 research assistantships with tuition reimbursements (averaging $13,976 per year), 26 teaching assistantships with tuition reimbursements (averaging $14,955 per year) were awarded; fellowships with tuition reimbursements, career-related internships or fieldwork, Federal Work-Study, scholarships/grants, health care benefits, and unspecified assistantships also available. Support available to part-time students. Financial award application deadline: 7/1; financial award applicants required to submit FAFSA. *Faculty research:* Plant-herbivore interactions, plant metabolic defenses, insect manufacture of glycerol, ice nucleators, structure and functions of arctic and subarctic freshwater ecosystems. *Unit head:* Christa Mulder, Department Chair, 907-474-7671, Fax: 907-474-6716, E-mail: fybio@uaf.edu. *Application contact:* Mike Earnest, Director of Admissions, 907-474-7500, Fax: 907-474-5379, E-mail: admissions@uaf.edu. Web site: http://www.bw.uaf.edu.

University of Alaska Fairbanks, School of Fisheries and Ocean Sciences, Program in Marine Sciences and Limnology, Fairbanks, AK 99775-7220. Offers marine biology (MS, PhD); oceanography (PhD), including biological oceanography, chemical oceanography, fisheries, geological oceanography, physical oceanography. Part-time programs available. *Faculty:* 6 full-time (4 women). *Students:* 40 full-time (29 women), 17 part-time (12 women); includes 7 minority (3 Asian, non-Hispanic/Latino; 4 Hispanic/Latino), 4 international. Average age 30. 61 applicants, 20% accepted, 12 enrolled. In 2011, 3 master's, 3

doctorates awarded. *Degree requirements:* For master's, comprehensive exam, thesis, oral defense; for doctorate, comprehensive exam, thesis/dissertation, oral defense. *Entrance requirements:* For master's and doctorate, GRE General Test. Additional exam requirements/recommendations for international students: Required—TOEFL (minimum score 550 paper-based; 213 computer-based; 80 iBT). *Application deadline:* For fall admission, 6/1 for domestic students, 3/1 for international students; for spring admission, 10/15 for domestic students, 8/1 for international students. Applications are processed on a rolling basis. Application fee: $60. Electronic applications accepted. *Expenses:* Tuition, state resident: full-time $6696; part-time $372 per credit. Tuition, nonresident: full-time $13,680; part-time $760 per credit. Tuition and fees vary according to course load and reciprocity agreements. *Financial support:* In 2011–12, 26 research assistantships with tuition reimbursements (averaging $11,484 per year), 7 teaching assistantships with tuition reimbursements (averaging $14,772 per year) were awarded; fellowships with tuition reimbursements, career-related internships or fieldwork, Federal Work-Study, scholarships/grants, health care benefits, and unspecified assistantships also available. Support available to part-time students. Financial award application deadline: 7/1; financial award applicants required to submit FAFSA. *Unit head:* Katrin Iken, Co-Chair, 907-474-7289, Fax: 907-474-5863, E-mail: academics@sfos.uaf.edu. *Application contact:* Christina Neumann, Academic Manager, 907-474-7289, Fax: 907-474-5863, E-mail: clneumann@alaska.edu. Web site: http://www.sfos.uaf.edu/academics/prospective/graduate.html.

The University of Arizona, College of Agriculture and Life Sciences, School of Natural Resources, Program in Wildlife, Fisheries Conservation, and Management, Tucson, AZ 85721. Offers MS, PhD. *Faculty:* 18 full-time (3 women), 4 part-time/adjunct (0 women). *Students:* 3 full-time (0 women), 2 part-time (0 women), 1 international. Average age 42. In 2011, 2 doctorates awarded. *Degree requirements:* For master's, thesis; for doctorate, comprehensive exam, thesis/dissertation. *Entrance requirements:* For master's, GRE General Test, GRE Subject Test (biology), minimum GPA of 3.0, 3 letters of recommendation; for doctorate, GRE General Test, GRE Subject Test (biology), minimum GPA of 3.0, 3 letters of recommendation, MA or MS. Additional exam requirements/recommendations for international students: Required—TOEFL (minimum score 550 paper-based; 213 computer-based). *Application deadline:* For fall admission, 8/1 priority date for domestic students, 12/1 for international students; for spring admission, 7/1 for international students. Applications are processed on a rolling basis. Application fee: $75. *Expenses:* Tuition, state resident: full-time $10,840. Tuition, nonresident: full-time $25,802. *Financial support:* Research assistantships with partial tuition reimbursements, teaching assistantships with partial tuition reimbursements, scholarships/grants, health care benefits, tuition waivers (partial), and unspecified assistantships available. *Faculty research:* Short-term effects of artificial oases on Arizona wildlife, elk response to cattle in northern Arizona, effect of reservoir operation on tailwaters, conservation of wildlife. *Unit head:* Dr. R. William Mannan, Chair, 520-621-7283, E-mail: mannan@ag.arizona.edu. *Application contact:* Cheryl L. Craddock, Academic Coordinator, 520-621-7260, Fax: 520-621-8801, E-mail: ccraddoc@email.arizona.edu. Web site: http://www.ag.arizona.edu/srnr/.

University of Arkansas at Pine Bluff, School of Agriculture, Fisheries and Human Sciences, Pine Bluff, AR 71601-2799. Offers aquaculture and fisheries (MS).

University of Delaware, College of Agriculture and Natural Resources, Department of Entomology and Wildlife Ecology, Newark, DE 19716. Offers entomology and applied ecology (MS, PhD), including avian ecology, evolution and taxonomy, insect biological control, insect ecology and behavior (MS), insect genetics, pest management, plant-insect interactions, wildlife ecology and management. Part-time programs available. *Degree requirements:* For master's, comprehensive exam, thesis, oral exam, seminar; for doctorate, comprehensive exam, thesis/dissertation, qualifying exam, seminar. *Entrance requirements:* For master's, GRE General Test, minimum GPA of 3.0 in field, 2.8 overall; for doctorate, GRE General Test, GRE Subject Test (biology), minimum GPA of 3.0 in field, 2.8 overall. Additional exam requirements/recommendations for international students: Required—TOEFL. Electronic applications accepted. *Faculty research:* Ecology and evolution of plant-insect interactions, ecology of wildlife conservation management, habitat restoration, biological control, applied ecosystem management.

University of Florida, Graduate School, College of Agricultural and Life Sciences, Department of Wildlife Ecology and Conservation, Gainesville, FL 32611. Offers MS, PhD. *Faculty:* 16 full-time (4 women), 1 part-time/adjunct (0 women). *Students:* 38 full-time (19 women), 12 part-time (6 women); includes 10 minority (4 Black or African American, non-Hispanic/Latino; 1 Asian, non-Hispanic/Latino; 5 Hispanic/Latino), 17 international. Average age 31. 45 applicants, 33% accepted, 12 enrolled. In 2011, 10 master's, 3 doctorates awarded. *Degree requirements:* For master's, comprehensive exam, thesis optional; for doctorate, comprehensive exam, thesis/dissertation. *Entrance requirements:* For master's and doctorate, GRE General Test, minimum GPA of 3.3. Additional exam requirements/recommendations for international students: Required—TOEFL (minimum score 550 paper-based; 213 computer-based; 80 iBT), IELTS (minimum score 6). *Application deadline:* For fall admission, 6/1 priority date for domestic students; for spring admission, 12/1 for domestic students. Applications are processed on a rolling basis. Application fee: $30. Electronic applications accepted. *Financial support:* Fellowships, research assistantships, teaching assistantships, and institutionally sponsored loans

516 facebook.com/petersonspublishing

Peterson's Graduate Programs in the Physical Sciences, Mathematics, Agricultural Sciences, the Environment & Natural Resources 2013

available. Financial award applicants required to submit FAFSA. *Faculty research:* Wildlife biology and management, tropical ecology and conservation, conservation biology, landscape ecology and restoration, conservation education. *Unit head:* Dr. John P. Hayes, Department Chair, 352-846-0552, E-mail: hayesj@ufl.edu. *Application contact:* Dr. Wiley Kitchens, Graduate Coordinator, 352-846-0536, Fax: 352-846-0841, E-mail: wiley01@ufl.edu. Web site: http://www.wec.ufl.edu/.

University of Idaho, College of Graduate Studies, College of Natural Resources, Department of Fish and Wildlife Resources, Moscow, ID 83844-1136. Offers natural resources (MS, PhD). *Faculty:* 12 full-time, 1 part-time/adjunct. *Students:* 4 part-time. Average age 28. In 2011, 5 master's, 1 doctorate awarded. *Degree requirements:* For doctorate, thesis/dissertation. *Entrance requirements:* For master's, minimum GPA of 2.8; for doctorate, minimum undergraduate GPA of 2.8, 3.0 graduate. *Application deadline:* For fall admission, 8/1 for domestic students; for spring admission, 12/15 for domestic students. Applications are processed on a rolling basis. Application fee: $60. Electronic applications accepted. *Expenses:* Tuition, state resident: full-time $3874; part-time $334 per credit hour. Tuition, nonresident: full-time $16,394; part-time $861 per credit hour. *Required fees:* $2808; $99 per credit hour. Tuition and fees vary according to program. *Financial support:* Research assistantships and teaching assistantships available. Financial award applicants required to submit FAFSA. *Faculty research:* Waterfowl and wetland ecology, lake restoration and management, sustainable aquaculture production, riparian ecology and river restoration, wildlife ecology and management. *Unit head:* Dr. Kerry Reese, Department Head, 208-885-6434, E-mail: fish_wildlife@uidaho.edu. *Application contact:* Erick Larson, Director of Graduate Admissions, 208-885-4723, E-mail: gadms@uidaho.edu. Web site: http://www.uidaho.edu/cnr/fishwild.

University of Maine, Graduate School, College of Natural Sciences, Forestry, and Agriculture, Department of Wildlife Ecology, Orono, ME 04469. Offers wildlife conservation (MWC); wildlife ecology (MS, PhD). Part-time programs available. *Faculty:* 7 full-time (3 women), 1 (woman) part-time/adjunct. *Students:* 13 full-time (5 women), 5 part-time (2 women); includes 2 minority (1 Asian, non-Hispanic/Latino; 1 Hispanic/Latino), 1 international. Average age 32. 22 applicants, 41% accepted, 6 enrolled. In 2011, 3 master's, 2 doctorates awarded. *Degree requirements:* For master's, thesis (for some programs); for doctorate, one foreign language, thesis/dissertation. *Entrance requirements:* For master's and doctorate, GRE General Test. Additional exam requirements/recommendations for international students: Required—TOEFL. *Application deadline:* For fall admission, 2/1 priority date for domestic students. Applications are processed on a rolling basis. Application fee: $65. Electronic applications accepted. *Expenses:* Tuition, state resident: full-time $5016. Tuition, nonresident: full-time $14,424. *Financial support:* In 2011–12, 19 research assistantships with full tuition reimbursements (averaging $18,500 per year), 2 teaching assistantships with full tuition reimbursements (averaging $13,600 per year) were awarded; career-related internships or fieldwork, Federal Work-Study, institutionally sponsored loans, and tuition waivers (full and partial) also available. Financial award application deadline: 3/1. *Faculty research:* Integration of wildlife and forest management; population dynamics; behavior, physiology and nutrition; wetland ecology and influence of environmental disturbances. *Total annual research expenditures:* $159,122. *Unit head:* Dr. James Gilbert, Chair, 207-581-2872, Fax: 207-581-2858. *Application contact:* Scott G. Delcourt, Associate Dean of the Graduate School, 207-581-3291, Fax: 207-581-3232, E-mail: graduate@maine.edu. Web site: http://www2.umaine.edu/graduate/.

University of Massachusetts Amherst, Graduate School, College of Natural Sciences, Department of Environmental Conservation, Amherst, MA 01003. Offers building systems (MS, PhD); environmental policy and human dimensions (MS, PhD); forest resources (MS, PhD); sustainability science (MS); water, wetlands and watersheds (MS, PhD); wildlife and fisheries conservation (MS, PhD). Part-time programs available. *Faculty:* 57 full-time (10 women). *Students:* 61 full-time (26 women), 34 part-time (13 women); includes 4 minority (1 Black or African American, non-Hispanic/Latino; 2 Hispanic/Latino; 1 Two or more races, non-Hispanic/Latino), 12 international. Average age 32. 84 applicants, 40% accepted, 22 enrolled. In 2011, 1 master's, 2 doctorates awarded. Terminal master's awarded for partial completion of doctoral program. *Degree requirements:* For master's, thesis or alternative; for doctorate, comprehensive exam, thesis/dissertation. *Entrance requirements:* For master's and doctorate, GRE General Test. Additional exam requirements/recommendations for international students: Required—TOEFL (minimum score 550 paper-based; 213 computer-based; 80 iBT), IELTS (minimum score 6.5). *Application deadline:* For fall admission, 2/1 for domestic and international students; for spring admission, 10/1 for domestic and international students. Applications are processed on a rolling basis. Application fee: $50 ($65 for international students). Electronic applications accepted. Tuition and fees vary according to course load, campus/location and program. *Financial support:* Fellowships with full and partial tuition reimbursements, research assistantships with full and partial tuition reimbursements, teaching assistantships with full and partial tuition reimbursements, career-related internships or fieldwork, Federal Work-Study, scholarships/grants, traineeships, health care benefits, tuition waivers (full and partial), and unspecified assistantships available. Support available to part-time students. Financial award application deadline: 2/1. *Unit head:* Dr. Kevin McGarigal, Graduate Program Director, 413-545-2257, Fax: 413-545-4358. *Application contact:* Lindsay DeSantis, Interim Supervisor of Admissions, 413-545-0721, Fax: 413-577-0100, E-mail: gradadm@grad.umass.edu. Web site: http://eco.umass.edu/.

University of Miami, Graduate School, Rosenstiel School of Marine and Atmospheric Science, Division of Marine Biology and Fisheries, Coral Gables, FL 33124. Offers MA, MS, PhD. Terminal master's awarded for partial completion of doctoral program. *Degree requirements:* For master's, comprehensive exam, thesis; for doctorate, comprehensive exam, thesis/dissertation. *Entrance requirements:* For master's and doctorate, GRE General Test. Additional exam requirements/recommendations for international students: Required—TOEFL (minimum score 550 paper-based; 213 computer-based). Electronic applications accepted. *Faculty research:* Biochemistry, physiology, plankton, coral, biology.

University of Missouri, Graduate School, School of Natural Resources, Department of Fisheries and Wildlife, Columbia, MO 65211. Offers conservation biology (Certificate); fisheries and wildlife (MS, PhD). *Faculty:* 10 full-time (1 woman). *Students:* 16 full-time (4 women), 15 part-time (9 women); includes 1 minority (Black or African American, non-Hispanic/Latino), 3 international. Average age 30. 14 applicants, 57% accepted, 6 enrolled. In 2011, 8 master's, 3 doctorates, 2 other advanced degrees awarded. *Degree requirements:* For doctorate, thesis/dissertation. *Entrance requirements:* For master's and doctorate, GRE General Test, minimum GPA of 3.0. Additional exam requirements/recommendations for international students: Required—TOEFL (minimum score 550 paper-based; 213 computer-based; 79 iBT). *Application deadline:* Applications are processed on a rolling basis. Application fee: $55 ($75 for international students). *Expenses:* Tuition, state resident: full-time $5881. Tuition, nonresident: full-time $15,183. *Required fees:* $952. Tuition and fees vary according to campus/location and program. *Financial support:* Fellowships, research assistantships, teaching assistantships, institutionally sponsored loans, and scholarships/grants available. *Faculty research:* Limnology; conservation biology; landscape ecology; natural resource policy and management; rare species conservation; Avian ecology; behavior and conservation; large river ecology; native fish ecology and restoration ecology; wildlife disease ecology; behavioral, population and community ecology; conservation biology; mammalian carnivores; fish bioenergetics; compensatory growth; fish population dynamics and aquaculture; endangered species recovery; wildlife stress physiology. *Unit head:* Dr. Jack Jones, Department Chair, E-mail: jonesj@missouri.edu. *Application contact:* Janice Faaborg, 573-882-9422, E-mail: faaborgj@missouri.edu. Web site: http://www.snr.missouri.edu/fw/academics/graduate-program.php.

The University of Montana, Graduate School, College of Forestry and Conservation, Missoula, MT 59812-0002. Offers ecosystem management (MEM, MS); fish and wildlife biology (PhD); forestry (MS, PhD); recreation management (MS); resource conservation (MS); wildlife biology (MS). *Degree requirements:* For doctorate, thesis/dissertation. *Entrance requirements:* For master's and doctorate, GRE General Test. Additional exam requirements/recommendations for international students: Required—TOEFL (minimum score 575 paper-based; 213 computer-based).

University of New Hampshire, Graduate School, College of Life Sciences and Agriculture, Department of Natural Resources, Durham, NH 03824. Offers environmental conservation (MS); forestry (MS); integrated coastal ecosystem science, policy, management (MS); natural resources (MS); water resources (MS); wildlife (MS). Part-time programs available. *Faculty:* 40 full-time. *Students:* 32 full-time (15 women), 24 part-time (13 women); includes 2 minority (1 Asian, non-Hispanic/Latino; 1 Hispanic/Latino), 1 international. Average age 29. 79 applicants, 49% accepted, 20 enrolled. In 2011, 10 master's awarded. *Degree requirements:* For master's, thesis or alternative. *Entrance requirements:* For master's, GRE General Test. Additional exam requirements/recommendations for international students: Required—TOEFL (minimum score 550 paper-based; 213 computer-based; 80 iBT). *Application deadline:* For fall admission, 6/1 for domestic students, 4/1 for international students; for spring admission, 12/1 for domestic students. Applications are processed on a rolling basis. Application fee: $65. Electronic applications accepted. *Expenses:* Tuition, state resident: full-time $12,360; part-time $687 per credit hour. Tuition, nonresident: full-time $25,680; part-time $1058 per credit hour. *International tuition:* $29,550 full-time. *Required fees:* $1666; $833 per course. $416.50 per semester. Tuition and fees vary according to course load and degree level. *Financial support:* In 2011–12, 35 students received support, including 3 fellowships, 13 research assistantships, 17 teaching assistantships; career-related internships or fieldwork, Federal Work-Study, scholarships/grants, and tuition waivers (full and partial) also available. Support available to part-time students. Financial award application deadline: 2/15. *Unit head:* Dr. Ted Howard, Chairperson, 603-862-2700, E-mail: natural.resources@unh.edu. *Application contact:* Nancy Brown, Administrative Assistant, 603-862-1022, E-mail: natural.resources@unh.edu. Web site: http://www.nre.unh.edu/academics/.

University of North Dakota, Graduate School, College of Arts and Sciences, Department of Biology, Grand Forks, ND 58202. Offers botany (MS, PhD); ecology (MS, PhD); entomology (MS, PhD); environmental biology (MS, PhD); fisheries/wildlife (MS, PhD); genetics (MS, PhD); zoology (MS, PhD). Terminal master's awarded for partial completion of doctoral program. *Degree requirements:* For master's, thesis, final exam; for doctorate, comprehensive exam, thesis/dissertation, final exam. *Entrance requirements:* For master's, GRE General Test, GRE Subject Test, minimum GPA of 3.0; for doctorate, GRE General Test, GRE Subject Test, minimum GPA of 3.5. Additional exam requirements/recommendations for international students: Required—TOEFL (minimum score 550 paper-based; 213 computer-based; 79 iBT), IELTS (minimum score 6.5). Electronic applications accepted. *Faculty research:*

Peterson's Graduate Programs in the Physical Sciences, Mathematics, Agricultural Sciences, the Environment & Natural Resources 2013

facebook.com/petersonspublishing **517**

Fish, Game, and Wildlife Management

Population biology, wildlife ecology, RNA processing, hormonal control of behavior.

University of Rhode Island, Graduate School, College of the Environment and Life Sciences, Department of Fisheries, Animal and Veterinary Science, Kingston, RI 02881. Offers animal health and disease (MS); animal science (MS); aquaculture (MS); aquatic pathology (MS); environmental sciences (PhD), including animal science, aquacultural science, aquatic pathology, fisheries science; fisheries (MS). *Faculty:* 10 full-time (4 women). *Students:* 14 full-time (7 women), 6 part-time (1 woman). In 2011, 5 degrees awarded. *Degree requirements:* For master's, comprehensive exam (for some programs), thesis optional; for doctorate, comprehensive exam, thesis/dissertation. *Entrance requirements:* For master's and doctorate, GRE, 2 letters of recommendation. Additional exam requirements/recommendations for international students: Required—TOEFL (minimum score 550 paper-based; 213 computer-based). *Application deadline:* For fall admission, 7/15 for domestic students, 2/1 for international students; for spring admission, 11/15 for domestic students, 7/15 for international students. Application fee: $65. Electronic applications accepted. *Expenses:* Tuition, state resident: full-time $10,432; part-time $580 per credit hour. Tuition, nonresident: full-time $23,130; part-time $1285 per credit hour. *Required fees:* $1362; $36 per credit hour. $35 per semester. One-time fee: $130. *Financial support:* In 2011–12, 3 research assistantships with full and partial tuition reimbursements (averaging $11,654 per year), 4 teaching assistantships with full and partial tuition reimbursements (averaging $12,214 per year) were awarded. Financial award application deadline: 7/15; financial award applicants required to submit FAFSA. *Unit head:* Dr. David Bengtson, Chair, 401-874-2668, Fax: 401-874-7575, E-mail: bengtson@uri.edu. *Application contact:* Dr. Marta Gomez-Chiarri, Director of Graduate Studies, 401-874-2917, Fax: 401-874-7575, E-mail: gomezchi@uri.edu. Web site: http://www.uri.edu/cels/favs/.

The University of Tennessee, Graduate School, College of Agricultural Sciences and Natural Resources, Department of Forestry, Wildlife, and Fisheries, Program in Wildlife and Fisheries Science, Knoxville, TN 37996. Offers MS. *Degree requirements:* For master's, thesis. *Entrance requirements:* For master's, GRE General Test, minimum GPA of 2.7. Additional exam requirements/recommendations for international students: Required—TOEFL. Electronic applications accepted. *Expenses:* Tuition, state resident: full-time $8332; part-time $464 per credit hour. Tuition, nonresident: full-time $25,174; part-time $1400 per credit hour. *Required fees:* $1162; $56 per credit hour. Tuition and fees vary according to program.

University of Washington, Graduate School, College of the Environment, School of Aquatic and Fishery Sciences, Seattle, WA 98195. Offers MS, PhD. *Degree requirements:* For master's, thesis; for doctorate, thesis/dissertation. *Entrance requirements:* For master's and doctorate, GRE General Test, minimum GPA of 3.0. Additional exam requirements/recommendations for international students: Required—TOEFL. Electronic applications accepted. *Faculty research:* Fish and shellfish ecology, fisheries management, aquatic ecology, conservation biology, genetics.

University of Washington, Graduate School, College of the Environment, School of Forest Resources, Seattle, WA 98195. Offers bioresource science and engineering (MS, PhD); environmental horticulture (MEH); environmental horticulture and urban forestry (MS, PhD); forest ecology (MS, PhD); forest management (MFR); forest soils (MS, PhD); forest systems and bioenergy (MS, PhD); restoration ecology (MS, PhD); social sciences (MS, PhD); sustainable resource management (MS, PhD); wildlife science (MS, PhD); MFR/MAIS; MPA/MS. *Accreditation:* SAF. *Degree requirements:* For master's, thesis (for some programs); for doctorate, comprehensive exam (for some programs), thesis/dissertation. *Entrance requirements:* For master's and doctorate, GRE, minimum GPA of 3.0. Additional exam requirements/recommendations for international students: Required—TOEFL. Electronic applications accepted. *Faculty research:* Ecosystem analysis, silviculture and forest protection, paper science and engineering, environmental horticulture and urban forestry, natural resource policy and economics.

University of Wisconsin–Madison, Graduate School, College of Agricultural and Life Sciences, Department of Forest and Wildlife Ecology, Program in Wildlife Ecology, Madison, WI 53706-1380. Offers MS, PhD. *Expenses:* Tuition, state resident: full-time $10,296; part-time $643.51 per credit. Tuition, nonresident: full-time $24,054; part-time $1503.40 per credit. *Required fees:* $70.06 per credit. Tuition and fees vary according to course load, campus/location, program and reciprocity agreements.

Utah State University, School of Graduate Studies, College of Natural Resources, Department of Watershed Sciences, Logan, UT 84322. Offers ecology (MS, PhD); fisheries biology (MS, PhD); watershed science (MS, PhD). *Degree requirements:* For master's, thesis (for some programs); for doctorate, thesis/dissertation. *Entrance requirements:* For master's and doctorate, GRE General Test, minimum GPA of 3.2. Additional exam requirements/recommendations for international students: Required—TOEFL. Electronic applications accepted. *Faculty research:* Behavior, population ecology, habitat, conservation biology, restoration, aquatic ecology, fisheries management, fluvial geomorphology, remote sensing, conservation biology.

Utah State University, School of Graduate Studies, College of Natural Resources, Department of Wildland Resources, Logan, UT 84322. Offers ecology (MS, PhD); forestry (MS, PhD); range science (MS, PhD); wildlife biology (MS, PhD). Part-time programs available. *Degree requirements:* For master's, thesis; for doctorate, comprehensive exam, thesis/dissertation. *Entrance requirements:* For master's and doctorate, GRE General Test, minimum GPA of 3.0. Additional exam requirements/recommendations for international students: Required—TOEFL. *Faculty research:* Range plant ecophysiology, plant community ecology, ruminant nutrition, population ecology.

Virginia Polytechnic Institute and State University, Graduate School, College of Natural Resources and Environment, Department of Fisheries and Wildlife Sciences, Blacksburg, VA 24061. Offers MS, PhD. *Degree requirements:* For master's, comprehensive exam (for some programs), thesis (for some programs); for doctorate, comprehensive exam (for some programs), thesis/dissertation (for some programs). *Entrance requirements:* For master's and doctorate, GRE. Additional exam requirements/recommendations for international students: Required—TOEFL (minimum score 550 paper-based; 213 computer-based). *Application deadline:* For fall admission, 7/1 for domestic and international students; for spring admission, 12/1 for domestic and international students. Applications are processed on a rolling basis. Application fee: $65. Electronic applications accepted. *Expenses:* Tuition, state resident: full-time $10,048; part-time $558.25 per credit hour. Tuition, nonresident: full-time $19,497; part-time $1083.25 per credit hour. *Required fees:* $405 per semester. Tuition and fees vary according to course load, campus/location and program. *Financial support:* Research assistantships with full tuition reimbursements, teaching assistantships with full tuition reimbursements, career-related internships or fieldwork, Federal Work-Study, scholarships/grants, health care benefits, and unspecified assistantships available. Financial award application deadline: 1/15. *Faculty research:* Fisheries management, wildlife management, wildlife toxicology and physiology, endangered species, computer applications. *Unit head:* Dr. Eric M. Hallerman, Unit Head, 540-231-5573, Fax: 540-231-7580, E-mail: ehallerm@vt.edu. *Application contact:* Steve McMullin, Information Contact, 540-231-8847, Fax: 540-231-7580, E-mail: smcmulli@vt.edu. Web site: http://www.fw.vt.edu/fisheries/.

West Virginia University, Davis College of Agriculture, Forestry and Consumer Sciences, Division of Forestry, Program in Wildlife and Fisheries Resources, Morgantown, WV 26506. Offers MS. Part-time programs available. *Degree requirements:* For master's, comprehensive exam, thesis. *Entrance requirements:* For master's, GRE, minimum GPA of 3.0. Additional exam requirements/recommendations for international students: Required—TOEFL. Electronic applications accepted. *Faculty research:* Managing habitat for game, nongame, and fish; fish ecology; wildlife ecology.

Forestry

Auburn University, Graduate School, School of Forestry and Wildlife Sciences, Auburn University, AL 36849. Offers forest economics (PhD); forestry (MS, PhD); natural resource conservation (MNR); wildlife sciences (MS, PhD). *Accreditation:* SAF. Part-time programs available. *Faculty:* 32 full-time (6 women), 2 part-time/adjunct (0 women). *Students:* 28 full-time (12 women), 36 part-time (15 women), 18 international. Average age 28. 28 applicants, 43% accepted, 10 enrolled. In 2011, 22 master's, 5 doctorates awarded. *Degree requirements:* For master's, thesis (MS); for doctorate, thesis/dissertation. *Entrance requirements:* For master's and doctorate, GRE General Test. *Application deadline:* For fall admission, 7/7 for domestic students; for spring admission, 11/24 for domestic students. Applications are processed on a rolling basis. Application fee: $50 ($60 for international students). Electronic applications accepted. *Expenses:* Tuition, state resident: full-time $7290; part-time $405 per credit hour. Tuition, nonresident: full-time $21,870; part-time $1215 per credit hour. *International*

tuition: $22,000 full-time. *Required fees:* $1402. *Financial support:* Fellowships, research assistantships, teaching assistantships, and Federal Work-Study available. Support available to part-time students. Financial award application deadline: 3/15; financial award applicants required to submit FAFSA. *Faculty research:* Forest nursery management, silviculture and vegetation management, biological processes and ecological relationships, growth and yield of plantations and natural stands, urban forestry, forest taxation, law and policy. *Unit head:* Dr. James P. Shepard, Dean, 334-844-4000, Fax: 334-844-1084, E-mail: brinker@forestry.auburn.edu. *Application contact:* Dr. George Flowers, Dean of the Graduate School, 334-844-2125. Web site: http://www.forestry.auburn.edu/.

California Polytechnic State University, San Luis Obispo, College of Agriculture, Food and Environmental Sciences, Department of Natural Resources Management and Environmental Sciences, San Luis Obispo, CA 93407. Offers

Peterson's Graduate Programs in the Physical Sciences, Mathematics, Agricultural Sciences, the Environment & Natural Resources 2013

forestry sciences (MS). Part-time programs available. *Students:* 2 full-time (0 women), 1 part-time (0 women); includes 1 minority (Hispanic/Latino). Average age 42. 4 applicants, 0% accepted, 0 enrolled. In 2011, 3 master's awarded. *Degree requirements:* For master's, comprehensive exam, thesis. *Entrance requirements:* For master's, minimum GPA of 2.75 in last 90 quarter units of course work. Additional exam requirements/recommendations for international students: Required—TOEFL (minimum score 550 paper-based; 213 computer-based) or IELTS (minimum score 6). *Application deadline:* For fall admission, 4/1 for domestic students, 11/30 for international students; for winter admission, 10/1 for domestic students, 6/30 for international students; for spring admission, 10/1 for domestic students. Applications are processed on a rolling basis. Application fee: $55. Electronic applications accepted. *Expenses:* Tuition, state resident: full-time $6738. Tuition, nonresident: full-time $17,898. *Required fees:* $2449. *Financial support:* Fellowships, research assistantships, career-related internships or fieldwork, Federal Work-Study, institutionally sponsored loans, scholarships/grants, and unspecified assistantships available. Support available to part-time students. Financial award application deadline: 3/2; financial award applicants required to submit FAFSA. *Faculty research:* Hydrology, biometrics, forest health and management, fire science, urban and community forestry. *Unit head:* Dr. Christopher Dicus, Department Head/Graduate Coordinator, 805-756-5104, Fax: 805-756-1402, E-mail: cdicus@calpoly.edu. *Application contact:* Dr. Mark Shelton, Associate Dean/Graduate Coordinator, 805-756-2161, Fax: 805-756-6577, E-mail: mshelton@calpoly.edu. Web site: http://nres.calpoly.edu/.

Clemson University, Graduate School, College of Agriculture, Forestry and Life Sciences, Department of Forestry and Natural Resources, Program in Forest Resources, Clemson, SC 29634. Offers MFR, MS, PhD. Part-time programs available. *Students:* 35 full-time (10 women), 4 part-time (2 women); includes 2 minority (both Two or more races, non-Hispanic/Latino), 7 international. Average age 30. 27 applicants, 78% accepted, 16 enrolled. In 2011, 11 master's, 3 doctorates awarded. *Degree requirements:* For master's, thesis; for doctorate, thesis/dissertation. *Entrance requirements:* For master's, GRE General Test, minimum B average in last 2 years of undergraduate course work; for doctorate, GRE General Test, minimum B average in graduate course work. Additional exam requirements/recommendations for international students: Required—TOEFL, IELTS. *Application deadline:* For fall admission, 3/1 priority date for domestic students, 4/15 for international students; for spring admission, 10/1 for domestic students, 9/15 for international students. Applications are processed on a rolling basis. Application fee: $70 ($80 for international students). Electronic applications accepted. *Expenses:* Contact institution. *Financial support:* In 2011–12, 19 students received support, including 3 fellowships with full and partial tuition reimbursements available (averaging $8,000 per year), 13 research assistantships with partial tuition reimbursements available (averaging $14,977 per year), 6 teaching assistantships with partial tuition reimbursements available (averaging $7,837 per year); career-related internships or fieldwork, institutionally sponsored loans, scholarships/grants, health care benefits, and unspecified assistantships also available. Support available to part-time students. Financial award application deadline: 5/1; financial award applicants required to submit FAFSA. *Faculty research:* Wetlands management, wood technology, forest management, silviculture, economics. *Unit head:* Dr. Patricia Layton, Chair, 864-656-3303, Fax: 864-656-3304, E-mail: playton@clemson.edu. *Application contact:* Dr. David Guynn, Graduate Program Coordinator, 864-656-4830, E-mail: dguynn@clemson.edu. Web site: http://www.clemson.edu/cafls/departments/forestry/.

Colorado State University, Graduate School, Warner College of Natural Resources, Department of Forest and Rangeland Stewardship, Fort Collins, CO 80523-1472. Offers forest sciences (MS, PhD); natural resources stewardship (MNRS); rangeland ecosystem science (MS, PhD); watershed science (MS). Part-time programs available. Postbaccalaureate distance learning degree programs offered (no on-campus study). *Faculty:* 12 full-time (2 women). *Students:* 32 full-time (15 women), 81 part-time (31 women); includes 5 minority (3 American Indian or Alaska Native, non-Hispanic/Latino; 2 Hispanic/Latino), 15 international. Average age 35. 33 applicants, 91% accepted, 27 enrolled. In 2011, 27 master's, 2 doctorates awarded. *Degree requirements:* For master's, thesis (for some programs); for doctorate, comprehensive exam, thesis/dissertation. *Entrance requirements:* For master's, GRE General Test (minimum score 1000 verbal and quantitative), minimum GPA of 3.0, 3 letters of recommendation; for doctorate, GRE General Test (combined minimum score of 1100 on the Verbal and Quantitative sections), minimum GPA of 3.0, 3 letters of recommendation, statement of research interest. Additional exam requirements/recommendations for international students: Required—TOEFL (minimum score 550 paper-based; 213 computer-based; 80 iBT), IELTS (minimum score 6.5). *Application deadline:* For fall admission, 2/15 priority date for domestic students, 2/15 for international students; for spring admission, 7/15 priority date for domestic students, 7/15 for international students. Applications are processed on a rolling basis. Application fee: $50. Electronic applications accepted. *Expenses:* Tuition, state resident: full-time $7992. Tuition, nonresident: full-time $19,592. *Required fees:* $1735; $58 per credit. *Financial support:* In 2011–12, 44 students received support, including 1 fellowship (averaging $19,360 per year), 31 research assistantships with full and partial tuition reimbursements available (averaging $17,090 per year), 12 teaching assistantships with full and partial tuition reimbursements available (averaging $6,607 per year); Federal Work-Study, scholarships/grants, and unspecified assistantships also available. Financial award application deadline: 2/15; financial award applicants required to submit FAFSA. *Faculty research:* Ecology, natural resource management, hydrology, restoration, human

dimensions. *Total annual research expenditures:* $2.9 million. *Unit head:* Dr. Frederick Smith, Interim Department Head, 970-491-7505, Fax: 970-491-6754, E-mail: fwsmith@colostate.edu. *Application contact:* Sonya LeFebre, Coordinator, 970-491-1907, Fax: 970-491-6754, E-mail: sonya.lefebre@colostate.edu. Web site: http://warnercnr.colostate.edu/frws-home/.

Cornell University, Graduate School, Graduate Fields of Agriculture and Life Sciences, Field of Natural Resources, Ithaca, NY 14853-0001. Offers aquatic science (MPS, MS, PhD); environmental management (MPS); fishery science (MPS, MS, PhD); forest science (MPS, MS, PhD); resource policy and management (MPS, MS, PhD); wildlife science (MPS, MS, PhD). *Faculty:* 39 full-time (7 women). *Students:* 52 full-time (21 women); includes 4 minority (1 American Indian or Alaska Native, non-Hispanic/Latino; 1 Asian, non-Hispanic/Latino; 1 Hispanic/Latino; 1 Two or more races, non-Hispanic/Latino), 15 international. Average age 32. 72 applicants, 21% accepted, 11 enrolled. In 2011, 2 master's, 5 doctorates awarded. *Degree requirements:* For master's, thesis (MS), project paper (MPS); for doctorate, comprehensive exam, thesis/dissertation. *Entrance requirements:* For master's and doctorate, GRE General Test, 2 letters of recommendation. Additional exam requirements/recommendations for international students: Required—TOEFL (minimum score 550 paper-based; 213 computer-based; 77 iBT). *Application deadline:* For spring admission, 10/30 for domestic students. Applications are processed on a rolling basis. Application fee: $95. Electronic applications accepted. *Financial support:* In 2011–12, 10 fellowships with full tuition reimbursements, 14 research assistantships with full tuition reimbursements, 28 teaching assistantships with full tuition reimbursements were awarded; institutionally sponsored loans, scholarships/grants, health care benefits, tuition waivers (full and partial), and unspecified assistantships also available. Financial award applicants required to submit FAFSA. *Faculty research:* Ecosystem-level dynamics, systems modeling, conservation biology/management, resource management's human dimensions, biogeochemistry. *Unit head:* Director of Graduate Studies, 607-255-2807, Fax: 607-255-0349. *Application contact:* Graduate Field Assistant, 607-255-2807, Fax: 607-255-0349, E-mail: nrgrad@cornell.edu. Web site: http://www.gradschool.cornell.edu/fields.php?id-54&a-2.

Duke University, Nicholas School of the Environment, Durham, NC 27708-0328. Offers coastal environmental management (MEM); DEL-environmental leadership (MEM); energy and environment (MEM); environmental economics and policy (MEM); environmental health and security (MEM); forest resource management (MF); global environmental change (MEM); resource ecology (MEM); water and air resources (MEM); JD/AM; JD/MEM; JD/MF; MAT/MEM; MBA/MEM; MBA/MF; MEM/MPP; MF/MPP. *Accreditation:* SAF (one or more programs are accredited). Part-time programs available. *Degree requirements:* For master's, thesis. *Entrance requirements:* For master's, GRE General Test, previous course work in biology or ecology, calculus, statistics, and microeconomics; computer familiarity with word processing and data analysis. Additional exam requirements/recommendations for international students: Required—TOEFL (minimum score 550 paper-based; 213 computer-based). Electronic applications accepted. *Expenses:* Contact institution. *Faculty research:* Ecosystem management, conservation ecology, earth systems, risk assessment.

Harvard University, Graduate School of Arts and Sciences, Department of Forestry, Cambridge, MA 02138. Offers forest science (MFS). *Degree requirements:* For master's, thesis. *Entrance requirements:* For master's, GRE General Test, bachelor's degree in biology or forestry. Additional exam requirements/recommendations for international students: Required—TOEFL. *Expenses: Tuition:* Full-time $36,304. *Required fees:* $1186. Full-time tuition and fees vary according to program. *Faculty research:* Forest ecology, planning, and physiology; forest microbiology.

Humboldt State University, Academic Programs, College of Natural Resources and Sciences, Programs in Natural Resources, Arcata, CA 95521-8299. Offers natural resources (MS), including fisheries, forestry, natural resources planning and interpretation, rangeland resources and wildland soils, wastewater utilization, watershed management, wildlife. *Students:* 45 full-time (26 women), 28 part-time (11 women); includes 4 minority (2 Asian, non-Hispanic/Latino; 1 Hispanic/Latino; 1 Two or more races, non-Hispanic/Latino), 1 international. Average age 30. 100 applicants, 22% accepted, 11 enrolled. In 2011, 25 master's awarded. *Degree requirements:* For master's, thesis or alternative. *Entrance requirements:* For master's, GRE, appropriate bachelor's degree, minimum GPA of 2.5, 3 letters of recommendation, resume. Additional exam requirements/recommendations for international students: Required—TOEFL (minimum score 500 paper-based; 173 computer-based). *Application deadline:* For fall admission, 2/1 for domestic and international students; for spring admission, 9/30 for domestic and international students. Applications are processed on a rolling basis. Application fee: $55. *Expenses:* Tuition, state resident: full-time $6734. Tuition, nonresident: full-time $15,662; part-time $372 per credit. *Required fees:* $903. Tuition and fees vary according to program. *Financial support:* Fellowships, career-related internships or fieldwork, and Federal Work-Study available. Support available to part-time students. Financial award application deadline: 3/1; financial award applicants required to submit FAFSA. *Faculty research:* Spotted owl habitat, pre-settlement vegetation, hardwood utilization, tree physiology, fisheries. *Unit head:* Dr. Robert Van Kirk, Coordinator, 707-826-3744, E-mail: rob.vankirk@humboldt.edu. *Application contact:* Julie Tucker, Administrative Support Coordinator, 707-826-3256, E-mail: jlt7002@humboldt.edu. Web site: http://www.humboldt.edu/cnrs/graduate_programs.

Peterson's Graduate Programs in the Physical Sciences, Mathematics, Agricultural Sciences, the Environment & Natural Resources 2013

facebook.com/petersonspublishing **519**

Iowa State University of Science and Technology, Department of Natural Resource Ecology and Management, Ames, IA 50011-3140. Offers forestry (MS, PhD); wildlife ecology (MS). *Entrance requirements:* For master's and doctorate, GRE General Test. Additional exam requirements/recommendations for international students: Required—TOEFL (minimum score 550 paper-based; 79 iBT), IELTS (minimum score 6.5). *Application deadline:* For fall admission, 4/1 priority date for domestic students, 4/1 for international students; for spring admission, 10/1 priority date for domestic students, 10/1 for international students. Application fee: $40 ($90 for international students). Electronic applications accepted. *Unit head:* Dr. Janette Thompson, Director of Graduate Education, 515-294-7400, Fax: 515-294-7406, E-mail: nremgradinfo@iastate.edu. *Application contact:* Kelly Kyle, Director of Graduate Education, 515-294-7400, Fax: 515-294-7406, E-mail: nremgradinfo@iastate.edu. Web site: http://www.nrem.iastate.edu/.

Iowa State University of Science and Technology, Program in Forestry, Ames, IA 50011-3140. Offers MS, PhD. *Entrance requirements:* For master's and doctorate, GRE. Additional exam requirements/recommendations for international students: Required—TOEFL (minimum score 550 paper-based; 79 iBT), IELTS (minimum score 6.5). *Application deadline:* For fall admission, 4/1 for domestic students; for spring admission, 10/1 for domestic students. Electronic applications accepted. *Unit head:* Janette Thompson, Director of Graduate Education, 515-294-7400, Fax: 515-294-7406, E-mail: nremgradinfo@iastate.edu. *Application contact:* Kelly Kyle, Application Contact, 515-294-7400, Fax: 515-294-7406, E-mail: nremgradinfo@iastate.edu. Web site: http://www.nrem.iastate.edu.

Lakehead University, Graduate Studies, Faculty of Natural Resources Management, Thunder Bay, ON P7B 5E1, Canada. Offers forest sciences (PhD); forestry (M Sc F). Part-time programs available. *Degree requirements:* For master's, thesis. *Entrance requirements:* For master's, minimum B average. Additional exam requirements/recommendations for international students: Required—TOEFL. *Faculty research:* Soils, silviculture, wildlife, ecology, genetics.

Louisiana State University and Agricultural and Mechanical College, Graduate School, College of Agriculture, School of Renewable Natural Resources, Baton Rouge, LA 70803. Offers fisheries (MS); forestry (MS, PhD); wildlife (MS); wildlife and fisheries science (PhD). *Faculty:* 31 full-time (5 women). *Students:* 53 full-time (13 women), 11 part-time (2 women); includes 2 minority (both Hispanic/Latino), 16 international. Average age 30. 21 applicants, 33% accepted, 7 enrolled. In 2011, 12 master's, 7 doctorates awarded. *Degree requirements:* For master's, thesis; for doctorate, thesis/dissertation. *Entrance requirements:* For master's, GRE General Test, minimum GPA of 3.0; for doctorate, GRE General Test, MS, minimum GPA of 3.0. Additional exam requirements/recommendations for international students: Required—TOEFL (minimum score 550 paper-based; 213 computer-based; 79 iBT), IELTS (minimum score 6.5). *Application deadline:* For fall admission, 1/25 priority date for domestic students, 5/15 for international students; for spring admission, 10/15 for international students. Applications are processed on a rolling basis. Application fee: $50 ($70 for international students). Electronic applications accepted. *Financial support:* In 2011–12, 61 students received support, including 52 research assistantships with partial tuition reimbursements available (averaging $19,938 per year), 1 teaching assistantship (averaging $22,000 per year); fellowships, Federal Work-Study, institutionally sponsored loans, scholarships/grants, health care benefits, tuition waivers (full and partial), and unspecified assistantships also available. Financial award application deadline: 4/15; financial award applicants required to submit FAFSA. *Faculty research:* Forest biology and management, aquaculture, fisheries biology and ecology, upland and wetlands wildlife. *Total annual research expenditures:* $47,156. *Unit head:* Dr. Allen Rutherford, Director, 225-578-4131, Fax: 225-578-4227, E-mail: druther@lsu.edu. *Application contact:* Dr. William Kelso, Coordinator of Graduate Studies, 225-578-4176, Fax: 225-578-4227, E-mail: wkelso@lsu.edu. Web site: http://www.fwf.lsu.edu/.

McGill University, Faculty of Graduate and Postdoctoral Studies, Faculty of Agricultural and Environmental Sciences, Department of Natural Resource Sciences, Montréal, QC H3A 2T5, Canada. Offers entomology (M Sc, PhD); environmental assessment (M Sc); forest science (M Sc, PhD); microbiology (M Sc, PhD); micrometeorology (M Sc, PhD); neotropical environment (M Sc, PhD); soil science (M Sc, PhD); wildlife biology (M Sc, PhD).

Michigan State University, The Graduate School, College of Agriculture and Natural Resources, Department of Forestry, East Lansing, MI 48824. Offers forestry (MS, PhD); forestry-environmental toxicology (PhD); plant breeding, genetics and biotechnology-forestry (MS, PhD). *Entrance requirements:* Additional exam requirements/recommendations for international students: Required—TOEFL (minimum score 550 paper-based; 213 computer-based), Michigan State University ELT (minimum score 85), Michigan English Language Assessment Battery (minimum score 83). Electronic applications accepted.

Michigan Technological University, Graduate School, School of Forest Resources and Environmental Science, Houghton, MI 49931. Offers applied ecology (MS); forest ecology and management (MS); forest science (PhD); forestry (MF, MS); molecular genetics and biotechnology (MS, PhD). *Accreditation:* SAF. Part-time programs available. *Faculty:* 26 full-time (5 women), 37 part-time/adjunct (13 women). *Students:* 67 full-time (37 women), 18 part-time (8 women), 15 international. Average age 30. 72 applicants, 39% accepted, 24 enrolled. In 2011, 24 degrees awarded. Terminal master's awarded for partial completion of doctoral program. *Degree requirements:* For master's,

comprehensive exam (for some programs), thesis (for some programs); for doctorate, comprehensive exam, thesis/dissertation. *Entrance requirements:* For master's and doctorate, GRE (minimum scores: 500 in verbal, 500 quantitative, 3.5 in analytical), statement of purpose, official transcripts, 3 letters of recommendation, resume/curriculum vitae. Additional exam requirements/recommendations for international students: Required—TOEFL (minimum score 79 iBT) or IELTS. *Application deadline:* Applications are processed on a rolling basis. Electronic applications accepted. *Expenses:* Tuition, state resident: full-time $12,636; part-time $702 per credit. Tuition, nonresident: full-time $12,636; part-time $702 per credit. *Required fees:* $226; $226 per year. *Financial support:* In 2011–12, 78 students received support, including 16 fellowships with full tuition reimbursements available (averaging $6,065 per year), 36 research assistantships with full tuition reimbursements available (averaging $6,065 per year), 2 teaching assistantships with full tuition reimbursements available (averaging $6,065 per year); career-related internships or fieldwork, Federal Work-Study, scholarships/grants, health care benefits, tuition waivers (partial), unspecified assistantships, and cooperative program also available. Financial award applicants required to submit FAFSA. *Faculty research:* Forest molecular genetics and biotechnology, forestry, forest ecology and management, applied ecology, wood science. *Total annual research expenditures:* $5.9 million. *Unit head:* Dr. Terry Sharik, Dean, 906-487-2352, Fax: 906-487-2915. *Application contact:* 906-487-2352, Fax: 906-487-2915. Web site: http://www.mtu.edu/forest/.

Mississippi State University, College of Forest Resources, Department of Forest Products, Mississippi State, MS 39762. Offers forest products (MS); forest resources (PhD), including forest products. *Faculty:* 12 full-time (2 women), 2 part-time/adjunct (0 women). *Students:* 25 full-time (10 women), 2 part-time (0 women); includes 2 minority (1 Asian, non-Hispanic/Latino; 1 Hispanic/Latino), 18 international. Average age 31. 16 applicants, 25% accepted, 3 enrolled. In 2011, 5 master's, 4 doctorates awarded. *Degree requirements:* For master's, thesis optional; for doctorate, comprehensive exam, thesis/dissertation. *Entrance requirements:* For master's, GRE (if undergraduate GPA of last two years less than 3.0); for doctorate, GRE if undergraduate GPA of last two years is below 3.0. Additional exam requirements/recommendations for international students: Required—TOEFL (minimum score 550 paper-based; 213 computer-based; 79 iBT); Recommended—IELTS (minimum score 6.5). *Application deadline:* For fall admission, 7/1 for domestic students, 5/1 for international students; for spring admission, 11/1 for domestic students, 9/1 for international students. Applications are processed on a rolling basis. Application fee: $40. Electronic applications accepted. *Expenses:* Tuition, state resident: full-time $5805; part-time $322.50 per credit hour. Tuition, nonresident: full-time $14,670; part-time $815 per credit hour. *Financial support:* In 2011–12, 21 research assistantships with full tuition reimbursements (averaging $13,220 per year), 1 teaching assistantship with full tuition reimbursement (averaging $12,270 per year) were awarded; Federal Work-Study, institutionally sponsored loans, and unspecified assistantships also available. Financial award application deadline: 4/1; financial award applicants required to submit FAFSA. *Faculty research:* Wood property enhancement and durability, environmental science and chemistry, wood-based composites, primary wood production, furniture manufacturing and management. *Unit head:* Dr. Robin Shmulsky, Department Head, 662-325-2243, Fax: 662-325-8126, E-mail: rshmulsky@cfr.msstate.edu. *Application contact:* Rachel Singleton, Coordinator of Student Services, 662-325-9376, Fax: 662-325-8726, E-mail: rsingleton@cfr.msstate.edu. Web site: http://www.cfr.msstate.edu/forestp/.

Mississippi State University, College of Forest Resources, Department of Forestry, Mississippi State, MS 39762. Offers forest resources (PhD); forestry (MS). Part-time programs available. *Faculty:* 17 full-time (2 women). *Students:* 24 full-time (6 women), 31 part-time (7 women); includes 4 minority (2 Black or African American, non-Hispanic/Latino; 1 Hispanic/Latino; 1 Native Hawaiian or other Pacific Islander, non-Hispanic/Latino), 10 international. Average age 31. 37 applicants, 59% accepted, 16 enrolled. In 2011, 12 master's, 9 doctorates awarded. *Degree requirements:* For master's, thesis optional, comprehensive oral or written exam; for doctorate, comprehensive exam, thesis/dissertation. *Entrance requirements:* For master's, GRE (if undergraduate GPA of last two years less than 3.0), minimum GPA of 2.5; for doctorate, minimum GPA of 3.1 on prior graduate courses. Additional exam requirements/recommendations for international students: Required—TOEFL (minimum score 550 paper-based; 213 computer-based; 79 iBT); Recommended—IELTS (minimum score 6.5). *Application deadline:* For fall admission, 7/1 for domestic students, 5/1 for international students; for spring admission, 11/1 for domestic students, 9/1 for international students. Applications are processed on a rolling basis. Application fee: $40. Electronic applications accepted. *Expenses:* Tuition, state resident: full-time $5805; part-time $322.50 per credit hour. Tuition, nonresident: full-time $14,670; part-time $815 per credit hour. *Financial support:* In 2011–12, 21 research assistantships with full tuition reimbursements (averaging $13,785 per year) were awarded; Federal Work-Study, institutionally sponsored loans, and unspecified assistantships also available. Financial award application deadline: 4/1; financial award applicants required to submit FAFSA. *Faculty research:* Forest hydrology, forest biometry, forest management/economics, forest biology, industrial forest operations. *Unit head:* Dr. Andrew Ezell, Professor/Head/Graduate Coordinator, 662-325-2949, Fax: 662-325-8126, E-mail: aezell@cfr.msstate.edu. *Application contact:* Rachel Singleton, Coordinator, Student Services, 662-325-9376, Fax: 662-325-8726, E-mail: rsingleton@cfr.msstate.edu. Web site: http://www.cfr.msstate.edu/forestry/.

Mississippi State University, College of Forest Resources, Department of Wildlife, Fisheries and Aquaculture, Mississippi State, MS 39762. Offers forest

520 facebook.com/petersonspublishing

Peterson's Graduate Programs in the Physical Sciences, Mathematics, Agricultural Sciences, the Environment & Natural Resources 2013

resources (PhD), including wildlife and fisheries; wildlife and fisheries science (MS). Part-time programs available. *Faculty:* 20 full-time (1 woman), 1 part-time/adjunct (0 women). *Students:* 64 full-time (19 women), 17 part-time (7 women); includes 4 minority (1 Black or African American, non-Hispanic/Latino; 2 Hispanic/Latino; 1 Two or more races, non-Hispanic/Latino), 8 international. Average age 28. 33 applicants, 45% accepted, 15 enrolled. In 2011, 16 master's, 3 doctorates awarded. *Degree requirements:* For master's, thesis, comprehensive oral or written exam; for doctorate, comprehensive exam, thesis/dissertation. *Entrance requirements:* For master's, GRE or minimum GPA of 3.0 on last 60 hours of undergraduate courses, bachelor's degree; for doctorate, GRE or minimum GPA of 3.2 on prior graduate studies, master's degree. Additional exam requirements/recommendations for international students: Required—TOEFL (minimum score 550 paper-based; 213 computer-based; 79 iBT); Recommended—IELTS (minimum score 6.5). *Application deadline:* For fall admission, 7/1 for domestic students, 5/1 for international students; for spring admission, 11/1 for domestic students, 9/1 for international students. Applications are processed on a rolling basis. Application fee: $40. Electronic applications accepted. *Expenses:* Tuition, state resident: full-time $5805; part-time $322.50 per credit hour. Tuition, nonresident: full-time $14,670; part-time $815 per credit hour. *Financial support:* In 2011–12, 56 research assistantships with partial tuition reimbursements (averaging $14,621 per year) were awarded; Federal Work-Study, institutionally sponsored loans, and unspecified assistantships also available. Financial award application deadline: 4/1; financial award applicants required to submit FAFSA. *Faculty research:* Spatial technology, habitat restoration, aquaculture, fisheries, wildlife management. *Unit head:* Dr. Bruce D. Leopold, Department Head and Graduate Coordinator, 662-325-2615, Fax: 662-325-8726, E-mail: bleopold@cfr.msstate.edu. *Application contact:* Dr. Eric Dibble, Professor and Coordinator of Graduate Studies, 662-325-7494, Fax: 662-325-8726, E-mail: edibble@cfr.msstate.edu. Web site: http://www.cfr.msstate.edu/wildlife/index.asp.

North Carolina State University, Graduate School, College of Natural Resources, Department of Forestry and Environmental Resources, Raleigh, NC 27695. Offers MF, MS, PhD. Part-time programs available. *Degree requirements:* For master's, thesis (for some programs), teaching experience; for doctorate, thesis/dissertation, teaching experience. *Entrance requirements:* For master's and doctorate, GRE General Test. Additional exam requirements/recommendations for international students: Required—TOEFL. Electronic applications accepted. *Faculty research:* Forest genetics, forest ecology and silviculture, forest economics/management/policy, international forestry, remote sensing/geographic information systems.

Northern Arizona University, Graduate College, College of Engineering, Forestry and Natural Sciences, School of Forestry, Flagstaff, AZ 86011. Offers forest science (MF, MSF); forestry (PhD). Part-time programs available. *Faculty:* 19 full-time (10 women). *Students:* 37 full-time (19 women), 6 part-time (4 women); includes 3 minority (2 Hispanic/Latino; 1 Two or more races, non-Hispanic/Latino), 1 international. Average age 33. 19 applicants, 74% accepted, 10 enrolled. In 2011, 24 master's, 4 doctorates awarded. *Degree requirements:* For master's, thesis optional; for doctorate, comprehensive exam, thesis/dissertation. *Entrance requirements:* For master's, GRE General Test; for doctorate, GRE General Test. Additional exam requirements/recommendations for international students: Required—TOEFL (minimum score 550 paper-based; 213 computer-based; 80 iBT), IELTS (minimum score 7). *Application deadline:* For fall admission, 3/15 priority date for domestic students, 3/15 for international students; for spring admission, 10/15 priority date for domestic students, 10/15 for international students. Applications are processed on a rolling basis. Application fee: $65. Electronic applications accepted. *Expenses:* Tuition, state resident: full-time $7190; part-time $355 per credit hour. Tuition, nonresident: full-time $18,092; part-time $1005 per credit hour. *Required fees:* $818; $328 per semester. *Financial support:* In 2011–12, 19 research assistantships (averaging $18,996 per year) were awarded; career-related internships or fieldwork, Federal Work-Study, scholarships/grants, traineeships, health care benefits, tuition waivers (full and partial), and unspecified assistantships also available. Financial award applicants required to submit FAFSA. *Faculty research:* Multiresource management, ecology, entomology, recreation, hydrology. *Total annual research expenditures:* $1.4 million. *Unit head:* Dr. James Allen, Chair, 928-523-5894, Fax: 928-523-1080, E-mail: james.allen@nau.edu. *Application contact:* E-mail: forestrygraduatestudies@xdl.nau.edu. Web site: http://nau.edu/cefns/forestry/.

Oklahoma State University, College of Agricultural Science and Natural Resources, Department of Natural Resource Ecology and Management, Stillwater, OK 74078. Offers M Ag, MS, PhD. *Faculty:* 31 full-time (4 women). *Students:* 6 full-time (2 women), 42 part-time (12 women); includes 9 minority (1 Black or African American, non-Hispanic/Latino; 3 American Indian or Alaska Native, non-Hispanic/Latino; 1 Asian, non-Hispanic/Latino; 4 Two or more races, non-Hispanic/Latino), 8 international. Average age 31. 11 applicants, 36% accepted, 3 enrolled. In 2011, 13 master's, 1 doctorate awarded. *Degree requirements:* For master's, comprehensive exam (for some programs), thesis; for doctorate, comprehensive exam, thesis/dissertation. *Entrance requirements:* For master's and doctorate, GRE or GMAT. Additional exam requirements/recommendations for international students: Required—TOEFL (minimum score 550 paper-based; 79 iBT). *Application deadline:* For fall admission, 3/1 for international students; for spring admission, 8/1 for international students. Applications are processed on a rolling basis. Application fee: $40 ($75 for international students). Electronic applications accepted. *Expenses:* Tuition, state resident: full-time $4044; part-time $168.50 per credit hour. Tuition, nonresident: full-time $16,008; part-time $667 per credit hour. *Required fees:* $2122; $88.45

per credit hour. One-time fee: $50. Tuition and fees vary according to course load and campus/location. *Financial support:* In 2011–12, 29 research assistantships (averaging $16,397 per year), 1 teaching assistantship (averaging $17,496 per year) were awarded; career-related internships or fieldwork, Federal Work-Study, scholarships/grants, health care benefits, tuition waivers (partial), and unspecified assistantships also available. Support available to part-time students. Financial award application deadline: 3/1; financial award applicants required to submit FAFSA. *Faculty research:* Forest ecology, upland bird ecology, forest ecophysiology, urban forestry, molecular forest genetics/biotechnology/tree breeding. *Unit head:* Dr. Keith Owens, Head, 405-744-5438, Fax: 405-744-3530. *Application contact:* Dr. Sheryl Tucker, Dean, 405-744-7099, Fax: 405-744-0355, E-mail: grad-i@okstate.edu. Web site: http://nrem.okstate.edu/.

Oregon State University, Graduate School, College of Forestry, Department of Forest Ecosystems and Society, Corvallis, OR 97331. Offers MAIS, MF, MS, PhD. *Accreditation:* SAF (one or more programs are accredited). Part-time programs available. *Degree requirements:* For master's, thesis (for some programs); for doctorate, thesis/dissertation. *Entrance requirements:* For master's and doctorate, GRE General Test, minimum GPA of 3.0 in last 90 hours. Additional exam requirements/recommendations for international students: Required—TOEFL. *Faculty research:* Ecosystem structure and function, nutrient cycling, biotechnology, vegetation management, integrated forest protection.

Oregon State University, Graduate School, College of Forestry, Department of Forest Engineering, Resources and Management, Corvallis, OR 97331. Offers forest engineering (MF, MS); forest hydrology (MF, MS, PhD); forest operations (MF); forest soil science (MF, MS, PhD); timber harvesting (PhD).

Oregon State University, Graduate School, College of Forestry, Department of Wood Science and Engineering, Corvallis, OR 97331. Offers forest products (MAIS, MF, MS, PhD); wood science and technology (MF, MS, PhD). *Accreditation:* SAF (one or more programs are accredited). Part-time programs available. *Degree requirements:* For master's, thesis (for some programs); for doctorate, thesis/dissertation. *Entrance requirements:* For master's and doctorate, GRE General Test, minimum GPA of 3.0 in last 90 hours. Additional exam requirements/recommendations for international students: Required—TOEFL. *Faculty research:* Biodeterioration and preservation, timber engineering, process engineering and control, composite materials science, anatomy, chemistry and physical properties.

Penn State University Park, Graduate School, College of Agricultural Sciences, School of Forest Resources, State College, University Park, PA 16802-1503. Offers forest resources (M Agr, MFR, MS, PhD); wildlife and fisheries science (M Agr, MFR, MS, PhD). *Unit head:* Dr. Bruce A. McPheron, Dean, 814-865-2541, Fax: 814-865-3103, E-mail: bam10@psu.edu. *Application contact:* Cynthia E. Nicosia, Director of Graduate Enrollment Services, 814-865-1834, E-mail: cey1@psu.edu. Web site: http://sfr.psu.edu/.

Purdue University, Graduate School, College of Agriculture, Department of Forestry and Natural Resources, West Lafayette, IN 47907. Offers fisheries and aquatic sciences (MS, MSF, PhD); forest biology (MS, MSF, PhD); natural resource social science (MS, PhD); natural resources social science (MSF); quantitative ecology (MS, MSF, PhD); wildlife science (MS, MSF, PhD); wood products and wood products manufacturing (MS, MSF, PhD). *Faculty:* 26 full-time (3 women), 9 part-time/adjunct (1 woman). *Students:* 67 full-time (31 women), 8 part-time (3 women); includes 3 minority (2 Hispanic/Latino; 1 Two or more races, non-Hispanic/Latino), 17 international. Average age 29. 58 applicants, 16% accepted, 8 enrolled. In 2011, 9 master's, 11 doctorates awarded. *Degree requirements:* For master's, thesis; for doctorate, thesis/dissertation. *Entrance requirements:* For master's and doctorate, GRE General Test with minimum score required: verbal >=50th percentile; Quantitative >= 50th percentile; Analytical writing = 4.0 or greater, minimum undergraduate GPA of 3.2 or equivalent. Additional exam requirements/recommendations for international students: Required—TOEFL (minimum score 550 paper-based; 77 iBT). *Application deadline:* For fall admission, 1/5 for domestic students, 1/15 for international students; for spring admission, 9/15 for domestic and international students. Applications are processed on a rolling basis. Application fee: $60 ($75 for international students). Electronic applications accepted. *Financial support:* In 2011–12, 10 research assistantships (averaging $15,259 per year) were awarded; fellowships, teaching assistantships, career-related internships or fieldwork, and scholarships/grants also available. Support available to part-time students. Financial award application deadline: 1/5; financial award applicants required to submit FAFSA. *Faculty research:* Wildlife management, forest management, forest ecology, forest soils, limnology. *Unit head:* Dr. Robert K. Swihart, Interim Head, 765-494-3590, Fax: 765-494-9461, E-mail: rswihart@purdue.edu. *Application contact:* Kelly J. Garrett, Graduate Secretary, 765-494-3572, Fax: 765-494-9461, E-mail: kgarrett@purdue.edu. Web site: http://www.fnr.purdue.edu/.

Southern Illinois University Carbondale, Graduate School, College of Agriculture, Department of Forestry, Carbondale, IL 62901-4701. Offers MS. Part-time programs available. *Faculty:* 10 full-time (2 women). *Students:* 10 full-time (6 women), 26 part-time (7 women); includes 2 minority (1 Black or African American, non-Hispanic/Latino; 1 Hispanic/Latino), 4 international. Average age 24. 9 applicants, 67% accepted, 5 enrolled. In 2011, 6 master's awarded. *Degree requirements:* For master's, thesis. *Entrance requirements:* For master's, minimum GPA of 2.7. Additional exam requirements/recommendations for international students: Required—TOEFL. *Application deadline:* Applications are

Peterson's Graduate Programs in the Physical Sciences, Mathematics, Agricultural Sciences, the Environment & Natural Resources 2013

facebook.com/petersonspublishing **521**

Forestry

processed on a rolling basis. Application fee: $0. *Financial support:* In 2011–12, 18 students received support, including 3 fellowships with full tuition reimbursements available, 10 research assistantships with full tuition reimbursements available, 3 teaching assistantships with full tuition reimbursements available; career-related internships or fieldwork, Federal Work-Study, institutionally sponsored loans, and tuition waivers (full) also available. Support available to part-time students. *Faculty research:* Forest recreation, forest ecology, remote sensing, forest management and economics. *Unit head:* Dr. John Phelps, Chair, 618-453-3341, E-mail: jphelps@siu.edu. *Application contact:* Patti Cludray, Administrative Clerk, 618-453-3341, E-mail: plc1@siu.edu.

Southern University and Agricultural and Mechanical College, Graduate School, College of Agricultural, Family and Consumer Sciences, Department of Urban Forestry, Baton Rouge, LA 70813. Offers MS. *Degree requirements:* For master's, thesis. *Entrance requirements:* For master's, GRE, minimum GPA of 3.0. Additional exam requirements/recommendations for international students: Required—TOEFL (minimum score 525 paper-based; 193 computer-based). *Faculty research:* Biology of plant pathogen, water resources, plant pathology.

State University of New York College of Environmental Science and Forestry, Department of Environmental and Forest Biology, Syracuse, NY 13210-2779. Offers applied ecology (MPS); chemical ecology (MPS, MS, PhD); conservation biology (MPS, MS, PhD); ecology (MPS, MS, PhD); entomology (MPS, MS, PhD); environmental interpretation (MPS, MS, PhD); environmental physiology (MPS, MS, PhD); fish and wildlife biology and management (MPS, MS, PhD); forest pathology and mycology (MPS, MS, PhD); plant biotechnology (MPS); plant science and biotechnology (MPS, MS, PhD). *Degree requirements:* For master's, thesis (for some programs); for doctorate, comprehensive exam, thesis/dissertation. *Entrance requirements:* For master's and doctorate, GRE General Test, GRE Subject Test, minimum GPA of 3.0. Additional exam requirements/recommendations for international students: Required—TOEFL (minimum score 550 paper-based; 213 computer-based; 80 iBT), IELTS (minimum score 6). *Application deadline:* For fall admission, 2/1 priority date for domestic students, 2/1 for international students; for spring admission, 11/1 priority date for domestic students, 11/1 for international students. Applications are processed on a rolling basis. Application fee: $60. *Expenses:* Tuition, state resident: full-time $8870; part-time $370 per credit hour. Tuition, nonresident: full-time $15,160; part-time $632 per credit hour. *Required fees:* $60; $370 per credit hour. $350 per semester. One-time fee: $85. *Financial support:* Fellowships with full and partial tuition reimbursements, research assistantships with full and partial tuition reimbursements, teaching assistantships with full and partial tuition reimbursements, Federal Work-Study, institutionally sponsored loans, scholarships/grants, health care benefits, and unspecified assistantships available. Financial award application deadline: 6/30. *Faculty research:* Ecology, fish and wildlife biology and management, plant science, entomology. *Total annual research expenditures:* $4.1 million. *Unit head:* Dr. Donald J. Leopold, Chair, 315-470-6760, Fax: 315-470-6934. *Application contact:* Dr. Dudley J. Raynal, Dean, Instruction and Graduate Studies, 315-470-6599, Fax: 315-470-6978, E-mail: esfgrad@esf.edu. Web site: http://www.esf.edu/efb/.

State University of New York College of Environmental Science and Forestry, Department of Forest and Natural Resources Management, Syracuse, NY 13210-2779. Offers ecology and ecosystems (MPS, MS, PhD); economics, governance and human dimensions (MPS, MS, PhD); environmental and natural resources policy (MPS, MS); forest and natural resources management (MPS, MS, PhD); monitoring, analysis and modeling (MPS, MS, PhD). *Accreditation:* SAF. *Degree requirements:* For master's, thesis (for some programs); for doctorate, comprehensive exam, thesis/dissertation. *Entrance requirements:* For master's and doctorate, GRE General Test, minimum GPA of 3.0. Additional exam requirements/recommendations for international students: Required—TOEFL (minimum score 550 paper-based; 213 computer-based; 80 iBT), IELTS (minimum score 6). *Application deadline:* For fall admission, 2/1 priority date for domestic students, 2/1 for international students; for spring admission, 11/1 priority date for domestic students, 11/1 for international students. Applications are processed on a rolling basis. Application fee: $60. *Expenses:* Tuition, state resident: full-time $8870; part-time $370 per credit hour. Tuition, nonresident: full-time $15,160; part-time $632 per credit hour. *Required fees:* $60; $370 per credit hour. $350 per semester. One-time fee: $85. *Financial support:* Fellowships with full and partial tuition reimbursements, research assistantships with full and partial tuition reimbursements, teaching assistantships with full and partial tuition reimbursements, career-related internships or fieldwork, Federal Work-Study, institutionally sponsored loans, scholarships/grants, health care benefits, and unspecified assistantships available. Financial award application deadline: 6/30; financial award applicants required to submit FAFSA. *Faculty research:* Silviculture recreation management, tree improvement, operations management, economics. *Total annual research expenditures:* $2.1 million. *Unit head:* Dr. David Newman, Chair, 315-470-6534, Fax: 315-470-6535. *Application contact:* Dr. Dudley J. Raynal, Dean, Instruction and Graduate Studies, 315-470-6599, Fax: 315-470-6978, E-mail: esfgrad@esf.edu. Web site: http://www.esf.edu/fnrm/.

State University of New York College of Environmental Science and Forestry, Department of Sustainable Construction Management and Engineering, Syracuse, NY 13210-2779. Offers construction management (MPS, MS, PhD); engineered wood products and structures (MPS, MS, PhD); sustainable construction (MPS, MS, PhD); tropical timbers (MPS, MS, PhD); wood anatomy and ultrastructure (MPS, MS, PhD); wood science and technology (MPS, MS, PhD); wood treatments (MPS, MS, PhD). *Degree requirements:* For

master's, thesis (for some programs); for doctorate, comprehensive exam, thesis/dissertation. *Entrance requirements:* For master's and doctorate, GRE General Test, minimum GPA of 3.0. Additional exam requirements/recommendations for international students: Required—TOEFL (minimum score 550 paper-based; 213 computer-based; 80 iBT), IELTS (minimum score 6). *Application deadline:* For fall admission, 2/1 priority date for domestic students, 2/1 for international students; for spring admission, 11/1 priority date for domestic students, 11/1 for international students. Applications are processed on a rolling basis. Application fee: $60. *Expenses:* Tuition, state resident: full-time $8870; part-time $370 per credit hour. Tuition, nonresident: full-time $15,160; part-time $632 per credit hour. *Required fees:* $60; $370 per credit hour. $350 per semester. One-time fee: $85. *Financial support:* Fellowships with full tuition reimbursements, research assistantships with full tuition reimbursements, teaching assistantships with full tuition reimbursements, career-related internships or fieldwork, Federal Work-Study, institutionally sponsored loans, scholarships/grants, health care benefits, and unspecified assistantships available. Financial award application deadline: 6/30; financial award applicants required to submit FAFSA. *Total annual research expenditures:* $160,385. *Unit head:* Dr. Susan E. Anagnost, Chair, 315-470-6880, Fax: 315-470-6879, E-mail: seanagno@esf.edu. *Application contact:* Dr. Dudley J. Raynal, Dean, Instruction and Graduate Studies, 315-470-6599, Fax: 315-470-6879, E-mail: esfgrad@esf.edu. Web site: http://www.esf.edu/scme/.

Stephen F. Austin State University, Graduate School, College of Forestry and Agriculture, Department of Forestry, Nacogdoches, TX 75962. Offers MF, MS, PhD. Part-time programs available. *Degree requirements:* For master's, thesis; for doctorate, thesis/dissertation. *Entrance requirements:* For master's and doctorate, GRE General Test. Additional exam requirements/recommendations for international students: Required—TOEFL. *Faculty research:* Wildlife management, basic plant science, forest recreation, multipurpose land management.

Texas A&M University, College of Agriculture and Life Sciences, Department of Ecosystem Science and Management, College Station, TX 77843. Offers forestry (MS, PhD); rangeland ecology and management (M Agr, MS, PhD). Part-time programs available. *Faculty:* 24. *Students:* 64 full-time (34 women), 34 part-time (16 women); includes 21 minority (3 Black or African American, non-Hispanic/Latino; 3 Asian, non-Hispanic/Latino; 14 Hispanic/Latino; 1 Two or more races, non-Hispanic/Latino), 17 international. Average age 27. In 2011, 8 master's, 4 doctorates awarded. Terminal master's awarded for partial completion of doctoral program. *Degree requirements:* For master's, thesis (for some programs); for doctorate, thesis/dissertation. *Entrance requirements:* For master's and doctorate, GRE General Test. Additional exam requirements/recommendations for international students: Required—TOEFL. *Application deadline:* For fall admission, 3/1 priority date for domestic students; for spring admission, 11/1 priority date for domestic students. Applications are processed on a rolling basis. Application fee: $50 ($75 for international students). Electronic applications accepted. *Expenses:* Tuition, state resident: full-time $5437; part-time $226.55 per credit hour. Tuition, nonresident: full-time $12,949; part-time $539.55 per credit hour. *Required fees:* $2741. *Financial support:* In 2011–12, fellowships with partial tuition reimbursements (averaging $15,000 per year), research assistantships with partial tuition reimbursements (averaging $15,000 per year), teaching assistantships with partial tuition reimbursements (averaging $15,000 per year) were awarded; career-related internships or fieldwork and institutionally sponsored loans also available. Support available to part-time students. Financial award application deadline: 3/1; financial award applicants required to submit FAFSA. *Faculty research:* Expert systems, geographic information systems, economics, biology, genetics. *Unit head:* Dr. Steve Whisenant, Professor and Head, 979-845-5000, Fax: 979-845-6049, E-mail: s-whisenant@tamu.edu. *Application contact:* Dr. Carol Loopstra, Associate Professor, 979-862-2200, Fax: 979-845-6049, E-mail: c-loopstra@tamu.edu. Web site: http://essm.tamu.edu.

Tropical Agriculture Research and Higher Education Center, Graduate School, Turrialba, Costa Rica. Offers agribusiness management (MS); agroforestry systems (PhD); development practices (MS); ecological agriculture (MS); environmental socioeconomics (MS); forestry in tropical and subtropical zones (PhD); integrated watershed management (MS); international sustainable tourism (MS); management and conservation of tropical rainforests and biodiversity (MS); tropical agriculture (PhD); tropical agroforestry (MS). *Entrance requirements:* For master's, GRE, 2 years of related professional experience, letters of recommendation; for doctorate, GRE, 4 letters of recommendation, letter of support from employing organization, master's degree in agronomy, biological sciences, forestry, natural resources or related field. Additional exam requirements/recommendations for international students: Required—TOEFL (minimum score 550 paper-based; 213 computer-based). Electronic applications accepted. *Faculty research:* Biodiversity in fragmented landscapes, ecosystem management, integrated pest management, environmental livestock production, biotechnology carbon balances in diverse land uses.

Université du Québec en Abitibi-Témiscamingue, Graduate Programs, Program in Environmental Sciences, Rouyn-Noranda, QC J9X 5E4, Canada. Offers biology (MS); environmental sciences (PhD); sustainable forest ecosystem management (MS).

Université Laval, Faculty of Forestry, Geography and Geomatics, Department of Wood and Forest Sciences, Programs in Forestry Sciences, Québec, QC G1K 7P4, Canada. Offers M Sc, PhD. Terminal master's awarded for partial completion of doctoral program. *Degree requirements:* For master's, thesis (for some programs); for doctorate, comprehensive exam, thesis/dissertation.

522 facebook.com/petersonspublishing

Peterson's Graduate Programs in the Physical Sciences, Mathematics, Agricultural Sciences, the Environment & Natural Resources 2013

Entrance requirements: For master's and doctorate, knowledge of French. Additional exam requirements/recommendations for international students: Required—TOEIC or TOEFL. Electronic applications accepted.

Université Laval, Faculty of Forestry, Geography and Geomatics, Department of Wood and Forest Sciences, Programs in Wood Sciences, Québec, QC G1K 7P4, Canada. Offers M Sc, PhD. Terminal master's awarded for partial completion of doctoral program. *Degree requirements:* For master's, thesis; for doctorate, comprehensive exam, thesis/dissertation. *Entrance requirements:* For master's and doctorate, knowledge of French. Electronic applications accepted.

Université Laval, Faculty of Forestry, Geography and Geomatics, Program in Agroforestry, Québec, QC G1K 7P4, Canada. Offers M Sc. *Degree requirements:* For master's, thesis (for some programs). *Entrance requirements:* For master's, English exam (comprehension of English), knowledge of French, knowledge of a third language. Electronic applications accepted.

University of Alberta, Faculty of Graduate Studies and Research, Department of Rural Economy, Edmonton, AB T6G 2E1, Canada. Offers agricultural economics (M Ag, M Sc, PhD); forest economics (M Ag, M Sc, PhD); rural sociology (M Ag, M Sc); MBA/M Ag. Part-time programs available. *Degree requirements:* For doctorate, thesis/dissertation. *Entrance requirements:* Additional exam requirements/recommendations for international students: Required—TOEFL. *Faculty research:* Agroforestry, development, extension education, marketing and trade, natural resources and environment, policy, production economics.

The University of Arizona, College of Agriculture and Life Sciences, School of Natural Resources, Watershed Resources Program, Tucson, AZ 85721. Offers MS, PhD. *Students:* 5 full-time (3 women), 3 part-time (0 women); includes 5 minority (3 Hispanic/Latino; 2 Two or more races, non-Hispanic/Latino). Average age 34. In 2011, 3 doctorates awarded. *Degree requirements:* For master's, thesis; for doctorate, comprehensive exam, thesis/dissertation. *Entrance requirements:* For master's, GRE General Test, minimum GPA of 3.0, 3 letters of recommendation; for doctorate, GRE General Test, minimum GPA of 3.0, 3 letters of recommendation, MA or MS. Additional exam requirements/recommendations for international students: Required—TOEFL (minimum score 550 paper-based; 213 computer-based). *Application deadline:* For fall admission, 8/1 priority date for domestic students, 12/1 for international students; for spring admission, 7/1 for international students. Applications are processed on a rolling basis. Application fee: $75. *Expenses:* Tuition, state resident: full-time $10,840. Tuition, nonresident: full-time $25,802. *Financial support:* Research assistantships with partial tuition reimbursements, teaching assistantships with partial tuition reimbursements, career-related internships or fieldwork, scholarships/grants, health care benefits, tuition waivers (partial), and unspecified assistantships available. *Faculty research:* Forest fuel characteristics, prescribed fire, tree ring-fire scar analysis, erosion, sedimentation. *Unit head:* Dr. Joseph G. Hiller, Chair, 520-621-7255, Fax: 520-621-8801, E-mail: jghiller@cals.arizona.edu. *Application contact:* Cheryl L. Craddock, Academic Coordinator, 520-621-7260, Fax: 520-621-8801, E-mail: ccraddoc@email.arizona.edu. Web site: http://www.ag.arizona.edu/srnr/.

University of Arkansas at Monticello, School of Forest Resources, Monticello, AR 71656. Offers MS. Part-time programs available. *Degree requirements:* For master's, comprehensive exam, thesis. *Entrance requirements:* For master's, GRE General Test, minimum GPA of 2.7. Additional exam requirements/recommendations for international students: Required—TOEFL (minimum score 550 paper-based; 213 computer-based). Electronic applications accepted. *Faculty research:* Geographic information systems/remote sensing, forest ecology, wildlife ecology and management.

The University of British Columbia, Faculty of Forestry, Vancouver, BC V6T 1Z1, Canada. Offers M Sc, MA Sc, MF, PhD. Part-time programs available. *Degree requirements:* For master's, thesis (for some programs); for doctorate, comprehensive exam, thesis/dissertation, thesis exam. *Entrance requirements:* Additional exam requirements/recommendations for international students: Required—TOEFL (minimum score 550 paper-based; 213 computer-based; 80 iBT). Electronic applications accepted. *Faculty research:* Forest sciences, forest resources management, forest operations, wood sciences, conservation, forests and society.

University of California, Berkeley, Graduate Division, College of Natural Resources, Department of Environmental Science, Policy, and Management, Berkeley, CA 94720-1500. Offers environmental science, policy, and management (MS, PhD); forestry (MF). Terminal master's awarded for partial completion of doctoral program. *Degree requirements:* For master's, thesis optional; for doctorate, thesis/dissertation, qualifying exam. *Entrance requirements:* For master's and doctorate, GRE General Test, minimum GPA of 3.0, 3 letters of recommendation. Additional exam requirements/recommendations for international students: Required—TOEFL. Electronic applications accepted. *Faculty research:* Biology and ecology of insects; ecosystem function and environmental issues of soils; plant health/interactions from molecular to ecosystem levels; range management and ecology; forest and resource policy, sustainability, and management.

University of Florida, Graduate School, College of Agricultural and Life Sciences, School of Forest Resources and Conservation, Gainesville, FL 32611. Offers MFAS, MFRC, MS, PhD, JD/MFRC, JD/MS, JD/PhD. Part-time and evening/weekend programs available. Postbaccalaureate distance learning degree programs offered. *Faculty:* 39 full-time (6 women), 6 part-time/adjunct (2

women). *Students:* 88 full-time (38 women), 40 part-time (17 women); includes 7 minority (3 Asian, non-Hispanic/Latino; 4 Hispanic/Latino), 27 international. Average age 32. 71 applicants, 45% accepted, 23 enrolled. In 2011, 20 master's, 11 doctorates awarded. Terminal master's awarded for partial completion of doctoral program. *Degree requirements:* For master's, comprehensive exam, thesis optional, project (for MFRC); for doctorate, comprehensive exam, thesis/dissertation. *Entrance requirements:* For master's, GRE General Test (minimum score of 1000), minimum GPA of 3.0; for doctorate, GRE General Test, minimum GPA of 3.25. Additional exam requirements/recommendations for international students: Required—TOEFL (minimum score 550 paper-based; 213 computer-based; 80 iBT), IELTS (minimum score 6). *Application deadline:* For fall admission, 1/3 priority date for domestic students, 1/3 for international students; for spring admission, 8/1 for domestic and international students. Applications are processed on a rolling basis. Application fee: $30. Electronic applications accepted. *Financial support:* Fellowships with full tuition reimbursements, research assistantships with full tuition reimbursements, teaching assistantships with full tuition reimbursements, Federal Work-Study, and institutionally sponsored loans available. Support available to part-time students. Financial award application deadline: 1/3; financial award applicants required to submit FAFSA. *Faculty research:* Forest biology and ecology; natural resource economics and management; human dimensions and resource policy; tropical forestry and agroforestry; geomatics: geospatial, GIS, and remote sensing. *Total annual research expenditures:* $3.4 million. *Unit head:* Dr. Tim White, Director, 352-846-0850, Fax: 352-392-1707, E-mail: tlwhite@ufl.edu. *Application contact:* Dr. Taylor Stein, Graduate Coordinator, 352-846-0860, Fax: 352-846-1277, E-mail: tstein@ufl.edu. Web site: http://www.sfrc.ufl.edu/.

University of Georgia, School of Forestry and Natural Resources, Athens, GA 30602. Offers MFR, MS, PhD. *Faculty:* 46 full-time (6 women), 8 part-time/adjunct (1 woman). *Students:* 162 full-time (73 women), 29 part-time (8 women); includes 9 minority (2 Black or African American, non-Hispanic/Latino; 3 Asian, non-Hispanic/Latino; 2 Hispanic/Latino; 2 Two or more races, non-Hispanic/Latino), 26 international. Average age 29. 104 applicants, 67% accepted, 45 enrolled. In 2011, 47 master's, 12 doctorates awarded. *Degree requirements:* For master's, thesis (MS); for doctorate, one foreign language, thesis/dissertation. *Entrance requirements:* For master's and doctorate, GRE General Test. *Application deadline:* For fall admission, 7/1 priority date for domestic students; for spring admission, 11/15 for domestic students. Application fee: $50. Electronic applications accepted. *Financial support:* Fellowships, research assistantships, teaching assistantships, and unspecified assistantships available. *Unit head:* Michael L. Clutter, Professor, 706-542-4741, Fax: 706-542-8356, E-mail: mclutter@warnell.uga.edu. *Application contact:* Dr. Laurence Schimleck, Graduate Coordinator, 706-542-0464, Fax: 706-542-8356, E-mail: lschimlect@warnell.uga.edu. Web site: http://www.warnell.uga.edu/.

University of Kentucky, Graduate School, College of Agriculture, Program in Forestry, Lexington, KY 40506-0032. Offers MSFOR. *Degree requirements:* For master's, comprehensive exam, thesis optional. *Entrance requirements:* For master's, GRE General Test, minimum undergraduate GPA of 2.75. Additional exam requirements/recommendations for international students: Required—TOEFL (minimum score 550 paper-based; 213 computer-based). Electronic applications accepted. *Faculty research:* Forest ecology, silviculture, watershed management, forest products utilization, wildlife habitat management.

University of Maine, Graduate School, College of Natural Sciences, Forestry, and Agriculture, Department of Forest Management and Forest Ecosystem Science, Orono, ME 04469. Offers forest resources (PhD); forestry (MF, MS). *Accreditation:* SAF (one or more programs are accredited). Part-time programs available. *Faculty:* 20 full-time (1 woman). *Students:* 37 full-time (12 women), 15 part-time (7 women), 13 international. Average age 29. 35 applicants, 57% accepted, 17 enrolled. In 2011, 11 master's, 2 doctorates awarded. *Degree requirements:* For master's, thesis; for doctorate, one foreign language, thesis/dissertation. *Entrance requirements:* For master's and doctorate, GRE General Test. Additional exam requirements/recommendations for international students: Required—TOEFL. *Application deadline:* For fall admission, 2/1 priority date for domestic students. Applications are processed on a rolling basis. Application fee: $65. Electronic applications accepted. *Expenses:* Tuition, state resident: full-time $5016. Tuition, nonresident: full-time $14,424. *Financial support:* In 2011–12, 28 research assistantships with full tuition reimbursements (averaging $20,447 per year), 7 teaching assistantships with full tuition reimbursements (averaging $13,600 per year) were awarded; career-related internships or fieldwork, Federal Work-Study, and institutionally sponsored loans also available. Financial award application deadline: 3/1. *Faculty research:* Forest economics, engineering and operations analysis, biometrics and remote sensing, timber management, wood technology. *Total annual research expenditures:* $336,195. *Unit head:* Dr. Robert Wagner, Chair, 207-581-4737. *Application contact:* Scott G. Delcourt, Associate Dean of the Graduate School, 207-581-3291, Fax: 207-581-3232, E-mail: graduate@maine.edu. Web site: http://www2.umaine.edu/graduate/.

University of Maine, Graduate School, College of Natural Sciences, Forestry, and Agriculture, Department of Plant, Soil, and Environmental Sciences, Orono, ME 04469. Offers biological sciences (PhD); ecology and environmental sciences (MS, PhD); forest resources (PhD); horticulture (MS); plant science (PhD); plant, soil, and environmental sciences (MS); resource utilization (MS). *Faculty:* 9 full-time (3 women), 7 part-time/adjunct (3 women). *Students:* 7 full-time (4 women), 2 part-time (0 women), 2 international. Average age 30. 14 applicants, 50% accepted, 5 enrolled. In 2011, 4 degrees awarded. *Entrance requirements:* For

Peterson's Graduate Programs in the Physical Sciences, Mathematics, Agricultural Sciences, the Environment & Natural Resources 2013

facebook.com/petersonspublishing **523**

master's and doctorate, GRE General Test. Additional exam requirements/recommendations for international students: Required—TOEFL. *Application deadline:* Applications are processed on a rolling basis. Application fee: $65. Electronic applications accepted. *Expenses:* Tuition, state resident: full-time $5016. Tuition, nonresident: full-time $14,424. *Financial support:* In 2011–12, 16 research assistantships with full tuition reimbursements (averaging $17,336 per year), 1 teaching assistantship with full tuition reimbursement (averaging $13,600 per year) were awarded; scholarships/grants, tuition waivers (full and partial), and unspecified assistantships also available. *Total annual research expenditures:* $179,065. *Unit head:* Dr. Gregory Porter, Chair, 207-581-2943, Fax: 207-581-3207. *Application contact:* Scott G. Delcourt, Associate Dean of the Graduate School, 207-581-3291, Fax: 207-581-3232, E-mail: graduate@maine.edu. Web site: http://www2.umaine.edu/graduate/.

University of Massachusetts Amherst, Graduate School, College of Natural Sciences, Department of Environmental Conservation, Amherst, MA 01003. Offers building systems (MS, PhD); environmental policy and human dimensions (MS, PhD); forest resources (MS, PhD); sustainability science (MS); water, wetlands and watersheds (MS, PhD); wildlife and fisheries conservation (MS, PhD). Part-time programs available. *Faculty:* 57 full-time (10 women). *Students:* 61 full-time (26 women), 34 part-time (13 women); includes 4 minority (1 Black or African American, non-Hispanic/Latino; 2 Hispanic/Latino; 1 Two or more races, non-Hispanic/Latino), 12 international. Average age 32. 84 applicants, 40% accepted, 22 enrolled. In 2011, 1 master's, 2 doctorates awarded. Terminal master's awarded for partial completion of doctoral program. *Degree requirements:* For master's, thesis or alternative; for doctorate, comprehensive exam, thesis/dissertation. *Entrance requirements:* For master's and doctorate, GRE General Test. Additional exam requirements/recommendations for international students: Required—TOEFL (minimum score 550 paper-based; 213 computer-based; 80 iBT), IELTS (minimum score 6.5). *Application deadline:* For fall admission, 2/1 for domestic and international students; for spring admission, 10/1 for domestic and international students. Applications are processed on a rolling basis. Application fee: $50 ($65 for international students). Electronic applications accepted. Tuition and fees vary according to course load, campus/location and program. *Financial support:* Fellowships with full and partial tuition reimbursements, research assistantships with full and partial tuition reimbursements, teaching assistantships with full and partial tuition reimbursements, career-related internships or fieldwork, Federal Work-Study, scholarships/grants, traineeships, health care benefits, tuition waivers (full and partial), and unspecified assistantships available. Support available to part-time students. Financial award application deadline: 2/1. *Unit head:* Dr. Kevin McGarigal, Graduate Program Director, 413-545-2257, Fax: 413-545-4358. *Application contact:* Lindsay DeSantis, Interim Supervisor of Admissions, 413-545-0721, Fax: 413-577-0100, E-mail: gradadm@grad.umass.edu. Web site: http://eco.umass.edu/.

University of Missouri, Graduate School, School of Natural Resources, Department of Forestry, Columbia, MO 65211. Offers MS, PhD. *Faculty:* 17 full-time (2 women), 1 part-time/adjunct (0 women). *Students:* 25 full-time (7 women), 10 part-time (3 women); includes 2 minority (both Two or more races, non-Hispanic/Latino), 7 international. Average age 30. 19 applicants, 74% accepted, 12 enrolled. In 2011, 8 master's, 2 doctorates awarded. Terminal master's awarded for partial completion of doctoral program. *Degree requirements:* For master's, thesis; for doctorate, thesis/dissertation. *Entrance requirements:* For master's and doctorate, GRE General Test, minimum GPA of 3.0. Additional exam requirements/recommendations for international students: Required—TOEFL (minimum score 500 paper-based; 173 computer-based; 61 iBT). *Application deadline:* Applications are processed on a rolling basis. Application fee: $55 ($75 for international students). *Expenses:* Tuition, state resident: full-time $5881. Tuition, nonresident: full-time $15,183. *Required fees:* $952. Tuition and fees vary according to campus/location and program. *Financial support:* Fellowships, research assistantships, teaching assistantships, institutionally sponsored loans, and scholarships/grants available. *Faculty research:* Spatial analysis of natural resource-based industries; forest industry corporate responsibility and environmental stewardship programs; consumer preferences for forest products; forest sector economic development; development of improved nut tree cultivars for use in agroforestry-based systems; hardwood tree improvement; tree growth-wood quality interactions; evaluation and development of forest management guidelines to improve forest health, sustainability and value; agroforestry. *Unit head:* Dr. Dave Larsen, Department Chair, 573-882-8835, E-mail: muzikar@missouri.edu. *Application contact:* Laura A. Gilpin, 573-882-7242, E-mail: gilpinl@missouri.edu. Web site: http://www.snr.missouri.edu/forestry/academics/graduate-program.php.

The University of Montana, Graduate School, College of Forestry and Conservation, Missoula, MT 59812-0002. Offers ecosystem management (MEM, MS); fish and wildlife biology (PhD); forestry (MS, PhD); recreation management (MS); resource conservation (MS); wildlife biology (MS). *Degree requirements:* For doctorate, thesis/dissertation. *Entrance requirements:* For master's and doctorate, GRE General Test. Additional exam requirements/recommendations for international students: Required—TOEFL (minimum score 575 paper-based; 213 computer-based).

University of New Brunswick Fredericton, School of Graduate Studies, Faculty of Forestry and Environmental Management, Fredericton, NB E3B 5A3, Canada. Offers ecological foundations of forest management (PhD); environmental management (MEM); forest engineering (M Sc FE, MFE); forest products

marketing (MBA); forest resources (M Sc F, MF, PhD). Part-time programs available. *Faculty:* 22 full-time (3 women), 1 part-time/adjunct (0 women). *Students:* 72 full-time (27 women), 15 part-time (12 women). In 2011, 13 master's, 4 doctorates awarded. *Degree requirements:* For master's, thesis; for doctorate, thesis/dissertation. *Entrance requirements:* For master's and doctorate, minimum GPA of 3.0. Additional exam requirements/recommendations for international students: Required—TWE (minimum score 4), TOEFL (minimum score 580 paper-based) or IELTS. *Application deadline:* For fall admission, 3/1 priority date for domestic students. Application fee: $50 Canadian dollars. Electronic applications accepted. *Financial support:* In 2011–12, 55 fellowships, 34 teaching assistantships were awarded. *Faculty research:* Forest machines, soils, and ecosystems; integrated forest management; forest meteorology; wood engineering; stream ecosystems dynamics; forest and natural resources policy; forest operations planning; wood technology and mechanics; forest road construction and engineering; forest, wildlife, insect, bird, and fire ecology; remote sensing; insect impacts; Silviculture; LiDAR analytics; integrated pest management; forest tree genetics; genetic resource conservation and sustainable management. *Unit head:* Dr. John Kershaw, Director of Graduate Studies, 506-453-4933, Fax: 506-453-3538, E-mail: kershaw@unb.ca. *Application contact:* Faith Sharpe, Graduate Secretary, 506-458-7520, Fax: 506-453-3538, E-mail: fsharpe@unb.ca. Web site: http://www.unb.ca/fredericton/forestry/.

University of New Hampshire, Graduate School, College of Life Sciences and Agriculture, Department of Natural Resources, Durham, NH 03824. Offers environmental conservation (MS); forestry (MS); integrated coastal ecosystem science, policy, management (MS); natural resources (MS); water resources (MS); wildlife (MS). Part-time programs available. *Faculty:* 40 full-time. *Students:* 32 full-time (15 women), 24 part-time (13 women); includes 2 minority (1 Asian, non-Hispanic/Latino; 1 Hispanic/Latino), 1 international. Average age 29. 79 applicants, 49% accepted, 20 enrolled. In 2011, 10 master's awarded. *Degree requirements:* For master's, thesis or alternative. *Entrance requirements:* For master's, GRE General Test. Additional exam requirements/recommendations for international students: Required—TOEFL (minimum score 550 paper-based; 213 computer-based; 80 iBT). *Application deadline:* For fall admission, 6/1 for domestic students, 4/1 for international students; for spring admission, 12/1 for domestic students. Applications are processed on a rolling basis. Application fee: $65. Electronic applications accepted. *Expenses:* Tuition, state resident: full-time $12,360; part-time $687 per credit hour. Tuition, nonresident: full-time $25,680; part-time $1058 per credit hour. *International tuition:* $29,550 full-time. *Required fees:* $1666; $833 per course. $416.50 per semester. Tuition and fees vary according to course load and degree level. *Financial support:* In 2011–12, 35 students received support, including 3 fellowships, 13 research assistantships, 17 teaching assistantships; career-related internships or fieldwork, Federal Work-Study, scholarships/grants, and tuition waivers (full and partial) also available. Support available to part-time students. Financial award application deadline: 2/15. *Unit head:* Dr. Ted Howard, Chairperson, 603-862-2700, E-mail: natural.resources@unh.edu. *Application contact:* Nancy Brown, Administrative Assistant, 603-862-1022, E-mail: natural.resources@unh.edu. Web site: http://www.nre.unh.edu/academics/.

The University of Tennessee, Graduate School, College of Agricultural Sciences and Natural Resources, Department of Forestry, Wildlife, and Fisheries, Program in Forestry, Knoxville, TN 37996. Offers MS. *Degree requirements:* For master's, thesis or alternative. *Entrance requirements:* For master's, GRE General Test, minimum GPA of 2.7. Additional exam requirements/recommendations for international students: Required—TOEFL. Electronic applications accepted. *Expenses:* Tuition, state resident: full-time $8332; part-time $464 per credit hour. Tuition, nonresident: full-time $25,174; part-time $1400 per credit hour. *Required fees:* $1162; $56 per credit hour. Tuition and fees vary according to program.

University of Toronto, School of Graduate Studies, Faculty of Forestry, Toronto, ON M5S 1A1, Canada. Offers M Sc F, MFC, PhD. *Degree requirements:* For master's, comprehensive exam, thesis, oral thesis/research paper defense; for doctorate, thesis/dissertation, oral defense of thesis. *Entrance requirements:* For master's, bachelor's degree in a related area, minimum B average in final year (M Sc F), final 2 years (MFC); resume, 3 letters of reference; for doctorate, writing sample, minimum A average, master's in a related area, 3 letters of reference, resume. Additional exam requirements/recommendations for international students: Required—TOEFL (minimum score 580 paper-based; 93 iBT), TWE (minimum score 5). Electronic applications accepted.

University of Vermont, Graduate College, The Rubenstein School of Environment and Natural Resources, Program in Natural Resources, Burlington, VT 05405. Offers natural resources (MS, PhD), including aquatic ecology and watershed science (MS), environment thought and culture (MS), environment, science and public affairs (MS), forestry (MS). *Students:* 104 (58 women); includes 10 minority (1 Black or African American, non-Hispanic/Latino; 2 American Indian or Alaska Native, non-Hispanic/Latino; 5 Asian, non-Hispanic/Latino; 2 Hispanic/Latino), 2 international. 148 applicants, 28% accepted, 19 enrolled. In 2011, 19 master's, 6 doctorates awarded. *Degree requirements:* For master's, thesis or alternative; for doctorate, thesis/dissertation. *Entrance requirements:* For master's and doctorate, GRE General Test. Additional exam requirements/recommendations for international students: Required—TOEFL (minimum score 550 paper-based; 213 computer-based; 80 iBT). *Application deadline:* For fall admission, 3/1 priority date for domestic students, 3/1 for international students. Applications are processed on a rolling basis. Application fee: $40. Electronic applications accepted. *Financial support:* Fellowships,

524 facebook.com/petersonspublishing

Peterson's Graduate Programs in the Physical Sciences, Mathematics, Agricultural Sciences, the Environment & Natural Resources 2013

research assistantships, and teaching assistantships available. Financial award application deadline: 3/1. *Unit head:* Clare Ginger, Chair, 802-656-2620. *Application contact:* Kimberly Wallin, Coordinator, 802-656-2620.

University of Washington, Graduate School, College of the Environment, School of Forest Resources, Seattle, WA 98195. Offers bioresource science and engineering (MS, PhD); environmental horticulture (MEH); environmental horticulture and urban forestry (MS, PhD); forest ecology (MS, PhD); forest management (MFR); forest soils (MS, PhD); forest systems and bioenergy (MS, PhD); restoration ecology (MS, PhD); social sciences (MS, PhD); sustainable resource management (MS, PhD); wildlife science (MS, PhD); MFR/MAIS; MPA/ MS. *Accreditation:* SAF. *Degree requirements:* For master's, thesis (for some programs); for doctorate, comprehensive exam (for some programs), thesis/ dissertation. *Entrance requirements:* For master's and doctorate, GRE, minimum GPA of 3.0. Additional exam requirements/recommendations for international students: Required—TOEFL. Electronic applications accepted. *Faculty research:* Ecosystem analysis, silviculture and forest protection, paper science and engineering, environmental horticulture and urban forestry, natural resource policy and economics.

University of Wisconsin–Madison, Graduate School, College of Agricultural and Life Sciences, Department of Forest and Wildlife Ecology, Program in Forestry, Madison, WI 53706-1380. Offers MS, PhD. *Expenses:* Tuition, state resident: full-time $10,296; part-time $643.51 per credit. Tuition, nonresident: full-time $24,054; part-time $1503.40 per credit. *Required fees:* $70.06 per credit. Tuition and fees vary according to course load, campus/location, program and reciprocity agreements.

Utah State University, School of Graduate Studies, College of Natural Resources, Department of Wildland Resources, Logan, UT 84322. Offers ecology (MS, PhD); forestry (MS, PhD); range science (MS, PhD); wildlife biology (MS, PhD). Part-time programs available. *Degree requirements:* For master's, thesis; for doctorate, comprehensive exam, thesis/dissertation. *Entrance requirements:* For master's and doctorate, GRE General Test, minimum GPA of 3.0. Additional exam requirements/recommendations for international students: Required— TOEFL. *Faculty research:* Range plant ecophysiology, plant community ecology, ruminant nutrition, population ecology.

Virginia Polytechnic Institute and State University, Graduate School, College of Natural Resources and Environment, Department of Forestry, Blacksburg, VA 24061. Offers forestry (MS, PhD); watershed management (Certificate). *Degree requirements:* For master's, comprehensive exam (for some programs), thesis (for some programs); for doctorate, comprehensive exam (for some programs), thesis/ dissertation (for some programs). *Entrance requirements:* For master's and doctorate, GRE. Additional exam requirements/recommendations for international students: Required—TOEFL (minimum score 550 paper-based; 213 computer-based). *Application deadline:* For fall admission, 7/1 for domestic and international students; for spring admission, 12/1 for domestic and international students. Applications are processed on a rolling basis. Application fee: $65. Electronic applications accepted. *Expenses:* Tuition, state resident: full-time $10,048; part-time $558.25 per credit hour. Tuition, nonresident: full-time $19,497; part-time $1083.25 per credit hour. *Required fees:* $405 per semester. Tuition and fees vary according to course load, campus/location and program. *Financial support:* Research assistantships with full tuition reimbursements, teaching assistantships with full tuition reimbursements, career-related internships or fieldwork, Federal Work-Study, scholarships/grants, health care benefits, and unspecified assistantships available. Financial award application deadline: 1/15. *Unit head:* Dr. Janaki Alavalapati, Unit Head, 540-231-5676, Fax: 540-231-3698, E-mail: jrra@vt.edu. *Application contact:* Peggy Quarterman, Information Contact, 540-231-5481, E-mail: pquarter@vt.edu. Web site: http://www.fw.vt.edu/forestry/.

Virginia Polytechnic Institute and State University, Graduate School, College of Natural Resources and Environment, Department of Wood Science and Forest Products, Blacksburg, VA 24061. Offers MF, MS, PhD. *Degree requirements:* For master's, comprehensive exam (for some programs), thesis (for some programs); for doctorate, comprehensive exam (for some programs), thesis/dissertation (for some programs). *Entrance requirements:* For master's and doctorate, GRE. Additional exam requirements/recommendations for international students: Required—TOEFL (minimum score 550 paper-based; 213 computer-based). *Application deadline:* For fall admission, 7/1 for domestic and international students; for spring admission, 12/1 for domestic and international students. Applications are processed on a rolling basis. Application fee: $65. Electronic applications accepted. *Expenses:* Tuition, state resident: full-time $10,048; part-time $558.25 per credit hour. Tuition, nonresident: full-time $19,497; part-time $1083.25 per credit hour. *Required fees:* $405 per semester. Tuition and fees vary according to course load, campus/location and program. *Financial support:* Research assistantships with full tuition reimbursements, teaching assistantships with full tuition reimbursements, career-related internships or fieldwork, Federal Work-Study, scholarships/grants, health care benefits, and unspecified assistantships available. Financial award application deadline: 1/15. *Faculty research:* Wood chemistry, wood engineering, wood composites, wood processing, forest products marketing/management, recycling. *Unit head:* Dr. Barry M. Goodell, Unit Head, 540-231-8854, Fax: 540-231-8176, E-mail: goodell@vt.edu. *Application contact:* Debbie Garnand, Information Contact, 540-231-8853, Fax: 540-231-8176, E-mail: garnandd@vt.edu. Web site: http:// sbio.vt.edu/.

West Virginia University, Davis College of Agriculture, Forestry and Consumer Sciences, Division of Forestry, Program in Forest Resource Science, Morgantown, WV 26506. Offers PhD. *Degree requirements:* For doctorate, comprehensive exam, thesis/dissertation. *Entrance requirements:* For doctorate, GRE, minimum GPA of 3.0. Additional exam requirements/recommendations for international students: Required—TOEFL. *Faculty research:* Impact of management on wildlife and fish, forest sampling designs, forest economics and policy, oak regeneration.

West Virginia University, Davis College of Agriculture, Forestry and Consumer Sciences, Division of Forestry, Program in Forestry, Morgantown, WV 26506. Offers MSF. *Degree requirements:* For master's, thesis. *Entrance requirements:* For master's, GRE, minimum GPA of 3.0. Additional exam requirements/ recommendations for international students: Required—TOEFL. *Faculty research:* Health and productivity on Appalachian forests, wood industries in Appalachian forests, role of forestry in regional economics.

Yale University, Graduate School of Arts and Sciences, Department of Forestry and Environmental Studies, New Haven, CT 06520. Offers environmental sciences (PhD); forestry (PhD). *Degree requirements:* For doctorate, thesis/ dissertation. *Entrance requirements:* For doctorate, GRE General Test.

Yale University, School of Forestry and Environmental Studies, New Haven, CT 06511. Offers MEM, MES, MF, MFS, PhD, JD/MEM, MBA/MEM, MBA/MF, MEM/ M Arch, MEM/MA, MEM/MPH, MF/MA. *Accreditation:* SAF (one or more programs are accredited). Part-time programs available. Terminal master's awarded for partial completion of doctoral program. *Degree requirements:* For master's, thesis (for some programs); for doctorate, thesis/dissertation. *Entrance requirements:* For master's, GRE General Test, GMAT or LSAT; for doctorate, GRE General Test. Additional exam requirements/recommendations for international students: Required—TOEFL (minimum score 600 paper-based; 250 computer-based; 100 iBT). Electronic applications accepted. *Expenses:* Contact institution. *Faculty research:* Environmental policy, social ecology, industrial environmental management, forestry, environmental health, urban ecology, water science policy.

Natural Resources

American University, School of International Service, Washington, DC 20016-8071. Offers comparative and international disability policy (MA); comparative and regional studies (Certificate); cross-cultural communication (Certificate); development management (MS); ethics, peace, and global affairs (MA); European studies (Certificate); global environmental policy (MA, Certificate); global information technology (Certificate); international affairs (MA), including comparative and international disability policy, comparative and regional studies, international economic relations, international politics, natural resources and sustainable development, U.S. foreign policy; international communication (MA, Certificate); international development (MA, Certificate); international economic policy (Certificate); international economic relations (Certificate); international media (MA); international peace and conflict resolution (MA, Certificate); international politics (Certificate); international relations (PhD); international service (MIS); peacebuilding (Certificate); social enterprise (MA); the Americas (Certificate); United States foreign policy (Certificate); JD/MA. Part-time and evening/weekend programs available. Postbaccalaureate distance learning degree programs offered (no on-campus study). *Faculty:* 108 full-time (45 women), 51 part-time/adjunct (23 women). *Students:* 595 full-time (375 women),

399 part-time (243 women); includes 201 minority (64 Black or African American, non-Hispanic/Latino; 6 American Indian or Alaska Native, non-Hispanic/Latino; 53 Asian, non-Hispanic/Latino; 66 Hispanic/Latino; 12 Two or more races, non-Hispanic/Latino), 153 international. Average age 27. 2,096 applicants, 63% accepted, 370 enrolled. In 2011, 331 master's, 2 doctorates, 2 other advanced degrees awarded. Terminal master's awarded for partial completion of doctoral program. *Degree requirements:* For master's, one foreign language, comprehensive exam, thesis or alternative; for doctorate, one foreign language, comprehensive exam, thesis/dissertation, research practicum; for Certificate, minimum 15 credit hours related course work. *Entrance requirements:* For master's, GRE, 24 credits of course work in related social sciences, minimum GPA of 3.5, 2 letters of recommendation, bachelor's degree, resume, statement of purpose; for doctorate, GRE, 3 letters of recommendation, 24 credits in related social sciences; for Certificate, bachelor's degree. Additional exam requirements/ recommendations for international students: Required—TOEFL (minimum score 600 paper-based; 250 computer-based; 100 iBT). *Application deadline:* For fall admission, 1/15 priority date for domestic students; for spring admission, 10/1 priority date for domestic students. Applications are processed on a rolling basis.

Peterson's Graduate Programs in the Physical Sciences, Mathematics, Agricultural Sciences, the Environment & Natural Resources 2013

facebook.com/petersonspublishing **525**

Application fee: $50. *Expenses: Tuition:* Full-time $24,264; part-time $1348 per credit hour. *Required fees:* $430. Tuition and fees vary according to course load and program. *Financial support:* Fellowships with partial tuition reimbursements, research assistantships with partial tuition reimbursements, teaching assistantships with partial tuition reimbursements, career-related internships or fieldwork, Federal Work-Study, institutionally sponsored loans, and scholarships/grants available. Financial award application deadline: 1/15. *Faculty research:* International intellectual property, international environmental issues, international law and legal order, international telecommunications/technology, international sustainable development. *Unit head:* Dr. James Goldgeier, Dean, 202-885-1603, Fax: 202-885-2494, E-mail: goldgeier@american.edu. *Application contact:* Amanda Taylor, Director of Graduate Admissions and Financial Aid, 202-885-2496, Fax: 202-885-1109, E-mail: ataylor@american.edu. Web site: http://www.american.edu/sis/.

Auburn University, Graduate School, School of Forestry and Wildlife Sciences, Auburn University, AL 36849. Offers forest economics (PhD); forestry (MS, PhD); natural resource conservation (MNR); wildlife sciences (MS, PhD). *Accreditation:* SAF. Part-time programs available. *Faculty:* 32 full-time (6 women), 2 part-time/adjunct (0 women). *Students:* 28 full-time (12 women), 36 part-time (15 women), 18 international. Average age 28. 28 applicants, 43% accepted, 10 enrolled. In 2011, 22 master's, 5 doctorates awarded. *Degree requirements:* For master's, thesis (MS); for doctorate, thesis/dissertation. *Entrance requirements:* For master's and doctorate, GRE General Test. *Application deadline:* For fall admission, 7/7 for domestic students; for spring admission, 11/24 for domestic students. Applications are processed on a rolling basis. Application fee: $50 ($60 for international students). Electronic applications accepted. *Expenses:* Tuition, state resident: full-time $7290; part-time $405 per credit hour. Tuition, nonresident: full-time $21,870; part-time $1215 per credit hour. *International tuition:* $22,000 full-time. *Required fees:* $1402. *Financial support:* Fellowships, research assistantships, teaching assistantships, and Federal Work-Study available. Support available to part-time students. Financial award application deadline: 3/15; financial award applicants required to submit FAFSA. *Faculty research:* Forest nursery management, silviculture and vegetation management, biological processes and ecological relationships, growth and yield of plantations and natural stands, urban forestry, forest taxation, law and policy. *Unit head:* Dr. James P. Shepard, Dean, 334-844-4000, Fax: 334-844-1084, E-mail: brinker@forestry.auburn.edu. *Application contact:* Dr. George Flowers, Dean of the Graduate School, 334-844-2125. Web site: http://www.forestry.auburn.edu/.

Ball State University, Graduate School, College of Sciences and Humanities, Department of Natural Resources, Muncie, IN 47306-1099. Offers MA, MS. *Faculty:* 8 full-time (2 women), 1 (woman) part-time/adjunct. *Students:* 14 full-time (10 women), 7 part-time (5 women); includes 1 minority (Hispanic/Latino). Average age 25. 24 applicants, 75% accepted, 10 enrolled. In 2011, 1 master's awarded. *Entrance requirements:* For master's, GRE General Test. Application fee: $50. Tuition and fees vary according to program and reciprocity agreements. *Financial support:* In 2011–12, 15 students received support, including 14 teaching assistantships with full tuition reimbursements available (averaging $9,334 per year); research assistantships with full tuition reimbursements available and career-related internships or fieldwork also available. Financial award application deadline: 3/1. *Faculty research:* Acid rain, indoor air pollution, land reclamation. *Unit head:* Dr. James Eflin, Chairman, 765-285-5780, Fax: 765-285-2606. *Application contact:* Dr. Robert Morris, Associate Provost for Research and Dean of the Graduate School, 765-285-1300, E-mail: rmorris@bsu.edu. Web site: http://www.bsu.edu/nrem/.

California Polytechnic State University, San Luis Obispo, College of Agriculture, Food and Environmental Sciences, Department of Natural Resources Management and Environmental Sciences, San Luis Obispo, CA 93407. Offers forestry sciences (MS). Part-time programs available. *Students:* 2 full-time (0 women), 1 part-time (0 women); includes 1 minority (Hispanic/Latino). Average age 42. 4 applicants, 0% accepted, 0 enrolled. In 2011, 3 master's awarded. *Degree requirements:* For master's, comprehensive exam, thesis. *Entrance requirements:* For master's, minimum GPA of 2.75 in last 90 quarter units of course work. Additional exam requirements/recommendations for international students: Required—TOEFL (minimum score 550 paper-based; 213 computer-based) or IELTS (minimum score 6). *Application deadline:* For fall admission, 4/1 for domestic students, 11/30 for international students; for winter admission, 10/1 for domestic students, 6/30 for international students; for spring admission, 10/1 for domestic students. Applications are processed on a rolling basis. Application fee: $55. Electronic applications accepted. *Expenses:* Tuition, state resident: full-time $6738. Tuition, nonresident: full-time $17,898. *Required fees:* $2449. *Financial support:* Fellowships, research assistantships, career-related internships or fieldwork, Federal Work-Study, institutionally sponsored loans, scholarships/grants, and unspecified assistantships available. Support available to part-time students. Financial award application deadline: 3/2; financial award applicants required to submit FAFSA. *Faculty research:* Hydrology, biometrics, forest health and management, fire science, urban and community forestry. *Unit head:* Dr. Christopher Dicus, Department Head/Graduate Coordinator, 805-756-5104, Fax: 805-756-1402, E-mail: cdicus@calpoly.edu. *Application contact:* Dr. Mark Shelton, Associate Dean/Graduate Coordinator, 805-756-2161, Fax: 805-756-6577, E-mail: mshelton@calpoly.edu. Web site: http://nres.calpoly.edu/.

Central Washington University, Graduate Studies and Research, College of the Sciences, Program in Resource Management, Ellensburg, WA 98926. Offers MS. *Faculty:* 26 full-time (7 women). *Students:* 34 full-time (17 women), 19 part-time (10 women); includes 9 minority (8 American Indian or Alaska Native, non-Hispanic/Latino; 1 Asian, non-Hispanic/Latino). 41 applicants, 66% accepted, 27 enrolled. In 2011, 20 master's awarded. *Degree requirements:* For master's, thesis. *Entrance requirements:* For master's, minimum GPA of 3.0. Additional exam requirements/recommendations for international students: Required—TOEFL (minimum score 550 paper-based; 213 computer-based; 79 iBT). *Application deadline:* For fall admission, 2/1 priority date for domestic students; for spring admission, 1/1 for domestic students. Applications are processed on a rolling basis. Application fee: $50. Electronic applications accepted. *Expenses:* Tuition, state resident: full-time $8112; part-time $270 per credit. Tuition, nonresident: full-time $18,069; part-time $602 per credit. *Required fees:* $924. *Financial support:* In 2011–12, 6 research assistantships with full and partial tuition reimbursements (averaging $9,234 per year), 14 teaching assistantships with full and partial tuition reimbursements (averaging $9,234 per year) were awarded; career-related internships or fieldwork, Federal Work-Study, health care benefits, and unspecified assistantships also available. Financial award application deadline: 3/1; financial award applicants required to submit FAFSA. *Unit head:* Dr. Karl Lillquist, Co-Director, 509-963-1188, Fax: 509-963-3224, E-mail: lillquis@cwu.edu. *Application contact:* Justine Eason, Admissions Program Coordinator, 509-963-3103, Fax: 509-963-1799, E-mail: masters@cwu.edu.

Colorado State University, Graduate School, Warner College of Natural Resources, Department of Forest and Rangeland Stewardship, Fort Collins, CO 80523-1472. Offers forest sciences (MS, PhD); natural resources stewardship (MNRS); rangeland ecosystem science (MS, PhD); watershed science (MS). Part-time programs available. Postbaccalaureate distance learning degree programs offered (no on-campus study). *Faculty:* 12 full-time (2 women). *Students:* 32 full-time (15 women), 81 part-time (31 women); includes 5 minority (3 American Indian or Alaska Native, non-Hispanic/Latino; 2 Hispanic/Latino), 15 international. Average age 35. 33 applicants, 91% accepted, 27 enrolled. In 2011, 27 master's, 2 doctorates awarded. *Degree requirements:* For master's, thesis (for some programs); for doctorate, comprehensive exam, thesis/dissertation. *Entrance requirements:* For master's, GRE General Test (minimum score 1000 verbal and quantitative), minimum GPA of 3.0, 3 letters of recommendation; for doctorate, GRE General Test (combined minimum score of 1100 on the Verbal and Quantitative sections), minimum GPA of 3.0, 3 letters of recommendation, statement of research interest. Additional exam requirements/recommendations for international students: Required—TOEFL (minimum score 550 paper-based; 213 computer-based; 80 iBT), IELTS (minimum score 6.5). *Application deadline:* For fall admission, 2/15 priority date for domestic students, 2/15 for international students; for spring admission, 7/15 priority date for domestic students, 7/15 for international students. Applications are processed on a rolling basis. Application fee: $50. Electronic applications accepted. *Expenses:* Tuition, state resident: full-time $7992. Tuition, nonresident: full-time $19,592. *Required fees:* $1735; $58 per credit. *Financial support:* In 2011–12, 44 students received support, including 1 fellowship (averaging $19,360 per year), 31 research assistantships with full and partial tuition reimbursements available (averaging $17,090 per year), 12 teaching assistantships with full and partial tuition reimbursements available (averaging $6,607 per year); Federal Work-Study, scholarships/grants, and unspecified assistantships also available. Financial award application deadline: 2/15; financial award applicants required to submit FAFSA. *Faculty research:* Ecology, natural resource management, hydrology, restoration, human dimensions. *Total annual research expenditures:* $2.9 million. *Unit head:* Dr. Frederick Smith, Interim Department Head, 970-491-7505, Fax: 970-491-6754, E-mail: fwsmith@colostate.edu. *Application contact:* Sonya LeFebre, Coordinator, 970-491-1907, Fax: 970-491-6754, E-mail: sonya.lefebre@colostate.edu. Web site: http://warnercnr.colostate.edu/frws-home/.

Colorado State University, Graduate School, Warner College of Natural Resources, Department of Human Dimensions of Natural Resources, Fort Collins, CO 80523-1480. Offers MS, PhD. Part-time programs available. Postbaccalaureate distance learning degree programs offered. *Faculty:* 11 full-time (3 women). *Students:* 43 full-time (24 women), 16 part-time (8 women); includes 8 minority (1 Black or African American, non-Hispanic/Latino; 6 Hispanic/Latino; 1 Two or more races, non-Hispanic/Latino), 6 international. Average age 31. 16 applicants, 50% accepted, 7 enrolled. In 2011, 10 master's, 2 doctorates awarded. Terminal master's awarded for partial completion of doctoral program. *Degree requirements:* For master's, comprehensive exam, thesis; for doctorate, comprehensive exam, thesis/dissertation. *Entrance requirements:* For master's, GRE General Test, minimum GPA of 3.0, 3 letters of recommendation, statement of interest; for doctorate, GRE General Test (combined minimum score of 1000 on the Verbal and Quantitative sections), minimum GPA of 3.0, 3 letters of recommendation, copy of master's thesis or professional paper, interview, statement of interest. Additional exam requirements/recommendations for international students: Required—TOEFL (minimum score 550 paper-based; 213 computer-based; 80 iBT). *Application deadline:* For fall admission, 2/1 priority date for domestic students, 2/1 for international students. Application fee: $50. Electronic applications accepted. *Expenses:* Tuition, state resident: full-time $7992. Tuition, nonresident: full-time $19,592. *Required fees:* $1735; $58 per credit. *Financial support:* In 2011–12, 27 students received support, including 2 fellowships (averaging $14,054 per year), 18 research assistantships with tuition reimbursements available (averaging $14,762 per year), 7 teaching assistantships with tuition reimbursements available (averaging $11,227 per year); career-related internships or fieldwork, Federal Work-Study, scholarships/grants, traineeships, and unspecified assistantships also available. Support available to part-time students. Financial award application deadline: 2/15;

526 facebook.com/petersonspublishing

Peterson's Graduate Programs in the Physical Sciences, Mathematics, Agricultural Sciences, the Environment & Natural Resources 2013

financial award applicants required to submit FAFSA. *Faculty research:* International tourism, wilderness preservation, resource interpretation, human dimensions in natural resources, protected areas management. *Total annual research expenditures:* $1.5 million. *Unit head:* Dr. Michael J. Manfredo, Head, 970-491-0474, Fax: 970-491-2255, E-mail: manfredo@cnr.colostate.edu. *Application contact:* Jacqie Hasan, Graduate Contact, 970-491-6591, Fax: 970-491-2255, E-mail: jacqie.hasan@colostate.edu. Web site: http://warnercnr.colostate.edu/hdnr-home.

Cornell University, Graduate School, Graduate Fields of Agriculture and Life Sciences, Field of Natural Resources, Ithaca, NY 14853-0001. Offers aquatic science (MPS, MS, PhD); environmental management (MPS); fishery science (MPS, MS, PhD); forest science (MPS, MS, PhD); resource policy and management (MPS, MS, PhD); wildlife science (MPS, MS, PhD). *Faculty:* 39 full-time (7 women). *Students:* 52 full-time (21 women); includes 4 minority (1 American Indian or Alaska Native, non-Hispanic/Latino; 1 Asian, non-Hispanic/Latino; 1 Hispanic/Latino; 1 Two or more races, non-Hispanic/Latino), 15 international. Average age 32. 72 applicants, 21% accepted, 11 enrolled. In 2011, 2 master's, 5 doctorates awarded. *Degree requirements:* For master's, thesis (MS), project paper (MPS); for doctorate, comprehensive exam, thesis/dissertation. *Entrance requirements:* For master's and doctorate, GRE General Test, 2 letters of recommendation. Additional exam requirements/recommendations for international students: Required—TOEFL (minimum score 550 paper-based; 213 computer-based; 77 iBT). *Application deadline:* For spring admission, 10/30 for domestic students. Applications are processed on a rolling basis. Application fee: $95. Electronic applications accepted. *Financial support:* In 2011–12, 10 fellowships with full tuition reimbursements, 14 research assistantships with full tuition reimbursements, 28 teaching assistantships with full tuition reimbursements were awarded; institutionally sponsored loans, scholarships/grants, health care benefits, tuition waivers (full and partial), and unspecified assistantships also available. Financial award applicants required to submit FAFSA. *Faculty research:* Ecosystem-level dynamics, systems modeling, conservation biology/management, resource management's human dimensions, biogeochemistry. *Unit head:* Director of Graduate Studies, 607-255-2807, Fax: 607-255-0349. *Application contact:* Graduate Field Assistant, 607-255-2807, Fax: 607-255-0349, E-mail: nrgrad@cornell.edu. Web site: http://www.gradschool.cornell.edu/fields.php?id-54&a-2.

Dalhousie University, Faculty of Management, Centre for Advanced Management Education, Halifax, NS B3H 3J5, Canada. Offers financial services (MBA); information management (MIM); management (MPA); natural resources (MBA). Part-time programs available. Postbaccalaureate distance learning degree programs offered. *Entrance requirements:* For master's, GMAT, minimum GPA of 3.0, resume. Additional exam requirements/recommendations for international students: Required—TOEFL, IELTS, CANTEST, CAEL, or Michigan English Language Assessment Battery. Electronic applications accepted.

Delaware State University, Graduate Programs, Department of Agriculture and Natural Resources, Program in Natural Resources, Dover, DE 19901-2277. Offers MS. *Entrance requirements:* For master's, GRE. Additional exam requirements/recommendations for international students: Required—TOEFL (minimum score 550 paper-based).

Duke University, Graduate School, Department of Environment, Durham, NC 27708. Offers natural resource economics/policy (PhD); natural resource science/ecology (PhD); natural resource systems science (PhD); JD/AM. Part-time programs available. *Faculty:* 28 full-time. *Students:* 53 full-time (32 women); includes 3 minority (1 Black or African American, non-Hispanic/Latino; 2 Asian, non-Hispanic/Latino), 16 international. 87 applicants, 20% accepted, 9 enrolled. In 2011, 10 doctorates awarded. *Degree requirements:* For doctorate, variable foreign language requirement, thesis/dissertation. *Entrance requirements:* For doctorate, GRE General Test. Additional exam requirements/recommendations for international students: Required—TOEFL (minimum score 550 paper-based; 83 iBT), IELTS (minimum score 7). *Application deadline:* For fall admission, 12/8 priority date for domestic students, 12/8 for international students. Application fee: $75. Electronic applications accepted. *Expenses:* Tuition: Full-time $40,720. *Required fees:* $3107. *Financial support:* Fellowships, research assistantships, teaching assistantships, and Federal Work-Study available. Financial award application deadline: 12/8. *Unit head:* Gaby Katul, Director of Graduate Studies, 919-613-8002, Fax: 919-613-8061, E-mail: meg.stephens@duke.edu. *Application contact:* Elizabeth Hutton, Director, Graduate Admissions, 919-684-3913, Fax: 919-684-2277, E-mail: grad-admissions@duke.edu. Web site: http://www.env.duke.edu/.

Duke University, Nicholas School of the Environment, Durham, NC 27708-0328. Offers coastal environmental management (MEM); DEL-environmental leadership (MEM); energy and environment (MEM); environmental economics and policy (MEM); environmental health and security (MEM); forest resource management (MF); global environmental change (MEM); resource ecology (MEM); water and air resources (MEM); JD/AM; JD/MEM; JD/MF; MAT/MEM; MBA/MEM; MBA/MF; MEM/MPP; MF/MPP. *Accreditation:* SAF (one or more programs are accredited). Part-time programs available. *Degree requirements:* For master's, thesis. *Entrance requirements:* For master's, GRE General Test, previous course work in biology or ecology, calculus, statistics, and microeconomics; computer familiarity with word processing and data analysis. Additional exam requirements/recommendations for international students: Required—TOEFL (minimum score 550 paper-based; 213 computer-based). Electronic applications accepted.

Expenses: Contact institution. *Faculty research:* Ecosystem management, conservation ecology, earth systems, risk assessment.

Georgia Institute of Technology, Graduate Studies and Research, College of Engineering, School of Chemical and Biomolecular Engineering, Atlanta, GA 30332-0001. Offers bioengineering (MS Bio E, PhD); chemical engineering (MS Ch E, PhD); paper science and engineering (MS, PhD); polymers (MS Poly). *Degree requirements:* For master's, thesis; for doctorate, comprehensive exam, thesis/dissertation. *Entrance requirements:* For master's and doctorate, GRE, minimum GPA of 3.0. Additional exam requirements/recommendations for international students: Required—TOEFL (minimum score 550 paper-based; 213 computer-based). Electronic applications accepted. *Faculty research:* Biochemical engineering; process modeling, synthesis, and control; polymer science and engineering; thermodynamics and separations; surface and particle science.

Humboldt State University, Academic Programs, College of Natural Resources and Sciences, Programs in Natural Resources, Arcata, CA 95521-8299. Offers natural resources (MS), including fisheries, forestry, natural resources planning and interpretation, rangeland resources and wildland soils, wastewater utilization, watershed management, wildlife. *Students:* 45 full-time (26 women), 28 part-time (11 women); includes 4 minority (2 Asian, non-Hispanic/Latino; 1 Hispanic/Latino; 1 Two or more races, non-Hispanic/Latino), 1 international. Average age 30. 100 applicants, 22% accepted, 11 enrolled. In 2011, 25 master's awarded. *Degree requirements:* For master's, thesis or alternative. *Entrance requirements:* For master's, GRE, appropriate bachelor's degree, minimum GPA of 2.5, 3 letters of recommendation, resume. Additional exam requirements/recommendations for international students: Required—TOEFL (minimum score 500 paper-based; 173 computer-based). *Application deadline:* For fall admission, 2/1 for domestic and international students; for spring admission, 9/30 for domestic and international students. Applications are processed on a rolling basis. Application fee: $55. *Expenses:* Tuition, state resident: full-time $6734. Tuition, nonresident: full-time $15,662; part-time $372 per credit. *Required fees:* $903. Tuition and fees vary according to program. *Financial support:* Fellowships, career-related internships or fieldwork, and Federal Work-Study available. Support available to part-time students. Financial award application deadline: 3/1; financial award applicants required to submit FAFSA. *Faculty research:* Spotted owl habitat, pre-settlement vegetation, hardwood utilization, tree physiology, fisheries. *Unit head:* Dr. Robert Van Kirk, Coordinator, 707-826-3744, E-mail: rob.vankirk@humboldt.edu. *Application contact:* Julie Tucker, Administrative Support Coordinator, 707-826-3256, E-mail: jlt7002@humboldt.edu. Web site: http://www.humboldt.edu/cnrs/graduate_programs.

Instituto Tecnologico de Santo Domingo, Graduate School, Area of Basic And Environmental Sciences, Santo Domingo, Dominican Republic. Offers environmental science (M En S), including environmental education, environmental management, marine resources, natural resources management; mathematics (MS, PhD); renewable energy technology (MS, Certificate).

Iowa State University of Science and Technology, Program in Biorenewable Resources and Technology, Ames, IA 50011. Offers MS, PhD. *Degree requirements:* For master's, thesis or alternative; for doctorate, thesis/dissertation. *Entrance requirements:* For master's and doctorate, GRE General Test. Additional exam requirements/recommendations for international students: Required—TOEFL (minimum score 550 paper-based; 79 iBT), IELTS (minimum score 6.5). *Application deadline:* For fall admission, 1/1 priority date for domestic students, 1/1 for international students; for spring admission, 9/1 for domestic and international students. Application fee: $40 ($90 for international students). Electronic applications accepted. *Unit head:* Dr. Robert Brown, Director of Graduate Education, 515-294-1033, Fax: 515-294-1123, E-mail: brtgrad@iastate.edu. *Application contact:* Kris Bell, Application Contact, 515-294-1033, Fax: 515-294-1123, E-mail: brtgrad@iastate.edu. Web site: http://www.biorenew.iastate.edu/.

Laurentian University, School of Graduate Studies and Research, School of Engineering, Sudbury, ON P3E 2C6, Canada. Offers mineral resources engineering (M Eng, MA Sc); natural resources engineering (PhD). Part-time programs available. *Faculty research:* Mining engineering, rock mechanics (tunneling, rockbursts, rock support), metallurgy (mineral processing, hydro and pyrometallurgy), simulations and remote mining, simulations and scheduling.

Louisiana State University and Agricultural and Mechanical College, Graduate School, College of Agriculture, School of Renewable Natural Resources, Baton Rouge, LA 70803. Offers fisheries (MS); forestry (MS, PhD); wildlife (MS); wildlife and fisheries science (PhD). *Faculty:* 31 full-time (5 women). *Students:* 53 full-time (13 women), 11 part-time (2 women); includes 2 minority (both Hispanic/Latino), 16 international. Average age 30. 21 applicants, 33% accepted, 7 enrolled. In 2011, 12 master's, 7 doctorates awarded. *Degree requirements:* For master's, thesis; for doctorate, thesis/dissertation. *Entrance requirements:* For master's, GRE General Test, minimum GPA of 3.0; for doctorate, GRE General Test, MS, minimum GPA of 3.0. Additional exam requirements/recommendations for international students: Required—TOEFL (minimum score 550 paper-based; 213 computer-based; 79 iBT), IELTS (minimum score 6.5). *Application deadline:* For fall admission, 1/25 priority date for domestic students, 5/15 for international students; for spring admission, 10/15 for international students. Applications are processed on a rolling basis. Application fee: $50 ($70 for international students). Electronic applications accepted. *Financial support:* In 2011–12, 61 students received support, including

Peterson's Graduate Programs in the Physical Sciences, Mathematics, Agricultural Sciences, the Environment & Natural Resources 2013

facebook.com/petersonspublishing **527**

Natural Resources

52 research assistantships with partial tuition reimbursements available (averaging $19,938 per year), 1 teaching assistantship (averaging $22,000 per year); fellowships, Federal Work-Study, institutionally sponsored loans, scholarships/grants, health care benefits, tuition waivers (full and partial), and unspecified assistantships also available. Financial award application deadline: 4/15; financial award applicants required to submit FAFSA. *Faculty research:* Forest biology and management, aquaculture, fisheries biology and ecology, upland and wetlands wildlife. *Total annual research expenditures:* $47,156. *Unit head:* Dr. Allen Rutherford, Director, 225-578-4131, Fax: 225-578-4227, E-mail: druther@lsu.edu. *Application contact:* Dr. William Kelso, Coordinator of Graduate Studies, 225-578-4176, Fax: 225-578-4227, E-mail: wkelso@lsu.edu. Web site: http://www.fwf.lsu.edu/.

Marylhurst University, Department of Business Administration, Marylhurst, OR 97036-0261. Offers finance (MBA); general management (MBA); government policy and administration (MBA); green development (MBA); health care management (MBA); marketing (MBA); natural and organic resources (MBA); nonprofit management (MBA); organizational behavior (MBA); real estate (MBA); renewable energy (MBA); sustainable business (MBA). Part-time and evening/weekend programs available. Postbaccalaureate distance learning degree programs offered (no on-campus study). *Faculty:* 3 full-time (0 women), 39 part-time/adjunct (6 women). *Students:* 29 full-time (15 women), 675 part-time (373 women); includes 178 minority (59 Black or African American, non-Hispanic/Latino; 6 American Indian or Alaska Native, non-Hispanic/Latino; 34 Asian, non-Hispanic/Latino; 46 Hispanic/Latino; 4 Native Hawaiian or other Pacific Islander, non-Hispanic/Latino; 29 Two or more races, non-Hispanic/Latino), 14 international. Average age 37. 262 applicants, 91% accepted, 194 enrolled. In 2011, 352 master's awarded. *Degree requirements:* For master's, comprehensive exam, capstone course. *Entrance requirements:* For master's, GMAT (if GPA less than 3.0 and fewer than 5 years of work experience), interview, resume, 2 letters of recommendation. Additional exam requirements/recommendations for international students: Recommended—TOEFL (minimum score 550 paper-based; 213 computer-based; 80 iBT). *Application deadline:* For fall admission, 9/11 priority date for domestic students, 9/11 for international students; for winter admission, 12/15 priority date for domestic students, 12/15 for international students; for spring admission, 3/15 priority date for domestic students, 3/17 for international students. Applications are processed on a rolling basis. Application fee: $50. Electronic applications accepted. *Expenses: Tuition:* Full-time $14,796; part-time $548 per quarter hour. Tuition and fees vary according to program. *Financial support:* Scholarships/grants available. Support available to part-time students. Financial award applicants required to submit FAFSA. *Unit head:* David McNamee, Interim Chair, 503-636-8141, Fax: 503-697-5597, E-mail: mba@marylhurst.edu. *Application contact:* Maruska Lynch, Graduate Admissions Specialist, 800-634-9982 Ext. 6322, Fax: 503-699-6320, E-mail: admissions@marylhurst.edu. Web site: http://www.marylhurst.edu/.

McGill University, Faculty of Graduate and Postdoctoral Studies, Faculty of Agricultural and Environmental Sciences, Department of Natural Resource Sciences, Montréal, QC H3A 2T5, Canada. Offers entomology (M Sc, PhD); environmental assessment (M Sc); forest science (M Sc, PhD); microbiology (M Sc, PhD); micrometeorology (M Sc, PhD); neotropical environment (M Sc, PhD); soil science (M Sc, PhD); wildlife biology (M Sc, PhD).

Michigan State University, The Graduate School, College of Agriculture and Natural Resources, Department of Community, Agriculture, Recreation, and Resource Studies, East Lansing, MI 48824. Offers MS, PhD. *Entrance requirements:* Additional exam requirements/recommendations for international students: Required—TOEFL. Electronic applications accepted.

Missouri State University, Graduate College, College of Natural and Applied Sciences, Department of Geography, Geology, and Planning, Springfield, MO 65897. Offers geospatial sciences (MS, MS Ed), including earth science (MS Ed), geology (MS), human geography and planning (MS), physical geography (MS Ed); natural and applied science (MNAS), including geography, geology and planning; secondary education (MS Ed), including geography. Part-time and evening/weekend programs available. *Faculty:* 19 full-time (4 women). *Students:* 19 full-time (9 women), 12 part-time (7 women), 2 international. Average age 31. 20 applicants, 80% accepted, 11 enrolled. In 2011, 15 master's awarded. *Degree requirements:* For master's, comprehensive exam, thesis (for some programs). *Entrance requirements:* For master's, GRE General Test (MS, MNAS), minimum undergraduate GPA of 3.0 (MS, MNAS), 9-12 teacher certification (MS Ed). Additional exam requirements/recommendations for international students: Required—TOEFL (minimum score 550 paper-based; 213 computer-based; 79 iBT). *Application deadline:* For fall admission, 7/20 priority date for domestic students, 5/1 for international students; for spring admission, 12/20 priority date for domestic students, 9/1 for international students. Applications are processed on a rolling basis. Application fee: $35 ($50 for international students). Electronic applications accepted. *Expenses: Tuition,* state resident: full-time $4086; part-time $227 per credit hour. Tuition, nonresident: full-time $8172; part-time $454 per credit hour. *Required fees:* $275 per semester. Tuition and fees vary according to course load, campus/location and program. *Financial support:* In 2011–12, 3 research assistantships with full tuition reimbursements (averaging $8,000 per year), 9 teaching assistantships with full tuition reimbursements (averaging $8,000 per year) were awarded; career-related internships or fieldwork, Federal Work-Study, institutionally sponsored loans, scholarships/grants, and unspecified assistantships also available. Financial award application deadline: 3/31; financial award applicants required to submit FAFSA. *Faculty*

research: Stratigraphy and ancient meteorite impacts, environmental geochemistry of karst, hyperspectral image processing, water quality, small town planning. *Unit head:* Dr. Thomas Plymate, Head, 417-836-5800, Fax: 417-836-6934, E-mail: tomplymate@missouristate.edu. *Application contact:* Misty Stewart, Coordinator of Graduate Recruitment, 417-836-6079, Fax: 417-836-6200, E-mail: mistystewart@missouristate.edu. Web site: http://geosciences.missouristate.edu/

Montana State University, College of Graduate Studies, College of Agriculture, Department of Land Resources and Environmental Sciences, Bozeman, MT 59717. Offers land rehabilitation (interdisciplinary) (MS); land resources and environmental sciences (MS), including land rehabilitation (interdisciplinary), land resources and environmental sciences. Part-time programs available. *Degree requirements:* For master's, comprehensive exam. *Entrance requirements:* For master's, GRE General Test. Additional exam requirements/recommendations for international students: Required—TOEFL (minimum score 550 paper-based; 213 computer-based). Electronic applications accepted. *Faculty research:* Soil nutrient management and plant nutrition, isotope biogeochemistry of soils, biodegradation of hydrocarbons in soils and natural waters, remote sensing, GIS systems, managed and natural ecosystems, microbial and metabolic diversity in geothermally heated soils, integrated management of weeds, diversified cropping systems, insect behavior and ecology, river ecology, microbial biogeochemistry, weed ecology.

North Carolina State University, Graduate School, College of Natural Resources, Department of Parks, Recreation and Tourism Management, Raleigh, NC 27695. Offers natural resource management (MPRTM, MS); park and recreation management (MPRTM, MS); parks, recreation and tourism management (PhD); recreational sport management (MPRTM, MS); spatial information science (MPRTM, MS); tourism policy and development (MPRTM, MS). *Degree requirements:* For master's, thesis (for some programs); for doctorate, thesis/dissertation. *Entrance requirements:* For master's and doctorate, GRE General Test. Additional exam requirements/recommendations for international students: Required—TOEFL. Electronic applications accepted. *Faculty research:* Tourism policy and development, spatial information systems, natural resource management, recreational sports management, park and recreation management.

North Carolina State University, Graduate School, College of Natural Resources and College of Agriculture and Life Sciences, Program in Natural Resources, Raleigh, NC 27695. Offers MNR, MS. *Degree requirements:* For master's, thesis optional. *Entrance requirements:* For master's, GRE. Electronic applications accepted.

North Dakota State University, College of Graduate and Interdisciplinary Studies, College of Agriculture, Food Systems, and Natural Resources, Department of Animal and Range Sciences, Fargo, ND 58108. Offers animal science (MS, PhD); natural resource management (MS, PhD); range sciences (MS, PhD). *Faculty:* 19 full-time (4 women), 1 part-time/adjunct (0 women). *Students:* 24 full-time (16 women), 9 part-time (5 women), 4 international. Average age 25. 15 applicants, 47% accepted, 4 enrolled. In 2011, 4 master's, 5 doctorates awarded. *Degree requirements:* For master's, thesis; for doctorate, comprehensive exam, thesis/dissertation. *Entrance requirements:* For master's and doctorate, GRE General Test. Additional exam requirements/recommendations for international students: Required—TOEFL (minimum score 71 iBT). *Application deadline:* Applications are processed on a rolling basis. Application fee: $35. *Financial support:* In 2011–12, 1 fellowship with tuition reimbursement (averaging $18,000 per year), 29 research assistantships with tuition reimbursements (averaging $13,000 per year) were awarded; teaching assistantships, Federal Work-Study, institutionally sponsored loans, and tuition waivers (partial) also available. Financial award application deadline: 3/15. *Faculty research:* Reproduction, nutrition, meat and muscle biology, breeding/genetics. *Unit head:* Dr. Gregory Lardy, Chair, 701-231-7641, Fax: 701-231-7590, E-mail: gregory.lardy@ndsu.edu. *Application contact:* Sonya Goergen, Marketing, Recruitment, and Public Relations Coordinator, 701-231-7033, Fax: 701-231-6524.

North Dakota State University, College of Graduate and Interdisciplinary Studies, College of Agriculture, Food Systems, and Natural Resources, Department of Entomology, Fargo, ND 58108. Offers entomology (MS, PhD); environment and conservation science (MS, PhD); natural resource management (MS, PhD). Part-time programs available. *Students:* 7 full-time (4 women), 3 part-time (1 woman), 3 international. Average age 34. 6 applicants, 0% accepted, 0 enrolled. In 2011, 1 master's awarded. *Degree requirements:* For master's, thesis; for doctorate, comprehensive exam, thesis/dissertation. *Entrance requirements:* For master's and doctorate, minimum GPA of 3.0. Additional exam requirements/recommendations for international students: Required—TOEFL (minimum score 550 paper-based; 213 computer-based; 79 iBT). *Application deadline:* For fall admission, 5/1 for international students; for winter admission, 8/1 for international students. Application fee: $35. Electronic applications accepted. *Financial support:* In 2011–12, 11 research assistantships with full tuition reimbursements (averaging $13,800 per year) were awarded; Federal Work-Study, institutionally sponsored loans, and unspecified assistantships also available. Financial award application deadline: 4/15. *Faculty research:* Insect systematics, conservation biology, integrated pest management, insect behavior, insect biology. *Unit head:* Dr. Frank Casey, Chair, 701-231-7582, Fax: 701-231-8557, E-mail: francis.casey@ndsu.edu. *Application contact:* Dr. Jason Harmon, Program

528 facebook.com/petersonspublishing

Peterson's Graduate Programs in the Physical Sciences, Mathematics, Agricultural Sciences, the Environment & Natural Resources 2013

Leader, 701-231-7033, Fax: 701-231-8557, E-mail: jason.harmon@ndsu.edu. Web site: http://www.ndsu.nodak.edu/entomology/.

North Dakota State University, College of Graduate and Interdisciplinary Studies, College of Agriculture, Food Systems, and Natural Resources, Department of Plant Sciences, Fargo, ND 58108. Offers crop and weed sciences (MS); horticulture (MS); natural resource management (MS); plant sciences (PhD). Part-time programs available. *Faculty:* 31 full-time (5 women). *Students:* 51 full-time (19 women), 16 part-time (6 women); includes 4 minority (2 Hispanic/Latino; 2 Two or more races, non-Hispanic/Latino), 36 international. Average age 26. 16 applicants, 69% accepted, 6 enrolled. In 2011, 9 master's, 3 doctorates awarded. *Degree requirements:* For master's, thesis; for doctorate, thesis/dissertation. *Entrance requirements:* Additional exam requirements/recommendations for international students: Required—TOEFL (minimum score 525 paper-based; 197 computer-based; 71 iBT). *Application deadline:* For fall admission, 5/1 for international students; for winter admission, 8/1 for international students. Applications are processed on a rolling basis. Application fee: $35. Electronic applications accepted. *Financial support:* In 2011–12, 2 fellowships (averaging $19,950 per year), 64 research assistantships were awarded; teaching assistantships, Federal Work-Study, and institutionally sponsored loans also available. Financial award application deadline:. 4/15. *Faculty research:* Biotechnology, weed control science, plant breeding, plant genetics, crop physiology. *Unit head:* Dr. Richard Horsley, Head, 701-231-7971, Fax: 701-231-8474, E-mail: richard.horsley@ndsu.edu. *Application contact:* Sonya Goergen, Marketing, Recruitment, and Public Relations Coordinator, 701-231-7033, Fax: 701-231-6524. Web site: http://www.ndsu.nodak.edu/.

North Dakota State University, College of Graduate and Interdisciplinary Studies, College of Agriculture, Food Systems, and Natural Resources, Department of Soil Science, Fargo, ND 58108. Offers environmental and conservation science (PhD); environmental conservation science (MS); natural resource management (MS, PhD); soil sciences (MS, PhD). Part-time programs available. *Students:* 7 full-time (5 women), 3 part-time (1 woman), 4 international. Average age 23. 4 applicants, 50% accepted, 0 enrolled. In 2011, 4 degrees awarded. *Degree requirements:* For master's, comprehensive exam, thesis, classroom teaching; for doctorate, comprehensive exam, thesis/dissertation, classroom teaching. *Entrance requirements:* Additional exam requirements/recommendations for international students: Required—TOEFL (minimum score 525 paper-based; 193 computer-based; 71 iBT). *Application deadline:* For fall admission, 5/1 for international students; for winter admission, 8/1 for international students. Applications are processed on a rolling basis. Application fee: $35. Electronic applications accepted. *Financial support:* In 2011–12, 7 research assistantships with full tuition reimbursements (averaging $14,300 per year) were awarded; fellowships, Federal Work-Study, institutionally sponsored loans, and scholarships/grants also available. Financial award application deadline: 3/15. *Faculty research:* Microclimate, nitrogen management, landscape studies, water quality, soil management. *Unit head:* Dr. Donald Kirby, Interim Chair, 701-231-8901, Fax: 701-231-7861. *Application contact:* Sonya Goergen, Marketing, Recruitment, and Public Relations Coordinator, 701-231-7033, Fax: 701-231-6524. Web site: http://www.ndsu.edu/ndsu/academic/factsheets/ag/soilsci.shtml.

North Dakota State University, College of Graduate and Interdisciplinary Studies, College of Science and Mathematics, Department of Biological Sciences, Fargo, ND 58108. Offers biology (MS); botany (MS, PhD); cellular and molecular biology (PhD); environmental and conservation sciences (MS, PhD); genomics (PhD); natural resources management (MS, PhD); zoology (MS, PhD). *Faculty:* 13 full-time (7 women), 3 part-time/adjunct (1 woman). *Students:* 20 full-time (10 women), 2 part-time (both women); includes 1 minority (American Indian or Alaska Native, non-Hispanic/Latino), 2 international. 12 applicants, 33% accepted, 4 enrolled. In 2011, 3 degrees awarded. *Degree requirements:* For master's, thesis; for doctorate, thesis/dissertation. *Entrance requirements:* For master's and doctorate, GRE General Test. Additional exam requirements/recommendations for international students: Required—TOEFL. *Application deadline:* For fall admission, 1/15 for domestic students. Applications are processed on a rolling basis. Application fee: $35. Electronic applications accepted. *Financial support:* Fellowships with full tuition reimbursements, research assistantships with full tuition reimbursements, teaching assistantships with full tuition reimbursements, career-related internships or fieldwork, Federal Work-Study, institutionally sponsored loans, scholarships/grants, tuition waivers (full), and unspecified assistantships available. Support available to part-time students. Financial award application deadline: 4/15; financial award applicants required to submit FAFSA. *Faculty research:* Comparative endocrinology, physiology, behavioral ecology, plant cell biology, aquatic biology. *Unit head:* Dr. Wendy Reed, Head, 701-231-7087, E-mail: wendy.reed@ndsu.edu. *Application contact:* Sonya Goergen, Marketing, Recruitment, and Public Relations Coordinator, 701-231-7033, Fax: 701-231-6524. Web site: http://biology.ndsu.nodak.edu/.

North Dakota State University, College of Graduate and Interdisciplinary Studies, Interdisciplinary Program in Natural Resources Management, Fargo, ND 58108. Offers MS, PhD. Part-time programs available. *Students:* 45 full-time (15 women), 17 part-time (5 women); includes 3 minority (2 Black or African American, non-Hispanic/Latino; 1 Two or more races, non-Hispanic/Latino), 6 international. 20 applicants, 65% accepted, 9 enrolled. In 2011, 11 master's, 3 doctorates awarded. *Degree requirements:* For master's, thesis; for doctorate, comprehensive exam, thesis/dissertation. *Entrance requirements:* Additional exam requirements/recommendations for international students: Required—

TOEFL (minimum score 525 paper-based; 197 computer-based; 71 iBT). *Application deadline:* Applications are processed on a rolling basis. Application fee: $35. Electronic applications accepted. *Financial support:* In 2011–12, 25 students received support. Research assistantships with full tuition reimbursements available and teaching assistantships with full tuition reimbursements available available. Support available to part-time students. Financial award application deadline: 3/15. *Faculty research:* Natural resources economics, wetlands issues, wildlife, prairie ecology, range management. *Unit head:* Dr. Carolyn E. Grygiel, Director, 701-231-8180, Fax: 701-231-7590, E-mail: carolyn.grygiel@ndsu.edu. *Application contact:* Sonya Goergen, Marketing, Recruitment, and Public Relations Coordinator, 701-231-7033, Fax: 701-231-6524. Web site: http://www.ag.ndsu.nodak.edu/nrm/grad.htm.

The Ohio State University, Graduate School, College of Food, Agricultural, and Environmental Sciences, School of Environment and Natural Resources, Columbus, OH 43210. Offers MS, PhD. *Faculty:* 35. *Students:* 72 full-time (40 women), 20 part-time (13 women); includes 8 minority (1 Black or African American, non-Hispanic/Latino; 2 Asian, non-Hispanic/Latino; 3 Hispanic/Latino; 2 Two or more races, non-Hispanic/Latino), 10 international. Average age 30. In 2011, 12 master's, 3 doctorates awarded. *Degree requirements:* For master's, thesis; for doctorate, thesis/dissertation. *Entrance requirements:* For master's and doctorate, GRE. Additional exam requirements/recommendations for international students: Required—TOEFL (minimum score 550 paper-based; 79 iBT), Michigan English Language Assessment Battery (minimum score 82). *Application deadline:* Applications are processed on a rolling basis. Application fee: $40 ($50 for international students). Electronic applications accepted. *Expenses:* Tuition, state resident: full-time $11,400. Tuition, nonresident: full-time $28,125. Tuition and fees vary according to course load, degree level, campus/location and program. *Unit head:* Ronald Hendrick, Director, 614-292-8522, E-mail: hendrick.15@osu.edu. *Application contact:* Amy Schmidt, Graduate Program Coordinator, 614-292-9883, Fax: 614-292-7432, E-mail: schmidt.442@osu.edu. Web site: http://senr.osu.edu/default.asp.

Oklahoma State University, College of Agricultural Science and Natural Resources, Stillwater, OK 74078. Offers M Ag, MS, PhD. Postbaccalaureate distance learning degree programs offered. *Faculty:* 238 full-time (54 women), 14 part-time/adjunct (2 women). *Students:* 163 full-time (79 women), 331 part-time (164 women); includes 53 minority (9 Black or African American, non-Hispanic/Latino; 15 American Indian or Alaska Native, non-Hispanic/Latino; 6 Asian, non-Hispanic/Latino; 10 Hispanic/Latino; 13 Two or more races, non-Hispanic/Latino), 178 international. Average age 29. 499 applicants, 29% accepted, 83 enrolled. In 2011, 120 master's, 33 doctorates awarded. *Degree requirements:* For master's, thesis (for some programs); for doctorate, comprehensive exam, thesis/dissertation. *Entrance requirements:* For master's and doctorate, GRE or GMAT. Additional exam requirements/recommendations for international students: Required—TOEFL (minimum score 550 paper-based; 79 iBT). *Application deadline:* For fall admission, 3/1 for international students; for spring admission, 8/1 for international students. Applications are processed on a rolling basis. Application fee: $40 ($75 for international students). Electronic applications accepted. *Expenses:* Tuition, state resident: full-time $4044; part-time $168.50 per credit hour. Tuition, nonresident: full-time $16,008; part-time $667 per credit hour. *Required fees:* $2122; $88.45 per credit hour. One-time fee: $50. Tuition and fees vary according to course load and campus/location. *Financial support:* In 2011–12, 281 research assistantships (averaging $16,006 per year), 23 teaching assistantships (averaging $14,476 per year) were awarded; fellowships, career-related internships or fieldwork, Federal Work-Study, scholarships/grants, health care benefits, tuition waivers (partial), and unspecified assistantships also available. Support available to part-time students. Financial award application deadline: 3/1; financial award applicants required to submit FAFSA. *Unit head:* Dr. Robert E. Whitson, Dean, 405-744-5398, Fax: 405-744-2480. *Application contact:* Dr. Sheryl Tucker, Dean, 405-744-7099, Fax: 405-744-0355, E-mail: grad-i@okstate.edu. Web site: http://www.dasnr.okstate.edu.

Purdue University, Graduate School, College of Agriculture, Department of Forestry and Natural Resources, West Lafayette, IN 47907. Offers fisheries and aquatic sciences (MS, MSF, PhD); forest biology (MS, MSF, PhD); natural resource social science (MS, PhD); natural resources social science (MSF); quantitative ecology (MS, MSF, PhD); wildlife science (MS, MSF, PhD); wood products and wood products manufacturing (MS, MSF, PhD). *Faculty:* 26 full-time (3 women), 9 part-time/adjunct (1 woman). *Students:* 67 full-time (31 women), 8 part-time (3 women); includes 3 minority (2 Hispanic/Latino; 1 Two or more races, non-Hispanic/Latino), 17 international. Average age 29. 58 applicants, 16% accepted, 8 enrolled. In 2011, 9 master's, 11 doctorates awarded. *Degree requirements:* For master's, thesis; for doctorate, thesis/dissertation. *Entrance requirements:* For master's and doctorate, GRE General Test with minimum score required: verbal >=50th percentile; Quantitative >= 50th percentile; Analytical writing = 4.0 or greater, minimum undergraduate GPA of 3.2 or equivalent. Additional exam requirements/recommendations for international students: Required—TOEFL (minimum score 550 paper-based; 77 iBT). *Application deadline:* For fall admission, 1/5 for domestic students, 1/15 for international students; for spring admission, 9/15 for domestic and international students. Applications are processed on a rolling basis. Application fee: $60 ($75 for international students). Electronic applications accepted. *Financial support:* In 2011–12, 10 research assistantships (averaging $15,259 per year) were awarded; fellowships, teaching assistantships, career-related internships or fieldwork, and scholarships/grants also available. Support available to part-time students. Financial award application deadline: 1/5; financial award applicants

Peterson's Graduate Programs in the Physical Sciences, Mathematics, Agricultural Sciences, the Environment & Natural Resources 2013

facebook.com/petersonspublishing **529**

Natural Resources

required to submit FAFSA. *Faculty research:* Wildlife management, forest management, forest ecology, forest soils, limnology. *Unit head:* Dr. Robert K. Swihart, Interim Head, 765-494-3590, Fax: 765-494-9461, E-mail: rswihart@purdue.edu. *Application contact:* Kelly J. Garrett, Graduate Secretary, 765-494-3572, Fax: 765-494-9461, E-mail: kgarrett@purdue.edu. Web site: http://www.fnr.purdue.edu/.

San Francisco State University, Division of Graduate Studies, College of Science and Engineering, Department of Geography and Human Environmental Studies, San Francisco, CA 94132-1722. Offers geographic information science (MS); geography (MA), including resource management and environmental planning. *Unit head:* Dr. Jerry Davis, Chair, 415-338-2049, E-mail: jerry@sfsu.edu. *Application contact:* Nancy Wilkinson, Graduate Coordinator, 415-338-2049. Web site: http://www.bss.sfsu.edu/geog.

State University of New York College of Environmental Science and Forestry, Department of Environmental Resources Engineering, Syracuse, NY 13210-2779. Offers ecological engineering (MS, PhD); environmental and resources engineering (MPS, MS, PhD); environmental management (MPS); geospatial information science and engineering (MS, PhD); mapping sciences (MPS); water resources engineering (MS, PhD). *Degree requirements:* For master's, thesis (for some programs); for doctorate, comprehensive exam, thesis/dissertation. *Entrance requirements:* For master's and doctorate, GRE General Test, minimum GPA of 3.0. Additional exam requirements/recommendations for international students: Required—TOEFL (minimum score 550 paper-based; 213 computer-based; 80 iBT), IELTS (minimum score 6). *Application deadline:* For fall admission, 2/1 priority date for domestic students, 2/1 for international students; for spring admission, 11/1 priority date for domestic students; 11/1 for international students. Applications are processed on a rolling basis. Application fee: $60. *Expenses:* Tuition, state resident: full-time $8870; part-time $370 per credit hour. Tuition, nonresident: full-time $15,160; part-time $632 per credit hour. *Required fees:* $60; $370 per credit hour. $350 per semester. One-time fee: $85. *Financial support:* Fellowships with full and partial tuition reimbursements, research assistantships with full and partial tuition reimbursements, teaching assistantships with full and partial tuition reimbursements, Federal Work-Study, institutionally sponsored loans, scholarships/grants, health care benefits, and unspecified assistantships available. Financial award application deadline: 6/30; financial award applicants required to submit FAFSA. *Faculty research:* Forest engineering, paper science and engineering, wood products engineering. *Total annual research expenditures:* $968,412. *Unit head:* Dr. Theodore Endreny, Chair, 315-470-6565, Fax: 315-470-6958, E-mail: te@esf.edu. *Application contact:* Dr. Dudley J. Raynal, Dean, Instruction and Graduate Studies, 315-470-6599, Fax: 315-470-6978, E-mail: esfgrad@esf.edu. Web site: http://www.esf.edu/ere.

State University of New York College of Environmental Science and Forestry, Department of Forest and Natural Resources Management, Syracuse, NY 13210-2779. Offers ecology and ecosystems (MPS, MS, PhD); economics, governance and human dimensions (MPS, MS, PhD); environmental and natural resources policy (MPS, MS); forest and natural resources management (MPS, MS, PhD); monitoring, analysis and modeling (MPS, MS, PhD). *Accreditation:* SAF. *Degree requirements:* For master's, thesis (for some programs); for doctorate, comprehensive exam, thesis/dissertation. *Entrance requirements:* For master's and doctorate, GRE General Test, minimum GPA of 3.0. Additional exam requirements/recommendations for international students: Required—TOEFL (minimum score 550 paper-based; 213 computer-based; 80 iBT), IELTS (minimum score 6). *Application deadline:* For fall admission, 2/1 priority date for domestic students, 2/1 for international students; for spring admission, 11/1 priority date for domestic students, 11/1 for international students. Applications are processed on a rolling basis. Application fee: $60. *Expenses:* Tuition, state resident: full-time $8870; part-time $370 per credit hour. Tuition, nonresident: full-time $15,160; part-time $632 per credit hour. *Required fees:* $60; $370 per credit hour. $350 per semester. One-time fee: $85. *Financial support:* Fellowships with full and partial tuition reimbursements, research assistantships with full and partial tuition reimbursements, teaching assistantships with full and partial tuition reimbursements, career-related internships or fieldwork, Federal Work-Study, institutionally sponsored loans, scholarships/grants, health care benefits, and unspecified assistantships available. Financial award application deadline: 6/30; financial award applicants required to submit FAFSA. *Faculty research:* Silviculture recreation management, tree improvement, operations management, economics. *Total annual research expenditures:* $2.1 million. *Unit head:* Dr. David Newman, Chair, 315-470-6534, Fax: 315-470-6535. *Application contact:* Dr. Dudley J. Raynal, Dean, Instruction and Graduate Studies, 315-470-6599, Fax: 315-470-6978, E-mail: esfgrad@esf.edu. Web site: http://www.esf.edu/fnrm/.

State University of New York College of Environmental Science and Forestry, Department of Sustainable Construction Management and Engineering, Syracuse, NY 13210-2779. Offers construction management (MPS, MS, PhD); engineered wood products and structures (MPS, MS, PhD); sustainable construction (MPS, MS, PhD); tropical timbers (MPS, MS, PhD); wood anatomy and ultrastructure (MPS, MS, PhD); wood science and technology (MPS, MS, PhD); wood treatments (MPS, MS, PhD). *Degree requirements:* For master's, thesis (for some programs); for doctorate, comprehensive exam, thesis/dissertation. *Entrance requirements:* For master's and doctorate, GRE General Test, minimum GPA of 3.0. Additional exam requirements/recommendations for international students: Required—TOEFL (minimum score 550 paper-based; 213 computer-based; 80 iBT), IELTS (minimum score 6). *Application deadline:* For fall

admission, 2/1 priority date for domestic students, 2/1 for international students; for spring admission, 11/1 priority date for domestic students, 11/1 for international students. Applications are processed on a rolling basis. Application fee: $60. *Expenses:* Tuition, state resident: full-time $8870; part-time $370 per credit hour. Tuition, nonresident: full-time $15,160; part-time $632 per credit hour. *Required fees:* $60; $370 per credit hour. $350 per semester. One-time fee: $85. *Financial support:* Fellowships with full tuition reimbursements, research assistantships with full tuition reimbursements, teaching assistantships with full tuition reimbursements, career-related internships or fieldwork, Federal Work-Study, institutionally sponsored loans, scholarships/grants, health care benefits, and unspecified assistantships available. Financial award application deadline: 6/30; financial award applicants required to submit FAFSA. *Total annual research expenditures:* $160,385. *Unit head:* Dr. Susan E. Anagnost, Chair, 315-470-6880, Fax: 315-470-6879, E-mail: seanagno@esf.edu. *Application contact:* Dr. Dudley J. Raynal, Dean, Instruction and Graduate Studies, 315-470-6599, Fax: 315-470-6879, E-mail: esfgrad@esf.edu. Web site: http://www.esf.edu/scme/.

Texas A&M University, College of Agriculture and Life Sciences, Department of Ecosystem Science and Management, College Station, TX 77843. Offers forestry (MS, PhD); rangeland ecology and management (M Agr, MS, PhD). Part-time programs available. *Faculty:* 24. *Students:* 64 full-time (34 women), 34 part-time (16 women); includes 21 minority (3 Black or African American, non-Hispanic/Latino; 3 Asian, non-Hispanic/Latino; 14 Hispanic/Latino; 1 Two or more races, non-Hispanic/Latino), 17 international. Average age 27. In 2011, 8 master's, 4 doctorates awarded. Terminal master's awarded for partial completion of doctoral program. *Degree requirements:* For master's, thesis (for some programs); for doctorate, thesis/dissertation. *Entrance requirements:* For master's and doctorate, GRE General Test. Additional exam requirements/recommendations for international students: Required—TOEFL. *Application deadline:* For fall admission, 3/1 priority date for domestic students; for spring admission, 11/1 priority date for domestic students. Applications are processed on a rolling basis. Application fee: $50 ($75 for international students). Electronic applications accepted. *Expenses:* Tuition, state resident: full-time $5437; part-time $226.55 per credit hour. Tuition, nonresident: full-time $12,949; part-time $539.55 per credit hour. *Required fees:* $2741. *Financial support:* In 2011–12, fellowships with partial tuition reimbursements (averaging $15,000 per year), research assistantships with partial tuition reimbursements (averaging $15,000 per year), teaching assistantships with partial tuition reimbursements (averaging $15,000 per year) were awarded; career-related internships or fieldwork and institutionally sponsored loans also available. Support available to part-time students. Financial award application deadline: 3/1; financial award applicants required to submit FAFSA. *Faculty research:* Expert systems, geographic information systems, economics, biology, genetics. *Unit head:* Dr. Steve Whisenant, Professor and Head, 979-845-5000, Fax: 979-845-6049, E-mail: s-whisenant@tamu.edu. *Application contact:* Dr. Carol Loopstra, Associate Professor, 979-862-2200, Fax: 979-845-6049, E-mail: c-loopstra@tamu.edu. Web site: http://essm.tamu.edu.

Texas A&M University, College of Agriculture and Life Sciences, Department of Recreation, Park and Tourism Sciences, College Station, TX 77843. Offers natural resources development (M Agr); recreation resources development (M Agr); recreation, park, and tourism sciences (MS, PhD). *Faculty:* 17. *Students:* 58 full-time (32 women), 19 part-time (11 women); includes 10 minority (5 Black or African American, non-Hispanic/Latino; 1 Asian, non-Hispanic/Latino; 3 Hispanic/Latino; 1 Two or more races, non-Hispanic/Latino), 30 international. Average age 28. In 2011, 12 master's, 6 doctorates awarded. *Degree requirements:* For master's, thesis (for some programs), internship and professional paper (M Agr); for doctorate, thesis/dissertation. *Entrance requirements:* For master's and doctorate, GRE General Test. Additional exam requirements/recommendations for international students: Required—TOEFL. *Application deadline:* For fall admission, 4/15 priority date for domestic students; for spring admission, 10/15 priority date for domestic students. Applications are processed on a rolling basis. Application fee: $50 ($75 for international students). Electronic applications accepted. *Expenses:* Tuition, state resident: full-time $5437; part-time $226.55 per credit hour. Tuition, nonresident: full-time $12,949; part-time $539.55 per credit hour. *Required fees:* $2741. *Financial support:* Fellowships, research assistantships, teaching assistantships, career-related internships or fieldwork, institutionally sponsored loans, and scholarships/grants available. Financial award application deadline: 4/15; financial award applicants required to submit FAFSA. *Faculty research:* Administration and tourism, outdoor recreation, commercial recreation, environmental law, system planning. *Unit head:* Dr. Gary Ellis, Head, 979-845-7324. *Application contact:* Graduate Admissions, 979-845-1044, E-mail: admissions@tamu.edu. Web site: http://rpts.tamu.edu/.

Texas Tech University, Graduate School, College of Agricultural Sciences and Natural Resources, Department of Natural Resources Management, Lubbock, TX 79409. Offers fisheries science (MS, PhD); range science (MS, PhD); wildlife, aquatic, and wildlands science and management (MS, PhD). Part-time programs available. *Faculty:* 11 full-time (1 woman). *Students:* 50 full-time (13 women), 3 part-time (0 women); includes 7 minority (1 American Indian or Alaska Native, non-Hispanic/Latino; 3 Hispanic/Latino; 3 Two or more races, non-Hispanic/Latino), 7 international. Average age 27. 20 applicants, 45% accepted, 8 enrolled. In 2011, 4 master's, 2 doctorates awarded. *Degree requirements:* For master's, thesis; for doctorate, thesis/dissertation. *Entrance requirements:* For master's and doctorate, GRE General Test, formal approval from departmental committee. Additional exam requirements/recommendations for international students: Required—TOEFL (minimum score 550 paper-based; 213 computer-based; 79 iBT). *Application deadline:* For fall admission, 6/1 priority date for domestic students, 1/15 for international students; for spring admission, 9/1 priority date for domestic students, 6/15 for international students. Applications are processed on a rolling basis. Application fee: $50 ($75 for international students). Electronic applications accepted. *Expenses:* Tuition, state resident: full-time $5899; part-time $245.80 per credit hour. Tuition, nonresident: full-time $13,411; part-time $558.80 per credit hour. *Required fees:* $2680.60; $86.50 per credit hour. $920.30 per semester. *Financial support:* In 2011–12, 17 students received support. Application deadline: 4/15; applicants required to submit FAFSA. *Faculty research:* Use of fire on range lands; big game, upland game, and waterfowl; playa lakes in the southern Great Plains; conservation biology; fish ecology and physiology. *Total annual research expenditures:* $2.1 million. *Unit head:* Dr. Mark Wallace, Interim Chairman, 806-742-2841, Fax: 806-742-2280, E-mail: mark.wallace@ttu.edu. *Application contact:* Renee Dillon, Senior Business Assistant, 806-742-2841, E-mail: renee.dillon@ttu.edu. Web site: http://www.rw.ttu.edu/dept/.

Universidad Metropolitana, School of Environmental Affairs, Program in Environmental Management, San Juan, PR 00928-1150. Offers MSEM. Part-time programs available. *Degree requirements:* For master's, thesis. Electronic applications accepted.

Universidad Nacional Pedro Henriquez Urena, Graduate School, Santo Domingo, Dominican Republic. Offers agricultural diversity (MS), including horticultural/fruit production, tropical animal production; conservation of monuments and cultural assets (M Arch); ecology and environment (MS); environmental engineering (MEE); international relations (MA); natural resource management (MS); political science (MA); project optimization (MPM); project feasibility (MPM); project management (MPM); sanitation engineering (ME); science for teachers (MS); tropical Caribbean architecture (M Arch).

Université du Québec à Montréal, Graduate Programs, Program in Earth Sciences, Montreal, QC H3C 3P8, Canada. Offers earth sciences (M Sc); mineral resources (PhD); non-renewable resources (DESS). Part-time programs available. Terminal master's awarded for partial completion of doctoral program. *Degree requirements:* For master's, thesis (for some programs); for doctorate, thesis/dissertation. *Entrance requirements:* For master's, appropriate bachelor's degree or equivalent, proficiency in French. *Faculty research:* Economic geology, structural geology, geochemistry, Quaternary geology, isotopic geochemistry.

Université du Québec en Abitibi-Témiscamingue, Graduate Programs, Program in Environmental Sciences, Rouyn-Noranda, QC J9X 5E4, Canada. Offers biology (MS); environmental sciences (PhD); sustainable forest ecosystem management (MS).

University of Alaska Fairbanks, School of Natural Resources and Agricultural Sciences, Fairbanks, AK 99775-7140. Offers natural resource and sustainability (PhD); natural resource management (MS); natural resource management and geography (MNRM, MS). Part-time programs available. *Faculty:* 33 full-time (10 women), 4 part-time/adjunct (3 women). *Students:* 21 full-time (15 women), 31 part-time (17 women); includes 4 minority (1 American Indian or Alaska Native, non-Hispanic/Latino; 2 Hispanic/Latino; 1 Two or more races, non-Hispanic/Latino), 6 international. Average age 33. 25 applicants, 28% accepted, 6 enrolled. In 2011, 7 master's awarded. *Degree requirements:* For master's, comprehensive exam, thesis or alternative. *Entrance requirements:* For master's, GRE General Test. Additional exam requirements/recommendations for international students: Required—TOEFL (minimum score 550 paper-based; 213 computer-based). *Application deadline:* For fall admission, 6/1 for domestic students, 3/1 for international students; for spring admission, 10/15 for domestic students, 9/1 for international students. Applications are processed on a rolling basis. Application fee: $60. Electronic applications accepted. *Expenses:* Tuition, state resident: full-time $6696; part-time $372 per credit. Tuition, nonresident: full-time $13,680; part-time $760 per credit. Tuition and fees vary according to course load and reciprocity agreements. *Financial support:* In 2011–12, 8 research assistantships (averaging $16,856 per year), 4 teaching assistantships (averaging $5,770 per year) were awarded; fellowships, career-related internships or fieldwork, Federal Work-Study, scholarships/grants, health care benefits, and unspecified assistantships also available. Support available to part-time students. Financial award application deadline: 2/15; financial award applicants required to submit FAFSA. *Faculty research:* Conservation biology, soil/water conservation, land use policy and planning in the arctic and subarctic, forest ecosystem management, subarctic agricultural production. *Total annual research expenditures:* $6.2 million. *Unit head:* Dr. Carol E. Lewis, Dean, 907-474-7083, Fax: 907-474-6567, E-mail: fysnras@uaf.edu. *Application contact:* Veazey David, Director of Enrollment Management, 907-474-5276, Fax: 907-474-6567, E-mail: dave.veazey@alaska.edu. Web site: http://www.uaf.edu/snras/.

University of Alberta, Faculty of Graduate Studies and Research, Department of Renewable Resources, Edmonton, AB T6G 2E1, Canada. Offers agroforestry (M Ag, M Sc, MF); conservation biology (M Sc, PhD); forest biology and management (M Sc, PhD); land reclamation and remediation (M Sc, PhD); protected areas and wildlands management (M Sc, PhD); soil science (M Ag, M Sc, PhD); water and land resources (M Ag, M Sc, PhD); wildlife ecology and management (M Sc, PhD); MBA/M Ag; MBA/MF. Part-time programs available. *Degree requirements:* For master's, thesis (for some programs); for doctorate, comprehensive exam, thesis/dissertation. *Entrance requirements:* For master's, minimum 2 years of relevant professional experiences, minimum GPA of 3.0; for doctorate, minimum GPA of 3.0. Additional exam requirements/recommendations for international students: Required—TOEFL (minimum score 550 paper-based;

213 computer-based). Electronic applications accepted. *Faculty research:* Natural and managed landscapes.

University of Alberta, Faculty of Graduate Studies and Research, Program in Business Administration, Edmonton, AB T6G 2E1, Canada. Offers international business (MBA); leisure and sport management (MBA); natural resources and energy (MBA); technology commercialization (MBA); MBA/LL B; MBA/M Ag; MBA/M Eng; MBA/MF; MBA/PhD. *Accreditation:* AACSB. Part-time and evening/weekend programs available. *Degree requirements:* For master's, thesis or alternative. *Entrance requirements:* For master's, GMAT. Additional exam requirements/recommendations for international students: Required—TOEFL (minimum score 600 paper-based; 250 computer-based). Electronic applications accepted. *Faculty research:* Natural resources and energy/management and policy/family enterprise/international business/healthcare research management.

The University of Arizona, College of Agriculture and Life Sciences, School of Natural Resources, Program in Natural Resources, Tucson, AZ 85721. Offers MS, PhD. *Faculty:* 18 full-time (3 women), 4 part-time/adjunct (0 women). *Students:* 72 full-time (38 women), 26 part-time (17 women); includes 19 minority (11 Hispanic/Latino; 8 Two or more races, non-Hispanic/Latino), 12 international. Average age 33. *Degree requirements:* For master's, thesis; for doctorate, comprehensive exam, thesis/dissertation. *Entrance requirements:* For master's and doctorate, GRE General Test, minimum GPA of 3.0. Additional exam requirements/recommendations for international students: Required—TOEFL (minimum score 550 paper-based; 213 computer-based). *Application deadline:* Applications are processed on a rolling basis. Application fee: $75. *Expenses:* Tuition, state resident: full-time $10,840. Tuition, nonresident: full-time $25,802. *Financial support:* Research assistantships, teaching assistantships, career-related internships or fieldwork, scholarships/grants, health care benefits, tuition waivers (partial), and unspecified assistantships available. *Faculty research:* Criteria for defining, mapping, and evaluating range sites; methods of establishing forage plants on southwestern range lands; plants for pollution and erosion control, beautification, and browse. *Unit head:* Dr. Lisa J. Graumlich, Director, 520-621-7257, E-mail: lisag@cals.arizona.edu. *Application contact:* Cheryl L. Craddock, Academic Coordinator, 520-621-7260, Fax: 520-621-8801, E-mail: ccraddoc@email.arizona.edu. Web site: http://grad.arizona.edu/live/programs/description/117.

University of Arkansas at Monticello, School of Forest Resources, Monticello, AR 71656. Offers MS. Part-time programs available. *Degree requirements:* For master's, comprehensive exam, thesis. *Entrance requirements:* For master's, GRE General Test, minimum GPA of 2.7. Additional exam requirements/recommendations for international students: Required—TOEFL (minimum score 550 paper-based; 213 computer-based). Electronic applications accepted. *Faculty research:* Geographic information systems/remote sensing, forest ecology, wildlife ecology and management.

The University of British Columbia, Program in Resource Management and Environmental Studies, Vancouver, BC, BC V6T 1Z4, Canada. Offers M Sc, MA, PhD. *Degree requirements:* For master's, thesis; for doctorate, comprehensive exam, thesis/dissertation. *Entrance requirements:* Additional exam requirements/recommendations for international students: Required—TOEFL (minimum score 600 paper-based; 250 computer-based; 100 iBT). Electronic applications accepted. *Faculty research:* Land management, water resources, energy, environmental assessment, risk evaluation.

University of California, Berkeley, Graduate Division, Group in Energy and Resources, Berkeley, CA 94720-1500. Offers MA, MS, PhD. *Degree requirements:* For master's, project or thesis; for doctorate, one foreign language, thesis/dissertation, qualifying exam. *Entrance requirements:* For master's and doctorate, GRE General Test, minimum GPA of 3.0, 3 letters of recommendation. *Faculty research:* Technical, economic, environmental, and institutional aspects of energy conservation in residential and commercial buildings; international patterns of energy use; renewable energy sources; assessment of valuation of energy and environmental resources pricing.

University of Connecticut, Graduate School, College of Agriculture and Natural Resources, Department of Natural Resources Management and Engineering, Storrs, CT 06269. Offers MS, PhD. Terminal master's awarded for partial completion of doctoral program. *Degree requirements:* For master's, comprehensive exam. *Entrance requirements:* For master's, GRE General Test, GRE Subject Test. Additional exam requirements/recommendations for international students: Required—TOEFL (minimum score 550 paper-based; 213 computer-based). Electronic applications accepted. *Faculty research:* Forest management, forest protection, water resources, biometeorology.

University of Delaware, College of Agriculture and Natural Resources, Department of Bioresources Engineering, Newark, DE 19716. Offers MS.

University of Denver, University College, Denver, CO 80208. Offers arts and culture (MLS, Certificate), including art, literature, and culture, arts development and program management (Certificate), creative writing; environmental policy and management (MAS, Certificate), including energy and sustainability (Certificate), environmental assessment of nuclear power (Certificate), environmental health and safety (Certificate), environmental management, natural resource management (Certificate); geographic information systems (MAS, Certificate); global affairs (MLS, Certificate), including translation studies, world history and culture; healthcare leadership (MPH, Certificate), including healthcare policy, law, and ethics, medical and healthcare information technologies, strategic

Peterson's Graduate Programs in the Physical Sciences, Mathematics, Agricultural Sciences, the Environment & Natural Resources 2013

facebook.com/petersonspublishing **531**

Natural Resources

management of healthcare; information and communications technology (MCIS, Certificate), including database design and administration (Certificate), geographic information systems (MCIS), information security systems security (Certificate), information systems security (MCIS), project management (MCIS, MPS, Certificate), software design and administration (Certificate), software design and programming (MCIS), technology management, telecommunications technology (MCIS), Web design and development; leadership and organizations (MPS, Certificate), including human capital in organizations, philanthropic leadership, project management (MCIS, MPS, Certificate), strategic innovation and change; organizational and professional communication (MPS, Certificate), including alternative dispute resolution, organizational communication, organizational development and training, public relations and marketing; security management (MAS, Certificate), including emergency planning and response, information security (MAS), organizational security; strategic human resource management (MPS, Certificate), including global human resources (MPS), human resource management and development (MPS). Part-time and evening/weekend programs available. Postbaccalaureate distance learning degree programs offered (no on-campus study). *Faculty:* 204 part-time/adjunct (80 women). *Students:* 56 full-time (26 women), 1,096 part-time (647 women); includes 196 minority (81 Black or African American, non-Hispanic/Latino; 7 American Indian or Alaska Native, non-Hispanic/Latino; 30 Asian, non-Hispanic/Latino; 66 Hispanic/Latino; 3 Native Hawaiian or other Pacific Islander, non-Hispanic/Latino; 9 Two or more races, non-Hispanic/Latino), 76 international. Average age 36. 572 applicants, 95% accepted, 410 enrolled. In 2011, 404 master's, 123 other advanced degrees awarded. *Degree requirements:* For master's, capstone project. *Entrance requirements:* For master's, two letters of recommendation, personal statement, resume. Additional exam requirements/recommendations for international students: Required—TOEFL (minimum score 550 paper-based; 80 iBT). *Application deadline:* For fall admission, 7/20 priority date for domestic students, 6/8 for international students; for winter admission, 10/26 priority date for domestic students, 9/14 for international students; for spring admission, 2/1 priority date for domestic students, 12/14 for international students. Applications are processed on a rolling basis. Application fee: $75. Electronic applications accepted. *Expenses:* Contact institution. *Financial support:* Applicants required to submit FAFSA. *Unit head:* Dr. James Davis, Dean, 303-871-2291, Fax: 303-871-4047, E-mail: jdavis@du.edu. *Application contact:* Information Contact, 303-871-3155, Fax: 303-871-4047, E-mail: ucolinfo@du.edu. Web site: http://www.universitycollege.du.edu/.

University of Florida, Graduate School, College of Agricultural and Life Sciences, School of Forest Resources and Conservation, Gainesville, FL 32611. Offers MFAS, MFRC, MS, PhD, JD/MFRC, JD/MS, JD/PhD. Part-time and evening/weekend programs available. Postbaccalaureate distance learning degree programs offered. *Faculty:* 39 full-time (6 women), 6 part-time/adjunct (2 women). *Students:* 88 full-time (38 women), 40 part-time (17 women); includes 7 minority (3 Asian, non-Hispanic/Latino; 4 Hispanic/Latino), 27 international. Average age 32. 71 applicants, 45% accepted, 23 enrolled. In 2011, 20 master's, 11 doctorates awarded. Terminal master's awarded for partial completion of doctoral program. *Degree requirements:* For master's, comprehensive exam, thesis optional, project (for MFRC); for doctorate, comprehensive exam, thesis/dissertation. *Entrance requirements:* For master's, GRE General Test (minimum score of 1000), minimum GPA of 3.0; for doctorate, GRE General Test, minimum GPA of 3.25. Additional exam requirements/recommendations for international students: Required—TOEFL (minimum score 550 paper-based; 213 computer-based; 80 iBT), IELTS (minimum score 6). *Application deadline:* For fall admission, 1/3 priority date for domestic students, 1/3 for international students; for spring admission, 8/1 for domestic and international students. Applications are processed on a rolling basis. Application fee: $30. Electronic applications accepted. *Financial support:* Fellowships with full tuition reimbursements, research assistantships with full tuition reimbursements, teaching assistantships with full tuition reimbursements, Federal Work-Study, and institutionally sponsored loans available. Support available to part-time students. Financial award application deadline: 1/3; financial award applicants required to submit FAFSA. *Faculty research:* Forest biology and ecology; natural resource economics and management; human dimensions and resource policy; tropical forestry and agroforestry; geomatics: geospatial, GIS, and remote sensing. *Total annual research expenditures:* $3.4 million. *Unit head:* Dr. Tim White, Director, 352-846-0850, Fax: 352-392-1707, E-mail: tlwhite@ufl.edu. *Application contact:* Dr. Taylor Stein, Graduate Coordinator, 352-846-0860, Fax: 352-846-1277, E-mail: tstein@ufl.edu. Web site: http://www.sfrc.ufl.edu/.

University of Florida, Graduate School, School of Natural Resources and Environment, Gainesville, FL 32611. Offers interdisciplinary ecology (MS, PhD). *Students:* 87 full-time (53 women), 25 part-time (11 women); includes 15 minority (3 Black or African American, non-Hispanic/Latino; 1 American Indian or Alaska Native, non-Hispanic/Latino; 3 Asian, non-Hispanic/Latino; 8 Hispanic/Latino), 39 international. Average age 33. 68 applicants, 19% accepted, 11 enrolled. In 2011, 14 master's, 17 doctorates awarded. *Degree requirements:* For master's, comprehensive exam, thesis; for doctorate, comprehensive exam, thesis/dissertation. *Entrance requirements:* For master's and doctorate, GRE General Test, minimum GPA of 3.0. Additional exam requirements/recommendations for international students: Required—TOEFL (minimum score 550 paper-based; 213 computer-based; 80 iBT), IELTS (minimum score 6). *Application deadline:* For fall admission, 2/1 priority date for domestic students, 2/1 for international students. Applications are processed on a rolling basis. Application fee: $30. Electronic applications accepted. *Financial support:* Fellowships, research assistantships,

and teaching assistantships available. Financial award applicants required to submit FAFSA. *Faculty research:* Natural sciences, social sciences, sustainability studies, research design and methods. *Unit head:* Dr. Stephen R. Humphrey, Director and Graduate Coordinator, 352-392-9230, Fax: 352-392-9748, E-mail: humphrey@ufl.edu. *Application contact:* Office of Graduate Admissions, 352-392-1365, E-mail: gradinfo@ufl.edu. Web site: http://www.snre.ufl.edu/.

University of Georgia, School of Forestry and Natural Resources, Athens, GA 30602. Offers MFR, MS, PhD. *Faculty:* 46 full-time (6 women), 8 part-time/adjunct (1 woman). *Students:* 162 full-time (73 women), 29 part-time (8 women); includes 9 minority (2 Black or African American, non-Hispanic/Latino; 3 Asian, non-Hispanic/Latino; 2 Hispanic/Latino; 2 Two or more races, non-Hispanic/Latino), 26 international. Average age 29. 104 applicants, 67% accepted, 45 enrolled. In 2011, 47 master's, 12 doctorates awarded. *Degree requirements:* For master's, thesis (MS); for doctorate, one foreign language, thesis/dissertation. *Entrance requirements:* For master's and doctorate, GRE General Test. *Application deadline:* For fall admission, 7/1 priority date for domestic students; for spring admission, 11/15 for domestic students. Application fee: $50. Electronic applications accepted. *Financial support:* Fellowships, research assistantships, teaching assistantships, and unspecified assistantships available. *Unit head:* Michael L. Clutter, Professor, 706-542-4741, Fax: 706-542-8356, E-mail: mclutter@warnell.uga.edu. *Application contact:* Dr. Laurence Schimleck, Graduate Coordinator, 706-542-0464, Fax: 706-542-8356, E-mail: lschimlect@warnell.uga.edu. Web site: http://www.warnell.uga.edu/.

University of Guelph, Graduate Studies, Ontario Agricultural College, Department of Land Resource Science, Guelph, ON N1G 2W1, Canada. Offers atmospheric science (M Sc, PhD); environmental and agricultural earth sciences (M Sc, PhD); land resources management (M Sc, PhD); soil science (M Sc, PhD). Part-time programs available. *Degree requirements:* For master's, thesis (for some programs), research project (non-thesis track); for doctorate, comprehensive exam, thesis/dissertation. *Entrance requirements:* For master's, minimum B average during previous 2 years of course work; for doctorate, minimum B average during previous 2 years of course work. Additional exam requirements/recommendations for international students: Required—TOEFL (minimum score 550 paper-based; 213 computer-based). Electronic applications accepted. *Faculty research:* Soil science, environmental earth science, land resource management.

University of Hawaii at Manoa, Graduate Division, College of Tropical Agriculture and Human Resources, Department of Natural Resources and Environmental Management, Honolulu, HI 96822. Offers MS, PhD. Part-time programs available. Terminal master's awarded for partial completion of doctoral program. *Degree requirements:* For master's, thesis optional; for doctorate, comprehensive exam, thesis/dissertation. *Entrance requirements:* For master's and doctorate, GRE General Test, minimum GPA of 3.0 in last 4 semesters of course work. Additional exam requirements/recommendations for international students: Required—TOEFL (minimum score 600 paper-based; 250 computer-based; 100 iBT), IELTS (minimum score 7). *Faculty research:* Bioeconomics, natural resource management.

University of Idaho, College of Graduate Studies, College of Natural Resources, Department of Conservation Social Sciences, Moscow, ID 83844-1139. Offers natural resources (MS, PhD). *Faculty:* 12 full-time. *Students:* 18 full-time, 1 part-time. Average age 25. In 2011, 4 master's awarded. *Degree requirements:* For doctorate, thesis/dissertation. *Entrance requirements:* For master's, minimum GPA of 2.8; for doctorate, minimum undergraduate GPA of 2.8, 3.0 graduate. *Application deadline:* For fall admission, 8/1 for domestic students; for spring admission, 12/15 for domestic students. Applications are processed on a rolling basis. Application fee: $60. Electronic applications accepted. *Expenses:* Tuition, state resident: full-time $3874; part-time $334 per credit hour. Tuition, nonresident: full-time $16,394; part-time $861 per credit hour. *Required fees:* $2808; $99 per credit hour. Tuition and fees vary according to program. *Financial support:* Research assistantships and teaching assistantships available. Financial award applicants required to submit FAFSA. *Faculty research:* Parks, wilderness and protected areas policy, planning and management, recreation and tourism planning, urban and community forestry, resource-based tourism, ecotourism, human dimensions of ecosystem management. *Unit head:* Dr. Edwin Krumpe, Department Chair, 208-885-7911, E-mail: css@uidaho.edu. *Application contact:* Erick Larson, Director of Graduate Admissions, 208-885-4723, E-mail: gadms@uidaho.edu. Web site: http://www.uidaho.edu/cnr/css.

University of Idaho, College of Graduate Studies, College of Natural Resources, Department of Fish and Wildlife Resources, Moscow, ID 83844-1136. Offers natural resources (MS, PhD). *Faculty:* 12 full-time, 1 part-time/adjunct. *Students:* 4 part-time. Average age 28. In 2011, 5 master's, 1 doctorate awarded. *Degree requirements:* For doctorate, thesis/dissertation. *Entrance requirements:* For master's, minimum GPA of 2.8; for doctorate, minimum undergraduate GPA of 2.8, 3.0 graduate. *Application deadline:* For fall admission, 8/1 for domestic students; for spring admission, 12/15 for domestic students. Applications are processed on a rolling basis. Application fee: $60. Electronic applications accepted. *Expenses:* Tuition, state resident: full-time $3874; part-time $334 per credit hour. Tuition, nonresident: full-time $16,394; part-time $861 per credit hour. *Required fees:* $2808; $99 per credit hour. Tuition and fees vary according to program. *Financial support:* Research assistantships and teaching assistantships available. Financial award applicants required to submit FAFSA. *Faculty research:* Waterfowl and wetland ecology, lake restoration and management, sustainable aquaculture production, riparian ecology and river restoration, wildlife ecology and management. *Unit head:* Dr. Kerry Reese, Department Head, 208-885-6434, E-mail: fish_wildlife@uidaho.edu. *Application contact:* Erick Larson, Director of Graduate Admissions, 208-885-4723, E-mail: gadms@uidaho.edu. Web site: http://www.uidaho.edu/cnr/fishwild.

University of Idaho, College of Graduate Studies, College of Natural Resources, Program in Natural Resources, Moscow, ID 83844-1138. Offers MNR, MS, PhD. *Faculty:* 5 full-time, 1 part-time/adjunct. *Students:* 118 full-time, 71 part-time. Average age 33. In 2011, 17 master's, 5 doctorates awarded. *Application deadline:* Applications are processed on a rolling basis. Application fee: $60. Electronic applications accepted. *Expenses:* Tuition, state resident: full-time $3874; part-time $334 per credit hour. Tuition, nonresident: full-time $16,394; part-time $861 per credit hour. *Required fees:* $2808; $99 per credit hour. Tuition and fees vary according to program. *Financial support:* Applicants required to submit FAFSA. *Unit head:* Dr. Kurt Scott Pregitzer, Dean, 208-885-8981, Fax: 208-885-5534, E-mail: cnr@uidaho.edu. *Application contact:* Erick Larson, Director of Graduate Admissions, 208-885-4723, E-mail: gadms@uidaho.edu. Web site: http://www.uidaho.edu/cnr.

University of Idaho, College of Graduate Studies, Program in Environmental Science, Moscow, ID 83844-3006. Offers environmental science (MS, PhD); natural resources and environmental science (PSM); water resources (MS, PhD). *Faculty:* 19 full-time, 1 part-time/adjunct. *Students:* 87 full-time, 57 part-time. Average age 32. In 2011, 20 master's, 2 doctorates awarded. *Application deadline:* For fall admission, 8/1 for domestic students; for spring admission, 12/15 for domestic students. Applications are processed on a rolling basis. Application fee: $60. Electronic applications accepted. *Expenses:* Tuition, state resident: full-time $3874; part-time $334 per credit hour. Tuition, nonresident: full-time $16,394; part-time $861 per credit hour. *Required fees:* $2808; $99 per credit hour. Tuition and fees vary according to program. *Financial support:* Research assistantships and teaching assistantships available. Financial award applicants required to submit FAFSA. *Unit head:* Dr. Jan Boll, Director, 208-885-6113, Fax: 208-885-4674, E-mail: envs@uidaho.edu. *Application contact:* Erick Larson, Director of Graduate Admissions, 208-885-4723, E-mail: gadms@uidaho.edu. Web site: http://www.uidaho.edu/cogs/envs.

University of Illinois at Urbana–Champaign, Graduate College, College of Agricultural, Consumer and Environmental Sciences, Department of Natural Resources and Environmental Science, Champaign, IL 61820. Offers MS, PhD, MS/JD. Part-time programs available. Postbaccalaureate distance learning degree programs offered (no on-campus study). *Faculty:* 21 full-time (6 women), 1 part-time/adjunct (0 women). *Students:* 62 full-time (26 women), 81 part-time (38 women); includes 9 minority (1 Black or African American, non-Hispanic/Latino; 1 American Indian or Alaska Native, non-Hispanic/Latino; 1 Asian, non-Hispanic/Latino; 5 Hispanic/Latino; 1 Two or more races, non-Hispanic/Latino), 19 international. 124 applicants, 40% accepted, 42 enrolled. In 2011, 21 master's, 3 doctorates awarded. *Entrance requirements:* For master's and doctorate, GRE, minimum GPA of 3.0. Additional exam requirements/recommendations for international students: Required—TOEFL (minimum score 600 paper-based; 250 computer-based). *Application deadline:* Applications are processed on a rolling basis. Application fee: $75 ($90 for international students). Electronic applications accepted. *Financial support:* In 2011–12, 7 fellowships, 66 research assistantships, 26 teaching assistantships were awarded; tuition waivers (full and partial) also available. *Unit head:* Jeffrey D. Brawn, Head, 217-244-5937, Fax: 217-244-3219, E-mail: jbrawn@illinois.edu. *Application contact:* Karen M. Claus, Secretary, 217-333-5824, Fax: 217-244-3219, E-mail: kclaus@illinois.edu. Web site: http://nres.illinois.edu/.

University of Maine, Graduate School, College of Natural Sciences, Forestry, and Agriculture, Department of Forest Management and Forest Ecosystem Science, Orono, ME 04469. Offers forest resources (PhD); forestry (MF, MS). *Accreditation:* SAF (one or more programs are accredited). Part-time programs available. *Faculty:* 20 full-time (1 woman). *Students:* 37 full-time (12 women), 15 part-time (7 women), 13 international. Average age 29. 35 applicants, 57% accepted, 17 enrolled. In 2011, 11 master's, 2 doctorates awarded. *Degree requirements:* For master's, thesis; for doctorate, one foreign language, thesis/dissertation. *Entrance requirements:* For master's and doctorate, GRE General Test. Additional exam requirements/recommendations for international students: Required—TOEFL. *Application deadline:* For fall admission, 2/1 priority date for domestic students. Applications are processed on a rolling basis. Application fee: $65. Electronic applications accepted. *Expenses:* Tuition, state resident: full-time $5016. Tuition, nonresident: full-time $14,424. *Financial support:* In 2011–12, 28 research assistantships with full tuition reimbursements (averaging $20,447 per year), 7 teaching assistantships with full tuition reimbursements (averaging $13,600 per year) were awarded; career-related internships or fieldwork, Federal Work-Study, and institutionally sponsored loans also available. Financial award application deadline: 3/1. *Faculty research:* Forest economics, engineering and operations analysis, biometrics and remote sensing, timber management, wood technology. *Total annual research expenditures:* $336,195. *Unit head:* Dr. Robert Wagner, Chair, 207-581-4737. *Application contact:* Scott G. Delcourt, Associate Dean of the Graduate School, 207-581-3291, Fax: 207-581-3232, E-mail: graduate@maine.edu. Web site: http://www2.umaine.edu/graduate/.

University of Maine, Graduate School, College of Natural Sciences, Forestry, and Agriculture, Department of Plant, Soil, and Environmental Sciences, Orono, ME 04469. Offers biological sciences (PhD); ecology and environmental sciences (MS, PhD); forest resources (PhD); horticulture (MS); plant science (PhD); plant, soil, and environmental sciences (MS); resource utilization (MS). *Faculty:* 9 full-

time (3 women), 7 part-time/adjunct (3 women). *Students:* 7 full-time (4 women), 2 part-time (0 women), 2 international. Average age 30. 14 applicants, 50% accepted, 5 enrolled. In 2011, 4 degrees awarded. *Entrance requirements:* For master's and doctorate, GRE General Test. Additional exam requirements/recommendations for international students: Required—TOEFL. *Application deadline:* Applications are processed on a rolling basis. Application fee: $65. Electronic applications accepted. *Expenses:* Tuition, state resident: full-time $5016. Tuition, nonresident: full-time $14,424. *Financial support:* In 2011–12, 16 research assistantships with full tuition reimbursements (averaging $17,336 per year), 1 teaching assistantship with full tuition reimbursement (averaging $13,600 per year) were awarded; scholarships/grants, tuition waivers (full and partial), and unspecified assistantships also available. *Total annual research expenditures:* $179,065. *Unit head:* Dr. Gregory Porter, Chair, 207-581-2943, Fax: 207-581-3207. *Application contact:* Scott G. Delcourt, Associate Dean of the Graduate School, 207-581-3291, Fax: 207-581-3232, E-mail: graduate@maine.edu. Web site: http://www2.umaine.edu/graduate/.

The University of Manchester, School of Materials, Manchester, United Kingdom. Offers advanced aerospace materials engineering (M Sc); advanced metallic systems (PhD); biomedical materials (M Phil, M Sc, PhD); ceramics and glass (M Phil, M Sc, PhD); composite materials (M Sc, PhD); corrosion and protection (M Phil, M Sc, PhD); materials (M Phil, PhD); metallic materials (M Phil, M Sc, PhD); nanostructural materials (M Phil, M Sc, PhD); paper science (M Phil, M Sc, PhD); polymer science and engineering (M Phil, M Sc, PhD); technical textiles (M Sc); textile design, fashion and management (M Phil, M Sc, PhD); textile science and technology (M Phil, M Sc, PhD); textiles (M Phil, PhD); textiles and fashion (M Ent).

University of Manitoba, Faculty of Graduate Studies, Clayton H. Riddell Faculty of Environment, Earth, and Resources, Natural Resources Institute, Winnipeg, MB R3T 2N2, Canada. Offers natural resources and environmental management (PhD); natural resources management (MNRM).

University of Maryland, College Park, Academic Affairs, College of Agriculture and Natural Resources, Department of Plant Science and Landscape Architecture, Natural Resource Sciences Program, College Park, MD 20742. Offers MS, PhD. In 2011, 1 master's awarded. *Expenses: Tuition, area resident:* Part-time $525 per credit hour. Tuition, state resident: part-time $525 per credit hour. Tuition, nonresident: part-time $1131 per credit hour. *Required fees:* $386.31 per term. Tuition and fees vary according to program. *Financial support:* Fellowships, research assistantships, and teaching assistantships available. *Faculty research:* Wetland soils, acid mine drainage, acid sulfate soil. *Unit head:* Dr. William Kenworthy, Chair, 301-405-6244, Fax: 301-314-9308, E-mail: wkenwort@umd.edu.

University of Michigan, School of Natural Resources and Environment, Ann Arbor, MI 48109. Offers environmental justice (Certificate); industrial ecology (Certificate); landscape architecture (MLA, PhD); natural resources and environment (MS, PhD), including aquatic sciences: research and management (MS), behavior, education and communication (MS), conservation biology (MS), conservation ecology (MS), environmental informatics (MS), environmental justice (MS), environmental policy and planning (MS), natural resources and environment (PhD), sustainable systems (MS), terrestrial ecosystems (MS); spatial analysis (Certificate); JD/MS; MBA/MS; MLA/M Arch; MLA/MBA; MLA/MUP; MPP/MS; MS/AM; MS/JD; MS/MBA; MS/MPP; MS/MSE. *Accreditation:* ASLA (one or more programs are accredited); SAF (one or more programs are accredited). *Faculty:* 45 full-time, 23 part-time/adjunct. *Students:* 474 (270 women); includes 66 minority (7 Black or African American, non-Hispanic/Latino; 2 American Indian or Alaska Native, non-Hispanic/Latino; 35 Asian, non-Hispanic/Latino; 16 Hispanic/Latino; 6 Two or more races, non-Hispanic/Latino), 71 international. Average age 28. 692 applicants. In 2011, 133 master's, 11 doctorates awarded. *Degree requirements:* For master's, thesis, practicum, or group project; for doctorate, comprehensive exam, thesis/dissertation, oral defense of dissertation, preliminary exam. *Entrance requirements:* For master's, GRE General Test; for doctorate, GRE General Test, master's degree. Additional exam requirements/recommendations for international students: Required—TOEFL (minimum score 560 paper-based; 220 computer-based; 84 iBT). *Application deadline:* For fall admission, 1/5 priority date for domestic students, 1/5 for international students. Applications are processed on a rolling basis. Application fee: $65 ($75 for international students). Electronic applications accepted. *Financial support:* Fellowships with tuition reimbursements, research assistantships with tuition reimbursements, teaching assistantships with tuition reimbursements, career-related internships or fieldwork, Federal Work-Study, institutionally sponsored loans, scholarships/grants, health care benefits, unspecified assistantships, and Peace Corps Fellows available. Support available to part-time students. Financial award application deadline: 1/5; financial award applicants required to submit FAFSA. *Faculty research:* Ecology, environmental policy, landscape architecture, climate change, Great Lakes, sustainable systems, environmental justice, conservation ecology. *Total annual research expenditures:* $4.1 million. *Unit head:* Dr. Marie Lynn Miranda, Dean, 734-764-2550, Fax: 734-763-8965, E-mail: mlmirand@umich.edu. *Application contact:* Adam D. Ancira, Recruiting and Admissions Coordinator, 734-764-6453, Fax: 734-936-2195, E-mail: snre.admissions@umich.edu. Web site: http://www.snre.umich.edu/.

University of Minnesota, Twin Cities Campus, Graduate School, College of Food, Agricultural and Natural Resource Sciences, Program in Natural Resources Science and Management, Minneapolis, MN 55455-0213. Offers MS, PhD. Part-time programs available. *Faculty:* 125 full-time (24 women). *Students:* 74 full-time

Peterson's Graduate Programs in the Physical Sciences, Mathematics, Agricultural Sciences, the Environment & Natural Resources 2013

facebook.com/petersonspublishing **533**

Natural Resources

(40 women), 5 part-time (1 woman); includes 3 minority (2 Asian, non-Hispanic/Latino; 1 Hispanic/Latino), 12 international. Average age 30. 93 applicants, 38% accepted, 16 enrolled. In 2011, 12 master's, 8 doctorates awarded. Terminal master's awarded for partial completion of doctoral program. *Degree requirements:* For master's, comprehensive exam, thesis; for doctorate, comprehensive exam, thesis/dissertation. *Entrance requirements:* For master's and doctorate, GRE General Test. Additional exam requirements/recommendations for international students: Required—TOEFL (minimum score 500 paper-based; 213 computer-based; 79 iBT), IELTS (minimum score 6.5), TOEFL preferred. *Application deadline:* For fall admission, 12/15 priority date for domestic students, 12/15 for international students; for spring admission, 10/15 for domestic and international students. Applications are processed on a rolling basis. Application fee: $75 ($95 for international students). Electronic applications accepted. *Financial support:* In 2011–12, fellowships with full tuition reimbursements (averaging $23,500 per year), research assistantships with full tuition reimbursements (averaging $19,000 per year), teaching assistantships with full tuition reimbursements (averaging $19,000 per year) were awarded; scholarships/grants, health care benefits, tuition waivers (partial), and unspecified assistantships also available. *Faculty research:* Paper science, forestry, recreation resource management, wildlife ecology, environmental education, hydrology, conservation, tourism, economics, policy, watershed management, GIS, forest products. *Total annual research expenditures:* $6 million. *Unit head:* Dr. Michael Kilgore, Director of Graduate Studies, 612-624-6298, E-mail: mkilgore@umn.edu. *Application contact:* Jennifer Welsh, Program Coordinator, 612-624-7683, Fax: 612-625-5212, E-mail: jwelsh@umn.edu. Web site: http://www.nrsm.umn.edu.

University of Missouri, Graduate School, School of Natural Resources, Natural Resources Master's Program, Columbia, MO 65211. Offers MNR. *Students:* 2 part-time (0 women). Average age 36. 2 applicants, 0% accepted. In 2011, 1 degree awarded. *Expenses:* Tuition, state resident: full-time $5881. Tuition, nonresident: full-time $15,183. *Required fees:* $952. Tuition and fees vary according to campus/location and program. *Unit head:* Dr. Bruce Cutter, Associate Director, 573-882-7045, E-mail: cutterb@missouri.edu. *Application contact:* E-mail: snr@missouri.edu. Web site: http://www.snr.missouri.edu/academics/graduate.php.

The University of Montana, Graduate School, College of Forestry and Conservation, Missoula, MT 59812-0002. Offers ecosystem management (MEM, MS); fish and wildlife biology (PhD); forestry (MS, PhD); recreation management (MS); resource conservation (MS); wildlife biology (MS). *Degree requirements:* For doctorate, thesis/dissertation. *Entrance requirements:* For master's and doctorate, GRE General Test. Additional exam requirements/recommendations for international students: Required—TOEFL (minimum score 575 paper-based; 213 computer-based).

University of Nebraska–Lincoln, Graduate College, College of Agricultural Sciences and Natural Resources, Department of Agricultural Economics, Lincoln, NE 68588. Offers agribusiness (MBA); agricultural economics (MS, PhD); community development (M Ag). *Degree requirements:* For master's, thesis optional; for doctorate, comprehensive exam, thesis/dissertation. *Entrance requirements:* For master's and doctorate, GRE General Test. Additional exam requirements/recommendations for international students: Required—TOEFL (minimum score 550 paper-based; 213 computer-based). Electronic applications accepted. *Faculty research:* Marketing and agribusiness, production economics, resource law, international trade and development, rural policy and revitalization.

University of Nebraska–Lincoln, Graduate College, College of Agricultural Sciences and Natural Resources, School of Natural Resources, Lincoln, NE 68588. Offers geography (PhD); natural resources (MS, PhD). *Degree requirements:* For master's, thesis optional. *Entrance requirements:* For master's, GRE General Test. Additional exam requirements/recommendations for international students: Required—TOEFL. Electronic applications accepted. *Faculty research:* Wildlife biology, aquatic sciences, landscape ecology, agroforestry.

University of New Brunswick Saint John, MBA Program, Saint John, NB E2L 4L5, Canada. Offers administration (MBA); electronic commerce (MBA); international business (MBA); natural resource management (MBA). Part-time programs available. *Faculty:* 19 full-time (4 women), 14 part-time/adjunct (8 women). *Students:* 58 full-time (24 women), 130 part-time (46 women). 93 applicants, 78% accepted, 25 enrolled. In 2011, 36 master's awarded. *Entrance requirements:* For master's, GMAT, minimum GPA of 3.0. Additional exam requirements/recommendations for international students: Required—TOEFL (minimum score 580 paper-based; 237 computer-based), IELTS (minimum score 7), TWE (minimum score 4.5). *Application deadline:* For fall admission, 5/15 for domestic and international students. Applications are processed on a rolling basis. Application fee: $100. Electronic applications accepted. *Expenses:* Contact institution. *Financial support:* In 2011–12, 4 students received support. Career-related internships or fieldwork and scholarships/grants available. *Faculty research:* Business use of weblogs and podcasts to communicate, corporate governance, high-involvement work systems, international competitiveness, supply chain management and logistics. *Unit head:* Henryk Sterniczuk, Director of Graduate Studies, 506-648-5573, Fax: 506-648-5574, E-mail: sternicz@unbsj.ca. *Application contact:* Tammy Morin, Secretary, 506-648-5746, Fax: 506-648-5574, E-mail: tmorin@unbsj.ca. Web site: http://www.mba.unbsj.ca.

University of New Hampshire, Graduate School, College of Life Sciences and Agriculture, Department of Natural Resources, Durham, NH 03824. Offers environmental conservation (MS); forestry (MS); integrated coastal ecosystem science, policy, management (MS); natural resources (MS); water resources (MS); wildlife (MS). Part-time programs available. *Faculty:* 40 full-time. *Students:* 32 full-time (15 women), 24 part-time (13 women); includes 2 minority (1 Asian, non-Hispanic/Latino; 1 Hispanic/Latino), 1 international. Average age 29. 79 applicants, 49% accepted, 20 enrolled. In 2011, 10 master's awarded. *Degree requirements:* For master's, thesis or alternative. *Entrance requirements:* For master's, GRE General Test. Additional exam requirements/recommendations for international students: Required—TOEFL (minimum score 550 paper-based; 213 computer-based; 80 iBT). *Application deadline:* For fall admission, 6/1 for domestic students, 4/1 for international students; for spring admission, 12/1 for domestic students. Applications are processed on a rolling basis. Application fee: $65. Electronic applications accepted. *Expenses:* Tuition, state resident: full-time $12,360; part-time $687 per credit hour. Tuition, nonresident: full-time $25,680; part-time $1058 per credit hour. *International tuition:* $29,550 full-time. *Required fees:* $1666; $833 per course. $416.50 per semester. Tuition and fees vary according to course load and degree level. *Financial support:* In 2011–12, 35 students received support, including 3 fellowships, 13 research assistantships, 17 teaching assistantships; career-related internships or fieldwork, Federal Work-Study, scholarships/grants, and tuition waivers (full and partial) also available. Support available to part-time students. Financial award application deadline: 2/15. *Unit head:* Dr. Ted Howard, Chairperson, 603-862-2700, E-mail: natural.resources@unh.edu. *Application contact:* Nancy Brown, Administrative Assistant, 603-862-1022, E-mail: natural.resources@unh.edu. Web site: http://www.nre.unh.edu/academics/.

University of New Hampshire, Graduate School, College of Life Sciences and Agriculture, Department of Resource Economics and Development, Program in Resource Administration, Durham, NH 03824. Offers MS. Part-time programs available. *Faculty:* 4 full-time (0 women), 1 (woman) part-time/adjunct. *Students:* 3 full-time (all women), 2 part-time (1 woman); includes 1 minority (Asian, non-Hispanic/Latino). Average age 28. 3 applicants, 67% accepted, 1 enrolled. In 2011, 1 master's awarded. *Degree requirements:* For master's, thesis or alternative. *Entrance requirements:* For master's, GRE General Test. Additional exam requirements/recommendations for international students: Required—TOEFL (minimum score 550 paper-based; 213 computer-based; 80 iBT). *Application deadline:* For fall admission, 6/1 priority date for domestic students, 4/1 for international students; for spring admission, 12/1 for domestic students. Applications are processed on a rolling basis. Application fee: $65. Electronic applications accepted. *Expenses:* Tuition, state resident: full-time $12,360; part-time $687 per credit hour. Tuition, nonresident: full-time $25,680; part-time $1058 per credit hour. *International tuition:* $29,550 full-time. *Required fees:* $1666; $833 per course. $416.50 per semester. Tuition and fees vary according to course load and degree level. *Financial support:* In 2011–12, 2 students received support, including 2 teaching assistantships; fellowships, research assistantships, career-related internships or fieldwork, Federal Work-Study, and scholarships/grants also available. Support available to part-time students. Financial award application deadline: 2/15. *Unit head:* Dr. Serita Frey, Chairperson, 603-862-3880. *Application contact:* Jennifer Bourgeault, Information Contact, 603-862-2227, E-mail: resecon.ms.program@unh.edu. Web site: http://www.dred.unh.edu.

University of New Hampshire, Graduate School, College of Life Sciences and Agriculture, Department of Resource Economics and Development, Program in Resource Economics, Durham, NH 03824. Offers MS. Part-time programs available. *Faculty:* 6 full-time. *Students:* 1 full-time (0 women). Average age 22. 4 applicants, 50% accepted, 1 enrolled. *Degree requirements:* For master's, thesis or alternative. *Entrance requirements:* For master's, GRE General Test. Additional exam requirements/recommendations for international students: Required—TOEFL (minimum score 550 paper-based; 213 computer-based; 80 iBT). *Application deadline:* For fall admission, 6/1 for domestic students, 4/1 for international students; for spring admission, 12/1 for domestic students. Applications are processed on a rolling basis. Application fee: $65. Electronic applications accepted. *Expenses:* Tuition, state resident: full-time $12,360; part-time $687 per credit hour. Tuition, nonresident: full-time $25,680; part-time $1058 per credit hour. *International tuition:* $29,550 full-time. *Required fees:* $1666; $833 per course. $416.50 per semester. Tuition and fees vary according to course load and degree level. *Financial support:* In 2011–12, 1 student received support, including 1 teaching assistantship; fellowships, research assistantships, career-related internships or fieldwork, and Federal Work-Study also available. Support available to part-time students. Financial award application deadline: 2/15. *Unit head:* Dr. Serita Frey, Chairperson, 603-862-3880. *Application contact:* Jennifer Bourgeault, Information Contact, 603-862-2227, E-mail: resecon.ms.program@unh.edu. Web site: http://www.dred.unh.edu.

University of New Hampshire, Graduate School, Interdisciplinary Programs, Doctoral Program in Natural Resources and Earth System Science, Durham, NH 03824. Offers earth and environmental science (PhD), including geology, oceanography; natural resources and environmental studies (PhD). *Faculty:* 59 full-time (11 women). *Students:* 53 full-time (28 women), 28 part-time (12 women); includes 4 minority (all Asian, non-Hispanic/Latino), 9 international. Average age 35. 36 applicants, 39% accepted, 10 enrolled. In 2011, 10 doctorates awarded. *Degree requirements:* For doctorate, thesis/dissertation. *Entrance requirements:* For doctorate, GRE (if from a non-US university). Additional exam requirements/recommendations for international students: Required—TOEFL (minimum score 550 paper-based; 213 computer-based; 80 iBT). *Application deadline:* For fall

534 facebook.com/petersonspublishing

Peterson's Graduate Programs in the Physical Sciences, Mathematics, Agricultural Sciences, the Environment & Natural Resources 2013

admission, 6/1 priority date for domestic students, 4/1 for international students; for spring admission, 12/1 for domestic students. Applications are processed on a rolling basis. Application fee: $65. Electronic applications accepted. *Expenses:* Tuition, state resident: full-time $12,360; part-time $687 per credit hour. Tuition, nonresident: full-time $25,680; part-time $1058 per credit hour. *International tuition:* $29,550 full-time. *Required fees:* $1666; $833 per course. $416.50 per semester. Tuition and fees vary according to course load and degree level. *Financial support:* In 2011–12, 48 students received support, including 8 fellowships, 26 research assistantships, 6 teaching assistantships; Federal Work-Study, scholarships/grants, and tuition waivers (full and partial) also available. Financial award application deadline: 2/15. *Faculty research:* Environmental and natural resource studies and management. *Unit head:* Dr. Serita Frey, Chairperson, 603-862-3880. *Application contact:* Dr. Jennifer Bourgeault, Administrative Assistant, 603-862-2227, E-mail: nress.phd.program@unh.edu. Web site: http://www.unh.edu/nressphd/.

University of New Mexico, Graduate School, College of Arts and Sciences, Department of Economics, Albuquerque, NM 87131-2039. Offers environmental/natural resources (MA, PhD); international/development (MA, PhD); labor/human resources (MA, PhD); public finance (MA, PhD). Part-time programs available. *Faculty:* 14 full-time (7 women), 8 part-time/adjunct (1 woman). *Students:* 37 full-time (9 women), 25 part-time (6 women); includes 10 minority (3 Asian, non-Hispanic/Latino; 6 Hispanic/Latino; 1 Two or more races, non-Hispanic/Latino), 17 international. Average age 35. 61 applicants, 49% accepted, 14 enrolled. In 2011, 10 master's, 3 doctorates awarded. Terminal master's awarded for partial completion of doctoral program. *Degree requirements:* For master's, comprehensive exam, thesis (for some programs); for doctorate, comprehensive exam, thesis/dissertation. *Entrance requirements:* For master's and doctorate, GRE General Test, 3 letters of recommendation, letter of intent, curriculum vitae. Additional exam requirements/recommendations for international students: Required—TOEFL (minimum score 520 paper-based; 190 computer-based; 68 iBT). *Application deadline:* For fall admission, 3/1 priority date for domestic students, 3/1 for international students. Applications are processed on a rolling basis. Application fee: $50. Electronic applications accepted. *Financial support:* In 2011–12, 47 students received support, including 3 fellowships with tuition reimbursements available (averaging $3,611 per year), 14 research assistantships with tuition reimbursements available (averaging $7,791 per year), 15 teaching assistantships with tuition reimbursements available (averaging $7,467 per year); career-related internships or fieldwork, Federal Work-Study, scholarships/grants, health care benefits, and unspecified assistantships also available. Support available to part-time students. Financial award application deadline: 3/1; financial award applicants required to submit FAFSA. *Faculty research:* Core theory, econometrics, public finance, international/development economics, labor/human resource economics, environmental/natural resource economics. *Total annual research expenditures:* $1.8 million. *Unit head:* Dr. Robert Berrens, Chair, 505-277-5304, Fax: 505-277-9445, E-mail: rberrens@unm.edu. *Application contact:* Rikk Murphy, Academic Advisor, 505-277-3056, Fax: 505-277-9445, E-mail: rikk@unm.edu. Web site: http://econ.unm.edu/.

University of Northern British Columbia, Office of Graduate Studies, Prince George, BC V2N 4Z9, Canada. Offers business administration (Diploma); community health science (M Sc); disability management (MA); education (M Ed); first nations studies (MA); gender studies (MA); history (MA); interdisciplinary studies (MA); international studies (MA); mathematical, computer and physical sciences (M Sc); natural resources and environmental studies (M Sc, MA, MNRES, PhD); political science (MA); psychology (M Sc, PhD); social work (MSW). Part-time and evening/weekend programs available. Postbaccalaureate distance learning degree programs offered (no on-campus study). *Degree requirements:* For master's, thesis; for doctorate, thesis/dissertation. *Entrance requirements:* For master's, GRE, minimum B average in undergraduate course work; for doctorate, candidacy exam, minimum A average in graduate course work.

University of Northern Iowa, Graduate College, College of Humanities, Arts and Sciences, Department of Biology, Cedar Falls, IA 50614. Offers biology (MA, MS); biotechnology (PSM); ecosystem management (PSM). Part-time programs available. *Students:* 30 full-time (11 women), 4 part-time (2 women); includes 1 minority (Asian, non-Hispanic/Latino), 4 international. 57 applicants, 60% accepted, 23 enrolled. In 2011, 19 master's awarded. *Degree requirements:* For master's, comprehensive exam (for some programs), thesis or alternative. *Entrance requirements:* For master's, minimum GPA of 3.0; 3 letters of recommendation. Additional exam requirements/recommendations for international students: Required—TOEFL (minimum score 500 paper-based; 180 computer-based; 61 iBT). *Application deadline:* For fall admission, 8/1 priority date for domestic students. Applications are processed on a rolling basis. Application fee: $50 ($70 for international students). Electronic applications accepted. *Expenses:* Tuition, state resident: full-time $7476. Tuition, nonresident: full-time $16,410. *Required fees:* $942. *Financial support:* Scholarships/grants available. Financial award application deadline: 2/1. *Unit head:* Dr. David Saunders, Head, 319-273-2456, Fax: 319-273-7125, E-mail: david.saunders@uni.edu. *Application contact:* Laurie S. Russell, Record Analyst, 319-273-2623, Fax: 319-273-2885, E-mail: laurie.russell@uni.edu. Web site: http://www.biology.uni.edu/.

University of Oklahoma, College of Earth and Energy, School of Petroleum and Geological Engineering, Program in Petroleum Engineering, Norman, OK 73019. Offers natural gas engineering and management (MS); petroleum engineering

(MS, PhD). Part-time programs available. *Students:* 64 full-time (12 women), 26 part-time (3 women); includes 5 minority (all Black or African American, non-Hispanic/Latino), 76 international. Average age 28. 237 applicants, 12% accepted, 19 enrolled. In 2011, 31 master's, 5 doctorates awarded. Terminal master's awarded for partial completion of doctoral program. *Degree requirements:* For master's, thesis optional, industrial team project or thesis; for doctorate, thesis/dissertation. *Entrance requirements:* For master's, GRE General Test, bachelor's degree in engineering, 3 letters of recommendation, minimum GPA of 3.0 during final 60 hours of undergraduate course work; for doctorate, GRE General Test, minimum GPA of 3.0, 3 letters of recommendation. Additional exam requirements/recommendations for international students: Required—TOEFL (minimum score 550 paper-based; 79 iBT). *Application deadline:* For fall admission, 6/1 priority date for domestic students, 3/1 for international students; for spring admission, 11/1 for domestic students, 9/1 for international students. Applications are processed on a rolling basis. Application fee: $40 ($90 for international students). Electronic applications accepted. *Expenses:* Tuition, state resident: full-time $4087; part-time $170.30 per credit hour. Tuition, nonresident: full-time $14,875; part-time $619.80 per credit hour. *Required fees:* $2659; $100.25 per credit hour. Tuition and fees vary according to course load and degree level. *Financial support:* In 2011–12, 83 students received support. Traineeships available. Financial award applicants required to submit FAFSA. *Faculty research:* Petrophysics, shale gas, reservoir simulation coiled tubing, poro-mechanics, enhanced oil recovery. *Unit head:* Dr. Chandra Rai, Director, 405-325-2921, Fax: 405-325-7477, E-mail: crai@ou.edu. *Application contact:* Shalli Young, Executive Assistant to the Graduate Liaison, 405-325-2921, Fax: 405-325-7477, E-mail: syoung@ou.edu. Web site: http://mpge.ou.edu/.

University of Rhode Island, Graduate School, College of the Environment and Life Sciences, Department of Environmental and Natural Resource Economics, Kingston, RI 02881. Offers MESM, MS, PhD. Part-time programs available. *Faculty:* 7 full-time (2 women). *Students:* 37 full-time (17 women), 4 part-time (2 women); includes 2 minority (1 Asian, non-Hispanic/Latino; 1 Hispanic/Latino), 15 international. In 2011, 3 doctorates awarded. *Degree requirements:* For master's, comprehensive exam (for some programs), thesis optional; for doctorate, comprehensive exam, thesis/dissertation. *Entrance requirements:* For master's, GRE, 2 letters of recommendation; for doctorate, GRE, 3 letters of recommendation. Additional exam requirements/recommendations for international students: Required—TOEFL (minimum score 550 paper-based; 213 computer-based). *Application deadline:* For fall admission, 7/15 for domestic students, 2/1 for international students; for spring admission, 11/15 for domestic students, 7/15 for international students. Application fee: $65. Electronic applications accepted. *Expenses:* Tuition, state resident: full-time $10,432; part-time $580 per credit hour. Tuition, nonresident: full-time $23,130; part-time $1285 per credit hour. *Required fees:* $1362; $36 per credit hour. $35 per semester. One-time fee: $130. *Financial support:* In 2011–12, 2 research assistantships with partial tuition reimbursements (averaging $10,698 per year), 6 teaching assistantships with full and partial tuition reimbursements (averaging $11,113 per year) were awarded. Financial award application deadline: 7/15; financial award applicants required to submit FAFSA. *Faculty research:* Policy Simulation Laboratory: utilizes computer technologies to help understand the consequences of policy actions, experimental economics. *Unit head:* Dr. James Opaluch, Chair, 401-874-4590, Fax: 401-874-4766, E-mail: jimo@uri.edu. *Application contact:* Dr. James Opaluch, Graduate Admission Committee, 401-874-4590, Fax: 401-874-4766, E-mail: jimo@uri.edu. Web site: http://www.uri.edu/cels/enre/.

University of Rhode Island, Graduate School, College of the Environment and Life Sciences, Department of Natural Resources Science, Kingston, RI 02881. Offers MESM, MS, PhD. Part-time programs available. *Faculty:* 10 full-time (1 woman), 1 (woman) part-time/adjunct. *Students:* 34 full-time (22 women), 9 part-time (8 women); includes 5 minority (1 Black or African American, non-Hispanic/Latino; 1 Asian, non-Hispanic/Latino; 3 Hispanic/Latino), 5 international. In 2011, 10 master's, 4 doctorates awarded. *Degree requirements:* For master's, comprehensive exam (for some programs), thesis optional; for doctorate, comprehensive exam, thesis/dissertation. *Entrance requirements:* For master's and doctorate, GRE, 2 letters of recommendation. Additional exam requirements/recommendations for international students: Required—TOEFL (minimum score 550 paper-based; 213 computer-based). *Application deadline:* For fall admission, 7/15 for domestic students, 2/1 for international students; for spring admission, 11/15 for domestic students, 7/15 for international students. Application fee: $65. Electronic applications accepted. *Expenses:* Tuition, state resident: full-time $10,432; part-time $580 per credit hour. Tuition, nonresident: full-time $23,130; part-time $1285 per credit hour. *Required fees:* $1362; $36 per credit hour. $35 per semester. One-time fee: $130. *Financial support:* In 2011–12, 2 research assistantships with full and partial tuition reimbursements (averaging $9,263 per year), 4 teaching assistantships with full and partial tuition reimbursements (averaging $11,298 per year) were awarded. Financial award application deadline: 7/15; financial award applicants required to submit FAFSA. *Faculty research:* Spatial data modeling, ecological mapping, data integration for environmental applications. *Unit head:* Dr. Scott McWilliams, Chair, 401-874-7531, Fax: 401-874-4561, E-mail: srmcwilliams@uri.edu. *Application contact:* Dr. Graham Forrester, Director of Graduate Studies, 401-874-7054, Fax: 401-874-4561, E-mail: gforrester@mail.uri.edu. Web site: http://nrs.uri.edu/.

University of San Francisco, College of Arts and Sciences, Environmental Management Program, San Francisco, CA 94117-1080. Offers MS. Evening/weekend programs available. *Faculty:* 7 full-time (3 women), 8 part-time/adjunct (1 woman). *Students:* 68 full-time (33 women), 21 part-time (10 women); includes

Peterson's Graduate Programs in the Physical Sciences, Mathematics, Agricultural Sciences, the Environment & Natural Resources 2013

facebook.com/petersonspublishing **535**

Natural Resources

26 minority (2 Black or African American, non-Hispanic/Latino; 13 Asian, non-Hispanic/Latino; 7 Hispanic/Latino; 1 Native Hawaiian or other Pacific Islander, non-Hispanic/Latino; 3 Two or more races, non-Hispanic/Latino), 3 international. Average age 30. 124 applicants, 43% accepted, 39 enrolled. In 2011, 36 master's awarded. *Degree requirements:* For master's, thesis, project. *Entrance requirements:* For master's, 3 semesters of course work in chemistry, minimum GPA of 2.7, work experience in environmental field. *Application deadline:* For fall admission, 3/1 priority date for domestic students. Applications are processed on a rolling basis. Application fee: $55 ($65 for international students). *Expenses:* Tuition: Full-time $20,070; part-time $1115 per unit. Tuition and fees vary according to course load, campus/location and program. *Financial support:* In 2011–12, 31 students received support. Teaching assistantships and career-related internships or fieldwork available. Financial award application deadline: 3/2; financial award applicants required to submit FAFSA. *Faculty research:* Problems of environmental managers, water quality, hazardous materials, environmental health. *Unit head:* Dr. Stephanie Oshita, Chair, 415-422-5927, Fax: 415-422-6387. *Application contact:* Information Contact, 415-422-5135, Fax: 415-422-2217, E-mail: asgraduate@usfca.edu. Web site: http://www.usfca.edu/artsci/msem/.

University of South Africa, College of Agriculture and Environmental Sciences, Pretoria, South Africa. Offers agriculture (MS); consumer science (MCS); environmental management (MA, MS, PhD); environmental science (MA, MS, PhD); geography (MA, MS, PhD); horticulture (M Tech); human ecology (MHE); life sciences (MS); nature conservation (M Tech).

The University of Texas at Austin, Graduate School, Cockrell School of Engineering, Department of Petroleum and Geosystems Engineering, Program in Energy and Earth Resources, Austin, TX 78712-1111. Offers MA. *Degree requirements:* For master's, thesis, seminar. *Entrance requirements:* For master's, GRE General Test. Additional exam requirements/recommendations for international students: Required—TOEFL. *Application deadline:* For fall admission, 4/30 priority date for domestic students. Applications are processed on a rolling basis. Application fee: $50 ($75 for international students). Electronic applications accepted. *Unit head:* Stephen P. Grand, Chair, 512-471-3005, E-mail: steveg@geo.utexas.edu. *Application contact:* Philip Guerrero, Graduate Coordinator, 512-471-6098, E-mail: philipg@mail.utexas.edu. Web site: http://www.jsg.utexas.edu/eer/.

University of Vermont, Graduate College, The Rubenstein School of Environment and Natural Resources, Program in Natural Resources, Burlington, VT 05405. Offers natural resources (MS, PhD), including aquatic ecology and watershed science (MS), environment thought and culture (MS), environment, science and public affairs (MS), forestry (MS). *Students:* 104 (58 women); includes 10 minority (1 Black or African American, non-Hispanic/Latino; 2 American Indian or Alaska Native, non-Hispanic/Latino; 5 Asian, non-Hispanic/Latino; 2 Hispanic/Latino), 2 international. 148 applicants, 28% accepted, 19 enrolled. In 2011, 19 master's, 6 doctorates awarded. *Degree requirements:* For master's, thesis or alternative; for doctorate, thesis/dissertation. *Entrance requirements:* For master's and doctorate, GRE General Test. Additional exam requirements/recommendations for international students: Required—TOEFL (minimum score 550 paper-based; 213 computer-based; 80 iBT). *Application deadline:* For fall admission, 3/1 priority date for domestic students, 3/1 for international students. Applications are processed on a rolling basis. Application fee: $40. Electronic applications accepted. *Financial support:* Fellowships, research assistantships, and teaching assistantships available. Financial award application deadline: 3/1. *Unit head:* Clare Ginger, Chair, 802-656-2620. *Application contact:* Kimberly Wallin, Coordinator, 802-656-2620.

University of Washington, Graduate School, College of the Environment, School of Forest Resources, Seattle, WA 98195. Offers bioresource science and engineering (MS, PhD); environmental horticulture (MEH); environmental horticulture and urban forestry (MS, PhD); forest ecology (MS, PhD); forest management (MFR); forest soils (MS, PhD); forest systems and bioenergy (MS, PhD); restoration ecology (MS, PhD); social sciences (MS, PhD); sustainable resource management (MS, PhD); wildlife science (MS, PhD); MFR/MAIS; MPA/MS. *Accreditation:* SAF. *Degree requirements:* For master's, thesis (for some programs); for doctorate, comprehensive exam (for some programs), thesis/dissertation. *Entrance requirements:* For master's and doctorate, GRE, minimum GPA of 3.0. Additional exam requirements/recommendations for international students: Required—TOEFL. Electronic applications accepted. *Faculty research:* Ecosystem analysis, silviculture and forest protection, paper science and engineering, environmental horticulture and urban forestry, natural resource policy and economics.

University of Wisconsin–Madison, Graduate School, Gaylord Nelson Institute for Environmental Studies, Environment and Resources Program, Madison, WI 53706-1380. Offers MS, PhD. Part-time programs available. *Faculty:* 16 full-time (5 women), 57 part-time/adjunct (14 women). *Students:* 86 full-time, 21 part-time; includes 7 minority (2 Black or African American, non-Hispanic/Latino; 1 American Indian or Alaska Native, non-Hispanic/Latino; 2 Asian, non-Hispanic/Latino; 2 Hispanic/Latino), 18 international. Average age 34. 180 applicants, 26% accepted, 19 enrolled. In 2011, 16 master's, 10 doctorates awarded. *Degree requirements:* For master's, thesis; for doctorate, thesis/dissertation. *Entrance requirements:* For master's and doctorate, GRE General Test. Additional exam requirements/recommendations for international students: Required—TOEFL (minimum score 550 paper-based; 213 computer-based; 80 iBT). *Application deadline:* For fall admission, 1/15 for domestic and international students; for spring admission, 10/15 for domestic and international students. Application fee: $56. Electronic applications accepted. *Expenses:* Tuition, state resident: full-time $10,296; part-time $643.51 per credit. Tuition, nonresident: full-time $24,054; part-time $1503.40 per credit. *Required fees:* $70.06 per credit. Tuition and fees vary according to course load, campus/location, program and reciprocity agreements. *Financial support:* In 2011–12, 74 students received support, including 12 fellowships with full tuition reimbursements available (averaging $18,567 per year), 28 research assistantships with full tuition reimbursements available (averaging $20,400 per year), 19 teaching assistantships with full tuition reimbursements available (averaging $9,392 per year); career-related internships or fieldwork, Federal Work-Study, scholarships/grants, traineeships, health care benefits, unspecified assistantships, and project assistantships also available. Financial award application deadline: 1/2. *Faculty research:* Land use issues, soil science/watershed management, geographic information systems, environmental law/justice, waste management, restoration ecology, agroecology, energy resources. *Unit head:* Patrick D. Eagan, Chair, 608-263-7429, Fax: 608-262-2273, E-mail: eagan@engr.wisc.edu. *Application contact:* Jim Miller, Student Services Coordinator, 608-263-4373, Fax: 608-262-2273, E-mail: jemiller@wisc.edu. Web site: http://nelson.wisc.edu/graduate_degrees/er.

University of Wisconsin–Stevens Point, College of Natural Resources, Stevens Point, WI 54481-3897. Offers MS. Part-time programs available. *Degree requirements:* For master's, thesis or alternative. *Entrance requirements:* For master's, GRE. *Faculty research:* Wildlife management, environmental education, fisheries, forestry, resource policy and planning.

University of Wyoming, College of Agriculture and Natural Resources, Department of Renewable Resources, Laramie, WY 82070. Offers agroecology (MS); entomology (MS, PhD); entomology/water resources (MS, PhD); rangeland ecology and watershed management (MS, PhD), including soil sciences (PhD), soil sciences and water resources (MS); rangeland ecology and watershed management/water resources (MS, PhD); soil science (MS); soil science/water resources (PhD). Part-time programs available. *Degree requirements:* For master's, comprehensive exam, thesis, oral examination; for doctorate, comprehensive exam, thesis/dissertation, preliminary oral and written exam, oral final exam. *Entrance requirements:* For master's and doctorate, GRE General Test, minimum GPA of 3.0. Additional exam requirements/recommendations for international students: Required—TOEFL. Electronic applications accepted. *Faculty research:* Plant control, grazing management, riparian restoration, riparian management, reclamation.

University of Wyoming, College of Arts and Sciences, Department of Geography, Program in Rural Planning and Natural Resources, Laramie, WY 82070. Offers community and regional planning and natural resources (MP). *Degree requirements:* For master's, thesis or alternative. *Entrance requirements:* For master's, GRE General Test, minimum GPA of 3.0. Additional exam requirements/recommendations for international students: Required—TOEFL. *Faculty research:* Rural and small town planning, public land management.

Utah State University, School of Graduate Studies, College of Natural Resources, Interdisciplinary Program in Natural Resources, Logan, UT 84322. Offers MNR. *Entrance requirements:* For master's, GRE General Test, minimum GPA of 3.0. Additional exam requirements/recommendations for international students: Required—TOEFL. *Faculty research:* Ecosystem management, human dimensions, quantitative methods, informative management.

Virginia Polytechnic Institute and State University, Graduate School, College of Natural Resources and Environment, Program in Natural Resources, Blacksburg, VA 24061. Offers MNR, Certificate. *Degree requirements:* For master's, comprehensive exam (for some programs), thesis (for some programs). *Entrance requirements:* For master's, GRE. Additional exam requirements/recommendations for international students: Required—TOEFL (minimum score 550 paper-based; 213 computer-based). *Application deadline:* For fall admission, 7/1 for domestic and international students; for spring admission, 12/1 for domestic and international students. Applications are processed on a rolling basis. Application fee: $65. Electronic applications accepted. *Expenses:* Tuition, state resident: full-time $10,048; part-time $558.25 per credit hour. Tuition, nonresident: full-time $19,497; part-time $1083.25 per credit hour. *Required fees:* $405 per semester. Tuition and fees vary according to course load, campus/location and program. *Financial support:* Research assistantships with full tuition reimbursements, career-related internships or fieldwork, Federal Work-Study, scholarships/grants, health care benefits, and unspecified assistantships available. Financial award application deadline: 1/15. *Unit head:* Dr. Paul M. Winistorfer, Unit Head, 540-231-5481, Fax: 540-231-5481, E-mail: pwinisto@vt.edu. *Application contact:* Peggy Quarterman, Information Contact, 540-231-5481, Fax: 540-231-5481, E-mail: pquarter@vt.edu. Web site: http://www.cnr.vt.edu/.

Virginia Polytechnic Institute and State University, VT Online, Blacksburg, VA 24061. Offers advanced transportation systems (Certificate); aerospace engineering (MS); agricultural and life sciences (MSLFS); business information systems (Graduate Certificate); career and technical education (MS); civil engineering (MS); computer engineering (M Eng, MS); decision support systems (Graduate Certificate); eLearning leadership (MA); electrical engineering (M Eng, MS); engineering administration (MEA); environmental engineering (Certificate); environmental politics and policy (Graduate Certificate); environmental sciences and engineering (MS); foundations of political analysis (Graduate Certificate); health product risk management (Graduate Certificate); industrial and systems

536 facebook.com/petersonspublishing

Peterson's Graduate Programs in the Physical Sciences, Mathematics, Agricultural Sciences, the Environment & Natural Resources 2013

engineering (MS); information policy and society (Graduate Certificate); information security (Graduate Certificate); information technology (MIT); instructional technology (MA); integrative STEM education (MA Ed); liberal arts (Graduate Certificate); life sciences: health product risk management (MS); natural resources (MNR, Graduate Certificate); networking (Graduate Certificate); nonprofit and nongovernmental organization management (Graduate Certificate); ocean engineering (MS); political science (MA); security studies (Graduate Certificate); software development (Graduate Certificate). *Expenses:* Tuition, state resident: full-time $10,048; part-time $558.25 per credit hour. Tuition, nonresident: full-time $19,497; part-time $1083.25 per credit hour. *Required fees:* $405 per semester. Tuition and fees vary according to course load, campus/ location and program. *Application contact:* Graduate School Applications General Assistance, 540-231-8636, Fax: 540-231-2039, E-mail: gradappl@vt.edu. Web site: http://www.vto.vt.edu/.

Washington State University, Graduate School, College of Agricultural, Human, and Natural Resource Sciences, Department of Natural Resource Sciences, Pullman, WA 99164. Offers MS. *Faculty:* 15. *Students:* 9 full-time (5 women), 2 part-time (1 woman); includes 1 minority (Hispanic/Latino). Average age 27. 18 applicants, 28% accepted, 5 enrolled. In 2011, 5 master's awarded. *Degree requirements:* For master's, comprehensive exam (for some programs), thesis (for some programs), oral exam. *Entrance requirements:* For master's, GRE General Test, official copies of all college transcripts, three letters of recommendation. Additional exam requirements/recommendations for international students: Required—TOEFL, IELTS. *Application deadline:* For fall admission, 1/10 priority date for domestic students, 1/10 for international students; for spring admission, 7/1 for domestic and international students. Applications are processed on a rolling basis. Application fee: $75. *Financial support:* In 2011–12, fellowships (averaging $2,333 per year), research assistantships with full and partial tuition reimbursements (averaging $13,917 per year), teaching assistantships with full and partial tuition reimbursements (averaging $13,056 per year) were awarded; career-related internships or fieldwork, Federal Work-Study, institutionally sponsored loans, tuition waivers (partial), and unspecified assistantships also available. Financial award application deadline: 2/15; financial award applicants required to submit FAFSA. *Faculty research:* Restoration ecology, landscape ecology, controlled and uncontrolled wild-land fire. *Total annual research expenditures:* $967,000. *Unit head:* Dr. Keith A. Blatner, Chair, 509-335-6166, E-mail: blatner@wsu.edu. *Application contact:* Graduate School Admissions, 800-GRADWSU, Fax: 509-335-1949, E-mail: gradsch@wsu.edu. Web site: http://www.natural-resources.wsu.edu/.

Washington State University, Graduate School, College of Sciences, School of Earth and Environmental Sciences, Program in Environmental and Natural Resource Sciences, Pullman, WA 99164. Offers PhD. *Students:* 13 full-time (9 women), 3 part-time (all women); includes 1 minority (Hispanic/Latino), 4 international. Average age 30. 25 applicants, 48% accepted, 12 enrolled. In 2011, 4 doctorates awarded. Application fee: $75. *Unit head:* Dr. Keith A. Blatner, Chair, 509-335-6166, E-mail: blatner@wsu.edu. *Application contact:* Graduate School Admissions, 800-GRADWSU, Fax: 509-335-1949, E-mail: gradsch@wsu.edu.

Washington State University, Graduate School, College of Sciences, School of Earth and Environmental Sciences, Program in Environmental Science, Pullman, WA 99164. Offers environmental and natural resource sciences (PhD); environmental science (MS). *Faculty:* 7. *Students:* 10 full-time (6 women), 1 part-time (0 women); includes 1 minority (Asian, non-Hispanic/Latino), 1 international. Average age 29. 43 applicants, 47% accepted, 13 enrolled. In 2011, 8 master's awarded. *Degree requirements:* For master's, comprehensive exam (for some programs), thesis (for some programs), oral exam; for doctorate, comprehensive exam, thesis/dissertation, oral exam, written exam. *Entrance requirements:* For master's, 3 undergraduate semester hours each in sociology or cultural anthropology, environmental science, biological sciences, and calculus or statistics; 4 in general ecology; and 6 in general chemistry or general physics; for doctorate, minimum GPA of 3.0. Additional exam requirements/recommendations for international students: Required—TOEFL, IELTS. *Application deadline:* For fall

admission, 1/10 priority date for domestic students, 1/10 for international students. Applications are processed on a rolling basis. Application fee: $75. *Financial support:* In 2011–12, 16 students received support, including 1 fellowship (averaging $3,000 per year), 4 research assistantships with full and partial tuition reimbursements available (averaging $13,917 per year), 4 teaching assistantships with full and partial tuition reimbursements available (averaging $13,506 per year); Federal Work-Study, institutionally sponsored loans, and tuition waivers (partial) also available. Financial award application deadline: 2/15; financial award applicants required to submit FAFSA. *Unit head:* Dr. John A. Wolff, Head, 509-335-2825, E-mail: jawolff@mail.wsu.edu. *Application contact:* Graduate School Admissions, 800-GRADWSU, Fax: 509-335-1949, E-mail: gradsch@wsu.edu. Web site: http://esrp.wsu.edu/.

Washington State University Tri-Cities, Graduate Programs, Program in Environmental Science, Richland, WA 99352-1671. Offers environmental and natural resource sciences (PhD); environmental science (MS). Part-time programs available. *Faculty:* 40. *Students:* 9 full-time (2 women), 33 part-time (18 women); includes 4 minority (2 Black or African American, non-Hispanic/Latino; 1 Asian, non-Hispanic/Latino; 1 Hispanic/Latino), 1 international. Average age 30. 8 applicants, 100% accepted, 8 enrolled. In 2011, 10 degrees awarded. *Degree requirements:* For master's, comprehensive exam, thesis (for some programs), oral exam; for doctorate, comprehensive exam, thesis/dissertation. *Entrance requirements:* For master's, GRE General Test, minimum GPA of 3.0, 3 letters of recommendation. Additional exam requirements/recommendations for international students: Required—TOEFL (minimum score 550 paper-based; 213 computer-based). *Application deadline:* For fall admission, 1/10 priority date for domestic students, 1/10 for international students; for spring admission, 7/1 priority date for domestic students, 7/1 for international students. Application fee: $75. *Financial support:* In 2011–12, 8 students received support, including research assistantships with full and partial tuition reimbursements available (averaging $14,634 per year), teaching assistantships with full and partial tuition reimbursements available (averaging $13,383 per year); fellowships, Federal Work-Study, scholarships/grants, health care benefits, and unspecified assistantships also available. Financial award application deadline: 1/15. *Faculty research:* Radiation ecology, cytogenetics. *Unit head:* John Strand, Graduate Advisor, 509-372-7326, E-mail: jstrand@tricity.wsu.edu. *Application contact:* Bonnie Bates, Graduate School Admissions, 800-GRADWSU, Fax: 509-372-7171, E-mail: bbates@tricity.wsu.edu. Web site: http://www.tricity.wsu.edu/science/environmental.html.

West Virginia University, College of Business and Economics, Division of Economics and Finance, Morgantown, WV 26506. Offers business analysis (MA); developmental financial economics (PhD); environmental and resource economics (PhD); international economics (PhD); mathematical economics (MA); monetary economics (PhD); public finance (PhD); public policy (MA); regional and urban economics (PhD); statistics and economics (MA). Terminal master's awarded for partial completion of doctoral program. *Degree requirements:* For master's, thesis optional; for doctorate, comprehensive exam, thesis/dissertation. *Entrance requirements:* For master's and doctorate, GRE General Test, minimum GPA of 3.0; course work in intermediate microeconomics, intermediate macroeconomics, calculus, and statistics. Additional exam requirements/recommendations for international students: Required—TOEFL. Electronic applications accepted. *Faculty research:* Financial economics, regional/urban development, public economics, international trade/international finance/development economics, monetary economics.

West Virginia University, Davis College of Agriculture, Forestry and Consumer Sciences, Division of Resource Management and Sustainable Development, Program in Resource Management and Sustainable Development, Morgantown, WV 26506. Offers PhD. Part-time programs available. *Degree requirements:* For doctorate, thesis/dissertation. *Entrance requirements:* For doctorate, GRE General Test. Additional exam requirements/recommendations for international students: Required—TOEFL.

Range Science

Colorado State University, Graduate School, Warner College of Natural Resources, Department of Forest and Rangeland Stewardship, Fort Collins, CO 80523-1472. Offers forest sciences (MS, PhD); natural resources stewardship (MNRS); rangeland ecosystem science (MS, PhD); watershed science (MS). Part-time programs available. Postbaccalaureate distance learning degree programs offered (no on-campus study). *Faculty:* 12 full-time (2 women). *Students:* 32 full-time (15 women), 81 part-time (31 women); includes 5 minority (3 American Indian or Alaska Native, non-Hispanic/Latino; 2 Hispanic/Latino), 15 international. Average age 35. 33 applicants, 91% accepted, 27 enrolled. In 2011, 27 master's, 2 doctorates awarded. *Degree requirements:* For master's, thesis (for some programs); for doctorate, comprehensive exam, thesis/dissertation. *Entrance requirements:* For master's, GRE General Test (minimum score 1000 verbal and quantitative), minimum GPA of 3.0, 3 letters of recommendation; for doctorate, GRE General Test (combined minimum score of 1100 on the Verbal and

Quantitative sections), minimum GPA of 3.0, 3 letters of recommendation, statement of research interest. Additional exam requirements/recommendations for international students: Required—TOEFL (minimum score 550 paper-based; 213 computer-based; 80 iBT), IELTS (minimum score 6.5). *Application deadline:* For fall admission, 2/15 priority date for domestic students, 2/15 for international students; for spring admission, 7/15 priority date for domestic students, 7/15 for international students. Applications are processed on a rolling basis. Application fee: $50. Electronic applications accepted. *Expenses:* Tuition, state resident: full-time $7992. Tuition, nonresident: full-time $19,592. *Required fees:* $1735; $58 per credit. *Financial support:* In 2011–12, 44 students received support, including 1 fellowship (averaging $19,360 per year), 31 research assistantships with full and partial tuition reimbursements available (averaging $17,090 per year), 12 teaching assistantships with full and partial tuition reimbursements available (averaging $6,607 per year); Federal Work-Study, scholarships/grants, and

Peterson's Graduate Programs in the Physical Sciences, Mathematics, Agricultural Sciences, the Environment & Natural Resources 2013

facebook.com/petersonspublishing **537**

unspecified assistantships also available. Financial award application deadline: 2/15; financial award applicants required to submit FAFSA. *Faculty research:* Ecology, natural resource management, hydrology, restoration, human dimensions. *Total annual research expenditures:* $2.9 million. *Unit head:* Dr. Frederick Smith, Interim Department Head, 970-491-7505, Fax: 970-491-6754, E-mail: fwsmith@colostate.edu. *Application contact:* Sonya LeFebre, Coordinator, 970-491-1907, Fax: 970-491-6754, E-mail: sonya.lefebre@colostate.edu. Web site: http://warnercnr.colostate.edu/frws-home/.

Kansas State University, Graduate School, College of Agriculture, Department of Agronomy, Manhattan, KS 66506. Offers crop science (MS, PhD); plant breeding and genetics (MS, PhD); range management (MS, PhD); soil science (MS, PhD); weed science (MS, PhD). Part-time programs available. *Faculty:* 28 full-time (4 women), 11 part-time/adjunct (1 woman). *Students:* 62 full-time (18 women), 10 part-time (4 women); includes 4 minority (2 Black or African American, non-Hispanic/Latino; 1 Asian, non-Hispanic/Latino; 1 Hispanic/Latino), 34 international. Average age 31. 31 applicants, 42% accepted, 9 enrolled. In 2011, 8 master's, 4 doctorates awarded. Terminal master's awarded for partial completion of doctoral program. *Degree requirements:* For master's, thesis or alternative, oral exam; for doctorate, thesis/dissertation, preliminary exams. *Entrance requirements:* For master's, minimum GPA of 3.0 in BS; for doctorate, minimum GPA of 3.5 in master's program. Additional exam requirements/recommendations for international students: Required—TOEFL (minimum score 500 paper-based; 250 computer-based). *Application deadline:* For fall admission, 2/1 priority date for domestic students, 2/1 for international students; for spring admission, 8/1 priority date for domestic students, 8/1 for international students. Applications are processed on a rolling basis. Application fee: $40 ($55 for international students). Electronic applications accepted. *Financial support:* In 2011–12, 64 research assistantships (averaging $21,705 per year), 7 teaching assistantships with partial tuition reimbursements (averaging $18,200 per year) were awarded; institutionally sponsored loans and scholarships/grants also available. Support available to part-time students. Financial award application deadline: 3/1; financial award applicants required to submit FAFSA. *Faculty research:* Range and forage science, soil and environmental science, crop physiology, weed science, plant breeding and genetics. *Total annual research expenditures:* $5.5 million. *Unit head:* Dr. William Schapaugh, Head, 785-532-6101, Fax: 785-532-6094, E-mail: wts@ksu.edu. *Application contact:* Dr. Scott Staggenborg, Graduate Coordinator, 785-532-7214, Fax: 785-532-6094, E-mail: sstaggen@ksu.edu. Web site: http://www.agronomy.k-state.edu/DesktopDefault.aspx.

Montana State University, College of Graduate Studies, College of Agriculture, Department of Animal and Range Sciences, Bozeman, MT 59717. Offers MS, PhD. Part-time programs available. *Degree requirements:* For master's, comprehensive exam; for doctorate, comprehensive exam, thesis/dissertation. *Entrance requirements:* For master's, GRE, minimum GPA of 3.0; undergraduate coursework in animal science, range science or closely-related field; faculty adviser; for doctorate, GRE. Additional exam requirements/recommendations for international students: Required—TOEFL (minimum score 550 paper-based; 213 computer-based; 80 iBT). Electronic applications accepted. *Faculty research:* Rangeland ecology, wildlife habitat management, residual feed intake, post-partum effect of bulls, increasing efficiency of sheep production systems.

New Mexico State University, Graduate School, College of Agricultural, Consumer and Environmental Sciences, Department of Animal and Range Sciences, Las Cruces, NM 88003-8001. Offers animal science (MS, PhD); domestic animal biology (M Ag); range science (M Ag, MS, PhD). Part-time programs available. *Faculty:* 15 full-time (3 women). *Students:* 33 full-time (19 women), 5 part-time (3 women); includes 4 minority (all Hispanic/Latino), 7 international. Average age 28. 23 applicants, 30% accepted, 4 enrolled. In 2011, 7 master's, 3 doctorates awarded. *Degree requirements:* For master's, thesis, seminar, experimental statistics; for doctorate, thesis/dissertation, research tool. *Entrance requirements:* For master's, minimum GPA of 3.0 in last 60 hours of undergraduate course work (MS); for doctorate, minimum graduate GPA of 3.2. Additional exam requirements/recommendations for international students: Required—TOEFL (minimum score 530 paper-based; 0 computer-based; 71 iBT), IELTS (minimum score 6). *Application deadline:* For fall admission, 7/1 priority date for domestic students, 7/1 for international students; for spring admission, 11/1 for domestic and international students. Applications are processed on a rolling basis. Application fee: $40 ($50 for international students). Electronic applications accepted. *Expenses:* Tuition, state resident: full-time $5004; part-time $208.50 per credit. Tuition, nonresident: full-time $17,446; part-time $726.90 per credit. *Financial support:* In 2011–12, 31 students received support, including 1 fellowship (averaging $3,754 per year), 8 research assistantships (averaging $21,980 per year), 19 teaching assistantships (averaging $22,750 per year); career-related internships or fieldwork, Federal Work-Study, scholarships/grants, traineeships, health care benefits, and unspecified assistantships also available. Support available to part-time students. Financial award application deadline: 3/15. *Faculty research:* Reproductive physiology, ruminant nutrition, nutrition toxicology, range ecology, wildland hydrology. *Unit head:* Dr. Tim Ross, Interim Head, 575-646-2514, Fax: 575-646-5441, E-mail: tross@nmsu.edu. *Application contact:* Dr. Tim Ross, Interim Head, 575-646-2514, Fax: 575-646-5441, E-mail: tross@nmsu.edu. Web site: http://aces.nmsu.edu/academics/anrs.

North Dakota State University, College of Graduate and Interdisciplinary Studies, College of Agriculture, Food Systems, and Natural Resources, Department of Animal and Range Sciences, Fargo, ND 58108. Offers animal science (MS, PhD); natural resource management (MS, PhD); range sciences (MS, PhD). *Faculty:* 19 full-time (4 women), 1 part-time/adjunct (0 women). *Students:* 24 full-time (16 women), 9 part-time (5 women), 4 international. Average age 25. 15 applicants, 47% accepted, 4 enrolled. In 2011, 4 master's, 5 doctorates awarded. *Degree requirements:* For master's, thesis; for doctorate, comprehensive exam, thesis/dissertation. *Entrance requirements:* For master's and doctorate, GRE General Test. Additional exam requirements/recommendations for international students: Required—TOEFL (minimum score 71 iBT). *Application deadline:* Applications are processed on a rolling basis. Application fee: $35. *Financial support:* In 2011–12, 1 fellowship with tuition reimbursement (averaging $18,000 per year), 29 research assistantships with tuition reimbursements (averaging $13,000 per year) were awarded; teaching assistantships, Federal Work-Study, institutionally sponsored loans, and tuition waivers (partial) also available. Financial award application deadline: 3/15. *Faculty research:* Reproduction, nutrition, meat and muscle biology, breeding/genetics. *Unit head:* Dr. Gregory Lardy, Chair, 701-231-7641, Fax: 701-231-7590, E-mail: gregory.lardy@ndsu.edu. *Application contact:* Sonya Goergen, Marketing, Recruitment, and Public Relations Coordinator, 701-231-7033, Fax: 701-231-6524.

Oregon State University, Graduate School, College of Agricultural Sciences, Department of Rangeland Ecology and Management, Corvallis, OR 97331. Offers M Agr, MAIS, MS, PhD. Terminal master's awarded for partial completion of doctoral program. *Degree requirements:* For master's, thesis (for some programs); for doctorate, thesis/dissertation. *Entrance requirements:* For master's and doctorate, GRE, minimum GPA of 3.0 in last 90 hours of course work. Additional exam requirements/recommendations for international students: Required—TOEFL. *Faculty research:* Range ecology, watershed science, animal grazing, agroforestry.

Sul Ross State University, Division of Agricultural and Natural Resource Science, Program in Range and Wildlife Management, Alpine, TX 79832. Offers M Ag, MS. Part-time programs available. *Degree requirements:* For master's, thesis (for some programs). *Entrance requirements:* For master's, GRE General Test, minimum undergraduate GPA of 2.5 in last 60 hours.

Texas A&M University, College of Agriculture and Life Sciences, Department of Ecosystem Science and Management, College Station, TX 77843. Offers forestry (MS, PhD); rangeland ecology and management (M Agr, MS, PhD). Part-time programs available. *Faculty:* 24. *Students:* 64 full-time (34 women), 34 part-time (16 women); includes 21 minority (3 Black or African American, non-Hispanic/Latino; 3 Asian, non-Hispanic/Latino; 14 Hispanic/Latino; 1 Two or more races, non-Hispanic/Latino), 17 international. Average age 27. In 2011, 8 master's, 4 doctorates awarded. Terminal master's awarded for partial completion of doctoral program. *Degree requirements:* For master's, thesis (for some programs); for doctorate, thesis/dissertation. *Entrance requirements:* For master's and doctorate, GRE General Test. Additional exam requirements/recommendations for international students: Required—TOEFL. *Application deadline:* For fall admission, 3/1 priority date for domestic students; for spring admission, 11/1 priority date for domestic students. Applications are processed on a rolling basis. Application fee: $50 ($75 for international students). Electronic applications accepted. *Expenses:* Tuition, state resident: full-time $5437; part-time $226.55 per credit hour. Tuition, nonresident: full-time $12,949; part-time $539.55 per credit hour. *Required fees:* $2741. *Financial support:* In 2011–12, fellowships with partial tuition reimbursements (averaging $15,000 per year), research assistantships with partial tuition reimbursements (averaging $15,000 per year), teaching assistantships with partial tuition reimbursements (averaging $15,000 per year) were awarded; career-related internships or fieldwork and institutionally sponsored loans also available. Support available to part-time students. Financial award application deadline: 3/1; financial award applicants required to submit FAFSA. *Faculty research:* Expert systems, geographic information systems, economics, biology, genetics. *Unit head:* Dr. Steve Whisenant, Professor and Head, 979-845-5000, Fax: 979-845-6049, E-mail: s-whisenant@tamu.edu. *Application contact:* Dr. Carol Loopstra, Associate Professor, 979-862-2200, Fax: 979-845-6049, E-mail: c-loopstra@tamu.edu. Web site: http://essm.tamu.edu.

Texas A&M University–Kingsville, College of Graduate Studies, College of Agriculture and Home Economics, Program in Range and Wildlife Management, Kingsville, TX 78363. Offers MS. *Degree requirements:* For master's, comprehensive exam, thesis or alternative. *Entrance requirements:* For master's, GRE General Test, minimum GPA of 3.0. Additional exam requirements/recommendations for international students: Required—TOEFL.

Texas Tech University, Graduate School, College of Agricultural Sciences and Natural Resources, Department of Natural Resources Management, Lubbock, TX 79409. Offers fisheries science (MS, PhD); range science (MS, PhD); wildlife, aquatic, and wildlands science and management (MS, PhD). Part-time programs available. *Faculty:* 11 full-time (1 woman). *Students:* 50 full-time (13 women), 3 part-time (0 women); includes 7 minority (1 American Indian or Alaska Native, non-Hispanic/Latino; 3 Hispanic/Latino; 3 Two or more races, non-Hispanic/Latino), 7 international. Average age 27. 20 applicants, 45% accepted, 8 enrolled. In 2011, 4 master's, 2 doctorates awarded. *Degree requirements:* For master's, thesis; for doctorate, thesis/dissertation. *Entrance requirements:* For master's and doctorate, GRE General Test, formal approval from departmental committee. Additional exam requirements/recommendations for international students: Required—TOEFL (minimum score 550 paper-based; 213 computer-based; 79 iBT). *Application deadline:* For fall admission, 6/1 priority date for domestic students, 1/15 for international students; for spring admission, 9/1 priority date for

538 facebook.com/petersonspublishing

Peterson's Graduate Programs in the Physical Sciences, Mathematics, Agricultural Sciences, the Environment & Natural Resources 2013

domestic students, 6/15 for international students. Applications are processed on a rolling basis. Application fee: $50 ($75 for international students). Electronic applications accepted. *Expenses:* Tuition, state resident: full-time $5899; part-time $245.80 per credit hour. Tuition, nonresident: full-time $13,411; part-time $558.80 per credit hour. *Required fees:* $2680.60; $86.50 per credit hour. $920.30 per semester. *Financial support:* In 2011–12, 17 students received support. Application deadline: 4/15; applicants required to submit FAFSA. *Faculty research:* Use of fire on range lands; big game, upland game, and waterfowl; playa lakes in the southern Great Plains; conservation biology; fish ecology and physiology. *Total annual research expenditures:* $2.1 million. *Unit head:* Dr. Mark Wallace, Interim Chairman, 806-742-2841, Fax: 806-742-2280, E-mail: mark.wallace@ttu.edu. *Application contact:* Renee Dillon, Senior Business Assistant, 806-742-2841, E-mail: renee.dillon@ttu.edu. Web site: http://www.rw.ttu.edu/dept/.

The University of Arizona, College of Agriculture and Life Sciences, School of Natural Resources, Program in Natural Resources, Tucson, AZ 85721. Offers MS, PhD. *Faculty:* 18 full-time (3 women), 4 part-time/adjunct (0 women). *Students:* 72 full-time (38 women), 26 part-time (17 women); includes 19 minority (11 Hispanic/Latino; 8 Two or more races, non-Hispanic/Latino), 12 international. Average age 33. *Degree requirements:* For master's, thesis; for doctorate, comprehensive exam, thesis/dissertation. *Entrance requirements:* For master's and doctorate, GRE General Test, minimum GPA of 3.0. Additional exam requirements/recommendations for international students: Required—TOEFL (minimum score 550 paper-based; 213 computer-based). *Application deadline:* Applications are processed on a rolling basis. Application fee: $75. *Expenses:* Tuition, state resident: full-time $10,840. Tuition, nonresident: full-time $25,802. *Financial support:* Research assistantships, teaching assistantships, career-related internships or fieldwork, scholarships/grants, health care benefits, tuition waivers (partial), and unspecified assistantships available. *Faculty research:* Criteria for defining, mapping, and evaluating range sites; methods of establishing forage plants on southwestern range lands; plants for pollution and erosion control, beautification, and browse. *Unit head:* Dr. Lisa J. Graumlich, Director, 520-621-7257, E-mail: lisag@cals.arizona.edu. *Application contact:* Cheryl L. Craddock, Academic Coordinator, 520-621-7260, Fax: 520-621-8801, E-mail: ccraddoc@email.arizona.edu. Web site: http://grad.arizona.edu/live/programs/description/117.

University of California, Berkeley, Graduate Division, College of Natural Resources, Group in Range Management, Berkeley, CA 94720-1500. Offers MS. *Degree requirements:* For master's, thesis. *Entrance requirements:* For master's, GRE General Test, minimum GPA of 3.0, 3 letters of recommendation. Additional exam requirements/recommendations for international students: Required—TOEFL. *Faculty research:* Grassland and savannah ecology, wetland ecology, oak woodland classification, wildlife habitat management.

University of Wyoming, College of Agriculture and Natural Resources, Department of Renewable Resources, Laramie, WY 82070. Offers agroecology (MS); entomology (MS, PhD); entomology/water resources (MS, PhD); rangeland ecology and watershed management (MS, PhD), including soil sciences (PhD), soil sciences and water resources (MS); rangeland ecology and watershed management/water resources (MS, PhD); soil science (MS); soil science/water resources (PhD). Part-time programs available. *Degree requirements:* For master's, comprehensive exam, thesis, oral examination; for doctorate, comprehensive exam, thesis/dissertation, preliminary oral and written exam, oral final exam. *Entrance requirements:* For master's and doctorate, GRE General Test, minimum GPA of 3.0. Additional exam requirements/recommendations for international students: Required—TOEFL. Electronic applications accepted. *Faculty research:* Plant control, grazing management, riparian restoration, riparian management, reclamation.

Utah State University, School of Graduate Studies, College of Natural Resources, Department of Wildland Resources, Logan, UT 84322. Offers ecology (MS, PhD); forestry (MS, PhD); range science (MS, PhD); wildlife biology (MS, PhD). Part-time programs available. *Degree requirements:* For master's, thesis; for doctorate, comprehensive exam, thesis/dissertation. *Entrance requirements:* For master's and doctorate, GRE General Test, minimum GPA of 3.0. Additional exam requirements/recommendations for international students: Required—TOEFL. *Faculty research:* Range plant ecophysiology, plant community ecology, ruminant nutrition, population ecology.

Water Resources

Albany State University, College of Arts and Humanities, Albany, GA 31705-2717. Offers English education (M Ed); public administration (MPA), including community and economic development administration, criminal justice administration, general administration, health administration and policy, human resources management, public policy, water resources management; social work (MSW). Part-time programs available. *Faculty:* 13 full-time (6 women). *Students:* 47 full-time (38 women), 38 part-time (22 women); includes 77 minority (all Black or African American, non-Hispanic/Latino). Average age 35. 43 applicants, 70% accepted, 23 enrolled. In 2011, 20 master's awarded. *Degree requirements:* For master's, comprehensive exam, professional portfolio (for MPA), internship, capstone report. *Entrance requirements:* For master's, GRE, MAT, minimum GPA of 3.0, official transcript, pre-medical record/certificate of immunization, letters of reference. *Application deadline:* For fall admission, 6/1 for domestic students, 5/1 for international students; for spring admission, 11/1 for domestic students, 10/1 for international students. Applications are processed on a rolling basis. Application fee: $20. Electronic applications accepted. *Expenses:* Tuition, state resident: full-time $3204; part-time $178 per credit hour. Tuition, nonresident: full-time $12,816; part-time $712 per credit hour. *Required fees:* $379 per semester. *Financial support:* Application deadline: 4/15; applicants required to submit FAFSA. *Faculty research:* HIV prevention for minority students. *Total annual research expenditures:* $2,000. *Unit head:* Dr. Leroy Bynum, Dean, 229-430-1877, Fax: 229-430-4296, E-mail: leroy.bynum@asurams.edu. *Application contact:* Jeffrey Pierce, II, Graduate Admissions Counselor, 229-430-4646, Fax: 229-430-4105, E-mail: jeffrey.pierce@asurams.edu. Web site: http://asu-sacs.asurams.edu/ASUCatalog/Graduate/index.html.

California State University, Monterey Bay, College of Science, Media Arts and Technology, Program in Coastal and Watershed Science and Policy, Seaside, CA 93955-8001. Offers MS, PSM. Part-time programs available. *Degree requirements:* For master's, thesis, thesis defense. *Entrance requirements:* For master's, GRE, recommendations, interview. Additional exam requirements/recommendations for international students: Required—TOEFL (minimum score 525 paper-based; 213 computer-based; 71 iBT). Electronic applications accepted. *Faculty research:* Remote sensing and geospatial technology, MPA design, efficacy and management, marine science and ecology, watershed process, hydrology, restoration, sedimentology, ecosystem modeling.

Colorado State University, Graduate School, Warner College of Natural Resources, Department of Forest and Rangeland Stewardship, Fort Collins, CO 80523-1472. Offers forest sciences (MS, PhD); natural resources stewardship (MNRS); rangeland ecosystem science (MS, PhD); watershed science (MS). Part-time programs available. Postbaccalaureate distance learning degree programs offered (no on-campus study). *Faculty:* 12 full-time (2 women). *Students:* 32 full-time (15 women), 81 part-time (31 women); includes 5 minority (3 American Indian or Alaska Native, non-Hispanic/Latino; 2 Hispanic/Latino), 15 international. Average age 35. 33 applicants, 91% accepted, 27 enrolled. In 2011, 27 master's, 2 doctorates awarded. *Degree requirements:* For master's, thesis (for some programs); for doctorate, comprehensive exam, thesis/dissertation. *Entrance requirements:* For master's, GRE General Test (minimum score 1000 verbal and quantitative), minimum GPA of 3.0, 3 letters of recommendation; for doctorate, GRE General Test (combined minimum score of 1100 on the Verbal and Quantitative sections), minimum GPA of 3.0, 3 letters of recommendation, statement of research interest. Additional exam requirements/recommendations for international students: Required—TOEFL (minimum score 550 paper-based; 213 computer-based; 80 iBT), IELTS (minimum score 6.5). *Application deadline:* For fall admission, 2/15 priority date for domestic students, 2/15 for international students; for spring admission, 7/15 priority date for domestic students, 7/15 for international students. Applications are processed on a rolling basis. Application fee: $50. Electronic applications accepted. *Expenses:* Tuition, state resident: full-time $7992. Tuition, nonresident: full-time $19,592. *Required fees:* $1735; $58 per credit. *Financial support:* In 2011–12, 44 students received support, including 1 fellowship (averaging $19,360 per year), 31 research assistantships with full and partial tuition reimbursements available (averaging $17,090 per year), 12 teaching assistantships with full and partial tuition reimbursements available (averaging $6,607 per year); Federal Work-Study, scholarships/grants, and unspecified assistantships also available. Financial award application deadline: 2/15; financial award applicants required to submit FAFSA. *Faculty research:* Ecology, natural resource management, hydrology, restoration, human dimensions. *Total annual research expenditures:* $2.9 million. *Unit head:* Dr. Frederick Smith, Interim Department Head, 970-491-7505, Fax: 970-491-6754, E-mail: fwsmith@colostate.edu. *Application contact:* Sonya LeFebre, Coordinator, 970-491-1907, Fax: 970-491-6754, E-mail: sonya.lefebre@colostate.edu. Web site: http://warnercnr.colostate.edu/frws-home/.

Duke University, Nicholas School of the Environment, Durham, NC 27708-0328. Offers coastal environmental management (MEM); DEL-environmental leadership (MEM); energy and environment (MEM); environmental economics and policy (MEM); environmental health and security (MEM); forest resource management (MF); global environmental change (MEM); resource ecology (MEM); water and air resources (MEM); JD/AM; JD/MEM; JD/MF; MAT/MEM; MBA/MEM; MBA/MF; MEM/MPP; MF/MPP. *Accreditation:* SAF (one or more programs are accredited). Part-time programs available. *Degree requirements:* For master's, thesis. *Entrance requirements:* For master's, GRE General Test, previous course work in biology or ecology, calculus, statistics, and microeconomics; computer familiarity with word processing and data analysis. Additional exam requirements/recommendations for international students: Required—TOEFL (minimum score

Peterson's Graduate Programs in the Physical Sciences, Mathematics, Agricultural Sciences, the Environment & Natural Resources 2013

facebook.com/petersonspublishing **539**

550 paper-based; 213 computer-based). Electronic applications accepted. *Expenses:* Contact institution. *Faculty research:* Ecosystem management, conservation ecology, earth systems, risk assessment.

Eastern Michigan University, Graduate School, College of Arts and Sciences, Department of Biology, Ypsilanti, MI 48197. Offers cell and molecular biology (MS); community college biology teaching (MS); ecology and organismal biology (MS); general biology (MS); water resources (MS). Part-time and evening/weekend programs available. Postbaccalaureate distance learning degree programs offered (minimal on-campus study). *Faculty:* 20 full-time (4 women). *Students:* 12 full-time (7 women), 40 part-time (21 women); includes 3 minority (1 Black or African American, non-Hispanic/Latino; 1 Asian, non-Hispanic/Latino; 1 Two or more races, non-Hispanic/Latino), 12 international. Average age 27. 70 applicants, 43% accepted, 12 enrolled. In 2011, 19 degrees awarded. *Entrance requirements:* For master's, GRE General Test, GRE Subject Test. Additional exam requirements/recommendations for international students: Required—TOEFL. *Application deadline:* Applications are processed on a rolling basis. Application fee: $35. *Expenses:* Tuition, state resident: full-time $10,367; part-time $432 per credit hour. Tuition, nonresident: full-time $20,435; part-time $851 per credit hour. *Required fees:* $39 per credit hour. $46 per semester. One-time fee: $100. Tuition and fees vary according to course level, degree level and reciprocity agreements. *Financial support:* Fellowships, research assistantships with full tuition reimbursements, teaching assistantships with full tuition reimbursements, career-related internships or fieldwork, Federal Work-Study, institutionally sponsored loans, scholarships/grants, tuition waivers (partial), and unspecified assistantships available. Support available to part-time students. Financial award applicants required to submit FAFSA. *Unit head:* Dr. Marianne Laporte, Department Head, 734-487-4242, Fax: 734-487-9235, E-mail: mlaporte@emich.edu. *Application contact:* Graduate Admissions, 734-487-2400, Fax: 734-487-6559, E-mail: graduate.admissions@emich.edu. Web site: http://www.emich.edu/biology.

Eastern Michigan University, Graduate School, College of Arts and Sciences, Department of Geography and Geology, Programs in Geography and Geology, Ypsilanti, MI 48197. Offers geography (MA, MS); water resources (Graduate Certificate). Part-time and evening/weekend programs available. Postbaccalaureate distance learning degree programs offered (minimal on-campus study). *Students:* 1 part-time (0 women). Average age 28. 1 applicant, 100% accepted, 0 enrolled. *Degree requirements:* For master's, thesis optional. *Entrance requirements:* Additional exam requirements/recommendations for international students: Required—TOEFL. *Application deadline:* Applications are processed on a rolling basis. Application fee: $35. *Expenses:* Tuition, state resident: full-time $10,367; part-time $432 per credit hour. Tuition, nonresident: full-time $20,435; part-time $851 per credit hour. *Required fees:* $39 per credit hour. $46 per semester. One-time fee: $100. Tuition and fees vary according to course level, degree level and reciprocity agreements. *Financial support:* Fellowships, research assistantships with full tuition reimbursements, teaching assistantships with full tuition reimbursements, career-related internships or fieldwork, Federal Work-Study, institutionally sponsored loans, traineeships, and unspecified assistantships available. Support available to part-time students. Financial award applicants required to submit FAFSA. *Unit head:* Dr. Richard Sambrook, Department Head, 734-487-0218, Fax: 734-487-6979, E-mail: rsambroo@emich.edu. *Application contact:* Dr. Andrew Nazzaro, Program Advisor, 734-487-8486, Fax: 734-487-6979, E-mail: andrew.nazzaro@emich.edu.

Humboldt State University, Academic Programs, College of Natural Resources and Sciences, Programs in Natural Resources, Arcata, CA 95521-8299. Offers natural resources (MS), including fisheries, forestry, natural resources planning and interpretation, rangeland resources and wildland soils, wastewater utilization, watershed management, wildlife. *Students:* 45 full-time (26 women), 28 part-time (11 women); includes 4 minority (2 Asian, non-Hispanic/Latino; 1 Hispanic/Latino; 1 Two or more races, non-Hispanic/Latino), 1 international. Average age 30. 100 applicants, 22% accepted, 11 enrolled. In 2011, 25 master's awarded. *Degree requirements:* For master's, thesis or alternative. *Entrance requirements:* For master's, GRE, appropriate bachelor's degree, minimum GPA of 2.5, 3 letters of recommendation, resume. Additional exam requirements/recommendations for international students: Required—TOEFL (minimum score 500 paper-based; 173 computer-based). *Application deadline:* For fall admission, 2/1 for domestic and international students; for spring admission, 9/30 for domestic and international students. Applications are processed on a rolling basis. Application fee: $55. *Expenses:* Tuition, state resident: full-time $6734. Tuition, nonresident: full-time $15,662; part-time $372 per credit. *Required fees:* $903. Tuition and fees vary according to program. *Financial support:* Fellowships, career-related internships or fieldwork, and Federal Work-Study available. Support available to part-time students. Financial award application deadline: 3/1; financial award applicants required to submit FAFSA. *Faculty research:* Spotted owl habitat, pre-settlement vegetation, hardwood utilization, tree physiology, fisheries. *Unit head:* Dr. Robert Van Kirk, Coordinator, 707-826-3744, E-mail: rob.vankirk@humboldt.edu. *Application contact:* Julie Tucker, Administrative Support Coordinator, 707-826-3256, E-mail: jlt7002@humboldt.edu. Web site: http://www.humboldt.edu/cnrs/graduate_programs.

Marquette University, Graduate School, College of Engineering, Department of Civil and Environmental Engineering, Milwaukee, WI 53201-1881. Offers construction and public works management (MS, PhD); construction engineering and management (Certificate); environmental/water resources engineering (MS, PhD); structural design (Certificate); structural/geotechnical engineering (MS, PhD); transportation planning and engineering (MS, PhD); waste and wastewater treatment processes (Certificate). Part-time and evening/weekend programs available. *Faculty:* 13 full-time (0 women), 5 part-time/adjunct (0 women). *Students:* 26 full-time (5 women), 11 part-time (0 women); includes 2 minority (1 Black or African American, non-Hispanic/Latino; 1 Asian, non-Hispanic/Latino), 12 international. Average age 27. 74 applicants, 62% accepted, 9 enrolled. In 2011, 6 master's, 3 doctorates awarded. Terminal master's awarded for partial completion of doctoral program. *Degree requirements:* For master's, comprehensive exam (for some programs), thesis or alternative; for doctorate, thesis/dissertation. *Entrance requirements:* For master's, GRE General Test (recommended), minimum GPA of 3.0, official transcripts from all current and previous colleges/universities except Marquette, three letters of recommendation; for doctorate, GRE General Test, minimum GPA of 3.0, official transcripts from all current and previous colleges/universities except Marquette, three letters of recommendation, brief statement of purpose, submission of any English language publications authored by applicant (strongly recommended). Additional exam requirements/recommendations for international students: Required—TOEFL (minimum score 530 paper-based; 78 computer-based). *Application deadline:* For fall admission, 6/1 priority date for domestic students. Applications are processed on a rolling basis. Application fee: $50. Electronic applications accepted. *Expenses:* Tuition: Full-time $17,010; part-time $945 per credit hour. Tuition and fees vary according to program. *Financial support:* In 2011–12, 21 students received support, including 6 fellowships with partial tuition reimbursements available (averaging $9,177 per year), 1 research assistantship with full tuition reimbursement available (averaging $13,745 per year), 7 teaching assistantships with full tuition reimbursements available (averaging $13,902 per year); scholarships/grants, health care benefits, tuition waivers (partial), and unspecified assistantships also available. Support available to part-time students. Financial award application deadline: 2/15. *Faculty research:* Highway safety, highway performance, and intelligent transportation systems; surface mount technology; watershed management. *Total annual research expenditures:* $826,608. *Unit head:* Dr. Thomas Wenzel, Chair, 414-288-7030, Fax: 414-288-7521, E-mail: thomas.wenzel@marquette.edu. *Application contact:* Dr. Stephen M. Heinrich, Director of Graduate Studies, 414-288-5466, E-mail: stephen.heinrich@marquette.edu. Web site: http://www.marquette.edu/engineering/pages/AllYouNeed/Civil_Environmental/civil.html.

Missouri University of Science and Technology, Graduate School, Department of Geological Sciences and Engineering, Rolla, MO 65409. Offers geological engineering (MS, DE, PhD); geology and geophysics (MS, PhD), including geochemistry, geology, geophysics, groundwater and environmental geology; petroleum engineering (MS, DE, PhD). Part-time programs available. *Degree requirements:* For master's, thesis optional; for doctorate, comprehensive exam, thesis/dissertation. *Entrance requirements:* For master's, GRE General Test (minimum score 600 quantitative, writing 3.5), minimum GPA of 3.0 in last 4 semesters; for doctorate, GRE General Test (minimum: Q 600, GRE WR 3.5). Additional exam requirements/recommendations for international students: Required—TOEFL. Electronic applications accepted. *Faculty research:* Digital image processing and geographic information systems, mineralogy, igneous and sedimentary petrology-geochemistry, sedimentology groundwater hydrology and contaminant transport.

Nova Scotia Agricultural College, Research and Graduate Studies, Truro, NS B2N 5E3, Canada. Offers agriculture (M Sc), including air quality, animal behavior, animal molecular genetics, animal nutrition, animal technology, aquaculture, botany, crop management, crop physiology, ecology, environmental microbiology, food science, horticulture, nutrient management, pest management, physiology, plant biotechnology, plant pathology, soil chemistry, soil fertility, waste management and composting, water quality. Program offered jointly with Dalhousie University. Part-time programs available. *Degree requirements:* For master's, thesis, ATC Exam Teaching Assistantship. *Entrance requirements:* For master's, honors B Sc, minimum GPA of 3.0. Additional exam requirements/recommendations for international students: Required—TOEFL (minimum score 580 paper-based; 237 computer-based; 92 iBT), IELTS, Michigan English Language Assessment Battery, CanTEST, CAEL. *Faculty research:* Bio-product development, organic agriculture, nutrient management, air and water quality, agricultural biotechnology.

Rutgers, The State University of New Jersey, New Brunswick, Graduate School-New Brunswick, Department of Environmental Sciences, Piscataway, NJ 08854-8097. Offers air pollution and resources (MS, PhD); aquatic biology (MS, PhD); aquatic chemistry (MS, PhD); atmospheric science (MS, PhD); chemistry and physics of aerosol and hydrosol systems (MS, PhD); environmental chemistry (MS, PhD); environmental microbiology (MS, PhD); environmental toxicology (PhD); exposure assessment (PhD); fate and effects of pollutants (MS, PhD); pollution prevention and control (MS, PhD); water and wastewater treatment (MS, PhD); water resources (MS, PhD). Terminal master's awarded for partial completion of doctoral program. *Degree requirements:* For master's, comprehensive exam, thesis or alternative, oral final exam; for doctorate, comprehensive exam, thesis/dissertation, thesis defense, qualifying exam. *Entrance requirements:* For master's and doctorate, GRE General Test. Additional exam requirements/recommendations for international students: Required—TOEFL. Electronic applications accepted. *Faculty research:* Biological waste treatment; contaminant fate and transport; air, soil and water quality.

State University of New York College of Environmental Science and Forestry, Program in Environmental Science, Syracuse, NY 13210-2779. Offers

540 facebook.com/petersonspublishing

Peterson's Graduate Programs in the Physical Sciences, Mathematics, Agricultural Sciences, the Environment & Natural Resources 2013

biophysical and ecological economics (MPS); coupled natural and human systems (MPS); ecosystem restoration (MPS); environmental and community land planning (MPS, MS); environmental and natural resources policy (PhD); environmental communication and participatory processes (MPS, MS); environmental monitoring and modeling (MPS); environmental policy and democratic processes (MPS, MS); environmental systems and risk management (MS); water and wetland resource studies (MPS, MS). Part-time programs available. *Degree requirements:* For master's, thesis (for some programs); for doctorate, comprehensive exam, thesis/dissertation. *Entrance requirements:* For master's and doctorate, GRE General Test, minimum GPA of 3.0. Additional exam requirements/recommendations for international students: Required—TOEFL (minimum score 550 paper-based; 213 computer-based; 80 iBT), IELTS (minimum score 6). *Application deadline:* For fall admission, 2/1 priority date for domestic students, 2/1 for international students; for spring admission, 11/1 priority date for domestic students, 11/1 for international students. Applications are processed on a rolling basis. Application fee: $60. *Expenses:* Tuition, state resident: full-time $8870; part-time $370 per credit hour. Tuition, nonresident: full-time $15,160; part-time $632 per credit hour. *Required fees:* $60; $370 per credit hour. $350 per semester. One-time fee: $85. *Financial support:* Fellowships with full and partial tuition reimbursements, research assistantships with full and partial tuition reimbursements, teaching assistantships with full and partial tuition reimbursements, career-related internships or fieldwork, Federal Work-Study, institutionally sponsored loans, scholarships/grants, health care benefits, and unspecified assistantships available. Support available to part-time students. Financial award application deadline: 6/30; financial award applicants required to submit FAFSA. *Faculty research:* Environmental education/communications, water resources, land resources, waste management. *Total annual research expenditures:* $169,919. *Unit head:* Dr. Ruth Yanai, Coordinator, 315-470-6955, Fax: 315-470-6700, E-mail: rdyanai@esf.edu. *Application contact:* Dr. Dudley J. Raynal, Dean, Instruction and Graduate Studies, 315-470-6599, Fax: 315-470-6978, E-mail: esfgrad@esf.edu. Web site: http://www.esf.edu/environmentalscience/.

Tropical Agriculture Research and Higher Education Center, Graduate School, Turrialba, Costa Rica. Offers agribusiness management (MS); agroforestry systems (PhD); development practices (MS); ecological agriculture (MS); environmental socioeconomics (MS); forestry in tropical and subtropical zones (PhD); integrated watershed management (MS); international sustainable tourism (MS); management and conservation of tropical rainforests and biodiversity (MS); tropical agriculture (PhD); tropical agroforestry (MS). *Entrance requirements:* For master's, GRE, 2 years of related professional experience, letters of recommendation; for doctorate, GRE, 4 letters of recommendation, letter of support from employing organization, master's degree in agronomy, biological sciences, forestry, natural resources or related field. Additional exam requirements/recommendations for international students: Required—TOEFL (minimum score 550 paper-based; 213 computer-based). Electronic applications accepted. *Faculty research:* Biodiversity in fragmented landscapes, ecosystem management, integrated pest management, environmental livestock production, biotechnology carbon balances in diverse land uses.

University of Alaska Fairbanks, College of Engineering and Mines, Department of Civil and Environmental Engineering, Program in Environmental Engineering, Fairbanks, AK 99775-5900. Offers engineering (PhD), including environmental engineering; environmental engineering (MS), including environmental contaminants, environmental science and management, water supply and waste treatment. Part-time programs available. *Students:* 3 full-time (0 women), 1 (woman) part-time. Average age 26. 5 applicants, 60% accepted, 1 enrolled. In 2011, 2 degrees awarded. *Degree requirements:* For master's, comprehensive exam, thesis or alternative; for doctorate, comprehensive exam, thesis/dissertation, oral exam, oral defense. *Entrance requirements:* For master's, basic computer techniques; for doctorate, GRE General Test. Additional exam requirements/recommendations for international students: Required—TOEFL (minimum score 575 paper-based; 213 computer-based). *Application deadline:* For fall admission, 6/1 for domestic students, 3/1 for international students; for spring admission, 10/15 for domestic students, 9/1 for international students. Applications are processed on a rolling basis. Application fee: $60. Electronic applications accepted. *Expenses:* Tuition, state resident: full-time $6696; part-time $372 per credit. Tuition, nonresident: full-time $13,680; part-time $760 per credit. Tuition and fees vary according to course load and reciprocity agreements. *Financial support:* In 2011–12, 1 research assistantship (averaging $16,834 per year), 2 teaching assistantships (averaging $6,390 per year) were awarded; fellowships, career-related internships or fieldwork, Federal Work-Study, scholarships/grants, health care benefits, and unspecified assistantships also available. Support available to part-time students. Financial award application deadline: 7/1; financial award applicants required to submit FAFSA. *Unit head:* Dr. David Barnes, Department Chair, 907-474-7241, Fax: 907-474-6087, E-mail: fyeqe@uaf.edu. *Application contact:* Mike Earnest, Director of Admissions, 907-474-7500, Fax: 907-474-5379, E-mail: admissions@uaf.edu. Web site: http://www.alaska.edu/uaf/cem/cee/env/.

The University of Arizona, College of Agriculture and Life Sciences, Department of Soil, Water and Environmental Science, Tucson, AZ 85721. Offers MS, PhD. *Faculty:* 10 full-time (3 women), 1 (woman) part-time/adjunct. *Students:* 50 full-time (32 women), 7 part-time (2 women); includes 15 minority (2 Black or African American, non-Hispanic/Latino; 1 American Indian or Alaska Native, non-Hispanic/Latino; 1 Asian, non-Hispanic/Latino; 8 Hispanic/Latino; 3 Two or more races, non-Hispanic/Latino), 15 international. Average age 31. 37 applicants, 54%

accepted, 13 enrolled. In 2011, 10 master's, 11 doctorates awarded. *Degree requirements:* For master's, thesis; for doctorate, comprehensive exam, thesis/dissertation. *Entrance requirements:* For master's, GRE (recommended), minimum GPA of 3.0, letter of interest, 3 letters of recommendation; for doctorate, GRE (recommended), MS, minimum GPA of 3.0, letter of interest, 3 letters of recommendation. Additional exam requirements/recommendations for international students: Required—TOEFL (minimum score 550 paper-based; 213 computer-based; 80 iBT). *Application deadline:* For fall admission, 6/1 for domestic students, 12/1 for international students; for spring admission, 10/1 for domestic students, 6/1 for international students. Applications are processed on a rolling basis. Application fee: $75. *Expenses:* Tuition, state resident: full-time $10,840. Tuition, nonresident: full-time $25,802. *Financial support:* In 2011–12, 14 students received support, including 24 research assistantships with full and partial tuition reimbursements available (averaging $18,526 per year), 2 teaching assistantships with full and partial tuition reimbursements available (averaging $18,529 per year); fellowships, Federal Work-Study, institutionally sponsored loans, scholarships/grants, health care benefits, tuition waivers (full and partial), and unspecified assistantships also available. Financial award application deadline: 5/1. *Faculty research:* Plant production, environmental microbiology, contaminant flow and transport, aquaculture. *Total annual research expenditures:* $3.4 million. *Unit head:* Dr. Jeffery C. Silvertooth, Head, 520-621-7228, Fax: 520-621-1647, E-mail: silver@ag.arizona.edu. *Application contact:* Alicia Velasquez, 520-621-1606, Fax: 520-621-1647, E-mail: avelasqu@ag.arizona.edu. Web site: http://ag.arizona.edu/SWES/.

The University of Arizona, College of Agriculture and Life Sciences, School of Natural Resources, Watershed Resources Program, Tucson, AZ 85721. Offers MS, PhD. *Students:* 5 full-time (3 women), 3 part-time (0 women); includes 5 minority (3 Hispanic/Latino; 2 Two or more races, non-Hispanic/Latino). Average age 34. In 2011, 3 doctorates awarded. *Degree requirements:* For master's, thesis; for doctorate, comprehensive exam, thesis/dissertation. *Entrance requirements:* For master's, GRE General Test, minimum GPA of 3.0, 3 letters of recommendation; for doctorate, GRE General Test, minimum GPA of 3.0, 3 letters of recommendation, MA or MS. Additional exam requirements/recommendations for international students: Required—TOEFL (minimum score 550 paper-based; 213 computer-based). *Application deadline:* For fall admission, 8/1 priority date for domestic students, 12/1 for international students; for spring admission, 7/1 for international students. Applications are processed on a rolling basis. Application fee: $75. *Expenses:* Tuition, state resident: full-time $10,840. Tuition, nonresident: full-time $25,802. *Financial support:* Research assistantships with partial tuition reimbursements, teaching assistantships with partial tuition reimbursements, career-related internships or fieldwork, scholarships/grants, health care benefits, tuition waivers (partial), and unspecified assistantships available. *Faculty research:* Forest fuel characteristics, prescribed fire, tree ring-fire scar analysis, erosion, sedimentation. *Unit head:* Dr. Joseph G. Hiller, Chair, 520-621-7255, Fax: 520-621-8801, E-mail: jghiller@cals.arizona.edu. *Application contact:* Cheryl L. Craddock, Academic Coordinator, 520-621-7260, Fax: 520-621-8801, E-mail: ccraddoc@email.arizona.edu. Web site: http://www.ag.arizona.edu/srnr/.

The University of Arizona, College of Science, Department of Hydrology and Water Resources, Tucson, AZ 85721. Offers MS, PhD. Part-time programs available. *Faculty:* 15 full-time (1 woman). *Students:* 45 full-time (12 women), 8 part-time (1 woman); includes 9 minority (1 American Indian or Alaska Native, non-Hispanic/Latino; 1 Asian, non-Hispanic/Latino; 4 Hispanic/Latino; 3 Two or more races, non-Hispanic/Latino), 12 international. Average age 31. 66 applicants, 14% accepted, 9 enrolled. In 2011, 7 master's, 5 doctorates awarded. *Degree requirements:* For master's, thesis; for doctorate, thesis/dissertation. *Entrance requirements:* For master's, GRE General Test, 3 letters of recommendation, bachelor's degree in related field; for doctorate, GRE General Test, minimum undergraduate GPA of 3.2, graduate 3.4; 3 letters of recommendation; master's degree in related field; master's thesis abstract. Additional exam requirements/recommendations for international students: Required—TOEFL (minimum score 550 paper-based; 213 computer-based; 79 iBT). *Application deadline:* For fall admission, 5/1 for domestic students, 12/1 for international students; for spring admission, 10/1 for domestic students, 6/1 for international students. Applications are processed on a rolling basis. Application fee: $75. Electronic applications accepted. *Expenses:* Tuition, state resident: full-time $10,840. Tuition, nonresident: full-time $25,802. *Financial support:* In 2011–12, 21 research assistantships with full tuition reimbursements (averaging $23,223 per year), 5 teaching assistantships with full tuition reimbursements (averaging $23,586 per year) were awarded; institutionally sponsored loans, scholarships/grants, health care benefits, and unspecified assistantships also available. Financial award application deadline: 1/31. *Faculty research:* Subsurface and surface hydrology, hydrometeorology/climatology, applied remote sensing, water resource systems, environmental hydrology and water quality. *Total annual research expenditures:* $1.2 million. *Unit head:* Dr. Kevin Lansey, Department Head, 520-621-7120, E-mail: lansey@email.arizona.edu. *Application contact:* Terrie Thompson, Academic Advising Coordinator, 520-621-3131, Fax: 520-621-1422, E-mail: programs@hwr.arizona.edu. Web site: http://www.hwr.arizona.edu/.

University of California, Riverside, Graduate Division, Environmental Sciences Department, Riverside, CA 92521-0102. Offers MS, PhD. *Faculty:* 27 full-time (4 women). *Students:* 27 full-time (12 women); includes 4 minority (1 Asian, non-Hispanic/Latino; 3 Hispanic/Latino), 11 international. Average age 29. In 2011, 5 master's, 1 doctorate awarded. *Degree requirements:* For doctorate, thesis/

Peterson's Graduate Programs in the Physical Sciences, Mathematics, Agricultural Sciences, the Environment & Natural Resources 2013

facebook.com/petersonspublishing **541**

dissertation. *Entrance requirements:* For master's and doctorate, minimum GPA of 3.2. Additional exam requirements/recommendations for international students: Required—TOEFL (minimum score 550 paper-based; 213 computer-based; 80 iBT). *Application deadline:* For fall admission, 5/1 for domestic students, 2/1 for international students; for winter admission, 9/1 for domestic students, 7/1 for international students; for spring admission, 12/1 for domestic students, 10/1 for international students. Application fee: $80 ($100 for international students). Electronic applications accepted. *Financial support:* Fellowships with tuition reimbursements and research assistantships with tuition reimbursements available. *Faculty research:* Environmental chemistry and ecotoxicology, environmental microbiology, environmental and natural resource economics and policy, soil and water sciences, environmental sciences and management. *Unit head:* Dr. Michael Anderson, Chair, 951-827-3757. *Application contact:* John Herring, Program Assistant, 951-827-2441, E-mail: soilwater@ucr.edu. Web site: http://envisci.ucr.edu/.

University of Colorado Denver, College of Liberal Arts and Sciences, Department of Geography and Environmental Sciences, Denver, CO 80217. Offers environmental sciences (MS), including air quality, ecosystems, environmental health, environmental science education, geo-spatial analysis, hazardous waste, water quality. Part-time and evening/weekend programs available. *Students:* 42 full-time (25 women), 6 part-time (5 women); includes 6 minority (2 Black or African American, non-Hispanic/Latino; 1 Asian, non-Hispanic/Latino; 2 Hispanic/Latino; 1 Two or more races, non-Hispanic/Latino), 10 international. Average age 29. 31 applicants, 68% accepted, 13 enrolled. In 2011, 24 master's awarded. *Degree requirements:* For master's, thesis or alternative, 30 credits including 21 of core requirements and 9 of environmental science electives. *Entrance requirements:* For master's, GRE General Test, BA in one of the natural/physical sciences or engineering (or equivalent background); prerequisite coursework in calculus and physics (one semester each), general chemistry with lab and general biology with lab (two semesters each), three letters of recommendation. Additional exam requirements/recommendations for international students: Required—TOEFL (minimum score 525 paper-based; 197 computer-based). *Application deadline:* For fall admission, 4/1 for domestic and international students; for spring admission, 10/1 for domestic and international students. Application fee: $50 ($75 for international students). Electronic applications accepted. *Financial support:* Research assistantships, teaching assistantships, and Federal Work-Study available. Financial award application deadline: 4/1; financial award applicants required to submit FAFSA. *Faculty research:* Air quality, environmental health, ecosystems, hazardous waste, water quality, geo-spatial analysis and environmental science education. *Unit head:* Dr. Brian K. Page, Department Chair, 303-556-8332, Fax: 303-556-6197, E-mail: john.wyckoff@cudenver.edu. *Application contact:* Sue Eddleman, Program Assistant, 303-556-6197, E-mail: sue.eddleman@ucdenver.edu. Web site: http://www.ucdenver.edu/academics/colleges/CLAS/Departments/ges/Pages/Geography.aspx.

University of Florida, Graduate School, College of Agricultural and Life Sciences, Department of Soil and Water Science, Gainesville, FL 32611. Offers MS, PhD. Part-time and evening/weekend programs available. Postbaccalaureate distance learning degree programs offered (no on-campus study). *Faculty:* 20 full-time (3 women). *Students:* 68 full-time (35 women), 53 part-time (21 women); includes 9 minority (1 Black or African American, non-Hispanic/Latino; 1 American Indian or Alaska Native, non-Hispanic/Latino; 3 Asian, non-Hispanic/Latino; 4 Hispanic/Latino), 39 international. Average age 33. 71 applicants, 46% accepted, 25 enrolled. In 2011, 22 master's, 8 doctorates awarded. Terminal master's awarded for partial completion of doctoral program. *Degree requirements:* For master's, thesis optional; for doctorate, comprehensive exam, thesis/dissertation. *Entrance requirements:* For master's and doctorate, GRE General Test (minimum score 1000 taken within last 5 years), minimum GPA of 3.0. Additional exam requirements/recommendations for international students: Required—TOEFL (minimum score 550 paper-based; 213 computer-based; 80 iBT), IELTS (minimum score 6). *Application deadline:* For fall admission, 3/1 priority date for domestic students, 3/1 for international students; for spring admission, 10/1 for domestic and international students. Applications are processed on a rolling basis. Application fee: $30. Electronic applications accepted. *Financial support:* Fellowships, research assistantships, teaching assistantships, career-related internships or fieldwork, Federal Work-Study, institutionally sponsored loans, and unspecified assistantships available. Support available to part-time students. Financial award applicants required to submit FAFSA. *Faculty research:* Nutrient, pesticide, and waste management; soil, water, and aquifer remediation; carbon dynamics and ecosystem services; landscape analysis and modeling; wetlands and aquatic ecosystems. *Unit head:* Dr. K. Ramesh Reddy, Chair, 352-392-1804 Ext. 317, Fax: 352-392-3399, E-mail: krr@ufl.edu. *Application contact:* Dr. Andrew Ogram, Graduate Coordinator, 352-392-1951 Ext. 211, Fax: 352-392-3902, E-mail: aogram@ufl.edu. Web site: http://soils.ifas.ufl.edu/.

University of Idaho, College of Graduate Studies, Program in Environmental Science, Moscow, ID 83844-3006. Offers environmental science (MS, PhD); natural resources and environmental science (PSM); water resources (MS, PhD). *Faculty:* 19 full-time, 1 part-time/adjunct. *Students:* 87 full-time, 57 part-time. Average age 32. In 2011, 20 master's, 2 doctorates awarded. *Application deadline:* For fall admission, 8/1 for domestic students; for spring admission, 12/15 for domestic students. Applications are processed on a rolling basis. Application fee: $60. Electronic applications accepted. *Expenses:* Tuition, state resident: full-time $3874; part-time $334 per credit hour. Tuition, nonresident: full-time $16,394; part-time $861 per credit hour. *Required fees:* $2808; $99 per credit

hour. Tuition and fees vary according to program. *Financial support:* Research assistantships and teaching assistantships available. Financial award applicants required to submit FAFSA. *Unit head:* Dr. Jan Boll, Director, 208-885-6113, Fax: 208-885-4674, E-mail: envs@uidaho.edu. *Application contact:* Erick Larson, Director of Graduate Admissions, 208-885-4723, E-mail: gadms@uidaho.edu. Web site: http://www.uidaho.edu/cogs/envs.

University of Maine, Graduate School, College of Natural Sciences, Forestry, and Agriculture, Department of Biological Sciences, Program in Ecology and Environmental Science, Orono, ME 04469. Offers water resources (PhD). Part-time programs available. *Students:* 40 full-time (31 women), 14 part-time (6 women). Average age 31. 72 applicants, 25% accepted, 12 enrolled. In 2011, 7 master's, 5 doctorates awarded. *Degree requirements:* For doctorate, thesis/dissertation. *Entrance requirements:* For master's and doctorate, GRE General Test. Additional exam requirements/recommendations for international students: Required—TOEFL. *Application deadline:* For fall admission, 2/1 priority date for domestic students. Applications are processed on a rolling basis. Application fee: $65. Electronic applications accepted. *Expenses:* Tuition, state resident: full-time $5016. Tuition, nonresident: full-time $14,424. *Financial support:* Career-related internships or fieldwork, Federal Work-Study, institutionally sponsored loans, and tuition waivers (full) available. Financial award application deadline: 3/1. *Unit head:* Dr. Mark Anderson, Coordinator, 207-581-3198. *Application contact:* Scott G. Delcourt, Associate Dean of the Graduate School, 207-581-3291, Fax: 207-581-3232, E-mail: graduate@maine.edu. Web site: http://www2.umaine.edu/graduate/.

University of Maine, Graduate School, College of Natural Sciences, Forestry, and Agriculture, Department of Earth Sciences, Orono, ME 04469. Offers water resources (MS, PhD). Part-time programs available. *Faculty:* 9 full-time (2 women), 3 part-time/adjunct (0 women). *Students:* 23 full-time (12 women), 10 part-time (5 women), 3 international. Average age 28. 32 applicants, 66% accepted, 17 enrolled. In 2011, 6 master's, 4 doctorates awarded. *Degree requirements:* For master's, thesis; for doctorate, one foreign language, thesis/dissertation. *Entrance requirements:* For master's and doctorate, GRE General Test. Additional exam requirements/recommendations for international students: Required—TOEFL. *Application deadline:* For fall admission, 2/1 priority date for domestic students. Applications are processed on a rolling basis. Application fee: $65. Electronic applications accepted. *Expenses:* Tuition, state resident: full-time $5016. Tuition, nonresident: full-time $14,424. *Financial support:* In 2011–12, 5 research assistantships with full tuition reimbursements (averaging $16,950 per year), 6 teaching assistantships with full tuition reimbursements (averaging $13,600 per year) were awarded; Federal Work-Study, institutionally sponsored loans, and tuition waivers (full and partial) also available. Financial award application deadline: 3/1. *Faculty research:* Appalachian bedrock geology, Quaternary studies, marine geology. *Unit head:* Dr. Joseph Kelley, Chair, 207-581-2162, Fax: 207-581-2202. *Application contact:* Scott G. Delcourt, Associate Dean of the Graduate School, 207-581-3291, Fax: 207-581-3232, E-mail: graduate@maine.edu. Web site: http://www2.umaine.edu/graduate/.

University of Massachusetts Amherst, Graduate School, College of Natural Sciences, Department of Environmental Conservation, Amherst, MA 01003. Offers building systems (MS, PhD); environmental policy and human dimensions (MS, PhD); forest resources (MS, PhD); sustainability science (MS); water, wetlands and watersheds (MS, PhD); wildlife and fisheries conservation (MS, PhD). Part-time programs available. *Faculty:* 57 full-time (10 women). *Students:* 61 full-time (26 women), 34 part-time (13 women); includes 4 minority (1 Black or African American, non-Hispanic/Latino; 2 Hispanic/Latino; 1 Two or more races, non-Hispanic/Latino), 12 international. Average age 32. 84 applicants, 40% accepted, 22 enrolled. In 2011, 1 master's, 2 doctorates awarded. Terminal master's awarded for partial completion of doctoral program. *Degree requirements:* For master's, thesis or alternative; for doctorate, comprehensive exam, thesis/dissertation. *Entrance requirements:* For master's and doctorate, GRE General Test. Additional exam requirements/recommendations for international students: Required—TOEFL (minimum score 550 paper-based; 213 computer-based; 80 iBT), IELTS (minimum score 6.5). *Application deadline:* For fall admission, 2/1 for domestic and international students; for spring admission, 10/1 for domestic and international students. Applications are processed on a rolling basis. Application fee: $50 ($65 for international students). Electronic applications accepted. Tuition and fees vary according to course load, campus/location and program. *Financial support:* Fellowships with full and partial tuition reimbursements, research assistantships with full and partial tuition reimbursements, teaching assistantships with full and partial tuition reimbursements, career-related internships or fieldwork, Federal Work-Study, scholarships/grants, traineeships, health care benefits, tuition waivers (full and partial), and unspecified assistantships available. Support available to part-time students. Financial award application deadline: 2/1. *Unit head:* Dr. Kevin McGarigal, Graduate Program Director, 413-545-2257, Fax: 413-545-4358. *Application contact:* Lindsay DeSantis, Interim Supervisor of Admissions, 413-545-0721, Fax: 413-577-0100, E-mail: gradadm@grad.umass.edu. Web site: http://eco.umass.edu/.

University of Minnesota, Twin Cities Campus, Graduate School, College of Food, Agricultural and Natural Resource Sciences, Program in Water Resources Science, Minneapolis, MN 55455-0213. Offers MS, PhD. Part-time programs available. *Faculty:* 122 full-time (25 women). *Students:* 30 full-time (16 women), 5 part-time (3 women), 2 international. Average age 30. 52 applicants, 50% accepted, 17 enrolled. In 2011, 8 master's, 7 doctorates awarded. *Degree*

542 facebook.com/petersonspublishing

Peterson's Graduate Programs in the Physical Sciences, Mathematics, Agricultural Sciences, the Environment & Natural Resources 2013

requirements: For master's, comprehensive exam, thesis; for doctorate, comprehensive exam, thesis/dissertation. *Entrance requirements:* For master's and doctorate, GRE, minimum GPA of 3.0, calculus, chemistry, biology, physics. Additional exam requirements/recommendations for international students: Required—TOEFL (minimum score 550 paper-based; 213 computer-based; 79 iBT), IELTS (minimum score 6.5), TOEFL preferred. *Application deadline:* For fall admission, 12/15 priority date for domestic students, 12/15 for international students; for spring admission, 12/15 priority date for domestic students, 12/15 for international students. Applications are processed on a rolling basis. Application fee: $75 ($95 for international students). Electronic applications accepted. *Financial support:* In 2011–12, fellowships with full tuition reimbursements (averaging $23,500 per year), research assistantships with full and partial tuition reimbursements (averaging $19,000 per year) were awarded; scholarships/grants, health care benefits, and unspecified assistantships also available. Financial award application deadline: 12/15. *Faculty research:* Hydrology, limnology, water policy and economics, water quality, water chemistry. *Total annual research expenditures:* $442,254. *Unit head:* Dr. Deb Swackhamer, Director of Graduate Studies, 612-625-0279, E-mail: dswack@umn.edu. *Application contact:* Bonnie R. Anderson, Assistant to Director of Graduate Studies, 612-624-7456, Fax: 612-625-1263, E-mail: ander742@umn.edu.

University of Nevada, Las Vegas, Graduate College, College of Science, Program in Water Resources Management, Las Vegas, NV 89154-4029. Offers MS. Part-time programs available. *Faculty:* 16 full-time (2 women), 4 part-time/adjunct (0 women). *Students:* 2 full-time (1 woman), 7 part-time (4 women); includes 1 minority (Hispanic/Latino), 1 international. Average age 34. 9 applicants, 44% accepted, 2 enrolled. In 2011, 4 master's awarded. *Degree requirements:* For master's, comprehensive exam, thesis. *Entrance requirements:* For master's, GRE Subject Test. Additional exam requirements/recommendations for international students: Required—TOEFL (minimum score 550 paper-based; 213 computer-based; 80 iBT), IELTS (minimum score 7). *Application deadline:* For fall admission, 2/1 priority date for domestic students, 5/1 for international students; for spring admission, 10/1 priority date for domestic students, 10/1 for international students. Applications are processed on a rolling basis. Application fee: $60 ($95 for international students). Electronic applications accepted. *Financial support:* In 2011–12, 3 students received support, including 1 research assistantship with partial tuition reimbursement available (averaging $6,000 per year), 2 teaching assistantships with partial tuition reimbursements available (averaging $10,500 per year); institutionally sponsored loans, scholarships/grants, health care benefits, and unspecified assistantships also available. Financial award application deadline: 3/1. *Faculty research:* Hydrogeology, water conservation, environmental chemistry, water resources planning, hydrology, waste management: hazardous materials management. *Unit head:* Dr. Michael Nicholl, Chair/Associate Professor, 702-895-4616, Fax: 702-895-4064, E-mail: michael.nicholl@unlv.edu. *Application contact:* Graduate College Admissions Evaluator, 702-895-3320, Fax: 702-895-4180, E-mail: gradcollege@unlv.edu. Web site: http://graduatecollege.unlv.edu/programs/all/index.html?waterresources.

University of New Brunswick Fredericton, School of Graduate Studies, Faculty of Engineering, Department of Civil Engineering, Fredericton, NB E3B 5A3, Canada. Offers construction engineering and management (M Eng, M Sc E, PhD); environmental engineering (M Eng, M Sc E, PhD); environmental studies (M Eng); geotechnical engineering (M Eng, M Sc E, PhD); groundwater/hydrology (M Eng, M Sc E, PhD); materials (M Eng, M Sc E, PhD); pavements (M Eng, M Sc E, PhD); structures (M Eng, M Sc E, PhD); transportation (M Eng, M Sc E, PhD). Part-time programs available. *Faculty:* 13 full-time (1 woman), 7 part-time/adjunct (1 woman). *Students:* 31 full-time (7 women), 17 part-time (2 women). In 2011, 11 master's, 2 doctorates awarded. *Degree requirements:* For master's, thesis, proposal; for doctorate, comprehensive exam, thesis/dissertation, qualifying exam; proposal; 27 credit hours of courses. *Entrance requirements:* For master's, minimum GPA of 3.0; B Sc E in civil engineering or related engineering degree; for doctorate, minimum GPA of 3.0; graduate degree in engineering or applied science. Additional exam requirements/recommendations for international students: Required—TWE (minimum score 4), TOEFL (minimum score 580 paper-based; 237 computer-based) or IELTS (minimum score 7.5). *Application deadline:* For fall admission, 5/1 priority date for domestic students; for winter admission, 11/1 priority date for domestic students. Applications are processed on a rolling basis. Application fee: $50 Canadian dollars. *Financial support:* In 2011–12, 14 fellowships, 30 research assistantships (averaging $7,000 per year), 42 teaching assistantships (averaging $2,000 per year) were awarded; career-related internships or fieldwork and scholarships/grants also available. *Faculty research:* Construction engineering and management; materials and infrastructure renewal; highway and pavement research; structures and solid mechanics; geotechnical, soil; structure interaction; transportation and planning; environment, solid waste management. *Unit head:* Dr. Eric Hildebrand, Director of Graduate Studies, 506-453-5113, Fax: 506-453-3568, E-mail: edh@unb.ca. *Application contact:* Joyce Moore, Graduate Secretary, 506-452-6127, Fax: 506-453-3568, E-mail: civil-grad@unb.ca. Web site: http://www.unbf.ca/eng/civil/.

University of New Hampshire, Graduate School, College of Life Sciences and Agriculture, Department of Natural Resources, Durham, NH 03824. Offers environmental conservation (MS); forestry (MS); integrated coastal ecosystem science, policy, management (MS); natural resources (MS); water resources (MS); wildlife (MS). Part-time programs available. *Faculty:* 40 full-time. *Students:* 32 full-time (15 women), 24 part-time (13 women); includes 2 minority (1 Asian, non-Hispanic/Latino; 1 Hispanic/Latino), 1 international. Average age 29. 79

applicants, 49% accepted, 20 enrolled. In 2011, 10 master's awarded. *Degree requirements:* For master's, thesis or alternative. *Entrance requirements:* For master's, GRE General Test. Additional exam requirements/recommendations for international students: Required—TOEFL (minimum score 550 paper-based; 213 computer-based; 80 iBT). *Application deadline:* For fall admission, 6/1 for domestic students, 4/1 for international students; for spring admission, 12/1 for domestic students. Applications are processed on a rolling basis. Application fee: $65. Electronic applications accepted. *Expenses:* Tuition, state resident: full-time $12,360; part-time $687 per credit hour. Tuition, nonresident: full-time $25,680; part-time $1058 per credit hour. *International tuition:* $29,550 full-time. *Required fees:* $1666; $833 per course. $416.50 per semester. Tuition and fees vary according to course load and degree level. *Financial support:* In 2011–12, 35 students received support, including 3 fellowships, 13 research assistantships, 17 teaching assistantships; career-related internships or fieldwork, Federal Work-Study, scholarships/grants, and tuition waivers (full and partial) also available. Support available to part-time students. Financial award application deadline: 2/15. *Unit head:* Dr. Ted Howard, Chairperson, 603-862-2700, E-mail: natural.resources@unh.edu. *Application contact:* Nancy Brown, Administrative Assistant, 603-862-1022, E-mail: natural.resources@unh.edu. Web site: http://www.nre.unh.edu/academics/.

University of New Mexico, Graduate School, Water Resources Program, Albuquerque, NM 87131-2039. Offers hydroscience (MWR); policy management (MWR). Part-time programs available. *Faculty:* 1 full-time (0 women). *Students:* 16 full-time (12 women), 33 part-time (18 women); includes 16 minority (1 Black or African American, non-Hispanic/Latino; 6 American Indian or Alaska Native, non-Hispanic/Latino; 2 Asian, non-Hispanic/Latino; 6 Hispanic/Latino; 1 Two or more races, non-Hispanic/Latino). Average age 36. 29 applicants, 62% accepted, 11 enrolled. In 2011, 8 degrees awarded. *Degree requirements:* For master's, professional project. *Entrance requirements:* For master's, minimum GPA of 3.0 during last 2 years of undergraduate work, 3 letters of reference. Additional exam requirements/recommendations for international students: Required—TOEFL (minimum score 550 paper-based; 213 computer-based). *Application deadline:* For fall admission, 7/15 for domestic students; for spring admission, 11/15 for domestic students. Applications are processed on a rolling basis. Application fee: $50. Electronic applications accepted. *Financial support:* In 2011–12, 24 students received support, including 3 research assistantships with full and partial tuition reimbursements available (averaging $5,791 per year); career-related internships or fieldwork, institutionally sponsored loans, scholarships/grants, and unspecified assistantships also available. Financial award application deadline: 3/1; financial award applicants required to submit FAFSA. *Faculty research:* Sustainable water resources, transboundary water resources, economics, water law, hydrology, developing countries, hydrogeology. *Total annual research expenditures:* $150,557. *Unit head:* Dr. Bruce M. Thomson, Director, 505-277-5249, Fax: 505-277-5226, E-mail: bthomson@unm.edu. *Application contact:* Annamarie Cordova, Administrative Assistant II, 505-277-7759, Fax: 505-277-5226, E-mail: acordova@unm.edu. Web site: http://www.unm.edu/~wrp/.

University of Southern California, Graduate School, Viterbi School of Engineering, Sonny Astani Department of Civil Engineering, Los Angeles, CA 90089. Offers applied mechanics (MS); civil engineering (MS, PhD); computer-aided engineering (ME, Graduate Certificate); construction management (MCM); engineering technology commercialization (Graduate Certificate); environmental engineering (MS, PhD); environmental quality management (ME); structural design (ME); sustainable cities (Graduate Certificate); transportation systems (MS, Graduate Certificate); water and waste management (MS). Part-time and evening/weekend programs available. Terminal master's awarded for partial completion of doctoral program. *Degree requirements:* For master's, thesis optional; for doctorate, thesis/dissertation. *Entrance requirements:* For master's and doctorate, GRE General Test. Additional exam requirements/recommendations for international students: Recommended—TOEFL. Electronic applications accepted. *Faculty research:* Geotechnical engineering, transportation engineering, structural engineering, construction management, environmental engineering, water resources.

University of the Pacific, McGeorge School of Law, Sacramento, CA 95817. Offers advocacy (JD); criminal justice (JD); experiential law teaching (LL M); intellectual property (JD); international legal studies (JD); international water resources law (LL M, JSD); law (JD); public law and policy (JD); public policy and law (LL M); tax (JD); transnational business practice (LL M); JD/MBA; JD/MPPA. *Accreditation:* ABA. Part-time and evening/weekend programs available. *Faculty:* 48 full-time (20 women), 59 part-time/adjunct (18 women). *Students:* 704 full-time (325 women), 255 part-time (122 women); includes 254 minority (19 Black or African American, non-Hispanic/Latino; 19 American Indian or Alaska Native, non-Hispanic/Latino; 151 Asian, non-Hispanic/Latino; 65 Hispanic/Latino), 41 international. Average age 27. 3,564 applicants, 38% accepted, 228 enrolled. In 2011, 36 master's, 307 doctorates awarded. *Degree requirements:* For master's, thesis (for some programs); for doctorate, thesis/dissertation (for some programs). *Entrance requirements:* For master's, JD; for doctorate, LSAT (for JD), LL M (for JSD). Additional exam requirements/recommendations for international students: Required—TOEFL (minimum score 600 paper-based; 250 computer-based; 100 iBT). *Application deadline:* For fall admission, 3/15 priority date for domestic students. Applications are processed on a rolling basis. Application fee: $50. Electronic applications accepted. *Expenses:* Contact institution. *Financial support:* Fellowships, research assistantships, teaching assistantships, career-related internships or fieldwork, Federal Work-Study, institutionally sponsored loans, and scholarships/grants available. Support available to part-time students. Financial

Peterson's Graduate Programs in the Physical Sciences, Mathematics, Agricultural Sciences, the Environment & Natural Resources 2013

facebook.com/petersonspublishing **543**

award applicants required to submit FAFSA. *Faculty research:* International legal studies, public policy and law, advocacy, intellectual property law, taxation, criminal law. *Unit head:* Elizabeth Rindskopf Parker, Dean, 916-739-7151, E-mail: elizabeth@pacific.edu. *Application contact:* 916-739-7105, Fax: 916-739-7301, E-mail: mcgeorge@pacific.edu. Web site: http://www.mcgeorge.edu/.

University of Wisconsin–Madison, Graduate School, Gaylord Nelson Institute for Environmental Studies, Water Resources Management Program, Madison, WI 53706-1380. Offers MS. Part-time programs available. *Faculty:* 2 full-time (0 women), 8 part-time/adjunct (3 women). *Students:* 22 full-time, 3 part-time; includes 2 minority (1 Asian, non-Hispanic/Latino; 1 Hispanic/Latino). Average age 28. 44 applicants, 68% accepted, 9 enrolled. In 2011, 13 master's awarded. *Degree requirements:* For master's, summer practicum workshop. *Entrance requirements:* For master's, GRE General Test. Additional exam requirements/recommendations for international students: Required—TOEFL (minimum score 550 paper-based; 213 computer-based; 80 iBT). *Application deadline:* For fall admission, 1/15 for domestic and international students; for spring admission, 10/15 for domestic and international students. Application fee: $56. Electronic applications accepted. *Expenses:* Tuition, state resident: full-time $10,296; part-time $643.51 per credit. Tuition, nonresident: full-time $24,054; part-time $1503.40 per credit. *Required fees:* $70.06 per credit. Tuition and fees vary according to course load, campus/location, program and reciprocity agreements. *Financial support:* In 2011–12, 11 students received support, including 1 fellowship with full tuition reimbursement available (averaging $20,400 per year), 6 teaching assistantships with full tuition reimbursements available (averaging $9,392 per year); research assistantships with full tuition reimbursements available, career-related internships or fieldwork, Federal Work-Study, scholarships/grants, health care benefits, unspecified assistantships, and project assistantships also available. Financial award application deadline: 1/2. *Faculty research:* Geology, hydrogeology, water chemistry, limnology, oceanography, aquatic ecology, rural sociology, water law and policy. *Unit head:* Kenneth W. Potter, Chair, 608-262-0040, Fax: 608-262-2273, E-mail: kwpotter@wisc.edu. *Application contact:* Jim Miller, Student Services Coordinator, 608-263-4373, Fax: 608-262-2273, E-mail: jemiller@wisc.edu. Web site: http://nelson.wisc.edu/graduate_degrees/wrm.

University of Wisconsin–Milwaukee, Graduate School, School of Freshwater Sciences, Milwaukee, WI 53201-0413. Offers freshwater sciences (PhD); freshwater sciences and technology (MS). *Faculty:* 12 full-time (3 women). *Students:* 21 full-time (6 women), 6 part-time (3 women); includes 2 minority (1 Black or African American, non-Hispanic/Latino; 1 Asian, non-Hispanic/Latino), 1 international. Average age 32. 37 applicants, 51% accepted, 12 enrolled. Application fee: $56 ($96 for international students). One-time fee: $506.10 full-time. Tuition and fees vary according to course load and reciprocity agreements. *Financial support:* Fellowships, research assistantships, teaching assistantships, and unspecified assistantships available. Financial award applicants required to submit FAFSA. *Total annual research expenditures:* $6.3 million. *Unit head:* David Garman, Founding Dean, 414-382-1700, E-mail: garmand@uwm.edu. *Application contact:* General Information Contact, 414-229-4982, Fax: 414-229-6967, E-mail: gradschool@uwm.edu. Web site: http://www4.uwm.edu/freshwater/.

University of Wyoming, College of Agriculture and Natural Resources, Department of Renewable Resources, Laramie, WY 82070. Offers agroecology (MS); entomology (MS, PhD); entomology/water resources (MS, PhD); rangeland ecology and watershed management (MS, PhD), including soil sciences (PhD), soil sciences and water resources (MS); rangeland ecology and watershed management/water resources (MS, PhD); soil science (MS); soil science/water resources (PhD). Part-time programs available. *Degree requirements:* For master's, comprehensive exam, thesis, oral examination; for doctorate, comprehensive exam, thesis/dissertation, preliminary oral and written exam, oral final exam. *Entrance requirements:* For master's and doctorate, GRE General Test, minimum GPA of 3.0. Additional exam requirements/recommendations for international students: Required—TOEFL. Electronic applications accepted. *Faculty research:* Plant control, grazing management, riparian restoration, riparian management, reclamation.

Utah State University, School of Graduate Studies, College of Natural Resources, Department of Watershed Sciences, Logan, UT 84322. Offers ecology (MS, PhD); fisheries biology (MS, PhD); watershed science (MS, PhD). *Degree requirements:* For master's, thesis (for some programs); for doctorate, thesis/dissertation. *Entrance requirements:* For master's and doctorate, GRE General Test, minimum GPA of 3.2. Additional exam requirements/recommendations for international students: Required—TOEFL. Electronic applications accepted. *Faculty research:* Behavior, population ecology, habitat, conservation biology, restoration, aquatic ecology, fisheries management, fluvial geomorphology, remote sensing, conservation biology.

Virginia Polytechnic Institute and State University, Graduate School, College of Natural Resources and Environment, Department of Forestry, Blacksburg, VA 24061. Offers forestry (MS, PhD); watershed management (Certificate). *Degree requirements:* For master's, comprehensive exam (for some programs), thesis (for some programs); for doctorate, comprehensive exam (for some programs), thesis/dissertation (for some programs). *Entrance requirements:* For master's and doctorate, GRE. Additional exam requirements/recommendations for international students: Required—TOEFL (minimum score 550 paper-based; 213 computer-based). *Application deadline:* For fall admission, 7/1 for domestic and international students; for spring admission, 12/1 for domestic and international students. Applications are processed on a rolling basis. Application fee: $65. Electronic applications accepted. *Expenses:* Tuition, state resident: full-time $10,048; part-time $558.25 per credit hour. Tuition, nonresident: full-time $19,497; part-time $1083.25 per credit hour. *Required fees:* $405 per semester. Tuition and fees vary according to course load, campus/location and program. *Financial support:* Research assistantships with full tuition reimbursements, teaching assistantships with full tuition reimbursements, career-related internships or fieldwork, Federal Work-Study, scholarships/grants, health care benefits, and unspecified assistantships available. Financial award application deadline: 1/15. *Unit head:* Dr. Janaki Alavalapati, Unit Head, 540-231-5676, Fax: 540-231-3698, E-mail: jrra@vt.edu. *Application contact:* Peggy Quarterman, Information Contact, 540-231-5481, E-mail: pquarter@vt.edu. Web site: http://www.fw.vt.edu/forestry/.

544 facebook.com/petersonspublishing

Peterson's Graduate Programs in the Physical Sciences, Mathematics, Agricultural Sciences, the Environment & Natural Resources 2013

APPENDIXES

Institutional Changes Since the 2012 Edition

Following is an alphabetical listing of institutions that have recently closed, merged with other institutions, or changed their names or status. In the case of a name change, the former name appears first, followed by the new name.

Adams State College (Alamosa, CO): name changed to Adams State University

Andrew Jackson University (Birmingham, AL): name changed to New Charter University

The Art Institute of Atlanta (Atlanta, GA): no longer offers graduate degrees

The Art Institute of Boston at Lesley University (Boston, MA): merged into a single entry for Lesley University (Cambridge, MA)

The Art Institute of California–San Francisco (San Francisco, CA): name changed to The Art Institute of California, a college of Argosy University, San Francisco

Atlantic Union College (South Lancaster, MA): currently not accepting applications

Babel University School of Translation (Honolulu, HI): name changed to Babel University Professional School of Translation

Baldwin-Wallace College (Berea, OH): name changed to Baldwin Wallace University

Baltimore International College (Baltimore, MD): name changed to Stratford University

Bethany University (Scotts Valley, CA): closed

Bethesda Christian University (Anaheim, CA): name changed to Bethesda University of California

Broadview University (West Jordan, UT): name changed to Broadview University–West Jordan

City of Hope National Medical Center/Beckman Research Institute (Duarte, CA): name changed to Irell & Manella Graduate School of Biological Sciences

City University of New York School of Law at Queens College (Flushing, NY): name changed to City University of New York School of Law

Cleveland Chiropractic College–Los Angeles Campus (Los Angeles, CA): closed

College of Notre Dame of Maryland (Baltimore, MD): name changed to Notre Dame of Maryland University

College of the Humanities and Sciences, Harrison Middleton University (Tempe, AZ): name changed to Harrison Middleton University

Colorado Technical University Denver (Greenwood Village, CO): name changed to Colorado Technical University Denver South

Concordia University (Ann Arbor, MI): name changed to Concordia University Ann Arbor

Cornell University, Joan and Sanford I. Weill Medical College and Graduate School of Medical Sciences (New York, NY): name changed to Weill Cornell Medical College

Daniel Webster College–Portsmouth Campus (Portsmouth, NH): closed

Edward Via Virginia College of Osteopathic Medicine (Blacksburg, VA): name changed to Edward Via College of Osteopahtic Medicine–Virginia Campus

Evangelical Theological Seminary (Myerstown, PA): name changed to Evangelical Seminary

Everest University (Lakeland, FL): no longer offers graduate degrees

Faith Evangelical Lutheran Seminary (Tacoma, WA): name changed to Faith Evangelical College & Seminary

Franklin Pierce Law Center (Concord, NH): name changed to University of New Hampshire School of Law

Frontier School of Midwifery and Family Nursing (Hyden, KY): name changed to Frontier Nursing University

Globe University (Woodbury, MN): name changed to Globe University–Woodbury

Harding University Graduate School of Religion (Memphis, TN): name changed to Harding School of Theology

Kol Yaakov Torah Center (Monsey, NY): closed

Long Island University at Riverhead (Riverhead, NY): name changed to Long Island University–Riverhead

Long Island University, Brentwood Campus (Brentwood, NY): name changed to Long Island University–Brentwood Campus

Long Island University, Brooklyn Campus (Brooklyn, NY): name changed to Long Island University–Brooklyn Campus

Long Island University, C.W. Post Campus (Brookville, NY): name changed to Long Island University–C. W. Post Campus

Long Island University, Rockland Graduate Campus (Orangeburg, NY): name changed to Long Island University–Hudson at Rockland

Long Island University, Westchester Graduate Campus (Purchase, NY): name changed to Long Island University–Hudson at Westchester

Lourdes College (Sylvania, OH): name changed to Lourdes University

Lutheran Theological Seminary (Saskatoon, SK, Canada): name changed to Lutheran Theological Seminary Saskatoon

Mars Hill Graduate School (Seattle, WA): name changed to The Seattle School of Theology and Psychology

Mesa State College (Grand Junction, CO): name changed to Colorado Mesa University

Michigan Theological Seminary (Plymouth, MI): name changed to Moody Theological Seminary–Michigan

Midwest University (Wentzville, MO): no longer accredited by agency recognized by USDE or CHEA

National Defense Intelligence College (Washington, DC): name changed to National Intelligence University

National-Louis University (Chicago, IL): name changed to National Louis University

National Theatre Conservatory (Denver, CO): closed

The New School: A University (New York, NY): name changed to The New School

Northeastern Ohio Universities Colleges of Medicine and Pharmacy (Rootstown, OH): name changed to Northeastern Ohio Medical University

Northwest Baptist Seminary (Tacoma, WA): name changed to Corban University School of Ministry

Northwood University (Midland, MI): name changed to Northwood University, Michigan Campus

OGI School of Science & Engineering at Oregon Health & Science University (Beaverton, OR): merged into a single entry for Oregon Health & Science University (Portland, OR) by request from the institution

Parker College of Chiropractic (Dallas, TX): name changed to Parker University

Philadelphia Biblical University (Langhorne, PA): name changed to Cairn University

Piedmont Baptist College and Graduate School (Winston-Salem, NC): name changed to Piedmont International University

Pikeville College (Pikeville, KY): name changed to University of Pikeville

Polytechnic Institute of NYU (Brooklyn, NY): name changed to Polytechnic Institute of New York University

Ponce School of Medicine (Ponce, PR): name changed to Ponce School of Medicine & Health Sciences

Rivier College (Nashua, NH): name changed to Rivier University

Saint Bernard's School of Theology and Ministry (Rochester, NY): name changed to St. Bernard's School of Theology and Ministry

St. Charles Borromeo Seminary, Overbrook (Wynnewood, PA): name changed to Saint Charles Borromeo Seminary, Overbrook

Saint Francis Seminary (St. Francis, WI): name changed to Saint Francis de Sales Seminary

Saint Joseph College (West Hartford, CT): name changed to University of Saint Joseph

Saint Vincent de Paul Regional Seminary (Boynton Beach, FL): name changed to St. Vincent de Paul Regional Seminary

Schiller International University (London, United Kingdom): closed

Silver Lake College (Manitowoc, WI): name changed to Silver Lake College of the Holy Family

Trinity (Washington) University (Washington, DC): name changed to Trinity Washington University

TUI University (Cypress, CA): name changed to Trident University International

University of Phoenix (Phoenix, AZ): name changed to University of Phoenix–Online Campus

University of Phoenix–Phoenix Campus (Phoenix, AZ): name changed to University of Phoenix–Phoenix Main Campus

The University of Tennessee–Oak Ridge National Laboratory Graduate School of Genome Science and Technology (Oak Ridge, TN): name changed to The University of Tennessee–Oak Ridge National Laboratory

The University of Texas Southwestern Medical Center at Dallas (Dallas, TX): name changed to The University of Texas Southwestern Medical Center

University of Trinity College (Toronto, ON, Canada): name changed to Trinity College

Washington Theological Union (Washington, DC): closed

West Virginia University Institute of Technology (Montgomery, WV): no longer offers graduate degrees.

548 facebook.com/petersonspublishing

Peterson's Graduate Programs in the Physical Sciences, Mathematics, Agricultural Sciences, the Environment & Natural Resources 2013

Abbreviations Used in the Guides

The following list includes abbreviations of degree names used in the profiles in the 2013 edition of the guides. Because some degrees (e.g., Doctor of Education) can be abbreviated in more than one way (e.g., D.Ed. or Ed.D.), and because the abbreviations used in the guides reflect the preferences of the individual colleges and universities, the list may include two or more abbreviations for a single degree.

DEGREES

A Mus D	Doctor of Musical Arts
AC	Advanced Certificate
AD	Artist's Diploma
	Doctor of Arts
ADP	Artist's Diploma
Adv C	Advanced Certificate
Adv M	Advanced Master
AGC	Advanced Graduate Certificate
AGSC	Advanced Graduate Specialist Certificate
ALM	Master of Liberal Arts
AM	Master of Arts
AMBA	Accelerated Master of Business Administration
	Aviation Master of Business Administration
AMRS	Master of Arts in Religious Studies
APC	Advanced Professional Certificate
APMPH	Advanced Professional Master of Public Health
App Sc	Applied Scientist
App Sc D	Doctor of Applied Science
AstE	Astronautical Engineer
Au D	Doctor of Audiology
B Th	Bachelor of Theology
CAES	Certificate of Advanced Educational Specialization
CAGS	Certificate of Advanced Graduate Studies
CAL	Certificate in Applied Linguistics
CALS	Certificate of Advanced Liberal Studies
CAMS	Certificate of Advanced Management Studies
CAPS	Certificate of Advanced Professional Studies
CAS	Certificate of Advanced Studies
CASPA	Certificate of Advanced Study in Public Administration
CASR	Certificate in Advanced Social Research
CATS	Certificate of Achievement in Theological Studies
CBHS	Certificate in Basic Health Sciences
CBS	Graduate Certificate in Biblical Studies
CCJA	Certificate in Criminal Justice Administration
CCSA	Certificate in Catholic School Administration
CCTS	Certificate in Clinical and Translational Science
CE	Civil Engineer
CEM	Certificate of Environmental Management
CET	Certificate in Educational Technologies
CGS	Certificate of Graduate Studies
Ch E	Chemical Engineer
CM	Certificate in Management
CMH	Certificate in Medical Humanities
CMM	Master of Church Ministries
CMS	Certificate in Ministerial Studies
CNM	Certificate in Nonprofit Management
CPASF	Certificate Program for Advanced Study in Finance
CPC	Certificate in Professional Counseling
	Certificate in Publication and Communication
CPH	Certificate in Public Health
CPM	Certificate in Public Management
CPS	Certificate of Professional Studies
CScD	Doctor of Clinical Science

CSD	Certificate in Spiritual Direction
CSS	Certificate of Special Studies
CTS	Certificate of Theological Studies
CURP	Certificate in Urban and Regional Planning
D Admin	Doctor of Administration
D Arch	Doctor of Architecture
D Be	Doctor in Bioethics
D Com	Doctor of Commerce
D Couns	Doctor of Counseling
D Div	Doctor of Divinity
D Ed	Doctor of Education
D Ed Min	Doctor of Educational Ministry
D Eng	Doctor of Engineering
D Engr	Doctor of Engineering
D Ent	Doctor of Enterprise
D Env	Doctor of Environment
D Law	Doctor of Law
D Litt	Doctor of Letters
D Med Sc	Doctor of Medical Science
D Min	Doctor of Ministry
D Miss	Doctor of Missiology
D Mus	Doctor of Music
D Mus A	Doctor of Musical Arts
D Phil	Doctor of Philosophy
D Prof	Doctor of Professional Studies
D Ps	Doctor of Psychology
D Sc	Doctor of Science
D Sc D	Doctor of Science in Dentistry
D Sc IS	Doctor of Science in Information Systems
D Sc PA	Doctor of Science in Physician Assistant Studies
D Th	Doctor of Theology
D Th P	Doctor of Practical Theology
DA	Doctor of Accounting
	Doctor of Arts
DA Ed	Doctor of Arts in Education
DAH	Doctor of Arts in Humanities
DAOM	Doctorate in Acupuncture and Oriental Medicine
DAT	Doctorate of Athletic Training
DATH	Doctorate of Art Therapy
DBA	Doctor of Business Administration
DBH	Doctor of Behavioral Health
DBL	Doctor of Business Leadership
DBS	Doctor of Buddhist Studies
DC	Doctor of Chiropractic
DCC	Doctor of Computer Science
DCD	Doctor of Communications Design
DCL	Doctor of Civil Law
	Doctor of Comparative Law
DCM	Doctor of Church Music
DCN	Doctor of Clinical Nutrition
DCS	Doctor of Computer Science
DDN	Diplôme du Droit Notarial
DDS	Doctor of Dental Surgery
DE	Doctor of Education
	Doctor of Engineering
DED	Doctor of Economic Development
DEIT	Doctor of Educational Innovation and Technology
DEL	Doctor of Executive Leadership
DEM	Doctor of Educational Ministry
DEPD	Diplôme d'Etudes Spécialisées
DES	Doctor of Engineering Science
DESS	Diplôme d'Etudes Supérieures Spécialisées

DFA	Doctor of Fine Arts
DGP	Diploma in Graduate and Professional Studies
DH Ed	Doctor of Health Education
DH Sc	Doctor of Health Sciences
DHA	Doctor of Health Administration
DHCE	Doctor of Health Care Ethics
DHL	Doctor of Hebrew Letters
	Doctor of Hebrew Literature
DHS	Doctor of Health Science
DHSc	Doctor of Health Science
Dip CS	Diploma in Christian Studies
DIT	Doctor of Industrial Technology
DJ Ed	Doctor of Jewish Education
DJS	Doctor of Jewish Studies
DLS	Doctor of Liberal Studies
DM	Doctor of Management
	Doctor of Music
DMA	Doctor of Musical Arts
DMD	Doctor of Dental Medicine
DME	Doctor of Music Education
DMEd	Doctor of Music Education
DMFT	Doctor of Marital and Family Therapy
DMH	Doctor of Medical Humanities
DML	Doctor of Modern Languages
DMP	Doctorate in Medical Physics
DMPNA	Doctor of Management Practice in Nurse Anesthesia
DN Sc	Doctor of Nursing Science
DNAP	Doctor of Nurse Anesthesia Practice
DNP	Doctor of Nursing Practice
DNP-A	Doctor of Nursing PracticeAnesthesia
DNS	Doctor of Nursing Science
DO	Doctor of Osteopathy
DOT	Doctor of Occupational Therapy
DPA	Doctor of Public Administration
DPC	Doctor of Pastoral Counseling
DPDS	Doctor of Planning and Development Studies
DPH	Doctor of Public Health
DPM	Doctor of Plant Medicine
	Doctor of Podiatric Medicine
DPPD	Doctor of Policy, Planning, and Development
DPS	Doctor of Professional Studies
DPT	Doctor of Physical Therapy
DPTSc	Doctor of Physical Therapy Science
Dr DES	Doctor of Design
Dr NP	Doctor of Nursing Practice
Dr PH	Doctor of Public Health
Dr Sc PT	Doctor of Science in Physical Therapy
DRSc	Doctor of Regulatory Science
DS	Doctor of Science
DS Sc	Doctor of Social Science
DSJS	Doctor of Science in Jewish Studies
DSL	Doctor of Strategic Leadership
DSW	Doctor of Social Work
DTL	Doctor of Talmudic Law
DV Sc	Doctor of Veterinary Science
DVM	Doctor of Veterinary Medicine
DWS	Doctor of Worship Studies
EAA	Engineer in Aeronautics and Astronautics
EASPh D	Engineering and Applied Science Doctor of Philosophy
ECS	Engineer in Computer Science
Ed D	Doctor of Education
Ed DCT	Doctor of Education in College Teaching
Ed L D	Doctor of Education Leadership
Ed M	Master of Education
Ed S	Specialist in Education
Ed Sp	Specialist in Education
EDB	Executive Doctorate in Business

EDM	Executive Doctorate in Management
EE	Electrical Engineer
EJD	Executive Juris Doctor
EMBA	Executive Master of Business Administration
EMFA	Executive Master of Forensic Accounting
EMHA	Executive Master of Health Administration
EMIB	Executive Master of International Business
EML	Executive Master of Leadership
EMPA	Executive Master of Public Administration
EMS	Executive Master of Science
EMTM	Executive Master of Technology Management
Eng	Engineer
Eng Sc D	Doctor of Engineering Science
Engr	Engineer
Ex Doc	Executive Doctor of Pharmacy
Exec Ed D	Executive Doctor of Education
Exec MBA	Executive Master of Business Administration
Exec MPA	Executive Master of Public Administration
Exec MPH	Executive Master of Public Health
Exec MS	Executive Master of Science
G Dip	Graduate Diploma
GBC	Graduate Business Certificate
GCE	Graduate Certificate in Education
GDM	Graduate Diploma in Management
GDPA	Graduate Diploma in Public Administration
GDRE	Graduate Diploma in Religious Education
GEMBA	Global Executive Master of Business Administration
GEMPA	Gulf Executive Master of Public Administration
GM Acc	Graduate Master of Accountancy
GMBA	Global Master of Business Administration
GP LL M	Global Professional Master of Laws
GPD	Graduate Performance Diploma
GSS	Graduate Special Certificate for Students in Special Situations
IEMBA	International Executive Master of Business Administration
IM Acc	Integrated Master of Accountancy
IMA	Interdisciplinary Master of Arts
IMBA	International Master of Business Administration
IMES	International Master's in Environmental Studies
Ingeniero	Engineer
JCD	Doctor of Canon Law
JCL	Licentiate in Canon Law
JD	Juris Doctor
JSD	Doctor of Juridical Science
	Doctor of Jurisprudence
	Doctor of the Science of Law
JSM	Master of Science of Law
L Th	Licenciate in Theology
LL B	Bachelor of Laws
LL CM	Master of Laws in Comparative Law
LL D	Doctor of Laws
LL M	Master of Laws
LL M in Tax	Master of Laws in Taxation
LL M CL	Master of Laws (Common Law)
M Ac	Master of Accountancy
	Master of Accounting
	Master of Acupuncture
M Ac OM	Master of Acupuncture and Oriental Medicine
M Acc	Master of Accountancy
	Master of Accounting
M Acct	Master of Accountancy
	Master of Accounting
M Accy	Master of Accountancy
M Actg	Master of Accounting
M Acy	Master of Accountancy

550 facebook.com/petersonspublishing

Peterson's Graduate Programs in the Physical Sciences, Mathematics, Agricultural Sciences, the Environment & Natural Resources 2013

M Ad	Master of Administration
M Ad Ed	Master of Adult Education
M Adm	Master of Administration
M Adm Mgt	Master of Administrative Management
M Admin	Master of Administration
M ADU	Master of Architectural Design and Urbanism
M Adv	Master of Advertising
M Aero E	Master of Aerospace Engineering
M AEST	Master of Applied Environmental Science and Technology
M Ag	Master of Agriculture
M Ag Ed	Master of Agricultural Education
M Agr	Master of Agriculture
M Anesth Ed	Master of Anesthesiology Education
M App Comp Sc	Master of Applied Computer Science
M App St	Master of Applied Statistics
M Appl Stat	Master of Applied Statistics
M Aq	Master of Aquaculture
M Arc	Master of Architecture
M Arch	Master of Architecture
M Arch I	Master of Architecture I
M Arch II	Master of Architecture II
M Arch E	Master of Architectural Engineering
M Arch H	Master of Architectural History
M Bioethics	Master in Bioethics
M Biomath	Master of Biomathematics
M Ch	Master of Chemistry
M Ch E	Master of Chemical Engineering
M Chem	Master of Chemistry
M Cl D	Master of Clinical Dentistry
M Cl Sc	Master of Clinical Science
M Comp	Master of Computing
M Comp Sc	Master of Computer Science
M Coun	Master of Counseling
M Dent	Master of Dentistry
M Dent Sc	Master of Dental Sciences
M Des	Master of Design
M Des S	Master of Design Studies
M Div	Master of Divinity
M Ec	Master of Economics
M Econ	Master of Economics
M Ed	Master of Education
M Ed T	Master of Education in Teaching
M En	Master of Engineering
	Master of Environmental Science
M En S	Master of Environmental Sciences
M Eng	Master of Engineering
M Eng Mgt	Master of Engineering Management
M Engr	Master of Engineering
M Ent	Master of Enterprise
M Env	Master of Environment
M Env Des	Master of Environmental Design
M Env E	Master of Environmental Engineering
M Env Sc	Master of Environmental Science
M Fin	Master of Finance
M Geo E	Master of Geological Engineering
M Geoenv E	Master of Geoenvironmental Engineering
M Geog	Master of Geography
M Hum	Master of Humanities
M Hum Svcs	Master of Human Services
M IBD	Master of Integrated Building Delivery
M IDST	Master's in Interdisciplinary Studies
M Kin	Master of Kinesiology
M Land Arch	Master of Landscape Architecture
M Litt	Master of Letters
M Mat SE	Master of Material Science and Engineering
M Math	Master of Mathematics
M Mech E	Master of Mechanical Engineering
M Med Sc	Master of Medical Science
M Mgmt	Master of Management
M Mgt	Master of Management
M Min	Master of Ministries
M Mtl E	Master of Materials Engineering
M Mu	Master of Music
M Mus	Master of Music
M Mus Ed	Master of Music Education
M Music	Master of Music
M Nat Sci	Master of Natural Science
M Oc E	Master of Oceanographic Engineering
M Pet E	Master of Petroleum Engineering
M Pharm	Master of Pharmacy
M Phil	Master of Philosophy
M Phil F	Master of Philosophical Foundations
M Pl	Master of Planning
M Plan	Master of Planning
M Pol	Master of Political Science
M Pr Met	Master of Professional Meteorology
M Prob S	Master of Probability and Statistics
M Psych	Master of Psychology
M Pub	Master of Publishing
M Rel	Master of Religion
M Sc	Master of Science
M Sc A	Master of Science (Applied)
M Sc AC	Master of Science in Applied Computing
M Sc AHN	Master of Science in Applied Human Nutrition
M Sc BMC	Master of Science in Biomedical Communications
M Sc CS	Master of Science in Computer Science
M Sc E	Master of Science in Engineering
M Sc Eng	Master of Science in Engineering
M Sc Engr	Master of Science in Engineering
M Sc F	Master of Science in Forestry
M Sc FE	Master of Science in Forest Engineering
M Sc Geogr	Master of Science in Geography
M Sc N	Master of Science in Nursing
M Sc OT	Master of Science in Occupational Therapy
M Sc P	Master of Science in Planning
M Sc Pl	Master of Science in Planning
M Sc PT	Master of Science in Physical Therapy
M Sc T	Master of Science in Teaching
M SEM	Master of Sustainable Environmental Management
M Serv Soc	Master of Social Service
M Soc	Master of Sociology
M Sp Ed	Master of Special Education
M Stat	Master of Statistics
M Sys E	Master of Systems Engineering
M Sys Sc	Master of Systems Science
M Tax	Master of Taxation
M Tech	Master of Technology
M Th	Master of Theology
M Tox	Master of Toxicology
M Trans E	Master of Transportation Engineering
M Urb	Master of Urban Planning
M Vet Sc	Master of Veterinary Science
MA	Master of Accounting
	Master of Administration
	Master of Arts
MA Comm	Master of Arts in Communication
MA Ed	Master of Arts in Education
MA Ed Ad	Master of Arts in Educational Administration
MA Ext	Master of Agricultural Extension
MA Islamic	Master of Arts in Islamic Studies
MA Min	Master of Arts in Ministry
MA Miss	Master of Arts in Missiology
MA Past St	Master of Arts in Pastoral Studies
MA Ph	Master of Arts in Philosophy

Peterson's Graduate Programs in the Physical Sciences, Mathematics, Agricultural Sciences, the Environment & Natural Resources 2013

facebook.com/petersonspublishing **551**

MA Psych	Master of Arts in Psychology
MA Sc	Master of Applied Science
MA Sp	Master of Arts (Spirituality)
MA Th	Master of Arts in Theology
MA-R	Master of Arts (Research)
MAA	Master of Administrative Arts
	Master of Applied Anthropology
	Master of Applied Arts
	Master of Arts in Administration
MAAA	Master of Arts in Arts Administration
MAAAP	Master of Arts Administration and Policy
MAAE	Master of Arts in Art Education
MAAT	Master of Arts in Applied Theology
	Master of Arts in Art Therapy
MAB	Master of Agribusiness
MABC	Master of Arts in Biblical Counseling
	Master of Arts in Business Communication
MABE	Master of Arts in Bible Exposition
MABL	Master of Arts in Biblical Languages
MABM	Master of Agribusiness Management
MABMH	bioethics and medical humanities
MABS	Master of Arts in Biblical Studies
MABT	Master of Arts in Bible Teaching
MAC	Master of Accountancy
	Master of Accounting
	Master of Arts in Communication
	Master of Arts in Counseling
MACC	Master of Arts in Christian Counseling
	Master of Arts in Clinical Counseling
MACCM	Master of Arts in Church and Community Ministry
MACCT	Master of Accounting
MACD	Master of Arts in Christian Doctrine
MACE	Master of Arts in Christian Education
MACFM	Master of Arts in Children's and Family Ministry
MACH	Master of Arts in Church History
MACI	Master of Arts in Curriculum and Instruction
MACIS	Master of Accounting and Information Systems
MACJ	Master of Arts in Criminal Justice
MACL	Master of Arts in Christian Leadership
MACM	Master of Arts in Christian Ministries
	Master of Arts in Christian Ministry
	Master of Arts in Church Music
	Master of Arts in Counseling Ministries
MACN	Master of Arts in Counseling
MACO	Master of Arts in Counseling
MAcOM	Master of Acupuncture and Oriental Medicine
MACP	Master of Arts in Christian Practice
	Master of Arts in Counseling Psychology
MACS	Master of Applied Computer Science
	Master of Arts in Catholic Studies
	Master of Arts in Christian Studies
MACSE	Master of Arts in Christian School Education
MACT	Master of Arts in Christian Thought
	Master of Arts in Communications and Technology
MAD	Master in Educational Institution Administration
	Master of Art and Design
MAD-Crit	Master of Arts in Design Criticism
MADR	Master of Arts in Dispute Resolution
MADS	Master of Animal and Dairy Science
	Master of Applied Disability Studies
MAE	Master of Aerospace Engineering
	Master of Agricultural Economics
	Master of Agricultural Education
	Master of Architectural Engineering
	Master of Art Education
	Master of Arts in Education

	Master of Arts in English
MAEd	Master of Arts Education
MAEL	Master of Arts in Educational Leadership
MAEM	Master of Arts in Educational Ministries
MAEN	Master of Arts in English
MAEP	Master of Arts in Economic Policy
MAES	Master of Arts in Environmental Sciences
MAET	Master of Arts in English Teaching
MAF	Master of Arts in Finance
MAFE	Master of Arts in Financial Economics
MAFLL	Master of Arts in Foreign Language and Literature
MAFM	Master of Accounting and Financial Management
MAFS	Master of Arts in Family Studies
MAG	Master of Applied Geography
MAGU	Master of Urban Analysis and Management
MAH	Master of Arts in Humanities
MAHA	Master of Arts in Humanitarian Assistance
	Master of Arts in Humanitarian Studies
MAHCM	Master of Arts in Health Care Mission
MAHG	Master of American History and Government
MAHL	Master of Arts in Hebrew Letters
MAHN	Master of Applied Human Nutrition
MAHSR	Master of Applied Health Services Research
MAIA	Master of Arts in International Administration
	Master of Arts in International Affairs
MAIB	Master of Arts in International Business
MAIDM	Master of Arts in Interior Design and Merchandising
MAIH	Master of Arts in Interdisciplinary Humanities
MAIOP	Master of Arts in Industrial/Organizational Psychology
MAIPCR	Master of Arts in International Peace and Conflict Management
MAIS	Master of Arts in Intercultural Studies
	Master of Arts in Interdisciplinary Studies
	Master of Arts in International Studies
MAIT	Master of Administration in Information Technology
	Master of Applied Information Technology
MAJ	Master of Arts in Journalism
MAJ Ed	Master of Arts in Jewish Education
MAJCS	Master of Arts in Jewish Communal Service
MAJE	Master of Arts in Jewish Education
MAJPS	Master of Arts in Jewish Professional Studies
MAJS	Master of Arts in Jewish Studies
MAL	Master in Agricultural Leadership
MALA	Master of Arts in Liberal Arts
MALD	Master of Arts in Law and Diplomacy
MALER	Master of Arts in Labor and Employment Relations
MALM	Master of Arts in Leadership Evangelical Mobilization
MALP	Master of Arts in Language Pedagogy
MALPS	Master of Arts in Liberal and Professional Studies
MALS	Master of Arts in Liberal Studies
MAM	Master of Acquisition Management
	Master of Agriculture and Management
	Master of Applied Mathematics
	Master of Arts in Ministry
	Master of Arts Management
	Master of Avian Medicine
MAMB	Master of Applied Molecular Biology
MAMC	Master of Arts in Mass Communication
	Master of Arts in Ministry and Culture
	Master of Arts in Ministry for a Multicultural Church
	Master of Arts in Missional Christianity

552 facebook.com/petersonspublishing

Peterson's Graduate Programs in the Physical Sciences, Mathematics, Agricultural Sciences, the Environment & Natural Resources 2013

MAME	Master of Arts in Missions/Evangelism	MAST	Master of Arts in Science Teaching
MAMFC	Master of Arts in Marriage and Family Counseling	MASW	Master of Aboriginal Social Work
		MAT	Master of Arts in Teaching
MAMFCC	Master of Arts in Marriage, Family, and Child Counseling		Master of Arts in Theology
			Master of Athletic Training
MAMFT	Master of Arts in Marriage and Family Therapy		Master's in Administration of Telecommunications
MAMHC	Master of Arts in Mental Health Counseling	Mat E	Materials Engineer
MAMI	Master of Arts in Missions	MATCM	Master of Acupuncture and Traditional Chinese Medicine
MAMS	Master of Applied Mathematical Sciences		
	Master of Arts in Ministerial Studies	MATDE	Master of Arts in Theology, Development, and Evangelism
	Master of Arts in Ministry and Spirituality		
MAMT	Master of Arts in Mathematics Teaching	MATDR	Master of Territorial Management and Regional Development
MAN	Master of Applied Nutrition		
MANT	Master of Arts in New Testament	MATE	Master of Arts for the Teaching of English
MAOL	Master of Arts in Organizational Leadership	MATESL	Master of Arts in Teaching English as a Second Language
MAOM	Master of Acupuncture and Oriental Medicine		
	Master of Arts in Organizational Management	MATESOL	Master of Arts in Teaching English to Speakers of Other Languages
MAOT	Master of Arts in Old Testament	MATF	Master of Arts in Teaching English as a Foreign Language/Intercultural Studies
MAP	Master of Applied Psychology		
	Master of Arts in Planning	MATFL	Master of Arts in Teaching Foreign Language
	Master of Psychology	MATH	Master of Arts in Therapy
	Master of Public Administration	MATI	Master of Administration of Information Technology
MAP Min	Master of Arts in Pastoral Ministry		
MAPA	Master of Arts in Public Administration	MATL	Master of Arts in Teacher Leadership
MAPC	Master of Arts in Pastoral Counseling		Master of Arts in Teaching of Languages
	Master of Arts in Professional Counseling		Master of Arts in Transformational Leadership
MAPE	Master of Arts in Political Economy	MATM	Master of Arts in Teaching of Mathematics
MAPM	Master of Arts in Pastoral Ministry	MATS	Master of Arts in Theological Studies
	Master of Arts in Pastoral Music		Master of Arts in Transforming Spirituality
	Master of Arts in Practical Ministry	MATSL	Master of Arts in Teaching a Second Language
MAPP	Master of Arts in Public Policy	MAUA	Master of Arts in Urban Affairs
MAPPS	Master of Arts in Asia Pacific Policy Studies	MAUD	Master of Arts in Urban Design
MAPS	Master of Arts in Pastoral Counseling/Spiritual Formation	MAURP	Master of Arts in Urban and Regional Planning
		MAWSHP	Master of Arts in Worship
	Master of Arts in Pastoral Studies	MAYM	Master of Arts in Youth Ministry
	Master of Arts in Public Service	MB	Master of Bioinformatics
MAPT	Master of Practical Theology		Master of Biology
MAPW	Master of Arts in Professional Writing	MBA	Master of Business Administration
MAR	Master of Arts in Reading	MBA-AM	Master of Business Administration in Aviation Management
	Master of Arts in Religion		
Mar Eng	Marine Engineer	MBA-EP	Master of Business AdministrationNExperienced Professionals
MARC	Master of Arts in Rehabilitation Counseling		
MARE	Master of Arts in Religious Education	MBA/MGPS	Master of Business Administration/Master of Global Policy Studies
MARL	Master of Arts in Religious Leadership		
MARS	Master of Arts in Religious Studies	MBAA	Master of Business Administration in Aviation
MAS	Master of Accounting Science	MBAE	Master of Biological and Agricultural Engineering
	Master of Actuarial Science		
	Master of Administrative Science		Master of Biosystems and Agricultural Engineering
	Master of Advanced Study		
	Master of Aeronautical Science	MBAH	Master of Business Administration in Health
	Master of American Studies	MBAi	Master of Business AdministrationNInternational
	Master of Applied Science		
	Master of Applied Statistics	MBAICT	Master of Business Administration in Information and Communication Technology
	Master of Archival Studies		
MASA	Master of Advanced Studies in Architecture	MBATM	Master of Business Administration in Technology Management
MASD	Master of Arts in Spiritual Direction	MBC	Master of Building Construction
MASE	Master of Arts in Special Education	MBE	Master of Bilingual Education
MASF	Master of Arts in Spiritual Formation		Master of Bioengineering
MASJ	Master of Arts in Systems of Justice		Master of Bioethics
MASLA	Master of Advanced Studies in Landscape Architecture		Master of Biological Engineering
			Master of Biomedical Engineering
MASM	Master of Aging Services Management		Master of Business and Engineering
	Master of Arts in Specialized Ministries		Master of Business Economics
MASP	Master of Applied Social Psychology		Master of Business Education
	Master of Arts in School Psychology	MBEE	Master in Biotechnology Enterprise and Entrepreneurship
MASPAA	Master of Arts in Sports and Athletic Administration		
		MBET	Master of Business, Entrepreneurship and Technology
MASS	Master of Applied Social Science		
	Master of Arts in Social Science	MBIOT	Master of Biotechnology

Peterson's Graduate Programs in the Physical Sciences, Mathematics, Agricultural Sciences, the Environment & Natural Resources 2013

facebook.com/petersonspublishing **553**

MBiotech	Master of Biotechnology
MBL	Master of Business Law
	Master of Business Leadership
	Master in Business Logistics Engineering
MBLE	
MBMI	Master of Biomedical Imaging and Signals
MBMSE	Master of Business Management and Software Engineering
MBOE	Master of Business Operational Excellence
MBS	Master of Biblical Studies
	Master of Biological Science
	Master of Biomedical Sciences
	Master of Bioscience
	Master of Building Science
	Master of Business and Science
MBST	Master of Biostatistics
MBT	Master of Biblical and Theological Studies
	Master of Biomedical Technology
	Master of Biotechnology
	Master of Business Taxation
MC	Master of Communication
	Master of Counseling
	Master of Cybersecurity
MC Ed	Master of Continuing Education
MC Sc	Master of Computer Science
MCA	Master of Arts in Applied Criminology
	Master of Commercial Aviation
MCAM	Master of Computational and Applied Mathematics
MCC	Master of Computer Science
MCCS	Master of Crop and Soil Sciences
MCD	Master of Communications Disorders
	Master of Community Development
MCE	Master in Electronic Commerce
	Master of Christian Education
	Master of Civil Engineering
	Master of Control Engineering
MCEM	Master of Construction Engineering Management
MCH	Master of Chemical Engineering
MCHE	Master of Chemical Engineering
MCIS	Master of Communication and Information Studies
	Master of Computer and Information Science
	Master of Computer Information Systems
MCIT	Master of Computer and Information Technology
MCJ	Master of Criminal Justice
MCJA	Master of Criminal Justice Administration
MCL	Master in Communication Leadership
	Master of Canon Law
	Master of Comparative Law
MCM	Master of Christian Ministry
	Master of Church Music
	Master of City Management
	Master of Communication Management
	Master of Community Medicine
	Master of Construction Management
	Master of Contract Management
	Master of Corporate Media
MCMP	Master of City and Metropolitan Planning
MCMS	Master of Clinical Medical Science
MCN	Master of Clinical Nutrition
MCOL	Master of Arts in Community and Organizational Leadership
MCP	Master of City Planning
	Master of Community Planning
	Master of Counseling Psychology
	Master of Cytopathology Practice
	Master of Science in Quality Systems and Productivity

MCPC	Master of Arts in Chaplaincy and Pastoral Care
MCPD	Master of Community Planning and Development
MCR	Master in Clinical Research
MCRP	Master of City and Regional Planning
MCRS	Master of City and Regional Studies
MCS	Master of Christian Studies
	Master of Clinical Science
	Master of Combined Sciences
	Master of Communication Studies
	Master of Computer Science
	Master of Consumer Science
MCSE	Master of Computer Science and Engineering
MCSL	Master of Catholic School Leadership
MCSM	Master of Construction Science/Management
MCST	Master of Science in Computer Science and Information Technology
MCTP	Master of Communication Technology and Policy
MCTS	Master of Clinical and Translational Science
MCVS	Master of Cardiovascular Science
MD	Doctor of Medicine
MDA	Master of Development Administration
	Master of Dietetic Administration
MDB	Master of Design-Build
MDE	Master of Developmental Economics
	Master of Distance Education
	Master of the Education of the Deaf
MDH	Master of Dental Hygiene
MDM	Master of Design Methods
	Master of Digital Media
MDP	Master in Sustainable Development Practice
	Master of Development Practice
MDR	Master of Dispute Resolution
MDS	Master of Dental Surgery
	Master of Design Studies
ME	Master of Education
	Master of Engineering
	Master of Entrepreneurship
	Master of Evangelism
ME Sc	Master of Engineering Science
MEA	Master of Educational Administration
	Master of Engineering Administration
MEAP	Master of Environmental Administration and Planning
MEBT	Master in Electronic Business Technologies
MEC	Master of Electronic Commerce
MECE	Master of Electrical and Computer Engineering
Mech E	Mechanical Engineer
MED	Master of Education of the Deaf
MEDS	Master of Environmental Design Studies
MEE	Master in Education
	Master of Electrical Engineering
	Master of Energy Engineering
	Master of Environmental Engineering
MEEM	Master of Environmental Engineering and Management
MEENE	Master of Engineering in Environmental Engineering
MEEP	Master of Environmental and Energy Policy
MEERM	Master of Earth and Environmental Resource Management
MEH	Master in Humanistic Studies
	Master of Environmental Horticulture
MEHP	Master of Education in the Health Professions
MEHS	Master of Environmental Health and Safety
MEIM	Master of Entertainment Industry Management
MEL	Master of Educational Leadership
	Master of English Literature
MELP	Master of Environmental Law and Policy

MEM	Master of Ecosystem Management		Master of Governmental Administration
	Master of Electricity Markets	MGC	Master of Genetic Counseling
	Master of Engineering Management	MGD	Master of Graphic Design
	Master of Environmental Management	MGE	Master of Geotechnical Engineering
	Master of Marketing	MGEM	Master of Global Entrepreneurship and Management
MEME	Master of Engineering in Manufacturing Engineering		
		MGIS	Master of Geographic Information Science
	Master of Engineering in Mechanical Engineering		Master of Geographic Information Systems
MENG	Master of Arts in English	MGM	Master of Global Management
MENVEGR	Master of Environmental Engineering	MGP	Master of Gestion de Projet
MEP	Master of Engineering Physics	MGPS	Master of Global Policy Studies
MEPC	Master of Environmental Pollution Control	MGPS/MA	Master of Global Policy Studies/Master of Arts
MEPD	Master of EducationNProfessional Development	MGPS/MPH	Master of Global Policy Studies/Master of Public Health
	Master of Environmental Planning and Design	MGREM	Master of Global Real Estate Management
MER	Master of Employment Relations	MGS	Master of Gerontological Studies
MERE	Master of Entrepreneurial Real Estate		Master of Global Studies
MES	Master of Education and Science	MH	Master of Humanities
	Master of Engineering Science	MH Ed	Master of Health Education
	Master of Environment and Sustainability	MH Sc	Master of Health Sciences
	Master of Environmental Science	MHA	Master of Health Administration
	Master of Environmental Studies		Master of Healthcare Administration
	Master of Environmental Systems		Master of Hospital Administration
	Master of Special Education		Master of Hospitality Administration
MESM	Master of Environmental Science and Management	MHAD	Master of Health Administration
		MHB	Master of Human Behavior
MET	Master of Educational Technology	MHCA	Master of Health Care Administration
	Master of Engineering Technology	MHCI	Master of Health Care Informatics
	Master of Entertainment Technology		Master of Human-Computer Interaction
	Master of Environmental Toxicology	MHCL	Master of Health Care Leadership
METM	Master of Engineering and Technology Management	MHE	Master of Health Education
			Master of Human Ecology
MEVE	Master of Environmental Engineering	MHE Ed	Master of Home Economics Education
MF	Master of Finance	MHEA	Master of Higher Education Administration
	Master of Forestry	MHHS	Master of Health and Human Services
MFA	Master of Fine Arts	MHI	Master of Health Informatics
MFAM	Master in Food Animal Medicine		Master of Healthcare Innovation
MFAS	Master of Fisheries and Aquatic Science	MHIIM	Master of Health Informatics and Information Management
MFAW	Master of Fine Arts in Writing		
MFC	Master of Forest Conservation	MHIS	Master of Health Information Systems
MFCS	Master of Family and Consumer Sciences	MHK	Master of Human Kinetics
MFE	Master of Financial Economics	MHL	Master of Hebrew Literature
	Master of Financial Engineering	MHM	Master of Healthcare Management
	Master of Forest Engineering	MHMS	Master of Health Management Systems
MFG	Master of Functional Genomics	MHP	Master of Health Physics
MFHD	Master of Family and Human Development		Master of Heritage Preservation
MFM	Master of Financial Management		Master of Historic Preservation
	Master of Financial Mathematics	MHPA	Master of Heath Policy and Administration
MFMS	Master's in Food Microbiology and Safety	MHPE	Master of Health Professions Education
MFPE	Master of Food Process Engineering	MHR	Master of Human Resources
MFR	Master of Forest Resources	MHRD	Master in Human Resource Development
MFRC	Master of Forest Resources and Conservation	MHRIR	Master of Human Resources and Industrial Relations
MFS	Master of Food Science		
	Master of Forensic Sciences	MHRLR	Master of Human Resources and Labor Relations
	Master of Forest Science		
	Master of Forest Studies	MHRM	Master of Human Resources Management
	Master of French Studies	MHS	Master of Health Science
MFST	Master of Food Safety and Technology		Master of Health Sciences
MFT	Master of Family Therapy		Master of Health Studies
	Master of Food Technology		Master of Hispanic Studies
MFWB	Master of Fishery and Wildlife Biology		Master of Human Services
MFWCB	Master of Fish, Wildlife and Conservation Biology		Master of Humanistic Studies
		MHSA	Master of Health Services Administration
MFWS	Master of Fisheries and Wildlife Sciences	MHSM	Master of Health Systems Management
MFYCS	Master of Family, Youth and Community Sciences	MI	Master of Information
			Master of Instruction
MG	Master of Genetics	MI Arch	Master of Interior Architecture
MGA	Master of Global Affairs	MIA	Master of Interior Architecture
			Master of International Affairs

Peterson's Graduate Programs in the Physical Sciences, Mathematics, Agricultural Sciences, the Environment & Natural Resources 2013

facebook.com/petersonspublishing **555**

MIAA	Master of International Affairs and Administration
MIAM	Master of International Agribusiness Management
MIAPD	Master of Interior Architecture and Product Design
MIB	Master of International Business
MIBA	Master of International Business Administration
MICM	Master of International Construction Management
MID	Master of Industrial Design
	Master of Industrial Distribution
	Master of Interior Design
	Master of International Development
MIDC	Master of Integrated Design and Construction
MIE	Master of Industrial Engineering
MIH	Master of Integrative Health
MIHTM	Master of International Hospitality and Tourism Management
MIJ	Master of International Journalism
MILR	Master of Industrial and Labor Relations
MiM	Master in Management
MIM	Master of Industrial Management
	Master of Information Management
	Master of International Management
MIMLAE	Master of International Management for Latin American Executives
MIMS	Master of Information Management and Systems
	Master of Integrated Manufacturing Systems
MIP	Master of Infrastructure Planning
	Master of Intellectual Property
	Master of International Policy
MIPA	Master of International Public Affairs
MIPER	Master of International Political Economy of Resources
MIPP	Master of International Policy and Practice
	Master of International Public Policy
MIPS	Master of International Planning Studies
MIR	Master of Industrial Relations
	Master of International Relations
MIRHR	Master of Industrial Relations and Human Resources
MIS	Master of Industrial Statistics
	Master of Information Science
	Master of Information Systems
	Master of Integrated Science
	Master of Interdisciplinary Studies
	Master of International Service
	Master of International Studies
MISE	Master of Industrial and Systems Engineering
MISKM	Master of Information Sciences and Knowledge Management
MISM	Master of Information Systems Management
MIT	Master in Teaching
	Master of Industrial Technology
	Master of Information Technology
	Master of Initial Teaching
	Master of International Trade
	Master of Internet Technology
MITA	Master of Information Technology Administration
MITM	Master of Information Technology and Management
MITO	Master of Industrial Technology and Operations
MJ	Master of Journalism
	Master of Jurisprudence
MJ Ed	Master of Jewish Education
MJA	Master of Justice Administration

MJM	Master of Justice Management
MJS	Master of Judicial Studies
	Master of Juridical Science
MKM	Master of Knowledge Management
ML	Master of Latin
ML Arch	Master of Landscape Architecture
MLA	Master of Landscape Architecture
	Master of Liberal Arts
MLAS	Master of Laboratory Animal Science
	Master of Liberal Arts and Sciences
MLAUD	Master of Landscape Architecture in Urban Development
MLD	Master of Leadership Development
MLE	Master of Applied Linguistics and Exegesis
MLER	Master of Labor and Employment Relations
MLHR	Master of Labor and Human Resources
MLI Sc	Master of Library and Information Science
MLIS	Master of Library and Information Science
	Master of Library and Information Studies
MLM	Master of Library Media
MLRHR	Master of Labor Relations and Human Resources
MLS	Master of Leadership Studies
	Master of Legal Studies
	Master of Liberal Studies
	Master of Library Science
	Master of Life Sciences
MLSP	Master of Law and Social Policy
MLT	Master of Language Technologies
MLTCA	Master of Long Term Care Administration
MM	Master of Management
	Master of Ministry
	Master of Missiology
	Master of Music
MM Ed	Master of Music Education
MM Sc	Master of Medical Science
MM St	Master of Museum Studies
MMA	Master of Marine Affairs
	Master of Media Arts
	Master of Musical Arts
MMAE	Master of Mechanical and Aerospace Engineering
MMAL	Master of Maritime Administration and Logistics
MMAS	Master of Military Art and Science
MMB	Master of Microbial Biotechnology
MMBA	Managerial Master of Business Administration
MMC	Master of Manufacturing Competitiveness
	Master of Mass Communications
	Master of Music Conducting
MMCM	Master of Music in Church Music
MMCSS	Master of Mathematical Computational and Statistical Sciences
MME	Master of Manufacturing Engineering
	Master of Mathematics Education
	Master of Mathematics for Educators
	Master of Mechanical Engineering
	Master of Medical Engineering
	Master of Mining Engineering
	Master of Music Education
MMF	Master of Mathematical Finance
MMFT	Master of Marriage and Family Therapy
MMG	Master of Management
MMH	Master of Management in Hospitality
	Master of Medical Humanities
MMI	Master of Management of Innovation
MMIS	Master of Management Information Systems
MMM	Master of Manufacturing Management
	Master of Marine Management

556 facebook.com/petersonspublishing

Peterson's Graduate Programs in the Physical Sciences, Mathematics, Agricultural Sciences, the Environment & Natural Resources 2013

	Master of Medical Management		MPA	Master of Physician Assistant
MMME	Master of Metallurgical and Materials Engineering			Master of Professional Accountancy
				Master of Professional Accounting
MMP	Master of Management Practice			Master of Public Administration
	Master of Marine Policy			Master of Public Affairs
	Master of Medical Physics		MPAC	Master of Professional Accounting
	Master of Music Performance		MPAID	Master of Public Administration and International Development
MMPA	Master of Management and Professional Accounting		MPAP	Master of Physician Assistant Practice
				Master of Public Affairs and Politics
MMQM	Master of Manufacturing Quality Management		MPAS	Master of Physician Assistant Science
MMR	Master of Marketing Research			Master of Physician Assistant Studies
MMRM	Master of Marine Resources Management		MPC	Master of Pastoral Counseling
MMS	Master of Management Science			Master of Professional Communication
	Master of Management Studies			Master of Professional Counseling
	Master of Manufacturing Systems		MPCU	Master of Planning in Civic Urbanism
	Master of Marine Studies		MPD	Master of Product Development
	Master of Materials Science			Master of Public Diplomacy
	Master of Medical Science		MPDS	Master of Planning and Development Studies
	Master of Medieval Studies		MPE	Master of Physical Education
MMSE	Master of Manufacturing Systems Engineering			Master of Power Engineering
	Multidisciplinary Master of Science in Engineering		MPEM	Master of Project Engineering and Management
MMSM	Master of Music in Sacred Music		MPH	Master of Public Health
MMT	Master in Marketing		MPHE	Master of Public Health Education
	Master of Music Teaching		MPHTM	Master of Public Health and Tropical Medicine
	Master of Music Therapy		MPI	Master of Product Innovation
	Master's in Marketing Technology		MPIA	Master in International Affairs
MMus	Master of Music			Master of Public and International Affairs
MN	Master of Nursing		MPM	Master of Pastoral Ministry
	Master of Nutrition			Master of Pest Management
MN NP	Master of Nursing in Nurse Practitioner			Master of Policy Management
MNA	Master of Nonprofit Administration			Master of Practical Ministries
	Master of Nurse Anesthesia			Master of Project Management
MNAL	Master of Nonprofit Administration and Leadership			Master of Public Management
MNAS	Master of Natural and Applied Science		MPNA	Master of Public and Nonprofit Administration
MNCM	Master of Network and Communications Management		MPO	Master of Prosthetics and Orthotics
MNE	Master of Network Engineering		MPOD	Master of Positive Organizational Development
	Master of Nuclear Engineering		MPP	Master of Public Policy
MNL	Master in International Business for Latin America		MPPA	Master of Public Policy Administration
				Master of Public Policy and Administration
MNM	Master of Nonprofit Management		MPPAL	Master of Public Policy, Administration and Law
MNO	Master of Nonprofit Organization		MPPM	Master of Public and Private Management
MNPL	Master of Not-for-Profit Leadership			Master of Public Policy and Management
MNpS	Master of Nonprofit Studies		MPPPM	Master of Plant Protection and Pest Management
MNR	Master of Natural Resources			
MNRES	Master of Natural Resources and Environmental Studies		MPRTM	Master of Parks, Recreation, and Tourism Management
MNRM	Master of Natural Resource Management		MPS	Master of Pastoral Studies
MNRS	Master of Natural Resource Stewardship			Master of Perfusion Science
MNS	Master of Natural Science			Master of Planning Studies
MO	Master of Oceanography			Master of Political Science
MOD	Master of Organizational Development			Master of Preservation Studies
MOGS	Master of Oil and Gas Studies			Master of Professional Studies
MOH	Master of Occupational Health			Master of Public Service
MOL	Master of Organizational Leadership		MPSA	Master of Public Service Administration
MOM	Master of Oriental Medicine		MPSRE	Master of Professional Studies in Real Estate
MOR	Master of Operations Research		MPT	Master of Pastoral Theology
MOT	Master of Occupational Therapy			Master of Physical Therapy
MP	Master of Physiology			Master of Practical Theology
	Master of Planning		MPVM	Master of Preventive Veterinary Medicine
MP Ac	Master of Professional Accountancy		MPW	Master of Professional Writing
MP Acc	Master of Professional Accountancy			Master of Public Works
	Master of Professional Accounting		MQM	Master of Quality Management
	Master of Public Accounting		MQS	Master of Quality Systems
MP Aff	Master of Public Affairs		MR	Master of Recreation
MP Aff/MPH	Master of Public Affairs/Master of Public Health			Master of Retailing
			MRA	Master in Research Administration
MP Th	Master of Pastoral Theology		MRC	Master of Rehabilitation Counseling

Peterson's Graduate Programs in the Physical Sciences, Mathematics, Agricultural Sciences, the Environment & Natural Resources 2013

facebook.com/petersonspublishing **557**

MRCP	Master of Regional and City Planning
	Master of Regional and Community Planning
MRD	Master of Rural Development
MRE	Master of Real Estate
	Master of Religious Education
MRED	Master of Real Estate Development
MREM	Master of Resource and Environmental Management
MRLS	Master of Resources Law Studies
MRM	Master of Resources Management
MRP	Master of Regional Planning
MRS	Master of Religious Studies
MRSc	Master of Rehabilitation Science'
MS	Master of Science
MS Cmp E	Master of Science in Computer Engineering
MS Kin	Master of Science in Kinesiology
MS Acct	Master of Science in Accounting
MS Accy	Master of Science in Accountancy
MS Aero E	Master of Science in Aerospace Engineering
MS Ag	Master of Science in Agriculture
MS Arch	Master of Science in Architecture
MS Arch St	Master of Science in Architectural Studies
MS Bio E	Master of Science in Bioengineering
	Master of Science in Biomedical Engineering
MS Bm E	Master of Science in Biomedical Engineering
MS Ch E	Master of Science in Chemical Engineering
MS Chem	Master of Science in Chemistry
MS Cp E	Master of Science in Computer Engineering
MS Eco	Master of Science in Economics
MS Econ	Master of Science in Economics
MS Ed	Master of Science in Education
MS El	Master of Science in Educational Leadership and Administration
MS En E	Master of Science in Environmental Engineering
MS Eng	Master of Science in Engineering
MS Engr	Master of Science in Engineering
MS Env E	Master of Science in Environmental Engineering
MS Exp Surg	Master of Science in Experimental Surgery
MS Int A	Master of Science in International Affairs
MS Mat E	Master of Science in Materials Engineering
MS Mat SE	Master of Science in Material Science and Engineering
MS Met E	Master of Science in Metallurgical Engineering
MS Mgt	Master of Science in Management
MS Min	Master of Science in Mining
MS Min E	Master of Science in Mining Engineering
MS Mt E	Master of Science in Materials Engineering
MS Otal	Master of Science in Otalrynology
MS Pet E	Master of Science in Petroleum Engineering
MS Phys	Master of Science in Physics
MS Poly	Master of Science in Polymers
MS Psy	Master of Science in Psychology
MS Pub P	Master of Science in Public Policy
MS Sc	Master of Science in Social Science
MS Sp Ed	Master of Science in Special Education
MS Stat	Master of Science in Statistics
MS Surg	Master of Science in Surgery
MS Tax	Master of Science in Taxation
MS Tc E	Master of Science in Telecommunications Engineering
MS-R	Master of Science (Research)
MS/CAGS	Master of Science/Certificate of Advanced Graduate Studies
MSA	Master of School Administration
	Master of Science Administration
	Master of Science in Accountancy
	Master of Science in Accounting
	Master of Science in Administration

	Master of Science in Aeronautics
	Master of Science in Agriculture
	Master of Science in Anesthesia
	Master of Science in Architecture
	Master of Science in Aviation
	Master of Sports Administration
MSA Phy	Master of Science in Applied Physics
MSAA	Master of Science in Astronautics and Aeronautics
MSAAE	Master of Science in Aeronautical and Astronautical Engineering
MSABE	Master of Science in Agricultural and Biological Engineering
MSAC	Master of Science in Acupuncture
MSACC	Master of Science in Accounting
MSAE	Master of Science in Aeronautical Engineering
	Master of Science in Aerospace Engineering
	Master of Science in Applied Economics
	Master of Science in Applied Engineering
	Master of Science in Architectural Engineering
MSAH	Master of Science in Allied Health
MSAL	Master of Sport Administration and Leadership
MSAM	Master of Science in Applied Mathematics
MSANR	Master of Science in Agriculture and Natural Resources Systems Management
MSAPM	Master of Security Analysis and Portfolio Management
MSAS	Master of Science in Applied Statistics
	Master of Science in Architectural Studies
MSAT	Master of Science in Accounting and Taxation
	Master of Science in Advanced Technology
	Master of Science in Athletic Training
MSB	Master of Science in Bible
	Master of Science in Biotechnology
	Master of Science in Business
	Master of Sustainable Business
MSBA	Master of Science in Business Administration
	Master of Science in Business Analysis
MSBAE	Master of Science in Biological and Agricultural Engineering
	Master of Science in Biosystems and Agricultural Engineering
MSBC	Master of Science in Building Construction
MSBCB	bioinformatics and computational biology
MSBE	Master of Science in Biological Engineering
	Master of Science in Biomedical Engineering
MSBENG	Master of Science in Bioengineering
MSBIT	Master of Science in Business Information Technology
MSBM	Master of Sport Business Management
MSBME	Master of Science in Biomedical Engineering
MSBMS	Master of Science in Basic Medical Science
MSBS	Master of Science in Biomedical Sciences
MSC	Master of Science in Commerce
	Master of Science in Communication
	Master of Science in Computers
	Master of Science in Counseling
	Master of Science in Criminology
MSCC	Master of Science in Christian Counseling
	Master of Science in Community Counseling
MSCD	Master of Science in Communication Disorders
	Master of Science in Community Development
MSCE	Master of Science in Civil Engineering
	Master of Science in Clinical Epidemiology
	Master of Science in Computer Engineering
	Master of Science in Continuing Education
MSCEE	Master of Science in Civil and Environmental Engineering
MSCF	Master of Science in Computational Finance
MSCH	Master of Science in Chemical Engineering

Peterson's Graduate Programs in the Physical Sciences, Mathematics, Agricultural Sciences, the Environment & Natural Resources 2013

MSChE	Master of Science in Chemical Engineering		Master of Science in Environmental Management
MSCI	Master of Science in Clinical Investigation	MSENE	Master of Science in Environmental Engineering
	Master of Science in Curriculum and Instruction	MSEO	Master of Science in Electro-Optics
MSCIS	Master of Science in Computer and Information Systems	MSEP	Master of Science in Economic Policy
	Master of Science in Computer Information Science	MSEPA	Master of Science in Economics and Policy Analysis
	Master of Science in Computer Information Systems	MSES	Master of Science in Embedded Software Engineering
MSCIT	Master of Science in Computer Information Technology		Master of Science in Engineering Science
MSCJ	Master of Science in Criminal Justice		Master of Science in Environmental Science
MSCJA	Master of Science in Criminal Justice Administration		Master of Science in Environmental Studies
MSCJS	Master of Science in Crime and Justice Studies	MSESM	Master of Science in Engineering Science and Mechanics
MSCLS	Master of Science in Clinical Laboratory Studies	MSET	Master of Science in Educational Technology
MSCM	Master of Science in Church Management		Master of Science in Engineering Technology
	Master of Science in Conflict Management	MSEV	Master of Science in Environmental Engineering
	Master of Science in Construction Management	MSEVH	Master of Science in Environmental Health and Safety
MScM	Master of Science in Management		
MSCM	Master of Supply Chain Management	MSF	Master of Science in Finance
MSCNU	Master of Science in Clinical Nutrition		Master of Science in Forestry
MSCP	Master of Science in Clinical Psychology		Master of Spiritual Formation
	Master of Science in Community Psychology	MSFA	Master of Science in Financial Analysis
	Master of Science in Computer Engineering	MSFAM	Master of Science in Family Studies
	Master of Science in Counseling Psychology	MSFCS	Master of Science in Family and Consumer Science
MSCPE	Master of Science in Computer Engineering	MSFE	Master of Science in Financial Engineering
MSCPharm	Master of Science in Pharmacy	MSFOR	Master of Science in Forestry
MSCPI	Master in Strategic Planning for Critical Infrastructures	MSFP	Master of Science in Financial Planning
MSCR	Master of Science in Clinical Research	MSFS	Master of Science in Financial Sciences
MSCRP	Master of Science in City and Regional Planning		Master of Science in Forensic Science
	Master of Science in Community and Regional Planning	MSFSB	Master of Science in Financial Services and Banking
MSCRP/MP Aff	Master of Science in Community and Regional Planning/Master of Public Affairs	MSFT	Master of Science in Family Therapy
		MSGC	Master of Science in Genetic Counseling
MSCRP/MSSD	Master of Science in Community and Regional Planning/Master of Science in Sustainable Design	MSH	Master of Science in Health
			Master of Science in Hospice
			Master of Science in Health Administration
MSCRP/MSUD	Master of Science in Community and Regional Planning/Masters of Science in Urban Design	MSHA	
		MSHCA	Master of Science in Health Care Administration
MSCS	Master of Science in Clinical Science	MSHCI	Master of Science in Human Computer Interaction
	Master of Science in Computer Science		
MSCSD	Master of Science in Communication Sciences and Disorders	MSHCPM	Master of Science in Health Care Policy and Management
MSCSE	Master of Science in Computer Science and Engineering	MSHE	Master of Science in Health Education
		MSHES	Master of Science in Human Environmental Sciences
MSCTE	Master of Science in Career and Technical Education	MSHFID	Master of Science in Human Factors in Information Design
MSD	Master of Science in Dentistry	MSHFS	Master of Science in Human Factors and Systems
	Master of Science in Design		
	Master of Science in Dietetics	MSHI	Master of Science in Health Informatics
MSE	Master of Science Education	MSHP	Master of Science in Health Professions
	Master of Science in Economics		Master of Science in Health Promotion
	Master of Science in Education	MSHR	Master of Science in Human Resources
	Master of Science in Engineering	MSHRL	Master of Science in Human Resource Leadership
	Master of Science in Engineering Management		
	Master of Software Engineering	MSHRM	Master of Science in Human Resource Management
	Master of Special Education		
	Master of Structural Engineering	MSHROD	Master of Science in Human Resources and Organizational Development
MSECE	Master of Science in Electrical and Computer Engineering	MSHS	Master of Science in Health Science
MSED	Master of Sustainable Economic Development		Master of Science in Health Services
MSEE	Master of Science in Electrical Engineering		Master of Science in Health Systems
	Master of Science in Environmental Engineering		Master of Science in Homeland Security
		MSHT	Master of Science in History of Technology
MSEH	Master of Science in Environmental Health	MSI	Master of Science in Information
MSEL	Master of Science in Educational Leadership		Master of Science in Instruction
MSEM	Master of Science in Engineering Management		Master of System Integration
	Master of Science in Engineering Mechanics	MSIA	Master of Science in Industrial Administration

Peterson's Graduate Programs in the Physical Sciences, Mathematics, Agricultural Sciences, the Environment & Natural Resources 2013

facebook.com/petersonspublishing **559**

	Master of Science in Information Assurance and Computer Security
MSIB	Master of Science in International Business
MSIDM	Master of Science in Interior Design and Merchandising
MSIDT	Master of Science in Information Design and Technology
MSIE	Master of Science in Industrial Engineering
	Master of Science in International Economics
MSIEM	Master of Science in Information Engineering and Management
MSIID	Master of Science in Information and Instructional Design
MSIM	Master of Science in Information Management
	Master of Science in International Management
MSIMC	Master of Science in Integrated Marketing Communications
MSIR	Master of Science in Industrial Relations
MSIS	Master of Science in Information Science
	Master of Science in Information Studies
	Master of Science in Information Systems
	Master of Science in Interdisciplinary Studies
MSIS/MA	Master of Science in Information Studies/ Master of Arts
MSISE	Master of Science in Infrastructure Systems Engineering
MSISM	Master of Science in Information Systems Management
MSISPM	Master of Science in Information Security Policy and Management
MSIST	Master of Science in Information Systems Technology
MSIT	Master of Science in Industrial Technology
	Master of Science in Information Technology
	Master of Science in Instructional Technology
MSITM	Master of Science in Information Technology Management
MSJ	Master of Science in Journalism
	Master of Science in Jurisprudence
MSJC	Master of Social Justice and Criminology
MSJE	Master of Science in Jewish Education
MSJFP	Master of Science in Juvenile Forensic Psychology
MSJJ	Master of Science in Juvenile Justice
MSJPS	Master of Science in Justice and Public Safety
MSJS	Master of Science in Jewish Studies
MSK	Master of Science in Kinesiology
MSL	Master of School Leadership
	Master of Science in Leadership
	Master of Science in Limnology
	Master of Strategic Leadership
	Master of Studies in Law
MSLA	Master of Science in Landscape Architecture
	Master of Science in Legal Administration
MSLD	Master of Science in Land Development
MSLFS	Master of Science in Life Sciences
MSLP	Master of Speech-Language Pathology
MSLS	Master of Science in Library Science
MSLSCM	Master of Science in Logistics and Supply Chain Management
MSLT	Master of Second Language Teaching
MSM	Master of Sacred Ministry
	Master of Sacred Music
	Master of School Mathematics
	Master of Science in Management
	Master of Science in Organization Management
	Master of Security Management
MSMA	Master of Science in Marketing Analysis
MSMAE	Master of Science in Materials Engineering
MSMC	Master of Science in Mass Communications
MSME	Master of Science in Mathematics Education

	Master of Science in Mechanical Engineering
MSMFE	Master of Science in Manufacturing Engineering
MSMFT	Master of Science in Marriage and Family Therapy
MSMIS	Master of Science in Management Information Systems
MSMIT	Master of Science in Management and Information Technology
MSMLS	Master of Science in Medical Laboratory Science
MSMOT	Master of Science in Management of Technology
MSMS	Master of Science in Management Science
	Master of Science in Medical Sciences
MSMSE	Master of Science in Manufacturing Systems Engineering
	Master of Science in Material Science and Engineering
	Master of Science in Mathematics and Science Education
MSMT	Master of Science in Management and Technology
MSMus	Master of Sacred Music
MSN	Master of Science in Nursing
MSN-R	Master of Science in Nursing (Research)
MSNA	Master of Science in Nurse Anesthesia
MSNE	Master of Science in Nuclear Engineering
MSNED	Master of Science in Nurse Education
MSNM	Master of Science in Nonprofit Management
MSNS	Master of Science in Natural Science
	Master of Science in Nutritional Science
MSOD	Master of Science in Organizational Development
MSOEE	Master of Science in Outdoor and Environmental Education
MSOES	Master of Science in Occupational Ergonomics and Safety
MSOH	Master of Science in Occupational Health
MSOL	Master of Science in Organizational Leadership
MSOM	Master of Science in Operations Management
	Master of Science in Oriental Medicine
MSOR	Master of Science in Operations Research
MSOT	Master of Science in Occupational Technology
	Master of Science in Occupational Therapy
MSP	Master of Science in Pharmacy
	Master of Science in Planning
	Master of Science in Psychology
	Master of Speech Pathology
MSPA	Master of Science in Physician Assistant
	Master of Science in Professional Accountancy
MSPAS	Master of Science in Physician Assistant Studies
MSPC	Master of Science in Professional Communications
	Master of Science in Professional Counseling
MSPE	Master of Science in Petroleum Engineering
MSPG	Master of Science in Psychology
MSPH	Master of Science in Public Health
MSPHR	Master of Science in Pharmacy
MSPM	Master of Science in Professional Management
	Master of Science in Project Management
MSPNGE	Master of Science in Petroleum and Natural Gas Engineering
MSPS	Master of Science in Pharmaceutical Science
	Master of Science in Political Science
	Master of Science in Psychological Services
MSPT	Master of Science in Physical Therapy
MSpVM	Master of Specialized Veterinary Medicine
MSR	Master of Science in Radiology
	Master of Science in Reading
MSRA	Master of Science in Recreation Administration

MSRC	Master of Science in Resource Conservation		Master of Teaching Arts
MSRE	Master of Science in Real Estate		Master of Tourism Administration
	Master of Science in Religious Education	MTCM	Master of Traditional Chinese Medicine
MSRED	Master of Science in Real Estate Development	MTD	Master of Training and Development
MSRLS	Master of Science in Recreation and Leisure Studies	MTE	Master in Educational Technology
MSRMP	Master of Science in Radiological Medical Physics	MTESOL	Master in Teaching English to Speakers of Other Languages
MSRS	Master of Science in Rehabilitation Science	MTHM	Master of Tourism and Hospitality Management
MSS	Master of Science in Software	MTI	Master of Information Technology
	Master of Security Studies	MTIM	Master of Trust and Investment Management
	Master of Social Science	MTL	Master of Talmudic Law
	Master of Social Services	MTM	Master of Technology Management
	Master of Software Systems		Master of Telecommunications Management
	Master of Sports Science		Master of the Teaching of Mathematics
	Master of Strategic Studies	MTMH	Master of Tropical Medicine and Hygiene
MSSA	Master of Science in Social Administration	MTOM	Master of Traditional Oriental Medicine
MSSCP	Master of Science in Science Content and Process	MTP	Master of Transpersonal Psychology
		MTPC	Master of Technical and Professional Communication
MSSD	Master of Science in Sustainable Design	MTR	Master of Translational Research
MSSE	Master of Science in Software Engineering	MTS	Master of Theatre Studies
	Master of Science in Space Education		Master of Theological Studies
	Master of Science in Special Education	MTSC	Master of Technical and Scientific Communication
MSSEM	Master of Science in Systems and Engineering Management	MTSE	Master of Telecommunications and Software Engineering
MSSI	Master of Science in Security Informatics		
	Master of Science in Strategic Intelligence	MTT	Master in Technology Management
MSSL	Master of Science in School Leadership	MTX	Master of Taxation
	Master of Science in Strategic Leadership	MUA	Master of Urban Affairs
MSSLP	Master of Science in Speech-Language Pathology	MUCD	Master of Urban and Community Design
		MUD	Master of Urban Design
MSSM	Master of Science in Sports Medicine	MUDS	Master of Urban Design Studies
MSSP	Master of Science in Social Policy	MUEP	Master of Urban and Environmental Planning
MSSPA	Master of Science in Student Personnel Administration	MUP	Master of Urban Planning
		MUPDD	Master of Urban Planning, Design, and Development
MSSS	Master of Science in Safety Science		
	Master of Science in Systems Science	MUPP	Master of Urban Planning and Policy
MSST	Master of Science in Security Technologies	MUPRED	Master of Urban Planning and Real Estate Development
MSSW	Master of Science in Social Work		
MSSWE	Master of Science in Software Engineering	MURP	Master of Urban and Regional Planning
MST	Master of Science and Technology		Master of Urban and Rural Planning
	Master of Science in Taxation	MURPL	Master of Urban and Regional Planning
	Master of Science in Teaching	MUS	Master of Urban Studies
	Master of Science in Technology	MUSA	Master of Urban Spatial Analytics
	Master of Science in Telecommunications	MVM	Master of VLSI and Microelectronics
	Master of Science Teaching	MVP	Master of Voice Pedagogy
MSTC	Master of Science in Technical Communication	MVPH	Master of Veterinary Public Health
	Master of Science in Telecommunications	MVS	Master of Visual Studies
MSTCM	Master of Science in Traditional Chinese Medicine	MWC	Master of Wildlife Conservation
		MWE	Master in Welding Engineering
MSTE	Master of Science in Telecommunications Engineering	MWPS	Master of Wood and Paper Science
		MWR	Master of Water Resources
	Master of Science in Transportation Engineering	MWS	Master of Women's Studies
			Master of Worship Studies
MSTM	Master of Science in Technical Management	MZS	Master of Zoological Science
	Master of Science in Technology Management	Nav Arch	Naval Architecture
	Master of Science in Transfusion Medicine	Naval E	Naval Engineer
MSTOM	Master of Science in Traditional Oriental Medicine	ND	Doctor of Naturopathic Medicine
		NE	Nuclear Engineer
MSUD	Master of Science in Urban Design	Nuc E	Nuclear Engineer
MSW	Master of Social Work	OD	Doctor of Optometry
MSWE	Master of Software Engineering	OTD	Doctor of Occupational Therapy
MSWREE	Master of Science in Water Resources and Environmental Engineering	PBME	Professional Master of Biomedical Engineering
		PC	Performer's Certificate
MSX	Master of Science in Exercise Science	PD	Professional Diploma
MT	Master of Taxation	PGC	Post-Graduate Certificate
	Master of Teaching	PGD	Postgraduate Diploma
	Master of Technology	Ph L	Licentiate of Philosophy
	Master of Textiles	Pharm D	Doctor of Pharmacy
MTA	Master of Tax Accounting		

Peterson's Graduate Programs in the Physical Sciences, Mathematics, Agricultural Sciences, the Environment & Natural Resources 2013

facebook.com/petersonspublishing **561**

PhD	Doctor of Philosophy	SLPD	Doctor of Speech-Language Pathology
PhD Otal	Doctor of Philosophy in Otalrynology	SM	Master of Science
PhD Surg	Doctor of Philosophy in Surgery	SM Arch S	Master of Science in Architectural Studies
PhDEE	Doctor of Philosophy in Electrical Engineering	SMACT	Master of Science in Art, Culture and Technology
PMBA	Professional Master of Business Administration	SMBT	Master of Science in Building Technology
PMC	Post Master Certificate	SP	Specialist Degree
PMD	Post-Master's Diploma	Sp C	Specialist in Counseling
PMS	Professional Master of Science	Sp Ed	Specialist in Education
	Professional Master's	Sp LIS	Specialist in Library and Information Science
Post-Doctoral MS	Post-Doctoral Master of Science	SPA	Specialist in Arts
Post-MSN Certificate	Post-Master of Science in Nursing Certificate	SPCM	Specialist in Church Music
PPDPT	Postprofessional Doctor of Physical Therapy	Spec	Specialist's Certificate
Pro-MS	Professional Science Master's	Spec M	Specialist in Music
PSM	Professional Master of Science	SPEM	Specialist in Educational Ministries
	Professional Science Master's	Spt	Specialist Degree
Psy D	Doctor of Psychology	SPTH	Specialist in Theology
Psy M	Master of Psychology	SSP	Specialist in School Psychology
Psy S	Specialist in Psychology	STB	Bachelor of Sacred Theology
Psya D	Doctor of Psychoanalysis	STD	Doctor of Sacred Theology
Rh D	Doctor of Rehabilitation	STL	Licentiate of Sacred Theology
S Psy S	Specialist in Psychological Services	STM	Master of Sacred Theology
Sc D	Doctor of Science	TDPT	Transitional Doctor of Physical Therapy
Sc M	Master of Science	Th D	Doctor of Theology
SCCT	Specialist in Community College Teaching	Th M	Master of Theology
ScDPT	Doctor of Physical Therapy Science	VMD	Doctor of Veterinary Medicine
SD	Doctor of Science	WEMBA	Weekend Executive Master of Business Administration
	Specialist Degree	XMA	Executive Master of Arts
SJD	Doctor of Juridical Science		

562 facebook.com/petersonspublishing

Peterson's Graduate Programs in the Physical Sciences, Mathematics, Agricultural Sciences, the Environment & Natural Resources 2013

INDEXES

Displays and Close-Ups

Directories and Subject Areas

Following is an alphabetical listing of directories and subject areas. Also listed are cross-references for subject area names not used in the directory structure of the guides, for example, "City and Regional Planning (see Urban and Regional Planning)."

Graduate Programs in the Humanities, Arts & Social Sciences

Addictions/Substance Abuse Counseling
Administration (see Arts Administration; Public Administration)
African-American Studies
African Languages and Literatures (see African Studies)
African Studies
Agribusiness (see Agricultural Economics and Agribusiness)
Agricultural Economics and Agribusiness
Alcohol Abuse Counseling (see Addictions/Substance Abuse Counseling)
American Indian/Native American Studies
American Studies
Anthropology
Applied Arts and Design—General
Applied Behavior Analysis
Applied Economics
Applied History (see Public History)
Applied Psychology
Applied Social Research
Arabic (see Near and Middle Eastern Languages)
Arab Studies (see Near and Middle Eastern Studies)
Archaeology
Architectural History
Architecture
Archives Administration (see Public History)
Area and Cultural Studies (see African-American Studies; African Studies; American Indian/Native American Studies; American Studies; Asian-American Studies; Asian Studies; Canadian Studies; Cultural Studies; East European and Russian Studies; Ethnic Studies; Folklore; Gender Studies; Hispanic Studies; Holocaust Studies; Jewish Studies; Latin American Studies; Near and Middle Eastern Studies; Northern Studies; Pacific Area/Pacific Rim Studies; Western European Studies; Women's Studies)
Art/Fine Arts
Art History
Arts Administration
Arts Journalism
Art Therapy
Asian-American Studies
Asian Languages
Asian Studies
Behavioral Sciences (see Psychology)
Bible Studies (see Religion; Theology)
Biological Anthropology
Black Studies (see African-American Studies)
Broadcasting (see Communication; Film, Television, and Video Production)
Broadcast Journalism Building Science Canadian Studies Celtic Languages
Ceramics (see Art/Fine Arts)
Child and Family Studies Child Development
Chinese
Chinese Studies (see Asian Languages; Asian Studies)
Christian Studies (see Missions and Missiology; Religion; Theology)
Cinema (see Film, Television, and Video Production)
City and Regional Planning (see Urban and Regional Planning)
Classical Languages and Literatures (see Classics)
Classics
Clinical Psychology

Clothing and Textiles
Cognitive Psychology (see Psychology—General; Cognitive Sciences)
Cognitive Sciences
Communication—General
Community Affairs (see Urban and Regional Planning; Urban Studies)
Community Planning (see Architecture; Environmental Design; Urban and Regional Planning; Urban Design; Urban Studies)
Community Psychology (see Social Psychology)
Comparative and Interdisciplinary Arts
Comparative Literature
Composition (see Music)
Computer Art and Design
Conflict Resolution and Mediation/Peace Studies
Consumer Economics
Corporate and Organizational Communication
Corrections (see Criminal Justice and Criminology)
Counseling (see Counseling Psychology; Pastoral Ministry and Counseling)
Counseling Psychology Crafts (see Art/Fine Arts)
Creative Arts Therapies (see Art Therapy; Therapies—Dance, Drama, and Music)
Criminal Justice and Criminology
Cultural Anthropology Cultural Studies Dance
Decorative Arts
Demography and Population Studies
Design (see Applied Arts and Design; Architecture; Art/Fine Arts; Environmental Design; Graphic Design; Industrial Design; Interior Design; Textile Design; Urban Design)
Developmental Psychology Diplomacy (see International Affairs)
Disability Studies
Drama Therapy (see Therapies—Dance, Drama, and Music)
Dramatic Arts (see Theater)
Drawing (see Art/Fine Arts)
Drug Abuse Counseling (see Addictions/Substance Abuse Counseling)
Drug and Alcohol Abuse Counseling (see Addictions/Substance Abuse Counseling)
East Asian Studies (see Asian Studies)
East European and Russian Studies Economic Development
Economics
Educational Theater (see Theater; Therapies—Dance, Drama, and Music)
Emergency Management
English
Environmental Design
Ethics
Ethnic Studies
Ethnomusicology (see Music)
Experimental Psychology
Family and Consumer Sciences—General
Family Studies (see Child and Family Studies)
Family Therapy (see Child and Family Studies; Clinical Psychology; Counseling Psychology; Marriage and Family Therapy)
Filmmaking (see Film, Television, and Video Production)
Film Studies (see Film, Television, and Video Production)
Film, Television, and Video Production
Film, Television, and Video Theory and Criticism
Fine Arts (see Art/Fine Arts)
Folklore
Foreign Languages (see specific language)
Foreign Service (see International Affairs; International Development)
Forensic Psychology
Forensic Sciences
Forensics (see Speech and Interpersonal Communication)
French
Gender Studies
General Studies (see Liberal Studies)
Genetic Counseling
Geographic Information Systems
Geography
German

Gerontology
Graphic Design
Greek (*see* Classics)
Health Communication
Health Psychology
Hebrew (*see* Near and Middle Eastern Languages)
Hebrew Studies (*see* Jewish Studies)
Hispanic and Latin American Languages
Hispanic Studies
Historic Preservation
History
History of Art (*see* Art History)
History of Medicine
History of Science and Technology
Holocaust and Genocide Studies
Home Economics (*see* Family and Consumer Sciences—General)
Homeland Security
Household Economics, Sciences, and Management (*see* Family and Consumer Sciences—General)
Human Development
Humanities
Illustration
Industrial and Labor Relations
Industrial and Organizational Psychology
Industrial Design
Interdisciplinary Studies
Interior Design
International Affairs
International Development
International Economics
International Service (*see* International Affairs; International Development)
International Trade Policy
Internet and Interactive Multimedia
Interpersonal Communication (*see* Speech and Interpersonal Communication)
Interpretation (*see* Translation and Interpretation)
Islamic Studies (*see* Near and Middle Eastern Studies; Religion)
Italian
Japanese
Japanese Studies (*see* Asian Languages; Asian Studies; Japanese)
Jewelry (*see* Art/Fine Arts)
Jewish Studies
Journalism
Judaic Studies (*see* Jewish Studies; Religion)
Labor Relations (*see* Industrial and Labor Relations)
Landscape Architecture
Latin American Studies
Latin (*see* Classics)
Law Enforcement (*see* Criminal Justice and Criminology)
Liberal Studies
Lighting Design
Linguistics
Literature (*see* Classics; Comparative Literature; specific language)
Marriage and Family Therapy
Mass Communication
Media Studies
Medical Illustration
Medieval and Renaissance Studies
Metalsmithing (*see* Art/Fine Arts)
Middle Eastern Studies (*see* Near and Middle Eastern Studies)
Military and Defense Studies
Mineral Economics
Ministry (*see* Pastoral Ministry and Counseling; Theology)
Missions and Missiology
Motion Pictures (*see* Film, Television, and Video Production)
Museum Studies
Music
Musicology (*see* Music)
Music Therapy (*see* Therapies—Dance, Drama, and Music)
National Security
Native American Studies (*see* American Indian/Native American Studies)
Near and Middle Eastern Languages
Near and Middle Eastern Studies
Near Environment (*see* Family and Consumer Sciences)

Northern Studies
Organizational Psychology (*see* Industrial and Organizational Psychology)
Oriental Languages (*see* Asian Languages)
Oriental Studies (*see* Asian Studies)
Pacific Area/Pacific Rim Studies Painting (*see* Art/Fine Arts)
Pastoral Ministry and Counseling
Philanthropic Studies
Philosophy
Photography
Playwriting (*see* Theater; Writing)
Policy Studies (*see* Public Policy)
Political Science
Population Studies (*see* Demography and Population Studies)
Portuguese
Printmaking (*see* Art/Fine Arts)
Product Design (*see* Industrial Design)
Psychoanalysis and Psychotherapy Psychology—General
Public Administration
Public Affairs
Public History
Public Policy
Public Speaking (*see* Mass Communication; Rhetoric; Speech and Interpersonal Communication)
Publishing
Regional Planning (*see* Architecture; Urban and Regional Planning; Urban Design; Urban Studies)
Rehabilitation Counseling
Religion
Renaissance Studies (*see* Medieval and Renaissance Studies)
Rhetoric
Romance Languages
Romance Literatures (*see* Romance Languages)
Rural Planning and Studies
Rural Sociology
Russian
Scandinavian Languages
School Psychology
Sculpture (*see* Art/Fine Arts)
Security Administration (*see* Criminal Justice and Criminology)
Slavic Languages
Slavic Studies (*see* East European and Russian Studies; Slavic Languages)
Social Psychology Social Sciences Sociology
Southeast Asian Studies (*see* Asian Studies)
Soviet Studies (*see* East European and Russian Studies; Russian)
Spanish
Speech and Interpersonal Communication
Sport Psychology
Studio Art (*see* Art/Fine Arts)
Substance Abuse Counseling (*see* Addictions/Substance Abuse Counseling)
Survey Methodology
Sustainable Development
Technical Communication
Technical Writing
Telecommunications (*see* Film, Television, and Video Production)
Television (*see* Film, Television, and Video Production)
Textile Design
Textiles (*see* Clothing and Textiles; Textile Design)
Thanatology
Theater
Theater Arts (*see* Theater)
Theology
Therapies—Dance, Drama, and Music
Translation and Interpretation
Transpersonal and Humanistic Psychology
Urban and Regional Planning
Urban Design
Urban Planning (*see* Architecture; Urban and Regional Planning; Urban Design; Urban Studies)
Urban Studies
Video (*see* Film, Television, and Video Production)
Visual Arts (*see* Applied Arts and Design; Art/Fine Arts; Film, Television, and Video Production; Graphic Design; Illustration; Photography)

568 facebook.com/petersonspublishing

Peterson's Graduate Programs in the Physical Sciences, Mathematics, Agricultural Sciences, the Environment & Natural Resources 2013

Western European Studies
Women's Studies
World Wide Web (*see* Internet and Interactive Multimedia)
Writing

Graduate Programs in the Biological/ Biomedical Sciences & Health Related/ Medical Professions

Acupuncture and Oriental Medicine
Acute Care/Critical Care Nursing Administration (*see* Health Services Management and Hospital Administration; Nursing and Healthcare Administration; Pharmaceutical Administration)
Adult Nursing
Advanced Practice Nursing (*see* Family Nurse Practitioner Studies)
Allied Health—General
Allied Health Professions (*see* Clinical Laboratory Sciences/Medical Technology; Clinical Research; Communication Disorders; Dental Hygiene; Emergency Medical Services; Occupational Therapy; Physical Therapy; Physician Assistant Studies; Rehabilitation Sciences)
Allopathic Medicine
Anatomy
Anesthesiologist Assistant Studies
Animal Behavior
Bacteriology
Behavioral Sciences (*see* Biopsychology; Neuroscience; Zoology)
Biochemistry
Bioethics
Biological and Biomedical Sciences—General Biological Chemistry (*see* Biochemistry)
Biological Oceanography (*see* Marine Biology)
Biophysics
Biopsychology
Botany
Breeding (*see* Botany; Plant Biology; Genetics)
Cancer Biology/Oncology
Cardiovascular Sciences
Cell Biology
Cellular Physiology (*see* Cell Biology; Physiology)
Child-Care Nursing (*see* Maternal and Child/Neonatal Nursing)
Chiropractic
Clinical Laboratory Sciences/Medical Technology
Clinical Research
Community Health
Community Health Nursing
Computational Biology
Conservation (*see* Conservation Biology; Environmental Biology)
Conservation Biology
Crop Sciences (*see* Botany; Plant Biology)
Cytology (*see* Cell Biology)
Dental and Oral Surgery (*see* Oral and Dental Sciences)
Dental Assistant Studies (*see* Dental Hygiene)
Dental Hygiene
Dental Services (*see* Dental Hygiene)
Dentistry
Developmental Biology Dietetics (*see* Nutrition)
Ecology
Embryology (*see* Developmental Biology)
Emergency Medical Services Endocrinology (*see* Physiology)
Entomology
Environmental Biology
Environmental and Occupational Health
Epidemiology
Evolutionary Biology
Family Nurse Practitioner Studies
Foods (*see* Nutrition)
Forensic Nursing
Genetics
Genomic Sciences

Gerontological Nursing
Health Physics/Radiological Health
Health Promotion
Health-Related Professions (*see* individual allied health professions)
Health Services Management and Hospital Administration
Health Services Research
Histology (*see* Anatomy; Cell Biology)
HIV/AIDS Nursing
Hospice Nursing
Hospital Administration (*see* Health Services Management and Hospital Administration)
Human Genetics
Immunology
Industrial Hygiene
Infectious Diseases
International Health
Laboratory Medicine (*see* Clinical Laboratory Sciences/Medical Technology; Immunology; Microbiology; Pathology)
Life Sciences (*see* Biological and Biomedical Sciences)
Marine Biology
Maternal and Child Health
Maternal and Child/Neonatal Nursing
Medical Imaging
Medical Microbiology
Medical Nursing (*see* Medical/Surgical Nursing)
Medical Physics
Medical/Surgical Nursing
Medical Technology (*see* Clinical Laboratory Sciences/Medical Technology)
Medical Sciences (*see* Biological and Biomedical Sciences)
Medical Science Training Programs (*see* Biological and Biomedical Sciences)
Medicinal and Pharmaceutical Chemistry
Medicinal Chemistry (*see* Medicinal and Pharmaceutical Chemistry)
Medicine (*see* Allopathic Medicine; Naturopathic Medicine; Osteopathic Medicine; Podiatric Medicine)
Microbiology
Midwifery (*see* Nurse Midwifery)
Molecular Biology
Molecular Biophysics
Molecular Genetics
Molecular Medicine
Molecular Pathogenesis
Molecular Pathology
Molecular Pharmacology
Molecular Physiology
Molecular Toxicology
Naturopathic Medicine
Neural Sciences (*see* Biopsychology; Neurobiology; Neuroscience)
Neurobiology
Neuroendocrinology (*see* Biopsychology; Neurobiology; Neuroscience; Physiology)
Neuropharmacology (*see* Biopsychology; Neurobiology; Neuroscience; Pharmacology)
Neurophysiology (*see* Biopsychology; Neurobiology; Neuroscience; Physiology)
Neuroscience
Nuclear Medical Technology (*see* Clinical Laboratory Sciences/Medical Technology)
Nurse Anesthesia
Nurse Midwifery
Nurse Practitioner Studies (*see* Family Nurse Practitioner Studies)
Nursing Administration (*see* Nursing and Healthcare Administration)
Nursing and Healthcare Administration
Nursing Education Nursing—General Nursing Informatics
Nutrition
Occupational Health (*see* Environmental and Occupational Health; Occupational Health Nursing)
Occupational Health Nursing
Occupational Therapy
Oncology (*see* Cancer Biology/Oncology)
Oncology Nursing
Optometry
Oral and Dental Sciences
Oral Biology (*see* Oral and Dental Sciences)
Oral Pathology (*see* Oral and Dental Sciences)

Peterson's Graduate Programs in the Physical Sciences, Mathematics, Agricultural Sciences, the Environment & Natural Resources 2013

facebook.com/petersonspublishing **569**

Organismal Biology (see Biological and Biomedical Sciences; Zoology)
Oriental Medicine and Acupuncture (see Acupuncture and Oriental Medicine)
Orthodontics (see Oral and Dental Sciences)
Osteopathic Medicine
Parasitology Pathobiology Pathology
Pediatric Nursing
Pedontics (see Oral and Dental Sciences)
Perfusion
Pharmaceutical Administration
Pharmaceutical Chemistry (see Medicinal and Pharmaceutical Chemistry)
Pharmaceutical Sciences
Pharmacology
Pharmacy
Photobiology of Cells and Organelles (see Botany; Cell Biology; Plant Biology)
Physical Therapy
Physician Assistant Studies
Physiological Optics (see Vision Sciences)
Podiatric Medicine
Preventive Medicine (see Community Health and Public Health)
Physiological Optics (see Physiology)
Physiology
Plant Biology
Plant Molecular Biology
Plant Pathology
Plant Physiology
Pomology (see Botany; Plant Biology)
Psychiatric Nursing
Public Health—General
Public Health Nursing (see Community Health Nursing)
Psychiatric Nursing
Psychobiology (see Biopsychology)
Psychopharmacology (see Biopsychology; Neuroscience; Pharmacology)
Radiation Biology
Radiological Health (see Health Physics/Radiological Health)
Rehabilitation Nursing
Rehabilitation Sciences
Rehabilitation Therapy (see Physical Therapy)
Reproductive Biology
School Nursing
Sociobiology (see Evolutionary Biology)
Structural Biology
Surgical Nursing (see Medical/Surgical Nursing)
Systems Biology
Teratology
Therapeutics
Theoretical Biology (see Biological and Biomedical Sciences)
Therapeutics (see Pharmaceutical Sciences; Pharmacology; Pharmacy)
Toxicology
Transcultural Nursing
Translational Biology
Tropical Medicine (see Parasitology)
Veterinary Medicine
Veterinary Sciences
Virology
Vision Sciences
Wildlife Biology (see Zoology)
Women's Health Nursing
Zoology

Graduate Programs in the Physical Sciences, Mathematics, Agricultural Sciences, the Environment & Natural Resources

Acoustics
Agricultural Sciences

Agronomy and Soil Sciences
Analytical Chemistry
Animal Sciences
Applied Mathematics
Applied Physics
Applied Statistics
Aquaculture
Astronomy
Astrophysical Sciences (see Astrophysics; Atmospheric Sciences; Meteorology; Planetary and Space Sciences)
Astrophysics
Atmospheric Sciences
Biological Oceanography (see Marine Affairs; Marine Sciences; Oceanography)
Biomathematics
Biometry
Biostatistics
Chemical Physics
Chemistry
Computational Sciences
Condensed Matter Physics
Dairy Science (see Animal Sciences)
Earth Sciences (see Geosciences)
Environmental Management and Policy
Environmental Sciences
Environmental Studies (see Environmental Management and Policy)
Experimental Statistics (see Statistics)
Fish, Game, and Wildlife Management
Food Science and Technology
Forestry
General Science (see specific topics)
Geochemistry
Geodetic Sciences
Geological Engineering (see Geology)
Geological Sciences (see Geology)
Geology
Geophysical Fluid Dynamics (see Geophysics)
Geophysics
Geosciences
Horticulture
Hydrogeology
Hydrology
Inorganic Chemistry
Limnology
Marine Affairs
Marine Geology
Marine Sciences
Marine Studies (see Marine Affairs; Marine Geology; Marine Sciences; Oceanography)
Mathematical and Computational Finance
Mathematical Physics
Mathematical Statistics (see Applied Statistics; Statistics)
Mathematics
Meteorology
Mineralogy
Natural Resource Management (see Environmental Management and Policy; Natural Resources)
Natural Resources
Nuclear Physics (see Physics)
Ocean Engineering (see Marine Affairs; Marine Geology; Marine Sciences; Oceanography)
Oceanography
Optical Sciences
Optical Technologies (see Optical Sciences)
Optics (see Applied Physics; Optical Sciences; Physics)
Organic Chemistry
Paleontology
Paper Chemistry (see Chemistry)
Photonics
Physical Chemistry
Physics
Planetary and Space Sciences
Plant Sciences
Plasma Physics
Poultry Science (see Animal Sciences)
Radiological Physics (see Physics)

570 facebook.com/petersonspublishing

Peterson's Graduate Programs in the Physical Sciences, Mathematics, Agricultural Sciences, the Environment & Natural Resources 2013

Range Management (*see* Range Science)
Range Science
Resource Management (*see* Environmental Management and Policy; Natural Resources)
Solid-Earth Sciences (*see* Geosciences)
Space Sciences (*see* Planetary and Space Sciences)
Statistics
Theoretical Chemistry
Theoretical Physics
Viticulture and Enology
Water Resources

Graduate Programs in Engineering & Applied Sciences

Aeronautical Engineering (*see* Aerospace/Aeronautical Engineering)
Aerospace/Aeronautical Engineering
Aerospace Studies (*see* Aerospace/Aeronautical Engineering)
Agricultural Engineering
Applied Mechanics (*see* Mechanics)
Applied Science and Technology Architectural Engineering
Artificial Intelligence/Robotics
Astronautical Engineering (*see* Aerospace/Aeronautical Engineering)
Automotive Engineering
Aviation
Biochemical Engineering
Bioengineering Bioinformatics
Biological Engineering (*see* Bioengineering)
Biomedical Engineering
Biosystems Engineering
Biotechnology
Ceramic Engineering (*see* Ceramic Sciences and Engineering)
Ceramic Sciences and Engineering
Ceramics (*see* Ceramic Sciences and Engineering)
Chemical Engineering
Civil Engineering
Computer and Information Systems Security
Computer Engineering
Computer Science
Computing Technology (*see* Computer Science)
Construction Engineering
Construction Management
Database Systems
Electrical Engineering
Electronic Materials
Electronics Engineering (*see* Electrical Engineering)
Energy and Power Engineering
Energy Management and Policy
Engineering and Applied Sciences
Engineering and Public Affairs (*see* Technology and Public Policy)
Engineering and Public Policy (*see* Energy Management and Policy; Technology and Public Policy)
Engineering Design
Engineering Management
Engineering Mechanics (*see* Mechanics)
Engineering Metallurgy (*see* Metallurgical Engineering and Metallurgy)
Engineering Physics
Environmental Design (*see* Environmental Engineering)
Environmental Engineering
Ergonomics and Human Factors
Financial Engineering
Fire Protection Engineering
Food Engineering (*see* Agricultural Engineering)
Game Design and Development
Gas Engineering (*see* Petroleum Engineering)
Geological Engineering
Geophysics Engineering (*see* Geological Engineering)
Geotechnical Engineering
Hazardous Materials Management
Health Informatics

Health Systems (*see* Safety Engineering; Systems Engineering)
Highway Engineering (*see* Transportation and Highway Engineering)
Human-Computer Interaction
Human Factors (*see* Ergonomics and Human Factors)
Hydraulics
Hydrology (*see* Water Resources Engineering)
Industrial Engineering (*see* Industrial/Management Engineering)
Industrial/Management Engineering
Information Science
Internet Engineering
Macromolecular Science (*see* Polymer Science and Engineering)
Management Engineering (*see* Engineering Management; Industrial/ Management Engineering)
Management of Technology
Manufacturing Engineering
Marine Engineering (*see* Civil Engineering)
Materials Engineering
Materials Sciences
Mechanical Engineering Mechanics
Medical Informatics
Metallurgical Engineering and Metallurgy
Metallurgy (*see* Metallurgical Engineering and Metallurgy)
Mineral/Mining Engineering
Modeling and Simulation
Nanotechnology
Nuclear Engineering
Ocean Engineering
Operations Research
Paper and Pulp Engineering
Petroleum Engineering
Pharmaceutical Engineering
Plastics Engineering (*see* Polymer Science and Engineering)
Polymer Science and Engineering
Public Policy (*see* Energy Management and Policy; Technology and Public Policy)
Reliability Engineering
Robotics (*see* Artificial Intelligence/Robotics)
Safety Engineering
Software Engineering
Solid-State Sciences (*see* Materials Sciences)
Structural Engineering
Surveying Science and Engineering
Systems Analysis (*see* Systems Engineering)
Systems Engineering
Systems Science
Technology and Public Policy
Telecommunications
Telecommunications Management
Textile Sciences and Engineering
Textiles (*see* Textile Sciences and Engineering)
Transportation and Highway Engineering
Urban Systems Engineering (*see* Systems Engineering)
Waste Management (*see* Hazardous Materials Management)
Water Resources Engineering

Graduate Programs in Business, Education, Information Studies, Law & Social Work

Accounting
Actuarial Science
Adult Education
Advertising and Public Relations
Agricultural Education
Alcohol Abuse Counseling (*see* Counselor Education)
Archival Management and Studies
Art Education
Athletics Administration (*see* Kinesiology and Movement Studies)
Athletic Training and Sports Medicine
Audiology (*see* Communication Disorders)

Peterson's Graduate Programs in the Physical Sciences, Mathematics, Agricultural Sciences, the Environment & Natural Resources 2013

facebook.com/petersonspublishing **571**

Aviation Management
Banking (*see* Finance and Banking)
Business Administration and Management—General
Business Education
Communication Disorders
Community College Education
Computer Education
Continuing Education (*see* Adult Education)
Counseling (*see* Counselor Education)
Counselor Education
Curriculum and Instruction
Developmental Education
Distance Education Development
Drug Abuse Counseling (*see* Counselor Education)
Early Childhood Education
Educational Leadership and Administration
Educational Measurement and Evaluation
Educational Media/Instructional Technology
Educational Policy
Educational Psychology
Education—General
Education of the Blind (*see* Special Education)
Education of the Deaf (*see* Special Education)
Education of the Gifted
Education of the Hearing Impaired (*see* Special Education)
Education of the Learning Disabled (*see* Special Education)
Education of the Mentally Retarded (*see* Special Education)
Education of the Physically Handicapped (*see* Special Education)
Education of Students with Severe/Multiple Disabilities
Education of the Visually Handicapped (*see* Special Education)
Electronic Commerce
Elementary Education
English as a Second Language
English Education
Entertainment Management
Entrepreneurship
Environmental Education
Environmental Law
Exercise and Sports Science
Exercise Physiology (*see* Kinesiology and Movement Studies)
Facilities and Entertainment Management
Finance and Banking
Food Services Management (*see* Hospitality Management)
Foreign Languages Education
Foundations and Philosophy of Education
Guidance and Counseling (*see* Counselor Education)
Health Education
Health Law
Hearing Sciences (*see* Communication Disorders)
Higher Education
Home Economics Education
Hospitality Management
Hotel Management (*see* Travel and Tourism)
Human Resources Development
Human Resources Management
Human Services
Industrial Administration (*see* Industrial and Manufacturing Management)
Industrial and Manufacturing Management
Industrial Education (*see* Vocational and Technical Education)
Information Studies
Instructional Technology (*see* Educational Media/Instructional Technology)
Insurance
Intellectual Property Law
International and Comparative Education
International Business
International Commerce (*see* International Business)
International Economics (*see* International Business)
International Trade (*see* International Business)
Investment and Securities (*see* Business Administration and Management; Finance and Banking; Investment Management)
Investment Management

Junior College Education (*see* Community College Education)
Kinesiology and Movement Studies
Law
Legal and Justice Studies
Leisure Services (*see* Recreation and Park Management)
Leisure Studies
Library Science
Logistics
Management (*see* Business Administration and Management)
Management Information Systems
Management Strategy and Policy
Marketing
Marketing Research
Mathematics Education
Middle School Education
Movement Studies (*see* Kinesiology and Movement Studies)
Multilingual and Multicultural Education
Museum Education Music Education Nonprofit Management
Nursery School Education (*see* Early Childhood Education)
Occupational Education (*see* Vocational and Technical Education)
Organizational Behavior
Organizational Management
Parks Administration (*see* Recreation and Park Management)
Personnel (*see* Human Resources Development; Human Resources Management; Organizational Behavior; Organizational Management; Student Affairs)
Philosophy of Education (*see* Foundations and Philosophy of Education)
Physical Education
Project Management
Public Relations (*see* Advertising and Public Relations)
Quality Management
Quantitative Analysis
Reading Education
Real Estate
Recreation and Park Management
Recreation Therapy (*see* Recreation and Park Management)
Religious Education
Remedial Education (*see* Special Education)
Restaurant Administration (*see* Hospitality Management)
Science Education
Secondary Education
Social Sciences Education
Social Studies Education (*see* Social Sciences Education)
Social Work
Special Education
Speech-Language Pathology and Audiology (*see* Communication Disorders)
Sports Management
Sports Medicine (*see* Athletic Training and Sports Medicine)
Sports Psychology and Sociology (*see* Kinesiology and Movement Studies)
Student Affairs
Substance Abuse Counseling (*see* Counselor Education)
Supply Chain Management
Sustainability Management
Systems Management (*see* Management Information Systems)
Taxation
Teacher Education (*see* specific subject areas)
Teaching English as a Second Language (*see* English as a Second Language)
Technical Education (*see* Vocational and Technical Education)
Transportation Management
Travel and Tourism
Urban Education
Vocational and Technical Education
Vocational Counseling (*see* Counselor Education)

572 facebook.com/petersonspublishing

Peterson's Graduate Programs in the Physical Sciences, Mathematics, Agricultural Sciences, the Environment & Natural Resources 2013

Directories and Subject Areas in This Book

NOTES

NOTES

NOTES

NOTES

NOTES